Xmas 1987

LONGMAN
—— FAMILY ——
DICTIONARY

LONGMAN
—FAMILY—
DICTIONARY

CHANCELLOR
PRESS

First published in Great Britain in 1984 by
Chancellor Press
59 Grosvenor Street
London W1

Reprinted 1985, 1986, 1987

This edition © Merriam-Webster Inc., and
Longman Group Limited 1984

This dictionary is based on the Longman New Universal Dictionary,
first published 1982 © G. & C. Merriam Company and Longman
Group Limited 1982.

ISBN 0 907486 45 2

Printed in Czechoslovakia

Headwords that the editors have reason to believe constitute trademarks
have been described as such. However, neither the presence nor absence of
such description should be regarded as affecting the legal status of any
trademark.

50526/6

How to use this Dictionary

1 How to find the word you want

All the words defined in this dictionary are entered as main entries in alphabetical order. Words that are not defined are entered under their base form (see 1.2). Idiomatic phrases are entered under the main word in the phrase (see 1.3).

1.1 Main entries

Alphabetical order of entry, letter by letter, applies to all main entries, whether they are single words, hyphenated words, or compounds consisting of two or more individual words. This means that, for example, **question mark** comes between **questionable** and **question-master**.

A compound written as a single word comes before the same compound written with a hyphen, which in turn comes before the same compound written as two or more separate words; hence **rundown** precedes **run-down** and **run down**.

Many words that share the same spelling have a different pronunciation or a different history, or are different in grammar. Such words are shown separately, with small numbers in front to distinguish them; see, for example, the entries at **lead**. These words are listed in historical order, according to when they first appeared in English.

1.2 Undefined words

Words whose meaning can easily be guessed, because they consist of a base form plus an added ending, are not given definitions. These words (run-ons) are shown at the end of the definition for their base form:

charitable...*adj*...–**charitableness** *n*, **charitably** *adv*

This indicates that the meaning of **charitableness** can be guessed from the meaning of **charitable** plus the meaning of the ending **-ness**, which can be found at its own place in the dictionary. Sometimes the undefined entry has the same form as its base, but a different part of speech:

²**chink** *n* a short sharp sound – **chink** *vb*

This means that the verb **chink** is obviously related to the noun **chink** – 'to make, or cause to make, a short sharp sound'.

Words whose meaning can be guessed because they consist of a base form plus something added at the beginning are shown at their own place in the dictionary, but with no definition; see, for instance, **unannounced** and **unchecked**.

1.3 Idiomatic phrases

An idiom is a fixed phrase whose meaning cannot be guessed from the meanings of the individual words from which it is made up. Idioms are shown at the end of an entry, after any undefined words:

¹**call** *vi* ... – **call a spade a spade** to speak frankly and usu bluntly

Compound verbs that end in a preposition are treated as idioms; although those that end in an adverb, such as **put up** and **give away**, are main entries.

Idioms are entered at the first meaningful word they contain. Hence **live it up** is entered at **live, on the ball** appears at **ball**, and **in spite of** is shown at **spite**. When an idiom has more than one accepted form, it is entered at the first invariable meaningful word it contains. The alternative form is shown after an oblique (/):

¹**seed** ... *n* ... – **go/run to seed** ...

2 Alternative versions of words

Many words come in pairs, or even trios, that are nearly identical. They may differ only in spelling (eg **judgment, judgement**), or in their ending (eg **excellence, excellency**), or even in the presence or absence of a complete word in a compound (eg **silk screen**, **silk-screen printing**). In this dictionary, common variant forms of a word are shown immediately after the main entry. When the variant is preceded by a comma, it is about as common as the main entry in current standard usage; when the variant is preceded by *also*, it is rather less common. These alternative forms are shown separately as main entries only if they fall more than ten places away from their main form in the alphabetical list.

Variant spellings of the **-ize/-ise** type are shown in abbreviated form at the main entry:

computerize, -ise *vt*

This means that **computerize** can also be spelt **computerise**.

Feminine forms of words are shown in the same way as other variants:

author ... *fem* **authoress** ... *n*

Individual meanings, as well as whole main entries, can have variant forms:

excellence ... *n* 1 ... 2 ... 3 **Excellency, Excellence** – used as a title for certain high dignitaries (eg ambassadors)

Variant forms that are entirely or partially restricted to British or American English are labelled *Br* or *NAm*:

jail, *Br also* **gaol** ... *n* ...
gaol ... *vb or n, chiefly Br* (to) jail

This means that the spelling **jail** is used everywhere in the English-speaking world, but British English also uses **gaol** (see 8.2).

If the variable part of a pair of words is shown as a main entry in its own right, then this variation is *not* shown in the entry for the word formed from it. Hence **hemorrhage**, the American variant spelling of **haemorrhage**, is not shown because **hemo-** is already entered as the American variant of **haemo-**.

3 Parts of speech

These are the various word classes to which the entries in this dictionary belong:

adj	adjective:	**energetic, durable**
adv	adverb:	**very, happily**
comb form	combining form:	**Anglo-, mal-**
conj	conjunction:	**but, insofar as**
interj	interjection:	**hey, bravo**
n	noun:	**dynamite, bird of paradise**
prefix		**pre-, trans-**
prep	preposition:	**for, according to**
pron	pronoun:	**herself, ours**
suffix		**-ful, -ness**
trademark		**Hoover**
vb	verb (both transitive and intransitive):	**agglomerate, americanize**
vb impersonal	impersonal verb:	**methinks**
verbal auxiliary		**can, must**
vi	intransitive verb:	**arise, arrive**
vt	transitive verb:	**indicate, thank**

Sometimes two parts of speech are combined:

yelp . . . *vi or n* (to utter) a sharp quick shrill cry

4 Inflections

The dictionary shows inflections only if they are irregular, and may therefore cause difficulty. They are written out in full, unless they involve merely the doubling of a consonant or the change of **-c** to **-ck-**:

¹**swat** . . . *vt* **-tt-**
picnic . . . *vi* **-ck-**

This means that the present participle and past of **swat** are **swatting** and **swatted**, and those of **picnic** are **picnicking** and **picnicked**.

4.1 Nouns
Regular plurals of nouns (eg **cats, matches, spies**) are not shown. All other plurals (eg **louse, lice; sheep, sheep**) are given. Sometimes alternative plurals are possible:

salmon . . . *n, pl* **salmon**, *esp for different types* **salmons**

Nouns that are always plurals are shown as follows:

environs . . . *n pl* . . .

Sometimes an individual sense of a noun is exclusively plural:

¹**victual** . . . *n* . . . **2** *pl* supplies of food; provisions

Not all plural nouns always take a plural verb. This is shown as follows:

genetics *n pl but sing in constr* . . .
forty winks *n pl but sing or pl in constr* . . .

This means that one says 'Genetics is . . .' but one says either 'Forty winks is . . .' or 'Forty winks are . . .'

Some nouns in apparently singular form can take a plural verb:

police *n* . . . **2a** . . . **b** *pl in constr* policemen
crew *n sing or pl in constr* . . .

This means that one says 'Several police are . . .' but one says either 'The crew is . . .' or '. . . are . . .'

Some nouns are used with the same meaning in the plural. They are shown like this:

latitude . . . *n* . . . a region as marked by its latitude – often pl with sing. meaning

This means that one can say 'It's very hot at this latitude' or '. . . at these latitudes.'

4.2 Verbs
Regular verb forms (eg **halted, cadged, carrying**) are not shown. All other verb inflections (eg **ring, rang, rung**) are shown, including those for verbs ending in a vowel other than *-e*, for verbs which keep a final *-e* before inflections, and for verbs having alternative inflections.

Inflections are shown in the following order:

present: 1st, 2nd, and 3rd person singular; plural; present subjunctive; present participle; past: 1st, 2nd, and 3rd person singular; plural; past subjunctive; past participle.

Only the irregular inflections are shown. Certain forms (eg the entire past tense, or the past tense and the past participle) are combined if they are identical. Thus in

run . . . *vb* **-nn-; ran; run**

the present participle is **running**, the entire past tense is **ran**, and the past participle is **run**.

Irregular American and archaic inflections are listed as separate entries, but are not shown at the main form of the verb.

4.3 Adjectives and adverbs
Adjectives and adverbs whose comparative and superlative are formed with **more** and **most**, or by adding **-(e)r** and **-(e)st** (eg **nicer, fastest, happier**), are not shown.

All other inflections (eg **good** . . . **better** . . . **best**) are shown, including alternatives (eg **shy** . . . **shier, shyer; shiest, shyest**).

4.4 Pronouns
Inflections of pronouns are entered at their alphabetical place and cross-referred to their main form:

²**her** *pron, objective case of* SHE

5 Capitalization

Some words, or meanings of words, can be used with or without a capital letter, and we show this with the notes *often cap* and *often not cap*. In the case of compound words, the note specifies which parts are capitalized:

pop art *n, often cap P&A* . . .

6 How the meaning of words is shown

Sometimes, instead of giving a definition, the dictionary describes how a word is used:

²**after** *prep* ... **3** – used to indicate the goal or purpose of an action <*go ~ gold*>

Trademarked terms are also treated in this way:

Hoover *trademark* – used for a vacuum cleaner

Most words, however, are given ordinary dictionary definitions, with one or more meanings.

6.1 The numbering of meanings

The main meanings of a word are numbered:

tress ... *n* **1** a plait of hair **2** a long lock of hair – usu pl

When a numbered main meaning of a word is divided into subsenses, they are introduced by letters:

quite ... *adv or adj* **1a** wholly, completely ... **b** positively, certainly ...
    Divisions of a subsense are indicated by bracketed numbers:

¹**take** ... *vb* ... **1a** ... **c(1)** to capture and remove from play ... **(2)** to win in a card game

When a definition is followed by a colon and two or more subsenses, this indicates that the meaning of the subsenses is covered by the introductory definition. The colon may be followed by *eg* when the subsenses are a representative sample rather than a complete list of meanings:

activate *vt* **1** to make (more) active or reactive, esp in chemical or physical properties: eg **a** to make (a substance) radioactive **b** to aerate (sewage) ...

Sometimes an introductory definition is simply the common element shared by the following subsenses:

cheapen ... *vb* to make or become **a** cheap in price or value **b** lower in esteem **c** tawdry, vulgar, or inferior

This indicates that **cheapen** means 'to make or become cheap in price and value', 'to make or become lower in esteem', and 'to make or become tawdry, vulgar, or inferior'.
    When two meanings of a word are very closely related, they are not separated off with numbers or letters, but run together, with the word *esp*, *specif*, *also*, or *broadly* between them to show the way in which they are related:

aggression ... *n* ... **2** attack, encroachment; *esp* unprovoked violation by one country of the territory of another

6.2 The order in which senses are shown

Those meanings that would be understood anywhere in the English-speaking world are shown first, in their historical order: the older senses before the newer. After these come the meanings whose usage is restricted in some way (eg because they are used in only one area, or have gone out of current use).

6.3 Brackets

Round brackets are used in four main ways in definitions:
They enclose the object of a verb:

²**contract** *vt* ... **2a** to catch (an illness)

They give extra information:

³**nap** *n* a hairy or downy surface (eg on a woven fabric)

They separate the parts of a combined definition that relate to different parts of speech:

cheep ... *vi or n* (to utter) a faint shrill sound characteristic of a young bird

They enclose optional wording:

afloat ... *adj or adv* **1a** borne (as if) on the water or air

This indicates that **afloat** means both 'borne on the water or air' and 'borne as if on the water or air'.

7 Examples

Definitions, particularly of words with several senses, may be followed by a phrase or sentence illustrating a typical use of the word in context. Many of these are quotations from a written or spoken source; in such cases the author or source is named.
    Examples are printed in italics between angle brackets (< >). Occasionally the word being illustrated is written out in full, but usually it is represented by a swung dash (~). When an inflected form of the main entry is being illustrated, it is usually shown by a swung dash followed by the inflection:

¹**dare** ... *vt* to confront boldly; defy <~d *the anger of her family*>

The complete example is therefore 'dared the anger of her family'.

8 Usage

There is more to a complete description of a word than a definition of its meaning; many words have peculiarities of usage that a dictionary must take account of. They may be restricted to a particular geographical area; they may be colloquial or slang, or felt to be 'incorrect'; they may have fallen out of use; and there may be limitations on the sort of context they can be used in.
    This dictionary shows such restrictions in two different ways. Words, or meanings, that are limited to a particular period or area are identified by an italic label:

fain ... *adv, archaic* **1** with pleasure ...

When an italic label comes between the main entry and the first definition it refers to all meanings of the word; otherwise, it applies to all subsenses of the number or letter it follows.
    All other information on usage is given in a note at the end of a definition:

tootsy ... *n* FOOT **1** – used chiefly to children

When such a note applies to all or several meanings of

a word, it follows the last definition, and is introduced by the word *USE*.

8.1 Words that are no longer in current use
The label *obs* for 'obsolete' means there is no evidence of use for a word or meaning since 1755 (the date of publication of Samuel Johnson's Dictionary); this label is a comment on the word being defined, not on the thing it designates.

The label *archaic* means that a word or meaning once in common use is found today only in special contexts, such as poetry or historical fiction, where it is used to introduce a flavour of the past.

Some of the more common archaisms that tend to linger on in poetic diction are treated more explicitly by means of a note:

e'en ... *adv* even – chiefly poetic

Similar treatment is given to comparatively modern terms which have become old-fashioned:

matron ... *n* ... **3** a woman in charge of the nursing in a hospital – not now used technically
cripes ... *interj*, *Br* – used to express surprise; no longer in vogue

8.2 Words that are not used throughout the English-speaking world
A word or sense limited in use to one or more of the countries of the English-speaking world is labelled accordingly:

³**crook** *adj*, *Austr & NZ* **1** ill, sick ...

The label *Br* indicates that a word or meaning is used in Britain and also usually in the Commonwealth countries of Australasia. The label *NAm* indicates the use of a word or meaning in both the USA and Canada.

The label *dial* for 'dialect' indicates that a word or meaning belongs to the common local speech of several different places.

8.3 Words that suggest a particular style, attitude, or level of formality
Most English words can be generally used in both speech and writing, but some would be traditionally described as 'colloquial' or 'slang', and others, perhaps, as 'formal'.

Words of this sort are identified by notes at the end of definitions. It is always hard to apply such descriptions consistently, since the status of these words is constantly shifting with the passage of time, and they are also frequently used in an incongruous setting for stylistic effect.

The note '– infml' is used for words or senses that are characteristic of conversational speech and casual writing (eg between friends and contemporaries) rather than of official or 'serious' speech or writing.

The note '– slang' is used for words or meanings usually found in contexts of extreme informality. Such words may be, or may have been until recently, used by a particular social group such as criminals or drug users. They often refer to topics that are thought of as risqué or 'low'.

At the opposite end of the scale, the note '– fml', for 'formal', is used for words or meanings characteristic of written rather than spoken English, and particularly of official or academic writings.

Other notes describe the attitude or tone of the user of a word:

egghead ... *n* an intellectual, highbrow – derog or humor
pass away *vi* ... **2** to die – euph

8.4 Words that are not 'correct'
It is not the role of a responsible modern dictionary to dictate usage; it can only make statements, based on reference to a large stock of spoken and written data, as to how a word is being used by the community at large. Where appropriate it can also warn that a use of a word is likely to arouse controversy or disapproval. Many people would disapprove of the use of some of the words we have described as 'slang' or 'informal', and there are of course many contexts in which their use would be inappropriate; but there is a further distinct class of words that are generally felt to be 'incorrect'.

The note '– nonstandard' is used for words or meanings that are quite commonly used in English but are considered incorrect by many speakers:

flaunt ... *vt* ... **2** to flout – nonstandard

Certain highly controversial words or meanings have the warning note '– disapproved of by some speakers':

disinterested *adj* **1** uninterested – disapproved of by some speakers

The note '– substandard' is used for words or meanings that are widely used but are not part of standard English:

learn ... *vb* ... **2** to teach – substandard

8.5 The context in which a word can appear
Many words or meanings can be used only in certain contexts within a sentence: some verbs are used only in the passive; some words can appear only in the negative, along with **not**, **never**, etc; others are always used with particular prepositions or adverbs, or in certain fixed phrases. Such restrictions are shown in a note following a definition:

abide ... *vb* **1** to bear patiently; tolerate – used negatively
agree ... *vi* ... **2a** to be of one mind – often + *with* <*I ~ with you*>
dumps ... *n pl* a gloomy state of mind; despondency – esp in *in the dumps*

Sometimes a word that is commonly used with the main entry word in a sentence is printed in italic within the definition:

allude ... *vi* to make indirect, casual, or implicit reference *to*
²**altogether** *n* the nude <*posed in the ~*> – infml

This means that **allude** is almost always used in the phrase **allude to**, and that the noun **altogether** is almost always used with **the**.

9 Cross-references

Cross-references draw attention to a related word in another part of the dictionary. Any word printed in SMALL CAPITAL letters is a cross-reference.

An entire definition may take the form of a cross-reference. This happens either when the word used in the definition has more than one meaning, and it is necessary to specify which meaning is referred to:

²**flash** *n* . . . **6a** . . . **c** FLASHLIGHT 2

or when the word used in the definition is a compound that is a main entry in the dictionary:

rubella . . . *n* GERMAN MEASLES

Variant forms of prefixes and combining forms – that is to say, alternative spellings used when combining with different base forms (eg the **im-** form of **in-** in words like **impossible**) – are shown as follows in the alphabetical list:

con- – see COM-
oestro- – see OESTR-

Full information about them may be found at the main entry.

10 Prefixes, suffixes, and combining forms

Word elements that can be used to form new words in English are entered at their alphabetical place in the dictionary. These elements are prefixes (eg **pre-**, **un-**), suffixes (eg **-ous**, **-ly**), and combining forms (eg **Anglo-**, **-logy**).

Suffixes and combining forms added to the end of a word may alter the grammatical function as well as the meaning of the word. Where appropriate, this change of part of speech is indicated as follows:

-ful *suffix* (*n→adj*) full of <*eventful*> <*colourful*>

This means that the suffix **-ful** is added to nouns to make adjectives.

11 Abbreviations

Abbreviations are listed in an appendix on p 821. Some abbreviations that are frequently used as 'words' are entered in the main body of the text. Examples of these are **sae** and **PVC**, which are shown in the main alphabetical list as nouns.

Abbreviations and symbols used in the dictionary itself are listed on p viii.

Abbreviations used in this Dictionary

A

A ampere
ab about
abbr abbreviation
AD Anno Domini
adj adjective
adv adverb
am ante meridiem
amt amount
apprec appreciative
approx approximate, approximately
arch archaic
attrib attributive
Austr Australian
AV Authorized Version

B

BC before Christ
Br British
Btu British thermal unit

C

c centi-
c century
C Celsius, centigrade
C coulomb
Can Canadian
cap capital, capitalized
cgs centimetre-gram-second
cm centimetre
comb combining
compar comparative
conj conjunction
constr construction
ctl cental
cwt hundredweight

D

Dan Daniel
derog derogatory
dial. dialect
dr dram

E

E East, Eastern
E English
eg for example
Eng English, England
esp especially
etc etcetera
euph euphemistic

F

f femto-
F Fahrenheit
F Farad
fem feminine
fl oz fluid ounce
fml formal
ft foot

G

gall gallon
Gen Genesis
gr grain

H

h hour
ha hectare
hp horsepower
humor humorous
Hz hertz

I

ie that is
imper imperative
in inch
Ind Indian
indef indefinite
indic indicative
infin infinitive
infml informal
interj interjection
interrog interrogative
Isa Isaiah

J

J joule
Jer Jeremiah
journ journalistic

K

k kilo-
kg kilogram
km kilometre

L

l litre
lat latitude
lb pound
Lk Luke
long longitude

M

m metre
m milli-
M mega-
masc masculine
MHz megahertz
mi mile
Mid Eng Midlands
Mid US Mid United States
mil military
min minute
ml millilitre
mm millimetre
mph miles per hour
Mt Matthew
Mt Mount

N

n noun
N North, Northern
N Newton
NAm North American
naut nautical
NE Eng North East England
neg negative
N Eng North England
neut neuter
New Eng US New England, United States
NW Eng North West England
NW US North West United States
NZ New Zealand

O

obs obsolete
occas occasionally
orig original, originally
oz ounce

P

p pence
Pa pascal
part participle
pass passive
perf perfect
pers person
phr(s) phrase(s)
pl plural
pm post meridiem
pp past participle
prep preposition
pres present
prob probably
pron pronoun
prp present participle
pt pint

Q

qr quarter
qt quart

R

RC Roman Catholic
refl reflexive
rel relative
Rom Roman
RSV Revised Standard Version
RV Revised Version

S

s second
S South, Southern
SAfr South Africa, South African

sby somebody
Sc Scots
Scot Scotland, Scottish
SEU S Survey of English Usage (Spoken)
SEU W Survey of English Usage (Written)
Shak Shakespeare
SI Système International d'Unités
sing. singular
specif specifically
st stone
St Saint
Ste Sainte
sthg something
subj subjunctive
substand substandard
superl superlative
S US Southern United States
SW Eng South Western England
SW US South Western United States

T

tech technical
TES Times Educational Supplement
THES Times Higher Education Supplement
TLS Times Literary Supplement
trans translation

U

UK United Kingdom
US United States
USA United States of America
usu usually

V

V volt
va verbal auxiliary
var variant
vb verb
vi verb intransitive
voc vocative
vt verb transitive
vulg vulgar

W

W watt
W West, Western
WI West Indian
W US Western United States
WWI World War 1
WWII World War 2

Y

yd yard

A

¹a *n, pl* **a's, as** *often cap* **1a** (a graphic representation of or device for reproducing) the 1st letter of the English alphabet **b** a speech counterpart of orthographic *a* **2** the 6th note of a C-major scale **3** one designated *a*, esp as the 1st in order or class **4** a grade rating a student's work as superior

²a *indefinite article* **1** one – used before singular nouns when the referent is unspecified ⟨~ *man overboard*⟩ and before number collectives and some numbers ⟨~ *great many*⟩ **2** the same ⟨*birds of* ~ *feather*⟩ ⟨*swords all of* ~ *length*⟩ **3a**(1) any ⟨~ *bicycle has 2 wheels*⟩ **(2)** one single ⟨*can't see* ~ *thing*⟩ **b** one particular ⟨*glucose is* ~ *simple sugar*⟩ **c** – used before the gerund or infinitive of a verb to denote a period or occurrence of the activity concerned ⟨*had* ~ *little weep*⟩ ⟨*heard* ~ *crashing of gears*⟩ **4** – used before a proper name to denote (1) membership of a class ⟨*I was* ~ *Burton before my marriage* – *SEU S*⟩ (2) resemblance ⟨~ *Daniel come to judgment*⟩ (3) one named but not otherwise known ⟨~ *Mrs Jones*⟩ **5** – used before a pair of items to be considered as a unit ⟨~ *cap and gown*⟩ *USE* used before words or letter sequences with an initial consonant sound; compare ¹AN 1

³a *prep* **1** PER **2** ⟨*twice* ~ *week*⟩ **2** *chiefly dial* on, in, at *USE* used before words or letter sequences with an initial consonant sound

⁴a *prep* of – often attached to the preceding word ⟨*kinda*⟩ ⟨*lotta*⟩

A *n or adj* (a film that is) certified in Britain as suitable for all ages but requiring parental guidance for children under 14

¹a- *prefix* **1** on; in; at; to ⟨*abed*⟩ ⟨*ajar*⟩ **2** in (such) a state or condition ⟨*ablaze*⟩ **3** in (such) a manner ⟨*aloud*⟩ **4** in the act or process of ⟨*gone a-hunting*⟩ ⟨*atingle*⟩ *USE* in predicative adjectives and adverbs

²a-, an- *prefix* not; without ⟨*asexual*⟩ ⟨*amoral*⟩ – a- usu before consonants other than *h*, an- before vowels and usu before *h* ⟨*anaesthetic*⟩ ⟨*anhedral*⟩

-a *suffix* (→ *n*) oxide ⟨*thoria*⟩ ⟨*alumina*⟩

A1 *adj* **1** *of a ship* having the highest possible classification of seaworthiness for insurance purposes **2** of the finest quality; first-rate

AA *n or adj* (a film that is) certified in Britain as suitable for people over 14

ab- *prefix* from; away; off ⟨*abaxial*⟩ ⟨*abduct*⟩

aback *adv* **1** unintentionally in a position to catch the wind on what is normally the leeward side – used with reference to a sail **2** by surprise – + take ⟨*was taken* ~ *by her sharp retort*⟩

abacus *n, pl* **abaci, abacuses** **1** a slab that forms the uppermost part of the capital of a column **2** an instrument for performing calculations by sliding counters along rods or in grooves

¹abandon *vt* **1** to give up completely, esp with the intention of never resuming or reclaiming ⟨~ed *his studies*⟩ ⟨*slow to* ~ *their native language*⟩ **2** to leave, often in the face of danger ⟨~ *ship*⟩ **3** to forsake or desert, esp in spite of an allegiance, duty, or responsibility ⟨*endure the ignominy of his* ~ing *her* – D H Lawrence⟩ ⟨~ed *to a humble death*⟩ **4** to give (oneself) over unrestrainedly *to* an emotion or activity – **abandoner** *n*, **abandonment** *n*

²abandon *n* freedom from constraint or inhibitions ⟨*danced with gay* ~⟩

abandoned *adj* wholly free from restraint ⟨*an* ~ *party*⟩

abase *vt* to bring lower in rank, office, prestige, or esteem – **abasement** *n*

abash *vt* to destroy the self-possession or self-confidence of; disconcert – usu pass – **abashment** *n*

abate *vt* **1** to put an end to; abolish ⟨~ *a nuisance*⟩ **2** to reduce in amount, intensity, or degree; moderate ⟨~ *a tax*⟩ ~ *vi* to decrease in force or intensity ⟨*the wind has* ~d⟩ – **abatement** *n*, **abater** *n*

abattoir *n* a slaughterhouse

abbess *n* the female superior of a convent of nuns

abbey *n* **1** a religious community governed by an abbot or abbess **2** the buildings, esp the church, of a (former) monastery ⟨*Westminster* ~⟩

abbot *n* the superior of an abbey of monks

abbreviate *vt* to make briefer; *esp* to reduce to a shorter form intended to stand for the whole – **abbreviator** *n*

abbreviation *n* a shortened form of a written word or phrase ⟨*amt is an* ~ *for* amount⟩

ABC *n, pl* **ABC's, ABCs** **1** the alphabet **2** the rudiments of a subject – usu pl with sing. meaning in NAm

abdicate *vt* to relinquish (e g sovereign power) formally ~ *vi* to renounce a throne, dignity, etc – **abdicator** *n*, **abdicable** *adj*, **abdication** *n*

abdomen *n* **1** (the cavity of) the part of the body between the thorax and the pelvis that contains the liver, gut, etc **2** the rear part of the body behind the thorax in an insect or other arthropod – **abdominal** *adj*, **abdominally** *adv*

abduct *vt* **1** to carry off secretly or by force **2** to draw away (e g a limb) from a position near or parallel to the main part of the body – **abductor** *n*, **abduction** *n*

abeam *adv or adj* on a line at right angles to the length of a ship or aircraft

abed *adv or adj* in bed

aberrant *adj* **1** deviating from the right or normal way ⟨~ *behaviour*⟩ **2** diverging from the usual or natural type – **aberrance** *n*, **aberrancy** *n*, **aberrantly** *adv*

aberration *n* **1** being aberrant, esp with respect to a moral standard or normal state **2** the failure of a mirror, lens, etc to produce exact correspondence between an object and its image **3** (an instance of) unsoundness or disorder of the mind **4** a small periodic change of apparent position in celestial bodies due to the combined effect of the motion of light and the motion of the observer **5** an aberrant organ or individual; SPORT 5 – **aberrational** *adj*

abet *vt* **-tt-** to give active encouragement or approval to ⟨*aided and* ~ted *in the crime by his wife*⟩ – **abetment** *n*, **abettor, abetter** *n*

abeyance *n* temporary inactivity; suspension ⟨*a rule in* ~ *since 1935*⟩

abhor *vt* **-rr-** to regard with extreme repugnance; loathe – **abhorrer** *n*

abhorrent *adj* **1** opposed, contrary *to* **2** causing horror; repugnant ⟨*acts* ~ *to every right-minded person*⟩ – **abhorrence** *n*, **abhorrently** *adv*

abide *vb* **abode, abided** *vt* to bear patiently; tolerate – used negatively ⟨*can't* ~ *such bigots*⟩ ~ *vi* **1** to remain stable or fixed in a state **2** *archaic* to dwell – **abider** *n* – **abide by** to remain true to; comply with ⟨*abide by the rules*⟩ ⟨*abide by one's word*⟩

abiding *adj* enduring ⟨*an* ~ *interest in nature*⟩ – **abidingly** *adv*

ability *n* **1a** being able; *esp* physical, mental, or legal power to perform ⟨*doubted her* ~ *to walk so far*⟩ **b** natural or acquired competence in doing; skill ⟨*a man of great* ~⟩ **2** a natural talent; aptitude – usu pl

-ability *also* **-ibility** *suffix* (*vb, adj* → *n*) capacity, suitability, or tendency to (so act or be acted on) ⟨*readability*⟩ ⟨*excitability*⟩

abject adj 1 showing utter hopelessness; wretched, miserable ⟨~ poverty⟩ 2 despicable, degraded 3 very humble, esp to the point of servility ⟨an ~ apology⟩ – **abjection** n, **abjectly** adv, **abjectness** n

abjure vt to renounce on oath or reject formally (e g a claim, opinion, or allegiance) – **abjurer** n, **abjuration** n

ablative n (a form in) a grammatical case expressing typically separation, source, cause, or instrument – **ablative** adj

ablaut n a systematic variation of vowels in the same root, esp in the Indo-European languages, usu accompanied by differences in use or meaning (e g in sing, sang, sung, song)

ablaze adj or adv 1 on fire 2 radiant with light or bright colour

able adj 1 having sufficient power, skill, resources, or qualifications to ⟨with more money I was better ~ to help⟩ 2 marked by intelligence, knowledge, skill, or competence ⟨the ~st lawyer in London⟩ – **ably** adv

-able also **-ible** suffix 1 (vb → adj) fit for, able to, liable to, or worthy to (so act or be acted on) ⟨breakable⟩ ⟨reliable⟩ ⟨get-at-able⟩ 2 (n → adj) marked by, providing, or possessing (a specified quality or attribute) ⟨knowledgeable⟩ ⟨comfortable⟩ – **-ably** suffix (vb, n → adv)

able-bodied adj physically strong and healthy; fit

able seaman, able-bodied seaman n a trained person ranking below noncommissioned officer in the British navy

ablution n the washing of (a part of) one's body, esp in a ritual purification – **ablutionary** adj

abnegation n renunciation, self-denial

abnormal adj deviating from the normal or average; esp markedly and disturbingly irregular ⟨~ behaviour⟩ – **abnormally** adv, **abnormality** n

abo n, pl **abos** often cap, Austr an Australian aborigine – chiefly derog – **abo** adj

aboard adv or prep 1 on, onto, or within (a ship, aircraft, train, or road vehicle) ⟨climb ~⟩ ⟨they were ~ a plane bound for Rome⟩ 2 alongside

abode n a home, residence – fml

abolish vt to do away with (e g a law or custom) wholly; annul – **abolishable** adj, **abolisher** n, **abolishment** n, **abolition** n, **abolitionary** adj

A-bomb n ATOM BOMB

abominable adj 1 worthy of or causing disgust or hatred; detestable 2 very disagreeable or unpleasant – esp in colloquial exaggeration ⟨~ weather⟩ – **abominably** adv

abominable snowman n, often cap A&S a large manlike animal reported as existing high in the Himalayas

abominate vt to hate or loathe intensely and unremittingly; abhor – **abominator** n

abomination n 1 sthg abominable; esp a detestable or shameful action 2 extreme disgust and hatred; loathing

¹aboriginal adj 1 indigenous 2 of esp Australian aborigines – **aboriginally** adv

²aboriginal n an (Australian) aborigine

aborigine n 1 an indigenous inhabitant, esp as contrasted with an invading or colonizing people; specif, often cap a member of the indigenous people of Australia 2 pl the original fauna and flora of an area

¹abort vi 1 to expel a premature nonviable foetus 2 to fail to develop completely; shrink away ~ vt 1 to induce the abortion of (a foetus) 2a to end prematurely ⟨~ a project⟩ b to stop in the early stages ⟨~ a disease⟩

²abort n the premature termination of a mission or procedure involving a military aircraft or spacecraft

abortion n 1 the spontaneous or induced expulsion of a

foetus 2 a monstrosity ⟨monstrously carved ~s – Country Life⟩ 3 (the result of) an arresting of development of a part, process, etc – **abortionist** n

abortive adj 1 fruitless, unsuccessful ⟨an ~ attempt⟩ 2 imperfectly formed or developed – **abortively** adv, **abortiveness** n

abound vi 1 to be present in large numbers or in great quantity ⟨wild animals ~⟩ 2 to be amply supplied – + in ⟨the old edition ~ed in coloured pictures – TLS⟩ 3 to be crowded or infested with ⟨the attics ~ with rats⟩

¹about adv 1 ROUND 2, 3c 2 in succession or rotation; alternately ⟨turn and turn ~⟩ 3 approximately ⟨cost ~ £5⟩ 4 almost ⟨~ starved⟩ ⟨~ as interesting as a wet Sunday⟩ 5 in the vicinity ⟨there was nobody ~⟩

²about prep 1 on every side of; surrounding ⟨the wall ~ the prison⟩ 2a in the vicinity of b on or near the person of ⟨have you a match ~ you?⟩ c in the make-up of ⟨a mature wisdom ~ him⟩ d at the command of ⟨has his wits ~ him⟩ 3a engaged in ⟨knows what she's ~⟩ b on the verge of – + to ⟨~ to join the army⟩ 4a with regard to, concerning ⟨a story ~ rabbits⟩ b intimately concerned with ⟨politics is ~ capturing votes⟩ 5 over or in different parts of ⟨walked ~ the streets⟩ 6 chiefly NAm – used with the negative to express intention or determination ⟨is not ~ to quit⟩

³about adj 1 moving from place to place; specif out of bed 2 in existence, evidence, or circulation ⟨skateboards weren't ~ long⟩

about-face vi or n, chiefly NAm (to) about-turn

about-turn n 1 a 180° turn to the right, esp as a drill movement 2 chiefly Br a reversal of direction, policy, or opinion ⟨a massive ~ on the Stock Exchange – Daily Mirror⟩ – **about-turn** vi

¹above adv 1a in the sky overhead b in or to heaven 2a in or to a higher place b higher on the same or an earlier page c upstairs ⟨the flat ~⟩ 3 in or to a higher rank or number ⟨30 and ~⟩ 4 upstage 5 archaic besides; IN ADDITION

²above prep 1 higher than the level of ⟨rose ~ the clouds⟩ ⟨shout ~ the noise⟩ 2 OVER 3 ⟨values safety ~ excitement⟩ ⟨nothing ~ £5⟩ 3 beyond, transcending ⟨~ criticism⟩ ⟨the lecture was ~ me⟩ 4a superior to (e g in rank) b too proud or honourable to stoop to 5 upstream from – **above oneself** excessively self-satisfied

³above n, pl **above** 1a sthg (written) above ⟨the ~ are the main facts⟩ b a person whose name is written above 2a a higher authority b heaven

⁴above adj written higher on the same, or on a preceding, page

aboveboard adj free from all traces of deceit or dishonesty – **above board** adv

abovementioned adj aforementioned

abracadabra n a magical charm or incantation – used interjectionally as an accompaniment to conjuring tricks

abrade vt to roughen, irritate, or wear away, esp by friction – **abradable** adj, **abrader** n

abrasion n 1 a wearing, grinding, or rubbing away by friction 2 an abraded area of the skin or mucous membrane

¹abrasive adj tending to abrade; causing irritation ⟨an ~ personality⟩ – **abrasively** adv, **abrasiveness** n

²abrasive n a substance (e g emery) that may be used for grinding away, smoothing, or polishing

abreast adv or adj 1 side by side and facing in the same direction ⟨columns of men 5 ~⟩ 2 up-to-date in attainment or information ⟨keeps ~ of the latest trends⟩

abridge vt 1 to reduce in scope; curtail ⟨attempts to ~

the right of free speech⟩ **2** to shorten by omission of words without sacrifice of sense; condense – **abridger** *n*

abridgment, abridgement *n* a shortened form of a work retaining the sense and unity of the original

abroad *adv or adj* **1** over a wide area; widely **2** away from one's home; out of doors ⟨*few people ~ at this hour*⟩ **3** beyond the boundaries of one's country **4** in wide circulation; about ⟨*the idea has got ~*⟩

abrogate *vt* to abolish by authoritative action; annul, repeal – **abrogation** *n*

abrupt *adj* **1** ending as if sharply cut off; truncated ⟨*~ plant filaments*⟩ **2a** occurring without warning; unexpected ⟨*~ weather changes*⟩ **b** unceremoniously curt ⟨*an ~ manner*⟩ **c** marked by sudden changes in subject matter **3** rising or dropping sharply; steep – **abruptly** *adv*, **abruptness** *n*

abscess *n* a pocket of pus surrounded by inflamed tissue – **abscessed** *adj*

abscond *vi* to depart secretly, esp so as to evade retribution ⟨*~ed with the funds*⟩ – **absconder** *n*

absence *n* **1** the state of being absent **2** the period of time that one is absent **3** a lack ⟨*an ~ of detail*⟩

absence of mind *n* inattention to present surroundings or occurrences

¹**absent** *adj* **1** not present or attending; missing **2** not existing; lacking **3** preoccupied – **absently** *adv*

²**absent** *vt* to take or keep (oneself) away – usu + *from* ⟨*~ed himself from morning prayers*⟩

absentee *n* one who is absent or who absents him-/herself – **absentee** *adj*

absenteeism *n* persistent and deliberate absence from work or duty

absentminded *adj* lost in thought and unaware of one's surroundings or actions; forgetful; *also* given to absence of mind – **absentmindedly** *adv*, **absentmindedness** *n*

absinthe, absinth *n* **1** WORMWOOD¹ **2** a green liqueur flavoured with wormwood or a substitute, aniseed, and other aromatics

absolute *adj* **1a** perfect ⟨*~ bliss*⟩ **b** (relatively) pure or unmixed ⟨*~ alcohol*⟩ **c** outright, unmitigated ⟨*an ~ lie*⟩ **2** completely free from constitutional or other restraint ⟨*an ~ monarch*⟩ **3** standing apart from a usual syntactic relation with other words or sentence elements **4** having no restriction, exception, or qualification ⟨*~ ownership*⟩ **5** positive, unquestionable ⟨*~ proof*⟩ **6** being self-sufficient and free of external references or relationships ⟨*an ~ term in logic*⟩ **7** relating to a temperature scale that has absolute zero as its lower reference point ⟨*10° ~*⟩ – **absolute** *n*, **absoluteness** *n*

absolutely *adv* totally, completely – often used to express emphatic agreement

absolute zero *n* the lowest temperature theoretically possible at which there is a complete absence of heat and which is equivalent to about –273.16°C or 0°K

absolution *n* the act of absolving; *specif* a declaration of forgiveness of sins pronounced by a priest

absolutism *n* (the theory favouring) government by an absolute ruler or authority – **absolutist** *n or adj*, **absolutistic** *adj*

absolve *vt* **1** to set free *from* an obligation or the consequences of guilt **2** to declare (a sin) of (a person) forgiven by absolution – **absolver** *n*

absorb *vt* **1** to take in and make part of an existing whole; incorporate **2a** to suck up or take up ⟨*plant roots ~ water*⟩ **b** to assimilate; TAKE IN **3** to engage or occupy wholly ⟨*~ed in thought*⟩ **4** to receive and transform (sound, radiant energy, etc) without reflecting or transmitting ⟨*the earth ~s the sun's rays*⟩ ⟨*a sound-absorbing surface*⟩ – **absorbable** *adj*, **absorber** *n*, **absorbability** *n*

absorbent *also* **absorbant** *n or adj* (sthg) able to absorb a liquid, gas, etc – **absorbency** *n*

absorbing *adj* engaging one's full attention; engrossing – **absorbingly** *adv*

absorption *n* **1** absorbing or being absorbed **2** total involvement of the mind ⟨*~ in his work*⟩ – **absorptive** *adj*

abstain *vi* **1** to refrain deliberately, and often with an effort of self-denial, *from* ⟨*resolved to ~ from intoxicating liquor*⟩ **2** to refrain from using one's vote – **abstainer** *n*

abstemious *adj* sparing, esp in eating or drinking; marked by abstinence – **abstemiously** *adv*

abstention *n* **1** abstaining – often + *from* **2** an instance of withholding a vote – **abstentious** *adj*

abstinence *also* **abstinency** *n* **1** voluntary forbearance, esp from indulgence of appetite or from eating some foods – often + *from* **2** habitual abstaining from intoxicating beverages – esp in *total abstinence* – **abstinent** *adj*, **abstinently** *adv*

¹**abstract** *adj* **1a** detached from any specific instance or object ⟨*~ entity*⟩ **b** difficult to understand; abstruse ⟨*~ problems*⟩ **c** ideal ⟨*~ justice*⟩ **2** *of a noun* naming a quality, state, or action rather than a thing; not concrete ⟨*the word poem is concrete, poetry is ~*⟩ **3** theoretical rather than practical ⟨*~ science*⟩ **4** having little or no element of pictorial representation – **abstractly** *adv*, **abstractness** *n*

²**abstract** *n* **1** a summary of points (e g of a piece of writing) **2** an abstract concept or state **3** an abstract composition or creation

³**abstract** *vt* **1** to remove, separate **2** to consider in the abstract **3** to make an abstract of; summarize **4** to draw away the attention of **5** to steal, purloin – *euph* – **abstractor, abstracter** *n*

abstracted *adj* preoccupied, absentminded ⟨*the ~ look of a professor*⟩ – **abstractedly** *adv*, **abstractedness** *n*

abstraction *n* **1** an abstract idea or term stripped of its concrete manifestations **2** absentmindedness **3** ²ABSTRACT 3 – **abstractionism** *n*, **abstractionist** *n*, **abstractive** *adj*

abstruse *adj* difficult to understand; recondite – **abstrusely** *adv*, **abstruseness** *n*

¹**absurd** *adj* **1** ridiculously unreasonable or incongruous; silly **2** lacking order or value; meaningless – **absurdity** *n*, **absurdly** *adv*, **absurdness** *n*

²**absurd** *n* the state or condition in which human beings exist in an irrational and meaningless universe, and in which their life has no meaning outside their own existence – **absurdism** *n*, **absurdist** *n or adj*

abundance *n* **1** an ample quantity; a profusion **2** affluence, wealth **3** the relative degree of plentifulness of a living organism, substance, etc in an area

abundant *adj* **1a** marked by great plenty (e g of resources) ⟨*a fair and ~ land*⟩ **b** amply supplied *with*; abounding *in* **2** occurring in abundance ⟨*~ rainfall*⟩ – **abundantly** *adv*

¹**abuse** *vt* **1** to attack in words; revile **2** to put to a wrong or improper use ⟨*~ a privilege*⟩ **3** to use so as to injure or damage; maltreat ⟨*~ a dog*⟩ – **abuser** *n*

²**abuse** *n* **1** a corrupt practice or custom **2** improper use or treatment; misuse ⟨*drug ~*⟩ **3** vehemently expressed condemnation or disapproval ⟨*greeted them with a torrent of ~*⟩ **4** physical maltreatment – **abusive** *adj*, **abusively** *adv*, **abusiveness** *n*

abut *vb* **-tt-** *vi* **1** *of an area* to touch along a boundary; border – + *on* or *upon* ⟨*land ~s on the road*⟩ **2** *of a structure* **a** to terminate at a point of contact; be adjacent – + *on* or *against* ⟨*the town hall ~s on the church*⟩ **b** to

lean for support – + *on* or *upon* ⟨*the neighbours' shed* ~s *on our wall*⟩ – *vt* to border on; touch – **abutter** *n*
abutment *n* **1** the place at which abutting occurs **2** the part of a structure that directly receives thrust or pressure (e g of an arch)
abysmal *adj* **1** deplorably great ⟨~ *ignorance*⟩ **2** immeasurably bad ⟨*standard of writing was* ~ – *Punch*⟩ – **abysmally** *adv*
abyss *n* **1** the infernal regions or chaos of the old cosmogonies, thought of as a bottomless pit **2a** an immeasurably deep gulf **b** moral or emotional depths ⟨*an* ~ *of hopelessness*⟩
¹**-ac** *suffix* (→ *n*) one affected with ⟨*maniac*⟩ ⟨*haemophiliac*⟩
²**-ac** *suffix* (→ *adj*) of or relating to ⟨*cardiac*⟩ ⟨*iliac*⟩
acacia *n* **1** any of a genus of woody leguminous plants of warm regions with white or yellow flowers **2** GUM ARA-BIC
¹**academic** *also* **academical** *adj* **1a** of an institution of higher learning **b** scholarly **c** very learned but inexperienced in practical matters ⟨~ *thinkers*⟩ **2** conventional, formal ⟨*an* ~ *painting*⟩ **3** theoretical with no practical or useful bearing ⟨*an* ~ *question*⟩ **4** chiefly NAm of liberal rather than technical or vocational studies – **academically** *adv*, **academicize** *vt*
²**academic** *n* a member (of the teaching staff) of an institution of higher learning
academician *n* a member of an academy for the advancement of science, art, or literature
academy *n* **1** *cap* **a** the school for advanced education founded by Plato **b** the philosophical doctrines associated with Plato's Academy **2a** a secondary school; *esp* a private high school – now only in names **b** a college in which special subjects or skills are taught ⟨*an* ~ *of music*⟩ **3** a society of learned people organized to promote the arts or sciences
accede *vi* **1** to become a party (e g to a treaty) **2** to express approval or give consent, often in response to urging **3** to enter on an office or position; *esp* to become monarch ⟨~ *to the throne*⟩ *USE* usu + *to*
accelerate *vt* **1** to bring about at an earlier time **2** to increase the speed of **3** to hasten the progress, development, or growth of ~ *vi* **1** to move faster; gain speed **2** to increase more rapidly ⟨*believed inflation was* accelerating⟩ – **accelerative** *adj*
acceleration *n* (the rate of) change, specif increase, of velocity ⟨*this car has good* ~⟩
accelerator *n* **1a** a pedal in a motor vehicle that controls the speed of the motor **2** a substance that speeds up a chemical reaction **3** an apparatus for giving high velocities to charged particles (e g electrons)
¹**accent** *n* **1** a distinctive manner of expression; *specif* a distinctive pattern in inflection, tone, or choice of words, esp as characteristic of a regional or national area **2a** prominence given to 1 syllable over others by stress or a change in pitch **b** greater stress given to 1 musical note **c** rhythmically significant stress on the syllables of a verse **3a** *accent*, **accent mark** a mark added to a letter (e g in *à*, *ñ*, *ç*) to indicate how it should be pronounced **b** a symbol used to indicate musical stress **4** a sharply contrasting detail ⟨*special concern or attention; emphasis* ⟨*an* ~ *on youth*⟩ – **accentless** *adj*
²**accent** *vt* **1a** to pronounce (a vowel, syllable, or word) with accent; stress **b** to mark with a written or printed accent **2** to make more prominent; emphasize
accentuate *vt* to accent, emphasize – **accentuation** *n*
accept *vt* **1a** to agree to receive ⟨~ *a gift*⟩ ⟨~ *a suitor*⟩; *also* to agree to ⟨~ *an invitation*⟩ **b** to be able or designed to take or hold (sthg applied or inserted) ⟨*machine* ~s

only pennies⟩ **2** to give admittance or approval to ⟨~ *her as one of the group*⟩ **3a** to endure without protest; accommodate oneself to ⟨~ *poor living conditions*⟩ **b** to regard as proper, normal, or inevitable **c** to recognize as true, factual, or adequate ⟨*refused to* ~ *my explanation*⟩ **4** to undertake the responsibility of ⟨~ *a job*⟩ ~ *vi* to receive favourably sthg offered
acceptable *adj* **1** capable or worthy of being accepted; satisfactory **2** welcome or pleasing to the receiver ⟨*compliments are always* ~⟩ **3** tolerable – **acceptableness** *n*, **acceptably** *adv*, **acceptability** *n*
acceptance *n* **1** accepting, approval **2** acceptability **3** agreement to the act or offer of another so that the parties become legally bound
¹**access** *n* **1** a fit of intense feeling; an outburst ⟨*an* ~ *of rage*⟩ **2a** freedom to approach, reach, or make use of sthg ⟨~ *to classified information*⟩ **b** a means (e g a doorway or channel) of access **c** the state of being readily reached or obtained ⟨*the building is not easy of* ~⟩
²**access** *vt* to get at; gain access to ⟨*accumulator and index registers can be* ~ed *by the programmer* – *Datamation*⟩
accessible *adj* **1** capable of being reached ⟨~ *by rail*⟩ **2** of a form that can be readily grasped intellectually **3** able to be influenced ⟨~ *to persuasion*⟩ – **accessibly** *adv*, **accessibility** *n*
¹**accession** *n* **1** sthg added; an acquisition; *specif* a book added to a library **2** becoming joined **3** the act by which a nation becomes party to an agreement already in force **4a** an increase due to sthg added **b** acquisition of property by addition to existing property **5** the act of entering on a high office ⟨*his* ~ *to the Papacy*⟩ **6** assent, agreement – *fml* – **accessional** *adj*
²**accession** *vt* to record (e g books) in order of acquisition
¹**accessory** *n* an inessential object or device that adds to the beauty, convenience, or effectiveness of sthg else ⟨*car accessories*⟩ ⟨*clothing accessories*⟩
²**accessory** *adj* aiding or contributing in a secondary way; supplementary, subordinate
accidence *n* the part of grammar that deals with inflections
accident *n* **1a** an event occurring by chance or arising from unknown causes **b** lack of intention or necessity; chance ⟨*met by* ~ *rather than by design*⟩ **2** an unexpected happening causing loss or injury **3** a nonessential property or condition of sthg **4** an irregularity of a surface (e g of the moon)
¹**accidental** *adj* **1** arising incidentally; nonessential **2a** occurring unexpectedly or by chance **b** happening without intent or through carelessness and often with unfortunate results – **accidentally** *adv*, **accidentalness** *n*
²**accidental** *n* **1** ACCIDENT 3 **2** (a sign indicating) a note altered to sharp, flat, or natural and foreign to a key indicated by a key signature
accident-prone *adj* having personality traits that predispose to accidents
¹**acclaim** *vt* **1** to applaud, praise **2** to hail or proclaim by acclamation ⟨~ed *her Queen*⟩ – **acclaimer** *n*
²**acclaim** *n* ACCLAMATION 1
acclamation *n* **1** a loud expression of praise, goodwill, or assent **2** an overwhelming affirmative vote by cheers or applause rather than by ballot ⟨*motion was carried by* ~⟩
acclimatize, -ise *vb* to adapt to a new climate or situation – **acclimatizer** *n*, **acclimatization** *n*
acclivity *n* an ascending slope
accolade *n* **1** a ceremony marking the conferral of knighthood, in which each of the candidate's shoulders is

touched with a sword **2a** a mark of acknowledgment or honour; an award **b** an expression of strong praise
accommodate *vt* **1** to make fit, suitable, or congruous *to* **2** to bring into agreement or concord; reconcile **3a** to give help to; oblige *with* **b** to provide with lodgings; house **4** to have or make adequate room for **5** to give consideration to; allow for – **accommodative** *adj*, **accommodativeness** *n*
accommodating *adj* helpful, obliging – **accommodatingly** *adv*
accommodation *n* **1a** lodging, housing – usu pl with sing. meaning in NAm **b** space, premises ⟨*office* ~⟩ **2a** sthg needed or desired for convenience; a facility **b** an adaptation, adjustment **c** a settlement, agreement **d** a bank loan **e** the (range of) automatic adjustment of the eye, esp by changes in the amount by which the lens bends light, for seeing at different distances – **accommodational** *adj*
accompaniment *n* **1** a subordinate instrumental or vocal part supporting or complementing a principal voice or instrument **2** an addition intended to give completeness; a complement
accompany *vt* **1** to go with as an escort or companion **2** to perform an accompaniment to or for **3a** to make an addition to; supplement *with* **b** *of a thing* to happen, exist, or be found with ⟨*the pictures that* ~ *the text*⟩ ~ *vi* to perform an accompaniment – **accompanist** *n*
accomplice *n* sby who collaborates with another, esp in wrongdoing
accomplish *vt* **1** to bring to a successful conclusion; achieve **2** to complete, cover (a measure of time or distance) – **accomplishable** *adj*, **accomplisher** *n*
accomplished *adj* **1** fully effected; completed ⟨*an* ~ *fact*⟩ **2a** skilled, proficient ⟨*an* ~ *dancer*⟩ **b** having many social accomplishments
accomplishment *n* **1** completion, fulfilment **2** an achievement **3** an acquired ability or esp social skill
¹**accord** *vt* **1** to grant, concede ⟨~ed *them permission*⟩ **2** to give, award ⟨~ed *her a warm welcome*⟩ ~ *vi* to be consistent *with*
²**accord** *n* **1a** ACCORDANCE **1 b** a formal treaty of agreement **2** balanced interrelationship (e g of colours or sounds); harmony – **of one's own accord** of one's own volition; unbidden – **with one accord** with the consent or agreement of all
accordance *n* **1** agreement, conformity ⟨*in* ~ *with a rule*⟩ **2** the act of granting
according as *conj* **1** in accordance with the way in which **2** depending on how or whether
accordingly *adv* **1** as suggested; appropriately **2** consequently, so
according to *prep* **1** in conformity with **2** as declared by **3** depending on
accordion *n* a portable keyboard wind instrument in which the wind is forced past free reeds by means of a hand-operated bellows – **accordionist** *n*
accost *vt* **1** to approach and speak to, esp boldly or challengingly **2** *of a prostitute* to solicit
¹**account** *n* **1** a record of debits and credits relating to a particular item, person, or concern **2** a list of items of expenditure to be balanced against income – usu pl ⟨*doing her monthly* ~ s⟩ **3a** a periodically rendered calculation listing purchases and credits ⟨*a grocery* ~⟩ **b** business, patronage ⟨*glad to get that customer's* ~⟩ **4** a business arrangement whereby money is deposited in, and may be withdrawn from, a bank, building society, etc **5** a commission to carry out a particular business operation (e g an advertising campaign) given by one company to another **6** value, importance ⟨*a man of no* ~⟩ **7** profit, advantage

⟨*turned his wit to good* ~⟩ **8** careful thought; consideration ⟨*left nothing out of* ~⟩ **9a** a statement explaining one's conduct ⟨*render an* ~⟩ **b** a statement of facts or events; a relation ⟨*a newspaper* ~⟩ **10** hearsay, report – usu pl ⟨*by all* ~ s *a rich man*⟩ **11** a version, rendering ⟨*the pianist's sensitive* ~ *of it*⟩ – **on account of** due to; BECAUSE OF – **on no account** *or* **not on any account** under no circumstances – **on one's own account 1** on one's own behalf **2** at one's own risk – **on somebody's account** for sby's sake
²**account** *vt* to think of as; consider ⟨~ s *himself lucky*⟩ – **account for 1** to give an explanation or reason for **2** to be the sole or primary explanation for **3** to bring about the defeat, death, or destruction of ⟨accounted for **3** *of the attackers*⟩
accountable *adj* **1** responsible, answerable **2** explicable – **accountableness** *n*, **accountably** *adv*, **accountability** *n*
accountancy *n* the profession or practice of accounting
accountant *n* one who practises and is usu qualified in accounting
accoutrement, *NAm also* **accouterment** *n* equipment, trappings; *specif* a soldier's outfit excluding clothes and weapons – usu pl
accredit *vt* **1a** to give official authorization to or approval of **b** to send (esp an envoy) with credentials **c** to recognize or vouch for as conforming to a standard **2** to credit *with*, attribute *to* – **accreditable** *adj*, **accreditation** *n*
accretion *n* **1a** an increase in size caused by natural growth or the external adhesion or addition of matter **b** sthg added or stuck extraneously **2a** an increase in area of land owned, caused esp by the action of natural forces **b** an increase in an inheritor's share of an estate caused by a co-inheritor not claiming his/her share **3** the growth of separate particles or parts (e g of a plant) into one; concretion – **accretionary** *adj*, **accretive** *adj*
accrue *vi* **1** to come as an increase or addition to sthg; arise as a growth or result **2** to be periodically accumulated ⟨*interest has* ~ d *over the year*⟩ ~ *vt* to collect, accumulate – **accruable** *adj*, **accruement** *n*
accumulate *vt* to collect together gradually; amass ~ *vi* to increase in quantity or number
accumulation *n* **1** increase or growth caused by esp repeated or continuous addition; *specif* increase in capital from interest payments **2** sthg that has accumulated
accumulative *adj* **1** cumulative **2** tending or given to accumulation, esp of money – **accumulatively** *adv*, **accumulativeness** *n*
accumulator *n* **1** a part (e g in a computer) where numbers are added or stored **2** *Br* a rechargeable secondary electric cell; *also* a connected set of these **3** *Br* a bet whereby the winnings from one of a series of events are staked on the next event
accurate *adj* **1** free from error, esp as the result of care ⟨*an* ~ *estimate*⟩ **2** conforming precisely to truth or a measurable standard; exact ⟨~ *instruments*⟩ – **accurately** *adv*, **accurateness** *n*, **accuracy** *n*
accursed, accurst *adj* **1** under a curse; ill-fated **2** damnable, detestable – **accursedly** *adv*, **accursedness** *n*
accusation *n* a charge of wrongdoing; an allegation
¹**accusative** *adj* of or being the grammatical accusative
²**accusative** *n* (a form (e g *me*) in) a grammatical case expressing the direct object of a verb or of some prepositions
accuse *vt* to charge with a fault or crime; blame ⟨~ d *him of murder*⟩ – **accuser** *n*, **accusingly** *adv*
accused *n, pl* **accused** the defendant in a criminal case
accustom *vt* to make used *to* through use or experience; habituate – **accustomation** *n*

accustomed *adj* **1** customary, habitual **2** in the habit of; used *to* ⟨~ *to making decisions*⟩ – **accustomedness** *n*

¹ace *n* **1** a die face, playing card, or domino marked with 1 spot or pip; *also* the single spot or pip on any of these **2** (a point scored by) a shot, esp a service in tennis, that an opponent fails to touch **3** a combat pilot who has brought down at least 5 enemy aircraft **4** an expert or leading performer in a specified field ⟨a soccer ~⟩ – **ace in the hole** an effective argument or resource held in reserve – **within an ace of** on the point of; very near to ⟨*came within an ace of winning*⟩

²ace *vt* to score an ace against (an opponent)

³ace *adj* great, excellent – *infml* ⟨*their new album's really* ~⟩

acerbic *adj* **1** bitter or sour in taste **2** sharp or vitriolic in speech, temper, or manner – **acerbically** *adv*, **acerbity** *n*

acetate *n* **1** a salt or ester of acetic acid **2** (a textile fibre or gramophone record made from) cellulose acetate

acetic *adj* of or producing acetic acid or vinegar

acetic acid *n* a pungent liquid acid that is the major acid in vinegar

acetylene *n* a colourless unsaturated hydrocarbon gas used esp as a fuel (e g in oxyacetylene torches) – **acetylenic** *adj*

¹ache *vi* **1a** to suffer a usu dull persistent pain **b** to feel anguish or distress ⟨*heart* ~d *for her*⟩ **2** to yearn, long ⟨*aching to see you*⟩ – **achingly** *adv*

²ache *n* a usu dull persistent pain

achieve *vt* **1** to carry out successfully; accomplish **2** to obtain by effort; win – **achievable** *adj*, **achiever** *n*

achievement *n* **1** successful completion; accomplishment **2** sthg accomplished, esp by resolve, persistence, or courage; a feat **3** performance in a test or academic course **4** a coat of arms with its formal accompaniments (e g helm, crest, and supporters)

Achilles' heel *n* a person's only vulnerable point

Achilles tendon *n* the strong tendon joining the muscles in the calf to the heelbone

¹acid *adj* **1a** sour or sharp to the taste **b** sharp, biting, or sour in speech, manner, or disposition; caustic ⟨*an* ~ *wit*⟩ **2** of, like, containing, or being an acid ⟨~ *soil*⟩; *specif* having a pH of less than 7 **3** of, being, or made by a steelmaking process in which the furnace is lined with acidic material **4** *of rock* rich in silica – **acidly** *adv*, **acidness** *n*, **acidity** *n*

²acid *n* **1** a sour substance; *specif* any of various typically water-soluble and sour compounds having a pH of less than 7 that are capable of giving up a hydrogen ion to or accepting an unshared pair of electrons from a base to form a salt **2** LSD – *infml*

acidic *adj* **1** acid-forming **2** acid

acidify *vt* to make or convert into (an) acid – **acidifier** *n*, **acidification** *n*

acid test *n* a severe or crucial test (e g of value or suitability)

acidulate *vt* to make (slightly) acid – **acidulation** *n*

acidulous *adj* somewhat acid in taste or manner; caustic – **acidulosity** *n*

ack-ack *adj* antiaircraft

acknowledge *vt* **1** to admit knowledge of; concede to be true or valid **2** to recognize the status or claims of **3a** to express gratitude or obligation for **b** to show recognition of (e g by smiling or nodding) **c** to confirm receipt of – **acknowledgeable** *adj*

acknowledgment *also* **acknowledgement** *n* **1** recognition or favourable reception of an act or achievement **2** a thing done or given in recognition of sthg received **3** a declaration or avowal of a fact **4** an author's list of people

to whom he/she is indebted, usu appearing at the front of a book – usu pl with sing. meaning

acme *n* the highest point or stage; esp a perfect representative of a specified class or thing ⟨*was the* ~ *of courtesy*⟩

acne *n* a skin disorder found esp among adolescents, characterized by inflammation of the skin glands and hair follicles and causing red pustules, esp on the face and neck – **acned** *adj*

acolyte *n* **1** an assistant performing minor duties in a liturgical service **2** one who attends or assists; a follower

aconite *n* (a drug obtained from) monkshood – **aconitic** *adj*

acorn *n* the nut of the oak, usu seated in a hard woody cup

¹acoustic *also* **acoustical** *adj* **1** of sound, the sense of hearing, or acoustics **2** of or being a musical instrument whose sound is not electronically modified – **acoustically** *adv*

²acoustic *n* **1** *pl but sing in constr* the science of sound **2** the properties of a room, hall, etc that govern the quality of sound heard – usu pl with sing. meaning – **acoustician** *n*

acquaint *vt* to cause to know; make familiar *with* sthg ⟨~ *oneself with the law*⟩

acquaintance *n* **1** personal knowledge; familiarity **2a** *sing or pl in constr* the people with whom one is acquainted **b** a person whom one knows but who is not a particularly close friend – **acquaintanceship** *n* – **make the acquaintance of** to come to know; meet

acquiesce *vi* to submit or comply tacitly or passively – often + *in* – **acquiescence** *n*, **acquiescent** *adj*, **acquiescently** *adv*

acquire *vt* **1a** to gain or come into possession of, often by unspecified means; *also* to steal – *euph* **b** to gain as a new characteristic or ability, esp as a result of skill or hard work **2** to locate and hold (an object) in a detector ⟨~ *a target by radar*⟩ – **acquirable** *adj*, **acquirement** *n*

acquisition *n* **1** acquiring, gaining **2** sby or sthg acquired or gained, esp to one's advantage – **acquisitional** *adj*, **acquisitor** *n*

acquisitive *adj* keen or tending to acquire and possess – **acquisitively** *adv*, **acquisitiveness** *n*

acquit *vt* **-tt-** **1** to free from responsibility or obligation; *specif* to declare not guilty ⟨*the court* ~ted *him of the charge*⟩ **2** to conduct (oneself) in a specified, usu favourable, manner – **acquitter** *n*

acquittal *n* a judicial release from a criminal charge

acre *n* **1** *pl* lands, fields **2** a unit of area equal to 4840yd² (4046.86m²) **3** *pl* great quantities – *infml*

acreage *n* area in acres

acrid *adj* **1** unpleasantly pungent in taste or smell **2** violently bitter in manner or language; acrimonious – **acridly** *adv*, **acridness** *n*, **acridity** *n*

acrimony *n* caustic sharpness of manner or language resulting from anger or ill nature – **acrimonious** *adj*, **acrimoniously** *adv*, **acrimoniousness** *n*

acrobat *n* **1** one who performs gymnastic feats requiring skilful control of the body **2** one who nimbly and often too readily changes his position or viewpoint ⟨*a political* ~⟩

acrobatic *adj* **1** of or like an acrobat **2** very mobile ⟨~ *eyebrows* – *Punch*⟩ – **acrobatically** *adv*

acrobatics *n pl* **1** *sing or pl in constr* the art, performance, or activity of an acrobat **2** a spectacular performance involving great agility ⟨*contralto's vocal* ~⟩

acronym *n* a word (e g *radar*) formed from the initial letters of other words – **acronymic** adj, **acronymically** adv

¹across adv **1** from one side to the other crosswise **2** to or on the opposite side **3** so as to be understandable, acceptable, or successful

²across prep **1** from one side to the other of ⟨walk ~ the lawn⟩ **b** on the opposite side of ⟨lives ~ the street⟩ **2** so as to intersect at an angle ⟨sawed ~ the grain of the wood⟩ **3** into transitory contact with

acrostic n **1** a composition, usu in verse, in which sets of letters (e g the first of each line) form a word or phrase **2** a series of words of equal length arranged to read the same horizontally or vertically – **acrostic** also **acrostical** adj, **acrostically** adv

acrylic fibre n a synthetic textile fibre made by polymerization of acrylonitrile usu with other polymers

¹act n **1** a thing done; a deed **2** STATUTE 1; also a decree, edict **3** the process of doing ⟨caught in the very ~⟩ **4** often cap a formal record of sthg done or transacted **5a** any of the principal divisions of a play or opera **b** any of the successive parts or performances in an entertainment (e g a circus) **6** a display of affected behaviour; a pretence – **be/get in on the act** to be or deliberately become involved in a situation or undertaking, esp for one's own advantage

²act vt **1** to represent by action, esp on the stage **2** to feign, simulate **3** to play the part of (as if) in a play ⟨~ the fool⟩ ⟨~ Hamlet⟩ **4** to behave in a manner suitable to ⟨~ your age⟩ ~ vi **1a** to perform on the stage; engage in acting **b** to behave insincerely **2** to function or behave in a specified manner ⟨~ed generously⟩ **3** to perform a specified function; serve as **4** to be a substitute or representative for **5** to produce an effect ⟨wait for the medicine to ~⟩ – **actable** adj, **actability** n

¹acting adj holding a temporary rank or position ⟨~ president⟩

²acting n the art or practice of representing a character in a dramatic production

actinism n the property of esp visible radiant energy by which chemical changes are produced (e g in photography) – **actinic** adj

¹action n **1** a civil legal proceeding **2** the process of acting or working, esp to produce alteration by force or through a natural agency **3a** the mode of movement of the body **b** a function of (a part of) the body **4** a voluntary act; a deed ⟨know him by his ~s⟩ **5a** the state of functioning actively ⟨machine is out of ~⟩ **b** practical, often militant, activity, often directed towards a political end ⟨an ~ group⟩ **c** energetic activity; enterprise ⟨a man of ~⟩ **6a(1)** an engagement between troops or ships **(2)** ²COMBAT **3 b** (the unfolding of) the events in a play or work of fiction **7** an operating mechanism (e g of a gun or piano); also the manner in which it operates **8** (the most) lively or productive activity ⟨go where the ~ is⟩ – infml

²action vt to take action on; implement

actionable adj giving grounds for an action at law – **actionably** adv

action painting n abstract art in which spontaneous techniques (e g dribbling or smearing) are used to apply paint

activate vt **1** to make (more) active or reactive, esp in chemical or physical properties: e g **a** to make (a substance) radioactive **b** to aerate (sewage) so as to favour the growth of organisms that decompose organic matter **2** NAm to equip or put (troops) on active duty – **activator** n, **activation** n

active adj **1** characterized by practical action rather than by contemplation or speculation ⟨take an ~ interest in⟩ **2** quick in physical movement; lively **3a** marked by or

requiring vigorous activity ⟨~ sports⟩ **b** full of activity; busy ⟨an ~ life⟩ **4** having practical operation or results; effective ⟨an ~ law⟩ **5** of a volcano liable to erupt; not extinct **6** of a verb form or voice having as the subject the person or thing doing the action **7** of, in, or being full-time service, esp in the armed forces ⟨on ~ duty⟩ **8** capable of acting or reacting; liveliness **9** of an electronic device containing and sometimes directing a power source – **actively** adv, **activeness** n

²active n **1** an active verb form **2** the active voice of a language

activism n a doctrine or practice that emphasizes vigorous action (e g the use of mass demonstrations) in controversial, esp political, matters – **activist** n or adj, **activistic** adj

activity n **1** the quality or state of being active **2** vigorous or energetic action; liveliness **3** a pursuit in which a person is active – usu pl ⟨social activities⟩

act of God n a sudden event, esp a catastrophe, brought about by uncontrollable natural forces

actor, fem **actress** n one who represents a character in a dramatic production; esp one whose profession is acting – **actorish** adj

act out vt **1a** to represent in action ⟨children act out what they read⟩ **b** to translate into action ⟨unwilling to act out what they believe⟩ **2** to express (repressed or unconscious impulses) unwittingly in overt behaviour

Acts n pl but sing in constr the fifth book of the New Testament narrating the beginnings of the Church

actual adj **1** existing in fact or reality; real ⟨~ and imagined conditions⟩ **2** existing or occurring at the time; current ⟨caught in the ~ commission of a crime⟩ – **actualize** vt, **actualization** n

actuality n an existing circumstance; a real fact – often pl ⟨possible risks which have been seized upon as actualities – T S Eliot⟩

actually adv **1** really; IN FACT ⟨nominally but not ~ independent⟩ **2** at the present moment ⟨the party ~ in power⟩ **3** strange as it may seem; even ⟨she ~ spoke Latin⟩

actuary n a statistician who calculates insurance risks and premiums – **actuarial** adj, **actuarially** adv

actuate vt **1** to put into action or motion **2** to incite to action ⟨~d by greed⟩ – **actuation** n, **actuator** n

act up vi **1** to behave in an unruly manner; PLAY UP **2** to give pain or trouble ⟨this typewriter is acting up again⟩ USE infml

acuity n keenness of mental or physical perception – fml

acumen n keenness and depth of discernment or discrimination, esp in practical matters

acupuncture n an orig Chinese practice of puncturing the body at particular points with needles to cure disease, relieve pain, produce anaesthesia, etc – **acupuncturist** n

acute adj **1a** of an angle measuring less than 90° **b** composed of acute angles ⟨~ triangle⟩ **2a** marked by keen discernment or intellectual perception, esp of subtle distinctions ⟨an ~ thinker⟩ **b** responsive to slight impressions or stimuli ⟨~ eyesight⟩ **3** intensely felt or perceived ⟨~ pain⟩ **4** esp of an illness having a sudden severe onset and short course – contrasted with chronic **5** demanding urgent attention; severe ⟨an ~ housing shortage⟩ **6** marked with, having the pronunciation indicated by, or being an accent mark written´ – **acutely** adv, **acuteness** n

ad n an advertisement – infml

ad-, ac-, af-, ag-, al-, ap-, as-, at- prefix **1** to; towards – usu ac- before c, k, or q ⟨acculturation⟩, af- before f, ag- before g ⟨aggrade⟩, al- before l ⟨alliteration⟩, ap- before p

⟨*approximate*⟩, *as-* before *s* ⟨*assuage*⟩, *at-* before *t* ⟨*attune*⟩, and *ad-* before other sounds, but sometimes *ad-* even before one of the listed consonants ⟨ad*sorb*⟩ 2 near; adjacent to – in this sense always in the form *ad-* ⟨*adrenal*⟩

-ad *suffix* (→ *adv*) in the direction of; towards ⟨*cephalad*⟩

adage *n* a maxim or proverb that embodies a commonly accepted observation

¹**adagio** *adv or adj* in an easy slow graceful manner – used in music

²**adagio** *n, pl* **adagios** 1 a musical composition or movement in adagio tempo 2 ballet dancing, esp a pas de deux, involving difficult feats of balance

¹**adamant** *n* a stone formerly believed to be of impenetrable hardness and sometimes identified with the diamond; *broadly* any very hard unbreakable substance

²**adamant** *adj* unshakable in determination; unyielding – **adamancy** *n*, **adamantly** *adv*

Adam's apple *n* the projection in the front of the neck formed by the largest cartilage of the larynx

adapt *vb* to make or become fit, often by modification – **adaptable** *adj*, **adaptability** *n*, **adaptedness** *n*

adaptation *n* 1 adjustment to prevailing or changing conditions: e g **a** adjustment of a sense organ to the intensity or quality of stimulation **b** modification of (the parts of) an organism fitting it better for existence and successful breeding 2 a composition rewritten in a new form or for a different medium – **adaptational** *adj*, **adaptationally** *adv*

adapter *also* **adaptor** *n* 1 a writer who adapts sthg 2 a device a for connecting 2 pieces of apparatus not orig intended to be joined **b** for converting a tool or piece of apparatus to some new use **c** for connecting several pieces of electrical apparatus to a single power point, or connecting a plug of one type to a socket of a different type

add *vt* 1 to join so as to bring about an increase or improvement ⟨*wine* ~ s *a creative touch to cooking*⟩ 2 to say or write further 3 to combine (numbers) into a single number – often + *up* ~ *vi* **1a** to perform addition **b** to come together or unite by addition 2 to make or serve as an addition *to* – **addable, addible** *adj*

addendum *n, pl* **addenda** a supplement to a book – often pl with sing. meaning but sing. in constr

¹**adder** *n* the common European venomous viper or other ground-living viper

²**adder** *n* a device (e g in a computer) that performs addition

¹**addict** *vt* 1 to devote or surrender (oneself) to sthg habitually or obsessively – usu pass 2 to cause (an animal or human) to become physiologically dependent upon a habit-forming drug – **addictive** *adj*, **addiction** *n*

²**addict** *n* 1 one who is addicted to a drug 2 DEVOTEE 2 ⟨*a detective-novel* ~⟩

addition *n* 1 sthg or sby added, esp as an improvement 2 the act or process of adding, esp adding numbers 3 direct chemical combination of substances to form a single product – **in addition** also, furthermore ⟨*a telephone in the kitchen* in addition *to the one in the hall*⟩

additional *adj* existing by way of addition; supplementary – **additionally** *adv*

¹**additive** *adj* of or characterized by addition – **additively** *adv*, **additivity** *n*

²**additive** *n* a substance added to another in relatively small amounts to impart desirable properties or suppress undesirable ones ⟨*food* ~ s⟩

addle *vb* **addling** *vt* to throw into confusion ~ *vi* 1 *of an egg* to become rotten 2 to become confused or muddled

¹**address** *vt* 1 to direct the efforts or attention of (oneself) ⟨~ *himself to the problem*⟩ **2a** to communicate directly ⟨~ es *his thanks to his host*⟩ **b** to speak or write directly to; *esp* to deliver a formal speech to 3 to mark directions for delivery on ⟨~ *a letter*⟩ 4 to greet by a prescribed form ⟨~ ed *him as 'My Lord'*⟩ 5 to take one's stance and adjust the club before hitting (a golf ball) ~ *vi obs* to direct one's speech or attentions – **addresser** *n*, **addressee** *n*

²**address** *n* 1 dutiful and courteous attention, esp in courtship – usu pl ⟨*paid his* ~ es *to her*⟩ 2 readiness and capability for dealing (e g with a person or problem) skilfully and smoothly; adroitness 3 a formal communication; *esp* a prepared speech delivered to an audience 4 a place of residence (where a person or organization may be communicated with); *also* a detailed description of its location (e g on an envelope) 5 a location (e g in the memory of a computer) where particular information is stored; *also* the digits that identify such a location

adduce *vt* to offer as example, reason, or proof in discussion or analysis – *fml* – **adducer** *n*, **adduction** *n*

add up *vi* 1 to amount *to* in total or substance ⟨*the play* adds up *to a lot of laughs*⟩ 2 to come to the expected total ⟨*the bill doesn't* add up⟩ 3 to be internally consistent; make sense ~ *vt* SIZE UP

-ade *suffix* (→ *n*) **1a** act or action of ⟨*block*ade⟩ ⟨*escap*ade⟩ **b** individual or group of people involved in (a specified action) ⟨*caval*cade⟩ ⟨*renegade*⟩ 2 product; *esp* sweet drink made from (a specified fruit) ⟨*lime*ade⟩

adenoid *adj or n* (of) an enlarged mass of lymphoid tissue at the back of the pharynx, often obstructing breathing – usu pl with sing. meaning

adenoidal *adj* of (sby with enlarged) adenoids – **adenoidally** *adv*

adept *adj or n* (being) a highly skilled expert *at* – **adeptly** *adv*, **adeptness** *n*

adequate *adj* sufficient for a specific requirement ⟨~ *grounds for divorce*⟩; *esp* barely sufficient or satisfactory – **adequacy** *n*, **adequately** *adv*, **adequateness** *n*

adhere *vi* 1 to give continued support, observance, or loyalty ⟨~ *to the treaty*⟩ 2 to hold or stick fast (as if) by gluing, suction, grasping, or fusing ~ *vt* to cause to stick fast – **adherent** *adj*, **adherence** *n*

adherent *n* a supporter of a leader, faction, etc

adhesion *n* 1 the action or state of adhering 2 (the tissues united by) an abnormal union of tissues that are usu separated in the body – **adhesional** *adj*

¹**adhesive** *adj* causing or prepared for sticking; sticky – **adhesively** *adv*, **adhesiveness** *n*

²**adhesive** *n* an adhesive substance (e g glue or cement)

ad hoc *adj or adv* with respect to the particular purpose at hand and without consideration of wider application ⟨*an* ~ *investigation*⟩

adieu *n, pl* **adieus, adieux** a farewell – often used interjectionally; usu poetic

ad infinitum *adv or adj* without end or limit

adipose *adj* of animal fat; fatty – **adiposity** *n*

adjacent *adj* having a common border; *broadly* neighbouring, nearby – **adjacency** *n*, **adjacently** *adv*

adjectival *adj* relating to or characterized by the use of adjectives – **adjectivally** *adv*

¹**adjective** *adj* 1 adjectival 2 *of a dye* requiring a mordant

²**adjective** *n* a word that modifies a noun or pronoun by describing a particular characteristic of it

adjoin *vb* to be next to or in contact with (one another) – **adjoining** *adj*

adjourn *vb* to suspend (a session) until a later stated time – **adjournment** *n*

adjudge *vt* **1a** to adjudicate **b** to pronounce formally ⟨~ *him guilty*⟩ **2** to pronounce to be; deem ⟨~ *the book a success*⟩

adjudicate *vt* to make a judicial decision on ~ *vi* to act as judge (e g in a competition) – **adjudicative** *adj*, **adjudicator** *n*

adjunct *n* **1** sthg joined to another thing as an incidental accompaniment but not essentially a part of it **2** a word or phrase (e g an adverb or prepositional phrase) that can be left out and still leave the sentence grammatically complete **3** a person, usu in a subordinate or temporary capacity, assisting another to perform some duty or service – **adjunct** *adj*, **adjunctly** *adv*, **adjunctive** *adj*, **adjunctively** *adv*

adjure *vt* **1** to charge or command solemnly (as if) under oath or penalty of a curse **2** to entreat or advise earnestly *USE fml* – **adjuration** *n*, **adjuratory** *adj*

adjust *vt* **1** to bring to a more satisfactory or conformable state by minor change or adaptation; regulate, correct, or modify **2** to determine the amount to be paid under an insurance policy in settlement of (a loss) ~ *vi* to adapt or conform oneself (e g to climate) – **adjustable** *adj*, **adjustive** *adj*, **adjustability** *n*

adjustment *n* **1** a correction or modification to reflect actual conditions **2** a means (e g a mechanism) by which things are adjusted one to another **3** a settlement of a disputed claim or debt – **adjustmental** *adj*

adjutant *n* an officer who assists the commanding officer and is responsible for correspondence and for ensuring that his orders are carried out – **adjutancy** *n*

ad-lib *adj* spoken, composed, or performed without preparation – *infml*

ad-lib *vb* **-bb-** to say (e g lines or a speech) spontaneously and without preparation; improvise – **ad-lib** *n*

ad lib *adv* without restraint or limit

adman *n* a member of the advertising profession – *infml*

admass *n*, *chiefly Br* a society in which the drive to consume material goods is promoted by mass-media advertising – **admass** *adj*

administer *vt* **1** to manage, supervise **2a** to mete out; dispense ⟨~ *punishment*⟩ **b** to give or perform ritually ⟨~ *the last rites*⟩ **c** to give remedially ~ *vi* to perform the office of administrator; manage affairs – **administrable** *adj*, **administrant** *n*

administration *n* **1** the act or process of administering **2** performance of executive duties; management **3** the execution of public affairs as distinguished from the making of policy **4a** a body of people who administer **b** *cap* GOVERNMENT **5** – **administrate** *vb*, **administrational** *adj*, **administrationist** *n*

administrative *adj* of (an) administration – **administratively** *adv*

administrator *n* sby who administers esp business, school, or governmental affairs

admirable *adj* deserving the highest respect; excellent – **admirableness** *n*, **admirably** *adv*, **admirability** *n*

admiral *n* the commander in chief of a navy

admiralty *n* **1** *sing or pl in constr*, *cap* the executive department formerly having authority over naval affairs **2** the court having jurisdiction over maritime questions

admiration *n* **1** a feeling of delighted or astonished approval **2** the object of admiring respect

admire *vt* to think highly of; express admiration for – sometimes sarcastically ⟨*I ~ your cheek*⟩ – **admiringly** *adv*

admirer *n* a woman's suitor

admissible *adj*, *esp of legal evidence* capable of being allowed or conceded; permissible – **admissibility** *n*

admission *n* **1** acknowledgment that a fact or allegation is true **2a** allowing or being allowed to enter sthg (e g a secret society) **b** a fee paid at or for admission – **admissive** *adj*

admit *vb* **-tt-** *vt* **1a** to allow scope for; permit **b** to concede as true or valid **2** to allow to enter sthg (e g a place or fellowship) ~ *vi* **1** to give entrance or access **2a** to allow, permit – often + *of* **b** to make acknowledgment – + *to*

admittance *n* **1** permission to enter a place **2** access, entrance

admittedly *adv* as must reluctantly be admitted

admixture *n* **1** mixing or being mixed **2** an ingredient added by mixing, or the resulting mixture – **admix** *vt*

admonish *vt* **1a** to indicate duties to **b** to warn about remissness or error, esp gently **2** to give friendly earnest advice or encouragement to – **admonisher** *n*, **admonishingly** *adv*, **admonishment** *n*

admonition *n* (a) gentle friendly reproof, counsel, or warning

admonitory *adj* expressing admonition; warning – **admonitorily** *adv*

ad nauseam *adv* in an extremely tedious manner; enough to make one sick

ado *n* fussy bustling excitement, esp over trivia; to-do

adobe *n* **1** a building brick of sun-dried earth and straw **2** a heavy clay used in making adobe bricks – **adobe** *adj*

adolescent *n* sby in the period of life between puberty and maturity – **adolescent** *adj*, **adolescence** *n*

adopt *vt* **1** to take by choice into a new relationship; *specif* to bring up voluntarily (a child of other parents) as one's own child **2** to take up and practise; take to oneself **3** to vote to accept ⟨~ *a constitutional amendment*⟩ **4** *of a constituency* to nominate as a Parliamentary candidate **5** *Br, of a local authority* to assume responsibility for the maintenance of (e g a road) – **adopter** *n*, **adoptable** *adj*, **adoptability** *n*, **adoption** *n*, **adoptee** *n*

adoptive *adj* made or acquired by adoption ⟨*one's ~ country*⟩ ⟨*the ~ father*⟩ – **adoptively** *adv*

adorable *adj* sweetly lovable; charming – **adorableness** *n*, **adorably** *adv*, **adorability** *n*

adore *vt* **1** to worship or honour as a deity **2** to regard with reverent admiration and devotion **3** to like very much – *infml* – **adorer** *n*, **adoration** *n*

adorn *vt* **1** to decorate, esp with ornaments **2** to add to the pleasantness or attractiveness of – **adornment** *n*

adrenal gland *n* an endocrine gland near the front of each kidney with an outer part that secretes steroid hormones and an inner part that secretes adrenalin

adrenalin, adrenaline *n* a hormone produced by the adrenal gland that occurs as a neurotransmitter in the sympathetic nervous system and that stimulates the heart and causes constriction of blood vessels and relaxation of smooth muscle

adrift *adv or adj* **1** afloat without motive power or mooring and at the mercy of winds and currents **2** in or into a state of being unstuck or unfastened; loose – esp in *come adrift* **3** astray – *infml* ⟨*his reasoning's gone completely ~*⟩

adroit *adj* **1** dexterous, nimble **2** marked by shrewdness, readiness, or resourcefulness in coping with difficulty or danger – **adroitly** *adv*, **adroitness** *n*

adulate *vt* to flatter or admire excessively or slavishly – **adulator** *n*, **adulation** *n*, **adulatory** *adj*

¹**adult** *adj* **1** fully developed and mature; grown-up **2** of or befitting adults ⟨*an ~ approach to a problem*⟩ **3** suitable only for adults; *broadly* salacious, pornographic ⟨~ *magazines*⟩ – **adulthood** *n*, **adultlike** *adj*, **adultness** *n*

²adult *n* a grown-up person or creature; *esp* a human being after an age specified by law (in Britain, 18)

¹adulterate *vt* to corrupt or make impure by the addition of a foreign or inferior substance – **adulterant** *n or adj*, **adulterator** *n*, **adulteration** *n*

²adulterate *adj* being adulterated, debased, or impure

adulterer, *fem* **adulteress** *n* sby who commits adultery

adultery *n* (an act of) voluntary sexual intercourse between a married person and sby other than his/her spouse – **adulterous** *adj*, **adulterously** *adv*

adumbrate *vt* 1 to foreshadow (a future event) vaguely 2 to outline broadly without details *USE* fml – **adumbration** *n*, **adumbrative** *adj*, **adumbratively** *adv*

¹advance *vt* 1 to bring or move forwards in position or time ⟨~ *the date of the meeting*⟩ 2 to accelerate the growth or progress of; further 3 to raise in rank; promote 4 to supply (money or goods) ahead of time or as a loan 5 to bring (an opinion or argument) forward for notice; propose ~ *vi* 1 to go forwards; proceed 2 to make progress 3 to rise in rank, position, or importance – **advancer** *n*

²advance *n* 1a a moving forward b (a signal for) forward movement (of troops) 2a progress in development; an improvement ⟨*an ~ in medical technique*⟩ b ADVANCEMENT 1a 3 a friendly or *esp* an amorous approach – usu pl ⟨*her attitude discouraged all ~s*⟩ 4 (a provision of) money or goods supplied before a return is received – **in advance** beforehand

³advance *adj* 1 made, sent, or provided ahead of time 2 going or situated ahead of others ⟨*an ~ party of soldiers*⟩

advanced *adj* 1 far on in time or course ⟨*a man ~ in years*⟩ 2 beyond the elementary; more developed ⟨*~ chemistry*⟩

Advanced level *n, often cap L* an examination that is the second of the 3 levels of the British General Certificate of Education and is a partial qualification for university entrance

advancement *n* 1a (a) promotion or elevation to a higher rank or position b furtherance towards perfection or completeness ⟨*the ~ of knowledge*⟩ 2 an advance of money or value

advantage *n* 1 superiority of position or condition ⟨*higher ground gave the enemy the ~*⟩ – often + *of* or *over* 2 a benefit, gain; *esp* one resulting from some course of action ⟨*a mistake which turned out to his ~*⟩ 3 (the score of) the first point won in tennis after deuce – **to advantage** so as to produce a favourable impression or effect

advantageous *adj* furnishing an advantage; favourable – **advantageously** *adv*

Advent *n* 1 the 4-week period before Christmas, observed by some Christians as a season of prayer and fasting ⟨*the second Sunday in ~*⟩ 2 the coming of Christ to earth as a human being 3 *not cap* a coming into being; an arrival ⟨*the ~ of spring*⟩

Adventism *n* the doctrine that the second coming of Christ and the end of the world are near at hand – **Adventist** *adj or n*

adventitious *adj* 1 coming accidentally or casually from another source; extraneous 2 occurring sporadically or in an unusual place ⟨*~ buds on a plant*⟩ – **adventitiously** *adv*, **adventitiousness** *n*

¹adventure *n* 1 an undertaking involving danger, risks, and uncertainty of outcome; *broadly* (an) exciting or remarkable experience 2 an enterprise involving financial risk – **adventuresome** *adj*, **adventurous** *adj*, **adventurously** *adv*, **adventurousness** *n*

²adventure *vt* to venture, risk ~ *vi* 1 to hazard oneself; dare to go or enter 2 to take a risk

adventurer, *fem* **adventuress** *n* 1 sby who takes part in an adventure; *esp* SOLDIER OF FORTUNE 2 sby who seeks wealth or position by unscrupulous means

adverb *n* a word that modifies a verb, an adjective, another adverb, a preposition, a phrase, a clause, or a sentence, and that answers such questions as how?, when? where?, etc

adverbial *adj* of or functioning as an adverb – **adverbial** *n*, **adverbially** *adv*

adversary *n* an enemy, opponent, or opposing faction

adverse *adj* 1 acting against or in a contrary direction ⟨*hindered by ~ winds*⟩ 2 unfavourable ⟨*~ criticism*⟩ – **adversely** *adv*, **adverseness** *n*

adversity *n* a condition of suffering, affliction, or hardship

¹advert *vi* to make a (glancing) reference or refer casually *to* – fml

²advert *n, chiefly Br* an advertisement

advertise *vt* 1 to make publicly and generally known ⟨*~d her presence by sneezing*⟩ 2 to announce (e g a article for sale or a vacancy) publicly, esp in the press to encourage sales or patronage of, esp by emphasizing desirable qualities ~ *vi* 1 to encourage sales or patronage esp by description in the mass media 2 to seek *for* b means of advertising – **advertiser** *n*

advertisement *n* a public notice; *esp* one published broadcast, or displayed publicly to advertise a product service, etc

advertising *n* 1 the action of calling sthg to the attention of the public, esp by paid announcements 2 advertisements ⟨*the magazine contains much ~*⟩ 3 the profession of preparing advertisements for publication or broadcast

advice *n* 1 recommendation regarding a decision of course of conduct ⟨*my ~ to you is: don't do it*⟩ communication, esp from a distance; intelligence – usu p 3 an official notice concerning a business transaction ⟨*remittance ~*⟩

advisable *adj* fitting to be advised or done; prudent – **advisability** *n*, **advisably** *adv*

advise *vt* 1a to give advice to ⟨*~ her to try a drie climate*⟩ b to caution, warn ⟨*~ him against going*⟩ 2 give information or notice to; inform ⟨*~ his friends of h intentions*⟩ ~ *vi* to give advice – **adviser, advisor** *n*

advised *adj* 1 thought out; considered – chiefly i *ill-advised, well-advised* 2 informed – in *keep someon advised* – **advisedly** *adv*

advisory *adj* 1 having or exercising power to advise containing or giving advice

advocacy *n* 1 active support or pleading ⟨*her ~ reform*⟩ 2 the function of an advocate

¹advocate *n* 1 a professional pleader before a tribunal of court 2 one who defends or supports a cause or propo sal

²advocate *vt* to plead in favour of – **advocator** *n*, **advoc tory** *adj*

adze, *NAm chiefly* **adz** *n* a tool that has the blade at rig angles to the handle for cutting or shaping wood

aegis *n* auspices, sponsorship ⟨*under the ~ of the educa tion department*⟩

aeon, eon *n* 1 an immeasurably or indefinitely long peric of time 2 a unit of geological time equal to 1000 millic years

aer-, aero- *comb form* 1 air; atmosphe ⟨*aerate*⟩ ⟨*aerobiology*⟩ 2 gas ⟨*aerosol*⟩ 3 aircraft ⟨*aer drome*⟩

aerate *vt* 1 to combine, supply, charge, or impregna

with a gas, esp air, oxygen, or carbon dioxide 2 to make effervescent – **aerator** n, **aeration** n

¹**aerial** adj **1a** of or occurring in the air or atmosphere **b** consisting of air ⟨~ *particles*⟩ **c** growing in the air rather than in the ground or water ⟨~ *roots*⟩ **d** operating overhead on elevated cables or rails ⟨*an* ~ *railway*⟩ **2** lacking substance; thin **3a** of aircraft ⟨~ *navigation*⟩ **b** by or from an aircraft ⟨~ *photo*⟩ **4** lofty ⟨~ *spires*⟩ – poetic **5** ethereal ⟨*visions of* ~ *joy* – P B Shelley⟩ – poetic – **aerially** adv

²**aerial** n a conductor (e g a wire) or arrangement of conductors designed to radiate or receive radio waves

aerie n an eyrie

aero adj of aircraft or aeronautics ⟨*an* ~ *engine*⟩

aerobatics n pl but sing or pl in constr the performance of feats (e g rolls) in an aircraft – **aerobatic** adj

aerodrome n, chiefly Br an airfield

aerodynamics n pl but sing or pl in constr the dynamics of the motion of (solid bodies moving through) gases (e g air) – **aerodynamic** adj, **aerodynamically** adv, **aerodynamicist** n

aerofoil n, chiefly Br a body (e g an aircraft wing) designed to provide an aerodynamic reaction

aeronautics n pl but sing in constr the art or science of flight – **aeronautical** adj, **aeronautically** adv

aeroplane n, chiefly Br an aircraft that is heavier than air, has nonrotating wings from which it derives its lift, and is mechanically propelled (e g by a propeller or jet engine)

¹**aerosol** n **1** a suspension of fine solid or liquid particles in gas (e g fog or smoke) **2** a substance dispersed from a pressurized container as an aerosol **3** AEROSOL CONTAINER

²**aerosol** vt **-ll-** to write with an aerosol ⟨*a slogan* ~led *on a wall*⟩

aerosol container n a metal container for substances in aerosol form

¹**aerospace** n **1** (a branch of physical science dealing with) the earth's atmosphere and the space beyond **2** the aerospace industry

²**aerospace** adj of or relating to aerospace, to vehicles used in aerospace or the manufacture of such vehicles, or to travel in aerospace ⟨~ *research*⟩ ⟨~ *medicine*⟩

Aertex trademark – used for a cellular cotton fabric

aesthete, NAm also **esthete** n **1** one who has or professes a developed sensitivity to the beautiful in art or nature **2** one who affects concern for the arts and indifference to practical affairs

aesthetic also **aesthetical** NAm also **esthetic** also **esthetical** adj **1a** of or dealing with aesthetics or the appreciation of the beautiful ⟨~ *theories*⟩ **b** artistic ⟨*a work of* ~ *value*⟩ **2** having a developed sense of beauty – **aesthetically** adv

aesthetics, NAm also **esthetics** n pl but sing or pl in constr a branch of philosophy dealing with the nature of the beautiful, with judgments concerning beauty and taste, and with theories of criticism in the arts – **aesthetician** n

aether n ETHER 1, 2

aetiology, chiefly NAm **etiology** n (the study of) the causes or origin, specif of a disease or abnormal condition – **aetiologic**, **aetiological** adj, **aetiologically** adv

afar adv or n (from, to, or at) a great distance ⟨*saw her* ~ *off*⟩ ⟨*saw him from* ~⟩

affable adj **1** being pleasant and relaxed in talking to others **2** characterized by ease and friendliness; benign – **affably** adv, **affability** n

affair n **1a** pl commercial, professional, or public business or matters ⟨*world* ~s⟩ **b** a particular or personal concern ⟨*that's my* ~, *not yours*⟩ **2a** a procedure, action, or occasion only vaguely specified **b** a social event; a party ⟨*a catered* ~⟩ **3** also **affaire, affaire de coeur** a romantic or passionate attachment between 2 people who are not married to each other, often of considerable but limited duration **4** a matter causing public anxiety, controversy, or scandal ⟨*the Dreyfus* ~⟩ **5** an object or collection of objects only vaguely specified – used with a descriptive or qualifying term; infml ⟨*the house was a 2-storey* ~⟩

¹**affect** n the conscious subjective aspect of an emotion considered apart from bodily changes

²**affect** vt **1** to be given to ⟨~ *flashy clothes*⟩ **2** to put on a pretence of (being); feign ⟨~ *indifference*⟩ ⟨~ *the experienced traveller*⟩

³**affect** vt **1** to have a material effect on or produce an alteration in ⟨*paralysis* ~ed *his limbs*⟩ **2** to act on (e g a person or his/her mind or feelings) so as to effect a response ⟨*was deeply* ~ed *by the news*⟩

affectation n **1** an insincere display (e g of a quality not really possessed) ⟨*the* ~ *of righteous indignation*⟩ **2** a deliberately assumed peculiarity of speech or conduct; artificiality

affected adj **1** inclined, disposed towards – chiefly in well-affected, ill-affected **2a** given to affectation **b** assumed artificially or falsely; pretended ⟨*an* ~ *interest in art*⟩ – **affectedly** adv, **affectedness** n

affecting adj evoking a strong emotional response; moving – **affectingly** adv

¹**affection** n **1** emotion as compared with reason – often pl with sing. meaning **2** tender and lasting attachment; fondness ⟨*she had a deep* ~ *for her parents*⟩ – **affectional** adj, **affectionally** adv

²**affection** n a disease, malady, or other bodily condition

affectionate adj **1** showing affection or warm regard; loving **2** proceeding from affection; tender ⟨~ *care*⟩ – **affectionately** adv

affiance vt to promise (oneself or another) solemnly in marriage; betroth

affidavit n a sworn written statement for use as judicial proof

¹**affiliate** vt to attach as a member or branch – + to or with ⟨*the union is* ~d *to the TUC*⟩ ~ vi to connect or associate oneself with another, often in a dependent or subordinate position; combine – **affiliation** n

²**affiliate** n an affiliated person or organization

affiliation order n a legal order that the father of an illegitimate child must pay towards its maintenance

affinity n **1** SYMPATHY **2a** ⟨*this mysterious* ~ *between us*⟩ **2** an attraction, esp between substances, causing them to combine chemically **3** resemblance based on relationship or causal connection

affirm vt **1a** to validate, confirm **b** to state positively **2** to assert (e g a judgment of a lower court) as valid; ratify ~ vi **1** to testify by affirmation **2** to uphold a judgment or decree of a lower court – **affirmable** adj, **affirmance** n

affirmation n **1** sthg affirmed; a positive assertion **2** a solemn declaration made by sby who conscientiously declines taking an oath

¹**affirmative** adj **1** asserting or answering that the fact is so ⟨*gave an* ~ *nod*⟩ **2** favouring or supporting a proposition or motion ⟨*an* ~ *vote*⟩ **3** chiefly NAm positive ⟨*an* ~ *responsibility*⟩ – **affirmatively** adv

²**affirmative** n **1** an expression (e g the word yes) of agreement or assent **2** an affirmative proposition

¹**affix** vt **1** to attach (physically) ⟨~ *a stamp to a letter*⟩; esp to add in writing ⟨~ *a signature*⟩ **2** to impress ⟨~ed

his seal⟩ – **affixable** *adj*, **affixment, affixation, affixture** *n*

²**affix** *n* **1** an addition to the beginning or end of or an insertion in a word or root to produce a derivative word or inflectional form **2** an appendage – **affixal, affixial** *adj*

afflict *vt* **1** to distress so severely as to cause persistent suffering **2** to trouble ⟨~ed *with shyness*⟩

affliction *n* **1** great suffering **2** a cause of persistent pain or distress

affluent *adj* **1** flowing in abundance **2** having a generously sufficient supply of material possessions; wealthy ⟨*our* ~ *society*⟩ – **affluence, affluency** *n*, **affluently** *adv*

afford *vt* **1a** to be able to do or to bear without serious harm – esp + *can* ⟨*you can't* ~ *to neglect your health*⟩ **b** to be able to bear the cost of ⟨~ *a new coat*⟩ **2** to provide, supply ⟨*her letters* ~ *no clue to her intentions*⟩ – **affordable** *adj*

afforest *vt* to establish or plant forest cover on – **afforestation** *n*

affray *n* a (public) brawl

affricate *n* a composite speech sound consisting of a stop and an immediately following fricative (e g the /t/ and /sh/ that are the constituents of the /tsh/ in *why choose*) – **affrication** *n*, **affricative** *n or adj*

affront *vt* to insult by openly insolent or disrespectful behaviour or language; give offence to – **affront** *n*

Afghan *n* **1** a native or inhabitant of Afghanistan **2** Pashto **3** *not cap* a blanket or shawl of coloured wool knitted or crocheted in strips or squares **4 Afghan, Afghan hound** a tall hunting dog with a coat of silky thick hair – **Afghan** *adj*

aficionado, *fem* **aficionada** *n, pl* **aficionados,** *fem* **aficionadas** a devotee, fan ⟨~s *of the bullfight*⟩

afield *adv* **1** to, in, or on the field **2** (far) away from home; abroad **3** out of the way; astray ⟨*irrelevant remarks that carried us far* ~⟩

afire *adj or adv* on fire ⟨~ *with enthusiasm*⟩

aflame *adj or adv* afire

afloat *adj or adv* **1a** borne (as if) on the water or air **b** at sea or on ship **2** free of debt **3** circulating about; rumoured ⟨*nasty stories were* ~⟩ **4** flooded with or submerged under water

afoot *adv or adj* **1** on foot **2** (in the process of) happening; astir ⟨*there's trouble* ~⟩

aforementioned *adj* mentioned previously

aforesaid *adj* aforementioned

aforethought *adj* premeditated, deliberate – fml; esp in *with malice aforethought*

a fortiori *adv* with still greater reason or certainty – used in drawing a conclusion that is inferred to be even more certain than another ⟨*if he can afford a house,* ~, *he can afford a tent*⟩

afraid *adj* **1** filled with fear or apprehension ⟨~ *of machines*⟩ ⟨~ *for his job*⟩ **2** regretfully of the opinion – in apology for an utterance ⟨*I'm* ~ *I won't be able to go*⟩

afresh *adv* anew, again

African *n or adj* (a native or inhabitant) of Africa – **Africanness** *n*

Afrikaans *n* a language of S Africa developed from 17th-c Dutch

Afrikaner *n* an Afrikaans-speaking S African of European, esp Dutch, descent

Afro *n or adj, pl* **Afros** (a hairstyle) shaped into a round curly bushy mass

Afro-, Afr- *comb form* African ⟨*Afro-American*⟩; African and ⟨*Afro-Asiatic*⟩

¹**aft** *adv* near, towards, or in the stern of a ship or the tail of an aircraft

²**aft** *adj* rearward; ⁴AFTER 2 ⟨*the* ~ *decks*⟩

¹**after** *adv* **1** BEHIND 1b ⟨*mourners follow* ~ – *SEU S*⟩ **2** afterwards

²**after** *prep* **1** behind in place or order ⟨*shut the door* ~ *you*⟩ – used in yielding precedence ⟨~ *you!*⟩ or in asking for the next turn ⟨~ *you with the pencil*⟩ **2a** following in time; later than ⟨~ *breakfast*⟩ **b** continuously succeeding ⟨*saw play* ~ *play*⟩ **c** in view or in spite of (sthg preceding) ⟨~ *all our advice*⟩ **3** – used to indicate the goal or purpose of an action ⟨*go* ~ *gold*⟩ **4** so as to resemble: e g **a** in accordance with **b** in allusion to the name of **c** in the characteristic manner of **d** in imitation of **5** about, concerning ⟨*ask* ~ *his health*⟩

³**after** *conj* later than the time when

⁴**after** *adj* **1** later, subsequent ⟨*in* ~ *years*⟩ **2** located towards the rear or stern of a ship, aircraft, etc

after all *adv* **1** in spite of everything **2** it must be remembered ⟨*he can't swim but,* ~, *he's only 2*⟩

afterbirth *n* the placenta and foetal membranes expelled after delivery of a baby, young animal, etc

aftercare *n* the care, treatment, etc given to people discharged from a hospital or other institution

aftereffect *n* an effect that follows its cause after an interval of time

afterglow *n* **1** a glow remaining (e g in the sky) where a light source has disappeared **2** a vestige of past splendour, success, or happy emotion

afterlife *n* **1** an existence after death **2** a later period in one's life

aftermath *n* **1** a second growth of forage after the harvest of an earlier crop **2** a consequence, result **3** the period immediately following a usu ruinous event ⟨*in the* ~ *of the war*⟩

afternoon *n* the time between noon and sunset – **afternoon** *adj*

afternoons *adv*, chiefly NAm in the afternoon repeatedly; on any afternoon ⟨~ *he usually slept*⟩

afters *n pl*, Br a dessert – infml

after-shave *n* (a) usu scented lotion for use on the face after shaving

aftertaste *n* persistence of a flavour or impression ⟨*the bitter* ~ *of a quarrel*⟩

afterthought *n* **1** an idea occurring later **2** sthg added later

afterwards *adv* after that; subsequently, thereafter ⟨*for years* ~⟩

again *adv* **1** so as to be as before ⟨*put it back* ~⟩ **2** another time; once more **3** on the other hand ⟨*he might go, and* ~ *he might not*⟩ **4** further; IN ADDITION ⟨*could eat as much* ~⟩

¹**against** *prep* **1a** in opposition or hostility to ⟨*the rule* ~ *smoking*⟩ **b** unfavourable to ⟨*his appearance is* ~ *him*⟩ **c** as a defence or protection from ⟨*warned them* ~ *opening the box*⟩ **2** compared or contrasted with ⟨*cost only £2, as* ~ *£3 at home*⟩ **3a** in preparation or provision for ⟨*saving* ~ *his retirement*⟩ **b** with respect to; towards ⟨*customs which had the force of law* ~ *both landlord and tenant*⟩ **4** (in the direction of and) in contact with ⟨*rain beat* ~ *the windows*⟩ ⟨*leaning* ~ *the wall*⟩ **5** in a direction opposite to the motion or course of; counter to ⟨*swam* ~ *the tide*⟩ **6** in exchange for

²**against** *adj* **1** opposed to a motion or measure **2** unfavourable to a specified degree; esp unfavourable to a win ⟨*the odds are 2 to 1* ~⟩

¹**agape** *adj* **1** wide open; gaping **2** in a state of wonder ⟨~ *with expectation*⟩

²**agape** *n* LOVE FEAST – **agapeic** *adj*

agar-agar *n* a gelatinous extract from any of various red algae used esp in culture media or as a gelling agent in foods

agate *n* 1 a mineral used as a gem composed of quartz of various colours, often arranged in bands 2 sthg made of or fitted with agate

¹age *n* **1a** the length of time a person has lived or a thing existed ⟨*a boy 10 years of* ~⟩ **b** the time of life at which some particular qualification, power, or capacity arises ⟨*the voting* ~ *is 18*⟩ **c** a stage of life ⟨*the 7* ~*s of man*⟩ 2 a generation ⟨*the* ~*s to come*⟩ 3 a period of time dominated by a central figure or prominent feature ⟨*the* ~ *of Pericles*⟩: e g **a** a period in history ⟨*the steam* ~⟩ **b** a cultural period marked by the prominence of a specified item ⟨*the atomic* ~⟩ **c** a division of geological time, usu shorter than an epoch 4 an individual's development in terms of the years required by an average individual for similar development ⟨*a mental* ~ *of 6*⟩ 5 a long time – usu pl with sing. meaning; *infml* ⟨*haven't seen him for* ~*s*⟩ – **of age** of legal adult status

²age *vb* **aging, ageing** *vi* 1 to become old; show the effects of increasing age ⟨*he's* ~*d terribly since you last saw him*⟩ 2 to become mellow or mature; ripen ⟨*this cheese has* ~*d for nearly 2 years*⟩ ~ *vt* 1 to cause to seem old, esp prematurely ⟨*illness has* ~*d him*⟩ 2 to bring to a state fit for use or to maturity

-age *suffix* (→ *n*) 1 aggregate or collection of ⟨*baggage*⟩ ⟨*acreage*⟩ **2a** action or process of ⟨*haulage*⟩ **b** cumulative result of ⟨*breakage*⟩ ⟨*spillage*⟩ **c** rate or amount of ⟨*dosage*⟩ 3 house or place of ⟨*orphanage*⟩ 4 condition or rank of ⟨*bondage*⟩ ⟨*peerage*⟩ 5 fee or charge for ⟨*postage*⟩ ⟨*wharfage*⟩

aged *adj* 1 grown old: e g **a** of an advanced age **b** having attained a specified age ⟨*a man* ~ *40 years*⟩ 2 typical of old age ⟨*his* ~ *steps*⟩ – **agedness** *n*

ageless *adj* 1 never growing old or showing the effects of age 2 timeless, eternal ⟨~ *truths*⟩ – **agelessly** *adv*, **agelessness** *n*

agency *n* 1 a power or force through which a result is achieved; instrumentality ⟨*communicated through the* ~ *of his ambassador*⟩ 2 the function or place of business of an agent or representative 3 an establishment that does business for another ⟨*an advertising* ~⟩

agenda *n* 1 a list of items to be discussed or business to be transacted (e g at a meeting) 2 a plan of procedure; a programme – **agendaless** *adj*

agent *n* **1a** sthg or sby that produces an effect or that acts or exerts power **b** a chemically, physically, or biologically active substance 2 a person who acts for or in the place of another by authority from him/her: e g **a** a business representative **b** one employed by or controlling an agency ⟨*my literary* ~⟩ **3a** a representative of a government **b** a spy

agent provocateur *n, pl* **agents provocateurs** a person employed to incite suspected people to some open action that will make them liable to punishment

age of consent *n* the age at which one is legally competent to give consent; *specif* that at which a person, esp a female, may consent to sexual intercourse

agglomerate *vb* to (cause to) gather into a cluster or disorderly mass

agglomerate *adj* gathered into a ball, mass, or cluster

agglomerate *n* 1 a disorderly mass or collection 2 a rock composed of irregular volcanic fragments

agglutination *n* 1 the formation of compound words by combining (parts of) other words which already have a single definite meaning 2 the collection of red blood cells or other minute suspended particles into clumps, esp as a response to a specific antibody – **agglutinative** *adj*

aggrandize, -ise *vt* 1 to give a false air of greatness to; praise highly ⟨~*d the one and disparaged the other*⟩ 2 to enhance the power, wealth, position, or reputation of – **aggrandizement** *n*

aggravate *vt* 1 to make worse or more severe 2 to annoy, irritate – **aggravation** *n*

¹aggregate *adj* formed by the collection of units or particles into a body, mass, or amount: e g **a** of a flower clustered in a dense mass or head **b** of a fruit formed from the several ovaries of a single flower **c** taking all units as a whole; total ⟨~ *earnings*⟩ ⟨~ *sales*⟩ – **aggregately** *adv*, **aggregateness** *n*

²aggregate *vt* 1 to bring together into a mass or whole 2 to amount to (a specified total) – **aggregative** *adj*, **aggregation** *n*, **aggregational** *adj*

³aggregate *n* 1 a mass of loosely associated parts; an assemblage 2 the whole amount; the sum total **3a** a rock composed of closely packed mineral crystals **b** sand, gravel, etc for mixing with cement to make concrete **c** a clustered mass of individual particles of various shapes and sizes that is considered to be the basic structural unit of soil

aggression *n* 1 a hostile attack; *esp* one made without just cause 2 attack, encroachment; *esp* unprovoked violation by one country of the territory of another 3 hostile, injurious, or destructive behaviour or outlook – **aggressor** *n*

aggressive *adj* **1a** tending towards or practising aggression ⟨*an* ~ *foreign policy*⟩ **b** ready to attack ⟨*an* ~ *fighter*⟩ 2 forceful, dynamic ⟨*an* ~ *salesman*⟩ – **aggressively** *adv*, **aggressiveness** *n*

aggrieved *adj* showing or expressing resentment; hurt – **aggrievedly** *adv*

aggro *n, chiefly Br* 1 provocation, hostility 2 deliberate aggression or violence *USE infml*

aghast *adj* suddenly struck with terror or amazement; shocked ⟨*stood by* ~ *as the building collapsed*⟩

agile *adj* 1 quick, easy, and graceful in movement 2 mentally quick and resourceful – **agilely** *adv*, **agility** *n*

agitate *vt* 1 to move, shake 2 to excite and often trouble the mind or feelings of; disturb ~ *vi* to work to arouse public feeling for or against a cause ⟨~*d for better schools*⟩ – **agitatedly** *adv*, **agitation** *n*, **agitational** *adj*

agitator *n* 1 sby who stirs up public feeling on controversial issues ⟨*political* ~*s*⟩ 2 a device or apparatus for stirring or shaking

aglow *adj* radiant with warmth or excitement

¹agnostic *n* sby who holds the view that any ultimate reality is unknown and prob unknowable; *also* one who doubts the existence of God – **agnosticism** *n*

²agnostic *adj* of or being an agnostic or the beliefs of agnostics

Agnus Dei *n* a liturgical prayer addressed to Christ as Saviour, often set to music ⟨*the* ~ *from Bach's B Minor Mass*⟩

ago *adj or adv* earlier than now ⟨*10 years* ~⟩ ⟨*how long* ~ *did they leave?*⟩

agog *adj* full of intense anticipation or excitement; eager ⟨*the court was* ~ *with gossip, scandal and intrigue* – *TLS*⟩

agonize, -ise *vt* to cause to suffer agony ~ *vi* 1 to suffer agony or anguish 2 to make a great effort

agonized, -ised *adj* characterized by, suffering, or expressing agony

agonizing, -ising *adj* causing agony; painful ⟨*an* ~ *reappraisal of his policies*⟩ – **agonizingly** *adv*

agony *n* 1 intense and often prolonged pain or suffering of mind or body; anguish 2 the struggle that precedes death ⟨*his last* ~⟩

agoraphobia *n* abnormal dread of being in open spaces – **agoraphobic** *n or adj*, **agoraphobe** *n*

¹**agrarian** *adj* 1 of or relating to (the tenure of) fields 2 (characteristic) of farmers or agricultural life or interests

²**agrarian** *n* a member of an agrarian party or movement

agree *vt* 1 to admit, concede – usu + a clause ⟨*I ~ that you're right*⟩ 2 to bring into harmony 3 *chiefly Br* to come to terms on, usu after discussion; accept by mutual consent ⟨*the following articles were ~*d – Winston Churchill⟩ ~ *vi* 1 to give assent; accede – often + *to* ⟨*~ to your proposal*⟩ 2a to be of one mind – often + *with* ⟨*I ~ with you*⟩ b to get along together c to decide together ⟨*~ on blue for the kitchen*⟩ 3a to correspond b to be consistent 4 to suit the health – + *with* ⟨*onions don't ~ with me*⟩ 5 to correspond in grammatical gender, number, case, or person

agreeable *adj* 1 to one's liking; pleasing 2 willing to agree or consent – **agreeableness** *n*, **agreeably** *adv*

agreement *n* 1a harmony of opinion or feeling b correspondence ⟨*~ between the copy and the original*⟩ 2a an arrangement laying down terms, conditions, etc b a treaty 3 (the language or document embodying) a legally binding contract

agriculture *n* the theory and practice of cultivating and producing crops from the soil and of raising livestock – **agricultural** *adj*, **agriculturally** *adv*, **agriculturist, agriculturalist** *n*

agronomy *n* a branch of agriculture dealing with field-crop production and soil management – **agronomic** *adj*, **agronomically** *adv*, **agronomist** *n*

aground *adv or adj* on or onto the shore or the bottom of a body of water ⟨*the ship ran ~*⟩

ague *n* a (malarial) fever with regularly recurring attacks of chills and sweating – **aguish** *adj*

ah *interj* – used to express delight, relief, regret, or contempt

aha *interj* – used to express surprise, triumph, derision, or amused discovery

ahead *adv or adj* 1a in a forward direction b in front ⟨*the road ~*⟩ 2 in, into, or for the future ⟨*plan ~*⟩ 3 in or towards a better position ⟨*get ~ of the rest*⟩

ahem *interj* – used esp to attract attention or express mild disapproval

ahoy *interj* – used chiefly by seamen as a greeting or warning ⟨*land ~*⟩

¹**aid** *vt* 1 to give assistance to; help 2 to bring about the accomplishment of; facilitate ⟨*~ his recovery*⟩ – **aider** *n*

²**aid** *n* 1 help; assistance; *specif* tangible means of assistance (e g money or supplies) 2a a helper b sthg that helps or supports ⟨*a visual ~*⟩; *specif* a hearing aid 3 a tribute paid by a vassal to his lord – **in aid of** 1 in order to aid; for the use of ⟨*sold her jewels* in aid of *charity*⟩ 2 *Br* for the purpose of ⟨*what's this* in aid of?⟩ – infml

aide *n* 1 an aide-de-camp 2 *chiefly NAm* an assistant

aide-de-camp *n, pl* **aides-de-camp** an officer in the armed forces acting as a personal assistant to a senior officer

ail *vt* to give pain, discomfort, or trouble to ~ *vi* to be unwell

aileron *n* a movable control surface of an aircraft wing or a movable aerofoil external to the wing at the trailing edge for giving a rolling motion and providing lateral control

ailment *n* a bodily disorder or chronic disease

¹**aim** *vi* 1 to direct a course; *specif* to point a weapon at an object 2 to channel one's efforts; aspire 3 to have the intention; mean ⟨*~s to marry a duke*⟩ ~ *vt* 1 to direct

or point (e g a weapon) at a target 2 to direct at or towards a specified goal; intend ⟨*shows ~*ed at *children*⟩

²**aim** *n* 1a the pointing of a weapon at a mark b the ability to hit a target c a weapon's accuracy or effectiveness 2 a clear intention or purpose – **aimless** *adj*, **aimlessly** *adv*, **aimlessness** *n*

ain't 1 are not 2 is not 3 am not 4 have not 5 has not USE chiefly nonstandard or humor in Br but acceptable in *ain't I* meaning 'am I not' in NAm

¹**air** *n* 1a the mixture of invisible odourless tasteless gases, containing esp nitrogen and oxygen, that surrounds the earth b a light breeze 2a empty unconfined space b nothingness ⟨*vanished into thin ~*⟩ 3a(1) aircraft ⟨*go by ~*⟩ (2) aviation ⟨*~ safety*⟩ b the supposed medium of transmission of radio waves; *also* radio, television ⟨*went on the ~*⟩ 4a the appearance or bearing of a person; demeanour ⟨*an ~ of dignity*⟩ b *pl* an artificial or affected manner; haughtiness ⟨*to put on ~*s⟩ c outward appearance of a thing ⟨*an ~ of luxury*⟩ d a surrounding or pervading influence; an atmosphere ⟨*an ~ of mystery*⟩ 5 a tune, melody – **in the air** 1 not yet settled; uncertain 2 being generally spread round or hinted at ⟨*rumours* in the air *that he will be promoted*⟩

²**air** *vt* 1 to expose to the air for drying, freshening, etc; ventilate 2 to expose to public view or bring to public notice 3 *chiefly Br* to expose to heat so as to warm or finish drying ⟨*~ the sheets round the fire*⟩ ~ *vi* to become exposed to the open air

air bed *n, chiefly Br* an inflatable mattress

airborne *adj* supported or transported by air

air brake *n* 1 a brake operated by compressed air 2 a movable surface projected into the air for slowing an aircraft

air brick *n* a building brick or brick-sized metal box perforated to allow ventilation

airbus *n* a subsonic jet passenger aeroplane designed for short intercity flights

air chief marshal *n* an officer holding the second highest rank in the Royal Air Force

air commodore *n* an officer in the Royal Air Force ranking below air vice-marshal

air-condition *vt* to equip (e g a building) with an apparatus for cleaning air and controlling its humidity and temperature; *also* to subject (air) to these processes – **air conditioner** *n*, **air conditioning** *n*

air-cool *vt* to cool the cylinders of (an internal-combustion engine) directly by air

aircraft *n, pl* **aircraft** a weight-carrying structure that can travel through the air and is supported either by its own buoyancy or by the dynamic action of the air against its surfaces

aircraft carrier *n* a warship designed so that aircraft can be operated from it

aircraftman *n* a person holding the lowest rank in the Royal Air Force

airdrop *n* a delivery of cargo or personnel by parachute from an aircraft – **air-drop** *vt*, **air-droppable** *adj*

Airedale, Airedale terrier *n* any of a breed of large terrier with a hard wiry coat that is dark on the back and side and tan elsewhere

airfield *n* an area of land maintained for the landing and takeoff of aircraft

airflow *n* the motion of air round a moving or stationary object (e g in wind)

air force *n* the branch of a country's armed forces for air warfare

air gun *n* 1 a gun from which a projectile is propelled by compressed air 2 any of various hand tools that work by compressed air

air hole *n* a hole to admit or discharge air

air hostess *n* a stewardess on an airliner

airily *adv* in an airy manner; jauntily, lightly

airing cupboard *n* a heated cupboard in which esp household linen is aired and kept dry

air lane *n* a path customarily followed by aeroplanes

airless *adj* **1** still, windless **2** lacking fresh air; stuffy – **airlessness** *n*

air letter *n* **1** an airmail letter **2** a sheet of airmail stationery that can be folded and sealed with the message inside and the address outside

airlift *n* the transport of cargo or passengers by air, usu to an otherwise inaccessible area – **airlift** *vt*

airline *n* an organization that provides regular public air transport

air line *n, chiefly NAm* a beeline

airliner *n* a passenger aircraft operated by an airline

air lock *n* **1** an airtight intermediate chamber (e g in a spacecraft or submerged caisson) which allows movement between 2 areas of different pressures or atmospheres **2** a stoppage of flow caused by air being in a part where liquid ought to circulate

airmail *n* (the postal system using) mail transported by aircraft – **airmail** *vt*

airman *n, pl* **airmen** a civilian or military pilot, aircraft crew member, etc

air marshal *n* an officer in the Royal Air Force ranking below air chief marshal

airplane *n, chiefly NAm* an aeroplane

air pocket *n* a region of down-flowing or rarefied air that causes an aircraft to drop suddenly

airport *n* a fully-equipped airfield that is used as a base for the transport of passengers and cargo by air

air raid *n* an attack by armed aircraft on a surface target

airship *n* a gas-filled lighter-than-air self-propelled aircraft that has a steering system

airsick *adj* suffering from the motion sickness associated with flying – **airsickness** *n*

airspace *n* the space lying above the earth or a certain area of land or water; *esp* the space lying above a nation and coming under its jurisdiction

airspeed *n* the speed (e g of an aircraft) relative to the air

airstrip *n* LANDING STRIP

airtight *adj* **1** impermeable to air **2** unassailable – **airtightness** *n*

air-to-air *adj* (launched) from one aircraft in flight at another

air vice-marshal *n* an officer in the Royal Air Force ranking below air marshal

airway *n* **1** a passage for air in a mine **2** a designated route along which aircraft fly

airworthy *adj* fit for operation in the air – **airworthiness** *n*

airy *adj* **1a** not having solid foundation; illusory ⟨~ *promises*⟩ **b** showing lack of concern; flippant **2** being light and graceful in movement or manner **3** delicately thin in texture **4** open to the free circulation of air; breezy **5** high in the air; lofty – poetic – **airiness** *n*

aisle *n* **1** the side division of a church separated from the nave by columns or piers **2** *chiefly NAm* a gangway – **aisleless** *adj*

aitch *n* the letter *h*

aitchbone *n* (the cut of beef containing) the hipbone, esp of cattle

ajar *adj or adv, esp of a door* slightly open

akimbo *adj or adv* having the hands on the hips and the elbows turned outwards

akin *adj* **1** descended from a common ancestor **2** essentially similar, related, or compatible *USE* often + *to*

al- – see AD-

¹-al, -ial *suffix* (*n* → *adj*) (having the character) of ⟨*directional*⟩⟨*fictional*⟩

²-al *suffix* (*vb* → *n*) action or process of ⟨*rehearsal*⟩⟨*withdrawal*⟩

³-al *suffix* (→ *n*) **1** aldehyde ⟨*butanal*⟩ **2** acetal ⟨*butyral*⟩

à la *prep* **1** in the manner of **2** prepared, flavoured, or served with ⟨*spinach* ~ *crème*⟩

alabaster *n* a fine-textured usu white and translucent chalky stone often carved into ornaments – **alabaster, alabastrine** *adj*

à la carte *adv or adj* according to a menu that prices each item separately

alack *interj, archaic* – used to express sorrow or regret

alacrity *n* promptness or cheerful readiness – *fml*

à la mode *adj* fashionable, stylish

¹alarm *n* **1** a signal (e g a loud noise or flashing light) that warns or alerts; *also* an automatic device that alerts or rouses **2** the fear resulting from the sudden sensing of danger

²alarm *vt* **1** to give warning to **2** to strike with fear – **alarmingly** *adv*

alarm clock *n* a clock that can be set to sound an alarm at a desired time

alarmism *n* the often unwarranted or excessive arousing of fears; scaremongering – **alarmist** *n or adj*

alas *interj* – used to express unhappiness, pity, or disappointment

albatross *n, pl* **albatrosses**, *esp collectively* **albatross** any of various (very) large web-footed seabirds related to the petrels

albeit *conj* even though – *fml*

albino *n, pl* **albinos** an organism with (congenitally) deficient pigmentation; *esp* a human being or other animal with a (congenital) lack of pigment resulting in a white or translucent skin, white or colourless hair, and eyes with a pink pupil – **albinic** *adj*, **albinism** *n*

album *n* **1** a book with blank pages used for making a collection (e g of stamps or photographs) **2** a recording or collection of recordings issued on 1 or more long-playing gramophone records or cassettes

albumen *n* **1** the white of an egg **2** albumin

albumin *n* any of numerous proteins that occur in large quantities in blood plasma, milk, egg white, plant fluids, etc and are coagulated by heat

alchemy *n* **1** a medieval chemical science and philosophical doctrine aiming to achieve the transmutation of the base metals into gold, a cure for disease, and immortality **2** the transformation of sthg common into sthg precious – **alchemist** *n*, **alchemic, alchemical** *adj*

alcohol *n* **1** a colourless volatile inflammable liquid that is the intoxicating agent in fermented and distilled drinks and is used also as a solvent **2** any of various organic compounds, specif derived from hydrocarbons, containing the hydroxyl group **3** intoxicating drink containing alcohol; *esp* spirits

¹alcoholic *adj* **1** of, containing, or caused by alcohol **2** affected with alcoholism – **alcoholically** *adv*

²alcoholic *n* sby affected with alcoholism

alcoholism *n* (a complex chronic psychological and nutritional disorder associated with) excessive and usu compulsive use of alcoholic drinks

alcove *n* **1a** a nook or recess off a larger room **b** a niche or arched opening (e g in a wall or hedge) **2** *archaic* a summerhouse

alder *n* any of a genus of trees or shrubs of the birch family that grow in moist ground

alderman *n, pl* **aldermen** **1** a person governing a kingdom, district, or shire as viceroy for an Anglo-Saxon king **2** a senior member of a county or borough council elected by the other councillors – not used officially in Britain after 1974 – **aldermanic** *adj*

ale *n* **1** beer **2** a malted and hopped alcoholic drink that is usually more bitter, stronger, and heavier than beer

¹alert *adj* **1** watchful, aware **2** active, brisk – **alertly** *adv*, **alertness** *n*

²alert *n* **1** an alarm or other signal that warns of danger (e g from hostile aircraft) **2** the danger period during which an alert is in effect – **on the alert** on the lookout, esp for danger or opportunity

³alert *vt* **1** to call to a state of readiness; warn **2** to cause to be aware (e g of a need or responsibility)

A level *n* ADVANCED LEVEL

alfalfa *n, NAm* lucerne

alfresco *also* **al fresco** *adj or adv* taking place in the open air ⟨*an ~ lunch*⟩

alga *n, pl* **algae** *also* **algas** any of a group of chiefly aquatic nonvascular plants (e g seaweeds and pond scums) – **algal** *adj*, **algoid** *adj*

algebra *n* a branch of mathematics in which letters, symbols, etc representing various entities are combined according to special rules of operation – **algebraist** *n*, **algebraic** *adj*

algorithm *n* a systematic procedure for solving a mathematical problem in a finite number of steps; *broadly* a step-by-step procedure for solving a problem or accomplishing some end – **algorithmic** *adj*

¹alias *adv* otherwise called or known as ⟨*Hancock ~ Jones*⟩

²alias *n* an assumed name

alibi *n* **1** (evidence supporting) the plea of having been elsewhere when a crime was committed **2** a plausible excuse, usu intended to avert blame or punishment

¹alien *adj* **1a** of or belonging to another person, place, or thing; strange **b** foreign ⟨*~ property*⟩ **2** differing in nature or character, esp to the extent of being opposed – + *to* ⟨*ideas quite ~ to ours*⟩

²alien *n* **1** a person from another family, race, or nation; *also* an extraterrestrial being **2** a foreign-born resident who has not been naturalized; *broadly* a foreign-born citizen – **alienage** *n*, **alienism** *n*

alienate *vt* **1** to convey or transfer (e g property or a right) to another, usu by a specific act **2** to make hostile or indifferent, esp in cases where attachment formerly existed ⟨*~d from their mothers*⟩ **3** to cause to be withdrawn or diverted – **alienator** *n*

alienation *n* **1** a conveyance of property to another **2** (a feeling of) withdrawal from or apathy towards one's former attachments or whole social existence

alienist *n* **1** *NAm* a specialist in legal aspects of psychiatry **2** *archaic* one who treats diseases of the mind

¹alight *vi* **alighted** *also* **alit** **1** to come down from sthg: e g **a** to dismount **b** to disembark **2** to descend from the air and settle; land – **alightment** *n*

²alight *adj* **1** animated, alive ⟨*see the place ~ with merriment* – *Punch*⟩ **2** *chiefly Br* on fire; ignited ⟨*paper caught ~*⟩

align *also* **aline** *vt* **1** to bring into proper relative position or state of adjustment; *specif* to place (3 or more points) in a straight line **2** to array or position on the side of or against a party or cause ⟨*nations ~ed against fascism*⟩ **~** *vi* **1** to join with others in a common cause **2** to be in or come into alignment – **alignment** *n*

¹alike *adj* showing close resemblance without being identical ⟨*~ in their beliefs*⟩

²alike *adv* in the same manner, form, or degree; equally ⟨*peasants and nobility ~ – SEU W*⟩

alimentary *adj* of nourishment or nutrition

alimentary canal *n* the tubular passage that extends from the mouth to the anus and functions in the digestion and absorption of food

alimony *n* **1** means of living; maintenance **2** *chiefly NAm* MAINTENANCE 3

alive *adj* **1** having life **2a** still in existence, force, or operation; active **b** LIVE 3b **3** realizing the existence of sthg; aware of sthg ⟨*~ to the danger*⟩ **4** marked by alertness **5** showing much activity or animation; swarming ⟨*sea was ~ with large whales* – Herman Melville⟩ **6** of all those living – used as an intensive following the noun ⟨*the proudest mother ~*⟩ – **aliveness** *n*

alkali *n, pl* **alkalies, alkalis** any of various chemical bases, esp a hydroxide or carbonate of an alkali metal

alkali metal *n* any of the univalent metals lithium, sodium, potassium, rubidium, caesium, and francium that comprise group 1A of the periodic table

alkaline *adj* (having the properties) of an alkali; *specif* having a pH of more than 7 – **alkalinity** *n*

alkaloid *n* any of numerous nitrogen-containing organic compounds (e g morphine) that are usu chemical bases, occur esp in flowering plants, and are extensively used as drugs – **alkaloidal** *adj*

alkane *n* any of a series of saturated open-chain hydrocarbons (e g methane, ethane, propane, or butane)

¹all *adj* **1a** the whole amount or quantity of ⟨*sat up ~ night*⟩ ⟨*~ the year round*⟩ **b** as much as possible ⟨*spoke in ~ seriousness*⟩ **2a** every one of (more than 2) **b** – used in logic as a verbalized equivalent of the universal quantifier **3** the whole number or sum of ⟨*~ dogs love aniseed*⟩ **4** every ⟨*~ manner of hardship*⟩ **5** any whatever ⟨*beyond ~ doubt*⟩ **6a** given to or displaying only ⟨*was ~ attention*⟩ **b** having or seeming to have (some physical feature) conspicuously or excessively ⟨*~ thumbs*⟩ ⟨*~ ears*⟩ – **all there** not mentally subnormal; esp shrewd – *infml* – **all very well** – used in rejection of advice or sympathy ⟨*it's all very well for you to talk*⟩

²all *adv* **1** wholly, altogether ⟨*sat ~ alone*⟩ ⟨*I'm ~ for it*⟩ **2** to a supreme degree – usu in combination ⟨*all-powerful*⟩ **3** for each side ⟨*the score is 2 ~*⟩

³all *pron, pl* **all** **1** the whole number, quantity, or amount ⟨*it was ~ I could do not to cry*⟩ **2** everybody, everything ⟨*sacrificed ~ for love*⟩ – **all in all** **1** generally; ON THE WHOLE 1 **2** supremely important ⟨*she was all in all to him*⟩ – **all of** fully; AT LEAST ⟨*lost all of £50*⟩ – **all the same** JUST THE SAME

⁴all *n* one's total resources ⟨*gave his ~ for the cause*⟩ – **in all** ALL TOLD

all-, allo- *comb form* **1** other; different; atypical ⟨*allogamous*⟩ ⟨*allopathy*⟩ **2** being one of a (specified) group whose members together constitute a structural unit, esp of a language ⟨*allophone*⟩

Allah *n* GOD 1 – used by Muslims or in reference to the Islamic religion

allay *vt* **1** to reduce the severity of; alleviate **2** to make quiet; pacify

all clear *n* a signal that a danger has passed or that it is safe to proceed

allegation *n* a statement of what one undertakes to prove

allege *vt* to assert without proof or before proving – **alleged** *adj*

allegedly *adv* according to allegation – used in reporting statements that have not been verified

allegiance n 1 the obligation of a subject or citizen to his/her sovereign or government 2 dedication to or dutiful support of a person, group, or cause

allegorical, allegoric adj 1 (having the characteristics) of allegory 2 having hidden spiritual meaning that transcends the literal sense of a sacred text – **allegorically** adv, **allegoricalness** n

allegory n 1a the expression by means of symbolic figures and actions of truths or generalizations about human existence b an instance (e g Spenser's *Faery Queene*) of such expression 2 a symbolic representation; an emblem

allegretto adv or adj faster than andante but not so fast as allegro – used in music

allegro n, adv, or adj, pl **allegros** (a musical composition or movement to be played) in a brisk lively manner

alleluia interj hallelujah

allergic adj 1 of or inducing allergy 2 averse, antipathetic to – infml ⟨~ to marriage⟩

allergy n 1 altered bodily reactivity to an antigen in response to a first exposure ⟨his bee-venom ~ may make a second sting fatal⟩ 2 exaggerated reaction by sneezing, itching, skin rashes, etc to substances that have no such effect on the average individual 3 a feeling of antipathy or aversion – infml

alleviate vt to relieve (a troublesome situation, state of mind, etc) – **alleviative alleviatory** adj, **alleviation** n

¹**alley** n 1 a garden walk bordered by trees or a hedge 2 a bowling alley 3 a narrow back street or passageway between buildings – **up/down one's alley** chiefly NAm UP ONE'S STREET

²**alley** n a playing marble (of superior quality)

alleyway n ALLEY 3

all fours n pl 1 all 4 legs of a quadruped 2 hands and knees ⟨crawling on ~⟩

alliance n 1 a union of families by marriage 2 a confederation of nations by formal treaty 3 a tie, connection ⟨a closer ~ between government and industry⟩

allied adj 1 in close association; united 2 joined in alliance by agreement or treaty 3a related by resemblance or common properties; associated ⟨heraldry and ~ subjects⟩ b related genetically 4 cap of the Allies

alligator n 1 either of 2 crocodilians with broad heads that do not taper towards the snout 2 leather made from alligator hide

all-in adj 1 chiefly Br all-inclusive; esp including all costs ⟨an ~ holiday in Greece⟩ 2 Br, of wrestling having almost no holds barred

all in adj tired out; exhausted – infml

alliteration n the repetition of usu initial consonant sounds in neighbouring words or syllables (e g threatening throngs of threshers) – **alliterative** adj, **alliteratively** adv

allocate vt 1a to apportion and distribute (e g money or responsibility) in shares b to assign (sthg limited in supply) to as a share ⟨we've been ~d the top flat⟩ 2 to earmark, designate ⟨~ a section of the building for research purposes⟩ – **allocatable** adj, **allocator** n, **allocation** n

allopathy n conventional medical practice using all effective treatments, esp when producing effects different from those of the disease being treated – **allopathic** adj, **allopathically** adv

allot vt -tt- to allocate – **allotter** n

allotment n, Br a small plot of land let out to an individual (e g by a town council) for cultivation

all-out adj using maximum effort and resources ⟨an ~ effort to win the contest⟩

all out adv with maximum determination and effort; FLAT OUT – chiefly in go all out

allover adj covering the whole extent or surface ⟨a sweater with an ~ pattern⟩

all over adv 1 over the whole extent or surface ⟨decorated ~ with a flower pattern⟩ 2 in every respect ⟨that's Paul ~⟩

allow vt 1a(1) to assign as a share or suitable amount (e g of time or money) ⟨~ an hour for lunch⟩ (2) to grant as an allowance ⟨~ed him £500 a year⟩ b to reckon as a deduction or an addition ⟨~ a gallon for leakage⟩ 2a to admit as true or valid; acknowledge b to admit the possibility of ⟨the facts ~ only one explanation⟩ 3 to permit: e g a to make it possible for; enable ⟨the gift will ~ me to buy a car⟩ b to fail to prevent; let ⟨~ herself to get fat⟩ ~ vi 1 to admit the possibility of ⟨evidence that ~s of only one conclusion⟩ 2 to make allowance for ⟨~ for expansion⟩

allowable adj 1 permissible 2 assigned as an allowance ⟨expenses ~ against tax⟩

¹**allowance** n 1a a (limited) share or portion allotted or granted; a ration b a sum granted as a reimbursement or bounty or for expenses c a reduction from a list price or stated price 2 a handicap (e g in a race) 3a permission, sanction b acknowledgment ⟨~ of your claim⟩ 4 the taking into account of mitigating circumstances – often pl with sing. meaning ⟨make ~s for his youth⟩

²**allowance** vt 1 to put on a fixed allowance 2 to provide in a limited quantity

¹**alloy** n 1 a solid substance composed of a mixture of metals or a metal and a nonmetal thoroughly intermixed 2 a metal mixed with a more valuable metal 3 an addition that impairs or debases

²**alloy** vt 1 to reduce the purity or value of by adding sthg 2 to mix so as to form an alloy 3a to impair or debase by addition b to temper, moderate

all-powerful adj having complete or sole power; omnipotent

all-purpose adj suited for many purposes or uses

¹**all right** adv 1 well enough ⟨does ~ in school⟩ 2 beyond doubt; certainly ⟨he has pneumonia ~⟩

²**all right** adj 1 satisfactory, acceptable ⟨the film is ~ for children⟩ 2 safe, well ⟨he was ill but he's ~ now⟩ 3 agreeable, pleasing – used as a generalized term of approval

³**all right** interj 1 – used for giving assent ⟨~, let's go⟩ 2 – used in indignant or menacing response ⟨~! Just you wait⟩

all-round adj 1 competent in many fields ⟨an ~ athlete⟩ 2 having general utility 3 encompassing all aspects; comprehensive ⟨an ~ reduction in price⟩

all round adv 1 by, for, or to everyone present ⟨ordered drinks ~⟩ 2 in every respect

allspice n (a mildly pungent spice prepared from) the berry of a W Indian tree belonging to the myrtle family

all-star adj composed wholly or chiefly of stars of the theatre, cinema, etc ⟨an ~ cast⟩

all-time adj exceeding all others yet known ⟨an ~ best seller⟩

all told adv with everything taken into account

allude vi to make indirect, casual, or implicit reference to

¹**allure** vt to entice by charm or attraction – **allurement** n

²**allure** n power of attraction or fascination; charm

allusion n 1 alluding or hinting 2 (the use of) implied or indirect reference, esp in literature – **allusive** adj, **allusively** adv, **allusiveness** n

alluvium *n, pl* **alluviums, alluvia** clay, silt, or similar detrital material deposited by running water – **alluvial** *adj*

¹**ally** *vt* **1** to join, unite *with/to* ⟨allied *himself with a wealthy family by marriage*⟩ **2** to relate *to* by resemblance or common properties ⟨*its beak allies it to the finches*⟩ ~ *vi* to form or enter into an alliance *with*

²**ally** *n* **1** a sovereign or state associated with another by treaty or league **2** a helper, auxiliary

-ally *suffix* (*adj* → *adv*) ²-LY ⟨*terrifically*⟩

alma mater *n* a school, college, or university which one has attended

almanac, almanack *n* **1** a usu annual publication containing statistical, tabular, and general information **2** *chiefly Br* a publication containing astronomical and meteorological data arranged according to the days, weeks, and months of a given year

¹**almighty** *adj* **1** *often cap* having absolute power over all ⟨Almighty *God*⟩ **2** having relatively unlimited power ⟨*the* ~ *dollar*⟩ **3** great in extent, seriousness, force, etc ⟨*an* ~ *crash*⟩ – infml – **almightiness** *n, often cap,* **almightiest** *adj*

²**almighty** *adv* to a great degree; mighty – infml

Almighty *n* GOD **1** – + *the*

almond *n* (the edible oval nut of) a small tree of the rose family

almond-eyed *adj* having narrow slanting almond-shaped eyes

almoner *n* **1** one who distributes alms **2** a social worker attached to a British hospital – not now used technically

almost *adv* very nearly but not exactly or entirely

alms *n sing or pl in constr* money, food, etc given to help the poor – **almsgiver** *n*, **almsgiving** *n*

almshouse *n, Br* a privately endowed house in which a poor person can live

aloe *n* **1** any of a large genus of succulent plants of the lily family with tall spikes of flowers **2** the dried juice of the leaves of various aloes used esp as a purgative – usu pl but sing. in constr

aloft *adv* **1** at or to a great height **2** at, on, or to the masthead or the upper rigging of a ship

alone *adj or adv* **1** considered without reference to any other; *esp* unassisted ⟨*the children* ~ *would eat that much*⟩ **2** separated from others; isolated ⟨*stands* ~⟩ **3** exclusive of other factors ⟨*time* ~ *will show*⟩ **4** free from interference ⟨*leave my bag* ~⟩ – **aloneness** *n*

¹**along** *prep* **1** in a line parallel with the length or direction of **2** in the course of (a route or journey) **3** in accordance with ⟨*something* ~ *these lines*⟩

²**along** *adv* **1** forward, on ⟨*move* ~⟩ **2** as a necessary or pleasant addition; with one ⟨*take your flute* ~⟩ **3** in company and simultaneously *with* ⟨*pay a penny a week* ~ *with all the other village boys* – SEU S⟩ **4** also; IN ADDITION ⟨*a bill came* ~ *with the parcel*⟩ **5** on hand, there ⟨*I'll be* ~ *in 5 minutes*⟩ – **all along** all the time ⟨*knew the truth all along*⟩

¹**alongside** *adv* along or at the side

²**alongside, alongside of** *prep* **1** side by side with; *specif* parallel to **2** concurrently with

¹**aloof** *adv* at a distance; out of involvement

²**aloof** *adj* distant in interest or feeling; reserved, unsympathetic – **aloofly** *adv*, **aloofness** *n*

alopecia *n* usu abnormal baldness in humans or loss of wool, feathers, etc in animals – **alopecic** *adj*

aloud *adv* with the speaking voice

alpaca *n* **1** (the fine long woolly hair of) a type of domesticated llama found in Peru **2** a thin cloth made of or containing this wool

alpenhorn *n* a long straight wooden horn used, esp formerly, by Swiss herdsmen to call sheep and cattle

alpenstock *n* a long iron-pointed staff, now superseded by the ice axe, for use in mountain climbing

¹**alpha** *n* **1** the 1st letter of the Greek alphabet **2** sthg that is first; a beginning **3** – used to designate the chief or brightest star of a constellation **4** ¹A **4**

²**alpha, α-** *adj* alphabetical ⟨~ *order*⟩

Alpha, Alfa – a communications code word for the letter *a*

alpha and omega *n* the beginning and ending

alphabet *n* a set of characters, esp letters, used to represent 1 or more languages, esp when arranged in a conventional order; *also* a system of signs and signals that can be used in place of letters

alphabetical, alphabetic *adj* **1** of or employing an alphabet **2** in the order of the letters of the alphabet – **alphabetically** *adv*

alpha particle *n* a positively charged nuclear particle identical with the nucleus of a helium atom ejected at high speed by some radioactive substances

alpine *n* an (ornamental) plant native to alpine or northern parts of the northern hemisphere

Alpine *adj* **1** *often not cap* of, growing in, or resembling the Alps; *broadly* of or resembling any mountains **2** *often not cap* of or growing in the elevated slopes above the tree line **3** of or being competitive ski events comprising slalom and downhill racing

already *adv* **1** no later than now or then; even by this or that time ⟨*he had* ~ *left*⟩ **2** before, previously ⟨*had seen the film* ~⟩

alright *adv, adj, or interj* ALL RIGHT – nonstandard

Alsatian *n* (any of) a breed of large intelligent dogs often used as guard dogs

also *adv* as an additional circumstance; besides

also-ran *n* **1** an entrant, esp a horse, that finishes outside the first 3 places in a race **2** a person of little importance

altar *n* **1** a usu raised structure or place on which sacrifices are offered or incense is burnt in worship **2** a table on which the bread and wine used at communion are consecrated or which serves as a centre of worship or ritual

altarpiece *n* a work of art that decorates the space above and behind an altar

alter *vt* **1** to make different without changing into sthg else **2** *chiefly NAm* to castrate, spay – euph ~ *vi* to become different – **alterer** *n*, **alterable** *adj*, **alterably** *adv*, **alteration** *n*, **alterability** *n*

altercation *n* a heated quarrel; *also* quarrelling

alter ego *n* a second self; *esp* a trusted friend

¹**alternate** *adj* **1** occurring or succeeding each other by turns ⟨*a day of* ~ *sunshine and rain*⟩ **2a** *of plant parts* arranged singly first on one side and then on the other of an axis **b** arranged one above or alongside the other **3** every other; every second ⟨*he works on* ~ *days*⟩ **4** of an angle being either of a pair on opposite sides of a transverse line at its intersection with 2 other lines **5** *NAm* ¹ALTERNATIVE **2** – **alternately** *adv*

²**alternate** *vt* to interchange with sthg else in turn ⟨~ *work with sleep*⟩ ~ *vi* **1** *of 2 things* to occur or succeed each other by turns ⟨*work and sleep* ~⟩ **2** to undergo or consist of repeated change from one thing to another ⟨*he* ~ *s between work and sleep*⟩ – **alternation** *n*

alternating current *n* an electric current that reverses its direction at regularly recurring intervals

¹**alternative** *adj* **1** affording a choice, esp between 2 mutually exclusive options **2** constituting an alternative **3**

..f or catering for the alternative society ⟨~ *technology*⟩ - **alternatively** *adv*

...ternative *n* 1 an opportunity or need for deciding ..etween 2 or more possibilities 2 either of 2 possibilities ..etween which a choice is to be made; *also* any of more ..han 2 such possibilities

...ternator *n* an electric generator for producing alternat..ng current

...though *also* **altho** *conj* in spite of the fact or possibility ..hat; though

...timeter *n* an instrument for measuring altitude – **altim-** ..try *n*

...titude *n* 1 the angular elevation of a celestial object ..bove the horizon 2 the height of an object (e g an ..ircraft), esp above sea level 3 the perpendicular distance ..rom the base of a geometrical figure to the vertex or the ..ide parallel to the base – **altitudinal** *adj*

...to *n, pl* **altos** 1a a countertenor b a contralto 2 the ..cond highest part in 4-part harmony 3 a member of a ..amily of instruments having a range between the treble or ..prano and the tenor – **alto** *adj*

...together *adv* 1 wholly, thoroughly ⟨*an* ~ *different* ..roblem*⟩ 2 ALL TOLD 3 in the main; ON THE WHOLE 4 in ..very way ⟨*more complicated* ~⟩

...together *n* the nude ⟨*posed in the* ~⟩ – *infml*

...truism *n* unselfish regard for or devotion to the welfare ..f others – **altruist** *n*, **altruistic** *adj*, **altruistically** *adv*

...um *n* (any of various double salts with a similar crystal ..ructure to) a sulphate of aluminium with potassium or ..mmonium, used esp as an emetic and astringent

...uminium *n* a bluish silver-white malleable light tri-..alent metallic element with good electrical and thermal ..nductivity and resistance to oxidation

...mnus, *fem* **alumna** *n, pl* **alumni,** *fem* **alumnae** *chiefly Am* a former student of a particular school, college, or ..iversity; *broadly* a former member of any organiza-..on

...eolar *adj* 1 of, resembling, made up of, or having ..veoli or an alveolus 2 articulated with the tip of the ..ngue touching or near the ridge of flesh behind the front ..eth ⟨*an* ~ *consonant*⟩

...eolus *n, pl* **alveoli** a small cavity or pit: e g a a socket ..r a tooth b an air cell of the lungs c a cell or compart-..ent of a honeycomb

...ays *adv* 1a at all times ⟨*have* ~ *lived here*⟩ b in all ..ses ⟨*they* ~ *have long tails*⟩ 2 on every occasion; ..peatedly ⟨*he's* ~ *complaining*⟩ 3 forever, perpetually ..ill ~ *love you*⟩ 4 as a last resort; at any rate ⟨*they* ..uld ~ *eat cake*⟩

...ssum *n* 1 any of a genus of Old World yellow-flowered ..ants of the mustard family 2 an annual or perennial ..ropean plant of the mustard family that has clusters of ..all fragrant usu white flowers

..**𝟏** *pres 1 sing of* BE

𝟏 *adj* of or being a broadcasting or receiving system ..ng amplitude modulation

...algam *n* 1 an alloy of mercury with another metal (e g ..ed in making dental fillings) 2 a mixture of different ..ments

...algamate *vt* to unite (as if) in an amalgam; *esp* ..mbine into a single body

...anuensis *n, pl* **amanuenses** sby employed to write ..m dictation or to copy manuscript

...ass *vt* 1 to collect for oneself; accumulate ⟨~ *a great* ..tune*⟩ 2 to bring together into a mass; gather

...ateur *n* 1 one who engages in a pursuit as a pastime ..her than as a profession; *esp* a sportsman who has never ..npeted for money 2 one who practises an art or science

unskilfully; a dabbler – **amateur** *adj*, **amateurish** *adj*, **amateurishly** *adv*, **amateurishness** *n*, **amateurism** *n*

amatory *adj* of or expressing sexual love

amaze *vt* to fill with wonder; astound – **amazement** *n*

amazing *adj* – used as a generalized term of approval ⟨*she has the most* ~ *vintage car*⟩

amazon *n, often cap* a tall strong athletic woman

ambassador *n* 1 an official envoy: e g a a top-ranking diplomat accredited to a foreign government or sovereign as a resident representative b one similarly appointed for a special and often temporary diplomatic assignment 2 a representative, messenger – **ambassadorship** *n*, **ambassadorial** *adj*

amber *n* 1 a hard yellowish to brownish translucent fossil resin used chiefly for ornaments and jewellery 2 the colour of amber 3 a yellow traffic light meaning 'caution' – **amber** *adj*

ambergris *n* a waxy substance found floating in tropical waters, believed to originate in the intestines of the sperm whale, and used in perfumery as a fixative

ambi- *prefix* both; two ⟨ambi*valent*⟩ ⟨ambi*guous*⟩

ambidextrous *adj* 1 able to use either hand with equal ease 2 unusually skilful; versatile 3 characterized by deceitfulness and double-dealing – **ambidextrously** *adv*, **ambidexterity** *n*

ambience, ambiance *n* a surrounding or pervading atmosphere; an environment, milieu

𝟏ambient *adj* surrounding on all sides; encompassing – fml

𝟐ambient *n* ambience – *fml*

ambiguity *n* 1 (a word or expression with) the quality of being ambiguous or imprecise in meaning 2 uncertainty of meaning or relative position ⟨*the basic* ~ *of her political stance*⟩

ambiguous *adj* 1 vague, indistinct, or difficult to classify 2 capable of 2 or more interpretations – **ambiguously** *adv*, **ambiguousness** *n*

ambit *n* 1 a limiting circumference 2 the bounds or limits of a place; the precincts 3 a sphere of influence; a scope

ambition *n* 1a a strong desire for status, wealth, or power b a desire to achieve a particular end 2 an object of ambition – **ambitionless** *adj*

ambitious *adj* 1a having or controlled by ambition b desirous *of*, aspiring 2 resulting from or showing ambition ⟨*an* ~ *attempt*⟩ 3 elaborate ⟨*cooked nothing more* ~ *than boiled eggs*⟩ – **ambitiously** *adv*, **ambitiousness** *n*

ambivalence *n* the state of having 2 opposing and contradictory attitudes or feelings towards an object, person, etc – **ambivalent** *adj*, **ambivalently** *adv*

𝟏amble *vi* **ambling** to move at an amble

𝟐amble *n* 1 an easy gait of a horse in which the legs on the same side of the body move together 2 an easy gait 3 a leisurely stroll

ambrosia *n* 1 the food of the Greek and Roman gods 2 sthg extremely pleasing to the taste or smell – **ambrosial** *adj*

ambulance *n* a vehicle equipped to transport the injured or ill

𝟏ambush *vt* to attack from an ambush; waylay ~ *vi* to lie in wait; lurk – **ambushment** *n*

𝟐ambush *n* 1 the concealment of soldiers, police, etc in order to carry out a surprise attack from a hidden position 2 people stationed in ambush; *also* their concealed position

ameba *n, chiefly NAm* an amoeba – **amebic** *also* **ameban** *adj*, **ameboid** *adj*

ameliorate *vb* to make or become better or more tolerable – **ameliorative** *adj*, **amelioration** *n*

amen *interj* – used to express solemn ratification (e g of an expression of faith) or hearty approval (e g of an assertion)

amenable *adj* **1** liable to be brought to account; answerable **2a** capable of submission (e g to judgment or test) **b** readily persuaded to yield or agree; tractable – **amenably** *adv*, **amenability** *n*

amend *vt* **1** to put right; *specif* to make emendations in (e g a text) **2a** to change or modify for the better; improve **b** to alter (e g a document) formally ⟨~ *the constitution*⟩

amendment *n* **1** the act of amending, esp for the better **2** an alteration proposed or effected by amending ⟨*several* ~s *to the Bill*⟩

amends *n pl but sing or pl in constr* compensation for a loss or injury; recompense ⟨*make* ~⟩

amenity *n* **1** sthg (e g a public facility) conducive to material comfort – often *pl* ⟨*urban amenities: roads, water, sewerage, and power – National Times (Sydney)*⟩ **2** sthg (e g a conventional social gesture) conducive to ease of social intercourse – usu *pl* **3** pleasantness, esp of environment – *fml*

¹American *n* **1** a N or S American Indian **2** a native or inhabitant of N or S America **3** a citizen of the USA **4** English as typically spoken and written in the USA

²American *adj* **1** (characteristic) of N or S America **2** (characteristic) of the USA **3** of the N and S American Indians

American Indian *n* a member of any of the indigenous peoples of N, S, or central America excluding the Eskimos

Americanism *n* **1** a characteristic feature (e g a custom or belief) of Americans or American culture **2a** adherence or attachment to America and its culture **b** the promotion of American policies

americanize, -ise *vb, often cap* to (cause to) have or acquire American customs, characteristics, etc – **americanization**, *often cap*

amethyst *n* a semiprecious gemstone of clear purple or violet quartz – **amethystine** *adj*

amiable *adj* **1** (seeming) agreeable and well-intentioned; inoffensive **2** friendly, congenial – **amiableness** *n*, **amiably** *adv*, **amiability** *n*

amicable *adj* characterized by friendly goodwill; peaceable – **amicableness** *n*, **amicably** *adv*, **amicability** *n*

amid *prep* in or to the middle of – poetic

amidships *adv* in or towards the middle part (of a ship)

amino acid *n* any of various organic acids containing an amino group and occurring esp in linear chains as the chief components of proteins

amir *n* an emir

amiss *adv or adj* **1** astray **2** out of order; at fault **3** out of place in given circumstances – usu + a negative ⟨*a few pertinent remarks may not come* ~ *here*⟩

amity *n* friendship

ammeter *n* an instrument for measuring electric current in amperes

ammo *n* ammunition – *infml*

ammonia *n* a pungent colourless·gas that is a compound of nitrogen and hydrogen and is very soluble in water, forming an alkaline solution

ammonite *n* a flat spiral fossil shell of a mollusc abundant esp in the Mesozoic age – **ammonitic** *adj*

ammunition *n* **1** the projectiles, together with their propelling charges, used in the firing of guns; *also* bombs, grenades, etc containing explosives **2** material used to defend or attack a point of view ⟨*his indiscretions provided* ~ *for the press*⟩

amnesia *n* a (pathological) loss of memory – **amnesia** **amnesic** *adj or n*, **amnestic** *adj*

amnesty *n* the act of pardoning a large group of indivi uals, esp for political offences – **amnesty** *vt*

amoeba, *chiefly NAm* **ameba** *n, pl* **amoebas, amoebae** *o* of various protozoans with lobed pseudopodia and wit out permanent organelles that are widely distributed water and wet places – **amoebic** *also* **amoeban** *adj*

amok, amuck *adv* **1** in a murderous frenzy; raging vic ently **2** OUT OF HAND 2 *USE* chiefly in *run amok*

among *prep* **1** in or through the midst of; surrounded b ⟨*living* ~ *artists*⟩ **2** by or through the whole group ⟨*discontent* ~ *the poor*⟩ **3** in the number or class of ⟨ *other things he was head boy*⟩ **4** between – used for mo than 2 ⟨*divided* ~ *the heirs*⟩ ⟨*quarrel* ~ *themselves*⟩ through the joint action of ⟨*made a fortune* ~ *the* selves⟩

amoral *adj* **1** being neither moral nor immoral; spe lying outside the sphere of ethical judgments **2** having understanding of, or unconcerned with, morals – **amor ism** *n*, **amorally** *adv*, **amorality** *n*

amorous *adj* **1** of or relating to love **2** moved by inclined to love or desire – **amorously** *adv*, **amorou ness** *n*

amorphous *adj* **1a** having no definite form; shapeless without definite character; unclassifiable **2** not crystalli – **amorphously** *adv*, **amorphousness** *n*

amortize, -ise *vt* to provide for the gradual extinguis ment of (e g a mortgage), usu by periodic contributions a sinking fund – **amortizable** *adj*, **amortization** *n*

¹amount *vi* to be equal in number, quantity, or signi cance *to*

²amount *n* **1** the total quantity **2** the quantity at hand under consideration ⟨*has an enormous* ~ *of energy*⟩

amour *n* a love affair, esp when illicit

amp *n* **1** an ampere **2** an amplifier *USE* infml

AMP *n* a mononucleotide of adenine that is reversi converted in cells to ADP and ATP

amperage *n* the strength of a current of electric expressed in amperes

ampere *n* the basic SI unit of electric current equal t constant current that when maintained in 2 straight par lel conductors of infinite length and negligible circu cross-section 1 metre apart in a vacuum produces betwe the conductors a force equal to 2×10^{-7} newton per me of length

ampersand *n* a sign, typically &, standing for the w *and*

amphetamine *n* (any of several derivatives of) a s· thetic stimulant of the brain which is a common drug abuse

amphibian *n, pl* **amphibians,** (*l*) **amphibians,** *esp coll tively* **amphibia** **1** an amphibious organism; *esp* a fr toad, newt, or other member of a class of cold-bloo vertebrates intermediate in many characteristics betw fishes and reptiles **2** an aeroplane, tank, etc adapted operate on or from both land and water – **amphib** *adj*

amphibious *adj* **1** able to live both on land and in wa **2a** relating to or adapted for both land and water ‹ *vehicles*⟩ **b** involving or trained for coordinated actio land, sea, and air forces organized for invasion **3** com· ing 2 positions or qualities – **amphibiously** *adv*, **amph ousness** *n*

amphitheatre *n* **1** an oval or circular building w rising tiers of seats ranged about an open space **2** semicircular gallery in a theatre **b** a flat or gently slop area surrounded by abrupt slopes **3** a place of pu games or contests

amphora *n, pl* **amphorae, amphoras** a 2-handled oval jar or vase with a narrow neck and base, orig used by the ancient Greeks and Romans for holding oil or wine

ample *adj* **1** generous in size, scope, or capacity **2** abundant, plentiful ⟨*they had* ~ *money for the trip*⟩ **3** buxom, 'portly – chiefly euph – **ampleness** *n*, **amply** *adv*

amplifier *n* a device usu employing valves or transistors to obtain amplification of voltage, current, or power

amplify *vt* **1** to expand (e g a statement) by the use of detail, illustration, etc **2** to make larger or greater; increase **3** to increase the magnitude of (a signal or other input of power) ~ *vi* to expand *on* one's remarks or ideas – **amplification** *n*

amplitude *n* **1** largeness of **a** dimensions **b** scope; abundance **2** the extent of a vibration or oscillation measured from the mean to a maximum

ampoule, *chiefly NAm* ampul, ampule *n* a hermetically sealed small bulbous glass vessel used esp to hold a sterile solution for hypodermic injection

amputate *vt* to cut or lop off; *esp* to cut (e g a damaged or diseased limb) from the body – **amputator** *n*, **amputation** *n*

amputee *n* sby who has had a limb amputated

amuck *adv* amok

amulet *n* a small object worn as a charm against evil

amuse *vt* **1** to entertain or occupy in a light or pleasant manner ⟨~ *the child with a story*⟩ **2** to appeal to the sense of humour of ⟨*the joke doesn't* ~ *me*⟩ – **amuser** *n*, **musing** *adj*, **amusingly** *adv*, **amusingness** *n*, **amusedly** *adv*

amusement *n* a means of entertaining or occupying; a pleasurable diversion

amusement arcade *n, chiefly Br* a covered area containing coin-operated games machines for recreation

amusement park *n* an enclosed park where various amusements (e g roundabouts, sideshows, etc) are permanently set up

an *indefinite article* ²A – used (1) before words with an initial vowel sound ⟨~ *oak*⟩⟨~ *honour*⟩ (2) frequently, esp formerly or in the USA, before words whose initial *h/* sound is often lost before the *an* ⟨~ *hotel*⟩ (3) sometimes, esp formerly in British writing, before words like *union* or *European* whose initial sound is */y/*

an, an' *conj* **1** and – *infml* **2** *archaic* if

an *prep* ³A – used under the same conditions as ¹AN

an- – see ²A-

-an, -ian *also* **-ean** *suffix* (→ *n*) **1** one who is of or belonging to ⟨*Mancunian*⟩⟨*republican*⟩ **2** one skilled in or specializing in ⟨*phonetician*⟩

-an, -ian *also* **-ean** *suffix* (→ *adj*) **1** of or belonging to ⟨*American*⟩⟨*Christian*⟩ **2** characteristic of; resembling ⟨*Mozartean*⟩⟨*Shavian*⟩

anachronism *n* **1** an error in chronology; *esp* a chronological misplacing of people, events, objects, or customs **2** sby who or sthg that seems chronologically out of place – **anachronistic** *also* **anachronic, anachronous** *adj*, **anachronistically** *also* **anachronously** *adv*

anaconda *n* a large semiaquatic S American snake of the boa family that crushes its prey in its coils

anaemia, *chiefly NAm* anemia *n* **1a** a condition in which the blood is deficient in red blood cells, haemoglobin, or total volume **b** ischaemia **2** lack of vitality – **anaemic** *adj*, **anaemically** *adv*

anaesthesia, *chiefly NAm* anesthesia *n* loss of sensation, esp loss of sensation of pain, resulting either from injury or a disorder of the nerves or from the action of drugs

anaesthetic, *chiefly NAm* anesthetic *n* a substance that produces anaesthesia, e g so that surgery can be carried out painlessly – **anaesthetic** *adj*, **anaesthetically** *adv*

anaesthetize, -ise, *chiefly NAm* anesthetize *vt* to subject to anaesthesia, esp for purposes of surgery – **anaesthetist** *n*

anagram *n* a word or phrase made by rearranging the letters of another – **anagrammatic, anagrammatical** *adj*, **anagrammatically** *adv*, **anagrammatize** *vt*

anal *adj* **1** of or situated near the anus **2** of or characterized by (parsimony, meticulousness, or other personality traits typical of) the stage of sexual development during which the child is concerned esp with faeces – **anally** *adv*, **anality** *n*

analgesia *n* insensibility to pain without loss of consciousness – **analgesic** *adj or n*, **analgetic** *adj or n*

analogize, -ise *vb* to compare by or use analogy

analogous *adj* **1** corresponding by analogy **2** being or related to as an analogue – **analogously** *adv*, **analogousness** *n*

¹analogue, *NAm chiefly* analog *n* sthg analogous or parallel to sthg else

²analogue, *NAm chiefly* analog *adj* of an analogue computer

analogue computer *n* a computer that operates with numbers represented by directly measurable quantities (e g voltages or mechanical rotations)

analogy *n* **1** inference from a parallel case **2** resemblance in some particulars; similarity **3** the tendency for new words or linguistic forms to be created in imitation of existing patterns **4** correspondence in function between anatomical parts of different structure and origin – **analogic, analogical** *adj*, **analogically** *adv*

analyse, *NAm chiefly* analyze *vt* **1** to subject to analysis **2** to determine by analysis the constitution or structure of **3** to psychoanalyse – **analysable** *adj*

analysis *n, pl* **analyses 1a** examination and identification of the components of a whole **b** a statement of such an analysis **2** the use of function words instead of inflectional forms as a characteristic device of a language **3** psychoanalysis

analyst *n* **1** a person who analyses or is skilled in analysis **2** a psychoanalyst

analytic, analytical *adj* **1** of analysis **2** skilled in or using analysis, esp in reasoning ⟨*a keenly* ~ *man*⟩ **3** asserting of a subject a predicate that is part of the meaning of that subject; *broadly* logically necessary; tautologous ⟨*"all women are female" is an* ~ *truth*⟩ **4** characterized by analysis rather than inflection ⟨~ *languages*⟩ **5** psychoanalytic – **analytically** *adv*, **analyticity** *n*

anapaest, *NAm chiefly* anapest *n* a metrical foot consisting of 2 short syllables followed by 1 long – **anapaestic** *adj or n*

anarchism *n* **1** a political theory holding all forms of governmental authority to be undesirable **2** the attacking of the established social order or laws; rebellion

anarchist *n* **1** one who attacks the established social order or laws; a rebel **2** a believer in or (violent) promoter of anarchism or anarchy – **anarchist, anarchistic** *adj*

anarchy *n* **1a** absence of government **b** lawlessness; (political) disorder **c** a utopian society with complete freedom and no government **2** anarchism – **anarchic** *adj*, **anarchically** *adv*

anathema *n* **1a** (the object of) a ban or curse solemnly pronounced by ecclesiastical authority and accompanied by excommunication **b** a vigorous denunciation; a curse **2** sby or sthg despised ⟨*his opinions are* ~ *to me*⟩ – **anathematize** *vt*

anatomist *n* **1** a student of anatomy (skilled in dissection) **2** one who analyses minutely and critically ⟨*an ~ of urban society*⟩

anatomy *n* **1** (a treatise on) the biology of the structure of organisms **2** dissection **3** structural make-up, esp of (a part of) an organism **4** an analysis **5** the human body – **anatomic, anatomical** *adj*, **anatomically** *adv*

-ance *suffix* (→ *n*) **1** action or process of ⟨*further*ance⟩; *also* instance of (a specified action or process) ⟨*perform*ance⟩ **2** quality or state of ⟨*brilli*ance⟩; *also* instance of (a specified quality or state) ⟨*protuber*ance⟩ **3** amount or degree of ⟨*conduct*ance⟩

ancestor, *fem* **ancestress** *n* **1a** one from whom a person is descended, usu more distant than a grandparent **b** FOREFATHER 2 **2** a progenitor of a more recent (species of) organism – **ancestral** *adj*, **ancestrally** *adv*

ancestry *n* a line of esp noble descent; a lineage

¹anchor *n* **1** a usu metal device dropped to the bottom from a ship or boat to hold it in a particular place **2** sby or sthg providing support and security; a mainstay **3** sthg that serves to hold an object firmly – **anchorless** *adj*

²anchor *vt* **1** to hold in place in the water by an anchor **2** to secure firmly; fix ~ *vi* **1** to cast anchor **2** to become fixed; settle

anchorage *n* **1** a place (suitable) for vessels to anchor **2** a source of reassurance **3** sthg that provides a secure hold or attachment

anchorite, *fem* **anchoress, anchress** *n* one who lives in seclusion, usu for religious reasons – **anchoritic** *adj*

anchovy *n*, *pl* **anchovies**, *esp collectively* **anchovy** a common small Mediterranean fish resembling a herring and used esp in appetizers and as a garnish; *also* any of various small fish related to this

¹ancient *adj* **1** having existed for many years **2** of (those living in) a remote period, specif that from the earliest known civilizations to the fall of the western Roman Empire in AD 476 **3** old-fashioned, antique

²ancient *n* **1a** sby who lived in ancient times **b** *pl the* members of a civilized, esp a classical, nation of antiquity **2** *archaic* an aged person

¹ancillary *adj* **1** subordinate, subsidiary **2** auxiliary, supplementary

²ancillary *n*, *Br* one who assists; a helper

-ancy *suffix* (→ *n*) quality or state of ⟨*piqu*ancy⟩ ⟨*expect*ancy⟩

and *conj* **1** – used to join coordinate sentence elements of the same class or function expressing addition or combination ⟨*cold ~ hungry*⟩ ⟨*John ~ I*⟩ **2** – used, esp in Br speech, before the numbers 1-99 after the number 100 ⟨*three hundred ~ seventeen*⟩; used also orig between tens and units ⟨*five ~ twenty blackbirds*⟩ **3** plus ⟨*three ~ three make six*⟩ **4** – used to introduce a second clause expressing temporal sequence ⟨*came to tea ~ stayed to dinner*⟩, consequence ⟨*water the seeds ~ they will grow*⟩, contrast ⟨*he's old ~ I'm young*⟩, or supplementary explanation ⟨*she's ill ~ can't travel*⟩ **5** – used to join repeated words expressing continuation or progression ⟨*ran ~ ran*⟩ ⟨*waited hours ~ hours*⟩ ⟨*came nearer ~ nearer*⟩ **6** – used to join words expressing contract of type or quality ⟨*there are aunts ~ aunts*⟩ ⟨*gynaecology of one sort ~ another* – Jan Morris⟩ **7** – used instead of *to* to introduce an infinitive after *come, go, run, try, stop* ⟨*come ~ look*⟩ – **and all that, and all** AND SO FORTH – **and how** – used to emphasize the preceding idea; infml – **and so forth, and so on 1** and others or more of the same kind **2** and further in the same manner **3** and the rest. **4** and other things – **and that** *chiefly Br* AND SO FORTH – nonstandard

andante *n*, *adv*, *or adj* (a musical composition or movement to be played) moderately slow

andiron *n* either of a pair of metal stands used on a hearth to support burning wood

androgynous *adj* having characteristics of both the male and female forms – **androgyny** *n*

anecdotal *adj* consisting of or depicting an anecdote ⟨*~ art*⟩ – **anecdotally** *adv*

anecdote *n* a usu short narrative about an interesting or amusing person or incident – **anecdotist, anecdotalist** *n*, **anecdotic, anecdotical** *adj*

anemia *n*, *chiefly NAm* anaemia – **anemic** *adj*, **anemically** *adv*

anemometer *n* an instrument for measuring the force or speed of the wind – **anemometry** *n*, **anemometric** *also* **anemometrical** *adj*

anemone *n* **1** any of a large genus of plants of the buttercup family with lobed or divided leaves and showy flowers **2** SEA ANEMONE

aneroid *adj* containing no liquid or operated without the use of liquid ⟨*an ~ barometer*⟩

anesthesia *n*, *chiefly NAm* anaesthesia – **anesthetic** *n or adj*, **anesthetist** *n*, **anesthetize** *vt*

anew *adv* **1** again, afresh **2** in a new form or way

angel *n* **1** a spiritual being, usu depicted as being winged, serving as God's intermediary or acting as a heavenly worshipper **2** an attendant spirit or guardian **3** a messenger, harbinger ⟨*~ of death*⟩ **4** a very kind or loving person, esp a woman or girl **5** a financial backer of a theatrical venture or other enterprise – chiefly infml – **angelic, angelical** *adj*, **angelically** *adv*

angelica *n* (the candied stalks used esp as a decoration on cakes and desserts, of) a biennial plant of the carrot family

Angelus *n* (a bell rung to mark) a devotion of the Western church said at morning, noon and evening to commemorate the incarnation

¹anger *n* a strong feeling of displeasure and usu antagonism – **angerless** *adj*

²anger *vb* to make or become angry

angina pectoris *n* brief attacks of intense chest pain, esp on exertion, precipitated by deficient oxygenation of the heart muscles

¹angle *n* **1** a corner **2a** the figure formed by 2 lines extending from the same point or by 2 surfaces diverging from the same line **b** a measure of the amount of turning necessary to bring one line of an angle to coincide with the other at all points **3a** a precise viewpoint; an aspect **b** special approach or technique for accomplishing an objective **4** a divergent course or position; a slant – esp in *an angle* – **angled** *adj*

²angle *vt* **1** to place, move, or direct obliquely **2** to present (e g a news story) from a particular or prejudiced point of view; slant ~ *vi* to turn or proceed at an angle

³angle *vi* **1** to fish with a hook and line **2** to use artful means to attain an objective ⟨*~d for an invitation*⟩ – **angler** *n*

angle bracket *n* either of a pair of punctuation marks ⟨ ⟩ used to enclose matter

Anglican *adj* of the body of churches including the established episcopal Church of England and churches of similar faith in communion with it – **Anglican** *n*, **Anglicanism** *n*

anglicism *n*, *often cap* **1** a characteristic feature of English occurring in another language **2** adherence or attachment to England, English culture, etc

anglicize, -ise *vt*, *often cap* **1** to make English in tastes or characteristics **2** to adapt (a foreign word or phrase) to English usage – **anglicization** *n*, *often cap*

angling *n* (the sport of) fishing with a hook and line – **angler** *n*

Anglo- *comb form* English nation, people, or culture ⟨Anglo*phobia*⟩; English and ⟨Anglo-*Japanese*⟩

Anglo-American *n or adj* (a) N American, esp of the USA, of English origin or descent

Anglo-Catholic *adj* of a High Church movement in Anglicanism fostering Catholic dogmatic and liturgical traditions – **Anglo-Catholic** *n*, **Anglo-Catholicism** *n*

Anglo-Indian *n* 1 a British person domiciled for a long time in India 2 a Eurasian of mixed British and Indian birth or descent – **Anglo-Indian** *adj*

anglophile *also* **anglophil** *n, often cap* a foreigner who is greatly interested in and admires England and things English – **anglophilia** *n, often cap* **anglophilic** *adj, often cap*, **anglophilism** *n, often cap*, **anglophily** *n*

anglophobe *n, often cap* a foreigner who is averse to England and things English – **anglophobia** *n, often cap*, **anglophobic** *adj, often cap*

Anglo-Saxon *n* 1 a member of the Germanic peoples who conquered England in the 5th c AD and formed the ruling group until the Norman conquest 2 sby of English, esp Anglo-Saxon descent 3 OLD ENGLISH – **Anglo-Saxon** *adj*

angora *n* 1 the hair of the Angora rabbit or goat 2 a fabric or yarn made (in part) of Angora rabbit hair, used esp for knitting 3 *cap* an Angora cat, goat or rabbit

Angora cat *n* a long-haired domestic cat

Angora goat *n* (any of) a breed of the domestic goat raised for its long silky hair which is the true mohair

Angora rabbit *n* a long-haired usu white domestic rabbit

angostura bark *n* the aromatic bitter bark of a S American tree of the rue family used as a bitter and formerly as a tonic

angry *adj* 1 feeling or showing anger ⟨~ *with his brother*⟩⟨~ *at his rude remark*⟩ 2 seeming to show or typify anger ⟨*an* ⟨ *sky*⟩ 3 painfully inflamed ⟨*an* ~ *rash*⟩ – **angrily** *adv*, **angriness** *n*

angst *n* anxiety and anguish, caused esp by considering the state of the world and the human condition

anguish *n* extreme physical pain or mental distress

anguished *adj* suffering or expressing anguish

angular *adj* 1a having 1 or more angles b forming an angle; sharp-cornered 2 measured by an angle ⟨~ *distance*⟩⟨~ *separation*⟩ 3a stiff in character or manner; awkward b lean, bony – **angularly** *adv*, **angularity** *n*

aniline *n* a liquid amine used chiefly in organic chemical synthesis (e g of dyes)

animadversion *n* 1 a critical and usu censorious remark 2 hostile criticism *USE* fml

animadvert *vi* to comment critically or adversely *on* – fml

¹animal *n* 1 any of a kingdom of living things typically differing from plants in their capacity for spontaneous movement, esp in response to stimulation 2a any of the lower animals as distinguished from human beings b a mammal – not in technical use 3 a person considered as a purely physical being; a creature – **animallike** *adj*, **animalness** *n*

²animal *adj* 1 of or derived from animals 2 of the body as opposed to the mind or spirit – chiefly derog – **animally** *adv*

animalcule *n* a minute usu microscopic organism – **animalcular** *adj*

animalism *n* 1a that state of having qualities typical of animals; lack of spiritual feeling b preoccupation with the satisfaction of physical drives; sensuality 2 a theory that human beings are nothing more than animals – **animalist** *n*, **animalistic** *adj*

animal kingdom *n* that one of the 3 basic groups of natural objects that includes all living and extinct animals

¹animate *adj* 1 possessing life; alive 2 of animal life 3 lively – **animately** *adv*, **animateness** *n*

²animate *vt* 1 to give spirit and support to; encourage 2 to give life or vigour to 3 to produce in the form of an animated cartoon – **animatedly** *adv*

animated cartoon *n* a film that creates the illusion of movement by photographing successive positional changes (e g of drawings)

animation *n* 1 vigorous liveliness 2 (the preparation of) an animated cartoon

animism *n* attribution of conscious life, spirits, or souls to nature or natural objects or phenomena – **animist** *n*, **animistic** *adj*

animosity *n* powerful often active ill will or resentment

animus *n* 1 a pervading attitude or spirit 2 ill will, animosity 3 an inner masculine part of the female personality – used in Jungian psychology

anise *n* a plant of the carrot family with aromatic seeds of a liquorice-like flavour; *also* aniseed

aniseed *n* the seed of anise used esp as a flavouring (e g in liqueurs)

ankle *n* 1 the (region of the) joint between the foot and the leg; the tarsus 2 the joint between the cannon bone and pastern of a horse or related animal

anklet *n* an ornamental band or chain worn round the ankle

annals *n pl* 1 a record of events, activities, etc, arranged in yearly sequence 2 historical records; chronicles

anneal *vt* 1 to toughen or relieve internal stresses in (steel, glass, etc) by heating and usu gradually cooling 2 to temper, toughen

¹annex *vt* 1 to subjoin, append 2 to take possession of; *esp* to incorporate (a country or other territory) within the domain of a state – **annexation** *n*, **annexational** *adj*, **annexationist** *n*

²annex, *chiefly Br* **annexe** *n* 1 sthg, esp an addition to a document, annexed or appended 2 a separate or attached extra structure; *esp* a building providing extra accommodation

annihilate *vt* 1 to destroy (almost) entirely 2 to defeat conclusively; rout ⟨*his team was* ~ d *in the quarterfinals*⟩ – **annihilation** *n*, **annihilative** *adj*, **annihilatory** *adj*, **annihilation** *n*

anniversary *n* (the celebration of) a day marking the annual recurrence of the date of a notable event

anno Domini *adv, often cap A* – used to indicate that a year or century comes within the Christian era

annotate *vt* to provide (e g a literary work) with notes – **annotative** *adj*, **annotator** *n*, **annotation** *n*

announce *vt* 1 to make known publicly; proclaim 2a to give notice of the arrival, presence, or readiness of b to indicate in advance; foretell 3 to give evidence of; indicate by action or appearance ~ *vi NAm* to serve as an announcer – **announcement** *n*

announcer *n* one who introduces television or radio programmes, makes commercial announcements, reads news summaries, or gives station identification

annoy *vt* 1 to disturb or irritate, esp by repeated acts; vex – often pass + *with* or *at* 2 to harass ~ *vi* to be a source of annoyance – **annoyance** *n*, **annoyer** *n*, **annoying** *adj*, **annoyingly** *adv*

¹annual *adj* 1 covering or lasting for the period of a year ⟨~ *rainfall*⟩ 2 occurring or performed once a year; yearly ⟨*an* ~ *reunion*⟩ 3 *of a plant* completing the life cycle in 1 growing season – **annually** *adv*

²**annual** *n* **1** a publication appearing yearly **2** sthg lasting 1 year or season; *specif* an annual plant

annual ring *n* the layer of wood produced by a single year's growth of a woody plant

annuity *n* **1** an amount payable at a regular (e g yearly) interval **2** (a contract embodying) the right to receive or the obligation to pay an annuity

annul *vt* **-ll-** **1** to reduce to nothing; obliterate, cancel **2** to declare (e g a marriage) legally invalid – **annulment** *n*

annular *adj* of or forming a ring – **annularly** *adv*, **annularity** *n*

Annunciation *n* (March 25 observed as a church festival commemorating) the announcement of the Incarnation to the Virgin Mary related in Luke 1:26–28

anode *n* **1** the electrode by which electrons leave a device and enter an external circuit; *specif* the negative terminal of a primary or secondary cell that is delivering current **2** a positive electrode used to accelerate electrons in an electron gun – **anodal** *adj*, **anodally** *adv*, **anodic** *adj*, **anodically** *adv*

¹**anodyne** *adj* **1** easing pain **2** mentally or emotionally soothing

²**anodyne** *n* **1** an analgesic drug **2** sthg that soothes or calms – **anodynic** *adj*

anoint *vt* **1** to smear or rub with oil or a similar substance **2a** to apply oil to as a sacred rite, esp for consecration **b** to designate (as if) through the rite of anointment; consecrate – **anointer** *n*, **anointment** *n*

anomalous *adj* **1** deviating from a general rule or standard; irregular, abnormal **2** incongruous – **anomalously** *adv*, **anomalousness** *n*

anomaly *n* **1** the angular distance of **a** a planet from its last perihelion **b** a satellite from its last perigee **2** deviation from the common rule; an irregularity, incongruity **3** sthg anomalous – **anomalistic** *adj*

anon *adv*, *archaic* **1** soon, presently **2** at another time

anonymous *adj* **1** having or giving no name ⟨*an ~ author*⟩ **2** of unknown or unnamed origin or authorship ⟨*~ gifts*⟩ **3** nondescript – **anonymously** *adv*, **anonymousness** *n*, **anonymity** *n*

anopheles *n* any of the genus of mosquitoes that includes all those which transmit malaria to human beings – **anopheline** *adj or n*

anorak *n*, *chiefly Br* a short weatherproof coat with a hood

anorexia *n* (prolonged) loss of appetite; *specif* ANOREXIA NERVOSA – **anorectic** *adj or n*, **anorexigenic** *adj*

anorexia nervosa *n* pathological aversion to food induced by emotional disturbance and typically accompanied by emaciation

¹**another** *adj* **1** being a different or distinct one ⟨*the same scene viewed from ~ angle*⟩ **2** some other ⟨*do it ~ time*⟩ **3** being one additional ⟨*have ~ piece of pie*⟩ **4** patterned after ⟨*~ Napolean*⟩

²**another** *pron*, *pl* **others** **1** an additional one; one more **2** a different one ⟨*he loved ~*⟩ ⟨*for one reason or ~*⟩

¹**answer** *n* **1** a spoken or written reply to a question, remark, etc **2** an esp correct solution to a problem **3** a response or reaction ⟨*his only ~ was to walk out*⟩ **4** sby or sthg intended to be a close equivalent or rival of another ⟨*Scotland's ~ to Andy Williams*⟩

²**answer** *vi* **1** to speak, write, or act in reply **2a** to be responsible or accountable *for* **b** to make amends; atone *for* **3** to correspond *to* **4** to be adequate or usable *~ vt* **1a** to speak or write in reply to **b** to reply to in justification or explanation ⟨*~ a charge*⟩ **2a** to correspond to **b** to be adequate or usable for **3** to act in response to (a sound or

other signal) ⟨*~ the telephone*⟩ **4** to offer a solution for; *esp* to solve ⟨*~ a riddle*⟩ – **answerer** *n*

answerable *adj* **1** responsible **2** capable of being answered or refuted – **answerability** *n*

answer back *vb*, *esp of a child* to reply rudely (to)

ant *n* any of a family of insects that live in large social groups having a complex organization and hierarchy

ant- – see ANTI-

¹**-ant** *suffix* (→ *n*) **1** sby or sthg that performs (a specified action) ⟨*claim*ant⟩ ⟨*deodor*ant⟩ **2** thing that causes (a specified action or process) ⟨*expector*ant⟩ **3** thing that is used or acted upon (in a specified manner) ⟨*inhal*ant⟩

²**-ant** *suffix* (→ *adj*) **1** performing (a specified action) or being (in a specified condition) ⟨*repent*ant⟩ ⟨*somnambul*ant⟩ **2** causing (a specified action or process) ⟨*expector*ant⟩

antacid *adj* that corrects excessive acidity, esp in the stomach – **antacid** *n*

antagonism *n* **1** hostility or antipathy, esp when actively expressed **2** opposition in physiological or biochemical action, esp between an agonist and an antagonist – **antagonistic** *adj*; **antagonistically** *adv*

antagonist *n* **1** an opponent, adversary **2** a drug that opposes the action of another or of a substance (e g a neurotransmitter) that occurs naturally in the body

antagonize, -ise *vt* **1** to oppose or counteract **2** to provoke the hostility of

antarctic *adj*, *often cap* of the South Pole or surrounding region

antarctic circle *n*, *often cap A&C* the parallel of latitude approx 66½° south of the equator that circumscribes the south polar region

¹**ante** *n* **1** a poker stake usu put up before the deal **2** an amount paid ⟨*these improvements would raise the ~*⟩ – *infml*

²**ante** *vt* anteing to put up (an ante)

ante- *prefix* **1a** prior; before ⟨*antecedent*⟩ ⟨*antedate*⟩ **b** prior to; earlier than ⟨*antediluvian*⟩ **2** anterior; situated before ⟨*anteroom*⟩

anteater *n* any of several mammals that feed (chiefly) on ants and termites

¹**antecedent** *n* **1** a word,phrase, or clause functioning as a noun and referred to by a pronoun **2** the premise of a conditional proposition (e g *if A* in 'if A, then B') **3** the first term of a mathematical ratio **4** a preceding thing, event, or circumstance **5a** a model or stimulus for later developments ⟨*the boneshaker was the ~ of the modern bicycle*⟩ **b** *pl* family origins; parentage

²**antecedent** *adj* **1** prior in time or order **2** causally or logically prior – **antecedently** *adv*

antechamber *n* an anteroom

antedate *vt* **1** to attach or assign a date earlier than the true one to (e g a document), esp with intent to deceive **2** to precede in time ⟨*his death ~d his brother's*⟩

antediluvian *adj* **1** of the period before the flood described in the Bible **2** completely out-of-date; antiquated ⟨*an ~ car*⟩ – **antediluvian** *n*

antelope *n*, *pl* **antelopes**, *esp collectively* **antelope** **1** any of various Old World ruminant mammals that are lighter and more graceful than the true oxen **2** leather made from antelope hide

ante meridiem *adj* being before noon – *abbr* **am**

antenatal *adj* of or concerned with an unborn child, pregnancy, or a pregnant woman; prenatal ⟨*an ~ clinic*⟩

antenna *n*, *pl* **antennae, antennas** **1** a movable segmented sense organ on the head of insects, myriapods, and crustaceans **2** an aerial – chiefly used in Br with reference to complex aerials – **antennal** *adj* anterior *adj* 1 before in time 2 situated before or towards the front: e g a *of an animal part* near the head; cephalic b *of the human body or its parts* ventral 3 *of a plant part* (on the side) facing away from the stem or axis; *also* INFERIOR 4a – anteriorly *adv*

anteroom *n* an outer room that leads to another usu more important one, often used as a waiting room

ante up *vb*, *chiefly NAm* PAY UP

anthem *n* 1a an antiphon b a piece of church music for voices usu set to a biblical text 2 a song or hymn of praise or gladness

anther *n* the part of a stamen that contains and releases pollen – antheral *adj*

anthill *n* 1 a mound thrown up by ants or termites in digging their nest 2 a place (e g a city) that is overcrowded and constantly busy ⟨*the human* ~ – H G Wells⟩

anthology *n* 1 a collection of selected literary pieces or passages 2 a collection of selected non-literary works ⟨*a fine* ~ *of Byzantine icons*⟩ – anthologist *n*

anthracite *n* a hard slow-burning coal containing little volatile matter – anthracitic *adj*

anthrax *n* an often fatal infectious disease of warm-blooded animals (e g cattle, sheep, or human beings) caused by a spore-forming bacterium

anthrop-, anthropo- *comb form* human being ⟨anthropology⟩

anthropocentric *adj* considering human beings to be the most significant entities of the universe – anthropocentrically *adv*, anthropocentricity *n*

anthropoid *adj* 1 resembling human beings or the anthropoid apes (e g in form or behaviour); apelike 2 resembling an ape ⟨~ *gangsters*⟩

anthropoid ape *n* APE 1

anthropology *n* the scientific study of human beings, esp in relation to physical characteristics, social relations and culture, and the origin and distribution of races – anthropologist *n*, anthropological *adj*, anthropologically *adv*

anthropomorphic, anthropomorphous *adj* 1 having a human form or human attributes ⟨~ *deities*⟩ 2 ascribing human characteristics to nonhuman things – anthropomorphically *adv*, anthropomorphously *adv*

anthropomorphism *n* the ascribing of human behaviour, form, etc to what is not human (e g a god or animal); humanization – anthropomorphist *n*, anthropomorphize *vt*

anthropophagous *adj* feeding on human flesh – anthropophagy *n*

¹anti *n*, *pl* antis an opponent of a practice or policy

²anti *prep* opposed or antagonistic to

anti-, ant-, anth- *prefix* 1a of the same kind but situated opposite; in the opposite direction to ⟨antipodes⟩ ⟨anticlockwise⟩ b opposite in kind to ⟨anticlimax⟩ ⟨anti-hero⟩ 2a opposing or hostile to in opinion, sympathy, or practice ⟨anti-Semite⟩ ⟨antislavery⟩ b opposing in effect or activity; preventing ⟨antiseptic⟩ ⟨anti-thief device⟩ 3 being the antimatter counterpart of ⟨antineutrino⟩ 4 combatting or defending against ⟨antiaircraft⟩ ⟨antitank⟩

antibiotic *n* a substance produced by a microorganism and able in dilute solution to inhibit the growth of or kill another microorganism – antibiotic *adj*, antibiotically *adv*

antibody *n* a protein (e g an immunoglobulin) that is produced by the body in response to a specific antigen and that counteracts its effects (e g by neutralizing toxins or grouping bacteria into clumps)

antic *n* a ludicrous act or action; a caper – usu *pl* ⟨*childish* ~s⟩

anticipate *vt* 1 to give advance thought, discussion, or treatment to 2 to foresee and deal with in advance; forestall 3 to use, expend, or act on before the right or natural time 4 to act before (another) often so as to thwart 5 to look forward to as certain; expect ~*vi* to speak or write in knowledge or expectation of sthg due to happen – anticipator *n*, anticipatable *adj*, anticipative *adj*, anticipatively *adv*, anticipatory *adj*

anticipation *n* an act of looking forward; *specif* pleasurable expectation

anticlerical *adj* opposed to the influence of the clergy or church in secular affairs – anticlerical *n*, anticlericalism *n*, anticlericalist *n*

anticlimax *n* 1 (an instance of) the usu sudden and ludicrous descent in writing or speaking from a significant to a trivial idea 2 an event (e g at the end of a series) that is strikingly less important or exciting than expected – anticlimactic, anticlimactical *adj*, anticlimactically *adv*

anticlockwise *adj or adv* in a direction opposite to that in which the hands of a clock rotate when viewed from the front

anticyclone *n* 1 a system of winds that rotates about a centre of high atmospheric pressure 2 ³HIGH 1 – anticyclonic *adj*

antidote *n* 1 a remedy that counteracts the effects of poison 2 sthg that relieves or counteracts ⟨*an* ~ *to the mechanization of our society*⟩ – antidotal *adj*

antifreeze *n* a substance added to a liquid (e g the water in a car radiator) to lower its freezing point

antigen *n* a protein, carbohydrate, etc that stimulates the production of an antibody when introduced into the body – antigenic *adj*, antigenically *adv*, antigenicity *n*

anti-hero, *fem* anti-heroine *n* a protagonist who lacks traditional heroic qualities (e g courage) – anti-heroic *adj*

antihistamine *n* any of various compounds that oppose the actions of histamine and are used esp for treating allergies and motion sickness – antihistaminic *adj or n*

antiknock *n* a substance added to fuel to prevent knocking in an internal-combustion engine

antilogarithm *n* the number corresponding to a given logarithm

antimacassar *n* a usu protective cover put over the backs or arms of upholstered seats

antimatter *n* matter composed of antiparticles (e g antiprotons instead of protons, positrons instead of electrons, and antineutrons instead of neutrons)

antimony *n* a trivalent and pentavalent brittle usu metallic metalloid element used esp as a constituent of alloys – antimonial *adj*, antimonious *adj*

antipathetic *adj* 1 feeling or causing aversion or opposition 2 opposed in nature or character *to* – antipathetically *adv*

antipathy *n* a fixed aversion or dislike; a distaste

antipersonnel *adj*, *of a weapon* (designed) for use against people

antiphon *n* a verse, usu from Scripture, said or sung usu before and after a canticle, psalm, or psalm verse as part of the liturgy – antiphonal *adj*

antipodal *adj* 1 of the antipodes; *specif* situated at the opposite side of the earth or moon ⟨*an* ~ *meridian*⟩ ⟨*an* ~ *continent*⟩ 2 diametrically opposite ⟨*an* ~ *point on a sphere*⟩

antipodes *n pl* the region of the earth diametrically opposite; *specif*, *often cap* Australasia – antipodean *adj*

¹antiquarian *n* one who collects or studies antiquities

²antiquarian *adj* 1 of antiquarians or antiquities 2 *of books or prints* old (and rare) – antiquarianism *n*

antiquary *n* an antiquarian

antiquated *adj* **1** outmoded or discredited by reason of age; out-of-date **2** advanced in age

¹antique *adj* **1** belonging to or surviving from earlier, esp classical, times; ancient ⟨*ruins of an ~ city*⟩ **2** old-fashioned **3** made in an earlier period and therefore valuable ⟨*~ mirrors*⟩; *also* suggesting the style of an earlier period

²antique *n* **1** *the* ancient Greek or Roman style in art **2** a relic or object of ancient times **3** a work of art, piece of furniture, or decorative object made at an earlier period and sought by collectors

antiquity *n* **1** ancient times; *esp* the period before the Middle Ages **2** the quality of being ancient **3** *pl* relics or monuments of ancient times

antirrhinum *n* any of a large genus of plants (e g the snapdragon or a related plant) of the figwort family with bright-coloured 2-lipped flowers

anti-Semitism *n* hostility towards Jews – **anti-Semitic** *adj*, **anti-Semite** *n*

¹antiseptic *adj* **1a** opposing sepsis (in living tissue), specif by arresting the growth of microorganisms, esp bacteria **b** of, acting or protecting like, or using an antiseptic **2a** scrupulously clean; aseptic **b** extremely neat or orderly, esp to the point of being bare or uninteresting **3** impersonal, detached – **antiseptically** *adv*

²antiseptic *n* an antiseptic substance; *also* a germicide

antisocial *adj* **1** hostile or harmful to organized society **2a** averse to the society of others; unsociable **b** *Br* UNSOCIAL 2

antithesis *n*, *pl* **antitheses 1a** a contrast of ideas expressed by a parallel arrangement of words (e g in 'action, not words') **b** opposition, contrast **c** the direct opposite ⟨*his ideas are the ~ of mine*⟩ **2** the second stage of a reasoned argument, in contrast to the thesis

antithetical, antithetic *adj* **1** constituting or marked by antithesis **2** directly opposed – **antithetically** *adv*

antitoxin *n* (a serum containing) an antibody capable of neutralizing the specific toxin that stimulated its production in the body – **antitoxic** *adj*

antler *n* (a branch of) the solid periodically shed (much branched) horn of an animal of the deer family – **antlered** *adj*

antonym *n* a word having the opposite meaning – **antonymous** *adj*, **antonymy** *n*

anus *n* the rear excretory opening of the alimentary canal

anvil *n* **1** a heavy, usu steel-faced, iron block on which metal is shaped **2** a towering anvil-shaped cloud **3** the incus

anxiety *n* **1a** apprehensive uneasiness of mind, usu over an impending or anticipated ill **b** an ardent or earnest wish ⟨*~ to please*⟩ **c** a cause of anxiety **2** an abnormal overwhelming sense of apprehension and fear, often with doubt about one's capacity to cope with the threat

anxious *adj* **1** troubled, worried **2** causing anxiety; worrying **3** ardently or earnestly wishing *to* – **anxiously** *adv*, **anxiousness** *n*

¹any *adj* **1** one or some indiscriminately; whichever is chosen ⟨*~ plan is better than none*⟩ **2** one, some, or all; whatever: e g **a** of whatever number or quantity; being even the smallest number or quantity of ⟨*have you ~ money?*⟩ ⟨*never get ~ letters*⟩ **b** no matter how great ⟨*at ~ cost*⟩ **c** no matter how ordinary or inadequate ⟨*wear just ~ old thing*⟩ **3** being an appreciable number, part, or amount of – not in positive statements ⟨*not for ~ length of time*⟩

²any *pron, pl any* **1** any person; anybody ⟨*~ of us*⟩ **2a** any thing **b** any part, quantity, or number ⟨*hardly ~ of it*⟩

³any *adv* to any extent or degree; AT ALL ⟨*not feeling ~ better*⟩

anybody *pron* any person ⟨*has ~ lost their glasses?*⟩

anyhow *adv* **1** in a haphazard manner ⟨*thrown down all ~*⟩ **2** anyway

anyone *pron* anybody

anyplace *adv, NAm* anywhere

anyroad *adv, Br* anyway – nonstandard

¹anything *pron* any thing whatever ⟨*do ~ for a quiet life*⟩ – **anything but** not at all; far from

²anything *adv* in any degree; AT ALL ⟨*isn't ~ like so cold*⟩

anyway *adv* **1** in any case, inevitably ⟨*going to be hanged ~*⟩ **2** – used when resuming a narrative ⟨*well, ~, I rang the bell*⟩

¹anywhere *adv* **1** in, at, or to any place ⟨*too late to go ~*⟩ **2** to any extent; AT ALL ⟨*isn't ~ near ready*⟩ **3** – used to indicate limits of variation ⟨*~ from 40 to 60*⟩

²anywhere *n* any place

aorta *n*, *pl* **aortas, aortae** the great artery that carries blood from the left side of the heart to be distributed by branch arteries throughout the body – **aortal** *adj*, **aortic** *adj*

apace *adv* at a quick pace; swiftly

apanage *n* a grant made to a dependent member of the royal family or a principal liege man

apart *adv* **1a** at a distance (from one another in space or time) ⟨*tried to keep ~ from the family squabbles*⟩ ⟨*towns 20 miles ~*⟩ **b** at a distance in character or opinions ⟨*their ideas are worlds ~*⟩ **2** so as to separate one from another ⟨*can't tell the twins ~*⟩ **3** excluded from consideration ⟨*joking ~, what shall we do?*⟩ **4** in or into 2 or more parts ⟨*had to take the engine ~*⟩

apart from *prep* **1** in addition to; besides ⟨*haven't time, quite ~ the cost*⟩ **2** EXCEPT FOR ⟨*excellent ~ a few blemishes*⟩

apartheid *n* racial segregation; *specif* a policy of segregation and discrimination against non-Europeans in the Republic of S Africa

apartment *n* **1** a single room in a building **2** a suite of rooms used for living quarters ⟨*the Royal ~s*⟩ **3** *chiefly NAm* a flat – **apartmental** *adj*

apartment house *n, NAm* a block of flats

apathetic *adj* **1** having or showing little or no feeling; spiritless **2** lacking interest or concern; indifferent – **apathetically** *adv*

apathy *n* **1** lack of feeling or emotion; impassiveness **2** lack of interest or concern; indifference

¹ape *n* **1** a (large semierect tailless or short-tailed Old World) monkey: **a** a chimpanzee **b** a gorilla **c** any similar primate **2a** a mimic **b** a large uncouth person – **apelike** *adj*

²ape *vt* to imitate closely but often clumsily and ineptly – **aper** *n*

aperient *n or adj* (a) laxative

aperitif *n* an alcoholic drink taken before a meal to stimulate the appetite

aperture *n* **1** an open space; a hole, gap **2a** (the diameter of) the opening in an optical (photographic) system through which the light passes **b** the diameter of the objective lens or mirror of a telescope

apex *n*, *pl* **apexes, apices 1a** the uppermost peak; the vertex ⟨*the ~ of a mountain*⟩ **b** the narrowed or pointed end; the tip ⟨*the ~ of the tongue*⟩ **2** the highest or culminating point ⟨*the ~ of his career*⟩

aphasia *n* (partial) loss of the power to use or understand words, usu resulting from brain damage – **aphasiac** *adj*, **aphasic** *n or adj*

aphid *n* a greenfly or related small sluggish insect that sucks the juices of plants

aphorism *n* a concise pithy formulation of a truth; an adage – **aphorize** *vi*, **aphorist** *n*, **aphoristic** *adj*, **aphoristically** *adv*

aphrodisiac *n or adj* (a substance) that stimulates sexual desire – **aphrodisiacal** *adj*

apiarist *n* a beekeeper

apiary *n* a place where (hives or colonies of) bees are kept, esp for their honey

apices *pl of* APEX

apiculture *n* the keeping of bees, esp on a large scale – **apicultural** *adj*, **apiculturist** *n*

apiece *adv* for each one; individually

apish *adj* resembling an ape: e g **a** slavishly imitative **b** extremely silly or affected – **apishly** *adv*, **apishness** *n*

aplomb *n* complete composure or self-assurance; poise

apocalypse *n* **1a** any of a number of early Jewish and Christian works, written esp under an assumed name, and characterized by symbolic imagery, which describe the establishment of God's kingdom **b** *cap* REVELATION 2 – usu + *the* **2** sthg viewed as a prophetic revelation

apocalyptic *also* **apocalyptical** *adj* **1** of or resembling an apocalypse **2** forecasting the ultimate destiny of the world; prophetic **3** foreboding imminent disaster; terrible – **apocalyptically** *adv*

apocrypha *n* **1** (a collection of) writings or statements of dubious authenticity **2** *sing or pl in constr*, *cap* books included in the Septuagint and Vulgate but excluded from the Jewish and Protestant canons of the Old Testament – usu + *the*

apocryphal *adj* **1** *often cap* of or resembling the Apocrypha **2** of doubtful authenticity – **apocryphally** *adv*, **apocryphalness** *n*

apogee *n* **1** the point farthest from a planet or other celestial body reached by any object orbiting it **2** the farthest or highest point; the culmination ⟨*Aegean civilization reached its ~ in Crete*⟩ – **apogean** *adj*

apologetic *adj* **1a** offered in defence or vindication **b** offered by way of excuse or apology ⟨*an ~ smile*⟩ **2** regretfully acknowledging fault or failure; contrite – **apologetically** *adv*

apologetics *n pl but sing or pl in constr* **1** systematic reasoned argument in defence (e g of a doctrine) **2** a branch of theology devoted to the rational defence of Christianity

apologia *n* a reasoned defence in speech or writing, esp of a faith, cause, or institution

apologist *n* the author of an apologia

apologize, -ise *vi* to make an apology

apology *n* **1a** an apologia **b** EXCUSE 1 **2** an admission of error or discourtesy accompanied by an expression of regret **3** a poor substitute *for*

apophthegm *n* a short, pithy, and instructive saying – **apophthegmatic, apophthegmatical** *adj*, **apophthegmatically** *adv*

apoplectic *adj* **1** of, causing, affected with, or showing symptoms of apoplexy **2** violently excited (e g from rage) – **apoplectically** *adv*

apoplexy *n* ²STROKE 5

apostasy *n* **1** renunciation of a religious faith **2** abandonment of a previous loyalty; defection

apostate *n* one who commits apostasy – **apostate** *adj*

apostatize, -ise *vi* to commit apostasy

a posteriori *adj* **1** inductive **2** relating to or derived by reasoning from observed facts – **a posteriori** *adv*

apostle *n* **1** one sent on a mission; *esp* any of an authoritative New Testament group sent out to preach the gospel and made up esp of Jesus's original 12 disciples and

Paul **2a** one who first advocates an important belief or system **b** an ardent supporter; an adherent ⟨*an ~ of liberal tolerance*⟩ – **apostleship** *n*

apostolic *adj* **1** of an apostle or the New Testament apostles **2a** of the divine authority vested in the apostles held (e g by Roman Catholics, Anglicans, and Eastern Orthodox) to be handed down through the successive ordinations of bishops **b** of the pope as the successor to the apostolic authority vested in St Peter – **apostolicity** *n*

¹**apostrophe** *n* the addressing, rhetorically, of a usu absent person or a usu personified thing – **apostrophize** *vb*, **apostrophic** *adj*

²**apostrophe** *n* a mark ' used to indicate the omission of letters or figures, the possessive case, or the plural of letters or figures – **apostrophic** *adj*

apothecaries' weight *n* the series of units of weight used formerly by pharmacists and based on the ounce of 8 drachms and the drachm of 3 scruples or 60 grains

apothecary *n*, *archaic or NAm* **1** a pharmacist **2** PHARMACY 2

apothegm *n*, *NAm* an apophthegm

apotheosis *n*, *pl* **apotheoses** **1** deification **2** *the* perfect example ⟨*she is the ~ of womanhood*⟩ – **apotheosize** *vt*

appal, *NAm chiefly* **appall** *vt* **-ll-** to overcome with consternation, horror, or dismay – **appalling** *adj*, **appallingly** *adv*

appanage *n* **1** apanage **2** a usual accompaniment

apparatus *n*, *pl* **apparatuses, apparatus** **1a** (a piece of) equipment designed for a particular use, esp for a scientific operation **b** a group of organs having a common function **2** the administrative bureaucracy of an organization, esp a political party

¹**apparel** *vt* **-ll-** (*NAm* **-l-, -ll-**) **1** to put clothes on; dress – *chiefly fml* **2** to adorn, embellish – *chiefly poetic*

²**apparel** *n* **1** garments, clothing – *chiefly fml* **2** sthg that clothes or adorns ⟨*the bright ~ of spring*⟩ – *chiefly poetic*

apparent *adj* **1** easily seen or understood; plain, evident **2** seemingly real but not necessarily so **3** having an absolute right to succeed to a title or estate ⟨*the heir ~*⟩ – **apparently** *adv*

apparition *n* **1a** an unusual or unexpected sight; a phenomenon **b** a ghostly figure **2** the act of becoming visible; appearance – **apparitional** *adj*

¹**appeal** *n* **1** a legal proceeding by which a case is brought to a higher court for review **2a**(1) an application (e g to a recognized authority) for corroboration, vindication, or decision (2) a call by members of the fielding side in cricket, esp by the bowler, for the umpire to decide whether a batsman is out **b** an earnest plea for aid or mercy; an entreaty **3** the power of arousing a sympathetic response; attraction ⟨*the theatre has lost its ~ for him*⟩

²**appeal** *vt* to take (a case) to a higher court ~ *vi* **1** to take a case to a higher court **2a** to call on another for corroboration, vindication, or decision **b** to make an appeal in cricket **3** to make an earnest plea or request **4** to arouse a sympathetic response *USE* often + *to* – **appealer** *n*, **appealable** *adj*, **appealability** *n*

appealing *adj* **1** having appeal; pleasing **2** marked by earnest entreaty; imploring – **appealingly** *adv*

appear *vi* **1a** to be or become visible ⟨*the sun ~s on the horizon*⟩ **b** to arrive ⟨*~s promptly at 8 each day*⟩ **2** to come formally before an authoritative body **3** to give the impression of being; seem ⟨*~s happy enough*⟩ **4** to come into public view ⟨*first ~ed on a television variety show*⟩

appearance *n* **1** the coming into court of a party in an action or his/her lawyer **2** a visit or attendance that is seen or noticed by others ⟨*put in an ~ at the party*⟩ **3a** an outward aspect; a look ⟨*had a fierce ~*⟩ **b** an external show; a semblance ⟨*although hostile, he tried to preserve an ~ of neutrality*⟩ **c** *pl* an outward or superficial indication that hides the real situation ⟨*would do anything to keep up ~*s⟩

appease *vt* **1** to pacify, calm **2** to cause to subside; allay ⟨*~ his hunger*⟩ **3** to conciliate (esp an aggressor) by concessions – **appeasable** *adj*, **appeasement** *n*, **appeaser** *n*

¹**appellant** *adj* appellate

²**appellant** *n* one who appeals against a judicial decision

appellate *adj* of or recognizing appeals ⟨*an ~ court*⟩

appellation *n* an identifying name or title

append *vt* to attach or add, esp as a supplement or appendix

appendage *n* **1** sthg appended to sthg larger or more important **2** a limb, seta, or other subordinate or derivative body part

appendectomy *n*, *NAm* an appendicectomy

appendicitis *n* inflammation of the vermiform appendix

appendix *n*, *pl* **appendixes, appendices 1** a supplement (e g containing explanatory or statistical material), usu attached at the end of a piece of writing **2** the vermiform appendix or similar bodily outgrowth

appertain *vi* to belong or be connected as a rightful or customary part, possession, or attribute; pertain – usu + *to*

appetite *n* **1** a desire to satisfy an internal bodily need; *esp* an (eager) desire to eat **2** a strong desire demanding satisfaction; an inclination – **appetitive** *adj*

appetizer, -iser *n* a food or drink that stimulates the appetite and is usu served before a meal

appetizing, -ising *adj* appealing to the appetite, esp in appearance or aroma – **appetizingly** *adv*

applaud *vb* to express approval (of), esp by clapping the hands – **applaudable** *adj*, **applauder** *n*

applause *n* **1** approval publicly expressed (e g by clapping the hands) **2** praise

apple *n* **1** (the fleshy, edible, usu rounded, red, yellow, or green fruit of) a tree of the rose family **2** a fruit or other plant structure resembling an apple – **apple of someone's** eye sby or sthg greatly cherished ⟨*his daughter is the* apple of his eye⟩ – **she's apples** *Austr* everything's fine – infml

apple-pie order *n* perfect order

appliance *n* **1** an instrument or device designed for a particular use; *esp* a domestic machine or device powered by gas or electricity (e g a food mixer, vacuum cleaner, or cooker) **2** BRACE 4e

applicable *adj* appropriate – **applicability** *n*

applicant *n* one who applies

application *n* **1a** an act of applying **b** a use to which sthg is put **c** close attention; diligence **2** a request, petition **3** a lotion **4** capacity for practical use; relevance – **applicative** *adj*, **applicatory** *adj*

applied *adj* put to practical use; *esp* applying general principles to solve definite problems ⟨*~ sciences*⟩

¹**appliqué** *n* a cutout decoration fastened (e g by sewing) to a larger piece of material; *also* the decorative work formed in this manner

²**appliqué** *vt* **appliquéing** to apply (e g a decoration or ornament) to a larger surface

apply *vt* **1a** to bring to bear; put to use, esp for some practical purpose ⟨*~ pressure*⟩ ⟨*~ the brakes*⟩ **b** to lay or spread on ⟨*~ varnish to a table*⟩ **2** to devote (e g

oneself) with close attention or diligence – usu + *to* ⟨*should ~ himself to his work*⟩ *~vi* **1** to have relevance – usu + *to* ⟨*this rule applies to new members only*⟩ **2** to make a request, esp in writing ⟨*~ for a job*⟩ – **applier** *n*

appoint *vt* **1** to fix or name officially **2** to select for an office or position **3** to declare the disposition of (an estate) to sby

appointed *adj* equipped, furnished

appointment *n* **1** an act of appointing; a designation ⟨*fill a vacancy by ~*⟩ **2** an office or position held by sby who has been appointed to it rather than voted into it **3** an arrangement for a meeting **4** *pl* equipment, furnishings

apportion *vt* to divide and share out in just proportion or according to a plan; allot – **apportionment** *n*

apposite *adj* highly pertinent or appropriate; apt – **appositely** *adv*, **appositeness** *n*

apposition *n* a grammatical construction in which 2 usu adjacent nouns or noun phrases have the same referent and stand in the same syntactic relation to the rest of a sentence (e g *the poet* and *Burns* in 'a biography of the poet Burns') – **appositional** *adj*, **appositionally** *adv*

appraisal *n* an act or instance of appraising; *specif* a valuation of property by an authorized person

appraise *vt* to evaluate the worth, significance, or status of; *esp* to give an expert judgment of the value or merit of – **appraisement** *n*, **appraiser** *n*, **appraising** *adj*, **appraisingly** *adv*

appreciable *adj* **1** capable of being perceived or measured **2** fairly large ⟨*an ~ distance*⟩ – **appreciably** *adv*

appreciate *vt* **1a** to understand the nature, worth, quality, or significance of **b** to recognize with gratitude; value or admire highly **2** to increase the value of *~vi* to increase in value – **appreciative** *adj*, **appreciatively** *adv*, **appreciator** *n*, **appreciatory** *adj*

appreciation *n* **1a** sensitive awareness; *esp* recognition of aesthetic values **b** a judgment, evaluation; *esp* a favourable critical estimate **c** an expression of admiration, approval, or gratitude **2** an increase in value

apprehend *vt* **1** to arrest, seize ⟨*~ a thief*⟩ **2** to understand, perceive *~vi* to understand

apprehension *n* **1** the act or power of comprehending ⟨*a man of dull ~*⟩ **2** arrest, seizure – used technically in Scottish law **3** anxiety or fear, esp of future evil; foreboding

apprehensive *adj* viewing the future with anxiety, unease, or fear – often + *for* or *of* – **apprehensively** *adv*, **apprehensiveness** *n*

¹**apprentice** *n* **1** one who is learning an art or trade **a** from an employer to whom he/she is bound by indenture **b** by practical experience under skilled workers **2** an inexperienced person; a novice – **apprenticeship** *n*

²**apprentice** *vt* to set at work as an apprentice

apprise *vt* to give notice to; tell – usu + *of*; fml

appro *n*, *Br* – **on appro** ON APPROVAL – infml

¹**approach** *vt* **1a** to draw closer to **b** to come very near to in quality, character, etc **2a** to make advances to, esp in order to create a desired result ⟨*was ~ed by several film producers*⟩ **b** to begin to consider or deal with ⟨*~ the subject with an open mind*⟩ *~vi* to draw nearer

²**approach** *n* **1a** an act or instance of approaching **b** an approximation **2** a manner or method of doing sthg, esp for the first time ⟨*a highly individual ~ to language*⟩ **3** a means of access ⟨*the ~es to the city*⟩ **4a** a golf shot from the fairway towards the green **b** (the steps taken on) the part of a tenpin bowling alley from which a bowler must deliver the ball **5** the final part of an aircraft flight before

landing **6** an advance made to establish personal or business relations – usu pl

approachable adj easy to meet or deal with – **approachability** n

approbation n formal or official approval; sanction – **approbatory** adj

¹appropriate vt **1** to take exclusive possession of **2** to set apart (specif money) for a particular purpose or use **3** to take or make use of without authority or right – **appropriable** adj, **appropriator** n

²appropriate adj especially suitable or compatible; fitting – **appropriately** adv, **appropriateness** n

appropriation n sthg appropriated; specif money set aside by formal action for a particular use – **appropriative** adj

approval n **1** a favourable opinion or judgment **2** formal or official permission – **on approval** of goods supplied commercially to be returned without payment if found unsatisfactory

approve vt **1** to have or express a favourable opinion of **2a** to accept as satisfactory **b** to give formal or official sanction to; ratify ⟨Parliament ~d the proposed policy⟩ ~ vi to take a favourable view – often + of ⟨doesn't ~ of fighting⟩ – **approvingly** adv

¹approximate adj nearly correct or exact – **approximately** adv

²approximate vt **1** to bring near or close – often + to **2** to come near to; approach, esp in quality or number ~ vi to come close – usu + to

approximation n sthg that is approximate; esp a mathematical quantity that is close in value but not equal to a desired quantity – **approximative** adj, **approximatively** adv

appurtenance n an accessory – **appurtenant** adj or n

apricot n **1** (the oval orange-coloured fruit of) a temperate-zone tree of the rose family closely related to the peach and plum **2** an orange pink colour

April n the 4th month of the Gregorian calendar

April fool n the victim of a joke or trick played on April Fools' Day

a priori adj **1a** relating to or derived by reasoning from self-evident propositions; deductive **b** of or relating to sthg that can be known by reason alone **c** true or false by definition or convention alone ⟨~ statements⟩ **2** without examination or analysis; presumptive – **a priori** adv, **apriority** n

apron n **1** a garment usu tied round the waist and used to protect clothing **2** sthg that suggests or resembles an apron in shape, position, or use: e g **a** the part of a stage that projects in front of the curtain **b** the extensive paved area by an airport terminal or in front of aircraft hangars

apron strings n pl dominance, esp of a man by his mother or wife ⟨still tied to his mother's ~⟩

¹apropos adv **1** at an opportune time **2** BY THE WAY

²apropos adj both relevant and opportune

³apropos prep APROPOS OF

apropos of prep concerning; WITH REGARD TO

apse n **1** a projecting part of a building (e g a church) that is usu semicircular or polygonal and vaulted **2** APSIS 1

apsis n, pl **apsides 1** the point in an astronomical orbit at which the distance of the body from the centre of attraction is either greatest or least **2** APSE 1

apt adj **1** ordinarily disposed; likely – usu + to **2** suited to a purpose; relevant **3** keenly intelligent and responsive ⟨an ~ pupil⟩ – **aptly** adv, **aptness** n

aptitude n **1** a natural ability; a talent, esp for learning **2** general fitness or suitability – usu + for – **aptitudinal** adj, **aptitudinally** adv

aqualung n cylinders of compressed air, oxygen, etc carried on the back and connected to a face mask for breathing underwater

aquamarine n **1** a transparent blue to green beryl used as a gemstone **2** a pale blue to light greenish blue colour

¹aquaplane n a board towed behind a fast motorboat and ridden by sby standing on it

²aquaplane vi **1** to ride on an aquaplane **2** of a car to go out of control by sliding on water lying on the surface of a wet road – **aquaplaner** n

aquarium n, pl **aquariums, aquaria 1** a glass tank, artificial pond, etc in which living aquatic animals or plants are kept **2** an establishment where collections of living aquatic organisms are exhibited

Aquarius n (sby born under) the 11th sign of the zodiac in astrology, which is pictured as a man pouring water – **Aquarian** adj or n

¹aquatic adj **1** growing, living in, or frequenting water **2** taking place in or on water ⟨~ sports⟩ – **aquatically** adv

²aquatic n **1** an aquatic animal or plant **2** pl but sing or pl in constr water sports

aquatint n (a print made by) a method of etching a printing plate that enables tones similar to watercolour washes to be reproduced – **aquatint** vt, **aquatinter** n, **aquatintist** n

aqua vitae n **1** ALCOHOL 1 **2** a strong spirit (e g brandy or whisky)

aqueduct n a conduit, esp an arched structure over a valley, for carrying water

aqueous adj of, resembling, or made from, with, or by water – **aqueously** adv

aquiline adj **1** of or like an eagle **2** of the human nose hooked – **aquilinity** n

¹-ar suffix (n → adj) of, relating to, or being ⟨molecular⟩ ⟨spectacular⟩; resembling ⟨oracular⟩

²-ar suffix (→ n) ²-ER ⟨beggar⟩ ⟨scholar⟩

Arab n **1a** a member of a Semitic people orig of the Arabian peninsula and now widespread throughout the Middle East and N Africa **b** a member of an Arabic-speaking people **2** not cap **a** a homeless vagabond; esp an outcast boy or girl **b** a mischievous or annoying child **3** a typically intelligent, graceful, and swift horse of an Arabian stock – **Arab** adj

¹arabesque adj (in the style) of arabesque

²arabesque n **1** a decorative design or style that combines natural motifs (e g flowers or foliage) to produce an intricate pattern **2** a posture in ballet in which the dancer is supported on one leg with one arm extended forwards and the other arm and leg backwards

Arabian n **1** a native or inhabitant of Arabia **2** ARAB 3 – **Arabian** adj

¹Arabic adj **1** (characteristic) of Arabia, Arabians, or the Arabs **2** of or being Arabic

²Arabic n a Semitic language, now the prevailing speech of Arabia, Jordan, Lebanon, Syria, Iraq, Egypt, and parts of N Africa

Arabic numeral n, often not cap A any of the number symbols 0, 1, 2, 3, 4, 5, 6, 7, 8, 9

arable n or adj (land) being or fit to be farmed for crops – **arability** n

arachnid n any of a class (e g spiders, mites, ticks, and scorpions) of arthropods whose bodies have 2 segments of which the front bears 4 pairs of legs – **arachnid** adj

arbiter n a person or agency with absolute power of judging and determining

arbitrary adj **1** depending on choice or discretion **2a** arising from unrestrained exercise of the will **b** selected at

random and without reason **3** despotic, tyrannical –
arbitrarily *adv*, **arbitrariness** *n*

arbitrate *vi* to act as arbitrator ~ *vt* **1** to act as arbiter
upon **2** to submit for decision to an arbitrator – **arbitrative** *adj*

arbitration *n* the settlement of a disputed issue by an
arbitrator – **arbitrational** *adj*

arbitrator *n* **1** sby chosen to settle differences between 2
parties in dispute **2** an arbiter

arboreal *adj* of, resembling, inhabiting, or frequenting a
tree or trees – **arboreally** *adv*

arboretum *n*, *pl* **arboretums, arboreta** a place where trees
and shrubs are cultivated for study and display

arbour, *NAm chiefly* **arbor** *n* a bower of (latticework
covered with) shrubs, vines, or branches

¹**arc** *n* **1** the apparent path described by a celestial body **2**
sthg arched or curved **3** a sustained luminous discharge
of electricity across a gap in a circuit or between electrodes; *also* ARC LAMP **4** a continuous portion of a curve
(e g of a circle or ellipse)

²**arc** *vi* to form an electric arc

³**arc** *adj* INVERSE **2** – used with the trigonometric and
hyperbolic functions ⟨~ *sine*⟩ ⟨*if y is the cosine of θ then*
θ is the ~ *cosine of* y⟩

arcade *n* **1** a long arched gallery or building **2** a passageway or avenue (e g between shops) – **arcaded** *adj*

Arcadia *n* a usu idealized rural region or scene of simple
pleasure and quiet – **Arcadian** *adj*

arcane *adj* known or knowable only to an initiate; secret

¹**arch** *n* **1** a typically curved structural member spanning
an opening and resisting lateral or vertical pressure (e g of
a wall) **2** sthg (e g the vaulted bony structure of the foot)
resembling an arch in form or function **3** an archway

²**arch** *vt* **1** to span or provide with an arch **2** to form or
bend into an arch ~ *vi* to form an arch

³**arch** *adj* **1** principal, chief ⟨*an arch-villain*⟩ ⟨*an* ~ *rebel*⟩
2a cleverly sly and alert **b** playfully saucy – **archly** *adv*,
archness *n*

¹**arch-** *prefix* **1** chief; principal ⟨arch*bishop*⟩ **2** extreme;
most fully embodying the qualities of (a specified usu
undesirable human type) ⟨arch*rogue*⟩ ⟨arch*enemy*⟩

²**arch-** – see ARCHI-

-arch *comb form* (→ *n*) ruler; leader
⟨*matri*arch⟩ ⟨*olig*arch⟩

archaeology *n* the scientific study of material remains
(e g artefacts and dwellings) of past human life and activities – **archaeological** *adj*, **archaeologically** *adv*, **archaeologist** *n*

archaic *adj* **1** (characteristic) of an earlier or more primitive time; antiquated **2** no longer used in ordinary speech
or writing – **archaically** *adv*

archaism *n* **1** the use of archaic diction or style **2** an
instance of archaic usage; *esp* an archaic word or
expression **3** sthg outmoded or old-fashioned – **archaist**
n, **archaize** *vb*, **archaistic** *adj*

archangel *n* a chief angel – **archangelic** *adj*

archbishop *n* a bishop at the head of an ecclesiastical
province, or one of equivalent honorary rank – **archbishopric** *n*

archdeacon *n* a clergyman having the duty of assisting
a diocesan bishop, esp in administrative work – **archdeaconate** *n*

archdiocese *n* the diocese of an archbishop – **archdiocesan** *adj*

archduke *n* a sovereign prince – **archducal** *adj*, **archduchy** *n*, **archdukedom** *n*

archer *n* one who practises archery

archery *n* the art, practice, skill, or sport of shooting
arrows from a bow

archetype *n* **1** an original pattern or model; a prototype
2 IDEA **1a** **3** an inherited idea or mode of thought
derived from the collective unconscious – **archetypal**,
archetypical *adj*, **archetypally archetypically** *adv*

archi-, arch- *prefix* **1** chief; principal ⟨archi*trave*⟩ **2**
primitive; original; primary

archimandrite *n* a dignitary in the Eastern church ranking below a bishop

archipelago *n*, *pl* **archipelagoes, archipelagos** (an
expanse of water with) a group of scattered islands –
archipelagic *adj*

architect *n* **1** sby who designs buildings and superintends
their construction **2** sby who devises, plans, and achieves
a difficult objective

architecture *n* **1** the art, practice, or profession of
designing and erecting buildings; *also* a method or style of
building **2** product or work of architecture ⟨*the beautiful*
~ *of Prague*⟩ – **architectural** *adj*, **architecturally** *adv*

architrave *n* **1** the lowest part of an entablature resting
immediately on the capital of the column **2** the moulded
frame round a rectangular recess or opening (e g a
door)

archive *n* a place in which public records or historical
documents are preserved; *also* the material preserved –
often pl with sing. meaning

archivist *n* sby in charge of archives

archway *n* (an arch over) a way or passage that runs
beneath arches

-archy *comb form* (→ *n*) rule; government ⟨*mon*archy⟩

arc lamp *n* a type of electric lamp that produces light by
an arc made when a current passes between two incandescent electrodes surrounded by gas

arctic *adj* **1** often cap of the N Pole or the surrounding
region **2a** extremely cold; frigid **b** cold in temper or
mood

arctic circle *n*, often cap A&C the parallel of latitude
approx 66 ½ degrees north of the equator that circumscribes the north polar region

-ard *suffix* (→ *n*) one characterized by or associated with
(a usu undesirable specified action, state, or quality)
⟨*dull*ard⟩

ardent *adj* characterized by warmth of feeling; eager,
zealous – **ardency** *n*, **ardently** *adv*

ardour, *NAm chiefly* **ardor** *n* **1** (transitory) warmth of
feeling **2** extreme vigour or intensity; zeal

arduous *adj* **1** hard to accomplish or achieve; difficult,
strenuous **2** hard to climb; steep – **arduously** *adv*, **arduousness** *n*

¹**are** *pres 2 sing or pres pl of* BE

²**are** *n* a metric unit of area equal to 100m²

area *n* **1** a level piece of ground **2** a particular extent of
space or surface, or one serving a special function **3** the
extent, range, or scope of a concept, operation, or activity;
a field – **areal** *adj*, **areally** *adv*

arena *n* **1** (a building containing) an enclosed area used
for public entertainment **2** a sphere of interest or activity;
a scene

aren't **1** are not **2** am not – used in questions

arête *n* a sharp-crested mountain ridge

argent *n* **1** a silver colour; *also* white – used in heraldry
2 *archaic* the metal or colour silver – **argent** *adj*

argon *n* a noble gaseous element found in the air and
volcanic gases and used esp as a filler for vacuum tubes
and electric light bulbs

argot *n* a (more or less secret) vocabulary peculiar to a
particular group

arguably *adv* as can be argued ⟨~ *the best black cellist around at present*⟩

argue *vi* **1** to give reasons for or against sthg; reason **2** to contend or disagree in words ~ *vt* **1** to give evidence of; indicate **2** to consider the reasons for and against; discuss **3** to (try to) prove by giving reasons; maintain **4** to persuade by giving reasons ⟨~d *him out of going*⟩ **5** to give reasons or arguments in favour of ⟨*his letter* ~s *restraint*⟩ – **arguable** *adj*, **arguer** *n*

argument *n* **1** a reason given in proof or rebuttal **2a** the act or process of arguing; debate **b** a coherent series of reasons offered **c** a quarrel, disagreement **3** an abstract or summary, esp of a literary work **4a** any of the variables which determine the value of a function **b** the angle indicating the direction of a complex number from the origin of the Argand diagram ⟨*if* a + ib *is written as* re^i Cθ *or* r(cosθ + isinθ) *then* θ *is the* ~⟩

argumentative *adj* given to argument; disputatious – **argumentatively** *adv*

argy-bargy, argie-bargie *n, chiefly Br* (a) lively discussion; (a) dispute – *infml*

aria *n, pl* **arias** an accompanied melody sung (e g in an opera) by 1 voice

-arian *suffix* (→ *n*) **1** believer in ⟨*Unitarian*⟩; advocate of ⟨*vegetarian*⟩ **2** one who pursues (a specified interest or activity) ⟨*antiquarian*⟩ ⟨*librarian*⟩ **3** one who is (so many decades) old ⟨*octogenarian*⟩

arid *adj* **1** excessively dry; *specif* having insufficient rainfall to support agriculture **2** lacking in interest and life – **aridity** *n*, **aridness** *n*

Aries *n* (sby born under) the 1st sign of the zodiac in astrology, which is pictured as a ram – **Arian** *adj or n*

aright *adv* rightly, correctly

arise *vi* **arose; arisen 1a** to originate from a source – often + *from* **b** to come into being or to attention **2** to get up, rise – chiefly fml

aristocracy *n* **1** (a state with) a government in which power is vested in a small privileged usu hereditary noble class **2** *sing or pl in constr* a (governing) usu hereditary nobility **3** *sing or pl in constr* the whole group of those believed to be superior (e g in wealth, rank, or intellect)

aristocrat *n* **1** a member of an aristocracy; *esp* a noble **2** one who has the bearing and viewpoint typical of the aristocracy

aristocratic *adj* belonging to, having the qualities of, or favouring aristocracy – **aristocratically** *adv*

arithmetic *n* **1** a branch of mathematics that deals with real numbers and calculations with them **2** computation, calculation – **arithmetic, arithmetical** *adj*, **arithmetically** *adv*, **arithmetician** *n*

arithmetic mean *n* a value found by dividing the sum of a set of terms by the number of terms

arithmetic progression *n* a sequence (e g 3, 5, 7, 9) in which the difference between any term and its predecessor is constant

ark *n* **1** a ship; *esp* (one like) the one built by Noah to escape the Flood **2a** the sacred chest representing to the Hebrews the presence of God among them **b** a repository for the scrolls of the Torah

¹arm *n* **1** (the part between the shoulder and the wrist of) the human upper limb **2** sthg like or corresponding to an arm: e g **a** the forelimb of a vertebrate animal **b** a limb of an invertebrate animal **3** an inlet of water (e g from the sea) **4** might, authority ⟨*the long* ~ *of the law*⟩ **5** a support (e g on a chair) for the elbow and forearm **6** a sleeve **7** a functional division of a group or activity – **armed** *adj*, **armful** *n*, **armless** *adj*, **armlike** *adj* – **at arm's length** far enough away to avoid intimacy

²arm *vt* **1** to supply or equip with weapons **2** to provide

with sthg that strengthens or protects **3** to fortify morally **4** to equip for action or operation ⟨~ *a bomb*⟩ ~ *vi* to prepare oneself for struggle or resistance

³arm *n* **1a** a weapon; *esp* a firearm – usu pl **b** a combat branch (e g of an army) **2** *pl* the heraldic insignia of a group or body (e g a family or government) **3** *pl* **a** active hostilities **b** military service or profession – **up in arms** angrily rebellious and protesting strongly ⟨*the entire community are* up in arms *about the proposed motorway*⟩

armada *n, pl* **armadas** a fleet of warships; *specif, cap* that sent against England by Spain in 1588

armadillo *n, pl* **armadillos** any of several burrowing chiefly nocturnal S American mammals with body and head encased in an armour of small bony plates

armament *n* **1** a military or naval force **2** the military strength, esp in arms and equipment, of a ship, fort, or combat unit, nation, etc **3** the process of preparing for war

armature *n* **1** an offensive or defensive structure in a plant or animal (e g teeth or thorns) **2a** the central rotating part of an electric motor or generator **b** a framework on which a modeller in clay, wax, etc builds up his/her work

¹armchair *n* a chair with armrests

²armchair *adj* **1** remote from direct dealing with practical problems ⟨~ *strategists*⟩ **2** sharing vicariously in another's experiences ⟨*an* ~ *traveller*⟩

armhole *n* an opening for the arm in a garment

armistice *n* a temporary suspension of hostilities; a truce

armlet *n* **1** a band (e g of cloth or metal) worn round the upper arm **2** a small arm (e g of the sea)

armorial *adj* of or bearing heraldic arms – **armorially** *adv*

armour, Nam chiefly armor *n* **1a** a defensive covering for the body; *esp* a covering (e g of metal) worn in combat **b** a usu metallic protective covering (e g for a ship, fort, aircraft, or car) **2** armoured forces and vehicles (e g tanks) – **armour, armourless** *adj*

armour-clad *adj* sheathed in or protected by armour

armoured *adj* consisting of or equipped with vehicles protected with armour plate

armourer *n* **1** sby who makes or looks after armour or arms **2** sby who repairs, assembles, and tests firearms

armour plate *n* a defensive covering of hard metal plates for combat vehicles and vessels

armoury *n* (a collection of or place for storing) arms and military equipment

armpit *n* the hollow beneath the junction of the arm and shoulder

army *n* **1a** a large organized force for war on land **b** *often cap* the complete military organization of a nation for land warfare **2** a great multitude **3** a body of people organized to advance a cause ⟨*the Salvation* Army⟩

aroma *n, pl* **aromas 1a** a distinctive, pervasive, and usu pleasant or savoury smell **b** the bouquet of a wine **2** a distinctive quality or atmosphere

¹aromatic *adj* **1** of or having an aroma: **a** fragrant **b** having a strong esp pungent or spicy smell **2** *of a chemical compound* having a molecular structure containing a ring, specif containing (a group like) a benzene ring – **aromatically** *adv*, **aromaticity** *n*, **aromaticness** *n*, **aromatize** *vt*, **aromatization** *n*

²aromatic *n* sthg aromatic

arose *past of* ARISE

¹around *adv, chiefly NAm* **1** round **2** ABOUT (3, 5)

²around *prep, chiefly NAm* **1** round **2** ABOUT (1, 2a, 5)

³around *adj, chiefly NAm* **1** ABOUT 1 ⟨*has been up and* ~

for 2 days⟩ **2** in existence, evidence, or circulation ⟨*the most intelligent of the artists ~ today* – R M Coates⟩
arouse *vt* **1** to awaken from sleep **2** to rouse to action; excite, esp sexually – **arousal** *n*
arpeggio *n, pl* **arpeggios** (the sounding of) a chord whose notes are played in succession, not simultaneously
arquebus *n* a heavy but portable matchlock gun usu fired from a support – **arquebusier** *n*
arrack, arak *n* an Asian alcoholic spirit that is a distillation of the fermented mash of rice and molasses and to which has been added the fermented sap of the coconut palm
arraign *vt* **1** to charge before a court **2** to accuse of wrong, inadequacy, or imperfection – **arraignment** *n*
arrange *vt* **1** to put in order or into sequence or relationship **2** to make preparations for; plan **3** to bring about an agreement concerning; settle ⟨*~ an exchange of prisoners of war*⟩ **4** to adapt (a musical composition) by scoring for different voices or instruments *~vi* to make plans ⟨*~ to go on holiday*⟩ – **arranger** *n*
arrangement *n* **1a** a preliminary measure; a preparation ⟨*travel ~s*⟩ **b** an adaptation of a musical composition for different voices or instruments **c** an informal agreement or settlement, esp on personal, social, or political matters **d** an agreement with a bank that allows one to draw money without notice from a branch other than that at which one has one's account ⟨*have you got an ~?*⟩ **2** sthg made by arranging constituents or things together ⟨*a floral ~*⟩
arrant *adj* notoriously without moderation; extreme ⟨*an ~ fool*⟩ – **arrantly** *adv*
arras *n, pl* **arras** a wall hanging or screen made of tapestry
¹array *vt* **1** to set or place in order; marshal **2** to dress or decorate, esp in splendid or impressive clothes; adorn – **arrayer** *n*
²array *n* **1** military order ⟨*forces in ~*⟩ **2a** clothing, garments **b** rich or beautiful apparel; finery **3** an imposing group; a large number **4** a number of mathematical elements arranged in rows and columns **5** an arrangement of computer memory elements (e g magnetic cores) in a single plane
arrear *n* **1** an unfinished duty **2** an unpaid and overdue debt *USE* usu pl with sing. meaning – **arrearage** *n* – **in arrears** behind in the discharge of obligations
¹arrest *vt* **1a** to bring to a stop ⟨*sickness ~ed his activities*⟩ **b** to make inactive **2** to seize, capture; *specif* to take or keep in custody by authority of law **3** to catch and fix or hold ⟨*~ the attention*⟩ – **arrester, arrestor** *n*, **arrestment** *n*
²arrest *n* **1a** the act of stopping **b** the condition of being stopped ⟨*cardiac ~*⟩ **2** the taking or detaining of sby in custody by authority of law **3** a device for arresting motion – **under arrest** in legal custody
arrival *n* **1** the attainment of an end or state **2** sby or sthg that has arrived
arrive *vi* **1** to reach a destination **2** to come ⟨*the moment has ~d*⟩ **3** to achieve success – **arriver** *n* – **arrive at** to reach by effort or thought ⟨*have arrived at a decision*⟩
arrogance *n* aggressive conceit – **arrogant** *adj*, **arrogantly** *adv*
arrogate *vt* to claim or seize without justification, on behalf of oneself or another – **arrogation** *n*
¹arrow *n* **1** a projectile shot from a bow, usu having a slender shaft, a pointed head, and feathers at the end **2** sthg shaped like an arrow; *esp* a mark to indicate direction
²arrow *vt* to indicate with an arrow ⟨*the location is ~ed on the map*⟩
arrowhead *n* **1** the pointed front part of an arrow **2** sthg

shaped like an arrowhead **3** any of several related (water) plants with leaves shaped like arrowheads
arrowroot *n* (a tropical American plant whose roots yield) a nutritive starch used esp as a thickening agent in cooking
arse *n* **1** the buttocks **2** the anus *USE* vulg
arsenal *n* **1** an establishment for the manufacture or storage of arms and military equipment; an armoury **2** a store, repertory
arsenic *n* **1** a trivalent and pentavalent semimetallic steel-grey poisonous element **2** an extremely poisonous trioxide of arsenic, used esp as an insecticide – **arsenic** *adj*, **arsenical** *adj or n*, **arsenious** *adj*
arson *n* the criminal act of setting fire to property in order to cause destruction – **arsonist** *n*
¹art *archaic pres 2 sing of* BE
²art *n* **1** a skill acquired by experience, study, or observation **2** *pl* the humanities as contrasted with science **3a** the conscious use of skill and creative imagination, esp in the production of aesthetic objects; *also* works so produced **b** (any of the) fine arts or graphic arts **4** decorative or illustrative elements in printed matter
³art *adj* **1** composed, designed, or created with conscious artistry ⟨*an ~ song*⟩ **2** designed for decorative purposes ⟨*~ pottery*⟩
artefact, artifact *n* **1a** a usu simple object (e g a tool or ornament) produced by human workmanship **b** a product of civilization ⟨*an ~ of the jet age*⟩ **2** sthg (e g a structure seen in the microscope) unnaturally present through extraneous influences (e g from defects in the staining procedure) – **artefactual** *adj*
arterial *adj* **1** of or (being the bright red blood) contained in an artery **2** of or being a main road – **arterially** *adv*
arteriosclerosis *n* abnormal thickening and hardening of the arterial walls – **arteriosclerotic** *adj or n*
artery *n* **1** any of the branching elastic-walled blood vessels that carry blood from the heart to the lungs and through the body **2** an esp main channel (e g a river or road) of transport or communication
artesian well *n* a well by which water reaches the surface with little or no pumping
artful *adj* adroit in attaining an end, often by deceitful or indirect means; crafty – **artfully** *adv*, **artfulness** *n*
arthritis *n, pl* **arthritides** usu painful inflammation of 1 or more joints
arthropod *n* any of a phylum of invertebrate animals (e g insects, arachnids, and crustaceans) with a jointed body and limbs and usu an outer skin made of chitin and moulted at intervals
artichoke *n* **1a** a tall composite plant like a thistle **b** the partly edible flower head of the artichoke, used as a vegetable **2** JERUSALEM ARTICHOKE
¹article *n* **1a(1)** a separate clause, item, provision, or point in a document **(2)** *pl* a written agreement specifying conditions of apprenticeship **b** a piece of nonfictional prose, usu forming an independent part of a magazine, newspaper, etc **2** an item of business; a matter **3** a word or affix (e g *a, an,* and *the*) used with nouns to give indefiniteness or definiteness **4a** a particular or separate object or thing, esp viewed as a member of a class of things ⟨*several ~s of clothing*⟩ ⟨*~s of value*⟩ **b** a thing of a particular and distinctive kind ⟨*the genuine ~*⟩
²article *vt* to bind by articles (e g of apprenticeship)
¹articulate *adj* **1a** divided into syllables or words meaningfully arranged **b** having the power of speech **c** expressing oneself readily, clearly, or effectively; *also* expressed in this manner **2** jointed – **articulacy** *n*, **articulately** *adv*, **articulateness** *n*

²articulate *vt* **1a** to utter distinctly **b** to give clear and effective utterance to ⟨ ~ *one's grievances*⟩ **2** to unite with a joint ~ *vi* **1** to utter articulate sounds **2** to become united or connected (as if) by a joint – **articulative** *adj*, **articulator** *n*, **articulatory** *adj*

articulated *adj, chiefly Br* having 2 parts flexibly connected and intended to operate as a unit ⟨*an ~ lorry*⟩

articulation *n* **1a** the action or manner of jointing or interrelating **b** the state of being jointed or interrelated **2 a** (movable) joint (between plant or animal parts) **3a** the (verbal) expression of thoughts and feelings **b** the act or manner of articulating sounds **4** the fitting together of teeth with the cusps of opposing teeth when the mouth is closed

artifact *n* an artefact – **artifactual** *adj*

artifice *n* **1** an artful device, expedient, or stratagem; a trick **2** clever or artful skill; ingenuity

artificer *n* **1** a skilled or artistic worker or craftsman **2** a military or naval mechanic

artificial *adj* **1** made by human skill and labour, often to a natural model; man-made ⟨*an ~ limb*⟩ ⟨*~ diamonds*⟩ **2a** lacking in natural quality; affected **b** imitation, sham – **artificiality** *n*, **artificially** *adv*, **artificialness** *n*

artificial insemination *n* introduction of semen into the uterus or oviduct by other than natural means

artificial respiration *n* the rhythmic forcing of air into and out of the lungs of sby whose breathing has stopped

artillery *n* **1** large-calibre mounted firearms (e g guns, howitzers, missile launchers, etc) **2** *sing or pl in constr* a branch of an army armed with artillery

artisan *n* **1** a skilled manual worker (e g a carpenter, plumber, or tailor) **2** a member of the urban proletariat

artist *n* **1a** one who professes and practises an imaginative art **b** a person skilled in a fine art **2** a skilled performer; *specif* an artiste **3** one who is proficient in a specified and usu dubious activity; an expert ⟨*rip-off ~*⟩ – *infml* **4** *Austr & NAm* a fellow or character, esp of a specified sort – *infml*

artiste *n* a skilled public performer; *specif* a musical or theatrical entertainer

artistic *adj* **1** concerning or characteristic of art or artists **2** showing imaginative skill in arrangement or execution – **artistically** *adv*

artistry *n* **1** artistic quality **2** artistic ability

artless *adj* **1** free from artificiality; natural ⟨*~ grace*⟩ **2** free from deceit, guile, or craftiness; sincerely simple – **artlessly** *adv*, **artlessness** *n*

art nouveau *n, often cap A&N* a decorative style of late 19th-c origin, characterized esp by curved lines and plant motifs

arty *adj* showily or pretentiously artistic ⟨*~ lighting and photography*⟩ – **artily** *adv*, **artiness** *n*

arty-crafty *adj* arty; *esp* affectedly simple or rustic in style – *infml*

¹-ary *suffix* (→ *n*) **1** thing belonging to or connected with ⟨*ovary*⟩; *esp* place or repository of or for ⟨*library*⟩ ⟨*aviary*⟩ **2** one belonging to, connected with, or engaged in ⟨*functionary*⟩ ⟨*missionary*⟩

²-ary *suffix* (→ *adj*) of or connected with ⟨*budgetary*⟩ ⟨*military*⟩

¹as *adv* **1** to the same degree or amount; equally ⟨*~ deaf as a post*⟩ **2** when considered in a specified form or relation – usu used before a preposition or participle ⟨*my opinion ~ distinguished from his*⟩

²as *conj* **1a** to the same degree that ⟨*deaf ~ a post* ⟩ – usu used as a correlative after *as* or *so* to introduce a comparison ⟨*as long ago ~ 1930*⟩ or as a result ⟨*so clearly guilty*

~ *to leave no doubt*⟩ **b** – used after *same* or *such* to introduce an example or comparison ⟨*in the same building ~ my brother*⟩ ⟨*such trees ~ oak or pine*⟩ **c** – used after *so* to introduce the idea of purpose ⟨*he hid so ~ not to get caught*⟩ **2** in the way that ⟨*do ~ I say, not ~ I do*⟩ – used before *so* to introduce a parallel ⟨*~ the French like their wine, so the British like their beer*⟩ **3** in accordance with what ⟨*quite good ~ boys go*⟩ ⟨*late, ~ usual*⟩ **4** while, when ⟨*spilt the milk ~ she got up*⟩ **5** regardless of the fact that; though ⟨*naked ~ I was, I rushed out*⟩ **6** for the reason that; seeing ⟨*~ it's raining, let's make toffee*⟩ – **as is** in the present condition without modification ⟨*bought the clock at an auction* as is⟩ – *infml* – **as it is** IN REALITY – **as it were** SO TO SPEAK – **as often as not** at least half the time

³as *pron* **1** a fact that; and this ⟨*is ill, ~ you can see*⟩ ⟨*unaccustomed ~ I am to public speaking*⟩ **2** which also; and so ⟨*plays football, ~ do his brothers*⟩

⁴as *prep* **1** LIKE 1a, **2** in the capacity, character, role, or state of ⟨*works ~ an editor*⟩ ⟨*they regard her ~ clever*⟩

⁵as *n, pl* **asses** (a unit of value represented by) a bronze coin of ancient Rome

as- – see AD-

asbestos *n* either of 2 minerals composed of thin flexible fibres, used to make noncombustible, nonconducting, or chemically resistant materials

ascend *vi* **1** to move or slope gradually upwards; rise **2a** to rise from a lower level or degree ⟨*~ to power*⟩ **b** to go back in time or in order of genealogical succession ~ *vt* **1** to go or move up **2** to succeed to; begin to occupy – esp in *ascend the throne* – **ascendable, ascendible** *adj*, **ascending** *adj*

ascendancy *also* **ascendency** *n* controlling influence; domination

¹ascendant *also* **ascendent** *n* **1** the degree of the zodiac that rises above the eastern horizon at any moment (e g at one's birth) **2** a state or position of dominant power or importance – esp in *in the ascendant* **3** an ancestor

²ascendant *also* **ascendent** *adj* **1** rising **2** superior, dominant – **ascendantly** *adv*

ascension *n* the act or process of ascending

Ascension Day *n* the Thursday 40 days after Easter observed in commemoration of Christ's ascension into Heaven

ascent *n* **1a** the act of going, climbing, or travelling up **b** a way up; an upward slope or path **2** an advance in social status or reputation; progress

ascertain *vt* to find out or learn with certainty – **ascertainable** *adj*

ascetic *also* **ascetical** *adj* **1** practising strict self-denial as a spiritual discipline **2** austere in appearance, manner, or attitude – **ascetic** *n*, **ascetically** *adv*, **asceticism** *n*

ascribe *vt* to refer or attribute (sthg) *to* a supposed cause or source – **ascribable** *adj*

ascription *n* the act of ascribing; attribution

asepsis *n* **1** the condition of being aseptic **2** the methods of making or keeping sthg aseptic

aseptic *adj* **1** preventing infection ⟨*~ techniques*⟩ **2** free or freed from disease-causing microorganisms ⟨*an ~ operating theatre*⟩ – **aseptically** *adv*

asexual *adj* **1** lacking sex (organs) **2** produced without sexual action or differentiation **3** without expression of or reference to sexual interest – **asexually** *adv*

as for *prep* concerning; IN REGARD TO – used esp in making a contrast ⟨*~ the others, they'll arrive later*⟩

as from *prep* not earlier or later than ⟨*takes effect ~ July 1st*⟩

¹ash *n* **1** (the tough elastic wood of) any of a genus of tall pinnate-leaved trees of the olive family **2** the ligature *K* used in Old English to represent a low front vowel

²**ash** *n* **1a** the solid residue left when material is thoroughly burned or oxidized **b** fine particles of mineral matter from a volcano **2** *pl* the remains of sthg destroyed by fire ⟨*a new city built on the ~es of the old*⟩ **3** *pl* the remains of a dead body after cremation or disintegration – **ashless** *adj*

ashamed *adj* **1** feeling shame, guilt, or disgrace **2** restrained by fear of shame ⟨*was ~ to beg*⟩ – **ashamedly** *adv*

ash can *n*, *NAm* a dustbin

¹**ashen** *adj* of or made from the wood of the ash tree

²**ashen** *adj* **1** consisting of or resembling ashes **2** deadly pale; blanched ⟨*his face was ~ with fear*⟩

Ashes *n pl* a trophy played for in a series of cricket test matches between England and Australia – + *the*

ashore *adv* on or to the shore

ashtray *n* a (small) receptacle for tobacco ash and cigar and cigarette ends

Ash Wednesday *n* the first day of Lent

ashy *adj* **1** of ashes **2** ²ASHEN 2

Asian *adj* (characteristic) of the continent of Asia or its people – **Asian** *n*

Asiatic *adj* Asian – **Asiatic** *n*

¹**aside** *adv or adj* **1** to or towards the side ⟨*stepped ~*⟩ **2** out of the way ⟨*put his work ~*⟩ **3** apart; IN RESERVE **4** APART 3

²**aside** *n* **1** an utterance meant to be inaudible; *esp* an actor's speech supposedly not heard by other characters on stage **2** a digression

aside from *prep*, *chiefly NAm* APART FROM

as if *conj* **1** as it would be if ⟨*it was ~ he had lost his best friend*⟩ **2** as one would do if ⟨*shook his head ~ to say no*⟩ **3** that ⟨*it's not ~ she's poor*⟩ **4** – used in emphatic repudiation of a notion ⟨*~ I cared!*⟩

asinine *adj* stupid – **asininely** *adv*, **asininity** *n*

ask *vt* **1a** to call on for an answer ⟨*I ~ed him about his trip*⟩ **b** to put a question about ⟨*I ~ed his whereabouts*⟩ **c** to put or frame (a question) ⟨*~ a question of him*⟩ **2a** to make a request of ⟨*she ~ed her teacher for help*⟩ **b** to make a request for ⟨*she ~ed help from her teacher*⟩ **3** to behave in such a way as to provoke (an unpleasant response) ⟨*just ~ing to be given a good hiding*⟩ **4** to set as a price ⟨*~ed £1500 for the car*⟩ **5** to invite ⟨*~ him to dinner*⟩ **~** *vi* to seek information ⟨*he ~ed after the old man's health*⟩ – **asker** *n*

askance *adv* with disapproval or distrust – esp in *look askance*

askew *adv or adj* awry – **askewness** *n*

asking price *n* the price set by the seller

aslant *prep*, *adv*, *or adj* (over or across) in a slanting direction

asleep *adj* **1** in a state of sleep **2** dead – euph **3** lacking sensation; numb

as long as *conj* **1** providing, while; SO LONG AS **2** *chiefly NAm* since; INASMUCH AS ⟨*~ you're going, I'll go too*⟩

as of *prep*, *chiefly NAm* AS FROM

asp *n* a small venomous snake of Egypt, variously identified as a cobra or cerastes

asparagus *n* (any of a genus of Old World perennial plants of the lily family including) a tall plant widely cultivated for its edible young shoots

aspect *n* **1a** the position of planets or stars with respect to one another, held by astrologers to influence human affairs; *also* the apparent position (e g conjunction) of a body in the solar system with respect to the sun **b** a position facing a particular direction ⟨*the house has a southern ~*⟩ **c** the manner of presentation of an aerofoil, hydrofoil, etc to a gas or liquid through which it is moving

2a appearance to the eye or mind **b** a particular feature of a situation, plan, or point of view **3** (a set of inflected verb forms that indicate) the nature of an action as to its beginning, duration, completion, or repetition (e g in *I swim* and *I am swimming*) – **aspectual** *adj*

aspen *n* any of several poplars with leaves that flutter in the lightest wind

asperity *n* **1** rigour, hardship **2** roughness of surface; unevenness **3** roughness of manner or temper; harshness

aspersion *n* **1** a sprinkling with water, esp in religious ceremonies **2** a calumnious or unwarranted doubt ⟨*he cast ~s on her integrity*⟩

asphalt *n* **1** a brown to black bituminous substance found in natural beds and also obtained as a residue in petroleum or coal tar refining **2** an asphaltic composition used for surfacing roads and footpaths – **asphaltic** *adj*

asphodel *n* any of various Old World plants of the lily family with long spikes of flowers

asphyxia *n* a lack of oxygen in the body, usu caused by interruption of breathing, and resulting in unconsciousness or death – **asphyxiate** *vb*, **asphyxiation** *n*, **asphyxiator** *n*

aspic *n* a clear savoury jelly (e g of fish or meat stock) used as a garnish or to make a meat, fish, etc mould

aspidistra *n* any of various Asiatic plants of the lily family with large leaves, often grown as house plants

¹**aspirate, aspirated** *adj* pronounced with aspiration

²**aspirate** *vt* **1** to pronounce (a vowel, consonant, or word) with an *h*-sound **2** to draw or remove (e g blood) by suction

³**aspirate** *n* **1** (a character, esp *h*, representing) an independent /h/ sound **2** an aspirated consonant (e g the p of pit) **3** material removed by aspiration

aspiration *n* **1** the pronunciation or addition of an aspirate **2** a drawing of sthg in, out, up, or through (as if) by suction: e g **a** the act of breathing (sthg in) **b** the withdrawal of fluid from the body **3a** a strong desire to achieve sthg high or great **b** an object of such desire

aspire *vi* to seek to attain or accomplish a particular goal – usu + *to* ⟨*~d to a career in medicine*⟩ – **aspirant** *n or adj*, **aspirer** *n*

aspirin *n*, *pl* **aspirin**, **aspirins** (a tablet containing) a derivative of salicylic acid used for relief of pain and fever

as regards *prep* with respect to; IN REGARD TO

¹**ass** *n* **1** the donkey or a similar long-eared hardy gregarious mammal related to and smaller than the horse **2** a stupid, obstinate, or perverse person or thing ⟨*saying that the law is an ~*⟩

²**ass** *n*, *chiefly NAm* the arse

assail *vt* **1** to attack violently with blows or words **2** to prey on ⟨*~ed by doubts*⟩ – **assailable** *adj*, **assailant** *n*

assassin *n* **1** *cap* any of a secret order of Muslims who at the time of the Crusades committed secret murders **2** a murderer; *esp* one who murders a politically important person, for money or from fanatical motives

assassinate *vt* to murder suddenly or secretly, usu for political reasons – **assassination** *n*, **assassinator** *n*

¹**assault** *n* **1** a violent physical or verbal attack **2a** an attempt to do or immediate threat of doing unlawful personal violence **b** rape **3** an attempt to attack a fortification by a sudden rush

²**assault** *vt* **1** to make an (indecent) assault on **2** to rape – **assaulter** *n*, **assaultive** *adj*

¹**assay** *n* analysis of an ore, drug, etc to determine the presence, absence, or quantity of 1 or more components

²**assay** *vt* **1a** to analyse (e g an ore) for 1 or more valuable

components **b** to judge the worth or quality of **2** to try, attempt – *fml* – **assayer** *n*

assegai, assagai *n* a slender iron-tipped hardwood spear used in southern Africa

assemblage *n* **1** a collection of people or things; a gathering **2** a three-dimensional collage made from scraps, junk, and odds and ends (e g of cloth, wood, stone etc)

assemble *vb* **assembling** *vt* **1** to bring together (e g in a particular place or for a particular purpose) **2** to fit together the parts of ∼ *vi* to gather together; convene – **assembler** *n*

assembly *n* **1** a company of people gathered for deliberation and legislation, entertainment, or worship; *specif* a morning gathering of a school for prayers and/or for the giving out of notices **2** *cap* a legislative body **3a** an assemblage **b** assembling or being assembled **4** a bugle, drum, etc signal for troops to assemble or fall in **5** (a collection of parts assembled by) the fitting together of manufactured parts into a complete machine, structure, etc

assembly line *n* **1** an arrangement of machines, equipment, and usu workers in which work passes through successive operations until the product is assembled **2** a process for turning out a finished product in a mechanically efficient but often cursory manner

¹**assent** *vi* to agree to sthg – **assentor, assenter** *n*

²**assent** *n* acquiescence, agreement

assert *vt* **1** to state or declare positively and often forcefully **2** to demonstrate the existence of – **assertor** *n* – **assert oneself** to compel recognition of esp one's rights

assertion *n* a declaration, affirmation

assertive *adj* characterized by bold assertion; dogmatic – **assertively** *adv*, **assertiveness** *n*

assess *vt* **1a** to determine the rate or amount of (e g a tax) **b** to impose (e g a tax) according to an established rate **2** to make an official valuation of (property) for the purposes of taxation **3** to determine the importance, size, or value of – **assessable** *adj*, **assessment** *n*

assessor *n* **1** a specialist who advises a court **2** an official who assesses property for taxation **3** *chiefly Br* sby who investigates and values insurance claims

asset *n* **1a** *pl* the total property of a person, company, or institution; *esp* that part which can be used to pay debts **b** a single item of property **2** an advantage, resource **3** *pl* the items on a balance sheet showing the book value of property owned

asseverate *vt* to affirm solemnly – *fml* – **asseveration** *n*, **asseverative** *adj*

assiduity *n* **1** diligence **2** solicitous or obsequious attention to a person

assiduous *adj* marked by careful unremitting attention or persistent application; sedulous – **assiduously** *adv*, **assiduousness** *n*

¹**assign** *vt* **1** to transfer (property) to another, esp in trust or for the benefit of creditors **2** to appoint to a post or duty **3** to fix authoritatively; specify, designate – **assignability** *n*, **assignable** *adj*, **assigner, assignor** *n*

²**assign** *n* **1** ASSIGNEE 1, 2 **2** sby to whom property or a right is legally assigned

assignation *n* **1** the act of assigning; *also* the assignment made **2** a meeting, esp a secret one with a lover ⟨*returned from an* ∼ *with his mistress* – W B Yeats⟩ – **assignational** *adj*

assignee *n* **1** a person to whom an assignment is made **2** a person appointed to act for another **3** ASSIGN 2

assignment *n* **1a** a position, post, or job to which one is assigned **b** a specified task or amount of work assigned by

authority **2** (a document effecting) the legal transfer of property

assimilate *vt* **1a** to take in or absorb into the system (as nourishment) **b** to absorb; *esp* to take into the mind and fully comprehend **2a** to make similar – usu + *to* or *with* **b** to absorb into a cultural tradition **3** to compare, liken – usu + *to* or *with* ∼ *vi* to become assimilated – **assimilable** *adj*, **assimilative** *adj*, **assimilator** *n*, **assimilatory** *adj*

assimilation *n* adaptation of a sound to an adjacent sound (e g the *p* in *cupboard*)

¹**assist** *vi* **1** to give support or aid **2** to be present as a spectator ∼ *vt* to give support or aid to – **assistance** *n*, **assistant** *n*

²**assist** *n* the officially recorded action of a player who by throwing a ball in baseball or by passing a ball or puck in basketball, lacrosse, or ice hockey enables a teammate to put an opponent out or score a goal

assize *n*, *often cap* the periodical sessions of the superior courts formerly held in every English county for trial of civil and criminal cases – usu pl with sing. meaning

¹**associate** *vt* **1** to join as a friend, companion, or partner in business ⟨∼ *ourselves with a larger firm*⟩ **2** to bring together in any of various ways (e g in memory, thought, or imagination) ∼ *vi* **1** to come together as partners, friends, or companions **2** to combine or join with other parts; unite **3** often + *with* – **associatory** *adj*

²**associate** *adj* **1** closely connected (e g in function or office) with another **2** having secondary or subordinate status ⟨∼ *membership in a society*⟩

³**associate** *n* **1** a fellow worker; partner, colleague **2** a companion, comrade **3** sthg closely connected with or usu accompanying another **4** one admitted to a subordinate degree of membership ⟨*an* ∼ *of the Royal Academy*⟩ – **associateship** *n*

association *n* **1** an organization of people having a common interest; a society, league **2** sthg linked in memory, thought, or imagination with a thing or person; a connotation **3** the formation of mental connections between sensations, ideas, memories, etc **4** the formation of polymers by loose chemical linkage (e g through hydrogen bonds) **5** an ecological community with usu 2 or more dominant species uniformly distributed – **associational** *adj*

association football *n* soccer

assonance *n* **1** resemblance of sound in words or syllables **2** repetition of esp only the vowel sounds (e g in *stony* and *holy*) or only the consonant sounds, as an alternative to rhyme – **assonant** *adj or n*

as soon as *conj* immediately at or just after the time that

assort *vt* to distribute into groups of a like kind; classify ∼ *vi* to suit or match well or ill with sthg – **assortative** *adj*, **assorter** *n*

assorted *adj* **1** consisting of various kinds **2** suited by nature, character, or design; matched ⟨*an ill*-assorted *pair*⟩

assortment *n* a collection of assorted things or people

assuage *vt* to lessen the intensity of (pain, suffering, desire, etc); ease – **assuagement** *n*

assume *vt* **1a** to take to or upon oneself; undertake **b** to invest oneself formally with (an office or its symbols) **2** to seize, usurp **3** to pretend to have or be; feign **4** to take as granted or true; suppose – often + *that* – **assumability** *n*, **assumable** *adj*, **assumably** *adv*

assumption *n* **1a** the taking up of a person into heaven **b** *cap* August 15 observed in commemoration of the assumption of the Virgin Mary **2** the act of laying claim to or taking possession of sthg **3a** the supposition that sthg is true **b** a fact or statement (e g a proposition, axiom, or postulate) taken for granted

assurance *n* **1a** a pledge, guarantee **b** *chiefly Br* (life) insurance **2a** the quality or state of being sure or certain; freedom from doubt **b** confidence of mind or manner; *also* excessive self-confidence; brashness **3** sthg that inspires or tends to inspire confidence

assure *vt* **1** to make safe; insure (esp life or safety) **2** to give confidence to; reassure **3** to inform positively **4** to guarantee the happening or attainment of; ensure

¹assured *adj* **1** characterized by self-confidence ⟨*an ~ dancer*⟩ **2** satisfied as to the certainty or truth of a matter; convinced – **assuredly** *adv*, **assuredness** *n*

²assured *n, pl* **assured, assureds** an insured person

aster *n* any of various chiefly autumn-blooming leafy-stemmed composite plants with often showy heads

-aster *suffix* (*n → n*) one who is an inferior, worthless, or false kind of ⟨*criticaster*⟩ ⟨*poetaster*⟩

¹asterisk *n* a sign * used as a reference mark, esp to denote the omission of letters or words or to show that sthg is doubtful or absent

²asterisk *vt* to mark with an asterisk; star

astern *adv or adj* **1** behind the stern; to the rear **2** at or towards the stern of a ship **3** backwards ⟨*the captain signalled full ~*⟩

¹asteroid *n* any of thousands of small planets mostly between Mars and Jupiter – **asteroidal** *adj*

²asteroid *adj* **1** starlike **2** of or like a starfish

asthma *n* (an allergic condition marked by attacks of) laboured breathing with wheezing and usu coughing, gasping, and a sense of constriction in the chest – **asthmatic** *adj or n*, **asthmatically** *adv*

as though *conj* AS IF

astigmatic *adj* affected with, relating to, or correcting astigmatism – **astigmatically** *adv*

astigmatism *n* a defect of an optical system (e g a lens or the eye) in which rays from a single point fail to meet in a focal point, resulting in a blurred image

astir *adj* **1** in a state of bustle or excitement **2** out of bed; up

as to *prep* **1a** with regard or reference to; about – used esp with questions and speculations **b** AS FOR **2** by; ACCORDING TO ⟨*graded ~ size and colour*⟩

astonish *vt* to strike with sudden wonder or surprise – **astonishing** *adj*, **astonishingly** *adv*, **astonishment** *n*

astound *vt* to fill with bewilderment and wonder – **astounding** *adj*, **astoundingly** *adv*

astr-, astro- *comb form* star; heavens; outer space ⟨*astrophysics*⟩

astrakhan, astrachan *n, often cap* **1** karakul of Russian origin **2** a woollen fabric with curled and looped pile

astral *adj* **1** (consisting) of stars **2** (consisting) of a spiritual substance held in theosophy to be the material of which sby's supposed second body is made up, that can be seen by specially gifted people – **astrally** *adv*

astray *adv or adj* **1** off the right path or route **2** in error; away from a proper or desirable course or development

¹astride *adv* with the legs wide apart

²astride *prep* **1** on or above and with 1 leg on each side of **2** extending over or across; spanning

¹astringent *adj* **1** capable of making firm the soft tissues of the body; styptic **2** rigidly severe; austere – **astringency** *n*, **astringently** *adv*

²astringent *n* an astringent substance

astro- – see ASTR-

astrolabe *n* an instrument used, before the invention of the sextant, to observe the position of celestial bodies

astrology *n* the art or practice of determining the sup-

posed influences of the planets on human affairs – **astrologer** *n*, **astrological** *adj*, **astrologically** *adv*

astronaut *n* sby who travels beyond the earth's atmosphere

astronautics *n pl but sing or pl in constr* the science of the construction and operation of vehicles for travel in space – **astronautic, astronautical** *adj*, **astronautically** *adv*

astronomer *n* sby who is skilled in or practises astronomy

astronomical, astronomic *adj* enormously or inconceivably large – *infml* – **astronomically** *adv*

astronomy *n* a branch of science dealing with the celestial bodies

astrophysics *n pl but sing or pl in constr* a branch of astronomy dealing with the physical and chemical constitution of the celestial bodies – **astrophysical** *adj*, **astrophysicist** *n*

astute *adj* shrewdly perspicacious – **astutely** *adv*, **astuteness** *n*

asunder *adv or adj* **1** into parts ⟨*torn ~*⟩ **2** apart from each other in position ⟨*wide ~*⟩

asylum *n* **1** a place of refuge for criminals, debtors, etc; a sanctuary **2** a place of retreat and security; a shelter **3a** the protection from the law or refuge afforded by an asylum **b** protection from arrest and extradition given by a nation to political refugees **4** an institution for the care of the destitute or afflicted, esp the insane

asymmetric, asymmetrical *adj* **1** not symmetrical **2** *of an atom or group* bonded to several different atoms or groups – **asymmetrically** *adv*, **asymmetry** *n*

at *prep* **1** – used to indicate presence or occurrence in, on, or near a place imagined as a point ⟨*~ a hotel*⟩ ⟨*sick ~ heart*⟩; compare IN 1a(3) **2** – used to indicate the goal or direction of an action or motion ⟨*aim ~ the target*⟩; compare TO 1 **3a** – used to indicate occupation or employment ⟨*~ the controls*⟩ ⟨*~ tea*⟩ **b** when it comes to (an occupation or employment) ⟨*an expert ~ chess*⟩ **4** – used to indicate situation or condition ⟨*~ liberty*⟩ ⟨*~ risk*⟩ **5** in response to ⟨*laugh ~ his jokes*⟩ **6** – used to indicate position on a scale (e g of cost, speed, or age) ⟨*~ 90 mph*⟩ **7** – used to indicate position in time ⟨*~ 3 o'clock*⟩ ⟨*~ weekends*⟩ **8** from a distance of ⟨*shot him ~ 30 paces*⟩ – **at a** as a result of only 1; by or during only 1 ⟨*drank it at a gulp*⟩ ⟨*reduce prices at a stroke*⟩ ⟨*2 at a time*⟩ – **at it** doing it; esp busy ⟨*been hard at it all day*⟩ – **at that 1** at that point and no further ⟨*let it go at that*⟩ **2** which makes it more surprising; IN ADDITION ⟨*she says sack him, and maybe I will at that*⟩

at- – see AD-

at all *adv* to the least extent or degree; under any circumstances ⟨*not ~ far*⟩ ⟨*very seldom if ~*⟩ – **not at all** – used in answer to thanks or to an apology

atavism *n* (an individual or character showing) recurrence in (the parts of) an organism of a form typical of ancestors more remote than the parents – **atavist** *n*, **atavistic** *adj*, **atavistically** *adv*

ate *past of* EAT

¹-ate *suffix* (*→ n*) **1** product of (a specified process) ⟨*distillate*⟩ ⟨*condensate*⟩ ⟨*initiate*⟩ **2** chemical compound or complex anion derived from (a specified compound or element) ⟨*phenolate*⟩ ⟨*ferrate*⟩; esp salt or ester of (a specified acid with a name ending in *-ic* and not beginning with *hydro-*) ⟨*sulphate*⟩

²-ate *suffix* (*→ n*) **1** office, function, or rank of ⟨*consulate*⟩ ⟨*doctorate*⟩ **2** individual or group of people holding (a specified office or rank) or having (a specified function) ⟨*electorate*⟩ ⟨*candidate*⟩

³-ate, -ated *suffix* (*→ adj*) **1** being in or brought to (a specified state) ⟨*passionate*⟩ ⟨*inanimate*⟩ **2** marked by having ⟨*craniate*⟩ ⟨*loculated*⟩ **3** resembling; having the shape of ⟨*pinnate*⟩ ⟨*foliate*⟩

⁴**-ate** *suffix* (→ *vb*) **1** act (in a specified way) ⟨*pontificate*⟩ ⟨*remonstrate*⟩ **2** act (in a specified way) upon ⟨*insulate*⟩ ⟨*assassinate*⟩ **3** cause to become; cause to be modified or affected by ⟨*activate*⟩ ⟨*pollinate*⟩ **4** provide with ⟨*substantiate*⟩ ⟨*aerate*⟩

atelier *n* an artist's or designer's studio or workroom

atheism *n* the belief or doctrine that there is no deity – **atheist** *n*, **atheistic, atheistical** *adj*, **atheistically** *adv*

athlete *n* sby who is trained in, skilled in, or takes part in exercises, sports, etc that require physical strength, agility, or stamina

athlete's foot *n* ringworm of the feet

athletic *adj* **1** of athletes or athletics **2** characteristic of an athlete; *esp* vigorous, active – **athletically** *adv*, **athleticism** *n*

athletics *n pl but sing or pl in constr, Br* competitive walking, running, throwing, and jumping sports collectively

at home *n* a reception given at one's home

¹**athwart** *adv* **1** across, esp in an oblique direction **2** in opposition to the right or expected course

²**athwart** *prep* **1** across **2** in opposition to

-ation *suffix* (*vb* → *n*) **1** action or process of ⟨*flirtation*⟩ ⟨*computation*⟩ **2** result or product of (a specified action or process) ⟨*alteration*⟩ ⟨*plantation*⟩ **3** state or condition of ⟨*elation*⟩ ⟨*agitation*⟩

-ative *suffix* (*vb, n* → *adj*) **1** of, relating to, or connected with ⟨*authoritative*⟩ **2** tending to; disposed to ⟨*talkative*⟩ ⟨*laxative*⟩

atlas *n* **1** *cap* one who bears a heavy burden **2** a bound collection of maps, charts, or tables **3** the first vertebra of the neck

atmosphere *n* **1** a mass of gas enveloping a celestial body (e g a planet); *esp* all the air surrounding the earth **2** the air of a locality **3** a surrounding influence or environment **4** a unit of pressure chosen to be a typical pressure of the air at sea level and equal to $101,325N/m^2$ (about $14.7lb/in^2$) **5** a dominant aesthetic or emotional effect or appeal – **atmosphered** *adj*

atmospheric *adj* **1** of, occurring in, or like the atmosphere **2** having, marked by, or contributing aesthetic or emotional atmosphere ⟨~ *music*⟩ – **atmospherically** *adv*

atmospherics *n pl* (the electrical phenomena causing) audible disturbances produced in a radio receiver by electrical atmospheric phenomena (e g lightning)

atoll *n* a coral reef surrounding a lagoon

atom *n* **1** any of the minute indivisible particles of which according to ancient materialism the universe is composed **2** a tiny particle; a bit ⟨*not an ~ of truth in it*⟩ **3** the smallest particle of an element that can exist either alone or in combination, consisting of various numbers of electrons, protons, and neutrons **4** nuclear power

atom bomb *n* **1** a bomb whose violent explosive power is due to the sudden release of atomic energy derived from the splitting of the nuclei of plutonium, uranium, etc by neutrons in a very rapid chain reaction **2** HYDROGEN BOMB – **atom-bomb** *vt*

atomic *adj* **1** of or concerned with atoms, atom bombs, or atomic energy **2** *of a chemical element* existing as separate atoms – **atomically** *adv*

atomic energy *n* energy liberated in an atom bomb, nuclear reactor, etc by changes in the nucleus of an atom

atomic number *n* the number of protons in the nucleus of an atom which is characteristic of a chemical element and determines its place in the periodic table

atomic pile *n* REACTOR 2

atomic weight *n* the ratio of the average mass of an atom of an element to the mass of an atom of the most abundantly occurring isotope of carbon

atomize, -ise *vt* to reduce to minute particles or to a fine spray – **atomization** *n*

atonal *adj* organized without reference to a musical key and using the notes of the chromatic scale impartially – **atonalism** *n*, **atonalist** *n*, **atonally** *adv*, **atonalistic** *adj*, **atonality** *n*

atone *vi* to supply satisfaction *for*; make amends *for* ⟨*the atoning death of Christ*⟩ – **atonement** *n*

-ator *suffix* (→ *n*) ¹-OR ⟨*commentat*or⟩

atrium *n, pl* **atria** *also* **atriums 1** an inner courtyard open to the sky (e g in a Roman house) **2** an anatomical cavity or passage; *specif* a chamber of the heart that receives blood from the veins and forces it into a ventricle or ventricles – **atrial** *adj*

atrocious *adj* **1** extremely wicked, brutal, or cruel; barbaric **2** of very poor quality ⟨~ *handwriting*⟩ – **atrociously** *adv*, **atrociousness** *n*

atrocity *n* **1** being atrocious **2** an atrocious act, object, or situation

¹**atrophy** *n* **1** (sometimes natural) decrease in size or wasting away of a body part or tissue **2** a wasting away or progressive decline; degeneration – **atrophic** *adj*

²**atrophy** *vb* to (cause to) undergo atrophy

attach *vt* **1** to seize by legal authority **2** to bring (oneself) into an association **3** to appoint to serve with an organization for special duties or for a temporary period **4** to fasten **5** to ascribe, attribute ~ *vi* to become attached; stick *USE* often + *to* – **attachable** *adj*

attaché *n* a technical expert on a diplomatic staff

attaché case *n* a small thin case used esp for carrying papers

attachment *n* **1** a seizure by legal process **2a** fidelity – often + *to* ⟨~ *to a cause*⟩ **b** an affectionate regard **3** a device attached to a machine or implement **4** the physical connection by which one thing is attached to another

¹**attack** *vt* **1** to set upon forcefully in order to damage, injure, or destroy **2** to take the initiative against in a game or contest **3** to assail with unfriendly or bitter words **4** to begin to affect or to act on injuriously **5** to set to work on, esp vigorously ~ *vi* to make an attack – **attacker** *n*

²**attack** *n* **1** the act of attacking; an assault **2** a belligerent or antagonistic action or verbal assault – often + *on* **3** the beginning of destructive action (e g by a chemical agent) **4** the setting to work on some undertaking **5** a fit of sickness or (recurrent) disease **6a** an attempt to score or to gain ground in a game **b** *sing or pl in constr* the attacking players in a team or the positions occupied by them; *specif* the bowlers in a cricket team ⟨*the Yorkshire ~ gave nothing away*⟩ **7** the act or manner of beginning a musical tone or phrase ⟨*a sharp ~*⟩

attain *vt* to reach as an end; achieve ~ *vi* to come or arrive by motion, growth, or effort – + *to* – **attainable** *adj*, **attainableness, attainability** *n*

attainder *n* a penalty enforced until 1870 by which sby sentenced to death or outlawry forfeited his/her property and civil rights

attainment *n* sthg attained; an accomplishment

attar *n* a fragrant essential oil (e g from rose petals); *also* a fragrance

¹**attempt** *vt* to make an effort to do, accomplish, solve, or effect, esp without success – **attemptable** *adj*

²**attempt** *n* **1** the act or an instance of attempting; *esp* an unsuccessful effort **2** an attack, assault – often + *on*

attend *vt* **1** to take charge of; LOOK AFTER **2** to go or stay with as a companion, nurse, or servant **3** to be present with; accompany, escort **4** to be present at ~ *vi* **1a** to apply oneself ⟨ ~ *to your work*⟩ **b** to deal with **2** to apply the mind or pay attention; heed *USE* – often + *to* – **attender** *n*

attendance *n* **1** the number of people attending **2** the number of times a person attends, usu out of a possible maximum

¹**attendant** *adj* accompanying or following as a consequence

²**attendant** *n* one who attends another to perform a service; *esp* an employee who waits on customers ⟨*a car park* ~⟩

attention *n* **1** attending, esp through application of the mind to an object of sense or thought **2** consideration with a view to action **3a** an act of civility or courtesy, esp in courtship – usu pl **b** sympathetic consideration of the needs and wants of others **4** a formal position of readiness assumed by a soldier – usu as a command – **attentional** *adj*

attentive *adj* **1** mindful, observant **2** solicitous **3** paying attentions (as if) in the role of a suitor – **attentively** *adv*, **attentiveness** *n*

¹**attenuate** *vt* **1** to make thin **2** to lessen the amount, force, or value of; weaken **3** to reduce the severity, virulence, or vitality of ~ *vi* to become thin or fine; diminish – **attenuation** *n*

²**attenuate** *adj* tapering gradually ⟨*an* ~ *leaf*⟩

attest *vt* **1a** to affirm to be true **b** to authenticate esp officially **2** to be proof of; bear witness to **3** to put on oath ~ *vi* to bear witness, testify – often + *to* – **attester** *n*, **attestation** *n*

attic *n* a room or space immediately below the roof of a building

¹**Attic** *adj* (characteristic) of Attica or Athens

²**Attic** *n* a Greek dialect of ancient Attica which became the literary language of the Greek-speaking world

¹**attire** *vt* to put garments on; dress, array; *esp* to clothe in fancy or rich garments

²**attire** *n* dress, clothes; *esp* splendid or decorative clothing

attitude *n* **1** the arrangement of the parts of a body or figure; a posture **2** a feeling, emotion, or mental position with regard to a fact or state **3** a manner assumed for a specific purpose **4** a ballet position in which one leg is raised at the back and bent at the knee **5** the position of an aircraft or spacecraft relative to a particular point of reference (e g the horizon) – **attitudinal** *adj*

attitudinize, -ise *vi* to assume an affected mental attitude; pose

attorney *n* **1** sby with legal authority to act for another **2** *NAm* a lawyer – **attorneyship** *n*

attorney general *n, pl* **attorneys general, attorney generals** *often cap* A&G the chief legal officer of a nation or state

attract *vt* to cause to approach or adhere: e g **a** to pull to or towards oneself or itself ⟨*a magnet* ~ s *iron*⟩ **b** to draw by appeal to interest, emotion, or aesthetic sense ⟨ ~ *attention*⟩ ~ *vi* to possess or exercise the power of attracting sthg or or sby ⟨*opposites* ~⟩ – **attractable** *adj*, **attractor** *n*, **attractive** *adj*, **attractively** *adv*, **attractiveness** *n*

attraction *n* **1** a characteristic that elicits interest or admiration – usu pl **2** the action or power of drawing forth a response (e g interest or affection); an attractive quality **3** a force between unlike electric charges, unlike magnetic poles, etc, resisting separation **4** sthg that

attracts or is intended to attract people by appealing to their desires and tastes

¹**attribute** *n* **1** an inherent characteristic **2** an object closely associated with a usu specified person, thing, or office **3** a subordinate word or phrase that grammatically limits the meaning of another; *esp* an adjective

²**attribute** *vt* to reckon as originating in an indicated fashion – usu + *to* – **attributable** *adj*, **attributer** *n*, **attribution** *n* – **attribute to** **1** to explain by indicating as a cause **2** to regard as a characteristic of (a person or thing)

attributive *adj* **1** relating to or of the nature of an attribute **2** directly preceding a modified noun (e g *city* in *city streets*) – **attributive** *n*, **attributively** *adv*

attrition *n* **1** sorrow for one's sins arising from fear of punishment **2** the act of rubbing together; friction; *also* the act of wearing or grinding down by friction **3** the act of weakening or exhausting by constant harassment or abuse ⟨*war of* ~⟩ – **attritional** *adj*

attune *vt* to bring into harmony; tune – **attunement** *n*

atypical *adj* not typical; irregular – **atypically** *adv*, **atypicality** *n*

aubergine **1** (the edible usu smooth dark purple ovoid fruit of) the eggplant **2** a deep reddish purple colour

aubrietia *n* any of various trailing spring-flowering rock plants of the mustard family

auburn *adj or n* (of) a reddish brown colour

¹**auction** *n* **1a** a public sale of property to the highest bidder **2** the act or process of bidding in some card games

²**auction** *vt* to sell at an auction – often + *off* ⟨ ~ ed *off the silver*⟩

auction bridge *n* a form of bridge differing from contract bridge in that tricks made in excess of the contract are scored towards game

auctioneer *n* an agent who sells goods at an auction – **auctioneer** *vt*

audacious *adj* **1a** intrepidly daring; adventurous **b** recklessly bold; rash **2** insolent – **audaciously** *adv*, **audaciousness** *n*, **audacity** *n*

audible *adj* heard or capable of being heard – **audibly** *adv*, **audibility** *n*

audience *n* **1a** a formal hearing or interview ⟨*an* ~ *with the pope*⟩ **b** an opportunity of being heard ⟨*the court refused him* ~⟩ **2** *sing or pl in constr* a group of listeners or spectators

¹**audio** *adj* **1** of or being acoustic, mechanical, or electrical frequencies corresponding to those of audible sound waves, approx 20 to 20,000Hz **2a** of sound or its reproduction, esp high-fidelity reproduction **b** relating to or used in the transmission or reception of sound

²**audio** *n* the transmission, reception, or reproduction of sound

audio- *comb form* **1** hearing ⟨*audiometer*⟩ **2** sound ⟨*audiophile*⟩ **3** auditory and ⟨*audiovisual*⟩

audiometer *n* an instrument for measuring the sharpness of hearing – **audiometry** *n*, **audiometric** *adj*

audiovisual *adj* of (teaching methods using) both hearing and sight

¹**audit** *n* (the final report on) a formal or official examination and verification of an account book

²**audit** *vt* to perform an audit on – **auditable** *adj*

¹**audition** *n* **1** the power or sense of hearing **2** the act of hearing; *esp* a critical hearing **3** a trial performance to appraise an entertainer's abilities

²**audition** *vt* to test (e g for a part) in an audition ~ *vi* to give a trial performance – usu + *for*

auditor *n* **1** one who hears or listens; *esp* a member of an audience **2** one authorized to perform an audit

auditorium *n, pl* **auditoria, auditoriums** the part of a public building where an audience sits

auditory *adj* of or experienced through hearing

au fait *adj* **1** fully competent; capable **2** fully informed; familiar *with*

auger *n* **1** a tool for boring holes in wood consisting of a shank with a central tapered screw and a pair of cutting lips with projecting spurs that cut the edge of the hole **2** any of various instruments or devices shaped like an auger

¹aught *pron* **1** all ⟨*for ~ I care*⟩ **2** *archaic* anything

²aught *n* a zero, cipher

¹augment *vi* to become greater, increase ~ *vt* **1** to make greater, more numerous, larger, or more intense **2** to add an augment to – **augmentable** *adj*, **augmenter, augmentor** *n*, **augmentation** *n*

²augment *n* a prefixed or lengthened initial vowel marking past tense, esp in Greek and Sanskrit verbs

¹augur *n* one held to foretell events by omens; a soothsayer; *specif* an official diviner of Ancient Rome

²augur *vt* **1** to foretell, esp from omens **2** to give promise of; presage ~ *vi* to predict the future, esp from omens

augury *n* **1** predicting the future from omens or portents **2** an omen, portent

august *adj* marked by majestic dignity or grandeur – **augustly** *adv*, **augustness** *n*

August *n* the 8th month of the Gregorian calendar

auk *n* a puffin, guillemot, razorbill, or related short-necked diving seabird of the northern hemisphere

auld lang syne *n* the good old times

aunt *n* **1a** the sister of one's father or mother **b** the wife of one's uncle **2** – often used as a term of affection for a woman who is a close friend of a young child or its parents

Aunt Sally *n* **1** an effigy of a woman at which objects are thrown at a fair **2** *Br* an easy target of criticism or attack

¹au pair *n* a foreign girl who does domestic work for a family in return for room and board and the opportunity to learn the language of the family

²au pair *vi* to work as an au pair

aura *n* **1** a distinctive atmosphere surrounding a given source **2** a luminous radiation; a nimbus **3** a sensation experienced before an attack of a brain disorder, esp epilepsy

aural *adj* of the ear or the sense of hearing – **aurally** *adv*

aureole, aureola *n* **1** a radiant light surrounding the head or body of a representation of a holy figure **2** the halo surrounding the sun, moon etc when seen through thin cloud – **aureole** *vt*

au revoir *n* goodbye – often used interjectionally

auricle *n* **1a** PINNA 2 **b** an atrium of the heart – not now in technical use **2** an ear-shaped lobe

auricular *adj* **1** of or using the ear or the sense of hearing **2** told privately ⟨*an ~ confession*⟩ **3** understood or recognized by the sense of hearing **4** of an auricle

auriferous *adj* gold-bearing

aurora *n, pl* **auroras, aurorae** dawn – **auroral** *adj*, **aurorean** *adj*

aurora australis *n* a phenomenon in the S hemisphere corresponding to the aurora borealis

aurora borealis *n* a luminous electrical phenomenon in the N hemisphere, esp at high latitudes, that consists of streamers or arches of light in the sky

auscultation *n* the act of listening to the heart, lungs, etc as a medical diagnostic aid – **auscultate** *vt*

auspice *n* **1** a (favourable) prophetic sign **2** *pl* kindly patronage and guidance

auspicious *adj* **1** affording a favourable auspice; propitious **2** attended by good auspices; prosperous – **auspiciously** *adv*, **auspiciousness** *n*

Aussie *n* an Australian – *infml*

austere *adj* **1** stern and forbidding in appearance and manner **2** rigidly abstemious; self-denying **3** unadorned, simple – **austerely** *adv*, **austereness** *n*

austerity *n* **1** an austere act, manner, or attitude **2** enforced or extreme economy

¹Austr-, Austro- *comb form* south; southern ⟨*Austroasiatic*⟩

²Austr-, Austro- *comb form* Austrian and ⟨*Austro-Hungarian*⟩

Australasian *n or adj* (a native or inhabitant) of Australasia

¹Australian *n* **1** a native or inhabitant of Australia **2** the speech of the aboriginal inhabitants of Australia **3** English as spoken and written in Australia

²Australian *adj* **1** (characteristic) of Australia **2** of or being a biogeographic region that comprises Australia and the islands north of it from the Celebes eastwards, Tasmania, New Zealand, and Polynesia

aut-, auto- *comb form* **1** self; same one; of or by oneself ⟨*autobiography*⟩ ⟨*autodidact*⟩ **2** automatic; self-acting; self-regulating ⟨*autodyne*⟩

autarchy *n* absolute sovereignty

autarky *also* **autarchy** *n* national (economic) self-sufficiency and independence – **autarkic, autarkical** *adj*

authentic *adj* **1** worthy of belief as conforming to fact or reality; trustworthy **2** not imaginary, false, or imitation; genuine – **authentically** *adv*, **authenticity** *n*

authenticate *vt* to (serve to) prove the authenticity of – **authenticator** *n*, **authentication** *n*

author, *fem* **authoress** *n* **1a** the writer of a literary work **b** (the books written by) sby whose profession is writing **2** sby or sthg that originates or gives existence; a source – **authorial** *adj*

authoritarian *adj* of or favouring submission to authority rather than personal freedom – **authoritarian** *n*, **authoritarianism** *n*

authoritative *adj* **1a** having or proceeding from authority; official **b** entitled to credit or acceptance; conclusive **2** dictatorial, peremptory – **authoritatively** *adv*, **authoritativeness** *n*

authority *n* **1a** a book, quotation, etc referred to for justification of one's opinions or actions **b** a conclusive statement or set of statements **c** an individual cited or appealed to as an expert **2a** power to require and receive submission; the right to expect obedience **b** power to influence or command **c** a right granted by sby in authority; authorization **3a** *pl the* people in command **b** persons in command; *specif* government **c** *often cap* a governmental administrative body **4a** grounds, warrant ⟨*had excellent ~ for his strange actions*⟩ **b** convincing force; weight ⟨*his strong tenor lent ~ to the performance*⟩

authorize, -ise *vt* **1** to invest with authority or legal power; empower – often + infin **2** to establish (as if) by authority; sanction – **authorizer** *n*, **authorization** *n*

Authorized Version *n* an English version of the Bible prepared under James I, published in 1611, and widely used by Protestants

authorship *n* **1** the profession or activity of writing **2** the identity of the author of a literary work ⟨*the ~ of Hamlet is not seriously disputed*⟩

autism *n* a disorder of childhood development marked esp by inability to form relationships with other people – **autistic** *adj*

auto n, pl **autos** chiefly NAm MOTOR CAR
¹**auto-** – see AUT-
²**auto-** comb form self-propelling; automotive ⟨**auto**cycle⟩
autobahn n a German motorway
autobiography n the biography of a person written by him-/herself; also such writing considered as a genre – **autobiographer** n, **autobiographic, autobiographical** adj
autocracy n government by an autocrat
autocrat n 1 one who rules with unlimited power 2 a dictatorial person – **autocratic** adj, **autocratically** adv
autoeroticism n autoerotism – **autoerotic** adj, **autoerotically** adv
autoerotism n sexual gratification obtained by oneself without the participation of another person – **autoerotic** adj **autoerotically** adv
¹**autograph** n an identifying mark, specif a person's signature, made by the individual him-/herself – **autography** n
²**autograph** vt to write one's signature in or on
automate vt 1 to operate by automation 2 to convert to largely automatic operation ~ vi to undergo automation – **automatable** adj
¹**automatic** adj 1a acting or done spontaneously or unconsciously b resembling an automaton; mechanical 2 having a self-acting or self-regulating mechanism ⟨an ~ car with ~ transmission⟩ 3 of a firearm repeatedly ejecting the empty cartridge shell, introducing a new cartridge, and firing it – **automatically** adv, **automaticity** n
²**automatic** n an automatic machine or apparatus; esp an automatic firearm or vehicle
automatic pilot n a device for automatically steering a ship, aircraft, or spacecraft
automation n 1 the technique of making an apparatus, process, or system operate automatically 2 automatic operation of an apparatus, process, or system by mechanical or electronic devices that take the place of human operators
automatism n 1 an automatic action 2 a theory that conceives of the body as a machine, with consciousness being merely an accessory – **automatist** n
automaton n, pl **automatons, automata** 1 a mechanism having its own power source; also a robot 2 a person who acts in a mechanical fashion
automobile n, NAm MOTOR CAR – **automobile** vi, **automobilist** n
autonomous adj self-governing, independent – **autonomously** adv
autonomy n 1 self-determined freedom and esp moral independence 2 self-government; esp the degree of political independence possessed by a minority group, territorial division, etc – **autonomist** n
autopsy n a postmortem examination – **autopsy** vt
autostrada n, pl **autostradas, autostrade** an Italian motorway
autosuggestion n an influencing of one's attitudes, behaviour, or physical condition by mental processes other than conscious thought – **autosuggest** vt
autumn n 1 the season between summer and winter, extending, in the northern hemisphere, from the September equinox to the December solstice 2 a period of maturity or the early stages of decline – **autumnal** adj, **autumnally** adv
¹**auxiliary** adj 1 subsidiary 2 being a verb (e g be, do, or may) used typically to express person, number, mood, voice, or tense, usu accompanying another verb 3 supplementary
²**auxiliary** n 1 an auxiliary person, group, or device 2 an

auxiliary verb 3 a member of a foreign force serving a nation at war
¹**avail** vb to be of use or advantage (to) – **avail oneself of** to make use of; take advantage of
²**avail** n benefit, use – chiefly after of or to and in negative contexts ⟨of little ~⟩ ⟨to no ~⟩
available adj 1 present or ready for immediate use 2 accessible, obtainable 3 qualified or willing to do sthg or to assume a responsibility ⟨~ candidates⟩ 4 present in such chemical or physical form as to be usable (e g by a plant) ⟨~ nitrogen⟩ ⟨~ water⟩ – **availableness** n, **availably** adv, **availability** n
¹**avalanche** n 1 a large mass of snow, rock, ice, etc falling rapidly down a mountain 2 a sudden overwhelming rush or accumulation of sthg
²**avalanche** vi to descend in an avalanche ~ vt to overwhelm, flood
¹**avant-garde** n the group of people who create or apply new ideas and techniques in any field, esp the arts; also such a group that is extremist, bizarre, or arty and affected – **avant-gardism** n, **avant-gardist** n
²**avant-garde** adj of the avant-garde or artistic work that is new and experimental
avarice n excessive or insatiable desire for wealth or gain; cupidity – **avaricious** adj, **avariciously** adv, **avariciousness** n
avatar n 1 an earthly incarnation of a Hindu deity 2a an incarnation in human form b an embodiment (e g of a concept or philosophy), usu in a person
avenge vt 1 to take vengeance on behalf of 2 to exact satisfaction for (a wrong) by punishing the wrongdoer – **avenger** n
avenue n 1 a line of approach 2 a broad passageway bordered by trees 3 an often broad street or road 4 chiefly Br a tree-lined walk or driveway to a large country house situated off a main road
aver vt -rr- 1 to allege, assert 2 to declare positively – fml – **averment** n
¹**average** n 1 a partial loss or damage sustained by a ship or cargo; also a charge arising from this, usu distributed among all chargeable with it 2 a single value representative of a set of other values; esp ARITHMETIC MEAN 3 a level (e g of intelligence) typical of a group, class, or series 4 a ratio expressing the average performance of a sports team or sportsman as a fraction of the number of opportunities for successful performance
²**average** adj 1 equalling an arithmetic mean 2a about midway between extremes b not out of the ordinary; common – **averagely** adv, **averageness** n
³**average** vi to be or come to an average ⟨the gain ~d out to 20 per cent⟩ ~ vt 1 to do, get, or have on average or as an average sum or quantity ⟨~s 12 hours of work a day⟩ 2 to find the arithmetic mean of 3 to bring towards the average 4 to have an average value of ⟨a colour averaging a pale purple⟩
averse adj having an active feeling of repugnance or distaste – + to or from – **aversely** adv, **averseness** n
aversion n 1 a feeling of settled dislike for sthg; antipathy 2 chiefly Br an object of aversion; a cause of repugnance – **aversive** adj
avert vt 1 to turn away or aside (e g the eyes) in avoidance 2 to see coming and ward off; avoid, prevent
aviary n a place for keeping birds
aviation n 1 the operation of heavier-than-air aircraft 2 aircraft manufacture, development, and design
aviator n, fem **aviatrix** n the pilot of an aircraft
avid adj urgently or greedily eager; keen – **avidly** adv, **avidness** n, **avidity** n
avocado n, pl **avocados** also **avocadoes** (a tropical Ameri-

can tree of the laurel family bearing) a pulpy green or purple pear-shaped edible fruit

avocation n a subordinate occupation pursued in addition to one's vocation, esp for enjoyment; a hobby – **avocational** adj, **avocationally** adv

avocet n a black and white wading bird with webbed feet and a slender upward-curving bill

avoid vt **1a** to keep away from; shun **b** to prevent the occurrence or effectiveness of **c** to refrain from **2** to make legally void – **avoidable** adj, **avoidably** adv, **avoidance** n, **avoider** n

avoirdupois, avoirdupois weight n the series of units of weight based on the pound of 16 ounces and the ounce of 16 drams

avow vt **1** to declare assuredly **2** to acknowledge openly, bluntly, and without shame – **avower** n, **avowal** n, **avowedly** adv

avuncular adj **1** of an uncle **2** kindly, genial

await vt **1** to wait for **2** to be in store for

¹**awake** vb **awoke** also **awaked; awoken** vi **1** to emerge from sleep or a sleeplike state **2** to become conscious or aware of sthg – usu + to ⟨awoke to their danger⟩ ~ vt **1** to arouse from sleep or a sleeplike state **2** to make active; stir up ⟨awoke old memories⟩

²**awake** adj **1** roused (as if) from sleep **2** fully conscious; aware – usu + to

awaken vb to awake – **awakener** n

¹**award** vt **1** to give by judicial decree **2** to confer or bestow as being deserved or needed – **awardable** adj, **awarder** n

²**award** n **1** a final decision; esp the decision of arbitrators in a case submitted to them **2** sthg that is conferred or bestowed, esp on the basis of merit or need

aware adj having or showing realization, perception, or knowledge; conscious – often + of – **awareness** n

awash adj **1** covered with water; flooded **2** marked by an abundance

¹**away** adv **1** on the way; along ⟨get ~ early⟩ **2** from here or there; hence, thence ⟨go ~ and leave me alone!⟩ **3a** in a secure place or manner ⟨locked ~⟩ ⟨tucked ~⟩ **b** in another direction; aside ⟨looked ~⟩ **4** out of existence; to an end ⟨echoes dying ~⟩ ⟨laze ~ the afternoon⟩ **5** from one's possession ⟨gave ~ a fortune⟩ **6a** on, uninterruptedly ⟨clocks ticking ~⟩ **b** without hesitation or delay ⟨do it right ~⟩ **7** by a long distance or interval; far ⟨~ back in 1910⟩

²**away** adj **1** absent from a place; gone ⟨~ for the weekend⟩ **2** distant ⟨a lake 10 miles ~⟩ **3** played on an opponent's grounds ⟨an ~ game⟩

awe vt or n (to inspire with) an emotion compounded of dread, veneration, and wonder

awesome adj inspiring or expressing awe – **awesomely** adv, **awesomeness** n

awestruck also **awestricken** adj filled with awe

¹**awful** adj **1** extremely disagreeable or objectionable **2** exceedingly great ⟨an ~ lot to do⟩ – used as an intensive; chiefly infml – **awfully** adv, **awfulness** n

²**awful** adv very, extremely – nonstandard

awkward adj **1** lacking dexterity or skill, esp in the use of hands; clumsy **2** lacking ease or grace (e g of movement or expression) **3a** lacking social grace and assurance **b** causing embarrassment ⟨an ~ moment⟩ **4** poorly adapted for use or handling **5** requiring caution ⟨an ~ diplomatic situation⟩ **6** deliberately obstructive – **awkwardly** adv, **awkwardness** n

awl n a pointed instrument for marking surfaces or making small holes (e g in leather)

awning n **1** an often canvas rooflike cover, used to protect sthg (e g a shop window or a ship's deck) from sun

or rain **2** a shelter resembling an awning – **awninged** adj

awoken past part of AWAKE

AWOL adj, often not cap absent without leave

awry adv or adj **1** in a turned or twisted position or direction; askew **2** out of the right or hoped-for course; amiss

¹**axe, NAm chiefly ax** n **1** a tool that has a cutting edge parallel to the handle and is used esp for felling trees and chopping and splitting wood **2** drastic reduction or removal (e g of personnel) – **axe to grind** an ulterior often selfish purpose to further

²**axe, NAm chiefly ax** vt **1a** to hew, shape, dress, or trim with an axe **b** to chop, split, or sever with an axe **2** to remove abruptly (e g from employment or from a budget)

axiom n **1** a principle, rule, or maxim widely accepted on its intrinsic merit; a generally recognized truth **2a** a proposition regarded as a self-evident truth **b** a postulate

axiomatic adj of or having the nature of an axiom; esp self-evident – **axiomatically** adv

axis n, pl **axes 1a** a straight line about which a body or a geometric figure rotates or may be supposed to rotate **b** a straight line with respect to which a body or figure is symmetrical **c** any of the reference lines of a coordinate system **2a** the second vertebra of the neck on which the head and first vertebra pivot **b** any of various parts that are central, fundamental, or that lie on or constitute an axis **3** a plant stem **4** any of several imaginary reference lines used in describing a crystal structure **5** a partnership or alliance (e g the one between Germany and Italy in WW II)

axle n **1** a shaft on or with which a wheel revolves **2** a rod connecting a pair of wheels of a vehicle; also an axletree

axolotl n any of several salamanders of mountain lakes of Mexico

ayah n a native nurse or maid in India

¹**aye** also **ay** adv ever, always, continually

²**aye** also **ay** adv yes – used as the correct formal response to a naval order ⟨~,~, sir⟩

³**aye** also **ay** n an affirmative vote or voter

azalea n any of a group of rhododendrons with funnel-shaped flowers and usu deciduous leaves

azimuth n **1** an arc of the horizon expressed as the clockwise angle measured between a fixed point (e g true N or true S) and the vertical circle passing through the centre of an object **2** horizontal direction – **azimuthal** adj, **azimuthally** adv

azure n **1a** sky blue **b** blue – used in heraldry **2** archaic LAPIS LAZULI – **azure** adj

B

b n, pl **b's, bs** often cap **1a** (a graphic representation of or device for reproducing) the 2nd letter of the English alphabet **b** a speech counterpart of orthographic b **2** the 7th note of a C-major scale **3** one designated b, esp as the 2nd in order or class **4** a grade rating a student's work as good but short of excellent **5** sthg that is the supporting item of 2 things ⟨a ~-movie⟩ **6** – used euphemistically for any offensive word beginning with the letter b

baa, ba vi or n (to make) the bleat of a sheep

babble vb **babbling** vi **1a** to utter meaningless or unintelligible sounds **b** to talk foolishly; chatter **2** to make a continuous murmuring sound ~ *vt* **1** to utter in an incoherently or meaninglessly repetitious manner **2** to reveal by talk that is too free – **babble** *n*, **babblement** *n*, **babbler** *n*

babe *n* **1** a naive inexperienced person **2a** an infant, baby – chiefly poetic **b** a girl, woman – slang; usu as a noun of address

Babel *n, often not cap* **1** a confusion of sounds or voices **2** a scene of noise or confusion

baboon *n* any of several large African and Asiatic primates having doglike muzzles and usu short tails – **baboonish** *adj*

babu *n* **1** a Hindu gentleman – a form of address corresponding to *Mr* **2** an Indian with some education in English – chiefly derog

¹baby *n* **1a(1)** an extremely young child; *esp* an infant **(2)** an unborn child ⟨*my ~ started kicking before I was 4 months pregnant*⟩ **(3)** an extremely young animal **b** the youngest of a group **2** an infantile person **3** a person or thing for which one feels special responsibility or pride **4** a person; *esp* a girl, woman – slang; usu as a noun of address – **babyish** *adj*, **babyhood** *n*

²baby *adj* very small ⟨*use ~ mushrooms*⟩

³baby *vt* to tend or indulge with often excessive or inappropriate care

baby-minder *n chiefly Br* a childminder for babies or preschool children – **baby-minding** *n*

baby-sit *vi* **-tt-; baby-sat** to care for a child, usu for a short period while the parents are out – **baby-sitter** *n*

baby talk *n* the imperfect speech used by or to small children

baccalaureate *n* the academic degree of bachelor

baccarat *n* a card game in which 3 hands are dealt and players may bet on either or both hands against the dealer's

bacchanal *n* **1a** a devotee of Bacchus; *esp* one who celebrates the Bacchanalia **b** a reveller **2** drunken revelry or carousal; bacchanalia – **bacchanal** *adj*

bacchanalia *n, pl* **bacchanalia 1** *pl, cap* a Roman festival of Bacchus celebrated with dancing, song, and revelry **2** a drunken feast; an orgy – **bacchanalian** *adj or n*

baccy *n, chiefly Br* tobacco – infml

bachelor *n* **1** a recipient of what is usu the lowest degree conferred by a college or university ⟨*~ of arts*⟩ **2a** an unmarried man **b** a man past the usual age for marrying or one who seems unlikely to marry **3** a male animal (e g a fur seal) without a mate during breeding time – **bachelordom** *n*, **bachelorhood** *n*

bachelor girl *n* an unmarried girl or woman who lives independently

bacillus *n, pl* **bacilli** a usu rod-shaped bacterium; *esp* one that causes disease

¹back *n* **1a** the rear part of the human body, esp from the neck to the end of the spine **b** the corresponding part of a quadruped or other lower animal **2a** the side or surface behind the front or face; the rear part; *also* the farther or reverse side **b** sthg at or on the back for support ⟨*the ~ of a chair*⟩ **3** (the position of) a primarily defensive player in some games (e g soccer) – **backless** *adj* – **with one's back to the wall** in a situation from which one cannot retreat and must either fight or be defeated

²back *adv* **1a(1)** to, towards, or at the rear ⟨*tie one's hair ~*⟩ **(2)** away (e g from the speaker) ⟨*stand ~ and give him air*⟩ **b** in or into the past or nearer the beginning; ago ⟨*3 years ~*⟩ **c** in or into a reclining position ⟨*lie ~*⟩ **d** in or into a delayed or retarded condition ⟨*set them ~ on the schedule*⟩ **2a** to, towards, or in a place from which sby or sthg came ⟨*put it ~ on the shelf*⟩ **b** to or towards a

former state ⟨*thought ~ to his childhood*⟩ **c** in return or reply ⟨*ring me ~*⟩ – **back and forth** backwards and forwards repeatedly

³back *adj* **1a** at or in the back ⟨*~ door*⟩ **b** distant from a central or main area; remote ⟨*~ roads*⟩ **c** articulated at or towards the back of the oral passage **2** being in arrears ⟨*~ pay*⟩ **3** not current ⟨*~ number of a magazine*⟩

⁴back *vt* **1a** to support by material or moral assistance – often + *up* **b** to substantiate – often + *up* ⟨*~ up an argument with forceful illustrations*⟩ **c(1)** to countersign, endorse **(2)** to assume financial responsibility for ⟨*~ an enterprise*⟩ **2** to cause to go back or in reverse **3a** to provide with a back **b** to be at the back of **4** to place a bet on (e g a horse) ~ *vi* **1** to move backwards **2** *of the wind* to shift anticlockwise **3** to have the back in the direction of sthg ⟨*my house ~s onto the golf course*⟩

backache *n* a (dull persistent) pain in the back

back away *vi* to move back (e g from a theoretical position); withdraw

back bench *n* any of the benches in Parliament on which rank and file members sit – usu pl – **back-bencher** *n*

backbite *vb* **backbit; backbitten** to say mean or spiteful things about (sby) – **backbiter** *n*

backbone *n* **1** SPINAL COLUMN **2a** a chief mountain ridge, range, or system **b** the foundation or most substantial part of sthg **3** a firm and resolute character

backbreaking *adj* physically taxing or exhausting

backchat *n, chiefly Br* impudent or argumentative talk made in reply, esp by a subordinate – infml

backcloth *n, Br* **1** a painted cloth hung across the rear of a stage **2** BACKGROUND 1a, 3

backcomb *vt* to comb (the hair) against the direction of growth starting with the short underlying hairs in order to produce a bouffant effect

backdate *vt* to apply (e g a pay rise) retrospectively

back down *vi* to retreat from a commitment or position

backdrop *n* a backcloth

backer *n* **1** one who supports, esp financially **2** *Br* one who has placed a bet

¹backfire *n* a premature explosion in the cylinder or an explosion in the exhaust system of an internal-combustion engine

²backfire *vi* **1** to make or undergo a backfire **2** to have the reverse of the desired or expected effect

back-formation *n* the formation of a word by subtraction from an existing word; *also* a word so formed (e g *burgle* from *burglar*)

backgammon *n* a board game played with dice and counters in which each player tries to move his/her counters along the board and at the same time to block or capture his/her opponent's counters

background *n* **1a** the scenery or ground behind sthg **b** the part of a painting or photograph that depicts what lies behind objects in the foreground **2** an inconspicuous position ⟨*in the ~*⟩ **3a** the conditions that form the setting within which sthg is experienced **b** information essential to the understanding of a problem or situation **c** the total of a person's experience, knowledge, and education

¹backhand *n* **1** a stroke in tennis, squash, etc made with the back of the hand turned in the direction of movement; *also* the side of the body on which this is made **2** handwriting whose strokes slant downwards from left to right

²backhand, backhanded *adv* with a backhand

³backhand *vt* to do, hit, or catch backhand

backhanded *adj* **1** using or made with a backhand **2** of *writing* being backhand **3** indirect, devious; *esp* sarcastic ⟨*a ~ compliment*⟩ – **backhandedly** *adv*

backhander *n* **1** a backhanded blow or stroke **2** *Br* a backhanded remark **3** a bribe – *infml*

backing *n* **1** sthg forming a back **2a** support, aid **b** endorsement

backlash *n* **1** a sudden violent backward movement or reaction **2** a strong adverse reaction – **backlasher** *n*

backlog *n* **1** a reserve **2** an accumulation of tasks not performed, orders unfulfilled, or materials not processed

backmost *adj* farthest back

back number *n* sby or sthg that is out of date; *esp* an old issue of a periodical or newspaper

back of beyond *n* a remote inaccessible place ⟨*an old house in the ~*⟩

back off *vi* BACK DOWN

back out *vi* to withdraw, esp from a commitment or contest

back passage *n, chiefly Br* the rectum – *euph*

backpedal *vi* **1** to move backwards (e g in boxing) **2** to back down from or reverse a previous opinion or stand

backroom *adj* of or being a directing group that exercises its authority in an inconspicuous and indirect way

back seat *n* an inferior position ⟨*won't take a ~ to anyone*⟩

back-seat driver *n* a passenger in a motor car who offers unwanted advice to the driver

backside *n* the buttocks

backslide *vi* -**slid**; -**slid**, -**slidden** to lapse morally or in the practice of religion – **backslider** *n*

backspace *vi* to press a key on a typewriter which causes the carriage to move back 1 space

¹**backstage** *adv* **1** in or to a backstage area **2** in private, secretly

²**backstage** *adj* **1** of or occurring in the parts of a theatre that cannot be seen by the audience **2** of the inner working or operation (e g of an organization)

backstairs *adj* **1** secret, furtive ⟨*~ political deals*⟩ **2** sordid, scandalous ⟨*~ gossip*⟩

backstay *n* a stay extending aft from a masthead to the stern or side of a ship

backstreet *adj* made, done, or acting illegally or surreptitiously ⟨*~ abortion*⟩

backstroke *n* a swimming stroke executed on the back – **backstroker** *n*

backtrack *vi* **1** to retrace a path or course **2** to reverse a position or stand

backup *n* **1** sby or sthg that serves as a substitute, auxiliary, or alternative **2** sby or sthg that gives support

back up *vt* to support (sby), esp in argument or in playing a team game ~ *vi* to back up a teammate

backward *adj* **1a** directed or turned backwards **b** done or executed backwards ⟨*a ~ somersault*⟩ **2** retarded in development **3** of or occupying a fielding position in cricket behind the batsman's wicket **4** *chiefly NAm* diffident, shy – **backwardly** *adv*, **backwardness** *n*

backwards, *chiefly NAm* **backward** *adv* **1** towards the back **2** with the back foremost **3** in a reverse direction; towards the beginning ⟨*say the alphabet ~*⟩ **4** perfectly; BY HEART ⟨*knows it all ~*⟩ **5** towards the past **6** towards a worse state – **bend/fall/lean over backwards** to make extreme efforts, esp in order to please or conciliate

backwash *n* **1a** a backward movement in air, water, etc produced by a propelling force (e g the motion of oars) **b** the backward movement of a receding wave **2** a usu unwelcome consequence or by-product of an event; an aftermath

backwater *n* **1** a stagnant pool or inlet kept filled by the opposing current of a river; *broadly* a body of water turned back in its course **2** a place or condition that is isolated or backward, esp intellectually

backwoods *n, pl but sing or pl in constr* a remote or culturally backward area – usu + *the* – **backwoodsman** *n*

bacon *n* (the meat cut from) the cured and often smoked side of a pig

bacteria *pl of* BACTERIUM

bacteriology *n* **1** a science that deals with bacteria **2** bacterial life and phenomena ⟨*the ~ of a water supply*⟩ – **bacteriologist** *n*, **bacteriologic, bacteriological** *adj*, **bacteriologically** *adv*

bacterium *n, pl* **bacteria** any of a group of microscopic organisms that live in soil, water, organic matter, or the bodies of plants and animals and are important to human beings because of their chemical effects and because many of them cause diseases – **bacterial** *adj*, **bacterially** *adv*

Bactrian camel *n* CAMEL 1b

¹**bad** *adj* **worse**; **worst** **1a** failing to reach an acceptable standard; poor, inadequate **b** unfavourable **c** no longer acceptable, because of decay or disrepair ⟨*~ fish*⟩ ⟨*the house was in ~ condition*⟩ **2a** morally objectionable **b** mischievous, disobedient **3** unskilful, incompetent – often + *at* ⟨*~ at crosswords*⟩ **4** disagreeable, unpleasant ⟨*~ news*⟩ **5a** injurious, harmful ⟨*smoking is ~ for your health*⟩ **b** worse than usual; severe ⟨*a ~ cold*⟩ **6** incorrect, faulty ⟨*~ grammar*⟩ **7a** suffering pain or distress; unwell ⟨*he felt ~ because of his cold*⟩ **b** unhealthy, diseased ⟨*~ teeth*⟩ **8** sorry, unhappy ⟨*felt ~ after slighting a friend*⟩ **9** invalid, worthless ⟨*a ~ cheque*⟩ ⟨*a ~ coin*⟩ **10** *of a debt* not collectible – **bad** *adv*, **badly** *adv*, **badness** *n* – **in someone's bad books** out of favour with sby

²**bad** *n* an evil or unhappy state

bad blood *n* ill feeling; bitterness

bade *past of* BID

badge *n* **1** a device or token, esp of membership in a society or group **2** a characteristic mark **3** an emblem awarded rfor a particular accomplishment – **badge** *vt*

¹**badger** *n* (the pelt or fur of) any of several sturdy burrowing nocturnal mammals widely distributed in the northern hemisphere

²**badger** *vt* to harass or annoy persistently

badinage *n* playful repartee; banter

badly off *adj* in an unsatisfactory condition; *esp* not having enough money

badminton *n* a court game played with light long-handled rackets and a shuttle volleyed over a net

¹**baffle** *vt* **baffling** to throw into puzzled confusion; perplex – **bafflement** *n*, **baffler** *n*, **bafflingly** *adv*

²**baffle** *n* **1** a device (e g a plate, wall, or screen) to deflect, check, or regulate flow (e g of a fluid or light) **2** a structure that reduces the exchange of sound waves between the front and back of a loudspeaker

¹**bag** *n* **1a** a usu flexible container for holding, storing, or carrying sthg **b** a handbag or shoulder bag **2** sthg resembling a bag; *esp* a sagging in cloth **3a** a quantity of game (permitted to be) taken **b** spoils, loot **4** *pl chiefly Br* lots, masses – *infml* ⟨*has ~ s of money*⟩ **5** a slovenly unattractive woman ⟨*silly old ~*⟩ – slang **6** a way of life – slang – **bagful** *n* – **bag and baggage 1** with all one's belongings **2** entirely, wholesale – **in the bag** as good as achieved; already certain before the test – *infml*

²**bag** *vb* -**gg**- *vi* **1** to swell out; bulge **2** to hang loosely ~ *vt* **1** to cause to swell **2** to put into a bag **3a** to take (animals) as game **b** to get possession of, seize; *also* to steal

bagatelle *n* **1** TRIFLE 1 **2** a game in which balls must be put into or through cups or arches at one end of an oblong table

baggage n 1 portable equipment, esp of a military force 2 superfluous or useless things, ideas, or practices 3 NAm luggage, esp for travel by sea or air 4 a good-for-nothing woman; a pert girl – infml

baggy adj loose, puffed out, or hanging like a bag 〈~ trousers〉 – **baggily** adv, **bagginess** n

bagpipe n a wind instrument consisting of a leather bag, mouth tube, chanter, and drone pipes – often pl with sing. meaning but sing. or pl in constr – **bagpiper** n .

bah interj – used to express disdain

¹bail n 1 security deposited as a guarantee that sby temporarily freed from custody will return to stand trial 2 temporary release on bail 3 one who provides bail

²bail vt 1 to deliver (property) in trust to another for a special purpose and for a limited period 2 to release on bail 3 to procure the release of (a person in custody) by giving bail – often + out – **bailable** adj, **bailee** n, **bailment** n, **bailor** n

³bail n 1 either of the 2 crosspieces that lie on the stumps to form the wicket in cricket 2 chiefly Br a device for confining or separating animals

⁴bail, Br also **bale** n a container used to remove water from a boat

⁵bail, Br also **bale** vt to clear (water) from a boat by collecting in a bail, bucket etc and throwing over the side ~ vi to parachute from an aircraft USE (vt & vi) usu + out – **bailer** n

bailey n (the space enclosed by) the outer wall of a castle or any of several walls surrounding the keep

Bailey bridge n a prefabricated bridge built from interchangeable latticed steel panels

bailiff n 1 an official employed by a sheriff to serve writs, make arrests, etc 2 chiefly Br one who manages an estate or farm – **bailiffship** n

bail out, Br also **bale out** vt to help from a predicament; release from difficulty

bairn n, chiefly Scot & N Eng a child

¹bait vt 1 to provoke, tease, or exasperate with unjust, nagging, or persistent remarks 2 to harass (e g a chained animal) with dogs, usu for sport 3 to provide with bait 〈~ a hook〉 – **baiter** n

²bait n 1a sthg used in luring, esp to a hook or trap b a poisonous material placed where it will be eaten by pests 2 a lure, temptation

baize n a woollen cloth, resembling felt, used chiefly for covering and lining sthg (e g table tops or drawers)

¹bake vt 1 to cook (e g food) by dry heat, esp in an oven 2 to dry or harden by subjecting to heat ~ vi 1 to cook food (e g bread and cakes) by baking 2 to become baked 3 to become extremely hot 〈I'll have to stop sunbathing, I'm baking〉 – **baker** n

²bake n, NAm a social gathering at which (baked) food is served

Bakelite trademark – used for any of various synthetic resins and plastics

baker's dozen n thirteen

bakery n a place for baking or selling baked goods, esp bread and cakes

baking powder n a powder that consists of a bicarbonate and an acid substance used in place of yeast as a raising agent in making scones, cakes, etc

baksheesh n, pl **baksheesh** money given as a tip

balaclava, **balaclava helmet** n, often cap B a knitted pull-on hood that covers the ears, neck, and throat

balalaika n a musical instrument of Russian origin, usu having 3 strings and a triangular body which is played by plucking

¹balance n 1 an instrument for weighing: e g a a centrally-supported beam that has 2 scalepans of equal weight suspended from its ends b any device that measures weight and force 2 a counterbalancing weight, force, or influence 3 stability produced by even distribution of weight on each side of a vertical axis 4a equilibrium between contrasting, opposing, or interacting elements b equality between the totals of the 2 sides of an account 5 an aesthetically pleasing integration of elements 6 the ability to retain one's physical equilibrium 7 the weight or force of one side in excess of another 〈the ~ of the evidence lay on the side of the defendant〉 8a (a statement of) the difference between credits and debits in an account b sthg left over; a remainder c an amount in excess, esp on the credit side of an account 9 mental and emotional steadiness 10 the point on the trigger side of a rifle at which the weight of the ends balance each other – **balanced** adj – **in the balance** in an uncertain critical position; with the fate or outcome about to be determined – **on balance** all things considered

²balance vt 1a(1) to compute the difference between the debits and credits of (an account) (2) to pay the amount due on b to arrange so that one set of elements exactly equals another 〈~ a mathematical equation〉 2a to counterbalance, offset b to equal or equalize in weight, number, or proportion 3 to compare the relative importance, value, force, or weight of; ponder 4 to bring to a state or position of balance ~ vi 1 to become balanced or established in balance 〈sat balancing on the fence〉 2 to be an equal counterpoise – often + with 3 to waver, hesitate 〈a mind that ~s and deliberates〉 – **balancer** n

balance of payments n the difference over a period of time between a country's payments to and receipts from abroad

balance of power n an equilibrium of power sufficient to prevent one nation from imposing its will upon another

balance sheet n a statement of financial condition at a given date

balcony n 1 a platform built out from the wall of a building and enclosed by a railing or low wall 2 a gallery inside a building (e g a theatre) – **balconied** adj

bald adj 1a lacking a natural or usual covering (e g of hair, vegetation, or nap) b having little or no tread 〈~ tyres〉 2 unadorned, undisguised 〈the ~ truth〉 3 of an animal marked with white, esp on the head or face – **baldish** adj, **baldly** adv, **baldness** n

balderdash n nonsense – often as a generalized expression of disagreement

balding adj becoming bald

baldric n an often ornamented belt worn over one shoulder and across the body to support a sword, bugle, etc

¹bale n a large bundle of goods; specif a large closely pressed package of merchandise bound and usu wrapped for storage or transportation – **bale** vt

²bale n or vb, Br ⁴/⁵BAIL

baleful adj 1 deadly or pernicious in influence 2 gloomily threatening – **balefully** adv, **balefulness** n

bale out vt, Br BAIL OUT

¹balk, chiefly Br **baulk** n 1 a ridge of land left unploughed 2 a roughly squared beam of timber 3 the area behind the balk lines on a billiard table

²balk, chiefly Br **baulk** vt to check or stop (as if) by an obstacle; hinder, thwart ~ vi 1 to stop short and refuse to proceed 2 to refuse abruptly – often + at 〈~ed at the suggestion〉 – **balker** n

¹ball n 1 a round or roundish body or mass: a a solid or hollow spherical or egg-shaped body used in a game or sport b a spherical or conical projectile; also projectiles used in firearms ⟨*powder and* ~⟩ **c** the rounded slightly raised fleshy area at the base of a thumb or big toe **2 a** delivery or play of the ball in cricket, baseball, etc ⟨*bowled by a good* ~⟩ **3** a game in which a ball is thrown, kicked, or struck; *specif, NAm* baseball **4a** a testis – usu *pl*; *vulg* **b** *pl* nonsense – often used interjectionally; *vulg* – **on the ball** marked by being knowledgeable and competent; alert – *infml* – **start/set/keep the ball rolling** to begin/continue sthg

²**ball** *vb* **1** to form or gather into a ball **2** to have sexual intercourse (with) – *vulg*

³**ball** *n* **1** a large formal gathering for social dancing **2** a very pleasant experience; a good time – *infml*

ballad *n* **1** a narrative composition in rhythmic verse suitable for singing **2 a** (slow, romantic or sentimental) popular, esp narrative, song – **balladic** *adj*

ballade *n* a fixed verse form of usu 3 stanzas with recurrent rhymes, a short concluding verse, and an identical refrain for each part

¹**ballast** *n* **1a** heavy material carried in a ship to improve stability **b** heavy material that is carried on a balloon or airship to steady it and can be jettisoned to control the rate of descent **2** sthg that gives stability, esp in character or conduct **3** gravel or broken stone laid in a bed for railway lines or the lower layer of roads

²**ballast** *vt* **1** to steady or equip (as if) with ballast **2** to fill in (e g a railway bed) with ballast

ball bearing *n* a bearing having minimal friction in which hardened steel balls roll easily in a groove between a shaft and a support; *also* any of the balls in such a bearing

ball cock *n* an automatic valve (e g in a cistern) controlled by the rise and fall of a float at the end of a lever

ballerina *n* a female, esp principal, ballet dancer

ballet *n* **1** (a group that performs) artistic dancing in which the graceful flowing movements are based on conventional positions and steps **2** a theatrical art form using ballet dancing, music, and scenery to convey a story, theme, or atmosphere – **balletic** *adj*

ballistic *adj* **1** of ballistics **2** actuated by a sudden impulse (e g one due to an electric discharge) – **ballistically** *adv*

ballistics *n pl but sing or pl in constr* **1** the science dealing with the motion of projectiles in flight **2** (the study of) the individual characteristics of and firing processes in a firearm or cartridge

ball lightning *n* a rare form of lightning consisting of luminous balls that may move along solid objects or float in the air

ballock *n* a bollock

balloon *n* **1** an envelope filled with hot air or a gas lighter than air so as to rise and float in the atmosphere **2** an inflatable usu brightly coloured rubber bag used as a toy **3** a line enclosing words spoken or thought by a character, esp in a cartoon

balloon *vt* to inflate, distend ~ *vi* **1** to ascend or travel in a balloon **2** to swell or puff out; expand – often + *out* **3** to increase rapidly **4** to travel in a high curving arc

balloon *adj* relating to, resembling, or suggesting a balloon ⟨*a* ~ *sleeve*⟩

ballooning *n* the act or sport of riding in a balloon – **balloonist** *n*

ballot *n* **1** (a sheet of paper, or orig a small ball, used in) secret voting **2** the right to vote **3** the number of votes cast

ballot *vi* to vote by ballot ~ *vt* to ask for a vote from ⟨*the union* ~ *ed the members*⟩ – **balloter** *n*

ballpoint, ballpoint pen *n* a pen having as the writing point a small rotating metal ball that inks itself by contact with an inner magazine

balls-up, *NAm* **ball-up** *n* a state of muddled confusion caused by a mistake – slang

balls up, *NAm* **ball up** *vb* to make or become badly muddled or confused – slang

bally *adj or adv, Br* ¹BLOODY 4, ³BLOODY – euph

ballyhoo *n, pl* **ballyhoos** **1** a noisy demonstration or talk **2** flamboyant, exaggerated, or sensational advertising or propaganda – **ballyhoo** *vt*

balm *n* **1** an aromatic and medicinal resin **2** an aromatic preparation (e g a healing ointment) **3** any of various aromatic plants of the mint family **4** sthg that soothes, relieves, or heals physically or emotionally

balmy *adj* **1a** having the qualities of balm; soothing **b** mild **2** barmy – **balmily** *adv*, **balminess** *n*

baloney *n* nonsense – often as a generalized expression of disagreement

balsa *n* (the strong very light wood of) a tropical American tree

balsam *n* **1** (a preparation containing) an oily and resinous substance flowing from various plants **2a** any of several trees yielding balsam **b** any of a widely distributed genus of watery-juiced annual plants (e g touch-me-not) **3** BALM 4 – **balsamic** *adj*

baluster *n* an upright, rounded, square, or vase-shaped support (e g for the rail of a staircase balustrade)

balustrade *n* a row of balusters topped by a rail; *also* a usu low parapet or barrier

bamboo *n, pl* **bamboos** any of various chiefly tropical giant grasses including some with strong hollow stems used for building, furniture, or utensils – **bamboo** *adj*

bamboo curtain *n, often cap B&C* a political, military, and ideological barrier between China and the capitalist world

bamboozle *vt* to deceive by trickery – **bamboozlement** *n*

¹**ban** *vt* **-nn-** to prohibit, esp by legal means or social pressure

²**ban** *n* **1** an ecclesiastical curse, excommunication **2** a legal or social prohibition

banal *adj* lacking originality, freshness, or novelty; trite, hackneyed – **banally** *adv*, **banality** *n*

banana *n* (a tropical tree that bears) an elongated usu tapering fruit with soft pulpy flesh enclosed in a soft usu yellow rind that grows in bunches reminiscent of the fingers of a hand

banana republic *n* a small tropical country that is politically unstable and usu economically underdeveloped – derog

¹**band** *n* **1** a strip or belt serving to join or hold things together **2** a ring of elastic **3** a more or less well-defined range of wavelengths, frequencies, or energies of light waves, radio waves, sound waves, etc **4** an elongated surface or section with parallel or roughly parallel sides **5** a narrow strip serving chiefly as decoration: e g **a** a narrow strip of material applied as trimming to an article of dress **b** *pl* 2 cloth strips sometimes worn at the front of the neck as part of clerical, legal, or academic dress **6** a strip distinguishable in some way (e g by colour, texture, or composition) **7** *Br* a group of pupils assessed as being of broadly similar ability

²**band** *vt* **1** to fasten a band to or tie up with a band **2** to gather together for a purpose; unite **3** *Br* to divide (pupils) into bands ~ *vi* **1** to unite for a common purpose; confederate – often + *together* ⟨*they all* ~ *ed together to fight the enemy*⟩ **2** to divide pupils into bands – **bander** *n*

³**band** *n sing or pl in constr* a group of people, animals, or things; *esp* a group of musicians organized for ensemble playing and using chiefly woodwind, brass, and percussion instruments

¹bandage *n* a strip of fabric used esp to dress and bind up wounds

²bandage *vt* to bind, dress, or cover with a bandage – **bandager** *n*

Band-Aid *trademark* – used for a small adhesive plaster with a gauze pad

bandanna, bandana *n* a large colourful patterned handkerchief

bandbox *n* a usu cylindrical box of cardboard or thin wood used esp for holding hats

bandeau *n, pl* **bandeaux** a band of material worn round the head to keep the hair in place

bandit *n, pl* **bandits** *also* **banditti** 1 an outlaw; *esp* a member of a band of marauders 2 a political terrorist – **banditry** *n*

bandmaster *n* a conductor of an esp military band

bandolier *n* a belt worn over the shoulder and across the chest with pockets or loops for cartridges

bandsman *n* a member of a musical band

bandstand *n* a usu roofed stand or platform for a band to perform on outdoors

bandwagon *n* a party, faction, or cause that attracts adherents by its timeliness, momentum, etc – **jump/climb on the bandwagon** to attach oneself to a successful cause or enterprise in the hope of personal gain

¹bandy *vt* 1 to exchange (words) in an argumentative, careless, or lighthearted manner 2 to use in a glib or offhand manner – often + *about*

²bandy *n* a game similar to ice hockey played esp in the Baltic countries

³bandy *adj* 1 *of legs* bowed 2 bowlegged – **bandy-legged** *adj*

bane *n* 1 poison – esp in combination ⟨*rats*bane⟩ 2 a cause of death, ruin, or trouble – **baneful** *adj*

¹bang *vt* 1 to strike sharply; bump ⟨*fell and* ~ed *his knee*⟩ 2 to knock, beat, or strike hard, often with a sharp noise 3 to have sexual intercourse with – vulg ~*vi* 1 to strike with a sharp noise or thump ⟨*the falling chair* ~ed *against the wall*⟩ 2 to produce a sharp often explosive noise or noises

²bang *n* 1 a resounding blow; a thump 2 a sudden loud noise – often used interjectionally 3 a quick burst of energy ⟨*start off with a* ~⟩ 4 an act of sexual intercourse – vulg

³bang *adv* 1 right, directly 2 exactly ⟨*arrived* ~ *on 6 o'clock*⟩ USE infml

⁴bang *n* a short squarely-cut fringe of hair – usu pl with sing. meaning

banger *n, Br* 1 a firework that explodes with a loud bang 2 a sausage 3 an old usu dilapidated car USE (2&3) infml

bangle *n* a rigid usu ornamental bracelet or anklet slipped or clasped on

bang-on *adj or adv, Br* just what is needed; first-rate – infml

bang up *vt, chiefly Br* to raise ⟨*to* bang up *an executive's salary*⟩ – infml

banian *n* a banyan

banish *vt* 1 to require by authority to leave a place, esp a country 2 to dispel – **banisher** *n,* **banishment** *n*

banister *also* **bannister** *n* a handrail with its upright supports guarding the edge of a staircase – often pl with sing. meaning

banjo *n, pl* **banjos** *also* **banjoes** a stringed instrument with a drumlike body that is strummed with the fingers – **banjoist** *n*

¹bank *n* 1a a mound, pile, or ridge (e g of earth or snow) b a piled up mass of cloud or fog c an undersea elevation rising esp from the continental shelf 2 the rising ground bordering a lake or river or forming the edge of a cut or hollow 3 the lateral inward tilt of a surface along a curve or of a vehicle when following a curved path

²bank *vt* 1 to surround with a bank 2 to keep *up* to ensure slow burning 3 to build (a road or railway) with the outer edge of a curve higher than the inner ~*vi* 1 to rise in or form a bank – often + *up* 2a to incline an aircraft laterally when turning **b(1)** *of an aircraft* to incline laterally **(2)** to follow a curve or incline, specif in racing

³bank *n* 1 a bench for the rowers of a galley 2 a row of keys on an alphabetic keyboard (e g of a typewriter)

⁴bank *n* 1 an establishment for the custody, loan, exchange, or issue of money and for the transmission of funds 2 a person conducting a gambling house or game; *specif* the banker in a game of cards 3 a supply of sthg held in reserve: e g **a** the money, chips, etc held by the bank or banker for use in a gambling game **b** the pool of pieces belonging to a game (e g dominoes) from which the players draw 4 a place where data, human organs, etc are held available for use when needed

⁵bank *vi* to deposit money or have an account in a bank ⟨*where do you* ~?⟩ ~*vt* to deposit in a bank – **bank on** to depend or rely on; COUNT ON

bankbook *n* the depositor's book in which a bank enters a record of his/her account

¹banker *n* 1 one who engages in the business of banking 2 the player who keeps the bank in various games

²banker *n* a man or boat employed in the cod fishery on the Newfoundland banks

banker's card *n, Br* CHEQUE CARD

bank holiday *n* 1 *often cap B&H* a public holiday in the British Isles on which banks and most businesses are closed by law 2 *NAm* a period when banks are closed often by government fiat

banking *n* the business of a bank or a banker

bank note *n* a promissory note issued by a bank, payable to the bearer on demand without interest, and acceptable as money

¹bankrupt *n* 1a an insolvent person whose estate is administered under the bankruptcy laws for the benefit of his/her creditors **b** one who becomes insolvent 2 one who is destitute of a usu specified quality or thing ⟨*a moral* ~⟩

²bankrupt *vt* 1 to reduce to bankruptcy 2 to impoverish

³bankrupt *adj* 1 reduced to a state of financial ruin; *specif* legally declared a bankrupt 2a broken, ruined ⟨*a* ~ *professional career*⟩ **b** destitute – + *of* or *in*

bankruptcy *n* 1 being bankrupt 2 utter failure, impoverishment, or destitution

banner *n* 1a a usu square flag bearing heraldic arms; *broadly* ⁴FLAG 1 **b** an ensign displaying a distinctive or symbolic device or legend; *esp* one presented as an award of honour or distinction 2 a headline in large type running across a newspaper page 3 a strip of cloth on which a sign is painted 4 a name, slogan, or goal associated with a particular group or ideology – often + *under*

bannock *n* a usu unleavened flat bread or biscuit made with oatmeal or barley meal

banns *n pl* the public announcement, esp in church, of a proposed marriage – chiefly in *publish/read the banns*

¹banquet *n* an elaborate ceremonial meal for numerous people often in honour of a person; a feast

²banquet *vb* to provide with or partake of a banquet – **banqueter** *n*

banshee *n* a female spirit in Gaelic folklore whose wailing warns of approaching death in a household

¹bantam *n* any of numerous small domestic fowl

²bantam *adj* small, diminutive

bantamweight *n* a boxer who weighs not more than 8st 6lb (about 53.5kg) if professional or more than 51kg (about 8st) but not more than 54kg (about 8st 7lb) if amateur

¹**banter** *vi* to speak or act playfully or wittily – **banterer** *n*, **banteringly** *adv*

²**banter** *n* good-natured repartee; badinage

banyan *n* an Indian tree of the fig family with branches that send out shoots which grow down to the soil and root to form secondary trunks

baobab *n* a broad-trunked Old World tropical tree with an edible acid fruit resembling a gourd and bark used in making paper, cloth, and rope

baptism *n* **1** the ritual use of water for purification, esp in the Christian sacrament of admission to the church **2** an act, experience, or ordeal by which one is purified, sanctified, initiated, or named – **baptismal** *adj*, **baptismally** *adv*

baptist *n* **1** one who baptizes **2** *cap* a member of a Protestant denomination which reserves baptism to full believers, – **Baptist** *adj*

baptize, -ise *vt* **1** to administer baptism to **2a** to purify or cleanse spiritually, esp by a purging experience or ordeal **b** to initiate, launch **3** to give a name to (as if) at baptism; christen ~ *vi* to administer baptism – **baptizer** *n*

¹**bar** *n* **1a** a straight piece (e g of wood or metal), that is longer than it is wide and has any of various uses (e g as a lever, support, barrier, or fastening) **b** a solid piece or block of material that is usu rectangular and considerably longer than it is wide **c** a usu rigid piece (e g of wood or metal) longer than it is wide that is used as a handle or support; *specif* a barre **2** sthg that obstructs or prevents passage, progress, or action: e g **a** the extinction of a claim in law **b** an intangible or nonphysical impediment **c** a submerged or partly submerged bank (e g of sand) along a shore or in a river, often obstructing navigation **3a** ⁶DOCK; *also* the railing that encloses the dock **b** *often cap* (1) *sing or pl in constr* the whole body of barristers (2) the profession of barrister **c** a barrier beyond which nonmembers of Parliament may not pass **4** a straight stripe, band, or line much longer than it is wide: e g **a** any of 2 or more horizontal stripes on a heraldic shield **b** STRIPE 2 **c** a strip of metal attached to a military medal to indicate an additional award of the medal **5a(1)** a counter at which food or esp alcoholic drinks are served (2) a room or establishment whose main feature is a bar for the serving of alcoholic drinks **b** a place where goods, esp a specified commodity, are sold or served across a counter ⟨a shoe ~⟩ **6** (a group of musical notes and rests that add up to a prescribed time value, bounded on each side on the staff by) a bar line **7** a small loop or crosspiece of oversewn threads used, esp on garments, as a fastening (e g for a hook), for joining, or for strengthening sthg

²**bar** *vt* **-rr-** **1a** to fasten with a bar **b** to place bars across to prevent movement in, out, or through **2** to mark with stripes **3a** to shut in or out (as if) by bars **b** to set aside the possibility of; RULE OUT **4a** to interpose legal objection to **b** to prevent, forbid ⟨no holds ~red⟩

³**bar** *prep* except

⁴**bar** *adv*, *of odds in betting* being offered for all the unnamed competitors ⟨20 to 1 ~⟩

⁵**bar** *n* a unit of pressure equal to 100,000N/m² (about 14.5lb/in²)

bar-, baro- *comb form* weight; pressure ⟨baro*meter*⟩

barb *n* **1a** a sharp projection extending backwards from the point of an arrow, fishhook, etc, and preventing easy extraction **b** a biting or pointedly critical remark or comment **2** any of the side branches of the shaft of a feather **3** a plant hair or bristle ending in a hook

²**barb** *vt* to provide (e g an arrow) with a barb

³**barb** *n* any of a northern African breed of horses that are noted for speed and endurance and are related to Arabs

barbarian *adj* **1** of a land, culture, or people alien and usu believed to be inferior to and more savage than one's own **2** lacking refinement, learning, or artistic or literary culture – **barbarian** *n*, **barbarianism** *n*

barbaric *adj* **1** (characteristic) of barbarians; *esp* uncivilized **2** savage, barbarous – **barbarically** *adv*

barbarism *n* **1** (use of) a word or action unacceptable by contemporary standards; *also* the practice or display of barbarian ideas, acts, or attitudes **2** a barbarian or barbarous social or intellectual condition; backwardness

barbarity *n* **1** barbarism **2** (an act or instance of) barbarous cruelty; inhumanity

barbarize, -ise *vb* to make or become barbarous – **barbarization** *n*

barbarous *adj* **1** uncivilized **2** lacking culture or refinement **3** mercilessly harsh or cruel – **barbarously** *adv*, **barbarousness** *n*

¹**barbecue** *n* **1** a (portable) fireplace over which meat and fish are roasted **2** meat roasted over an open fire or barbecue pit **3** a social gathering, esp in the open air, at which barbecued food is served

²**barbecue** *vt* to roast or grill on a rack over hot coals or on a revolving spit in front of or over a source of cooking heat, esp an open fire – **barbecuer** *n*

barbed *adj* **1** having barbs **2** characterized by pointed and biting criticism – **barbedness** *n*

barbed wire *n* twisted wires armed at intervals with sharp points

¹**barbel** *n* a European freshwater fish with 4 barbels on its upper jaw

²**barbel** *n* a slender tactile projecting organ on the lips of certain fishes (e g catfish) used in locating food

barber *n* sby, esp a man, whose occupation is cutting and dressing men's hair and shaving – **barber** *vb*

barber's pole *n* a red and white striped pole fixed to the front of a barber's shop

barbican *n* an outer defensive work; *esp* a tower at a gate or bridge

barbiturate *n* **1** a salt or ester of barbituric acid **2** any of several derivatives of barbituric acid (e g thiopentone and phenobarbitone) that are used esp in the treatment of epilepsy and were formerly much used in sleeping pills

barbituric acid *n* an acid used in the manufacture of barbiturate drugs and plastics

barcarole, barcarolle *n* (music imitating) a Venetian boat song with a beat suggesting a rowing rhythm

¹**bard** *n* **1** sby, *specif* a Celtic poet-singer, who composed, sang, or recited verses on heroes and their deeds **2** a poet; *specif* one recognized or honoured at an eisteddfod **3** *cap* – used as an epithet for Shakespeare; + *the* – **bardic** *adj*

²**bard, barde** *n* a strip of pork fat, bacon, etc for covering lean meat before roasting – **bard** *vt*

¹**bare** *adj* **1** lacking a natural, usual, or appropriate covering, esp clothing **2** open to view; exposed – often in *lay bare* **3a** unfurnished, empty ⟨the cupboard was ~⟩ **b** destitute *of* **4a** having nothing left over or added; scant, mere ⟨the ~ necessities⟩ **b** undisguised, unadorned ⟨the ~ facts⟩ – **bareness** *n*

²**bare** *vt* to make or lay bare; uncover, reveal

bareback, barebacked *adv or adj* on the bare back of a horse without a saddle

barefaced *adj* lacking scruples; shameless – **barefacedly** *adv*, **barefacedness** *n*

barefoot, **barefooted** *adv or adj* without shoes, socks, stockings, etc; with the feet bare

bareheaded *adv or adj* without a covering for the head – **bareheadedness** *n*

barely *adv* **1** scarcely, hardly **2** in a meagre manner; scantily ⟨*a ~ furnished room*⟩

¹bargain *n* **1** an agreement between parties concerning the terms of a transaction between them or the course of action each pursues in respect to the other **2** an advantageous purchase **3** a transaction, situation, or event regarded in the light of its good or bad results ⟨*make the best of a bad ~*⟩ – **into the bargain** also

²bargain *vi* **1** to negotiate over the terms of a purchase, agreement, or contract **2** to come to terms; agree – **bargainer** *n* – **bargain for** to be at all prepared for; EXPECT 2a

¹barge *n* **1a** a flat-bottomed boat used chiefly for the transport of goods on inland waterways or between ships and the shore; *also* NARROW BOAT **b** a flat-bottomed coastal sailing vessel with leeboards instead of a keel **2a** a large naval motorboat used by flag officers **b** an ornate carved vessel used on ceremonial occasions

²barge *vi* **1** to move in a headlong or clumsy fashion **2** to intrude *in or into*

bargee *n, Br* sby who works on a barge

baritone *n* **1** (a person with) a male singing voice between bass and tenor **2** a member of a family of instruments having a range next below that of the tenor – **baritone** *adj*, **baritonal** *adj*

barium *n* a soft bivalent metallic element of the alkaline-earth group – **baric** *adj*

barium meal *n* a solution of barium sulphate swallowed by a patient to make the stomach or intestines visible in X-ray pictures

¹bark *vi* **1** to make (a sound similar to) the short loud cry characteristic of a dog **2** to speak in a curt, loud, and usu angry tone; snap *~ vt* to utter in a curt, loud, and usu angry tone – **barker** *n* – **bark up the wrong tree** to proceed under a misapprehension

²bark *n* **1** (a sound similar to) the sound made by a barking dog **2** a short sharp peremptory utterance – **barkless** *adj*

³bark *n* the tough exterior covering of a woody root or stem – **barkless** *adj*

⁴bark *vt* to abrade the skin of

⁵bark *n* **1** *NAm* a barque **2** a boat – poetic

barley *n* a widely cultivated cereal grass whose seed is used to make malt and in foods (e g breakfast cereals and soups) and stock feeds

barley wine *n* a strong ale

barm *n* yeast formed during the fermenting of beer

barman, *fem* **barmaid** *n* one who serves drinks in a bar

bar mitzvah *n, often cap B&M* (the initiatory ceremony of) a Jewish youth of 13 who assumes adult religious duties and responsibilities

barmy *adj* **1** frothy with barm **2** slightly mad; foolish – infml

barn *n* **1** a usu large farm building for storage, esp of feed, cereal products, etc **2** an unusually large and usu bare building ⟨*a great ~ of a house*⟩ – **barny** *adj*

barnacle *n* any of numerous marine crustaceans that are free-swimming as larvae but fixed to rocks or floating objects as adults – **barnacled** *adj*

barn dance *n* a type of country dance, esp a round dance or a square dance with called instructions; *also* a social gathering for such dances

barn door *n* a movable flap on a (theatre) light used to control the shape of the beam

barnstorm *vb, chiefly NAm* *vi* **1** to tour in theatrical performances **2** to pilot an aeroplane on sightseeing flights or in exhibition stunts, esp in rural districts *~ vt* to travel across while barnstorming – **barnstormer** *n*

barnyard *n* a farmyard

barograph *n* a recording barometer – **barographic** *adj*

barometer *n* **1** an instrument for determining the pressure of the atmosphere and hence for assisting in predicting the weather or measuring the height of an ascent **2** sthg that serves to register fluctuations (e g in public opinion) – **barometry** *n*, **barometric**, **barometrical** *adj*, **barometrically** *adv*

baron *n* **1a** a feudal tenant holding his rights and title by military or other honourable service directly from a sovereign ruler **b** a lord of the realm **2a** a member of the lowest rank of the peerage in Britain **b** a European nobleman **3** a man of great power or influence in a specified field of activity **4** a joint of meat consisting of 2 loins or sirloins joined by the backbone ⟨*a ~ of beef*⟩

baroness *n* **1** the wife or widow of a baron **2** a woman having in her own right the rank of a baron

baronet *n* the holder of a rank of honour below a baron and above a knight

baronetcy *n* the rank of a baronet

baronial *adj* **1** of or befitting a baron or the baronage **2** stately, ample

barony *n* the domain or rank of a baron

baroque *adj* (typical) of a style of artistic expression prevalent esp in the 17th c that is marked by extravagant forms and elaborate and sometimes grotesque ornamentation – **baroquely** *adv*

barque *NAm chiefly* **bark** *n* a sailing vessel with the rearmost of usu 3 masts fore-and-aft rigged and the others square-rigged

¹barrack *n* **1** (a set or area of) buildings for lodging soldiers in garrison – often pl with sing. meaning but sing. or pl in constr **2** a large building characterized by extreme plainness or dreary uniformity with others – usu pl with sing. meaning but sing. or pl in constr

²barrack *vt* to lodge in barracks

³barrack *vi* **1** *chiefly Br* to jeer, scoff **2** *chiefly Austr & NZ* to root, cheer – usu + *for ~ vt* **1** *chiefly Br* to shout at derisively; jeer **2** *chiefly Austr & NZ* to support (e g a sports team), esp by shouting encouragement – **barracker** *n*

barracuda *n, pl* **barracuda**, *esp for different types* **barracudas** any of several predatory fishes of warm seas that include excellent food fishes as well as forms regarded as poisonous

¹barrage *n* an artificial dam placed in a watercourse or estuary

²barrage *n* **1** a barrier, esp of intensive artillery fire, to hinder enemy action **2** a rapid series (e g of questions) – **barrage** *vt*

¹barrel *n* **1** an approximately cylindrical vessel with bulging sides and flat ends constructed from wooden staves bound together with hoops; *also* any similar vessel **2** a drum or cylindrical part: e g **a** the discharging tube of a gun **b** the part of a fountain pen or pencil containing the ink or lead **c** a cylindrical or tapering housing containing the lenses, iris diaphragm, etc of a camera or other piece of optical equipment **3** the trunk, esp of a quadruped – **barrelled**, *NAm* **barreled** *adj* – **over a barrel** at a disadvantage; in an awkward situation so that one is helpless ⟨*he had me over a barrel so I had to give in*⟩ – infml

²barrel *vt* **-ll-** (*NAm* **-l-, -ll-**) to put or pack in a barrel

barrel organ *n* a musical instrument consisting of a

revolving cylinder studded with pegs that open a series of valves to admit air from a bellows to a set of pipes

barren adj **1** not reproducing: e g **a** of a female or mating incapable of producing offspring **b** habitually failing to fruit **2** not productive; esp producing inferior or scanty vegetation **3** lacking, devoid of **4** lacking interest, information, or charm – **barrenly** adv, **barrenness** n

¹**barricade** vt **1** to block off, stop up, or defend with a barricade **2** to prevent access to by means of a barricade

²**barricade** n **1** an obstruction or rampart thrown up across a way or passage to check the advance of the enemy **2** a barrier, obstacle

barrier n **1** a material object (e g a stockade, fortress, or railing) or set of objects that separates, demarcates, or serves as a barricade **2** sthg immaterial that impedes or separates ⟨~s of reserve⟩ **3** a factor that tends to restrict the free movement, mingling, or interbreeding of individuals or populations

barring prep excepting

barrister, barrister-at-law n a lawyer who has the right to plead as an advocate in an English or Welsh superior court

¹**barrow** n a large mound of earth or stones over the remains of the dead; a tumulus

²**barrow** n a male pig castrated before sexual maturity

³**barrow** n a cart with a shallow box body, 2 wheels, and shafts for pushing it

barrow boy n a man or boy who sells goods (e g fruit or vegetables) from a barrow

bar sinister n **1** an imaginary heraldic shape or representation indicating bastardy **2** the condition of being of illegitimate birth

bartender n, chiefly NAm a barman

barter vi to trade by exchanging one commodity for another without the use of money ~ vt **1** to exchange (as if) by bartering **2** to part with unwisely or for an unworthy return – + away – **barterer** n

barter n the carrying on of trade by bartering

basal adj **1** of, situated at, or forming the base **2** of the foundation, base, or essence; fundamental – **basally** adv

basalt n a dense to fine-grained dark igneous rock consisting essentially of a feldspar and usu pyroxene – **basaltic** adj

base n **1a** the bottom of sthg; a foundation **b** the lower part of a wall, pier, or column considered as a separate architectural feature **c** a side or face of a geometrical figure on which it is regarded as standing **d** that part of an organ by which it is attached to another structure nearer the centre of a living organism **2a** a main ingredient **b** a supporting or carrying ingredient **3** the fundamental part of sthg; a basis **4a** a centre from which a start is made in an activity or from which operations proceed **b** a line in a survey which serves as the origin for computations **c** the locality or installations on which a military force relies for supplies or from which it starts operations **d(1)** the number with reference to which a number system is constructed **(2)** a number with reference to which logarithms are computed **e** ROOT 6 **5a** the starting place or goal in various games **b** any of the stations at each of the 4 corners of the inner part of a baseball field to which a batter must run in turn in order to score a run **6** the middle region of a transistor that controls the current flow **7** any of various typically water-soluble and acrid or brackish tasting chemical compounds that are capable of taking up a hydrogen ion from or donating an unshared pair of electrons to an acid to form a salt **8** also **base component** that part of a transformational grammar that

consists of rules and a lexicon and that generates the deep structures of a language – **based** adj, **baseless** adj

²**base** vt **1** to make, form, or serve as a base for **2** to use as a base or basis for; establish, found – usu + on or upon

³**base** adj constituting or serving as a base

⁴**base** adj **1a** of a metal of comparatively low value and having relatively inferior properties (e g resistance to corrosion) **b** containing a larger than usual proportion of base metals **2** lacking higher values; degrading ⟨a drab ~ way of life⟩ **3** of relatively little value – **basely** adv, **baseness** n

baseball n (the ball used in) a game played with a bat and ball between 2 teams of 9 players each on a large field centring on 4 bases arranged in a square that mark the course a batter must run to score

baseboard n, NAm SKIRTING BOARD

baseborn adj **1** of humble or illegitimate birth **2** archaic mean, ignoble

baseline n the back line at each end of a court in tennis, badminton, etc

basement n the part of a building that is wholly or partly below ground level – **basementless** adj

¹**bash** vt **1** to strike violently; also to injure or damage by striking; smash – often + in or up **2** to make a violent attack on USE infml – **basher** n

²**bash** n **1** a forceful blow **2** chiefly Br a try, attempt ⟨have a ~ at it⟩ **3** NAm a festive social gathering; a party USE infml

bashful adj **1** socially shy or timid **2** characterized by, showing, or resulting from extreme sensitiveness or self-consciousness – **bashfully** adv, **bashfulness** n

¹**basic** adj **1** of or forming the base or essence; fundamental **2** constituting or serving as the minimum basis or starting point **3a** of, containing, or having the character of a chemical base **b** having an alkaline reaction; being an alkali **4** of rock containing relatively little silica **5** of, being, or made by a steelmaking process in which the furnace is lined with material containing relatively little silica – **basically** adv, **basicity** n

²**basic** n sthg basic; a fundamental

BASIC n a high-level computer language for programming and interacting with a computer in a wide variety of applications

Basic English n a simplified version of English with a vocabulary of 850 words designed for teaching and international communication

basil n any of several plants of the mint family

basilica n **1** an oblong building used in ancient Rome as a place of assembly or as a lawcourt and usu ending in an apse **2** an early Christian church similar to a Roman basilica **3** a Roman Catholic church given certain ceremonial privileges – **basilican** adj

basilisk n **1** a mythical reptile whose breath and glance were fatal **2** any of several crested tropical American lizards related to the iguanas – **basilisk** adj

basin n **1a** a round open usu metal or ceramic vessel with a greater width than depth and sides that slope or curve inwards to the base, used typically for holding water for washing **b** a bowl with a greater depth than width esp for holding, mixing, or cooking food ⟨a pudding ~⟩ **c** the contents of a basin **2a** a dock built in a tidal river or harbour **b** a (partly) enclosed water area, esp for ships **3a** a depression in the surface of the land or ocean floor **b** the region drained by a river and its tributaries **4** an area of the earth in which the strata dip from the sides towards the centre – **basinal** adj, **basined** adj

basis n, pl **bases 1** a foundation **2** the principal component of sthg **3** a basic principle or way of proceeding

bask _vi_ **1** to lie in, or expose oneself to, a pleasant warmth or atmosphere **2** to enjoy sby's favour or approval – usu + _in_

basket _n_ **1a** a rigid or semirigid receptacle made of interwoven material (e g osiers, cane, wood, or metal) **b** any of various lightweight usu wood containers **c** the contents of a basket **2** sthg that resembles a basket, esp in shape or use **3** a net open at the bottom and suspended from a metal ring that constitutes the goal in basketball **4** a collection, group ⟨_the ~ of major world currencies_⟩ **5** _Br_ a person of a specified type ⟨_she's a nice old ~_⟩ – infml – **basketful** _n_, **basketlike** _adj_

basketball _n_ (the ball used in) an indoor court game between 2 teams of 5 players each who score by tossing a large ball through a raised basket

basketry _n_ (the art or craft of making) baskets or objects woven like baskets

basketwork _n_ basketry

bas-relief _n_ sculptural relief in which the design projects very slightly from the surrounding surface

¹bass _n, pl_ **bass**, _esp for different types_ **basses** any of numerous edible spiny-finned fishes

²bass _adj_ **1** deep or grave in tone **2a** of low pitch **b** of or having the range or part of a bass

³bass _n_ **1** the lowest part in 4-part harmony **2a** (a person with) the lowest adult male singing voice **b** a member of a family of instruments having the lowest range; _esp_ a double bass or bass guitar

⁴bass _n_ a coarse tough fibre from palm trees

bass clef _n_ a clef placing the F below middle C on the fourth line of the staff

basset, basset hound _n_ (any of) a breed of short-legged hunting dogs with very long ears

bassoon _n_ a double-reed woodwind instrument with a usual range 2 octaves lower than the oboe – **bassoonist** _n_

bast _n_ **1** phloem **2** a strong woody fibre obtained chiefly from the phloem of certain plants

¹bastard _n_ **1** an illegitimate child **2** sthg spurious, irregular, inferior, or of questionable origin **3a** an offensive or disagreeable person – often + _you_ as a generalized term of abuse **b** a fellow of a usu specified type ⟨_poor old ~_⟩ – infml – **bastardly** _adj_

²bastard _adj_ **1** illegitimate **2** of an inferior or less typical type, stock, or form **3** lacking genuineness or authority; false

bastardize, -ise _vt_ **1** to declare illegitimate **2** to debase – **bastardization** _n_

bastardy _n_ the quality or state of being a bastard; illegitimacy

¹baste _vt_ TACK 1b – **baster** _n_

²baste _vt_ to moisten (e g meat) at intervals with melted butter, dripping, etc during cooking, esp roasting – **baster** _n_

³baste _vt_ to beat severely or soundly; thrash

bastinado _n, pl_ **bastinadoes** **1** (a blow or beating with) a stick or cudgel **2** the punishment of beating the soles of the feet with a stick – **bastinado** _vt_

bastion _n_ **1** a projecting part of a fortification **2** a fortified area or position **3** sthg considered a stronghold; a bulwark – **bastioned** _adj_

¹bat _n_ **1** a stout solid stick; a club **2** a sharp blow; a stroke **3** a (wooden) implement used for hitting the ball in cricket, baseball, table tennis, etc **4a** a batsman **b** a turn at batting in cricket, baseball, etc **5** a hand-held implement shaped like a table-tennis bat for guiding aircraft when landing or taxiing – **off one's own bat** through one's own efforts, esp without being prompted

²bat _vb_ **-tt-** _vt_ **1** to strike or hit (as if) with a bat ~ _vi_ **1** to

strike a ball with a bat **2** to take one's turn at batting, esp in cricket

³bat _n_ any of an order of nocturnal flying mammals with forelimbs modified to form wings

⁴bat _vt_ **-tt-** to blink, esp in surprise or emotion ⟨_never ~ted an eyelid_⟩

batch _n_ **1** the quantity baked at 1 time **2a** the quantity of material produced at 1 operation or for use at 1 time **b** a group of jobs to be run on a computer at 1 time with the same program ⟨_~ processing_⟩ **3** a group of people or things; a lot

bate _vt, archaic_ to restrain – **with bated breath** anxiously, worriedly

¹bath _n, pl_ **baths** **1** a washing or soaking (e g in water or steam) of all or part of the body **2a** water used for bathing ⟨_run a ~_⟩ **b** a vessel for bathing in; _esp_ one that is permanently fixed in a bathroom **c** (a vat, tank, etc holding) a specified type of liquid used for a special purpose (e g to keep samples at a constant temperature) **3a** a building containing an apartment or a series of rooms designed for bathing **b** SWIMMING POOL – usu pl with sing. meaning but sing. or pl in constr **c** a spa **4** _NAm_ a bathroom USE (3a&3c) usu pl with sing. meaning

²bath _vb, Br_ _vt_ to give a bath to ~ _vi_ to take a bath

bath-, batho- _comb form_ depth ⟨_bathometer_⟩

bath chair _n, often cap B_ a usu hooded wheelchair

¹bathe _vt_ **1** to wash or soak in a liquid (e g water) **2** to moisten **3** to apply water or a liquid medicament to **4** to suffuse, esp with light ~ _vi_ **1** to take a bath **2** to swim (e g in the sea or a river) for pleasure **3** to become immersed or absorbed – **bather** _n_

²bathe _n, Br_ an act of bathing, esp in the sea

bathing beauty _n_ a woman in a swimming costume who is a contestant in a beauty contest

bathing suit _n_ SWIMMING COSTUME

bath mat _n_ **1** a usu washable mat, often of absorbent material, placed beside a bath **2** a mat of nonslip material, esp rubber, placed in a bath to prevent the bather from slipping

bathos _n_ **1** a sudden descent from the sublime to the commonplace or absurd; an anticlimax **2** exceptional commonplaceness; triteness

bathrobe _n_ a loose usu absorbent robe worn before and after having a bath

bathroom _n_ **1** a room containing a bath or shower and usu a washbasin and toilet **2** a toilet – chiefly euph

bathysphere _n_ a strongly built diving sphere for deep-sea observation

batik _n_ (a fabric or design printed by) an Indonesian method of hand-printing by coating with wax the parts to be left undyed

batiste _n_ a fine soft sheer fabric of plain weave made of various fibres

batman _n_ a British officer's servant

baton _n_ **1** a cudgel, truncheon **2** a staff borne as a symbol of office **3** a wand with which a conductor directs a band or orchestra **4** a stick or hollow cylinder passed by each member of a relay team to the succeeding runner

bats _adj, chiefly Br_ batty ⟨_he's gone ~_⟩ – infml

batsman _n_ sby who bats or is batting, esp in cricket – **batsmanship** _n_

battalion _n sing or pl in constr_ **1** a large body of organized troops **2** a military unit composed of a headquarters and 2 or more companies **3** a large group

¹batten _vi_ – **batten on** **1** to make oneself selfishly dependent on (sby) ⟨_battened on his rich relatives_⟩ **2** to seize on (an excuse, argument, etc)

²batten _n_ **1** a thin narrow strip of squared timber **2a** a thin strip of wood, plastic, etc inserted into a sail to keep it fla and taut **b** a slat used to secure the tarpaulins and hatch covers of a ship **3** a strip holding a row of floodlights

³batten *vt* to provide or fasten (e g hatches) with battens – often + *down*

¹batter *vt* **1** to beat persistently or hard so as to bruise, shatter, or demolish **2** to wear or damage by hard usage or blows ⟨*a* ~ed *old hat*⟩ ~ *vi* to strike heavily and repeatedly; beat

²batter *n* a mixture that consists essentially of flour, egg, and milk or water and is thin enough to pour or drop from a spoon; *also* batter mixture (e g that used for coating fish) when cooked

³batter *vi* to slope upwards and backwards ~ *vt* to cause (e g a wall) to slope upwards and backwards

⁴batter *n* an upwards and backwards slope of the outer face of a structure

⁵batter *n* the player who is batting in baseball

battering ram *n* an ancient military siege engine consisting of a large wooden beam with a head of iron used for beating down walls

battery *n* **1a** the act of battering **b** the unlawful application of any degree of force to a person without his/her consent **2** a grouping of similar artillery guns (e g for tactical purposes) **3** *sing or pl in constr* a tactical and administrative army artillery unit equivalent to an infantry company **4** one or more cells connected together to provide an electric current: e g **a** STORAGE CELL **b** DRY CELL; *also* a connected group of dry cells **5a** a number of similar articles, items, or devices arranged, connected, or used together; a set, series **b(1)** a large number of small cages in which egg-laying hens are kept **(2)** a series of cages or compartments for raising or fattening animals, esp poultry **c** an impressive or imposing group; an array **6** the position of readiness of a gun for firing

¹battle *n* **1** a general hostile encounter between armies, warships, aircraft, etc **2** a combat between 2 people **3** an extended contest, struggle, or controversy

²battle *vb* **battling** *vi* **1** to engage in battle; fight **2** to contend with full strength, craft, or resources; struggle ~ *vt* **1** to fight against **2** to force (e g one's way) by battling – **battler** *n*

battle-axe *n* a quarrelsome domineering woman

battle cruiser *n* a large heavily-armed warship faster than a battleship

battlement *n* a parapet with indentations that surmounts a wall and is used for defence or decoration – **battlemented** *adj*

battle royal *n, pl* **battles royal, battle royals 1** a fight or contest between more than 2 opponents, esp until only the winner remains on his/her feet or in the ring **2** a violent struggle or heated dispute

battleship *n* the largest and most heavily armed and armoured type of warship

batty *adj* mentally unstable; crazy – *infml* – **battiness** *n*

bauble *n* **1** a trinket or trifle **2** a jester's staff

baulk *vb or n, chiefly Br* (to) balk

bauxite *n* a mineral that is an impure mixture of earthy hydrous aluminium oxides and hydroxides and is the principal ore of aluminium – **bauxitic** *adj*

bawd *n* a woman who keeps a house of prostitution; a madam

bawdy *adj* boisterously or humorously indecent – **bawdily** *adv*, **bawdiness** *n*

bawdy *n* suggestive, coarse, or obscene language

bawl *vb* **1** to yell, bellow **2** to cry, wail – **bawler** *n*

bawl *n* a loud prolonged cry

bawl out *vt, chiefly NAm* to reprimand loudly or severely – *infml*

¹bay *adj, esp of a horse* of the colour bay

²bay *n* **1** a horse with a bay-coloured body and black mane, tail, and points **2** a reddish brown colour

³bay *n* **1** any of several shrubs or trees resembling the laurel **2** an honorary garland or crown, esp of laurel, given for victory or excellence

⁴bay *n* **1** a division of a part of a building (e g the walls or roof) or of the whole building **2** a main division of a structure; *esp* a compartment in the fuselage of an aircraft ⟨*the forward instrument* ~⟩

⁵bay *vi* to bark with prolonged tones

⁶bay *n* **1** the position of one unable to retreat and forced to face a foe or danger ⟨*brought his quarry to* ~⟩ **2** the position of one kept off or repelled with difficulty ⟨*police kept the rioters at* ~⟩

⁷bay *n* (a land formation resembling) an inlet of a sea, lake, etc, usu smaller than a gulf

bay leaf *n* the leaf of the European laurel used dried in cooking

¹bayonet *n* a blade attached to the muzzle of a firearm and used in hand-to-hand combat

²bayonet *vt* to stab or drive (as if) with a bayonet ~ *vi* to use a bayonet

bay rum *n* a fragrant cosmetic and medicinal liquid from the (oil of the) leaves of a W Indian tree of the myrtle family

bay window *n* a window or series of windows projecting outwards from the wall

bazaar *n* **1** an (Oriental) market consisting of rows of shops or stalls selling miscellaneous goods **2** a fair for the sale of miscellaneous articles, esp for charitable purposes

bazooka *n* an individual infantry antitank rocket launcher

be *vb, pres 1 sing* **am**; *2 sing* **are**; *3 sing* **is**; *pl* **are**; *pres subjunctive* **be**; *pres part* **being**; *past 1&3 sing* **was**; *2 sing* **were** ; *pl* **were**; *past subjunctive* **were**; *past part* **been** *vi* **1a** to equal in meaning; have the same connotation as ⟨*January is the first month*⟩ ⟨*let* x ~ *10*⟩ **b** to represent, symbolize ⟨*God* is *love*⟩ ⟨*Olivier* was *Hamlet*⟩ ⟨*Valentino* was *romance*⟩ **c** to have identity with ⟨*it's me*⟩ ⟨*the first person I met* was *my brother*⟩ ⟨*the difficulty is finding them*⟩ **d** to belong to the class of ⟨*the fish is a trout*⟩ **e** to occupy a specified position in space ⟨*the book* is *on the table*⟩ ⟨*where* are *the Grampians?*⟩ **f** to take place at a specified time; occur ⟨*the concert* was *last night*⟩ **g** to have a specified qualification ⟨*the leaves* are *green*⟩ ⟨~ *quick*⟩, destination ⟨~ *off*⟩, origin ⟨*she is from India*⟩, occupation ⟨*what's he up to?*⟩, function or purpose ⟨*it's for you*⟩ ⟨*it's to cut with*⟩, cost or value ⟨*the book* is *£5*⟩, or standpoint ⟨~ *against* terrorism⟩ **2** to have reality or actuality; exist ⟨*I think, therefore I* am⟩ ⟨*once upon a time there* was *a castle*⟩ ~ *va* **1** – used with the past participle of transitive verbs as a passive-voice auxiliary ⟨*the money* was *found*⟩ ⟨*the house is* ~ing *built*⟩ **2** – used as the auxiliary of the present participle in progressive tenses expressing continuous action ⟨*he is* reading⟩ ⟨*I have* been *sleeping*⟩ or arrangement in advance ⟨*we are* leaving *tomorrow*⟩ **3** – used with the past participle of some intransitive verbs as an auxiliary forming archaic perfect tenses ⟨*my father* is come – Jane Austen⟩ **4** – used with *to* and an infinitive to express destiny ⟨*he was to become famous*⟩ ⟨*they* were *to have been married*⟩, arrangement in advance ⟨*I am to interview him today*⟩, obligation or necessity ⟨*you are not to smoke*⟩, or possibility ⟨*it* was *nowhere to be found*⟩ ⟨*you weren't to know*⟩ USE *vi* (*1*) used regularly as the linking verb of simple predication; used in the past subjunctive or often in the indicative to express unreal

conditions ⟨*if I were you*⟩ ⟨*if I was*n't *a Catholic* – *Daily Mirror*⟩; often in British English used of groups in the plural form ⟨*Somerset were 28 for 2* – *The Observer*⟩
be- *prefix* **1** (*vb* → *vb*) on; round; all over ⟨be*daub*⟩ ⟨be*smear*⟩ **2** (*vb* → *vb*) to a great or greater degree; thoroughly ⟨be*fuddle*⟩ ⟨be*rate*⟩ ⟨be*labour*⟩ **3** (*adj* → *adj*) wearing (a specified article of dress) ⟨be*wigged*⟩ ⟨be*ribboned*⟩ ⟨be*spectacled*⟩ **4** (*vb* → *vb*) about; to; at; upon; against; across ⟨be*stride*⟩ ⟨be*speak*⟩ **5** (*adj, n* → *vb*) make; cause to be; treat as ⟨be*little*⟩ ⟨be*fool*⟩ ⟨be*friend*⟩ **6** (*n* → *vb*) affect, afflict, provide, or cover with, esp excessively ⟨be*calmed*⟩ ⟨be*devil*⟩
¹beach *n* a (gently sloping) seashore or lakeshore usu covered by sand or pebbles; *esp* the part of this between the high and low water marks
²beach *vt* to run or drive ashore
beachcomber *n* one who searches along a shore for useful or salable flotsam and jetsam; *esp* a white man on the islands of the S Pacific who earns a living by doing this – **beachcomb** *vb*
beachhead *n* an area on a hostile shore occupied to secure further landing of troops and supplies
beacon *n* **1** a signal fire commonly on a hill, tower, or pole; *also, Br* a high conspicuous hill suitable for or used in the past for such a fire **2a** a signal mark used to guide shipping **b** a radio transmitter emitting signals for the guidance of aircraft **3** a source of light or inspiration
¹bead *n* **1** a small ball (e g of wood or glass) pierced for threading on a string or wire **2** *pl* (a series of prayers and meditations made with) a rosary **3** a small ball-shaped body: e g **a** a drop of liquid **b** a small metal knob on a firearm used as a front sight **4** a projecting rim, band, or moulding
²bead *vt* **1** to adorn or cover with beads or beading **2** to string together like beads ~ *vi* to form into a bead
beading *n* **1** material adorned with or consisting of beads **2a** a narrow moulding of rounded often semicircular cross section **b** a moulding that resembles a string of beads **3** a narrow openwork insertion or trimming (e g on lingerie)
beadle *n* a minor parish official whose duties include ushering and preserving order at services
beady *adj, esp of eyes* small, round, and shiny with interest or greed
beagle *n* (any of) a breed of small short-legged smooth-coated hounds
beagling *n* hunting on foot with beagles – **beagler** *n*
beak *n* **1a** the bill of a bird; *esp* the bill of a bird of prey adapted for striking and tearing **b** any of various rigid projecting mouth structures (e g of a turtle); *also* the long sucking mouth of some insects **2** a pointed structure or formation: **a** a metal-tipped beam projecting from the bow of an ancient galley for ramming an enemy ship **b** the pouring spout of a vessel **c** a projection suggesting the beak of a bird **3** the human nose – *infml* **4** *chiefly Br* **a** a magistrate – *slang* **b** a schoolmaster – *slang* – **beaked** *adj*
beaker *n* **1** a large drinking cup with a wide mouth; a mug **2** a cylindrical flat-bottomed vessel usu with a pouring lip that is used esp by chemists and pharmacists
be-all and end-all *n the* chief factor; *the* essential element – often derog
¹beam *n* **1a** a long piece of heavy often squared timber suitable for use in construction **b** the part of a plough to which the handles, standard, and coulter are attached **c** the bar of a balance from which scales hang **d** any of the principal horizontal supporting members of a building or across a ship **e** the width of a ship at its widest part **f** an oscillating lever joining an engine piston rod to a crank, esp in one type of stationary steam engine (a ~ engine) **2a** a ray or shaft of radiation, esp light **b** a collection of nearly parallel rays (e g X rays) or of particles (e g electrons) moving in nearly parallel paths **c** (the course indicated by) a radio signal transmitted continuously in one direction as an aircraft navigation aid **3** the main stem of a deer's antler **4** the width of the buttocks ⟨*broad in the* ~⟩ – *infml* – **off (the) beam** wrong, irrelevant – **on the beam** proceeding or operating correctly
²beam *vt* **1** to emit in beams or as a beam, esp of light **2** to aim (a broadcast) by directional aerials ~ *vi* to smile with joy
beam-ends *n pl, Br* buttocks – *infml* – **on her beam-ends** *of a ship* about to capsize
bean *n* **1a** (the often edible seed of) any of various erect or climbing leguminous plants **b** a bean pod used when immature as a vegetable **c** (a plant producing) any of various seeds or fruits that resemble beans or bean pods **2a** a valueless item ⟨*not worth a* ~⟩ **b** the smallest possible amount of money ⟨*gave up my job and haven't a* ~⟩ *USE* (2) infml
beanpole *n* a very tall thin person – *infml*
¹bear *n, pl* **bears**, *(1)* **bears** *or esp collectively* **bear 1** any of a family of large heavy mammals that have long shaggy hair and a short tail and feed largely on fruit and insects as well as on flesh **2** a surly, uncouth, or shambling person **3** one who sells securities or commodities in expectation of a fall in price
²bear *vb* **bore**; **borne** *also* **born** *vt* **1a** to carry, transport ⟨~ *gifts*⟩ – often in combination ⟨*airborne troops*⟩ **b** to carry or own as equipment ⟨~ *arms*⟩ **c** to entertain mentally ⟨~ *malice*⟩ **d** to behave, conduct **e** to have or show as a feature ⟨~ *scars*⟩ ⟨~ *no relationship*⟩ **f** to give as testimony ⟨~ *false witness*⟩ **g** to have as an identification ⟨bore *the name of John*⟩ **2a** to give birth to **b** to produce as yield ⟨~ *apples*⟩ **c** to contain – often in combination ⟨oil-bearing *shale*⟩ **3a** to support the weight of **b** to accept the presence of; tolerate ⟨~ *pain*⟩ ⟨*couldn't* ~ *his wife's family*⟩ **c** to sustain, incur ⟨~ *the cost*⟩ ⟨~ *the responsibility*⟩ **d** to admit of; allow ⟨*it won't* ~ *repeating*⟩ ~ *vi* **1a** to become directed ⟨*bring guns to* ~ *on a target*⟩ **b** to go or extend in a usu specified direction ⟨*the road* ~s *to the right*⟩ **2** to apply, have relevance ⟨*facts* ~ing *on the situation*⟩ **3** to support weight or strain **4** to produce fruit; yield – **bear fruit** to come to satisfying fruition or production – **bear in mind** to think of, esp as a warning; remember – **bear with** to show patience or indulgence towards ⟨bear with *the old bore for a while longer*⟩
¹beard *n* **1** the hair that grows on the lower part of a man's face, usu excluding the moustache **2** a hairy or bristly appendage or tuft (e g on a goat's chin) – **bearded** *adj*, **beardedness** *n*, **beardless** *adj*
²beard *vt* to confront and oppose with boldness, resolution, and often effrontery; defy
bear down *vt* to overcome, overwhelm ~ *vi* **1** to exert full strength and concentrated attention **2** *of a woman in childbirth* to exert concentrated downward pressure in an effort to expel the child from the womb – **bear down on 1** to weigh heavily on **2** to come towards purposefully or threateningly
bearer *n* **1** a porter **2** a plant yielding fruit **3** a pallbearer **4** one holding an order for payment, esp a bank note or cheque
bear hug *n* a rough tight embrace
bearing *n* **1** the manner in which one bears or conducts oneself **2** the act, power, or time of bringing forth offspring or fruit **3a** an object, surface, or point that supports

b a machine part in which another part turns or slides – often pl with sing. meaning **4** an emblem or figure on a heraldic shield **5a** the compass direction of one point (with respect to another) **b** a determination of position **c** pl comprehension of one's position, environment, or situation ⟨*lost his* ~ s⟩ **d** a relation, connection, significance – usu + *on* ⟨*has no* ~ *on the matter*⟩

bearish *adj* marked by, tending to cause, or fearful of falling prices (e g in a stock market) – **bearishly** *adv*, **bearishness** *n*

bear out *vt* to confirm, substantiate ⟨*research* bore out *his theory*⟩

bearskin *n* an article made of the skin of a bear; *esp* a tall black military hat worn by the Brigade of Guards

bear up *vt* to support, encourage ~ *vi* to summon up courage, resolution, or strength ⟨bearing up *under the strain*⟩

beast *n* **1a** an animal as distinguished from a plant **b** a 4-legged mammal as distinguished from human beings, lower vertebrates, and invertebrates **c** an animal under human control **2** a contemptible person

beastly *adj* **1** bestial **2** abominable, disagreeable ⟨~ *weather*⟩ – **beastliness** *n*

beastly *adv* very ⟨*a* ~ *cold day*⟩ – infml

beast of burden *n* an animal employed to carry heavy material or perform other heavy work (e g pulling a plough)

beat *vb* beat; beaten, beat *vt* **1** to strike repeatedly: **a** to hit repeatedly so as to inflict pain – often + *up* **b** to strike directly against (sthg) forcefully and repeatedly ⟨*shores* ~ en *by heavy waves*⟩ **c** to flap or thrash at vigorously ⟨a *trapped bird* ~ ing *the air*⟩ **d** to strike at or range over (as if) in order to rouse game **e** to mix (esp food) by stirring; whip **f** to strike repeatedly in order to produce music or a signal **2a** to drive or force by blows ⟨*to* ~ *off the savage dogs*⟩ **b** to pound into a powder, paste, or pulp **c** to make by repeated treading or driving over ⟨~ *a path*⟩ **d(1)** to dislodge by repeated hitting ⟨~ *the dust from the carpet*⟩ **(2)** to lodge securely by repeated striking ⟨~ *a stake into the ground*⟩ **e** to shape by beating; *esp* to flatten thin by blows ⟨*gold* ~ en *into foil*⟩ **f** to sound or express, esp by drumbeat ⟨~ *a tattoo*⟩ **3** to cause to strike or tap repeatedly ⟨~ *his foot nervously on the ground*⟩ **4a** to overcome, defeat; *also* to surpass **b** to prevail despite ⟨~ *the odds*⟩ **c** to leave dispirited, irresolute, or hopeless ⟨a *failure at*⟩ – en *man*⟩ **d** to be or to bowl a ball that is too good for (a batsman) to hit **5** to act ahead of, usu so as to forestall – chiefly in *beat someone to it* **6** to indicate by beating **7** to bewilder, baffle – infml ~ *vi* **1a** to dash, strike ⟨*the rain was* ~ ing *on the roof*⟩ **b** to glare or strike with oppressive intensity ⟨*the sun was* ~ ing *down*⟩ **2a** to pulsate, throb **b** to sound on being struck ⟨*the drums were* ~ ing⟩ **3a** to strike the air; flap ⟨*the birds wings* ~ *frantically*⟩ **b** to strike cover or range (as if) in order to find or rouse game **4** to progress with much difficulty; *specif, of a sailing vessel* to make way at sea against the wind by a series of alternate tacks across the wind – **beat about the bush** to fail to come to the point in conversation by talking indirectly or evasively – **beat it** to hurry away; scram – infml – **beat one's brains out** to try intently to resolve sthg difficult by thinking

beat *n* **1a** a single stroke or blow, esp in a series; *also* a pulsation, throb **b** a sound produced (as if) by beating **2** each of the pulsations of amplitude produced by the mixing of sine waves (e g sound or radio waves) having different frequencies **3a** (the rhythmic effect of) a metrical or rhythmic stress in poetry or music **b** the tempo indicated to a musical performer **4** an area or route

regularly patrolled, esp by a policeman **5** TACK 3b **6 a** deadbeat – infml – **beatless** *adj*

beat *adj* **1** of or being beatniks ⟨~ *poets*⟩ **2** exhausted – infml

beat *n* a beatnik

beaten *adj* **1** hammered into a desired shape ⟨~ *gold*⟩ **2** defeated

beater *n* **1a** any of various hand-held implements for whisking or beating ⟨a *carpet* ~⟩ ⟨*an egg* ~⟩ **b** a rotary blade attached to an electric mixer **c** a stick for beating a gong **2** one who strikes bushes or other cover to rouse game

beatific *adj* **1** of, possessing, or imparting beatitude **2** having a blissful or benign appearance; saintly, angelic ⟨a ~ *smile*⟩ – **beatifically** *adv*

beatify *vt* **1** to make supremely happy **2** to authorize the veneration of (a dead person) by Catholics by giving the title 'Blessed' – **beatification** *n*

beating *n* **1** injury or damage inflicted by striking with repeated blows **2** a throbbing **3** a defeat

beatitude *n* **1a** a state of utmost bliss **b** – used as a title for a primate, esp of an Eastern church **2** any of a series of sayings of Jesus beginning in the Authorized version of the Bible 'Blessed are'

beatnik *n* a person, esp in the 1950s and 1960s, who rejected the moral attitudes of established society (e g by unconventional behaviour and dress)

beau *n, pl* beaux, beaus **1** a lover **2** *archaic* a dandy

Beaujolais *n* a chiefly red table wine made in southern Burgundy in France

beaut *n, chiefly Austr & NZ* BEAUTY 3 – infml

beaut *adj, Austr & NZ* fine, marvellous – infml

beauteous *adj, archaic* beautiful – **beauteously** *adv*, **beauteousness** *n*

beautician *n* sby who gives beauty treatments

beautiful *adj* **1** having qualities of beauty; exciting aesthetic pleasure or keenly delighting the senses **2** generally pleasing; excellent – **beautifully** *adv*, **beautifulness** *n*

beautify *vt* to make beautiful; embellish – **beautifier** *n* **beautification** *n*

beauty *n* **1** the qualities in a person or thing that give pleasure to the senses or pleasurably exalt the mind or spirit; loveliness **2** a beautiful person or thing; *esp* a beautiful woman **3** a brilliant, extreme, or conspicuous example or instance ⟨*that mistake was a* ~⟩ **4** a particularly advantageous or excellent quality ⟨*the* ~ *of my idea is that it costs so little*⟩

beauty sleep *n* sleep considered as being beneficial to a person's beauty

beauty spot *n* a beautiful scenic area

beaver *n, pl* beavers, (1a) beavers *or esp collectively* beaver **1a** a large semiaquatic rodent mammal that has webbed hind feet, a broad flat tail, and builds dams and underwater lodges **b** the fur or pelt of the beaver **2** a hat made of beaver fur or a fabric imitation **3** a heavy fabric of felted wool napped on both sides **4** an energetic hard-working person

beaver *vi* to work energetically ⟨~ ing *away at the problem*⟩

beaver *n* **1** a piece of armour protecting the lower part of the face **2** a helmet visor

bebop *n* bop – **bebopper** *n*

becalm *vt* to keep motionless by lack of wind – usu pass

because *conj* **1** for the reason that; since ⟨*he rested* ~ *he was tired*⟩ **2** and the proof is that ⟨*they must be in,* ~ *the light's on*⟩

because *adv* because of sthg forgotten or unmentionable – infml ⟨*I did it, well, just* ~⟩

because of *prep* **1** as a result of **2** for the sake of
¹beck *n*, *NEng* a brook; *esp* a pebbly mountain stream
²beck *n* – **at someone's beck and call** in continual readiness
to obey any command from sby
beckon *vi* **1** to summon or signal, typically with a wave
or nod **2** to appear inviting ~*vt* to beckon to –
beckon *n*
become *vb* **became; become** *vi* **1** to come into existence
2 to come to be ⟨~ *sick*⟩ ⟨became *party leader*⟩ ~*vt* to
suit or be suitable to ⟨*her clothes* ~ *her*⟩ – **become of** to
happen to ⟨*what* became of *that girl who always came
top?*⟩
becoming *adj* suitable, fitting; *esp* attractively suitable –
becomingly *adv*
¹bed *n* **1a** a piece of furniture on or in which one may lie
and sleep and which usu includes bedstead, mattress, and
bedding **b** a place of sexual relations; *also* LOVEMAKING **2**
c a place for sleeping or resting **d** sleep; *also* a time for
sleeping ⟨*took a walk before* ~⟩ **e** the use of a bed for the
night **2** a flat or level surface: e g **a** (plants grown in) a
plot of ground, esp in a garden, prepared for plants **b** the
bottom of a body of water; *also* an area of sea or lake
bottom supporting a heavy growth of a specified organism
⟨*an oyster* ~⟩ **3** a supporting surface or structure; *esp* the
foundation that supports a road or railway **4** STRATUM **1a**
5 a mass or heap resembling a bed ⟨*a* ~ *of ashes*⟩; *esp* a
heap on which sthg else is laid ⟨*coleslaw on a* ~ *of
lettuce*⟩ – **in bed** in the act of sexual intercourse ⟨*found
him* in bed *with another woman*⟩
²bed *vb* **-dd-** *vt* **1a** to provide with a bed or bedding; settle
in sleeping quarters **b** to go to bed with, usu for sexual
intercourse **2a** to embed **b** to plant or arrange (garden
plants, vegetable plants, etc) in beds – often + *out* **c** to
base, establish **3** to lay flat or in a layer ~*vi* **1a** to find
or make sleeping accommodation **b** to go to bed **2** to form
a layer **3** to lie flat or flush *USE* (*vt 1a; vi 1, 2*) often +
down
bed and breakfast *n*, *Br* a night's lodging and breakfast
the following morning
bedbug *n* a wingless bloodsucking bug that sometimes
infests beds
bedclothes *n pl* the covers (e g sheets and blankets) used
on a bed
¹bedding *n* **1** bedclothes **2** a bottom layer; a foundation
3 material to provide a bed for livestock **4** a stratified rock
formation
²bedding *adj*, *of a plant* appropriate or adapted for culture
in open-air beds
bedeck *vt* to clothe with finery; deck out
bedevil *vt* **1** to possess (as if) with a devil; bewitch **2** to
change for the worse; spoil, frustrate **3** to torment
maliciously; harass – **bedevilment** *n*
bedfellow *n* **1** one who shares a bed **2** a close associate;
an ally ⟨*political* ~s⟩
bedlam *n* a place, scene, or state of uproar and confusion
– **bedlam** *adj*
bed linen *n* the sheets and pillowcases used on a bed
bedouin, beduin *n*, *pl* **bedouins**, *esp collectively* **bedouin**
often cap a nomadic Arab of the Arabian, Syrian, or N
African deserts
bedpan *n* a shallow vessel used by a person in bed for
urination or defecation
bedpost *n* a usu turned or carved post of a bedstead
bedraggled *adj* **1** left wet and limp (as if) by rain **2** soiled
and stained (as if) by trailing in mud
bedridden *adj* confined (e g by illness) to bed
bedrock *n* **1** the solid rock underlying unconsolidated
surface materials (e g soil) **2** the basis of sthg – **bedrock**
adj

¹bedroom *n* a room furnished with a bed and intended
primarily for sleeping
²bedroom *adj* dealing with, suggestive of, or inviting
sexual relations ⟨a ~ *farce*⟩
bedside *adj* **1** of or conducted at the bedside **2** suitable
for a person in bed ⟨~ *reading*⟩
bedside manner *n* the manner with which a medical
doctor deals with his/her patients
bed-sitter *n*, *Br* a single room serving as both bedroom
and sitting room
bedsore *n* a sore caused by prolonged pressure on the
tissue of a bedridden invalid
bedspread *n* a usu ornamental cloth cover for a bed
bedstead *n* the framework of a bed
bee *n* **1** a social 4-winged insect often kept in hives for the
honey that it produces; *broadly* any of numerous insects
that differ from the related wasps, esp in the heavier
hairier body and legs and in sometimes having a pollen
basket **2** *NAm* a gathering of people for a usu specified
purpose ⟨a *sewing* ~⟩ – **beelike** *adj* – **bee in one's bonnet**
an obsession about a specified subject or idea
beech *n*, *pl* **beeches, beech** (the wood of) any of a genus
of hardwood deciduous trees with smooth grey bark and
small edible triangular nuts – **beechen** *adj*
beech mast *n* the nuts of the beech (when lying on the
ground)
¹beef *n*, *pl* **beefs**, (2a) **beeves, beef**, *NAm chiefly* **beefs**
the flesh of a bullock, cow, or other adult domestic bovine
animal **2a** an ox, cow, or bull in a (nearly) full-grown
state; *esp* a bullock or cow fattened for food ⟨a *herd of
good* ~⟩ **b** a dressed carcass of a beef animal **3** muscular
flesh; brawn **4** a complaint – *infml*
²beef *vt* to add weight, strength, or power to – usu + *up*
~ *vi* to complain – *infml*
beefcake *n* a photographic display of muscular male
physiques – *infml*; compare CHEESECAKE
beefeater *n* YEOMAN OF THE GUARD – not used technically
beefy *adj* **1** full of beef **2** brawny, powerful
beehive *n* **1** HIVE **1 2** a scene of crowded activity –
beehive *adj*
beeline *n* a straight direct course
been *past part of* BE; *specif* paid a visit ⟨*has the postman* ~?⟩
beer *n* **1** an alcoholic drink brewed from fermented malt
flavoured with hops **2** a carbonated nonalcoholic or
fermented slightly alcoholic drink flavoured with roots or
other plant parts ⟨*ginger* ~⟩
beery *adj* **1** affected or caused by beer ⟨~ *voices*⟩ **2**
smelling or tasting of beer ⟨a ~ *tavern*⟩
beeswax *n* a yellowish plastic substance secreted by bees
that is used by them for constructing honeycombs and
used as a wood polish
beet *n* **1** any of various plants of the goosefoot family with
a swollen root used as a vegetable, as a source of sugar,
or for forage **2** *NAm* beetroot
¹beetle *n* **1** any of an order of insects that have 4 wings of
which the front pair are modified into stiff coverings that
protect the back pair at rest **2** a game in which the player
attempt to be the first to complete a stylized drawing of
a beetle in accordance with the throwing of a dice
²beetle *vi* **beetling** *Br* to move swiftly ⟨~d *off down the
road*⟩ – *infml*
³beetle *n* a heavy wooden tool for hammering or ramming
beetling *adj* prominent and overhanging ⟨~ *brows*⟩
beetroot *n*, *pl* **beetroot, beetroots** *chiefly Br* a cultivated
beet with a red edible root that is a common salad
vegetable

befall *vb* befell; befallen to happen (to), esp as if by fate

befit *vt* -tt- to be proper or becoming to

befitting *adj* suitable, appropriate – **befittingly** *adv*

¹before *adv* **1** so as to be in advance of others; ahead **2** earlier in time; previously ⟨*haven't we met* ~*?*⟩ ⟨*had left a week* ~⟩

²before *prep* **1a** IN FRONT OF **b** under the jurisdiction or consideration of ⟨*the case* ~ *the court*⟩ **2** preceding in time; earlier than **3** in a higher or more important position than ⟨*put quantity* ~ *quality*⟩ **4** under the onslaught of

³before *conj* **1** earlier than the time when **2** rather than

beforehand *adv or adj* **1** in anticipation **2** ahead of time – **beforehandedness** *n*

befriend *vt* to become a friend of purposely; show kindness and understanding to

befuddle *vb* befuddling **1** to muddle or stupefy (as if) with drink **2** to confuse, perplex – **befuddlement** *n*

beg *vb* -gg- *vt* **1** to ask for as a charity ⟨~ ged *alms*⟩ **2** to ask earnestly (for); entreat ⟨~ a *favour*⟩ ⟨~ ged *her to stay*⟩ **3a** to evade, sidestep ⟨~ ged *the real problems*⟩ **b** to assume as established or proved without justification ⟨~ *the question*⟩ ~ *vi* **1** to ask for alms or charity **2a** to ask earnestly ⟨~ ged *for mercy*⟩ **b** to ask permission – usu + an infinitive ⟨*I* ~ *to differ*⟩ **3** of a dog to sit up and hold out the forepaws

beget *vt* -tt-; begot, *archaic* begat; begotten, begot **1** to procreate as the father; sire **2** to produce as an effect; cause – **begetter** *n*

¹beggar *n* **1** one who lives by asking for gifts **2** a pauper **3** a person; esp a fellow – infml ⟨*lucky* ~⟩

²beggar *vt* **1** to reduce to beggary **2** to exceed the resources or abilities of ⟨*it* ~s *description*⟩

beggarly *adj* **1** marked by extreme poverty **2** contemptibly mean, petty, or paltry – **beggarliness** *n*

beggary *n* poverty, penury

begin *vb* -nn-; began; begun *vi* **1a** to do the first part of an action; start ⟨*if you're all ready, we'll* ~⟩ **b** to undergo initial steps ⟨*work on the project began in May*⟩ **2a** to come into existence; arise ⟨*the war began in 1939*⟩ **b** to have a starting point ⟨*the alphabet* ~s *with* A⟩ ~ *vt* **1** to set about the activity of ⟨*the children began laughing*⟩ **2** to call into being; found ⟨~ *a dynasty*⟩ **3** to come first in ⟨A ~s *the alphabet*⟩ **4** to do or succeed in, in the least degree ⟨*can't* ~ *to describe her beauty*⟩ – **beginner** *n*

beginning *n* **1** the point at which sthg begins; the start **2** the first part **3** the origin, source **4** a rudimentary stage or early period – usu pl

beg off *vi* to ask to be released from sthg

begone *vi* to go away; depart – usu in the infin or esp the imperative

begonia *n* any of a large genus of tropical plants that have asymmetrical leaves and are widely cultivated as ornamental garden and house plants

begorra *interj, Irish* – used as a mild oath

begrudge *vt* **1** to give or concede reluctantly ⟨*he* ~d *every minute taken from his work*⟩ **2** to envy the pleasure or enjoyment of ⟨*they* ~ *him his wealth*⟩ – **begrudger** *n*, **begrudgingly** *adv*

beguile *vt* **1** to deceive, hoodwink **2** to while away, esp by some agreeable occupation **3** to please or persuade by the use of wiles; charm ⟨*her ways* ~d *him*⟩ ~ *vi* to deceive by wiles – **beguilement** *n*, **beguiler** *n*, **beguilingly** *adv*

behalf *n* – on behalf of, NAm in behalf of in the interest of; as a representative of

behave *vb* **1** to conduct (oneself) in a specified way ⟨*she has been* behaving *badly*⟩ **2** to conduct (oneself) properly

⟨*you must learn to* ~ *yourself in company*⟩ – **behaver** *n*

behaviour, NAm chiefly behavior *n* **1a** anything that an organism does involving action and response to stimulation **b** the response of an individual, group, or species to its environment **2** the way in which sthg (e g a machine) functions – **behavioural** *adj*, **behaviourally** *adv*

behaviourism *n* a theory holding that the proper concern of psychology is the objective study of behaviour and that information derived from introspection is not admissible psychological evidence

behead *vt* to cut off the head of; decapitate

behest *n* an urgent prompting or insistent request ⟨*returned home at the* ~ *of his friends*⟩

¹behind *adv* **1a** in the place, situation, or time that is being or has been departed from ⟨*I've left the keys* ~ – *SEU S*⟩ **b** in, to, or towards the back ⟨*look* ~⟩ **2a** in a secondary or inferior position **b** IN ARREARS ⟨~ *in his payments*⟩ **c** slow

²behind *prep* **1a(1)** at or to the back or rear of ⟨*look* ~ *you*⟩ **(2)** remaining after (sby who has departed) ⟨*left a great name* ~ *him*⟩ **b** obscured by ⟨*malice* ~ *the mask of friendship*⟩ **2** – used to indicate backwardness ⟨~ *his classmates in performance*⟩, delay ⟨~ *schedule*⟩, or deficiency ⟨*lagged* ~ *last year's sales*⟩ **3a** in the background of ⟨*the conditions* ~ *the strike*⟩ **b** in a supporting position at the back of ⟨*solidly* ~ *their candidate*⟩ – behind the times old-fashioned, out-of-date

³behind *n* the buttocks – slang

behindhand *adj* **1** behind schedule; IN ARREARS ⟨*he was* ~ *with the rent*⟩ **2** lagging behind the times; backward

behold *vb* beheld *vt* to see, observe ~ *vi archaic* – used in the imper to call attention – **beholder** *n*

beholden *adj* under obligation for a favour or gift; indebted *to*

behove *vb* to be incumbent (on), or necessary, proper, or advantageous (for) ⟨*it* ~s *us to fight*⟩

beige *n* a yellowish grey colour – **beige** *adj*, **beigy** *adj*

¹being *n* **1a** the quality or state of having existence **b** conscious existence; life ⟨*the mother who gave him his* ~⟩ **2** the qualities that constitute an existent thing; the essence; esp personality **3** a living thing; esp a person

²being *adj* – for the time being for the moment

belabour *vt* **1** to work on or at to absurd lengths ⟨~ *the obvious*⟩ **2a** to beat soundly **b** to assail, attack

belated *adj* delayed beyond the usual time – **belatedly** *adv*, **belatedness** *n*

¹belay *vt* **1** to secure or make fast (e g a rope) by turns round a support or bitt **2** to stop **3a** to secure (a person) at the end of a rope **b** to secure (a rope) to a person or object ~ *vi* **1** to be belayed **2** to stop; LEAVE OFF – in the imper ⟨~ *there*⟩ **3** to make a rope fast

²belay *n* **1** a method or act of belaying a rope or person in mountain climbing **2** (sthg to which is attached) a mountain climber's belayed rope

belch *vi* **1** to expel gas suddenly from the stomach through the mouth **2** to erupt, explode, or detonate violently **3** to issue forth spasmodically; gush ~ *vt* **1** to eject or emit violently **2** to expel (gas) suddenly from the stomach through the mouth – **belch** *n*

beleaguer *vt* **1** to surround with an army so as to prevent escape; besiege **2** to beset, harass

belfry *n* (a room in which a bell is hung in) a bell tower, esp when associated with a church

belie *vt* belying **1** to give a false impression of **2** to show (sthg) to be false – **belier** *n*

belief *n* **1** trust or confidence in sby or sthg **2** sthg believed; specif a tenet or body of tenets held by a group

3 conviction of the truth of some statement or the reality of some being, thing, or phenomenon, esp when based on examination of evidence

believe *vi* **1a** to have a firm religious faith **b** to accept sthg trustfully and on faith ⟨*people who* ~ *in the natural goodness of man*⟩ **2** to have a firm conviction as to the reality or goodness of sthg ⟨~ *in exercise*⟩ ~*vt* **1** to consider to be true or honest ⟨~ *the reports*⟩ **2** to hold as an opinion; think ⟨*I* ~ *it will rain soon*⟩ USE (*vi*) often + *in* – **believable** *adj*, **believer** *n*

Belisha beacon *n* a flashing light in an amber globe mounted on a usu black and white striped pole that marks a zebra crossing

belittle *vt* **belittling** to undermine the value of ⟨~s *her efforts*⟩ – **belittlement** *n*, **belittler** *n*

¹bell *n* **1** a hollow metallic device, usu cup-shaped with a flaring mouth if operated manually, and saucer-shaped if part of an electrical or clockwork device, that vibrates and gives forth a ringing sound when struck **2** *the* sound of a bell as a signal; *specif* one to mark the start of the last lap in a running or cycling race or the start or end of a round in boxing, wrestling, etc **3a** a bell rung to tell the hour **b** a half-hour subdivision of a watch on shipboard indicated by the strokes of a bell **4** sthg bell-shaped: e g **a** the corolla of any of many flowers **b** the flared end of a wind instrument

²bell *vt* **1** to provide with a bell **2** to make bell-mouthed ~ *vi* to take the form of a bell; flare

³bell *vi, of a stag or hound* to make a resonant bellowing or baying sound

belladonna *n* (an atropine-containing extract of) deadly nightshade

bell-bottoms *n pl* trousers with wide flaring bottoms – **bell-bottom** *adj*

bellboy *n, chiefly NAm* ¹PAGE

belle *n* a popular and attractive girl or woman ⟨*bathing* ~s⟩ ⟨*the* ~ *of the ball*⟩

belles lettres *n pl but sing in constr* (light, entertaining, usu sophisticated) literature that has no practical or informative function – **belletrist** *n*

bellflower *n* any of a genus of plants (e g the harebell) having usu showy bell-shaped flowers

bellicose *adj* disposed to or fond of quarrels or wars – **bellicosely** *adv*, **bellicoseness** *n*, **bellicosity** *n*

-bellied *comb form* (*adj* → *adj*) having (such) a belly ⟨*a big-bellied man*⟩

belligerence, belligerency *n* **1** an aggressive or truculent attitude, atmosphere, or disposition **2** the state of being at war or in conflict; *specif* the status of a legally recognized belligerent

belligerent *adj* **1** engaged in legally recognized war **2** inclined to or exhibiting assertiveness, hostility, or combativeness – **belligerent** *n*, **belligerently** *adv*

bellow *vi* **1** to make the loud deep hollow sound characteristic of a bull **2** to shout in a deep voice ~ *vt* to bawl ⟨~s *the orders*⟩ – **bellow** *n*

bellows *n, pl* **bellows 1** a device that by alternate expansion and contraction supplies a current of air – often pl with sing. meaning **2** a pleated expandable part in a camera

bell push *n* a button that is pushed to ring a bell

¹belly *n* **1a** ABDOMEN 1 **b(1)** the undersurface of an animal's body **(2)** a cut of pork consisting of this part of the body **c** the womb, uterus **d** the stomach and associated organs **2** an internal cavity; the interior **3** a surface or object curved or rounded like a human belly

²belly *vb* to swell, fill ⟨*the sails* bellied⟩

¹bellyache *n* colic

²bellyache *vi* to complain whiningly or peevishly; find fault – infml – **bellyacher** *n*

belly button *n* NAVEL 1 – infml

belly dance *n* a usu solo dance emphasizing movements of the belly – **belly dance** *vi*, **belly dancer** *n*

belly flop *n* a dive into water in which the front of the body strikes flat against the surface – **belly flop** *vi*

bellyful *n* an excessive amount ⟨*a* ~ *of advice*⟩ – infml

belly-land *vi* to land an aircraft on its undersurface without the use of landing gear – **belly landing** *n*

belly laugh *n* a deep hearty laugh

belong *vi* **1** to be in a proper situation (e g according to ability or social qualification), position, or place **2** to be attached or bound *to* by birth, allegiance, dependency, or membership **3** to be an attribute, part, or function of a person or thing ⟨*nuts and bolts* ~ *to a car*⟩ **4** to be properly classified ⟨*whales* ~ *among the mammals*⟩ – **belong to** to be the property of

belonging *n* **1** a possession – usu pl **2** close or intimate relationship ⟨*a sense of* ~⟩

beloved *n or adj, pl* **beloved** (sby) dearly loved – usu in fml or religious contexts

¹below *adv* **1** in, on, or to a lower place, floor, or deck; *specif* on earth or in or to Hades or hell **2** UNDER 2 **3** under the surface of the water or earth

²below *prep* **1** in or to a lower place than; under **2** inferior to (e g in rank) **3** not suitable to the rank of; BENEATH 2 **4** covered by; underneath **5** downstream from **6** UNDER 4 ⟨~ *the age of 18*⟩

³below *n, pl* **below** *the* thing or matter written or discussed lower on the same page or on a following page

⁴below *interj* – used by a climber to warn others below to beware of falling stones or rocks

¹belt *n* **1** a strip of material worn round the waist or hips or over the shoulder for decoration or to hold sthg (e g clothing or a weapon) **2** an endless band of tough flexible material for transmitting motion and power or conveying materials **3** an area characterized by some distinctive feature (e g of culture, geology, or life forms); *esp* one suited to a specified crop – **belted** *adj*, **beltless** *adj* – **below the belt** in an unfair way ⟨*alluding to his past misdeeds in that way was really hitting below the belt*⟩ – **under one's belt** as part of one's experience; having been attained

²belt *vt* **1a** to encircle or fasten with a belt **b** to strap on **2a** to beat (as if) with a belt; thrash **b** to strike, hit – infml **3** to sing in a forceful manner or style – usu + *out*; infml ~ *vi* to move or act in a vigorous or violent manner – infml

³belt *n* a jarring blow; a whack – infml

belting *n* **1** belts collectively **2** material for belts

belt up *vi, Br* SHUT UP – infml

beltway *n, chiefly NAm* RING ROAD

bemoan *vt* to express regret, displeasure, or deep grief over; lament

bemuse *vt* to make confused; bewilder – **bemusedly** *adv*, **bemusement** *n*

¹bench *n* **1a** a long usu backless seat (e g of wood or stone) for 2 or more people **b** a thwart in a boat **2a** *often cap* **(1)** a judge's seat in court **(2)** the office of judge or magistrate ⟨*appointed to the* ~⟩ **b** *sing or pl in constr* the judges (**1**) hearing a particular case **(2)** collectively **3a(1)** a seat for an official (e g a judge or magistrate) **(2)** the office or dignity of such an official **b** any of the long seats on which members sit in Parliament **4** a long worktable

²bench *vt* **1** to exhibit (a dog) at a show **2** *NAm* to remove from or keep out of a game

bencher *n, Br* any of the chief or governing members of any of the Inns of Court

benchmark *n* **1** a point of reference (e g a mark on a permanent object indicating height above sea level) from which measurements may be made, esp in surveying **2** sthg that serves as a standard by which others may be measured

¹bend *n* any of various knots for fastening one rope to another or to an object

²bend *vb* **bent** *vt* **1** to force into or out of a curve or angle **2** to fasten ⟨~ *a sail to its yard*⟩ **3** to make submissive; subdue **4a** to cause to turn from a course; deflect **b** to guide or turn towards sthg; direct ⟨*he bent his steps homewards*⟩ **5** to direct strenuously or with interest; apply ⟨bent *themselves to the task*⟩ **6** to alter or modify to make more acceptable, esp to oneself ⟨~ *the rules*⟩ ~ *vi* **1** to move or curve out of a straight line or position **2** to incline the body, esp in submission; bow **3** to yield, compromise – **bend over backwards** to make extreme efforts

³bend *n* **1** bending or being bent **2** a curved part, esp of a road or stream **3** *pl but sing or pl in constr* CAISSON DISEASE ⟨*a case of the* ~ s⟩ – **round the bend** mad, crazy – *infml* ⟨*thought his friends must have gone* round the bend⟩

¹beneath *adv* **1** in or to a lower position; below **2** directly under; underneath

²beneath *prep* **1a** in or to a lower position than; below **b** directly under, esp so as to be close or touching **2** not suitable to; unworthy of ⟨~ *contempt*⟩ **3** under the control, pressure, or influence of

Benedictine *n* **1** a monk or a nun of any of the congregations following the rule of St Benedict and devoted esp to scholarship **2** often not cap a brandy-based liqueur made orig by French Benedictine monks – **Benedictine** *adj*

benediction *n* **1** the invocation of a blessing; *esp* the short blessing with which public worship is concluded **2** often cap a Roman Catholic or Anglo-Catholic devotion including the exposition of the Host and the blessing of the people with it

Benedictus *n* **1** a liturgical text from Mt 21:9 beginning 'Blessed is he that cometh in the name of the Lord' **2** a canticle from Lk 1:68 beginning 'Blessed be the Lord God of Israel'

benefaction *n* **1** the act of doing good, esp by generous donation **2** a benefit conferred; *esp* a charitable donation

benefactor, *fem* **benefactress** *n* one who gives aid; *esp* one who makes a gift or bequest to a person, institution, etc

benefice *n* an ecclesiastical office to which an income is attached – **benefice** *vt*

beneficent *adj* doing or producing good; *esp* performing acts of kindness and charity – **beneficently** *adv*, **beneficence** *n*

beneficial *adj* **1** conferring benefits; conducive to personal or social well-being **2** receiving or entitling one to receive advantage or profit, esp from property ⟨*the* ~ *owner of an estate*⟩ – **beneficially** *adv*, **beneficialness** *n*

beneficiary *n* **1** one who benefits from sthg **2** one who receives the income or proceeds of a trust, will, or insurance policy – **beneficiary** *adj*

¹benefit *n* **1a** sthg that promotes well-being; an advantage **b** good, welfare ⟨*did it for his* ~⟩ **2a** financial help in time of need (e g sickness, old age, or unemployment) **b** a payment or service provided for under an annuity, pension scheme, or insurance policy **3** an entertainment, game, or social event to raise funds for a person or cause

²benefit *vb* **-t-** (*NAm* **-t-, -tt-**) *vt* to be useful or profitable to ~ *vi* to receive benefit

benefit of clergy 1 the former clerical privilege of being tried in an ecclesiastical court **2** the ministration or sanction of the church – chiefly humor ⟨*a couple living together without* ~⟩

benefit of the doubt *n* the assumption of innocence in the absence of complete proof of guilt

benevolent *adj* **1** marked by or disposed to doing good; charitable **2** indicative of or characterized by goodwill ⟨~ *smiles*⟩ – **benevolence** *n*, **benevolently** *adv*, **benevolentness** *n*

benighted *adj* intellectually, morally, or socially unenlightened – **benightedly** *adv*, **benightedness** *n*

benign *adj* **1** gentle, gracious **2** favourable, mild ⟨*a* ~ *climate*⟩ **3** of a tumour not malignant – **benignly** *adv*, **benignity** *n*

¹bent *n* **1a** a reedy grass **b** a stalk of stiff coarse grass **2** any of a genus of grasses including important pasture and lawn grasses

²bent *adj* **1** changed from an original straight or even condition by bending; curved **2** set *on* ⟨*was* ~ *on winning*⟩ **3** *Br* homosexual – slang **4** *Br* corrupt; CROOKED 2 – slang

³bent *n* **1** a strong inclination or interest; a bias **2** a special ability or talent ⟨*a* ~ *for art*⟩

benumb *vt* to make inactive or numb; deaden

Benzedrine *trademark* – used for a type of amphetamine

benzene *n* an inflammable poisonous liquid hydrocarbon used in the synthesis of organic chemical compounds and as a solvent – **benzenoid** *adj*

benzine *n* any of various volatile inflammable petroleum distillates used esp as solvents or motor fuels

bequeath *vt* **1** to give or leave (sthg, esp personal property) by will **2** to transmit; HAND DOWN ⟨*ideas* ~ ed *to us by the 19th c*⟩ – **bequeathal** *n*

bequest *n* **1** the act of bequeathing **2** a legacy

berate *vt* to scold or condemn vehemently

bereave *vt* **bereaved, bereft** to rob or deprive *of* sby or sthg held dear, esp through death – **bereavement** *n*

bereaved *n or adj, pl* **bereaved** (*the* person) suffering the death of a loved one

bereft *adj* **1** deprived or robbed *of*; completely without sthg ⟨~ *of all hope*⟩ **2** bereaved

beret *n* a cap with a tight headband, a soft full flat top, and no peak

beriberi *n* a deficiency disease marked by degeneration of the nerves and caused by a lack of or inability to assimilate vitamin B_1

berk *n, Br* a burk – slang

¹berry *n* **1a** a small, pulpy, and usu edible fruit (e g a strawberry or raspberry) **b** a simple fruit (e g a currant, grape, tomato, or banana) with a pulpy or fleshy pericarp – used technically in botany **2** an egg of a fish or lobster – **berried** *adj*, **berrylike** *adj*

²berry *vi* **1** to bear or produce berries **2** to gather or seek berries

¹berserk *n* any of a type of ancient Scandinavian warrior who fought in a wild frenzy

²berserk *adj* frenzied, esp with anger; crazed – usu in *go berserk* – **berserk** *adv*

¹berth *n* **1** safe distance for manoeuvring maintained between a ship and another object **2** an allotted place for a ship when at anchor or at a wharf **3** a place for sleeping (e g a bunk), esp on a ship or train **4a** a place, position ⟨*earned the number 2* ~⟩ **b** a job, post – infml – **give a wide berth to** to remain at a safe distance from; avoid

²berth vt **1** to bring into a berth; dock **2** to allot a berth to ~ vi to come into a berth

beryl n a mineral that is a silicate of beryllium and aluminium, occurs as green, yellow, pink, or white crystals, and is used as a gemstone

beryllium n a light strong bivalent metallic element

beseech vt **besought, beseeched 1** to beg for urgently or anxiously ⟨besought a favour of her⟩ **2** to request earnestly; implore ⟨do not go, I ~ you⟩ – **beseechingly** adv

beset vt **1** to trouble or assail constantly ⟨~ by fears⟩ **2** to surround and (prepare to) attack ⟨~ by the enemy⟩ – **besetment** n

besetting adj constantly causing temptation or difficulty; continuously present ⟨a ~ sin⟩

beside prep **1a** by the side of ⟨walk ~ me⟩ **b** in comparison with **c** on a par with **d** unconnected with; wide of ⟨~ the point⟩ **2** besides – **beside oneself** in a state of extreme agitation or excitement

¹besides adv **1** as an additional factor or circumstance ⟨has a wife and 6 children ~⟩ **2** moreover, furthermore

²besides prep **1** other than; unless we are to mention ⟨who ~ John would say that?⟩ **2** as an additional circumstance to ⟨~ being old, she is losing her sight⟩

besiege vt **1** to surround with armed forces **2a** to crowd round; surround closely **b** to press with questions, requests, etc; importune – **besieger** n

besmirch vt to sully, soil

besom n BROOM 2; esp one made of twigs

besotted adj **1** made dull or foolish, esp by infatuation **2** drunk, intoxicated

bespatter vt to spatter

bespeak vt **bespoke; bespoken 1** to hire, engage, or claim beforehand **2** to indicate, signify ⟨her performance ~s considerable practice⟩ USE fml

bespoke adj, Br **1** made-to-measure; broadly made or arranged according to particular requirements **2** dealing in or producing articles that are made to measure ⟨a ~ tailor⟩

¹best adj, superlative of GOOD **1** excelling all others (e g in ability, quality, integrity, or usefulness) ⟨the ~ student⟩ **2** most productive of good ⟨what is the ~ thing to do⟩ **3** most, largest ⟨for the ~ part of a week⟩ **4** reserved for special occasions ⟨got out the ~ sherry glasses⟩

²best adv, superlative of WELL **1** in the best manner; to the best extent or degree ⟨a Wednesday would suit me ~ – SEU S⟩ **2** BETTER 2 ⟨is ~ avoided⟩ ⟨we'd ~ go⟩ – **as best** in the best way ⟨climbed over as best he could⟩

³best n, pl **best 1** the best state or part ⟨never at my ~ before breakfast⟩ ⟨the ~ of life is over at 20⟩ **2** sby or sthg that is best ⟨can ride with the ~ of them⟩ **3** the greatest degree of good or excellence ⟨always demand the ~ of my pupils⟩ **4** one's maximum effort ⟨did my ~⟩ **5** best clothes ⟨Sunday ~⟩ **6** a winning majority ⟨the ~ of 3 games⟩ – **at best** even under the most favourable circumstances; seen in the best light – **make the best of** to cope with an unfavourable situation in the best and most optimistic manner possible

⁴best vt to get the better of; outdo

bestial adj **1** of beasts **2** marked by brutal or inhuman instincts or desires; specif sexually depraved – **bestialize** vt, **bestially** adv

bestiality n bestial behaviour; specif sexual relations between a human being and an animal

bestiary n a medieval allegorical or moralizing work about real or imaginary animals

bestir vt to stir up; rouse to action

best man n the principal attendant of a bridegroom at a wedding

bestow vt to present as a gift – usu + on or upon – **bestowal** n

bestrew vt **bestrewed; bestrewed, bestrewn 1** to strew **2** to lie scattered over

bestride vt **bestrode; bestridden 1** to ride, sit, or stand astride; straddle **2** to tower over; dominate

best-seller n **1** sthg, esp a book, which has sold in very large numbers, usu over a given period **2** an author or performer whose works sell in very large numbers – **best-selling** adj

¹bet n **1a** the act of risking a sum of money or other stake on the forecast outcome of a future event (e g a race or contest), esp in competition with a second party **b** a stake so risked **c** an outcome or result on which a stake is gambled **2** an opinion, belief ⟨my ~ is it will pour with rain⟩ **3** a plan of action; course ⟨your best ~ is to call a plumber⟩ – infml

²bet vb bet also **betted; -tt-** vt **1** to stake as a bet – usu + on or against **2** to make a bet with (sby) **3** to be convinced that ⟨I ~ they don't turn up⟩ – infml ~ vi to lay a bet – **bet one's bottom dollar** to be virtually certain – infml – **you bet** you may be sure; certainly – slang

beta n **1a** the 2nd letter of the Greek alphabet **b** Β **4 2** – used to designate the second brightest star of a constellation

betake vt **betook; betaken** to cause (oneself) to go – fml

betel n a climbing pepper whose leaves are chewed together with betel nut and lime, esp by SE Asians, to stimulate the flow of saliva

betel nut n the astringent seed of the betel palm

bête noire n, pl **bêtes noires** a person or thing strongly detested

bethel n **1** a Nonconformist chapel **2** a place of worship for seamen

bethink vt **bethought** archaic to cause (oneself) to be reminded or to consider – usu + of

betide vt to happen to; befall ⟨woe ~ them if they're late!⟩ ~ vi to happen, esp as if by fate ⟨we shall remain friends, whatever may ~⟩ USE fml or poetic; used only in the 3rd pers sing. pres subj and infin

betoken vt **1** to give evidence of; show **2** to presage, portend

betray vt **1** to deceive, lead astray **2a** to deliver to an enemy by treachery **b** to be a traitor to ⟨~ ed his people⟩ **3a** to fail or desert, esp in time of need **b** to disappoint the hopes, expectation, or confidence of **4a** to be a sign of (sthg one would like to hide) **b** to disclose, deliberately or unintentionally, in violation of confidence – **betrayal** n, **betrayer** n

betroth vt **betrothed, betrothing** to promise to marry or give in marriage

betrothal n a mutual promise or contract for a future marriage

betrothed n the person to whom one is betrothed

¹better adj, comparative of GOOD or of WELL **1** more than half ⟨for the ~ part of a month⟩ **2** improved in health; recovered **3** of greater quality, ability, integrity, usefulness, etc

²better adv, comparative of WELL **1** in a better manner; to a better extent or degree **2a** to a higher degree ⟨he knows the story ~ than you do⟩ **b** more wisely or usefully ⟨is ~ avoided⟩ ⟨I'd ~ not go round at lunchtime – SEU S⟩

³better n, pl **better, (1b) betters 1a** sthg better **b** one's superior, esp in merit or rank – usu pl **2** the advantage, victory ⟨*get the* ~ *of him*⟩ – **for better or for worse** whatever the outcome

better *vt* **1** to make better: e g **a** to make more tolerable or acceptable ⟨*trying to* ~ *the lot of slum dwellers*⟩ **b** to make more complete or perfect **2** to surpass in excellence; excel ~ *vi* to become better

betterment *n* an improvement

between *prep* **1a** through the common action of; jointly engaging ⟨~ *them, they managed to lay the carpet*⟩ **b** in shares to each of ⟨*divided* ~ *his 4 children*⟩ **2a** in or into the time, space, or interval that separates ⟨*in* ~ *the rafters*⟩ **b** in intermediate relation to ⟨*a colour* ~ *blue and grey*⟩ **3a** from one to the other of ⟨*travelling* ~ *London and Paris*⟩ **b** serving to connect or separate ⟨*dividing line* ~ *fact and fancy*⟩ **4** in point of comparison of ⟨*not much to choose* ~ *them*⟩ **5** taking together the total effect of; WHAT WITH ⟨*kept very busy* ~ *cooking, writing, and gardening*⟩ – **between you and me** in confidence

between *adv* in or into an intermediate space or interval

betwixt *adv or prep, archaic* between

betwixt and between *adv or adj* in a midway position; neither one thing nor the other

bevel *n* **1** the angle or slant that one surface or line makes with another when they are not at right angles **2** an instrument consisting of 2 rules or arms jointed together and opening to any angle for drawing angles or adjusting surfaces to be given a bevel

bevel *vb* **-ll-** (*NAm* **-l-, -ll-**), *vt* to cut or shape to a bevel ~ *vi* to incline, slant

bevel gear *n* (a system of gears having) a pair of toothed wheels that work shafts inclined to each other

beverage *n* a liquid for drinking; *esp* one that is not water

bevy *n* a group or collection, esp of girls

bewail *vt* to express deep sorrow for; lament

beware *vb* to be wary (of) ⟨~ *the Ides of March!*⟩ ⟨~ *of the dog!*⟩ – usu in imper and infin

bewilder *vt* to perplex or confuse, esp by a complexity, variety, or multitude of objects or considerations – **bewilderedly** *adv*, **bewilderingly** *adv*, **bewilderment** *n*

bewitch *vt* **1a** to influence or affect, esp injuriously, by witchcraft **b** to cast a spell over **2** to attract as if by the power of witchcraft; enchant ⟨~ed *by her beauty*⟩ – **bewitchingly** *adv*, **bewitchment** *n*

beyond *adv* **1** on or to the farther side; farther **2** as an additional amount; besides

beyond *prep* **1** on or to the farther side of; at a greater distance than **2a** out of the reach or sphere of ⟨~ *repair*⟩ **b** in a degree or amount surpassing ⟨~ *my wildest dreams*⟩ **c** out of the comprehension of **3** BESIDES 2 **4** later than; except

beyond *n* **1** sthg that lies beyond **2** sthg that lies outside the scope of ordinary experience; *specif* ²HEREAFTER

bezique *n* (the combination of the queen of spades and jack of diamonds held in) a card game for 2 people that is played with a double pack of 64 cards

bhang *n* a mild form of cannabis used esp in India

bi- *prefix* **1a** two ⟨*biparous*⟩ ⟨*bilingual*⟩ **b** appearing or occurring every 2 ⟨*bimonthly*⟩ ⟨*biweekly*⟩ **c** into two parts ⟨*bisect*⟩ **2a** twice; doubly; on both sides ⟨*biconvex*⟩ ⟨*biserrate*⟩ **b** appearing or occurring twice in ⟨*biweekly*⟩ – often disapproved of in this sense because of the likelihood of confusion with sense 1b; compare SEMI- **3** located between, involving, or affecting **2** (specified symmetrical parts) ⟨*biaural*⟩ **4** DI- 2 ⟨*biphenyl*⟩ **5** acid salt ⟨*bicarbonate*⟩

²**bi-, bio-** *comb form* life ⟨*biography*⟩; living organisms or tissue ⟨*biology*⟩

¹**bias** *n* **1** a line diagonal to the grain of a fabric, often used in the cutting of garments for smoother fit – usu + *the* ⟨*cut on the* ~⟩ **2a** an inclination of temperament or outlook; *esp* a personal prejudice **b** a bent, tendency **c** a tendency of an estimate to deviate in one direction from a true value (e g because of non-random sampling) **3** (the property of shape or weight causing) the tendency of a bowl used in the game of bowls to take a curved path when rolled **4** a voltage applied to a device (e g the grid of a thermionic valve) to enable it to function normally – **on the bias** askew, obliquely

²**bias** *adj, esp of fabrics and their cut* diagonal, slanting – **bias** *adv*

³**bias** *vt* **-s-, -ss-** **1a** to give a prejudiced outlook to **b** to influence unfairly **2** to apply an electrical bias to

bib *n* **1** a covering (e g of cloth or plastic) placed over a child's front to protect his/her clothes **2** a small rectangular section of a garment (e g an apron or dungarees) extending above the waist

bible *n* **1a** *cap* the sacred book of Christians comprising the Old Testament and the New Testament **b** any book containing the sacred writings of a religion **2** *cap* a copy or an edition of the Bible **3** an authoritative book ⟨*the fisherman's* ~⟩

biblical *adj* **1** of or in accord with the Bible **2** suggestive of the Bible or Bible times – **biblically** *adv*

biblio- *comb form* book ⟨*bibliography*⟩

bibliography *n* **1** the history, identification, or description of writings and publications **2** a list of writings relating to a particular topic, written by a particular author, issued by a particular publisher, etc **3** a list of the works referred to in a text or consulted by the author in its production – **bibliographer** *n*, **bibliographic, bibliographical** *adj*, **bibliographically** *adv*

bibliophile *n* a lover or collector of books – **bibliophilic** *adj*, **bibliophilism** *n*, **bibliophilist** *n*, **bibliophily** *n*

bibulous *adj* prone to over-indulgence in alcoholic drinks – **bibulously** *adv*, **bibulousness** *n*

bicameral *adj* having 2 legislative chambers – **bicameralism** *n*

bicarb *n* SODIUM BICARBONATE – *infml*

bicarbonate *n* an acid carbonate; *esp* SODIUM BICARBONATE

bicentenary *n or adj* (the celebration) of a 200th anniversary

bicentennial *n or adj* (a) bicentenary

biceps *n* the large muscle at the front of the upper arm that bends the arm at the elbow when it contracts; *broadly* any muscle attached in 2 places at one end

bicker *vi* to engage in petulant or petty argument – **bicker** *n*, **bickerer** *n*

bicycle *vi or n* bicycling (to ride) a 2 wheeled pedal-driven vehicle with handlebars and a saddle – **bicycler** *n*, **bicyclist** *n*

¹**bid** *vb* bade, bid, (3) bid; bidden, bid *also* bade; **-dd-** *vt* **1a** to issue an order to; tell ⟨*he did as he was* ~⟩ **b** to invite to come **2** to give expression to ⟨*bade* *him a tearful farewell*⟩ **3a** to offer (a price) for payment or acceptance (e g at an auction) **b** to make a bid of or in (a suit at cards) ~ *vi* to make a bid – **bidder** *n* – **bid fair** to seem likely; show promise ⟨*she bids fair to become extremely attractive*⟩

²**bid** *n* **1a** the act of one who bids **b** a statement of what one will give or take for sthg; *esp* an offer of a price **c** sthg offered as a bid **2** an opportunity to bid **3** (an announcement of) the amount of tricks to be won, suit to be played

in, etc in a card game **4** an attempt to win or achieve sthg ⟨*a ~ for power*⟩

biddable *adj* **1** easily led or controlled; docile **2** capable of being reasonably bid – **biddably** *adv*, **biddability** *n*

bidding *n* order, command ⟨*came at my ~*⟩

bide *vi* **bode, bided; bided** *archaic or dial* to remain awhile; stay – **bider** *n* – **bide one's time** to wait until the appropriate time comes to initiate action or to proceed

bidet *n* a low fixture used esp for bathing the external genitals and the anus

biennial *adj* **1** occurring every 2 years **2** *of a plant* growing vegetatively during the first year and fruiting and dying during the second – **biennial** *n*, **biennially** *adv*

bier *n* a stand on which a corpse or coffin is placed; *also* a coffin together with its stand

biff *n* a whack, blow – *infml* – **biff** *vt*

bifocal *adj* **1** having 2 focal lengths **2** having 1 part that corrects for near vision and 1 for distant vision ⟨*a ~ lens*⟩

bifocals *n pl* glasses with bifocal lenses

bifurcate *vi* to divide into 2 branches or parts – **bifurcate** *adj*, **bifurcation** *n*

¹**big** *adj* **-gg-** **1** of great force ⟨*a ~ storm*⟩ **2a** large in bulk or extent; *also* large in number or amount ⟨*a ~ house*⟩ ⟨*a ~ fleet*⟩ **b** conducted on a large scale ⟨*~ business*⟩ **c** important in influence, standing, or wealth ⟨*the ~ 4 banks*⟩ **3a** advanced in pregnancy ⟨*~ with child*⟩ **b** full to bursting; swelling ⟨*~ with rage*⟩ **4** *of the voice* loud and resonant **5a** elder ⟨*my ~ sister*⟩ **b** older, grown-up ⟨*when I'm a ~ girl, I'm going to be a nurse*⟩ **6a** chief, outstanding ⟨*the ~ issue of the campaign*⟩ ⟨*his ~ moment*⟩ **b** of great importance or significance ⟨*a ~ decision*⟩ **7a** pretentious, boastful ⟨*~ talk*⟩ **b** magnanimous, generous ⟨*that's very ~ of you*⟩ **8** popular ⟨*Frank Sinatra is very ~ in Las Vegas*⟩ – *infml* – **biggish** *adj*, **bigness** *n*

²**big** *adv* **1a** outstandingly ⟨*made it ~ in New York*⟩ **b** on a grand scale ⟨*think ~!*⟩ **2** pretentiously ⟨*he talks ~*⟩ USE *infml*

bigamy *n* the crime of going through a marriage ceremony with one person while legally married to another – **bigamist** *n*, **bigamous** *adj*, **bigamously** *adv*

big bang theory *n* a theory in cosmology: the universe originated from the explosion of a single mass of material so that the components are still flying apart

Big Brother *n* (the leader of) a ruthless all-powerful government

big dipper *n* **1** *often cap B&D, Br* ROLLER COASTER **2** *cap B&D, NAm* URSA MAJOR

big end *n* the end of an engine's connecting rod nearest the crankpin

big game *n* **1** large animals hunted or fished for sport **2** an important objective; *esp* one involving risk

bighead *n* a conceited person – *infml*

big head *n* an exaggerated opinion of one's importance – *infml* – **bigheaded** *adj*

bight *n* **1a** the middle part of a slack rope **b** a loop in a rope **2** (a hollow formed by) a bend of a river, coast, mountain chain, etc

big name *n* a very famous or important performer or personage – **big-name** *adj*

bigot *n* one who is obstinately or intolerantly devoted to his/her own religion, opinion, etc – **bigoted** *adj*, **bigotedly** *adv*, **bigotry** *n*

big stick *n* (the threat of using) force – *infml*

big time *n* *the* highest rank, esp among entertainers – *infml* – **big-time** *adj*, **big-timer** *n*

big top *n* the main tent of a circus

big tree *n* a very large Californian evergreen tree of the pine family

bigwig *n* an important person – *infml*

¹**bijou** *n, pl* **bijous, bijoux** a small dainty usu ornamental piece of delicate workmanship; a jewel

²**bijou** *adj, esp of a house* desirably elegant and usu small

bike *vi or n* (to ride) **1** a bicycle **2** a motorcycle

bikini *n* a woman's brief 2-piece garment resembling bra and pants worn for swimming or sunbathing

bilabial *n or adj* (a consonant) produced with both lips (e g /b, p, m/)

bilateral *adj* **1** having 2 sides **2** BIPARTITE **2** – **bilateralism** *n*, **bilaterally** *adv*, **bilateralness** *n*

bilberry *n* (the bluish edible fruit of) a dwarf bushy European shrub of the heath family that grows on moorland

bile *n* **1** a yellow or greenish fluid secreted by the liver into the intestines to aid the digestion of fats **2** inclination to anger

¹**bilge** *n* **1** the (space inside the) lowest usu rounded part of a ship's hull between the keel and the vertical sides **2** stale or worthless remarks or ideas – *infml*

²**bilge** *vt* to damage (a ship) in the bilge *~vi* to suffer damage in the bilge

bilingual *adj* **1** of, containing, or expressed in 2 languages **2** using or able to use 2 languages with the fluency of a native speaker – **bilingual** *n*, **bilingualism** *n*, **bilingually** *adv*

bilious *adj* **1** marked by or suffering from disordered liver function, esp excessive secretion of bile **2** peevish, ill-natured **3** *of colours* extremely distasteful; sickly ⟨*a ~ green*⟩ – *infml* – **biliously** *adv*, **biliousness** *n*

bilk *vt* to cheat out of what is due – **bilker** *n*

¹**bill** *n* **1** (a mouthpart resembling) the jaws of a bird together with variously shaped and coloured horny coverings and often specialized for a particular diet **2** a projection of land like a beak

²**bill** *vi* to caress affectionately – chiefly in **bill and coo**

³**bill** *n* **1** a long staff with a hook-shaped blade used as a weapon up to the 18th c **2** a billhook

⁴**bill** *n* **1** a draft of a law presented to a legislature **2** a paper carrying a statement of particulars **3a** (an itemized account of) charges due for goods or services **b** a statement of a creditor's claim **4a** a written or printed notice advertising an event of interest to the public (e g a theatrical entertainment) **b** an item (e g a film or play) in a programme entertainment **5** *chiefly NAm* ²NOTE **3c**

⁵**bill** *vt* **1** to submit a bill of charges to **2a** to advertise, esp by posters or placards **b** to arrange for the presentation of as part of a programme

billboard *n, chiefly NAm* HOARDING **2**

¹**billet** *n* **1a** an official order directing that a member of a military force be provided with board and lodging (e g in a private home) **b** quarters assigned (as if) by a billet **2** a position, job ⟨*a lucrative ~*⟩

²**billet** *vt* to provide (e g soldiers) with a billet

³**billet** *n* **1** a small thick piece of wood (e g for firewood) **2** a usu small bar of iron, steel, etc **3** a Romanesque architectural moulding or ornamentation consisting of raised short cylinders or square pieces placed at regular intervals

billet-doux *n, pl* **billets-doux** a love letter

billfold *n, NAm* WALLET **1**

billhook *n* a cutting tool, used esp for pruning, that has a blade with a hooked point

billiards *n pl but sing in constr* any of several games played on an oblong table by driving small balls against one another or into pockets with a cue; *specif* one with 3

balls in which scores are made by causing a cue ball to hit 2 object balls in succession – **billiard** adj
billion n 1 a thousand millions (10^9) 2 an indefinitely large number – often pl with sing. meaning 3 Br a million millions (10^{12}) – **billion** adj, **billionth** adj or n
bill of exchange n an unconditional written order from one person to another to pay a specified sum of money to a designated person
bill of fare n a menu
bill of lading n a receipt signed usu by the agent or owner of a ship listing goods (to be) shipped
bill of rights n, often cap B&R a summary in law (e g the English Statute of 1689) of fundamental rights and privileges guaranteed by the state
bill of sale n a formal document for the conveyance or transfer of title to goods and personal property
¹billow n 1 a great wave, esp in the open sea 2 a rolling swirling mass (e g of flame or smoke) – **billowy** adj
²billow vb to (cause to) rise, roll, bulge, or swell out (as if) in billows
billposter n one who pastes up advertisements and public notices on hoardings – **billposting** n
¹billy, billy club n, NAm TRUNCHEON 2
²billy, chiefly Austr **billycan** n a can of metal or enamelware with an arched handle and a lid, used for outdoor cooking or carrying food or liquid
billy goat n a male goat – infml
billy-o n – like **billy-o/billy-oh** very much; vigorously ⟨was raining like billy-o⟩
biltong n, chiefly SAfr strips of lean meat dried in the sun
bimetallic adj (of or being a device with a part) composed of 2 different metals, esp ones that expand by different amounts when heated – **bimetal** adj or n
bimonthly adj or adv (occurring) every 2 months or twice a month
¹bin n 1 a container used for storage (e g of flour, grain, bread, or coal) 2 a partitioned case or stand for storing and aging bottles of wine 3 Br a wastepaper basket, dustbin, or similar container for rubbish
²bin vt -nn- to put or store (esp bottled wine) in a bin
bin- comb form ¹BI- ⟨binaural⟩
binary adj 1 consisting of or marked by 2 things or parts 2a of, being, or belonging to a system of numbers having 2 as its base ⟨the ~ digits 0 and 1⟩ b involving a choice or condition of 2 alternatives (e g on or off) ⟨~ logic⟩ 3 having 2 musical subjects or 2 complementary sections – form⟩ – **binary** n
¹bind vb **bound** vt **1a** to make secure by tying (e g with cord) or tying together **b** to confine or restrict (as if) with bonds ⟨he was bound and thrown into prison⟩ **c** to put under a (legal) obligation ⟨we are all bound to keep the law⟩ 2 to wrap round with sthg (e g cloth) so as to enclose or cover 3 to encircle, gird **4a** to cause to stick together ⟨add an egg to ~ the mixture⟩ **b** to take up and hold (e g by chemical forces); combine with ⟨enzymes ~ their substrates⟩ 5 to constipate 6 to make binding; settle ⟨a deposit ~s the sale⟩ 7 to protect, strengthen, cover, or decorate with (a) binding 8 to cause to be attached (e g by gratitude or affection) ~ vi 1 to form a cohesive mass 2 to become hindered from free operation; jam 3 to complain – infml
²bind n a nuisance, bore – infml – **in a bind** chiefly NAm in trouble or difficulty – infml
binder n 1 a person who binds books 2 a usu detachable cover (e g for holding sheets of paper) 3 sthg (e g tar or cement) that produces or promotes cohesion in loosely assembled substances
¹binding n a material or device used to bind: e g **a** a

covering that fastens the leaves of a book **b** a narrow strip of fabric used to finish raw edges
²binding adj imposing an obligation ⟨a ~ promise⟩
bind over vt to impose a specific legal obligation on ⟨he was bound over to keep the peace⟩
bindweed n any of various twining plants with usu large showy trumpet-shaped flowers
binge n an unrestrained indulgence in sthg; esp a drunken revel – infml
¹bingo interj 1 – used to express the suddenness or unexpectedness of an event 2 – used as an exclamation to show that one has won a game of bingo
²bingo n a game of chance played with cards having numbered squares corresponding to numbers drawn at random and won by covering or marking off all or a predetermined number of such squares
binnacle n a case, stand, etc containing a ship's compass
binocular adj of, using, or adapted to the use of both eyes ⟨good ~ vision⟩ – **binocularly** adv
binoculars n pl, pl **binoculars** a binocular optical instrument; esp field glasses or opera glasses
binomial n or adj (a mathematical expression) consisting of 2 terms connected by a plus sign or minus sign – **binomially** adv
bio- – see ²BI-
biochemistry n chemistry that deals with the chemical compounds and processes occurring in organisms – **biochemist** n, **biochemical** adj, **biochemically** adv
biodegradable adj capable of being broken down, esp into simpler harmless products, by the action of living beings (e g microorganisms) – **biodegradability** n, **biodegrade** vb, **biodegradation** n
biogeographical adj of or being a geographical region viewed in terms of its plants and animals
biography n 1 a usu written account of a person's life 2 biographical writing as a literary genre – **biographer** n, **biographical, biographic** adj, **biographically** adv
biological warfare n warfare involving the use of (disease-causing) living organisms, or chemicals harmful to plants
biology n 1 a science that deals with the structure, function, development, distribution, and life processes of living organisms 2a the plant and animal life of a region or environment **b** the biology of an organism or group – **biologist** n, **biological** adj, **biologically** adv
bionic adj 1 involving bionics; also having or being a bionically designed part (e g a limb) 2 having exceptional abilities or powers – not used technically – **bionically** adv
bionics n pl but sing or pl in constr 1 a science concerned with the application of biological systems to engineering problems 2 the use of mechanical parts to replace or simulate damaged parts of a living thing
biosphere n the part of the world in which life exists
bipartisan adj of or involving 2 parties
bipartite adj 1 being in 2 parts 2 of a treaty, contract, etc between 2 parties **a** having 2 correspondent parts, one for each party **b** affecting both parties in the same way 3 cleft (almost) into 2 parts ⟨a ~ leaf⟩ – **bipartitely** adv, **bipartition** n
biped n a 2-footed animal – **biped, bipedal** adj
biplane n an aeroplane with 2 pairs of wings placed one above and usu slightly forward of the other
¹birch n 1 (the hard pale close-grained wood of) any of a genus of deciduous usu short-lived trees or shrubs typically having a layered outer bark that peels readily 2 a birch rod or bundle of twigs for flogging – **birch, birchen** adj

²**birch** *vt* to whip (as if) with a birch

bird *n* **1** any of a class of warm-blooded vertebrates with the body more or less completely covered with feathers and the forelimbs modified as wings **2a** a (peculiar) fellow – chiefly infml **b** *chiefly Br* a girl – infml **3** a hissing or jeering expressive of disapproval or derision – chiefly in *give somebody the bird/get the bird*; infml **4** *Br* TIME 5b – slang – **birdlike** *adj* – **for the birds** trivial, worthless – infml

birdbrain *n* a silly or stupid person – infml – **birdbrained** *adj*

bird dog *n*, *NAm* a gundog trained to hunt or retrieve birds

¹**birdie** *n* **1** a (little) bird – used esp by or to children **2** a golf score of 1 stroke less than par on a hole

²**birdie** *vt* **birdieing** to play (a hole in golf) in 1 stroke under par

birdlime *n* **1** a sticky substance that is smeared on twigs to snare small birds **2** the droppings of birds

bird of paradise *n* any of numerous brilliantly coloured plumed birds of the New Guinea area

bird of passage *n* **1** a migratory bird **2** a person who leads a wandering or unsettled life

bird of prey *n* a hawk, vulture, or other bird that feeds on carrion or on meat taken by hunting

birdseed *n* a mixture of hemp, millet, and other seeds used for feeding caged and wild birds

bird's-eye view *n* **1** a view from above; an aerial view **2** a brief and general summary; an overview

bird-watching *n* the observation or identification of birds in their natural environment – **bird-watcher** *n*

biretta *n* a square cap with 3 ridges on top worn by (Roman Catholic) clergy

Biro *trademark* – used for a ballpoint pen

birth *n* **1a** the emergence of a new individual from the body of its parent **b** the act or process of bringing forth young from within the body **2** the fact of being born, esp at a particular time or place ⟨*a Frenchman by* ∼⟩ **3** (noble) lineage or extraction ⟨*marriage between equals in* ∼⟩ **4** a beginning, start ⟨*the* ∼ *of an idea*⟩ **5** natural or inherited tendency ⟨*an artist by* ∼⟩

birth control *n* control of the number of children born, esp by preventing or lessening the frequency of conception; *broadly* contraception

birthday *n* **1a** the day of a person's birth **b** a day of origin **2** an anniversary of a birth ⟨*her 21st* ∼⟩

birthmark *n* a usu red or brown blemish on the skin at birth

birthrate *n* the number of (live) births per unit of population (e g 1000 people) in a period of time (e g 1 year)

birthright *n* sthg (e g a privilege or possession) to which a person is entitled by birth

biscuit *n* **1** earthenware or porcelain after the first firing and before glazing **2** a light yellowish brown colour **3** *Br* any of several variously-shaped small usu unleavened thin dry crisp bakery products that may be sweet or savoury **4** *NAm* a soft cake or bread (e g a scone) made without yeast

bisect *vt* to divide into 2 (equal) parts ∼*vi* to cross, intersect – **bisection** *n*

bisexual *adj* **1a** possessing characteristics of both sexes **b** sexually attracted to both sexes **2** of or involving both sexes – **bisexual** *n*, **bisexually** *adv*, **bisexuality** *n*

bishop *n* **1** a clergyman ranking above a priest, having authority to ordain and confirm, and typically governing a diocese **2** either of 2 chess pieces of each colour allowed to move diagonally across any number of consecutive unoccupied squares – **bishophood** *n*

bishopric *n* **1** a diocese **2** the office of bishop

bismuth *n* a heavy chiefly trivalent metallic element – **bismuthic** *adj*

bison *n*, *pl* **bison 1** a large shaggy-maned European bovine mammal that is now nearly extinct **2** BUFFALO 2

¹**bisque** *n* an advantage (e g an extra turn in croquet) allowed to an inferior player

²**bisque** *n* a thick cream soup (e g of shellfish or game)

³**bisque** *n* BISCUIT 1; *esp* a type of white unglazed ceramic ware

bistro *n*, *pl* **bistros** a small bar, restaurant, or tavern

¹**bit** *n* **1** a bar of metal or occas rubber attached to the bridle and inserted in the mouth of a horse **2** the biting or cutting edge or part of a tool; *also* a replaceable drilling, boring, etc part of a compound tool **3** sthg that curbs or restrains **4** the part of a key that enters the lock and acts on the bolt and tumblers

²**bit** *vt* **-tt-** to put a bit in the mouth of (a horse)

³**bit** *n* **1a** a small piece or quantity of anything (e g food) ⟨*a* ∼ *of cake*⟩ ⟨*a* ∼ *of string*⟩ ⟨*a little* ∼ *more*⟩ **b(1)** a usu specified small coin ⟨*a fivepenny* ∼⟩ **(2)** a money unit worth ⅛ of a US dollar **c** a part, section ⟨*couldn't hear the next* ∼⟩ **2** sthg small or unimportant of its kind: e g **a** a brief period; a while **b(1)** an indefinite usu small degree, extent, or amount ⟨*is a* ∼ *of a rascal*⟩ ⟨*every* ∼ *as powerful*⟩ **(2)** an indefinite small fraction ⟨*3 inches and a* ∼⟩ – infml **3** all the items, situations, or activities appropriate to a given style, role, etc ⟨*rejected the whole love and marriage* ∼⟩ **4** a small but necessary piece of work ⟨*doing their* ∼ *for Britain by refusing a pay rise*⟩ **5** a young woman – slang – **a bit 1** somewhat, rather ⟨*a bit difficult*⟩ – infml **2** the smallest or an insignificant amount or degree ⟨*not a bit sorry*⟩ – infml – **a bit much** a little more than one wants to endure – **a bit of all right** *Br* sby or sthg very pleasing; *esp* a sexually attractive person – infml – **bit by bit** little by little – **bit on the side** (a person with whom one has) occasional sexual intercourse usu outside marriage – **to bits** TO PIECES

⁴**bit** *n* (the physical representation in a computer or electronic memory of) a unit of computer information equivalent to the result of a choice between 2 alternatives (e g *on* or *off*)

¹**bitch** *n* **1** the female of the dog or similar flesh-eating animals **2** a malicious, spiteful, and domineering woman **3** a complaint – infml

²**bitch** *vi* to complain – infml

bitchy *adj* characterized by malicious, spiteful, or arrogant behaviour – **bitchily** *adv*, **bitchiness** *n*

¹**bite** *vb* **bit**; **bitten** *also* **bit** *vt* **1a** to seize with teeth or jaws, so that they enter, grip, or wound **b** to sting with a fang or other specialized part of the body ⟨*the midges are biting me*⟩ **c** to remove or sever with the teeth **2** to cut or pierce (as if) with an edged weapon **3** to cause sharp pain or stinging discomfort to **4** to take strong hold of; grip ∼*vi* **1** to bite or have the habit of biting sthg ⟨*does that dog* ∼*?*⟩ **2** of a weapon or tool to cut, pierce **3** to have a sharp penetrating effect ⟨*the sauce really* ∼s⟩ **4** of fish to take a bait **5** to take or maintain a firm hold – **biter** *n* – **bite off more than one can chew** to undertake more than one can perform – **bite the dust 1** to fall dead, esp in battle **2** to be finished or defeated ⟨*another of his schemes has bitten the dust*⟩

²**bite** *n* **1a** the amount of food taken with 1 bite; a morsel **b** a small amount of food; a snack **2** a wound made by biting **3** the hold or grip by which friction is created or purchase is obtained **4** a sharp incisive quality or effect

biting *adj* having the power to bite ⟨*a* ∼ *wind*⟩; *esp* sharp, cutting ⟨∼ *irony*⟩ – **bitingly** *adv*

bit part *n* a small acting part, usu with spoken lines

bitt *n* either of a pair of posts on a ship's deck for securing ropes

¹**bitter** *adj* **1a** being or inducing an acrid, astringent, or-disagreeable taste similar to that of quinine that is one of the 4 basic taste sensations **b** distressing, galling ⟨*a ~ sense of shame*⟩ **2a** intense, severe ⟨*~ enemies*⟩ **b** very cold ⟨*a ~ winter*⟩ **c** cynical, rancorous ⟨*~ contempt*⟩ **3** expressive of severe grief or regret ⟨*~ tears*⟩ – **bitterish** *adj*, **bitterly** *adv*, **bitterness** *n*

²**bitter** *adv*, *NAm* bitterly

³**bitter** *n* **1** *pl but sing or pl in constr* a usu alcoholic solution of bitter and often aromatic plant products used esp in preparing mixed drinks or as a mild tonic **2** *Br* a very dry beer heavily flavoured with hops

bittern *n* any of various small or medium-sized herons with a characteristic booming cry

¹**bittersweet** *n* a rambling poisonous nightshade with purple-and-yellow flowers

²**bittersweet** *adj* bitter and sweet at the same time; *esp* pleasant but with elements of suffering or regret ⟨*a ~ ballad*⟩ – **bittersweetly** *adv*, **bittersweetness** *n*

bitty *adj* scrappy, disjointed – **bittily** *adv*

bitumen *n* any of various mixtures of hydrocarbons (e g tar) that occur naturally or as residues after heating petroleum, coal, etc – **bituminoid** *adj*, **bituminize** *vt*, **bituminization** *n*

bituminous *adj* resembling, containing, or impregnated with bitumen

bivalent *adj* **1** having a valency of 2 **2** *of chromosomes* that become associated in pairs during meiotic cell division – **bivalent** *n*

bivalve *n or adj* (a mollusc) having a shell composed of 2 valves

¹**bivouac** *n* a usu temporary encampment under little or no shelter

²**bivouac** *vi* -ck- to make a bivouac; camp

biweekly *n, adj, or adv* (a publication) issued or occurring **a** every 2 weeks **b** twice a week

bizarre *adj* **1** odd, extravagant, eccentric **2** involving sensational contrasts or incongruities – **bizarrely** *adv*, **bizarreness** *n*

blab *vb* -bb- *vt* to reveal (a secret) ~ *vi* to talk indiscreetly or thoughtlessly – **blab** *n*

blabber *vi* to babble ~ *vt* to say indiscreetly – **blabber** *n*

blabbermouth *n* one who talks too much

¹**black** *adj* **1a** of the colour black **b** very dark in colour ⟨*his face was ~ with rage*⟩ **2** *often cap* **a** having dark pigmentation; *esp* of the Negro race ⟨*~ Americans*⟩ **b** of black people or culture ⟨*~ literature*⟩ **3** dressed in black ⟨*the ~ Prince*⟩ **4** dirty, soiled ⟨*hands ~ with dirt*⟩ **5a** having or reflecting little or no light ⟨*~ water*⟩ ⟨*a ~ night*⟩ **b** *of coffee* served without milk or cream **6a** thoroughly sinister or evil ⟨*a ~ deed*⟩ **b** indicative of hostility, disapproval, or discredit ⟨*met only with ~ looks*⟩ **7a** very dismal or calamitous ⟨*~ despair*⟩ **b** marked by the occurrence of disaster ⟨*~ Friday*⟩ **8** showing a profit ⟨*a ~ financial statement*⟩ **9** characterized by grim, distorted, or grotesque humour **10** bought, sold, or operating illegally and esp in contravention of official economic regulations ⟨*the ~ economy*⟩ ⟨*~ food*⟩ **11** *chiefly Br* subject to boycott by trade-union members – **blackish** *adj*, **blackly** *adv*, **blackness** *n*

²**black** *n* **1** a black pigment or dye **2** the colour of least lightness that belongs to objects that neither reflect nor transmit light **3** sthg black; *esp* black clothing ⟨*looks good in ~*⟩ **4** one who belongs wholly or partly to a dark-skinned race; *esp* a Negro **5** (the player playing) the dark-coloured pieces in a board game (e g chess) for 2

players **6** (nearly) total absence of light ⟨*the ~ of night*⟩ **7** the condition of being financially in credit or solvent or of making a profit – usu + *in the*; compare RED 3

³**black** *vt* **1** to make black **2** *chiefly Br* to declare (e g a business or industry) subject to boycott by trade-union members

blackamoor *n*, *archaic* BLACK 4

black-and-blue *adj* darkly discoloured from blood that has leaked under the skin by bruising

Black and Tan *n* a member of the Royal Irish Constabulary resisting the armed movement for Irish independence in 1921

black-and-white *adj* **1** reproducing visual images in tones of grey rather than in colours ⟨*~ television*⟩ **2a** sharply divided into 2 groups or sides **b** evaluating things as either all good or all bad ⟨*~ morality*⟩

black and white *n* **1** writing, print **2** a drawing or print done in black and white or in monochrome **3** black-and-white reproduction of visual images, esp by photography or television

blackball *vt* **1** to vote against (esp a candidate for membership of a club) **2** to ostracize – **blackball** *n*

black belt *n* (one who has) a rating of expert in judo, karate, etc

blackberry *n* (the usu black seedy edible fruit of) any of various prickly shrubs of the rose family

black bile *n* the one of the 4 humours in medieval physiology that was believed to be secreted by the kidneys or spleen and to cause melancholy

blackbird *n* **1** a common Old World thrush the male of which is black with an orange beak and eye rim **2** any of several American birds

blackboard *n* a hard smooth usu dark surface for writing or drawing on with chalk

black box *n* **1** a usu electronic device, esp one that can be plugged in or removed as a unit, whose internal mechanism is hidden from or mysterious to the user **2** FLIGHT RECORDER

blackcap *n* a small Old World warbler with a black crown

black cap *n* a black head-covering formerly worn by a judge in Britain when passing the death sentence

blackcurrant *n* (the small black edible fruit of) a widely cultivated European currant

black death *n*, *often cap B&D* a form of plague epidemic in Europe and Asia in the 14th c

blacken *vi* to become dark or black ⟨*the sky ~s*⟩ ~ *vt* **1** to make dark or black **2** to defame, sully – **blackener** *n*

black eye *n* a discoloration of the skin round the eye from bruising

blackguard *n* a coarse or unscrupulous person; a scoundrel – now often humor – **blackguardism** *n*, **blackguardly** *adj or adv*

blackhead *n* a small usu dark-coloured oily plug blocking the duct of a sebaceous gland, esp on the face

black hole *n* a celestial body, prob formed from a collapsed star, with a very high density and an intense gravitational field, from which no radiation can escape

black ice *n*, *Br* transparent slippery ice (e g on a road)

blacking *n* **1** a paste, polish, etc applied to an object to make it black **2** a boycotting of business, industry, etc by trade-union members

¹**blackjack** *n* **1** ²PONTOON **2** *NAm* a cosh

²**blackjack** *vt*, *NAm* to strike with a blackjack

black lead *n* graphite

blackleg *n*, *chiefly Br* a worker hostile to trade unionism or acting in opposition to union policies black letter *n* a heavier angular style of type or lettering used esp by early European printers

blacklist *n* a list of people or organizations who are disapproved of or are to be punished or boycotted – blacklist *vt*

black magic *n* magic performed with the aim of harming or killing sby or sthg

blackmail *n* 1 (money obtained by) extortion by threats, esp of exposure of secrets that would lead to loss of reputation, prosecution, etc 2 political, industrial, or moral pressure to do sthg that is considered undesirable – blackmail *vt*

Black Maria *n* an enclosed motor vehicle used by police to carry prisoners

black market *n* illicit trade in commodities or currencies in violation of official regulations (e g rationing)

black marketeer *n* one who trades on a black market

Black Mass *n* a travesty of the Christian mass ascribed to worshippers of Satan

Black Muslim *n* a member of an exclusively black chiefly US Muslim sect that advocates a strictly separate black community

blackout *n* 1 a period of darkness enforced as a precaution against air raids, or caused by a failure of electrical power 2 a temporary loss or dulling of vision, consciousness, or memory 3 a holding back or suppression of sthg ⟨~ *of news about the invasion*⟩ 4 a usu temporary loss of radio signal (e g during the reentry of a spacecraft)

black out *vi* 1 to become enveloped in darkness 2 to undergo a temporary loss of vision, consciousness, or memory 3 to extinguish or screen all lights for protection, esp against air attack ~ *vt* 1 to cause to black out 2 to suppress, esp by censorship ⟨*black out the news*⟩

Black Panther *n* a member of a militant organization of US blacks

black pepper *n* a pungent condiment prepared from the dried black-husked berries of an E Indian plant used either whole or ground

black power *n* the mobilization of the political and economic power of US blacks, esp to further racial equality

black pudding *n, chiefly Br* a very dark sausage made from suet and a large proportion of pigs blood

black sheep *n* a disreputable member of a respectable group, family, etc

Blackshirt *n* a member of a fascist organization having a black shirt as part of its uniform

blacksmith *n* one who works iron, esp at a forge – blacksmithing *n*

black spot *n, Br* a stretch of road on which accidents occur frequently

blackthorn *n* a European spiny shrub of the rose family with hard wood and small white flowers

black-tie *adj* characterized by or requiring the wearing of semiformal evening dress by men including a dinner jacket and a black bow tie ⟨*a ~ dinner*⟩

blackwater fever *n* a severe form of malaria in which the urine becomes dark-coloured

bladder *n* 1a a membranous sac in animals that serves as the receptacle of a liquid or contains gas; *esp* the urinary bladder b VESICLE 1a 2 a bag filled with a liquid or gas (e g the air-filled rubber one inside a football)

blade *n* 1 (the flat expanded part, as distinguished from the stalk, of) a leaf, esp of a grass, cereal, etc 2a the broad flattened part of an oar, paddle, bat, etc b an arm of a screw propeller, electric fan, steam turbine, etc c the broad flat or concave part of a machine (e g a bulldozer) that comes into contact with material to be moved d a broad flat body part; *specif* the scapula – used chiefly in

naming cuts of meat 3a the cutting part of a knife, razor, etc b a sword c the runner of an ice skate 4 *archaic* a dashing lively man – now usu humor

blaeberry *n, Scot* the bilberry

blah *n* silly or pretentious chatter or nonsense – infml

¹blame *vt* 1 to find fault with; censure 2a to hold responsible for sthg reprehensible ⟨~ *him for everything*⟩ b to place responsibility for (sthg reprehensible) – + *on* ⟨~s *it on me*⟩ – blamable *adj*, blamably *adv*, blamer *n*

²blame *n* 1 an expression of disapproval or reproach 2 responsibility for sthg reprehensible ⟨*they must share the ~ for the crime*⟩ – blameful *adj*, blamefully *adv*, blameless *adj*, blamelessly *adv*, blamelessness *n*

blameworthy *adj* deserving blame – blameworthiness *n*

blanch *vt* 1 to take the colour out of: a to bleach (a growing plant) by excluding light b to scald or parboil (e g almonds or food for freezing) in water or steam in order to remove the skin from, whiten, or stop enzymatic action 2 to make ashen or pale ⟨*fear ~es the cheek*⟩ ~ *vi* to become white or pale ⟨~ed *when he heard the news*⟩ – blancher *n*

blancmange *n* a usu sweetened and flavoured dessert made from gelatinous or starchy substances (e g cornflour) and milk

bland *adj* 1a smooth, soothing ⟨*a ~ smile*⟩ b unperturbed ⟨*a ~ confession of guilt*⟩ 2a not irritating or stimulating; mild ⟨*a ~ diet*⟩ b dull, insipid ⟨~ *stories with little plot or action*⟩ – blandly *adv*, blandness *n*

blandishment *n* a coaxing or flattering act or utterance – often pl – blandish *vb*

¹blank *adj* 1a dazed, nonplussed ⟨*stared in ~ dismay*⟩ b expressionless ⟨*a ~ stare*⟩ 2a lacking interest, variety, or change ⟨*a ~ prospect*⟩ b devoid of covering or content; esp free from writing ⟨~ *paper*⟩ c not filled in ⟨*a ~ cheque*⟩ 3 absolute, unqualified ⟨*a ~ refusal*⟩ 4 having a plain or unbroken surface where an opening is usual ⟨*a ~ arch*⟩ – blankly *adv*, blankness *n*

²blank *n* 1 an empty space 2a a void ⟨*my mind was a ~ during the test*⟩ b a vacant or uneventful period ⟨*a long ~ in history*⟩ 3 a dash substituted for an omitted word 4a a piece of material prepared to be made into sthg (e g a key or coin) by a further operation b a cartridge loaded with powder but no bullet

³blank *vt* 1a to make blank – usu + *out* b to block – usu + *off* ⟨~ed off *the tunnel*⟩ 2 NAm to keep (an opposing team) from scoring

blank cheque *n* 1 a signed cheque with the amount unspecified 2 complete freedom of action or control; CARTE BLANCHE

¹blanket *n* 1 a large thick usu rectangular piece of fabric (e g woven from wool or acrylic yarn) used esp as a bed covering or a similar piece of fabric used as a body covering (e g for a horse) 2 a thick covering or layer ⟨*a ~ of snow*⟩

²blanket *vt* to cover (as if) with a blanket ⟨*new grass ~s the slope*⟩

³blanket *adj* applicable in all instances or to all members of a group or class

blank verse *n* unrhymed verse, esp in iambic pentameters

blare *vi* to emit loud and harsh sound ~ *vt* 1 to sound loudly and usu harshly 2 to proclaim loudly or sensationally ⟨*headlines ~d his defeat*⟩ – blare *n*

blarney *n* 1 smooth wheedling talk; flattery 2 nonsense – blarney *vb*

blasé *adj* indifferent to pleasure or excitement as a result of excessive indulgence or enjoyment; *also* sophisticated

bless

blaspheme *vb* to speak of or address (God or sthg sacred) with impiety – **blasphemer** *n*
blasphemy *n* (the act of showing) contempt or lack of reverence for God or sthg (considered) sacred – **blasphemous** *adj*, **blasphemously** *adv*, **blasphemousness** *n*
¹blast *n* **1** a violent gust of wind **2** the sound produced by air blown through a wind instrument or whistle **3a** a stream of air or gas forced through a hole **b** a violent outburst **c** the continuous draught forced through a blast furnace **4** a sudden pernicious influence or effect 〈*the ~ of a huge epidemic*〉 **5** (a violent wave of increased atmospheric pressure followed by a wave of decreased atmospheric pressure produced in the vicinity of) an explosion or violent detonation **6** speed, capacity 〈*going full ~ down the road*〉 **7** the utterance of the word *blast* as a curse
²blast *vi* **1** to produce loud harsh sounds **2a** to use an explosive **b** to shoot **3** to shrivel, wither ~ *vt* **1** to injure (as if) by the action of wind; blight **2** to shatter, remove, or open (as if) with an explosive 〈*~ a new course for the stream*〉 **3** to apply a forced draught to **4** to cause to blast off 〈*will ~ themselves from the moon's surface*〉 **5a** to denounce vigorously 〈*judge ~s police methods*〉 **b** to curse, damn **c** to hit vigorously and effectively **6** to defeat decisively 〈*they ~ed the home team*〉 – **blaster** *n*, **blasting** *n or adj*
³blast *interj*, *Br* – used to express annoyance; slang
blast-, blasto- *comb form* bud; embryo; germ 〈*blastocyst*〉 〈*blastula*〉
-blast *comb form* (→ *n*) formative cell; cell layer 〈*erythroblast*〉; *also* formative unit, esp of living matter
blasted *adj* **1a** withered **b** damaged (as if) by an explosive, lightning, or the wind **2** confounded, detestable 〈*this ~ weather*〉 – *infml*
blast furnace *n* a furnace, esp for converting iron ore into iron, in which combustion is forced by a current of air under pressure
blast off *vi*, *esp of rocket-propelled missiles and vehicles* TAKE OFF **3** – **blast-off** *n*
blatant *adj* **1** noisy, esp in a vulgar or offensive manner **2** completely obvious, conspicuous, or obtrusive, esp in a crass or offensive manner – **blatantly** *adv*, **blatancy** *n*
blather *n* foolish voluble talk – **blather** *vi*, **blatherer** *n*
¹blaze *n* **1a** an intensely burning flame or sudden fire **b** intense direct light, often accompanied by heat 〈*the ~ of noon*〉 **2a** a dazzling display 〈*a ~ of flowers*〉 **b** a sudden outburst 〈*a ~ of fury*〉 **c** brilliance 〈*the ~ of the jewels*〉 **3** *pl* HELL **2a** – used as an interjection or as a generalized term of abuse 〈*go to ~s*〉
²blaze *vi* **1a** to burn intensely 〈*the sun ~d overhead*〉 **b** to flare up 〈*he suddenly ~d with anger*〉 **2** to be conspicuously brilliant or resplendent **3** to shoot rapidly and repeatedly 〈*~d away at the target*〉 – **blazingly** *adv*
³blaze *vt* to make public or conspicuous – chiefly in *blaze abroad*
⁴blaze *n* **1** a broad white mark on the face of an animal, esp a horse **2** a trail marker; *esp* a mark made on a tree by cutting off a piece of the bark
⁵blaze *vt* **1** to mark (e g a trail) with blazes **2** to lead or pioneer in (some direction or activity) – chiefly in *blaze the trail*
blazer *n* a jacket, esp with patch pockets, that is for casual wear or is part of a school uniform
¹blazon *n* **1** COAT OF ARMS **2** the proper formal description of heraldic arms or charges
²blazon *vt* **1** to proclaim widely – often + *forth* **2** to describe (heraldic arms or charges) in technical terms – **blazoner** *n*, **blazoning** *n*
blazonry *n* **1** blazon **2** dazzling display

¹bleach *vt* **1** to remove colour or stains from **2** to make whiter or lighter, esp by physical or chemical removal of colour ~ *vi* to grow white or lose colour – **bleachable** *adj*
²bleach *n* **1** a preparation used in bleaching **2** the degree of whiteness obtained by bleaching
bleaching powder *n* a white powder consisting chiefly of calcium hydroxide, calcium chloride, and calcium hypochlorite used as a bleach, disinfectant, or deodorant
¹bleak *adj* **1** exposed, barren, and often windswept **2** cold, raw **3a** lacking in warmth or kindness **b** not hopeful or encouraging 〈*a ~ outlook*〉 **c** severely simple or austere – **bleakish** *adj*, **bleakly** *adv*, **bleakness** *n*
²bleak *n* a small European river fish
bleary *adj* **1** of the eyes or vision dull or dimmed, esp from fatigue or sleep **2** poorly outlined or defined – **blearily** *adv*, **bleariness** *n*
¹bleat *vi* **1** to make (a sound like) the cry characteristic of a sheep or goat **2a** to talk complainingly or with a whine **b** to blather ~ *vt* to utter in a bleating manner – **bleater** *n*
²bleat *n* (a sound like) the characteristic cry of a sheep or goat
¹bleed *vb* **bled** *vi* **1a** to emit or lose blood **b** to die or be wounded, esp in battle 〈*men who bled for their country*〉 **2** to feel anguish, pain, or sympathy **3** to lose some constituent (e g sap or dye) by exuding it or by diffusion **4** to be printed so as to run off an edge of a page after trimming ~ *vt* **1** to remove or draw blood from **2** to extort money from **3** to draw sap from (a tree) **4** to extract or let out some of (a contained substance) from (a container) **5** to cause (e g a printed illustration) to bleed; *also* to trim (e g a page) so that some of the printing bleeds **6** to extract or drain the vitality or lifeblood from 〈*high taxes ~ing private enterprise*〉
²bleed *n* an act or instance of bleeding, esp by a haemophiliac
bleeder *n* **1** a haemophiliac **2** a worthless person – slang
bleeding *adj or adv* ¹BLOODY **4**, ³BLOODY – slang
bleeding heart *n* any of various plants of the fumitory family with usu red or pink heart-shaped flowers
¹bleep *n* **1** a short high-pitched sound (e g from electronic equipment) **2** a bleeper
²bleep *vt* **1** to call (sby) by means of a bleeper **2** to replace (recorded words) with a bleep or other sound – usu + *out* 〈*all the obscenities were ~ed out*〉 ~ *vi* to emit a bleep
bleeper *n* a portable radio receiver that emits a bleep as a signal that the wearer is required
blemish *vt or n* (to spoil the perfection of by) a noticeable imperfection
blench *vi* to draw back or flinch from lack of courage
¹blend *vb* **blended** *also* **blent** *vt* **1** to mix; esp to combine or associate so that the separate constituents cannot be distinguished **2** to prepare by thoroughly intermingling different varieties or grades ~ *vi* **1a** to mix or intermingle thoroughly **b** to combine into an integrated whole **2** to produce a harmonious effect
²blend *n* **1** an act or product of blending 〈*our own ~ of tea*〉 **2** a word (e g *brunch*) produced by combining other words or parts of words
blender *n* an electric appliance for grinding or mixing; *specif* a liquidizer
bless *vt* **blessed** *also* **blest** **1** to hallow or consecrate by religious rite, esp by making the sign of the cross **2** to invoke divine care for **3a** to praise, glorify 〈*~ His holy name*〉 **b** to speak gratefully of 〈*~ed him for his kindness*〉 **4** to confer prosperity or happiness on **5** – used in

exclamations chiefly to express mild or good-humoured surprise ⟨~ *my soul, what's happened now?*⟩ **6** *archaic* to protect, preserve

blessed *adj* **1a** *often cap* holy; venerated ⟨*the Blessed Sacrament*⟩ **b** *cap* – used as a title for a beatified person ⟨*Blessed Oliver Plunket*⟩ **2** – used as an intensive ⟨*no one gave us a ~ penny*⟩ – **blessedly** *adv*, **blessedness** *n*

blessing *n* **1a** the invocation of God's favour upon a person ⟨*the congregation stood for the ~*⟩ **b** approval **2** sthg conducive to happiness or welfare **3** grace said at a meal

blether *vi or n* (to) blather

blew *past of* BLOW

¹blight *n* **1** (an organism that causes) a disease or injury of plants resulting in withering, cessation of growth, and death of parts without rotting **2** sthg that impairs, frustrates, or destroys **3** a condition of disorder or decay ⟨*urban ~*⟩

²blight *vt* **1** to affect (e g a plant) with blight **2** to impair, frustrate ~ *vi* to suffer from or become affected with blight

blighter *n, chiefly Br* a fellow; *esp* one held in low esteem – *infml*

blimey *interj, chiefly Br* – used for expressing surprise; *slang*

blimp *n* **1** a nonrigid airship **2** *cap* COLONEL BLIMP – **blimpish** *adj*, **blimpishly** *adv*, **blimpishness** *n*

¹blind *adj* **1a** unable to see; sightless **b** of or designed for sightless people **2a** unable or unwilling to discern or judge ⟨*~ to all arguments*⟩ **b** not based on reason, evidence, or knowledge ⟨*~ faith*⟩ **3** completely insensible ⟨*in a ~ stupor*⟩ **4** without sight or knowledge of anything that could serve for guidance beforehand **5** performed solely by the use of instruments within an aircraft ⟨*a ~ landing*⟩ **6** hidden from sight; concealed ⟨*a ~ corner*⟩ ⟨*~ stitch*⟩ **7** having only 1 opening or outlet ⟨*a ~ alley*⟩ **8** having no opening for light or passage ⟨*a ~ wall*⟩ – **blindly** *adv*, **blindness** *n*

²blind *vt* **1** to make blind **2** to rob of judgment or discernment **3** to dazzle ~ *vi Br* to swear ⟨*cursing and ~ing*⟩ – *infml* – **blindingly** *adv* – **blind with science** to impress or overwhelm with a display of usu technical knowledge

³blind *n* **1** sthg to hinder sight or keep out light: e g **a** a window shutter **b** *chiefly Br* an awning **c** a flexible screen (e g a strip of cloth) usu mounted on a roller for covering a window **d** a curtain **e** VENETIAN BLIND **2** a cover, subterfuge **3** *NAm* ³HIDE

⁴blind *adv* **1** to the point of insensibility ⟨*~ drunk*⟩ **2** without seeing outside an aircraft ⟨*to fly ~*⟩ **3** – used as an intensive ⟨*swore ~ he wouldn't escape*⟩

blind alley *n* a fruitless or mistaken course or direction

blind date *n* a date between people who have not previously met

blinder *n* **1** *Br* sthg outstanding; *esp* an outstanding piece of play in cricket or football – *infml* **2** *NAm* BLINKER 3

blindfold *vt or n* **1** (to cover the eyes of with) a piece of material (e g a bandage) for covering the eyes to prevent sight **2** (to hinder from seeing or esp understanding with) sthg that obscures vision or mental awareness

blindman's buff *n* a group game in which a blindfolded player tries to catch and identify another player

blind spot *n* **1a** the point in the retina where the optic nerve enters that is not sensitive to light **b** a part of a visual field that cannot be seen or inspected ⟨*the car has a bad ~*⟩ **2** an area in which one lacks knowledge, understanding, or discrimination

¹blink *vi* **1** to close and open the eyes involuntarily **2** to shine intermittently **3a** to wink *at* **b** to look with surprise or dismay *at* ~ *vt* **1** to cause (one's eyes) to blink **2** to evade, shirk

²blink *n* **1** a glimmer, sparkle **2** a usu involuntary shutting and opening of the eye **3** iceblink – **on the blink** not working properly ⟨*the light switch is* on the blink⟩ – *infml*

blinker *n* **1** a warning or signalling light that flashes on and off **2** *pl* an obstruction to sight or discernment **3** *chiefly Br* either of two flaps, one on each side of a horse's bridle, allowing only frontal vision – **blinker** *vt*, **blinkered** *adj*

blinking *adj or adv*, *Br* ¹BLOODY 4, ³BLOODY – *euph*

blip *n* **1** a bleep **2** an image on a radar screen

bliss *n* **1** complete happiness **2** paradise, heaven – **blissful** *adj*, **blissfully** *adv*, **blissfulness** *n*

¹blister *n* **1** a raised part of the outer skin containing watery liquid **2** an enclosed raised spot (e g in paint) resembling a blister **3** a disease of plants marked by large swollen patches on the leaves **4** any of various structures that bulge out ⟨*an aircraft's radar ~*⟩ – **blistery** *adj*

²blister *vi* to become affected with a blister ~ *vt* **1** to raise a blister on **2** to attack harshly

blistering *adj* **1** extremely intense or severe **2** *of speed* extremely high – **blisteringly** *adv*

blithe *adj* **1** lighthearted, merry, cheerful ⟨*hail to thee, ~ spirit* – P B Shelley⟩ **2** casual, heedless ⟨*~ unconcern*⟩ – **blithely** *adv*

blithering *adj* talking nonsense; babbling; *broadly* utterly stupid ⟨*you ~ idiot!*⟩ – *infml*

blitz *n* **1a** a blitzkrieg **b** an intensive aerial bombardment; *specif, often cap* the bombardment of British cities by the German air force in 1940 and 1941 **2** an intensive non-military campaign ⟨*a ~ against the unions*⟩ – chiefly *journ* – **blitz** *vb*

blitzkrieg *n* a violent swift surprise campaign conducted by coordinated air and ground forces

blizzard *n* **1** a long severe snowstorm **2** an intensely strong cold wind filled with fine snow **3** an overwhelming rush or deluge ⟨*the ~ of mail at Christmas*⟩ – **blizzardy** *adj*

bloated *adj* **1** unpleasantly swollen **2** much larger than is warranted ⟨*a ~ estimate*⟩

bloater *n* a large herring or mackerel lightly salted and briefly smoked

blob *n* **1a** a small drop of liquid ⟨*a ~ of ink*⟩ **b** a small drop or lump of sthg viscous or thick **2** sthg ill-defined or amorphous

bloc *n* a (temporary) combination of individuals, parties, or nations for a common purpose

¹block *n* **1** a compact usu solid piece of substantial material (e g wood or stone): e g **a** a mould or form on which articles are shaped or displayed **b** a rectangular building unit that is larger than a brick **c** a usu cubical and solid wooden or plastic building toy that is usu provided in sets **d** the metal casting that contains the cylinders of an internal-combustion engine **2** HEAD 1 – *slang* **3a** an obstacle **b** an obstruction of an opponent's play in sports, esp in football, hockey, etc **c** interruption of the normal physiological function (e g transmission of nerve impulses) of a tissue or organ **4** a wooden or metal case enclosing 1 or more pulleys **5** (a ballet shoe with) a solid toe on which a dancer can stand on points **6a** a quantity or number of things dealt with as a unit **b** a part of a building or set of buildings devoted to a particular use **c** *chiefly NAm* (the distance along 1 side of) a usu rectangular space (e g in a town) enclosed by streets and usu occupied by buildings **d** BLOCK SECTION **7** a piece of engraved or etched material (e g wood or metal) from which impressions are printed

²**block** vt **1a** to make unsuitable for passage or progress by obstruction **b** to hinder the passage, progress, or accomplishment of (as if) by interposing an obstruction **c** to shut off from view ⟨*trees* ~ing *the sun*⟩ **d** to obstruct or interfere usu legitimately with (e g an opponent) in various games or sports **e** to prevent normal functioning of **2** to make (2 or more lines of writing or type) flush at the left or at both margins **3** to arrange (e g a school timetable) in long continuous periods ~ vi to block an opponent in sports – **blockage** n, **blocker** n

¹**blockade** n **1** the surrounding or blocking of a particular enemy area to prevent passage of people or supplies **2** an obstruction

²**blockade** vt to subject to a blockade – **blockader** n

block and tackle n an arrangement of pulley blocks with associated rope or cable for hoisting or hauling

blockbuster n **1** a huge high-explosive demolition bomb **2** sby or sthg particularly outstanding or effective *USE* infml

blockhead n an extremely dull or stupid person

blockhouse n **1** a building made of heavy timbers with loopholes for firing through, observation, etc, formerly used as a fort **2** an observation post built to withstand heat, blast, radiation, etc

block in vt to sketch the outlines of, in a design

block letter n a simple capital letter ⟨*write in* block letters, *please*⟩

block section n a length of railway track of defined limits, the use of which is governed by block signals

bloke n, *chiefly Br* a man – infml

¹**blond** adj **1a** of hair of a flaxen, golden, light auburn, or pale yellowish brown colour **b** of a pale white or rosy white colour ⟨~ skin⟩ **c** being a blond ⟨a handsome ~ youth⟩ **2a** of a light colour **b** of the colour blond – **blondish** adj

²**blond** n **1** sby with blond hair and often a light complexion and blue or grey eyes **2** a light yellowish brown to dark greyish yellow colour

¹**blood** n **1a** the usu red fluid that circulates in the heart, arteries, capillaries, and veins of a vertebrate animal, carrying nourishment and oxygen to, and bringing away waste products from, all parts of the body **b** a comparable fluid of an invertebrate animal **2a** lifeblood; *broadly* life **b** human lineage; *esp* the royal lineage **c** kinship **d** descent from parents **3a** temper, passion **b** the one of the 4 humours in medieval physiology that was believed to cause sanguinity **4** people or ideas of the specified, esp innovative, kind ⟨need some fresh ~ in the organization⟩ **5** archaic a dashing lively esp young man; a rake – now usu humor

²**blood** vt **1** to stain or wet with blood; esp to mark the face of (an inexperienced fox hunter) with the blood of the fox **2** to give an initiating experience to (sby new to a particular field of activity)

bloodbath n a great slaughter; a massacre

blood brother n either of 2 men pledged to mutual loyalty, esp by a ceremonial mingling of each other's blood – **blood brotherhood** n

blood count n (the determination of) the number of blood cells in a definite volume of blood

bloodcurdling adj arousing horror ⟨~ screams⟩ – **bloodcurdlingly** adv

-blooded comb form (→ adj) having (such) blood or (such) a temperament ⟨cold-blooded⟩ ⟨warm-blooded⟩

blood feud n a murderous feud between clans or families

blood group n any of the classes into which human beings can be separated on the basis of the presence or absence of specific antigens in their blood

blood heat n a temperature approximating to that of the human body; about 37°C or 98°F

bloodhound n **1** a large powerful hound of European origin remarkable for its acuteness of smell and poor sight **2** a person (e g a detective) who is keen in pursuing or tracking sby or sthg down

bloodless adj **1** deficient in or free from blood **2** not accompanied by the shedding of blood ⟨a ~ victory⟩ **3** lacking in spirit or vitality **4** lacking in human feeling ⟨~ statistics⟩ – **bloodlessly** adv, **bloodlessness** n

bloodletting n **1** phlebotomy **2** bloodshed

blood money n **1** money obtained at the cost of another's life **2** money paid to the next of kin of a slain person

blood poisoning n septicaemia

blood pressure n pressure that is exerted by the blood on the walls of the blood vessels, esp arteries, and that varies with the age and health of the individual

blood red adj having the colour of blood

blood-relation n a person related by consanguinity

bloodshed n **1** the shedding of blood **2** the taking of life

bloodshot adj, of an eye having the white part tinged with red

blood sport n a field sport (e g fox hunting or beagling) in which animals are killed – derog; not used technically

bloodstain n a discoloration caused by blood – **bloodstained** adj

bloodstock n sing or pl in constr horses of Thoroughbred breeding, esp when used for racing

bloodstream n the flowing blood in a circulatory system

bloodsucker n **1** a leech **2** a person who extorts money from another – **bloodsucking** adj

bloodthirsty adj eager for bloodshed – **bloodthirstily** adv, **bloodthirstiness** n

blood type n BLOOD GROUP

blood vessel n any of the vessels through which blood circulates in an animal

¹**bloody** adj **1** smeared, stained with, or containing blood **2** accompanied by or involving bloodshed **3a** murderous, bloodthirsty **b** merciless, cruel **4** – used as an intensive; slang – **bloodily** adv, **bloodiness** n

²**bloody** vt to make bloody

³**bloody** adv – used as an intensive; slang ⟨not ~ likely!⟩

Bloody Mary n, pl **Bloody Marys** a cocktail consisting chiefly of vodka and tomato juice

bloody-minded adj deliberately obstructive or unhelpful – **bloody-mindedness** n

¹**bloom** n a thick bar of hammered or rolled iron or steel

²**bloom** n **1a** a flower **b** the flowering state ⟨the roses in ~⟩ **c** an excessive growth of phytoplankton **2** a time of beauty, freshness, and vigour ⟨the ~ of youth⟩ **3a** a delicate powdery coating on some fruits and leaves **b** cloudiness on a film of varnish or lacquer **c** a mottled surface that appears on chocolate, often due to incorrect temperatures in manufacture or storage **4** a rosy or healthy appearance – **bloomy** adj

³**bloom** vi **1a** to produce or yield flowers **b** to support abundant plant life ⟨make the desert ~⟩ **2a** to flourish ⟨~ing with health⟩ **b** to reach maturity; blossom ⟨their friendship ~ed over the weeks⟩ **3** of a body of water to become densely populated with microorganisms, esp plankton

bloomer n a stupid blunder – infml

bloomers *n pl* a woman's undergarment with full loose legs gathered at the knee

blooming *adj, chiefly Br* – used as a generalized intensive; euph ⟨*that* ~ *idiot*⟩

¹blossom *n* **1a** the flower of a plant; *esp* the flower that produces edible fruits **b** the mass of bloom on a single plant **2a** a high point or stage of development – **blossomy** *adj*

²blossom *vi* **1** to bloom **2** to come into one's own; develop ⟨*a* ~ ing *talent*⟩

¹blot *n* **1** a soiling or disfiguring mark; a spot **2** a mark of reproach; a blemish

²blot *vb* **-tt-** *vt* **1** to spot, stain, or spatter with a discolouring substance **2** to dry or remove with an absorbing agent (e g blotting paper) ~ *vi* **1** to make a blot **2** to become marked with a blot – **blot one's copybook** to mar one's previously good record or standing

³blot *n* a backgammon counter exposed to capture

blotch *n* **1** an imperfection, blemish **2** an irregular spot or mark (e g of colour or ink) – **blotch** *vt*, **blotchily** *adv*, **blotchy** *adj*

blot out *vt* **1** to obscure, eclipse **2** to destroy; WIPE OUT

blotter *n* a piece of blotting paper

blotting paper *n* a spongy unsized paper used to absorb ink

blotto *adj, Br* extremely drunk – slang

blouse *n* a usu loose-fitting woman's upper garment that resembles a shirt or smock and is waist-length or longer

¹blow *vb* blew; blown *vi* **1** of air to move with speed or force ⟨*it's* ~ ing *hard tonight*⟩ **2** to send forth a current of gas, esp air ⟨blew *on his cold hands*⟩ **3** to make a sound by blowing ⟨*the whistle* blew⟩ **4** to boast **5a** to pant **b** *of a whale* to eject moisture-laden air from the lungs through the blowhole **6** *of an electric fuse* to melt when overloaded **7** *of a tyre* to lose the contained air through a spontaneous puncture – usu + *out* ~ *vt* **1a** to set (gas or vapour) in motion **b** to act on with a current of gas or vapour **2** to damn, disregard – infml ⟨~ *the expense*⟩ **3** to produce or shape by the action of blown or injected air ⟨~ ing *bubbles*⟩⟨~ ing *glass*⟩ **4** to deposit eggs or larvae on or in – used with reference to an insect **5** to shatter, burst, or destroy by explosion **6** to cause (a fuse) to blow **7** to rupture by too much pressure ⟨blew *a gasket*⟩ **8** to squander (money or an advantage) ⟨blew *£50 on a dress*⟩ ⟨blew *his chance*⟩ – slang **9** to leave hurriedly ⟨blew *town*⟩ – slang – **blow hot and cold** to act changeably by alternately favouring and rebuffing – **blow off steam** to release pent-up emotions – **blow one's own trumpet** to praise oneself; boast – **blow one's top** to become furious; explode with anger – infml – **blow the gaff** *Br* to let out a usu discreditable secret – **blow someone's mind 1** to cause sby to hallucinate – slang **2** to amaze sby – infml – **blow the whistle on 1** to bring (sthg secret) into the open – slang **2** to inform against – slang

²blow *n* **1** a strong wind or windy storm **2** an act or instance of blowing **3** a walk or other outing in the fresh air – infml

³blow *vt* blew; blown to cause (e g flowers or blossom) to open out, usu just before dropping ⟨*these roses are* ~ n⟩

⁴blow *n* ²BLOOM 1b ⟨*lilacs in full* ~⟩ – poetic

⁵blow *n* **1** a hard stroke delivered with a part of the body or with an instrument **2** *pl* a hostile or aggressive state – esp in **come to blows** **3** a forcible or sudden act or effort ⟨*a* ~ *for freedom*⟩ **4** a shock or misfortune

blowback *n* a recoil-operated action of a firearm in which no locking or inertia mechanism hinders the rearward

motion of the bolt or breechblock; *also* an automatic firearm using such an action

blow-by-blow *adj* minutely detailed ⟨*a* ~ *account*⟩

blower *n* **1** sby or sthg that blows or is blown **2** a device for producing a current of air or gas **3** *Br the* telephone – infml

blowfly *n* any of various 2-winged flies that deposit their eggs or maggots esp on meat or in wounds; *esp* a bluebottle

blowgun *n* BLOWPIPE 2

blowhard *n* a braggart

blowhole *n* **1** a nostril in the top of the head of a whale, porpoise, or dolphin **2** a hole in the ice to which aquatic mammals (e g seals) come to breathe

blow in *vi* to arrive casually or unexpectedly – infml

blowlamp *n* a small portable burner that produces an intense flame and has a pressurized fuel tank

blown *adj* **1** swollen **2** flyblown

blowout *n* **1** a large meal –infml **2** a bursting of a container (e g a tyre) by pressure of the contents on a weak spot **3** an uncontrolled eruption of an oil or gas well

blow out *vi* **1** to become extinguished by a gust **2** *of an oil or gas well* to erupt out of control ~ *vt* to extinguish by a gust

blow over *vi* to pass away without effect

blowpipe *n* **1** a small tube for blowing air, oxygen, etc into a flame to direct and increase the heat **2** a tube for propelling a projectile (e g a dart) by blowing **3** a long metal tube used by a glassblower

blowsy *also* **blowzy** *adj* **1** having a coarse ruddy complexion **2** *esp of a woman* slovenly in appearance and usu fat

blowup *n* **1** an explosion **2** an outburst of temper **3** a photographic enlargement

blow up *vt* **1** to shatter or destroy by explosion **2** to build up or exaggerate to an unreasonable extent **3** to fill up with a gas, esp air ⟨blow up *a balloon*⟩ **4** to make a photographic enlargement of ~ *vi* **1a** to explode **b** to be disrupted or destroyed (e g by explosion) **c** to become violently angry **2a** to become filled with a gas, esp air **b** to become expanded to unreasonable proportions **3** to come into being; arise

blowy *adj* windy ⟨*a* ~ *March day*⟩

¹blubber *n* the fat of large marine mammals, esp whales – **blubbery** *adj*

²blubber *vi* to weep noisily ~ *vt* to utter while weeping USE infml

³blubber *adj* puffed out; thick ⟨~ *lips*⟩

¹bludgeon *n* a short club used as a weapon

²bludgeon *vt* **1** to hit or beat with a bludgeon **2** to overcome by aggressive argument

¹blue *adj* **1** of the colour blue **2** discoloured through cold, anger, bruising, or fear **3** bluish grey ⟨*a* ~ *cat*⟩ **4a** low in spirits **b** depressing, dismal **5** CONSERVATIVE 1 **6a** obscene, pornographic ⟨*a* ~ *film*⟩ **b** off-colour, risqué ⟨~ *jokes*⟩ – **bluely** *adv*, **blueness** *n* – **once in a blue moon** very rarely – **until one is blue in the face** unsuccessfully for ever ⟨*you can complain* until you're blue in the face *but no one will listen*⟩

²blue *n* **1** a colour whose hue is that of the clear sky and lies between green and violet in the spectrum **2a** a blue pigment or dye **b** a blue preparation used to whiten clothes in laundering **3** blue clothing ⟨*dressed in* ~⟩ **4a(1)** the sky **(2)** the far distance **b** the sea **5** any of numerous small chiefly blue butterflies **6** *often cap, Br* a usu notional award given to sby who has played in a sporting contest between Oxford and Cambridge universities; *also* sby who has been given such an award **7** *Austr* a quarrel, row – infml – **out of the blue** without warning;

unexpectedly ⟨*she just turned up* out of the blue *expecting a meal*⟩

³**blue** *vb* **blueing, bluing** to (cause to) turn blue

⁴**blue** *vt* **blueing, bluing** *Br* to spend lavishly and wastefully – *infml*

blue baby *n* a baby with a bluish tint, usu from a congenital heart defect

bluebeard *n* a man who marries and kills one wife after another

bluebell *n* **1** any of various plants of the lily family bearing blue bell-shaped flowers; *esp* the wild hyacinth **2** *chiefly Scot* the harebell

blueberry *n* (the edible blue or blackish berry of) any of several shrubs of the heath family

bluebird *n* any of several small N American songbirds

blue-black *adj* dark blue

blue blood *n* high or noble birth – **blue-blooded** *adj*

blue book *n* an official parliamentary report or document

bluebottle *n* **1** CORNFLOWER 2 **2** any of several blowflies of which the abdomen or the whole body is iridescent blue, that make a loud buzzing noise in flight **3** *Austr & SAfr* a small blue jellyfish with 1 tentacle

blue cheese *n* cheese marked with veins of greenish blue mould

blue chip *n* a stock issue of high investment quality that usu pertains to a substantial well-established company and enjoys public confidence in its worth and stability – **blue-chip** *adj*

blue-collar *adj* of or being the class of manual wage-earning employees whose duties call for the wearing of work clothes or protective clothing

bluefish *n* an active voracious fish that is found in all warm seas

blue gum *n* any of several Australian eucalyptuses grown for their wood

blue-pencil *vt* to edit by correcting or deleting – **blue penciller** *n*

blue peter *n* a blue signal flag with a white square in the centre, used to indicate that a merchant vessel is ready to sail

blueprint *n* **1** a photographic print in white on a bright blue ground, used esp for copying maps and plans **2** a detailed programme of action ⟨*a ~ for victory*⟩ – **blueprint** *vt*

blue ribbon *n* a ribbon of blue fabric worn as an honour or award, esp by members of the Order of the Garter

blues *n, pl* **blues 1** *sing or pl in constr* low spirits; melancholy – + *the* **2** (a song in) a melancholy style of music characterized by flattened thirds or sevenths where a major interval would be expected in the melody and harmony ⟨*singing the ~*⟩ – **bluesy** *adj*

bluestocking *n* a woman with intellectual or literary interests – *derog*

¹**bluff** *adj* **1** rising steeply with a broad, flat, or rounded front **2** good-naturedly frank and outspoken – **bluffly** *adv*, **bluffness** *n*

²**bluff** *n* a high steep bank; a cliff

³**bluff** *vt* **1** to deceive (an opponent) in cards by a bold bet on an inferior hand with the result that the opponent withdraws a winning hand **2** to deceive by pretence or an outward appearance of strength, confidence, etc *~ vi* to bluff sby – **bluffer** *n*

⁴**bluff** *n* an act or instance of bluffing

¹**blunder** *vi* **1** to move unsteadily or confusedly **2** to make a blunder – **blunderer** *n*, **blunderingly** *adv*

²**blunder** *n* a gross error or mistake resulting from stupidity, ignorance, or carelessness

blunderbuss *n* an obsolete short firearm with a large bore and usu a flaring muzzle

¹**blunt** *adj* **1** insensitive, dull **2** having an edge or point that is not sharp **3a** aggressively outspoken **b** direct, straightforward – **bluntly** *adv*, **bluntness** *n*

²**blunt** *vt* to make less sharp or definite

¹**blur** *n* **1** a smear or stain **2** sthg vague or indistinct – **blurry** *adj*, **blurriness** *n*

²**blur** *vb* **-rr-** *vt* **1** to obscure or blemish by smearing **2** to make indistinct or confused *~ vi* to become vague, indistinct, or confused – **blurringly** *adv*

blurb *n* a short publicity notice, esp on a book cover

blurt out *vt* to utter abruptly and impulsively

¹**blush** *vi* **1** to become red in the face, esp from shame, modesty, or embarrassment **2** to feel shame or embarrassment – **blushingly** *adv*

²**blush** *n* **1** a reddening of the face, esp from shame, confusion, or embarrassment **2** a red or rosy tint – **blushful** *adj*

¹**bluster** *vi* **1** to blow in stormy gusts **2** to talk or act in a noisily self-assertive or boastful manner – **blusterer** *n*, **blusteringly** *adv*

²**bluster** *n* **1** a violent blowing **2** loudly boastful or threatening talk – **blusterous** *adj*, **blustery** *adj*

bo *n, chiefly NAm* a fellow – used chiefly in infml address

BO *n* a disagreeable smell, esp of stale perspiration, given off by a person's body

boa *n* **1** a large snake (e g the boa constrictor, anaconda, or python) that crushes its prey **2** a long fluffy scarf of fur, feathers, or delicate fabric

boar *n* **1a** an uncastrated male pig **b** the male of any of several mammals (e g a guinea pig or badger) **2** the Old World wild pig from which most domestic pigs derive – **boarish** *adj*

¹**board** *n* **1** the distance that a sailing vessel makes on 1 tack **2a** a usu long thin narrow piece of sawn timber **b** *pl* STAGE 2a(2), (3) **3a** a table spread with a meal **b** daily meals, esp when provided in return for payment **4** *sing or pl in constr* **a** a group of people having managerial, supervisory, or investigatory powers ⟨*~ of directors*⟩ ⟨*~ of examiners*⟩ **b** an official body ⟨*the gas ~*⟩ **5** a flat usu rectangular piece of material designed or marked for a special purpose (e g for playing chess, ludo, backgammon, etc or for use as a blackboard or surfboard) **6a** any of various wood pulps or composition materials formed into stiff flat rectangular sheets **b** cardboard **7** *archaic* TABLE 1 – **boardlike** *adj* – **on board** aboard

²**board** *vt* **1** to come up against or alongside (a ship), usu to attack **2** to go aboard (e g a ship, train, aircraft, or bus) **3** to cover with boards – + *over* or *up* ⟨*~ up a window*⟩ **4** to provide with regular meals and usu lodging for a fixed price *~ vi* to take one's meals, usu as a paying customer

boarder *n* **1** a lodger **2** a resident pupil at a boarding school

boardinghouse *n* a lodging house that supplies meals

boarding school *n* a school at which meals and lodging are provided

board out *vb* to (cause to) receive regular board and usu lodging away from home ⟨*boarded the cat out while they were on holiday*⟩

boardroom *n* a room in which board meetings are held

boardwalk *n, NAm* a walk often constructed of planking, usu beside the sea

¹**boast** *n* **1** an act of boasting **2** a cause for pride – **boastful** *adj*, **boastfully** *adv*, **boastfulness** *n*

²**boast** *vi* to praise oneself *~ vt* **1** to speak of or assert with

excessive pride **2** to have or display as notable or a source of pride – **boaster** *n*

³boast *n* a usu defensive shot in squash made from a rear corner of the court and hitting a side wall before the front wall

¹boat *n* **1** a small open vessel or craft for travelling across water **2** a usu small ship ⟨*left England on the Calais ~*⟩ **3** a boat-shaped utensil or dish ⟨*a gravy ~*⟩ – **in the same boat** in the same situation or predicament

²boat *vi* to use a boat, esp for recreation

boater *n* a stiff straw hat with a shallow flat crown and a brim

boathook *n* a pole with a hook at one end, used esp for fending off or holding boats alongside

boathouse *n* a shed for boats

boatman *n* one who works with or hires out esp pleasure boats – **boatmanship, boatsmanship** *n*

boatswain *n* a petty officer on a merchant vessel or warrant officer in the navy who supervises all work done on deck and is responsible esp for routine maintenance of the ship's structure

boat train *n* an express train that takes people to or from a ship

¹bob *vb* **-bb-** *vt* **1** to move up and down in a short quick movement ⟨*~ one's head*⟩ **2** to perform (a respectful gesture, esp a curtsy) briefly ~ *vi* **1** to move down and up briefly or repeatedly ⟨*a cork ~bed in the water*⟩ **2** to curtsy briefly **3** to try to seize a suspended or floating object with the teeth ⟨*~ for apples at a Halloween party*⟩ – **bobber** *n*

²bob *n* **1** a short quick down-and-up motion **2** (a method of bell ringing using) a modification of the order in change ringing

³bob *n* **1a** *Scot* a nosegay **b** a knot or twist (e g of ribbons or hair) **c** a haircut for a woman or girl in which the hair hangs loose just above the shoulders **2** FLOAT 1a **3** a hanging ball or weight on a plumb line or kite's tail **4** *pl* a small insignificant item ⟨*bits and ~s*⟩

⁴bob *vt* **-bb-** **1** to cut shorter; crop ⟨*~ a horse's tail*⟩ **2** to cut (hair) in a bob

⁵bob *n, pl* **bob** *Br* a shilling; *also* the sum of 5 new pence – *infml*

bobbin *n* **1** a cylinder or spindle on which yarn or thread is wound (e g for use in spinning, sewing, or lacemaking) **2** a coil of insulated wire or the reel it is wound on

bobby *n, Br* a policeman – *infml*

bobcat *n* a common N American lynx

bobsleigh *n* **1** either of a pair of short sledges joined by a coupling **2** a large usu metal sledge for 2 or 4 people used in racing

bobtail *n* a horse or dog with a bobbed tail – **bobtail, bobtailed** *adj*

bob up *vi* to emerge, arise, or appear suddenly or unexpectedly ⟨*the question bobbed up again*⟩

bod *n* a person – *infml* ⟨*an odd ~*⟩

bode *vt* to augur, presage ⟨*this ~s ill for the future*⟩ – **bodement** *n*

bodice *n* the part of a dress that is above the waist

-bodied *comb form* (*adj, n → adj*) having (such) a body ⟨*full-bodied*⟩ ⟨*glass-bodied*⟩

¹bodily *adj* of the body ⟨*~ comfort*⟩ ⟨*~ organs*⟩

²bodily *adv* **1** IN THE FLESH, IN PERSON **2** as a whole; altogether

bodkin *n* **1a** a small sharp slender instrument for making holes in cloth **b** a long ornamental hairpin **2** a blunt thick needle with a large eye used to draw tape or ribbon through a loop or hem **3** *archaic* a dagger, stiletto

body *n* **1a(1)** the organized physical substance of a living animal or plant **(2)** a corpse **b** a human being; a person

2a the main part of a plant or animal body, esp as distinguished from limbs and head **b** the main, central, or principal part: e g **(1)** the nave of a church **(2)** the part of a vehicle on or in which the load is placed **3a** the part of a garment covering the body or trunk **b** the central part of printed or written matter **c** the sound box or pipe of a musical instrument **4a** a mass of matter distinct from other masses ⟨*a ~ of water*⟩ **b** any of the 7 planets in old astronomy **c** sthg that embodies or gives concrete reality to a thing; *specif* a material object in physical space **5** *sing or pl in constr* a group of people or things: e g **a** a fighting unit **b** a group of individuals organized for some purpose ⟨*a legislative ~*⟩ **6a** compactness or firmness of texture **b** comparative richness of flavour in wine

body blow *n* a serious setback

bodyguard *n* an escort whose duty it is to protect a person from bodily harm

bodyline bowling *n* intimidatory fast bowling in cricket aimed persistently at the batsman's body and directed esp towards the leg side

body politic *n* a group of people under a single government

body snatcher *n* one who formerly dug up corpses illegally for dissection

bodywork *n* the structure or form of a vehicle body

Boer *n* a S African of Dutch descent

boffin *n, chiefly Br* a scientific expert; *esp* one involved in technological research – *infml*

bog *n* **1** (an area of) wet spongy poorly-drained ground **2** *Br* TOILET 2 – *slang* – **boggy** *adj*

bog asphodel *n* either of 2 bog plants of the lily family

bog down *vb* **-gg-** *vt* to cause to sink (as if) into a bog; impede ~ *vi* to become impeded

bogey *also* **bogy, bogie** *n, pl* **bogeys** *also* **bogies** **1** a spectre, ghost **2** a source of fear, perplexity, or harassment **3** a golf score of 1 stroke over par on a hole

¹boggle *vi* **boggling** **1** to be startled or amazed ⟨*the mind ~s*⟩ **2** to hesitate because of doubt, fear, or scruples – **boggle** *n*

²boggle *n* a bogle

bogie *also* **bogey, bogy** *n, pl* **bogies** *also* **bogeys** *chiefly Br* a swivelling framework with 1 or more pairs of wheels and springs to carry and guide 1 end of a railway vehicle

bogle *n, dial Br* a goblin, spectre; *also* an object of fear or loathing

bogus *adj* spurious, sham – **bogusness** *n*

Bohemian *n* **1a** a native or inhabitant of Bohemia **b** the group of Czech dialects used in Bohemia **2** a person (e g a writer or artist) living an unconventional life – **bohemian** *adj, often cap*

¹boil *n* a localized pus-filled swelling of the skin resulting from infection in a skin gland

²boil *vi* **1a** *of a fluid* to change into (bubbles of) a vapour when heated **b** to come to the boiling point (of the contents) ⟨*the kettle's ~ing*⟩ **2** to bubble or foam violently; churn **3** to be excited or stirred ⟨*made his blood ~*⟩ **4** to undergo the action of a boiling liquid (e g in cooking) ~ *vt* **1** to subject to the action of a boiling liquid (e g in cooking) ⟨*~ eggs*⟩ **2** to heat to the boiling point (of the contents)

³boil *n* the act or state of boiling; BOILING POINT ⟨*keep it on the ~*⟩

boil down *vt* **1** to reduce in bulk by boiling **2** to condense or summarize ~ *vi* to amount to ⟨*her speech boiled down to a plea for more money*⟩

boiler *n* **1** a vessel used for boiling **2** the part of a steam generator in which water is converted into steam under pressure 3 a tank in which water is heated or hot water is stored

boiler suit n, chiefly Br a one-piece outer garment combining shirt and trousers, worn chiefly to protect clothing

boiling point n 1 the temperature at which a liquid boils 2 the point at which a person loses his/her self-control

boil over vi 1 to overflow while boiling 2 to lose one's temper

boil up vi to rise towards a dangerous level (e g of unrest)

boisterous adj 1 noisily and cheerfully rough 2 stormy, wild – **boisterously** adv, **boisterousness** n

¹**bold** adj 1 showing or requiring a fearless adventurous spirit 2 impudent, presumptuous 3 departing from convention or tradition 4 standing out prominently; conspicuous 5 (set) in boldface – **boldly** adv, **boldness** n

²**bold** n boldface

boldface n (printing in) the thickened form of a typeface used to give prominence or emphasis

bole n the trunk of a tree

bolero n, pl **boleros** 1 (music for) a type of Spanish dance 2 a loose waist-length jacket open at the front

boll n the seed pod of cotton or similar plants

bollard n 1 a post on a wharf round which to fasten mooring lines 2 a bitt 3 Br a short post (e g on a kerb or traffic island) to guide vehicles or forbid access

bollock n, Br 1 a testicle – usu pl 2 pl nonsense, rubbish – often used interjectionally USE vulg

boll weevil n a weevil that infests the cotton plant

boloney n baloney

Bolshevik n, pl **Bolsheviks** also **Bolsheviki** 1 a member of the more radical wing of the Russian Social Democratic party that seized power in Russia in 1917 2 COMMUNIST 1 – derog – **Bolshevik** adj, **bolshevism** n, often cap, **bolshevize** vt, **Bolshevization** n

bolshie, bolshy n a Bolshevik – infml

¹**bolster** n 1 a long pillow or cushion placed across the head of a bed, usu under other pillows 2 a structural part (e g in machinery) that eliminates friction or provides support

²**bolster** vt to give support to; reinforce ⟨~ ed up his pride⟩ – **bolsterer** n

¹**bolt** n 1a a short stout usu blunt-headed arrow shot from a crossbow b a lightning stroke; a thunderbolt 2a a sliding bar or rod used to fasten a door b the part of a lock that is shot or withdrawn by the key 3 a roll of cloth or wallpaper of a standard length 4a a metal rod or pin for fastening objects together b a screw-bolt with a head suitable for turning with a spanner 5 a rod or bar that closes the breech of a breech-loading firearm

²**bolt** vi 1 to move rapidly; dash ⟨she ~ed for the door⟩ 2a to dart off or away; flee b to break away from control 3 to produce seed prematurely 4 NAm to break away from or oppose one's political party ~ vt 1 to flush, start ⟨~ rabbits⟩ 2 to secure with a bolt 3 to attach or fasten with bolts 4 to swallow (e g food) hastily or without chewing – **bolter** n

³**bolt** adv in a rigidly erect position ⟨sat ~ upright⟩

⁴**bolt** n a dash, run

⁵**bolt** vt to sift (e g flour) – **bolter** n

bolt-hole n 1 a hole into which an animal runs for safety 2 a means of rapid escape or place of refuge

⁶**bomb** n 1a any of several explosive or incendiary devices typically detonated by impact or a timing mechanism and usu dropped from aircraft, thrown or placed by hand, or fired from a mortar b ATOM BOMB; broadly nuclear weapons – + the 2 a rounded mass of lava exploded from a volcano 3 Br a large sum of money ⟨she's made a ~⟩ –

infml 4 NAm a failure, flop – infml – **a bomb** Br very successfully – infml ⟨our act goes down a bomb in Britain – News of the World⟩

²**bomb** vt to attack with bombs; bombard ~ vi to fail; FALL FLAT – infml

bombard vt 1 to attack with heavy artillery or with bombers 2 to attack vigorously or persistently (e g with questions) 3 to subject to the impact of electrons, alpha rays, or other rapidly moving particles – **bombardment** n

bombardier n 1 a noncommissioned officer in the British artillery 2 a US bomber-crew member who aims and releases the bombs

bombast n pretentious inflated speech or writing – **bombastic** adj, **bombastically** adv

bomb bay n a bomb-carrying compartment in the underside of a combat aircraft

bomber n 1 an aircraft designed for bombing 2 sby who throws or places bombs

bombshell n 1 BOMB 1a 2 sby or sthg that has a stunning or devastating effect ⟨the book was a political ~⟩

bombsight n a sighting device for aiming bombs

bombsite n an area of ground on which buildings have been destroyed by bombing, esp from the air

bona fide adj genuine, sincere

bona fides n sing or pl in constr honest intentions; sincerity

bonanza n 1 an exceptionally large and rich mass of ore in a mine 2 sthg (unexpectedly) considered valuable, profitable, or rewarding ⟨the oil ~⟩

bonbon n SWEET 2b; specif one with a chocolate or fondant coating and fondant centre that sometimes contains fruits and nuts

¹**bond** n 1 sthg (e g a fetter) that binds or restrains 2 a binding agreement 3a a mechanism by means of which atoms, ions, or groups of atoms are held together in a molecule or crystal b an adhesive or cementing material 4 sthg that unites or binds ⟨the ~s of friendship⟩ 5a a legally enforceable agreement to pay b a certificate of intention to pay the holder a specified sum, with or without interest, on a specified date 6 the system of overlapping bricks in a wall 7 the state of imported goods retained by customs authorities until duties are paid 8 a strong durable paper, now used esp for writing and typing

²**bond** vt 1 to overlap (e g bricks) for solidity of construction 2 to put (goods) in bond until duties and taxes are paid 3a to cause to stick firmly b to hold together in a molecule or crystal by chemical bonds ~ vi to cohere (as if) by means of a bond – **bondable** adj, **bonder** n

bondage n 1 the tenure or service of a villein, serf, or slave 2a slavery, serfdom b subjugation to a controlling person or force c a form of sexual gratification involving the physical restraint of one partner ⟨~ fantasies⟩

bonded adj 1 used for or being goods in bond ⟨a ~ warehouse⟩ 2 composed of 2 or more layers of fabric held together by an adhesive ⟨~ fabrics⟩

bondholder n one who holds a government or company bond

¹**bone** n 1a (any of the hard body structures composed of) the largely calcium-containing connective tissue of which the adult skeleton of most vertebrate animals is chiefly composed b (a structure made of) baleen, ivory, or another hard substance resembling bone 2 the essential or basic part or level; the core ⟨cut expenses to the ~⟩ 3 pl the core of one's being ⟨I felt in my ~s that she was lying⟩ 4 a subject or matter of dispute ⟨a ~ of contention⟩ 5a pl thin bars of bone, ivory, or wood held in pairs between

the fingers and used to produce musical rhythms **b** a strip of whalebone or steel used to stiffen a corset or dress **c** *pl* dice **d** a domino – **boned** *adj*, **boneless** *adj* – **bone to pick** a matter to argue or complain about

²bone *vt* **1** to remove the bones from **2** to stiffen (a garment) with bones – **boner** *n*

³bone *adv* absolutely, utterly – chiefly in *bone dry, bone idle*

bone china *n* a type of translucent and durable white hard-paste porcelain made from a mixture of bone ash and kaolin

bonehead *n* a stupid person – *infml* – **boneheaded** *adj*

bone meal *n* fertilizer or feed made of crushed or ground bone

bonesetter *n* a person, esp one who is not a licensed physician, who sets broken or dislocated bones

bone shaker *n* an early bicycle with solid tyres

bone up *vi* to try to master necessary information in a short time, esp for a special purpose ⟨*better* bone up *on those theories before the exam*⟩ – *infml*

bonfire *n* a large fire built in the open air

¹bongo *n*, *pl* bongos, *esp collectively* bongo any of 3 large striped antelopes of tropical Africa

²bongo *n*, *pl* bongos *also* bongoes either of a pair of small tuned drums played with the hands – **bongoist** *n*

bonhomie *n* good-natured friendliness

bonito *n*, *pl* bonitos, *esp collectively* bonito any of various medium-sized tunas

bonkers *adj*, *chiefly Br* mad, crazy – *infml*

bon mot *n*, *pl* bons mots, bon mots a witticism

bonnet *n* **1** a cloth or straw hat tied under the chin, now worn chiefly by children **2** *Br* the hinged metal covering over the engine of a motor vehicle

bonny *adj*, *chiefly Br* attractive, comely – **bonnily** *adv*

bonsai *n*, *pl* bonsai (the art of growing) a potted plant dwarfed by special methods of culture

bonus *n* **1** sthg given in addition to what is usual or strictly due **2** money or an equivalent given in addition to an employee's usual remuneration

bon vivant *n*, *pl* bons vivants, bon vivants a person with cultivated and refined tastes, esp in regard to food and drink

bony, boney *adj* **1** consisting of or resembling bone **2a** full of bones **b** having large or prominent bones **3** skinny, scrawny

¹boo *interj* – used to express contempt or disapproval or to startle or frighten

²boo *n*, *pl* boos a shout of disapproval or contempt

³boo *vb* to show scorn or disapproval (of) by uttering 'boo'

¹boob *n* **1** a stupid mistake; a blunder – *infml* **2** BREAST 1 – *slang*

²boob *vi* to make a stupid mistake – *infml*

¹booby *n* **1** an awkward foolish person **2** any of several small gannets of tropical seas **3** the poorest performer in a group

²booby *n* BREAST 1 – *vulg*

booby hatch *n*, *NAm* MADHOUSE 1

booby prize *n* an award for the poorest performance in a contest

booby trap *n* **1** a trap for the unwary or unsuspecting **2** a harmless-looking object concealing an explosive device that is set to explode by remote control or if touched – **booby-trap** *vt*

boodle *n* money, esp when stolen or used for bribery – *slang*

¹book *n* **1a** a set of written, printed, or blank sheets bound together into a volume **b** a long written or printed literary composition **c** a major division of a treatise or literary

work **d** a record of business transactions – usu pl ⟨*their* ~s *show a profit*⟩ **2** *cap the* Bible **3** sthg regarded as a source of enlightenment or instruction **4** a packet of (paper, cardboard, etc) commodities (e g tickets, stamps, or matches) bound together **5** the bets registered by a bookmaker **6** the number of tricks that must be won at cards before any trick can have scoring value – **bookful** *n*, **booklet** *n* – **by/according to the book** by following previously laid down instructions and not using personal initiative ⟨*it's safer to go* by the book *than risk making a mistake*⟩ – **in one's book** in one's own opinion ⟨in my book *this is the way to handle it*⟩ – **one for the book** an act or occurrence worth noting

²book *vt* **1** to reserve or make arrangements for in advance ⟨~ *2 seats at the theatre*⟩ **2a** to take the name of with a view to prosecution **b** to enter the name of (a player) in a book for a violation of the rules usu involving foul play – used with reference to a rugby or soccer player ~ *vi* **1** to reserve sthg in advance ⟨~ *up through your travel agent*⟩ **2** *chiefly Br* to register in a hotel – **booker** *n*

³book *adj* **1** derived from books; theoretical **2** shown by books of account

bookable *adj*, *chiefly Br* **1** that may be reserved in advance **2** that makes a player liable to be booked by a referee

bookbinding *n* the craft or trade of binding books – **bookbinder** *n*, **bookbindery** *n*

bookcase *n* a piece of furniture consisting of a set of shelves to hold books

bookend *n* a support placed at the end of a row of books

booking *n* **1** an engagement or scheduled performance **2** a reservation **3** an instance of being booked by a referee

booking office *n*, *chiefly Br* an office where tickets are sold and bookings made, esp at a railway station

bookish *adj* **1** relying on theoretical knowledge rather than practical experience **2** literary as opposed to colloquial – **bookishly** *adv*, **bookishness** *n*

bookkeeper *n* one who records the accounts or transactions of a business – **bookkeeping** *n*

bookmaker *n* sby who determines odds and receives and pays off bets – **bookmaking** *n*

bookmark, bookmarker *n* sthg used to mark a place in a book

bookplate *n* a label that is usu placed inside the cover of a book to identify the owner

bookseller *n* sby who sells books; *specif* the owner or manager of a bookshop

bookshop *n* a shop where books are the main items offered for sale

bookstall *n* a stall where books, magazines, and newspapers are sold

book token *n* a gift token exchangeable for books

book up *vt* to reserve all the accommodation in or services of – usu pass

bookworm *n* **1** any of various insect larvae that feed on the binding and paste of books **2** a person unusually fond of reading and study

¹boom *n* **1** a spar at the foot of the mainsail in fore-and-aft rig that is attached at its fore end to the mast **2** a long movable arm used to manipulate a microphone **3** a barrier across a river or enclosing an area of water to keep logs together; *also* the enclosed logs **4** a cable or line of spars extended across a river or the mouth of a harbour as a barrier to navigation

²boom *vi* **1** to make a deep hollow sound or cry **2** to experience a rapid increase in activity or importance ⟨*business was* ~ing⟩ ~ *vt* to cause to resound

³boom *n* **1** a booming sound or cry **2a** rapid settlement and development (e g of a town) **b** a rapid growth or increase in a specified area ⟨*the baby* ~⟩ **c** a rapid widespread expansion of economic activity

boomerang *n* **1** a bent piece of wood shaped so that it returns to its thrower and used by Australian aborigines as a hunting weapon **2** an act or utterance that backfires on its originator – **boomerang** *vi*

¹boon *n* **1** a benefit or favour, esp when given in answer to a request **2** a timely benefit; a blessing

²boon *adj* close, intimate, and convivial – esp in *boon companion*

boor *n* a coarse, ill-mannered, or insensitive person – **boorish** *adj*

¹boost *vt* **1** to push or shove up from below **2** to increase, raise ⟨*plans to* ~ *production*⟩ **3** to encourage, promote ⟨*extra pay to* ~ *morale*⟩ **4** to increase the force, pressure, or amount of; *esp* to raise the voltage of or across (an electric circuit)

²boost *n* **1** a push upwards **2** an increase in amount **3** an act that promotes or encourages

booster *n* **1** an auxiliary engine which assists (e g at take-off) by providing a large thrust for a short time **2** a supplementary dose increasing or renewing the effectiveness of a medicament

¹boot *n* – **to boot** besides

²boot *n* **1a** an outer covering for the human foot that extends above the ankle and has a stiff or thick sole and heel **b** a stout shoe, esp for sports ⟨*football* ~s⟩ **2** an instrument of torture that crushes the leg and foot **3** a blow or kick delivered (as if) by a booted foot **4** *Br* the major luggage compartment of a motor car **5** summary discharge or dismissal – slang; chiefly in *give/get the boot* – **booted** *adj* – **put/stick the boot in** *chiefly Br* to cause added distress to one who is already defeated – infml **2** to act with brutal decisiveness – infml

³boot *vt* to kick

bootblack *n* sby who cleans and shines shoes

bootee, bootie *n* **1** a short boot **2** an infant's sock worn in place of a shoe

booth *n, pl* **booths** **1** a stall or stand for the sale or exhibition of goods **2** a small enclosure affording privacy (e g for telephoning, dining, etc)

bootlace *n, Br* a long stout shoelace

¹bootleg *adj or n, chiefly NAm* (being) smuggled or illegally produced alcoholic drink

²bootleg *vb, chiefly NAm* to manufacture, sell, or transport for sale (esp alcoholic drink) contrary to law

bootless *adj* useless, unprofitable – fml – **bootlessly** *adv*, **bootlessness** *n*

boot out *vt* to eject or discharge summarily ⟨*was booted out of office*⟩ – infml

boots *n, pl* **boots** *Br* a servant who polishes shoes and carries luggage, esp in a hotel

bootstraps *n* – **haul/pull oneself up by one's own bootstraps** to improve oneself or one's situation by one's own unaided efforts

booty *n* **1** plunder taken (e g in war) **2** a rich gain or prize

¹booze *vi* to drink intoxicating liquor to excess – slang – **boozily** *adv*, **boozy** *adj*

²booze *n* **1** intoxicating drink; *esp* spirits **2** a drinking spree *USE* slang

boozer *n* a public house – slang

booze-up *n* **1** BOOZE **2 2** a drunken party *USE* slang

¹bop *vt or n* -pp- (to strike with) a blow (e g of the fist) – infml

²bop *n* jazz characterized by unusual chord structures, syncopated rhythm, and harmonic complexity and innovation – **bopper** *n*

³bop *vi* -pp- to dance (e g in a disco) in a casual and unrestricted manner, esp to popular music – infml

boracic acid *n* BORIC ACID

borage *n* a coarse hairy blue-flowered European herb

borax *n* natural or synthetic hydrated sodium borate used esp as a flux, cleansing agent, and water softener

Bordeaux *n, pl* **Bordeaux** a red or white wine of the Bordeaux region of France

bordello *n, pl* **bordellos** a brothel

¹border *n* **1** an outer part or edge **2** a boundary, frontier ⟨*crossed the* ~ *into Italy*⟩ **3** a narrow bed of planted ground (e g beside a path) **4** an ornamental design at the edge of sthg (e g printed matter, fabric, or a rug) – **bordered** *adj*

²border *vt* **1** to put a border on **2** to adjoin at the edge or boundary – **borderer** *n* – **border on 1** BORDER 2 ⟨*the USA borders on Canada*⟩ **2** to resemble closely ⟨*his devotion borders on the ridiculous*⟩

Border collie *n* (any of) a breed of rough-haired, often black-and-white, stocky dogs commonly used in Britain for herding sheep

borderline *adj* **1** verging on one or other place or state without being definitely assignable to either **2** not quite meeting accepted standards (e g of morality or good taste) ⟨*a* ~ *joke*⟩

border line *n* a line of demarcation

¹bore *vt* **1** to pierce (as if) with a rotary tool **2** to form or construct by boring ~ *vi* **1a** to make a hole by boring **b** to drill a mine or well **2** to make one's way steadily or laboriously

²bore *n* **1** a hole made (as if) by boring **2a** an interior cylindrical cavity ⟨*the* ~ *of a thermometer*⟩ **b** ¹BARREL 2a **3a** the size of a hole **b** the interior diameter of a tube **c** the diameter of an engine cylinder

³bore *past of* BEAR

⁴bore *n* a tidal flood that moves swiftly as a steep-fronted wave in a channel, estuary, etc

⁵bore *n* a tedious person or thing

⁶bore *vt* to weary by being dull or monotonous – **boring** *adj*, **boringly** *adv*, **boredom** *n*

borehole *n* a hole drilled in the earth to obtain water, oil, etc

borer *n* a tool used for boring

boric acid *n* a white solid acid used esp as a weak antiseptic

born *adj* **1a** brought into existence (as if) by birth **b** by birth; native ⟨*British-born*⟩ **2** having a specified character or situation from birth ⟨*a* ~ *leader*⟩ ⟨*nobly* ~⟩

borne *past part of* BEAR

boron *n* a trivalent metalloid element found in nature only in combination – **boronic** *adj*

borough *n* **1** a British urban constituency **2a** a municipal corporation in certain states of the USA **b** any of the 5 political divisions of New York City

borrow *vt* **1** to take or receive with the intention of returning ⟨~ *a book*⟩ **2a** to appropriate for one's own use **b** to copy or imitate **3** to take (1) from a figure of the minuend in subtraction and add it as 10 to the next lowest figure ~ *vi* to borrow sthg ⟨*English* ~s *from other languages*⟩ – **borrower** *n*

borscht *n* a soup made primarily from beetroots and served hot or cold, often with sour cream

borstal *n, often cap, Br* a penal institution for young offenders

borzoi *n* any of a breed of large long-haired dogs developed in Russia, esp for pursuing wolves

bosh *n* nonsense – infml

¹bosom n **1** the front of the human chest; *esp* the female breasts **2a** the breast considered as the centre of secret thoughts and emotions **b** close relationship ⟨*in the ~ of her family*⟩ **3** the part of a garment covering the breast

²bosom adj close, intimate ⟨*~ friends*⟩

bosomy adj having large breasts

¹boss n **1a** a protuberant part or body ⟨*a ~ of granite*⟩ ⟨*a ~ on an animal's horn*⟩ **b** a raised ornamentation **c** a carved ornament concealing the intersection of the ribs of a vault or panelled ceiling **2** the enlarged part of a shaft, esp on which a wheel is mounted

²boss n **1** one who exercises control or authority; *specif* one who directs or supervises workers **2** a politician who controls a party organization (e g in the USA)

³boss vt **1** to act as director or supervisor of **2** ORDER 2a – often + *about* or *around* USE infml

boss-eyed adj *Br* having a squint; cross-eyed – infml

bossy adj domineering, dictatorial – infml – **bossiness** n

bosun n a boatswain

botanize, -ise vi to collect plants for botanical investigation; *also* to study plants, esp on a field trip

botany n **1** a branch of biology dealing with plant life **2a** the plant life (of a region) **b** the properties and life phenomena exhibited by a plant, plant type, or plant group – **botanist** n, **botanic** adj, **botanical** adj, **botanically** adv

¹botch vt **1** to repair, patch, or assemble in a makeshift or inept way **2** to foul up hopelessly; bungle USE infml – **botcher** n

²botch n **1** sthg botched; a mess **2** a clumsy patchwork USE infml – **botchy** adj

¹both adj being the 2; affecting or involving the one as well as the other ⟨*~ his feet*⟩

²both pron pl in constr the one as well as the other ⟨*~ of the books*⟩ ⟨*we're ~ well*⟩

³both conj – used to indicate and stress the inclusion of each of 2 or more things specified by coordinated words or word groups ⟨*she ~ speaks and writes Swahili*⟩

¹bother vt **1** to cause to be troubled or perplexed **2a** to annoy or inconvenience **b** – used as a mild interjection of annoyance ~ vi **1** to feel mild concern or anxiety **2** to take pains; take the trouble

²bother n **1** (a cause of) mild discomfort, annoyance, or worry **2** unnecessary fussing **3** a minor disturbance ⟨*there was a spot of ~ here today*⟩

botheration n **1** bothering or being bothered **2** – used as a mild interjection of annoyance

bothersome adj causing bother; annoying

¹bottle n **1a** a rigid or semirigid container, esp for liquids, usu of glass or plastic, with a comparatively narrow neck or mouth **b** the contents of a bottle **2a** intoxicating drink – slang ⟨*hit the ~*⟩ **b** bottled milk used to feed infants **3** *Br* NERVE 3b – slang – **bottleful** n

²bottle vt bottling **1** to put into a bottle **2** *Br* to preserve (e g fruit) by storage in glass jars – **bottler** n

bottle-feed vt bottle-fed to feed (e g an infant) by means of a bottle

bottle green adj or n very dark green

bottleneck n **1a** a narrow stretch of road **b** a point or situation where free movement or progress is held up **2** a style of guitar playing using an object (e g a metal bar or the neck of a bottle) pressed against the strings to produce the effect of one note sliding into another

bottle up vt to confine as if in a bottle; restrain ⟨*bottling up their anger*⟩

¹bottom n **1a** the underside of sthg **b** a surface on which sthg rests **c** the buttocks, rump **2** the ground below a body of water **3** the part of a ship's hull lying below the water **4a** the lowest, deepest, or farthest part or place **b** the bottom – usu + *out* – **bottomer** n

³bottom adj **1** of or situated at the bottom **2** frequenting the bottom ⟨*~ fishes*⟩ – **bottommost**

bottom drawer n, *Br* (a drawer for storing) a young woman's collection of clothes and esp household articles, kept in anticipation of her marriage

bottomless adj **1** extremely deep **2** boundless, unlimited – **bottomlessly** adv, **bottomlessness** n

botulism n acute often fatal food poisoning caused by botulin in (preserved) food

boudoir n a woman's dressing room, bedroom, or private sitting room

bouffant adj puffed out ⟨*a ~ hairstyle*⟩ ⟨*~ sleeves*⟩

bougainvillaea n any of a genus of ornamental tropical American woody climbing plants with brilliant purple or red floral bracts

bough n a (main) branch of a tree – **boughed** adj

bought past of BUY

bouillabaisse n a highly seasoned fish stew made with at least 2 kinds of fish

bouillon n a thin clear soup made usu from lean beef

boulder n a large stone or mass of rock

boulevard n a broad avenue, usu lined by trees

¹bounce vt **1** to cause to rebound ⟨*~ a ball*⟩ **2** to return (a cheque) as not good because of lack of funds in the payer's account – infml ~ vi **1** to rebound after striking **2** to move violently, noisily, or with a springing step ⟨*~ into the room*⟩ **3** to be returned by a bank as not good – infml

²bounce n **1a** a sudden leap or bound **b** a rebound **2** verve, liveliness

bounce back vi to recover quickly from a blow or defeat

bouncer n **1** a man employed in a public place to restrain or remove disorderly people **2** a fast intimidatory short-pitched delivery of a cricket ball that passes or hits the batsman at above chest height after bouncing

bouncing adj enjoying good health; robust

bouncy adj **1** buoyant, exuberant **2** that bounces readily – **bouncily** adv

¹bound adj going or intending to go ⟨*~ for home*⟩ ⟨*college-bound*⟩

²bound n **1** a limiting line; a boundary **2** sthg that limits or restrains ⟨*beyond the ~s of decency*⟩ USE usu pl with sing. meaning

³bound vt **1** to set limits to **2** to form the boundary of USE usu pass

⁴bound adj **1a** confined ⟨*desk-bound*⟩ **b** certain, sure *to* ⟨*~ to rain soon*⟩ **2** placed under legal or moral obligation ⟨*I'm ~ to say*⟩ ⟨*duty-bound*⟩ **3** held in chemical or physical combination ⟨*~ water in a molecule*⟩ **4** always occurring in combination with another linguistic form (e g *un-* in *unknown* and *-er* in *speaker*)

⁵bound n **1** a leap, jump **2** a bounce

⁶bound vi **1** to move by leaping **2** to rebound, bounce

boundary n **1** sthg, esp a dividing line, that indicates or fixes a limit or extent **2a** the marked limits of a cricket field **b** (the score of 4 or 6 made by) a stroke in cricket that sends the ball over the boundary

bounden *adj* made obligatory; binding – esp in *bounden duty*

bounder *n* a cad – not now in vogue

boundless *adj* limitless – **boundlessly** *adv*, **boundlessness** *n*

bounteous *adj* giving or given freely – **bounteously** *adv*, **bounteousness** *n*

bountiful *adj* **1** generous, liberal **2** abundant, plentiful ⟨*a ~ harvest*⟩ – **bountifully** *adv*, **bountifulness** *n*

bounty *n* **1** generosity **2** sthg given generously **3a** a financial inducement or reward, esp when offered by a government for some act or service **b** a payment to encourage the killing of vermin or dangerous animals

bouquet *n* **1** a bunch of flowers fastened together **2** a distinctive and characteristic fragrance (e g of wine)

bouquet garni *n* a small bunch of herbs (e g thyme, parsley, and a bay leaf) for use in flavouring stews and soups

bourbon *n* **1** *cap* a member of a royal dynasty who ruled in France, Spain, etc **2** a whisky distilled from a mash made up of not less than 51 per cent maize plus malt and rye **3** *often cap, chiefly NAm* an extreme political reactionary – **bourbonism** *n, often cap*

bourgeois *n, pl* **bourgeois 1** a middle-class person **2** one whose behaviour and views are influenced by bourgeois values or interests **3** *pl* the bourgeoisie

bourgeois *adj* **1** middle-class **2** marked by a narrow-minded concern for material interests and respectability **3** capitalist

bourgeoisie *n sing or pl in constr* MIDDLE CLASS

bourn, bourne *n* a small stream

bourn, bourne *n, archaic* a boundary, limit

bourse *n* EXCHANGE 4a; *specif* a European stock exchange

bout *n* **1** a spell of activity ⟨*a ~ of work*⟩ **2** an athletic match (e g of boxing) **3** an outbreak or attack of illness, fever, etc

boutique *n* a small fashionable shop selling specialized goods; *also* a small shop within a large department store

bouzouki *also* **bousouki** *n* a long-necked Greek stringed instrument that resembles a mandolin

bovine *adj* **1** of oxen or cows **2** like an ox or cow (e g in being slow, stolid, or dull)

Bovril *trademark* – used for a concentrated beef extract

bovver *n, Br* rowdy or violent disturbance; aggro ⟨*~ boys*⟩

bow *vi* **1** to submit, yield **2** to bend the head, body, or knee in respect, submission, or greeting ~ *vt* **1** to incline (e g the head), esp in respect, submission, or shame **2** to express by bowing – **bow and scrape** to act in an obsequious manner

bow *n* a bending of the head or body in respect, submission, or greeting

bow *n* **1** a bend, arch **2** a strip of wood, fibreglass, or other flexible material held bent by a strong cord connecting the 2 ends and used to shoot an arrow **3** an often ornamental slipknot (e g for tying a shoelace) **4** (a stroke made with) a resilient wooden rod with horsehairs stretched from end to end, used in playing an instrument of the viol or violin family

bow *vb* **1** to (cause to) bend into a curve **2** to play (a stringed instrument) with a bow

bow *n* **1** the forward part of a ship – often pl with sing. meaning **2** ²BOWMAN; *specif* one who rows in the front end of a boat

bowdlerize, -ise *vt* to expurgate (e g a book) by omitting or modifying parts considered vulgar – **bowdlerizer** *n*, **bowdlerization** *n*

bowel *n* **1** (a specified division of) the intestine or gut – usu pl with sing. meaning **2** *pl* the innermost parts ⟨*~s of the earth*⟩ – **bowelless** *adj*

bower *n* **1** an attractive dwelling or retreat **2** a (garden) shelter made with tree boughs or vines twisted together **3** a boudoir – poetic – **bowery** *adj*

bower *n* a ship's principal anchor carried in the bows

bowie knife *n* a stout hunting knife with a sharpened part on the back edge curved concavely to the point

bowl *n* **1** any of various round hollow vessels used esp for holding liquids or food or for mixing food **2** the contents of a bowl **3a** the hollow of a spoon or tobacco pipe **b** the receptacle of a toilet **4a** a bowl-shaped geographical region or formation **b** *NAm* a bowl-shaped structure; *esp* a sports stadium – **bowled** *adj*, **bowlful** *n*

bowl *n* **1** a ball used in bowls that is weighted or shaped to give it a bias **2** *pl but sing in constr* a game played typically outdoors on a green, in which bowls are rolled at a target jack in an attempt to bring them nearer to it than the opponent's bowls

bowl *vi* **1a** to participate in a game of bowling **b** to play or roll a ball in bowls or bowling **c** to play as a bowler in cricket **2** to travel in a vehicle smoothly and rapidly – often + *along* ~ *vt* **1a** to roll (a ball) in bowling **b** to score by bowling ⟨*~s 150*⟩ **2a** to deliver (a ball) to a batsman in cricket **b** to dismiss (a batsman in cricket) by breaking the wicket – used with reference to a bowled ball or a bowler

bowlegged *adj* having legs that are bowed outwards at the knees – **bowlegs** *n pl*

bowler *n* the person who bowls in a team sport; *specif* a member of the fielding side who bowls (as a specialist) the ball in cricket

bowler, bowler hat *n* a stiff felt hat with a rounded crown and a narrow brim

bowline *n* **1** a rope attached to a square sail that is used to keep the windward edge of the sail taut and at a steady angle to the wind **2** a knot used to form a non-slipping loop at the end of a rope

bowling *n* any of several games in which balls are rolled at 1 or more objects

bowling alley *n* (a building or room containing) a long narrow enclosure or lane with a smooth usu wooden floor for bowling or playing skittles

bowling green *n* a smooth close-cut area of turf for playing bowls

bowl over *vt* **1** to strike with a swiftly moving object **2** to overwhelm with surprise

bowman *n* an archer

bowman *n* a boatman, oarsman, etc in the front of a boat

bow out *vi* to retire, withdraw

bowsprit *n* a spar projecting forwards from the bow of a ship

bow tie *n* a short tie fastened in a bow

bow window *n* a curved bay window

bowwow *n* **1** the bark of a dog – often used imitatively **2** a dog – used esp by or to children

box *n, pl* **box, boxes** any of several evergreen shrubs or small trees used esp for hedges

box *n* **1a** a rigid container having 4 sides, a bottom, and a cover **b** the contents of a box **2a** a small compartment (e g for a group of spectators in a theatre) **b(1)** PENALTY AREA **(2)** PENALTY BOX **3a** a boxlike protective case (e g for machinery) **b** a shield to protect the genitals, worn esp by batsmen and wicketkeepers in cricket **c** a structure that contains a telephone for use by members of a specified organization ⟨*police ~*⟩ ⟨*AA or RAC ~*⟩ **4** a small simple sheltering or enclosing structure **5** *Br* a gift given

box 76

to tradesmen at Christmas **6** *Br television; specif* a television set – + *the*; *infml* – **boxful** *n*, **boxy** *adj*, **boxiness** *n*

³**box** *vt* **1** to provide with a box **2** to enclose (as if) in a box – + *in* or *up* **3** to hem in (e g an opponent in soccer) – usu + *in* – **box the compass 1** to name the 32 points of the compass in their order **2** to make a complete reversal

⁴**box** *n* a punch or slap, esp on the ear

⁵**box** *vt* **1** to slap (e g the ears) with the hand **2** to engage in boxing with ~ *vi* to engage in boxing

Box and Cox *adv or adj, Br* alternating; IN TURN

¹**boxer** *n* one who engages in the sport of boxing

²**boxer** *n* a compact medium-sized short-haired dog of a breed originating in Germany

Boxer *n* a member of a Chinese secret society which was opposed to foreign influence in China and whose rebellion was suppressed in 1900

boxing *n* the art of attack and defence with the fists practised as a sport

Boxing Day *n* December 26, observed as a public holiday in Britain (apart from Scotland) and elsewhere in the Commonwealth, on which service workers (e g postmen) were traditionally given Christmas boxes

boxing glove *n* a heavily padded leather mitten worn in boxing

box kite *n* a tailless kite consisting of 2 or more open-ended connected boxes

box number *n* the number of a box or pigeon hole at a newspaper or post office where arrangements are made for replies to advertisements or other mail to be sent

box office *n* **1** an office (e g in a theatre) where tickets of admission are sold **2** sthg that enhances ticket sales ⟨*the publicity is all good* ~⟩

box spanner *n* a spanner that is shaped to enclose a nut, bolt head, etc

boxwood *n* the very close-grained heavy tough hard wood of the box tree

¹**boy** *n* **1a** a male child from birth to puberty **b** a son **c** an immature male; a youth **d** a boyfriend **2** a fellow, person ⟨*the* ~*s at the office*⟩ **3** a male servant – sometimes taken to be offensive – **boyhood** *n*, **boyish** *adj*, **boyishly** *adv*, **boyishness** *n*

²**boy** *interj, chiefly NAm* – used to express esp excitement or surprise

boycott *vt* to engage in a concerted refusal to have dealings with (e g a person, shop, or organization), usu to express disapproval or to force acceptance of certain conditions – **boycott** *n*, **boycotter** *n*

boyfriend *n* **1** a frequent or regular male companion of a girl or woman **2** a male lover

boy scout *n* SCOUT **4** – no longer used technically

bra *n, pl* **bras** a woman's closely fitting undergarment with cups for supporting the breasts

¹**brace** *n, pl* **braces**, (*1*) **braces**, *after a determiner* **brace 1** two of a kind; a pair ⟨*several* ~ *of quail*⟩ **2** sthg (e g a clasp) that connects or fastens **3** a crank-shaped instrument for turning a drilling bit **4a** a diagonal piece of structural material that serves to strengthen **b** a rope attached to a yard on a ship that swings the yard horizontally to trim the sail **c** *pl* straps worn over the shoulders to hold up trousers **d** an appliance for supporting a weak leg or other body part **e** a dental fitting worn to correct irregular teeth **5a** a mark { or } used to connect words or items to be considered together **b** (this mark connecting) 2 or more musical staves the parts of which are to be performed simultaneously

²**brace** *vt* **1a** to prepare for use by making taut **b** to prepare, steel ⟨~ *yourself for the shock*⟩ **2** to turn (a sail

yard) by means of a brace **3** to provide or support with a brace ⟨*heavily* ~d *because of polio*⟩

bracelet *n* **1** an ornamental band or chain worn round the wrist **2** sthg (e g handcuffs) resembling a bracelet

brace up *vb* to (cause to) have more courage, spirit, and cheerfulness

bracing *adj* refreshing, invigorating ⟨*a* ~ *breeze*⟩

bracken *n* (a dense growth of) a common large coarse fern of esp moorland, that is poisonous to grazing animals

¹**bracket** *n* **1** an overhanging projecting fixture or member that is designed to support a vertical load or strengthen an angle **2a** PARENTHESIS 1b **b** either of a pair of marks ( ) used in writing and printing to enclose matter or in mathematics and logic to show that a complex expression should be treated as a single unit **c** ANGLE BRACKET **d** BRACE 5b **3** (the distance between) a pair of shots fired usu in front of and beyond a target to aid in range-finding **4** any of a graded series of income groups ⟨*the £20,000 income* ~⟩

²**bracket** *vt* **1** to place (as if) within brackets **2** to provide or fasten with brackets **3** to put in the same category; associate – usu + *together* **4a** to get a range by firing in front of and behind (a target) **b** to establish a margin on either side of (e g an estimation)

brackish *adj* slightly salty ⟨~ *water*⟩ – **brackishness** *n*

bract *n* **1** a usu small leaf near a flower or floral axis **2** a leaf borne on a floral axis – **bracteal** *adj*, **bracteate** *adj*, **bracted** *adj*

bradawl *n* an awl; *esp* one used by a woodworker

brae *n, chiefly Scot* a hillside, esp along a river

¹**brag** *n* a card game resembling poker

²**brag** *vb* -gg- to talk or assert boastfully – **bragger** *n*

braggadocio *n* empty boasting

braggart *n* a loud arrogant boaster – **braggart** *adj*

Brahman *n* **1a** a Hindu of the highest caste traditionally assigned to the priesthood **b** the impersonal ground of all being in Hinduism **2** any of an Indian breed of humped cattle; *also* a large vigorous heat-resistant and tick-resistant animal developed in the USA by interbreeding Indian cattle – **Brahmanic** *adj*

¹**braid** *vt* **1** *chiefly NAm* PLAIT 2 **2** to ornament, esp with ribbon or braid – **braider** *n*

²**braid** *n* **1** a narrow piece of fabric, esp plaited cord or ribbon, used for trimming **2** *chiefly NAm* a length of plaited hair

braille *n, often cap* a system of writing or printing for the blind that uses characters made up of raised dots

¹**brain** *n* **1a** the portion of the vertebrate central nervous system that constitutes the organ of thought and neural coordination, is made up of neurons and supporting and nutritive structures, is enclosed within the skull, and is continuous with the spinal cord **b** a nervous centre in invertebrates comparable in position and function to the vertebrate brain **2a**(1) an intellect, mind ⟨*has a good* ~⟩ (2) intellectual endowment; intelligence – often pl with sing. meaning ⟨*plenty of* ~s *in that family*⟩ **b**(1) a very intelligent or intellectual person (2) the chief planner of an organization or enterprise – usu pl with sing. meaning but sing. in constr **3** an automatic device (e g a computer) that performs 1 or more of the functions of the human brain for control or computation – **on the brain** as an obsession; continually in mind ⟨*I've got that tune* on the brain *again*⟩

²**brain** *vt* **1** to kill by smashing the skull **2** to hit hard on the head – *infml*

brainchild *n* a product of one's creative imagination

brain drain *n the* loss of highly qualified workers and professionals through emigration

-brained *comb form* (*adj, n → adj*) having (such) a brain ⟨*feather*brained⟩

brainless *adj* stupid, foolish – **brainlessly** *adv*, **brainlessness** *n*

brainstorm *n* **1** a fit of insanity **2** *chiefly NAm* BRAIN WAVE 2

brains trust *n sing or pl in constr, chiefly Br* a group of expert advisers, esp assembled to answer questions of immediate or current interest

brainwashing *n* a systematic attempt to instil beliefs into sby, often in place of beliefs already held – **brainwash** *vt*, **brainwash** *n*, **brainwasher** *n*

brain wave *n* **1** a rhythmic fluctuation of voltage between parts of the brain **2** a sudden bright idea

brainy *adj* intelligent, clever – *infml* – **braininess** *n*

braise *vt* to cook (e g meat) slowly by first sautéeing in hot fat and then simmering gently in very little liquid in a closed container

'brake *n* **1** a device for arresting usu rotary motion, esp by friction **2** sthg that slows down or stops movement or activity – **brakeless** *adj*

'brake *vt* to slow or stop by a brake ~ *vi* **1** to operate, manage, or apply a brake, esp on a vehicle **2** to become slowed by a brake

'brake *n* an area of overgrown rough or marshy land – **braky** *adj*

'brake *n* ESTATE CAR

brake horsepower *n* the useful power of an engine as calculated from the resistance to a brake or dynamometer applied to the shaft or flywheel

bramble *n* a rough prickly shrub, esp a blackberry – **brambly** *adj*

bran *n* the broken husk of cereal grain separated from the flour or meal by sifting

branch *n* **1** a secondary shoot or stem (e g a bough) arising from a main axis (e g of a tree) **2a** TRIBUTARY 2 **b** a side road or way **c** a slender projection (e g the tine of an antler) **3** a distinct part of a complex whole: e g **a** a division of a family descending from a particular ancestor **b** a distinct area of knowledge ⟨*pathology is a ~ of medicine*⟩ **c** a division or separate part of an organization – **branched** *adj*, **branchless** *adj*, **branchlet** *n*, **branchy** *adj*

'branch *vi* **1** to put forth branches **2** to spring out (e g from a main stem)

branch out *vi* to extend activities ⟨*the business is branching out all over the state*⟩

'brand *n* **1** a charred piece of wood **2a** a mark made by burning with a hot iron, or with a stamp or stencil, to identify manufacture or quality or to designate ownership (e g of cattle) **b(1)** a mark formerly put on criminals with a hot iron **(2)** a mark of disgrace ⟨*the ~ of poverty*⟩ **3a** a class of goods identified by name as the product of a single firm or manufacturer **b** a characteristic or distinctive kind ⟨*a lively ~ of humour*⟩ **4** a tool used to produce a brand **5** a sword – *poetic*

'brand *vt* **1** to mark with a brand **2** to stigmatize **3** to impress indelibly – **brander** *n*

brandish *vt* to shake or wave (e g a weapon) menacingly or ostentatiously

brand-new *adj* conspicuously new and unused

brandy *n* a spirit distilled from wine or fermented fruit juice ⟨*plum ~*⟩

brandy snap *n* a very thin cylindrical ginger biscuit sometimes flavoured with brandy

brash *n* a mass of fragments (e g of ice)

brash *adj* **1** impetuous, rash **2** uninhibitedly energetic or demonstrative **3** aggressively self-assertive; impudent – **brashly** *adv*, **brashness** *n*

brass *n* **1** an alloy of copper and zinc **2a** *sing or pl in constr* the brass instruments of an orchestra or band **b** a usu brass memorial tablet **c** bright metal fittings or utensils **3** brazen self-assurance **4** *sing or pl in constr* BRASS HATS **5** *chiefly N Eng* money USE (*3, 4, & 5*) *infml* – **brass** *adj*

brass band *n* a band consisting (chiefly) of brass and percussion instruments

brasserie *n* a restaurant that serves beer

brass hat *n* a high-ranking military officer – *infml*

brassiere *n* a bra – *fml*

brass tacks *n pl* details of immediate practical importance – esp in *get down to brass tacks*

brassy *adj* **1** shamelessly bold; brazen **2** resembling brass, esp in colour – **brassily** *adv*, **brassiness** *n*

brat *n* an (ill-mannered) child

bravado *n, pl* **bravadoes, bravados** (a display of) blustering swaggering conduct

'brave *adj* **1** courageous, fearless **2** excellent, splendid ⟨*a ~ new world*⟩ – **bravely** *adv*

'brave *vt* to face or endure with courage

'brave *n* a N American Indian warrior

bravery *n* courage, valour

'bravo *n, pl* **bravos, bravoes** a villain, desperado; *esp* a hired assassin

'bravo *n, pl* **bravos** a shout of approval – often used interjectionally in applauding a performance

Bravo *n* – a communications code word for the letter *b*

bravura *n* **1** a flamboyant brilliant style **2** a musical passage requiring exceptional agility and technical skill in execution **3** a show of daring or brilliance

'brawl *vi* **1** to quarrel or fight noisily **2** *of water* to make a loud confused bubbling sound – **brawler** *n*

'brawl *n* **1** a noisy quarrel or fight **2** a brawling noise

brawn *n* **1a** strong muscles **b** muscular strength **2** pork trimmings, esp the meat from a pig's head, boiled, chopped, and pressed into a mould

brawny *adj* muscular, strong – **brawnily** *adv*, **brawniness** *n*

'bray *vi* to utter the loud harsh cry characteristic of a donkey ~ *vt* to utter or play loudly, harshly, or discordantly – **bray** *n*

'bray *vt* to crush or grind finely

'brazen *adj* **1** resembling or made of brass **2** sounding harsh and loud like struck brass **3** contemptuously bold – **brazenly** *adv*, **brazenness** *n*

'brazen *vt* to face with defiance or impudence – esp in *brazen it out*

'brazier *n* one who works in brass

'brazier *n* a receptacle or stand for holding burning coals

'breach *n* **1** infraction or violation (e g of a law, obligation, or standard) ⟨*~ of contract*⟩ **2** a gap (e g in a wall) made by battering **3** a break in customarily friendly relations **4** a leap, esp of a whale out of water

'breach *vt* to make a breach in ⟨*~ the city walls*⟩ **2** to break, violate ⟨*~ an agreement*⟩

breach of promise *n* violation of a promise, esp to marry

breach of the peace *n* an instance of disorderly conduct

'bread *n* **1** a food consisting essentially of flour or meal which is baked and usu leavened, esp with yeast **2** food, sustenance ⟨*our daily ~*⟩ **3a** livelihood ⟨*earns his daily ~ as a labourer*⟩ **b** money – *slang* – **bread upon the waters** resources chanced or charitable deeds performed without expectation of return

'bread *vt* to cover with breadcrumbs ⟨*a ~ed pork chop*⟩

bread-and-butter *adj* **1a** basic, fundamental ⟨*wages, housing, and other ~ issues*⟩ **b** dependable, routine ⟨*the ~ repertoire of an orchestra*⟩ **2** sent or given as thanks for hospitality ⟨*a ~ letter*⟩
bread and butter *n* a means of sustenance or livelihood
breadbasket *n* the stomach – slang
¹breadcrumb *n* a small fragment of bread
²breadcrumb *vt* ²BREAD
breadfruit *n* the large starchy fruit of a tropical tree that has white flesh with a breadlike texture
breadline *n* **1** *Br* the level of income required for subsistence **2** *chiefly NAm* a queue of people waiting to receive food given in charity
breadth *n* **1** distance from side to side **2a** sthg of full width ⟨*a ~ of cloth*⟩ **b** a wide expanse ⟨*~s of grass*⟩ **3a** catholicity, scope **b** liberality of views or taste
breadthways, breadthwise *adv or adj* in the direction of the breadth ⟨*a course of bricks laid ~*⟩
breadwinner *n* one whose wages are a family's livelihood – breadwinning *n*
¹break *vb* broke; broken *vt* **1a** to separate into parts with suddenness or violence **b** to fracture ⟨*~ an arm*⟩ **c** to rupture ⟨*~ the skin*⟩ **2** to violate, transgress ⟨*~ the law*⟩ **3a** to force a way through or into ⟨*the silence was broken by a dog barking*⟩ **b** to escape by force from ⟨*he broke jail*⟩ **4** to make or effect by cutting or forcing through ⟨*~ a trail through the woods*⟩ **5** to disrupt the order or compactness of ⟨*~ ranks*⟩ **6a** to defeat utterly; destroy **b** to crush the spirit of **c(1)** to train (an animal, esp a horse) for the service of human beings **(2)** to inure, accustom ⟨*a horse broken to the saddle*⟩ **d** to exhaust in health, strength, or capacity **7a** to ruin financially **b** to reduce in rank **8a** to reduce the force or intensity of ⟨*the bushes will ~ his fall*⟩ **b** to cause failure and discontinuance of (a strike) by measures outside bargaining processes **9** to exceed, surpass ⟨*~ a record*⟩ ⟨*~ the speed limit*⟩ **10** to ruin the prospects of ⟨*could make or ~ her career*⟩ **11a** to stop or interrupt **b** to open and bring about suspension of operation ⟨*~ an electric circuit*⟩ **c** to destroy the unity or completeness of ⟨*they must be kept together; I don't want to ~ the collection*⟩ **d** to destroy the uniformity of ⟨*the straight line of the horizon was broken by a rocky outcrop*⟩ **12** to cause to discontinue a habit ⟨*tried to ~ him of smoking*⟩ **13** to make known; tell ⟨*~ the bad news gently*⟩ **14a** to solve (a code or cipher system); CRACK 3a **b** to demonstrate the falsity of (an alibi) **15** to split into smaller units, parts, or processes; divide ⟨*~ a £10 note*⟩ – often + up or down **16** to open the operating mechanism of (a gun) ~ *vi* **1** to escape with sudden forceful effort – often + out or away ⟨*~ out of jail*⟩ ⟨*broke away from the main bunch*⟩ **2a** to come into being, esp suddenly ⟨*day was ~ing*⟩ ⟨*the storm broke*⟩ **b** to come to pass; occur ⟨*report news stories as they ~*⟩ **3** to effect a penetration ⟨*~ through enemy lines*⟩ **4** to take a different course; depart ⟨*~ from tradition*⟩ **5** to make a sudden dash ⟨*~ for cover*⟩ **6** to separate after a clinch in boxing **7** to come apart or split into pieces; burst, shatter **8** *of a wave* to curl over and disintegrate in surf or foam **9** *of weather* to change suddenly, esp after a fine spell **10** to give way in disorderly retreat **11a** to fail in health, strength, or control ⟨*may ~ under questioning*⟩ **b** to become inoperative because of damage, wear, or strain **12** to end a relationship, agreement, etc *with* **13** *esp of a ball bowled in cricket* to change direction of forward travel on bouncing **14** *of a voice* to alter sharply in tone, pitch, or intensity; *esp* to shift abruptly from one register to another ⟨*her voice ~ing with emotion*⟩ ⟨*boys' voices ~ at puberty*⟩ **15** *of a horse* to fail to keep a prescribed gait **16** to interrupt

one's activity for a brief period ⟨*~ for lunch*⟩ **17** to make the opening shot of a game of snooker, billiards, or pool **18a** to fold, lift, or come apart at a seam, groove, or joint **b** *of cream* to separate during churning into liquid and fat **19** *chiefly NAm* to happen, develop ⟨*for the team to succeed, everything has to ~ right*⟩ – **breakable** *adj or n* – **break a leg** to be successful in a performance – used in the theatre to wish another luck – **break cover** to emerge abruptly from a hiding place ⟨*the hunted fox broke cover*⟩ – **break even** to achieve a balance between expenditure and income; *esp* to recover precisely what one spends ⟨*the church fete only broke even this year*⟩ – **break into 1a** to begin abruptly ⟨*the horse breaks into a gallop*⟩ **b** to give voice or expression to abruptly ⟨*she broke into song*⟩ ⟨*broke into a laugh*⟩ **2** to enter by force ⟨*thieves broke into the house*⟩ **3** to make entry or entrance into ⟨*trying to break into show business*⟩ **4** to interrupt ⟨*kept breaking into the conversation*⟩ – **break new ground** to make or show new discoveries; pioneer ⟨*breaking new ground in genetic engineering*⟩ – **break service/break someone's service** to win a game against the server (e g in tennis) – **break someone's heart** to cause sby heartbreak – **break the back** to do or overcome the largest or hardest part – **break the ice** to overcome initial reserve – **break wind** to expel gas from the intestine through the anus
²break *n* **1** an act or action of breaking **2a** a condition produced (as if) by breaking; a gap ⟨*a ~ in the clouds*⟩ **b** a rupture in previously good relations **c** a gap in an otherwise continuous electric circuit **3** the action or act of breaking in, out, or forth ⟨*a jail ~*⟩ **4** a dash, rush ⟨*make a ~ for it*⟩ **5** the act of separating after a clinch in boxing **6a** a change or interruption in a continuous process or trend ⟨*it makes a ~*⟩ **b** a change from the status quo ⟨*a sharp ~ with tradition*⟩ **c** a respite from work or duty; *specif* a daily pause for play and refreshment at school **d** a planned interruption in a radio or television programme ⟨*a ~ for the commercial*⟩ **7a** the opening shot in a game of snooker, billiards, or pool **b** change in direction of forward travel, esp of a cricket ball on bouncing because of spin imparted by the bowler **c** a slow ball bowled in cricket that deviates in a specified direction on bouncing ⟨*an off ~*⟩ **d** the act or an instance of breaking an opponent's service in tennis **e** failure of a horse to maintain a prescribed gait **f** (a score made by) a sequence of successful shots or strokes (e g in snooker) **8** a notable variation in pitch, intensity, or tone in the voice **9** a place, situation, or time at which a break occurs: e g **a** the point where one musical register changes to another **b** a short ornamental passage inserted between phrases in jazz **10a** a stroke of esp good luck **b** an opportunity, chance ⟨*give me a ~*⟩
breakage *n* **1** sthg broken – usu pl **2** allowance for things broken (e g in transit)
¹breakaway *n* **1** sby or sthg that breaks away **2** a breaking away (e g from a group or tradition); a withdrawing
²breakaway *adj* **1** favouring independence from an affiliation; withdrawing ⟨*a ~ faction formed a new party*⟩ **2** *chiefly NAm* made to break or bend easily ⟨*~ road signs for highway safety*⟩
breakdown *n* **1** a failure to function **2** a physical, mental, or nervous collapse **3** failure to progress or have effect ⟨*a ~ of negotiations*⟩ **4** the process of decomposing ⟨*~ of food during digestion*⟩ **5** a division into categories; a classification **6** a whole analysed into parts; *specif* an account in which the transactions are recorded under various categories
break down *vt* **1a** to cause to fall or collapse by breaking

or shattering **b** to make ineffective ⟨break down *legal barriers*⟩ **c** to put an end to; suppress ⟨*he tried to* break down *their opposition*⟩ **2a** to divide into parts or categories **b** to separate into simpler substances **c** to take apart, esp for storage or shipment ~ *vi* **1a** to become inoperative through breakage or wear **b** to become inapplicable or ineffective; deteriorate ⟨*relations began to* break down⟩ **2a** to be susceptible to analysis or subdivision ⟨*the outline* breaks down *into 3 parts*⟩ **b** to undergo decomposition **3** to lose one's composure completely ⟨*he* broke down *and wept*⟩

breaker *n* **1** a wave breaking into foam **2** a user of Citizens' Band radio – *slang*

breaker *n* a small water cask

break-even *adj or n* (of or being) the point at which profit equals loss

breakfast *n* (food prepared for) the first meal of the day, esp when taken in the morning – **breakfast** *vb*, **breakfaster** *n*

break in *vi* **1** to enter a house or building by force **2a** to interrupt a conversation **b** to intrude ~ *vt* **1** to accustom to a certain activity ⟨break in *a new reporter*⟩ **2** to use or wear until comfortable or working properly

breakneck *adj* extremely dangerous ⟨~ *speed*⟩

break off *vi* **1** to become detached; separate **2** to stop abruptly ⟨break off *in the middle of a sentence*⟩ ~ *vt* to discontinue ⟨break off *diplomatic relations*⟩

breakout *n* a violent or forceful breaching of a restraint (e g imprisonment or siege)

break out *vi* **1** to become affected with a skin eruption ⟨broke out *in a rash*⟩ **2** to develop or emerge with suddenness and force ⟨*a riot* broke out⟩ **3** to escape ~ *vt* **1** to take from shipboard stowage ready for use **2** to unfurl (a flag) at the mast

breakthrough *n* **1** an act or point of breaking through an obstruction **2** an attack that penetrates enemy lines **3** a sudden advance, esp in knowledge or technique ⟨*a medical* ~⟩

breakup *n* **1** a dissolution, disruption ⟨*the* ~ *of a marriage*⟩ **2** a division into smaller units **3** *chiefly Can* the spring thaw

break up *vt* **1** to disrupt the continuity of ⟨*too many footnotes can* break up *a text*⟩ **2** to decompose ⟨break up *a chemical*⟩ **3** to bring to an end ⟨*it* broke up *their marriage*⟩ **4a** to break into pieces (e g for salvage); scrap **b** to crumble **5a** to distress ⟨*his wife's death really* broke *him* up⟩ – *infml* **b** *chiefly NAm* to cause to laugh heartily – *infml* ~ *vi* **1a** to come to an end ⟨*their partnership* broke up⟩ **b** to separate, split up ⟨*Simon and Mary have* broken up⟩ **2** to lose morale or composure ⟨*he is likely to* break up *under attack*⟩; *also* to give way to laughter **3** *Br, of a school* to disband for the holidays

breakwater *n* an offshore structure (e g a wall) used to protect a harbour or beach from the force of waves

bream *n, pl* bream, esp for *different types* breams **1** any of various European freshwater fishes related to the carps and minnows **2** any of various freshwater sunfishes

bream *vt* ³GRAVE

breast *n* **1** either of 2 protuberant milk-producing glandular organs situated on the front of the chest in the human female and some other mammals; *broadly* a discrete mammary gland **2** the fore part of the body between the neck and the abdomen **3** sthg (e g a swelling or curve) resembling a breast **4** the seat of emotion and thought; the bosom – *fml*

breast *vt* **1** to contend with resolutely; confront ⟨~ *the rush-hour traffic*⟩ **2a** to meet or lean against with the breast or front ⟨*the swimmer* ~ed *the waves*⟩ **b** to thrust

the chest against ⟨*the sprinter* ~ed *the tape*⟩ **3** *chiefly Br* to climb, ascend

breastbone *n* the sternum

breast-feed *vt* to feed (a baby) with the milk from the breast rather than a bottle

breastplate *n* **1** a metal plate worn as defensive armour for the chest **2** PLASTRON 2

breaststroke *n* a swimming stroke executed on the front by thrusting the arms forwards while kicking outwards and backwards with the legs, then sweeping the arms backwards – **breaststroker** *n*

breastwork *n* a temporary fortification, usu consisting of a low parapet

breath *n* **1a** a slight fragrance or smell **b** a slight indication; a suggestion ⟨*the faintest* ~ *of scandal*⟩ **2a** the faculty of breathing **b** an act of breathing **c** opportunity or time to breathe; respite **3** a slight movement of air **4** air inhaled and exhaled in breathing **5** spirit, animation – **out of breath** breathing very rapidly (e g from strenuous exercise) – **under one's breath** in a whisper

breathalyse *also* **breathalyze** *vt* to test (e g a driver) for the level of alcohol in exhaled breath

breathalyser *also* **breathalyzer** *n* a device used to test the alcohol content in the blood of a motorist, usu consisting of a plastic bag into which the subject blows through crystals which turn green if the alcohol level is too high

breathe *vi* **1** to draw air into and expel it from the lungs **2** to live **3** to pause and rest before continuing **4** *of wind* to blow softly **5** *of wine* to be exposed to the beneficial effects of air after being kept in an airtight container (e g a bottle) ~ *vt* **1a** to send out by exhaling ⟨~d *garlic over him*⟩ **b** to instil (as if) by breathing ⟨~ *new life into the movement*⟩ **2a** to utter, express ⟨*don't* ~ *a word of it to anyone*⟩ **b** to make manifest; display ⟨*the novel* ~s *despair*⟩ **3** to allow (e g a horse) to rest after exertion **4** to inhale – **breathe down someone's neck** to keep sby under constant or too close surveillance ⟨*parents always* breathing down his neck⟩ – **breathe easily/freely** to enjoy relief (e g from pressure or danger)

breather *n* **1** a small vent in an otherwise airtight enclosure (e g a crankcase) **2** a break in activity for rest or relief – *infml*

breathing *n* either of the marks ' and ' used in writing Greek to indicate aspiration or its absence

breathing space *n* a pause in a period of activity, esp for rest and recuperation

breathless *adj* **1** not breathing; esp holding one's breath due to excitement or suspense **2a** gasping; OUT OF BREATH **b** gripping, intense ⟨~ *tension*⟩ **3** without any breeze; stuffy ⟨*a* ~ *summer's afternoon*⟩ – **breathlessly** *adv*, **breathlessness** *n*

breathtaking *adj* **1** making one breathless **2** exciting, thrilling ⟨*a* ~ *stock car race*⟩ – **breathtakingly** *adv*

breathy *adj* characterized or accompanied by the audible passage of breath – **breathily** *adv*, **breathiness** *n*

breech *n* **1** the buttocks **2** the part of a firearm at the rear of the barrel

breeches *n pl* **1** knee-length trousers, usu closely fastened at the lower edges **2** jodhpurs that are baggy at the thigh and close fitting and fastened with buttons from the knee to the ankle

breeches buoy *n* a seat in the form of a pair of canvas breeches hung from a life buoy running on a rope leading to a place of safety for use in rescue at sea

breechloader *n* a firearm that is loaded at the breech – **breech-loading** *adj*

¹**breed** *vb* bred *vt* **1a** to produce (offspring) by hatching or gestation **b** to rear; BRING UP 1 ⟨*born and* bred *in Somer-*

set⟩ **2** to produce, engender ⟨*despair often* ~s *violence*⟩ **3** to propagate (plants or animals) sexually and usu under controlled conditions **4** to inculcate by training ⟨~ *good behaviour*⟩ **5** to produce (a fissile element) in a nuclear chain reaction ~ *vi* **1** to produce offspring by sexual union **2** to propagate animals or plants – **breeder** *n*

²**breed** *n* **1** a group of animals or plants, often specially selected, visibly similar in most characteristics **2** race, lineage **3** class, kind ⟨*a new* ~ *of radicals*⟩

breeding *n* **1** ancestry **2** behaviour; *esp* that showing good manners **3** the sexual propagation of plants or animals

breeding ground *n* a place or set of circumstances favourable to the propagation of certain ideas, movements, etc

¹**breeze** *n* **1** a light gentle wind; *also* a wind of between 4 and 31 mph **2** a slight disturbance or quarrel – infml **3** chiefly *NAm* sthg easily done; a cinch – infml – **breezeless** *adj*

²**breeze** *vi* **1** to come in or into, or move along, swiftly and airily ⟨*she* ~d *in as if nothing had happened*⟩ **2** to make progress quickly and easily ⟨~ *through the books*⟩ – infml

³**breeze** *n* ashy residue from the making of coke or charcoal

breeze-block *n* a rectangular building block made of breeze mixed with sand and cement

breezy *adj* **1** windy, fresh **2** brisk, lively **3** insouciant, airy – **breezily** *adv*, **breeziness** *n*

Bren gun *n* a gas-operated magazine-fed light machine gun

brethren *pl of* BROTHER – chiefly in fml address or in referring to the members of a profession, society, or sect

breve *n* **1** a curved mark⁻ used to indicate a short vowel or a short or unstressed syllable **2** a note equal in time value to 2 semibreves or 4 minims

¹**brevet** *n* a commission giving a military officer higher nominal rank than that for which he receives pay

²**brevet** *vt* -tt-, -t- to confer a usu specified rank on by brevet

breviary *n*, *often cap* **1** a book containing the prayers, hymns, psalms, and readings for the canonical hours **2** DIVINE OFFICE

brevity *n* **1** shortness of duration; the quality of being brief **2** expression in few words; conciseness

¹**brew** *vt* **1** to prepare (e g beer or ale) by steeping, boiling, and fermentation or by infusion and fermentation **2** to contrive, plot – often + *up* ⟨~ *up a plan*⟩ **3** to prepare (e g tea) by infusion in hot water ~ *vi* **1** to brew beer or ale **2** to be in the process of formation ⟨*a storm is* ~ing *in the east*⟩ – often + *up* **3** chiefly *Br* to undergo infusion ⟨*left the tea to* ~⟩ – **brewer** *n*

²**brew** *n* **1a** a brewed beverage **b(1)** an amount brewed at once **(2)** the quality of what is brewed ⟨*likes a nice strong* ~⟩ **c** a product of brewing **2** the process of brewing

brewer's droop *n*, *Br* an inability to achieve penile erection after drinking too much alcohol – slang

brewery *n* an establishment in which beer or ale is brewed

brew up *vi*, *Br* to make tea

¹**briar** *n* ¹BRIER

²**briar** *n* **1** ²BRIER **2** a tobacco pipe made from the root of a brier

¹**bribe** *vt* to induce or influence (as if) by bribery ~ *vi* to practise bribery – **bribable** *adj*, **briber** *n*

²**bribe** *n* sthg, esp money, given or promised to influence the judgment or conduct of a person

bribery *n* the act or practice of giving or taking a bribe

bric-a-brac *n* miscellaneous small articles, usu of ornamental or sentimental value; curios

¹**brick** *n* **1** a usu rectangular unit for building or paving purposes, typically not exceeding 215mm x 102mm x 65mm (about 8in × 3¾in × 2¼in) and made of moist clay hardened by heat **2** a rectangular compressed mass (e g of ice cream) **3** a reliable stout hearted person; a stalwart ⟨*Angela, you're a real* ~⟩ – infml

²**brick** *vt* to close, face, or pave with bricks – usu + *up* ⟨~ ed *up a disused entrance*⟩

brickbat *n* **1** a fragment of a hard material (e g a brick); *esp* one used as a missile **2** a critical remark

brickfield *n*, *Br* a place where bricks are made

bricklayer *n* a person who is employed to lay bricks – **bricklaying** *n*

brickwork *n* (the part of) a structure made from bricks and mortar

bridal *adj* of or for a bride or wedding; nuptial

bride *n* a woman at the time of her wedding

bridegroom *n* a man at the time of his wedding

bridesmaid *n* an unmarried girl or woman who attends a bride

¹**bridge** *n* **1a** a structure spanning a depression or obstacle and supporting a roadway, railway, canal, or path **b** a time, place, or means of connection or transition **2a** the upper bony part of the nose **b** an arch serving to raise the strings of a musical instrument **c** a raised platform on a ship from which it is directed **d** the support for a billiards or snooker cue formed esp by the hand **3a** sthg (e g a partial denture permanently attached to adjacent natural teeth) that fills a gap **b** a connection (e g an atom or bond) that joins 2 different parts of a molecule (e g opposite sides of a ring)

²**bridge** *vt* to make a bridge over or across; *also* to cross (e g a river) by a bridge – **bridgeable** *adj*

³**bridge** *n* any of various card games for usu 4 players in 2 partnerships in which players bid for the right to name a trump suit, and in which the hand of the declarer's partner is exposed and played by the declarer; *speci* CONTRACT BRIDGE

bridgehead *n* **1a** a fortification protecting the end of a bridge nearest an enemy **b** the area round the end of a bridge **2** an advanced position, usu beyond a bridge, (to be) seized in hostile territory as a foothold for further advance

bridgework *n* a dental bridge

¹**bridle** *n* **1** a framework of leather straps buckled together round the head of a draught or riding animal, including the bit and reins, used to direct and control it **2** a length of secured cable, esp on a boat, to which a second cable can be attached (e g for mooring) **3** a curb, restraint ⟨*se a* ~ *on his power*⟩

²**bridle** *vb* **bridling** *vt* **1** to put a bridle on **2** to restrain or control (as if) with a bridle ⟨*you must learn to* ~ *you tongue*⟩ ~ *vi* to show hostility or resentment (e g because of an affront), esp by drawing back the head and chin

bridle path *n* a track or right of way suitable for horse back riding

Brie *n* a large round cream-coloured soft cheese ripene through bacterial action

¹**brief** *adj* **1** short in duration or extent **2** in few words concise – **briefly** *adv*, **briefness** *n*

²**brief** *n* **1** a papal directive, less binding than a bull **2a** synopsis, summary **b(1)** a statement of a client's cas drawn up for the instruction of counsel **(2)** a case, or piec of employment, given to a barrister **c** a set of instruction outlining what is required, and usu setting limits to one' powers (e g in negotiating) ⟨*her* ~ *was to reduce Britis*

payments⟩ **3** *pl* short close-fitting pants – **in brief** in a few words; briefly

³brief *vt* **1** to provide with final instructions or necessary information ⟨~ *journalists about the situation*⟩ **2** *Br* to retain (a barrister) as legal counsel

briefcase *n* a flat rectangular case for carrying papers or books

briefing *n* (a meeting to give out) final instructions or necessary information

¹brier, briar *n* a plant with a woody, thorny, or prickly stem – **briery** *adj*

²brier, briar *n* a heath of S Europe with a root used for making pipes

¹brig *n* a 2-masted square-rigged sailing vessel

²brig *n* a prison in the US Navy

¹brigade *n* **1** a large section of an army usu composed of a headquarters, several fighting units (e g infantry battalions or armoured regiments), and supporting units **2** an organized or uniformed group of people (e g firemen)

²brigade *vt* to form or unite into a brigade

brigadier *n* an officer in the British army ranking below a major general and commanding a brigade

brigadier general *n* an officer in the US airforce or army ranking below a major general

brigand *n* one who lives by plunder, usu as a member of a group; a bandit – **brigandage** *n*, **brigandism** *n*

brigantine *n* a 2-masted square-rigged sailing vessel differing from a brig in not carrying a square mainsail

bright *adj* **1a** radiating or reflecting light; shining **b** radiant with happiness ⟨~ *faces*⟩ **2** *of a colour* of high saturation or brilliance **3a** intelligent, clever **b** lively, charming ⟨*be ~ and jovial among your guests* – *Shak*⟩ **c** promising, talented – **bright** *adv*, **brightly** *adv*, **brightness** *n*

brighten *vb* to make or become bright or brighter – often + *up* – **brightener** *n*

Bright's disease *n* any of several kidney diseases marked by albumin in the urine

brill *n, pl* **brill** (a European flatfish related to) the turbot

¹brilliant *adj* **1** very bright; glittering **2a** striking, distinctive ⟨*a ~ example*⟩ **b** having great intellectual ability **3** of high quality; good – *infml* – **brilliance** *n*, **brilliancy** *n*, **brilliantly** *adv*

²brilliant *n* a gem, esp a diamond, cut with numerous facets for maximum brilliance

brilliantine *n* a preparation for making hair glossy and smooth

¹brim *n* **1** the edge or rim of a hollow vessel, a natural depression, or a cavity **2** the projecting rim of a hat – **brimless** *adj*

²brim *vi* **-mm-** to be full to the brim

brimful *adj* full to the brim; ready to overflow

-brimmed *comb form* (→ *adj*) having (such) a brim ⟨*a wide-brimmed hat*⟩

brim over *vi* to overflow a brim

brimstone *n* SULPHUR 1

brindled *adj* having obscure dark streaks or flecks on a grey or tawny ground

¹brine *n* water (almost) saturated with common salt – **briny** *adj*, **brininess** *n*

²brine *vt* to treat with brine (e g by soaking)

bring *vt* **brought 1a** to convey (sthg) to a place or person; come with or cause to come **b(1)** to attract ⟨*his screams brought the neighbours*⟩ **(2)** to force, compel ⟨*cannot ~ myself to do it*⟩ **(3)** to cause to achieve a particular condition ⟨~ *water to the boil*⟩ **2a** to cause to occur, lead to ⟨*winter will ~ snow and ice*⟩ **b** to initiate ⟨~ *legal action*⟩ **c** to offer, present ⟨~ *an argument*⟩ **3** PREFER 3

⟨~ *a charge*⟩ **4** to sell for (a price) ⟨*the car should ~ £800*⟩ – **bringer** *n* – **bring home** to make unmistakably clear to – **bring to bear 1** to put to use ⟨*bring knowledge to bear on the problem*⟩ **2** to apply, exert ⟨*bring pressure to bear on the management*⟩ – **bring to book 1** to put in a position in which one must answer for one's acts **2** to cause to be reproved – **bring to light** to disclose, reveal – **bring to mind** to cause to be recalled – **bring up the rear** to come last

bring about *vt* to cause to take place; effect

bring down *vt* **1** to cause to fall or come down **2** to kill by shooting ⟨*brought the bear* down *with one shot*⟩ **3** to reduce **4** to cause to be depressed – usu pass – **bring the house down** to win the enthusiastic approval of the audience

bring forth *vt* **1** to bear ⟨*brought forth fruit*⟩ **2** to give birth to; produce **3** to offer, present ⟨*brought forth arguments to justify her conduct*⟩

bring forward *vt* **1** to produce to view; introduce **2** to carry (a total) forward (e g to the top of the next page)

bring in *vt* **1** to produce as profit or return ⟨*this will* bring in *the money*⟩ **2** to introduce **3** to pronounce (a verdict) in court **4** to earn ⟨*she* brings in *a good salary*⟩

bring off *vt* to carry to a successful conclusion; achieve, accomplish

bring on *vt* **1** to cause to appear or occur **2** to improve, help

bring out *vt* **1** to make clear **2a** to present to the public; *specif* to publish **b** to introduce (a young woman) formally to society **3** to utter **4** to cause (sby) to be afflicted with a rash, spots, etc – usu + *in* **5** to encourage to be less reticent – esp in **bring somebody out of** *him-/herself* **6** *chiefly Br* to instruct or cause (workers) to go on strike

bring round *vt* **1** to cause to adopt a particular opinion or course of action; persuade **2** to restore to consciousness; revive

bring to *vt* **1** to cause (a boat) to lie to or come to a standstill **2** BRING ROUND 2

bring up *vt* **1** to educate, rear **2** to cause to stop suddenly **3** to bring to attention; introduce **4** to vomit

brink *n* **1** an edge; *esp* the edge at the top of a steep place **2** *the* verge, onset ⟨*on the ~ of war*⟩

brinkmanship *n* the art of going to the very brink of conflict, danger, etc before drawing back

brioche *n* a light slightly sweet bread roll made with a rich yeast dough

briquette, briquet *n* a compacted block, usu of coal-dust

brisk *adj* **1** keenly alert; lively **2** fresh, invigorating ⟨~ *weather*⟩ **3** energetic, quick ⟨*a ~ pace*⟩ **4** sharp in tone or manner – chiefly euph – **briskly** *adv*, **briskness** *n*

brisket *n* a joint of beef cut from the breast; *broadly* the breast or lower chest of a 4-legged animal

¹bristle *n* a short stiff coarse hair or filament

²bristle *vb* **bristling** *vi* **1a** to rise and stand stiffly erect ⟨*quills* bristling *in all directions*⟩ **b** to raise the bristles (e g in anger) **2** to take on an aggressive attitude or appearance (e g in response to a slight) **3** to be filled or thickly covered (*with* sthg suggestive of bristles) ~ *vt* **1** to provide with bristles **2** to make bristly; ruffle

bristly *adj* **1a** consisting of or resembling bristles **b** thickly covered with bristles **2** tending to bristle easily; belligerent

bristols *n pl, Br* breasts – vulg

Brit *n* a British person – infml

britches *n pl* breeches

¹British *n* **1** the Celtic language of the ancient Britons **2** *pl in constr* the people of Britain **3** *chiefly NAm* English as typically spoken and written in Britain

²**British** *adj* of Britain, its people, or their language – **Britishness** *n*

Britisher *n*, chiefly *NAm* BRITON 2

British thermal unit *n* the quantity of heat required to raise the temperature of 1lb of water by 1°F under standard conditions

Briton *n* **1** a member of any of the peoples inhabiting Britain before the Anglo-Saxon invasions **2** a native, inhabitant, or subject of Britain

brittle *adj* **1a** easily broken or cracked **b** insecure, frail ⟨*a ~ friendship*⟩ **2** easily hurt or offended; sensitive ⟨*a ~ personality*⟩ **3** sharp, tense ⟨*a ~ sound*⟩ **4** lacking warmth or depth of feeling ⟨*~ gaiety*⟩ – **brittlely** *adv*, **brittleness** *n*

¹**broach** *n* **1** any of various pointed or tapered tools: e g **a** a bit for boring holes **b** a tool for tapping casks **2** a spit for roasting meat

²**broach** *vt* **1a** to pierce (a container, esp a cask or bottle) prior to using the contents; tap **b** to open up or break into (e g a store or stock of sthg) and start to use **2** to open up (a subject) for discussion

³**broach** *vi*, *of a boat* to change direction dangerously, esp so as to lie broadside to the waves – usu + *to* ~ *vt* to cause (a boat) to broach

¹**broad** *adj* **1a** having ample extent from side to side or between limits ⟨*~ shoulders*⟩ **b** in width; across ⟨*made the path 10 feet ~*⟩ **2** extending far and wide; spacious ⟨*the ~ plains*⟩ **3a** open, full – esp in *broad daylight* **b** plain, obvious ⟨*a ~ hint*⟩ **4** marked by lack of restraint or delicacy; coarse **5a** liberal, tolerant **b** widely applicable or applied; general **6** relating to the main points ⟨*~ outlines*⟩ **7** dialectal, esp in pronunciation **8** *of a vowel* open – used specif of *a* pronounced as /ah/ – **broadly** *adv*

²**broad** *adv* in a broad manner; fully

³**broad** *n* **1** the broad part ⟨*~ of his back*⟩ **2** often cap, *Br* a large area of fresh water formed by the broadening of a river – usu pl; used chiefly with reference to such formations found in E Anglia **3** a prostitute – slang **4** chiefly *NAm* a woman – slang

broad bean *n* (the large flat edible seed of) a widely cultivated Old World leguminous plant

¹**broadcast** *adj* cast or scattered in all directions

²**broadcast** *n* **1** the act of transmitting by radio or television **2** a single radio or television programme

³**broadcast** *vb* **broadcast** *also* **broadcasted** *vt* **1** to scatter or sow (seed) broadcast **2** to make widely known **3** to transmit as a broadcast, esp for widespread reception ~ *vi* **1** to transmit a broadcast **2** to speak or perform on a broadcast programme – **broadcaster** *n*

⁴**broadcast** *adv* to or over a broad area

Broad Church *adj* of 19th-c liberal Anglicanism

broadcloth *n* a twilled napped woollen or worsted fabric with a smooth lustrous finish and dense texture

broaden *vb* to make or become broad

broad jump *n*, *NAm* LONG JUMP

broadloom *n or adj* (a carpet) woven on a wide loom

broad-minded *adj* tolerant of varied views, unconventional behaviour, etc; liberal – **broad-mindedly** *adv*, **broad-mindedness** *n*

broadsheet *n* **1** a large sheet of paper printed on 1 side only; *also* sthg (e g an advertisement) printed on a broadsheet **2** a newspaper whose page depth is the full size of a rotary press plate

¹**broadside** *n* **1** the side of a ship above the waterline **2** a broadsheet **3a** (the simultaneous firing of) all the guns on 1 side of a ship **b** a forceful verbal or written attack

²**broadside** *adv* with the broadside or broader side towards a given object or point

broadsword *n* a sword with a broad blade for cutting rather than thrusting

brocade *n* a rich (silk) fabric woven with raised patterns – **brocade** *vt*, **brocaded** *adj*

broccoli *n* **1** a large hardy cauliflower **2** broccoli, **sprouting broccoli** a branching form of cauliflower whose young shoots are used for food

brochure *n* a small pamphlet

¹**brogue** *n* a stout walking shoe characterized by decorative perforations on the uppers

²**brogue** *n* a dialect or regional pronunciation; *esp* an Irish accent

broil *vt* to cook by direct exposure to radiant heat (e g over a fire); *specif*, *NAm* to grill ~ *vi* to become extremely hot

broiler *n* a bird suitable for grilling; *esp* a young chicken

¹**broke** *past of* BREAK

²**broke** *adj* penniless – *infml*; compare STONY-BROKE

broken *adj* **1** violently separated into parts; shattered **2a** having undergone or been subjected to fracture ⟨*a ~ leg*⟩ **b** *of a land surface* irregular, interrupted, or full of obstacles ⟨*~ ground*⟩ **c** not fulfilled; violated ⟨*a ~ promise*⟩ **d** discontinuous, interrupted **3a** made weak or infirm **b** subdued completely; crushed ⟨*a ~ spirit*⟩ **c** not working; defective **4a** cut off; disconnected **b** adversely affected or disrupted by marital separation or divorce ⟨*~ marriage*⟩ ⟨*a ~ home*⟩ **c** imperfect ⟨*~ English*⟩ – **brokenly** *adv*, **brokenness** *n*

broken-down *adj* **1** in a state of disrepair; wrecked, dilapidated **2** spiritually or physically ill or exhausted

brokenhearted *adj* overcome by grief or despair

broken wind *n* a chronic respiratory disease of horses marked by a persistent cough and heaving of the flanks – **broken-winded** *adj*

broker *n* **1** one who acts as an intermediary (e g in a business deal) **2** an agent who negotiates contracts of purchase and sale (e g of commodities or securities)

brolly *n*, chiefly *Br* an umbrella – *infml*

bromide *n* **1** a compound of bromine with another element or radical; *esp* any of various bromides formerly used as sedatives **2** a commonplace or hackneyed statement or notion

bromine *n* a nonmetallic element, usu occurring as a deep red corrosive toxic liquid

bronchial *adj* of the bronchi or their ramifications in the lungs – **bronchially** *adv*

bronchitis *n* (a disease marked by) acute or chronic inflammation of the bronchial tubes accompanied by a cough and catarrh – **bronchitic** *adj*

bronco *n*, *pl* **broncos** an unbroken or imperfectly broken horse of western N America

brontosaurus *n* any of various large 4-legged and prob plant-eating dinosaurs

¹**bronze** *vt* **1** to give the appearance of bronze to **2** to make brown or tanned

²**bronze** *n* **1** any of various copper-base alloys; *esp* one containing tin **2** a sculpture or artefact made of bronze **3** a yellowish-brown colour **4** BRONZE MEDAL ⟨*won a ~ in the 100 metres*⟩ – **bronze** *adj*, **bronzy** *adj*

Bronze Age *n* the period of human culture characterized by the use of bronze or copper tools and weapons

bronze medal *n* a medal of bronze awarded to sby who comes third in a competition – **bronze medallist** *n*

brooch *n* an ornament worn on clothing and fastened by means of a pin

¹**brood** *n* **1a** young birds, insects, etc hatched or cared for

at one time **b** the children in one family – humor **2** a group having a common nature or origin

brood *vi* **1** *of a bird* to sit on eggs in order to hatch them **2a** to dwell gloomily *on*; worry *over* or *about* **b** to be in a state of depression – **broodingly** *adv*

brood *adj* kept for breeding ⟨*a ~ mare*⟩

broody *adj* **1** *of fowl* being in a state of readiness to brood eggs **2** given or conducive to introspection; contemplative, moody **3** *of a woman* feeling a strong desire or urge to be a mother – *infml* – **broodiness** *n*

brook *vt* to tolerate; STAND FOR ⟨*she would ~ no interference with her plans*⟩

brook *n* a usu small freshwater stream

broom *n* **1** any of various leguminous shrubs with long slender branches, small leaves, and usu showy yellow flowers **2** a brush for sweeping composed of a bundle of firm stiff twigs, bristles, or fibres (e g of nylon) bound to or set on a long handle

broomstick *n* the long thin handle of a broom

broth *n* **1a** the stock in which meat, fish, cereal grains, or vegetables have been cooked **b** a thin soup made from stock **2** a liquid medium for culturing esp bacteria

brothel *n* a premises (e g a house) in which the services of prostitutes can be bought

brother *n*, *pl* **brothers**, *(3, 4, & 5)* **brothers** *also* **brethren 1** a male having the same parents as another person; *also* a half brother or stepbrother **2a** a kinsman **b** one, esp a male, who shares with another a common national or racial origin **3** a fellow member – used as a title in some evangelical denominations **4** one, esp a male, who is related to another by a common tie or interest **5** a member of a men's religious order who is not in holy orders ⟨*a lay ~*⟩

brotherhood *n* **1** the quality or state of being brothers **2a** an association (e g a religious body) for a particular purpose **b** (an idea of) fellowship between all human beings ⟨*universal ~*⟩

brother-in-law *n*, *pl* **brothers-in-law 1** the brother of one's spouse **2** the husband of one's sister

brotherly *adj* **1** of, resembling, or appropriate to brothers, esp in feeling or showing platonic affection **2** filled with fellow feeling, sympathy, or compassion ⟨*she was overwhelmed with ~ love for the homeless*⟩ – **brotherliness** *n*, **brotherly** *adv*

brougham *n* a light closed 4-wheeled horse-drawn carriage

brought *past of* BRING

brouhaha *n* a hubbub, uproar

brow *n* **1a** an eyebrow **b** the forehead **2** the top or edge of a hill, cliff, etc

browbeat *vt* **browbeat; browbeaten** to intimidate, coerce, or bully by a persistently threatening or dominating manner ⟨*union members ~en into accepting a cut in salary*⟩

brown *adj* **1** of the colour brown; *esp* of dark or tanned complexion **2** (made with ingredients that are) partially or wholly unrefined or unpolished ⟨*~ sugar*⟩

brown *n* any of a range of dark colours between red and yellow in hue – **brownish** *adj*, **browny** *adj*

brown *vb* to make or become brown (e g by sautéing)

browned off *adj*, *chiefly Br* annoyed; FED UP – *infml*

brownie *n* **1** a good-natured goblin believed to perform household chores at night **2 brownie guide, brownie** a member of the most junior section of the (British) Guide movement for girls aged from 7 to 10 **3** *chiefly NAm* a small square or rectangle of rich chocolate cake containing nuts

brown study *n* a state of serious absorption or abstraction; a reverie

browse *n* **1** tender shoots, twigs, and leaves of trees and shrubs that provide food for animals (e g deer) **2** a period of time spent browsing ⟨*had a good ~ in the library*⟩

browse *vt* to feed on (browse) ~ *vi* **1** *of animals* to nibble at leaves, grass, or other vegetation **2** to read or search idly *through* a book or a mass of things (e g in a shop), in the hope of finding sthg interesting – **browser** *n*

brucellosis *n* a serious long-lasting disease, esp of human beings and cattle, caused by a bacterium

bruin *n* – used chiefly in stories as a name for the bear

bruise *vt* **1** to inflict a bruise on **2** to crush (e g leaves or berries) by pounding **3** to wound, injure; *esp* to inflict psychological hurt on ~ *vi* **1** to be damaged by a bruise ⟨*tomatoes ~ easily*⟩

bruise *n* **1a** an injury involving rupture of small blood vessels and discoloration without a break in the skin **b** an injury to plant tissue involving underlying damage and discoloration without a break in the skin **2** an injury, esp to the feelings

bruiser *n* a large burly man; *specif* a prizefighter

brunch *n* a meal, usu taken in the middle of the morning, that combines a late breakfast and an early lunch

brunette, *NAm also* **brunet** *n or adj* (sby, esp a young adult woman,) having dark hair and usu a relatively dark complexion

brunt *n* the principal force or stress (e g of an attack) – esp in *bear the brunt of*

brush *n* **1** (land covered with) scrub vegetation **2** *chiefly NAm & Austr* brushwood

brush *n* **1** an implement composed of filaments (e g of hair, bristle, nylon, or wire) set into a firm piece of material and used esp for grooming hair, painting, sweeping, or scrubbing **2** a bushy tail, esp of a fox **3** a conductor (e g a piece of carbon or braided copper wire) that makes electrical contact between a stationary and a moving part **4** an act of brushing **5** a quick light touch or momentary contact in passing ⟨*felt the ~ of her coat*⟩

brush *vt* **1a** to apply a brush to **b** to apply with a brush **2** to remove with sweeping strokes (e g of a brush) – usu + *away* or *off* ⟨*~ ed the dirt off her coat*⟩ **3** to pass lightly over or across; touch gently against in passing

brush *vi* to move lightly, heedlessly, or rudely – usu + *by* or *past*

brush *n* a brief antagonistic encounter or skirmish ⟨*had a ~ with authority*⟩

brush-off *n* a quietly curt or disdainful dismissal; a rebuff – *infml*

brush off *vt* to dispose of in an offhand way; dismiss

brush up *vi* to tidy one's clothes, hair, etc ⟨*wanted to wash and brush up when they arrived*⟩ ~ *vt* to renew one's skill in; refresh one's memory of ⟨*she'll have to brush up her French*⟩ – **brushup** *n* – **brush up on** BRUSH UP *vt*

brushwood *n* **1** twigs or small branches, esp when cut or broken **2** a thicket of shrubs and small trees

brushwork *n* (a particular artist's) technique of applying paint with a brush

brusque *adj* blunt or abrupt in manner or speech, often to the point of rudeness – **brusquely** *adv*, **brusqueness** *n*

brussels sprout *n*, *often cap B* (any of the many edible small green buds that grow on the stem of) a plant of the mustard family

brutal *adj* **1** grossly ruthless or unfeeling ⟨*a ~ slander*⟩ **2** cruel, cold-blooded ⟨*a ~ attack*⟩ **3** harsh, severe ⟨*~ weather*⟩ **4** unpleasantly accurate and incisive ⟨*~ truth*⟩ – **brutally** *adv*, **brutality** *n*

brutalize, **-ise** *vt* **1** to make brutal, unfeeling, or inhuman ⟨*people ~d by poverty and disease*⟩ **2** to beat brutally – **brutalization** *n*

¹brute *adj* **1** characteristic of an animal in quality, action, or instinct: e g **a** cruel, savage **b** not working by reason; mindless ⟨~ *instinct*⟩ **2** purely physical ⟨~ *strength*⟩
²brute *n* **1** a beast **2** a brutal person – **brutish** *adj*, **brutishly** *adv*
¹bubble *vi* **bubbling 1** to form or produce bubbles **2** to make a sound like the bubbles rising in liquid ⟨*a brook bubbling over rocks*⟩ **3** to be highly excited or overflowing (with a feeling) ⟨*bubbling over with happiness*⟩
²bubble *n* **1a** a usu small body of gas within a liquid or solid **b** a thin spherical usu transparent film of liquid inflated with air or vapour **c** a transparent dome **2** sthg that lacks firmness or reality; *specif* an unreliable or speculative scheme **3** a sound like that of bubbling
bubble and squeak *n, chiefly Br* a dish consisting of usu leftover potato, cabbage, and sometimes meat, fried together
bubble gum *n* a chewing gum that can be blown into large bubbles
¹bubbly *adj* **1** full of bubbles **2** overflowing with good spirits or liveliness; vivacious ⟨*a ~ personality*⟩
²bubbly *n* champagne; *broadly* any sparkling wine – *infml*
bubo *n, pl* **buboes** an inflamed swelling of a lymph gland, esp in the groin or armpit – **bubonic** *adj*
bubonic plague *n* plague characterized by the formation of buboes
buccaneer *n* **1** a freebooter preying on Spanish ships and settlements, esp in the W Indies in the 17th c; *broadly* a pirate **2** an unscrupulous adventurer, esp in politics or business – **buccaneer** *vi*
¹buck *n, pl* **bucks**, (*1*) **bucks**, *esp collectively* **buck 1a** a male animal, esp a male deer, antelope, rabbit, rat, etc **b** an antelope **2** a dashing fellow; a dandy **3** VAULTING HORSE **4** *NAm* DOLLAR **2** – slang
²buck *vi* **1** *of a horse or mule* to spring into the air with the back curved and come down with the forelegs stiff and the head lowered **2** to refuse assent; balk **3** *chiefly NAm* to move or react jerkily ~ *vt* **1** to throw (e g a rider) by bucking **2** to fail to comply with; run counter to ⟨~ *the system*⟩
³buck *n* **1** an object formerly used in poker to mark the next player to deal; *broadly* sthg used as a reminder **2** *the* responsibility – esp in *pass the buck*
buckboard *n, NAm* a 4-wheeled horse-drawn vehicle with a sprung platform
bucked *adj* pleased, encouraged ⟨*felt very ~ to hear the news*⟩
¹bucket *n* **1** a large open container, usu round, with tapering sides and a semicircular handle on top, used esp for holding or carrying liquids **2** sthg resembling a bucket, esp in shape or function: e g **a** the scoop of an excavating machine **b** any of the receptacles on the rim of a waterwheel **c** any of the vanes of a turbine rotor **3** *pl* large quantities ⟨~ s *of blood*⟩ – *infml*
²bucket *vt* to draw or lift in buckets ~ *vi* **1** to move about jerkily or recklessly **2** *chiefly Br* BUCKET DOWN
bucket down *vi, chiefly Br* **1** *of rain* to fall heavily **2** to rain very hard ⟨*it's been bucketing down all day*⟩
bucket seat *n* a round-backed separate seat for 1 person in a motor car, aircraft, etc
¹buckle *n* a fastening consisting of a rigid rim, usu with a hinged pin, used to join together **2** loose ends (e g of a belt or strap) or for ornament
²buckle *vb* **buckling 1** to fasten with a buckle **2** to cause to bend, give way, or crumple ~ *vi* **1** to bend, warp ⟨*the pavement ~d in the heat*⟩ **2** to yield; GIVE WAY ⟨*one who does not ~ under pressure*⟩
³buckle *n* a distorted formation due to buckling

buckle down *vi* to apply oneself vigorously ⟨*about time she buckled down to her work*⟩
buckler *n* a small round shield held by a handle at arm's length
buckle to *vi* to brace oneself or gather up one's strength to put effort into work ⟨*we must buckle to and start writing the dictionary*⟩
buckram *n* a fabric of cotton or linen, with a stiff finish, used for interlinings in garments, for stiffening in hats, and in bookbinding
buckshee *adj or adv, Br* without charge; free – slang
buckshot *n* a coarse lead shot used esp for shooting large animals
buckskin *n* a soft pliable usu suede-finished leather – **buckskin** *adj*
bucktooth *n* a large projecting front tooth – **buck-toothed** *adj*
buck up *vi* **1** to become encouraged **2** to hurry up ~ *vt* **1** to improve, smarten **2** to raise the morale or spirits of ⟨*the news bucked her up no end*⟩
buckwheat *n* **1** any of a genus of plants of the dock family that have pinkish white flowers and triangular seeds **2** the seed of a buckwheat, used as a cereal grain
bucolic *adj* **1** of shepherds or herdsmen; pastoral **2** (typical) of rural life – **bucolically** *adv*
¹bud *n* **1** a small protuberance on the stem of a plant that may develop into a flower, leaf, or shoot **2** sthg not yet mature or fully developed: e g **a** an incompletely opened flower **b** an outgrowth of an organism that becomes a new individual
²bud *vb* **-dd-** *vi* **1** *of a plant* to put forth buds **2** to develop by way of outgrowth **3** to reproduce asexually by forming and developing buds ~ *vt* **1** to produce or develop from buds **2** to graft a bud into (a plant of another kind), usu in order to propagate a desired variety
Buddhism *n* an eastern religion growing out of the teaching of Gautama Buddha that one can be liberated from the suffering inherent in life by mental and moral self-purification – **Buddhist** *n or adj*
budding *adj* being in an early and usu promising stage of development ⟨~ *novelists*⟩
buddy *n, chiefly NAm* **1** a companion, partner **2** ¹MATE **1c** *USE* infml
budge *vb* **1** to (cause to) move or shift ⟨*the mule wouldn't* ~⟩ **2** to (force or cause to) change an opinion or yield ⟨*couldn't ~ her on the issue*⟩
budgerigar *n* a small Australian bird that belongs to the same family as the parrots and is often kept in captivity
¹budget *n* **1** a statement of a financial position for a definite period of time (e g for the following year), that is based on estimates of expenditures and proposals for financing them **2** a plan of how money will be spent or allocated ⟨*a weekly* ~⟩ **3** the amount of money available for, required for, or assigned to a particular purpose – **budgetary** *adj*
²budget *vt* to plan or provide for the use of (e g money, time, or manpower) in detail ~ *vi* to arrange or plan a budget
¹buff *n* **1** a strong supple oil-tanned leather produced chiefly from cattle hides **2** *the* bare skin – chiefly in *in the buff* **3** (a) pale yellowish brown **4** a device (e g a stick or pad) with a soft absorbent surface used for polishing sthg **5** one who has a keen interest in and wide knowledge of a specified subject; an enthusiast ⟨*a film* ~⟩ – **buff** *adj*
²buff *vt* **1** to polish, shine **2** to give a velvety surface like that of buff to (leather) – **buffer** *n*
buffalo *n, pl* **buffaloes** *also* **buffalos**, *esp collectively* **buffalo 1** WATER BUFFALO **2** a large N American wild ox

with short horns, heavy forequarters, and a large muscular hump; *also* any similar wild ox

buffer *n* an (ineffectual) fellow – chiefly in *old buffer*; infml

²buffer *n* **1** any of various devices for reducing the effect of an impact; *esp, Br* a spring-loaded metal disc on a railway vehicle or at the end of a railway track **2** a device that serves to protect sthg, or to cushion against shock **3** a person who shields another, esp from annoying routine matters **4** (a solution containing) a substance capable in solution of neutralizing both acids and bases and thereby maintaining the original acidity or basicity of the solution **5** a temporary storage unit (e g in a computer); *esp* one that accepts information at one rate and delivers it at another

buffer *vt* **1** to lessen the shock of; cushion **2** to add a buffer to (e g a solution); *also* to buffer a solution of (a substance)

buffer state *n* a small neutral state lying between 2 larger potentially rival powers

buffet *n* **1** a blow, esp with the hand **2** sthg that strikes with telling force

buffet *vt* **1** to strike sharply, esp with the hand; cuff **2** to strike repeatedly; batter ⟨*the waves* ~ed *the shore*⟩ **3** to use roughly; treat unpleasantly ⟨~ed *by life*⟩

buffet *n* **1** a sideboard or cupboard often used for the display of tableware **2** a counter for refreshments **3** a meal set out on tables or a sideboard for diners to help themselves **4** *chiefly Br* a self-service restaurant or snack bar

buffoon *n* **1** a ludicrous figure; a clown **2** a rough and noisy fool – **buffoonery** *n*

bug *n* **1** any of several insects commonly considered obnoxious; *esp* a bedbug **2** an unexpected defect or imperfection ⟨*we'll need to iron the* ~s *out*⟩ **3** a disease-producing germ; *also* a disease caused by it – not used technically **4** a concealed listening device **5** a temporary enthusiasm; a craze – infml

bug *vt* **-gg- 1a** to plant a concealed listening device in **b** to eavesdrop on by means of a mechanical bug **2** to bother, annoy – infml ⟨*don't* ~ *me with petty details*⟩

bugaboo *n, pl* **bugaboos** *chiefly NAm* a bugbear

bugbear *n* an object or (persistent) source of fear, concern, or difficulty ⟨*this national* ~ *of inflation*⟩

bugger *n* **1** a sodomite **2a** a worthless or contemptible person, esp male **b** a creature; *esp* a man ⟨*poor* ~⟩ **3** *chiefly Br* a cause of annoyance or difficulty *USE* (*except 1*) vulg

bugger *vt* **1** to practise sodomy on **2a** – used interjectionally to express contempt or annoyance ⟨~ *Tom! We'll go without him*⟩ **b** to damage or ruin, usu because of incompetence – often + *up* **3** to exhaust; WEAR OUT **4** *Br* to be evasive with or misleading to – + *around* or *about* ⟨*don't* ~ *me about*⟩ ~*vi Br* to fool *around* or *about*, esp by dithering or being being indecisive *USE* (*except 1*) vulg

bugger off *vi, Br* to go away – vulg

buggery *n* sodomy

buggy *adj* infested with bugs

buggy *n* a light one-horse carriage

bugle *n* a European annual plant of the mint family that has spikes of blue flowers

bugle *n* a valveless brass instrument that is used esp for military calls

bugle *vi* to sound a bugle – **bugler** *n*

buhl, boulle *n* inlaid decoration of tortoiseshell or ornamental metalwork (e g brass) used in cabinetwork

build *vb* **built** *vt* **1** to construct by putting together materials gradually into a composite whole **2** to cause to be constructed **3** to develop according to a systematic plan, by a definite process, or on a particular base **4** to increase or enlarge ~*vi* **1** to engage in building **2a** to increase in intensity ⟨~ *to a climax*⟩ **b** to develop in extent ⟨*outside the arena a queue was already* ~ing⟩

²build *n* the physical proportions of a person or animal; *esp* a person's figure of a usu specified type ⟨*an athletic* ~⟩

builder *n* sby who contracts to build and supervises building operations

build in *vt* to construct or develop as an integral part

building *n* **1** a permanent structure (e g a school or house) usu having walls and a roof **2** the art, business, or act of assembling materials into a structure

building society *n* any of various British organizations in which the public can invest money, and which advance money for house purchase

buildup *n* **1** sthg produced by building up ⟨*deal with the* ~ *of traffic*⟩ **2** praise or publicity, esp given in advance ⟨*sales were slow in spite of the* ~ *the product received*⟩

build up *vt* **1** to develop gradually by increments ⟨*built up a library*⟩ **2** to promote the esteem of; praise ~*vi* **to** accumulate or develop appreciably ⟨*clouds building up on the horizon*⟩

built *adj* proportioned or formed in a specified way ⟨*a slightly* ~ *girl*⟩

built-in *adj* **1** forming an integral part of a structure ⟨~ *cupboards*⟩ **2** inherent

built-up *adj* **1** made of several sections or layers fastened together **2** well-filled or fully covered with buildings ⟨*a* ~ *area*⟩

bulb *n* **1a** a short stem base of a plant (e g the lily, onion, or hyacinth), with 1 or more buds enclosed in overlapping membranous or fleshy leaves, that is formed underground as a resting stage in the plant's development **b** a tuber, corm, or other fleshy structure resembling a bulb in appearance **c** a plant having or developing from a bulb **2** INCANDESCENT LAMP **3** a rounded or swollen anatomical structure

bulbous *adj* **1** growing from or bearing bulbs **2** resembling a bulb, esp in roundness ⟨*a* ~ *nose*⟩ – **bulbously** *adv*

bulbul *n* any of various songbirds of Asia and Africa that live in groups

bulge *n* **1** BILGE 1 **2** a swelling or convex curve on a surface, usu caused by pressure from within or below **3** a sudden and usu temporary expansion (e g in population) – **bulgy** *adj*

²bulge *vi* to jut out; swell ⟨*eaten so much I'm bulging*⟩

bulk *n* **1a** spatial dimension; *esp* volume **b** roughage **2a** voluminous or ponderous mass – often used with reference to the shape or size of a corpulent person **b** a structure, esp when viewed as a mass of material ⟨*the shrouded* ~s *of snow-covered cars*⟩ **3** the main or greater part of – **in bulk** in large amounts or quantities; *esp, of goods bought and sold* in amounts or quantities much larger than as usu packaged or purchased

²bulk *vt* **1** to cause to swell or to be thicker or fuller; pad – often + *out* ⟨*had to* ~ *the text out to 20,000 words*⟩ **2** to gather into a mass ~*vi* to appear as a factor; loom ⟨*a consideration that* ~s *large in everyone's thinking*⟩

³bulk *adj* (of materials) in bulk ⟨~ *cement*⟩

bulkhead *n* a partition or wall separating compartments (e g in an aircraft or ship)

bulky *adj* **1** having too much bulk; *esp* unwieldy **2** corpulent – chiefly euph – **bulkily** *adv*, **bulkiness** *n*

bull *n* **1a** an adult male bovine animal **b** an adult male elephant, whale, or other large animal **2** one who buys securities or commodities in expectation of a price rise or who acts to effect such a rise **3** BULL'S-EYE 3a

²bull *adj* BULLISH 1

³bull *vt* to try to increase the price of (e g stocks) or in (a market)

⁴bull *n* **1** a papal edict on a subject of major importance **2** an edict, decree

⁵bull *n* **1** empty boastful talk; nonsense **2** *Br* unnecessary or irksome fatigues or discipline, esp in the armed forces *USE* slang

bulldog *n* **1** a thickset muscular short-haired dog of an English breed that has widely separated forelegs and a short neck **2** a proctor's attendant at Oxford or Cambridge

bulldoze *vt* **1** to bully **2** to move, clear, gouge out, or level off with a bulldozer **3** to force insensitively or ruthlessly

bulldozer *n* a tractor-driven machine with a broad blunt horizontal blade that is used for clearing land, building roads, etc

bullet *n* **1** a small round or elongated missile designed to be fired from a firearm; *broadly* CARTRIDGE 1a **2** sthg resembling a bullet – **bulletproof** *adj*

bulletheaded *adj* **1** having a rounded solid-looking head **2** bullheaded

bulletin *n* **1** a brief public notice; *specif* a brief news item intended for immediate publication **2** a short programme of news items on radio or television

bulletin board *n, NAm* a notice-board

bullfight *n* a spectacle (in an arena) in which bulls are ceremonially excited, fought with, and in Hispanic tradition killed, for public entertainment – **bullfighter** *n*

bullfinch *n* a European finch, the male of which has a rosy red breast and throat

bullfrog *n* a heavy-bodied deep-voiced frog

bullheaded *adj* stupidly stubborn; headstrong – **bullheadedly** *adv*, **bullheadedness** *n*

bullion *n* gold or silver (in bars) that has not been minted

bullish *adj* **1** suggestive of a bull (e g in brawniness) **2** marked by, tending to cause, or hopeful of rising prices (e g in a stock market)

bull neck *n* a thick short powerful neck – **bullnecked** *adj*

bullock *n* **1** a young bull **2** a castrated bull

bullring *n* an arena for bullfights

bull's-eye *n* **1** a small thick disc of glass inserted (e g in a ship's deck) to let in light **2** a very hard round usu peppermint sweet **3a** (a shot that hits) the centre of a target **b** sthg that precisely attains a desired end **4** (a lantern having) a simple lens of short focal distance

bullshit *n* nonsense – vulg

bull terrier *n* a short-haired terrier of a breed originated in England by crossing the bulldog with a breed of terrier

¹bully *n* **1** a browbeating person; *esp* one habitually cruel to others weaker than him-/herself **2** a hired ruffian

²bully *adj* – **bully for** – used to congratulate a specified person, sometimes ironically 〈*well bully for you!*〉

³bully *vt* to treat abusively; intimidate

⁴bully, bully-off *n* a procedure for starting play in a hockey match in which 2 opposing players face each other and alternately strike the ground and the opponent's stick 3 times before attempting to gain possession of the ball

⁵bully *vt* to put (a hockey ball) in play with a bully ~ *vi* to start or restart a hockey match with a bully – usu + *off*

bullyboy *n* a rough man, esp a hired thug

bulrush *n* **1** any of a genus of annual or perennial sedges

2 the papyrus – used in the Bible **3** *Br* either of 2 reedmaces

bulwark *n* **1a** a solid wall-like structure raised for defence; a rampart **b** a breakwater, seawall **2a** a strong support or protection 〈*education as a ~ of democracy*〉 **b** a defence 〈*a pay rise of 30 per cent would be a ~ against inflation*〉 **3** the side of a ship above the upper deck – usu pl with sing. meaning

¹bum *n, chiefly Br* the buttocks – slang

²bum *vt* **-mm-** *Br* to have anal intercourse with – vulg

³bum *vb* **-mm-** *vi* to spend time idly and often travelling casually 〈*~ med around for 3 years before she got a job*〉 – usu + *around*; slang ~ *vt* to obtain by begging; cadge 〈*can I ~ a fag off you?*〉 – slang

⁴bum *n* **1** *NAm* an idler, loafer; *specif* a vagrant, tramp **2** *chiefly NAm* an incompetent worthless person **3** *NAm* one who devotes his/her time to a specified recreational activity 〈*a ski ~*〉〈*a beach ~*〉 *USE* slang

⁵bum *adj, chiefly NAm* **1** inferior, worthless 〈*~ advice*〉 **2** disabled 〈*a ~ knee*〉 *USE* slang

¹bumble *vi* **bumbling** DRONE 1

²bumble *vi* **bumbling 1** to speak in a faltering manner **2** to proceed unsteadily; stumble – often + *along* – **bumbler** *n*, **bumblingly** *adv*

bumblebee *n* any of numerous large robust hairy bees

bumboat *n* a boat that brings commodities for sale to larger ships

bumf, bumph *n, Br* (undesirable or superfluous) paperwork – infml

¹bummer *n, chiefly NAm* 'BUM 1

²bummer *n* an unpleasant experience (e g a bad reaction to a hallucinogenic drug) – infml

¹bump *vt* **1** to strike or knock with force **2** to collide with **3** to dislodge with a jolt ~ *vi* **1** to knock against sthg with a forceful jolt – often + *into* **2** to proceed in a series of bumps – **bump into** to encounter, esp by chance

²bump *n* **1** a sudden forceful blow or jolt **2** a rounded projection from a surface: e g **a** a swelling of tissue **b** a natural protuberance of the skull **3** a thrusting of the hips forwards in an erotic manner **4** *pl the* act of holding a child by his/her arms and legs and swinging him/her into the air and back to the ground 〈*gave her the ~s on her birthday*〉

¹bumper *n* **1** a brimming cup or glass **2** sthg unusually large

²bumper *adj* unusually large 〈*a ~ crop*〉

³bumper *n* **1** a metal or rubber bar, usu at either end of a motor vehicle, for absorbing shock or minimizing damage in collision **2** a bouncer

bumpkin *n* an awkward and unsophisticated rustic 〈*a country ~*〉

bump off *vt* to murder – slang

bumptious *adj* self-assertive in a presumptuous, obtuse and often noisy manner; obtrusive – **bumptiously** *adv*, **bumptiousness** *n*

bumpy *adj* **1** having or covered with bumps; uneven 〈*a ~ road*〉 **2** marked by jolts 〈*a ~ ride*〉 – **bumpily** *adv*, **bumpiness** *n*

bun *n* **1** any of various usu sweet and round small bread rolls that may contain added ingredients (e g currants or spice) **2** a usu tight knot of hair worn esp on the back of the head **3** *chiefly N Eng* a small round sweet cake often made from a sponge-cake mixture – **bun in the oven** a child in the womb 〈*she's got a bun in the oven*〉

¹bunch *n* **1** a compact group formed by a number of things of the same kind, esp when growing or held together; a cluster **2** *sing or pl in constr* the main group (e g of cyclists) in a race **3** *pl, Br* a style in which the hair is divided into 2 lengths and tied, usu one on each side of th head **4** *sing or pl in constr* a group of people – *infml* – bunchy *adj*

²bunch *vb* to form (into) a group or cluster – often + *up*

¹bundle *n* **1a** a collection of things held loosely together **b** a package **c** a collection, conglomerate **2** a small band of mostly parallel nerve or other fibres **3** a great deal; mass ⟨*that will be a ~ of fun*⟩ ⟨*he's a ~ of nerves*⟩ **4** a sizable sum of money – *slang*

²bundle *vt* **bundling 1** to make into a bundle or package **2** to hustle or hurry unceremoniously ⟨*~ d the children off to school*⟩ **3** to hastily deposit or stuff *into* a suitcase, box, drawer, etc

bundle up *vb* to dress warmly

¹bung *n* the stopper in the bunghole of a cask; *broadly* sthg used to plug an opening

²bung *vt* **1** to plug, block, or close (as if) with a bung – often + *up* **2** *chiefly Br* to throw, toss **3** *Br* to put ⟨*~ that record on*⟩ USE (except 1) *infml*

bungalow *n* a usu detached or semidetached 1-storied house

bunghole *n* a hole for emptying or filling a cask

bungle *vt* **bungling** to perform clumsily; mishandle, botch – bungler *n*, bungling *adj*

bunion *n* an inflamed swelling at the side of the foot on the first joint of the big toe

¹bunk *n* **1** a built-in bed (e g on a ship) that is often one of a tier of berths **2** a sleeping place – *infml*

²bunk *vi* to sleep or bed *down*, esp in a makeshift bed

³bunk *n* – do a bunk *chiefly Br* to make a hurried departure, esp in order to escape – *slang*

⁴bunk *n* nonsense, humbug ⟨*history is ~* – Henry Ford⟩

bunk bed *n* either of 2 single beds usu placed one above the other

¹bunker *n* **1** a bin or compartment for storage; *esp* one on a ship for storing fuel **2a** a protective embankment or dugout; *esp* a fortified chamber mostly below ground **b** a golf course hazard that is an area of sand-covered bare ground with 1 or more embankments

²bunker *vt* to place or store (esp fuel) in a bunker

bunkum *n* insincere or foolish talk; nonsense

bunny *n* RABBIT 1 – usu used by or to children

Bunsen burner *n* a gas burner in which air is mixed with the gas to produce an intensely hot blue flame

¹bunting *n* any of various birds that have short strong beaks and are related to the finches

²bunting *n* (flags or decorations made of) a lightweight loosely woven fabric

¹buoy *n* a distinctively shaped and marked float moored to the bottom **a** as a navigational aid to mark a channel or hazard **b** for mooring a ship

²buoy *vt* **1** to mark (as if) by a buoy **2a** to keep afloat **b** to support, sustain **3** to raise the spirits of ⟨*hope ~s him up*⟩ USE (2 & 3) usu + *up*

buoyancy *n* **1a** the tendency of a body to float or to rise when submerged in a fluid **b** the power of a fluid to exert an upward force on a body placed in it **2** resilience, vivacity – buoyant *adj*, buoyantly *adv*

bur *n* ¹BURR

burble *vi* **burbling 1** to make a bubbling sound; gurgle **2** to babble, prattle **3** *of airflow* to become turbulent – burble *n*

¹burden *n* **1a** sthg that is carried; a load **b** a duty, responsibility **2** sthg oppressive or wearisome; an encumbrance **3** capacity for carrying cargo ⟨*a ship of a hundred tons ~*⟩

²burden *vt* to load, oppress

³burden *n* **1** a chorus, refrain **2** a central topic; a theme

burden of proof *n* the duty of proving an assertion

burdensome *adj* imposing or constituting a burden; oppressive

burdock *n* any of a genus of coarse composite plants bearing prickly spherical flower heads

bureau *n*, *pl* bureaus *also* bureaux **1a** a specialized administrative unit; *esp* a government department **b** an establishment for exchanging information, making contacts, or coordinating activities **2** *Br* a writing desk; *esp* one with drawers and a sloping top

bureaucracy *n* **1** government characterized by specialization of functions, adherence to fixed rules, and a hierarchy of authority; *also* the body of appointed government officials **2** a system of public administration marked by excessive officialism – bureaucratize *vt*, bureaucratization *n*, bureaucratic *adj*, bureaucratically *adv*

bureaucrat *n* a member of a bureaucracy; *esp* a government official who follows a rigid routine

burgeon *vi* **1** to send forth new growth (e g buds or branches) **2** to grow and expand rapidly

burgess *n*, *archaic* a citizen of a British borough

burgh *n* a borough; *specif* a town in Scotland that has a charter

burgher *n* an inhabitant of an esp medieval borough or a town

burglar *n* sby who commits burglary – burglarize *vt*, *chiefly NAm*

burglary *n* the offence of unlawfully entering a building with criminal intent, esp to steal

burgle *vt* **burgling** to commit an act of burglary against

burgomaster *n* the mayor of a town in certain European countries

Burgundy *n* a red or white table wine from the Burgundy region of France

burial *n* the act, process, or ceremony of burying esp a dead body

burlap *n* a coarse heavy plain-woven fabric, usu of jute or hemp, used for sacking and in furniture and linoleum manufacture

¹burlesque *n* **1** a literary or dramatic work that uses exaggeration or imitation to ridicule **2** mockery, usu by caricature **3** a US stage show usu consisting of short turns, comic sketches, and striptease acts – burlesque *adj*

²burlesque *vt* to imitate in a humorous or derisive manner; mock

burly *adj* strongly and heavily built – burliness *n*

¹burn *n*, *chiefly Scot* a small stream

²burn *vb* **burnt, burned** *vi* **1a** to consume fuel and give off heat, light, and gases **b** to undergo combustion **c** to undergo nuclear fission or nuclear fusion **d** to give off light ⟨*a light ~ing in the window*⟩ **2a** *of the ears or face* to become very red and feel uncomfortably hot **b** to produce or undergo a painfully stinging or smarting sensation ⟨*fingers ~ing from the cold*⟩ **c** to receive sunburn ⟨*kind of skin that ~s easily*⟩ **d(1)** to long passionately ⟨¹DIE 3 ⟨*~ing to tell the story*⟩ (2) to be filled *with*; experience sthg strongly ⟨*~ing with fury*⟩ **3** to become charred, scorched, or destroyed by fire or the action of heat ⟨*the potatoes are ~ing*⟩ ~ *vt* **1a** to cause to undergo combustion; *esp* to destroy by fire ⟨*~ed the rubbish*⟩ **b** to use as fuel **2a** to transform by exposure to heat or fire ⟨*~ clay to bricks*⟩ **b** to produce by burning ⟨*~ a hole in the sleeve*⟩ **3a** to injure or damage by exposure to fire, heat, radiation, caustic chemicals, or electricity **b** to execute by burning ⟨*~ heretics at the stake*⟩ **c** to char or scorch by exposing to fire or heat **4**

to harm, exploit – often pass – **burnable** *adj* – **burn one's bridges/boats** to cut off all means of retreat – **burn the candle at both ends** to use one's resources or energies to excess; *esp* to be active at night as well as by day – **burn the midnight oil** to work or study far into the night

³burn *n* **1a** injury or damage resulting (as if) from burning **b** a burned area ⟨*a* ~ *on the table top*⟩ **c** a burning sensation ⟨*the* ~ *of iodine on a cut*⟩ **2** a firing of a spacecraft rocket engine in flight

burner *n* the part of a fuel-burning device (e g a stove or furnace) where the flame is produced

burning *adj* **1a** on fire **b** ardent, intense ⟨~ *enthusiasm*⟩ **2a** affecting (as if) with heat ⟨*a* ~ *fever*⟩ **b** resembling that produced by a burn ⟨*a* ~ *sensation on the tongue*⟩ **3** of fundamental importance; urgent ⟨*one of the* ~ *issues of our time*⟩ – **burningly** *adv*

burnish *vt* to make shiny or lustrous, esp by rubbing; polish – **burnishing** *adj or n*

burnous *n* a hooded cloak traditionally worn by Arabs and Moors

burn out *vt* **1** to cause to be no longer active, having completed a course of development ⟨*the disease had* burnt *itself* out⟩ **2** to exhaust by excessive physical or mental activity ⟨*she was a* burnt-out *case at 30*⟩ **3** to cause to burn out ~ *vi* to cease to conduct electricity when the enclosed filament or conducting wire has melted

burn up *vt* to drive along extremely fast ⟨burn up *the motorway*⟩ – infml – **burn-up** *n*

¹burp *n* a belch – infml

²burp *vb* to (cause to) belch – infml

¹burr, bur *n* **1** a rough or prickly covering of a fruit or seed **2** sthg that sticks or clings **3** a thin rough edge left after cutting or shaping metal, plastic, etc **4** the pronunciation of /r/ in a W country or Northumberland accent **5** a small drill; *also* a bit used in a dentist's or surgeon's burr **6** a rough whirring sound – burred *adj*, **burry** *adj*

²burr *vi* to make a whirring sound ~ *vt* to pronounce with a burr

burro *n*, *pl* **burros** *chiefly NAm* a small donkey (used as a pack animal)

¹burrow *n* a hole or excavation in the ground made by a rabbit, fox, etc for shelter and habitation

²burrow *vt* **1** to construct or excavate by tunnelling ⟨~ ed *its way beneath the hill*⟩ **2** to make a motion suggestive of burrowing with; nestle ⟨*she* ~ ed *her grubby hand into mine*⟩ ~ *vi* **1** to conceal oneself (as if) in a burrow **2a** to make a burrow **b** to progress (as if) by digging **3** to make a motion suggestive of burrowing; snuggle, nestle ⟨~ ed *against her back for warmth*⟩ **4** to make a search as if by digging ⟨~ ed *into her pocket for a 10p piece*⟩ – **burrower** *n*

bursa *n*, *pl* **bursas, bursae** a small sac or pouch (between a tendon and a bone) – **bursal** *adj*

bursar *n* **1** an officer (e g of a monastery or college) in charge of funds **2** *chiefly Scot* the holder of a bursary

bursary *n* **1** a bursar's office **2** a grant of money to a needy student

¹burst *vb* **burst** *vi* **1** to break open, apart, or into pieces, usu from impact or because of pressure from within **2a** to give way from an excess of emotion ⟨*his heart will* ~ *with grief*⟩ **b** to give vent suddenly to a repressed emotion ⟨~ *into tears*⟩ **3a** to emerge or spring suddenly ⟨~ *out of a house*⟩ **b** to launch, plunge ⟨~ *into song*⟩ **4** to be filled to breaking point or to the point of overflowing ~ *vt* **1** to cause to break open or into pieces, usu by means of pressure from within **2** to produce (as if) by bursting – **burst at the seams** to be large or full to the point of discomfort

²burst *n* **1** a sudden usu temporary outbreak **2** an explo-

sion, eruption **3** a sharp temporary increase (of speed, energy, etc) **4** a volley of shots

burst out *vi* to begin suddenly ⟨*he* burst out *laughing*⟩ ~ *vt* to exclaim suddenly

bury *vt* **1** to dispose of by depositing (as if) in the earth; *esp* to inter **2** to conceal, hide ⟨*the report was* buried *under miscellaneous papers*⟩ **3** to put completely out of mind; HAVE DONE WITH ⟨~ ing *their differences*⟩ **4** to submerge, engross – usu + *in* ⟨buried *herself in her books*⟩ – **bury the hatchet** to settle a disagreement; become reconciled

¹bus *n*, *pl* **-s-**, *chiefly NAm* **-ss-** **1** a large motor-driven passenger vehicle operating usu according to a timetable along a fixed route **2** a busbar

²bus *vb* **-s-**, **-ss-** *vi* to travel by bus ~ *vt* to transport by bus; *specif*, *chiefly NAm* to transport (children) by bus to a school in another district where the pupils are of a different race, in order to create integrated classes

busbar *n* a conductor or an assembly of conductors connected to several similar circuits in an electrical or electronic system

busby *n* **1** a military full-dress fur hat worn esp by hussars **2** the bearskin worn by the Brigade of Guards – not used technically

¹bush *n* **1a** a (low densely branched) shrub **b** a close thicket of shrubs **2** a large uncleared or sparsely settled area (e g in Africa or Australia), usu scrub-covered or forested **3a** a bushy tuft or mass ⟨*a* ~ *of black hair*⟩ **b** ²BRUSH 2

²bush *vt* to support, protect, etc with bushes ~ *vi* to extend like or resemble a bush

³bush, bushing *n* a usu removable cylindrical lining for an opening used to limit the size of the opening, resist abrasion, or serve as a guide

⁴bush *vt* to provide (a bearing, shaft, etc) with a bush

bush baby *n* a member of either of 2 genera of small active nocturnal tree-dwelling African primates

bushed *adj* **1** perplexed, confused **2** *chiefly Austr* lost, esp in the bush **3** tired, exhausted – infml

bushel *n* **1** any of various units of dry capacity **2** a container holding a bushel

bush telegraph *n* the rapid unofficial communication of news, rumours, etc by word of mouth

bushwhack *vi* **1** to clear a path through thick woods **2** to live or hide out in the woods **3** to fight in or attack from the bush ~ *vt* to ambush – **bushwhacker** *n*, **bushwhacking** *n*

bushy *adj* **1** full of or overgrown with bushes **2** growing thickly or densely – **bushily** *adv*, **bushiness** *n*

business *n* **1a** a role, function **b** an immediate task or objective; a mission **c** a particular field of endeavour ⟨*the best in the* ~⟩ **2a** a usu commercial or mercantile activity engaged in as a means of livelihood **b** one's regular employment, profession, or trade **c** a commercial or industrial enterprise ⟨*sold her* ~ *and retired*⟩; *also* such enterprises ⟨~ *seldom acts as a unit*⟩ **d** economic transactions or dealings ⟨*ready to take his* ~ *elsewhere unless service improved*⟩ **3** an affair, matter ⟨*a strange* ~⟩ **4** movement or action performed by an actor **5a** personal concern ⟨*none of your* ~⟩ **b** proper motive; justifying right ⟨*you have no* ~ *asking me that*⟩ **6** serious activity ⟨*immediately got down to* ~⟩ – **like nobody's business** extraordinarily well

businesslike *adj* **1** (briskly) efficient **2** serious, purposeful

businessman, fem businesswoman *n* **1** sby professionally engaged in commercial transactions; *esp* a business executive **2** sby with financial flair ⟨*I'm not much of a* ~⟩

busk *vi, chiefly Br* to sing or play an instrument in the street (e g outside a theatre) in order to earn money – **busker** *n*

busman *n, chiefly Br* sby who works on a bus

busman's holiday *n* a holiday spent doing one's usual work

bus-stop *n* a place, usu marked by a standardized sign, where people may board and alight from buses

¹**bust** *n* 1 a sculpture of the upper part of the human figure including the head, neck, and usu shoulders 2 the upper part of the human torso between neck and waist; *esp* the (size of the) breasts of a woman

²**bust** *vb* busted *also* bust *vt* 1a to break, smash; *also* to make inoperative ⟨~ *my watch this morning*⟩ b to bring to an end; BREAK UP 3 – often + *up* 2a to arrest b to raid ⟨*police* ~ *ed the flat below looking for heroin*⟩ ~ *vi* 1a to burst ⟨*laughing fit to* ~⟩ b BREAK DOWN 1a 2 to lose a game or turn by exceeding a limit (e g the count of 21 in pontoon) USE (*vt; vi 1*) infml – **bust a gut** to exert oneself; make a great effort – infml

³**bust** *n* a police raid or arrest – infml

⁴**bust** *adj* 1 broken – chiefly infml 2 bankrupt – chiefly in **go bust**; infml

bustard *n* any of a family of usu large Old World and Australian game birds

buster *n* 1 sby or sthg that breaks or breaks up ⟨*crime* ~s⟩ 2 chiefly NAm PAL 2a – usu as a form of address ⟨*thanks a million,* ~⟩

¹**bustle** *vi* bustling to move briskly and often ostentatiously – bustling *adj*, bustlingly *adv*

²**bustle** *n* noisy and energetic activity ⟨*the hustle and* ~ *of the big city*⟩

³**bustle** *n* a pad or framework worn to expand and support fullness at the back of a woman's skirt

bust-up *n* 1 a breaking up or apart ⟨*the* ~ *of their marriage*⟩ 2 a quarrel USE infml

¹**busy** *adj* 1 engaged in action; occupied 2 full of activity; bustling ⟨*a* ~ *seaport*⟩ 3 foolishly or intrusively active; meddlesome 4 full of detail ⟨*a* ~ *design*⟩ 5 NAm, esp of a telephone in use – busily *adv*, busyness *n*

²**busy** *vt* to make (esp oneself) busy; occupy ⟨*he busied himself with the ironing*⟩

busybody *n* an officious or inquisitive person

¹**but** *conj* 1a were it not ⟨*would collapse* ~ *for your help*⟩ b without the necessary accompaniment that – used after a negative ⟨*it never rains* ~ *it pours*⟩ c otherwise than; that not ⟨*I don't know* ~ *what I'll go*⟩ 2a on the contrary; on the other hand – used to join coordinate sentence elements of the same class or function expressing contrast ⟨*I meant to tell you* ~ *you weren't here*⟩ b and nevertheless; and yet ⟨*poor* ~ *proud*⟩ c – introducing an expression of protest or enthusiasm ⟨~ *that's ridiculous*⟩ or embarking on a new topic ⟨~ *to continue B*⟩

²**but** *prep* 1a with the exception of; barring ⟨*we're all here* ~ *Mary*⟩ b other than ⟨*this letter is nothing* ~ *an insult*⟩ c not counting ⟨*the next house* ~ *2*⟩ 2 Scot without, lacking

³**but** *adv* 1 only, merely ⟨*he is* ~ *a child*⟩ 2 to the contrary ⟨*who knows* ~ *that he may succeed*⟩ 3 – used for emphasis ⟨*get there* ~ *fast*⟩ 4 NE Eng & Austr however, though ⟨*it's pouring with rain, warm* ~⟩

⁴**but** *n* a doubt, objection ⟨*there are no* ~s *about it*⟩

butane *n* an inflammable gaseous hydrocarbon of the alkane series used esp as a fuel (e g in cigarette lighters)

¹**butch** *n, chiefly Br* a male or female homosexual who plays the masculine role in a relationship

²**butch** *adj, chiefly Br* aggressively masculine in appearance

– used, often disparagingly, of both women and (esp homosexual) men

¹**butch** *n* 1a sby who slaughters animals or dresses their flesh b sby who deals in meat 2 sby who kills ruthlessly or brutally

²**butcher** *vt* 1 to slaughter and prepare for market 2 to kill in a barbarous manner 3 to spoil, ruin – **butcherer** *n*

butchery *n* 1 the preparation of meat for sale 2 cruel and ruthless slaughter of human beings 3 the action of spoiling or ruining 4 chiefly Br a slaughterhouse

butler *n* 1 a manservant in charge of the wines and spirits 2 the chief male servant of a household

¹**butt** *vb* to strike or shove (sthg) with the head or horns

²**butt** *n* a blow or thrust, usu with the head or horns

³**butt** *n* 1a a backstop for catching missiles shot at a target b a target c *pl* a range, specif for archery or rifle practice d a low mound, wall, etc from behind which sportsmen shoot at game birds 2 an object of abuse or ridicule; a victim

⁴**butt** *vi* to abut – usu + *against* or *onto* ~ *vt* 1 to place end to end or side to side without overlapping 2 to join by means of a butt joint

⁵**butt** *n* 1 the end of a plant or tree nearest the roots 2 the thicker or handle end of a tool or weapon 3 an unused remainder; *esp* the unsmoked remnant of a cigar or cigarette

⁶**butt** *n* a large cask, esp for wine, beer, or water

¹**butter** *n* 1 a pale yellow solid emulsion of fat globules, air, and water made by churning milk or cream and used as food 2a any of various vegetable oils remaining solid or semisolid at ordinary temperatures ⟨*cocoa* ~⟩ b any of various food spreads made with or having the consistency of butter ⟨*peanut* ~⟩ – **butterless** *adj*

²**butter** *vt* to spread or cook with butter

butter bean *n* 1 a (large dried) lima bean 2 SIEVA BEAN

buttercup *n* any of many plants with usu bright yellow flowers that commonly grow in fields and as weeds

butterfat *n* the natural fat of milk and chief constituent of butter

butterfingers *n, pl* butterfingers a butterfingered person – infml

butterfly *n* 1 any of numerous slender-bodied day-flying insects with large broad often brightly coloured wings 2 a person chiefly occupied with the pursuit of pleasure 3 a swimming stroke executed on the front by moving both arms together forwards out of the water and then sweeping them back through the water 4 *pl* queasiness caused esp by nervous tension – infml

buttermilk *n* 1 the liquid left after butter has been churned from milk or cream 2 cultured milk made by the addition of suitable bacteria to milk

butterscotch *n* (the flavour of) a brittle toffee made from brown sugar, syrup, butter, and water

butter up *vt* to charm with lavish flattery; cajole – infml

¹**buttery** *n* a room (e g in a college) in which food and drink are served or sold

²**buttery** *adj* similar to or containing butter

butt in *vi* 1 to meddle, intrude 2 to interrupt

buttock *n* the back of a hip that forms one of the 2 fleshy parts on which a person sits

¹**button** *n* 1 a small knob or disc secured to an article (e g of clothing) and used as a fastener by passing it through a buttonhole or loop 2 an immature whole mushroom 3 a guard on the tip of a fencing foil 4 PUSH BUTTON 5 sthg of little value ⟨*not worth a* ~⟩ – **buttonless** *adj*

²**button** *vt* to close or fasten (as if) with buttons – often +

up ⟨~ *up your overcoat*⟩ ~ *vi* to have buttons for fastening ⟨*this dress* ~s *at the back*⟩

button-down *adj, of a collar* having the ends fastened to the garment with buttons

¹buttonhole *n* **1** a slit or loop through which a button is passed **2** *chiefly Br* a flower worn in a buttonhole or pinned to the lapel

²buttonhole *vt* **1** to provide with buttonholes **2** to sew with buttonhole stitch – **buttonholer** *n*

³buttonhole *vt* to detain in conversation

buttonhook *n* a hook for drawing small buttons through buttonholes

buttons *n, pl* **buttons** *Br* a bellboy – *infml*

buttress *n* **1** a structure built against a wall or building to provide support or reinforcement **2** a projecting part of a mountain **3** sthg that supports or strengthens ⟨*a* ~ *of the cause of peace*⟩ – **buttress** *vt*, **buttressed** *adj*

buxom *adj* attractively or healthily plump; *specif* full-bosomed – **buxomness** *n*

¹buy *vb* **bought** *vt* **1** to acquire possession or rights to the use of by payment, esp of money; purchase **2** to obtain, often by some sacrifice ⟨bought *peace with their lives*⟩ **3** to bribe, hire **4** to be the purchasing equivalent of ⟨*the pound* ~s *less today than it used to*⟩ **5** to believe, accept ⟨*OK, I'll* ~ *that*⟩ – *slang* ~ *vi* to make a purchase – **buy time** to delay an imminent action or decision; stall

²buy *n* an act of buying; a purchase

buyer *n* one who selects and buys stock to be sold in an esp large shop

buyer's market *n* a market in which supply exceeds demand, buyers have a wide range of choice, and prices tend to be low

buy in *vt* to obtain (a stock or supply of sthg) by purchase, esp in anticipation of need; *also* to complete an outstanding securities transaction by purchase against the account of (a delaying or defaulting speculator or dealer) – **buy-in** *n*

buy off *vt* to make a payment to in order to avoid some undesired course of action (e g prosecution)

buy out *vt* **1** to purchase the share or interest of ⟨bought out *his partner*⟩ **2** to free (e g from military service) by payment – usu + *of* ⟨bought *himself* out *of the army*⟩

buy up *vt* **1** to purchase a controlling interest in (e g a company), esp by acquiring shares **2** to buy the entire available supply of

¹buzz *vi* **1** to make a low continuous vibratory sound like that of a bee **2** to be filled with a confused murmur ⟨*the room* ~ed *with excitement*⟩ **3** to make a signal with a buzzer ~ *vt* **1** to cause to buzz **2** to fly over or close to in order to threaten or warn ⟨*the airliner was* ~ed *by fighters during its approach*⟩ **3** to summon or signal with a buzzer

²buzz *n* **1** a persistent vibratory sound **2a** a confused murmur or flurry of activity **b** rumour, gossip **3** a signal conveyed by a buzzer or bell; *specif* a telephone call – *infml* **4** *chiefly NAm* a pleasant stimulation; a kick – *infml*

buzzard *n* **1** a contemptible, greedy, or grasping person **2** *chiefly Br* a common large European hawk with soaring flight, or a similar related bird **3** *chiefly NAm* a (large) bird of prey (e g the turkey buzzard)

buzzer *n* an electric signalling device that makes a buzzing sound

buzz off *vi* to go away quickly – slang

¹by *prep* **1a** in proximity to; near ⟨*standing* ~ *the window*⟩ **b** on the person or in the possession of ⟨*keep a spare set* ~ *me*⟩ **2a** through (the medium of); via ⟨*enter* ~ *the door*⟩ ⟨*delivered* ~ *hand*⟩ **b** 11°15′ in the direction of (another compass point up to 90° away) ⟨*north* ~ *east*⟩

c up to and then beyond; past ⟨*went right* ~ *him*⟩ **3a** in the circumstances of; during ⟨*studied* ~ *night*⟩ **b** not later than ⟨*in bed* ~ *2 am*⟩ **4a**(1) through the instrumentality or use of ⟨~ *bus*⟩ ⟨*what did he mean* ~ *that?*⟩ **(2)** through the action or creation of ⟨*a trio* ~ *Mozart*⟩ **b(1)** sired by **(2)** with the participation of (the other parent) ⟨*his daughter* ~ *his first wife*⟩ **5** with the witness or sanction of ⟨*swear* ~ *Heaven*⟩ **6a** in conformity with ⟨*acted* ~ *the rules*⟩ ⟨*opened it* ~ *mistake*⟩ **b** in terms of ⟨*paid* ~ *the hour*⟩ ⟨*called her* ~ *name*⟩ **c** from the evidence of ⟨*judge* ~ *appearances*⟩ **d** with the action of ⟨*began* ~ *scolding her*⟩ ⟨*alarmed him* ~ *driving too fast*⟩ **7** with respect to ⟨*French* ~ *birth*⟩ **8** to the amount or extent of ⟨*better* ~ *far*⟩ **9** in successive units or increments of ⟨~ *inches*⟩ ⟨*day* ~ *day*⟩ ⟨*succeeded little* ~ *little*⟩ **10** – used in division as the inverse of *into* ⟨*divide 70* ~ *35*⟩, in multiplication ⟨*multiply 10* ~ *4*⟩, and in measurements ⟨*a room 15ft* ~ *20ft*⟩ **11** *chiefly Scot* in comparison with; beside – **by oneself 1** alone, unaccompanied ⟨*standing* by himself *watching the others playing*⟩ **2** unaided ⟨*did her shoes up all* by herself⟩

²by *adv* **1a** close at hand; near ⟨*when nobody was* ~⟩ **b** at or to another's home ⟨*stop* ~ *for a chat*⟩ **2** past ⟨*saw him go* ~⟩ **3** aside, away; in or into reserve ⟨*keep a few bottles* ~⟩

by and by *adv* soon

by and large *adv* ON THE WHOLE, IN GENERAL

¹bye, by *n* **1** sthg of secondary importance **2** the passage to the next round of a tournament allowed to a competitor without an opponent **3** a run scored in cricket off a ball that passes the batsman without striking the bat or body – **by the bye** BY THE WAY

²bye, by *interj* – used to express farewell

bye-bye, by-by *interj* – used to express farewell

by-election *also* **bye-election** *n* a special election to fill a vacancy

¹bygone *adj* earlier, past; *esp* outmoded

²bygone *n* an esp domestic artefact of an early and disused type – **let bygones be bygones** to forgive and forget past quarrels

bylaw, byelaw *n* a local or secondary law or regulation

by-line *n* **1** a secondary line; a sideline **2** the author's name printed with a newspaper or magazine article

¹bypass *n* **1** a passage to one side; *esp* a road built so that through traffic can avoid a town centre **2** a channel carrying a fluid round a part and back to the main stream

²bypass *vt* **1** to avoid by means of a bypass **2** to neglect or ignore, usu intentionally; circumvent

byplay *n* action engaged in on the side while the main action proceeds (e g during a dramatic production)

by-product *n* sthg produced (e g in manufacturing) in addition to a principal product

byre *n, chiefly Br* a cow shed

bystander *n* one present but not involved in a situation or event

byte *n* a string of adjacent binary digits that is often shorter than a word and is processed by a computer as a unit; *esp* one that is 8 bits long

byway *n* **1** a little-used road **2** a secondary or little known aspect ⟨*the author takes us down the* ~s *of medieval literature*⟩

byword *n* **1** a proverb **2** (the name of) sby or sthg taken as representing some usu bad quality ⟨*a* ~ *for cruelty*⟩

Byzantine *adj* **1** (characteristic) of the ancient city of Byzantium or its empire **2** of or in a style of architecture developed in the Byzantine Empire in the 5th and 6th c, featuring a central dome carried over a square space and much use of mosaics **3** intricately tortuous; labyrinthine – **Byzantine** *n*

C

c *n, pl* **c's, cs** **1** (a graphic representation of or device for reproducing) the 3rd letter of the English alphabet **2** a speech counterpart of orthographic *c* **3** the keynote of a C-major scale **4** one designated *c*, esp as the 3rd in order or class **5** a grade rating a student's work as fair or mediocre in quality **6a** one hundred **b** *chiefly NAm* a sum of $100 – slang

ca' *vb or n, Scot* (to) call

cab *n* **1** a taxi **2** the part of a locomotive, lorry, crane, etc that houses the driver and operating controls

cabal *vi or n* **-ll-** (to unite in or form) a clandestine or unofficial faction, esp in political intrigue – **cabalist** *n*

cabaret *n* a stage show or series of acts provided at a nightclub, restaurant, etc

cabbage *n* **1** a cultivated plant that has a short stem and a dense globular head of usu green leaves used as a vegetable **2a** one who has lost control of his/her esp mental and physical faculties as the result of illness or accident **b** an inactive and apathetic person *USE* (2) infml

cabby, cabbie *n* a taxi driver – infml

caber *n* a roughly trimmed tree trunk that is tossed for distance in a Scottish sport

¹cabin *n* **1a** a room or compartment on a ship or boat for passengers or crew **b** a compartment in an aircraft for cargo, crew, or passengers **2** a small usu single-storied dwelling of simple construction **3** *chiefly Br* CAB 2

²cabin *vt* to confine – chiefly poetic

cabin boy *n* a boy employed as a servant on board a ship

cabin class *n* a class of accommodation on a passenger ship superior to tourist class and inferior to first class

cabin cruiser *n* a private motorboat with living accommodation

¹cabinet *n* **1a** a case for storing or displaying articles **b** an upright case housing a radio or television set **2** *sing or pl in constr, often cap* a body of advisers of a head of state, who formulate government policy

²cabinet *adj* of a governmental cabinet

cabinetmaker *n* a craftsman who makes fine furniture in wood – **cabinetmaking** *n*

¹cable *n* **1a** a strong thick rope **b** a wire rope or metal chain of great tensile strength **2** an assembly of electrical conductors insulated from each other and surrounded by a sheath **3** a cablegram **4** **cable, cable length** a nautical unit of length equal to about **a** *Br* 185m (202yd) **b** *NAm* 219m (240yd)

²cable *vb* **cabling** *vt* **1** to fasten or provide with a cable or cables **2a** to transmit (a message) by submarine cable **b** to communicate with or inform (a person) by cablegram **3** to make into (a form resembling) a cable ~ *vi* to communicate by means of a cablegram

cable car *n* a carriage made to be moved on a cable railway or along an overhead cable

cablegram *n* a message sent by a submarine cable

cable railway *n* a railway along which the carriages are pulled by an endless cable operated by a stationary motor; ²FUNICULAR

caboodle *n* a collection, lot ⟨*sell the whole* ~⟩ – infml

caboose *n* **1** a ship's galley **2** *NAm* a wagon attached to a goods train, usu at the rear, mainly for the use of the train crew

cabriolet *n* a light 2-wheeled 1-horse carriage with upward-curving shafts

cacao *n, pl* **cacaos** (a S American tree bearing) the fatty seeds which are used, partly fermented and dried, in making cocoa, chocolate, and cocoa butter

cache *n* **1** a hiding place, esp for provisions or weapons **2** sthg hidden or stored in a cache – **cache** *vt*

cachet *n* **1** ³SEAL 1; *esp* one used as a mark of official approval **2** (a characteristic feature or quality conferring) prestige **3** sthg other than the postmark that is stamped by hand on a postal item

cachou *n* **1** catechu **2** a pill or lozenge used to sweeten the breath

cackle *vi* **cackling** **1** to make the sharp broken noise or cry characteristic of a hen, esp after laying **2** to laugh in a way suggestive of a hen's cackle **3** ¹CHATTER 2 – **cackle** *n*, **cackler** *n*

cacophony *n* harsh or discordant sound; dissonance – **cacophonous** *adj*

cactus *n, pl* **cacti, cactuses** any of a family of plants that have fleshy stems and scaly or spiny branches instead of leaves and are found esp in dry areas (e g deserts)

cad *n* an unscrupulous or dishonourable man – derog; not now in vogue – **caddish** *adj*

cadaver *n* a corpse, usu intended for dissection

cadaverous *adj* **1** (suggestive) of a corpse **2a** unhealthily pale; pallid, livid **b** gaunt, emaciated – **cadaverously** *adv*

caddie, caddy *n* one who assists a golfer, esp by carrying clubs – **caddie, caddy** *vi*

caddy *n* a small box or tin used esp for holding tea

cadence, cadency *n* **1a** the rhythm and intonations in language **b** a falling inflection of the voice **2** a concluding strain; *specif* a musical chord sequence moving to a harmonic close or point of rest and giving the sense of harmonic completion **3** the modulated and rhythmic recurrence of a sound – **cadenced** *adj*, **cadential** *adj*

cadenza *n* a technically showy sometimes improvised solo passage in a concerto

cadet *n* **1a** a younger brother or son **b** (a member of) a younger branch of a family **2** sby training to be an officer in the armed forces or a policeman **3** a young person receiving basic military training, esp at school – **cadetship** *n*

cadge *vb* to get (sthg) by asking and usu imposing on sby's hospitality or good nature – infml – **cadger** *n*

cadi *n* a judge in a Muslim community

cadmium *n* a bluish-white soft toxic bivalent metallic element used esp in platings and bearing metals

cadre *n* **1** a permanent nucleus of an esp military organization, capable of rapid expansion if necessary **2** (a member of) a group of activists working for the Communist party cause

caecum, *NAm chiefly* cecum *n* a cavity open at 1 end; *esp* the pouch in which the large intestine begins and into which the ileum opens – **caecal** *adj*, **caecally** *adv*

Caerphilly *n* a mild white moist cheese

caesarean, caesarean section, caesarian, *NAm* cesarean *n* a surgical incision of the abdominal and uterine walls for the delivery of offspring

caesura *n, pl* **caesuras, caesurae** a break or pause in usu the middle of a line of verse – **caesural** *adj*

café *n* **1** *chiefly Br* a small restaurant or coffeehouse serving light meals and nonalcoholic drinks **2** *NAm* BAR 5a(2)

cafeteria *n* a restaurant in which the customers serve

themselves or are served at a counter and take the food to tables to eat

caffeine *n* an alkaloid found esp in tea and coffee that acts as a stimulant and diuretic – **caffeinic** *adj*

caftan, kaftan *n* a loose ankle-length garment with long sleeves, traditionally worn by Arabs

¹cage *n* **1** a box or enclosure of open construction for animals **2** a barred cell or fenced area for prisoners **3** a framework serving as a support ⟨*the steel* ~ *of a skyscraper*⟩ **4** an enclosure resembling a cage in form or purpose

²cage *vt* to put or keep (as if) in a cage

cagey *also* **cagy** *adj* **1** hesitant about committing oneself **2** wary of being trapped or deceived; shrewd *USE* infml – **cagily** *adv*, **caginess** *also* **cageyness** *n*

cahoot *n* a partnership, league – usu pl with sing. meaning; infml; usu in *in cahoots*

caiman *n*, *pl* **caimans**, *esp collectively* **caiman** a cayman

cairn *n* a pile of stones built as a memorial or landmark – **cairned** *adj*

caisson *n* **1** a chest or wagon for artillery ammunition **2a** a watertight chamber used for construction work under water or as a foundation **b** a float for raising a sunken vessel **c** a hollow floating box or a boat used as a floodgate for a dock or basin **3** COFFER 4

caisson disease *n* pain, paralysis, and often collapse caused by the release of gas bubbles in tissue on too rapid reduction of pressure (e g in deep-sea diving)

cajole *vt* to persuade or deceive with deliberate flattery, esp in the face of reluctance – **cajolement** *n*, **cajoler** *n*, **cajolery** *n*

¹cake *n* **1a** a usu fried or baked often unleavened breadlike food – usu in combination ⟨*oatcake*⟩ **b** (a shaped mass of) any of various sweet baked foods made from a basic mixture of flour and sugar, usu with fat, eggs, and a raising agent **c** a flattened usu round mass of (baked or fried) food ⟨*a fish* ~⟩ **2** a block of compressed or congealed matter ⟨*a* ~ *of ice*⟩

²cake *vt* to encrust ~*vi* to form or harden into a mass

calabash *n* (a container or utensil made from the hard shell of) a gourd

calaboose *n*, *dial NAm* a (local) jail

calamine *n* a pink powder of zinc oxide or carbonate with a small amount of ferric oxide, used in soothing or cooling lotions

calamity *n* **1** a state of deep distress caused by misfortune or loss **2** an extremely grave event; a disaster – **calamitous** *adj*, **calamitously** *adv*, **calamitousness** *n*

calcify *vb* **1** to make or become hardened by deposition of calcium salts, esp calcium carbonate **2** to make or become inflexible or unchangeable – **calcific** *adj*, **calcification** *n*

calcine *vt* to heat (e g inorganic materials) without melting usu in order to drive off volatile matter or to bring about oxidation or powdering of the material ~*vi* to be calcined – **calcination** *n*

calcium *n* a silver-white bivalent metallic element of the alkaline-earth group occurring only in combination

calcium carbide *n* a usu dark grey compound that produces acetylene when mixed with water

calculable *adj* subject to or ascertainable by calculation – **calculably** *adv*, **calculability** *n*

calculate *vt* **1** to determine by mathematical processes **2** to reckon by exercise of practical judgment; estimate ~*vi* **1** to make a calculation **2** to forecast consequences **3** to count, rely – + *on* or *upon*

calculating *adj* **1** used for making calculations ⟨*a* ~

machine⟩ **2** marked by shrewd consideration of self-interest; scheming – **calculatingly** *adv*

calculation *n* **1** (the result of) the process or an act of calculating **2** studied care in planning, esp to promote self-interest – **calculative** *adj*

calculator *n* **1** an electronic or mechanical machine for performing mathematical operations **2** a set or book of tables used in calculating

calculus *n*, *pl* **calculi** *also* **calculuses 1a** an abnormal hard stony mass (e g of cholesterol) in the kidney, gall bladder, or other hollow organ **b** ¹TARTAR 2 **2a** a method of computation or calculation in a special symbolic notation **b** the mathematical methods comprising differential and integral calculus

caldron *n* a cauldron

¹calendar *n* **1** a system for fixing the beginning, length, and divisions of the civil year and arranging days and longer divisions of time (e g weeks and months) in a definite order **2** a tabular display of the days of 1 year **3** a chronological list of events or activities

²calendar *vt* to enter in a calendar

calender *n* a machine for pressing cloth, rubber, paper, etc between rollers or plates (e g for smoothing and glazing) – **calender** *vt*

calends, kalends *n pl but sing or pl in constr* the first day of the ancient Roman month

¹calf *n*, *pl* **calves** *also* **calfs**, *(2)* **calfs 1a** the young of the domestic cow or a closely related mammal (e g a bison) **b** the young of some large animals (e g the elephant and whale) **2** calfskin ⟨*the book was bound in fine* ~⟩ **3** a small mass of ice broken off from a coastal glacier, iceberg, etc – **calflike** *adj* – **in calf** *of a cow* pregnant

²calf *n*, *pl* **calves** the fleshy back part of the leg below the knee

calf love *n* PUPPY LOVE

calfskin *n* a high-quality leather made from the skin of a calf

calibrate *vt* **1** to determine the calibre of (e g a thermometer tube) **2** to determine, adjust, or mark the graduations of (e g a thermometer) **3** to determine the correct reading of (an arbitrary or inaccurate scale or instrument) by comparison with a standard – **calibrator** *n*

calibration *n* a set of graduations that indicate values or positions –usu pl with sing. meaning

calibre, NAm chiefly caliber *n* **1** the internal or external diameter of a round body (e g a bullet or other projectile) or a hollow cylinder (e g a gun barrel) **2a** degree of mental capacity or moral quality **b** degree of excellence or importance

calico *n*, *pl* **calicoes, calicos 1** white unprinted cotton cloth of medium weight, orig imported from India **2** *NAm* brightly printed cotton fabric – **calico** *adj*

caliper *vt or n*, *chiefly NAm* (to) calliper

caliph, calif *n* a secular and spiritual head of Islam claiming descent from Muhammad – **caliphal** *adj*, **caliphate** *n*

calisthenics *n pl but sing or pl in constr*, *chiefly NAm* callisthenics – **calisthenic** *adj*

calk *vt* to caulk – **calker** *n*

¹call *vt* **1a** to speak loudly or distinctly so as to be heard at a distance; shout **b** to make a request or demand ⟨~ *for an investigation*⟩ **c** *of an animal* to utter a characteristic note or cry **2** to make a demand in card games (e g for a particular card or for a show of hands) **3** *of a batsman* to indicate vocally to one's batting partner whether one intends to take a run or not **4** to make a brief visit – often + *in* or *by* ⟨~ed *in at the pub*⟩ **5** *chiefly NAm* to (try to) get into communication by telephone – often + *up* ~*vt* **1a** to utter or announce in a loud distinct voice - often + *out* **b** to read aloud (e g a list of names) ⟨*the teacher* ∼ed *the register every morning*⟩ **2a** to command or request to come or be present ⟨∼ed *to testify*⟩ **b** to cause to come; bring ⟨∼s *to mind an old saying*⟩ **c** to summon to a particular activity, employment, or office ⟨*was* ∼ed *to active duty*⟩ **d** to invite or command to meet; convoke ⟨∼ *a meeting*⟩ **3** to rouse from sleep **4** to give the order for; bring into action ⟨∼ *a strike against the company*⟩ **5a** to make a demand in bridge for (a card or suit) **b** to require (a player) to show the hand in poker by making an equal bet **6** to attract (e g game) by imitating a characteristic cry **7a** to rule on the status of (e g a tennis serve) ⟨*the serve was* ∼ed *out by the umpire*⟩ **b** of a cricket umpire to pronounce the bowling delivery to be illegal ⟨*Griffin was* ∼ed *for throwing*⟩ **8** to give the calls for (a square dance) **9** to suspend ⟨*time was* ∼ed⟩ **10** to speak of or address by a specified name; give a name to ⟨∼ *her Kitty*⟩ **11a** to regard or characterize as a certain kind; consider ⟨*can hardly be* ∼ed *generous*⟩ **b** to consider for purposes of an estimate or for convenience ⟨∼ *it an even quid*⟩ **12** to predict, guess ⟨∼ *the toss of a coin*⟩ **13** chiefly NAm to (try to) get into communication with by telephone –often + *up* – **callable** *adj*, **caller** *n* – **call a spade a spade** to speak frankly and usu bluntly – **called to the bar** admitted as a barrister – **call for 1** to call to get; collect **2** to require as necessary or appropriate ⟨*it called for all her strength*⟩ **3** to demand, order ⟨*legislation calling for the establishment of new schools*⟩ – **call in/into question** to cast doubt upon ⟨*called in question the validity of his statement*⟩ – **call it a day** to stop whatever one has been doing at least for the present – **call it quits 1** CALL IT A DAY **2** to acknowledge that the advantage is now even – **call on/upon 1** to require, oblige ⟨*may be called on to do several jobs*⟩ **2** to appeal to; invoke ⟨*universities are called upon to meet the needs of a technological world*⟩ – **call someone's bluff** to challenge and expose an empty pretence or threat – **call the shots/the tune** to be in charge or control; determine the policy or procedure – **call to account** to hold responsible; reprimand ⟨*called to account for violation of the rules*⟩ – **call to order** to order (a meeting) to observe the customary rules

²**call** *n* **1a** an act of calling with the voice **b** the cry of an animal (e g a bird) **c** (an instrument used to produce) an imitation of an animal's cry made to attract the animal **2a** a request or command to come or assemble **b** a summons or signal on a drum, bugle, or pipe **c** a summoning of actors to the stage (e g for rehearsal) **3a** admission to the bar as a barrister **b** a divine vocation **c** a strong inner prompting to a course of action **d** the attraction or appeal of a particular activity or place ⟨*the* ∼ *of the wild*⟩ **4a** a demand, request **b** need, justification ⟨*there was no* ∼ *for such rudeness*⟩ **5** a short usu formal visit ⟨*a courtesy* ∼⟩ **6** the name (e g of a suit in a card game) or thing called **7** the act of calling in a card game **8** the act of telephoning **9** a direction or a succession of directions for a square dance rhythmically called to the dancers **10** a usu vocal ruling made by an official of a sports contest – **on call 1** available for use ⟨*the company car is always* on call *for you*⟩ **2** ready to respond to a summons or command ⟨*a doctor* on call⟩ – **within call** within hearing or reach of a call or summons

calla,calla lily *n* any of several plants of the arum family; *esp* a European plant that grows in wet places

call box *n, Br* a public telephone box

callboy *n* **1** a person who tells actors when it is time to go on stage **2** chiefly NAm a hotel page

call down *vt* to invoke, request ⟨call down *a blessing on the crops*⟩

call girl *n* a prostitute who accepts appointments by telephone

calligraphy *n* (beautiful or elegant) handwriting – **calligrapher, calligraphist** *n*, **calligraphic** *adj*, **calligraphically** *adv*

call in *vt* **1a** to withdraw from an advanced position ⟨call in *the outposts*⟩ **b** to withdraw from circulation ⟨call in *bank notes and issue new ones*⟩ **2** to summon to one's aid or for consultation ⟨call in *an arbitrator to settle the dispute*⟩

calling *n* **1** a strong inner impulse towards a particular course of action, esp when accompanied by conviction of divine influence **2** a vocation, profession

¹**calliper**, chiefly NAm **caliper** *n* **1** a measuring instrument with 2 arms that can be adjusted to determine thickness, diameter, or distance between surfaces – usu pl with sing. meaning ⟨*a pair of* ∼s⟩ **2** a support for the human leg extending from the knee or thigh to the foot

²**calliper**, chiefly NAm **caliper** *vt* to measure (as if) with callipers

callisthenics, chiefly NAm **calisthenics** *n pl but sing or pl in constr* (the art or practice of) systematic rhythmic bodily exercises performed usu without apparatus – **callisthenic** *adj*

call off *vt* **1** to draw away; divert ⟨call *the dogs* off!⟩ **2** to cancel ⟨call *the trip* off⟩

callous *adj* **1** hardened and thickened **2** unfeeling; *esp* unsympathetic – **callously** *adv*, **callousness** *n*

call out *vt* **1** to summon into action ⟨call out *the guard*⟩ **2** to challenge to a duel **3** to order a strike of ⟨call out *the steelworkers*⟩

callow *adj* **1** of a bird not yet fully fledged **2** lacking adult attitudes; immature ⟨∼ *youth*⟩ – **callowness** *n*

call sign *n* the combination of letters or letters and numbers assigned to an operator, activity, or station for identification of a radio broadcast

call-up *n* an order to report for military service

call up *vt* **1** to bring to mind; evoke **2** to summon before an authority **3** to summon together or collect (e g for a united effort) ⟨call up *all his forces for the attack*⟩ **4** to summon for active military duty

callus *n* **1** a hard thickened area on skin or bark **2** a mass of connective tissue formed round a break in a bone and changed into bone during healing **3** soft tissue that forms over a cut plant surface **4** a tumour of plant tissue

¹**calm** *n* **1a** the absence of winds or rough water; stillness **b** a state in which the wind has a speed of less than 1km/h (about ⅝mph) **2** a state of repose free from agitation

²**calm** *adj* **1** marked by calm; still ⟨*a* ∼ *sea*⟩ **2** free from agitation or excitement ⟨*a* ∼ *manner*⟩ – **calmly** *adv*, **calmness** *n*

³**calm** *vb* to make or become calm

calomel *n* MERCUROUS CHLORIDE

Calor gas *trademark* – used for butane gas in liquid form that is contained in portable cylinders and used as a fuel (e g for domestic heating)

calorie *also* **calory** *n* **1a** the quantity of heat required to raise the temperature of 1g of water by 1°C under standard conditions **b** a kilocalorie; *also* an equivalent unit expressing the energy-producing value of food when oxidized **2** an amount of food having an energy-producing value of 1 kilocalorie

calorific *adj* of heat production

calumet *n* a long highly ornamented pipe of the N American Indians smoked esp on ceremonial occasions in token of peace

calumniate *vt* to slander – fml – **calumniator** *n*, **calumniation** *n*

calumny *n* (the act of uttering) a false charge or misrepresentation maliciously calculated to damage another's reputation – **calumnious** *adj*, **calumniously** *adv*

calvary *n* **1** an open-air representation of the crucifixion of Christ **2** an experience of intense mental suffering

calve *vb* **1** to give birth to (a calf) **2** *of an ice mass* to release (a calf)

calves *pl of* CALF

Calvinism *n* the theological system of Calvin and his followers, marked by emphasis on the sovereignty of God and esp by the doctrine of predestination – **Calvinist** *n or adj*, **Calvinistic** *adj*, **Calvinistically** *adv*

calypso *n, pl* **calypsos** *also* **calypsoes** an improvised ballad, usu satirizing current events, in a style originating in the W Indies – **calypsonian** *n or adj*

calyx *n, pl* **calyxes, calyces** **1** the outer usu green or leafy part of a flower or floret, consisting of sepals **2 calyx, calix** a cuplike animal structure – **calyceal** *adj*

cam *n* a mechanical device (e g a wheel attached to an axis at a point other than its centre) that transforms circular motion into intermittent or back-and-forth motion

camaraderie *n* friendly good humour amongst comrades

¹camber *vb* to (cause to) curve upwards in the middle

²camber *n* **1** a slight convexity or arching (e g of a beam or road) **2** an arrangement of the wheels of a motor vehicle so as to be closer together at the bottom than at the top

cambric *n* a fine thin white linen or cotton fabric

¹came *past of* COME

²came *n* a slender grooved lead rod used to hold together panes of glass, esp in a lattice or stained-glass window

camel *n* **1** either of 2 large ruminant mammals used as draught and saddle animals in (African and Asian) desert regions: **a** the 1-humped Arabian camel **b** the 2-humped Bactrian camel **2** a float used to lift submerged ships **3** a light yellowish brown colour

camel hair *n* cloth, usu of a light tan colour with a soft silky texture, made from the hair of a camel or a mixture of this and wool

camellia *also* **camelia** *n* an ornamental greenhouse shrub with glossy evergreen leaves and roselike flowers, or a related shrub or tree of the tea family

Camembert *n* a round thin-rinded soft rich cheese

cameo *n, pl* **cameos** **1a** a gem carved in relief; *esp* a small piece of sculpture cut in relief in one layer with another contrasting layer serving as background **b** a small medallion with a profiled head in relief **2** a usu brief part in literature or film that reveals or highlights character, plot, or scene **3** a small dramatic role often played by a well-known actor – **cameo** *adj or vt*

camera *n* **1** *often cap* the treasury department of the papal curia **2** a lightproof box having an aperture, and esp a lens, for recording the image of an object on a light-sensitive material: e g **a** one containing photographic film for producing a permanent record **b** one containing a device which converts the image into an electrical signal (e g for television transmission)

cameraman *n* one who operates a (television) camera

camiknickers *n pl in constr, pl* **camiknickers** *Br* a one-piece close-fitting undergarment worn by women, that combines a camisole and knickers – **camiknicker** *adj*

camisole *n* a short bodice worn as an undergarment by women

camomile, chamomile *n* any of several strong-scented composite plants whose flower heads are used in herbal remedies

¹camouflage *n* **1** the disguising of esp military equipment or installations with nets, paint, etc **2a** concealment by means of disguise **b** sthg (e g a disguise) designed to deceive or conceal

²camouflage *vt* to conceal or disguise by camouflage – **camouflageable** *adj*

¹camp *n* **1a** a ground on which temporary shelters (e g tents) are erected **b** a temporary shelter or group of shelters erected on such ground **c** a new settlement (e g in a lumbering or mining region) **2** *sing or pl in constr* a group of people engaged in promoting or defending a theory or position ⟨*Liberal and Conservative* ~s⟩ **3a** military service or life **b** a place where troops are housed or trained

²camp *vi* **1** to pitch or occupy a camp **2** to live temporarily in a camp or outdoors

³camp *adj* **1** homosexual **2** exaggeratedly effeminate **3** deliberately and outrageously artificial, affected, or inappropriate, esp to the point of tastelessness *USE* infml – **campily** *adv*, **campness** *n*, **campy** *adj*

⁴camp *vi or n* (to engage in) a camp style, manner, etc – infml –**camp it up** to act or behave in an affected or esp exaggeratedly effeminate manner – infml

¹campaign *n* **1** a connected series of military operations forming a distinct phase of a war **2** active military life; ¹CAMP 3a **3** a connected series of operations designed to bring about a particular result

²campaign *vi* to go on, engage in, or conduct a campaign – **campaigner** *n*

campanile *n, pl* **campaniles, campanili** a usu freestanding bell tower

campanology *n* the art of bell ringing – **campanologist** *n*

campanula *n* a bellflower

camp bed *n* a small collapsible bed, usu of fabric stretched over a frame

camper *n* **1** a person who temporarily stays in a tent, caravan, etc **2** a motor vehicle equipped for use as temporary accommodation (e g while holidaying)

camp follower *n* **1** a civilian, esp a prostitute, who follows a military unit to attend or exploit military personnel **2** a follower who is not of the main body of adherents

camphor *n* a tough gummy volatile fragrant compound obtained esp from the wood and bark of an evergreen tree and used as a liniment, plasticizer, and insect repellent – **camphoraceous** *adj*, **camphoric** *adj*

camphorate *vt* to impregnate or treat with camphor

campion *n* any of several Eurasian plants of the pink family with small red or white flowers

campus *n* the grounds and buildings of a geographically self-contained university

camshaft *n* a shaft to which a cam is fastened

¹can *verbal auxiliary, pres sing & pl* **can**; *past* **could 1a** to know how to ⟨*he* ~ *read*⟩ **b** be physically or mentally able to ⟨*I* ~'*t think why*⟩ **c** may perhaps – chiefly in questions ⟨*what* ~ *they want?*⟩ **d** be logically inferred or supposed to – chiefly in negatives ⟨*he* ~ *hardly have meant that*⟩; compare ¹MUST 4 **e** be permitted by conscience or feeling to ⟨~ *hardly blame him*⟩ **f** be inherently able or designed to ⟨*everything that money* ~ *buy*⟩ **g** be logically able to ⟨*2 + 2* ~ *also be written 3 + 1*⟩ **h** be enabled by law, agreement, or custom to **2** have permission to – used interchangeably with *may* **3** will – used in questions with the force of a request ⟨~ *you hold on a minute, please?*⟩ **4** will have to ⟨*if you don't like it you* ~ *lump it*⟩ – **can keep it** – used in rejection of sthg distasteful ⟨*if that's their famous temple they can keep it*⟩

²can *n* **1** a usu cylindrical receptacle: **a** a vessel for holding liquids **b** TIN 2a; *esp* a tin containing a beverage (e g beer)

2 *NAm* TOILET **2** – *infml* **3** *chiefly NAm* jail – slang – **canful** *adj* – **in the can** of a film or videotape completed and ready for release

³can *vt* **-nn- 1** to pack or preserve in a tin **2** *chiefly NAm* to put a stop or end to – slang – **canner** *n*

Canadian *n or adj* (a native or inhabitant) of Canada

canal *n* **1** a channel, watercourse **2** a tubular anatomical channel **3** an artificial waterway for navigation, drainage, or irrigation

canalize, -ise *vt* **1** to provide with or make into a canal or channel **2** to direct into preferred channels – **canalization** *n*

canapé *n* an appetizer consisting of a piece of bread, biscuit, etc, topped with a savoury spread

canard *n* **1** a false or unfounded report or story; a hoax **2** (an aeroplane with) a small surface providing stability or control mounted in front of the main supporting surface on an aeroplane or hydrofoil

canary *n* a small usu green to yellow finch of the Canary islands, widely kept as a cage bird

canasta *n* **1** a form of rummy usu for 4 players using 2 full packs plus jokers **2** a combination of 7 cards of the same rank in canasta

cancan *n* a dance performed by women, characterized by high kicking usu while holding up the front of a full ruffled skirt

¹cancel *vb* **-ll-** (*NAm* **-l-, -ll-**), *vt* **1a** to mark or strike out for deletion **b** to omit, delete **2a** to make void; countermand, annul ⟨~ *a magazine subscription*⟩ **b** to bring to nothingness; destroy **c** to match in force or effect; offset – often + *out* ⟨*his irritability* ~ led *out his natural kindness* – Osbert Sitwell⟩ **3** to call off, usu without intending to reschedule to a later time **4a** to remove (a common divisor) from a numerator and denominator **b** to remove (equivalents) on opposite sides of an equation or account **5** to deface (a stamp), usu with a set of parallel lines, so as to invalidate reuse to neutralize each other's strength or effect; counterbalance – usu + *out* – **cancellable** *adj*, **canceller** *n*

²cancel *n* a cancellation

cancellation, *NAm also* **cancelation** *n* **1** sthg cancelled, esp a seat in an aircraft, theatre performance, etc **2** a mark made to cancel sthg (e g a postage stamp)

cancer *n* **1** *cap* (sby born under) the 4th zodiacal constellation, pictured as a crab **2** (a condition marked by) a malignant tumour of potentially unlimited growth **3** a source of evil or anguish ⟨*the* ~ *of hidden resentment* – *Irish Digest*⟩ – **cancerous** *adj*, **cancerously** *adv*

candela *n* the SI unit of luminous intensity

candelabrum *n, pl* **candelabra** *also* **candelabrums** a branched candlestick or lamp with several lights

candid *adj* **1** indicating or suggesting complete sincerity **2** disposed to criticize severely; blunt – **candidly** *adv*, **candidness** *n*

candidate *n* **1** one who is nominated or qualified for, or aspires to an office, membership, or award **2** one who is taking an examination **3** sthg suitable for a specified action or process – **candidacy** *n*

candidature *n, chiefly Br* being a candidate; *esp* standing for election

¹candle *n* **1** a usu slender cylindrical mass of tallow or wax enclosing a wick that is burnt to give light **2** sthg resembling a candle in shape or use ⟨*a sulphur* ~ *for fumigation*⟩ **3** a candela – **not worth the candle** *chiefly Br* not worth the effort; not justified by the result

²candle *vt* to examine (eggs) for staleness, blood clots, or fertility by holding between the eye and a light – **candler** *n*

Candlemas *n* February 2 observed as a church festival in commemoration of the presentation of Christ in the temple and the purification of the Virgin Mary

candlepower *n* luminous intensity expressed in candelas

candlestick *n* a holder with a socket for a candle

candlewick *n* a very thick soft cotton yarn; *also* fabric made with this yarn usu with a raised tufted pattern, used esp for bedspreads

candour, *NAm chiefly* **candor** *n* unreserved and candid expression; forthrightness

¹candy *n* **1** crystallized sugar formed by boiling down sugar syrup **2** *chiefly NAm* SWEET 2b – **candy** *adj*

²candy *vt* to encrust or glaze (e g fruit or fruit peel) with sugar

candy floss *n* a light fluffy mass of spun sugar, usu wound round a stick as a sweet

candytuft *n* any of a genus of plants of the mustard family cultivated for their white, pink, or purple flowers

¹cane *n* **1a** a hollow or pithy usu flexible jointed stem (e g of bamboo) **b** an elongated flowering or fruiting stem (e g of a raspberry) **c** any of various tall woody grasses or reeds; *esp* sugarcane **2a** a walking stick; *specif* one made of cane **b** (*the* use of) a cane or rod for flogging **c** a length of split rattan for use in basketry

²cane *vt* **1** to beat with a cane; *broadly* to punish **2** to weave or furnish with cane ⟨~ *the seat of a chair*⟩

¹canine *adj* of or resembling a dog or (members of) the family of flesh-eating mammals that includes the dogs, wolves, jackals, and foxes

²canine *n* **1** any of the 4 conical pointed teeth each of which lies between an incisor and the first premolar on each side of both the top and bottom jaws **2** DOG 1

canister *also* **cannister** *n* **1** a small usu metal box or tin for holding a dry product (e g tea or shot) **2** encased shot for close-range antipersonnel artillery fire

¹canker *n* **1a(1)** an erosive or spreading sore **(2)** an area of local tissue death in a plant **b** any of various inflammatory animal diseases **2** a source of corruption or debasement – **cankerous** *adj*

²canker *vt* to corrupt with a malignancy of mind or spirit ~ *vi* **1** to become infested with canker **2** to undergo corruption

cannabis *n* the dried flowering spikes of the female hemp plant, sometimes smoked in cigarettes for their intoxicating effect

canned *adj* **1** recorded for mechanical or electronic reproduction; *esp* prerecorded for addition to a sound track or a videotape ⟨~ *laughter*⟩⟨~ *music*⟩ **2** drunk – slang

cannelloni *n* large tubular rolls of pasta (filled with meat, cheese, etc)

cannery *n* a factory for canning foods

cannibal *n* **1** a human being who eats human flesh **2** an animal that eats its own kind – **cannibal** *adj*, **cannibalism** *n*, **cannibalistic** *adj*

cannibalize, -ise *vt* to dismantle (e g a machine) in order to provide spare parts for others – **cannibalization** *n*

¹cannon *n, pl* **cannons, cannon 1** a usu large gun mounted on a carriage **2** an automatic shell-firing gun mounted esp in an aircraft

²cannon *n, Br* a shot in billiards in which the cue ball strikes each of 2 object balls

³cannon *vi* **1a** to collide – usu + *into* **b** to collide with and be deflected *off* sthg **2** *Br* to make a cannon in billiards

cannonade *vb or n* (to attack with) heavy continuous artillery fire

cannonball *n* a round solid missile made for firing from an old type of cannon

cannon fodder *n* people regarded merely as material to be used in armed conflict

cannot can not – **cannot but/cannot help but** to be bound to; must ⟨could not but *smile at the answer*⟩

canny *adj* 1 cautious and shrewd; *specif* thrifty 2 *Scot & NE Eng* careful, steady 3 *NE Eng* agreeable, comely – **cannily** *adv*, **canniness** *n*

¹canoe *n* 1 a long light narrow boat with sharp ends and curved sides usu propelled by paddling 2 *chiefly Br* a kayak

²canoe *vi* to travel in or paddle a canoe, esp as a recreation or sport ∼ *vt* to transport in a canoe – **canoeist** *n*

¹canon *n* 1a a regulation or dogma decreed by a church council b a provision of canon law 2 the series of prayers forming the unvarying part of the Mass 3a an authoritative list of books accepted as Holy Scripture b the authentic works of a writer 4a an accepted principle, rule, or criterion b a body of principles, rules, or standards 5 a musical composition for 2 or more voice parts in which the melody is repeated by the successively entering voices

²canon *n* 1 a clergyman belonging to the chapter of a cathedral or collegiate church 2 CANON REGULAR

cañon *n* a canyon

canonical, canonic *adj* 1 of an esp ecclesiastical or musical canon 2 conforming to a general rule; orthodox 3 accepted as forming the canon of scripture 4 reduced to the simplest or clearest equivalent form ⟨*a* ∼ *matrix*⟩ – **canonically** *adv*, **canonicity** *n*

canonicals *n pl* the vestments prescribed by canon for an officiating clergyman

canonize, -ise *vt* 1 to recognize officially as a saint 2 to attribute authoritative sanction or approval to – **canonization** *n*

canon law *n* the usu codified law governing a church

canon regular *n, pl* **canons regular** a member of any of several Roman Catholic open religious communities

canoodle *vi* **canoodling** to caress or cuddle (with sby) – *infml*

¹canopy *n* 1a a cloth covering suspended over a bed b a cover (e g of cloth) fixed or carried above a person of high rank or a sacred object c an awning, marquee d anything which seems like a cover ⟨*the* ∼ *of the heavens*⟩ ⟨*a* ∼ *of branches*⟩ 2 an ornamental rooflike structure 3a the transparent enclosure over an aircraft cockpit b the lifting or supporting surface of a parachute

²canopy *vt* to cover (as if) with a canopy

canst *archaic pres 2 sing of* ¹CAN

¹cant *n* 1a a sudden thrust that produces some displacement b the displacement so caused 2 an oblique or slanting surface; a slope

²cant *vt* 1 to give a cant or oblique edge to; bevel 2 to set at an angle; tip or tilt up or over ∼ *vi* 1 to pitch to one side; lean 2 to slope

³cant *vi* to speak in cant or jargon

⁴cant *n* 1 jargon; *specif* the argot of the underworld 2 a set or stock phrase 3 the insincere expression of platitudes or sentiments, esp those suggesting piety

can't can not

Cantabrigian *n* a student or graduate of Cambridge University

cantaloupe, cantaloup *n* a muskmelon with a hard ridged rind and reddish orange flesh

cantankerous *adj* ill-natured, quarrelsome – **cantankerously** *adv*, **cantankerousness** *n*

cantata *n* a usu religious choral composition comprising choruses, solos, recitatives, and interludes

canteen *n* 1 a shop providing supplies in a camp 2 a

dining hall 3 a partitioned chest or box for holding cutlery 4 a usu cloth-covered flask carried by a soldier, traveller, etc and containing a liquid, esp drinking water

¹canter *vi* to progress or ride at a canter ∼ *vt* to cause to canter

²canter *n* 1 a 3-beat gait of a quadruped, specif a horse, resembling but smoother and slower than the gallop 2 a ride at a canter

canticle *n* a song; *specif* any of several liturgical songs (e g the Magnificat) taken from the Bible

cantilever *n* a projecting beam or member supported at only 1 end: e g a a bracket-shaped member supporting a balcony or a cornice b either of the 2 beams or trusses that when joined directly or by a suspended connecting member form a span of a cantilever bridge

canto *n, pl* **cantos** a major division of a long poem

¹canton *n* 1 a small territorial division of a country (e g Switzerland or France) 2 a rectangle in the right chief corner of a heraldic shield – **cantonal** *adj*

²canton *vt* 1 to divide into cantons 2 ²BILLET

cantonment *n* (a group of usu temporary structures for) the housing of troops

cantor *n* a singer who leads liturgical music (e g in a synagogue)

canvas *also* **canvass** *n* 1 a firm closely woven cloth usu of linen, hemp, or cotton used for clothing, sails, tents etc 2 a set of sails; sail 3 a cloth surface suitable for painting on in oils; *also* the painting on such a surface 4 a coarse cloth so woven as to form regular meshes as a basis for embroidery or tapestry 5 the floor of a boxing or wrestling ring – **canvaslike** *adj* – **under canvas** living in a tent

canvass *also* **canvas** *vt* 1 to examine in detail; *specif, NAm* to examine (votes) officially for authenticity 2 to discuss, debate 3 to visit (e g a voter) in order to solicit political support or to ascertain opinions ∼ *vi* to seek orders or votes; solicit – **canvass** *n*, **canvasser** *also* **canvaser** *n*

canyon, cañon *n* a deep valley or gorge

¹cap *n* 1a a soft usu flat head covering with a peak and no brim b (one who has gained) a head covering awarded to a player selected for a special, specif national, sports team or who is a regular member of esp a cricket team 2 a natural cover or top: e g a a usu unyielding overlying rock or soil layer b the pileus c (a patch of distinctively coloured feathers on) the top of a bird's head 3 sthg that serves as a cover or protection, esp for the end or top of an object 4 a mortarboard ⟨*students dressed in* ∼ *and gown*⟩ 5 the uppermost part; the top 6 a small container holding an explosive charge (e g for a toy pistol or for priming the charge in a firearm) 7 the symbol ∩ indicating the intersection of 2 sets 8 *Br* DUTCH CAP – **capful** *n*

²cap *vt* **-pp-** 1a to provide or protect with a cap b to give a cap to as a symbol of honour or rank 2 to form a cap over; crown ⟨*the mountains were* ∼ *ped with mist* – John Buchan⟩ 3 to follow with sthg more noticeable or significant; outdo

capability *n* 1 being capable 2 a feature or faculty capable of development; potential 3 the capacity for an indicated use or development

capable *adj* 1 susceptible ⟨*a remark* ∼ *of being misunderstood*⟩ 2 having the attributes or traits required to perform a specified deed or action ⟨*he is* ∼ *of murder*⟩ 3 able ⟨*her* ∼ *fingers*⟩ USE (*except* 3) + *of* – **capableness** *n*, **capably** *adv*

capacious *adj* able to hold a great deal – **capaciously** *adv*, **capaciousness** *n*

capacitor *n* a component in an electrical circuit that provides ability to store a charge of electricity and usu consists of an insulator sandwiched between 2 oppositely charged conductors

capacity *n* **1a** the ability to receive, accommodate, or deal with sthg **b** an ability to contain ⟨*a jug with a ~ of 2pt*⟩ **c** the maximum amount that can be contained or produced ⟨*working at ~*⟩⟨*a ~ crowd*⟩ **2** legal competence or power **3a** ability, calibre **b** POTENTIAL **1** **4** a position or role assigned or assumed ⟨*in his ~ as judge*⟩

cap and bells *n, pl* **caps and bells** the traditional dress of a court jester

caparison *n* **1** an ornamental covering for a horse, esp a warhorse in former times **2** rich clothing; adornment – **caparison** *vt*

¹**cape** *n* a peninsula or similar land projection jutting out into water

²**cape** *n* a sleeveless outer (part of a) garment that fits closely at the neck and hangs loosely from the shoulders

Cape Coloured *n* a person of mixed black and white ancestry in S Africa – **Cape Coloured** *adj*

¹**caper** *n* **1** any of a genus of low prickly shrubs of the Mediterranean region **2** a greenish flower bud or young berry of the caper, pickled and used as a seasoning, garnish, etc

²**caper** *vi* to leap about in a carefree way; prance

³**caper** *n* **1** a joyful leap **2** a high-spirited escapade; a prank **3** *chiefly NAm* an illegal enterprise; a crime – *infml*

capillarity *n* the elevation or depression of the surface of a liquid in contact with a solid (e g in a fine-bore tube) that depends on the relative attraction of the molecules of the liquid for each other and for those of the solid

¹**capillary** *adj* **1a** resembling a hair, esp in slender elongated form **b** *of a tube, passage, etc* having a very fine bore **2** involving, held by, or resulting from surface tension **3** of capillaries or capillarity

²**capillary** *n* a capillary tube; *esp* any of the smallest blood vessels connecting arteries with veins and forming networks throughout the body

¹**capital** *adj* **1a** punishable by death ⟨*a ~ crime*⟩ **b** involving execution ⟨*~ punishment*⟩ **2** *of a letter* of or conforming to the series (e g A, B, C rather than a, b, c) used to begin sentences or proper names **3a** of the greatest importance or influence ⟨*the ~ importance of criticism in the work of creation itself* – T S Eliot⟩ **b** being the seat of government **4** excellent ⟨*a ~ book*⟩ – not now in vogue

²**capital** *n* **1a** (the value of) a stock of accumulated goods, esp at a particular time and in contrast to income received during a particular period **b** accumulated possessions calculated to bring in income **c** *sing or pl in constr* people holding capital **d** a sum of money saved **2** an esp initial capital letter **3** a city serving as a seat of government – **make capital of/out of** to turn (a situation) to one's advantage

³**capital** *n* the top part or piece of an architectural column

capital assets *n pl* tangible or intangible long-term assets

capital gain *n* the profit from the sale of a capital asset (e g a house) – usu pl with sing. meaning ⟨*capital-gains tax*⟩

capitalism *n* an economic system characterized by private ownership and control of the means of production, distribution, and exchange and by the profit motive

¹**capitalist** *n* **1** a person with (invested) capital; *broadly* a very wealthy person **2** one who favours capitalism

²**capitalist, capitalistic** *adj* **1** owning capital ⟨*the ~ class*⟩ **2** practising, advocating, or marked by capitalism ⟨*~ nations*⟩ – **capitalistically** *adv*

capitalize, -ise *vt* **1** to write or print in capitals or with an initial capital **2** to convert into capital ⟨*~ the company's reserve fund*⟩ **3** to convert (a periodic payment) into an equivalent capital sum ⟨*~d annuities*⟩ **4** to supply capital for ~ *vi* to gain by turning sthg to advantage – usu + *on* – **capitalization** *n*

capitation *n* a uniform payment or charge made per person

capitol *n* **1** a building in which a US legislative body meets **2** *cap* the building in which Congress meets at Washington

capitulate *vi* **1** to surrender, often after negotiation of terms **2** to cease resisting; acquiesce

capitulation *n* **1** an agreement between governments **2** the act or agreement of sby who surrenders **3** a surrender, acquiescence

capon *n* a castrated male chicken – **caponize** *vt*

caprice *n* **1a** a sudden and seemingly unmotivated change of mind **b** a sudden and unpredictable change or series of changes ⟨*the ~s of the weather*⟩ **2** a disposition to change one's mind impulsively

capricious *adj* governed or characterized by caprice; apt to change suddenly or unpredictably – **capriciously** *adv*, **capriciousness** *n*

Capricorn *n* (sby born under) the 10th zodiacal constellation, pictured as a creature resembling a goat with the tail of a fish – **Capricornian** *adj or n*

capsicum *n* (the many-seeded usu fleshy-walled fruit of) any of a genus of tropical herbaceous plants and shrubs of the nightshade family

capsize *vb* to (cause to) overturn ⟨*~ a canoe*⟩

capstan *n* **1** a mechanical device consisting of an upright drum round which a rope, hawser, etc is fastened, used for moving or raising heavy weights **2** a rotating shaft that drives tape at a constant speed in a tape recorder

capsule *n* **1** a membrane or sac **a** enclosing a body part **b** surrounding a microorganism **2** a closed plant receptacle containing spores or seeds **3** a usu gelatin shell enclosing a drug for swallowing **4** a compact usu rounded container **5** a detachable pressurized compartment, esp in a spacecraft or aircraft, containing crew and controls; *also* a spacecraft **6** a usu metal, wax, or plastic covering that encloses the top of a bottle, esp of wine, and protects the cork – **capsular** *adj*

¹**captain** *n* **1a(1)** an officer in the army or US airforce ranking below major **(2)** an officer in the navy ranking below commodore **b** an officer in charge of a ship **c** a pilot of a civil aircraft **2** a distinguished military leader **3** a leader of a team, esp a sports team **4** a dominant figure ⟨*~s of industry*⟩ **5** *Br* the head boy or girl at a school **6** *NAm* a fire or police officer – **captaincy** *n*, **captainship** *n*

²**captain** *vt* to be captain of

caption *n* **1** a heading or title, esp of an article or document **2** a comment or description accompanying a pictorial illustration **3** a film subtitle – **caption** *vt*, **captionless** *adj*

captious *adj* marked by an often ill-natured inclination to stress faults and raise objections – **captiously** *adv*, **captiousness** *n*

captivate *vt* to fascinate or charm irresistibly – **captivatingly** *adv*, **captivation** *n*

captive *adj* **1a** taken and held as prisoner, esp by an enemy in war **b** kept within bounds; confined **c** held under control **2** in a situation that makes departure or inattention difficult ⟨*a ~ audience*⟩ – **captive** *n*, **captivity** *n*

captor n one who or that which holds another captive

¹capture n 1 the act of gaining control or possession 2 one who or that which has been captured 3 the acquisition by an atom, molecule, ion, or nucleus of an additional elementary particle, often with associated emission of radiation

²capture vt 1 to take captive; win, gain ⟨~ a city⟩ 2 to preserve in a relatively permanent form ⟨how well the scene was ~d on film⟩ 3 to remove (e g a chess piece) from the playing board according to the rules of a game 4 to bring about the capture of (an elementary particle)

car n 1 a vehicle moving on wheels: **a** a chariot of war or of triumph – chiefly poetic **b** a railway carriage; esp one used for a specific purpose ⟨buffet ~⟩ ⟨sleeping ~⟩ **c** MOTOR CAR 2 the passenger compartment of an airship or balloon 3 NAm the cage of a lift

carafe n a (glass) bottle used to hold water or wine, esp at table

caramel n 1 a brittle brown somewhat bitter substance obtained by heating sugar and used as a colouring and flavouring agent 2 a chewy usu quite soft caramel-flavoured toffee – **caramelize** vb

carapace n a hard case (e g of chitin) covering (part of) the back of a turtle, crab, etc

carat n 1 a unit of weight for precious stones equal to 200mg 2 NAm chiefly **karat** a unit of fineness for gold equal to ½₄ part of pure gold in an alloy

¹caravan n **1a** sing or pl in constr a company of travellers on a journey through desert or hostile regions; also a train of pack animals **b** a group of vehicles travelling together 2 Br a covered vehicle designed to be towed by a motor car or horse and to serve as a dwelling when parked

²caravan vi -nn- (NAm -n-, -nn-) to have a holiday in a caravan

caravanserai, NAm chiefly **caravansary** n, pl **caravanserais, caravanserai** a usu large inn in Eastern countries that is built round a courtyard and used as a resting place for caravans

caraway n a usu white-flowered aromatic plant with pungent seeds used as a flavouring

carbide n a compound of carbon with a more electropositive element; esp CALCIUM CARBIDE

carbine n 1 a short light rifle or musket orig carried by cavalry 2 a short light gas-operated magazine-fed automatic rifle

carbohydrate n any of various compounds of carbon, hydrogen, and oxygen (e g sugars, starches, and celluloses) formed by green plants and constituting a major class of energy-providing animal foods

carbolic acid n phenol

carbon n 1 a nonmetallic chiefly tetravalent element occurring as diamond, graphite, charcoal, coke, etc and as a constituent of coal, petroleum, carbonates (e g limestone), and organic compounds **2a** a sheet of carbon paper **b** CARBON COPY 1 3 a piece of carbon used as an element in a voltaic cell – **carbonless** adj

¹carbonate n a salt or ester of carbonic acid

²carbonate vt 1 to convert into a carbonate 2 to impregnate with carbon dioxide; aerate ⟨a ~d beverage⟩ – **carbonation** n

carbon black n carbon as a colloidal black substance (e g soot)

carbon copy n 1 a copy made with carbon paper 2 a duplicate or exact replica

carbon dating n the dating of ancient material (e g an archaeological specimen) by recording the amount of carbon 14 remaining

carbon dioxide n a heavy colourless gas that does not support combustion, is formed esp by the combustion and decomposition of organic substances, and is absorbed from the air by plants in photosynthesis

carbonic acid n a weak acid that is a solution of carbon dioxide in water and whose salts are carbonates

carboniferous adj 1 producing or containing carbon or coal 2 cap of or being the period of the Palaeozoic era between the Devonian and the Permian in which coal deposits formed – **Carboniferous** n

carbonize, -ise vt to convert into carbon or a carbon-containing residue to become carbonized; char – **carbonization** n

carbon monoxide n a colourless odourless very toxic gas formed as a product of the incomplete combustion of carbon

carbon paper n (a sheet of) thin paper coated on 1 side with dark pigment, used to make copies by placing between 2 sheets of paper, so that the pigment is transferred to the lower sheet by the pressure of writing or typing on the upper

Carborundum trademark – used for various abrasives

carboy n a large usu roughly spherical glass or plastic container for liquids

carbuncle n 1 a red gemstone, usu a garnet, cut in a domed shape without facets 2 a painful local inflammation of the skin and deeper tissues with multiple openings for the discharge of pus – **carbuncled** adj, **carbuncular** adj

carburettor, NAm **carburetor** n an apparatus for supplying an internal-combustion engine with vaporized fuel mixed with air in an explosive mixture

carcass, Br also **carcase** n 1 a dead body; esp the dressed body of a meat animal 2 the decaying or worthless remains of a structure ⟨the half-submerged ~ of a wrecked vessel⟩ 3 a framework; esp the framework of a tyre as distinct from the tread

carcinogen n sthg (e g a chemical compound) that causes cancer – **carcinogenesis** n, **carcinogenic** adj, **carcinogenically** adv, **carcinogenicity** n

¹card vt to cleanse and disentangle (fibres) by the use of a carding machine preparatory to spinning – **carder** n

²card n an implement or machine for carding fibres or raising a nap on cloth

³card n 1 PLAYING CARD 2 pl but sing or pl in constr a game played with cards 3 a valuable asset or right for use in negotiations 4 a flat stiff usu small and rectangular piece of paper or thin cardboard: e g **a** a postcard **b** VISITING CARD **c** PROGRAMME 1a; esp one for a sporting event **d** GREETINGS CARD 5 pl, Br the National Insurance and other papers of an employee, held by his/her employer 6 a comical or amusing fellow 7 Br a person of a specified type ⟨a knowing ~⟩ USE (6&7) infml – **on the cards** quite possible; likely to occur – **get/ask for one's cards** to be dismissed/resign from employment

cardamom n (an E Indian plant that bears) an aromatic capsular fruit containing seeds used as a spice or condiment

¹cardboard n material of similar composition to paper but thicker and stiffer

²cardboard adj 1 made (as if) of cardboard 2 unreal, insubstantial ⟨the story has too many ~ characters⟩

card-carrying adj being a fully paid-up member, esp of the Communist party

cardi-, cardio- comb form heart; cardiac ⟨cardiogram⟩ ⟨cardiograph⟩ ⟨cardiology⟩; cardiac and ⟨cardiovascular⟩

¹cardiac adj 1 of, situated near, or acting on the heart 2 of the oesophageal end of the stomach

²cardiac n sby suffering from heart disease

cardigan *n* a knitted garment for the upper body that opens down the front and is usu fastened with buttons

¹**cardinal** *adj* of primary importance; fundamental – **cardinally** *adv*

²**cardinal** *n* a member of a body of high officials of the Roman Catholic church whose powers include the election of a new pope – **cardinalate** *n*, **cardinalship** *n*

cardinal number *n* a number (e g 1, 2, 3) that is used in simple counting and that indicates how many elements there are in a collection

cardinal point *n* any of the 4 principal compass points north, south, east, and west

card index *n*, *Br* a filing system in which each item is entered on a separate card – **card-index** *vt*

cardsharp, cardsharper *n* one who habitually cheats at cards

¹**care** *n* **1** a cause for anxiety ⟨*the ~s of the world*⟩ **2** close attention; effort ⟨*took ~ over the drawing*⟩ **3** change, supervision ⟨*under the doctor's ~*⟩; *specif, Br* guardianship and supervision of children by a local authority **4** sby or sthg that is an object of attention, anxiety, or solicitude ⟨*the flower garden was her special ~*⟩

²**care** *vi* **1a** to feel trouble or anxiety **b** to feel interest or concern – often + *about* **2** to give care ⟨*~ for the sick*⟩ **3** to have a liking or taste *for* ~ *vt* **1** to be concerned about ⟨*nobody ~s what I do*⟩ **2** to wish ⟨*if you ~ to go*⟩

careen *vt* **1** to cause (a boat) to lean over on one side **2** to clean, caulk, or repair (a boat) in this position ~ *vi* **1a** to careen a boat **b** to undergo this process **2** to heel over **3** *chiefly NAm* to career

¹**career** *n* **1** the course of (a particular sphere of) a person's life ⟨*Churchill's ~ as a politician*⟩ **2** a field of employment in which one expects to remain; *esp* such a field which requires special qualifications and training

²**career** *vi* to move swiftly in an uncontrolled fashion ⟨*the car ~ed off the road*⟩

³**career** *adj* of or engaged in an occupation which offers a long-term series of opportunities for advancement, usu within some specified organization or business ⟨*a ~ diplomat*⟩

career girl *adj* a woman who puts advancement in her career or profession before marriage or motherhood

careerist *n* one who is intent on advancing his/her career, often at the expense of personal integrity – **careerism** *n*

carefree *adj* free from anxiety or responsibility ⟨*~ holidays*⟩

careful *adj* **1** exercising or taking care **2a** marked by attentive concern **b** cautious, prudent ⟨*be ~ of the horses*⟩ – often + *to* and an infinitive ⟨*be ~ to switch off the machine*⟩ – **carefully** *adv*, **carefulness** *n*

careless *adj* **1** not taking care **2a** negligent, slovenly ⟨*writing that is ~ and full of errors*⟩ **b** unstudied, spontaneous ⟨*~ grace*⟩ **3a** free from care; untroubled ⟨*~ days*⟩ **b** indifferent, unconcerned ⟨*~ of the consequences*⟩ – **carelessly** *adv*, **carelessness** *n*

¹**caress** *n* **1** a kiss **2** a caressing touch or stroke

²**caress** *vt* **1** to touch or stroke lightly and lovingly **2** to touch or affect gently or soothingly ⟨*music that ~es the ear*⟩ – **caresser** *n*, **caressingly** *adv*

caret *n* a mark or V or ⟩ used on written or printed matter to indicate an insertion to be made

caretaker *n* **1** one who takes care of the house or land of an owner, esp during his/her absence **2** one who keeps clean a large and/or public building (e g a school or office), looks after the heating system, and carries out minor repairs **3** sby or sthg temporarily installed in office ⟨*a ~ government*⟩

careworn *adj* showing the effects of grief or anxiety ⟨*a ~ face*⟩

cargo *n, pl* **cargoes, cargos** the goods conveyed in a ship, aircraft, or vehicle; freight

caribou *n, pl* **caribous, *esp collectively*** **caribou** any of several large N American antlered deer

¹**caricature** *n* **1** exaggeration of features or characteristics, often to a ludicrous or grotesque degree **2** a comic or satirical representation, esp in literature or art, that has the qualities of caricature **3** a distortion so gross or inferior as to seem like a caricature – **caricatural** *adj*, **caricaturist** *n*

²**caricature** *vt* to make or draw a caricature of; represent in caricature

caries *n, pl* **caries** progressive decay of a tooth or sometimes a bone, caused by microorganisms

carillon *n* a set of bells sounded by hammers controlled from a keyboard

carious *adj* affected with caries

Carmelite *n* a member of the Roman Catholic mendicant Order of Our Lady of Mount Carmel founded in the 12th c – **Carmelite** *adj*

carmine *n* **1** a rich crimson or scarlet pigment **2** a vivid red

carnage *n* great slaughter (e g in battle)

carnal *adj* **1** given to or marked by physical and esp sexual pleasures and appetites **2** temporal, worldly – **carnality** *n*, **carnally** *adv*

carnation *n* **1** light red or pink **2** any of numerous cultivated usu double-flowered pinks

carnelian *n* (a) cornelian

carnival *n* **1** a period of merrymaking before Lent, esp in Roman Catholic countries **2** an instance of merrymaking or feasting **3a** an exhibition or organized programme of entertainment; a festival **b** *chiefly NAm* a travelling circus or funfair

carnivore *n* a flesh-eating animal; *esp* any of an order of flesh-eating mammals

carnivorous *adj* **1** of or being a carnivore; *specif* flesh-eating **2** *of a plant* feeding on nutrients obtained from animal tissue, esp insects – **carnivorously** *adv*, **carnivorousness** *n*

carob *n* (the edible pod of) a Mediterranean evergreen leguminous tree with red flowers

¹**carol** *n* a popular seasonal usu religious song or ballad; *esp* a Christmas song or hymn

²**carol** *vb* **-ll-** (*NAm* **-l-**; **-ll-**) to sing (joyfully)

carotid *adj or n* (of or being) the chief artery or pair of arteries that supply the head with blood

carousal *n* a carouse

¹**carouse** *n* a drunken revel

²**carouse** *vi* **1** to drink alcoholic beverages heavily or freely **2** to take part in a drinking bout

carousel, *NAm also* **carrousel** *n* **1** a rotating stand or delivery system ⟨*a luggage ~ at the airport*⟩ **2** *chiefly NAm* a merry-go-round

¹**carp** *vi* to find fault or complain querulously and often unnecessarily – *infml*; usu + *at*

²**carp** *n, pl* **carps, *esp collectively*** **carp** (a fish resembling or related to) a large Old World soft-finned freshwater fish often farmed for food

carp-, carpo- *comb form* fruit ⟨*carpology*⟩

-carp *comb form* (→ *n*) part of a fruit ⟨*mesocarp*⟩; fruit ⟨*schizocarp*⟩

car park *n*, *chiefly Br* an area or building set aside for parking motor vehicles

carpel *n* any of the structures of a flowering plant that constitute the female (innermost) part of a flower and usu consist of an ovary, style, and stigma – **carpellary** *adj*, **carpellate** *adj*

¹**carpenter** *n* a woodworker; *esp* one who builds or repairs large-scale structural woodwork

²**carpenter** *vi* to follow the trade of a carpenter ⟨~ed *when he was young*⟩ ~ *vt* to put together, often in a mechanical manner

carpentry *n* **1** the art or trade of a carpenter; *specif* the art of shaping and assembling structural woodwork **2** timberwork constructed by a carpenter

¹**carpet** *n* **1** a heavy woven or felted material used as a floor covering; *also* a floor covering made of this fabric **2** a surface resembling or suggesting a carpet ⟨a ~ *of leaves*⟩ – **on the carpet** before an authority for censure or reprimand

²**carpet** *vt* **1** to cover (as if) with a carpet ⟨*snowdrops* ~ *the lawn*⟩ **2** to reprimand – *infml*

carpetbag *n* a bag made of carpet fabric, common in the 19th c

carpetbagger *n* **1** a Northerner who went to the American South after the Civil War in search of personal gain **2** a nonresident who meddles in the politics of a locality

carpeting *n* (material for) carpets

carport *n* a usu open-sided shelter for cars

carpus *n, pl* **carpi** (the bones of) the wrist – **carpal** *adj*

carriage *n* **1** the act of carrying **2** the manner of bearing the body; posture **3** the price or cost of carrying ⟨~ *paid*⟩ **4** a wheeled vehicle; *esp* a horse-drawn passenger-carrying vehicle designed for private use **5** a movable part of a machine that supports some other part ⟨a *typewriter* ~⟩ **6** *Br* a railway passenger vehicle; a coach

carriageway *n, Br* the part of a road used by vehicular traffic; *specif* LANE 2b

carrier *n* **1** a bearer, messenger **2** an individual or organization that contracts to transport goods, messages, etc **3a** a container for carrying **b** a device, platform, machine, etc that carries ⟨a *luggage* ~ *on a bicycle*⟩ **4** a bearer and transmitter of a causative agent of disease; *esp* one who is immune to the disease **5a** a usu inactive accessory substance; VEHICLE 1 **b** a substance (e g a catalyst) by whose agency some element or group is transferred from one compound to another **6** a radio or electrical wave of relatively high frequency that can be modulated by a signal (e g representing sound or vision information), esp in order to transmit that signal **7** a mobile hole or electron capable of carrying an electric charge in a semiconductor **8** AIRCRAFT CARRIER

carrier bag *n, Br* a bag of plastic or thick paper used for carrying goods, esp shopping

carrier pigeon *n* a homing pigeon (used to carry messages)

carrion *n* **1** dead and putrefying flesh **2** sthg corrupt or rotten

carrion crow *n* the common European black crow

carrot *n* **1** (a biennial plant with) a usu orange spindle-shaped root eaten as a vegetable **2** a promised and often illusory reward or advantage ⟨*offered them the* ~ *of promotion*⟩

carroty *adj* bright orange-red in colour

¹**carry** *vt* **1** to support and move (a load); transport **2a** to convey, conduct **b** to support ⟨*this beam* carries *the weight of the upper storeys*⟩ **3** to lead or influence by appeal to the emotions **4** to transfer from one place to another; *esp* to transfer (a digit corresponding to a multiple of 10) to the next higher power of 10 in addition **5a** to wear or have on one's person ⟨*I never* ~ *money on me*⟩ **b** to bear on or within oneself ⟨*is* ~ ing *an unborn child*⟩ **c** to have as a mark, attribute, or property ⟨~ *a scar*⟩ **6** to have as a consequence, esp in law; involve ⟨*the crime* carried *a heavy penalty*⟩ **7** to hold (e g one's

person) in a specified manner ⟨carries *himself well*⟩ **8** to sing with reasonable correctness of pitch ⟨~ *a tune*⟩ **9a** to keep in stock for sale **b** to provide sustenance for; support ⟨*land* ~ing *100 head of cattle*⟩ **10** to maintain through financial support or personal effort ⟨*he carried the magazine single-handedly*⟩ **11** to extend or prolong in space, time, or degree ⟨~ *a principle too far*⟩ **12** to gain victory for **13a** to broadcast **b** to publish ⟨*newspapers* ~ *weather reports*⟩ **14** to perform with sufficient ability to make up for the poor performance of (e g a partner or teammate) **15** to hoist and maintain (a sail) in use ~ *vi* **1** to act as a bearer **2a** to reach or penetrate to a distance ⟨*voices* ~ *well*⟩ **b** to convey itself to a reader or audience **3** to undergo or allow carriage in a specified way – **carry a torch** to be in love, esp without reciprocation; cherish a longing or devotion ⟨*she still* carries a torch *for him even though their engagement is broken*⟩ – **carry the can** to bear the responsibility; accept the blame – *infml* – **carry the day** to win, prevail

²**carry** *n* **1** the range of a gun or projectile or of a struck or thrown ball **2** portage

carry away *vt* to arouse to a high and often excessive degree of emotion or enthusiasm – usu passive

carrycot *n, chiefly Br* a small lightweight boxlike bed, usu with 2 handles, in which a baby can be carried

carry forward *vt* to transfer (e g a total) to the succeeding column, page, or book relating to the same account

carrying-on *n, pl* **carryings-on** rowdy, excited, or improper behaviour – *infml*

carry off *vt* **1** to cause the death of ⟨*the plague* carried off *thousands*⟩ **2** to perform easily or successfully ⟨*the leading lady* carried off *her part brilliantly*⟩ **3** to gain possession or control of; capture ⟨carried off *the prize*⟩

carryon *n, NAm* a piece of luggage suitable for a passenger to carry on board an aircraft

carry-on *n* an instance of rowdy, excited, or improper behaviour; a to-do – *infml*

carry on *vt* to conduct, manage ⟨carry on *a business*⟩ *vi* **1** to behave in a rowdy, excited, or improper manner ⟨*embarrassed by the way he* carries on⟩ **2** to continue one's course or activity, esp in spite of obstacles or discouragement **3** *Br* to flirt; *also* to have a love affair – usu + *with*

carryout *n* **1** *chiefly Scot* food or esp alcoholic drink bought to be consumed off the premises **2** *chiefly NAm & Scot* a takeaway

carry out *vt* **1** to put into execution ⟨carry out *a plan*⟩ **2** to bring to a successful conclusion; complete, accomplish

carry over *vt* CARRY FORWARD ~ *vi* to persist from one stage or sphere of activity to another

carry through *vt* CARRY OUT ~ *vi* to survive, persist ⟨*feelings that* carry through *to the present*⟩

carsick *adj* suffering from the motion sickness associated with travelling by car – **carsickness** *n*

¹**cart** *n* **1** a heavy 2-wheeled or 4-wheeled vehicle used for transporting bulky or heavy loads (e g goods or animal feed) **2** a lightweight 2-wheeled vehicle drawn by a horse, pony, or dog **3** a small wheeled vehicle

²**cart** *vt* **1** to carry or convey (as if) in a cart **2** to take or drag away without ceremony or by force – *infml*; usu + *off* ⟨*they* ~ed *him off to jail*⟩ **3** to carry by hand – *infml* – **carter** *n*

cartage *n* the act of carting; *also* the charge for this

carte blanche *n* full discretionary power ⟨*was given* ~ *to furnish the house*⟩

cartel *n* a combination of independent commercial enterprises designed to limit competition

cart horse n any large powerful draught horse (e g a Clydesdale)

cartilage n (a structure composed of) a translucent elastic tissue that makes up most of the skeleton of very young vertebrates and becomes mostly converted into bone in adult higher vertebrates – **cartilaginous** adj

cartography n map making – **cartographer** n, **cartographic, cartographical** adj

carton n a box or container made of plastic, cardboard, etc

cartoon n 1 a preparatory design, drawing, or painting (e g for a fresco) 2a a satirical drawing commenting on public and usu political matters b STRIP CARTOON 3 ANI-MATED CARTOON – **cartoon** vb, **cartoonist** n

cartridge n 1a a tube of metal, paper, etc containing a complete charge, a primer, and often the bullet or shot for a firearm b a case containing an explosive charge for blasting 2 the part of the arm of a record player holding the stylus and the mechanism that converts movements of the stylus into electrical signals 3 a case containing a reel of magnetic tape designed for insertion into a tape recorder

cartridge belt n a belt with a series of loops for holding cartridges

cartridge paper n a stiff rough-surfaced close-grained paper (e g for drawing)

¹**cartwheel** n a sideways handspring with arms and legs extended

²**cartwheel** vi to perform cartwheels

carve vt 1a to cut so as to shape b to produce by cutting ⟨~d his initials in the soft sandstone⟩ 2 to make or acquire (a career, reputation, etc) through one's own efforts – often + out ⟨~d out a place for himself in the firm⟩ 3 to cut (food, esp meat) into pieces or slices ~ vi 1 to cut up and serve meat 2 to work as a sculptor or engraver

carver 1 a long sharp knife used for carving meat 2 pl a knife and fork used for carving and serving meat

carve-up n 1 a competitive event in which the result has been irregularly decided beforehand – infml 2 a division into parts; esp the sharing out of loot – slang

carve up vt 1 to divide into parts or shares ⟨carved up the inheritance between them⟩ 2 to wound with a knife – slang

carving n 1 the act or art of one who carves 2 a carved object or design

caryatid n, pl **caryatids, caryatides** a draped female figure used as a column to support an entablature

¹**cascade** n 1 a steep usu small fall of water; esp one of a series of such falls 2a sthg arranged in a series or in a succession of stages so that each stage derives from or acts on the product of the preceding stage ⟨a ~ amplifier⟩ b an arrangement of fabric (e g lace) that falls in a wavy line 3 sthg falling or rushing forth in profusion ⟨a ~ of flowers⟩

²**cascade** vi to fall (as if) in a cascade ~ vt to connect in a cascade arrangement

cascara n 1 **cascara, cascara buckthorn** a buckthorn of the Pacific coast of the USA 2 **cascara, cascara sagrada** the dried bark of cascara buckthorn, used as a mild laxative

¹**case** n 1a a set of circumstances or conditions; a situation b a situation or object requiring investigation or action 2 an (inflectional) form of a noun, pronoun, or adjective indicating its grammatical relation to other words 3a a suit or action that reaches a court of law b(1) the evidence supporting a conclusion ⟨the ~ for bringing back hanging⟩ (2) an argument; esp one that is convincing 4a an instance of disease or injury; also a patient suffering from

a specific illness b an instance that directs attention to a situation or exhibits it in action; an example 5 a peculiar person; a character – infml – **in any case** without regard to or in spite of other considerations; whatever else is done or is the case ⟨war is inevitable in any case⟩ – **in case** 1 as a precaution; as a precaution against the event that ⟨take a towel anyway just in case you want to swim⟩ 2 chiefly NAm if – **in case of** 1 in the event of ⟨in case of trouble, yell⟩ 2 for fear of; as a precaution against ⟨posted sentries in case of attack⟩

²**case** n 1 a box or receptacle for holding sthg: e g a a glass-panelled box for the display of specimens (e g in a museum) b chiefly Br a suitcase c a box together with its contents 2 a pair – chiefly with reference to pistols 3a an outer covering ⟨a pastry ~⟩ b a stiff book cover that is made apart from the book and glued onto it 4 a shallow divided tray for holding printing type

³**case** vt 1 to enclose in or cover with a case; encase 2 to inspect or study (e g a house), esp with intent to rob – slang

casebook n a book containing records of illustrative cases for reference (e g in law or medicine)

case history n a record of history, environment, and relevant details (e g of individual behaviour or condition), esp for use in analysis, illustration, or diagnosis

casein n a protein in milk that is precipitated by (lactic) acid or rennet, is the chief constituent of cheese, and is used in making plastics

case law n law established by previous judicial decisions

casement n (a window with) a sash that opens on hinges at the side

case study n an analysis of a person, institution, or community based on details concerning development, environment, etc

casework n social work involving direct consideration of the problems of individual people or families – **case-worker** n

¹**cash** n 1 ready money 2 money or its equivalent paid promptly at the time of purchase

²**cash** vt 1 to pay or obtain cash for ⟨~ a cheque⟩ 2 to lead and win a bridge trick with (the highest remaining card of a suit)

³**cash** n, pl **cash** (a money unit equivalent to) a small Chinese or Indian coin

cash-and-carry adj sold for cash and collected by the purchaser

cash crop n a crop (e g cotton or sugar beet) produced for sale rather than for use by the grower

cash desk n a desk (e g in a shop) where payment for purchases is taken

cashew n (the edible kidney-shaped nut of) a tropical American tree of the sumach family

¹**cashier** vt to dismiss, usu dishonourably, esp from service in the armed forces

²**cashier** 1 one employed to receive cash from customers, esp in a shop 2 one who collects and records payments (e g in a bank)

cash in vt to convert into cash ⟨cashed in all his bonds⟩ ~ vi to exploit a financial or other advantage – usu + on ⟨cashing in on the success of recent peace initiatives⟩

cashmere n (yarn or fabric made from) fine wool from the undercoat of the Kashmir goat

cash register n a machine that has a drawer for cash and is used to record and display the amount of each purchase and the money received

casing n sthg that encases; material for encasing

casino n, pl **casinos** a building or room used for social amusements, specif gambling

cask *n* **1** a barrel-shaped container, usu for holding liquids **2** a cask and its contents; *also* the quantity contained in a cask

casket *n* **1** a small usu ornamental chest or box (e g for jewels) **2** *NAm* a coffin

casque *n* a helmet

cassava *n* (the fleshy edible starch-yielding rootstock of) any of several tropical plants of the spurge family

¹casserole *n* **1** a heatproof dish with a cover in which food may be baked and served **2** the savoury food cooked and served in a casserole

²casserole *vt* to cook (food) slowly in a casserole

cassette, casette *n* **1** a lightproof container for holding film or plates that can be inserted into a camera **2** a small case containing magnetic tape that can be inserted into a tape recorder

cassock *n* an ankle-length garment worn by the Roman Catholic and Anglican clergy or by laymen assisting in services

cassowary *n* any of several large flightless Australasian birds closely related to the emu

¹cast *vb* **cast** *vt* **1a** to cause to move by throwing ⟨∼ *a fishing line*⟩ **b** to direct ⟨∼ *a shadow*⟩ ⟨∼ *doubt on the enterprise*⟩ **c(1)** to send forth; emit ⟨*the fire* ∼*s a warm glow*⟩ **(2)** to place as if by throwing ⟨∼ *a spell*⟩ ⟨*was* ∼ *into prison*⟩ **d** to deposit (a vote) formally **e(1)** to throw off or away ⟨*the horse* ∼ *a shoe*⟩ **(2)** to shed, moult **(3)** *of an animal* to give birth to (prematurely) **2** to calculate (a horoscope) by means of astrology **3a** to arrange into a suitable form or order **b** to assign a part for (e g a play) or to (e g an actor) **4a** to shape (e g metal or plastic) by pouring into a mould when molten **b** to form by casting ∼*vi* **1** to throw out a line and lure with a fishing rod **2** to look round; seek − + *about* or *around* ⟨*she* ∼ *around uncertainly for somewhere to sit*⟩ **3** to veer **4** to take form in a mould − **cast anchor** to lower the anchor; to anchor − **cast lots** DRAW LOTS

²cast *n* **1a** an act of casting **b** a throw of a (fishing) line or net **2** *sing or pl in constr* the set of performers in a dramatic production **3** the distance to which sthg can be thrown **4a** a turning of the eye in a particular direction **b** a slight squint in the eye **5a** a reproduction (e g of a statue) formed by casting **b** an impression taken from an object with a molten or plastic substance **c** ¹PLASTER 3 **6a** a modification of a colour by a trace of some added colour ⟨*grey with a greenish* ∼⟩ **b** a tinge, suggestion **7** a shape, appearance ⟨*the delicate* ∼ *of her features*⟩ **8** the excrement of an earthworm

castanet *n* either of a pair of small usu wooden or plastic shells clicked together in the hand and used esp by dancers − usu pl

castaway *n* a person who is cast adrift or ashore as a result of a shipwreck or as a punishment − **castaway** *adj*

cast away *vt* to cause (a person or vessel) to be shipwrecked − usu passive

caste *n* **1** any of the hereditary social groups in Hinduism that restrict the occupations of their members and their association with members of other castes **2a** a social class **b** the prestige conferred by caste **3** the system of social division by castes **4** a specialized form of a social insect (e g a soldier or worker ant) adapted to carry out a particular function in the colony

castellated *adj* having battlements like a castle

caster *n* **1** a machine that casts type ²CASTOR 1, 2

caster sugar *n* finely granulated white sugar

castigate *vt* to punish or reprimand severely − fml − **castigator** *n*, **castigation** *n*

casting *n* **1** sthg cast in a mould **2** sthg cast out or off

casting vote *n* a deciding vote cast in the event of a tie

cast-iron *adj* **1** capable of withstanding great strain; strong, unyielding ⟨*a* ∼ *stomach*⟩ **2** impossible to disprove or falsify ⟨*a* ∼ *alibi*⟩

cast iron *n* a hard brittle alloy of iron, carbon, and silicon cast in a mould

¹castle *n* **1** a large fortified building or set of buildings **2** a stronghold **3** ³ROOK

²castle *vb* **castling** to move (a chess king) 2 squares towards a rook and then place the rook on the square on the other side of the king

castoff *n* **1** a cast-off article (e g of clothing) − usu pl **2** an estimate of the space that will be required for a given amount of text when printed

cast-off *adj* thrown away or discarded, esp because outgrown or no longer wanted ⟨∼ *clothes*⟩ ⟨*a* ∼ *lover*⟩

cast off *vt* **1** to unfasten or untie (a boat or line) **2** to remove (a stitch or stitches) from a knitting needle in such a way as to prevent unravelling **3** to get rid of; discard ⟨cast off *all restraint*⟩ **4** to measure (an amount of text) to determine the space it will take up when printed ∼*vi* **1** to unfasten or untie a boat or a line **2** to finish a knitted article by casting off all the stitches

cast on *vb* to place (a stitch or stitches) on a knitting needle for beginning or enlarging a knitted article

¹castor *n* a strong-smelling substance consisting of dried glands taken from near the anus of the beaver, used esp in making perfume

²castor, caster *n* **1** a small wheel set in a swivel mounting on the base of a piece of furniture, machinery, etc **2** a container with a perforated top for sprinkling powdered or granulated foods, esp sugar

castor oil *n* a pale viscous oil from the beans of a tropical Old World plant, used esp as a purgative

cast out *vt* to drive out; expel

castrate *vt* **1** to deprive of sexual organs: **a** to remove the testes of; geld **b** to remove the ovaries of; spay **2** to deprive of vitality or vigour; emasculate − **castrate** *n*, **castration** *n*

¹casual *adj* **1** subject to, resulting from, or occurring by chance **2a** occurring without regularity; occasional **b** employed for irregular periods ⟨*a* ∼ *labourer*⟩ **3a** feeling or showing little concern; nonchalant **b** informal, natural; *also* designed for informal wear − **casually** *adv*, **casualness** *n*

²casual *n* a casual or migratory worker

casualty *n* **1** a member of a military force killed or wounded in action **2** a person or thing injured, lost, or destroyed ⟨*small firms will be the first* casualties *of these policies*⟩

casuistry *n* **1** a method or doctrine dealing with particular ethical problems **2** the false application of general principles to particular instances, esp with regard to morals or law − **casuist** *n*, **casuistic, casuistical** *adj*

casus belli *n*, *pl* **casus belli** an event or action that brings about a war

¹cat *n* **1a** a small domesticated flesh-eating mammal kept as a pet or for catching rats and mice **b** any of a family of carnivores that includes the domestic cat, lion, tiger, leopard, jaguar, cougar, lynx, and cheetah **2** a malicious woman **3** a cat-o'-nine-tails **4** a player or devotee of jazz − slang **5** a (male) person − slang

²cat *n* CATAMARAN 2 − infml

cata-, cat-, cath- *prefix* down ⟨*catapult*⟩ ⟨*catarrh*⟩

cataclysm *n* **1** a flood, deluge **2** a violent geological change of the earth's surface **3** a momentous event marked by violent upheaval and destruction – **cataclysmal, cataclysmic** adj

catacomb n 1 a galleried subterranean cemetery with recesses for tombs 2 an underground passageway or group of passageways; a labyrinth *USE* often pl with sing. meaning

catafalque n an ornamental structure supporting or bearing a coffin (e g during a lying in state)

catalepsy n a trancelike state associated with schizophrenia in which the body remains rigid and immobile for prolonged periods – **cataleptic** adj or n

¹**catalogue, NAm chiefly catalog** 1 (a pamphlet or book containing) a complete list of items arranged systematically with descriptive details 2 a list, series ⟨a ~ of disasters⟩

²**catalogue, NAm chiefly catalog** vt 1 to enter in a catalogue; esp to classify (books or information) descriptively 2 to make a catalogue of

catalysis n, pl **catalyses** a change, esp an increase, in the rate of a chemical reaction induced by a catalyst

catalyst n 1 a chemical agent that causes catalysis 2 a substance (e g an enzyme) that changes, esp increases, the rate of a chemical reaction but itself remains chemically unchanged 3 sby or sthg whose action inspires further and usu more important events

catamaran n 1 a raft made of logs or pieces of wood lashed together 2 a boat with twin hulls side by side

cat-and-mouse adj consisting of continuous chasing and near captures and escapes

¹**catapult** n 1 an ancient military device for hurling missiles 2 a device for launching an aeroplane at flying speed (e g from an aircraft carrier) 3 Br a Y-shaped stick with a piece of elastic material fixed between the 2 prongs, used for shooting small objects (e g stones)

²**catapult** vb 1 to throw or launch (a missile) by means of a catapult 2 to (cause to) move suddenly or abruptly ⟨was ~ed from rags to riches overnight⟩

cataract n 1 clouding of (the enclosing membrane of) the lens of the eye; also the clouded area 2a (a large steeply-descending) waterfall b steep rapids in a river c a downpour, deluge

catarrh n (the mucus resulting from) inflammation of a mucous membrane, esp in the human nose and air passages – **catarrhal** adj

catastrophe n 1 a momentous, tragic, and unexpected event of extreme gravity 2 CATACLYSM 2 – **catastrophic** adj, **catastrophically** adv

catatonia n (a psychological disorder, esp schizophrenia, marked by) catalepsy – **catatonic** adj or n

cat burglar n, Br a burglar who enters buildings by climbing up walls, drainpipes, etc

catcall n a loud or raucous cry expressing disapproval – **catcall** vb

¹**catch** vb **caught** vt **1a** to capture or seize, esp after pursuit **b** to take or entangle (as if) in a snare ⟨caught in a web of deceit⟩ **c** to discover unexpectedly; surprise ⟨caught in the act⟩ **d** to check suddenly or momentarily **e** to cause to become entangled, fastened, or stuck ⟨~ a sleeve on a nail⟩ **2a** to seize; esp to intercept and keep hold of (a moving object), esp in the hands ⟨~ the ball⟩ **b** to dismiss (a batsman in cricket) by catching the ball after it has been hit and before it has touched the ground **3a** to contract; become infected with ⟨~ a cold⟩ **b** to hit, strike ⟨~ the mood of the occasion⟩ **c** to receive the force or impact of **4** to attract, arrest ⟨tried to ~ his attention⟩ **5** to take or get momentarily or quickly ⟨~ a glimpse of her friend⟩ **6** to be in time for ⟨~ the bus⟩ ⟨~ the last post⟩ **7** to grasp with the senses or the mind ~ vi **1** to become caught **2** of a fire to start to burn **3** BURN 3 ⟨the sugar caught on

the bottom of the pan⟩ – **catchable** adj – **catch a crab** to make a faulty stroke in rowing – **catch it** to incur blame, reprimand, or punishment – infml – **catch one's breath** 1 to rest long enough to restore normal breathing 2 to stop breathing briefly, usu under the influence of strong emotion – **catch someone on the hop** to find sby unprepared – infml

²**catch** n 1 sthg caught; esp the total quantity caught at one time ⟨a large ~ of fish⟩ 2 a game in which a ball is thrown and caught 3 sthg that retains or fastens ⟨the safety ~ of her brooch was broken⟩ 4 an often humorous or coarse round for 3 or more voices 5 a concealed difficulty; a snag ⟨there must be a ~ in it somewhere⟩ 6 an eligible marriage partner – infml

catch crop n a crop planted between the rows of the main crop or grown between the harvesting of a main crop and the planting of another

catcher n a baseball player who stands behind the batter to catch balls that the batter fails to hit

catching adj 1 infectious, contagious 2 alluring, attractive

catchment area n 1 the area from which a lake, reservoir, etc gets its rainwater 2 a geographical area from which people are drawn to attend a particular school, hospital, etc

catch on vi 1 to become popular ⟨the new fashion quickly caught on in Britain⟩ 2 to understand, learn – often + to; infml

catch out vt to expose or detect in wrongdoing or error – usu passive

catchpenny n or adj (sthg) worthless but designed to appear attractive, esp by being showy – derog

catchphrase n an arresting phrase that enjoys short-lived popularity

catchup n, chiefly NAm ketchup

catch up vt 1a to pick up, often abruptly ⟨caught the child up in her arms⟩ b to ensnare, entangle – usu + up; usu passive c to engross, absorb – usu + in; usu passive 2 to act or move fast enough to draw level with ⟨we'll catch you up later⟩ ~ vi 1 to act or move fast enough to draw level ⟨we'll catch up with you later⟩ 2 to acquaint oneself or deal with sthg belatedly – + on or with ⟨I must catch up on the bookkeeping⟩

catchword n 1 a word placed so as to assist a reader when turning a page 2 a word or expression associated with some school of thought or political movement; a slogan

catchy adj 1 tending to attract the interest or attention ⟨a ~ title⟩ 2 easy to remember and reproduce ⟨a ~ tune⟩

catechism n 1 instruction by question and answer 2 a manual for catechizing; specif a summary of religious doctrine, often in the form of questions and answers 3 a set of formal questions put as a test – **catechismal** adj

catechize, -ise vt 1 to teach systematically, esp by using question and answer; specif to teach the articles of faith of a religion in such a manner 2 to question systematically or searchingly – **catechist** n, **catechizer** n, **catechization** n

categorical also **categoric** adj absolute, unqualified ⟨a ~ denial⟩ – **categorically** adv

categorize, -ise vt to put into a category; classify – **categorization** n

category n 1 a general or fundamental form or class of terms, things, or ideas (e g in philosophy) 2 a division within a system of classification

cater vi 1 to provide and serve a supply of usu prepared food 2 to supply what is required or desired – usu + for or to ⟨~ed to her whims all day long⟩ – **caterer** n

caterpillar *n* a wormlike larva, specif of a butterfly or moth

Caterpillar *trademark* – used for a tractor designed to travel over rough or soft ground and propelled by 2 endless metal belts

caterwaul *vi* to cry noisily – **caterwaul** *n*

catfish *n* any of numerous large-headed fishes with long barbels

catgut *n* a tough cord usu made from sheep intestines and used esp for the strings of musical instruments and tennis rackets and for surgical sutures

catharsis *n, pl* **catharses 1** purgation **2** purification or purgation of the emotions through drama **3** the process of bringing repressed ideas and feelings to consciousness and expressing them, esp during psychoanalysis – **cathartic** *adj*

cathedral *n* a church that is the official seat of a diocesan bishop

catherine wheel *n, often cap C* a firework in the form of a wheel that spins as it burns

catheter *n* a tubular device for insertion into a hollow body part (e g a blood vessel), usu to inject or draw off fluids or to keep a passage open – **catheterize** *vt*

cathode *n* the electrode by which electrons leave an external circuit and enter a device; *specif* the positive terminal of a primary cell or of a storage battery that is delivering current – **cathodal** *adj*, **cathodic** *adj*

cathode-ray tube *n* a vacuum tube in which a beam of electrons is projected onto a fluorescent screen to provide a visual display (e g a television picture)

catholic *adj* **1** comprehensive, universal; *esp* broad in sympathies or tastes **2** *cap* **a** of or forming the entire body of worshippers that constitutes the Christian church **b** of or forming the ancient undivided Christian church or a church claiming historical continuity from it; *specif* ROMAN CATHOLIC – **catholicism** *n*, **catholicize** *vb*

Catholic *n* a member of a Catholic church; *specif* ROMAN CATHOLIC

catholicity *n* **1** liberality of sentiments or views **2** universality

catkin *n* a hanging spike-shaped densely crowded group of flowers without petals (e g in a willow)

catnap *n* a brief period of sleep, esp during the day – **catnap** *vi*

catnip *n* catmint

cat-o'-nine-tails *n, pl* **cat-o'-nine-tails** a whip made of usu 9 knotted cords fastened to a handle

cat's cradle *n* a game in which a string looped in a pattern on the fingers of one person's hands is transferred to the hands of another so as to form a different figure

cat's-eye *n, pl* **cat's-eyes 1** any of various gems (e g a chrysoberyl or a chalcedony) that reflect a narrow band of light from within **2** a small reflector set in a road, usu in a line with others, to reflect vehicle headlights

cat's-paw *n, pl* **cat's-paws 1** a light breeze that ruffles the surface of water in irregular patches **2** sby used by another as a tool or dupe **3** a hitch in a rope onto which a tackle may be hooked

catsuit *n* a tightly fitting 1-piece garment combining top and trousers

catsup *n, chiefly NAm* ketchup

cattle *n, pl* bovine animals kept on a farm, ranch, etc

cattle grid *n, Br* a shallow ditch in a road covered by parallel bars spaced far enough apart to prevent livestock from crossing

catty *adj* slyly spiteful; malicious – **cattily** *adv*, **cattiness** *n*

catwalk *n* **1** a narrow walkway (e g round a machine) **2** a narrow stage in the centre of a room on which fashion shows are held

Caucasian *adj* **1** of Caucasus or its inhabitants **2** of the white race of mankind as classified according to physical features – **Caucasian** *n*, **Caucasoid** *adj or n*

caucus *n* a closed political meeting to decide on policy, select candidates, etc

caudal *adj* **1** of or being a tail **2** situated at or directed towards the hind part of the body

caught *past of* CATCH

caul *n* **1** the large fatty fold of membrane covering the intestines **2** the inner foetal membrane of higher vertebrates, esp when covering the head at birth

cauldron, caldron *n* **1** a large open metal pot used for cooking over an open fire **2** sthg that resembles a boiling cauldron ⟨a ~ *of intense emotions*⟩

cauliflower *n* (a plant closely related to the cabbage with) a compact head of usu white undeveloped flowers eaten as a vegetable

caulk, calk *vt* to stop up and make watertight (e g the seams of a boat, cracks in wood, etc) by filling with a waterproof material – **caulker** *n*

causal *adj* **1** expressing or indicating cause; causative ⟨a ~ *clause introduced by* since *or* because⟩ **2** of or being a cause ⟨*the* ~ *agent of a disease*⟩ – **causally** *adv*

causality *n* **1** a causal quality or agency **2** the relation between a cause and its effect

causation *n* **1** the act or process of causing **2** the act or agency by which an effect is produced

causative *adj* **1** effective or operating as a cause or agent **2** expressing causation – **causative** *n*, **causatively** *adv*

¹**cause** *n* **1a** sby or sthg that brings about an effect **b** an agent that brings sthg about **c** a reason for an action or condition; a motive **2** a ground for legal action **3** a principle or movement worth defending or supporting – **causeless** *adj*

²**cause** *vt* to serve as the cause or occasion of – **causer** *n*

'**cause** *conj* because – nonstandard

cause célèbre *n, pl* **causes célèbres 1** a legal case that excites widespread interest **2** a notorious incident or episode

causeway *n* a raised road or path, esp across wet ground or water

¹**caustic** *adj* **1** capable of destroying or eating away by chemical action; corrosive **2** incisive, biting ⟨~ *wit*⟩ **3** of or being the envelope of rays reflected or refracted by a curved surface – **caustically** *adv*, **causticity** *n*

²**caustic** *n* a curve or surface formed by (the intersection of) the envelope of rays reflected or refracted by a curved surface

cauterize, -ise *vt* to sear or destroy (e g a wound or body tissue) with a cautery, esp in order to rid of infection – **cauterization** *n*

¹**caution** *n* **1** a warning, admonishment; *specif* an official warning given to sby who has committed a minor offence **2** prudent forethought intended to minimize risk; care **3** sby or sthg that causes astonishment or amusement – *infml* ⟨*she's a proper* ~⟩ – **cautionary** *adj*

²**caution** *vt* **1a** to advise caution to; warn; *specif* to warn (sby under arrest) that his/her words will be recorded and may be used in evidence **b** to admonish, reprove; *specif* to give an official warning to ⟨~ ed *for disorderly conduct*⟩ **2** of a soccer referee ²BOOK 2b ~ *vi* to urge, warn ⟨~ ed *against an excess of alcohol*⟩

cautious *adj* careful, prudent – **cautiously** *adv*, **cautiousness** *n*

cavalcade *n* **1** PROCESSION 1; *esp* one of riders or carriages **2** a dramatic sequence or procession; a series

¹**cavalier** *n* **1** a gentleman of former times trained in arms and horsemanship; *specif* a mounted soldier **2** a gallant gentleman of former times; *esp* one in attendance on a lady **3** *cap* an adherent of Charles I of England, esp during the Civil War

²**cavalier** *adj* **1** debonair **2** given to or characterized by offhand dismissal of important matters **3** *cap* of the party of Charles I of England – **cavalierly** *adv*

cavalry *n, sing or pl in constr* **1** a branch of an army consisting of mounted troops **2** a branch of a modern army consisting of armoured vehicles

¹**cave** *n* **1** a natural chamber (e g underground or in the side of a hill or cliff) having a usu horizontal opening on the surface **2** *Br* a formal withdrawing or group of people withdrawing from a political party

²**cave** *vt* to form a cave in or under; hollow out ~ *vi* to explore cave or pothole systems – **caver** *n*

³**cave** *interj, Br* – used as a warning call among schoolchildren, esp at public school; compare KEEP CAVE

caveat *n* **1** a cautionary remark or statement; a warning – *fml* an official notice to a court to suspend a proceeding until the opposition has been heard

caveat emptor *n* the principle in commerce which states that without a guarantee the buyer takes the risk of quality upon him-/herself

cave dweller *n* one who dwells in a cave

cave in *vt* to cause to fall in or collapse ~ *vi* **1** to fall in or collapse **2** to cease to resist; submit – *infml*

caveman *n* **1** a cave dweller, esp of the Stone Age **2** a man who acts in a rough primitive manner, esp towards women

cavern *n* a large usu underground chamber or cave – **cavernous** *adj*, **cavernously** *adv*

caviar, caviare *n* **1** the salted roe of large fish (e g sturgeon) eaten as a delicacy **2** sthg considered too delicate or lofty for mass appreciation ⟨*will be* ~ *to the multitude*⟩

cavil *vi* -ll- (*NAm* -l-, -ll-), to raise trivial and frivolous objections – **cavil** *n*, **caviller** *n*

cavity *n* an empty or hollowed-out space within a mass; *specif* a decaying hollow in a tooth

cavity wall *n* a wall built in 2 thicknesses, the air space between providing insulation

cavort *vi* **1** to prance **2** to engage in extravagant behaviour

cavy *n* a guinea pig or related short-tailed S American rodent

caw *vi* to utter (a sound like) the harsh raucous cry of the crow – **caw** *n*

cay *n* a low island or reef of sand or coral

cayenne pepper *n* **1** a pungent red condiment consisting of the ground dried pods and seeds of hot peppers **2** a hot pepper, esp a cultivated capsicum

cayman, caiman *n, pl* **caymans**, *esp collectively* **cayman** any of several Central and S American crocodilians related to the alligators

¹**cease** *vt* to bring to an end; terminate ⟨~ *this noise!*⟩ ~ *vi* **1** to come to an end ⟨*when will this quarrelling* ~ *?*⟩ **2** to bring an activity or action to an end; discontinue ⟨*cried for hours without ceasing*⟩

²**cease** *n* stopping, cessation ⟨*without* ~⟩

cease-fire *n* (a military order for) a cessation of firing or of active hostilities

ceaseless *adj* continuing endlessly; constant – **ceaselessly** *adv*, **ceaselessness** *n*

cedar *n* (the fragrant wood of) any of a genus of usu tall evergreen coniferous trees of the pine family

cede *vt* to yield or surrender (e g territory), usu by treaty – **ceder** *n*

cedilla *n* a mark‚ placed under a letter (e g ç in French) to indicate an alteration or modification of its usual phonetic value (e g in the French *façade*)

ceiling *n* **1** the overhead inside surface of a room **2** the height above the ground of the base of the lowest layer of clouds **3** a prescribed or actual maximum height at which an aircraft can fly **4** an upper usu prescribed limit ⟨*a* ~ *on rents and wages*⟩

celandine *n* **1** *also* **greater celandine** a yellow-flowered biennial plant of the poppy family **2** *also* **lesser celandine** a common yellow-flowered European perennial plant of the buttercup family

celebrant *n* the priest officiating at the Eucharist

celebrate *vt* **1** to perform (a sacrament or solemn ceremony) publicly and with appropriate rites ⟨~ *the mass*⟩ **2a** to mark (a holy day or feast day) ceremonially **b** to mark (a special occasion) with festivities or suspension of routine activities **3** to hold up for public acclaim; extol ⟨*his poetry* ~ *s the glory of nature*⟩ ~ *vi* **1** to officiate at a religious ceremony **2** to observe a special occasion, usu with festivities – **celebration** *n*, **celebrator** *n*, **celebratory** *adj*

celebrated *adj* widely known and often referred to – **celebratedness** *n*

celebrity *n* **1** the state of being famous **2** a well-known and widely acclaimed person

celerity *n* rapidity of motion or action – *fml*

celery *n* a European plant of the carrot family with leafstalks eaten cold or hot as a vegetable

celestial *adj* **1** of or suggesting heaven or divinity; divine **2** of or in the sky or visible heavens ⟨*a* ~ *body*⟩ – **celestially** *adv*

celestial sphere *n* an imaginary sphere of infinite radius against which the celestial bodies appear to be projected

celibate *n* one who is unmarried and does not have sexual intercourse, esp because of a religious vow – **celibacy** *n*, **celibate** *adj*

cell *n* **1** a 1-room dwelling occupied esp by a hermit or recluse **2a** a barely furnished room for 1 person (e g in a convent or monastery) **b** a small room in a prison for 1 or more inmates **3** a small compartment (e g in a honeycomb), receptacle, cavity (e g one containing seeds in a plant ovary), or bounded space **4** the smallest structural unit of living matter consisting of nuclear and cytoplasmic material bounded by a semipermeable membrane and capable of functioning either alone or with others in all fundamental life processes **5a** a vessel (e g a cup or jar) containing electrodes and an electrolyte either for generating electricity by chemical action or for use in electrolysis **b** a single unit in a device for producing an electrical effect as a result of exposure to radiant energy **6** the primary unit of a political, esp Communist, organization **7** a basic subdivision of a computer memory that is addressable and can hold 1 unit (e g a word) of a computer's basic operating data

¹**cellar** *n* **1** an underground room; *esp* one used for storage **2** an individual's stock of wine

²**cellar** *vt* to store or place (e g wine) in a cellar

cellarage *n* **1** cellar space, esp for storage **2** the charge made for storage in a cellar

cell division *n* the process by which 2 daughter cells are formed from a parent cell

cello *n, pl* **cellos** a large stringed instrument of the violin family tuned an octave below the viola – **cellist** *n*

cellophane *n* regenerated cellulose in the form of thin transparent sheets, used esp for wrapping goods

cellular *adj* **1** of, relating to, or consisting of cells **2**

containing cavities; porous **3** having a very open weave ⟨*a ~ blanket*⟩ – **cellularly** *adv*, **cellularity** *n*
celluloid *n* film for the cinema; *also* FILM **3** – **celluloid** *adj*
Celluloid *trademark* – used for a tough inflammable thermoplastic composed essentially of cellulose nitrate and camphor
cellulose *n* **1** a polysaccharide of glucose units that constitutes the chief part of plant cell walls, occurs naturally in cotton, kapok, etc, and is the raw material of many manufactured goods (e g paper, rayon, and cellophane) **2** paint or lacquer of which the main constituent is cellulose nitrate or acetate
Celsius *adj* relating to, conforming to, or being a scale of temperature on which water freezes at 0° and boils at 100° under standard conditions
Celt, Kelt *n* **1** a member of a division of the early Indo-European peoples extending at various times from the British Isles and Spain to Asia Minor **2** a modern Gael, Highland Scot, Irishman, Welshman, Cornishman, Manxman, or Breton
¹Celtic, Keltic *adj* (characteristic) of the Celts or their languages
²Celtic, Keltic *n* a branch of Indo-European languages comprising Welsh, Cornish, Breton, Irish, Scots Gaelic, and Manx, which is now confined to Brittany and parts of the British Isles – **Celticist** *n*
¹cement *n* **1** a powder consisting of alumina, silica, lime, iron oxide, and magnesia pulverized together and burnt in a kiln, that is used as the binding agent in mortar and concrete **2** a substance (e g a glue or adhesive) used for sticking objects together **3** sthg serving to unite firmly ⟨*a common tradition is the ~ which holds the community together*⟩ **4** cementum **5** an adhesive preparation used for filling teeth, attaching dental crowns, etc **6** concrete – not used technically – **cementitious** *adj*
²cement *vt* **1** to unite or make firm (as if) by the application of cement **2** to overlay with concrete
cemetery *n* a burial ground; *esp* one not in a churchyard
cenotaph *n* a tomb or monument erected in honour of a person or group of people whose remains are elsewhere; *specif*, *cap* that standing in Whitehall in London in memory of the dead of WWs I and II
¹censor *n* **1** either of 2 magistrates of early Rome who acted as census takers, inspectors of morals, etc **2** an official who examines publications, films, letters, etc and has the power to suppress objectionable (e g obscene or libellous) matter **3** a supposed mental agency that represses certain unacceptable ideas and desires before they reach consciousness – **censorial** *adj*
²censor *vt* to subject to censorship
censorious *adj* severely critical; given to censure – **censoriously** *adv*, **censoriousness** *n*
censorship *n* **1** the act, practice, or duties of a censor; *esp* censorial control **2** the office, power, or term of a Roman censor **3** the repression in the mind of unacceptable ideas and desires
¹censure *n* **1** a judgment involving condemnation **2** the act of blaming or condemning sternly **3** an official reprimand
²censure *vt* to find fault with and criticize as blameworthy – **censurable** *adj*, **censurer** *n*
census *n* **1** a periodic counting of the population and gathering of related statistics (e g age, sex, or social class) carried out by government **2** a usu official count or tally
cent *n* (a coin or note representing) a unit worth ¹/₁₀₀ of

the basic money unit of certain countries (e g the American dollar)
centaur *n* any of a race of mythological creatures having the head, arms, and upper body of a man, and the lower body and back legs of a horse
centavo *n*, *pl* **centavos** (a coin or note representing) a unit worth ¹/₁₀₀ of the basic money unit of certain Spanish or Portuguese-speaking countries (e g Chile, Cuba, Mexico, Portugal)
centenarian *n* sby who is (more than) 100 years old – **centenarian** *adj*
centenary *n* (the celebration of) a 100th anniversary – **centenary** *adj*
centennial *n*, *chiefly NAm* a centenary – **centennial** *adj*, **centennially** *adv*
center *vb or n*, *NAm* (to) centre
centi- *comb form* **1** hundred ⟨*centipede*⟩ **2** one hundredth (10⁻²) part of (a specified unit) ⟨*centimetre*⟩
centigrade *adj* Celsius
centigram *n* one hundredth of a gram
centime *n* (a note or coin representing) a unit worth ¹/₁₀₀ of the basic money unit of certain French-speaking countries (e g Algeria, Belgium, France)
centimetre *n* one hundredth of a metre (about 0.4in)
centipede *n* any of a class of many-segmented arthropods with each segment bearing 1 pair of legs
central *adj* **1** containing or constituting a centre **2** of primary importance; principal ⟨*the ~ character of the novel*⟩ **3a** at, in, or near the centre ⟨*the plains of ~ N America*⟩ **b** easily accessible; convenient ⟨*our house is very ~ for the shops*⟩ **4** having overall power or control ⟨*decided by the ~ committee*⟩ **5** of, originating in, or comprising the central nervous system – **centrally** *adv*, **centrality** *n*
central heating *n* a system of heating whereby heat is produced at a central source (e g a boiler) and carried by pipes to radiators or air vents throughout a building (e g a house or office block)
centralism *n* the practice or principle of concentrating power and control in a central authority – **centralist** *n or adj*, **centralistic** *adj*
centralize, -ise *vi* to come to or gather round a centre; *specif* to gather under central control (e g of government) ~*vt* to bring to a centre; consolidate; *specif* to bring (power, authority, etc) under central control – **centralizer** *n*, **centralization** *n*
central nervous system *n* the part of the nervous system which in vertebrates consists of the brain and spinal cord and which coordinates the activity of the entire nervous system
¹centre, *NAm chiefly* center *n* **1** the point round which a circle or sphere is described; *broadly* the centre of symmetry **2a** a place, esp a collection of buildings, round which a usu specified activity is concentrated ⟨*a shopping ~*⟩ **b** sby or sthg round which interest is concentrated ⟨*the ~ of the controversy*⟩ **c** a source from which sthg originates ⟨*a propaganda ~*⟩ **d** a region of concentrated population ⟨*an urban ~*⟩ **3** a group of nerve cells having a common function ⟨*respiratory ~*⟩ **4** the middle part (e g of a stage) **5** *often cap* a group, party, etc holding moderate political views ⟨*the possible formation of a new ~ party*⟩ **6a** a player occupying a middle position in the forward line of a team (e g in football or hockey) **b** an instance of passing the ball from a wing to the centre of a pitch or court (e g in football) **7** (a recess containing) a rod with a conical end which supports a workpiece in a lathe or grinding machine and about or with which the workpiece revolves **8** a temporary wooden framework on which an arch is supported during construction

²**centre,** *NAm chiefly* **center** *vi* **1** to have a centre; focus – usu + *round* or *on* **2** to come to or towards a centre or central area **3** to centre a ball, puck, etc ~ *vt* **1** to place or fix in or at a centre or central area ⟨~ *the picture on the wall*⟩ **2** to gather to a centre; concentrate ⟨~s *her hopes on her son*⟩ **3** to adjust (e g lenses) so that the axes coincide **4** to pass (e g a ball or puck) from either side towards the middle of the playing area

centreboard *n* a retractable keel used esp in small yachts

centre-forward *n* (the position of) a player in hockey, soccer, etc positioned in the middle of the forward line

centre of gravity *n* **1** CENTRE OF MASS **2** the point at which the entire weight of a body may be considered as concentrated so that if supported at this point the body would remain in equilibrium in any position

centre of mass *n* the point at which the entire mass of a body or system of bodies may be considered as concentrated

centrepiece *n* **1** an ornament (e g of flowers) placed in the centre of a table **2** the most important or outstanding item

centrifugal *adj* **1** proceeding or acting in a direction away from a centre or axis **2** using or acting by centrifugal force ⟨*a* ~ *pump*⟩ **3** tending away from centralization; separatist ⟨~ *tendencies in modern society*⟩

centrifugal force *n* the force that appears to act outwardly from the centre of rotation of an object moving along a circular path

centrifuge *vt or n* (to subject to centrifugal action, esp in) a machine using centrifugal force, esp for separating substances of different densities – **centrifugation** *n*

centripetal *adj* **1** proceeding or acting in a direction towards a centre or axis **2** tending towards centralization; unifying – **centripetally** *adv*

centrist *n*, *often cap* a member of a moderate party; *broadly* one holding moderate political views – **centrism** *n*

centurion *n* an officer commanding a Roman century

century *n* **1** a subdivision of the ancient Roman legion orig consisting of 100 men **2** a group, sequence, or series of 100 like things; *specif* 100 runs made by a cricketer in 1 innings **3** a period of 100 years; *esp* any of the 100-year periods reckoned forwards or backwards from the conventional date of the birth of Christ

cephalic *adj* **1** of or relating to the head **2** directed towards or situated on, in, or near the head – **cephalically** *adv*

-cephalic, -cephalous *comb form* (→ *adj*) having (such) a head or (so many) heads ⟨brachycephalic⟩

cephalopod *n* any of a class of tentacled molluscs that includes the squids, cuttlefishes, and octopuses – **cephalopod**, **cephalopodan** *adj or n*

¹**ceramic** *adj* of or being (the manufacture of) a product (e g porcelain or brick) made from a nonmetallic mineral (e g clay) by firing at high temperatures

²**ceramic** *n* **1** *pl but sing in constr* the art or process of making ceramic articles **2** a product of ceramic manufacture – **ceramist, ceramicist** *n*

¹**cereal** *adj* of or relating to (the plants that produce) grain

²**cereal** *n* **1** (a grass or other plant yielding) grain suitable for food **2** a food made from grain and usu eaten with milk and sugar at breakfast

cerebellum *n*, *pl* **cerebellums, cerebella** a large part of the back of the brain which projects outwards and is concerned esp with coordinating muscles and maintaining equilibrium – **cerebellar** *adj*

cerebral *adj* **1a** of the brain or the intellect **b** of or being

the cerebrum **2a** appealing to the intellect ⟨~ *drama*⟩ **b** primarily intellectual in nature ⟨*a* ~ *society*⟩ – **cerebrally** *adv*

cerebrate *vi* to use the mind; think – *fml* – **cerebration** *n*

cerebrum *n*, *pl* **cerebrums, cerebra 1** BRAIN 1a **2** the expanded front portion of the brain that in higher mammals overlies the rest of the brain and consists of the 2 cerebral hemispheres

¹**ceremonial** *adj* marked by, involved in, or belonging to ceremony – **ceremonialism** *n*, **ceremonialist** *n*, **ceremonially** *adv*

²**ceremonial** *n* **1a** a ceremonial act or action **b** a usu prescribed system of formalities or rituals **2** (a book containing) the order of service in the Roman Catholic church

ceremonious *adj* **1** ceremonial **2** devoted to form and ceremony; punctilious – **ceremoniously** *adv*, **ceremoniousness** *n*

ceremony *n* **1** a formal act or series of acts prescribed by ritual, protocol, or convention ⟨*the marriage* ~⟩ **2** (observance of) established procedures of civility or politeness

cerise *n or adj* (a) light purplish red

cert *n*, *Br* CERTAINTY 1; *esp* a horse that is sure to win a race – *infml* ⟨*a dead* ~ *for the 4.30*⟩

¹**certain** *adj* **1** fixed, settled ⟨*guaranteed a* ~ *percentage of the profit*⟩ **2a** of a particular but unspecified character, quantity, or degree ⟨*the house has a* ~ *charm*⟩ **b** named but not known ⟨*a* ~ *Bill Clarke*⟩ **3a** established beyond doubt or question; definite ⟨*it is* ~ *that we exist*⟩ **b** unerring, dependable ⟨*her discernment was* ~⟩ **4a** inevitable ⟨*the* ~ *advance of age and decay*⟩ **b** incapable of failing; sure – + infinitive ⟨*she is* ~ *to do well*⟩ **5a** assured in mind; convinced ⟨*I'm* ~ *she saw me*⟩ **b** assured in action; sure ⟨*be* ~ *you catch your train*⟩ – **certainly** *adv* – **for certain** as a certainty; assuredly

²**certain** *pron*, *pl in constr* certain ones ⟨~ *of the questions raised were thought to be irrelevant*⟩

certainty *n* **1** sthg certain **2** the quality or state of being certain

¹**certificate** *n* a document containing a certified statement; *esp* one declaring the status or qualifications of the holder ⟨*a birth* ~⟩

²**certificate** *vt* to testify to, authorize by, or award with a certificate – **certification** *n*, **certificatory** *adj*

certify *vt* **1a** to confirm, esp officially in writing **b** to declare officially as being true or as meeting a standard **c** to declare officially the insanity of **2** to certificate, license ⟨*a certified teacher*⟩ **3** *chiefly NAm* to guarantee the payment or value of (a cheque) by endorsing on the front – **certifiable** *adj*, **certifiably** *adv*, **certifier** *n*

certitude *n* the state of being or feeling certain

cerulean *adj* deep sky blue in colour

cerumen *n* the yellow waxy secretion from the outer ear – **ceruminous** *adj*

cervical *adj* of a neck or cervix

cervix *n*, *pl* **cervices, cervixes 1** (the back part of) the neck **2** a constricted portion of an organ or body part; *esp* the narrow outer end of the uterus

cesarean *also* **cesarian** *n*, *NAm* a caesarean – **cesarean** *also* **cesarian** *adj*

cessation *n* a temporary or final stop; an ending

cession *n* the act or an instance of yielding rights, property, or esp territory

cesspit *n* **1** a pit for the disposal of refuse (e g sewage) **2** a corrupt or squalid place

cesspool *n* an underground basin for liquid waste (e g household sewage)

cetacean *n* any of an order of aquatic, mostly marine, mammals that includes the whales, dolphins, and porpoises – **cetacean** *adj*, **cetaceous** *adj*

Chablis *n, pl* **Chablis** a very dry white table wine produced in northern Burgundy

cha-cha, cha-cha-cha *n* (a piece of music for performing) a fast rhythmic ballroom dance of Latin American origin – **cha-cha** *vi*

chaconne *n* 1 an old Spanish dance tune resembling the passacaglia 2 a musical composition in 3₄ time typically consisting of variations on a repeated succession of chords

¹**chafe** *vt* 1 to irritate, vex 2 to warm (part of the body) by rubbing 3a to rub so as to wear away b to make sore (as if) by rubbing ~ *vi* 1 to feel irritation or discontent; fret ⟨~s *at his restrictive desk job*⟩ 2 to become sore or uncomfortable as a result of rubbing

²**chafe** *n* (injury or wear caused by) friction

¹**chaff** *n* 1 the seed coverings and other debris separated from the seed in threshing grain 2 worthless matter – esp in *separate the wheat from the chaff* 3 chopped straw, hay, etc used for animal feed 4 material (e g strips of foil) ejected into the air to reflect enemy radar waves and so prevent detection – **chaffy** *adj*

²**chaff** *n* light jesting talk; banter

³**chaff** *vt* to tease good-naturedly ~ *vi* to jest, banter

chaffinch *n* a European finch with a reddish breast, bluish head, and white wing bars

chafing dish *n* a dish for cooking or keeping food warm, esp over a spirit burner at the table

chagrin *vt or n* (to subject to) mental distress caused by humiliation, disappointment, or failure

¹**chain** *n* 1a a series of usu metal links or rings connected to or fitted into one another and used for various purposes (e g support or restraint) b an ornament or badge of office consisting of such a series of links c(1) a measuring instrument of 100 links used in surveying (2) a unit of length equal to 66ft (about 20.12m) 2 sthg that confines, restrains, or secures – usu pl ⟨*the* ~s *of ignorance*⟩ 3a a series of linked or connected things ⟨*a* ~ *of events*⟩ ⟨*a mountain* ~⟩ b a group of associated establishments (e g shops or hotels) under the same ownership ⟨*a* ~ *of supermarkets*⟩ c a number of atoms or chemical groups united like links in a chain

²**chain** *vt* to fasten, restrict, or confine (as if) with a chain – often + *up* or *down*

chain gang *n, sing or pl in constr* a gang of convicts chained together, usu while doing hard labour outside prison

chain letter *n* a letter containing a request that copies of it, sometimes together with money or goods, be sent to a specified number of other people who should then repeat the process

chain mail *n* flexible armour of interlinked metal rings

chain reaction *n* 1 a series of events so related to each other that each one initiates the next 2 a self-sustaining chemical or nuclear reaction yielding energy or products that cause further reactions of the same kind

chain saw *n* a portable power saw that has teeth linked together to form a continuous revolving chain

chain-smoke *vb* to smoke (esp cigarettes) continually, usu by lighting one cigarette from the previous one smoked

chain stitch *n* an ornamental embroidery or crochet stitch that resembles a linked chain

chain store *n* any of several usu retail shops under the same ownership and selling the same lines of goods

¹**chair** *n* 1 a seat for 1 person, usu having 4 legs and a back and sometimes arms 2a an office or position of authority

or dignity; *specif* a professorship ⟨*holds a university* ~⟩ b a chairman 3 SEDAN CHAIR 4 a deep-grooved metal block fastened to a sleeper to hold a rail in place

²**chair** *vt* 1 to install in office 2 to preside as chairman of 3 *chiefly Br* to carry shoulder-high in acclaim ⟨*the time you won your town the race we* ~ed *you through the market place* –A E Housman⟩

chair lift *n* a ski lift with seats for passengers

chairman, *fem* **chairlady, chairwoman** *n* 1 one who presides over or heads a meeting, committee, organization, or board of directors 2 a radio or television presenter; *esp* one who coordinates unscripted or diverse material 3 a carrier of a sedan chair – **chairmanship** *n*

chairperson *n, pl* **chairpersons** a chairman or chairwoman

chaise *n* a light carriage, usu having 2 wheels and a folding top

chaise longue *n, pl* **chaise longues** *also* **chaises longues** a low sofa with only 1 armrest, on which one may recline

chalcedony *n* a translucent quartz that is often pale blue or grey and is used as a gemstone – **chalcedonic** *adj*

chalet *n* 1 a hut used by herdsmen in the Alps 2a a small wooden house with a steeply sloping roof and widely overhanging eaves, common esp in Switzerland b a small house or hut used esp for temporary accommodation (e g at a holiday camp)

chalice *n* 1 a drinking cup; a goblet 2 an esp gold or silver cup used to hold the wine at communion

¹**chalk** *n* 1 a soft white, grey, or buff limestone composed chiefly of the shells of small marine organisms 2 a short stick of chalk or chalky material used esp for writing and drawing – **chalky** *adj*

²**chalk** *vt* 1 to rub or mark with chalk 2 to write or draw with chalk 3 to set down or add up (as if) with chalk – usu + *up* ⟨~ *up the score*⟩, ~ *vi Br* to act as scorer for a darts match

chalk out *vt* to delineate roughly; sketch ⟨chalk out *a plan of action*⟩

chalk up *vt* 1 to ascribe, credit; *specif* to charge to sby's account ⟨chalk *it up to me*⟩ 2 to attain, achieve ⟨chalked up *a record score for the season*⟩

¹**challenge** *vt* 1 to order to halt and prove identity ⟨*the sentry* ~d *the stranger at the gates*⟩ 2 to dispute, esp as being unjust, invalid, or outmoded; impugn ⟨uncovered *new data that* ~s *old assumptions*⟩ 3 to question formally the legality or legal qualifications of (e g a juror) 4a to defy boldly; dare b to call out to duel, combat, or competition 5 to stimulate by testing the skill of (sby or sthg) ⟨*maths* ~s *him*⟩ 6 to administer infective (antigenic) material to (an organism) in order to ascertain whether experimental immunization has been effective – **challenger** *n*, **challenging** *adj*, **challengingly** *adv*

²**challenge** *n* 1a a calling to account or into question; a protest b a command given by a sentry, watchman, etc to halt and prove identity c a questioning of right or validity 2a a summons that is threatening or provocative; *specif* a call to a duel b an invitation to compete 3 (sthg having) the quality of being demanding or stimulating ⟨*the job presented a real* ~⟩ 4 a test of immunity by reexposure to infective (antigenic) material after specific immunization with it

¹**chamber** *n* 1 a natural or artificial enclosed space or cavity 2a(1) a room where a judge hears private cases – usu pl with sing. meaning (2) *pl* a set of rooms used by a group of barristers b a reception room in an official or state building 3 (a hall used by) a legislative or judicial body; *esp* either of 2 houses of a legislature 4 the part of

a gun that holds the charge or cartridge **5** *archaic* a room; *esp* a bedroom

²chamber *vt* to accommodate (e g a charge) in the chamber of a firearm

chamberlain *n* **1** a chief officer of a royal or noble household **2** a treasurer (e g of a corporation)

chambermaid *n* a maid who cleans bedrooms and makes beds (e g in a hotel)

chamber music *n* music written for a small group of instruments

Chamber of Commerce *n* an association of businessmen to promote commercial and industrial interests in the community

chamber orchestra *n* a small orchestra, usu with 1 player for each instrumental part

chamber pot *n* a bowl-shaped receptacle for urine and faeces, used chiefly in the bedroom

chameleon *n* **1** any of a group of Old World lizards with a long tongue, a prehensile tail, and the ability to change the colour of the skin **2** sby or sthg changeable; *specif* a fickle person – **chameleonic** *adj*

chamois *n*, *pl* **chamois** *also* **chamoix** **1** a small goatlike antelope of Europe and the Caucasus **2** a soft pliant leather prepared from the skin of the chamois or sheep, used esp as a cloth for polishing

chamomile *n* camomile

¹champ *vt* **1** to munch (food) noisily **2** to gnaw, bite ~ *vi* **1** to make biting or gnashing movements **2** to eat noisily **3** to show impatience or eagerness – usu in *champ at the bit* ⟨*the children were* ~ing *at the bit to get on board*⟩

²champ *n* a champion – infml

champagne *n* a white sparkling wine made in the old province of Champagne in France

champaign *n* an expanse of level open country; a plain – **champaign** *adj*

¹champion *n* **1** a militant supporter of, or fighter for, a cause or person ⟨*an outspoken* ~ *of civil rights*⟩ **2** one who shows marked superiority; *specif* the winner of a competitive event

²champion *vt* to protect or fight for as a champion

³champion *adj*, *chiefly N Eng* superb, splendid – infml

championship *n* **1** the act of championing; defence ⟨*his* ~ *of freedom of speech*⟩ **2** a contest held to determine a champion

¹chance *n* **1a** an event without discernible human intention or observable cause ⟨*this is a strange* ~ *that throws you and me together* – Charles Dickens⟩ **b** the incalculable (assumed) element in existence; that which determines unaccountable happenings ⟨*we met by* ~⟩ **2** a situation favouring some purpose; an opportunity **3** an opportunity of dismissing a batsman in cricket **4a** the possibility of a specified or favourable outcome in an uncertain situation ⟨*we have almost no* ~ *of winning*⟩ **b** *pl* the more likely indications ⟨~s *are he's already heard the news*⟩ **5** a risk ⟨*took a* ~ *on it*⟩ – **chance** *adj*, **chanceless** *adj*

²chance *vi* **1** to take place or come about by chance; happen ⟨*it* ~d *that the street was empty*⟩ **2** to come or light *on* or *upon* by chance ⟨~d *on the idea*⟩ ~ *vt* to accept the hazard of; risk

chancel *n* the part of a church containing the altar and seats for the clergy and choir

chancellery, chancellory *n* **1** the position or department of a chancellor **2** the office or staff of an embassy or consulate

chancellor *n* **1a** the secretary of a nobleman, prince, or king **b** LORD CHANCELLOR **c** a Roman Catholic priest heading a diocesan chancery **2** the titular head of a British university **3** a usu lay legal officer of an Anglican diocese

4 the chief minister of state in some European countries – **chancellorship** *n*

chancery *n* **1a** **Chancery Division, Chancery** a division of the High Court having jurisdiction over causes in equity **b** a US court of equity **2** a record office for public archives or those of ecclesiastical, legal, or diplomatic proceedings **3a** a chancellor's court or office **b** the office in which the business of a Roman Catholic diocese is transacted and recorded **c** CHANCELLERY 2

chancy *adj* uncertain in outcome or prospect; risky – **chancily** *adj*, **chanciness** *n*

chandelier *n* a branched often ornate lighting fixture suspended from a ceiling

chandler *n* a retail dealer in supplies and equipment of a specified kind ⟨*a ship's* ~⟩ ⟨*a corn* ~⟩

¹change *vt* **1a** to make different **b** to give a different position, direction, status, or aspect to ⟨*we* ~d *our thinking on the matter*⟩ ⟨*stop* changing *your mind*⟩ **c** to exchange, reverse – often + *over* or *round* ⟨*just* ~ *the speaker leads over*⟩ **2a** to replace with another ⟨*let's* ~ *the subject*⟩ **b** to move from one to another ⟨~ *sides*⟩ **c** to exchange for an equivalent sum or comparable item **d** to undergo a loss or modification of ⟨*foliage* changing *colour*⟩ **e** to put fresh clothes or covering on ⟨~ *a bed*⟩ ~ *vi* **1** to become different ⟨*her mood* ~s *every hour*⟩ **2** *of the moon* to pass from one phase to another **3** to go from one vehicle of a public transport system to another **4** *of the (male) voice* to shift to a lower register; BREAK 9a **5** to undergo transformation, transition, or conversion ⟨*winter* ~d *to spring*⟩ ⟨*most industries have* ~d *to the metric system*⟩ **6** to put on different clothes **7** to engage in giving sthg and receiving sthg in return – usu + *with* – **changer** *n* – **change hands** to pass from the possession of one person to that of another

²change *n* **1a** a (marked) alteration ⟨*has undergone a* ~ *since he was married*⟩ **b** a substitution ⟨*a* ~ *of players*⟩ **c** the passage of the moon from one phase to another; *specif* the coming of the new moon **2** an alternative set, esp of clothes **3a** money of lower denominations received in exchange for an equivalent sum of higher denominations ⟨*have you got* ~ *for a pound?*⟩ **b** money returned when a payment exceeds the amount due **c** coins of low denominations ⟨*a pocketful of* ~⟩ **4** an order in which a set of bells is struck in change ringing – **changeful** *adj*, **changefully** *adv*, **changefulness** *n*, **changeless** *adj*, **changelessly** *adv*, **changelessness** *n*

changeable *adj* **1** able or apt to vary **2** capable of being altered or exchanged **3** fickle – **changeableness** *n*, **changeably** *adv*, **changeability** *n*

changeling *n* a child secretly exchanged for another in infancy; *specif* a half-witted or ugly elf-child left in place of a human child by fairies

change of life *n* the menopause

change-over *n* a conversion to a different system or function

change ringing *n* the art or practice of ringing a set of tuned (church) bells in continually varying order

¹channel *n* **1a** the bed where a stream of water runs **b** the deeper part of a river, harbour, or strait **c** a narrow region of sea between 2 land masses **d** a path along which information passes or can be stored (e g on a recording tape) ⟨*there is no sound coming from the left* ~ *of the stereo*⟩ **e** a course or direction of thought, action, or communication – often *pl* with sing. meaning ⟨*used official* ~s *to air his grievance*⟩ **f(1)** a band of frequencies of sufficient width for a transmission (e g from a radio or television station) **(2)** a television station ⟨*switch over to another* ~⟩ **2** a usu tubular passage, esp for liquids **3** a long gutter, groove, or furrow

²**channel** vt -ll- (NAm -l-, -ll-), **channelling 1** to form or wear a channel in **2** to convey into or through a channel; direct ⟨~ his energy into constructive activities⟩

¹**chant** vi **1** to sing a chant **2** to recite in a monotonous tone ~ vt to utter as in chanting

²**chant** n **1** (the music or performance of) a repetitive melody used for liturgical singing in which as many syllables are assigned to each note as required **2** a rhythmic monotonous utterance or song

chanterelle n a rich-yellow edible mushroom

chanticleer n – used as a poetic name of the domestic cock

chantry n (a chapel or altar founded under) an endowment for the chanting of masses for the founder's soul

chaos n **1** often cap the confused unorganized state of primordial matter before the creation of distinct forms **2a** a state of utter confusion **b** a confused mass – **chaotic** adj, **chaotically** adv

¹**chap** n a man, fellow – infml

²**chap** vb -pp- to (cause to) open in slits or cracks ⟨~ped lips⟩

³**chap** n a crack in the skin caused by exposure to wind or cold

⁴**chap** n **1** (the fleshy covering of) a jaw **2** the lower front part of the face USE usu pl with sing. meaning

¹**chapel** n **1a** a place of worship serving a residence or institution **1** a room or bay in a church for prayer or minor religious services **2** a choir of singers belonging to a chapel **3** a chapel service or assembly **4** sing or pl in constr the members of a trade union, esp in a printing office **5** a place of worship used by a Christian group other than an established church ⟨a nonconformist ~⟩

²**chapel** adj, chiefly Br belonging to a Nonconformist church

¹**chaperon, chaperone** n one delegated to ensure propriety; esp a married or older woman who accompanies a younger woman on social occasions

²**chaperon, chaperone** vt to act as chaperon to; escort – **chaperonage** n

chapfallen adj depressed, dejected

chaplain n **1** a clergyman in charge of a chapel **2** a clergyman officially attached to a branch of the armed forces, an institution, or a family or court – **chaplaincy** n, **chaplainship** n

chaplet n **1a** a wreath to be worn on the head **2a** a string of beads **b** a part of a rosary comprising 5 decades – **chapleted** adj

chaps n pl leather leggings worn over the trousers, esp by N American ranch hands

chapter n **1a** a major division of a book **b** sthg resembling a chapter in being a significant specified unit ⟨breaking his leg was the final event in a ~ of accidents⟩ **2** (a regular meeting of) the canons of a cathedral or collegiate church, or the members of a religious house **3** a local branch of a society or fraternity

chapter house n the building or rooms where a chapter meets

¹**char, charr** n, pl **chars**, esp collectively **char** any of a genus of small-scaled trouts

²**char** vb -rr- vt **1** to convert to charcoal or carbon, usu by heat; burn **2** to burn slightly; scorch ~ vi to become charred

³**char** vi -rr- to work as a cleaning woman

⁴**char** n, Br a charwoman – infml

⁵**char, cha** n, Br TEA 2 – infml

charabanc n, Br an (old-fashioned) motor coach used for sightseeing

character n **1a** a distinctive mark, usu in the form of a stylized graphic device **b** a graphic symbol (e g a hieroglyph or alphabet letter) used in writing or printing **c(1)** style of writing or printing **(2)** CIPHER 2 **2a** (any of) the mental or ethical qualities that make up and distinguish the individual **b(1)** (a group or kind distinguished by) a feature used to categorize things (e g organisms) **(2)** an inherited characteristic **(3)** the sum of the distinctive qualities characteristic of a breed, type, etc; the (distinctive) main or essential nature of sthg ⟨a wine of great ~⟩ ⟨the unique ~ of the town⟩ **3a** a person, esp one marked by notable or conspicuous traits ⟨one of the real ~s in Westminster today⟩ **b** any of the people portrayed in a novel, film, play, etc ⟨he plays the main ~ in the film⟩ **4** (good) reputation ⟨~ assassination⟩ **5** moral strength; integrity ⟨a man of ~⟩ – **characterless** adj – **in/out of character** in/not in accord with a person's usual qualities, traits, or behaviour

¹**characteristic** adj serving to reveal and distinguish the individual character; typical – **characteristically** adv

²**characteristic** n **1** a distinguishing trait, quality, or property **2** the integral part of a common logarithm

characterize, -ise vt **1** to describe the character or quality of; delineate ⟨~d him as soft-spoken yet ambitious⟩ **2** to be a characteristic of; distinguish ⟨a cool light fragrance ~s the cologne⟩ – **characterization** n

charade n **1** pl but sing or pl in constr a game in which one team acts out each syllable of a word or phrase while the other tries to guess what is being represented **2** a ridiculous pretence

charcoal n **1** a dark or black porous carbon prepared by partly burning vegetable or animal substances (e g wood or bone) **2** fine charcoal used in pencil form for drawing

chard n a beet with large edible dark green leaves and succulent stalks

¹**charge** vt **1a(1)** to place a usu powder charge in (a firearm) **(2)** to load or fill to capacity ⟨~ the blast furnace with ore⟩ **b(1)** to restore the active materials in (a storage battery) by the passage of a direct current in the opposite direction to that of discharge **(2)** to give an electric charge to **c** to place a heraldic charge on **d** to fill with (passionate) emotion, feeling, etc ⟨the music is ~d with excitement⟩ ⟨a highly ~d issue⟩ **2** to command or exhort with right or authority ⟨I ~ you not to leave⟩ **3a** to blame ⟨~s him as the instigator⟩ **b** to make an assertion against; accuse ⟨~s him with armed robbery⟩ **c** to place the blame for ⟨~ her failure to negligence⟩ **d** to assert as an accusation ⟨~s that he distorted the data⟩ **4** to rush violently at; attack; also to rush into (an opponent), usu illegally, in soccer, basketball, etc **5a(1)** to impose a financial obligation on ⟨~ his estate with debts incurred⟩ **(2)** to impose as financial obligation ⟨~ debts to an estate⟩ **b(1)** to fix or ask as fee or payment **(2)** to ask payment of (a person) ⟨~ a client for expenses⟩ **c** to record (an item) as an expense, debt, obligation, or liability ⟨~ it to my account⟩ ~ vi **1** to rush forwards (as if) in assault **2** to ask or set a price – **chargeable** adj – **charge with** to impose (a task or responsibility) on

²**charge** n **1** a shape, representation, or design depicted on a heraldic achievement **2a** the quantity that an apparatus is intended to receive and fitted to hold; esp the quantity of explosive for a gun or cannon **b** power, force ⟨the emotional ~ of the drama⟩ **c(1)** a basic property of matter that occurs in discrete natural units and is considered as negative (e g when belonging to an electron) or positive (e g when belonging to a proton) **(2)** a definite quantity of electricity; esp the charge that a storage battery is capable of yielding **3a** an obligation, requirement **b** control, supervision ⟨has ~ of the home office⟩ ⟨I leave you in ~⟩ **c** sby or sthg committed to the care of

another **4a** an instruction, command **b** instructions given by a judge to a jury **5** the price demanded or paid for sthg ⟨*no admission* ~⟩ **6** an accusation, indictment, or statement of complaint **7** a violent rush forwards (e g in attack)

chargé d'affaires *n*, *pl* **chargés d'affaires 1** a diplomat who substitutes for an ambassador **2** a diplomatic representative inferior in rank to an ambassador

¹charger *n* a large flat meat dish

²charger *n* a horse for battle or parade

charge sheet *n* a police record of charges made and people to be tried in a magistrate's court

chariot *n* **1** a light 4-wheeled pleasure or state carriage **2** a 2-wheeled horse-drawn vehicle of ancient times used in warfare and racing

charioteer *n* the driver of a chariot

charisma *n* the special magnetic appeal, charm, or power of an individual (e g a political leader) that inspires popular loyalty and enthusiasm – **charismatic** *adj*

charitable *adj* **1a** liberal in giving to the poor; generous **b** of or giving charity ⟨~ *institutions*⟩ **2** merciful or kind in judging others; lenient – **charitableness** *n*, **charitably** *adv*

charity *n* **1** benevolent goodwill towards or love of humanity **2a** kindly generosity and helpfulness, esp towards the needy or suffering; *also* aid given to those in need **b** an institution engaged in relief of the poor, sick, etc **c** public provision for the relief of the needy **3a** a gift for public benevolent purposes **b** an institution (e g a hospital) funded by such a gift **4** lenient judgment of others

charlady *n*, *Br* a charwoman

charlatan *n* **1** QUACK 1 **2** one who pretends, usu ostentatiously, to have special knowledge or ability; a fraud – **charlatanism, charlatanry** *n*

Charleston *vi or n* (to dance) a lively ballroom dance in which the heels are swung sharply outwards on each step

charlock *n* a wild mustard that is a weed of cultivated ground

¹charm *n* **1** an incantation **2** sthg worn to ward off evil or to ensure good fortune **3a** a quality that fascinates, allures, or delights **b** *pl* physical graces or attractions, esp of a woman **4** a small ornament worn on a bracelet or chain **5** a quantum property postulated to account for unexpectedly long lifetimes of particles that have quantum numbers identical to other elementary particles – **charmless** *adj*

²charm *vt* **1a** to affect (as if) by magic; bewitch **b** to soothe or delight by compelling attraction ⟨~s *the women with his suave manner*⟩ **2** to control (an animal) by the use of rituals (e g the playing of music) held to have magical powers ⟨~ *a snake*⟩ ~ *vi* to have the effect of a charm; fascinate

charmer *n* an attractive or captivating person – chiefly infml

charming *adj* extremely pleasing or delightful; entrancing – **charmingly** *adv*

charnel house *n* a building or chamber in which bodies or bones are deposited

¹chart *n* **1a** an outline map showing the geographical distribution of sthg (e g climatic or magnetic variations) **b** a navigator's map **2a** a sheet giving information in tabular form; *esp*, *pl* *the* list of best-selling popular gramophone records (produced weekly) **b** ¹GRAPH **c** a schematic, usu large, diagram **d** a sheet of paper ruled and graduated for use in a recording instrument (e g on an electrocardiograph)

²chart *vt* **1** to make a chart of **2** to lay out a plan for **3** to display or mark (as if) on a chart

¹charter *n* **1** a formal written instrument or contract **2a** a document that creates and defines the rights of a city, educational institution, or company **b** CONSTITUTION 4 **3** a special privilege, immunity, or exemption **4** a total or partial lease of a ship, aeroplane, etc for a particular use or group of people ⟨*low-cost travel on* ~ *flights to Greece and Spain*⟩

²charter *vt* **1a** to establish or grant by charter **b** to certify as qualified ⟨*a* ~ed *accountant*⟩ ⟨*a* ~ed *surveyor*⟩ **2** to hire or lease for usu exclusive and temporary use ⟨~ed *a boat*⟩ – **charterer** *n*

chartered accountant *n*, *Br* a professionally qualified accountant

charter member *n* an original member of a society or corporation

Chartreuse *trademark* – used for an aromatic usu green or yellow liqueur

charwoman *n* a cleaning woman; *esp*, *Br* one employed in a private house

chary *adj* **1** cautious; *esp* wary of taking risks **2** slow to grant or accept ⟨*a man very* ~ *of compliments*⟩ – **charily** *adv*, **chariness** *n*

¹chase *vt* **1a** to follow rapidly or persistently; pursue ⟨*he's too old to* ~ *women*⟩ **b** to hunt **2** to cause to depart or flee; drive ⟨~ *the dog out of the pantry*⟩ **3** *chiefly Br* to investigate (a matter) or contact (a person, company, etc) in order to obtain information or (hasten) results – usu + *up* ~ *vi* **1** to chase an animal, person, or thing – usu + *after* **2** to rush, hasten ⟨~d *all over town looking for a place to stay*⟩

²chase *n* **1a** the act of chasing; pursuit **b** *the* hunting of wild animals **2** sthg pursued; a quarry **3** a tract of unenclosed land set aside for the breeding of animals for hunting and fishing **4** a steeplechase

³chase *vt* **1** to ornament (metal) by indenting with a hammer and tools that have no cutting edge **2** to make by such ornamentation ⟨~ *a monogram*⟩

⁴chase *n* **1** a groove cut in a surface for a pipe, wire, etc **2** the part of a cannon enclosing the barrel between the trunnions and the mouth of the muzzle

⁵chase *n* a rectangular steel or iron frame into which printing type or blocks are locked for printing or plate-making

chaser *n* **1** a glass or swallow of a mild drink (e g beer) taken after spirits; *also* a drink of spirits taken after a mild drink (e g beer) **2** a horse that is a steeplechaser

chasm *n* **1** a deep cleft in the earth **2** an apparently unbridgeable gap ⟨*a political* ~ *between the 2 countries*⟩

chassis *n*, *pl* **chassis 1** a supporting framework for the body of a vehicle (e g a car) **2** the frame on which the electrical parts of a radio, television, etc are mounted

chaste *adj* **1** abstinent from (unlawful or immoral) sexual intercourse; celibate **2** pure in thought and act; modest **3** severely simple in design or execution; austere ⟨*he wrote in a pure* ~ *style*⟩ – **chastely** *adv*, **chasteness** *n*, **chastity** *n*

chasten *vt* **1** to correct by punishment or suffering; discipline **2** to subdue, restrain – **chastener** *n*

chastise *vt* **1** to inflict punishment on, esp by whipping **2** to subject to severe reproof or criticism – **chastisement** *n*, **chastiser** *n*

chastity belt *n* a device consisting of a belt with an attachment passing between the legs, designed to prevent sexual intercourse on the part of the woman wearing it

chasuble *n* a sleeveless outer vestment worn by the officiating priest at mass

¹chat *vi* **-tt-** to talk in an informal or familiar manner

²chat *n* **1** (an instance of) light familiar talk; *esp* (a) conversation **2** a stonechat, whinchat, or related bird

château *n*, *pl* **châteaus**, **châteaux** **1** a feudal castle or large country house in France **2** a French vineyard estate

chatelaine *n* **1** the mistress of a castle or large house **2** a clasp with a short chain formerly used to attach small articles (e g keys) to a woman's belt

chattel *n* an item of personal property – usu in *goods and chattels*

¹chatter *vi* **1** to produce rapid successive inarticulate sounds suggestive of language ⟨*squirrels* ~ed *angrily*⟩ **2** to talk idly, incessantly, or fast; jabber **3a** *esp of teeth* to click repeatedly or uncontrollably (e g from cold) **b** *of a cutting tool (e g a drill)* to vibrate rapidly whilst cutting – **chatterer** *n*

²chatter *n* **1** the sound or (vibrating) action of chattering **2** idle talk; prattle

chatterbox *n* one who engages in much idle talk – *infml*

chatty *adj* **1** fond of chatting; talkative **2** having the style and manner of light familiar conversation ⟨*a* ~ *letter*⟩ USE *infml* – **chattily** *adv*, **chattiness** *n*

chat up *vt*, *Br* to engage (sby) in friendly conversation for an ulterior motive, esp with amorous intent – *infml*

¹chauffeur *n* a person employed to drive a private passenger-carrying motor vehicle, esp a car

²chauffeur *vi* to work as a chauffeur ~ *vt* to transport (a person) or drive (e g a car) as (if) a chauffeur

chauvinism *n* **1** excessive or blind patriotism **2** undue attachment to one's group, cause, or place ⟨*male* ~⟩ – **chauvinist** *n*, **chauvinistic** *adj*, **chauvinistically** *adv*

¹cheap *n* – **on the cheap** at minimum expense; cheaply ⟨*schools that are run* on the cheap⟩

²cheap *adj* **1a** (relatively) low in price; *esp* purchasable below the market price or the real value **b** charging a low price ⟨*a* ~ *supermarket*⟩ **c** depreciated in value (e g by currency inflation) ⟨~ *dollars*⟩ **2** gained with little effort ⟨*a* ~ *victory*⟩; *esp* gained by contemptible means ⟨~ *laughs*⟩ ⟨~ *thrill*⟩ **3a** of inferior quality or worth; tawdry, sleazy **b** contemptible because of lack of any fine or redeeming qualities ⟨~ *election gimmickry*⟩ **4** *of money* obtainable at a low rate of interest **5** *NAm* stingy – **cheap**, **cheaply** *adv*, **cheapish** *adj*, **cheapness** *n*

cheapen *vb* to make or become a cheap in price or value **b** lower in esteem **c** tawdry, vulgar, or inferior

¹cheap-jack *n* sby, esp a pedlar, who sells cheap wares

²cheap-jack *adj* **1** inferior, cheap, or worthless ⟨~ *film companies*⟩ **2** characterized by unscrupulous opportunism ⟨~ *speculators*⟩

cheapskate *n*, *chiefly NAm* a miserly or stingy person

¹cheat *n* **1** a fraudulent deception; a fraud **2** one who cheats; a pretender, deceiver

²cheat *vt* **1** to deprive of sthg valuable by deceit or fraud **2** to influence or lead by deceit or fraud **3** to defeat the purpose or blunt the effects of ⟨~ *winter of its dreariness* – Washington Irving⟩ ~ *vi* **1a** to practise fraud or deception **b** to violate rules dishonestly (e g at cards or in an exam) **2** to be sexually unfaithful – usu + *on* – **cheater** *n*

¹check *n* **1** exposure of a chess king to an attack from which it must be protected or moved to safety – often used interjectionally **2** a sudden stoppage of a forward course or progress; an arrest **3** a sudden pause or break in a progression **4** one who or that which arrests, limits, or restrains; a restraint **5a** a standard for testing and evaluation; a criterion **b** an inspection, examination, test, or verification **6a** (a square in) a pattern of squares (of alternating colours) **b** a fabric woven or printed with such a design **7** a crack or break, esp in a piece of timber **8** *NAm* a cheque **9a** *chiefly NAm* a ticket or token showing ownership or identity or indicating payment made ⟨*luggage* ~⟩ **b** *NAm* a counter in various games **c** *NAm* a bill, esp for food and drink in a restaurant **10** *NAm* ²TICK **2** – **in check** under restraint or control ⟨*held the enemy* in check⟩

²check *vt* **1** to put (a chess opponent's king) in check **2a** to slow or bring to a stop; brake **b** to block the progress of (e g an ice-hockey player) **3a** to restrain or diminish the action or force of; control **b** to ease off and then secure again (e g a rope) **4a** to compare with a source, original, or authority; verify **b** to inspect for satisfactory condition, accuracy, safety, or performance – sometimes + *out* or *over* **5** to mark into squares; chequer – usu in past part **6** *chiefly NAm* to note or mark with a tick – often + *off* **7a** *NAm* CHECK IN **2** **b** *chiefly NAm* to leave or accept for safekeeping in a cloakroom or left-luggage office – often + *in* **8** *chiefly dial* to rebuke, reprimand ~ *vi* **1a** *of a dog* to stop in a chase, esp when scent is lost **b** to halt through caution, uncertainty, or fear **2a** to investigate and make sure ⟨~ed *on the passengers' safety*⟩ **b** *chiefly NAm* to correspond point for point; tally ⟨*the description* ~s *with the photograph*⟩ – often + *out* ⟨*his story* ~ed *out*⟩ – **checkable** *adj*, **checker** *n* – **check into** to check in at ⟨check into a *hotel*⟩ – **check up on 1** to examine for accuracy or truth, esp in order to corroborate information ⟨check up on the *facts*⟩ **2** to make thorough inquiries about ⟨*police* checked up on *her*⟩

¹checker *n* **1** *chiefly NAm* a chequer **2** *NAm* a draughtsman

²checker *vt*, *chiefly NAm* to chequer

checkers *n pl but sing in constr*, *NAm* the game of draughts

check in *vi* to report one's presence or arrival; *esp* to arrive and register at a hotel or airport ~ *vt* **1** to return or accept the return of ⟨check in *the equipment after use*⟩ **2** to deposit (luggage) for transport, esp by air

checklist *n* an inventory, catalogue; *esp* a complete list of checks to be made

¹checkmate *vt* **1** to thwart or counter completely **2** to check (a chess opponent's king) so that escape is impossible

²checkmate *n* **1a** the act of checkmating **b** the situation of a checkmated king **2** complete defeat USE (*1*) often used interjectionally

checkout *n* a cash desk equipped with a cash register in a self-service shop

check out *vi* to complete the formalities for leaving, esp at a hotel ~ *vt* to have the removal of (sthg) recorded ⟨check out *a library book*⟩

checkpoint *n* a location where inspection (e g of travellers) may take place

checkrein *n* a short rein attached from the bit to the saddle to prevent a horse from lowering its head

checkroom *n*, *NAm* a room in which luggage, parcels, or coats may be left for safekeeping

checkup *n* a (general physical) examination

Cheddar *n* a hard smooth-textured cheese with a flavour that ranges from mild to strong as the cheese matures

¹cheek *n* **1** the fleshy side of the face below the eye and above the side of the mouth **2** either of 2 paired facing parts (e g the jaws of a vice) **3** insolent boldness; impudence **4** a buttock – *infml*

²cheek *vt* to speak rudely or impudently to – *infml*

cheekbone *n* (the bone forming) the prominence below the eye

-cheeked *comb form* (→ *adj*) having (such) cheeks ⟨*rosy*-cheeked⟩

cheeky *adj* impudent, insolent – **cheekily** *adv*, **cheekiness** *n*

cheep *vi or n* (to utter) a faint shrill sound characteristic of a young bird

¹cheer *n* **1** state of mind or heart; spirit ⟨*be of good* ~ – Matthew 9:2(AV)⟩ **2** happiness, gaiety **3** sthg that gladdens **4** a shout of applause or encouragement – **cheerless** *adj*, **cheerlessly** *adv*, **cheerlessness** *n*

²cheer *vt* **1a** to instil with hope or courage; comfort **b** to make glad or happy **2** to urge *on* or encourage, esp by shouts ⟨~ed *the team on*⟩ **3** to applaud with shouts ~ *vi* **1** to grow or be cheerful; rejoice **2** to utter a shout of applause or triumph *USE* (*vt 1*; *vi 1*) usu + *up* – **cheerer** *n*

cheerful *adj* **1a** full of good spirits; merry **b** ungrudging ⟨~ *obedience*⟩ **2** conducive to good cheer; likely to dispel gloom ⟨*a* ~ *sunny room*⟩ – **cheerfully** *adv*, **cheerfulness** *n*

cheerio *interj*, *chiefly Br* – used to express farewell

cheerleader *n* one, esp a female, who leads organized cheering (e g at a N American football game)

cheers *interj* – used as a toast and sometimes as an informal farewell or expression of thanks

cheery *adj* marked by or causing good spirits; cheerful – **cheerily** *adv*, **cheeriness** *n*

¹cheese *n* **1** (an often cylindrical cake of) a food consisting of coagulated, compressed, and usu ripened milk curds **2** sthg resembling cheese in consistency or a cylindrical cake of cheese **3** a fruit preserve with the consistency of cream cheese – **cheesy** *adj*, **cheesiness** *n*

²cheese *n* an important person; a boss – slang; chiefly in *big cheese*

cheesecake *n* **1** a baked or refrigerated dessert consisting of a soft filling, usu containing cheese, in a biscuit or pastry case **2** a photographic display of shapely and scantily clothed female figures – infml; compare BEEF-CAKE

cheesecloth *n* a very fine unsized cotton gauze

cheesed off *adj*, *chiefly Br* browned-off – slang

cheeseparing *n* miserly or petty economizing; stinginess – **cheeseparing** *adj*

cheetah *n* a long-legged spotted swift-moving African and formerly Asiatic cat with nonretractile claws

chef *n* a skilled cook; esp the chief cook in a restaurant or hotel

chef d'oeuvre *n*, *pl* **chefs d'oeuvre** an (artistic or literary) masterpiece

chem-, chemo- *also* **chemi-** *comb form* **1** chemical; chemistry ⟨*chemo*therapy⟩⟨*chemo*taxis⟩ **2** chemically ⟨*chemi*sorb⟩

¹chemical *adj* **1** of, used in, or produced by chemistry **2** acting, operated, or produced by chemicals – **chemically** *adv*

²chemical *n* a substance (e g an element or chemical compound) obtained by a chemical process or used for producing a chemical effect

chemise *n* **1** a woman's one-piece undergarment **2** a usu loose straight-hanging dress

chemist *n* **1** one who is trained in chemistry **2** *Br* (a pharmacist, esp in) a retail shop where medicines and miscellaneous articles (e g cosmetics and films) are sold

chemistry *n* **1** a science that deals with the composition, structure, and properties of substances and of the transformations they undergo **2a** the composition and chemical properties of a substance **b** chemical processes and phenomena (e g of an organism) ⟨*blood* ~⟩

chemotherapy *n* the use of chemical agents in the treatment or control of disease – **chemotherapeutic** *adj*, **chemotherapist** *n*

chenille *n* a (wool, cotton, silk, or rayon) yarn with protruding pile; *also* a fabric with a pile face and a chenille yarn weft

cheque *n*, *chiefly Br* a written order for a bank to pay money as instructed; *also* a printed form on which such an order is usually written

chequebook *n* a book containing unwritten cheques

cheque card *n* a card issued to guarantee that the holder's cheques up to a specific amount will be honoured by the issuing bank

¹chequer, *chiefly NAm* **checker** *n* ¹CHECK 6a

²chequer, *chiefly NAm* **checker** *vt* **1** to variegate with different colours or shades; *esp* to mark with squares of (2) alternating colours **2** to vary with contrasting elements or situations ⟨*a* ~ed *career*⟩ *USE* usu in past part

cherish *vt* **1a** to hold dear; feel or show affection for **b** to keep or cultivate with care and affection; nurture **2** to keep in the mind deeply and with affection ⟨*still* ~es *that memory*⟩ – **cherishable** *adj*

cheroot *n* a cigar cut square at both ends

cherry *n* **1** (the wood or small pale yellow to deep red or blackish fruit of) any of numerous trees and shrubs of the rose family, often cultivated for their fruit or ornamental flowers **2** light red – **cherry** *adj*, **cherrylike** *adj*

cherub *n*, *pl* **cherubs**, (*1*) **cherubim 1** a biblical attendant of God or of a holy place, often represented as a being with large wings, a human head, and an animal body **2a** a beautiful usu winged child in painting and sculpture **b** an innocent-looking usu chubby and pretty person – **cherubic** *adj*

chervil *n* an aromatic plant of the carrot family whose leaves are used as a herb

chess *n* a game for 2 players each of whom moves his/her 16 chessmen according to fixed rules across a chessboard and tries to checkmate his/her opponent's king

chessboard *n* a board used in chess, draughts, etc that is divided into usu 64 equal squares of 2 alternating colours

chessman *n*, *pl* **chessmen** any of the pieces (1 king, 1 queen, 2 rooks, 2 bishops, 2 knights, and 8 pawns) used by each side in playing chess

chest *n* **1a** a box with a lid used esp for the safekeeping of belongings **b** a usu small cupboard used esp for storing medicines or first-aid supplies **c** a case in which a commodity (e g tea) is shipped **2** the part of the body enclosed by the ribs and breastbone – **chestful** *n*

-chested *comb form* (→ *adj*) having (such) a chest ⟨*flat*-chested⟩ ⟨*deep*-chested⟩

chesterfield *n* a heavily padded usu leather sofa

¹chestnut *n* **1** (the nut or wood of) a tree or shrub of the beech family; *esp* SPANISH CHESTNUT **2** reddish brown **3** HORSE CHESTNUT **4** a chestnut-coloured animal, specif a horse **5** the small callus on the inner side of a horse's leg **6** an often repeated joke or story; *broadly* anything repeated excessively

²chestnut *adj* of the colour chestnut

chest of drawers *n* a piece of furniture containing a set of drawers (e g for holding clothes)

chesty *adj* **1** of, inclined to, symptomatic of, or suffering from disease of the chest ⟨*a* ~ *cough*⟩ – not used technically **2** having prominent breasts – slang

cheval glass *n* a full-length mirror in a frame by which it may be tilted

chevalier *n* a member of certain orders of merit (e g the French Legion of Honour)

chevron *n* a figure, pattern, or object having the shape of an (inverted) V; *esp* a sleeve badge that usu consists of 1 or more chevron-shaped stripes and indicates the wearer's rank

¹chew *vb* to crush, grind, or gnaw (esp food) (as if) with the teeth – **chewable** *adj*, **chewer** *n*, **chewy** *adj*

²chew *n* 1 the act of chewing 2 sthg for chewing ⟨*a ~ of tobacco*⟩

chewing gum *n* a flavoured usu sweetened insoluble material (e g chicle) for chewing

chew over *vt* to meditate on; think about reflectively – infml

chi *n* the 22nd letter of the Greek alphabet

Chianti *n* a dry (red) Italian table wine

chiaroscuro *n*, *pl* **chiaroscuros** 1 pictorial representation in terms of light and shade 2 the arrangement or treatment of light and shade in a painting

chic *adj or n* (having or showing) elegance and sophistication, esp of dress or manner – **chicly** *adv*, **chicness** *n*

chicanery *n* 1 deception by the use of fallacious or irrelevant arguments 2 a piece of sharp practice or legal trickery – **chicane** *vb*

chichi *adj or n* 1 showy, frilly, or elaborate (ornamentation) 2 unnecessarily elaborate or affected (behaviour, style, etc)

chick *n* 1 a young bird; *esp* a (newly hatched) chicken 2 a young woman – slang

¹chicken *n* 1 the common domestic fowl, esp when young; *also* its flesh used as food 2 a young person – chiefly in *he/she is no chicken* 3a a contest in which the participants put themselves in danger to see who is most brave b a coward – slang *USE (2&3a)* infml

²chicken *adj* scared – infml

chicken feed *n* a small and insignificant amount, esp of money – infml

chickenhearted *adj* timid, cowardly

chicken out *vi* to lose one's nerve – infml

chicken pox *n* an infectious virus disease, esp of children, that is marked by mild fever and a rash of small blisters

chick-pea *n* (the hard edible seed of) an Asiatic leguminous plant

chickweed *n* any of various low-growing small-leaved plants of the pink family that occur commonly as weeds

chicle *n* a gum from the latex of the sapodilla used as the chief ingredient of chewing gum

chicory *n* a usu blue-flowered European perennial composite plant widely grown for its edible thick roots and as a salad plant; *also* the ground roasted root used as a coffee additive

chide *vb* **chid, chided; chid, chidden, chided** to rebuke (sby) angrily; scold – **chidingly** *adv*

¹chief *n* 1 (a broad band across) the upper part of a heraldic field 2 the head of a body of people or an organization; a leader ⟨*~ of police*⟩ – **chiefdom, chiefship** *n*

²chief *adj* 1 accorded highest rank or office ⟨*~ librarian*⟩ 2 of greatest importance or influence ⟨*the ~ reasons*⟩

chief justice *n* the presiding judge of a supreme court of justice (e g the US Supreme Court)

chiefly *adv* 1 most importantly; principally; especially 2 for the most part; mostly, mainly

chief of staff *n* the senior officer of an armed forces staff that serves a commander

chieftain, *fem* **chieftainess** *n* a chief, esp of a band, tribe, or clan – **chieftainship** *n*

chiffon *n* a sheer (silk) fabric

chiffonier *n* a high narrow chest of drawers

chigger *n* a chigoe

chignon *n* a usu large smooth knot of hair worn esp at the nape of the neck

Chihuahua *n* a very small round-headed large-eared dog of Mexican origin

chilblain *n* an inflammatory sore, esp on the feet or hands, caused by exposure to cold

child *n*, *pl* **children** 1 an unborn or recently born person 2a a young person, esp between infancy and youth b a childlike or childish person c(1) a person not yet of (a legally specified) age (2) sby under the age of 14 – used in English law 3a a son or daughter ⟨*left the estate to her ~ren*⟩ b a descendant ⟨*the* Children *of David*⟩ 4 one strongly influenced by another or by a place or state of affairs ⟨*a ~ of the depression*⟩ 5 a product, result ⟨*dreams; which are the ~ren of an idle brain* – Shak⟩ – **childless** *adj*, **childlessness** *n* – **with child** of a woman PREGNANT 3

child benefit *n* a (weekly) allowance paid through the post office for each child in the family

childbirth *n* parturition

childhood *n* 1 the state or period of being a child 2 an early period in the development of sthg ⟨*there was a ~ of religion as there was a ~ of science* – TLS⟩

childish *adj* 1 of or befitting a child or childhood 2 marked by or suggestive of immaturity ⟨*a ~ spiteful remark*⟩ – **childishly** *adv*, **childishness** *n*

childlike *adj* marked by innocence and trust

child's play *n* an extremely simple task or act

¹chill *vi* 1 to become cold 2 to catch a chill 3 of a metal to become surface-hardened by sudden cooling ~ *vt* 1a to make cold or chilly b to make (esp food or drink) cool, esp without freezing 2 to affect as if with cold; dispirit 3 to harden the surface of (metal) by sudden cooling – **chillingly** *adv*

²chill *adj* CHILLY 1, 2 – **chillness** *n*

³chill *n* 1a a (disagreeable) sensation of coldness b COMMON COLD 2 a moderate but disagreeable degree of cold 3 coldness of manner ⟨*felt the ~ of his opponent's stare*⟩

chilli, chili *n*, *pl* **chillies, chilies** the pod of a hot pepper used either whole or ground as a pungent condiment

chilly *adj* 1 noticeably (unpleasantly) cold 2 lacking warmth of feeling; distant, unfriendly 3 tending to arouse fear or apprehension ⟨*~ details*⟩ – **chilliness** *n*

¹chime *n* 1a a musically tuned set of bells b a set of objects (e g hanging metal bars or tubes) that sound like bells when struck 2a the sound of a set of bells – usu pl with sing. meaning b a musical sound like that of bells

²chime *vi* 1 to make the sounds of a chime 2 to be or act in accord ⟨*the music and the mood* ~d *well together*⟩ ~ *vt* 1 to cause to chime 2 to signal or indicate by chiming ⟨*the clock* ~d *midnight*⟩ – **chimer** *n*

³chime, chimb *n* the projecting rim of a barrel

chime in *vi* 1 to break into a conversation or discussion, esp in order to express an opinion 2 to combine harmoniously – often + *with*

chimera *n* 1a *cap* a fire-breathing female mythological monster that had a lion's head, a goat's body, and a serpent's tail b an imaginary monster made up of incongruous parts 2a an illusion or fabrication of the mind; *esp* an unrealizable dream b a terror that exists only in the mind 3 an individual, organ, or part consisting of tissues of diverse genetic constitution and occurring esp in plants and most frequently at a graft union – **chimeric, chimerical** *adj*, **chimerically** *adv*

chimney *n* 1 a vertical structure incorporated into a building and enclosing a flue or flues for carrying off smoke; *esp* the part of such a structure extending above a roof 2 a structure through which smoke and gases (e g from a furnace or steam engine) are discharged **3** a tube, usu of glass, placed round a flame (e g of an oil lamp) to serve as a shield **4** a narrow cleft, vent, etc (e g in rock)

chimney breast *n* the wall that encloses a chimney and projects into a room

chimney corner *n* a seat by or within a large open fireplace

chimneypiece *n* a mantelpiece

chimney pot *n* a usu earthenware pipe at the top of a chimney

chimney stack *n* **1** a masonry, brickwork, etc chimney rising above a roof and usu containing several flues **2** a tall chimney, typically of circular section, serving a factory, power station, etc

chimney sweep *n* one whose occupation is cleaning soot from chimney flues

chimpanzee *n* a tree-dwelling anthropoid ape of equatorial Africa that is smaller and less fierce than the gorilla

chin *n* the lower portion of the face lying below the lower lip and including the prominence of the lower jaw

china *n* **1** porcelain; *also* vitreous porcelain ware (e g dishes and vases) for domestic use **2** chinaware; *broadly* crockery ⟨*set the table with the good* ~⟩ **3** *chiefly Br* BONE CHINA

china clay *n* kaolin

Chinatown *n* the Chinese quarter of a city

chinaware *n* tableware made of china

chinchilla *n* **1** (the soft pearly-grey fur of) a S American rodent the size of a large squirrel **2** (any of) a breed of domestic rabbit with long white or greyish fur; *also* (any of) a breed of cat with similar fur

¹chine *n, Br* a steep-sided ravine, esp in Dorset or the Isle of Wight

²chine *n* **1** (a cut of meat including the whole or part of) the backbone **2** a (mountain) ridge **3** the intersection of the bottom and sides of a boat

³chine *vt* to separate the backbone from the ribs of (a joint of meat); *also* to cut through the backbone of (a carcass)

Chinese *n, pl* **Chinese** **1** a native or inhabitant of China **2** a group of related Sino-Tibetan tone languages used by the people of China; *specif* Mandarin – **Chinese** *adj*

¹chink *n* **1** a small slit or fissure ⟨*a* ~ *in the curtain*⟩ **2** a means of evasion or escape; a loophole ⟨*a* ~ *in the law*⟩

²chink *n* a short sharp sound – **chink** *vb*

Chink *n* a native of China – derog

chinless *adj, Br* lacking firmness of purpose; ineffectual – infml

chinook *n* **1** a warm moist southwesterly wind of the NW coast of the USA **2** a warm dry westerly wind of the E slopes of the Rocky mountains

chintz *n* a (glazed) printed plain-weave fabric, usu of cotton

chin-wag *n* a conversation, chat – infml

¹chip *n* **1a** a small usu thin and flat piece (e g of wood or stone) cut, struck, or flaked off **b** a small thin slice or piece of fruit, chocolate, etc **2** a counter used as a token for money in gambling games **3** a flaw left after a chip is removed **4** (the small piece of semiconductor, esp silicon, on which is constructed) an integrated circuit **5** CHIP SHOT **6a** *chiefly Br* a strip of potato fried in deep fat **b** *NAm & Austr* ³CRISP – **chip off the old block** a child that resembles either of his/her parents – **chip on one's shoulder** a challenging, belligerent, or embittered attitude – **when the chips are down** when the crucial or critical point has been

reached ⟨*when the chips are down you have only yourself to depend on*⟩

²chip *vb* **-pp-** *vt* **1a** to cut or hew with an edged tool **b(1)** to cut or break (a small piece) from sthg **(2)** to cut or break a fragment from **2** to kick or hit (a ball, pass, etc) in a short high arc ~ *vi* **1** to break off in small pieces **2** to play a chip shot

chipboard *n* an artificial board made from compressed wood chips and glue

chip in *vi* **1** to contribute ⟨*everyone* chipped in *for the gift*⟩ **2** to interrupt or add a comment to a conversation between other people ~ *vt* to contribute ⟨chipped in *£1 for the gift*⟩ *USE* infml

chipmunk *n* any of numerous small striped American squirrels

Chippendale *adj or n* (of or being) an 18th-c English furniture style characterized by graceful outline and fine ornamentation

chippy *n* **1** a carpenter **2** *Br* a shop selling fish and chips *USE* infml

chip shot *n* a short shot in golf that lofts the ball to the green and allows it to roll

chiromancy *n* palmistry – **chiromancer** *n*

chiropody *n* the care and treatment of the human foot in health and disease – **chiropodist** *n*

chiropractic *n* a system of healing disease that employs manipulation and adjustment of body structures (e g the spinal column) – **chiropractor** *n*

chirp *vi or n* (to make or speak in a tone resembling) the characteristic short shrill sound of a small bird or insect

chirpy *adj* lively, cheerful – infml – **chirpily** *adv*, **chirpiness** *n*

¹chisel *n* a metal tool with a cutting edge at the end of a blade used in dressing, shaping, or working wood, stone, metal, etc

²chisel *vb* **-ll-** (*NAm* **-l-**, **-ll-**), **1** to cut or work (as if) with a chisel **2** to trick, cheat, or obtain (sthg) by cheating ⟨*he's* ~ led *me out of my prize*⟩ – slang – **chiseller** *n*

¹chit *n* an immature often disrespectful young woman, usu of slight build ⟨*a mere* ~ *of a girl*⟩

²chit *n* a small slip of paper with writing on it; *esp* an order for goods

chitchat *vi or n* **-tt-** (to make) small talk; gossip – infml

chivalrous *adj* **1** having the characteristics (e g valour or gallantry) of a knight **2** (characteristic) of knight-errantry **3a** honourable, generous **b** graciously courteous and considerate, esp to women – **chivalrously** *adv*, **chivalrousness** *n*

chivalry *n* **1** the system, spirit, or customs of medieval knighthood **2** the qualities (e g courage, integrity, and consideration) of an ideal knight; chivalrous conduct **3** *archaic, sing or pl in constr* mounted men-at-arms – **chivalric** *adj*

chive *n* a perennial plant related to the onion and used esp to flavour and garnish food – usu pl with sing. meaning

chivvy, chivy *vt* **1** to tease or annoy with persistent petty attacks; harass **2** to rouse to activity – often + *up* or *along* *USE* infml

chloride *n* a compound of chlorine with another element or radical; *esp* a salt or ester of hydrochloric acid

chlorinate *vt* to treat or cause to combine with (a compound of) chlorine – **chlorinator** *n*, **chlorination** *n*

chlorine *n* a halogen element that is isolated as a pungent heavy greenish yellow gas

chloroform *vt or n* (to anaesthetize with) a colourless volatile liquid used esp as a solvent and formerly as a general anaesthetic

chlorophyll n 1 the green photosynthetic colouring matter of plants found in the chloroplasts 2 a waxy green chlorophyll-containing substance extracted from green plants and used as a colouring agent or deodorant

chloroplast n a chlorophyll-containing organelle that is the site of photosynthesis and starch formation in plant cells

choc-ice n, Br a bar of ice cream covered in chocolate

¹chock n a wedge or block placed under a door, barrel, wheel, etc to prevent movement

²chock vt 1 to provide, stop, or make fast (as if) with chocks 2 to raise or support on blocks

³chock adv as closely or as completely as possible

chock-a-block adj or adv tightly packed; in a very crowded condition

chocolate n 1 a paste, powder, or solid block of food prepared from (sweetened or flavoured) ground roasted cacao seeds 2 a beverage made by mixing chocolate with usu hot water or milk 3 a sweet made or coated with chocolate 4 dark brown – **chocolate** adj

¹choice n 1 the act of choosing; selection 2 the power of choosing; an option 3a sby or sthg chosen b the best part; the elite 4 a sufficient number and variety to choose among

²choice adj 1 worthy of being chosen 2 selected with care; well chosen 3 of high quality – **choicely** adv, **choiceness** n

choir n 1 sing or pl in constr an organized company of singers 2 the part of a church occupied by the singers or the clergy; specif the part of the chancel between the sanctuary and the nave

choirboy n a boy singer in a (church) choir

choir school n a school primarily intended for the boys of a cathedral or college choir

¹choke vt 1 to check the normal breathing of by compressing or obstructing the windpipe, or by poisoning available air 2 to stop or suppress expression of or by; silence ⟨a ban designed to ~ discussion⟩ – often + back or down **3a** to restrain the growth or activity of ⟨the flowers were ~ d by the weeds⟩ b to obstruct by filling up or clogging ⟨leaves ~ d the drain⟩ c to fill completely; jam ~ vi 1 to become choked in breathing **2a** to become obstructed or checked b to become speechless or incapacitated, esp from strong emotion – usu + up 3 to lose one's composure and fail to perform effectively in a critical situation

²choke n sthg that obstructs passage or flow: e g **a** a valve in the carburettor of a petrol engine for controlling the amount of air in a fuel air mixture b an inductor c a narrowing towards the muzzle in the bore of a gun d a device allowing variation of the choke of a shotgun

³choke n the fibrous (inedible) central part of a globe artichoke

choker n 1 a high stiff (clerical) collar 2 a short necklace or decorative band that fits closely round the throat

chokey, choky n, Br PRISON 2 – slang

choler n 1 anger, irascibility – fml **2a** archaic YELLOW BILE b obs BILE 1a 3 obs the state of being bilious

cholera n (any of several diseases of human beings and domestic animals similar to) an often fatal infectious epidemic disease caused by a bacterium and marked by severe gastrointestinal disorders – **choleraic** adj

choleric adj 1 easily moved to (excessive) anger; irascible 2 angry, irate USE fml

cholesterol n a hydroxy steroid that is present in animal and plant cells and is a possible factor in hardening of the arteries

chomp vb to champ

choose vb **chose; chosen** vt **1a** to select freely and after consideration b to decide on; esp to elect ⟨chose her as leader⟩ **2a** to decide ⟨chose to go by train⟩ b to wish ⟨I ~ not to do it⟩ ~ vi to make a selection – **chooser** n

choosy, choosey adj fastidiously selective; particular

¹chop vb -pp- vt **1a** to cut into or sever, usu by a blow or repeated blows of a sharp instrument ⟨~ down a tree⟩ b to cut into pieces – often + up 2 to strike (a ball) so as to impart backspin 3 to subject to the action of a chopper ⟨~ a beam of light⟩ ~ vi to make a quick stroke or repeated strokes (as if) with a sharp instrument

²chop n 1 a forceful usu slanting blow or stroke (as if) with an axe or cleaver 2 a small cut of meat often including part of a rib 3 an uneven motion of the sea, esp when wind and tide are opposed 4 abrupt removal; esp ¹SACK 4 – + the; infml

³chop vi -pp- esp of the wind to change direction – **chop and change** to keep changing one's mind, plans, etc – **chop logic** to argue with minute oversubtle distinctions

⁴chop n (a licence validated by) a seal or official stamp such as was formerly used in China or India

chop-chop adv or interj without delay; quickly – infml

chophouse n a restaurant specializing in meat dishes, esp chops or steaks

chopper n 1 a short-handled axe or cleaver 2 a device that interrupts an electric current or a beam of radiation (e g light) at short regular intervals 3 a helicopter – infml

choppy adj, of the sea or other expanse of water rough with small waves

chopstick n either of 2 slender sticks held between thumb and fingers, used chiefly in oriental countries to lift food to the mouth

chopsuey n a Chinese dish of shredded meat or chicken with bean sprouts and other vegetables, usu served with rice and soy sauce

choral adj accompanied with or designed for singing (by a choir) – **chorally** adv

chorale also **choral** n 1 (music composed for) a usu German traditional hymn or psalm for singing in church 2 sing or pl in constr a chorus, choir

¹chord n a combination of notes sounded together

²chord n 1 CORD 3a 2 a straight line joining 2 points on a curve 3 an individual emotion or disposition ⟨touch the right ~⟩ 4 the straight line joining the leading and trailing edges of an aerofoil

chore n 1 a routine task or job 2 a difficult or disagreeable task

choreography n 1 the art of representing dance steps and sequences in symbols 2 stage dancing as distinguished from social or ballroom dancing 3 the composition and arrangement of a ballet or other dance for the stage – **choreographer** n, **choreograph** vb, **choreographic** adj, **choreographically** adv

chorister n a singer in a choir; specif a choirboy

chortle vi **chortling** to laugh or chuckle, esp in satisfaction or exultation – **chortle** n, **chortler** n

¹chorus n 1 (the part of a drama sung or spoken by) a character (e g in Elizabethan drama) or group of singers and dancers (e g in Greek drama) who comment on the action 2 sing or pl in constr **a** an organized company of singers who sing in concert; specif a body of singers who sing the choral parts of a work (e g in opera) b a group of dancers and singers supporting the featured players in a musical or revue ⟨a ~ girl⟩ **3a** a part of a song or hymn recurring at intervals b a composition sung by a chorus 4 sthg performed, sung, or uttered simultaneously by a number of people or animals – **in chorus** in unison

²chorus vb to sing or utter in chorus

chose *past of* CHOOSE

chosen *adj* selected or marked for favour or special privilege ⟨*granted to a ~ few*⟩

chosen *n pl in constr* the people who are the object of divine favour

chough *n* an Old World bird of the crow family that has red legs, a red beak, and glossy black plumage

choux pastry *n* a light pastry made with an egg-enriched dough and used for profiteroles, eclairs, etc

chow *n* food – *infml*

chow *also* **chow chow** *n* a heavy-coated broad-headed dog with a blue-black tongue

chowder *n* a thick (clam or other seafood) soup or stew

chow mein *n* a Chinese dish of fried noodles usu mixed with shredded meat or poultry and vegetables

Christ *n* 1 the Messiah 2 Jesus – **Christlike** *adj*

christen *vt* 1a BAPTIZE 1, 3 b to name at baptism 2 to name or dedicate (e g a ship or bell) by a ceremony suggestive of baptism 3 to name 4 to use for the first time – *infml*

Christendom *n* the community of people or nations professing Christianity

christening *n* the ceremony of baptizing and naming a child

Christian *n* 1a an adherent of Christianity b a member of a Christian denomination, esp by baptism 2 a good or kind person regardless of religion

Christian *adj* 1 of or consistent with Christianity or Christians 2 commendably decent or generous ⟨*has a very ~ concern for others*⟩ – **Christianize** *vt*, **Christianization** *n*, **Christianly** *adv*

Christian era *n* the period dating from the birth of Christ

Christianity *n* 1 the religion based on the life and teachings of Jesus Christ and the Bible 2 conformity to (a branch of) the Christian religion

Christian name *n* 1 a name given at christening (or confirmation) 2 a forename

Christian Science *n* a religion founded by Mary Baker Eddy in 1866 that includes a practice of spiritual healing – **Christian Scientist** *n*

Christmas *n* 1 a festival of the western Christian churches on December 25 that commemorates the birth of Christ and is usu observed as a public holiday 2 **Christmas**, **Christmastide** the festival season from Christmas Eve till the Epiphany (January 6) – **Christmassy** *adj*

Christmas Eve *n* the (evening of the) day before Christmas day

Christmas tree *n* an evergreen or artificial tree decorated with lights, tinsel, etc at Christmas

chromatic *adj* 1a of colour sensation or (intensity of) colour b highly coloured 2a of or giving all the notes of the chromatic scale b characterized by frequent use of intervals or notes outside the diatonic scale – **chromatically** *adv*, **chromaticism** *n*

chrome *n* 1 (a pigment formed from) chromium 2 (sthg with) a plating of chromium

chrome *comb form* (→ *n, adj*) 1 coloured thing ⟨*heliochrome*⟩; coloured ⟨*polychrome*⟩ 2 colouring matter ⟨*urochrome*⟩

chromium *n* a blue-white metallic element found naturally only in combination and used esp in alloys and in electroplating

chromosome *n* any of the gene-carrying bodies that contain DNA and protein and are found in the cell nucleus – **chromosomal** *adj*, **chromosomally** *adv*

chron-, chrono- *comb form* time ⟨*chronology*⟩

chronic *adj* 1a *esp of an illness* marked by long duration or frequent recurrence – usu contrasted with ACUTE 4 b suffering from a chronic disease 2a always present or encountered; *esp* constantly troubling ⟨*~ financial difficulties*⟩ b habitual, persistent ⟨*a ~ grumbler*⟩ 3 Br bad, terrible – *infml* – **chronically** *adv*, **chronicity** *n*

chronicle *n* 1 a usu continuous and detailed historical account of events arranged chronologically without analysis or interpretation 2 a narrative

chronicle *vt* **chronicling** 1 to record (as if) in a chronicle 2 to list, describe – **chronicler** *n*

chronograph *n* an instrument for accurately measuring and recording time intervals – **chronographic** *adj*, **chronography** *n*

chronological *also* **chronologic** *adj* of or arranged in or according to the order of time ⟨*~ tables of British history*⟩ – **chronologically** *adv*

chronology *n* 1 (the scientific study or use of) a method for setting past events in order of occurrence 2 an arrangement in order of occurrence; *specif* such an arrangement presented in tabular or list form – **chronologer**, **chronologist** *n*, **chronologize** *vt*

chronometer *n* an instrument for measuring time; *esp* one designed to keep time with great accuracy

chrysalis *n, pl* **chrysalides**, **chrysalises** 1 (the case enclosing) a pupa, esp of a butterfly or moth 2 a sheltered state or stage of being or growth ⟨*ready to emerge from the ~ of adolescence*⟩

chrysanthemum *n* any of various (cultivated) composite plants with brightly coloured often double flower heads

chub *n, pl* **chub**, *esp for different types* **chubs** (a marine or freshwater fish similar to) a European freshwater fish of the carp family

chubby *adj* of large proportions; plump ⟨*a ~ boy*⟩ – **chubbiness** *n*

chuck *n* – used as a term of endearment

chuck *vt* 1 to pat, tap ⟨*~ed her under the chin*⟩ 2a to toss, throw b to discard – often + *out* or *away* 3 to leave; GIVE UP 2 ⟨*~ed his job*⟩ – often + *in* or *up* USE (*except 1*) *infml*

chuck *n* 1 a pat or nudge under the chin 2 a throw – *infml*

chuck *n* 1 a cut of beef that includes most of the neck and the area about the shoulder blade 2 a device for holding a workpiece (e g for turning on a lathe) or tool (e g in a drill)

chuckle *vi* **chuckling** to laugh inwardly or quietly – **chuckle** *n*, **chucklesome** *adj*, **chucklingly** *adv*

chuck out *vt* to eject (a person) from a place or an office; dismiss – *infml* – **chucker-out** *n*

chug *vi or n* -**gg**- (to move or go with) a usu repetitive dull explosive sound made (as if) by a labouring engine

chukker *n* any of the periods of play in a polo game

chum *n* a close friend; a mate – *infml*; no longer in vogue

chum *vi* -**mm**- to form a friendship, esp a close one – usu + (*up*) *with*; no longer in vogue

chummy *adj* friendly, intimate – *infml* – **chummily** *adv*, **chumminess** *n*

chump *n* 1 a cut of meat taken from between the loin and hindleg, esp of a lamb, mutton, or pork carcass 2 a fool, duffer – *infml* – **off one's chump** OFF ONE'S HEAD

chunk *n* 1 LUMP 1; *esp* one of a firm or hard material (e g wood) 2 a (large) quantity ⟨*put a sizable ~ of money on the race*⟩ – *infml*

chunky *adj* 1 stocky 2 filled with chunks ⟨*~ marmalade*⟩ 3 *of materials, clothes, etc* thick and heavy – **chunkily** *adv*, **chunkiness** *n*

¹church *n* **1** a building for public (Christian) worship; *esp* a place of worship used by an established church **2** *often cap* institutionalized religion; *esp* the established Christian religion of a country **3** *cap* a body or organization of religious believers: e g **a** the whole body of Christians **b** DENOMINATION 2 **c** CONGREGATION 2 **4** an occasion for public worship ⟨goes to ~ every Sunday⟩ **5** the clerical profession ⟨considered the ~ as a possible career⟩ – **churchly** *adj*, **churchman**, *fem* **churchwoman** *n*
²church *adj* **1** of a church **2** *chiefly Br* being a member of the established state church
churching *n* a ceremony in which a woman after childbirth is received and blessed in church – **church** *vt*
Church of England *n* the established episcopal church of England
Church of Scotland *n* the established presbyterian church of Scotland
churchwarden *n* **1** either of 2 lay parish officers in Anglican churches with responsibility esp for parish property and alms **2** a long-stemmed (clay) tobacco pipe
churchyard *n* an enclosed piece of ground surrounding a church; *esp* one used as a burial ground
churl *n* **1a** a rude ill-bred person **b** a mean morose person **2** *archaic* a rustic, countryman
churlish *adj* **1** lacking refinement or sensitivity **2** rudely uncooperative; surly – **churlishly** *adv*, **churlishness** *n*
¹churn *n* **1** a vessel used in making butter in which milk or cream is agitated to separate the oily globules from the watery medium **2** *Br* a large metal container for transporting milk
²churn *vt* **1** to agitate (milk or cream) in a churn in order to make butter **2** to stir or agitate violently ~ *vi* **1** to work a churn **2** to produce or be in violent motion
churn out *vt* to produce prolifically and mechanically, usu without great concern for quality – chiefly infml
chute *n* **1** a waterfall, rapid, etc **2** an inclined plane, channel, or passage down which things may pass **3** a parachute – infml
chutney *n* a thick condiment or relish of Indian origin that contains fruits, sugar, vinegar, and spices
cicada *n* any of a family of insects that have large transparent wings and whose males produce a shrill singing noise
cicatrice *n* a cicatrix
cicatrix *n, pl* **cicatrices** **1** a scar resulting after a flesh wound has healed **2** a mark resembling a scar: e g a mark left on a stem after the fall of a leaf or bract – **cicatricial** *adj*
cicerone *n, pl* **ciceroni** one who acts as a guide to antiquities; *broadly* a guide, mentor
-cide *comb form* (→ *n*) **1** killer ⟨insecticide⟩ **2** killing ⟨suicide⟩ – **-cidal** *comb form* (→ *adj*)
cider, *Br also* **cyder** *n* fermented often sparkling apple juice
cigar *n* a small roll of tobacco leaf for smoking
cigarette, *NAm also* **cigaret** *n* a narrow cylinder of cut tobacco enclosed in paper for smoking; *also* a similar roll of a herbal or narcotic substance
¹cinch *n* **1** *NAm* GIRTH 1 **2a** a task performed with ease **b** sthg certain to happen USE (2) infml
²cinch *vt* **1** *NAm* to fasten or tighten a girth round (a horse) – often + *up* **2** to make certain of; assure – infml
cinchona *n* (the dried quinine-containing bark of) any of a genus of S American trees and shrubs of the madder family
cincture *n* a girdle, belt; *esp* a cloth cord or sash worn round an ecclesiastical vestment or the habit of a religious order

cinder *n* **1** (a fragment of) slag (e g from a blast furnace or volcano) **2** a fragment of ash **3** a piece of partly burned material (e g coal) that will burn further but will not flame – **cindery** *adj*
Cinderella *n* **1** sby or sthg that suffers undeserved neglect **2** sby or sthg that is suddenly raised from obscurity to honour or importance
cine- *comb form* relating to the cinema ⟨cinecamera⟩ ⟨cinefilm⟩
cinema *n* **1a** films considered esp as an art form, entertainment, or industry – usu + *the* **b** the art or technique of making films; *also* the effects appropriate to film **2** *chiefly Br* a theatre where films are shown
cinematic *adj* **1** made and presented as a film ⟨~ fantasies⟩ **2** of or suitable for (the making of) films – **cinematically** *adv*
cinematograph *n, chiefly Br* a film camera or projector
cinematography *n* the art or science of cinema photography – **cinematographer** *n*, **cinematographic** *adj*, **cinematographically** *adv*
cinnamon *n* **1** (any of several trees of the laurel family with) an aromatic bark used as a spice **2** light yellowish brown – **cinnamic** *adj*
cinquefoil *n* **1** any of a genus of plants of the rose family with 5-lobed leaves **2** a design enclosed by 5 joined arcs arranged in a circle
¹cipher *also* **cypher** *n* **1a** ZERO 1 **b** sby who or sthg that has no worth or influence; a nonentity **2a** a method of transforming a text in order to conceal its meaning **b** a message in code **3** any of the Arabic numerals **4** a combination of symbolic letters; *esp* a monogram
²cipher *also* **cypher** *vt* **1** to encipher **2** to compute arithmetically
circa *prep* at, in, or of approximately – used esp with dates ⟨born ~ 1600⟩
circadian *adj* being, having, characterized by, or occurring in approximately day-long periods or cycles (e g of biological activity or function) ⟨~ rhythms⟩⟨~ leaf movements⟩
¹circle *n* **1a** a closed plane curve every point of which is equidistant from a fixed point within the curve **b** the plane surface bounded by such a curve **2** sthg in the form of (an arc of) a circle: e g **a** a balcony or tier of seats in a theatre **b** a circle formed on the surface of a sphere (e g the earth) by the intersection of a plane **3** cycle, round ⟨the wheel has come full ~⟩ **4** *sing or pl in constr* a group of people sharing a common interest, activity, or leader ⟨the gossip of court ~s⟩
²circle *vb* **circling** *vt* **1** to enclose (as if) in a circle **2** to move or revolve round ~ *vi* to move (as if) in a circle – **circler** *n*
circlet *n* a little circle; *esp* a circular ornament
circuit *n* **1** a closed loop encompassing an area **2a** a course round a periphery **b** a racetrack **3a** a regular tour (e g by a judge) round an assigned area or territory **b** the route travelled **c** a group of church congregations with 1 pastor (e g in the Methodist church) **4a** the complete path of an electric current, usu including the source of energy **b** an array of electrical components connected so as to allow the passage of current **c** a 2-way communication path between points (e g in a computer) **5a** an association or league of similar groups **b** a chain of theatres at which productions are presented successively – **circuital** *adj*
circuit breaker *n* a switch that automatically interrupts an electric circuit under an infrequent abnormal condition
circuitous *adj* indirect in route or method; roundabout – **circuitously** *adv*, **circuitousness**, **circuity** *n*

circular adj 1 having the form of a circle 2 moving in or describing a circle or spiral 3 marked by the fallacy of assuming sthg which is to be demonstrated ⟨~ arguments⟩ 4 marked by or moving in a cycle 5 intended for circulation – **circularity** n, **circularly** adv, **circularness** n

circular n a paper (e g a leaflet or advertisement) intended for wide distribution

circularize, -ise vt 1 to send circulars to 2 to publicize, esp by means of circulars – **circularization** n

circular saw n a power-driven saw that has its teeth set on the edge of a revolving metal disc

circulate vi 1 to move in a circle, circuit, or orbit; esp to follow a course that returns to the starting point ⟨blood ~s through the body⟩ 2 to pass from person to person or place to place; e g a to flow without obstruction b to become well known or widespread ⟨rumours ~d through the town⟩ c to go from group to group at a social gathering d to come into the hands of readers; specif to become sold or distributed ~vt to cause to circulate – **circulatable** adj, **circulative** adj, **circulator** n, **circulatory** adj

circulation n 1 a flow 2 orderly movement through a circuit; esp the movement of blood through the vessels of the body induced by the pumping action of the heart 3a passage or transmission from person to person or place to place; esp the interchange of currency ⟨coins in ~⟩ b the extent of dissemination; esp the average number of copies of a publication sold over a given period

circulatory system n the system of blood, blood and lymphatic vessels, and heart concerned with the circulation of the blood and lymph

circum- prefix round; about ⟨circumnavigate⟩

circumcise vt to cut off the foreskin of (a male) or the clitoris of (a female) – **circumciser** n

circumcision n 1 a Jewish rite of circumcising performed on male infants as a sign of inclusion in the Jewish religious community 2 cap January 1 observed as a church festival in commemoration of the circumcision of Jesus

circumference n 1 the perimeter of a circle 2 the external boundary or surface of a figure or object – **circumferential** adj

circumflex adj marked with or having the sound indicated by a circumflex

circumflex n an accent mark ˆ , , or ̄ used in various languages to mark length, contraction, or a particular vowel quality

circumlocution n 1 the use of an unnecessarily large number of words to express an idea 2 evasive speech – **circumlocutious** adj, **circumlocutory** adj

circumnavigate vt to go round; esp to travel completely round (the earth), esp by sea – **circumnavigator** n, **circumnavigation** n

circumscribe vt 1 to surround by a physical or imaginary line 2 to restrict the range or activity of definitely and clearly 3 to draw round (a geometrical figure) so as to touch at as many points as possible

circumscription n (a) circumscribing or being circumscribed; esp (the act of imposing) a restriction

circumspect adj careful to consider all circumstances and possible consequences; prudent – **circumspection** n, **circumspectly** adv

circumstance n 1 a condition or event that accompanies, causes, or determines another; also the sum of such conditions or events ⟨economic ~⟩ 2a a state of affairs; an occurrence ⟨open rebellion was a rare ~⟩ – often pl with sing. meaning ⟨a victim of ~s⟩ b pl situation with regard to material or financial welfare ⟨he was in easy

~s⟩ 3 attendant formalities and ceremony ⟨pomp and ~⟩ 4 an incident viewed as part of a narrative or course of events; a fact – **in/under the circumstances** because of the conditions; considering the situation

circumstantial adj 1 belonging to, consisting in, or dependent on circumstances 2 pertinent but not essential; incidental – **circumstantiality** n, **circumstantially** adv

circumvent vt to check or evade, esp by ingenuity or stratagem – **circumvention** n

circus n 1a a large circular or oval stadium used esp for sports contests or spectacles b a public spectacle 2a (the usu covered arena housing) an entertainment in which a variety of performers (e g acrobats and clowns) and performing animals are involved in a series of unrelated acts b an activity suggestive of a circus (e g in being a busy scene of noisy or frivolous action) 3 Br a road junction in a town partly surrounded by a circle of buildings – usu in proper names ⟨Piccadilly Circus⟩ – **circusy** adj

cirque n 1 a deep steep-walled basin on a mountain 2 archaic CIRCUS 1a

cirrhosis n, pl **cirrhoses** hardening (of the liver) caused by excessive formation of connective tissue – **cirrhotic** adj or n

cirrus n, pl **cirri** 1 TENDRIL 1 2 a slender usu flexible (invertebrate) animal appendage 3 a wispy white cloud formation usu of minute ice crystals formed at high altitudes

cissy, sissy n, Br 1 an effeminate boy or man 2 a cowardly person USE infml – **cissy** adj

Cistercian n a member of an austere Benedictine order founded by St Robert of Molesme in 1098 at Cîteaux in France – **Cistercian** adj

cistern n an artificial reservoir for storing liquids, esp water: e g a a tank at the top of a house or building b a water reservoir for a toilet c chiefly NAm a usu underground tank for storing rainwater

citadel n 1 a fortress; esp one that commands a city 2 a stronghold

citation n 1a an act of citing or quoting b a quotation 2 a mention; specif specific reference in a military dispatch to meritorious conduct – **citational** adj

cite vt 1 to call upon to appear before a court 2 to quote by way of example, authority, precedent, or proof ⟨~ Biblical passages⟩ 3 to refer to or name; esp to mention formally in commendation or praise – **citable** adj

citizen n 1 an inhabitant of a city or town; esp a freeman 2 a (native or naturalized) member of a state – **citizenly** adj, **citizenship** n

citizenry n sing or pl in constr the whole body of citizens

citric acid n an acid occurring in lemons, limes, etc, formed as an intermediate in cell metabolism, and used as a flavouring

citron n 1 a (tree that bears) fruit like the lemon but larger and with a thicker rind 2 the preserved rind of the citron, used esp in cakes and puddings

citrus n, pl **citrus, citruses** any of several often thorny trees and shrubs of the rue family grown in warm regions for their edible thick-rinded juicy fruit (e g the orange or lemon) – **citrus** adj

city n 1a a large town b an incorporated British town that has a cathedral or has had civic status conferred on it c a usu large chartered municipality in the USA 2 a city-state 3a the financial and commercial area of London b cap, sing or pl in constr the influential financial interests of the British economy

city father n an important official or prominent citizen of a city

city hall n the chief administrative building of a city

city-state *n* an autonomous state consisting of a city and surrounding territory

civet *n* a thick yellowish musky-smelling substance extracted from a pouch near the sexual organs of the civet cat and used in perfumery

civet cat *n* a long-bodied short-legged flesh-eating African mammal from which civet is obtained

civic *adj* of a citizen, a city, or citizenship – **civically** *adv*

civics *n pl but sing or pl in constr* a social science dealing with the rights and duties of citizens

civies *n pl* civvies

civil *adj* **1** of citizens ⟨~ *liberties*⟩ **2** adequately courteous and polite; not rude **3** relating to private rights as distinct from criminal proceedings **4** *of time* based on the sun and legally recognized for use in ordinary affairs **5** of or involving the general public as distinguished from special (e g military or religious) affairs – **civilly** *adv*

civil defence *n, often cap C&D* protective measures organized by and for civilians against hostile attack, esp from the air, or natural disaster

civil disobedience *n* refusal to obey governmental demands (e g payment of tax) as a means of forcing concessions

civil engineer *n* an engineer whose training or occupation is in the designing and construction of large-scale public works (e g roads or bridges) – **civil engineering** *n*

civilian *n* one who is not in the army, navy, air force, or other uniformed public body – **civilian** *adj*, **civilianize** *vt*, **civilianization** *n*

civility *n* **1** courtesy, politeness **2** a polite act or expression – usu pl

civilization, -isation *n* **1a** a relatively high level of cultural and technological development **b** the culture characteristic of a particular time or place **2** the process of becoming civilized **3** life in a place that offers the comforts of the modern world; *specif* life in a city – often humor

civilize, -ise *vt vi* **1** to cause to develop out of a primitive state; *specif* to bring to a technically advanced and rationally ordered stage of cultural development **2** to educate, refine – **civilizable** *adj*, **civilizer** *n*

civil law *n, often cap C&L* **1** ROMAN LAW **2** the body of private law developed from Roman law as distinct from common law **3** the law established by a nation or state for its own jurisdiction (e g as distinct from international law) **4** the law of private rights

civil liberty *n* a right or freedom of the individual citizen in relation to the state (e g freedom of speech); *also* such rights or freedoms considered collectively – **civil libertarian** *n*

civil list *n* an annual allowance by Parliament for the expenses of the monarch and royal family

civil marriage *n* a marriage involving a civil contract but no religious rite

civil rights *n pl* CIVIL LIBERTIES; *esp* those of status equality between races or groups – **civil righter, civil rightist** *n*

civil servant *n* a member of a civil service

civil service *n sing or pl in constr* the administrative service of a government or international agency, exclusive of the armed forces

civil war *n* a war between opposing groups of citizens of the same country

civvies, civies *n pl* civilian as distinguished from military clothes – slang

civvy street *n, often cap C&S, Br* civilian life as opposed to life in the services – slang

¹clack *vi* **1** CHATTER **2** – infml **2** to make an abrupt striking sound or sounds ~*vt* to cause to make a clatter – **clacker** *n*

²clack *n* **1** rapid continuous talk; chatter – infml **2** a sound of clacking

¹clad *adj* being covered or clothed ⟨*ivy*-clad *buildings*⟩ ⟨~ *in tweeds*⟩

²clad *vt* **-dd-; clad** to cover with cladding

³clad *n* cladding

¹claim *vt* **1a** to ask for, esp as a right ⟨~ ed *Supplementary Benefit*⟩ **b** to require, demand **c** to take; ACCOUNT FOR 3 ⟨*plague* ~ed *thousands of lives*⟩ **2** to take as the rightful owner **3** to assert in the face of possible contradiction; maintain ⟨~ed *that he'd been cheated*⟩ – **claimable** *adj*, **claimer** *n*

²claim *n* **1** a demand for sthg (believed to be) due ⟨*insurance* ~⟩ **2a** a right or title to sthg **b** an assertion open to challenge ⟨*a* ~ *to fame*⟩ **3** sthg claimed; *esp* a tract of land staked out

claimant *n* one who asserts a right or entitlement

clairvoyance *n* **1** the power or faculty of discerning objects not apparent to the physical senses **2** the ability to perceive matters beyond the range of ordinary perception – **clairvoyant** *adj or n*

clam *n* **1** any of numerous edible marine molluscs (e g a scallop) living in sand or mud **2** a freshwater mussel

clambake *n, NAm* **1** an outdoor party; *esp* a seashore outing where food is cooked on heated rocks covered by seaweed **2** a gathering characterized by noisy sociability; *esp* a political rally

clamber *vi* to climb awkwardly or with difficulty – **clamberer** *n*

clammy *adj* being damp, clinging, and usu cool – **clammily** *adv*, **clamminess** *n*

clamour, *NAm chiefly* clamor *vi or n* **1** (to engage in) noisy shouting **2** (to make) a loud continuous noise **3** (to make) insistent public expression (e g of support or protest) ⟨*the* ~ *for representation*⟩ – **clamorous** *adj*, **clamorously** *adv*, **clamourousness** *n*

¹clamp *n* **1** a device that holds or compresses 2 or more parts firmly together **2** a heap of wooden sticks or bricks for burning, firing, etc

²clamp *vt* **1** to fasten (as if) with a clamp ⟨~ *an artery*⟩ **2** to hold tightly

³clamp *n, Br* a heap of potatoes, turnips, etc covered over with straw or earth

clamp down *vi* to impose restrictions; *also* to make restrictions more stringent – **clamp-down** *n*

clam up *vi* to become silent – infml

clan *n* **1a** a (Highland Scots) Celtic group of households descended from a common ancestor **b** a group of people related by family ⟨*the Kennedy* ~⟩ **2** a usu close-knit group united by a common interest or common characteristics – **clansman** *n*

clandestine *adj* held in or conducted with secrecy; surreptitious – **clandestinely** *adv*

clang *vi* **1** to make a loud metallic ringing sound ⟨*anvils* ~ed⟩ **2** *esp of a crane or goose* to utter a harsh cry ~*vt* to cause to clang ⟨~ *a bell*⟩ – **clang** *n*

clanger *n, Br* a blunder – infml

clangour, *NAm chiefly* clangor *vi or n* (to make) a resounding clang or medley of clangs ⟨*the* ~ *of hammers*⟩ – **clangorous** *adj*, **clangorously** *adv*

¹clank *vb* to (cause to) make a clank or series of clanks – **clankingly** *adv*

²clank *n* a sharp brief metallic sound

clannish *adj* tending to associate only with a select group of similar background, status, or interests – **clannishly** *adv*, **clannishness** *n*

¹clap *vb* **-pp-** *vt* **1** to strike (e g 2 flat hard surfaces) together so as to produce a loud sharp percussive noise **2a** to strike (the hands) together repeatedly, usu in applause **b** to applaud **3** to strike with the flat of the hand in a friendly way **4** to place, put, or set, esp energetically – infml ⟨~ *him in irons*⟩ ⟨*finest vessel I ever* ~*ped eyes on*⟩ ~*vi* **1** to produce a sharp percussive noise **2** to applaud

clap *n* **1** a loud sharp percussive noise, specif of thunder **2** a friendly slap ⟨*a* ~ *on the shoulder*⟩ **3** the sound of clapping hands; *esp* applause

clap *n* VENEREAL DISEASE; *esp* gonorrhoea – slang

clapboard *n*, *NAm* weatherboard – **clapboard** *vt*

clapped out *adj*, *chiefly Br*, *esp of machinery* (old and) worn-out; liable to break down irreparably – infml

clapper *n* the tongue of a bell – **like the clappers** *Br* as fast as possible – infml; + *run* or *go*

clapper-board *n* a hinged board containing identifying details of the scene to be filmed that is held before the camera and banged together to mark the beginning and end of each take

claptrap *n* pretentious nonsense; rubbish – infml

claque *n sing or pl in constr* **1** a group hired to applaud at a performance **2** a group of self-interested obsequious flatterers

claret *n* **1** a dry red Bordeaux **2** a dark purplish red colour – **claret** *adj*

clarify *vt* **1** to make (e g a liquid) clear or pure, usu by freeing from suspended matter **2** to make free from confusion **3** to make understandable ~*vi* to become clear – **clarification** *n*, **clarifier** *n*

clarinet *n* a single-reed woodwind instrument with a usual range from D below middle C upwards for 3½ octaves – **clarinettist**, *NAm chiefly* **clarinetist** *n*

clarion *n* (the sound of) a medieval trumpet

clarion *adj* brilliantly clear ⟨*a* ~ *call to action*⟩

clarity *n* the quality or state of being clear

clash *vi* **1** to make a clash ⟨*cymbals* ~*ed*⟩ **2a** to come into conflict **b** to form a displeasing combination; not match ⟨*these colours* ~⟩ ~*vt* to cause to clash – **clasher** *n*

clash *n* **1** a noisy usu metallic sound of collision **2a** a hostile encounter **b** a sharp conflict ⟨*a* ~ *of opinions*⟩

clasp *n* **1** a device for holding objects or parts of sthg together ⟨*the* ~ *of a necklace*⟩ **2** a holding or enveloping (as if) with the hands or arms

clasp *vt* **1** to fasten (as if) with a clasp **2** to enclose and hold with the arms; *specif* to embrace **3** to seize (as if) with the hands; grasp

clasp knife *n* a large single-bladed folding knife having a catch to hold the blade open

class *n* **1a** *sing or pl in constr* a group sharing the same economic or social status in a society consisting of several groups with differing statuses – often pl with sing. meaning ⟨*the labouring* ~*es*⟩ **b(1)** social rank **(2)** the system of differentiating society by classes **c** high quality; elegance **2** *sing or pl in constr* a body of students meeting regularly to study the same subject **3** a group, set, or kind sharing common attributes: e g **a** a category in biological classification ranking above the order and below the phylum or division **b** a grammatical category **4a** a division or rating based on grade or quality **b** *Br* a level of university honours degree awarded to a student according to merit ⟨*what* ~ *did she get?*⟩

class *vt* to classify

class-conscious *adj* **1** actively aware of one's common status with others in a particular class **2** taking part in class war – **class-consciousness** *n*

classic *adj* **1a** of recognized value or merit; serving as a standard of excellence **b** both traditional and enduring ⟨*a* ~ *heritage*⟩ **c** characterized by simple tailored and elegant lines that remain in fashion year after year ⟨*a* ~ *suit*⟩ **2** CLASSICAL 2 **3a** authoritative, definitive **b** being an example that shows clearly the characteristics of some group of things or occurrences; archetypal

classic *n* **1a** a literary work of ancient Greece or Rome **b** *pl* Greek and Latin literature, history, and philosophy considered as an academic subject **2a** (the author of) a work of lasting excellence **b** an authoritative source **3** a classic example; archetype **4** an important long-established sporting event; *specif*, *Br* any of 5 flat races for horses (e g the Epsom Derby)

classical *adj* **1** standard, classic **2** of the (literature, art, architecture, or ideals of the) ancient Greek and Roman world **3a** of or being (a composer of) music of the late 18th c and early 19th c characterized by an emphasis on simplicity, objectivity, and proportion **b** of or being music in the educated European tradition that includes such forms as chamber music, opera, and symphony as distinguished from folk, popular music, or jazz **4a** both authoritative and traditional **b(1)** of or being systems or methods that constitute an accepted although not necessarily modern approach to a subject ⟨~ *Mendelian genetics*⟩ **(2)** not involving relativity, wave mechanics, or quantum theory ⟨~ *physics*⟩ **5** concerned with instruction in the classics

classicism, classicalism *n* **1a** the principles or style embodied in classical literature, art, or architecture **b** a classical idiom or expression **2** adherence to traditional standards (e g of simplicity, restraint, and proportion) that are considered to have universal and lasting worth – **classicalist, classicist** *n*, **classicistic** *adj*

classification *n* **1** classifying **2a** systematic arrangement in groups according to established criteria; *specif* taxonomy **b** a class, category – **classificatorily** *adv*, **classificatory** *adj*

classified *adj* withheld from general circulation for reasons of national security ⟨~ *information*⟩

classify *vt* **1** to arrange in classes **2** to assign to a category – **classifiable** *adj*, **classifier** *n*

classless *adj* **1** free from class distinction ⟨*a* ~ *society*⟩ **2** belonging to no particular social class – **classlessness** *n*

classmate *n* a member of the same class in a school or college

classroom *n* a room where classes meet

class war *n* the struggle for power between workers and property owners assumed by Marxist theory to develop in a capitalist society

classy *adj* elegant, stylish – infml – **classiness** *n*

clatter *vi* **1** to make a clatter ⟨*the dishes* ~*ed on the shelf*⟩ **2** to move or go with a clatter ⟨~*ed down the stairs*⟩ **3** to prattle ~*vt* to cause to clatter – **clatterer** *n*, **clatteringly** *adv*

clatter *n* **1** a rattling sound (e g of hard bodies striking together) ⟨*the* ~ *of pots and pans*⟩ **2** a commotion ⟨*the midday* ~ *of the business district*⟩ – **clattery** *adj*

clause *n* **1** a distinct article or condition in a formal document **2** a phrase containing a subject and predicate and functioning either in isolation or as a member of a complex or compound sentence – **clausal** *adj*

claustrophobia *n* abnormal dread of being in closed or confined spaces – **claustrophobic** *adj*

clavichord *n* an early usu rectangular keyboard instrument – **clavichordist** *n*

clavicle *n* a bone of the vertebrate shoulder typically linking the shoulder blade and breastbone; the collarbone – **clavicular** *adj*

claw *n* **1** (a part resembling or limb having) a sharp usu slender curved nail on an animal's toe **2** any of the pincerlike organs on the end of some limbs of a lobster, scorpion, or similar arthropod **3** sthg (e g the forked end of a claw hammer) resembling a claw – **clawed** adj

²claw vt to rake, seize, dig, or make (as if) with claws ~ vi to scrape, scratch, dig, or pull (as if) with claws

claw hammer n a hammer with one end of the head forked for pulling out nails

clay n **1a** (soil composed chiefly of) an earthy material that is soft when moist but hard when fired, is composed mainly of fine particles of aluminium silicates, and is used for making brick, tile, and pottery **b** thick and clinging earth or mud **2a** a substance that resembles clay and is used for modelling **b** the human body as distinguished from the spirit – **clayey** adj, **clayish** adj

claymore n a large single-edged broadsword formerly used by Scottish Highlanders

clay pigeon n a saucer-shaped object usu made of baked clay and hurled into the air as a target for shooting at with a shotgun

¹clean adj **1a** (relatively) free from dirt or pollution ⟨changed into ~ clothes⟩ **b** free from contamination or disease **c** relatively free from radioactive fallout ⟨a ~ atomic explosion⟩ **2** unadulterated, pure **3a** free from illegal, immoral, or disreputable activities ⟨a ~ record⟩ **b** free from the use of obscenity ⟨I just don't know any ~ jokes!⟩ **c** observing the rules; fair ⟨a ~ fight⟩ **4** thorough, complete ⟨a ~ break with the past⟩ **5** relatively free from error or blemish; clear; specif legible ⟨~ copy⟩ **6a** characterized by clarity, precision, or deftness ⟨architecture with ~ almost austere lines⟩ **b** not jagged; smooth ⟨a ~ edge⟩ **c** of a ship or aircraft well streamlined – **cleanly** adv, **cleanness** n

²clean adv **1a** so as to leave clean ⟨a new broom sweeps ~⟩ **b** in a clean manner ⟨fight ~⟩ **2** all the way; completely ⟨the bullet went ~ through his arm⟩

³clean vt **1** to make clean – often + up **2a** to strip, empty **b** to deprive of money or possessions – often + out ⟨they ~ed him out completely⟩; infml ~ vi to undergo cleaning – **cleanable** adj

⁴clean n an act of cleaning away dirt

clean-cut adj **1** cut so that the surface or edge is smooth and even **2** sharply defined **3** of wholesome appearance

cleaner n **1** sby whose occupation is cleaning rooms or clothes **2** a substance, implement, or machine for cleaning – **to the cleaners** to or through the experience of being deprived of all one's money – infml

cleanliness n fastidiousness in keeping things or one's person clean – **cleanly** adj

cleanse vb to clean

cleanser n a preparation (e g a scouring powder or skin cream) used for cleaning

clean-shaven adj with the hair, specif of the beard and moustache, shaved off

clean up vi to make a large esp sweeping gain (e g in business or gambling) ~ vt to remove by cleaning – **cleanup** n

¹clear adj **1a** bright, luminous **b** free from cloud, mist, haze, or dust ⟨a ~ day⟩ **c** untroubled, serene ⟨a ~ gaze⟩ **2** clean, pure: e g **a** free from blemishes **b** easily seen through; transparent **3a** easily heard **b** easily visible; plain **c** free from obscurity or ambiguity; easily understood **4a** capable of sharp discernment; keen ⟨this problem needs a ~ mind⟩ **b** free from doubt; sure ⟨we are not ~ what to do⟩ **5** free from guilt ⟨a ~ conscience⟩ **6a** net ⟨a ~ profit⟩ **b** unqualified, absolute ⟨a ~ victory⟩ **c** free from obstruction or entanglement **d** full ⟨6 ~ days⟩ – **clearly** adv, **clearness** n

²clear adv **1** clearly ⟨to cry loud and ~⟩ **2** chiefly NAm all the way ⟨can see ~ to the mountains today⟩

³clear vt **1a** to make transparent or translucent **b** to free from unwanted material – often + out ⟨~ out that cupboard⟩ **2a** to free from accusation or blame; vindicate **b** to certify as trustworthy ⟨~ a man for top secret military work⟩ **3a** to rid (the throat) of phlegm; also to make a rasping noise in (the throat) **b** to erase accumulated totals or stored data from (e g a calculator or computer memory) **4** to authorize or cause to be authorized **5a** to free from financial obligation **b(1)** to settle, discharge ⟨~ an account⟩ **(2)** to deal with until finished or settled ⟨~ the backlog of work⟩ **c** to gain without deduction ⟨~ a profit⟩ **d** to put through a clearinghouse **6a** to get rid of; remove ⟨~ the plates from the table⟩ – often + off, up, or away ⟨~ away the rubbish⟩ **b** to kick or pass (the ball) away from the goal as a defensive measure in soccer **7** to go over without touching ⟨the horse ~ed the jump⟩ ~ vi **1a** to become clear – often + up ⟨it ~ed up quickly after the rain⟩ **b** to go away; vanish ⟨the symptoms ~ed gradually⟩ – sometimes + off, out ⟨told him to ~ out⟩, or away ⟨after the mist ~ed away⟩ **c** to sell **2** to pass through a clearinghouse – **clearable** adj, **clearer** n – **clear the air** to remove elements of hostility, tension, confusion, or uncertainty from the mood or temper of the time – **clear the decks** to get things ready for action

⁴clear n a high long arcing shot in badminton – **in the clear 1** free from guilt or suspicion **2** in plaintext; not in code or cipher

clearance n **1a** an authorization **b** a sale to clear out stock **c** the removal of buildings, people, etc from the space they previously occupied ⟨the Highland ~s⟩ ⟨slum ~⟩ **d** a clearing of the ball in soccer **2** the distance by which one object clears another, or the clear space between them

clear-cut adj **1** sharply outlined; distinct **2** free from ambiguity or uncertainty

clearheaded adj **1** not confused; sensible, rational **2** having no illusions about a state of affairs; realistic – **clearheadedly** adv, **clearheadedness** n

clearing n an area of land cleared of wood and brush

clearinghouse n an establishment maintained by banks for settling mutual claims and accounts

clear-sighted adj CLEARHEADED 2; esp having perceptive insight – **clear-sightedly** adv, **clear-sightedness** n

clear up vt **1** to tidy up **2** to explain ⟨clear up the mystery⟩

clearway n, Br a road on which vehicles may stop only in an emergency

cleat n **1a** a wedge-shaped piece fastened to sthg and serving as a support or check **b** a wooden or metal fitting, usu with 2 projecting horns, round which a rope may be made fast **2a** a projecting piece (e g on the bottom of a shoe) that provides a grip **b** pl shoes equipped with cleats

cleavage n **1** the property of a crystal or rock (e g slate) of splitting along definite planes **2 (a)** division **3** CELL DIVISION **4** the splitting of a molecule into simpler molecules **5** (the space between) a woman's breasts, esp when exposed by a low-cut garment

¹cleave vi cleaved, clove to stick firmly and closely or loyally and steadfastly – usu + to

²cleave vb cleaved also cleft, clove; cleaved also cleft, cloven vt to divide or pass through (as if) by a cutting blow; split ~ vi to split, esp along the grain – **cleavable** adj

cleaver n a butcher's implement for cutting animal carcasses into joints or pieces

clef *n* a sign placed on a musical staff to indicate the pitch represented by the notes following it

cleft *n* **1** a space or opening made by splitting; a fissure **2** a usu V-shaped indented formation; a hollow between ridges or protuberances

cleft palate *n* a congenital fissure of the roof of the mouth

clematis *n* a usu climbing or scrambling plant of the buttercup family with 3 leaflets on each leaf and usu white, pink, or purple flowers

clemency *n* disposition to be merciful, esp to moderate the severity of punishment due

clement *adj* **1** inclined to be merciful; lenient ⟨*a ~ judge*⟩ **2** *of weather* pleasantly mild – **clemently** *adv*

clench *vt* **1** CLINCH 1, 2 **2** to hold fast; clutch **3** to set or close tightly ⟨*~ed his teeth*⟩ ⟨*~ his fists*⟩

clerestory, clearstory *n* **1** the part of an outside wall of a room or building that rises above an adjoining roof ⟨*~ windows*⟩ **2** *chiefly NAm* a raised ventilating section of a railway carriage roof

clergy *n sing or pl in constr* a group ordained to perform pastoral or sacerdotal functions in an organized religion, esp a Christian church

clergyman *n* an ordained minister

cleric *n* a member of the clergy; *specif* one in orders below the grade of priest

¹clerical *adj* **1** (characteristic) of the clergy, a clergyman, or a cleric **2** of a clerk or office worker – **clerically** *adv*

²clerical *n* **1** a clergyman **2** an adherent of clericalism **3** *pl* clerical clothes

clerical collar *n* a narrow stiff upright white collar fastening at the back and worn by clergymen

clerihew *n* a witty pseudo-biographical 4-line verse

¹clerk *n* **1** a cleric **2a** sby whose occupation is keeping records or accounts or doing general office work ⟨*a filing ~*⟩ **b** *NAm* SHOP ASSISTANT – **clerkly** *adj*, **clerkship** *n*

²clerk *vi* to act or work as a clerk

clerk of the works *n* the person in charge of building works in a particular place

clever *adj* **1a** skilful or adroit *with* the hands or body; nimble **b** mentally quick and resourceful; intelligent **2** marked by wit or ingenuity; *also* thus marked but lacking depth or soundness – **cleverish** *adj*, **cleverly** *adv*, **cleverness** *n*

clever-dick *n*, *Br* SMART ALEC – *infml*

¹clew *n* **1** CLUE 1 **2** *also* **clue** (a metal loop attached to) the lower or after corner of a sail

²clew *vt* **1** CLUE 2 **2** *also* **clue** to haul (a sail) by ropes through the clews

cliché *n* **1** a hackneyed phrase or expression; *also* the idea expressed by it **2** a hackneyed theme or situation – **cliché** *adj*, **clichéd** *adj*

¹click *n* **1** a slight sharp sound **2** a sharp speech sound in some languages made by the sudden inrush of air at the release of an occlusion in the mouth

²click *vt* to strike, move, or produce with a click ⟨*~ed his heels together*⟩ ~ *vi* **1** to operate with or make a click **2a** to strike up an immediately warm friendship, esp with sby of the opposite sex **b** to succeed ⟨*a film that ~s*⟩ **c** *Br* to cause sudden insight or recognition ⟨*the name ~ed*⟩ – sometimes in *click into place* USE (2) infml

client *n* **1** a vassal, state, etc under the protection of another ⟨*~ states*⟩ **2a** sby who engages or receives the advice or services of a professional person or organization **b** a customer – **clientage** *n*, **cliental** *adj*

clientele *n sing or pl in constr* a body of clients ⟨*a shop that caters to an exclusive ~*⟩

cliff *n* a very steep high face of rock, earth, ice, etc – **cliffy** *adj*

cliff-hanger *n* **1** an adventure serial or melodrama, usu presented in instalments each ending in suspense **2** a contest or situation whose outcome is in doubt to the very end

¹climacteric *adj* of or being a critical period (e g of life)

²climacteric *n* **1** a major turning point or critical stage; *specif* one supposed to occur at intervals of 7 years **2** the menopause; *also* a corresponding period in the male during which sexual activity and competence are reduced

climactic *adj* of or being a climax – **climactically** *adv*

climate *n* **1** (a region of the earth having a specified) average course or condition of the weather over a period of years as shown by temperature, wind, rain, etc **2** the prevailing state of affairs or feelings of a group or period; a milieu ⟨*a ~ of fear*⟩ – **climatic** *adj*, **climatically** *adv*

climatology *n* a branch of meteorology dealing with climates – **climatological** *adj*, **climatologically** *adv*, **climatologist** *n*

¹climax *n* **1a** the highest point; a culmination **b** the point of highest dramatic tension or a major turning point in some action (e g of a play) **c** an orgasm **2** a relatively stable final stage reached by a (plant) community in its ecological development

²climax *vi* to come to a climax

climb *vi* **1a** to go gradually upwards; rise ⟨*watching the smoke ~*⟩ **b** to slope upwards ⟨*the road ~s steadily*⟩ **2a** to go up, down, etc on a more or less vertical surface using the hands to grasp or give support **b** *of a plant* to ascend in growth (e g by twining) **3** to get *into* or *out of* clothing, usu with some haste or effort ~ *vt* **1** to go upwards on or along, to the top of, or over ⟨*~ a hill*⟩ **2** to draw or pull oneself up, over, or to the top of, by using hands and feet ⟨*~ a tree*⟩ **3** to grow up or over – **climb** *n*, **climbable** *adj*, **climber** *n*

climb down *vi* BACK DOWN – **climb-down** *n*

climbing iron *n* a crampon

clime *n* CLIMATE 1 – usu *pl* with *sing.* meaning; chiefly poetic

¹clinch *vt* **1** to turn over or flatten the protruding pointed end of (e g a driven nail) **2** to fasten in this way ~ *vi* to hold an opponent (e g in boxing) at close quarters – **clinchingly** *adv*

²clinch *n* **1** a fastening by means of a clinched nail, rivet, or bolt **2** an act or instance of clinching in boxing

clincher *n* a decisive fact, argument, act, or remark

cline *n* a graded series of differences in shape or physiology shown by a group of related organisms, usu along a line of environmental or geographical transition; *broadly* a continuum – **clinal** *adj*, **clinally** *adv*

-cline *comb form* (→ *n*) slope ⟨*monocline*⟩ – **-clinal** *comb form* (→ *adj*), **-clinic** *comb form* (→ *adj*)

cling *vi* **clung 1a** to stick as if glued firmly **b** to hold (on) tightly or tenaciously **2a** to have a strong emotional attachment or dependence **b** *esp of a smell* to linger – **clingy** *adj*

clinic *n* **1** a class of medical instruction in which patients are examined and discussed **2** a meeting held by an expert or person in authority, to which people bring problems for discussion and resolution ⟨*an MP's weekly ~ for her constituents*⟩ **3a** a facility (e g of a hospital) for the diagnosis and treatment of outpatients **b** a usu private hospital

clinical *adj* **1** involving, based on, or noticeable from direct observation of the patient ⟨*~ psychology*⟩ **2** analytic, detached – **clinically** *adv*

¹clink vb to (cause to) give out a slight sharp short metallic sound – **clink** n

²clink n PRISON 2 – slang

clinker n stony matter fused by fire; slag

clinker-built adj having the lower edge of each external plank or plate overlapping the upper edge of the one below it ⟨a ~ boat⟩

¹clip vt **-pp-** to clasp or fasten with a clip

²clip n **1** any of various devices that grip, clasp, or hold **2** (a device to hold cartridges for charging) a magazine from which ammunition is fed into the chamber of a firearm **3** a piece of jewellery held in position by a spring clip

³clip vb **-pp-** vt **1a** to cut (off) (as if) with shears **b** to cut off the end or outer part of **c** ³EXCISE **2** to abbreviate in speech or writing **3** to hit with a glancing blow; also to hit smartly ⟨~ped him round the ear⟩ – infml ~ vi to clip sthg

⁴clip n **1a** the product of (a single) shearing (e g of sheep) **b** a section of filmed material **2a** an act of clipping **b** the manner in which sthg is clipped **3** a sharp blow **4** a rapid rate of motion USE (3&4) infml

clipboard n a small writing board with a spring clip for holding papers

clip joint n **1** a place of public entertainment (e g a nightclub) that defrauds, overcharges, etc **2** a business establishment that makes a practice of overcharging USE slang

clip-on adj of or being sthg that clips on ⟨~ earrings⟩

clip on vi to be capable of being fastened by an attached clip

clipper n **1** an implement for cutting or trimming hair or nails – usu pl with sing. meaning **2** a fast sailing ship, esp with long slender lines, a sharply raked bow, and a large sail area

clippie n, Br a female bus conductor – infml

clipping n, chiefly NAm CUTTING 2

clique n sing or pl in constr a highly exclusive and often aloof group of people held together by common interests, views, etc – **cliquey, cliquy** adj, **cliquish** adj, **cliquishly** adv, **cliquishness** n

clitoris n a small erectile organ at the front or top part of the vulva that is a centre of sexual sensation in females – **clitoral, clitoric** adj

cloaca n, pl **cloacae 1** a conduit for sewage **2** the chamber into which the intestinal, urinary, and generative canals discharge, esp in birds, reptiles, amphibians, and many fishes – **cloacal** adj

¹cloak n **1** a sleeveless outer garment that usu fastens at the neck and hangs loosely from the shoulders **2** sthg that conceals; a pretence, disguise

²cloak vt to cover or hide (as if) with a cloak

cloak-and-dagger adj dealing in or suggestive of melo- dramatic intrigue and action usu involving espionage

cloakroom n **1** a room in which outdoor clothing or luggage may be left during one's stay **2** chiefly Br a room with a toilet – euph

¹clobber n, Br gear, paraphernalia; esp clothes worn for a usu specified purpose or function – infml

²clobber vt **1** to hit with force **2** to defeat overwhelmingly USE infml

cloche n **1** a translucent cover used for protecting out- door plants **2** a woman's usu soft close-fitting hat with a deeply rounded crown and narrow brim

¹clock n **1** a device other than a watch for indicating or measuring time **2** a recording or metering device with a dial and indicator attached to a mechanism: e g **a** a speedometer **b** Br a milometer **3** Br a face – slang – **clocklike** adj – **round the clock 1** continuously for 24

hours; day and night without cessation **2** without relax- ation and heedless of time

²clock vt **1** to time with a stopwatch or electric timing device – used chiefly in sports **2a** to register on a mech- anical recording device **b** Br to attain a time, speed, etc, of – often + up; infml **3** to hit ⟨~ed him on the jaw⟩ – infml – **clocker** n

³clock n an ornamental pattern on the outside ankle or side of a stocking or sock

clock in vi to record the time of one's arrival or com- mencement of work by punching a card in a time clock

clock out vi to record the time of one's departure or stopping of work by punching a card in a time clock

clock-watcher n a person (e g a worker) who keeps close watch on the passage of time in order not to work a single moment longer than he/she has to – **clock-watching** n

clockwise adv in the direction in which the hands of a clock rotate as viewed from in front – **clockwise** adj

clockwork n machinery that operates in a manner similar to that of a mechanical clock; specif machinery powered by a coiled spring ⟨a ~ toy⟩ – **like clockwork** smoothly and with no hitches

clod n **1** a lump or mass, esp of earth or clay **2** an oaf, dolt **3** a gristly cut of beef taken from the neck – **cloddish** adj, **cloddishness** n, **cloddy** adj

clodhopper n **1** a clodhopping person – infml **2** a large heavy shoe – chiefly humor

¹clog n **1** a weight attached, esp to an animal, to hinder motion **2** a shoe, sandal, or overshoe with a thick typically wooden sole

²clog vb **-gg-** vt **1** to halt or retard the progress, operation, or growth of **2a** to obstruct so as to hinder motion in or through **b** to block ⟨the drain is ~ged up⟩ ~ vi to become blocked up

cloisonné adj or n (in) a style of enamel decoration in which the enamel is fired in raised sections separated by fine wire or thin metal strips

cloister n **1a** a monastic establishment **b** the monastic life **2** a covered passage on the side of an open court, usu having one side walled and the other an open arcade or colonnade

¹clone n **1** an individual that is asexually produced and is therefore identical to its parent **2** all such progeny of a single parent – used technically – **clonal** adj, **clonally** adv

²clone vt to cause to grow (as if) as a clone

clop n a sound made (as if) by a hoof or shoe against a hard surface – **clop** vi

¹close vt **1a** to move so as to bar passage ⟨~ the gate⟩ **b** to deny access to ⟨~ the park⟩ **c** to suspend or stop the operations of; also to discontinue or dispose of (a business) permanently – often + down **2a** to bring to an end ⟨~ an account⟩ **b** to conclude discussion or negotiation about ⟨the question is ~d⟩; also to bring to agreement or settlement ⟨~ a deal⟩ **3** to bring or bind together the parts or edges of ⟨a ~d fist⟩ ~ vi **1a** to contract, swing, or slide so as to leave no opening ⟨the door ~d quietly⟩ **b** to cease operation ⟨the factory ~d down⟩ ⟨the shops ~ at 9 pm⟩; specif, Br to stop broadcasting – usu + down **2** to draw near, esp in order to fight – usu + with **3** to come to an end – **closable, closeable** adj, **closer** n – **close one's doors 1** to refuse admission ⟨the nation closed its doors to immigrants⟩ **2** to go out of business ⟨after nearly 40 years he had to close his doors for lack of trade⟩ – **close one's eyes to** to ignore deliberately – **close ranks** to unite in a concerted stand, esp to meet a challenge – **close the door** to be uncompromisingly obstructive ⟨his attitude closed the door to further negotiation⟩

²**close** *n* a conclusion or end in time or existence ⟨*the decade drew to a* ~⟩

³**close** *n* 1 a road closed at one end 2 *Br* the precinct of a cathedral

⁴**close** *adj* 1 having no openings; closed 2a confined, cramped ⟨~ *quarters*⟩ b articulated with some part of the tongue close to the palate ⟨*a* ~ *vowel*⟩ 3 restricted, closed ⟨*the* ~ *season*⟩ 4 secretive, reticent ⟨*she was very* ~ *about her past*⟩ 5 strict, rigorous ⟨*keep* ~ *watch*⟩ ⟨*under* ~ *arrest*⟩ 6 hot and stuffy 7 having little space between items or units; compact, dense ⟨~ *texture*⟩ 8 very short or near to the surface ⟨*he barber gave him a* ~ *shave*⟩ 9 near; *esp* adjacent ⟨*he and I are* ~ *relations*⟩ 10 intimate, familiar ⟨~ *collaboration*⟩ 11a searching, minute ⟨*a* ~ *study*⟩ b faithful to an original ⟨*a* ~ *copy*⟩ 12 evenly contested or having a (nearly) even score ⟨*a* ~ *game*⟩ – **closely** *adv*, **closeness** *n* – **close to home** within one's personal interests so that one is strongly affected ⟨*the audience felt that the speaker's remarks hit pretty close to home*⟩

⁵**close** *adv* in or into a close position or manner; near ⟨*come* ~ *to ruining us*⟩ – **close on** almost ⟨*close on 500 people*⟩

close call *n* a narrow escape

close-cropped *adj* clipped short ⟨~ *hair*⟩

closed *adj* 1a not open b enclosed ⟨*a* ~ *porch*⟩ 2a forming a self-contained unit allowing no additions ⟨~ *system*⟩ b(1) traced by a moving point that returns to its starting point without retracing its path ⟨*a* ~ *curve*⟩; *also* so formed that every plane section is a closed curve ⟨*a* ~ *surface*⟩ (2) characterized by mathematical elements that when subjected to an operation produce only elements of the same set ⟨*the set of whole numbers is* ~ *under addition and multiplication*⟩ (3) containing all the limit points of every subset ⟨*a* ~ *set*⟩ 3a confined to a few ⟨~ *membership*⟩ b rigidly excluding outside influence ⟨*a* ~ *mind*⟩

closed circuit *n* 1 a television installation in which the signal is transmitted by wire to a limited number of receivers, usu in 1 location 2 a connected array of electrical components that will allow the passage of current – **closed-circuit** *adj*

closedown *n* the act or result of closing down; *esp* the end of a period of broadcasting

closed shop *n* an establishment which employs only union members

closefisted *adj* tightfisted

close-hauled *adj or adv* with the sails set for sailing as near directly into the wind as possible

close in *vi* 1 to gather in close all round with an oppressing effect ⟨*despair closed in on her*⟩ 2 to approach from various directions to close quarters, esp for an attack or arrest ⟨*at dawn the police closed in*⟩ 3 to grow dark ⟨*the short November day was already closing in* – Ellen Glasgow⟩

close-knit *adj* bound together by close ties

close out *vb*, *NAm* to (attempt to) dispose of (goods), esp by selling at reduced prices

close season *n*, *Br* a period during which it is illegal to kill or catch certain game or fish

¹**closet** *n* 1 a small or private room 2 WATER CLOSET 3 *chiefly NAm* a cupboard

²**closet** *vt* to shut (oneself) up (as if) in a closet 2 to take into a closet for a secret interview

close-up *n* 1 a photograph or film shot taken at close range 2 a view or examination of sthg from a small distance away

¹**closure** *n* 1 closing or being closed 2 the ending of a side's

innings in cricket by declaration 3 the closing of debate in a legislative body, esp by calling for a vote

²**closure** *vt* to close (a debate) by closure

¹**clot** *n* 1a a roundish viscous lump formed by coagulation of a portion of liquid (e g cream) b a coagulated mass produced by clotting of blood 2 *Br* a stupid person – infml

²**clot** *vb* -tt- *vi* 1 to become a clot; form clots 2 *of blood* to undergo a sequence of complex chemical and physical reactions that results in conversion from liquid form into a coagulated mass ~ *vt* to cause to clot

cloth *n*, *pl* **cloths** 1 a pliable material made usu by weaving, felting, or knitting natural or synthetic fibres and filaments 2 a piece of cloth adapted for a particular purpose: e g a a tablecloth b a dishcloth c a duster 3 (the distinctive dress of) a profession or calling distinguished by its dress; *specif* the clergy

clothe *vt* **clothed, clad** 1a to cover (as if) with clothing; dress b to provide with clothes 2 to express or enhance by suitably significant language

clothes *n pl* 1 articles of material (e g cloth) worn to cover the body, for warmth, protection, or decoration 2 bedclothes

clothes basket *n* a basket used for storing clothes that are to be washed

clotheshorse *n* 1 a frame on which to hang clothes, esp for drying or airing indoors 2 *chiefly NAm* a conspicuously dressy person – derog

clothesline *n* a line (e g of cord or nylon) on which clothes may be hung to dry, esp outdoors

clothes moth *n* any of several small yellowish moths whose larvae eat wool, fur, hair, etc

clothes peg *n* a wooden or plastic clip or forked device used for holding clothes or washing on a line

clothier *n* sby who makes or sells cloth or clothing

clothing *n* clothes

cloture *n*, *NAm* CLOSURE 3 – **cloture** *vt*

¹**cloud** *n* 1a a visible mass of particles of water or ice at a usu great height in the air b a light filmy, puffy, or billowy mass seeming to float in the air 2 any of many masses of opaque matter in interstellar space 3 a great crowd or multitude; a swarm, esp of insects ⟨~ *s of mosquitoes*⟩ 4 sthg that obscures or blemishes ⟨*their reputation is under a* ~⟩ – **cloudless** *adj*, **cloudlet** *n*

²**cloud** *vi* 1 to grow cloudy – usu + *over* or *up* 2a *of facial features* to become troubled, apprehensive, etc b to become blurred, dubious, or ominous ~ *vt* 1a to envelop or obscure (as if) with a cloud b to make opaque or murky by condensation, smoke, etc 2 to make unclear or confused 3 to taint, sully ⟨*a* ~ *ed reputation*⟩ 4 to cast gloom over

cloudburst *n* a sudden very heavy fall of rain

cloud chamber *n* a vessel containing saturated water vapour whose sudden expansion reveals the passage of an ionizing particle (e g an alpha particle) by a trail of visible droplets

cloud nine *n* a feeling of extreme well-being or elation – usu + *on*; infml

cloudy *adj* 1 (having a sky) overcast with clouds 2 not clear or transparent ⟨~ *beer*⟩ ⟨*a* ~ *mirror*⟩ – **cloudily** *adv*, **cloudiness** *n*

¹**clout** *n* 1 *dial chiefly N Eng & Scot* CLOTH 2; *specif* a piece of cloth or rag used for household tasks (e g polishing or cleaning) – often in combination ⟨*dish*clout⟩ 2 a blow or lusty hit with the hand, cricket bat, etc 3 influence; *esp* effective political power USE (2&3) infml

²**clout** *vt* to hit forcefully – infml

¹**clove** *n* any of the small bulbs (e g in garlic) developed as parts of a larger bulb

²clove past of CLEAVE
³clove n (a tree of the myrtle family that bears) a flower bud that is used dried as a spice
clove hitch n a knot used to secure a rope temporarily to a spar or another rope
cloven past part of ²CLEAVE
cloven foot n a foot (e g of a sheep) divided into 2 parts at the end farthest from the body – **cloven-footed** adj
cloven hoof n CLOVEN FOOT – **cloven-hoofed** adj
clover n any of a genus of leguminous plants having leaves with 3 leaflets and flowers in dense heads – **in clover** in prosperity or in pleasant circumstances
cloverleaf n, pl **cloverleafs, cloverleaves** a road junction whose plan resembles the arrangement of leaves in a 4-leaved clover and that connects 2 major roads at different levels
clown n 1 a jester in an entertainment (e g a play); specif a grotesquely dressed comedy performer in a circus 2 one who habitually plays the buffoon; a joker – **clown** vi, **clownery** n, **clownish** adj, **clownishly** adv, **clownishness** n
cloy vt to surfeit with an excess, usu of sthg orig pleasing ~ vi to cause surfeit – **cloyingly** adv
¹club n 1a a heavy stick thicker at one end than the other and used as a hand weapon b a stick or bat used to hit a ball in golf and other games c a light spar 2a a playing card marked with 1 or more black figures in the shape of a cloverleaf b pl but sing or pl in constr the suit comprising cards identified by this figure 3a sing or pl in constr (1) an association of people for a specified object, usu jointly supported and meeting periodically ⟨judo ~⟩ (2) an often exclusive association of people that has premises available as a congenial place of retreat or temporary residence or for dining at b the meeting place or premises of a club c a group of people who agree to make regular payments or purchases in order to secure some advantage ⟨book ~⟩ d a nightclub – **in the club** of a woman pregnant – infml
²club vb -bb- vt to beat or strike (as if) with a club ~ vi to combine to share a common expense or object – usu + together
clubbable, clubable adj sociable
clubfoot n a misshapen foot twisted out of position from birth – **clubfooted** adj
¹cluck vi 1 to make a cluck 2 to express fussy interest or concern – usu + over; infml ~ vt to call with a cluck
²cluck n the characteristic guttural sound made by a hen
¹clue n 1 also **clew** sthg that guides via intricate procedure to the solution of a problem 2 CLEW 2
²clue vt **clueing, cluing** 1 CLEW 2 2 also **clew** to inform – usu + in or up; infml ⟨~ me in on how it happened⟩
clueless adj, Br hopelessly ignorant or lacking in sense – infml
¹clump n 1 a compact group of things of the same kind, esp trees or bushes; a cluster 2 a compact mass 3 a heavy tramping sound – **clumpy** adj
²clump vi 1 to tread clumsily and noisily 2 to form clumps ~ vt to arrange in or cause to form clumps
clumsy adj 1a awkward and ungraceful in movement or action b lacking tact or subtlety ⟨a ~ joke⟩ 2 awkwardly or poorly made; unwieldy – **clumsily** adv, **clumsiness** n
clung past of CLING
¹cluster n a compact group formed by a number of similar things or people; a bunch: e g a a group of faint stars or galaxies that appear close together and have common properties (e g distance and motion) b the group of 4 cups that connect the teats of a cow to a milking machine – **clustery** adj

²cluster vt to collect into a cluster ~ vi to grow or assemble in a cluster
¹clutch vt to grasp or hold (as if) with the hand or claws, esp tightly or suddenly ~ vi 1 to seek to grasp and hold – often + at 2 to operate the clutch on a motor vehicle
²clutch n 1 (the claws or a hand in) the act of grasping or seizing firmly 2 (a lever or pedal operating) a coupling used to connect and disconnect a driving and a driven part of a mechanism
³clutch n a nest of eggs or a brood of chicks; broadly a group, bunch
¹clutter vt to fill or cover with scattered or disordered things – often + up
²clutter n 1a a crowded or confused mass or collection b scattered or disordered material 2 interfering echoes visible on a radar screen caused by reflection from objects other than the target
co- prefix 1 with; together; joint ⟨coexist⟩ ⟨coheir⟩ ⟨coeducation⟩ 2 in or to the same degree ⟨coextensive⟩ 3a associate; fellow ⟨coauthor⟩ ⟨co-star⟩ b deputy; assistant ⟨copilot⟩
¹coach n 1a a large usu closed four-wheeled carriage b a railway carriage c a usu single-deck bus used esp for long-distance or charter work 2a a private tutor b sby who instructs or trains a performer, sportsman, etc
²coach vt 1 to train intensively by instruction, demonstration, and practice 2 to act as coach to ~ vi 1 to go in a coach 2 to instruct, direct, or prompt as a coach – **coacher** n
coachman n a man who drives or whose business is to drive a coach or carriage
coachwork n the bodywork of a road or rail vehicle
coadjutor n an assistant; specif a bishop assisting a diocesan bishop and often having the right of succession – **coadjutor** adj
coagulant n sthg that produces coagulation
coagulate vb to (cause to) become viscous or thickened into a coherent mass; curdle, clot – **coagulable** adj, **coagulability** n, **coagulation** n
coal n 1 a piece of glowing, burning, or burnt carbonized material (e g partly burnt wood) 2 a (small piece or broken up quantity of) black or blackish solid combustible mineral consisting chiefly of carbonized vegetable matter and widely used as a natural fuel
coalesce vi to unite into a whole; fuse – **coalescence** n, **coalescent** adj
coalfield n a region in which deposits of coal occur
coal gas n gas made from burning coal; esp gas made by carbonizing bituminous coal and used for heating and lighting
coalhole n 1 a hole or chute for receiving coal 2 Br a compartment for storing coal
coalition n 1a an act of coalescing; a union b a body formed by the union of orig distinct elements 2 sing or pl in constr a temporary alliance (e g of political parties) for joint action (e g to form a government) – **coalitionist** n
coal tar n tar obtained by the distilling of bituminous coal and used esp in making dyes and drugs
coarse adj 1 of ordinary or inferior quality or value; common 2a(1) composed of relatively large particles ⟨~ sand⟩ (2) rough in texture or tone ⟨~ cloth⟩ ⟨a ~ bell⟩ b adjusted or designed for heavy, fast, or less delicate work ⟨a ~ saw with large teeth⟩ c not precise or detailed with respect to adjustment or discrimination 3 crude or unrefined in taste, manners, or language – **coarsely** adv, **coarseness** n
coarse fish n, chiefly Br any freshwater fish not belonging to the salmon family – **coarse fishing** n

coarsen vb to make or become coarse

¹coast n the land near a shore; the seashore – **coastal** adj, **coastally** adv, **coastwards** adv

²coast vt to sail along the shore of ~ vi **1** to sail along the shore **2a** to slide, glide, etc downhill by the force of gravity **b** to move along (as if) without further application of propulsive power **c** to proceed easily without special application of effort or concern

coaster n **1** a small vessel trading from port to port along a coast **2a** a tray or stand, esp of silver, for a decanter **b** a small mat used, esp under a drinks glass, to protect a surface

coastguard n (a member of) a force responsible for maintaining lookout posts round the coast of the UK for mounting rescues at sea, preventing smuggling, etc

coastline n the outline or shape of a coast

¹coat n **1** an outer garment that has sleeves and usu opens the full length of the centre front **2** the external covering of an animal **3** a protective layer; a coating – **coated** adj

²coat vt to cover or spread with a protective or enclosing layer – **coater** n

coat hanger n ²HANGER

coating n a layer of one substance covering another

coat of arms n, pl **coats of arms** (a tabard or surcoat embroidered with) a set of distinctive heraldic shapes or representations, usu depicted on a shield, that is the central part of a heraldic achievement

coat tails n pl two long tapering skirts at the back of a man's coat

coax vt **1** to influence or gently urge by caresses or flattery; wheedle **2** to draw or gain by means of gentle urging or flattery ⟨~ed an answer out of her⟩ **3** to manipulate with great perseverance and skill towards a desired condition

¹cob n **1** a male swan **2** CORNCOB 1 **3** (any of) a breed of short-legged stocky horses **4** Br a small rounded usu crusty loaf – **cobby** adj

²cob n a building material used chiefly in SW England and consisting of natural clay or chalk mixed with straw or hair as a binder; also a house built of cob

cobalt n a tough bivalent or trivalent silver-white magnetic metallic element – **cobaltic** adj, **cobaltous** adj

cobber n, Austr a man's male friend; a mate – infml

¹cobble vt **cobbling** **1** to repair (esp shoes); also to make (esp shoes) **2** to make or assemble roughly or hastily – usu + together

²cobble n a naturally rounded stone of a size suitable for paving a street

³cobble vt to pave with cobblestones

cobbler n **1** a mender or maker of leather goods, esp shoes **2** pl, Br nonsense, rubbish – often used interjectionally; infml

cobblestone n a cobble – **cobblestoned** adj

cobra n any of several venomous Asiatic and African snakes that have grooved fangs and when excited expand the skin of the neck into a hood

cobweb n **1** (a) spider's web **2** a single thread spun by a spider – **cobwebbed** adj, **cobwebby** adj

coca n (the dried cocaine-containing leaves of) a S American shrub

cocaine n an alkaloid that is obtained from coca leaves, has been used as a local anaesthetic, and is a common drug of abuse that can result in psychological dependence – **cocainism** n

coccyx n, pl **coccyges** also **coccyxes** the end of the spinal column below the sacrum in human beings and the tailless apes – **coccygeal** adj

cochineal n a red dyestuff consisting of the dried bodies of female cochineal insects, used esp as a colouring agent for food

cochlea n, pl **cochleas, cochleae** a coiled part of the inner ear of higher vertebrates that is filled with liquid through which sound waves are transmitted to the auditory nerve – **cochlear** adj

¹cock n **1a** the (adult) male of various birds, specif the domestic fowl **b** the male of fish, crabs, lobsters, and other aquatic animals **2** a device (e g a tap or valve) for regulating the flow of a liquid **3** the hammer of a firearm or its position when cocked ready for firing **4** Br – used as a term of infml address to a man **5** the penis – vulg **6** Br nonsense, rubbish – slang

²cock vi to set the hammer of a firearm ready for firing ~ vt **1a** to draw back and set the hammer of (a firearm) for firing **b** to draw or bend back in preparation for throwing or hitting **2a** to set erect ⟨the dog ~ed its ears⟩ **b** to turn, tip, or tilt, usu to one side ⟨~ed his head inquiringly⟩ **3** to turn up (e g the brim of a hat) – **cock a snook** to react with disdain or defiance ⟨cock a snook at authority⟩

³cock n a small pile (e g of hay)

⁴cock vt to put (e g hay) into cocks

cockade n an ornament (e g a rosette or knot of ribbon) worn on the hat as a badge – **cockaded** adj

cock-a-hoop adj triumphantly boastful; exulting – infml

cock-a-leekie n a chicken and leek soup

cockatoo n, pl **cockatoos** any of numerous large noisy usu showy and crested chiefly Australasian parrots

cockchafer n a large European beetle destructive to vegetation

cockcrow n dawn

cocked hat n a hat with brim turned up at 3 places to give a 3-cornered shape

cockerel n a young male domestic fowl

cocker spaniel n a small spaniel with long ears and silky coat

cockeyed adj **1** having a squint **2a** askew, awry **b** somewhat foolish or mad ⟨a ~ scheme⟩ USE infml – **cockeyedly** adv, **cockeyedness** n

¹cockle n CORN COCKLE

²cockle n (the ribbed shell of) a (common edible) bivalve mollusc

³cockle n a pucker or wrinkle – **cockle** vb

cockleshell n **1** the shell of a cockle, scallop, or similar mollusc **2** a light flimsy boat

cockney n **1** a native of London and now esp the E End of London **2** the dialect of (the E End of) London – **cockney** adj, **cockneyfy** vt, **cockneyish** adj, **cockneyism** n

cockpit n **1a** a pit or enclosure for cockfights **b** a place noted for bloody, violent, or prolonged conflict **2a** the rear part of the lowest deck of a sailing warship used as officers' quarters and for treating the wounded **b** a recess below deck level from which a small vessel (e g a yacht) is steered **c** a space in the fuselage of an aeroplane for the pilot (and crew) **d** the driver's compartment in a racing or sports car

cockroach n any of numerous omnivorous usu dark brown chiefly nocturnal insects that include some that are domestic pests

cocksure adj cocky – infml – **cocksurely** adv, **cocksureness** n

¹cocktail n **1a** a drink of mixed spirits or of spirits mixed with flavourings **b** sthg resembling or suggesting such a drink; esp a mixture of diverse elements **2a** an appetizer of tomato juice, shellfish, etc **b** a dish of finely chopped mixed fruits

²cocktail *adj* of, appropriate to accompany, or set aside for cocktails or a cocktail party ⟨*the ~ hour*⟩ ⟨*a ~ dress*⟩

cock up *vt, chiefly Br* to spoil or render a failure by bungling or incompetence – *slang* – **cock-up** *n*

¹cocky *adj* marked by overconfidence or presumptuousness – *infml* – **cockily** *adv*, **cockiness** *n*

²cocky *n, Austr & NZ* one who owns a small farm

coco *n, pl* **cocos** COCONUT PALM

cocoa *n* 1 the cacao tree 2a powdered ground roasted cacao seeds from which some fat has been removed **b** a beverage made by mixing cocoa with usu hot milk

coconut *also* **cocoanut** *n* the large oval fruit of the coconut palm whose outer fibrous husk yields coir and whose nut contains thick edible meat and a thick sweet milk; *also* COCONUT PALM

coconut palm *n* a tall (American) tropical palm

coconut shy *n* a stall at a funfair where one throws balls at coconuts on stands

¹cocoon *n* 1 (an animal's protective covering similar to) a (silk) envelope which an insect larva forms about itself and in which it passes the pupa stage 2 a (protective) covering like a cocoon (e g for an aeroplane in storage) 3 a sheltered or insulated state of existence

²cocoon *vt* to wrap or envelop, esp tightly, (as if) in a cocoon

¹cod, codfish *n, pl* **cod** (the flesh of) a soft-finned N Atlantic food fish or related Pacific fish

²cod *n, Br* nonsense – *slang*

coda *n* 1 a concluding musical section that is formally distinct from the main structure 2 sthg that serves to round out or conclude sthg, esp a literary or dramatic work, and that has an interest of its own

coddle *vt* **coddling** 1 to cook (esp eggs) slowly in a liquid just below the boiling point 2 to treat with extreme care; pamper – **coddler** *n*

¹code *n* 1 a systematic body of laws, esp with statutory force 2 a system of principles or maxims ⟨*moral ~*⟩ 3a a system of signals for communication **b** a system of symbols used to represent assigned and often secret meanings – **codeless** *adj*

²code *vt* 1 to put into the form or symbols of a code 2 to specify (an amino acid, protein, etc) in terms of the genetic code ~*vi* to be or contain the genetic code *for* an amino acid, protein, etc – **codable** *adj*, **coder** *n*

codeine *n* a derivative of morphine that is weaker in action than morphine and is given orally to relieve pain and coughing

codex *n, pl* **codices** a manuscript book, esp of biblical or classical texts

codger *n* an old and mildly eccentric man – esp in *old codger*; *infml*

codicil *n* 1 a modifying clause added to a will 2 an appendix, supplement – **codicillary** *adj*

codify *vt* 1 to reduce to a code 2 to express in a systematic form – **codifiable** *adj*, **codifiability** *n*, **codification** *n*

¹codling *n* a young cod

²codling *n* any of several elongated greenish cooking apples

cod-liver oil *n* an oil obtained from the liver of the cod and closely related fishes and used as a source of vitamins A and D

codpiece *n* a flap or bag concealing an opening in the front of men's breeches, esp in the 15th and 16th c

codswallop *n, chiefly Br* nonsense – *slang*

coed *n* 1 a coeducational school 2 *NAm* a female student in a coeducational institution *USE* infml – **coed** *adj*

coeducation *n* the education of students of both sexes at the same institution – **coeducational** *adj*, **coeducationally** *adv*

coefficient *n* 1 any of the factors, esp variable quantities, that are multiplied together in a mathematical product considered in relation to a usu specified factor ⟨*in the expression* 5xy *the ~ of* xy *is* 5⟩ 2 a number that serves as a measure of some property or characteristic (e g of a device or process) ⟨*~ of expansion of a metal*⟩

coelacanth *n* any of a family of mostly extinct fishes – **coelacanthine, coelacanthous** *adj*

coelenterate *n* any of a phylum of invertebrate animals including the corals, sea anemones, and jellyfishes – **coelenterate** *adj*

coenzyme *n* a nonprotein compound that combines with a protein to form an active enzyme and whose activity cannot be destroyed by heat – **coenzymatic** *adj*, **coenzymatically** *adv*

coerce *vt* 1 to restrain or dominate by authority or force 2 to compel to an act or choice – often + *into* 3 to enforce or bring about by force or threat – **coercible** *adj*, **coercive** *adj*, **coercion** *n*

coeval *adj* of the same or equal age, antiquity, or duration – **coeval** *n*, **coevality** *n*

coexist *vi* 1 to exist together or at the same time 2 to live in peace with each other – **coexistence** *n*, **coexistent** *adj*

coextensive *adj* having the same scope or boundaries in space or time – **coextensively** *adv*

coffee *n* 1a a beverage made by percolation, infusion, or decoction from the roasted seeds of a coffee tree; *also* these seeds either green or roasted **b** COFFEE TREE 2 a cup of coffee 3 a time when coffee is drunk

coffeehouse *n* an establishment that sells refreshments and commonly serves as an informal club

coffee-table *adj, of a publication* being outsize and lavishly produced (e g with extensive use of full-colour illustrations) as if for display on a coffee table ⟨*a pompous ~ tome – TLS*⟩

coffee table *n* a low table usu placed in a living room

coffee tree *n* a large African evergreen shrub or small tree of the madder family, widely cultivated in warm regions for its seeds

coffer *n* 1 a chest, box; *esp* a strongbox 2 a treasury, exchequer; *broadly* a store of wealth – usu pl with sing. meaning 3a a caisson **b** a cofferdam 4 a recessed decorative panel in a vault, ceiling, etc

cofferdam *n* a watertight enclosure from which water is pumped to allow construction or repair (e g of a pier or ship's hull)

coffin *n* 1 a box or chest for the burial of a corpse 2 the horny body forming the hoof of a horse's foot – **coffin** *vt*

¹cog *n* 1 a tooth on the rim of a wheel or gear 2 a subordinate person or part – **cogged** *adj*

²cog *vt* **-gg-** to direct the fall of (dice) fraudulently

cogent *adj* appealing forcibly to the mind or reason; convincing ⟨*~ evidence*⟩ – **cogency** *n*, **cogently** *adv*

cogitate *vi* to ponder, usu intently and objectively; meditate ~ *vt* to cogitate on *USE* fml – **cogitation** *n*, **cogitative** *adj*

cognac *n* a French brandy, specif one from the departments of Charente and Charente-Maritime distilled from white wine

¹cognate *adj* 1 related by blood, esp on the mother's side 2a related by derivation or borrowing or by descent from the same ancestral language ⟨*German* vater *is ~ with* father⟩ **b** *of a noun* related in form and meaning to the verb of which it is the object 3 of the same or similar nature – **cognately** *adv*, **cognateness, cognation** *n*

²cognate *n* sthg (e g a word) cognate with another

cognition *n* (a product of) the act or process of knowing

cold sweat

that involves the processing of sensory information and includes perception, awareness, and judgment – **cognitional** adj, **cognitive** adj

cognizance, -isance n 1 jurisdiction, control 2 the ability to perceive or understand 3 notice, heed ⟨take ~ of a fault⟩ USE fml or technical

cognizant, -isant adj having special or certain knowledge, often from firsthand sources – fml or technical

cognomen n, pl **cognomens, cognomina** 1 a surname; esp the family (and usu 3rd) name of sby named in the ancient Roman fashion 2 a name; esp a descriptive nickname – fml or humor – **cognominal** adj

cognoscente n, pl **cognoscenti** a person having or claiming expert knowledge; a connoisseur

cogwheel n a wheel with cogs or teeth

cohabit vi to live or exist together, specif as husband and wife – **cohabitant** n, **cohabitation** n

cohere vi 1 to hold together firmly as parts of the same mass; broadly to stick, adhere 2a to become united in ideas or interests b to be logically or aesthetically consistent

coherent adj 1 having the quality of cohering 2a logically consistent ⟨a ~ argument⟩ b showing a unity of thought or purpose 3 relating to, composed of, or producing (electromagnetic) waves in phase with each other ⟨~ light⟩ – **coherence, coherency** n, **coherently** adv

cohesion n the act or process of cohering – **cohesionless** adj, **cohesive** adj, **cohesively** adv, **cohesiveness** n

cohort n 1a a group of soldiers; esp, sing or pl in constr a division of a Roman legion b a band, group c a group of individuals having age, class membership, or other statistical factors in common in a study of the population 2 chiefly NAm a companion, accomplice

¹**coif** n a close-fitting cap: e g a a hoodlike bonnet worn by nuns under a veil b a protective usu metal skullcap formerly worn under a hood of mail

²**coif** vt **-ff-** 1 to cover or dress (as if) with a coif 2 to arrange (hair) by brushing, combing, or curling

coiffeur n a hairdresser

coiffure n a hairstyle – **coiffured** adj

¹**coil** vt to wind into rings or spirals ~ vi 1 to move in a circular, spiral, or winding course 2 to form or lie in a coil – **coilability** n

²**coil** n 1a (a length of rope, cable, etc gathered into) a series of loops; a spiral b a single loop of a coil 2 a number of turns of wire, esp in spiral form, usu for electromagnetic effect or for providing electrical resistance 3 a series of connected pipes in rows, layers, or windings 4 (a stamp from) a roll of postage stamps

¹**coin** n 1 a usu thin round piece of metal issued as money 2 metal money

²**coin** vt 1a to make (a coin), esp by stamping; mint b to convert (metal) into coins 2 to create, invent ⟨~ a phrase⟩ 3 to make or earn (money) rapidly and in large quantity – often in coin it

coinage n 1 coining or (a large number of) coins 2 sthg (e g a word) made up or invented

coincide vi 1 to occupy the same place in space or time 2 to correspond in nature, character, function, or position 3 to be in accord or agreement; concur

coincidence n 1 the act or condition of coinciding; a correspondence 2 (an example of) the chance occurrence at the same time or place of 2 or more events that appear to be related or similar – **coincidental** adj, **coincidentally** adv

coincident adj 1 occupying the same space or time ⟨~ points⟩ 2 of similar nature; harmonious – **coincidently** adv

coir n a stiff coarse fibre from the husk of a coconut

coitus n the natural conveying of semen to the female reproductive tract; broadly SEXUAL INTERCOURSE – **coital** adj, **coitally** adv

coitus interruptus n coitus which is purposely interrupted in order to prevent ejaculation of sperm into the vagina

¹**coke** n a solid porous fuel that remains after gases have been driven from coal by heating

²**coke** vt to convert (coal) into coke

³**coke** n cocaine – slang

col n a depression or pass in a mountain ridge or range

¹**col-** – see COM-

²**col-, coli-, colo-** comb form 1 colon ⟨colitis⟩ ⟨colostomy⟩ 2 colon bacillus ⟨coliform⟩ ⟨coliphage⟩

¹**cola** pl of ¹ ²COLON

²**cola** also **kola** n a carbonated soft drink flavoured with extract from coca leaves, kola nut, sugar, caramel, and acid and aromatic substances

colander, cullender n a perforated bowl-shaped utensil for washing or draining food

¹**cold** adj 1 having a low temperature, often below some normal temperature or below that compatible with human comfort 2a marked by lack of warm feeling; unemotional; also unfriendly ⟨a ~ stare⟩ b marked by deliberation or calculation ⟨a ~ act of aggression⟩ 3a previously cooked but served cold ⟨~ meats⟩ b not (sufficiently) hot or heated c made cold ⟨~ drinks⟩ d of a process performed on an unheated material ⟨~ conditioning of steel prior to rolling⟩ 4a depressing, cheerless b producing a sensation of cold; chilling ⟨~ blank walls⟩ c COOL 5 5a dead b unconscious ⟨knocked out ~⟩ 6a retaining only faint scents, traces, or clues ⟨a ~ trail⟩ b far from a goal, object, or solution sought c stale, uninteresting ⟨~ news⟩ 7 presented or regarded in a straightforward way; impersonal ⟨the ~ facts⟩ 8 unprepared 9 intense yet without the usual outward effects ⟨a ~ fury⟩ – **coldish** adj, **coldly** adv, **coldness** n – **in cold blood** with premeditation; deliberately

²**cold** n 1a a condition of low temperature b cold weather 2 bodily sensation produced by relative lack of heat; chill 3 a bodily disorder popularly associated with chilling; specif COMMON COLD 4 a state of neglect or deprivation – esp in come/bring in out of the cold

³**cold** adv with utter finality; absolutely ⟨was turned down ~⟩

cold-blooded adj 1a done or acting without consideration or compunction; ruthless ⟨~ murder⟩ b concerned only with the facts; emotionless 2 having a body temperature not internally regulated but approximating to that of the environment – **cold-bloodedly** adv, **cold-bloodedness** n

cold chisel n a chisel made of steel of a strength and temper suitable for chipping or cutting cold metal

cold comfort n scant consolation

cold cream n a thick oily often perfumed cream for cleansing and soothing the skin of the neck, face, etc

cold feet n pl apprehension or doubt strong enough to prevent a planned course of action

cold frame n a usu glass-covered frame without artificial heat used to protect plants and seedlings

cold front n an advancing edge of a cold air mass

cold shoulder n intentionally cold or unsympathetic treatment – usu + the – **cold-shoulder** vt

cold sore n (herpes simplex when occurring as) 1 or more blisters appearing round or inside the mouth

cold storage n a condition of being held or continued without being acted on; abeyance

cold sweat n concurrent perspiration and chill, usu associated with fear, pain, or shock

cold war *n* **1** a conflict carried on by methods short of military action **2** a hostile but nonviolent relationship – **cold warrior** *n*

coleslaw *n* a salad of raw sliced or chopped white cabbage

coley *n, pl* **coley,** *esp for different types* **coleys** *Br* an important N Atlantic food fish closely related to the cod

colic *n* a paroxysm of abdominal pain localized in the intestines or other hollow organ and caused by spasm, obstruction, or twisting – **colicky** *adj*

colitis *n* inflammation of the colon

collaborate *vi* **1** to work together or with another (e g in an intellectual endeavour) **2** to cooperate with an enemy of one's country – **collaborator** *n,* **collaborative** *adj,* **collaboration** *n*

collage *n* **1** an (abstract) composition made of pieces of paper, wood, cloth, etc fixed to a surface **2** an assembly of diverse fragments ⟨*a ~ of ideas*⟩ – **collagist** *n*

¹**collapse** *vi* **1** to break down completely; disintegrate **2** to fall in or give way abruptly and completely (e g through compression) **3** to lose force, value, or effect suddenly **4** to break down in energy, stamina, or self-control through exhaustion or disease; *esp* to fall helpless or unconscious **5** to fold down into a more compact shape ⟨*a telescope that ~s*⟩ ~*vt* to cause to collapse – **collapsible** *adj,* **collapsibility** *n*

²**collapse** *n* **1a** an (extreme) breakdown in energy, strength, or self-control **b** an airless state of (part of) a lung **2** the act or an instance of collapsing

¹**collar** *n* **1** a band, strip, or chain worn round the neck: e g **a** a band that serves to finish or decorate the neckline of a garment; *esp* one that is turned over **b** a band fitted about the neck of an animal **c** a part of the harness of draught animals that fits over the shoulders and takes the strain when a load is drawn **d** a protective or supportive device worn round the neck **2** sthg resembling a collar (e g a ring or round flange to restrain motion or hold sthg in place) **3** any of various animal structures or markings similar to a collar in appearance or form **4** a cut of bacon from the neck of a pig – **collared** *adj,* **collarless** *adj*

²**collar** *vt* **1a** to seize by the collar or neck; *broadly* to apprehend **b** to get control of **2** to buttonhole *USE infml*

collarbone *n* the clavicle

collate *vt* **1** to collect and compare carefully in order to verify and often to integrate or arrange in order **2** to appoint (a priest) to a Church of England benefice of which the bishop is the patron **3** to assemble in proper order ⟨*~ printed sheets*⟩ – **collator** *n*

¹**collateral** *adj* **1** accompanying as secondary or subordinate **2** belonging to the same ancestral stock but not in a direct line of descent – usu contrasted with *lineal* **3** parallel or corresponding in position, time, or significance **4** of or being collateral – **collaterally** *adv,* **collaterality** *n*

²**collateral** *n* **1** a collateral relative **2** property pledged by a borrower to protect the interests of the lender

collation *n* **1** a light meal; *esp* one allowed on fast days in place of lunch or supper **2** the act, process, or result of collating

colleague *n* a fellow worker, esp in a profession

¹**collect** *n* a short prayer comprising an invocation, petition, and conclusion; *specif, often cap* one preceding the Epistle read at Communion

²**collect** *vt* **1a** to bring together into 1 body or place; *specif* to assemble a collection of **b** to gather or exact from a number of sources ⟨*~ taxes*⟩ **2** to accumulate, gather ⟨*books ~ dust*⟩ **3** to gain or regain control of ⟨*~ his*

thoughts⟩ **4** to claim as due and receive possession or payment of ⟨*~ social security*⟩ **5** to provide transport or escort for ⟨*~ the children from school*⟩ **6** *chiefly Br* to gain, obtain ~*vi* **1** to come together in a band, group, or mass; gather ⟨*the troops ~ed*⟩ **2a** to assemble a collection **b** to receive payment ⟨*~ing on his insurance*⟩ – **collectible, collectable** *adj*

³**collect** *adv or adj, NAm* to be paid for by the receiver ⟨*send the package ~*⟩ ⟨*a ~ telephone call*⟩

collected *adj* **1** exhibiting calmness and composure **2** *of a gait or horse* (performed) in a state of collection – **collectedly** *adv,* **collectedness** *n*

collection *n* **1** sthg collected; *esp* an accumulation of objects gathered for study, comparison, or exhibition **2** a standard pose of a well-schooled and responsive riding horse with its head arched and its hocks well under the body

¹**collective** *adj* **1** denoting a number of individuals considered as 1 group ⟨*flock is a ~ word*⟩ **2** of a fruit MULTIPLE **4** **3** of, made, or held in common by a group of individuals ⟨*~ responsibility*⟩ **4** collectivized ⟨*a ~ farm*⟩ – **collectively** *adv*

²**collective** *n* **1** *sing or pl in constr* a collective body; a group **2** a cooperative organization; *specif* a collective farm

collective bargaining *n* negotiation between an employer and union representatives usu on wages, hours, and working conditions

collectivism *n* a political or economic theory advocating collective control, esp over production and distribution – **collectivist** *adj or n,* **collectivistic** *adj,* **collectivistically** *adv*

collectivize, -ise *vt* to organize under collective control – **collectivization** *n*

collector *n* **1a** an official who collects funds, esp money **b** one who makes a collection ⟨*a stamp ~*⟩ **2** a conductor maintaining contact between moving and stationary parts of an electric circuit **3** a region in a transistor that collects charge carriers – **collectorship** *n*

colleen *n* **1** an Irish girl **2** *Irish* a girl

college *n* **1** a building used for an educational or religious purpose **2a** a self-governing endowed constituent body of a university offering instruction and often living quarters but not granting degrees **b** an institution offering vocational or technical instruction ⟨*business ~*⟩ ⟨*art ~*⟩ **3** an organized body of people engaged in a common pursuit **4** *chiefly Br* a public school or private secondary school; *also* a state school for older pupils ⟨*a Sixth-form ~*⟩ *USE* (except 1) sing. or pl in constr – **college** *adj*

collegiate *adj* **1** of a collegiate church **2** of or comprising a college – **collegiately** *adv*

collegiate church *n* a church other than a cathedral that has a chapter of canons

collide *vi* **1** to come together forcibly **2** to come into conflict

collie *n* a large dog of any of several varieties of a breed developed in Scotland, esp for use in herding sheep and cattle

collier *n* **1** a coal miner **2** a ship for transporting coal

colliery *n* a coal mine and its associated buildings

collision *n* **1** an act or instance of colliding; a clash **2** an encounter between particles (e g atoms or molecules) resulting in exchange or transformation of energy – **collisional** *adj*

collision course *n* a course or approach that would result in collision or conflict if continued unaltered

collocate *vt* to set or arrange in a place or position; *esp* to set side by side – *fml* ~*vi, of a linguistic element* to form part of a collocation

collocation *n* the act or result of placing or arranging together; *specif* a noticeable arrangement or joining together of linguistic elements (e g words) – **collocational** *adj*

colloid *n* **1a** a substance composed of particles that are too small to be seen with a light microscope but too large to form a true solution and that will typically diffract a beam of light **b** a system consisting of a colloid together with the gaseous, liquid, or solid medium in which it is dispersed **2** a gelatinous substance found in tissues, esp in disease – **colloidal** *adj*, **colloidally** *adv*

colloquial *adj* used in, characteristic of, or using the style of familiar and informal conversation; conversational – **colloquial** *n*, **colloquially** *adv*, **colloquiality** *n*

colloquialism *n* **1** a colloquial expression **2** colloquial style

colloquy *n* a formal conversation or dialogue

collude *vi* to conspire, plot

collusion *n* secret agreement or cooperation for an illegal or deceitful purpose – **collusive** *adj*, **collusively** *adv*

collywobbles *n pl* **1** stomachache **2** qualms, butterflies USE + *the*; *infml*

cologne *n* TOILET WATER – **cologned** *adj*

¹colon *n*, *pl* **colons, cola** the part of the large intestine that extends from the caecum to the rectum – **colonic** *adj*

²colon *n*, *pl* **colons, cola** **1** a punctuation mark : used chiefly to direct attention to matter that follows, to introduce the words of a speaker (e g in a play), in various references (e g in John 4:10), and, esp in NAm, between the parts of an expression of time in hours and minutes **2** the sign : used in a ratio where it is usu read as 'to' (e g in 4:1), or in phonetic transcription (e g in i:) where it signals a change in length and in vowel quality

colonel *n* an officer in the army or US airforce ranking below brigadier or brigadier general – **colonelcy** *n*

Colonel Blimp *n* a pompous person with out-of-date or ultraconservative views; *broadly* a reactionary – **Colonel Blimpism** *n*

¹colonial *adj* **1** (characteristic) of a colony **2** *often cap* made or prevailing in America before 1776 ⟨~ *architecture*⟩ **3** possessing or composed of colonies ⟨*Britain's* ~ *empire*⟩ – **colonialize** *vt*, **colonially** *adv*, **colonialness** *n*

²colonial *n* a member or inhabitant of a (British Crown) colony

colonialism *n* (a policy based on) control by a state over a dependent area or people – **colonialist** *n or adj*, **colonialistic** *adj*

colonist *n* **1** a member or inhabitant of a colony **2** one who colonizes or settles in a new country

colonize, -ise *vt* to establish a colony in, on, or of to make or establish a colony; settle – **colonizer** *n*, **colonization** *n*

colonnade *n* a row of columns, usu supporting an entablature – **colonnaded** *adj*

colony *n* **1** a body of settlers living in a new territory but subject to control by the parent state; *also* their territory **2** a distinguishable localized population within a species ⟨*a* ~ *of termites*⟩ **3a** a mass of microorganisms, usu growing in or on a solid medium **b** all the units of a compound animal (e g a coral) **4** (the area occupied by) a group of individuals with common interests living close together ⟨*an artists'* ~⟩ **5** a group of people segregated from the general public ⟨*a leper* ~⟩ ⟨*a penal* ~⟩

color *vb or n, chiefly NAm* (to) colour

Colorado beetle *n* a black-and-yellow striped beetle that feeds on the leaves of the potato

coloration, *Br also* **colouration** *n* **1** COLOURING 1c(1), COMPLEXION 1 ⟨*the dark* ~ *of his skin*⟩ **2** use or choice of colours (e g by an artist) **3** an arrangement or range of colours ⟨*the brilliant* ~ *of a butterfly's wing*⟩

coloratura *n* (a singer who uses) elaborate embellishment in vocal music

colossal *adj* of or like a colossus; *esp* of very great size or degree ⟨*a* ~ *building*⟩ ⟨*a* ~ *blunder*⟩ – **colossally** *adv*

colossus *n, pl* **colossuses, colossi** **1** a statue of gigantic size **2** sby or sthg remarkably preeminent

colostrum *n* the milk that is secreted for a few days after giving birth and is characterized by high protein and antibody content – **colostral** *adj*

¹colour, *NAm chiefly* **color** *n* **1a** the visual sensation (e g red or grey) caused by the wavelength of perceived light that enables one to differentiate otherwise identical objects **b** the aspect of objects and light sources that may be described in terms of hue, lightness, and saturation for objects and hue, brightness, and saturation for light sources **c** a hue, esp as opposed to black, white, or grey **2** an outward often deceptive show; an appearance (of authenticity) ⟨*his wounds gave* ~ *to his story*⟩ **3** the tint characteristic of good health **4a** an identifying badge, pennant, or flag (e g of a ship or regiment) **b** coloured clothing distinguishing one as a member of a usu specified group or as a representative of a usu specified person or thing **c** any of the 5 principal heraldic tinctures azure, vert, sable, gules, and purpure **5** character, nature ⟨*showed himself in his true* ~ s⟩ **6** the use or combination of colours (e g by painters) **7** vitality, interest ⟨*the play had a good deal of* ~ *to it*⟩ **8** a pigment **9** tonal quality in music **10** skin pigmentation other than white, characteristic of race **11** *Br* the award made to a regular member of a team ⟨*got my cricket* ~ s⟩ USE (4a, 4b, 5, & 11) usu pl with sing. meaning

²colour, *NAm chiefly* **color** *vt* **1a** to give colour to **b** to change the colour of **2** to change as if by dyeing or painting: e g **a** to misrepresent, distort **b** to influence, affect ⟨~ *his judgment*⟩ ~ *vi* to take on or impart colour; *specif* to blush – **colourant** *n*

colour bar *n* a social or legal barrier that prevents coloured people from participating with whites in various activities or restricts their opportunities

colour-blind *adj* (partially) unable to distinguish 1 or more colours – **colour blindness** *n*

¹coloured *adj* **1** having colour **2** marked by exaggeration or bias **3a** of a race other than the white; *esp* BLACK **2 b** *often cap* of mixed race – esp of S Africans of mixed descent

²coloured *n, pl* **coloureds, coloured** *often cap* a coloured person

colourfast *adj* having colour that will not fade or run – **colourfastness** *n*

colourful *adj* **1** having striking colours **2** full of variety or interest – **colourfully** *adv*, **colourfulness** *n*

colouring 1a (the effect produced by combining or) applying colours **b** sthg that produces colour **c**(1) natural colour (2) COMPLEXION 1 ⟨*her dark* ~⟩ **2** an influence, bias **3** a timbre, quality

colourless *adj* lacking colour: e g **a** pallid **b** dull, uninteresting – **colourlessly** *adv*, **colourlessness** *n*

colour scheme *n* a systematic combination of colours ⟨*the* ~ *of a room*⟩

colt *n* **1** a young male horse that is either sexually immature or has not attained an arbitrarily designated age **2** a novice; *esp* a cricketer or rugby player in a junior team

coltish *adj* **1** frisky, playful **2** of or resembling a colt – **coltishly** *adv*, **coltishness** *n*

columbine *n* any of a genus of plants of the buttercup family with showy spurred flowers

column n **1a** a vertical arrangement of items or a vertical section of printing on a page ⟨a ~ of figures⟩ **b** a special and usu regular feature in a newspaper or periodical **2** a pillar that usu consists of a round shaft, a capital, and a base **3** sthg resembling a column in form, position, or function ⟨a ~ of water⟩ **4** a long narrow formation of soldiers, vehicles, etc in rows – **columned** adj

columnist n one who writes a newspaper or magazine column

com-, col-, con- prefix with; together; jointly – usu com- before b, p, or m ⟨commingle⟩, col- before l ⟨collinear⟩, and con- before other sounds ⟨concentrate⟩

¹coma n a state of deep unconsciousness caused by disease, injury, etc

²coma n, pl **comae** **1** the head of a comet, usu containing a nucleus **2** an optical aberration in which the image of a point source becomes a comet-shaped blur – **comatic** adj

comatose adj **1** of or suffering from coma **2** characterized by lethargy and sluggishness; torpid ⟨a ~ economy⟩

¹comb n **1a** a toothed instrument used esp for adjusting, cleaning, or confining hair **b** a structure resembling such a comb; esp any of several toothed devices used in handling or ordering textile fibres **c** a currycomb **2** a fleshy crest on the head of a domestic fowl or a related bird **3** a honeycomb – **combed** adj, **comblike** adj

²comb vt **1** to draw a comb through for the purpose of arranging or cleaning **2** to pass across with a scraping or raking action **3a** to eliminate (e g with a comb) by a thorough going over – usu + out **b** to search or examine systematically **4** to use with a combing action ~vi, of a wave to roll over or break into foam

¹combat vb **-tt-** (NAm **-t-, -tt-**) vi to engage in combat; fight ~vt **1** to fight with; battle **2** to struggle against; esp to strive to reduce or eliminate ⟨~ inflation⟩

²combat n **1** a fight or contest between individuals or groups **2** a conflict, controversy **3** active fighting in a war – **combat** adj

combatant n a person, nation, etc that is (ready to be) an active participant in combat – **combatant** adj

combative adj marked by eagerness to fight or contend – **combatively** adv, **combativeness** n

comber n ROLLER 2

combination n **1a** a result or product of combining **b** a group of people working as a team **2** any of the different sets of a usu specified number of individuals that can be chosen from a group and are considered without regard to order within the set **3** pl any of various 1-piece undergarments for the upper and lower parts of the body and legs **4** a (process of) combining, esp to form a chemical compound – **combinational** adj

combination lock n a lock with a mechanism operated by the selection of a specific combination of letters or numbers

combinatorial adj **1** of or involving combinations **2** of or relating to the manipulation of mathematical elements within finite sets ⟨~ mathematics⟩

¹combine vt **1a** to bring into such close relationship as to obscure individual characters; merge **b** to cause to unite into a chemical compound **2** to cause to mix together **3** to possess in combination ~vi **1a** to become one **b** to unite to form a chemical compound **2** to act together – **combiner** n, **combinable** adj, **combinability** n

²combine n **1** a combination of people or organizations, esp in industry or commerce, to further their interests **2** **combine, combine harvester** a harvesting machine that cuts, threshes, and cleans grain while moving over a field

combining form n a linguistic form (e g Franco-) that cannot stand alone but forms compounds with other free or bound forms

combo n, pl **combos** a usu small jazz or dance band

combustible adj **1** capable of (easily) being set on fire **2** easily excited – **combustible** n, **combustibly** adv, **combustibility** n

combustion n **1** a chemical reaction, esp an oxidation, in which light and heat are evolved **2** a slower chemical oxidation – **combustive** adj

¹come vb **came; come** vi **1a** to move towards sthg nearer, esp towards the speaker; approach ⟨~ here⟩ ⟨came running to her mother⟩ **b** to move or journey nearer, esp towards or with the speaker, with a specified purpose ⟨he came to see us⟩ ⟨~ and see what's going on⟩ **c**(1) to reach a specified position in a progression ⟨now we ~ to the section on health⟩ ⟨came short of his goal⟩ (2) to arrive, appear,occur ⟨the time has ~⟩ ⟨they came by train⟩ – used in the subjunctive mood before an expression of future time ⟨a year ago ~ March⟩ **d**(1) to approach, reach, or fulfil a specified condition ⟨this ~s near perfection⟩ – often + to ⟨came to his senses⟩ ⟨~ to the throne⟩ ⟨what are things coming to?⟩ (2) – used with a following infinitive to express arrival at a condition ⟨came to regard him as a friend⟩ or chance occurrence ⟨how did you ~ to be invited?⟩ **2a** to happen, esp by chance ⟨no harm will ~ to you⟩ ⟨~ what may⟩ ⟨how ~s it that you're at home?⟩ **b**(1) to extend, reach ⟨her dress came to her ankles⟩ (2) to amount ⟨that ~s to 75p exactly⟩ **c** to originate, arise, or be the result of ⟨wine ~s from grapes⟩ ⟨~s of sturdy stock⟩ ⟨this ~s of not changing your socks⟩ **d** to fall within the specified limits, scope, or jurisdiction ⟨rabbits ~ under rodents⟩ ⟨this ~s within the terms of the treaty⟩ **e** to issue from ⟨a sob came from her throat⟩ **f** to be available or turn out, usu as specified ⟨this model ~s in several sizes⟩ ⟨good clothes ~ expensive⟩ **g** to be or belong in a specified place or relation ⟨the address ~s above the date⟩; also TAKE PLACE ⟨Monday ~s after Sunday⟩ **h** to take form ⟨the story won't ~⟩ to become ⟨it came untied⟩ ⟨the handle came off⟩; esp to reach a culminating state ⟨it all came right in the end⟩ **4** to experience orgasm – infml ~vt **1a** to move nearer by traversing ⟨has ~ several miles⟩ **b** to reach some state after traversing ⟨has ~ a long way from humble beginnings⟩ **2** to take on the aspect of; play the role of – infml ⟨don't ~ the old soldier with me⟩ – **as it comes** without stipulated additions; specif NEAT 1a – **come a cropper 1** chiefly Br to have a fall or an accident – infml **2** to fail completely – slang – **come across** to meet with or find by chance ⟨came across an interesting problem⟩ – **come by** to get possession of; acquire ⟨good jobs are hard to come by⟩ – **come clean** to tell the whole story; confess – infml – **come home to roost** to rebound upon the perpetrator – **come into** to acquire as a possession or inheritance ⟨came into a fortune⟩ – **come it** chiefly Br to act with bold disrespect ⟨don't come it over me⟩ – slang – **come off it** to cease foolish or pretentious talk or behaviour – usu used imperatively; infml – **come one's way** to fall to one's lot – **come over** to seize suddenly and strangely ⟨what's come over you?⟩ – **come through** to survive (e g an illness) – **come to** to be to be a question of ⟨hopeless when it comes to arithmetic⟩ – **come to a head** to arrive at a culminating point or crisis – **come to grief** to end badly; fail – **come to oneself 1** COME TO **2** to regain self-control – **come to pass** HAPPEN **2** – fml – **come unstuck** COME TO GRIEF ⟨the government came unstuck over food prices⟩ – infml – **come upon** to meet with or find by chance – **to come in** the future; coming ⟨in years to come⟩ – **whether one is coming or going** – used to suggest frenetic disorder and bewilderment ⟨*don't know* whether I'm coming or going⟩

²**come** *interj* – used to express encouragement or to urge reconsideration ⟨~, ~, *it's not as bad as that*⟩

come about *vi* **1** to occur; TAKE PLACE **2** to change direction ⟨*the wind has* come about *into the north*⟩ **3** *of a ship* to turn onto a new tack

come across *vi* **1** to provide sthg demanded or expected, esp sex or money **2** to produce an impression ⟨*he comes* across *as a persuasive speaker*⟩

come again *interj* – used as a request for a remark to be repeated; infml

come along *vi* **1** to appear ⟨*wouldn't just marry the first man that* came along⟩ **2** to hurry – usu imperative

comeback *n* **1a** a means of redress **b** a retrospective criticism of a decision **2** a return to a former state or condition **3** a sharp or witty reply; a retort – infml

come back *vi* **1** to return to memory ⟨*it's all coming* back *to me now*⟩ **2** to reply, retort **3** to regain a former condition or position

Comecon *n* an economic organization formed in 1949 by the countries of the Soviet bloc to coordinate their economies, and promote mutual aid

comedian, *fem* **comedienne** *n* **1** an actor who plays comic roles **2** one, esp a professional entertainer, who aims to be amusing

comedown *n* a striking descent in rank or dignity – infml

come down *vi* **1** to formulate and express one's opinion or decision ⟨came down *in favour of abortion on demand*⟩ **2** *of an aircraft, missile, etc* to land; *esp* to crash **3** to become ill ⟨*they* came down *with measles*⟩ **4** *Br* to return from a university

comedy *n* **1a** a drama of light and amusing character, typically with a happy ending **b** (a work in) the genre of (dramatic) literature dealing with comic or serious subjects in a light or satirical manner **2** a ludicrous or farcical event or series of events **3** the comic aspect of sthg

come-hither *adj* sexually inviting ⟨*that ~ look in his eyes*⟩

come in *vi* **1** to arrive ⟨*I was there when the train* came in⟩ **2** to finish as specified, esp in a competition ⟨came in *third*⟩ **3a** to function in a specified manner; be of use ⟨*to* come in *handy*⟩ **b** to make reply to a signal ⟨came in *loud and clear*⟩ **4** to assume a role or function ⟨*that's where you* come in⟩ – **come in for** to become subject to ⟨coming in for *increasing criticism*⟩

comely *adj* of pleasing appearance; not plain – **comeliness** *n*

come off *vi* **1** to finish or emerge from sthg in a specified condition ⟨came off *well in the contest*⟩ **2** to succeed ⟨*that didn't quite* come off⟩ **3** to happen, occur **4** to become detached

come-on *n* **1** *chiefly NAm* an attraction or enticement (e g in sales promotion) to induce an action **2** an instance of sexually provocative enticement – infml

come on *vi* **1** to advance or begin by degrees ⟨*as darkness* came on, *it got harder to see*⟩ **2** – used in cajoling, pleading, defiance, or encouraging ⟨come on, *you can do it*⟩ **3** COME ALONG 2 **4** to appear on the radio, television, or stage **5** *chiefly NAm* to project a specified appearance ⟨comes on *as a Liberal in his speeches*⟩

come out *vi* **1a** to come to public notice; be published **b** to become evident ⟨*this will* come out *in the full analysis*⟩ **2a** to declare oneself, esp in public utterance ⟨came out *in favour of the popular candidate*⟩ **b** to present oneself openly as homosexual **3** to end up; TURN OUT ⟨*everything will* come out *right*⟩ **4** to make a debut; *specif* to make one's first appearance in society as a debutante – **come out**

in the wash 1 to become known in the course of time **2** to reach a satisfactory conclusion – **come out with** to utter or say, usu unexpectedly

come over *vi* **1a** to change from one side (e g of a controversy) to the other **b** to drop in casually ⟨come over *any time; we're always in*⟩ **2** COME ACROSS 2 ⟨*she* comes over *as a very sincere person*⟩ **3** *Br* to become ⟨*she* came over *all queer*⟩

comer *n* **1** sby who comes or arrives ⟨*all* ~s⟩ **2** *chiefly NAm* sby making rapid progress or showing promise

come round *vi* **1** COME TO **2** to accede to a particular opinion or course of action **3** COME ABOUT 2

comestible *n* food – usu pl with sing. meaning; fml

comet *n* a celestial body that follows a usu highly elliptical orbit round the sun and consists of an indistinct head usu surrounding a bright nucleus, often with a long tail which points away from the sun – **cometary** *adj*

come through *vi* **1** to do what is needed or expected **2** to become communicated

come to *vi* to recover consciousness

come up *vi* **1** to rise in rank or status ⟨*an officer who* came up *from the ranks*⟩ **2** to arise inevitably or by chance ⟨*any problems that* come up⟩ **3** to appear before a magistrate ⟨*he* came up *for speeding*⟩ **4** to become, esp after cleaning ⟨*the table* came up *like new*⟩ – **come up with** to provide, esp in dealing with a problem or challenge ⟨came up with *a better solution*⟩

come-uppance *n* a deserved rebuke or penalty

comfit *n* a sweetmeat consisting of a nut, seed, piece of fruit, etc coated and preserved with sugar

¹**comfort** *n* **1** (sby or sthg that provides) consolation or encouragement in time of trouble or worry **2** contented well-being – **comfortless** *adj*

²**comfort** *vt* **1** to cheer up **2** to ease the grief or trouble of; console – **comfortingly** *adv*

comfortable *adj* **1a** providing or enjoying contentment and security ⟨*a ~ income*⟩ **b** providing or enjoying physical comfort ⟨*a ~ armchair*⟩ **2a** causing no worry or doubt ⟨*~ assumptions that require no thought*⟩ **b** free from stress or tension ⟨*a ~ routine*⟩ – **comfortably** *adv*

comforter *n* **1** *cap* HOLY SPIRIT **2a** a knitted scarf **b** *chiefly NAm* a quilt, eiderdown

comfort station *n*, *NAm* a public toilet (e g at a petrol station) – euph

comfrey *n* any of a genus of (tall) plants of the borage family whose coarse hairy leaves are much used in herbal medicine

comfy *adj* comfortable – infml

¹**comic** *adj* **1** of or marked by comedy **2** causing laughter or amusement; funny

²**comic** *n* **1** a comedian **2** a magazine consisting mainly of strip-cartoon stories **3** *pl, NAm* the part of a newspaper devoted to strip cartoons

comical *adj* being of a kind to excite laughter, esp because of a startlingly or unexpectedly humorous impact ⟨*he thought her hat was* ~⟩ – **comically** *adv*

comic opera *n* opera with humorous episodes and usu some spoken dialogue and a sentimental plot

comic strip *n* STRIP CARTOON

Cominform *n* an organization operating from 1947 to 1956 to coordinate the activities of 9 European Communist parties

¹**coming** *n* an act or instance of arriving ⟨*~s and goings*⟩

²**coming** *adj* **1** immediately due in sequence or development; next ⟨*the ~ year*⟩ **2** gaining in importance; up-and-coming

Comintern *n* an international of Socialist organizations operating from 1919 to 1943

comity *n* harmony, fellowship; *specif* the recognition by courts of one jurisdiction of the laws and decisions of another

comity of nations *n* the courtesy and friendship of nations, marked esp by recognition of each other's laws

comma *n* 1 a punctuation mark , used esp as a mark of separation within the sentence 2 a butterfly with a silvery comma-shaped mark on the underside of the hind wing

¹**command** *vt* 1 to direct authoritatively; order 2a to have at one's immediate disposal **b** to be able to ask for and receive ⟨~s a high fee⟩ **c** to overlook or dominate (as if) from a strategic position **d** to have military command of as senior officer ~ *vi* to be commander; be supreme – **commandable** *adj*

²**command** *n* 1 an order given 2 (the activation of a device by) an electrical signal 3a the ability or power to control; the mastery **b** the authority or right to command ⟨the officer in ~⟩ **c** facility in use ⟨a good ~ of French⟩ 4 sing or pl in constr the unit, personnel, etc under a commander

³**command** *adj* done on command or request ⟨a ~ performance⟩

commandant *n* a commanding officer

commandeer *vt* 1 to seize for military purposes 2 to take arbitrary or forcible possession of

commander *n* an officer in the navy ranking below captain – **commandership** *n*

commander-in-chief *n* one who is in supreme command of an armed force

commanding *adj* 1 having command; being in charge ⟨a ~ officer⟩ 2 dominating or having priority ⟨a ~ position of a castle⟩ ⟨a ~ lead⟩ 3 deserving or expecting respect and obedience ⟨a ~ voice⟩ – **commandingly** *adv*

commandment *n* sthg commanded; *specif* any of the biblical Ten Commandments

commando *n, pl* **commandos, commandoes** (a member of) a usu small military unit for surprise raids

command paper *n* a government report laid before Parliament at the command of the crown

command post *n* the headquarters of a military unit in the field

comme il faut *adj* conforming to accepted standards; proper

commemorate *vt* 1 to call to formal remembrance 2 to mark by some ceremony or observation; observe 3 to serve as a memorial of – **commemorative** *adj,* **commemoration** *n*

commence *vb* to start, begin – *fml* – **commencement** *n*

commend *vt* 1 to entrust for care or preservation 2 to recommend as worthy of confidence or notice – **commendable** *adj,* **commendably** *adv*

commendation *n* sthg (e g a formal citation) that commends – **commendatory** *adj*

commensurable *adj* having a common measure; *esp* divisible by a common unit an integral number of times – **commensurably** *adv,* **commensurability** *n*

commensurate *adj* 1 (approximately) equal in measure or extent; coextensive 2 corresponding in size, extent, amount, or degree; proportionate ⟨was given a job ~ with his abilities⟩ – **commensurately** *adv,* **commensuration** *n*

¹**comment** *n* 1 a note explaining or criticizing the meaning of a piece of writing ⟨~s printed in the margin⟩ 2a an observation or remark expressing an opinion or attitude **b** a judgment expressed indirectly ⟨this film is a ~ on current moral standards⟩

²**comment** *vi* to explain or interpret sthg by comment; *broadly* to make a comment ⟨~ed on the match⟩

commentary *n* 1 a systematic series of explanations or interpretations (e g of a piece of writing) 2 a series of spoken remarks and comments used as a broadcast description of some event ⟨a running ~ on the match⟩

commentate *vi* to act as a commentator; *esp* to give a broadcast commentary

commentator *n* a person who provides a commentary; *specif* one who reports and discusses news or sports events on radio or television

commerce *n* the exchange or buying and selling of commodities, esp on a large scale

¹**commercial** *adj* 1a(1) engaged in work designed for the market (2) (characteristic) of commerce (3) having or being a good financial prospect ⟨found oil in ~ quantities⟩ **b**(1) *esp of a chemical* average or inferior in quality (2) producing work to a standard determined only by market criteria 2a viewed with regard to profit ⟨a ~ success⟩ **b** designed for a large market 3 supported by advertisers ⟨~ TV⟩ – **commercially** *adv*

²**commercial** *n* an advertisement broadcast on radio or television

commercialism *n* 1 commercial spirit, institutions, or methods 2 excessive emphasis on profit – **commercialist** *n,* **commercialistic** *adj*

commercialize, -ise *vt* 1a to manage on a business basis for profit **b** to make commercial 2 to exploit for profit – **commercialization** *n*

commercial traveller *n, Br* SALES REPRESENTATIVE

commie *n* a communist – chiefly derog

commiserate *vi* to feel or express sympathy *with* sby; condole ⟨~ over their hard luck⟩ – **commiserative** *adj,* **commiseration** *n*

commissar *n* 1 a Communist party official assigned to a military unit to teach party principles and ideals 2 the head of a government department in the USSR until 1946

commissariat *n* 1 the department of an army that organizes food supplies 2 a government department in the USSR until 1946

commissary *n* 1 an officer in charge of military supplies 2 *NAm* (a store for) equipment, food supplies, etc, esp of a military force

¹**commission** *n* 1a a formal warrant granting various powers **b** (a certificate conferring) military rank above a certain level 2 an authorization or command to act in a prescribed manner or to perform prescribed acts; a charge 3 authority to act as agent for another; *also* sthg to be done by an agent 4a *sing or pl in constr* a group of people directed to perform some duty **b** *often cap* a government agency 5 an act of committing sthg 6 a fee, esp a percentage, paid to an agent or employee for transacting a piece of business or performing a service – **in/into commission** 1 of a ship ready for active service 2 in use or in condition for use – **on commission** with commission serving as partial or full pay for work done – **out of commission** 1 out of active service or use 2 out of working order

²**commission** *vt* 1a to confer a formal commission on **b** to order, appoint, or assign to perform a task or function ⟨the writer who was ~ed to do the biography⟩ 2 to put (a ship) in commission

commissionaire *n, chiefly Br* a uniformed attendant at a cinema, theatre, office, etc

commissioner *n* 1 a member or the head of a commission 2 the government representative in a district, province, etc – **commissionership** *n*

commit *vt* **-tt-** 1a to entrust **b** to place in a prison or mental institution **c** to transfer, consign ⟨~ *something to paper*⟩ **2** to carry out (a crime, sin, etc) **3a** to obligate, bind **b** to assign to some particular course or use ⟨*all available troops were ~ted to the attack*⟩ – **committable** *adj*

commitment *n* **1** an act of committing to a charge or trust; *esp* a consignment to an institution **2a** an agreement or pledge to do sthg in the future **b** sthg pledged **c** loyalty to a system of thought or action

committal *n* commitment or consignment (e g to prison or the grave)

committee *n sing or pl in constr* a body of people delegated **a** to report on, investigate, etc some matter ⟨*a parliamentary ~*⟩ **b** to organize or administrate a society, event, etc ⟨*the fête ~*⟩ – **committeeman** *n*, **committee-woman** *n*

committee stage *n* the stage in parliamentary procedure between the second reading and the third reading when a bill is discussed in detail in committee

commode *n* **1** a low chest of drawers **2** a boxlike structure or chair with a removable seat covering a chamber pot

commodious *adj* comfortably or conveniently spacious; roomy – *fml* – **commodiously** *adv*, **commodiousness** *n*

commodity *n* **1** sthg useful or valuable **2a** a product possessing utility; sthg that can be bought and sold **b** an article of trade or commerce, esp when delivered for shipment

commodore *n* **1** an officer in the navy ranking below rear admiral **2** the senior captain of a merchant shipping line **3** the chief officer of a yacht club

¹**common** *adj* **1** of the community at large; public ⟨*work for the ~ good*⟩ **2a** belonging to or shared by 2 or more individuals or by all members of a group **b** belonging equally to 2 or more quantities ⟨*a ~ denominator*⟩⟨*a ~ factor*⟩ **3a** occurring or appearing frequently; familiar ⟨*a ~ sight*⟩ **b** of the familiar kind **4a** widespread, general ⟨*being ~ knowledge*⟩ **b** characterized by a lack of privilege or special status ⟨*the ~ people*⟩ **c** simply satisfying accustomed criteria (and no more); elementary ⟨*~ decency*⟩ **5a** falling below ordinary standards; second-rate **b** lacking refinement **6** either masculine or feminine in gender – **commonly** *adv*, **commonness** *n*

²**common** *n* **1** *pl* the common people – used chiefly in a historical context **2** *pl* food or provisions (shared jointly by all members of an institution) – esp in *short commons* **3** *pl but sing or pl in constr*, *often cap* the political group or estate made up of commoners **b** HOUSE OF COMMONS **4** a right which sby may have on another's land **5** a piece of land open to use by all: e g **a** undivided land used esp for pasture **b** a more or less treeless expanse of undeveloped land available for recreation **6a** a religious service suitable for any of various festivals **b** the ordinary of the Mass **7** *Br* COMMON SENSE – slang – **in common** shared together – used esp of shared interests, attitudes, or experience ⟨*we had a lot in common*⟩

commonalty *n* (the political estate formed by) the common people

common cold *n* inflammation of the mucous membranes of the nose, throat, mouth, etc caused by a virus and lasting for a short time

commoner *n* **1** a member of the common people; sby not of noble rank **2** a student (e g at Oxford) who is not supported by the college endowments

common-law *adj* **1** of the common law **2** recognized in law without solemnization of marriage ⟨*his ~ wife*⟩

common law *n* the body of uncodified English law that forms the basis of the English legal system

common market *n* an economic unit formed to remove trade barriers among its members; *specif*, *often cap C&M* the European economic community

common noun *n* a noun that may occur with limiting modifiers (e g *a* or *an*, *some*, *every*, and *my*) and that designates any one of a class of beings or things

common or garden *adj* ordinary, everyday – *infml*

¹**commonplace** *n* **1** an obvious or trite observation **2** sthg taken for granted

²**commonplace** *adj* routinely found; ordinary, unremarkable – **commonplaceness** *n*

common room *n* a room or set of rooms in a school, college, etc for the recreational use of the staff or students

common sense *n* sound and prudent (but often unsophisticated) judgment – **commonsense** *adj*, **commonsensical** *adj*

commonwealth *n* **1** a political unit: e g **a** one founded on law and united by agreement of the people for the common good **b** one in which supreme authority is vested in the people **2** *cap* the English state from 1649 to 1660 **3** a state of the USA **4** *cap* a federal union of states – used officially of Australia **5** *often cap* a loose association of autonomous states under a common allegiance; *specif* an association consisting of Britain and states that were formerly British colonies

commotion *n* **1** a state of civil unrest or insurrection **2** a disturbance, tumult **3** noisy confusion and bustle

communal *adj* **1** of a commune or communes **2** of a community **3** shared ⟨*~ activity*⟩ – **communalize** *vt*, **communally** *adv*, **communality** *n*

¹**commune** *vi* **1** to receive Communion **2** to communicate intimately

²**commune** *n* **1** the smallest administrative district of many (European) countries **2** *sing or pl in constr* an often rural community of unrelated individuals or families organized on a communal basis

communicable *adj*, *esp of a disease* transmittable – **communicableness** *n*, **communicably** *adv*, **communicability** *n*

communicant *n* **1** a church member who receives or is entitled to receive Communion **2** an informant – **communicant** *adj*

communicate *vt* **1** to convey knowledge of or information about; make known **2** to cause to pass from one to another *~ vi* **1** to receive Communion **2** to transmit information, thought, or feeling so that it is satisfactorily received or understood **3** to give access to each other; connect ⟨*the rooms ~*⟩ – **communicator** *n*, **communicatory** *adj*

communication *n* **1** a verbal or written message **2** (the use of a common system of symbols, signs, behaviour, etc for the) exchange of information **3** *pl* **a** a system (e g of telephones) for communicating **b** a system of routes for moving troops, supplies, etc **4** *pl but sing or pl in constr* techniques for the effective transmission of information, ideas, etc – **communicational** *adj*

communication cord *n*, *Br* a device (e g a chain or handle) in a railway carriage that may be pulled in an emergency to sound an alarm

communicative *adj* **1** tending to communicate; talkative **2** of communication – **communicatively** *adv*, **communicativeness** *n*

communion *n* **1a** *often cap* the religious service celebrating the Eucharist in Protestant churches **b** the act of receiving the Eucharist **2** intimate fellowship or rapport **3** a body of Christians having a common faith and discipline

communiqué *n* BULLETIN 1

communism *n* **1a** a theory advocating elimination of

private property **b** a system in which goods are held in common and are available to all as needed **2** *cap* **a** a doctrine based on revolutionary Marxian socialism and Marxism-Leninism that is the official ideology of the USSR **b** a totalitarian system of government in which a single party controls state-owned means of production

communist *n, often cap* **1** an adherent or advocate of Communism **2** a left-wing revolutionary – **communist** *adj, often cap*, **communistic** *adj, often cap*

community *n* **1** *sing or pl in constr* **a** a group of people living in a particular area **b** all the interacting populations of various living organisms in a particular area **c** a group of individuals with some common characteristic (e g profession, religion, or status) **d** a body of people or nations having a common history or common interests ⟨*the international* ∼⟩ **2** society in general **3a** joint ownership or participation **b** common character; likeness ⟨*bound by* ∼ *of interests*⟩ **c** social ties; fellowship **d** the state or condition of living in a society

community centre *n* a building or group of buildings for the educational and recreational activities of a community

community chest *n, NAm* a general fund accumulated from subscriptions to pay for social-welfare requirements in a community

commutation *n* **1** a replacement; *specif* a substitution of one form of payment or charge for another **2** an act or process of commuting **3** the process of converting an alternating current to a direct current

commutation ticket *n, NAm* a ticket sold, usu at a reduced rate, for a fixed number of trips over the same route during a limited period

commutative *adj* **1** of or showing commutation **2** combining elements to produce a result that is independent of the order in which the elements are taken ⟨*a* ∼ *group*⟩ ⟨*addition of the positive integers is* ∼⟩

commutator *n* a device for reversing the direction of an electric current; *esp* a device on a motor or generator that converts alternating current to direct current

commute *vt* **1** to convert (e g a payment) into another form **2** to exchange (a penalty) for another less severe ∼ *vi* **1** to travel back and forth regularly (e g between home and work) **2** *of 2 mathematical operators* to give a commutative result – **commutable** *adj*, **commuter** *n*

¹**compact** *adj* **1** having parts or units closely packed or joined **2** succinct, terse ⟨*a* ∼ *statement*⟩ **3** occupying a small volume because of efficient use of space ⟨*a* ∼ *camera*⟩ – **compactly** *adv*, **compactness** *n*

²**compact** *vt* **1a** to knit or draw together; combine, consolidate **b** to press together; compress **2** to make up by connecting or combining; compose – **compactible** *adj*, **compaction** *n*, **compactor** *n*

³**compact** *n* sthg compact or compacted: e g **a** a small slim case for face powder **b** a medium-sized US motor car

⁴**compact** *n* an agreement, contract

¹**companion** *n* one who accompanies another; a comrade – **companionate** *adj*, **companionship** *n*

²**companion** *n* (a covering at the top of) a companionway

companionable *adj* marked by, conducive to, or suggestive of companionship; sociable – **companionableness** *n*, **companionably** *adv*

companionway *n* a ship's stairway from one deck to another

company *n* **1a** friendly association with another; fellowship ⟨*I enjoy her* ∼⟩ **b** companions, associates ⟨*know a person by the* ∼ *he keeps*⟩ **c** *sing or pl in constr* visitors, guests ⟨*having* ∼ *for dinner*⟩ **2** *sing or pl in constr* **a** a group of people or things ⟨*a* ∼ *of horsemen*⟩ **b** a unit of

soldiers composed usu of a headquarters and 2 or more platoons **c** an organization of musical or dramatic performers **d** the officers and men of a ship **3a** *sing or pl in constr* an association of people for carrying on a commercial or industrial enterprise **b** those members of a partnership firm whose names do not appear in the firm name ⟨*John Smith and* Company⟩

company secretary *n* a senior officer of a company who typically supervises its financial and legal aspects

comparable *adj* **1** capable of or suitable for comparison **2** approximately equivalent; similar ⟨*fabrics of* ∼ *quality*⟩ – **comparableness** *n*, **comparably** *adv*, **comparability** *n*

¹**comparative** *adj* **1** of or constituting the degree of grammatical comparison expressing increase in quality, quantity, or relation **2** considered as if in comparison to sthg else as a standard; relative ⟨*a* ∼ *stranger*⟩ **3** characterized by the systematic comparison of phenomena ⟨∼ *anatomy*⟩ – **comparatively** *adv*, **comparativeness** *n*

²**comparative** *n* the comparative degree or form in a language

¹**compare** *vt* **1** to represent as similar; liken **2** to examine the character or qualities of, esp in order to discover resemblances or differences **3** to inflect or modify (an adjective or adverb) according to the degrees of comparison ∼ *vi* **1** to bear being compared ⟨*it just doesn't* ∼⟩ **2** to be equal or alike – + *with*

²**compare** *n* COMPARISON **1b** ⟨*beauty beyond* ∼⟩

comparison *n* **1a** the representing of one thing or person as similar to or like another **b** an examination of 2 or more items to establish similarities and dissimilarities **2** identity or similarity of features ⟨*several points of* ∼ *between the 2 authors*⟩ **3** the modification of an adjective or adverb to denote different levels of quality, quantity, or relation

compartment *n* **1** any of the parts into which an enclosed space is divided **2** a separate division or section – **compartment** *vt*, **compartmental** *adj*

compartmentalize, -ise *vt* to separate into isolated compartments; *also* to keep in isolated categories ⟨∼ d knowledge⟩ – **compartmentalization** *n*

¹**compass** *vt* **1** to devise or contrive often with craft or skill; plot **2a** to encompass **b** to travel entirely round ⟨∼ *the earth*⟩ **3** to achieve; BRING ABOUT **4** to comprehend *USE fml* – **compassable** *adj*

²**compass** *n* **1a** a boundary, circumference ⟨*within the* ∼ *of the city walls*⟩ **b** range, scope ⟨*the* ∼ *of a voice*⟩ **2a** an instrument that indicates directions, typically by means of a freely-turning needle pointing to magnetic north **b** an instrument for drawing circles or transferring measurements that consists of 2 legs joined at 1 end by a pivot – usu pl with sing. meaning

compass card *n* the circular card attached to the needles of a mariner's compass showing the 32 points of the compass

compassion *n* sympathetic consciousness of others' distress together with a desire to alleviate it – **compassionless** *adj*

compassionate *adj* **1** having or showing compassion; sympathetic **2** granted because of unusual, distressing circumstances affecting an individual – used of special privileges (e g extra leave of absence) – **compassionately** *adv*, **compassionateness** *n*

compatible *adj* **1** capable of existing together in harmony **2a** being or relating to a television system in which colour transmissions may be received on unmodified black-and-white sets **b** being or relating to an audio system allowing stereo signals to be treated as mono by unmodified mono equipment – **compatibleness** *n*, **compatibly** *adv*, **compatibility** *n*

compatriot *n* a fellow countryman – **compatriotic** *adj*

compeer *n* an equal, peer

compel *vt* **-ll-** **1** to drive or force irresistibly *to* do sthg ⟨*poverty* ~led *him to work*⟩ **2** to cause to occur by overwhelming pressure ⟨*exhaustion of ammunition* ~led *their surrender*⟩ – **compellable** *adj*

compendious *adj* comprehensive but relatively brief – **compendiously** *adv*, **compendiousness** *n*

compendium *n*, *pl* **compendiums, compendia** **1** a brief summary of a larger work or of a field of knowledge; an abstract **2** a collection of indoor games and puzzles

compensate *vt* **1** to have an equal and opposite effect to; counterbalance **2** to make amends to, esp by appropriate payment ⟨~ *a neighbour for damage to his property*⟩ ~*vi* to supply an equivalent *for* – **compensative** *adj*, **compensator** *n*, **compensatory** *adj*

compensation *n* **1a** increased functioning or development of one organ to compensate for a defect in another **b** the alleviation of feelings of inferiority, frustration, failure, etc in one field by increased endeavour in another **2** a recompense; *specif* payment for damage or loss – **compensational** *adj*

¹**compere** *n*, *Br* the presenter of a radio or television programme, esp a light entertainment programme

²**compere** *vb*, *Br* to act as compere (for)

compete *vi* to strive consciously or unconsciously for an objective; *also* to be in a state of rivalry

competence *also* **competency** *n* **1** the quality or state of being competent **2** the innate human capacity to acquire, use, and understand language **3** a sufficiency of means for the necessities and conveniences of life – fml

competent *adj* **1a** having requisite or adequate ability ⟨*a* ~ *workman*⟩ **b** showing clear signs of production by a competent agent (e g a workman or writer) ⟨*a* ~ *novel*⟩ **2** legally qualified – **competently** *adv*

competition *n* **1** the act or process of competing; rivalry **2** a usu organized test of comparative skill, performance, etc; *also*, *sing or pl in constr* the others competing with one ⟨*keep ahead of the* ~⟩ **3** the competing of 2 or more parties to do business with a third party **4** competing demand by 2 or more (kinds of) organisms for some environmental resource in short supply

competitive *adj* **1** relating to, characterized by, or based on competition; *specif*, *of wages and prices* at least as good as those offered by competitors **2** inclined or desiring to compete – **competitively** *adv*, **competitiveness** *n*

competitor *n* sby who or sthg that competes; a rival

compilation *n* sthg compiled

compile *vt* **1** to collect into 1 work **2** to compose out of materials from other documents

complacency *also* **complacence** *n* self-satisfaction accompanied by unawareness of actual dangers or deficiencies

complacent *adj* self-satisfied ⟨*a* ~ *smile*⟩ – **complacently** *adv*

complain *vi* **1** to express feelings of discontent ⟨~ed *about the heat*⟩ ⟨~ed *it was too hot*⟩ **2** to make a formal accusation or charge – **complainer** *n*, **complainingly** *adv*

complainant *n* one who makes a complaint; *specif* the party in a legal action or proceeding who makes a complaint

complaint *n* **1** an expression of discontent **2a** sthg that is the cause or subject of protest or outcry **b** a bodily ailment or disease

complaisant *adj* **1** marked by an inclination to please or comply **2** tending to consent to others' wishes – **complaisance** *n*, **complaisantly** *adv*

¹**complement** *n* **1a** sthg that fills up or completes **b** the quantity required to make sthg complete; *specif* COMPANY

2d c either of 2 mutually completing parts; a counterpart **2a** an angle or arc that when added to a given angle or arc equals 90° **b** a number that when added to another number of the same sign yields zero if the significant digit farthest to the left is discarded **3** an added word or expression by which a predication is made complete (e g *president* in 'they elected him president') **4** the protein in blood serum that in combination with antibodies causes the destruction of antigens (e g bacteria) – **complemental** *adj*

²**complement** *vt* to be complementary to

complementary *adj* **1** serving to fill out or complete **2** mutually supplying each other's lack **3** of or constituting either of a pair of contrasting colours that produce a neutral colour when combined **4** of the precise pairing of bases between 2 strands of DNA or RNA such that the sequence of bases on one strand determines that on the other **5** *of a pair of angles* having the sum of 90° – **complementary** *n*, **complementariness** *n*, **complementarily** *adv*, **complementarity** *n*

¹**complete** *adj* **1** having all necessary parts, elements, or steps **2** whole or concluded ⟨*after 2* ~ *revolutions about the sun*⟩ **3** thoroughly competent; highly proficient **4a** fully carried out; thorough ⟨*a* ~ *renovation*⟩ **b** total, absolute ⟨~ *silence*⟩ – **completely** *adv*, **completeness** *n*, **completive** *adj*

²**complete** *vt* **1** to bring to an end; *esp* to bring to a perfected state ⟨~ *a painting*⟩ **2a** to make whole or perfect ⟨*the church* ~s *the charm of this village*⟩ **b** to mark the end of ⟨*a rousing chorus* ~s *the show*⟩ **c** to execute, fulfil ⟨~ *a contract*⟩ – **completion** *n*

¹**complex** *adj* **1a** composed of 2 or (many) more parts **b**(1) *of a word* having a bound form as 1 or both of its immediate constituents (e g *unmanly*) (2) *of a sentence* consisting of a main clause and 1 or more subordinate clauses **2** hard to separate, analyse, or solve **3** of or being a complex number – **complexly** *adv*, **complexity** *n*

²**complex** *n* **1** a whole made up of complicated or interrelated parts ⟨*a shopping* ~⟩ **2a** a group of repressed related desires and memories that usu adversely affects personality and behaviour **b** an exaggerated reaction to sthg ⟨*has a* ~ *about flying*⟩

complexion *n* **1** the appearance of the skin, esp of the face **2** overall aspect or character ⟨*that puts a different* ~ *on things*⟩ – **complexional** *adj*, **complexioned** *adj*

complex number *n* a number containing both real and imaginary parts

compliance *n* **1** the act or process of complying (readily) with the wishes of others **2** a disposition to yield to others **3** (a measure of) the ease of overcoming a restoring force (e g a spring) – **compliant** *adj*, **compliantly** *adv*,

complicate *vt* **1** to combine, esp in an involved or inextricable manner **2** to make complex or difficult

complicated *adj* **1** consisting of parts intricately combined **2** difficult to analyse, understand, or explain – **complicatedly** *adv*, **complicatedness** *n*

complication *n* **1a** intricacy, complexity **b** an instance of making difficult, involved, or intricate **c** a complex or intricate feature or element **d** a factor or issue that occurs unexpectedly and changes existing plans, methods, or attitudes – often *pl* **2** a secondary disease or condition developing in the course of a primary disease

complicity *n* (an instance of) association or participation (as if) in a wrongful act

¹**compliment** *n* **1** an expression of esteem, affection, or admiration; *esp* a flattering remark **2** *pl* best wishes; regards

²**compliment** *vt* **1** to pay a compliment to **2** to present with a token of esteem

complimentary *adj* 1 expressing or containing a compliment 2 given free as a courtesy or favour ⟨∼ *tickets*⟩ – **complimentarily** *adv*

compline *n, often cap* the last of the canonical hours, said before retiring at night

comply *vi* to conform or adapt one's actions to another's wishes or to a rule – **complier** *n*

¹**component** *n* 1 a constituent part; an ingredient 2 any of the vector terms added to form a vector sum or resultant – **componential** *adj*

²**component** *adj* serving or helping to constitute; constituent

comport *vi* to be fitting; accord ⟨*acts that* ∼ *with ideals*⟩ ∼ *vt* to behave (oneself) in a manner conformable to what is right, proper, or expected *USE fml*

compose *vt* 1a to form by putting together ⟨∼ *a collage with those pictures*⟩ b to form the substance of; MAKE UP – chiefly passive ⟨∼d *of many ingredients*⟩ c SET 11c 2a to create by mental or artistic labour; produce ⟨∼ *a sonnet*⟩ b to formulate and write (a piece of music) 3 to settle (a point of disagreement) 4 to free from agitation; calm, settle ⟨∼ *oneself*⟩ ∼ *vi* to practise composition

composer *n* a person who writes music

composing stick *n* a tray with an adjustable slide into which type is set

¹**composite** *adj* 1 made up of distinct parts: e g a *cap* of a Roman order of architecture that combines Ionic with Corinthian b of or belonging to a very large family of plants, including the dandelion, daisy, and sunflower, typically having florets arranged in dense heads that resemble single flowers 2 combining the typical or essential characteristics of individuals making up a group ⟨*a* ∼ *portrait of mystics known to the painter*⟩ – **compositely** *adv*

²**composite** *n* sthg composite; a compound

composition *n* 1a the act or process of composing; *specif* arrangement into proper proportion or relation and esp into artistic form b (the production of) an arrangement of type for printing 2 the factors or parts which go to make sthg; *also* the way in which the factors or parts make up the whole 3 an agreement by which a creditor accepts partial payment 4 a product of mixing or combining various elements or ingredients 5 an intellectual creation: e g a a piece of writing; *esp* a school essay b a written piece of music, esp of considerable size and complexity – **compositional** *adj*, **compositionally** *adv*

compositor *n* sby who sets type

compos mentis *adj* of sound mind, memory, and understanding

¹**compost** *n* a mixture of decayed organic matter used for fertilizing and conditioning land

²**compost** *vt* to convert (e g plant debris) to compost – **composter** *n*

composure *n* calmness or repose, esp of mind, bearing, or appearance

compote *n* a dessert of fruit cooked in syrup and usu served cold

¹**compound** *vt* 1 to put together (parts) so as to form a whole; combine ⟨∼ *ingredients*⟩ 2 to form by combining parts ⟨∼ *a medicine*⟩ 3a to pay (interest) on both the accumulated interest and the principal b to add to; augment ⟨*to* ∼ *an error*⟩ 4 to agree for a consideration not to prosecute (an offence) ⟨∼ *a felony*⟩ ∼ *vi* to become joined in a compound – **compoundable** *adj*, **compounder** *n*

²**compound** *adj* 1 composed of or resulting from union of (many similar) separate elements, ingredients, or parts 2 involving or used in a combination 3 *of a sentence* having 2 or more main clauses

³**compound** *n* 1 a word consisting of components that are words, combining forms, or affixes (e g *houseboat, anthropology*) 2 sthg formed by a union of elements or parts; *specif* a distinct substance formed by combination of chemical elements in fixed proportion by weight

⁴**compound** *n* a fenced or walled-in area containing a group of buildings, esp residences

compound eye *n* an arthropod eye consisting of a number of separate visual units

compound fracture *n* a bone fracture produced in such a way as to form an open wound

compound interest *n* interest computed on the original principal plus accumulated interest

comprehend *vt* 1 to grasp the nature, significance, or meaning of; understand 2 to include ⟨*the park* ∼s *all of the land beyond the river*⟩ – *fml* – **comprehendible** *adj*

comprehensible *adj* capable of being comprehended; intelligible – **comprehensibleness** *n*, **comprehensibly** *adv*, **comprehensibility** *n*

comprehension *n* 1a grasping with the intellect; understanding b knowledge gained by comprehending c the capacity for understanding fully 2 a school exercise testing understanding of a passage

¹**comprehensive** *adj* 1 covering completely or broadly; inclusive ⟨∼ *insurance*⟩ 2 having or exhibiting wide mental grasp ⟨∼ *knowledge*⟩ 3 *chiefly Br* of or being the principle of educating in 1 unified school nearly all children above the age of 11 from a given area regardless of ability ⟨∼ *education*⟩ – **comprehensively** *adv*, **comprehensiveness** *n*

²**comprehensive** *n, Br* a comprehensive school

¹**compress** *vt* 1 to press or squeeze together 2 to reduce in size or volume as if by squeezing ∼ *vi* to be compressed – **compressible** *adj*, **compressibility** *n*

²**compress** *n* a pad pressed on a body part (e g to ease the pain and swelling of a bruise)

compression *n* 1 a compressing or being compressed 2 (the quality of) the process of compressing the fuel mixture in a cylinder of an internal-combustion engine – **compressional** *adj*

compressor *n* sthg that compresses; *esp* a machine for compressing gases

comprise *vt* 1 to include, contain 2 to be made up of 3 to make up, constitute

¹**compromise** *n* 1a the settling of differences through arbitration or through consent reached by mutual concessions b a settlement reached by compromise c sthg blending qualities of 2 different things ⟨*a* ∼ *solution*⟩ 2 a concession to sthg disreputable or prejudicial ⟨*a* ∼ *of principles*⟩

²**compromise** *vt* 1 to adjust or settle by mutual concessions 2 to expose to discredit or scandal ∼ *vi* to come to agreement by mutual concession – **compromiser** *n*

Comptometer *trademark* – used for a calculating machine

comptroller *n* CONTROLLER 1 – **comptrollership** *n*

compulsion *n* 1a compelling or being compelled b a force or agency that compels 2 a strong impulse to perform an irrational act

compulsive *adj* of, caused by, like, or suffering from a psychological compulsion or obsession – **compulsively** *adv*, **compulsiveness** *n*

compulsory *adj* 1 mandatory, enforced ⟨∼ *arbitration*⟩ 2 involving compulsion or obligation; coercive ⟨∼ *legislation*⟩ – **compulsorily** *adv*

compunction *n* 1 anxiety arising from awareness of guilt; remorse 2 a twinge of misgiving; a scruple ⟨*cheated without* ∼⟩ – **compunctious** *adj*

computation *n* 1 the use or operation of a computer 2

(a system of) calculating; *also* the amount calculated – **computational** *adj*

compute *vt* to determine, esp by mathematical means; *also* to determine or calculate by means of a computer ~ *vi* **1** to make calculation; reckon **2** to use a computer – **computable** *adj*, **computability** *n*

computer *n* a programmable electronic device that can store, retrieve, and process data

computerize, -ise *vt* **1** to carry out, control, or conduct by means of a computer **2** to equip with computers – **computerization** *n*

comrade *n* **1a** an intimate friend or associate; a companion **b** a fellow soldier **2** a communist – **comradely** *adj*, **comradeliness** *n*, **comradeship** *n*

¹**con**, *NAm chiefly* **conn** *vt* **-nn-** to conduct or direct the steering of (e g a ship)

²**con**, *NAm chiefly* **conn** *n* the control exercised by one who cons a ship

³**con** *adv* on the negative side; in opposition ⟨*so much has been written pro and* ~⟩

⁴**con** *n* (sby holding) the opposing or negative position

⁵**con** *vt* **-nn-** **1** to swindle, trick **2** to persuade, cajole *USE* slang – **con** *n*

⁶**con** *n* a convict – slang

⁷**con** *prep* with – used in music ⟨~ *sordini*⟩

con- – see COM-

concatenate *vt* to link together in a series or chain – fml – **concatenation** *n*

concave *adj* hollowed or rounded inwards like the inside of a bowl – **concavely** *adv*

concavity *n* **1** a concave line or surface or the space included in it **2** the quality or state of being concave

conceal *vt* **1** to prevent disclosure or recognition of **2** to place out of sight – **concealable** *adj*, **concealer** *n*, **concealingly** *adv*, **concealment** *n*

concede *vt* **1** to grant as a right or privilege **2a** to accept as true, valid, or accurate **b** to acknowledge grudgingly or hesitantly **3** to allow involuntarily ⟨~d *2 more goals*⟩ – chiefly journ ~ *vi* **1** to make concession; yield – **conceder** *n*

conceit *n* **1** excessively high opinion of oneself **2a** a fanciful idea **b** an elaborate, unusual, and cleverly expressed figure of speech

conceited *adj* having an excessively high opinion of oneself – **conceitedly** *adv*, **conceitedness** *n*

conceivable *adj* capable of being conceived; imaginable – **conceivableness** *n*, **conceivably** *adv*, **conceivability** *n*

conceive *vt* **1** to become pregnant with (young) **2a** to cause to originate in one's mind ⟨~ *a prejudice against him*⟩ **b** to form a conception of; evolve mentally; visualize **3** to be of the opinion – fml ~ *vi* **1** to become pregnant **2** to have a conception *of* – **conceiver** *n*

¹**concentrate** *vt* **1a** to bring or direct towards a common centre or objective; focus **b** to gather into 1 body, mass, or force ⟨*power* ~d *in a few able hands*⟩ **2a** to make less dilute **b** to express or exhibit in condensed form ⟨*the author* ~s *his message in the last paragraph*⟩ ~ *vi* **1** to draw towards or meet in a common centre **2** to gather, collect **3** to concentrate one's powers, efforts, or attention ⟨~ *on a problem*⟩ – **concentrative** *adj*, **concentrator** *n*

²**concentrate** *n* sthg concentrated; *esp* a feed for animals rich in digestible nutrients

concentration *n* **1** direction of attention to a single object **2** a concentrated mass or thing **3** the relative content of a (chemical) component; strength

concentration camp *n* a camp where political prisoners, refugees, etc are confined; *esp* any of the Nazi camps for the internment or mass execution of (Jewish) prisoners during WW II

concentric *adj* having a common centre ⟨~ *circles*⟩ – **concentrically** *adv*, **concentricity** *n*

concept *n* **1** sthg conceived in the mind; a thought, notion **2** a generic idea abstracted from particular instances – **conceptual** *adj*, **conceptually** *adv*

conception *n* **1a** conceiving or being conceived **b** an embryo, foetus **2** a general idea; a concept **3** the originating of sthg in the mind – **conceptional** *adj*, **conceptive** *adj*

conceptualize, -ise *vt* to form a concept of – **conceptualization** *n*

¹**concern** *vt* **1** to relate to; be about ⟨*the novel* ~s *3 soldiers*⟩ **2** to have an influence on; involve; *also* to be the business or affair of ⟨*the problem* ~s *us all*⟩ **3** to be a care, trouble, or distress to ⟨*his ill health* ~s *me*⟩ **4** to engage, occupy ⟨~s *himself with trivia*⟩

²**concern** *n* **1** sthg that relates or belongs to one ⟨*it's not my* ~⟩ **2** matter for consideration **3** marked interest or regard, usu arising through a personal tie or relationship **4** a business or manufacturing organization or establishment

concerned *adj* **1** anxious ⟨~ *for his safety*⟩⟨~ *to discover the truth*⟩ **2a** interestedly engaged ⟨~ *with books and music*⟩ **b** (culpably) involved ⟨*arrested all* ~⟩

concerning *prep* relating to; with reference to

concert *n* **1** an instance of working together; an agreement – esp in *in concert (with)* **2** a public performance of music or dancing; *esp* a performance, usu by a group of musicians, that is made up of several individual compositions

concerted *adj* **1a** planned or done together; combined ⟨*a* ~ *effort*⟩ **b** performed in unison ⟨~ *artillery fire*⟩ **2** arranged in parts for several voices or instruments – **concertedly** *adv*, **concertedness** *n*

concert grand *n* a grand piano of the largest size for concerts

¹**concertina** *n* a small hexagonal musical instrument of the accordion family

²**concertina** *vi* **concertinaed**; **concertinaing** *Br* to become compressed in the manner of a concertina being closed, esp as a result of a crash

concertmaster *n*, *chiefly NAm* LEADER 5a

concerto *n*, *pl* **concerti**, **concertos** a piece for 1 or more soloists and orchestra, usu with 3 contrasting movements

concert pitch *n* **1** a tuning standard of usu 440 Hz for A above middle C **2** a high state of fitness, tension, or readiness

concession *n* **1** the act or an instance of conceding **2** a grant of land, property, or a right made, esp by a government, in return for services or for a particular use **3** a reduction of demands or standards made esp to accommodate shortcomings – **concessional** *adj*, **concessionally** *adv*, **concessionary** *adj*

concessionaire *n* the owner or beneficiary of a concession

concessive *adj* denoting the yielding or admitting of a point ⟨*a* ~ *clause beginning with 'although'*⟩ – **concessively** *adv*

conch *n*, *pl* **conches**, **conchs** **1** (the spiral shell of) any of various large marine gastropod molluscs **2** (the plain semidome of) an apse

conch-, **concho-** *comb form* shell ⟨*concho*logy⟩

conchology *n* the branch of zoology that deals with shells – **conchologist** *n*

concierge *n* sby who is employed as doorkeeper, caretaker, etc, esp in France

conciliate vt 1 to reconcile 2 to appease – **conciliator** n, **conciliative** adj, **conciliatory** adj, **conciliation** n
concise adj marked by brevity of expression or statement; free from all elaboration and superfluous detail – **concisely** adv, **conciseness** n
concision n conciseness
conclave n a private meeting or secret assembly; esp the assembly of Roman Catholic cardinals secluded continuously while electing a pope
conclude vt 1 to bring to an end, esp in a particular way or with a particular action ⟨~ a meeting with a prayer⟩ 2a to arrive at as a logically necessary inference ⟨~d that her argument was sound⟩ b to decide ⟨~d he would wait a little longer⟩ c to come to an agreement on; effect ⟨~ a sale⟩ ~ vi END 1
conclusion n 1 a reasoned judgment; an inference; specif the inferred proposition of a syllogism 2a a result, outcome b a final summing up (e g of an essay) 3 an act or instance of concluding
conclusive adj putting an end to debate or question, esp by reason of irrefutability – **conclusively** adv, **conclusiveness** n
concoct vt to prepare (e g a meal, story, etc) by combining diverse ingredients – **concocter** n, **concoctive** adj, **concoction** n
¹**concomitant** adj accompanying, esp in a subordinate or incidental way – **concomitance** n, **concomitantly** adv
²**concomitant** n sthg that accompanies or is collaterally connected with sthg else; an accompaniment
concord n 1a a state of agreement; harmony b a harmonious combination of simultaneously heard notes 2 a treaty, covenant 3 grammatical agreement
concordance n 1 an alphabetical index of the principal words in a book or an author's works, with their immediate contexts 2 agreement
concordant adj consonant, harmonious – **concordantly** adv
concordat n a compact, covenant; specif one between a pope and a sovereign or government
concourse n 1 a coming, gathering, or happening together ⟨a large ~ of people⟩ 2a an open space where roads or paths meet b an open space or main hall (e g in a station)
¹**concrete** adj 1 of a noun naming a thing rather than a quality, state, or action 2a characterized by or belonging to immediate experience of actual things or events b specific, particular ⟨~ proposals⟩ c real, tangible ⟨~ evidence⟩ 3 relating to or made of concrete – **concretely** adv, **concreteness** n
²**concrete** n a hard strong building material made by mixing a cementing material (e g portland cement) and a mineral aggregate (e g sand and gravel) with sufficient water to cause the cement to set and bind the entire mass
³**concrete** vt 1 to form into a solid mass; solidify 2 to cover with, form of, or set in concrete ~ vi to become concreted
concretion n 1 a hard usu inorganic mass formed (abnormally) in a living body 2 a mass of deposited mineral matter in a rock – **concretionary** adj
concubinage n being or having a concubine
concubine n a woman who lives with a man as his wife; MISTRESS 5; esp a woman who lives with a man in addition to his lawful wife or wives
concupiscence n strong desire; esp lust – **concupiscent** adj
concur vi -rr- 1 to happen together; coincide 2 to act together to a common end or single effect 3 to express agreement ⟨~ with an opinion⟩

concurrence n 1a agreement or union in action b(1) agreement in opinion or design (2) consent 2 a coming together; a conjunction
concurrent adj 1a meeting or intersecting in a point b running parallel 2 operating or occurring at the same time – **concurrent** n, **concurrently** adv
concuss vt to affect with concussion
concussion n 1 a hard blow or collision 2 (a jarring injury to the brain often resulting in unconsciousness caused by) a stunning or shattering effect from a hard blow – **concussive** adj, **concussively** adv
condemn vt 1 to declare to be utterly reprehensible, wrong, or evil, usu after considering evidence 2a to prescribe punishment for; specif to sentence to death b to sentence, doom 3 to declare unfit for use or consumption 4 to declare (e g contraband) convertible to public use – **condemnable** adj, **condemnatory** adj
condemnation n 1 censure, blame 2 the act of judicially convicting 3 the state of being condemned
condemned cell n a prison cell for people condemned to death
condensation n 1a chemical combination between molecules with elimination of a simple molecule (e g water) to form a new, more complex compound b a change to a denser form (e g from vapour to liquid) 2 a product of condensing; specif an abridgment of a literary work – **condensational** adj
condense vt to make denser or more compact; esp to subject to condensation ~ vi to undergo condensation – **condensable** adj
condenser n 1a a lens or mirror used to concentrate light on an object b an apparatus for condensing gas or vapour 2 a capacitor – now used chiefly in the motor trade
condescend vi to waive the privileges of rank ⟨~ ed to eat with subordinates⟩; broadly to descend to less formal or dignified action or speech
condescension n 1 voluntary descent from one's rank or dignity in relations with an inferior 2 a patronizing attitude
condign adj deserved, appropriate ⟨~ punishment⟩ – fml – **condignly** adv
condiment n sthg used to enhance the flavour of food; esp seasoning
¹**condition** n 1 sthg essential to the appearance or occurrence of sthg else; a prerequisite ⟨one of the necessary ~s for producing a pure chemical acid is clean apparatus⟩ 2 a protasis 3 a favourable or unfavourable state of sthg ⟨delayed by the ~ of the road⟩ 4a a state of being b social status; rank c a usu defective state of health or appearance ⟨a heart ~⟩ d a state of physical fitness or readiness for use ⟨the car was in good ~⟩ ⟨exercising to get into ~⟩ e pl attendant circumstances ⟨under present ~s⟩
²**condition** vt 1 to put into a proper or desired state for work or use 2 to give a certain condition to 3a to adapt to a surrounding culture b to modify so that an act or response previously associated with one stimulus becomes associated with another – **conditionable** adj, **conditioner** n
conditional adj 1 subject to, implying, or dependent on a condition ⟨a ~ promise⟩ 2 expressing, containing, or implying a supposition ⟨the ~ clause if he speaks⟩ 3 CONDITIONED 3 – **conditional** n, **conditionally** adv, **conditionality** n
conditioned adj 1 CONDITIONAL 1 2 brought or put into a specified state 3 esp of a reflex determined or established by conditioning
condole vi to express sympathetic sorrow ⟨we ~ with you in your misfortune⟩ – **condolatory** adj

condolence *n* (an expression of) sympathy with another in sorrow

condom *n* a sheath, usu of rubber, worn over the penis (e g to prevent conception or venereal infection during sexual intercourse)

condominium *n* 1 (a territory under) joint sovereignty by 2 or more nations 2 *NAm* (individual ownership of) a unit in a multi-unit structure (e g a block of flats)

condone *vt* to pardon or overlook voluntarily; tacitly accept; *esp* to treat as if harmless or of no importance ⟨~ *corruption in politics*⟩ – **condoner** *n*, **condonable** *adj*, **condonation** *n*

condor *n* a very large vulture of the high Andes with bare head and neck

conduce *vi* to lead or tend *to* a particular and usu desirable result; contribute – **conducive** *adj*

¹conduct *n* 1 the act, manner, or process of carrying on; management 2 a mode or standard of personal behaviour, esp as based on moral principles

²conduct *vt* 1 to bring (as if) by leading; guide ⟨~ *tourists through a museum*⟩ 2 to carry on or out, usu from a position of command or control ⟨~ *a siege*⟩ ⟨~ *an experiment*⟩ 3a to convey in a channel, pipe, etc b to act as a medium for transmitting (e g heat or light) 4 to behave in a specified manner ⟨~ed *himself appallingly*⟩ 5 to direct the performance or execution of (e g a musical work or group of musicians) ~ *vi* 1 to act as leader or director, esp of an orchestra 2 to have the property of transmitting heat, sound, electricity, etc – **conductible** *adj*, **conductive** *adj*, **conductibility** *n*

conduction *n* 1 the act of conducting or conveying 2 transmission through or by means of a conductor 3 the transmission of an electrical impulse through (nerve) tissue

conductivity *n* the quality or power of conducting or transmitting

conductor *n* 1 a collector of fares on a public conveyance, esp a bus 2 one who directs the performance of musicians 3 a substance or body capable of transmitting electricity, heat, sound, etc 4 *chiefly NAm* GUARD 6 – **conductorial** *adj*

conductor rail *n* a rail for conducting current to an electric locomotive or train

conduit *n* 1 a channel through which sthg (e g a fluid) is conveyed 2 a pipe, tube, or tile for protecting electric wires or cables

cone *n* 1 a mass of overlapping woody scales that, esp in trees of the pine family, are arranged on an axis and bear seeds between them; *broadly* any of several similar flower or fruit clusters 2a a solid generated by rotating a right-angled triangle about a side other than its hypotenuse b a solid figure tapering evenly to a point from a circular base 3a any of the relatively short light receptors in the retina of vertebrates that are sensitive to bright light and function in colour vision b any of many somewhat conical tropical gastropod molluscs c the apex of a volcano d a crisp cone-shaped wafer for holding a portion of ice cream

cone *vt* 1 to bevel like the slanting surface of a cone 2 to mark off (e g a road) with cones

coney *n* 1 a cony 2 rabbit fur

confabulate *vi* 1 to chat 2 to hold a discussion *USE* humor – **confabulatory** *adj*, **confabulation** *n*

confection *n* a fancy or rich dish (e g a cream cake or preserve) or sweetmeat – **confectionary** *adj*

confectioner *n* a manufacturer of or dealer in confectionery

confectionery *n* 1 confections, sweets 2 the confectioner's art or business 3 a confectioner's shop

confederacy *n* 1 a league or compact for mutual support or common action; an alliance 2 an unlawful association; a conspiracy 3 a league or alliance for common action; *esp*, *cap* the 11 states withdrawing from the USA in 1860 and 1861 – **confederal** *adj*, **confederalist** *n*

¹confederate *adj* 1 united in a league; allied 2 *cap* of or relating to the Confederacy

²confederate *n* 1 an ally, accomplice 2 *cap* an adherent of the Confederacy

³confederate *vt* to unite in a confederacy ~ *vi* to band together – **confederative** *adj*

confederation *n* a league

confer *vb* **-rr-** *vt* to bestow (as if) from a position of superiority ~ *vi* to come together to compare views or take counsel; consult – **conferrable** *adj*, **conferral** *n*, **conferrer** *n*, **conferee** *n*

conference *n* 1a a usu formal interchange of views; a consultation b a meeting of 2 or more people for the discussion of matters of common concern 2 a representative assembly or administrative organization of a denomination, organization, association, etc – **conferential** *adj*

confess *vt* 1 to make known (e g sthg wrong or damaging to oneself); admit 2a to acknowledge (sin) to God or a priest b to receive the confession of (a penitent) 3 to declare faith in or adherence to ~ *vi* 1a to acknowledge one's sins or the state of one's conscience to God or a priest b to hear a confession 2 to admit – **confessable** *adj*, **confessor** *n*

confession *n* 1 a disclosure of one's sins 2 a statement of what is confessed: e g a a written acknowledgment of guilt by a party accused of an offence b a formal statement of religious beliefs 3 an organized religious body having a common creed – **confessional** *adj*, **confessionalism** *n*, **confessionalist** *n*, **confessionally** *adv*

confessional *n* 1 a place where a priest hears confessions 2 *the* practice of confessing to a priest

confetti *n* small bits of brightly coloured paper meant to be thrown (e g at weddings)

confidant, *fem* **confidante** *n* one to whom secrets are entrusted; *esp* an intimate

confide *vi* to show confidence *in* by imparting secrets ~ *vt* to tell confidentially

confidence *n* 1 faith, trust ⟨*their* ~ *in God's mercy*⟩ 2 a feeling or consciousness of one's powers being sufficient, or of reliance on one's circumstances 3 the quality or state of being certain ⟨*they had every* ~ *of success*⟩ 4a a relationship of trust or intimacy ⟨*took his friend into his* ~⟩ b reliance on another's discretion ⟨*their story was told in strictest* ~⟩ c legislative support ⟨*vote of* ~⟩ 5 sthg said in confidence; a secret

confidence trick *n* a swindle performed by a person who pretends to be sthg that he/she is not

confident *adj* 1 characterized by assurance; *esp* self-reliant 2 full of conviction; certain – **confidently** *adv*

confidential *adj* 1 private, secret 2 marked by intimacy or willingness to confide ⟨*a* ~ *tone*⟩ – **confidentially** *adv*, **confidentialness** *n*, **confidentiality** *n*

configuration *n* 1a (relative) arrangement of parts b sthg (e g a figure, contour, pattern, or apparatus) produced by such arrangement c the relative positions in space of the atoms in a chemical compound 2 a gestalt ⟨*personality* ~⟩ – **configurational** *adj*, **configurationally** *adv*, **configurative** *adj*

¹confine *vt* 1 to keep within limits; restrict 2a to shut up; imprison b to keep indoors or in bed, esp just before childbirth ⟨*she was* ~d *2 days before the baby was due*⟩ – usu passive – **confiner** *n*

²**confine** n **1** bounds, borders **2** outlying parts; limits *USE* usu pl with sing. meaning

confinement n confining or being confined, esp in child-birth

confirm vt **1** to make firm or firmer; strengthen **2** to give approval to; ratify ⟨~ *a treaty*⟩ **3** to administer the rite of confirmation to **4** to make certain of; remove doubt about by authoritative act or indisputable fact ⟨*I* ~ *our offer of the job*⟩ ⟨*served to* ~ *me in my suspicions*⟩ – **confirmable** adj, **confirmability** n

confirmation n **1** a rite admitting a person to full membership of a church **2** confirming proof; corroboration – **confirmational** adj, **confirmatory** adj

confirmed adj **1a** made firm; strengthened **b** being so fixed in habit as to be unlikely to change ⟨*a* ~ *bachelor*⟩ **2** having received the rite of confirmation – **confirmedly** adv, **confirmedness** n

confiscate vt to seize (as if) by authority – **confiscator** n, **confiscation** n, **confiscatory** adj

conflagration n a (large disastrous) fire

conflate vt to bring together; fuse ⟨~ *2 texts into 1*⟩ – **conflation** n

¹**conflict** n **1** a sharp disagreement or clash (e g between divergent ideas, interests, or people) **2** (distress caused by) mental struggle resulting from incompatible impulses **3** a hostile encounter (e g a fight, battle, or war)

²**conflict** vi to be in opposition (to another or each other); disagree – **confliction** n

confluence, confluency n **1** a coming or flowing together; a meeting or gathering at 1 point **2** the (place of) union of 2 or more streams

conform vt to give the same shape, outline, or contour to; bring into harmony or accord ~ vi **1** to be similar or identical **2** to be obedient or compliant; *esp* to adapt oneself to prevailing standards or customs – **conformer** n, **conformism** n, **conformist** n

conformable adj **1** corresponding in form or character; similar – usu + *to* **2** of geological strata following in unbroken sequence – **conformably** adv

conformation n **1** adaptation **2a** CONFORMITY 1 **b** the way in which sthg is formed; shape, structure – **conformational** adj

conformity n **1** correspondence in form, manner, or character; agreement ⟨*behaved in* ~ *with his beliefs*⟩ **2** an act or instance of conforming **3** action in accordance with a specified standard or authority; obedience ⟨~ *to social custom*⟩

confound vt **1** to put to shame; discomfit ⟨*a performance that* ~ed *his critics*⟩ **2** to refute ⟨*sought to* ~ *his arguments*⟩ **3** to damn – used as a mild interjection of annoyance ⟨~ *him!*⟩ **4** to throw into confusion or perplexity **5** to increase the confusion of ⟨*confusion worse* ~ed – John Milton⟩ – **confounder** n

confounded adj damned ⟨*that* ~ *cat!*⟩ – **confoundedly** adv

confraternity n a society devoted to a religious or charitable cause

confront vt **1** to face, esp in challenge; oppose **2a** to cause to meet; bring face to face with ⟨~ *a reader with statistics*⟩ **b** to be faced with ⟨*the problems that one* ~s *are enormous*⟩ – **confronter** n

confrontation n **1** a face-to-face meeting **2** (an instance of) the clashing of forces or ideas; a conflict ⟨*sit-ins,* ~s *and riot* – Power & Authority in British Universities⟩ – **confrontational** adj, **confrontationism** n, **confrontationist** n

Confucian adj of the Chinese philosopher Confucius †479 BC or his teachings or followers – **Confucian** n, **Confucianism** n

confuse vt **1a** to make embarrassed; abash **b** to disturb or muddle in mind or purpose ⟨*his question* ~d *me*⟩ **2a** to make indistinct; blur ⟨*stop confusing the issue*⟩ **b** to mix indiscriminately; jumble **c** to fail to differentiate from another often similar or related thing ⟨~ *Socialism with Communism*⟩ **3** archaic to bring to ruin – **confused** adj, **confusedly** adv, **confusing** adj, **confusingly** adv

confusion n **1** an instance of confusing or being confused **2** (a) disorder, muddle

confute vt to overwhelm in argument; refute conclusively – **confutation** n

conga n **1** a dance involving 3 steps followed by a kick and performed by a group, usu in single file **2** a tall narrow bass drum beaten with the hands

congeal vt **1** to bring from a fluid to a solid state (as if) by cold; to coagulate **2** to make rigid, inflexible, or immobile ~ vi to become congealed – **congealable** adj, **congealment** n

congenial adj **1** existing or associated together harmoniously – often + *with* **2** pleasant; *esp* agreeably suited to one's nature, tastes, or outlook – **congenially** adv, **congeniality** n

congenital adj **1a** existing at or dating from birth ⟨~ *idiocy*⟩ **b** constituting an essential characteristic; inherent ⟨~ *fear of snakes*⟩ **2** being such by nature ⟨*a* ~ *liar*⟩ – **congenitally** adv

conger, conger eel n any of various related (large) edible sea eels

congest vt **1** to cause an excessive fullness of the blood vessels of (e g an organ) **2** to clog ⟨*traffic* ~ed *the highways*⟩ – **congestion** n, **congestive** adj

¹**conglomerate** adj made up of parts from various sources or of various kinds

²**conglomerate** vt to accumulate ~ vi to gather into a mass or coherent whole ⟨*numbers of dull people* ~d *round her* – Virginia Woolf⟩ – **conglomerator** n, **conglomerative** adj

³**conglomerate** n **1** a composite mixture; *specif* (a) rock composed of variously-sized rounded fragments in a cement **2** a widely diversified business company – **conglomeratic** adj

conglomeration n a mixed coherent mass

congrats n pl congratulations – infml

congratulate vt to express pleasure to (a person) on account of success or good fortune – **congratulator** n, **congratulatory** adj

congratulation n a congratulatory expression – usu pl with sing. meaning

congregate vb to (cause to) gather together

congregation n **1** an assembly of people; *esp* such an assembly for religious worship **2** a religious community; *esp* an organized body of believers in a particular locality

congregational adj **1** of a congregation **2** *often cap* of (a body of) Protestant churches governed by the assembly of the local congregation – **congregationalism** n, *often cap*, **congregationalist** n or adj, *often cap*

congress n **1** a formal meeting of delegates for discussion and usu action on some question **2** the supreme legislative body of a nation; *esp, cap* that of the USA **3** an association, usu made up of delegates from constituent organizations **4** the act or action of coming together and meeting – fml – **congressional** adj, **congressionally** adv

congressman, fem congresswoman n a member of a congress

congruent adj **1** congruous **2** being exactly the same in size and shape ⟨~ *triangles*⟩ – **congruently** adv

congruity n being congruent or congruous

congruous adj **1** in agreement, harmony, or correspondence **2** conforming to the circumstances or requirements of a situation; appropriate – *fml* ⟨*a ~ room to work in* – G B Shaw⟩ – **congruously** *adv*, **congruousness** *n*

conic, conic section *n* **1** a plane curve, line, or point that is the intersection of a plane and a cone **2** a curve generated by a point which moves so that the ratio of its distance from a fixed point to its distance from a fixed line is constant

conical, conic *adj* **1** resembling a cone in shape **2** of a cone – **conically** *adv*, **conicity** *n*

conifer *n* any of an order of mostly evergreen trees and shrubs including pines, cypresses, and yews, that bear ovules naked on the surface of scales rather than enclosed in an ovary – **coniferous** *adj*

conjectural *adj* of the nature of or involving or based on conjecture – **conjecturally** *adv*

¹conjecture *n* **1** the drawing of conclusions from inadequate evidence **2** a conclusion reached by surmise or guesswork

²conjecture *vt* **1** to arrive at by conjecture **2** to make conjectures as to *~ vi* to form conjectures – **conjecturer** *n*

conjoin *vi* to join together, esp for a common purpose

conjoint *adj* related to, made up of, or carried by 2 or more in combination; joint, united – **conjointly** *adv*

conjugal *adj* of the married state or married people and their relationship – **conjugally** *adv*, **conjugality** *n*

¹conjugate *adj* **1** having features in common but opposite or inverse in some particular **2** derived from the same root ⟨*~ words*⟩ – **conjugately** *adv*, **conjugateness** *n*

²conjugate *vt* to give in prescribed order the various inflectional forms of (a verb) *~ vi* **1** to become joined together **2** to pair and fuse in genetic conjugation

³conjugate *n* sthg conjugate; a product of conjugating

conjugation *n* **1a** (a diagrammatic arrangement of) the inflectional forms of a verb **b** a class of verbs having the same type of inflectional forms **2a** fusion of (similar) gametes with union of their nuclei that in algae, fungi, etc replaces the typical fertilization of higher forms **b** the one-way transfer of DNA between bacteria in cellular contact – **conjugational** *adj*, **conjugationally** *adv*, **conjugative** *adj*

conjunction *n* **1** joining together; being joined together **2** occurrence together in time or space; concurrence **3** the apparent meeting or passing of 2 or more celestial bodies **4** a word (e g *and* or *when*) that joins together sentences, clauses, phrases, or words – **conjunctional** *adj*, **conjunctionally** *adv*

conjunctiva *n*, *pl* **conjunctivas, conjunctivae** the mucous membrane that lines the inner surface of the eyelids and is continued over part of the eyeball – **conjunctival** *adj*, **conjunctivitis** *n*

conjunctive *adj* **1** connective **2** being or functioning like a conjunction – **conjunctive** *n*, **conjunctively** *adv*

conjuncture *n* a combination of circumstances or events usu producing a crisis; a juncture

conjure *vt* **1a** to summon by invocation or by uttering a spell, charm, etc **b(1)** to affect or effect (as if) by magical powers **(2)** to imagine, contrive – often + *up* ⟨*to ~ up imaginary dangers*⟩ **2** *archaic* to charge or entreat earnestly or solemnly *~ vi* **1** to make use of magical powers **2** to use a conjurer's tricks

conjurer, conjuror *n* one who performs tricks by sleight of hand or illusion

conk *n* (a punch on) the nose – *infml*

conk *vt* to hit (someone) on the head, esp the nose – *infml*

conk *vi* **1** to break down; *esp* to stall ⟨*the motor suddenly ~ed out*⟩ **2** to faint *USE* usu + *out*; *infml*

conker *n* **1** *pl but sing in constr* a British game in which each player in turn swings a conker on a string to try to break one held on its string by his/her opponent **2** the large seed of the horse chestnut, esp as used in playing conkers

connect *vt* **1** to join or fasten together, usu by some intervening thing **2** to place or establish in relationship *~ vi* **1** to be or become joined ⟨*the 2 rooms ~ through a hallway*⟩ **2** to make a successful hit or shot – **connectable** *also* **connectible** *adj*, **connector** *also* **connecter** *n*

connected *adj* **1** joined or linked together **2** having a social, professional, or commercial relationship – **connectedly** *adv*, **connectedness** *n*

connecting rod *n* a rod that transmits power from a part of a machine in reciprocating motion (e g a piston) to another that is rotating (e g a crankshaft)

connection, chiefly Br connexion *n* **1a** causal or logical relationship ⟨*the ~ between 2 ideas*⟩ **b** contextual relations or associations ⟨*in this ~ the word has a different meaning*⟩ **2a** sthg that connects; a link ⟨*a loose ~ in the wiring*⟩ **b** an arrangement that assists communication or transport; *specif* a train, aeroplane, etc that one should transfer to at a particular station, airport, etc ⟨*missed their ~ at Crewe*⟩ **3** a person connected with others, esp by marriage, kinship, or common interest ⟨*has powerful ~s in high places*⟩ **4** a social, professional, or commercial relationship: e g **a** an arrangement to execute orders or advance interests of another ⟨*a firm's foreign ~s*⟩ **b** a source of contraband (e g illegal drugs) **5** a religious denomination – **connectional** *adj* – **in connection with** with reference to; concerning

¹connective *adj* tending to connect – **connectively** *adv*, **connectivity** *n*

²connective *n* sthg that connects; *esp* a conjunction

conning tower *n* a raised observation tower and usu entrance on the deck of a submarine

connivance *n* knowledge of and active or passive consent to wrongdoing

connive *vi* **1** to pretend ignorance of or fail to take action against sthg one ought to oppose **2a** to be indulgent or in secret sympathy **b** to cooperate secretly or have a secret understanding; conspire *USE* often + *at* – **conniver** *n*

connoisseur *n* **1** an expert judge in matters of taste or appreciation (e g of art) **2** one who enjoys with discrimination and appreciation of subtleties ⟨*a ~ of fine wines*⟩ – **connoisseurship** *n*

connote *vt* **1** to convey in addition to exact explicit meaning ⟨*all the misery that poverty ~s*⟩ **2** to be associated with or inseparable from as a consequence or accompaniment ⟨*the remorse so often ~d by guilt*⟩ **3** to imply or indicate as a logically essential attribute of sthg denoted – **connotation** *n*, **connotational, connotative** *adj*

connubial *adj* conjugal – **connubially** *adv*, **connubiality** *n*

conquer *vt* **1** to gain or acquire by force of arms; subjugate ⟨*~ed England*⟩ **2** to overcome by force of arms; vanquish ⟨*~ed Harold*⟩ **3** to gain mastery over ⟨*~ed the mountain*⟩ ⟨*~ed his fear*⟩ *~ vi* to be victorious ⟨*we will ~ or die*⟩ – **conqueror** *n*

conquest *n* **1** conquering **2a** sthg conquered; *esp* territory appropriated in war – often *pl* **b** a person who has been won over, esp by love or sexual attraction

conquistador *n*, *pl* **conquistadores, conquistadors** one who conquers; *specif* any of the Spanish conquerors of America

consanguineous *adj* of the same blood or origin; *specif* descended from the same ancestor – **consanguineously** *adv*, **consanguinity** *n*

conscience *n* **1** the consciousness of the moral quality of one's own conduct or intentions, together with a feeling of obligation to refrain from doing wrong 2 conformity to the dictates of conscience; conscientiousness ⟨~ *argues against it*⟩ – **conscienceless** *adj* – **in all conscience** by any standard of fairness

conscience clause *n* a clause in a law exempting those who object on moral or religious grounds

conscience money *n* money paid usu anonymously to relieve the conscience

conscientious *adj* 1 governed by or conforming to the dictates of conscience; scrupulous 2 meticulous or careful, esp in one's work; *also* hard-working – **conscientiously** *adv*, **conscientiousness** *n*

conscientious objector *n* one who refuses to serve in the armed forces or bear arms, esp on moral or religious grounds – **conscientious objection** *n*

¹**conscious** *adj* 1 perceiving with a degree of controlled thought or observation 2 personally felt 3 capable of or marked by thought, will, intention, or perception 4 having mental faculties undulled by sleep, faintness, or stupor; awake 5 done or acting with critical awareness ⟨*made a ~ effort to avoid the same mistakes*⟩ 6 marked by awareness of or concern for sthg specified ⟨*a fashion-conscious shopper*⟩ – **consciously** *adv*

²**conscious** *n* CONSCIOUSNESS 3 – used in Freudian psychology

consciousness *n* 1 concern, awareness ⟨*class ~*⟩ 2 the totality of conscious states of an individual 3 the upper level of mental life of which sby is aware, as contrasted with unconscious processes

¹**conscript** *n or adj* (sby) conscripted

²**conscript** *vt* to enlist compulsorily, esp for military service – **conscription** *n*

consecrate *vt* 1 to ordain to a religious office, esp that of bishop 2a to make or declare sacred by a solemn ceremony b to prepare (bread and wine used at communion) to be received as Christ's body and blood c to devote to a purpose with deep solemnity or dedication 3 to make inviolable or venerable ⟨*principles ~d by the weight of history*⟩ – **consecrator** *n*, **consecration** *n*, **consecratory** *adj*

consecutive *adj* following one after the other in order without gaps – **consecutively** *adv*, **consecutiveness** *n*

consensus *n* 1 general agreement; unanimity 2 the judgment arrived at by most of those concerned

¹**consent** *vi* to give assent or approval; agree *to* – **consenter** *n*, **consentingly** *adv*

²**consent** *n* compliance with or approval of what is done or proposed by another; acquiescence

consequence *n* 1 sthg produced by a cause or necessarily following from a set of conditions 2 a conclusion arrived at by reasoning 3a importance in terms of power to produce an effect; moment b social importance – **in consequence** as a result; consequently

consequent *adj* following as a result or effect

consequential *adj* 1 consequent 2 of the nature of a secondary result; indirect 3 having significant consequences; important ⟨*a grave and ~ event*⟩ – **consequentially** *adv*, **consequentialness**, **consequentiality** *n*

consequently *adv* as a result; in view of the foregoing

conservancy *n* 1a conservation b (an area protected by) an organization designated to conserve and protect the environment 2 *Br* a board regulating a river or port

conservation *n* careful preservation and protection, esp of a natural resource, the quality of the environment, or plant or animal species, to prevent exploitation, destruction, etc – **conservational** *adj*, **conservationist** *n*

conservatism *n* 1 (a political philosophy based on) the disposition to preserve what is established 2 *cap* the

principles and policies of a Conservative party 3 the tendency to prefer an existing situation to change

¹**conservative** *adj* 1a of or being a philosophy of conservatism; traditional b *cap* advocating conservatism; *specif* of or constituting a British political party associated with support of established institutions and opposed to radical change 2a moderate, cautious ⟨*a ~ estimate*⟩ b marked by or relating to traditional norms of taste, elegance, style, or manners ⟨*a ~ suit*⟩ – **conservatively** *adv*, **conservativeness** *n*

²**conservative** *n* 1 *cap* a supporter of a Conservative party 2 one who keeps to traditional methods or views

conservatoire *n* a school specializing in any one of the fine arts ⟨*a ~ of music*⟩

conservatory *n* 1 a greenhouse, usu forming a room of a house, for growing or displaying ornamental plants 2 *chiefly NAm* a conservatoire

¹**conserve** *vt* 1a to keep in a state of safety or wholeness ⟨*~ wild life*⟩ b to avoid wasteful or destructive use of ⟨*~ natural resources*⟩ 2 to preserve, esp with sugar 3 to maintain (mass, energy, momentum, etc) constant during a process of chemical or physical change – **conserver** *n*

²**conserve** *n* a preserve of fruit boiled with sugar that is used like jam

consider *vt* 1 to think about with care or caution 2 to gaze on steadily or reflectively 3 to think of as specified; regard as being ⟨*~ thrift essential*⟩ ⟨*their works are well ~ed abroad*⟩ 4 to have as an opinion ⟨*~ed that he was wrong*⟩ ~ *vi* to reflect, deliberate ⟨*paused a moment to ~*⟩

considerable *adj* 1 worth consideration; significant 2 large in extent or degree ⟨*a ~ number*⟩ – **considerably** *adv*

considerate *adj* marked by or given to consideration of the rights and feelings of others – **considerately** *adv*, **considerateness** *n*

consideration *n* 1 continuous and careful thought ⟨*after long ~*⟩ 2a sthg considered as a basis for thought or action; a reason b a taking into account 3 thoughtful and sympathetic or solicitous regard 4a a recompense, payment ⟨*for a small ~*⟩ b an element of inducement that distinguishes a legally binding contract from a mere promise – **in consideration of** 1 in recompense or payment for 2 ON ACCOUNT OF, BECAUSE OF

considered *adj* matured by extended thought ⟨*his ~ opinion*⟩

¹**considering** *prep* taking into account ⟨*he did well ~ his limitations*⟩

²**considering** *conj* in view of the fact that ⟨*~ he was new at the job, he did quite well*⟩

consign *vt* 1 to give over to another's care 2 to give, transfer, or deliver into the hands or control of another; *also* to assign *to* sthg as a destination or end – **consignable** *adj*, **consignor** *n*

consignee *n* one to whom sthg is consigned

consignment *n* sthg consigned, esp in a single shipment

consist *vi* 1 to lie, reside *in* ⟨*liberty ~s in the absence of obstructions* – A E Housman⟩ 2 to be made up or composed *of* ⟨*breakfast ~ed of cereal, milk, and fruit*⟩

consistency *also* **consistence** *n* 1 internal constancy of constitution or character; persistency 2 degree of resistance of a a liquid to movement ⟨*the ~ of thick syrup*⟩ b a soft solid to deformation ⟨*the ~ of clay*⟩ 3a agreement or harmony of parts or features to one another or a whole; *specif* ability to be asserted together without contradiction b harmony of conduct or practice with past performance or stated intent ⟨*followed his own advice with ~*⟩

consistent *adj* **1** marked by harmonious regularity or steady continuity; free from irregularity, variation, or contradiction ⟨*a ~ style in painting*⟩ **2** converging to the true value of a statistical parameter estimated as the sample becomes large ⟨*a ~ estimator*⟩ – **consistently** *adv*

consistory *n* a church tribunal or governing body; *esp* one made up of the Pope and cardinals – **consistorial** *adj*

consol *n* an interest-bearing government bond having no maturity date but redeemable on call – usu pl

consolation prize *n* a prize given to one who just fails to gain a major prize in a contest

console *vt* to alleviate the grief or sense of loss of – **consolingly** *adv*, **consolable** *adj*, **consolation** *n*, **consolatory** *adj*

console *n* **1** a carved bracket projecting from a wall to support a shelf or cornice **2** the desk containing the keyboards, stops, etc of an organ **3a** a control panel; *also* a cabinet in which a control panel is mounted **b** the part of a computer used for communication between the operator and the computer **4** a cabinet (e g for a radio or television set) designed to rest directly on the floor

console table *n* a table fixed to a wall and supported by brackets

consolidate *vt* **1** to join together into 1 whole; unite ⟨*~ several small school districts*⟩ **2** to make firm or secure; strengthen ⟨*~ their hold on first place*⟩ **3** to form into a compact mass *~ vi* to become consolidated; *specif* to merge ⟨*the 2 companies ~* d⟩ – **consolidator** *n*

consommé *n* a thin clear meat soup made from meat broth

consonance *n* **1a** correspondence or recurrence of sounds, esp in words; assonance **b** an agreeable combination of musical notes in harmony **2** harmony or agreement among components – *fml*

consonant *n* (a letter or other symbol representing) any of a class of speech sounds (e g /p/, /g/, /n/, /l/, /s/, /r/) characterized by constriction or closure at 1 or more points in the breath channel – **consonantal** *adj*

consonant *adj* **1** marked by musical consonances **2** having similar sounds ⟨*~ words*⟩ **3** in agreement or harmony; free from elements making for discord – *fml* – **consonantly** *adv*

consort *n* **1** an associate **2** a spouse

consort *n* **1** a conjunction, association ⟨*he ruled in ~ with his father*⟩ **2a** a group of musicians performing esp early music **b** a set of musical instruments (e g viols or recorders) of the same family played together

consort *vi* **1** to keep company *with* ⟨*~* ing *with criminals*⟩ **2** to accord, harmonize *with* ⟨*the illustrations ~ admirably with the text – TLS*⟩ *USE* fml

consortium *n, pl* **consortia** *also* **consortiums** a business or banking agreement or combination

conspectus *n, pl* **conspectuses** a survey, summary; *esp* a brief one providing an overall view

conspicuous *adj* **1** obvious to the eye or mind **2** attracting attention; striking – **conspicuously** *adv*, **conspicuousness** *n*

conspiracy *n* **1** (the offence of) conspiring together ⟨*~ to murder*⟩ **2a** an agreement among conspirators **b** *sing or pl in constr* a group of conspirators

conspiracy of silence *n* an agreement to keep silent, esp in order to promote or protect selfish interests

conspirator *n* one who conspires; a plotter

conspiratorial *adj* (suggestive) of a conspiracy or conspirator – **conspiratorially** *adv*

conspire *vi* **1a** to join in a plot **b** to scheme **2** to act together ⟨*circumstances ~* d *to defeat his efforts*⟩

constable *n* **1** a high officer of a medieval royal or noble household **2** the warden or governor of a royal castle or a fortified town **3** *Br* a policeman; *specif* one ranking below sergeant

constabulary *n sing or pl in constr* **1** the police force of a district or country **2** an armed police force organized on military lines ⟨*the Royal Ulster* Constabulary⟩

constabulary *adj* of a constable or constabulary

constancy *n* **1** fidelity, loyalty **2** freedom from change

constant *adj* **1** marked by steadfast resolution or faithfulness; exhibiting constancy of mind or attachment ⟨*his ~ friend for years*⟩ **2** invariable, uniform **3** continually occurring or recurring; regular – **constantly** *adv*

constant *n* sthg invariable or unchanging: e g **a** a number that has a fixed value in a given situation or universally or that is characteristic of some substance or instrument **b** a number that is assumed not to change value in a given mathematical discussion **c** a term in logic with a fixed designation

constellation *n* **1** any of many arbitrary configurations of stars supposed to fill the outlines of usu mythical figures **2** a cluster, group, or configuration; *esp* a large or impressive one – **constellatory** *adj*

consternation *n* amazed dismay that hinders or throws into confusion

constipate *vt* to cause constipation in

constipation *n* **1** abnormally delayed or infrequent passage of faeces **2** impairment or blockage of proper functioning

constituency *n* (the residents in) an electoral district

constituent *n* **1** an essential part; a component **2** a resident in a constituency

constituent *adj* **1** serving to form, compose, or make up a unit or whole; component **2** having the power to frame or amend a constitution ⟨*a ~ assembly*⟩ – **constituently** *adv*

constitute *vt* **1** to appoint to an often specified office, function, or dignity ⟨*~* d *authorities*⟩ ⟨*~* d *himself their representative*⟩ **2** to establish; SET UP: e g **a** to establish formally **b** to give legal form to **3** to form, make, be ⟨*12 months ~ a year*⟩ ⟨*unemployment ~* s *a major problem*⟩

constitution *n* **1** the act of establishing, making, or setting up **2a** the physical and mental structure of an individual **b** the factors or parts which go to make sthg; composition; *also* the way in which these parts or factors make up the whole **3** the way in which a state or society is organized **4** (a document embodying) the fundamental principles and laws of a nation, state, or social group

constitutional *adj* **1** relating to, inherent in, or affecting the constitution of body or mind **2** being in accordance with or authorized by the constitution of a state or society ⟨*a ~ government*⟩ **3** regulated according to a constitution ⟨*a ~ monarchy*⟩ **4** of a constitution – **constitutionalize** *vt*, **constitutionality** *n*

constitutional *n* a walk taken for one's health

constitutionalism *n* adherence to constitutional principles; *also* a constitutional system of government – **constitutionalist** *n*

constitutionally *adv* **1a** in accordance with one's mental or bodily constitution ⟨*~ unable to grasp subtleties*⟩ **b** in structure, composition, or physical constitution **2** in accordance with a constitution ⟨*was not ~ eligible to fill the office*⟩

constitutive *adj* having the power to enact or establish – **constitutively** *adv*

constrain *vt* **1** to force by imposed stricture or limitation ⟨*necessity ~* s *me to work*⟩ ⟨*the evidence ~* s *belief*⟩ **2** to

force or produce in an unnatural or strained manner ⟨*a ~ed smile*⟩ **3** to hold within narrow confines; *also* to clasp tightly – **constrainedly** *adv*
constraint *n* **1a** constraining or being constrained **b** a constraining agency or force; a check ⟨*put legal ~s on the board's activities*⟩ **2a** repression of one's own feelings, behaviour, or actions **b** a sense of being constrained; embarrassment
constrict *vt* **1a** to make narrow **b** to compress, squeeze ⟨*~ a nerve*⟩ **2** to set or keep within limits – **constrictive** *adj*, **constriction** *n*
constrictor *n* **1** a muscle that contracts a cavity or orifice or compresses an organ **2** a snake (e g a boa constrictor) that kills prey by compressing it in its coils
¹construct *vt* **1** to make or form by combining parts; build **2** to set in logical order **3** to draw (a geometrical figure) with suitable instruments and under given conditions – **constructible** *adj*, **constructor** *n*
²construct *n* sthg constructed, esp mentally
construction *n* **1** the arrangement and connection of morphemes, words, or groups of words into some higher unit (e g a phrase or clause) **2** the process, art, or manner of constructing; *also* sthg constructed **3** the act or result of construing, interpreting, or explaining – **constructional** *adj*, **constructionally** *adv*
constructive *adj* **1** (judicially) implied rather than explicit ⟨*~ permission*⟩ **2** of or involved in construction **3** suggesting improvement or development ⟨*~ criticism*⟩ – **constructively** *adv*, **constructiveness** *n*
construe *vt* **1** to analyse the syntax of (e g a sentence or sentence part) **2** to understand or explain the sense or intention of ⟨*~d my actions as hostile*⟩ **3** to translate closely – *~ vi* to construe a sentence or sentence part, esp in connection with translating – **construable** *adj*
consubstantiation *n* (the Anglican doctrine of) the actual presence and combination of the body and blood of Christ with the bread and wine used at Communion
consul *n* **1a** either of 2 elected chief magistrates of the Roman republic **b** any of 3 chief magistrates of France from 1799 to 1804 **2** an official appointed by a government to reside in a foreign country to look after the (commercial) interests of citizens of the appointing country – **consulship** *n*, **consular** *adj*
consulate *n* **1** a government by consuls **2** the residence, office, or jurisdiction of a consul
consult *vt* **1** to ask the advice or opinion of ⟨*~ a doctor*⟩ **2** to refer to ⟨*~ a dictionary*⟩ – *~ vi* **1** to deliberate together; confer **2** to serve as a consultant – **consulter** *n*
consultancy *n* **1** an agency that provides consulting services **2** consultation
consultant *n* **1** one who consults sby or sthg **2** an expert who gives professional advice or services **3** the most senior grade of British hospital doctor, usu having direct clinical responsibility for hospital patients – **consultantship** *n*
consultation *n* **1** a council, conference **2** the act of consulting or conferring
consultative *adj* of or intended for consultation; advisory ⟨*a ~ committee*⟩
consulting *adj* **1** providing professional or expert advice ⟨*a ~ architect*⟩ **2** of a (medical) consultation or consultant
consume *vt* **1** to do away with completely; destroy ⟨*fire ~d several buildings*⟩ **2a** to spend wastefully; squander **b** to use or use up ⟨*work ~s time*⟩⟨*furnaces ~ fuel*⟩ **3** to eat or drink, esp in great quantity or eagerly **4** to engage fully; engross ⟨*she was ~d with curiosity*⟩ – *~ vi* to waste

or burn away; perish – **consumable** *adj*, **consumingly** *adv*
consumer *n* **1** a customer for goods or services **2** an organism requiring complex organic compounds for food, which it obtains by preying on other organisms or by eating particles of organic matter – **consumership** *n*
¹consummate *adj* **1** extremely skilled and accomplished ⟨*a ~ liar*⟩ **2** of the highest degree ⟨*~ skill*⟩⟨*~ cruelty*⟩ – **consummately** *adv*
²consummate *vt* to make (a marriage) complete by sexual intercourse – **consummative** *adj*, **consummator** *n*
consummation *n* **1** the consummating of a marriage **2** the ultimate end; a goal
consumption *n* **1** the act or process of consuming **2** the utilization of economic goods in the satisfaction of wants or in the process of production, resulting chiefly in their destruction, deterioration, or transformation **3** (a progressive wasting of the body, esp from) lung tuberculosis
consumptive *adj* of or affected with consumption (of the lungs) – **consumptive** *n*, **consumptively** *adv*
¹contact *n* **1a** (an instance of) touching **b** (a part made to form) the junction of 2 electrical conductors through which a current passes **2a** association, relationship ⟨*she needs human ~*⟩ **b** connection, communication ⟨*keep in ~!*⟩ **c** the act of establishing communication with sby or observing or receiving a significant signal from a person or object ⟨*radar ~ with Mars*⟩ **3** one serving as a carrier or source ⟨*our ~ in Berlin*⟩
²contact *vt* **1** to bring into contact **2a** to enter or be in contact with; join **b** to get in communication with ⟨*~ your local agent*⟩ – *~ vi* to make contact
³contact *adj* maintaining, involving, or activated or caused by contact ⟨*~ explosives*⟩
contact lens *n* a thin lens designed to fit over the cornea of the eye, esp for the correction of a visual defect
contagion *n* **1a** the transmission of a disease by (indirect) contact **b** (a virus, bacterium, etc that causes) a contagious disease **2** corrupting influence or contact
contagious *adj* **1** communicable by contact; catching **2** bearing contagion **3** exciting similar emotions or conduct in others ⟨*~ enthusiasm*⟩ – **contagiously** *adv*, **contagiousness** *n*
contain *vt* **1** to keep within limits; hold back or hold down: e g **a** to restrain, control ⟨*~ yourself!*⟩ **b** to check, halt ⟨*~ the enemy's attack*⟩ **c** to follow successfully a policy of containment towards **d** to prevent (an enemy, opponent, etc) from advancing or attacking **2a** to have within; hold **b** to comprise, include ⟨*the bill ~s several new clauses*⟩ **3** to be divisible by, usu without a remainder – **containable** *adj*
container *n* a receptacle for the shipment of goods; *specif* a metal packing case, standardized for mechanical handling, usu forming a single lorry or rail-wagon load
containerize, -ise *vt* **1** to ship by containerization **2** to convert to the use of containers ⟨*plans to ~ the ports*⟩
container ship *n* a ship for carrying cargo in containers
containment *n* preventing the expansion of a hostile power or ideology
contaminate *vt* **1a** to soil, stain, or infect by contact or association **b** to make inferior or impure by adding sthg ⟨*iron ~d with phosphorus*⟩ **2** to make unfit for use by the introduction of unwholesome or undesirable elements – **contaminator** *n*, **contamination** *n*, **contaminative** *adj*
contemplate *vt* **1** to view or consider with continued attention; meditate on **2** to have in view as contingent or probable or as an end or intention ⟨*what do you ~ doing?*⟩ – *~ vi* to ponder, meditate – **contemplator** *n*

contemplation n 1 meditation on spiritual things as a private devotion 2 an act of considering with attention; a study 3 the act of regarding steadily

contemplative adj 1 of or involving contemplation 2 of a religious order devoted to prayer and penance – **contemplative** n, **contemplatively** adv, **contemplativeness** n

contemporaneous adj CONTEMPORARY 1 – **contemporaneously** adv, **contemporaneousness**, **contemporaneity** n

¹**contemporary** adj 1 happening, existing, living, or coming into being during the same period of time 2 marked by characteristics of the present period; modern – **contemporarily** adv

²**contemporary** n sby or sthg contemporary with another; specif one of about the same age as another

contempt n 1a the act of despising; the state of mind of one who despises b lack of respect or reverence for sthg 2 the state of being despised ⟨*he is held in* ∼ ⟩ 3 obstruction of the administration of justice in court; esp wilful disobedience to or open disrespect of a court

contemptible adj worthy of contempt – **contemptibleness** n, **contemptibly** adv

contemptuous adj manifesting, feeling, or expressing contempt – **contemptuously** adv, **contemptuousness** n

contend vi 1 to strive or vie in contest or rivalry or against difficulties 2 to strive in debate; argue ∼ vt to maintain, assert ⟨∼ed *that he was right*⟩ – **contender** n

¹**content** adj happy, satisfied ⟨∼ *to wait quietly*⟩ – **contentment** n

²**content** vt 1 to appease the desires of; satisfy 2 to limit (oneself) in requirements, desires, or actions – usu + with

³**content** n freedom from care or discomfort; satisfaction

⁴**content** n 1a that which is contained – usu pl with sing. meaning ⟨*the jar's* ∼s⟩ ⟨*the drawer's* ∼s⟩ b pl the topics or matter treated in a written work ⟨*table of* ∼s⟩ 2a the substance, gist ⟨∼ *as opposed to form*⟩ b the events, physical detail, and information in a work of art 3 the matter dealt with in a field of study 4 the amount of specified material contained; proportion ⟨*the lead* ∼ *of paint*⟩

contented adj marked by satisfaction with one's possessions, status, or situation; happy – **contentedly** adv, **contentedness** n

contention n 1 (an act or instance of) contending 2 a point advanced or maintained in a debate or argument

contentious adj 1 exhibiting an often perverse and wearisome tendency to quarrels and disputes 2 likely to cause contention ⟨*a* ∼ *argument*⟩ – **contentiously** adv, **contentiousness** n

¹**contest** vt to make the subject of dispute, contention, or litigation ∼ vi to strive, vie – **contestable** adj, **contester** n

²**contest** n 1 a struggle for superiority or victory 2 a competitive event; COMPETITION 2; esp one adjudicated by a panel of specially chosen judges

contestant n 1 one who participates in a contest 2 one who contests an award or decision

context n 1 the parts surrounding a written or spoken word or passage that can throw light on its meaning 2 the interrelated conditions in which sthg exists or occurs – **contextual** adj, **contextually** adv

contiguous adj 1 in actual contact; touching along a boundary or at a point 2 next or near in time or sequence – **contiguously** adv, **contiguousness** n, **contiguity** n

continence n 1 self-restraint from yielding to impulse or desire 2 ability to refrain from a bodily activity; the state of being continent

¹**continent** adj 1 exercising continence 2 not suffering from incontinence of the urine or faeces – **continently** adv

²**continent** n 1 any of the (7) great divisions of land on the globe 2 cap the continent of Europe as distinguished from the British Isles

¹**continental** adj (characteristic) of a continent, esp Europe – **continental** adv

²**continental** n an inhabitant of a continent, esp Europe

continental breakfast n a light breakfast, typically of bread rolls with preserves and coffee

continental drift n the (supposed) drifting apart of the continents from being a solid land mass

continental quilt n a duvet

continental shelf n the gently sloping part of the ocean floor that borders a continent and ends in a steeper slope to the ocean depths

contingency n 1 an event that may occur; esp an undesirable one 2 an event that is liable to accompany another event

¹**contingent** adj 1 happening by chance or unforeseen causes 2 dependent on or conditioned by sthg else 3 not logically necessary; esp empirical – **contingently** adv

²**contingent** n a quota or share, esp of people supplied from or representative of an area, group, or military force

continual adj 1 continuing indefinitely without interruption ⟨∼ *fear*⟩ 2 recurring in steady rapid succession – **continually** adv

continuance n 1 the act or process of continuing in a state, condition, or course of action 2 NAm adjournment of court proceedings

continuation n 1 the act or process of continuing in a state or activity 2 resumption after an interruption 3 sthg that continues, increases, or adds

continue vi 1 to maintain a condition, course, or action without interruption 2 to remain in existence; endure 3 to remain in a place or condition; stay 4 to resume an activity after interruption ∼ vt 1a to maintain (a condition, course, or action) without interruption; CARRY ON ⟨∼s *walking*⟩ b to prolong; specif to resume after interruption 2 to cause to continue 3 to say further ⟨'*We must fight for freedom*', ∼d *the speaker*⟩ 4 NAm to postpone (a legal proceeding) – **continuer** n

continuity n 1a uninterrupted connection, succession, or union b persistence without essential change c uninterrupted duration in time 2 sthg that has, displays, or provides continuity: e g a a script or scenario in the performing arts; esp one giving the details of the sequence of individual shots b speech or music used to link parts of an entertainment, esp a radio or television programme 3 an example of the property characteristic of a continuous mathematical function

continuo n, pl **continuos** a bass part for a keyboard or stringed instrument written as a succession of bass notes with figures that indicate the required chords; also (the instruments playing) a continuo accompaniment

continuous adj 1 marked by uninterrupted extension in space, time, or sequence 2 of a function having an arbitrarily small numerical difference between the value at any one point and the value at any other point sufficiently near the first point – **continuously** adv, **continuousness** n

continuum n, pl **continua**, **continuums** 1 sthg (e g duration or extension) absolutely continuous and homogeneous that can be described only by reference to sthg else (e g numbers) 2a sthg in which a fundamental common character is discernible amid a series of impercetible or indefinite variations ⟨*the ~ of experience*⟩ **b** an uninterrupted ordered sequence

contort *vb* to twist in a violent manner; deform ⟨*his features ~*ed *with fury*⟩⟨*~ spelling and grammar*⟩ – **contortive** *adj*, **contortion** *n*

contortionist *n* **1** an acrobat who specializes in unnatural body postures **2** one who extricates him-/herself from a dilemma by complicated but doubtful arguments – **contortionistic** *adj*

¹**contour** *n* **1** (a line representing) an outline, esp of a curving or irregular figure **2 contour, contour line** a line (e g on a map) connecting points of equal elevation or height

²**contour** *vt* **1a** to shape the contour of **b** to shape so as to fit contours **2** to construct (e g a road) in conformity to a contour

contra- *prefix* **1** against; contrary; contrasting ⟨contra*distinction*⟩⟨contra*ception*⟩ **2** pitched below normal ⟨contra*bass*⟩

contraband *n* goods or merchandise whose import, export, or possession is forbidden; *also* smuggled goods – **contraband** *adj*

contrabass *n* DOUBLE BASS

contraception *n* prevention of conception or impregnation – **contraceptive** *adj*

contraceptive *n* a method or device used in preventing conception; *esp* a condom

¹**contract** *n* **1a** (a document containing) a legally binding agreement between 2 or more people or parties **b** a betrothal **2** an undertaking to win a specified number of tricks in bridge

²**contract** *vt* **1** to undertake by contract **2a** to catch (an illness) **b** to incur as an obligation ⟨*~ a debt*⟩ **3** to knit, wrinkle ⟨*a frown ~*ed *his brow*⟩ **4** to reduce to a smaller size (as if) by squeezing or forcing together **5** to shorten (e g a word) *~vi* **1** to make a contract **2** to draw together so as to become smaller or shorter ⟨*metal ~*s *on cooling*⟩⟨*muscles ~ involuntarily in tetanus*⟩ – **contractible** *adj*, **contractibility** *n*

contract bridge *n* a form of bridge in which overtricks do not count towards game bonuses

contractile *adj* having the power or property of contracting ⟨*a ~ protein*⟩ – **contractility** *n*

contract in *vb* to agree to inclusion (of) in a particular scheme

contraction *n* **1** the shortening and thickening of a muscle (fibre) **2** (a form produced by) a shortening of a word, syllable, or word group – **contractional** *adj*, **contractive** *adj*

contractor *n* one who contracts to perform work, esp building work, or to provide supplies, usu on a large scale

contract out *vb* to agree to exclusion (of) from a particular scheme

contractual *adj* of or constituting a contract – **contractually** *adv*

contradict *vt* **1** to state the contrary of (a statement or speaker) **2** to deny the truthfulness of (a statement or speaker) – **contradictable** *adj*, **contradictor** *n*

contradiction *n* **1** a logical inconsistency ⟨*a ~ in terms*⟩ **2** an opposition or conflict inherent in a system or situation

¹**contradictory** *n* a proposition so related to another that if one is true the other must be false and if one is false the other must be true

²**contradictory** *adj* **1** given to or marked by contradiction **2** serving to contradict – **contradictorily** *adv*, **contradictoriness** *n*

contradistinction *n* distinction by contrast – **contradistinctive** *adj*, **contradistinctively** *adv*

contrail *n* a streak of condensed water vapour created in the air by the passage of an aircraft or rocket at high altitudes

contraindicate *vt* to make (a treatment of procedure) inadvisable ⟨*a drug that is ~*d *in pregnancy*⟩ – **contraindication** *n* **contraindicative** *adj*

contralto *n*, *pl* **contraltos 1** (a person with) the lowest female singing voice **2** the part sung by a contralto

contraption *n* a newfangled or complicated device; a gadget

contrapuntal *adj* of counterpoint – **contrapuntally** *adv*

contrariety *n* opposition, disagreement – fml

contrariwise *adv* conversely; VICE VERSA

¹**contrary** *n* **1** a fact or condition incompatible with another **2** either of a pair of opposites **3** either of 2 terms (e g true and false) that cannot both simultaneously be said to be true of the same subject – **on the contrary** just the opposite; no – **to the contrary 1** to the opposite effect ⟨*if I hear nothing* to the contrary *I'll accept that explanation*⟩ **2** notwithstanding

²**contrary** *adj* **1** completely different or opposed **2** opposite in position, direction, or nature **3** *of wind or weather* unfavourable **4** obstinately self-willed; inclined to oppose the wishes of others – **contrarily** *adv*, **contrariness** *n*

contrary to *prep* in opposition to

¹**contrast** *n* **1a** juxtaposition of dissimilar elements (e g colour, tone, or emotion) in a work of art **b** degree of difference between the lightest and darkest parts of a painting, photograph, television picture, etc **2** comparison of similar objects to set off their dissimilar qualities **3** a person or thing against which another may be contrasted – **contrastive** *adj*, **contrastively** *adv*

²**contrast** *vi* to exhibit contrast – *vt* **1** to put in contrast **2** to compare in respect to differences – **contrastable** *adj*

contravene *vt* to go or act contrary to ⟨*~ a law*⟩ – **contravener** *n*

contravention *n* a violation or infringement

contretemps *n*, *pl* **contretemps** a minor setback, disagreement, or confrontation

contribute *vt* **1** to give in common with others **2** to supply (e g an article) for a publication *~vi* **1** to help bring about an end or result **2** to supply articles to a publication – **contributive** *adj*, **contributively** *adv*, **contributor** *n*

contribution *n* the act of contributing; *also* sthg contributed

¹**contributory** *adj* **1** contributing to a common fund or enterprise **2** of or forming a contribution **3** financed by contributions; *specif*, *of an insurance or pension plan* contributed to by both employers and employees

²**contributory** *n* sby liable in British law to contribute towards meeting the debts of a bankrupt company

contrite *adj* **1** grieving and penitent for sin or shortcoming **2** showing contrition – **contritely** *adv*, **contriteness** *n*

contrition *n* sorrow for one's sins, arising esp from the love of God rather than fear of punishment

contrivance *n* **1** contriving or being contrived **2** sthg contrived; *esp* a mechanical device

contrive *vt* **1a** to devise, plan **b** to create in an inventive or resourceful manner **2** to bring about; manage – **contriver** *n*

contrived *adj* unnatural and forced

¹**control** *vt* **-ll- 1** to check, test, or verify **2a** to exercise

restraining or directing influence over **b** to have power over; rule – **controllable** *adj*, **controllability** *n*

²**control** *n* **1** power to control, direct, or command **2a** (an organism, culture, etc used in) an experiment in which the procedure or agent under test in a parallel experiment is omitted and which is used as a standard of comparison in judging experimental effects **b** a mechanism used to regulate or guide the operation of a machine, apparatus, or system – often pl **c** an organization that directs a space flight ⟨*mission* ∼⟩ **d** a personality or spirit believed to be responsible for the actions of a spiritualistic medium at a séance

controller *n* **1a** a public-finance official **b** a chief financial officer, esp of a business enterprise **2** one who controls or has power to control – **controllership** *n*

controversial *adj* of, given to, or arousing controversy – **controversialism** *n*, **controversialist** *n*, **controversially** *adv*

controversy *n* (a) debate or dispute, esp in public or in the media

controvert *vt* to deny or dispute – fml – **controverter** *n*, **controvertible** *adj*

contumacious *adj* stubbornly disobedient; rebellious – fml – **contumaciously** *adv*, **contumacy** *n*

contumely *n* abusive and contemptuous language or treatment – fml – **contumelious** *adj*, **contumeliously** *adv*

contuse *vt* to bruise (tissue) – **contusion** *n*

conundrum *n* **1** a riddle; *esp* one whose answer is or involves a pun **2** an intricate and difficult problem

conurbation *n* a grouping of several previously separate towns to form 1 large community

convalesce *vi* to recover gradually after sickness or weakness – **convalescence** *n*, **convalescent** *adj or n*

convection *n* (the transfer of heat by) the circulatory motion that occurs in a gas or liquid at a nonuniform temperature owing to the variation of density with temperature – **convect** *vb*, **convectional** *adj*, **convective** *adj*

convector *n* a heating unit from which heated air circulates by convection

convene *vi* to come together in a body ∼ *vt* **1** to summon before a tribunal **2** to cause to assemble

convenience *n* **1** fitness or suitability **2** an appliance, device, or service conducive to comfort **3** a suitable time; an opportunity ⟨*at your earliest* ∼⟩ **4** personal comfort or advantage **5** *Br* PUBLIC CONVENIENCE

convenient *adj* **1** suited to personal comfort or to easy use **2** suited to a particular situation **3** near at hand; easily accessible – **conveniently** *adv*

convent *n* a local community or house of a religious order or congregation; *esp* an establishment of nuns

conventicle *n* **1** an (irregular or unlawful) assembly or meeting **2** a (clandestine) assembly for religious worship **3** a meetinghouse – **conventicler** *n*

convention *n* **1a** an agreement or contract, esp between states or parties **b** an agreement between enemies (e g concerning the exchange of prisoners) **2** a generally agreed principle or practice **3** an assembly **4a** (an) accepted social custom or practice **b** an established artistic technique or practice ⟨*the* ∼s *of the stream-of-consciousness novel*⟩ **c** an agreed system of bidding or playing that conveys information between partners in bridge or another card game

conventional *adj* **1a** conforming to or sanctioned by convention **b** lacking originality or individuality **2** of *warfare* not using atom or hydrogen bombs – **conventionalism** *n*, **conventionalist** *n*, **conventionalize** *vt*, **conventionally** *adv*, **conventionality** *n*

converge *vi* **1** to move together towards a common point;

meet **2** to come together in a common interest or focus **3** *of (the value of a term in) a mathematical series* to approach a limit as the number of terms increases without limit ∼ *vt* to cause to converge

conversant *adj* having knowledge or experience; familiar with – **conversantly** *adv*

conversation *n* **1** (an instance of) informal verbal exchange of feelings, opinions, or ideas **2** an exchange similar to conversation; *esp* real-time interaction with a computer, esp through a keyboard – **conversational** *adj*, **conversationally** *adv*

conversationalist *n* one who converses a great deal or who excels in conversation

conversazione *n, pl* **conversaziones**, **conversazioni** a meeting for informal discussion of intellectual or cultural matters

¹**converse** *vi* **1** to exchange thoughts and opinions in speech; talk **2** to carry on an exchange similar to a conversation; *esp* to interact with a computer

²**converse** *n* conversation – fml

³**converse** *adj* reversed in order, relation, or action; opposite – **conversely** *adv*

⁴**converse** *n* sthg converse to another; *esp* a proposition in logic in which the subject and predicate terms have been interchanged ⟨'*no P is S*' *is the* ∼ *of* '*no S is P*'⟩

conversion *n* **1** converting or being converted **2** (an experience associated with) a definite and decisive adoption of a religious faith **3** sthg converted from one use to another **4** the unlawful exercising of rights to personal property belonging to another **5** the alteration of a building to a different purpose; *also* a building so altered **6** (the score resulting from) an opportunity to kick a goal awarded to the scoring team after a try in rugby **7** **conversion, conversion hysteria** bodily symptoms (e g paralysis) appearing as a result of mental conflict without a physical cause – **conversional** *adj*

¹**convert** *vt* **1a** to win over from one persuasion or party to another **b** to bring about a religious conversion in **2a** to alter the physical or chemical nature or properties of, esp in manufacturing **b** to change from one form or function to another; *esp* to make (structural) alterations to (a building or part of a building) **c** to exchange for an equivalent **3** to complete (a try) in rugby by successfully kicking a conversion ∼ *vi* to undergo conversion – **converter** *n*

²**convert** *n* a person who has experienced an esp religious conversion

¹**convertible** *adj* **1** capable of being converted **2** *of a motor vehicle* having a top that may be lowered or removed ⟨*a* ∼ *sports car*⟩ **3** capable of being exchanged for a specified equivalent (e g another currency) – **convertibleness** *n*, **convertibly** *adv*

²**convertible** *n* a convertible motor car

convex *adj* curved or rounded outwards like the outside of a bowl – **convexly** *adv*

convexity *n* a convex line, surface, or part

convey *vt* **1** to take or carry from one place to another **2** to impart or communicate (e g feelings or ideas) **3** to transmit, transfer; *specif* to transfer (property or the rights to property) to another

conveyance *n* **1** a document by which rights to property are transferred **2** a means of transport; a vehicle

conveyancing *n* the act or business of transferring rights to property – **conveyancer** *n*

conveyer, conveyor *n* a mechanical apparatus for carrying articles or bulk material (e g by an endless moving belt)

¹**convict** *vt* **1** to find or prove to be guilty **2** to convince of error or sinfulness

²**convict** *n* a person serving a (long-term) prison sentence

conviction *n* 1 convicting or being convicted, esp in judicial proceedings 2a a strong persuasion or belief b the state of being convinced

convince *vt* to cause to believe; persuade

convincing *adj* having the power to overcome doubt or disbelief; plausible – **convincingly** *adv*, **convincingness** *n*

convivial *adj* relating to or fond of eating, drinking, and good company – **convivially** *adv*, **conviviality** *n*

convocation *n* 1 an assembly of people called together: e g a either of the 2 provincial assemblies of bishops and representative clergy of the Church of England ⟨the ~ of York⟩ b a ceremonial assembly of graduates of a college or university 2 the act of calling together – **convocational** *adj*

convoke *vt* to call together to a formal meeting

convoluted *adj* 1 having convolutions 2 involved, intricate ⟨a ~ argument⟩

convolution *n* 1 any of the irregular ridges on the surface of the brain, esp of the cerebrum of higher mammals 2 sthg intricate or complicated – **convolutional** *adj*

convolvulus *n*, *pl* **convolvuluses, convolvuli** any of a genus of usu twining plants (e g bindweed)

¹**convoy** *vt* to accompany or escort, esp for protection

²**convoy** *n* 1 convoying or being convoyed 2 *sing or pl in constr* a group of ships, military vehicles, etc moving together, esp with a protective escort; *also* such an escort

convulse *vt* 1 to shake or agitate violently, esp (as if) with irregular spasms 2 to cause to laugh helplessly

convulsion *n* 1 an abnormal violent and involuntary contraction or series of contractions of the muscles 2a a violent disturbance b an uncontrolled fit; a paroxysm – **convulsionary** *adj*

convulsive *adj* constituting, producing, or affected with a convulsion – **convulsively** *adv*, **convulsiveness** *n*

cony, coney *n* 1 a rabbit 2 a pika 3 a hyrax

¹**coo** *vi* cooed, coo'd 1 to make (a sound similar to) the low soft cry characteristic of a dove or pigeon 2 to talk lovingly or appreciatively – **coo** *n*

²**coo** *interj*, *Br* – used to express surprise; infml

¹**cook** *n* sby who prepares food for eating

²**cook** *vi* 1 to prepare food for eating, esp by subjection to heat 2 to undergo the process of being cooked ⟨the rice is ~ ing now⟩ 3 to occur, happen – infml ⟨what's ~ ing?⟩ ~ *vt* 1 to prepare (e g food) for eating by a heating process 2 to subject to the action of heat or fire – **cook someone's goose** to ruin sby irretrievably – **cook the books** to falsify financial accounts in order to deceive

cooker *n* 1 an apparatus, appliance, etc for cooking; *esp* one typically consisting of an oven, hot plates or rings, and a grill fixed in position 2 a variety, esp of fruit, not usu eaten raw

cookery *n* the art or practice of cooking

cookery book *n* a book of recipes and instructions for preparing and cooking food

cookhouse *n* a kitchen set up outdoors, at a campsite, or on board ship

cookie, cooky *n* 1a *Scot* a plain bun b *NAm* a sweet flat or slightly leavened biscuit 2 chiefly *NAm* a person, esp of a specified type – infml ⟨a tough ~⟩

cooking *adj* suitable for or used in cooking ⟨~ apples⟩ ⟨~ utensils⟩

cookout *n*, chiefly *NAm* (the meal eaten at) an outing at which food is cooked and served in the open

cook up *vt* to concoct, improvise – infml

¹**cool** *adj* 1 moderately cold; lacking in warmth 2a dispassionately calm and self-controlled b lacking friendliness or enthusiasm c of or being an understated, restrained, and melodic style of jazz 3 disrespectful, impudent ⟨a ~ reply⟩ 4 bringing or suggesting relief from heat ⟨a ~ dress⟩ 5 of a colour producing an impression of being cool; *specif* in the range blue to green 6 showing sophistication by a restrained or detached manner 7 – used as an intensive; infml ⟨paid a ~ million for it⟩ 8 very good; excellent – slang – **coolish** *adj*, **coolly** also **cooly** *adv*, **coolness** *n*

²**cool** *vi* 1 to become cool; lose heat or warmth 2 to lose enthusiasm or passion ~ *vt* 1 to make cool; impart a feeling of coolness to – often + off or down 2 to moderate the excitement, force, or activity of – **cool it** to become calm or quiet; relax – infml ⟨just cool it, will you, so I can think⟩ – **cool one's heels** to wait or be kept waiting for a long time, esp (as if) from disdain or discourtesy

³**cool** *n* 1 a cool atmosphere or place 2 poise, composure – infml ⟨don't lose your ~⟩

⁴**cool** *adv* in a casual and nonchalant manner – infml ⟨play it ~⟩

coolant *n* a liquid or gas used in cooling, esp in an engine

cool down *vi* to allow a violent emotion (e g rage) to pass

cooler *n* 1a a container for cooling liquids b *NAm* a refrigerator 2 a prison cell – slang

coolheaded *adj* not easily excited

coolie *n* an unskilled labourer or porter, usu in or from the Far East, hired for low or subsistence wages

coon *n* 1 chiefly *NAm* a raccoon 2 a Negro – derog

¹**coop** *n* 1 a cage or small enclosure or building, esp for housing poultry 2 a confined space

²**coop** *vt* 1 to confine in a restricted space – usu + up 2 to place or keep in a coop – often + up

co-op *n* a cooperative

cooper *n* a maker or repairer of barrels, casks, etc – **cooper** *vb*, **cooperage** *n*

cooperate *vi* to act or work with another or others for a common purpose – **cooperator** *n*

cooperation *n* 1 a common effort 2 association for common benefit

¹**cooperative** *adj* 1 showing cooperation or a willingness to work with others 2 of, or organized as, a cooperative – **cooperatively** *adv*, **cooperativeness** *n*

²**cooperative** *n* an enterprise (e g a shop) or organization (e g a society) owned by and operated for the benefit of those using its services ⟨a housing ~⟩

co-opt *vt* 1 to choose or elect as a member; *specif, of a committee* to draft onto itself as an additional member 2 to gain the participation or services of; assimilate – **co-optation** *n*, **co-optative** *adj*, **co-option** *n*, **co-optive** *adj*

¹**coordinate** *adj* 1 equal in rank, quality, or significance 2 relating to or marked by coordination – **coordinately** *adv*, **coordinateness** *n*

²**coordinate** *n* 1 any of a set of numbers used in specifying the location of a point on a line, on a surface, or in space 2 *pl* outer garments, usu separates, in harmonizing colours, materials, and pattern

³**coordinate** *vt* to combine in a common action; harmonize ~ *vi* to be or become coordinate, esp so as to act together harmoniously – **coordination** *n*, **coordinative** *adj*, **coordinator** *n*

coot *n* 1 any of various slaty-black water birds of the rail family that somewhat resemble ducks 2 a foolish person – infml

¹**cop** *vt* -pp- to get hold of; catch; *specif, Br* to arrest – slang – **cop it** *Br* to be in serious trouble – slang

²cop *n*, *Br* a capture, arrest – esp in a *fair cop*; slang **– not much cop** *chiefly Br* fairly bad; worthless – slang

³cop *n* a policeman – infml

¹cope *n* a long ecclesiastical vestment resembling a cape, worn on special occasions (e g processions)

²cope *vt* to supply or cover with a cope or coping

³cope *vi* to deal with a problem or task effectively – usu + **with**

copeck *n* a kopeck

Copernican *adj* of Copernicus or the belief that the earth rotates daily on its axis and the planets revolve in orbits round the sun – **Copernican** *n*, **Copernicanism** *n*

copier *n* a machine for making copies, esp by photocopying or xeroxing

co-pilot *n* a qualified aircraft pilot who assists or relieves the pilot but is not in command

coping *n* the final, usu sloping, course of brick, stone, etc on the top of a wall

copingstone *n*, *chiefly Br* a stone forming (part of) a coping

copious *adj* 1 plentiful, lavish ⟨*a ~ harvest*⟩ 2 profuse in words or expression – **copiously** *adv*, **copious ness** *n*

cop-out *n* an act of copping out – infml

cop out *vi* to avoid an unwanted responsibility or commitment – infml

¹copper *n* 1 a common reddish metallic element that is ductile and malleable and one of the best conductors of heat and electricity 2 a coin or token made of copper or bronze and usu of low value 3 any of various small butterflies with usu copper-coloured wings 4 *chiefly Br* a large metal vessel used, esp formerly, for boiling clothes – **coppery** *adj*

²copper *n* a policeman – infml

copper beech *n* a variety of beech with copper-coloured leaves

copper-bottomed *adj*, *chiefly Br* completely safe; reliable ⟨*a ~ currency*⟩ ⟨*a ~ promise*⟩ – infml

copperplate *n* handwriting modelled on engravings in copper and marked by lines of sharply contrasting thickness; *broadly* formal and ornate handwriting

coppersmith *n* sby who works in, or produces articles of, copper

coppice *n* a thicket, grove, etc of small trees (originating mainly from shoots or root suckers rather than seed) – **coppice** *vb*

copra *n* dried coconut meat yielding coconut oil

Copt *n* a member of a people descended from the ancient Egyptians

Coptic *adj* of the Copts, their Afro-Asiatic liturgical language, or their church – **Coptic** *n*

copula *n* a verb (e g a form of *be* or *seem*) that links a subject and a complement

copulate *vi* to engage in sexual intercourse – **copulation** *n*, **copulatory** *adj*

¹copulative *adj* 1a joining together coordinate words or word groups and expressing addition of their meanings b functioning as a copula 2 of copulation – **copulatively** *adv*

²copulative *n* a copulative word

¹copy *n* 1 an imitation, transcript, or reproduction of an original work 2 any of a series of esp mechanical reproductions of an original impression 3 (newsworthy) material ready to be printed or photoengraved

²copy *vt* 1 to make a copy of 2 to model oneself on ~ *vi* 1 to make a copy 2 to undergo copying ⟨*the document did not ~ well*⟩

copybook *n* a book formerly used in teaching penmanship and containing models for imitation

copy-book *adj*, *Br* completely correct; proper

copycat *n* one who slavishly imitates the behaviour or practices of another – used chiefly by children

copy-edit *vb* to prepare (manuscript copy) for printing, esp by correcting errors and specifying style – **copy editor** *n*

copyhold *n* (land held by) a former type of land tenure in England established by a transcript of the manorial records – **copyholder** *n*

copyist *n* one who makes copies

¹copyright *n* the exclusive legal right to reproduce, publish, and sell a literary, musical, or artistic work – **copyright** *adj*

²copyright *vt* to secure a copyright on

copywriter *n* a writer of advertising or publicity copy

coquetry *n* flirtatious behaviour or attitude

coquette *n* a woman who tries to gain the attention and admiration of men without sincere affection – **coquettish** *adj*

cor *interj*, *Br* – used to express surprise or incredulity; slang

coracle *n* a small (nearly) circular boat of a traditional Welsh or Irish design made by covering a wicker frame with waterproof material

coral *n* 1 (the hard esp red deposit produced as a skeleton chiefly by) a colony of anthozoan polyps 2 a piece of (red) coral 3a a bright reddish mass of ovaries (e g of a lobster or scallop) b deep orange-pink – **coral** *adj*, **coralloid**, **coralloidal** *adj*

cor anglais *n* a double-reed woodwind instrument similar to, and with a range a fifth lower than, the oboe

¹corbel *n* a projection from a wall which supports a weight; *esp* one stepped upwards and outwards from a vertical surface

²corbel *vt* -ll- (*NAm* -l-, -ll-) to supply with or make into a corbel

¹cord *n* 1 (a length of) long thin flexible material consisting of several strands (e g of thread or yarn) woven or twisted together 2 a moral, spiritual, or emotional bond 3a an anatomical structure (e g a nerve) resembling a cord b an electric flex 4 a unit of cut wood usu equal to 128ft³ (about 3.63m³); *also* a stack containing this amount of wood 5a a rib like a cord on a textile b(1) a fabric made with such ribs (2) *pl* trousers made of corduroy

²cord *vt* 1 to provide, bind, or connect with a cord 2 to pile up (wood) in cords – **corder** *n*

cordage *n* ropes, esp in a ship's rigging

¹cordial *adj* 1 warmly and genially affable ⟨*a most ~ welcome*⟩ 2 sincerely or deeply felt – **cordially** *adv*, **cordialness**, **cordiality** *n*

²cordial *n* 1 a stimulating medicine 2 a nonalcoholic sweetened fruit drink; a fruit syrup

cordillera *n* (any of the ranges in) a parallel series of mountain ranges – **cordilleran** *adj*

cordite *n* a smokeless explosive for propelling bullets, shells, etc made from nitroglycerine, guncotton, and petroleum jelly

¹cordon *n* 1a *sing or pl in constr* a line of troops, police, etc enclosing an area b a line or ring of people or objects 2 a plant, esp a fruit-tree, trained to a single stem by pruning off all side shoots

²cordon *vt* to form a protective or restrictive cordon round – often + **off**

cordon bleu *adj or n* (typical of or being) sby with great skill or distinction in (classical French) cookery ⟨*~ cooking*⟩

corduroy *n* 1 a durable usu cotton pile fabric with lengthways ribs or wales 2 *chiefly NAm* a road built of logs laid side by side

¹core *n* 1 a central or interior part, usu distinct from an

enveloping part: e g **a** the usu inedible central part of an apple, pineapple, etc **b** the portion of a foundry mould that shapes the interior of a hollow casting **c** a cylindrical portion removed from a mass for inspection; *specif* such a portion of rock got by boring **d**(1) a piece of ferromagnetic material (e g iron) serving to concentrate and intensify the magnetic field resulting from a current in a surrounding coil (2) a tiny ring-shaped piece of magnetic material (e g ferrite) used in computer memories (3) **core, core memory, core storage** a computer memory consisting of an array of cores strung on fine wires **e** the central part of a planet, esp the earth **f** a piece of stone (e g flint) from which flakes have been struck for making primitive weapons or tools **g** a conducting wire with its insulation in an electric cable **h** a subject which is central in a course of studies **2** the essential, basic, or central part (e g of an individual, class, or entity)

²**core** *vt* to remove a core from – **corer** *n*

co-respondent *n* a person claimed to have committed adultery with the respondent in a divorce case

corgi *n, pl* **corgis** (any of) either of 2 varieties of short-legged long-backed dogs with fox-like heads, orig developed in Wales

coriander *n* (the aromatic ripened dried fruits used for flavouring of) an Old World plant of the carrot family

Corinthian *adj* 1 (characteristic) of (inhabitants of) Corinth 2 of the lightest and most ornate of the 3 Greek orders of architecture characterized esp by a bell-shaped capital decorated with acanthus leaves – **Corinthian** *n*

¹**cork** *n* **1a** the elastic tough outer tissue of the cork oak used esp for stoppers and insulation **b** the phellem of a plant **2** a usu cork stopper, esp for a bottle **3** an angling float – **corky** *adj*

²**cork** *vt* to fit or close with a cork

corkage *n* a charge made for serving alcoholic drink, esp wine, in a restaurant; *esp* one made for serving drink bought elsewhere

corked *adj, of wine* having an unpleasant smell and taste as a result of being kept in a bottle sealed with a leaky cork

corker *n* sthg or sby astonishing or superlative – *infml*; no longer in vogue – **corking** *adj or adv*

¹**corkscrew** *n* an implement for removing corks from bottles, typically consisting of a pointed spiral piece of metal attached to a handle

²**corkscrew** *vt* to twist into a spiral ~ *vi* to move in a winding course

³**corkscrew** *adj* spiral ⟨*a ~ staircase*⟩

corm *n* a rounded thick underground plant stem base with buds and scaly leaves

cormorant *n* a common dark-coloured web-footed European seabird with a long neck, hooked bill, and white throat and cheeks; *also* any of several related seabirds

¹**corn** *n* **1** a small hard seed **2** (the seeds of) the important cereal crop of a particular region (e g wheat and barley in Britain) **3** SWEET CORN **4** sthg corny – *infml*

²**corn** *vt* to preserve or season with salt or brine ⟨*~ed beef*⟩

³**corn** *n* a local hardening and thickening of skin (e g on the top of a toe)

corncob *n* **1** the axis on which the edible kernels of sweet corn are arranged **2** an ear of sweet corn

corn cockle *n* a poisonous annual purple-flowered plant of the pink family that is a now rare weed of cornfields

corncrake *n* a common Eurasian short-billed rail

cornea *n* the hard transparent part of the coat of the eyeball that covers the iris and pupil – **corneal** *adj*

cornelian *n* a hard reddish chalcedony used in jewellery

¹**corner** *n* **1a** the point where converging lines, edges, or sides meet; an angle **b** the place of intersection of 2 streets or roads **c** a piece designed to form, mark, or protect a corner (e g of a book) **2** the angular space between meeting lines, edges, or borders: e g **a** the area of a playing field or court near the intersection of the sideline and the goal line or baseline **b** any of the 4 angles of a boxing ring; *esp* that in which a boxer rests between rounds **3** *sing or pl in constr* a contestant's group of supporters, adherents, etc **4** CORNER KICK; *also* CORNER HIT **5a** a private, secret, or remote place ⟨*a quiet ~ of a small Welsh town*⟩ ⟨*a hole and ~ business*⟩ **b** a difficult or embarrassing situation; a position from which escape or retreat is difficult ⟨*talked himself into a tight ~*⟩ **6** control or ownership of enough of the available supply of a commodity or security to permit manipulation of esp the price **7** a point at which significant change occurs – often in **turn a corner** – **cornered** *adj* – **round the corner** imminent; AT HAND ⟨*promised that good times were just round the corner*⟩

²**corner** *vt* **1a** to drive into a corner **b** to catch and hold the attention of, esp so as to force into conversation **2** to get a corner on ⟨*~ the wheat market*⟩ ~ *vi* to turn a corner ⟨*this car ~ s well*⟩

-cornered *comb form* (→ *adj*) **1** having such or so many corners **2** having so many participants or contestants

corner hit *n* a free hit, esp in hockey or shinty, awarded to the attacking side when a member of the defending side has sent the ball over his/her own goal line

corner kick *n* a free kick in soccer that is taken from the corner of the field and is awarded to the attacking team when a member of the defending team has sent the ball behind his/her own goal line

cornerstone *n* **1** a block of stone forming a part of a corner or angle in a wall; *specif* FOUNDATION STONE **2** the most basic element; a foundation

¹**cornet** *n* **1** a valved brass instrument resembling a trumpet but with a shorter tube and less brilliant tone **2** sthg shaped like a cone: e g **a** a piece of paper twisted for use as a container **b** an ice cream cone – **cornetist, cornettist** *n*

²**cornet** *n* the former fifth commissioned officer of a British cavalry troop who carried the standard

cornflakes *n pl* toasted flakes of maize eaten as a breakfast cereal

cornflour *n* a finely ground flour made from maize, rice, etc and used esp as a thickening agent in cooking

cornflower *n* **1** CORN COCKLE **2** a usu bright-blue-flowered European composite (garden) plant

cornice *n* **1a** the ornamental projecting piece that forms the top edge of a building, pillar, etc; *esp* the top projecting part of an entablature **b** an ornamental plaster moulding between wall and ceiling **2** a decorative band of metal or wood used to conceal curtain fixtures **3** an overhanging mass of snow, ice, etc on a mountain – **corniced** *adj*

¹**Cornish** *adj* (characteristic) of Cornwall

²**Cornish** *n* the ancient Celtic language of Cornwall

Corn Laws *n pl* a series of laws in force in Britain before 1846 restricting the import of foreign grain

corn pone *n, S & Mid US* a bread made with maize and baked or fried

cornucopia *n* **1** a goat's horn overflowing with fruit and corn used to symbolize abundance **2** an inexhaustible store; an abundance **3** a vessel shaped like a horn or cone – **cornucopian** *adj*

corny *adj* **1** tiresomely simple and sentimental; trite **2** hackneyed – *infml* – **cornily** *adv*, **corniness** *n*

corolla *n* the petals of a flower constituting the inner floral envelope – **corollate** *adj*

corollary *n* **1** a direct conclusion from a proved proposition 2 sthg that naturally follows or accompanies – **corollary** *adj*

corona *n* 1 the concave moulding on the upper part of a classical cornice 2a a usu coloured circle of usu diffracted light seen round and close to a luminous celestial body (e g the sun or moon) b the tenuous outermost part of the atmosphere of the sun and other stars appearing as a halo round the moon's black disc during a total eclipse of the sun c the upper portion of a bodily part (e g a tooth or the skull) d a circular appendage on the inner side of the corolla in the daffodil, jonquil, etc 3 a long straight-sided cigar with a roundly blunt sealed mouth end

¹coronary *adj* (of or being the arteries or veins) of the heart

²coronary *n* CORONARY THROMBOSIS

coronary thrombosis *n* the blocking of a coronary artery of the heart by a blood clot, usu causing death of heart muscle tissue

coronation *n* the act or ceremony of investing a sovereign or his/her consort with the royal crown

coroner *n* a public officer whose principal duty is to inquire into the cause of any death which there is reason to suppose might not be due to natural causes

coronet *n* 1 a small crown 2 an ornamental wreath or band for the head 3 the lower part of a horse's pastern where the horn ends in skin

corpora *pl of* CORPUS

¹corporal *adj* of or affecting the body ⟨~ *punishment*⟩ – **corporality** *n*, **corporally** *adv*

²corporal *n* a noncommissioned officer in the army, marines, or Royal Air Force, ranking below sergeant

corporate *adj* 1a INCORPORATED 2 b of a company 2 of or formed into a unified body of individuals 3 **corporate**, **corporative** (formed according to the principles) of corporatism ⟨*a ~ state*⟩ – **corporately** *adv*

corporation *n* 1 *sing or pl in constr* the municipal authorities of a town or city 2 a body made up of more than 1 person which is formed and authorized by law to act as a single person with its own legal identity, rights, and duties 3 an association of employers and employees or of members of a profession in a corporate state 4 a potbelly – *humor*

corporation tax *n* tax levied on the profits of limited companies

corporeal *adj* having, consisting of, or relating to a physical material body: e g a not spiritual b not immaterial or intangible; substantial – **corporealness** *n*, **corporeally** *adv*, **corporeality** *n*

corps *n*, *pl* **corps** 1 *sing or pl in constr* an army unit usu consisting of 2 or more divisions (organized for a particular purpose) 2 any of various associations of German university students

corps de ballet *n*, *pl* **corps de ballet** the ensemble of a ballet company

corpse *n* a dead (human) body

corpulence, corpulency *n* the state of being excessively fat; obesity – **corpulent** *adj*

corpus *n*, *pl* **corpora** 1 the body or corpse of a human or animal 2 the main body or corporeal substance of a thing; *esp* the main part of a bodily structure or organ ⟨*the ~ of the uterus*⟩ 3a a collection or body of writings or works (e g of 1 author or artist), esp of a particular kind or on a particular subject b a body of spoken and/or written language for linguistic study

corpuscle *n* 1 a minute particle 2a a living (blood) cell b any of various very small multicellular parts of an organism – **corpuscular** *adj*

corpus delicti *n*, *pl* **corpora delicti** the body of facts

showing that a breach of the law has taken place; *esp* the body of the victim in a case of murder

¹corral *n* 1 a pen or enclosure for confining livestock 2 an enclosure made with wagons for defence of an encampment

²corral *vt* -ll- 1 to enclose in a corral 2 to arrange (wagons) so as to form a corral

¹correct *vt* 1 to alter or adjust so as to counteract some imperfection or failing 2a to punish (e g a child) with a view to reforming or improving b to point out the faults of ⟨~*ing essays*⟩ – **correctable** *adj*, **corrective** *adj or n*, **correctively** *adv*, **corrector** *n*

²correct *adj* 1 conforming to an approved or conventional standard 2 true, right – **correctly** *adv*, **correctness** *n*

correction *n* 1a an amendment to a rebuke, punishment 2a sthg substituted, esp written, in place of what is wrong b a quantity applied by way of correcting (e g in adjusting an instrument) – **correctional** *adj*

¹correlate *n* either of 2 things so related that one directly implies the other (e g husband and wife) – **correlate** *adj*

²correlate *vi* to have reciprocal or mutual relationship ~ *vt* 1 to establish a mutual or reciprocal relation of 2 to relate so that to each member of one set or series a corresponding member of another is assigned – **correlatable** *adj*

correlation *n* 1 a relation of phenomena as invariable accompaniments of each other 2 an interdependence between mathematical variables, esp in statistics – **correlational** *adj*

correlative *adj* naturally related; corresponding – **correlative** *n*, **correlatively** *adv*

correspond *vi* 1a to be in conformity or agreement; suit, match – usu + *to* or *with* b to be equivalent or parallel 2 to communicate *with* a person by exchange of letters

correspondence *n* 1a the agreement of things with one another b a particular similarity c an association of 1 or more members of one set with each member of another set 2a (communication by) letters b the news, information, or opinion contributed by a correspondent to a newspaper or periodical

¹correspondent *adj* 1 corresponding 2 fitting, conforming *USE* + *with* or *to*

²correspondent *n* 1 one who communicates with another by letter 2 one who has regular commercial relations with another 3 one who contributes news or comment to a publication or radio or television network ⟨*a war ~*⟩

corresponding *adj* 1a agreeing in some respect (e g kind, degree, position, or function) b related, accompanying 2 participating at a distance and by post ⟨*a ~ member of the society*⟩ – **correspondingly** *adv*

corridor *n*, 1 a passage (e g in a hotel or railway carriage) onto which compartments or rooms open 2 a usu narrow passageway or route: e g a a narrow strip of land through foreign-held territory b a restricted path for air traffic 3 a strip of land that by geographical characteristics is distinct from its surroundings

corrie *n*, *chiefly Scot* a steep-sided bowl-like valley in the side of a mountain; a cwm, cirque

corrigendum *n*, *pl* **corrigenda** an error in a printed work, shown with its correction on a separate sheet

corroborate *vt* to support with evidence or authority; make more certain – **corroborative, corroboratory** *adj*, **corroborator** *n*, **corroboration** *n*

corroboree *n* 1 a nocturnal Australian aboriginal festivity with songs and symbolic dances to celebrate important events 2 *Austr* a a noisy festivity b a tumult

corrode *vt* 1 to eat or wear (esp metal) away gradually, esp by chemical action **2** to weaken or destroy (as if) by corrosion ~ *vi* to undergo corroding – **corrodible** *adj*

corrosion *n* the action or process of corroding; *also* the product of such a process

corrosive *adj* **1** corroding ⟨~ *acids*⟩⟨~ *action*⟩ **2** bitingly sarcastic – **corrosive** *n*, **corrosively** *adv*, **corrosiveness** *n*

corrugate *vb* to shape or become shaped into alternating ridges and grooves; furrow ⟨~ d *cardboard*⟩⟨~ d *iron*⟩ – **corrugation** *n*

¹corrupt *vt* **1a** to change from good to bad in morals, manners, or actions; *also* to influence by bribery **b** to degrade with unsound principles or moral values **2** to alter from the original or correct form or version ~ *vi* to become corrupt – **corrupter, corruptor** *n*, **corruptible** *adj*, **corruptibly** *adv*, **corruptibility** *n*, **corruptive** *adj*

²corrupt *adj* **1a** morally degenerate and perverted **b** characterized by bribery **2** having been vitiated by mistakes or changes ⟨*a* ~ *text*⟩ – **corruptly** *adv*, **corruptness** *n*

corruption *n* **1** impairment of integrity, virtue, or moral principle **2** decay, decomposition **3** inducement by bribery to do wrong **4** a departure from what is pure or correct

corsage *n* an arrangement of flowers to be worn by a woman, esp on the bodice

corsair *n* a pirate; *esp* a privateer of the Barbary coast

corselette, corselet *n*, a one-piece undergarment combining girdle and bra

¹corset *n* a boned supporting undergarment for women, extending from beneath the bust to below the hips, and designed to give shape to the figure; *also* a similar garment worn by men and women, esp in cases of injury

²corset *vt* to restrict closely

cortege *also* **cortège** *n* **1** a train of attendants; a retinue **2** a procession; *esp* a funeral procession

cortex *n*, *pl* **cortices, cortexes** **1** a plant bark (e g cinchona) used medicinally **2** the outer part of the kidney, adrenal gland, a hair, etc; *esp* the outer layer of grey matter of the brain **3** the layer of (parenchymatous) tissue between the inner vascular tissue and the outer epidermal tissue of a green plant

cortisone *n* a glucocorticoid steroid hormone that is produced by the cortex of the adrenal gland

corundum *n* a very hard natural or synthetic mineral that consists of aluminium oxide, exists in various colours, and is used as an abrasive and a gemstone

coruscate *vi* to sparkle, flash ⟨*her* coruscating *wit*⟩ – **coruscation** *n*

corvée *n* labour exacted in lieu of taxes by public authorities

corvette *n* **1** a small sailing warship with a flush deck **2** a small highly manoeuvrable armed escort ship

¹cos *conj* because – used in writing to represent a casual or childish pronunciation

²cos, cos lettuce *n* a long-leaved variety of lettuce

cosh *vt or n*, *chiefly Br* (to strike with) a short heavy rod often enclosed in a softer material and used as a hand weapon

cosine *n* the trigonometric function that for an acute angle in a right-angled triangle is the ratio between the side adjacent to the angle and the hypotenuse

¹cosmetic *n* a cosmetic preparation for external use

²cosmetic *adj* of or intended to improve beauty (e g of the hair or complexion) ⟨~ *surgery*⟩; *broadly* intended to improve the outward appearance – **cosmetically** *adv*, **cosmetology** *n*, **cosmetologist** *n*

cosmetician *n* sby who is professionally trained in the use of cosmetics

cosmic *also* **cosmical** *adj* **1** of the universe in contrast to the earth alone **2** great in extent, intensity, or comprehensiveness – **cosmically** *adv*

cosmic dust *n* very fine particles of solid matter in any part of the universe

cosmic ray *n* a stream of highly energetic radiation reaching the earth's atmosphere from space – usu pl with sing. meaning

cosmogony *n* (a theory of) the creation or origin of the universe – **cosmogonist** *n*, **cosmogonic, cosmogonical** *adj*

cosmology *n* **1** a theoretical account of the nature of the universe **2** astronomy dealing with the origin, structure, and space-time relationships of the universe – **cosmologic, cosmological** *adj*, **cosmologically** *adv*, **cosmologist** *n*

cosmonaut *n* a usu Soviet astronaut

¹cosmopolitan *adj* **1** having worldwide rather than provincial scope or bearing **2** marked by a sophistication that comes from wide and often international experience **3** composed of people, constituents, or elements from many parts of the world **4** *of a plant, animal, etc* found in most parts of the world and under varied ecological conditions – **cosmopolitanism** *n*

²cosmopolitan *n* a cosmopolite

cosmos *n* **1** an orderly universe **2** a complex and orderly system that is complete in itself **3** any of a genus of tropical American composite plants grown for their yellow or red flower heads

cosset *vt* to treat as a pet; pamper

¹cost *n* **1a** the price paid or charged for sthg **b** the expenditure (e g of effort or sacrifice) made to achieve an object **2** the loss or penalty incurred in gaining sthg **3** *pl* expenses incurred in litigation – **costless** *adj* – **at all costs** regardless of the price or difficulties – **to one's cost** to one's disadvantage or loss

²cost *vb* **cost**, (*vt* 2) **costed** *vi* **1** to require a specified expenditure ⟨*the best goods* ~ *more*⟩ **2** to require the specified effort, suffering, or loss ~ *vt* **1** to cause to pay, suffer, or lose ⟨*frequent absences* ~ *him his job*⟩⟨*your suggestion would* ~ *us too much time*⟩ **2** to estimate or set the cost of

co-star *n* a star who has equal billing with another leading performer in a film or play – **co-star** *vb*

costermonger *n*, *Br* a seller of articles, esp fruit or vegetables, from a street barrow or stall

costive *adj* affected with or causing constipation – **costively** *adv*, **costiveness** *n*

costly *adj* **1** valuable, expensive **2** made at great expense or with considerable sacrifice – **costliness** *n*

cost of living *n* the cost of purchasing those goods and services which are included in an accepted standard level of consumption

¹costume *n* **1** a distinctive fashion in coiffure, jewellery, and apparel of a period, country, class, or group **2** a set of garments suitable for a specified occasion, activity, or season **3** a set of garments belonging to a specific time, place or character, worn in order to assume a particular role (e g in a play or at a fancy-dress party) – **costumey** *adj*

²costume *vt* **1** to provide with a costume **2** to design costumes for ⟨~ *a play*⟩

³costume *adj* characterized by the use of costumes ⟨*a* ~ *ball*⟩⟨*a* ~ *drama*⟩

costume jewellery *n* inexpensive jewellery typically worn attached to clothing rather than on the body

costumier, costumer *n* sby who deals in or makes costumes (e g for theatrical productions)

¹cosy, NAm chiefly cozy *adj* **1** enjoying or affording warmth and ease; snug **2a** marked by the intimacy of the family or a close group **b** self-satisfied, complacent – **cosily** adv

²**cosy, NAm chiefly cozy** n a covering, esp for a teapot, designed to keep the contents hot

¹**cot** n a small house; a cottage – poetic

²**cot** n **1** a lightweight bedstead **2** a small bed with high enclosing sides, esp for a child **3** chiefly NAm CAMP BED

cotangent n the trigonometric function that is the reciprocal of the tangent

cote n a shed or coop for small domestic animals, esp pigeons

coterie n a close group of people with a unifying common interest or purpose

coterminous adj **1** having the same boundaries ⟨~ states⟩ **2** coextensive in scope or duration ⟨~ interests⟩ – **coterminously** adv

cotillion also **cotillon** n **1** an elaborate French dance with frequent changing of partners **2** NAm a formal ball

cottage n a small house, esp in the country – **cottager** n, **cottagey** adj

cottage cheese n a soft white bland cheese made from the curds of skimmed milk

cottage hospital n, Br a small hospital without resident doctors

cottage industry n an industry whose work force consists of family units working at home with their own equipment

cottage pie n a shepherd's pie esp made with minced beef

¹**cotton** n **1** (a plant producing or grown for) a soft usu white fibrous substance composed of the hairs surrounding the seeds of various tropical plants of the mallow family **2a** fabric made of cotton **b** yarn spun from cotton

²**cotton** vi to come to understand; CATCH ON **2** – usu + on or onto; infml

cotton gin n a machine for separating the seeds, seed cases, and foreign material from cotton

cotton wool n **1** raw cotton; esp cotton pressed into sheets used esp for lining, cleaning, or as a surgical dressing **2** an overprotected comfortable environment

cotyledon n **1** a lobule of the placenta of a mammal **2** the first leaf or either of the first pair or whorl of leaves developed by the embryo of a seed plant – **cotyledonal** adj, **cotyledonary, cotyledonous** adj

¹**couch** vt **1** to lower to and hold in an attacking position ⟨~ed his lance⟩ **2** to treat (a cataract) by displacing the lens of the eye **3** to phrase in a specified manner ⟨~ed in hostile terms⟩ – fml ~ vi, of an animal to lie down to sleep; also to lie in ambush

²**couch** n **1** a piece of furniture for sitting or lying on **a** with a back and usu armrests **b** with a low back and raised head-end **2** a long upholstered seat with a headrest for patients to lie on during medical examination or psychoanalysis **3** the den of an animal (e g an otter)

couchette n a seat in a railway-carriage compartment that converts into a bunk

couch grass n any of several grasses that spread rapidly by long creeping underground stems and are difficult to eradicate

cougar n, pl **cougars**, esp collectively **cougar** chiefly NAm a puma

¹**cough** vi **1** to expel air from the lungs suddenly with an explosive noise **2** to make a noise like that of coughing ~ vt to expel by coughing ⟨~ up mucus⟩

²**cough** n **1** a condition marked by repeated or frequent coughing **2** an act or sound of coughing

cough up vb to produce or hand over (esp money or information) unwillingly – infml

could verbal auxiliary **1** past of CAN – used in the past ⟨he found he ~ go⟩, in the past conditional ⟨he said he would go if he ~⟩, as an alternative to can suggesting less force or certainty ⟨you ~ be right⟩, as a polite form in the present ⟨~ you do this for me⟩, as an alternative to might expressing purpose in the past ⟨wrote it down so that I ~ remember it⟩, and as an alternative to ought or should ⟨you ~ at least apologize⟩ **2** feel impelled to ⟨I ~ wring her neck⟩

couldn't could not

coulter n a blade or sharp disc attached to the beam of a plough that makes a vertical cut in the ground in front of the ploughshare

¹**council** n **1** an assembly, meeting **2a** sing or pl in constr an elected or appointed body with administrative, legislative, or advisory powers **b** a locally-elected body having power over a parish, district, county, etc

²**council** adj **1** used by a council ⟨a ~ chamber⟩ **2** Br provided, maintained, or operated by local government ⟨~ flats⟩

councillor, NAm also **councilor** n a member of a council

¹**counsel** n, pl **counsels**, (4) **counsel** **1** advice **2** deliberation, consultation **3** thoughts or intentions – chiefly in keep one's own counsel **4a** a barrister engaged in the trial of a case in court **b** a lawyer appointed to advise a client

²**counsel** vt -ll- (NAm -l, -ll-), to advise

counsellor, NAm chiefly counselor n **1** an adviser **2** NAm a lawyer; specif a counsel

¹**count** vt **1a** to reckon or name by units or groups so as to find the total number of units involved – often + up **b** to name the numbers in order up to and including **c** to include in a tallying and reckoning ⟨about 100 copies if you ~ the damaged ones⟩ **2** to consider ⟨~ yourself lucky⟩ **3** to include or exclude (as if by counting ⟨~ me in⟩ ~ vi **1a** to name the numbers in order by units or groups ⟨~ in tens⟩ **b** to count the units in a group **2** to rely on or upon sby or sthg **3** to have value or significance ⟨these are the men who really ~⟩ – **countable** adj – **count on** to look forward to as certain; anticipate ⟨counted on winning⟩

²**count** n **1a** the action or process of counting **b** a total obtained by counting **2a** an allegation in an indictment ⟨guilty on all ~s⟩ **b** a specific point under consideration; an issue ⟨disagreed on several ~s⟩ **3** the total number of individual things in a given unit or sample ⟨blood ~⟩ **4** the calling out of the seconds from 1 to 10 when a boxer has been knocked down during which he must rise or be defeated **5** any of various measures of the fineness of a textile yarn **6** chiefly NAm the score

³**count** n a European nobleman corresponding in rank to a British earl

countdown n a continuous counting backwards to zero of the time remaining before an event, esp the launching of a space vehicle – **count down** vi

¹**countenance** n **1** composure ⟨keep one's ~⟩ **2** a face; esp the face as an indication of mood, emotion, or character **3** moral support; sanction USE fml

²**countenance** vt to extend approval or support to – fml

¹**counter** n **1** a small disc of metal, plastic, etc used in counting or in games **2** sthg of value in bargaining; an asset **3** a level surface (e g a table) over which transactions are conducted or food is served or on which goods are displayed – **over the counter** without a prescription ⟨cough mixture available over the counter⟩ – **under the**

counter by surreptitious means; in an illicit and private manner

²counter *n* a device for indicating a number or amount

³counter *vt* **1** to act in opposition to; oppose **2** to nullify the effects of; offset ⟨*tried to ~ the trend towards bureaucratization*⟩ *~ vi* to meet attacks or arguments with defensive or retaliatory steps

⁴counter *adv* in an opposite, contrary, or wrong direction

⁵counter *n* **1** the contrary, opposite **2** an overhanging stern of a vessel **3a** the (blow resulting from the) making of an attack while parrying (e g in boxing or fencing) **b** an agency or force that offsets; a check

⁶counter *adj* **1** marked by or tending towards an opposite direction or effect **2** showing opposition, hostility, or antipathy

counter- *prefix* **1a** contrary; in the opposite direction ⟨*countermarch*⟩ **b** opposing; retaliatory ⟨*counteroffensive*⟩ **2** complementary; corresponding ⟨*counterpart*⟩ **3** duplicate; substitute ⟨*counterfoil*⟩

counteract *vt* to lessen or neutralize the usu ill effects of by an opposing action – **counteraction** *n*, **counteractive** *adj*

counterattack *vb* to make an attack (against) in reply to an enemy's attack – **counterattack** *n*

counterattraction *n* an attraction that competes with another

¹counterbalance *n* **1** a weight that balances another **2** a force or influence that offsets or checks an opposing force

²counterbalance *vt* to oppose or balance with an equal weight or force

counterblast *n* an energetic and often vociferous reaction or response

counterclaim *n* an opposing claim, esp in law – **counterclaim** *vi*

counterclockwise *adj or adv, chiefly NAm* anticlockwise

counterespionage *n* espionage directed towards detecting and thwarting enemy espionage

¹counterfeit *vb* to imitate or copy (sthg) closely, esp with intent to deceive or defraud – **counterfeiter** *n*

²counterfeit *adj* **1** made in imitation of sthg else with intent to deceive or defraud **2** insincere, feigned ⟨*~ sympathy*⟩

³counterfeit *n* **1** a forgery **2** sthg likely to be mistaken for sthg of higher value

counterfoil *n* a detachable part of a cheque, ticket, etc usu kept as a record or receipt

counterintelligence *n* organized activity of an intelligence service designed to block an enemy's sources of information

counterirritant *n* sthg applied locally to produce surface inflammation with the object of reducing inflammation in tissue underneath – **counterirritant** *adj*

¹countermand *vt* **1** to revoke (a command) by a contrary order **2** to order back (e g troops) by a superseding contrary order

²countermand *n* (the giving of) a contrary order revoking an earlier one

countermarch *n* a movement in marching by which a unit of troops reverses direction while keeping the same order – **countermarch** *vi*

countermeasure *n* a measure designed to counter another action or state of affairs

counteroffensive *n* a military offensive undertaken from a previously defensive position

counterpane *n* a bedspread

counterpart *n* **1** a duplicate **2** sthg that completes; a

complement **3** one having the same function or characteristics as another; an equivalent

¹counterpoint *n* **1a** one or more independent melodies added above or below a given melody **b** the combination of 2 or more independent melodies into a single harmonic texture **2a** a complementing or contrasting item **b** use of contrast or interplay of elements in a work of art

²counterpoint *vt* **1** to compose or arrange in counterpoint **2** to set off or emphasize by contrast or juxtaposition

counterpoise *n* **1** a counterbalance **2** a state of balance; equilibrium – **counterpoise** *vt*

counterrevolution *n* a revolution directed towards overthrowing the system established by a previous revolution – **counterrevolutionary** *adj or n*, **counterrevolutionist** *n*

¹countersign *n* a password or secret signal given by one wishing to pass a guard

²countersign *vt* to add one's signature to (a document) as a witness of another signature – **countersignature** *n*

countersink *vt* **countersunk 1** to enlarge (a hole), esp by bevelling, so that the head of a bolt, screw, etc will fit below or level with the surface **2** to set the head of (e g a screw) below or level with the surface

countertenor *n* (a person with) an adult male singing voice higher than tenor

countervail *vt* to counterbalance, offset

countess *n* **1** the wife or widow of an earl or count **2** a woman having in her own right the rank of an earl or count

countinghouse *n* a building, room, or office used for keeping account books and transacting business

countless *adj* too numerous to be counted; innumerable

countrified *also* **countryfied** *adj* **1** rural, rustic **2** unsophisticated

country *n* **1** an indefinite usu extended expanse of land; a region **2a** the land of a person's birth, residence, or citizenship **b** a political state or nation or its territory **3** *sing or pl in constr* **a** the populace **b** the electorate ⟨*the government was forced to go to the ~* ⟩ **4** rural as opposed to urban areas **5** COUNTRY MUSIC

country and western *n* COUNTRY MUSIC

country club *n* a sporting or social club set in a rural area

country cousin *n* one who is unaccustomed to or confused by the bustle and sophistication of city life

country dance *n* any of various native or folk dances for several pairs of dancers typically arranged in square or circular figures or in 2 long rows facing a partner

countryman, *fem* **countrywoman** *n* **1** an inhabitant or native of a specified country **2** a compatriot **3** one living in the country or having country ways

country music *n* music derived from or imitating the folk style of the southern USA or the Western cowboy

country seat *n* a mansion or estate in the country that is the hereditary property of 1 family

countryside *n* a rural area

¹county *n* **1a** any of the territorial divisions of Britain and Ireland constituting the chief units for administrative, judicial, and political purposes **b** *sing or pl in constr* the people of a county **2** the largest local government unit in various countries (e g the USA)

²county *adj* **1** of a county **2** *Br* characteristic of or belonging to the English landed gentry ⟨*a ~ accent*⟩

county borough *n* a borough which until 1974 had the local-government powers of a county

county court *n, often cap 1st C* a local civil court in England which is presided over by a judge and deals with relatively minor claims

county town *n, chiefly Br* a town that is the seat of the government of a county

¹coup *vb, chiefly Scot* to overturn, upset

²coup *n, pl* **coups** **1** a brilliant, sudden, and usu highly successful stroke or act **2** COUP D'ETAT

coup de grâce *n, pl* **coups de grâce** **1** a fatal blow or shot administered to end the suffering of a mortally wounded person or animal **2** a decisive finishing stroke

coup d'é tat *n, pl* **coups d'état** the violent overthrow of an existing government by a small group

coupe *n* (a cold dessert of fruit and ice cream served in) a small goblet-shaped dish

coupé, coupe *n* **1** a 4-wheeled horse-drawn carriage for 2 passengers with an outside seat for the driver **2** a closed 2-door motor car for usu 2 people

¹couple *vb* **coupling** *vt* **1** to unite or link ⟨~d *his praise with a request*⟩ **2a** to fasten together; connect **b** to bring (2 electric circuits) into such close proximity as to permit mutual influence **3** to join in marriage ~ *vi* **1** to copulate **2** to join

²couple *n, pl* **couples, couple** **1** *sing or pl in constr* 2 people paired together; *esp* a married or engaged couple **2a** 2 things considered together; a pair **b** an indefinite small number; a few ⟨a ~ *of days ago*⟩ – *infml* **3** 2 equal and opposite forces that act along parallel lines and cause rotation

³couple *adj* two – + a ⟨a ~ *more drinks*⟩

couplet *n* a unit of 2 successive, usu rhyming, lines of verse

coupling *n* a device that serves to connect the ends of adjacent parts or objects

coupon *n* a form handed over in order to obtain an article, service, or accommodation: e g **a** a detachable ticket or certificate that entitles the holder to sthg **b** a voucher given with a purchase that can be exchanged for goods **c** a part of a printed advertisement to be cut off for use as an order form or enquiry form **d** a printed entry form for a competition, esp the football pools

courage *n* mental or moral strength to confront and withstand danger, fear, or difficulty; bravery – **courageous** *adj*, **courageously** *adv*

courgette *n* (the plant that bears) a variety of small vegetable marrow cooked and eaten as a vegetable

courier *n* **1a** a member of a diplomatic service who carries state or embassy papers **b** one who carries secret information, contraband, etc **2** a tourist guide employed by a travel agency

¹course *n* **1** the act or action of moving in a path from point to point **2** the path over which sthg moves: e g **a** a racecourse **b** the direction of travel, usu measured as a clockwise angle from north **c** WATERCOURSE **d** GOLF COURSE **3a** usual procedure or normal action ⟨*the law must take its* ~⟩ **b** a chosen manner of conducting oneself; a plan of action ⟨*our wisest* ~ *is to retreat*⟩ **c** progression through a series of acts or events or a development or period ⟨*in the* ~ *of the year*⟩ **4a** a series of educational activities relating to a subject, esp when constituting a curriculum ⟨a *management* ~⟩ **b** a particular medical treatment administered over a designated period **5a** a part of a meal served at one time **b** a row; *esp* a continuous horizontal layer of brick or masonry throughout a wall – **of course 1** as might be expected; naturally **2** admittedly; TO BE SURE

²course *vt* **1** to hunt or pursue (e g hares) with dogs that follow by sight **2** to follow close upon; pursue ~ *vi of a liquid* to run or pass rapidly (as if) along an indicated path ⟨*blood* coursing *through his veins*⟩

³course *adv* OF COURSE – *infml*

courser *n* any of various African and Asian birds noted for their swift running

¹court *n* **1a** the residence or establishment of a dignitary, esp a sovereign **b** *sing or pl in constr* **(1)** the sovereign and his officers and advisers who are the governing power **(2)** the family and retinue of a sovereign **c** a reception held by a sovereign **2a** a manor house or large building (e g a block of flats) surrounded by usu enclosed grounds – archaic except in proper names ⟨Hampton Court⟩ ⟨Withdean Court⟩ **b** a space enclosed wholly or partly by a building **c** (a division of) a rectangular space walled or marked off for playing lawn tennis, squash, basketball, etc **d** a yard surrounded by houses, with only 1 opening onto a street **3a** (a session of) an official assembly for the transaction of judicial business **b** *sing or pl in constr* judicial officers in session **4** *sing or pl in constr* an assembly with legislative or administrative powers **5** conduct or attention intended to win favour ⟨*pay* ~ *to the king*⟩

²court *vt* **1** to act so as to invite or provoke ⟨~s *disaster*⟩ **2a** to seek the affections of; woo **b** *of an animal* to perform actions to attract (a mate) **3** to seek to win the favour of ~ *vi of a man and woman* to be involved in a relationship that may lead to marriage

court card *n* a king, queen, or jack in a pack of cards

courteous *adj* showing respect and consideration for others – **courteously** *adv*, **courteousness** *n*

courtesan *n* a prostitute with a courtly, wealthy, or upper-class clientele

¹courtesy *n* **1** courteous behaviour **2** a courteous act or expression – **by courtesy of** through the kindness, generosity, or permission granted by (a person or organization)

²courtesy *adj* granted, provided, or performed by way of courtesy ⟨*made a* ~ *call on the ambassador*⟩

courthouse *n, chiefly NAm* a building in which courts of law are regularly held

courtier *n* one in attendance at a royal court

courtly *adj* of a quality befitting the court; elegant, refined – **courtliness** *n*

¹court-martial *n, pl* **courts-martial** *also* **court-martials** (a trial by) a court of commissioned officers that tries members of the armed forces

²court-martial *vt* **-ll-** (*NAm* **-l-**, **-ll-**) to try by court-martial

court of inquiry *n* a board of people appointed to ascertain the causes of an accident, disaster, etc

Court of Session *n* the highest civil court in Scotland

courtship *n* the act, process, or period of courting

courtyard *n* an open court or enclosure adjacent to a building

couscous *n* a N African dish of crushed or coarsely ground wheat steamed and served with meat, vegetables, and spices

cousin *n* **1a** a child of one's uncle or aunt **b** a relative descended from one's grandparent or more remote ancestor in a different line **2** formerly used as a title by a sovereign in addressing a nobleman – **cousinhood** *n*, **cousinship** *n*

couture *n* **1** the business of designing and making fashionable custom-made women's clothing; *also* the designers and establishments engaged in this business **2** HAUTE COUTURE

¹cove *n* **1** a small sheltered area; *esp* an inlet or bay **2** a (deep) recess in (the side of) a mountain **3** a concave moulding, esp at the point where a wall meets a ceiling or floor

²cove *vt* to make in a hollow concave form

³cove *n, Br* a man, fellow – slang; no longer in vogue

coven *n sing or pl in constr* an assembly or band of witches

¹covenant *n* **1** a solemn agreement **2** a written promise

²covenant *vb* to promise by or enter into a covenant

Coventry *n* a state of ostracism or exclusion – chiefly in *send to Coventry*

¹cover *vt* **1a** to guard from attack **b(1)** to have within the range of one's guns **(2)** to hold within range of an aimed firearm **c(1)** to insure **(2)** to afford protection against or compensation for **d** to mark (an opponent) in order to obstruct play **e** to make sufficient provision for (a demand or charge) by means of a reserve or deposit ⟨*his balance was insufficient to ~ his cheque*⟩ **2a** to hide from sight or knowledge; conceal – usu + *up* ⟨*~ up a scandal*⟩ **b** to lie or spread over; envelop ⟨*snow ~ed the ground*⟩ **3** to lay or spread sthg over **4** to extend thickly or conspicuously over the surface of ⟨*~ed in spots*⟩ **5** to place or set a cover or covering over **6a** *of a male animal* to copulate with (a female animal) **b** to sit on and incubate (eggs) **7** to invest with a large or excessive amount of sthg ⟨*~s himself with glory*⟩ **8** to play a higher-ranking card on (a previously played card) **9** to include, consider, or take in ⟨*this book ~s the whole Renaissance*⟩ **10a** to have as one's territory or field of activity ⟨*one salesman ~s the whole county*⟩ **b** to report news about **11** to pass over; traverse ⟨*~ed 5 miles at great speed*⟩ **~ vi 1** to conceal sthg illicit, blameworthy, or embarrassing from notice – usu + *up* **2** to act as a substitute or replacement during an absence – chiefly in *cover for someone* – **cover one's tracks** to conceal evidence of one's past actions in order to elude pursuit or investigation – **cover the ground 1** to cover a distance with adequate speed **2** to deal with an assignment or examine a subject thoroughly

²cover *n* **1** sthg that protects, shelters, or guards: e g **a** natural shelter for an animal **b(1)** a position affording shelter from attack **(2)** (the protection offered by) a force supporting a military operation **2** COVERAGE 3a **2** sthg that is placed over or about another thing: **a** a lid, top **b** (the front or back part of) a binding or jacket of a book **c** an overlay or outer layer (e g for protection) ⟨*a chair ~*⟩ **d** a roof **e** a cloth (e g a blanket) used on a bed ⟨*threw back the ~s*⟩ **f** sthg (e g vegetation or snow) that covers the ground **g** the extent to which clouds obscure the sky **3a** sthg that conceals or obscures ⟨*under ~ of darkness*⟩ **b** a masking device; a pretext **4** an envelope or wrapper for postal use ⟨*under separate ~*⟩ **5a** cover-point, extra cover, or a cricket fielding position between them **b** *pl* the fielding positions in cricket that lie between point and mid-off

coverage *n* **1** the act or fact of covering **2** inclusion within the scope of discussion or reporting ⟨*news ~*⟩ **3a** the total range of risks covered by the terms of an insurance contract **b** the number or percentage of people reached by a communications medium

cover charge *n* a charge (e g for service) made by a restaurant or nightclub in addition to the charge for food and drink

cover girl *n* an attractive girl whose picture appears on a magazine cover

¹covering *n* sthg that covers or conceals

²covering *adj* containing an explanation of an accompanying item ⟨*a ~ letter*⟩

coverlet *n* a bedspread

cover note *n, Br* a provisional insurance document providing cover between acceptance of a risk and issue of a full policy

cover-point *n* a fielding position in cricket further from

the batsman than point and situated between mid-off and point

¹covert *adj* not openly shown; secret – **covertly** *adv*, **covertness** *n*

²covert *n* **1a** a hiding place; a shelter **b** a thicket affording cover for game **2** a feather covering the bases of the wing or tail feathers of a bird

cover-up *n* a device or course of action that conceals sthg (e g sthg illegal)

covet *vt* to desire (what belongs to another) inordinately or culpably

covetous *adj* showing an inordinate desire for esp another's wealth or possessions – **covetously** *adv*, **covetousness** *n*

covey *n* **1** a mature bird or pair of birds with a brood of young; *also* a small flock **2** a company, group

¹cow *n* **1** the mature female of cattle or of any animal the male of which is called *bull* **2** a domestic bovine animal regardless of sex or age **3** a woman; *esp* one who is unpleasant **4** *chiefly Austr* a cause of annoyance or difficulty *USE* (3&4) vulg – **till the cows come home** FOREVER 1

²cow *vt* to intimidate with threats or a show of strength

coward *n* one who lacks courage or resolve

cowardice *n* lack of courage or resolve

¹cowardly *adv* in a cowardly manner

²cowardly *adj* resembling or befitting a coward ⟨*a ~ retreat*⟩ – **cowardliness** *n*

cowbell *n* a bell hung round the neck of a cow to make a sound by which it can be located

cowboy, *fem* **cowgirl** *n* **1** one who tends or drives cattle; *esp* a usu mounted cattle ranch hand in N America **2a** one who employs irregular or unscrupulous methods, esp in business **b** a person who uses underhand or dubious means to get his own way *USE* (2) infml

cowcatcher *n, chiefly NAm* an apparatus on the front of a locomotive or tram for removing obstacles from the track

cower *vi* to crouch down or shrink away (e g in fear) from sthg menacing

cowhand *n* a cowherd or cowboy

cowherd *n* one who tends cows

cowhide *n* **1** leather made from the hide of a cow **2** *NAm* a coarse leather whip

cowl *n* **1a** a hood or long hooded cloak, esp of a monk **b** a draped neckline on a garment resembling a folded-down hood **2a** a chimney covering designed to improve ventilation **b** a cowling – **cowled** *adj*

cowlick *n* a tuft of hair that sticks up, esp over the forehead

cowling *n* a removable metal covering over an engine, esp in an aircraft

cowman *n* a cowherd or cowboy

co-worker *n* a fellow worker

cowpat *n* a small heap of cow dung

cowpox *n* a mild disease of the cow that when communicated to humans gives protection against smallpox

cowrie, **cowry** *n* any of numerous marine gastropod molluscs with glossy and often brightly coloured shells, formerly used as money in parts of Africa and Asia

cowslip *n* a common European plant of the primrose family with fragrant yellow or purplish flowers

cox *vb or n* (to) coxswain – **coxless** *adj*

coxcomb *n* a conceited foolish person; a fop

coy *adj* **1a** (affectedly) shy **b** provocatively playful or coquettish **2** showing reluctance to make a definite commitment or face unpalatable facts – **coyly** *adv*, **coyness** *n*

coyote *n, pl* **coyotes,** *esp collectively* **coyote** a small N American wolf

coypu *n, pl* **coypus,** *esp collectively* **coypu** a S American aquatic rodent with webbed feet now commonly found in E Anglia

¹**cozy** *adj, NAm* cosy

²**cozy** *n, chiefly NAm* a cosy

¹**crab** *n* 1 any of numerous chiefly marine crustaceans usu with the front pair of limbs modified as grasping pincers and a short broad flattened carapace; *also* the flesh of this cooked and eaten as food 2 *pl* infestation with crab lice

²**crab** *vb* -bb- *vt* 1 to cause to move sideways or in an indirect or diagonal manner 2 to head (an aircraft) by means of the rudder into a crosswind to counteract drift ~ *vi* to move sideways indirectly or diagonally

³**crab** *n* CRAB APPLE

⁴**crab** *vb* -bb- *vt* to make sullen; sour ⟨*old age has* ~ *bed his nature*⟩ ~ *vi* to carp, grouse ⟨*always* ~s *about the weather*⟩ – *infml*

⁵**crab** *n* an ill-tempered person – *infml*

crab apple *n* (a tree that bears) a small usu wild sour apple

crabbed *adj* 1 morose, peevish 2 difficult to read or understand ⟨~ *handwriting*⟩ – **crabbedly** *adv,* **crabbedness** *n*

crabby *adj* cross, ill-tempered – *infml*

crabgrass *n* a grass with freely rooting creeping stems that grows as a weed in lawns

crab louse *n* a sucking louse that infests the pubic region of the human body

crabwise *adv* 1 sideways 2 in a sidling or cautiously indirect manner

¹**crack** *vi* 1 to make a sudden sharp explosive noise ⟨*the whip* ~s⟩ 2a to break or split apart b to develop fissures 3a to lose control or effectiveness under pressure – often + up b to fail in tone, volume, etc ⟨*his voice* ~ed⟩ 4 *esp of hydrocarbons* to break up into simpler chemical compounds when heated, usu with a catalyst ~ *vt* 1a to break so that fissures appear on the surface ⟨~ *a mirror*⟩ b to break with a crack ⟨~ *nuts*⟩ 2 to tell (a joke) 3a to puzzle out and expose, solve, or reveal the mystery of ⟨~ *a code*⟩ b to break into ⟨~ *a safe*⟩ c to break through (e g a barrier) so as to gain acceptance or recognition 4 to cause to make a sudden sharp noise ⟨~ *one's knuckles*⟩ 5a to subject (esp heavy hydrocarbons) to cracking, esp to produce petrol b to produce (e g petrol) by cracking 6 to open (e g a can or bottle) for drinking – *infml*

²**crack** *n* 1 a sudden sharp loud noise ⟨*the* ~ *of rifle fire*⟩ 2a a line or narrow opening that marks a break; a fissure ⟨*a* ~ *in the ice*⟩ b a narrow opening; a chink ⟨*leave the door open a* ~⟩ 3 a broken tone of the voice 4 a sharp resounding blow ⟨*gave him a* ~ *on the head*⟩ 5 a witty remark; a quip – *infml* 6 an attempt, try *at* – *infml*

³**crack** *adj* of superior quality or ability ⟨*a* ~ *shot*⟩ – *infml*

crackdown *n* an act or instance of cracking down

crack down *vi* to take regulatory or disciplinary action – usu + *on*

cracked *adj* 1 marked by harshness, dissonance, or failure to sustain a tone ⟨*a* ~ *voice*⟩ 2 mentally disordered; crazy – *infml*

cracker *n* 1a a (folded) usu paper cylinder containing an explosive that is discharged to make a noise b a brightly coloured paper and cardboard tube that makes a cracking noise when pulled sharply apart and usu contains a toy, paper hat, or other party item 2 *pl* a nutcracker 3 a thin often savoury biscuit 4 the equipment in which cracking, esp of petroleum, is carried out 5 *Br* sthg or sby excep-

tional; *esp* an outstandingly attractive girl or woman – *infml*

crackers *adj, chiefly Br* mad, crazy – *infml*

¹**crackle** *vb* **crackling** *vi* 1 to make a crackle ⟨*the fire* ~s *on the hearth*⟩ 2 CRAZE ~ *vt* 1 to crush or crack with a snapping sound 2 CRAZE 1

²**crackle** *n* 1 the noise of repeated small cracks or reports 2 a network of fine cracks on an otherwise smooth surface – **crackly** *adj*

crackling *n* 1 the crisp skin of roast meat, esp pork 2 the crisp residue left after the rendering of animal fat, esp lard – usu pl with sing. meaning

crackpot *n* sby with eccentric ideas; a crank – *infml* – **crackpot** *adj*

cracksman *n* a burglar – *infml*

crack-up *n* 1 a mental collapse; NERVOUS BREAKDOWN 2 a collapse, breakdown

crack up *vt* to present in (excessively) favourable terms ⟨*wasn't all that it was* cracked up *to be*⟩ – *infml* ~ *vi* to undergo a physical or mental collapse

-cracy *comb form* (→ *n*) 1 rule; government ⟨*democracy*⟩ 2 powerful or dominant social or political class ⟨*aristocracy*⟩ 3 state having a (specified) government or ruling class ⟨*meritocracy*⟩

¹**cradle** *n* 1a a baby's bed or cot, usu on rockers b a framework of wood or metal used as a support, scaffold, etc 2a the earliest period of life; infancy ⟨*from the* ~ *to the grave*⟩ b a place of origin ⟨~ *of civilization*⟩

²**cradle** *vt* **cradling** 1 to place or keep (as if) in a cradle 2 to shelter or hold protectively

¹**craft** *n, pl* **crafts,** (5) **craft** *also* **crafts** 1 skill in planning, making, or executing; dexterity – often in combination ⟨*stagecraft*⟩ 2 an activity or trade requiring manual dexterity or artistic skill; *broadly* a trade, profession 3 skill in deceiving to gain an end 4 *sing or pl in constr* the members of a trade or trade association 5a a (small) boat b an aircraft c a spacecraft

²**craft** *vt* to make (as if) using skill and dexterity ⟨*a beautifully* ~ed *novel*⟩

craftsman, *fem* **craftswoman** *n* 1 a workman who practises a skilled trade or handicraft 2 one who displays a high degree of manual dexterity or artistic skill – **craftsmanlike** *adj,* **craftsmanship** *n*

crafty *adj* showing subtlety and guile – **craftily** *adv,* **craftiness** *n*

crag *n* a steep rugged rock or cliff

craggy *adj* rough, rugged ⟨*a* ~ *face*⟩ – **cragginess** *n*

crake *n* a (short-billed) rail (e g the corncrake)

cram *vb* -mm- *vt* 1 to pack tight; jam ⟨~ *a suitcase with clothes*⟩ 2 to thrust forcefully 3 to prepare hastily for an examination 4 to eat voraciously; bolt – *infml* ~ *vi* 1 to study hastily and intensively for an examination 2 to eat greedily or until uncomfortably full – *infml*

cram-full *adj* as full as can be

crammer *n, Br* a school or teacher that prepares students intensively for an examination – *infml*

¹**cramp** *n* 1 a painful involuntary spasmodic contraction of a muscle 2 *pl* severe abdominal pain

²**cramp** *n* 1 a usu metal device bent at the ends and used to hold timbers or blocks of stone together 2 a clamp

³**cramp** *vt* 1 to affect with cramp 2a to confine, restrain b to restrain from free expression – esp in *cramp someone's style* 3 to fasten or hold with a clamp

crampon *n* 1 a hooked mechanical device for lifting heavy objects – usu pl with sing. meaning 2 a metal frame with downward- and forward-pointing spikes that is fixed to the sole of a boot for climbing slopes of ice or hard snow

cranberry *n* any of various plants of the heath family; *also* the red acid berry of such plants used in making sauces and jellies

¹crane n **1** any of a family of tall wading birds **2** a machine for moving heavy weights by means of a projecting swinging arm or a hoisting apparatus supported on an overhead track

²crane vt **1** to raise or lift (as if) by a crane **2** to stretch (e g the neck), esp in order to see better ~ vi to stretch one's neck, esp in order to see better ⟨I ~d out of the window⟩

crane fly n any of numerous long-legged slender two-winged flies that resemble large mosquitoes but do not bite

cranium n, pl **craniums, crania** the skull; specif the part that encloses the brain – **cranial** adj

¹crank n **1** a part of an axle or shaft bent at right angles by which reciprocating motion is changed into circular motion or vice versa **2** an eccentric person; also one who is excessively enthusiastic or fastidious about sthg

²crank vi to turn a crank (e g in starting an engine) ~ vt **1** to bend into the shape of a crank **2** to provide or fasten with a crank **3a** to move or operate (as if) by a crank **b** to start by use of a crank – often + up

³crank adj, of a boat easily capsized

crankshaft n a shaft driven by or driving a crank

cranky adj **1** of machinery working erratically; unpredictable **2** ECCENTRIC 2 **3** NAm bad-tempered – **crankily** adv, **crankiness** n

cranny n a small crack or slit; a chink – **crannied** adj

¹crap n **1a** excrement **b** an act of defecation **2** nonsense, rubbish – slang; sometimes used as an interjection USE (1) vulg

²crap vi **-pp-** to defecate – vulg

crappy adj of very poor quality – slang

craps n pl but sing or pl in constr a gambling game played with 2 dice – **crap** adj

¹crash vt **1a** to break violently and noisily; smash **b** to damage (an aircraft) in landing **c** to damage (a vehicle) by collision **2a** to cause to make a crashing sound ⟨~ the cymbals together⟩ **b** to force (e g one's way) with loud crashing noises **3** to enter without invitation or payment ⟨~ the party⟩ – infml **4** to cause (e g a computer system or program) to crash ~ vi **1a** to break or go to pieces (as if) with violence and noise **b** to crash an aircraft or vehicle **c** to be involved in a crash **2** to make a crashing noise **3** to move or go (as if) with a crash **4** to spend the night in a (makeshift) place; go to sleep ⟨can I ~ on your floor tonight?⟩ – sometimes + out; slang **5** esp of a computer system or program to become (suddenly) completely inoperative

²crash n **1** a loud noise (e g of things smashing) ⟨a ~ of thunder⟩ **2** a breaking to pieces (as if) by collision; also an instance of crashing ⟨a plane ~⟩ **3** a sudden decline or failure (e g of a business) ⟨the Wall Street ~⟩

³crash adj designed to achieve an intended result in the shortest possible time ⟨a ~ diet⟩

⁴crash n a coarse fabric made orig of linen, used for draperies, clothing, etc

crash barrier n a barrier to prevent vehicles accidentally colliding or leaving the road

crash-dive vb (to cause) to descend or dive steeply and quickly – used esp with reference to an aircraft or submarine – **crashdive** n

crash helmet n a helmet that is worn (e g by motorcyclists) to protect the head in the event of an accident

crashing adj utter, absolute ⟨a ~ bore⟩

crash-land vb to land (an aircraft) under emergency conditions, usu with some damage to the craft – **crash landing** n

crass adj **1** insensitive, coarse ⟨~ behaviour⟩ **2** deplorably great; complete ⟨~ stupidity⟩ – **crassitude** n, **crassly** adv, **crassness** n

-crat comb form (→ n) **1** advocate or partisan of (a specified form of government) ⟨democrat⟩ **2** member of (a specified ruling class) ⟨plutocrat⟩ ⟨technocrat⟩ – **-cratic** comb form (→ adj)

¹crate n **1** a usu wooden framework or box for holding goods (e g fruit, bottles, etc), esp during transit **2** the contents of a crate

²crate vt to pack in a crate

¹crater n **1 a** (bowl-shaped) depression: e g **a** round the mouth of a volcano **b** formed by the impact of a meteorite **2** a hole in the ground made by an explosion **3** a jar or vase with a wide mouth used in classical antiquity for mixing wine and water

²crater vt to form craters in

cravat n a decorative band or scarf worn round the neck, esp by men

crave vt **1** to have a strong or urgent desire for **2** to ask for earnestly; beg ⟨I ~ the court's indulgence⟩ – fml ~ vi to have a strong desire; yearn ⟨~s after affection⟩

craven adj completely lacking in courage; cowardly – **craven** n, **cravenly** adv, **cravenness** n

craving n a great desire or longing ⟨a ~ for tobacco⟩

¹crawl vi **1** to move slowly in a prone position (as if) without the use of limbs **2** to move or progress slowly or laboriously **3** CREEP 3b **4a** to be alive or swarming (as if) with creeping things **b** to have the sensation of insects creeping over one ⟨the story made her flesh ~⟩ **5** to behave in a servile manner – infml ~ vt to move upon (as if) in a creeping manner ⟨the meanest man who ever ~ed the earth⟩

²crawl n **1a** crawling **b** slow or laborious motion ⟨traffic moving at a ~⟩ **2** the fastest swimming stroke, executed lying on the front and consisting of alternating overarm strokes combined with kicks with the legs

crawler n **1** a vehicle (e g a crane) that travels on endless metal belts **2** a servile person – infml

crayfish n **1** any of numerous freshwater crustaceans resembling the lobster but usu much smaller **2** SPINY LOBSTER

crayon vt or n (to draw or colour with) a stick of coloured chalk or wax used for writing or drawing

¹craze vt **1** to produce minute cracks on the surface or glaze of **2** to make (as if) insane ⟨~d by pain and fear⟩ ~ vi to develop a mesh of fine cracks

²craze n **1** an exaggerated and often short-lived enthusiasm; a fad **2** fine cracks in a surface or coating of glaze, enamel, etc

crazy adj **1** mad, insane **2a** impractical ⟨a ~ idea⟩ **b** unusual, eccentric **3** extremely enthusiastic about; very fond – **crazily** adv, **craziness** n – **like crazy** to an extreme degree ⟨everyone dancing like crazy⟩ – infml

crazy paving n, Br a paved surface made up of irregularly shaped paving stones

¹creak vi to make a prolonged grating or squeaking noise

²creak n a prolonged rasping, grating, or squeaking noise (e g of an unoiled hinge) – **creaky** adj, **creakily** adv

¹cream n **1** the yellowish part of milk containing butterfat, that forms a surface layer when milk is allowed to stand **2a** a food (e g a sauce or cake filling) prepared with or resembling cream in consistency, richness, etc **b** a biscuit, chocolate, etc filled with (a soft preparation resembling) whipped cream **c** sthg with the consistency of thick cream; esp a usu emulsified medicinal or cosmetic preparation ⟨skin ~⟩ **3** the choicest part **4** a pale yellowish white colour – **creamily** adv, **creaminess** n, **creamy** adj

²**cream** *vi* 1 to form cream or a surface layer like the cream on milk 2 to break into a creamy froth ~ *vt* 1a SKIM 1c b to take away (the choicest part) – usu + *off* ⟨~ *off the brightest students*⟩ 2 to provide, prepare, or treat with cream or a cream sauce 3 to work or blend to the consistency of cream ⟨~ *butter and sugar*⟩ 4 to cause to form a surface layer of or like cream 5 NAm to defeat completely – infml

cream cheese *n* a mild white soft unripened cheese made from whole milk enriched with cream

creamer *n* 1 a device for separating cream from milk 2 a small vessel (e g a jug) for serving cream

creamery *n* an establishment where butter and cheese are made or where milk and milk products are prepared or sold

cream of tartar *n* potassium hydrogen tartrate occurring as a white powder and used esp in baking powder

¹**crease** *n* 1 a line or mark made (as if) by folding a pliable substance 2a an area surrounding the goal in lacrosse, hockey, etc into which an attacking player may not precede the ball or puck b the bowling crease, popping crease, or return crease of a cricket pitch – **creaseless** *adj*

²**crease** *vt* 1 to make a crease in or on; wrinkle 2 *chiefly Br* a to cause much amusement to – often + *up* b to tire out ~ *vi* to become creased USE (2) infml

create *vt* 1 to bring into existence ⟨*God* ~ d *the heaven and the earth* – Gen 1:1 (AV)⟩ 2a to invest with a new form, office, or rank ⟨*was* ~ d *a peer of the realm*⟩ b to produce, cause ⟨~ d *a disturbance*⟩ 3 to design, invent ~ *vi Br* to make a loud fuss about sthg – infml

creation *n* 1 *often cap* the act of bringing the world into ordered existence 2 sthg created: e g a the world b creatures singly or collectively c an original work of art d a product of some minor art or craft (e g dressmaking or cookery) showing unusual flair or immagination – often derog ⟨*a hideous* ~ *in mauve and magneta tulle*⟩

creative *adj* 1 marked by or requiring the ability or power to create; given to creating 2 having the quality of sthg imaginatively created ⟨*the* ~ *arts*⟩ – **creatively** *adv*, **creativeness** *n*

creator *n* a person who creates, usu by bringing sthg new or original into being; *esp, cap* GOD 1

creature *n* 1a sthg created ⟨~s *of fantasy*⟩ b a lower animal ⟨*the* ~s *of the woods*⟩ 2a an animate being; *esp* a non-human one b a human being; a person 3 one who is the servile dependant or tool of another – **creatural** *adj*, **creatureliness** *n*, **creaturely** *adj*

creature comforts *n pl* material things that give bodily comfort

crèche *n* 1 a representation of the Nativity scene 2 *chiefly Br* a centre where children under school age are looked after while their parents are at work

credence *n* acceptance of sthg as true or real ⟨*give* ~ *to gossip*⟩

credential *n* sthg, esp a letter, that gives proof of identity, status, or authority – usu pl with sing. meaning

credibility gap *n* (a lack of credibility arising from) a discrepancy between what is claimed and what is perceived to be true

credible *adj* offering reasonable grounds for belief – **credibly** *adv*, **credibility** *n*

¹**credit** *n* 1a the balance in a person's favour in an account b an amount or sum placed at a person's disposal by a bank and usu to be repaid with interest c time given for payment for goods or services provided but not immediately paid for ⟨*long-term* ~⟩ d an entry on the right-hand side of an account constituting an addition to a revenue, net worth, or liability account 2 credence 3 influence

derived from enjoying the confidence of others; standing 4 a source of honour or repute ⟨*a* ~ *to her parents*⟩ 5 acknowledgment, approval ⟨~ *where* ~ *is due*⟩ 6a a line, note, or name that acknowledges the source of an item b an acknowledgment of a contributor by name that appears at the beginning or end of a film or television programme 7a recognition that a student has fulfilled a course requirement b the passing of an examination at a level well above the minimum though not with distinction –**on credit** with the cost charged to one's account and paid later ⟨*bought his new tape recorder* on credit⟩

²**credit** *vt* 1 to believe 2a to enter on the credit side of an account b to place to the credit of ⟨~ *an account*⟩ 3a to ascribe some usu favourable characteristic to – + *with* ⟨~ *me with some intelligence*⟩ b to attribute *to* some person ⟨*they* ~ *the invention to him*⟩

creditable *adj* 1 worthy of esteem or praise 2 NAm capable of being attributed *to* – **creditably** *adv*

credit card *n* a card provided by a bank, agency, or business allowing the holder to obtain goods and services on credit

creditor *n* one to whom a debt is owed

credo *n, pl* **credos** 1 a creed 2 *cap* a musical setting of the creed in a sung mass

credulity *n* undue willingness to believe; gullibility

credulous *adj* ready to believe, esp on slight evidence – **credulously** *adv*, **credulousness** *n*

creed *n* 1 a brief conventionalized statement of religious belief; *esp* such a statement said or sung as part of Christian worship 2 a set of fundamental beliefs – **creedal** *adj*, **credal** *adj*

creek *n* 1 *chiefly Br* a small narrow inlet of a lake, sea, etc 2 *chiefly NAm & Austr* a brook – **up the creek** 1 in trouble – infml 2 wrong, mistaken – infml

Creek *n* a member, or the Muskogean language, of a confederacy of American Indian peoples of Alabama, Georgia, and Florida

creel *n* a wickerwork container (e g for newly caught fish)

¹**creep** *vi* **crept** 1 to move along with the body prone and close to the ground 2a to go very slowly ⟨*the hours* crept *by*⟩ b to go timidly or cautiously so as to escape notice c to enter, advance, or develop gradually or slowly ⟨*a note of irritation* crept *into her voice*⟩ 3a CRAWL 4b b *of a plant* to spread or grow over a surface by clinging with tendrils, roots, etc or rooting at intervals 4 to change shape permanently due to prolonged stress or exposure to high temperatures

²**creep** *n* 1 a movement of or like creeping 2 the slow change of dimensions of an object due to prolonged exposure to high temperature or stress 3 a distressing sensation, esp of apprehension or disgust, like that caused by insects creeping over one's flesh – usu pl with sing. meaning ⟨*gives me the* ~s⟩; infml 4 *Br* an obnoxious or ingratiatingly servile person – infml

creeper *n* 1a a creeping plant b a bird (e g a tree creeper) that creeps about on trees or bushes c a creeping insect or reptile 2 a grapnel

creepy *adj* producing a sensation of shivery apprehension ⟨*a* ~ *horror story*⟩

creepy-crawly *n, Br* a small creeping or scuttling creature (e g a spider) – infml

cremate *vt* to reduce (a dead body) to ashes by burning – **cremation** *n*

crematorium *n, pl* **crematoriums, crematoria** a place where cremation is carried out

crème de menthe *n* a sweet green or white mint-flavoured liqueur

crenellated *adj* having battlements

creole *adj, often cap* of Creoles or their language
Creole *n* 1 a person of European descent in the W Indies
or Spanish America 2 a white descendant of early French
or Spanish settlers of the Gulf States of the USA 3 a
person of mixed French or Spanish and Negro descent 4
not cap a language based on 2 or more languages that
serves as the native language of its speakers
¹creosote *n* 1 a clear or yellowish oily liquid obtained
from wood tar and used as an antiseptic 2 a brownish oily
liquid obtained from coal tar and used esp as a wood
preservative
²creosote *vt* to treat with creosote
crepe, crêpe *n* 1 a light crinkled fabric woven from any
of various fibres 2 a small very thin pancake – crepey,
crepy *adj*
crepe paper *n* thin paper with a crinkled or puckered
texture
crept *past of* CREEP
crepuscular *adj* 1 active in the twilight ⟨~ *insects*⟩ 2
of or resembling twilight; dim – *fml*
¹crescendo *n, pl* crescendos, crescendoes 1 a gradual
increase; *esp* a gradual increase in volume in a musical
passage 2 a crescendo musical passage – crescendo *vi*
²crescendo *adv or adj* with an increase in volume – used
in music
crescent *n* 1 the figure of the moon at any stage between
new moon and first quarter or last quarter and the
succeeding new moon 2 sthg shaped like a crescent and
consisting of a concave and a convex curve
cress *n* any of numerous plants of the mustard family that
have mildly pungent leaves and are used in salads and as
a garnish
¹crest *n* 1a a showy tuft or projection on the head of an
animal, esp a bird b the plume, emblem, etc worn on a
knight's helmet c(1) a symbol of a family, office, etc that
appears as a figure on top of the helmet in a heraldic
achievement (2) COAT OF ARMS – not used technically in
heraldry d the upper muscular ridge of a horse's neck
from which the mane grows 2 the ridge or top, esp of a
wave, roof, or mountain 3 *the* climax, culmination ⟨*at the
~ of his fame*⟩ – crestless *adj*
²crest *vt* 1 to provide with a crest; crown 2 to reach the
crest of ~ *vi of waves* to rise to a crest
crested *adj* 1 having a crest 2 marked or decorated with
a crest ⟨~ *crockery*⟩
crestfallen *adj* disheartened, dejected
cretaceous *adj* 1 resembling or containing chalk 2 *cap*
of or being the last period of the Mesozoic era – cretaceous *n*, cretaceously *adv*
cretin *n* sby afflicted with cretinism; *broadly* an imbecile,
idiot – cretinous *adj*
cretinism *n* (congenital) physical stunting and mental
retardation caused by severe deficiency of the thyroid
gland in infancy
cretonne *n* a strong unglazed cotton or linen cloth used
esp for curtains and upholstery
crevasse *n* a deep fissure, esp in a glacier
crevice *n* a narrow opening resulting from a split or
crack
¹crew *chiefly Br past of* CROW
²crew *n sing or pl in constr* 1 a company of men working
on 1 job or under 1 foreman 2a the personnel of a ship
or boat (excluding the captain and officers) b members of
a crew ⟨*the captain and 50 ~*⟩ c the people who man an
aircraft in flight 3 a number of people temporarily associated – *infml* – crewless *adj*, crewman *n*
³crew *vb* to serve as a member of a crew (on)
crew cut *n* a very short bristly haircut, esp for a man
¹crib *n* 1 a manger for feeding animals 2 an enclosure, esp

with barred or slatted sides: e g a a stall for a stabled
animal b CRADLE 1a c a bin for storage 3a a set of cards
contributed to equally by each player in cribbage for the
dealer to use in scoring b cribbage 4 a literal translation;
esp one used surreptitiously by students 5 *Br* a building
considered with a view to unlawful entry 6 *chiefly NAm*
COT 2
²crib *vb* -bb- *vt* 1 to confine, cramp 2 to provide with or
put into a crib 3 to pilfer, steal; *esp* to plagiarize ~ *vi* 1
to steal, plagiarize 2 to use a crib; cheat – cribber *n*
cribbage *n* a card game for 2 to 4 players each attempting
to form various counting combinations of cards
¹crick *n* a painful spasmodic condition of the muscles of the
neck, back, etc
²crick *vt* to cause a crick in (the neck, back, etc)
¹cricket *n* a leaping insect noted for the chirping sounds
produced by the male
²cricket *n* a game played with a bat and ball on a large field
with 2 wickets near its centre by 2 sides of 11 players each
– cricketer *n* – not cricket against the dictates of fair play;
not honourable
crier *n* an officer who makes announcements in a court
crikey *interj, chiefly Br* – used to express surprise; no
longer in vogue
crime *n* 1 (a) violation of law 2 a grave offence, esp
against morality 3 criminal activity 4 sthg deplorable,
foolish, or disgraceful ⟨*it's a ~ to waste good food*⟩ –
infml
¹criminal *adj* 1 involving or being a crime 2 relating to
crime or its punishment ⟨~ *law*⟩⟨*a ~ court*⟩ 3 guilty of
crime 4 disgraceful, deplorable – *infml* – criminally *adv*,
criminality *n*
²criminal *n* one who has committed or been convicted of
a crime
criminology *n* the study of crime, criminals, and penal
treatment – criminologist *n*, criminological *adj*
¹crimp *vt* 1 to make wavy, or curly ⟨~ *her hair*⟩ 2 to roll
or curl the edge of (e g a steel panel) 3 to pinch or press
together in order to seal or join – crimp *n*, crimper *n*
²crimp *n or vt* (one employed) to entrap or force (men) into
joining the army or navy
Crimplene *trademark* – used for a textured continuous-
filament polyester yarn
¹crimson *adj or n* (a) deep purplish red
²crimson *vb* to make or become crimson
cringe *vi* 1 to shrink or wince, esp in fear or servility 2
to behave with fawning self-abasement
¹crinkle *vb* crinkling *vi* 1 to wrinkle 2 to rustle ~ *vt* to
cause to crinkle
²crinkle *n* a wrinkle – crinkly *adj*
crinoid *n* any of a large class of echinoderms having a
cup-shaped body with 5 or more feathery arms – crinoid
adj
crinoline *n* (a padded or hooped petticoat supporting) a
full skirt as worn by women in the 19th c
cripes *interj, Br* – used to express surprise; no longer in
vogue
¹cripple *n* a lame or partly disabled person or animal
²cripple *vt* crippling 1 to make a cripple; lame 2 to deprive
of strength, efficiency, wholeness, or capability for service
crisis *n, pl* crises 1a the turning point for better or worse
in an acute disease (e g pneumonia) b a sudden attack of
pain, distress, etc 2 an unstable or crucial time or situation; *esp* TURNING POINT
¹crisp *adj* 1a easily crumbled; brittle b desirably firm and
fresh ⟨*a ~ apple*⟩ c newly made or prepared ⟨*a ~ pound
note*⟩ 2 sharp, clean-cut, and clear ⟨*a ~ illustration*⟩ 3

decisive, sharp ⟨a ~ *manner*⟩ **4** *of weather* briskly cold; fresh; *esp* frosty – **crisply** *adv*, **crispness** *n*

²crisp *vt* **1** to curl, crimp **2** to make or keep crisp ⟨~ *the bread in the oven*⟩ ~ *vi* to become crisp – **crisper** *n*

³crisp *n, chiefly Br* a thin slice of (flavoured or salted) fried potato, usu eaten cold

crispy *adj* crisp – **crispiness** *n*

¹crisscross *adj or n* (marked or characterized by) crisscrossing or a crisscrossed pattern

²crisscross *vt* **1** to mark with intersecting lines **2** to pass back and forth through or over ~ *vi* to go or pass back and forth

criterion *n, pl* **criteria** *also* **criterions** a standard on which a judgment or decision may be based – **criterial** *adj*

critic *n* one who criticizes: e g **a** one who evaluates works of art, literature, or music, esp as a profession **b** one who tends to judge harshly or to be over-critical of minor faults

critical *adj* **1a** inclined to criticize severely and unfavourably **b** consisting of or involving criticism ⟨~ *writings*⟩ **c** exercising or involving careful judgment or judicious evaluation **2a** relating to or being a measurement, point, etc at which some quality, property, or phenomenon undergoes a marked change ⟨~ *temperature*⟩ **b** crucial, decisive ⟨~ *test*⟩ **c** being in or approaching a state of crisis **3** *of a nuclear reactor* sustaining an energy-producing chain reaction – **critically** *adv*, **criticality** *n*

criticism *n* **1a** the act of criticizing, usu unfavourably **b** a critical observation or remark **c** a critique **2** the art or act of analysing and evaluating esp the fine arts, literature, or literary documents

criticize, -ise *vt* **1** to consider the merits and demerits of and judge accordingly; evaluate **2** to stress the faults of ~ *vi* to criticize sthg or sby

critique *n* an act of criticizing; *esp* a critical estimate or discussion (e g an article or essay)

critter *n, dial* a creature

¹croak *vi* **1a** to make a croak **b** to speak in a hoarse throaty voice **2** to die – slang ~ *vt* **1** to utter (gloomily) in a hoarse raucous voice ⟨*the raven that ~s the fatal entrance of Duncan* – Shak⟩ **2** to kill – slang

²croak *n* a deep hoarse cry characteristic of a frog or toad; *also* a similar sound – **croaky** *adj*

¹crochet *n* crocheted work

²crochet *vt* to form (e g a garment or design) by drawing a single continuous yarn or thread into a pattern of interlocked loops using a hooked needle ~ *vi* to do or make crochet work – **crocheter** *n*

¹crock *n* **1** a thick earthenware pot or jar **2** a piece of broken earthenware used esp to cover the bottom of a flowerpot

²crock *n* **1** an old (broken-down) vehicle **2** an (elderly) disabled person *USE* infml

³crock *vt* to cause to become disabled ~ *vi* BREAK DOWN 1a *USE* (*vt & vi*) sometimes + *up*; infml

crockery *n* earthenware or china tableware, esp for everyday domestic use

crocodile *n* **1** any of several tropical or subtropical large voracious thick-skinned long-bodied aquatic reptiles; *broadly* a crocodilian **2** the skin of a crocodile; *also* leather prepared from this **3** *Br* a line of people (e g schoolchildren) walking in pairs

crocodile tears *n pl* false or affected tears; hypocritical sorrow

crocus *n, pl* **crocuses** any of a large genus of usu early-flowering plants of the iris family bearing a single usu brightly-coloured long-tubed flower

croft *n, chiefly Br* **1** a small enclosed field usu adjoining a house **2** a small farm on often poor land, esp in Scotland, worked by a tenant – **crofter** *n*

croissant *n* a usu flaky rich crescent-shaped roll of bread or yeast- leavened pastry

cromlech *n* a dolmen

crone *n* a withered old woman

crony *n* a close friend, esp of long standing; a chum – infml; often derog ⟨*old* cronies *down at the pub*⟩

¹crook *n* **1** an implement or part of sthg having a bent or hooked shape **2** a shepherd's staff **3** a bend, curve ⟨*she carried the parcel in the ~ of her arm*⟩ **4** a person given to criminal practices; a thief, swindler – infml

²crook *vt* BEND 1 ⟨*I ~ed my neck so I could see*⟩ ~ *vi* to curve, wind

³crook *adj, Austr & NZ* **1** ill, sick **2** not in correct working order **3** bad, unpleasant *USE* infml

crooked *adj* **1** having a crook or curve; bent **2** not morally straightforward; dishonest **3** *Austr* bad-tempered; angry – **crookedly** *adv*, **crookedness** *n*

croon *vi* to sing usu sentimental popular songs in a low or soft voice ~ *vt* to sing in a crooning manner – **croon** *n*, **crooner** *n*

¹crop *n* **1** (the stock or handle of) a riding whip, esp with a short stock and a loop on the end **2** a pouched enlargement of the gullet of many birds in which food is stored and prepared for digestion **3** a short haircut **4a** (the total production of) a plant or animal product that can be grown and harvested extensively ⟨*a large apple ~*⟩ **b** a group or quantity appearing at any one time ⟨*a new ~ of students*⟩

²crop *vb* **-pp-** *vt* **1a** to remove the upper or outer parts of ⟨~ *a hedge*⟩ **b** to harvest ⟨~ *trout*⟩ **c** to cut short; trim **2** to grow as or to cause (land) to bear a crop ⟨~ *more wheat next year*⟩ ~ *vi* **1** to feed by cropping sthg **2** to yield or bear a crop

¹cropper *n* a plant that yields a crop of a usu specified quality or amount

²cropper *n* **1** a severe fall **2** a sudden or complete disaster *USE* chiefly in *come a cropper*; infml

crop up *vi* to happen or appear unexpectedly or casually – infml

croquet *n* **1** a game in which wooden balls are driven by mallets through a series of hoops set out on a lawn **2** the driving away of an opponent's croquet ball by striking one's own ball placed against it – **croquet** *vt*

croquette *n* a small (rounded) piece of minced meat, vegetable, etc coated with egg and breadcrumbs and fried in deep fat

crore *n, pl* **crores** *also* **crore** a money unit worth 10 million rupees or 100 lakhs

crosier, crozier *n* a staff resembling a shepherd's crook carried by bishops as a symbol of office

¹cross *n* **1a** an upright stake with a transverse beam used, esp by the ancient Romans, for execution **b** *often cap* the cross on which Jesus was crucified **2a** the Crucifixion **b** an affliction, trial **3** a figure or design consisting of an upright bar intersected by a horizontal one; *specif* one used as a Christian emblem **4** a monument shaped like or surmounted by a cross ⟨*the market ~*⟩ **5** a mark formed by 2 intersecting lines crossing at their midpoints that is used as a signature, to mark a position, to indicate that sthg is incorrect, or to indicate a kiss in a letter **6** a badge, emblem, or decoration shaped like a cross **7a** the crossing of dissimilar individuals; *also* the resulting hybrid **b** sby who or sthg that combines characteristics of 2 different types or individuals **8** a hook delivered over the opponent's lead in boxing **9** the act of crossing the ball in soccer – **on the cross** on the bias; diagonally

²cross *vt* **1a** to lie or be situated across **b** to intersect **2**

to make the sign of the cross on or over **3** to cancel by marking a cross on or drawing a line through **4** to place or fold crosswise ⟨~ *the arms*⟩ **5** to run counter to; oppose **6** to go across **7a** to draw a line across ⟨~ *one's t's*⟩ **b** to draw 2 parallel lines across (a cheque) so that it can only be paid directly into a bank account **8** to cause (an animal or plant) to interbreed with one of a different kind; hybridize **9** to kick or pass (the ball) across the field in soccer, specif from the wing into the goal area ~ *vi* **1** to move, pass, or extend across sthg – usu + *over* **2** *of letters, travellers, etc* to meet and pass **3** to interbreed, hybridize **4** to cross the ball in soccer – **cross the floor** *of a member of parliament* to transfer allegiance to the opposing party – **cross swords** to come into conflict – **cross one's mind** to occur to one

³**cross** *adj* **1** lying or moving across **2** mutually opposed ⟨~ *purposes*⟩ **3** involving mutual interchange; reciprocal **4a** irritable, grumpy **b** angry, annoyed **5** crossbred, hybrid – **crossly** *adv*, **crossness** *n*

⁴**cross** *adv* not parallel; crosswise

crossbar *n* a transverse bar (e g between goalposts)

cross-bench *n* any of the benches in the House of Lords for members who belong to neither government nor opposition parties – usu pl – **crossbencher** *n*

crossbones *n pl* 2 leg or arm bones placed or depicted crosswise

crossbow *n* a short bow mounted crosswise near the end of a wooden stock and used to fire bolts and stones – **crossbowman** *n*

crossbred *adj* hybrid; *specif* produced by interbreeding 2 pure but different breeds, strains, or varieties – **crossbred** *n*

¹**crossbreed** *vb* **crossbred** *vt* to hybridize or cross (esp 2 varieties or breeds of the same species) ~ *vi* to undergo crossbreeding

²**crossbreed** *n* a hybrid

cross-check *vb* to check (information) for validity or accuracy by reference to more than 1 source – **cross-check** *n*

¹**cross-country** *adj* **1** proceeding over countryside and not by roads **2** racing or travelling over the countryside instead of over a track or run – **cross-country** *adv*

²**cross-country** *n* cross-country running, horse riding, etc

crosscurrent *n* a conflicting tendency – usu pl ⟨*political* ~*s*⟩

crosscut *vt* to intersperse with contrasting images – **crosscut** *n*

crosscut saw *n* a saw designed to cut across the grain of wood

crosse *n* the long-handled netted stick used in lacrosse

cross-examine *vt* to question closely (esp a witness in a law court) in order to check answers or elicit new information – **cross-examination** *n*, **cross-examiner** *n*

cross-fertilization, -isation *n* **1a** fertilization by the joining of ova with pollen or sperm from a different individual **b** cross-pollination **2** interaction, esp of a broadening or productive nature – **cross-fertilize** *vb*

crossfire *n* **1** firing from 2 or more points in crossing directions **2** rapid or heated interchange

cross-grained *adj* **1** having the grain or fibres running diagonally, transversely, or irregularly **2** difficult to deal with; intractable

crosshatch *vt* to shade with a series of intersecting parallel lines – **cross-hatching** *n*

crossing *n* **1** a traversing or travelling across **2a** a place or structure (e g on a street or over a river) where pedestrians or vehicles may cross **b** LEVEL CROSSING **c** a place where railway lines, roads, etc cross each other

cross-legged *adv or adj* **1** with legs crossed and knees spread wide apart ⟨*sat* ~ *on the floor*⟩ **2** with one leg placed over and across the other

crosspatch *n* a bad-tempered person – *infml*

crosspiece *n* a horizontal member (e g of a structure)

crossply *n or adj* (a tyre) with the cords arranged crosswise to strengthen the tread

cross-purposes *n pl* – **at cross purposes** having a mutual misunderstanding or deliberately conflicting approach

cross-refer *vb* **-rr-** *vt* **1** to direct (a reader) from one page or entry (e g in a book) to another **2** to refer from (a secondary entry) to a main entry ~ *vi* to make a cross-reference

¹**cross-reference** *n* an indication at one place (e g in a book or filing system) of the existence of relevant information at another place

²**cross-reference** *vb* to cross-refer

crossroad *n* **1** the place where 2 or more roads intersect **2a** a central meeting place ⟨*the* ~s *of the world*⟩ **b** a crucial point, esp where a decision must be made ⟨*at a* ~s *in her career*⟩ USE usu pl with sing. meaning but sing. or pl in constr

cross-section *n* **1** (a drawing of) a surface made by cutting across sthg, esp at right angles to its length **2** the probability of an encounter between particles (resulting in a specified effect) ⟨*the ionization* ~⟩ **3** a representative sample ⟨*a* ~ *of society*⟩ – **cross-sectional** *adj*

cross-stitch *n* (needlework using) a stitch in the shape of an X formed by crossing one stitch over another – **cross-stitch** *vb*

cross-talk *n* **1** unwanted signals in a communication channel that come from another channel **2** *Br* rapid exchange of repartee (e g between comedians)

crosstrees *n pl* a pair of horizontal crosspieces on a mast to which supporting ropes are attached

crosswind *n* a wind blowing in a direction not parallel to the course of a vehicle, aircraft, etc

crosswise *adv* so as to cross sthg; across ⟨*logs laid* ~⟩

crossword puzzle *n* a puzzle in which words are entered in a pattern of numbered squares in answer to correspondingly numbered clues in such a way that the words read across and down

crotch *n* **1** an angle formed where 2 branches separate off from a tree trunk **2** the angle between the inner thighs where they meet the human body – **crotched** *adj*

crotchet *n* a musical note with the time value of half a minim or 2 quavers

crotchety *adj* bad-tempered ⟨*a* ~ *old man*⟩ – *infml* – **crotchetiness** *n*

crouch *vi* to lower the body by bending the legs – **crouch** *n*

¹**croup** *n* the rump of a quadruped

²**croup** *n* a spasmodic laryngitis, esp of infants, marked by periods of difficult breathing and a hoarse cough – **croupous** *adj*, **croupy** *adj*

croupier *n* an employee of a gambling casino who collects and pays out bets at the gaming tables

crouton *n* a small cube of crisp toasted or fried bread served with soup or used as a garnish

¹**crow** *n* **1** the carrion or hooded crow or a related large usu entirely glossy black bird **2** a crowbar – **as the crow flies** in a straight line

²**crow** *vi* **crowed**, (*1*) **crowed** *also* **crew 1** to make the loud shrill cry characteristic of a cock **2** *esp of an infant* to utter sounds of happiness or pleasure **3a** to exult gloatingly, esp over another's misfortune **b** to brag exultantly or blatantly

³crow *n* **1** the characteristic cry of the cock **2** a triumphant cry

crowbar *n* an iron or steel bar for use as a lever that is wedge-shaped at the working end

¹crowd *vi* **1** to press close ⟨*people* ~ing *through the narrow gates*⟩ **2** to collect in numbers; throng ~ *vt* **1a** to fill by pressing or thronging together ⟨*people* ~ed *the hall*⟩ **b** to force or thrust into a small space ⟨~ed *books onto the shelves*⟩ **2** to push, force ⟨~ed *us off the pavement*⟩ **3** to hoist more (sail) than usual for greater speed – usu + *on* **4** to press close to; jostle **5** to put pressure on – infml

²crowd *n sing or pl in constr* **1** a large number of people gathered together without order; a throng **2** people in general – + *the* **3** a large number of things close together and in disorder **4** a specified social group ⟨*the in* ~⟩

crowded **1** filled with numerous people, things, or events **2** pressed or forced into a small space ⟨~ *spectators*⟩

crowd out *vt* **1** to exclude by depriving of space or time **2** to fill to capacity by coming or collecting together

crowfoot *n, pl* **crowfoots** any of numerous plants, esp of the buttercup family, with lobed leaves shaped like a crow's foot

¹crown *n* **1** a reward of victory or mark of honour; *esp* the title representing the championship in a sport **2** a (gold and jewel-encrusted) headdress worn as a symbol of sovereignty **3a** the topmost part of the skull or head **b** the summit of a slope, mountain, etc **c** the upper part of the foliage of a tree or shrub **d** the part of a hat or cap that covers the crown of the head **e** (an artificial substitute for) the part of a tooth visible outside the gum **4** a wreath, band, or circular ornament for the head, esp worn as a symbol of victory **5** *often cap* **a** the sovereign as head of state; *also* sovereignty **b** the government under a constitutional monarchy **6** the high point or culmination **7a** a British coin worth 25 pence (formerly 5 shillings) **b** a size of paper usu 20 x 15in (508 × 381mm) **8a** a koruna **b** a krona **c** a krone **9** the part of a flowering plant at which stem and root merge – **crowned** *adj*

²crown *vt* **1a** to place a crown on the head of, esp as a symbol of investiture ⟨~ed *her queen*⟩ **b** to recognize, usu officially, as (the leader in a particular field) **2** to bestow sthg on as a mark of honour or reward **3** to surmount, top; *esp* to put a draughtsman on top of (another draughtsman) to make a king **4** to bring to a successful conclusion **5** to put an artificial crown on (a tooth) **6** to hit on the head – infml

crown colony *n, often cap C&C* a colony of the Commonwealth over which the British government retains some control

Crown Court *n* a local criminal court in England and Wales having jurisdiction over serious offences

crown jewels *n pl* the jewels (e g crown and sceptre) belonging to a sovereign's regalia

crown prince *n* an heir apparent to a crown or throne

crown princess *n* **1** the wife of a crown prince **2** a female heir apparent or heir presumptive to a crown or throne

crow's-foot *n, pl* **crow's-feet 1** any of the wrinkles round the outer corners of the eyes – usu pl **2** crowfoot

crow's nest *n* a partly enclosed high lookout platform (e g on a ship's mast)

crozier *n* a crosier

crucial *adj* **1** important or essential to the resolving of a crisis; decisive **2** of the greatest importance or significance – **crucially** *adv*

crucible *n* **1** a vessel for melting and calcining a substance at a very high temperature **2** a severe test

crucifix *n* a representation of Christ on the cross

crucifixion *n* **1** the act of crucifying **2** *cap* the crucifying of Christ

cruciform *adj* forming or arranged in a cross – **cruciformly** *adv*

crucify *vt* **1** to execute by nailing or binding the hands and feet to a cross and leaving to die **2** to treat cruelly; torture, persecute

¹crude *adj* **1** existing in a natural state and unaltered by processing **2** vulgar, gross **3** rough or inexpert in plan or execution **4** tabulated without being broken down into classes ⟨~ *death rate*⟩ – **crudely** *adv*, **crudeness** *n*

²crude *n* a substance, esp petroleum, in its natural unprocessed state

crudity *n* **1** being crude **2** sthg crude

cruel *adj* **-ll-** (*NAm* **-l-, -ll-**) **1** liking to inflict pain or suffering; pitiless **2** causing suffering; painful – **cruelly** *adv*, **cruelness** *n*

cruelty *n* **1** being cruel **2** (an instance of) cruel behaviour

cruet *n* **1** a vessel to hold wine or water for the Eucharist **2** a small usu glass bottle or jug that holds oil or vinegar for use at table **3** a small container (e g a pot or shaker) for holding a condiment, esp salt, pepper, or mustard, at table **4** a set of cruets, usu on a stand

¹cruise *vi* **1** to travel by sea for pleasure **2** to go about or patrol the streets without any definite destination ⟨*a cruising taxi*⟩ **3a** of an aircraft to fly at the most efficient operating speed **b** *of a vehicle* to travel at an economical speed that can be maintained for a long distance **4** to make progress easily **5** to search (e g in public places) for an esp homosexual partner – slang

²cruise *n* an act or instance of cruising; *esp* a sea voyage for pleasure

cruiser *n* **1** CABIN CRUISER **2** a large fast lightly armoured warship

¹crumb *n* **1** a small fragment, esp of bread **2** a small amount ⟨*a* ~ *of comfort*⟩ **3a** (loose crumbly soil or other material resembling) the soft part of bread inside the crust **b** a small lump consisting of soil particles **4** a worthless person – slang

²crumb *vt* **1** to break up into crumbs **2** to cover or thicken with crumbs

¹crumble *vb* **crumbling** to break or fall into small pieces; disintegrate – often + *away* – **crumbly** *adj*

²crumble *n* a dessert of stewed fruit topped with a crumbly mixture of fat, flour, and sugar

crummy, crumby *adj* **1** miserable, filthy **2** of poor quality; worthless *USE* slang

crumpet *n* **1** a small round cake made from an unsweetened leavened batter that is cooked on a griddle and usu toasted before serving **2** *Br* women collectively as sexual objects – slang ⟨*a piece of* ~⟩

¹crumple *vb* **crumpling** *vt* to press, bend, or crush out of shape; rumple ~ *vi* **1** to become crumpled **2** to collapse ⟨*her face* ~d *at the news*⟩ – often + *up*

²crumple *n* a wrinkle or crease made by crumpling

¹crunch *vb* **1** to chew or bite (sthg) with a noisy crushing sound **2** to (cause to) make a crushing sound **3** to make (one's way) with a crushing sound

²crunch *n* **1** an act or sound of crunching **2** *the* critical or decisive situation or moment – infml

crupper *n* a leather loop passing under a horse's tail and buckled to the saddle to prevent the saddle from slipping forwards

crusade *n* **1** *cap* any of the medieval Christian military expeditions to win the Holy Land from the Muslims **2** a reforming enterprise undertaken with zeal and enthusiasm – **crusade** *vi*

cruse *n* a small earthenware jar or pot for holding oil, water, etc

¹**crush** *vt* 1 to alter or destroy the structure of by pressure or compression 2 to reduce to particles by pounding or grinding 3 to subdue, overwhelm ⟨~ed *the revolt*⟩⟨a ~ing *remark*⟩ 4 to crowd, push ~ *vi* to become crushed ⟨*eggshells* ~ *easily*⟩ – **crushable** *adj*, **crusher** *n*

²**crush** *n* 1 a crowding together, esp of many people 2 (the object of) an intense usu brief infatuation – *infml*

crush barrier *n* a barrier erected to control crowds

crust *n* 1a the hardened exterior of bread b a piece of this or of bread grown dry or hard 2 the pastry cover of a pie 3a a hard or brittle surface layer (e g of soil or snow) b the outer rocky layer of the earth c a deposit built up on the inside of a wine bottle during long aging d a hard deposit (on the skin); *esp* a scab 4 a superficial hardness of behaviour ⟨*break through her* ~ *of reserve*⟩ – **crust** *vb*, **crustal** *adj*

crustacean *n*, *pl* **crustaceans, crustacea** any of a large class of mostly aquatic arthropods with a carapace, a pair of appendages on each segment, and 2 pairs of antennae, including the lobsters, crabs, woodlice, etc – **crustacean** *adj*

crusty *adj* 1 having a hard well-baked crust 2 surly, uncivil – **crustily** *adv*, **crustiness** *n*

crutch *n* 1a a staff of wood or metal typically fitting under the armpit to support a disabled person in walking b a prop, stay 2 the crotch of an animal or human 3 the part of a garment that covers the human crotch

crux *n*, *pl* **cruxes** *also* **cruces** 1 a puzzling or difficult problem 2 an essential or decisive point ⟨*the* ~ *of the matter*⟩

¹**cry** *vi* 1 to call loudly; shout (e g in fear or pain) 2 to weep, sob 3 *of a bird or animal* to utter a characteristic sound or call 4 to require or suggest strongly a remedy – usu + *out for*; *infml* ~ *vt* 1 to utter loudly; shout 2 to proclaim publicly; advertise ⟨~ *their wares*⟩ – **cry over spilt milk** to express vain regrets for what cannot be recovered or undone – **cry wolf** to raise a false alarm and risk the possibility that a future real need will not be taken seriously – **for crying out loud** used to express exasperation and annoyance; *infml*

²**cry** *n* 1 an inarticulate utterance of distress, rage, pain, etc 2 a loud shout 3 a watchword, slogan ⟨*'death to the invader' was the* ~⟩ 4 a general public demand or complaint 5 a spell of weeping ⟨*have a good* ~⟩ 6 the characteristic sound or call of an animal or bird 7 pursuit – **in** *in full cry*

cry-, cryo- *comb form* cold; low temperature; freezing ⟨*cryogen*⟩

crybaby *n* one who cries or complains too easily or frequently – *infml*

cry down *vt* to disparage, depreciate

crying *adj* calling for notice ⟨*a* ~ *shame*⟩

cry off *vt* to call off (e g an agreement) ~ *vi*, *chiefly Br* to withdraw; BACK OUT

crypt *n* a chamber (e g a vault) wholly or partly underground; *esp* a vault under the main floor of a church – **cryptal** *adj*

crypt-, crypto- *comb form* 1 hidden; obscure ⟨*cryptogenic*⟩ 2 secret; unavowed ⟨*cryptofascist*⟩

cryptic *adj* 1 secret, occult 2 intended to be obscure or mysterious 3 serving to conceal ⟨~ *coloration in animals*⟩ 4 making use of cipher or code – **cryptically** *adv*

crypto *n*, *pl* **cryptos** one who supports or belongs secretly to a party, sect, or other group

cryptogram *n* a communication in cipher or code – **cryptogrammic** *adj*

cryptography *n* 1 secret writing; cryptic symbolization 2 the preparation of cryptograms, ciphers, or codes – **cryptographer** *n*, **cryptographic** *adj*

¹**crystal** *n* 1 (almost) transparent and colourless quartz 2 sthg resembling crystal in transparency and colourlessness 3 a chemical substance in a form that has a regularly repeating internal arrangement of atoms and often regularly arranged external plane faces 4 (an object made of) a clear colourless glass of superior quality 5 the transparent cover over a watch or clock dial 6 an electronic component containing crystalline material used as a frequency-determining element

²**crystal** *adj* 1 consisting of or resembling crystal; clear, lucid 2 relating to or using a crystal ⟨*a* ~ *microphone*⟩

crystal gazing *n* 1 the art or practice of concentrating on a crystal ball to aid divination 2 the attempt to predict future events or make difficult judgments, esp without adequate data – **crystal gazer** *n*

crystalline *adj* composed of crystal or crystals – **crystallinity** *n*

crystallize, -ise *also* **crystalize, -ise** *vt* 1 to cause to form crystals or assume crystalline form 2 to cause to take a definite form ⟨*tried to* ~ *his thoughts*⟩ 3 to coat (e g fruit) with (sugar) crystals ~ *vi* to become crystallized – **crystallizable** *adj*, **crystallized** *adj*, **crystallizer** *n*, **crystallization** *n*

cry up *vt* to praise highly; extol

cub *n* 1 the young of a flesh-eating mammal (e g a bear or lion) 2 an inexperienced newspaper reporter 3 CUB SCOUT

cubby, cubby hole *n* a snug or cramped space

¹**cube** *n* 1a the regular solid of 6 equal square sides b a block of anything so shaped ⟨*a bouillon* ~⟩ 2 the product got by multiplying together 3 equal numbers

²**cube** *vt* 1 to raise to the third power 2 to cut into cubes – **cuber** *n*

cube root *n* a number whose cube is a given number

cubic *adj* 1 cube-shaped 2 of or being a crystal system characterized by 3 equal axes at right angles 3a three-dimensional b being the volume of a cube whose edge is a specified unit ⟨~ *metre*⟩ 4 of or involving (terms of) the third power or order – **cubicly** *adv*, **cubic** *n*, **cubically** *adv*

cubical *adj* cubic; *esp* shaped like a cube – **cubically** *adv*

cubicle *n* 1 a sleeping compartment partitioned off from a large room 2 a small partitioned space or compartment

cubism *n* a 20th-c art movement that stresses abstract form, esp by displaying several aspects of the same object simultaneously – **cubist** *n*, **cubist**, **cubistic** *adj*

cubit *n* any of various ancient units of length based on the length of the forearm from the elbow to the tip of the middle finger

cub scout *n* a member of the most junior section of the (British) Scout movement

¹**cuckold** *n* a man whose wife is adulterous

²**cuckold** *vt* to make a cuckold of (a husband) – **cuckolder** *n*, **cuckoldry** *n*

¹**cuckoo** *n*, *pl* **cuckoos** 1 (any of a large family of birds including) a greyish brown European bird that lays its eggs in the nests of other birds which hatch them and rear the offspring 2 the characteristic call of the cuckoo

²**cuckoo** *adj* deficient in sense or intelligence; silly – *infml*

cuckoo clock *n* a clock that announces the hours by sounds resembling a cuckoo's call

cuckoo spit n (a frothy secretion exuded on plants by the larva of) a froghopper

cucumber n (a climbing plant with) a long green edible fruit cultivated as a garden vegetable and eaten esp in salads

cud n food brought up into the mouth by a ruminating animal from its first stomach to be chewed again

cuddle vb **cuddling** vt to hold close for warmth or comfort or in affection ~ vi to lie close; nestle, snuggle

cuddle n an act of cuddling

cuddlesome /-s(M)m/ adj cuddly

cuddly adj suitable for cuddling; lovable

cudgel n a short heavy club

cudgel vt **-ll-** (NAm **-l-**, **-ll-**), to beat (as if) with a cudgel

cue n **1a** a signal to a performer to begin a specific speech or action **b** sthg serving a comparable purpose; a hint **2** a feature of sthg that determines the way in which it is perceived

cue vt **cuing, cueing** to give a cue to; prompt

cue n a leather-tipped tapering rod for striking the ball in billiards, snooker, etc

cue vb **cuing, cueing** vt to strike with a cue ~ vi to use a cue

cuff n **1** a fold or band at the end of a sleeve which encircles the wrist **2** a turned-up hem of a trouser leg **3** a handcuff – usu pl; infml – **cuffless** adj – **off the cuff** without preparation

cuff vt to strike, esp (as if) with the palm of the hand

cuff n a blow with the hand, esp when open; a slap

cuff link n a usu ornamental device consisting of 2 linked parts used to fasten a shirt cuff

cuirass n a piece of armour consisting of a (joined backplate and) breastplate

cuisine n a manner of preparing or cooking food; also the food prepared

cul-de-sac n, pl **culs-de-sac** also **cul-de-sacs** **1** an (anatomical) pouch or tube with only 1 opening **2** a street, usu residential, closed at 1 end

culinary adj of the kitchen or cookery

cull vt **1** to select from a group; choose **2** to identify and remove the rejects from (a flock, herd, etc) **3** to control the size of a population of (animals) by killing a limited number – **culler** n

cull n **1** culling **2** a culled animal

cullender n a colander

culminate vi **1** of a celestial body to be at the meridian; be directly overhead **2** to reach the highest or a climactic or decisive point – often + in – **culmination** n

culottes n pl short trousers having the appearance of a skirt and worn by women – **culotte** adj

culpable adj meriting condemnation or blame ⟨~ negligence⟩ – **culpableness** n, **culpably** adv, **culpability** n

culprit n one guilty of a crime or a fault

cult n **1** (the body of adherents of) **a** a system of religious beliefs and ritual ⟨the ~ of the Virgin Mary⟩ **b** a religion regarded as unorthodox or spurious **2** (a group marked by) great devotion, often regarded as a fad, to a person, idea, or thing – **cultic** adj, **cultism** n, **cultist** n

cultivate vt **1** to prepare or use (land, soil, etc) for the growing of crops; also to break up the soil about (growing plants) **2a** to foster the growth of (a plant or crop) **b** CULTURE 2a **c** to improve by labour, care, or study; refine ⟨~ the mind⟩ **3** to further, encourage ⟨~ a friendship⟩ – **cultivable** adj, **cultivation** n

cultivated adj refined, educated

cultivator n an implement to break up the soil (while crops are growing)

culture n **1** cultivation, tillage **2** the development of the

mind, esp by education **3a** enlightenment and excellence of taste acquired by intellectual and aesthetic training **b** intellectual and artistic enlightenment as distinguished from vocational and technical skills **4a** the socially transmitted pattern of human behaviour that includes thought, speech, action, institutions, and artefacts **b** the customary beliefs, social forms, etc of a racial, religious, or social group **5** (a product of) the cultivation of living cells, tissue, viruses, etc in prepared nutrient media – **cultural** adj, **culturally** adv

culture vt **1** to cultivate **2a** to grow (bacteria, viruses, etc) in a culture **b** to start a culture from ⟨~ a specimen of urine⟩

cultured adj cultivated

culvert n a construction that allows water to pass over or under an obstacle (e g a road or canal)

cum prep with; combined with; along with ⟨lounge ~ dining room⟩

cumber vt **1** to clutter up; hamper **2** to burden USE fml

cumbersome adj unwieldy because of heaviness and bulk – **cumbersomely** adv, **cumbersomeness** n

cumin n a plant of the carrot family cultivated for its aromatic seeds used as a flavouring

cummerbund n a broad waistsash worn esp with men's formal evening wear

cumulative adj **1a** made up of accumulated parts **b** increasing by successive additions **2** formed by adding new material of the same kind ⟨a ~ book index⟩ – **cumulatively** adv, **cumulativeness** n

cumulonimbus n a cumulus cloud formation often in the shape of an anvil, extending to great heights and characteristic of thunderstorm conditions

cumulus n, pl **cumuli** a massive cloud formation with a flat base and rounded outlines often piled up like a mountain

cuneiform adj **1** wedge-shaped **2** composed of or written in the wedge-shaped characters used in ancient Assyrian, Babylonian, and Persian inscriptions ⟨~ alphabet⟩

cuneiform n **1** cuneiform writing **2** a cuneiform part

cunnilingus n oral stimulation of the vulva or clitoris

cunning adj **1** dexterous, ingenious **2** devious, crafty **3** NAm prettily appealing; cute – **cunningly** adv, **cunningness** n

cunning n craft, slyness

cunt n **1** the female genitals **2** sexual intercourse – used by men **3** Br an unpleasant person USE vulg

cup n **1** a small open drinking vessel that is usu bowl-shaped and has a handle on 1 side **2** the consecrated wine of the Communion **3** that which comes to one in life (as if) by fate ⟨~ of happiness⟩ **4** (a competition or championship with) an ornamental usu metal cup offered as a prize **5a** sthg resembling a cup **b** either of 2 parts of a garment, esp a bra, that are shaped to fit over the breasts **6** any of various usu alcoholic and cold drinks made from mixed ingredients ⟨cider ~⟩ **7** the capacity of a cup; specif, chiefly NAm CUPFUL 2 **8** the symbol indicating the union of 2 sets – **cuplike** adj – **in one's cups** ²DRUNK 1

cup vt **-pp-** **1** to treat or draw blood from by cupping **2** to form into the shape of a cup ⟨~ped his hands⟩

cupboard n a shelved recess or freestanding piece of furniture with doors, for storage of utensils, food, clothes, etc

cupboard love n insincere love professed for the sake of gain

cupful n, pl **cupfuls** also **cupsful** **1** as much as a cup will hold **2** chiefly NAm a unit of measure equal to 8 fl oz (about 0.23l)

Cupid *n* 1 the Roman god of erotic love 2 *not cap* a representation of Cupid as a winged naked boy often holding a bow and arrow

cupidity *n* inordinate desire for wealth; avarice, greed

cupola *n* 1 a small domed structure built on top of a roof 2 a vertical cylindrical furnace for melting pig iron

cuppa *n, chiefly Br* a cup of tea – infml

cupping *n* the application to the skin of a previously heated glass vessel, in which a partial vacuum develops, in order to draw blood to the surface (e g for bleeding)

cupric *adj* of or containing (bivalent) copper

cup-tie *n* a match in a knockout competition for a cup

cur *n* 1 a mongrel or inferior dog 2 a surly or cowardly fellow

curaçao *also* **curaçoa** *n* a liqueur flavoured with the peel of bitter oranges

curacy *n* the (term of) office of a curate

curate *n* a clergyman serving as assistant (e g to a rector) in a parish

curative *adj* relating to or used in the cure of diseases – **curative** *n*, **curatively** *adv*

curator *n* sby in charge of a place of exhibition (e g a museum or zoo) – **curatorship** *n*, **curatorial** *adj*

¹**curb** *n* 1a a chain or strap that is used to restrain a horse and is attached to the sides of the bit and passes below the lower jaw b a bit used esp with a curb chain or strap, usu in a double bridle 2 a sprain in a ligament just below a horse's hock 3 a check, restraint 4 an edge or margin that strengthens or confines 5 *chiefly NAm* a kerb

²**curb** *vt* 1 to put a curb on 2 to check, control

curd *n* 1 the thick casein-rich part of coagulated milk used as a food or made into cheese 2 a rich thick fruit preserve made with eggs, sugar, and butter 3 the edible head of a cauliflower or a similar related plant – **curdy** *adj*

curdle *vb* **curdling** 1 to form curds (in); *specif* to separate into solid curds and liquid ⟨*overheating* ~d *the milk*⟩ 2 to spoil, sour

¹**cure** *n* 1 spiritual or pastoral charge 2 (a drug, treatment, etc that gives) relief or esp recovery from a disease 3 sthg that corrects a harmful or troublesome situation; a remedy 4 a process or method of curing – **cureless** *adj*

²**cure** *vt* 1a to restore to health, soundness, or normality b to bring about recovery from 2a to rectify b to free (sby) from sthg objectionable or harmful 3 to prepare by chemical or physical processing; *esp* to preserve (meat, fish, etc) by salting, drying, smoking, etc ~ *vi* 1 to undergo a curing process 2 to effect a cure – **curable** *adj*, **curableness** *n*, **curably** *adv*, **curer** *n*, **curability** *n*

curé *n* a French parish priest

cure-all *n* a remedy for all ills; a panacea

curettage *n* a surgical scraping or cleaning (e g of the womb) by means of a curette

curfew *n* 1 a regulation imposed on all or particular people, esp during times of civil disturbance, requiring their withdrawal from the streets by a stated time 2 a signal (e g the sounding of a bell) announcing the beginning of a time of curfew 3a the hour at which a curfew becomes effective b the period during which a curfew is in effect

curia *n, pl* **curiae** 1 a division of an ancient Roman tribe 2 *often cap* the administration and governmental apparatus of the Roman Catholic church – **curial** *adj*

curio *n, pl* **curios** sthg considered novel, rare, or bizarre

curiosity *n* 1 desire to know 2 inquisitiveness, nosiness 3 a strange, interesting, or rare object, custom, etc

curious *adj* 1 eager to investigate and learn 2 inquisitive, nosy 3 strange, novel, or odd – **curiously** *adv*, **curiousness** *n*

¹**curl** *vt* 1 to form into waves or coils 2 to form into a curved shape; twist 3 to provide with curls ~ *vi* 1a to grow in coils or spirals b to form curls or twists 2 to move or progress in curves or spirals 3 to play the game of curling

²**curl** *n* 1 a curled lock of hair 2 sthg with a spiral or winding form; a coil 3 curling or being curled ⟨*a* ~ *of the lip*⟩ 4 a (plant disease marked by the) rolling or curling of leaves

curler *n* a small cylinder on which hair is wound for curling

curlew *n, pl* **curlews**, *esp collectively* **curlew** any of various largely brownish (migratory) wading birds with long legs and a long slender down-curved bill

curlicue *also* **curlycue** *n* a decorative curve or flourish (e g in handwriting)

curling *n* a game in which 2 teams, of 4 players each, slide heavy round flat-bottomed stones over ice towards a target circle marked on the ice – **curler** *n*

curly *adj* tending to curl; having curls – **curliness** *n*

curmudgeon *n* a crusty ill-tempered (old) man – **curmudgeonly** *adj*

currant *n* 1 a small seedless type of dried grape used in cookery 2 (a shrub of the gooseberry family bearing) a redcurrant, blackcurrant, or similar acid edible fruit

currency *n* 1a circulation as a medium of exchange ⟨*sixpences are no longer in* ~⟩ b (the state of being in) general use, acceptance, or prevalence 2 sthg (e g coins and bank notes) that is in circulation as a medium of exchange

¹**current** *adj* 1a elapsing now ⟨*during the* ~ *week*⟩ b occurring in or belonging to the present time 2 used as a medium of exchange 3 generally accepted, used, or practised at the moment – **currently** *adv*, **currentness** *n*

²**current** *n* 1a the part of a body of gas or liquid that moves continuously in a certain direction b the swiftest part of a stream c a (tidal) movement of lake, sea, or ocean water 2 a tendency to follow a certain or specified course 3 a flow of electric charge; *also* the rate of such flow

current account *n, chiefly Br* a bank account against which cheques may be drawn and on which interest is usu not payable

curriculum *n, pl* **curricula** *also* **curriculums** the courses offered by an educational institution or followed by an individual or group – **curricular** *adj*

curriculum vitae *n, pl* **curricula vitae** a summary of sby's career and qualifications, esp as relevant to a job application

currish *adj* ignoble – **currishly** *adv*

¹**curry** *vt* 1 to dress the coat of (e g a horse) with a currycomb 2 to dress (tanned leather) – **currier** *n* – **curry favour** to seek to gain favour by flattery or attention

²**curry** *also* **currie** *n* a food or dish seasoned with a mixture of spices or curry powder

³**curry** *vt* to flavour or cook with curry powder or sauce

currycomb *n* a metal comb with rows of teeth or serrated ridges, used esp to clean grooming brushes or to curry horses – **currycomb** *vt*

curry powder *n* a condiment consisting of several pungent ground spices (e g cayenne pepper, fenugreek, and turmeric)

¹**curse** *n* 1 an utterance (of a deity) or a request (to a deity) that invokes harm or injury; an imprecation 2 an evil or misfortune that comes (as if) in response to imprecation or as retribution 3 a cause of misfortune 4 menstruation – + *the*; infml

²**curse** *vt* 1 to call upon divine or supernatural power to cause harm or injury to; *also* to doom, damn 2 to use

profanely insolent language against **3** to bring great evil upon; afflict ~ *vi* to utter curses; swear

cursed *also* **curst** *adj* under or deserving a curse – **cursedly** *adv*, **cursedness** *n*

¹**cursive** *adj* running, coursing; *esp* written in flowing, usu slanted, strokes with the characters joined in each word – **cursively** *adv*, **cursiveness** *n*

²**cursive** *n* cursive writing

cursory *adj* rapid and often superficial; hasty – **cursorily** *adv*, **cursoriness** *n*

curt *adj* marked by rude or peremptory shortness; brusque – **curtly** *adv*, **curtness** *n*

curtail *vt* to cut short, limit – **curtailer** *n*, **curtailment** *n*

¹**curtain** *n* **1** a hanging fabric screen that can usu be drawn back or up; *esp* one used at a window **2** a device or agency that conceals or acts as a barrier **3a** a castle wall between 2 neighbouring bastions **b** an exterior wall that carries no load **4a** the movable screen separating the stage from the auditorium of a theatre **b** the ascent or opening (e g at the beginning of a play) of a stage curtain; *also* its descent or closing **c** CURTAIN CALL **d** *pl* the end; *esp* death – infml

²**curtain** *vt* **1** to furnish (as if) with curtains **2** to veil or shut off (as if) with a curtain

curtain call *n* an appearance by a performer after the final curtain of a play in response to the applause of the audience

curtain raiser *n* **1** a short play presented before the main full-length drama **2** a usu short preliminary to a main event

¹**curtsy, curtsey** *n* an act of respect on the part of a woman, made by bending the knees and lowering the head and shoulders

²**curtsy, curtsey** *vi* to make a curtsy

curvaceous *also* **curvacious** *adj, of a woman* having a pleasingly well-developed figure with attractive curves – infml

curvature *n* **1** (a measure or amount of) curving or being curved **2a** an abnormal curving (e g of the spine) **b** a curved surface of an organ (e g the stomach)

¹**curve** *vi* to have or make a turn, change, or deviation from a straight line without sharp breaks or angularity ~ *vt* to cause to curve

²**curve** *n* **1** a curving line or surface **2** sthg curved (e g a curving line of the human body) **3** a representation on a graph of a varying quantity (e g speed, force, or weight) **4** a distribution indicating the relative performance of individuals measured against one another – **curvy** *adj*

¹**cushion** *n* **1** a soft pillow or padded bag; *esp* one used for sitting, reclining, or kneeling on **2** a bodily part resembling a pad **3** a pad of springy rubber along the inside of the rim of a billiard table off which balls bounce **4** sthg serving to mitigate the effects of disturbances or disorders – **cushionless** *adj*, **cushiony** *adj*

²**cushion** *vt* **1** to furnish with a cushion **2a** to mitigate the effects of **b** to protect against force or shock **3** to slow gradually so as to minimize the shock or damage to moving parts

cushy *adj* entailing little hardship or effort; easy ⟨*a ~ job*⟩ – infml – **cushily** *adv*, **cushiness** *n*

cusp *n* a point, apex: e g **a** either horn of a crescent moon **b** a pointed projection formed by or arising from the intersection of 2 arcs or foils **c(1)** a point on the grinding surface of a tooth **(2)** a fold or flap of a heart valve – **cuspate** *adj*

cuspidor *n* a spittoon

¹**cuss** *n* **1** a curse **2** a fellow ⟨*a harmless old ~*⟩ USE infml

²**cuss** *vb* to curse – infml – **cusser** *n*

cussed *adj* **1** cursed **2** obstinate, cantankerous USE infml – **cussedly** *adv*, **cussedness** *n*

custard *n* **1** a semisolid usu sweetened and often baked mixture made with milk and eggs **2** a sweet sauce made with milk and eggs or a commercial preparation of coloured cornflour

custodial *adj* **1** of guardianship or custody **2** of or involving legal detention ⟨*a ~ sentence*⟩

custodian *n* one who guards and protects or maintains; *esp* the curator of a public building – **custodianship** *n*

custody *n* **1a** the state of being cared for or guarded **b** imprisonment, detention **2** the act or right of caring for a minor, esp when granted by a court of law; guardianship

¹**custom** *n* **1a** an established socially accepted practice **b** long-established practice having the force of law **c** the usual practice of an individual **d** the usages that regulate social life **2a** *pl* duties or tolls imposed on imports or exports **b** *pl but sing or pl in constr* the agency, establishment, or procedure for collecting such customs **3** *chiefly Br* business patronage

²**custom** *adj, Nam* made or performed according to personal order ⟨*~ clothes*⟩

customary *adj* established by or according to custom; usual – **customarily** *adv*, **customariness** *n*

customer *n* **1** one who purchases a commodity or service **2** an individual, usu having some specified distinctive trait ⟨*a tough ~*⟩

customshouse *n* a building where customs are collected and where vessels are entered and cleared

¹**cut** *vb* **-tt-**; **cut** *vt* **1a(1)** to penetrate (as if) with an edged instrument **(2)** to castrate (a usu male animal) **b** to hurt the feelings of ⟨*his cruel remark ~ me deeply*⟩ **c** ¹CHOP **2 d** to experience the emergence of (a tooth) through the gum **2a** to trim, pare **b** to shorten by omissions **c** to dilute, adulterate ⟨*~ the whisky with water*⟩ **d** to reduce in amount ⟨*~ costs*⟩ **e** EDIT **1b 3a** to mow or reap ⟨*~ hay*⟩ **b(1)** to divide into parts with an edged instrument ⟨*~ bread*⟩ **(2)** to fell, hew ⟨*~ timber*⟩ **c** to play a cut in cricket at (a ball) or at the bowling of (a bowler) **4a** to divide into segments **b** to intersect, cross **c** to break, interrupt ⟨*~ our supply lines*⟩ **d(1)** to divide (a pack of cards) into 2 portions **(2)** to draw (a card) from the pack **5a** to refuse to recognize (an acquaintance) **b** to stop (a motor) by opening a switch **c** to terminate the filming of (a scene in a film) **6a** to make or give shape to (as if) with an edged tool ⟨*~ stone*⟩ ⟨*~ a diamond*⟩ **b** to record sounds on (a gramophone record) **7a** to perform, make ⟨*~ a caper*⟩ ⟨*~ a dash*⟩ **b** to give the appearance or impression of ⟨*~ a fine figure*⟩ **8a** to stop, cease ⟨*~ the nonsense*⟩ – infml **b** to absent oneself from (e g a class) – infml ~ *vi* **1a** to function (as if) as an edged tool **b** to be able to be separated, divided, or marked with a sharp instrument ⟨*cheese ~s easily*⟩ **c** to perform the operation of dividing, severing, incising, or intersecting **d(1)** to make a stroke with a whip, sword, etc **(2)** to play a cut in cricket **e** to wound feelings or sensibilities **f** to cause constriction or chafing **g** to be of effect, influence, or significance ⟨*an analysis that ~s deep*⟩ **2a** to cut a pack of cards, esp in order to decide who deals **b** to draw a card from the pack **3a** to move swiftly ⟨*a yacht ~ting through the water*⟩ **b** to describe an oblique or diagonal line **c** to change sharply in direction; swerve **d** to make an abrupt transition from one sound or image to another in film, radio, or television **4** to stop filming or recording – **cut corners** to perform some action in the quickest, easiest, or cheapest way – **cut no ice** to fail to impress; have no importance or influence – infml – **cut short 1** to abbreviate **2** INTERRUPT **1**

²**cut** *n* **1** sthg cut (off): e g **a** a length of cloth varying from 40 to 100yd (44 to 109m) in length **b** the yield of products cut, esp during 1 harvest **c** a (slice cut from a) piece from a meat carcass or a fish **d** a share ⟨*took his ~ of the profits*⟩ **2a** a canal, channel, or inlet made by excavation or worn by natural action **b(1)** an opening made with an edged instrument **(2)** a gash, wound **c** a surface or outline left by cutting **d** a passage cut as a roadway **3a** a gesture or expression that hurts the feelings **b** a stroke or blow with the edge of sthg sharp **c** a lash (as if) with a whip **d** the act of reducing or removing a part ⟨*a ~ in pay*⟩ **e** (the result of) a cutting of playing cards **4a** a sharp downward blow or stroke; *also* backspin **b** an attacking stroke in cricket played with the bat held horizontally and sending the ball on the off side **5** an abrupt transition from one sound or image to another in film, radio, or television **6a** the shape and style in which a thing is cut, formed, or made ⟨*clothes of a good ~*⟩ **b** a pattern, type **c** a haircut **– a cut above** superior (to); of higher quality or rank (than)

cut-and-dried *adj* completely decided; not open to further discussion

cutaway *adj* having or showing parts cut away or absent

cutback *n* **1** sthg cut back **2** a reduction

cut back *vt* **1** to shorten by cutting; prune ⟨cut back *a rose tree*⟩ **2** to reduce, decrease ⟨cut back *expenditure*⟩ *~ vi* **1** to interrupt the sequence of a plot (e g of a film) by returning to events occurring previously **2** CUT DOWN; *esp* to economize

cut down *vt* **1** to strike down and kill or incapacitate **2** to reduce, curtail ⟨cut down *expenses*⟩ *~ vi* to reduce or curtail volume or activity ⟨cut down *on his smoking*⟩ **– cut down to size** to reduce from an exaggerated importance to true or suitable stature

cute *adj* attractive or pretty, esp in a dainty or delicate way – infml **– cutely** *adv*, **cuteness** *n*

cut glass *n* glass ornamented with patterns cut into its surface by an abrasive wheel and then polished

cuticle *n* a skin or outer covering: e g **a** the (dead or horny) epidermis of an animal **b** a thin fatty film on the external surface of many higher plants **– cuticular** *adj*

cut in *vi* **1** to thrust oneself into a position between others or belonging to another **2** to join in sthg suddenly ⟨cut in *on the conversation*⟩ **3** to take 1 of a dancing couple as one's partner **4** to become automatically connected or started in operation *~ vt* **1** to introduce into a number, group, or sequence **2** to include, esp among those benefiting or favoured ⟨cut *them* in *on the profits*⟩

cutlass *also* **cutlas** *n* a short curved sword, esp as used formerly by sailors

cutler *n* one who deals in, makes, or repairs cutlery

cutlery *n* **1** edged or cutting tools; *esp* implements (e g knives, forks, and spoons) for cutting and eating food **2** the business of a cutler

cutlet *n* **1** (a flat mass of minced food in the shape of) a small slice of meat from the neck of lamb, mutton, or veal **2** a cross-sectional slice from between the head and centre of a large fish

cutoff *n* **1** (a device for) cutting off **2** the point, date, or period for a cutoff **– cutoff** *adj*

cut off *vt* **1** to strike off; sever **2** to bring to an untimely end **3** to stop the passage of ⟨cut off *supplies*⟩ **4** to shut off, bar ⟨*the fence* cut off *his view*⟩ **5** to separate, isolate ⟨cut *himself* off *from his family*⟩ **6** to disinherit **7a** to stop the operation of; turn off **b** to stop or interrupt while in communication ⟨*the operator* cut *me* off⟩

cutout *n* **1** sthg cut out or off from sthg else **2** a device

that cuts out; *esp* one that is operated automatically by an excessive electric current **– cutout** *adj*

¹**cut out** *vt* **1** to form or shape by cutting, erosion, etc **2** to take the place of; supplant **3** to put an end to; desist from ⟨cut out *smoking*⟩ **4a** to remove or exclude (as if) by cutting **b** to make inoperative *~ vi* to cease operating

²**cut out** *adj* naturally fitted or suited ⟨*not ~ to be an actor*⟩

cut-price *adj* selling or sold at a discount

cutter *n* **1a** one whose work is cutting or involves cutting (e g of cloth or film) **b** an instrument, machine, machine part, or tool that cuts **2a** a ship's boat for carrying stores or passengers **b** a fore-and-aft rigged sailing boat with a single mast and 2 foresails **c** a small armed boat in the US coastguard

¹**cutthroat** *n* a murderous thug

²**cutthroat** *adj* **1** murderous, cruel **2** ruthless, unprincipled ⟨*~ competition*⟩

¹**cutting** *n* **1** sthg cut (off or out): e g **a** a part of a plant stem, leaf, root, etc capable of developing into a new plant **b** a harvest **c** *chiefly Br* an excavation or cut, esp through high ground, for a canal, road, etc **d** *chiefly Br* an item cut out of a publication **2** sthg made by cutting

²**cutting** *adj* **1** designed for cutting; sharp, edged **2** *of wind* marked by sharp piercing cold **3** likely to wound the feelings of another; *esp* sarcastic **– cuttingly** *adv*

cuttlefish *n* a 10-armed marine cephalopod mollusc differing from the related squids in having a hard internal shell

¹**cut up** *vt* **1** to cut into parts or pieces **2** to subject to hostile criticism; censure *~ vi NAm* to behave in a comic, boisterous, or unruly manner **– cut up rough** to express often obstreperous resentment

²**cut up** *adj* deeply distressed; grieved – infml

cutworm *n* any of various chiefly nocturnal caterpillars (that feed on plant stems near ground level)

cwm *n* CIRQUE 1

-cy *suffix* (*n, adj* → *n*) **1** action or practice of ⟨*mendicancy*⟩ ⟨*piracy*⟩ **2** rank or office of ⟨*baronetcy*⟩ ⟨*papacy*⟩ **3** body or class of ⟨*magistracy*⟩ **4** quality or state of ⟨*accuracy*⟩ ⟨*bankruptcy*⟩ *USE* often replacing a final *-t* or *-te* of the base word

cyanide *n* (a usu extremely poisonous salt of hydrocyanic acid or a nitrile, containing) the univalent chemical radical -CN

cybernetics *n pl but sing or pl in constr* the comparative study of the automatic control systems formed by the nervous system and brain and by mechanical-electrical communication systems **– cybernetic** *adj*

cyclamate *n* a synthetic compound used, esp formerly, as an artificial sweetener

cyclamen *n* any of a genus of plants of the primrose family with showy drooping flowers

¹**cycle** *n* **1a** (the time needed to complete) a series of related events happening in a regularly repeated order **b** one complete performance of a periodic process (e g a vibration or electrical oscillation) **2** a group of poems, plays, novels, or songs on a central theme **3** a bicycle, motorcycle, tricycle, etc

²**cycle** *vi* **cycling 1a** to pass through a cycle **b** to recur in cycles **2** to ride a cycle; *specif* to bicycle **– cycler** *n*

cyclic, cyclical *adj* **1** of or belonging to a cycle **2** of or containing a ring of atoms ⟨*benzene is a ~ compound*⟩ **– cyclically, cyclicly** *adv*

cyclist *n* one who rides a cycle

cyclone *n* **1a** a storm or system of winds that rotates about a centre of low atmospheric pressure, advances at high speeds, and often brings abundant rain **b** a tornado

c ^{3}LOW 1b **2** any of various centrifugal devices for separating materials (e g solid particles from gases or liquids) – **cyclonic** *adj*, **cyclonically** *adv*

cyclopedia, cyclopaedia *n* an encyclopedia – **cyclopedic** *adj*

^{1}**cyclostyle** *n* a machine for making multiple copies that uses a stencil cut by a pen whose tip is a small rowel

^{2}**cyclostyle** *vt* to make multiple copies of by using a cyclostyle

cyclotron *n* a particle accelerator in which protons, ions, etc are propelled by an alternating electric field in a constant magnetic field

cyder *n, Br* cider

cygnet *n* a young swan

cylinder *n* **1a** a surface traced by a straight line moving in a circle or other closed curve round and parallel to a fixed straight line **b** the space bounded by a cylinder and 2 parallel planes that cross it **c** a hollow or solid object with the shape of a cylinder and a circular cross-section **2a** the piston chamber in an engine **b** any of various rotating parts (e g in printing presses) **c** a cylindrical clay object inscribed with cuneiform characters – **cylindered** *adj*

cylindrical, cylindric *adj* (having the form) of a cylinder – **cylindrically** *adv*

cymbal *n* a concave brass plate that produces a clashing tone when struck with a drumstick or against another cymbal – **cymbalist** *n*

cynic *n* **1** *cap* an adherent of an ancient Greek school of philosophers who held that virtue is the highest good and that its essence lies in mastery over one's desires and wants **2a** one who is habitually pessimistic or sardonic **b** one who sarcastically doubts the existence of human sincerity or of any motive other than self-interest – **cynic, cynical** *adj*, **cynically** *adv*, **cynicism** *n*

cynosure *n* a centre of attraction or attention

cypher *vb* or *n, chiefly Br* (to) cipher

cypress *n* (the wood of) any of a genus of evergreen gymnospermous trees with aromatic overlapping leaves resembling scales

Cyrillic *adj* of or constituting an alphabet used for writing various Slavic languages (e g Old Church Slavonic and Russian)

cyst *n* **1** a closed sac (e g of watery liquid or gas) with a distinct membrane, developing (abnormally) in a plant or animal **2** a body resembling a cyst: e g **a** (a capsule formed about) a microorganism in a resting or spore stage **b** a resistant cover about a parasite when inside the host – **cystoid** *adj or n*

cyst-, cysti-, cysto- *comb form* bladder ⟨cyst*itis*⟩; sac ⟨cysto*carp*⟩

-cyst *comb form* (→ *n*) bladder; sac ⟨blasto*cyst*⟩

cystitis *n* inflammation of the urinary bladder

cytology *n* the biology of (the structure, function, multiplication, pathology, etc of) cells – **cytologist** *n*, **cytological, cytologic** *adj*, **cytologically** *adv*

cytoplasm *n* the substance of a plant or animal cell outside the organelles (e g the nucleus and mitochondria) – **cytoplasmic** *adj*, **cytoplasmically** *adv*

czar *n* a tsar

Czech *n* **1** a native or inhabitant of Czechoslovakia; *specif* a Slav of W Czechoslovakia **2** the Slavonic language of the Czechs – **Czech** *adj*

D

d *n, pl* **d's, ds** *often cap* **1** (a graphic representation of or device for reproducing) the 4th letter of the English alphabet **2** five hundred **3** the 2nd note of a C-major scale **4** one designated *d*, esp as the 4th in order or class, or as a mark of lesser quality than *a, b,* or *c* **5** sthg shaped like the letter D: e g **a** a semicircle on a billiard table used chiefly when returning a potted cue ball to the table **b** the metal loop on the cheek piece of the bit of a bridle

d- *prefix* dextrorotatory ⟨d-*tartaric acid*⟩

^{1}**-d** *suffix* **1** – used to form the past participle of regular weak verbs that end in *e* ⟨*loved*⟩ ⟨*faded*⟩; compare ^{1}-ED 1 **2** – used to form adjectives of identical meaning from Latin-derived adjectives ending in -*ate* ⟨*crenulated*⟩ **3** ^{1}-ED 2 – used to form adjectives from nouns ending in *e* ⟨*brogued*⟩ ⟨*bow-tied*⟩

^{2}**-d** *suffix* (→ *vb*) – used to form the past tense of regular weak verbs that end in *e*; compare ^{2}-ED

^{3}**-d** *suffix* (→ *adj*), *NAm* – used after the figure 2 or 3 to indicate the ordinal number second or third ⟨2d⟩ ⟨53d⟩

d' *vb* do ⟨d'*you know*⟩

'd *vb* **1** had **2** would **3** did ⟨*when'd she go?*⟩ – used in questions; infml

^{1}**dab** *n* **1a** a sudden feeble blow or thrust; a poke **2** a gentle touch or stroke (e g with a sponge); a pat

^{2}**dab** *vb* **-bb-** *vt* **1** to touch lightly, and usu repeatedly; pat **2** to apply lightly or irregularly; daub ~*vi* to make a dab

^{3}**dab** *n* **1** a daub, patch **2** *pl, Br* fingerprints – infml

^{4}**dab** *n* a flatfish; *esp* any of several flounders

^{5}**dab** *n* DAB HAND – infml

dabble *vb* **dabbling** *vt* to wet slightly or intermittently by dipping in a liquid ⟨*she* ~d *her fingers in the river*⟩ ~*vi* **1** to paddle, splash, or play (as if) in water **2** to work or concern oneself superficially ⟨~s *in art*⟩

dabchick *n* any of several small grebes

dab hand *n, chiefly Br* sby skilful *at*; an expert – infml

dace *n, pl* **dace** a small freshwater European fish

dachshund *n* (any of) a breed of dogs of German origin with a long body, short legs, and long drooping ears

dactyl *n* a metrical foot consisting of 1 long and 2 short, or 1 stressed and 2 unstressed, syllables (e g in *tenderly*) – **dactylic** *adj or n*

dad *n* a father – infml

daddy *n* a father – infml

daddy longlegs *n, pl* **daddy longlegs 1** CRANE FLY **2** *NAm* a harvestman

dado *n, pl* **dadoes 1** the part of a pedestal or plinth between the base and the cornice **2** the lower part of an interior wall when specially decorated or faced; *also* the decoration adorning this part of a wall

daemon *n* **1** an attendant power or spirit; a genius **2** a supernatural being of Greek mythology **3** DEMON 1

daffodil *n* any of various plants with flowers that have a large typically yellow corona elongated into a trumpet shape; *also* a related bulb-forming plant

daft *adj* **1** silly, foolish **2** *chiefly Br* fanatically enthusiastic ⟨~ *about football*⟩ USE infml – **daft** *adv*, **daftly** *adv*, **daftness** *n*

dagger *n* **1** a short sharp pointed weapon for stabbing **2** a sign † used as a reference mark or to indicate a death date – **at daggers drawn** in bitter conflict

dago *n, pl* **dagos, dagoes** sby of Italian, Spanish, or Portuguese birth or descent – derog

daguerreotype *n* an early photograph produced on a

silver or a silver-covered copper plate – **daguerreotype** *vt*

dahlia *n* any of an American genus of composite (garden) plants with showy flower heads and roots that form tubers

Dáil, Dáil Eireann *n* the lower house of parliament in the Irish Republic

¹**daily** *adj* **1a** occurring, made, or acted on every day **b** *of a newspaper* issued every weekday **c** of or providing for every day **2** covering the period of or based on a day ⟨~ *statistics*⟩ – **dailiness** *n*

²**daily** *adv* every day; every weekday

³**daily** *n* **1** a newspaper published daily from Monday to Saturday **2** *Br* a charwoman who works on a daily basis

daily dozen *n* a series of physical exercises to be performed daily

¹**dainty** *n* sthg particularly nice to eat; a delicacy

²**dainty** *adj* **1** attractively prepared and served **2** delicately beautiful **3a** fastidious **b** showing avoidance of anything rough – **daintily** *adv*, **daintiness** *n*

daiquiri *n* a cocktail made of rum, lime juice, and sugar

¹**dairy** *n* **1** a room, building, etc where milk is processed and butter or cheese is made **2** farming concerned with the production of milk, butter, and cheese **3** an establishment for the sale or distribution of milk and milk products

²**dairy** *adj* of or concerned with (the production of) milk (products)

dairying *n* the business of operating a dairy or producing milk products

dairyman, *fem* dairymaid *n* one who operates or works for a dairy (farm)

dais *n* a raised platform; *esp* one at the end of a hall

daisy *n* a composite plant with well-developed ray flowers in its flower head: e g **a** a common short European plant with a yellow disc and white or pink ray flowers **b** OXEYE DAISY

Dalai Lama *n* the spiritual head of Tibetan Buddhism

dale *n* a vale, valley

dalliance *n* a dallying: e g **a** amorous or erotically stimulating activity **b** a frivolous action

dally *vi* **1a** to act playfully; *esp* to flirt **b** to deal lightly; toy **2** to waste time; dawdle – **dallier** *n*

dalmatian *n, often cap* (any of) a breed of medium-sized dogs with a white short-haired coat with black or brown spots

¹**dam** *n* a female parent – used esp with reference to domestic animals

²**dam** *n* **1** a barrier preventing the flow of a fluid; *esp* a barrier across a watercourse **2** a body of water confined by a dam

³**dam** *vt* **-mm-** **1** to provide or restrain with a dam **2** to stop up; block

¹**damage** *n* **1** loss or harm resulting from injury to person, property, or reputation **2** *pl* compensation in money imposed by law for loss or injury **3** expense, cost – *infml* ⟨*what's the* ~?⟩

²**damage** *vt* to cause damage to – ~*vi* to become damaged – **damager** *n*

¹**damascene** *n* the characteristic markings of Damascus steel

²**damascene** *vt* to ornament (e g iron or steel) with wavy patterns like those of watered silk or with inlaid work of precious metals

¹**damask** *n* **1** a reversible lustrous fabric (e g of linen, cotton, or silk) having a plain background woven with patterns **2** greyish red

²**damask** *adj* **1** made of or resembling damask **2** of the colour damask

damask rose *n* a large fragrant pink rose cultivated esp as a source of attar of roses

dame *n* **1** a woman of rank, station, or authority: e g **a** the wife or daughter of a lord **b** a female member of an order of knighthood – used as a title preceding the Christian name **2a** an elderly woman; *specif* a comic one in pantomime played usu by a male actor **b** *chiefly NAm* a woman – *infml*

dame school *n* a school in which reading and writing were taught by a woman in her home

¹**damn** *vt* **1** to condemn to a punishment or fate; *esp* to condemn to hell **2** to condemn as a failure by public criticism **3** to bring ruin on **4** to curse – often used as an interjection to express annoyance ⟨~ *it all!*⟩ ~*vi* to curse, swear – **I'll be damned** – used to express astonishment – **I'll be damned if** I emphatically do not or will not ⟨I'll be damned if *I'll go*⟩

²**damn** *n* **1** the utterance of the word *damn* as a curse **2** the slightest bit ⟨*I couldn't care a* ~⟩ – chiefly in negative phrases

³**damn** *adj or adv* – used as an intensive – **damn well** beyond doubt or question; certainly ⟨*better* damn well *marry that boy* – Spare Rib⟩

damnable *adj* **1** liable to or deserving condemnation **2** very bad; detestable ⟨~ *weather*⟩ – **damnableness** *n*, **damnably** *adv*

damnation *n* damning or being damned

damnedest, damndest *n* utmost, best – chiefly in *do one's damnedest* ⟨*doing her* ~ *to succeed*⟩; infml

damning *adj* causing or leading to condemnation or ruin ⟨*presented some* ~ *testimony*⟩ – **damningly** *adv*

¹**damp** *n* **1** a noxious gas, esp in a coal mine **2** moisture, humidity **3** DAMPER **2** ⟨*the bad news cast a* ~ *on his spirits*⟩ **4** *archaic* fog, mist – **damp-proof** *adj*

²**damp** *vt* **1a** to diminish the activity or intensity of ⟨~ *the fire in the furnace*⟩ – often + *down* **b** to reduce progressively the vibration or oscillation of (e g sound waves) **2** to dampen ~*vi* to diminish progressively in vibration or oscillation

³**damp** *adj* slightly or moderately wet – **damply** *adv*, **dampness** *n*, **dampish** *adj*

damp course *n* a horizontal damp-resistant layer near the ground in a masonry wall

dampen *vt* **1** to check or diminish the activity or vigour of (esp feelings) ⟨*nothing could* ~ *his spirits*⟩ **2** to make damp **3** DAMP **1b** – **dampener** *n*

damper *n* **1** a device that damps: e g **a** a valve or plate (e g in the flue of a furnace) for regulating the draught **b** a small felted block which prevents or stops the vibration of a piano string **c** a device (e g a shock absorber) designed to bring a mechanism to rest with minimum oscillation **2** a dulling or deadening influence ⟨*put a* ~ *on the celebration*⟩ **3** *Austr & NZ* unleavened bread made with flour and water and baked in the ashes of a fire

damsel *n, archaic* a young woman; a girl

damson *n* (the small acid purple fruit of) an Asiatic plum that is a cultivated bullace

¹**dance** *vi* **1** to engage in or perform a dance **2** to move quickly up and down or about ~*vt* **1** to perform or take part in as a dancer **2** to bring or accompany into a specified condition by dancing ⟨~*d her way to fame*⟩ – **danceable** *adj*, **dancer** *n*

²**dance** *n* **1** (an act or instance or the art of) a series of rhythmic and patterned bodily movements usu performed to music **2** a social gathering for dancing **3** a piece of music for dancing to

dandelion *n* any of a genus of yellow-flowered composite plants including one that occurs virtually worldwide as a weed

dander n anger, temper – chiefly in *have/get one's dander up*; infml

dandify vt to cause to resemble a dandy – **dandification** n

dandle vt **dandling** to move (e g a baby) up and down in one's arms or on one's knee in affectionate play

dandruff n a scurf that comes off the scalp in small white or greyish scales – **dandruffy** adj

¹**dandy** n a man who gives exaggerated attention to dress and demeanour – **dandyish** adj, **dandyishly** adv, **dandyism** n

²**dandy** adj, NAm very good; first-rate – infml; not now in vogue

danger n **1** exposure to the possibility of injury, pain, or loss **2** a case or cause of danger ⟨*the* ~s *of mining*⟩

danger money n extra pay for dangerous work

dangerous adj **1** exposing to or involving danger **2** able or likely to inflict injury – **dangerously** adv, **dangerousness** n

dangle vb **dangling** vi to hang or swing loosely ~vt **1** to cause to dangle; swing **2** to display enticingly ⟨~d *the possibility before them*⟩ – **dangler** n, **danglingly** adv

¹**Danish** adj (characteristic) of Denmark

²**Danish** n the Germanic language of the Danes

Danish pastry n (a piece of) confectionery made from a rich yeast dough with a sweet filling

dank adj unpleasantly moist or wet – **dankly** adv, **dankness** n

dapper adj, *esp of a small man* neat and spruce as regards clothing and demeanour – **dapperly** adv, **dapperness** n

dapple vb to mark or become marked with rounded patches of varying shade – **dapple** n

Darby and Joan n a happily married elderly couple

¹**dare** vb **dared**, archaic **durst** vi to have sufficient courage or impudence (to) ⟨*no one* ~d *say a word*⟩⟨*try it if you* ~⟩ ~vt **1a** to challenge to perform an action, esp as a proof of courage ⟨~d *him to jump*⟩ **b** to confront boldly; defy ⟨~d *the anger of her family*⟩ **2** to have the courage to contend against, venture, or try – **darer** n

²**dare** n a challenge to a bold act ⟨*foolishly took a* ~⟩

daredevil n or adj (sby) recklessly bold – **daredevilry** n

daren't dare not

daresay vb pres I sing venture to say (so); think (it) probable; suppose (so)

¹**daring** adj adventurously bold in action or thought ⟨~ *acrobats*⟩⟨~ *crimes*⟩ – **daringly** adv, **daringness** n

²**daring** n venturesome boldness

¹**dark** adj **1** (partially) devoid of light **2a** (partially) black **b** *of a colour* of (very) low lightness **3a** arising from or showing evil traits or desires; evil **b** dismal, sad ⟨*took a* ~ *view of the future*⟩ **c** lacking knowledge or culture **4** not fair; swarthy ⟨*her* ~ *good looks*⟩ **5** secret ⟨*kept his plans* ~⟩ **6** *of a theatre* temporarily not presenting any production – **darkish** adj, **darkly** adv, **darkness** n

²**dark** n **1a** the absence of light; darkness **b** a place or time of little or no light; night, nightfall ⟨*after* ~⟩ **2** a dark or deep colour – **in the dark** in ignorance ⟨*kept the public in the dark about the agreement*⟩

Dark Ages n pl the period from about AD 476 to about 1000

darken vb to make or become dark or darker – **darkener** n

dark horse n sby or sthg (e g a contestant) little known, but with a potential much greater than the evidence would suggest

darkroom n a room with no light or with a safelight for

handling and processing light-sensitive photographic materials

darky, darkey n a Negro – derog

¹**darling** n **1a** a dearly loved person **b** DEAR 1b **2** a favourite ⟨*the critics'* ~⟩

²**darling** adj **1** dearly loved; favourite **2** charming ⟨*a* ~ *little house*⟩ – used esp by women

¹**darn** vt to mend (sthg) with interlacing stitches woven across a hole or worn part ⟨~ *a sock*⟩ – **darner** n

²**darn** n a place that has been darned ⟨*a sweater full of* ~s⟩

³**darn** vb to damn – **darned** adj or adv

⁴**darn** adj or adv damned

¹**dart** n **1a** a small projectile with a pointed shaft at one end and flights of feather, plastic, etc at the other **b** pl but sing in constr a game in which darts are thrown at a dartboard **2** sthg with a slender pointed shaft or outline; specif a stitched tapering fold put in a garment to shape it to the figure **3** a quick movement; a dash

²**dart** vt **1** to throw with a sudden movement **2** to thrust or move with sudden speed **3** to put a dart or darts in (a garment or part of a garment) ~vi to move suddenly or rapidly ⟨~ed *across the road*⟩

dartboard n a circular target used in darts that is divided, usu by wire, into different scoring areas

¹**dash** vt **1** to strike or knock violently **2** to break by striking or knocking **3** to destroy, ruin ⟨*the news* ~ed *her hopes*⟩ **4** Br DAMN 4 – euph ⟨~ *it all*⟩ ~vi **1** to move with sudden speed ⟨~ed *through the rain*⟩ **2** to smash

²**dash** n **1** (the sound produced by) a sudden burst or splash **2a** a stroke of a pen **b** a punctuation mark – used esp to indicate a break in the thought or structure of a sentence **3** a small but significant addition ⟨*a* ~ *of salt*⟩ **4** liveliness of style and action; panache **5** a sudden onset, rush, or attempt **6** a signal (e g a flash or audible tone) of relatively long duration that is one of the 2 fundamental units of Morse code **7** Br PRIME 5

dashboard n a panel extending across a motor car, aeroplane, or motorboat below the windscreen and usu containing dials and controls

dashing adj **1** marked by vigorous action; spirited **2** marked by smartness, esp in dress and manners – **dashingly** adv

dash off vt to complete or execute (e g writing or drawing) hastily ⟨dash off *a letter*⟩

data n pl but sing or pl in constr factual information (e g measurements or statistics) used as a basis for reasoning, discussion, or calculation ⟨*all the essential* ~ *are here* – TLS⟩⟨*any* ~ *he could glean was valuable* – TLS⟩

data bank n a collection of data organized esp for rapid search and retrieval (e g by computer)

data processing n the conversion (e g by computer) of crude information into usable or storable form – **data processor** n

¹**date** n (the oblong edible fruit of) a tall palm

²**date** n **1a** the time reckoned in days or larger units at which an event occurs ⟨*the* ~ *of her birth*⟩ **b** a statement of such a time ⟨*the* ~ *on the letter*⟩ **2** the period of time to which sthg belongs **3a** an appointment for a specified time; esp a social engagement between 2 people of opposite sex – infml **b** NAm a person of the opposite sex with whom one has a date – infml – **to date** up to the present moment

³**date** vt **1** to determine the date of ⟨~ *an antique*⟩ **2** to record the date of **3a** to mark with characteristics typical of a particular period **b** to show up plainly the age of ⟨*his knickerbockers* ~ *him*⟩ **4** chiefly NAm to make or have a date with (a person of the opposite sex) – infml ~vi **1** to have been in existence – usu + *from* **2** to become

old-fashioned ⟨*clothes that never* ∼⟩ – **datable, dateable** *adj*, **dater** *n*

dated *adj* **1** provided with a date ⟨*a* ∼ *document*⟩ **2** out-of-date, old-fashioned – **datedly** *adv*, **datedness** *n*

dateless *adj* **1** having no date **2** timeless

dateline *n* **1** a line in a written document or publication giving the date and place of composition or issue **2** INTERNATIONAL DATE LINE – **dateline** *vt*

dative *n* (a form in) a grammatical case expressing typically the indirect object of a verb, the object of some prepositions, or a possessor – **dative** *adj*

¹**daub** *vt* **1** to cover or coat with soft adhesive matter; plaster **2** to coat with a dirty substance **3** to apply (e g colouring material) crudely (to) ∼*vi* to paint without much skill – **dauber** *n*

²**daub** *n* **1** material used to daub walls ⟨*wattle and* ∼⟩ **2** a daubing **3** sthg daubed on; a smear **4** a crude picture

¹**daughter** *n* **1a** a human female having the relation of child to parent **b** a female descendant – often pl **2a** a human female having a specified origin or affiliation ⟨*a* ∼ *of the Church*⟩ **b** sthg considered as a daughter ⟨*French is a* ∼ *(language) of Latin*⟩ **3** an isotope formed as the immediate product of the radioactive decay of an element – **daughterless** *adj*, **daughterly** *adj*

²**daughter** *adj* **1** having the characteristics or relationship of a daughter **2** of the first generation of offspring, molecules, etc produced by reproduction, division, or replication ⟨*the* ∼ *cells*⟩

daughter-in-law *n*, *pl* **daughters-in-law** the wife of one's son

daunt *vt* to lessen the courage of; inspire awe in

dauntless *adj* fearless ⟨*a* ∼ *hero*⟩ – **dauntlessly** *adv*, **dauntlessness** *n*

dauphin *n*, *often cap* the eldest son of a king of France

davit *n* any of 2 or more projecting arms on a vessel which are used as cranes, esp for lowering boats

Davy Jones's locker *n* the bottom of the sea

Davy lamp *n* an early safety lamp used in mines

dawdle *vi* **dawdling** *vi* **1** to spend time idly ⟨∼ *over one's coffee*⟩ **2** to move lackadaisically – **dawdle** *n*, **dawdler** *n*

¹**dawn** *vi* **1** to begin to grow light as the sun rises **2** to begin to appear or develop **3** to begin to be perceived or understood ⟨*the truth finally* ∼ed *on him*⟩

²**dawn** *n* **1** the first appearance of light in the morning **2** a first appearance; a beginning ⟨*the* ∼ *of the space age*⟩

day *n* **1** the time of light when the sun is above the horizon between one night and the next **2** the time required by a celestial body, specif the earth, to turn once on its axis **3** the solar day of 24 hours beginning at midnight **4** a specified day or date ⟨*wash* ∼⟩ **5** a specified time or period ⟨*in grandfather's* ∼⟩ **6** the conflict or contention of the day ⟨*played hard and won the* ∼⟩ **7** the time established by usage or law for work, school, or business ⟨*an 8-hour* ∼⟩ **8** an era – **day in, day out** DAY AFTER DAY – **from day to day** ²DAILY

day after day *adv* for an indefinite or seemingly endless number of successive days

daybreak *n* DAWN 1

daydream *n* a visionary, usu wish-fulfilling, creation of the waking imagination – **daydream** *vi*

daylight *n* **1** DAWN 1 **2** knowledge or understanding of sthg that has been obscure ⟨*began to see* ∼ *on the problem*⟩ **3** *pl* mental soundness or stability; wits ⟨*scared the* ∼s *out of her*⟩ – infml

daylight saving time *n*, *chiefly NAm* time usu 1 hour ahead of standard time and used esp during the summer

day nursery *n* a public centre for the care of young children

day of reckoning *n* a time when the results of mistakes or misdeeds are felt, or when offences are punished

day-return *n*, *Br* a ticket sold for a return journey on the same day and usu at a reduced rate if used outside rush hours

days *adv*, *chiefly NAm* by day repeatedly; on any day

day-to-day *adj* **1** taking place, made, or done in the course of successive days ⟨∼ *problems*⟩ **2** providing for a day at a time with little thought for the future ⟨*lived an aimless* ∼ *existence*⟩

daze *vt* to stupefy, esp by a blow; stun – **daze** *n*, **dazedly** *adv*, **dazedness** *n*

dazzle *vb* **dazzling** *vi* **1** to lose clear vision, esp from looking at bright light **2a** to shine brilliantly **b** to arouse admiration by an impressive display ∼*vt* **1** to overpower or temporarily blind (the sight) with light **2** to impress deeply, overpower, or confound with brilliance ⟨∼d *the crowd with her oratory*⟩ – **dazzle** *n*, **dazzler** *n*, **dazzlingly** *adv*

D day *n* a day set for launching an operation; *specif* June 6, 1944, on which the Allies began the invasion of France in WW II

DDT *n* a synthetic chlorinated water-insoluble insecticide that tends to accumulate in food chains and is poisonous to many vertebrates

de- *prefix* **1a** do the opposite of (a specified action) ⟨*depopulate*⟩ ⟨*decompose*⟩ **b** reverse of ⟨*de-emphasis*⟩ ⟨*deindustrialization*⟩ **2a** remove (sthg specified) from ⟨*delouse*⟩ ⟨*decapitate*⟩ **b** remove from (sthg specified) ⟨*dethrone*⟩ **3** reduce ⟨*devalue*⟩ **4** alight from (a specified thing) ⟨*detrain*⟩

deacon *n* a subordinate officer in a Christian church: e g **a** a clergyman ranking below a priest and, in the Anglican and Roman Catholic churches, usu a candidate for ordination as priest **b** an assistant minister in a Lutheran parish **c** any of a group of laymen with administrative and sometimes spiritual duties in various Protestant churches

¹**dead** *adj* **1** deprived of life; having died **2a(1)** having the appearance of death; deathly ⟨*in a* ∼ *faint*⟩ **(2)** lacking power to move, feel, or respond; numb **b** very tired **c** grown cold; extinguished ⟨∼ *coals*⟩ **3a** inanimate, inert ⟨∼ *matter*⟩ **b** barren, infertile ⟨∼ *soil*⟩ **4a(1)** no longer having power or effect ⟨*a* ∼ *law*⟩ ⟨*a* ∼ *battery*⟩ **(2)** no longer having interest, relevance, or significance ⟨*a* ∼ *issue*⟩ **b** no longer used; obsolete ⟨*a* ∼ *language*⟩ **c** no longer existing ⟨*charity is* ∼⟩ **d** lacking in activity **e** lacking elasticity or springiness **f** out of action or use; *specif* free from any connection to a source of voltage and free from electric charges **g** temporarily out of play ⟨*a* ∼ *ball*⟩ **5** not imparting motion or power although otherwise functioning ⟨*a* ∼ *rear axle*⟩ **6** lacking warmth, odour, vigour, or taste **7a** absolutely uniform ⟨∼ *level*⟩ **b** exact ⟨∼ *centre of the target*⟩ **c** abrupt ⟨*brought to a* ∼ *stop*⟩ **d** complete, absolute ⟨*a* ∼ *silence*⟩⟨*a* ∼ *loss*⟩⟨*a* ∼ *giveaway*⟩ **8** lacking in gaiety or animation – chiefly infml – **deadness** *n*

²**dead** *n* **1** *pl in constr* dead people or animals **2** the state of being dead ⟨*raised him from the* ∼ – Col 2:12(RSV)⟩ **3** the time of greatest quiet or inactivity ⟨*the* ∼ *o night*⟩

³**dead** *adv* **1** absolutely, utterly ⟨∼ *certain* ⟩ **2** suddenly and completely ⟨*stopped* ∼⟩ **3** directly, exactly ⟨∼ *ahead*⟩⟨∼ *on time*⟩ **4** *Br* very, extremely ⟨∼ *lucky*⟩ – infml

deadbeat n, chiefly NAm a loafer

deaden vt 1 to deprive of liveliness, brilliance, sensation, or force 2 to make (eg a wall) impervious to sound – **deadener** n, **deadeningly** adv

dead-end adj 1a lacking opportunities for advancement ⟨a ~ job⟩ b lacking an exit ⟨a ~ street⟩ 2 made aggressively antisocial by a dead-end existence ⟨~ kids⟩

dead end n 1 an end (eg of a street) without an exit 2 a position, situation, or course of action that leads no further

dead heat n an inconclusive finish to a race or other contest, in which the fastest time, highest total, etc is achieved by more than one competitor – **dead-heat** vi

dead letter n 1 a law that has lost its force without being formally abolished 2 an undeliverable and unreturnable letter

deadline n 1 a boundary beyond which it is not possible or permitted to pass 2 a date or time before which sthg (eg the presentation of copy for publication) must be done

deadlock n 1 a lock that can be opened and shut only by a key 2 inaction or neutralization resulting from the opposition of equally powerful and uncompromising people or factions; a standstill 3 a tied score – **deadlock** vt

deadly adj 1 likely to cause or capable of producing death ⟨a ~ disease⟩ ⟨a ~ instrument⟩ 2a aiming to kill or destroy; implacable ⟨a ~ enemy⟩ b unerring ⟨~ accuracy⟩ c marked by determination or extreme seriousness ⟨she was in ~ earnest⟩ 3 lacking animation; dull ⟨~ bores⟩ ⟨a ~ conversation⟩ 4 intense, extreme ⟨~ fear⟩ – **deadliness** n

deadly adv 1 suggesting death ⟨~ pale⟩ 2 extremely ⟨~ serious⟩

deadly nightshade n a European poisonous nightshade that has dull purple flowers and black berries

dead man's handle n, Br a handle that requires constant pressure to allow operation (eg of a train or tram)

deadpan adj impassive, expressionless

deadpan adv in a deadpan manner

dead reckoning n the calculation without celestial observations of the position of a ship or aircraft, from the record of the courses followed, the distance travelled, etc – **dead reckon** vb, **dead reckoner** n

deadweight n 1 the unrelieved weight of an inert mass 2 a ship's total weight including cargo, fuel, stores, crew, and passengers

deadwood n useless personnel or material

deaf adj 1 (partially) lacking the sense of hearing 2 unwilling to hear or listen to; not to be persuaded ⟨~ to reason⟩ – **deafish** adj, **deafly** adv, **deafness** n

deaf-aid n, Br HEARING AID

deafen vt to make deaf ~vi to cause deafness or stun sby with noise – **deafeningly** adv

deaf-mute n or adj (one who is) deaf and dumb

deal n 1 a usu large or indefinite quantity or degree; a lot ⟨a great ~ of support⟩ ⟨a good ~ faster⟩ 2a the act or right of distributing cards to players in a card game b HAND 9b

deal vb dealt vt 1a to give as sby's portion; apportion b to distribute (playing cards) to players in a game 2 to administer, bestow ⟨~t him a blow⟩ ~vi 1 to distribute the cards in a card game 2 to concern oneself or itself ⟨the book ~s with education⟩ 3a to trade b to sell or distribute sthg as a business ⟨~ in insurance⟩ 4 to take action with regard to sby or sthg ⟨~ with an offender⟩

deal n 1 a transaction 2 treatment received ⟨a raw ~⟩ 3 an arrangement for mutual advantage

deal n (a sawn piece of) fir or pine timber – **deal** adj

dealer n 1 sby who deals in goods or services 2 sby or sthg that deals playing cards

dealing n 1 pl friendly or business interactions 2 a method of business; a manner of conduct

dean, dene n, Br a narrow wooded valley containing a stream

dean n 1a the head of the chapter of a collegiate or cathedral church – often used as a title b RURAL DEAN 2 the head of a university division, faculty, or school 3 a doyen – **deanship** n

deanery n the office, jurisdiction, or official residence of a clerical dean

dear adj 1 highly valued; much loved – often used in address ⟨~ Sir⟩ 2 expensive 3 heartfelt ⟨her ~est wish⟩ – **dear** adv, **dearly** adv, **dearness** n

dear n 1a a loved one; a sweetheart b – used as a familiar or affectionate form of address 2 a lovable person

dear interj – used typically to express annoyance or dismay ⟨oh ~⟩

dearth n an inadequate supply; a scarcity

deary n a dear person – used chiefly in address

death n 1 a permanent cessation of all vital functions; the end of life 2 the cause or occasion of loss of life ⟨drinking was the ~ of him⟩ 3 cap death personified, usu represented as a skeleton with a scythe 4 the state of being dead 5 extinction, disappearance – **at death's door** seriously ill – **to death** beyond all acceptable limits; excessively ⟨bored to death⟩

deathbed n – **on one's deathbed** near the point of death

deathblow n a destructive or killing stroke or event

death duty n, chiefly Br tax levied on the estate of a dead person – often pl with sing. meaning

deathless adj immortal, imperishable ⟨~ fame⟩ – **deathlessly** adv, **deathlessness** n

deathly adj (suggestive) of death ⟨a ~ pallor⟩ – **deathly** adv

death mask n a cast taken from the face of a dead person

death rate n the number of deaths per 1000 people in a population over a given period

death rattle n a gurgling sound produced by air passing through mucus in the lungs and throat of a dying person

death's-head n a human skull symbolic of death

death trap n a potentially lethal structure or place

death warrant n a warrant for the execution of a death sentence

deathwatch n a vigil kept with the dead or dying

death-wish n a usu unconscious desire for the death of another or oneself

deb n a debutante – infml – **debby** adj

debacle n 1 a tumultuous breakup of ice in a river 2 a violent disruption (eg of an army); a rout 3 a complete failure; a fiasco

debar vt -rr- to bar from having, doing, or undergoing sthg; preclude – **debarment** n

debark vt to remove the bark from (a tree)

debase vt 1 to lower in status, esteem, quality, or character 2a to reduce the intrinsic value of (a coin) by increasing the content of low-value metal b to reduce the exchange value of (a monetary unit) – **debasement** n, **debaser** n

debatable adj 1 claimed by more than 1 country ⟨~ territory⟩ 2 open to debate; questionable

debate n a contention by words or arguments; esp the formal discussion of a motion a in parliament b between 2 opposing sides

²**debate** *vi* **1a** to contend in words **b** to discuss a question by considering opposed arguments **2** to participate in a debate ~*vt* **1** to argue about **2** to consider – **debater** *n*

¹**debauch** *vt* **1** to lead away from virtue or excellence **2** to make excessively intemperate or sensual – **debaucher** *n*

²**debauch** *n* **1** an act or occasion of debauchery **2** an orgy

debauchee *n* one given to debauchery

debauchery *n* excessive indulgence in the pleasures of the flesh

debenture *n*, *Br* a loan secured on the assets of a company in respect of which the company must pay a fixed interest before any dividends are paid to its own shareholders

debilitate *vt* to impair the strength of; enfeeble – **debilitation** *n*

debility *n* a weakness or infirmity

¹**debit** *n* **1a** (an entry in an account that is) a record of money owed **b** the sum of the items so entered **2** a charge against a bank account

²**debit** *vt* **1** to enter as a debit **2** to charge to the debit of ⟨~ *an account*⟩

debonair *adj* **1** suave, urbane **2** lighthearted, nonchalant – **debonairly** *adv*, **debonairness** *n*

debouch *vi* to emerge or issue, esp from a narrow place into a wider place

debrief *vt* to interrogate (a person) on return from a mission in order to obtain useful information

debris *n* **1** the remains of sthg broken down or destroyed **2a** an accumulation of fragments of rock **b** accumulated rubbish or waste

debt *n* **1** a state of owing ⟨*heavily in* ~⟩ **2** sthg owed; an obligation ⟨*couldn't pay her* ~s⟩ – **debtless** *adj* – **in someone's debt** owing sby gratitude; indebted to sby

debtor *n* one who owes a debt

debug *vt* **-gg- 1** to eliminate errors in or malfunctions of ⟨~ *a computer program*⟩ **2** to remove a concealed microphone or wiretapping device from

debunk *vt* to expose the falseness of – **debunker** *n*

debut *n* **1** a first public appearance **2** a formal entrance into society – **debut** *vi*

debutante *n* a woman making a debut; *esp* a young woman making her formal entrance into society

deca-, dec-, deka-, dek- *comb form* ten (10^1) ⟨*deca*merous⟩ ⟨*deca*thlon⟩

decade *n* **1** a group, set, or sequence of 10 **2** a period of 10 years **3** a division of the rosary containing 10 Hail Marys

decadence *n* **1** being decadent **2** a period of decline

decadent *adj* **1** marked by decay or decline, esp in moral or cultural standards **2** tending to gratify one's desires, appetites, or whims in an excessive or unrestrained manner – **decadently** *adv*

Decalogue *n* TEN COMMANDMENTS

decamp *vi* **1** to break up a camp **2** to depart suddenly; abscond – **decampment** *n*

decant *vt* **1** to pour from one vessel into another, esp a decanter **2** to draw off without disturbing the sediment – **decantation** *n*

decanter *n* an ornamental glass bottle used for serving an alcoholic drink, esp wine

decapitate *vt* to cut off the head of – **decapitator** *n*, **decapitation** *n*

decathlon *n* a men's athletic contest in which each competitor competes in 10 running, jumping, and throwing events

¹**decay** *vi* **1** to decline from a sound or prosperous condi-tion **2** to decrease gradually in quantity, activity, or force; *specif* to undergo radioactive decay **3** to fall into ruin **4** to decline in health, strength, or vigour **5** to undergo decomposition ~*vt* to destroy by decomposition – **decayer** *n*

²**decay** *n* **1** a gradual decline in strength, soundness, prosperity, or quality **2** a wasting or wearing away; ruin **3** (a product of) rot; *specif* decomposition of organic matter (e g proteins), chiefly by bacteria in the presence of oxygen **4** a decline in health or vigour **5** decrease in quantity, activity, or force; *esp* spontaneous disintegration of an atom or particle (e g a meson) usu with the emission of radiation

decease *n* death – *fml* – **decease** *vi*

deceased *n or adj*, *pl* **deceased** (sby) no longer living; *esp* (sby) recently dead

deceit *n* **1** the act or practice of deceiving; deception **2** the quality of being deceitful

deceitful *adj* having a tendency or disposition to deceive: **a** not honest **b** deceptive, misleading – **deceitfully** *adv*, **deceitfulness** *n*

deceive *vt* to cause to accept as true or valid what is false or invalid; delude ~*vi* to practise deceit – **deceivable** *adj*, **deceiver** *n*, **deceivingly** *adv*

decelerate *vb* to (cause to) move at decreasing speed – **decelerator** *n*, **deceleration** *n*

December *n* the 12th month of the Gregorian calendar

decency *n* **1** propriety, decorum **2** a standard of propriety – usu pl

decent *adj* **1** conforming to standards of propriety, good taste, or morality; *specif* clothed according to standards of propriety **2** free from obscenity **3** adequate, tolerable ⟨~ *wages*⟩ ⟨~ *housing*⟩ ⟨*grow a* ~ *beard*⟩ **4** *chiefly Br* obliging, considerate ⟨*jolly* ~ *of you*⟩ – *infml* – **decently** *adv*

decentralization, -isation *n* **1** the distribution of functions and powers from a central authority to regional authorities, departments, etc **2** the redistribution of population and industry from urban centres to outlying areas – **decentralizationist** *n*

decentralize, -ise *vt* to bring about the decentralization of ~*vi* to undergo decentralization

deception *n* **1a** the act of deceiving **b** the fact or condition of being deceived **2** sthg that deceives; a trick – **deceptional** *adj*

deceptive *adj* tending or having power to deceive; misleading – **deceptively** *adv*, **deceptiveness** *n*

deci- *comb form* one tenth part of (a specified unit) ⟨*deci*litre⟩

decibel *n* **1** a unit for expressing the ratio of 2 amounts of electric or acoustic signal power equal to 10 times the common logarithm of this ratio **2** a unit for expressing the intensity of sounds on a scale from zero for the average least perceptible sound to about 130 for the average pain level

decide *vt* **1** to arrive at a solution that ends uncertainty or dispute about ⟨~ *the borderline issues*⟩ **2** to bring to a definitive end **3** to induce to come to a choice ~*vi* to make a choice or judgment – **decider** *n*, **decidable** *adj*, **decidability** *n*

decided *adj* **1** unquestionable ⟨*a* ~ *advantage*⟩ **2** free from doubt or hesitation ⟨*a woman of* ~ *opinions*⟩ – **decidedly** *adv*, **decidedness** *n*

deciduous *adj* **1** (having parts) that fall off or are shed seasonally or at a particular stage in development ⟨~ *teeth*⟩ ⟨*a* ~ *tree*⟩ **2** ephemeral, transitory – *fml* – **deciduously** *adv*, **deciduousness** *n*

¹**decimal** *adj* **1** numbered or proceeding by tens: **a** based

on the number 10 **b** subdivided into units which are tenths, hundredths, etc of another unit **c** expressed in a decimal fraction **2** using a decimal system (e g of coinage) ⟨*when Britain went* ∼⟩ – **decimally** *adv*

decimal, decimal fraction *n* a fraction that is expressed as a sum of integral multiples of powers of $^1/_{10}$ by writing a dot followed by 1 digit for the number of tenths, 1 digit for the number of hundredths, and so on (e g 0.25 = $^{25}/_{100}$)

decimalize, -ise *vt* to convert to a decimal system ⟨∼ *currency*⟩ – **decimalization** *n*

decimal point *n* the dot at the left of a decimal fraction

decimate *vt* **1** to kill every tenth man of (e g mutinous soldiers) **2** to destroy a large part of – **decimation** *n*

decipher *vt* **1a** to convert into intelligible form **b** to decode **2** to make out the meaning of despite obscurity – **decipherable** *adj*, **decipherer** *n*, **decipherment** *n*

decision *n* **1a** deciding **b** a conclusion arrived at after consideration **2** a report of a conclusion ⟨*the* ∼ *appeared in all the newspapers*⟩ **3** promptness and firmness in deciding ⟨*a man of courage and* ∼⟩ – **decisional** *adj*

decisive *adj* **1** having the power or quality of deciding; conclusive **2** marked by or indicative of determination or firmness; resolute **3** unmistakable, unquestionable ⟨*a* ∼ *victory*⟩ – **decisively** *adv*, **decisiveness** *n*

deck *n* **1** a platform in a ship serving usu as a structural element and forming the floor for its compartments **2** sthg resembling the deck of a ship: e g **a** a level or floor of a bus with more than 1 floor **b** the roadway of a bridge **c** TAPE DECK **d** RECORD DECK **3** *NAm* a pack of playing cards **4** *the* ground – *infml*; chiefly in *hit the deck* – **decked** *adj*

deck *vt* to array, decorate – often + *out*

deck chair *n* an adjustable folding chair made of canvas stretched over a wooden frame

decker *n* sthg with a deck or a specified number of levels, floors, or layers – often in combination ⟨*double*-decker *bus*⟩

deckhand *n* a seaman who performs manual duties

deckle edge *n* a rough untrimmed edge of paper – **deckle-edged** *adj*

declaim *vi* **1** to speak rhetorically **2** to speak pompously or bombastically ∼ *vt* to deliver rhetorically; *specif* to recite in elocution – **declaimer** *n*, **declamation** *n*

declaration *n* **1** sthg declared **2** a document containing such a declaration

declare *vt* **1** to make known formally or explicitly **2** to make evident; show **3** to state emphatically; affirm ⟨∼ s *his innocence*⟩ **4** to make a full statement of (one's taxable or dutiable income or property) **5a** to announce (e g a trump suit) in a card game **b** to meld (a combination of playing cards) in canasta, rummy, etc ∼ *vi* **1** to make a declaration **2** to avow one's support **3** *of a captain or team* to announce one's decision to end one's side's innings in cricket before all the batsmen are out – **declarable** *adj* – **declare war** to commence hostilities; *specif* to make a formal declaration of intention to go to war

declassify *vt* to declare (e g information) no longer secret

declension *n* **1** a schematic arrangement of noun, adjective, or pronoun inflections **2** a class of nouns or adjectives having the same type of inflectional forms – **declensional** *adj*

declination *n* **1** angular distance (e g of a star) N or S from the celestial equator **2** a formal refusal **3** the angle between a compass needle and the geographical meridian, equal to the difference between magnetic and true north – **declinational** *adj*

¹decline *vi* **1a** to slope downwards; descend **b** to bend down; droop **2a** *of a celestial body* to sink towards setting **b** to draw towards a close; wane **3** to refuse ∼ *vt* **1** to give in prescribed order the grammatical forms of (a noun, pronoun, or adjective) **2a** to refuse to undertake, engage in, or comply with ⟨∼ *battle*⟩ **b** to refuse courteously ⟨∼ *an invitation*⟩ – **declinable** *adj*

²decline *n* **1** the process of declining: **a** a gradual physical or mental decay **b** a change to a lower state or level **2** the period during which sthg is approaching its end **3** a downward slope

declivity *n* **1** downward inclination **2** a descending slope *USE* fml – **declivitous** *adj*

decoct *vt* **1** to extract the essence of by boiling **2** to boil down; concentrate – **decoction** *n*

decode *vt* to convert (a coded message) into intelligible language – **decoder** *n*

décolletage *n* the low-cut neckline of a dress

décolleté *adj* **1** wearing a strapless or low-necked dress **2** low-necked

decolonize, -ise *vt* to free from colonial status – **decolonization** *n*

decompose *vt* **1** to separate into constituent parts, elements, atoms, etc **2** to rot ∼ *vi* to undergo chemical breakdown; decay, rot – **decomposer** *n*, **decomposable** *adj*, **decomposability** *n*, **decomposition** *n*, **decompositional** *adj*

decompress *vt* to release from pressure or compression – **decompression** *n*

decongestant *n* sthg (e g a drug) that relieves congestion

decontaminate *vt* to rid of contamination (e g radioactivity) – **decontamination** *n*

decor, décor *n* **1** the style and layout of interior decoration and furnishings **2** a stage setting

decorate *vt* **1a** to add sthg ornamental to **b** to apply new coverings of paint, wallpaper, etc to the interior or exterior surfaces of **2** to award a mark of honour to

decoration *n* **1** an ornament ⟨*Christmas* ∼s⟩ **2** a badge of honour (e g a medal)

decorative *adj* serving to decorate; *esp* purely ornamental rather than functional – **decoratively** *adv*, **decorativeness** *n*

decorator *n* one who designs or executes interior decoration and furnishings

decorous *adj* marked by propriety and good taste; correct – **decorously** *adv*, **decorousness** *n*

decorum *n* propriety and good taste in conduct or appearance

¹decoy *n* **1** a pond into which wild fowl are lured for capture **2** sthg used to lure or lead another into a trap **3** sby or sthg used to distract or divert the attention (e g of an enemy)

²decoy *vt* to lure or entice (as if) by a decoy

¹decrease *vb* to (cause to) grow progressively less (e g in size, amount, number, or intensity) – **decreasingly** *adv*

²decrease *n* **1** the process of decreasing **2** the amount by which sthg decreases

¹decree *n* **1** an order usu having legal force **2a** a religious rule made by a council or titular head **b** a foreordaining will **3** a judicial decision, esp in an equity, probate, or divorce court

²decree *vt* to command or impose by decree ⟨∼ *an amnesty*⟩ – **decreer** *n*

decree nisi *n* a provisional decree of divorce that is made absolute after a fixed period unless cause to the contrary is shown

decrepit *adj* **1** wasted and weakened (as if) by the

infirmities of old age **2a** worn-out **b** fallen into ruin or disrepair – **decrepitly** adv, **decrepitude** n

decry vt **1** to depreciate (e g a coin) officially or publicly **2** to express strong disapproval of – **decrier** n

dedicate vt **1** CONSECRATE **2A 2a** to set apart to a definite use **b** to assign permanently to a goal or way of life **3** to inscribe or address (a book, song, etc) to somebody or something as a mark of esteem or affection ⟨~ a book to a friend⟩ – **dedicator** n, **dedicatee** n

dedicated adj **1** devoted to a cause, ideal, or purpose; zealous ⟨a ~ scholar⟩ **2** given over to a particular purpose ⟨a ~ process control computer⟩ – **dedicatedly** adv

dedication n **1** a devoting or setting aside for a particular, specif religious, purpose **2** a phrase or sentence that dedicates **3** self-sacrificing devotion – **dedicative** adj, **dedicatory** adj

deduce vt to establish by deduction; specif to infer from a general principle – **deducible** adj

deduct vt to subtract (an amount) from a total – **deductible** adj, **deductibility** n

deduction n ·**1a** an act of taking away **b** sthg that is or may be subtracted **2** (the deriving of) a necessary conclusion reached by reasoning; specif an inference in which a particular conclusion is drawn from general premises

deductive adj **1** of or employing mathematical or logical deduction **2** capable of being deduced from premises; inferential – **deductively** adv

¹**deed** n **1** sthg that is done ⟨evil ~s⟩ **2** an illustrious act or action; a feat, exploit **3** the act of performing ⟨never mistake the word for the ~⟩ **4** a signed (and sealed) written document containing some legal transfer, bargain, or contract – **deedless** adj

²**deed** vt, NAm to convey or transfer by deed

deed poll n, pl **deeds poll** a deed made and executed by 1 party only

deem vt to judge, consider – fml ⟨would ~ it an honour⟩

¹**deep** adj **1** extending far from some surface or area: e g **a** extending far downwards ⟨a ~ well⟩ **b** (extending) far from the surface of the body **c** extending well back from a front surface ⟨a ~ cupboard⟩ **d(1)** near the outer limits of the playing area or far from an attacking movement **(2)** of or occupying a fielding position in cricket far from the batsman **2** having a specified extension in an implied direction ⟨shelf 20 inches ~⟩⟨cars parked 3-deep⟩ **3a** difficult to understand ⟨may be true, but it's too ~ for me⟩ **b** capable of profound thought ⟨a ~ thinker⟩ **c** engrossed, involved ⟨a man ~ in debt⟩ **d** intense, extreme ⟨~ sleep⟩⟨~ sin⟩ **4a** of a colour high in saturation and low in lightness **b** having a low musical pitch or pitch range **5** remote in time or space – **deeply** adv, **deepness** n – **in deep water** in difficulty or distress; unable to manage

²**deep** adv **1a(1)** to a great depth ⟨still waters run ~⟩ **(2)** deep to a specified degree – usu in combination ⟨ankle-deep in mud⟩ **b** well within the boundaries ⟨a house ~ in the woods⟩ **2** far on; late ⟨danced ~ into the night⟩ **3** in a deep position ⟨the wingers were playing ~⟩ **4** far back in space or time ⟨had its roots ~ in the Dark Ages⟩

³**deep** n **1** a vast or immeasurable extent; an abyss **2a** the sea **b** any of the very deep portions of a body of water, esp the sea

deepen vb to make or become deeper or more profound

deep-freeze vt -**froze; -frozen** to freeze or store (e g food) in a freezer

deep freeze n a freezer

deep-fry vt to fry (food) by complete immersion in hot fat or oil – **deep-fryer** n

deep-rooted adj firmly established ⟨a ~ loyalty⟩

deep-seated adj **1** situated far below the surface ⟨a ~ inflammation⟩ **2** firmly established ⟨~ tradition⟩

deer n, pl **deer** also **deers 1** any of several ruminant mammals of which most of the males and some of the females bear antlers **2** archaic an animal; esp a small mammal

deerstalker n a close-fitting hat with peaks at the front and the back and flaps that may be folded down as coverings for ears

deface vt to mar the external appearance of – **defacement** n, **defacer** n

¹**de facto** adv in reality; actually

²**de facto** adj existing in fact; effective ⟨a ~ state of war⟩

defame vt to injure the reputation of by libel or slander – **defamation** n, **defamatory** adj, **defamer** n

¹**default** n failure to act, pay, appear, or compete – **in default of** in the absence of

²**default** vi to fail to meet an esp financial obligation ~ vt **1** to fail to perform, pay, or make good **2** to declare to be in default – **defaulter** n

¹**defeat** vt **1a** to nullify ⟨~ an estate⟩ **b** to frustrate ⟨~ a hope⟩ **2** to win victory over ⟨~ the opposing team⟩

²**defeat** n **1** an overthrow, esp of an army in battle **2** the loss of a contest

defeatism n acceptance of or resignation to defeat – **defeatist** n or adj

defecate, Br also **defaecate** vb to discharge (esp faeces) from the bowels – **defecation** n

¹**defect** n **1** an imperfection that impairs worth or usefulness ⟨a hearing ~⟩ **2** an irregularity (e g a foreign atom) in the lattice of a crystal

²**defect** vi to desert a cause or party, often in order to espouse another – **defector** n, **defection** n

¹**defective** adj **1** lacking sthg essential; faulty ⟨a ~ pane of glass⟩⟨~ eyesight⟩ **2** lacking 1 or more of the usual grammatical inflections – **defectively** adv, **defectiveness** n

²**defective** n one who is subnormal physically or mentally

defence, NAm chiefly **defense** n **1** the act or action of defending **2a** a means or method of defending; also, pl a defensive structure **b** an argument in support or justification **c** a defendant's denial, answer, or strategy **3** sing or pl in constr **a** a defending party or group (e g in a court of law) **b** defensive players, acts, or moves in a game or sport **4** the military resources of a country ⟨~ budget⟩ – **defenceless** adj, **defencelessly** adv, **defencelessness** n

defend vt **1a** to protect from attack **b** to maintain by argument in the face of opposition or criticism **c** to attempt to prevent an opponent from scoring in (e g a goal) **2** to act as legal representative in court for ~ vi **1** to take action against attack or challenge **2** to play or be in defence – **defendable** adj

defendant n a person, company, etc against whom a criminal charge or civil claim is made

defensible adj capable of being defended – **defensibly** adv, **defensibility** n

¹**defensive** adj **1** serving to defend **2a** devoted to resisting or preventing aggression or attack; also disposed (as if) to ward off expected criticism or critical inquiry **b** of or relating to the attempt to keep an opponent from scoring – **defensively** adv, **defensiveness** n

²**defensive** n – **on the defensive** being prepared for expected aggression, attack, or criticism

defer *vt* -rr- to delay; PUT OFF 2a – **deferment** *n*, **deferrable** *adj*, **deferral** *n*, **deferrer** *n*

defer *vi* -rr- *vi* to submit *to* another's opinion, usu through deference or respect

deference *n* respect and esteem due a superior or an elder – **in deference to** because of respect for

defiance *n* a disposition to resist; contempt of opposition – **defiant** *adj*, **defiantly** *adv* – **in defiance of** despite; CONTRARY TO

deficiency *n* 1 being deficient 2 a shortage of substances necessary to health

deficiency disease *n* a disease (e g scurvy) caused by a lack of essential vitamins, minerals, etc in the diet

deficient *adj* 1 lacking in some necessary quality or element 2 not up to a normal standard or complement – **deficiently** *adv*

deficit *n* 1 a deficiency in amount or quality 2 an excess of expenditure over revenue

defile *vt* 1 to make unclean or impure 2 to deprive of virginity – **defilement** *n*, **defiler** *n*

defile *vi* to march off in a file

defile *n* a narrow passage or gorge

define *vt* 1a to fix or mark the limits of; demarcate b to make clear or precise in outline ⟨*the issues aren't too well* ~ d⟩ 2a to be the essential quality or qualities of; identify ⟨*whatever* ~ s *us as human*⟩ b to set forth the meaning of ⟨~ *a word*⟩ ~ *vi* to make a definition – **definable** *adj*, **definer** *n*

definite *adj* 1 having distinct or certain limits 2a free of all ambiguity, uncertainty, or obscurity b unquestionable, decided ⟨*a* ~ *advantage*⟩ 3 designating an identified or immediately identifiable person or thing ⟨*the* ~ *article* the⟩ – **definitely** *adv*, **definiteness** *n*

definition *n* 1a a word or phrase expressing the essential nature of a person, word, or thing; a meaning b the action or process of stating such a meaning 2a the action or power of making definite and clear b(1) distinctness of outline or detail (e g in a photograph) (2) clarity, esp of musical sound in reproduction – **definitional** *adj*

definitive *adj* 1 serving to provide a final solution ⟨*a* ~ *victory*⟩ 2 authoritative and apparently exhaustive ⟨*a* ~ *biography*⟩ 3 *of a postage stamp* issued as one of the normal stamps of the country or territory of use – **definitively** *adv*, **definitiveness** *n*

deflate *vt* 1 to release air or gas from 2a to reduce in size or importance b to reduce in self-confidence or self-importance, esp suddenly 3 to reduce (a price level) or cause (the availability of credit or the economy) to contract ~ *vi* to lose firmness (as if) through the escape of contained gas – **deflator** *n*

deflation *n* 1a a contraction in the volume of available money and credit, and thus in the economy, esp as a result of government policy b a decline in the general level of prices 2 the erosion of soil by the wind – **deflationary** *adj*

deflect *vb* to turn from a straight course or fixed direction – **deflective** *adj*, **deflector** *n*

deflection, Br also **deflexion** *n* (the amount or degree of) deflecting

deflower *vt* to deprive of virginity; ravish – **deflowerer** *n*

defoliant *n* a chemical applied to plants to cause the leaves to drop off prematurely – **defoliate** *vt or adj*, **defoliation** *n*, **defoliator** *n*

deforest *vt* to clear of forests – **deforestation** *n*

deform *vt* 1 to spoil the form or appearance of 2 to make hideous or monstrous 3 to alter the shape of by stress ~ *vi* to become misshapen or changed in shape – **deformation** *n*, **deformational** *adj*

deformity *n* 1 the state of being deformed 2 a physical blemish or distortion; a disfigurement

defraud *vt* to cheat of sthg – **defrauder** *n*, **defraudation** *n*

defray *vt* to provide for the payment of – **defrayable** *adj*, **defrayal** *n*

defrock *vt* to unfrock

defrost *vt* 1 to thaw out from a frozen state ⟨~ *meat*⟩ 2 to free from ice ⟨~ *the refrigerator*⟩ 3 *NAm* to demist ~ *vi* to thaw out, esp from a deep-frozen state – **defroster** *n*

deft *adj* marked by facility and skill – **deftly** *n*, **deftness** *n*

defunct *adj* no longer existing or in use; *esp* dead

defuse *vt* 1 to remove the fuse from (a mine, bomb, etc) 2 to make less harmful, potent, or tense ⟨~ *the crisis*⟩

defy *vt* 1 to challenge to do sthg considered impossible; dare 2 to face with assured power of resistance; show no fear of nor respect for ⟨~ *public opinion*⟩ 3 to resist attempts at ⟨*the paintings* ~ *classification*⟩ – **defier** *n*

degauss *vt* to demagnetize; *esp* to demagnetize (a steel ship), esp as a protection against magnetic mines – **degausser** *n*

¹degenerate *adj* 1a having declined in nature, character, structure, function, etc from an ancestral or former state b having sunk to a condition below that which is normal to a type; *esp* having sunk to a lower and usu peculiarly corrupt state 2 characterized by or made of atoms stripped of their electrons and packed very densely ⟨*a* ~ *star*⟩ – **degenerately** *adv*, **degenerateness** *n*, **degeneracy** *n*

²degenerate *n* sthg or esp sby degenerate; *esp* one showing signs of reversion to an earlier cultural or evolutionary stage

³degenerate *vi* 1 to pass from a higher to a lower type or condition; deteriorate. 2 to sink into a low intellectual or moral state 3 to decline from a former thriving or healthy condition 4 to evolve or develop into a less autonomous or complex form ⟨~ d *into parasites*⟩ – **degenerative** *adj*, **degeneration** *n*

degrade *vt* 1a to lower in grade, rank, or status; demote b to reduce the quality of; *specif* to impair with respect to some physical property 2 to bring to low esteem or into disrepute ⟨*degrading vices*⟩ 3 ERODE 1c 4 to decompose (a chemical compound) ~ *vi* 1 to degenerate 2 *of a chemical compound* to decompose – **degradable** *adj*, **degrader** *n*, **degradingly** *adv*, **degradation** *n*

degree *n* 1 a step or stage in a process, course, or order of classification ⟨*advanced by* ~ s⟩ 2a the extent or measure of an action, condition, or relation b any of the (sets of) forms used in the comparison of an adjective or adverb c a legal measure of guilt or negligence ⟨*guilty of murder in the first* ~ ⟩ d a positive and esp considerable amount ⟨*eccentric to a* ~ ⟩ 3 the civil condition or status of a person ⟨*people of high* ~ ⟩ 4 an academic title conferred a on students in recognition of proficiency b honorarily 5 a division or interval of a scale of measurement; *specif* any of various units for measuring temperature 6 a 360th part of the circumference of a circle 7a the rank of algebraic expression that for a monomial term is the sum of the exponents of the variable factors and for a polynomial is the sum of the exponents of the variable factors of the highest degree ⟨x^2y^3z and $x^6 + y^2 + 2z$ are both of the 6th degree⟩ b the greatest power of the derivative of highest order in a differential equation – **degreed** *adj* – **to a degree** 1 to a remarkable extent 2 in a small way

dehumanize, -**ise** *vt* to divest of human qualities or personality – **dehumanization** *n*

dehydrate *vt* 1 to remove (bound) water from (a chemical compound, foods, etc) 2 to make dry and uninteresting in style or character ~ *vi* to lose water or body fluids (abnormally) – **dehydrator** *n*, **dehydration** *n*

deify *vt* 1a to make a god of **b** to take as an object of worship 2 to glorify as of supreme worth ⟨~ *money*⟩ – **deification** *n*

deign *vi* to condescend ⟨*she barely* ~ed *to acknowledge their greeting*⟩ ~ *vt* to condescend to give or offer

deism *n*, *often cap* a movement or system of thought advocating natural religion based on human reason rather than revelation; *specif* a chiefly 18th-c doctrine asserting that although God created the universe he does not intervene in its functioning – **deist** *n*, *often cap*, **deistic** *adj*, **deistically** *adv*

deity *n* 1a the rank or essential nature of a god **b** *cap the* Supreme Being; GOD 1 2 a god or goddess ⟨*the* deities *of ancient Greece*⟩ 3 one exalted or revered as supremely good or powerful

déjà vu *n* 1 the illusion of remembering scenes and events when they are experienced for the first time 2 sthg excessively or unpleasantly familiar

dejected *adj* cast down in spirits; depressed – **dejectedly** *adv*, **dejectedness** *n*

dejection *n* lowness of spirits

de jure *adv or adj* by (full legal) right ⟨*recognition extended* ~ *to the new government*⟩

dekko *n*, *Br* a look, glance – *slang*

¹delay *n* 1 delaying or (an instance of) being delayed 2 the time during which sthg is delayed

²delay *vt* 1 to postpone 2 to stop, detain, or hinder for a time ~ *vi* 1 to move or act slowly 2 to pause momentarily – **delayer** *n*, **delaying** *adj*

delectable *adj* 1 highly pleasing; delightful 2 delicious – **delectableness** *n*, **delectably** *adv*, **delectability** *n*

delectation *n* 1 DELIGHT 1 2 enjoyment

delegacy *n* 1a the act of delegating **b** an appointment as delegate 2 *sing or pl in constr* a body of delegates; a board

¹delegate *n* a person delegated to act for another; *esp* a representative to a conference

²delegate *vt* 1 to entrust (e g a duty or responsibility) to another 2 to appoint as one's representative ~ *vi* to assign responsibility or authority

delegation *n* 1 the act of empowering to act for another 2 *sing or pl in constr* a group of people chosen to represent others

delete *vt* to eliminate, esp by blotting out, cutting out, or erasing

deleterious *adj* harmful, detrimental – *fml* – **deleteriously** *adv*, **deleteriousness** *n*

deletion *n* sthg deleted

delft *n* tin-glazed Dutch earthenware with blue and white or polychrome decoration

¹deliberate *adj* 1 characterized by or resulting from careful and thorough consideration 2 characterized by awareness of the consequences; wilful 3 slow, unhurried ⟨*walked with a* ~ *step*⟩ – **deliberately** *adv*, **deliberateness** *n*

²deliberate *vt* to think about deliberately and often with formal discussion before reaching a decision ~ *vi* to ponder issues and decisions carefully

deliberation *n* 1 deliberating or being deliberate 2 a discussion and consideration of pros and cons – **deliberative** *adj*, **deliberatively** *adv*, **deliberativeness** *n*

delicacy *n* 1 sthg pleasing to eat that is considered rare or luxurious 2 the quality or state of being dainty ⟨*lace of great* ~⟩ 3 frailty, fragility 4 precise and refined perception or discrimination 5a refined sensibility in feeling or conduct **b** avoidance of anything offensive or disturbing

delicate *adj* 1a pleasing to the senses in a mild or subtle way **b** marked by daintiness or charm of colour, line, or proportion 2a marked by keen sensitivity or subtle discrimination ⟨~ *perception*⟩ **b** fastidious, squeamish 3a marked by extreme precision **b** having or showing extreme sensitivity ⟨*a* ~ *instrument*⟩ 4 calling for or involving meticulously careful treatment ⟨*the* ~ *balance of power*⟩ 5a very finely made **b**(1) fragile (2) weak, sickly **c** marked by or requiring tact ⟨*touches on a* ~ *subject*⟩ – **delicately** *adv*, **delicateness** *n*

delicatessen *n* 1 *pl in constr* (delicacies and foreign) foods ready for eating (e g cooked meats) 2 a shop where delicatessen are sold

delicious *adj* 1 affording great pleasure; delightful 2 highly pleasing to one of the bodily senses, esp of taste or smell – **deliciously** *adv*, **deliciousness** *n*

¹delight *n* 1 great pleasure or satisfaction; joy 2 sthg that gives great pleasure ⟨*a* ~ *to behold*⟩

²delight *vi* to take great pleasure *in* doing sthg ~ *vt* to give enjoyment or satisfaction to ⟨~ed *the audience with his performance*⟩ – **delighter** *n*

delightful *adj* highly pleasing – **delightfully** *adv*, **delightfulness** *n*

delimit *vt* to fix the limits of ⟨~ *a boundary*⟩

delineate *vt* 1 to show by drawing lines in the shape of 2 to describe in usu sharp or vivid detail – **delineator** *n*, **delineative** *adj*, **delineation** *n*

delinquency *n* (the practice of engaging in) antisocial or illegal conduct – used esp when emphasis is placed on maladjustment rather than criminal intent

¹delinquent *n* a delinquent person

²delinquent *adj* 1 guilty of wrongdoing or of neglect of duty 2 marked by delinquency ⟨~ *behaviour*⟩ – **delinquently** *adv*

deliquesce *vi* to melt away; *specif, of a compound* to dissolve gradually in water attracted and absorbed from the air – **deliquescence** *n*, **deliquescent** *adj*

delirious *adj* (characteristic) of or affected by delirium – **deliriously** *adv*, **deliriousness** *n*

delirium *n* 1 confusion, frenzy, disordered speech, hallucinations, etc occurring as a (temporary) mental disturbance 2 frenzied excitement

delirium tremens *n* a violent delirium with tremors induced by chronic alcoholism

deliver *vt* 1 to set free 2 to hand over; convey ⟨~ *the milk*⟩ 3a to assist in giving birth ⟨*she was* ~ed *of a fine boy*⟩ **b** to aid in the birth of **c** to give birth to 4 to utter ⟨~ed *her speech effectively*⟩ 5 to aim or guide (e g a blow) to an intended target or destination ~ *vi* to produce the promised, desired, or expected results – *infml* – **deliverable** *adj*, **deliverer** *n*

deliverance *n* 1 liberation, rescue 2 an opinion or verdict expressed publicly

delivery *n* 1 DELIVERANCE 1 2a the act of handing over **b** a physical or legal transfer **c** sthg delivered at 1 time or in 1 unit ⟨*milk* deliveries⟩ 3 the act of giving birth 4 the uttering of a speech; *also* the manner or style of uttering in speech or song 5 the act or manner or an instance of sending forth, throwing, or bowling

deliveryman *n*, *pl* **deliverymen** a van driver who delivers wholesale or retail goods to customers, usu over a regular local route

dell *n* a small secluded hollow or valley, esp in a forest

delouse *vt* to remove lice from

Delphic, Delphian *adj* 1 of ancient Delphi or its oracle 2a ambiguous **b** obscure, enigmatic – **delphically** *adv*

delphinium *n* any of a genus of plants of the buttercup

family with deeply cut leaves and flowers in showy
spikes

delta *n* **1a** the 4th letter of the Greek alphabet **b** 'D 4 **2**
a triangular alluvial deposit at the mouth of a river **3** an
increment of a variable – **deltaic** *adj*

Delta – a communications code word for the letter *d*

delta wing *n* an approximately triangular aircraft wing
with a (nearly) straight rearmost edge – **delta-winged**
adj

delude *vt* to mislead the mind or judgment of; deceive,
trick – **deluder** *n*, **deludingly** *adv*

deluge *n* **1a** a great flood; *specif, cap the* Flood recorded
in the Old Testament (Gen 6:8) **b** a drenching fall of rain
2 an overwhelming amount or number ⟨*a ∼ of
criticism*⟩ ⟨*a ∼ of letters*⟩

deluge *vt* **1** to overflow with water; inundate **2** to
overwhelm, swamp

delusion *n* **1** deluding or being deluded **2a** sthg delusively believed **b** (a mental state characterized by) a false
belief (about the self or others) that persists despite the
facts and occurs esp in psychotic states – **delusional** *adj*,
delusionary *adj*

delusive *adj* **1** likely to delude **2** constituting a delusion
– **delusively** *adv*, **delusiveness** *n*

de luxe *adj* notably luxurious or elegant

delve *vi* **1** to dig or work (as if) with a spade **2** to make
a careful or detailed search for information ⟨*∼d into the
past*⟩ – **delver** *n*

demagnetize, -ise *vt* to cause not to have magnetic
properties or a magnetic field – **demagnetizer** *n*, **demag-
netization** *n*

demagogue, *NAm also* **demagog** *n* **1** a leader of the
common people in ancient times **2** an agitator who makes
use of popular prejudices in order to gain power –
demagoguery *n*, **demagogy** *n*, **demagogic** , **demagogical**
adj, **demagogically** *adv*

demand *n* **1** an act of demanding or asking, esp with
authority; a claim **2a** an expressed desire for ownership
or use **b** willingness and ability to purchase a commodity
or service **c** the quantity of a commodity or service
wanted at a specified price and time **3** a desire or need *for*;
the state of being sought after ⟨*gold is in great ∼*⟩ ⟨*a great
∼ for teachers*⟩ – **on demand** whenever the demand is
made ⟨*feed the baby on demand*⟩

demand *vi* to make a demand; ask *∼ vt* **1** to ask or call
for with authority; claim as due or just ⟨*∼ payment of a
debt*⟩ **2** to call for urgently, peremptorily, or insistently
3 to ask authoritatively or earnestly to be informed of ⟨*∼
the reason for her visit*⟩ **4** to require – **demandable** *adj*,
demander *n*

demanding *adj* exacting – **demandingly** *adv*

demarcate *vt* **1** to mark the limits of **2** to set apart;
separate

demarcation *also* **demarkation** *n* the marking of limits or
boundaries, esp between areas of work to be carried out
by members of particular trade unions ⟨*a ∼ dispute*⟩

demean *vt* to degrade, debase

demeanour, *NAm chiefly* **demeanor** *n* behaviour
towards others; outward manner

demented *adj* insane; *also* crazy – **dementedly** *adv*,
dementedness *n*

demerara sugar *n* brown crystallized unrefined cane
sugar from the W Indies

demerit *n* **1** a quality that deserves blame or lacks merit;
a fault, defect **2** *NAm* a bad mark given to an
offender

demesne *n* **1** legal possession of land as one's own **2** land
actually occupied by the owner and not held by tenants **3a**

the land attached to a mansion **b** landed property; an
estate **c** a region, realm

demi- *prefix* **1** half ⟨*demisemiquaver*⟩ **2** partly belonging
to (a specified type or class) ⟨*demigod*⟩

demigod, *fem* **demigoddess** *n* **1a** a mythological superhuman being with less power than a god **b** an offspring
of a union between a mortal and a god **2** a person so
outstanding that he/she seems to approach the divine

demijohn *n* a narrow-necked large bottle of glass or
stoneware

demilitarize, -ise *vt* to strip of military forces, weapons,
etc – **demilitarization** *n*

demise *vt* **1** to convey (e g an estate) by will or lease **2**
to transmit by succession or inheritance *∼ vi* to pass by
descent or bequest ⟨*the property ∼d to the king*⟩

demise *n* **1** the conveyance of an estate or transfer of
sovereignty by demising **2a** death – technical, euph, or
humor **b** a cessation of existence or activity – fml or
humor

demist *vt*, *Br* to remove mist from (e g a car windscreen)
– **demister** *n*

demo *n*, *pl* **demos** **1** DEMONSTRATION 4 **2** *cap NAm*
DEMOCRAT 2

demob *vt*, *chiefly Br* to demobilize

demob *n*, *chiefly Br* a demobilization

demobilize, -ise *vt* **1** to disband **2** to discharge from
military service – **demobilization** *n*

democracy *n* **1a** government by the people **b** (a political
unit with) a government in which the supreme power is
exercised by the people directly or indirectly through a
system of representation usu involving free elections **2** the
absence of class distinctions or privileges

democrat *n* **1a** an adherent of democracy **b** one who
practises social equality **2** *cap* a member of the Democratic party of the USA

democratic *adj* **1** of or favouring democracy or social
equality **2** *often cap* of or constituting a political party of
the USA associated with policies of social reform and
internationalism – **democratically** *adv*, **democratize** *vt*,
democratization *n*, **democratizer** *n*

démodé *adj* no longer fashionable; out-of-date

demography *n* the statistical study of human populations, esp with reference to size and density, distribution,
and vital statistics – **demographer** *n*, **demographic** *adj*,
demographically *adv*

demolish *vt* **1** to destroy, smash, or tear down **2** to eat
up – infml – **demolisher** *n*

demolition *n* the act or an instance of demolishing –
demolitionist *n*

demon *n* **1a** an evil spirit **b** an evil or undesirable
emotion, trait, or state **2** DAEMON 1, 2 **3** one who has
unusual drive or effectiveness ⟨*a ∼ for work*⟩ – **demon-
ism** *n*, **demonize** *vt*, **demonization** *n*, **demonology** *n*

demonetize, -ise *vt* to stop using (a metal) as a money
standard – **demonetization** *n*

demoniac *also* **demoniacal** *adj* **1** possessed or influenced
by a demon **2** demonic – **demoniacally** *adv*

demonic *also* **demonical** *adj* (suggestive) of a demon;
fiendish ⟨*∼ cruelty*⟩ – **demonically** *adv*

demonstrable *adj* **1** capable of being demonstrated **2**
apparent, evident – **demonstrableness** *n*, **demonstrably**
adv, **demonstrability** *n*

demonstrate *vt* **1** to show clearly **2a** to prove or make
clear by reasoning or evidence **b** to illustrate and explain,
esp with many examples **3** to show or prove the application, value, or efficiency of to a prospective buyer *∼ vi* **1**
to make or give a demonstration **2** to take part in a
demonstration ⟨*demonstrating against the abortion
bill*⟩

demonstration n 1 an outward expression or display 2a(1) conclusive evidence; proof (2) a proof in which the conclusion is the immediate sequence of reasoning from premises b a showing and explanation of the merits of a product to a prospective buyer c a display of an action or process ⟨*cooking* ~⟩ 3 a show of armed force 4 a mass meeting, procession, etc to display group feelings (e g about grievances or political issues) – **demonstrational** adj

¹**demonstrative** adj 1 demonstrating sthg to be real or true 2 pointing out the one referred to and distinguishing it from others of the same class ⟨~ *pronouns*⟩ 3 given to or marked by display of feeling – **demonstratively** adv, **demonstrativeness** n

²**demonstrative** n a demonstrative word or morpheme

demonstrator n one who demonstrates: e g a a junior staff member who demonstrates experiments in a university science department b sby who participates in a demonstration ⟨*the* ~s *were given a police escort*⟩

demoralize, -ise vt to weaken the morale or self-respect of; discourage, dispirit – **demoralizingly** adv, **demoralization** n

demote vt to reduce to a lower grade or rank – **demotion** n

demotic adj 1 of the people 2 of or written in a simplified form of the ancient Egyptian hieratic writing 3 of the Modern Greek vernacular – **demotic** n

¹**demur** vi -rr- 1 to put in a demurrer 2 to take exception; (mildly) object – **demurral** n, **demurrable** adj

²**demur** n 1 a hesitation ⟨*men who follow fashion without* ~⟩ 2 objection, protest

demure adj 1 reserved, modest 2 affectedly modest, reserved, or serious; coy – **demurely** adv, **demureness** n

demystify vt to eliminate the mystery from; clarify ⟨~ *the law*⟩ – **demystification** n

den n 1 the lair of a wild, usu predatory, animal 2 a centre of secret, esp unlawful, activity ⟨*an opium* ~⟩ 3 a comfortable usu secluded room

denationalize, -ise vt 1 to divest of national status, character, or rights 2 to remove from ownership or control by the state – **denationalization** n

denial n 1 a refusal to satisfy a request or desire 2a a refusal to admit the truth or reality (e g of a statement or charge) b an assertion that an allegation is false 3 a refusal to acknowledge sby or sthg; a disavowal

denier n a unit of fineness for silk, rayon, or nylon yarn equal to the fineness of a yarn weighing 1g for each 9000m

denigrate vt 1 to cast aspersions on; defame 2 to belittle – **denigrator** n, **denigratory** adj, **denigration** n

denim n 1 a firm durable twilled usu blue cotton fabric used esp for jeans 2 pl denim trousers; esp blue jeans

denizen n 1 an inhabitant 2 a naturalized plant or animal

denominate vt to give a name to – fml

denomination n 1 a name, designation; esp a general name for a category 2 a religious organization or sect 3 a grade or degree in a series of values or sizes (e g of money)

denominational adj of a particular religious denomination ⟨*a* ~ *school*⟩ – **denominationally** adv

denominator n the part of a vulgar fraction that is below the line and that in fractions with 1 as the numerator indicates into how many parts the unit is divided; a divisor

denotation n 1 a direct specific meaning as distinct from a connotation 2 a denoting term; a name 3 the totality of subjects of which a term may be predicated, esp in logic

denote vt 1 to indicate ⟨*the swollen bellies that* ~ *starvation*⟩ 2 to be a sign or mark for ⟨*red* ~s *danger*⟩ 3 to have the meaning of; mean – **denotative** adj

denouement n 1 the resolution of the main complication in a literary work 2 the outcome of a complex sequence of events

denounce vt 1 to condemn, esp publicly, as deserving censure or punishment 2 to inform against; accuse 3 to announce formally the termination of (e g 'a treaty) – **denouncement** n, **denouncer** n

dense adj 1 marked by high density, compactness, or crowding together of parts ⟨~ *undergrowth*⟩ ⟨*a* ~ *fog*⟩ 2 sluggish of mind; stupid 3 demanding concentration to follow or comprehend ⟨~ *prose*⟩ – **densely** adv, **denseness** n

density n 1 the quantity per unit volume, unit area, or unit length: e g a the mass of a substance or distribution of a quantity per unit of volume or space b the average number of individuals or units per unit of space ⟨a population ~⟩ 2 the degree of opaqueness of sthg translucent

¹**dent** n 1 a depression or hollow made by a blow or by pressure 2 an adverse effect ⟨*made a* ~ *in the weekly budget*⟩

²**dent** vt to make a dent in or on

dent-, denti-, dento- comb form tooth; teeth ⟨*dentiform*⟩ ⟨*dentifrice*⟩

¹**dental** adj 1 of the teeth or dentistry 2 articulated with the tip or blade of the tongue against or near the upper front teeth – **dentalize** vt, **dentally** adv

²**dental** n a dental consonant

dentifrice n a powder, paste, or liquid for cleaning the teeth

dentist n one who treats diseases, malformations, and injuries to the teeth, mouth, etc and who makes and inserts false teeth – **dentistry** n

denture n an artificial replacement for 1 or more teeth esp, pl a set of false teeth

denude vt 1a to strip of all covering b to lay bare by erosion 2 to remove an important possession or quality from; strip ⟨~d *of his dignity*⟩ – **denudation** n

denunciation n a (public) condemnation

deny vt 1 to declare to be untrue or invalid; refuse to accept 2 to disown, repudiate 3a to give a negative answer to b to refuse to grant ⟨~ *a request*⟩ c to restrain (oneself) from self-indulgence

deodorant n a preparation that destroys or masks unpleasant smells – **deodorant** adj

deodorize, -ise vt to destroy or prevent the unpleasant smell of – **deodorizer** n, **deodorization** n

depart vi 1 to go away; leave 2 to turn aside; deviate from ~ vt to go away from; leave

departed adj 1 bygone 2 having died, esp recently – euph

department n 1a a major division of a government b a division of an institution or business that provides a specified service or deals with a specified subject ⟨*sale* ~⟩ c a major administrative subdivision (e g in France d a section of a department store 2 a distinct sphere (e of activity or thought) – infml ⟨*that's not my* ~⟩ – **departmental** adj, **departmentally** adv, **departmentalize** v **departmentalization** n

department store n a large shop, selling a wide variet of goods, arranged in several departments

departure n 1a the act of going away b a setting out (e on a new course of action) 2 the distance due east or west travelled by a ship in its course 3 deviation, divergenc

depend vi 1 to be determined by or based on som condition or action 2a to place reliance or trust b to b

dependent, esp for financial support **3** to hang down *USE (1&2)* + *on* or *upon*

dependable *adj* reliable – **dependableness** *n*, **dependably** *adv*, **dependability** *n*

dependant, *NAm chiefly* **dependent** *n* a person who relies on another for esp financial support

dependence *also* **dependance** *n* **1** being influenced by or subject to another **2** reliance, trust **3** a need for or reliance on a drug: **a** compulsive physiological need for a habit-forming drug (e g heroin); addiction **b** psychological need for a drug after a period of use; habituation

dependency *n* sthg that is dependent on sthg else; *specif* a territorial unit under the jurisdiction of a nation but not formally annexed to it

dependent *adj* **1** determined or conditioned by another; contingent **2** relying on another for support **3** subject to another's jurisdiction **4** SUBORDINATE **3** *USE (1&2)* + *on* or *upon* – **dependently** *adv*

depict *vt* **1** to represent by a picture **2** to describe – **depicter** *n*, **depiction** *n*

depilate *vt* to remove hair from – **depilation** *n*, **depilatory** *adj or n*

deplete *vt* to reduce in amount by using up; exhaust, esp of strength or resources – **depletion** *n*

deplorable *adj* **1** lamentable ⟨*a ~ accident*⟩ **2** extremely bad – **deplorableness** *n*, **deplorably** *adv*

deplore *vt* **1** to feel or express grief for **2** to regret or disapprove of strongly – **deploringly** *adv*

deploy *vt* **1** to spread out (e g troops or ships), esp in battle formation **2** to utilize or arrange as if deploying troops – *~vi* to move in being deployed – **deployable** *adj*, **deployment** *n*

1deponent *adj, of a verb* occurring with passive or middle voice forms but with active voice meaning

2deponent *n* **1** a deponent verb **2** one who gives (written) evidence

depopulate *vt* to reduce greatly the population of – *~vi* to decrease in population – **depopulator** *n*, **depopulation** *n*

deport *vt* **1a** to expel (e g an alien) legally from a country **b** to transport (e g a convicted criminal) to a penal colony or place of exile **2** to behave or conduct (oneself) in a specified manner – *fml* – **deportation** *n*, **deportee** *n*

deportment *n* **1** *Br* the manner in which one stands, sits, or walks; posture **2** *NAm* behaviour, conduct

depose *vt* **1** to remove from a position of authority (e g a throne) **2** to testify under oath or by affidavit – *~vi* to bear witness

1deposit *vt* **1** to place, esp for safekeeping or as a pledge; *esp* to put in a bank **2a** to lay down; place **b** to let fall (e g sediment) – **depositor** *n*

2deposit *n* **1** depositing or being deposited **2a** money deposited in a bank **b** money given as a pledge or down payment **3** a depository **4** sthg laid down; *esp* (an accumulation of) matter deposited by a natural process

deposit account *n, chiefly Br* an account (e g in a bank) on which interest is usu payable and from which withdrawals can be made usu only by prior arrangement

deposition *n* **1** removal from a position of authority **2** a (written and sworn) statement presented as evidence **3** an act or process of depositing – **depositional** *adj*

depository *n* **1** a depositary **2** a place where sthg is deposited, esp for safekeeping

1depot *n* **1a** a place for the storage of military supplies **b** a place for the reception and training of military recruits; a regimental headquarters **2a** a place for storing goods **b** a store, depository **3a** *Br* an area (e g a garage) in which buses or trains are stored, esp for maintenance **b** *NAm* a railway station

2depot *adj, of a (dose of a) drug* designed to act over a long period

deprave *vt* to corrupt morally; pervert – **depravedly** *adv*, **depraver** *n*, **depravation** *n*

depravity *n* (an instance of) moral corruption

deprecate *vt* to express disapproval of, esp mildly or regretfully – **deprecatingly** *adv*, **deprecation** *n*

deprecatory *adj* **1** apologetic **2** disapproving – **deprecatorily** *adv*

depreciate *vt* **1** to lower the price or estimated value of **2** to belittle, disparage – *~vi* to lessen in value; fall – **depreciable** *adj*, **depreciator** *n*, **depreciative** , **depreciatory** *adj*, **depreciation**

depredate *vb* to plunder, ravage – **depredator** *n*, **depredatory** *adj*, **depredation** *n*

depress *vt* **1** to push or press down ⟨*~ a typewriter key*⟩ **2** to lessen the activity or strength of **3** to sadden, dispirit **4** to decrease the market value or marketability of – **depressingly** *adv*

depressed *adj* **1** low in spirits; sad **2** lowered or sunken, esp in the centre **3** suffering from economic depression ⟨*a ~ area*⟩

depression *n* **1** the angular distance of a celestial body below the horizon **2a** a pressing down; a lowering **b** (a mental disorder marked by inactivity, difficulty in thinking and concentration, and esp by) sadness or dejection **c** a lowering of activity, vitality, amount, force, etc **3** a depressed place or part; a hollow **4** ³LOW 1b **5** a period of low general economic activity marked esp by rising levels of unemployment

deprivation *n* **1** an act of depriving; a loss **2** being deprived; privation

deprive *vt* **1** to take sthg away from **2** to remove (e g a clergyman) from office **3** to withhold sthg from ⟨*he threatened to ~ them of their rights*⟩ *USE (1&3)* + *of*

deprived *adj* lacking the necessities of life or a good environment ⟨*culturally ~ children*⟩

depth *n* **1a(1)** a deep place in a body of water ⟨*found in the ~s of the ocean*⟩ **(2)** a part that is far from the outside or surface ⟨*the ~s of the woods*⟩ **b(1)** a profound or intense state (e g of thought or feeling) ⟨*the ~s of despair*⟩ **(2)** the worst, most intensive, or severest part ⟨*the ~s of winter*⟩ **2a** the perpendicular measurement downwards from a surface **b** the distance from front to back **3** the quality of being deep **4** the degree of intensity ⟨*~ of a colour*⟩ *USE (1)* often pl with sing. meaning – **in depth** with great thoroughness ⟨*haven't studied it in depth*⟩ – **out of one's depth 1** in water that is deeper than one's height **2** beyond one's ability to understand

depth charge *n* an explosive projectile for use underwater, esp against submarines

deputation *n sing or pl in constr* a group of people appointed to represent others

1depute *vt* to delegate

2depute *n, Scot* a deputy

deputize, -ise *vi* to act as a deputy for

deputy *n* **1** a person (e g a second-in-command) appointed as a substitute with power to act for another **2** a member of the lower house of some legislative assemblies

derail *vt* to cause (e g a train) to leave the rails – *~vi* to be derailed – **derailment** *n*

derange *vt* to disturb the operation or functions of – **derangement** *n*

derby *n* **1** *cap* a flat race for 3-year-old horses over 1½mi (about 2.9km) held annually at Epsom in England **2** a usu informal race or contest for a specified category of contestant ⟨*a donkey ~*⟩ **3** a sporting match against a major local rival **4** *chiefly NAm* ²BOWLER

¹derelict adj 1 left to decay 2 chiefly NAm lacking a sense of duty; negligent

²derelict n 1 sthg voluntarily abandoned; specif a ship abandoned on the high seas 2 a down-and-out

dereliction n 1 (intentional) abandonment or being abandoned 2 a recession of water leaving permanently dry land 3a conscious neglect ⟨~ of duty⟩ b a fault, short-coming

deride vt to mock, scorn

de rigueur adj required by fashion, etiquette, or custom

derision n deriding or being derided

derisive adj showing derision; mocking, scornful – **derisively** adv

derisory adj 1 derisive 2 worthy of derision; ridiculous; specif contemptibly small ⟨a ~ pay offer⟩

derivation n 1a the formation of a word from another word or root, esp with an affix b an act of tracing or stating the derivation of a word c ETYMOLOGY 1 2a the source, origin b descent ⟨a family of Scottish ~⟩ 3 DERIVATIVE 2 4 an act of deriving – **derivational** adj

¹derivative adj 1 formed by derivation 2 made up of derived elements; not original – **derivatively** adv

²derivative n 1 a word formed by derivation 2 sthg derived 3 the limit of the ratio of the change in a function to the corresponding change in its independent variable as the latter change approaches zero 4 a chemical related structurally to and (theoretically) derivable from another

derive vt 1a to obtain or receive, esp from a specified source b to obtain (a chemical) from a parent substance 2 to infer, deduce 3a to trace the derivation of b to form by derivation ~ vi to come as a derivative from – **derivable** adj

derm n 1 the dermis 2 SKIN 2a

derm-, derma-, dermo- comb form dermat- ⟨dermal⟩

-derm comb form (→ n) skin; layer ⟨ectoderm⟩ ⟨pachyderm⟩

dermatitis n a disease or inflammation of the skin

dermatology n a branch of medicine dealing with (diseases of) the skin – **dermatologist** n, **dermatologic, dermatological** adj

dermis n (the sensitive vascular inner layer of) the skin – **dermal** adj

derogate vb – **derogation** n, **derogative** adj – **derogate from** to impair by taking away a part; detract from – fml

derogatory adj expressing a low opinion; disparaging – **derogatorily** adv

derrick n 1 a hoisting apparatus employing a tackle rigged at the end of a beam 2 a framework over an oil well or similar hole, for supporting drilling tackle

derring-do n daring action ⟨deeds of ~⟩

derv n fuel oil for diesel engines

dervish n a member of a Muslim religious order noted for devotional exercises (e g bodily movements leading to a trance)

desalinate vt to remove salt from (esp sea water) – **desalinator** n, **desalination** n

¹descant n a counterpoint superimposed on a simple melody and usu sung by some or all of the sopranos

²descant vi 1 to sing or play a descant 2 to talk or write at considerable length on or upon

descend vi 1 to pass from a higher to a lower level 2 to pass from the general to the particular 3 to pass by inheritance 4 to incline, lead, or extend downwards ⟨the road ~ s to the river⟩ 5a to come down or make a sudden attack – usu + on or upon b to make a sudden disconcerting visit or appearance – usu + on or upon; chiefly humor 6 to proceed from higher to lower in a sequence or gradation 7 to sink in status or dignity; stoop ~ vt to pass, move, or extend down or down along ⟨he ~ ed the steps⟩

descendant, descendent NAm also n sby or sthg descended or deriving from another

descended adj having as an ancestor; sprung from

descent n 1 the act or process of descending 2 a downward step (e g in status or value) 3a derivation from an ancestor; birth, lineage b transmission of an estate by inheritance c a transmission from a usu earlier source; a derivation 4a a downward inclination; a slope b a descending way (e g a staircase) 5 a sudden hostile raid or attack

describe vt 1 to give an account of in words 2 to trace the outline of – **describable** adj

description n 1 an account intended to convey a mental image of sthg experienced 2 kind, sort ⟨people of every ~⟩

descriptive adj 1 serving to describe, esp vividly 2 of a modifier expressing the quality, kind, or condition of what is denoted by the modified term; not limiting or demonstrative (e g hot in 'hot water') – **descriptively** adv

descry vt to notice or see, esp at a distance – fml

desecrate vt to violate the sanctity of; profane – **desecrator** n, **descration** n

desegregate vt to eliminate (racial) segregation in – **desegregation** n

desensitize, -ise vt 1 to make (sby previously sensitive) insensitive or nonreactive to a sensitizing agent 2 to make (a photographic material) less sensitive or completely insensitive to radiation – **desensitizer** n, **desensitization** n

¹desert n 1 (a desolate region like) a dry barren region incapable of supporting much life 2 an area or place that is deprived of or devoid of sthg important ⟨a cultural ~⟩ – **desertic** adj

²desert n deserved reward or punishment – usu pl with sing. meaning ⟨got her just ~ s⟩

³desert vt 1 to leave, usu without intending to return 2a to abandon or forsake, esp in time of need b to abandon (military service) without leave ~ vi to quit one's post, (military) service, etc without leave or justification – **deserter** n

Desert trademark – used for an ankle-high laced suede boot with a rubber sole

desertion n the abandonment of a post or relationship and the moral and legal obligations attached to it ⟨sued for divorce on grounds of ~⟩

deserve vb to be worthy of or suitable for (some recompense or treatment) – **deservedly** adv

deserving adj meriting (financial) aid

deshabille, déshabillé n the state of being only partially or carelessly dressed

desiccate vt 1 to dry up 2 to preserve (a food) by drying to dehydrate – **desiccant** n, **desiccator** n, **desiccative** adj, **desiccation** n

desideratum n, pl **desiderata** sthg desired as necessary – fml

¹design vt 1a to conceive and plan out in the mind b to devise for a specific function or end 2a to draw the plans for b to create or execute according to a plan; devise ~ vi 1 to conceive or execute a plan 2 to draw, lay out, or prepare a design – **designer** n, **designedly** adv

²design n 1 a mental plan or scheme 2a a particular purpose held in view b deliberate purposeful planning ⟨more by accident than by ~⟩ 3 pl dishonest, hostile, or acquisitive intent – + on 4 (the act of producing) a drawing, plan, or pattern showing the details of how sthg is to be constructed **5** the arrangement of the elements of a work of art or artefact **6** a decorative pattern

¹designate *adj* chosen for an office but not yet installed ⟨*ambassador* ∼⟩

²designate *vt* **1** to indicate; POINT OUT **2** to call by a distinctive name or title **3** to nominate for a specified purpose, office, or duty – **designator** *n*, **designatory** *adj*

designation *n* **1** the act of indicating or identifying **2** a distinguishing name or title **3** appointment to an office, post, or service

designing *adj* crafty, scheming

desirable *adj* **1** causing (sexual) desire; attractive **2** worth seeking or doing as advantageous, beneficial, or wise – **desirableness** *n*, **desirably** *adv*, **desirability** *n*

¹desire *vt* **1** to long or hope for **2** to express a wish for; request **3** to wish to have sexual relations with

²desire *n* **1** a conscious impulse towards an object or experience promising enjoyment or satisfaction **2** a (sexual) longing or craving **3** a formal request or petition **4** sthg desired

desirous *adj* eagerly wanting; desiring – *fml*

desist *vi* to cease to proceed or act – *fml* – **desistance** *n*

desk *n* **1a** a table with a sloping or horizontal surface and often drawers and compartments, that is designed esp for writing and reading **b** a church lectern **c** a table, counter, or booth at which cashiers, clerks, etc work **d** a music stand **2** a division of an organization specializing in a usu specified phase of activity

¹desolate *adj* **1** deserted, uninhabited **2** forsaken, forlorn **3** barren, lifeless ⟨*a* ∼ *landscape*⟩ – **desolately** *adv*, **desolateness** *n*

²desolate *vt* **1** to deprive of inhabitants **2** to lay waste – **desolator** *n*

¹despair *vi* to lose all hope or confidence ⟨∼ *of winning*⟩ – **despairingly** *adv*

²despair *n* **1** utter loss of hope **2** a cause of hopelessness ⟨*that child is the* ∼ *of his parents*⟩

despatch *vb or n* (to) dispatch

desperado *n, pl* **desperadoes, desperados** a bold, reckless, or violent person, esp a criminal

desperate *adj* **1** being (almost) beyond hope **2a** reckless because of despair **b** undertaken as a last resort ⟨*a* ∼ *remedy*⟩ **3** suffering extreme need or anxiety ⟨∼ *for money*⟩ **4** fraught with extreme danger or impending disaster – **desperately** *adv*, **desperateness** *n*

desperation *n* **1** loss of hope and surrender to despair **2** extreme recklessness caused by despair

despicable *adj* morally contemptible – **despicableness** *n*, **despicably** *adv*

despise *vt* **1** to regard with contempt or distaste **2** to regard as negligible or worthless – **despiser** *n*

despite *prep* notwithstanding; IN SPITE OF ⟨*ran* ∼ *her injury*⟩

despoil *vt* to plunder, pillage – **despoiler** *n*, **despoilment** *n*

despondent *adj* feeling extreme discouragement or dejection – **despondently** *adv*, **despondency** *n*

despot *n* **1** a ruler with absolute power **2** a person exercising power abusively or tyrannically – **despotic** *adj*, **despotically** *adv*

despotism *n* **1** rule by a despot; absolutism **2** despotic exercise of power

dessert *n* a usu sweet course or dish served at the end of a meal

dessertspoon *n* **1** a spoon intermediate in size between a teaspoon and a tablespoon and used for eating dessert **2** a dessertspoonful

dessertspoonful *n* **1** as much as a dessertspoon can hold

2 a unit of measure equal to about 8.9cm³ (about 2½ fluid drachms)

dessert wine *n* a usu sweet wine often served with dessert

destination *n* a place which is set for the end of a journey or to which sthg is sent

destine *vt* **1** to designate or dedicate in advance **2** to direct or set apart for a specified purpose or goal ⟨*freight* ∼d *for English ports*⟩ USE usu pass

destiny *n* **1** the power or agency held to determine the course of events **2** sthg to which a person or thing is destined; fortune **3** a predetermined course of events

destitute *adj* **1** lacking sthg necessary or desirable – + *of* ⟨*a heart* ∼ *of feeling*⟩ **2** lacking the basic necessities of life; extremely poor – **destitution** *n*

destroy *vt* **1** to demolish, ruin **2a** to put an end to; kill **b** to make ineffective; neutralize

destroyer *n* a fast multi-purpose warship smaller than a cruiser

destruction *n* **1** destroying or being destroyed **2** a cause of ruin or downfall·

destructive *adj* **1** causing destruction **2** designed or tending to destroy; negative ⟨∼ *criticism*⟩ – **destructively** *adv*, **destructiveness** *n*, **destructivity** *n*

desuetude *n* discontinuance from use; disuse – *fml*

desultory *adj* passing aimlessly from one subject or activity to another – **desultorily** *adv*, **desultoriness** *n*

detach *vt* **1** to separate, esp from a larger mass and usu without causing damage **2** to separate from a parent organization for a special purpose ⟨∼ *a ship from the fleet*⟩ – **detachable** *adj*, **detachably** *adv*, **detachability** *n*

detached *adj* **1** standing by itself; *specif* not sharing any wall with another building **2** free from prejudice or emotional involvement; aloof – **detachedly** *adv*

detachment *n* **1** a detaching, separation **2** *sing or pl in constr* a body of troops, ships, etc separated from the main body for a special mission **3** freedom from bias

¹detail *n* **1** extended treatment of or attention to particular items **2a** a small and subordinate part; *specif* part of a work of art considered or reproduced in isolation **b** a part considered separately from the whole **c** an individual relevant part or fact – usu *pl* ⟨*can you let me have the* ∼s *by tonight*⟩ **3a** *sing or pl in constr* a small military detachment selected for a particular task **b** the task to be performed by a military detail – **in detail** item by item; thoroughly

²detail *vt* **1** to report in detail **2** to assign to a particular task or place

detailed *adj* marked by abundant detail or thorough treatment

detain *vt* **1** to hold or retain (as if) in custody ⟨∼ed *in hospital overnight*⟩ **2** to delay; HOLD BACK 1

detainee *n* a person held in custody, esp for political reasons

detect *vt* to discover the existence or presence of – **detectable** *adj*, **detection** *n*, **detectability** *n*

¹detective *adj* **1** used in detecting sthg **2** of detectives or their work ⟨*a* ∼ *novel*⟩

²detective *n* a policeman or other person engaged in investigating crimes, detecting lawbreakers, or getting information that is not readily accessible

detector *n* an electrical circuit for separating an (audio) signal from a (radio) carrier

détente, detente *n* a relaxation of strained relations (e g between ideologically opposed nations)

detention *n* **1** detaining or being detained, esp in custody **2** *chiefly Br* the keeping in of a pupil after school hours as a punishment

deter *vt* **-rr-** to discourage or prevent from acting – **determent** *n*, **deterable** *adj*

detergent *n* a cleansing agent; *specif* any of various synthetic (water-soluble) compounds that are chemically different from soaps and are able to keep oils, dirt, etc in suspension and act as wetting agents

deteriorate *vb* to grow or make or worse – **deteriorative** *adj*, **deterioration** *n*

determinant *n* **1** sthg that determines, fixes, or conditions **2** an array of symbols or numbers written in the form of a square matrix bordered on either side by a vertical line; *also* a value assigned to a determinant obtained by manipulating its elements according to a certain rule **3** a gene

determination *n* **1** a judicial decision settling a controversy **2a** firm intention **b** the ability to make and act on firm decisions; resoluteness

determine *vt* **1a** to fix conclusively or authoritatively **b** to settle, decide ⟨~ *the rights and wrongs of a case*⟩ **2a** to fix beforehand **b** to regulate ⟨*demand* ~ *s the price*⟩ **3a** to ascertain the intent, nature, or scope of **b** to set an end to ⟨~ *an estate*⟩ ~ *vi* **1** to come to a decision **2** to come to an end or become void

determined *adj* **1** decided, resolved ⟨*was* ~ *to learn to drive*⟩ **2** firm, resolute ⟨*a very* ~ *woman*⟩ – **determinedly** *adv*, **determinedness** *n*

determiner *n* a word that limits the meaning of a noun and comes before a descriptive adjective modifying the same noun (e g *his* in 'his new car')

determinism *n* **1** a doctrine that all phenomena are determined by preceding occurrences; *esp* the doctrine that all human acts, choices, etc are causally determined and that free will is illusory **2** a belief in predestination – **determinist** *n* or *adj*, **deterministic** *adj*, **deterministically** *adv*

¹deterrent *adj* serving to deter – **deterrence** *n*, **deterrently** *adv*

²deterrent *n* sthg that deters; *esp* a (nuclear) weapon that is held in readiness by one nation or alliance in order to deter another from attacking

detest *vt* to feel intense dislike for; loathe – **detestable** *adj*, **detestably** *adv*

dethrone *vt* DEPOSE 1 – **dethronement** *n*

detonate *vb* to (cause to) explode with sudden violence ⟨~ *an atom bomb*⟩ – **detonatable** *adj*, **detonative** *adj*

detonation *n* **1** the action or process of detonating **2** premature combustion in an internal-combustion engine that results in knocking

detonator *n* **1** a device used for detonating a high explosive **2** a device, clipped on to a railway line, that detonates as a train passes to warn of esp fog or emergency

¹detour *n* a deviation from a course or procedure; *specif* a way that is an alternative to a shorter or planned route

²detour *vi* to make a detour ~ *vt* to send by a roundabout route

detract *vi* to take away sthg desirable – usu + *from*

detractor *n* one who denigrates sby or his/her ideas or beliefs ⟨*her* ~s *were more vociferous than her followers*⟩

detrain *vb* to alight or remove from a railway train – **detrainment** *n*

detriment *n* (a cause of) injury or damage

detrimental *adj* harmful, damaging – **detrimentally** *adv*

detritus *n, pl* **detritus 1** loose material (e g rock fragments or organic particles) produced by disintegration **2** debris caused by disintegration – **detrital** *adj*

de trop *adj* not wanted or needed; superfluous

deuce *n* **1** a playing card or the face of a dice representing the number 2 **2** a tie in a game (e g tennis) after which a side must score 2 consecutive clear points to win **3a** the devil, the dickens – formerly used as an interjection or intensive **b** sthg very bad or remarkable of its kind ⟨*a* ~ *of a mess*⟩

deuced *adj* damned, confounded – **deuced, deucedly** *adv*

Deuteronomy *n* the fifth book of the Old Testament containing Mosaic laws and narrative

devaluation *n* **1** a reduction in the exchange value of a currency **2** a lessening, esp of status or stature

devalue, devaluate *vt* **1** to reduce the exchange value of (money) **2** to lessen the value or reputation of ~ *vi* to institute devaluation

devastate *vt* **1** to reduce to ruin; lay waste **2** to have a shattering effect on; overwhelm ⟨*a devastating attack on his work*⟩ – **devastatingly** *adv*, **devastator** *n*, **devastation** *n*

develop *vt* **1a** to unfold gradually or in detail; expound **b** to show signs of ⟨~ *an illness*⟩ **c** to subject (exposed photograph material) esp to chemicals, in order to produce a visible image; *also* to make visible by such a method **d** to elaborate by the unfolding of a musical idea and by the working out of rhythmic and harmonic changes in the theme **2** to bring out the possibilities of **3a** to promote the growth of ⟨~ed *her muscles*⟩ **b** to make more available or usable ⟨~ *its resources*⟩ **c** to build on or change the use of (a tract of land) **d** to move (a chess piece) to a position providing more opportunity for effective use **4** to cause to grow, mature, or increase **5** to acquire gradually ⟨~ *a taste for good wine*⟩ ~ *vi* **1a** to go through a process of natural growth, differentiation, or evolution by successive changes **b** to evolve; *broadly* to grow **2** to become gradually visible or apparent **3** to develop one's pieces in chess – **developable** *adj*

developer *n* **1** a chemical used to develop exposed photographic materials **2** a person who develops real estate; *esp* sby who improves and subdivides land and builds and sells houses on it

development *n* **1** the act, process, or result of developing **2** being developed – **developmental** *adj*, **developmentally** *adv*

¹deviant *adj* **1** deviating, esp from a norm **2** characterized by deviation – **deviance** *n*, **deviancy** *n*

²deviant *n* a person whose behaviour differs markedly from the norm

¹deviate *vi* to stray, esp from a topic, principle, or accepted norm or from a straight course – **deviator** *n*, **deviatory** *adj*

²deviate *n, chiefly NAm* a deviant

deviation *n* **1** deflection of a compass needle caused by local magnetic influences **2** the difference between a value in a frequency distribution and a fixed number **3** departure from an established party line **4** departure from accepted norms of behaviour ⟨*sexual* ~⟩ – **deviationism** *n*, **deviationist** *n*

device *n* **1a** a scheme to trick or deceive **b** sthg elaborate or intricate in design **c** sthg (e g a figure of speech or a dramatic convention) designed to achieve a particular artistic effect **d** a piece of equipment or a mechanism designed for a special purpose or function **2** *pl* desire, will ⟨*left to her own* ~s⟩ **3a** an emblematic design used in a heraldic achievement **b** a motto

¹devil *n* **1** *often cap* the supreme spirit of evil in Jewish and Christian belief, the tempter of mankind, the leader of all apostate angels, and the ruler of hell **2** a malignant spirit; a demon **3** an extremely cruel or wicked person; a fiend **4** a high-spirited, reckless, or energetic person **5** a junior

legal counsel working without payment to gain experience
6a a person of the specified type ⟨*poor* ~⟩ ⟨*lucky* ~⟩ **b**
sthg provoking, difficult, or trying ⟨*this type of bottle is
the very* ~ *to open*⟩ **c** – used as an interjection or
intensive ⟨*what the* ~ *is that?*⟩ *USE* (6) infml
²**devil** *vb* -ll- (*NAm* -l-, -ll-), *vt* to season (food) highly, esp
with peppery condiments ⟨~ led *kidneys*⟩ ~ *vi* to serve or
function as a legal devil
devilish *adj* (characteristic) of a devil ⟨~ *tricks*⟩ –
devilishly *adv*
devil-may-care *adj* heedless of authority or convention
devilment *n* wild mischief
devil's advocate *n* **1** the Roman Catholic official who
presents the possible objections to claims to canonization
or to the title 'Blessed' **2** a person who champions the less
accepted or approved cause, esp for the sake of argument
devious *adj* **1** deviating from a fixed or straight course **2**
deviating from a right, accepted, or common course **3** not
straightforward or wholly sincere – **deviously** *adv*, **devi-
ousness** *n*
¹**devise** *vt* **1a** to formulate in the mind; invent **b** to plan,
plot **2** to give or leave (real property) by will – **devisable**
adj, **devisal** *n*, **diviser** *n*
²**devise** *n* **1** a devising act or clause **2** property devised by
will
devitalize, -ise *vt* to deprive of life, vigour, or effectiveness
devoid *adj* not having or using; lacking – + *of*
devolution *n* **1** the passage of rights, property, etc to a
successor **2** delegation or conferral to a subordinate **3** the
surrender of functions and powers to regional or local
authorities by a central government; *specif* such a surrender of powers to Scottish and Welsh authorities by the UK
government – **devolutionary** *adj*, **devolutionist** *n*
devolve *vt* **1** to transfer from one person to another; HAND
DOWN 1, 2 **2** to surrender by devolution ~ *vi* **1** to pass
by transmission or succession **2** to fall or be passed, usu
as an obligation or responsibility *USE* (*vi*) usu + *on* or
upon
devote *vt* **1** to set apart for a special purpose; dedicate *to*
2 to give (oneself) over wholly *to*
devoted *adj* loyally attached ⟨*a* ~ *friend*⟩ – **devotedly**
adv
devotee *n* **1** a deeply religious person **2** a keen follower
or supporter; an enthusiast ⟨*a* ~ *of opera*⟩
devotion *n* **1a** piety **b** a special act of prayer or supplication – usu pl **2a** devoting or being devoted **b** ardent love,
affection, or dedication – **devotional** *adj*, **devotionally**
adv
devour *vt* **1** to eat up greedily or ravenously **2** to swallow
up; consume ⟨~ ed *by fire*⟩ **3** to preoccupy, absorb ⟨~ ed
by guilt⟩ **4** to take in eagerly through the mind or senses
⟨~ s *books*⟩ – **devourer** *n*
devout *adj* **1** devoted to religion; pious **2** sincere, genuine
⟨*a* ~ *hope*⟩ – **devoutly** *adv*, **devoutness** *n*
dew *n* moisture that condenses on the surfaces of cool
bodies, esp at night
dewlap *n* a hanging fold of skin under the neck of an
animal (e g a cow) – **dewlapped** *adj*
dew pond *n* a shallow usu artificial pond thought to be
filled by the condensation of dew
dewy *adj* moist (as if) with dew – **dewily** *adv*, **dewi-
ness** *n*
dexterity *n* **1** skill and ease in using the hands **2** mental
quickness
dexterous, dextrous *adj* **1** skilful with the hands **2**
mentally adroit – **dexterously** *adv*
dextrose *n* dextrorotatory glucose

dhoti *n*, *pl* **dhotis** a loincloth worn by Hindu men
dhow *n* an Arab lateen-rigged boat, usu having a long
overhanging bow and a high poop
di- *comb form* **1** twice; twofold; double ⟨*dichromatic*⟩ **2**
containing 2 atoms, groups, or chemical equivalents in the
molecular structure ⟨*dichloride*⟩
dia- *also* **di-** *prefix* through ⟨*diapositive*⟩; across ⟨*diameter*⟩
diabetes *n* any of various abnormal conditions characterized by the secretion and excretion of excessive amounts
of urine; *specif* DIABETES MELLITUS
diabetes mellitus *n* a disorder of the process by which
the body uses sugars and other carbohydrates in which not
enough insulin is produced or the cells become resistant
to its action and which is characterized typically by
abnormally great amounts of sugar in the blood and
urine
¹**diabetic** *adj* **1** of diabetes or diabetics **2** affected with
diabetes
²**diabetic** *n* a person affected with diabetes
diabolic *adj* **1** (characteristic) of the devil; fiendish **2**
DIABOLICAL 2 – **diabolically** *adv*, **diabolicalness** *n*
diabolical *adj* **1** DIABOLIC 1 **2** *chiefly Br* dreadful, appalling ⟨*it's* ~ *the way he treats his wife*⟩ ⟨*that meal was* ~⟩
– infml
diacritic *n* a mark near or through an orthographic or
phonetic character or combination of characters indicating a changed phonetic value
diacritical *also* **diacritic** *adj* **1** serving as a diacritic **2**
serving to distinguish; distinctive
diadem *n* **1** a crown; *specif* a headband worn as a badge
of royalty **2** regal power or dignity
diaeresis, *chiefly NAm* **dieresis** *n*, *pl* **diaereses** **1** a mark
placed over a vowel to indicate pronunciation as a
separate syllable (e g in *naïve*) **2** the break in a verse
caused by the coincidence of the end of a foot with the end
of a word – **diaeretic** *adj*
diagnose *vt* to recognize (e g a disease) by signs and
symptoms – **diagnosable, diagnoseable** *adj*
diagnosis *n*, *pl* **diagnoses** **1** the art or act of identifying
a disease from its signs and symptoms **2** (a statement
resulting from) the investigation of the cause or nature of
a problem or phenomenon
¹**diagnostic** *also* **diagnostical** *adj* of or involving diagnosis
– **diagnostically** *adv*
²**diagnostic** *n* the art or practice of diagnosis – often pl
with sing. meaning – **diagnostician** *n*
¹**diagonal** *adj* **1** joining 2 nonadjacent angles of a polygon
or polyhedron **2** running in an oblique direction from a
reference line (e g the vertical) – **diagonalize** *vt*, **diagonally** *adv*
²**diagonal** *n* **1** a diagonal straight line or plane **2** a
diagonal direction **3** SOLIDUS 2
¹**diagram** *n* **1** a line drawing made for mathematical or
scientific purposes **2** a drawing or design that shows the
arrangement and relations (e g of parts) – **diagrammatic**
also **diagrammatical** *adj*, **diagrammatically** *adv*
²**diagram** *vt* -mm- (*NAm* -m-, -mm-) to represent in the
form of a diagram
¹**dial** *n* **1** a sundial **2** the graduated face of a timepiece **3a**
a face on which some measurement is registered, usu by
means of numbers and a pointer **b** a disc-shaped control
on an electrical or mechanical device ⟨*a telephone* ~⟩ **4**
Br a person's face – slang
²**dial** *vb* -ll- (*NAm* -l-, -ll-) *vt* to operate a dial so as to select
⟨~ led *the number*⟩ ~ *vi* **1** to manipulate a dial **2** to make
a call on a dial telephone
dialect *n* a regional, social, or subordinate variety of a

language, usu differing distinctively from the standard or original language – **dialectal** adj, **dialectally** adv
dialectic n **1a** development through the stages of thesis, antithesis, and synthesis in accordance with (systems derived from) Hegel's logic **b** the theoretical application of dialectical materialism, esp in Marxist investigation of economics and the social sciences **2** a systematic reasoning, exposition, or argument that juxtaposes opposed or contradictory ideas and usu seeks to resolve their conflict **3** the dialectical tension or opposition between 2 interacting forces or elements USE (1a&2) usu pl with sing. meaning but sing. or pl in constr
dialectical also **dialectic** adj **1** of or in accordance with dialectic **2** (characteristic) of a dialect – **dialectically** adv
dialectical materialism n the Marxist theory that the material basis of a reality constantly changes in a dialectical process that is independent of thought
dialectician n **1** one who is skilled in or practises dialectic **2** a student of dialects
dialogue, NAm also **dialog** n **1** a literary work in conversational form **2a** a conversation between 2 or more people or between a person and sthg else (e g a computer) **b** an exchange of ideas and opinions **3** the conversational element of literary or dramatic composition **4** discussion or negotiation between 2 nations, factions, groups, etc with conflicting interests ⟨the continuing governmental policy of ~ between East and West⟩
diameter n **1** a line passing through the centre of a geometrical figure or body **2** the length of a straight line through the centre of an object (e g a circle) – **diametral** adj
diametric, diametrical adj **1** of or constituting a diameter **2** completely opposed or opposite – **diametrically** adv
¹diamond n **1a** (piece of) very hard crystalline carbon that is highly valued as a precious stone, esp when flawless and transparent, and is used industrially as an abrasive and in rock drills **2** a square or rhombus orientated so that the diagonals are horizontal and vertical **3a** a playing card marked with 1 or more red diamond-shaped figures **b** pl but sing or pl in constr the suit comprising cards identified by this figure **4** the entire playing field or the area enclosed by the bases in baseball – **diamondiferous** adj
²diamond adj of, marking, or being a 60th or 75th anniversary ⟨~ wedding⟩
¹diaper n **1** a soft usu white linen or cotton fabric used for tablecloths or towels **2** an ornamental pattern consisting of one or more small repeated units of design (e g geometric figures) **3** chiefly NAm a nappy
²diaper vt to ornament with diaper designs
diaphanous adj so fine as to be almost transparent – **diaphanously** adv, **diaphanousness** n
diaphragm n **1** the partition separating the chest and abdominal cavities in mammals **2** a dividing membrane or thin partition, esp in a tube **3** a partition in a plant or the body or shell of an invertebrate animal **4** a device that limits the aperture of a lens or optical system **5** a thin flexible disc that is free to vibrate (e g in an earphone) **6** DUTCH CAP – **diaphragmatic** adj, **diaphragmatically** adv
diarist n one who keeps a diary
diarrhoea, NAm chiefly **diarrhea** n abnormally frequent intestinal evacuations with more or less fluid faeces – **diarrhoeal, diarrhoeic** also **diarrhoetic** adj
diary n **1** (a book containing) a daily record of personal experiences or observations **2** chiefly Br a book with dates marked in which memoranda can be noted
Diaspora n **1** the settling, or area of settlement, of Jews outside Palestine after the Babylonian exile **2** sing or pl

in constr the Jews living outside Palestine or modern Israel
diatom n any of a class of minute single-celled algae with hard shell-like skeletons that are composed of silica – **diatomaceous** adj
diatonic adj relating to a major or minor musical scale of 8 notes to the octave without chromatic deviation – **diatonically** adv
diatribe n a (lengthy) piece of bitter and abusive criticism
¹dibble n a small pointed hand implement used to make holes in the ground for plants, seeds, or bulbs
²dibble vt **1** to plant with a dibble **2** to make holes in (soil) (as if) with a dibble
¹dice n, pl **dice 1a** a small cube that is marked on each face with from 1 to 6 spots so that spots on opposite faces total 7 and that is used to determine arbitrary values in various games **b** a gambling game played with dice **2** a small cubical piece (e g of food) – **no dice** of no avail; no use – infml
²dice vt **1a** to cut (e g food) into small cubes **b** to ornament with square markings **2** to gamble using dice ⟨~ his money away⟩ ~ vi **1** to play games with dice **2** to take a chance ⟨~ with death⟩ – **dicer** n
dicey adj risky, unpredictable – infml
dichotomy n **1** a division into 2 esp mutually exclusive or contradictory groups **2** a (repeated) branching (into 2 branches)
dick n **1** chiefly Br a person ⟨clever ~⟩ **2** a detective **3** the penis – vulg USE (1&2) infml
dickens n devil, deuce – used as an interjection or intensive
dicker vi **1** to bargain, haggle **2** to hesitate, dither
dickeybird n **1** a small bird – used by or to children **2** so much as a single word ⟨never said a ~⟩ – infml
dicky adj, Br in a weak or unsound condition – infml ⟨~ heart⟩
Dictaphone trademark – used for a dictating machine
¹dictate vi **1** to give dictation **2** to speak or act with authority; prescribe ~ vt **1** to speak or read for a person to transcribe or for a machine to record **2** to impose, pronounce, or specify with authority
²dictate n **1** an authoritative rule, prescription, or command **2** a ruling principle – usu pl ⟨according to the ~s of his conscience⟩
dictation n **1** PRESCRIPTION **2** **2a** the act or manner of uttering words to be transcribed **b** material that is dictated or transcribed
dictator n **1** a person granted absolute emergency power, esp in ancient Rome **2** an absolute ruler; esp one who has seized power unconstitutionally and uses it oppressively
dictatorial adj **1** of a dictator **2** arrogantly domineering – **dictatorially** adv, **dictatorialness** n
dictatorship n **1** the office of dictator **2** total or absolute control; leadership, rule **3** a state or form of government where absolute power is concentrated in one person or a small clique
diction n **1** choice of words, esp with regard to correctness or clearness **2** pronunciation and enunciation of words in speaking or singing – **dictional** adj, **dictionally** adv
dictionary n **1** a reference book containing words, terms, or names, usu alphabetically arranged, together with information about them, esp their forms, pronunciations, functions, etymologies, meanings, syntactic and idiomatic uses, and applications **2** a reference book giving for words of one language equivalents in another **3** a list (e g of synonyms or hyphenation instructions) stored in machine-readable form (e g on a computer disk) for refer-

ence by an automatic system (e g for computerized type-setting)

dictum *n*, *pl* **dicta** *also* **dictums** 1 an authoritative statement on some topic; a pronouncement 2 OBITER DICTUM 1

did *past of* DO

didactic *adj* 1 intended to teach sthg, esp a moral lesson 2 having a tendency to teach in an authoritarian manner – **didactically** *adv*, **didacticism** *n*

diddle *vt* diddling to cheat, swindle – infml – **diddler** *n*

didn't did not

didst *archaic past 2 sing of* DO

¹**die** *vi* dying 1 to stop living; suffer the end of physical life 2 to pass out of existence, cease ⟨*his anger* ~d *at these words*⟩ 3 to long keenly or desperately ⟨*dying to go*⟩ 4 to stop ⟨*the motor* ~d⟩

²**die** *n*, *pl* (*1*) **dice**, (*2&3*) **dies** 1 a dice 2 DADO 1 3 any of various tools or devices for giving a desired shape, form, or finish to a material or for impressing an object or material – **the dice are loaded** all the elements of a situation are combined to work – usu + *against* or *in favour of* ⟨*I will never get the job,* the dice are loaded *in favour of him*⟩ – **the die is cast** the irrevocable decision or step has been taken

die down *vi* 1 *of a plant* to undergo death of the parts lying above ground 2 to diminish, subside

die-hard *n or adj* (one) strongly resisting change – **die-hardism** *n*

die out *vi* to become extinct

dieresis *n*, *chiefly NAm* a diaeresis

diesel *n* 1 (a vehicle driven by) a diesel engine 2 **diesel, diesel oil** a heavy mineral oil used as fuel in diesel engines

diesel engine *n* an internal-combustion engine in which fuel is ignited by air compressed to a sufficiently high temperature

¹**diet** *n* 1 the food and drink habitually taken by a group, animal, or individual 2 the kind and amount of food prescribed for a person or animal for a special purpose (e g losing weight)

²**diet** *vb* to (cause to) eat and drink sparingly or according to prescribed rules – **dieter** *n*

³**diet** *n* any of various national or provincial legislatures

¹**dietary** *n* the kinds and amounts of food available to or eaten by an individual, group, or population

²**dietary** *adj* of (the rules of) a diet – **dietarily** *adv*

dietetic *adj* 1 of diet 2 adapted for use in special diets – **dietetically** *adv*

dietetics *n pl but sing or pl in constr* the application of the principles of nutrition to feeding

dietitian, dietician *n* a specialist in dietetics

differ *vi* 1a to be unlike; be distinct *from* b to change from time to time; vary 2 to disagree ⟨*people who* ~ *on religious matters*⟩

difference *n* 1a unlikeness between 2 or more people or things b the degree or amount by which things differ 2 a disagreement, dispute; dissension ⟨*unable to settle their* ~s⟩ 3 the degree or amount by which things differ in quantity or measure; *specif* REMAINDER 2b(1) 4 a significant change in or effect on a situation

different *adj* 1 partly or totally unlike; dissimilar – + *from*, chiefly Br *to*, or chiefly NAm *than* 2a distinct b various c another 3 unusual, special – **differently** *adv*, **differentness** *n*

¹**differential** *adj* 1a of or constituting a difference b based on or resulting from a differential ⟨~ *freight charges*⟩ c functioning or proceeding differently or at a different rate 2 of or involving a differential or differentiation 3 of quantitative differences – **differentially** *adv*

²**differential** *n* 1 the product of the derivative of a function of one variable with the increment of the independent variable ⟨*for a function* f(x) *the* ~ *is* f(x)dx⟩ 2 the amount of a difference between comparable individuals or classes; *specif* the amount by which the remuneration of distinct types of worker differs 3 (a case covering) a differential gear

differential calculus *n* a branch of mathematics dealing chiefly with the rate of change of functions with respect to their variables

differential gear *n* an arrangement of gears in a vehicle that allows one of the wheels imparting motion to turn (e g in going round a corner) faster than the other

differentiate *vt* 1 to obtain the mathematical derivative of 2 to mark or show a difference in 3 to cause differentiation of in the course of development 4 to express the specific difference of ~ *vi* 1 to recognize a difference *between* 2 to become distinct or different in character 3 to undergo differentiation – **differentiability** *n*, **differentiable** *adj*

differentiation *n* 1 development into more complex, numerous, or varied forms 2a modification of body parts for performance of particular functions b all the processes whereby apparently similar cells, tissues, and structures attain their adult forms and functions

difficult *adj* 1 hard to do, make, carry out, or understand ⟨*a* ~ *climb*⟩⟨*a* ~ *text*⟩ 2a hard to deal with, manage, or please ⟨*a* ~ *child*⟩ b puzzling – **difficultly** *adv*

difficulty *n* 1 being difficult 2 an obstacle or impediment 3 a cause of (financial) trouble or embarrassment – usu pl with sing. meaning

diffident *adj* 1 lacking in self-confidence 2 reserved, unassertive – **diffidently** *adv*, **diffidence** *n*

diffract *vt* to cause (a beam of light) to become a set of light and dark or coloured bands in passing by the edge of an opaque body, through narrow slits, etc – **diffraction** *n*

¹**diffuse** *adj* 1 not concentrated or localized; scattered 2 lacking conciseness; verbose – **diffusely** *adv*, **diffuseness** *n*

²**diffuse** *vt* 1 to spread out freely in all directions 2 to break up and distribute (incident light) by reflection ~ *vi* 1 to spread out or become transmitted 2 to undergo diffusion – **diffuser** *n*, **diffusible** *adj*, **diffusive** *adj*

diffusion *n* 1 diffusing or being diffused 2 being long-winded 3a the process whereby particles of liquids, gases, or solids intermingle as the result of their spontaneous movement b reflection of light by a rough reflecting surface – **diffusional** *adj*

¹**dig** *vb* **-gg-; dug** *vi* 1 to turn up, loosen, or remove earth 2 to understand ~ *vt* 1 to break up, turn, or loosen (earth) with an implement 2 to bring to the surface (as if) by digging; unearth 3 to hollow out by removing earth; excavate ⟨~ *a hole*⟩ 4 to drive down into; thrust 5 to poke, prod ⟨~ *him in the ribs*⟩ 6a to pay attention to; notice b to understand, appreciate USE (*vi 2*; *vt 6*) slang

²**dig** *n* 1a a thrust, poke b a cutting or snide remark 2 an archaeological excavation (site) 3 *pl*, *chiefly Br* LODGING 2b

¹**digest** *n* 1 a systematic compilation of laws 2 a literary abridgment

²**digest** *vt* 1 to distribute or arrange systematically 2 to convert (food) into a form the body can use 3 to assimilate mentally 4 to soften or decompose or extract soluble ingredients from by heat and moisture or chemicals 5 to compress into a short summary ~ *vi* to become digested – **digester** *n*, **digestible** *adj*, **digestibility** *n*

digestion *n* the process or power of digesting sthg, esp food

¹digestive *n* sthg that aids digestion

²digestive *adj* of, causing, or promoting digestion – **digestively** *adv*, **digestiveness** *n*

digger *n* 1 a tool or machine for digging 2 a private soldier from Australia or New Zealand, esp in WW I – *infml*

diggings *n pl* 1 material dug out 2 a place of excavating, esp for ore, metals, or precious stones

dig in *vt* to incorporate by burying in the soil ~ *vi* 1 to dig defensive positions 2 to hold stubbornly to a position; defend doggedly (e g when batting in cricket) 3 to begin eating – *infml* – **dig one's heels in** to refuse to move or change one's mind; be stubborn

digit *n* 1a any of the Arabic numerals from 1 to 9, usu also including 0 b any of the elements that combine to form numbers in a system other than the decimal system 2 a finger or toe 3 a unit of measurement equal to ¾ in (about 1.9cm)

digital *adj* 1 of or with the fingers or toes 2 of calculation by numerical methods which use discrete units 3 of data in the form of numerical digits 4 *of an automatic device* presenting information in the form of numerical digits – **digitally** *adv*

digital computer *n* a computer that operates with numbers expressed as discrete pulses representing digits

dignified *adj* showing or having dignity

dignify *vt* to confer dignity or distinction on

dignitary *n* a person of high rank or holding a position of dignity or honour – **dignitary** *adj*

dignity *n* 1 being worthy, honoured, or esteemed 2 high rank, office, or position 3 stillness of manner; gravity

dig out *vt* to find, unearth

digraph *n* a group of 2 successive letters, esp whose phonetic value is a single sound – **digraphic** *adj*, **digraphically** *adv*

digress *vi* to turn aside, esp from the main subject in writing or speaking – **digressive** *adj*, **digressively** *adv*, **digressiveness** *n*

digression *n* (an instance of) digressing – **digressional** *adj*, **digressionary** *adj*

¹dike *vb or n* (to) dyke

²dike *n* a lesbian – *derog*

dilapidated *adj* decayed or fallen into partial ruin, esp through neglect or misuse – **dilapidation** *n*

dilate *vt* to distend ~ *vi* 1 to comment at length *on* or *upon* 2 to become wide – **dilatable** *adj*, **dilator** *n*, **dilative** *adj*, **dilatability** *n*

dilatory *adj* 1 tending or intended to cause delay 2 slow, tardy – **dilatorily** *adv*, **dilatoriness** *n*

dildo *n*, *pl* **dildos** an object serving as an artificial penis for inserting into the vagina

dilemma *n* 1 an argument in which an opponent's position is refuted by being shown to lead to 2 or more unacceptable alternatives 2 a situation involving choice between 2 equally unsatisfactory alternatives – **dilemmatic** *adj*

dilettante *n*, *pl* **dilettanti dilettantes** a person with a superficial interest in an art or a branch of knowledge – **dilettante** *adj*, **dilettantish** *adj*, **dilettantism** *n*

diligence *n* steady application and effort

diligent *adj* showing steady application and effort – **diligently** *adv*

dill *n* a European plant with aromatic foliage and seeds, both of which are used in flavouring foods (e g pickles)

dillydally *vi* to waste time by loitering; dawdle – *infml*

¹dilute *vt* 1 to make thinner or more liquid by adding another liquid 2 to diminish the strength or brilliance of by adding more liquid, light, etc 3 to attenuate – **diluter**, **dilutor** *n*, **dilutive** *adj*, **dilution** *n*

²dilute *adj* weak, diluted – **diluteness** *n*

¹dim *adj* -mm- 1 giving out a weak or insufficient light 2a seen indistinctly ⟨a ~ *shape loomed out of the fog*⟩ b characterized by an unfavourable or pessimistic attitude – esp in *take a dim view of* 3 not seeing clearly ⟨*the old man's eyes were* ~⟩ 4 lacking intelligence; stupid – *infml* – **dimly** *adv*, **dimness** *n*

²dim *vb* -mm- *vt* 1 to make dim 2 *NAm* DIP 4 ~ *vi* to become dim

dime *n* a coin worth ¹/₁₀ of a US dollar

¹dimension *n* 1a(1) extension in 1 direction (2) any of a group of parameters necessary and sufficient to determine uniquely each element of a system of usu mathematical entities ⟨*the surface of a sphere has 2* ~ s⟩ b the size of extension in 1 or all directions c the range over which sthg extends; the scope – usu pl with sing. meaning d an aspect ⟨*gave a whole new* ~ *to the problem*⟩ 2 any of the fundamental quantities, specif mass, length, and time, which combine to make a derived unit – usu pl ⟨*velocity has the* ~ s *of length divided by time*⟩ – **dimensional** *adj*, **dimensionally** *adv*, **dimensionless** *adj*, **dimensionality** *n*

²dimension *vt* to indicate the dimensions on (a drawing)

diminish *vt* 1 to make or cause to appear less 2 to lessen the reputation of; belittle ~ *vi* to become gradually less; dwindle – **diminishable** *adj*, **diminishment** *n*

diminuendo *n*, *adv*, *or adj*, *pl* **diminuendos** (a musical passage played) with a decrease in volume

diminution *n* a diminishing or decrease – **diminutional** *adj*

¹diminutive *n* a diminutive word, affix, or name

²diminutive *adj* 1 indicating small size and sometimes lovableness or triviality – used in connection with affixes and words formed with them (e g *duckling*), with clipped forms (e g *Jim*), and with altered forms (e g *Peggy*) 2 exceptionally small; tiny – **diminutively** *adv*, **diminutiveness** *n*

dimity *n* a corded cotton fabric woven with checks or stripes

¹dimple *n* 1 a slight natural indentation in the cheek or another part of the human body 2 a depression or indentation on a surface – **dimply** *adj*

²dimple *vb* to mark with or form dimples

dimwit *n* a stupid or mentally slow person – *infml* – **dim-witted** *adj*, **dim-wittedly** *adv*, **dim-wittedness** *n*

¹din *n* a loud continued discordant noise

²din *vi* -nn- to make a din ⟨*the music* ~ned *in their ears*⟩ – **din into** to instil into by perpetual repetition

dinar *n* (a coin or note representing) a money unit of certain Arab countries and Yugoslavia

dine *vi* to eat dinner ~ *vt* to entertain to dinner ⟨*wined and* ~ d *us splendidly*⟩ – **dine off/on/upon** to eat (sthg) as one's meal, esp one's dinner

diner *n* 1 sby who is dining 2a *NAm* a small restaurant, often beside the road b *chiefly NAm* DINING CAR

¹dingdong *n* 1 the ringing sound produced by repeated strokes, esp on a bell 2 a rapid heated exchange of words or blows – *infml*

²dingdong *adj* 1 of or resembling the sound of a bell 2 with the advantage (e g in an argument or race) passing continually back and forth from one participant, side, etc to the other – *infml*

dinghy *n* 1 a small boat often carried on a ship and used esp as a lifeboat or to transport passengers to and from shore 2 a small open sailing boat 3 a rubber life raft

dingle *n* a small narrow wooded valley

dingo *n*, *pl* **dingoes** a wild dog of Australia

dingy *adj* **1** dirty, discoloured **2** shabby, squalid – **dingily** *adv*, **dinginess** *n*

dining car *n* a railway carriage where meals are served

dining room *n* a room set aside for eating meals in

dinkum *adj*, *Austr* real, genuine – *infml*

dinky *adj* **1** *chiefly Br* neat and dainty **2** *chiefly NAm* small, insignificant *USE infml*

dinner *n* **1** (the food eaten for) the principal meal of the day taken either in the evening or at midday **2** a formal evening meal or banquet

dinner jacket *n* a usu black jacket for men's semiformal evening wear

dinosaur *n* **1** any of a group of extinct, typically very large flesh- or plant-eating reptiles, most of which lived on the land; *broadly* any large extinct reptile **2** an organization or institution that is unwieldy and outdated ⟨*Britain's industrial* ~s⟩ – **dinosaurian** *adj or n*, **dinosauric** *adj*

dint *n* – **by dint of** by means or application of

diocese *n* the area under the jurisdiction of a bishop – **diocesan** *adj*

dioxide *n* an oxide containing 2 atoms of oxygen

¹dip *vb* **-pp-** *vt* **1a** to plunge or immerse in a liquid (e g in order to moisten or dye) **b** to immerse (e g a sheep) in an antiseptic or parasite-killing solution **2** to lift up (water, grain.etc) by scooping or ladling **3** to lower and then raise again ⟨~ *a flag in salute*⟩ **4** to lower (the beam of a vehicle's headlights) so as to reduce glare ~ *vi* **1a** to plunge into a liquid and quickly emerge **b** to immerse sthg in a processing liquid or finishing material **2** to drop down or decrease suddenly **3** to reach inside or below sthg, esp so as to take out part of the contents – usu + *in* or *into* **4** to incline downwards from the plane of the horizon – **dip into 1** to make inroads into for funds ⟨dipped into *the family's savings*⟩ **2** to read superficially or in a random manner ⟨dipped into *a book while he was waiting*⟩

²dip *n* **1** a brief bathe for sport or exercise **2a** a sharp downward course; a drop **b** the angle that a stratum or similar geological feature makes with a horizontal plane **3** the angle formed with the horizon by a magnetic needle rotating in the vertical plane **4** a hollow, depression **5a** a sauce or soft mixture into which food is dipped before being eaten **b** a liquid preparation into which an object or animal may be dipped (e g for cleaning or disinfecting) **6** a pickpocket – *slang*

diphtheria *n* an acute infectious disease caused by a bacterium and marked by fever and the formation of a false membrane, esp in the throat, causing difficulty in breathing – **diphtherial, diphtherian** *adj*, **diphtheritic** *adj*, **diphtheroid** *adj*

diphthong *n* **1** a gliding monosyllabic vowel sound (e g /oy/ in toy) that starts at or near the articulatory position for one vowel and moves to or towards the position of another **2** a digraph **3** either of the ligatures K or – **diphthongal** *adj*

diploma *n* **1** an official or state document **2** a document conferring some honour or privilege **3** (a certificate of) a qualification, usu in a more specialized subject or at a lower level than a degree

diplomacy *n* **1** the art and practice of conducting international relations **2** skill and tact in handling affairs

diplomat *n* **1** one (e g an ambassador) employed in diplomacy **2** one skilled in dealing with people tactfully and adroitly

diplomatic *adj* **1** exactly reproducing the original ⟨*a ~ edition*⟩ **2** of diplomats or international relations **3** employing tact and conciliation – **diplomatically** *adv*

diplomatist *n* a person skilled or employed in diplomacy

dipper *n* **1** sthg (e g a long-handled cup) used for dipping **2** any of several diving birds **3** *cap*, *chiefly NAm* **a** Dipper, Big Dipper URSA MAJOR **b** URSA MINOR

dipsomania *n* an uncontrollable craving for alcoholic drinks – **dipsomaniac** *n*, **dipsomaniacal** *adj*

dipstick *n* a graduated rod for measuring the depth of a liquid (e g the oil in a car's engine)

diptych *n* **1** a 2-leaved hinged writing tablet **2** a painting or carving done on 2 hinged panels and used esp as an altarpiece

dire *adj* **1** dreadful, awful **2** warning of disaster; ominous ⟨*a ~ forecast*⟩ **3** desperately urgent ⟨~ *need*⟩ – **direly** *adv*, **direness** *n*

¹direct *vt* **1a** to mark (e g a letter or parcel) with a name and address **b** to address or aim (e g a remark) **2** to cause to turn, move, point, or follow a straight course ⟨~ed *her eyes heavenward*⟩ **3** to show or point out the way for **4a** to control and regulate the activities or course of **b** to control the organization and performance of; supervise ⟨~ed *the latest science fiction film*⟩ **c** to order or instruct with authority ⟨*police* ~ed *the crowd to move back*⟩ **d** to train and usu lead performances of; *specif, chiefly NAm* to conduct ⟨~ed *the orchestra in a new work*⟩ ~ *vi* to act as director

²direct *adj* **1a** going from one point to another in time or space without deviation or interruption; straight **b** going by the shortest way ⟨*the ~ route*⟩ **2a** stemming immediately from a source, cause, or reason ⟨~ *result*⟩ **b** passing in a straight line of descent from parent to offspring ⟨~ *ancestor*⟩ **3** frank, straightforward **4a** operating without an intervening agency **b** effected by the action of the people or the electorate and not by representatives **5** consisting of or reproducing the exact words of a speaker or writer ⟨~ *speech*⟩ **6** diametric, exact ⟨*was a ~ contradiction of all he'd said before*⟩ **7** of a celestial body moving in the general planetary direction from W to E; not retrograde – **directness** *n*

³direct *adv* **1** from point to point without deviation; by the shortest way ⟨*write to him* ~⟩ **2** without an intervening agency or stage

direct action *n* action that seeks to achieve an end by the most immediately effective means (e g boycott or strike)

direct current *n* an electric current flowing in 1 direction only; *esp* such a current that is substantially constant in value

direction *n* **1** guidance or supervision of action **2a** the act, art, or technique of directing an orchestra, film, or theatrical production **b** a word, phrase, or sign indicating the appropriate tempo, mood, or intensity of a passage or movement in music **3** *pl* explicit instructions on how to do sthg or get to a place ⟨*read the* ~s *on the packet*⟩ ⟨*asked for* ~s *to King's Cross*⟩ **4a** the line or course along which sby or sthg moves or is aimed ⟨*drove off in the* ~ *of London*⟩ **b** the point towards which sby or sthg faces ⟨*which* ~ *does this house face?*⟩ **5a** a tendency, trend **b** a guiding or motivating purpose ⟨*had a new sense of* ~⟩

directional *adj* **1** of or indicating direction in space: e g **a** suitable for detecting the direction from which radio signals come, or for sending out signals in 1 direction only ⟨*a ~ aerial*⟩ **b** of or being a device that operates more efficiently in one direction than in others **2** relating to direction or guidance, esp of thought or effort – **directionality** *n*

direction finder *n* an aerial used to determine the direction of incoming radio waves

¹directive *adj* **1** serving to direct, guide, or influence **2** serving to provide a direction

²**directive** *n* an authoritative instruction issued by a high-level body or official

¹**directly** *adv* **1** in a direct manner **2a** without delay; immediately **b** soon, shortly

²**directly** *conj, chiefly Br* immediately after; as soon as – *infml*

direct object *n* a grammatical object representing the primary goal or the result of the action of its verb (e g *me* in 'he hit me' and *house* in 'we built a house')

director *n* **1** the head of an organized group or administrative unit **2** a member of a governing board entrusted with the overall direction of a company **3** sby who has responsibility for supervising the artistic and technical aspects of a film or play – **directorship** *n*, **directorial** *adj*

directorate *n* **1** the office of director **2** a board of directors (e g of a company)

directory *n* **1** a book or collection of directions or rules, esp concerning forms of worship **2** an alphabetical or classified list (e g of names, addresses, telephone numbers, etc)

direct tax *n* a tax (e g income tax) exacted directly from the person, organization, etc on whom it is levied

dirge *n* **1** a song or hymn of grief or lamentation, esp intended to accompany funeral or memorial rites **2** a slow mournful piece of music

¹**dirigible** *adj* capable of being steered

²**dirigible** *n* an airship

dirk *n* a long straight-bladed dagger, used esp by Scottish Highlanders

dirndl *n* a full skirt with a tight waistband

dirt *n* **1a** excrement **b** a filthy or soiling substance (e g mud or grime) **c** sby or sthg worthless or contemptible **2** ³SOIL **2a 3a** obscene or pornographic speech or writing **b** scandalous or malicious gossip

¹**dirty** *adj* **1a** not clean or pure; marked or contaminated with dirt **b** causing sby or sthg to become soiled or covered with dirt ⟨~ *jobs*⟩ **2a** base, sordid ⟨*war is a* ~ *business*⟩ **b** unsportsmanlike, unfair ⟨~ *players*⟩ **c** low, despicable ⟨~ *tricks*⟩ **3a** indecent, obscene ⟨~ *language*⟩ **b** sexually illicit ⟨*a* ~ *weekend*⟩ **4** of weather rough, stormy **5** *of colour* not clear and bright; dull ⟨*drab dirty-pink walls*⟩ **6** conveying resentment or disgust ⟨*gave him a* ~ *look*⟩ **7** producing considerable fallout ⟨~ *bombs*⟩ – **dirtily** *adv*, **dirtiness** *n*

²**dirty** *vb* to make or become dirty

dis- *prefix* **1a** do the opposite of (a specified action) ⟨*disestablish*⟩⟨*disappear*⟩ **b** deprive of, remove (sthg specified) from ⟨*disarm*⟩⟨*dismember*⟩ **c** exclude or expel from ⟨*disbar*⟩ **2** opposite or absence of ⟨*disarray*⟩⟨*disbelief*⟩ **3** not ⟨*disagreeable*⟩⟨*dishonest*⟩ **4** completely ⟨*disannul*⟩⟨*disgruntled*⟩ **5** dys- ⟨*disfunction*⟩

disability *n* **1a** the condition of being disabled; *specif* inability to do sthg (e g pursue an occupation) because of physical or mental impairment **b** sthg that disables; a handicap **2** a legal disqualification

disable *vt* **1** to deprive of legal right, qualification, or capacity **2** to make incapable or ineffective; *esp* to deprive of physical soundness; cripple – **disablement** *n*

disabuse *vt* to free from a mistaken impression or judgment

¹**disadvantage** *n* **1** loss or damage, esp to reputation or finances **2a** an unfavourable, inferior, or prejudicial situation ⟨*we were at a* ~⟩ **b** sby or sthg which causes one to be in an unfavourable condition or position; a handicap ⟨*her poor health is a great* ~ *to her*⟩

²**disadvantage** *vt* to place at a disadvantage

disadvantageous *adj* **1** prejudicial, unfavourable **2** derogatory, disparaging – **disadvantageously** *adv*, **disadvantageousness** *n*

disaffect *vt* to alienate the affection or loyalty of – **disaffection** *n*

disaffected *adj* discontented and resentful, esp towards authority

disaffiliate *vb* to end, or separate from, an affiliation or connection – **disaffiliation** *n*

disagree *vi* **1** to be unlike or at variance **2** to differ in opinion – usu + *with* **3** to have a bad effect – usu + *with* ⟨*fried foods* ~ *with me*⟩

disagreeable *adj* **1** unpleasant, objectionable **2** peevish, ill-tempered – **disagreeableness** *n*, **disagreeably** *adv*, **disagreeability** *n*

disagreement *n* **1** a lack of correspondence; a disparity **2** a difference of opinion; an argument

disallow *vt* to refuse to admit or recognize – **disallowance** *n*

disappear *vi* **1** to pass from view suddenly or gradually **2** to cease to be or to be known **3** to leave or depart, esp secretly – *infml* – **disappearance** *n*

disappoint *vt* to fail to meet the expectation or hope of; *also* to sadden by so doing – **disappointing** *adj*, **disappointingly** *adv*

disappointed *adj* defeated in expectation or hope; thwarted – **disappointedly** *adv*

disappointment *n* **1** disappointing or being disappointed **2** sby or sthg that disappoints

disapprobation *n* disapproval – *fml*

disapproval *n* unfavourable opinion; censure

disapprove *vt* to refuse approval to; reject – *vi* to have or express an unfavourable opinion *of* – **disapprover** *n*, **disapprovingly** *adv*

disarm *vt* **1a** to deprive of a weapon or weapons **b** to deprive of a means of attack or defence **c** to make (e g a bomb) harmless, esp by removing a fuse or warhead **2** to dispel the hostility or suspicion of – *vi* **1** to lay aside arms **2** to reduce or abolish weapons and armed forces – **disarmament** *n*

disarrange *vt* to disturb the arrangement or order of – **disarrangement** *n*

¹**disarray** *n* a lack of order or sequence; disorder

²**disarray** *vt* to throw or place into disorder

disassociate *vt* to dissociate – **disassociation** *n*

disaster *n* **1** a sudden event bringing great damage, loss, or destruction; *broadly* an unfortunate occurrence **2** a failure ⟨*was a complete* ~ *as a teacher*⟩ – *infml* – **disastrous** *adj*, **disastrously** *adv*

disavow *vt* to deny knowledge of or responsibility for; repudiate – *fml* – **disavowal** *n*

disband *vb* to (cause to) break up and separate; disperse – **disbandment** *n*

disbar *vt* to deprive (a barrister) of the right to practise; expel from the bar – **disbarment** *n*

disbelief *n* mental rejection of sthg as untrue

disbelieve *vb* to reject or withhold belief (in) – **disbeliever** *n*

disburden *vt* to unburden – **disburdenment** *n*

disburse *vt* **1** to pay out, esp from a fund **2** to make a payment in settlement of; defray – *fml* – **disbursement** *n*, **disburser** *n*

disc, *NAm chiefly* **disk** *n* **1a** a thin flat circular object **b** an apparently flat figure or surface (e g of a planet) ⟨*the solar* ~⟩ **2** any of various round flat anatomical structures; *esp* any of the cartilaginous discs between the spinal vertebrae ⟨*suffering from a slipped* ~⟩ **3** a gramophone record **4** DISK **1a 5** any of the sharp-edged concave circular cutting blades of a harrow

¹**discard** *vt* **1a** to throw out (a playing card) from one's

hand **b** to play (any card from a suit different from the one led except a trump) when unable to follow suit **2** to get rid of as useless or superfluous ~*vi* to discard a playing card

²**discard** *n* **1** the act of discarding in a card game **2** sby or sthg discarded; *esp* a discarded card

disc brake *n* a brake that operates by the friction of a calliper pressing against the sides of a rotating disc

discern *vt* **1** to detect with one of the senses, esp vision **2** to perceive or recognize mentally – **discerner** *n*, **discernible** *also* **discernable** *adj*, **discernibly** *adv*

discerning *adj* showing insight and understanding; discriminating – **discerningly** *adv*

discernment *n* skill in discerning; keen insight

¹**discharge** *vt* **1a** to unload **b** to release from an obligation **2a** to shoot ⟨~ *a gun*⟩ **b** to release from custody or care **c** to send or pour out; emit **3a** to dismiss from employment or service **b** to fulfil (e g a debt or obligation) by performing an appropriate action **c** to annul legally **4** to remove an electric charge from or reduce the electric charge of ~*vi* **1** to throw off or deliver a load, charge, or burden **2a** *of a gun* to be fired **b** to pour out (fluid) contents **3** to lose or reduce an electric charge – **dischargeable** *adj*, **dischargee** *n*, **discharger** *n*

²**discharge** *n* **1a** the relieving of an obligation, accusation, or penalty **b** a certificate of release or payment **2** the act of discharging or unloading **3a** legal release from confinement **b** an acquittal **4** the act or an instance of firing a missile or missiles ⟨*an artillery* ~⟩ **5a** a flowing or pouring out **b** sthg that is discharged or emitted ⟨*a purulent* ~⟩ **6** release or dismissal, esp from an office or employment **7a** a usu brief flow of an electric charge through a gas, usu with associated light emission **b** the conversion of the chemical energy of a battery into electrical energy

disciple *n* **1** one who accepts and assists in spreading another's doctrines; a follower **2** any of the followers of Christ during his life on earth; *esp* any of Christ's 12 appointed followers – **discipleship** *n*, **discipular** *adj*

disciplinarian *n* one who enforces or advocates (strict) discipline or order – **disciplinarian** *adj*

disciplinary *adj* **1** of or involving discipline; corrective ⟨~ *action*⟩ **2** of a particular field of study

¹**discipline** *n* **1a** a field of study **2** training of the mind and character designed to produce obedience and self-control **3** punishment, chastisement **4a** order obtained by enforcing obedience (e g in a school or army) **b** self-control **5** a system of rules governing conduct – **disciplinal** *adj*

²**discipline** *vt* **1** to punish or penalize for the sake of discipline **2** to train by instruction and exercise, esp in obedience and self-control **3** to bring (a group) under control ⟨~ *troops*⟩ – **disciplinable** *adj*, **discipliner** *n*

disc jockey *n* one who introduces records of popular usu contemporary music (e g on a radio programme or at a discotheque)

disclaim *vi* to make a disclaimer ~*vt* **1** to renounce a legal claim to **2** to deny, disavow

disclaimer *n* **1** a denial of legal responsibility **2** a denial, repudiation

disclose *vt* **1** to expose to view **2** to make known; reveal to public knowledge – **discloser** *n*

disclosure *n* **1** (an instance of) disclosing; an exposure **2** sthg disclosed; a revelation

disco *n*, *pl* **discos 1** a collection of popular records together with the equipment for playing them **2** a discotheque – *infml*

discolour *vb* to (cause to) change colour for the worse; stain – **discoloration** *n*

discomfit *vt* **1** to frustrate the plans of; thwart **2** to cause

perplexity and embarrassment to; disconcert – **discomfiture** *n*

¹**discomfort** *vt* to make uncomfortable or uneasy

²**discomfort** *n* (sthg causing) mental or physical unease

discompose *vt* to destroy the composure of – *fml* – **discomposure** *n*

disconcert *vt* to disturb the composure of; fluster – **disconcerting** *adj*, **disconcertingly** *adv*

disconnect *vt* to sever the connection of or between; *specif* CUT OFF 7B – **disconnection** *n*

disconnected *adj* disjointed, incoherent – **disconnectedly** *adv*, **disconnectedness** *n*

disconsolate *adj* dejected, downcast – **disconsolately** *adv*, **disconsolateness** *n*, **disconsolation** *n*

¹**discontent** *n* **1** lack of contentment; dissatisfaction **2** one who is discontented; a malcontent

²**discontent** *vt* to make discontented

discontented *also* **discontent** *adj* restlessly unhappy; dissatisfied

discontinue *vt* to cease, stop; *specif* to cease production of ⟨*this line has been* ~d⟩ ~*vi* to come to an end – **discontinuance** *n*

discontinuous *adj* lacking sequence, coherence, or continuity – **discontinuously** *adv*, **discontinuity** *n*

discord *n* **1** lack of agreement or harmony; conflict **2a** dissonance **b** a harsh unpleasant combination of sounds

discordant *adj* **1** disagreeing; AT VARIANCE **2** relating to a discord; dissonant ⟨~ *tones*⟩ – **discordance**, **discordancy** *n*, **discordantly** *adv*

discotheque *n* a nightclub for dancing to usu recorded music

¹**discount** *n* a reduction made from the gross amount or value of sthg: e g **a** a reduction in the price of goods, accorded esp to special or trade customers **b** a reduction in the amount due on a bill of exchange, debt, etc when paid promptly or before the specified date – **at a discount** below the usual price

²**discount** *vt* **1a** to make a deduction from, usu for cash or prompt payment **b** to sell or offer for sale at a discount **c** to buy or sell (a bill of exchange) before maturity at below the stated price **2a** to leave out of account as unimportant, unreliable, or irrelevant; disregard **b** to underestimate the importance of; minimize **3** to take (e g a future event) into account in present arrangements or calculations – **discountable** *adj*

discountenance *vt* **1** to abash, disconcert **2** to discourage by showing disapproval – *fml*

discourage *vt* **1** to deprive of confidence; dishearten **2a** to hinder, deter *from* **b** to attempt to prevent, esp by showing disapproval – **discouragement** *n*

¹**discourse** *n* **1** a talk, conversation **2** (orderly expression of ideas in) a formal speech or piece of writing

²**discourse** *vi* **1** to express one's ideas in speech or writing **2** to talk, converse *USE* usu + *on* or *upon* – **discourser** *n*

discourteous *adj* rude, impolite – **discourteously** *adv*, **discourteousness** *n*

discourtesy *n* (an instance of) rudeness; (an) incivility

discover *vt* **1** to obtain sight or knowledge of for the first time **2** to make known or visible – *fml* – **discoverable** *adj*, **discoverer** *n*

discovery *n* **1a** the act or an instance of discovering or revealing **b** an obligatory disclosure of documents or facts by a party to a legal action **2** sby or sthg discovered

¹**discredit** *vt* **1** to refuse to accept as true or accurate **2** to cast doubt on the accuracy, authority, or reputation of

²**discredit** n 1 (sby or sthg causing) loss of credit or reputation 2 loss of belief or confidence; doubt

discreditable adj bringing discredit or disgrace – **discreditably** adv

discreet adj 1 judicious in speech or conduct; esp capable of maintaining a prudent silence 2 unpretentious, modest ⟨the house was furnished with ~ elegance⟩ – **discreetly** adv, **discreetness** n

discrepant adj disagreeing; AT VARIANCE – **discrepancy** n, **discrepantly** adv

discrete adj 1 individually distinct 2 consisting of distinct or unconnected elements – **discretely** adv, **discreteness** n

discretion n 1 the quality of being discreet 2 the ability to make responsible decisions 3a individual choice or judgment ⟨left the decision to his ~⟩ b power of free decision within legal bounds ⟨reached the age of ~⟩

discretionary adj 1 left to or exercised at one's own discretion ⟨~ powers⟩ 2 subject to the discretion of another

discriminate vt to distinguish (e g objects or ideas) by noting differences ⟨~ good from bad⟩ ~vi 1a to make a distinction ⟨~ between fact and fancy⟩ b to show good judgment or discernment 2 to treat sby differently and esp unfavourably on the grounds of race, sex, religion, etc – **discriminator** n

discriminating adj 1 discerning, judicious 2 discriminatory – **discriminatingly** adv

discrimination n 1 the act or process of responding to different sensory stimuli in different ways 2 discernment and good judgment, esp in matters of taste 3 prejudicial treatment (e g on the grounds of race or sex) – **discriminational** adj

discriminatory adj showing esp unfavourable discrimination ⟨a ~ law⟩ – **discriminatorily** adv

discursive adj 1 passing usu unmethodically from one topic to another; digressive 2 proceeding by logical argument or reason – **discursively** adv, **discursiveness** n

discus n, pl **discuses** (the athletic field event involving the throwing of) a solid disc, between 180mm and 219mm (about 7 to 9in) in diameter, that is thicker in the centre than at the edge

discuss vt to consider or examine (a topic) in speech or writing – **discussable, discussible** adj

discussion n (an instance of) consideration of a question in open debate or conversation

¹**disdain** n contempt for sthg regarded as worthless or insignificant; scorn

²**disdain** vt 1 to regard with disdain 2 to refuse or abstain from because of disdain ⟨she ~ed to answer him⟩

disdainful adj feeling or showing disdain – **disdainfully** adv, **disdainfulness** n

disease n 1 a condition of (a part of) a living animal or plant body that impairs the performance of a vital function; (a) sickness, malady 2 a harmful or corrupt development, situation, condition, etc ⟨the ~ of prejudice⟩ – **diseased** adj

disembark vb to (cause to) alight from a ship, plane, etc – **disembarkation** n

disembody vt to divest of a body or material existence

disembowel vt to remove the bowels or entrails of; eviscerate – **disembowelment** n

disembroil vt to free from a confused or entangled state or situation

disenchant vt to rid of an illusion – **disenchanter** n, disenchanting adj, disenchantingly adv, **disenchantment** n

disencumber vt to free from an encumbrance

disendow vt to strip of an endowment – **disendowment** n

disengage vt 1 to release or detach from sthg that engages or entangles 2 to remove (e g troops) from combat areas ~vi 1 to detach or release oneself; specif, esp of troops to withdraw 2 to move one's fencing sword to the other side of an opponent's sword in order to attack – **disengagement** n

disentangle vb to (cause to) become free from entanglements: unravel – **disentanglement** n

disequilibrium n loss or lack of equilibrium

disestablish vt to deprive (esp a national church) of established status – **disestablishment** n

¹**disfavour** n 1 disapproval, dislike 2 the state of being disapproved of ⟨fell into ~⟩

²**disfavour** vt to regard or treat with disfavour

disfigure vt to spoil the appearance or quality of; mar – **disfigurement** n

disfranchise vt to disenfranchise – **disfranchisement** n

disfrock vt to unfrock

disgorge vt 1a to discharge with force; specif to vomit b to give up on request or under pressure 2 to discharge the contents of (e g one's stomach) ~vi to discharge contents ⟨where the river ~s into the sea⟩

¹**disgrace** vt 1 to bring reproach or shame to 2 to cause to lose favour or standing

²**disgrace** n 1a loss of favour, honour, or respect; shame b the state of being out of favour ⟨she's in ~⟩ 2 sby or sthg shameful ⟨his manners are a ~⟩

disgraceful adj shameful, shocking – **disgracefully** adv, **disgracefulness** n

disgruntled adj aggrieved and dissatisfied

¹**disguise** vt 1 to change the appearance or nature of in order to conceal identity ⟨~d himself as a tramp⟩ 2 to hide the true state or character of – **disguisedly** adv, **disguisement** n

²**disguise** n 1 (the use of) sthg (e g clothing) to conceal one's identity 2 an outward appearance that misrepresents the true nature of sthg ⟨a blessing in ~⟩

¹**disgust** n strong aversion aroused by sby or sthg physically or morally distasteful

²**disgust** vt to arouse repugnance or aversion in – **disgusted** adj, **disgustedly** adv

¹**dish** n 1a a shallow open often circular or oval vessel used esp for holding or serving food; broadly any vessel from which food is eaten or served b a dishful c pl the utensils and tableware used in preparing, serving, and eating a meal ⟨wash the ~es⟩ 2 a type of food prepared in a particular way ⟨a delicious meat ~⟩ 3 sthg resembling a dish in shape: e g a a directional aerial, esp for receiving radio or television transmissions or microwaves, having a concave usu parabolic reflector b a hollow or depression 4 an attractive person – infml

²**dish** vt 1 to make concave like a dish 2 chiefly Br to ruin or spoil (e g a person or his/her hopes) – infml

dishabille n deshabille

disharmony n lack of harmony; discord – **disharmonious** adj

dishcloth n a cloth for washing or drying dishes

dishearten vt to cause to lose enthusiasm or morale; discourage – **disheartening** adj, **dishearteningly** adv, **disheartenment** n

dishevel vt -ll- (NAm -l-, -ll-) to make untidy or disordered

dishevelled, NAm chiefly **disheveled** adj, esp of a person's hair or appearance unkempt, untidy

dishful n the amount a dish contains or will hold

dishonest adj not honest, truthful, or sincere – **dishonestly** adv

dishonesty *n* (an instance of) lack of honesty or integrity

¹dishonour *n* **1** (sby or sthg causing) loss of honour or reputation **2** a state of shame or disgrace

²dishonour *vt* **1** to treat in a degrading or disrespectful manner **2** to bring shame on **3** to refuse to accept or pay (e g a cheque)

dishonourable *adj* base, shameful – **dishonourably** *adv*

dish out *vt* to give or distribute freely ⟨*always* dishing out *advice*⟩ – infml

dish up *vt* **1** to put (a meal, food, etc) onto dishes; serve **2** to produce or present (e g facts) ⟨*has been* dishing up *the same lessons for years*⟩ – infml ~ *vi* to put food onto dishes ready to be eaten ⟨*I'm* dishing up *now*⟩

dishwasher *n* a person or electrical machine that washes dishes

dishwater *n* water in which dishes have been washed

dishy *adj*, *chiefly Br*, *of a person* attractive – infml

¹disillusion *n* the state of being disillusioned

²disillusion *vt* to reveal the usu unpleasant truth (e g about sby or sthg admired) to; disenchant – **disillusionment** *n*

disillusioned *adj* bitter or depressed as a result of having been disillusioned ⟨*feeling very* ~ *with government policies*⟩

disincentive *n* sthg that discourages action or effort; a deterrent

disinclination *n* (an) unwillingness to do sthg; mild dislike

disinclined *adj* unwilling

disinfect *vt* to cleanse of infection, esp by destroying harmful microorganisms – **disinfection** *n*

disinfectant *n* a chemical that destroys harmful microorganisms

disinfest *vt* to rid of insects, rodents, or other pests – **disinfestation** *n*

disingenuous *adj* insincere; *also* falsely frank or naive in manner – **disingenuously** *adv*, **disingenuousness** *n*

disinherit *vt* to deprive (an heir) of the right to inherit; *broadly* to deprive of a special right or privilege – **disinheritance** *n*

disintegrate *vt* **1** to break up into fragments or constituent elements **2** to destroy the unity or cohesion of ~ *vi* **1** to break into fragments or constituent elements **2** to lose unity or cohesion **3** *esp of a nucleus* to undergo a change in composition (e g by emitting radioactive particles or dividing into smaller units) – **disintegrator** *n*, **disintegrative** *adj*, **disintegration** *n*

disinter *vt* **1** to remove from a grave or tomb **2** to bring to light; unearth – **disinterment** *n*

disinterested *adj* **1** uninterested – disapproved of by some speakers **2** free from selfish motive or interest; impartial – **disinterestedly** *adv*, **disinterestedness** *n*

disjoint *vt* **1** to disturb the orderly arrangement of **2** to take apart at the joints

disjointed *adj* lacking orderly sequence; incoherent – **disjointedly** *adv*, **disjointedness** *n*

¹disjunctive *n* a disjunctive conjunction

²disjunctive *adj* **1a** being, belonging to, or characterizing a logical disjunction **b** expressing an alternative or opposition between the meanings of the words connected (e g in the question 'Is he old or young?', *or* is a disjunctive conjunction) **2** marked by breaks or separation – fml – **disjunctively** *adv*

disk *n* **1a** *Br also* **disc** a round flat plate coated with a magnetic substance on which data for a computer is stored **b disk**, **disk pack** a computer storage device consisting of a stack of disks rotating at high speed, each disk having

its own head to read and write data **2** *chiefly NAm* a disc

¹dislike *vt* to regard with dislike

²dislike *n* (an object of) a feeling of aversion or disapproval

dislocate *vt* **1** to put out of place; *esp* to displace (e g a bone or joint) from normal connection **2** to put (plans, machinery, etc) out of order; disrupt

dislocation *n* **1** displacement of 1 or more bones at a joint **2** a discontinuity in the lattice structure of a crystal **3** disruption of an established order or course

dislodge *vt* to force out of or remove from a fixed or entrenched position

disloyal *adj* untrue to obligations or ties; unfaithful – **disloyally** *adv*, **disloyalty** *n*

dismal *adj* causing or expressing gloom or sadness – **dismally** *adv*, **dismalness** *n*

dismantle *vt* **1** to strip of furniture, equipment, etc **2** to take to pieces – **dismantlement** *n*

dismast *vt* to remove or break off the mast of (a ship)

¹dismay *vt* to fill with dismay – **dismayingly** *adv*

²dismay *n* sudden consternation or apprehension

dismember *vt* **1** to cut or tear off the limbs or members of **2** to divide up (e g a territory) into parts – **dismemberment** *n*

dismiss *vt* **1** to allow to leave; send away **2** to remove or send away from employment or service **3a** to put out of one's mind; reject as unworthy of serious consideration **b** to put out of judicial consideration; refuse a further hearing to (e g a court case) **4** to bowl out (a batsman or side) in cricket – **dismissal** *n*, **dismissible** *adj*

dismount *vi* to alight from a horse, bicycle, etc ~ *vt* **1** to throw down or remove from horseback **2** to remove from a mounting

disobedient *adj* refusing or failing to obey – **disobedience** *n*, **disobediently** *adv*

disobey *vb* to fail to obey

disoblige *vt* **1** to go counter to the wishes of **2** to inconvenience

¹disorder *vt* **1** to throw into confusion or disorder **2** to disturb the good health of; upset

²disorder *n* **1** lack of order; confusion **2** breach of the peace or public order ⟨*troubled times marked by social* ~s⟩ **3** an abnormal physical or mental condition; an ailment

disorderly *adj* **1a** untidy, disarranged **b** unruly, violent **2** offensive to public order ⟨*charged with being drunk and* ~⟩ – **disorderliness** *n*

disorderly house *n* a brothel

disorganize, **-ise** *vt* to throw into disorder or confusion – **disorganization** *n*

disorientate *vt* **1** to deprive of the normal sense of position, relationship, or identity **2** to confuse – **disorientation** *n*

disown *vt* **1** to refuse to acknowledge as one's own **2** to repudiate any connection with

disparage *vt* to speak slightingly of; belittle – **disparagement** *n*, **disparaging** *adj*, **disparagingly** *adv*

disparate *adj* markedly distinct in quality or character – **disparately** *adv*, **disparateness** *n*

disparity *n* (a) difference or inequality

dispassionate *adj* not influenced by strong feeling; *esp* calm, impartial – **dispassionately** *adv*, **dispassionateness** *n*

¹dispatch *vt* **1** to send off or away promptly, esp to a particular place or to carry out a particular, usu official, task **2a** to carry out or complete (e g a task) rapidly or efficiently **b** to get through; consume quickly – infml

⟨*soon* ~ed *that chocolate cake*⟩ 3 to kill, esp with quick efficiency – euph – **dispatcher** *n*

²**dispatch** *n* 1 a sending off (e g of a communication or messenger) 2a a message; *esp* an important official diplomatic or military message b a news item sent in by a correspondent to a newspaper 3 promptness and efficiency 4 an act of killing; *specif* a murder – euph

dispel *vt* -ll- to drive away; disperse

dispensable *adj* that can be dispensed with; inessential – **dispensability** *n*

dispensary *n* a part of a hospital or chemist's shop where drugs, medical supplies, etc are dispensed

dispensation *n* 1a an esp divine ordering of human affairs b a particular arrangement or provision made by God, providence, or nature c a usu specified religious system, esp considered as controlling human affairs during a particular period 2a an exemption from a law, vow, etc; *specif* permission to disregard or break a rule of Roman Catholic church law b a formal authorization – **dispensational** *adj*

dispense *vt* 1a to deal out, distribute b to administer (e g law or justice) 2 to give a dispensation to; exempt *from* 3 to prepare and give out (drugs, medicine, etc on prescription) – **dispense with** 1 DISCARD 2 2 to do without

dispenser *n* 1 a container or machine that dispenses items (e g of food) or usu fixed quantities (e g of drink) 2 a person who dispenses medicines

disperse *vt* 1a to cause to break up or scatter ⟨*they* ~d *the meeting*⟩ b to spread over a wide area c to cause to evaporate or vanish 2a to subject (e g light) to dispersion b to distribute (e g fine particles) more or less evenly throughout a liquid ~ *vi* 1 to break up in random fashion; scatter 2 to become dispersed; dissipate – **dispersal** *n*, **dispersedly** *adv*, **disperser** *n*, **dispersible** *adj*, **dispersive** *adj*, **dispersively** *adv*, **dispersiveness** *n*

dispersion *n* 1 *cap the* Diaspora 2 the extent to which the values of a frequency distribution are scattered around an average 3 the separation of light into colours by refraction or diffraction with formation of a spectrum; *also* the separation of nonhomogeneous radiation into components in accordance with some characteristic (e g energy, wavelength, or mass) 4a a dispersed substance b a system consisting of a dispersed substance and the medium in which it is dispersed; COLLOID 1b

dispirit *vt* to dishearten, discourage – **dispirited** *adj*, **dispiritedly** *adv*, **dispiritedness** *n*

displace *vt* 1a to remove from or force out of the usual or proper place b to remove from office 2 to take the place of; replace; *specif* to take the place of (e g an atom) in a chemical reaction – **displaceable** *adj*

displaced person *n* sby who has been forced to leave his/her country because of war, revolution, etc; a refugee

displacement *n* 1a the volume or weight of a fluid (e g water) displaced by a body (e g a ship) of equal weight floating in it b the difference between the initial position of a body and any later position 2 the transfer of emotions from the object that orig evoked them to a substitute (e g in dreams)

¹**display** *vt* 1 to expose to view; show 2 to exhibit, esp ostentatiously ~ *vi* to make a breeding display

²**display** *n* 1a(1) a presentation or exhibition of sthg in open view ⟨*a fireworks* ~⟩ (2) an esp ostentatious show or demonstration b an arrangement of type or printing designed to catch the eye (e g in headlines and title pages) c an eye-catching arrangement exhibiting sthg (e g goods for sale) d a device (e g a cathode-ray tube screen) that presents information in visual form ⟨*a visual* ~ *unit*⟩ 2

a pattern of behaviour exhibited esp by male birds in the breeding season

displease *vb* to cause annoyance or displeasure (to)

displeasure *n* disapproval, annoyance

disport *vt* to divert or amuse (oneself) actively ~ *vi* to frolic, gambol

¹**disposable** *adj* 1 available for use; *specif* remaining after deduction of taxes ⟨~ *income*⟩ 2 designed to be used once and then thrown away – **disposability** *n*

²**disposable** *n* a disposable article

disposal *n* 1a orderly arrangement or distribution b management, administration c bestowal d the act or action of getting rid of sthg; *specif* the destruction or conversion of waste matter 2 the power or right to use freely ⟨*the car was at my* ~⟩

dispose *vt* 1 to incline *to* – ⟨~d *to ill-health*⟩ 2 to put in place; arrange 3 to cause to have a specified attitude *towards* ⟨*unfavourably* ~d *towards her in-laws*⟩ ~ *vi* to settle a matter finally – **dispose of** 1 to get rid of (e g by finishing, selling, eating, or killing) 2 to deal with conclusively ⟨*disposed of the matter efficiently*⟩

disposition *n* 1a final arrangement; settlement b transfer of property, esp by will or deed c orderly arrangement 2a natural temperament b a tendency, inclination

dispossess *vt* to deprive of possession or occupancy – **dispossessor** *n*, **dispossession** *n*

disproof *n* 1 the act or action of disproving 2 evidence that disproves

disproportion *n* (a) lack of proportion, symmetry, or proper relation – **disproportional** *adj*

disproportionate *adj* out of proportion – **disproportionately** *adv*

disprove *vt* to prove to be false; refute – **disprovable** *adj*

disputant *n* one engaged in a dispute

disputation *n* 1 a debate, argument 2 the oral defence of a thesis by formal logic

disputatious *adj* inclined to dispute; argumentative – **disputatiously** *adv*, **disputatiousness** *n*

¹**dispute** *vi* to argue, esp angrily and persistently – often + *about* ~ *vt* 1a to make the subject of disputation; discuss angrily b to call into question 2a to struggle against; resist b to struggle over; contest – **disputable** *adj*, **disputably** *adv*, **disputer** *n*

²**dispute** *n* 1 controversy, debate ⟨*his honesty is beyond* ~⟩ 2 a quarrel, disagreement

disqualification *n* 1 disqualifying or being disqualified 2 sthg that disqualifies

disqualify *vt* 1 to make or declare unfit or unsuitable to do sthg 2 to declare ineligible (e g for a prize) because of violation of the rules

disquiet *vt or n* (to cause) anxiety or worry – **disquieting** *adj*, **disquietingly** *adv*

disquietude *n* disquiet – fml

disquisition *n* a long or elaborate discussion or essay on a subject

¹**disregard** *vt* 1 to pay no attention to 2 to treat as not worthy of regard or notice

²**disregard** *n* lack of attention or regard; neglect – **disregardful** *adj*

disremember *vt, chiefly NAm* to forget

disrepair *n* the state of being in need of repair

disreputable *adj* 1 having a bad reputation; not respectable 2 dirty or untidy in appearance – **disreputableness** *n*, **disreputably** *adv*, **disreputability** *n*

disrepute *n* lack of good reputation or respectability

disrespect *n* lack of respect or politeness – **disrespectful** *adj*, **disrespectfully** *adv*, **disrespectfulness** *n*

disrobe *vi* to take off (esp ceremonial outer) clothing – fml or humor

disrupt *vt* **1** to break apart forcibly; rupture **2a** to throw into disorder **b** to interrupt the continuity of – **disruption** *n*, **disruptive** *adj*, **disruptively** *adv*, **disruptiveness** *n*

dissatisfaction *n* lack of satisfaction; discontent – **dissatisfactory** *adj*

dissatisfy *vt* to make displeased, discontented, or disappointed

dissect *vt* **1** to cut (e g an animal or plant) into pieces, esp for scientific examination **2** to analyse and interpret in detail – **dissection** *n*, **dissector** *n*

dissemble *vt* to disguise, conceal ~ *vi* to conceal facts, intentions, or feelings under some pretence – **dissembler** *n*

disseminate *vt* to spread about freely or widely 〈~ *ideas*〉 – **disseminator**, **dissemination** *n*

dissension *n* disagreement in opinion; discord

¹**dissent** *vi* **1** to withhold assent **2** to differ in opinion; *specif* to reject the doctrines of an established church – **dissenter** *n*

²**dissent** *n* difference of opinion; *esp* religious or political nonconformity

Dissenter *n* an English Nonconformist

dissenting *adj*, *often cap* Nonconformist

dissertation *n* a long, detailed, usu written treatment of a subject; *specif* one submitted for a (higher) degree

disservice *n* an action or deed which works to sby's disadvantage

dissever *vb* to (cause to) separate or come apart – fml – **disseverance** *n*, **disseverment** *n*

dissident *n or adj* (sby) disagreeing strongly or rebelliously with an established opinion, group, government, etc 〈*political* ~ s〉 – **dissidence** *n*

dissimilar *adj* not similar; unlike – **dissimilarly** *adv*, **dissimilarity** *n*

dissimulate *vb* to dissemble – **dissimulator** *n*, **dissimulation** *n*

dissipate *vt* **1a** to cause to disappear or scatter; dispel **b** to lose (e g heat or electricity) irrecoverably **2** to spend or use up (money, energy, etc) aimlessly or foolishly ~ *vi* to separate and scatter or vanish – **dissipater** *n*, **dissipative** *adj*

dissipated *adj* given to dissipation; dissolute – **dissipatedly** *adv*, **dissipatedness** *n*

dissipation *n* **1** dispersion, diffusion **2** wasteful expenditure **3** dissolute living; debauchery; *specif* excessive indulgence in alcohol

dissociate *vt* **1** to separate from association or union with sby or sthg else; disconnect **2** to subject to chemical dissociation ~ *vi* to undergo dissociation

dissociation *n* **1** the process by which a chemical combination breaks up into simpler constituents, esp as a result of the action of heat or a solvent **2** the separation of a more or less autonomous group of ideas or activities from the mainstream of consciousness, esp in cases of mental disorder – **dissociative** *adj*

dissoluble *adj* capable of being dissolved or disintegrated – **dissolubility** *n*

dissolute *adj* loose in morals; debauched – **dissolutely** *adv*, **dissoluteness** *n*

dissolution *n* **1** separation into component parts **2** disintegration, decay **3** the termination of an association, union, etc **4** the breaking up or dispersal of a group, assembly, etc

¹**dissolve** *vt* **1a** to terminate officially 〈*the marriage was* ~ d〉 **b** to cause to break up; dismiss 〈*Parliament was* ~ d *before the election*〉 **2a** to cause to pass into solution 〈~ *sugar in water*〉 **b** to melt, liquefy **3** to fade out (one film

or television scene) whilst fading in another ~ *vi* **1a** to pass into solution **b** to become fluid; melt **2** to fade away; disperse 〈*the vision* ~ d *before his eyes*〉 **3** to be emotionally overcome – **dissolvable** *adj*, **dissolver** *n*

²**dissolve** *n* an effect used in films and television in which one scene is dissolved into the next

dissonance *n* **1** a combination of discordant sounds **2** lack of agreement **3** (the sound produced by playing) an unresolved musical note or chord; *specif* an interval not included in a major or minor triad or its inversions

dissonant *adj* **1** marked by dissonance **2** incongruous – **dissonantly** *adv*

dissuade *vt* to deter or discourage *from* a course of action by persuasion

distaff *n* **1** a staff for holding the flax, tow, wool, etc in spinning **2** woman's work or domain

distal *adj*, *esp of an anatomical part* far from the centre or point of attachment or origin; terminal – **distally** *adv*

¹**distance** *n* **1a** (the amount of) separation in space or time between 2 points or things **b** an extent of space or an advance along a route measured linearly; *specif* a usu particular length covered in a race 〈*a world class runner over all* ~ s〉 **c** a distant point or place **2a** remoteness in space **b** reserve, coldness **c** difference, disparity

²**distance** *vt* **1** to place or keep physically or mentally at a distance **2** to outstrip

distant *adj* **1a** separated in space or time by a specified distance 〈*a few miles* ~ 〉 **b** far-off or remote in space or time 〈*the* ~ *hills*〉 **2** not closely related 〈*a* ~ *cousin*〉 **3** different in kind **4** reserved, aloof **5** coming from or going to a remote place 〈~ *voyages*〉 – **distantly** *adv*, **distantness** *n*

distaste *n* (a) dislike, aversion

distasteful *adj* showing or causing distaste; offensive – **distastefully** *adv*, **distastefulness** *n*

¹**distemper** *n* any of various animal diseases; *esp* a highly infectious virus disease occurring esp in dogs and marked by fever and disorder of the respiratory and sometimes the nervous systems

²**distemper** *vt* to paint in or with distemper

³**distemper** *n* **1** a method of painting in which pigments are mixed with white or yolk of egg or size, esp for mural decoration **2** the paint used in the distemper process; *broadly* any of numerous water-based paints for general, esp household, use

distend *vb* to (cause to) swell from internal pressure – **distensible** *adj*, **distensibility** *n*, **distension** *n*

distil, *NAm chiefly* **distill** *vb* -ll- *vt* **1** to cause to fall or exude in drops or a fine mist **2a** to subject to or transform by distillation **b** to obtain or separate *out or off* (as if) by distillation **c** to extract the essence of (e g an idea or subject) ~ *vi* **1** to undergo distillation **2** to condense or drop from a still after distillation **3** to appear slowly or in small quantities at a time

distillate *n* **1** a product of distillation **2** a concentrated form

distillation *n* a process that consists of condensing the gas or vapour obtained from heated liquids or solids and that is used esp for purification, fractionation, or the formation of new substances

distiller *n* a person or company that makes alcohol, esp spirits, by distilling – **distillery** *n*

distinct *adj* **1** different, separate *from* **2** readily perceptible to the senses or mind; clear **3** definite, decided 〈*a* ~ *possibility of rain*〉 – **distinctly** *adv*, **distinctness** *n*

distinction *n* **1a** discrimination, differentiation **b** a difference made or marked; a contrast **2** a distinguishing quality or mark **3a** outstanding merit, quality, or worth

⟨*a writer of some* ∼⟩ **b** special honour or recognition ⟨*passed her exam with* ∼⟩
distinctive *adj* clearly marking sby or sthg as different from others; characteristic – **distinctively** *adv*, **distinctiveness** *n*
distinguish *vt* **1a** to mark or recognize as separate or different – often + *from* **b** to separate into kinds, classes, or categories **c** to make (oneself) outstanding or noteworthy **d** to mark as different; characterize **2** to discern; MAKE OUT **3, 5** ∼ *vi* to recognize the difference *between* – **distinguishable** *adj*, **distinguishably** *adv*, **distinguishability** *n*
distinguished *adj* **1** marked by eminence, distinction, or excellence **2** dignified in manner, bearing, or appearance
distort *vt* **1** to alter the true meaning of; misrepresent **2** to cause to take on an unnatural or abnormal shape **3** to reproduce or broadcast (radio sound, a television picture, etc) poorly or inaccurately owing to a change in the wave form of the original signal – **distortion** *n*, **distortional** *adj*
distract *vt* **1** to turn aside; divert **2** to draw (e g one's attention) to a different object – **distractingly** *adv*, **distractible** *adj*, **distractibility** *n*
distracted *adj* **1** confused, perplexed **2** agitated – **distractedly** *adv*
distraction *n* **1** extreme agitation or mental confusion ⟨*drove him to* ∼ *with her taunts*⟩ **2** sthg that distracts; *esp* an amusement – **distractive** *adj*
distrain *vb* to impose a distress (upon); *also* to seize (goods, property, etc) by way of distress – **distrainable** *adj*, **distrainer** *n*, **distrainment** *n*, **distrainee** *n*
distraint *n* distraining; DISTRESS 1a
distrait *adj* absentminded
distraught *adj* mentally agitated; frantic – **distraughtly** *adv*
¹**distress** *n* **1a** (a) seizure of goods, property, etc as a pledge or to obtain satisfaction of a claim **b** sthg distrained **2a** mental or physical anguish **b** hardship or suffering caused esp by lack of money or the necessities of life **3** a state of danger or desperate need ⟨*a ship in* ∼⟩ – **distressful** *adj*
²**distress** *vt* to cause distress to – **distressingly** *adv*
distribute *vt* **1** to divide among several or many **2a** to disperse or scatter over an area **b** to give out, deliver **3** to return (e g used type) to the proper storage places
distribution *n* **1a** distributing, apportioning **b** sthg distributed **2a** the position, arrangement, or frequency of occurrence (e g of the members of a group) over a usu specified area or length of time **b** the natural geographical range of an organism **3** an arrangement of statistical data that shows the frequency of occurrence of the values of a variable **4** the transport and marketing of goods between manufacturer or wholesaler and retailer – **distributional** *adj*
¹**distributive** *adj* **1** of distribution **2** denoting a word (e g *each, either*, or *none*) referring singly to all the members of a group – **distributively** *adv*, **distributiveness** *n*
²**distributive** *n* a distributive word
distributor *n* **1** sby employed to manage the distribution of goods **2** an apparatus for directing current to the various sparking plugs of an internal-combustion engine
district *n* **1** a territorial division made esp for administrative purposes **2** an area or region with a specified character or feature ⟨*a residential* ∼⟩
distrust *vt or n* (to view with) suspicion or lack of trust – **distrustful** *adj*, **distrustfully** *adv*, **distrustfulness** *n*
disturb *vt* **1a** to break in upon; interrupt **b** to alter the position or arrangement of **2a** to destroy the peace of

mind or composure of **b** to throw into disorder *vt* **c** to put to inconvenience – **disturbingly** *adv*
disturbance *n* **1** disturbing or being disturbed **2** sthg that disturbs
disturbed *adj* having or showing symptoms of emotional or mental instability
disunion *n* **1** the termination of union; separation **2** disunity
disunite *vt* to divide, separate
disunity *n* lack of unity; *esp* dissension
disuse *n* the state of no longer being used ⟨*that word has fallen into* ∼⟩
disused *adj* no longer used; abandoned
¹**ditch** *n* a long narrow excavation dug in the earth for defence, drainage, irrigation, etc
²**ditch** *vt* **1a** to enclose with a ditch **b** to dig a ditch in **2** to make a forced landing of (an aircraft) on water **3** to get rid of; abandon USE (2&3) *infml* – **ditch** *n*
¹**dither** *vi* to act nervously or indecisively; vacillate – **ditherer** *n*
²**dither** *n* a state of indecision or nervous excitement ⟨*all of a* ∼⟩ – **dithery** *adj*
¹**ditto** *n* **1** a thing mentioned previously or above; the same – used to avoid repeating a word **2** *also* **ditto mark** a mark „ or ' used as a sign indicating repetition usu of a word directly above in a previous line
²**ditto** *vt* to repeat the action or statement of
ditty *n* a short simple song
diuretic *n or adj* (a drug) acting to increase the flow of urine – **diuretically** *adv*
diurnal *adj* **1** having a daily cycle **2a** occurring during the day or daily **b** opening during the day and closing at night ⟨∼ *flowers*⟩ **c** active during the day – **diurnally** *adv*
divagate *vi* to wander from one place or subject to another; stray – *fml* – **divagation** *n*
divan *n* **1** the privy council of the Ottoman Empire **2** a council chamber in some Muslim countries, esp Turkey **3a** a long low couch, usu without arms or back, placed against a wall **b** a bed of a similar style without a head or foot board
¹**dive** *vb* **dived**, NAm *also* **dove** *vi* **1a** to plunge into water headfirst **b** to engage in the sport of prescribed dives into water **c** to submerge ⟨*the submarine* ∼ d⟩ **2a** to descend or fall steeply **b** to plunge one's hand quickly *into* **c** *of an aircraft* to descend in a dive **3** to lunge or dash headlong ⟨∼ d *for cover*⟩ ∼ *vt* **1** to cause to descend ⟨∼ d *his plane through the sound barrier*⟩ **2** to dip or plunge (one's hand) *into*
²**dive** *n* **1a**(1) a headlong plunge into water; *esp* one executed in a prescribed manner (2) an act or instance of submerging (e g by a submarine) (3) a steep descent of an aeroplane at greater than the maximum horizontal speed **b** a sharp decline **2a** a disreputable bar, club, etc **3** a faked knockout – chiefly in *take a dive* **4** a ploy in soccer in which a player makes it appear that he has been fouled by falling over deliberately after a tackle USE (*except* 1a) *infml*
dive-bomb *vt* to bomb from an aeroplane while making a steep dive towards the target – **dive-bomber** *n*
diver *n* **1** sby who dives; *esp* a person who works or explores underwater for long periods, either carrying a supply of air or having it sent from the surface **2** any of various diving birds; *specif* a loon
diverge *vi* **1a** to move in different directions from a common point **b** to differ in character, form, or opinion – often + *from* **2** to turn aside from a path or course – often + *from* **3** to be mathematically divergent
divergence *also* **divergency** *n* **1a** (an instance of) diverging or being divergent **b** the amount by which sthg

diverges; DIFFERENCE 3 2 the acquisition of dissimilar characteristics by related organisms living in different environments

divergent adj 1 diverging or differing from each other 2 of a mathematical series having a sum that continues to increase or decrease as the number of terms increases without limit 3 causing divergence of rays ⟨a ~ lens⟩ – **divergently** adv

divers adj, archaic various

diverse adj 1 different, unlike 2 varied, assorted – **diversely** adv, **diverseness** n

diversify vt 1 to make diverse; vary 2 to divide (e g investment of funds) among different securities to reduce risk ~ vi to engage in varied business operations in order to reduce risk – **diversifier** n, **diversification** n

diversion n 1 a turning aside from a course, activity, or use; specif a detour used by traffic when the usual route is closed 2 an amusement, pastime 3 sthg that draws the attention away from the main scene of activity or operations – **diversionary** adj

diversity n 1 the condition of being different or having differences 2 a variety, assortment

divert vt 1 to turn aside from one course or use to another b to distract 2 to entertain, amuse

divertimento n, pl **divertimenti, divertimentos** an instrumental chamber work in several movements and usu light in character

divertissement n, pl **divertissements** 1 a ballet suite serving as an interlude 2 a divertimento 3 a diversion, entertainment

divest vt 1a to deprive or dispossess of property, authority, title, etc b to rid or free (oneself) of c to strip of clothing, equipment, etc 2 to take away (e g property or vested rights) USE (1c&2) fml – **divestiture** n, **divestment** n

¹divide vt 1 to separate into 2 or more parts, categories, divisions, etc 2a to give out in shares; distribute b to set aside for different purposes ⟨~d his time between work and play⟩ 3a to cause to be separate; serve as a boundary between b to separate into opposing sides or parties c to cause (a parliamentary body) to vote by division 4a to mark divisions on ⟨~ a sextant⟩ b to determine how many times (a number or quantity) contains another number or quantity by means of a mathematical operation ⟨~ 42 by 14⟩ ~ vi 1 to perform mathematical division 2a(1) to become separated into parts (2) to diverge b to vote by division – **dividable** adj – **divide into** to use as a divisor of ⟨divide 14 into 42⟩

²divide n 1 WATERSHED 1 2 a point or line of division

dividend n 1 (a pro rata share in) the part of a company's profits payable to shareholders 2 a reward, benefit ⟨her action will pay great ~s⟩ 3a a number to be divided by another b a sum or fund to be divided and distributed

divider n 1 pl a compasslike instrument with 2 pointed ends used for measuring or marking off lines, angles, etc 2 a partition or screen used to separate parts of a room, hall, etc

divination n 1 the art or practice that seeks to foresee the future or discover hidden knowledge (e g by using supernatural powers) 2 (an instance of) unusual insight or perception – **divinatory** adj

¹divine adj 1a of, being, or proceeding directly from God or a god b devoted to the worship of God or a god; sacred 2 delightful, superb – infml – **divinely** adv, **divineness** n

²divine n a clergyman; esp one skilled in theology

³divine vt 1 to discover, perceive, or foresee intuitively or by supernatural means 2 to discover or locate (e g water

or minerals) by means of a divining rod ~ vi to practise divination – **divinable** adj, **diviner** n

Divine Office n the prescribed forms of prayer and ritual for daily worship used by Roman Catholic priests

divine right n the right of a sovereign to rule, held to derive directly from God ⟨~ of kings⟩; broadly a right which cannot be transferred

divine service n an esp nonsacramental service of Christian worship

diving bell n a bell-shaped metal container open only at the bottom and supplied with compressed air through a tube, in which a person can be let down under water

diving suit n a waterproof diver's suit with a helmet that is supplied with air pumped through a tube

divining rod n a forked rod (e g a twig) believed to dip downwards when held over ground concealing water or minerals

divinity n 1 the quality or state of being divine 2a often cap GOD 1 b a male or female deity 3 theology

divisible adj capable of being divided, esp without a remainder – **divisibility** n

division n 1a dividing or being divided b (a) distribution 2 any of the parts or sections into which a whole is divided 3 sing or pl in constr a a major army formation having the necessary tactical and administrative services to act independently b a naval unit of men under a single command 4a an administrative territorial unit b an administrative or operating unit of an organization 5 a group of organisms forming part of a larger group; specif a primary category of the plant kingdom equivalent to a phylum of the animal kingdom 6 a competitive class or category (e g of a soccer league) 7 sthg that divides, separates, or marks off 8 disagreement, disunity 9 the physical separation into different lobbies of the members of a parliamentary body voting for and against a question 10 the mathematical operation of dividing one number by another – **divisional** adj

division of labour n the distribution of various parts of the process of production among different people, groups, or machines, each specializing in a particular job, to increase efficiency

divisive adj tending to cause disunity or dissension – **divisively** adv, **divisiveness** n

divisor n the number by which another number or quantity is divided

¹divorce n 1 (a decree declaring) a legal dissolution of a marriage 2 a separation, severance

²divorce vt 1a to end marriage with (one's spouse) by divorce b to dissolve the marriage between 2 to end the relationship or union of; separate – usu + from ~ vi to obtain a divorce

divorcé, fem **divorcée** n a divorced person

divot n 1 a piece of turf dug out in making a golf shot 2 Scot a piece of turf

divulge vt to make known (e g a confidence or secret); reveal – **divulgence** n

divvy n, Br DIVIDEND 1; esp one paid by a Cooperative Wholesale Society – infml

dixie n, Br a large metal pot in which food and drink is made or carried, esp by soldiers

Dixie n the Southern states of the USA

dixieland n jazz music in duple time characterized by collective improvisation

¹dizzy adj 1a experiencing a whirling sensation in the head with a tendency to lose balance b mentally confused 2 causing or feeling giddiness or mental confusion ⟨a ~ height⟩ 3 foolish, silly – infml – **dizzily** adv, **dizziness** n

²dizzy vt to make dizzy; bewilder – **dizzyingly** adv

DJ *n* **1** DISC JOCKEY **2** DINNER JACKET
djin, djinn *n, pl* **djin, djinn** a jinn
DNA *n* any of various nucleic acids that are found esp in
cell nuclei, are constructed of a double helix held together
by hydrogen bonds between purine and pyrimidine bases
which project inwards from 2 chains containing alternate
links of deoxyribose and phosphate, and are responsible
for transmitting genetic information
¹**do** *vb* **does; did; done** *vt* **1** to carry out the task of; effect,
perform ⟨~ *some washing*⟩ ⟨~ *overtime*⟩ **2** to put into
a specified condition ⟨~ *him to death*⟩ **3** to have as a
function ⟨*what's that book* ~ing *on the floor?*⟩ **4** to
cause, impart ⟨*sleep will* ~ *you good*⟩ **5** to bring to an
esp unwanted conclusion; finish – used esp in the past
participle ⟨*that's* done *it*⟩; compare DONE 2 **6** to expend,
exert ⟨*did their damnedest to hog the game*⟩ **7a** to
provide ⟨*they* ~ *a mail-order service*⟩ **b** to have available
for purchase; sell ⟨*they* ~ *teas here*⟩ **8** to bring into
existence; produce ⟨~ *a biography of the general*⟩ **9a** to
put on; perform ⟨*are* ~ing *'The Merchant of Venice'*
tomorrow night⟩ **b** to play the part of; act ⟨*can* ~ *Harold*
Wilson very well⟩ **c** to behave like ⟨*did a Houdini and*
escaped from his chains⟩ **10a** to put in order; arrange ⟨~
the garden⟩ ⟨*had his hair* done⟩ **b** to clean, wash ⟨~ *the*
dishes⟩ **c** to cook ⟨*likes her steak well* done⟩ **d** to
decorate, furnish ⟨*did the living room in blue*⟩ **11a** to
execute an artistic representation of ⟨*did her in oils*⟩ **b** to
perform the appropriate professional service or services
for ⟨*the barber will* ~ *you now*⟩ ⟨~ *you very well at that*
hotel⟩ **12a** to work at, esp as a course of study or
occupation ⟨~ *classics*⟩ ⟨*what are you* ~ing *nowadays?*⟩
b to solve; WORK OUT ⟨~ *a sum*⟩ **13a** to pass over; cover
⟨~ *30 miles to the gallon*⟩ **b** to travel at a (maximum)
speed of ⟨~ *70 on the motorway*⟩ ⟨*this car* ~es *80*⟩ **14**
to see the sights of; tour ⟨~ *12 countries in 12 days*⟩ **15**
to serve out, esp as a prison sentence ⟨*did 3 years*⟩ **16** to
suffice, suit ⟨*worms will* ~ *us for bait*⟩ **17** – used as a
substitute verb to avoid repetition ⟨*if you must make such*
a racket, ~ *it somewhere else*⟩ **18a** *chiefly Br* to arrest,
convict – *slang* ⟨*get* done *for theft*⟩ **b** *chiefly Br* to attack,
hurt – *slang* **c** to treat unfairly; *esp* to cheat, deprive ⟨*did*
him out of his inheritance⟩ – *infml* **d** to rob – *slang* ⟨~
a shop⟩ **19** to have sexual intercourse with (a woman or
passive partner) – *slang* ~ *vi* **1** to act, behave ⟨~ *as I say*⟩
2a to fare; GET ALONG ⟨~ *well at school*⟩ ⟨*how do you*
~ *?*⟩ **b** to carry on business or affairs; manage ⟨*we can* ~
without your help⟩ **3** to be in progress; happen ⟨*there's*
nothing ~ing⟩ **4** to come to or make an end; finish – used
in the past participle ⟨*have you* done *with the news-*
paper?⟩; compare DONE 2 **5** to be active or busy ⟨*let us*
then be up and ~ing – H W Longfellow⟩ **6** to suffice,
serve ⟨*half of that will* ~⟩ **7** to be fitting; conform to
custom or propriety ⟨*won't* ~ *to be late*⟩ **8a** – used as a
substitute verb to avoid repetition ⟨*you sing,* ~ *you?*⟩
and, esp in British English, after a modal auxiliary
⟨*haven't heard of her yet but you will* ~⟩ **b** – used as a
substitute for verb and object ⟨*he likes it and so* ~ *I*⟩ **9**
– used in the imperative after another imperative to add
emphasis ⟨*be quiet,* ~⟩ – used with the infinitive without
to **a** to form present and past tenses in legal and parliamentary language ⟨~ *hereby bequeath*⟩ and in poetry
⟨*give what she did crave* – Shak⟩ **b** to form present and
past tenses in declarative sentences with inverted word
order ⟨*fervently* ~ *we pray* – Abraham Lincoln⟩ or in
questions or negative sentences ⟨*did you hear that?*⟩ ⟨*we*
don't know⟩ ⟨*don't go*⟩ **c** to form present and past tenses
expressing emphasis ⟨*it* ~es *hurt*⟩ ⟨~ *be careful*⟩ –
doable *adj* – **do away with** **1** to put an end to; abolish **2**
to put to death; kill – **do by** to deal with; treat ⟨*afraid*

you've been rather hard done *by*⟩ – **do duty for** to act as
a substitute for; serve as – **do for** **1** *chiefly Br* to keep
house for **2a** to wear out, exhaust **b** to bring'about the
death or ruin of – **do justice (to)** **1a** to treat fairly or
adequately **b** to show due appreciation for **2** to show in
the best light ⟨*I hope he* did *himself* justice *in the exam-*
inations⟩ – **do one's bit** *Br* to make one's personal
contribution, esp to a cause – **do one's block** *Austr* DO
ONE'S NUT – *infml* – **do one's nut** to become frantic or angry
– *infml* – **do proud** to treat or entertain splendidly – **do**
the dirty on to play a sly trick on – **do something for** to
improve the appearance of ⟨*that dress really* does *some-*
thing for you⟩ – **do the trick** to achieve the desired result
– *infml* ⟨*castor oil should* do *the trick*⟩ – **to do with**
concerned with; of concern to ⟨*a job* to do *with plastics*⟩
⟨*nothing* to do *with you*⟩
²**do** *n, pl* **dos, do's** **1** sthg one ought to do – usu *pl* ⟨*gave*
her a list of ~s *and don'ts*⟩ **2** *chiefly Br* a festive party
or occasion – *infml*
³**do, doh** *n* the 1st note of the diatonic scale in solmization
dobbin *n* – used chiefly as a familiar name for a farm
horse
doc *n* a doctor – often used as an informal term of
address
docile *adj* easily led or managed; tractable – **docilely** *adv*,
docility *n*
¹**dock** *n* any of a genus of coarse weeds whose leaves are
used to alleviate nettle stings
²**dock** *n* the solid bony part of an animal's tail as distinguished from the hair
³**dock** *vt* **1a** to remove part of the tail of **b** to cut (e g a tail)
short **2** to make a deduction from (e g wages) **3** to take
away (a specified amount) *from*
⁴**dock** *n* **1a** a usu artificially enclosed body of water in a
port or harbour, where a ship can moor (e g for repair
work to be carried out) **b** *pl* the total number of such
enclosures in a harbour, together with wharves, sheds, etc
2 *chiefly NAm* a wharf – **in dock** in a garage or repair
shop ⟨*my car's in dock at the moment*⟩
⁵**dock** *vt* **1** to haul or guide into a dock **2** to join (e g 2
spacecraft) together while in space ~ *vi* **1** to come or go
into dock **2** *of spacecraft* to join together while in
space
⁶**dock** *n* the prisoner's enclosure in a criminal court – **in**
the dock on trial ⟨*always found himself* in the dock *for his*
opinions⟩
docker *n* sby employed in loading and unloading ships,
barges, etc
¹**docket** *n* **1** a brief written summary of a document **2a** a
document recording the contents of a shipment or the
payment of customs duties **b** a label attached to goods
bearing identification or instructions **c** (a copy of) a
receipt **3a** *NAm* **(1)** a formal record of legal proceedings
(2) a list of legal causes to be tried **b** *chiefly NAm* a list
of business matters to be acted on
²**docket** *vt* **1** to put an identifying statement or label on **2**
to make an abstract of (e g legal proceedings) **3** *NAm* to
place on the docket for legal action
dockyard *n* a place or enclosure in which ships are built
or repaired
¹**doctor** *n* **1a** *also* **Doctor of the Church,** *often cap* a
theologian whose doctrines the Roman Catholic church
holds to be authoritative **b** a holder of the highest level of
academic degree conferred by a university **2a** one qualified to practise medicine; a physician or surgeon **b** *NAm*
a licensed dentist or veterinary surgeon **3** sby skilled in
repairing or treating a usu specified type of machine,

vehicle, etc **4** *archaic* a learned or authoritative teacher – **doctoral** *adj*, **doctorate** *n*, **doctorship** *n*

²doctor *vt* **1a** to give medical treatment to **b** to repair, mend **2a** to adapt or modify for a desired end ⟨~ed *the play to suit the audience*⟩ **b** to alter in a dishonest way **3** to castrate or spay – *euph* ~ *vi* to practise medicine – *infml*

doctrinaire *n or adj* (one) concerned with abstract theory to the exclusion of practical considerations – chiefly *derog* – **doctrinairism** *n*

doctrinal *adj* of or concerned with doctrine – **doctrinally** *adv*

doctrine *n* **1** sthg that is taught **2** a principle or the body of principles in a branch of knowledge or system of belief

¹document *n* an original or official paper that gives information about or proof of sthg

²document *vt* **1** to provide documentary evidence of **2a** to support with factual evidence, references, etc **b** to be or provide a documentary account of **3** to provide (a ship) with papers required by law recording ownership, cargo, etc

¹documentary *adj* **1** being or consisting of documents; contained or certified in writing ⟨~ *evidence*⟩ **2** presenting or based on factual material – **documentarily** *adv*

²documentary *n* a broadcast or film that presents a factual account of a person or topic using a variety of techniques (e g narrative and interview) – **documentarist** *n*

documentation *n* (the provision or use of) documents or documentary evidence – **documentational** *adj*

¹dodder *n* any of a genus of leafless plants of the bindweed family that are wholly parasitic on other plants

²dodder *vi* **1** to tremble or shake from weakness or age **2** to walk feebly and unsteadily – **dodderer** *n*

doddering, doddery *adj* weak, shaky, and slow, esp because of old age

doddle *n, chiefly Br* a very easy task – *infml*

¹dodge *vi* to shift position suddenly and usu repeatedly (e g to avoid a blow or a pursuer) ~ *vt* **1** to evade (e g a duty) usu by trickery **2a** to avoid by a sudden or repeated shift of position **b** to avoid an encounter with

²dodge *n* **1** a sudden movement to avoid sthg **2** a clever device to evade or trick ⟨*a tax* ~⟩

dodgem, dodgem car *n, Br* any of a number of small electric cars designed to be steered about and bumped into one another as a fun-fair amusement

dodger *n* one who uses clever and often dishonest methods, esp to avoid payment (e g of taxes) or responsibility

dodgy *adj, chiefly Br* **1** shady, dishonest ⟨*a* ~ *person*⟩ **2** risky, dangerous ⟨*a* ~ *plan*⟩ **3** liable to collapse, fail, or break down ⟨*that chair's a bit* ~⟩ *USE* infml

dodo *n, pl* **dodoes, dodos** an extinct heavy flightless bird that formerly lived on the island of Mauritius

do down *vt, chiefly Br* **1** to cheat **2** to speak badly of; belittle

doe *n, pl* **does**, *esp collectively* **doe** the adult female fallow deer; *broadly* the adult female of any of various mammals (e g the rabbit) or birds (e g the guinea fowl) of which the male is called a buck

doer *n* one who takes action or participates actively in sthg, rather than theorizing

does *pres 3rd sing of* DO

doeskin *n* **1** (leather made from) the skin of a doe **2** a smooth closely woven woollen fabric

doff *vt* to take off (one's hat) in greeting or as a sign of respect

¹dog *n* **1a** a 4-legged flesh-eating domesticated mammal occurring in a great variety of breeds and prob descended from the common wolf **b** any of a family of carnivores to which the dog belongs **c** a male dog **2a** any of various usu simple mechanical devices for holding, fastening, etc that consist of a spike, rod, or bar **b** an andiron **3a** SUN DOG **b** a fogbow **4** *chiefly NAm* sthg inferior of its kind **5** an esp worthless man or fellow ⟨*a lazy* ~⟩ **6** *pl* feet **7** *pl* ruin ⟨*go to the* ~ s⟩ *USE* (5, 6, &7) infml – **doglike** *adj*

²dog *vt* **-gg-** to pursue closely like a dog; hound

³dog *adj* male ⟨*a* ~ *fox*⟩

dog biscuit *n* a hard dry biscuit for dogs

dog collar *n* CLERICAL COLLAR – infml

dog days *n pl* the hottest days in the year

doge *n* the chief magistrate of the former republics of Venice and Genoa

dog-eared *adj* having dog-ears; *broadly* worn, shabby

dog-eat-dog *adj* marked by ruthless self-interest; cut-throat

dogfight *n* **1** a viciously fought contest **2** a fight between aircraft, usu at close quarters – **dogfight** *vi*

dogfish *n* any of various small sharks

dogged *adj* stubbornly determined – **doggedly** *adv*, **doggedness** *n*

doggerel *n* (an example of) verse that is loosely styled and irregular in measure, esp for comic effect

doggo *adv, Br* in hiding and without moving – infml; chiefly in *lie doggo*

doggoned, doggone *adj or adv, chiefly NAm* damned – euph

¹doggy *adj* **1** resembling or suggestive of a dog ⟨*a* ~ *odour*⟩ **2** concerned with or fond of dogs ⟨*a* ~ *person*⟩ *USE* infml

²doggy, doggie *n* a dog – used esp by or to children

doghouse *n, chiefly NAm* a dog kennel – **in the doghouse** in a state of disfavour – infml

¹dogleg *n* **1** a sharp bend (e g in a road) **2** an angled fairway on a golf course

²dogleg *adj* bent like a dog's hind leg

dogma *n* **1** an authoritative tenet or principle **2** a doctrine or body of doctrines formally and authoritatively stated by a church **3** a point of view or tenet put forth as authoritative without adequate grounds – chiefly *derog*

dogmatic *also* **dogmatical** *adj* **1** of dogma or dogmatics **2** characterized by or given to the use of dogmatism – chiefly *derog* – **dogmatically** *adv*, **dogmaticalness** *n*

dogmatics *n pl but sing or pl in constr* a branch of theology that seeks to interpret the dogmas of a religious faith

dogmatism *n* (unwarranted or arrogant) assertion of opinion – **dogmatist** *n*

do-gooder *n* an earnest often naive and ineffectual humanitarian or reformer

dog paddle *n* an elementary form of swimming (e g for learners) in which the arms paddle and the legs kick – **dog-paddle** *vi*

dogsbody *n, chiefly Br* a person who carries out routine or menial work – infml

dog-tired *n* extremely tired – infml

dogtooth *n* an Early English moulding or architectural ornamentation consisting of a series of 4 leaves radiating from a raised centre

dogwood *n* any of several trees and shrubs with heads of small flowers

doh *n* ³DO

doily, doyley, doyly *n* a small decorative mat, esp of paper, cloth, or plastic openwork, often placed under food, esp cakes, on a plate or stand

do in *vt* **1** to kill ⟨*tried to do him in with a club*⟩ **2** to wear out, exhaust ⟨*walking all day nearly did us in*⟩ USE infml

doings *n, pl* **doings** *also* **doingses,** *chiefly Br* a small object, esp one whose name is forgotten or not known ⟨*screw up that little ~ on the top*⟩ – infml

doldrums *n pl* **1** a depressed state of mind; *the* blues **2** an equatorial ocean region where calms, squalls, and light shifting winds prevail **3** a state of stagnation or slump

dole *n* **1** a distribution of food, money, or clothing to the needy **2** *the* government unemployment benefit

doleful *adj* sad, mournful – **dolefully** *adv,* **dolefulness** *n*

dole out *vt* to give, distribute, or deliver, esp in small portions

doll *n* **1** a small-scale figure of a human being used esp as a child's toy **2a** a (pretty but often silly) young woman – infml **b** an attractive person – slang – **dollish** *adj,* **dollishly** *adv*

dollar *n* **1** a taler **2** (a coin or note representing) the basic money unit of the USA, Canada, Australia, etc **3** *Br* 5 shillings (25p) – slang; no longer in vogue

¹dollop *n* a soft shapeless blob; *esp* a serving of mushy or semiliquid food ⟨*a ~ of mashed potato*⟩

²dollop *vt* to serve *out* carelessly or clumsily

doll's house *n* a child's small-scale toy house

doll up *vt* to dress prettily or showily – infml

¹dolly *n* **1** DOLL 1 – used chiefly by or to children **2** a wooden-pronged instrument for beating and stirring clothes while washing them in a tub **3a** a platform on a roller or on wheels or castors for moving heavy objects **b** a wheeled platform for a film or television camera

²dolly *vi* to move a film or television camera on a dolly towards or away from a subject – usu + *in* or *out*

dolly bird *n, chiefly Br* a pretty young woman, esp one who is a slavish follower of fashion and not regarded as intelligent

dolmen *n* a prehistoric monument consisting of 2 or more upright stones supporting a horizontal slab

dolorous *adj* causing or expressing misery or grief – **dolorously** *adv,* **dolorousness** *n*

dolour, *NAm chiefly* **dolor** *n* mental suffering or anguish

dolphin *n* **1** any of various small toothed whales with the snout elongated into a beak to varying extents **2** a spar or buoy for mooring boats

dolt *n* an extremely dull or stupid person – **doltish** *adj,* **doltishly** *adv,* **doltishness** *n*

Dom *n* **1** – used as a title for Benedictine, Carthusian, and Cistercian monks and some canons regular **2** – used formerly as a title preceding the Christian name of a Portuguese or Brazilian man of rank

-dom *suffix* (→ *n*) **1a** rank or office of ⟨*duke*dom⟩ **b** realm or jurisdiction of ⟨*king*dom⟩ ⟨*Christen*dom⟩ **2** state or fact of being ⟨*free*dom⟩ ⟨*bore*dom⟩ **3** group or class of people having (a specified office, occupation, interest, or character) ⟨*official*dom⟩ ⟨*film*dom⟩

domain *n* **1** a territory over which control is exercised **2** a sphere of influence or activity **3** the set of values to which a variable is limited; *esp* the set of values that the independent variable of a function may take on **4** any of the small randomly oriented regions of uniform magnetization in a ferromagnetic substance

¹dome *n* **1** a (nearly) hemispherical roof or vault **2** a dome-shaped (geological) structure **3** *archaic* a stately building; a mansion – **domal** *adj*

²dome *vt* to cover with or form into a dome

Domesday Book *n* a record of a survey of English lands made by order of William I about 1086

¹domestic *adj* **1** of or devoted to the home or the family

2 of one's own or some particular country; not foreign ⟨*~ politics*⟩ **3a** living near or about the habitations of human beings **b** tame; *also* bred by human beings for some specific purpose (e g food, hunting, etc) – **domestically** *adv*

²domestic *n* a household servant

domesticate *vt* **1** to bring (an animal or species) under human control for some specific purpose (e g for carrying loads, hunting, food, etc) **2** to cause to be fond of or adapted to household duties or pleasures – **domestication**

domestic fowl *n* a chicken, turkey, or other bird developed from the jungle fowl, esp for meat or egg production

domesticity *n* (devotion to) home or family life

domestic science *n* instruction in the household arts

¹domicile *also* **domicil** *n* a home; *esp* a person's permanent and principal home for legal purposes

²domicile *vt* to establish in or provide with a domicile

domiciliary *adj* **1** of or being a domicile **2** taking place or attending in the home ⟨*~ visit*⟩

¹dominant *adj* **1** commanding, controlling, or prevailing over all others **2** overlooking and commanding from a superior height **3** being the one of a pair of bodily structures that is the more effective or predominant in action ⟨*the ~ eye*⟩ **4** being the one of a pair of (genes determining) contrasting inherited characteristics that predominates – **dominance** *n,* **dominantly** *adv*

²dominant *n* **1** a socially dominant individual **2** the fifth note of a diatonic scale

dominate *vt* **1** to exert controlling influence or power over **2** to overlook from a superior height **3** to occupy a commanding or preeminent position in ~ *vi* **1** to have or exert mastery or control **2** to occupy a higher or superior position – **dominator** *n,* **dominative** *adj,* **domination** *n*

domineer *vi* to exercise arbitrary or overbearing control ⟨*a ~ing husband*⟩ – **domineeringly** *adv*

Dominican *n or adj* (a member) of a preaching order of mendicant friars founded by St Dominic in 1215

dominion *n* **1** the power or right to rule; sovereignty **2** absolute ownership **3** *often cap* a self-governing nation of the Commonwealth other than the United Kingdom

domino *n, pl* **dominoes, dominos 1a(1)** a long loose hooded cloak worn with a mask as a masquerade costume **(2)** a half mask worn with a masquerade costume **b** sby wearing a domino **2a** a flat rectangular block whose face is divided into 2 equal parts that are blank or bear from 1 to usu 6 dots arranged as on dice faces **b** *pl but usu sing in constr* any of several games played with a set of usu 28 dominoes

¹don *n* **1** a Spanish nobleman or gentleman – used preceding the Christian name **2** a head, tutor, or fellow in a college of Oxford or Cambridge university; *broadly* a university teacher

²don *vt* **-nn-** PUT ON 1a, b

donate *vb* **1** to make a gift or donation (of), esp to a public or charitable cause **2** to give off or transfer (e g electrons) – **donator** *n*

donation *n* **1** the act of donating **2** sthg donated

¹done 1 *past part of* DO **2** *chiefly dial & NAm past of* DO

²done *adj* **1** conformable to social convention ⟨*it's not ~ to eat peas off your knife*⟩ **2** arrived at or brought to an end; completed **3** physically exhausted; spent **4** no longer involved; through ⟨*I'm ~ with the Army*⟩ **5** doomed to failure, defeat, or death **6** cooked sufficiently **7** arrested, imprisoned – slang ⟨*robbed a bank and got ~ for 10 years*⟩

³done *interj* – used in acceptance of a bet or transaction

done in *adj* physically exhausted – infml

donjon *n* a massive inner tower in a medieval castle

Don Juan *n* a promiscuous man; *broadly* a lady-killer

donkey *n* **1** the domestic ass **2** a stupid or obstinate person

donkey engine *n* a small, usu portable, auxiliary engine

donkey jacket *n* a thick hip-length hard-wearing jacket, usu blue and with a strip of (imitation) leather across the shoulders

donkey's years *n pl, chiefly Br* a very long time – infml

donkeywork *n* hard, monotonous, and routine work – infml

donnish *adj* pedantic – **donnishly** *adv*, **donnishness** *n*

donor *n* **1** a person who gives, donates, or presents **2** sby used as a source of biological material ⟨*a blood ~*⟩ **3a** a compound capable of giving up a part (e g an atom, radical, or elementary particle) for combination with an acceptor **b** an impurity that is added to a semiconductor to increase the number of mobile electrons

¹don't **1** do not **2** does not – nonstandard, though sometimes used by educated speakers ⟨*there are simply certain things he ~ know* – Ezra Pound⟩

²don't *n* a prohibition – usu pl ⟨*a list of dos and ~s*⟩

doodle *vi or n* **doodling** (to make) an aimless scribble or sketch – **doodler** *n*

doodlebug *n* FLYING BOMB – infml

¹doom *n* **1** a law in Anglo-Saxon England **2a** JUDGMENT 2a; *also, archaic* a judicial condemnation **b** JUDGMENT DAY **3a** an (unhappy) destiny **b** unavoidable death or destruction; *also* environmental catastrophe – often in combination ⟨*The road forward does not lie through the despair of doomwatching   B – New Scientist*⟩

²doom *vt* **1** to destine, esp to failure or destruction **2** *archaic* to give judgment against; condemn

doomsday *n, often cap* JUDGMENT DAY; *broadly* some remote point in the future ⟨*if you expect people to work harder for less money, you'll have to wait* from now till ~⟩

door *n* **1** a usu swinging or sliding barrier by which an entry is closed and opened; *also* a similar part of a piece of furniture **2** a doorway **3** a means of access – **doorless** *adj* – **at someone's door** as a charge against sby as being responsible ⟨*laid the blame* at our door⟩

doorframe *n* **1** a frame round the opening in which a door is fitted **2** the framework in which the panels of a door are fitted

doorkeeper *n* a person who guards the main door to a building and lets people in and out

doorknob *n* a knob that when turned releases a door latch

doorman *n* a (uniformed) person who tends the entrance to a hotel, theatre, etc and assists people (e g in calling taxis)

doormat *n* **1** a mat (e g of bristles) placed before or inside a door for wiping dirt from the shoes **2** a person who submits to bullying and indignities – infml

doornail *n* a large-headed nail formerly used for the strengthening or decoration of doors – chiefly in *dead as a doornail*

doorstep *n* **1** a step in front of an outer door **2** *Br* a very thick slice of bread – infml

door-to-door *adj* **1** making a usu unsolicited call (e g for selling or canvassing) at every home in an area **2** providing delivery to a s specified address

doorway *n* an entrance into a building or room that is closed by means of a door

do over *vt, Br* to attack and injure – slang

¹dope *n* **1a** a thick liquid or pasty preparation **b** a preparation for giving a desired quality to a substance or surface **c** a coating (e g a cellulose varnish) applied to a surface or fabric (e g of an aeroplane or balloon) to improve strength, impermeability, or tautness **2** absorbent or adsorbent material used in various manufacturing processes (e g the making of dynamite) **3a** marijuana, opium, or another drug **b** a preparation given illegally to a racing horse, greyhound, etc to make it run faster or slower **4** a stupid person – infml **5** information, esp from a reliable source – infml

²dope *vt* **1** to treat or affect with dope; *esp* to give a narcotic to **2** to add an impurity to (a semiconductor) so as to give the required electrical properties ~*vi* to take dope – **doper** *n*

dopey, dopy *adj* **1a** dulled by alcohol or a narcotic **b** stupefied (e g by a drug or sleep) **2** dull, stupid – infml – **dopiness** *n*

¹Doric *adj* **1** (characteristic) of the Dorians or their language **2** of the oldest and simplest of the 3 Greek orders of architecture

²Doric *n* **1** a dialect of ancient Greek **2** a broad rustic dialect of English, esp a Scots one

dormant *adj* **1** marked by a suspension of activity: e g **a** temporarily devoid of external activity ⟨*a ~ volcano*⟩ **b** temporarily in abeyance ⟨*the report lay ~ for several years until its suggestions were taken up by a new administration*⟩ **2** (appearing to be) asleep or inactive, esp throughout winter – **dormancy** *n*

dormer *n* a window set vertically in a structure projecting through a sloping roof

dormitory *n* **1** a large room containing a number of beds **2** a residential community from which the inhabitants commute to their places of employment ⟨*a ~ town*⟩

dormouse *n* any of numerous small Old World rodents having a long bushy tail

dorsal *adj* relating to or situated near or on the back or top surface esp of an animal or aircraft or of any of its parts – **dorsally** *adv*

dosage *n* **1a** the amount of a dose of medicine **b** the giving of such a dose **2** the presence and relative representation or strength of a factor or agent

dose *n* **1a** the measured quantity of medicine to be taken at one time **b** the quantity of radiation administered or absorbed **2** a part of an experience to which one is exposed ⟨*a ~ of hard work*⟩ **3** an infection with a venereal disease – slang – **dose** *vt*

²dose *vt* to give a dose, esp of medicine, to

doss *n, chiefly Br* **1** a crude or makeshift bed, esp one in a dosshouse **2** a short sleep *USE* slang

doss down *vi, chiefly Br* to sleep or bed down in a makeshift bed – infml

dosser *n, chiefly Br* a down-and-out, esp one who is forced to sleep in dosshouses

dosshouse *n, chiefly Br* a hostel for derelicts

dossier *n* a file of papers containing a detailed report or information

dost *archaic pres 2 sing of* DO

¹dot *n* **1** a small spot; a speck **2a(1)** a small point made with a pointed instrument **(2)** a small round mark used in spelling or punctuation **b(1)** a point after a note or rest in music indicating augmentation of the time value by one half **(2)** a point over or under a note indicating that it is to be played staccato **3** a precise point, esp in time ⟨*arrived at 6 on the ~*⟩ **4** a signal (e g a flash or audible tone) of relatively short duration that is one of the 2 fundamental units of Morse code

²dot *vb* **-tt-** *vt* **1** to mark with a dot **2** to intersperse with dots or objects scattered at random ⟨*boats* ~ *ting the lake*⟩ ~*vi* to make a dot

dotage *n* a state or period of senile mental decay resulting in feeblemindedness

dote *vi* **1** to exhibit mental decline of or like that of old age **2** to show excessive or foolish fondness – usu + *on* – **doter** *n*, **dotingly** *adv*

doth *archaic pres 3 sing of* DO

dottle *n* (partially) unburnt tobacco left in the bowl of a pipe

dotty *adj* **1** crazy, mad **2** amiably eccentric or absurd USE *infml* – **dottily** *adv*, **dottiness** *n*

¹double *adj* **1** twofold, dual **2** consisting of 2, usu combined, similar members or parts ⟨*an egg with a* ~ *yolk*⟩ **3** being twice as great or as many ⟨~ *the number of expected applicants*⟩ **4** marked by duplicity; deceitful **5** folded in 2 **6** of twofold or extra size, strength, or value ⟨*a* ~ *Scotch*⟩ ⟨*a* ~ *room*⟩ **7** *of a plant or flower* having more than the normal number of petals or ray flowers – **doubleness** *n*

²double *n* **1** a double amount; *esp* a double measure of spirits **2a** a living person who closely resembles another living person **b** a wraith; a doppelgänger **c(1)** an understudy **(2)** one who resembles an actor and takes his/her place in scenes calling for special skills **3** a sharp turn or twist **4a** a bet in which the winnings and stake from a first race are bet on a second race **b** two wins in or on horse races, esp in a single day's racing **5** an act of doubling in a card game **6** the outermost narrow ring on a dartboard counting double the stated score; *also* a throw in darts that lands there – **at the double** at a fast rate between running and walking; *specif, of a military order to move* in double time

³double *adv* **1** to twice the extent or amount **2** two together

⁴double *vb* **doubled; doubling** *vt* **1a** to increase by adding an equal amount **b** to amount to twice the number of **c** to make a call in bridge that increases the value of tricks won or lost on (an opponent's bid) **2a** to make into 2 thicknesses; fold **b** to clench ⟨~d *his fist*⟩ **c** to cause to stoop or bend over – usu + *up* or *over* **3** to cause (troops) to move in double time **4** to cause (a billiard ball) to rebound ~*vi* **1a** to become twice as much or as many **b** to double a bid (e g in bridge) **2** to turn back on one's course – usu + *back* **3** to become bent or folded, usu in the middle – usu + *up* or *over* **4** to serve an additional purpose – usu + *as* **5** to hurry along; *esp, of troops* to move in double time **6** *of a billiard ball* to rebound

double-barrelled *adj* **1** *of a firearm* having 2 barrels **2** having a double purpose ⟨*asked a* ~ *question*⟩ **3** *of a surname* having 2 parts

double bass *n* the largest instrument in the violin family tuned a fifth below the cello – **double bassist** *n*

double bed *n* a bed for 2 people

double-breasted *adj* having a front fastening with one half of the front overlapping the other and usu a double row of buttons and a single row of buttonholes ⟨*a* ~ *coat*⟩

double check *vb or n* (to make or subject to) a careful check, esp for a second time

double chin *n* a chin with a fleshy fold under it

double cream *n* thick heavy cream that contains 48 per cent butterfat and is suitable for whipping

double-cross *vt or n* (to deceive by) an act of betraying or cheating – **double-crosser** *n*

double-dealing *adj or n* underhand or deceitful (action) – **double-dealer** *n*

double-decker *n* sthg that has 2 decks, levels, or layers; *esp* a bus with seats on 2 floors

double declutch *vi, Br* to change gear in a motor vehicle by disengaging the gear twice, first to pass to neutral, then to pass to the desired gear

double dutch *n, often cap 2nd D* unintelligible or nonsensical speech or writing; gibberish – *infml*

double-edged *adj* having 2 purposes or possible interpretations; *specif, of a remark* seeming innocent, but capable of a malicious interpretation

double entendre *n, pl* **double entendres** an ambiguous word or expression one of whose meanings is usu risqué

double first *n, Br* first-class honours gained in 2 university examinations or subjects

double glazing *n* a system of glazing in which 2 panes of glass are separated by an air space providing heat and sound insulation; *also* the 2 panes of glass so used – **double-glaze** *vt*

double-jointed *adj* having or being a joint that permits an exceptional degree of flexibility of the parts joined

double-park *vi* to park beside a row of vehicles already parked parallel to the kerb

double-quick *adj* very quick – **double-quick** *adv*

doubles *n, pl* **doubles** a game between 2 pairs of players

double stopping *n* the simultaneous playing of 2 strings of a bowed instrument (e g a violin)

doublet *n* **1** a man's close-fitting jacket, with or without sleeves, worn in Europe, esp in the 15th to 17th c **2** two thrown dice showing the same number on the upper face **3** either of a pair; *specif* either of 2 words (e g *guard* and *ward*) in a language having the same derivation but a different meaning

double take *n* a delayed reaction to a surprising or significant situation – esp in *do a double take*

double-talk *n* involved and often deliberately ambiguous language – **double-talk** *vi*, **double-talker** *n*

doublethink *n* a simultaneous belief in 2 contradictory ideas

double time *n* **1** a rate of marching of twice the number of steps per minute as the normal slow rate **2** payment of a worker at twice his/her regular wage rate

double up *vi* to share accommodation designed for one

doubloon *n* a former gold coin of Spain and Spanish America

doubly *adv* **1** to twice the degree ⟨~ *pleased*⟩ **2** in 2 ways

¹doubt *vt* **1** to be in doubt about ⟨*he* ~s *everyone's word*⟩ **2a** to lack confidence in; distrust **b** to consider unlikely ~*vi* to be uncertain – **doubtable** *adj*, **doubter** *n*, **doubtingly** *adv*

²doubt *n* **1** (a state of) uncertainty of belief or opinion **2** a lack of confidence; distrust **3** an inclination not to believe or accept; a reservation – **in doubt** uncertain – **no doubt** doubtless

doubtful *adj* **1** causing doubt; open to question **2a** lacking a definite opinion; hesitant **b** uncertain in outcome; not settled **3** of questionable worth, honesty, or validity – **doubtfully** *adv*, **doubtfulness** *n*

doubting Thomas *n* a habitually doubtful person

doubtless *adv* **1** without doubt **2** probably

douche *n* (a device for giving) a jet or current of fluid, directed against a part or into a cavity of the body, esp the vagina – **douche** *vb*

dough *n* **1** a mixture that consists essentially of flour or meal and milk, water, or another liquid and is stiff enough to knead or roll **2** money – slang – **doughlike** *adj*

doughnut *n* a small round or ring-shaped cake that is often made with a yeast dough, filled with jam, and deep-fried

doughty *adj* valiant, bold – poetic – **doughtily** *adv*, **doughtiness** *n*

doughy *adj* unhealthily pale; pasty

do up *vt* 1 to repair, restore ⟨do up *old furniture*⟩ 2 to wrap up ⟨do up *a parcel*⟩ 3 to fasten (clothing or its fastenings) together ⟨*she* did *her blouse* up⟩ 4 to make more beautiful or attractive ⟨*she's* done *herself* up *for the party*⟩ – infml

dour *adj* 1 stern, harsh 2 gloomy, sullen – **dourly** *adv*, **dourness** *n*

douse, dowse *vt* to take (a sail) in or down

douse, dowse *vt* 1 to plunge into or drench with water 2 to extinguish ⟨~ *the lights*⟩ – **douser** *n*

dove *n* 1 any of various (smaller and slenderer) types of pigeon 2 an advocate of negotiation and compromise; *esp* an opponent of war – usu contrasted with *hawk* – **dovish** *adj*, **dovishness** *n*

dove *NAm past of* DIVE

dovecot, dovecote *n* a small compartmented raised house or box for domestic pigeons

dovetail *n* a tenon like a dove's tail and the mortise into which it fits to form a joint

dovetail *vb* 1 to join (as if) by means of dovetails 2 to fit skilfully together to form a whole

dowager *n* 1 a widow holding property or a title received from her deceased husband 2 a dignified elderly woman

dowdy *adj* 1 not neat or smart in appearance 2 old-fashioned, frumpy – **dowdily** *adv*, **dowdiness** *n*, **dowdyish** *adj*

dowel *n* a usu metal or wooden pin fitting into holes in adjacent pieces to preserve their relative positions; *also* rods of wood or metal for sawing into such pins

dowel *vt* -ll- (*NAm* -l-, -ll-) to fasten by dowels

dower *n* a widow's legal share during her life of her deceased husband's property – no longer used technically

down *n* (a region of) undulating treeless usu chalk uplands, esp in S England – usu pl with sing. meaning

down *adv* 1a at or towards a relatively low level ⟨~ *into the cellar*⟩ ⟨*the river is* ~⟩ b downwards from the surface of the earth or water c below the horizon d downstream e in or into a lying or sitting position ⟨*lie* ~⟩ f to or on the ground, surface, or bottom ⟨*house burnt* ~⟩ ⟨*telephone wires are* ~⟩ g so as to conceal a particular surface ⟨*turned it face* ~⟩ h downstairs 2 ON THE SPOT 2; *esp* as an initial payment ⟨*paid £10* ~⟩ 3a(1) in or into a relatively low condition or status ⟨*family has come* ~ *in the world*⟩ – sometimes used interjectionally to express opposition ⟨~ *with the oppressors!*⟩ (2) to prison – often + *go* or *send* b(1) in or into a state of relatively low intensity or activity ⟨*calm* ~⟩ ⟨*turn the radio* ~⟩ (2) into silence ⟨*shouted him* ~⟩ (3) into a slower pace or lower gear ⟨*changed* ~ *into second*⟩ c lower in amount, price, figure, or rank ⟨*prices are coming* ~⟩ d behind an opponent ⟨*we're 3 points* ~⟩ 4a so as to be known, recognized, or recorded, esp on paper ⟨*scribbled it* ~⟩ ⟨*you're* ~ *to speak next*⟩ – compare SET DOWN, PUT DOWN b so as to be firmly held in position ⟨*stick* ~ *the flap of the envelope*⟩ ⟨*don't like to feel tied* ~⟩ c to the moment of catching or discovering ⟨*track the criminal* ~⟩ 5 in a direction conventionally the opposite of up: e g a to leeward b in or towards the south c *chiefly Br* away from the capital of a country or from a university city ⟨~ *in Wiltshire*⟩ d to or at the front of a theatrical stage 6 DOWNWARDS 3, 4 ⟨*jewels handed* ~ *in the family*⟩ 7a to a concentrated state ⟨*got his report* ~ *to 3 pages*⟩ b so as to be flattened, reduced, eroded, or diluted ⟨*water* ~

the gin⟩ ⟨*heels worn* ~⟩ c completely from top to bottom ⟨*hose the car* ~⟩

down *adj* 1 directed or going downwards ⟨*the* ~ *escalator*⟩ 2a depressed, dejected b ill ⟨~ *with flu*⟩ 3 having been finished or dealt with ⟨*eight* ~ *and two to go*⟩ 4 with the rudder to windward – used with reference to a ship's helm 5 *chiefly Br* bound in a direction regarded as down; *esp* travelling away from a large town, esp London

down *prep* 1a down along, round, through, towards, in, into, or on b at the bottom of ⟨*the bathroom is* ~ *those stairs*⟩ 2 *Br* down to; to ⟨*going* ~ *the shops*⟩ – nonstandard

down *n* a grudge, prejudice – often in *have a down on*

down *vt* 1 to cause to go or come down 2 to drink down; swallow quickly – infml 3 to defeat – infml – **down tools** *chiefly Br* to stop working; esp ¹STRIKE 7

down *n* a covering of soft fluffy feathers

down-and-out *n or adj* (sby) destitute or impoverished

downbeat *n* the principally accented (e g the first) note of a bar of music

downbeat *adj* 1 pessimistic, gloomy 2 relaxed, informal

downcast *adj* 1 dejected, depressed 2 directed downwards ⟨*with* ~ *eyes*⟩

downdraught *n* a downward movement of gas, esp air (e g in a chimney)

downer *n* a depressing experience or situation – infml

downfall *n* 1 (a cause of) a sudden fall (e g from high rank or power) 2 an often heavy fall of rain or esp snow – **downfallen** *adj*

downgrade *vt* 1 to lower in rank, value, or importance 2 to alter the status of (a job) so as to lower the rate of pay

downhearted *adj* downcast, dejected – **downheartedly** *adv*, **downheartedness** *n*

downhill *n* a skiing race downhill against time

downhill *adv* 1 towards the bottom of a hill 2 towards a lower or inferior state or level – in *go downhill*

downhill *adj* sloping downhill

Downing Street *n* the British government; *also* (a spokesman for) the British prime minister ⟨*talks between Dublin and* ~⟩ ⟨~ *is expected to announce cabinet changes soon*⟩

down payment *n* a deposit paid at the time of purchase or delivery

downpour *n* a heavy fall of rain

downright *adv* thoroughly, outright ⟨~ *mean*⟩

downright *adj* 1 absolute, thorough ⟨*a* ~ *lie*⟩ 2 plain, blunt ⟨*a* ~ *man*⟩ – **downrightly** *adv*, **downrightness** *n*

Down's syndrome *n* a form of congenital mental deficiency in which a child is born with slanting eyes, a broad short skull, and broad hands with short fingers; mongolism

downstage *adv or adj* at the front of a theatrical stage; *also* towards the audience or camera

downstairs *adv* down the stairs; on or to a lower floor

downstairs *adj* situated on the main, lower, or ground floor of a building

downstairs *n, pl* **downstairs** the lower floor of a building

downstream *adv or adj* in the direction of the flow of a stream

down-to-earth *adj* practical, realistic

downtown *adv, adj, or n, chiefly NAm* (to, towards, or in) the lower part or main business district of a town or city

downtrodden *adj* oppressed by those in power

downward *adj* 1 moving or extending downwards ⟨*the ~ path*⟩ 2 descending to a lower pitch 3 descending from a head, origin, or source – **downwardly** *adv,* **downwardness** *n*

downwards *adv* 1a from a higher to a lower place or level; in the opposite direction from up ⟨*sun sank ~*⟩ b downstream c so as to conceal a particular surface ⟨*turned it face ~*⟩ 2a from a higher to a lower condition b going down in amount, price, figure, or rank ⟨*from the fourth form ~*⟩ 3 from an earlier time 4 from an ancestor or predecessor

downwind *adv or adj* in the direction that the wind is blowing

downy *adj* 1 resembling or covered in down 2 made of down

dowry *n* the money, goods, or estate that a woman brings to her husband in marriage

¹**dowse** *vt* to douse

²**dowse** *vi* to search for hidden water or minerals with a divining rod

dowsing rod *n* a divining rod

doxology *n* a liturgical expression of praise to God

doyen, *fem* **doyenne** *n* the senior or most experienced member of a body or group ⟨*Dan Maskell, ~ of tennis commentators*⟩

doyley, doyly *n* a doily

doze *vi* 1 to sleep lightly 2 to fall into a light sleep – usu + *off* – **doze** *n,* **dozer** *n*

doze away *vt* to pass (time) drowsily

dozen *n, pl* **dozens, dozen** 1 a group of 12 2 an indefinitely large number – usu pl with sing. meaning ⟨*I've ~s of things to do*⟩ – **dozen** *adj,* **dozenth** *adj*

dozy *adj* 1 drowsy, sleepy 2 *chiefly Br* stupid and slow-witted – *infml* – **doziness** *n*

¹**drab** *adj* **-bb-** 1 of a dull brown colour 2 dull, cheerless – **drably** *adv,* **drabness** *n*

²**drab** *n* – see DRIBS AND DRABS

drachm *n* 1 a drachma 2 a unit of weight equal to ⅛oz apothecary (about 3.89g)

drachma *n, pl* **drachmas, drachmae, drachmai** 1 any of various ancient Greek units of weight 2a an ancient Greek silver coin equivalent to 6 obols

draconian, draconic *adj, often cap, esp of a law* extremely severe; drastic

¹**draft** *n* 1 the act, result, or plan of drawing out or sketching: e g a a construction plan b a preliminary sketch, outline, or version ⟨*a rough ~ of a book*⟩ 2a a group of individuals selected for a particular job b (the group of individuals resulting from) the selecting of certain animals from a herd or flock 3a an order for the payment of money drawn by one person or bank on another b (an instance of) drawing from or making demands on sthg 4 *chiefly NAm* conscription – usu + *the* 5 *NAm* a draught

²**draft** *adj* 1 *esp of livestock* chosen from a group 2 *NAm* draught

³**draft** *vt* 1 to draw the preliminary sketch, version, or plan of 2 *NAm* to conscript for military service – **draftable** *adj,* **draftee** *n,* **drafter** *n*

draftsman *n* sby who draws up legal documents or other writings

¹**drag** *n* 1 a device for dragging under water to search for objects 2a sthg that retards motion, action, or progress b the retarding force acting on a body (e g an aircraft) moving through a fluid (e g air), parallel and opposite to the direction of motion c a burden, encumbrance 3 an object drawn over the ground to leave a scented trail (e g for dogs to follow) 4a a drawing along or over a surface with effort or pressure b motion effected with slowness or

difficulty c a drawing into the mouth of pipe, cigarette, or cigar smoke – *infml* 5a woman's clothing worn by a man – *slang;* often in *in drag* b clothing – *slang* 6 a dull or boring person or experience – *slang*

²**drag** *vb* **-gg-** *vt* 1a to draw slowly or heavily; haul b to cause to move with painful or undue slowness or difficulty 2a to search (a body of water) with a drag b to catch with a dragnet or trawl 3 to bring by force or compulsion – *infml* ⟨*had to ~ her husband to the opera*⟩ ~ *vi* 1 to hang or lag behind 2 to trail along on the ground 3 to move or proceed laboriously or tediously – *infml* ⟨*the book ~s*⟩ 4 to draw tobacco smoke into the mouth – usu + *on* ⟨~ *on a cigarette*⟩; *infml* – **draggingly** *adv* – **drag one's feet/heels** to act in a deliberately slow, dilatory, or ineffective manner

³**drag** *adj* of drag racing

draggle *vt* to make wet and dirty ~ *vi* 1 to trail on the ground 2 to straggle

draggy *adj* dull or boring ⟨*spent a really ~ evening with relations*⟩

dragnet *n* 1 a net drawn along the bottom of a body of water or the ground to catch fish or small game 2 a network of measures for apprehension (e g of criminals)

dragoman *n, pl* **dragomans, dragomen** an interpreter, chiefly of Arabic, Turkish, or Persian, employed esp in the Near East

dragon *n* 1 a mythical winged and clawed monster, often breathing fire 2 a fierce, combative, or very strict person – **dragonish** *adj*

dragonfly *n* any of a suborder of long slender-bodied often brightly coloured insects that have a fine network of veins in their wings and often live near water

¹**dragoon** *n* a member of a European military unit formerly composed of mounted infantrymen armed with carbines

²**dragoon** *vt* 1 to reduce to subjection by harsh use of troops 2 to (attempt to) force into submission by persecution

¹**drain** *vt* 1a to draw off (liquid) gradually or completely b to exhaust physically or emotionally 2a to make gradually dry ⟨~ *a swamp*⟩ b to carry away the surface water of c to deplete or empty (as if) by drawing off gradually ⟨*war that ~s a nation of youth and wealth*⟩ d to empty by drinking the contents of ⟨~ *ed his glass*⟩ ~ *vi* 1 to flow off gradually 2 to become gradually dry – **drainer** *n*

²**drain** *n* 1 a means (e g a pipe) by which usu liquid matter is drained away 2 a gradual outflow or withdrawal 3 sthg that causes depletion; a burden – **down the drain** being used wastefully or brought to nothing ⟨*years of work went down the drain in the fire at his studio*⟩

drainage *n* 1a draining b sthg drained off 2 a system of drains

draining board *n, Br* a usu grooved and often slightly sloping surface at the side of a sink unit on which washed dishes are placed to drain

drainpipe *n* a pipe that carries waste, liquid sewage, excess water, etc away from a building

drainpipe trousers, drainpipes *n pl* tight trousers with narrow legs

¹**drake** *n* a mayfly; *esp* an artificial one used as bait in angling

²**drake** *n* a male duck

dram *n* 1 a unit of mass equal to ¹/₁₆oz avoirdupois (about 1.77g) 2 *chiefly Scot* a tot of spirits, usu whisky

drama *n* 1 a composition in verse or prose intended to portray life or character or to tell a story through action and dialogue; *specif* a play 2 dramatic art, literature, or affairs 3 a situation or set of events having the qualities of a drama

dramatic *adj* 1 of drama 2a suitable to or characteristic of drama; vivid **b** striking in appearance or effect – **dramatically** *adv*

dramatic irony *n* incongruity between a situation developed in a play and the accompanying words or actions that is understood by the audience but not by the characters

dramatics *n pl* **1** *sing or pl in constr* the study or practice of theatrical arts (e g acting and stagecraft) **2** dramatic behaviour; *esp* an exaggerated display of emotion

dramatis personae *n pl* (a list of) the characters or actors in a play

dramatist *n* a playwright

dramatize, -ise *vt* **1** to adapt (e g a novel) for theatrical presentation **2** to present in a dramatic manner – *vi* **1** to be suitable for dramatization **2** to behave dramatically – **dramatizable** *adj*, **dramatization** *n*

drank *past of* DRINK

drape *vt* **1** to cover or decorate (as if) with folds of cloth **2** to hang or stretch loosely or carelessly ⟨~*d his legs over the chair*⟩ **3** to arrange in flowing lines or folds – **drapable** *also* **drapeable** *adj*, **drapability** *also* **drapeability** *n*

drape *n* a piece of drapery; *esp, chiefly NAm* a curtain

draper *n, chiefly Br* a dealer in cloth and sometimes also in clothing, haberdashery, and soft furnishings

drapery *n* **1a** (a piece of) cloth or clothing arranged or hung gracefully, esp in loose folds **b** cloth or textile fabrics used esp for clothing or soft furnishings; *also, NAm* hangings of heavy fabric used as a curtain **2** the draping or arranging of materials **3a** *Br* the trade of a draper **b** the goods sold by a draper

drastic *adj* **1** acting rapidly or violently ⟨a ~ *purgative*⟩ **2** radical in effect or action; severe – **drastically** *adv*

drat *vt* -**tt**- to damn – euph; used as a mild oath

draught, NAm chiefly draft *n* **1** (the quantity of fish taken by) the act of drawing a net **2** a team of animals together with what they draw **3** the act or an instance of drinking; *also* the portion drunk in such an act **4** the act of drawing (e g from a cask); *also* a quantity of liquid so drawn **5** the depth of water a ship requires to float in, esp when loaded **6** a current of air in a closed-in space – **on draught** *of beer or cider* ready to be served from the cask or barrel with or without the use of added gas in serving

draught, NAm chiefly draft *adj* **1** used for drawing loads ⟨~ *oxen*⟩ **2** served from the barrel or cask ⟨~ *beer*⟩

draughtboard *n* a chessboard

draughts *n pl but sing or pl in constr, Br* a game for 2 players each of whom moves his/her usu 12 draughtsmen according to fixed rules across a chessboard usu using only the black squares

draughtsman *n* **1a** an artist skilled in drawing **b** *fem* **1draughtswoman** sby who draws plans and sketches (e g of machinery or structures) **2** *Br* a disc-shaped piece used in draughts

draughty *adj* having a cold draught blowing through

draw *vb* **drew; drawn** *vt* **1** to pull, haul **2** to cause to go in a certain direction ⟨drew *him aside*⟩ **3a** to attract ⟨honey ~s *flies*⟩ **b** to bring in, gather, or derive from a specified source ⟨a college that ~s *its students from many towns*⟩ ⟨drew *inspiration from his teacher*⟩ **c** to bring on oneself; provoke ⟨drew *enemy fire*⟩ **d** to bring out by way of response; elicit ⟨drew *cheers from the audience*⟩ **4** to inhale ⟨drew *a deep breath*⟩ **5a** to bring or pull out, esp with effort ⟨~ *a tooth*⟩ ⟨~ *a sword*⟩ **b** to extract the essence from ⟨~ *tea*⟩ **c** to disembowel ⟨pluck and ~ a goose⟩ **d** to cause (blood) to flow **6** to require (a specified depth) to float in **7a** to accumulate, gain ⟨~ing *interest*⟩ **b** to take (money) from a place of deposit – often + out

c to use in making a cash demand ⟨~ing *a cheque on his account*⟩ **d** to receive regularly, esp from a particular source ⟨~ *a salary*⟩ **8a** to take (cards) from a dealer or pack **b** to receive or take at random ⟨drew *a winning number*⟩ **9** to bend (a bow) by pulling back the string **10** to strike (a ball) so as to impart a curved motion or backspin **11** to leave undecided or have equal scores in (a contest) **12** to produce a likeness of (e g by making lines on a surface); portray, delineate **13** to formulate or arrive at by reasoning ⟨~ *a conclusion*⟩ ⟨~ *comparisons*⟩ **14** to pull together and close (e g curtains) **15** to stretch or shape (esp metal) by pulling through dies; *also* to produce (e g a wire) thus **16** to drive game out of – *vi* **1** to come or go steadily or gradually ⟨night ~s *near*⟩ **2** to advance as far as a specified position ⟨drew *level*⟩ ⟨drew *up to the front door*⟩ **3a** to pull back a bowstring **b** to bring out a weapon **4a** to produce or allow a draught ⟨the chimney ~s *well*⟩ **b** *of a sail* to swell out in a wind **5** to steep, infuse ⟨give the tea time to ~⟩ **6** to sketch **7** to finish a competition or contest without either side winning **8a** to make a written demand for payment of money on deposit **b** to obtain resources (e g of information) ⟨~ing *from a common fund of knowledge*⟩ **9** *chiefly NAm* to suck in sthg, esp tobacco smoke – usu + *on* – **draw a blank** to fail to gain the desired object (e g information sought) – **draw lots** to decide an issue by lottery in which objects of unequal length or with different markings are used – **draw on/upon** to use as source of supply ⟨drawing on the whole community for support⟩ – **draw rein** to bring a horse to a stop while riding – **draw stumps** to end play in a cricket match – **draw the/a line 1** to fix an arbitrary boundary between things that tend to merge ⟨the difficulty of drawing a line between art and pornography⟩ **2** to fix a boundary excluding what one will not tolerate or engage in – usu + *at*

draw *n* **1a** a sucking pull on sthg held between the lips ⟨took a ~ *on his pipe*⟩ **b** *the* removing of a handgun from its holster in order to shoot **2** a drawing of lots; a raffle **3** a contest left undecided; a tie **4** sthg that draws public attention or patronage **5** the usu random assignment of starting positions in a competition, esp a competitive sport **6** *NAm* the movable part of a drawbridge

draw away *vi* to move ahead (e g of an opponent in a race) gradually

drawback *n* an objectionable feature; a disadvantage

draw back *vi* to avoid an issue or commitment; retreat

drawbridge *n* a bridge made to be raised up, let down, or drawn aside so as to permit or hinder passage

drawer *n* **1** one who draws a bill of exchange or order for payment or makes a promissory note **2** an open-topped box in a piece of furniture which to open and close slides back and forth in its frame **3** *pl* an undergarment for the lower body – now usu humor

draw in *vt* **1** to cause or entice to enter or participate **2** to sketch roughly ⟨drawing *in the first outlines*⟩ – *vi* **1** *of a train* to come into a station **2** *of successive days* to grow shorter (e g in winter)

drawing *n* **1** the art or technique of representing an object, figure, or plan by means of lines **2** sthg drawn or subject to drawing: e g **a** an amount drawn from a fund **b** a representation formed by drawing

drawing board *n* **1** a board to which paper is attached for drawing on **2** a planning stage ⟨a project still on the ~⟩ ⟨back to the ~⟩

drawing pin *n, Br* a pin with a broad flat head for fastening esp sheets of paper to boards

drawing room *n* **1** a formal reception room **2** LIVING ROOM – fml

¹drawl *vb* to speak or utter slowly and often affectedly, with vowels greatly prolonged – **drawler** *n*, **drawlingly** *adv*

²drawl *n* a drawling manner of speaking – **drawly** *adj*

draw off *vt* to remove (liquid) ~ *vi of troops* to move apart (and form new groups)

draw on *vi* to approach ⟨*night* draws on⟩ ~ *vt* 1 to cause; BRING ON 1 2 to put on ⟨*she* drew on *her gloves*⟩

draw out *vt* 1 to remove, extract 2 to extend beyond a minimum in time; prolong 3 to cause to speak freely

drawstring *n* a string or tape threaded through fabric, which when pulled closes an opening (e g of a bag) or gathers material (e g of curtains or clothes)

draw up *vt* 1 to bring (e g troops) into array 2 DRAFT 1 3 to straighten (oneself) to an erect posture, esp as an assertion of dignity or resentment 4 to bring to a halt ~ *vi* to come to a halt

¹dray *n* a strong low cart or wagon without sides, used esp by brewers

²dray a drey

¹dread *vt* 1 to fear greatly 2 to be extremely apprehensive about

²dread *n* (the object of) great fear, uneasiness, or apprehension

³dread *adj* causing or inspiring dread

dreadful *adj* 1 inspiring dread; causing great and oppressive fear 2a extremely unpleasant or shocking b very disagreeable (e g through dullness or poor quality) 3 extreme ⟨~ *disorder*⟩ – **dreadfully** *adv*, **dreadfulness** *n*

dreadnought *n* a battleship whose main armament consists of big guns of the same calibre

¹dream *n* 1 a series of thoughts, images, or emotions occurring during sleep 2 a daydream, reverie ⟨*walked round in a* ~ *all day*⟩ 3 sthg notable for its beauty, excellence, or enjoyable quality ⟨*the new car goes like a* ~⟩ 4 a strongly desired goal; an ambition ⟨*his* ~ *of becoming president*⟩; *also* a realization of an ambition – often used attributively ⟨*a* ~ *house*⟩ – **dreamful** *adj*, **dreamfully** *adv*, **dreamfulness** *n*, **dreamless** *adj*, **dreamlessly** *adv*, **dreamlessness** *n*, **dreamlike** *adj*

²dream *vb* **dreamed, dreamt** *vi* 1 to have a dream 2 to indulge in daydreams or fantasies ⟨~ing *of a better future*⟩ ~ *vt* 1 to have a dream of 2 to consider as a possibility; imagine 3 to pass (time) in reverie or inaction – usu + *away* – **dreamer** *n* – **dream of** to consider even the possibility of – in neg constructions ⟨*wouldn't* dream *of disturbing you*⟩

dreamboat *n* a highly attractive person of the opposite sex – *infml*; no longer in vogue

dreamland *n* an unreal delightful region existing only in imagination or in fantasy; NEVER-NEVER LAND

dream up *vt* to devise, invent – *infml*

dreamy *adj* 1 pleasantly abstracted from immediate reality 2 given to dreaming or fantasy ⟨*a* ~ *child*⟩ 3a suggestive of a dream in vague or visionary quality b delightful, pleasing; *esp, of a man* sexually attractive – *infml* – **dreamily** *adv*, **dreaminess** *n*

drear *adj* dreary – *poetic*

dreary *adj* causing feelings of cheerlessness or gloom; dull – **drearily** *adv*, **dreariness** *n*

¹dredge *n* 1 an oblong frame with an attached net for gathering fish, shellfish, etc from the bottom of the sea, a river, etc 2 a machine for removing earth, mud, etc usu by buckets on an endless chain or a suction tube

²dredge *vt* **1a** to dig, gather, or pull out with a dredge – often + *up* or *out* **b** to deepen (e g a waterway) with a dredging machine 2 to bring to light by thorough searching – usu + *up* ⟨dredging *up memories*⟩; *infml* ~ *vi* to use a dredge

³dredge *vt* to coat (e g food) by sprinkling (e g with flour) – **dredger** *n*

dredger *n* a barge with an apparatus for dredging harbours, waterways, etc

dreg *n* 1 sediment; lees 2 the most undesirable part ⟨*the* ~s *of society*⟩ USE usu pl with sing. meaning

¹drench *n* a poisonous or medicinal drink, esp put down the throat of an animal

²drench *vt* 1 to administer a drench to (an animal) 2 to make thoroughly wet (e g with falling water or by immersion); saturate

¹dress *vt* 1 to arrange (e g troops) in the proper alignment **2a** to put clothes on **b** to provide with clothing 3 to add decorative details or accessories to; embellish ⟨~ a *Christmas tree*⟩ 4 to prepare for use or service; *esp* to prepare (e g a chicken) for cooking or eating **5a** to apply dressings or medicaments to (e g a wound) **b(1)** to arrange (the hair) **(2)** to groom and curry (an animal) **c** to kill and prepare for market **d** to cultivate, esp by applying manure or fertilizer **e** to finish the surface of (e g timber, stone, or textiles) **f** to arrange goods on a display in (e g a shop window) ~ *vi* **1a** to put on clothing **b** to put on or wear formal, elaborate, or fancy clothes ⟨*guests were expected to* ~ *for dinner*⟩ 2 to align oneself properly in a line 3 *of a man* to have one's genitals lying on a specified side of the trouser crutch ⟨*do you* ~ *to the right or left, sir?*⟩

²dress *n* 1 utilitarian or ornamental covering for the human body; *esp* clothing suitable for a particular purpose or occasion 2 a 1-piece outer garment including both top and skirt usu for a woman or girl 3 covering, adornment, or appearance appropriate or peculiar to a specified time ⟨*18th-century* ~⟩

³dress *adj* of, being, or suitable for an occasion requiring or permitting formal dress ⟨*a* ~ *affair*⟩

dressage *n* the execution by a trained horse of precise movements in response to its rider

dress circle *n* the first or lowest curved tier of seats in a theatre

dress down *vt* to reprove severely – **dressing down** *n*

¹dresser *n* 1 a piece of kitchen furniture resembling a sideboard with a high back and having compartments and shelves for holding dishes and cooking utensils 2 *chiefly NAm* a chest of drawers or bureau with a mirror

²dresser *n* a person who looks after stage costumes and helps actors to dress

dressing *n* 1 a seasoning, sauce, or stuffing 2 material applied to cover a wound, sore, etc 3 manure or compost to improve the growth of plants

dressing gown *n* a loose robe worn esp over nightclothes or when not fully dressed

dressing table *n* a table usu fitted with drawers and a mirror for use while dressing and grooming oneself

dressmaker *n* sby who makes dresses – **dressmaking** *n*

dress rehearsal *n* 1 a full rehearsal of a play in costume and with stage props shortly before the first performance 2 a full-scale practice; DRY RUN 2

dress up *vt* **1a(1)** to clothe in best or formal clothes **(2)** to make suitable for a formal occasion (e g by adding accessories) ⟨*dressing up a smock with a gilt belt and scarves*⟩ **b** to dress in clothes suited to a particular assumed role 2 to present or cause to appear in a certain light (e g by distortion or exaggeration) ~ *vi* to get dressed up

dressy *adj* 1 *of a person* showy in dress 2 *of clothes* stylish, smart 3 overly elaborate in appearance – **dressiness** *n*

drew *past of* DRAW

¹dribble *vb* **dribbled; dribbling** *vi* **1** to fall or flow in drops or in a thin intermittent stream; trickle **2** to let saliva trickle from the mouth; drool **3** to come or issue in piecemeal or disconnected fashion **4a** to dribble a ball or puck **b** to proceed by dribbling **c** *of a ball* to move with short bounces ~ *vt* to propel (a ball or puck) by successive slight taps or bounces with hand, foot, or stick – **dribbler** *n*

²dribble *n* **1** a small trickling stream or flow **2** a tiny or insignificant bit or quantity **3** an act or instance of dribbling

dribs and drabs *n pl* small usu scattered amounts – infml

dried-up *adj* wizened, shrivelled

drier *also* **dryer** *n* **1** a substance that accelerates drying (e g of oils and printing inks) **2** any of various machines for drying sthg (e g the hair or clothes)

¹drift *n* sthg driven, propelled, or urged along or drawn (as if) by a natural agency: e g **1a** a mass of sand, snow, etc deposited (as if) by wind or water **b** rock debris deposited by natural wind, water, etc; *specif* a deposit of clay, sand, gravel, and boulders transported by (running water from) a glacier **2** a general underlying tendency or meaning, esp of what is spoken or written **3** a tool for ramming down or driving sthg, usu into or out of a hole **4** the motion or action of drifting: e g **a** a ship's deviation from its course caused by currents **b** a slow-moving ocean current **c** the lateral motion of an aircraft due to air currents **d** an easy, moderate, more or less steady flow along a spatial course **e** a gradual shift in attitude, opinion, or emotion **f** an aimless course, with no attempt at direction or control **g** a deviation from a true reproduction, representation, or reading **5** a nearly horizontal mine passage on or parallel to a vein or rock stratum **6** a gradual change in a supposedly constant characteristic of a device, esp an electrical one – **drifty** *adj*

²drift *vi* **1a** to become driven or carried along by a current of water or air **b** to move or float smoothly and effortlessly **2a** to move in a random or casual way **b** to become carried along aimlessly ⟨*the conversation* ~*ed from one topic to another*⟩ **3** to pile up under the force of wind or water **4** to deviate from a set adjustment ~ *vt* to pile up in a drift

drifter *n* **1** sby or sthg that travels or moves about aimlessly **2** a coastal fishing boat equipped with drift nets

drift net *n* a large fishing net that hangs vertically and is arranged to drift with the tide, currents, etc

driftwood *n* wood cast up on a shore or beach

¹drill *vt* **1a** to bore or drive a hole in (as if) by the piercing action of a drill **b** to make (e g a hole) by piercing action **2a** to instruct and exercise by repeating **b** to train or exercise in military drill ~ *vi* **1** to make a hole with a drill **2** to engage in esp military drill – **drillable** *adj*

²drill *n* **1** (a device or machine for rotating) a tool with an edged or pointed end for making a hole in a solid substance by revolving or by a succession of blows **2** training in marching and the manual of arms **3** a physical or mental exercise aimed at improving facility and skill by regular practice **4** a marine snail that bores through oyster shells and eats the flesh **5** *chiefly Br* the approved or correct procedure for accomplishing sthg efficiently – infml

³drill *n* **1a** a shallow furrow into which seed is sown **b** a row of seed sown in such a furrow **2** a planting implement that makes holes or furrows, drops in the seed and sometimes fertilizer, and covers them with earth

⁴drill *vt* **1** to sow (seeds) by dropping along a shallow

furrow **2** to sow with seed or set with seedlings inserted in drills

⁵drill *n* a durable cotton fabric in twill weave

drily *adv* dryly

¹drink *vb* **drank; drunk, drank** *vt* **1a** to swallow (a liquid); *also* to swallow the liquid contents of (e g a cup) **b** to take in or suck up; absorb ⟨~ing *air into his lungs*⟩ **c** to take in or receive avidly – usu + *in* ⟨drank *in every word of the lecture*⟩ **2** to join in (a toast) **3** to bring to a specified state by taking drink ⟨drank *himself into oblivion*⟩ ~ *vi* **1** to take liquid into the mouth for swallowing **2** to drink alcoholic beverages, esp habitually or to excess – **drink like a fish** to habitually drink alcohol to excess – **drink to** to drink a toast to

²drink *n* **1a** liquid suitable for swallowing **b** alcoholic drink ⟨*a* ~s *cupboard*⟩ **2** a draught or portion of liquid for drinking **3** excessive consumption of alcoholic beverages ⟨*drove him to* ~⟩ **4** OCEAN 1; *broadly* any sizable body of water – + *the*; infml

drinkable *adj* suitable or safe for drinking

drinker *n* one who drinks alcoholic beverages to excess

¹drip *vb* **-pp-** *vt* to let fall in drops ~ *vi* **1a** to let fall drops of moisture or liquid **b** to overflow (as if) with moisture ⟨*a novel that* ~s *with sentimentality*⟩ **2** to fall (as if) in drops – **dripper** *n*

²drip *n* **1a** the action or sound of falling in drops **b** liquid that falls, overflows, or is forced out in drops **2** a projection for throwing off rainwater **3a** a device for the administration of a liquid at a slow rate, esp into a vein **b** a substance administered by means of a drip ⟨*a saline* ~⟩ **4** a dull or inconsequential person – infml – **dripless** *adj*, **drippy** *adj*

¹drip-dry *vb* to dry with few or no wrinkles when hung dripping wet

²drip-dry *adj* made of a washable fabric that drip-dries

dripping *n* the fat that runs out from meat during roasting

¹drive *vb* **drove; driven** *vt* **1a** to set in motion by physical force **b** to force into position by blows ⟨~ *a nail into the wall*⟩ **c** to repulse or cause to go by force, authority, or influence ⟨~ *the enemy back*⟩ ⟨drove *the thought from my mind*⟩ **d** to set or keep in motion or operation ⟨~ *machinery by electricity*⟩ **2a** to control and direct the course of (a vehicle or draught animal) **b** to convey or transport in a vehicle **3** to carry on or through energetically ⟨driving *a hard bargain*⟩ **4a** to exert inescapable or persuasive pressure on; force **b** to compel to undergo or suffer a change (e g in situation, awareness, or emotional state) ⟨drove *him crazy*⟩ **c** to urge relentlessly to continuous exertion **5** to cause (e g game or cattle) to move in a desired direction **6** to bore (e g a tunnel or passage) **7a** to propel (an object of play) swiftly **b** to play a drive in cricket at (a ball) or at the bowling of (a bowler) ~ *vi* **1** to rush or dash rapidly or with force against an obstruction ⟨*rain driving against the windscreen*⟩ **2** to operate a vehicle **3** to drive an object of play (e g a golf ball) – **drive at** to imply as an ultimate meaning or conclusion ⟨*couldn't work out what she was* driving *at*⟩ – **drive up the wall** to infuriate or madden (sby)

²drive *n* **1** an act of driving: e g **a** a trip in a carriage or motor vehicle **b** a shoot in which the game is driven within the range of the guns **2** a private road giving access from a public way to a building on private land **3** a (military) offensive, aggressive, or expansionist move **4** a strong systematic group effort; a campaign **5a** a motivating instinctual need or acquired desire ⟨*a sexual* ~⟩ ⟨*a* ~ *for perfection*⟩ **b** great zeal in pursuing one's ends **6a** the means for giving motion to a machine (part) ⟨*a chain* ~⟩ **b** the means by or position from which the movement of a motor vehicle is controlled or directed **7** a device including a transport and heads for reading information from or writing information onto a tape, esp magnetic tape, or disc **8** the act or an instance of driving an object of play; *esp* an attacking cricket stroke played conventionally with a straight bat and designed to send the ball in front of the batsman's wicket

drive-in *adj or n* (being) a place (e g a bank, cinema, or restaurant) that people can use while remaining in their cars

¹drivel *vi* -**ll**- (*NAm* -**l**-, -**ll**-), **1** to let saliva dribble from the mouth or mucus run from the nose **2** to talk stupidly and childishly or carelessly – **driveller** *n*

²drivel *n* foolish or childish nonsense

driver *n* **1** a coachman **2** the operator of a motor vehicle **3** an implement (e g a hammer) for driving **4** a mechanical piece for imparting motion to another piece **5** a golf club with a wooden head used in hitting the ball long distances, esp off the tee – **driverless** *adj*

driveway *n* DRIVE 2

driving *adj* **1** that communicates force ⟨*a ~ wheel*⟩ **2a** having great force ⟨*~ rain*⟩ **b** acting with vigour; energetic

¹drizzle *vb* **drizzling** *vi* to rain in very small drops or very lightly ~ *vt* to shed or let fall in minute drops

²drizzle *n* a fine misty rain – **drizzly** *adj*

drogue *n* **1** SEA ANCHOR **2** a small parachute for stabilizing or decelerating sthg or for pulling a larger parachute out of stowage

droll *adj* humorous, whimsical, or odd – **drollness** *n*, **drolly** *adv*

drollery *n* **1** the act or an instance of jesting or droll behaviour **2** droll humour

-drome *comb form* (→ *n*) **1** sthg that runs in (such) a direction ⟨*palindrome*⟩ ⟨*loxodrome*⟩ **2** racecourse ⟨*motor*-drome⟩ ⟨*hippo*drome⟩ **3** large place specially prepared for ⟨*aerodrome*⟩ – **-dromous** *comb form* (→ *adj*)

dromedary *n* a (1-humped) camel bred esp for riding

¹drone *n* **1** the male of a bee (e g the honeybee) that has no sting and gathers no honey **2** sby who lives off others **3** a remotely-controlled pilotless aircraft, missile, or ship

²drone *vi* **1** to make a sustained deep murmuring or buzzing sound **2** to talk in a persistently monotonous tone – **droner** *n*, **droningly** *adv*

³drone *n* **1** any of the usu 3 pipes on a bagpipe that sound fixed continuous notes **2** a droning sound **3** an unvarying sustained bass note

drool *vi* **1a** to secrete saliva in anticipation of food **b** DRIVEL 1 **2** to make a foolishly effusive show of pleasure ~ *vt* to express sentimentally or effusively

¹droop *vi* **1** to hang or incline downwards **2** to become depressed or weakened; languish ~ *vt* to let droop – **droopingly** *adv*

²droop *n* the condition or appearance of drooping – **droopy** *adj*

¹drop *n* **1a(1)** the quantity of fluid that falls in 1 spherical mass **(2)** *pl* a dose of medicine measured by drops **b** a minute quantity ⟨*not a ~ of pity in him*⟩ **2** sthg that resembles a liquid drop: e g **a** an ornament that hangs from a piece of jewellery (e g an earring) **b** a small globular often medicated sweet or lozenge ⟨*pear ~*⟩ ⟨*cough ~*⟩ **3a** the act or an instance of dropping; a fall **b** a decline in quantity or quality **c** (the men or equipment dropped by) a parachute descent **4a** the distance from a higher to a lower level or through which sthg drops **b** a decrease of electric potential **5** sthg that drops, hangs, or falls: e g **a** an unframed piece of cloth stage

scenery **b** a hinged platform on a gallows **6** *NAm* a central point or depository to which sthg (e g mail) is brought for distribution **7** a small quantity of drink, esp alcohol; *broadly* an alcoholic drink – infml **8** (a secret place used for the deposit and collection of) letters or stolen or illegal goods – slang – **droplet** *n* – **at the drop of a hat** without hesitation; promptly – **have/get the drop on** *NAm* to have or get at a disadvantage – slang

²drop *vb* -**pp**- *vi* **1** to fall in drops **2a(1)** to fall, esp unexpectedly or suddenly **(2)** to descend from one level to another ⟨*his voice ~ped*⟩ **b** to fall in a state of collapse or death ⟨*he'll work until he ~s*⟩ **c** *of a card* to become played by reason of the obligation to follow suit **3a** to cease to be of concern; lapse ⟨*let the matter ~*⟩ **b** to become less ⟨*production ~ped*⟩ ~ *vt* **1a** to let fall; cause to fall **b** to drop a catch offered by (a batsman) **2a** to lower from one level or position to another **b** to cause to score (a goal) with a dropkick **5a** to give up (a plan or idea) **b** to leave incomplete; cease ⟨*~ped what he was doing*⟩ **c** to break off an association or connection with ⟨*~ped his old friends*⟩; *also* to leave out of a team or group **6** to leave (a letter representing a speech sound) unsounded ⟨*~ the h in have*⟩ **7a** to utter or mention in a casual way ⟨*~ a hint*⟩ **b** to send through the post ⟨*~ us a line soon*⟩ **8** to lose ⟨*~ped £500 on the stock market*⟩ – infml – **drop a brick/clanger** to make an embarrassing error or mistaken remark – infml

drop behind *vb* to fail to keep up (with)

drop hammer *n* a power hammer raised and then released to drop on metal resting on an anvil or die

drop in *vi* to pay a usu brief, casual, or unexpected visit

dropkick *n* a kick made (e g in rugby) by dropping a football to the ground and kicking it at the moment it starts to rebound – **drop-kick** *vb*, **drop kicker** *n*

drop-off *n* a marked dwindling or decline ⟨*a ~ in attendance*⟩

drop off *vi* **1** to fall asleep **2** to decline, slump

dropout *n* **1** one who rejects or withdraws from participation in conventional society **2** a student who fails to complete or withdraws from a course, usu of higher education **3** a spot on a magnetic tape from which data has disappeared **4** a dropkick awarded to the defending team in rugby (e g after an unconverted try)

drop out *vi* **1** to withdraw from participation **2** to make a dropout in rugby

dropper *n* a short usu glass tube fitted with a rubber bulb and used to measure or administer liquids by drops – **dropperful** *n*

droppings *n pl* animal dung

dropsy *n* oedema – **dropsical** *adj*

dross *n* **1** the scum on the surface of molten metal **2** waste, rubbish, or foreign matter; impurities – **drossy** *adj*

drought *n* **1** a prolonged period of dryness **2** a prolonged shortage of sthg – **droughty** *adj*

¹drove *n* **1** a group of animals driven or moving in a body **2** a crowd of people moving or acting together

²drove *past of* DRIVE

drover *n* one who drives cattle or sheep

drown *vi* to become drowned ~ *vt* **1a** to suffocate by submergence, esp in water **b** to submerge, esp by a rise in the water level **c** to wet thoroughly; drench ⟨*~ed the chips with ketchup*⟩ **2** to engage (oneself) deeply and strenuously ⟨*~ed himself in work*⟩ **3** to blot out (a sound) by making a loud noise ⟨*his speech was ~ed out*⟩

by boos – New Yorker⟩ **4** to destroy (e g a sensation or an idea) as if by drowning ⟨~ed *his sorrows in drink*⟩
drowse *vi* to doze ~*vt* to pass (time) drowsily or in dozing – usu + *away*
drowse *n* the act or an instance of dozing
drowsy *adj* **1a** sleepy **b** tending to induce sleepiness ⟨*a ~ summer afternoon*⟩ **c** indolent, lethargic **2** giving the appearance of peaceful inactivity – **drowsily** *adv*, **drowsiness** *n*
drub *vt* **-bb- 1** to beat severely **2** to defeat decisively
drudge *vi* to do hard, menial, routine, or monotonous work – **drudger** *n*, **drudgery** *n*
drudge *n* one who drudges
drug *n* **1** a substance used as (or in the preparation of) a medication **2** a substance that causes addiction or habituation
drug *vt* **-gg- 1** to affect or adulterate with a drug **2** to administer a drug to **3** to lull or stupefy (as if) with a drug
drugget *n* a coarse durable cloth used chiefly as a floor covering
druggist *n* **1** one who deals in or dispenses drugs and medicines; a pharmacist **2** *NAm* the owner or manager of a drugstore
drugstore *n*, *chiefly NAm* a chemist's shop; *esp* one that also sells sweets, magazines, and refreshments
druid, *fem* **druidess** *n*, *often cap* **1** a member of a pre-Christian Celtic order of priests associated with a mistletoe cult **2** an officer of the Welsh Gorsedd **3** MANDARIN 1b – **druidic**, **druidical** *adj*, *often cap*
drum *n* **1** a percussion instrument usu consisting of a hollow cylinder with a drumhead stretched over each end, that is beaten with a stick or a pair of sticks in playing **2** the tympanic membrane of the ear **3** the sound made by striking a drum; *also* any similar sound **4** sthg resembling a drum in shape: e g **a** a cylindrical machine or mechanical device or part; *esp* a metal cylinder coated with magnetic material on which data (e g for a computer) may be recorded **b** a cylindrical container; *specif* a large usu metal container for liquids **5** a dwelling; PAD **6** – slang – **drumlike** *adj*
drum *vb* **-mm-** *vi* **1** to beat a drum **2** to make a succession of strokes, taps, or vibrations that produce drumlike sounds **3** to throb or sound rhythmically ⟨*blood* ~med *in his ears*⟩ ~*vt* **1** to summon or enlist (as if) by beating a drum ⟨~med *them into service*⟩ **2** to instil (an idea or lesson) by constant repetition – usu + *into* or *out of* ⟨~med *the idea into them*⟩ **3a** to strike or tap repeatedly **b** to produce (rhythmic sounds) by such action
drum *n* **1** a drumlin **2** *chiefly Scot* a long narrow hill or ridge
drumbeat *n* a stroke on a drum or its sound
drumfire *n* artillery fire so continuous as to sound like a roll on a drum
drumhead *n* the material stretched over the end of a drum
drumhead court-martial *n* a summary court-martial
drum major *n* the marching leader of a band
drummer *n* **1** one who plays a drum **2** *chiefly NAm* SALES REPRESENTATIVE
drum out *vt* to dismiss ignominiously; expel ⟨drummed *him out of the army*⟩
drumstick *n* **1** a stick for beating a drum **2** the part of a fowl's leg between the thigh and tarsus when cooked as food
drum up *vt* **1** to bring about by persistent effort ⟨drum up *some business*⟩ **2** to invent, originate ⟨drum up *a new time-saving method*⟩
drunk *past part of* DRINK

²drunk *adj* **1** under the influence of alcohol **2** dominated by an intense feeling ⟨~ *with power*⟩ **3** DRUNKEN 2b
³drunk *n* a person who is (habitually) drunk
drunkard *n* a person who is habitually drunk
drunken *adj* **1** DRUNK 1 **2a** given to habitual excessive use of alcohol **b** of, characterized by, or resulting from alcoholic intoxication ⟨*a ~ brawl*⟩ **3** unsteady or lurching as if from alcoholic intoxication – **drunkenly** *adv*, **drunkenness** *n* – **drunk in charge** driving while intoxicated
drupe *n* a fruit (e g a cherry or almond) that has a stone enclosed by a fleshy layer and is covered by a flexible or stiff outermost layer – **drupaceous** *adj*
¹dry *adj* **1a** (relatively) free from a liquid, esp water **b** not in or under water ⟨~ *land*⟩ **c** lacking precipitation or humidity ⟨*a ~ climate*⟩ **2a** characterized by exhaustion of a supply of water or liquid ⟨*a ~ well*⟩ ⟨*the barrel ran ~*⟩ **b** devoid of natural moisture ⟨~ *mouth*⟩; *also* thirsty **c** no longer sticky or damp ⟨*the paint is ~*⟩ **d** *of a mammal* not giving milk ⟨*a ~ cow*⟩ **e** lacking freshness; stale **f** anhydrous **3a** marked by the absence or scantiness of secretions ⟨*a ~ cough*⟩ **b** not shedding or accompanied by tears ⟨*no ~ eyes*⟩ **4** prohibiting the manufacture or distribution of alcoholic beverages ⟨*a ~ county*⟩ **5** lacking sweetness; sec **6** solid as opposed to liquid ⟨~ *groceries*⟩ **7** functioning without lubrication ⟨*a ~ clutch*⟩ **8** built or constructed without a process which requires water: **a** using no mortar ⟨~ *masonry*⟩ **b** using prefabricated materials (e g plasterboard) rather than a construction involving plaster or mortar ⟨~ *wall construction*⟩ **9a** not showing or communicating warmth, enthusiasm, or feeling; impassive **b** uninteresting ⟨~ *passages of description*⟩ **c** lacking embellishment, bias, or emotional concern; plain ⟨*the ~ facts*⟩ **10** not yielding what is expected or desired; unproductive ⟨*a ~ oil field*⟩ **11** marked by a matter-of-fact, ironic, or terse manner of expression ⟨~ *wit*⟩ – **dryish** *adj*, **dryishly** *adv*, **dryly** *adv*, **dryness** *n*
²dry *vb* to make or become dry – often + *out* – **dryable** *adj*
³dry *n*, *pl* **drys** sthg dry: e g **a** a dry place **b** *chiefly Austr* the dry season
dryad *n* a nymph of the woods in Greek mythology
dry cell *n* a primary cell whose electrolyte is not a liquid
dry-clean *vb* to subject to or undergo dry cleaning – **dry-cleanable** *adj*, **dry cleaner** *n*
dry cleaning *n* **1** the cleaning of fabrics or garments with organic solvents, esp chlorinated hydrocarbons, and without water **2** that which is dry-cleaned
dry dock *n* a dock from which the water can be pumped to allow ships to be repaired
dryer *n* a drier
dry goods *n pl*, *NAm* drapery as distinguished esp from hardware and groceries
dry ice *n* solidified carbon dioxide
dry out *vi* to undergo treatment for alcoholism or drug addiction
dry rot *n* **1** (a fungus causing) a decay of seasoned timber in which the cellulose of wood is consumed leaving a soft skeleton which is readily reduced to powder **2** decay from within, caused esp by resistance to new forces ⟨*art infected by the ~ of formalism* – D G Mandelbaum⟩
dry run *n* **1** a firing practice without ammunition **2** a practice exercise; a rehearsal, trial
dry-shod *adj* having or keeping dry shoes or feet
dry up *vi* **1** to disappear or cease to yield (as if) by evaporation, draining, or the cutting off of a source of supply **2** to wither or die through gradual loss of vitality

3 to wipe dry dishes, cutlery, etc by hand after they have been washed **4** to stop talking; SHUT UP – infml ~ *vt* to cause to dry up

dt's *n pl, often cap* D&T DELIRIUM TREMENS

dual *adj* **1** *of grammatical number* denoting reference to 2 **2a** consisting of 2 (like) parts or elements **b** having a double character or nature – **dual** *n*, **duality** *n*, **dualize** *vt*, **dually** *adv*

dual carriageway *n, chiefly Br* a road that has traffic travelling in opposite directions separated by a central reservation

¹dub *vt* **-bb-** **1a** to confer knighthood on **b** to call by a descriptive name or epithet; nickname **2** *Br* to dress (a fishing fly) – **dubber** *n*

²dub *vt* **-bb-** **1** to make alterations to the original sound track of (a film): e g **a** to provide with a sound track in which the voices are not those of the actors on the screen **b** to provide with a sound track in a new language ⟨*in Europe, American films are usually ~bed into the local language*⟩ **2** to transpose (a previous recording) to a new record **3** *chiefly Br* MIX 1b(2) – **dubber** *n*

dubbin *also* **dubbing** *n* a dressing of oil and tallow for leather – **dubbin** *vt*

dubiety *n* **1** the state of being doubtful **2** a doubtful matter *USE* fml

dubious *adj* **1** giving rise to doubt; uncertain ⟨*they considered our scheme a little ~*⟩ **2** unsettled in opinion; undecided ⟨*they were a little ~ about our plan*⟩ **3** of uncertain outcome ⟨*a rather ~ experiment*⟩ **4** of questionable value, quality, or origin ⟨*won by ~ means*⟩ – **dubiously** *adv*, **dubiousness** *n*

ducal *adj* of or relating to a duke or duchy – **ducally** *adv*

ducat *n* a usu gold coin formerly used in many European countries

duchess *n* **1** the wife or widow of a duke **2** a woman having in her own right the rank of a duke

duchy *n* a dukedom

¹duck *n, pl* **ducks**, (*1a*) **ducks**, *esp collectively* **duck** **1a** any of various swimming birds in which the neck and legs are short, the bill is often broad and flat, and the sexes are almost always different from each other in plumage **b** the flesh of any of these birds used as food **2** a female duck **3** *chiefly Br* DEAR 1b – often pl with sing. meaning but sing. in constr; infml

²duck *vt* **1** to thrust momentarily under water **2** to lower (e g the head), esp quickly as a bow or to avoid being hit **3** to avoid, evade ⟨*~ the issue*⟩ ~ *vi* **1** to plunge at least one's head under the surface of water **2a** to move the head or body suddenly; dodge **b** to bow, bob **3** to evade a duty, question, or responsibility – **duck** *n*

³duck *n* a durable closely woven usu cotton fabric

⁴duck *n* a score of nought, esp in cricket

duckbilled platypus *n* the platypus

duckboard *n* a usu wooden board or slat used to make a path over wet or muddy ground – usu pl

ducking stool *n* a seat attached to a plank and formerly used to plunge culprits into water

duckling *n* a young duck

ducks and drakes *n pl but sing in constr* the pastime of skimming flat stones or shells along the surface of calm water

duckweed *n* any of several small free-floating stemless plants that often cover large areas of the surface of still water

¹ducky *adj* darling, sweet – infml

²ducky, duckie *n* DEAR 1b – infml

¹duct *n* **1** a bodily tube or vessel, esp when carrying the secretion of a gland **2a** a pipe, tube, or channel that conveys a substance **b** a pipe or tubular runway for carrying an electric power line, telephone cables, or other conductors **3** a continuous tube in plant tissue – **ducting** *n*

²duct *vt* to convey (e g a gas) through a duct

ductile *adj* **1** capable of being easily fashioned into a new form **2** *of metals* capable of being drawn out or hammered thin **3** easily led or influenced; tractable ⟨*the ~ masses*⟩ – infml – **ductility** *n*

ductless gland *n* ENDOCRINE 2

¹dud *n* **1** a bomb, missile, etc that fails to explode **2** *pl* personal belongings; *esp* clothes **3** a failure **4** a counterfeit, fake *USE* (*2, 3, & 4*) infml

²dud *adj* valueless ⟨*~ cheques*⟩ – infml

dude *n, chiefly NAm* **1** a dandy **2** a city-dweller; *esp* a man from the eastern USA holidaying (on a ranch) in the western USA *USE* infml – **dudish** *adj*, **dudishly** *adv*

dude ranch *n* an American cattle ranch converted into a holiday centre, offering typical ranch activities such as camping and riding

dudgeon *n* indignation, resentment – esp in *in high dudgeon*

¹due *adj* **1** owed or owing as a debt **2a** owed or owing as a natural or moral right ⟨*got his ~ reward*⟩ **b** appropriate ⟨*after ~ consideration*⟩ **3a** (capable of) satisfying a need, obligation, or duty **b** regular, lawful ⟨*~ proof of loss*⟩ **4** ascribable – + *to* ⟨*this advance is partly ~ to a few men of genius* –A N Whitehead⟩ **5** payable **6** required or expected in the prearranged or normal course of events ⟨*~ to arrive at any time*⟩ – **in due course** after a normal passage of time; in the expected or allocated time

²due *n* sthg due or owed: e g **a** sthg esp nonmaterial that rightfully belongs to one ⟨*I don't like him, but to give him his ~ he's a good singer*⟩ **b** *pl* fees, charges

³due *adv* directly, exactly – used before points of the compass ⟨*~ north*⟩

¹duel *n* **1** a formal combat with weapons fought between 2 people in the presence of witnesses in order to settle a quarrel **2** a conflict between usu evenly matched antagonistic people, ideas, or forces

²duel *vi* **-ll-** (*NAm* **-l-, -ll-**) to fight a duel – **dueller** *n*, **duellist** *n*

duenna *n* **1** an older woman serving as governess and companion to the younger ladies in a Spanish or Portuguese family **2** a chaperon – **duennaship** *n*

duet *n* a (musical) composition for 2 performers

due to *prep* BECAUSE OF **1** – though disapproved by many, now used by numerous educated speakers and writers; compare ¹DUE 4

¹duff *n* a boiled or steamed pudding, often containing dried fruit

²duff *adj, Br* not working; worthless, useless – slang

duffel, duffle *n* a coarse heavy woollen material with a thick nap

duffel bag *n* a cylindrical fabric bag, closed by a drawstring, used for carrying personal belongings

duffel coat *n* a coat made of duffel that is usu thigh- or knee-length, hooded, and fastened with toggles

duffer *n* an incompetent, ineffectual, or clumsy person

¹dug *past of* DIG

²dug *n* an udder; *also* a teat – usu used with reference to animals but derog when used of a woman

dugout *n* **1** a boat made by hollowing out a large log **2** a shelter dug in the ground or in a hillside, esp for troops

duke *n* **1** a sovereign ruler of a European duchy **2** a nobleman of the highest hereditary rank; *esp* a member of the highest rank of the British peerage **3** a fist – usu pl slang – **dukedom** *n*

dulcet *adj, esp of sounds* sweetly pleasant or soothing ⟨~ *tones*⟩ – **dulcetly** *adv*

dulcimer *n* a stringed instrument having strings of graduated length stretched over a sounding board and played with light hammers

¹dull *adj* **1** mentally slow; stupid **2a** slow in perception or sensibility; insensible **b** lacking zest or vivacity; listless **3** lacking sharpness of cutting edge or point; blunt **4** not resonant or ringing ⟨a ~ *booming sound*⟩ **5** *of a colour* low in saturation and lightness **6** cloudy, overcast **7** boring, uninteresting – **dullness, dulness** *n*, **dully** *adv*

²dull *vb* to make or become dull ⟨*eyes and ears* ~ *ed by age*⟩

dullard *n* a stupid or insensitive person

duly *adv* in a due manner, time, or degree; properly ⟨*your suggestion has been* ~ *noted*⟩

dumb *adj* **1** devoid of the power of speech **2** naturally incapable of speech ⟨~ *animals*⟩ **3** not expressed in uttered words ⟨~ *insolence*⟩ **4a** not willing to speak **b** temporarily unable to speak (e g from astonishment) ⟨*struck* ~⟩ **5** lacking some usual attribute or accompaniment **6** stupid – **dumbly** *adv*, **dumbness** *n*

dumbbell *n* **1** a short bar with adjustable weights at each end used usu in pairs for weight training **2** *NAm* DUMMY **6**

dumbfound, dumfound *vt* to strike dumb with astonishment; amaze

dumb show *n* (a play or part of a play presented by) movement, signs, and gestures without words

dumb waiter *n* **1** a movable table or stand often with revolving shelves for holding food or dishes **2** a small lift for conveying food and dishes (e g from the kitchen to the dining area of a restaurant)

dumdum *n* a bullet that expands on impact and inflicts a severe wound

¹dummy *n* **1** the exposed hand in bridge played by the declarer in addition to his/her own hand; *also* the player whose hand is a dummy **2** an imitation or copy of sthg used to reproduce some of the attributes of the original; e g **a** *chiefly Br* a rubber teat given to babies to suck in order to soothe them **b** a large puppet in usu human form, used by a ventriloquist **c** a model of the human body, esp the torso, used for fitting or displaying clothes **3** a person or corporation that seems to act independently but is in reality acting for or at the direction of another **4** a pattern for a printing job showing the position of typographic elements (e g text and illustrations) **5** an instance of dummying an opponent in sports **6** a dull or stupid person – *infml*

²dummy *adj* resembling or being a dummy: e g **a** sham, artificial **b** existing in name only; fictitious ⟨*bank accounts held in* ~ *names*⟩

³dummy *vi* **1** to deceive an opponent (e g in rugby or soccer) by pretending to pass or release the ball while still retaining possession of it **2** *NAm* to refuse to talk – usu + *up*; slang ~ *vt* to deceive (an opponent) by dummying

dummy run *n* a rehearsal; TRIAL RUN

¹dump *vt* **1a** to unload or let fall in a heap or mass **b** to get rid of unceremoniously or irresponsibly; abandon **2** to sell in quantity at a very low price; *specif* to sell abroad at less than the market price at home **3** to copy (data in a computer's internal storage) onto an external storage medium – **dumper** *n*

²dump *n* **1a** an accumulation of discarded materials (e g refuse) **b** a place where such materials are dumped **2** a quantity of esp military reserve materials accumulated in 1 place ⟨*arms* ~⟩ **3** an instance of dumping data stored

in a computer **4** a disorderly, slovenly, or dilapidated place – *infml*

dumper truck, dump truck *n* a lorry whose body may be tilted to empty the contents

dumpling *n* **1** a small usu rounded mass of leavened dough cooked by boiling or steaming often in stew **2** a short round person – *humor*

dumps *n pl* a gloomy state of mind; despondency – esp in *in the dumps*; *infml*

dumpy *adj* short and thick in build; squat – **dumpily** *adv*, **dumpiness** *n*

¹dun *adj* **1** of the colour dun **2** *of a horse* having a greyish or light brownish colour

²dun *n* **1** a dun horse **2** a slightly brownish dark grey **3** (an artificial fly tied to imitate) a mayfly that has not acquired all the typical adult characteristics

³dun *vt* **-nn-** to make persistent demands upon for payment

⁴dun *n* **1** one who duns **2** an urgent request; *esp* a demand for payment

⁵dun *n* an Irish or Scottish stronghold protected by usu 2 encircling mounds or a mound and a palisade

dunce *n* a dull or stupid person

dunce's cap *n* a conical cap formerly used to humiliate slow learners at school

dunderhead *n* a dunce, blockhead – **dunderheaded** *adj*

dune *n* a hill or ridge of sand piled up by the wind

¹dung *n* the excrement of an animal – **dungy** *adj*

²dung *vt* to fertilize or dress with manure ~ *vi, of an animal* to defecate

dungaree *n* a heavy coarse durable cotton twill woven from coloured yarns; *specif* blue denim

dungarees *n pl* a 1-piece outer garment consisting of trousers and a bib with shoulder straps fastened at the back – **dungaree** *adj*

dungeon *n* a dark usu underground prison or vault, esp in a castle

dunghill *n* a heap of dung (e g in a farmyard)

dunk *vt* to dip (e g a piece of bread) into liquid (e g soup) before eating

duo *n, pl* **duos** a pair (of performers); *also* a piece (e g of music) written for 2 players

duo- *comb form* two

duodecimal *adj* proceeding by or based on the number of 12 – **duodecimal** *n*

duodenum *n, pl* **duodena, duodenums** the first part of the small intestine extending from the stomach to the jejunum – **duodenal** *adj*

duologue *n* a (theatrical) dialogue between 2 people

¹dupe *n* one who is easily deceived or cheated

²dupe *vt* to make a dupe of; deceive – **duper** *n*, **dupery** *n*

duple *adj* **1** having 2 elements; twofold **2** marked by 2 or a multiple of 2 beats per bar of music

¹duplex *adj* **1** double, twofold **2** allowing telecommunication in opposite directions simultaneously

²duplex *n* sthg duplex: e g **a** *NAm* a 2-family house **b** *NAm* a flat on 2 floors

¹duplicate *adj* **1a** consisting of or existing in 2 corresponding or identical parts or examples ⟨~ *invoices*⟩ **b** being the same as another ⟨a ~ *key*⟩ **2** being a card game, *specif* bridge, in which different players play identical hands in order to compare scores

²duplicate *n* **1** either of 2 things that exactly resemble each other; *specif* an equally valid copy of a legal document **2** a copy – **in duplicate** with an original and 1 copy ⟨*typed* ~⟩; *also* with 2 identical copies

³duplicate *vt* **1** to make double or twofold **2** to make an exact copy of ⟨~ *the document*⟩ ~ *vi* to replicate ⟨*DNA in chromosomes* ~ s⟩ – **duplication** *n*, **duplicative** *adj*

duplicator *n* a machine for making copies, esp by means other than photocopying or xeroxing

duplicity *n* malicious deception in thought, speech, or action – **duplicitous** *adj*, **duplicitously** *adv*

durable *adj* able to exist or be used for a long time without significant deterioration – **durableness** *n*, **durably** *adv*, **durability** *n*

duration *n* 1 continuance in time 2 the time during which sthg exists or lasts

durbar *n* a reception held in former times by an Indian prince or a British governor or viceroy in India

duress *n* 1 forcible restraint or restriction 2 compulsion by threat, violence, or imprisonment

Durex *trademark* – used for a condom

during *prep* 1 throughout the whole duration of ⟨*swims every day* ~ *the summer*⟩ 2 at some point in the course of ⟨*takes his holiday* ~ *July*⟩

dusk *n* (the darker part of) twilight ⟨*lights go on at* ~⟩

dusky *adj* 1 somewhat dark in colour; *esp* dark-skinned 2 shadowy, gloomy – **duskily** *adv*, **duskiness** *n*

¹**dust** *n* 1 fine dry particles of any solid matter, esp earth; *specif* the fine particles of waste that settle esp on household surfaces 2 the particles into which sthg, esp the human body, disintegrates or decays 3 sthg worthless ⟨*worldly success was* ~ *to him*⟩ 4 the surface of the ground 5a a cloud of dust ⟨*the cars raised quite a* ~⟩ b confusion, disturbance – esp in *kick up/raise a dust* – **dustless** *adj*, **dustlike** *adj*

²**dust** *vt* 1 to make free of dust (e g by wiping or beating) 2 to prepare to use again – usu + *down* or *off* 3a to sprinkle with fine particles ⟨~ *a cake with icing sugar*⟩ b to sprinkle in the form of dust ⟨~ *sugar over a cake*⟩ ~ *vi* 1 *of a bird* to work dust into the feathers 2 to remove dust (e g from household articles), esp by wiping or brushing

dustbin *n*, *Br* a container for holding household refuse until collection

dust bowl *n* a region that suffers from prolonged droughts and dust storms

dustcart *n*, *Br* a vehicle for collecting household waste

dustcoat *n*, *chiefly Br* a loose lightweight coat worn to protect clothing

duster *n* sthg that removes dust; *specif* a cloth for removing dust from household articles

dust jacket *n* a removable outer paper cover for a book

dustman *n*, *Br* one employed to remove household refuse

dustpan *n* a shovel-like utensil with a handle into which household dust and litter is swept

dustsheet *n* a large sheet (e g of cloth) used as a cover to protect sthg, esp furniture, from dust

dust-up *n* a quarrel, row – infml

dusty *adj* 1 covered with or full of dust 2 consisting of dust; powdery 3 resembling dust, esp in consistency or colour 4 lacking vitality; dry ⟨~ *scholarship*⟩ – **dustily** *adv*, **dustiness** *n* – **not so dusty** fairly good

¹**dutch** *adv*, *often cap* with each person paying for him-/herself ⟨*we always go* ~⟩

²**dutch** *n*, *Br* one's wife – slang

Dutch *n* 1 the Germanic language of the Netherlands 2 *pl in constr* the people of the Netherlands – **Dutch** *adj*, **Dutchman** *n*

Dutch auction *n* an auction in which the auctioneer gradually reduces the bidding price until a bid is received

Dutch barn *n* a large barn with open sides used esp for storage of hay

Dutch cap *n* a moulded cap, usu of thin rubber, that fits over the uterine cervix to act as a mechanical contraceptive barrier

Dutch courage *n* courage produced by intoxication rather than inherent resolution

Dutch elm disease *n* a fatal disease of elms caused by a fungus, spread from tree to tree by a beetle, and characterized by yellowing of the foliage and defoliation

Dutch oven *n* 1 a 3-walled metal shield used for roasting before an open fire 2 a brick oven in which food is cooked by heat radiating from the prewarmed walls

Dutch treat *n* a meal or entertainment for which each person pays for him-/herself

Dutch uncle *n* one who admonishes sternly and bluntly

dutiable *adj* subject to a duty ⟨~ *imports*⟩

dutiful *adj* 1 filled with or motivated by a sense of duty ⟨*a* ~ *son*⟩ 2 proceeding from or expressive of a sense of duty ⟨~ *affection*⟩ – **dutifully** *adv*, **dutifulness** *n*

duty *n* 1 conduct due to parents and superiors; respect 2a tasks, conduct, service, or functions that arise from one's position, job, or moral obligations b assigned (military) service or business 3a a moral or legal obligation b the force of moral obligation 4 a tax, esp on imports 5 a measure of efficiency expressed in terms of the amount of work done in relation to the energy consumed

duty-free *adj* exempted from duty

duvet *n* a large quilt filled with insulating material (e g down, feathers, or acrylic fibre), usu placed inside a removable fabric cover and used in place of bedclothes

¹**dwarf** *n*, *pl* **dwarfs**, **dwarves** 1 a person of unusually small stature; *esp* one whose bodily proportions are abnormal 2 an animal or plant much below normal size 3 a small manlike creature in esp Norse and Germanic mythology who was skilled as a craftsman – **dwarfish** *adj*, **dwarfishness** *n*, **dwarflike** *adj*, **dwarfness** *n*

²**dwarf** *vt* 1 to stunt the growth of 2 to cause to appear smaller ⟨*the other buildings are* ~ed *by the skyscraper*⟩

dwell *vi* **dwelt**, **dwelled** 1 to remain for a time 2 to keep the attention directed, esp in speech or writing; linger – + *on* or *upon* ⟨*dwelt on the weaknesses in his opponent's arguments*⟩ 3 to live as a resident; reside – fml – **dweller** *n*

dwelling *n* a place (e g a house or flat) in which people live – fml or humor

dwindle *vi* **dwindling** to become steadily less in quantity; shrink, diminish

dyarchy, diarchy *n* a government in which power is vested in 2 rulers

¹**dye** *n* 1 a colour or tint produced by dyeing 2 a soluble or insoluble colouring matter

²**dye** *vt* **dyeing** to impart a new and often permanent colour to, esp by impregnation with a dye – **dyer** *n*, **dyeable** *adj*, **dyeability** *n*

dyed-in-the-wool *adj* thoroughgoing, uncompromising ⟨*a* ~ *conservative*⟩

dyestuff *n* DYE 2

¹**dyke, dike** *n* 1 an artificial watercourse; a ditch 2 a bank, usu of earth, constructed to control or confine water 3 a barrier preventing passage, esp of sthg undesirable 4 a raised causeway 5 a body of intrusive igneous rock running across the strata 6 *chiefly Br* a natural watercourse 7 *dial Br* a wall or fence of turf or stone

²**dyke, dike** *vt* to surround or protect with a dyke

¹**dynamic** *adj* 1a of physical force or energy in motion b

of dynamics **2a** marked by continuous activity or change ⟨*a ~ population*⟩ **b** energetic, forceful ⟨*a ~ personality*⟩ – **dynamical** *adj*, **dynamically** *adv*

²**dynamic** *n* a dynamic force

dynamics *n pl but sing or pl in constr* **1** a branch of mechanics that deals with forces and their relation to the motion of bodies **2** a pattern of change or growth ⟨*population ~*⟩ **3** variation and contrast in force or intensity (e g in music)

dynamism *n* **1a** a philosophical system that describes the universe in terms of the interplay of forces **b** DYNAMICS 2 **2** dynamic quality – **dynamist** *n*, **dynamistic** *adj*

¹**dynamite** *n* **1** a blasting explosive that is made of nitro-glycerine absorbed in a porous material **2** sby or sthg that has explosive force or effect – infml

²**dynamite** *vt* to destroy with dynamite – **dynamiter** *n*

dynamo *n, pl* **dynamos** **1** a machine by which mechanical energy is converted into electrical energy; *specif* such a device that produces direct current (e g in a motor car) **2** a forceful energetic person

dynasty *n* a succession of hereditary rulers; *also* the time during which such a dynasty rules – **dynastic** *adj*, **dynastically** *adv*

dys- *prefix* **1** abnormal; impaired ⟨dys*function*⟩ ⟨dys*plasia*⟩ **2** difficult; painful ⟨dys*uria*⟩ ⟨dys*menorrhoea*⟩

dysentery *n* any of several infectious diseases character-ized by severe diarrhoea, usu with passing of mucus and blood – **dysenteric** *adj*

dyslexia *n* a maldevelopment of reading ability in other-wise normal children due to a neurological disorder – **dyslexic** *adj*

dyspepsia *n* indigestion

dyspeptic *adj* **1** relating to or having dyspepsia **2** show-ing a sour disposition; ill-tempered – **dyspeptic** *n*, **dyspeptically** *adv*

E

---

e *n, pl* **e's, es** *often cap* **1a** (a graphic representation of or device for reproducing) the 5th letter of the English alphabet **b** a speech counterpart of orthographic *e* **2** the 3rd note of a C-major scale **3** one designated e: e g **a** the 5th in order or class **b** the base of the system of natural logarithms having the approximate numerical value 2.71828 **4** a mark rating a student's work as poor or failing

e- *prefix* **1a** deprive of; remove (a specified quality or thing) ⟨*emasculate*⟩ ⟨*eviscerate*⟩ **b** lacking; without ⟨*edentate*⟩ ⟨*ecaudate*⟩ **2** out; on the outside ⟨*evert*⟩ **3** forth ⟨*emanate*⟩ ⟨*ejaculate*⟩

¹**each** *adj* being one of 2 or more distinct individuals considered separately and often forming a group ⟨*~ foot in turn*⟩ ⟨*they ~ want something different*⟩

²**each** *pron* each one ⟨*~ of us*⟩ ⟨*~ is equally attrac-tive*⟩

³**each** *adv* to or for each; apiece ⟨*tickets at £1 ~*⟩

each other *pron* each of 2 or more in reciprocal action or relation – not used as subject of a clause ⟨*wore each other's shirts*⟩ ⟨*looked at ~ in surprise*⟩

each way *adj or adv, Br, of a bet* backing a horse, dog, etc to finish in the first two, three, or four in a race as well as to win

eager *adj* marked by keen, enthusiastic, or impatient

desire or interest ⟨*always ~ to help*⟩ – **eagerly** *adv*, **eagerness** *n*

eagle *n* **1** any of various large birds of prey noted for their strength, size, gracefulness, keenness of vision, and powers of flight **2** any of various emblematic or symbolic rep-resentations of an eagle: e g **a** the standard of the ancient Romans **b** the seal or standard of a nation (e g the USA) having an eagle as emblem **3** a 10-dollar gold coin of the USA **4** a golf score for 1 hole of 2 strokes less than par

eagle-eyed *adj* **1** having very good eyesight **2** looking very keenly at sthg ⟨*watched ~ while the cashier counted out the money*⟩ **3** good at noticing details; observant ⟨*an ~ employer who spots the smallest mistake*⟩

eaglet *n* a young eagle

¹**ear** *n* **1a** (the external part of) the characteristic vertebrate organ of hearing and equilibrium **b** any of various organs capable of detecting vibratory motion **2** the sense or act of hearing **3** sensitivity to musical tone and pitch **4** sthg resembling an ear in shape or position; *esp* a projecting part (e g a lug or handle) **5a** sympathetic attention ⟨*gained the ~ of the managing director*⟩ **b** *pl* notice, awareness ⟨*it has come to my ~s that you are discon-tented*⟩ – **by ear** from memory of the sound without having seen the written music – **in one ear and out the other** through one's mind without making an impression ⟨*everything you say to him goes* in one ear and out the other⟩ – **up to one's ears** deeply involved; heavily impli-cated

²**ear** *n* the fruiting spike of a cereal, including both the seeds and protective structures

earache *n* an ache or pain in the ear

eardrum *n* TYMPANIC MEMBRANE

eared *adj* having ears, esp of a specified kind or number ⟨*long-eared owl*⟩

earful *n* **1** an outpouring of news or gossip **2** a sharp verbal reprimand *USE* infml

earl *n* a member of the British peerage ranking below a marquess and above a viscount – **earldom** *n*

earlobe *n* the pendent part of the ear of humans or of some fowls

¹**early** *adv* **1** at or near the beginning of a period of time, a development, or a series ⟨*earlier on in the experiment*⟩ **2** before the usual or proper time ⟨*got up ~*⟩

²**early** *adj* **1a** of or occurring near the beginning of a period of time, a development, or a series **b(1)** distant in past time **(2)** primitive **2a** occurring before the usual time **b** occurring in the near future **c** maturing or producing sooner than related forms ⟨*an ~ peach*⟩ – **earliness** *n*

early closing *n* **1** the closing of shops in a British town or district on 1 afternoon a week **2** the day on which shops close early

¹**earmark** *n* **1** a mark of identification on the ear of an animal **2** a distinguishing or identifying characteristic

²**earmark** *vt* **1** to mark (livestock) with an earmark **2** to designate (e g funds) for a specific use or owner

earmuffs *n pl* a pair of ear coverings connected by a flexible band and worn as protection against cold or noise

earn *vt* **1** to receive (e g money) as return for effort, esp for work done or services rendered **2** to bring in as income ⟨*my shares ~ed nothing last year*⟩ **3a** to gain or deserve because of one's behaviour or qualities ⟨*Alexander ~ed the title 'The Great' by his victories in war*⟩ **b** to make worthy of or obtain for ⟨*Alexander's victories in war ~ed him the title 'The Great'*⟩

¹**earnest** *n* a serious and intent mental state – esp in *in earnest*

²**earnest** adj determined and serious – **earnestly** adv, **earnestness** n

³**earnest** n 1 sthg of value, esp money, given by a buyer to a seller to seal a bargain 2 a token of what is to come; a pledge

earnings n pl money earned; esp gross revenue

earphone n a device that converts electrical energy into sound waves and is worn over or inserted into the ear

earpiece n a part of an instrument (e g a telephone) to which the ear is applied for listening; esp an earphone

earplug n a device inserted into the outer opening of the ear for protection against water, loud noise, etc

earring n an ornament for the ear that is attached to the earlobe

earshot n the range within which sthg, esp the unaided voice, may be heard

¹**earth** n 1 ³SOIL 2a 2 the sphere of mortal or worldly existence as distinguished from spheres of spiritual life 3a areas of land as distinguished from sea and air **b** the solid ground 4 often cap the planet on which we live that is third in order from the sun 5 the people of the planet earth 6 the lair of a fox, badger, etc 7 a metallic oxide formerly classed as an element 8 chiefly Br **a** an electrical connection to earth **b** a large conducting body (e g the earth) used as the arbitrary zero of potential 9 a huge amount of money ⟨his suit must have cost the ~!⟩ – infml – **earthlike** adj, **earthward** adj or adv, **earthwards** adv – **on earth** – used to intensify an interrogative pronoun ⟨where on earth is it?⟩

²**earth** vt 1 to drive (e g a fox) to hiding in its earth 2 to draw soil about (plants) – usu + up 3 chiefly Br to connect electrically with earth ~ vi, of a hunted animal to hide in its lair

earthbound adj **1a** restricted to the earth **b** heading or directed towards the planet earth ⟨an ~ spaceship⟩ **2a** bound by worldly interests; lacking spiritual quality **b** pedestrian, unimaginative

earthen adj made of earth or baked clay

earthenware n ceramic ware made of slightly porous opaque clay fired at a low temperature

earthling n an inhabitant of the earth, esp as contrasted with inhabitants of other planets

¹**earthly** adj **1a** characteristic of or belonging to this earth **b** relating to human beings' actual life on this earth; worldly 2 possible – usu + neg or interrog ⟨there is no ~ reason for such behaviour⟩ – **earthliness** n

²**earthly** n a chance of success – usu + neg; infml

earthnut n the pignut

earthquake n a (repeated) usu violent earth tremor caused by volcanic action or processes within the earth's crust

earthshaking adj having tremendous importance or a widespread often violent effect – chiefly infml

earthwork n (the construction of) an embankment, field fortification, etc made of earth

earthworm n any of numerous widely distributed hermaphroditic worms that live in the soil

earthy adj **1** consisting of, resembling, or suggesting earth ⟨an ~ flavour⟩ 2 crude, coarse ⟨~ humour⟩ – **earthily** adv, **earthiness** n

earwig n any of numerous insects that have slender many-jointed antennae and a pair of appendages resembling forceps

¹**ease** n **1** being comfortable: e g **a** freedom from pain, discomfort, or anxiety **b** freedom from labour or difficulty **c** freedom from embarrassment or constraint; naturalness 2 facility, effortlessness 3 easing or being eased – **easeful** adj, **easefully** adv – **at ease 1** free from pain or discomfort 2 free from restraint or formality ⟨he's quite at his ease in

any kind of company⟩ 3 standing with the feet apart and usu 1 or both hands behind the body – used esp as a military command

²**ease** vt **1** to free from sthg that pains, disquiets, or burdens – + of 2 to alleviate 3 to lessen the pressure or tension of, esp by slackening, lifting, or shifting 4 to make less difficult 5 to manoeuvre gently or carefully in a specified way ⟨~d the heavy block into position⟩ 6 to put the helm of (a ship) towards the lee ~ vi **1** to decrease in activity, intensity, or severity – often + off or up ⟨the rain is easing off⟩ 2 to manoeuvre oneself gently or carefully ⟨~d through a hole in the fence⟩

easel n a frame for supporting sthg (e g an artist's canvas)

easily adv **1** without difficulty ⟨my car will do a hundred ~⟩ 2 without doubt; by far ⟨~ the best⟩

¹**east** adj or adv towards, at, belonging to, or coming from the east ⟨a biting ~ wind⟩ ⟨we headed ~⟩

²**east** n **1** (the compass point corresponding to) the direction 90° to the right of north that is the general direction of sunrise **2a** often cap regions or countries lying to the east of a specified or implied point of orientation **b** cap regions lying to the east of Europe **3** the altar end of a church **4** sby (e g a bridge player) occupying a position designated east – **eastward** adj or n, **eastwards** adv

Easter n a feast that commemorates Christ's resurrection and is observed on the first Sunday after the first full moon following March 21

Easter egg n a (chocolate or painted and hard-boiled) egg given as a present and eaten at Easter

¹**easterly** adj or adv east ⟨in an ~ direction⟩ ⟨an ~ wind⟩

²**easterly** n a wind from the east

eastern adj **1** often cap (characteristic) of a region conventionally designated east **2** east **3 Eastern, Eastern Orthodox** ORTHODOX 2a – **easternmost** adj

Easterner n, chiefly NAm a native or inhabitant of the East, esp the E USA

¹**easy** adj **1** causing or involving little difficulty or discomfort ⟨an ~ problem⟩ **2a** not severe; lenient **b** readily prevailed on; compliant: e g **(1)** not difficult to deceive or take advantage of ⟨~ prey⟩ **(2)** readily persuaded to have sexual relations – infml **3a** plentiful in supply at low or declining interest rates ⟨~ money⟩ **b** less in demand and usu lower in price ⟨gilts were easier⟩ **4a** marked by peace and comfort ⟨the ~ course of his life⟩ **b** not hurried or strenuous ⟨an ~ pace⟩ **c** free from pain, annoyance, or anxiety **5** marked by social ease ⟨~ manners⟩ **6** not burdensome or straitened ⟨bought on ~ terms⟩ **7** marked by ready facility and freedom from constraint ⟨an ~ flowing style⟩ **8** chiefly Br not having marked preferences on a particular issue – infml – **easiness** n – **easy on 1** lenient with ⟨be easy on the boy⟩ 2 attractive to ⟨easy on the eyes⟩

²**easy** adv **1** easily ⟨promises come ~⟩ 2 without undue speed or excitement; slowly, cautiously ⟨take it ~⟩ – **easy on 1** leniently with ⟨go easy on the boy⟩ 2 not too lavishly with ⟨go easy on the ice, bartender⟩

easy chair n a large usu upholstered armchair designed for comfort and relaxation

easygoing adj taking life easily: e g **a** placid and tolerant **b** indolent and careless – **easygoingness** n

eat vb ate; eaten vt **1** to take in through the mouth and swallow as food 2 to consume gradually; corrode ⟨the acid has ~ en away the battery terminals⟩ 3 to vex, bother – infml ⟨what's ~ing you?⟩ ~ vi to take food or a meal – **eatable** adj, **eater** n – **eat humble pie** to apologize or retract under pressure humble pie alter. of umble pie, fr umbles – **eat one's heart out** to grieve bitterly, esp for sthg desired but unobtainable – **eat one's words** to retract what one has said – **eat out of someone's hand** to accept sby's domination

eatables *n pl* food

eats *n pl* food – *infml*

eau de cologne *n, pl* **eaux de cologne** TOILET WATER

eaves *n pl* the lower border of a roof that overhangs the wall

eavesdrop *vi* to listen secretly to what is said in private – **eavesdropper** *n*

¹ebb, ebb tide *n* **1** the flowing out of the tide towards the sea **2** a point or condition of decline ⟨*relations were at a low ~*⟩

²ebb *vi* **1** *of tidal water* to recede from the flood state **2** to decline from a higher to a lower level or from a better to a worse state

¹ebony *n* (any of various tropical trees that yield) a hard heavy black wood

²ebony *adj* **1** made of or resembling ebony **2** black, dark – *usu apprec*

ebullience, ebulliency *n* the quality of being full of liveliness and enthusiasm; exuberance

ebullient *adj* **1** boiling, agitated **2** characterized by ebullience – **ebulliently** *adv*

¹eccentric *adj* **1** not having the same centre ⟨*~ spheres*⟩ **2** deviating from established convention; odd ⟨*~ behaviour*⟩ **3a** deviating from a circular path ⟨*an ~ orbit*⟩ **b** located elsewhere than at the geometrical centre; *also* having the axis or support so located ⟨*an ~ wheel*⟩ – **eccentrically** *adv*

²eccentric *n* **1** a mechanical device using eccentrically mounted parts to transform circular into reciprocating motion **2** an eccentric person

eccentricity *n* **1** being eccentric **2** a number that for a given conic section is the ratio of the distances from any point on the curve to the focus and the directrix

ecclesiastic *n* a clergyman

ecclesiastical *adj* **1** of a church, esp as a formal and established institution ⟨*~ law*⟩ **2** suitable for use in a church ⟨*~ vestments*⟩ – **ecclesiastically** *adv*

¹echelon *n* **1** an arrangement of units (e g of troops or ships) resembling a series of steps **2** a particular division of a headquarters or supply organization in warfare **3** any of a series of levels or grades (e g of authority or responsibility) in some organized field of activity

²echelon *vt* to form or arrange in an echelon

echinoderm *n* any of a phylum of radially symmetrical marine animals consisting of the starfishes, sea urchins, and related forms – **echinodermatous** *adj*

¹echo *n, pl* **echoes 1a** the repetition of a sound caused by the reflection of sound waves **b** the repeated sound due to such reflection **2** sby or sthg that repeats or imitates another ⟨*his opinions were just an ~ of his superiors'*⟩ **3** a repercussion, result **4** a soft repetition of a musical phrase **5a** the reflection by an object of transmitted radar signals **b** a blip – **echoey** *adj*

²echo *vi* **1** to resound with echoes **2** to produce an echo ~ *vt* **1** to repeat, imitate **2** to send back or repeat (a sound) as an echo

Echo – a communications code word for the letter *e*

éclair *n* a small light oblong cake of choux pastry that is split and filled with cream and usu topped with (chocolate) icing

éclat *n* **1** ostentatious display **2** brilliant or conspicuous success **3** acclaim, applause

¹eclectic *adj* **1** selecting or using elements from various doctrines, methods, or styles **2** composed of elements drawn from various sources – **eclectically** *adv*, **eclecticism** *n*

²eclectic *n* one who uses an eclectic method or approach

¹eclipse *n* **1a** the total or partial obscuring of one celestial body by another **b** passage into the shadow of a celestial body **2** a falling into obscurity or decay; a decline **3** the state of being in eclipse plumage ⟨*a mallard in ~*⟩

²eclipse *vt* to cause an eclipse of: e g **a** to obscure, darken **b** to surpass

¹ecliptic *n* **1** the plane of the earth's orbit extended to meet the celestial sphere **2** a great circle drawn on a terrestrial globe making an angle of about 23° 27′ with the equator and used for illustrating and solving astronomical problems

²ecliptic *adj* of the ecliptic or an eclipse

eclogue *n* a short poem; *esp* a pastoral dialogue

ecology *n* (a science concerned with) the interrelationship of living organisms and their environments – **ecological** *adj*, **ecologically** *adv*, **ecologist** *n*

economic *adj* **1** of economics **2** of or based on the production, distribution, and consumption of goods and services **3** of an economy **4** having practical or industrial significance or uses; affecting material resources ⟨*~ pests*⟩ **5** profitable – **economically** *adv*

economical *adj* thrifty – **economically** *adv*

economics *n pl but sing or pl in constr* **1** a social science concerned chiefly with the production, distribution, and consumption of goods and services **2** economic aspect or significance – **economist** *n*

economize, -ise *vi* to practise economy; be frugal – often + *on* ⟨*~ on oil*⟩ ~ *vt* to use more economically; save ⟨*~ oil*⟩ – **economizer** *n*

economy *n* **1** thrifty and efficient use of material resources; frugality in expenditure; *also* an instance or means of economizing ⟨*the government implemented drastic economies*⟩⟨*bought an economy-size packet of soap powder*⟩⟨*booked an ~ flight to Greece*⟩ **2** efficient and sparing use of nonmaterial resources (e g effort, language, or motion) **3** the structure of economic life in a country, area, or period; *specif* an economic system

ecosystem *n* a complex consisting of a community and its environment functioning as a reasonably self-sustaining ecological unit in nature

ecru *adj or n* (of) a pale fawn colour

ecstasy *n* **1** a state of very strong feeling, esp of joy or happiness **2** a (mystic or prophetic) trance

ecstatic *adj* subject to, causing, or in a state of ecstasy – **ecstatic** *n*, **ecstatically** *adv*

ect-, ecto- *comb form* outside; external ⟨*ectopic*⟩ ⟨*ectoderm*⟩

ectoderm *n* **1** the outer cellular membrane of an animal having only 2 germ layers in the embryo (e g a jellyfish) **2** (a tissue derived from) the outermost of the 3 primary germ layers of an embryo – **ectodermal, ectodermic** *adj*

ectoplasm *n* **1** the outer relatively rigid granule-free layer of the cytoplasm of a cell **2** a substance supposed to emanate from a spiritualist medium in a state of trance – **ectoplasmic** *adj*

ecumenical *also* **oecumenical** *adj* **1** of or representing the whole of a body of churches ⟨*an ~ council*⟩ **2** promoting or tending towards worldwide Christian unity or cooperation ⟨*~ discussions*⟩ – **ecumenicalism** *n*, **ecumenically** *adv*, **ecumenism** *n*, **ecumenist** *n*

eczema *n* an inflammatory condition of the skin characterized by itching and oozing blisters – **eczematous** *adj*

¹-ed *suffix* **1** – used to form the past participle of regular weak verbs that end in a consonant ⟨*ended*⟩ ⟨*dropped*⟩, a vowel other than *e* ⟨*haloed*⟩, or a final *y* that changes to *i* ⟨*cried*⟩; compare **¹-D 1 2a** having; characterized by; provided with ⟨*polo-necked*⟩ ⟨*2-legged*⟩ **b** wearing;

dressed in ⟨*bowler-hatted*⟩ ⟨*jodhpured*⟩ **c** having the characteristics of ⟨*bigoted*⟩ *USE* (2) used to form adjectives from nouns that end in a consonant, a vowel other than *e*, or a final *y* that changes to *i*; compare ¹-D 2

²-ed *suffix* – used to form the past tense of regular weak verbs that end in a consonant, a vowel other than *e*, or a final *y* that changes to *i*; compare ²-D

Edam *n* a yellow mild cheese of Dutch origin usu made in flattened balls coated with red wax

¹eddy *n* **1** a current of water or air running contrary to the main current; *esp* a small whirlpool **2** sthg (e g smoke or fog) moving in the manner of an eddy or whirlpool

²eddy *vb* to (cause to) move in or like an eddy ⟨*the crowd eddied about in the marketplace*⟩

edelweiss *n* a small perennial plant that is covered in dense fine white hairs and grows high in the Alps

Eden *n* **1** the garden where, according to the account in Genesis, Adam and Eve lived before the Fall **2** PARADISE 2 – **Edenic** *adj*

¹edge *n* **1a** the cutting side of a blade **b** the (degree of) sharpness of a blade **c** penetrating power; keenness ⟨*an ~ of sarcasm in his voice*⟩ ⟨*took the ~ off the criticism*⟩ **2a** the line where an object or area begins or ends; a border ⟨*the town stands on the ~ of a plain*⟩ **b** the narrow part adjacent to a border; the brink, verge **c** a point that marks a beginning or transition; a threshold – esp in *on the edge of* ⟨*felt herself to be on the ~ of insanity*⟩ **d** a favourable margin; an advantage ⟨*had the ~ on the competition*⟩ **3** a line where 2 planes or 2 plane faces of a solid body meet or cross **4** the edging of a cricket ball – **on edge** anxious, nervous

²edge *vt* **1** to give or supply an edge to **2** to move or force gradually in a specified way ⟨*~d him off the road*⟩ ⟨*~d her out of the leadership*⟩ **3** to incline (a ski) sideways so that 1 edge cuts into the snow **4** to hit (a ball) or the bowling of (a bowler) in cricket with the edge of the bat ~ *vi* to advance cautiously (e g by short sideways steps) ⟨*the climbers ~d along the cliff*⟩ ⟨*the car ~d round the corner*⟩ – **edger** *n*

edged *adj* having a specified kind of edge, boundary, or border or a specified number of edges – usu in combination ⟨*rough-edged*⟩ ⟨*two-edged*⟩

edgeways, edgewise *adv* with the edge foremost; sideways

edging *n* sthg that forms an edge or border

edgy *adj* tense, irritable; ON EDGE – **edgily** *adv*, **edginess** *n*

edible *adj* fit to be eaten as food – **edible** *n*, **edibleness** *n*, **edibility** *n*

edict *n* **1** an official public decree **2** the order or command of an authority – **edictal** *adj*

edification *n* the improvement of character or the mind – *fml* – **edificatory** *adj*

edifice *n* **1** a building; *esp* a large or massive structure **2** a large abstract structure or organization ⟨*the keystone which holds together the social ~* – R H Tawney⟩

edify *vt* to instruct and improve, esp in moral and spiritual knowledge

edit *vt* **1a** to prepare an edition of ⟨*~ed Pope's works*⟩ **b** to assemble (e g a film or tape recording) by deleting, inserting, and rearranging material **c** to alter or adapt (e g written or spoken words), esp to make consistent with a particular standard or purpose **2** to direct the publication of ⟨*~s the local newspaper*⟩ **3** to delete – usu + *out* – **editable** *adj*

edition *n* **1a** the form in which a text is published ⟨*paperback ~*⟩ **b** the whole number of copies published at one time ⟨*an ~ of 50,000*⟩ **c** the issue of a newspaper or periodical for a specified time or place ⟨*the late*

~⟩ ⟨*the Manchester ~*⟩ **2** the whole number of articles of one style put out at one time ⟨*a limited ~ of collectors' pieces*⟩ **3** a copy, version ⟨*she's a friendlier ~ of her mother*⟩

editor *n* **1** one who edits written material, films, etc, esp as an occupation **2** a person responsible for the editorial policy and content of a (section of a) newspaper or periodical ⟨*sports ~*⟩ – **editorship** *n*

¹editorial *adj* of or written by an editor ⟨*~ policy*⟩ ⟨*an ~ statement*⟩ – **editorially** *adv*

²editorial *n* a newspaper or magazine article that gives the opinions of the editors or publishers

editorialize, -ise *vi* **1** to express an opinion in the form of an editorial **2** to introduce personal opinion into an apparently objective report (e g by direct comment or hidden bias) – **editorializer** *n*, **editorialization** *n*

educate *vt* **1** to provide schooling for **2** to develop mentally or morally, esp by instruction **3** to train or improve (faculties, judgment, skills, etc) – **educable** *adj*, **educative** *adj*, **educator** *n*

educated *adj* **1** having an education, esp one beyond the average **2a** trained, skilled ⟨*an ~ palate*⟩ **b** befitting sby educated ⟨*~ conversation*⟩ **c** based on some knowledge of fact ⟨*an ~ guess*⟩ – **educatedly** *adv*, **educatedness** *n*

education *n* **1** educating or being educated **2** the field of study that deals with methods of teaching and learning – **educational** *adj*, **educationally** *adv*

educationalist, educationist *n* an educational theorist or administrator

educe *vt* **1** to elicit, develop **2** to arrive at through a consideration of the facts or evidence; infer *USE* fml – **educible** *adj*, **eduction** *n*

ee *n*, *pl* **een** *Scot* an eye

¹-ee *suffix* **1** (*vt → n*) one to whom (a specified action) is done ⟨*appointee*⟩ ⟨*trainee*⟩ **2** (*n, adj, vb → n*) one who acts (in a specified way) ⟨*escapee*⟩ ⟨*absentee*⟩

²-ee *suffix* (*n → n*) a particular, esp small, kind of ⟨*bootee*⟩

eel *n* any of numerous long snakelike fishes with a smooth slimy skin and no pelvic fins – **eellike** *adj*, **eely** *adj*

-een *suffix* (*n → n*) inferior fabric resembling (a specified fabric); imitation ⟨*velveteen*⟩

e'en *adv* even – chiefly poetic

-eer *suffix* (*n → n*) person engaged in (a specified occupation or activity) ⟨*auctioneer*⟩ ⟨*buccaneer*⟩ – often derog ⟨*profiteer*⟩ ⟨*racketeer*⟩

e'er *adv* ever – chiefly poetic

eerie *also* **eery** *adj* frighteningly strange or gloomy; weird – **eerily** *adv*, **eeriness** *n*

efface *vt* **1** to eliminate or make indistinct (as if) by wearing away a surface; obliterate ⟨*coins with dates ~d by wear*⟩ **2** to make (oneself) modestly or shyly inconspicuous – **effaceable** *adj*, **effacement** *n*, **effacer** *n*

¹effect *n* **1a** the result of a cause or agent **b** the result of purpose or intention ⟨*employed her knowledge to good ~*⟩ **2** the basic meaning; intent – esp in *to that effect* **3** power to bring about a result; efficacy **4** *pl* personal movable property; goods **5a** a distinctive impression on the human senses ⟨*the use of colour produces a very striking ~*⟩ **b** the creation of an often false desired impression ⟨*her tears were purely for ~*⟩ **c** sthg designed to produce a distinctive or desired impression – often *pl* ⟨*special lighting ~s*⟩ **6** the quality or state of being operative; operation ⟨*the law comes into ~ next week*⟩ **7** an experimental scientific phenomenon named usu after its discoverer – **in effect** for all practical purposes; actually although not appearing so – **to the effect** with the meaning ⟨*issued a statement to the effect that he would resign*⟩

²**effect** vt 1 to bring about, often by surmounting obstacles; accomplish ⟨~ a settlement of a dispute⟩ 2 to put into effect; CARRY OUT ⟨the duty of the legislature to ~ the will of the citizens⟩

¹**effective** adj 1a producing a decided, decisive, or desired effect b impressive, striking 2 ready for service or action ⟨~ manpower⟩ 3 actual, real ⟨the ~ strength of the army⟩ 4 being in effect; operative ⟨the tax becomes ~ next year⟩ – **effectiveness** n

²**effective** n a soldier equipped and fit for duty

effectively adv for all practical purposes; IN EFFECT

effectual adj producing or able to produce a desired effect; adequate, effective – **effectualness** n, **effectuality** n

effectually adv for all practical purposes; IN EFFECT

effectuate vt – **effectuation** n

effeminate adj 1 of a man having qualities usu thought of as feminine; not manly in appearance or manner 2 marked by an unbecoming delicacy or lack of vigour ⟨~ art⟩ – **effeminate** n, **effeminacy** n

effendi n, pl **effendis** a man of property, authority, or education in an eastern Mediterranean country

effervesce vi 1 of a liquid to bubble, hiss, and foam as gas escapes 2 to show liveliness or exhilaration – **effervescence** n, **effervescent** adj, **effervescently** adv

effete adj 1 worn out; exhausted 2 marked by weakness or decadent overrefinement ⟨an ~ civilization⟩ – **effetely** adv, **effeteness** n

efficacious adj having the power to produce a desired effect – **efficacity** n, **efficacy** n, **efficaciously** adv, **efficaciousness** n

efficiency n 1 the quality or degree of being efficient 2a efficient operation b the ratio of the useful energy delivered by a dynamic system to the energy supplied to it

efficient adj 1 of a person able and practical; briskly competent 2 productive of desired effects, esp with minimum waste ⟨an ~ method of generating electricity⟩ – **efficiently** adv

effigy n an image or representation, esp of a person; specif a crude figure representing a hated person

efflorescence n 1 the period or state of flowering 2 the action, process, period, or result of developing and unfolding as if coming into flower; blossoming ⟨periods of intellectual and artistic ~ – Julian Huxley⟩ 3 the process or product of efflorescing chemically 4 a redness of the skin; an eruption – **efflorescent** adj

¹**effluent** adj flowing out; emanating ⟨an ~ river⟩

²**effluent** n sthg that flows out: e g a an outflowing branch of a main stream or lake b smoke, liquid industrial refuse, sewage, etc discharged into the environment, esp when causing pollution

efflux n an effluence, esp of liquid or gas – **effluxion** n

effort n 1 conscious exertion of physical or mental power 2 a serious attempt; a try 3 sthg produced by exertion or trying ⟨the novel was his most ambitious ~⟩ 4 the force applied (e g to a simple machine) as distinguished from the force exerted against the load – **effortful** adj, **effortless** adj, **effortlessly** adv, **effortlessness** n

effrontery n the quality of being shamelessly bold; insolence ⟨the ~ to propound three such heresies – TLS⟩

effulgence n radiant splendour; brilliance – fml – **effulgent** adj

effusion n 1 an act of effusing 2 unrestrained expression of words or feelings 3 the escape of a fluid from a containing vessel; also the fluid that escapes

effusive adj 1 unduly emotionally demonstrative; gushing 2 of rock characterized or formed by a nonexplosive outpouring of lava – **effusively** adv, **effusiveness** n

eft n a newt

egalitarian adj marked by or advocating egalitarianism – **egalitarian** n

¹**egg** vt to incite to action – usu + on ⟨~ed the mob on to riot⟩

²**egg** n 1a the hard-shelled reproductive body produced by a bird; esp that produced by domestic poultry and used as a food b an animal reproductive body consisting of an ovum together with its nutritive and protective envelopes that is capable of developing into a new individual c an ovum 2 sthg resembling an egg in shape 3 a person – infml; not now in vogue ⟨he's a good ~!⟩

eggcup n a small cup without a handle used for holding a boiled egg

egghead n an intellectual, highbrow – derog or humor – **eggheaded** adj

eggnog n a drink consisting of eggs beaten up with sugar, milk or cream, and often spirits (e g rum or brandy)

eggplant n a widely cultivated plant of the nightshade family; also, chiefly NAm its fruit, the aubergine

¹**eggshell** n the hard exterior covering of an egg

²**eggshell** adj 1 esp of china thin and fragile 2 esp of paint having a slight sheen

egg timer n an instrument like a small hourglass that runs for about 3 minutes and is used for timing the boiling of eggs

egis n an aegis

eglantine n sweetbrier

ego n, pl **egos** 1 the self, esp as contrasted with another self or the world 2 SELF-ESTEEM 1 3 the one of the 3 divisions of the mind in psychoanalytic theory that serves as the organized conscious mediator between the person and reality, esp in the perception of and adaptation to reality

egocentric adj limited in outlook or concern to one's own activities or needs; self-centred, selfish – **egocentric** n, **egocentrically** adv, **egocentricity** n, **egocentrism** n

egoism n 1 (conduct based on) a doctrine that individual self-interest is or should be the foundation of morality 2 egotism

egoist n 1 a believer in egoism 2 an egocentric or egotistic person – **egoistic** also **egoistical** adj, **egoistically** adv

egotism n 1 the practice of talking about oneself too much 2 an extreme sense of self-importance – **egotist** n, **egotistic**, **egotistical** adj, **egotistically** adv

ego trip n an act or series of acts that selfishly enhances and satisfies one's ego – infml – **ego-trip** vi, **ego-tripper** n

egregious adj conspicuously or shockingly bad; flagrant ⟨an ~ mistake⟩ – fml – **egregiously** adv, **egregiousness** n

egress n 1 going or coming out; specif the emergence of a celestial object from eclipse, transit, or occultation 2 a place or means of going out; an exit – fml – **egress** vi, **egression** n

egret n any of various herons that bear long plumes during the breeding season

¹**Egyptian** adj (characteristic) of Egypt

²**Egyptian** n 1 a native or inhabitant of Egypt 2 the Afro-Asiatic language of the ancient Egyptians to about the 3rd c AD

eh interj – used to ask for confirmation or to express inquiry

eiderdown n 1 the down of the eider duck 2 a thick warm quilt filled with eiderdown or other insulating material

eight n 1 (the number) 8 2 the eighth in a set or series 3 sthg having 8 parts or members or a denomination of 8; esp (the crew of) an 8-person racing boat – **eight** adj or pron, **eightfold** adj or adv

eighteen n (the number) 18 – **eighteen** adj or pron, **eighteenth** adj or n

eighth adj or n (of or being) number eight in a countable series

eighth note n, NAm a quaver

eightsome reel n a Scottish reel for eight dancers

eighty n **1** (the number) 80 **2** pl the numbers 80 to 89; specif a range of temperatures, ages, or dates within a century characterized by those numbers – **eightieth** adj or n, **eighty** adj or pron, **eightyfold** adj or adv

eisteddfod n, pl **eisteddfods**, **eisteddfodau** a Welsh-language competitive festival of the arts, esp music and poetry – **eisteddfodic** adj

¹**either** adj **1** being the one and the other of 2 ⟨flowers blooming on ~ side of the path⟩ **2** being the one or the other of 2 ⟨take ~ road⟩

²**either** pron the one or the other ⟨could be happy with ~ of them⟩ ⟨don't want ~⟩

³**either** conj – used before 2 or more sentence elements of the same class or function joined usu by or to indicate that what immediately follows is the first of 2 or more alternatives ⟨~ sink or swim⟩ ⟨~ coffee, tea, or whisky⟩

⁴**either** adv for that matter, likewise – used for emphasis after a negative or implied negation ⟨not wise or handsome ~⟩ ⟨I can't swim, ~⟩

either-or adj or n (involving) an unavoidable choice between only 2 possibilities

¹**ejaculate** vt **1** to eject from a living body; specif to eject (semen) in orgasm **2** to utter suddenly and vehemently – fml – **ejaculation** n, **ejaculatory** adj

²**ejaculate** n the semen released by a single ejaculation

eject vt **1** to drive out, esp by physical force ⟨the hecklers were ~ed⟩ **2** to evict from property ~ vi to escape from an aircraft by using the ejector seat – **ejectable** adj, **ejection** n, **ejective** adj, **ejector** n

ejector seat n an emergency escape seat that propels an occupant out and away from an aircraft by means of an explosive charge

eke out vt **1a** to make up for the deficiencies of; supplement ⟨eked out his income by getting a second job⟩ **b** to make (a supply) last by economy **2** to make (e g a living) by laborious or precarious means

el n, NAm an elevated railway

¹**elaborate** adj **1** planned or carried out with great care and attention to detail ⟨~ preparations⟩ **2** marked by complexity, wealth of detail, or ornateness; intricate ⟨a highly ~ coiffure⟩ – **elaborately** adv, **elaborateness** n

²**elaborate** vt **1** to build up (complex organic compounds) from simple ingredients **2** to work out in detail; develop ~ vi to go into detail; add further information ⟨need I ~?⟩ – often + on ⟨urged him to ~ on his scheme⟩ – **elaboration** n, **elaborative** adj

élan n vigorous spirit or enthusiasm; verve

eland n either of 2 large African antelopes

elapse vi, of a period of time to pass by ⟨4 years ~d before he returned⟩

¹**elastic** adj **1a** of a solid capable of recovering size and shape after deformation **b** of a gas capable of indefinite expansion **2** buoyant, resilient **3** capable of being easily stretched or expanded and resuming its former shape **4** capable of ready change; flexible, adaptable ⟨an ~ conscience⟩ ⟨~ rules⟩ ⟨~ demand for goods⟩ – **elastically** adv, **elasticity** n, **elasticize** vt

²**elastic** n **1** an elastic fabric usu made of yarns containing rubber **2** easily stretched rubber, usu prepared in cords, strings, or bands

elastic band n, Br RUBBER BAND

Elastoplast trademark – used for an elastic adhesive plaster

elate vt to fill with joy or pride; put in high spirits – **elated** adj, **elatedly** adv, **elation** n

¹**elbow** n **1a** the joint between the human forearm and upper arm **b** a corresponding joint in the forelimb of a vertebrate animal **2** an elbow-like pipe fitting **3** the part of a garment that covers the elbow – **out at elbows 1** shabbily dressed **2** POOR 1 – **up to the elbows in/with** busily engaged in

²**elbow** vt **1** to push or shove aside (as if) with the elbow; jostle ⟨~ed him out of the way⟩ **2** to force (e g one's way) rudely or roughly (as if) by pushing with the elbow ⟨~ed his way into the best circles⟩ ~ vi to advance by elbowing one's way

elbow grease n hard physical effort – infml

elbowroom n adequate space or scope for movement, work, or operation

¹**elder** n any of several shrubs or small trees of the honeysuckle family

²**elder** adj of earlier birth or greater age, esp than another related person or thing ⟨his ~ brother⟩

³**elder** n **1** one who is older; a senior ⟨the child trying to please his ~s⟩ **2** one having authority by virtue of age and experience ⟨the village ~s⟩ **3** an official of the early church or of a Presbyterian congregation – **eldership** n

elderberry n (the edible black or red berry of) an elder

elderly adj rather old – **elderliness** n

elder statesman n an eminent senior or retired member of a group whose advice is often sought unofficially

eldest adj of the greatest age or seniority; oldest

El Dorado n a place of fabulous wealth, abundance, or opportunity

¹**elect** adj **1** SELECT 1, 2 **2** chosen for salvation through divine mercy **3** chosen for office or position but not yet installed ⟨the president-elect⟩

²**elect** vt **1** to select by vote for an office, position, or membership ⟨~ed him president⟩ **2** of God to choose or predestine (sby) to receive salvation **3** chiefly NAm to make a selection of ~ vi to choose, decide – fml – **election** n

electioneer vi to work for a candidate or party in an election – **electioneer** n

elective adj **1a** chosen or filled by popular election ⟨an ~ office⟩ **b** of election **2** permitting a choice; optional – **electively** adv, **electiveness** n

elector n **1** sby qualified to vote in an election **2** sby entitled to participate in an election: e g **a** often cap any of the German princes entitled to elect the Holy Roman Emperor **b** a member of the electoral college in the USA

electoral adj of (an) election or electors

electoral college n sing or pl in constr a body of electors chosen in each state to elect the president and vice-president of the USA

electorate n **1** often cap the territory, jurisdiction, etc of a German elector **2** sing or pl in constr a body of electors

electr-, electro- comb form **1a** (caused by) electricity ⟨electromagnetism⟩ ⟨electrochemistry⟩ **b** electric ⟨electrode⟩; electric and ⟨electrochemical⟩ ⟨electromechanical⟩; electrically ⟨electropositive⟩ **2** electrolytic ⟨electroanalysis⟩ ⟨electrodeposition⟩ **3** electron ⟨electrophile⟩

Electra complex n the Oedipus complex when it occurs in a female

¹**electric** adj **1a** of, being, supplying, producing, or produced by electricity ⟨~ current⟩ ⟨an ~ plug⟩ **b** operated by or using electricity ⟨an ~ motor⟩ **2** producing an intensely stimulating effect; thrilling ⟨an ~ performance⟩

3 *of a musical instrument* electronically producing or amplifying sound ⟨an ~ organ⟩
²**electric** *n* **1** *pl* electrical parts; electric circuitry **2** electricity – sometimes pl with sing. meaning; infml
electrical *adj* **1** of or connected with electricity ⟨~ output⟩ ⟨~ engineering⟩ **2** ELECTRIC 1 ⟨~ appliances⟩ – **electrically** *adv*
electric blanket *n* a blanket containing an electric heating element that is used to warm a bed
electric chair *n* **1** a chair used in legal electrocution **2** *the* penalty of death by electrocution
electric eye *n* PHOTOELECTRIC CELL
electrician *n* one who installs, maintains, operates, or repairs electrical equipment
electricity *n* **1** (the study of) the phenomena due to (the flow or accumulation of) positively and negatively charged particles (e g protons and electrons) **2** electric current; *also* electric charge
electric ray *n* any of various rays found in warm seas that can give elctric shocks
electric shock *n* ²SHOCK 4
electrify *vt* **1a** to charge (a body) with electricity **b** to equip for use of or supply with electric power **2** to excite, thrill – **electrification** *n*
electro- – see ELECTR-
electrocardiogram *n* the tracing made by an electrocardiograph
electrocardiograph *n* an instrument for recording the changes of electrical potential difference occurring during the heartbeat – **electrocardiographic** *adj*, **electrocardiographically** *adv*, **electrocardiography** *n*
electroconvulsive therapy *n* a treatment for serious mental disorder, esp severe depression, in which a fit is induced by passing an electric current through the brain
electrocute *vt* to execute or kill by electricity – **electrocution** *n*
electrode *n* a conductor used to establish electrical contact with a nonmetallic part of a circuit (e g the acid in a car battery)
electroencephalogram *n* the tracing made by an electroencephalograph
electroencephalograph *n* an instrument for detecting and recording brain waves – **electroencephalographic** *adj*, **electroencephalography** *n*
electrolysis *n* **1** the passage of an electric current through an electrolyte to generate a gas, deposit a metal on (an object serving as) an electrode, etc **2** the destruction of hair roots, warts, moles, etc by means of an electric current – **electrolyse** *vt*
electrolyte *n* **1** a nonmetallic electric conductor (e g a salt solution) in which current is carried by the movement of ions **2** a substance that becomes an ionic conductor when dissolved in a suitable solvent or melted
electromagnetic spectrum *n* the entire range of wavelengths or frequencies of electromagnetic radiation extending from gamma rays to the longest radio waves and including visible light
electron *n* a negatively charged elementary particle that occurs in atoms outside the nucleus and the mass movement of which constitutes an electric current in a metal
electronic *adj* **1** of electrons **2** of, being, or using devices constructed or working by the methods or principles of electronics – **electronically** *adv*
electronics *n pl but sing in constr* physics or technology dealing with the emission, behaviour, and effects of electrons in thermionic valves, transistors, or other electronic devices
electron microscope *n* an instrument in which a beam of electrons is used to produce an enormously enlarged image of a minute object – **electron microscopist** *n*, **electron microscopy** *n*
electron tube *n* an electronic device (e g a thermionic valve) consisting of a sealed container containing a vacuum or gas through which the flow of electrons is controlled
electroplate *vt* to plate with a continuous metallic coating by electrolysis
electroshock therapy *n* ELECTROCONVULSIVE THERAPY
eleemosynary *adj* of, supported by, or giving charity
elegant *adj* **1** gracefully refined or dignified (e g in manners, taste, or style) **2** tastefully rich or luxurious, esp in design or ornamentation ⟨~ furnishings⟩ **3** *of ideas* neat and simple ⟨an ~ piece of reasoning⟩ ⟨an ~ mathematical proof⟩ – **elegance** *n*, **elegantly** *adv*
elegiac couplet *n* a classical verse form in which dactylic hexameters alternate with pentameters
elegy *n* **1a** a song, poem, or other work expressing sorrow or lamentation, esp for one who is dead **b** a pensive or reflective poem that is usu nostalgic or melancholy **2** a poem in elegiac couplets – **elegize** *vb*, **elegiac** *adj*, **elegiacal** *adj*, **elegiacally** *adv*
element *n* **1a** any of the 4 substances air, water, fire, and earth formerly believed to constitute the physical universe **b** *pl* forces of nature; *esp* violent or severe weather **c** the state or sphere natural or suited to sby or sthg ⟨at school she was in her ~⟩ **2** a constituent part: e g **a** *pl* the simplest principles of a subject of study; the rudiments **b** any of the numbers or symbols in an array (e g a matrix) **c** a constituent of a mathematical set **d** a specified group within a human community ⟨the rowdy ~ in the classroom⟩ ⟨the smart ~⟩ – often pl with sing. meaning **e** any of the factors determining an outcome **f** a distinct part of a composite device; *esp* a resistor in an electric heater, kettle, etc **3** any of more than 100 fundamental substances that consist of atoms of only one kind **4** *pl* the bread and wine used at Communion
elemental *adj* **1** existing as an uncombined chemical element **2** of or resembling a great force of nature ⟨~ passions⟩ – **elemental** *n*, **elementally** *adv*
elementary *adj* **1** of or dealing with the basic elements or principles of sthg; simple ⟨can't handle the most ~ decision-making⟩ **2** ELEMENTAL 1 – **elementarily** *adv*, **elementariness** *n*
elementary particle *n* any of the constituents of matter and energy (e g the electron, proton, or photon) whose nature has not yet been proved to be due to the combination of other more fundamental entities
elephant *n* a very large nearly hairless mammal having the snout prolonged into a muscular trunk and 2 upper incisors developed into long tusks which provide ivory
elephantiasis *n*, *pl* **elephantiases** enormous enlargement of a limb or the scrotum caused by lymphatic obstruction, esp by filarial worms
elephantine *adj* **1a** huge, massive **b** clumsy, ponderous **2** of an elephant
elevate *vt* **1** to lift up; raise **2** to raise in rank or status; exalt **3** to improve morally, intellectually, or culturally **4** to raise the spirits of; elate
elevated *adj* **1** raised, esp above a surface (e g the ground) ⟨an ~ road⟩ **2** morally or intellectually on a high plane; lofty ⟨~ thoughts⟩ **3** exhilarated in mood or feeling **4** slightly tipsy – not now in vogue
elevation *n* **1** the height to which sthg is elevated: e g **a** the angle to which a gun is aimed above the horizon **b** the height above sea level **2** (the ability to achieve) a ballet dancer's or a skater's leap and seeming suspension in the air **3** an elevated place **4** being elevated **5** a geometrical

projection (e g of a building) on a vertical plane – **elevational** adj

elevator n 1 sby or sthg that raises or lifts sthg up: e g a an endless belt or chain conveyer for raising grain, liquids, etc b chiefly NAm LIFT 9 c NAm a building for elevating, storing, discharging, and sometimes processing grain 2 a movable horizontal control surface, usu attached to the tailplane of an aircraft for controlling climb and descent

eleven n 1 (the number) 11 2 the eleventh in a set or series 3 sing or pl in constr sthg having 11 parts or members or a denomination of 11; esp a cricket, soccer, or hockey team – **eleven** adj or pron, **elevenfold** adj or adv, **eleventh** adj or n

eleven-plus, 11-plus n an examination taken, esp formerly, at the age of 10-11 to determine which type of British state secondary education a child should receive

elevenses n pl but sometimes sing in constr, Br light refreshment taken in the middle of the morning

eleventh hour n the latest possible time ⟨won his reprieve at the ∼⟩ – **eleventh-hour** adj

elf n, pl **elves** a (mischievous) fairy – **elfish** adj, **elfishly** adv

elfin adj of or resembling an elf, esp in being small, sprightly, or impish

elicit vt 1 to draw forth or bring out (sthg latent or potential) 2 to call forth or draw out (a response or reaction); evoke – **elicitor** n, **elicitation** n

elide vt to suppress or alter (e g a vowel or syllable) by elision

eligible adj 1 qualified to be chosen; also entitled ⟨∼ for promotion⟩ ⟨∼ to retire⟩ 2 worthy or desirable, esp as a marriage partner ⟨an ∼ young bachelor⟩ – **eligible** n, **eligibly** adv, **eligibility** n

eliminate vt 1a to cast out or get rid of completely; eradicate ⟨the need to ∼ poverty⟩ b to set aside as unimportant; ignore 2 to expel (e g waste) from the living body 3a to kill (a person), esp so as to remove as an obstacle b to remove (a competitor, team, etc) from a competition, usu by defeat – **elimination** n, **eliminative** adj, **eliminator** n

élite, elite n 1 sing or pl in constr a small superior group; esp one that has a power out of proportion to its size 2 a typewriter type producing 12 characters to the inch – **élite** adj

élitism, elitism n (advocacy of) leadership by an élite – **élitist** n or adj

elixir n 1 an alchemist's substance supposedly capable of changing base metals into gold 2a elixir, elixir of life a substance held to be capable of prolonging life indefinitely b a cure-all 3 a sweetened liquid (e g a syrup) containing a drug or medicine

Elizabethan adj (characteristic) of (the age of) Elizabeth I – **Elizabethan** n

elk n, pl **elks**, esp collectively **elk** 1 the largest existing deer of Europe and Asia 2 NAm the wapiti

elkhound n any of a large Norwegian breed of hunting dogs with a very heavy coat

ellipse n a closed plane curve generated by a point moving in such a way that the sums of its distances from 2 fixed points is a constant; a closed plane curve obtained by plane section of a right circular cone

ellipsis n, pl **ellipses** 1 the omission of 1 or more words needed to make a construction grammatically complete 2 marks or a mark (e g ... or *** or –) indicating the omission of letters or words

elliptical, elliptic adj 1a of or shaped like an ellipse b of or marked by ellipsis or an ellipsis 2 of speech or writing

extremely or excessively concise – **elliptically** adv, **ellipticity** n

elm n (the wood of) any of a genus of large graceful trees

elocution n the art of effective public speaking, esp of good diction – **elocutionary** adj, **elocutionist** n

¹**elongate** vt to extend the length of to grow in length

²**elongate, elongated** adj long in proportion to width – used esp in botany and zoology

elongation n the angular distance of one celestial body from another round which it revolves or from a particular point in the sky as viewed from earth

elope vi to run away secretly with the intention of getting married or cohabiting, usu without parental consent – **elopement** n, **eloper** n

eloquent adj 1 characterized by fluent, forceful, and persuasive use of language 2 vividly or movingly expressive or revealing ⟨put his arm around her in an ∼ gesture of reassurance⟩ – **eloquence** n, **eloquently** adv

else adv 1 apart from the person, place, manner, or time mentioned or understood ⟨how ∼ could he have acted⟩ ⟨everybody ∼ but me⟩ 2 also, besides ⟨who ∼ did you see⟩ ⟨there's nothing ∼ to eat⟩ 3 if not, otherwise ⟨do what you are told or ∼ you'll be sorry⟩ ⟨they must be coming; they'd have phoned ∼⟩ – used absolutely to express a threat ⟨do what I tell you or ∼⟩

elsewhere adv in or to another place ⟨took his business ∼⟩

elucidate vb to make (sthg) lucid, esp by explanation – **elucidative** adj, **elucidator** n, **elucidation** n

elude vt 1 to avoid cunningly or adroitly 2 to escape the memory, understanding, or notice of

elusive adj tending to elude – **elusively** adv, **elusiveness** n, **elusion** n

elver n a young eel

elves pl of ELF

elvish adj elfish

Elysium n, pl **Elysiums, Elysia** 1 the home of the blessed after death in Greek mythology 2 PARADISE 2 – **Elysian** adj

em, m n 1 the width of the body of a piece of type bearing the letter M used as a unit of measure of printed matter 2 ¹PICA 2

em- – see EN-

'**em** pron them – used in writing to suggest casual speech

emaciate vt to make or become excessively thin or feeble – **emaciation** n

emanate vi to come out from a source ⟨a foul smell ∼d from the sewer⟩ ⟨rumours emanating from high places⟩ ∼ vt EMIT 1

emancipate vt to free from restraint, control, or esp slavery – **emancipator** n, **emancipation** n, **emancipationist** n

emasculate vt 1 to castrate 2 to deprive of strength, vigour, or spirit; weaken – **emasculate** adj, **emasculation** n, **emasculator** n

embalm vt 1 to treat (a dead body) so as to give protection against decay 2 to preserve from oblivion – **embalmer** n, **embalmment** n

embankment n a raised structure to hold back water or to carry a roadway or railway – **embank** vt

embargo n, pl **embargoes** 1 an order of a government prohibiting the departure or entry of commercial ships 2 a legal prohibition on commerce ⟨an ∼ on arms shipments⟩ 3 a stoppage, impediment; esp a prohibition – **embargo** vt

embark vi 1 to go on board a boat or aircraft 2 to make a start; commence – usu + on or upon ⟨∼ed on a new *career*⟩ ~*vt* to cause to go on board a boat or aircraft – **embarkment** *n*, **embarkation** *n*

embarrass *vt* 1 to involve in financial difficulties, esp debt 2 to cause to experience a state of self-conscious distress; disconcert ⟨*smutty stories* ~ed *her*⟩ – **embarrassedly** *adv*, **embarrassingly** *adv*, **embarrassment** *n*

embassy *n* 1a the position of an ambassador b an ambassador's official mission abroad 2 (the residence of) a diplomatic body headed by an ambassador

embattled *adj* involved in battle or conflict

embed *vt* -dd- to place or fix firmly (as if) in surrounding matter ⟨*a splinter was* ~ded *in his finger*⟩

embellish *vt* 1 to make beautiful by adding ornaments; decorate 2 to make (speech or writing) more interesting by adding fictitious or exaggerated detail – **embellisher** *n*, **embellishment** *n*

ember *n* 1 a glowing fragment (e g of coal or wood) in a (dying) fire 2 *pl* the smouldering remains of a fire 3 *pl* slowly fading emotions, memories, ideas, or responses

ember day *n* a day set aside for fasting and prayer in Anglican and Roman Catholic churches that falls on the Wednesday, Friday, or Saturday following the first Sunday in Lent, Whitsunday, September 14, or December 13

embezzle *vt* embezzling to appropriate (e g property entrusted to one's care) fraudulently to one's own use – **embezzlement** *n*, **embezzler** *n*

embitter *vt* 1 to make bitter 2 to excite bitter feelings in – **embitterment** *n*

emblazon *vt* 1 to display conspicuously 2a(1) to deck in bright colours (2) to inscribe, adorn, or embellish (as if) with heraldic bearings or devices b to celebrate, extol – **emblazonment** *n*, **emblazonry** *n*

emblem *n* 1 an object or a typical representation of an object symbolizing another object or idea 2 a device, symbol, or figure adopted and used as an identifying mark

emblematic *also* **emblematical** *adj* of or constituting an emblem; symbolic – **emblematically** *adv*

embody *vt* 1 to give a body to (a spirit); incarnate 2 to make (e g ideas or concepts) concrete and perceptible ⟨*a chapter which embodies his new theory*⟩ 3 to make (e g connected ideas or principles) a part of a body or system; incorporate, include – usu + *in* ⟨*their way of life is embodied in their laws*⟩ 4 to represent in human or animal form; personify ⟨*men who embodied the idealism of the revolution*⟩ – **embodier** *n*, **embodiment** *n*

embolden *vt* to make bold or courageous

embolism *n* (the sudden obstruction of a blood vessel by) an embolus – **embolismic** *adj*

emboss *vt* 1 to ornament with raised work 2 to raise in relief from a surface – **embosser** *n*, **embossment** *n*

¹**embrace** *vt* 1 to take and hold closely in the arms as a sign of affection; hug 2 to encircle, enclose 3a to take up, esp readily or eagerly; adopt ⟨~ *a cause*⟩ b to avail oneself of; welcome ⟨~d *the opportunity to study further*⟩ 4 to include as a part or element of a more inclusive whole ~*vi* to join in an embrace; hug one another – **embracer** *n*, **embracingly** *adv*, **embracive** *adj*

²**embrace** *n* an act of embracing or gripping ⟨*a loving* ~⟩⟨*helpless in the* ~ *of terror*⟩

embrasure *n* 1 a door or window aperture, esp with splayed sides that increase the width of the opening on the inside 2 an opening with sides flaring outwards in a wall or parapet, usu for a gun

embrocation *n* a liniment

embroider *vt* 1a to ornament (e g cloth or a garment) with decorative stitches made by hand or machine b to form (e g a design or pattern) in ornamental needlework 2 to elaborate on (a narrative); embellish with exaggerated or fictitious details ~*vi* 1 to do or make embroidery 2 to provide embellishments; elaborate – + *on* or *upon* – **embroiderer** *n*, **embroidery** *n*

embroil *vt* 1 to throw (e g a person or affairs) into disorder or confusion 2 to involve in conflict or difficulties – **embroilment** *n*

embryo *n*, *pl* **embryos** 1a an animal in the early stages of growth before birth or hatching b the developing human individual during the first 8 weeks after conception 2 a rudimentary plant within a seed 3a sthg as yet undeveloped b a beginning or undeveloped state of sthg – esp in *in embryo* ⟨*plans still in* ~⟩

embryonic *also* **embryonal** *adj* 1 of an embryo 2 in an early stage of development – **embryonically** *adv*

emend *vt* to correct, usu by textual alterations – **emendable** *adj*, **emender** *n*

emendation *n* (an alteration made by) the act of emending

emerald *adj or n* (of the bright green colour of) a beryl used as a gemstone

emerge *vi* 1 to rise (as if) from an enveloping fluid; come out into view 2 to become manifest or known 3 to rise from an obscure or inferior condition

emergence *n* a superficial outgrowth of plant tissue (e g the thorn of a rose)

emergency *n* an unforeseen occurrence or combination of circumstances that calls for immediate action

emergent *adj* emerging; *esp* in the early stages of formation or development ⟨*the* ~ *countries of the world*⟩

emeritus, *fem* **emerita** *adj* holding an honorary title after retirement

emery *n* a dark granular mineral consisting mainly of corundum which is used for grinding and polishing

emetic *n or adj* (sthg) that induces vomiting – **emetically** *adv*

emigrant *n* one who emigrates – **emigrant** *adj*

emigrate *vi* to leave one's home or country for life or residence elsewhere – **emigration** *n*

émigré, **emigré** *n* a (political) emigrant

eminence *n* 1 a position of prominence or superiority – used as a title for a cardinal 2 sby or sthg high, prominent, or lofty: e g a a person of high rank or attainments b a natural geographical elevation; a height

eminent *adj* 1 standing out so as to be readily seen or noted; conspicuous, notable 2 exhibiting eminence, esp in position, fame, or achievement – **eminently** *adv*

emir *n* 1 a ruler of any of various Muslim states 2 a high-ranking Turkish official of former times 3 a male descendant of Muhammad

emirate *n* the position, state, power, etc of an emir

emissary *n* one sent on an often secret mission as the agent of another

emission *n* 1 an act or instance of emitting 2a sthg (e g electromagnetic waves, smoke, electrons, noise, etc) sent forth by emitting b an effluvium – **emissive** *adj*

emit *vt* -tt- 1a to throw or give off or out (e g light) b to send out; eject 2 to give utterance or voice to ⟨~ted *a groan*⟩

Emmenthal *n* a pale yellow Swiss cheese with many holes that form during ripening

emollient *n or adj* (a substance) that makes soft or gives relief

emolument *n* the returns arising from office or employment; a salary

emote *vi* to give expression to emotion, esp theatrically

emotion *n* 1 excitement 2 a mental and physical reaction (e g anger, fear, or joy) marked by strong feeling and often physiological changes that prepare the body for immediate vigorous action – **emotionless** adj

emotional adj **1** of the emotions ⟨an ~ disorder⟩ **2** inclined to show (excessive) emotion **3** EMOTIVE 2 – **emotionalism** n, **emotionalist** n, **emotionalize** vt, **emotionally** adv, **emotionality** n

emotive adj **1** EMOTIONAL 1 **2** appealing to, expressing, or arousing emotion rather than reason ⟨executions were an ~ issue⟩ – **emotively** adv, **emotivity** n

empanel vt **-ll-** (NAm **-l-, -ll-**), to enrol in or on a panel ⟨~ a jury⟩

empathy n **1** the imaginative projection of a subjective state into an object, esp a work of art, so allowing it to be better understood and appreciated **2** the capacity for participation in another's feelings or ideas – **empathize** vi, **empathic** adj

emperor n the supreme ruler of an empire – **emperorship** n

emphasis n, pl **emphases** **1a** force or intensity of expression that gives special impressiveness or importance to sthg ⟨writing with ~ on the need for reform⟩ **b** a particular prominence given in speaking or writing to 1 or more words or syllables **2** special consideration of or stress on sthg ⟨the school's ~ on examinations⟩

emphasize, -ise vt to give emphasis to; place emphasis or stress on ⟨~d the need for reform⟩

emphatic adj **1** spoken with or marked by emphasis **2** tending to express oneself in forceful speech or to take decisive action – **emphatically** adv

emphysema n a disorder characterized by air-filled expansions of body tissues, esp in the lungs

empire n **1a** (the territory of) a large group of countries or peoples under 1 authority **b** sthg resembling a political empire; esp an extensive territory or enterprise under single domination or control **2** imperial sovereignty

Empire adj (characteristic) of a style (e g of furniture or interior decoration) popular during the first French Empire (1804-14); specif of a style of women's dress having a high waistline

empirical also **empiric** adj originating in, based, or relying on observation or experiment rather than theory ⟨~ data⟩ ⟨~ laws⟩ – **empirically** adv

empiricism n **1** quackery **2** the practice of discovery by observation and experiment **3** a theory that all knowledge is dependent on experience of the external world – **empiricist** n

emplacement n **1** the situation or location of sthg **2** a prepared position for weapons or military equipment ⟨radar ~ s ⟩ – **emplace** vt

emplane vb to (cause to) board an aircraft

¹employ vt **1a** to use in a specified way or for a specific purpose **b** to spend (time) **c** to use **2a** to engage the services of **b** to provide with a job that pays wages or a salary USE (1b,c) fml – **employable** adj, **employer** n, **employability** n

²employ n the state of being employed, esp for wages or a salary ⟨in the government's ~ ⟩ – fml

employee, NAm also **employe** n one employed by another, esp for wages or a salary and in a position below executive level

employment n (an) activity in which one engages or is employed

employment agency n an agency whose business is to find jobs for people seeking them or to find people to fill vacant jobs

employment exchange n LABOUR EXCHANGE

emporium n, pl **emporiums, emporia** a place of trade; esp a commercial centre or large shop

empower vt to give official authority or legal power to – **empowerment** n

empress n **1** the wife or widow of an emperor **2** a woman having in her own right the rank of emperor

¹empty adj **1a** containing nothing; esp lacking typical or expected contents **b** not occupied, inhabited, or frequented ⟨~ house⟩ ⟨~ streets⟩ **2a** lacking reality or substance; hollow ⟨an ~ pleasure⟩ **b** lacking effect, value, or sincerity ⟨~ threats⟩ ⟨an ~ gesture⟩ **c** lacking sense; foolish ⟨his ~ ideas⟩ **3** hungry – infml – **emptily** adv, **emptiness** n – **on an empty stomach** not having eaten anything

²empty vt **1a** to make empty; remove the contents of **b** to deprive, divest ⟨acting emptied of all emotion⟩ **c** to discharge (itself) of contents **2** to remove from what holds, encloses, or contains **3** to transfer by emptying ⟨emptied the biscuits onto the plate⟩ ~ vi **1** to become empty **2** to discharge contents ⟨the river empties into the ocean⟩ – **emptier** n

³empty n a bottle, container, vehicle, etc that has been emptied

empty-handed adj having or bringing nothing, esp because nothing has been gained or obtained ⟨returned ~ ⟩

empty-headed adj foolish, silly

empyreal adj celestial

empyrean adj or n (of) the highest heavenly sphere in ancient and medieval cosmology

emu n a swift-running Australian flightless bird

emulate vt **1** RIVAL 2 **2** to imitate closely; approach equality with; specif to imitate by means of an emulator – **emulation** n, **emulative** adj

emulsify vt to convert (e g an oil) into an emulsion – **emulsifiable** adj, **emulsifier** n, **emulsification** n

¹emulsion n **1** (the state of) a substance (e g fat in milk) consisting of one liquid dispersed in droplets throughout another liquid ⟨~ paint⟩ **2** SUSPENSION 2b; esp a suspension of a silver compound in a gelatin solution or other solid medium for coating photographic plates, film, etc – **emulsive** adj

²emulsion vt to paint (e g a wall) with emulsion paint

en, n n the width of the body of a piece of type bearing the letter n used as a unit of measure of printed matter; one half of an em

¹en- also **em-** prefix (→ vb) **1** put into or onto ⟨embed⟩ ⟨enthrone⟩; go into or onto ⟨embus⟩ ⟨entram⟩ **2** cause to be ⟨enslave⟩ ⟨enrich⟩ **3** provide with ⟨empower⟩ ⟨enfranchise⟩ **4** so as to cover ⟨engulf⟩; thoroughly ⟨entangle⟩ USE usu em before b, m, or p

²en- also **em-** prefix in; within ⟨energy⟩ – usu em- before b, m, or p ⟨empathy⟩

¹-en also **-n** suffix (n → adj) made of; consisting of ⟨earthen⟩ ⟨wooden⟩

²-en suffix (n, adj → vb) **1a** cause to be ⟨sharpen⟩ ⟨embolden⟩ **b** cause to have ⟨heighten⟩ **2a** become ⟨steepen⟩ **b** come to have ⟨lengthen⟩

enable vt **1** to provide with the means or opportunity **2** to make possible, practical, or easy

enact vt **1** to make into law **2** to act out, play – **enaction** n, **enactment** n

¹enamel vt **-ll-** (NAm **-l-, -ll-**), to cover, inlay, or decorate with enamel – **enameler** n, **enamelist** n

²enamel n **1** a usu opaque glassy coating applied to the surface of metal, glass, or pottery **2** sthg enamelled; esp enamelware **3** a substance composed of calcium phosphate that forms a thin hard layer capping the teeth **4** a paint that dries with a glossy appearance **5** chiefly NAm an often coloured coating applied to the nails to give them a smooth or glossy appearance; nail varnish

enamelware *n* metal household or kitchen utensils coated with enamel

enamour, *NAm chiefly* **enamor** *vt* to inspire with love or liking – usu pass + *of*

encamp *vt* to place or establish in a camp ~ *vi* to set up or occupy a camp

encampment *n* the place where a group (e g a body of troops) is encamped; a camp

encapsulate *vt* 1 to enclose (as if) in a capsule 2 to epitomize, condense ~ *vi* to become encapsulated – **encapsulation** *n*

encase *vt* to enclose (as if) in a case – **encasement** *n*

encaustic *n* (a decorative technique using) a paint made from pigment mixed with melted beeswax and resin and fixed by heat after application – **encaustic** *adj*

-ence *suffix* (*vb → n*) 1 action or process of ⟨*emergence*⟩; *also* instance of (a specified action or process) ⟨*reference*⟩ ⟨*reminiscence*⟩ 2 quality or state of ⟨*dependence*⟩ ⟨*somnolence*⟩ – **-ent** *suffix* (*vb → adj* or *n*)

encephalitis *n, pl* **encephalitides** inflammation of the brain, usu caused by infection – **encephalitic** *adj*

enchant *vt* 1 to bewitch 2 to attract and move deeply; delight – **enchantment** *n*

enchanter *n* a sorcerer

enchanting *adj* charming – **enchantingly** *adv*

encipher *vt* to convert (a message) into a cipher

encircle *vt* 1 to form a circle round; surround 2 to move or pass completely round – **encirclement** *n*

enclave *n* a territorial or culturally distinct unit enclosed within foreign territory

enclose *also* **inclose** *vt* 1a(1) to close in completely; surround ⟨~d *the field with a high fence*⟩ (2) to fence off (common land) for individual use **b** to hold in; confine 2 to include in a package or envelope, esp along with sthg else ⟨*a cheque is* ~d *herewith*⟩

enclosure *n* 1 enclosing or being enclosed 2 sthg that encloses 3 sthg enclosed: e g **a** sthg included in the same envelope or package as a letter **b** an area of enclosed ground; *esp* one reserved for a certain class of spectator in a sports ground

encode *vt* to convert (e g a body of information) from one system of communication into another; *esp* to convert (a message) into code – **encoder** *n*

encomium *n, pl* **encomiums**, **encomia** a usu formal expression of warm or high praise; a eulogy

encompass *vt* 1 to form a circle about; enclose 2 to include ⟨*a plan that* ~es *a number of aims*⟩ – **encompassment** *n*

¹encore *n* (an audience's appreciative demand for) a performer's reappearance to give an additional or repeated performance

²encore *vt* to call for an encore of or by

¹encounter *vt* **1a** to meet as an adversary or enemy **b** to engage in conflict with 2 to meet or come across, esp unexpectedly

²encounter *n* 1 a meeting or clash between hostile factions or people 2 a chance meeting

encounter group *n* a group of people who meet to try and develop greater sensitivity to their own and one another's feelings

encourage *vt* 1 to inspire with courage, spirit, or hope 2 to spur on ⟨*they were* ~d *to paint by their parents*⟩ 3 to give help or patronage to (a process or action); promote ⟨*many companies* ~ *union membership*⟩ – **encouragement** *n*, **encouragingly** *adv*

encroach *vi* 1 to enter gradually or by stealth into the possessions or rights of another; intrude, trespass 2 to

advance beyond the usual or proper limits *USE* usu + *on* or *upon* – **encroachment** *n*

encrust *also* **incrust** *vt* to cover, line, or overlay with a crust, esp of jewels or precious metal ~ *vi* to form a crust

encumber *vt* 1 to weigh down, burden 2 to impede or hamper the function or activity of 3 to burden with a legal claim ⟨~ *an estate*⟩

encumbrance *n* 1 sthg that encumbers; an impediment 2 a claim (e g a mortgage) against property

-ency *suffix* (→ *n*) quality or state of ⟨*despond*ency⟩

encyclical *n* a papal letter to the bishops of the church as a whole or to those in 1 country

encyclopedia, **encyclopaedia** *n* a work containing general information on all branches of knowledge or comprehensive information on 1 branch, usu in articles arranged alphabetically by subject – **encyclopedist** *n*

encyclopedic, **encyclopaedic** *adj* (suggestive) of an encyclopedia or its methods of treating a subject; comprehensive ⟨*an* ~ *memory*⟩ – **encyclopedically** *adv*

¹end *n* **1a** the part of an area that lies at the boundary ⟨*the north* ~ *of the village*⟩; *also* the farthest point from where one is ⟨*it's at the other* ~ *of the garden*⟩ **b(1)** the point that marks the extent of sthg in space or time; the limit ⟨*at the* ~ *of the day*⟩ **(2)** the point where sthg ceases to exist ⟨*world without* ~⟩ **c** either of the extreme or last parts lengthways of an object that is appreciably longer than it is broad ⟨*a pencil with a point at either* ~⟩ **2a** (the events, sections, etc immediately preceding) the cessation of action, activity, or existence ⟨*the* ~ *of the play was its weakest part*⟩ ⟨*at the* ~ *of the war*⟩ **b** the final condition; *esp* death ⟨*the* ~ *being oblivion*⟩ 3 sthg left over; remnant 4 an aim or purpose 5 sthg or sby extreme of a kind; *the* ultimate **6a** either half of a games pitch, court, etc ⟨*change* ~s *at halftime*⟩ **b** a period of action or turn to play in bowls, curling, etc 7 a particular part of an undertaking or organization ⟨*the advertising* ~ *of a business*⟩ *USE* (5 & 7) infml – **ended** *adj* – **in the end** ultimately – **no end** 1 exceedingly 2 an endless amount; a huge quantity – **on end** 1 ²UPRIGHT ⟨*turned the table* on end *to get it through the door*⟩ 2 without a stop or letup ⟨*it rained for days* on end⟩

²end *vt* 1 to bring to an end 2 to destroy ~ *vi* 1 to come to an end 2 to reach a specified ultimate situation, condition, or rank – often + ⟨~ed *up as a colonel*⟩

³end *adj* final, ultimate ⟨~ *results*⟩ ⟨~ *markets*⟩

end-, **endo-** *comb form* 1 within; inside ⟨endo*skeleton*⟩ 2 taking in; absorbing ⟨endo*thermal*⟩

endanger *vt* to bring into or expose to danger or peril – **endangerment** *n*

endear *vt* to cause to become beloved or admired – often + *to* – **endearingly** *adv*

endearment *n* a word or act (e g a caress) expressing affection

¹endeavour, *NAm chiefly* **endeavor** *vt* to attempt by exertion or effort; TRY 4 – usu + infin; fml ⟨~ing *to control her disgust*⟩

²endeavour, *NAm chiefly* **endeavor** *n* serious determined effort ⟨*fields of* ~⟩; *also* an instance of this – fml

¹endemic *adj* 1 belonging or native to a particular people or region; not introduced or naturalized ⟨~ *diseases*⟩ ⟨*an* ~ *species of plant*⟩ 2 regularly occurring in or associated with a particular topic or sphere of activity – **endemically** *adv*, **endemicity** *n*, **endemism** *n*

²endemic *n* an endemic disease or species

end game *n* the final stage of a (specif chess) game, esp when forces have been greatly reduced

ending *n* 1 the last part of a book, film, etc 2 one or more letters or syllables added to a word base, esp as an inflection

endive n **1** an annual or biennial composite plant that resembles a lettuce and has bitter leaves used in salads **2** NAm the developing crown of chicory when blanched for use as a salad plant

endless adj **1** (seeming) without end **2** extremely numerous **3** of a belt, chain, etc that is joined to itself at its ends – **endlessly** adv, **endlessness** n

¹endocrine adj **1** producing secretions that are discharged directly into the bloodstream ⟨~ system⟩ **2** of or being an endocrine gland or its secretions ⟨~ hormone⟩

²endocrine n **1** a hormone – no longer in technical use **2** endocrine, **endocrine gland** the thyroid, pituitary, or other gland that produces an endocrine secretion

endogenous also **endogenic** adj **1** growing from or on the inside **2** originating within the body – **endogenously** adv

endorse vt **1a** to write on the back of **b** to write (one's signature) on a cheque, bill, or note **2** to express approval of; support; specif, chiefly NAm to express support for (e g a political candidate) publicly **3** Br to record on (e g a driving licence) particulars of an offence committed by the holder – **endorsable** adj, **endorsement** n, **endorser** n, **endorsee** n

endosperm n a nourishing tissue in seed plants that is formed within the embryo sac – **endospermic** adj, **endospermous** adj

endow vt **1** to provide with a continuing source of income ⟨~ a hospital⟩ **2a** to provide with an ability or attribute ⟨~ed with a natural grace⟩ **b** CREDIT **3a** – usu + with

¹endowment n **1** sthg endowed; specif the part of an institution's income derived from donations **2** a natural quality with which a person is endowed

²endowment adj of, being, or involving life insurance under which a certain sum is paid to the insured at the end of an agreed period or to a specified beneficiary if the insured dies within that period ⟨an ~ policy⟩⟨an ~ mortgage⟩

endpaper n a folded sheet of paper forming the front or back inside cover and flyleaf of a book

endue vt to provide, endow; also to imbue – usu pass + with; fml

endurance n the ability to withstand hardship, adversity, or stress

endure vi to continue in the same state; last ~ vt **1** to undergo (e g a hardship), esp without giving in **2** to tolerate, permit – **endurable** adj, **endurably** adv

endways, endwise adv or adj **1** with the end forwards (e g towards the observer) **2** in or towards the direction of the ends; lengthways **3** upright; ON END ⟨boxes set ~⟩ **4** end to end ⟨put the tables together ~⟩

enema n, pl **enemas** also **enemata 1** injection of liquid into the intestine by way of the anus (e g to ease constipation) **2** material for injection as an enema

enemy n **1** one who is antagonistic to another; esp one seeking to injure, overthrow, or confound an opponent **2** sthg harmful or deadly **3a** sing or pl in constr a military adversary ⟨the ~ undertook guerrilla warfare⟩ **b** a hostile military unit or force

energetic adj **1** marked by energy, activity, or vigour **2** operating with power or effect; forceful **3** of energy ⟨~ equation⟩ – **energetically** adv

energize, -ise vt **1** to give energy to; make energetic or vigorous **2** to apply energy to so as to facilitate normal operation – **energizer** n

energy n **1** the capacity of acting or being active ⟨great intellectual ~⟩ **2** natural power vigorously exerted

⟨devoted all his energies to it⟩ **3** the capacity for doing work ⟨solar ~⟩

enervate vt to lessen the mental or physical strength or vitality of; weaken – **enervate, enervated** adj, **enervation** n

en famille adv all together as a family

enfant terrible n, pl **enfants terribles** a person whose remarks or unconventional actions cause embarrassment

enfeeble vt to make feeble – **enfeeblement** n

enfilade vt or n (to subject to) gunfire directed along the length of an enemy battle line

enfold vt **1** to wrap up; envelop **2** to clasp in the arms; embrace

enforce vt **1** to give greater force to (e g an argument); reinforce **2** to impose, compel ⟨~ obedience from them⟩ **3** to cause (a rule or law) to be carried out effectively – **enforceable** adj, **enforcement** n, **enforcer** n, **enforceability** n

enfranchise vt **1** to set free (e g from slavery) **2a** to admit to the right of voting **b** to admit (a municipality) to political privileges, esp the right of Parliamentary representation – **enfranchisement** n

engage vt **1a** to attract and hold (sby's thoughts, attention, etc) **b** to interlock with; cause to mesh **2a** to arrange to employ (sby) **b** to arrange to obtain the services of **c** to order (a room, seat, etc) to be kept for one; reserve **3a** to hold the attention of; engross ⟨her work ~s her completely⟩ **b** to induce to participate, esp in conversation **4a** to enter into contest with ⟨~ the enemy fleet⟩ **b** to bring together or interlock (e g weapons) ~ vi **1** to pledge oneself; promise **2** to occupy one's time; participate ⟨at university he ~d in gymnastics⟩ **3** to enter into conflict ⟨the fleets ~d in the Atlantic⟩ **4** to be or become interlocked or meshed

engagé adj actively involved or committed (politically)

engaged adj **1** involved in activity; occupied **2** pledged to be married **3** chiefly Br **a** in use ⟨the telephone is ~⟩ **b** reserved, booked ⟨this table is ~⟩

engagement n **1** an agreement to marry; a betrothal **2** a pledge **3a** a promise to be present at a certain time and place **b** employment, esp for a stated time **4** a hostile encounter between military forces

engaging adj attractive, pleasing – **engagingly** adv

engender vt to cause to exist or develop; produce ⟨angry words ~ strife⟩

engine n **1** a mechanical tool ⟨a terrible ~ of war⟩ **2** a machine for converting any of various forms of energy into mechanical force and motion **3** a railway locomotive – **engineless** adj

-engined comb form (→ adj) having (such or so many) engines ⟨front-engined cars⟩ ⟨four-engined planes⟩

¹engineer n **1** a soldier who carries out engineering work **2a** a designer or builder of engines **b** a person who is trained in or follows as a profession a branch of engineering **c** a person who starts or carries through an enterprise, esp by skilful or artful contrivance ⟨the ~ of the agreement⟩ **3** a person who runs or supervises an engine or apparatus

²engineer vt **1** to lay out, construct, or manage as an engineer **2** to contrive, plan, or guide, usu with subtle skill and craft

engineering n **1** the art of managing engines **2** the application of science and mathematics by which the properties of matter and the sources of energy in nature are made useful to human beings

¹English adj (characteristic) of England – **Englishman** n, **Englishness** n

²English n **1a** the Germanic language of the people of

entangle

Britain, the USA, and most Commonwealth countries **b** English language, literature, or composition as an academic subject **2** *pl in constr* the people of England

English horn *n, chiefly NAm* COR ANGLAIS

English setter *n* any of a breed of gundogs characterized by a moderately long silky coat

engrave *vt* **1a** to cut (a design or lettering) on a hard surface (e g metal or stone) with a sharp tool **b** to impress deeply, as if by engraving ⟨*the incident was* ~d *in his memory*⟩ **2a** to cut a design or lettering on (a hard surface) for printing; *also* to print from an engraved plate **b** to photoengrave – **engraver** *n*

engraving *n* (a print made from) an engraved printing surface

engross *vt* **1a** to copy or write in a large hand **b** to prepare the final text of (an official document) **2** to occupy fully the time and attention of; absorb ⟨*a scholar* ~ed *in research*⟩⟨*an* ~ing *problem*⟩ – **engrosser** *n*, **engrossment** *n*

engulf *vt* **1** to flow over and enclose; overwhelm ⟨*the mounting seas threatened to* ~ *the island*⟩ **2** *of an amoeba, phagocytic cell, etc* to take in (food) by flowing over and enclosing – **engulfment** *n*

enhance *vt* to improve (e g in value, desirability, or attractiveness); heighten – **enhancement** *n*

enigma *n* **1** intentionally obscure speech or writing; a riddle **2** sby or sthg hard to understand or explain; a puzzle – **enigmatic** *adj*, **enigmatically** *adv*

enjoin *vt* **1** to order (sby) to do sthg; command **2** to impose (a condition or course of action) on sby **3** to forbid by law; prohibit *USE* fml

enjoy *vt* **1** to take pleasure or satisfaction in **2a** to have the use or benefit of **b** to experience ⟨*he* ~ed *good health*⟩ – **enjoyable** *adj*, **enjoyableness** *n*, **enjoyably** *adv*, **enjoyment** *n*

enlarge *vt* **1** to make larger **2** to reproduce in a larger form; *specif* to make a photographic enlargement of ~ *vi* **1** to grow larger **2** to speak or write at length; elaborate – often + *on* or *upon* – **enlarger** *n*

enlargement *n* a photographic print that is larger than the negative

enlighten *vt* to cause to understand; free from false beliefs

enlightenment *n* **1** *cap* an 18th-c movement marked by a belief in universal human progress and the importance of reason and the sciences – + *the* **2** NIRVANA 1

enlist *vt* **1** to engage (a person) for duty in the armed forces **2a** to secure the support and aid of ⟨~ *you in a good cause*⟩ ~ *vi* to enrol oneself in the armed forces – **enlistment** *n*

enlisted man *n* a person in the US armed forces ranking below a commissioned or warrant officer

enliven *vt* to give life, action, spirit, or interest to; animate – **enlivenment** *n*

en masse *adv* in a body; as a whole

enmesh *vt* to catch or entangle (as if) in a net or mesh – **enmeshment** *n*

enmity *n* (a state of) hatred or ill will

ennoble *vt* **1** to make noble; elevate ⟨*believes that hard work* ~s *the human spirit*⟩ **2** to raise to the rank of the nobility – **ennoblement** *n*

ennui *n* weariness and dissatisfaction resulting from lack of interest or boredom

enormity *n* **1** great wickedness ⟨*the sheer* ~ *of the crime*⟩ **2** a terribly wicked or evil act **3** the quality or state of being enormous

enormous *adj* marked by extraordinarily great size, number, or degree – **enormously** *adv*, **enormousness** *n*

¹enough *adj* fully adequate in quantity, number, or degree ⟨*not* ~ *beer*⟩⟨*was fool* ~ *to believe him*⟩

²enough *adv* **1** to a fully adequate degree; sufficiently ⟨*not cooked long* ~⟩ **2** to a tolerable degree ⟨*he understands well* ~⟩

³enough *pron, pl* **enough** a sufficient quantity or number ⟨~ *were present to constitute a quorum*⟩⟨*had* ~ *of their foolishness*⟩

en passant *adv* in passing – used in chess of the capture of a pawn as it makes a first move of 2 squares by an enemy pawn in a position to threaten the first of these squares

enplane *vi, chiefly NAm* to emplane

enquire *vb* to inquire

enquiry *n* an inquiry

enrage *vt* to fill with rage; anger

enrapture *vt* to fill with delight

enrich *vt* **1** to make rich or richer, esp in some desirable quality ⟨*the experience greatly* ~ed *his life*⟩ **2** to adorn, ornament ⟨~ing *the ceiling with frescoes*⟩ **3a** to make (soil) more fertile **b** to improve (a food) in nutritive value by adding nutrients (lost in processing) **c** to increase the proportion of a valuable or desirable ingredient in ⟨~ *uranium with uranium 235*⟩; *also* to add a desirable substance to ⟨~ *natural gas*⟩ – **enricher** *n*, **enrichment** *n*

enrol, NAm also enroll *vb* -ll- *vt* **1** to enter on a list, roll, etc **2** to prepare a final perfect copy of (a bill passed by a legislature) in written or printed form ~ *vi* to enrol oneself ⟨~ *in the history course*⟩ – **enrolment** *n*

en route *adv or adj* on or along the way ⟨*soon they were* ~ *to the border*⟩

ensconce *vt* to settle (e g oneself) comfortably or snugly ⟨*the cat* ~d *itself in the basket*⟩

ensemble *n* **1** a group constituting an organic whole or together producing a single effect: e g **a** a concerted music of 2 or more parts **b** a complete outfit of matching garments **c** *sing or pl in constr* (1) the musicians engaged in the performance of a musical ensemble (2) a group of supporting players, singers, or dancers **2** the quality of togetherness in performance ⟨*the quartet's* ~ *was poor*⟩

enshrine *vt* **1** to enclose (as if) in a shrine **2** to preserve or cherish, esp as sacred ⟨*they* ~d *their leader's memory in their hearts*⟩ – **enshrinement** *n*

enshroud *vt* to shroud

ensign *n* **1** a flag that is flown (e g by a ship) as the symbol of nationality **2a** a standard-bearer **b** an officer of the lowest rank in the US navy

enslave *vt* to reduce (as if) to slavery; subjugate – **enslavement** *n*, **enslaver** *n*

ensnare *vt* to take (as if) in a snare

ensue *vi* to take place afterwards or as a result

ensure *vt* to make sure, certain, or safe; guarantee

ent-, ento- *comb form* inner; within ⟨ento*blast*⟩⟨ento*zoa*⟩

entablature *n* the upper section of a wall or storey, usu supported on columns or pilasters, and in classical orders consisting of architrave, frieze, and cornice

¹entail *vt* **1** to settle (property) so that sale or bequeathal is not permitted and inheritance is limited to (a specified class of) the owner's lineal descendants **2** to involve or imply as a necessary accompaniment or result ⟨*the project will* ~ *considerable expense*⟩ – **entailer** *n*, **entailment** *n*

²entail *n* **1** (the rule fixing) an entailing **2** sthg entailed

entangle *vt* **entangling** **1** to make tangled, complicated, or confused **2** to involve in a tangle ⟨*become* ~d *in a ruinous lawsuit*⟩ – **entangler** *n*

entanglement *n* 1 sthg that entangles, confuses, or ensnares 2 the condition of being deeply involved

entente *n* 1 a friendly relationship between 2 or more countries 2 *sing or pl in constr* the countries having an entente

enter *vi* 1 to go or come in 2 to register as candidate in a competition ⟨*decided to ~ for the race*⟩ 3 to make a beginning ⟨*~ing upon a career*⟩ *~ vt* 1 to go or come into ⟨*~ a room*⟩⟨*~ing her early thirties*⟩ 2 to inscribe, register ⟨*~ the names of qualified voters in the rolls*⟩ 3 to cause to be received, admitted, or considered – often + *for* ⟨*~ a child for a public school*⟩ 4 to put in; insert 5 to become a member of or an active participant in ⟨*~ university*⟩⟨*~ a race*⟩⟨*~ politics*⟩ 6 to put on record ⟨*~ a complaint against his partner*⟩ – **enterable** *adj* – **enter into** 1 to make oneself a party to or in ⟨*enter into an important agreement*⟩ 2 to participate or share in ⟨*cheerfully entering into the household tasks*⟩

enter-, entero- *comb form* intestine ⟨*enteritis*⟩

enteritis *n* inflammation of the intestines, esp the human ileum, usu marked by diarrhoea

enteron *n* the alimentary canal or system, esp of the embryo

enterprise *n* 1 a (difficult or complicated) project or undertaking 2 a unit of economic organization or activity; *esp* a business organization 3 readiness to engage in enterprises – **enterpriser** *n*

enterprising *adj* marked by initiative and readiness to engage in enterprises

entertain *vt* 1 to show hospitality to 2 to be ready and willing to think about (an idea, doubt, suggestion, etc) 3 to hold the attention of, usu pleasantly or enjoyably; divert 4 to play against (an opposing team) on one's home ground *~ vi* to invite guests to esp one's home – **entertainer** *n*

entertainment *n* 1 sthg entertaining, diverting, or engaging 2 a public performance

enthral, *NAm also* **enthrall** *vt* **-ll-** to hold the complete interest and attention of; captivate – **enthralment** *n*

enthrone *vt* to seat, esp ceremonially, (as if) on a throne – **enthronement** *n*

enthuse *vt* to make enthusiastic ⟨*proposals which shocked the orthodox and ~d the rebellious – TLS*⟩ *~ vi* to show enthusiasm

enthusiasm *n* 1 keen and eager interest and admiration – usu + *for* or *about* 2 an object of enthusiasm

enthusiast *n* sby filled with enthusiasm; *esp* sby ardently attached to a usu specified cause, object, or pursuit ⟨*a cycling ~*⟩ – **enthusiastic** *adj*, **enthusiastically** *adv*

entice *vt* to tempt or persuade by arousing hope or desire – **enticement** *n*

entire *adj* 1 having no element or part left out ⟨*was alone the ~ day*⟩ 2 complete in degree; total ⟨*his ~ devotion to his family*⟩ 3a consisting of 1 piece; homogeneous ⟨*the book is ~ in style*⟩ **b** intact ⟨*strove to keep the collection ~*⟩ 4 not castrated – **entire** *adv*, **entireness** *n*

entirely *adv* 1 wholly, completely ⟨*agreed with me ~*⟩ 2 in an exclusive manner; solely ⟨*it is his fault ~*⟩

entirety *n* 1 the state of being entire or complete 2 the whole or total

entitle *vt* 1 to title 2 to give (sby) the right *to* (do or have) sthg ⟨*this ticket ~s the bearer to free admission*⟩ – **entitlement** *n*

entity *n* **1a** being, existence; *esp* independent, separate, or self-contained existence **b** the existence of a thing as contrasted with its attributes 2 sthg that has separate and distinct existence

entomb *vt* 1 to deposit (as if) in a tomb; bury 2 to serve as a tomb for – **entombment** *n*

entomology *n* zoology that deals with insects – **entomologist** *n*, **entomological** *adj*, **entomologically** *adv*

entourage *n* *sing or pl in constr* a group of attendants or associates, esp of sby of high rank

entr'acte *n* (a performance or interlude in) the interval between 2 acts of a play

entrails *n pl* internal parts; *esp* the intestines

¹**entrain** *vt*, *of a fluid* to draw in and transport (e g solid particles or gas) – **entrainment** *n*

²**entrain** *vb* to put or go aboard a train

¹**entrance** *n* 1 the act of entering 2 the means or place of entry 3 power or permission to enter; admission 4 an arrival of a performer onto the stage or before the cameras

²**entrance** *vt* 1 to put into a trance 2 to fill with delight, wonder, or rapture – **entrancement** *n*

entrant *n* sby or sthg that enters or is entered; *esp* one who enters a contest

entrap *vt* **-pp-** 1 to catch (as if) in a trap 2 to lure into a compromising statement or act – **entrapment** *n*

entreat *vt* to ask urgently or plead with (sby) *for* (sthg); beg ⟨*~ed the judge for another chance*⟩⟨*~ his help*⟩ *~ vi* to make an earnest request; plead – **entreatingly** *adv*, **entreatment** *n*

entreaty *n* an act of entreating; a plea

entrée, entree *n* 1 freedom of entry or access ⟨*had an ~ into the highest circles*⟩ **2a** *chiefly Br* a dish served between the usual (fish and meat) courses of a dinner **b** *chiefly NAm* the principal dish of a meal

entrench *vt* **1a** to surround with a (defensive) trench **b** to place (oneself) in a strong defensive position 2 to establish solidly, esp so as to make change difficult *~ vi* to dig or occupy a (defensive) trench – **entrenchment** *n*

entrepôt *n* a seaport, warehouse, or other intermediary centre of trade and transshipment

entrepreneur *n* one who organizes, manages, and assumes the risks of a business or enterprise – **entrepreneurial** *adj*, **entrepreneurship** *n*

entresol *n* a mezzanine

entropy *n* 1 a measure of the unavailable energy in a closed thermodynamic system 2 a measure of the amount of information in a message that is based on the logarithm of the number of possible equivalent messages 3 the degradation of the matter and energy in the universe to an ultimate state of inert uniformity – **entropic** *adj*

entrust *vt* 1 to confer a trust on; *esp* to deliver sthg in trust to – + *with* ⟨*~ed the bank with his savings*⟩ 2 to commit to another with confidence – + *to* ⟨*~ed his savings to the bank*⟩ – **entrustment** *n*

entry *n* 1 the act of entering; entrance 2 the right or privilege of entering 3 a door, gate, hall, vestibule, or other place of entrance **4a** the act of registering a record **b** a record made in a diary, account book, index, etc **c** a dictionary headword, often with its definition 5 a person, thing, or group entered in a contest; an entrant 6 the total of those entered or admitted ⟨*double the annual ~ to our medical schools*⟩

entwine *vb* to twine together or round

enumerate *vt* 1 to count 2 to specify one after another; list – **enumerator** *n*, **enumerative** *adj*, **enumeration** *n*

enunciate *vt* **1a** to make a definite or systematic statement of; formulate **b** to announce, proclaim ⟨*~d the principles to be followed by the new administration*⟩ 2 to articulate, pronounce *~ vi* to utter articulate sounds – **enunciator** *n*, **enunciable** *adj*, **enunciation** *n*

envelop *vt* 1 to enclose or enfold completely (as if) with a covering 2 to surround so as to cut off communication or retreat ⟨*~ the enemy*⟩ – **envelopment** *n*

envelope *n* 1 sthg that envelops; a wrapper, covering 2 a flat container, usu of folded and gummed paper (e g for a letter) **3** a membrane or other natural covering that encloses **4** a curve tangent to each of a family of curves **5** the performance limits of a machine, aircraft, etc ⟨*the flight ~ of the prototype fighter was explored*⟩

envenom *vt* **1** to put poison into or onto ⟨*~ a weapon*⟩ **2** to embitter ⟨*jealousy ~ing his mind*⟩

enviable *adj* highly desirable – **enviableness** *n*, **enviably** *adv*

envious *adj* feeling or showing envy ⟨*~ looks*⟩⟨*~ of a neighbour's wealth*⟩ – **enviously** *adv*, **enviousness** *n*

environ *vt* to encircle, surround – *fml*

environment *n* **1** the circumstances, objects, or conditions by which one is surrounded **2** the complex of climatic, soil, and biological factors that acts upon an organism or an ecological community – **environmental** *adj*, **environmentally** *adv*

environmentalist *n* **1** an advocate of environmentalism **2** sby concerned about the quality of the human environment

environs *n pl* the neighbourhood surrounding sthg, esp a town

envisage *vt* to have a mental picture of; visualize, esp in advance of an expected or hoped-for realization ⟨*~s an entirely new system of education*⟩

¹envoy, envoi *n* the concluding remarks to a poem, essay, or book; *specif* a short fixed final stanza of a ballade

²envoy *n* **1** a diplomatic agent, esp one who ranks immediately below an ambassador **2** a messenger, representative

¹envy *n* painful, resentful, or admiring awareness of an advantage enjoyed by another, accompanied by a desire to possess the same advantage; *also* an object of such a feeling

²envy *vt* to feel envy towards or on account of – **envier** *n*, **envyingly** *adv*

enzyme *n* any of numerous complex proteins that are produced by living cells and catalyse specific biochemical reactions at body temperatures – **enzymatic** *adj*, **enzymatically** *adv*, **enzymic** B *adv*

eon *n* an aeon

epaulette, *NAm chiefly* **epaulet** *n* an ornamental (fringed) strip or pad attached to the shoulder of a garment, esp a military uniform

épée *n* (the sport of fencing with) a sword having a bowl-shaped guard and a rigid tapering blade of triangular cross-section with no cutting edge – **épéeist** *n*

ephemeral *adj* **1** lasting 1 day only ⟨*an ~ fever*⟩ **2** lasting a very short time ⟨*~ pleasures*⟩ – **ephemerally** *adv*, **ephemerality** *n*

¹epic *adj* **1** (having the characteristics) of an epic **2a** extending beyond the usual or ordinary, esp in size or scope ⟨*his genius was ~ – TLS*⟩ **b** heroic – **epical** *adj*, **epically** *adv*

²epic *n* **1** a long narrative poem recounting the deeds of a legendary or historical hero **2** a series of events or body of legend or tradition fit to form the subject of an epic ⟨*that great environmental ~, the wreck of the Torrey Canyon – The Guardian*⟩

epicentre *n* **1** the part of the earth's surface directly above the place of origin of an earthquake **2** CENTRE 2 – **epicentral** *adj*

epicure *n* sby with sensitive and discriminating tastes, esp in food or wine – **epicurism** *n*

Epicurean *n or adj* **1** (a follower) of the doctrine of the Greek philosopher Epicurus who advocated the superiority of emotional calm and intellectual pleasures **2** *often not cap* (of or suited to) an epicure – **Epicureanism** *n*

epidemic *n or adj* (an outbreak of a disease) affecting

many individuals within a population, community, or region at the same time ⟨*typhoid was ~*⟩ – **epidemical** *adj*, **epidemically** *adv*, **epidemicity** *n*

epidermis *n* **1a** the thin outer epithelial layer of the animal body that is derived from ectoderm and forms in vertebrates an insensitive layer over the dermis **b** any of various covering layers resembling the epidermis **2** a thin surface layer of tissue in higher plants – **epidermal** *adj*, **epidermic** *adj*, **epidermoid** *adj*

epidiascope *n* a projector for images of opaque objects or for transparencies

epiglottis *n* a thin plate of flexible cartilage in front of the glottis that folds back over and protects the glottis during swallowing – **epiglottal** *also* **epiglottic** *adj*

epigram *n* **1** a short often satirical poem **2** a neat, witty, and often paradoxical remark or saying – **epigrammatic, epigrammatical** *adj*, **epigrammatically** *adv*, **epigrammatism** *n*, **epigrammatist** *n*, **epigrammatize** *vb*

epigraph *n* **1** an engraved inscription **2** a quotation at the beginning of a book, chapter, etc suggesting its theme

epilepsy *n* any of various disorders marked by disturbed electrical rhythms of the brain and spinal chord and typically manifested by convulsive attacks often with clouding of consciousness

epileptic *adj* of, affected with, or having the characteristics of epilepsy – **epileptic** *n*, **epileptically** *adv*

epilogue *n* **1** a concluding section of a literary or dramatic work that comments on or summarizes the main action or plot **2** a speech or poem addressed to the audience by an actor at the end of a play

epiphany *n* **1** *cap* (January 6 observed as a church festival in commemoration of) the coming of the Magi **2** a usu sudden manifestation or perception of the essential nature or meaning of sthg – **epiphanic** *adj*

episcopacy *n* **1** government of the church by bishops or by a hierarchy **2** an episcopate

episcopal *adj* **1** of a bishop **2** of, having, or constituting government by bishops **3** *cap* Anglican; *esp* of an Anglican church that is not established (e g in the USA or Scotland) – **episcopally** *adv*, **Episcopalian** *n or adj*, **Episcopalianism** *n*

episode *n* **1a** the part of an ancient Greek tragedy between 2 choric songs **b** a developed situation or incident that is integral to but separable from a continuous narrative (e g a play or novel) **c** the part of a serial presented at 1 performance **2** an event that is distinctive and separate although part of a larger series (e g in history or in sby's life)

episodic *also* **episodical** *adj* **1** made up of separate, esp loosely connected, episodes ⟨*an ~ narrative*⟩ **2** of or limited in duration or significance to a particular episode **3** occasional, sporadic – **episodically** *adv*

epistle *n* **1** *cap* (a liturgical reading from) any of the letters (e g of St Paul) adopted as books of the New Testament **2** an esp formal letter

epistolary *adj* **1** of or suitable to a letter **2** carried on by or in the form of letters ⟨*an endless sequence of ~ love affairs – TLS*⟩ **3** written in the form of a series of letters ⟨*~ novel*⟩

epitaph *n* **1** a commemorative inscription on a tombstone or monument **2** a brief statement commemorating a deceased person or past event

epithet *n* **1** a descriptive word or phrase accompanying or occurring in place of the name of a person or thing **2** a disparaging or abusive word or phrase – **epithetic, epithetical** *adj*

epitome *n* **1** a condensed account or summary, esp of a literary work **2** a typical or ideal example; an embodiment ⟨*the British monarchy itself is the ~ of tradition*⟩

epitomize, -ise *vt* to make or serve as an epitome of

epoch *n* **1** a date or time selected as a point of reference (e g in astronomy) **2** a memorable event or date; *esp* TURNING POINT **3a** an extended period of time, usu characterized by a distinctive development or by a memorable series of events **b** a division of geological time less than a period and greater than an age – **epochal** *adj*, **epochally** *adv*

epoch-making *adj* uniquely or highly significant ⟨*the steam engine was an ~ invention*⟩

eponym *n* the person after whom sthg is (believed to be) named – **eponymic** *adj*, **eponymous** *adj*

Epsom salts *n pl but sing or pl in constr* hydrated magnesium sulphate used as a purgative

equable *adj* uniform, even; *esp* free from extremes or sudden changes ⟨*an ~ temperament*⟩ ⟨*an ~ climate*⟩ – **equably** *adv*, **equability** *n*

¹**equal** *adj* **1a** of the same quantity, amount, or number as another **b** identical in value; equivalent **2a** like in quality, nature, or status **b** like for each member of a group, class, or society ⟨*provide ~ employment opportunities*⟩ ⟨*~ rights*⟩ **3** evenly balanced or matched ⟨*the 2 opponents were ~*⟩ **4** capable of meeting the requirements of sthg (e g a situation or task) – + *to* ⟨*he is quite ~ to the job*⟩

²**equal** *n* sby or sthg equal ⟨*she is anyone's ~*⟩

³**equal** *vt* **-ll-** (*NAm* **-l-, -ll-**) **1** to be equal to; *esp* to be identical in value to **2** to make or produce sthg equal to

equalitarian *n or adj* (an) egalitarian – **equalitarianism** *n*

equality *n* the quality or state of being equal

equalize, -ise *vt* **1** to make equal **2** to make uniform; *esp* to distribute evenly or uniformly ~ *vi chiefly Br* to make sthg equal; *esp* to bring the scores level (e g in a football match) – **equalizer** *n*, **equalization** *n*

equally *adv* **1** in an equal or uniform manner; evenly **2** to an equal degree; alike ⟨*respected ~ by young and old*⟩

equanimity *n* evenness of mind or temper, esp under stress

equate *vt* **1** to make or set equal **2** to treat, represent, or regard as equal, equivalent, or comparable ⟨*~ s dissension with disloyalty*⟩

equation *n* **1** equating or being equated **2** a statement of the equality of 2 mathematical expressions – **equational** *adj*, **equationally** *adv*

equator *n* **1** the great circle of the celestial sphere whose plane is perpendicular to the rotational axis of the earth **2** GREAT CIRCLE; *specif* the one that is equidistant from the 2 poles of the earth and divides the earth's surface into the northern and southern hemispheres **3** a circle or circular band dividing the surface of a body into 2 usu equal and symmetrical parts ⟨*the ~ of a dividing cell*⟩ – **equatorward** *adj or adv*, **equatorwards** *adv*

equatorial *adj* **1a** of, at, or in the plane of the (earth's) equator **b** *of the climate* characterized by consistently high temperatures and rainfall throughout the year **2** being or having a support (e g for a telescope) that includes 2 axles at right angles to each other and allows a celestial body to be kept in view as the earth rotates

equerry *n* **1** an officer of a prince or noble charged with the care of horses **2** an officer of the British royal household in personal attendance on a member of the royal family

¹**equestrian** *adj* **1a** of or featuring horses, horsemen, or horsemanship **b** representing a person on horseback **2** (composed) of knights – **equestrianism** *n*

²**equestrian** *n* sby who rides or performs on horseback

equi- *comb form* equal ⟨*equipoise*⟩; equally ⟨*equiprobable*⟩

equidistant *adj* equally distant – **equidistantly** *adv*, **equidistance** *n*

equilateral *adj* having all sides equal ⟨*~ triangle*⟩

equilibrium *n, pl* **equilibriums, equilibria 1** a state of balance between opposing forces, actions, or processes (e g in a reversible chemical reaction) **2a** a state of adjustment between opposing or divergent influences or elements **b** a state of intellectual or emotional balance **3** the normal state of the animal body in respect to its environment that involves adjustment to changing conditions

equine *adj* of or resembling the horse (family) – **equine** *n*, **equinely** *adv*

¹**equinoctial** *adj* **1** relating to (the time when the sun passes) an equinox **2** relating to the regions or climate of the equinoctial line or equator

²**equinoctial, equinoctial circle** *n* EQUATOR 1

equinox *n* **1** either of the 2 times each year that occur about March 21st and September 23rd when the sun crosses the equator and day and night are of equal length everywhere on earth **2** either of the 2 points on the celestial sphere where the celestial equator intersects the ecliptic

equip *vt* **-pp-** **1** to make ready for service, action, or use; provide with appropriate supplies **2** to dress, array

equipage *n* **1** material or articles used in equipment **2a** an etui **b** trappings **3** a horse-drawn carriage (with its servants)

equipment *n* **1** the set of articles, apparatus, or physical resources serving to equip a person, thing, enterprise, expedition, etc **2** mental or emotional resources

equipoise *n* **1** a state of equilibrium **2** a counterbalance

equitable *adj* **1** fair and just **2** valid in equity as distinguished from law – **equitableness** *n*, **equitably** *adv*, **equitability** *n*

equitation *n* the act or art of riding on horseback

equity *n* **1** justice according to natural law or right; fairness **2** a system of justice originally developed in the Chancery courts on the basis of conscience and fairness to supplement or override the more rigid common law **3a** a right, claim, or interest existing or valid in equity **b** the money value of a property or of an interest in a property in excess of claims against it **4** a share that does not bear fixed interest – usu pl

equivalent *adj* **1** equal in force, amount, or value **2** corresponding or virtually identical, esp in effect, function, or meaning **3** having the same chemical combining capacity ⟨*~ quantities of 2 elements*⟩ – **equivalence** *also* **equivalency** *n*, **equivalent** *n*, **equivalently** *adv*

equivocal *adj* **1** subject to 2 or more interpretations; ambiguous ⟨*~ evidence*⟩ **2** questionable, suspicious – **equivocally** *adv*, **equivocalness** *n*, **equivocality** *n*

equivocate *vi* to use equivocal language, esp with intent to deceive or avoid committing oneself – **equivocation** *n*, **equivocator** *n*

er, ur *interj* – used to express hesitation or doubt

¹**-er** *suffix* (→ *adj or adv*) – used to form the comparative degree of adjectives and adverbs of 1 syllable, and of some adjectives and adverbs of 2 or more syllables, that end in a consonant ⟨*hotter*⟩, a vowel other than *e*, or a final *y* that changes to *i* ⟨*drier*⟩; compare ¹-R

²**-er, -ar, -ier, -r, -yer** *suffix* **1** (*n → n*) **a** one engaged in the occupation of ⟨*furrier*⟩ ⟨*lawyer*⟩ ⟨*geographer*⟩ **b** one belonging to or associated with ⟨*sixth-former*⟩ **c** native of; resident of ⟨*cottager*⟩ ⟨*Londoner*⟩ **d** sthg that has ⟨*three-wheeler*⟩ ⟨*four-poster*⟩ **2** (*vb → n*) **a** one who or that which does or performs (a specified action)

⟨*reporter*⟩ ⟨*eye-opener*⟩ – sometimes added to both elements of a compound ⟨*builder-upper*⟩ **b** sthg that is a suitable object of (a specified action) ⟨*broiler*⟩ ⟨*cooker*⟩ **3** (*adj → n*) sby or sthg that is ⟨*foreigner*⟩ *USE* -yer in a few words after *w, -ier* in a few words after other letters, *-r* in words after *e,* otherwise *-er*

era *n* **1** a system of chronological notation computed from a given date as a basis ⟨*Christian* ~⟩ **2** EPOCH 2 **3a** a usu historical period set off or typified by some distinctive figure or characteristic feature ⟨*the* ~ *of space flight*⟩ **b** any of the 5 major divisions of geological time ⟨*Palaeozoic* ~⟩

eradicate *vt* **1** to pull up by the roots **2** to eliminate; DO AWAY WITH ⟨~ *ignorance by better teaching*⟩ – **eradicator** *n,* **eradicable** *adj,* **eradication** *n,* **eradicative** *adj,*

erase *vt* **1a** to obliterate or rub out (e g written, painted, or engraved letters) **b** to remove (recorded matter) from a magnetic tape or wire **c** to delete from a computer storage device **2** to remove from existence or memory as if by erasing ~ *vi* to yield to being erased ⟨*pencil* ~s *easily*⟩ – **erasability** *n,* **erasable** *adj,* **erasure** *n*

eraser *n* ¹RUBBER 1b

¹**ere** *prep* ²BEFORE 2 – poetic

²**ere** *conj* before – poetic

¹**erect** *adj* **1a** vertical in position; upright **b** standing up or out from the body ⟨~ *hairs*⟩ **c** characterized by firm or rigid straightness (e g in bodily posture) ⟨*an* ~ *bearing*⟩ **2** in a state of physiological erection – **erectly** *adv,* **erectness** *n*

²**erect** *vt* **1a** to put up by the fitting together of materials or parts; build **b** to fix in an upright position **2** to elevate in status ⟨~s *a few odd notions into a philosophy*⟩ **3** to establish; SET UP 6a **4** to construct (a perpendicular) on a given base – **erectable** *adj,* **erector** *n*

erectile *adj* **1** capable of being raised to an erect position; esp, of animal tissue capable of becoming swollen with blood to bring about the erection of a body part **2** of or involving the erection of the penis – **erectility** *n*

erection *n* **1** (an occurrence in the penis or clitoris of) the dilation with blood and resulting firmness of a previously flaccid body part **2** sthg erected

eremite *n* a usu Christian hermit or recluse – **eremitic, eremitical** *adj*

erg *n* the cgs unit of work or energy; 10 Q7J

erg-, ergo- *comb form* work ⟨*ergonomics*⟩

ergo *adv* therefore, hence

ergo- *comb form* ergot ⟨*ergosterol*⟩

ergonomics *n pl but sing or pl in constr* a science concerned with the relationship between human beings, the machines they use, and the working environment – **ergonomic** *adj,* **ergonomist** *n*

ermine *n, pl* ermines, *esp collectively* ermine (the winter fur of) a stoat or related weasel that has a white winter coat usu with black on the tail

erode *vt* **1a** to diminish or destroy by degrees **b** to eat into or away by slow destruction of substance; corrode **c** to wear away by the action of water, wind, glacial ice, etc **2** to produce or form by eroding ~ *vi* to undergo erosion – **erodible** *adj*

erogenous *also* **erogenic** *adj* of or producing sexual excitement (when stimulated) ⟨~ *zones*⟩

erosion *n* (an instance or product of) eroding or being eroded – **erosional** *adj,* **erosionally** *adv,* **erosive** *adj*

erotic *adj* **1** of, concerned with, or tending to arouse sexual desire ⟨~ *art*⟩ **2** strongly affected by sexual desire – **erotic** *n,* **erotical** *adj,* **erotically** *adv,* **eroticize** *vt*

erotica *n pl but sing or pl in constr* literature or art with an erotic theme or quality

eroticism *n* **1** an erotic theme, quality, or character

EROTISM 1 **3** (insistent) sexual impulse or desire – **eroticist** *n*

erotism *n* **1** sexual exitement or arousal **2** EROTICISM 1, 3

err *vi* **1a** to make a mistake **b** to do wrong; sin **2** to be inaccurate or incorrect

errand *n* (the object or purpose of) a short trip taken to attend to some business, often for another

errant *adj* **1** (given to) travelling, esp in search of adventure **2** going astray ⟨*an* ~ *calf*⟩; esp doing wrong; erring ⟨*an* ~ *child*⟩ – **errant** *n,* **errantly** *adv*

erratic *adj* **1** having no fixed course ⟨*an* ~ *comet*⟩ **2** esp of a boulder transported from an original resting place, esp by a glacier **3** characterized by lack of consistency, regularity, or uniformity, esp in behaviour – **erratic** *n,* **erratically** *adv,* **erraticism** *n*

erratum *n, pl* **errata** a corrigendum

erroneous *adj* containing or characterized by error; incorrect ⟨~ *assumptions*⟩ – **erroneously** *adv,* **erroneousness** *n*

error *n* **1a** a mistake or inaccuracy in speech, opinion, or action ⟨*a typing* ~⟩ **b** the state of being wrong in behaviour or beliefs ⟨*he realized the* ~ *of his ways*⟩ **c** an act that fails to achieve what was intended **2** the difference between an observed or calculated value and a true value – **errorless** *adj* – **in error** by mistake

ersatz *adj* being a usu artificial and inferior substitute; an imitation – **ersatz** *n*

Erse *n* Scottish Gaelic – no longer used technically – **Erse** *adj*

eructation *n* belching

erudite *adj* possessing or displaying extensive or profound knowledge; learned ⟨*an* ~ *scholar*⟩ – **eruditely** *adv,* **erudition** *n*

erupt *vi* **1a** esp of a volcano to release lava, steam, etc suddenly and usu violently **b**(1) to burst violently from limits or restraint (2) of a tooth to emerge through the gum **c** to become suddenly active or violent; explode ⟨*will terrorism* ~ *again?*⟩ **2** to break out (e g in a rash) ~ *vt* to force out or release suddenly or violently – **eruptible** *adj,* **eruptive** *adj,* **eruptively** *adv*

eruption *n* (a product of) erupting

-ery, -ry *suffix* (→ *n*) **1** quality or state of having (a specified trait or mode of behaviour) ⟨*snobbery*⟩ ⟨*treachery*⟩ **2** art or practice of ⟨*cookery*⟩ ⟨*skulduggery*⟩ **3** place of doing, keeping, producing, or selling (a specified thing) ⟨*fishery*⟩ ⟨*bakery*⟩ **4a** collection or body of ⟨*finery*⟩ ⟨*greenery*⟩ **b** class of (specified) goods ⟨*ironmongery*⟩ ⟨*confectionery*⟩ **5** state or condition of ⟨*slavery*⟩ **6** all that is concerned with or characteristic of – chiefly derog ⟨*popery*⟩ ⟨*tomfoolery*⟩ *USE* -ry often after *d, t, l, n,* otherwise *-ery*

erysipelas *n* a feverish disease with intense deep red local inflammation of the skin, caused by infection by a streptococcal bacterium

¹**-es** *suffix* (→ *n pl*) **1** – used to form the plural of most nouns that end in *s* ⟨*glasses*⟩, *z* ⟨*fuzzes*⟩, *sh* ⟨*bushes*⟩, *ch* ⟨*peaches*⟩, or a final *y* that changes to *i* ⟨*ladies*⟩ and some nouns ending in *f* that changes to *v* ⟨*loaves*⟩; compare ¹-s 1 2 ¹-s 2

²**-es** *suffix* (→ *vb*) – used to form the third person singular present of most verbs that end in *s* ⟨*blesses*⟩, *z* ⟨*fizzes*⟩, *sh* ⟨*hushes*⟩, *ch* ⟨*catches*⟩, or a final *y* that changes to *i* ⟨*defies*⟩; compare ²-s

escalate *vi* **1** EXPAND 1a ⟨*the matter has* ~d *into something like a major scandal – Sunday Times Magazine*⟩ **2** RISE 10b ⟨*escalating prices*⟩ ~ *vt* EXPAND 1 – **escalation** *n,* **escalatory** *adj*

escalator *n* a power-driven set of stairs arranged like an endless belt that ascend or descend continuously

escalope *n* a thin boneless slice of meat; *esp* a slice of veal from the leg

escapade *n* a wild, reckless, and often mischievous adventure, esp one that flouts rules or convention

¹**escape** *vi* **1a** to get away, esp from confinement or restraint ⟨~d *from the burning building*⟩ ⟨*fantasy allows us to ~ from reality*⟩ **b** of gases, liquids, *etc* to leak out gradually; seep **c** *of a plant* to run wild from cultivation **2** to avoid a threatening evil ~ *vt* **1** to get or stay out of the way of; avoid ⟨~ *death*⟩ **2** to fail to be noticed or recallable by ⟨*his name* ~s *me*⟩ **3** to be produced or made by (esp a person), usu involuntarily ⟨*a yawn* ~d *him*⟩ – **escapable** *adj*, **escaper** *n*, **escapee** *n*

²**escape** *n* **1** an act or instance of escaping **2** a means of escape **3** a cultivated plant run wild

³**escape** *adj* **1** providing a means of escape ⟨*an* ~ *hatch*⟩ ⟨~ *literature*⟩ **2** providing a means of evading a regulation, claim, or commitment ⟨*an* ~ *clause in a contract*⟩

escapement *n* a device in a timepiece through which the energy of the power source is delivered to the regulatory mechanism that controls the motion of the cogwheels

escape velocity *n* the minimum velocity that a moving body (e g a rocket) must have to escape from the gravitational field of the earth or of a celestial body

escapism *n* habitual diversion of the mind to purely imaginative activity or entertainment as an escape from reality or routine – **escapist** *adj or n*

escapology *n* the art or practice of escaping, esp as a theatrical performance – **escapologist** *n*

escarpment *n* a long cliff or steep slope separating 2 more gently sloping surfaces

eschatology *n* **1** a branch of theology or religious belief concerned with the ultimate destiny of the universe or of mankind **2** the Christian doctrine concerning death, judgment, heaven, and hell – **eschatological** *adj*, **eschatologically** *adv*

eschew *vt* to avoid habitually, esp on moral or practical grounds; shun – *fml*

¹**escort** *n* **1** a person, group of people, ship, aircraft, *etc* accompanying sby or sthg to give protection or show courtesy **2** one who accompanies another socially

²**escort** *vt* to accompany as an escort

escort agency *n* an organization that provides usu female social escorts

escritoire *n* a writing table or desk

escutcheon *n* **1** a shield on which a coat of arms is displayed **2** a protective or ornamental shield or plate (e g round a keyhole)

¹**-ese** *suffix* (*n* → *adj*) of or originating in (a specified place or country) ⟨*Japan*ese⟩ ⟨*Vienn*ese⟩

²**-ese** *suffix* (*n* → *n*), *pl* **-ese 1** inhabitant of ⟨*Chin*ese⟩ **2a** language of ⟨*Portugu*ese⟩ ⟨*Canton*ese⟩ **b** speech, literary style, or diction peculiar to (a specified place, person, or group) – chiefly derog ⟨*journal*ese⟩ ⟨*official*ese⟩

Eskimo *also* **Esquimau** *n, pl* **Eskimos**, *esp collectively* **Eskimo** (a member or the language of) any of a group of peoples of N Canada, Greenland, Alaska, and E Siberia – **Eskimoan** *adj*

Eskimo dog *n* (any of) a breed of broad-chested powerful sledge dogs native to Greenland and Labrador

esoteric *adj* **1** designed for, understood by, or restricted to a small group, esp of the specially initiated ⟨~ *knowledge*⟩ ⟨~ *pursuits*⟩ **2** private, confidential ⟨*an* ~ *purpose*⟩ – **esoterically** *adv*, **esotericism** *n*

ESP *n* extrasensory perception

espalier *n* (a fruit tree or shrub trained to grow flat against) a railing, trellis, etc

especial *adj* (distinctively or particularly) special – **especially** *adv*

Esperanto *n* an artificial international language largely based on words common to the chief European languages – **Esperantist** *n or adj*

espionage *n* spying or the use of spies to obtain information ⟨*industrial* ~⟩

esplanade *n* a level open stretch of paved or grassy ground, esp along a shore

espousal *n* **1** a betrothal; *also* a marriage – often pl with sing. meaning; *fml* **2** the adoption or support of a cause or belief

espouse *vt* **1** to marry – *fml* **2** to take up and support as a cause; become attached to ⟨~ *the problems of minority groups*⟩ – **espouser** *n*

espresso *n, pl* **espressos** (an apparatus for making) coffee brewed by forcing steam through finely ground coffee beans

esprit de corps *n* the common spirit and loyalty existing among the members of a group

espy *vt* to catch sight of

-esque *suffix* (*n* → *adj*) in the manner or style of; like ⟨*statu*esque⟩ ⟨*Kafka*esque⟩ ⟨*roman*esque⟩

-ess *suffix* (*n* → *n*) female ⟨*actr*ess⟩ ⟨*lion*ess⟩ – often derog ⟨*Negr*ess⟩ ⟨*poet*ess⟩

¹**essay** *vt* to attempt – *fml* – **essayer** *n*

²**essay** *n* **1** a usu short piece of prose writing on a specific topic **2** an (initial tentative) effort or attempt – *fml* – **essayist** *n*, **essayistic** *adj*

essence *n* **1a** the real or ultimate nature of an individual being or thing, esp as opposed to its existence or its accidental qualities **b** the properties or attributes by means of which sthg can be categorized or identified **2** sthg that exists, esp in an abstract form; an entity **3a** an alcoholic solution or other preparation of) an extract, essential oil, etc possessing the special qualities of a plant, drug, etc in concentrated form **b** an odour, perfume **c** one who or that which resembles an extract in possessing a quality in concentrated form – **in essence** in or by its very nature; essentially – **of the essence** of the utmost importance; essential ⟨*time was of the essence*⟩

¹**essential** *adj* **1** of or being (an) essence; inherent **2** of the utmost importance; basic, necessary ⟨~ *foods*⟩ ⟨*an* ~ *requirement for admission to university*⟩ **3** idiopathic – **essentially** *adv*, **essentialness, essentiality** *n*

²**essential** *n* sthg basic, indispensable, or fundamental ⟨*the* ~s *of astronomy*⟩

¹**-est** *suffix* (*adj or adv* → *adj or adv*) – used to form the superlative degree of adjectives and adverbs of 1 and sometimes 2 or more syllables that end in a consonant ⟨*fatt*est⟩ ⟨*dear*est⟩, a vowel other than *e*, or a final *y* that changes to *i* ⟨*dreari*est⟩; compare ¹-ST

²**-est, -st** *suffix* (→ *vb*) – used to form the archaic second person singular of verbs (with *thou*)

establish *vt* **1** to make firm or stable **2** to enact permanently ⟨~ *a law*⟩ **3** to bring into existence; found ⟨~ed *a republic*⟩ **4a** to set on a firm basis; place (e g oneself) in a permanent or firm usu favourable position ⟨~ed *himself as the leader*⟩ **b** to gain full recognition or acceptance of ⟨*she* ~ed *her fame as an actress*⟩ **5** to make (a church or religion) a national institution supported by civil authority **6** to put beyond doubt; prove ⟨~ed *his innocence*⟩ **7** to cause (a plant) to grow and multiply in a place where previously absent – **establishable** *adj*, **establisher** *n*

establishment *n* **1** sthg established: e g **a** a usu large organization or institution **b** a place of business or residence with its furnishings and staff **2** an established order of society: e g **a** *sing or pl in constr, often cap the* entrenched social, economic, and political leaders of a nation **b** *often cap* a controlling group ⟨*the literary* ~⟩

estaminet *n, pl* **estaminets** a small café

estate *n* **1** a social or political class (e g the nobility, clergy, or commons) **2a(1)** the whole of sby's real or personal property **(2)** the assets and liabilities left by sby at death **b** a large landed property, esp in the country, usu with a large house on it **3** *Br* a part of an urban area devoted to a particular type of development ⟨*a housing* ~ *next to an industrial* ~⟩; *specif* one devoted to housing ⟨*a council* ~⟩ **4** a state, condition – *fml* ⟨*men of low* ~⟩

estate agent *n, Br* **1** an agent who is involved in the buying and selling of land and property (e g houses) **2** one who manages an estate; a steward

estate car *n, Br* a relatively large motor car with a nearly vertical rear door and 1 compartment in which both passengers and bulky luggage can be carried

¹esteem *n* favourable regard ⟨*held in high* ~ *by his colleagues*⟩

²esteem *vt* **1** to consider, deem ⟨*would* ~ *it a privilege*⟩ **2** to set a high value on; regard highly and prize accordingly

ester *n* a (fragrant) compound formed by the reaction between an acid and an alcohol usu with elimination of water

esthete *n, NAm* an aesthete – **esthetic** *adj,* **esthetics** *n*

estimable *adj* worthy of esteem – **estimableness** *n*

¹estimate *vt* **1a** to judge approximately the value, worth, or significance of **b** to determine roughly the size, extent, or nature of **c** to produce a statement of the approximate cost of **2** to judge, conclude – **estimative** *adj,* **estimator** *n*

²estimate *n* **1** the act of appraising or valuing; a calculation **2** an opinion or judgment of the nature, character, or quality of sby or sthg **3** (the numerical value of) a rough or approximate calculation **4** a statement of the expected cost of a job

estimation *n* **1** ESTIMATE 2 **2a** estimating **b** the value, amount, or size arrived at in an estimate **3** esteem

estrange *vt* to arouse enmity or indifference in (sby) in place of affection; alienate – usu + *from* ⟨~d *from her husband*⟩ – **estrangement** *n,* **estranger** *n*

estuary *n* a water passage where the tide meets a river; *esp* a sea inlet at the mouth of a river

et al *adv* and others

etc *adv* ET CETERA

et cetera *adv* and other things, esp of the same kind; broadly and so forth

¹etch *vt* **1a** to produce (e g a picture or letters), esp on a plate of metal or glass, by the corrosive action of an acid **b** to subject (metal, glass, etc) to such etching **2** to delineate or impress clearly ⟨*scenes that are indelibly* ~ed *in our minds*⟩ ~ *vi* to practise etching – **etcher** *n*

²etch *n* (the action or effect of) an etching acid (on a surface)

etching *n* **1** the art of producing pictures or designs by printing from an etched metal plate **2** an impression from an etched plate

¹eternal *adj* **1** having infinite duration; everlasting ⟨~ *life*⟩ **2** incessant, interminable **3** timeless ⟨*the* ~ *truths*⟩ – **eternalize** *vt,* **eternally** *adv,* **eternalness** *n,* **eternize** *vt*

²eternal *n cap* GOD 1 – + *the* **2** sthg eternal

eternal triangle *n* a conflict that results from the sexual attraction between 2 people of one sex and 1 person of the other

eternity *n* **1** the quality or state of being eternal **2** infinite

time **3** the eternal life after death **4** a (seemingly) endless or immeasurable time ⟨*we waited an* ~ *for the train*⟩

ethane *n* an odourless gaseous hydrocarbon of the alkane group found in natural gas and used esp as a fuel

ether *n* **1** ether, aether (the rarefied element formerly believed to fill) the upper regions of space; the heavens **2** ether, aether a medium formerly held to permeate all space and transmit electromagnetic waves (e g light and radio waves) **3a** a volatile inflammable liquid used esp as a solvent and formerly as a general anaesthetic **b** any of various organic compounds characterized by an oxygen atom attached to 2 carbon atoms – **etherish** *adj,* **etheric** *adj*

ethereal *adj* **1** of the regions beyond the earth **2a** lacking material substance; intangible **b** marked by unusual delicacy, lightness, and refinement **3** of, containing, or resembling a chemical ether **4** celestial, heavenly – *poetic* – **ethereally** *adv,* **ethereality, etherealness** *n,* **etherealize** *vt,* **etherealization** *n*

ethic *n* **1** *pl but sing or pl in constr* inquiry into the nature and basis of moral principles and judgments **2** a set of moral principles or values ⟨*the current materialistic* ~⟩ **3** *pl but sing or pl in constr* the principles of conduct governing an individual or a group ⟨*professional* ~s⟩

ethical *also* **ethic** *adj* **1** conforming to accepted, esp professional, standards of conduct or morality **2** of a drug available to the general public only on a doctor's or dentist's prescription – **ethically** *adv,* **ethicality, ethicalness** *n*

¹ethnic *adj* **1** of or being human races or large groups classed according to common traits ⟨~ *minorities*⟩ ⟨~ *groups*⟩ **2** of an exotic, esp peasant, culture ⟨~ *restaurants*⟩ – **ethnicity** *n*

²ethnic *n, chiefly NAm* a member of an ethnic (minority) group

ethnical *adj* **1** ethnic **2** ethnological – **ethnically** *adv*

ethnography *n* ethnology; *specif* descriptive anthropology – **ethnographer** *n,* **ethnographic, ethnographical** *adj,* **ethnographically** *adv*

ethnology *n* a science that deals with the various forms of social relationships (e g kinship, law, religion, etc) found in esp preliterate human societies – **ethnologist** *n,* **ethnologic, ethnological** *adj,* **ethnologically** *adv*

ethos *n* the distinguishing character or guiding beliefs of a person, institution, etc

ethyl *n* a univalent hydrocarbon radical C_2H_5 derived from ethane

ethyl alcohol *n* ALCOHOL 1

ethylene *n* **1** an inflammable gaseous unsaturated hydrocarbon of the alkene group, found in coal gas and used esp in organic chemical synthesis **2** a bivalent hydrocarbon radical C_2H_4 derived from ethane – **ethylenic** *adj*

etiolate *vt* **1** to bleach and alter the natural development of (a green plant) by excluding sunlight **2** to make weak, pale, or sickly – **etiolation** *n*

etiology *n, NAm* aetiology – **etiologic, etiological** *adj,* **etiologically** *adv*

etiquette *n* the conventionally accepted standards of proper social or professional behaviour ⟨*medical* ~⟩

-ette *suffix* (*n* → *n*) **1** small or lesser kind of ⟨*kitchenette*⟩ ⟨*cigarette*⟩ **2** female ⟨*suffragette*⟩ ⟨*usherette*⟩ **3** imitation; substitute ⟨*leatherette*⟩ ⟨*flannelette*⟩

etymology *n* **1** the history of the origin and development of a word or other linguistic form **2** a branch of linguistics dealing with etymologies – **etymologist** *n,* **etymological** *adj,* **etymologically** *adv*

eucalyptus *n, pl* **eucalyptuses, eucalypti** any of a genus of mostly Australian evergreen trees of the myrtle family that are widely cultivated for their gums, resins, oils, and wood

Eucharist *n* (the bread and wine consecrated in) the Christian sacrament in which bread and wine, being or representing the body and blood of Christ, are ritually consumed in accordance with Christ's injunctions at the Last Supper – **eucharistic** *adj, often cap*

euclidean *adj, often cap* of or being the geometry of Euclid that describes euclidean space

eugenic *adj* 1 relating to or fit for the production of good offspring 2 of eugenics – **eugenically** *adv*

eugenics *n pl but sing in constr* a science dealing with the improvement (e g by control of human mating) of the hereditary qualities of a race or breed – **eugenicist** *n*

eulogize, -ise *vt* to extol – **eulogizer** *n*

eulogy *n* 1 a (formal) speech or piece of writing in praise of a person or thing 2 high praise – **eulogist** *n*, **eulogistic** *adj*, **eulogistically** *adv*

eunuch *n* 1 a castrated man employed, esp formerly, in a harem or as a chamberlain in a palace 2 a man or boy deprived of the testes or external genitals – **eunuchism** *n*, **eunuchoid** *adj or n*

euphemism *n* the substitution of a mild, indirect, or vague expression for an offensive or unpleasant one; *also* the expression so substituted ⟨fall asleep *is a* ~ *for* die⟩ – **euphemistic** *adj*, **euphemistically** *adv*

euphonious *adj* pleasing to the ear – **euphoniously** *adv*, **euphonize** *vt*

euphonium *n* a brass instrument smaller than but resembling a tuba and having a range from B flat below the bass staff upwards for 3 octaves

euphony *n* a pleasing or sweet sound, esp in speech – **euphonic** *adj*, **euphonically** *adv*

euphoria *n* an (inappropriate) feeling of well-being or elation – **euphoric** *adj*, **euphorically** *adv*

euphuism *n* an artificial and ornate style of writing or speaking – **euphuist** *n*, **euphuistic** *adj*, **euphuistically** *adv*

Eurasian *adj* 1 of, growing in, or living in Europe and Asia 2 of mixed European and Asian origin – **Eurasian** *n*

eureka *interj* – used to express triumph at a discovery

eurhythmic, eurythmic *adj* 1 harmonious 2 of eurhythmics

eurhythmics, eurythmics *n pl but sing or pl in constr* the art of harmonious bodily movement, esp through expressive timed movements in response to music

euro *n, pl* **euros** *Austr* a large reddish grey kangaroo

Eurocrat *n* a staff member of the administrative commission of the European Economic Community – *infml*

Eurodollar *n* a US dollar held (e g by a bank) outside the USA, esp in Europe

¹European *adj* 1 native to Europe 2 of European descent or origin 3 concerned with or affecting the whole of Europe 4 advocating European unity or alliance – **Europeanism** *n*, **Europeanize** *vt*, **Europeanization** *n*

²European *n* a native or inhabitant of (the mainland of) Europe

eustachian tube *n, often cap E* a tube connecting the middle ear with the pharynx that equalizes air pressure on both sides of the eardrum

euthanasia *n* the act or practice of killing (hopelessly sick or injured) individuals for reasons of mercy – **euthanasic** *adj*

evacuate *vt* 1 EMPTY 1a 2 to discharge from the body as waste 3 to remove gas, water, etc from, esp by pumping; *esp* to produce a vacuum in 4a to remove, esp from a dangerous area b to withdraw from military occupation of c to vacate ⟨*rapidly* ~d *the burning building*⟩ ~ *vi* 1

to withdraw from a place in an organized way, esp for protection 2 to pass urine or faeces from the body – **evacuation** *n*, **evacuative** *adj*

evacuee *n* a person evacuated from a dangerous place

evade *vi* to take refuge by evading sthg ~ *vt* 1 to get away from or avoid, esp by deception 2a to avoid facing up to ⟨~d *the issue*⟩ b to fail to pay ⟨~ *taxes*⟩ 3 to baffle, foil ⟨*the problem* ~s *all efforts at solution*⟩ – **evadable** *adj*, **evader** *n*

evaluate *vt* to determine the amount, value, or significance of, esp by careful appraisal and study – **evaluation** *n*, **evaluative** *adj*, **evaluator** *n*

evanescent *adj* tending to dissipate or vanish like vapour – **evanescence** *n*, **evanesce** *vi*

evangelical *also* **evangelic** *adj* 1 of or in agreement with the Christian message as presented in the 4 Gospels 2 *often cap* Protestant; *specif* of the German Protestant church 3 *often cap* (of or being a usu Protestant denomination) emphasizing salvation by faith in the atoning death of Jesus Christ, personal conversion, and the authority of Scripture 4a of, adhering to, or marked by fundamentalism b LOW CHURCH 5 evangelistic, zealous ⟨~ *ardour*⟩ – **Evangelical** *n*, **Evangelicalism** *n*, **evangelically** *adv*

evangelist *n* 1 *often cap* a writer of any of the 4 Gospels 2 one who evangelizes; *specif* a Protestant minister or layman who preaches at special services

evangelize, -ise *vb* to preach the Christian gospel (to), esp with the intention of converting to Christianity – **evangelization** *n*

evaporate *vi* 1a to pass off in vapour b to pass off or away; disappear, fade ⟨*his fears* ~d⟩ 2 to give out vapour ~ *vt* 1 to convert into vapour 2a to expel moisture, esp water, from ⟨~d *milk*⟩ b to cause to disappear or fade – **evaporatable** *adj*, **evaporation** *n*, **evaporative** *adj*, **evaporator** *n*

evasion *n* an act, instance, or means of evading ⟨*suspected of tax* ~⟩

evasive *adj* tending or intended to evade; equivocal ⟨~ *answers*⟩ – **evasively** *adv*, **evasiveness** *n*

eve *n* 1 the evening or the day before a special day, esp a religious holiday ⟨*Christmas* ~⟩ 2 the period immediately preceding an event ⟨*the* ~ *of the election*⟩ 3 the evening – chiefly poetic

¹even *n, archaic* the evening – poetic

²even *adj* 1a having a horizontal surface; flat, level ⟨~ *ground*⟩ b without break or irregularity; smooth c in the same plane or line – + *with* ⟨~ *with the ground*⟩ 2a without variation; uniform ⟨*an* ~ *disposition*⟩ ⟨*an* ~ *grey sky*⟩ b LEVEL 3 3a equal ⟨*we were* ~ *after the 4th game, having won 2 each*⟩; *also* fair ⟨*an* ~ *exchange*⟩ b being in equilibrium 4 exactly divisible by 2 ⟨*an* ~ *number*⟩ 5 exact, precise ⟨*an* ~ *pound*⟩ 6 fifty-fifty ⟨*she stands an* ~ *chance of winning*⟩ – **evenly** *adv*, **evenness** *n*

³even *adv* 1 at the very time – + *as* 2a – used as an intensive to emphasize the contrast with a less strong possibility ⟨*he looks content*, ~ *happy*⟩ ⟨*can't* ~ *walk, let alone run*⟩ b – used as an intensive to emphasize the comparative degree ⟨~ *better than last time*⟩ – **even if** in spite of the possibility or fact that – **even now** 1 at this very moment 2 in spite of what has happened – **even so** in spite of that

⁴even *vb* to make or become even – often + *up* or *out* – **evener** *n*

evenhanded *adj* fair, impartial – **evenhandedly** *adv*, **evenhandedness** *n*

evening *n* 1 the latter part of the day and the early part of the night; the time between sunset and bedtime 2 a late period (e g of time or life); the end **3** (the period of) an evening's entertainment

evening dress *n* **1** clothes for formal or semiformal evening occasions **2** a dress, esp with a floor-length skirt, for wear on formal or semiformal occasions

evening prayer *n, often cap E&P* the daily evening office of the Anglican church

evenings *adv, chiefly NAm* in the evening repeatedly; on any evening

evening star *n* a bright planet, specif Venus, seen in the western sky at sunset

evensong *n, often cap* **1** VESPERS 1 **2** EVENING PRAYER

event *n* **1a** a qualitative or quantitative change or complex of changes located in a restricted portion of time and space **b** a (noteworthy or important) happening or occurrence **c** a social occasion or activity **2** a contingency, case – esp in *in the event of* ⟨*in the ~ of my death*⟩ and (*chiefly NAm*) *in the event that* ⟨*in the ~ that I die*⟩ **3** any of the contests in a sporting programme or tournament – **eventful** *adj*, **eventfully** *adv*, **eventfulness** *n*, **eventless** *adj* – **in any event, at all events** ANYWAY 1 – **in the event** *Br* when it actually happens or happened

eventide *n* the evening – chiefly poetic

eventual *adj* taking place at an unspecified later time; ultimately resulting ⟨*they counted on his ~ success*⟩ – **eventually** *adv*

eventuality *n* a possible, esp unwelcome, event or outcome

eventuate *vi* to result – fml

ever *adv* **1** always – now chiefly in certain phrases and in combination ⟨*~ yours, John*⟩ ⟨*an ever-growing need*⟩ **2** at any time ⟨*faster than ~*⟩ – chiefly in negatives and questions ⟨*have you ~ met?*⟩ ⟨*he won't ~ do it*⟩ **3** – used as an intensive ⟨*looks ~ so angry*⟩ ⟨*as quick as ~ I can*⟩ ⟨*~ since Monday*⟩ ⟨*why ~ not?*⟩ – **ever so/such** chiefly *Br* very much – infml ⟨*ever such a nice girl*⟩ ⟨*thanks ever so*⟩

evergreen *adj* **1** having leaves that remain green and functional through more than 1 growing season **2** always retaining freshness, interest, or popularity ⟨*the ~ items of the American popular repertoire* – Benny Green⟩

evergreen *n* an evergreen plant; *also* a conifer

everlasting *adj* **1** lasting or enduring through all time **2a(1)** continuing long or indefinitely; perpetual **(2)** *of a plant* retaining its form or colour for a long time when dried **b** tediously persistent; ETERNAL 2 **3** lasting or wearing for a long time; durable – **everlastingly** *adv*, **everlastingness** *n*

everlasting *n* **1** *cap* GOD **1** – + *the* **2** eternity

evermore *adv* **1** always, forever **2** in the future

every *adj* **1** being each member without exception, of a group larger than 2 ⟨*~ word counts*⟩ ⟨*enjoyed ~ minute*⟩ ⟨*his ~ word*⟩ **2** being each or all possible ⟨*was given ~ chance*⟩ ⟨*have ~ confidence in him*⟩ **3** being once in each ⟨*go ~ third day*⟩ ⟨*change the oil ~ 5000 miles*⟩ – **every now and then/again, every so often** at intervals; occasionally

everybody *pron* every person ⟨*~ decides they're a bit hungry* – SEU S⟩

everyday *adj* encountered or used routinely or typically; ordinary ⟨*clothes for ~ wear*⟩ – **everydayness** *n*

everyone *pron* everybody

everything *pron* **1a** all that exists **b** all that is necessary or that relates to the subject ⟨*my new car has ~*⟩ **2** sthg of the greatest importance; all that counts ⟨*he meant ~ to her*⟩

everywhere *adv or n* (in, at, or to) every place or the whole place

every which way *adv, NAm* in every direction; all over the place

evict *vt* **1a** to recover (property) from a person by a legal process **b** to remove (a tenant) from rented accommodation or land by a legal process **2** to force out – **evictor** *n*, **eviction** *n*

¹evidence *n* **1** an outward sign; an indication **2** sthg, esp a fact, that gives proof or reasons for believing or agreeing with sthg; *specif* information used (by a tribunal) to arrive at the truth – **evidential** *adj*, **evidentially** *adv*, **evidentiary** *adj* – **in evidence** to be seen; conspicuous

²evidence *vt* to offer evidence of; show

evident *adj* clear to the vision or understanding

evidently *adv* **1** clearly, obviously **2** on the basis of available evidence; as seems evident

¹evil *adj* -**ll**- (*NAm* -**l**-, -**ll**-) **1a** not good morally; sinful, wicked ⟨*a thoroughly ~ doctrine*⟩ **b** arising from bad character or conduct ⟨*a man of ~ reputation*⟩ **2a** causing discomfort or repulsion; offensive ⟨*an ~ smell*⟩ **b** disagreeable ⟨*an ~ temper*⟩ **3a** pernicious, harmful **b** marked by misfortune ⟨*an ~ day*⟩ – **evil** *adv, archaic*, **evilly** *adv*, **evilness** *n*

²evil *n* **1** sthg evil; sthg that brings sorrow, distress, or calamity **2a** the fact of suffering, misfortune, or wrongdoing **b** wickedness, sin

evil eye *n* (a spell put on sby with) a look believed to be capable of inflicting harm

evince *vt* to show clearly; reveal – fml – **evincible** *adj*

eviscerate *vt* **1** to disembowel **2** to remove an organ from (a patient); *also* to remove the contents of (an organ) **3** to deprive of vital content or force – fml – **evisceration** *n*

evoke *vt* to call forth or up: e g **a** CONJURE 1a **b** to cite, esp with approval or for support; invoke **c** to bring to mind or recollection, esp imaginatively or poignantly ⟨*this place ~s memories of happier years*⟩ – **evocation** *n*, **evocative** *adj*, **evocatively** *adv*, **evocator** *n*

evolution *n* **1a** a process of change and development, esp from a lower or simpler state to a higher or more complex state **b** the action or an instance of forming and giving sthg off; emission **c** a process of gradual and relatively peaceful social, political, economic, etc advance **d** sthg evolved **2** the process of working out or developing **3a** the historical development of a biological group (e g a race or species) **b** a theory that the various types of animals and plants derived from preexisting types and that the distinguishable differences are due to natural selection – **evolutionism** *n*, **evolutionist** *n or adj*, **evolutionary** *adj*, **evolutionarily** *adv*

evolve *vt* **1** EMIT 1a **2a** to work out, develop **b** to produce by natural evolutionary processes ~ *vi* to undergo evolutionary change – **evolvable** *adj*, **evolvement** *n*

ewe *n* the female of the (mature) sheep or a related animal

Ewe *n* a Kwa language of Ghana and Togo

ewer *n* a wide-mouthed pitcher or jug; *esp* one used to hold water for washing or shaving

¹ex *adj* former ⟨*~ president Nixon*⟩ – often in combination ⟨*the ex-president*⟩

²ex *prep* **1** from a specified place or source **2a** *esp of securities* without an indicated value or right **b** free of charges until the time of removal from (a place) ⟨*~ dock*⟩

³ex *n* a former spouse, boyfriend, or girl friend – infml

¹ex- *prefix* **1** out of; outside ⟨*exclude*⟩ ⟨*exodus*⟩ **2** cause to be ⟨*exacerbate*⟩ ⟨*exalt*⟩ **3** not ⟨*exanimate*⟩ **4** deprive of ⟨*expropriate*⟩ ⟨*excommunicate*⟩

²ex- see EXO-

exacerbate *vt* to make (sthg bad) worse; aggravate – **exacerbation** *n*

¹exact *vt* to demand and obtain by force, threats, etc; require ⟨*from them has been* ~ed *the ultimate sacrifice* – D D Eisenhower⟩ – **exactable** *adj*, **exactor** *also* **exacter** *n*

²exact *adj* **1** exhibiting or marked by complete accordance with fact **2** marked by thorough consideration or minute measurement of small factual details – **exactness** *n*

exacting *adj* making rigorous demands; *esp* requiring careful attention and precise accuracy – **exactingly** *adv*, **exactingness** *n*

exaction *n* **1a** exacting **b** extortion **2** sthg exacted; *esp* a fee, reward, or contribution demanded or levied with severity or injustice

exactly *adv* **1** altogether, entirely ⟨*not* ~ *what I had in mind*⟩ **2** quite so – used to express agreement

exaggerate *vt* **1** to say or believe more than the truth about **2** to make greater or more pronounced than normal; overemphasize ⟨*he* ~d *his line to gain sympathy*⟩ ~ *vi* to make an exaggeration – **exaggeratedly** *adv*, **exaggeratedness** *n*, **exaggerative**, **exaggeratory** *adj*, **exaggerator** *n*, **exaggeration** *n*

exalt *vt* **1** to raise high, esp in rank, power, or character **2** to praise highly; glorify – **exaltedly** *adv*, **exalter** *n*

exaltation *n* an excessively intensified sense of well-being, power, or importance

exam *n* an examination

examination *n* **1** (an) examining ⟨*a medical* ~⟩ **2** (the taking by a candidate for a university degree, Advanced level, Ordinary level, etc of) a set of questions designed to test knowledge **3** a formal interrogation (in a law court) – **examinational** *adj*, **examinatorial** *adj*

examine *vt* **1** to inspect closely; investigate **2a** to interrogate closely ⟨~ *a prisoner*⟩ **b** to test (e g a candidate for a university degree) by an examination in order to determine knowledge – **examinable** *adj*, **examinee** *n*, **examiner** *n*

example *n* **1** sthg representative of all of the group or type to which it belongs **2** sby or sthg that may be copied by other people ⟨*a good or bad* ~⟩ ⟨*set an* ~⟩ **3** (the recipient of) a punishment inflicted as a warning to others ⟨*make an* ~ *of them*⟩ **4** a problem to be solved to illustrate a rule (e g in arithmetic) – **for example** as an example ⟨*there are many sources of air pollution; exhaust fumes,* for example⟩

exasperate *vt* to anger or irritate (sby) – **exasperatedly** *adv*, **exasperatingly** *adv*, **exasperation** *n*

ex cathedra *adv or adj* with authority ⟨~ *pronouncements*⟩

excavate *vt* **1** to form a cavity or hole in **2** to form by hollowing **3** to dig out and remove **4** to expose to view by digging away a covering ~ *vi* to make excavations – **excavator** *n*, **excavation** *n*

exceed *vt* **1** to extend beyond **2** to be greater than or superior to **3** to act or go beyond the limits of ⟨~ *the speed limit*⟩

exceedingly, **exceeding** *adv* very, extremely

excel *vb* **-ll-** to be superior (to); surpass (others) in accomplishment or achievement – often + *at* or *in*

excellence *n* **1** *also* **excellency** being excellent **2** *also* **excellency** an excellent or valuable quality; a virtue **3** **Excellency**, **Excellence** – used as a title for certain high dignitaries (e g ambassadors) of state and church

excellent *adj* outstandingly good – **excellently** *adv*

¹except *vt* to take or leave out from a number or a whole; exclude

²except *also* **excepting** *prep* with the exclusion or excep-

tion of ⟨*daily* ~ *Sundays*⟩ ⟨*can do everything* ~ *cook*⟩

³except *also* **excepting** *conj* **1** only, but ⟨*would go* ~ *it's too far*⟩ ⟨*would have protested* ~ *that he was afraid*⟩ **2** unless ⟨~. *you repent*⟩ – *fml*

except for *prep* **1** but for; were it not for ⟨*couldn't have done it* ~ *your help*⟩ **2** with the exception of ⟨*all here* ~ *Mary*⟩

exception *n* **1** excepting or excluding **2** sby or sthg excepted; *esp* a case to which a rule does not apply **3** question, objection ⟨*witnesses whose authority is beyond* ~ – T B Macaulay⟩

exceptionable *adj* likely to cause objection; objectionable – **exceptionably** *adv*, **exceptionability** *n*

exceptional *adj* **1** forming an exception; unusual ⟨*an* ~ *number of rainy days*⟩ **2** not average; *esp* superior – **exceptionally** *adv*, **exceptionality** *n*

¹excerpt *vt* **1** to select (a passage) for quoting, copying, or performing **2** to take excerpts from (e g a book) – **excerpter** *also* **excerptor** *n*, **excerption** *n*

²excerpt *n* a passage taken from a book, musical composition, etc

¹excess *n* **1a** the exceeding of usual, proper, or specified limits **b** the amount or degree by which one thing or quantity exceeds another **2** (an instance of) undue or immoderate indulgence; intemperance **3** an amount an insured person agrees to pay him-/herself out of each claim made on an insurance policy in return for a lower premium – **excessive** *adj*, **excessively** *adv*, **excessiveness** *n* – **in excess of** more than

²excess *adj* more than the usual, proper, or specified amount; extra ⟨*charges for* ~ *baggage*⟩

¹exchange *n* **1a** the act of exchanging one thing for another; a trade ⟨*an* ~ *of prisoners*⟩ **b** a usu brief interchange of words or blows ⟨*had an acrimonious* ~ *with the manager*⟩ **2** sthg offered, given, or received in an exchange **3a** (the system of settling, usu by bills of exchange rather than money) debts payable currently, esp in a foreign country **b(1)** change or conversion of one currency into another **(2)** **exchange**, **exchange rate** the value of one currency in terms of another **4** a place where things or services are exchanged: e g **a** an organized market for trading in securities or commodities **b** a centre or device controlling the connection of telephone calls between many different lines

²exchange *vt* **1a** to part with, give, or transfer in return for sthg received as an equivalent ⟨*where can I* ~ *my dollars for pounds?*⟩ ⟨*John* ~d *books with Peter*⟩ ⟨*exchanging freedom for security*⟩ **b** of 2 parties to give and receive (things of the same type) ⟨*2 armies* ~d *prisoners*⟩ ⟨*they* ~d *blows*⟩ **2** to replace by other goods ⟨*will they* ~ *clothes that don't fit?*⟩ ~ *vi* **1** to pass or become received in exchange **2** to engage in an exchange – **exchangeable** *adj*, **exchanger** *n*, **exchangeability** *n*

exchequer *n* **1** *cap* a former civil court having jurisdiction primarily over revenue and now merged with the Queen's Bench Division **2** *often cap* the department of state in charge of the national revenue **3** the (national or royal) treasury

¹excise *n* **1** an internal tax levied on the manufacture, sale, or consumption of a commodity within a country **2** any of various taxes on privileges, often levied in the form of a licence that must be bought

²excise *vt* to impose an excise on – **excisable** *adj*

³excise *vt* to remove (as if) by cutting out – **excision** *n*

excitable *adj* capable of being readily activated or roused into a state of excitement or irritability; *specif* capable of being activated by and reacting to stimuli – **excitableness, excitability** n

excite vt **1a** to provoke or stir up (action) ⟨~ *a rebellion*⟩ **b** to rouse to strong, esp pleasurable, feeling **c** to arouse (e g an emotional response) ⟨*the plight of the refugees* ~d *their pity*⟩ ⟨*her late arrival* ~d *much curiosity*⟩ **2** to induce a magnetic field or electric current in; *also* to induce (e g a magnetic field or an electric current) **3** to raise (e g an atom or a molecule) to a higher energy level – **excitant** n *or adj*, **excitative, excitatory** adj, **excitedly** adv, **excitement** n, **exciter** n, **exciting** adj, **excitingly** adv, **excitation** n

exclaim vi to cry out or speak in strong or sudden emotion ⟨~ed *in delight*⟩ ~ vt to utter sharply, passionately, or vehemently – **exclaimer** n

exclamation n exclaiming or the words exclaimed – **exclamatory** adj

exclamation mark n a punctuation mark ! used esp after an interjection or exclamation

exclude vt **1a** to shut out **b** to bar from participation, consideration, or inclusion **2** to expel, esp from a place or position previously occupied – **excludable** adj, **excluder** n, **exclusion** n, **exclusionary** adj

¹exclusive adj **1a** excluding or having power to exclude **b** limiting or limited to possession, control, use, etc by a single individual, group, etc ⟨*an* ~ *contract*⟩ ⟨*an* ~ *interview*⟩ **2a** excluding others (considered to be inferior) from participation, membership, or entry ⟨*an* ~ *club*⟩ **b** snobbishly aloof **3** stylish and expensive **4a** SOLE 1, 2 ⟨~ *jurisdiction*⟩ **b** whole, undivided ⟨*his* ~ *attention*⟩ **5** not inclusive ⟨*Monday to Friday* ~⟩ – **exclusively** adv, **exclusiveness** n, **exclusivity** n

²exclusive n **1** a newspaper story printed by only 1 newspaper **2** an exclusive right (e g to sell a particular product in a certain area)

excogitate vt to think out; devise – fml – **excogitative** adj, **excogitation** n

¹excommunicate vt **1** to deprive officially of the rights of church membership **2** to exclude from fellowship of a group or community – **excommunicative, excommunicatory** adj, **excommunication** n

²excommunicate n *or adj* (one who is) excommunicated

excoriate vt **1** to wear away the skin of; abrade **2** to censure scathingly – fml – **excoriation** n

excrement n faeces or other waste matter discharged from the body – **excremental** adj, **excrementitious** adj

excrescence, excrescency n an excessive or abnormal outgrowth or enlargement – **excrescent** adj

excreta n pl excrement – **excretal** adj

excrete vt to separate and eliminate or discharge (waste) from blood or living tissue – **excreter** n, **excretory** adj, **excretion** n

excruciating adj **1** causing great pain or anguish; agonizing, tormenting ⟨*an* ~ *migraine*⟩ **2** very intense; extreme ⟨~ *pain*⟩ – **excruciate** vt, **excruciatingly** adv, **excrutiation** n

exculpate vt to clear from alleged fault, blame, or guilt – **exculpation** n, **exculpatory** adj

excursion n **1a** (a brief) pleasure trip, usu at reduced rates **2** a deviation from a direct, definite, or proper course; *esp* a digression ⟨*needless* ~s *into abstruse theory*⟩ **3** (the distance travelled in) a movement outwards and back or from a mean position or axis – **excursionist** n

excuse vt **1a** to make apology for ⟨*quietly* ~d *his clumsiness*⟩ **b** to try to remove blame from ⟨~d *himself for being so careless*⟩ **2** to forgive entirely or overlook as unimportant ⟨*she graciously* ~d *his thoughtlessness*⟩ **3** to allow to leave; dismiss ⟨*the class was* ~d⟩ **4** to be an

acceptable reason for; justify – usu neg ⟨*nothing can* ~ *his cruelty*⟩ **5** Br to free from (a duty) – usu pass ⟨*the class was* ~d *homework*⟩ – **excusal** n, **excusable** adj, **excusably** adv, **excusatory** adj, **excuser** n

²excuse n **1** sthg offered as grounds for being excused ⟨*he had a good* ~ *for being late*⟩ **2** pl an expression of regret for failure to do sthg or esp for one's absence ⟨*make my* ~s *at the party tomorrow*⟩

ex-directory adj, Br intentionally not listed in a telephone directory

execrable adj detestable, appalling ⟨~ *behaviour*⟩ ⟨~ *taste*⟩ – chiefly fml – **execrably** adv

execrate vt **1** to declare to be evil or detestable; denounce **2** to detest utterly; abhor USE chiefly fml – **execrator** n, **execration** n, **execrative** adj

executant n one who executes or performs; *esp* one skilled in the technique of an art

execute vt **1** to carry out fully; put completely into effect **2** to put to death (legally) as a punishment **3** to make or produce (e g a work of art), esp by carrying out a design **4** to (do what is required to) make valid ⟨~ *a deed*⟩ **5** to play, perform ⟨~ *a piece of music*⟩ – **executable** adj

execution n **1** a putting to death as a punishment **2** a judicial writ directing the enforcement of a judgment **3** the act, mode, or result of performance ⟨*the* ~ *was perfect but the piece lacked expression*⟩

executioner n one who puts to death; *specif* one legally appointed to perform capital punishment

¹executive adj **1** concerned with making and carrying out laws, decisions, etc; *specif*, Br of or concerned with the detailed application of policy or law rather than its formulation **2** of, for, or being an executive ⟨*the* ~ *offices are on the top floor*⟩

²executive n **1** the executive branch of a government **2** an individual or group that controls or directs an organization **3** one who holds a position of administrative or managerial responsibility

executor, fem **executrix** n, pl **executors**, fem **executrices** one appointed to carry out the provisions of a will – **executory, executorial** adj

exegesis n, pl **exegeses** an explanation or critical interpretation of an esp biblical text; *broadly* an exposition – **exegetic, exegetical** adj

exemplar n sthg that serves as a model or example; *also* a copy of a book or text

exemplary adj **1** deserving imitation; commendable ⟨*his conduct was* ~⟩ **2** serving as a warning ⟨~ *punishments*⟩ **3** serving as an example, instance, or illustration – **exemplarily** adv, **exemplariness, exemplarity** n

exemplify vt **1** to show or illustrate by example **2** to be an instance of or serve as an example of; typify, embody – **exemplification** n

¹exempt adj freed from some liability or requirement to which others are subject ⟨~ *from jury service*⟩

²exempt vt to make exempt; excuse ⟨~ed *from jury service*⟩ – **exemption** n

¹exercise n **1** the use of a specified power or right ⟨*the* ~ *of his authority*⟩ **2a** regular or repeated use of a faculty or body part **b** bodily exertion for the sake of developing and maintaining physical fitness **3** sthg performed or practised in order to develop, improve, or display a specific power or skill **4** a manoeuvre or drill carried out for training and discipline

²exercise vt **1** to make effective in action; use, exert ⟨*didn't* ~ *good judgment*⟩ **2a** to use repeatedly in order to strengthen or develop **b** to train (e g troops) by drills and manoeuvres **c** to give exercise to ⟨~ *the horses*⟩ **3a** to engage the attention and effort of ⟨*the problem greatly* ~d *his mind*⟩ **b** to cause anxiety, alarm, or indignation in ⟨*citizens* ~d *about pollution*⟩ ~ *vi* to take exercise; *esp* to train – **exercisable** *adj*, **exerciser** *n*

exert *vt* **1** to bring (e g strength or authority) to bear, esp with sustained effort; employ, wield **2** to take upon (oneself) the effort of doing sthg ⟨*he never* ~s *himself to help anyone*⟩ – **exertion** *n*

exeunt – used as a stage direction to specify that all or certain named characters leave the stage

ex gratia *adj or adv* as a favour; not compelled by legal right ⟨~ *payments*⟩

exhalation *n* **1** exhaling **2** sthg exhaled or given off; an emanation

exhale *vt* **1** to breathe out **2** to give forth (gas or vapour); emit ~ *vi* **1** to rise or be given off as vapour **2** to emit breath or vapour

¹**exhaust** *vt* **1a** to draw off or let out completely **b** to empty by drawing off the contents; *specif* to create a vacuum in **2a** to consume entirely; USE UP ⟨~ ed *our funds in a week*⟩ **b** to tire out ⟨~ed *by their efforts*⟩ **3a** to develop or deal with (a subject) to the fullest possible extent **b** to try out the whole number of ⟨~ed *all the possibilities*⟩ – **exhauster** *n*, **exhaustible** *adj*, **exhaustibility** *n*

²**exhaust** *n* **1** (the escape of) used gas or vapour from an engine **2** the conduit or pipe through which used gases escape

exhaustion *n* extreme tiredness

exhaustive *adj* comprehensive, thorough ⟨*conducted an* ~ *investigation*⟩ – **exhaustively** *adv*, **exhaustiveness** *n*, **exhaustivity** *n*

¹**exhibit** *vt* to present to view: e g **a** to show or display outwardly, esp by visible signs or actions; reveal, manifest ⟨~ed *no fear*⟩ **b** to show publicly, esp for purposes of competition or demonstration ~*vi* to display sthg for public inspection – **exhibitive** *adj*, **exhibitor** *n*, **exhibitory** *adj*

²**exhibit** *n* **1** sthg exhibited **2** sthg produced as evidence in a lawcourt **3** *chiefly NAm* EXHIBITION 1

exhibition *n* **1** an act or instance of exhibiting ⟨*an* ~ *of ill-temper*⟩ **2** a public showing (e g of works of art or objects of manufacture) **3** *Br* a grant drawn from the funds of a school or university to help to maintain a student

exhibitionism *n* **1** a perversion marked by a tendency to indecent exposure **2** the act or practice of behaving so as to attract attention to oneself – **exhibitionist** *n or adj*, **exhibitionistic** *adj*

exhilarate *vt* **1** to make cheerful **2** to enliven, invigorate – **exhilarative** *adj*, **exhilaration** *n*

exhort *vt* to urge or advise strongly ⟨~ed *them to behave well*⟩ ~ *vi* to give warnings or advice; make urgent appeals – **exhortative** *adj*, **exhorter** *n*

exhortation *n* language intended to incite and encourage; *esp* an inspiring or encouraging speech or passage of writing

exhume *vt* **1** to disinter **2** to bring back from neglect or obscurity – **exhumer** *n*, **exhumation** *n*

exigency, exigence *n* **1** an exigent state of affairs; an emergency ⟨*the cabinet must be free to act in any* ~⟩ **2** such need or necessity as belongs to the occasion; a requirement – usu pl with sing. meaning *USE fml*

exigent *adj* **1** requiring immediate aid or action **2** exacting, demanding *USE fml* – **exigently** *adv*

exiguous *adj* excessively scanty; inadequate, meagre – fml – **exiguously** *adv*, **exiguousness** *n*, **exiguity** *n*

¹**exile** *n* **1** enforced or voluntary absence from one's country or home **2** one who is exiled voluntarily or by authority

²**exile** *vt* to send into exile

exist *vi* **1a** to have being in the real world; be ⟨*do unicorns* ~?⟩ **b** to have being in specified conditions ⟨*some chemical compounds* ~ *only in solution*⟩ **2** to continue to be ⟨*Nazism still* ~s⟩ **3a** to have life or the functions of vitality ⟨*man cannot* ~ *without water*⟩ **b** to live at an inferior level or under adverse circumstances ⟨*starving people* ~ing *from one day to the next*⟩

existence *n* **1a** the totality of existent things **b** the state or fact of existing; life ⟨*death is an elementary fact of* ~⟩ **2** manner of living or being ⟨*pursued a solitary* ~⟩

existent *adj* **1** having being; existing **2** extant – **existent** *n*

existential *adj* **1** of or grounded in existence ⟨~ *propositions*⟩ **2** existentialist – **existentially** *adv*

existentialism *n* a philosophical movement characterized by inquiry into human beings' experience of themselves in relation to the world, esp with reference to their freedom, responsibility, and isolation and the experiences (e g of anxiety and despair) in which these are revealed

¹**exit** – used as a stage direction to specify who goes off stage

²**exit** *n* **1** a departure of a performer from a scene **2** the act of going out or away **3** a way out of an enclosed place or space **4** death – euph – **exit** *vi*

ex libris *n, pl* **ex libris** a bookplate

exo-, ex- *comb form* **1** outside ⟨*exogamy*⟩; outer ⟨*exoskeleton*⟩ **2** giving off; releasing ⟨*exocrine*⟩

exodus *n* **1** *cap* the second book of the Old Testament relating the flight of the Israelites from Egypt **2** a mass departure; an emigration

ex officio *adv or adj* by virtue or because of an office ⟨*the president is an* ~ *member of the committee*⟩

exogamy *n* marriage outside one's tribe – **exogamous**, **exogamic** *adj*

exonerate *vt* **1** to relieve of a responsibility, obligation, or hardship **2** to free from blame; exculpate USE usu + *from* ⟨~ d *him from a charge of corruption*⟩ – **exonerative** *adj*, **exoneration** *n*

exorbitant *adj*, of prices, demands, etc much greater than is reasonable; excessive – **exorbitance** *n*, **exorbitantly** *adv*

exorcise, -ize *vt* **1a** to expel (an evil spirit) by solemn command (e g in a religious ceremony) **b** to get rid of (e g an unpleasant thought or emotion) as if by exorcism **2** to free (e g a person or place) of an evil spirit – **exorciser** *n*

exorcism *n* (a spell used in) the act of exorcising – **exorcist** *n*

exotic *adj* **1** introduced from another country; not native to the place where found ⟨*an* ~ *plant*⟩ **2** strikingly or excitingly different or unusual ⟨*an* ~ *dish*⟩ – **exotic** *n*, **exotically** *adv*, **exoticness** *n*, **exoticism** *n*

expand *vt* **1a** to increase the size, extent, number volume, or scope of ⟨*the company has* ~ed *its interests overseas*⟩ **b** to introduce gas into (a plastic or resin) ⟨~ ed *vinyl*⟩ **2** to express in detail or in full ⟨~ *an argument*⟩ ~ *vi* **1** to become expanded ⟨*iron* ~s *when heated*⟩ **2** ENLARGE 2 **3** to grow genial; become more sociable ⟨*only* ~s *among friends*⟩ – **expandable** *adj*

expanse *n* **1** sthg spread out, esp over a wide area **2** the extent to which sthg is spread out

expansion *n* **1** expanding or being expanded ⟨*territoria* ~⟩ **2** the increase in volume of working fluid (e g steam in an engine cylinder **3** sthg expanded: e g **a** an expanded part **b** a fuller treatment of an earlier theme or work **4** the expanding of a mathematical expression or function in a series – **expansional** *adj*, **expansionary** *adj*

expansive *adj* **1** having a capacity or tendency to expand or cause expansion **2** freely communicative; genial, effus ive ⟨*she grew* ~ *after dinner*⟩ **3** having wide expanse or extent **4** characterized by largeness or magnificence of scale ⟨~ *living*⟩ – **expansively** *adv*, **expansiveness** *n*, **expansivity** *n*

ex parte *adv or adj* from or in the interests of 1 side only – used of legal proceedings

expatiate *vi* to speak or write at length or in detail, usu on a single subject – usu + *on* or *upon* – **expatiation** *n*

expatriate *vt* **1** to exile, banish **2** to withdraw (oneself) from residence in or allegiance to one's native country – **expatriation** *n*

expatriate *n* one who lives in a foreign country – **expatriate** *adj*

expect *vi* **1** to look forward with anticipation **2** to be pregnant ~ *vt* **1** to anticipate or look forward to ⟨~ed *a telephone call*⟩ **2a** to consider (an event) probable or certain ⟨~ *to be forgiven*⟩ **b** to consider reasonable, due, or necessary ⟨*he* ~ed *respect from his children*⟩ **c** to consider bound in duty or obligated ⟨*they* ~ed *him to pay his dues*⟩ **3** to suppose, think ⟨*I* ~ *that's true*⟩ – infml – **expectable** *adj*, **expectably** *adv*, **expectance, expectancy** *n*, **expectedly** *adv*, **expectedness** *n*

expectant *adj* **1** characterized by expectation **2** *of a pregnant woman* expecting the birth of a child – **expectantly** *adv*

expectant *n* one (e g a candidate for a position) who is expectant

expectation *n* **1** expecting or sthg expected **2** prospects of inheritance – usu pl with sing. meaning **3** an expected amount or number (e g of years of life) based on statistical probability

expectorate *vb* **1** to eject (matter) from the throat or lungs by coughing or spitting **2** to spit (e g saliva) – **expectoration** *n*

expediency *n* **1** expediency, **expedience** suitability, fitness **2** cultivation of or adherence to expedient means and methods **3** an expedient

expedient *adj* **1** suitable for achieving a particular end **2** characterized by concern with what is opportune and esp by self-interest, rather than by concern with what is moral – **expediently** *adv*

expedient *n* a means to an end; *esp* one devised or used in case of urgent need

expedite *vt* **1** to execute promptly **2** to hasten the process or progress of; facilitate *USE* fml – **expediter** *n*

expedition *n* **1** a journey or excursion undertaken for a specific purpose (e g for war or exploration) **2** efficient promptness; speed – fml

expeditionary *adj* of or constituting an expedition; *also* sent on military service abroad ⟨*an* ~ *force*⟩

expeditious *adj* speedy – fml – **expeditiously** *adv*, **expeditiousness** *n*

expel *vt* **-ll-** **1** to drive or force out ⟨~led *air from the lungs*⟩ **2** to drive away; *esp* to deport **3** to cut off from membership ⟨~led *from school*⟩ – **expellable** *adj*, **expeller** *n*, **expellee** *n*

expend *vt* **1** to pay out ⟨*the new roads on which so much public money is* ~ed⟩ **2** to consume (e g time, care, or attention) by use; *USE UP* ⟨*projects on which he* ~ed *great energy*⟩ – **expender** *n*

expendable *adj* **1** normally used up in service; not intended to be kept or reused ⟨~ *supplies like pencils and paper*⟩ **2** regarded as available for sacrifice or destruction in order to accomplish an objective ⟨~ *troops*⟩ – **expendability** *n*

expenditure *n* **1** the act or process of expending **2** the amount expended

expense *n* **1a** sthg expended to secure a benefit or bring about a result **b** financial burden or outlay **c** *pl* the

charges incurred by an employee in performing his/her duties **d** an item of business outlay chargeable against revenue in a specific period **2** a cause or occasion of usu high expenditure ⟨*a car is a great* ~⟩ – **at somebody's expense** in a manner that causes sby to be ridiculed ⟨*made a joke* at my *expense*⟩ – **at the expense of** to the detriment of ⟨*develop a boy's physique* at the expense of *his intelligence* – Bertrand Russell⟩

expense account *n* an account of expenses reimbursable to an employee – **expense-account** *adj*

expensive *adj* **1** involving great expense ⟨*an* ~ *hobby*⟩ **2** commanding a high price; dear – **expensively** *adv*, **expensiveness** *n*

¹experience *n* **1** (the facts or events perceived by) the usu conscious perception or apprehension of reality or of an external, bodily, or mental event **2** (the knowledge, skill, or practice derived from) direct participation or observation **3** the sum total of conscious events that make up an individual life or the collective past of a community, nation, or humankind generally **4** sthg personally encountered or undergone ⟨*a terrifying* ~⟩

²experience *vt* to have experience of ⟨~d *severe hardships as a child*⟩

experienced *adj* skilful or wise as a result of experience of a particular activity or of life as a whole ⟨*an* ~ *driver*⟩

experiment *n* **1** a tentative procedure or policy that is on trial **2** an operation carried out under controlled conditions in order to test or establish a hypothesis or to illustrate a known law ⟨*a scientific* ~⟩ **3** the process of making experiments – **experiment** *vi*, **experimentation** *n*, **experimenter** *n*

experimental *adj* **1** experiential **2** based on or derived from experiment – **experimentalism** *adj*, **experimentally** *adv*

expert *n or adj* (sby or sthg) having or showing special skill or knowledge derived from training or experience – **expertly** *adv*, **expertness** *n*

expertise *n* skill in or knowledge of a particular field; know-how ⟨*technical* ~⟩

expiate *vt* **1a** to eradicate the guilt incurred by (e g a sin) **b** to pay the penalty for (e g a crime) **2** to make amends for – **expiation** *n*, **expiator** *n*, **expiatory** *adj*

expiration *n* **1** the release of air from the lungs through the nose or mouth **2** expiry, termination

expire *vi* **1** to come to an end ⟨*his term of office* ~s *this year*⟩ **2** to emit the breath **3** to die – fml ~ *vt* to breathe out (as if) from the lungs

explain *vt* **1** to make plain or understandable **2** to give the reason for or cause of ⟨*unwilling to* ~ *his conduct*⟩ ~ *vi* to make sthg plain or understandable – **explainable** *adj*, **explainer** *n* – **explain oneself** to clarify one's statements or the reasons for one's conduct

explain away *vt* to avoid blame for or cause to appear insignificant by making excuses ⟨*tried to* explain away *the corruption in his department*⟩

explanation *n* the act or process of explaining; sthg, esp a statement, that explains

explanatory *adj* serving to explain ⟨~ *notes*⟩ – **explanatorily** *adv*

¹expletive *adj* serving to fill up ⟨~ *phrases*⟩

²expletive *n* **1** a word, phrase, etc inserted to fill a space without adding to the sense **2** a usu meaningless exclamatory word or phrase; *specif* one that is obscene or profane

explicable *adj* capable of being explained – **explicably** *adv*

explicate *vt* **1** to give a detailed explanation of **2** to

develop the implications of; analyse logically – **explicator**
n, **explicative** *adj*, **explicatory** *adj*, **explication** *n*
explicit *adj* 1 clear, unambiguous ⟨~ *instructions*⟩; *also*
graphically frank ⟨~ *sex scenes*⟩ 2 fully developed or
formulated – **explicitly** *adv*, **explicitness** *n*
explode *vt* 1 to bring (e g a belief or theory) into discredit
by demonstrating falsity ⟨~ *a rumour*⟩ 2 to cause to
explode or burst noisily ~*vi* 1 to give expression to
sudden, violent, and usu noisy emotion ⟨~ *with anger*⟩
2a to undergo a rapid chemical or nuclear reaction with
the production of noise, heat, and violent expansion of
gases **b** to burst or expand violently as a result of pressure
⟨*the boiler* ~d⟩ ⟨*the* exploding *population*⟩ –
exploder *n*
exploded *adj* showing the parts separated but in correct
relationship to each other ⟨*an* ~ *view of a carburettor*⟩
¹**exploit** *n* a deed, act; *esp* a notable or heroic one
²**exploit** *vt* 1 to turn to economic account ⟨~ *a mine*⟩; *also*
to utilize 2 to take unfair advantage of for financial or
other gain ⟨~s *the workers by paying low wages*⟩ –
exploitable *adj*, **exploiter** *n*, **exploitive** *adj*,
exploitively *adj*, **exploitability** *n*
exploitation *n* 1 exploiting or being exploited 2 cashing
in on a topical theme ⟨~ *movie*⟩ – **exploitative** *adj*,
exploitatively *adv*
explore *vt* 1 to examine or inquire into thoroughly ⟨~
the possibilities of reaching an agreement⟩ 2 to examine
minutely, esp for diagnostic purposes 3 to travel into or
through for purposes of geographical discovery ~*vi* to
make or conduct a search – **explorer** *n*, **exploration** *n*,
explorative *adj*, **exploratively** *adv*, **exploratory** *adj*
explosion *n* 1 exploding: e g **a** a rapid large-scale expansion, increase, or upheaval ⟨*the population* ~⟩ **b** a
sudden violent outburst of emotion 2 plosion
¹**explosive** *adj* 1 tending or threatening to burst forth with
sudden violence or noise ⟨*an* ~ *substance*⟩ ⟨*an* ~ *situation*⟩ 2 tending to arouse strong reactions; controversial
⟨*the play's* ~ *topicality*⟩ – **explosively** *adv*, **explosive-
ness** *n*
²**explosive** *n* 1 an explosive substance 2 a plosive, stop
expo *n*, *pl* **expos** EXPOSITION 3
exponent *n* 1 a symbol written above and to the right of
a mathematical expression to indicate the operation of
raising to a power ⟨*in the expression* a³, *the* ~ 3 *indicates
that* a *is cubed*⟩ 2a sby or sthg that expounds or interprets
b sby who advocates or exemplifies USE (2) usu + *of*
exponential *adj* 1 involving a variable in an exponent
⟨10ˣ *is an* ~ *expression*⟩ 2 expressible or approximately
expressible in terms of exponential functions ⟨*an* ~
growth rate⟩
¹**export** *vt* to carry or send (e g a commodity) to some other
place (e g another country) for purposes of trade ~*vi* to
export sthg abroad – **exportable** *adj*, **exportability** *n*,
exporter *n*
²**export** *n* 1 sthg exported 2 an act of exporting
exportation *n* an act of exporting; *also, chiefly NAm* a
commodity exported
expose *vt* 1a to deprive of shelter or protection; lay open
to attack or distressing influence ⟨~s *himself to ridicule*⟩
b to submit or subject to an action or influence; *specif* to
subject (a photographic film, plate, or paper) to the action
of radiant energy **c** to abandon (an infant) in an unshel-
tered place 2 to lay open to view; display: e g **a** to exhibit
for public veneration **b** to reveal the face of (a playing
card) **c** to engage in indecent exposure of (oneself) 3 to
bring (sthg shameful) to light ⟨~d *their trickery*⟩ –
exposer *n*
exposé, expose *n* 1 a formal recital or exposition of facts;

a statement 2 an exposure of sthg discreditable ⟨*a newspaper* ~ *of organized crime*⟩
exposition *n* 1 the art or practice of expounding or
explaining the meaning or purpose of sthg (e g a text) 2a
a detailed explanation or elucidation, esp of sthg difficult
to understand ⟨*a brilliant* ~ *of existentialism*⟩ **b** the first
part of a musical composition in which the theme is
presented 3 a usu international public exhibition or show
(e g of industrial products) – **expositional** *adj*, **expositor**
n, **expository** *adj*
ex post facto *adj or adv* 1 after the fact ⟨~ *approval*⟩
2 applied retrospectively ⟨~ *laws*⟩
expostulate *vi* to reason earnestly *with* sby in order to
dissuade or remonstrate – *fml* – **expostulation** *n*
exposure *n* 1a a disclosure, esp of a weakness or sthg
shameful or criminal; an exposé, unmasking ⟨*continued
his* ~ *of electoral frauds*⟩ **b** presentation or exposition,
esp to the public by means of the mass media **c**(1) the act
of exposing a sensitized photographic film, plate, or paper;
also the duration of such an exposure (2) a section of a
film with 1 picture on it 2a being exposed, specif to the
elements **b** the specified direction in which a building,
room, etc faces ⟨*a house with a western* ~⟩
expound *vt* to set forth, esp in careful or elaborate detail;
state, explain – **expounder** *n*
¹**express** *adj* 1 firmly and explicitly stated ⟨*he disobeyed
my* ~ *orders*⟩ 2 of a particular sort; specific ⟨*he came for
that* ~ *purpose*⟩ 3a (adapted or suitable for) travelling at
high speed ⟨*an* ~ *highway*⟩ **b** *Br* designated to be
delivered without delay by special messenger ⟨~ *mail*⟩
²**express** *adv* by express
³**express** *n* 1 an express vehicle 2 *Br* express mail
⁴**express** *vt* 1a to show or represent, esp in words; state
b to make known the opinions, feelings, etc of (oneself)
⟨~es *himself through his work*⟩ **c** to represent by a sign
or symbol 2 to force out (e g the juice of a fruit) by
pressure – **expresser** *n*, **expressible** *adj*
expression *n* 1a expressing, esp in words ⟨*freedom of*
~⟩ **b**(1) an outward manifestation or symbol ⟨*this gift is
an* ~ *of my admiration for you*⟩ (2) a significant word
or phrase (3) a mathematical or logical symbol or combination of symbols serving to express sthg 2a a means or
manner of expressing sthg; *esp* sensitivity and feeling in
communicating or performing ⟨*read the poem with* ~⟩
b(1) the quality or fact of being expressive (2) facial aspect
or vocal intonation indicative of feeling 3 (a product of)
pressing out – **expressional** *adj*, **expressionless** *adj*,
expressionlessly *adv*, **expressionlessness** *n*
expressionism *n* a mode of artistic expression that
attempts to depict the artist's subjective emotions and
responses to objects and events – **expressionist** *n or adj*,
expressionistic *adj*, **expressionistically** *adv*
expressive *adj* 1 of expression ⟨*the* ~ *function of
language*⟩ 2 serving to express or represent ⟨*he used foul
and novel terms* ~ *of rage* – H G Wells⟩ 3 full of
expression; significant ⟨*an* ~ *silence*⟩ – **expressively** *adv*,
expressiveness *n*, **expressivity** *n*
expressly *adv* 1 explicitly ⟨*I* ~ *told you not to do that*⟩
2 for the express purpose; specially ⟨*needed a clinic* ~ *for
the treatment of addicts*⟩
expressway *n, chiefly NAm* a motorway
expropriate *vt* 1 to dispossess 2 to transfer to one's own
possession ⟨~d *all the land within a 10-mile radius*⟩ –
expropriator *n*, **expropriation** *n*
expulsion *n* expelling or being expelled – **expulsive**
adj
expunge *vt* 1 to strike out; obliterate, erase 2 to efface
completely; destroy ⟨*nothing can* ~ *his shame*⟩ USE *fml*
– **expunction** *n*, **expunger** *n*

expurgate vt to rid of sthg morally offensive; *esp* to remove objectionable parts from, before publication or presentation – **expurgator** n, **expurgation** n, **expurgatorial** adj, **expurgatory** adj

exquisite adj **1a** marked by flawless, beautiful, and usu delicate craftsmanship **b** keenly sensitive, esp in feeling; discriminating ⟨~ *taste*⟩ **2a** extremely beautiful; delightful ⟨*an* ~ *white blossom*⟩ **b** acute, intense ⟨~ *pain*⟩ – **exquisitely** adv, **exquisiteness** n

extant adj still or currently existing ⟨~ *manuscripts*⟩

extemporaneous adj **1** done, spoken, performed, etc on the spur of the moment; impromptu ⟨*gave a witty* ~ *speech*⟩ **2** provided, made, or put to use as an expedient; makeshift – **extemporaneously** adv, **extemporaneousness** n, **extemporaneity** n

extempore adj or adv (spoken or done) in an extemporaneous manner ⟨*speaking* ~⟩

extemporize, -ise vi to speak, or perform sthg, extemporaneously; improvise ~ vt to compose, perform, or utter extemporaneously – **extemporizer** n, **extemporization** n

extend vt **1** to spread or stretch forth; unfold ⟨~ ed *both her arms*⟩ **2a** to stretch out to fullest length ⟨~ ed *the sail*⟩ **b** to exert (e g a horse or oneself) to full capacity ⟨*won the race without* ~ ing *himself*⟩ **3** to give or offer, usu in response to need; proffer ⟨~ ing *aid to the needy*⟩ **4a** to cause to reach (e g in distance or scope) ⟨*national authority was* ~ ed *over new territories*⟩ ⟨~ ed *the road to the coast*⟩ **b** to prolong in time **c** to advance, further ⟨~ ing *human knowledge*⟩ **5a** to enlarge **b** to increase the scope, meaning, or application of; broaden ~ vi **1** to stretch out in distance, space, or time ⟨*his jurisdiction* ~ ed *over the whole area*⟩ **2** to reach in scope or application – **extendable, extendible** adj

extension n **1a** extending or being extended **b** sthg extended **2** extent, scope **3** a straightening of (a joint between the bones of) a limb **4** an increase in length of time **5** a programme of instruction for nonresident students of a university **6a** a part added (e g to a building) **b** an extra telephone connected to the principal line

extensive adj **1** having wide or considerable extent ⟨~ *reading*⟩ **2** of or being farming in which large areas of land are used with minimum outlay and labour – **extensively** adv, **extensiveness** n

extent n **1** the range or distance over which sthg extends ⟨*the* ~ *of the forest*⟩ ⟨*the* ~ *of his knowledge*⟩ **2** the point or limit to which sthg extends ⟨*the* ~ *of our patience*⟩

extenuate vt to (try to) lessen the seriousness or extent of (e g a crime) by giving excuses – **extenuator** n, **extenuatory** adj, **extenuation** n

exterior adj **1** on the outside or an outside surface; external **2** suitable for use on outside surfaces – **exteriorize** vt, **exteriorly** adv, **exteriorization** n, **exteriority** n

exterior n **1a** an exterior part or surface; outside **b** an outward manner or appearance ⟨*a deceptively friendly* ~⟩ **2** a representation of an outdoor scene

exterminate vt to destroy completely; esp to kill all of ⟨~ d *the mice*⟩ – **exterminator** n, **extermination** n, **exterminatory** adj

external adj **1a** capable of being perceived outwardly ⟨~ *signs of a disease*⟩ **b**(1) superficial (2) not intrinsic or essential ⟨~ *circumstances*⟩ **2** of, connected with, or intended for the outside or an outer part **3a**(1) situated outside, apart, or beyond (2) arising or acting from outside ⟨*an* ~ *force*⟩ **b** of dealings with foreign countries **c** having existence independent of the mind ⟨~ *reality*⟩ – **externally** adv, **externality** n

external n an external feature or aspect – usu pl

externalize, -ise vt **1** to make external or externally

visible **2** to attribute to causes outside the self; rationalize ⟨~ s *his failure*⟩ – **externalization** n

exterritorial adj extraterritorial – **exterritoriality** n

extinct adj **1a** no longer burning **b** no longer active ⟨*an* ~ *volcano*⟩ **2** no longer existing ⟨*an* ~ *animal*⟩ **3** having no qualified claimant ⟨*an* ~ *title*⟩

extinction n **1** making or being extinct or (causing to be) extinguished **2** elimination or reduction of a conditioned response by not reinforcing it – **extinctive** adj

extinguish vt **1a** to cause to cease burning; quench **b** to bring to an end ⟨*hope for their safety was slowly* ~ ed⟩ **c** to cause extinction of (a conditioned response) **2a** to make void ⟨~ *a claim*⟩ **b** to abolish (a debt) by payment – **extinguishable** adj, **extinguisher** n, **extinguishment** n

extirpate vt **1** to destroy completely (as if) by uprooting; annihilate **2** to cut out by surgery – **extirpator** n, **extirpation** n, **extirpative** adj

extol, NAm also **extoll** vt **-ll-** to praise highly; glorify – **extoller** n, **extolment** n

extort vt to obtain from sby by force or threats ⟨~ *money*⟩ ⟨~ *a confession*⟩ – **extorter** n, **extortive** adj

extortion n extorting; specif the unlawful extorting of money – **extortioner** n, **extortionist** n

extortionate adj excessive, exorbitant – **extortionately** adv

¹**extra** adj **1** more than is due, usual, or necessary; additional ⟨~ *work*⟩ **2** subject to an additional charge ⟨*room service is* ~⟩

²**extra** n sthg or sby extra or additional: e g **a** an added charge **b** a specified edition of a newspaper ⟨*late night* ~⟩ **c** a run in cricket (e g a bye, leg bye, no-ball, or wide) that is not scored by a stroke of the bat and is not credited to a batsman's individual score **d** an additional worker; specif one hired to act in a group scene in a film or stage production

³**extra** adv beyond or above the usual size, extent, or amount ⟨*to work* ~ *hard*⟩ ⟨*they charge* ~ *for single rooms*⟩

extra- prefix outside; beyond ⟨extra*judicial*⟩ ⟨extra*mural*⟩

¹**extract** vt **1** to draw forth or pull out, esp against resistance or with effort ⟨~ ed *a wisdom tooth*⟩ ⟨~ ed *a confession*⟩ **2** to withdraw (e g a juice or fraction) by physical or chemical process; also to treat with a solvent so as to remove a soluble substance **3** to separate (a metal) from an ore **4** to find (a mathematical root) by calculation **5** to excerpt – **extractable, extractible** adj, **extractor** n, **extractability** n

²**extract** n **1** an excerpt **2** extract, **extractive** /ik1straktiv/ (a solution of) the essential constituents of a complex material (e g an aromatic plant) prepared by extraction

extraction n **1** extracting **2** ancestry, origin **3** sthg extracted

extracurricular adj **1** not falling within the scope of a regular curriculum **2** lying outside one's normal activities

extraditable adj liable to or warranting extradition ⟨*an* ~ *offence*⟩

extradite vt **1** to hand over for extradition **2** to obtain by extradition

extradition n the surrender of an alleged criminal by one state to another having jurisdiction to try the charge

extrajudicial adj **1** not forming part of regular legal proceedings ⟨*an* ~ *investigation*⟩ **2** in contravention of law ⟨*an* ~ *execution*⟩ – **extrajudicially** adv

extramarital adj, esp of sexual relations involving sby other than one's spouse

extramural adj **1** outside (the walls or boundaries of) a place or organization **2** chiefly Br of extension courses or facilities ⟨*university* ~ *department*⟩ – **extramurally** *adv*

extraneous *adj* **1** on or coming from the outside **2** not forming an essential or vital part; irrelevant ⟨*an* ~ *scene that added nothing to the play*⟩ – **extraneously** *adv*, **extraneousness** *n*

extraordinary *adj* **1a** going beyond what is usual, regular, or customary ⟨*an Act that gave him* ~ *powers*⟩ **b** highly exceptional; remarkable ⟨~ *beauty*⟩ **2** on or for a special function or service ⟨*an ambassador* ~ ⟩ ⟨*an* ~ *general meeting*⟩ – **extraordinarily** *adv*, **extraordinariness** *n*

extrapolate *vt* **1** to infer (values of a variable in an unobserved interval) from values within an already observed interval **2a** to use or extend (known data or experience) in order to surmise or work out sthg unknown **b** to predict by extrapolating known data or experience – **extrapolator** *n*, **extrapolative** *adj*, **extrapolation** *n*

extrasensory *adj* residing beyond or outside the ordinary physical senses ⟨*instances of* ~ *perception*⟩

extraterrestrial *adj* originating, existing, or occurring outside the earth or its atmosphere

extraterritorial *adj* outside the territorial limits of a jurisdiction

extravagance, extravagancy *n* **1** an extravagant act; *specif* an excessive outlay of money **2** sthg extravagant

extravagant *adj* **1a** lacking in moderation, balance, and restraint; excessive ⟨~ *praise*⟩ **b** excessively elaborate or showy **2a** wasteful, esp of money **b** profuse **3** exorbitant – **extravagantly** *adv*

extravaganza *n* **1** a literary or musical work marked by extreme freedom of style and structure **2** a lavish or spectacular show or event

extravert *n or adj* (an) extrovert

¹**extreme** *adj* **1a** existing in a very high degree ⟨~ *poverty*⟩ **b** going to great or exaggerated lengths; not moderate ⟨*an* ~ *right-winger*⟩ **c** exceeding the usual or expected; severe ⟨*took* ~ *measures*⟩ **2** situated at the farthest possible point from a centre or the nearest to an end ⟨*the country's* ~ *north*⟩ **3a** most advanced or thoroughgoing ⟨*the* ~ *avant-garde*⟩ **b** maximum ⟨*the* ~ *penalty*⟩ – **extremely** *adv*, **extremeness** *n*

²**extreme** *n* **1a** sthg situated at or marking one or other extreme point of a range ⟨~ s *of heat and cold*⟩ **b** the first term or the last term of a mathematical proportion **2** a very pronounced or extreme degree ⟨*his enthusiasm was carried to an* ~ ⟩ **3** an extreme measure or expedient ⟨*going to* ~ s⟩ – **in the extreme** to the greatest possible extent ⟨*boring in the extreme*⟩

extreme unction *n* the (Roman Catholic) sacrament of anointing and praying over sby who is dying

extremism *n* advocacy of extreme political measures; radicalism – **extremist** *n or adj*

extremity *n* **1a** the most extreme part, point, or degree **b** a (human) hand, foot, or other limb **2** (a moment marked by) extreme misfortune and esp danger of destruction or death **3** a drastic or desperate act or measure

extricate *vt* to disentangle, esp with considerable effort ⟨*managed to* ~ *himself from a tricky situation*⟩ – **extricable** *adj*, **extrication** *n*

extrinsic *adj* **1** not forming part of or belonging to a thing; extraneous **2** originating from or on the outside – **extrinsically** *adv*

extrovert *also* **extravert** *n* one whose attention and interests are directed wholly or predominantly towards what is outside the self – **extrovert** *adj*, **extroverted** *adj*, **extroversion** *n*

extrude *vt* **1** to force or push out **2** to shape (e g metal or plastic) by forcing through a die ~ *vi* to become

extruded – **extruder** *n*, **extrudable** *adj*, **extrudability** *n*, **extrusion** *n*

exuberant *adj* **1a** joyously unrestrained and enthusiastic ⟨~ *high spirits*⟩ **b** lavish and flamboyant ⟨~ *metaphors*⟩ **2** great or extreme in degree, size, or extent **3** abundant, luxuriant ⟨~ *vegetation*⟩ – **exuberance** *n*, **exuberantly** *adv*

exude *vi* to ooze out ⟨*moisture* ~ d *from the damp wall*⟩ ~ *vt* **1** to allow or cause to ooze or spread out in all directions ⟨~ *sweat*⟩ **2** to radiate an air of ⟨~ s *charm*⟩ – **exudation** *n*

exult *vi* to be extremely joyful; rejoice openly – usu + *at, in,* or *over* – **exultance** *n*, **exultancy** *n*, **exultant** *adj*, **exultingly** *adv*, **exultation** *n*, **exultantly** *adv*

-ey – see ¹y-

¹**eye** *n* **1a** any of various usu paired organs of sight; *esp* a nearly spherical liquid-filled organ that is lined with a light-sensitive retina and housed in a bony socket in the skull **b** the visible parts of the eye with its surrounding structures (e g eyelashes and eyebrows) **c(1)** the faculty of seeing with eyes ⟨*a keen* ~ *for detail*⟩ **(2)** the faculty of intellectual or aesthetic perception or appreciation ⟨*an* ~ *for beauty*⟩ **d** a gaze, glance ⟨*caught his* ~ ⟩ **e** view, attention ⟨*in the public* ~ ⟩ **2a** the hole through the head of a needle **b** a (nearly) circular mark (e g on a peacock's tail) **c** a loop; *esp* one of metal or thread into which a hook is inserted **d** an undeveloped bud (e g on a potato) **e** a calm area in the centre of a tropical cyclone **f** the (differently coloured or marked) centre of a flower **3** the centre, nub ⟨*the* ~ *of the problem* – Norman Mailer⟩ **4** the direction from which the wind is blowing – **eyeless** *adj*, **eyelike** *adj* – **in the eye/eyes of** in the judgment or opinion of ⟨*beauty is* in the eye of *the beholder*⟩ – **my eye** – used to express mild disagreement or sometimes surprise ⟨*a diamond*, my eye! *That's glass*⟩; *infml* – **set/clap eyes on** to catch sight of – **with an eye to** having as an aim or purpose

²**eye** *vt* **eyeing, eying** to watch closely – **eyer** *n*

eyeball *n* the capsule of the eye of a vertebrate formed by the sclera and cornea that cover it, together with the structures they contain

eyebrow *n* (hair growing on) the ridge over the eye

eye-catching *adj* strikingly visually attractive – **eye-catcher** *n*

eyed *adj* having an eye or eyes, esp of a specified kind or number – often in combination ⟨*an almond-*eyed *girl*⟩

eyeful *n* a pleasing sight; *specif* an attractive woman – *infml*

eyeglass *n* **1** an eyepiece **2** a lens worn to aid vision; *specif* a monocle **3** *pl* glasses, spectacles

eyelash *n* (a single hair of) the fringe of hair edging the eyelid

eyelet *n* **1** a small usu reinforced hole designed so that a cord, lace, etc may be passed through it, or used in embroidery **2** a small typically metal ring to reinforce an eyelet; a grommet

eyelid *n* a movable lid of skin and muscle that can be closed over the eyeball

eyeliner *n* a cosmetic for emphasizing the contours of the eyes

eye-opener *n* **1** chiefly NAm a drink intended to stop one feeling sleepy on waking up **2** sthg surprising and esp revelatory – *infml* ⟨*his behaviour was a real* ~ *to me*⟩ – **eye-opening** *adj*

eyepiece *n* the lens or combination of lenses at the eye end of an optical instrument

eye shadow *n* a coloured cream or powder applied to the eyelids to accentuate the eyes

eyesight *n* SIGHT 5

eyesore *n* sthg offensive to the sight

eyetooth *n* a canine tooth of the upper jaw

eyewash *n* deceptive statements or actions; rubbish, claptrap – *infml*

eyewitness *n* one who sees an occurrence and can bear witness to it (e g in court)

eyot *n* an ait

eyrie *n* **1** the nest of a bird (of prey) on a cliff or a mountain top **2** a room or dwelling situated high up ⟨*sat in his seventh floor ~ in Mayfair*⟩

F

---

f *n*, *pl* **f's, fs** *often cap* **1** (a graphic representation of or device for reproducing) the 6th letter of the English alphabet **2** the 4th note of a C-major scale **3** a grade rating a student's work as failing

fa, fah *n* the 4th note of the diatonic scale in solmization

FA *n*, *Br* fuck-all – *euph*; often in *sweet FA*

Fabian *adj* of or being a society founded in England in 1884 to work for the gradual establishment of socialism – **Fabian** *n*, **Fabianism** *n*

fable *n* **1a** a legendary story of supernatural happenings **b** myths or legendary tales collectively **2** a fictitious account; a lie **3** a story intended to convey a moral; *esp* one in which animals speak and act like human beings

fabled *adj* **1** fictitious **2** told or celebrated in fables; legendary

fabric *n* **1a** the basic structure of a building ⟨*the ~ of the theatre*⟩ **b** an underlying structure; a framework ⟨*the ~ of society*⟩ **2** an act of constructing; an erection **3** texture, quality – used chiefly with reference to textiles **4a** CLOTH 1 **b** a material that resembles cloth

fabricate *vt* **1** to construct or manufacture from many parts **2** to invent or create, esp in order to deceive – **fabricator** *n*, **fabrication** *n*

fabulous *adj* **1** resembling things told of in fables, esp in incredible or exaggerated quality; extraordinary ⟨*~ wealth*⟩ **2** told in or based on fable **3** marvellous, great – *infml* ⟨*a ~ party*⟩ – **fabulously** *adv*, **fabulousness** *n*

facade *also* **façade** *n* **1** a face, esp the front or principal face, of a building given special architectural treatment **2** a false or superficial appearance

face *n* **1** the front part of the (human) head including the chin, mouth, nose, eyes, etc and usu the forehead **2a** a facial expression; *specif* a grimace ⟨*he pulled a ~*⟩ **b** MAKE-UP 2a, b ⟨*she put her ~ on*⟩ **3a** an outward appearance ⟨*put a good ~ on it*⟩ **b** effrontery, impudence ⟨*had the ~ to ask for his money back*⟩ **c** dignity, reputation ⟨*afraid to lose ~*⟩ ⟨*we must save ~ at all costs*⟩ **4a(1)** a front, upper, or outer surface **(2)** the front of sthg with 2 or 4 sides **(3)** an exposed surface of rock **(4)** any of the plane surfaces of a geometric solid **b** a surface specially prepared: e g **(1)** the right side (e g of cloth or leather) **(2)** an inscribed, printed, or marked surface **c** the surface (e g of type) that receives the ink and transfers it to the paper **5** the exposed working surface of a mine, drift, or excavation – **in the face of/in face of** in opposition to; despite ⟨*succeed in the face of great difficulties*⟩ – **to someone's face** candidly in sby's presence and to his/her knowledge

¹face *vt* **1** to meet or deal with firmly and without evasion ⟨*~ the situation calmly*⟩ **2a** to apply a facing to **b** to cover the front or surface of ⟨*~d the building with*

marble⟩ **3** to have the face towards ⟨*~ the wall*⟩; *also* to front on ⟨*a house facing the park*⟩ **4** to turn (e g a playing card) face-up **5** to make the surface of (e g a stone) flat or smooth **6** to cause (troops) to face in a particular direction on command ~ *vi* **1** to have the face or front turned in a specified direction ⟨*the house ~s towards the east*⟩ **2** to turn the face in a specified direction – **face the music** to confront and endure the unpleasant consequences of one's actions – **face up to** to confront without shrinking – **face with** to confront with ⟨*faced him with the evidence*⟩

facecloth *n* FLANNEL 3

-faced *comb form* (adj, *n* → adj) having (such) a face or (so many) faces ⟨*two-faced*⟩

faceless *adj* lacking identity; anonymous ⟨*~ bureaucrats*⟩ – **facelessness** *n*

face-lift *n* **1** plastic surgery to remove facial defects (e g wrinkles) typical of aging **2** an alteration intended to improve appearance or utility – **face-lift** *vt*

face out *vt* to confront defiantly or impudently ⟨*faced out the opposition*⟩

face-pack *n* a cream, paste, etc applied to the face to improve the complexion and remove impurities

face-saving *adj* serving to preserve one's dignity or reputation – **face-saver** *n*

facet *n* **1** a small plane surface (e g of a cut gem) **2** any of the aspects from which sthg specified may be considered ⟨*another ~ of his genius*⟩ **3** the external surface of any of the usu many optical elements of the compound eye of an insect or other arthropod – **faceted, facetted** *adj*

facetious *adj* **1** inappropriately lacking seriousness in manner; flippant ⟨*a ~ question*⟩ **2** intended to be amusing – **facetiously** *adv*, **facetiousness** *n*

face-to-face *adj* in each other's usu hostile presence ⟨*a ~ encounter*⟩

face to face *adv* **1** in or into the usu hostile presence of (one) another **2** in or into confrontation with sthg which calls for immediate action ⟨*came ~ with the problem*⟩

face value *n* **1** the value indicated on the face (e g of a postage stamp or a share certificate) **2** the apparent value or significance ⟨*if their results may be taken at ~*⟩

¹facial *adj* of the face – **facially** *adv*

²facial *n* a facial beauty treatment

facile *adj* **1a** easily or readily accomplished or performed ⟨*a ~ victory*⟩ **b** specious, superficial ⟨*I am not concerned with offering any ~ solution for so complex a problem* – T S Eliot⟩ **2** used, done, or understood with ease – **facilely** *adv*, **facileness** *n*

facilitate *vt* to make easier – *fml* – **facilitative** *adj*, **facilitator** *n*

facility *n* **1** the quality of being easily performed **2** the ability to perform sthg easily; aptitude **3** sthg (e g equipment) that promotes the ease of an action or operation – usu *pl* ⟨*provide books and other facilities for independent study*⟩

facing *n* **1a** a lining at the edge of sthg, esp a garment, for stiffening or ornament **b** *pl* the collar, cuffs, and trimmings of a uniform coat **2** an ornamental or protective layer **3** material used for facing

facsimile *n* **1** an exact copy, esp of printed material **2** the transmission and reproduction of graphic material (e g typescript or pictures) by wire or radio – **facsimile** *vt*

fact *n* **1** a thing done; *esp* a criminal act **2** the quality of having actual existence in the real world; *also* sthg having such existence **3** an event, esp as distinguished from its legal effect **4** a piece of information presented as having objective reality ⟨*that's a ~*⟩ – **factless** *adj*, **facticity** *n* –

in fact 1 really; AS A MATTER OF FACT **2** briefly; IN SHORT

¹faction n **1** a party or minority group within a party **2** dissension with a party or group – **factional** adj, **factionalism** n, **factionally** adv

²faction n the dramatized reconstruction of some real historical situation or event ⟨~ has actually been around for quite some time   Shakespeare was the first great ~ writer in his history plays – The Guardian⟩

-faction comb form (→ n) **1** making; **-fication** ⟨liquefaction⟩ **2** state ⟨satisfaction⟩ – **-factive** comb form (→ adj)

factious adj **1** caused by or inclined to faction **2** seditious – **factiously** adv, **factiousness** n

factitious adj **1** produced by human beings rather than by natural forces **2** produced artificially; sham, unreal ⟨created a ~ demand by spreading rumours of shortage⟩ – **factitiously** adv, **factitiousness** n

fact of life n, pl **facts of life 1** pl the processes and behaviour involved in (human) sex and reproduction **2** sthg that exists and must be taken into consideration

¹factor n **1** one who acts for another; an agent **2** a condition, force, or fact that actively contributes to a result **3** a gene **4** any of the numbers or symbols that when multiplied together form a product – **factorship** n

²factor vt to express as the product of factors – **factorable** adj

factorize, -ise vt to factor – **factorization** n

factory n a building or set of buildings with facilities for manufacturing

factotum n a servant employed to carry out many types of work

factual adj **1** of facts **2** restricted to or based on fact – **factually** adv, **factualness** n, **factuality** n

faculty n **1a** an inherent capability, power, or function of the body ⟨the ~ of hearing⟩ **b** a natural aptitude; a talent ⟨has a ~ for saying the right things⟩ **2** a group of related subject departments in a university **3** sing or pl in constr the members of a profession **4** (conferred) power or prerogative

fad n **1** a usu short-lived but enthusiastically pursued practice or interest; a craze **2** an idiosyncratic taste or habit ⟨cats that have ~s about food⟩ – **faddish** adj, **faddishness** n, **faddism** n, **faddist** n, **faddy** adj

¹fade vi **1** to lose freshness or vigour; wither **2** of a brake to lose braking power gradually, esp owing to prolonged use **3** to lose freshness or brilliance of colour **4** to disappear gradually; vanish – often + away ⟨the smile ~d from his face⟩ **5** to change gradually in loudness, strength, or visibility – often used of electronic signals or sounds; usu + in or out ~ vt to cause to fade

²fade n an effect consisting of a fade-out or a fade-in or a combination of both

fade-in n the gradual appearance of a sound or picture, usu in broadcasting or on film

fade-out n the gradual disappearance of esp a sound or picture, usu in broadcasting or on film

faeces, NAm chiefly **feces** n pl bodily waste discharged through the anus – **faecal** adj

faerie also **faery** n **1** fairyland **2** a fairy USE poetic – **faery** adj

¹fag vi **-gg- 1** to act as a fag, esp in a British public school **2** to work hard; toil – infml

²fag n **1** a British public-school pupil who acts as servant to an older schoolmate **2** chiefly Br a tiring or boring task ⟨it's a real ~⟩ – infml

³fag n a cigarette – infml

⁴fag n, chiefly NAm FAGGOT 2

fag end n **1** a poor or worn-out end; a remnant **2** the extreme end ⟨the ~ of one quarrel – William Golding⟩ USE infml

fagged out adj tired, exhausted – infml

¹faggot n **1** NAm chiefly **fagot** **a** a bundle: e g (1) a bundle of sticks (2) a bundle of pieces of wrought iron to be shaped by hammering or rolling at high temperature (3) a bunch of herbs tied together; BOUQUET GARNI **b** a round mass of minced meat (e g pig's liver) mixed with herbs and usu breadcrumbs **2** chiefly NAm a usu male homosexual – derog

²faggot, NAm chiefly **fagot** vt **1** to make a faggot of; bind together into a bundle ⟨~ed sticks⟩ **2** to ornament with faggoting

Fahrenheit adj relating to, conforming to, or being a scale of temperature on which water freezes at 32° and boils at 212° under standard conditions

faience, faïence n tin-glazed decorated earthenware

¹fail vi **1a** to lose strength; weaken ⟨her health was ~ing⟩ **b** to fade or die away ⟨until the light ~s⟩ **c** to stop functioning **2a** to fall short ⟨~ed in his duty⟩ **b** to be or become absent or inadequate ⟨the water supply ~ed⟩ **c** to be unsuccessful (e g in passing a test) **d** to become bankrupt or insolvent ~ vt **1a** to disappoint the expectations or trust of ⟨his friends ~ed him⟩ **b** to prove inadequate for or incapable of carrying out an expected service or function for ⟨for once his wit ~ed him⟩ **2** to be deficient in; lack **3** to leave undone; neglect **4a** to be unsuccessful in passing (e g a test) **b** to grade (e g a student) as not passing – **failingly** adv

²fail n **1** failure – chiefly in without fail **2** an examination failure

¹failing n a usu slight or insignificant defect in character; broadly a fault, imperfection

²failing prep in absence or default of ⟨~ specific instructions, use your own judgment⟩

failsafe adj designed so as to counteract automatically the effect of an anticipated possible source of failure

failure n **1a** nonoccurrence or nonperformance; specif a failing to perform a duty or expected action **b** inability to perform a normal function ⟨heart ~⟩ **2** lack of success **3a** a falling short; a deficiency ⟨a ~ in the supply of raw materials⟩ **b** deterioration, decay **4** sby or sthg unsuccessful

fain adv, archaic **1** with pleasure **2** rather

¹faint adj **1** cowardly, timid – chiefly in faint heart **2** weak, dizzy, and likely to faint ⟨felt ~⟩ **3** performed, offered, or accomplished weakly or languidly; feeble ⟨made a ~ attempt at a smile⟩ **4** lacking distinctness; esp dim ⟨a ~ light⟩ – **faintly** adv, **faintness** n

²faint vi to lose consciousness because of a temporary decrease in the blood supply to the brain (e g through exhaustion or shock)

³faint n (a condition of) fainting

fainthearted adj lacking courage or resolution; timid – **faintheartedly** adv, **faintheartedness** n

¹fair adj **1** attractive, beautiful **2** superficially pleasing; specious ⟨she trusted his ~ promises⟩ **3** clean, clear ⟨a ~ copy⟩ **4** not stormy or foul; fine ⟨~ weather⟩ **5a** free from self-interest or prejudice; honest **b** conforming with the established rules; allowed ⟨a ~ tackle⟩ **6** favourable to a ship's course ⟨a ~ wind⟩ **7** light in colour; blond **8** moderately good or large; adequate ⟨a ~ understanding of the work⟩ **9** real, perfect – infml ⟨a ~ treat to watch him – New Republic⟩; compare FAIR AND SQUARE – **fairness** n – **in a fair way to** likely to

²fair adv fairly

³fair vi , of the weather to clear ~ vt to join so that the external surfaces blend smoothly

¹**air** *n* **1** a periodic gathering of buyers and sellers at a particular place and time for trade or a competitive exhibition, usu accompanied by entertainment and amusements **2a** *Br* FUN FAIR **b** an exhibition usu designed to acquaint prospective buyers or the general public with a product **3** a sale of a collection of articles usu for a charitable purpose

¹**air and square** *adv* **1** in an honest manner ⟨won the match ∼⟩ **2** exactly, directly ⟨hit him ∼ on the nose⟩ – **fair and square** *adj*

¹**air game** *n* sby or sthg open to legitimate pursuit, attack, or ridicule ⟨he was ∼ for our criticism⟩

¹**airground** *n* an area where outdoor fairs, circuses, or exhibitions are held

¹**airly** *adv* **1** completely, quite ⟨∼ bursting with pride⟩ **2a** in a proper or legal manner ⟨∼ priced stocks⟩ **b** impartially, honestly ⟨a story told ∼ and objectively⟩ **3** to a full degree or extent; plainly, distinctly ⟨had ∼ caught sight of him⟩ **4** for the most part; quite ⟨a ∼ easy job⟩

¹**air play** *n* equitable or impartial treatment; justice

¹**airway** *n* **1** a navigable channel in a river, bay, or harbour **2** the mowed part of a golf course between a tee and a green

¹**air-weather** *adj* present or loyal only in untroubled times – chiefly in *fair-weather friend*

¹**airy** *n* **1** a small mythical being having magic powers and usu human form **2** an effeminate male (homosexual) – derog – **fairy** *adj*, **fairylike** *adj*

fairyland *n* **1** the land of fairies **2** a place of magical charm

fairy lights *n pl, chiefly Br* small coloured electric lights for decoration, esp outdoors or on a Christmas tree

fairy-tale *adj* marked by **a** an unusual grace or beauty **b** apparently magical success or good fortune ⟨a ∼ start to his career⟩

fairy tale *n* **1** a story which features supernatural or imaginary forces and beings **2** a made-up story, usu designed to mislead; a fabrication

fait accompli *n, pl* **faits accomplis** sthg already accomplished and considered irreversible

faith *n* **1a** allegiance to duty or a person; loyalty – chiefly in *good/ bad faith* **b** fidelity to one's promises – chiefly in *keep/ break faith* **2a** belief and trust in and loyalty to God or the doctrines of a religion **b(1)** firm belief in sthg for which there is no objective proof **(2)** complete confidence **3** sthg believed with strong conviction; *esp* a system of religious beliefs

¹**faithful** *adj* **1** showing faith; loyal, steadfast; *specif* loyal to one's spouse in having no sexual relations outside marriage **2** firm in adherence to promises or in observance of duty; conscientious **3** true to the facts or to an original; accurate ⟨the portrait is a ∼ likeness⟩ – **faithfully** *adv*, **faithfulness** *n*

²**faithful** *n pl* **1** *the* full church members **2** *the* body of adherents of a religion (e g Islam) **3** faithful, faithfuls loyal followers or members ⟨party ∼s⟩

faith healing *n* a practice of attempting the cure of illnesses by prayer rather than medical techniques – **faith healer** *n*

faithless *adj* **1a** lacking faith, esp religious faith **b** heedless of duty or allegiance; disloyal **2** that may not be relied on; untrustworthy ⟨a ∼ friend⟩ – **faithlessly** *adv*, **faithlessness** *n*

¹**fake** *vt* to coil in fakes

²**fake** *n* any of the loops of a coiled rope or cable

³**fake** *vt* **1** to alter or treat so as to impart a false character or appearance; falsify ⟨∼d all the results to suit his theories⟩ **2a** to counterfeit, simulate **b** to feign ⟨∼d a nervous breakdown – Michael Billington⟩ ∼*vi* **1** to

engage in faking sthg; pretend **2** *NAm* to dummy – **faker** *n*, **fakery** *n*

⁴**fake** *n* **1** a worthless imitation passed off as genuine **2** an impostor, charlatan

⁵**fake** *adj* counterfeit, phoney

fakir *n* **1** a Muslim mendicant **2** an itinerant Hindu ascetic holy man

falcon *n* **1** any of various hawks distinguished by long wings **2** ¹HAWK 1

falconer *n* one who hunts with hawks or who breeds or trains hawks for hunting

falconry *n* the art of training or the sport of using falcons to pursue game

¹**fall** *vi* **fell; fallen 1a** to descend freely by the force of gravity **b** to hang freely ⟨her hair ∼s over her shoulders⟩ **c** to come as if by descending ⟨a hush fell on the audience⟩ **2a** to become less or lower in degree, level, pitch, or volume ⟨their voices fell to a whisper⟩ **b** to be uttered; issue ⟨let ∼ a remark⟩ **c** to look down ⟨her glance fell on me⟩ **3a** to come down from an erect to a usu prostrate position suddenly and esp involuntarily ⟨slipped and fell on the ice⟩ **b** to enter an undesirable state, esp unavoidably or unwittingly; stumble, stray ⟨fell into error⟩ ⟨fell ill⟩ **c** to drop because wounded or dead; *esp* to die in battle – euph **d** to suffer military capture ⟨after a long siege the city fell⟩ **e** to lose office ⟨the government fell⟩ **f** to suffer ruin or defeat ⟨we must stand or ∼ together⟩ **4a** to yield to temptation; sin **b** *of a woman* to lose one's virginity, esp outside marriage **5a** to move or extend in a downward direction – often + *off* or *away* ⟨the land ∼s away to the east⟩ **b** to decline in quality or quantity; abate, subside – often + *off* or *away* ⟨production fell off because of the strike⟩ **c** to assume a look of disappointment or dismay ⟨his face fell⟩ **d** to decline in financial value ⟨shares fell sharply today⟩ **6a** to occur at a specified time or place ⟨the accent ∼s on the second syllable⟩ ⟨Christmas ∼s on a Thursday this year⟩ **b** to come (as if) by chance – + *in* or *into* **c** to come or pass by lot, assignment, or inheritance; devolve – usu + *on, to,* or *upon* ⟨it fell to me to break the news⟩ **7** to come within the limits, scope, or jurisdiction of sthg ⟨∼s within our borders⟩ **8** to pass, esp involuntarily and suddenly, into a new state or condition ⟨∼ in love⟩ ⟨the book fell apart⟩ **b** to begin heartily or actively – usu + *to* ⟨fell to work⟩ – **fall behind** DROP BEHIND – **fall between two stools** to fail because of inability to choose between or reconcile **2** alternative or conflicting courses of action – **fall flat** to produce no response or result ⟨the joke fell flat⟩ – **fall for 1** to fall in love with **2** to be deceived by ⟨he fell for the trick⟩ – **fall foul of** to arouse aversion in; clash with – **fall on/upon 1** to descend upon; attack ⟨fell hungrily on the pie⟩ **2** to meet with ⟨he fell on hard times⟩ **3** to hit on – **fall over oneself** to display almost excessive eagerness – **fall short** to fail to attain a goal or target

²**fall** *n* **1** the act of falling by the force of gravity **2a** a falling out, off, or away; a dropping ⟨a ∼ of snow⟩ **b** sthg or a quantity that falls or has fallen ⟨a ∼ of rock⟩ **c** the quantity born – used esp with reference to lambs **3** a rope or chain for a hoisting tackle **4a** a loss of greatness or power; a collapse ⟨the ∼ of the Roman Empire⟩ **b** the surrender or capture of a besieged place ⟨the ∼ of Troy⟩ **c** *often cap* mankind's loss of innocence through the disobedience of Adam and Eve **5a** a downward slope – in CATARACT **2a** – usu pl with sing. meaning but sing. or pl in constr **6** a decrease in size, quantity, degree, or value **7** the distance which sthg falls **8a** an act of forcing a wrestler's shoulders to the mat for a prescribed time **b** a bout of wrestling **9** *chiefly NAm* autumn

fall about *vi* to be convulsed (with laughter) – infml

fallacy n 1 deceptive appearance or nature; deception, delusiveness 2 a false idea ⟨*the popular ~ that scientists are illiterate*⟩ 3 an argument failing to satisfy the conditions of valid inference – **fallacious** adj, **fallaciously** adv, **fallaciousness** n

fall back vi to retreat, recede – **fallback** n – **fall back on/upon** to have recourse to ⟨*when facts were scarce he fell back on his imagination*⟩

fall down vi to fail to meet expectations or requirements; be inadequate ⟨*she fell down on the job*⟩ – infml

fall guy n 1 one who is easily cheated or tricked 2 a scapegoat USE infml

fallible adj capable of being or likely to be wrong – **fallibly** adv, **fallibility** n

fall in vi 1 to sink or collapse inwards ⟨*the roof fell in*⟩ 2 to take one's proper place in a military formation – **fall in with** to concur with ⟨*had to fall in with her wishes*⟩

falling star n a meteor when falling into the earth's atmosphere and producing a bright streak of light

falloff n a decline, esp in quantity or quality ⟨*a ~ in exports*⟩

fallopian tube n, often cap F either of the pair of tubes conducting the egg from the ovary to the uterus in mammals

fallout n 1a polluting particles, esp radioactive particles resulting from a nuclear explosion, descending through the atmosphere b descent of fallout through the atmosphere 2 secondary results or products ⟨*the war produced its own literary ~: a profusion of books – Newsweek*⟩

fall out vi 1 to have a disagreement; quarrel ⟨*they fell out with one another over money*⟩ 2 to leave one's place in the ranks of a military formation 3 to happen; COME ABOUT – fml or poetic ⟨*as it fell out upon a day*⟩

¹**fallow** adj light yellowish brown

²**fallow** n 1 (ploughed and harrowed) land that is allowed to lie idle during the growing season 2 (the period of) being fallow

³**fallow** vt to plough, harrow, etc (land) without seeding, esp so as to destroy weeds

⁴**fallow** adj 1 of land left unsown after ploughing 2 dormant, inactive – chiefly in to lie fallow – **fallowness** n

fallow deer n a small European deer with broad antlers and a pale yellow coat spotted with white in the summer

fall through vi to fail to be carried out

fall to vi to begin doing sthg (e g working or eating), esp vigorously – often imper

false adj 1 not genuine ⟨*~ documents*⟩ 2a intentionally untrue; lying ⟨*~ testimony*⟩ b adjusted or made so as to deceive ⟨*a suitcase with a ~ bottom*⟩ 3 not based on reality; untrue ⟨*~ premises*⟩⟨*a ~ sense of security*⟩ 4 disloyal, treacherous ⟨*a ~ friend*⟩ 5a fitting over a main part as strengthening, protection, or disguise b appearing forced or artificial; unconvincing 6 resembling or related to a more widely known kind ⟨*~ oats*⟩ 7 inaccurate in pitch or vowel length 8 imprudent, unwise ⟨*a ~ move*⟩ – **falsely** adv, **falseness** n, **falsity** n

false alarm n an occurrence that raises but fails to meet expectations

falsehood n 1 an untrue statement; a lie 2 absence of truth or accuracy; falsity 3 the practice of telling lies

false start n 1 an incorrect and esp illegally early start by a competitor in a race 2 an abortive beginning to an activity or course of action

falsetto n, pl **falsettos** (a singer who uses) an artificially high voice, specif an artificially produced male singing voice that extends above the range of the singer's full voice – **falsetto** adv

falsies n pl pads of foam rubber or other material worn to enlarge the apparent size of the breasts

falsify vt 1 to prove or declare false 2a to make false by fraudulent alteration ⟨*his accounts were falsified to conceal a theft*⟩ b to represent falsely; misrepresent – **falsifier** n, **falsification** n

falter vi 1 to walk or move unsteadily or hesitatingly; stumble 2 to speak brokenly or weakly; stammer 3a to hesitate in purpose or action; waver b to lose strength, purpose, or effectiveness; weaken ⟨*the business was ~ing*⟩ ~ vt to utter in a hesitant or broken manner – **falterer** n, **falteringly** adv

fame n 1 public estimation; reputation 2 popular acclaim; renown

famed adj well-known, famous

familial adj 1 (characteristic) of a family or its members 2 tending to occur in more members of a family than expected by chance alone ⟨*a ~ disorder*⟩

¹**familiar** n 1 an intimate associate; a companion 2 FAMILIAR SPIRIT

²**familiar** adj 1 closely acquainted; intimate ⟨*a subject I am ~ with*⟩ 2a casual, informal b too intimate and unrestrained; presumptuous 3 frequently seen or experienced; common – **familiarly** adv, **familiarness** n

familiarity n 1a absence of ceremony; informality b an unduly informal act or expression; an impropriety 2 close acquaintance with or knowledge of sthg

familiarize, -ise vt 1 to make known or familiar 2 to make well acquainted ⟨*~ yourselves with the rules*⟩ – **familiarization** n

familiar spirit n a spirit or demon that waits on an individual (e g a witch)

¹**family** n sing or pl in constr 1 a group of people united by their common convictions (e g of religion or philosophy); a fellowship, brotherhood 2 a group of people of common ancestry or deriving from a common stock 3 a group of people living under 1 roof; esp a set of 2 or more adults living together and rearing their children 4a a closely related series of elements or chemical compounds b a group of related languages descended from a single ancestral language 5 a category in the biological classification of living things ranking above a genus and below an order 6 a set of curves or surfaces whose equations differ only in certain constant terms

²**family** adj of or suitable for a family or all of its members ⟨*~ entertainment*⟩

family allowance n CHILD BENEFIT

family man n 1 a man with a wife and children dependent on him 2 a man of domestic habits

family planning n a system of achieving planned parenthood by contraception; BIRTH CONTROL

family tree n (a diagram of) a genealogy

famine n an extreme scarcity of food; broadly any great shortage

famish vt to cause to suffer severely from hunger – usu pass ⟨*I'm ~ed*⟩

famous adj 1 well-known 2 excellent, first-rate ⟨*~ weather for a walk*⟩ – infml; no longer in vogue – **famously** adv, **famousness** n

¹**fan** n 1 a device for winnowing grain 2 an instrument for producing a current of air: e g a a folding circular or semicircular device that consists of material (e g paper or silk) mounted on thin slats that is waved to and fro by hand to produce a cooling current of air b a device, usu a series of vanes radiating from a hub rotated by a motor, for producing a current of air – **fanlike** adj

²**fan** vb -nn- vt 1a to winnow (grain) b to eliminate (e g chaff) by winnowing 2 to move or impel (air) with a fan 3a to direct or blow a current of air on (as if) with a fan

b to stir up to activity as if by fanning a fire; stimulate ⟨*he was ~ning the mob's fury with an emotive speech*⟩ **4** to spread like a fan ⟨*~ned the pack of cards*⟩ **5** to fire (a revolver) by squeezing the trigger and striking the hammer to the rear with the free hand ~ *vi* **1** to move like a fan; flutter **2** to spread like a fan – often + *out* ⟨*tanks ~ning out across the plain*⟩

³fan *n* an enthusiastic supporter or admirer (e g of a sport, pursuit, or celebrity) ⟨*a football ~*⟩ ⟨*a Presley ~*⟩

fanatic *n or adj* (one who is) excessively and often uncritically enthusiastic, esp in religion or politics – **fanatical** *adj*, **fanatically** *adv*, **fanaticism** *n*, **fanaticize** *vt*

fan belt *n* an endless belt driving a cooling fan for a radiator

fancier *n* one who breeds or grows a usu specified animal or plant for points of excellence ⟨*a pigeon ~*⟩

fanciful *adj* **1** given to or guided by fancy or imagination rather than by reason and experience **2** existing in fancy only; imaginary **3** marked by fancy or whim; *specif* elaborate, contrived – **fancifully** *adv*, **fancifulness** *n*

¹fancy *n* **1** a liking based on whim rather than reason; an inclination ⟨*took a ~ to her*⟩ **2a** a notion, whim **b** a mental image or representation of sthg **3a** imagination, esp of a capricious or delusive sort **b** the power of mental conception and representation, used in artistic expression (e g by a poet) **4a** *sing or pl in constr* the group of fanciers or of devotees of a particular sport, esp boxing **b** sby or sthg considered likely to do well (e g in a race) – infml

²fancy *vt* **1** to believe without knowledge or evidence ⟨*I ~ I've seen you somewhere before*⟩ **2a** to have a fancy for; like, desire ⟨*I really ~ blond men*⟩ **b** to consider likely to do well ⟨*which horse do you ~?*⟩ **3** to form a conception of; imagine – often imper ⟨*just ~ that!*⟩ USE (2&3) infml – **fanciable** *adj*

³fancy *adj* **1** based on fancy or the imagination; whimsical **2a** not plain or ordinary ⟨*~ cakes*⟩; *esp* fine, quality **b** ornamental ⟨*~ goods*⟩ **c** of an animal or plant bred esp for bizarre or ornamental qualities **d** parti-coloured ⟨*~ carnations*⟩ **3** extravagant, exorbitant ⟨*~ prices*⟩ – infml

fancy dress *n* unusual or amusing dress (e g representing a historical or fictional character) worn for a party or other special occasion

fancy-free *adj* free to do what one wants, esp because not involved in a relationship – chiefly in *footloose and fancy-free*

fancy man *n* a woman's lover – derog; infml

fancy woman *n* **1** MISTRESS 4 – derog **2** a prostitute USE infml

fancywork *n* decorative needlework

fandango *n*, *pl* **fandangos** (music for) a lively Spanish dance, usu performed by a couple to the accompaniment of guitar and castanets

fanfare *n* **1** a flourish of trumpets **2** a showy outward display

fang *n* **1a** a tooth by which an animal's prey is seized and held or torn **b** any of the long hollow or grooved teeth of a venomous snake **2** the root of a tooth or any of the prongs into which a root divides **3** a projecting tooth or prong – **fanged** *adj*

fanlight *n* an esp semicircular window with radiating divisions over a door or window

fanny *n* **1** *Br* the female genitals – vulg **2** *NAm* the buttocks – infml

fantasia *n* a free instrumental or literary composition not in strict form (comprising familiar tunes)

fantastic *adj* **1a** unreal, imaginary **b** so extreme as to challenge belief; incredible; *specif* exceedingly large or great **2** marked by extravagant fantasy or eccentricity **3** – used as a generalized term of approval ⟨*looked ~ in his velvet jacket*⟩ – **fantastical** *adj*, **fantastically** *adv*, **fantasticalness** *n*, **fantasticality** *n*

¹fantasy *n* **1** unrestricted creative imagination; fancy **2a** a creation of the unrestricted imagination whether expressed or merely conceived (e g a fantastic design or idea) **b** a fantasia **c** imaginative fiction or drama characterized esp by strange, unrealistic, or grotesque elements **3** (the power or process of creating) a usu extravagant mental image or daydream

²fantasy *vb* to fantasize

¹far *adv* **farther, further; farthest, furthest** **1** to or at a considerable distance in space ⟨*wandered ~ into the woods*⟩ **2a** by a broad interval ⟨*the ~ distant future*⟩ **b** in total contrast – + *from* ⟨*~ from criticizing you, I'm delighted*⟩ **3** to or at an extent or degree ⟨*as ~ as I know*⟩ **4a** to or at a considerable distance or degree ⟨*a bright student will go ~*⟩ **b** MUCH 1c ⟨*~ too hot*⟩ ⟨*~ better methods*⟩ **5** to or at a considerable distance in time ⟨*worked ~ into the night*⟩ ⟨*parties are few and ~ between*⟩ – **by far** FAR AND AWAY – **far and away** by a considerable margin ⟨*was far and away the best team*⟩ – **how far** to what extent, degree, or distance ⟨*didn't know how far to trust him*⟩ – **so far 1** to a certain extent, degree, or distance ⟨*when the water rose so far, the villagers sought higher ground*⟩ **2** up to the present ⟨*has written only one novel so far*⟩

²far *adj* **farther, further; farthest, furthest** **1** remote in space, time, or degree ⟨*in the ~ distance*⟩ **2** long ⟨*a ~ journey*⟩ **3** being the more distant of 2 ⟨*the ~ side of the lake*⟩ **4** of a political position extreme ⟨*the ~ left*⟩

faraway *adj* **1** lying at a great distance; remote **2** dreamy, abstracted ⟨*a ~ look in her eyes*⟩

farce *n* **1** forcemeat **2** a comedy with an improbable plot that is concerned more with situation than characterization **3** the broad humour characteristic of farce **4** a ridiculous or meaningless situation or event – **farcical** *adj*, **farcically** *adv*, **farcicality** *n*

¹fare *vi* to get along; succeed, do ⟨*how did you ~ in your exam?*⟩

²fare *n* **1a** the price charged to transport sby **b** a paying passenger **2** food provided for a journey ⟨*good simple ~*⟩

¹farewell *interj* goodbye

²farewell *n* **1** a parting wish for good luck; a goodbye **2** an act of departure or leave-taking – **farewell** *adj*

³farewell *vt*, *NAm*, *Austr*, *& NZ* to bid farewell

farfetched *adj* not easily or naturally deduced; improbable ⟨*a ~ example*⟩ – **farfetchedness** *n*

far-flung *adj* **1** widely spread or distributed **2** remote ⟨*a ~ outpost of the Empire*⟩

far-gone *adj* in an advanced state, esp of sthg unpleasant (e g drunkenness or madness)

farina *n* **1** a starchy flour or fine meal of vegetable matter (e g cereal grains) used chiefly as a cereal or for making puddings **2** any of various powdery or mealy substances – **farinaceous** *adj*

¹farm *n* **1** an area of land devoted to growing crops or raising (domestic) animals **2** FISH FARM

²farm *vt* **1a** to collect and take the proceeds of (e g taxation or a business) on payment of a fixed sum **b** to give up the proceeds of (e g an estate or a business) to another on condition of receiving in return a fixed sum **2a** to cultivate or rear (crops or livestock) on a farm **b** to manage and cultivate (land) as farmland or as a farm **3** to attempt to receive (all the balls bowled) (e g so as to protect the other batsman from dismissal) ~ *vi* to engage in the production of crops or livestock

farmer n 1 sby who pays a fixed sum for some privilege or source of income 2 sby who cultivates land or crops or raises livestock

farmhand n a farm worker

farmhouse n a dwelling house on a farm

farm out vt 1 to turn over for performance or use, usu on contract 2 to put (e g children) into sby's care in return for a fee

farmyard n the area round or enclosed by farm buildings

far-off adj remote in time or space

far-out adj 1 extremely unconventional; weird ⟨~ clothes⟩ 2 – used as a generalized term of approval ⟨~, man!⟩ USE infml; no longer in vogue – **far-outness** n

farrago n, pl **farragoes** a confused collection; a hotch-potch

far-reaching adj having a wide range, influence, or effect

farrier n 1 a horse doctor 2 a blacksmith who shoes horses – **farriery** n

¹**farrow** vb to give birth to (pigs) – often + down

²**farrow** n (farrowing) a litter of pigs

farsighted adj 1a seeing or able to see to a great distance b having foresight or good judgment; sagacious 2 hypermetropic – **farsightedly** adv, **farsightedness** n

¹**fart** vi to expel wind from the anus – vulg

²**fart** n 1 an expulsion of intestinal wind 2 an unpleasant person USE vulg

¹**farther** adv 1 at or to a greater distance or more advanced point ⟨~ down the corridor⟩ 2 ¹FURTHER 3

²**farther** adj 1a more distant; remoter b FAR 3 ⟨the ~ side⟩ 2 ²FURTHER 2

¹**farthest** adj most distant in space or time

²**farthest** adv 1 to or at the greatest distance in space, time, or degree 2 by the greatest degree or extent; most

farthing n 1 (a coin representing) a former British money unit worth ¼ of an old penny 2 sthg of small value; a mite

fascia n, pl **fasciae, fascias** 1a a flat horizontal piece (e g of stone or board) under projecting eaves b a nameplate over the front of a shop 2 a broad well-defined band of colour 3 (a sheet of) connective tissue covering or binding together body structures 4 Br the dashboard of a motor car – **fascial** adj

fascinate vt 1 to transfix by an irresistible mental power ⟨believed that the serpent could ~ its prey⟩ 2 to attract strongly, esp by arousing interest; captivate ~ vi to be irresistibly attractive – **fascinator** n, **fascinatingly** adv, **fascination** n

fascism n 1 a political philosophy, movement, or regime that is usu hostile to socialism, exalts nation and race, and stands for a centralized government headed by a dictatorial leader, severe regimentation, and forcible suppression of opposition 2 brutal dictatorial control – **fascist** n or adj, often cap, **fascistic** adj, often cap

¹**fashion** n 1 the make or form of sthg 2 a manner, way ⟨the people assembled in an orderly ~⟩ 3a a prevailing and often short-lived custom or style b the prevailing style or custom, esp in dress c an affluent and fashionable life style ⟨women of ~⟩ – **after a fashion** in an approximate or rough way ⟨became an artist after a fashion⟩

²**fashion** vt 1 to give shape or form to, esp by using ingenuity; mould, construct 2 to mould into a particular character by influence or training; transform, adapt – **fashioner** n

-fashion comb form (n → adv) in the manner of a ⟨wore the scarf turban-fashion⟩

fashionable adj 1 conforming to the latest custom or

fashion 2 of the world of fashion; used or patronized by people of fashion ⟨~ shops⟩ – **fashionableness** n, **fashionably** adv

¹**fast** adj 1a firmly fixed or attached b tightly closed or shut 2 firm, steadfast – chiefly in fast friends **3a**(1) moving or able to move rapidly; swift (2) taking a comparatively short time (3) of a suburban train EXPRESS 3a (4) accomplished quickly (5) quick to learn b conducive to rapidity of play or action or quickness of motion ⟨a ~ pitch⟩ c indicating in advance of what is correct ⟨the clock was ~⟩ d having or being a high photographic speed ⟨~ film⟩ ⟨~ lens⟩ 4 of a colour permanently dyed; not liable to fade 5a dissipated, wild ⟨a very ~ set⟩ b esp of a woman FORWARD 3b; also promiscuous 6 resistant to change from destructive action, fading, etc – often in combination ⟨colourfast⟩ ⟨acid-fast bacteria⟩ 7 dishonest, shady; also acquired by dishonest means or with little effort – infml ⟨made a ~ buck⟩

²**fast** adv 1 in a firm or fixed manner 2 sound, deeply ⟨fell ~ asleep⟩ 3a in a rapid manner; quickly b in quick succession ⟨orders came in thick and ~⟩ 4 in a reckless or dissipated manner 5 ahead of a correct time or posted schedule

³**fast** vi to abstain from some or all foods or meals ~ vt to deprive of food ⟨the animals were ~ ed for 24 hours before the experiment⟩

⁴**fast** n an act or time of fasting

fasten vt 1 to attach or secure, esp by pinning, tying, or nailing 2 to fix or direct steadily ⟨~ed his eyes on the awful sight⟩ 3 to attach, impose on ⟨~ed the blame on me⟩ ~ vi to become fast or fixed – **fastener** n – **fasten on/upon/onto** 1 to take a firm grip or hold on 2 to focus attention on

fastening n a fastener

fastidious adj 1 excessively difficult to satisfy or please 2 showing or demanding great delicacy or care – **fastidiously** adv, **fastidiousness** n

fastness n 1a the quality of being fixed b colourfast quality 2 a fortified, secure, or remote place ⟨he spent the weekend in his mountain ~⟩

¹**fat** adj -tt- 1 having an unusually large amount of fat: a plump b obese c of a meat animal fattened for market 2a well filled out; thick, big ⟨a ~ volume of verse⟩ b prosperous, wealthy ⟨grew ~ on the war – Time⟩ 3 richly rewarding or profitable; substantial ⟨a ~ part in a new play⟩ 4 productive, fertile ⟨a ~ year for crops⟩ 5 practically nonexistent ⟨a ~ chance⟩ ⟨a ~ lot of good it did him⟩ – infml 6 foolish, thick ⟨get that idea out of your ~ head⟩ – infml – **fatly** adv, **fatness** n, **fattish** adj

²**fat** n 1 (animal tissue consisting chiefly of cells distended with) greasy or oily matter 2a any of numerous compounds of carbon, hydrogen, and oxygen that are a major class of energy-rich food and are soluble in organic solvents (e g ether) but not in water b a solid or semisolid fat as distinguished from an oil 3 the best or richest part ⟨the ~ of the land⟩ 4 excess ⟨we must trim the ~ off this budget⟩

³**fat** vt -tt- to fatten

fatal adj 1 fateful, decisive 2a of fate b like fate in proceeding according to a fixed sequence; inevitable 3a causing death b bringing ruin c productive of disagreeable or contrary results – infml ⟨it's ~ to offer him a drink⟩

fatalism n the belief that all events are predetermined and outside the control of human beings – **fatalist** n, **fatalistic** adj, **fatalistically** adv

fatality n 1 sthg established by fate 2a the quality or state of causing death or destruction b the quality or condition of being destined for disaster 3 FATE 1 4a death resulting from a disaster **b** one who experiences or is subject to a fatal outcome

fatally *adv* **1** in a fatal manner; *esp* mortally ⟨~ *wounded*⟩ **2** as is or was fatal

fat cat *n, chiefly NAm* a wealthy, privileged, and usu influential person; *esp* one who contributes to a political campaign fund

¹fate *n* **1** the power beyond human control that determines events; destiny **2a** a destiny apparently determined by fate **b** a disaster; *esp* death **3a** an outcome, end; *esp* one that is adverse and inevitable **b** the expected result of normal development ⟨*prospective ~ of embryonic cells*⟩

²fate *vt* to destine; *also* to doom – usu *pass* ⟨*the plan was ~d to fail*⟩

fateful *adj* **1** having a quality of ominous prophecy ⟨*a ~ remark*⟩ **2a** having momentous and often unpleasant consequences; decisive ⟨*the ~ decision to declare war*⟩ **b** deadly, catastrophic **3** controlled by fate; foreordained – **fatefully** *adv*, **fatefulness** *n*

Fates *n pl* the 3 goddesses of classical mythology who determine the course of human life

fathead *n* a slow-witted or stupid person; a fool – *infml* – **fatheaded** *adj*, **fatheadedly** *adv*, **fatheadedness** *n*

¹father *n* **1a** a male parent of a child; *also* SIRE **3 b** *cap* **(1)** GOD **1 (2)** the first person of the Trinity **2** a forefather **3a** a man who relates to another in a way suggesting the relationship of father and child, esp in receiving filial respect **b** *often cap* **(1)** an old man – used as a respectful form of address **(2)** sthg personified as an old man ⟨*Father Time*⟩ ⟨*Father Thames*⟩ **4** *often cap* an early Christian writer accepted by the church as authoritative **5a** sby who originates or institutes ⟨*the ~ of radio*⟩ **b** a source, origin **6** a priest of the regular clergy – used esp as a title in the Roman Catholic church **7** any of the leading men (e g of a city) – usu *pl* – **fatherhood** *n*, **fatherless** *adj*, **fatherly** *adj*

²father *vt* **1a** to beget **b** to give rise to; initiate **c** to accept responsibility for **2** to fix the paternity of *on*

Father Christmas *n, Br* an old man with a white beard and red suit believed by children to deliver their presents at Christmas time

father-in-law *n, pl* **fathers-in-law** the father of one's spouse

¹fathom *n* a unit of length equal to 6ft (about 1.83m) used esp for measuring the depth of water

²fathom *vt* **1** to measure by a sounding line **2** to penetrate and come to understand – often + *out* – **fathomable** *adj*

fathomless *adj* incapable of being fathomed – **fathomlessly** *adv*, **fathomlessness** *n*

¹fatigue *n* **1a** physical or nervous exhaustion **b** the temporary loss of power to respond induced in a sensory receptor or motor end organ by continued stimulation **2a** manual or menial military work **b** *pl* the uniform or work clothing worn on fatigue **3** the tendency of a material to break under repeated stress

²fatigue *vt* **1** to weary, exhaust **2** to induce a condition of fatigue in ~ *vi, esp of a metal* to suffer fatigue – **fatigable** *adj*, **fatigability** *n*, **fatiguingly** *adv*

³fatigue *adj* being part of fatigues ⟨*a ~ cap*⟩

fatten *vt* **1** to make fat, fleshy, or plump; *esp* to feed (e g a stock animal) for slaughter – often + *up* **2** to make fertile ~ *vi* to become fat – **fattener** *n*

¹fatty *adj* **1** containing (large amounts of) fat; *also* corpulent **2** GREASY **2** ⟨~ *food*⟩ **3** derived from or chemically related to fat – **fattiness** *n*

²fatty *n* a fat person or animal – *infml*

fatuous *adj* complacently or inanely foolish; idiotic – **fatuously** *adv*, **fatuousness** *n*, **fatuity** *n*

faucet *n, NAm* a tap

¹fault *n* **1a** a failing **b** an imperfection, defect ⟨*a ~ in the computer*⟩ **c** an action, esp a service that does not land in the prescribed area, which loses a rally in tennis, squash, etc **2a** a misdemeanour **b** a mistake **3** responsibility for wrongdoing or failure ⟨*the accident was the driver's ~*⟩ **4** a fracture in the earth's crust accompanied by displacement (e g of the strata) along the fracture line – **faultless** *adj*, **faultlessly** *adv*, **faultlessness** *n*, **faulty** *adj*, **faultily** *adv*, **faultiness** *n* – **at fault** in the wrong; liable for blame

²fault *vi* **1** to commit a fault; err **2** to produce a geological fault ~ *vt* **1** to find a fault in ⟨*can't ~ his logic*⟩ **2** to produce a geological fault in

faultfinding *adj* overinclined to criticize – **faultfinder** *n*, **faultfinding** *n*

fauna *n, pl* **faunas** *also* **faunae** the animals or animal life of a region, period, or special environment – **faunal** *adj*, **faunally** *adv*, **faunistic** *adj*

faux pas *n, pl* **faux pas** an esp social blunder

¹favour, NAm chiefly favor *n* **1a(1)** friendly regard shown towards another, esp by a superior **(2)** approving consideration or attention; approbation ⟨*looked with ~ on our project*⟩ **b** partiality, favouritism **c** popularity **2** (an act of) kindness beyond what is expected or due **3** a token of allegiance or love (e g a ribbon or badge), usu worn conspicuously **4** consent to sexual activities, esp given by a woman – usu *pl* with *sing. meaning*; *euph* ⟨*granted her ~s*⟩ – **in favour of 1** in agreement or sympathy with; on the side of **2** to the advantage of ⟨*John gave up his rights in the house* in favour of *his wife*⟩ **3** in order to choose; out of preference for ⟨*he refused a job in industry* in favour of *an academic appointment*⟩ – **in someone's favour 1** liked or esteemed by sby ⟨*doing extra work to get back in his boss's favour*⟩ **2** to sby's advantage ⟨*the odds were* in his favour⟩ – **out of favour** unpopular, disliked

²favour, NAm chiefly favor *vt* **1a** to regard or treat with favour **b** to do a favour or kindness for; oblige – usu + *by* or *with* ⟨*Wilson ~ed them with a kindly smile – The Listener*⟩ **2** to show partiality towards; prefer **3a** to give support or confirmation to; sustain ⟨*this evidence ~s my theory*⟩ **b** to afford advantages for success to; facilitate ⟨*good weather ~ed the outing*⟩ **4** to look like (e g a relation) ⟨*he ~s his father*⟩

favourable *adj* **1a** disposed to favour; partial **b** expressing or winning approval; *also* giving a result in one's favour ⟨*a ~ comparison*⟩ **2a** tending to promote; helpful, advantageous ⟨~ *wind*⟩ **b** successful – **favourably** *adv*

favoured *adj* **1** endowed with special advantages or gifts **2** having an appearance or features of a specified kind – usu in combination ⟨*an ill-favoured child*⟩ **3** receiving preferential treatment

¹favourite *n* **1** sby or sthg favoured or preferred above others; *specif* one unduly favoured, esp by a person in authority ⟨*teachers should not have ~s*⟩ **2** the competitor judged most likely to win, esp by a bookmaker

²favourite *adj* constituting a favourite

favouritism *n* the showing of unfair favour; partiality

¹fawn *vi* **1** *esp of a dog* to show affection **2** to court favour by acting in a servilely flattering manner USE usu + *on* or *upon* – **fawner** *n*, **fawningly** *adv*

²fawn *n* **1** a young (unweaned) deer **2** light greyish brown

fay *n* a fairy – *poetic*

faze *vt, chiefly NAm* to disturb the composure of; disconcert, daunt – *infml*

fealty *n* **1** fidelity to one's feudal lord **2** allegiance, faithfulness

¹fear *n* **1** (an instance of) an unpleasant often strong emotion caused by anticipation or awareness of (a specified) danger; *also* a state marked by this emotion ⟨*in ~ of their lives*⟩ **2** anxiety, solicitude **3** profound reverence and awe, esp towards God **4** reason for alarm; danger – **fearless** *adj*, **fearlessly** *adv*, **fearlessness** *n* – **for fear of** because of anxiety about; IN CASE OF ⟨*for fear of losing electoral support*⟩

²fear *vt* **1** to have a reverential awe of ⟨*~ God*⟩ **2** to be afraid of; consider or expect with alarm *~ vi* to be afraid or apprehensive – **fearer** *n*

fearful *adj* **1** causing or likely to cause fear **2a** full of fear ⟨*~ of reprisals*⟩ **b** showing or arising from fear ⟨*a ~ glance*⟩ **c** timid, timorous ⟨*a ~ child*⟩ **3** extremely bad, large, or intense ⟨*a ~ waste*⟩ – infml – **fearfully** *adv*, **fearfulness** *n*

fearsome *adj* FEARFUL 1, 2c – **fearsomely** *adv*, **fearsomeness** *n*

feasible *adj* **1** capable of being done or carried out ⟨*a ~ plan*⟩ **2** capable of being used or dealt with successfully; suitable ⟨*our ~ sources of energy are limited*⟩ **3** reasonable, likely – **feasibleness** *n*, **feasibly** *adv*, **feasibility** *n*

¹feast *n* **1a** an elaborate often public meal, sometimes accompanied by a ceremony or entertainment; a banquet **b** sth that gives abundant pleasure ⟨*a ~ for the eyes*⟩ **2** a periodic religious observance commemorating an event or honouring a deity, person, or thing

²feast *vi* to have or take part in a feast *~ vt* **1** to give a feast for **2** to delight, gratify ⟨*~ your eyes on her beauty*⟩ – **feaster** *n*

feat *n* **1** a notable and esp courageous act or deed **2** an act or product of skill, endurance, or ingenuity

¹feather *n* **1a** any of the light horny outgrowths that form the external covering of a bird's body and consist of a shaft that bears 2 sets of barbs that interlock to form a continuous vane **b** the vane of an arrow **2** plumage **3** the act of feathering an oar – **feathered** *adj*, **feathery** *adj* –**a feather in one's cap** a deserved honour or mark of distinction in which one can take pride

²feather *vt* **1a** to fit (e g an arrow) with feathers **b** to cover, clothe, or adorn with feathers **2a** to turn (an oar blade) almost horizontal when lifting from the water **b** to change the angle at which (a propeller blade) meets the air so as to have the minimum wind resistance; *also* to feather the propeller blades attached to (a propeller or engine) **3** to reduce the edge of to a featheredge **4** to cut (e g air) (as if) with a wing *~ vi* **1** *of ink or a printed impression* to soak in and spread; blur **2** to feather an oar or an aircraft propeller blade – **feather one's nest** to provide for oneself, esp dishonestly, through a job in which one is trusted

featherbed *vt* **-dd-** **1** to cushion or protect from hardship, worry, etc; to pamper **2** to assist (e g an industry) with government subsidies

feather bed *n* (a bed with) a feather mattress

featherbrain *n* a foolish scatterbrained person – **featherbrained** *adj*

featherweight *n* **1** a boxer who weighs not more than 9st (57.2kg) if professional or more than 54kg (about 8st 7lb) but not more than 57kg (about 8st 13lb) if amateur **2** sby or sthg of limited importance or effectiveness

¹feature *n* **1a** the make-up or appearance of the face or its parts ⟨*gentle of ~*⟩ **b** a part of the face ⟨*her nose was not her best ~*⟩; *also*, *pl* the face ⟨*an embarrassed look on his ~s*⟩ **2** a prominent or distinctive part or characteristic **3a** a full-length film; *esp* the main film on a cinema programme **b** a distinctive article, story, or special section in a newspaper or magazine **c** *Br* a radio documentary, often one about cultural rather than political matters – **featureless** *adj*

²feature *vt* **1** to give special prominence to (e g in a performance or newspaper) **2** to have as a characteristic or feature *~ vi* to play an important part; be a feature – usu + *in*

febrile *adj* of fever; feverish

February *n* the 2nd month of the Gregorian calendar

feces *n pl*, *NAm* faeces – **fecal** *adj*

feckless *adj* **1** ineffectual, weak **2** worthless, irresponsible – **fecklessly** *adv*, **fecklessness** *n*

fecund *adj* **1** fruitful in offspring or vegetation; prolific **2** very intellectually productive or inventive to a marked degree *USE* fml – **fecundity** *n*

¹fed *past of* FEED

²fed *n*, *often cap*, *NAm* a federal agent or officer – infml

federal *adj* **1a** formed by agreement between political units that surrender their individual sovereignty to a central authority but retain limited powers of government; *also* of or constituting a government so formed **b** of the central government of a federation as distinguished from those of the constituent units **2** of or loyal to the federal government of the USA in the American Civil War – **federally** *adv*

Federal *n* a supporter or soldier of the North in the American Civil War

federalism *n*, *often cap* (advocacy of) the federal principle

federate *vt* to join in a federation – **federative** *adj*

federation *n* **1** federating; *esp* the formation of a federal union **2** sthg formed by federating: e g **a** a country formed by the federation of separate states **b** a union of organizations

fed up *adj* discontented, bored ⟨*~ with the 9-to-5 day*⟩ – infml

¹fee *n* **1a** an estate in land held in feudal law from a lord **b** an inherited or heritable estate in land **2a(1)** a sum of money paid esp for entrance or for a professional service – often pl with sing. meaning **(2)** money paid for education – usu pl with sing. meaning **b** a gratuity – **in fee** in absolute and legal possession

²fee *vt* **1** to give a fee to **2** *chiefly Scot* to hire for a fee

feeble *adj* **1** lacking in strength or endurance; weak ⟨*a ~ old man*⟩ **2** deficient in authority, force, or effect ⟨*a ~ joke*⟩ ⟨*a ~ excuse*⟩ – **feebleness** *n*, **feeblish** *adj*, **feebly** *adv*

feebleminded *adj* **1** mentally deficient **2** foolish, stupid – **feeblemindedly** *adv*, **feeblemindedness** *n*

¹feed *vb* fed *vt* **1a** to give food to **b** to give as food **2** to provide sthg essential to the growth, sustenance, maintenance, or operation of **3** to produce or provide food for **4a** to satisfy, gratify **b** to support, encourage **5a(1)** to supply for use, consumption, or processing, esp in a continuous manner ⟨fed *the tape into the machine*⟩ **(2)** to supply material to (e g a machine), esp in a continuous manner **b** to supply (a signal or power) to an electronic circuit **6** to act as a feed for **7** to pass or throw a ball or puck to (a teammate) *~ vi* **1a** to consume food; eat **b** to prey **2** to become nourished or satisfied as if by food **3** to be moved into a machine or opening for use, processing, or storage ⟨*the grain* fed *into the silo*⟩ *USE* (*vi 1*) usu + *off*, *on*, or *upon*

²feed *n* **1** an act of eating **2a** (a mixture or preparation of) food for livestock **b** the amount given at each feeding **3a** material supplied (e g to a furnace) **b** a mechanism by which the action of feeding is effected **4** one who supplies cues for another esp comic performer's lines or actions **5** an esp large meal – infml

feedback *n* **1** the return to the input of a part of the output of a machine, system, or process **2** (the return to a source of) information about the results of an action or process, usu in response to a request

feeder n **1** a device or apparatus for supplying food (e g to a caged animal) **2a** a device feeding material into or through a machine **b** a heavy wire conductor supplying electricity to a point of an electric distribution system **c** a transmission line running from a radio transmitter to an antenna **d** a road, railway, airline, or aircraft that links remote areas with the main transport system **3** an animal being fattened or suitable for fattening

feeding bottle n a bottle with a teat, designed to hold milk and used for feeding babies

feed up vt to fatten by plentiful feeding

¹**feel** vb felt vt **1a** to handle or touch in order to examine or explore **b** to perceive by a physical sensation coming from discrete end organs (e g of the skin or muscles) ⟨~ a draught⟩ **2** to experience actively or passively; be affected by ⟨he shall ~ my wrath⟩ ⟨try to ~ the music⟩ **3** to ascertain or explore by cautious trial ⟨~ing their way⟩ – often + out ⟨felt out the opposition⟩ **4a** to be aware of by instinct or by drawing conclusions from the evidence available ⟨felt the presence of a stranger in the room⟩ **b** to believe, think ⟨is generally felt that such action is inadvisable⟩ ~ vi **1a** to (be able) to receive the sensation of touch **b** to search for sthg by using the sense of touch **2a** to be conscious of an inward impression, state of mind, or physical condition ⟨~s much better now⟩ **b** to believe oneself to be ⟨I did ~ a fool⟩ **3** to have sympathy or pity ⟨really ~s for the underprivileged⟩ – **feel like 1** to resemble or seem to be on the evidence of touch ⟨it feels like velvet⟩ **2** to wish for; be in the mood for ⟨do you feel like a drink?⟩

²**feel** n **1** the sense of feeling; touch **2** sensation, feeling **3a** the quality of a thing as imparted through touch ⟨the material had a velvety ~⟩ **b** typical or peculiar quality or atmosphere ⟨the ~ of an old country pub⟩ **4** intuitive skill, knowledge, or ability – usu + for ⟨a ~ for words⟩

feeler n **1** a tactile appendage (e g a tentacle) of an animal **2** sthg (e g a proposal) ventured to ascertain the views of others

¹**feeling** n **1a** (a sensation experienced through) the one of the 5 basic physical senses by which stimuli, esp to the skin and mucous membranes, are interpreted by the brain as touch, pressure, and temperature **b** generalized bodily consciousness, sensation, or awareness ⟨experienced a ~ of safety⟩ ⟨a good ~⟩ **2a** an emotional state or reaction ⟨a ~ of loneliness⟩ **b** pl susceptibility to impression; sensibility ⟨the remark hurt her ~s⟩ **3** a conscious recognition; a sense ⟨the harsh sentence left him with a ~ of injustice⟩ **4a** an opinion or belief, esp when unreasoned; a sentiment ⟨what are your ~s on the matter?⟩ **b** a presentiment ⟨I've a ~ he won't come⟩ **5** capacity to respond emotionally, esp with the higher emotions ⟨a man of noble ~⟩ **6** FEEL 3, 4 **7** the quality of a work of art that embodies and conveys the emotion of the artist

²**feeling** adj **1a** having the capacity to feel or respond emotionally; sensitive **b** easily moved emotionally; sympathetic **2** expressing emotion or sensitivity – **feelingly** adv

feet pl of ¹FOOT

feign vt to give a false appearance or impression of deliberately ⟨~ death⟩; also to pretend ~ vi to pretend, dissemble – **feigner** n

¹**feint** n sthg feigned; specif a mock blow or attack directed away from the point one really intends to attack

²**feint** vi to make a feint ~ vt to make a pretence of ⟨he ~ed an attack and continued on his way⟩

³**feint** adj, of rulings on paper faint, pale

feldspar, felspar n any of a group of minerals that consist of aluminium silicates with either potassium, sodium, calcium, or barium, and are an essential constituent of nearly all crystalline rocks

felicitate vt to offer congratulations or compliments to – usu + on or upon; fml – **felicitator** n, **felicitation** n

felicitous adj **1** very well suited or expressed; apt ⟨a ~ remark⟩; also marked by or given to such expression ⟨a ~ speaker⟩ **2** pleasant, delightful USE fml – **felicitously** adv, **felicitousness** n

felicity n **1** (sthg causing) great happiness **2** a felicitous faculty or quality, esp in art or language; aptness **3** a felicitous expression USE fml

feline adj **1** of cats or the cat family **2** resembling a cat; having the characteristics generally attributed to cats, esp grace, stealth, or slyness – **feline** n, **felinely** adv, **felinity** n

¹**fell** vt **1** to cut, beat, or knock down ⟨~ing trees⟩ **2** to kill – **fellable** adj, **feller** n

²**fell** past of FALL

³**fell** n a steep rugged stretch of high moorland, esp in northern England and Scotland – often pl with sing. meaning

⁴**fell** adj **1** fierce, cruel **2** very destructive; deadly USE poetic – **fellness** n, **felly** adv – **at one fell swoop** all at once; also with a single concentrated effort

fellah n, pl **fellahin, fellaheen** a peasant or agricultural labourer in an Arab country

fellatio n oral stimulation of the penis – **fellate** vt, **fellation** n, **fellator** n

¹**fellow** n **1** a comrade, associate – usu pl **2a** an equal in rank, power, or character; a peer **b** either of a pair; a mate **3** a member of an incorporated literary or scientific society **4** a man; also a boy **5** an incorporated member of a collegiate foundation **6** a person appointed to a salaried position allowing for advanced research **7** a boyfriend – infml

²**fellow** adj being a companion or associate; belonging to the same group – used before a noun ⟨~ traveller⟩

fellow feeling n a feeling of community of interest or of mutual understanding; specif sympathy

fellowship n **1** the condition of friendly relations between people; companionship **2a** community of interest, activity, feeling, or experience **b** the state of being a fellow or associate **3** sing or pl in constr a group of people with similar interests; an association **4a** the position of a fellow (e g of a university) **b** (a foundation for the provision of) the salary of a fellow

fellow traveller n a nonmember who sympathizes with and often furthers the ideals and programme of an organized group, esp the Communist party – chiefly derog

felon n **1** sby who has committed a felony **2** a whitlow

felony n a grave crime (e g murder or arson) that was formerly regarded in law as more serious than a misdemeanour and involved forfeiture of property in addition to any other punishment – **felonious** adj, **feloniously** adv

felspar n feldspar

¹**felt** n **1** a nonwoven cloth made by compressing wool or fur often mixed with natural or synthetic fibres **2** an article made of felt **3** a material resembling felt

²**felt** vt **1** to make into or cover with felt **2** to cause to stick and mat together

³**felt** past of FEEL

felucca n a narrow lateen-rigged sailing ship, chiefly of the Mediterranean area

¹**female** n **1** an individual that bears young or produces

eggs; *esp* a woman or girl as distinguished from a man or boy **2** a plant or flower with an ovary but no stamens

²female *adj* **1** of or being a female **2** designed with a hole or hollow into which a corresponding male part fits ⟨*a ~ plug*⟩ – **femaleness** *n*

¹feminine *adj* **1** of or being a female person **2** characteristic of, appropriate to, or peculiar to women; womanly **3** of or belonging to the gender that normally includes most words or grammatical forms referring to females **4a** having or occurring in an extra unstressed final syllable ⟨*~ rhyme*⟩ **b** having the final chord occurring on a weak beat – **femininely** *adv*, **feminineness** *n*, **femininity** *n*

²feminine *n* **1** the feminine principle in human nature – *esp* in *eternal feminine* **2** (a word or morpheme of) the feminine gender

feminism *n* the advocacy or furtherance of women's rights, interests, and equality with men in political, economic, and social spheres – **feminist** *n or adj*, **feministic** *adj*

femme fatale *n, pl* **femmes fatales** a seductive and usu mysterious woman; *esp* one who lures men into dangerous or compromising situations

femur *n, pl* **femurs, femora** **1** the bone of the hind or lower limb nearest the body; the thighbone **2** the third segment of an insect's leg counting from the base – **femoral** *adj*

fen *n* an area of low wet or flooded land

¹fence *n* **1** a barrier (e g of wire or boards) intended to prevent escape or intrusion or to mark a boundary ⟨*a garden ~*⟩ **2a** a receiver of stolen goods **b** a place where stolen goods are bought – **fenceless** *adj* – **on the fence** in a position of neutrality or indecision

²fence *vt* **1a** to enclose with a fence – usu + *in* **b** to separate *off* or keep *out* (as if) with a fence **2** to provide a defence for; shield, protect **3** to receive or sell (stolen goods) – *vi* **1a** to practise fencing **b(1)** to use tactics of attack and defence (e g thrusting and parrying) resembling those of fencing **(2)** *of a batsman* to play at and miss the ball in cricket, esp outside the off stump – usu + *at* **2** to deal in stolen goods – **fencer** *n*

fencing *n* **1** the art of attack and defence with a sword (e g the foil, épée, or sabre) **2** (material used for building) fences

fend *vi* – **fend for** to provide a livelihood for; support

fender *n* a device that protects: e g **a** a cushion (e g of rope or wood) hung over the side of a ship to absorb impact **b** a low metal guard for a fire used to confine the coals **c** *NAm* a wing or mudguard

fend off *vt* to keep or ward off; repel

fennel *n* a European plant of the carrot family cultivated for its aromatic seeds and foliage

feral *adj* **1** (suggestive) of a wild beast; savage **2a** not domesticated or cultivated; WILD 1a **b** having escaped from domestication and become wild ⟨*~ pigeons*⟩

¹ferment *vb* **1** to (cause to) undergo fermentation **2** to (cause to) be in a state of agitation or intense activity – **fermentable** *adj*, **fermenter** *n*

²ferment *n* **1** an agent (e g an enzyme or organism) capable of bringing about fermentation **2a** FERMENTATION 1 **b** a state of unrest or upheaval; agitation, tumult

fermentation *n* **1a** a chemical change with effervescence **b** an enzymatically controlled anaerobic breakdown of an energy-rich compound (e g a carbohydrate to carbon dioxide and alcohol); *broadly* an enzymatically controlled transformation of an organic compound **2** FERMENT 2b – **fermentative** *adj*

fern *n* any of a class of flowerless seedless lower plants; *esp* any of an order resembling flowering plants in having a

root, stem, and leaflike fronds but differing in reproducing by spores – **fernlike** *adj*, **ferny** *adj*

ferocious *adj* extremely fierce or violent – **ferociously** *adv*, **ferociousness** *n*

ferocity *n* the quality or state of being ferocious

¹ferret *n* **1** a partially domesticated usu albino European polecat used esp for hunting small rodents (e g rats) **2** an active and persistent searcher – **ferrety** *adj*

²ferret *vi* **1** to hunt with ferrets **2** to search *about* or *around* – *infml* ~ *vt* **1** to hunt (e g rats) with ferrets **2** to drive (game), esp from covert or burrows – **ferreter** *n*

ferret out *vt* to find and bring to light by searching ⟨*ferret out the answers*⟩ – *infml*

ferric *adj* of, containing, or being (trivalent) iron

ferro- *comb form* **1** (containing) iron ⟨*ferroconcrete*⟩; iron and ⟨*ferronickel*⟩ – chiefly in names of alloys **2** ferrous iron ⟨*ferrocyanide*⟩

ferrous *adj* of, containing, or being (bivalent) iron

ferrule *n* **1** a ring or cap, usu of metal, strengthening a cane, tool handle, etc **2** a short tube or bush for making a tight joint (e g between pipes)

¹ferry *vt* **1** to carry by boat over a body of water **2** to convey (e g by car) from one place to another ~ *vi* to cross water in a boat

²ferry *n* (a boat used at) a place where people or things are carried across a body of water (e g a river)

fertile *adj* **1a** (capable of) producing or bearing fruit (in great quantities); productive **b** characterized by great resourcefulness and activity; inventive ⟨*a ~ imagination*⟩ **2a(1)** capable of sustaining abundant plant growth ⟨*~ soil*⟩ **(2)** affording abundant possibilities for development ⟨*a ~ area for research*⟩ **b** capable of growing or developing ⟨*~ egg*⟩ **c** capable of breeding or reproducing **3** capable of being converted into fissile material – **fertilely** *adv*, **fertileness** *n*, **fertility** *n*

fertilize, -ise *vt* to make fertile: e g **a(1)** to inseminate, impregnate, or pollinate **(2)** to make (an ovule, egg, etc) capable of developing into a new individual by uniting with a male germ cell **b** to apply a fertilizer to ⟨*~ land*⟩ – **fertilizable** *adj*, **fertilization** *n*, **fertilizational** *adj*

fertilizer, -iser *n* a substance (e g manure) used to make soil more fertile

ferule *n* a flat ruler used to punish children

fervent *adj* exhibiting deep sincere emotion; ardent ⟨*a ~ believer in free speech*⟩ – **fervently** *adv*

fervid *adj* passionately intense; ardent – **fervidly** *adv*, **fervidness** *n*

fervour, *NAm chiefly* **fervor** *n* the quality or state of being fervent or fervid

festal *adj* festive – **festally** *adv*

fester *vi* **1** to generate pus **2** to putrefy, rot **3** to rankle ~ *vt* to make inflamed or corrupt

¹festival *adj* of, appropriate to, or set apart as a festival

²festival *n* **1a** a time marked by special (e g customary) celebration **b** FEAST 2 **2** a usu periodic programme or season of cultural events or entertainment ⟨*the Edinburgh ~*⟩ **3** gaiety, conviviality

festive *adj* **1** of or suitable for a feast or festival **2** joyous, gay – **festively** *adv*, **festiveness** *n*

festivity *n* **1** FESTIVAL 1 **2** festive activity – often pl with sing. meaning

¹festoon *n* a decorative chain or strip hanging between 2 points; *also* a carved, moulded, or painted ornament representing this

²festoon *vt* **1** to hang or form festoons on **2** to cover profusely and usu gaily

fetal *adj* foetal

¹fetch *vt* **1** to go or come after and bring or take back **2a** to cause to come; bring **b** to produce as profit or return;

realize **3** to reach by sailing, esp against the wind or tide and without having to tack **4** to strike or deal (a blow, slap, etc) ⟨~ed *him one in the face*⟩ – infml ~ *vi* **1** to go after sthg and bring it back **2** to take a roundabout way **3** to hold course on a body of water – **fetcher** *n*

²**fetch** *n* **1** the distance along open water or land over which the wind blows **2** the distance traversed by waves without obstruction

fetching *adj* attractive, becoming – **fetchingly** *adv*

fetch up *vt* **1** to bring up or out; produce **2** to bring to a stop **3** to vomit ~ *vi* to come to a specified standstill, stopping place, or result; arrive *USE* infml

¹**fete, fête** *n* **1** a festival **2** *Br* a usu outdoor bazaar or other entertainment held esp to raise money for a particular purpose

²**fete, fête** *vt* to honour or commemorate (sby or sthg) with a fete or other ceremony

fetid, foetid *adj* having a heavy offensive smell; stinking – **fetidly** *adv*, **fetidness** *n*

fetish *also* **fetich** *n* **1** an object believed among a primitive people to have magical power; *broadly* a material object regarded with superstitious trust or reverence **2** an object of irrational reverence or obsessive devotion **3** an object or bodily part whose presence in reality or fantasy is psychologically necessary for sexual gratification

fetishism *also* **fetichism** *n* **1** belief in magical fetishes **2** the displacement of erotic interest and satisfaction to a fetish – **fetishist** *n*, **fetishistic** *adj*

fetlock *n* **1** a projection bearing a tuft of hair on the back of the leg above the hoof of an animal of the horse family **2** the joint of the limb or tuft of hair at the fetlock

¹**fetter** *n* **1** a shackle for the feet **2** sthg that confines; a restraint – usu pl with sing. meaning

²**fetter** *vt* **1** to put fetters on **2** to bind (as if) with fetters; shackle, restrain

¹**fettle** *vt* **fettling 1** to line with fettling **2** to trim the rough joints or edges of (e g unfired pottery or a metal casting)

²**fettle** *n* a state of physical or mental fitness or order; condition ⟨*in fine* ~⟩

fetus *n* a foetus

feud *n* a lasting state of hostilities, esp between families or clans, marked by violent attacks for the purpose of revenge – **feud** *vi*

feudal *adj* of feudalism or a medieval fee; *also* suggestive of feudalism (e g in servility) – **feudally** *adv*, **feudalize** *vt*, **feudalization** *n*

feudalism *n* a medieval system of political organization involving the relationship of lord to vassal with all land held in fee, homage, the service of tenants under arms and in court, wardship, and forfeiture – **feudalist** *n*, **feudalistic** *adj*

feudatory *adj* **1** owing feudal allegiance **2** under a foreign overlord

¹**fever** *n* **1** (any of various diseases characterized by) a rise of body temperature above the normal **2a** a state of intense emotion or activity ⟨*in a* ~ *of impatience*⟩ **b** a contagious usu transient enthusiasm; a craze ⟨*football* ~ *raged throughout the world*⟩

²**fever** *vt* to throw into a fever; agitate

feverish *also* **feverous** *adj* **1a** having the symptoms of a fever **b** indicating, relating to, or caused by (a) fever **c** tending to cause or infect with fever **2** marked by intense emotion, activity, or instability – **feverishly** *adv*, **feverishness** *n*, **feverously** *adv*

fever pitch *n* a state of intense excitement and agitation ⟨*raised the crowd to* ~⟩

¹**few** *adj* **1** amounting to only a small number ⟨*one of his*

~ *pleasures*⟩ **2** at least some though not many – + *a* ⟨*a good* ~ *drinks*⟩ ⟨*caught a* ~ *more fish*⟩ – **fewness** *n*

²**few** *n pl in constr* **1** not many ⟨~ *were present*⟩ ⟨*all the* ~ *that remained*⟩ ⟨~ *of his stories were true*⟩ **2** at least some though not many – + *a* ⟨*a* ~ *of them*⟩ **3** a select or exclusive group of people; an elite ⟨*the* ~⟩

fey *adj* **1** able to see into the future **b** marked by an otherworldly and irresponsible air **2** *chiefly Scot* **a** fated to die; doomed **b** marked by an excited or elated state – **feyness** *n*

fez *n, pl* **-zz-** *also* **-z-** a brimless hat shaped like a truncated cone, usu red and with a tassel, which is worn by men in southern and eastern Mediterranean countries

fiancé, fem fiancée *n* sby engaged to be married

fiasco *n, pl* **fiascoes** a complete and ignominious failure

fiat *n* an authoritative and often arbitrary order; a decree ⟨*government by* ~⟩

fib *vi or n* **-bb-** (to tell) a trivial or childish lie – infml – **fibber** *n*

fibre, NAm *chiefly* **fiber** *n* **1a** an elongated tapering supportive thick-walled plant cell **b(1)** NERVE **2 (2)** any of the filaments composing most of the intercellular matrix of connective tissue **(3)** any of the elongated contractile cells of muscle tissue **c** a slender natural or man-made thread or filament (e g of wool, cotton, or asbestos) **2** material made of fibres **3** essential structure or character ⟨*the very* ~ *of his being*⟩; *also* strength, fortitude ⟨*a man of great moral* ~⟩

fibreboard *n* a material made by compressing fibres (e g of wood) into stiff boards

fibreglass *n* **1** glass in fibrous form used in making various products (e g textiles and insulation materials) **2** a combination of synthetic resins and fibreglass

fibrositis *n* a painful muscular condition prob resulting from inflammation of fibrous tissue (e g muscle sheaths)

fibrous *adj* **1a** containing, consisting of, or resembling fibres **b** characterized by fibrosis **c** capable of being separated into fibres ⟨*a* ~ *mineral*⟩ **2** tough, stringy – **fibrously** *adv*, **fibrousness** *n*

fibula *n, pl* **fibulae, fibulas 1** an ornamented clasp used esp by the ancient Greeks and Romans **2** the (smaller) outer of the 2 bones of the hind limb of higher vertebrates between the knee and ankle – **fibular** *adj*

fichu *n* a woman's light triangular scarf draped over the shoulders and fastened at the bosom

fickle *adj* lacking steadfastness or constancy; capricious – **fickleness** *n*

fiction *n* **1a** sthg invented by the imagination; *specif* an invented story ⟨*distinguish fact from* ~⟩ **b** literature (e g novels or short stories) describing imaginary people and events **2** an assumption of a possibility as a fact, irrespective of the question of its truth ⟨*a legal* ~⟩ **3** the action of feigning or creating with the imagination – **fictionist** *n*, **fictional** *adj*, **fictionally** *adv*, **fictionality** *n*, **fictionalize** *vt*, **fictionalization** *n*

fictitious *adj* **1** (characteristic) of fiction **2** *of a name* false, assumed **3** not genuinely felt; feigned – **fictitiously** *adv*, **fictitiousness** *n*

¹**fiddle** *n* **1** a violin **2** a device to keep objects from sliding off a table on board ship **3** fiddlesticks – used as an interjection; infml **4** *Br* a dishonest practice; a swindle – infml **5** *Br* an activity involving intricate manipulation ⟨*a bit of a* ~ *to get all these wires back in place*⟩ – infml

²**fiddle** *vb* **fiddling** *vi* **1** to play on a fiddle **2a** to move the hands or fingers restlessly **b** to spend time in aimless or fruitless activity – often + *about* or *around* ~ *vt* **1** *Br* to falsify (e g accounts), esp so as to gain financial advantage

2 *Br* to get or contrive by cheating or deception ⟨~d *an extra 10 pounds on his expenses*⟩ USE (*vi 2 & vt*) infml – **fiddler** *n* – **fiddle with** to tamper or meddle with – infml

fiddle-faddle *n* nonsense – often used as an interjection; infml

fiddlesticks /ˈfidlˌstiks/ *n pl* nonsense – used as an interjection; infml

fiddling *adj* trifling, petty ⟨made some ~ *excuse*⟩

fidelity *n* **1a** the quality or state of being faithful; loyalty **b** accuracy in details; exactness **2** the degree of similarity between some reproduced (e g recorded) material and its original source

¹fidget *n* **1** uneasiness or restlessness shown by nervous movements – usu pl with sing. meaning **2** sby who fidgets USE infml

²fidget *vb* to (cause to) move or act restlessly or nervously – **fidgety** *adj*

fie *interj, archaic* – used to express disgust or shock

fief *n* **1** a feudal estate **2** sthg over which one has rights or exercises control ⟨a *politician's* ~⟩ – **fiefdom** *n*

¹field *n* **1a** an (enclosed) area of land free of woods and buildings (used for cultivation or pasture) **b** an area of land containing a natural resource ⟨coal ~⟩ **c** (the place where) a battle is fought; *also* a battle **d** a large unbroken expanse (e g of ice) **2a** an area or division of an activity ⟨a *lawyer eminent in his* ~⟩ **b** the sphere of practical operation outside a place of work (e g a laboratory) ⟨geologists *working in the* ~⟩⟨~ *research*⟩ **c** an area in which troops are operating (e g in an exercise or theatre of war) **d**(1) an area constructed, equipped, or marked for sports (2) the part of a sports area enclosed by the running track and used for athletic field events **3** a space on which sthg is drawn or projected; *esp* the surface, esp a shield, on which a coat of arms is displayed **4** the participants in a sports activity, esp with the exception of the favourite or winner **5a** a set of mathematical elements that is closed under 2 binary operations, the second of which is distributive relative to the first, and that is a commutative group under the first operation and also under the second if the identity element under the first is omitted **b** a region in which a mathematical quantity (e g a scalar or vector) is associated with every point **c** a region or space·in which a given effect (e g magnetism) exists **6** *also* **field of view** the area visible through the lens of an optical instrument

²field *vt* **1a** to stop and pick up (a batted ball) **b** to deal with by giving an impromptu answer ⟨the Minister ~ed the reporters' questions⟩ **2** to put into the field of play or battle ⟨~ *a team*⟩ ~ *vi* to play as a fielder in cricket, baseball, etc

field day *n* **1a** a day for military exercises or manoeuvres **b** an outdoor meeting or social gathering **2** a time of unusual pleasure and unrestrained action ⟨the newspaper had a ~ *with the scandal*⟩

fielder *n* any of the players whose job is to field the ball (e g in cricket)

field event *n* an athletic event (e g discus, javelin, or jumping) other than a race

field glasses *n pl* an optical instrument usu consisting of 2 telescopes on a single frame with a focussing device

field hockey *n, chiefly NAm* HOCKEY 1

field marshal *n* an officer holding the highest rank in the British army

field mouse *n* any of various mice or voles that inhabit fields

field officer *n* a commissioned army officer of the rank of colonel, lieutenant colonel, or major

fieldwork *n* **1** a temporary fortification in the field **2** work done in the field (e g by students) to gain practical experience through firsthand observation **3** the gathering of data in anthropology, sociology, etc through the observation or interviewing of subjects in the field – **field-worker** *n*

fiend *n* **1a** DEVIL 1 **b** a demon **c** a person of great wickedness or cruelty **2** sby excessively devoted to a specified activity or thing; a fanatic, devotee ⟨a golf ~⟩⟨a fresh-air ~⟩ **3** one who uses immoderate quantities of sthg (specified); an addict ⟨a dope ~⟩ **4** sby remarkably clever at a specified activity; WIZARD 2 ⟨a ~ *at arithmetic*⟩ USE (2 & 4) infml

fiendish *adj* **1** perversely diabolical **2** extremely cruel or wicked **3** excessively bad, unpleasant, or difficult – **fiendishly** *adv*, **fiendishness** *n*

fierce *adj* **1** violently hostile or aggressive; combative, pugnacious **2a** lacking restraint or control; violent, heated ⟨a ~ *argument*⟩ **b** extremely intense or severe ⟨~ *pain*⟩ **3** furiously active or determined ⟨make a ~ *effort*⟩ **4** wild or menacing in appearance – **fiercely** *adv*, **fierceness** *n*

fiery *adj* **1a** consisting of fire **b** burning, blazing ⟨~ *cross*⟩ **c** liable to catch fire or explode ⟨make a ~ *chilli sauce*⟩ **3** of the colour of fire; *esp* red **4a** full of or exuding strong emotion or spirit; passionate ⟨a ~ *speech*⟩ **b** easily provoked; irascible ⟨a ~ *temper*⟩ **5** of a cricket pitch allowing the bowled ball to bounce dangerously high and fast – **fierily** *adv*, **fieriness** *n*

fiesta *n* a saint's day in Spain and Latin America, often celebrated with processions and dances

fife *n* a small flute used chiefly to accompany the drum

fifteen *n* **1** (the number) 15 **2** the fifteenth in a set or series **3** *sing or pl in constr* sthg having 15 parts or members or a denomination of 15; *esp* a Rugby Union football team – **fifteen** *adj or pron*, **fifteenth** *adj or n*

fifth *n* . **1** number five in a countable series **2a** (the combination of 2 notes at) a musical interval of 5 diatonic degrees **b** DOMINANT 2 – **fifth** *adj or adv*, **fifthly** *adv*

fifth column *n* a group within a nation or faction that sympathizes with and works secretly for an enemy or rival – **fifth columnist** *n*

fifty *n* **1** (the number) 50 **2** *pl* the numbers 50 to 59; *specif* a range of temperatures, ages, or dates within a century characterized by those numbers – **fiftieth** *adj or n*, **fifty** *adj or pron*, **fiftyfold** *adj or adv*

¹fifty-fifty *adv* evenly, equally ⟨they shared the money ~⟩

²fifty-fifty *adj* half favourable and half unfavourable; even ⟨a ~ *chance*⟩

¹fig *n* **1** (any of a genus of trees that bear) a many-seeded fleshy usu pear-shaped or oblong edible fruit **2** a contemptibly worthless trifle ⟨not worth a ~⟩

²fig *n* dress, array ⟨in full Regency ~ – The Listener⟩

¹fight *vb* fought *vi* **1a** to contend in battle or physical combat; *esp* to strive to overcome a person by blows or weapons **b** 'BOX **2** to strive, struggle ⟨~ing *for his life*⟩ ~ *vt* **1a**(1) to contend against (as if) in battle or physical combat (2) to engage in a boxing match with **b** to attempt to prevent the success, effectiveness, or development of ⟨the company fought *the strike for months*⟩ **2a** to wage ⟨~ *a war*⟩ **b** to take part in (a boxing match) **c** to stand as a candidate for (e g a constituency) in an election **3** to struggle to endure or surmount ⟨he fought *his illness for a year before he died*⟩ **4a** to make (one's way) by fighting **b** to resolve or control by fighting – + *out* or *down* ⟨fought down *her fear*⟩ – **fight shy of** to avoid facing or meeting

²fight *n* **1a** an act of fighting; a battle, combat **b** a boxing match **c** a verbal disagreement; an argument **2** a usu protracted struggle for an objective ⟨a ~ *for justice*⟩ **3**

strength or disposition for fighting; pugnacity ⟨*still full of* ~⟩

fight back *vi* to struggle to recover from a losing or disadvantageous position; resist – **fightback** *n*

fighter *n* **1a** a pugnacious or boldly determined individual **b** ¹BOXER **2** a fast manoeuvrable aeroplane designed to destroy enemy aircraft

fighting chance *n* a small chance that may be realized through struggle ⟨*a* ~ *of getting to the final*⟩

fight off *vt* to ward off (as if) by fighting; repel

fight out *vt* to settle (e g an argument) by fighting – esp in *fight it out*

figment *n* sthg fabricated or imagined ⟨*a* ~ *of the author's imagination*⟩

figurative *adj* **1a** representing by a figure or likeness; emblematic **b** representational ⟨~ *sculpture*⟩ **2** characterized by or using figures of speech, esp metaphor – **figuratively** *adv*, **figurativeness** *n*

¹**figure** *n* **1a** an (Arabic) number symbol ⟨*a salary running into 6* ~s⟩ **b** *pl* arithmetical calculations ⟨*good at* ~s⟩ **c** a written or printed character **d** value, esp as expressed in numbers ⟨*the house sold at a low* ~⟩ **2** bodily shape or form, esp of a person ⟨*a slender* ~⟩ **3a** the graphic representation of an esp human form **b** a diagram or pictorial illustration in a text **c** a geometrical diagram or shape **4** an intentional deviation from the usual form or syntactic relation of words **5** the form of a syllogism with respect to the position of the middle term **6** an often repetitive pattern in a manufactured article (e g cloth) or natural substance (e g wood) **7** an appearance made; a usu favourable impression produced ⟨*the couple cut quite a* ~⟩ **8a** a series of movements in a dance **b** an outline representation of a form traced by a series of evolutions (e g by a skater on an ice surface) **9** a personage, personality ⟨*great political* ~s⟩ **10** a short musical phrase

²**figure** *vt* **1** to represent (as if) by a figure or outline; portray **2a** to decorate with a pattern **b** to write figures over or under (the bass) in order to indicate the accompanying chords **3** to indicate or represent by numerals **4a** to calculate **b** *chiefly NAm* to conclude, decide ⟨*he* ~d *there was no use in further effort*⟩ **c** *chiefly NAm* to regard, consider ~ *vi* **1** to take an esp important or conspicuous part – often + *in* **2** to calculate **3** to seem reasonable or expected – *infml*; esp in *that figures* – **figurer** *n* – **figure on** *NAm* to take into consideration (e g in planning) ⟨figure on *$50 a month extra income*⟩

figured *adj* **1** represented, portrayed **2** adorned with or formed into a figure ⟨~ *muslin*⟩ ⟨~ *wood*⟩ **3** indicated by figures

figured bass *n* a continuo

figurehead *n* **1** an ornamental carved figure on a ship's bow **2** a head or chief in name only

figure of eight *n* sthg (e g a skater's figure) resembling the Arabic numeral 8 in form or shape

figure of speech *n* a form of expression (e g a hyperbole or metaphor) used to convey meaning or heighten effect

figure out *vt* **1** to discover, determine ⟨*try to* figure out *a solution*⟩ **2** to solve, fathom ⟨*I just can't* figure *him* out⟩

figurine *n* a statuette

filament *n* a single thread or a thin flexible threadlike object or part: e g **a** a slender conductor (e g in an electric light bulb) made incandescent by the passage of an electric current; *specif* such a conductor that heats the cathode of a thermionic device **b** an elongated thin series of attached cells or a very long thin single cell (e g of some algae, fungi, or bacteria) **c** the anther-bearing stalk of a stamen – **filamentary** *adj*, **filamentous** *adj*

filbert *n* (the sweet thick-shelled nut of) either of 2 European hazels

filch *vt* to steal (sthg of small value); pilfer

¹**file** *n* a tool, usu of hardened steel, with many cutting ridges for shaping or smoothing objects or surfaces

²**file** *vt* to rub, smooth, or cut away (as if) with a file

³**file** *vt* **1** to arrange in order (e g alphabetically) for preservation and reference **2** to submit or record officially ⟨~ *a lawsuit*⟩ ~ *vi* to place items, esp papers, in a file

⁴**file** *n* **1** a folder, cabinet, etc in which papers are kept in order **2** a collection of papers or publications on a subject, usu arranged or classified

⁵**file** *n* **1** a row of people, animals, or things arranged one behind the other **2** any of the rows of squares that extend across a chessboard from white's side to black's side

⁶**file** *vi* to march or proceed in file

¹**filet** *n* a lace with a square mesh and geometric designs

²**filet** *n*, *chiefly NAm* a fillet

filial *adj* **1** of or befitting a son or daughter, esp in his/her relationship to a parent ⟨~ *obedience*⟩ **2** having or assuming the relation of a child or offspring – **filially** *adv*

filibuster *vi or n*, *chiefly NAm* (to engage in) the use of extreme delaying tactics in a legislative assembly

filigree *vt or n* (to decorate with) a ornamental openwork of delicate or intricate design **b** a pattern or design resembling such openwork ⟨*a* ~ *of frost on a window*⟩

filing *n* a usu metal fragment rubbed off in filing – usu pl ⟨*iron* ~s⟩

¹**fill** *vt* **1a** to put into as much as can be held or conveniently contained ⟨~ *a cup with water*⟩ **b** to supply with a full complement ⟨*the class is already* ~ed⟩ **c(1)** to cause to swell or billow ⟨*wind* ~ed *the sails*⟩ **(2)** to trim (a sail) to catch the wind **d** to repair the cavities of (a tooth) **e** to stop up; obstruct, plug **2a** to feed, satiate **b** to satisfy, fulfil ⟨~s *all requirements*⟩ **3a** to occupy the whole of ⟨*smoke* ~ed *the room*⟩ **b** to spread through **4a** to possess and perform the duties of; hold ⟨~ *an office*⟩ **b** to place a person in ⟨~ *a vacancy*⟩ ~ *vi* to become full – **fill somebody's shoes** to take over sby's job, position, or responsibilities – **fill the bill** to suffice

²**fill** *n* **1a** the quantity needed to fill sthg ⟨*a* ~ *of pipe tobacco*⟩; esp as much as one can eat or drink ⟨*eat your* ~⟩ **b** as much as one can bear ⟨*I've had my* ~ *of them for today*⟩ **2** material used to fill a receptacle, cavity, passage, or low place

filler *n* **1** a substance added to a product (e g to increase bulk or strength) **2** a composition or material used to fill holes before painting or varnishing **3** a piece (e g a plate) used to cover or fill a space between 2 parts of a structure

¹**fillet**, *chiefly NAm* **filet** *n* **1** a ribbon or narrow strip of material used esp as a headband **2a** a thin narrow strip of material **b(1)** a fleshy boneless piece of meat cut from the hind loin or upper hind leg **(2)** a long slice of boneless fish **3a** a junction in which the interior angle is rounded off or partly filled in **b** a usu triangular piece that partly fills such an interior **4** a narrow flat architectural moulding; *esp* the raised band between 2 flutes in a shaft

²**fillet** *vt* **1** to bind, provide, or adorn (as if) with a fillet **2a** to cut (meat or fish) into fillets **b** to remove the bones from (esp fish) **3** to remove inessential parts from

fill in *vt* **1** to give necessary or recently acquired information to ⟨*friends* filled *him* in *on the latest gossip*⟩ **2** to add what is necessary to complete; MAKE OUT **2** ⟨fill in *this form, please*⟩ **3** to enrich (e g a design) with detail ~ *vi* to take sby's place, usu temporarily; substitute ⟨*he often* filled in *in emergencies*⟩

filling *n* **1** sthg used to fill a cavity, container, or depression ⟨a ~ for a tooth⟩ **2** a food mixture used to fill cakes, sandwiches, etc **3** chiefly NAm weft

filling station n a retail establishment for selling fuel, oil, etc to motorists

¹**fillip** n sthg that arouses or boosts; a stimulus ⟨this should give a ~ to sales⟩

²**fillip** vt to stimulate

fill out vi to put on flesh ~vt, chiefly NAm FILL IN 2

filly n **1** a young female horse, usu of less than 4 years **2** a young woman; a girl – infml

¹**film** n **1a** a thin skin or membranous covering **b** (dimness of sight resulting from) an abnormal growth on or in the eye **2a** a thin layer or covering ⟨a ~ of ice on the pond⟩ **b**(1) a thin flexible transparent sheet (e g of plastic) used as a wrapping (2) a roll or strip of cellulose acetate or cellulose nitrate coated with a light-sensitive emulsion for taking photographs **3a** a series of pictures recorded on film for the cinema and projected rapidly onto a screen so as to create the illusion of movement **b** a representation (e g of an incident or story) on film **c** CINEMA 2 – often pl with sing. meaning – **filmic** adj, **filmically** adv, **filmy** adj, **filminess** n

²**film** vt to make a film of or from ~vi **1** to be suitable for photographing **2** to make a film

filmstrip n a strip of film containing photographs, diagrams, or graphic matter for still projection

¹**filter** n **1** a porous article or mass (e g of paper, sand, etc) through which a gas or liquid is passed to separate out matter in suspension **2** an apparatus containing a filter medium ⟨a car's oil ~⟩ **3a** a device or material for suppressing or minimizing waves or oscillations of certain frequencies (e g of electricity, light, or sound) **b** a transparent material (e g coloured glass) that absorbs light of certain colours selectively

³**filter** vt **1** to subject to the action of a filter **2** to remove by means of a filter ~vi **1** to pass or move (as if) through a filter **2** to move gradually ⟨the children ~ed out of assembly⟩ **3** to become known over a period of time ⟨the news soon ~ed through to the public⟩ **4** Br, of traffic to turn left or right in the direction of the green arrow while the main lights are still red – **filterable** also **filtrable** adj, **filterability** n

filter tip n (a cigar or cigarette with) a tip of porous material that filters the smoke before it enters the smoker's mouth – **filter-tipped** adj

filth n **1** foul or putrid matter, esp dirt or refuse **2** sthg loathsome or vile; esp obscene or pornographic material

filthy adj **1** covered with or containing filth; offensively dirty **2** vile, obscene – **filthily** adv, **filthiness** n

¹**fin** n **1** an external membranous part of an aquatic animal (e g a fish or whale) used in propelling or guiding the body **2a**(1) an appendage of a boat (e g a submarine) (2) a vertical aerofoil attached to an aircraft for directional stability **b** FLIPPER 1 **c** any of the projecting ribs on a radiator or an engine cylinder – **finlike** adj, **finned** adj

²**fin** vb **-nn-** vi to lash or move through the water (as if) using fins ~vt to equip with fins

¹**final** adj **1** not to be altered or undone; conclusive **2** being the last; occurring at the end ⟨the ~ chapter of a book⟩ **3** of or relating to the ultimate purpose or result of a process ⟨the ~ goal of life⟩ – **finally** adv

²**final** n **1** a deciding match, game, trial, etc in a sport or competition; also, pl a round made up of these **2** the last examination in a course – usu pl

finale n **1** the last section of an instrumental musical composition **2** a final scene or number in (an act of) a public performance **3** the last and often climactic event or item in a sequence

finalist n a contestant in the finals of a competition

finality n **1** the condition of being at an ultimate point, esp of development or authority **2** a fundamental fact, action, or belief

finalize, -ise vt **1** to put in final or finished form **2** to give final approval to – **finalization** n

¹**finance** n **1** pl resources of money **2** the system that includes the circulation of money and involves banking, credit, and investment **3** the science of the management of funds **4** the obtaining of funds – **financial** adj, **financially** adv

²**finance** vt to raise or provide money for

financier n one skilled in dealing with finance or investment

finch n any of numerous songbirds with a short stout conical beak adapted for crushing seeds

¹**find** vb **found** vt **1a** to come upon, esp accidentally; encounter **b** to meet with (a specified reception) ⟨hoped to ~ favour⟩ **2a** to come upon or discover by searching, effort, or experiment; obtain **b** to obtain by effort or management ⟨~ the time to study⟩ **c** to attain, reach ⟨water ~s its own level⟩ **3a** to experience, feel ⟨found much pleasure in their company⟩ **b** to perceive (oneself) to be in a specified place or condition ⟨found himself in a dilemma⟩ **c** to gain or regain the use or power of ⟨trying to ~ his tongue⟩ **d** to bring (oneself) to a realization of one's powers or of one's true vocation ⟨he must be helped to ~ himself as an individual⟩ **4** to provide, supply ⟨the parents must ~ all the school fees themselves⟩ **5** to determine and announce ⟨~ a verdict⟩ ~vi to determine a case judicially by a verdict ⟨~ for the defendant⟩ – **find fault** to criticize unfavourably

²**find** n **1** an act or instance of finding sthg, esp sthg valuable **2** sby or sthg found; esp a valuable object or talented person discovered ⟨the new player was a real ~⟩

finder n a small astronomical telescope attached to a larger telescope for finding an object

fin de siècle adj (characteristic) of the close of the 19th c and esp its literary and artistic climate of sophisticated decadence and world-weariness

finding n **1** FIND 2 **2a** the result of a judicial inquiry **b** the result of an investigation – usu pl with sing. meaning ⟨the ~s of the welfare committee⟩ **3** pl, NAm small tools and materials used by a craftsman

find out vt **1** to learn by study, observation, or search; discover **2a** to detect in an offence ⟨the culprits were soon found out⟩ **b** to ascertain the true character or identity of; unmask ~vi to discover, learn, or verify sthg

¹**fine** n **1** a sum payable as punishment for an offence **2** a forfeiture or penalty paid to an injured party in a civil action – **in fine** IN SHORT

²**fine** vt to punish by a fine

³**fine** adj **1** free from impurity **2a** very thin in gauge or texture ⟨~ thread⟩⟨~ nib⟩ **b** consisting of relatively small particles **c** very small ⟨~ print⟩ **d** keen, sharp ⟨a knife with a ~ edge⟩ **3a**(1) having a delicate or subtle quality ⟨a wine of ~ bouquet⟩ (2) subtle or sensitive in perception or discrimination ⟨a ~ distinction⟩ **b** performed with extreme care and accuracy ⟨~ workmanship⟩ **4** in, at, or through a fielding position in cricket behind the batsman and near an extension of the line between the wickets **5a** superior in quality, conception, or appearance; excellent ⟨a ~ musician⟩ **b** bright and sunny ⟨the weather will be ~ in all parts of the country⟩ **6** marked by or affecting often excessive elegance or refinement ⟨~ manners⟩ **7** very well ⟨feel ~⟩ **8** awful – used as an intensive ⟨a ~ mess we're in!⟩ – **fine** adv, **finely** adv, **fineness** n

⁴**fine** *vt* **1** to purify, clarify – often + *down* **2** to make finer in quality or size – often + *down* ~ *vi* **1** to become pure or clear ⟨*the ale will* ~⟩ **2** to become finer or smaller in lines or proportions; diminish – often + *away* or *down*

fine art *n* (an) art (e g painting, sculpture, or music) concerned primarily with beauty rather than utility – usu pl

finery *n* dressy or showy clothing and jewels

fines herbes *n pl* a mixture of finely chopped herbs used esp as a seasoning

¹**finesse** *n* **1** refinement or delicacy of workmanship **2** skilful handling of a situation; adroitness **3** the withholding of one's highest card in the hope that a lower card will take the trick because the only opposing higher card is in the hand of an opponent who has already played

²**finesse** *vi* to make a finesse in playing cards ~ *vt* **1** to play (a card) in a finesse **2a** to bring about by finesse **b** to evade or trick by finesse

¹**finger** *n* **1** any of the 5 parts at the end of the hand or forelimb; *esp* one other than the thumb **2a** sthg that resembles a finger, esp in being long, narrow, and often tapering in shape ⟨*a* ~ *of toast*⟩ **b** a part of a glove into which a finger is inserted **3** the breadth of a finger – **fingered** *adj*, **fingerlike** *adj* – **have a finger in the/every pie** to be involved or have an interest in sthg/everything – *infml* – **pull/take one's finger out** *Br* to start working hard; get cracking – *slang*

²**finger** *vt* **1a** to play (a musical instrument) with the fingers **b** to play (e g notes or chords) with a specific fingering **c** to mark fingerings on (a music score) as a guide in playing **2** to touch or feel with the fingers; handle **3** *chiefly NAm* to point out, identify ⟨~ ed *his associates to the police*⟩ – *infml* ~ *vi* to touch or handle sthg ⟨~ s *through the cards*⟩

fingerboard *n* the part of a stringed instrument against which the fingers press the strings to vary the pitch

finger bowl *n* a small water bowl for rinsing the fingers at table

¹**fingering** *n* (the marking indicating) the use or position of the fingers in sounding notes on an instrument

²**fingering** *n* a fine wool yarn for knitting, used esp in the manufacture of stockings

finger painting *n* (a picture produced by) spreading pigment on wet paper chiefly with the fingers

fingerplate *n* a protective plate fastened to a door usu near the handle to protect the door surface from finger marks

fingerpost *n* a signpost whose signs are or terminate in the shape of a pointing finger

fingerprint *n* **1** the impression of a fingertip on any surface; *esp* an ink impression of the lines upon the fingertip taken for purposes of identification **2** unique distinguishing characteristics (e g of a recording machine or infrared spectrum) **3** the characteristic pattern produced by chromatography or electrophoresis of a particular partially broken down protein or other macromolecule – **fingerprint** *vt*, **fingerprinting** *n*

fingerstall *n* a protective cover for an injured finger

fingertip *adj* readily accessible; being in close proximity

finicky *adj* **1** excessively exacting or meticulous in taste or standards; fussy **2** requiring delicate attention to detail ⟨*a* ~ *job*⟩ – **finickiness** *n*

finis *n* the end, conclusion – used esp to mark the end of a book or film

¹**finish** *vt* **1a** to end, terminate **b** to eat, drink, or use entirely – often + *off* or *up* **2a** to bring to completion or issue; complete, perfect ⟨~ ed *her new novel*⟩ – often + *off* **b** to put a final coat or surface on **c** to neaten (the raw edge of a piece of sewing) to prevent fraying **d** to complete the schooling of (a girl), esp in the social graces **3a** to bring to an end the significance or effectiveness of ⟨*the scandal* ~ ed *his career*⟩ **b** to bring about the death of ~ *vi* **1** to end, terminate **2a** to come to the end of a course, task, or undertaking in a specified manner ⟨~ ed *with a song*⟩ **b** to come to the end of a relationship ⟨*David and I have* ~ ed⟩ **3** to arrive, end, or come to rest in a specified position or manner – often + *up* ⟨*we* ~ ed *up in Paris*⟩ ⟨*the car* ~ ed *upside down in a ditch*⟩; *specif* to end a competition in a specified manner or position ⟨~ ed *third in the race*⟩ – **finisher** *n* – **finish with** to end a relationship or affair with

²**finish** *n* **1a** the final stage; the end **b** the cause of one's ruin; downfall **2** the texture or appearance of a surface, esp after a coating has been applied **3** the result or product of a finishing process **4** the quality or state of being perfected, esp in the social graces

finishing school *n* a private school for girls that prepares its students esp for social activities

finite *adj* **1a** having definite or definable limits ⟨*a* ~ *number of possibilities*⟩ **b** subject to limitations, esp those imposed by the laws of nature ⟨~ *beings*⟩ **2** completely determinable in theory or in fact by counting, measurement, or thought ⟨*a* ~ *distance*⟩ ⟨*the* ~ *velocity of light*⟩ **3** neither infinite nor infinitesimal **4** of a verb form showing distinction of grammatical person and number – **finite** *n*, **finitely** *adv*, **finiteness** *n*, **finitude** *n*

fink *n*, *NAm* **1** an informer **2** a contemptible person *USE infml*

finnan haddie *n*, *chiefly Scot* FINNAN HADDOCK

finnan haddock *n* a haddock that is split and smoked until pale yellow

¹**Finnish** *adj* (characteristic) of Finland

²**Finnish** *n* a Finno-Ugric language of Finland, Karelia, and parts of Sweden and Norway

fiord, fjord *n* a narrow inlet of the sea between cliffs (e g in Norway)

fipple flute *n* a tubular wind instrument characterized mainly by a whistle mouthpiece and finger holes

fir *n* (the wood of) any of various related evergreen trees of the pine family that have flattish leaves and erect cones

¹**fire** *n* **1a** the phenomenon of combustion manifested in light, flame, and heat **b(1)** burning passion or emotion; ardour **(2)** liveliness of imagination; inspiration **2** fuel in a state of combustion (e g in a fireplace or furnace) **3a** a destructive burning (e g of a building or forest) **b** a severe trial or ordeal **4** brilliance, luminosity ⟨*the* ~ *of a diamond*⟩ **5** the discharge of firearms **6** *Br* a small usu gas or electric domestic heater – **fireless** *adj* – **on fire** eager, burning – **under fire** under attack

²**fire** *vt* **1a** to set on fire; kindle; *also* to ignite ⟨~ *a rocket engine*⟩ **b(1)** to give life or spirit to; inspire ⟨~ d *the poet's imagination*⟩ **(2)** to fill with passion; inflame **c** to light up as if by fire **2a** to drive out or away (as if) by fire – usu + *out* **b** to dismiss from a position **3a(1)** to cause to explode **(2)** to propel (as if) from a gun ⟨~ *a rocket*⟩ **b** to throw with speed; hurl **4** to apply fire or fuel to: e g **a** to process by applying heat **b** to feed or serve the fire of ~ *vi* **1a** to catch fire; ignite **b** *of an internal-combustion engine* to undergo ignition of the explosive charge **2** to become filled with excitement or anger – often + *up* **3a** to discharge a firearm **b** to emit or let fly an object – **firer** *n*

firearm *n* a weapon from which a shot is discharged by gunpowder – usu used only with reference to small arms

fire away *vi* to go ahead; begin – usu imper; *infml*

fireball *n* **1** a large brilliant meteor **2** BALL LIGHTNING **3** the bright cloud of vapour and dust created by a nuclear explosion **4** a highly energetic person – infml

firebomb *n* an incendiary bomb – **firebomb** *vt*

firebox *n* a chamber (e g of a furnace or steam boiler) that contains a fire

firebrand *n* **1** a piece of burning material, esp wood **2** one who creates unrest or strife; an agitator, troublemaker

firebreak *n* a strip of cleared or unplanted land intended to check a forest or grass fire

firebrick *n* a brick that is resistant to high temperatures and is used in furnaces, fireplaces, etc

fire brigade *n* an organization for preventing or extinguishing fires; *esp* one maintained in Britain by local government

firebug *n* a pyromaniac, fire-raiser – infml

fireclay *n* clay that is resistant to high temperatures and is used esp for firebricks and crucibles

fire control *n* the planning, preparation, and delivery of gunfire

firedamp *n* (the explosive mixture of air with) a combustible mine gas that consists chiefly of methane

firedog *n* an andiron

fire drill *n* a practice drill in extinguishing or escaping from fires

fire-eater *n* **1** a performer who pretends to eat fire **2** one who is quarrelsome or violent – **fire-eating** *adj*

fire engine *n* a vehicle equipped with fire-fighting equipment

fire escape *n* a device, esp an external staircase, for escape from a burning building

fire extinguisher *n* an apparatus for putting out fires with chemicals

fire fighter *n* sby who fights fires – **fire fighting** *n*

firefly *n* any of various night-flying beetles that produce a bright intermittent light

fireguard *n* a protective metal framework placed in front of an open fire

fire irons *n pl* utensils (e g tongs, poker, and shovel) for tending a household fire

firelight *n* the light of a fire, esp of one in a fireplace

fire lighter *n* a piece of inflammable material used to help light a fire (e g in a grate)

fireman *n, pl* **firemen 1** sby employed to extinguish fires **2** sby who tends or feeds fires or furnaces

fireplace *n* a usu framed opening made in a chimney to hold a fire; a hearth

firepower *n* the capacity (e g of a military unit) to deliver effective fire on a target

fireproof *adj* proof against or resistant to fire; *also* heatproof ⟨∼ *dishes*⟩ – **fireproof** *vt*, **fireproofing** *n*

fire-raising *n, Br* arson – **fire-raiser** *n*

fireside *n* **1** a place near the fire or hearth **2** home – **fireside** *adj*

fire station *n* a building housing fire apparatus and usu firemen

fire storm *n* a huge uncontrollable fire that is started typically by bombs and that causes and is kept in being by an inrush of high winds

firetrap *n* a building difficult to escape from in case of fire

fire-watcher *n* sby who watches for the outbreak of fire (e g during an air raid) – **fire-watching** *n*

firewater *n* strong alcoholic drink – infml

firewood *n* wood cut for fuel

firework *n* **1** a device for producing a striking display (e g of light or noise) by the combustion of explosive or inflammable mixtures **2** *pl* a display of fireworks **3** *pl* **a** a display of temper or intense conflict **b** PYROTECHNICS **2**

firing line *n* **1** a line from which fire is delivered against a target; *also* the troops stationed in a firing line **2** the forefront of an activity, esp one involving risk or difficulty – esp in *in the firing line*

firing squad *n* a detachment detailed to fire a salute at a military burial or carry out an execution

firkin *n* **1** a small wooden vessel or cask of usu 9 gall capacity **2** any of various British units of capacity usu equal to a quarter of a barrel (about 41l)

¹firm *adj* **1a** securely or solidly fixed in place **b** not weak or uncertain; vigorous ⟨*a* ∼ *handshake*⟩ **c** having a solid or compact structure that resists stress or pressure **2** not subject to change, unsteadiness, or disturbance; steadfast ⟨*a* ∼ *price*⟩ **3** indicating firmness or resolution ⟨*a* ∼ *mouth*⟩ – **firm** *adv*, **firmish** *adj*, **firmly** *adv*, **firmness** *n*

²firm *vt* **1** to make solid, compact, or firm ⟨∼ ing *his grip on the racket*⟩ **2** to put into final form; settle ⟨∼ *a contract*⟩ **3** to support, strengthen ⟨*help* ∼ *up the franc*⟩ ∼ *vi* **1** to become firm; harden **2** to recover from a decline; improve ⟨*the market* ∼ ed *slightly*⟩ USE (*vt* 2 & 3, *vi*) often + *up*

³firm *n* a business partnership not usu recognized as a legal person distinct from the members composing it; *broadly* any business unit or enterprise

firmament *n* the vault or arch of the sky; the heavens – **firmamental** *adj*

¹first *adj* **1** preceding all others in time, order, or importance: e g **a** earliest **b** being the lowest forward gear or speed of a motor vehicle **c** relating to or having the (most prominent and) usu highest part among a group of instruments or voices **2** least, slightest ⟨*hasn't the* ∼ *idea what to do*⟩ – **at first hand** directly from the original source

²first *adv* **1** before anything else; at the beginning ⟨*came* ∼ *and left last*⟩ ⟨∼ *of all we had cocktails*⟩ **2** for the first time **3** in preference to sthg else ⟨*I'll see him dead* ∼⟩

³first *n, pl* (2a) **first**, (2b, c, & d) **firsts 1** number one in a countable series **2** sthg or sby that is first: e g **a** the first occurrence or item of a kind ⟨*was one of the* ∼ *to know*⟩ **b** the first and lowest forward gear or speed of a motor vehicle **c** the winning place in a contest **d first, first class** *often cap* the highest level of British honours degree ⟨*got a* ∼ *in history*⟩ – **at first** at the beginning; initially – **from the first** from the beginning

first aid *n* **1** emergency care or treatment given to an ill or injured person before proper medical aid can be obtained **2** temporary emergency measures taken to alleviate a problem before a permanent solution can be found – **first-aider** *n*

firstborn *adj* born before all others; eldest – **firstborn** *n*

¹first class *n* the first or highest group in a classification: e g **a** the highest of usu 3 classes of travel accommodation **b** FIRST **2d** – **first-class** *adj*

²first class *adv* **1** in the highest quality of accommodation ⟨*travel* ∼⟩ **2** as mail that is delivered as fast as possible ⟨*send a letter* ∼⟩

first floor *n* **1** *Br* the floor immediately above the ground floor **2** *NAm* GROUND FLOOR

firstfruits *n pl* **1** agricultural produce offered to God in thanksgiving **2** the earliest products or results of an enterprise

firsthand *adj* of or coming directly from the original source – **firsthand** *adv*

first lady *n, often cap F&L* the wife or hostess of a US president or state governor

first lieutenant *n* an officer holding the second lowest rank in the US army, airforce, or marines

firstly *adv* in the first place; first

first name *n* the name that stands first in a person's full name

first night *n* the night on which a theatrical production is first performed at a given place

first offender *n* sby convicted of an offence for the first time

first person *n* (a member of) a set of linguistic forms (e g verb forms and pronouns) referring to the speaker or writer of the utterance in which they occur

first-rate *adj* of the first or greatest order of size, importance, or quality – **first-rater** *n*

firth *n* a sea inlet or estuary (e g in Scotland)

¹fiscal *adj* of taxation, public revenues, or public debt ⟨~ policy⟩ – **fiscally** *adv*

²fiscal *n* a procurator-fiscal

¹fish *n, pl* **fish, fishes 1a** an aquatic animal – usu in combination ⟨star*fish*⟩ ⟨cuttle*fish*⟩ **b** (the edible flesh of) any of numerous cold-blooded aquatic vertebrates that typically have an elongated scaly body, limbs, when present, in the form of fins, and gills **2** a person; *esp* a fellow – usu derog ⟨a queer ~⟩ – **fishless** *adj*, **fishlike** *adj* – **fish out of water** a person who is out of his/her proper sphere or element

²fish *vi* **1** to try to catch fish **2** to seek sthg by roundabout means ⟨~ing *for compliments*⟩ **3a** to search for sthg underwater ⟨~ *for pearls*⟩ **b** to search (as if) by groping or feeling ⟨~ing *around under the bed for his shoes*⟩ ~ *vt* **1a** to (try to) catch (fish in) ⟨~ *the stream*⟩ ⟨~ *salmon*⟩ **b** to use (e g a net, type of rod, or bait) in fishing **2** to draw out as if fishing *USE* (*vi 2 & 3*) usu + *for*; (*vi 2 & 3b, vt 2*) infml – **fisher** *n*

³fish *n* a piece of wood or iron fastened alongside another member to strengthen it

fisherman *n* **1** *fem* **1fisher0woman** one who engages in fishing as an occupation or for pleasure **2** a ship used in commercial fishing

fishery *n* **1** the activity or business of catching fish and other sea animals **2** a place or establishment for catching fish and other sea animals

fish farm *n* a tract of water used for the artificial cultivation of an aquatic life form (e g fishes)

fish finger *n* a small oblong of fish coated with breadcrumbs

fishing *n* the sport or business of or a place for catching fish

fishmonger *n, chiefly Br* a retail fish dealer

fish out *vt* to exhaust the supply of fish in by overfishing

fishplate *n* a usu metal plate used to lap a butt joint

fish slice *n* **1** a broad-bladed knife for cutting and serving fish at table **2** a kitchen implement with a broad blade and long handle used esp for turning or lifting food in frying

fishwife *n* **1** a woman who sells or guts fish **2** a vulgar abusive woman

fishy *adj* **1** of or like fish, esp in taste or smell **2** creating doubt or suspicion; questionable – infml

fissile *adj* **1** capable of being split or cleft; having the property of cleavage **2** capable of undergoing (nuclear) fission – **fissility** *n*

fission *n* **1** a splitting or breaking up into parts **2** reproduction by spontaneous division into 2 or more parts each of which grows into a complete organism **3** the splitting of an atomic nucleus with the release of large amounts of energy – **fission** *vb*, **fissionable** *adj*, **fissional** *adj*, **fissionability** *n*

¹fissure *n* **1** a narrow, long, and deep opening, usu caused by breaking or parting **2** a natural cleft between body parts or in the substance of an organ (e g the brain)

²fissure *vb* to break into fissures

¹fist *n* **1** the hand clenched with the fingers doubled into the palm and the thumb across the fingers **2** HAND 1a ⟨get your ~s off my book⟩ **3** an attempt that meets with the specified degree of success *USE* (*2 & 3*) infml

²fist *vt* to hit with the fist ⟨the goalkeeper ~ed the ball clear⟩

-fisted *comb form* (*adj, n → adj*) having (such or so many) fists ⟨two-fisted⟩ ⟨tightfisted⟩

fisticuffs *n pl* the act or practice of fighting with the fists – no longer in vogue; humor

fistula *n, pl* **fistulas, fistulae** an abnormal or surgically made passage leading from an abscess or hollow organ to the body surface or between hollow organs

¹fit *n, archaic* a division of a poem or song

²fit *n* **1a** a sudden violent attack of a disease (e g epilepsy), esp when marked by convulsions or unconsciousness **b** a sudden but transient attack of a specified physical disturbance ⟨a ~ of shivering⟩ **2** a sudden outburst or flurry, esp of a specified activity or emotion ⟨a ~ of letter-writing⟩ – **by/in fits and starts** in a jerky, impulsive, or irregular manner

³fit *adj* **-tt- 1a**(1) adapted or suited to an end or purpose (2) adapted to the environment so as to be capable of surviving **b** acceptable from a particular viewpoint (e g of competence, morality, or qualifications) **2a** in a suitable state; ready **b** in such a distressing state as to be ready to do or suffer sthg specified ⟨so tired I was ~ to drop⟩ **3** HEALTHY 1 – **fitly** *adv*, **fitness** *n*

⁴fit *vb* **fitted** *also* **fit; -tt-** *vt* **1** to be suitable for or to; harmonize with **2a** to be of the correct size or shape for **b** to insert or adjust until correctly in place **c**(1) to cause to try on (clothes) in order to make adjustments in size (2) to make or find clothes of the right size for ⟨it's difficult to ~ him because he's so short⟩ **d** to make a place or room for; accommodate **3** to be in agreement or accord with ⟨the theory ~s all the facts⟩ **4a** to put into a condition of readiness **b** to bring to a required form and size; adjust **c** to cause to conform to or suit sthg **5** to supply, equip –often + *out* **6** to adjust (a smooth curve of a specified type) to a given set of points **7** *archaic* to befit ~ *vi* **1** to conform to a particular shape or size **2** to be in harmony or accord; belong

⁵fit *n* **1** the manner in which clothing fits the wearer **2** the degree of closeness with which surfaces are brought together in an assembly of parts **3** the conformity between an experimental result and theoretical expectation or between data and an approximating curve

fitful *adj* having a spasmodic or intermittent character; irregular ⟨~ sleep⟩ – **fitfully** *adv*, **fitfulness** *n*

fitment *n* **1** a piece of equipment; *esp* an item of built-in furniture **2** *pl* FITTINGS 2

fitter *n* sby who assembles or repairs machinery or appliances ⟨a gas ~⟩

¹fitting *adj* appropriate to the situation ⟨made a ~ answer⟩ – **fittingly** *adv*, **fittingness** *n*

²fitting *n* **1** a trying on of clothes which are in the process of being made or altered **2** a small often standardized part ⟨a plumbing ~⟩ ⟨an electrical ~⟩

fit up *vt* **1** FIX UP **2** *Br* FRAME 4a ⟨was fitted up for the murder of the policeman⟩ – slang – **fit-up** *n*

five *n* **1** (the number) 5 **2** the fifth in a set or series ⟨the ~ of clubs⟩ **3** sthg having 5 parts or members or a denomination of 5 **4** *pl but sing in constr* any of several games in which players hit a ball with their hands against the front wall of a 3- or 4-walled court – **five** *adj or pron*, **fivefold** *adj or adv*

five o'clock shadow *n* a just visible beard-growth

fiver *n* a £5 or $5 note; *also* the sum of £5 – infml

¹**fix** *vt* **1a** to make firm, stable, or stationary **b(1)** to change into a stable compound or available form ⟨*bacteria that ~ nitrogen*⟩ **(2)** to kill, harden, and preserve for microscopic study **(3)** to make the image of (a photographic film) permanent by removing unused sensitive chemicals **c** to fasten, attach **2** to hold or direct steadily ⟨*~es his eyes on the horizon*⟩ **3a** to set or place definitely; establish **b** to assign ⟨*~ the blame*⟩ **4** to set in order; adjust **5a** to repair, mend ⟨*~ the clock*⟩ **b** to restore, cure **c** to spay, castrate **6** *chiefly NAm* to get ready or prepare (esp food or drink) ⟨*can I ~ you a drink?*⟩ **7a** to get even with – infml **b** to influence by illicit means ⟨*the jury had been ~ed*⟩ – infml *~ vi* **1** to become firm, stable, or fixed **2** *chiefly NAm* to get ready; be about to ⟨*we're ~ing to leave soon*⟩ – **fixable** *adj*

²**fix** *n* **1** a position of difficulty or embarrassment; a trying predicament **2** (a determination of) the position (e g of a ship) found by bearings, radio, etc **3** sthg influenced by illicit means ⟨*the election was a ~*⟩ – infml **4** a shot of a narcotic – slang

fixation *n* **1** an (obsessive or unhealthy) attachment or preoccupation **2** a concentration of the libido on infantile forms of gratification ⟨*~ at the oral stage*⟩

fixative *n* sthg that fixes or sets: e g **a** a substance added to a perfume, esp to prevent too rapid evaporation **b** a varnish used esp to protect crayon drawings **c** a substance used to fix living tissue – **fixative** *adj*

fixed *adj* **1a** securely placed or fastened; stationary **b** formed into a chemical compound ⟨*~ nitrogen*⟩ **c** not subject to or capable of change or fluctuation; settled ⟨*a ~ income*⟩ **d** intent; IMMOBILE 2 ⟨*a ~ stare*⟩ **2** supplied with sthg needed or desirable (e g money) ⟨*how are you ~?*⟩ – infml – **fixedly** *adv*, **fixedness** *n* –**no fixed abode** no regular home

fixed star *n* any of the stars so distant that they appear to remain fixed relative to one another

fixity *n* the quality or state of being fixed or stable

fixture *n* **1** fixing or being fixed **2a** sthg fixed (e g to a building) as a permanent appendage or as a structural part **b** sthg so annexed to land or a building that it is regarded as legally a part of it **3** sby or sthg invariably present in a specified setting or long associated with a specified place or activity ⟨*now a ~ as the England wicket keeper*⟩ **4** (an esp sporting event held on) a settled date or time

fix up *vt* to provide *with*; make the arrangements for – infml ⟨*she fixed him up with a good job*⟩

¹**fizz** *vi* to make a hissing or sputtering sound

²**fizz** *n* **1a** a fizzing sound **b** spirit, liveliness **2** an effervescent beverage (e g champagne) – infml – **fizzy** *adj*

fizzle *vi or n* **fizzling** (to make) a weak fizzing sound

fizzle out *vi* to fail or end feebly, esp after a promising start – infml

fjord *n* a fiord

flabbergast *vt* to overwhelm with shock or astonishment – infml

flabby *adj* **1** (having flesh) lacking resilience or firmness **2** ineffective, feeble – **flabbily** *adv*, **flabbiness** *n*

flaccid *adj* **1a** lacking normal or youthful firmness; flabby ⟨*~ muscles*⟩ **b** LIMP 1 **2** lacking vigour or force – **flaccidly** *adv*, **flaccidity** *n*

¹**flag** *n* a (wild) iris or similar plant of damp ground with long leaves

²**flag** *n* a (slab of) hard evenly stratified stone that splits into flat pieces suitable for paving

³**flag** *vt* **-gg-** to lay (e g a pavement) with flags

⁴**flag** *n* **1** a usu rectangular piece of fabric of distinctive design that is used as a symbol (e g of a nation) or as a signalling device; *esp* one flown from a single vertical staff **2** NATIONALITY 3; *esp* the nationality of registration of a ship, aircraft, etc

⁵**flag** *vt* **-gg-** **1** to put a flag on (e g for identification) **2a** to signal to (as if) with a flag **b** to signal to stop – usu + *down*

⁶**flag** *vi* **-gg-** **1** to hang loose without stiffness **2** to become feeble, less interesting, or less active; decline

flag day *n*, *Br* a day on which charitable contributions are solicited in exchange for small paper flags on pins or, more recently, stickers

flagellant *n* **1** a person who scourges him-/herself as a public penance **2** a person who responds sexually to being beaten by or to beating another person – **flagellant** *adj*, **flagellantism** *n*

¹**flagellate** *vt* to whip or flog, esp as a religious punishment or for sexual gratification – **flagellation** *n*

²**flagellate, flagellated** *adj* **1** having flagella **2** shaped like a flagellum

³**flagellate** *n* a protozoan or algal cell that has a flagellum

flagellum *n*, *pl* **flagella** *also* **flagellums** any of various elongated filament-shaped appendages of plants or animals; *esp* one that projects singly or in groups and powers the motion of a microorganism – **flagellar** *adj*

¹**flageolet** *n* a small fipple flute

²**flageolet** *n* FRENCH BEAN

flag of convenience *n* the flag of a country in which a ship is registered in order to avoid the taxes and regulations of the ship-owner's home country

flagon *n* **1a** a large usu metal or pottery vessel with handle and spout and often a lid, used esp for holding liquids at table **b** a large squat short-necked bottle, often with 1 or 2 ear-shaped handles, in which cider, wine, etc are sold **2** the contents of or quantity contained in a flagon

flagrant *adj* conspicuously scandalous; outrageous ⟨*~ neglect of duty*⟩ – **flagrance, flagrancy** *n*, **flagrantly** *adv*

flagship *n* **1** the ship that carries the commander of a fleet or subdivision of a fleet and flies his flag **2** the finest, largest, or most important one of a set

flag-waving *n* passionate appeal to patriotic or partisan sentiment; jingoism – **flag-waver** *n*

¹**flail** *n* a threshing implement consisting of a stout short free-swinging stick attached to a wooden handle

²**flail** *vt* **1a** to strike (as if) with a flail **b** to swing or beat as though wielding a flail ⟨*~ing his arms to ward off the insects*⟩ **2** to thresh (grain) with a flail *~ vi* to wave, thrash – often + *about*

flair *n* **1** discriminating sense; intuitive discernment, esp in a specified field ⟨*a ~ for style*⟩ **2** natural aptitude; talent ⟨*shows little ~ for the subject*⟩ **3** a uniquely attractive quality; *esp* sophistication or smartness ⟨*she has a certain ~ about her*⟩ USE (1 & 2) usu + *for*

flak *n* **1** the fire from antiaircraft guns **2** heavy criticism or opposition – infml

¹**flake** *n* a platform, tray, etc for drying fish or produce

²**flake** *n* **1** a small loose mass or particle **2** a thin flattened piece or layer; a chip **3** a pipe tobacco of small irregularly cut pieces

³**flake** *vi* to come away in flakes – usu + *off* *~ vt* **1** to form or separate into flakes; chip **2** to cover (as if) with flakes – **flaker** *n*

flake out *vi* to collapse or fall asleep from exhaustion – infml

flaky *adj* **1** consisting of flakes **2** tending to flake – **flakiness** *n*

flambeau *n, pl* **flambeaux, flambeaus** a flaming torch; *broadly* TORCH 1

¹**flamboyant** *adj* **1** *often cap, of architecture* character-ized by waving curves suggesting flames **2** ornate, florid; *also* resplendent **3** given to dashing display; ostentatious – **flamboyance, flamboyancy** *n,* **flamboyantly** *adv*

²**flamboyant** *n* a showy tropical tree with scarlet and orange flowers

¹**flame** *n* **1** (a tongue of) the glowing gaseous part of a fire **2a** a state of blazing usu destructive combustion – often *pl* with sing. meaning ⟨*the whole city was in* ~s⟩ **b** a condition or appearance suggesting a flame, esp in having red, orange, or yellow colour **c** bright reddish orange **2** brilliance, brightness **3** burning passion or love **4** a sweetheart – usu in *old flame* – **flameless** *adj,* **flameproof** *adj or vt,* **flamy** *adj*

²**flame** *vi* **1** to burn with a flame; blaze **2** to break out violently or passionately ⟨*flaming with indignation*⟩ **3** to shine brightly like flame; glow ~ *vt* **1** to treat or affect with flame: e g **a** to cleanse, sterilize, or destroy by fire **b** to flambé – **flamer** *n*

flamenco *n, pl* **flamencos** (music suitable for) a vigorous rhythmic dance (style) of the Andalusian gypsies

flamethrower *n* a weapon that expels a burning stream of liquid

flaming *adj* **1** being in flames or on fire; blazing **2** resembling or suggesting a flame in colour, brilliance, or shape ⟨~ *red hair*⟩ **3** ardent, passionate ⟨*had a* ~ *row with the boss*⟩ **4** BLOODY 4 – slang – **flamingly** *adv*

flamingo *n, pl* **flamingos** *also* **flamingoes** any of several web-footed broad-billed aquatic birds with long legs and neck and rosy-white plumage with scarlet and black markings

flammable *adj* INFLAMMABLE 1 – **flammable** *n,* **flamma-bility** *n*

flan *n* **1** a pastry or cake case containing a sweet or savoury filling **2** the metal disc from which a coin, medal, etc is made

¹**flange** *n* a rib or rim for strength, for guiding, or for attachment to another object ⟨*a* ~ *on a pipe*⟩

²**flange** *vt* to provide with a flange – **flanger** *n*

¹**flank** *n* **1** the (fleshy part of the) side, esp of a quadruped, between the ribs and the hip **2a** a side **b** the right or left of a formation

²**flank** *vt* **1** to protect a flank of **2** to attack or threaten the flank of **3** to be situated at the side of; border

¹**flannel** *n* **1a** a twilled loosely woven wool or worsted fabric with a slightly napped surface **b** a stout cotton fabric usu napped on 1 side **2** *pl* garments of flannel; *esp* men's trousers **3** *Br* a cloth used for washing the skin, esp of the face **4** *chiefly Br* flattering talk; *also* nonsense – infml – **flannel** *adj,* **flannelly** *adj*

²**flannel** *vb* **-ll-** (*NAm* **-l-, -ll-**) *chiefly Br vi* to speak or write flannel, esp with intent to deceive ~ *vt* to make (one's way) or persuade (sby) to one's advantage by flannelling *USE* infml

flannelette *n* a napped cotton flannel

¹**flap** *n* **1** a stroke with sthg broad; a slap **2** sthg broad or flat, flexible or hinged, and usu thin, that hangs loose or projects freely: e g **a** an extended part forming a closure (e g of an envelope or carton) **b** a movable control surface on an aircraft wing for increasing lift or lift and drag **3** the motion of sthg broad and flexible (e g a sail); *also* an instance of the up-and-down motion of a wing (e g of a bird) **4** a state of excitement or panicky confusion; an uproar – infml

²**flap** *vb* **-pp-** *vt* **1** to beat (as if) with a flap **2** to (cause to) move in flaps ~ *vi* **1** to sway loosely, usu with a noise of striking and esp when moved by the wind **2a** to beat (sthg suggesting) wings **b** *esp of wings* to beat **c** to progress by flapping **d** to flutter ineffectively **3** to be in a flap or panic – infml

flapjack *n* **1** a thick pancake **2** a biscuit made with oats and syrup

flapper *n* **1a** an implement that can be flapped (e g to scare birds or swat flies) **b** FLIPPER 1 **2** a young woman; *specif* an emancipated girl of the period of WW I and the twenties – infml

¹**flare** *vi* **1** to burn with an unsteady flame **2a** to shine or blaze with a sudden flame **b** to become suddenly and often violently excited, angry, or active **3** to open or spread outwards; *esp* to widen gradually towards the lower edge ~ *vt* **1** to cause to flare **2** to provide with a flare ⟨*a* ~d *skirt*⟩ *USE* (*vi* 2) usu + up

²**flare** *n* **1** a (sudden) unsteady glaring light or flame **2a** (a device or substance used to produce) a fire or blaze of light used to signal, illuminate, or attract attention **b** a tempor-ary outburst of energy **(1)** from a small area of the sun's surface **(2)** from a star **3** a sudden outburst (e g of sound, excitement, or anger) **4** a spreading outwards; *also* a place or part that spreads ⟨*jeans with wide* ~s⟩ **5** light result-ing from reflection (e g between lens surfaces)

flare-up *n* an instance of sudden activity, emotion, etc ⟨*a new* ~ *of border disputes*⟩

¹**flash** *vi* **1** *of flowing water* to rush, dash **2a** to burst violently into flames **b** to break forth in or like a sudden flame or flare ⟨*lightning* ~ing *in the sky*⟩ **3a** to appear suddenly ⟨*an idea* ~es *into her mind*⟩ **b** to move (as if) with great speed ⟨*the days* ~ *by*⟩ **4a** to break forth or out so as to make a sudden display ⟨*the sun* ~ed *from behind a cloud*⟩ **b** to act or speak vehemently and suddenly, esp in anger – often + out **5a** to give off light suddenly or in transient bursts **b** to glow or gleam, esp with animation or passion ⟨*his eyes* ~ed *in a sinister fashion*⟩ **6** to commit the offence of indecent exposure – slang ~ *vt* **1a** to cause the sudden appearance or reflection of (esp light) **b(1)** to cause (e g a mirror) to reflect light **(2)** to cause (a light) to flash **c** to convey by means of flashes of light **2a** to make known or cause to appear with great speed ⟨~ *a message on the screen*⟩ **b** to display ostentatiously ⟨*always* ~ing *his money around*⟩ **c** to expose to view suddenly and briefly ⟨~ing *a shy smile*⟩

²**flash** *n* **1** a sudden burst of light ⟨*a* ~ *of lightning*⟩ **2** a sudden burst of perception, emotion, etc ⟨*had a* ~ *of intuition*⟩ **3** a short time ⟨*I'll be back in a* ~⟩ **4** an esp vulgar or ostentatious display **5** a rush of water released to permit passage of a boat **6a** a brief look; a glimpse **b** a brief news report, esp on radio or television **c** FLASH-LIGHT 2; *also* flashlight photography **d** a quick-spreading flame or momentary intense outburst of radiant heat **7** a thin ridge on a cast or forged article, resulting from the hot metal, plastic, etc penetrating between the 2 parts of the mould **8** an immediate brief pleasurable feeling result-ing from an intravenous injection (e g of heroin) **9** an indecent exposure of the genitals *USE* (8 & 9) slang

³**flash** *adj* **1** of sudden origin or onset and usu short duration ⟨*a* ~ *fire*⟩; *also* carried out very quickly ⟨~ *freezing*⟩ **2** flashy, showy – infml

flashback *n* **1** (an) interruption of chronological sequence in a literary, theatrical, or cinematic work by the evocation of earlier events **2** a burst of flame back or out to an unwanted position (e g in a furnace)

flashbulb *n* an electric flash lamp in which metal foil or wire is burned

flashcube *n* a small cube incorporating 4 flashbulbs for taking 4 photographs in succession

flasher *n* **1a** a light (e g a traffic signal or car light) that catches the attention by flashing **b** a device for automatically flashing a light **2** one who commits the offence of indecent exposure – slang

flashgun *n* a device for holding and operating a photographic flashlight

flashlight *n* **1** a usu regularly flashing light used for signalling (e g in a lighthouse) **2** (a photograph taken with) a sudden bright artificial light used in taking photographic pictures **3** *chiefly NAm* an electric torch

flash point *n* **1** the temperature at which vapour from a volatile substance ignites **2** a point at which sby or sthg bursts suddenly into (violent) action

flashy *adj* **1** superficially attractive; temporarily brilliant or bright **2** ostentatious or showy, esp beyond the bounds of good taste – **flashily** *adv*, **flashiness** *n*

flask *n* **1** a broad flat bottle, usu of metal or leather-covered glass, used to carry alcohol or other drinks on the person **2** any of several conical, spherical, etc narrow-necked usu glass containers used in a laboratory **3** VACUUM FLASK

¹flat *adj* **-tt-** **1** having a continuous horizontal surface **2a** lying at full length or spread out on a surface; prostrate **b** resting with a surface against sthg **3** having a broad smooth surface and little thickness; *also* shallow ⟨*a ~ dish*⟩ **4a** clearly unmistakable; downright ⟨*gave a ~ denial*⟩ **b**(1) fixed, absolute ⟨*charged a ~ rate*⟩ (2) exact ⟨*got to work in 10 minutes ~*⟩ **5a** lacking animation; dull, monotonous; *also* inactive ⟨*trade is a bit ~ just now*⟩ **b** having lost effervescence or sparkle ⟨*~ beer*⟩ **6a** *of a tyre* lacking air; deflated **b** *of a battery* completely or partially discharged **7a** *of a musical note* lowered a semitone in pitch **b** lower than the proper musical pitch **8a** having a low trajectory ⟨*threw a fast ~ ball*⟩ **b** *of a tennis ball or shot* hit squarely without spin **9a** uniform in colour **b** *of a painting* lacking illusion of depth **c**(1) *of a photograph* lacking contrast (2) *of lighting for photography* not emphasizing shadows or contours **d** *esp of paint* having a matt finish – **flatly** *adv*, **flatness** *n*, **flattish** *adj*

²flat *n* **1** an area of level ground; a plain – often pl with sing. meaning **2** a flat part or surface ⟨*the ~ of one's hand*⟩ **3** (a character indicating) a musical note 1 semitone lower than a specified or particular note **4a** a flat piece of theatrical scenery **b** any of the sides of a nut or bolt head **5** a flat tyre **6** *often cap* the flat-racing season ⟨*the end of the ~*⟩

³flat *adv* **1** positively, uncompromisingly ⟨*turned the offer down ~*⟩ **2a** on or against a flat surface **b** so as to be spread out; at full length ⟨*fell ~ on the ground*⟩ **3** below the proper musical pitch **4** wholly, completely ⟨*~ broke*⟩ – infml

⁴flat *vb* **-tt-** to flatten

⁵flat *n* a self-contained set of rooms used as a dwelling – **flatlet** *n*

flatfish *n* any of an order of marine fishes (e g the flounders and soles) that swim on one side of the flattened body and have both eyes on the upper side

flatfoot *n, pl* **flatfeet** a policeman – slang

flat-footed *adj* affected with flat feet – **flat-footedly** *adv*

flatiron *n* IRON 2c; *esp* one heated on a fire, stove, etc

flat out *adv* at maximum speed, capacity, or performance – **flat-out** *adj*, *chiefly Br*

flat race *n* a race, usu for horses, on a level course without obstacles – **flat-racing** *n*

flat spin *n* **1** an aerial manoeuvre or flight condition consisting of a spin in which the aircraft is roughly horizontal **2** a state of extreme agitation – infml

flatten *vt* **1** to make flat **2** to lower in pitch, esp by a semitone **3** to beat or overcome utterly ⟨*got ~ed in the*

annual cricket match⟩ – infml ~*vi* to become flat or flatter: e g **a** to extend in or into a flat position or form ⟨*hills ~ ing into coastal plains*⟩ – often + *out* **b** to become uniform or stabilized, often at a new lower level – usu + *out* – **flattener** *n*

flatter *vt* **1** to praise excessively, esp from motives of self-interest or in order to gratify another's vanity **2** to raise the hope of or gratify, often groundlessly or with intent to deceive ⟨*I was ~ ed by the invitation*⟩ **3a**(1) to portray or represent (too) favourably ⟨*always paints pictures that ~ his subjects*⟩ (2) to display to advantage ⟨*candlelight often ~ s the face*⟩ **b** to judge (oneself) (too) favourably ⟨*I ~ myself I am not a fool*⟩ ~*vi* to flatter sby or sthg – **flatterer** *n*, **flatteringly** *adv*, **flattery** *n*

flattop *n*, *chiefly NAm* AIRCRAFT CARRIER

flatulent *adj* **1** causing, marked by, or affected with accumulation of gas in the stomach or intestines **2** pretentious without real worth or substance; turgid – **flatulence**, **flatulency** *n*, **flatulently** *adv*

flaunt *vi* **1** to wave or flutter proudly ⟨*the flag ~ s in the breeze*⟩ **2** to parade or display oneself to public notice ~*vt* **1** to display ostentatiously or impudently; parade ⟨*~ ing his superiority*⟩ **2** to flout – nonstandard – **flauntingly** *adv*, **flaunty** *adj*

flautist *n* one who plays a flute

¹flavour, *NAm chiefly* **flavor** *n* **1** the blend of taste and smell sensations evoked by a substance in the mouth; *also* a distinctive flavour ⟨*condiments give ~ to food*⟩ **2** characteristic or predominant quality ⟨*the newspaper retains a sporting ~*⟩ – **flavourful** *adj*, **flavourless** *adj*, **flavoursome** *adj*

²flavour, *NAm chiefly* **flavor** *vt* to give or add flavour to – **flavouring** *n*

flaw *n* **1** a blemish, imperfection **2** a usu hidden defect (e g a crack) that may cause failure under stress ⟨*a ~ in a bar of steel*⟩ **3** a weakness in sthg immaterial ⟨*a ~ in his argument*⟩ **4** a fault in a legal paper that may invalidate it – **flaw** *vb*, **flawless** *adj*, **flawlessly** *adv*, **flawlessness** *n*

flax *n* **1** (a plant related to or resembling) a slender erect blue-flowered plant cultivated for its strong woody fibre and seed **2** the fibre of the flax plant, esp when prepared for spinning

flaxen *adj* **1** made of flax **2** resembling flax, esp in being a pale soft straw colour ⟨*~ hair*⟩

flay *vt* **1** to strip off the skin or surface of; *also* to whip savagely **2a** to strip of possessions; SKIN 3 **b** to criticize or censure harshly

flea *n* **1** any of an order of wingless bloodsucking jumping insects that feed on warm-blooded animals **2** FLEA BEETLE – **with a flea in one's ear** with a usu embarrassing reprimand ⟨*sent off with a flea in his ear*⟩

fleabag *n* **1** a dirty or neglected person or animal **2** *chiefly NAm* an inferior hotel or lodging USE infml

flea beetle *n* a small jumping beetle that feeds on foliage

fleabite *n* a trifling problem or expense – infml

flea market *n* a usu open-air market selling secondhand articles and antiques

fleapit *n*, *chiefly Br* a shabby cinema or theatre – infml or humor

¹fleck *vt* to mark or cover with flecks; streak

²fleck *n* **1** a small spot or mark, esp of colour **2** a grain, particle

fledge *vt* **1** to rear until ready for flight or independent activity **2** to cover (as if) with feathers or down **3** to feather (esp an arrow)

fledgling, fledgeling *n* **1** a young bird just fledged **2** an inexperienced person

flee *vb* **fled** *vi* **1** to run away from danger, evil, etc **2** to pass away swiftly; vanish ⟨*mists* ~ing *before the rising sun*⟩ ~*vt* to run away from; shun

¹fleece *n* **1a** the coat of wool covering a sheep or similar animal **b** the wool obtained from a sheep at 1 shearing **2a** a soft or woolly covering like a sheep's fleece ⟨*a* ~ *of snow lay on the ground*⟩ **b** a soft bulky deep-piled fabric used chiefly for lining coats – **fleeced** *adj*, **fleecy** *adj*

²fleece *vt* to strip of money or property, usu by fraud or extortion; *esp* to overcharge – *infml*

¹fleet *vi* to fly swiftly; pass rapidly ⟨*clouds* ~ing *across the sky*⟩

²fleet *n* **1** a number of warships under a single command **2** *often cap* a country's navy – usu + *the* **3** a group of ships, aircraft, lorries, etc owned or operated under one management

³fleet *adj* swift in motion; nimble – **fleetly** *adv*, **fleetness** *n*

fleet admiral *n* an officer holding the highest rank in the US navy

fleeting *adj* passing swiftly; transitory – **fleetingly** *adv*, **fleetingness** *n*

Fleet Street *n* the national London-based press

¹flesh *n* **1a** the soft, esp muscular, parts of the body of a (vertebrate) animal as distinguished from visceral structures, bone, hide, etc **b** excess weight; fat **2** the edible parts of an animal; *esp* the muscular tissue of any animal usu excluding fish and sometimes fowl **3a** the physical being of humans ⟨*the spirit indeed is willing, but the* ~ *is weak* – Mt 26:41 (AV)⟩ **b** the physical or sensual aspect of human nature ⟨*pleasures of the* ~⟩ **4a** human beings; humankind – esp in *all flesh* **b** living beings generally **c** kindred, stock ⟨*one's own* ~⟩ **5** a fleshy (edible) part of a plant or fruit – **in the flesh** in bodily form; IN PERSON

²flesh *vt* **1** to feed (e g a hawk or hound) with flesh from the kill to encourage interest in the chase; *broadly* to initiate or habituate, esp by giving a foretaste **2** to clothe or cover (as if) with flesh; *broadly* to give substance to ⟨~ed *his argument out with solid fact*⟩ – usu + *out* ~*vi* to become (more) fleshy or substantial – usu + *out*

fleshings *n pl* flesh-coloured tights worn by dancers and actors

fleshly *adj* carnal

fleshpot *n* **1** *pl* bodily comfort or good living; luxury – usu + *the* **2** a nightclub or similar place of entertainment ⟨*a tour of the city's* ~s⟩ – usu pl

flesh wound *n* an injury involving penetration of body muscle without damage to bones or internal organs

fleshy *adj* **1a** consisting of or resembling flesh **b** marked by (abundant) flesh; *esp* corpulent **2** succulent, pulpy – **fleshiness** *n*

fleur-de-lis, fleur-de-lys *n, pl* **fleurs-de-lis, fleurs-de-lys, fleur-de-lis, fleur-de-lys** **1** IRIS **2** **2** a conventionalized iris in art and heraldry

flew *past of* FLY

¹flex *vt* **1** BEND 1 **2a** to bend (a limb or joint) **b** to move (a muscle or muscles) so as to flex a limb or joint

²flex *n, chiefly Br* a length of flexible insulated electrical cable used in connecting a portable electrical appliance to a socket

flexible *adj* **1** capable of being bent; pliant **2** yielding to influence; tractable **3** capable of changing in response to new conditions; versatile ⟨*a highly* ~ *curriculum*⟩ – **flexibility** *n*, **flexibly** *adv*

flibbertigibbet *n* a flighty or garrulous woman – *infml*

¹flick *n* a light jerky movement or blow

²flick *vt* **1a** to strike lightly with a quick sharp motion **b** to remove with flicks – usu + *away* or *off* **2** to cause to move with a flick ⟨*the cow* ~ed *its tail from side to side*⟩ ~*vi* **1** to move lightly or jerkily; dart **2** to direct a flick at sthg – **flick through** LEAF THROUGH

³flick *n* **1** FILM 4b **2** (a showing of a film at) a cinema – + *the*; usu pl USE *infml*

¹flicker *vi* **1** to move irregularly or unsteadily; quiver **2** to burn fitfully or with a fluctuating light **3** to appear or be present irregularly or indistinctly **4** *of a light* to fluctuate in intensity ~*vt* to cause to flicker – **flickeringly** *adv*

²flicker *n* **1** a flickering (movement or light) **2** a momentary quickening or stirring ⟨*a* ~ *of interest*⟩ – **flickery** *adj*

flick-knife *n* a pocket knife with a blade that flicks open when required

flier, flyer *n* **1** sby or sthg that moves very fast **2** airman

¹flight *n* **1a** a passage through the air using wings **b** the ability to fly **2a(1)** a passage or journey through air or space; *specif* any such flight scheduled by an airline **(2)** the distance covered in such a flight **b** the trajectory of a struck or bowled ball; *esp* a relatively high curve imparted to a bowled ball in cricket **c** swift movement **3** a group of similar creatures or objects flying through the air **4** a brilliant, imaginative, or unrestrained exercise or display ⟨*a* ~ *of fancy*⟩ **5** (a series of locks, hurdles, etc resembling) a continuous series of stairs from one landing or floor to another **6** any of the vanes or feathers at the tail of a dart, arrow, etc that provide stability **7** a small unit of (military) aircraft or personnel in the Royal Air Force – **flightless** *adj*

²flight *vt* **1** ¹FLUSH 2 **2** to impart flight to (a bowled ball)

³flight *n* an act or instance of fleeing

flight deck *n* **1** the deck of a ship used for the takeoff and landing of aircraft **2** the compartment housing the controls and those crew who operate them in an aircraft

flight lieutenant *n* an officer in the Royal Air Force ranking below squadron leader

flight recorder *n* a robust device fitted to an aircraft that records details of its flight, esp for use in investigating accidents

flight sergeant *n* a high-ranking noncommissioned officer in the Royal Air Force

flighty *adj* **1** easily excited or upset; skittish **2** irresponsible, silly; *also* flirtatious – **flightily** *adv*, **flightiness** *n*

¹flimsy *adj* **1a** lacking in strength or substance **b** of inferior materials or workmanship; easily destroyed or broken **2** having little worth or plausibility ⟨*a* ~ *excuse*⟩ – **flimsily** *adj*, **flimsiness** *n*

²flimsy *n* (a document printed on) a lightweight paper used esp for multiple copies

flinch *vi* to shrink (as if) from physical pain; *esp* to tense the muscles involuntarily in fear – **flinch** *n*, **flinchingly** *adv*

¹fling *vb* **flung** *vi* **1** to move in a hasty or violent manner ⟨~ing *out of the room in a rage*⟩ **2** *of an animal* to kick or plunge vigorously – usu + *out* ~*vt* **1** to throw or cast (aside), esp with force or recklessness ⟨flung *the books on the table*⟩ ⟨~ing *his arms out*⟩ ⟨flung *off all restraint*⟩ **2** to place or send suddenly and unceremoniously ⟨*the attack* flung *the enemy force into confusion*⟩ **3** to ejaculate or utter vigorously **4** to cast or direct (oneself or one's efforts) vigorously or unrestrainedly ⟨flung *herself into her work*⟩

²fling *n* **1** a period devoted to self-indulgence ⟨*determined to have one last* ~ *before settling down*⟩ **2** a casual attempt – chiefly *infml*

flint *n* **1** a hard quartz found esp in chalk or limestone **2**

a flint implement used by primitive human beings **3** a material (e g an alloy of iron and cerium) used for producing a spark (e g in a cigarette lighter) – **flintlike** *adj*, **flinty** *adj*

flintlock *n* (a gun having) a gunlock used in the 17th and 18th c, in which the charge is ignited by sparks struck from flint

¹**flip** *vb* **-pp-** *vt* **1** to toss or cause to move with a sharp movement, esp so as to be turned over in the air ⟨~ *a coin*⟩ **2** FLICK 1a **3** to turn *over* ~ *vi* **1** to lose one's sanity or self-control **2** to become extremely enthusiastic; go wild ⟨*I just* ~ped *over that new record*⟩ USE (*vi*) slang – **flip through** LEAF THROUGH

²**flip** *n* **1** a (motion used in) flipping or a flick **2** a somersault, esp when performed in the air **3** a mixed drink usu consisting of a sweetened spiced alcoholic drink to which beaten eggs have been added

³**flip** *adj* **-pp-** flippant, impertinent – *infml*

flip-flop *n* **1** a backward handspring **2** a usu electronic device or circuit (e g in a computer) capable of assuming either of 2 stable states **3** a rubber sandal consisting of a sole and a strap fixed between the toes – **flip-flop** *vi*

flippant *adj* lacking proper respect or seriousness, esp in the consideration of grave matters – **flippancy** *n*, **flippantly** *adv*

flipper *n* **1** a broad flat limb (e g of a seal) adapted for swimming **2** a flat rubber shoe with the front expanded into a paddle used for underwater swimming

flipping *adj or adv*, *Br* ¹BLOODY 4, ²BLOODY – euph

flip side *n* the side of a gramophone record which is not the principal marketing attraction

¹**flirt** *vi* to behave amorously without serious intent – **flirty** *adj*, **flirtation** *n*, **flirtatious** *adj*, **flirtatiously** *adv*, **flirtatiousness** *n* – **flirt with** to show superficial or casual interest in or liking for

²**flirt** *n* **1** an act or instance of flirting **2** one, esp a woman, who flirts

flit *vi* **-tt-** **1** to pass lightly and quickly or irregularly from one place or condition to another; *esp* to fly in this manner **2** *chiefly Scot & NEng* to move house, esp rapidly and secretly – **flit** *n*

flitch *n* **1** a salted and often smoked side of pork **2** a longitudinal section of a log

¹**float** *n* **1a** a cork or other device used to keep the baited end of a fishing line afloat **b** a floating platform for swimmers or boats **c** sthg (e g a hollow ball) that floats at the end of a lever in a cistern, tank, or boiler and regulates the liquid level **d** a sac containing air or gas and buoying up the body of a plant or animal **e** a watertight structure enabling an aircraft to float on water **2** a tool for smoothing a surface of plaster, concrete, etc **3** (a vehicle with) a platform supporting an exhibit in a parade **4** a sum of money available for day-to-day use (e g for expenses or for giving change)

²**float** *vi* **1** to rest on the surface of or be suspended in a fluid **2a** to drift (as if) on or through a liquid ⟨*yellow leaves* ~ed *down*⟩ **b** to wander aimlessly **3** to lack firmness of purpose; vacillate **4** *of a currency* to find a level in the international exchange market in response to the law of supply and demand and without artificial support or control ~ *vt* **1** to cause to float in or on the surface of a liquid; *also* to carry along in this manner **2** to smooth (e g plaster) with a float **3** to present (e g an idea) for acceptance or rejection **4** to cause (currency) to float

floatation *n* flotation

floating *adj* **1** located out of the normal position ⟨*a* ~ *kidney*⟩ **2a** continually changing position or abode ⟨*a large* ~ *population*⟩ **b** not presently committed or

invested ⟨~ *capital*⟩ **c** short-term and usu not funded ⟨~ *debt*⟩ **3** connected or constructed so as to operate and adjust smoothly

floating dock *n* a floating dry dock that can be partly submerged under a ship and then raised

floating rib *n* a rib (e g any of the last 2 pairs in human beings) that has no attachment to the sternum

¹**flock** *n sing or pl in constr* **1** a group of birds or mammals assembled or herded together **2** a church congregation, considered in relation to its pastor **3** a large group ⟨*a whole* ~ *of tourists*⟩

²**flock** *vi* to gather or move in a crowd ⟨*they* ~ed *to the beach*⟩

³**flock** *n* **1** a tuft of wool or cotton fibre **2** woollen or cotton refuse used for stuffing furniture, mattresses, etc **3** very short or pulverized fibre used esp to form a velvety pattern on cloth or paper or a protective covering on metal **4** FLOC 1

⁴**flock** *vt* to decorate with flock – **flocking** *n*

floe *n* (a sheet of) floating ice, esp on the sea

flog *vt* **-gg-** **1** to beat severely with a rod, whip, etc **2** to force into action; drive **3** to repeat (sthg) so frequently as to make uninteresting – esp in *flog something to death*; *infml* **4** *Br* SELL 2a – *slang* – **flog a dead horse** to waste time or energy on worn-out or previously settled subjects

¹**flood** *n* **1** an overflowing of a body of water, esp onto normally dry land **2** FLOW 2 **3** an overwhelming quantity or volume ⟨*a* ~ *of letters*⟩ **4** a floodlight

²**flood** *vt* **1** to cover with a flood; inundate **2a** to fill abundantly or excessively ⟨*strawberries* ~ed *the market and prices dropped*⟩ **b** to supply (a carburettor) with an excess of fuel **3** to drive *out* of a house, village, etc by flooding ~ *vi* **1** to pour forth in a flood **2** to become filled with a flood

floodgate *n* **1** a gate for shutting out or admitting water **2** sthg serving to restrain an outburst

floodlight *n* (a source of) a broad beam of light for artificial illumination – **floodlight** *vt*

flood tide *n* the tide while flowing in or at its highest point

¹**floor** *n* **1** the level base of a room **2a** the lower inside surface of a hollow structure (e g a cave or bodily part) **b** a ground surface ⟨*the ocean* ~⟩ **3** a structure between 2 storeys of a building; *also* a storey **4a** the part of an assembly in which members sit and speak **b** the members of an assembly ⟨*concluded by calling for questions from the* ~⟩ **c** the right to address an assembly ⟨*the member for Blackpool North has the* ~⟩ **5** a lower limit – **flooring** *n*

²**floor** *vt* **1** to cover with a floor **2a** to knock to the floor or ground **b** to reduce to silence or defeat; nonplus USE (2) *infml*

floor show *n* a series of acts presented in a nightclub

floorwalker *n*, *chiefly NAm* a shopwalker

floozy, floozie, floosie *n* **1** a (disreputable) woman or girl **2** a female companion – derog

¹**flop** *vi* **-pp-** **1** to swing or hang loosely but heavily **2** to fall, move, or drop in a heavy, clumsy, or relaxed manner ⟨~ped *into the chair with a sigh of relief*⟩ **3** to relax completely; slump **4** to fail completely ⟨*in spite of good reviews the play* ~ped⟩ USE (3&4) *infml*

²**flop** *n* **1** (the dull sound of) a flopping motion ⟨*fell with a* ~⟩ **2** a complete failure – *infml*

³**flop** *adv* with a flop

floppy *adj* tending to hang loosely; *esp* being both soft and flexible – **floppily** *adv*, **floppiness** *n*

flora *n*, *pl* **floras** *also* **florae** **1** a treatise on, or a work used to identify, the plants of a region **2** plant life (of a region, period, or special environment)

floral *adj* of flowers or a flora – **florally** *adv*

floret *n* any of the small flowers forming the head of a (composite) plant

florid *adj* **1** excessively flowery or ornate in style **2** tinged with red; ruddy ⟨*a ~ complexion*⟩ – **floridly** *adv*, **floridness** *n*, **floridity** *n*

florin *n* **1** any of various former gold coins of European countries **2** a former British or Commonwealth silver coin worth 2 shillings **3** a gulden

florist *n* one who deals in or grows flowers and ornamental plants for sale – **floristry** *n*

floss *n* **1** waste or short silk or silky fibres, esp from the outer part of a silkworm's cocoon **2** soft thread of silk or mercerized cotton for embroidery – **flossy** *adj*

flotation, floatation *n* **1** the act, process, or state of floating **2** the launching, esp by financing, of a company, enterprise, etc **3** the separation of particles of a material (e g pulverized ore) according to their relative capacity for floating on a liquid

flotilla *n* a small fleet of ships, esp warships

flotsam and jetsam *n* **1** vagrants **2** unimportant miscellaneous material; ODDS AND ENDS

flounce *vi* **1** to move in a violent or exaggerated fashion **2** to go in such a way as to attract attention, esp when angry ⟨*slapped him and ~*d *out of the room*⟩ – **flounce** *n*, **flouncy** *adj*

flounce *n* a wide gathered strip of fabric attached by the gathered edge (e g to the hem of a skirt or dress) – **flouncy** *adj*

flounce *vt* to trim with a flounce or flounces

flounder *n, pl* **flounder,** esp for *different types* **flounders** any of various flatfishes including some marine food fishes

flounder *vi* **1** to struggle to move or obtain footing **2** to proceed or act clumsily or ineffectually ⟨*~*ing *through a poor lecture*⟩ – **flounder** *n*

flour *n* **1** finely ground meal, esp of wheat **2** a fine soft powder – **floury** *adj*

flour *vt* **1** to coat (as if) with flour **2** to make (e g grain) into flour

flourish *vi* **1** to grow luxuriantly; thrive **2a** to achieve success; prosper **b** to be in good health **c** to reach a height of activity, development, or influence ~ *vt* to wave or wield with dramatic gestures; brandish

flourish *n* **1** a showy or flowery embellishment (e g in literature or handwriting) or passage (e g in music) **2a** an act of brandishing **b** an ostentatious or dramatic action

flout *vt* to treat with contemptuous disregard; scorn ⟨*openly ~*ing *the rules*⟩ – **flouter** *n*

flow *vi* **1a** to issue or move (as if) in a stream ⟨*rivers ~*ing *to the sea*⟩ ⟨*wealth ~*ing *from the oil industry*⟩ **b** to circulate ⟨*blood ~*ing *round the body*⟩ **2** of the tide to rise **3** to abound ⟨*~*ing *with milk and honey*⟩ **4a** to proceed smoothly and readily ⟨*conversation began to ~*⟩ **b** to have a smooth graceful continuity ⟨*the ~*ing *lines of the car*⟩ **5** to hang loose or freely **6** *of a plastic solid (e g rock)* to deform under stress without cracking or rupturing

flow *n* **1** a flowing **2** the flowing in of the tide towards the land **3a** a smooth uninterrupted movement or supply ⟨*a steady ~ of ideas*⟩ **b** a stream or gush of fluid **c** the direction of (apparent) movement **4** the quantity that flows in a certain time **5** menstruation **6a** the motion characteristic of fluids **b** a continuous transfer of energy

flow diagram *n* a flowchart

flower *n* **1a** a blossom, inflorescence **b** a shoot of a higher

plant bearing leaves modified for reproduction to form petals, sepals, ovaries, and anthers **c** a plant cultivated for its blossoms **2a** the finest or most perfect part or example ⟨*the ~ of a nation's youth destroyed in war*⟩ **b** the finest most vigorous period; prime **c** a state of blooming or flourishing – esp in *in flower* **3** *pl* a finely divided powder produced esp by condensation or sublimation ⟨*~*s *of sulphur*⟩ – **flowered** *adj*, **flowerless** *adj*

flower *vi* **1** to produce flowers; blossom **2** to reach a peak condition; flourish ~ *vt* **1** to cause to bear flowers **2** to decorate with a floral design – **flowerer** *n*, **flowering** *adj*

flower girl *n* a girl or woman who sells flowers, esp in a market or the street

flowerpot *n* a pot, typically the shape of a small bucket, in which to grow plants

flowery *adj* **1** of or resembling flowers **2** containing or using highly ornate language – **floweriness** *n*

flown *past part of* FLY

flu *n* influenza

fluctuate *vi* **1** to rise and fall; swing back and forth **2** to change continually and irregularly; waver – **fluctuant** *adj*, **fluctuation** *n*

flue *n* **1** a channel in a chimney for flame and smoke **2** a pipe for conveying heat (e g to water in a steam boiler)

fluent *adj* **1** capable of flowing; fluid **2a** able to speak or write with facility; *also* spoken or written in this way ⟨*his Welsh is ~*⟩ **b** effortlessly smooth and rapid; polished ⟨*a ~ performance*⟩ – **fluency** *n*, **fluently** *adv*

flue pipe *n* an organ pipe whose tone is produced by an air current striking the lip and causing the air within to vibrate

fluff *n* **1a** small loose bits of waste material (e g hairs and threads) that stick to clothes, carpets, etc **b** soft light fur, down, etc **2** a blunder; *esp* an actor's lapse of memory – chiefly *infml*

fluff *vi* **1** to become fluffy – often + *out* or *up* **2** to make a mistake, esp in a performance ~ *vt* **1** to make fluffy – often + *out* or *up* ⟨*the bird ~*ed *out its feathers*⟩ **2a** to fail to perform or achieve successfully; bungle ⟨*he ~*ed *his exam*⟩ **b** to deliver badly or forget (one's lines) in a play *USE (vi 2; vt 2)* chiefly *infml*

fluffy *adj* **1** like or covered with fluff **2** light and soft or airy ⟨*a ~ sponge cake*⟩ – **fluffiness** *n*

fluid *adj* **1a** having particles that easily change their relative position without separation of the mass; able to flow **b** likely or tending to change or move; not fixed **2** characterized by or employing a smooth easy style ⟨*the ballerina's ~ movements*⟩ **3a** available for a different use **b** easily converted into cash ⟨*~ assets*⟩ – **fluidly** *adv*, **fluidity** *also* **fluidness** *n*

fluid *n* **1** sthg capable of flowing to conform to the outline of its container; *specif* a liquid or gas **2** a liquid in the body of an animal or plant ⟨*cerebrospinal ~*⟩ – **fluidal** *adj*

fluid ounce, *NAm* **fluidounce** *n* **1** a British unit of liquid capacity equal to $\frac{1}{20}$ imperial pt (about 28.41cm³) **2** a US unit of liquid capacity equal to $\frac{1}{16}$ US pt (about 29.54cm³)

fluke *n* **1** a flatfish **2** a liver fluke or related trematode worm

fluke *n* **1** the part of an anchor that digs into the sea, river, etc bottom **2** a barbed end (e g of a harpoon) **3** either of the lobes of a whale's tail

fluke *n* **1** an accidentally successful stroke or action **2** a stroke of luck ⟨*the discovery was a ~*⟩

fluky *also* **flukey** *adj* **1** happening by or depending on chance rather than skill **2** *esp of wind* unsteadily, changeable

flume *n* an inclined channel for conveying water (e g for power generation)

flummery *n* 1 a sweet dish typically made with flour or oatmeal, eggs, honey, and cream 2 pretentious humbug

flummox *vt* to bewilder or confuse completely

flung *past of* FLING

flunk *vb, chiefly NAm vi* 1 to fail, esp in an examination or course 2 to be turned *out* of a school or college for failure ~ *vt* 1 to give a failing mark to 2 to get a failing mark in *USE* infml

flunky, flunkey *n* 1 a liveried servant 2 a yes-man 3 *chiefly NAm* a person performing menial duties 〈*worked as a* ~ *in a cookhouse*〉

fluorescence *n* the emitting of electromagnetic radiation, usu as visible light, as a result of the simultaneous absorption of radiation of shorter wavelength; *also* the radiation emitted – **fluoresce** *vi*, **fluorescer** *n*

fluorescent *adj* 1 of or having fluorescence 2 bright and glowing as a result of fluorescence 〈*a* ~ *pink*〉

fluoridate *vt* to add a fluoride to (e g drinking water) – **fluoridation** *n*

fluoride *n* a compound of fluorine

fluorine *n* a nonmetallic univalent halogen element that is normally a pale yellowish toxic gas

¹**flurry** *n* 1a a gust of wind b a brief light fall of snow 2 a state of nervous excitement or bustle 3 a short-lived outburst of trading activity

²**flurry** *vb* to (cause to) become agitated and confused

¹**flush** *vi* to take wing suddenly ~ *vt* 1 to cause (a bird) to flush 2 to expose or chase from a place of concealment – often + *out* 〈~ *out the criminals*〉

²**flush** *n* 1 (a cleansing with) a sudden flow, esp of water 2a a sudden increase, esp of new plant growth b a surge of emotion 〈*felt a* ~ *of anger at the insult*〉 3a a tinge of red, esp in the cheeks; a blush b a fresh and vigorous state 〈*in the first* ~ *of womanhood*〉 4 a transitory sensation of extreme heat; *specif* HOT FLUSH 5 *Br* a device for flushing toilets or drains

³**flush** *vi* 1 to flow and spread suddenly and freely 2a to glow brightly with a ruddy colour b to blush 3 to produce new growth 〈*the plants* ~ed *twice during the year*〉 ~ *vt* 1a to cause to flow or be carried along on a stream of liquid; *specif* to dispose of thus b to pour liquid over or through; *esp* to cleanse (as if) with a rush of liquid 〈~ *the toilet*〉 2 to inflame, excite – usu pass 〈*was* ~ed *with victory*〉 3 to cause to blush

⁴**flush** *adj* 1 filled to overflowing 2a having or forming a continuous edge or plane surface; not indented, recessed, or projecting 〈*panelling* ~ *with the wall*〉 b arranged edge to edge so as to fit snugly 3 readily available; abundant – chiefly infml 4 having a plentiful supply of money – infml – **flushness** *n*

⁵**flush** *adv* 1 so as to form a level or even surface or edge 2 squarely 〈*hit him* ~ *on the chin*〉

⁶**flush** *vt* to make flush 〈~ *the headings on a page*〉

⁷**flush** *n* a hand of playing cards, esp in a gambling game, all of the same suit

¹**fluster** *vb* to make or become agitated, nervous, or confused

²**fluster** *n* a state of agitated confusion

¹**flute** *n* 1 a keyed woodwind instrument that consists of a cylindrical tube stopped at one end, is played by blowing air across a side hole, and has a range from middle C upwards for 3 octaves 2a a grooved pleat b any of the vertical parallel grooves on the shaft of a classical column – **fluting** *n*

²**flute** *vi* to produce a flutelike sound ~ *vt* 1 to utter with a flutelike sound 2 to form flutes in – **fluter** *n*

flutist *n, chiefly NAm* a flautist

¹**flutter** *vi* 1 to flap the wings rapidly 2a to move with quick wavering or flapping motions 〈*flags* ~ing *in the wind*〉 b to beat or vibrate in irregular spasms 〈*his pulse* ~ed〉 3 to move about or behave in an agitated aimless manner ~ *vt* to cause to flutter – **flutterer** *n*, **fluttery** *adj*

²**flutter** *n* 1 a fluttering 2a a state of (nervous) confusion, excitement, or commotion b abnormal spasmodic fluttering of a body part 3 a distortion in reproduced sound similar to but at a faster rate than wow 4 an unwanted oscillation (e g of an aircraft part or bridge) set up by natural forces 5 *chiefly Br* a small gamble or bet

fluvial *adj* of, produced by, or living in a stream or river

¹**flux** *n* 1 a continuous flow or flowing 2a an influx b continual change; fluctuation 〈*the programme was in a state of* ~〉 3 a substance used to promote fusion of metals (e g in soldering or brazing) 4 the rate of transfer of a fluid, particles, or energy across a given surface 5 *archaic* an (abnormal) flowing of fluid, esp excrement from the body

²**flux** *vt* 1 to cause to become fluid 2 to treat with a flux ~ *vi* to become fluid

¹**fly** *vb* **flew; flown** *vi* 1a to move in or through the air by means of wings b to move through the air or space 〈*flags* ~ing *at half-mast*〉 2a to take flight; flee b to fade and disappear; vanish 〈*the shadows have* flown〉 3a to move, act, or pass swiftly 〈*he flew past me*〉 b to move or pass suddenly and violently into a specified state 〈*flew into a rage*〉 c to seem to pass quickly 〈*our holiday simply* flew〉 4 to operate or travel in an aircraft or spacecraft 5 to depart in haste; dash – chiefly infml ~ *vt* 1a to cause to fly 〈~ *a kite*〉 b to operate (a flying machine or spacecraft) in flight c to journey over by flying 〈~ *the Atlantic*〉 2 to flee or escape from 3 to transport by aircraft 4 to use (a specified airline) for travelling 〈*I always* ~ *British Airways*〉 – **flyable** *adj*, **flying** *n* – **fly at/on, fly out at** to assail suddenly and violently – **fly in the face/teeth of** to act in open defiance or disobedience of – **fly off the handle** to lose one's temper, esp suddenly

²**fly** *n* 1 an act or process of flying 2 *pl* the space over a stage where scenery and equipment can be hung 3a a (garment) opening concealed by a fold of cloth extending over the fastener; *esp, pl* such an opening in the front of a pair of trousers b FLY SHEET 2 c(1) the length of an extended flag from its staff or support (2) the outer or loose end of a flag 4 *chiefly Br* a light covered horse-drawn carriage

³**fly** *adj, chiefly Br* keen, artful – infml

⁴**fly** *n* 1 a winged insect – often in combination 〈*mayfly*〉 2 TWO-WINGED FLY 3 a natural or artificial fly attached to a fishhook for use as bait – **fly in the ointment** a detracting factor or element

flyaway *adj* 1 lacking practical sense; flighty 2 *esp of the hair* tending not to stay in place

flyblown *adj* 1 infested with flyblows 2 impure, tainted; *also* not new; used

flyby *n, pl* **flybys** 1 a flypast 2 a flight of a spacecraft close to a celestial body (e g Mars), esp to obtain scientific data

¹**fly-by-night** *n* 1 one who seeks to evade responsibilities or debts by flight 2 a shaky business enterprise *USE* chiefly infml

²**fly-by-night** *adj* 1 given to making a quick profit, usu by disreputable or irresponsible acts; *broadly* untrustworthy 2 transitory, passing 〈~ *fashions*〉 *USE* chiefly infml

flycatcher *n* any of several small birds that feed on insects caught while flying

foggy

flyer *n* a flier

fly-fishing *n* fishing (e g for salmon or trout) using artificial flies as bait

fly-half *n* STAND-OFF HALF

flying *adj* **1a** (capable of) moving in the air **b** rapidly moving ⟨~ *feet*⟩ **c** very brief; hasty ⟨*a* ~ *visit*⟩ **2** intended for ready movement or action ⟨~ *pickets*⟩ **3** of (the operation of) or using an aircraft **4** (to be) traversed after a flying start – **with flying colours** with complete or eminent success ⟨*passed the exam* with flying colours⟩

flying boat *n* a seaplane with a hull adapted for floating

flying bomb *n* a pilotless aircraft carrying explosives; *esp* a V-1

flying buttress *n* a projecting arched structure that supports a wall or building

flying fish *n* any of numerous (tropical) fishes that have long pectoral fins and are able to glide some distance through the air

flying fox *n* FRUIT BAT

flying officer *n* an officer in the Royal Air Force ranking below flight lieutenant

flying saucer *n* any of various unidentified flying objects reported as being saucer- or disc-shaped

flying squad *n*, *often cap F&S* a standby group of people, esp police, ready to move or act swiftly in an emergency

flying start *n* **1** a start to a race in which the participants are already moving when they cross the starting line or receive the starting signal **2** a privileged or successful beginning ⟨*she got off to a* ~ *at school*⟩

flyleaf *n* a blank leaf at the beginning or end of a book that is fastened to the cover

flyover *n*, *Br* (the upper level of) a crossing of 2 roads, railways, etc at different levels

flypaper *n* paper coated with a sticky, often poisonous, substance for killing flies

flypast *n*, *Br* a ceremonial usu low-altitude flight by (an) aircraft over a person or public gathering

fly sheet *n* **1** a small pamphlet or circular **2** an outer protective sheet covering a tent

flyswatter *n* a implement for killing insects that consists of a flat piece of usu rubber or plastic attached to a handle

flyweight *n* a boxer who weighs not more than 8st (50.8kg) if professional or more than 48kg (about 7st 7lb) but not more than 51kg (about 8st) if amateur

flywheel *n* a wheel with a heavy rim that when revolving can either reduce speed fluctuations in the rotation of an engine or store energy

FM *adj* of or being a broadcasting or receiving system using frequency modulation and usu noted for lack of interference

foal *n* a young animal of the horse family

foal *vb* to give birth to (a foal)

foam *n* **1a** (a substance in the form of) a light frothy mass of fine bubbles formed in or on the surface of a liquid (e g by agitation or fermentation) **b** a frothy mass formed in salivating or sweating **c** a chemical froth discharged from fire extinguishers **2** a material in a lightweight cellular form resulting from introduction of gas bubbles during manufacture **3** *the sea* – poetic – **foamless** *adj*, **foamy** *adj*, **foamily** *adv*, **foaminess** *n*

foam *vi* **1a** to produce or form foam **b** to froth at the mouth, esp in anger; *broadly* to be angry **2** to gush out in foam **3** to become covered (as if) with foam ⟨*streets* - ~ *ing with life* – Thomas Wolfe⟩ ~ *vt* **1** to cause air bubbles to form in **2** to convert (e g a plastic) into a foam

foam rubber *n* fine-textured spongy rubber made by introducing air bubbles before solidification

fob *n* **1** a small pocket on or near the waistband of a man's trousers, orig for holding a watch **2** a short strap or chain attached to a watch carried in a fob or a waistcoat pocket

fob off *vt* **-bb-** **1** to put off with a trick or excuse – usu + *with* **2** to pass or offer (sthg spurious or inferior) as genuine or perfect – usu + *on*

fob watch *n* a large circular watch often with a cover for the face that is usu carried in a (fob) pocket

focal length *n* the distance between the optical centre of a lens or mirror and the focal point

focal point *n* **1** the focus for a beam of incident rays parallel to the axis of a lens or mirror **2** FOCUS 5 ⟨*the fireplace was the* ~ *of the room*⟩

fo'c'sle *n* a forecastle

¹focus *n*, *pl* **focuses, foci** **1a** a point at which rays (e g of light, heat, or sound) converge or from which they (appear to) diverge after reflection or refraction **b** the point at which an object must be placed for an image formed by a lens or mirror to be sharp **2a** FOCAL LENGTH **b** adjustment (e g of the eye) necessary for distinct vision **c** a state in which sthg must be placed in order to be clearly perceived ⟨*tried to bring the issues into* ~⟩ **3** a fixed point that together with a straight line forms a reference system for generating a conic section in plane geometry; *also* either of 2 fixed points used in generating an ellipse or hyperbola **4** a localized area of disease or the chief site of a generalized disease **5** a centre of activity or attention ⟨*the* ~ *of the meeting was drug abuse*⟩ **6** the place of origin of an earthquake – **focal** *adj*, **focally** *adv* – **out of/in focus** not/having or giving the proper sharpness of outline due to good focussing

²focus *vb* **-ss-**, **-s-** *vt* **1** to bring to a focus **2** to cause to be concentrated ⟨~ *sed their attention on the most urgent problems*⟩ **3a** to adjust the focus of **b** to bring into focus ~ *vi* **1** to come to a focus; converge **2** to bring one's eyes or a camera to a focus

fodder *n* **1** (coarse) food for cattle, horses, sheep, or other domestic animals **2** sthg used to supply a constant demand ⟨*collected data which became computer* ~⟩ – **fodder** *vt*

foe *n* an enemy, adversary

foetus, fetus *n* an unborn or unhatched vertebrate; *specif* a developing human from usu 3 months after conception to birth – **foetal** *adj*

¹fog *n* **1** dead or decaying grass on land in the winter **2** a second growth of grass; an aftermath

²fog *n* **1** (a murky condition of the atmosphere caused esp by) fine particles, specif of water, suspended in the lower atmosphere **2a** a state of confusion or bewilderment **b** sthg that confuses or obscures ⟨*hid behind a* ~ *of rhetoric*⟩ **3** cloudiness on a developed photograph caused by chemical action or radiation (e g from X rays)

³fog *vb* **-gg-** *vt* **1** to envelop or suffuse (as if) with fog **2** to make confused or confusing **3** to produce fog on (e g a photographic film) during development ~ *vi* **1** to become covered or thick with fog **2** to become blurred (as if) by a covering of fog or mist

fogbound *adj* **1** covered with or surrounded by fog ⟨*a* ~ *coast*⟩ **2** unable to move because of fog

fogey, fogy *n* a person with old-fashioned ideas – chiefly in *old fogey*; chiefly *infml* – **fogeyish** *adj*, **fogeyism** *n*

foggy *adj* **1a** thick with fog **b** covered or made opaque by moisture or grime **2** blurred, obscured ⟨*hadn't the foggiest notion what they were voting for*⟩ – **foggily** *adv*, **fogginess** *n*

foghorn n 1 a horn (e g on a ship) sounded in a fog to give warning 2 a loud hoarse voice – infml

foible n 1 the part of a sword blade between the middle and point 2 a minor weakness or shortcoming in personal character or behaviour; *also* a quirk

foie gras n the fatted liver of an animal, esp a goose, usu in the form of a pâté

¹foil vt 1 *esp of a hunted animal* to spoil (a trail or scent) by crossing or retracing 2 to prevent from attaining an end; frustrate, defeat

²foil n 1 (fencing with) a light fencing sword with a circular guard and a flexible blade tapering to a blunted point 2 *archaic* the track or trail of an animal

³foil n 1a a curved recess between cusps (e g in Gothic tracery) b any of several arcs that enclose a complex design 2a very thin sheet metal ⟨*silver* ~⟩ b a thin coat of tin or silver laid on the back of a mirror 3 a thin piece of metal put under a gem or inferior stone to add colour or brilliance 4 sby or sthg that serves as a contrast to another ⟨*acted as a* ~ *for a comedian*⟩ 5 a hydrofoil

⁴foil vt to back or cover with foil

foist vt 1a to introduce or insert surreptitiously or without warrant – + *in* or *into* b to force another to accept or tolerate, esp by stealth or deceit 2 to pass off as genuine or worthy *USE* (*1b&2*) usu + *off on, on,* or *upon*

¹fold n 1 an enclosure for sheep; *also* a flock of sheep 2 *sing or pl in constr* a group of people adhering to a common faith, belief, or enthusiasm

²fold vt 1 to pen (e g sheep) in a fold 2 to pen sheep for the fertilization of (land)

³fold vt 1 to lay one part of over another part 2 to reduce the length or bulk of by doubling over – often + *up* 3a to clasp together; entwine ⟨~ed *his arms*⟩ b to bring (limbs) to rest close to the body ⟨*the bird* ~ed *its wings*⟩ 4a to clasp closely; embrace b to wrap, envelop 5 to bend (e g a layer of rock) into folds 6 to gently incorporate (a food ingredient) into a mixture without thorough stirring or beating – usu + *in* ~ *vi* 1 to become or be capable of being folded ⟨*a* ~ing *chair*⟩ 2 to fail completely; *esp* to stop production or operation because of lack of business or capital – often + *up*; chiefly infml 3 to succumb to fatigue – infml – **foldable** adj

⁴fold n 1 (a crease made by) a doubling or folding over 2 a part doubled or laid over another part; a pleat 3 (a hollow inside) sthg that is folded or that enfolds 4a a bend in rock strata produced usu by compression b *chiefly Br* an undulation in the landscape

-fold suffix (→ adj or adv) 1 multiplied by (a specified number); times ⟨*a twelve*fold *increase*⟩ ⟨*repay you ten*fold⟩ 2 having (so many) parts ⟨*three*fold *aspect of the problem*⟩

foldaway adj designed to fold out of the way or out of sight ⟨*a* ~ *bed*⟩

folder n a folded cover or large envelope for holding or filing loose papers

foliage n 1 the leaves of a plant or clump of plants 2 (an ornamental representation of) a cluster of leaves, branches, etc – **foliaged** adj, **foliar** adj

¹foliate adj 1 having leaves or leaflets; *also* leaf-shaped – often in combination ⟨*tri*foliate⟩ 2 foliated

²foliate vt to beat (metal) into a leaf or thin foil to number the leaves of (e g a manuscript) to decorate (e g an arch or pedestal) with foils ~*vi* to divide into thin layers or leaves – **foliation** n

¹folio n, pl **folios** 1a a leaf of a manuscript or book b a page or leaf number 2a(1) (the size of each of the 2 leaves formed from) a sheet of paper folded once (2) a book printed on pages of this size b a book of the largest size 3 a case or folder for loose papers 4 a certain number of words taken as a unit in measuring the length of a document

²folio vt **folios; folioing; folioed** FOLIATE 2

¹folk n 1 pl in constr the great proportion of a people that tends to preserve its customs, superstitions, etc 2 pl in constr a specified kind or class of people ⟨*old* ~⟩ – often pl with sing. meaning ⟨*just plain* ~s⟩ 3 simple music, usu song, of traditional origin or style 4 pl in constr people generally – infml; often pl with sing. meaning 5 pl the members of one's own family; relatives – infml

²folk adj 1 originating or traditional with the common people 2 of (the study of) the common people

folk etymology n the transformation of words so as to bring them into an apparent relationship with other more familiar words (e g in the change of Spanish *cucaracha* to *cockroach*)

folklore n 1 traditional customs and beliefs of a people preserved by oral tradition 2 the study of the life and spirit of a people through their folklore – **folklorist** n, **folkloric** adj

folksy adj 1 informal or familiar in manner or style 2 having or affecting a lack of sophistication – chiefly derog *USE* infml – **folksily** adv, **folksiness** n

folkway n a traditional social custom

follicle n 1a a small anatomical cavity or deep narrow depression b GRAAFIAN FOLLICLE 2 a dry 1-celled many-seeded fruit that has a single carpel and opens along 1 line only – **follicular, folliculate** *also* **folliculated** adj

follow vt 1 to go, proceed, or come after ⟨~ed *the guide*⟩ 2a to pursue, esp in an effort to overtake b to seek to attain; strive after ⟨~ *knowledge*⟩ 3a to accept as a guide or leader b to obey or act in accordance with ⟨*he* ~ed *the advice*⟩ 4 to copy, imitate 5a to walk or proceed along ⟨~ *a path*⟩ b to engage in as a calling or way of life; pursue (e g a course of action) 6a to come or take place after in time or order b to cause to be followed – usu + *with* ⟨~ed *dinner with a liqueur*⟩ 7 to come into existence or take place as a result or consequence of 8a to watch steadily ⟨~ed *the ball over the fence*⟩ b to keep the mind on ⟨~ *a speech*⟩ c to attend closely to; keep abreast of ⟨*she* ~ed *his career with interest*⟩ d to understand the logic of (e g an argument) ⟨*I don't quite* ~ *you*⟩ ~*vi* 1 to go or come after sby or sthg in place, time, or sequence 2 to result or occur as a consequence or inference 3 chiefly Br to understand the logic of a line of thought – **follow one's nose** to go in a straight or obvious course – **follow suit** 1 to play a card of the same suit as the card led 2 to follow an example set

follower n 1a one who follows the opinions or teachings of another b one who imitates another 2 ²FAN

¹following adj 1 next after; succeeding ⟨*the* ~ *day*⟩ 2 now to be stated ⟨*trains will leave at the* ~ *times*⟩ 3 *of a wind* blowing in the direction in which sthg is travelling

²following n, pl (1) **following,** (2) **followings** 1 sthg that comes immediately after or below in writing or speech 2 *sing or pl in constr* a group of followers, adherents, or partisans

³following prep subsequent to ⟨~ *the lecture tea was served*⟩

follow-my-leader n, Br 1 a game in which the actions of a designated leader must be copied by the other players 2 the slavish following by the majority of people of an example set by an individual

follow on vi, *of a side in cricket* to bat a second time immediately after making a score that is less, by more than a predetermined limit, than that of the opposing team in its first innings – **follow-on** n

follow through vi to continue the movement of a stroke

after a cricket, golf, etc ball has been struck ~ *vt* to pursue (an activity or process), esp to a conclusion – **follow-through** *n*

follow up *vt* **1a** to follow with sthg similar, related, or supplementary ⟨following up *his promises with action*⟩ **b** to take appropriate action about ⟨follow up *complaints and customer suggestions*⟩ **2** to maintain contact with or reexamine (a person) at usu prescribed intervals in order to evaluate a diagnosis or treatment – **follow-up** *n*

folly *n* **1** lack of good sense or prudence **2** a foolish act or idea **3** (criminally or tragically) foolish actions or conduct **4** a usu fanciful structure (e g a summerhouse) built esp for scenic effect or to satisfy a whim

foment *vt* **1** to treat with moist heat (e g for easing pain) **2** to promote the growth or development of; incite ⟨~ *a rebellion*⟩ – **fomenter** *n*

fomentation *n* **1** (the application to the body of) hot moist substances **2** fomenting, instigation

fond *adj* **1** foolish, silly ⟨~ *pride*⟩ **2** having an affection or liking for sthg specified – + *of* ⟨~ *of music*⟩ **3a** foolishly tender; indulgent **b** affectionate, loving **4** doted on; cherished ⟨*his* ~est *hopes*⟩ – **fondness** *n*

fondant *n* (a sweet made from) a soft creamy preparation of flavoured sugar and water

fondle *vb* **fondling** *vt* to handle tenderly or lingeringly ~ *vi* to show affection or desire by caressing

fondly *adv* **1** affectionately **2** in a willingly credulous manner ⟨government ~ *imagine that cutting taxes will reduce wage demands*⟩

fondue *n* a dish consisting of a hot liquid (e g oil or a thick sweet or savoury sauce) into which small pieces of food are dipped for cooking or coating; *esp* one made with melted cheese and usu white wine

¹**font** *n* **1a** a receptacle for holy water; *esp* one used in baptism **b** a receptacle for oil in a lamp **2** *chiefly NAm* ¹FOUNT – **fontal** *adj*

²**font** *n*, *chiefly NAm* ²FOUNT

food *n* **1a** (minerals, vitamins, etc together with) material consisting essentially of protein, carbohydrate, and fat taken into the body of a living organism and used to provide energy and sustain processes (e g growth and repair) essential for life **b** inorganic substances absorbed (e g in gaseous form or in solution) by plants **2** nutriment in solid form **3** sthg that sustains or supplies ⟨~ *for thought*⟩

food poisoning *n* an acute gastrointestinal disorder caused by (the toxic products of) bacteria or by chemical residues in food

foodstuff *n* a substance with food value; *esp* the raw material of food before or after processing

fool *n* **1** a person lacking in prudence, common sense, or understanding **2a** a jester **b** a person who is victimized or made to appear foolish; a dupe **3** a cold dessert of fruit puree mixed with whipped cream or custard – **foolery** *n*

fool *vi* **1a** to act or spend time idly or aimlessly **b(1)** to meddle, play, or trifle *with* ⟨*a dangerous man to* ~ *with*⟩ **(2)** to philander *with* ⟨*stop* ~ing *about with my wife*⟩ **2** to play or improvise a comic role; *specif* to joke ~ *vt* to make a fool of; deceive *USE* (*vi 1*) often + *around* or *about*

fool *adj* foolish, silly ⟨*barking his* ~ *head off*⟩ – infml

foolhardy *adj* foolishly adventurous and bold; rash – **foolhardily** *adv*, **foolhardiness** *n*

foolish *adj* **1** marked by or proceeding from folly **2** absurd, ridiculous – **foolishly** *adv*, **foolishness** *n*

foolproof *adj* so simple or reliable as to leave no opportunity for error, misuse, or failure ⟨*a* ~ *plan*⟩

foolscap *n* a size of paper usu 17 × 13½in (432 × 343mm)

fool's errand *n* a needless or fruitless errand

fool's gold *n* IRON PYRITES

fool's paradise *n* a state of illusory happiness

¹**foot** *n*, *pl* **feet**, *(3)* **feet** *also* **foot**, *(9)* **foot 1** the end part of the vertebrate leg on which an animal stands **2** an organ of locomotion or attachment of an invertebrate animal, esp a mollusc **3** a unit of length equal to ⅓yd (0.305m) ⟨*a 10-foot pole*⟩⟨*6 feet tall*⟩ **4** the basic unit of verse metre consisting of any of various fixed combinations of stressed and unstressed or long and short syllables **5** manner or motion of walking or running; step ⟨*fleet of* ~⟩ **6a** the lower end of the leg of a chair, table, etc **b** the piece on a sewing machine that presses the cloth against the feed **7** the lower edge or lowest part; the bottom ⟨*the* ~ *of a page*⟩⟨*the* ~ *of the stairs*⟩ **8a** the end that is opposite the head or top or nearest to the human feet ⟨*the* ~ *of the bed*⟩ **b** the part (e g of a stocking) that covers the human foot **9** *chiefly Br*, *sing or pl in constr* the infantry – **footless** *adj* – **my foot** MY EYE – infml – **on foot** by walking or running ⟨*tour the city on foot*⟩ – **on one's feet 1** standing **2** in a recovered condition (e g from illness) **3** in an impromptu manner ⟨*good debaters can think* on their feet⟩

²**foot** *vi* to dance ~ *vt* **1a** to perform the movements of (a dance) **b** to walk, run, or dance on, over, or through **2** to pay or stand credit for ⟨*agreed to* ~ *the bill*⟩ **3** to make or renew the foot of (e g a stocking) – **foot it 1** to dance **2** to travel on foot

footage *n* **1** length or quantity expressed in feet **2** (the length in feet of) exposed film

foot and mouth, foot and mouth disease *n* a contagious virus disease, esp of cloven-footed animals, marked by small ulcers in the mouth, about the hoofs, and on the udder and teats

football *n* **1** (the inflated round or oval ball used in) any of several games, esp soccer, that are played between 2 teams on a usu rectangular field having goalposts at each end and whose object is to get the ball over a goal line or between goalposts by running, passing, or kicking **2** sthg treated as a basis for contention rather than on its intrinsic merits ⟨*the bill became a political* ~ *in Parliament*⟩ – **footballer** *n*

football pools *n* a form of organized gambling based on forecasting the results of football matches

footbath *n* a bath for cleansing, warming, or disinfecting the feet

footboard *n* **1** a narrow platform on which to stand or brace the feet **2** a board forming the foot of a bed

footbridge *n* a bridge for pedestrians

footed *adj* having a foot or feet, esp of a specified kind or number – usu in combination ⟨*a* 4-footed *animal*⟩

footer *n*, *chiefly Br* soccer – infml; no longer in vogue

-footer *comb form* (→ *n*) sby or sthg that is a (specified) number of feet in height, length, or breadth

footfall *n* the sound of a footstep

foot fault *vi or n* (to make) a fault in tennis made when a server's feet are not behind the baseline

foothill *n* a hill at the foot of mountains

foothold *n* **1** FOOTING 1 **2** an (established) position or basis from which to progress ⟨*secured a* ~ *in the plastics market*⟩

footing *n* **1** a stable position or placing of or for the feet **2** a (condition of a) surface with respect to its suitability for walking or running on **3a** an established position; FOOTHOLD **2 b** a position or rank in relation to others ⟨*they all started off on an equal* ~⟩ **4** an enlargement at the lower end of a foundation, wall, pier, or column to

distribute the load; *also* a trench dug to accommodate this
– often pl ⟨*the ~ must be excavated to a minimum depth
of 4ft*⟩

footle *vi* **footling** to mess or potter *around* or *about*; *also*
to waste time – *infml*

footlights *n pl* a row of lights set across the front of a
stage floor

footling *adj* **1** bungling, inept ⟨*~ amateurs who understand nothing* – E R Bentley⟩ **2** unimportant, trivial; *also*
pettily fussy *USE infml*

footloose *adj* having no ties; free to go or do as one
pleases

footman *n* a servant in livery hired chiefly to wait, receive
visitors, etc

footnote *n* **1** a note of reference, explanation, or comment typically placed at the bottom of a printed page **2**
sthg subordinately related to a larger event or work ⟨*that
biography is an illuminating ~ to the history of our
times*⟩ – **footnote** *vt*

[1]footpad *n, archaic* one who robs a pedestrian

[2]footpad *n* a broad foot on the leg of a spacecraft

footpath *n* a narrow path for pedestrians; *also* PAVE-
MENT *n*

footplate *n, Br* the platform on which the crew stand in
a locomotive

footprint *n* **1** an impression left by the foot **2** an area
within which a spacecraft is intended to land

foot rot *n* a progressive inflammation of the feet of sheep
or cattle

footrule *n* a ruler 1ft long; *also* a ruler graduated in feet
and inches

footsie *n* **1** surreptitious amorous caresses with the feet
2 clandestine dealings *USE* chiefly in *play footsie with*;
infml

footslog *vi* **-gg-** to march or tramp laboriously – *infml* –
footslog *n,* **footslogger** *n*

footsore *adj* having sore or tender feet (e g from much
walking) – **footsoreness** *n*

footstep *n* **1a** the sound of a step or tread **b** distance
covered by a step **2** FOOTPRINT 1 **3** a way of life, conduct,
or action – usu pl with sing. meaning ⟨*followed in his
father's ~ s*⟩

footwear *n* articles (e g shoes or boots) worn on the
feet

footwork *n* **1** the control and placing of the feet, esp in
sport (e g in boxing or batting) **2** the activity of moving
from place to place on foot ⟨*the investigation entailed a
lot of ~*⟩

fop *n* a dandy – **foppish** *adj*, **foppishly** *adv*, **foppish-
ness** *n*

[1]for *prep* **1a** – used to indicate purpose ⟨*a grant ~ studying
medicine*⟩ ⟨*an operation ~ cancer*⟩ ⟨*what's this knob
~?*⟩, goal or direction ⟨*left ~ home*⟩ ⟨*acted ~ the
best*⟩ ⟨*getting on ~ 5*⟩, or that which is to be had or
gained ⟨*now ~ a good rest*⟩ ⟨*run ~ your life*⟩ ⟨*an eye ~
a bargain*⟩ **b** to belong to ⟨*the flowers are ~ you*⟩ **2** as
being or constituting ⟨*take him ~ a fool*⟩ ⟨*ate it ~
breakfast*⟩ ⟨*I ~ one don't care*⟩ **3a** BECAUSE OF 1 ⟨*cried
~ joy*⟩ ⟨*feel better ~ a holiday*⟩ **b** because of the hindrance of ⟨*couldn't speak ~ laughing*⟩ ⟨*if it weren't ~
you I'd leave*⟩ **4a** in place of ⟨*change ~ a pound*⟩ **b** on
behalf of; representing ⟨*acting ~ my client*⟩ ⟨*red ~
danger*⟩ **c** in support of; IN FAVOUR OF 1 ⟨*he played ~
England*⟩ **5** considered as; considering ⟨*tall ~ her
age*⟩ ⟨*cold ~ April*⟩ **6** with respect to; concerning
⟨*famous ~ its scenery*⟩ ⟨*a stickler ~ detail*⟩ ⟨*eggs are
good ~ you*⟩ **7** – used to indicate cost, payment, equivalence, or correlation ⟨*£7 ~ a hat*⟩ ⟨*all out ~ 342
runs*⟩ ⟨*punished ~ talking*⟩ ⟨*wouldn't hurt her ~ the

world*⟩ ⟨*5 duds ~ every good one*⟩ **8** – used to indicate
duration of time or extent of space ⟨*~ 10 miles*⟩ ⟨*the
worst accident ~ months*⟩ **9** on the occasion or at the
time of ⟨*came home ~ Christmas*⟩ ⟨*invited them ~ 9
o'clock*⟩ **10** – used to introduce a clause with a nonfinite
verb ⟨*no need ~ you to worry*⟩ ⟨*it's dangerous ~ George
to hurry*⟩ **11** chiefly NAm AFTER 5 – **for all 1** IN SPITE
OF ⟨*couldn't open it for all their efforts*⟩ **2** to the extent
that ⟨*dead for all I know*⟩ **3** considering how little
⟨*might as well stop talking for all the good it does*⟩ – **for
all one is worth** with all one's might – **for it** chiefly Br
likely to get into trouble – *infml* – **for what it is worth**
without guarantee of wisdom or accuracy – **for you** – used
after *there* or *that* in exclamations of enthusiasm or
exasperation ⟨*that's country hotels for you!*⟩

[2]for *conj* **1** and the reason is that **2** BECAUSE 2

[3]for *adj* being in favour of a motion or measure

for- *prefix* **1a** so as to involve prohibition or exclusion
⟨*forbid*⟩ ⟨*forfend*⟩ **b** so as to involve omission, refraining,
or neglect ⟨*forgo*⟩ ⟨*forsake*⟩ ⟨*forget*⟩ ⟨*forswear*⟩ **2**
destructively; detrimentally ⟨*fordo*⟩ **3** completely; excessively ⟨*forspent*⟩ ⟨*forlorn*⟩

[1]forage *n* **1** food for animals, esp when taken by browsing
or grazing **2** a foraging for provisions; *broadly* a
search

[2]forage *vt* **1** to collect or take provisions or forage from
2 to secure by foraging ⟨*~ d a chicken for the feast*⟩ ~ *vi*
1 to wander in search of forage or food **2** to make a search
for; rummage – **forager** *n*

forasmuch as *conj, archaic* in view of the fact that;
since

[1]foray *vi* to make a raid or incursion – **forayer** *n*

[2]foray *n* **1** a sudden invasion, attack, or raid **2** a brief
excursion or attempt, esp outside one's accustomed sphere
⟨*the teacher's ~ into politics*⟩

[1]forbear *vb* **forbore; forborne** *vt* to hold oneself back from,
esp with an effort of self-restraint ⟨*he forbore to answer
the slander*⟩ ~ *vi* **1** to hold back, abstain – usu + *from* ⟨*he
forbore from expressing his disagreement*⟩ **2** to control
oneself when provoked; be patient – chiefly *fml*

[2]forbear *n* a forebear

forbearance *n* **1** a refraining from the enforcement of
sthg (e g a debt, right, or obligation) that is due **2** patience
3 leniency

forbid *vt* **forbidding; forbade, forbad; forbidden 1a** to
refuse (e g by authority) to allow; command against ⟨*the
law ~ s shops to sell alcohol to minors*⟩ **b** to refuse access
to or use of ⟨*her father forbade him the house*⟩ **2** to make
impracticable; hinder, prevent ⟨*space ~ s further treatment of the subject here*⟩ – **forbidder** *n*

forbidden *adj, of quantum phenomena* not conforming to
the usual selection principles

forbidding *adj* **1** having a menacing or dangerous
appearance ⟨*~ mountains*⟩ **2** unfriendly ⟨*his father was
a stern ~ figure*⟩ – **forbiddingly** *adv*, **forbiddingness** *n*

[1]force *n* **1a** strength or energy exerted or brought to bear;
active power ⟨*the ~ s of nature*⟩ **b** moral or mental
strength **c** capacity to persuade or convince ⟨*couldn't
resist the ~ of his argument*⟩ **d** (legal) validity; operative
effect ⟨*an agreement having the ~ of law*⟩ **2a**(1) a body
(e g of troops or ships) assigned to a military purpose **b**(1) a
pl the armed services of a nation or commander **b**(1) a
body of people or things fulfilling an often specified
function ⟨*a labour ~*⟩ (2) POLICE FORCE – often + *the* **c**
an individual or group having the power of effective action
⟨*he was the driving ~ behind the passing of that bill*⟩ **3**
violence, compulsion, or constraint exerted on or against
a person or thing **4a** (the intensity of) an agency that is
applied to a free body results chiefly in an acceleration o

the body and sometimes in elastic deformation and other effects **b** an agency or influence analogous to a physical force ⟨*economic* ~s⟩ **5** the quality of conveying impressions intensely in writing or speech **6** *cap* a measure of wind strength as expressed by a number on the Beaufort scale ⟨*a Force 9 gale*⟩ – **in force 1** in great numbers ⟨*police were summoned* in force⟩ **2** valid, operative ⟨*the new law is now* in force⟩

²**force** *vt* **1** to compel by physical, moral, or intellectual means ⟨~d *labour*⟩ **2** to make or cause through natural or logical necessity ⟨*his arguments* ~d *them to admit he was right*⟩ **3a** to press, drive, or effect against resistance or inertia ⟨~ *a bill through Parliament*⟩ ⟨~d *his way through the crowd*⟩ **b** to impose or thrust urgently, importunately, or inexorably ⟨~ *unwanted attentions on a woman*⟩ **4a** to capture or penetrate by force ⟨~ *a castle*⟩ ⟨~d *the mountain passes*⟩ **b** to break open or through ⟨~ *a lock*⟩ **5a** to raise or accelerate to the utmost ⟨forcing *the pace*⟩ **b** to produce only with unnatural or unwilling effort ⟨*she* ~d *a smile in spite of her distress*⟩ ⟨*a* ~d *laugh*⟩ **6** to hasten the growth, onset of maturity, or rate of progress of ⟨forcing *rhubarb*⟩ **7** to induce (e g a particular bid from one's partner) in a card game by some conventional act, bid, etc **8** *of a batsman in cricket* to play an aggressive shot at (a delivery), esp off the back foot – **forcedly** *adv*, **forcer** *n* – **force someone's hand** to cause sby to act precipitously or reveal his/her purpose or intention

force-feed *vt* to feed forcibly

forceful *adj* possessing or filled with force; effective – **forcefully** *adv*, **forcefulness** *n*

force majeure *n* a disruptive event (e g war) that cannot be reasonably anticipated

forcemeat *n* a savoury highly seasoned stuffing, esp of breadcrumbs and meat

forceps *n, pl* **forceps** an instrument used (e g in surgery and watchmaking) for grasping, holding firmly, or pulling – usu pl with sing. meaning

forcible *adj* **1** effected by force used against opposition or resistance **2** powerful, forceful ⟨*a* ~ *argument*⟩ – **forcibleness** *n*, **forcibly** *adv*

ford *n* a shallow part of a river or other body of water that can be crossed by wading, in a vehicle, etc

ford *vt* to cross (a river, stream, etc) at a ford – **fordable** *adj*

fore *adj or adv* (situated) in, towards, or adjacent to the front

fore *n* sthg that occupies a forward position – **to the fore** in or into a position of prominence

fore *interj* – used by a golfer to warn anyone in the probable line of flight of his/her ball

²**fore-** *comb form* **1** (occurring) earlier or beforehand ⟨fore*payment*⟩ ⟨fore*see*⟩ **2a** situated at the front; in front ⟨fore*leg*⟩ **b** front part of ⟨fore*arm*⟩

²**fore-and-aft** *adj* **1** lying, running, or acting in the general line of the length of a ship or other construction **2** having no square sails

fore and aft *adv* from stem to stern

forearm *vt* to arm in advance; prepare

forearm *n* (the part in other vertebrates corresponding to) the human arm between the elbow and the wrist

forebear, forbear *n* an ancestor, forefather

forebode *vt* **1** to foretell, portend **2** to have a premonition of (evil, misfortune, etc) – **foreboder** *n*

foreboding *n* an omen, prediction, or presentiment, esp of coming evil

forecast *vb* **forecast, forecasted** *vt* **1** to estimate or predict (some future event or condition), esp as a result of rational study and analysis of available pertinent data **2**

to serve as a forecast of; presage ⟨*such events may* ~ *peace*⟩ ~ *vi* to calculate or predict the future – **forecaster** *n*

²**forecast** *n* a prophecy, estimate, or prediction of a future happening or condition; esp a weather forecast

forecastle, fo'c's'le *n* **1** a short raised deck at the bow of a ship **2** a forward part of a merchant ship having the living quarters

foreclose *vt* **1** to take away the right to redeem (e g a mortgage), usu because of nonpayment **2** to take away the right to redeem a mortgage or other debt from ~ *vi* to foreclose a mortgage or other debt – **foreclosure** *n*

forecourt *n* an open or paved area in front of a building; *esp* that part of a petrol station where the petrol pumps are situated

forefather *n* **1** ANCESTOR 1a **2** a person of an earlier period and common heritage

forefinger *n* the finger next to the thumb

forefoot *n* the forward part of a ship where the stem and keel meet

forefront *n* the foremost part or place; the vanguard ⟨*was in the* ~ *of the progressive movement*⟩

forego *vt* **foregoes; foregoing; forewent; foregone** to forgo

foregoing *adj* going before; that immediately precedes ⟨*the* ~ *statement is open to challenge*⟩

foregone conclusion *n* an inevitable result; a certainty ⟨*the victory was a* ~⟩

foreground *n* **1** the part of a picture or view nearest to and in front of the spectator **2** a position of prominence; the forefront

¹**forehand** *n* **1** the part of a horse in front of the rider **2** a forehand stroke in tennis, squash, etc; *also* the side or part of the court on which such strokes are made

²**forehand** *adj or adv* (made) with the palm of the hand turned in the direction of movement

forehead *n* the part of the face above the eyes

foreign *adj* **1** (situated) outside a place or country; *esp* (situated) outside one's own country **2** born in, belonging to, or characteristic of some place or country other than the one under consideration **3** of or proceeding from some other person or material thing than the one under consideration **4** alien in character; not connected or pertinent to **5** of, concerned with, or dealing with other nations ⟨~ *affairs*⟩ ⟨~ *minister*⟩ ⟨~ *trade*⟩ **6** occurring in an abnormal situation in the living body and commonly introduced from outside – **foreignism** *n*, **foreignness** *n*

foreign aid *n* (economic) assistance provided by one nation to another

foreigner *n* **1** a person belonging to or owing allegiance to a foreign country; an alien **2** *chiefly dial* STRANGER 1b; *esp* a person not native to a community

foreign office *n* the government department for foreign affairs

foreknow *vt* **foreknew; foreknown** to have previous knowledge of; know beforehand, esp by paranormal means or by revelation – **foreknowledge** *n*

foreland *n* a promontory, headland

foreleg *n* a front leg, esp of a quadruped

forelimb *n* an arm, fin, wing, or leg that is (homologous to) a foreleg

forelock *n* a lock of hair growing just above the forehead

foreman, fem forewoman *n, pl* **foremen 1** the chairman and spokesman of a jury **2** a person, often a chief worker, who supervises a group of workers, a particular operation, or a section of a plant

foremast *n* the (lower part of the) mast nearest the bow of a ship

¹foremost *adj* **1** first in a series or progression **2** of first rank or position; preeminent

²foremost *adv* most importantly ⟨*first and ~*⟩

forename *n* a name that precedes a person's surname

forenoon *n* the morning – *fml*

forensic *adj* **1** belonging to or used in courts of law **2** of or being the scientific investigation of crime – **forensically** *adv*

foreordain *vt* to settle, arrange, or appoint in advance; predestine – **foreordination** *n*

forepart *n* the front part of sthg

foreplay *n* erotic stimulation preceding sexual intercourse

forerunner *n* **1** a premonitory sign or symptom **2a** a predecessor, forefather **b** PROTOTYPE 1

foresail *n* **1** the lowest square sail on the foremast of a square-rigged ship **2** the principal fore-and-aft sail set on a schooner's foremast

foresee *vt* **foreseeing; foresaw; foreseen** to be aware of (e g a development) beforehand – **foreseeable** *adj*, **foreseer** *n*

foreshadow *vt* to represent or typify beforehand; prefigure, suggest ⟨*present trends ~ future events*⟩ – **foreshadower** *n*

foreshore *n* **1** a strip of land bordering a body of water **2** the part of a seashore between high-tide and low-tide marks

foreshorten *vt* **1** to shorten (a detail in a drawing or painting) so as to create an illusion of depth **2** to make more compact

foresight *n* **1** foreseeing, prescience **2** provident care; prudence ⟨*had the ~ to invest his money wisely*⟩ **3** the sight nearest the muzzle on a firearm – **foresighted** *adj*, **foresightedly** *adv*, **foresightedness** *n*

foreskin *n* a fold of skin that covers the glans of the penis

¹forest *n* **1** a tract of wooded land in Britain formerly owned by the sovereign and used for hunting game **2** a dense growth of trees and underbrush covering a large tract of land **3** sthg resembling a profusion of trees ⟨*a ~ of TV aerials*⟩

²forest *vt* to cover with trees or forest – **forestation** *n*

forestall *vt* **1** to exclude, hinder, or prevent by prior measures **2** to get ahead of; anticipate – **forestaller** *n*, **forestallment** *n*

forester *n* **1** a person trained in forestry **2** a person, animal, moth, etc that inhabits forest land

forestry *n* **1** forest land **2** the scientific cultivation or management of forests

foretaste *n* **1** an advance indication or warning **2** a small anticipatory sample

foretell *vt* **foretold** to tell beforehand; predict – **foreteller** *n*

forethought *n* **1** a thinking or planning out in advance; premeditation **2** consideration for the future

¹forever *adv* **1** forever, forevermore for all future time; indefinitely ⟨*wants to live ~*⟩ **2** persistently, incessantly ⟨*is ~ whistling out of tune*⟩

²forever *n* a seemingly endless length of time ⟨*took her ~ to find the answer*⟩

forewarn *vt* to warn in advance

forewoman *n, pl* **forewomen** a woman who acts as a foreman

foreword *n* a preface; *esp* one written by sby other than the author of the text

¹forfeit *n* **1** sthg lost, taken away, or imposed as a penalty **2** the loss or forfeiting of sthg, esp of civil rights **3a** an article deposited or a task performed in the game of forfeits **b** *pl but sing or pl in constr* a game in which

articles are deposited (e g for making a mistake) and then redeemed by performing a silly task – **forfeit** *adj*

²forfeit *vt* **1** to lose the right to by some error, offence, or crime **2** to subject to confiscation as a forfeit – **forfeitable** *adj*, **forfeiture** *n*

forgather, foregather *vi* to come together; assemble

¹forge *n* (a workshop with) an open furnace where metal, esp iron, is heated and wrought

²forge *vt* **1** to shape (metal or a metal object) by heating and hammering or with a press **2** to form or bring into being, esp by an expenditure of effort ⟨*made every effort to ~ party unity*⟩ **3** to counterfeit (esp a signature, document, or bank note) *~ vi* to commit forgery – **forgeable** *adj*, **forger** *n*

³forge *vi* **1** to move forwards slowly and steadily but with effort ⟨*the great ship ~d through the waves*⟩ **2** to move with a sudden increase of speed and power ⟨*the horse ~d ahead to win the race*⟩

forgery *n* **1** (the crime of) forging **2** a forged document, bank note, etc

forget *vb* **forgetting; forgot; forgotten,** *archaic or NAm* **forgot** *vt* **1** to fail to remember; lose the remembrance of ⟨*I ~ his name*⟩ **2** to fail to give attention to; disregard ⟨*forgot his old friends*⟩ **3a** to disregard intentionally; overlook ⟨*we will ~ our differences*⟩ **b** to reject the possibility of ⟨*as for going out tonight, ~ it!*⟩ *~ vi* **1** to cease remembering or noticing ⟨*forgive and ~*⟩ **2** to fail to remember at the proper time – usu + *about* ⟨*~ about paying the bill*⟩ – **forgetter** *n* – **forget oneself** to lose one's dignity, temper, or self-control; act unsuitably or unworthily

forgetful *adj* **1** likely or apt to forget **2** characterized by negligent failure to remember; neglectful – usu + *of* ⟨*~ of his manners*⟩ **3** inducing oblivion ⟨*~ sleep*⟩ – *poetic* – **forgetfully** *adv*, **forgetfulness** *n*

forget-me-not *n* any of a genus of small plants of the borage family with white or bright blue flowers usu arranged in a spike

forgive *vb* **forgave; forgiven** *vt* **1** to cease to resent ⟨*~ an insult*⟩ ⟨*~ one's enemies*⟩ **2** to pardon ⟨*~ us our trespasses*⟩ *~ vi* to grant forgiveness – **forgivable** *adj*, **forgivably** *adv*, **forgiver** *n*, **forgiving** *adj*, **forgivingly** *adv*

forgiveness *n* forgiving or being forgiven; pardon

forgo, forego *vt* **forgoes; forgoing; forwent; forgone** to abstain or refrain from ⟨*~ immediate gratification for the sake of future gains*⟩

¹fork *n* **1** a tool or implement with 2 or more prongs set on the end of a handle: e g **a** an agricultural or gardening tool for digging, carrying, etc **b** a small implement for eating or serving food **2a** a forked part, or piece of equipment **b** a forked support for a cycle wheel – often pl with sing. meaning **3** (a part containing) a division into branches **4** any of the branches into which sthg forks **5** an attack by a chess piece (e g a knight) on 2 pieces simultaneously – **forkful** *n*

²fork *vi* **1** to divide into 2 or more branches ⟨*where the road ~s*⟩ **2** to make a turn into one of the branches of a fork ⟨*we ~ed left at the inn*⟩ **3** to make a payment or contribution – + *out* or *up ~ vt* **1** to raise, pitch, dig, or work with a fork ⟨*~ hay*⟩ **2** to attack (2 chessmen simultaneously **3** to pay, contribute – + *out, over,* or *up* ⟨*~ed out half of his salary for a new car*⟩ USE (*vi 3; vt 3*) *infml*

forked *adj* having one end divided into 2 or more branches or points ⟨*~ lightning*⟩

forklift, forklift truck *n* a vehicle for hoisting and transporting heavy objects by means of steel prongs inserted under the load

forlorn *adj* **1a** bereft or forsaken *of* **b** sad and lonely

because of isolation or desertion; desolate **2** in poor condition; miserable, wretched ⟨~ *tumbledown buildings*⟩ **3** nearly hopeless ⟨*a* ~ *attempt*⟩ – **forlornly** *adv*
forlorn hope *n* a desperate or extremely difficult enterprise
¹form *n* **1a** the shape and structure of sthg as distinguished from its material **b** a body (e g of a person), esp in its external appearance or as distinguished from the face **2** the essential nature of a thing as distinguished from the matter in which it is embodied **3a** established or correct method of proceeding or behaving ⟨*I must ask for your name as a matter of* ~⟩ **b** a prescribed and set order of words ⟨*the* ~ *of the marriage service*⟩ **4** a printed or typed document; *esp* one with blank spaces for insertion of required or requested information ⟨*income-tax* ~ s⟩ **5a** conduct regulated by external controls (e g custom or etiquette); ceremony ⟨*the rigid* ~ *of the imperial court*⟩ **b** manner or conduct of a specified sort, as tested by a prescribed or accepted standard ⟨*rudeness is simply bad* ~⟩ **6a** the bed or nest of a hare **b** a long seat; a bench **7** sthg (e g shuttering) that holds, supports, and determines shape **8a** the way in which sthg is arranged, exists, or shows itself ⟨*written in the* ~ *of a letter*⟩ **b** a kind, variety ⟨*one* ~ *of respiratory disorder*⟩ **9a** orderly method of arrangement (e g in the presentation of ideas); manner of coordinating elements (e g of an artistic production or line of reasoning) ⟨*his work lacks* ~⟩ **b** the structural element, plan, or design of a work of art **10** *sing or pl in constr* a class organized for the work of a particular year, esp in a British school **11a** the past performances of a competitor considered as a guide to its future performance ⟨*a singer at the top of his* ~⟩ **c** condition suitable for performing, esp in sports – often + *in*, *out of*, or *off* ⟨*was out of* ~ *all season*⟩ **12a** LINGUISTIC FORM **b** any of the ways in which a word may be written or spoken as a result of inflection or change of spelling or pronunciation ⟨*verbal* ~ s⟩ **13** NAm a forme **14** Br a criminal record – slang – **formless** *adj*, **formlessly** *adv*, **formlessness** *n*
form *vt* **1** to give form, shape, or existence to; fashion ⟨~ ed *from clay*⟩ ⟨~ *a judgment*⟩ **2a** to give a particular shape to; shape or mould into a certain state or after a particular model ⟨~ ed *the dough into various shapes*⟩ ⟨*a state* ~ ed *along the lines of the Roman Republic*⟩ **b** to arrange themselves in ⟨*the women* ~ ed *a line*⟩ **c** to model or train by instruction and discipline ⟨*a mind* ~ ed *by classical education*⟩ **3** to develop, acquire ⟨~ *a habit*⟩ **4** to serve to make up or constitute; be a usu essential or basic element of **5a** to produce (e g a tense) by inflection ⟨~ s *the past in* -ed⟩ **b** to combine to make (a compound word) **6** to arrange in order; DRAW UP **1** ~ *vi* **1** to become formed or shaped ⟨*a scab* ~ ed *over the wound*⟩ **2** to take (a definite) form; come into existence ⟨*thunderclouds were* ~ ing *over the hills*⟩ – **formable** *adj*
form- *comb form* **form** *formic* *acid* ⟨*formaldehyde*⟩ ⟨*formate*⟩
form, -iform *comb form* (→ *adj*) having the form or shape of; resembling ⟨*cruciform*⟩
¹formal *adj* **1a** determining or being the essential constitution or structure ⟨~ *cause*⟩ **b** of, concerned with, or being the (outward) form of sthg as distinguished from its content **2** following or according with established form, custom, or rule; conventional ⟨*lacked* ~ *qualifications for the job*⟩ **3a** based on conventional forms and rules ⟨~ *landscaping*⟩ **b** characterized by punctilious respect for correct procedure ⟨*very* ~ *in all his dealings*⟩ **c** rigidly ceremonious; prim **4** having the appearance without the substance; ostensible ⟨~ *Christians who go to church only at Easter*⟩ – **formally** *adv*

formaldehyde *n* a pungent irritating gas used chiefly as a disinfectant and preservative and in chemical synthesis
formalin *n* a clear aqueous solution of formaldehyde
formalism *n* the practice or doctrine of strict adherence to or sole consideration of prescribed or external forms (e g in mathematics, religion, or art) – **formalist** *n or adj*, **formalistic** *adj*
formality *n* **1** compliance with or observance of formal or conventional rules **2** an established form that is required or conventional
formalize, -ise *vt* **1** to make formal **2** to give formal status or approval to – **formalization** *n*
¹format *n* **1** the shape, size, and general make-up (e g of a book) **2** the general plan of organization or arrangement
²format *vt* **-tt-** to arrange (e g a book or data) in a particular format or style
formation *n* **1** giving form or shape to sthg or taking form; development **2** sthg formed ⟨*new word* ~ s⟩ **3** the manner in which a thing is formed; structure **4** a body or series of rocks represented as a unit in geological mapping **5** an arrangement of a group of people or things in some prescribed manner or for a particular purpose; *also, sing or pl in constr* such a group – **formational** *adj*
¹formative *adj* **1a** (capable of) giving form; constructive ⟨*a* ~ *influence*⟩ **b** used in word formation or inflection ⟨*a* ~ *affix*⟩ **2** capable of alteration by growth and development ⟨~ *tissues*⟩ **3** of or characterized by formative effects or formation ⟨~ *years*⟩ – **formatively** *adv*
²formative *n* a formative affix
forme, NAm **form** *n* a frame enclosing metal type or blocks ready for printing
¹former *adj* **1** of or occurring in the past ⟨*in* ~ *times*⟩ **2** preceding in time or order ⟨*the* ~ *Prime Minister*⟩ **3** first of 2 things (understood to have been) mentioned
²former *n, pl* **former** the first mentioned; first ⟨*of puppies and kittens the* ~ *are harder to train*⟩
³former *n, chiefly Br* a member of a specified school form or year ⟨*a sixth* ~⟩ – often in combination
⁴former *n* a frame or core on which an electrical coil is wound
formerly *adv* at an earlier time; previously
Formica *trademark* – used for any of various laminated plastics used for surfaces, esp on wood
formic acid *n* a pungent corrosive liquid acid naturally produced by ants
formidable *adj* **1** causing fear, dread, or apprehension ⟨*a* ~ *prospect*⟩ **2** difficult to overcome; discouraging approach **3** tending to inspire respect or awe – **formidableness** *n*, **formidably** *adv*
formula *n, pl* **formulas**, **formulae** **1a** a set form of words for use in a ceremony or ritual **b** (a conventionalized statement intended to express) a truth, principle, or procedure, esp as a basis for negotiation or action ⟨*the 2 sides worked out a peace* ~⟩ ⟨*the* ~ *for a good marriage*⟩ **2** (a list of ingredients used in) a recipe **3a** a fact, rule, or principle expressed in symbols **b** a symbolic expression of the chemical composition of a substance **c** a group of numerical symbols associated to express a single concept **4** a prescribed or set form or method (e g of writing); an established rule or custom ⟨*unimaginative television programmes written to a* ~⟩ **5** a classification of racing cars specifying eng size, weight, and engine capacity – **formulaic** *adj*, **formulaically** *adv*
formulate *vt* **1** to state in or reduce to a formula **2** to devise or develop ⟨~ *policy*⟩ ⟨~ d *a new soap*⟩ – **formulation** *n*, **formulator** *n*
fornicate *vi* to commit fornication – **fornicator** *n*

fornication *n* voluntary sexual intercourse outside marriage

forsake *vt* **forsook ; forsaken 1** to renounce (e g sthg once cherished) without intent to recover or resume ⟨*forsook her family ties*⟩ **2** to desert, abandon ⟨*false friends ~ us in adversity*⟩

forsooth *adv* indeed, actually – now often used to imply contempt or doubt

forswear *vb* **forswear; forsworn** *vt* **1a** to reject or deny under oath **b** to (solemnly) renounce **2** to make a liar of (oneself) (as if) under oath ~*vi* to swear falsely

forsythia *n* any of a genus of ornamental shrubs of the olive family with bright yellow bell-shaped flowers appearing in early spring before the leaves

fort *n* a strong or fortified place

¹forte *n* **1** the area or skill in which a person excels **2** the strongest part of a sword blade being between the middle and the hilt

²forte *n, adv, or adj* (a note or passage played) in a loud and often forceful manner – used in music

forth *adv* **1** onwards in time, place, or order; forwards ⟨*from that day ~*⟩ **2** out into notice or view ⟨*put ~ leaves*⟩ **3** away from a centre; abroad ⟨*went ~ to preach*⟩

forthcoming *adj* **1** approaching **2a** made available ⟨*new funds will be ~ next year*⟩ **b** willing to give information; responsive

forthright *adj* going straight to the point without ambiguity or hesitation – **forthrightly** *adv*, **forthrightness** *n*

forthwith *adv* immediately

fortification *n* **1a** fortifying **b** the science or art of providing defensive works **2** sthg that fortifies, defends, or strengthens; *esp* works erected to defend a place or position

fortified wine *n* a wine to which alcohol has been added during or after fermentation

fortify *vt* to make strong: e g **a** to strengthen and secure by military defences **b** to give strength, courage, or endurance to; strengthen **c** to add material to for strengthening or enriching ~*vi* to erect fortifications – **fortifier** *n*

fortissimo *adv or adj* very loud – used in music

fortitude *n* patient courage in pain or adversity

fortnight *n, chiefly Br* two weeks

¹fortnightly *adj* occurring or appearing once a fortnight

²fortnightly *adv, chiefly Br* once in a fortnight; every fortnight

³fortnightly *n* a publication issued fortnightly

fortress *n* a fortified place; *esp* a large and permanent fortification, sometimes including a town

fortuitous *adj* **1** occurring by chance **2** fortunate, lucky – **fortuitously** *adv*, **fortuitousness** *n*

fortunate *adj* **1** unexpectedly bringing some good; auspicious **2** lucky – **fortunately** *adv*, **fortunateness** *n*

fortune *n* **1** *often cap* a supposed (personified) power that unpredictably determines events and issues **2a** prosperity attained partly through luck **b** LUCK 1 **c** *pl* the favourable or unfavourable events that accompany the progress of an individual or thing ⟨*tracing the ~s of a rags-to-riches hero*⟩ ⟨*the declining ~s of the film industry*⟩ **3** destiny, fate ⟨*tell his ~ with cards*⟩ **4a** material possessions or wealth **b** a very large sum of money ⟨*won a ~ on the pools*⟩ – infml

fortune hunter *n* a person who seeks wealth, esp by marriage

fortune-teller *n* a person who claims to foretell future events – **fortune-telling** *n or adj*

forty *n* **1** (the number) 40 **2** *pl* the numbers 40 to 49;

specif a range of temperatures, ages, or dates in a century characterized by those numbers – **fortieth** *adj or n*, **forty** *adj or pron*, **fortyfold** *adj or adv*

forty-five *n* **1** (the number) 45 **2** a gramophone record that plays at 45 revolutions per minute – usu written 45 – **forty-five** *adj or pron*

forty winks *n pl but sing or pl in constr* ²NAP – infml

forum *n, pl* **forums** *also* **fora 1a** the marketplace or public place of an ancient Roman city forming the public centre **b** a public meeting place or medium for open discussion **2a** a public meeting or lecture involving audience discussion **b** a programme (e g on radio or television) based around the discussion of problems

¹forward *adj* **1a** located at or directed towards the front **b** situated in advance **2** of or occupying a fielding position in cricket in front of the batsman's wicket **3a** eager, ready **b** lacking modesty or reserve; pert **4** advanced in development; precocious **5** moving, tending, or leading towards a position in (or at the) front **6** advocating an advanced policy in the direction of what is considered progress **7** of or getting ready for the future ⟨*~ planning*⟩ – **forwardly** *adv*, **forwardness** *n*

²forward *adv* **1** to or towards what is ahead or in front ⟨*from that time ~*⟩ ⟨*moved slowly ~ through the crowd*⟩ **2** to or towards an earlier time ⟨*bring the date of the meeting ~*⟩ **3** into prominence

³forward *n* a mainly attacking player in hockey, soccer, etc stationed at or near the front of his/her side or team

⁴forward *vt* **1** to help onwards; promote **2a** to send (forwards) ⟨*will ~ the goods on payment*⟩ **b** to send onwards from an intermediate point in transit – **forwarder** *n*

fosse, foss /fos/ *n* a ditch, moat

¹fossil *n* **1a** a relic of an animal or plant of a past geological age, preserved in the earth's crust **2a** a person with outmoded views **b** sthg that has become rigidly fixed – **fossiliferous** *adj*

²fossil *adj* **1a** extracted from the earth and derived from the remains of living things ⟨*coal is a ~ fuel*⟩ **b** preserved in a mineralized or petrified form from a past geological age **2** outmoded

fossilize, -ise *vt* **1** to convert into a fossil **2** to make outmoded, rigid, or fixed ~*vi* to become fossilized – **fossilization** *n*

¹foster *adj* giving, receiving, or sharing parental care though not related by blood ⟨*a ~ child*⟩

²foster *vt* **1** to give parental care to; nurture **2** to promote the growth or development of – **fosterer** *n*

fought *past of* FIGHT

¹foul *adj* **1a** offensive to the senses **b** dirty, stained ⟨*~ linen*⟩ **2** notably unpleasant or distressing; detestable **3** obscene, abusive ⟨*~ language*⟩ **4a** treacherous, dishonourable ⟨*fair means or ~*⟩ **b** constituting a foul in a game or sport **5** defaced by changes ⟨*~ manuscript*⟩ **6** encrusted, clogged, or choked with a foreign substance ⟨*a ~ ship's bottom*⟩ **7** polluted ⟨*~ air*⟩ **8** entangled ⟨*a ~ anchor*⟩ – **foulness** *n*

²foul *n* **1** an entanglement or collision in angling, sailing, etc **2** an infringement of the rules in a game or sport

³foul *vi* **1** to become or be foul; *esp* to become clogged, choked up, or entangled **2** to commit a foul in a sport or game ~*vt* **1a** to pollute **b** to become entangled with **c** to encrust with a foreign substance **d** to obstruct, block **2** to dishonour, discredit **3** to commit a foul against

foulmouthed *adj* given to the use of obscene, profane, or abusive language

foul play *n* violence; *esp* murder

foul-up *n* **1** a state of confusion caused by ineptitude, carelessness, or mismanagement **2** a mechanical difficulty USE infml

oul up vt **1** chiefly NAm to contaminate **2** chiefly NAm to spoil or confuse by making mistakes or using poor judgment **3** to entangle, block ⟨fouled up the communications⟩ USE (2 & 3) infml

ound past of FIND

ound adj having all usual, standard, or reasonably expected equipment ⟨the boat comes fully ∼, ready to go⟩

ound vt **1** to take the first steps in building **2** to set or ground on sthg solid – often + on or upon **3** to establish (e g an institution), often with provision for continued financial support – **founder** n

ound vt to melt (metal) and pour into a mould – **founder** n

oundation n **1** the act of founding **2** the basis on which thg stands or is supported **3** an organization or institution established by endowment with provision for future maintenance **4** an underlying natural or prepared base or support; esp the whole masonry substructure on which a building rests **5** a body or ground on which sthg is built up or overlaid **6** a cream, lotion, etc applied as a base for other facial make-up – **foundational** adj, **foundationally** adv, **foundationless** adj

oundation garment n a girdle, corset, or other supporting undergarment

oundation stone n a stone in the foundation of a building, esp when laid with public ceremony

ounder vi **1** to become disabled; esp to go lame **2** to collapse; GIVE WAY 3a **3** to sink **4** to come to grief; fail ∼ vt o disable (e g a horse), esp by overwork

ounding father n **1** a founder **2** cap both Fs a member of the American Constitutional Convention of 1787

oundling n an infant found abandoned by unknown parents

oundry n (a place for) casting metals

ount n a fountain, source

ount, chiefly NAm **font** n, Br a complete set of matrices of characters (e g for photocomposition) in 1 style

ountain n **1** a spring of water issuing from the earth **2** source **3** (the structure providing) an artificially produced jet of water **4** a reservoir containing a supply of liquid (e g in a lamp or printing press)

ountain vb to (cause to) flow or spout like a fountain

ountainhead n **1** a spring that is the source of a stream **a** principal source

ountain pen n a pen containing a reservoir that automatically feeds the nib with ink

our n **1** (the number) 4 **2** the fourth in a set or series ⟨the ∼ of hearts⟩ **3** sthg having 4 parts or members or a denomination of 4; esp (the crew of) a 4-person racing rowing boat **4** a shot in cricket that crosses the boundary after having hit the ground and scores 4 runs – **four** adj or pron, **fourfold** adj or adv

our-in-hand n (a vehicle drawn by) a team of 4 horses driven by 1 person

our-leaf clover, four-leaved clover n a clover leaf that has 4 leaflets instead of 3 and is held to bring good luck

our-letter word n any of a group of vulgar or obscene words typically made up of 4 letters

ourpenny adj costing or worth fourpence

our-poster n a bed with 4 tall often carved corner posts designed to support curtains or a canopy

oursquare adj forthright

oursquare adv **1** in a solidly based and steady way **2** absolutely

fourteen n (the number) 14 – **fourteen** adj or pron, **fourteenth** adj or n

fourth n **1** number four in a countable series **2a** (the combination of 2 notes at) a musical interval of 4 diatonic degrees **b** a subdominant **3** the 4th and usu highest forward gear or speed of a motor vehicle – **fourth** adj or adv, **fourthly** adv

fourth dimension n **1** a dimension in addition to length, breadth, and depth; specif a coordinate in addition to 3 rectangular coordinates, esp when interpreted as the time coordinate in a space-time continuum **2** sthg outside the range of ordinary experience – **fourth-dimensional** adj

fourth estate n, often cap F&E PRESS 6a

¹fowl n, pl fowls, esp collectively fowl **1** BIRD 1 **2** DOMESTIC FOWL; esp an adult hen **3** the flesh of birds used as food

²fowl vi to hunt, catch, or kill wildfowl – **fowler** n

fowling piece n a light gun for shooting birds or small animals

fowl pest n a fatal infectious virus disease of domestic poultry

¹fox n, pl foxes, esp collectively fox **1** (the fur of) a red fox or related flesh-eating mammal of the dog family with a pointed muzzle, large erect ears, and a long bushy tail **2** a clever crafty person **3** cap a member, or the language, of an American Indian people who once lived in Wisconsin

²fox vt **1** to outwit **2** to baffle

foxglove n a common tall European plant that has showy white or purple tubular flowers and is a source of digitalis

foxhole n a pit dug, usu hastily, for individual cover against enemy fire

foxhound n any of various large swift powerful hounds of great endurance used in hunting foxes

foxhunting n the practice of hunting foxes on horseback with a pack of hounds – **foxhunter** n

fox terrier n a small lively smooth-haired or wirehaired terrier formerly used to dig out foxes

Foxtrot – a communications code word for the letter f

fox-trot vi or n (to dance) a ballroom dance that includes slow walking and quick running steps

foxy adj **1** cunningly shrewd in conniving and contriving **2** warmly reddish brown **3** NAm physically attractive – **foxily** adv, **foxiness** n

foyer n an anteroom or lobby (e g of a theatre); also an entrance hallway

fracas n, pl fracas, NAm fracases a noisy quarrel; a brawl

fraction n **1a** a number (e g ¾, ⅝, 0.234) that is expressed as the quotient of 2 numbers **b** a (small) portion or section **2** an act of breaking up; specif the breaking of the bread by a priest in the Eucharist **3** a tiny bit; a little ⟨a ∼ closer⟩ **4** any of several portions (e g of a distillate) separable by fractionation

fractional adj **1** of or being a fraction **2** relatively tiny or brief **3** of or being a process for separating components of a mixture through differences in physical or chemical properties ⟨∼ distillation⟩

fractionally adv to a very small extent

fractionate vt to separate (e g a mixture) into different portions – **fractionation** n, **fractionator** n

fractious adj irritable and restless; hard to control – **fractiously** adv, **fractiousness** n

¹fracture n **1** a break or breaking, esp of hard tissue (e g bone) **2** the appearance of a broken surface of a mineral **3a** the substitution of a diphthong for an orig simple vowel, esp under the influence of a following consonant **b** a diphthong thus substituted

²**fracture** vt 1 to cause a fracture in 2 to damage or destroy as if by breaking apart; break up ~vi to undergo fracture

fragile adj 1 easily shattered 2 lacking in strength; delicate – **fragility** n

¹**fragment** n an incomplete, broken off, or detached part

²**fragment** vt to break up or apart into fragments ~vi to fall to pieces – **fragmentation** n

fragmentary adj consisting of fragments; incomplete – **fragmentarily** adv, **fragmentariness** n

fragrance n 1 (the quality or state of having) a sweet or pleasant smell 2 the smell of perfume, cologne, or toilet water – **fragrant** adj, **fragrantly** adv

frail adj 1 morally or physically weak 2 easily broken or destroyed 3 slight, insubstantial – **fraily** adv, **frailness** n

frailty n a (moral) fault due to weakness

¹**frame** vt 1a to plan; WORK OUT 1b, c b to shape, construct 2 to fit or adjust for a purpose 3 to construct by fitting and uniting the parts of 4a to contrive evidence against (an innocent person) b to prearrange the outcome of (e g a contest) – **framer** n

²**frame** n 1 sthg composed of parts fitted together and joined; esp the physical structure of a human body 2 a structure that gives shape or strength (e g to a building) 3a an open case or structure made for admitting, enclosing, or supporting sthg ⟨a window ~⟩ b a machine built on or within a framework ⟨a spinning ~⟩ c the rigid part of a bicycle d the outer structure of a pair of glasses that holds the lenses 4a an enclosing border b the matter or area enclosed in such a border: e g (1) any of the squares in which scores for each round are recorded (e g in bowling) (2) a box of a strip cartoon (3) a single picture of the series on a length of film (4) a single complete television picture made up of lines c a limiting, typical, or esp appropriate set of circumstances; a framework 5 a minimal unit of programmed instruction or stimulus calling for a response by the student 6 one round of play in snooker, bowling, etc 7 a frame-up – infml

³**frame** adj having a wooden frame ⟨~ houses⟩

frame of mind n a particular mental or emotional state

frame of reference n 1 an arbitrary set of axes used as a reference to describe the position or motion of sthg or to formulate physical laws 2 a set or system of facts, ideas, etc serving to orient or give particular meaning to a statement, a point of view, etc

frame-up n a conspiracy to frame sby or sthg – infml

framework n 1 a skeletal, openwork, or structural frame 2 a basic structure (e g of ideas)

franc n (a note or coin representing) the basic money unit of France, Belgium, Switzerland, and certain other French-speaking countries

¹**franchise** n 1 freedom from some burden or restriction 2a a special privilege granted to an individual or group b a right or privilege; specif the right to vote c the right granted to an individual or group to market a company's goods or services in a particular territory; also the territory involved in such a right

²**franchise** vt to grant a franchise to

Franciscan n a member of the Order of missionary friars founded by St Francis of Assisi in 1209 – **Franciscan** adj

Franco- comb form 1 French nation, people, or culture ⟨Francophile⟩ 2 French and ⟨Franco-German⟩

¹**frank** adj marked by free, forthright, and sincere expression ⟨a ~ reply⟩; also undisguised ⟨~ admiration⟩ – **frankness** n

²**frank** vt 1a to send (a piece of mail) without charge b to put a frank on (a piece of mail) 2 to enable to pass or go freely or easily ⟨the delegates will ~ the policy⟩

³**frank** n 1 an official signature or sign on a piece of mail indicating exemption from postal charges 2 a mark or stamp on a piece of mail indicating postage paid 3 a franked envelope

Frank n a member of a W Germanic people that established themselves in the Netherlands and Gaul and on the Rhine in the 3rd and 4th c – **Frankish** adj

frankfurter n a cured cooked, usu beef and pork, sausage

frankincense n a fragrant gum resin chiefly from African or Arabian trees that is burnt as incense

franklin n a medieval English landowner of free but not noble birth

frankly adv to tell the truth; actually ⟨~, I couldn't care less⟩

frantic adj 1 emotionally out of control ⟨~ with anger and frustration⟩ 2 marked by fast and nervous, disordered, or anxiety-driven activity – **frantically** adv, **franticly** adv, **franticness** n

frappé n or adj (a drink that is) chilled or partly frozen

fraternal adj 1a of or involving brothers b of or being fraternity or society 2 of twins derived from 2 ova – friendly, brotherly – **fraternalism** n, **fraternally** adv

fraternity n 1 sing or pl in constr a group of people associated or formally organized for a common purpose, interest, or pleasure: e g a a fraternal order b a club for male students in some American universities 2 brotherliness 3 sing or pl in constr men of the same usu specified class, profession, character, or tastes ⟨the racing ~⟩

fraternize, -ise vi 1 to associate or mingle on friendly terms 2 to associate on close terms with citizens or troops of a hostile country – **fraternization** n

fratricide n (the act of) sby who kills his/her brother or sister – **fratricidal** adj

Frau n, pl **Frauen** a German-speaking married woman used as a title equivalent to Mrs

fraud n 1a deception, esp for unlawful gain b a trick 2 a person who is not what he/she pretends to be b sthg that is not what it seems or is represented to be

fraudulent adj characterized by, involving, or done by fraud – **fraudulence** n, **fraudulently** adv

fraught adj 1 filled or charged with sthg specified ⟨the situation is ~ with danger⟩ 2 Br characterized by anxieties and tensions ⟨~ and complex relationships⟩

fräulein n an unmarried German-speaking woman – used as a title equivalent to Miss

¹**fray** n a brawl, fight

²**fray** vt 1 to separate the threads at the edge of (e g fabric) 2 to strain, irritate ⟨his temper became a bit ~ed⟩ ~vi to wear out or into shreds

¹**frazzle** vt to put in a state of extreme physical or nervous fatigue; upset – infml

²**frazzle** n a frazzled condition ⟨worn to a ~⟩ – infml

¹**freak** n 1a a sudden and odd or seemingly pointless idea or whim b a seemingly capricious action or event 2 a person or animal with a physical oddity who appears in a circus, funfair, etc 3 a person seen as being highly unconventional, esp in dress or ideas 4 an ardent enthusiast ⟨a jazz ~⟩ 5a a sexual pervert b HEAD 19 – often in combination ⟨speedfreak⟩; slang USE (3 & 4) infml

²**freak** vb FREAK OUT – slang

freakish adj whimsical, capricious – **freakishly** adv, **freakishness** n

freak of nature n FREAK 2

freak-out n a drug-induced state of mind – slang

freak out *vt* **1** to put under the influence of a (hallucinogenic) drug **2** to put into a state of intense excitement ~ *vi* **1** to experience hallucinations or withdraw from reality, esp by taking drugs **2** to behave in an irrational, uncontrolled, or unconventional manner (as if) under the influence of drugs *USE* slang

freckle *n* any of the small brownish spots on the skin, esp of white people, that increase in number and intensity on exposure to sunlight – **freckly** *adj*

freckle *vb* to mark or become marked with freckles or small spots

free *adj* **1a** enjoying civil and political liberty **b** politically independent **c** not subject to the control or domination of another **2a** not determined by external influences ⟨*a ~ agent*⟩ **b** voluntary, spontaneous **3a** exempt, relieved, or released ⟨*as* from an unpleasant or unwanted condition or obligation ⟨*~ from pain*⟩ – often in combination ⟨*trouble*-free⟩ ⟨*duty*-free⟩ **b** not bound, confined, or detained by force ⟨*prisoner was now ~*⟩ **4a** having no trade restrictions **b** not subject to government regulation **5** having or taken up with no obligations or commitments ⟨*I'll be ~ this evening*⟩ **6** having an unrestricted scope ⟨*a ~ variable*⟩ **7a** not obstructed or impeded **b** not being used or occupied ⟨*used a ~ hand*⟩ **c** not hampered or restricted; unfettered ⟨*~ speech*⟩ **8** not fastened ⟨*the ~ end of the rope*⟩ **9a** lavish, unrestrained ⟨*very ~ with her praises*⟩ **b** outspoken **c** too familiar or forward **10** not costing or charging anything **11a** not (permanently) united with, attached to, or combined with sthg else; separate ⟨*~ oxygen*⟩ **b** capable of being used alone as a meaningful linguistic form ⟨*hats is a ~ form*⟩ **12a** not literal or exact ⟨*~ translation*⟩ **b** not restricted by or conforming to conventional forms ⟨*~ jazz*⟩ **13** open to all comers – **freely** *adv*

free *adv* **1** in a free manner **2** without charge ⟨*admitted ~*⟩ **3** not close-hauled ⟨*sailing ~*⟩

free *vt* **1** to cause to be free **2** to relieve or rid of sthg that restrains, confines, restricts, or embarrasses ⟨*~ her husband from debt*⟩ **3** to disentangle, clear – **freer** *n*

free association *n* the expression of conscious thoughts, ideas, etc used esp in psychoanalysis to reveal unconscious processes; *esp* (the reporting of) the first thought, image, etc that comes to mind in response to a given stimulus (e g a word)

freebie, freebee *n, chiefly NAm* sthg (e g a theatre ticket) given or received without charge – *infml*

freeboard *n* the vertical distance between the waterline and the deck of a ship

freebooter *n* a pirate, plunderer

freeborn *adj* not born in slavery

Free Church *n, chiefly Br* a British Nonconformist church

freedman, fem freedwoman *n* sby freed from slavery

freedom *n* **1a** the absence of necessity or constraint in choice or action **b** liberation from slavery or restraint **c** being exempt or released *from* sthg (onerous) ⟨*~ from care*⟩ **2a** ease, facility **b** being frank, open, or outspoken **c** improper familiarity **3** boldness of conception or execution **4** unrestricted use of ⟨*gave him the ~ of their home*⟩ **5** a right or privilege, esp political

free enterprise *n* an economic system that relies on private business operating competitively for profit to satisfy consumer demands and in which government action is restricted to protecting public interest and to keeping the national economy in balance

free-fall *n* **1** (the condition of) unrestrained motion in a gravitational field **2** the part of a parachute jump before the parachute opens

free-floating *adj* relatively uncommitted to a particular course of action, party, etc

free-for-all *n* **1** a fight or competition open to all comers and usu with no rules **2** an often vociferous quarrel or argument involving several participants

freehand *adj* done without the aid of drawing or measuring instruments – **freehand** *adv*

free hand *n* freedom of action or decision ⟨*gave her a ~*⟩

freehanded *adj* openhanded, generous – **freehandedly** *adv*

freehold *n* a tenure in absolute possession; *also* a property held by such tenure – **freeholder** *n*

free house *n* a public house in Britain that is entitled to sell drinks supplied by more than 1 brewery

free kick *n* an unhindered kick in soccer, rugby, etc awarded because of a breach of the rules by an opponent

freelance *n* a person who pursues a profession without long-term contractual commitments to any one employer – **free-lance** *adj*

freelance *vi* to act as a freelance

free lance *n* a mercenary knight

free-living *adj, of a living organism* neither parasitic nor symbiotic – **free-liver** *n*

freeload *vi* to take advantage of another's generosity or hospitality without sharing in the cost or responsibility involved – *infml* – **freeloader** *n*

free love *n* the concept or practice of sexual relations without legal, financial, etc commitment

freeman *n* **1** sby enjoying civil or political liberty **2** sby who has the full rights of a citizen

Freemason *n* a member of an ancient and widespread secret fraternity called Free and Accepted Masons

freemasonry *n* **1** *cap* the principles, institutions, or practices of Freemasons **2** natural or instinctive fellowship or sympathy

free port *n* an enclosed (section of a) port where goods are received and shipped free of customs duty

free-range *adj* of, being, or produced by poultry reared in the open air rather than in a battery

free rein *n* unrestricted liberty or scope ⟨*give ~ to one's feelings*⟩

freesia *n* any of a genus of sweet-scented African plants of the iris family with red, white, yellow, or purple flowers

freestanding *adj* standing without lateral support or attachment ⟨*a ~ column*⟩

freestone *n* **1** a stone that can be cut without splitting **2** (a fruit with) a stone to which the flesh does not cling

freestyle *n* **1** (a style used in) a competition in which a contestant uses a style (e g of swimming) of his/her choice **2** catch-as-catch-can **3** CRAWL 2

freethinker *n* a person who forms opinions on the basis of reason; *esp* one who rejects religious dogma – **freethinking** *n* or *adj*

free thought *n* freethinking; *specif* 18th-c deism

free trade *n* trade based on the unrestricted international exchange of goods

free verse *n* verse without fixed metrical form

freeway *n, NAm* a motorway

freewheel *n* a device fitted to a vehicle wheel allowing forward motion when the motive power is removed

freewheel *vi* **1** *of a bicycle, cyclist, or motor car* to coast freely without power from the pedals or engine **2** to move, live, or drift along freely or irresponsibly – **freewheeler** *n*

free will *n* the power of choosing without the constraint of divine necessity or causal law

¹**freeze** *vb* **froze; frozen** *vi* **1** to become congealed into a solid (e g ice) by cold **2** to become chilled with cold ⟨*almost* froze *to death*⟩ **3** to stick solidly (as if) by freezing **4** to become clogged with ice ⟨*the water pipes* froze⟩ **5** to become fixed or motionless; *esp* to abruptly cease acting or speaking **6** to be capable of undergoing freezing for preservation ⟨*do strawberries* ~ *well?*⟩ ~ *vt* **1** to convert from a liquid to a solid by cold **2** to make extremely cold **3a** to act on, usu destructively, by frost **b** to anaesthetize (as if) by cold ⟨*the injection* froze *her gum*⟩ **4** to cause to become fixed, immovable, or unalterable, as if paralysed **5** to immobilize the expenditure, withdrawal, or exchange of (foreign-owned bank balances) by government regulation **6** to preserve (e g food) by freezing the water content and maintaining at a temperature below 0°C – **freezingly** *adv*

²**freeze** *n* **1** freezing cold weather **2a** an act or period of freezing sthg, esp wages or prices at a certain level **b** being frozen

freeze-dry *vb* to dehydrate (sthg) while in a frozen state in a vacuum, esp for preservation – **freeze-dried** *adj*

freeze out *vt* to deliberately ignore or fail to respond to (sby) – infml

freezer *n* an apparatus that freezes or keeps cool; *esp* an insulated cabinet or room for storing frozen food or for freezing food rapidly

freeze-up *n* a spell of very cold weather – infml

¹**freight** *n* **1** the charge made for transporting goods **2 a** cargo **3** a goods train

²**freight** *vt* to load (esp a ship) with goods for transport

freighter *n* **1** a person or company that (charters and) loads a ship **2** a ship or aircraft used chiefly to carry freight

freightliner *n, Br* a train designed for carrying container-ized cargo

¹**French** *adj* of France, its people, or their language – **Frenchman** *n*, **Frenchness** *n*

²**French** *n* **1** the Romance language of the people of France and of parts of Belgium, Switzerland, and Canada **2** *pl in constr* the people of France **3** language full of swear words and mild profanities – infml ⟨*I wish we'd never heard of the bugger, pardon my* ~ – Alan Coren⟩

French bean *n, chiefly Br* (the seed or pod of) a common bean often cultivated for its slender edible green pods

French bread *n* crusty white bread made in long thin loaves

French chalk *n* a soft white granular variety of soapstone used esp for drawing lines on cloth and as a dry lubri-cant

French dressing *n* a salad dressing of oil, vinegar, and seasonings

french fry *n, chiefly NAm* ¹CHIP 6a – usu pl

French horn *n* a circular valved brass instrument with a usual range from B below the bass staff upwards for more than 3 octaves

French kiss *n* a kiss made with open mouths and usu with tongue-to-tongue contact – **French-kiss** *vb*

French leave *n* leave taken without permission

French letter *n, Br* a condom – infml

French-polish *vt* to apply French polish to (wood or furniture) in order to obtain a high gloss finish

French polish *n* a solution of shellac used as a wood polish

French windows *n pl* a pair of doors with full length glazing

frenetic *adj* frenzied, frantic – **frenetically** *adv*

frenzied *adj* marked by frenzy ⟨*the dog's* ~ *barking*⟩ – **frenziedly** *adv*

frenzy *n* **1** a temporary madness **2** (a spell of) wild, compulsive, or agitated behaviour

frequency *n* **1** frequency, frequence the fact or condition of occurring frequently **2a** the number of times that a periodic function repeats the same sequence of values during a unit variation of the independent variable **b** the number or proportion of individuals in a single class when objects are classified according to variations in a set of attributes **3a** the number of complete alternations per second of an alternating current **b** the number of sound waves per second produced by a sounding body **c** the number of complete oscillations per second of an electro-magnetic wave

¹**frequent** *adj* **1** often repeated or occurring **2** habitual, persistent – **frequently** *adv*

²**frequent** *vt* to be in or visit often or habitually – **frequenter** *n*, **frequentation** *n*

fresco *n, pl* **frescoes, frescos** (a painting made by) the application of water colours to moist plaster

¹**fresh** *adj* **1a** not salt ⟨~ *water*⟩ **b** free from taint; clean **c** *of wind* rather strong **d** *of weather* cool and windy **2a** *of food* not preserved **b** refreshed ⟨*rose* ~ *from a good night's sleep*⟩ **c** not stale, sour, or decayed **3a** (different or alternative and) new ⟨*make a* ~ *start*⟩ **b** newly or just come or arrived ⟨~ *from school*⟩ **4** too forward with a person of the opposite sex ⟨*slapped his face when he got* ~ *with me*⟩ – infml – **freshly** *adv*, **freshness** *n*

²**fresh** *adv* **1** just recently; newly ⟨*a* ~ *laid egg*⟩ **2** *chiefly NAm* as of a very short time ago ⟨*we're* ~ *out of tomatoes*⟩

freshen *vi* **1** *of wind* to increase in strength **2** *of water* to lose saltiness ~ *vt* to make fresh; *also* to refresh, revive – often + *up*

freshen up *vb* to make (oneself) fresher or more comfortable, esp by washing, changing one's clothes, etc

fresher *n, chiefly Br* a student in the first term at college or university – infml

freshet *n* STREAM 1

freshwater *adj* of or living in fresh water

¹**fret** *vb* **-tt-** *vt* **1** to torment with anxiety or worry; vex **2** to eat or gnaw into; corrode **b** to rub, chafe **c** to make (e g a channel) by wearing away **3** to agitate, ripple ~ *vi* **1** to eat into sthg; corrode **2** to chafe **3a** to become vexed or worried **b** *of running water* to become agitated

²**fret** *n* **1** (a spot that has been subject to) wearing away **2** a state of (querulous) mental agitation or irritation

³**fret** *vt* **-tt-** **1** to decorate with interlaced designs **2** to decorate (e g a ceiling) with embossed or carved patterns

⁴**fret** *n* an ornamental pattern or decoration consisting of small straight bars intersecting usu at right angles

⁵**fret** *n* any of a series of ridges fixed across the fingerboard of a stringed musical instrument (e g a guitar)

fretful *adj* **1** tending to fret; in a fret **2** *of water* having the surface agitated – **fretfully** *adv*, **fretfulness** *n*

fretsaw *n* a narrow-bladed fine-toothed saw held under tension in a frame and used for cutting intricate patterns in thin wood

fretwork *n* **1** decoration consisting of frets **2** ornamental openwork, esp in thin wood; *also* ornamental work in relief

Freudian *adj* of or conforming to the psychoanalytic theories or practices of S Freud – **Freudian** *n*

Freudian slip *n* a slip of the tongue that is held to reveal some unconscious aspect of the speaker's mind

friable *adj* easily crumbled – **friableness** *n*, **friability** *n*

friar *n* a member of a religious order combining monast life with outside religious activity and orig owning neither personal nor community property

friary *n* (a building housing) a community of friars

fricassee *n* a dish of small pieces of stewed chicken, rabbit, etc served in a white sauce – **fricassee** *vt*

fricative *n* a consonant (e g /f, th, sh/) made by forcing air through a narrow opening formed by placing the tongue or lip close to another part of the mouth, or in languages other than English, esp Arabic, also by constricting the pharynx – **fricative** *adj*

friction *n* **1a** the rubbing of one body against another **b** resistance to relative motion between 2 bodies in contact **2** disagreement between 2 people or parties of opposing views – **frictional** *adj*, **frictionless** *adj*

Friday *n* the day of the week following Thursday – **Fridays** *adv*

fridge *n, chiefly Br* a refrigerator

friend *n* **1a** a person whose company, interests, and attitudes one finds sympathetic and to whom one is not closely related **b** an acquaintance **2a** sby or sthg not hostile **b** sby or sthg of the same nation, party, or group **c** sby or sthg that favours or encourages sthg (e g a charity) ⟨*a ~ of the poor*⟩ **3** *cap* a Quaker – **friendless** *adj*

¹**friendly** *adj* **1a** having the relationship of friends ⟨*Billy is ~ with Dave*⟩ **b** showing interest and goodwill ⟨*~ neighbours*⟩ **c** not hostile ⟨*~ nations*⟩ **d** inclined to be favourable – usu + *to* **2** cheerful, comforting **3** engaged in only for pleasure or entertainment and not hotly contested ⟨*a ~ game of poker*⟩ – **friendliness** *n*

²**friendly** *n, chiefly Br* a match played for practice or pleasure and not as part of a competition

friendly society *n, often cap F&S, Br* a mutual insurance association providing its subscribers with benefits during sickness, unemployment, and old age

friendship *n* being friends or being friendly

frier *n* a fryer

¹**frieze** *n* a heavy coarse fabric made of wool and shoddy

²**frieze** *n* **1** the part of an entablature between the architrave and the cornice **2** a sculptured or ornamented band (e g on a building)

frig *vi* **-gg-** **1** to masturbate **2** to have sexual intercourse *USE vulg*

frigate *n* **1** a square-rigged 3-masted warship next in size below a ship of the line **2** a general-purpose naval escort vessel between a corvette and a cruiser in size

¹**fright** *n* **1** fear excited by sudden danger or shock **2** sthg unsightly, strange, ugly, or shocking ⟨*she looks a ~*⟩ – infml

²**fright** *vt* to frighten – chiefly poetic

frighten *vt* **1** to make afraid; scare **2** to force by frightening ⟨*~ ed them into confessing*⟩ *~ vi* to become frightened – **frighteningly** *adv*

frightful *adj* **1** causing intense fear, shock, or horror **2** unpleasant, difficult ⟨*had a ~ morning*⟩ – infml – **frightfully** *adv*

frigid *adj* **1a** intensely cold **b** lacking warmth or intensity of feeling **2** *esp of a woman* abnormally averse to sexual contact, esp intercourse – **frigidly** *adv*, **frigidness** *n*, **frigidity** *n*

¹**frill** *vt* to provide or decorate with a frill

²**frill** *n* **1a** a gathered or pleated fabric edging used on clothing **b** a small fringed or fluted roll of paper for decorating the bone end of a chop, chicken leg, etc **2** a ruff of hair or feathers round the neck of an animal **3a** an affectation, air **b** sthg decorative but not essential *USE* (*3*) usu pl – **frilly** *adj*

¹**fringe** *n* **1** an ornamental border (e g on a curtain or garment) consisting of straight or twisted threads or tassels **2a** sthg resembling a fringe; a border **b** the hair that falls over the forehead **c** any of the alternating light or dark bands produced by interference or diffraction of light **3a** sthg marginal, additional, or secondary **b** *sing or pl in constr* a group with marginal or extremist views **c** *often cap* a part of the British professional theatre featuring small-scale avant-garde productions

²**fringe** *vt* **1** to provide or decorate with a fringe **2** to serve as a fringe for ⟨*a clearing ~d with trees*⟩

fringe benefit *n* a benefit (e g a pension) granted by an employer to an employee that involves a money cost without affecting basic wage rates

¹**frippery** *n* **1** nonessential ornamentation, esp of a showy or tawdry kind **2** affected elegance

²**frippery** *adj* trifling, tawdry

Frisbee *trademark* – used for a plastic disc thrown between players by a flip of the wrist

Frisian *n* **1** a member of a Germanic people inhabiting Friesland and the Frisian islands **2** the language of the Frisian people – **Frisian** *adj*

¹**frisk** *vi* to leap, skip, or dance in a lively or playful way *~ vt* to search (a person) for sthg, esp a hidden weapon, by passing the hands over his/her body – infml

²**frisk** *n* **1** a gambol, romp **2** an act of frisking

frisky *adj* lively, playful – **friskiness** *n*

frisson *n, pl* **frissons** a shudder, thrill

fritter *n* a piece of fried batter often containing fruit, meat, etc

fritter away *vt* to waste bit by bit ⟨*fritters away all her money on clothes*⟩

frivolous *adj* **1** lacking in seriousness; irresponsibly self-indulgent **2** lacking practicality or serious purpose; unimportant – **frivolity** *n*, **frivolously** *adv*, **frivolousness** *n*

frizz *n* (hair in) a mass of small tight curls – **frizz** *vb*, **frizzy** *adj*, **frizziness** *n*

¹**frizzle** *vb* **frizzling** to frizz or curl (the hair) – **frizzle** *n*, **frizzly** *adj*

²**frizzle** *vt* **1** to fry (e g bacon) until crisp and curled **2** to burn, scorch *~ vi* to cook with a sizzling noise

fro *prep, dial* from

frock *n* **1** a monk's or friar's habit **2** a workman's outer shirt; *esp* SMOCK FROCK **3** a woman's dress

frock coat *n* a usu double-breasted coat with knee-length skirts worn by men, esp in the 19th c

frog *n* **1** any of various tailless smooth-skinned web-footed largely aquatic leaping amphibians **2** the triangular horny pad in the middle of the sole of a horse's foot **3a** a loop attached to a belt to hold a weapon or tool **b** a usu ornamental fastening for the front of a garment consisting of a button and a loop **4** a device permitting the wheels on one rail of a track to cross an intersecting rail **5** a condition in the throat that produces hoarseness ⟨*had a ~ in her throat*⟩ – infml **6** *often cap* a French person – chiefly derog; infml **7** the hollow in either or both faces of a brick to take mortar

frogman *n* a person equipped with face mask, flippers, rubber suit, etc and an air supply for swimming underwater for extended periods

frogmarch *vt* **1** to carry (a person) face downwards by the arms and legs **2** to force (a person) to move forwards with the arms held firmly behind

frogspawn *n* (a gelatinous mass of) frog's eggs

¹**frolic** *vi* **-ck-** **1** to play and run about happily **2** to make merry

²**frolic** *n* **1** (a) playful expression of high spirits; gaiety **2** a lighthearted entertainment or game – **frolicsome** *adj*

from *prep* **1** – used to indicate a starting point: e g **a** a place where a physical movement, or an action or condition suggestive of movement, begins ⟨came here ~ the city⟩ ⟨shot ~ above⟩ ⟨translated ~ French⟩ **b** a starting point in measuring or reckoning or in a statement of extent or limits ⟨cost ~ £5 to £10⟩ ⟨lives 5 miles ~ the coast⟩ ⟨~ 60 to 80 people⟩ **c** a point in time after which a period is reckoned ⟨a week ~ today⟩ **d** a viewpoint ⟨seen ~ my window⟩ ⟨~ a practical standpoint⟩ **2** – used to indicate separation: e g **a** a physical separation ⟨absent ~ school⟩ ⟨took the toy away ~ the baby⟩ **b** removal, refraining, exclusion, release, or differentiation ⟨protection ~ the sun⟩ ⟨relief ~ pain⟩ ⟨kept the news ~ her⟩ ⟨saved ~ drowning⟩ ⟨refrain ~ smoking⟩ ⟨don't know one ~ the other⟩ **3** – used to indicate the source, cause, agent, or basis ⟨a call ~ my lawyer⟩ ⟨a friend ~ Oxford⟩ ⟨made ~ flour⟩ ⟨worked hard ~ necessity⟩ ⟨suffering ~ mumps⟩ ⟨~ what I hear, he's quite rich⟩

frond n (a shoot or thallus resembling) a leaf, esp of a palm or fern – **fronded** adj

¹front n **1** (feigned) demeanour or bearing, esp in the face of a challenge, danger, etc ⟨put up a brave ~⟩ **2a** the vanguard **b** often cap a zone of conflict between armies **c** the lateral space occupied by a military unit **3a** a sphere of activity ⟨progress on the educational ~⟩ **b** a movement linking divergent elements to achieve certain common objectives; esp a political coalition **4a** the (main) face of a building **b** the forward part or surface: e g **(1)** the part of the human body opposite to the back **(2)** the part of a garment covering the chest **c** a frontage **d** the beach promenade at a seaside resort **5** the boundary between 2 dissimilar air masses **6a** a position ahead of a person or of the foremost part of a thing **b** a position of importance, leadership, or advantage **7a** a person, group, or thing used to mask the identity or true character of the actual controlling agent **b** a person who serves as the nominal head or spokesman of an enterprise or group to lend it prestige **8** the forehead – poetic – **in front of** 1 directly ahead of ⟨watching the road in front of him⟩ **2** in the presence of ⟨don't swear in front of the children⟩ – **out front** in the audience

²front vi **1** to face – often + on or onto ⟨garden ~ing on a lake⟩ **2** to serve as a front – often + for **3** Austr & NZ to appear; TURN UP **2** – often + up ~ vt **1** to be in front of **2** to supply a front to **3** to face towards ⟨the house ~s the street⟩ **4** to articulate (a sound) with the tongue farther forward

³front adj **1** of or situated at the front **2** articulated at or towards the front of the mouth ⟨~ vowels⟩ – **front** adv

frontage n **1a** a piece of land that fronts **b** the land between the front of a building and the street **2** (the width of) the front face of a building

¹frontal n a facade

²frontal adj **1** of or adjacent to the forehead ⟨~ bone⟩ **2a** of, situated at, or showing the front ⟨full ~ nudity⟩ **b** direct ⟨~ assault⟩ **3** of a meteorological front – **frontally** adv

front bench n either of 2 rows of benches in Parliament on which party leaders sit

frontier n **1** a border between 2 countries **2** the boundary between the known and the unknown – often pl with sing. meaning ⟨the ~s of medicine⟩ **3** NAm a region that forms the margin of settled or developed territory – **frontier** adj

frontiersman n a man living on the frontier

frontispiece n an illustration preceding and usu facing the title page of a book or magazine

front line n **1** a military front **2** the most advanced,

responsible, or significant position in a field of activity – **front-line** adj

front-page adj very newsworthy

front-runner n **1** a contestant who runs best when in the lead **2** a leading contestant in a competition

¹frost n **1a** (the temperature that causes) freezing **b** a covering of minute ice crystals on a cold surface **2a** coldness of attitude or manner **b** a failure – chiefly infml

²frost vt **1a** to cover (as if) with frost **b** to produce a fine-grained slightly roughened surface on (metal, glass, etc) **c** to cover (e g a cake or grapes) with sugar; also, chiefly NAm to ice (a cake) **2** to injure or kill (e g plants) by frost ~ vi to freeze – often + over

frostbite n (gangrene or other local effect of a partial) freezing of some part of the body

frostbitten adj afflicted with frostbite

frosting n **1** a dull or roughened finish on metal or glass **2a** Br thick fluffy cooked icing **b** chiefly NAm icing

frosty adj **1** marked by or producing frost **2** (appearing as if) covered with frost **3** marked by coolness or extreme reserve in manner – **frostily** adv, **frostiness** n

¹froth n **1a** a mass of bubbles formed on or in a liquid **b** a foamy saliva sometimes accompanying disease or exhaustion **2** sthg insubstantial or of little value

²froth vt to cause to foam – often + up ~ vi to produce or emit froth – often + up

frothy adj gaily frivolous or light – **frothily** adv, **frothiness** n

¹frown vi **1** to contract the brow in a frown **2** to give evidence of displeasure or disapproval – often + on or upon ~ vt to express by frowning – **frowner** n, **frowningly** adv

²frown n **1** a wrinkling of the brow in displeasure, concentration, or puzzlement **2** an expression of displeasure

frowst vi, chiefly Br to remain indoors in a hot airless room

frowsty adj, chiefly Br STUFFY 1a

frowsy, frowzy adj **1** having a slovenly or uncared-for appearance **2** musty, stale

froze past of FREEZE

frozen adj **1a** treated, affected, solidified, or crusted over by freezing **b** subject to long and severe cold ⟨the ~ north⟩ **2a** drained or incapable of emotion **b** incapable of being changed, moved, or undone **c** not available for present use ⟨~ capital⟩ – **frozenly** adv, **frozenness** n

fructification n **1** forming or producing fruit **2** FRUIT 1d

fructify vi to bear fruit – fml ~ vt to make fruitful or productive ⟨social philosophy fructified the political thinking of liberals – TLS⟩ – fml

frugal adj economical in the expenditure of resources; sparing – **frugally** adv, **frugality** n

¹fruit n **1a** a product of plant growth (e g grain or vegetables) ⟨the ~s of the field⟩ **b(1)** the (edible) reproductive body of a flowering plant; esp one having a sweet pulp associated with the seed **(2)** a succulent edible plant part used chiefly in a dessert or sweet dish **c** a dish, quantity, or diet of fruits ⟨please pass the ~⟩ **d** the ripened fertilized ovary of a flowering plant together with its contents **2** offspring, progeny **3a** the state of bearing fruit ⟨a tree in ~⟩ **b** a (favourable) product or result – often pl with sing. meaning **4** Br a fellow – in old fruit; infml – **fruited** adj

²fruit vb to (cause to) bear fruit

fruit bat n any of various large Old World fruit-eating bats of warm regions

fruiterer n one who deals in fruit

fruit fly *n* any of various small flies whose larvae feed on fruit or decaying vegetable matter

fruitful *adj* **1** (conducive to) yielding or producing (abundant) fruit **2** abundantly productive – **fruitfully** *adv*, **fruitfulness** *n*

fruition *n* **1** bearing fruit **2** realization, fulfilment

fruitless *adj* **1** lacking or not bearing fruit **2** useless, unsuccessful – **fruitlessly** *adv*, **fruitlessness** *n*

fruit machine *n*, *Br* a coin-operated gambling machine that pays out according to different combinations of symbols (e g different types of fruit) visible on wheels

fruity *adj* **1** having the flavour of the unfermented fruit ⟨~ *wine*⟩ **2** *of a voice* marked by richness and depth **3** amusing in a sexually suggestive way ⟨*a ~ story*⟩ – *infml* – **fruitily** *adv*, **fruitiness** *n*

frump *n* **1** a dowdy unattractive girl or woman **2** a staid drab old-fashioned person *USE* chiefly *infml* – **frumpish** *adj*, **frumpy** *adj*

frustrate *vt* **1a** to balk or defeat in an endeavour; foil **b** to induce feelings of discouragement and vexation in **2** to make ineffectual; nullify – **frustrating** *adj*, **frustratingly** *adv*

frustration *n* **1a** frustrating or being frustrated **b** a deep sense of insecurity, tension, and dissatisfaction arising from unresolved problems or unfulfilled needs **2** sthg that frustrates

¹fry *vb* to cook in hot fat

²fry *n* **1** a dish of fried food **2** *NAm* a social gathering (e g a picnic) at which food is fried and eaten

³fry *n*, *pl* **fry** **1a** recently hatched or very small (adult) fishes **b** the young of other animals, esp when occurring in large numbers **2** a member of a group or class; *esp* a person ⟨*books for small* ~⟩

fryer *n* sthg intended for or used in frying; *esp* a deep vessel for frying foods

frying pan *n* a shallow metal pan with a handle that is used for frying foods – **out of the frying pan into the fire** clear of one difficulty only to fall into a greater one

fry-up *n*, *Br* (a dish prepared by) the frying of food for a simple impromptu meal – chiefly *infml*

fuchsia *n* any of a genus of decorative shrubs with showy nodding flowers usu in deep pinks, reds, and purples

¹fuck *vi* **1** to have sexual intercourse **2** to mess *about* or *around* ~ *vt* to have sexual intercourse with *USE* (*vi*, *vt*) *vulg*

²fuck *n* **1** an act of sexual intercourse **2** the slightest amount ⟨*didn't care a* ~⟩ *USE* vulg

³fuck *interj* – used to express annoyance; vulg

fucker *n* a fool – vulg

fuck off *vi* **1** to go away **2** *NAm* to fuck about *USE* vulg

fuddle *vt* **1** to make drunk **2** to make confused

fuddy-duddy *n* a person who is old-fashioned, pompous, unimaginative, or concerned about trifles – *infml* – **fuddy-duddy** *adj*

¹fudge *vi* to avoid commitment; hedge – usu + *on* ~ *vt* **1a** to devise or put together roughly or without adequate basis ⟨*she could always* ~ *up an excuse*⟩ **b** to falsify ⟨~ *d the figures*⟩ **2** to fail to come to grips with; dodge

²fudge *n* **1** a soft (creamy) sweet made typically of sugar, milk, butter, and flavouring **2** foolish nonsense – *infml*; sometimes used interjectionally

¹fuel *n* **1a** a material used to produce heat or power by combustion **b** nutritive material **c** a material from which atomic energy can be liberated, esp in a reactor **2** a source of sustenance, strength, or encouragement

²fuel *vb* **-ll-** (*NAm* **-l-**, **-ll-**) *vt* **1** to provide with fuel **2** to support, stimulate ⟨*inflation* ~led *by massive wage awards*⟩ ~ *vi* to take in fuel – often + *up*

fug *n* the stuffy atmosphere of a poorly ventilated space – chiefly *infml* – **fuggy** *adj*

¹fugitive *adj* **1** running away or trying to escape **2a** elusive **b** likely to change, fade, or disappear **3** fleeting, ephemeral – **fugitively** *adv*, **fugitiveness** *n*

²fugitive *n* a person who flees or tries to escape, esp from danger, justice, or oppression

fugue *n* **1** a musical composition in which 1 or 2 themes are repeated or imitated by successively entering voices and are developed in a continuous interweaving of the voice parts **2** a disturbed state in which a person performs acts of which on recovery he/she has no recollection and which usu involves disappearance from his/her usual environment – **fuguist** *n*

führer, fuehrer *n* **1** LEADER 2c(3) **2** a leader exercising tyrannical authority

¹-ful *suffix* **1** (*n* → *adj*) full of ⟨*eventful*⟩ ⟨*colourful*⟩ **2** (*n* → *adj*) characterized by ⟨*peaceful*⟩ ⟨*boastful*⟩ **3** (*n* → *adj*) having the qualities of ⟨*masterful*⟩ **4** (*vb* → *adj*) tending to or able to ⟨*mournful*⟩

²-ful *suffix* (*n* → *n*) number or amount that (a specified thing) holds or can hold ⟨*roomful*⟩ ⟨*handful*⟩

fulcrum *n*, *pl* **fulcrums, fulcra** the support about which a lever turns

fulfil, *NAm chiefly* **fulfill** *vt* **-ll-** **1a** to cause to happen as appointed or predicted – usu pass **b** to put into effect; CARRY OUT 1 **c** to measure up to; satisfy **2** to develop the full potential of – **fulfiller** *n*, **fulfilment** *n*

¹full *adj* **1** possessing or containing a great amount or as much or as many as is possible or normal **2a** complete, esp in detail, number, or duration **b** lacking restraint, check, or qualification ⟨~ *support*⟩ **c** having all distinguishing characteristics; enjoying all authorized rights and privileges **3a** at the highest or greatest degree; maximum **b** at the height of development ⟨~ *bloom*⟩ **4** rounded in outline; *also* well filled out or plump **5a** having an abundance of material (e g in the form of gathers or folds) ⟨*a ~ skirt*⟩ **b** rich in experience ⟨*a ~ life*⟩ **6** satisfied, esp with food or drink, often to the point of discomfort – usu + *up* **7** having both parents in common ⟨~ *sisters*⟩ **8a** with the attention completely occupied by or centred on sthg ⟨*always ~ of his own importance*⟩ **b** filled with excited anticipation or pleasure ⟨~ *of her plans for a holiday in Fiji*⟩ **9** possessing a rich or pronounced quality **10** – used as an intensive ⟨*won by a ~ 4 shots*⟩ – **fullness** *also* **fulness** *n* – **full of oneself** bumptiously self-centred or conceited

²full *adv* exactly, squarely

³full *n* **1** the highest or fullest state, extent, or degree **2** the requisite or complete amount – chiefly in **in full**

⁴full *vi*, *of the moon* to become full ~ *vt* to make full in sewing

⁵full *vt* to cleanse and finish (woollen cloth) by moistening, heating, and pressing – **fuller** *n*

fullback *n* a primarily defensive player in soccer, rugby, etc, usu stationed nearest the defended goal

full-blooded *adj* **1** of unmixed ancestry; purebred **2a** forceful, vigorous **b** virile **3** being the specified thing to a great extent ⟨*a ~ socialist*⟩ – **full-bloodedness** *n*

full-blown *adj* **1** at the height of bloom **2** fully developed or mature

full-bodied *adj* marked by richness and fullness, esp of flavour ⟨*a ~ wine*⟩

full circle *adv* through a series of developments that lead back to the original source, position, or situation

full-dress *adj* **1** complete, full-scale **2** of or being full dress ⟨~ *uniform*⟩

full dress *n* the style of dress prescribed for ceremonial or formal social occasions

fuller *n* a blacksmith's hammer for grooving and spreading iron

fuller's earth *n* a clayey substance used in fulling cloth and as a catalyst

full-fledged *adj, chiefly NAm* fully-fledged

full house *n* a poker hand containing 3 of a kind and a pair

full-length *adj* **1** showing or adapted to the entire length, esp of the human figure **2** having a normal or standard length; unabridged

full moon *n* the moon when its whole apparent disc is illuminated

full nelson *n* a wrestling hold in which both arms are thrust under the corresponding arms of an opponent and the hands clasped behind the opponent's head

full-scale *adj* **1** identical to an original in proportion and size **2** involving full use of available resources ⟨*a ~ biography*⟩

full stop *n* a punctuation mark . used to mark the end (e g of a sentence or abbreviation) – often used to express completion ⟨*They were just brave, clean, British success stories. Full stop. – Punch*⟩

full-time *adj* employed for or involving full time ⟨*~ employees*⟩ – **full time** *adv*

full time *n* **1** the amount of time considered the normal or standard amount for working during a given period, esp a week **2** the end of a sports, esp soccer, match

full toss *n* a throw, esp a bowled ball in cricket, that has not hit the ground by the time it arrives at the point at which it was aimed

fully *adv* **1** completely **2** AT LEAST **1** ⟨*~ nine tenths of us*⟩

fully-fashioned *adj* employing or produced by a knitting process for shaping to body lines ⟨*~ tights*⟩

fully-fledged, *NAm* **full-fledged** *adj* having attained complete status

fulmar *n* a seabird of colder regions closely related to the petrels

¹fulminate *vt* to utter or thunder out with denunciation ~ *vi* **1** to thunder forth censure or invective – usu + *against* or *at* **2** to be agitated or enraged (by feelings of indignation) ⟨*he ~*d *in silence*⟩ – **fulminator** *n*, **fulmination** *n*

²fulminate *n* an (explosive) salt (e g of mercury) containing the radical CNO

fulsome *adj* **1** overabundant, copious ⟨*described in ~ detail*⟩ **2a** unnecessarily effusive **b** obsequious – **fulsomely** *adv*, **fulsomeness** *n*

fumble *vb* **fumbling** *vi* **1a** to grope for or handle sthg clumsily or awkwardly **b** to make awkward attempts to do or find sthg **2** to feel one's way or move awkwardly ~ *vt* **1** to feel or handle clumsily **2** to deal with awkwardly or clumsily – **fumble** *n*, **fumbler** *n*, **fumblingly** *adv*

¹fume *n* **1** an (irritating or offensive) smoke, vapour, or gas – often pl with sing. meaning **2** a state of unreasonable excited irritation or anger ⟨*in a ~ of impatience*⟩ – **fumy** *adj*

²fume *vt* to expose to or treat with fumes ~ *vi* **1a** to emit fumes **b** to be in a state of excited irritation or anger ⟨*she fretted and ~*d *over the delay*⟩ **2** to rise (as if) in fumes

fumigate *vt* to apply smoke, vapour, or gas to, esp in order to disinfect or destroy pests – **fumigator** *n*, **fumigant** *n*, **fumigation** *n*

¹fun *n* **1** (a cause of) amusement or enjoyment **2** derisive jest; ridicule ⟨*made him a figure of ~*⟩ **3** violent or excited activity or argument ⟨*let a snake loose in the classroom; then the ~ began*⟩

²fun *adj, chiefly NAm* providing entertainment, amusement, or enjoyment ⟨*a ~ person to be with*⟩ – infml

¹function *n* **1** an occupational duty **2** the action characteristic of a person or thing or for which a thing exists ⟨*examining the ~ of poetry in modern society*⟩ **3** any of a group of related actions contributing to a larger action **4** an impressive, elaborate, or formal ceremony or social gathering **5a** a mathematical relationship between each element of one set and at least one element of the same or another set **b** a quality, trait, or fact dependent on and varying with another **c** a facility on a computer or similar device corresponding to a mathematical function or operation – **functionless** *adj*

²function *vi* **1** to have a function; serve ⟨*an attributive noun ~*s *as an adjective*⟩ **2** to operate ⟨*a government ~*s *through numerous divisions*⟩

functional *adj* **1a** of, connected with, or being a function **b** affecting physiological or psychological functions but not organic structure ⟨*~ heart disease*⟩ **2** designed or developed for practical use without ornamentation **3** (capable of) performing a function – **functionally** *adv*

functionalism *n* **1** a theory that stresses the interdependence of the institutions of a society **2** a theory or practice that emphasizes practical utility or functional relations to the exclusion of ornamentation – **functionalist** *n*, **functionalistic** *adj*

functionary *n* **1** sby who serves in a certain function **2** sby holding office

function word *n* a word (e g a preposition or conjunction) chiefly expressing grammatical relationship

¹fund *n* **1** an available quantity of material or intangible resources ⟨*~ of knowledge*⟩ **2** (an organization administering) a resource, esp a sum of money, whose principal or interest is set apart for a specific objective **3** *pl* an available supply of money

²fund *vt* **1** to make provision of resources for discharging the interest or principal of **2** to provide funds for ⟨*research ~*ed *by the government*⟩

¹fundamental *adj* **1** serving as a basis to support existence or to determine essential structure or function – often + *to* **2** of essential structure, function, or facts ⟨*~ change*⟩ **3** of, being, or produced by the lowest component of a complex vibration **4** of central importance; principal ⟨*~ purpose*⟩ **5** belonging to one's innate or ingrained characteristics – **fundamentally** *adv*

²fundamental *n* **1** a minimum constituent without which a thing or system would not be what it is **2** the prime tone of a harmonic series **3** the harmonic component of a complex wave that has the lowest frequency

fundamentalism *n* (adherence to) a belief in the literal truth of the Bible – **fundamentalist** *n or adj*

funeral *n* **1** (a procession connected with) a formal and ceremonial disposing of dead body, esp by burial or cremation; *also, NAm* a funeral service **2** a matter, esp a difficulty, that is of concern only to the specified person ⟨*if you get lost, that's your ~*⟩ – infml

funeral director *n* an undertaker

funeral parlour *n* an undertaker's establishment

funerary *adj* of, used for, or associated with burial ⟨*a pharaoh's ~ chamber*⟩

funereal *adj* **1** of a funeral **2** gloomy, solemn – **funereally** *adv*

fun fair *n, chiefly Br* a usu outdoor show offering amusements (e g sideshows, rides, or games of skill)

fungicide *n* a substance used for destroying or preventing fungus – **fungicidal** *adj*, **fungicidally** *adv*

fungoid *adj* resembling, characteristic of, or being a fungus – **fungoid** *n*

fungous *adj* of, like, or caused by a fungus or fungi

fungus *n, pl* fungi *also* **funguses** any of a major group of often parasitic organisms lacking chlorophyll and including moulds, rusts, mildews, smuts, mushrooms, and toadstools – **fungal** *adj*

¹**funicular** *adj* **1** dependent on the tension of a cord or cable **2** (of the form) of or associated with a cord

²**funicular** *n* a cable railway in which an ascending carriage counterbalances a descending carriage

¹**funk** *n* **1a** a state of paralysing fear **b** a fit of inability to face difficulty **2** a coward *USE* infml

²**funk** *vt* **1** to be afraid of **2** to avoid doing or facing (sthg) because of lack of determination *USE* infml

³**funk** *n* funky music – slang

funky *adj* **1** having an offensive smell – chiefly infml **2** having an earthy unsophisticated style and feeling (as in the blues) **3** having an earthily sexual quality **4** – used to approve sthg or sby, esp in pop culture *USE* (*2, 3, & 4*) slang – **funkiness** *n*

¹**funnel** *n* **1** a utensil usu having the shape of a hollow cone with a tube extending from the smaller end, designed to direct liquids or powders into a small opening **2** a shaft, stack, or flue for ventilation or the escape of smoke or steam

²**funnel** *vb* -ll- (*NAm* -l-, -ll-) *pres part vi* **1** to have or take the shape of a funnel **2** to pass (as if) through a funnel ⟨*the crowd* ∼ *led out of the football ground*⟩ ∼ *vt* **1** to form in the shape of a funnel ⟨∼*led his hands and shouted through them*⟩ **2** to move to a focal point or into a central channel ⟨*contributions were* ∼ *led into 1 account*⟩

¹**funny** *adj* **1** causing mirth and laughter; seeking or intended to amuse **2** peculiar, strange, or odd **3** involving trickery, deception, or dishonesty ⟨*told the prisoner not to try anything* ∼⟩ ⟨∼ *business*⟩ **4** unwilling to be helpful; difficult ⟨*at first he was a bit* ∼ *about it but in the end he agreed*⟩ **5a** slightly unwell **b** slightly mad ⟨∼ *in the head*⟩ **6** pleasantly amusing; nice – esp in *funny old* ⟨*look at that* ∼ *old dog*⟩ *USE* (*3, 4, 5, & 6*) infml – **funnily** *adv*, **funniness** *n*, **funny** *adv*

²**funny** *n* a comic strip or comic section in a periodical – usu pl

funny bone *n* the place at the back of the elbow where the nerve supplying the hand and forearm rests against the bone

funny farm *n, chiefly NAm* a mental hospital – chiefly humor

¹**fur** *vb* -rr- to (cause to) become coated or clogged (as if) with fur – often + *up*

²**fur** *n* **1** a piece of the dressed pelt of an animal used to make, trim, or line garments **2** an article of clothing made of or with fur **3** the hairy coat of a mammal, esp when fine, soft, and thick; *also* such a coat with the skin **4** a coating resembling fur: e g **a** a coating of dead cells on the tongue of sby who is unwell **b** the thick pile of a fabric (e g chenille) **c** a coating formed in vessels (e g kettles or pipes) by deposition of scale from hard water **5** any of the heraldic representations of animal pelts or their colours that have a stylized pattern of tufts or patches – **furless** *adj*, **furred** *adj*

furbelow *n* **1** a pleated or gathered piece of material; *specif* a flounce on women's clothing **2** sthg that suggests a furbelow, esp in being showy or superfluous – often in *frills and furbelows* – **furbelow** *vt*

furbish *vt* **1** to polish **2** to renovate – often + *up* – **furbisher** *n*

furious *adj* **1a** exhibiting or goaded by uncontrollable anger **b** giving a stormy or turbulent appearance ⟨∼ *bursts of flame from the fire*⟩ **c** marked by (violent) noise, excitement, or activity **2** INTENSE **1a** – **furiously** *adv*

furl *vt* to fold or roll (e g a sail or umbrella) close to or

round sthg ∼*vi* to curl or fold as in being furled – **furl** *n*

furlong *n* a unit of length equal to 220yd (about 0.201km)

¹**furlough** *n* a leave of absence from duty granted esp to a soldier

²**furlough** *vt, chiefly NAm* to grant a furlough to

furnace *n* an enclosed apparatus in which heat is produced (e g for heating a building or reducing ore)

furnish *vt* to provide or supply (with what is needed); *esp* to equip with furniture – **furnisher** *n*

furnishing *n* an object that tends to increase comfort or utility; *specif* an article of furniture for the interior of a building – usu pl

furniture *n* **1** necessary, useful, or desirable equipment: e g **a** the movable articles (e g tables, chairs, and beds) that make an area suitable for living in or use **b** accessories ⟨*door* ∼⟩ **c** the whole movable equipment of a ship (e g rigging, sails, anchors, and boats) **2** pieces of wood or metal less than type high placed in printing forms to fill in blank spaces

furore *n* an outburst of general excitement or indignation

furrier *n* a fur dealer

¹**furrow** *n* **1a** a trench in the earth made by a plough **b** rural land; a field **2** sthg like the track of a plough: e g **a** a groove **b** a deep wrinkle

²**furrow** *vb* to make or form furrows, grooves, lines, etc (in)

furry *adj* like, made of, or covered with fur

¹**further** *adv* **1** FARTHER **1** **2** moreover **3** to a greater degree or extent ⟨∼ *annoyed by a second interruption*⟩

²**further** *adj* **1** FARTHER **1** **2** extending beyond what exists or has happened; additional ⟨∼ *volumes*⟩ **3** coming after the one referred to ⟨*closed until* ∼ *notice*⟩

³**further** *vt* to help forward ⟨*this will* ∼ *your chances of success*⟩ – **furtherance** *n*, **furtherer** *n*

further education *n, Br* vocational, cultural, or recreational education for people who have left school

furthermore *adv* in addition to what precedes; moreover – used esp when introducing fresh matter for consideration

furthermost *adj* most distant

further to *prep* following up ⟨∼ *your letter of the 4th July*⟩

furthest *adv or adj* farthest

furtive *adj* expressing or done by stealth – **furtively** *adv*, **furtiveness** *n*

fury *n* **1** intense, disordered, and often destructive rage **2a** *cap* any of the 3 avenging deities who in Greek mythology punished crimes **b** (one who resembles) an avenging spirit **3** wild disordered force or activity **4** a frenzy

furze *n* gorse – **furzy** *adj*

¹**fuse** *n* **1** a combustible substance enclosed in a cord or cable for setting off an explosive charge by transmitting fire to it **2** *NAm chiefly* **fuze** the detonating device for setting off the charge in a projectile, bomb, etc

²**fuse**, *NAm also* **fuze** *vt* to equip with a fuse

³**fuse** *vt* **1** to reduce to a liquid or plastic state by heat **2** to blend thoroughly (as if) by melting together **3** to cause (e g a light bulb) to fail by fusing ∼*vi* **1** to become fluid with heat **2** to become blended (as if) by melting together **3** to fail because of the melting of a fuse – **fusible** *adj*, **fusibility** *n*

⁴**fuse** *n* (a device that includes) a wire or strip of fusible metal that melts and interrupts the circuit when the current exceeds a particular value

fuselage *n* the central body portion of an aeroplane

designed to accommodate the crew and the passengers or cargo

fusilier *n* a member of a British regiment formerly armed with fusils

¹fusillade *n* **1** a number of shots fired simultaneously or in rapid succession **2** a spirited outburst, esp of criticism

²fusillade *vt* to attack or shoot down by a fusillade

fusion *n* **1** fusing or rendering plastic by heat **2** a union (as if) by melting: e g **a** a merging of diverse elements into a unified whole **b** the union of light atomic nuclei to form heavier nuclei resulting in the release of enormous quantities of energy

¹fuss *n* **1a** needless or useless bustle or excitement **b** a show of (affectionate) attention – often in *make a fuss of* **2a** a state of agitation, esp over a trivial matter **b** an objection, protest ⟨*kicked up a ∼ about the new regulations*⟩

²fuss *vi* **1a** to create or be in a state of restless activity; *specif* to shower affectionate attentions **b** to pay close or undue attention to small details ⟨*∼ed with her hair*⟩ **2** to become upset; worry ∼ *vt* to agitate, upset – **fusser** *n*

fusspot *n* a person who fusses about trifles – infml

fussy *adj* **1** nervous and excitable (about small matters) **2a** showing too much concern over details **b** fastidious ⟨*not ∼ about food*⟩ **3** having too much or too detailed ornamentation – **fussily** *adv*, **fussiness** *n*

fustian *n* **1** a strong cotton or linen fabric (e g corduroy or velveteen), usu having a pile face and twill weave **2** pretentious and banal writing or speech – **fustian** *adj*

fusty *adj* **1** stale or musty from being left undisturbed for a long time **2** out-of-date **3** rigidly old-fashioned or reactionary – **fustily** *adv*, **fustiness** *n*

futile *adj* **1** completely ineffective **2** *of a person* ineffectual – **futilely** *adv*, **futileness** *n*, **futility** *n*

¹future *adj* **1** that is to be; *specif* existing after death **2** of or constituting the future tense

²future *n* **1a** time that is to come **b** that which is going to occur **2** likelihood of success ⟨*not much ∼ in trying to sell furs in a hot country*⟩ **3** sthg (e g a bulk commodity) bought for future acceptance or sold for future delivery – usu *pl* **4** (a verb form in) the future tense of a language – **futureless** *adj*

futurism *n* **1** *often cap* a movement in art, music, and literature begun in Italy about 1910 and seeking to express the dynamic energy and movement of mechanical processes **2** a point of view that finds meaning or fulfilment in the future rather than in the past or present – **futurist** *n or adj*

futuristic *adj* of the future or futurism; *esp* bearing no relation to known or traditional forms; ultramodern – **futuristically** *adv*

futurity *n* **1** FUTURE 1a **2** *pl* future events or prospects **3** *chiefly NAm* a competition, esp a horse race, for which entries are made well in advance of the event

¹fuzz *n* fine light particles or fibres (e g of down or fluff)

²fuzz *n sing or pl in constr* the police – slang

fuzzy *adj* **1** marked by or giving a suggestion of fuzz ⟨*a ∼ covering of felt*⟩ **2** not clear; indistinct – **fuzzily** *adv*, **fuzziness** *n*

-fy, -ify *suffix* (→ *vb*) **1** become or cause to be ⟨*purify*⟩ ⟨*mollify*⟩ ⟨*solidify*⟩ **2** fill with ⟨*stupefy*⟩ ⟨*horrify*⟩ **3** give the characteristics of; make similar to ⟨*countrify*⟩ ⟨*dandify*⟩ **4** engage in (a specified activity) ⟨*argufy*⟩ ⟨*speechify*⟩ – often humor or derog

---

G

g *n, pl* **g's, gs** *often cap* **1** (a graphic representation of or device for reproducing) the 7th letter of the English alphabet **2** the 5th note of a C-major scale **3** a unit of force equal to the force exerted by gravity on a body at rest and used to indicate the force to which a body is subjected when accelerated **4** *chiefly NAm* a sum of $1000 – slang

¹gab *vi* **-bb-** to chatter, blab – infml – **gabber** *n*

²gab *n* (idle) talk – infml

gabardine *n* **1** GABERDINE 1 **2a** a firm durable fabric (e g of wool or rayon) twilled with diagonal ribs on the right side **b** *chiefly Br* a waterproof coat made of gabardine

gabble *vb* gabbling to talk or utter rapidly or unintelligibly – **gabble** *n*, **gabbler** *n*

gaberdine *n* **1** a coarse long coat or smock worn chiefly by Jews in medieval times **2** GABARDINE 2

gable *n* the vertical triangular section of wall between 2 slopes of a pitched roof – **gabled** *adj*

gad *vi* **-dd-** to go or travel in an aimless or restless manner or in search of pleasure – usu + *about* – **gadder** *n*

gadfly *n* **1** any of various flies (e g a horsefly or botfly) that bite or annoy livestock **2** a usu intentionally annoying person who stimulates or provokes others, esp by persistent irritating criticism

gadget *n* a usu small and often novel mechanical or electronic device, esp on a piece of machinery – **gadgetry** *n*

Gaelic *adj* of or being (the Goidelic language of) the Celts in Ireland, the Isle of Man, and the Scottish Highlands – **Gaelic** *n*

¹gaff *n* **1a** a spear or spearhead for killing fish or turtles **b** a pole with a hook for holding or landing heavy fish **2** a spar on which the head of a fore-and-aft sail is extended

²gaff *vt* to strike or secure (e g a fish) with a gaff

gaffe *n* a social blunder; FAUX PAS

gaffer *n* **1** the chief lighting electrician in a film or television studio **2** *Br* a foreman or overseer **3** *dial* an old man

¹gag *vb* **-gg-** *vt* **1** to apply a gag to or put a gag in the mouth of (to prevent speech) **2** to cause to retch **3** to obstruct, choke ⟨*∼ a valve*⟩ **4** to prevent from having free speech or expression – chiefly journ ∼ *vi* **1** to heave, retch **2** to tell jokes

²gag *n* **1** sthg thrust into the mouth to keep it open or prevent speech or outcry **2** JOKE 1a **3** a hoax, trick **4** a check to free speech – chiefly journ

gaga *adj* **1a** senile **b** slightly mad **2** infatuated – often + *about* USE infml

¹gage *n* **1** a token of defiance; *specif* a glove, cap, etc thrown on the ground in former times as a challenge to a fight **2** sthg deposited as a pledge of performance

²gage *n* **1** GAUGE 3 **2** *NAm* GAUGE 1, 2, 4, 5, 6

³gage *vt, NAm* to gauge

⁴gage *n* a greengage

gaggle *n* **1** a flock (of geese) **2** *sing or pl in constr* a typically noisy or talkative group or cluster – chiefly infml

gaiety *n* **1** merrymaking; *also* festive activity **2** gay quality, spirits, manner, or appearance

gaily *adv* in a gay manner

¹gain *n* **1** resources or advantage acquired or increased; a profit **2** the obtaining of profit or possessions **3a** an increase in amount, magnitude, or degree ⟨*a ∼ in* *efficiency*⟩ **b** the ratio of output power to input power in an amplifier

²**gain** *vt* **1a**(1) to get possession of or win, usu by industry, merit, or craft **(2)** to increase a lead over or catch up a rival by (esp time or distance) ⟨*~ed 35yd on the third lap*⟩ **b** to get by a natural development or process ⟨*~ strength*⟩ **c** to acquire ⟨*~ a friend*⟩ **d** to arrive at ⟨*~ed the river that night*⟩ **2** to increase in ⟨*~ momentum*⟩ **3** *of a timepiece* to run fast by the amount of ⟨*the clock ~s a minute a day*⟩ *~ vi* **1** to get advantage; profit ⟨*hoped to ~ from his crime*⟩ **2** to increase, specif in weight **3** *of a timepiece* to run fast – **gainer** *n* – **gain ground** to make progress

gainful *adj* profitable ⟨*~ employment*⟩ – **gainfully** *adv*

gainsay *vt* **gainsays; gainsaid 1** to deny, dispute ⟨*couldn't ~ the statistics*⟩ **2** to oppose, resist – **gainsayer** *n*

gait *n* **1** a manner of walking or moving on foot **2** a sequence of foot movements (e g a walk, trot, or canter) by which a horse moves forwards

gaiter *n* a cloth or leather covering reaching from the instep to ankle, mid-calf, or knee

gal *n* a girl – used in writing to represent esp a US or upper-class pronunciation

gala *n* **1** a festive gathering (that constitutes or marks a special occasion) **2** *Br* a gala sports meeting ⟨*a swimming ~*⟩

galactic *adj* of a galaxy, esp the Milky Way galaxy

galantine *n* a cold dish of boned and usu stuffed cooked meat glazed with aspic

galaxy *n* **1a** *often cap* MILKY WAY **b** any of many independent systems composed chiefly of stars, dust, and gases and separated from each other in the universe by vast distances **2** an assemblage of brilliant or notable people or things

gale *n* **1** a strong wind; *specif* a moderate gale, strong gale, or esp fresh gale **2** a noisy outburst ⟨*~s of laughter*⟩

¹**gall** *n* **1a** BILE **1 b** sthg bitter to endure **c** rancour **2** brazen and insolent audacity

²**gall** *n* a skin sore caused by rubbing

³**gall** *vt* **1a** to wear (away) by rubbing; chafe **b** to cause feelings of mortification and irritation in; vex acutely **2** to harass ⟨*~ed by enemy fire*⟩ *~ vi* to become sore or worn by rubbing – **gallingly** *adv*

⁴**gall** *n* a diseased swelling of plant tissue produced by infection with fungi, insect parasites, etc

¹**gallant** *n* a (young) man of fashion (who is particularly attentive to women)

²**gallant** *adj* **1a** splendid, stately ⟨*a ~ ship*⟩ **b** nobly chivalrous and brave **2** courteously and elaborately attentive, esp to ladies – **gallantly** *adv*

gallantry *n* **1a** an act of marked courtesy **b** courteous attention to a lady **2** spirited and conspicuous bravery

gall bladder *n* a membranous muscular sac in which bile from the liver is stored

galleon *n* a heavy square-rigged sailing ship of the 15th to early 18th c used (by the Spanish) for war or commerce

gallery *n* **1** a covered passage for walking; a colonnade **2** an outdoor balcony **3a** a long and narrow passage, room, or corridor ⟨*a shooting ~*⟩ **b** a horizontal subterranean passage in a cave or (military) mining system **c** a passage, esp in the ground or wood, made by a mole or insect **4a** (a collection worthy of being displayed as if in) a room or building devoted to the exhibition of works of art ⟨*the National* Gallery⟩ ⟨*the novel contained a rich ~ of characters*⟩ **b** an institution or business exhibiting or dealing in works of art **5** *sing or pl in constr* **a** (the occupants of)

a balcony projecting from 1 or more interior walls of a hall, auditorium, or church, to accommodate additional people, or reserved for musicians, singers, etc **b** the undiscriminating general public ⟨*a politician who always plays to the ~*⟩ **c** the spectators at a tennis, golf, etc match – **galleried** *adj*

galley *n* **1** a large low usu single-decked ship propelled by oars and sails and used esp in the Mediterranean in the Middle Ages and in classical antiquity **2** a kitchen on a ship or aircraft **3a** a long oblong tray with upright sides for holding set type **b galley, galley proof** a proof in the form of a long sheet (taken from type on a galley)

galley slave *n* a drudge

Gallic *adj* (characteristic) of Gaul or France

gallicism *n, often cap* a characteristic French word or expression (occurring in another language)

gallivant *vi* to travel energetically or roam about for pleasure

gallon *n* either of 2 units of liquid capacity equal to 8pt: **a** a British unit equal to about 4.546l **b** a US unit equal to about 3.785l – **gallonage** *n*

¹**gallop** *n* **1** a fast bounding gait of a quadruped; *specif* the fastest natural 4-beat gait of the horse **2** a ride or run at a gallop **3** a rapid or hasty progression ⟨*rushed through the reports at a ~*⟩

²**gallop** *vb* to (cause to) progress or ride at a gallop – **galloper** *n*

galloping *adj* increasing rapidly; accelerating ⟨*~ inflation*⟩

gallows *n, pl* **gallows** *also* **gallowses 1 gallows, gallows tree** a frame, usu of 2 upright posts and a crosspiece, for hanging criminals **2** *the* punishment of hanging

gallows humour *n* grim humour that makes fun of a very serious or terrifying situation

gallstone *n* a calculus formed in the gall bladder or bile ducts

Gallup poll *n* a survey of public opinion frequently used as a means of forecasting sthg (e g an election result)

galore *adj* abundant, plentiful – used after a noun ⟨*bargains ~*⟩

galosh *n* a rubber overshoe – **galoshed** *adj*

galumph *vi* to move with a clumsy heavy tread – *infml*

galvanic *adj* **1** of, being, or producing a direct current of electricity resulting from chemical action ⟨*a ~ cell*⟩ **2** having an electric effect; stimulating vigorous activity or vitality – **galvanically** *adv*

galvanism *n* **1** (the therapeutic use of) direct electric current produced by chemical action **2** vital or forceful activity

galvanize, -ise *vt* **1** to subject to or stimulate, rouse, or excite (as if) by the action of an electric current ⟨*~ a muscle*⟩ ⟨*the candidate ~d his supporters into action*⟩ **2** to coat (iron or steel) with zinc as a protection from rust – **galvanizer** *n,* **galvanization** *n*

gambit *n* **1** a chess opening, esp in which a player risks (several) minor pieces to gain an advantage **2a** a remark intended to start a conversation or make a telling point **b** a calculated move; a stratagem

¹**gamble** *vb* **gambling** *vi* **1a** to play a game (of chance) for money or property **b** to bet or risk sthg on an uncertain outcome **2** SPECULATE **2** *~ vt* **1** to risk by gambling; wager **2** to venture, hazard – **gambler** *n*

²**gamble** *n* **1** the playing of a game (of chance) for stakes **2** (sthg involving) an element of risk

gamboge *n* **1** a gum resin from some SE Asian trees that is used as a yellow pigment **2** a strong yellow

gambol *vb or n* **-ll-** (*NAm* **-l-, -ll-**); **gambling** (to engage in) skipping or leaping about in play

¹game *n* **1a**(1) activity engaged in for diversion or amusement; play (2) the equipment for a particular esp indoor game **b** often derisive or mocking jesting ⟨*make ~ of a nervous player*⟩ **2a** a course or plan consisting of (secret) manoeuvres directed towards some end ⟨*playing a waiting ~*⟩ **b** a specified type of activity seen as competitive or governed by rules (and pursued for financial gain) ⟨*the newspaper ~*⟩ **3a**(1) (the quality of play in) a physical or mental competition conducted according to rules with the participants in direct opposition to each other; a match (2) a division of a larger contest (3) the number of points necessary to win a game **b** *pl* organized sports, esp athletics **c** a situation that involves contest, rivalry, or struggle ⟨*got into microelectronics early in the ~*⟩ **4a** animals under pursuit or taken in hunting; *specif* (the edible flesh of) certain wild mammals, birds, and fish (e g deer and pheasant), hunted for sport or food **b** an object of ridicule or attack – often in *fair game* **5** prostitution – slang; often in *on the game*

²game *vi* GAMBLE **1** *~vt archaic* to lose or squander by gambling

³game *adj* **1** having a resolute unyielding spirit ⟨*~ to the end*⟩ **2** ready to take risks or try sthg new – **gamely** *adv*, **gameness** *n*

⁴game *adj* injured, crippled, or lame ⟨*a ~ leg*⟩

gamekeeper *n* one who has charge of the breeding and protection of game animals or birds on a private preserve

gamesmanship *n* the art or practice of winning games by means other than superior skill without actually violating the rules

gamete *n* a mature germ cell with a single set of chromosomes capable of fusing with another gamete of the other sex to form a zygote from which a new organism develops – **gametic** *adj*, **gametically** *adv*

gamma *n* **1** the 3rd letter of the Greek alphabet **2** c **4**

gamma globulin *n* any of several immunoglobulins in blood or serum including most antibodies

gamma ray *n* (a quantum of) electromagnetic radiation of shorter wavelength than X rays emitted in some radioactive decay processes – usu *pl*

¹gammon *n* (the meat of) the lower end including the hind leg of a side of bacon removed from the carcass after curing with salt

²gammon *n* the winning of a backgammon game before the loser removes any men from the board – **gammon** *vt*

³gammon *n* nonsense, humbug – not now in vogue

gammy *adj, Br* 'GAME – infml

gamp *n, Br* a large, esp loosely tied, umbrella – infml

gamut *n* **1** the whole series of recognized musical notes **2** an entire range or series

gamy, gamey *adj* having the strong flavour or smell of game (that has been hung until high) – **gamily** *adv*, **gaminess** *n*

-gamy *comb form* (→ *n*) **1** marriage ⟨*polygamy*⟩ **2** possession of (such) reproductive organs or (such) a mode of fertilization ⟨*apogamy*⟩ – **-gamic, -gamous** *comb form* (→ *adj*)

¹gander *n* **1** an adult male goose **2** a simpleton

²gander *n* a look, glance – infml ⟨*talking and taking ~s at the girls – Life*⟩

¹gang *n* **1** a combination of similar implements or devices arranged to act together **2** *sing or pl in constr* a group of people **a** working together **b** associating for criminal, disreputable, etc ends; *esp* a group of adolescents who (disreputably) spend leisure time together **c** that have informal and usu close social relations ⟨*have the ~ over for a party*⟩

²gang *vt* to assemble or operate (e g mechanical parts) simultaneously as a group *~vi* to move or act as a gang ⟨*the children ~ed together*⟩

³gang *vi, Scot* to go

ganger *n, Br* the foreman of a gang of workmen

gangling, gangly *adj* tall, thin, and awkward in movement ⟨*a ~ gawky child*⟩

ganglion *n, pl* **ganglia** *also* **ganglions 1a** a small cyst on a joint membrane or tendon sheath **b** a mass of nerve cells outside the brain or spinal cord; *also* NUCLEUS 2b **2** a focus of strength, energy, or activity – **ganglionated** *adj*, **ganglionic** *adj*

gangplank *n* a movable board, plank, etc used to board a ship from a quay or another ship

¹gangrene *n* **1** local death of the body's soft tissues due to loss of blood supply **2** a pervasive moral evil – **gangrenous** *adj*

²gangrene *vb* to make or become gangrenous

gangster *n* a member of a criminal gang – **gangsterism** *n*

gang up *vi* **1** to combine as a group for a specific (disreputable) purpose **2** to make a joint assault *on*

gangway *n* **1a** a (temporary) passageway (constructed of planks) **2a** the opening in a ship's side or rail through which it is boarded **b** a gangplank **3** a clear passage through a crowd – often used interjectionally **4** *Br* a narrow passage between sections of seats in a theatre, storage bays in a warehouse, etc

gannet *n* **1** any of several related large fish-eating seabirds that breed in large colonies chiefly on offshore islands **2** a greedy person; a scavenger – **gannetry** *n*

gantry *n* **1** a frame for supporting barrels **2** a frame structure raised on side supports that spans over or round sthg and is used for railway signals, as a travelling crane, for servicing a rocket before launching, etc

gaol *vb or n, chiefly Br* (to) jail

gap *n* **1** a break in a barrier (e g a wall or hedge) **2a** a mountain pass **b** a ravine **3** an empty space between 2 objects or 2 parts of an object **4** a break in continuity ⟨*unexplained ~s in his story*⟩ **5** a disparity or difference ⟨*the ~ between imports and exports*⟩ **6** a wide difference in character or attitude ⟨*the generation ~*⟩ – **gappy, gapped** *adj*

¹gape *vi* **1a** to open the mouth wide **b** to open or part widely ⟨*holes ~d in the pavement*⟩ **2** to gaze stupidly or in openmouthed surprise or wonder **3** to yawn – **gapingly** *adv*

²gape *n* **1** an act of gaping; *esp* an openmouthed stare **2** the average width of the open mouth or beak **3** a fit of yawning **4** *pl* a disease of young birds characterized by constant gaping and caused by gapeworms infesting the windpipe

¹garage *n* **1** a building for the shelter of motor vehicles **2** an establishment for providing essential services (e g the supply of petrol or repair work) to motor vehicles

²garage *vt* to keep or put in a garage

garb *n* **1** a style of clothing; dress ⟨*arranged themselves in priestly ~*⟩ **2** an outward form; appearance – **garb** *vt*

garbage *n* **1** worthless writing or speech **2** *chiefly NAm* RUBBISH

garble *vt* to distort or confuse, giving a false impression of the facts ⟨*a ~d message*⟩ – **garbler** *n*

¹garden *n* **1a** a plot of ground where herbs, fruits, vegetables, or typically flowers are cultivated **b** a rich well-cultivated region ⟨*the ~ of England*⟩ **2a** a public recreation area or park ⟨*a botanical ~*⟩ **b** an open-air eating or drinking place ⟨*beer ~*⟩ – **gardenful** *n*

²**garden** *vi* to work in, cultivate, or lay out a garden – **gardener** *n*

³**garden** *adj* of a cultivated as distinguished from a wild kind grown in the open ⟨*a ~ plant*⟩

garden city *n* a planned town with spacious residential areas including public parks and considerable garden space

gardenia *n* any of a genus of Old World tropical trees and shrubs with showy fragrant white or yellow flowers

garden party *n* a usu formal party held on the lawns of a garden

gargantuan *adj, often cap* gigantic, colossal ⟨*a ~ meal*⟩

¹**gargle** *vb* **gargling** *vt* **1** to blow air from the lungs through (a liquid) held in the mouth or throat **2** to cleanse (the mouth or throat) in this manner ~ *vi* **1** to use a gargle **2** to speak or sing as if gargling

²**gargle** *n* **1** a liquid used in gargling **2** a bubbling liquid sound produced by gargling

gargoyle *n* a spout in the form of a grotesque human or animal figure projecting from a roof gutter to throw rainwater clear of a building – **gargoyled** *adj*

garish *adj* **1** excessively and gaudily bright or vivid **2** tastelessly showy – **garishly** *adv*, **garishness** *n*

¹**garland** *n* **1** a wreath of flowers or leaves worn as an ornament or sign of distinction **2** an anthology or collection

²**garland** *vt* to form into or deck with a garland

garlic *n* (the pungent compound bulb, much used as a flavouring in cookery, of) a European plant of the lily family – **garlicky** *adj*

garment *n* an article of clothing

¹**garner** *n* **1** a granary **2** a grain bin *USE fml or poetic*

²**garner** *vt* to gather, store – *fml or poetic*

garnet *n* **1** a hard brittle silicate mineral used as an abrasive and in its transparent deep red form as a gem **2** a dark red

¹**garnish** *vt* **1a** to decorate, embellish **b** to add decorative or savoury touches to (food) **2** to garnishee

²**garnish** *n* **1** an embellishment, ornament **2** an edible savoury or decorative addition (e g watercress) to a dish

garret *n* a small room just under the roof of a house

¹**garrison** *n* **1** a (fortified) town or place in which troops are stationed **2** *sing or pl in constr* the troops stationed at a garrison

²**garrison** *vt* **1** to station troops in **2a** to assign (troops) as a garrison **b** to occupy with troops

¹**garrotte, garotte**, *chiefly NAm* **garrote** *n* **1** (a Spanish method of execution using) an iron collar for strangling sby **2** strangling, esp with robbery as the motive

²**garrotte, garotte**, *chiefly NAm* **garrote** *vt* **1** to execute with a garrotte **2** to strangle and rob – **garrotter** *n*

garrulous *adj* excessively talkative, esp about trivial things – **garrulously** *adv*, **garrulousness** *n*, **garrulity** *n*

garter *n* **1** a band, usu of elastic, worn to hold up a stocking or sock **2** *cap* (the blue velvet garter that is the badge of) the Order of the Garter; *also* membership of the Order

¹**gas** *n, pl* **-s-** *also* **-ss- 1** a fluid (e g air) that has neither independent shape nor volume and tends to expand indefinitely **2a** a gas or gaseous mixture used to produce general anaesthesia, as a fuel, etc **b** a substance (e g tear gas or mustard gas) that can be used to produce a poisonous, asphyxiating, or irritant atmosphere **3** *NAm* petrol **4** empty talk – *chiefly infml* – **gaseous** *adj*, **gaseousness** *n*

²**gas** *vb* **-ss-** *vt* **1** to treat chemically with a gas **2** to poison or otherwise affect adversely with gas ~ *vi* **1** to give off gas **2** to talk idly – *chiefly infml*

gasbag *n* an idle talker – *infml*

gas chamber *n* a chamber in which prisoners are executed or animals killed by poison gas

¹**gash** *vt or n* (to injure with) a deep long cut or cleft, esp in flesh

²**gash** *n* sthg, specif rubbish on board ship, superfluous or extra – *infml*

gasholder *n* a gasometer

gasify *vb* to change into gas ⟨*~ coal*⟩ – **gasifier** *n*, **gasification** *n*

gasket *n* (a specially shaped piece of) sealing material for ensuring that a joint, esp between metal surfaces, does not leak liquid or gas

gaslight *n* (light from) a gas flame or gas lighting fixture

gas mask *n* a mask connected to a chemical air filter and used as a protection against noxious fumes or gases

gasoline, gasolene *n, NAm* petrol – **gasolinic** *adj*

gasp *vi* **1** to catch the breath suddenly and audibly (e g with shock) **2** to breathe laboriously ~ *vt* to utter with gasps – usu + *out* ⟨*he ~ed out his message*⟩ – **gasp** *n*

gas ring *n* a hollow metal perforated ring through which jets of gas issue and over which food is cooked

gassy *adj* full of, containing, or like gas ⟨*~ beer*⟩ – **gassiness** *n*

gastric *adj* of the stomach

gastroenteritis *n* inflammation of the lining of the stomach and the intestines, usu causing painful diarrhoea

gastronomy *n* the art or science of good eating – **gastronomic** *also* **gastronomical** *adj*, **gastronomically** *adv*

gastropod *n* any of a large class of molluscs (e g snails) usu with a distinct head bearing sensory organs – **gastropod** *adj*, **gastropodan** *adj or n*

gasworks *n, pl* **gasworks** a plant for manufacturing gas – often pl with sing. meaning

¹**gat** *archaic past of* GET

²**gat** *n* a firearm – *slang*

¹**gate** *n* **1** (the usu hinged frame or door that closes) an opening in a wall or fence **2** a city or castle entrance, often with defensive structures **3a** a means of entrance or exit **b** a mountain pass **c** a space between 2 markers through which a skier, canoeist, etc must pass in a slalom race **d** a mechanically operated barrier used as a starting device for a race **e** either of a pair of barriers that (**1**) let water in and out of a lock (**2**) close a road at a level crossing **4** an (electronic) device (e g in a computer) that produces a signal when specified input conditions are met ⟨*a logic ~*⟩ **5** the set of notches in a manually worked gearbox into which the gear lever is pushed to select the gears **6** the total admission receipts or the number of spectators at a sporting event

²**gate** *vt, Br* to punish by confinement to the premises of a school or college

gateau *n, pl* **gateaux, gateaus** any of various rich often filled elaborate (cream) cakes

gate-crasher *n* one who enters, attends, or participates without a ticket or invitation – **gate-crash** *vb*

gatehouse *n* **1** a structure above or beside a gate (e g of a city wall or castle) often used in former times as a guardroom or prison **2** a lodge at the entrance to the grounds of a large house **3** a building at a dam or lock from which the sluices or gates are controlled

gatekeeper *n* sby who or sthg that tends or guards a gate

gateleg table *n* a table with drop leaves supported by 2 movable legs

gatepost *n* the post on which a gate is hung or against which it closes

gateway *n* 1 an opening for a gate 2 GATE 3a

¹**gather** *vt* 1 to bring together; collect (*up*) 2 to pick, harvest 3a to summon up ⟨~ *his courage*⟩ b to accumulate ⟨~ *speed*⟩ c to prepare (e g oneself) for an effort 4a to bring together the parts of b to draw about or close to sthg ⟨~*ing her cloak about her*⟩ c to pull (fabric) together, esp along a line of stitching, to create small tucks 5 to reach a conclusion (intuitively from hints or through inferences) ⟨*I ~ you're ready to leave*⟩ ~ *vi* to come together in a body ⟨*a crowd had ~ed*⟩ – **gatherer** *n*

²**gather** *n* sthg gathered; *esp* a tuck in cloth made by gathering

gathering *n* 1 an assembly, meeting; *also* a compilation 2 an abscess 3 a gather or series of gathers in cloth 4 SECTION 11

gauche *adj* lacking social experience or grace – **gauchely** *adv*, **gaucheness** *n*

gaucherie *n* (an instance of) tactless or awkward manner or behaviour

gaucho *n, pl* **gauchos** a cowboy of the pampas

¹**gaudy** *adj* ostentatiously or tastelessly (and brightly) ornamented – **gaudily** *adv*, **gaudiness** *n*

²**gaudy** *n* a feast, esp a dinner for ex-students, in some British universities

¹**gauge, NAm** also **gage** *n* 1a measurement according to some standard or system b dimensions, size 2 an instrument for or a means of measuring or testing sthg (e g a dimension or quantity) 3 gauge, gage relative position of a ship with reference to another ship and the wind 4 the distance between the rails of a railway, wheels on an axle, etc 5 a measure of the size of the bore of a shotgun 6a the thickness of a thin sheet of metal, plastic, film, etc b the diameter of wire, a hypodermic needle, a screw, etc c (a measure of) the fineness of a knitted fabric

²**gauge, NAm** also **gage** *vt* 1a to measure (exactly) the size, dimensions, capacity, or contents of b to estimate, judge ⟨*can you ~ his reaction?*⟩ 2 to check for conformity to specifications or limits – **gaugeable** *adj*, **gaugeably** *adv*

gaunt *adj* 1 excessively thin and angular as if from suffering 2 barren, desolate – **gauntly** *adv*, **gauntness** *n*

¹**gauntlet** *n* 1 a glove to protect the hand, worn with medieval armour 2 a strong protective glove with a wide extension above the wrist, used esp for sports and in industry 3 a challenge to combat – esp in *take up/throw down the gauntlet* – **gauntleted** *adj*

²**gauntlet** *n* a double file of men armed with weapons with which to strike at sby made to run between them; *broadly* criticism or an ordeal or test – usu in *run the gauntlet*

gauze *n* 1a a thin often transparent fabric used chiefly for clothing or draperies b a loosely woven cotton surgical dressing c a fine mesh of metal or plastic filaments 2 a thin haze or mist – **gauzily** *adv*, **gauziness** *n*, **gauzy** *adj*

gave *past of* GIVE

gavel *n* a small mallet with which a chairman, judge, or auctioneer commands attention or confirms a vote, sale, etc

gavotte *n* 1 an 18th-c dance in which the feet are raised rather than slid 2 a composition or movement of music in moderately quick 4₄ time – **gavotte** *vi*

¹**gawk** *vi* to gawp – infml – **gawker** *n*

²**gawk** *n* a clumsy awkward person – **gawkish** *adj*, **gawkishly** *adv*, **gawkishness** *n*

gawky *adj* awkward and usu lanky ⟨*a ~ child*⟩ – **gawkily** *adv*, **gawky** *n*

gawp *vi* to gape or stare stupidly – infml

¹**gay** *adj* 1 happily excited 2 bright, attractive ⟨~ *sunny meadows*⟩ 3 given to social pleasures ⟨*the ~ life*⟩ 4 homosexual – **gay** *adv*, **gayness** *n*

²**gay** *n* a homosexual

gaze *vi or n* (to fix the eyes in) a steady and intent look – **gazer** *n*

gazebo *n, pl* **gazebos** a freestanding structure placed to command a view; *also* a belvedere

gazelle *n, pl* **gazelles**, *esp collectively* **gazelle** any of numerous small, graceful, and swift African and Asian antelopes noted for their soft lustrous eyes

¹**gazette** *n* 1 a newspaper – usu in newspaper titles 2 an official journal containing announcements of honours and government appointments

²**gazette** *vt, Br* to announce (the appointment or status of) in an official gazette ⟨*he was ~d major*⟩

gazetteer *n* a dictionary of place names

gazump *vb, Br* to thwart (a would-be house purchaser) by raising the price after agreeing to sell at a certain price – **gazumper** *n*

ge-, geo- *comb form* 1a ground; soil ⟨*geophyte*⟩ ⟨*geophagia*⟩ b earth; earth's surface ⟨*geophysics*⟩ geodesic⟩ 2 geographical; geography and ⟨*geopolitics*⟩

¹**gear** *n* 1a clothing, garments b movable property; goods 2 a set of equipment usu for a particular purpose ⟨*fishing ~*⟩ 3a(1) a mechanism that performs a specific function in a complete machine ⟨*the steering ~*⟩ (2) a toothed wheel (that is one of a set of interlocking wheels) (3) working relation, position, or adjustment ⟨*out of ~*⟩ ⟨*put the car in ~*⟩ b any of 2 or more adjustments of a transmission (e g of a bicycle or motor vehicle) that determine direction of travel or ratio of engine speed to vehicle speed – **gearless** *adj*

²**gear** *vt* 1a to provide with or connect by gearing b to put into gear 2 to adjust *to* so as to match, blend with, or satisfy sthg ⟨*an institution ~ed to the needs of the blind*⟩

gearbox *n* (a protective casing enclosing) a set of (car) gears

gear lever *n* a control, esp a rod, on a gear-changing mechanism (e g a gearbox) used to engage the different gears

gear up *vt* to make ready for effective operation; *also* to put (e g oneself) into a state of anxious excitement or nervous anticipation

gecko *n, pl* **geckos, geckoes** any of numerous small chiefly tropical lizards able to walk on vertical or overhanging surfaces

gee *interj, chiefly NAm* – used as an introductory expletive or to express surprise or enthusiasm

gee-gee *n* a horse – used esp by or to children or in racing slang

geese *pl of* GOOSE

gee-up *interj* – used as a direction, esp to a horse, to move ahead

geezer *n* a man (who is thought to be a little odd or peculiar) – chiefly infml; esp in *old geezer*

Geiger counter *n* an electronic instrument for detecting the presence and intensity of ionizing radiations (e g cosmic rays or particles from a radioactive substance)

geisha, geisha girl *n, pl* **geisha, geishas** a Japanese girl who is trained to provide entertaining and lighthearted company, esp for a man or a group of men

¹**gel** *n* 1 a colloid in a more solid form than a sol 2 JELLY 3

²**gel, chiefly NAm** jell *vb* -ll- 1 to change (from a sol) into

a gel **2** to (cause to) take shape or become definite – **gelable** *adj*, **gelation** *n*

³gel *n* a girl – used in writing to represent an upper-class pronunciation

gelatin, gelatine *n* **1** a glutinous material obtained from animal tissues by boiling; *esp* a protein used esp in food (e g to set jellies) and photography **2** a thin coloured transparent sheet used to colour a stage light – **gelatinize** *vb*, **gelatinization** *n*

gelatinous *adj* resembling gelatin or jelly, esp in consistency; viscous – **gelatinously** *adv*, **gelatinousness** *n*

geld *vt* to castrate – used esp with reference to male animals

gelding *n* a castrated male horse

gelignite *n* a dynamite in which the adsorbent base is a mixture of potassium or sodium nitrate usu with wood pulp

¹gem *n* **1** a precious or sometimes semiprecious stone, esp when cut and polished for use in jewellery **2** sby or sthg highly prized or much beloved – **gemmy** *adj*

²gem *vt* **-mm-** to adorn (as if) with gems

Gemini *n* (sby born under) the 3rd sign of the zodiac in astrology, which is pictured as twins – **Geminian** *adj or n*

gen *n, Br* the correct or complete information – infml

¹gen-, geno- *comb form* **1** race ⟨*genocide*⟩ **2** genus; kind ⟨*genotype*⟩

²gen-, geno- *comb form* gene ⟨*genome*⟩

-gen *also* **-gene** *comb form* (*n* → *n*) **1** sthg that produces ⟨*androgen*⟩⟨*carcinogen*⟩ **2** sthg that is (so) produced ⟨*phosgene*⟩

gendarme *n* **1** a member of a corps of armed police, esp in France **2** a policeman – chiefly humor

gender *n* **1** sex **2a** a system of subdivision within a grammatical class of a language (e g noun or verb), partly based on sexual characteristics, that determines agreement with and selection of other words or grammatical forms **b** (membership of) a subclass within such a system

gene *n* a unit of inheritance that is carried on a chromosome, controls transmission of hereditary characters, and consists of DNA or, in some viruses, RNA – **genic** *adj*, **genically** *adv*

genealogy *n* **1** (an account of) the descent of a person, family, or group from an ancestor or from older forms **2** the study of family pedigrees – **genealogist** *n*, **genealogical** *adj*, **genealogically** *adv*

genera *pl of* GENUS

¹general *adj* **1** involving or applicable to the whole **2** of, involving, or applicable to (what is common to) every member of a class, kind, or group **3a** applicable to or characteristic of the majority of individuals involved; prevalent **b** concerned or dealing with universal rather than particular aspects **4** approximate rather than strictly accurate **5** not confined by specialization or careful limitation **6** holding superior rank or taking precedence over others similarly titled ⟨*the* ~ *manager*⟩ – **in general** usually; FOR THE MOST PART

²general *n* **1** the chief of a religious order or congregation **2** a high-ranking officer in the army or US airforce

general election *n* an election in which candidates are elected in all constituencies of a nation or state

generalissimo *n, pl* **generalissimos** the supreme commander of several armies acting together or of a nation's armed forces

generality *n* **1** total applicability **2** generalization **3** *the* greatest part; *the* bulk

generalization, -isation *n* **1** generalizing **2** a general statement, law, principle, or proposition (that does not

take adequate account of the facts) **3** the occurring of a response to a stimulus similar but not identical to a reference stimulus

generalize, -ise *vt* **1** to give a general form to **2** to derive or induce (a general conception or principle) from particulars **3** to give general applicability to ⟨~ *a law*⟩ ~ *vi* to make generalizations or vague or indefinite statements – **generalizable** *adj*, **generalizer** *n*

generally *adv* **1** without regard to specific instances ⟨~ *speaking*⟩ **2** usually; AS A RULE ⟨*he* ~ *drinks tea*⟩ **3** collectively; AS A WHOLE ⟨*of interest to children* ~⟩

general practitioner *n* a medical doctor who treats all types of disease and is usu the first doctor consulted by a patient

general staff *n* a group of officers who aid a commander in administration, training, supply, etc

general strike *n* a strike in all or many of the industries of a region or country

generate *vt* **1** to bring into existence or originate (e g by a life-giving, physical, or chemical process); produce ⟨~ *electricity*⟩ **2** to define (a linguistic, mathematical, etc structure (e g a curve or surface)) by the application of 1 or more rules or operations to given quantities **3** to be the cause of (a situation, action, or state of mind)

generation *n* **1** *sing or pl in constr* **a** a group of living organisms constituting a single step in the line of descent from an ancestor **b** a group of individuals born and living at the same time **c** a group of individuals sharing a usu specified status for a limited period ⟨*the next* ~ *of students*⟩ **d** a type or class of objects usu developed from an earlier type ⟨*a new* ~ *of computers*⟩ **2** the average time between the birth of parents and that of their offspring **3a** the producing of offspring; procreation **b** the process of coming or bringing into being ⟨~ *of income*⟩ ⟨~ *of electricity*⟩ – **generational** *adj*

generative *adj* having the power or function of generating, originating, producing, reproducing, etc

generator *n* **1** an apparatus for producing a vapour or gas **2** DYNAMO 1; *also* an alternator

generic *adj* **1** (characteristic) of or applied to (members of) a whole group or class **2** (having the rank) of a biological genus – **generically** *adv*

generous *adj* **1** magnanimous, kindly **2** liberal in giving (e g of money or help) **3** marked by abundance, ample proportions, or richness – **generously** *adv*, **generousness** *n*, **generosity** *n*

genesis *n, pl* **geneses** the origin or coming into being of sthg

Genesis *n* the first book of the Old Testament

genetic *adj* **1** of or determined by the origin or development of sthg **2a** of or involving genetics **b** genic – **genetically** *adv*

-genetic *comb form* (→ *adj*) **-GENIC** 1, 2 ⟨*psychogenetic*⟩ ⟨*spermatogenetic*⟩

genetics *n pl but sing in constr* **1** the biology of (the mechanisms and structures involved in) the heredity and variation of organisms **2** the genetic make-up of an organism, type, group, or condition – **geneticist** *n*

¹genial *adj* **1** favourable to growth or comfort; mild ⟨~ *sunshine*⟩ **2** cheerfully good-tempered; kindly – **genially** *adv*, **genialness** *n*, **geniality** *n*

²genial *adj* of the chin

-genic *comb form* (→ *adj*) **1** producing; forming ⟨*erotogenic*⟩ **2** produced by; formed from ⟨*phytogenic*⟩ **3** well-suited to production or reproduction by (a specified medium) ⟨*photogenic*⟩ ⟨*telegenic*⟩

genie *n, pl* **genies** *also* **genii** a jinn

genital *adj* **1** of or being the genitalia or another sexual organ **2** of or characterized by the final stage of sexual development in which oral and anal impulses are replaced by gratification obtained from (sexual) relationships – **genitally** adv

genitalia n pl the (external) reproductive and sexual organs

genitals n pl the genitalia

genitive adj or n (of or in) a grammatical case expressing typically a relationship of possessor or source; also sthg in this case – **genitival** adj, **genitivally** adv

genius n, pl (1a) **genii**, (1b & 3) **genii** also **geniuses**, (4) **geniuses** also **genii** **1a** an attendant spirit of a person or place **b** one who influences another for good or bad **2a** a peculiar, distinctive, or identifying character or spirit ⟨optimism was the ~ of the Victorian era⟩ **b** the associations and traditions of a place **3** a spirit or jinn **4a** a single strongly marked capacity or aptitude ⟨had a ~ for teaching maths⟩ **b** (a person endowed with) extraordinary intellectual power (as manifested in creative activity)

genius loci n, pl **genii loci** the pervading spirit of a place

genocide n the deliberate murder of a racial or cultural group – **genocidal** adj

genre n **1** a sort, type **2** a category of artistic, musical, or literary composition characterized by a particular style, form, or content

gent n a gentleman – nonstandard or humor

genteel adj **1a** of or appropriate to (the status or manners of) the gentry or upper class **b** free from vulgarity or rudeness; polite **2a** maintaining or striving to maintain the appearance of superior social status or respectability **b** marked by false delicacy, prudery, or affectation – **genteelly** adv, **genteelness** n

gentian n any of several related esp mountain plants with showy usu blue flowers

gentile adj or n, often cap (of) a non-Jewish person

gentility n **1** sing or pl in constr the members of the upper class **2a** genteel attitudes, behaviour, or activity **b** superior social status or prestige indicated by manners, possessions, etc

¹**gentle** adj **1a** honourable, distinguished; specif of or belonging to a gentleman ⟨of ~ birth⟩ **b** kind, amiable ⟨bear with me, ~ reader⟩ **2** free from harshness, sternness, or violence; mild, soft; also tractable **3** MODERATE 1, 2a – **gentleness** n, **gently** adv

²**gentle** n a maggot, esp when used as bait for fish

³**gentle** vt to make mild, docile, soft, or moderate

gentlefolk also **gentlefolks** n pl people of good family and breeding

gentleman n, pl **gentlemen** **1a** a man belonging to the landed gentry or nobility **b** a man who is chivalrous, well-mannered, and honourable (and of good birth or rank) **c** a man of independent wealth who does not work for gain **2** a valet – usu in gentleman's gentleman **3** a man of any social class or condition ⟨ladies and gentlemen⟩ – often as a courteous reference ⟨show this ~ to a seat⟩ – **gentlemanlike** adj

gentleman-at-arms n, pl **gentlemen-at-arms** any of a bodyguard of 40 gentlemen who attend the British sovereign on state occasions

gentlemanly adj characteristic of or having the character of a gentleman – **gentlemanliness** n

gentleman's agreement, **gentlemen's agreement** n an unwritten agreement secured only by the honour of the participants

gentle sex n the female sex

gentlewoman n, pl **gentlewomen** **1a** a woman of noble or gentle birth **b** a woman attendant on a lady of rank **2** a lady

gentry n, sing or pl in constr **1** the upper class **2** a class whose members are (landed proprietors) entitled to bear a coat of arms though not of noble rank

gents n, pl **gents** often cap, Br a public lavatory for men – chiefly infml

genuflect vi to bend the knee, esp in worship or as a gesture of respect (to sacred objects) – **genuflector** n, **genuflection**, **genuflexion** n

genuine adj **1** actually produced by or proceeding from the alleged source or author or having the reputed qualities or character ⟨the signature is ~⟩ ⟨this is a ~ antique⟩ **2** free from pretence; sincere – **genuinely** adv, **genuineness** n

genus n, pl **genera** **1** a category in the classification of living things ranking between the family and the species **2** a class divided into several subordinate classes

geo- – see GE-

geocentric adj **1** measured from or observed as if from the earth's centre **2** having or relating to the earth as centre – **geocentrically** adv

geography n **1a** a science that deals with the earth and its life; esp the description of land, sea, air, and the distribution of plant and animal life including human beings and their industries **2** the geographical features of an area – **geographer** n, **geographic**, **geographical** adj, **geographically** adv

geology n **1a** a science that deals with the history of the earth's crust, esp as recorded in rocks **b** a study of the solid matter of a celestial body (e g the moon) **2** the geological features of an area – **geologist** n, **geologize** vi, **geological**, **geologic** adj, **geologically** adv

geometric, **geometrical** adj **1a** of or according to (the laws of) geometry **b** increasing in a geometric progression ⟨~ population growth⟩ **2a** cap of or being (a style of) ancient Greek pottery decorated with geometric patterns **b** using, being, or decorated with patterns formed from straight and curved lines – **geometrically** adv

geometric progression n a sequence (e g 1, ½, ¼) in which the ratio of any term to its predecessor is constant

geometry n **1a** a branch of mathematics that deals with the measurement, properties, and relationships of points, lines, angles, surfaces, and solids **b** a particular type or system of geometry **2** (surface) shape **3** an arrangement of objects or parts that suggests geometrical figures

geophysics n pl but sing or pl in constr the physics of the earth including meteorology, oceanography, seismology, etc – **geophysical** adj, **geophysically** adv, **geophysicist** n

geopolitics n pl but sing in constr the study of the influence of geography, economics, and demography on politics – **geopolitical** adj, **geopolitically** adv

georgette n a thin strong clothing crepe of silk or of other material with a dull pebbly surface

¹**Georgian** n or adj (a native or inhabitant or the language) of Georgia in the Caucasus

²**Georgian** n or adj (a native or inhabitant) of Georgia in the USA

³**Georgian** adj **1** (characteristic) of (the time of) the reigns of the first 4 Georges (1714 to 1830) **2** (characteristic) of the reign of George V (1910 to 1936) – **Georgian** n

geranium n **1** any of a widely distributed genus of plants having radially symmetrical flowers with glands that alternate with the petals **2** a pelargonium

geriatric adj **1** of geriatrics, the aged, or the process of aging **2** aged, decrepit – derog – **geriatric** n

geriatrics n pl but sing in constr a branch of medicine that deals with (the diseases of) old age – **geriatrician** n

germ n **1a** a small mass of cells capable of developing into (a part of) an organism **b** the embryo of a cereal grain that is usu separated from the starchy endosperm during milling **2** sthg that serves as an origin **3 a** (disease-causing) microorganism – **germproof** *adj*, **germy** *adj*

german *adj* having the same parents, or the same grand-parents, on either the maternal or paternal side – usu in comb ⟨*brother*-german⟩ ⟨*cousin*-german⟩

¹German *n* **1a** a native or inhabitant of Germany **b** one (e g a Swiss German) who speaks German as his/her native language outside Germany **2** the Germanic language of the people of Germany, Austria, and parts of Switzerland

²German *adj* (characteristic) of Germany, the Germans, or German

germane *adj* both relevant and appropriate – **germanely** *adv*

¹Germanic *adj* **1** German **2** (characteristic) of the Germanic-speaking peoples **3** of Germanic

²Germanic *n* a branch of the Indo-European language family containing English, German, Dutch, Afrikaans, Flemish, Frisian, the Scandinavian languages, and Gothic

German measles *n pl but sing or pl in constr* a virus disease that is milder than typical measles but is damaging to the foetus when occurring early in pregnancy

germicide *n* sthg that kills germs – **germicidal** *adj*, **germicidally** *adv*

germinal *adj* **1a** in the earliest stage of development **b** creative, seminal **2** (having the characteristics) of a germ cell or early embryo – **germinally** *adv*

Germinal *n* the 7th month of the French Revolutionary calendar corresponding to 22 March–20 April

germinate *vt* to cause to sprout or develop ~ *vi* **1** to begin to grow; sprout **2** to come into being – **germinative** *adj*, **germination** *n*

gerontology *n* the biology and medicine of aging and the problems of the aged – **gerontologist** *n*, **gerontological**, **gerontologic** *adj*

¹gerrymander *n* (a pattern of districts resulting from) gerrymandering

²gerrymander *vt* to divide (an area) into election districts to give one political party an electoral advantage – **gerrymandering** *n*

gerund *n* a verbal noun in Latin that expresses generalized or uncompleted action

gestalt *n, pl* **gestalten, gestalts** a structure, pattern, etc (e g a melody) that as an object of perception constitutes a functional unit with properties not derivable from the sum of its parts

gestapo *n, pl* **gestapos** a secret-police organization operating esp against suspected traitors; *specif, cap* that of Nazi Germany

gestation *n* **1** the carrying of young in the uterus; pregnancy **2** conception and development, esp in the mind – **gestational** *adj*

gesticulate *vi* to make expressive gestures, esp when speaking ⟨~d *to the waiter for the bill* – Rebecca West⟩ – **gesticulator** *n*, **gesticulative** *adj*, **gesticulatory** *adj*, **gesticulation** *n*

¹gesture *n* **1a** a movement, usu of the body or limbs, that expresses or emphasizes an idea, sentiment, or attitude **b** the use of gestures **2** sthg said or done for its effect on the attitudes of others or to convey a feeling (e g friendliness) – **gestural** *adj*

²gesture *vb* to make or express (by) a gesture

¹get *vb* **-tt-**; **got**; **got**, *NAm also* **gotten**; *nonstandard pres pl & 1 & 3 sing get* *vt* **1** to gain possession of: e g **a** to obtain by way of benefit or advantage ⟨~ *the better of an enemy*⟩ ⟨got *little for his trouble*⟩ **b** to obtain by con-

cession or entreaty ⟨~ *your mother's permission to go*⟩ **c** to seek out and fetch or provide ⟨~ *blackberries in the wood*⟩ ⟨~ *you a present*⟩ **d** to acquire by memorizing or calculation ⟨~ *the verse by heart*⟩ ⟨~ *the answer to a problem*⟩ **e** to seize **2a** to receive as a return; earn ⟨*he got a bad reputation for carelessness*⟩ **b** to become affected by; catch ⟨got *measles from his sister*⟩ **c** to be subjected to ⟨~ *the sack*⟩ **3** to beget **4a** to cause to come, go, or move ⟨*quickly* ~ *his luggage through customs*⟩ ⟨*grumbling won't* ~ *you anywhere*⟩ **b** to bring into a specified condition by direct action ⟨~ *my shoes mended*⟩ ⟨*let me* ~ *this clear*⟩ **c** to prevail on; induce ⟨~ *the Russians to give an English broadcast – SEU S*⟩ **5** to make ready; prepare ⟨~ *dinner*⟩ **6a** to overcome ⟨*I'll* ~ *him on that point*⟩ **b** to take vengeance on; *specif* to kill ⟨*out to* ~ *his man*⟩ **7a** to have – used in the present perfect tense form with present meaning ⟨*I've got no money*⟩ **b** to have as an obligation or necessity – used in the present perfect tense form with present meaning; + *to* and an understood or expressed infinitive ⟨*he has got to come*⟩ ⟨*I won't if I haven't got to*⟩ **8a** to hear ⟨*I didn't quite* ~ *that for the noise*⟩ **b** to establish communication with ⟨~ *her on the telephone*⟩ **9a** to puzzle ⟨*you've really got me there*⟩ **b** to irritate ⟨*his superior attitude really* ~s *me*⟩ **10** to hit ⟨~ *him on the ear with a potato*⟩ **11** to understand ⟨*don't* ~ *me wrong*⟩ **12** to affect emotionally ⟨*the sight of her tears got him*⟩ ~ *vi* **1** to reach or enter into the specified condition or activity ⟨~ *drunk*⟩ ⟨*food's* ~ting *cold*⟩ ⟨~ *moving*⟩ ⟨*you're* ~ting *a big girl now*⟩ ⟨*they* got *married last week*⟩ – used as a verbal auxiliary instead of *be* to form the passive ⟨*wouldn't take the slightest risk of* ~ting *trapped inside* – SEU W⟩ **2a** to reach, arrive ⟨*where's my pen got to?*⟩ **b** to succeed in coming or going ⟨~ *into my jeans*⟩ ⟨*at last we're* ~ting *somewhere*⟩ ⟨~ *to sleep after midnight*⟩ **c** to contrive by effort, luck, or permission – + *to* and an infinitive ⟨*when you* ~ *to know him*⟩ ⟨*she never* ~s *to drive the car*⟩ **USE** (*vt* 9a, 9b, 10, 11, & 12) *infml* – **get ahead** to achieve success ⟨*determined to get ahead in life*⟩ – **get a move on** to hurry up – **get at 1** to reach effectively ⟨*get at the truth*⟩ **2** to influence corruptly; bribe **3** to nag, tease **4** to mean, imply ⟨*what's he getting at?*⟩ – **get away with** to do (a reprehensible act) without criticism or penalty – **get cracking/weaving** to make a start; get going ⟨*ought to get cracking on the washing up*⟩ – *infml* – **get even with** to repay in kind; revenge oneself on – **get into** to possess, dominate ⟨*what's got into you?*⟩ – **get it** CATCH IT – **get off one's bike** *Austr* to become annoyed – *infml* – **get one's eye in** *chiefly Br* to get into practice; *specif* to gain ability to judge the speed and direction of a moving ball – **get one's goat** to make one angry or annoyed – *infml* – **get one's own back** to revenge oneself – **get on one's high horse** to adopt an unyielding and usu arrogant attitude – **get outside** to eat (sthg) – *infml* – **get over 1** to overcome, surmount **2** to recover from **3** to accept calmly ⟨*can't get over your beard*⟩ – **get rid of** to rid oneself of; disencumber oneself of by eliminating, dismissing, or clearing away – **get round 1** to circumvent, evade **2** to cajole, persuade – **get the better of** to overcome – **get there 1** to be successful **2** to understand what is meant – **get the wind up** to become frightened – *infml* – **get the wrong end of the stick** to misunderstand sthg – **get through 1** to reach the end of; complete **2a** USE UP **1** ⟨got through *a lot of money*⟩ **b** WHILE AWAY ⟨*hardly knew how to* get through *his days*⟩ – **get under one's skin** to cause one persistent and often troublesome irritation, stimulation, or excitement – **get up someone's nose** to irritate sby intensely – *infml* – **get wind of** to become aware of

²**get** n 1 sthg begotten 2 a successful return of a difficult shot in tennis, squash, etc 3 Br a git – slang

get about vi 1 to be up and about; be well enough to walk 2 to become circulated, esp orally ⟨the news soon got about⟩

get across vb to make or become clear or convincing

get along vi 1 to move away; leave for another destination 2 to manage 3 to be or remain on congenial terms

getaway n a departure, escape

get back vi to return, revert – **get back at** to gain revenge on; retaliate against

get by vi 1 to manage, survive ⟨we'll get by without your help⟩ 2 to succeed by a narrow margin; be just about acceptable

get down vi to leave or descend (e g from a vehicle) ~ vt 1 to depress ⟨the weather was getting her down⟩ 2 to swallow ⟨get this medicine down⟩ 3 to record in writing ⟨get down the details⟩ – **get down to** to apply serious attention or consideration to; concentrate one's efforts on

get off vi 1 to start, leave 2 to escape from a dangerous situation or from punishment ⟨won't get off lightly⟩ 3 to leave work with permission 4 Br to start an amorous or sexual relationship – often + with; slang ~ vt 1 to secure the release of or procure a modified penalty for ⟨his lawyers got him off with little difficulty⟩ 2 to send, post

get on vi 1 GET ALONG 2 to become late or old – **get on for** to come near; approach ⟨he's getting on for 90⟩

get out vi 1 to emerge, escape ⟨doubted that he would get out alive⟩ 2 to become known; LEAK 3 ⟨their secret got out⟩ ~ vt 1 to cause to emerge or escape 2 to bring before the public; esp to publish ⟨get a new book out⟩

get round vi GET ABOUT 2 – **get round to** to give esp overdue attention or consideration

get-together n an (informal social) gathering or meeting

get together vt to bring together; accumulate ~ vi 1 to come together; assemble 2 to unite in discussion or promotion of a project

getup n the outer appearance; specif an outfit, clothing – infml

get up vi 1a to arise from bed b to rise to one's feet 2 to go ahead or faster – used in the imperative as a command, esp to driven animals ~ vt 1 to organize ⟨got up a party for the newcomers⟩ 2 to arrange the external appearance of; dress 3 to acquire a knowledge of 4 to create in oneself ⟨can't get up an atom of sympathy for them⟩

geum n an avens

gewgaw n a bauble, trinket

geyser n 1 a spring that intermittently throws out jets of heated water and steam 2 Br an apparatus with a boiler in which water (e g for a bath) is rapidly heated by a gas flame and may be stored

gharry n a usu horse-drawn Indian taxi

ghastly adj 1a (terrifyingly) horrible ⟨a ~ crime⟩ b intensely unpleasant, disagreeable, or objectionable ⟨such a life seems ~ in its emptiness and sterility – Aldous Huxley⟩ 2 pale, wan – **ghastliness** n

ghat n a broad flight of steps providing access to an Indian river

ghee, ghi n a semifluid clarified butter made, esp in India, from cow's or buffalo's milk

gherkin n 1 (a slender annual climbing plant of the cucumber family that bears) a small prickly fruit used for pickling 2 the small immature fruit of the cucumber used for pickling

ghetto n, pl **ghettos, ghettoes** 1 part of a city in which Jews formerly lived 2 an often slum area of a city in which a minority group live, esp because of social, legal, or economic pressures; broadly an area with 1 predominant type of resident

¹**ghost** n 1 the seat of life or intelligence ⟨give up the ~⟩ 2 a disembodied soul; esp the soul of a dead person haunting the living 3a a faint shadowy trace ⟨a ~ of a smile⟩ b the least bit ⟨didn't have a ~ of a chance⟩ 4 a false image in a photographic negative or on a television screen 5 a ghost-writer 6 a red blood cell that has lost its haemoglobin – **ghostlike** adj

²**ghost** vb to ghostwrite

ghostly adj of, like, or being a ghost; spectral – **ghostliness** n

ghost town n a once-flourishing but now deserted town

ghoul n 1 a evil being of Arabic legend that robs graves and feeds on corpses 2 one who enjoys the macabre – **ghoulish** adj, **ghoulishly** adv, **ghoulishness** n

ghyll n ³GILL

¹**GI** adj (characteristic) of US military personnel or equipment

²**GI** n, pl **GI's, GIs** a member of the US army, esp a private

¹**giant** n 1 fem **giantess** /-tis/ a legendary humanoid being of great stature and strength 2 sby or sthg extraordinarily large 3 a person of extraordinary powers ⟨a literary ~⟩ – **giantlike** adj

²**giant** adj extremely large

giant panda n PANDA 2

¹**gibber** vi to make rapid, inarticulate, and usu incomprehensible utterances ⟨a ~ing idiot⟩

²**gibber** n, Austr a small stone; a pebble; also a boulder, rock

gibberish n unintelligible or meaningless language

gibbet vt or n (to execute or expose on) an upright post with an arm for hanging the bodies of executed criminals

gibbon n any of several tailless Asian anthropoid tree-dwelling apes

gibbous adj 1a of the moon or a planet seen with more than half but not all of the apparent disc illuminated b swollen on 1 side; convex, protuberant 2 having a hump; humpbacked – **gibbously** adv, **gibbousness** n, **gibbosity** n

gibe, jibe vb to jeer (at) – **gibe** n, **giber** n

giblets n pl a fowl's heart, liver, or other edible internal organs

giddy adj 1 lightheartedly frivolous 2a feeling, or causing to feel, a sensation of unsteadiness and lack of balance as if everything is whirling round b whirling rapidly – **giddily** adv, **giddiness** n

¹**gift** n 1 a natural capacity or talent 2 sthg freely given by one person to another 3 the act, right, or power of giving ⟨the regional fund is not in M Pompidou's ~ – The Times⟩ – **gift of the gab** the ability to talk glibly and persuasively – infml

²**gift** vt to present

gifted adj 1 having or revealing great natural ability 2 highly intelligent ⟨~ children⟩ – **giftedly** adv, **giftedness** n

¹**gig** n 1 a long light ship's boat propelled by oars, sails, etc 2 a light 2-wheeled one-horse carriage

²**gig** n a pronged spear for catching fish

³**gig** n a musician's engagement for a specified time; esp such an engagement for 1 performance

gigantic adj unusually great or enormous – **gigantically** adv

¹giggle *vi* to laugh with repeated short catches of the breath (and in a silly manner) – **giggler** *n*, **gigglingly** *adv*

²giggle *n* **1** an act or instance of giggling **2** *chiefly Br* sthg that amuses or diverts – chiefly infml ⟨*did it for a* ~⟩ – **giggly** *adj*

gigolo *n, pl* **gigolos 1** a man paid by a usu older woman for companionship or sex **2** a professional dancing partner or male escort

¹gild *vt* **gilded, gilt 1** to overlay (as if) with a thin covering of gold **2** to give an attractive but often deceptive appearance to – **gilder** *n*, **gilding** *n* – **gild the lily** to add unnecessary ornamentation to sthg beautiful in its own right

²gild *n* a guild

¹gill *n* a unit of liquid capacity equal to ¼ pint

²gill *n* **1** an organ, esp of a fish, for oxygenating blood using the oxygen dissolved in water **2** the flesh under or about the chin or jaws – usu pl with sing. meaning **3** any of the radiating plates forming the undersurface of the cap of some fungi (e g mushrooms) – **gilled** *adj*

³gill, ghyll *n, Br* **1** a ravine **2** a narrow mountain stream or rivulet

gillie, gilly, ghillie *n* an attendant to sby who is hunting or fishing in Scotland

¹gilt *adj* covered with gold or gilt; of the colour of gold

²gilt *n* **1** (sthg that resembles) gold laid on a surface **2** superficial brilliance; surface attraction **3** a gilt-edged security – usu pl

³gilt *n* a young female pig

gilt-edged, gilt-edge *adj* **1** of the highest quality or reliability **2** *of government securities* having a guaranteed fixed interest rate and redeemable at face value

gimcrack *n* a showy unsubstantial object of little use or value – **gimcrack** *adj*, **gimcrackery** *n*

¹gimlet *n* **1** a tool for boring small holes in wood, usu consisting of a crosswise handle fitted to a tapered screw **2** a cocktail consisting of lime juice, gin or vodka, and soda water

²gimlet *adj, of eyes* piercing, penetrating ⟨*give him a gimlet-eyed stare*⟩

gimmick *n* a scheme, device, or object devised to gain attention or publicity – **gimmickry** *n*, **gimmicky** *adj*

¹gin *n* any of various tools or mechanical devices: e g **a** a snare or trap for game **b** a machine for raising or moving heavy weights **c** COTTON GIN

²gin *vt* **-nn- 1** to snare **2** to separate (cotton fibre) from seeds and waste material – **ginner** *n*, **ginning** *n*

³gin *n* a spirit made by distilling a mash of grain with juniper berries

ginger *n* **1a** (any of several cultivated tropical plants with) a thickened pungent aromatic underground stem used (dried and ground) as a spice, or candied as a sweet **b** the spice usu prepared by drying and grinding ginger **2** a strong brown colour – **gingery** *adj*

ginger ale *n* a sweet yellowish carbonated nonalcoholic drink flavoured with ginger

gingerbread *n* a thick biscuit or cake made with treacle or syrup and flavoured with ginger

ginger group *n, Br* a pressure group (e g within a political party) urging stronger action

gingerly *adj* very cautious or careful – **gingerliness** *n*, **gingerly** *adv*

ginger nut *n* a hard brittle biscuit flavoured with ginger

ginger up *vt* to stir to activity; vitalize ⟨ginger up *boardroom attitudes* – Punch⟩

gingham *n* a plain-weave often checked clothing fabric usu of yarn-dyed cotton

ginkgo, gingko *n, pl* **ginkgoes, gingkoes** a showy (ornamental) Chinese gymnospermous tree with fan-shaped leaves and yellow fruit

gin palace *n, Br* a gaudy public house – derog

ginseng *n* (the aromatic root, widely valued as a tonic, of) a Chinese or American plant of the ivy family

gipsy, *NAm* **gypsy 1** *often cap* a member of a dark Caucasian people coming orig from India to Europe in the 14th or 15th c and leading a migratory way of life **2** a person who moves from place to place; a wanderer

giraffe *n, pl* **giraffes**, *esp collectively* **giraffe** a large African ruminant mammal with a very long neck and a beige coat marked with brown or black patches

gird *vb* **girded, girt** *vt* **1a** to encircle or bind with a flexible band (e g a belt) **b** to surround **2** to provide or equip with a sword **3** to prepare (oneself) for action ~ *vi* to prepare for action – **gird one's loins, gird up one's loins** to prepare for action; muster one's resources

girder *n* a horizontal main supporting beam

¹girdle *n* **1** sthg that encircles or confines: e g **a** a belt or cord encircling the body, usu at the waist **b** a woman's tightly fitting undergarment that extends from the waist to below the hips **c** a bony ring at the front and rear end of the trunk of vertebrates supporting the arms or legs **d** a ring made by the removal of the bark and cambium round a plant stem or tree trunk **2** the edge of a cut gem that is grasped by the setting

²girdle *vt* **girdling 1** to encircle (as if) with a girdle **2** to cut a girdle round (esp a tree), usu in order to kill

³girdle *n, Scot & dial Eng* a griddle

girl *n* **1a** a female child **b** a young unmarried woman **2a** a sweetheart, girlfriend **b** a daughter **3** a woman – chiefly infml – **girlhood** *n*, **girlish** *adj*, **girlishness** *n*

girl Friday *n* a female general assistant, esp in an office

girlfriend *n* **1** a frequent or regular female companion of a boy or man; *esp* one with whom he is romantically involved **2** a female friend

girl guide *n, chiefly Br* GUIDE 3 – not now used technically

girlie, girly *adj* featuring nude or scantily clothed young women ⟨~ *magazines*⟩

giro *n* a computerized low-cost system of money transfer comparable to a current account that is one of the national post office services in many European countries

girt *vb* to gird

¹girth *n* **1** a strap that passes under the body of a horse or other animal to fasten esp a saddle on its back **2** a measurement of thickness round a body

²girth *vt* **1** to encircle **2** to bind or fasten with a girth

gist *n* *the* main point of a matter; *the* essence

¹give *vb* **gave; given** *vt* **1** to make a present of ⟨~ *a doll to a child*⟩ **2a** to grant, bestow, or allot (by formal action) **b** to accord or yield to another ⟨~ *blood*⟩ ⟨~ *him her confidence*⟩ **3a** to administer as a sacrament or medicine **b** to commit to another as a trust or responsibility ⟨gave *her his coat to hold*⟩ **c** to convey or express to another ⟨~ *an order*⟩ ⟨~ *my regards to your family*⟩ **4a** to proffer, present (for another to use or act on) ⟨gave *his hand to the visitor*⟩ **b** to surrender (oneself) to a partner in sexual intercourse **5** to present to view or observation ⟨gave *a signal*⟩ ⟨gave *no sign of life*⟩ **6a** to present for, or provide by way of, entertainment ⟨~ *a party*⟩ **b** to present, perform, or deliver in public ⟨~ *a lecture*⟩ ⟨~ *a piano recital*⟩ **7** to propose as a toast ⟨*I* ~ *you the Queen*⟩ **8** to attribute, ascribe ⟨gave *all the glory to God*⟩ **9** to yield as a product or effect ⟨cows ~ *milk*⟩ ⟨*84 divided by 12* ~ *s 7*⟩ ⟨*she gave him two sons*⟩ **10** to make known; show ⟨*the thermometer* ~ *s the temperature*⟩ **11** to yield possession of by way of exchange; pay **12** to make, execute, or deliver (e g by some bodily action) ⟨gave *him a push*⟩ ⟨*the ship* gave *a lurch*⟩ ⟨gave *a hollow laugh*⟩ **13a** to inflict as punishment ⟨gave *the boy a whipping*⟩ **b** to cause to undergo; impose ⟨~ *them a spelling test*⟩ ⟨~ *it a try*⟩ **14a** to award by formal verdict ⟨~ *judgment against the plaintiff*⟩ **b** to make a specified ruling on the status of (a player) ⟨*Bowles was* ~ n *offside*⟩ **15a** to offer for consideration, acceptance, or use ⟨*don't* ~ *me that old line*⟩ **b** to agree to act in accordance with ⟨*I* ~ *you my word*⟩ ⟨~ *a legal undertaking*⟩ **16a** to cause or receive ⟨*mountains always* gave *him pleasure*⟩ **b** to cause to catch or contract ⟨*digging* ~s *me backache*⟩ **c** to cause (sby) (to think or wonder) ⟨*I was given to understand that he was ill*⟩ **17** to apply freely or fully; devote ⟨~ *one's time to the service of others*⟩ **18** to allow, concede ⟨*it's late, I* ~ *you that*⟩ **19** to care to the extent of ⟨*didn't* ~ *a hang*⟩ ~ *vi* **1** to make gifts **2** to yield or collapse in response to pressure ⟨*the fence* gave *under his weight*⟩ **3** to afford a view or passage; open ⟨*the door* ~s *directly upon the garden*⟩ **4** of weather to become mild **5** to impart information; talk – infml **6** to happen; GO ON **3** – slang ⟨*what* ~s?⟩ – **giver** *n* – **give a dog a bad name** to implant prejudice by slander – **give a good account of** to acquit (oneself) well – **give a miss** *chiefly Br* to avoid, bypass ⟨*language learners* give *Russian* a miss – *TES*⟩ – **give as good as one gets** to counterattack with equal vigour – **give birth to 1** to bring forth as a mother **2** to be the cause or origin of – **give chase** to go in pursuit – **give ground** to withdraw before superior force; retreat – **give me** I prefer ⟨give me *London any day!*⟩ – **give or take** allowing for a specified imprecision ⟨*three hours,* give or take *a few minutes either way*⟩ – **give place** to yield by way of being superseded ⟨*valves* give place *to transistors*⟩ – **give someone a wide berth** to stay at a safe distance from sby – **give someone best** *Br* to acknowledge sby's superiority – **give someone/something his/her/its head 1** to give sby or sthg greater freedom and responsibility **2** to allow (a horse) to gallop – **give someone rope** to give sby free scope – **give the lie to** to belie – **give way 1a** to retreat; GIVE GROUND **b** to yield the right of way ⟨gave way *to oncoming traffic*⟩ **2** to yield oneself without restraint or control ⟨give way *to tears*⟩ **3a** to yield (as if) to physical stress ⟨*the wind caused the roof to* give way⟩ **b** to yield to entreaty or insistence **4** GIVE PLACE

²give *n* the capacity or tendency to yield to pressure; resilience, elasticity ⟨*there's no* ~ *in this mattress*⟩ ⟨*there's no* ~ *in her political opinions*⟩

give-and-take *n* **1** the practice of making mutual concessions **2** the good-natured exchange of ideas or words

giveaway *n* **1** an unintentional revelation or betrayal **2** sthg given free or at a reduced price

give away *vt* **1** to make a present of **2** to hand over (a bride) to the bridegroom at a wedding **3a** to betray **b** to disclose, reveal – esp in **give the game/show away 4** to be at a disadvantage in a sporting contest by (e g a weight or age) compared with an opponent ⟨giving away *4 years to the junior champion*⟩

give in *vt* to hand in; deliver ⟨gave in *the money he'd found*⟩ ~ *vi* to yield under insistence or entreaty

given *adj* **1** prone, disposed ⟨~ *to swearing*⟩ **2** of an official document executed on the date specified **3a** fixed, specified ⟨*at a* ~ *time*⟩ **b** assumed as actual or hypothetical ⟨~ *that all men are equal before the law*⟩ – **given** *n*

given name *n, chiefly NAm* CHRISTIAN NAME

give off *vt* to emit ⟨gave off *an unpleasant smell*⟩

give out *vt* **1** to declare, publish ⟨giving out *that the doctor required a few days of complete rest* – Charles Dickens⟩ **2** to emit ⟨gave out *a constant hum*⟩ **3** to issue, distribute ⟨gave out *new uniforms*⟩ ~ *vi* **1** to come to an end; fail ⟨*finally their patience* gave out *and they came to blows*⟩

give over *vt* **1** to set apart for a particular purpose or use **2** to deliver to sby's care ~ *vi* **1** to bring an activity to an end ⟨*told him to* give over *and let me alone* – Brendan Behan⟩ – infml

give up *vt* **1** to surrender, esp as a prisoner ⟨*he* gave *himself* up⟩ **2** to desist from ⟨*refused to* give up *trying*⟩ **3a** to abandon (oneself) to a particular feeling, influence, or activity ⟨gave *himself* up *to despair*⟩ **b** to renounce ⟨*I must* give up *sugar*⟩ **4** to declare incurable or insoluble ⟨*the doctors* gave *her* up *for dead*⟩ **5** to stop having a relationship with ⟨*she's* given *me* up⟩ ~ *vi* to abandon an activity or course of action; *esp* to stop trying – **give up the ghost** to die

gizzard *n* **1** a muscular enlargement of the alimentary canal of birds that immediately follows the crop and has a tough horny lining for grinding food **2** a thickened part of the alimentary canal of some animals (e g an earthworm) similar in function to the crop of a bird

glacé *adj* **1** made or finished so as to have a smooth glossy surface ⟨~ *silk*⟩ **2** coated with a glaze; candied ⟨~ *cherries*⟩

glacial *adj* **1a** extremely cold ⟨*a* ~ *wind*⟩ **b** devoid of warmth and cordiality ⟨*a* ~ *smile*⟩ **2a** of or produced by glaciers **b** of or being any of those parts of geological time when much of the earth was covered by glaciers **3** resembling ice in appearance, esp when frozen ⟨~ *acetic acid*⟩ – **glacially** *adv*

glacier *n* a large body of ice moving slowly down a slope or spreading outwards on a land surface

¹glad *adj* **-dd- 1** expressing or experiencing pleasure, joy, or delight **2** very willing ⟨~ *to do it*⟩ **3** causing happiness and joy ⟨~ *tidings*⟩ – **gladden** *vt*, **gladly** *adv*, **gladness** *n*

²glad *n* a gladiolus – infml

glade *n* an open space within a wood or forest

glad eye *n* an amorous or sexually inviting look ⟨*he* gave *her the* ~⟩ – infml

glad hand *n* a warm welcome or greeting often prompted by ulterior motives – infml – **glad hand** *vt*

gladiator *n* **1** sby trained to fight in the arena for the entertainment of ancient Romans **2** sby engaging in a public fight or controversy – **gladiatorial** *adj*

gladiolus *n, pl* **gladioli** any of a genus of (African) plants of the iris family with spikes of brilliantly coloured irregular flowers

glad rags *n pl* smart clothes – infml

glamorize, -ise *also* **glamourize, -ise** *vt* **1** to make glamorous ⟨~ *the living room*⟩ **2** to romanticize ⟨*the novel* ~s *war*⟩

glamour, NAm *also* **glamor** *n* a romantic, exciting, and often illusory attractiveness; *esp* alluring or fascinating personal attraction – **glamorous** *also* **glamourous** *adj*, **glamorously** *also* **glamourously** *adv*

¹glance *vi* **1** to strike a surface obliquely so as to go off at an angle ⟨*the bullet* ~d *off the wall*⟩ – often + *off* **2a** to flash or gleam with intermittent rays of reflected light ⟨*brooks* glancing *in the sun*⟩ **b** to make sudden quick movements ⟨*dragonflies* glancing *over the pond*⟩ **3** to touch on a subject or refer to it briefly or indirectly ⟨*the work* ~s *at the customs of ancient cultures*⟩ **4a** of the eyes to move swiftly from one thing to another **b** to take a quick look at sthg ⟨~d *at his watch*⟩ ~ *vt* **1a** to cause to glance off a surface by throwing or shooting **b** to play a glance in cricket at (a ball) or at the bowling of (a bowler) **2** *archaic* to catch a glimpse of

²glance *n* **1** a quick intermittent flash or gleam **2 a** a deflected impact or blow **3a** a swift movement of the eyes **b** a quick or cursory look **4** an allusion **5** a stroke in cricket that barely deflects the ball from its line of flight – **at first glance** on first consideration 〈at first glance *the subject seems harmless enough*〉

³glance *n* any of several usu dark mineral sulphides with a metallic lustre

glancing *adj* having a slanting direction 〈*a ~ blow*〉 – **glancingly** *adv*

¹gland *n* **1** (an animal structure that does not secrete but resembles) an organ that selectively removes materials from the blood, alters them, and secretes them esp for further use in the body or for elimination **2** any of various secreting organs (e g a nectary) of plants – **glandless** *adj*

²gland *n* **1** a device for preventing leakage of fluid past a joint in machinery **2** the movable part of a stuffing box by which the packing is compressed

glandular *adj* of, involving, or being (the cells or products of) glands – **glandularly** *adv*

¹glare *vi* **1** to shine with a harsh uncomfortably brilliant light **2** to stare angrily or fiercely ~ *vt* to express (e g hostility) by staring fiercely

²glare *n* **1a** a harsh uncomfortably bright light; *specif* painfully bright sunlight **b** garishness **2** an angry or fierce stare

glaring *adj* painfully and obtrusively evident 〈*a ~ error*〉 – **glaringly** *adv*, **glaringness** *n*

¹glass *n* **1a** a hard brittle usu transparent or translucent inorganic substance formed by fusing a mixture of silica sand, metallic oxides, and other ingredients **b** a substance resembling glass, esp in hardness and transparency **c** a substance (e g pumice) produced by the quick cooling of molten rock from the earth's core **2a** sthg made of glass: e g **(1)** a glass drinking vessel (e g a tumbler or wineglass) **(2)** a mirror; LOOKING GLASS **(3)** a barometer **b(1)** an optical instrument (e g a magnifying glass) for viewing objects not readily seen **(2)** *pl* a pair of lenses together with a frame to hold them in place for correcting defects of vision or protecting the eyes **3** the quantity held by a glass container or drinking vessel **4** glassware – **glassful** *n*, **glassless** *adj*

²glass *vt* to enclose, case, or wall with glass 〈*the sun porch was ~ed in*〉

glassblowing *n* the art of shaping a mass of semimolten glass by blowing air into it through a tube – **glassblower** *n*

glasshouse *n, chiefly Br* **1** a greenhouse **2** a military prison – *slang*

glassware *n* articles made of glass

glass wool *n* glass fibres in a mass resembling wool used esp for thermal insulation

glassworks *n, pl* **glassworks** a place where glass is made – often pl with sing. meaning

glassy *adj* dull, lifeless 〈*~ eyes*〉 – **glassily** *adv*, **glassiness** *n*

glaucoma *n* increased pressure within the eyeball (leading to damage to the retina and gradual loss of vision)

glaucous *adj* **1a** pale yellowy green **b** *esp of plants or plant parts* of a dull blue or bluish-green colour **2** *of a plant or fruit* having a powdery or waxy coating giving a frosted appearance – **glaucousness** *n*

¹glaze *vt* **1** to provide or fit with glass **2** to coat (as if) with a glaze 〈*~ apple tarts*〉 **3** to give a smooth glossy surface to ~ *vi* **1** to become glazed or glassy 〈*his eyes ~d over*〉 **2** to form a glaze – **glazer** *n*

²glaze *n* **1a** a liquid preparation that gives a glossy coating to food **b** a mixture predominantly of oxides (e g silica and alumina) applied to the surface of ceramic wares as decoration and to make them nonporous **c** a transparent or translucent colour applied to a printed surface to modify its tone **d** a smooth glossy or lustrous surface or finish **2** a glassy film (e g of ice)

glazier *n* one who fits glass, esp into windows, as an occupation – **glaziery** *n*

¹gleam *n* **1a** a transient appearance of subdued or partly obscured light **b** a glint 〈*a ~ of anticipation in his eyes*〉 **2** a brief or faint appearance or occurrence 〈*a ~ of hope*〉 – **gleamy** *adj*

²gleam *vi* **1** to shine with subdued steady light or moderate brightness **2** to appear briefly or faintly

glean *vi* **1** to gather produce, esp grain, left by reapers **2** to gather material (e g information) bit by bit ~ *vt* **1a** to pick up (e g grain) after a reaper **b** to strip (e g a field) by gleaning **2a** to gather (e g information) bit by bit **b** to pick over in search of relevant material – **gleanable** *adj*, **gleaner** *n*

gleanings *n pl* things acquired by gleaning

glebe *n* **1** land belonging to an ecclesiastical benefice **2** *archaic* (a plot of cultivated) land

glee *n* **1** a feeling of merry high-spirited joy or delight **2** an unaccompanied song for 3 or more usu male solo voices – **gleeful** *adj*, **gleefully** *adv*, **gleefulness** *n*

glen *n* a secluded narrow valley

glengarry *n, often cap* a straight-sided woollen cap coming to a rounded point over the brow and having 2 short ribbons hanging down behind, worn esp as part of Highland military uniform

glib *adj* **-bb-** **1** showing little forethought or preparation; lacking depth and substance 〈*~ solutions to problems*〉 **2** marked by (superficial or dishonest) ease and fluency in speaking or writing – **glibly** *adv*, **glibness** *n*

¹glide *vi* **1** to move noiselessly in a smooth, continuous, and effortless manner **2** to pass gradually and imperceptibly **3a** *of an aircraft* to fly without the use of engines **b** to fly in a glider ~ *vt* to cause to glide

²glide *n* **1** the act or action of gliding **2a** a portamento **b** a transitional sound produced by the vocal organs passing from one articulatory position to another

glider *n* an aircraft similar to an aeroplane but without an engine

¹glimmer *vi* **1** to shine faintly or unsteadily **2** to appear indistinctly with a faintly luminous quality

²glimmer *n* **1** a feeble or unsteady light **2a** a dim perception or faint idea **b** a small sign or amount 〈*a ~ of intelligence*〉

glimmering *n* a glimmer

¹glimpse *vt* to get a brief look at

²glimpse *n* a brief fleeting view or look

¹glint *vi* **1** *of rays of light* to strike a reflecting surface obliquely and dart out at an angle **2** to shine with tiny bright flashes; sparkle or glitter, esp by reflection ~ *vt* to cause to glint

²glint *n* **1** a tiny bright flash of light; a sparkle **2** a brief or faint manifestation 〈*detected a ~ of recognition in her expression*〉

¹glissade *vi* to slide usu in a standing or squatting position down a slope, esp one that is snow-covered

²glissade *n* **1** the action of glissading **2** a gliding step in ballet

glissando *n, pl* **glissandi**, **glissandos** a rapid sliding up or down the musical scale

glisten *vi* to shine, usu by reflection, with a sparkling radiance or with the lustre of a wet or oiled surface

glister *vi* to glitter – chiefly poetic – **glister** *n*

¹glitter vi **1a** to shine by reflection with a brilliant or metallic lustre ⟨~ing sequins⟩ **b** to shine with a hard cold glassy brilliance ⟨~ing eyes⟩ **2** to be brilliantly attractive in a superficial or deceptive way ⟨the chance of success ~ed before them⟩ – **glitteringly** adv

²glitter n **1** sparkling brilliance, showiness, or attractiveness **2** small glittering particles used for ornamentation – **glittery** adj

gloaming n the twilight, dusk

¹gloat vi to observe or think about sthg with great and often malicious satisfaction, gratification, or relish – **gloater** n, **gloatingly** adv

²gloat n a gloating feeling

global adj **1** spherical **2** of or involving the entire world **3** general, comprehensive – **globally** adv

globe n sthg spherical or rounded: e g **a** a spherical representation of the earth, a heavenly body, or the heavens **b** EARTH 4

globe artichoke n ARTICHOKE 1b

globefish n any of a family of (tropical) poisonous marine fishes which can distend themselves to a globular form

globe-trotter n one who travels widely – **globe-trotting** n or adj

globular adj **1** globe- or globule-shaped ⟨~ proteins⟩ **2** having or consisting of globules – **globularly** adv, **globularness** n

globule n a tiny globe or ball (e g of liquid or melted solid)

glockenspiel n a percussion instrument consisting of a series of graduated metal bars played with 2 hammers

¹gloom vi **1** to mope **2** to loom up dimly or sombrely ⟨the castle ~ed before them⟩ ~vt to make dark, murky, or sombre

²gloom n **1** partial or total darkness **2a** lowness of spirits **b** an atmosphere of despondency ⟨a ~ fell over the household⟩

gloomy adj **1a** partially or totally dark; esp dismally and depressingly dark ⟨~ weather⟩ **b** low in spirits **2** causing gloom ⟨a ~ story⟩ – **gloomily** adv, **gloominess** n

glorify vt **1a** to make glorious by bestowing honour, praise, or admiration **b** to elevate to celestial glory **2** to shed radiance or splendour on **3** to cause to appear better, more appealing, or more important than in reality **4** to give glory to (e g in worship) – **glorifier** n, **glorification** n

glorious adj **1a** possessing or deserving glory **b** conferring glory **2** marked by great beauty or splendour **3** delightful, wonderful ⟨had a ~ weekend⟩ – **gloriously** adv, **gloriousness** n

¹glory n **1a** (sthg that secures) praise or renown **b** worshipful praise, honour, and thanksgiving ⟨giving ~ to God⟩ **2** a (most) commendable asset ⟨her hair was her crowning ~⟩ **3a** (sthg marked by) resplendence or magnificence ⟨the ~ that was Greece and the grandeur that was Rome – E A Poe⟩ **b** the splendour, blessedness, and happiness of heaven; broadly eternity **4** a state of great gratification or exaltation **5** a ring or spot of light: e g **a** an aureole **b** CORONA 2a, b

²glory vi to rejoice proudly ⟨~ing in their youth and vigour⟩

¹gloss n **1** (sthg that gives) surface lustre or brightness **2** a deceptively attractive outer appearance **3** paint to which varnish has been added to give a gloss finish

²gloss n **1a** a brief explanation (e g in the margin of a text) of a difficult word or expression **b** a false interpretation (e g of a text) **2a** a glossary **b** an interlinear translation **c** a continuous commentary accompanying a text

³gloss vt to supply glosses for

gloss-, glosso- comb form **1** tongue ⟨glossal⟩ ⟨glossitis⟩; tongue and ⟨glossopharyngeal⟩ **2** language ⟨glossology⟩

glossary n a list of terms (e g those used in a particular text or in a specialized field), usu with their meanings

gloss over vt **1** to make appear right and acceptable **2** to veil or hide by treating rapidly or superficially ⟨glossing over humiliations, gilding small moments of glory – TLS⟩

¹glossy adj **1** having a surface lustre or brightness **2** attractive in an artificially opulent, sophisticated, or smoothly captivating manner ⟨a ~ musical⟩ – **glossily** adv, **glossiness** n

²glossy n, chiefly Br a magazine expensively produced on glossy paper and often having a fashionable or sophisticated content

glottal stop n a speech sound produced by sudden closure of the glottis

glottis n, pl **glottises, glottides** (the structures surrounding) the elongated space between the vocal cords – **glottal** adj

¹glove n **1** a covering for the hand having separate sections for each of the fingers and the thumb and often extending part way up the arm **2** BOXING GLOVE

²glove vt to cover (as if) with a glove

glove compartment n a small storage compartment in the dashboard of a motor vehicle

¹glow vi **1** to shine (as if) with an intense heat **2a** to experience a sensation (as if) of heat; show a ruddy colour (as if) from being too warm ⟨~ing with rage⟩ **b** to show satisfaction or elation ⟨~ with pride⟩ – **glowingly** adv

²glow n **1** brightness or warmth of colour ⟨the ~ of his cheeks⟩ **2a** warmth of feeling or emotion **b** a sensation of warmth ⟨the drug produces a sustained ~⟩ **3a** the state of glowing with heat and light **b** light (as if) from sthg burning without flames or smoke

glower vi to look or stare with sullen annoyance or anger – **glower** n

glowworm n a luminescent wingless insect; esp a larva or wingless female of a firefly that emits light from the abdomen

glucose n a sweet (dextrorotatory form of a) sugar that occurs widely in nature and is the usual form in which carbohydrate is assimilated by animals

¹glue n **1** any of various strong adhesives; esp a gelatinous protein substance that forms a strongly adhesive solution and is obtained by boiling hides, bones, etc **2** a solution of glue used for sticking things together – **gluey** adj, **gluily** adv

²glue vt **gluing** also **glueing** **1** to cause to stick tightly with glue ⟨~ the wings onto the model aeroplane⟩ **2** to fix (e g the eyes) on an object steadily or with deep concentration ⟨kept her eyes ~d to the TV⟩

glum adj **-mm- 1** broodingly morose **2** dreary, gloomy – **glumly** adv, **glumness** n

¹glut vt **-tt- 1** to fill, esp with food, to beyond capacity **2** to flood (the market) with goods so that supply exceeds demand

²glut n an excessive supply (e g of a harvested crop) which exceeds market demand

gluten n an elastic protein substance, esp of wheat flour, that gives cohesiveness to dough – **glutenous** adj

glutinous adj (thick and) sticky; gummy – **glutinously** adv, **glutinousness** n

glutton n **1a** one given habitually to greedy and voracious eating and drinking **b** one who has a great capacity for accepting or enduring sthg ⟨he's a ~ for punishment⟩ **2** the wolverine – **gluttonous** adj, **gluttonousness** n

gluttony n excess in eating or drinking

glycerin, glycerine n glycerol

glycerol n a sweet syrupy alcohol usu obtained from fats and used esp as a solvent and plasticizer

glycoside n any of numerous sugar derivatives in which a nonsugar group is attached by an oxygen or nitrogen atom and that on hydrolysis yield a sugar – **glycosidic** adj, **glycosidically** adv

gnarled adj 1 full of or covered with knots or protuberances 2 crabbed in disposition, aspect, or character

gnash vt to strike or grind (esp the teeth) together – **gnash** n

gnat n any of various small usu biting 2-winged flies – **gnatty** adj

gnaw vt 1a to bite or chew on with the teeth; esp to wear away by persistent biting or nibbling ⟨a dog ~ing a bone⟩ b to make by gnawing ⟨rats ~ed a hole⟩ 2 to affect as if by continuous eating away; plague 3 to erode, corrode ~ vi 1 to bite or nibble persistently 2 to destroy or reduce sthg (as if) by gnawing ⟨waves ~ing away at the cliffs⟩ – **gnawer** n

gneiss n a metamorphic rock usu composed of light bands of feldspar and quartz and dark bands of mica or hornblende – **gneissic** adj, **gneissoid** adj, **gneissose** adj

gnocchi n pl small dumplings made from flour, semolina, potatoes, or choux pastry

gnome n a dwarf of folklore who lives under the earth and guards treasure – **gnomish** adj

gnu n, pl **gnus**, esp collectively **gnu** any of several large horned African antelopes with an oxlike head, a short mane, and a long tail

¹go vb **went; gone** vi 1 to proceed on a course ⟨~ slow⟩ ⟨went by train⟩ ⟨went to France⟩ 2a to move out of or away from a place; leave ⟨I must ~⟩ ⟨the ferry ~es every hour⟩ – sometimes used with a further verb to express purpose ⟨I went to see them⟩ ⟨I'll ~ and look⟩ b to make an expedition for a specified activity ⟨~ shopping⟩ ⟨~ skydiving⟩ 3a to pass by means of a specified process or according to a specified procedure ⟨your suggestion will ~ before the committee⟩ b(1) to proceed in a thoughtless or reckless manner – used to intensify a complementary verb ⟨don't ~ saying that⟩ ⟨why did she have to ~ and spoil everything?⟩ ⟨he's been and gone and told her⟩ (2) to proceed to do sthg surprising – used with and to intensify a complementary verb ⟨she went and won first prize⟩ c(1) to extend ⟨it's true as far as it ~es⟩ ⟨the field ~es as far as the stream⟩ (2) to speak, proceed, or develop in a specified direction or up to a specified limit ⟨you've gone too far⟩ ⟨don't let's ~ into details⟩ 4 to travel on foot or by moving the feet 5 to be, esp habitually ⟨~ bareheaded⟩ ⟨~ barefoot⟩ 6a to become lost, consumed, or spent ⟨my pen's gone⟩ ⟨half their income ~es in rent⟩ b to die c to elapse ⟨only three weeks to ~⟩ ⟨the evening went pleasantly enough⟩ d to be got rid of (e g by sale or removal) ⟨these slums must ~⟩ ⟨~ing cheap⟩ e to fail ⟨his hearing started to ~⟩ f to succumb; GIVE WAY ⟨at last the dam went⟩ 7a to happen, progress – often + on ⟨what's ~ing on⟩ ⟨how are things ~ing?⟩ b to be in general or on an average ⟨cheap, as yachts ~⟩ c to pass or be granted by award, assignment, or lot ⟨the prize went to a French girl⟩ d to turn out (well) ⟨worked hard to make the party ~⟩ 8 to put or subject oneself ⟨went to unnecessary expense⟩ 9a to begin an action, motion, or process ⟨here ~es⟩ ⟨ready, steady, ~!⟩ ⟨~ to court to recover damages⟩ b to maintain or perform an action or motion ⟨his tongue went nineteen to the dozen⟩ ⟨went like this with her eyebrows⟩ c to function in a proper or specified way ⟨trying to get the motor to ~⟩ ⟨felt ill, but tried to keep ~ing⟩ d to make a characteristic noise ⟨the telephone went⟩ e to perform a demonstrated action ⟨~ like this with your left

foot⟩ 10a to be known or identified as specified ⟨now ~es by another name⟩ b(1) to be in phrasing or content ⟨as the saying ~es⟩ ⟨the story ~es that the expedition was a failure⟩ (2) to be sung or played in a specified manner ⟨the song ~es to the tune of 'Greensleeves'⟩ 11a to act or occur in accordance or harmony ⟨a good rule to ~ by⟩ b to contribute to a total or result ⟨taxes that ~ for education⟩ 12 to be about, intending, or destined – + to and an infinitive ⟨is ~ing to leave town⟩ ⟨is it ~ing to rain?⟩ 13a to come or arrive at a specified state or condition ⟨~ to sleep⟩ ⟨~ to waste⟩ b to join a specified institution professionally or attend it habitually ⟨to ~ on the stage⟩ ⟨does she ~ to school?⟩ c to come to be; turn ⟨the tyre went flat⟩ ⟨he went broke⟩ d(1) to become voluntarily ⟨~ bail for his friend⟩ (2) to change to a specified system or tendency ⟨~ supersonic⟩ ⟨the company went public⟩ ⟨~ comprehensive⟩ e to continue to be; remain ⟨~ hungry⟩ ⟨~ without sugar⟩ ⟨jobs went unfilled⟩ 14 to be compatible with, harmonize ⟨claret ~es with beef⟩ 15a to be capable of passing, extending, or being contained or inserted ⟨it won't ~ round my waist⟩ ⟨3 into 2 won't ~⟩ b to belong ⟨these books ~ on the top shelf⟩ 16a to carry authority ⟨what she said went⟩ b to be acceptable, satisfactory, or adequate ⟨anything ~es here⟩ c to be the case; be valid ⟨and that ~es for you too⟩ 17 to empty the bladder or bowels ⟨always ~ after breakfast⟩ – euph ~ vt 1 to proceed along or according to ⟨~ one's own way⟩ 2 to traverse ⟨~ ten miles⟩ 3 to undertake by travelling ⟨~ errands⟩ 4 to emit (a sound) ⟨the bell ~es ding dong⟩ 5 to participate to the extent of ⟨~ shares⟩ ⟨~ halves⟩ 6 to perform, effect ⟨~ the limit⟩ 7 to change to; adopt ⟨you ~ wheels or you go bust – R A Keith⟩ 8 Br to say – nonstandard; used in direct speech ⟨so she ~es 'Don't you ever do that again!'⟩ – **go about** to undertake; SET ABOUT – **go after** to seek, pursue – **go against** 1 to act in opposition to; offend 2 to turn out unfavourably to – **go ahead** 1 to begin 2 to continue, advance – **go all the way** 1 to enter into complete agreement 2 to engage in actual sexual intercourse – **go along with** 1 to occur as a natural accompaniment of 2 to agree with; support – **go ape** to run amok; lose control – **go at** 1 to attack, assail 2 to undertake energetically – **go back on** 1 to fail to keep (e g a promise) 2 to be disloyal to; betray – **go begging** to be available but in little demand – **go by the board** to be discarded – **go crook** Aust & NZ to lose one's temper – **go for** 1 to serve or be accounted as ⟨pigs that go for pork⟩ ⟨it all went for nothing⟩ 2 to try to secure ⟨he went for the biggest mango⟩ 3a to favour, accept ⟨cannot go for your idea⟩ b to have an interest in or liking for ⟨she went for him in a big way⟩ 4 to attack, assail ⟨went for him when his back was turned⟩ – **go for a burton** Br to get lost, broken, or killed – slang – **go great guns** to achieve great success – **go hang** to cease to be of interest or concern – **go into** 1 to be contained in ⟨5 goes into 60 12 times⟩ 2 to investigate 3 to explain in depth ⟨the book doesn't go into the moral aspects⟩ – **go it** 1 to behave in a reckless, excited, or impromptu manner 2 to proceed rapidly or furiously 3 to conduct one's affairs; act ⟨insists on going it alone⟩ – **go missing** chiefly Br to disappear – **go off the deep end** 1 to enter recklessly on a course of action 2 to become very excited or perturbed – **go on** to be enthusiastic about ⟨we don't go much on cars – Len Deighton⟩ – compare GO ON vi – **go one better** to outdo or surpass another – **go out of one's way** to take extra trouble – **go over** 1 EXAMINE 1 2a REPEAT 1 b to study, revise – **go phut** chiefly Br to stop functioning – infml – **go places** to be on the way to success – **go slow** to hold a go-slow – **go steady** to be the constant and exclusive boyfriend or girl friend of another or each other – **go straight** to abandon a life of crime – **go the way of all flesh** to die – **go through** 1 to subject to thorough examination, study, or discussion; GO OVER 2 to experience, undergo 3 to perform ⟨went through *his work in a daze*⟩ – compare GO THROUGH *vi* – **go to bed with** to have sexual intercourse with – **go to one's head** 1 to make one confused, excited, or dizzy 2 to make one conceited or overconfident – **go to pieces** to become shattered (e g in nerves or health) – **go to pot** to deteriorate, collapse – infml ⟨*the office* went to pot *while his secretary was away*⟩ – **go to sleep** to lose sensation; become numb ⟨*my foot has* gone to sleep⟩ – **go to town** 1 to work or act rapidly or efficiently 2 to indulge oneself ostentatiously ⟨*the papers* went to town *on the hidden life of Leroy – Sunday Times*⟩ – **go walkabout** 1 *Austr* to go on a walkabout 2 *Br* to meet and hold a conversation informally with members of the public during an official engagement or tour ⟨*the Queen* going walkabout *in Milton Keynes*⟩ – **go west** to die or become destroyed or expended – humor – **go with** 1 GO ALONG WITH 1 ⟨*the responsibility that* goes with *parenthood*⟩ 2 to be the social or esp sexual companion of

²**go** *n, pl* **goes** 1 the act or manner of going 2 energy, vigour ⟨*full of get up and* ~⟩ 3a a turn in an activity (e g a game) b an attempt, try ⟨*have a* ~ *at painting*⟩ c chance, opportunity ⟨*a fair* ~ *at work for everyone* – The Listener⟩ 4 a spell of activity ⟨*finished the job at one* ~⟩ 5 a success ⟨*made a* ~ *of the business*⟩ 6 the height of fashion; *the* rage ⟨*shawls are all the* ~ *at the moment*⟩ – chiefly infml 7 an often unexpected or awkward turn of affairs – chiefly infml ⟨*it's a rum* ~⟩ – **on the go** constantly or restlessly active – infml

³**go** *adj* functioning properly ⟨*declared all systems* ~ *for the rocket launch*⟩

⁴**go** *n* an Oriental game of capture and territorial domination played by 2 players with counters on a board covered in a grid

go about *vi* to change tack when sailing

¹**goad** *n* 1 a pointed rod used to urge on an animal 2 sthg that pricks, urges, or stimulates (into action)

²**goad** *vt* 1 to drive (e g cattle) with a goad 2 to incite or rouse by nagging or persistent annoyance

¹**go-ahead** *adj* energetic and progressive

²**go-ahead** *n* a sign, signal, or authority to proceed

goal *n* 1 an end towards which effort is directed 2a an area or object through or into which players in various games attempt to put a ball or puck against the defence of the opposing side b (the points gained by) the act of putting a ball or puck through or into a goal

goalkeeper *n* a player who defends the goal in soccer, hockey, lacrosse, etc – **goalkeeping** *n*

goal line *n* a line at either end and usu running the width of a playing area on which a goal or goal post is situated

goalmouth *n* the area of a playing field directly in front of the goal

go along *vi* 1 to move along; proceed 2 to go or travel as a companion 3 to agree, cooperate ⟨*I'd* go along *with your suggestion*⟩

goalpost *n* either of usu 2 vertical posts that with or without a crossbar constitute the goal in soccer, rugby, etc

go around *vi* 1 to go here and there, esp in company ⟨*the friends she* goes around *with*⟩ 2 GO ROUND 1, 2

goat *n* 1 any of various long-legged (horned) ruminant mammals smaller than cattle and related to the sheep 2 a lecherous man 3 a foolish person – infml – **goatish** *adj*, **goatlike** *adj*

goatee *n* a small pointed beard

goatskin *n* (leather made from) the skin of a goat

¹**gob** *n* a shapeless or sticky lump

²**gob** *n, Br* MOUTH 1a – slang

gobbet *n* a piece, portion

¹**gobble** *vt* **gobbling** 1 to swallow or eat greedily or noisily 2 to take, accept, or read eagerly – often + *up*

²**gobble** *vi* to make the guttural sound of a male turkey or a similar sound – **gobble** *n*

gobbledygook, gobbledegook *n* wordy and generally unintelligible jargon

gobbler *n* a male turkey – infml

go-between *n* an intermediate agent

goblet *n* 1 a drinking vessel that has a usu rounded bowl, a foot, and a stem and is used esp for wine 2 the part of a liquidizer in which food is liquidized or ground by means of rotating blades

goblin *n* a grotesque mischievous elf

goby *n, pl* **gobies,** *esp collectively* **goby** any of numerous spiny-finned fishes with the pelvic fins often united to form a sucking disc

go-by *n* an act of avoidance; a miss ⟨*give them the* ~⟩

go by *vi* to pass ⟨*as time* goes by⟩

god *n* 1 *cap* the supreme or ultimate reality; the being perfect in power, wisdom, and goodness whom human beings worship as creator and ruler of the universe 2 a being or object believed to have more than natural attributes and powers (e g the control of a particular aspect of reality) and to require human beings' worship 3 sby or sthg of supreme value 4 a very influential person 5 *pl* the highest gallery in a theatre, usu with the cheapest seats – **godlike** *adj*

godchild *n* sby for whom sby else becomes sponsor at baptism

¹**goddamn, goddam** *n, often cap* a damn ⟨*he doesn't give a* ~ *about anything*⟩

²**goddamn, goddam** *vb, often cap* to damn ⟨*I'll be* ~ed⟩ ⟨*you feel like swearing and* ~ing *worse and worse* – Ernest Hemingway⟩

goddess *n* 1 a female deity 2 a woman whose great charm or beauty arouses adoration

God-fearing *adj* devout

godforsaken *adj* 1 remote, desolate 2 neglected, dismal

godhead *n* 1 divine nature or essence 2 *cap* a GOD 1 – usu + *the* b *the* nature of God, esp as existing in 3 persons

godless *adj* not acknowledging a deity; impious – **godlessness** *n*

godly *adj* 1 divine 2 pious, devout – **godliness** *n*

godown *n* a warehouse in an Asian country, esp India

go down *vi* 1a to fall (as if) to the ground ⟨*the plane* went down *in flames*⟩ b to go below the horizon ⟨*the sun* went down⟩ c to sink ⟨*the ship* went down *with all hands*⟩ 2 to be capable of being swallowed ⟨*the medicine* went down *easily*⟩ 3 to undergo defeat 4a to find acceptance ⟨*will the plan* go down *well with the farmers?*⟩ b to come to be remembered, esp by posterity ⟨*he will* go down *in history as a great general*⟩ 5a to undergo a decline or decrease ⟨*the market is* going down⟩ b *esp of a computer system or program* to crash 6 to become ill – usu + *with* ⟨*he* went down *with flu*⟩ 7 *Br* to leave a university 8 to be sent to prison – slang – **go down on** to perform fellatio or cunnilingus on – vulg

godparent *n* a sponsor at baptism

godsend *n* a desirable or needed thing or event that comes unexpectedly

Godspeed *n* a prosperous journey; success ⟨*bade him* ~⟩

goer *n* 1 a regular attender – usu in combination ⟨*a*

theatregoer⟩ **2** sby or sthg that moves or does things fast or actively; *esp* a swinger – *infml*

go-getter *n* an aggressively enterprising person – **go-getting** *adj or n*

goggle *vi* to stare with wide or protuberant eyes – **goggler** *n*

goggle-box *n, Br* a television set – *infml*

goggle-eyed *adj or adv* with the eyes wide or bulging (in amazement or fascination)

goggles *n pl* protective glasses set in a flexible frame that fits snugly against the face

go-go *adj* of or being the music or a style of dance performed or a dancer performing at a disco

go in *vi* **1** to enter **2** *of a celestial body* to become obscured by a cloud ⟨*the sun* went in *for 5 minutes*⟩ **3** to form a union or alliance – often + *with* ⟨*asked the rest of us to* go in *with them on the project*⟩ – **go in for 1** to engage in, esp as a hobby or for enjoyment **2** to enter and compete in (e g a test or race) ⟨*decided not to* go in for *her A-levels until the following year*⟩

¹going *n* **1** an act or instance of going – often in combination ⟨*theatregoing*⟩ **2** the condition of the ground (e g for horse racing) **3** advance, progress ⟨*found the* ∼ *too slow and gave up the job*⟩ **4** the depth of the tread of a stair

²going *adj* **1a** living, existing ⟨*the best novelist* ∼⟩ **b** available for use or enjoyment ⟨*asked if there were any jobs* ∼⟩ **2a** current, prevailing ⟨∼ *price*⟩ **b** profitable, thriving ⟨∼ *concern*⟩ – **going for** favourable to ⟨*had everything going for me*⟩

going-over *n, pl* **goings-over 1** a thorough examination or investigation **2** a severe scolding

goings-on *n pl* **1** actions, events ⟨*coming-out parties and sundry* ∼⟩ **2** reprehensible happenings or conduct ⟨*tales of scandalous* ∼ *in high circles*⟩

goitre, *NAm chiefly* **goiter** *n* an abnormal enlargement of the thyroid gland visible as a swelling of the front of the neck

go-kart *n* a tiny racing car with small wheels

gold *n* **1** a malleable ductile yellow metallic element that occurs chiefly free or in a few minerals and is used esp in coins and jewellery and as a currency reserve **2a(1)** gold coins **(2)** GOLD MEDAL ⟨*won a* ∼ *in the 100m*⟩ **b** money **c** GOLD STANDARD **d** gold as a commodity **3** a deep metallic yellow **4** sthg valued as excellent or the finest of its kind ⟨*a heart of* ∼⟩ **5** (a shot hitting) the golden or yellow centre spot of an archery target

goldbeater *n* sby who beats gold into gold leaf – **gold-beating** *n*

gold digger *n* a woman who uses charm to extract money or gifts from men – *infml*

golden *adj* **1** consisting of, relating to, or containing gold **2a** of the colour of gold **b** BLOND 1a **3** prosperous, flourishing ⟨∼ *days*⟩ **4** highly favoured and promising (worldly) success – often in *golden boy/girl* **5** favourable, advantageous ⟨*a* ∼ *opportunity*⟩ **6** of or marking a 50th anniversary ⟨∼ *wedding*⟩ – **goldenly** *adv*, **goldenness** *n*

golden age *n* a period of great happiness, prosperity, and achievement

golden handshake *n* a large ex gratia money payment given by a company to an employee, esp on retirement

golden mean *n* the medium between extremes; moderation

golden oriole *n* an Old World oriole of which the male is brilliant yellow

golden rule *n* **1** a rule of ethical conduct, recorded in Mt 7:12 and Lk 6:31, requiring one to treat others as one would wish to be treated by them **2** a guiding principle

golden syrup *n* the pale yellow syrup derived from cane sugar refining and used in cooking

goldfinch *n* a small red, black, yellow, and white European finch

goldfish *n* a small (golden yellow) fish related to the carps and widely kept in aquariums and ponds

gold leaf *n* gold beaten into very thin sheets and used esp for gilding

gold medal *n* a medal of gold awarded to sby who comes first in a competition

gold mine *n* a rich source of sthg desired (e g information)

gold rush *n* a rush to newly discovered goldfields in pursuit of riches

goldsmith *n* one who works in gold or deals in articles of gold

gold standard *n* a standard of money under which the basic unit of currency is defined by a stated quantity of gold of a fixed fineness

golf *n* a game in which a player using special clubs attempts to hit a ball into each of the 9 or 18 successive holes on a course with as few strokes as possible – **golf** *vi*

Golf – a communications code word for the letter *g*

golf course *n* an area of land laid out for playing golf consisting of a series of 9 or 18 holes each with a tee, fairway, and putting green

golfer *n* sby who plays golf

golf links *n* a golf course, esp near the sea – often pl with sing. meaning

Goliath *n* a giant

golliwog, gollywog *n* a child's doll made from soft material that is dressed as a man and has a black face and black hair standing out round its head

¹golly *interj* – used to express surprise

²golly *n* a golliwog

gon-, gono- *comb form* sexual; reproductive; gonad ⟨*gonidium*⟩

-gon *comb form* (→ *n*) geometrical figure having (so many) angles ⟨*decagon*⟩

gonad *n* any of the primary sex glands (e g the ovaries or testes) – **gonadal** *adj*

gondola *n* **1** a long narrow flat-bottomed boat used on the canals of Venice **2a** an enclosure suspended from a balloon for carrying passengers or instruments **b** a cabin suspended from a cable and used for transporting passengers (e g up a ski slope) **3** a fixture approachable from all sides used in self-service retail shops to display merchandise

gondolier *n* a boatman who propels a gondola

¹gone *adj* **1a** involved, absorbed ⟨*far* ∼ *in hysteria*⟩ **b** pregnant by a specified length of time ⟨*she's 6 months* ∼⟩ **c** infatuated – often + *on*; *infml* ⟨*was real* ∼ *on that man*⟩ **2** dead – *euph*

²gone *adv, Br* past, turned ⟨*it's* ∼ *3 o'clock*⟩

goner *n* one whose case or state is hopeless or lost – *infml*

gong *n* **1** a disc-shaped percussion instrument that produces a resounding tone when struck with a usu padded hammer **2** a flat saucer-shaped bell **3** a medal or decoration – slang – **gong** *vi*

gonna *verbal auxiliary pres* to be going to ⟨*I'm* ∼ *wash that man right out of my hair* – Oscar Hammerstein⟩ – nonstandard

gonorrhoea, *chiefly NAm* **gonorrhea** *n* a venereal disease in which there is inflammation of the mucous membranes of the genital tracts caused by gonococcal bacteria – **gonorrhoeal** *adj*

goo *n* **1** sticky matter **2** cloying sentimentality *USE* infml – **gooey** *adj*

¹**good** *adj* **better; best 1a(1)** of a favourable character or tendency ⟨~ *news*⟩ **(2)** bountiful, fertile ⟨~ *land*⟩ **(3)** handsome, attractive ⟨~ *looks*⟩ **b(1)** suitable, fit ⟨*it's a ~ day for planting roses*⟩ **(2)** free from injury or disease; whole ⟨*1 ~ arm*⟩ **(3)** not depreciated ⟨*bad money drives out ~*⟩ **(4)** commercially sound ⟨*a ~ risk*⟩ **(5)** certain to last or live ⟨~ *for another year*⟩ **(6)** certain to pay or contribute ⟨~ *for a few quid*⟩ **(7)** certain to elicit a specified result ⟨*always ~ for a laugh*⟩ **c(1)** agreeable, pleasant; *specif* amusing **(2)** beneficial to the health or character ⟨*spinach is ~ for you*⟩ **(3)** not rotten; fresh ⟨*the beef is still ~*⟩ **d** ample, full **e(1)** well-founded, true ⟨~ *reasons*⟩ **(2)** deserving of respect; honourable ⟨*in ~ standing*⟩ **(3)** legally valid ⟨~ *title*⟩ **f(1)** adequate, satisfactory; *also* strong, robust **(2)** conforming to a standard ⟨~ *English*⟩ **(3)** choice, discriminating ⟨~ *taste*⟩ **2a(1)** morally commendable; virtuous ⟨*a ~ man*⟩ **(2)** correct; *specif* well-behaved **(3)** kind, benevolent ⟨~ *intentions*⟩ **b** reputable; *specif* wellborn ⟨*a ~ family*⟩ **c** competent, skilful ⟨*a ~ doctor*⟩ **d** loyal ⟨*a ~ Catholic*⟩ – **goodish** *adj* – **as good as** virtually; IN EFFECT ⟨*as good as dead*⟩ – **as good as gold** extremely well-behaved ⟨*the child was as good as gold*⟩ – **good and** very, entirely – infml ⟨*should be good and ready by Tuesday*⟩ – **in someone's good books** in sby's favour

²**good** *n* **1a** sthg good ⟨*it's no ~ complaining*⟩ **b** the quality of being good ⟨*to know ~ from evil*⟩ **c** a good element or portion ⟨*recognized the ~ in him*⟩ **2** prosperity, benefit ⟨*for the ~ of the community*⟩ **3a** sthg that has economic utility or satisfies an economic want – usu pl **b** *pl* personal property having intrinsic value but usu excluding money, securities, and negotiable instruments **c** *pl* wares, merchandise ⟨*tinned ~s*⟩ **4** *pl but sing or pl in constr* the desired or necessary article ⟨*came up with the ~s*⟩ – infml **5** *pl* proof of wrongdoing – slang ⟨*the police have got the ~s on him*⟩ – **for good** forever, permanently – **to the good 1** for the best; beneficial ⟨*this rain is all to the good*⟩ **2** in a position of net gain or profit ⟨*he ended the game £10 to the good*⟩

³**good** *adv* well – infml

good book *n, often cap G&B* the Bible

¹**goodbye,** *NAm also* **goodby** *interj* – used to express farewell

²**goodbye,** *NAm also* **goodby** *n* a concluding remark or gesture at parting ⟨*time to say our ~s*⟩

¹**good-for-nothing** *adj* of no value; worthless

²**good-for-nothing** *n* an idle worthless person

Good Friday *n* the Friday before Easter, observed in churches as the anniversary of the crucifixion of Christ

good-humoured *adj* good-natured, cheerful – **good-humouredly** *adv*

good-looking *adj* having a pleasing or attractive appearance – **good-looker** *n*

goodly *adj* **1** significantly large in amount; considerable ⟨*a ~ number*⟩ **2** *archaic* pleasantly attractive; handsome

good-natured *adj* of a cheerful and cooperative disposition – **goodnaturedly** *adv*, **good-naturedness** *n*

goodness *n* the nutritious or beneficial part of sthg ⟨*boil all the ~ out of the meat*⟩

good offices *n pl* power or action that helps sby out of a difficulty – often in *through the good offices of*

goodwill *n* **1a** a kindly feeling of approval and support; benevolent interest or concern **b** the favour or prestige that a business has acquired beyond the mere value of

what it sells **2a** cheerful consent **b** willing effort – **goodwilled** *adj*

goody, goodie *n* **1** sthg particularly attractive, pleasurable, or desirable **2** a good person or hero *USE* infml

goody-goody *n or adj* (sby) affectedly or ingratiatingly prim or virtuous – infml

¹**goof** *n* **1** a ridiculous stupid person **2** *chiefly NAm* a blunder *USE* infml

²**goof** *vb, chiefly NAm vi* to make a goof; blunder ~ *vt* to make a mess of; bungle – often + *up USE* infml

go off *vi* **1** to explode **2** to go forth or away; depart **3** to undergo decline or deterioration; *specif, of food or drink* to become rotten or sour **4** to follow a specified course; proceed ⟨*the party went off well*⟩ **5** to make a characteristic noise; sound ⟨*the alarm went off*⟩

goofy *adj* silly, daft – infml – **goofily** *adv*, **goofiness** *n*

googly *n* a usu slow delivery by a right-handed bowler in cricket that is an off break as viewed by a right-handed batsman although apparently delivered with a leg-break action

goon *n* **1** *NAm* a man hired to terrorize or eliminate opponents **2** an idiot, dope – slang – **goony** *adj*

go on *vi* **1** to continue; CARRY ON **2** **2a** to proceed (as if) by a logical step ⟨*he went on to explain why*⟩ **b** of time to pass **3** to take place; happen ⟨*what's going on?*⟩ **4** to be capable of being put on ⟨*her gloves wouldn't* go on⟩ **5a** to talk, esp in an effusive manner ⟨*the way people* go on *about pollution*⟩ **b** to criticize constantly; nag ⟨*you're always* going on *at me*⟩ **6a** to come into operation, action, or production ⟨*the lights* went on *at sunset*⟩ **b** to appear on the stage **7** *Br* to manage; GET ALONG ⟨*how did you* go on *for money?*⟩

¹**goose** *n, pl (1 & 2)* **geese,** *(3)* **gooses 1** (the female of) any of numerous large long-necked web-footed waterfowl **2** a simpleton, dolt **3** a tailor's smoothing iron with a gooseneck handle – **goosey** *adj*

²**goose** *vt, chiefly NAm* to poke between the buttocks – vulg

gooseberry *n* **1** (the shrub that bears) an edible acid usu prickly green or yellow fruit **2** an unwanted companion to 2 lovers – chiefly in *to play gooseberry*

gooseflesh *n* a bristling roughness of the skin produced by erection of its papillae, usu from cold or fear

goose pimples *n pl* gooseflesh

goose step *n* a straight-legged marching step – **goose-stepper** *n*

go out *vi* **1a** to leave a room, house, country, etc **b** to fight in a duel **c** to travel to a distant place ⟨*they* went out *to Africa*⟩ **d** to work away from home ⟨*she* went out *charring*⟩ **2a** to become extinguished ⟨*the hall light* went out⟩ **b** to become obsolete or unfashionable **c** to play the last card of one's hand **3** to spend time regularly *with* sby of esp the opposite sex **4** to be broadcast ⟨*the programme* went out *at 9 o'clock*⟩

go over *vi* **1** to become converted (e g to a religion or political party) **2** to receive approval; succeed ⟨*my play should* go over *well in Scotland*⟩

gopher *n* **1** any of several American burrowing rodents that are the size of a large rat and have large cheek pouches **2** any of numerous small N American ground squirrels closely related to the chipmunks

Gordian knot *n* an intricate problem; *esp* one insoluble in its own terms

¹**gore** *n* (clotted) blood

²**gore** *n* a tapering or triangular piece of material (e g cloth) used to give shape to sthg (e g a garment or sail) – **gored** *adj*

³**gore** *vt* to pierce or wound with a horn or tusk

¹**gorge** *n* **1** the throat **2** the (contents of the) stomach or

belly **3** the entrance into an outwork of a fort **4** a narrow steep-walled valley, often with a stream flowing through it

²**gorge** *vi* to eat greedily or until full ~ *vt* **1** to fill completely or to the point of making distended ⟨*veins* ~ d *with blood*⟩ **2** to swallow greedily – **gorger** *n*

gorgeous *adj* **1** splendidly beautiful or magnificent **2** very fine; pleasant ⟨*it was a* ~ *day for a picnic*⟩ – **gorgeously** *adv*, **gorgeousness** *n*

gorgon *n* **1** *cap* any of 3 sisters in Greek mythology who had live snakes in place of hair and whose glance turned the beholder to stone **2** an ugly or repulsive woman – **Gorgonian** *adj*

Gorgonzola *n* a blue-veined strongly flavoured cheese of Italian origin

gorilla *n* **1** an anthropoid ape of western equatorial Africa related to the chimpanzee but less erect and much larger **2** an ugly or brutal man

gormandize, -ise *vb* to eat voraciously; gorge – **gorman-dizer** *n*

gormless *adj*, *Br* lacking understanding and intelligence; stupid – infml

go round *vi* **1** to spread, circulate ⟨*there's a rumour* going round⟩ **2** to satisfy demand; meet the need ⟨*not enough jobs to* go round⟩ **3** GO AROUND 1

gorse *n* a spiny yellow-flowered evergreen leguminous European shrub – **gorsy** *adj*

gory *adj* **1** covered with gore; bloodstained **2** full of violence; bloodcurdling ⟨*a* ~ *film*⟩

gosh *interj* – used to express surprise

gosling *n* a young goose

go-slow *n*, *Br* a deliberate slowing down of production by workers as a means of forcing management's compliance with their demands

¹**gospel** *n* **1** *often cap* the message of the life, death, and resurrection of Jesus Christ; *esp* any of the first 4 books of the New Testament, or any similar apocryphal book, relating this **2** *cap* a liturgical reading from any of the New Testament Gospels **3** the message or teachings of a religious teacher or movement **4a** sthg accepted as a guiding principle ⟨*the* ~ *of hard work*⟩ **b** sthg so authoritative as not to be questioned ⟨*they took his word as* ~⟩

²**gospel** *adj* **1** of the Christian gospel; evangelical **2** of or being usu evangelistic religious songs of American origin

gossamer *n* **1** a film of cobwebs floating in air in calm clear weather **2** sthg light, insubstantial, or tenuous – **gossamer** *adj*, **gossamery** *adj*

¹**gossip** *n* **1** sby who habitually reveals usu sensational facts concerning other people's actions or lives **2a** (rumour or report of) the facts related by a gossip **b** a chatty talk – **gossipry** *n*, **gossipy** *adj*

²**gossip** *vi* to relate gossip – **gossiper** *n*

got 1 *past of* GET **2** *pres pl & 1&2 sing of* GET ⟨*I* ~ *news for you*⟩ ⟨*we* ~ *to go*⟩ – nonstandard

¹**Gothic** *adj* **1** of the Goths, their culture, or Gothic **2** of a style of architecture prevalent from the middle of the 12th c to the early 16th c characterized by vaulting and pointed arches **3** *often not cap* of or like a class of novels of the late 18th and early 19th c dealing with macabre or mysterious events – **gothically** *adv*, **Gothicism** *n*, **gothicize** *vt*

²**Gothic** *n* **1** the E Germanic language of the Goths **2** Gothic architectural style **3a** BLACK LETTER **b** SANS SERIF

go through *vi* **1** to continue firmly or obstinately to the end – often + *with* ⟨*can't* go through *with the wedding*⟩

2a to receive approval or sanction **b** to come to a desired or satisfactory conclusion

¹**gotta** *vt pres* to have a ⟨*I* ~ *horse*⟩ – nonstandard

²**gotta** *verbal auxiliary pres* to have to; must ⟨*we* ~ *go*⟩ – nonstandard

gotten *NAm past part of* GET

gouache *n* a method of painting with opaque water-colours that have been ground in water and mixed with a gum preparation

Gouda *n* a mild cheese of Dutch origin that is similar to Edam but contains more fat

¹**gouge** *n* **1** a chisel with a curved cross section and bevel on the concave side of the blade **2** *chiefly NAm* over-charging, extortion – infml

²**gouge** *vt* **1** to scoop out (as if) with a gouge **2a** to force out (an eye), esp with the thumb **3** *chiefly NAm* to subject to extortion; overcharge – infml – **gouger** *n*

goulash *n* **1** a meat stew made usu with veal or beef and highly seasoned with paprika **2** a round in bridge played with hands dealt in lots of 5, 5, and 3 cards consecutively from a pack formed by the unshuffled arranged hands from a previous deal

go under *vi* to be destroyed or defeated; fail ⟨*empty order books and high interest charges forced the company to* go under⟩

go up *vi*, *Br* to enter or return to a university

gourd *n* (the fruit of) any of the cucumber family of typically tendril-bearing climbing plants (e g the melon, squash, and pumpkin); *esp* any of various hard-rinded inedible fruits used for ornament or for vessels and uten-sils

gourmand *n* one who is excessively fond of or heartily interested in food and drink – **gourmandism** *n*

gourmet *n* a connoisseur of food and drink – **gourmet** *adj*

gout *n* **1** painful inflammation of the joints, esp that of the big toe, resulting from a metabolic disorder in which there is an excessive amount of uric acid in the blood **2** a sticky blob – **gouty** *adj*

govern *vt* **1** to exercise continuous sovereign authority over **2a** to control, determine, or strongly influence ⟨*availability often* ~ s *choice*⟩ **b** to hold in check; restrain **3** to require (a word) to be in a usu specified case ⟨*in English a transitive verb* ~ s *a pronoun in the accusative*⟩ **4** to serve as a precedent or deciding principle for ⟨*habits and customs that* ~ *human decisions*⟩ ~ *vi* **1** to prevail **2** to exercise authority – **governable** *adj*

governance *n* governing or being governed – fml

governess *n* a woman entrusted with the private teaching and often supervision of a child

government *n* **1** governing; *specif* authoritative direction or control **2** the office, authority, or function of governing **3** policy making as distinguished from administration **4** the machinery through which political authority is exercised **5** *sing or pl in constr* the body of people that constitutes a governing authority – **governmental** *adj*, **governmentally** *adv*

governor *n* **1a** a ruler, chief executive, or nominal head of a political unit **b** a commanding officer **c** the managing director and usu the principal officer of an institution or organization **d** a member of a group (e g the governing body of a school) that controls an institution **2** a device giving automatic control of pressure, fuel, steam, etc, esp to regulate speed **3** sby (e g a father, guardian, or employer) looked on as governing – slang **b** Mister, Sir – slang; used as a familiar form of address – **governorate** *n*, **governorship** *n*

governor-general *n*, *pl* **governors-general, governor-generals** a governor of high rank; *esp* one representing the

Crown in a Commonwealth country – **governor-generalship** *n*

gown *n* **1a** a loose flowing robe worn esp by a professional or academic person when acting in an official capacity **b** a woman's dress, esp one that is elegant or for formal wear **c** an outer garment worn in an operating theatre **2** the body of students and staff of a college or university ⟨*riots between town and* ~⟩

goy *n, pl* **goyim, goys** a gentile – chiefly derog – **goyish** *adj*

Graafian follicle *n* a vesicle in the ovary of a mammal enclosing a developing egg

¹**grab** *vb* **-bb-** *vt* **1** to take or seize hastily or by a sudden motion or grasp **2** to obtain unscrupulously **3** to forcefully engage the attention of – infml ⟨*he* ~s *an audience*⟩ ~ *vi* to make a grab; snatch – **grabber** *n*

²**grab** *n* **1a** a sudden snatch **b** an unlawful or unscrupulous seizure **c** sthg intended to be grabbed – often in combination ⟨*a grab-rail*⟩ **2a** a mechanical device for clutching an object – **up for grabs** available for anyone to take or win – infml

¹**grace** *n* **1a** unmerited divine assistance given to human beings for their regeneration or sanctification **b** a state of being pleasing to God **2** a short prayer at a meal asking a blessing or giving thanks **3a** disposition to or an act or instance of kindness or clemency **b** a special favour ⟨*each in his place, by right, not* ~, *shall rule his heritage* – Rudyard Kipling⟩ **c** a temporary exemption; a reprieve **d** approval, favour **4a** a charming trait or accomplishment **b** an elegant appearance or effect; charm **c** ease and suppleness of movement or bearing **5** – used as a title for a duke, duchess, or archbishop **6** consideration, decency ⟨*had the* ~ *to blush*⟩ – **with bad/good grace** (un)willingly or (un)happily ⟨*took his defeat with good grace*⟩

²**grace** *vt* **1** to confer dignity or honour on **2** to adorn, embellish

graceful *adj* displaying grace in form, action, or movement – **gracefully** *adv*, **gracefulness** *n*

graceless *adj* **1** lacking a sense of propriety **2** devoid of elegance; awkward – **gracelessly** *adv*, **gracelessness** *n*

Graces *n pl* the 3 beautiful sister goddesses in Greek mythology who are the givers of charm and beauty

gracious *adj* **1a** marked by kindness and courtesy **b** marked by tact and delicacy **c** having those qualities (e g comfort, elegance, and freedom from hard work) made possible by wealth ⟨~ *living*⟩ **2** merciful, compassionate – used conventionally of royalty and high nobility – **graciously** *adv*, **graciousness** *n*

gradation *n* **1** (a step or place in) a series forming successive stages **2** a gradual passing from one tint or shade to another (e g in a painting) **3** ablaut – **gradational** *adj*, **gradationally** *adv*

¹**grade** *n* **1a(1)** a stage in a process **(2)** a position in a scale of ranks or qualities **b** a degree of severity of illness **2** a class of things of the same stage or degree **3** a gradient **4** a domestic animal with one parent purebred and the other of inferior breeding **5** *NAm* a school form; a class **6** *NAm* a mark indicating a degree of accomplishment at school – **gradeless** *adj*

²**grade** *vt* **1a** to arrange in grades; sort **b** to arrange in a scale or series **2** to improve (e g cattle) by breeding with purebred animals – often + **up 3** *NAm* to assign a mark to – **grader** *n*

-**grade** *comb form* (→ *adj*) walking ⟨*planti*grade⟩; moving ⟨*retro*grade⟩

grade crossing *n, chiefly NAm* LEVEL CROSSING

gradient *n* **1** the degree of inclination of a road or slope; *also* a sloping road or railway **2** change in the value of a (specified) quantity with change in a given variable, esp

distance ⟨*a vertical temperature* ~⟩⟨*a concentration* ~⟩

gradual *adj* proceeding or happening by steps or degrees – **gradually** *adv*, **gradualness** *n*

¹**graduate** *n* **1** the holder of an academic degree **2** a graduated cup, cylinder, or flask for measuring **3** *chiefly NAm* one who has completed a course of study

²**graduate** *adj* **1** holding an academic degree or diploma ⟨*a* ~ *secretary*⟩ **2** postgraduate

³**graduate** *vt* **1** to mark with degrees of measurement **2** to divide into grades or intervals ~ *vi* **1** to receive an academic degree **2** to move up to a usu higher stage of experience, proficiency, or prestige **3** to change gradually **4** *NAm* to complete a course of study – **graduator** *n*

graduation *n* **1** a mark (e g on an instrument or vessel) indicating degrees or quantity **2** the award of an academic degree

Graeco-, *chiefly NAm* **Greco-** *comb form* **1** Greek nation, people, or culture ⟨*Graeco*mania⟩ **2** Greek and ⟨*Graeco-Roman*⟩

graffito *n, pl* **graffiti** an inscription or drawing, usu of a crude or political nature, made on a wall, rock, etc – usu pl

¹**graft** *vt* **1a** to cause (a plant scion) to unite with a stock; *also* to unite (plants or scion and stock) to form a graft **b** to propagate (a plant) by grafting **2** to attach, add **3** to implant (living tissue) surgically ~ *vi* **1** to become grafted **2** to perform grafting **3** *NAm* to practise graft – **grafter** *n*

²**graft** *n* **1a** a grafted plant **b** (the point of insertion upon a stock of) a scion **2** (living tissue used in) grafting **3a** the improper use of one's position (e g public office) to one's private, esp financial, advantage **b** sthg acquired by graft

³**graft** *vi, Br* to work hard – slang – **graft** *n*

Grail *n* HOLY GRAIL

¹**grain** *n* **1** a seed or fruit of a cereal grass; *also* (the seeds or fruits collectively of) the cereal grasses or similar food plants **2a** a discrete (small hard) particle or crystal (e g of sand, salt, or a metal) **b** the least amount possible ⟨*not a* ~ *of truth in what he said*⟩ **c** fine crystallization (e g of sugar) **3** a fast dye **4a** a granular surface, nature, or appearance **b** the outer or hair side of a skin or hide (from which the hair has been removed) **5** a unit of weight equal to 0.0648 gram **6a** the arrangement of the fibres in wood **b** the direction, alignment, or texture of the constituent particles, fibres, or threads ⟨*the* ~ *of a rock*⟩⟨*the* ~ *of a fabric*⟩ **7** tactile quality **8** natural disposition or character; temper **9** (a brilliant scarlet dye made from) either kermes or cochineal – not now used technically – **grained** *adj*, **grainy** *adj*, **graininess** *n* – **against the grain** counter to one's inclination, disposition, or feeling

²**grain** *vt* **1** to form into grains; granulate **2** to paint in imitation of the grain of wood or stone ~ *vi* to become granular; granulate – **grainer** *n*

¹**gram** *n* a leguminous plant (e g the chick-pea) grown esp for its seed

²**gram, gramme** *n* one thousandth of a kilogram (about 0.04oz)

-**gram** *comb form* (→ *n*) drawing; writing; record ⟨*ideo*gram⟩⟨*tele*gram⟩⟨*chrono*gram⟩

¹**grammar** *n* **1** the study of the classes of words, their inflections, and their functions and relations in the sentence; *broadly* this study when taken to include that of phonology and sometimes of usage **2** the characteristic system of inflections and syntax of a language **3a** a grammar textbook **b** speech or writing evaluated according to its conformity to grammatical rules **4** the principles

or rules of an art, science, or technique – **grammarian** *n*

²**grammar** *adj* of the type of education provided at a grammar school ⟨*the ~ stream*⟩

grammar school *n* **1** a secondary school that emphasized the study of the classics **2** *Br* a secondary school providing an academic type of education from the age of 11 to 18

grammatical *adj* **1** of grammar **2** conforming to the rules of grammar – **grammatically** *adv*, **grammaticalness** *n*, **grammaticality** *n*

gramophone *n* a device for reproducing sounds from the vibrations of a stylus resting in a spiral groove on a rotating disc; *specif, chiefly Br* RECORD PLAYER

grampus *n* any of various (dolphinlike) small whales (e g the killer whale)

gran *n*, *chiefly Br* a grandmother – *infml*

granary *n* **1** a storehouse for threshed grain **2** a region producing grain in abundance

¹**grand** *adj* **1** having more importance than others; foremost **2** complete, comprehensive ⟨*the ~ total of all money paid out*⟩ **3** main, principal **4** large and striking in size, extent, or conception ⟨*a ~ design*⟩ **5a** lavish, sumptuous ⟨*a ~ celebration*⟩ **b** marked by regal form and dignity; imposing **c** lofty, sublime ⟨*writing in the ~ style*⟩ **6** intended to impress ⟨*a man of ~ gestures and pretentious statements*⟩ **7** very good; wonderful – *infml* ⟨*a ~ time*⟩ – **grandly** *adv*, **grandness** *n*

²**grand** *n* **1** GRAND PIANO **2a** *Br* a thousand pounds **b** *NAm* a thousand dollars *USE* (2) *slang*

grandchild *n* a child of one's son or daughter

granddad, grandad *n* a grandfather – *infml*

granddaughter *n* a daughter of one's son or daughter

grandee *n* a Spanish or Portuguese nobleman of the highest rank

grandeur *n* **1** the quality of being large or impressive; magnificence **2** personal greatness marked by nobility, dignity, or power

grandfather *n* the father of one's father or mother; *broadly* a male ancestor – **grandfatherly** *adj*

grandfather clock *n* a tall pendulum clock standing directly on the floor

grandiloquence *n* lofty or pompous eloquence; bombast – **grandiloquent** *adj*, **grandiloquently** *adv*

grandiose *adj* **1** impressive because of uncommon largeness, scope, or grandeur **2** characterized by affectation of grandeur or by absurd exaggeration – **grandiosely** *adv*, **grandioseness, grandiosity** *n*

grandma *n* a grandmother – *infml*

grand mal *n* (an attack of) the severe form of epilepsy

grand master *n* a chess player who has consistently scored higher than a standardized score in international competition

grandmother *n* the mother of one's father or mother; *broadly* a female ancestor – **grandmotherly** *adj*

Grand National *n* the major British steeplechase for horses that is run annually at Aintree near Liverpool

grand opera *n* opera with a serious dramatic plot and no spoken dialogue

grandpa *n* a grandfather – *infml*

grandparent *n* the parent of one's father or mother – **grandparenthood** *n*, **grandparental** *adj*

grand piano *n* a piano with horizontal frame and strings

grand prix *n*, *pl* **grand prix** *often cap G&P* any of a series of long-distance races for formula cars, held consecutively in different countries

grand slam *n* **1** the winning of all the tricks in 1 hand

of a card game, specif bridge **2** a clean sweep or total success, esp in a sport

grandson *n* a son of one's son or daughter

¹**grandstand** *n* a usu roofed stand for spectators at a racecourse, stadium, etc in an advantageous position for viewing the contest

²**grandstand** *vi, NAm* to play or act so as to impress onlookers – *infml* – **grandstander** *n*

grand tour *n* **1** an extended tour of the Continent, formerly a usual part of the education of young British gentlemen – usu + *the* **2** an extensive and usu educational tour

grange *n* a farm; *esp* a farmhouse with outbuildings

granite *n* **1** a very hard granular igneous rock formed of quartz, feldspar, and mica and used esp for building **2** unyielding firmness or endurance – **granitelike** *adj*, **granitoid** *adj*, **granitic** *adj*

¹**granny, grannie** *n* a grandmother – *infml*

²**granny, grannie** *adj* designed for use by an older relative – *infml* ⟨*~ flat*⟩

¹**grant** *vt* **1a** to consent to carry out or fulfil (e g a wish or request) ⟨*~ a child his wish*⟩ **b** to permit as a right, privilege, or favour ⟨*luggage allowances ~ed to passengers*⟩ **2** to bestow or transfer formally **3a** to be willing to concede **b** to assume to be true – **grantable** *adj*, **granter** *n*, **grantor** *n*

²**grant** *n* **1** sthg granted; *esp* a gift for a particular purpose **2** a transfer of property; *also* the property so transferred

granular *adj* (apparently) consisting of granules; having a grainy texture – **granularly** *adv*, **granularity** *n*

granulate *vt* to form or crystallize into grains or granules ⟨*~d sugar*⟩ *~ vi, esp of a wound* (to form minute granules of new capillaries while beginning) to heal – **granulator** *n*, **granulation** *n*, **granulative** *adj*

granule *n* a small grain

grape *n* **1** (any of a genus of widely cultivated woody vines that bear, in clusters,) a smooth-skinned juicy greenish white to deep red or purple berry eaten as a fruit or fermented to produce wine **2** grapeshot – **grapy** *adj*

grapefruit *n* (a small tree that bears) a large round citrus fruit with a bitter yellow rind and a somewhat acid juicy pulp

grapeshot *n* a cluster of small iron balls used as a charge for a cannon

grapevine *n* a secret or unofficial means of circulating information or gossip

¹**graph** *n* **1** a diagram (e g a series of points, a line, a curve, or an area) expressing a relation between quantities or variables **2** the collection of all points whose coordinates satisfy a given relation (e g the equation of a function)

²**graph** *vt* to plot on or represent by a graph

-graph *comb form* (→ *n*) **1** sthg written or represented ⟨*monograph*⟩ ⟨*pictograph*⟩ **2** instrument for recording or transmitting (sthg specified or by a specified means) ⟨*seismograph*⟩ ⟨*telegraph*⟩

¹**graphic** *also* **graphical** *adj* **1** formed by writing, drawing, or engraving **2** marked by clear and vivid description; sharply outlined **3a** of the pictorial arts **b** of or employing engraving, etching, lithography, photography, or other methods of reproducing material in the graphic arts **c** of or according to graphics **4** *of a rock or mineral surface* having marks resembling written characters **5** of or represented by a graph **6** of writing – **graphically** *adv*, **graphicness** *n*

²**graphic** *n* **1** a product of graphic art **2** a picture, map, or graph used for illustration or demonstration **3** a graphic representation displayed by a computer (e g on a VDU)

-graphic, -graphical *comb form* (→ *adj*) **1** written, represented, or transmitted in (such) a way ⟨*stylo*graphic⟩ ⟨*ideo*graphic⟩ **2** of writing on a (specified) subject ⟨*autobio*graphic⟩

graphite *n* a soft black lustrous form of carbon that conducts electricity and is used esp in lead pencils and as a lubricant – **graphitize** *vt*, **graphitic** *adj*

graphology *n* the study of handwriting, esp for the purpose of character analysis – **graphologist** *n*, **graphological** *adj*

graph paper *n* paper ruled for drawing graphs

grapnel *n* an instrument with several claws that is hurled with a line attached in order to hook onto a ship, the top of a wall, etc

¹grapple *n* **1** a grapnel **2** a hand-to-hand struggle

²grapple *vb* **grappling** *vt* to seize (as if) with a grapple ~ *vi* to come to grips *with*; wrestle – **grappler** *n*

¹grasp *vi* to make the motion of seizing; clutch ~ *vt* **1** to take, seize, or clasp eagerly (as if) with the fingers or arms **2** to succeed in understanding; comprehend – **graspable** *adj*, **grasper** *n*

²grasp *n* **1** a firm hold **2** control, power ⟨*he is in her* ~⟩ **3** the power of seizing and holding or attaining ⟨*success was just beyond his* ~⟩ **4** comprehension ⟨*showed a firm* ~ *of her subject*⟩

grasping *adj* eager for material possessions; avaricious – **graspingly** *adv*, **graspingness** *n*

¹grass *n* **1a** herbage suitable or used for grazing animals **b** pasture, grazing **2** any of a large family of plants with slender leaves and (green) flowers in small spikes or clusters, that includes bamboo, wheat, rye, corn, etc **3** land on which grass is grown ⟨*keep off the* ~⟩ **4** grass leaves or plants **5** cannabis; *specif* marijuana – slang **6** *Br* a police informer – slang – **grasslike** *adj* – **put/send out to grass** to cause (sby) to enter usu enforced retirement

²grass *vt* **1** to feed (livestock) on grass **2** to cover or seed with grass – often + *down* ~ *vi*, *Br* to inform the police; *esp* to betray sby to the police – slang

grasshopper *n* any of numerous plant-eating insects with hind legs adapted for leaping

grassland *n* **1** farmland used for grazing **2** land on which the natural dominant plant forms are grasses

grass roots *n pl but sing or pl in constr* **1** society at the local level as distinguished from the centres of political leadership **2** the fundamental level or source – **grass-roots** *adj*

grass widow *n* a woman whose husband is temporarily away from her

grassy *adj* **1** consisting of or covered with grass **2** (having a smell) like grass

¹grate *n* **1** a frame or bed of metal bars to hold the fuel in a fireplace, stove, or furnace **2** a fireplace

²grate *vt* **1** to reduce to small particles by rubbing on sthg rough ⟨~ *cheese*⟩ **2a** to gnash or grind noisily **b** to cause to make a rasping sound ~ *vi* **1** to rub or rasp noisily **2** to cause irritation; jar ⟨*his manner of talking* ~s *on my nerves*⟩ – **grater** *n*

grateful *adj* **1** feeling or expressing thanks **2** pleasing, comforting – **gratefully** *adv*, **gratefulness** *n*

graticule *n* **1** a network or scale visible when using a telescope, microscope, etc and used in locating or measuring objects **2** the network of latitude and longitude lines on which a map is drawn

gratification *n* **1** gratifying or being gratified **2** a source of satisfaction or pleasure

gratify *vt* **1** to be a source of or give pleasure or satisfaction to **2** to give in to; satisfy ⟨~ *a whim*⟩ – **gratifyingly** *adv*

grating *n* **1** a partition, covering, or frame of parallel bars or crossbars **2** a lattice used to close or floor any of various openings **3** a set of close parallel lines or bars ruled on a polished surface to produce (optical) spectra by diffraction

gratis *adv or adj* without charge or recompense; free

gratitude *n* the state or feeling of being grateful; thankfulness

gratuitous *adj* **1a** costing nothing; free **b** not involving a return benefit or compensation **2** not called for by the circumstances; unwarranted ⟨*the film contained scenes of* ~ *violence*⟩ – **gratuitously** *adv*, **gratuitousness** *n*

gratuity *n* sthg given voluntarily, usu in return for or in anticipation of some service; *esp* a tip

¹grave *vt* **graven, graved** to engrave

²grave *n* an excavation for burial of a body; *broadly* a tomb

³grave *vt* to clean and then tar (e g a ship's bottom)

⁴grave *adj* **1a** requiring serious consideration; important ⟨~ *problems*⟩ **b** likely to produce great harm or danger ⟨*a* ~ *mistake*⟩ **2** serious, dignified **3** drab in colour; sombre **4** *of a sound* low in pitch – **gravely** *adv*, **graveness** *n*

⁵grave *adj or n* (being or marked with) an accent˙ used to show that a vowel is pronounced with a fall of pitch (e g in ancient Greek) or has a certain quality (e g *è* in French)

¹gravel *n* **1** (a stratum or surface of) loose rounded fragments of rock mixed with sand **2** a sandy deposit of small stones in the kidneys and urinary bladder

²gravel *adj* GRAVELLY 2

³gravel *vt* **-ll-** (*NAm* **-l-, -ll-**), **1** to cover or spread with gravel **2** to perplex, confound

gravelly *adj* **1** of, containing, or covered with gravel **2** harsh, grating ⟨*a* ~ *voice*⟩

gravestone *n* a stone over or at one end of a grave, usu inscribed with the name and details of the dead person

graveyard *n* **1** a cemetery **2** a condition of final disappointment or failure ⟨*the* ~ *of their hopes*⟩

graving dock *n* DRY DOCK

gravitate *vb* to (cause to) move under the influence of gravitation – **gravitate towards** to move or be compulsively drawn towards

gravitation *n* (movement resulting from) the natural force of mutual attraction between bodies or particles – **gravitational** *adj*, **gravitationally** *adv*, **gravitative** *adj*

gravity *n* **1a** dignity or sobriety of bearing **b** significance; *esp* seriousness ⟨*he couldn't comprehend the* ~ *of the situation*⟩ **2** (the quality of having) weight **3** (the attraction of a celestial body for bodies at or near its surface resulting from) gravitation – **gravity** *adj*

gravure *n* **1** the process of printing from an intaglio plate of copper or wood **2** photogravure

gravy *n* the (thickened and seasoned) fat and juices from cooked meat used as a sauce

gray *vb, n, or adj, chiefly NAm* (to) grey

¹graze *vi* to feed on growing herbage ~ *vt* **1a** to crop and eat (growing herbage) **b** to feed on the herbage of (e g a pasture) **2** to put to graze ⟨~ *d the cows on the meadow*⟩ – **grazable** *adj*, **grazer** *n*

²graze *vt* **1** to touch lightly in passing **2** to abrade, scratch ⟨~ *d her elbow*⟩ ~ *vi* to touch or rub against sthg in passing ⟨*our bumpers just* ~ *d*⟩

³graze *n* (an abrasion, esp of the skin, made by) a scraping along a surface

¹grease *n* **1a** melted down animal fat **b** oily matter **c** a thick lubricant **2** oily wool as it comes from the sheep – **greaseless** *adj*, **greaseproof** *adj* – **in the grease** *of wool or fur* in the natural uncleaned condition

²grease *vt* **1** to smear, lubricate, or soil with grease **2** to

hasten or ease the process or progress of – **greaser** n – **grease the palm of** to bribe
greasepaint n theatrical make-up
greasy adj **1a** smeared or soiled with grease **b** oily in appearance, texture, or manner ⟨his ~ smile – Jack London⟩ **c** slippery **2** containing an unusual amount of grease ⟨~ food⟩ – **greasily** adv, **greasiness** n
great adj **1a** notably large in size or number **b** of a relatively large kind – in plant and animal names **c** elaborate, ample ⟨~ detail⟩ **2a** extreme in amount, degree, or effectiveness ⟨~ bloodshed⟩ **b** of importance; significant ⟨a ~ day in European history⟩ **3** full of emotion ⟨~ with anger⟩ **4a** eminent, distinguished ⟨a ~ poet⟩ **b** aristocratic, grand ⟨~ ladies⟩ **5** main, principal ⟨a reception in the ~ hall⟩ **6** removed in a family relationship by at least 3 stages directly or 2 stages indirectly – chiefly in combination ⟨great-grandfather⟩ **7** markedly superior in character or quality; esp noble **8a** remarkably skilled **b** enthusiastic, keen ⟨she was a ~ film-goer⟩ **9** archaic pregnant ⟨~ with child⟩ **10** – used as a generalized term of approval ⟨had a ~ time⟩; infml – **great** adv, **greatly** adv, **greatness** n – **no great shakes** not very good, skilful, effective, etc ⟨he's no great shakes as a boss⟩
great n, pl **great, greats** one who is great – usu pl ⟨the ~ s of the stage⟩
Great Bear n URSA MAJOR
great circle n a circle formed on the surface of a sphere, specif the earth, by the intersection of a plane that passes through the centre of the sphere
greatcoat n a heavy overcoat
Great Dane n any of a breed of massive powerful smooth-coated dogs
greater adj, often cap consisting of a central city together with adjacent areas that are geographically or administratively connected with it ⟨Greater London⟩
grebe n any of a family of swimming and diving birds closely related to the loons but having lobed instead of webbed toes
Grecian adj Greek – **Grecian** n, **grecianize** vt, often cap
Greco- comb form, chiefly NAm Graeco-
greed n **1** excessive acquisitiveness; avarice **2** excessive desire for or consumption of food
greedy adj **1** having a usu excessive desire for sthg, esp food or money **2** having a great need for ⟨plants ~ for water⟩ – **greedily** adv, **greediness** n
greedy-guts n, pl **greedy-guts** chiefly Br one who eats too much; a glutton – infml
Greek n **1** a native or inhabitant of Greece **2** the Indo-European language used by the Greeks **3** not cap sthg unintelligible ⟨it's all ~ to me⟩ – infml
Greek adj **1** of Greece, the Greeks, or Greek **2** **Greek, Greek Orthodox a** ORTHODOX 2a **b** of an Eastern church, esp the established Orthodox church of Greece using the Byzantine rite in Greek
green adj **1** of the colour green **2a** covered by green growth or foliage ⟨~ fields⟩ **b** consisting of green (edible) plants ⟨a ~ salad⟩ **3a** youthful, vigorous **b** not ripened or matured; immature ⟨~ apples⟩ **c** fresh, new **4** appearing pale, sickly, or nauseated **5** affected by intense envy or jealousy **6a** not aged ⟨a ~ ham⟩ **b** not dressed or tanned ⟨~ hides⟩ **c** of wood freshly sawn; unseasoned **7a** deficient in training, knowledge, or experience **b** lacking sophistication; naive **8** being an exchange unit that has a differential rate of exchange in relation to the specified currency and is used for paying agricultural producers in the European economic community ⟨the ~ pound⟩ – **greenly** adv, **greenness** n

²green vi to become green
³green n **1** a colour whose hue resembles that of growing fresh grass or the emerald and lies between blue and yellow in the spectrum **2** sthg of a green colour **3** pl green leafy vegetables (e g spinach and cabbage) the leaves and stems of which are often cooked **4a** a common or park in the centre of a town or village **b** a smooth area of grass for a special purpose (e g bowling or putting) – **greeny** adj
greenback n, NAm a legal-tender note issued by the US government – infml
green belt n a belt of parks, farmland, etc encircling an urban area and usu subject to restrictions on new building
greenery n green foliage or plants
green-eyed adj jealous
green fingers n pl an unusual ability to make plants grow – **green-fingered** adj
greenfly n, pl **greenflies**, esp collectively **greenfly** Br (an infestation by) any of various green aphids that are destructive to plants
greengage n any of several small rounded greenish cultivated plums
greengrocer n, chiefly Br a retailer of fresh vegetables and fruit – **greengrocery** n
greenhorn n **1** an inexperienced or unsophisticated (easily cheated) person **2** chiefly NAm a newcomer (e g to a country) unacquainted with local manners and customs
greenhouse n a glassed enclosure for the cultivation or protection of tender plants
greenish adj rather green – **greenishness** n
green light n authority or permission to undertake a project
green pepper n SWEET PEPPER
greenroom n a room in a theatre or concert hall where performers can relax when not on stage
green tea n tea that is light in colour from incomplete fermentation of the leaf before firing
green thumb n, NAm GREEN FINGERS – **green-thumbed** adj
Greenwich Mean Time n the mean solar time of the meridian of Greenwich used as the primary point of reference for standard time throughout the world
greenwood n a forest green with foliage
¹greet vt **1** to welcome with gestures or words **2** to meet or react to in a specified manner ⟨the candidate was ~ ed with catcalls⟩ **3** to be perceived by ⟨a surprising sight ~ ed her eyes⟩ – **greeter** n
²greet vi grat; grutten Scot to weep, lament
greeting n **1** a salutation at meeting **2** an expression of good wishes; regards – usu pl with sing. meaning
greetings card n a card containing a message of good will usu sent or given on some special occasion (e g an anniversary)
gregarious adj **1a** tending to associate with others of the same kind ⟨a ~ gull⟩ **b** marked by or indicating a liking for companionship; sociable **c** of a crowd, flock, or other group of people, animals, etc **2** of a plant growing in a cluster or a colony – **gregariously** adv, **gregariousness** n
Gregorian calendar n a revision of the Julian Calendar now in general use, that was introduced in 1582 by Pope Gregory XIII and adopted in Britain and the American colonies in 1752 and that restricts leap years to every 4th year except for those centenary years not divisible by 400
Gregorian chant n a rhythmically free liturgical chant in unison practised in the Roman Catholic church

gremlin *n* a mischievous creature said to cause malfunctioning of machinery or equipment

grenade *n* **1** a small missile that contains explosive, gas, incendiary chemicals, etc and is thrown by hand or launcher **2** a glass container of chemicals that bursts when thrown, releasing a fire extinguishing agent, tear gas, etc

grenadier *n* a member of a regiment or corps formerly specially trained in the use of grenades

grenadine *n* a syrup flavoured with pomegranates and used in mixed drinks

grew *past of* GROW

¹**grey, NAm chiefly gray** *adj* **1** of the colour grey **2a** dull in colour **b** having grey hair **3a** lacking cheer or brightness; dismal ⟨*a ~ day*⟩ **b** intermediate or unclear in position, condition, or character ⟨*a ~ area*⟩ **4** *of a textile* being in an unbleached undyed state as taken from the loom **5** *of a horse* having white hair but dark skin – **greyly** *adv*, **greyness** *n*

²**grey, NAm chiefly gray** *n* **1** any of a series of neutral colours ranging between black and white **2** sthg grey; *esp* grey clothes, paint, or horses

³**grey, NAm chiefly gray** *vb* to make or become grey

greybeard *n* an old man

greyhound *n* (any of) a tall slender smooth-coated breed of dogs characterized by swiftness and keen sight and used for coursing game and racing

greyish *adj*, *of a colour* low in saturation

grey matter *n* **1** brownish-grey nerve tissue, esp in the brain and spinal cord, containing nerve-cell bodies as well as nerve fibres **2** brains, intellect – *infml*

grid *n* **1** a grating **2a** a network of conductors for distribution of electric power **b** (sthg resembling) a network of uniformly spaced horizontal and perpendicular lines for locating points on a map **3** the starting positions of vehicles on a racetrack **4** GRILL 1 – **gridded** *adj*

griddle *n* a flat metal surface on which food is cooked by dry heat

gridiron *n* GRILL 1

grief *n* (a cause of) deep and poignant distress (e g due to bereavement) – **griefless** *adj*

grievance *n* **1** a cause of distress (e g unsatisfactory working conditions) felt to afford reason for complaint or resistance **2** the formal expression of a grievance; a complaint

¹**grieve** *vt* to cause to suffer grief ~ *vi* to suffer from grief, esp over a bereavement – often + *for* – **griever** *n*

²**grieve** *n*, *Scot* a farm or estate manager or overseer

grievous *adj* **1** causing or characterized by severe pain, suffering, or sorrow ⟨*a ~ loss*⟩ **2** serious, grave ⟨*~ fault*⟩ – **grievously** *adv*, **grievousness** *n*

griffin, griffon, gryphon *n* a mythical animal with the head and wings of an eagle and the body and tail of a lion

¹**grill** *vt* **1** to cook on or under a grill by radiant heat **2a** to torture (as if) with great heat **b** to subject to intense and usu long periods of questioning – *infml* ~ *vi* to become grilled – **griller** *n*

²**grill** *n* **1** a cooking utensil of parallel bars on which food is exposed to heat (e g from burning charcoal) **2** an article or dish of grilled food **3** grill, grillroom a usu informal restaurant or dining room, esp in a hotel **4** *Br* an apparatus on a cooker under which food is cooked or browned by radiant heat

grille, grill *n* **1** a grating forming a barrier or screen; *specif* an ornamental metal one at the front end of a motor vehicle **2** an opening covered with a grille

grim *adj* **-mm-** **1** fierce or forbidding in disposition, action, or appearance **2** unflinching, unyielding ⟨*~ determina-*

tion⟩ **3** ghastly or sinister in character **4** unpleasant, nasty ⟨*had a pretty ~ afternoon at the dentist's*⟩ – *infml* – **grimly** *adv*, **grimness** *n*

grimace *n* a distorted facial expression, usu of disgust, anger, or pain – **grimace** *vi*, **grimacer** *n*

grime *n* soot or dirt, esp when sticking to or embedded in a surface – **grime** *vt*, **grimy** *adj*, **griminess** *n*

grin *vi* **-nn-** to smile so as to show the teeth – **grin** *n*, **grinner** *n*

¹**grind** *vb* **ground** *vt* **1** to reduce to powder or small fragments by crushing between hard surfaces **2** to wear down, polish, or sharpen by friction; whet ⟨*~ an axe*⟩ **3a** to rub, press, or twist harshly ⟨ground *the cigarette out with a heel*⟩ ⟨ground *his fist into his opponent's stomach*⟩ **b** to press together with a rotating motion ⟨*~ the teeth*⟩ **4** to operate or produce by turning a crank ⟨*~ a hand organ*⟩ ~ *vi* **1** to perform the operation of grinding **2** to become pulverized, polished, or sharpened by friction **3** to move with difficulty or friction, esp so as to make a grating noise ⟨*~ing gears*⟩ **4** to work monotonously; *esp* to study hard ⟨*~ for an exam*⟩ **5** to rotate the hips in an erotic manner – **grindingly** *adv* – **grind into** to instil (knowledge, facts, etc) into (sby) with great difficulty

²**grind** *n* **1** dreary monotonous labour or routine **2** the result of grinding; *esp* material obtained by grinding to a particular degree of fineness **3a** the act of rotating the hips in an erotic manner **b** *Br* an act of sexual intercourse – *vulg* **4** *chiefly NAm* a swot – *infml*

grind down *vt* to oppress, harass

grinder *n* a molar tooth

grind out *vt* to produce in a mechanical way ⟨grind out *best-sellers*⟩ – *derog*

grindstone *n* **1** MILLSTONE 1 **2** a flat circular stone that revolves on an axle and is used for grinding, shaping, etc

gringo *n*, *pl* **gringos** an (English-speaking) foreigner in Spain or Latin America

¹**grip** *vb* **-pp-** *vt* **1** to seize or hold firmly **2** to attract and hold the interest of ⟨*a story that ~s the reader*⟩ ~ *vi* to take firm hold – **gripper** *n*, **grippingly** *adv*

²**grip** *n* **1a** a strong or tenacious grasp **b** manner or style of gripping **2a** control, mastery, power ⟨*he kept a good ~ on his pupils*⟩ **b** (power of) understanding or doing ⟨*she has a good ~ of the situation*⟩ **3** a part or device that grips ⟨*a hair ~*⟩ **4** a part by which sthg is grasped; *esp* a handle **5** one who handles scenery, properties, lighting, or camera equipment in a theatre or film or television studio **6** a travelling bag

¹**gripe** *vt* to cause intestinal gripes in ~ *vi* **1** to experience intestinal gripes **2** to complain persistently – *infml* – **griper** *n*

²**gripe** *n* **1** a stabbing spasmodic intestinal pain – usu pl **2** a grievance, complaint – *infml*

grippe *n* influenza – **grippy** *adj*

grisly *adj* inspiring horror, intense fear, or disgust; forbidding ⟨*houses that were dark and ~ under the blank, cold sky* – D H Lawrence⟩ – **grisliness** *n*

grist *n* **1** (a batch of) grain for grinding **2** the product obtained from grinding grain – **grist to the mill** sthg that can be put to use or profit

gristle *n* cartilage; *broadly* tough cartilaginous or fibrous matter, esp in cooked meat – **gristly** *adj*, **gristliness** *n*

¹**grit** *n* **1** a hard sharp granule (e g of sand or stone); *also* material composed of such granules **2** the structure or texture of a stone that adapts it to grinding **3** firmness of mind or spirit; unyielding courage – *infml*

²**grit** *vb* **-tt-** *vi* to give forth a grating sound ~ *vt* **1** to cover or spread with grit **2** to cause (esp one's teeth) to grind or grate

grits n pl but sing or pl in constr grain, esp oats, husked and usu coarsely ground

grizzle vi grizzling Br **1** of a child to cry quietly and fretfully **2** to complain in a self-pitying way – often + about USE infml

grizzled adj sprinkled or streaked with grey ⟨a ~ beard⟩

grizzly adj grizzled

grizzly, grizzly bear n a very large typically brownish yellow bear that lives in the highlands of western N America

groan vi **1** to utter a deep moan **2** to creak under strain ⟨the boards ~ed under our weight⟩ ~ vt to utter with groaning – **groan** n, **groaner** n

groat n hulled grain (broken into fragments larger than grits) – usu pl with sing. meaning but sing. or pl in constr

groat n a former British coin worth 4 old pence

grocer n a dealer in (packaged or tinned) staple foodstuffs, household supplies, and usu fruit, vegetables, and dairy products

grocery n **1** pl commodities sold by a grocer **2** a grocer's shop

grog n alcoholic drink; specif spirits (e g rum) mixed with water

groggy adj weak and dazed, esp owing to illness or tiredness – **groggily** adv, **grogginess** n

groin n **1a** the fold marking the join between the lower abdomen and the inner part of the thigh **b** the male genitals – euph **2** the line along which 2 intersecting vaults meet **3** chiefly NAm a groyne

groom n **1** one who is in charge of the feeding, care, and stabling of horses **2** a bridegroom **3** archaic a manservant

groom vt **1** to clean and care for (e g a horse) **2** to make neat or attractive ⟨an impeccably ~ed woman⟩ **3** to get into readiness for a specific objective; prepare ⟨was being ~ed as a Tory candidate⟩ ~ vi to groom oneself – **groomer** n

groove n **1a** a long narrow channel or depression **b** the continuous spiral track on a gramophone record whose irregularities correspond to the recorded sounds **2** a fixed routine; a rut **3** top form – infml ⟨a great talker when he is in the ~⟩ **4** an enjoyable or exciting experience – infml; no longer in vogue

groove vt **1** to make a groove in **2** to excite pleasurably – infml; no longer in vogue ~ vi **1** to form a groove **2** to enjoy oneself intensely; also to get on well – infml; no longer in vogue – **groover** n

groovy adj fashionably attractive or exciting – infml; no longer in vogue

grope vi **1** to feel about blindly or uncertainly for **2** to search blindly or uncertainly for or after ⟨groping for the right words⟩ ~ vt **1** to touch or fondle the body of (a person) for sexual pleasure **2** to find (e g one's way) by groping – **grope** n, **groper** n

gross adj **1** glaringly noticeable, usu because excessively bad or objectionable; flagrant ⟨~ error⟩ **2a** big, bulky, esp excessively fat **b** of vegetation dense, luxuriant **3** consisting of an overall total before deductions (e g for taxes) are made ⟨~ income⟩ **4** made up of material or perceptible elements; corporal ⟨the ~er part of human nature⟩ **5** coarse in nature or behaviour; specif crudely vulgar – **grossly** adv, **grossness** n

gross n an overall total exclusive of deductions

gross vt to earn or bring in (an overall total) exclusive of deductions – **grosser** n

gross n, pl **gross** a group of 12 dozen things ⟨a ~ of pencils⟩

grotesque n **1** a style of decorative art in which incongruous or fantastic human and animal forms are interwoven with natural motifs (e g foliage) **2** sby grotesque **3** SANS SERIF

grotesque adj (having the characteristics) of the grotesque: e g **a** fanciful, bizarre **b** absurdly incongruous **c** departing markedly from the natural, expected, or typical – **grotesquely** adv, **grotesqueness** n

grotto n, pl **grottoes** also **grottos 1** an esp picturesque cave **2** an excavation or structure made to resemble a natural cave

grotty adj, Br nasty, unpleasant – slang – **grottily** adv

grouch n **1** a bad-tempered complaint **2** a habitually irritable or complaining person; a grumbler – **grouch** vi, **grouchy** adj

ground n **1a** the bottom of a body of water **b** pl (1) SEDIMENT **1 (2)** ground coffee beans after brewing **2** a basis for belief, action, or argument – often pl with sing. meaning ⟨~s for complaint⟩ **3a** a surrounding area; a background **b** (material that serves as) a substratum **4a** the surface of the earth **b** an area used for a particular purpose ⟨parade ~⟩ ⟨football ~⟩ **c** pl the area round and belonging to a house or other building **d** an area to be won or defended (as if) in battle **e** an area of knowledge or special interest ⟨covered a lot of ~ in his lecture⟩ **5a** ³SOIL **2b b** chiefly NAm EARTH **8** – **off the ground** started and in progress ⟨the programme never got off the ground⟩ – **to ground** into hiding

ground vt **1** to bring to or place on the ground **2a** to provide a reason or justification for **b** to instruct in fundamentals (e g of a subject) **3** to restrict (e g a pilot or aircraft) to the ground **4** chiefly NAm to earth ~ vi to run aground

ground past of GRIND

groundbait n bait scattered on the water so as to attract fish

ground bass n a short bass passage continually repeated below constantly changing melody and harmony

ground floor n the floor of a house on a level with the ground

grounding n fundamental training in a field of knowledge

groundless adj having no foundation ⟨~ fears⟩ – **groundlessly** adv, **groundlessness** n

groundnut n **1** (a N American leguminous plant with) an edible tuberous root **2** chiefly Br the peanut

ground plan n **1** a plan of the ground floor of a building **2** a first or basic plan

ground rent n the rent paid by a lessee for the use of land, esp for building

ground rule n a basic rule of procedure

groundsel n a (plant related to a) European composite plant that is a common weed and has small yellow flower heads

groundsheet n a waterproof sheet placed on the ground (e g in a tent)

groundsman n sby who tends a playing field, esp a cricket pitch

groundstaff n the people who maintain a sports ground

ground swell n a sea swell caused by an often distant gale or ground tremor

groundwork n (work done to provide) a foundation or basis

group n **1** two or more figures or objects forming a complete unit in a composition **2** sing or pl in constr **a** a number of individuals or objects assembled together or having some unifying relationship **b** an operational and administrative unit belonging to a command of an air force **3a** an assemblage of atoms forming part of a molecule; a radical ⟨*a methyl* ~⟩ **b** all the (similar) chemical elements forming one of the vertical columns of the periodic table **4** a mathematical set that is closed under a binary associative operation, has an identity element, and has an inverse for every element

²group *vt* **1** to combine in a group **2** to assign to a group; classify ~ *vi* to form or belong to a group – **groupable** *adj*

group captain *n* an officer in the Royal Air Force ranking below air commodore

groupie *n* an ardent (female) fan of a famous person, esp a rock star, who follows the object of admiration on tour

grouping *n* a set of individuals or objects combined in a group

group practice *n* a practice run by a group of associated medical general practitioners

group therapy *n* the treatment of several individuals (with similar psychological problems) simultaneously through group discussion and mutual aid

¹grouse *n, pl* **grouse** any of several (important game) birds with a plump body and strong feathered legs

²grouse *vi or n* (to) grumble – *infml* – **grouser** *n*

grove *n* a small wood, group, or planting of trees

grovel *vi* -**ll**- (*NAm* -**l**-, -**ll**-) **1** to lie or creep with the body prostrate in token of subservience or abasement **2** to abase or humble oneself – **groveller** *n*, **grovellingly** *adv*

grow *vb* **grew; grown** *vi* **1a** to spring up and develop to maturity (in a specified place or situation) **b** to assume some relation (as if) through a process of natural growth ⟨*2 tree trunks* grown *together*⟩ **2a** to increase in size by addition of material (e g by assimilation into a living organism or by crystallization) **b** to increase, expand **3** to develop from a parent source ⟨*the book* grew *out of a series of lectures*⟩ **4** to become gradually ⟨grew *pale*⟩ ~ *vt* **1** to cause to grow; produce ⟨~ *roses*⟩ **2** DEVELOP **5** ⟨~ *wings*⟩ – **grower** *n*, **growingly** *adv* – **grow on** to have an increasing influence on; *esp* to become more pleasing to

growing pains *n pl* **1** pains in the legs of growing children that have no known cause **2** the early problems attending a new project or development

¹growl *vi* **1a** to rumble **b** to utter a growl **2** to complain angrily

²growl *n* a deep guttural inarticulate sound

grown *adj* **1** fully grown; mature ⟨~ *men*⟩ **2** overgrown or covered (*with*)

grown-up *n or adj* (an) adult

growth *n* **1a** (a stage in the process of) growing **b** progressive development **c** an increase, expansion **2a** sthg that grows or has grown **b** a tumour or other abnormal growth of tissue **3** the result of growth; a product

grow up *vi* **1** *of a person* to develop towards or arrive at a mature state **2** to arise and develop ⟨*the movement* grew up *in the 60s*⟩ **3** to begin to act sensibly – usu imper

groyne, *chiefly NAm* **groin** *n* a rigid structure built out from a shore, esp to check erosion of the beach

¹grub *vb* -**bb**- *vt* **1** to clear by digging up roots and stumps **2** to dig *up* or *out* (as if) by the roots ~ *vi* **1** to dig in the ground, esp for sthg that is difficult to find or extract **2** to search about; rummage – **grubber** *n*

²grub *n* **1** a soft thick wormlike larva of an insect **2** food – *infml*

grubby *adj* dirty, grimy ⟨~ *hands*⟩ – **grubbily** *adv*, **grubbiness** *n*

Grub Street *n* the world or life-style of needy literary hacks

¹grudge *vt* to be unwilling or reluctant to give or admit; begrudge ⟨~ d *the money to pay taxes*⟩ – **grudger** *n*

²grudge *n* a feeling of deep-seated resentment or ill will

grudging *adj* unwilling, reluctant – **grudgingly** *adv*

gruel *n* a thin porridge

gruelling, *NAm chiefly* **grueling** *adj* trying or taxing to the point of causing exhaustion; punishing ⟨*a* ~ *race*⟩

gruesome *adj* inspiring horror or repulsion; ⟨~ *scenes of torture*⟩ – **gruesomely** *adv*, **gruesomeness** *n*

gruff *adj* **1** brusque or stern in manner, speech, or aspect ⟨*a* ~ *reply*⟩ **2** deep and harsh ⟨*a* ~ *voice*⟩ – **gruffly** *adv*, **gruffness** *n*

grumble *vb* **grumbling** *vi* **1** to mutter in discontent **2** to rumble ~ *vt* to express in a moaning or discontented way – **grumble** *n*, **grumbler** *n*, **grumblingly** *adv*, **grumbly** *adj*

grumbling *adj* causing intermittent pain or discomfort ⟨~ *appendix*⟩

grumpy *adj* moodily cross; surly – **grumpily** *adv*, **grumpiness** *n*

Grundyism *n* prudery

¹grunt *vb* to utter (with) a grunt – **grunter** *n*

²grunt *n* the deep short guttural sound of a pig; *also* a similar sound

Gruyère *n* a Swiss cheese with smaller holes and a slightly fuller flavour than Emmenthal

gryphon *n* a griffin

G-string *n* a small piece of cloth, leather, etc covering the genitalia and held in place by thongs, elastic, etc that is passed round the hips and between the buttocks

guano *n* (an artificial fertilizer similar to) a phosphate-rich substance consisting chiefly of the excrement of seabirds and used as a fertilizer

¹guarantee *n* **1** one who guarantees **2** a written undertaking to answer for the payment of a debt or the performance of a duty of another in case of the other's default **3a** an agreement by which one person accepts responsibility for another's obligations, esp debts, in case of default **b** an assurance of the quality of or of the length of use to be expected from a product offered for sale, accompanied by a promise to replace it or pay the customer back **4** sthg given as security; a pledge

²guarantee *vt* **guaranteed; guaranteeing 1** to undertake to answer for the debt or default of **2a** to undertake to do or secure (sthg) ⟨*she* ~ d *delivery of the goods*⟩ **b** to engage for the existence, permanence, or nature of **3** to give security to

guarantor *n* **1** one who guarantees **2** one who makes or gives a guarantee

guaranty *n* GUARANTEE 2

¹guard *n* **1** a defensive position in boxing, fencing, etc **2** the act or duty of protecting or defending **3** a person or a body of men on sentinel duty **4a** a person or group whose duty is to protect a place, people, etc **b** *pl* HOUSEHOLD TROOPS **5** a protective or safety device; *esp* a device on a machine for protecting against injury **6** *Br* the person in charge of a railway train

²guard *vt* **1** to protect from danger, esp by watchful attention; make secure ⟨*policemen* ~ ing *our cities*⟩ **2** to watch over so as to prevent escape, entry, theft, etc; *also* to keep in check ⟨~ *your tongue*⟩ ~ *vi* to watch by way of caution or defence; stand guard – **guarder** *n* – **guard against** to attempt to prevent (sthg) by taking precautions

guarded *adj* marked by caution ⟨*a* ~ *reply*⟩ ⟨*a* ~ *look*⟩ – **guardedly** *adv*, **guardedness** *n*

guardhouse *n* a building used by soldiers on guard duty or as a prison

guardian *n* **1** one who or that which guards or protects **2** sby who has the care of the person or property of another; *specif* sby entrusted by law with the care of sby who is of unsound mind, not of age, etc – **guardianship** *n*

guardrail *n* a railing for guarding against danger or trespass

guardroom *n* a room serving as a guardhouse

guardsman *n* a member of a military body called *guard* or *guards*

guard's van *n*, *Br* a railway wagon or carriage attached usu at the rear of a train for the use of the guard

guava *n* (the sweet acid yellow edible fruit of) a shrubby tropical American tree

gubernatorial *adj* of a governor

¹gudgeon *n* **1** a pivot or journal **2** a socket for a rudder pintle

²gudgeon *n*, *pl* gudgeons, *esp collectively* gudgeon a small European freshwater fish used esp for food or bait

guelder rose *n* a (cultivated) shrub of the honeysuckle family with clusters of white flowers

guerrilla, guerilla *n* a member of a small independent fighting force which engages in sabotage, unexpected assaults, etc

¹guess *vt* **1** to form an opinion of with little or no consideration of the facts **2** to arrive at a correct conclusion about by conjecture, chance, or intuition ⟨~ed *the answer*⟩ **3** *chiefly NAm* to believe, suppose ⟨*I* ~ *you're right*⟩ – infml ~ *vi* to make a guess – **guesser** *n*

²guess *n* a surmise, estimate

guesswork *n* (judgment based on) the act of guessing

¹guest *n* **1a** a person entertained in one's home **b** a person taken out, entertained, and paid for by another **c** a person who pays for the services of an establishment (e g a hotel) **2** one who is present by invitation ⟨*a* ~ *star on a TV programme*⟩

²guest *vi* to appear as a guest

guesthouse *n* a private house used to accommodate paying guests

guffaw *vi or n* (to utter) a loud or boisterous laugh

guidance *n* **1** help, advice **2** the process of controlling the course of a projectile by a built-in mechanism

¹guide *n* **1a** one who leads or directs another **b** one who shows and explains places of interest to travellers, tourists, etc **c** sthg, esp a guidebook, that provides sby with information about a place, activity, etc **d** sthg or sby that directs a person in his/her conduct or course of life **2a** a bar, rod, etc for steadying or directing the motion of sthg **3** *often cap, chiefly Br* a member of a worldwide movement of girls and young women founded with the aim of forming character and teaching good citizenship through outdoor activities and domestic skills; *specif* a member of the intermediate section for girls aged from 10 to 15

²guide *vt* **1** to act as a guide to; direct in a way or course **2** to direct or supervise, usu to a particular end; *also* to supervise the training of ~ *vi* to act or work as a guide; give guidance – **guider** *n*, **guidable** *adj*

guideline *n* a line by which one is guided; *esp* an indication of policy or conduct

guild *n sing or pl in constr* an association of people with similar interests or pursuits; *esp* a medieval association of merchants or craftsmen – **guildship** *n*

guilder *n* a gulden

guildhall *n* a hall where a guild or corporation usu assembles; *esp* TOWN HALL

guild socialism *n* an early socialist theory advocating state ownership of industry with control by guilds of workers

guile *n* deceitful cunning; duplicity – **guileful** *adj*, **guilefully** *adv*, **guileless** *adj*, **guilelessly** *adv*

guillemot *n*, *pl* guillemots, *esp collectively* guillemot any of several narrow-billed auks of northern seas

guillotine *n* **1** a machine for beheading consisting of a heavy blade that slides down between grooved posts **2** an instrument (e g a paper cutter) that works like a guillotine **3** limitation of the discussion of legislative business by the imposition of a time limit – **guillotine** *vt*

guilt *n* **1** the fact of having committed a breach of conduct, esp one that violates law **2a** responsibility for a criminal or other offence **b** feelings of being at fault or to blame, esp for imagined offences or from a sense of inadequacy

guilty *adj* **1** justly answerable for an offence **2a** suggesting or involving guilt ⟨*a* ~ *deed*⟩ **b** feeling guilt ⟨*their* ~ *consciences*⟩ – **guiltily** *adv*, **guiltiness** *n*

guinea *n* **1** a former British gold coin worth 21 shillings **2** a money unit worth £1 and 5 new pence

guinea fowl *n* a W African bird with white-speckled slaty plumage that is related to the pheasants and is widely kept for food

guinea pig *n* **1** a small stout-bodied short-eared nearly tailless rodent often kept as a pet **2** sby or sthg used as a subject of (scientific) research or experimentation

guipure *n* a heavy large-patterned decorative lace on a fabric foundation

guise *n* **1** external appearance; aspect **2** assumed appearance; semblance – **in the guise of** masquerading as

guitar *n* a flat-bodied stringed instrument with a long fretted neck, plucked with a plectrum or the fingers – **guitarist** *n*

gulch *n*, *chiefly NAm* a ravine, esp with a torrent flowing through it

gulden *n*, *pl* guldens, gulden the standard unit of money in the Netherlands

¹gulf *n* **1** a partially landlocked part of the sea, usu larger than a bay **2** a deep chasm; an abyss **3** an unbridgeable gap ⟨*the* ~ *between theory and practice*⟩

²gulf *vt* to engulf

¹gull *n* any of numerous related long-winged web-footed largely white, grey, or black aquatic birds

²gull *vt* to trick, cheat, or deceive ⟨~ed *into a bad purchase*⟩

gullet *n* the oesophagus; *broadly* the throat

gullible *adj* easily deceived or cheated – **gullibility** *n*

¹gully *also* gulley *n* **1** a trench worn in the earth by running water after rain **2** a deep gutter or drain **3** a fielding position in cricket close to the batsman on the off side and between point and the slips

²gully *vt* to make gullies in

gulp *vt* to swallow hurriedly, greedily, or in 1 swallow – often + *down* ~ *vi* to make a sudden swallowing movement as if surprised or nervous – **gulp** *n*, **gulper** *n*

gulp back *vt* to keep back (as if) by swallowing; suppress ⟨gulped back *his tears*⟩

¹gum *n* (the tissue that surrounds the teeth and covers) the parts of the jaws from which the teeth grow

²gum *n* **1a** any of numerous sugary plant substances that are gelatinous when moist but harden on drying **b** any of various substances (e g a mucilage or gum resin) that exude from plants **2** a substance or deposit resembling a plant gum (e g in adhesive quality) **3** *Austr* a eucalyptus – **gummy** *adj*

³gum *vb* -**mm**- *vt* to smear or stick (as if) with gum ~ *vi* to exude or form gum – **gummer** *n*

⁴gum *n* God – esp in *by gum* as a mild oath

gum arabic *n* a water-soluble gum obtained from several acacias and used esp in the manufacture of adhesives and in pharmacy

gumbo *n* **1** a (meat and vegetable) soup thickened with okra pods **2** *often cap* a patois used by Negroes and Creoles, esp in Louisiana **3** *NAm* OKRA 1 – **gumbo** *adj*

gumboil *n* an abscess in the gum

gumboot *n* a strong waterproof rubber boot reaching usu to the knee

gumption *n* **1** shrewd practical common sense **2** initiative; *specif* boldness

gum up *vt* to prevent or impede the proper working or carrying out of – esp in *gum up the works*; *infml*

¹**gun** *n* **1a** a piece of ordnance, usu with a high muzzle velocity and a comparatively flat trajectory **b** a rifle, pistol, etc **c** a device that throws a projectile **2** a discharge of a gun **3a** sby who carries a gun in a shooting party **b** *NAm* one who is skilled with a gun; *esp* a gunman – **gunned** *adj*

²**gun** *vt* **-nn-** **1** to fire on **2** to shoot – often + *down* – **gun for** to search for in order to attack – *infml*

¹**gunboat** *n* a relatively heavily armed ship of shallow draught

²**gunboat** *adj* of or employing the high-handed use of naval or military power ⟨~ *diplomacy*⟩

guncotton *n* (an explosive highly nitrated with) cellulose nitrate

gundog *n* a dog trained to locate or retrieve game for hunters

gunfire *n* the (noise of) firing of guns

gunge *n, Br* an unpleasant, dirty, or sticky substance – slang – **gungy** *adj*

gunlock *n* the mechanism for igniting the charge of a firearm

gunman *n* a man armed with a gun; *esp* a professional killer

gunmetal *n* (a metal treated to imitate) a bronze formerly used for cannon – **gunmetal** *adj*

gunner *n* **1** a soldier or airman who operates a gun; *specif* a private in the Royal Artillery **2** sby who hunts with a gun **3** a warrant officer who supervises naval ordnance and ordnance stores

gunnery *n* the use of guns; *specif* the science of the flight of projectiles and of the effective use of guns

gunny *n* a coarse heavy material, usu of jute, used esp for sacking

gunpoint *n* – **at gunpoint** under threat of death

gunpowder *n* an explosive mixture of potassium nitrate, charcoal, and sulphur used in gunnery and blasting

gunrunner *n* one who carries or deals in contraband arms and ammunition – **gunrunning** *n*

gunshot *n* **1** a shot or projectile fired from a gun **2** the range of a gun ⟨*out of* ~⟩

gun-shy *adj, esp of a dog* afraid of the sound of a gun

gunsmith *n* sby who designs, makes, or repairs firearms

gunwale, gunnel *n* the upper edge of a ship's or boat's side

guppy *n, pl* **guppies,** *esp collectively* **guppy** a small (aquarium) fish native to the W Indies and S America

gurgle *vb* **gurgling** *vi* to make the sound (as if) of unevenly flowing water; *also* to flow or move with such a sound ~ *vt* to utter with a gurgling sound – **gurgle** *n*

guru *n, pl* **gurus** **1** a personal religious teacher and spiritual guide (e g in Hinduism) **2a** a spiritual and intellectual guide; a mentor **b** an acknowledged leader or chief proponent (e g of a cult or idea) – *infml* ⟨*the* ~ *of modern philosophical thought*⟩

¹**gush** *vi* **1** to issue copiously or violently **2** to emit a sudden copious flow **3** to make an effusive often affected display of sentiment or enthusiasm ⟨*women* ~ing *over the baby*⟩ ~ *vt* to emit in a copious free flow – **gushy** *adj*, **gushing** *adj*

²**gush** *n* **1** (sthg emitted in) a sudden outpouring **2** an effusive and usu affected display of sentiment or enthusiasm

gusher *n* an oil well with a copious natural flow

gusset *n* **1** a piece of material inserted in a seam (e g the crotch of an undergarment) to provide expansion or reinforcement **2** a plate or bracket for strengthening an angle in framework – **gusset** *vt*

¹**gust** *n* **1** a sudden brief rush of (rain carried by the) wind **2** a sudden outburst; a surge ⟨*a* ~ *of emotion*⟩ – **gustily** *adv*, **gustiness** *n*, **gusty** *adj*

²**gust** *vi* to blow in gusts ⟨*winds* ~ing *up to 40 mph*⟩

gustatory, gustative *adj* of, associated with, or being the sense of taste – **gustatorily** *adv*, **gustation** *n*

gusto *n* enthusiastic and vigorous enjoyment or vitality ⟨*he sang with great* ~⟩

¹**gut** *n* **1a** the basic emotionally or instinctively responding part of a person ⟨*a* ~ *feeling*⟩ **b** (a part of) the alimentary canal **c** the belly or abdomen **d** catgut **2** a narrow (water) passage **3** the sac of silk taken from a silkworm and drawn out into a thread for use in attaching a fish hook to a fishing line **4** *pl* the inner essential parts ⟨*the* ~s *of a car*⟩ – *infml* **5** *pl* courage, determination – *infml*

²**gut** *vt* **-tt-** **1** to eviscerate, disembowel **2a** to destroy the inside of ⟨*fire* ~ted *the building*⟩ **b** to destroy the essential power or effectiveness of ⟨*inflation* ~ting *the economy of a country*⟩ **3** to extract the essentials of ⟨~ *a novel*⟩

³**gut** *adj* arising from or concerning one's strongest emotions or instincts ⟨*her* ~ *reaction to their behaviour was one of disgust*⟩

gutless *adj* lacking courage; cowardly – *infml* – **gutlessness** *n*

gutsy *adj* **1** courageous **2** expressing or appealing strongly to the physical passions; lusty ⟨*belting out* ~ *rock*⟩ *USE* infml – **gutsiness** *n*

gutta-percha *n* a tough plastic substance obtained from the latex of several Malaysian trees and used esp for electrical insulation

¹**gutter** *n* **1** a trough just below the eaves or at the side of a street to catch and carry off rainwater, surface water, etc **2** a white space between 2 pages of a book, 2 postage stamps on a sheet, etc **3** *the* lowest or most vulgar level or condition of human life

²**gutter** *vt* to cut or wear gutters in ~ *vi* **1** to flow in rivulets **2a** *of a candle* to burn unevenly so that melted wax runs down one side **b** *of a flame* to burn fitfully or feebly; be on the point of going out

³**gutter** *adj* (characteristic) of the gutter; *esp* marked by extreme vulgarity or cheapness ⟨*the* ~ *press*⟩

guttersnipe *n* a deprived child living in poverty and usu dressed in ragged clothes

guttural *adj* **1** of the throat **2a** formed or pronounced in the throat ⟨~ *sounds*⟩ **b** velar or palatal – **gutturally** *adv*, **gutturalize** *vt*, **gutturalization** *n*

guv *n, Br* GOVERNOR 3 – slang

guvnor *n, Br* GOVERNOR 3 – slang

¹**guy** *n or n* (to steady or reinforce with) a rope, chain, rod, etc attached to sthg as a brace or guide

²**guy** *n* **1** *often cap* a humorous effigy of a man burnt in Britain on Guy Fawkes Night **2** a man, fellow – *infml*

³**guy** *vt* to make fun of; ridicule

Guy Fawkes Night *n* November 5 observed in Britain with fireworks and bonfires in commemoration of the arrest of Guy Fawkes in 1605 for attempting to blow up the Houses of Parliament

guzzle *vb* **guzzling** to consume (sthg) greedily, continually, or habitually – **guzzler** *n*

gym *n* **1** a gymnasium **2** development of the body by games, exercises, etc, esp in school

gymkhana *n* a sporting event featuring competitions and displays; *specif* a meeting involving competition in horse riding and carriage driving

gymnasium *n, pl* **gymnasiums, gymnasia 1** a large room or separate building used for indoor sports and gymnastic activities **2** a German or Scandinavian secondary school that prepares pupils for university

gymnast *n* sby trained in gymnastics – **gymnastic** *adj*

gymnastics *n pl but sing or pl in constr* **1** physical exercises developing or displaying bodily strength and coordination, often performed in competition **2** an exercise in intellectual or physical dexterity ⟨*verbal* ~⟩

gymnosperm *n* any of a class of woody vascular seed plants (e g conifers) that produce naked seeds not enclosed in an ovary – **gymnospermy** *n*, **gymnospermous** *adj*

¹gymslip *n, chiefly Br* a girl's tunic or pinafore dress that is worn usu with a belt as part of a school uniform

²gymslip *adj, chiefly Br* of a schoolgirl or a girl of school age ⟨*a* ~ *pregnancy*⟩ – infml

gyn-, gyno- *comb form* **1** woman ⟨gyno*cracy*⟩ **2** female reproductive organ; ovary ⟨gyno*phore*⟩; pistil ⟨gyno*ecium*⟩

gynaecology *n* a branch of medicine that deals with diseases and disorders (of the reproductive system) of women – **gynaecologist** *n*, **gynaecologic, gynaecological** *adj*

¹gyp *n* **1** *Br* a college servant at Cambridge university **2** *NAm* **a** a cheat, swindler **b** a fraud, swindle *USE* (2) infml

²gyp *vb* **-pp-** *NAm* to cheat – infml

³gyp *n* sharp pain – chiefly in *give one gyp*; infml

gypsum *n* hydrated calcium sulphate occurring as a mineral and used esp in plaster of paris – **gypseous** *adj*, **gypsiferous** *adj*

gypsy *n, chiefly NAm* a gipsy

gyrate *vb* **1** to revolve round a point or axis **2** to (cause to) move with a circular or spiral motion – **gyrator** *n*, **gyration** *n*, **gyrational** *adj*, **gyratory** *adj*

gyroscope *n* a wheel that is mounted to spin rapidly about an axis and is free to turn in various directions but that maintains constant orientation while spinning in the absence of applied forces – **gyroscopic** *adj*, **gyroscopically** *adv*

H

h *n, pl* **h's, hs** *often cap* **1** (a graphic representation of or device for reproducing) the 8th letter of the English alphabet **2** a speech counterpart of orthographic *h*

ha *interj* – used esp to express surprise, joy, triumph, etc

habeas corpus *n* a judicial writ requiring a detained person to be brought before a court so that the legality of his/her detention may be examined

haberdasher *n* **1** *Br* a dealer in buttons, thread, ribbon, etc used in making clothes **2** *NAm* a dealer in shirts, ties, and other minor articles of menswear

haberdashery *n* **1** goods sold by a haberdasher **2** a haberdasher's shop

habiliment *n* an article of clothing (characteristic of an occupation or occasion) – usu pl; fml

¹habit *n* **1** a costume characteristic of a calling, rank, or function ⟨*riding* ~⟩⟨*monk's* ~⟩ **2** bodily or mental make-up ⟨*a cheerful* ~ *of mind*⟩ **3a** a settled tendency or usual manner of behaviour **b** an acquired pattern or mode of behaviour **4** addiction ⟨*a drug* ~⟩ **5** characteristic mode of growth, occurrence, or appearance (e g of a plant or crystal)

²habit *vt* to clothe, dress – fml

habitable *adj* capable of being lived in – **habitableness** *n*, **habitably** *adv*, **habitability** *n*

habitat *n* **1** the (type of) place where a plant or animal naturally grows or lives **2** HABITATION 2

habitation *n* **1** the act of inhabiting; occupancy **2** a dwelling place; a residence, home

habitual *adj* **1** having the nature of a habit ⟨~ *smoking*⟩ **2** by force of habit ⟨~ *drunkard*⟩ **3** in accordance with habit; customary ⟨*gave his* ~ *end of term speech*⟩ – **habitually** *adv*, **habitualness** *n*

habituate *vt* to make used *to* ~ *vi* to cause habituation

habitué *n* one who frequents a specified place ⟨~ s *of the theatre*⟩

hacienda *n* (the main house of) a large estate or plantation, esp in a Spanish-speaking country

¹hack *vt* **1a** to cut (as if) with repeated irregular or unskilful blows **b** to sever with repeated blows **2** to clear by cutting away vegetation ⟨~ *a path*⟩ **3** to kick (an opposing player or the ball in football) **4** *chiefly NAm* to bear, tolerate – slang ~ *vi* **1** to make cutting blows or rough cuts **2** to cough in a short dry manner ⟨*a* ~ ing *cough*⟩ – **hacker** *n*

²hack *n* **1** a mattock, pick, etc **2** (a wound from) a kick in football **3** a hacking blow

³hack *n* **1** the board on which a falcon's meat is served **2** the state of partial liberty in which a young hawk is kept before training – usu + *at*

⁴hack *n* **1a** a riding horse let out for hire **b** ¹JADE 1 **c** a light easy saddle horse **2** an act of hacking; a ride **3** one who produces mediocre work for financial gain; *esp* a commercial writer **4** *NAm* a taxi

⁵hack *adj* **1** performed by, suited to, or characteristic of a hack ⟨~ *writing*⟩ **2** hackneyed, trite

⁶hack *vb* to ride (a horse) at an ordinary pace, esp over roads – **hacker** *n*

hackle *n* **1** a steel comb with long teeth for dressing flax or hemp **2a** any of the long narrow feathers on the neck of a domestic cock or other bird **b** *pl* the erectile hairs along the neck and back of esp a dog **3** an artificial fishing fly made from a cock's hackles

¹hackney *n* any of an English breed of rather compact English horses with a conspicuously high leg action

²hackney *adj* kept for public hire ⟨*a* ~ *cab*⟩

hackneyed *adj* lacking in freshness or originality; meaningless because used or done too often

hacksaw *n* a fine-toothed saw, esp for cutting metal – **hacksaw** *vt*

had *past of* HAVE

haddock *n, pl* **haddocks**, *esp collectively* **haddock** an important Atlantic food fish, usu smaller than the related common cod

Hades *n* **1** the underground abode of the dead in Greek mythology **2** *often not cap* hell – euph

hadji *n* a hajji

hadn't had not

haem-, haema-, haemo-, *NAm* **hem-, hema-, hemo-** *comb form* blood ⟨haemo*flagellate*⟩ ⟨haemo*philia*⟩

haemoglobin *n* an iron-containing protein that occurs in the red blood cells of vertebrates and is the means of oxygen transport from the lungs to the body tissues – **haemoglobinous** *adj*, **haemoglobinic** *adj*

haemophilia *n* delayed clotting of the blood with consequent difficulty in controlling bleeding even after minor injuries, occurring as a hereditary defect, usu in males – **haemophilic** adj

haemophiliac n or adj (sby) suffering from haemophilia

haemorrhage n a (copious) loss of blood from the blood vessels – **haemorrhage** vi, **haemorrhagic** adj

haemorrhoid n a mass of dilated veins in swollen tissue round or near the anus – usu pl with sing. meaning – **haemorrhoidal** adj

¹haft n the handle of a weapon or tool

²haft vt to fit with a haft

¹hag n 1 a witch 2 an ugly and usu ill-natured old woman – **haggish** adj

²hag n, Scot & NEng (a firm spot in) a bog

¹haggard adj 1 of a hawk not tamed 2 having a worn or emaciated appearance, esp through anxiety or lack of sleep – **haggardly** adv, **haggardness** n

²haggard n an adult hawk caught wild

haggis n a traditionally Scottish dish that consists of the heart, liver, and lungs of a sheep, calf, etc minced with suet, oatmeal, and seasonings and traditionally boiled in the stomach of the animal

haggle vi **haggling** to bargain, wrangle – **haggler** n

hagiography n 1 biography of saints or venerated people 2 idealizing or idolizing biography – **hagiographer** n, **hagiographic** adj, **hagiographical** adj, **hagiographically** adv

¹ha-ha interj – used to express or represent laughter or derision

²ha-ha n a fence or retaining wall sunk into a ditch and used as a boundary (e g of a park or grounds) so as to give an uninterrupted view

haiku n, pl **haiku** (a poem in) an unrhymed Japanese verse form of 3 lines containing 5, 7, and 5 syllables respectively

¹hail n 1 (precipitation in the form of) small particles of clear ice or compacted snow 2 a group of things directed at sby or sthg and intended to cause pain, damage, or distress ⟨a ~ of bullets⟩ ⟨a ~ of obscenities⟩

²hail vi 1 to precipitate hail 2 to pour down or strike like hail

³hail interj 1 – used to express acclamation ⟨~ to the chief – Sir Walter Scott⟩ 2 archaic – used as a salutation

⁴hail vt 1a to salute, greet b to greet with enthusiastic approval; acclaim as 2 to greet or summon by calling ⟨~ a taxi⟩ – vi to call (a greeting to a passing ship) – **hailer** n – **hail from** to be or have been a native or resident of

⁵hail n 1 a call to attract attention 2 hearing distance ⟨stayed within ~⟩ 3 archaic an exclamation of greeting or acclamation

hail-fellow-well-met adj heartily and often excessively informal from the first moment of meeting

hailstone n a pellet of hail

hair n 1a (a structure resembling) a slender threadlike outgrowth on the surface of an animal; esp, (any of) the many usu pigmented hairs that form the characteristic coat of a mammal b the coating of hairs, esp on the human head or other body part 2 haircloth 3 HAIR'S BREADTH ⟨won by a ~⟩ – **hairless** adj, **hairlessness** n, **hairlike** adj

hairbrush n a brush for the hair

haircut n (the result of) cutting and shaping of the hair – **haircutter** n, **haircutting** n

hairdo n, pl **hairdos** a hairstyle

hairdresser n sby whose occupation is cutting, dressing, and styling the hair – **hairdressing** n

haired adj having hair (of a specified kind) ⟨fair-haired⟩

hairgrip n, Br a flat hairpin with prongs that close together

hairline n 1 a very slender line; esp a tiny line or crack on a surface 2 (a fabric with) a design consisting of lengthways or widthways lines usu 1 thread wide 3 the line above the forehead beyond which hair grows – **hairline** adj

hairpiece n a section of false hair worn to enhance a hairstyle or make a person's natural hair seem thicker or more plentiful

¹hairpin n 1 a 2-pronged U-shaped pin of thin wire for holding the hair in place 2 a sharp bend in a road

²hairpin adj having the shape of a hairpin ⟨a ~ bend⟩

hair-raising adj causing terror or astonishment – **hair-raisingly** adv

hair's breadth n a very small distance or margin

hair shirt n a rough shirt worn next to the skin as a penance

hair-slide n, Br a (decorative) clip for the hair

hairsplitting n argument over unimportant differences and points of detail; quibbling – **hairsplitting** adj, **hairsplitter** n

hairspring n a slender spiral spring that regulates the motion of the balance wheel of a timepiece

hair-trigger adj immediately responsive to or disrupted by the slightest stimulus ⟨a ~ temper⟩

hair trigger n a trigger so adjusted that very slight pressure will fire the gun

hairy adj 1 covered with (material like) hair 2 made of or resembling hair 3 frighteningly dangerous ⟨a ~ crossing through mountainous waves⟩ – infml – **hairiness** n

hajji, hadji n one who has made a pilgrimage to Mecca – used as a title

hake n, pl **hakes**, esp collectively **hake** any of several marine food fishes related to the common Atlantic cod

halberd n a long-handled weapon combining a spear and battle-axe, used esp in the 15th and 16th c – **halberdier** n

¹halcyon n, a kingfisher – poetic

²halcyon adj calm, peaceful – esp in halcyon days

hale adj free from defect, disease, or infirmity; sound ⟨a ~ and hearty old man⟩

¹half n, pl **halves** 1a either of 2 equal parts into which sthg is divisible; also a part of a thing approximately equal to a half b half an hour – used in designation of time 2 either of a pair: e g a a partner ⟨my other ~⟩ b a school term – used esp at some British public schools 3 sthg of (approximately) half the value or quantity: e g a half a pint b a child's ticket c HALFPENNY 1 – **and a half** of remarkable quality – infml ⟨that was a party and a half⟩ – **by half** by a great deal – **by halves** half heartedly – **in half** into 2 (nearly) equal parts

²half adj 1a being one of 2 equal parts ⟨a ~ share⟩ ⟨~ a dozen⟩ b(1) amounting to approximately half ⟨~ the class⟩ ⟨a ~ mile⟩ ⟨~ my life⟩ (2) falling short of the full or complete thing ⟨~ measures⟩ ⟨a ~ smile⟩ 2 extending over or covering only half ⟨a ~ door⟩ ⟨~ sleeves⟩ 3 Br half past ⟨~ seven⟩ – **halfness** n

³half adv 1 in an equal part or degree ⟨she was ~ crying, ~ laughing⟩ 2 nearly but not completely ⟨~ cooked⟩ ⟨half-remembered stories from her childhood⟩ – **half as much again** one-and-a-half times as much

half-a-crown n HALF CROWN

half a dozen n a set of 6; also several

halfback n a player in rugby, soccer, hockey, etc positioned immediately behind the forward line – **halfback** adj

half-baked adj marked by or showing a lack of forethought or judgment; foolish ⟨*a ~ scheme for making money*⟩

half-breed *n* the offspring of parents of different races – **half-breed** *adj*

half brother *n* a brother related through 1 parent only

half-caste *n* a half-breed – **half-caste** *adj*

half cock *n* **1** the position of the hammer of a firearm when about half retracted and held by the safety catch so that it cannot be operated by a pull on the trigger **2** a state of inadequate preparation – esp in *go off at half cock*

half-cocked *adj* lacking adequate preparation or forethought

half crown *n* (a former British silver coin worth) 2 shillings and sixpence

half-hardy *adj, of a plant* able to withstand a moderately low temperature but injured by severe frost

halfhearted *adj* lacking enthusiasm or effort ⟨*~ attempts to start a conversation*⟩ – **halfheartedly** *adv*, **halfheartedness** *n*

half-holiday *n* a holiday of half a day, esp an afternoon

half-length *n* a portrait showing only the upper half of the body

half-mast *n* the position of a flag lowered halfway down the staff as a mark of mourning

half-moon *n* (sthg shaped like) the figure of the moon when half its disc is illuminated – **half-moon** *adj*

half nelson *n* a wrestling hold in which one arm is thrust under the corresponding arm of an opponent and the hand placed on the back of the opponent's neck

half note *n, NAm* a minim

halfpenny *n* **1** (a British bronze coin representing) one half of a penny **2** a small amount – **halfpenny** *adj*

halfpennyworth *n* as much as can be bought for 1 halfpenny; *broadly* a small amount

half sister *n* a sister related through 1 parent only

half term *n, chiefly Br* (a short holiday taken at) a period about halfway through a school term

half-timbered *adj* constructed of timber framework with spaces filled in by brickwork or plaster – **half-timbering** *n*

halftime *n* (an intermission marking) the completion of half of a game or contest

halftone *n* **1** any of the shades of grey between the darkest and the lightest parts of a photographic image **2** a photoengraving made from an image photographed through a screen and then etched so that the details of the image are reproduced in dots – **halftone** *adj*

half-track *n* (a vehicle with) a drive system of an endless chain or track at the back and wheels at the front – **half-track, half-tracked** *adj*

half-volley *n* **1** a shot in tennis made at a ball just after it has bounced **2** an easily-hit delivery of the ball in cricket that bounces closer than intended to the batsman

halfway *adj or adv* **1** midway between 2 points **2** (done or formed) partially – **halfway** *adv*

half-wit *n* a foolish or mentally deficient person – derog – **half-witted** *adj*, **half-wittedness** *n*

halibut *n, pl* **halibuts**, *esp collectively* **halibut** a large marine food flatfish

halitosis *n* (a condition of having) offensively smelling breath – **halitotic** *adj*

hall *n* **1a** the house of a medieval king or noble **b** the chief living room in a medieval house or castle **2** the manor house of a landed proprietor **3a** a building used by a college or university for some special purpose ⟨*a ~ of residence*⟩ **b** (a division of) a college at some universities **c** (a meal served in) the common dining room of an English college **4** the entrance room or passage of a

building **5** a large room for public assembly or entertainment **6** *NAm* a corridor or passage in a building

hallelujah *n or interj* (a shout, song, etc) used to express praise, joy, or thanks

halliard *n* a halyard

¹hallmark *n* **1** an official mark stamped on gold and silver articles in Britain after an assay test to testify to their purity **2** a distinguishing characteristic or object ⟨*the dramatic speeches which are the ~ of a barrister*⟩

²hallmark *vt* to stamp with a hallmark

¹hallo, halloa *vb, interj, or n* **halloing; hallooed; halloaing; halloaed; *pl* hallos; halloas** (to) hollo

²hallo *n or interj, pl* **hallos** *chiefly Br* (a) hello

hallow *vt* **1** to make holy or set apart for holy use **2** to respect and honour greatly; venerate

Halloween, Hallowe'en *n* October 31, the eve of All Saints' Day, observed by dressing up in disguise, party turns, etc

hallstand *n* a piece of furniture with pegs for holding coats, hats, and umbrellas

hallucinate *vt* to perceive or experience as a hallucination *~vi* to have hallucinations

hallucination *n* **1** the perception of sthg apparently real to the perceiver but which has no objective reality, *also* the image, object, etc perceived **2** a completely unfounded or mistaken impression or belief – **hallucinational** *adj*, **hallucinative** *adj*

hallucinatory *adj* **1** tending to produce hallucination ⟨*~ drugs*⟩ **2** resembling or being a hallucination

hallucinogen *n* a substance (e g LSD) that induces hallucinations – **hallucinogenic** *adj*

hallway *n* an entrance hall or corridor

¹halo *n, pl* **halos, haloes** **1** a circle of light appearing to surround the sun or moon and resulting from refraction or reflection of light by ice particles in the earth's atmosphere **2a** NIMBUS 1, 2 **b** a differentiated zone surrounding a central object **3** the aura of glory or veneration surrounding an idealized person or thing

²halo *vt* **haloing; haloed** to form into or surround with a halo

halogen *n* any of the 5 elements fluorine, chlorine, bromine, iodine, and astatine that form part of group VII A of the periodic table – **halogenate** *vt*, **halogenation** *n*, **halogenous** *adj*

¹halt *adj, archaic* lame

²halt *vi* **1** to hesitate between alternative courses; waver **2** to display weakness or imperfection (e g in speech or reasoning); falter

³halt *n* **1** a (temporary) stop or interruption **2** *Br* a railway stopping place, without normal station facilities, for local trains

⁴halt *vi* to come to a halt *~ vt* **1** to bring to a stop ⟨*the strike has ~ed tubes and buses*⟩ **2** to cause to stop; end ⟨*~ the slaughter of seals*⟩

¹halter *n* **1a** a rope or strap for leading or tying an animal **b** a band round an animal's head to which a lead may be attached **2** a noose for hanging criminals

²halter *vt* to put a halter on or catch (as if) with a halter

halter neck *n* (a garment having) a neckline formed by a strap passing from the front of a garment round the neck and leaving the shoulders and upper back bare

halting *adj* hesitant, faltering ⟨*the witness spoke in a ~ manner*⟩ – **haltingly** *adv*

halve *vt* **1a** to divide into 2 equal parts **b** to reduce to a half ⟨halving *the present cost*⟩ **2** to play (e g a hole or match in golf) in the same number of strokes as one's opponent

¹halves *pl of* HALF

²halves *adv* with equal half shares ⟨*let's go* ~⟩

halyard, halliard *n* a rope or tackle for hoisting or lowering

¹ham *n* **1** a buttock with its associated thigh – usu pl **2** (the meat of) the rear end of a bacon pig, esp the thigh, when removed from the carcass before curing with salt **3a** an inexpert but showy performer; *also* an actor performing in an exaggerated theatrical style **b** an operator of an amateur radio station – **ham** *adj*

²ham *vb* **-mm-** *vt* to execute with exaggerated speech or gestures; overact ~ *vi* to overplay a part

hamadryad *n* **1** a dryad **2a** KING COBRA **b** a baboon worshipped by the ancient Egyptians

hamburger *n* a round flat cake of minced beef; *also* a sandwich of a fried hamburger in a bread roll

ham-fisted *adj, chiefly Br* lacking dexterity with the hands; clumsy – infml

hamlet *n* a small village

¹hammer *n* **1a** a hand tool that consists of a solid head set crosswise on a handle and is used to strike a blow (e g to drive in a nail) **b** a power tool that substitutes a metal block or a drill for the hammerhead **2a** a lever with a striking head for ringing a bell or striking a gong **b** the part of the mechanism of a modern gun whose action ignites the cartridge **c** the malleus **d** a gavel **e**(1) a padded mallet in a piano action for striking a string (2) a hand mallet for playing various percussion instruments **3** (an athletic field event using) a metal sphere weighing 16lb (about 7.3kg) attached by a wire to a handle and thrown for distance – **under the hammer** for sale at auction

²hammer *vi* **1** to strike blows, esp repeatedly, (as if) with a hammer; pound **2** to make repeated efforts *at*; *esp* to reiterate an opinion or attitude ⟨*the lectures all* ~ed *away at the same points*⟩ ~ *vt* **1** to beat, drive, or shape (as if) with repeated blows of a hammer **2** to force as if by hitting repeatedly ⟨*wanted to* ~ *him into submission*⟩ **3** to declare formally that (a member of the Stock Exchange) is insolvent and is therefore forbidden to trade **4** to beat decisively – infml ⟨*we* ~ed *them at football*⟩ – **hammerer** *n* – **hammer into** to cause (sby) to learn or remember (sthg) by continual repetition

hammer and sickle *n* an emblem consisting of a crossed hammer and sickle used chiefly as a symbol of Communism

hammer out *vt* to produce or bring about through lengthy discussion ⟨hammered out *a new policy*⟩

hammock *n* a hanging bed, usu made of netting or canvas and suspended by cords at each end

¹hamper *vt* **1** to restrict the movement or operation of by bonds or obstacles; hinder **2** to interfere with; encumber

²hamper *n* a large basket with a cover for packing, storing, or transporting crockery, food, etc ⟨*picnic* ~⟩

hamster *n* any of numerous small Old World rodents with very large cheek pouches

¹hamstring *n* **1** either of 2 groups of tendons at the back of the human knee **2** a large tendon above and behind the hock of a quadruped

²hamstring *vt* **hamstrung 1** to cripple by cutting the leg tendons **2** to make ineffective or powerless; cripple

¹hand *n* **1a** (the segment of the forelimb of vertebrate animals corresponding to) the end of the forelimb of human beings, monkeys, etc when modified as a grasping organ **b** a part (e g the chela of a crustacean) serving the function of or resembling a hand **c** sthg resembling a hand: e g (1) a stylized figure of a hand used as a pointer or marker (2) a group of usu large leaves (e g of tobacco) reaped or tied together or of bananas growing together **d** a forehock of pork **e** an indicator or pointer on a dial **2a**

possession – usu pl with sing. meaning ⟨*the documents fell into the* ~s *of the enemy*⟩ **b** control, supervision – usu pl with sing. meaning ⟨*I'll leave the matter in your capable* ~s⟩ **3a** a side, direction ⟨*men fighting on either* ~⟩ **b** either of 2 sides or aspects of an issue or argument ⟨*on the one* ~ *we can appeal for peace, on the other declare war*⟩ **4** a pledge, esp of betrothal or marriage **5** handwriting **6a** skill, ability ⟨*tried her* ~ *at sailing*⟩ **b** an instrumental part ⟨*had a* ~ *in the crime*⟩ **7** a unit of measure equal to 4in (about 102mm) used esp for the height of a horse **8a** assistance or aid, esp when involving physical effort ⟨*lend a* ~⟩ **b** a round of applause **9a** (the cards or pieces held by) a player in a card or board game **b** a single round in a game **c** the force or solidity of one's position (e g in negotiations) **d** a turn to serve in a game (e g squash) in which only the server may score points and which lasts as long as the server can win points **10a** one who performs or executes a particular work ⟨*2 portraits by the same* ~⟩ **b** a worker, employee ⟨*employed over 100* ~s⟩; *esp* one employed at manual labour or general tasks ⟨*a field* ~⟩ **c** a member of a ship's crew ⟨*all* ~s *on deck*⟩ **d** one skilled in a particular action or pursuit ⟨*she's an old* ~ *at this job*⟩ **11a** handiwork **b** style of execution; workmanship ⟨*the* ~ *of a master*⟩ – **at hand** near in time or place – **at the hands of, at the hand of** by the act or instrumentality of – **by hand** with the hands, usu as opposed to mechanically – **in hand 1** not used up or lost and at one's disposal ⟨*they have a game in hand*⟩ **2** of a horse being led rather than being ridden **3** UNDER WAY ⟨*put the work in hand*⟩ – **off one's hands** out of one's care or charge – **on hand 1** ready to use **2** in attendance; present – **on one's hands** in one's possession, care, or management – **out of hand 1** without delay; without reflection or consideration ⟨*refused it* out of hand⟩ **2** out of control ⟨*that child has got quite* out of hand⟩ – **to hand** available and ready for use; *esp* within reach

²hand *vt* **1** to lead or assist with the hand ⟨*he* ~ed *her out of the car*⟩ **2** to give or pass (as if) with the hand ⟨*~ a letter to her*⟩ – **hand it to** to give credit to

handbag *n* a bag designed for carrying small personal articles and money, carried usu by women

handball *n* **1** (the small rubber ball used in) a game resembling fives and played in a walled court or against a single wall **2** an amateur indoor or outdoor game between 2 teams of 7 or 11 players whose object is to direct a soccer ball into the opponent's goal by throwing and catching

handbarrow *n* a flat rectangular frame with handles at both ends for carrying loads

handbill *n* a small printed sheet to be distributed (e g for advertising) by hand

handbook *n* a short reference book, esp on a particular subject

handcuff *vt* to apply handcuffs to; manacle

handcuffs *n pl* a pair of metal rings, usu connected by a chain or bar, for locking round prisoners' wrists

hand down *vt* **1** to transmit in succession (e g from father to son); bequeath **2** to give (an outgrown article of clothing) to a younger member of one's family **3** to deliver in court ⟨hand down *a judgment*⟩

-handed *comb form* (*adj* → *adj*) having or using a specified (kind of) hand or (number of) hands ⟨*a large*-handed *man*⟩ ⟨*right*-handed⟩ – **hander** *comb form* (*adj* → *n*)

handful *n, pl* **handfuls** *also* **handsful 1** as much or as many as the hand will grasp **2** a small quantity or number **3** sby or sthg (e g a child or animal) that is difficult to control – infml ⟨*that boy is a real* ~⟩

handgun *n* a firearm held and fired with 1 hand

handhold *n* sthg to hold on to for support (e g in mountain climbing)

¹**handicap** *n* **1** (a race or contest with) an artificial advantage or disadvantage given to contestants so that all have a more equal chance of winning **2** a (physical) disability or disadvantage that makes achievement unusually difficult

²**handicap** *vt* **-pp- 1** to assign handicaps to; impose handicaps on **2** to put at a disadvantage

handicraft *n* **1** (an occupation requiring) manual skill **2** articles fashioned by handicraft – **handicrafter** *n*

handiwork *n* **1** (the product of) work done by the hands **2** work done personally

handkerchief *n, pl* **handkerchiefs** *also* **handkerchieves** a small piece of cloth used for various usu personal purposes (e g blowing the nose or wiping the eyes) or as a clothing accessory

¹**handle** *n* **1** a part that is designed to be grasped by the hand **2** the feel of a textile **3** a title; *also* an esp aristocratic or double-barrelled name – *infml* – **handled** *adj*, **handleless** *adj* – **off the handle** into a state of sudden and violent anger

²**handle** *vb* **handling** *vt* **1a** to try or examine (e g by touching or moving) with the hand ⟨~ *silk to judge its weight*⟩ **b** to manage with the hands ⟨~ *a horse*⟩ **2a** to deal with (e g a subject or idea) in speech or writing, or as a work of art **b** to manage, direct ⟨*a solicitor* ~s *all my affairs*⟩ **3** to deal with, act on, or dispose of ⟨~d *the clients very well*⟩ **4** to engage in the buying, selling, or distributing of (a commodity) ~ *vi* to respond to controlling movements in a specified way ⟨*car that* ~s *well*⟩ – **handleable** *adj*

handlebar *n* a bar, esp on a cycle or scooter, for steering – often pl with sing. meaning

handler *n* one who is in immediate physical charge of an animal ⟨*a police dog* ~⟩

handmade *adj* made by hand rather than by machine

handmaiden *n* a personal maid or female servant

hand-me-down *n* a reach-me-down

hand on *vt* HAND DOWN

handout *n* **1** sthg (e g food, clothing, or money) distributed free, esp to people in need **2** a folder or circular of information for free distribution

hand-out *n* a player (e g in squash or badminton) who is not hand-in

hand out *vt* **1** to give freely or without charge **2** to administer ⟨hand out *a severe punishment*⟩

hand over *vb* to yield control or possession (of)

handpick *vt* **1** to pick by hand rather than by machine **2** to select personally and carefully

handrail *n* a narrow rail for grasping with the hand as a support, esp near stairs

handshake *n* a clasping and shaking of each other's usu right hand by 2 people (e g in greeting or farewell)

handsome *adj* **1** considerable, sizable ⟨*a painting that commanded a* ~ *price*⟩ **2** marked by graciousness or generosity; liberal ⟨~ *contributions to charity*⟩ **3a** *of a man* having a pleasing appearance; good-looking **b** *of a woman* attractive in a dignified statuesque way **4** *NAm* marked by skill or cleverness; adroit – **handsomely** *adv*, **handsomeness** *n*

handstand *n* an act of supporting and balancing the body on only the hands with the legs in the air

hand-to-hand *adj* involving physical contact; very close ⟨~ *fighting*⟩ – **hand to hand** *adv*

hand-to-mouth *adj* having or providing only just enough to live on; precarious ⟨*a* ~ *existence*⟩

handwork *n* work done with the hands and not by machine – **handworker** *n*

handwriting *n* writing done by hand; *esp* the style of writing peculiar to a particular person

handy *adj* **1a** convenient for use; useful **b** *of a vessel or vehicle* easily handled **2** clever in using the hands, esp in a variety of practical ways **3** conveniently near – *infml* – **handily** *adv*, **handiness** *n*

handyman *n* **1** sby who does odd jobs **2** sby competent in a variety of skills or repair work

¹**hang** *vb* **hung**, (1b) **hanged** *vt* **1a** to fasten to some elevated point by the top so that the lower part is free; suspend **b** to suspend by the neck until dead – often used as a mild oath ⟨*I'll be* ~ed⟩ **c** to fasten on a point of suspension so as to allow free motion within given limits ⟨~ *a door*⟩ ⟨~ *a pendulum*⟩ **d** to suspend (meat, esp game) before cooking to make the flesh tender and develop the flavour **2** to decorate, furnish, or cover by hanging sthg up (e g flags or bunting) ⟨*a room* hung *with tapestries*⟩ **3** to hold or bear in a suspended or inclined position ⟨hung *his head in shame*⟩ **4** to fasten (sthg, esp wallpaper) to a wall (e g with paste) **5** to display (pictures) in a gallery ~ *vi* **1a** to remain fastened at the top so that the lower part is free; dangle **b** to die by hanging **2** to remain poised or stationary in the air **3** to stay on; persist ⟨*the smell of the explosion* hung *in the afternoon air*⟩ **4** to be imminent; impend ⟨*doom* hung *over the nation*⟩ **5** to fall or droop from a usu tense or taut position ⟨*his mouth* hung *open*⟩ **6** to depend ⟨*election* ~s *on one vote*⟩ **7** to lean, incline, or jut over or downwards **8** to fall in flowing lines ⟨*the coat* ~s *well*⟩ – **hangable** *adj* – **hang fire 1** to be slow in the explosion of a charge after its primer has been discharged **2** to be delayed or held up – **hang in the balance** to be uncertain or at stake – **hang on 1** to pay close attention to ⟨hangs on *her every word*⟩ **2** to depend ⟨*the success of the whole enterprise* hangs on *your cooperation*⟩ **3** to be burdensome or oppressive ⟨*time* hangs on *his hands*⟩

²**hang** *n* **1** the manner in which a thing hangs **2** a downward slope; *also* a droop **3** the special method of doing, using, or dealing with sthg; the knack – chiefly in *get the hang of* **4** *Austr & NZ* an impressive amount ⟨*they got down in a* ~ *of a hurry* – Frank Sargeson⟩

hang about *vi, Br* **1** to wait or stay, usu without purpose or activity **2** to delay or move slowly *USE* infml

hangar *n* a shed; *esp* a large shed for housing aircraft

hang around *vi* HANG ABOUT 1

hang back *vi* to be reluctant to move or act; hesitate

hangdog *adj* ashamed; *also* abject

¹**hanger** *n* a wood growing on a steeply sloping hillside

²**hanger** *n* a device (e g a loop or strap) by which or to which sthg is hung or hangs; *esp* a hook and crosspiece to fit inside the shoulders of a dress, coat, etc to keep the shape of the garment when hung up

hanger-on *n, pl* **hangers-on** one who attempts to associate with a person, group, etc, esp for personal gain; a dependant

hang-glider *n* (sby who flies) a glider that resembles a kite and is controlled by the body movements of the harnessed person suspended beneath it – **hang-glide** *vi*

¹**hanging** *n* **1** (an) execution by suspension from a noose **2a** a curtain **b** a covering (e g a tapestry) for a wall

²**hanging** *adj* **1** situated or lying on steeply sloping ground ⟨~ *gardens*⟩ **2** jutting out; overhanging ⟨*a* ~ *rock*⟩ **3** adapted for sustaining a hanging object ⟨*a* ~ *rail*⟩ **4** deserving or liable to inflict hanging ⟨*a* ~ *matter*⟩ ⟨*a* ~ *judge*⟩

hangman *n* one who hangs a condemned person; a public executioner

hangnail *n* a bit of skin hanging loose at the side or root of a fingernail

hang on *vi* **1** to keep hold; hold onto sthg **2** to persist tenaciously ⟨*a cold that* hung on *all spring*⟩ **3** to wait for a short time ⟨hang on *a second*⟩ **4** to remain on the telephone ⟨*could you* hang on *please and I'll connect you*⟩ – **hang on to** to hold or keep tenaciously ⟨*learned to* hang on to *his money*⟩

hangout *n* a place where one is often to be seen – slang

hang out *vi* **1** to protrude, esp downwards **2** to live or spend much time – slang ⟨*the kids* hang out *on street corners*⟩

hangover *n* **1** sthg (e g a custom) that remains from the past **2** the disagreeable physical effects following heavy consumption of alcohol or use of other drugs

hang-up *n* a source of mental or emotional difficulty – infml

hang up *vt* **1** to place on a hook or hanger ⟨*told the child to* hang up *his coat*⟩ **2** to delay, suspend ⟨*the negotiations were* hung up *for a week*⟩ ~ *vi* to terminate a telephone conversation, often abruptly

hank *n* **1** a coil, loop; *specif* a coiled or looped bundle (e g of yarn, rope, or wire) usu containing a definite length **2** a ring attaching a jib or staysail to a stay

hanker *vi* to desire strongly or persistently – usu + *after* or *for* – **hankering** *n*

hankie, hanky *n* a handkerchief – infml

hanky-panky *n* mildly improper or deceitful behaviour – infml

Hansard *n* the official report of Parliamentary proceedings

hansom, hansom cab *n* a light 2-wheeled covered carriage with the driver's seat high up at the back

haphazard *adj* marked by lack of plan or order; aimless – **haphazard** *adv*, **haphazardly** *adv*, **haphazardness** *n*

hapless *adj* having no luck; unfortunate – **haplessly** *adv*, **haplessness** *n*

hap'orth, ha'porth, ha'p'orth *n* a halfpennyworth ⟨*doesn't make a* ~ *of difference*⟩

happen *vi* **happening 1** to occur by chance – often + *it* ⟨*it so* ~ s *I'm going your way*⟩ **2** to come into being as an event; occur **3** to have the luck or fortune *to*; chance ⟨*he* ~ ed *to overhear the plotters*⟩ – **happen on/upon** to see or meet (sthg or sby) by chance ⟨happened upon *an old acquaintance last week*⟩

happening *n* **1** sthg that happens; an occurrence **2a** the creation or presentation of a nonobjective work of art (e g an action painting) **b** a usu unscripted or improvised often multimedia public performance in which the audience participates

happily *adv* **1** by good fortune; luckily ⟨~, *he never knew*⟩ **2** in a happy manner or state ⟨*lived* ~ *ever after*⟩ **3** in an adequate or fitting manner; successfully ⟨*white wine goes* ~ *with fish*⟩

happy *adj* **1** favoured by luck or fortune; fortunate **2** well adapted or fitting; felicitous ⟨*a* ~ *choice*⟩ **3a** enjoying or expressing pleasure and contentment **b** glad, pleased ⟨*I was very* ~ *to hear from you*⟩ **4** characterized by a dazed irresponsible state – usu in combination ⟨*a punch*-happy *boxer*⟩ **5** impulsively quick or overinclined to use sthg – usu in combination ⟨*trigger*-happy⟩ **6** having or marked by an atmosphere of good fellowship; friendly **7** satisfied as to the fact; confident, sure ⟨*we're now quite* ~ *that the murder occurred at about 5.30*⟩ **8** tipsy – euph – **happiness** *n*

happy-go-lucky *adj* blithely unconcerned; carefree

hara-kiri *n* suicide by ritual disembowelment practised by the Japanese samurai, esp when disgraced or found guilty of a crime carrying the death penalty for commoners

¹harangue *n* **1** a speech addressed to a public assembly **2** a lengthy, ranting, and usu censorious speech or piece of writing

²harangue *vb* to make or address in a harangue

harass *vt* **1** to worry and impede by repeated raids ⟨~ ed *the enemy*⟩ **2** to annoy or worry persistently – **harasser** *n*, **harassment** *n*

harbinger *n* **1** one who pioneers or initiates a major change; a precursor **2** sthg that presages or foreshadows what is to come – **harbinger** *vt*

¹harbour, NAm chiefly harbor *n* **1** a place of security and comfort; a refuge **2** a part of a body of water providing protection and anchorage for ships ⟨*the ship came into* ~⟩

²harbour, NAm chiefly harbor *vt* **1** to give shelter or refuge to **2** to be the home or habitat of; contain ⟨*these cracks can* ~ *dangerous bacteria*⟩ **3** to have or keep (e g thoughts or feelings) in the mind ⟨~ ed *a grudge*⟩ ~ *vi* to take shelter (as if) in a harbour

¹hard *adj* **1** not easily penetrated or yielding to pressure; firm **2a** *of alcoholic drink* having a high percentage of alcohol **b** *of water* containing salts of calcium, magnesium, etc that inhibit lathering with soap **3a** of or being radiation of relatively high penetrating power ⟨~ *X rays*⟩ **b** having or producing relatively great photographic contrast ⟨*a* ~ *negative*⟩ **4a** metal as distinct from paper ⟨~ *money*⟩ **b** *of currency* stable in value; *also* soundly backed and readily convertible into foreign currencies without large discounts **c** being high and firm ⟨~ *prices*⟩ available to borrowers in limited supply and at high interest rates **5** firmly and closely twisted ⟨~ *yarns*⟩ **6a** physically fit or resistant to stress ⟨*the* ~ *men ran 100mi a week*⟩ **b** free of weakness or defects **7a**(1) firm, definite ⟨*reached a* ~ *agreement*⟩ (2) not speculative or conjectural; factual ⟨~ *evidence*⟩ **b** close, searching ⟨*gave a* ~ *look*⟩ **8a**(1) difficult to endure ⟨~ *times*⟩ (2) oppressive, inequitable ⟨*indirect taxes are* ~ *on the poor*⟩ **b** lacking consideration or compassion; ⟨*a* ~ *heart*⟩ **c**(1) harsh, severe ⟨*said some* ~ *things*⟩ (2) resentful ⟨~ *feelings*⟩ **d** inclement ⟨~ *winter*⟩ **e**(1) forceful, violent ⟨~ *blows*⟩ (2) demanding energy or stamina ⟨~ *work*⟩ (3) using or performing with great energy or effort ⟨*a* ~ *worker*⟩ **9a** sharply defined; stark ⟨*a* ~ *outline*⟩ **b** *of c and g* pronounced /k/ and /g/ respectively – not used technically **10a** difficult to do, understand, or explain ⟨~ *problems*⟩ **b** having difficulty in doing sthg ⟨~ *of hearing*⟩ **c** difficult to magnetize or demagnetize **11a** *of a drug* addictive and gravely detrimental to health ⟨*such* ~ *drugs as heroin*⟩ **b** *of pornography* HARD-CORE 2 **12** PERSISTENT 2b – **hardness** *n*

²hard *adv* **1a** with great or maximum effort or energy; strenuously ⟨*were* ~ *at work*⟩ **b** in a violent manner; fiercely **c** to the full extent – used in nautical directions ⟨*steer* ~ *aport*⟩ **d** in a searching or concentrated manner ⟨*stared* ~ *at him*⟩ **2a** in such a manner as to cause hardship, difficulty, or pain; severely **b** with bitterness or grief ⟨*took his defeat* ~⟩ **3** in a firm manner; tightly **4** to the point of hardness ⟨*the water froze* ~⟩ **5** close in time or space ⟨*the house stood* ~ *by the river*⟩ – **hard done by** unfairly treated

³hard *n, chiefly Br* a firm usu artificial foreshore or landing place

hard-and-fast *adj* fixed, strict ⟨*a* ~ *rule*⟩

hardback *n* a book bound in stiff covers – **hardback** *adj*

hard-bitten *adj* steeled by difficult experience; tough

hardboard *n* (a) composition board made by compressing shredded wood chips

hard-boiled *adj* devoid of sentimentality; tough

hard cash *n* money in the form of coin or bank notes as opposed to cheques or credit

hardcore *n*, *Br* compacted rubble or clinker used esp as a foundation for roads, paving, or floors

hard-core *adj* **1** of or constituting a hard core ⟨~ *Conservative supporters*⟩ **2** *of pornography* extremely explicit; *specif* showing real rather than simulated sexual acts

hard core *n sing or pl in constr* the unyielding or uncompromising members that form the nucleus of a group

harden *vt* **1** to make hard or harder **2** to confirm in disposition, feelings, or action; *esp* to make callous ⟨~ ed *his heart*⟩ **3a** to toughen, inure ⟨~ *troops*⟩ **b** to inure (e g plants) to cold or other unfavourable environmental conditions – often + *off* **4** to protect from blast or heat ⟨~ *a missile emplacement*⟩ ~ *vi* **1** to become hard or harder **2a** to become confirmed or strengthened ⟨*opposition began to* ~⟩ **b** to assume an appearance of harshness ⟨*her face* ~ ed *at the word*⟩ **3** to become higher or less subject to fluctuations downwards ⟨*prices* ~ ed *quickly*⟩ – **hardener** *n*

hardheaded *adj* **1** stubborn **2** sober, realistic ⟨~ *common sense*⟩ – **hardheadedly** *adv*, **hardheadedness** *n*

hardhearted *adj* lacking in sympathetic understanding; unfeeling – **hardheartedly** *adv*, **hardheartedness** *n*

hard labour *n* compulsory labour as part of prison discipline

hard-line *adj* advocating or involving a persistently firm course of action; unyielding ⟨*a* ~ *policy on unemployment*⟩ – **hard-liner** *n*

hard luck *n*, *chiefly Br* bad luck – often used as an interjection expressing mild sympathy

hardly *adv* **1** in a severe manner; harshly **2** with difficulty; painfully **3** only just; barely ⟨*I* ~ *knew her*⟩ **4** scarcely ⟨*that news is* ~ *surprising*⟩

hard-nosed *adj* **1** hard-bitten, stubborn **2** HARDHEADED **2** ⟨~ *budgeting*⟩

hard-of-hearing *adj* partially deaf

hard palate *n* the bony front part of the palate forming the roof of the mouth

hard sell *n* aggressive high-pressure salesmanship

hardship *n* (an instance of) suffering, privation

hard shoulder *n* either of 2 surfaced strips of land along a road, esp a motorway, on which stopping is allowed only in an emergency

hardtack *n* SHIP'S BISCUIT

hardtop *n* a motor car with a rigid top

hard up *adj* short of sthg, esp money ⟨*I'm very* ~ *for summer clothes*⟩ – infml

hardware *n* **1** items sold by an ironmonger **2** the physical components (e g electronic and electrical devices) of a vehicle (e g a spacecraft) or an apparatus (e g a computer) **3** tape recorders, closed-circuit television, etc used as instructional equipment

hardwearing *adj* durable

hardwood *n* (the wood of) a broad-leaved as distinguished from a coniferous tree – **hardwood** *adj*

hardy *adj* **1** bold, audacious **2a** inured to fatigue or hardships; robust **b** capable of withstanding adverse conditions; *esp* capable of living outdoors over winter without artificial protection ⟨~ *plants*⟩ – **hardiness** *n*

¹hare *n*, *pl* **hares**, *esp collectively* **hare** **1** any of various swift timid long-eared mammals like large rabbits with long hind legs **2** a figure of a hare moved mechanically along a dog track for the dogs to chase

²hare *vi* to run fast – infml

hare and hounds *n* PAPER CHASE

harebell *n* a slender plant with blue bell-shaped flowers that grows esp on heaths and in open woodlands

harebrained *adj* flighty, foolish – infml

harelip *n* a split in the upper lip like that of a hare occurring as a congenital deformity – **harelipped** *adj*

harem *n* **1a** a usu secluded (part of a) house allotted to women in a Muslim household **b** *sing or pl in constr* the women occupying a harem **2** a group of females associated with 1 male – used with reference to polygamous animals

haricot, haricot bean *n* FRENCH BEAN

hark *vi* to listen closely

hark back *vi* to return *to* an earlier topic or circumstance

harlequin *n* **1a** *cap* a stock character in comedy and pantomime **b** a buffoon **2** a variegated pattern (e g of a textile)

harlequinade *n* a part of a play or pantomime in which Harlequin has a leading role

harlot *n*, *archaic* a woman prostitute – **harlotry** *n*

¹harm *n* **1** physical or mental damage; injury **2** mischief, wrong – **harmful** *adj*, **harmfully** *adv*, **harmfulness** *n* – **out of harm's way** safe from danger

²harm *vt* to cause harm to

harmless *adj* **1** free from harm, liability, or loss **2** lacking capacity or intent to injure – **harmlessly** *adv*, **harmlessness** *n*

¹harmonic *adj* **1** of musical harmony, a harmonic, or harmonics **2** pleasing to the ear; harmonious **3** expressible in terms of sine or cosine functions ⟨~ *function*⟩ – **harmonically** *adv*, **harmonicalness** *n*

²harmonic *n* **1a** a tone in a harmonic series **b** a flutelike tone produced on a stringed instrument by touching a vibrating string at a point (e g the midpoint) which divides it into halves, thirds, etc **2** a component frequency of a harmonic motion that is an integral multiple of the fundamental frequency

harmonica *n* a small rectangular wind instrument with free reeds recessed in air slots from which notes are sounded by breathing out and in

harmonious *adj* **1** musically concordant **2** having the parts arranged so as to produce a pleasing effect ⟨*the patterns blended into a* ~ *whole*⟩ **3** marked by agreement – **harmoniously** *adv*, **harmoniousness** *n*

harmonium *n* a reed organ in which pedals operate a bellows that forces air through free reeds

harmonize, -ise *vi* **1** to be in harmony **2** to play or sing in harmony ~ *vt* **1** to bring into consonance or accord **2** to provide or accompany with harmony – **harmonizer** *n*, **harmonization** *n*

harmony *n* **1a** the (pleasant-sounding) combination of simultaneous musical notes in a chord **b** (the science of) the structure of music with respect to the composition and progression of chords **2a** pleasing or congruent arrangement of parts ⟨*a painting exhibiting* ~ *of colour and line*⟩ **b** agreement, accord ⟨*lives in* ~ *with her neighbours*⟩ **3** an arrangement of parallel literary passages (e g of the Gospels)

¹harness *n* **1a** the gear of a draught animal other than a yoke **b** (military) equipment (for a knight) **2** sthg that resembles a harness (e g in holding or fastening sthg) ⟨*a safety* ~⟩ **3** a part of a loom which holds and controls the heddles – **in harness 1** in one's usual work, surroundings, or routine ⟨*back* in harness *after a long illness*⟩ **2** in close association ⟨*working* in harness *with his colleagues*⟩

²harness *vt* **1a** to put a harness on (e g a horse) **b** to attach (e g a wagon) by means of a harness **2** to tie together; yoke **3** to utilize; *esp* to convert (a natural force) into energy

¹harp *n* a musical instrument that has strings stretched across an open triangular frame, plucked with the fingers – **harpist** *n*

²harp *vi* – **harp on** to dwell on or return to (a subject) tediously or monotonously

harpoon *n* a barbed spear used esp in hunting large fish or whales – **harpoon** *vt*, **harpooner** *n*

harpsichord *n* a chromatic keyboard instrument having a horizontal frame and strings and producing notes by the action of quills or leather points plucking the strings – **harpsichordist** *n*

harpy *n* **1** *cap* a rapacious creature of Greek mythology with the head of a woman and the body of a bird **2** a predatory person; *esp* a rapacious woman – derog

harquebus *n* an arquebus

harridan *n* an ill-tempered unpleasant woman

¹harrier *n* **1** a hunting dog resembling a small foxhound and used esp for hunting hares **2** a runner in a cross-country team

²harrier *n* any of various slender hawks with long angled wings

Harris tweed *trademark* – used for a loosely woven tweed made in the Outer Hebrides

¹harrow *n* a cultivating implement set with spikes, spring teeth, or discs and drawn over the ground esp to pulverize and smooth the soil

²harrow *vt* **1** to cultivate (ground or land) with a harrow **2** to cause distress to; agonize – **harrower** *n*

harry *vt* **1** to make a destructive raid on; ravage **2** to torment (as if) by constant attack; harass

harsh *adj* **1** having a coarse uneven surface; rough **2** disagreeable or painful to the senses ⟨*a ~ light*⟩ **3** unduly exacting; severe **4** lacking in aesthetic appeal or refinement; crude – **harshen** *vb*, **harshly** *adv*, **harshness** *n*

hart *n, chiefly Br* the male of the (red) deer, esp when over 5 years old

hartebeest *n* any of several large African antelopes with ridged horns that project upwards and outwards

harum-scarum *adj* reckless, irresponsible – infml – **harum-scarum** *adv*

¹harvest *n* **1** (the season for) the gathering in of agricultural crops **2** (the yield of) a mature crop of grain, fruit, etc **3** the product or reward of exertion

²harvest *vt* **1** to gather in (a crop); reap **2** to gather (a natural product) as if by harvesting ⟨*~ bacteria*⟩ ~ *vi* to gather in a food crop – **harvestable** *adj*, **harvester** *n*

Harvest Festival *n* a festival of thanksgiving for the harvest celebrated on a Sunday in September or October in British churches

harvest home *n* **1** the gathering or the time of harvest **2** a festival at the close of harvest

harvest moon *n* the full moon nearest the time of the September equinox

has *pres 3rd sing of* HAVE

has-been *n* sby or sthg that has passed the peak of effectiveness, success, or popularity – infml

¹hash *vt* to chop (e g meat and potatoes) into small pieces

²hash *n* **1** (a dish consisting chiefly of reheated cooked) chopped food, esp meat **2** a rehash **3** a muddle, mess ⟨*made a ~ of things*⟩ *USE*(2 & 3) infml

³hash *n* hashish – infml

hashish *n* the resin from the flowering tops of the female hemp plant that is smoked, chewed, etc for its intoxicating effect

hasn't has not

hasp *n* a device for fastening; *esp* a hinged metal strap that fits over a staple and is secured by a pin or padlock – **hasp** *vt*

¹hassle *n* **1** a heated often protracted argument; a wrangle

2 a trying problem; a struggle ⟨*it's such a ~ getting across London*⟩ *USE* infml

²hassle *vb* **hassling** *vi* to argue, fight ⟨*~d with the referee*⟩ ~ *vt* to subject to usu persistent harassment *USE* infml

hassock *n* **1** a tussock **2** a cushion for kneeling on, esp in church

hast *archaic pres 2 sing of* HAVE

¹haste *n* **1** rapidity of motion; swiftness **2** rash or head-long action; precipitateness ⟨*marry in ~, repent at leisure*⟩ – **make haste** to act quickly; hasten

²haste *vi* to move or act swiftly – fml

hasten *vt* **1** to cause to hurry ⟨*~ed her to the door* – A J Cronin⟩ **2** to accelerate ⟨*~ the completion of the project*⟩ ~ *vi* to move or act quickly; hurry – **hastener** *n*

hasty *adj* **1** done or made in a hurry **2** precipitate, rash **3** prone to or showing anger; irritable – **hastily** *adv*, **hastiness** *n*

hat *n* **1** a covering for the head usu having a shaped crown and brim **2** a role, position – infml ⟨*wearing his ministerial ~*⟩ – **hatless** *adj*

hatband *n* a fabric, leather, etc band round the crown of a hat just above the brim

¹hatch *n* **1** a small door or opening (e g in a wall or aircraft) **2a** (the covering for) an opening in the deck of a ship or in the floor or roof of a building **b** a hatchway

²hatch *vi* **1** to emerge from an egg or pupa **2** to incubate eggs; brood **3** to give forth young ⟨*the egg ~ed*⟩ ~ *vt* **1** to produce (young) from an egg by applying heat **2** to devise, esp secretly; originate – **hatchable** *adj*, **hatcher** *n*

³hatch *n* (a brood of young produced by) hatching

⁴hatch *vt* to mark (e g a drawing, map, or engraving) with fine closely spaced parallel lines – **hatching** *n*

hatchback *n* (a usu small motor car with) an upward-opening hatch giving entry to the luggage and passenger compartment

hatchery *n* a place for hatching (esp fish) eggs

hatchet *n* a short-handled axe

hatchet man *n* one hired for murder, coercion, or attack – slang

hatchway *n* a passage giving access (e g to a lower deck in a ship); *also* ¹HATCH 2a

¹hate *n* **1** intense hostility or dislike; loathing **2** an object of hatred – infml ⟨*one of my pet ~s*⟩

²hate *vb* to feel extreme enmity or aversion (towards) – **hater** *n* – **hate someone's guts** to hate sby with great intensity

hateful *adj* **1** full of hate; malicious **2** deserving of or arousing hate – **hatefully** *adv*, **hatefulness** *n*

hath *archaic pres 3 sing of* HAVE

hatred *n* hate

hat trick *n* three successes by 1 person or side in a usu sporting activity; *specif* the dismissing of 3 batsmen with 3 consecutive balls by a bowler in cricket

hauberk *n* a tunic of chain mail worn as defensive armour, esp from the 12th to the 14th c

haughty *adj* disdainfully proud; arrogant – **haughtily** *adv*, **haughtiness** *n*

¹haul *vt* **1a** to pull with effort; drag **b** to transport in a vehicle, esp a cart **2** to bring *up* (e g before an authority for judgment) – infml ⟨*~ed up before the magistrate for a traffic offence*⟩ ~ *vi* **1** to pull, drag ⟨*~ed on the rope*⟩ **2** of the wind to shift – **haulage** *n*

²haul *n* **1** the act or process of hauling **2a** an amount gathered or acquired; a take ⟨*the burglar's ~*⟩ **b** the fish taken in a single draught of a net **3a** transport by hauling or the load transported **b** the distance or route over which a load is transported ⟨*a long ~*⟩

haulier, *NAm* **hauler** *n* a person or commercial establishment whose business is transport by lorry

haulm *n* **1** the stems or tops of potatoes, peas, beans, etc (after the crop has been gathered) **2** *Br* an individual plant stem

haunch *n* **1** ²HIP 1a **2a** HINDQUARTER 2 – usu pl **b** HINDQUARTER 1 **3** the lower half of either of the sides of an arch – **on one's haunches** in a squatting position

¹**haunt** *vt* **1a** to visit often; frequent **b** to continually seek the company of (a person) **2a** to recur constantly and spontaneously to ⟨*the tune ~ed her all day*⟩ **b** to reappear continually in; pervade ⟨*a sense of tension that ~s his writing*⟩ **3** to visit or inhabit as a ghost ~ *vi* **1** to stay around or persist; linger **2** to appear habitually as a ghost – **haunter** *n*, **hauntingly** *adv*

²**haunt** *n* a place habitually frequented ⟨*the bar was a favourite ~ of criminals*⟩

hautboy, hautbois *n, archaic* an oboe

haute couture *n* (the houses or designers that create) exclusive and often trend-setting fashions for women

hauteur *n* arrogance, haughtiness

Havana *n* (a cigar made in Cuba or from) tobacco (of the type) grown in Cuba

¹**have** *vb* **has; had** *1* **1a** to hold in one's possession or at one's disposal ⟨*~ a car*⟩ ⟨*has only a little French*⟩ **b** to contain as a constituent or be characterized by ⟨*~ red hair*⟩ ⟨*coat has no pockets*⟩ ⟨*has it in him to win*⟩ **2** to own as an obligation or necessity – + *to* and an expressed or understood infinitive ⟨*~ to go*⟩ ⟨*don't ~ to if you don't want to*⟩ **3** to stand in relationship to ⟨*~ enemies*⟩ ⟨*~ 2 sisters*⟩ **4a** to get, obtain ⟨*these shoes are the best to be had*⟩ **b** to receive ⟨*had news*⟩ **c** to accept; *specif* to accept in marriage **d** to have sexual intercourse with (a woman or passive partner) **5** to display, show ⟨*had the impudence to refuse*⟩ ⟨*~ mercy on us*⟩ **6a** to experience, esp by undergoing or suffering ⟨*~ a cold*⟩ ⟨*~ my watch stolen*⟩ **b** to undertake and make or perform ⟨*~ a bath*⟩ ⟨*~ a look at that*⟩ **c** to entertain in the mind ⟨*~ an opinion*⟩ ⟨*~ a down on him*⟩ **d** to engage in; CARRY ON ⟨*~ sex*⟩ ⟨*~ a meeting*⟩ **7a** to cause to by persuasive or forceful means ⟨*~ the children stay*⟩ ⟨*so he would ~ us believe*⟩ **b** *chiefly Br* to bring into a specified condition by the action of another ⟨*~ my shoes mended*⟩ **c** to cause to be ⟨*soon ~ it finished*⟩ **d** to invite as a guest ⟨*~ them over for drinks*⟩ **8** to allow, permit ⟨*I'm not having any more of that*⟩ **9a** to hold in a position of disadvantage or certain defeat ⟨*we ~ him now*⟩ **b** to perplex, floor ⟨*you ~ me there*⟩ **10** to be able to exercise; be entitled to ⟨*I ~ my rights*⟩ **11a** to be pregnant with or be the prospective parents of ⟨*they're having a baby in August*⟩ **b** to give birth to ⟨*the cat's just had kittens*⟩ **12** to partake of; consume ⟨*~ dinner*⟩ ⟨*~ a cigar*⟩ **13** to take advantage of; fool ⟨*been had by his partner*⟩ – *infml* ~ *va* **1** – used with the past participle to form the present perfect ⟨*has gone home*⟩, the past perfect ⟨*had already eaten*⟩, the future perfect ⟨*will ~ finished dinner by then*⟩, or nonfinite perfective forms ⟨*having gone*⟩ ⟨*silly not to ~ gone*⟩; used with *got* to express obligation or necessity ⟨*~ got to go*⟩; used in the past tense with the past participle as a rather literary expression of the conditional ⟨*had I known*⟩ **2** WOULD 1b ⟨*I had as soon not*⟩ USE British speakers in particular often express the idea of momentary as opposed to habitual possession or experience with *have got* ⟨*have you got a cold?*⟩ ⟨*do you have many colds?*⟩ – **have a lot/enough on one's plate** to be (fully) occupied, often with a variety of tasks, problems, etc – **have an ear to the ground** to be in receipt of information not generally

known – **have a screw/slate loose** to be slightly cracked, feebleminded, or eccentric – **have a way with** to be good at dealing with ⟨*he has a way with old ladies*⟩ – **have a way with one** to be charming, esp persuasively – **have been around** to be sophisticated or well-informed – **have coming** to deserve or merit what one gets, benefits by, or suffers ⟨*he had that coming to him*⟩ – **have done with** to bring to an end; have no further concern with ⟨*let us have done with name-calling*⟩ – **have had it 1** to have had and missed one's chance – *infml* **2** to have passed one's prime; be obsolete, smashed, or dead ⟨*I'm afraid the car's had it*⟩ – **have it 1** to maintain, affirm ⟨*as rumour has it*⟩ **2** to live in the specified conditions ⟨*never had it so good*⟩ – **have it both ways** to exploit or profit from each of a pair of contradictory positions, circumstances, etc; *also* to maintain 2 contradictory views simultaneously – **have it coming to one** to deserve what one is going to get – **have it in for** to intend to do harm to – **have it off/away** to copulate *with* – *slang* – **have it out** to settle a matter of contention by discussion or a fight – **have no time for** to be unable or reluctant to spend time on; dislike – *infml* – **have one's eye on 1** to watch, esp constantly and attentively **2** to have as an objective – **have one's hands full** to be fully occupied ⟨*what with the triplets, 6 goldfish, 3 dogs, and the mushroom farm, he's got his hands full most days*⟩ – **have one's head screwed on** to be sensible, practical, or provident – **have one's work cut out** to be hard put to it – **have taped** to have the measure of; be in command or control of ⟨*soon have the problem taped*⟩ – **have the advantage of** to have superiority over; *specif* to have personal unreciprocated knowledge of – often used as an ironic disclaimer of acquaintanceship ⟨*I'm afraid you have the advantage of me*⟩ – **have the wind of** to be to windward of – **have to do with 1** to deal with **2** to have in the way of connection or relation with or effect on ⟨*the lawyer would have nothing to do with the case*⟩ – compare TO DO WITH – **have up one's sleeve** to have as an undeclared resource ⟨*he's got some new ideas up his sleeve*⟩ – **not have a clue** to know nothing; not to know – **what have you** any of various other things that might also be mentioned ⟨*paper clips, pins, and what have you*⟩

²**have** *n* a wealthy person – usu pl; esp in the *haves and have-nots*

haven *n* **1** a harbour, port **2** a place of safety or refuge

have-not *n* a poor person – usu pl; compare ²HAVE

haven't have not

have on *vt* **1** to be wearing ⟨*have a new suit on*⟩ **2** to have plans for ⟨*what do you have on for tomorrow?*⟩ **3** *chiefly Br* to deceive, tease – *infml*

haver *vi, chiefly Br* to be indecisive; hesitate

haversack *n* a knapsack

have up *vt* to bring before the authorities ⟨*he was had up in court for dangerous driving*⟩ – *infml*

havoc *n* **1** widespread destruction; devastation **2** great confusion and disorder ⟨*several small children can create ~ in a house*⟩

¹**haw** *n* (a berry of) hawthorn

²**haw** *n* (a domestic animal's inflamed) nictitating membrane

³**haw** *vi* to utter a sound resembling *haw*, esp in hesitation ⟨*hummed and ~ed before answering*⟩

⁴**haw** *interj* – often used to indicate hesitation

¹**hawk** *n* **1** any of numerous medium-sized birds of prey that have (short) rounded wings and long tails and that hunt during the day **2** a small board with a handle on the underside for holding mortar or plaster **3** one who takes a militant attitude; a supporter of a warlike policy – usu

contrasted with *dove* – **hawkish** *adj*, **hawkishly** *adv*, **hawkishness** *n*

²hawk *vi* **1** to hunt game with a trained hawk **2** to soar and strike like a hawk ⟨*birds* ~ ing *after insects*⟩ ~ *vt* to hunt on the wing like a hawk

³hawk *vt* to offer for sale in the street ⟨~ing *newspapers*⟩

⁴hawk *vi* to utter a harsh guttural sound (as if) in clearing the throat ~ *vt* to raise by hawking ⟨~ *up phlegm*⟩

⁵hawk *n* an audible effort to force up phlegm from the throat

¹hawker *n* a falconer

²hawker *n* sby who hawks wares

hawser *n* a large rope

hawthorn *n* any of a genus of spring-flowering spiny shrubs of the rose family with white or pink flowers and small red fruits

¹hay *n* herbage, esp grass, mowed and cured for fodder

²hay *vi* to cut, cure, and store grass for hay

³hay, hey *n* a rustic dance featuring winding and interweaving dance figures

haycock *n* a small conical pile of hay in a field

hay fever *n* nasal catarrh and conjunctivitis occurring usu in the spring and summer through allergy to pollen

haymaker *n* **1** one who tosses and spreads hay to dry after cutting **2** *chiefly NAm* a powerful blow – **haymaking** *n*

haystack *n* a relatively large sometimes thatched outdoor pile of hay

haywire *adj* **1** out of order ⟨*the radio went* ~⟩ **2** emotionally or mentally upset; crazy ⟨*went completely* ~ *after the accident*⟩ *USE* infml

¹hazard *n* **1** a game of chance played with 2 dice **2a** a risk, peril **b** a source of danger **3** a golf-course obstacle (e g a bunker)

²hazard *vt* **1** to expose to danger ⟨*a captain guilty of* ~ing *his ship*⟩ **2** to venture, risk ⟨~ *a guess*⟩

hazardous *adj* **1** depending on hazard or chance **2** involving or exposing one to risk (e g of loss or harm) ⟨*a* ~ *occupation*⟩ – **hazardously** *adv*, **hazardousness** *n*

¹haze *vb* to make or become hazy or cloudy

²haze *n* **1** vapour, dust, smoke, etc causing a slight decrease in the air's transparency **2** vagueness or confusion of mental perception

³haze *vt, chiefly NAm* to harass (a new student) with ridicule, criticism, etc – **hazer** *n*, **hazing** *n*

hazel *n* **1** (the wood or nut of) any of a genus of shrubs or small trees bearing nuts **2** a yellowish light to strong brown – **hazel** *adj*

hazy *adj* **1** obscured, cloudy ⟨*a* ~ *view of the mountains*⟩ **2** vague, indefinite ⟨*had only a* ~ *recollection of what happened*⟩ – **hazily** *adv*, **haziness** *n*

H-bomb *n* HYDROGEN BOMB

¹he *pron* **1** that male person or creature who is neither speaker nor hearer ⟨~ *is my father*⟩ – + cap in reference to God; compare SHE, HIM, HIS, IT, THEY **2** – used in a generic sense or when the sex of the person is unspecified ⟨~ *that hath ears to hear, let him hear* –Mt 11:15 (AV)⟩

²he *n* **1** a male person or creature ⟨*is the baby a* ~ *or a she?*⟩ ⟨*a* he-*goat*⟩ **2** ²IT 1

¹head *n, pl* **heads**, (4b) **head 1** the upper or foremost division of the body containing the brain, the chief sense organs, and the mouth **2a** the seat of the intellect; the mind ⟨*2* ~ s *are better than 1*⟩ **b** natural aptitude or talent ⟨*a good* ~ *for figures*⟩ **c** mental or emotional control; composure ⟨*a level* ~⟩ **d** a headache **3** the obverse of a coin – usu pl with sing. meaning; compare TAIL **5 4a** a person, individual ⟨*a* ~ *count*⟩ **b** a single individual

(domestic animal) out of a number – usu pl ⟨*500* ~ *of cattle*⟩ **5a** the end that is upper, higher, or opposite the foot ⟨*the* ~ *of the table*⟩ **b** the source of a stream, river, etc **c** either end of sthg (e g a cask or drum) whose 2 ends need not be distinguished **d** DRIFT 5 **6** a director, leader: e g **a** a school principal **b** one in charge of a department in an institution ⟨*the* ~ *of the English department*⟩ **7a** a capitulum **b** the foliaged part of a plant, esp when consisting of a compact mass of leaves or fruits **8** the leading part of a military column, procession, etc **9a** the uppermost extremity or projecting part of an object; the top **b** the striking part of a weapon, tool, implement, etc **10a** a body of water kept in reserve at a height **b** a mass of water in motion **11a** (the pressure resulting from) the difference in height between 2 points in a body of liquid **b** the pressure of a fluid ⟨*a good* ~ *of steam*⟩ **12a** (parts adjacent to) the bow of a ship **b** a (ship's) toilet – usu pl with sing. meaning in British English **13** a measure of length equivalent to a head ⟨*the horse won by a* ~⟩ **14** the place of leadership, honour, or command ⟨*at the* ~ *of his class*⟩ **15a** a word often in larger letters placed above a passage in order to introduce or categorize **b** a separate part or topic **16** the foam or froth that rises on a fermenting or effervescing liquid **17a** the part of a boil, pimple, etc at which it is likely to break **b** a culminating point; a crisis – esp in *come to a head* **18a** a part of a machine or machine tool containing a device (e g a cutter or drill); *also* the part of an apparatus that performs the chief or a particular function **b** any of at least 2 electromagnetic components which bear on the magnetic tape in a tape recorder, such that one can erase recorded material if desired and another may either record or play back **19** one who uses LSD, cannabis, etc habitually or excessively – often in combination; slang – **headless** *adj*, **headlessness** *n* – **off one's head** crazy, mad – **over someone's head 1** beyond sby's comprehension ⟨*I understand the gist but the technical language is* over my head⟩ **2** so as to pass over sby's superior standing or authority ⟨*went* over his *supervisor's* head *to complain*⟩

²head *adj* **1** principal, chief ⟨~ *cook*⟩⟨~ *office*⟩ **2** situated at the head

³head *vt* **1** to cut back or off the upper growth of (a plant) **2a** to provide with a head **b** to form the head or top of ⟨*tower* ~ed *by a spire*⟩ **3** to be at the head of; lead ⟨~ *a revolt*⟩ **4** to go round the head of (a stream) **5a** to put sthg at the head of (e g a list); *also* to provide with a heading **b** to stand as the first or leading member of ⟨~s *the list of heroes*⟩ **6** to set the course of ⟨~ *a ship northwards*⟩ **7** to drive (e g a soccer ball) with the head ~ *vi* **1** to form a head ⟨*this cabbage* ~s *early*⟩ **2** to point or proceed in a specified direction ⟨~ing *for disaster*⟩

headache *n* **1** pain in the head **2** a difficult situation or problem – **headachy** *adj*

headband *n* a band worn round the head, esp to keep hair out of the eyes

headboard *n* a board forming the head (e g of a bed)

headcheese *n* BRAWN 2

headdress *n* an often elaborate covering for the head

headed *adj* **1** having a head or a heading ⟨~ *notepaper*⟩ **2** having a head or heads of a specified kind or number – in combination ⟨*a cool*headed *businessman*⟩ ⟨*a round*headed *screw*⟩

header *n* **1** a brick or stone laid in a wall with its end towards the face of the wall **2** a headfirst fall or dive **3** a shot or pass in soccer made by heading the ball

headfirst *adv* with the head foremost; headlong ⟨*dived* ~ *into the waves*⟩ – **headfirst** *adj*

head-hunting *n* **1** decapitating and preserving the heads of enemies as trophies **2** searching for and recruitment of personnel, esp at executive level and often from other firms – **headhunter** *n*

heading *n* **1** the compass direction in which a ship or aircraft points **2a** an inscription, headline, or title standing at the top or beginning (e g of a letter or chapter) **b** a piece used in making either of the flat ends of a barrel **3** DRIFT 5

headland *n* **1** unploughed land near an edge of a field **2** a point of usu high land jutting out into a body of water

headlight *n* (the beam cast by) the main light mounted on the front of a motor vehicle

headline *n* a title printed in large type above a newspaper story or article; *also, pl, Br* a summary given at the beginning or end of a news broadcast

headlong *adv or adj* **1** headfirst **2** without deliberation **3** without pause or delay

headman *n* a chief of a primitive community

headmaster, *fem* **headmistress** *n* one who heads the staff of a school – **headmastership** *n*

head off *vt* to stop the progress of or turn aside by taking preventive action; block ⟨head *them* off *at the pass*⟩

head-on *adv or adj* **1** with the head or front making the initial contact ⟨*the cars collided* ~⟩ ⟨*a* ~ *collision*⟩ **2** in direct opposition ⟨*what happens when primitive and civilized man meet* ~?⟩ ⟨*a* ~ *confrontation*⟩

headphone *n* an earphone held over the ear by a band worn on the head – usu pl

headpiece *n* an ornamental printed device esp at the beginning of a chapter

headquarters *n, pl* **headquarters 1** a place from which a commander exercises command **2** the administrative centre of an enterprise *USE* often pl with sing. meaning

headrest *n* a support for the head; *esp* a cushioned pad supporting the head in a vehicle

headroom *n* vertical space (e g beneath a bridge) sufficient to allow passage or unrestricted movement

headset *n* an attachment for holding earphones and a microphone to one's head

headship *n* the position or office of a head (e g a headmaster); leadership

headshrinker *n* **1** a headhunter who shrinks the heads of his/her victims **2** a psychoanalyst or psychiatrist – humor

headstall *n* the part of a bridle or halter that encircles the head

head start *n* **1** an advantage granted or achieved at the beginning of a race, competition, etc **2** an advantageous or favourable beginning

headstone *n* a memorial stone placed at the head of a grave

headstrong *adj* wilful, obstinate ⟨*violent* ~ *actions*⟩

headway *n* **1a** (rate of) motion in a forward direction **b** advance, progress **2** headroom **3** the time interval between 2 vehicles travelling in the same direction on the same route

headwind *n* a wind blowing in a direction opposite to a course, esp of a ship or aircraft

headword *n* a word or term placed at the beginning (e g of a chapter or encyclopedia entry)

heady *adj* **1** violent, impetuous **2a** tending to make giddy or exhilarated; intoxicating **b** giddy, exhilarated ⟨~ *with his success*⟩ – **headily** *adv*, **headiness** *n*

heal *vt* **1a** to make sound or whole ⟨~ *a wound*⟩ **b** to restore to health **2** to restore to a sound or normal state; mend ⟨~ *a breach between friends*⟩ ~ *vi* to return to a sound or healthy state – **healer** *n*

health *n* **1a** soundness of body, mind, or spirit **b** the

general condition of the body ⟨*in poor* ~⟩ **2** condition ⟨*the economic* ~ *of the country is not good*⟩; *esp* a sound or flourishing condition; well-being **3** a toast to sby's health or prosperity

healthful *adj* **1** beneficial to health of body or mind **2** HEALTHY 1

healthy *adj* **1** enjoying or showing health and vigour of body, mind, or spirit **2** conducive to good health **3** prosperous, flourishing – **healthily** *adv*, **healthiness** *n*

¹**heap** *n* **1** a collection of things lying one on top of another; a pile **2** a great number or large quantity; a lot – *infml*; often pl with sing. meaning ⟨~s *more to say*⟩

²**heap** *vt* **1a** to throw or lay in a heap; pile *up* ⟨*his sole object was to* ~ *up riches*⟩ **b** to form or round into a heap ⟨~ed *the earth into a mound*⟩ **2** to supply abundantly *with*; *also* to bestow lavishly or in large quantities *upon*

hear *vb* **heard** *vt* **1** to perceive (sound) with the ear **2** to learn by hearing ⟨*I* ~d *you were leaving*⟩ **3a** to listen to with attention; heed ⟨~ *me out*⟩ **b** to attend ⟨~ *mass*⟩ **4** to give a legal hearing to ~ *vi* **1** to have the capacity of perceiving sound **2** to gain information; learn ⟨*I've* ~d *about what you did*⟩ **3** – often in the expression *Hear! Hear!* indicating approval (e g during a speech) – **hearer** *n* – **hear from** to receive a communication from – **hear of** to entertain the idea of – usu neg ⟨*wouldn't hear of it*⟩

hearing *n* **1a** the one of the 5 basic physical senses by which waves received by the ear are interpreted by the brain as sounds varying in pitch, intensity, and timbre **b** earshot **2a** an opportunity to be heard **b** a trial in court

hearing aid *n* an electronic device worn by a deaf person for amplifying sound before it reaches the ears

hearken *vi* to listen *to*; *also* to heed – poetic

hearsay *n* sthg heard from another; rumour

hearse *n* a vehicle for transporting a dead body in its coffin

¹**heart** *n* **1a** a hollow muscular organ that by its rhythmic contraction acts as a force pump maintaining the circulation of the blood **b** the breast, bosom **c** sthg resembling a heart in shape; *specif* a conventionalized representation of a heart **2a** a playing card marked with 1 or more red heart-shaped figures **b** *pl but sing or pl in constr* the suit comprising cards identified by this figure **c** *pl but sing in constr* a card game in which the object is to avoid taking tricks containing a heart or the queen of spades **3a** humane disposition; compassion ⟨*have you no* ~?⟩ **b** love, affections ⟨*lost his* ~ *to her*⟩ **c** courage, spirit ⟨*had no* ~ *for the task*⟩ **4** one's innermost character or feelings ⟨*a man after my own* ~⟩ **5a** the central or innermost part (of a lettuce, cabbage, etc) **b** the essential or most vital part ⟨*the* ~ *of the matter*⟩ – **by heart** by rote or from memory

²**heart** *vt, of a cabbage, lettuce, etc* to form a heart

heartache *n* mental anguish; sorrow

heart attack *n* an instance of abnormal functioning of the heart; *esp* CORONARY THROMBOSIS

heartbeat *n* a single complete pulsation of the heart

heartbreak *n* intense grief or distress

heartbreaking *adj* **1** causing intense sorrow or distress ⟨*a* ~ *waste of talent*⟩ **2** extremely trying or difficult ⟨*a* ~ *task*⟩ – **heartbreakingly** *adv*

heartbroken *adj* overcome by sorrow

heartburn *n* a burning pain behind the lower part of the breastbone usu resulting from spasm of the stomach or throat muscles

hearted *adj* having a heart, esp of a specified kind – usu in combination ⟨*a fainthearted leader*⟩ ⟨*a broken*hearted *lover*⟩

hearten *vt* to cheer, encourage – **hearteningly** *adv*

heart failure n (inability of the heart to perform adequately often leading to) cessation of the heartbeat and death

heartfelt adj deeply felt; earnest

hearth n **1a** a brick, stone, or cement area in front of the floor of a fireplace **b** the lowest section of a metal-processing furnace **2** home, fireside ⟨the comforts of ~ and home⟩

heartily adv **1a** with all sincerity; wholeheartedly ⟨I ~ recommend it⟩ **b** with zest; vigorously ⟨ate ~⟩ **2** quite, thoroughly ⟨~ sick of all this talk⟩

heartless adj unfeeling, cruel – **heartlessly** adv, **heartlessness** n

heartrending adj HEARTBREAKING 1 – **heartrendingly** adv

heartsease n any of various violas; esp the wild pansy

heartsick adj very despondent; depressed – **heartsickness** n

heartstrings n pl the deepest emotions or affections ⟨pulled at his ~⟩

heartthrob n one who is the object of or arouses infatuation

¹**heart-to-heart** adj sincere and intimate ⟨~ confidences⟩

²**heart-to-heart** n a frank or intimate talk – infml

heartwarming adj inspiring sympathetic feeling; cheering

heartwood n the older harder nonliving central wood in a tree, usu darker and denser than the surrounding sapwood

¹**hearty** adj **1a** enthusiastically or exuberantly friendly; jovial **b** unrestrained, vigorous ⟨a ~ laugh⟩ **2a** robustly healthy ⟨hale and ~⟩ **b** substantial, abundant ⟨a ~ meal⟩ – **heartiness** n

²**hearty** n **1** a sailor **2** chiefly Br a sporty outgoing person ⟨rugger hearties⟩

¹**heat** vb to make or become warm or hot – often + up – **heatable** adj, **heatedly** adv

²**heat** n **1a** the condition of being hot; warmth; also a marked degree of this **b** excessively high bodily temperature **c** the form of energy associated with the random motions of the molecules, atoms, etc of which matter is composed, transmitted by conduction, convection, or radiation **d** an esp high temperature ⟨at melting ~⟩ **e** any of a series of degrees of heating ⟨this iron has 4 ~s⟩ **2a** intensity of feeling or reaction ⟨the ~ of passion⟩ **b** the height or stress of an action or condition ⟨in the ~ of battle⟩ **c** readiness for sexual intercourse in a female mammal; specif oestrus – usu in on heat or (chiefly NAm) in heat **3** pungency of flavour **4a** a single round of a contest that has 2 or more rounds for each contestant **b** any of several preliminary contests whose winners go into the final **5** pressure, coercion ⟨his enemies turned the ~ on him⟩ – slang – **heatless** adj, **heatproof** adj

heated adj marked by anger ⟨a ~ argument⟩

heater n a device that gives off heat or holds sthg to be heated

heath n **1** any of various related evergreen plants that thrive on barren usu acid soil, with whorls of needlelike leaves and clusters of small flowers **2a** a tract of wasteland **b** a large area of level uncultivated land usu with poor peaty soil and bad drainage – **heathless** adj, **heathlike** adj, **heathy** adj

heathen n, pl **heathens**, **heathen 1** an unconverted member of a people or nation that does not acknowledge the God of the Bible – often pl + the ⟨the ~ say there is no God⟩ **2** an uncivilized or irreligious person – **heathen** adj, **heathenish** adj, **heathenism** n, **heathendom** n, **heathenize** vt

heather n a (common usu purplish-pink flowered northern) heath – **heather** adj

heat pump n an apparatus for transferring heat by mechanical means to a place of higher temperature (e g for heating or cooling a building)

heat rash n PRICKLY HEAT

heat sink n a means of absorbing or dissipating unwanted heat

heatstroke n overheating of the body resulting from prolonged exposure to high temperature and leading to (fatal) collapse

heat wave n a period of unusually hot weather

¹**heave** vb **heaved**, **hove** vt **1** to lift upwards or forwards, esp with effort **2** to throw, cast **3** to utter with obvious effort ⟨~d a sigh⟩ **4** to cause to swell or rise **5** to haul, draw ~ vi **1** to rise or become thrown or raised up **2a** to rise and fall rhythmically ⟨his chest ~ing with sobs⟩ **b** to pant **3** to vomit **4** to pull – **heaver** n – **heave in/into sight** to come into view

²**heave** n **1a** an effort to heave or raise **b** a throw, cast **2** an upward motion; esp a rhythmical rising ⟨the ~ of the sea⟩ **3** pl but sing or pl in constr BROKEN WIND

heaven n **1** (any of the spheres of) the expanse of space that surrounds the earth like a dome; the firmament – usu pl with sing. meaning **2** often cap the dwelling place of God, his angels, and the spirits of those who have received salvation; Paradise **3** cap GOD 1 **4** a place or condition of utmost happiness

heavenly adj **1** of heaven or the heavens; celestial ⟨the ~ choirs⟩ **2a** suggesting the blessed state of heaven; divine ⟨~ peace⟩ **b** delightful ⟨what a ~ idea⟩ – infml – **heavenliness** n

heaven-sent adj providential

heavenward adj directed towards heaven or the heavens – **heavenwards**, NAm chiefly **heavenward** adv

heave to vb to bring (a ship) to a stop with head to wind

heavily adv **1** slowly and laboriously; dully **2** to a great degree; severely

¹**heavy** adj **1a** having great weight **b** having great weight in proportion to size **c** of an isotope or compound having, being, or containing atoms of greater than normal mass ⟨~ hydrogen⟩ **2** hard to bear; specif grievous ⟨a ~ sorrow⟩ **3** of weighty import; serious ⟨a ~ book⟩ **4** emotionally intense; profound ⟨a ~ silence⟩ **5a** oppressed; burdened ⟨returned with ~ spirit from the meeting⟩ **b** pregnant; esp approaching parturition – often + with **6a** slow, sluggish ⟨~ movements⟩ **b** lacking sparkle or vivacity; dull ⟨the book made ~ reading⟩ **7** dulled with weariness; drowsy ⟨his eyelids felt ~ with sleep⟩ **8a** of an unusually large amount ⟨~ traffic⟩ **b** of great force ⟨~ seas⟩ **c** overcast ⟨a ~ sky⟩ **d** of ground or soil full of clay and inclined to hold water; impeding motion **e** loud and deep ⟨the ~ roll of thunder⟩ **f** laborious, difficult ⟨made ~ going of it⟩ **g** of large capacity or output **h** consuming in large quantities – usu + on ⟨this car is ~ on petrol⟩ **9a** digested with difficulty, usu because of excessive richness ⟨~ fruit cake⟩ **b** esp of bread not sufficiently raised or leavened **10** producing heavy usu large goods (e g coal, steel, or machinery) often used in the production of other goods ⟨~ industry⟩ **11a** of the larger variety ⟨a ~ howitzer⟩ **b** heavily armoured, armed, or equipped ⟨the ~ cavalry⟩ **12** of rock music loud and strongly rhythmic – slang **13** chiefly NAm frighteningly serious; specif threatening – slang; often used as an interjection – **heaviness** n – **with a heavy hand 1** with little mercy; sternly **2** without grace; clumsily

²**heavy** adv in a heavy manner; heavily ⟨time hangs ~ on us⟩

³**heavy** n **1** pl units (e g of bombers, artillery, or cavalry) of the heavy sort **2a** (an actor playing) a villain **b** sby of importance or significance – infml **3** a serious newspaper – usu pl; infml **4** one hired to compel or deter by means of threats or physical violence ⟨*set a gang of heavies on him*⟩ – slang

heavy-duty adj able or designed to withstand unusual strain or wear

heavy-handed adj **1** clumsy, awkward **2** oppressive, harsh – **heavy-handedly** adv, **heavy-handedness** n

heavyhearted adj despondent, melancholy – **heavy-heartedly** adv, **heavyheartedness** n

heavy water n water enriched esp with deuterium

heavyweight n **1** sby or sthg above average weight **2** one in the usu heaviest class of contestants: e g **a** a boxer whose weight is not limited if he is professional or is more than 81kg (about 12st 10lb) if he is amateur **b** a wrestler weighing over 100kg (about 15st 10lb) **c** a weight-lifter weighing over 110kg (about 17st 4lb) **3** an important or influential person ⟨*an intellectual* ∼⟩

hebdomadal adj weekly – fml – **hebdomadally** adv

Hebraic, Hebraistic adj of the Hebrews, their culture, or Hebrew – **Hebraically** adv, **Hebraistically** adv

Hebrew n **1** a member or descendant of any of a group of N Semitic peoples including the Israelites; *esp* an Israelite **2** the Semitic language of the ancient Hebrews; *also* a later form of Hebrew – **Hebrew** adj

hecatomb n **1** an ancient Greek and Roman sacrifice of 100 oxen or cattle **2** the sacrifice or slaughter of many victims

heck n HELL 2a – used as an interjection or intensive ⟨*what the* ∼!⟩ ⟨*a* ∼ *of a lot of money*⟩

heckle vt **heckling** to harass and try to disconcert (e g a speaker) with questions, challenges, or gibes – **heckler** n

hect-, hecto- comb form hundred (10²) ⟨*hectograph*⟩

hectare n a metric unit of area equal to 100 are (2.471 acres)

hectic adj **1** of, being, or suffering from a fluctuating fever (e g in tuberculosis) **2** filled with excitement or feverish activity ⟨*the* ∼ *days before Christmas*⟩ – **hectically** adv

hector vi to play the bully; swagger ∼ vt to intimidate by bullying or blustering – **hectoringly** adv

he'd he had; he would

¹**hedge** n **1a** a boundary formed by a dense row of shrubs or low trees **b** a barrier, limit **2** a means of protection or defence (e g against financial loss) **3** a calculatedly non-committal or evasive statement

²**hedge** vt **1** to enclose or protect (as if) with a hedge **2** to hem in or obstruct (as if) with a barrier; hinder **3** to protect oneself against losing (e g a bet), esp by making counterbalancing transactions ∼ vi **1** to plant, form, or trim a hedge **2** to avoid committing oneself to a definite course of action, esp by making evasive statements **3** to protect oneself financially: e g **a** to buy or sell commodity futures as a protection against loss due to price fluctuation – often + *against* **b** to minimize the risk of a bet – **hedger** n, **hedgingly** adv

hedgehog n any of a genus of small Old World spine-covered insect-eating mammals that are active at night

hedgehop vi **-pp-** to fly an aircraft close to the ground and rise over obstacles as they appear – **hedgehopper** n

hedgerow n a row of shrubs or trees surrounding a field

hedge sparrow n a dunnock

hedonism n (conduct based on) the doctrine that per-sonal pleasure is the sole or chief good – **hedonist** n, **hedonistic** adj, **hedonistically** adv

heebie-jeebies n pl *the* jitters, willies – infml

¹**heed** vb to pay attention (to)

²**heed** n attention, notice ⟨*take* ∼⟩

heedful adj attentive, mindful of – **heedfully** adv, **heedfulness** n

heedless adj inconsiderate, thoughtless – **heedlessly** adv, **heedlessness** n

hee-haw n **1** the bray of a donkey **2** a loud rude laugh; a guffaw – **hee-haw** vi

¹**heel** n **1** (the back part of the hind limb of a vertebrate corresponding to) the back of the human foot below the ankle and behind the arch or an anatomical structure resembling this **2** either of the crusty ends of a loaf of bread **3** the part of a garment or an article of footwear that covers or supports the human heel **4a** the lower end of a mast **b** the base of a tuber or cutting of a plant used for propagation **5** a backward kick with the heel in rugby, esp from a set scrum **6** a contemptible person – slang – **heeled** adj, **heelless** adj – **down at (the) heel** in or into a run-down or shabby condition – **on the heels of** immediately following; closely behind – **to heel 1** close behind – usu used in training a dog **2** into agreement or line; under control

²**heel** vt **1** to supply with a heel; esp to renew the heel of ⟨∼ *a sock*⟩ **2** to exert pressure on, propel, or strike (as if) with the heel; *specif* to kick (a rugby ball) with the heel, esp out of a scrum ∼ vi to move along at the heels of sby or close behind sthg ⟨*a dog that* 's *well*⟩ – **heeler** n

³**heel** vi to tilt to one side ∼ vt to cause (a boat) to heel

⁴**heel** n (the extent of) a tilt to one side

heelball n a mixture of wax and lampblack used to polish the heels of footwear and to take brass or stone rubbings

hefty adj **1** large or bulky and usu heavy **2** powerful, mighty ⟨*a* ∼ *blow*⟩ **3** impressively large ⟨*a* ∼ *price to pay*⟩ – **heftily** adv, **heftiness** n

hegemony n domination by one nation, group, etc over others

hegira also **hejira** n a journey, esp when undertaken to escape from a dangerous or undesirable situation; *specif*, cap the flight of Muhammad from Mecca to Medina in 622 AD, the event marking the beginning of the Muhammadan era

heifer n a young cow (that has at most 1 calf)

heigh-ho interj – used to express boredom, weariness, or sadness

height n **1** the highest or most extreme point; the zenith ⟨*at the* ∼ *of his powers*⟩ **2a** the distance from the bottom to the top of sthg standing upright **b** the elevation above a level **3** the condition of being tall or high **4a** a piece of land (e g a hill or plateau) rising to a considerable degree above the surrounding country – usu pl with sing. meaning **b** a high point or position

heighten vt **1a** to increase the amount or degree of; augment ⟨∼ed *his awareness of the problem*⟩ **b** to deepen, intensify ⟨*her colour was* ∼ed *by emotion*⟩ **2** to raise high or higher; elevate ⟨*the building was* ∼ed *by another storey*⟩ ∼ vi **1** to become great or greater in amount, degree, or extent **2** to intensify

heinous adj hatefully or shockingly evil; abominable ⟨*a* ∼ *crime*⟩ – **heinously** adv, **heinousness** n

heir n **1** sby who inherits or is entitled to succeed to an estate or rank **2** sby who receives or is entitled to receive some position, role, or quality passed on from a parent or predecessor – **heirless** adj, **heirship** n

heir apparent n, pl **heirs apparent 1** an heir who cannot be displaced so long as he/she outlives the person from whom he/she is to inherit **2** one whose succession, esp to a position or role, appears certain under existing circumstances

heiress n a female heir, esp to great wealth

heirloom n 1 a piece of valuable property handed down within a family for generations 2 sthg of special value handed on from one generation to another

heir presumptive n, pl **heirs presumptive** an heir who can be displaced only by the birth of a child with a superior claim

hejira n a hegira

held past of HOLD

helicopter n an aircraft which derives both lift and propulsive power from a set of horizontally rotating rotors or vanes and is capable of vertical takeoff and landing

heliograph n 1 a photoheliograph 2 an apparatus for signalling using the sun's rays reflected from a mirror

heliotrope n 1 any of a genus of plants of the borage family 2 (a) bloodstone 3 light purple

heliport n a place for helicopters to take off and land

helium n a noble gaseous element found in natural gases and used esp for inflating balloons and in low-temperature research

helix n, pl **helices** also **helixes** 1 sthg spiral in form (e g a coil formed by winding wire round a uniform tube) 2 the rim curved inwards of the external ear 3 a curve traced on a cylinder at a constant rate; broadly SPIRAL 1b – **helical** adj, **helically** adj

hell n 1a a nether world (e g Hades or Sheol) inhabited by the spirits of the dead b the nether realm of the devil in which the souls of those excluded from Paradise undergo perpetual torment c the home of the devil and demons in which the damned suffer punishment 2a a place or state of torment, misery, or wickedness – often as an interjection, an intensive, or as a generalized term of abuse ⟨one ~ of a mess⟩ ⟨go to ~⟩ b a place or state of chaos or destruction ⟨all ~ broke loose⟩ c a severe scolding ⟨got ~ for coming in late⟩ – **for the hell of it** for the intrinsic amusement or satisfaction of an activity – **hell to pay** serious trouble ⟨if he's late there'll be hell to pay⟩ – **like hell** 1 very hard or much ⟨worked like hell to get the job done on time⟩ 2 – used to intensify denial of a statement; slang ⟨'I did 4 hours overtime.' 'Like hell you did!'⟩ – **what the hell** it doesn't matter

he'll he will; he shall

hell-bent adj stubbornly and often recklessly determined ⟨civilization is ~ on self-destruction – R F Delderfield⟩

hellcat n a spiteful ill-tempered woman

Hellene n GREEK 1

Hellenic adj of Greece, its people, or its language

Hellenistic adj of Greek history, culture, or art after Alexander the Great

¹**hellish** adj of, resembling, or befitting hell; diabolical – **hellishly** adv, **hellishness** n

²**hellish** adv extremely, damnably ⟨a ~ cold day⟩

hello n, pl **hellos** an expression or gesture of greeting – used interjectionally in greeting, in answering the telephone, to express surprise, or to attract attention

¹**helm** n HELMET 1

²**helm** n 1 a tiller or wheel controlling the steering of a ship 2 the position of control; the head ⟨a new dean is at the ~ of the medical school⟩

³**helm** vt to steer (as if) with a helm

helmet n 1 a covering or enclosing headpiece of ancient or medieval armour 2 any of various protective head coverings, esp made of a hard material to resist impact 3 sthg, esp a hood-shaped petal or sepal, resembling a helmet – **helmeted** adj, **helmetlike** adj

helmsman n the person at the helm – **helmsmanship** n

helot n 1 cap a serf in ancient Sparta 2 a serf, slave – **helotry** n

¹**help** vt 1 to give assistance or support to ⟨~ a child to understand his lesson⟩ 2 to remedy, relieve ⟨took an aspirin to ~ her headache⟩ 3a to be of use to; benefit b to further the advancement of; promote ⟨~ing industry with loans⟩ 4a to refrain from ⟨couldn't ~ laughing⟩ b to keep from occurring; prevent ⟨they couldn't ~ the accident⟩ c to restrain (oneself) from taking action ⟨tried not to say anything, but couldn't ~ myself⟩ 5 to serve with food or drink, esp at a meal ⟨let me ~ you to some salad⟩ 6 to appropriate sthg for (oneself), esp dishonestly ⟨~ed himself to my pen⟩ ~ vi to be of use or benefit ⟨every little ~s⟩ – **helper** n – **help somebody on/off with** to help sby take off/put on (an article of clothing)

²**help** n 1 aid, assistance 2 remedy, relief ⟨there was no ~ for it⟩ 3a sby, esp a woman, hired to do work, esp housework ⟨a mother's ~⟩ b the services of a paid worker; also, chiefly NAm the workers providing such services ⟨~ wanted⟩

helpful adj of service or assistance; useful – **helpfully** adv, **helpfulness** n

helping n a serving of food

helpless adj 1 lacking protection or support; defenceless 2 lacking strength or effectiveness; powerless – **helplessly** adv, **helplessness** n

helpmate n one who is a companion and helper; esp a spouse

help out vb to give assistance or aid (to), esp when in great difficulty ⟨she helped me out when I was in hospital⟩

¹**helter-skelter** adj or adv (done) in a hurried and disorderly manner ⟨ran ~ down the stairs⟩

²**helter-skelter** n a spiral slide at a fairground

helve n a haft

¹**hem** n 1 the border of a cloth article when turned back and stitched down; esp the bottom edge of a garment finished in this manner 2 a similar border on an article of plastic, leather, etc

²**hem** vb -mm- vt 1a to finish (e g a skirt) with a hem b to border, edge 2 to enclose, confine – usu + in or about ⟨~med in by enemy troops⟩ ~ vi to make a hem in sewing – **hemmer** n

³**hem** interj – often used to indicate a pause in speaking

hem-, hema-, hemo- comb form, NAm **haem-**

he-man n a strong virile man – infml

hemisphere n 1a a half of the celestial sphere when divided into 2 halves by the horizon, the celestial equator, or the ecliptic b the northern or southern half of the earth divided by the equator or the eastern or western half divided by a meridian 2 either of the 2 half spheres formed by a plane that passes through the sphere's centre – **hemispheric, hemispherical** adj

hemline n the line formed by the lower hemmed edge of a garment, esp a dress

hemlock n 1 (a poison

hemlock n 1 (a poison obtained from) a very tall plant of the carrot family or a related very poisonous plant 2 (the soft light wood of) any of a genus of evergreen coniferous trees of the pine family

hemo- – see HAEM-

hemp n 1 (marijuana, hashish, or a similar drug obtained from) a tall widely cultivated plant from which a tough fibre used esp for making rope is prepared 2 the fibre of hemp or (a plant yielding) a similar fibre (e g jute) – **hempen** adj

hemstitch vt or n (to decorate with) drawnwork that consists of open spaces and embroidered groups of cross threads and is used esp on or next to the stitching line of hems

¹hen *n* **1a** a female bird, specif a domestic fowl (over a year old) **b** a female lobster, crab, fish, or other aquatic animal **2** an esp fussy woman – infml **3** *chiefly Scot* DEAR 1b – used to girls and women

²hen *adj* relating to or intended for women only ⟨a ~ party⟩

henbane *n* a poisonous fetid Old World plant of the nightshade family that contains hyoscyamine and scopolamine

hence *adv* **1** from this time; later than now **2** because of a preceding fact or premise ⟨born at Christmas; ~ the name Noel⟩ **3** from here; away – fml ⟨go ~⟩; sometimes + *from* ⟨depart from ~⟩; sometimes used as an interjection ⟨~! Depart!⟩

henceforth *adv* from this time or point on ⟨promise never to get drunk ~⟩

henchman *n* **1** a trusted follower; a right-hand man **2** a follower whose support is chiefly for personal advantage

¹henna *n* **1** an Old World tropical shrub or small tree with fragrant white flowers **2** a reddish brown dye obtained from the leaves of the henna plant and used esp on hair

²henna *vt* **hennaing; hennaed** to dye or tint (esp hair) with henna

henpecked *adj* cowed by persistent nagging ⟨~ husband⟩

hepatitis *n, pl* **hepatitides** (a condition marked by) inflammation of the liver: **a** INFECTIOUS HEPATITIS **b** SERUM HEPATITIS

heptagon *n* a polygon of 7 angles and 7 sides – **heptagonal** *adj*

¹her *adj* of her or herself, esp as possessor ⟨~ house⟩ ⟨~ fuselage⟩, agent ⟨~ research⟩, or object of an action ⟨~ rescue⟩ – used in titles of females ⟨~ Majesty⟩

²her *pron, objective case of* SHE

herald *n* **1a** an officer whose original duties of officiating at tournaments gave rise to other duties (e g recording names, pedigrees, and armorial bearings or tracing genealogies) **b** an official messenger between leaders, esp in war **c** an officer of arms ranking above a pursuivant and below a king of arms **2a** an official crier or messenger **b** sby or sthg that conveys news or proclaims ⟨it was the lark, the ~ of the morn – Shak⟩ **3** a harbinger, forerunner – **herald** *vt*

heraldic *adj* of a herald or heraldry – **heraldically** *adv*

heraldry *n* **1** the system, originating in medieval times, of identifying individuals by hereditary insignia; *also* the practice of granting, classifying, and creating these **2** the study of the history, display, and description of heraldry and heraldic insignia **3** pageantry

herb *n* **1** a seed plant that does not develop permanent woody tissue and dies down at the end of a growing season **2** a plant (part) valued for its medicinal, savoury, or aromatic qualities ⟨cultivated her ~ garden⟩ – **herbal** *adj*

herbaceous *adj* of, being, or having the characteristics of a (part of a) herb

herbage *n* (the succulent parts of) herbaceous plants (e g grass), esp when used for grazing

herbal *n* a book about (the medicinal properties of) plants

herbalist *n* sby who grows or sells herbs, esp for medicines

herbivore *n* a plant-eating animal – **herbivorous** *adj*

herculean *adj* of extraordinary strength, size, or difficulty ⟨a ~ task⟩

¹herd *n* **1** a number of animals of 1 kind kept together or living as a group **2a** *sing or pl in constr* a group of people usu having a common bond – often derog ⟨the ~ instinct⟩ **b** *the* masses – derog ⟨the common ~⟩ – **herdlike** *adj*

²herd *vi* to assemble or move in a herd or group ~ *vt* **1** to keep or move (animals) together **2** to gather, lead, or drive as if in a herd ⟨~ed his pupils into the hall⟩

herdsman *n* a manager, breeder, or tender of livestock

¹here *adv* **1** in or at this place ⟨turn ~⟩ – often interjectional, esp in answering a roll call **2** at or in this point or particular ⟨~ we agree⟩ **3** to this place or position ⟨come ~⟩ **4** – used when introducing, offering, or drawing attention ⟨~ she comes⟩ ⟨~ is the news⟩ ⟨~, take it⟩ **5** – used interjectionally to attract attention ⟨~, what's all this?⟩ – **here goes** – used to express resolution at the outset of a bold act; infml – **here's to** – used when drinking a toast – **here, there, and everywhere** scattered lavishly about – **here we go again** the same distressing events are repeating themselves – **here you are 1** what you wanted **2** you have arrived – **neither here nor there** of no consequence; irrelevant

²here *adj* **1** – used for emphasis, esp after a demonstrative ⟨this book ~⟩ ⟨ask my son ~⟩ **2** – used for emphasis between a demonstrative and the following noun; substandard ⟨this ~ book⟩

³here *n* this place or point ⟨full up to ~⟩

hereabouts *adv* in this vicinity

¹hereafter *adv* **1** after this **2** in some future time or state

²hereafter *n, often cap* **1** *the* future **2** an existence beyond earthly life

here and there *adv* **1** in one place and another **2** FROM TIME TO TIME

hereby *adv* by this means or pronouncement ⟨I ~ declare her elected⟩

hereditament *n* (real) property that can be inherited

hereditary *adj* **1a** genetically transmitted or transmissible from parent to offspring **b** characteristic of one's predecessors; ancestral ⟨~ pride⟩ **2a** received or passing by inheritance **b** having title through inheritance ⟨~ peer⟩ **3** traditional ⟨~ enemy⟩ **4** of inheritance or heredity – **hereditarily** *adv*

heredity *n* **1** the sum of the qualities and potentialities genetically derived from one's ancestors **2** the transmission of qualities from ancestor to descendant through a mechanism lying primarily in the chromosomes

herein *adv* in this – fml

hereinafter *adv* in the following part of this writing or document – fml

hereof *adv* of this – fml

heresy *n* **1** (adherence to) a religious belief or doctrine contrary to or incompatible with an explicit church dogma **2** an opinion or doctrine contrary to generally accepted belief

heretic *n* **1** a dissenter from established church dogma; *esp* a baptized member of the Roman Catholic church who disavows a revealed truth **2** one who dissents from an accepted belief or doctrine – **heretic, heretical** *adj*, **heretically** *adv*

hereto *adv* to this matter or document – fml

heretofore *adv* up to this time; hitherto – fml

hereunder *adv* under or in accordance with this writing or document – fml

hereupon *adv* **1** on this matter ⟨if all are agreed ~⟩ **2** immediately after this ⟨let us ~ adjourn⟩

herewith *adv* **1** hereby **2** with this; enclosed in this – fml

heritable *adj* **1** capable of being inherited **2** HEREDITARY 1a, 2a – **heritability** *n*

heritage *n* **1** sthg transmitted by or acquired from a predecessor; a legacy ⟨*a rich ~ of folklore*⟩ **2** a birthright ⟨*the ~ of natural freedom*⟩

hermaphrodite *n* **1** an animal or plant having both male and female reproductive organs **2** sthg that is a combination of 2 usu opposing elements – **hermaphrodite** *adj*, **hermaphroditism** *n*, **hermaphroditic** *adj*, **hermaphroditically** *adv*

hermetic *also* **hermetical** *adj* **1** *often cap* of or relating to the Gnostic and alchemical writings attributed to Hermes Trismegistus **2a** airtight ⟨*~ seal*⟩ **b** impervious to external influences **3** *often cap* abstruse, recondite – *infml* – **hermetically** *adv*

hermit *n* **1** one who retires from society and lives in solitude, esp for religious reasons **2** a recluse – **hermitism** *n*, **hermitic** *adj*

hermitage *n* **1** the habitation of one or more hermits **2** a secluded residence or private retreat; a hideaway

hernia *n*, *pl* **hernias, herniae** a protrusion of (part of) an organ through a wall of its enclosing cavity (e g the abdomen) – **hernial** *adj*, **herniated** *adj*

hero *n*, *pl* **heroes 1a** a mythological or legendary figure often of divine descent endowed with great strength or ability **b** an illustrious warrior **c** a person, esp a man, admired for noble achievements and qualities (e g courage) **2** the principal male character in a literary or dramatic work – **heroize** *vt*

heroic *also* **heroical** *adj* **1** of or befitting heroes **2a** showing or marked by courage **b** grand, noble **3** of impressive size, power, or effect; potent **4** of heroic verse – **heroically** *adv*

heroic couplet *n* a rhyming couplet in iambic pentameter

heroics *n pl* **1** HEROIC VERSE **2** extravagantly grand behaviour or language

heroic verse *n* the verse form employed in epic poetry (e g the heroic couplet in English)

heroin *n* a strongly physiologically addictive narcotic made from, but more potent than, morphine – **heroinism** *n*

heroism *n* heroic conduct or qualities; *esp* extreme courage

heron *n*, *pl* **herons,** *esp collectively* **heron** any of various long-necked long-legged wading birds with a long tapering bill, large wings, and soft plumage

heronry *n* a place where herons breed

herpes *n* herpes simplex or a similar inflammatory virus disease of the skin – **herpetic** *adj*

Herr *n*, *pl* **Herren** – used of a German-speaking man as a title equivalent to *Mr*

herring *n*, *pl* **herring,** *esp for different types* **herrings** a N Atlantic food fish that is preserved in the adult state by smoking or salting

¹herringbone *n* (sthg arranged in) a pattern made up of rows of parallel lines with any 2 adjacent rows slanting in opposite directions; *esp* a twilled fabric decorated with this pattern

²herringbone *vt* to make a herringbone pattern on – *vi* to ascend a (snow) slope by pointing the toes of the skis out

hers *pron*, *pl* **hers** that which or the one who belongs to her – used without a following noun as a pronoun equivalent in meaning to the adjective *her*; compare phrases at MINE 2

herself *pron* **1** that identical female person or creature used reflexively ⟨*she considers ~ lucky*⟩, for emphasis ⟨*she ~ did it*⟩ ⟨*Britain ~*⟩, or in absolute constructions ⟨*~ an orphan, she understood the situation*⟩ **2** her normal self ⟨*isn't quite ~*⟩

hertz *n*, *pl* **hertz** the SI unit of frequency equal to 1 cycle per second

he's he is; he has

hesitant *adj* tending to hesitate; irresolute – **hesitance, hesitancy** *n*, **hesitantly** *adv*

hesitate *vi* **1** to hold back, esp in doubt or indecision **2** to be reluctant or unwilling *to* **3** to stammer – **hesitater** *n*, **hesitatingly** *adv*, **hesitative** *adj*, **hesitation** *n*

Hesperus *n* EVENING STAR

hessian *n* **1** a coarse heavy plain-weave fabric, usu of jute or hemp, used esp for sacking **2** a lightweight material resembling hessian and used chiefly in interior decoration

heter-, hetero- *comb form* other; different; abnormal ⟨*heteromorphic*⟩

hetero *n*, *pl* **heteros** a heterosexual

heterodox *adj* **1** contrary to or different from established doctrines or opinions, esp in matters of religion ⟨*a ~ sermon*⟩ **2** holding opinions or doctrines which are not orthodox – **heterodoxy** *n*

heterogeneous *adj* consisting of dissimilar ingredients or constituents; disparate – **heterogeneously** *adv*, **heterogeneousness** *n*, **heterogeneity** *n*

heterosexual *adj or n* (of or being) sby having a sexual preference for members of the opposite sex – **heterosexually** *adv*, **heterosexuality** *n*

het up *adj* highly excited; upset – *infml*

¹heuristic *adj* **1** furthering investigation but otherwise unproved or unjustified ⟨*a ~ assumption*⟩ **2** of problem-solving techniques that proceed by trial and error ⟨*a ~ computer program*⟩ – **heuristically** *adv*

²heuristic *n* the study or practice of heuristic method

hew *vb* **hewed; hewed, hewn** *vt* **1** to strike, chop, or esp fell with blows of a heavy cutting instrument ⟨*~ed off a branch*⟩ ⟨*~ed down the tree*⟩ **2** to give form or shape to (as if) with heavy cutting blows – often + *out* ⟨*she ~ed out a career for herself*⟩ *~ vi* to make cutting blows – **hewer** *n*

¹hex *vb*, *NAm vi* to practise witchcraft *~ vt* to affect as if by an evil spell; jinx – **hexer** *n*

²hex *n*, *NAm* **1** a spell, jinx **2** a witch

hexagon *n* a polygon of 6 angles and 6 sides – **hexagonal** *adj*, **hexagonally** *adv*

hexagram *n* a 6-pointed star drawn by extending the sides of a regular hexagon

hexameter *n* a line of verse consisting of 6 metrical feet

¹hey *interj* – used esp to call attention or to express inquiry, surprise, or exultation

²hey *n* ¹HAY

heyday *n* the period of one's greatest vigour, prosperity, or fame

hey presto *interj* – used as an expression of triumph or satisfaction on completing or demonstrating sthg; *esp* used by conjurers about to reveal the outcome of a trick

hi *interj* – used esp to attract attention or, esp in the USA, as a greeting

¹hiatus *n* **1a** a break, gap **b** an (abnormal) anatomical gap or passage **2a** a lapse in continuity **b** the occurrence of 2 vowel sounds together without pause or intervening consonantal sound

²hiatus *adj* **1** involving a hiatus **2** *of a hernia* having a part that protrudes through the oesophageal opening of the diaphragm

hibernate *vi* **1** to pass the winter in a torpid or resting state **2** to be or become inactive or dormant – **hibernator** *n*, **hibernation** *n*

hibiscus *n* any of a genus of herbaceous plants, shrubs, or small trees of the mallow family with large showy flowers

¹hiccup also **hiccough** n **1** a spasmodic involuntary inhalation with closure of the glottis accompanied by a characteristic sharp sound **2** an attack of hiccuping – usu pl but sing. or pl in constr **3** chiefly Br a brief interruption or breakdown; a hitch ⟨a mistake due to a ~ in the computer⟩ – infml

²hiccup also **hiccough** vi -p-, -pp- to make a hiccup or hiccups

hick n, chiefly NAm an unsophisticated provincial person – **hick** adj

hickory n (the usu tough pale wood of) any of a genus of N American hardwood trees of the walnut family that often have sweet edible nuts – **hickory** adj

¹hide n any of various former English units of land area based on the amount of land that would support 1 free family and dependants

²hide vb **hid; hidden, hid** vt **1** to put out of sight; conceal **2** to keep secret ⟨hid the news from his parents⟩ **3** to screen from view ⟨house hidden by trees⟩ ~ vi **1** to conceal oneself **2** to remain out of sight – often + out – **hider** n

³hide n, chiefly Br a camouflaged hut or other shelter used for observation, esp of wildlife or game

⁴hide n the raw or dressed skin of an animal – used esp with reference to large heavy skins – **hide or/nor hair** the least vestige or trace – infml ⟨hadn't seen hide or hair of his wife for 20 years⟩

hide-and-seek n a children's game in which one player covers his/her eyes and then hunts for the other players who have hidden themselves

hideaway n a retreat, hideout

hidebound adj narrow or inflexible in character

hideous adj **1** offensive to the senses, esp the sight; exceedingly ugly **2** morally offensive; shocking – **hideously** adv, **hideousness** n

¹hiding n a state or place of concealment ⟨go into ~⟩

²hiding n a beating, thrashing ⟨gave him a good ~⟩; also a severe defeat – infml

hie vb **hying, hieing** archaic to hurry

hierarchy n **1** (church government by) a body of clergy organized according to rank, specif the bishops of a province or nation **2** a graded or ranked series

hieroglyph n a pictorial character used in hieroglyphics

hieroglyphics n pl but sing or pl in constr **1** a system of hieroglyphic writing; specif the picture script of various ancient peoples (e g the Egyptians) **2** sthg like hieroglyphics, esp in being difficult to decipher

hi-fi n **1** HIGH FIDELITY **2** equipment for the high-fidelity reproduction of sound *USE* infml

higgledy-piggledy adv in confusion; topsy-turvy – infml – **higgledy-piggledy** adj

¹high adj **1a** extending upwards for a considerable or above average distance ⟨rooms with ~ ceilings⟩ **b** situated at a considerable height above a base (e g the ground) ⟨a ~ plateau⟩ **c** of physical activity extending to or from, or taking place at a considerable height above, a base (e g the ground or water) ⟨~ diving⟩ **d** having a specified elevation; tall ⟨6 feet ~⟩ – often in combination ⟨sky-high⟩ **2** at the period of culmination or fullest development ⟨~ summer⟩ ⟨~ Gothic⟩ **3** elevated in pitch ⟨a ~ note⟩ **4** relatively far from the equator ⟨~ latitudes⟩ **5** of meat, esp game slightly decomposed or tainted **6a** exalted in character; noble ⟨~ principles⟩ **b** good, favourable ⟨has a very ~ opinion of her⟩ **7** of greater degree, amount, cost, value, or content than average ⟨~ prices⟩ ⟨food ~ in iron⟩ **8a** foremost in rank, dignity, or standing ⟨~

officials⟩ **b** critical, climactic ⟨the ~ point of the novel is the escape⟩ **c** marked by sublime or heroic events or subject matter ⟨~ tragedy⟩ **9** forcible, strong ⟨~ winds⟩ **10a** showing elation or excitement ⟨feelings ran ~⟩ **b** intoxicated by alcohol or a drug **11** advanced in complexity, development, or elaboration ⟨~er nerve centres⟩ ⟨~er mathematics⟩ ⟨~ technology⟩ **12** of a vowel CLOSE 2b **13** of a gear designed for fast speed **14** of words expressive of anger **15** rigidly traditionalist ⟨a ~ Tory⟩; specif HIGH CHURCH – **highly** adv – **on one's high horse** stubbornly or disdainfully proud ⟨gave up trying to reason with him when he got on his high horse⟩ .

²high adv at or to a high place, altitude, or degree ⟨threw the ball ~ in the air⟩

³high n **1** a region of high atmospheric pressure **2** a high point or level; a height ⟨sales have reached a new ~⟩ **3** NAm TOP **4** – **on high** in or to a high place, esp heaven

high-and-mighty adj arrogant, imperious

highball n a drink of spirits (e g whisky) and water or a carbonated beverage, served with ice in a tall glass

highborn adj of noble birth

highboy n, NAm TALLBOY 1

highbrow adj dealing with, possessing, or having pretensions to superior intellectual and cultural interests or activities ⟨a ~ radio programme⟩ – **highbrow** n, **highbrowed** adj, **highbrowism** n

high chair n a child's chair with long legs, a footrest, and usu a feeding tray

High Church adj tending, in the Anglican church, towards Roman Catholicism in liturgy, ceremonial, and dogma – **High Churchman** n

high-class adj superior, first-class

high commissioner n a principal commissioner; esp an ambassadorial representative of one Commonwealth country stationed in another

High Court n the lower branch of the Supreme Court of Judicature of England and Wales

higher education n education beyond the secondary level, at a college or university

higher-up n a person occupying a superior rank or position – infml

high explosive n an explosive (e g TNT) that explodes with extreme rapidity and has a shattering effect

highfalutin adj pretentious, pompous ⟨written in a ~ style⟩ – infml

high fidelity n the faithful reproduction of sound – **high-fidelity** adj

high-flier, high-flyer n a person who shows extreme ambition or outstanding promise

high-flown adj **1** excessively ambitious or extravagant **2** excessively elaborate or inflated; pretentious ⟨~ rhetoric⟩

high-flying adj **1** rising to considerable height **2** marked by extravagance, pretension, or excessive ambition

high-grade adj **1** of superior grade or quality ⟨~ bonds⟩ **2** being near the upper or most favourable extreme of a specified range

high-handed adj overbearingly arbitrary – **high-handedly** adv, **high-handedness** n

high jinks n pl high-spirited fun and games

high jump n (an athletic field event consisting of) a jump for height over a bar suspended between uprights – **high jumper** n, **high jumping** n – **for the high jump** about to receive a severe reprimand or punishment

highland n high or mountainous land – usu pl with sing. meaning – **highland** adj, **highlander** n

Highland adj **1** of the Highlands of Scotland **2** relating to or being a member of a shaggy long-haired breed of hardy beef cattle – **Highlander** *n*

Highland fling *n* a lively solo Scottish folk dance

Highlands *n pl the* northwest mountainous part of Scotland

high-level *adj* **1** occurring, done, or placed at a high level **2** of high importance or rank ⟨~ *diplomats*⟩ **3** *of a computer language* having each word equal to several machine code instructions and being easily understandable to humans

high life *n* luxurious living associated with the rich

¹highlight *n* **1** the lightest spot or area (e g in a painting or photograph) **2** an event or detail of special significance or interest ⟨~s *from the week's news*⟩ **3** a contrasting brighter part in the hair or on the face that reflects or gives the appearance of reflecting light

²highlight *vt* **1a** to focus attention on; emphasize **b** to emphasize (e g a figure) with light tones in painting, photography, etc **2** to give highlights to – **highlighter** *n*

highly *adv* **1** to a high degree; extremely ⟨~ *delighted*⟩ **2** with approval; favourably ⟨speak ~ *of someone*⟩

highly-strung, high-strung *adj* extremely nervous or sensitive

high mass *n, often cap H&M* an elaborate sung mass

high-minded *adj* having or marked by elevated principles and feelings – **high-mindedly** *adv*, **high-mindedness** *n*

Highness *n* – used as a title for a person of exalted rank (e g a king or prince)

high-octane *adj* having a high octane number and hence good antiknock properties ⟨~ *petrol*⟩

high-pitched *adj* **1** having a high pitch ⟨a ~ *voice*⟩ **2** marked by or exhibiting strong feeling; agitated ⟨a ~ *election campaign*⟩

high-powered *also* **high-power** *adj* having great drive, energy, or capacity; dynamic ⟨~ *executives*⟩

high-pressure *adj* **1** having or involving a (comparatively) high pressure, esp greatly exceeding that of the atmosphere **2a** using, involving, or being aggressive and insistent sales techniques ⟨~ *selling*⟩ **b** imposing or involving severe strain or tension ⟨~ *occupations*⟩

high priest *n* **1** a chief priest, esp of the ancient Jewish Levitical priesthood **2** the head or chief exponent of a movement – **high priesthood** *n*

high relief *n* sculptural relief in which at least half of the circumference of the design stands out from the surrounding surface

high-rise *adj* (situated in a building) constructed with a large number of storeys ⟨~ *flats*⟩ ⟨~ *blocks*⟩ – **high rise** *n*

highroad *n* **1** the easiest course *to* ⟨the ~ *to success*⟩ **2** chiefly *Br* a main road

high school *n* **1** chiefly *Br* secondary school; esp GRAMMAR SCHOOL – now chiefly in names **2** *NAm* a school usu for pupils aged about 15-18

high sea *n* the part of a sea or ocean outside territorial waters – usu pl with sing. meaning

high-sounding *adj* pompous, but meaningless

high-speed *adj* **1** (adapted to be) operated at high speed **2** relating to the production of photographs by very short exposures

high-spirited *adj* characterized by a bold or lively spirit; *also* highly-strung ⟨a ~ *horse*⟩ – **high-spiritedly** *adv*, **high-spiritedness** *n*

highspot *n* the most important or enjoyable feature of sthg ⟨the ~ *of his political career*⟩

high street *n, Br* a main or principal street, esp containing shops

high-strung *adj* highly-strung

high table *n, often cap H&T* a dining-room table, usu on a platform, used by the masters and fellows of a British college, or at a formal dinner or reception (e g by distinguished guests)

high tea *n, Br* a fairly substantial early evening meal (at which tea is served)

high-tension *adj* having a high voltage; *also* relating to apparatus to be used at high voltage

high tide *n* **1** (the time of) the tide when the water reaches its highest level **2** the culminating point; the climax

high-toned *adj* high in social, moral, or intellectual quality; dignified

high treason *n* TREASON 2

high water *n* HIGH TIDE 1

high-water mark *n* **1** a mark showing the highest level reached by the surface of a body of water **2** the highest point or stage

highway *n* **1** a public way; esp a main direct road **2** a busway

highway code *n, often cap H&C, Br* the official code of rules and advice for the safe use of roads

highwayman *n* a (mounted) robber of travellers on a road, esp in former times

hijack, high-jack *vt* **1a** to stop and steal from (a vehicle in transit) **b** to seize control of, and often divert, (a means of transport) by force ⟨gunmen ~ed *a plane bound for Frankfurt*⟩ **2** to steal, rob, or kidnap as if by hijacking – **hijack** *n*, **hijacker** *n*

¹hike *vi* to go on a hike – **hiker** *n*

²hike *n* **1** a long walk in the country, esp for pleasure or exercise **2** chiefly *NAm* an increase or rise ⟨a new wage ~⟩

hike up *vt, chiefly NAm* to move, pull, or raise with a sudden movement ⟨hiked *himself* up *on the wall*⟩ – infml

hilarious *adj* marked by or causing hilarity – **hilariously** *adv*, **hilariousness** *n*

hilarity *n* mirth, merriment

¹hill *n* **1** a usu rounded natural rise of land lower than a mountain **2** an artificial heap or mound (e g of earth) **3** an esp steep slope – **hilly** *adj* – **over the hill** past one's prime; too old

²hill *vt* to draw earth round the roots or base of (plants)

hillbilly *n, chiefly NAm* a person from a remote and culturally unsophisticated area

hillock *n* a small hill – **hillocky** *adj*

hilt *n* a handle, esp of a sword or dagger – **to the hilt** completely

him *pron, objective case of* HE

himself *pron* **1a** that identical male person or creature used reflexively ⟨he considers ~ *lucky*⟩, for emphasis ⟨he ~ *did it*⟩, or in absolute constructions ⟨~ *unhappy, he understood the situation*⟩ **b** – used reflexively when the sex of the antecedent is unspecified ⟨everyone must fend for ~⟩ **2** his normal self ⟨isn't quite ~ *today*⟩ **3** chiefly *NAm* oneself – used with one ⟨one should wash ~⟩

¹hind *n, pl* **hinds** *also* **hind** a female (red) deer

²hind *adj* situated at the back or behind; rear

¹hinder *vt* **1** to retard or obstruct the progress of; hamper **2** to restrain, prevent – often + *from* – **hinderer** *n*

²hinder *adj* situated behind or at the rear; posterior

hindmost *adj* furthest to the rear; last

hindquarter *n* **1** the back half of a side (of the carcass) of a quadruped **2** *pl* the hind legs (and adjoining structures) of a quadruped

hindrance *n* **1** the action of hindering **2** an impediment, obstacle

hindsight *n* the grasp or picture of a situation that one has after it has occurred

Hindu, *archaic* **Hindoo** *n* an adherent of Hinduism – **Hindu** *adj*

Hinduism *n* the dominant religion of India which involves belief in the illusory nature of the physical universe and in cycles of reincarnation, and is associated with a caste system of social organization

¹hinge *n* **1a** a jointed or flexible device on which a swinging part (e g a door or lid) turns **b** a flexible joint in which bones are held together by ligaments **c** a small piece of thin gummed paper used in fastening a postage stamp in an album **2** a point or principle on which sthg turns or depends

²hinge *vt* to attach by or provide with hinges ~*vi* **1** to hang or turn (as if) on a hinge ⟨*door* ~s *outwards*⟩ **2** to depend or turn *on* a single consideration or point

¹hint *n* **1** a brief practical suggestion or piece of advice ⟨~s *for home decorators*⟩ **2** an indirect or veiled statement; an insinuation **3** a slight indication or trace; a suggestion – usu + *of* ⟨*a* ~ *of irony in her voice*⟩

²hint *vt* to indicate indirectly or by allusion ⟨~ed *that something was up*⟩ ~*vi* to give a hint – **hint at** to imply or allude to (sthg)

hinterland *n* **1** a region lying inland from a coast **2** a region remote from urban or cultural centres

¹hip *n* the ripened fruit of a rose

²hip *n* **1a** the projecting region at each side of the lower or rear part of the mammalian trunk formed by the pelvis and upper part of the thigh **b** HIP JOINT **2** an external angle between 2 adjacent sloping sides of a roof

³hip *interj* – usu used to begin a cheer ⟨~ ~ *hooray*⟩

⁴hip *adj* **-pp-** keenly aware of or interested in the newest developments; *broadly* trendy – *infml* – **hipness** *n*

hip flask *n* a flat flask, usu for holding spirits, carried in a hip pocket

hip joint *n* the joint between the femur and the hipbone

hippie, hippy *n* a usu young person, esp during the 1960s, who rejected established mores, advocated a nonviolent ethic, and, in many cases, used psychedelic drugs; *broadly* a long-haired unconventionally dressed young person – **hippiehood** *n*, **hippie** *adj*, **hippiedom** *n*

Hippocratic oath *n* an oath embodying a code of medical ethics

hippodrome *n* **1** an arena for equestrian performances or circuses **2** a music hall, theatre, etc – esp in names

hippopotamus *n, pl* **hippopotamuses, hippopotami** any of several large plant-eating 4-toed chiefly aquatic mammals, with an extremely large head and mouth, very thick hairless skin, and short legs

hipster *n* **1** sby who is unusually aware of and interested in new and unconventional patterns, esp in jazz **2** *pl* trousers that start from the hips rather than the waist

¹hire *n* **1** payment for the temporary use of sthg **2** hiring or being hired

²hire *vt* **1a** to engage the services of for a set sum ⟨~ *a new crew*⟩ **b** to engage the temporary use of for an agreed sum ⟨~ *a hall*⟩ **2** to grant the services of or temporary use of for a fixed sum ⟨~ *themselves out*⟩ – **hirer** *n*

hireling *n* a person who works for payment, esp for purely mercenary motives – *derog*

hire purchase *n, chiefly Br* a system of paying for goods by instalments ⟨*bought their car on* ~⟩ ⟨*signed a* ~ *agreement*⟩

hirsute *adj* covered with (coarse stiff) hairs – **hirsuteness** *n*

¹his *adj* **1** of him or himself, esp as possessor ⟨~ *house*⟩ ⟨~ *tail*⟩, agent ⟨~ *writings*⟩, or object of an action ⟨~ *confirmation*⟩ – used in titles of males ⟨~

Majesty⟩ **2** *chiefly NAm* one's – used with *one* ⟨*one's duty to* ~ *public*⟩

²his *pron, pl* **his** that which or the one who belongs to him – used without a following noun as a pronoun equivalent in meaning to the adjective *his*; compare phrases at MINE 2

hiss *vi* to make a sharp voiceless sound like a prolonged *s,* esp in disapproval ~*vt* **1** to show disapproval of by hissing **2** to utter with a hiss – **hiss** *n*

hist *interj* – used to attract attention

hist-, histo- *comb form* tissue ⟨*histology*⟩

histamine *n* an amine that is a neurotransmitter in the autonomic nervous system and whose release under certain conditions causes an allergic reaction – **histaminic** *adj*

histology *n* (anatomy that deals with) the organization and microscopic structure of animal and plant tissues – **histologist** *n,* **histological** *adj,* **histologic** *adj,* **histologically** *adv*

historian *n* a student or writer of history

historic *adj* **1** (likely to be) famous or important in history ⟨*a* ~ *occasion*⟩ **2** *of a tense* expressive of past time

historical *adj* **1a** of or based on history **b** used in the past **2** famous in history **3** diachronic ⟨~ *linguistics*⟩ **4** dealing with or representing the events of history ⟨*a* ~ *novel*⟩ – **historically** *adv*

historic present *n* the present tense used to relate past events

history *n* **1** (a chronological record of) significant past events **2a** a treatise presenting systematically related natural phenomena ⟨*a* ~ *of British birds*⟩ **b** an account of sby's medical, sociological, etc background **3** a branch of knowledge that records the past **4a** past events ⟨*that's all* ~ *now*⟩ **b** an unusual or interesting past ⟨*this goblet has a* ~⟩ **c** previous treatment, handling, or experience

histrionic *adj* **1** of actors, acting, or the theatre **2** deliberately affected; theatrical – **histrionically** *adv*

histrionics *n pl but sing or pl in constr* deliberate display of emotion for effect

¹hit *vb* **-tt-;** **hit** *vt* **1a** to reach (as if) with a blow; strike ⟨~ *the ball*⟩ ⟨~ *by an attack of flu*⟩ **b** to make sudden forceful contact with ⟨*the car* ~ *the tree*⟩ **2a** to bring into contact ⟨~ *the stick against the railings*⟩ **b** to deliver, inflict ⟨~ *a severe blow*⟩ **3** to have a usu detrimental effect or impact on ⟨~ *hard by the drought*⟩ **4** to discover or meet, esp by chance ⟨*I seem to have* ~ *a snag*⟩ **5a** to reach, attain ⟨*prices* ~ *a new high*⟩ **b** to cause a propelled object to strike (e g a target), esp for a score in a contest **c** *of a batsman* to score (runs) in cricket; *also* to score runs off a ball bowled by (a bowler) **6** to indulge in, esp excessively ⟨~ *the bottle*⟩ **7** to arrive at or in ⟨~ *town*⟩ **8** to rob **9** *chiefly NAm* to kill ~*vi* **1** to strike a blow **2a** to come into forceful contact with sthg **b** to attack ⟨*wondered where the enemy would* ~ *next*⟩ **c** to happen or arrive, esp with sudden or destructive force ⟨*the epidemic* ~ *that summer*⟩ **3** to come, esp by chance; arrive at or find sthg – + *on* or *upon* ⟨~ *on a solution*⟩ USE (*vt 6 & 7*) *infml;* (*vt 8 & 9*) *slang* – **hit it off** to get along well – *infml* – **hit the jackpot** to be or become notably and unexpectedly successful – **hit the nail on the head** to be exactly right – **hit the road** to start on a journey – *infml* – **hit the roof** to give vent to a burst of anger or angry protest – *infml*

²hit *n* **1** a blow; *esp* one that strikes its target **2a** a stroke of luck **b** sthg (e g a popular tune) that enjoys great success ⟨*the song was a big* ~⟩ **3** a telling remark **4** a robbery **5** *chiefly NAm* an act of murder *USE (4 & 5)* slang

hit-and-run *adj* **1** being or involving a driver who does not stop after causing damage or injury **2** involving rapid action and immediate withdrawal ⟨~ *raids on coastal towns*⟩

¹hitch *vt* **1** to move by jerks **2** to catch or fasten (as if) by a hook or knot ⟨~ ed *his horse to the top rail of the fence*⟩ – often + *up* **3** to solicit and obtain (a free lift) in a passing vehicle ~ *vi* to hitchhike – *infml* – **hitcher** *n*

²hitch *n* **1** a sudden movement or pull; a jerk ⟨*gave his trousers a* ~⟩ **2** a sudden halt or obstruction; a stoppage ⟨*a* ~ *in the proceedings*⟩ **3** a knot used for a temporary fastening **4** *NAm* a period usu of military service – slang

hitchhike *vi* to travel by obtaining free lifts in passing vehicles – **hitchhiker** *n*

¹hither *adv* to or towards this place – *fml*

²hither *adj* NEAR 3a ⟨*the* ~ *side of the hill*⟩ – *fml*

hitherto *adv* up to this time; until now – *fml*

hit off *vt* to represent or imitate accurately

hit-or-miss *adj* showing a lack of planning or forethought; haphazard

hit out *vi* **1** to aim violent blows *at* **2** to aim angry verbal attacks *at*; speak violently *against*

hit parade *n* a group or listing of popular songs ranked in order of the number of records of each sold

¹hive *n* **1** (a structure for housing) a colony of bees **2** a place full of busy occupants ⟨*a* ~ *of industry*⟩

²hive *vt* to collect into a hive ~ *vi*, *of bees* to enter and take possession of a hive

hive off *vt* to separate from a group or larger unit; *specif* to assign (e g assets or responsibilities) to a subsidiary company or agency ~ *vi* **1** to become separated from a group; form a separate or subsidiary unit **2** to leave without warning ⟨hived off *at 4.30*⟩ – *infml*

hives *n pl but sing or pl in constr* urticaria

ho *interj* **1** – used esp to attract attention to sthg specified ⟨*land* ~⟩ **2** – used to express surprise or triumph

¹hoard *n* **1** an often secret supply (e g of money or food) stored up for preservation or future use **2** a cache of valuable archaeological remains

²hoard *vb* to lay up a hoard (of)

hoarding *n* **1** a temporary fence put round a building site **2** *Br* a large board designed to carry outdoor advertising

hoarfrost *n* FROST 1b

hoarse *adj* **1** rough or harsh in sound; grating ⟨~ *voice*⟩ **2** having a hoarse voice ⟨~ *with shouting*⟩ – **hoarsely** *adv*, **hoarseness** *n*, **hoarsen** *vb*

hoary *adj* **1a** grey or white with age; *also* grey-haired **b** having greyish or whitish hair, down, or leaves **2** impressively or venerably old; ancient **3** hackneyed ⟨*a* ~ *old joke*⟩ – **hoariness** *n*

¹hoax *vt* to play a trick on; deceive – **hoaxer** *n*

²hoax *n* an act of deception; a trick ⟨*the warning about the bomb was a* ~⟩

¹hob *n*, *dial Br* a goblin, elf

²hob *n* **1** a ledge near a fireplace on which sthg may be kept warm **2** a horizontal surface either on a cooker or installed as a separate unit that contains heating areas on which pans are placed

¹hobble *vi* to move along unsteadily or with difficulty; *esp* to limp ~ *vt* **1** to cause to limp **2** to fasten together the legs of (e g a horse) to prevent straying; fetter

²hobble *n* **1** a hobbling movement **2** sthg (e g a rope) used to hobble an animal

hobbledehoy *n* an awkward gawky youth

¹hobby *n* a leisure activity or pastime engaged in for interest or recreation – **hobbyist** *n*

²hobby *n* a small Old World falcon that catches small birds while in flight

hobbyhorse *n* **1** a figure of a horse fastened round the waist of a performer in a morris dance **2a** a toy consisting of an imitation horse's head attached to one end of a stick on which a child can pretend to ride **b** a toy horse on a merry-go-round **c** ROCKING HORSE **3** a topic to which one constantly returns

hobgoblin *n* **1** a goblin **2** a bugbear; BOGEY 2

hobnail *n* a short large-headed nail for studding shoe soles – **hobnailed** *adj*

hobnob *vi* -bb- **1** to associate familiarly **2** to talk informally *USE* usu + *with*; *infml*

hobo *n*, *pl* **hoboes** *also* **hobos 1** *chiefly NAm* a migratory worker **2** *NAm* TRAMP 1

Hobson's choice *n* an apparently free choice which offers no real alternative

¹hock *n* the tarsal joint of the hind limb of a horse or related quadruped that corresponds to the ankle in human beings

²hock *n*, *often cap*, *chiefly Br* a dry to medium-dry or sometimes sweet white table wine produced in the Rhine valley

³hock *n* **1** ¹PAWN 2 ⟨*got her watch out of* ~⟩ **2** DEBT 1 ⟨*in* ~ *to the bank*⟩ *USE infml*

⁴hock *vt* to pawn – *infml*

hockey *n* **1** a game played on grass between 2 teams of usu 11 players whose object is to direct a ball into the opponents' goal with a stick that has a flat-faced blade **2** *NAm* ICE HOCKEY

hocus-pocus *n* **1** SLEIGHT OF HAND **2** pointless activity or words, usu intended to obscure or deceive

hod *n* **1** a trough mounted on a pole handle for carrying mortar, bricks, etc **2** a coal scuttle; *specif* a tall one used to shovel fuel directly onto a fire

hodgepodge *n*, *chiefly NAm* a hotchpotch

¹hoe *n* any of various implements, esp one with a long handle and flat blade, used for tilling, weeding, etc

²hoe *vi* to work with a hoe ~ *vt* **1** to weed or cultivate (land or a crop) with a hoe **2** to remove (weeds) by hoeing

¹hog *n* **1** a hogg **2** a warthog or other wild pig **3** *Br* a castrated male pig raised for slaughter **4** *chiefly NAm* a domestic (fully grown) pig **5** a selfish, gluttonous, or filthy person – slang; compare ROAD HOG

²hog *vt* -gg- **1** to cut (a horse's mane) off or short **2** to appropriate a selfish or excessive share of; monopolize ⟨~ ged *the discussion*⟩ – *infml*

hoggish *adj* grossly selfish, gluttonous, or filthy

Hogmanay *n*, *Scot* the eve of New Year's Day

hogshead *n* **1** a large cask or barrel **2** any of several measures of capacity; *esp* a measure of 52½ imperial gallons (about 238l)

hogwash *n* **1** SWILL 1, SLOP 3a **2** sthg worthless; *specif* meaningless talk – slang

hoi polloi *n pl* *the* common people; *the* masses

¹hoist *vt* to raise into position (as if) by means of tackle; *broadly* to raise

²hoist *n* **1** an apparatus for hoisting **2a** the distance a flag extends along its staff or support **b** the end of a flag next to the staff

³hoist *adj* – **hoist with one's own petard** made a victim of or hurt by one's own usu malicious scheme

hoity-toity *adj* having an air of assumed importance; haughty – *infml*

¹hold *vb* **held** *vt* **1a** to have in one's keeping; possess ⟨~ *the title to the property*⟩ **b** to retain by force ⟨*troops* ~ *ing the ridge*⟩ **c** to keep by way of threat or coercion ⟨~ *ing* *the child for ransom*⟩ **2a** to keep under control; check ⟨held *her tongue*⟩ **b** to stop the action of temporarily; delay ⟨held *the presses to insert a late story*⟩ **c** to keep from advancing or from attacking successfully ⟨held *their opponents to a draw*⟩ **d** to restrict, limit ⟨~ *price increases to a minimum*⟩ **e** to bind legally or morally ⟨~ *a man to his word*⟩ **3a** to have, keep, or support in the hands or arms; grasp ⟨held *her to him*⟩ **b** to keep in a specified situation, position, or state ⟨~ *the ladder steady*⟩ **c** to support, sustain ⟨*the roof won't* ~ *much weight*⟩ **d** to retain ⟨*houses should* ~ *their value*⟩ **e** to keep in custody **f** to set aside; reserve ⟨~ *a room*⟩ **4** to bear, carry ⟨*the soldierly way he* ~s *himself*⟩ **5a** to keep up without interruption; continue ⟨*ship held its course*⟩ **b** to keep the uninterrupted interest or attention of ⟨held *the audience in suspense*⟩ **6a** to contain or be capable of containing ⟨*the can* ~s *5 gallons*⟩ **b** to have in store ⟨*what the future* ~s⟩ **7a** to consider to be true; believe **b** to have in regard ⟨*she* held *the matter to be of little importance*⟩ **8a** to engage in with sby else or with others ⟨~ *a conference*⟩ **b** to cause to be conducted; convene ⟨~ *a meeting of the council*⟩ **9a** to occupy as a result of appointment or election ⟨~s *a captaincy in the navy*⟩ **b** to have earned or been awarded ⟨~s *a PhD*⟩ ~ *vi* **1a** to maintain position ⟨*the defensive line is* ~ing⟩ **b** to continue unchanged; last ⟨*hopes the weather will* ~⟩ **2** to withstand strain without breaking or giving way ⟨*the anchor* held *in the rough sea*⟩ **3** to bear or carry oneself ⟨*asked her to* ~ *still*⟩ **4** to be or remain valid; apply ⟨*the rule* ~s *in most cases*⟩ **5** to maintain a course; continue ⟨held *south for several miles*⟩ – **hold a brief for** to be retained as counsel for – **hold forth** to speak at great length – **hold good** to be true or valid – **hold one's own** to maintain one's ground, position, or strength in the face of competition or adversity – **hold the fort** to cope with problems for or look after the work of sby who is absent – **hold to 1** to remain steadfast or faithful to; ABIDE BY **2** to cause to hold to ⟨held *him to his promise*⟩ – **hold water** to stand up under criticism or analysis – **hold with** to agree with or approve of ⟨*don't* hold with *such practices*⟩ – **not hold a candle to** to be much inferior to; not qualify for comparison with

²**hold** *n* **1a** a manner of grasping an opponent in wrestling **b** influence, control ⟨*his father had a strong* ~ *over him*⟩ **c** possession ⟨*tried to get* ~ *of a road map*⟩ **2** sthg that may be grasped as a support **3** a temporary stoppage of a countdown (e g in launching a spacecraft)

³**hold** *n* **1** a space below a ship's deck in which cargo is stored **2** the cargo compartment of a plane

holdall *n* a bag or case for miscellaneous articles

hold back *vt* **1** to hinder the progress of; restrain **2** to retain in one's keeping ~ *vi* to keep oneself in check

hold down *vt* **1** to keep within limits; *specif* to keep at a low level ⟨*try to* hold *prices* down⟩ **2** to hold and keep (a position of responsibility) ⟨holding down *2 jobs*⟩

holder *n* **1** a device that holds an often specified object ⟨*cigarette* ~⟩ **2a** an owner **b** a tenant **c** a person in possession of and legally entitled to receive payment of a bill, note, or cheque

holding *n* **1** land held **2** property (e g land or securities) owned – usu pl with sing. meaning

holding company *n* a company whose primary business is holding a controlling interest in the shares of other companies

hold off *vt* **1** to keep at a distance ⟨hold *the dogs* off⟩ **2** to resist successfully; withstand ⟨hold off *the enemy attack*⟩ **3** to defer action on; postpone ~ *vi* **1** to keep off or at a distance ⟨*hope the rain* holds off⟩ **2** to defer action; delay

hold on *vi* **1** to persevere in difficult circumstances **2** to wait; HANG ON ⟨hold on *a minute!*⟩ – **hold on to** to keep possession of

hold out *vt* to present as likely or realizable; proffer ⟨*the doctors* hold out *every hope of her recovery*⟩ ~ *vi* **1** LAST **2** ⟨*hope the car* holds out *till we get home*⟩ **2** to refuse to yield or give way ⟨*the garrison* held out *against the enemy attack*⟩ – **hold out for** to insist on as the price for an agreement – **hold out on** to withhold sthg (e g information) from – infml

hold over *vt* **1** to postpone **2** to prolong the engagement or tenure of ⟨*the show was* held over *for another week by popular demand*⟩

holdup *n* **1** an armed robbery **2** a delay

hold up *vt* **1** to delay, impede ⟨*got* held up *in the traffic*⟩ **2** to rob at gunpoint **3** to present, esp as an example ⟨*her work was* held up *as a model*⟩ ~ *vi* to endure a test; HOLD OUT

¹**hole** *n* **1** an opening into or through a thing **2a** a hollow place; *esp* a pit or cavity **b** a deep place in a body of water **c** a place in the crystal structure of a semiconductor, equivalent to a positively charged particle, where an electron has left its normal position **3** an animal's burrow **4** a serious discrepancy or flaw ⟨*picked* ~s *in his story*⟩ **5a** the unit of play from the tee to the hole in golf **b** a cavity in a putting green into which the ball is to be played in golf **6** a dirty or dingy place ⟨*lives in a dreadful* ~⟩ **7** an awkward position; a fix *USE* (*6 & 7*) infml – **holey** *adj*

²**hole** *vt* **1** to make a hole in **2** to drive into a hole ~ *vi* **1** to make a hole in sthg **2** to play one's ball into the hole in golf – usu + *out*

hole-and-corner *adj* clandestine, underhand

hole up *vi* to take refuge or shelter *in* ~ *vt* to place (as if) in a refuge or hiding place *USE* infml

¹**holiday** *n* **1** a day, often in commemoration of some event, on which no paid employment is carried out ⟨*Christmas Day is a public* ~⟩ **2** a period of relaxation or recreation spent away from home or work ⟨*went on* ~ *for a fortnight*⟩ – often pl with sing. meaning

²**holiday** *vi* to take or spend a holiday

holidaymaker *n* a person who is on holiday

holiness *n* **1** *cap* – used as a title for various high religious dignitaries ⟨*His* Holiness *Pope John Paul II*⟩ **2** sanctification

holland *n*, *often cap* a cotton or linen fabric in plain weave, usu heavily sized or glazed, that is used for window blinds, bookbinding, and clothing

holler *vb*, *chiefly NAm* to call out or shout (sthg) – **holler** *n*

¹**hollow** *adj* **1a** having a recessed surface; sunken **b** curved inwards; concave **2** having a cavity within ⟨~ *tree*⟩ **3** echoing like a sound made in or by beating on an empty container; muffled **4a** deceptively lacking in real value or significance ⟨*a* ~ *victory*⟩ **b** lacking in truth or substance; deceitful ⟨~ *promises*⟩ – **hollowly** *adv*, **hollowness** *n*

²**hollow** *vb* to make or become hollow

³**hollow** *n* **1** a depressed or hollow part of a surface; *esp* a small valley or basin **2** an unfilled space; a cavity

⁴**hollow** *adv* **1** in a hollow manner ⟨*his laughter rang* ~⟩ **2** completely, totally – infml ⟨*she beat me* ~⟩

hollow out *vt* to form a cavity or hole in; *also* to make in this way

holly *n* (the foliage of) any of a genus of trees and shrubs with thick glossy spiny-edged leaves and usu bright red berries

hollyhock *n* a tall orig Chinese plant of the mallow family with large coarse rounded leaves and tall spikes of showy flowers

Hollywood n the American film industry

holm oak n a S European evergreen oak

holocaust n **1** a sacrificial offering consumed by fire **2** an instance of wholesale destruction or loss of life **3** often cap the genocidal persecution of European Jewry by Hitler and the Nazi party during WW II

holograph n a document wholly in the handwriting of its author; also the handwriting itself – **holograph** adj, **holographic** adj

holstein n, chiefly NAm a Friesian

holster n a usu leather holder for a pistol

holy adj **1** set apart to the service of God or a god; sacred **2a** characterized by perfection and transcendence; commanding absolute adoration and reverence ⟨the ~ Trinity⟩ **b** spiritually pure; godly **3** evoking or worthy of religious veneration or awe ⟨the ~ cross⟩ **4** terrible, awful – used as an intensive ⟨a ~ terror⟩

Holy Communion n COMMUNION 1

Holy Grail n the cup or platter that according to medieval legend was used by Christ at the Last Supper and became the object of knightly quests

Holy See n the papacy

Holy Spirit n the 3rd person of the Trinity

Holy Week n the week before Easter during which the last days of Christ's life are commemorated

holy writ n, often cap H&W a writing or utterance of unquestionable authority

hom-, homo- comb form **1** one and the same; similar; alike ⟨homograph⟩ ⟨homosexual⟩ **2** containing one more CH_2 group than (the specified compound) ⟨homocysteine⟩

homage n **1a** a ceremony by which a man acknowledges himself the vassal of a lord **b** an act done or payment made by a vassal **2a** reverential regard; deference **b** flattering attention; tribute

homburg n a felt hat with a stiff curled brim and a high crown creased lengthways

¹home n **1a** a family's place of residence; a domicile **b** a house **2** the social unit formed by a family living together ⟨comes from a broken ~⟩ **3a** a congenial environment ⟨the theatre is my spiritual ~⟩ **b** a habitat **4a** a place of origin; also one's native country **b** the place where sthg originates or is based ⟨Lord's, ~ of cricket⟩ **5** an establishment providing residence and often care for children, convalescents, etc – **homeless** adj, **homelessness** n – **at home 1** relaxed and comfortable; AT EASE **2** ⟨felt completely at home on the stage⟩ **2** on familiar ground; knowledgeable ⟨teachers at home in their subjects⟩

²home adv **1** to or at home ⟨wrote ~⟩ **2** to a final, closed, or standard position ⟨drive a nail ~⟩ **3** to an ultimate objective (e g a finishing line) **4** to a vital sensitive core ⟨the truth struck ~⟩ **5** HOME AND DRY

³home adj **1** of or being a home, place of origin, or base of operations **2** prepared, carried out, or designed for use in the home ⟨~ cooking⟩ **3** operating or occurring in a home area ⟨the ~ team⟩

⁴home vi **1** to go or return home **2** of an animal to return accurately to one's home or birthplace from a distance – **home in on** to be directed at or head towards (a specified goal, target, etc)

home-, homeo- comb form, chiefly NAm homoe-

home and dry adv having safely or successfully achieved one's purpose

home brew n an alcoholic drink (e g beer) made at home

homecoming n a returning home

home economics n pl but sing or pl in constr DOMESTIC SCIENCE – **home economist** n

home from home n, Br a place as comfortable or congenial as one's own home

home front n the sphere of civilian activity in war

homegrown adj produced in, coming from, or characteristic of the home country or region ⟨~ vegetables⟩ ⟨~ politicians⟩

home help n, Br a person employed by a local authority to carry out household chores for the sick, elderly, or disabled

homeland n **1** one's native land **2** a Bantustan

homelike adj characteristic of one's own home, esp in being cheerful or cosy

homely adj **1** commonplace, familiar ⟨explained the problem in ~ terms⟩ **2** of a sympathetic character; kindly **3** simple, unpretentious ⟨a ~ meal of bacon and eggs⟩ **4** chiefly NAm not good-looking; plain – **homeliness** n

homemade adj made in the home, on the premises, or by one's own efforts ⟨~ cakes⟩

home office n, often cap H&O the government office concerned with internal affairs

home plate n a rubber slab at which a baseball batter stands

Homeric adj **1** (characteristic) of Homer, his age, or his writings **2** of epic proportions; heroic ⟨a ~ feat of endurance⟩

home rule n limited self-government by the people of a dependent political unit

home run n a hit in baseball that enables the batter to make a complete circuit of the bases and score a run

homesick adj longing for home and family while absent from them – **homesickness** n

¹homespun adj **1** made of homespun **2** lacking sophistication; simple ⟨~ prose⟩

²homespun n a loosely woven usu woollen or linen fabric orig made from yarn spun at home

homestead n **1** a house and adjoining land occupied by a family **2** Austr & NZ the owner's living quarters on a sheep or cattle station – **homesteader** n

home straight n the straight final part of a racecourse usu opposite the grandstand

homestretch n the final stage (e g of a project)

home truth n an unpleasant but true fact about a person's character or situation – often pl

homeward adj being or going towards home

homewards, chiefly NAm homeward adv towards home

homework n **1** work done in one's own home for pay **2** an assignment given to a pupil to be completed esp away from school **3** preparatory reading or research (e g for a discussion) ⟨she's done her ~ on the subject⟩ – **homeworker** n

homey adj homy

homicide n (the act of) sby who kills another – **homicidal** adj

homiletic, homiletical adj **1** of or resembling a homily **2** relating to homiletics

homiletics n pl but sing in constr the art of preaching

homily n **1** a sermon **2** a lecture on moral conduct

homing pigeon n a domesticated pigeon trained to return home

hominy n crushed or coarsely ground husked maize, esp when boiled with water or milk

¹homo n, pl homos any of a genus of primate mammals including recent man and various extinct ancestors

²homo n, pl homos a homosexual – chiefly derog

homoeopath n a practitioner of a system of disease treatment relying on the administration of minute doses of a remedy that produces symptoms like those of the disease – **homoeopathic** adj, **homoeopathy** n

homogeneous *adj* 1 of the same or a similar kind or nature 2 of uniform structure or composition throughout ⟨*a culturally ~ neighbourhood*⟩ 3 *of an equation, fraction, etc* having each term of the same degree when all variables are taken into account ⟨$x^2 + xy + y^2 = 0$ *is a ~ equation*⟩ – **homogeneously** *adv*, **homogeneousness** *n*

homogenize, -ise *vt* 1 to make homogeneous 2 to reduce the particles of so that they are uniformly small and evenly distributed; *esp* to break up the fat globules of (milk) into very fine particles ~ *vi* to become homogenized – **homogenizer** *n*, **homogenization** *n*

homograph *n* any of 2 or more words spelt alike but different in meaning, derivation, or pronunciation (e g the noun *conduct* and the verb *conduct*) – **homographic** *adj*

homonym *n* 1a a homophone b a homograph c any of 2 or more words that are both spelt and pronounced alike 2 a namesake – chiefly fml – **homonymic, homonymous** *adj*, **homonymously** *adv*, **homonymy** *n*

homophone *n* 1 any of 2 or more words pronounced alike but different in meaning, derivation, or spelling (e g *to*, *too*, and *two*) 2 a character or group of characters pronounced the same as another – **homophonous** *adj*

Homo sapiens *n* mankind

homosexual *adj or n* (of, for, or being) sby having a sexual preference for members of his/her own sex – **homosexuality** *n*

homy, homey *adj* homelike – chiefly infml

hone *vt or n* (to sharpen or make more keen or effective with or as if with) a stone for sharpening a cutting tool ⟨*finely ~ d sarcasm*⟩

honest *adj* 1 free from fraud or deception; legitimate, truthful 2 respectable or worthy 3a marked by integrity b frank, sincere ⟨*an ~ answer*⟩

honestly *adv* to speak in an honest way ⟨*~, I don't know why I bother*⟩

honesty *n* 1a upright and straightforward conduct; integrity b sincerity, truthfulness 2 any of a genus of European plants of the mustard family with large broad smooth semitransparent seed pods

honey *n* 1a (a pale golden colour like that typical of) a sweet viscous sticky liquid formed from the nectar of flowers in the honey sac of various bees b a sweet liquid resembling honey that is collected or produced by various insects 2 sthg sweet or agreeable; sweetness 3 *chiefly NAm* sweetheart, dear 4 a superlative example ⟨*a ~ of a girl* – Philip Roth⟩ – chiefly infml

honeybee *n* (a social honey-producing bee related to) a European bee kept for its honey and wax

¹**honeycomb** *n* 1 (sthg resembling in shape or structure) a mass of 6-sided wax cells built by honeybees in their nest to contain their brood and stores of honey 2 (tripe from) the second stomach of a cow or other ruminant mammal

²**honeycomb** *vt* 1 to cause to be chequered or full of cavities like a honeycomb 2 to penetrate into every part; riddle ⟨*the government is ~ed with spies* – T H White⟩

honeydew *n* a sweet deposit secreted on the leaves of plants usu by aphids

honeydew melon *n* a pale smooth-skinned muskmelon with greenish sweet flesh

honeyed *also* **honied** *adj* sweetened (as if) with honey ⟨*~ words*⟩

honeymoon *n* 1 the period immediately following marriage, esp when taken as a holiday by the married couple 2 a period of unusual harmony following the establish-

ment of a new relationship ⟨*the government's ~ with the public*⟩ – **honeymoon** *vi*, **honeymooner** *n*

honeysuckle *n* any of a genus of (climbing) shrubs usu with showy sweet-smelling flowers rich in nectar

¹**honk** *n* (a sound made by a car's electric horn like) the short loud unmusical tone that is the characteristic cry of the goose

²**honk** *vb* to (cause to) make a honk ⟨*the driver ~ed his horn*⟩ – **honker** *n*

honkie, honky *n, chiefly NAm* a white man – derog; used by Blacks

honky-tonk *n* 1 a form of ragtime piano playing 2 a cheap nightclub or dance hall – chiefly infml – **honky-tonk** *adj*

honorarium *n, pl* **honorariums, honoraria** a payment in recognition of professional services on which no price is set

honorary *adj* 1a conferred or elected in recognition of achievement, without the usual obligations ⟨*an ~ degree*⟩ b unpaid, voluntary ⟨*an ~ chairman*⟩ 2 depending on honour for fulfilment ⟨*an ~ obligation*⟩ – **honorarily** *adv*

¹**honorific** *adj* 1 conferring or conveying honour ⟨*~ titles*⟩ 2 belonging to or constituting a class of grammatical forms (e g in Chinese) used in speaking to or about a social superior – **honorifically** *adv*

²**honorific** *n* an honorific expression

¹**honour, NAm chiefly honor** *n* 1a good name or public esteem ⟨*his ~ was at stake*⟩ b outward respect; recognition 2 a privilege ⟨*I have the ~ to welcome you*⟩ 3 *cap* a person of superior social standing – now used esp as a title for a holder of high office (e g a judge in court) ⟨*if Your* Honour *pleases*⟩ 4 one who brings respect or fame ⟨*was an ~ to his profession*⟩ 5 a mark or symbol of distinction: e g a an exalted title or rank b a ceremonial rite or observance – usu pl ⟨*buried with full military ~s*⟩ 6 *pl* a course of study for a university degree more exacting and specialized than that leading to a pass degree 7 (a woman's) chastity or purity 8a a high standard of ethical conduct; integrity b one's word given as a pledge ⟨*~ bound*⟩ 9 *pl* social courtesies or civilities extended by a host ⟨*did the ~s at the table*⟩ 10a an ace, king, queen, or jack of the trump suit in whist; *also* these cards and the 10 in bridge or the 4 aces when the contract is no trumps b the privilege of playing first from the tee in golf awarded to the player who won the previous hole

²**honour, NAm chiefly honor** *vt* 1a to regard or treat with honour or respect b to confer honour on 2a to live up to or fulfil the terms of ⟨*~ a commitment*⟩ b to accept and pay when due ⟨*~ a cheque*⟩ 3 to salute (e g one's partner) with a bow in a country dance

honourable, NAm chiefly honorable *adj* 1 worthy of honour 2 performed or accompanied with marks of honour or respect 3 entitled to honour – used as a title for the children of certain British noblemen and for various government officials 4a bringing credit to the possessor or doer ⟨*an ~ performance*⟩ b consistent with an untarnished reputation ⟨*an ~ discharge from the army*⟩ 5 characterized by (moral) integrity ⟨*his intentions were ~*⟩

hooch *n, NAm* spirits, esp when inferior or illicitly made or obtained – slang

¹**hood** *n* 1a a loose often protective covering for the top and back of the head and neck that is usu attached to the neckline of a garment b a usu leather covering for a hawk's head and eyes 2a an ornamental scarf worn over an academic gown that indicates by its colour the wearer's university and degree b a hoodlike marking, crest, or expansion on the head of an animal (e g a cobra or seal)

3a a folding waterproof top cover for an open car, pram, etc **b** a cover or canopy for carrying off fumes, smoke, etc **4** *NAm* BONNET 2 – **hood** *vt*

²hood *n* a hoodlum or gangster – *infml*

-hood *suffix (adj or n → n)* **1** state or condition of ⟨*priest*hood⟩ ⟨*man*hood⟩ **2** quality or character of ⟨*likeli*hood⟩ **3** time or period of ⟨*child*hood⟩ **4** instance of (a specified quality or condition) ⟨*a false*hood⟩ **5** *sing or pl in constr* body or class of people sharing (a specified character or state) ⟨*brother*hood⟩ ⟨*priest*hood⟩

hooded *adj* **1** covered (as if) by a hood ⟨~ *eyes*⟩ **2** shaped like a hood

hoodlum *n* **1** a (violent) thug **2** a young rowdy – **hoodlumish** *adj*

¹hoodoo *n, pl* hoodoos *chiefly NAm* voodoo – **hoodooism** *n*

²hoodoo *vt, chiefly NAm* to cast an evil spell on; *broadly* to bring bad luck to

hoodwink *vt* to deceive, delude – *chiefly infml* – **hoodwinker** *n*

hooey *n* nonsense – *slang*

¹hoof *n, pl* hooves, hoofs (a foot with) a curved horny casing that protects the ends of the digits of a horse, cow, or similar mammal and that corresponds to a nail or claw – **hoofed** *adj* – **on the hoof** *of a meat animal* before being butchered; while still alive ⟨*50p a pound on the hoof*⟩

²hoof *vt* to kick ~ *vi* to go on foot – usu + *it*

hoo-ha *n* a fuss, to-do – *chiefly infml*

¹hook *n* **1** (sthg shaped like) a curved or bent device for catching, holding, or pulling **2a** (a flight of) a ball in golf that deviates from a straight course in a direction opposite to the dominant hand of the player propelling it **b** an attacking stroke in cricket played with a horizontal bat aimed at a ball of higher than waist height and intended to send the ball on the leg side **3** a short blow delivered in boxing with a circular motion while the elbow remains bent and rigid – **by hook or by crook** by any possible means – **hook, line, and sinker** completely ⟨*swallowed all the lies hook, line, and sinker*⟩

²hook *vt* **1** to form into a hook (shape) **2** to seize, make fast, or connect (as if) by a hook **3** to make (e g a rug) by drawing loops of yarn, thread, or cloth through a coarse fabric with a hook **4a** to hit or throw (a ball) so that a hook results **b** to play a hook in cricket at (a ball) or at the bowling of (a bowler) **5** to steal – *infml* ~ *vi* **1** to form a hook; curve **2** to become hooked **3** to play a hook in cricket or golf

hookah *n* a water pipe (with a single flexible tube by which smoke is drawn through water and into the mouth)

hooked *adj* **1** (shaped) like or provided with a hook **2** made by hooking ⟨*a ~ rug*⟩ **3a** addicted to drugs – *slang* **b** very enthusiastic or compulsively attached (to sthg specified) ⟨~ *on skiing*⟩ – *infml*

hooker *n* **1** (the position of) a player in rugby stationed in the middle of the front row of the scrum **2** *chiefly NAm* a woman prostitute – *slang*

hookup *n* (the plan of) a combination (e g of electronic circuits) used for a specific often temporary purpose (e g radio transmission)

hookworm *n* (infestation with or disease caused by) any of several parasitic nematode worms that have strong mouth hooks for attaching to the host's intestinal lining

hooky, hookey *n, chiefly NAm* truant – chiefly in *play hooky*; *infml*

hooligan *n* a young ruffian or hoodlum – **hooliganism** *n*

¹hoop *n* **1** a large (rigid) circular strip used esp for holding

together the staves of containers, as a child's toy, or to expand a woman's skirt **2** a circular figure or object **3** an arch through which balls must be hit in croquet

²hoop *vt* to bind or fasten (as if) with a hoop – **hooper** *n*

hoop-la *n* a (fairground) game in which prizes are won by tossing rings over them

hooray *interj* hurray

¹hoot *vi* **1** to utter a loud shout, usu in contempt **2a** to make (a sound similar to) the long-drawn-out throat noise of an owl **b** to sound the horn, whistle, etc of a motor car or other vehicle ⟨*the driver ~ed at me as he passed*⟩ **3** to laugh loudly – *infml* ~ *vt* **1** to assail or drive out by hooting ⟨~ *ed down the speaker*⟩ **2** to express in or by hooting ⟨~ *ed their disapproval*⟩

²hoot *n* **1** a sound of hooting **2** DAMN 2 ⟨*I couldn't care 2 ~ s*⟩ **3** a source of laughter or amusement ⟨*the play was an absolute ~*⟩ USE (2, 3) *infml*

hooter *n, chiefly Br* **1** a device (e g the horn of a car) for producing a loud hooting noise **2** the nose – *infml*

hoover *vb* to clean using a vacuum cleaner

Hoover *trademark* – used for a vacuum cleaner

¹hop *vb* **-pp-** *vi* **1** to move by a quick springy leap or in a series of leaps; *esp* to jump on 1 foot **2** to make a quick trip, esp by air **3** to board or leave a vehicle ⟨~ *onto a bus*⟩ ~ *vt* **1** to jump over ⟨~ *a fence*⟩ **2** *NAm* to ride on, esp without authorization ⟨~ *a train*⟩ USE (*vi* 2, 3) *infml* – **hop it** *Br* go away! – *infml*

²hop *n* **1a** a short leap, esp on 1 leg **b** a bounce, a rebound **2** a short or long flight between 2 landings ⟨*flew to Bangkok in 3 ~ s*⟩ **3** DANCE 2 – *infml*

³hop *n* **1** a climbing plant of the hemp family with inconspicuous green flowers of which the female ones are in cone-shaped catkins **2** *pl* the ripe dried catkins of a hop used esp to impart a bitter flavour to beer

⁴hop *vt* **-pp-** to impregnate (esp beer) with hops

¹hope *vi* to wish for with expectation of fulfilment ~ *vt* **1** to long for with expectation of obtainment **2** to expect with desire; trust – **hoper** *n* – **hope against hope** to hope without any basis for expecting fulfilment

²hope *n* **1** trust, reliance ⟨*all my ~ is in the Lord*⟩ **2a** desire accompanied by expectation of or belief in fulfilment ⟨*has high ~ s of an early recovery*⟩ **b** sby or sthg on which hopes are centred **c** sthg hoped for

hope chest *n, NAm* BOTTOM DRAWER

¹hopeful *adj* **1** full of hope ⟨*I'm ~ he'll come*⟩ **2** inspiring hope ⟨*the situation looks ~*⟩ – **hopefulness** *n*

²hopeful *n* a person who aspires to or is likely to succeed ⟨*young ~ s*⟩

hopefully *adv* **1** in a hopeful manner **2** it is hoped ⟨~ *he will arrive in time*⟩ – disapproved of by some speakers

hopeless *adj* **1** having no expectation of success **2a** giving no grounds for hope ⟨*a ~ case*⟩ **b** incapable of solution, management, or accomplishment ⟨*a ~ task*⟩ **3** incompetent, useless – *chiefly infml* ⟨*I'm ~ at sums*⟩ – **hopelessly** *adv*, **hopelessness** *n*

hopper *n* **1** a leaping insect; *specif* an immature hopping form of an insect **2a** a (funnel-shaped) receptacle for the discharging or temporary storage of grain, coal, etc **b** a goods wagon with a floor through which bulk materials may be discharged **c** a barge that can discharge dredged material through an opening bottom

hopscotch *n* a children's game in which a player tosses an object (e g a stone) into areas of a figure outlined on the ground and hops through the figure and back to regain the object

hop, skip, and jump *n* a short distance – *infml*

horde *n* **1 a** (Mongolian) nomadic people or tribe **2 a** crowd, swarm

horizon *n* **1a** the apparent junction of earth and sky **b**(1) the plane that is tangent to the earth's surface at an observer's position (2) (the great circle formed by the intersection with the celestial sphere of) the plane parallel to such a plane but passing through the earth's centre **c** range of perception, experience, or knowledge **2a** the geological deposit of a particular time, usu identified by distinctive fossils **b** any of the reasonably distinct soil or subsoil layers in a vertical section of land – **horizonal** *adj*

horizontal *adj* **1a** near the horizon **b** in the plane of or (operating in a plane) parallel to the horizon or a base line; level ⟨~ *distance*⟩⟨*a* ~ *engine*⟩ **2** of or concerning relationships between people of the same rank in different hierarchies – **horizontally** *adv*

hormone *n* (a synthetic substance with the action of) a product of living cells that usu circulates in body liquids (e g the blood or sap) and produces a specific effect on the activity of cells remote from its point of origin – **hormonal** *adj*, **hormonally** *adv*

horn *n* **1a**(1) any of the usu paired bony projecting parts on the head of cattle, giraffes, deer, and similar hoofed mammals and some extinct mammals and reptiles (2) a permanent solid pointed part consisting of keratin that is attached to the nasal bone of a rhinoceros **b** a natural projection from an animal (e g a snail or owl) resembling or suggestive of a horn **c** the tough fibrous material consisting chiefly of keratin that covers or forms the horns and hooves of cattle and related animals, or other hard parts (e g claws or nails) **d** a hollow horn used as a container **2** sthg resembling or suggestive of a horn: e g **a** either of the curved ends of a crescent **b** a horn-shaped body of land or water **3a** an animal's horn used as a wind instrument **b**(1) HUNTING HORN (2) FRENCH HORN **c** a wind instrument used in a jazz band; *esp* a trumpet **d** a device (e g on a motor car) for making loud warning noises ⟨*a fog* ~⟩ – **horn** *adj*, **horned** *adj*, **hornless** *adj*, **hornlike** *adj*

hornbeam *n* any of a genus of trees of the hazel family with smooth grey bark and hard white wood

hornbill *n* any of a family of large Old World birds with enormous bills

hornet *n* a large wasp with a black and yellow banded abdomen and a powerful sting

hornet's nest *n* an angry or hostile reaction – esp in *stir up a hornet's nest*

horn in *vi* to intrude – slang; often + *on*

hornpipe *n* (a piece of music for) a lively British folk dance typically associated with sailors

horn-rims *n pl* glasses with horn rims – **horn-rimmed** *adj*

horny *adj* **1** (made) of horn **2** sexually aroused – slang

horology *n* **1** the science of measuring time **2** the art of constructing instruments for indicating time – **horologer** *n*, **horologist** *n*, **horologic**, **horological** *adj*

horoscope *n* (an astrological forecast based on) a diagram of the relative positions of planets and signs of the zodiac at a specific time, esp sby's birth, used by astrologers to infer individual character and personality traits and to foretell events in a person's life

horrendous *adj* dreadful, horrible – **horrendously** *adv*

horrible *adj* **1** marked by or arousing horror ⟨*a* ~ *accident*⟩ **2** extremely unpleasant or disagreeable – chiefly infml ⟨~ *weather*⟩ – **horribleness** *n*, **horribly** *adv*

horrid *adj* **1** hor-ible, shocking **2** repulsive, nasty ⟨*a* ~ *little boy*⟩ – **horridly** *adv*, **horridness** *n*

horrific *adj* arousing horror; horrifying ⟨*a* ~ *account of the tragedy*⟩ – **horrifically** *adv*

horrify *vt* **1** to cause to feel horror **2** to fill with distaste; shock – **horrifyingly** *adv*

horror *n* **1a** intense fear, dread, or dismay **b** intense aversion or repugnance **2** (sby or sthg that has) the quality of inspiring horror ⟨*contemplating the* ~ *of their lives* – Liam O'Flaherty⟩ ⟨*that child is a perfect* ~⟩ **3** *pl* a state of horror, depression, or apprehension – chiefly infml

horror-struck, horror-stricken *adj* filled with horror

hors de combat *adv or adj* out of the fight; disabled

hors d'oeuvre *n, pl* **hors d'oeuvres** *also* **hors d'oeuvre** any of various savoury foods usu served as appetizers

¹**horse** *n, pl* **horses**, (3) **horse** **1a**(1) a large solid-hoofed plant-eating quadruped mammal domesticated by humans since prehistoric times and used as a beast of burden, a draught animal, or for riding (2) a racehorse ⟨*play the* ~ s⟩ **b** a male horse; a stallion or gelding **2a** a usu 4-legged frame for supporting sthg (e g planks) **b**(1) POMMEL HORSE (2) VAULTING HORSE **3** *sing or pl in constr* the cavalry **4** a mass of wall rock occurring in a vein **5** a rope suspended from the yard of a sailing ship, on which the seamen stand when working on the sails **6** heroin – slang – **from the horse's mouth** from the original source

²**horse** *vi* to engage in horseplay ⟨*horsing around*⟩ ~ *vt* to provide (a person or vehicle) with a horse

¹**horseback** *n* – **on horseback** mounted on a horse

²**horseback** *adv, chiefly NAm* ON HORSEBACK

horsebox *n* a lorry or closed trailer for transporting horses

horse chestnut *n* (the large glossy brown seed of) a large tree with 5-lobed leaves and erect conical clusters of showy flowers

horsefly *n* any of a family of swift usu large flies with bloodsucking females

horsehair *n* hair (from the mane or tail) of a horse; *also* cloth made from this

horselaugh *n* a loud boisterous laugh

horseman, *fem* **horsewoman** *n* **1** a rider on horseback **2** a (skilled) breeder, tender, or manager of horses – **horsemanship** *n*

horseplay *n* rough or boisterous play

horsepower *n* an imperial unit of power equal to about 746W

horseradish *n* **1** a tall coarse white-flowered plant of the mustard family **2** (a condiment prepared from) the pungent root of the horseradish

horse sense *n* COMMON SENSE

horseshit *n, chiefly NAm* bullshit – vulg

horseshoe *n* (sthg with a shape resembling) a shoe for horses, usu consisting of a narrow U-shaped plate of iron fitting the rim of the hoof – **horseshoe** *vt*, **horseshoer** *n*

horse-trading *n* negotiation accompanied by hard bargaining and reciprocal concessions

horsewhip *vt* to flog (as if) with a whip for horses

horsewoman *n* a female horseman

horsey, horsy *adj* **1** of or resembling a horse **2** very interested in horses, horse riding, or horse racing **3** characteristic of horsemen – **horsily** *adv*, **horsiness** *n*

hortative, hortatory *adj* giving encouragement – fml – **hortatively** *adv*

horticulture *n* the science and art of growing fruits, vegetables, and flowers – **horticultural** *adj*, **horticulturally** *adv*, **horticulturist** *n*

hosanna *interj or n* (used as) a cry of acclamation and adoration

¹**hose** *n, pl* **hose,** (1) **hose,** (2) **hoses 1** a leg covering that sometimes covers the foot: e g **a** short breeches reaching

to the knee ⟨*doublet and* ~⟩ **b** *pl, chiefly NAm* stockings; *also* tights **2** a flexible tube for conveying fluids (e g from a tap or in a car engine)

²hose *vt* to spray, water, or wash with a hose ⟨~ *down a stable floor*⟩

hosiery *n* socks, stockings, and tights in general

hospice *n* **1** a place of shelter for travellers or the destitute (run by a religious order) **2** *Br* a nursing home, esp for terminally ill patients

hospitable *adj* **1a** offering a generous and cordial welcome (to guests or strangers) **b** offering a pleasant or sustaining environment ⟨*a* ~ *climate*⟩ **2** readily receptive ⟨~ *to new ideas*⟩ – **hospitably** *adv*

hospital *n* **1** an institution where the sick or injured are given medical care – often used in British English without an article ⟨*the injured were taken to* ~⟩ **2** a repair shop for specified small objects ⟨*a doll's* ~⟩

hospitality *n* hospitable treatment or reception

hospitalize, -ise *vt* to place in a hospital as a patient – **hospitalization** *n*

¹host *n* **1** a very large number; a multitude **2** an army – chiefly poetic or archaic

²host *n* **1a** an innkeeper ⟨*mine* ~⟩ **b** one who receives or entertains guests socially or officially **c** sby or sthg that provides facilities for an event or function ⟨*our college served as* ~ *for the chess tournament*⟩ **2a** a living animal or plant on or in which a parasite or smaller organism lives **b** an individual into which a tissue or part is transplanted from another **3** a compere on a radio or television programme

³host *vt* to act as host at or of ⟨~ed *a series of TV programmes*⟩

⁴host *n, often cap* the bread consecrated in the Eucharist

hostage *n* a person held by one party as a pledge that promises will be kept or terms met by another party ⟨*hijackers took 3* ~s⟩

hostel *n* **1** *chiefly NAm* a supervised residential home: e g **a** an establishment providing accommodation for nurses, students, etc **b** an institution for junior offenders, ex-offenders, etc, encouraging social adaptation **2** YOUTH HOSTEL **3** an inn – chiefly poetic or archaic – **hosteller** *n*

hostelry *n* an inn, hotel

hostess *n* **1** a woman who entertains socially or acts as host **2a** a female employee on a ship, aeroplane, etc who manages the provisioning of food and attends to the needs of passengers **b** a woman who acts as a companion to male patrons, esp in a nightclub; *also* a prostitute

hostile *adj* **1** of or constituting an enemy **2** antagonistic, unfriendly **3** not hospitable ⟨*a* ~ *environment*⟩ – **hostile** *n*, **hostilely** *adv*

hostility *n* **1** *pl* overt acts of warfare **2** antagonism, opposition, or resistance

hostler *n, chiefly NAm* an ostler

¹hot *adj* -tt- **1a** having a relatively high temperature **b** capable of giving a sensation of heat or of burning, searing, or scalding **c** having a temperature higher than normal body temperature **2a** vehement, fiery ⟨*a* ~ *temper*⟩ **b** sexually excited; *also* sexually arousing **c** eager, enthusiastic ⟨~ *on the idea*⟩ **d** of or being an exciting style of jazz with strong rhythms **3** severe, stringent – usu + *on* ⟨*police are* ~ *on drunken drivers*⟩ **4** having or causing the sensation of an uncomfortable degree of body heat ⟨*felt too* ~⟩ **5a** very recent; fresh ⟨~ *off the press*⟩ **b** close to sthg sought ⟨*guess again, you're getting* ~⟩ **6a** suggestive of heat or of burning objects ⟨~ *colours*⟩ **b** pungent, peppery ⟨*a* ~ *curry*⟩ **7a** of intense and immediate interest; sensational **b** performing well or strongly fancied to

win (e g in a sport) ⟨~ *favourite*⟩ **c** currently popular; selling very well **d** very good – used as a generalized term of approval ⟨*his English is not so* ~⟩ **8** (of, being, or for material that is) radioactive **9a** recently and illegally obtained ⟨~ *jewels*⟩ **b** wanted by the police USE (2b, 2c, & 7d) infml, (9) slang – **hottish** *adj*, **hotness** *n*

²hot *adv* hotly

hot air *n* empty talk – chiefly infml

hotbed *n* **1** a bed of soil heated esp by fermenting manure and used for forcing or raising seedlings **2** an environment that favours rapid growth or development, esp of sthg specified ⟨*a* ~ *of crime*⟩

hot-blooded *adj* excitable, ardent – **hot–bloodedness** *n*

hotchpotch *n* a mixture composed of many usu unrelated parts; a jumble

hot cross bun *n* a yeast-leavened spicy bun marked with a cross and eaten esp on Good Friday

hot dog *n* a frankfurter or other sausage (heated and served in a bread roll)

hotel *n* a usu large establishment that provides meals and (temporary) accommodation for the public, esp for people travelling away from home

Hotel – a communications code word for the letter *h*

hotelier *n* a proprietor or manager of a hotel

hot flush *n* a sudden brief flushing and sensation of heat, usu associated with an imbalance of endocrine hormones occurring esp at the menopause

hotfoot *vi or adv* (to go) in haste – **hotfoot it** to hotfoot

hothead *n* a hotheaded person

¹hothouse *n* a heated greenhouse, esp for tropical plants

²hothouse *adj* delicate, overprotected

hot line *n* a direct telephone line kept in constant readiness for immediate communication (e g between heads of state)

hotly *adv* in a hot or fiery manner ⟨*a* ~ *debated issue*⟩

hot plate *n* a metal plate or spiral, usu on an electric cooker, on which food can be heated and cooked

hot pot *n* a (mutton, lamb, or beef and potato) stew cooked esp in a covered pot

hot potato *n* a controversial or sensitive question or issue – infml

hot rod *n* a motor vehicle rebuilt or modified for high speed and fast acceleration – **hot–rodder** *n*

hot seat *n* **1** a position involving risk, embarrassment, or responsibility for decision-making ⟨*in the* ~ *at the interview*⟩ – infml **2** ELECTRIC CHAIR – slang

hot spring *n* a spring of naturally hot water

hot stuff *n* **1** sby or sthg of outstanding ability or quality **2** sby or sthg sexually exciting ⟨*she's really* ~⟩ USE infml

Hottentot *n* a member, or the language, of a people of southern Africa apparently of mixed Bushman and Bantu origin

hot up *vi* to become hot; increase in activity, intensity, liveliness, excitement, etc ⟨*air raids began to* hot up *about the beginning of February* – George Orwell⟩ ~ *vt* to make hotter, livelier, or faster

hot water *n* a distressing predicament (likely to lead to punishment); trouble – infml

hot-water bottle *n* a usu flat rubber container that is filled with hot water and used esp to warm a (person in) bed

¹hound *n* **1** a dog; *esp* one of any of various hunting breeds typically with large drooping ears and a deep bark that track their prey by scent **2** a mean or despicable person **3** one who is devoted to the pursuit of sthg specified

²hound vt **1** to pursue (as if) with hounds **2** to harass persistently – **hounder** n

houndstooth check, hound's-tooth check n a small broken-check textile pattern

hour n **1** (any of the 7 times of day set aside for) a daily liturgical devotion **2** the 24th part of a day; a period of 60 minutes **3a** the time of day reckoned in hours and minutes by the clock; *esp* the beginning of each full hour measured by the clock ⟨*the train leaves on the* ∼⟩ **b** *pl* the time reckoned in one 24-hour period from midnight to midnight ⟨*attack at 0900* ∼s⟩ **4a** a fixed or customary period of time set aside for a usu specified purpose ⟨*the lunch* ∼⟩ – often *pl* ⟨*during office* ∼s⟩ **b** a particular, usu momentous, period or point of time ⟨*in his* ∼ *of need*⟩ **c** the present ⟨*the story of the* ∼⟩ **5** *pl* one's regular time of getting up or going to bed ⟨*kept late* ∼s⟩ **6** the work done or distance travelled at normal rate in an hour ⟨*the city was 2* ∼s *away*⟩ **7** *NAm* a unit of educational credit

¹hourglass n a glass or perspex instrument for measuring time consisting of 2 bulbs joined by a narrow neck from the uppermost of which a quantity of sand, water, etc runs into the lower in the space of an hour

²hourglass adj shapely with a narrow waist ⟨*an* ∼ *figure*⟩

hour hand n the short hand that marks the hours on the face of a watch or clock

houri n, *pl* **houris 1** any of the female virgin attendants of the blessed in the Muslim paradise **2** a voluptuously beautiful young woman

¹hourly adv **1** at or during every hour; *also* continually ⟨*we're expecting him* ∼⟩ **2** by the hour ⟨∼ *paid workers*⟩

²hourly adj **1** occurring or done every hour; *also* continual **2** reckoned by the hour

¹house n, *pl* **houses 1** a building designed for people to live in **2a** an animal's shelter or refuge (e g a nest or den) **b** a building in which sthg is housed or stored ⟨*a hen* ∼⟩ **c** a building used for a particular purpose, esp eating, drinking, or entertainment ⟨*a public* ∼⟩ **3** any of the 12 equal sectors into which the celestial sphere is divided in astrology **4a** *sing or pl in constr* the occupants of a house ⟨*you'll wake the whole* ∼⟩ **b** a family including ancestors, descendants, and kindred ⟨*the* ∼ *of Tudor*⟩ **5a** (a residence of) a religious community **b** any of several groups into which a British school may be divided for social purposes or games **6** (the chamber of) a legislative or deliberative assembly; *esp* a division of a body consisting of 2 chambers **7a** a business organization or establishment ⟨*a publishing* ∼⟩⟨∼ *style*⟩ **b** *cap* a large building used by a business or institution – used in names ⟨*Transport* House⟩ **c** (the audience in) a theatre or concert hall ⟨*a full* ∼⟩ – **houseful** n, **houseless** adj – **on the house** at the expense of an establishment or its management ⟨*have a drink* on the house⟩

²house vt **1** to provide with accommodation or storage space **2** to serve as shelter for; contain ⟨*a library* ∼s *thousands of books*⟩

house arrest n confinement to one's place of residence instead of prison

houseboat n an often permanently moored boat that is fitted out as a home

housebound adj confined to the house (e g because of illness)

housebreaking n an act of breaking into and entering the house of another with a criminal purpose – **housebreaker** n

housebroken adj, *chiefly NAm* housetrained

housecoat n a woman's light dressing gown for wear round the house; *also* a short overall

housecraft n **1** DOMESTIC SCIENCE **2** skill in running a household

housefather, *fem* **housemother** n sby in charge of a group of young people living in care (e g in a children's home)

housefly n a fly found in most parts of the world that frequents houses and carries disease

¹household n *sing or pl in constr* all the people who live together in a dwelling

²household adj **1** domestic **2** familiar, common ⟨*a* ∼ *name*⟩

householder n a person who occupies a dwelling as owner or tenant

household troops n *pl* troops appointed to guard a sovereign or his/her residence

housekeeper n sby, esp a woman, employed to take charge of the running of a house

housekeeping n **1** (money used for) the day-to-day running of a house and household affairs **2** the general management of an organization which ensures its smooth running (e g the provision of equipment, keeping of records, etc) **3** the routine tasks that have to be done in order for sthg to function properly

houselights n *pl* the lights that illuminate the auditorium of a theatre

housemaid n a female servant employed to do housework

housemaid's knee n a swelling over the knee due to an enlargement of the bursa in the front of the kneecap

houseman n (one holding) the most junior grade of British hospital doctor

house martin n a European martin with blue-black plumage and white rump that nests on cliffs and under the eaves of houses

housemaster, *fem* **housemistress** n a teacher in charge of a school house

housemother, *masc* **housefather** n sby in charge of a group of young people living in care (e g in a children's home)

house of cards n a precarious structure or situation

House of Commons n the lower house of the British and Canadian parliaments

House of Lords n **1** the upper house of Parliament **2** the body of Law Lords that constitutes the highest British court of appeal

House of Representatives n the lower house of the US Congress or Australian Parliament

house party n a party lasting for a day or more held at a large, usu country, house

house-proud adj (excessively) careful about the management and appearance of one's house

house sparrow n a brown Eurasian sparrow that lives esp in or near human settlements

house-to-house adj DOOR-TO-DOOR 1

housetop n a roof – **from the housetops** for all to hear; IN PUBLIC ⟨*shouting their grievances* from the housetops⟩

housetrain vt **1** *chiefly Br* to train (e g a pet) to defecate and urinate outdoors **2** to teach (e g a person) to behave acceptably – *humor*

housewarming n a party to celebrate moving into a new house or premises

housewife n **1** a usu married woman who runs a house **2** a small container for needlework articles (e g thread) – **housewifely** adj, **housewifery** n

housework n the work (e g cleaning) involved in maintaining a house

housing n **1** (the provision of) houses or dwelling-places collectively **2** a protective cover for machinery, sensitive instruments, etc

housing association n a nonprofitmaking society that constructs, renovates, and helps tenants to rent or buy housing

hove past of HEAVE

hovel n a small, wretched, and often dirty house or abode

hover vi **1** to hang in the air or on the wing **2a** to linger or wait restlessly around a place **b** to be in a state of uncertainty, irresolution, or suspense – **hover** n, **hoverer** n

hovercraft n, pl **hovercraft** a vehicle supported on a cushion of air provided by fans and designed to travel over both land and sea

¹how adv **1a** in what manner or way ⟨~ do you spell it?⟩ ⟨know ~ it works⟩ **b** with what meaning; to what effect ⟨~ can you explain it?⟩ **c** for what reason; why ⟨~ could you do it?⟩ **2** by what measure or quantity ⟨~ much does it cost?⟩ – often used in an exclamation as an intensive ⟨~ nice of you to come!⟩ **3** in what state or condition (e g of health) ⟨~ are you?⟩ ⟨~ is the market today?⟩ – **how about** what do you say to or think of ⟨how about going to London for the day?⟩ – **how come** how does it happen; why is it ⟨how come we never meet?⟩ – infml – **how do you do** – used as a formal greeting between people meeting for the first time – **how's that 1** – used to call attention to and invite comment on sthg ⟨how's that for enterprise?⟩ **2** please repeat **3** – used in cricket as an appeal to the umpire to give the batsman out

²how conj **1a** the way, manner, or state in which ⟨remember ~ they fought⟩ ⟨asked ~ he felt⟩ **b** that ⟨do you remember ~ he arrived right at the end⟩ **2** however, as ⟨do it ~ you like⟩

³how n the manner in which sthg is done ⟨the ~ and the why of it⟩

howdah n a usu canopied seat on the back of an elephant or camel

how-do-you-do, how d'ye do n a confused or embarrassing situation – infml

howdy n, chiefly NAm hello – infml

¹however conj in whatever manner or way ⟨can go ~ he likes⟩

²however adv **1** to whatever degree or extent; no matter how ⟨~ fast I eat⟩ **2** in spite of that; nevertheless ⟨would like to go; ~, I think I'd better not⟩ **3** how in the world ⟨~ did you manage it?⟩ – infml

howitzer n a short cannon usu with a medium muzzle velocity and a relatively high trajectory

howl vi **1a** esp of dogs, wolves, etc to make a loud sustained doleful cry **b** of wind to make a sustained wailing sound **2** to cry loudly and without restraint (e g with pain or laughter) ~ vt to utter with a loud sustained cry – **howl** n

howl down vt to express one's disapproval of (e g a speaker or his/her views), esp by shouting in order to prevent from being heard

howler n a stupid and comic blunder – infml

howling adj very great, extreme, or severe ⟨a ~ success⟩ – infml

hoyden n a boisterous girl – **hoydenish** adj

hub n **1** the central part of a wheel, propeller, or fan through which the axle passes **2** the centre of activity or importance

hubble-bubble n **1** WATER PIPE 2 **2** a flurry of noise or activity; a commotion

hubbub n a noisy confusion; uproar

hubby n a husband – infml

hubcap n a removable metal cap placed over the hub of a wheel

hubris n overweening pride, usu leading to retribution – **hubristic** adj

huckaback n an absorbent durable fabric of cotton, linen, or both, used chiefly for towels

huckleberry n **1** (an edible dark blue or black berry of) any of a genus of American shrubs of the heath family **2** a blueberry

¹huckster n **1** a hawker, pedlar **2** chiefly NAm one who writes advertising material, esp for radio or television

²huckster vi to haggle ~ vt **1** to deal in or bargain over **2** to promote or advertise, esp in an aggressive or underhand manner

¹huddle vb **huddling** vt **1** to crowd together **2** to draw or curl (oneself) up ~ vi **1** to gather in a closely-packed group **2** to curl up; crouch

²huddle n **1** a closely-packed group; a bunch **2** a secretive or conspiratorial meeting ⟨went into a ~ with his colleagues⟩

hue n **1** a complexion, aspect ⟨political factions of every ~⟩ **2** the attribute of colours that permits them to be classed as red, yellow, green, blue, or an intermediate between any adjacent pair of these colours; also a colour having this attribute

hue and cry n **1** a cry formerly used in pursuit of a criminal **2** a clamour of alarm or protest

¹huff vi **1** to emit loud puffs (e g of breath or steam) **2** to make empty threats ⟨management ~ed and puffed about the chances of a lockout⟩

²huff n – **huffily** adv, **huffiness** n, **huffish** adj, **huffy** adj – **in a huff** in a piqued and resentful mood

¹hug vt -gg- **1** to hold or press tightly, esp in the arms **2a** to feel very pleased with (oneself) **b** to cling to; cherish ⟨~ged his miseries like a sulky child – John Buchan⟩ **3** to stay close to ⟨thick smoke ~ged the ground⟩ – **huggable** adj

²hug n a tight clasp or embrace

huge adj great in size, scale, degree, or scope; enormous ⟨~ mountains⟩ ⟨a ~ success⟩ – **hugely** adv, **hugeness** n

hugely adv very much; enormously ⟨was ~ excited⟩

hugger-mugger n **1** secrecy **2** confusion, muddle – **hugger-mugger** adj or adv

huh interj – used to express surprise, disapproval, or inquiry

hula also **hula-hula** n a Polynesian dance involving swaying of the hips

hulk n **1a** the hull of a ship that is no longer seaworthy and is used as a storehouse or, esp formerly, as a prison **b** an abandoned wreck or shell, esp of a vessel **2** a person, creature, or thing that is bulky or unwieldy ⟨a big ~ of a man⟩

hulking adj bulky, massive

¹hull n **1a** the outer covering of a fruit or seed **b** the calyx that surrounds some fruits (e g the strawberry) **2** the main frame or body of a ship, flying boat, airship, etc **3** a covering, casing

²hull vt **1** to remove the hulls of **2** to hit or pierce the hull of (e g a ship) – **huller** n

hullabaloo n, pl **hullabaloos** a confused noise; uproar – infml

hullo interj or n, chiefly Br hello

¹hum vb -mm- vi **1a** to utter a prolonged /m/ sound **b** to make the characteristic droning noise of an insect in motion or a similar sound **2** to be lively or active – infml **3** to have an offensive smell – slang ~ vt **1** to sing with the lips closed and without articulation **2** to affect or express by humming – **hum** *n* – **hum and ha** *also* **hum and haw** to equivocate

²hum *interj* – used to express hesitation, uncertainty, disagreement, etc

¹human *adj* **1** (characteristic) of humans ⟨~ *voice*⟩ **2** consisting of men and women ⟨*the* ~ *race*⟩ ⟨*a* ~ *barrier*⟩ **3a** having the esp good attributes (e g kindness and compassion) thought to be characteristic of humans ⟨*is really very* ~⟩ **b** having, showing, or concerned with qualities or feelings characteristic of mankind ⟨*to err is* ~⟩ ⟨~ *interest*⟩ – **humanness** *n*

²human, human being *n* a man, woman, or child; a person

humane *adj* **1a** marked by compassion or consideration for other human beings or animals **b** causing the minimum pain possible ⟨~ *killing of animals*⟩ **2** characterized by broad humanistic culture; liberal ⟨~ *studies*⟩ – **humanely** *adv*, **humaneness** *n*

humanism *n* **1** a cultural movement dominant during the Renaissance that was characterized by a revival of classical learning and a shift of emphasis from religious to secular concerns; *broadly* literary culture **2** humanitarianism **3** a doctrine, attitude, or way of life based on human interests or values; *esp* a philosophy that asserts the intrinsic worth of man and that usu rejects religious belief – **humanist** *n or adj*, **humanistic** *adj*, **humanistically** *adv*

humanitarian *n* one who promotes human welfare and social reform; a philanthropist – **humanitarian** *adj*, **humanitarianism** *n*

humanity *n* **1** the quality of being humane **2** the quality or state of being human **3** *pl the* cultural branches of learning **4** mankind

humanize, -ise *vt* **1** to cause to be or seem human **2** to make humane – **humanization** *n*

humankind *n sing or pl in constr* human beings collectively

humanly *adv* **1a** from a human viewpoint **b** within the range of human capacity ⟨*as perfectly as is* ~ *possible*⟩ **2a** in a manner characteristic of humans, esp in showing emotion or weakness **b** with humaneness

humanoid *adj* having human form or characteristics – **humanoid** *n*

¹humble *adj* **1** having a low opinion of oneself; unassertive **2** marked by deference or submission ⟨*a* ~ *apology*⟩ **3a** ranking low in a hierarchy or scale ⟨*man of* ~ *origins*⟩ **b** modest, unpretentious ⟨*a* ~ *dwelling*⟩ – **humbleness** *n*, **humbly** *adv*

²humble *vt* **1** to make humble in spirit or manner; humiliate **2** to destroy the power, independence, or prestige of

¹humbug *n* **1a** sthg designed to deceive and mislead **b** an impostor, sham **2** pretence, deception **3** drivel, nonsense **4** a hard usu peppermint-flavoured striped sweet made from boiled sugar – **humbuggery** *n*

²humbug *vb* **-gg-** to deceive with a hoax

humdinger *n* an excellent or remarkable person or thing – *infml*

humdrum *adj* monotonous, dull – **humdrum** *n*

humerus *n, pl* **humeri** the long bone of the upper arm or forelimb extending from the shoulder to the elbow

humid *adj* containing or characterized by perceptible moisture ⟨*a* ~ *climate*⟩ – **humidly** *adv*

humidify *vt* to make humid – **humidification** *n*

humidity *n* (the degree of) moisture or dampness, esp in the atmosphere

humidor *n* a case or room in which cigars or tobacco can be kept moist

humiliate *vt* to cause to feel humble; lower the dignity or self-respect of – **humiliation** *n*

humility *n* the quality or state of being humble

hummingbird *n* any of numerous tiny brightly coloured usu tropical American birds related to the swifts, having a slender bill and narrow wings that beat rapidly making a humming sound

hummock *n* **1** a hillock **2** a ridge of ice – **hummocky** *adj*

humorist *n* a person specializing in or noted for humour in speech, writing, or acting – **humoristic** *adj*

humorous *adj* full of, characterized by, or expressing humour – **humorously** *adv*, **humorousness** *n*

¹humour, NAm chiefly humor *n* **1** any of the 4 fluids of the body (blood, phlegm, and yellow and black bile) formerly held to determine, by their relative proportions, a person's health and temperament **2** characteristic or habitual disposition ⟨*a man of cheerful* ~⟩ **3** a state of mind; a mood **4** a sudden inclination; a caprice **5a** (sthg having) the quality of causing amusement **b** the faculty of expressing or appreciating what is comic or amusing – **humourless** *adj*, **humourlessness** *n* – **out of humour** in a bad temper

²humour, NAm chiefly humor *vt* to comply with the mood or wishes of; indulge

¹hump *n* **1** a rounded protuberance: e g **a** a humped or crooked back **b** a fleshy protuberance on the back of a camel, bison, etc **c** a mound, knoll **2** a difficult, trying, or critical phase ⟨*we're over the* ~ *now*⟩ **3** *Br* a fit of depression or sulking – *infml*; + *the* ⟨*he's got the* ~⟩ – **humped** *adj*

²hump *vt* **1** to form or curve into a hump **2** *chiefly Br* to carry with difficulty ⟨~*ing suitcases around*⟩ **3** to have sexual intercourse with ~ *vi* **1** to rise in a hump **2** *Austr* to travel around or go on foot **3** to have sexual intercourse *USE* (*vt2; vi2*) infml; (*vt3; vi3*) slang

humpback *n* **1** a hunchback **2** *also* **humpback whale** a large whale related to the rorquals but having very long flippers – **humpbacked** *adj*

humph *vi or interj* (to utter) a gruntlike sound used to express doubt or contempt

humus *n* a brown or black organic soil material resulting from partial decomposition of plant or animal matter – **humic** *adj*

Hun *n, pl* **Huns** (**2b**) **Huns**, *esp collectively* **Hun 1** a member of a nomadic Mongolian people who overran a large part of central and E Europe under Attila during the 4th and 5th c AD **2a** *often not cap* a person who is wantonly destructive **b** a German; *esp* a German soldier in WW I or II – *derog* – **Hunnish** *adj*

¹hunch *vi* to assume a bent or crooked posture ~ *vt* to bend into a hump or arch ⟨~*ed his shoulders*⟩

²hunch *n* **1** HUMP 1 **2** a strong intuitive feeling

hunchback *n* (sby with) a humped back – **hunchbacked** *adj*

hundred *n, pl* **hundreds, hundred 1** (the number) 100 **2** the number occupying the position 3 to the left of the decimal point in Arabic notation; *also, pl* this position **3** 100 units or digits; *specif* £100 ⟨*must have cost* ~s⟩ **4** *pl the* numbers 100 to 999 **5** a score of 100 or more runs made by a batsman in cricket **6** *pl the* 100 years of a specified century ⟨*the 19* ~s⟩ **7** a historical subdivision of a county **8** an indefinitely large number – *infml*; often pl with sing. meaning – **hundred** *adj*, **hundredth** *adj or n*

hundredweight *n, pl* **hundredweight, hundredweights 1** a British unit of weight equal to 112lb (about 50.80kg) **2** *chiefly NAm* a US unit of weight equal to 100lb (about 4536kg)

hung past of HANG

¹hunger n **1** (a weakened condition or unpleasant sensation arising from) a craving or urgent need for food **2** a strong desire; a craving

²hunger vi **1** to feel or suffer hunger **2** to have an eager desire – usu + for or after

hunger strike n refusal, as an act of protest, to eat enough to sustain life – **hunger striker** n

hungry adj **1a** feeling hunger **b** characterized by or indicating hunger or appetite ⟨a ~ look⟩ **2** eager, avid ⟨~ for power⟩ **3** not rich or fertile; barren – **hungrily** adv, **hungriness** n

hunk n **1** a large lump or piece **2** a usu muscular sexually attractive man – infml

hunkers n pl the haunches – infml

¹hunt vt **1a** to pursue for food or enjoyment ⟨~ foxes⟩ **b** to use (e g hounds) in the search for game **2a** to pursue with intent to capture ⟨~ed the escaped prisoner⟩ **b** to search out; seek **3** to persecute or chase, esp by harrying **4** to traverse in search of prey ~ vi **1** to take part in a hunt, esp regularly **2** to attempt to find sthg **3** of a device, machine, etc to run alternately fast and slowly

²hunt n **1** the act, the practice, or an instance of hunting **2a** sing or pl in constr a group of usu mounted hunters and their hounds **b** the area hunted

hunter, fem (1a&2) **huntress** n **1a** sby who hunts game, esp with hounds **b** a usu fast strong horse used in hunting **2** a person who hunts or seeks sthg, esp overeagerly ⟨a fortune ~⟩ **3** a watch with a hinged metal cover to protect it

hunting n the pursuit of game on horseback with hounds

hunting ground n an area of usu fruitful search or exploitation ⟨the British Empire is now a favourite ~ for historians⟩

hunting horn n a signal horn used in the chase, usu consisting of a long coiled tube with a flared bell

hunting pink adj or n (of) the red colour of the coats worn by fox-hunters

huntsman n **1** HUNTER 1a **2** sby who looks after the hounds of a hunt

¹hurdle n **1a** a portable framework, usu of interlaced branches and stakes, used esp for enclosing land or livestock **b** a frame formerly used for dragging traitors to execution **2a** a light barrier jumped by men, horses, dogs, etc in certain races **b** pl any of various races over hurdles **3** a barrier, obstacle

²hurdle vb **hurdling** vt **1** to jump over, esp while running **2** to overcome, surmount ~ vi to run in hurdle races – **hurdler** n

hurdy-gurdy n a musical instrument in which the sound is produced by turning a crank; esp BARREL ORGAN

hurl vt **1** to drive or thrust violently **2** to throw forcefully **3** to utter or shout violently ⟨~ed insults at him⟩ ~ vi to rush, hurtle – **hurl** n, **hurler** n

hurling n an Irish game resembling hockey played between 2 teams of 15 players each

hurly-burly n (an) uproar, commotion

hurray interj – used to express joy, approval, or encouragement

hurricane n (a usu tropical cyclone with) a wind of a velocity greater than 117km/h (73 to 136mph)

hurricane lamp n a candlestick or oil lamp equipped with a glass chimney to protect the flame

hurried adj done in a hurry – **hurriedly** adv

¹hurry vt **1a** to transport or cause to go with haste; rush ⟨~ him to hospital⟩ **b** to cause to move or act with (greater) haste **2** to hasten the progress or completion of

⟨don't ~ this passage of the music⟩ ~ vi to move or act with haste – often + up

²hurry n **1** flurried and often bustling haste **2** a need for haste; urgency ⟨there's no ~ for it⟩ – **in a hurry 1** without delay; hastily **2** eager ⟨never in a hurry to get up⟩ **3** without difficulty; easily ⟨won't manage that in a hurry⟩ – infml

¹hurt vb hurt vt **1a** to afflict with physical pain; wound **b** to cause mental distress to; offend **2** to be detrimental to ⟨~ his chances of success⟩ ~ vi **1** to feel pain; suffer **2** to cause damage, distress, or pain

²hurt n **1** a bodily injury or wound **2** (a cause of) mental distress **3** wrong, harm – **hurtful** adj, **hurtfully** adv, **hurtfulness** n

hurtle vb **hurtling** vi to move rapidly or precipitately to hurl, fling

¹husband n a married man, esp in relation to his wife – **husbandly** adj

²husband vt to make the most economical use of; conserve ⟨~ one's strength⟩

husbandry n **1** the judicious management of resources **2** farming, esp of domestic animals

¹hush vb to make or become quiet or calm

²hush n a silence or calm, esp following noise

hush-hush adj secret, confidential – infml

hush money n money paid secretly to prevent disclosure of damaging information

hush up vt to keep secret; suppress ⟨hush the story up⟩

¹husk n **1** a dry or membranous outer covering (e g a shell or pod) of a seed or fruit **2** a useless outer layer of sthg

²husk vt to strip the husk from

¹husky adj of, resembling, or containing husks

²husky adj hoarse, breathy ⟨a ~ voice⟩ – **huskily** adv, **huskiness** n

³husky adj burly, hefty – infml

⁴husky n ESKIMO DOG

hussar n **1** a Hungarian horseman of the 15th c **2** often cap a member of any of various European cavalry regiments

hussy n an impudent or promiscuous woman or girl

hustings n pl but sing or pl in constr **1** a raised platform used until 1872 for the nomination of candidates for Parliament and for election speeches **2** a place where election speeches are made **3** the proceedings of an election campaign

hustle vb **hustling** vt **1a** to push or convey roughly, forcibly, or hurriedly ⟨~d him into a taxi⟩ **b** to impel, force ⟨~d her into accepting⟩ **2** to swindle, cheat out of – infml ~ vi **1** to hasten, hurry **2** chiefly NAm to make strenuous, often dishonest, efforts to secure money or business **3** chiefly NAm to engage in prostitution; solicit – **hustle** n, **hustler** n

hut n a small often temporary dwelling of simple construction

hutch n **1** a pen or cage for a small animal (e g a rabbit) **2** a shack, shanty – infml; derog

hutment n an encampment of huts

hyacinth n **1** a jacinth **2** a common garden plant with fragrant usu blue, pink, or white flowers that grow in spikes; also any of various related bulbous plants of the lily family **3** a colour varying from light violet to mid-purple – **hyacinth** adj, **hyacinthine** adj

hyaena n a hyena

hybrid n **1** an offspring of 2 animals or plants of different races, breeds, varieties, etc **2** a person of mixed cultural background **3a** sthg heterogeneous in origin or composition **b** a word (e g television) made up of elements from different languages – **hybrid** adj, **hybridism** n, **hybridist** n, **hybridize** vb, **hybridizable** adj, **hybridization**n, **hybridity** n

hydr-, hydro- comb form **1a** water ⟨**hydr**ous⟩ ⟨**hydro**electricity⟩ **b** liquid ⟨**hydro**kinetics⟩ ⟨**hydro**meter⟩ **2** hydrogen; containing or combined with hydrogen ⟨**hydro**carbon⟩ ⟨**hydro**chloric⟩

hydra n 1 a persistent evil that is not easily overcome **2** any of numerous small tubular freshwater polyps having a mouth surrounded by tentacles

hydrangea n any of a genus of shrubs which produce large clusters of white, pink, or pale blue flowers

hydrant n a discharge pipe with a valve and nozzle from which water may be drawn from a main

¹hydrate n a compound or complex ion formed by the union of water with another substance

²hydrate vt to cause to take up or combine with (the elements of) water – **hydrator** n, **hydration** n

hydraulic adj 1 operated, moved, or effected by means of liquid ⟨~ engineer⟩ **3** hardening or setting under water ⟨~ cement⟩ – **hydraulically** adv

hydraulics n pl but sing in constr a branch of physics that deals with the practical applications of liquid in motion

hydro- – see HYDR-

hydrocarbon n an organic compound (e g benzene) containing only carbon and hydrogen – **hydrocarbonous, hydrocarbonaceous, hydrocarbonic,** adj

hydrochloric acid n a solution of hydrogen chloride in water that is a strong corrosive acid and is naturally present in the gastric juice

hydrocyanic acid n a solution of hydrogen cyanide in water that is a highly poisonous weak acid

hydroelectric adj of or being the production of electricity by waterpower – **hydroelectrically** adv, **hydroelectricity** n

hydrofoil n (a ship or boat fitted with) an aerofoil-like device that, when attached to a ship, lifts the hull out of the water at speed

hydrogen n the simplest and lightest of the elements that is normally a highly inflammable gas – **hydrogenous** adj

hydrogen bomb n a bomb whose violent explosive power is due to the sudden release of atomic energy resulting from the nuclear fusion of hydrogen initiated by the explosion of an atom bomb

hydrogen peroxide n an unstable compound used esp as an oxidizing and bleaching agent, an antiseptic, and a rocket propellant

hydrophobia n 1 abnormal dread of water **2** rabies

hydroplane n 1 a speedboat fitted with hydrofoils or a stepped bottom so that the hull is raised wholly or partly out of the water when moving at speed **2** a horizontal surface on a submarine's hull, used to control movement upwards or downwards

hydroponics n pl but sing in constr the growing of plants in (a mechanically supporting medium containing) nutrient solutions rather than soil – **hydroponic** adj, **hydroponically** adv

hydrotherapy n the use of water in the treatment of disease; esp treatment using exercise in heated water

hydroxide n a compound of hydroxyl with an element or radical

hydroxyl n the univalent group or radical OH consisting of 1 hydrogen atom and 1 oxygen atom that is characteristic of hydroxides, alcohols, etc – **hydroxylate** vt, **hydroxylic** adj

hyena, hyaena n any of several large strong nocturnal flesh-eating Old World mammals that usu feed as scavengers

hygiene n (conditions or practices, esp cleanliness, conducive to) the establishment and maintenance of health – **hygienist** n, **hygienic** adj, **hygenics** n pl but sing in constr, **hygienically** adv

hymen n a fold of mucous membrane partly closing the opening of the vagina in virgins – **hymenal** adj

hymeneal adj nuptial – poetic

¹hymn n 1 a song of praise to God; esp a metrical composition that can be included in a religious service **2** a song of praise or joy

²hymn vt to praise or worship in hymns to sing a hymn

hymnal n (a book containing) a collection of church hymns

hyper adj overexcited, overwrought – slang

hyper- prefix **1** above; beyond; super- ⟨**hyper**physical⟩ **2a** excessively ⟨**hyper**sensitive⟩ ⟨**hyper**critical⟩ ⟨**hyper**active⟩ **b** excessive ⟨**hyper**aemia⟩ ⟨**hyper**tension⟩ **3** that exists in or is a space of more than 3 dimensions ⟨**hyper**cube⟩ ⟨**hyper**space⟩

hyperbola n, pl **hyperbolas, hyperbolae** a plane curve generated by a point so moving that the difference of its distances from 2 fixed points is a constant; the intersection of a double right circular cone with a plane that cuts both halves of the cone

hyperbole n a figure of speech based on extravagant exaggeration – **hyperbolist** n, **hyperbolize** vb

¹hyperbolic also **hyperbolical** adj of, characterized by, or given to hyperbole – **hyperbolically** adv

²hyperbolic also **hyperbolical** adj of or analogous to a hyperbola

hypermarket n a very large self-service retail store selling a wide range of household and consumer goods and usu situated on the outskirts of a major town or city

hypersensitive adj abnormally susceptible (e g to a drug or antigen) – **hypersensitiveness** n, **hypersensitivity** n

hypha n, pl **hyphae** any of the threads that make up the mycelium of a fungus – **hyphal** adj

¹hyphen n a punctuation mark - used to divide or to join together words, word elements, or numbers

²hyphen vt to hyphenate

hyphenate vt to join or separate with a hyphen – **hyphenation** n

hypnosis n, pl **hypnoses 1** any of various conditions that (superficially) resemble sleep; specif one induced by a person to whose suggestions the subject is then markedly susceptible **2** HYPNOTISM 1

hypnotic adj 1 tending to produce sleep; soporific **2** of hypnosis or hypnotism – **hypnotically** adv

hypnotism n 1 the induction of hypnosis **2** HYPNOSIS 1 – **hypnotist** n

hypnotize, -ise vt 1 to induce hypnosis in **2** to dazzle or overcome (as if) by suggestion; mesmerize ⟨drivers ~d by speed⟩ – **hypnotizable** adj, **hypnotization** n

¹hypo n, pl **hypos** sodium thiosulphate used as a fixing agent in photography

²hypo n, pl **hypos** a hypodermic

hypo-, hyp- prefix **1** under; beneath ⟨**hypo**blast⟩ ⟨**hypo**dermic⟩ **2** less than normal or normally ⟨**hyp**aesthesia⟩ ⟨**hypo**tension⟩ **3** in a lower state of oxidation ⟨**hypo**chlorous acid⟩

hypochondria also **hypochondriasis** n morbid concern about one's health

hypochondriac n or adj (sby) affected by hypochondria

hypocrisy n the feigning of virtues, beliefs, or standards, esp in matters of religion or morality

hypocrite *n* one given to hypocrisy – **hypocritical** *adj*, **hypocritically** *adv*

¹**hypodermic** *adj* 1 of the parts beneath the skin 2 adapted for use in or administered by injection beneath the skin – **hypodermically** *adv*

²**hypodermic** *n* 1 a hypodermic injection 2 HYPODERMIC SYRINGE

hypodermic syringe *n* a small syringe used with a hollow needle for injection or withdrawal of material beneath the skin

hypotenuse *n* the side of a right-angled triangle that is opposite the right angle

hypothermia *n* abnormally low body temperature – **hypothermic** *adj*

hypothesis *n, pl* **hypotheses** 1 a provisional assumption made in order to investigate its logical or empirical consequences 2 a proposition assumed for the sake of argument

hypothetical *adj* 1 involving logical hypothesis 2 of or depending on supposition; conjectural – **hypothetically** *adv*

hysterectomy *n* surgical removal of the uterus – **hysterectomize** *vt*

hysteria *n* 1 a mental disorder marked by emotional excitability and disturbances (e g paralysis) of the normal bodily processes 2 unmanageable emotional excess – **hysteric** *n*, **hysteric, hysterical** *adj*, **hysterically** *adv*

hysterics *n pl but sing or pl in constr* a fit of uncontrollable laughter or crying; hysteria

I

i *n, pl* **i's, is** *often cap* 1 (a graphic representation of or device for reproducing) the 9th letter of the English alphabet 2 one 3 – used as a symbol for the imaginary unit

I *pron* the one who is speaking or writing ⟨~ *feel fine*⟩ ⟨*my wife and* ~⟩

-i- – used as a connective vowel to join word elements, esp of Latin origin ⟨*matrilinear*⟩ ⟨*raticide*⟩

-ial – see ¹-AL

iamb *n* a metrical foot consisting of 1 short or unstressed syllable followed by 1 long or stressed syllable – **iambic** *adj or n*

-ian – see -AN

¹**Iberian** *n* a member of any of the ancient peoples inhabiting the Caucasus between the Black and Caspian seas – **Iberian** *adj*

²**Iberian** *n* 1a a member of any of the Caucasian peoples that in ancient times inhabited Spain and Portugal b a native or inhabitant of Spain or Portugal 2 any of the languages of the ancient Iberians – **Iberian** *adj*

ibex *n, pl* **ibexes,** *esp collectively* **ibex** any of several wild goats living chiefly in high mountain areas of the Old World and having large ridged backward-curving horns

ibidem *adv* in the same book, chapter, passage, etc as previously mentioned

-ibility – see -ABILITY

ibis *n, pl* **ibises,** *esp collectively* **ibis** any of several wading birds related to the herons but distinguished by a long slender downward-curving bill

-ible – see -ABLE

¹**-ic** *suffix* (*n → adj*) 1 having the character or form of; being ⟨*panoramic*⟩ ⟨*runic*⟩ 2a (characteristic) of or associated with ⟨*Homeric*⟩ ⟨*quixotic*⟩ b related to, derived from, or

containing ⟨*alcoholic*⟩ ⟨*oleic*⟩ 3 utilizing ⟨*electronic*⟩ ⟨*atomic*⟩ 4 exhibiting ⟨*nostalgic*⟩; affected with ⟨*allergic*⟩ 5 characterized by; producing ⟨*analgesic*⟩ 6 having a valency relatively higher than in (specified compounds or ions named with an adjective ending in *-ous*) ⟨*ferric iron*⟩ ⟨*mercuric*⟩

²**-ic** *suffix* (→ *n*) 1 one having the character or nature of ⟨*fanatic*⟩ 2 one belonging to or associated with ⟨*epic*⟩ 3 one affected by ⟨*alcoholic*⟩ 4 one that produces ⟨*emetic*⟩

-ical *suffix* (*n → adj*) -ic ⟨*symmetrical*⟩ ⟨*geological*⟩

ICBM *n, pl* **ICBM's, ICBMs** an intercontinental ballistic missile

¹**ice** *n* 1a frozen water b a sheet or stretch of ice 2 a substance reduced to the solid state by cold ⟨*ammonia* ~ *in the rings of Saturn*⟩ 3 (a serving of) a frozen dessert: e g a ICE CREAM b WATER ICE 4 *NAm* diamonds – slang – **iceless** *adj* – **on ice** in abeyance; in reserve for later use ⟨*kept their plans* on ice *for the time being*⟩

²**ice** *vt* 1a to coat with or convert into ice b to supply or chill with ice 2 to cover (as if) with icing ~ *vi* 1 to become ice-cold 2 to become covered or clogged with ice ⟨*the carburettor* ~ d *up*⟩

ice age *n* 1 a time of widespread glaciation 2 *cap I&A* the Pleistocene glacial epoch

ice axe *n* a combination pick and adze with a spiked handle used in climbing on snow or ice

ice bag *n* a bag of ice for application of cold to a part of the body

iceberg *n* 1 a large floating mass of ice detached from a glacier 2 an emotionally cold person

icebox *n* 1 *Br* the freezing compartment of a refrigerator 2 *NAm* a refrigerator

icebreaker *n* a ship equipped to make and maintain a channel through ice

ice cap *n* a lasting (extensive) cover of ice

ice cream *n* a sweet flavoured frozen food containing cream (substitute) and often eggs

ice hockey *n* a game played on an ice rink by 2 teams of 6 players on skates whose object is to drive a puck into the opponent's goal with a hockey stick

¹**Icelandic** *adj* (characteristic) of Iceland

²**Icelandic** *n* the N Germanic language of the Icelandic people

ice lolly *n* an ice cream or esp a flavoured piece of ice on a stick

iceman *n* 1 a man skilled in travelling on ice 2 one who sells or delivers ice, esp in the USA

ice pack *n* 1 an expanse of pack ice 2 ICE BAG

ice pick *n* a hand tool ending in a spike for chipping ice

ice skate *n* a shoe with a metal runner attached for skating on ice – **ice-skate** *vi*, **ice skater** *n*

ichneumon *n* 1 a mongoose 2 **ichneumon, ichneumon fly** any of various related 4-winged insects whose larvae are usu internal parasites of other insect larvae, esp caterpillars

icicle *n* a hanging tapering mass of ice formed by the freezing of dripping water

icing *n* a sweet (creamy) coating for cakes or other baked goods

icon, ikon *n* 1 a usu pictorial representation; an image 2 a conventional religious image typically painted on a small wooden panel and used in worship by the Eastern Christian Church – **iconic** *adj*, **iconically** *adv*, **iconicity** *n*

icon-, icono- *comb form* image; likeness ⟨*iconolater*⟩ ⟨*iconographer*⟩

iconoclast *n* 1 a person who destroys religious images or opposes their veneration 2 one who attacks established beliefs or institutions – **iconoclastic** *adj*, **iconoclastically** *adv*

-ics *suffix* (→ *n pl but sing or pl in constr*) 1 study, knowledge, skill, or practice of ⟨*linguist*ics⟩ ⟨*electron*ics⟩ 2 actions, activities, or mode of behaviour characteristic of (a specified person or thing) ⟨*histrion*ics⟩ ⟨*acrobat*ics⟩ 3 qualities, operations, or phenomena relating to ⟨*mechan*ics⟩ ⟨*acoust*ics⟩

icy *adj* **1a** covered with, full of, or consisting of ice **b** intensely cold **2** characterized by personal coldness ⟨*an* ~ *stare*⟩ – **icily** *adv*, **iciness** *n*

id *n* the one of the 3 divisions of the mind in psychoanalytic theory that is completely unconscious and is the source of psychic energy derived from instinctual needs and drives

¹-id *suffix* (→ *n*) 1 member of (a specified zoological family) ⟨*arachn*id⟩ 2 meteor associated with or radiating from (a specified constellation or comet) ⟨*Perse*id⟩

²-id *suffix* (→ *n*) (such) a body, particle, or structure ⟨*energ*id⟩ ⟨*pyram*id⟩

³-id *suffix* (→ *n*) -ide

I'd I had; I should; I would

ID card *n* IDENTITY CARD

ide *n* a European freshwater food fish of the carp family

-ide *suffix* (→ *n*) 1 binary chemical compound – added to the contracted name of the nonmetallic or more electronegative element ⟨*hydrogen sulph*ide⟩ or radical ⟨*cyan*ide⟩ 2 chemical compound derived from or related to (a specified compound) ⟨*glucos*ide⟩ ⟨*lanthan*ide⟩

idea *n* **1a** a transcendent entity of which existing things are imperfect representations **b** a plan of action **2a** an indefinite or vague impression ⟨*I'd an* ~ *you were coming*⟩ **b** sthg (e g a thought, concept, or image) actually or potentially present in the mind ⟨*the* ~ *of death never occurred to him*⟩ **3** a formulated thought or opinion **4** whatever is known or supposed about sthg **5** an individual's conception of the perfect or typical example of sthg specified ⟨*not my* ~ *of a good time*⟩ **6** the central meaning or aim of a particular action or situation ⟨*the* ~ *of the game is to score goals*⟩ – **idealess** *adj*

¹ideal *adj* **1a** existing only in the mind; *broadly* lacking practicality **b** relating to or constituting mental images, ideas, or conceptions **2** of or embodying an ideal; perfect ⟨*an* ~ *spot for a picnic*⟩

²ideal *n* **1** a standard of perfection, beauty, or excellence **2** one looked up to as embodying an ideal or as a model for imitation **3** an ultimate object or aim – **idealless** *adj*

idealism *n* **1a** a theory that the essential nature of reality lies in consciousness or reason **b** a theory that only what is immediately perceived (e g sensations or ideas) is real **2** the practice of living according to one's ideals **3** a literary or artistic theory or practice that affirms the preeminent value of imagination and representation of ideal types as compared with faithful copying of nature

idealist *n* **1** one who advocates or practises idealism in art or writing **2** sby guided by ideals; *esp* one who places ideals before practical considerations – **idealist, idealistic** *adj*, **idealistically** *adv*

idealize, -ise *vt* **1** to attribute qualities of excellence or perfection to **2** to represent in an ideal form to form ideals – **idealizer** *n*, **idealization** *n*

ideally *adv* **1** in accordance with an ideal; perfectly ⟨~ *suited for the job*⟩ **2** for best results ⟨~, *we should eat less sugar*⟩

idem *pron* the same as previously mentioned

identical *adj* **1** being the same ⟨*the* ~ *place we stopped before*⟩ **2** being very similar or exactly alike ⟨*the copy was* ~ *with the original*⟩ **3** *of twins, triplets, etc* derived from a single egg

identification *n* **1a** identifying or being identified **b** evidence of identity ⟨*employees must carry* ~ *at all times*⟩ **2a** the putting of oneself mentally in the position of another **b** the (unconscious) attribution of the characteristics of another to oneself in order to attain gratification, emotional support, etc

identification parade *n*, *chiefly Br* a line-up of people arranged by the police to allow a witness to identify a suspect

identify *vt* **1a** to cause to be or become identical **b** to associate or link closely ⟨*groups that are* identified *with conservation*⟩ **2** to establish the identity of ~ *vi* to experience psychological identification ⟨~ *with the hero of a novel*⟩ – **identifiable** *adj*, **identifiably** *adv*, **identifier** *n*

¹identikit *n*, *often cap* a set of alternative facial characteristics used by the police to build up a likeness, esp of a suspect; *also* a likeness constructed in this way

²identikit *adj*, *often cap* **1** of or produced by identikit **2** like many others of the same type ⟨*a middlebrow* ~ *novel*⟩

identity *n* **1** the condition of being exactly alike **2** the distinguishing character or personality of an individual **3** the condition of being the same as sthg or sby known or supposed to exist ⟨*establish the* ~ *of the stolen goods*⟩ **4** an algebraic equation that remains true whatever values are substituted for the symbols ⟨$(x+y)^2 = x^2 + 2xy + y^2$ *is an* ~⟩

identity card *n* a card bearing information that establishes the identity of the holder

ideogram *n* **1** a stylized picture or symbol used instead of a word or sound to represent a thing or idea **2** a logogram – **ideogramic, ideogrammic** *adj*, **ideogrammatic** *adj*

ideology *n* **1** a systematic body of concepts **2** a manner of thinking characteristic of an individual, group, or culture ⟨*medical* ~⟩ **3** the ideas behind a social, political, or cultural programme – **ideologist** *n*, **ideological** *also* **ideologic** *adj*, **ideologically** *adv*

ides *n pl but sing or pl in constr* (the week preceding) the 15th day of March, May, July, or October or the 13th day of any other month in the ancient Roman calendar

idiocy *n* **1** extreme mental deficiency **2** sthg notably stupid or foolish

idiom *n* **1a** the language peculiar to a people or to a district, community, or class **b** the syntactic, grammatical, or structural form peculiar to a language **2** an expression in the usage of a language that has a meaning that cannot be derived from the sum of the meanings of its elements **3** a characteristic style or form of artistic expression ⟨*the modern jazz* ~⟩

idiomatic *adj* of or conforming to idiom – **idiomatically** *adv*, **idiomaticity** *n*

idiosyncrasy *n* **1** characteristic peculiarity of habit or structure **2** a characteristic of thought or behaviour peculiar to an individual or group; *esp* an eccentricity – **idiosyncratic** *adj*, **idiosyncratically** *adv*

idiot *n* **1** an (ineducable) person afflicted with idiocy, esp from birth **2** a silly or foolish person – **idiot** *adj*, **idiotic** *adj*, **idiotically** *adv*

¹idle *adj* **1** having no particular purpose or value ⟨~ *curiosity*⟩ **2** groundless ⟨~ *rumour*⟩ **3** not occupied or employed: e g **a** not in use or operation ⟨*machines lying* ~⟩ **b** not turned to appropriate use ⟨~ *funds*⟩ **4** lazy – **idleness** *n*, **idly** *adv*

²idle *vb* **idling** *vi* **1a** to spend time in idleness **b** to move idly **2** *esp of an engine* to run without being connected to the part (e g the wheels of a car) that is driven, so that no useful work is done ~ *vt* **1** to pass in idleness **2** to cause to idle – **idler** *n*

idol *n* **1** an image or symbol used as an object of worship; *broadly* a false god **2** an object of passionate or excessive devotion ⟨*a pop* ~⟩

idolater *n* **1** a worshipper of idols **2** a passionate and often uncritical admirer

idolatry *n* **1** the worship of a physical object as a god **2** excessive attachment or devotion to sthg – **idolatrous** *adj*, **idolatrously** *adv*, **idolatrousness** *n*

idolize, -ise *vt* to worship idolatrously; *broadly* to love or admire to excess ~ *vi* to practise idolatry – **idolizer** *n*, **idolization** *n*

idyll, idyl *n* **1** a simple work in poetry or prose describing peaceful rustic life or pastoral scenes **2** an episode suitable for an idyll **3** a pastoral or romantic musical composition – **idyllic** *adj*, **idyllically** *adv*

-ie *suffix* (*n* → *n*) [4]-Y

-ier – see [2]-ER

[1]if *conj* **1a** in the event that ⟨~ *she should telephone, let me know*⟩ **b** supposing ⟨~ *you'd listened, you'd know*⟩ **c** on condition that **2** whether ⟨*asked* ~ *the mail had come*⟩ **3** – used to introduce an exclamation expressing a wish ⟨~ *it would only rain*⟩ **4** even if; although ⟨*an interesting* ~ *irrelevant point*⟩ **5** that – used after expressions of emotion ⟨*I don't care* ~ *she's cross*⟩ ⟨*it's not surprising* ~ *you're annoyed*⟩ **6** – used with a negative when an expletive introduces startling news ⟨*blow me* ~ *he didn't hit her!*⟩ – **if anything** on the contrary even; perhaps even ⟨if anything, *you ought to apologize*⟩

[2]if *n* **1** a condition, stipulation ⟨*the question depends on too many* ~ s⟩ **2** a supposition ⟨*a theory full of* ~ s⟩

-iform – see -FORM

-ify – see -FY

igloo *n*, *pl* **igloos 1** an Eskimo dwelling, usu made of snow blocks and in the shape of a dome **2** a structure shaped like a dome

igneous *adj* **1** fiery **2** relating to or formed by the flow or solidification of molten rock from the earth's core ⟨~ *rocks*⟩

ignis fatuus *n*, *pl* **ignes fatui** a will-o'-the-wisp

ignite *vt* **1a** to set fire to; *also* to kindle **b** to cause (a fuel mixture) to burn **2** to spark off; excite, esp suddenly ~ *vi* **1** to catch fire **2** to begin to glow **3** to burst forth suddenly into violence or conflict – **ignitable** *also* **ignitible** *adj*, **igniter, ignitor** *n*

ignition *n* **1** the act or action of igniting **2** the process or means (e g an electric spark) of igniting a fuel mixture

ignoble *adj* **1** of low birth or humble origin **2** base, dishonourable – **ignobleness** *n*, **ignobly** *adv*, **ignobility** *n*

ignominious *adj* **1** marked by or causing disgrace or discredit **2** humiliating, degrading ⟨*suffered an* ~ *defeat*⟩ – **ignominiously** *adv*, **ignominiousness** *n*

ignominy *n* **1** deep personal humiliation and disgrace **2** disgraceful or dishonourable conduct or quality

ignoramus *n* an ignorant person

ignorance *n* the state of being ignorant

ignorant *adj* **1** lacking knowledge, education, or comprehension (of sthg specified) **2** caused by or showing lack of knowledge **3** lacking social training; impolite – chiefly infml – **ignorantly** *adv*

ignore *vt* to refuse to take notice of; disregard – **ignorable** *adj*, **ignorer** *n*

iguana *n* any of various large lizards; *esp* a plant-eating (dark-coloured) tropical American lizard with a serrated crest on its back

ikon *n* an icon

il- – see IN-

ileum *n*, *pl* **ilea** the last division of the small intestine extending between the jejunum and the large intestine – **ileal** *adj*

ilex *n* **1** HOLM OAK **2** the holly

[1]ilk *pron, chiefly Scot that* same – esp in the names of landed families

[2]ilk *n* sort, kind ⟨*politicians and others of that* ~⟩

[3]ilk *adj, chiefly Scot* each, every

[1]ill *adj* **worse; worst 1a** bad: e g **a** morally evil ⟨~ *deeds*⟩ **b** malevolent, hostile ⟨~ *feeling*⟩ **c** attributing evil or an objectionable quality ⟨*held an* ~ *opinion of his neighbours*⟩ **2a** causing discomfort or inconvenience; disagreeable ⟨~ *effects*⟩ **b**(1) not normal or sound ⟨~ *health*⟩ (2) not in good health; *also* nauseated (3) *chiefly Br* hurt, wounded ⟨*still very* ~ *after the accident*⟩ **3** unlucky, disadvantageous ⟨*an* ~ *omen*⟩ ⟨~ *fortune*⟩ **4** socially improper ⟨~ *breeding*⟩ **5a** unfriendly, hostile ⟨~ *feeling*⟩ ⟨~ *will*⟩ **b** harsh ⟨~ *treatment*⟩

[2]ill *adv* **worse; worst 1a** with displeasure or hostility **b** in a harsh manner ⟨*used him* ~⟩ **c** so as to reflect unfavourably ⟨*spoke* ~ *of his neighbours*⟩ **2** in a reprehensible, harsh, or deficient manner ⟨*fared* ~⟩ ⟨ill-adapted to city life⟩ **3** hardly, scarcely ⟨~ *at ease*⟩ ⟨*can* ~ *afford such extravagances*⟩ **4a** in an unfortunate manner; badly, unluckily ⟨ill-*fated*⟩ **b** in a faulty, imperfect, or unpleasant manner ⟨ill-*equipped*⟩ *USE* often in combination

[3]ill *n* **1** the opposite of good; evil **2a** (a) misfortune, trouble ⟨*hope no more* ~ s *befall him*⟩ **b**(1) an ailment (2) sthg that disturbs or afflicts ⟨*economic and social* ~ s⟩ **3** sthg that reflects unfavourably ⟨*spoke no* ~ *of him*⟩

I'll I will; I shall

ill-advised *adj* showing lack of proper consideration or sound advice – **ill-advisedly** *adv*

ill at ease *adj* uneasy, uncomfortable

ill-bred *adj* having or showing bad upbringing; impolite

illegal *adj* not authorized by law – **illegally** *adv*, **illegality** *n*

illegible *adj* not legible – **illegibly** *adv*, **illegibility** *n*

illegitimate *adj* **1** not recognized as lawful offspring; *specif* born out of wedlock **2** wrongly deduced or inferred **3** departing from the regular; abnormal **4** illegal – **illegitimately** *adv*, **illegitimacy** *n*

ill-favoured *adj* **1** unattractive in physical appearance **2** offensive, objectionable

ill-gotten *adj* acquired by illicit or improper means – esp in *ill-gotten gains*

illiberal *adj* not liberal: e g **a** lacking culture and refinement **b** not broad-minded; bigoted **c** opposed to liberalism – **illiberalism** *n*, **illiberally** *adv*, **illiberalness, illiberality** *n*

illicit *adj* not permitted; unlawful ⟨~ *love affairs*⟩ – **illicitly** *adv*

illiterate *adj* **1** unable to read or write **2** showing lack of education – **illiterate** *n*, **illiterately** *adv*, **illiterateness, illiteracy** *n*

ill-mannered *adj* having bad manners

ill-natured *adj* having a disagreeable disposition; surly – **ill-naturedly** *adv*

illness *n* an unhealthy condition of body or mind

illogical *adj* **1** contrary to the principles of logic **2** devoid of logic; senseless – **illogically** *adv*, **illogicalness, illogicality** *n*

ill-tempered *adj* ill-natured – **ill-temperedly** *adv*

ill-timed *adj* badly timed; *esp* inopportune

ill-treat *vt* to treat cruelly or improperly – **ill-treatment** *n*

illuminate *vt* **1a**(1) to cast light on; fill with light (2) to brighten **b** to enlighten spiritually or intellectually **2** to elucidate **3** to decorate (a manuscript) with elaborate initial letters or marginal designs in gold, silver, and brilliant colours – **illuminatingly** adv, **illuminator** n, **illuminative** adj

illumination n **1** illuminating or being illuminated: e g **a** spiritual or intellectual enlightenment **b** decorative lighting or lighting effects ⟨the Blackpool ~s⟩ **c** decoration of a manuscript by the art of illuminating **2** the amount of light per unit area of a surface on which it falls **3** any of the decorative features used in the art of illuminating or in decorative lighting

illusion n **1** a false impression or notion ⟨I have no ~s about my ability⟩ **2a**(1) a misleading image presented to the vision (2) sthg that deceives or misleads intellectually **b**(1) perception of an object in such a way that it presents a misleading image ⟨an optical ~⟩ (2) HALLUCINATION 1 – **illusional** adj, **illusionist** n

illusory adj deceptive, unreal ⟨~ hopes⟩ – **illusorily** adv, **illusoriness** n

illustrate vt **1a** to clarify (by giving or serving as an example or instance) **b** to provide (e g a book) with visual material **2** to show clearly; demonstrate ~ vi to give an example or instance – **illustrator** n

illustration n **1** illustrating or being illustrated **2** sthg that serves to illustrate: e g **a** an example that explains or clarifies sthg **b** a picture or diagram that helps to make sthg clear or attractive – **illustrational** adj

illustrative adj serving or intended to illustrate ⟨~ examples⟩ – **illustratively** adv

illustrious adj marked by distinction or renown – **illustriously** adv, **illustriousness** n

ill will n unfriendly feeling

im- – see IN-

I'm I am

image n **1** a reproduction (e g a portrait or statue) of the form of a person or thing **2a** the optical counterpart of an object produced by a lens, mirror, etc or an electronic device **b** a likeness of an object produced on a photographic material **3a** exact likeness ⟨God created man in his own ~ – Gen 1:27 (RSV)⟩ **b** a person who strikingly resembles another specified person ⟨he's the ~ of his father⟩ **4** a typical example or embodiment (e g of a quality) ⟨he's the ~ of goodness⟩ **5a** a mental picture of sthg (not actually present) **b** an idea, concept **6** a figure of speech, esp a metaphor or simile **7** a conception created in the minds of people, esp the general public ⟨worried about his public ~⟩ **8** an element in the range of a mathematical function that corresponds to a particular element in the domain

imagery n **1** (the art of making) images **2** figurative language **3** mental images; esp the products of imagination

imaginable adj capable of being imagined – **imaginableness** n, **imaginably** adv

imaginary adj **1** existing only in imagination; lacking factual reality **2** containing or relating to (a multiple of) the positive square root of minus 1 – **imaginarily** adv, **imaginariness** n

imagination n **1** the act or power of forming a mental image of sthg not present to the senses or never before wholly perceived in reality **2** creative ability **3** a fanciful or empty notion

imaginative adj **1** of or characterized by imagination **2** given to imagining; having a lively imagination **3** of images; esp showing a command of imagery – **imaginatively** adv, **imaginativeness** n

imagine vt **1** to form a mental image of (sthg not present) **2** to suppose, think ⟨I ~ it will rain⟩ **3** to believe without

sufficient basis ⟨~s himself to be indispensable⟩ ~ vi to use the imagination

imam n **1** the leader of prayer in a mosque **2** cap a Shiite leader held to be the divinely appointed successor of Muhammad **3** a caliph; also any of various Islamic doctors of law or theology – **imamate** n

imbalance n lack of balance: e g **a** lack of functional balance in a physiological system ⟨hormonal ~⟩ **b** lack of balance between segments of a country's economy **c** numerical disproportion

imbecile n **1** MENTAL DEFECTIVE **2** a fool, idiot – **imbecile, imbecilic** adj

imbecility n **1** being (an) imbecile **2** (an instance of) utter foolishness or nonsense

imbed vb **-dd-** to embed

imbibe vt **1** to drink **2** to take in or up; absorb, assimilate ~ vi DRINK 2 – **imbiber** n

imbroglio n, pl **imbroglios** **1** a confused mass **2a** an intricate or complicated situation (e g in a drama) **b** a confused or complicated misunderstanding or disagreement

imbue vt **1** to tinge or dye deeply **2** to cause to become permeated ⟨a man ~d with a strong sense of duty⟩

imitate vt **1** to follow as a pattern, model, or example **2** to reproduce **3** to resemble **4** to mimic; TAKE OFF – **imitable** adj, **imitator** n

¹imitation n **1** an act or instance of imitating **2** sthg produced as a copy; a counterfeit **3** the repetition in one musical part of the melodic theme, phrase, or motive previously found in another musical part – **imitational** adj

²imitation adj made in imitation of sthg else that is usu genuine and of better quality

imitative adj **1a** marked by or given to imitation ⟨acting is an ~ art⟩ **b** onomatopoeic **2** imitating sthg superior – **imitatively** adv, **imitativeness** n

immaculate adj **1** without blemish; pure **2** free from flaw or error **3** spotlessly clean – **immaculately** adv, **immaculateness, immaculacy** n

Immaculate Conception n the conception of the Virgin Mary held in Roman Catholic dogma to have freed her from original sin

immanent adj **1** indwelling; esp having existence only in the mind **2** pervading nature or the souls of men ⟨belief in an ~ God⟩ – **immanence, immanency** n, **immanently** adv

immaterial adj **1** not consisting of matter; incorporeal **2** unimportant – **immaterially** adv, **immaterialness, immateriality** n, **immaterialize** vt

immature adj **1** lacking complete growth, differentiation, or development **2a** not having arrived at a definitive form or state ⟨a vigorous but ~ school of art⟩ **b** exhibiting less than an expected degree of maturity ⟨emotionally ~ adults⟩ – **immature** n, **immaturely** adv, **immatureness, immaturity** n

immeasurable adj indefinitely extensive – **immeasurableness, immeasurably** adv

immediacy n **1** the quality or state of being immediate **2** sthg requiring immediate attention – usu pl ⟨the immediacies of life⟩

immediate adj **1a** acting or being without any intervening agency or factor ⟨the ~ cause of death⟩ **b** involving or derived from a single premise ⟨an ~ inference⟩ **2** next in line or relationship ⟨only the ~ family was present⟩ **3** occurring at once or very shortly **4** in close or direct physical proximity ⟨the ~ neighbourhood⟩ **5** directly touching or concerning a person or thing – **immediateness** n

¹immediately adv **1** in direct relation or proximity;

directly ⟨*the parties ~ involved in the case*⟩ **2** without delay

²immediately *conj* AS SOON AS

immemorial *adj* extending beyond the reach of memory, record, or tradition ⟨*existing from time ~*⟩ – **immemorially** *adv*

immense *adj* very great, esp in size, degree, or extent – **immensely** *adv*, **immenseness, immensity** *n*

immerse *vt* **1** to plunge into sthg, esp a fluid, that surrounds or covers **2** to baptize by complete submergence **3** to engross, absorb ⟨*completely ~d in his work*⟩ – **immersible** *adj*

immersion *n* disappearance of a celestial body behind or into the shadow of another

immersion heater *n* an electrical apparatus for heating a liquid in which it is immersed; *esp* an electric water-heater fixed inside a domestic hot-water storage tank

immigrant *n* **1** one who comes to a country to take up permanent residence **2** a plant or animal that becomes established in an area where it was previously unknown – **immigrant** *adj*

immigrate *vi* to come into a country of which one is not a native for permanent residence ~ *vt* to bring in or send as immigrants – **immigration** *n*, **immigrational** *adj*

imminent *adj* about to take place; *esp* impending, threatening – **imminently** *adv*, **imminentness, imminence** *n*

immobile *adj* **1** incapable of being moved **2** motionless ⟨*keep the patient ~*⟩ – **immobility** *n*

immobilize, -ise *vt* **1** to prevent freedom of movement or effective use of **2** to reduce or eliminate motion of (sby or a body part) by mechanical means or by strict bed rest – **immobilizer** *n*, **immobilization** *n*

immoderate *adj* lacking in moderation; excessive – **immoderately** *adv*, **immoderacy, immoderateness, immoderation** *n*

immodest *adj* not conforming to standards of sexual propriety – **immodestly** *adv*, **immodesty** *n*

immolate *vt* **1** to kill as a sacrificial victim **2** to kill, destroy – **immolator** *n*, **immolation** *n*

immoral *adj* not conforming to conventional moral standards, esp in sexual matters – **immorally** *adv*, **immorality** *n*

¹immortal *adj* **1** exempt from death ⟨*the ~ gods*⟩ **2** enduring forever; imperishable ⟨*~ fame*⟩ – **immortally** *adv*, **immortalize** *vt*, **immortality** *n*

²immortal *n* **1a** one exempt from death **b** *pl, often cap* the gods of classical antiquity **2** a person of lasting fame

immovable *adj* **1** not moving or not intended to be moved **2a** steadfast, unyielding **b** incapable of being moved emotionally – **immovably** *adv*, **immovableness, immovability** *n*

immune *adj* **1** free, exempt ⟨*~ from prosecution*⟩ **2** having a high degree of resistance to a disease ⟨*~ to diphtheria*⟩ **3a** having or producing antibodies to a corresponding antigen ⟨*an ~ serum*⟩ **b** concerned with or involving immunity ⟨*an ~ response*⟩ – **immune** *n*, **immunize** *vt*, **immunization** *n*

immunity *n* being immune; *specif* the ability to resist the effects or development of a disease-causing parasite, esp a microorganism

immunoglobulin *n* a protein (e g an antibody) that is made up of light and heavy amino acid chains and usu binds specifically to a particular antigen

immure *vt* **1** to enclose (as if) within walls; imprison **2** to build into, or esp entomb in, a wall – **immurement** *n*

immutable *adj* not capable of or susceptible to change – **immutably** *adv*, **immutableness, immutability** *n*

¹imp *n* **1** a small demon **2** a mischievous child; a scamp

²imp *vt, archaic* to graft or repair (e g a falcon's wing or tail) with a feather to improve flight

¹impact *vt* to fix or press firmly (as if) by packing or wedging ~ *vi* to impinge or make contact, esp forcefully – **impactive** *adj*

²impact *n* **1a** an impinging or striking, esp of one body against another **b** (the impetus produced by or as if by) a violent contact or collision **2** a strong or powerful effect or impression ⟨*the ~ of modern science on our society*⟩

impacted *adj, of a tooth* not erupted as a result of lack of space in the jaw or of obstruction by bone or other teeth

impair *vt* to diminish in quality, strength, or amount – **impairer** *n*, **impairment** *n*

impala *n* a large brownish African antelope

impale *vt* **1** to pierce (as if) with sthg pointed; *esp* to torture or kill by fixing on a stake **2** to join (coats of arms) on a heraldic shield divided in half vertically – **impalement** *n*

impalpable *adj* **1** incapable of being sensed by the touch; intangible **2** not easily discerned or grasped by the mind – **impalpably** *adv*, **impalpability** *n*

impanel *vt* to empanel

impart *vt* **1** to convey, transmit ⟨*the flavour ~ed by herbs*⟩ **2** to make known; disclose – **impartable** *adj*, **impartment, impartation** *n*

impartial *adj* not biased – **impartially** *adv*, **impartiality** *n*

impassable *adj* incapable of being passed, traversed, or surmounted – **impassably** *adv*, **impassableness, impassability** *n*

impasse *n* **1** a predicament from which there is no obvious escape **2** DEADLOCK 2

impassion *vt* to arouse the feelings or passions of – **impassioned** *adj*

impassive *adj* **1** incapable of or not susceptible to emotion **2** showing no feeling or emotion – **impassively** *adv*, **impassiveness, impassivity** *n*

impatient *adj* **1a** restless or quickly roused to anger or exasperation **b** intolerant ⟨*~ of delay*⟩ **2** showing or caused by a lack of patience ⟨*an ~ reply*⟩ **3** eagerly desirous; anxious ⟨*~ to see her boyfriend*⟩ – **impatience** *n*, **impatiently** *adv*

impeach *vt* **1a** to bring an accusation against **b** to charge with a usu serious crime; *specif, chiefly NAm* to charge (a public official) with misconduct in office **2** to cast doubt on; *esp* to challenge the credibility or validity of ⟨*the testimony of a witness*⟩ – **impeachable** *adj*, **impeachment** *n*

impeccable *adj* **1** incapable of sinning **2** free from fault or blame; flawless – **impeccably** *adv*, **impeccability** *n*

impecunious *adj* having very little or no money – chiefly fml – **impecuniously** *adv*, **impecuniousness, impecuniosity** *n*

impedance *n* sthg that impedes; *esp* the opposition in an electrical circuit to the flow of an alternating current that is analogous to the opposition of an electrical resistance to the flow of a direct current

impede *vt* to interfere with or retard the progress of – **impeder** *n*

impediment *n* **1** sthg that impedes; *esp* a physiological speech defect **2** a hindrance to lawful marriage

impedimenta *n pl* **1** unwieldy baggage or equipment **2** things that impede; encumbrances

impel *vt* **-ll-** **1** to urge forward or force into action ⟨*felt ~led to speak his mind*⟩ **2** to propel

impend vi **1a** to hover threateningly; menace **b** to be about to happen **2** archaic to be suspended; hang

impenetrability n the inability of 2 portions of matter to occupy the same space at the same time

impenetrable adj **1a** incapable of being penetrated or pierced **b** inaccessible to intellectual influences or ideas **2** incapable of being comprehended **3** having the property of impenetrability – **impenetrableness** n, **impenetrably** adv

¹**imperative** adj **1a** of or being the grammatical mood that expresses command **b** expressive of a command, entreaty, or exhortation **c** having power to restrain, control, and direct **2** urgent ⟨an ~ duty⟩ – **imperatively** adv, **imperativeness** n

²**imperative** n **1** (a verb form expressing) the imperative mood **2** sthg imperative: e g **a** a command, order **b** an obligatory act or duty **c** an imperative judgment or proposition

imperceptible adj **1** not perceptible by the mind or senses **2** extremely slight, gradual, or subtle ⟨an ~ change in attitude⟩ – **imperceptibly** adv, **imperceptibility** n

¹**imperfect** adj **1** not perfect: e g **a** defective **b** not having the stamens and carpels in the same flower **2** of or being a verb tense expressing a continuing state or an incomplete action, esp in the past **3** of a cadence passing to a dominant chord from a tonic chord – **imperfectly** adv, **imperfectness** n, **imperfection** n

²**imperfect** n (a verb form expressing) the imperfect tense

¹**imperial** adj **1a** of or befitting an empire, emperor, or empress **b** of the British Empire **2a** sovereign, royal **b** regal, imperious **3** belonging to an official nonmetric British series of weights and measures – **imperially** adv

²**imperial** n a size of paper usu 30 × 22in (762 × 559mm)

imperialism n **1** government by an emperor **2** the policy, practice, or advocacy of extending the power and dominion of a nation, esp by territorial acquisition – **imperialist** n or adj, **imperialistic** adj, **imperialistically** adv

imperil vt **-ll-** (NAm **-l-**, **-ll-**) to endanger – **imperilment** n

imperious adj marked by arrogant assurance; domineering ⟨his ~ arbitrariness⟩ – **imperiously** adv, **imperiousness** n

imperishable adj **1** not perishable or subject to decay **2** enduring permanently ⟨~ fame⟩ – **imperishable** n, **imperishably** adv, **imperishableness**, **imperishability** n

impermanent adj transient – **impermanence**, **impermanency** n, **impermanently** adv

impermeable adj not permitting passage, esp of a fluid – **impermeably** adv, **impermeability** n

impersonal adj **1a** denoting verbal action with no expressed subject (e g methinks) or with a merely formal subject (e g rained in it rained) **b** of a pronoun indefinite **2a** having no personal reference or connection; objective **b** not involving or reflecting the human personality or emotions ⟨spoke in a flat ~ tone⟩ **c** not having personality ⟨an ~ deity⟩ – **impersonalize** vt, **impersonally** adv, **impersonality** n

impersonate vt to assume or act the character of – **impersonator** n, **impersonation** n

impertinent adj **1** not restrained within due or proper bounds ⟨~ curiosity⟩; also rude, insolent **2** irrelevant – chiefly fml – **impertinence** n, **impertinently** adv

imperturbable adj marked by extreme calm and composure – **imperturbably** adv, **imperturbability** n

impervious adj **1** impenetrable ⟨a coat ~ to rain⟩ **2** not capable of being affected or disturbed ⟨~ to criticism⟩ USE usu + to – **imperviously** adv, **imperviousness** n

impetigo n a contagious skin disease characterized by blisters and pustules – **impetiginous** adj

impetuous adj **1** marked by impulsive vehemence ⟨an ~ temperament⟩ **2** marked by forceful and violent movement – chiefly poetic – **impetuousness** n, **impetuously** adv, **impetuosity** n

impetus n **1a** a driving force **b** an incentive, stimulus ⟨gave a new ~ to the ailing economy⟩ **2** the energy possessed by a moving body

impiety n (an act showing) a lack of reverence

impinge vi **1** to strike, dash **2** to make an impression **3** to encroach, infringe ⟨~ on other people's rights⟩ USE usu + on or upon – **impingement** n

impious adj lacking in reverence or proper respect (e g for God); irreverent – **impiously** adv

impish adj mischievous – **impishly** adv, **impishness** n

implacable adj not capable of being appeased or pacified ⟨an ~ enemy⟩ – **implacableness** n, **implacably** adv, **implacability** n

¹**implant** vt **1a** to fix or set securely or deeply **b** to set permanently in the consciousness or habit patterns **2** to insert in the tissue of a living organism – **implantable** adj, **implanter** n, **implantation** n

²**implant** n sthg (e g a graft or hormone pellet) implanted in tissue

¹**implement** n **1** an article serving to equip ⟨the ~s of religious worship⟩ **2** (sby or sthg that serves as) a utensil or tool

²**implement** vt CARRY OUT; esp to give practical effect to ⟨plans not yet ~ed due to lack of funds⟩ – **implementation** n

implicate vt **1** to involve as a consequence, corollary, or inference; imply **2a** to bring into (incriminating) connection **b** to involve in the nature or operation of sthg; affect **3** archaic to entwine

implication n **1a** implicating or being implicated **b** incriminating involvement **2a** implying or being implied **b** a logical relation between 2 propositions such that if the first is true the second must be true **3** sthg implied – **implicative** adj

implicit adj **1a** implied rather than directly stated ⟨an ~ assumption⟩ **b** potentially present though not realized or visible **2** unquestioning, absolute ⟨~ obedience⟩ – **implicitly** adv, **implicitness** n

implore vt **1** to call on in supplication; beseech **2** to call or beg for earnestly; entreat

implosion n **1** imploding **2** the release of obstructed breath inwards that occurs in the articulation of one kind of stop consonant **3** the act or action of coming (as if) to a centre – **implosive** adj or n

imply vt **1** to involve or indicate as a necessary or potential though not expressly stated consequence **2** to express indirectly; hint at ⟨his silence implied consent⟩

impolite adj not polite; rude – **impolitely** adv, **impoliteness** n

impolitic adj unwise, ill-advised – chiefly fml – **impoliticly** adv

imponderable n or adj (sthg) incapable of being precisely weighed or evaluated – **imponderably** adv, **imponderability** n

¹**import** vt **1** to bring from a foreign or external source; esp to bring (e g merchandise) into a place or country from another country **2** to convey as meaning or portent; signify – chiefly fml – **importable** adj, **importer** n, **importation** n

²**import** n **1** sthg imported **2** importing, esp of merchandise **3** purport, meaning **4** (relative) importance ⟨it is

hard to determine the ~ of this decision⟩ USE (3 & 4) fml

importance n consequence, significance

important adj of considerable significance or consequence – **importantly** adv

importunate adj troublesomely urgent; extremely persistent in request or demand – chiefly fml – **importunately** adv, **importunity** n

importune vt 1 to press or urge with repeated requests; solicit with troublesome persistence 2 to solicit for purposes of prostitution ~ vi to beg, urge, or solicit importunately USE chiefly fml – **importuner** n

impose vt 1a to establish or apply as compulsory b to establish or make prevail by force 2 to arrange (typeset or plated pages) in order for printing 3 PALM OFF ⟨~ fake antiques on the public⟩ 4 to force into the company or on the attention of another ⟨~ oneself on others⟩ ~ vi to take unwarranted advantage ⟨~d on his good nature⟩; also to be an excessive requirement or burden USE (except vt 1 & 2) + on or upon – **imposer** n

imposing adj impressive because of size, bearing, dignity, or grandeur – **imposingly** adv

imposition n 1 the act of imposing 2 sthg imposed: e g a a levy, tax b an excessive or unwarranted requirement or burden

impossible adj 1a incapable of being or occurring; not possible b seemingly incapable of being done, attained, or fulfilled; insuperably difficult c difficult to believe ⟨an ~ story⟩ 2 extremely undesirable or difficult to put up with ⟨life became ~ because of lack of money⟩ – **impossibly** adv, **impossibility** n

impostor, imposter n one who assumes a false identity or title for fraudulent purposes

imposture n (an instance of) fraud, deception

impotent adj 1 lacking in efficacy, strength, or vigour 2a unable to copulate through an inability to maintain an erection of the penis b of a male STERILE 1 – not used technically – **impotence, impotency** n, **impotent** n, **impotently** adv

impound vt 1a to shut up (as if) in a pound; confine b to take and hold in legal custody 2 to collect and confine (water) (as if) in a reservoir – **impoundment** n

impoverish vt 1 to make poor 2 to deprive of strength, richness, or fertility – **impoverisher** n, **impoverishment** n

impracticable adj 1 incapable of being put into effect or carried out 2 impassable ⟨an ~ road⟩ – **impracticably** adv, **impracticableness, impracticability** n

impractical adj not practical: e g a incapable of dealing sensibly with practical matters b impracticable ⟨economically ~⟩ – **impracticality** n, **impractically** adv

imprecate vb to invoke evil (on); curse – **imprecatory** adj, **imprecation** n

impregnable adj 1 incapable of being taken by assault ⟨an ~ fortress⟩ 2 beyond criticism or question ⟨an ~ social position⟩ – **impregnably** adv, **impregnability** n

¹**impregnate** adj filled, saturated

²**impregnate** vt 1a to introduce sperm cells into b to make pregnant; fertilize 2a to cause to be imbued, permeated, or saturated b to permeate thoroughly – **impregnable** adj, **impregnation** n, **impregnator** n

impresario n, pl **impresarios** one who organizes, puts on, or sponsors a public entertainment (e g a sports event); esp the manager or conductor of an opera or concert company

¹**impress** vt 1a to apply with pressure so as to imprint b to mark (as if) by pressure or stamping 2a to fix strongly or deeply (e g in the mind or memory) b to produce a deep and usu favourable impression on 3 to transmit (force or

motion) by pressure ~ vi to produce a (favourable) impression ⟨performances that failed to ~⟩ – **impressible** n or adj

²**impress** n 1 the act of impressing 2 a mark made by pressure 3 an impression, effect

³**impress** vt 1 to force into naval service 2 to procure or enlist by forcible persuasion – **impressment** n

impression n 1 the act or process of impressing 2 the effect produced by impressing: e g a a stamp, form, or figure produced by physical contact b a (marked) influence or effect on the mind or senses; esp a favourable impression 3a an effect of alteration or improvement ⟨the settlement left little ~ on the wilderness⟩ b a telling image impressed on the mind or senses ⟨first ~s of Greece⟩ 4a the amount of pressure with which an inked printing surface deposits its ink on the paper b (a print or copy made from) the contact of a printing surface and the material being printed c all the copies of a publication (e g a book) printed in 1 continuous operation 5 a usu indistinct or imprecise notion or recollection 6 an imitation or representation of salient features in an artistic or theatrical medium; esp an imitation in caricature of a noted personality as a form of theatrical entertainment

impressionable adj 1 easily influenced 2 easily moulded – **impressionability** n

impressionism n 1 often cap an art movement, esp in late 19th-c France, that tries to convey the effects of actual reflected light on natural usu outdoor subjects 2 literary depiction that seeks to convey a general subjective impression rather than a detailed re-creation of reality – **impressionist** n or adj, often cap

impressionistic adj 1 of or being impressionism 2 based on or involving subjective impression as distinct from knowledge, fact, or systematic thought – **impressionistically** adv

impressive adj making a marked impression; stirring deep feelings, esp of awe or admiration – **impressively** adv, **impressiveness** n

imprimatur n 1 a licence granted, esp by Roman Catholic episcopal authority, to print or publish 2 sanction, approval

¹**imprint** vt 1 to mark (as if) by pressure 2 to fix indelibly or permanently (e g on the memory)

²**imprint** n 1 a mark or depression made by pressure ⟨the fossil ~ of a dinosaur's foot⟩ 2 a publisher's name printed at the foot of a title-page 3 an indelible distinguishing effect or influence ⟨their work bears a sort of regional ~ – Malcolm Cowley⟩

imprison vt to put (as if) in prison – **imprisonment** n

improbable adj unlikely to be true or to occur – **improbably** adv, **improbability** n

¹**impromptu** adj made, done, composed, or uttered (as if) on the spur of the moment ⟨an ~ change of plan⟩ – **impromptu** adv

²**impromptu** n 1 sthg impromptu 2 a musical composition suggesting improvisation

improper adj 1 not in accordance with fact, truth, or correct procedure ⟨~ inference⟩ 2 not suitable or appropriate 3 not in accordance with propriety or modesty; indecent – **improperly** adv

improper fraction n a fraction whose numerator is equal to, larger than, or of equal or higher degree than the denominator

impropriety n 1 being improper 2 an improper act or remark; esp an unacceptable use of a word

improve vt 1a to enhance in value or quality; make better b to increase the value of (land or property) by making better (e g by cultivation or the erection of buildings) 2 to use to good purpose ~ vi 1 to advance or make progress in what is desirable **2** to make useful additions or amendments ⟨*the new version* ~s *on the original*⟩

improvement *n* **1** improving or being improved **2** (sthg that gives) increased value or excellence ⟨~s *to an old house*⟩

improvident *adj* lacking foresight; not providing for the future – **improvidence** *n*, **improvidently** *adv*

improvise *vb* **1** to compose, recite, or perform impromptu or without a set script, musical score, etc **2** to make, devise, or provide (sthg) without preparation (from what is conveniently to hand) – **improviser** *n*, **improvisation** *n*, **improvisatory** *adj*

imprudent *adj* lacking discretion or caution – **imprudence** *n*, **imprudently** *adv*

impudent *adj* marked by contemptuous or cocky boldness or disregard of others – **impudence** *n*, **impudently** *adv*

impugn *vt* to assail by words or arguments; call into question the validity or integrity of – **impugnable** *adj*, **impugner** *n*

impulse *n* **1a** (motion produced by) the act of driving onwards with sudden force **b** a wave of excitation transmitted through a nerve that results in physiological (e g muscular) activity or inhibition **2a** a force so communicated as to produce motion suddenly **b** inspiration, stimulus ⟨*the creative* ~⟩ **3a** a sudden spontaneous inclination or incitement to some usu unpremeditated action **b** a propensity or natural tendency, usu other than rational **4a** the change in momentum produced by a (large) force **b** PULSE 4a

impulsion *n* **1a** impelling or being impelled **b** an impelling force **c** an impetus **2** IMPULSE 3

impulsive *adj* **1** having the power of driving or impelling **2** actuated by or prone to act on impulse **3** acting momentarily – **impulsively** *adv*, **impulsiveness** *n*

impunity *n* exemption or freedom from punishment, harm, or loss ⟨*trespassing with* ~⟩

impure *adj* not pure: e g **a** not chaste **b** containing sthg unclean ⟨~ *water*⟩ **c** ritually unclean **d** mixed; *esp* adulterated – **impurely** *adv*, **impurity** *n*

impute *vt* **1** to lay the responsibility or blame for, often unjustly **2** to credit to a person or a cause; *esp* to attribute unjustly – **imputable** *adj*, **imputative** *adj*, **imputation** *n*

¹in *prep* **1a(1)** – used to indicate location within or inside sthg three-dimensional ⟨*swimming* ~ *the lake*⟩ **(2)** – used to indicate location within or not beyond limits ⟨~ *reach*⟩ ⟨~ *sight*⟩ ⟨*wounded* ~ *the leg*⟩ **(3)** – used with the names of cities, countries, and places ⟨~ *London*⟩ **(4)** during ⟨~ *the summer*⟩ ⟨~ *1959*⟩ ⟨*lost* ~ *transit*⟩ **(5)** by or before the end of ⟨*wrote it* ~ *a week*⟩ ⟨*will come* ~ *an hour*⟩ **b** INTO 1a ⟨*went* ~ *the house*⟩ **2a** – used to indicate means, instrumentality, or medium of expression ⟨*drawn* ~ *pencil*⟩ ⟨*written* ~ *French*⟩ ⟨*drink your health* ~ *cider*⟩ **b** – used to describe costume ⟨*a child* ~ *gumboots*⟩ ⟨*a girl* ~ *red*⟩ **3a** – used to indicate qualification, manner, circumstance, or condition ⟨~ *fun*⟩ ⟨~ *public*⟩ ⟨~ *step*⟩ ⟨~ *his sleep*⟩ ⟨~ *a hurry*⟩ ⟨~ *pain*⟩ **b** so as to be ⟨*broke* ~ *pieces*⟩ **c** – used to indicate occupation or membership ⟨*a job* ~ *insurance*⟩ ⟨*everyone* ~ *the team*⟩ **4a** as regards ⟨*equal* ~ *distance*⟩ ⟨*weak* ~ *arithmetic*⟩ **b** by way of ⟨*said* ~ *reply*⟩ ⟨*the latest thing* ~ *shoes*⟩ **5a** – used to indicate division, arrangement, or quantity ⟨*standing* ~ *a circle*⟩ ⟨*arrived* ~ *their thousands*⟩ **b** – used to indicate the larger member of a ratio ⟨*one* ~ *six is eligible*⟩ ⟨*a tax of 40p* ~ *the £*⟩ **6** of an animal pregnant with ⟨~ *calf*⟩ **7** – used to introduce indirect objects ⟨*rejoice* ~⟩ or to form adverbial phrases; compare IN FACT, IN RETURN – **in it** of advantage (e g between competitors or alternatives)

⟨*there's not much in it between them*⟩ ⟨*what's in it for me?*⟩

²in *adv* **1a** to or towards the inside or centre ⟨*come* ~ *out of the rain*⟩ **b** so as to incorporate ⟨*mix* ~ *the flour*⟩ **c** to or towards home, the shore, or one's destination ⟨*3 ships came sailing* ~⟩ **d** at a particular place, esp at one's home or business ⟨*be* ~ *for lunch*⟩ **e** into concealment ⟨*the sun went* ~⟩ **2a** so as to be added or included ⟨*fit a piece* ~⟩ ⟨*write a paragraph* ~⟩ **b** in or into political power ⟨*voted them* ~⟩ **c(1)** on good terms ⟨~ *with the boss*⟩ **(2)** in a position of assured success **(3)** into a state of efficiency or proficiency ⟨*work a horse* ~⟩ **d** in or into vogue or fashion **e** in or into a centre, esp a central point of control ⟨*letters pouring* ~⟩ ⟨*after harvests are* ~⟩ ⟨*went* ~ *to bat*⟩ – **in for** certain to experience ⟨*in for trouble*⟩ – compare LET IN FOR – **in on** having a share in

³in *adj* **1a** located inside **b** being in operation or power ⟨*the fire's still* ~⟩ **c** shared by a select group ⟨*an* ~ *joke*⟩ **2** directed or serving to direct inwards ⟨*the* ~ *tray*⟩ **3** extremely fashionable ⟨*the* ~ *place to go*⟩

¹in-, il-, im-, ir- *prefix* not; non-; un- – usu *il-* before *l* ⟨*illogical*⟩, *im-* before *b,m*, or *p* ⟨*imbalance*⟩ ⟨*immoral*⟩ ⟨*impractical*⟩, *ir-* before *r* ⟨*irreducible*⟩, and *in-* before other sounds ⟨*inconclusive*⟩

²in-, il-, im-, ir- *prefix* **1** in; within; into; towards; on ⟨*influx*⟩ ⟨*immerse*⟩ ⟨*irradiance*⟩ – usu *il-* before *l*, *im-* before *b,m*, or *p*, *ir-* before *r*, and *in-* before other sounds **2** ¹EN- ⟨*imperil*⟩ ⟨*inspirit*⟩

¹-in *suffix* (→ *n*) chemical compound: e g **a** hydrolytic enzyme ⟨*pepsin*⟩ **b** antibiotic ⟨*streptomycin*⟩ **c** ²-INE ⟨*glycerin*⟩

²-in *comb form* (→ *n*) **1** organized public protest by means of or in favour of; demonstration ⟨*teach*-in⟩ ⟨*love*-in⟩ **2** public group activity ⟨*sing*-in⟩

inability *n* lack of sufficient power, resources, or capacity ⟨*his* ~ *to do maths*⟩

inaccessible *adj*

inaccurate *adj* faulty – **inaccurately** *adv*

inaction *n* lack of action or activity

inactive *adj* **1** not given to action or effort **2** out of use; not functioning **3** relating to members of the armed forces who are not performing or available for military duties **4** of a disease quiescent **5** chemically or biologically inert, esp because of the loss of some quality – **inactively** *adv*, **inactivate** *vt*, **inactivity** *n*

inadequate *adj* not adequate: e g **a** insufficient **b** characteristically unable to cope – **inadequacy** *n*, **inadequately** *adv*, **inadequateness** *n*

inadmissible *adj*

inadvertent *adj* **1** heedless, inattentive **2** unintentional – **inadvertently** *adv*

inalienable *adj* incapable of being alienated – **inalienably** *adv*, **inalienability** *n*

inamorata *n* a woman with whom one is in love or is having a sexual relationship

inane *adj* lacking significance, meaning, or point – **inanely** *adv*, **inaneness, inanity** *n*

inanimate *adj* **1** not endowed with life or spirit **2** lacking consciousness or power of motion – **inanimately** *adv*, **inanimateness** *n*

inanition *n* **1** the quality of being empty **2** the absence or loss of social, moral, or intellectual vitality or vigour USE *fml*

inapplicable *adj*

inappropriate *adj*

inapt *adj* not suitable or appropriate – **inaptly** *adv*, **inaptness** *n*

inaptitude *n* lack of aptitude

inarticulate adj **1a** not understandable as spoken words ⟨~ cries⟩ **b** incapable of (being expressed by) speech, esp under stress of emotion **2a** not giving or not able to give coherent, clear, or effective expression to one's ideas or feelings **b** not coherently, clearly, or effectively expressed ⟨an ~ speech⟩ **3** not jointed or hinged – **inarticulately** adv, **inarticulateness** n

inartistic adj **1** not conforming to the principles of art **2** not appreciative of art – **inartistically** adv

inasmuch as conj **1** INSOFAR AS **2** in view of the fact that; because

inattention n failure to pay attention; disregard

inattentive adj

inaudible adj

¹inaugural adj marking a beginning; first in a projected series

²inaugural n an address at inauguration

inaugurate vt **1** to induct ceremonially into office **2** to observe formally, or bring about, the beginning of – **inaugurator** n, **inauguration** n

inauspicious adj

inboard adv **1** towards the centre line of a vessel **2** in a position closer or closest to the long axis of an aircraft – **inboard** adj

inborn adj **1** born in or with one; forming part of one's natural make-up **2** hereditary, inherited

inbred adj **1** rooted and deeply ingrained in one's nature **2** subjected to or produced by inbreeding

inbreeding n **1** the interbreeding of closely related individuals, esp to preserve and fix desirable characters **2** confinement to a narrow range or a local or limited field of choice – **inbreed** vt, **inbreeder** n

incalculable adj **1** too large or numerous to be calculated **2** unpredictable, uncertain – **incalculably** adv, **incalculability** n

incandescent adj **1a** white, glowing, or luminous with intense heat **b** strikingly bright, radiant, or clear **2** of or being visible light produced by a (white) hot body – **incandesce** vb, **incandescence** n, **incandescently** adv

incandescent lamp n an electric lamp in which an electrically-heated filament gives off light

incantation n the use of spoken or sung spells in magic ritual; also a formula so used – **incantatory** adj

incapable adj lacking capacity, ability, or qualification for the purpose or end in view: e g **a** not in a state of or of a kind to admit of **b** not able or fit for the doing or performance of – **incapableness** n, **incapably** adv, **incapability** n

incapacitate vt **1** to deprive of capacity or natural power; disable **2** to disqualify legally – **incapacitation** n

incapacity n lack of ability or power or of natural or legal qualifications

incarcerate vt to imprison, confine – **incarceration** n

¹incarnate adj **1** invested with bodily, esp human, nature and form **2** that is the essence of; typified ⟨evil ~⟩

²incarnate vt to make incarnate

incarnation n **1** making or being incarnate **2a(1)** the embodiment of a deity or spirit in an earthly form **(2)** cap Christ's human manifestation **b** a quality or concept typified or made concrete, esp in a person **3** any of several successive bodily manifestations or lives

¹incendiary n **1a** one who deliberately sets fire to property **b** an incendiary agent (e g a bomb) **2** one who inflames or stirs up factions, quarrels, or sedition – **incendiarism** n

²incendiary adj **1** of the deliberate burning of property **2** tending to inflame or stir up trouble **3** (of, being, or involving the use of a missile containing a chemical) that ignites spontaneously on contact

¹incense n **1** material used to produce a fragrant smell when burned **2** the perfume given off by some spices and gums when burned; broadly a pleasing scent

²incense vt to arouse the extreme anger or indignation of

incentive n sthg that motivates or spurs one on (e g to action or effort) – **incentive** adj

inception n an act, process, or instance of beginning

incertitude n uncertainty, doubt

incessant adj continuing without interruption – **incessancy** n, **incessantly** adv

incest n sexual intercourse between people so closely related that they are forbidden by law to marry

incestuous adj **1** being, guilty of, or involving incest **2** unhealthily closed to outside influences – **incestuously** adv, **incestuousness** n

¹inch n **1** a unit of length equal to ⅓₆yd (about 25.4mm) **2** a small amount, distance, or degree **3** pl stature, height **4** a fall of rain, snow, etc enough to cover a surface to the depth of 1in – **every inch** to the utmost degree ⟨looks every inch a winner⟩ – **within an inch of one's life** very thoroughly; soundly ⟨thrashed him within an inch of his life⟩

²inch vb to move by small degrees

³inch n, chiefly Scot an island – usu in place-names

inchoate adj only partly in existence or operation; esp imperfectly formed or formulated ⟨an ~ longing⟩ – fml – **inchoately** adv, **inchoateness** n

incidence n **1a** an occurrence **b** the rate of occurrence or influence ⟨a high ~ of crime⟩ **2** the meeting of sthg (e g a projectile or a ray of light) with a surface

¹incident n **1** an occurrence of an action or situation that is a separate unit of experience **2** an occurrence that is a cause of conflict or disagreement ⟨a serious border ~⟩ **3** an event occurring as part of a series or as dependent on or subordinate to sthg else

²incident adj **1** that is a usual accompaniment or consequence ⟨the confusion ~ to moving house⟩ **2** dependent on another thing in law **3** falling or striking on sthg ⟨~ light rays⟩

¹incidental adj **1** occurring merely by chance **2** likely to ensue as a chance or minor consequence

²incidental n **1** sthg incidental **2** pl minor items (e g of expenses)

incidentally adv **1** by chance **2** BY THE WAY

incidental music n descriptive music played during a play to project a mood or to accompany stage action

incinerate vt to cause to burn to ashes – **incineration** n

incinerator n a furnace or container for incinerating waste materials

incipient adj beginning to come into being or to become apparent – **incipience, incipiency** n, **incipiently** adv

incise vt **1** to cut into **2a** to carve letters, figures, etc into; engrave **b** to carve (e g an inscription) into a surface

incision n **1a a** (marginal) notch **b** a cut or gash; specif one made, esp in surgery, into the body **2** an incising

incisive adj impressively direct and decisive (e g in manner or presentation) – **incisively** adv, **incisiveness** n

incisor n a cutting tooth; specif any of the cutting teeth in mammals in front of the canines

incite vt to move to action; stir up – **inciter** n, **incitement, incitation** n

incivility n **1** being uncivil **2** a rude or discourteous act

inclement adj physically severe; stormy – **inclemency** n, **inclemently** adv

inclination n **1a** a bow, nod **b** a tilting of sthg **2** a particular tendency or propensity; esp a liking **3a** (the degree of) a deviation from the vertical or horizontal **b** a slope **c** the angle between 2 lines or planes ⟨*the ~ of 2 rays of light*⟩ – **inclinational** *adj*

¹**incline** *vb* **1** to (cause to) lean, tend, or become drawn towards an opinion or course of conduct **2** to (cause to) deviate or move from a line, direction, or course, esp from the vertical or horizontal

²**incline** *n* an inclined surface; a slope

inclined plane *n* a plane surface that makes an angle with the plane of the horizon

inclose *vt* to enclose – **inclosure** *n*

include *vt* **1** to contain, enclose **2** to take in or comprise as a part of a larger group, set, or principle – **includable, includible** *adj*

inclusion *n* **1** including or being included **2** sthg included: e g **a** a gaseous, liquid, or solid foreign body enclosed in a mass, esp a mineral **b** sthg (e g a starch grain) taken up by, or stored within, a living cell

inclusive *adj* **1a** broad in orientation or scope **b** covering or intended to cover all or the specified items, costs, or services ⟨*~ of VAT*⟩ **2** including the stated limits or extremes ⟨*Monday to Friday ~*⟩ – **inclusively** *adv*, **inclusiveness** *n*

¹**incognito** *adv or adj* with one's identity concealed

²**incognito** *n, pl* **incognitos** the state or disguise of one who is incognito

incoherent *adj* lacking in logical connection or clarity of expression; unintelligible – **incoherence, incoherency** *n*, **incoherently** *adv*

incombustible *adj* incapable of being ignited or burned – **incombustibility** *n*

income *n* **1** a coming in; an input, influx **2** (the amount of) a usu periodic gain or recurrent benefit usu measured in money that derives from one's work, property, or investment

income tax *n* a tax on income

¹**incoming** *n* **1** a coming in, arrival **2** *pl* INCOME 2

²**incoming** *adj* **1** arriving or coming in ⟨*an ~ ship*⟩ ⟨*the ~ tide*⟩ **2** just starting, beginning, or succeeding ⟨*the ~ president*⟩

incommensurable *adj* lacking a common basis of comparison in respect to a quality normally subject to comparison; incapable of being compared – **incommensurably** *adv*, **incommensurability** *n*

incommensurate *adj* not adequate (in proportion) – **incommensurately** *adv*

incommode *vt* to inconvenience, trouble – fml

incommodious *adj* inconvenient or uncomfortable, esp because of being too small – fml – **incommodiously** *adv*, **incommodiousness** *n*

incommunicado *adv or adj* without means of communication; *also* in solitary confinement

incomparable *adj* **1** matchless **2** not suitable for comparison – **incomparableness** *n*, **incomparably** *adv*, **incomparability** *n*

incompatible *adj* **1** (incapable of association because) incongruous, discordant, or disagreeing **2** unsuitable for use together because of undesirable chemical or physiological effects ⟨*~ drugs*⟩ – **incompatibly** *adv*, **incompatibility** *n*

incompetent *adj* **1** lacking the qualities needed for effective action **2** not legally qualified ⟨*an ~ witness*⟩ **3** inadequate to or unsuitable for a particular purpose – **incompetence, incompetency** *n*, **incompetent** *n*, **incompetently** *adv*

incomplete *adj* **1** unfinished **2** lacking a part – **incompletely** *adv*, **incompleteness** *n*

incomprehensible *adj* impossible to comprehend or

understand – **incomprehensibleness** *n*, **incomprehensibly** *adv*, **incomprehensibility** *n*

incomprehension *n* lack of comprehension or understanding

inconceivable *adj* **1** beyond comprehension; unimaginable **2** unbelievable – **inconceivableness** *n*, **inconceivably** *adv*, **inconceivability** *n*

inconclusive *adj* leading to no conclusion or definite result – **inconclusively** *adv*, **inconclusiveness** *n*

incongruous *adj* out of place; discordant or disagreeing – **incongruously** *adv*, **incongruousness, incongruity** *n*

inconsequent *adj* **1** lacking reasonable sequence; illogical **2** irrelevant – **inconsequence** *n*, **inconsequently** *adv*

inconsequential *adj* **1** irrelevant **2** of no significance – **inconsequentially** *adv*, **inconsequentiality** *n*

inconsiderable *adj* trivial ⟨*exercised no ~ influence*⟩ – **inconsiderableness** *n*, **inconsiderably** *adv*

inconsiderate *adj* careless of the rights or feelings of others; thoughtless – **inconsiderately** *adv*, **inconsiderateness, inconsideration** *n*

inconsistent *adj* **1** not compatible; containing incompatible elements ⟨*an ~ argument*⟩ **2** not consistent or logical in thought or actions – **inconsistency, inconsistence** *n*, **inconsistently** *adv*

inconsolable *adj* incapable of being consoled; brokenhearted – **inconsolably** *adv*

inconspicuous *adj* not readily noticeable – **inconspicuously** *adv*, **inconspicuousness** *n*

inconstant *adj* **1** likely to change frequently without apparent reason **2** unfaithful ⟨*an ~ lover*⟩ – **inconstancy** *n*, **inconstantly** *adv*

incontestable *adj* not contestable; indisputable ⟨*~ proof*⟩ – **incontestably** *adv*, **incontestability** *n*

incontinent *adj* **1** lacking self-restraint (e g in sexual appetite) **2** suffering from lack of control of urination or defecation **3** not under control or restraint – **incontinence** *n*, **incontinently** *adv*

incontrovertible *adj* indisputable – **incontrovertibly** *adv*

inconvenience *vt or n* (to subject to) difficulty or discomfort or sthg that is inconvenient

inconvenient *adj* not convenient, esp in causing difficulty, discomfort, or annoyance – **inconveniently** *adv*

incorporate *vt* **1a** to unite thoroughly with or work indistinguishably into sthg **b** to admit to membership in a corporate body **2a** to combine thoroughly to form a consistent whole **b** to form into a legal corporation *~ vi* **1** to unite in or as 1 body **2** to form a legal corporation – **incorporator** *n*, **incorporable** *adj*, **incorporation** *n*

incorporated *also* **incorporate** *adj* **1** united in 1 body **2** formed into a legal corporation

incorporeal *adj* **1** having no material body or form **2** based upon property (e g bonds or patents) which has no intrinsic value – **incorporeally** *adv*, **incorporeity** *n*

incorrect *adj* **1** inaccurate; factually wrong **2** not in accordance with an established norm; improper – **incorrectly** *adv*, **incorrectness** *n*

incorrigible *adj* **1** incapable of being corrected or amended; *esp* incurably bad **2** unwilling or unlikely to change – **incorrigibly** *adv*, **incorrigibility** *also* **incorrigibleness** *n*

incorruptible *adj* **1** not subject to decay or dissolution **2** incapable of being bribed or morally corrupted – **incorruptibly** *adv*, **incorruptibility** *n*

¹**increase** *vi* **1** to become progressively greater (e g in size, amount, quality, number, or intensity) **2** to multiply by the production of young *~ vt* to make greater – **increasable** *adj*, **increasingly** *adv*

²**increase** *n* **1** (an) addition or enlargement in size, extent,

quantity, etc **2** sthg (e g offspring, produce, or profit) added to an original stock by addition or growth

incredible *adj* **1** too extraordinary and improbable to be believed; *also* hard to believe **2** – used as a generalized term of approval – **incredibly** *adv*, **incredibility** *n*

incredulous *adj* **1** unwilling to admit or accept what is offered as true **2** expressing disbelief – **incredulously** *adv*, **incredulity** *n*

increment *n* **1** (the amount of) an increase, esp in quantity or value **2a** any of a series of regular consecutive additions **b** a minute increase in the value of a variable (e g velocity) **3** a regular increase in pay resulting from an additional year's service – **incremental** *adj*, **incrementally** *adv*

incriminate *vt* to involve in or demonstrate involvement in a crime or fault – **incriminatory** *adj*, **incrimination** *n*

incrust *vb* to encrust

incrustation *n* **1** encrusting or being encrusted **2** (a growth or accumulation resembling) a crust or hard coating

incubate *vt* **1** to sit on so as to hatch (eggs) by the warmth of the body; *also* to maintain (e g an embryo or a chemically active system) under conditions favourable for hatching, development, or reaction **2** to cause (e g an idea) to develop ~ *vi* **1** to sit on eggs **2** to undergo incubation – **incubative, incubatory** *adj*

incubation *n* **1** incubating **2** the period between infection by a disease-causing agent and the manifestation of the disease

incubator *n* **1** an apparatus in which eggs are hatched artificially **2** an apparatus that maintains controlled conditions, esp for the housing of premature or sick babies or the cultivation of microorganisms

incubus *n, pl* **incubuses, incubi** **1** a male demon believed to have sexual intercourse with women in their sleep **2** (one who or that which oppresses or burdens like) a nightmare

inculcate *vt* to teach or instil by frequent repetition or warning ⟨~d *a sense of social responsibility in her children*⟩ ⟨*students* ~d *with a desire for knowledge*⟩ – **inculcator** *n*, **inculcation** *n*

inculpate *vt* to incriminate – **inculpatory** *adj*, **inculpation** *n*

incumbency *n* the sphere of action or period of office of an incumbent

¹**incumbent** *n* the holder of an office or Anglican benefice

²**incumbent** *adj* **1** imposed as a duty or obligation – usu + *on* or *upon* **2** occupying a specified office ⟨*the* ~ *caretaker*⟩

incur *vt* **-rr-** to become liable or subject to; bring upon oneself ⟨*she* ~red *several debts*⟩ – **incurrable** *adj*, **incurrence** *n*

incurable *adj*

incurious *adj* lacking a normal or usual curiosity ⟨*a blank* ~ *stare*⟩ – **incuriously** *adv*, **incuriosity** *n*

incursion *n* an unexpected or sudden usu brief invasion or entrance, esp into another's territory – **incursive** *adj*

incus *n, pl* **incudes** the middle bone of a chain of 3 small bones in the ear of a mammal; the anvil

Ind-, Indo- *comb form* **1** Indian ⟨Indo-*British*⟩; Indian and ⟨Indo-*African*⟩ **2** Indo-European ⟨Indo-*Hittite*⟩

indebted *adj* **1** owing money **2** owing gratitude or recognition to another – **indebtedness** *n*

indecent *adj* **1** hardly suitable; unseemly ⟨*he remarried with* ~ *haste*⟩ **2** morally offensive – **indecency** *n*, **indecently** *adv*

indecent assault *n* a sexual assault exclusive of rape

indecent exposure *n* intentional public exposure of part of one's body (e g the genitals) in violation of generally accepted standards of decency

indecision *n* a wavering between 2 or more possible courses of action

indecisive *adj* **1** giving an uncertain result ⟨*an* ~ *battle*⟩ **2** marked by or prone to indecision – **indecisively** *adv*, **indecisiveness** *n*

indecorous *adj*

indecorum *n* impropriety

indeed *adv* **1** without any question; truly ⟨*it is* ~ *remarkable*⟩ – often used in agreement ⟨~ *I will*⟩ **2** – used for emphasis after *very* and an adjective or adverb ⟨*very cold* ~⟩ **3** in point of fact; actually ⟨*I don't mind;* ~*, I'm pleased*⟩ ⟨*if* ~ *they come at all*⟩ **4** – expressing irony, disbelief, or surprise ⟨'*she wants to marry him.*' 'Indeed?' '*Does she* ~!'⟩

indefatigable *adj* tireless – **indefatigably** *adv*, **indefatigability** *n*

indefensible *adj* incapable of being defended or justified – **indefensibly** *adv*, **indefensibility** *n*

indefinable *adj* incapable of being precisely described or analysed – **indefinable** *n*, **indefinably** *adv*

indefinite *adj* **1** designating an unidentified or not immediately identifiable person or thing ⟨*the* ~ *articles a and* an⟩ **2** not precise; vague **3** having no exact limits – **indefinite** *n*, **indefinitely** *adv*, **indefiniteness** *n*

indelible *adj* (making marks difficult to remove or) incapable of being removed or erased – **indelibly** *adv*, **indelibility** *n*

indelicate *adj* offensive to good manners or refined taste – **indelicacy** *n*, **indelicately** *adv*

indemnify *vt* **1** to secure against harm, loss, or damage **2** to make compensation to for incurred harm, loss, or damage – **indemnification** *n*

indemnity *n* security against harm, loss, or damage

¹**indent** *vt* **1a** to cut or divide (a document) to produce sections with edges that can be matched for authentication **b** to draw up (e g a deed) in 2 or more exact copies **2** to notch the edge of **3** to set (e g a line of a paragraph) in from the margin **4** *chiefly Br* to requisition officially. ~ *vi* **1** to form an indentation **2** *chiefly Br* to make out an official requisition – **indenter** *n*

²**indent** *n* **1** an indenture **2** an indention **3** *chiefly Br* an official requisition

³**indent** *vt* (to force inwards so as) to form a depression in – **indenter** *n*

⁴**indent** *n* (an) indentation

indentation *n* **1a** an angular cut in an edge **b** a usu deep recess (e g in a coastline) **2** indention

indention *n* **1** indenting or being indented **2** the blank space produced by indenting

¹**indenture** *n* **1a** an indented document **b** a contract binding sby to work for another – usu pl with sing. meaning **2a** a formal certificate (e g an inventory or voucher) prepared for purposes of control **b** a document stating the terms under which a security (e g a bond) is issued

²**indenture** *vt* to bind (e g an apprentice) by indentures

independence *n* being independent

Independence Day *n* a day set aside for public celebration of the achievement of national independence; *esp* the public holiday observed in the USA on July 4 commemorating the Declaration of Independence in 1776

¹**independent** *adj* **1** not dependent: e g **a**(1) self-governing (2) not affiliated with a larger controlling unit **b**(1) not relying on sthg else ⟨*an* ~ *conclusion*⟩ (2) not committed to a political party **c**(1) not requiring or relying on, or allowing oneself to be controlled by, others (e g for guidance or care) (2) having or providing enough

money to live on, esp without working ⟨*a woman of ~ means*⟩ **2a** MAIN **4** ⟨*the ~ clause*⟩ **b** neither deducible from nor incompatible with another statement ⟨*~ postulates*⟩ – **independently** *adv*

²**independent** *n, often cap* sby not bound by a political party

indescribable *adj* **1** that cannot be described ⟨*an ~ sensation*⟩ **2** surpassing description ⟨*~ joy*⟩ – **indescribably** *adv*

indestructible *adj*

indeterminable *adj* incapable of being definitely decided or ascertained

indeterminate *adj* **1** not definitely or precisely determined or fixed **2** having an infinite number of solutions ⟨*a system of ~ equations*⟩ – **indeterminacy** *n*, **indeterminately** *adv*, **indeterminateness**, **indetermination** *n*

¹**index** *n, pl* **indexes, indices,** (4) *usu* **indices 1** a guide or list to aid reference: e g **a** an alphabetical list of items (e g topics or names) treated in a printed work that gives with each item the page number where it appears **b** CARD INDEX **2** sthg that points towards or demonstrates a particular state of affairs ⟨*the fertility of the land is an ~ of the country's wealth*⟩ **3** a list of restricted or prohibited material; *specif, cap* the list of books banned by the Roman Catholic church **4** a mathematical figure, letter, or expression; *esp* an exponent **5** a character **6** a number derived from a series of observations and used as an indicator or measure (e g of change in prices) – **indexical** *adj*

²**index** *vt* **1** to provide with or list in an index **2** to serve as an index of **3** to cause to be index-linked *~ vi* to prepare an index – **indexer** *n*

index finger *n* the forefinger

Indian *n* **1** a native or inhabitant of India **2a** a member of any of the indigenous peoples of N, Central, or S America excluding the Eskimos **b** any of the native languages of American Indians – **Indian** *adj*

Indian club *n* a club shaped like a large bottle that is swung for gymnastic exercise

Indian corn *n, chiefly NAm* maize

Indian file *n* SINGLE FILE

Indian hemp *n* HEMP 1

indian ink *n, often cap 1st I, Br* (an ink made from) a solid black pigment used in drawing and lettering

Indian summer *n* **1** a period of warm weather in late autumn or early winter **2** a happy or flourishing period occurring towards the end of sthg, esp of a person's life

india rubber *n, often cap I* ¹RUBBER 1b

indicate *vt* **1a**(1) to point to; point out (2) to show or demonstrate as or by means of a sign or pointer **b** to be a sign or symptom of **c** to demonstrate or suggest the necessity or advisability of – chiefly pass **2** to state or express briefly; suggest

indication *n* **1** the action of indicating **2a** sthg (e g a sign or suggestion) that serves to indicate **b** sthg indicated as advisable or necessary **3** the degree indicated on a graduated instrument

¹**indicative** *adj* **1** of or constituting the grammatical mood that represents the denoted act or state as an objective fact **2** serving to indicate ⟨*actions ~ of fear*⟩ – **indicatively** *adv*

²**indicative** *n* the indicative mood; *also* a verb form expressing it

indicator *n* **1a** a hand or needle on an instrument (e g a dial) **b** an instrument for giving visual readings attached to a machine or apparatus **c** a device (e g a flashing light) on a vehicle that indicates an intention to change direction **2a** a substance (e g litmus) that shows, esp by change of colour, the condition (e g acidity or alkalinity) of a sol-

ution **b** TRACER **2 3** a statistic (e g the level of industrial production) that gives an indication of the state of a national economy – **indicatory** *adj*

indices *pl of* INDEX

indict *vt* **1** to charge with an offence **2** to charge with a crime – **indicter, indictor** *n*

indictable *adj* (making one) liable to indictment

indictment *n* **1** indicting **2** a formal written accusation by a prosecuting authority **3** grounds for severe censure; condemnation – usu + *of* ⟨*a searing ~ of contemporary society*⟩

indifferent *adj* **1** that does not matter one way or the other **2** not interested in or concerned about sthg ⟨*completely ~ to the outcome*⟩ **3a** neither good nor bad; mediocre ⟨*does ~ work at the office*⟩ **b** not very good; inferior ⟨*a very ~ wine*⟩ **4** chemically, magnetically, etc neutral – **indifferently** *adv*, **indifference** *n*

indigenous *adj* **1** originating, growing, or living naturally in a particular region or environment ⟨*~ to Australia*⟩ **2** innate, inborn – **indigenously** *adv*, **indigenize** *vt*

indigent *adj* needy, poor – *fml* – **indigence** *n*, **indigent** *n*

indigestible *adj* not (easily) digested – **indigestibility** *n*

indigestion *n* (pain in the digestive system usu resulting from) difficulty in digesting sthg

indignant *adj* filled with or marked by indignation – **indignantly** *adv*

indignation *n* anger aroused by sthg judged unjust, unworthy, or mean

indignity *n* **1** an act that offends against a person's dignity or self-respect **2** humiliating treatment

indigo *n, pl* **indigos, indigoes 1** (any of several dyes related to) a blue dye with a coppery lustre formerly obtained from a plant and now made artificially **2** a dark greyish blue colour whose hue lies between violet and blue in the spectrum **3** a (leguminous) plant that yields indigo

indirect *adj* **1a** deviating from a direct line or course **b** not going straight to the point **2** not straightforward or open **3** not directly aimed at ⟨*~ consequences*⟩ **4** stating what a real or supposed original speaker said but with changes of tense, person, etc ⟨*~ speech*⟩ – **indirectly** *adv*, **indirectness** *n*

indirect object *n* a grammatical object representing the secondary goal of the action of its verb (e g *her* in *I gave her the book*)

indiscernible *adj* **1** that cannot be perceived or recognized **2** not recognizable as separate or distinct

indiscipline *n* lack of discipline – **indisciplined** *adj*

indiscreet *adj* not discreet; imprudent – **indiscreetly** *adv*

indiscretion *n* (an act or remark showing) lack of discretion

indiscriminate *adj* **1** not marked by careful distinction; lacking in discrimination and discernment **2** not differentiated; confused – **indiscriminately** *adv*, **indiscriminateness** *n*

indispensable *adj* that cannot be done without – **indispensable** *n*, **indispensableness** *n*, **indispensably** *adv*, **indispensability** *n*

indisposed *adj* **1** slightly ill **2** averse

indisposition *n* **1** disinclination **2** (a) slight illness

indisputable *adj* incontestable – **indisputableness** *n*, **indisputably** *adv*

indissoluble *adj* incapable of being dissolved, decomposed, undone, or annulled – **indissolubility** *n*, **indissolubly** *adv*

indistinct *adj* not distinct: e g **a** not sharply outlined or separable; not clearly seen **b** not clearly recognizable or understandable – **indistinctly** *adv*, **indistinctness** *n*

indistinguishable *adj* incapable of being **a** clearly perceived **b** discriminated – **indistinguishably** *adv*

¹**individual** *adj* **1a** of or being an individual **b** intended for 1 person ⟨*an ~ serving*⟩ **2** existing as a distinct entity; separate **3** having marked individuality ⟨*an ~ style*⟩ – **individually** *adv*

²**individual** *n* **1** a particular person, being, or thing (as distinguished from a class, species, or collection) **2** a person ⟨*an odd ~*⟩

individualism *n* (conduct guided by) **a** a doctrine that bases morality on the interests of the individual **b** a theory maintaining the independence of the individual and stressing individual initiative

individuality *n* **1** the total character peculiar to and distinguishing an individual from others **2** the tendency to pursue one's course with marked independence or self-reliance

individualize, -ise *vt* **1** to make individual in character **2** to treat or notice individually **3** to adjust or adapt to suit a particular individual – **individualization** *n*

indivisible *adj*

Indo- – see IND-

indoctrinate *vt* to imbue with a usu partisan or sectarian opinion, point of view, or ideology – **indoctrinator** *n*, **indoctrination** *n*

Indo-European *adj or n* (of or belonging to) a family of languages spoken in most of Europe, Asia as far east as N India, and N and S America

indolent *adj* **1a** causing little or no pain **b** slow to develop or heal ⟨*an ~ ulcer*⟩ **2a** averse to activity, effort, or movement **b** conducive to or exhibiting laziness – **indolence** *n*, **indolently** *adv*

indomitable *adj* incapable of being subdued – **indomitably** *adv*, **indomitability** *n*

Indonesian *n* **1** a native or inhabitant of Indonesia or the Malay archipelago **2** the official language of Indonesia – **Indonesian** *adj*

indoor *adj* **1** of the interior of a building **2** done, living, or belonging indoors ⟨*an ~ sport*⟩

indoors *adv* in or into a building

indorse *vt* to endorse

indrawn *adj* **1** drawn in **2** aloof, reserved

indubitable *adj* too evident to be doubted – **indubitably** *adv*, **indubitability** *n*

induce *vt* **1** to lead on to do sthg; move by persuasion or influence **2a** to cause to appear or to happen; BRING ON; *specif* to cause (labour) to begin by the use of drugs **b** to cause the formation of **c** to produce (e g an electric current) by induction **3** to establish by logical induction; *specif* to infer from particulars – **inducer** *n*, **inducible** *adj*

inducement *n* sthg that induces; *esp* a motive or consideration that encourages one to do sthg

induct *vt* **1** to place formally in office **2a** to introduce, initiate **b** *NAm* to enrol for military training or service

induction *n* **1a** the act or process of inducting (e g into office) **b** an initial experience; an initiation **2a** the act or an instance of reasoning from particular premises to a general conclusion; *also* a conclusion reached by such reasoning **b** mathematical demonstration of the validity of a law concerning all the positive integers, by proving that the law holds for the first integer and that if it holds for all the integers preceding a given integer it must hold for the given integer **3a** the act of causing or bringing on or about **b** the process by which an electrical conductor becomes electrified when near a charged body, by which a magnetizable body becomes magnetized when in a

magnetic field or in the magnetic flux set up by a magneto-motive force, or by which an electromotive force is produced in a circuit by varying the magnetic field linked with the circuit **c** the drawing of the fuel-air mixture from the carburettor into the combustion chamber of an internal-combustion engine

inductive *adj* **1** of or employing mathematical or logical induction **2** of inductance or electrical induction **3** introductory – **inductively** *adv*, **inductiveness** *n*

indue *vt* to endue

indulge *vt* **1a** to give free rein to (e g a taste) **b** to allow (oneself) to do sthg pleasurable or gratifying **2** to treat with great or excessive leniency, generosity, or consideration ~ *vi* to indulge oneself – **indulger** *n*

indulgence *n* **1** a remission of (part of) the purgatorial atonement for confessed sin in the Roman Catholic church **2** indulging or being indulgent **3** an indulgent act **4** sthg indulged in

indulgent *adj* indulging or characterized by indulgence – **indulgently** *adv*

¹**industrial** *adj* **1** of, involved in, or derived from industry **2** characterized by highly developed industries ⟨*an ~ nation*⟩ **3** used in industry ⟨*~ diamonds*⟩ – **industrially** *adv*

²**industrial** *n* a share or bond issued by an industrial enterprise – usu pl

industrial archaeology *n* the scientific study of the products and remains of past industrial activity

industrial estate *n* an area, usu at a distance from the centre of a city or town, designed esp for a community of industries and businesses

industrialism *n* social organization in which industries, esp large-scale industries, are dominant

industrialist *n* one who is engaged in the management of an industry

industrialize, -ise *vb* to make or become industrial; introduce industry (to) ⟨*~ an agricultural region*⟩ – **industrialization** *n*

industrial revolution *n* a rapid major development of an economy (e g in England in the late 18th c) marked by the general introduction of mechanized techniques and large-scale production

industrious *adj* **1** persistently diligent **2** constantly, regularly, or habitually occupied – **industriously** *adv*, **industriousness** *n*

industry *n* **1** diligence in an employment or pursuit **2a** systematic work, esp for the creation of value **b(1)** a usu specified group of productive or profit-making enterprises ⟨*the car ~*⟩ **(2)** an organized field of activity regarded in its commercial aspects ⟨*the Shakespeare ~*⟩ **c** manufacturing activity as a whole ⟨*the nation's ~*⟩

¹**-ine** *suffix* (→ *adj*) **1** of or resembling ⟨*equine*⟩ ⟨*feminine*⟩ **2** made of; like ⟨*opaline*⟩ ⟨*crystalline*⟩

²**-ine** *suffix* (→ *n*) **1** chemical compound: e g **a** carbon compound (e g an amino acid or alkaloid) that is a chemical base and contains nitrogen ⟨*atropine*⟩ ⟨*morphine*⟩ ⟨*leucine*⟩ ⟨*glycine*⟩ **b** mixture of compounds (e g of hydrocarbons) ⟨*kerosine*⟩ **c** usu gaseous hydride ⟨*arsine*⟩ **2** ¹-IN 2

inebriate *vt* to exhilarate or stupefy (as if) by liquor; intoxicate – **inebriant** *adj or n*, **inebriate** *adj or n*, **inebriation**, **inebriety** *n*

inedible *adj* not fit to be eaten

ineffable *adj* **1** unutterable **2** not to be uttered; taboo ⟨*the ~ name of Jehovah*⟩ – **ineffably** *adv*

ineffective *adj* **1** not producing an intended effect **2** not capable of performing efficiently or achieving results – **ineffectively** *adv*, **ineffectiveness** *n*

ineffectual *adj* **1** not producing or not able to give the proper or intended effect **2** unable to get things done; weak in character ⟨a very ~ person⟩ – **ineffectually** adv, **ineffectualness** n

inefficient adj not producing the effect intended or desired, esp in a capable or economical way – **inefficiency** n, **inefficiently** adv

inelastic adj **1** slow to react or respond to changing conditions **2** inflexible, unyielding – **inelasticity** n

inelegant adj lacking in refinement, grace, or good taste – **inelegance** n, **inelegantly** adv

ineligible adj not qualified or not worthy to be chosen or preferred – **ineligibility** n

ineluctable adj not to be avoided, changed, or resisted – fml – **ineluctably** adv

inept adj **1** not suitable or apt to the time, place, or occasion **2** lacking sense or reason **3** generally incompetent – **ineptitude** n, **ineptly** adv, **ineptness** n

inequality n **1a** social disparity **b** disparity of distribution or opportunity **2** an instance of being unequal **3** a formal statement of inequality between 2 expressions, usu with a sign of inequality (e g ⟨, ⟩, or signifying respectively is less than, is greater than, and is not equal to) between them

inequitable adj unfair – **inequitably** adv

inequity n (an instance of) injustice or unfairness

ineradicable adj incapable of being eradicated – **ineradicably** adv

inert adj **1** lacking the power to move **2** deficient in active (chemical or biological) properties **3** not moving; inactive, indolent – **inertly** adv, **inertness** n

inertia n **1** a property of matter by which it remains at rest or in uniform motion in the same straight line unless acted on by some external force **2** indisposition to motion, exertion, or change – **inertial** adj, **inertially** adv

inescapable adj unavoidable – **inescapably** adv

inessential n or adj (sthg) that is not essential

inestimable adj **1** too great to be estimated **2** too valuable or excellent to be measured – **inestimably** adv

inevitable adj incapable of being avoided or evaded; bound to happen or to confront one – **inevitableness** n, **inevitably** adv, **inevitability** n

inexact adj not precisely correct or true – **inexactitude** n, **inexactly** adv, **inexactness** n

inexcusable adj without excuse or justification – **inexcusableness** n, **inexcusably** adv

inexhaustible adj incapable of being used up or worn out – **inexhaustibly** adv, **inexhaustibility** n

inexorable adj **1** not to be persuaded or moved by entreaty **2** continuing inevitably; that cannot be averted – **inexorably** adv, **inexorability** n

inexpedient adj

inexpensive adj reasonable in price; cheap – **inexpensively** adv, **inexpensiveness** n

inexperience n **1** lack of (the skill gained from) experience **2** lack of knowledge of the ways of the world – **inexperienced** adj

inexpert adj unskilled – **inexpertly** adv, **inexpertness** n

inexplicable adj incapable of being explained, interpreted, or accounted for – **inexplicableness** n, **inexplicably** adv, **inexplicability** n

inexpressible adj beyond one's power to express – **inexpressibly** adv, **inexpressibility** n

inextinguishable adj unquenchable – **inextinguishably** adv

in extremis adv in extreme circumstances; esp at the point of death

inextricable adj **1** from which one cannot extricate oneself **2** incapable of being disentangled or untied ⟨an ~ knot⟩ – **inextricably** adv

infallible adj **1** incapable of error; esp, of the Pope incapable of error in defining dogma **2** not liable to fail – **infallibly** adv, **infallibility** n

infamous adj **1** having a reputation of the worst kind; notorious **2** disgraceful – **infamously** adv

infamy n **1** evil reputation brought about by sthg grossly criminal, shocking, or brutal **2** an extreme and publicly known criminal or evil act

infancy n **1** early childhood **2** a beginning or early period of existence ⟨when sociology was in its ~⟩ **3** the legal status of an infant

¹infant n **1** a child in the first period of life **2** a minor

²infant adj **1** in an early stage of development **2** concerned with or intended for young children, esp those aged from 5 to 7 or 8 ⟨an ~ teacher⟩

infanticide n (the act of) sby who kills an infant

infantile adj (suggestive) of infants or infancy ⟨~ behaviour⟩

infantile paralysis n poliomyelitis

infantry n sing or pl in constr (a branch of an army containing) soldiers trained, armed, and equipped to fight on foot

infantryman n an infantry soldier

infant school n, Br a kindergarten for children aged from 5 to 7 or 8

infatuate vt **1** to affect with folly **2** to inspire with powerful but superficial or short-lived feelings of love and desire – **infatuated** adj, **infatuation** n

infect vt **1** to contaminate (e g air or food) with a disease-causing agent **2a** to pass on a disease or a disease-causing agent to **b** to invade (an individual or organ), usu by penetration – used with reference to a pathogenic organism **3** to transmit or pass on sthg (e g an emotion) to – **infector** n

infection n **1** infecting **2** (an agent that causes) a contagious or infectious disease **3** the communication of emotions or qualities through example or contact

infectious adj **1a** infectious, infective capable of causing infection **b** communicable by infection **2** readily spread or communicated to others ⟨~ excitement⟩ – **infectiously** adv, **infectiousness** n

infectious hepatitis n a highly infectious liver inflammation caused by a virus

infectious mononucleosis n an acute infectious disease characterized by fever and swelling of lymph glands

infelicitous adj not apt; not suitably chosen for the occasion – **infelicitously** adv

infer vb -rr- vt **1** to derive as a conclusion from facts or premises **2** to suggest, imply – disapproved of by some speakers ~ vi to draw inferences – **inferable** adj

inference n **1a** the act of inferring **b** the act of passing from statistical sample data to generalizations (e g of the value of population parameters), usu with calculated degrees of certainty **2** sthg inferred; esp a proposition arrived at by inference

inferential adj deduced or deducible by inference

inferior adj **1** situated lower down **2** of low or lower degree or rank **3** of little or less importance, value, or merit **4a** of an animal or plant part situated below or at the base of another (corresponding) part **b(1)** of a calyx lying below the ovary **(2)** of an ovary lying below the petals or sepals **5** of or being a subscript **6** of a planet nearer the sun than the earth is – **inferior** n, **inferiorly** adv, **inferiority** n

inferiority complex n a sense of personal inferiority often resulting either in timidity or, through overcompensation, in exaggerated aggressiveness

infernal *adj* 1 of hell 2 hellish, diabolical 3 damned – infml ⟨*an ~ nuisance*⟩ – **infernally** *adv*

inferno *n, pl* **infernos** a place or a state that resembles or suggests hell, esp in intense heat or raging fire

infertile *adj* not fertile or productive ⟨*~ eggs*⟩ ⟨*~ fields*⟩ – **infertility** *n*

infest *vt* 1 to spread or swarm in or over in a troublesome manner ⟨*shark-infested waters*⟩ 2 to live in or on as a parasite – **infestation** *n*

infidel *n* **1a** an unbeliever in or opponent of a particular religion, esp of Christianity or Islam **b** sby who acknowledges no religious belief 2 a disbeliever in sthg specified or understood – **infidel** *adj*

infidelity *n* 1 lack of belief in a religion **2a** unfaithfulness, disloyalty **b** marital unfaithfulness

¹infield *n* (the fielding positions in) the area of a cricket or baseball field relatively near the wickets or bounded by the bases – **infielder** *n*

²infield *adv* away from the edge of a playing field

infighting *n* 1 fighting or boxing at close quarters 2 prolonged and often bitter dissension among members of a group or organization – **infighter** *n*

infiltrate *vt* 1 to cause (e g a liquid) to permeate sthg (e g by penetrating its pores or interstices) 2 to pass into or through (a substance) by filtering or permeating 3 to enter or become established in gradually or unobtrusively ~ *vi* to enter, permeate, or pass through a substance or area by filtering or by insinuating gradually – **infiltrative** *adj*, **infiltrator** *n*, **infiltration** *n*

¹infinite *adj* 1 subject to no limitation or external determination 2 extending indefinitely 3 immeasurably or inconceivably great or extensive **4a** extending beyond, lying beyond, or being greater than any arbitrarily chosen finite value, however large ⟨*there are an ~ number of positive integers*⟩ **b** extending to infinity ⟨*~ plane surface*⟩ – **infinitely** *adv*, **infiniteness** *n*

²infinite *n* 1 divineness, sublimity – + *the* 2 an incalculable or very great number 3 an infinite quantity or magnitude

¹infinitesimal *n* an infinitesimal variable or quantity

²infinitesimal *adj* 1 taking on values arbitrarily close to zero 2 immeasurably or incalculably small – **infinitesimally** *adv*

infinitive *adj or n* (using) a verb form that performs some functions of a noun and that in English is used with *to* (e g *go* in *I asked him to go*) except with auxiliary and various other verbs (e g *go* in *I must go*) – **infinitival** *adj or n*

infinitude *n* 1 the quality or state of being infinite 2 sthg infinite, esp in extent 3 an infinite number or quantity

infinity *n* **1a** the quality of being infinite **b** unlimited extent of time, space, or quantity 2 an indefinitely great number or amount 3 a distance so great that the rays of light from a point source at that distance may be regarded as parallel

infirm *adj* 1 physically feeble, esp from age 2 weak in mind, will, or character – **infirmly** *adv*

infirmary *n* HOSPITAL 1

infirmity *n* 1 being infirm or frail 2 a disease, malady

inflame *vt* 1 to set on fire **2a** to excite or arouse passion or excessive action or feeling in **b** to make more heated or violent 3 to cause to redden or grow hot 4 to cause inflammation in (bodily tissue) ~ *vi* 1 to burst into flame 2 to become excited or angered 3 to become affected with inflammation – **inflamer** *n*

inflammable *adj* 1 capable of being easily ignited and of burning rapidly 2 easily inflamed, excited, or angered – **inflammable** *n*, **inflammableness**, **inflammability** *n*

inflammation *n* 1 inflaming or being inflamed 2 a response to cellular injury marked by local redness, heat, and pain

inflammatory *adj* 1 tending to inflame ⟨*~ speeches*⟩ 2 accompanied by or tending to cause inflammation

inflatable *n* an inflatable boat, toy, etc

inflate *vt* 1 to swell or distend (with air or gas) 2 to increase (a price level) or cause (a volume of credit or the economy) to expand ~ *vi* to become inflated – **inflatable** *adj*, **inflator**, **inflater** *n*

inflated *adj* 1 bombastic, exaggerated 2 expanded to an abnormal or unjustifiable volume or level ⟨*~ prices*⟩ 3 swelled out; distended

inflation *n* inflating or being inflated; *esp* a substantial and continuing rise in the general level of prices, caused by or causing an increase in the volume of money and credit or an expansion of the economy – **inflationary** *adj*

inflect *vt* 1 to vary (a word) by inflection 2 to change or vary the pitch of (a voice or note) ~ *vi* to become modified by inflection – **inflective** *adj*

inflection, *Br also* **inflexion** *n* 1 change in pitch or loudness of the voice **2a** the change in the form of a word showing its case, gender, number, tense, etc **b** an element (e g a suffix) showing such variation 3 (a point on a curve of) change of curvature with respect to a fixed line from concave to convex or conversely – **inflectional** *adj*

inflexible *adj* rigidly firm: e g **a** lacking or deficient in suppleness **b** UNYIELDING 2 **c** incapable of change – **inflexibly** *adv*, **inflexibility** *n*

inflict *vt* to force or impose (sthg damaging or painful) on sby – **inflicter**, **inflictor** *n*, **infliction** *n*

inflow *n* a flowing in ⟨*a pipe taking the maximum rate of ~*⟩

¹influence *n* 1 an ethereal fluid supposed to flow from the stars and to affect the actions of human beings 2 the power to achieve sthg desired by using wealth or position 3 the act, power, or capacity of causing or producing an effect in indirect or intangible ways 4 sby or sthg that exerts influence; *esp* sby or sthg that tends to produce a moral or immoral effect on another – **under the influence** affected by alcohol; drunk ⟨*was arrested for driving under the influence*⟩

²influence *vt* to affect, alter, or modify by indirect or intangible means

influential *adj* exerting or possessing influence – **influentially** *adv*

influenza *n* 1 a highly infectious virus disease characterized by sudden onset, fever, severe aches and pains, and inflammation of the respiratory mucous membranes 2 any of numerous feverish usu virus diseases of domestic animals marked by respiratory symptoms

influx *n* a usu sudden increase in flowing in; the arrival of large amounts

info *n* information – infml

inform *vt* 1 to impart an essential quality or character to 2 to communicate knowledge to ~ *vi* 1 to give information or knowledge 2 to act as an informer *against* or *on* – **informant** *n*

informal *adj* marked by an absence of formality or ceremony; everyday – **informally** *adv*, **informality** *n*

information *n* 1 the communication or reception of facts or ideas **2a** knowledge obtained from investigation, study, or instruction **b** news **c** (significant) facts or data **d** a signal or character (e g in a radio transmission or computer) representing data **e** a quantitative measure of the content of information; *specif* a numerical quantity that measures the uncertainty in the outcome of an experiment to be performed 3 a formal accusation presented to a magistrate – **informational** *adj*

informative, informatory adj conveying facts or ideas; instructive – **informatively** adv, **informativeness** n

informed adj 1 possessing or based on possession of information 2 knowledgeable about matters of contemporary interest

informer n one who informs against another, esp to the police for a financial reward

infra adv lower on the same or a following page

infra- prefix 1 below ⟨infra*renal*⟩ ⟨infra*structure*⟩; less than ⟨infra*human*⟩ 2 within ⟨infra*specific*⟩ ⟨infra*territorial*⟩ 3 below in a scale or series ⟨infra*red*⟩

infraction n a violation, infringement

infra dig adj beneath one's dignity – infml

infrared adj or n (being, using, producing, or sensitive to) electromagnetic radiation with a wavelength between the red end of the visible spectrum and microwaves, that is commonly perceived as heat

infrastructure n 1 an underlying foundation or basic framework 2 the permanent installations required for military purposes

infrequent adj 1 rare 2 not habitual or persistent – **infrequency** n, **infrequently** adv

infringe vt to encroach on; violate – ~vi to encroach, trespass – **infringement** n

infuriate vt to make furious – **infuriate** adj, **infuriatingly** adv

infuse vt 1 to inspire, imbue 2 to steep in liquid without boiling so as to extract the soluble properties or constituents – **infuser** n

infusion n 1 infusing 2 the continuous slow introduction of a solution, esp into a vein 3 an extract obtained by infusing

¹-ing suffix (→ vb or adj) – used to form the present participle ⟨sai*ling*⟩ and sometimes to form an adjective resembling a present participle but not derived from a verb ⟨swashbuck*ling*⟩

²-ing suffix (→ n) 1 action or process of ⟨run*ning*⟩ ⟨sleep*ing*⟩; also instance of (a specified action or process) ⟨a meet*ing*⟩ – sometimes used to form a noun resembling a gerund but not derived from a verb ⟨skydiv*ing*⟩ 2 product or result of (a specified action or process) ⟨an engrav*ing*⟩ – often pl with sing. meaning ⟨earn*ings*⟩ 3 activity or occupation connected with ⟨boat*ing*⟩ ⟨bank*ing*⟩ 4a collection or aggregate of ⟨shipp*ing*⟩ ⟨hous*ing*⟩ b sthg connected with, consisting of, or used in making ⟨scaffold*ing*⟩ ⟨shirt*ing*⟩ 5 sthg related to (a specified concept) ⟨off*ing*⟩

ingenious adj marked by originality, resourcefulness, and cleverness – **ingeniously** adv

ingenue, ingénue n 1 a naive or artless young woman 2 (an actress playing) the stage role of an ingenue

ingenuity n (resourceful) cleverness; inventiveness

ingenuous adj showing innocent or childlike simplicity; frank, candid – **ingenuously** adv, **ingenuousness** n

ingest vt to take in (as if) for digestion; absorb – **ingestible** adj, **ingestion** n, **ingestive** adj

inglenook n (a seat in) an alcove by a large open fireplace

inglorious adj shameful, ignominious – **ingloriously** adv

ingoing adj entering

ingot n a (bar-shaped) mass of cast metal

ingrained adj firmly and deeply implanted; deep-rooted – **ingrainedly** adv

ingratiate vt to gain favour for (e g oneself) by deliberate effort ⟨~ *themselves with the public*⟩ – **ingratiatingly** adv, **ingratiatory** adj, **ingratiation** n

ingratitude n forgetfulness or scant recognition of kindness received

ingredient n sthg that forms a component part of a compound, combination, or mixture

ingress n 1 the act of entering; specif that of a celestial body into eclipse, occultation, or transit 2 the right of entrance or access

ingrowing, NAm chiefly ingrown adj growing inwards; specif having the free tip or edge embedded in the flesh ⟨an ~ toenail⟩

inhabit vt to occupy or be present in ⟨the hopes and fears that ~ the human mind⟩ – **inhabitable** adj, **inhabitancy** n, **inhabitant** n, **inhabitation** n

inhalation n (material for) inhaling

inhale vb to breathe in

inhaler n a device used for inhaling a medication

inharmonious adj 1 not harmonious 2 not congenial or compatible – **inharmoniously** adv

inhere vi to be inherent; belong ⟨power to make laws ~s in the state⟩

inherent adj intrinsic to the constitution or essence of sthg – **inherence** n, **inherently** adv

inherit vt 1 to receive a by right b from an ancestor at his/her death 2 to receive by genetic transmission ⟨~ a strong constitution⟩ to receive sthg by inheritance – **inheritor** n, **inheritress, inheritrix** n

inheritance n 1a inheriting property b the transmission of genetic qualities from parent to offspring c the acquisition of a possession, condition, or trait from past generations 2a sthg that is or may be inherited b sthg acquired or derived from the past

inhibit vt 1 to prohibit from doing sthg 2a to restrain b to discourage from free or spontaneous activity, esp by psychological or social controls to cause inhibition – **inhibitive** adj, **inhibitory** adj

inhibition n 1a inhibiting or being inhibited b sthg that forbids, debars, or restricts 2a a psychological restraint on another psychological or physical activity ⟨sexual ~s⟩ b a restraining of a function (e g of a bodily organ or enzyme)

inhospitable adj 1 not friendly or welcoming 2 providing no shelter or means of support – **inhospitableness** n, **inhospitably** adv

inhuman adj 1a inhumane b failing to conform to basic human needs 2 being other than human – **inhumanly** adv

inhumane adj lacking in kindness or compassion – **inhumanely** adv

inhumanity n 1 being pitiless or cruel 2 a cruel or barbarous act

inimical adj 1 hostile or indicating hostility 2 adverse in tendency, influence, or effects – **inimically** adv

inimitable adj defying imitation – **inimitableness** n, **inimitably** adv

iniquity n 1 gross injustice 2 a sin – **iniquitous** adj

¹initial adj 1 of the beginning ⟨the ~ symptoms of a disease⟩ 2 first ⟨the ~ number of a code⟩ – **initially** adv

²initial n 1 the first letter of a name 2 pl the first letter of each word in a full name

³initial vt -ll- (NAm -l-, -ll-) to put initials (indicating ownership or authorization) on

¹initiate vt 1 to cause or enable the beginning of; start 2 to instil with rudiments or principles (of sthg complex or obscure) 3 to induct into membership (as if) by formal rites – **initiator** n, **initiatory** adj

²initiate adj 1 initiated or properly admitted (e g to membership or an office) 2 instructed in some secret knowledge

³**initiate** *n* **1** sby who is undergoing or has undergone initiation **2** sby who is instructed or proficient in a complex or specialized field

initiation *n* **1** initiating or being initiated **2** the ceremony or formal procedure with which sby is made a member of a sect or society

¹**initiative** *adj* introductory, preliminary

²**initiative** *n* **1** a first step, esp in the attainment of an end or goal **2** energy or resourcefulness displayed in initiation of action **3** a procedure enabling voters to propose a law by petition – **on one's own initiative** without being prompted; independently of outside influence or control

inject *vt* **1a** to throw, drive, or force into sthg ⟨~ *fuel into an engine*⟩ **b** to force a fluid into **2** to introduce as an element or factor – **injector** *n*

injection *n* **1a** injecting **b** the placing of an artificial satellite or a spacecraft into an orbit or on a trajectory **2** sthg (e g a medication) that is injected

injudicious *adj* indiscreet, unwise – **injudiciously** *adv*, **injudiciousness** *n*

injunction *n* **1** an order, warning **2** a writ requiring sby to do or refrain from doing a particular act – **injunctive** *adj*

injure *vt* **1** to do injustice to **2a** to inflict bodily hurt on **b** to impair the soundness of **c** to inflict damage or loss on

injurious *adj* inflicting or tending to inflict injury – **injuriously** *adv*, **injuriousness** *n*

injury *n* **1** a wrong **2** hurt, damage, or loss sustained

injustice *n* (an act or state of) unfairness

¹**ink** *n* **1** a coloured liquid used for writing and printing **2** the black secretion of a squid or similar cephalopod mollusc that hides it from a predator or prey – **inky** *adj*

²**ink** *vt* to apply ink to

inkling *n* **1** a faint indication **2** a slight knowledge or vague idea

inkstand *n* a stand with fittings for holding ink and often pens

inkwell *n* a container (e g in a school desk) for ink

inlaid *adj* **1** set into a surface in a decorative design ⟨*tables with* ~ *marble*⟩ **2** decorated with a design or material set into a surface ⟨*a table with an* ~ *top*⟩

¹**inland** *adv or n* (into or towards) the interior part of a country

²**inland** *adj* **1** of the interior of a country **2** *chiefly Br* not foreign; domestic

Inland Revenue *n* the government department responsible for collecting taxes in Britain

in-law *n* a relative by marriage – *infml* ⟨*all her* ~s *turned up*⟩

¹**inlay** *vt* **inlaid 1** to set into a surface or ground material for decoration or reinforcement **2** to decorate with inlaid material

²**inlay** *n* **1** inlaid work or a decorative inlaid pattern **2** a dental filling shaped to fit a cavity

inlet *n* **1** a (long and narrow) recess in a shoreline or a water passage between 2 land areas **2** a means of entry; *esp* an opening for intake ⟨*a fuel* ~⟩

in loco parentis *adv* in the place of and esp having the responsibilities of a parent

inmate *n* any of a group occupying a place of residence, esp a prison or hospital

in memoriam *prep* in memory of

inmost *adj* **1** furthest within **2** most intimate

inn *n* **1a** an establishment (e g a small hotel) providing lodging and food, esp for travellers **b** PUBLIC HOUSE **2** a residence formerly provided for students in London

innards *n pl* **1** the internal organs of a human being or animal; *esp* the viscera **2** the internal parts of a structure or mechanism *USE* infml

innate *adj* **1a** existing in or belonging to an individual from birth **b** inherent **c** originating in the intellect **2** ENDOGENOUS 2 – **innately** *adv*, **innateness** *n*

inner *adj* **1a** situated within; internal ⟨*an* ~ *chamber*⟩ **b** situated near to a centre, esp of influence ⟨*an* ~ *circle of government ministers*⟩ **2** of the mind or soul ⟨*the* ~ *life of man*⟩ – **inner** *n*, **innermost** *adj*

inner light *n*, *often cap I&L* a divine influence held, esp in Quaker doctrine, to enlighten and guide the soul

inner tube *n* an inflatable tube inside the casing of a pneumatic tyre

inning *n* a baseball team's turn at batting or a division of a baseball game consisting of a turn at batting for each team

innings *n*, *pl* **innings 1a** any of the alternating divisions of a cricket match during which one side bats and the other bowls **b** the (runs scored in or quality of the) turn of 1 player to bat **c** an unplayed innings of a side ⟨*won by an* ~ *and 32 runs*⟩ **2a** a period in which sby has opportunity for action or achievements **b** *chiefly Br* the duration of sby's life ⟨*he had a good* ~⟩

innkeeper *n* the landlord of an inn

innocent *adj* **1a** free from guilt or sin; pure **b** harmless in effect or intention ⟨*an* ~ *conversation*⟩ **c** free from legal guilt **2** lacking or deprived of sthg ⟨*a face* ~ *of make-up*⟩ **3a** artless, ingenuous **b** ignorant, unaware – **innocence**, **innocency** *n*, **innocent** *n*, **innocently** *adv*

innocuous *adj* **1** having no harmful effects **2** inoffensive, insipid – **innocuously** *adv*, **innocuousness** *n*

innovate *vi* to make changes; introduce sthg new – **innovative** *adj*, **innovator** *n*, **innovatory** *adj*, **innovation** *n*

Inns of Court *n pl* (4 buildings housing) 4 societies of students and barristers in London which have the exclusive right of admission to the English Bar

innuendo *n*, *pl* **innuendos, innuendoes** an oblique allusion; *esp* a veiled slight on sby's character or reputation

innumerable *adj* countless – **innumerably** *adv*

inoculate *vt* **1a** to introduce a microorganism into ⟨~ *mice with anthrax*⟩ **b** to introduce (e g a microorganism) into a culture, animal, etc for growth **c** VACCINATE 2 **2** to imbue – **inoculative** *adj*, **inoculator** *n*, **inoculation** *n*

inoffensive *adj* **1** not causing any harm; innocuous **2** not objectionable to the senses – **inoffensively** *adv*, **inoffensiveness** *n*

inoperable *adj* **1** not suitable for surgery **2** impracticable

inoperative *adj* not functioning; having no effect

inopportune *adj* inconvenient, unseasonable – **inopportunely** *adv*, **inopportuneness** *n*

inordinate *adj* exceeding reasonable limits – **inordinately** *adv*

inorganic *adj* **1a** being or composed of matter other than plant or animal; mineral **b** of, being, or dealt with by a branch of chemistry concerned with inorganic substances **2** not arising through natural growth – **inorganically** *adv*

inpatient *n* a hospital patient who receives lodging and food as well as treatment

¹**input** *n* **1a** an amount coming or put in **b** sthg (e g energy, material, or data) supplied to a machine or system **c** a component of production (e g land, labour, or raw materials) **2** the point at which an input (e g of energy, material, or data) is made

²**input** *vt* -tt- to enter (e g data) into a computer or data-processing system

inquest *n* 1 a judicial inquiry, esp by a coroner, into the cause of a death 2 an inquiry or investigation, esp into sthg that has failed

inquietude *n* uneasiness, restlessness

inquire *vt* to ask about; ask to be told ~ *vi* 1 to seek information by questioning 2 to make a search or inquiry – **inquirer** *n*, **inquiringly** *adv* – **inquire after** to ask about the health of

inquiry *n* 1 a request for information 2 a systematic investigation

inquisition *n* 1 the act of inquiring 2 a judicial or official inquiry 3a *cap* a former Roman Catholic tribunal for the discovery and punishment of heresy b a ruthless investigation or examination – **inquisitional** *adj*

inquisitive *adj* 1 eager for knowledge or understanding 2 fond of making inquiries; *esp* unduly curious about the affairs of others – **inquisitively** *adv*, **inquisitiveness** *n*

inquisitor *n* one who inquires or conducts an inquisition (harshly or with hostility)

inquisitorial *adj* of a system of criminal procedure in which the judge is also the prosecutor – **inquisitorially** *adv*

inroad *n* 1 a raid 2 a serious or forcible encroachment or advance ⟨*an illness made* ~ s *on his savings*⟩

inrush *n* a crowding or flooding in

insalubrious *adj* unhealthy ⟨*an* ~ *climate*⟩ – **insalubriously** *adv*, **insalubrity** *n*

insane *adj* 1 mentally disordered; exhibiting insanity 2 typical of or intended for insane people ⟨*an* ~ *asylum*⟩ 3 utterly absurd – **insanely** *adv*, **insanity** *n*

insanitary *adj* unclean enough to endanger health; filthy, contaminated

insatiable *adj* incapable of being satisfied – **insatiably** *adv*, **insatiability** *n*

insatiate *adj* insatiable

inscribe *vt* 1a to write, engrave, or print (as a lasting record) b to enter on a list; enrol 2 to address or dedicate to sby, esp by a handwritten note 3 to draw within a figure so as to touch at as many points as possible ⟨*a regular polygon* ~ d *in a circle*⟩ – **inscriber** *n*

inscription *n* 1a a title, superscription b EPIGRAPH 2 c LEGEND 2a 2 a handwritten dedication in a book or on a work of art 3a the act of inscribing b the enrolment of a name (as if) on a list – **inscriptional** *adj*, **inscriptive** *adj*

inscrutable *adj* hard to interpret or understand; enigmatic – **inscrutableness** *n*, **inscrutably** *adv*, **inscrutability** *n*

insect *n* 1 any of a class of arthropods with a well-defined head, thorax, and abdomen, only 3 pairs of legs, and typically 1 or 2 pairs of wings 2 any of various small invertebrate animals (e g woodlice and spiders) – not used technically 3 a worthless or insignificant person

insecticide *n* sthg that destroys insects – **insecticidal** *adj*

insectivore *n* 1 any of an order of mammals including moles, shrews, and hedgehogs that are mostly small, nocturnal, and eat insects 2 an insect-eating plant or animal

insecure *adj* 1 lacking adequate protection or guarantee ⟨*an* ~ *job*⟩ 2 not firmly fixed or supported ⟨*the hinge is* ~⟩ 3a not stable or well-adjusted ⟨*an* ~ *marriage*⟩ b deficient in assurance; beset by fear and anxiety – **insecurely** *adv*, **insecurity** *n*

inseminate *vt* 1 sow 1b, 1c 2 to introduce semen into the genital tract of (a female) – **inseminator** *n*, **insemination** *n*

insensate *adj* 1 insentient 2 lacking in human feeling – **insensately** *adv*

insensible *adj* 1 incapable or bereft of feeling or sensation: e g a having lost consciousness b lacking or deprived of sensory perception ⟨~ *to pain*⟩ 2 incapable of being felt or sensed 3 lacking concern or awareness – **insensibly** *adv*, **insensibility** *n*

insensitive *adj* 1 lacking the ability to respond to or sympathize with the needs or feelings of others 2 not physically or chemically sensitive ⟨~ *to light*⟩ – **insensitively** *adv*, **insensitiveness, insensitivity** *n*

inseparable *adj* incapable of being separated – **inseparable** *n*, **inseparably** *adv*, **inseparability** *n*

¹**insert** *vt* 1 to put or thrust in ⟨~ *a coin in a slot machine*⟩ 2 to put or introduce into the body of sthg ⟨~ *an advertisement in a newspaper*⟩ 3 to set in and make fast; *esp* to insert by sewing between 2 cut edges ~ *vi*, *of a muscle* to be in attachment to a specified part ⟨*muscles* ~ *on bone*⟩ – **inserter** *n*

²**insert** *n* sthg (esp written or printed) inserted

insertion *n* 1 the mode or place of attachment of an organ or part 2 embroidery or needlework inserted as ornament between 2 pieces of fabric 3 a single appearance of an advertisement (e g in a newspaper) – **insertional** *adj*

in-service *adj*, *of training* undertaken in mid-career

¹**inset** *n* sthg set in: e g a a small illustration set within a larger one b a piece of cloth set into a garment for decoration, shaping, etc

²**inset** *vt* -tt-; inset, insetted to insert as an inset

inshore *adj or adv* (near or moving) towards the shore

¹**inside** *n* 1 an inner side or surface 2a an interior or internal part ⟨*fire destroyed the* ~ *of the house*⟩ b inward nature, thoughts, or feeling c the middle or main part of a division of time ⟨*the* ~ *of a week*⟩ d viscera, entrails – usu pl with sing. meaning 3 a position of confidence or of access to confidential information 4 the middle portion of a playing area 5 the side of a pavement nearer the wall

²**inside** *adj* 1 of, on, near, or towards the inside ⟨*an* ~ *toilet*⟩ 2 of or being the inner side of a curve or being near the side of the road nearest the kerb or hard shoulder ⟨*driving on the* ~ *lane*⟩

³**inside** *prep* 1a in or into the interior of b on the inner side of 2 within ⟨~ *an hour*⟩

⁴**inside** *adv* 1 to or on the inner side 2 in or into the interior 3 indoors 4 *chiefly Br* in or into prison – slang

inside of *prep* 1 in less time than 2 *chiefly NAm* inside USE *infml*

inside out *adv* 1 with the inner surface on the outside ⟨*turned his socks* ~⟩ 2 in a very thorough manner – *infml* ⟨*knows his subject* ~⟩

insider *n* sby recognized or accepted as a member of a group, category, or organization; *esp* one who has access to confidential information or is in a position of power

inside track *n* the inner lane of a curved racetrack

insidious *adj* 1 harmful but enticing 2a acting gradually and imperceptibly but with grave consequences b *of a disease* developing so gradually as to be well established before becoming apparent – **insidiously** *adv*, **insidiousness** *n*

insight *n* the power of or an act or result of discerning the true or underlying nature of sthg – **insightful** *adj*

insignia *n pl in constr*, *pl* insignia, insignias badges of authority or honour – sometimes treated as sing. in American English

insignificant *adj* 1 lacking meaning or import; inconsequential 2 very small in size, amount, or number – **insignificance, insignificancy** *n*, **insignificantly** *adv*

insincere adj hypocritical – **insincerely** adv, **insincerity** n

insinuate vt 1 to introduce (an idea) or suggest (sthg unpleasant) in a subtle or oblique manner 2 to gain acceptance for (e g oneself) by craft or stealth – **insinuative** adj, **insinuator** n

insinuation n a sly and usu derogatory reference

insipid adj 1 devoid of any definite flavour 2 devoid of interesting or stimulating qualities – **insipidly** adv, **insipidity** n

insist vi 1 to take a resolute stand 2 to place great emphasis or importance on sthg ~ vt to maintain persistently

insistent adj 1 insisting forcefully or repeatedly; emphatic 2 demanding attention – **insistence** n, **insistently** adv

in situ adv or adj in the natural or original position

insofar as conj to the extent or degree that ⟨I'll help you ~ I can⟩

insole n 1 an inside sole of a shoe 2 a strip the shape of the sole that is placed inside a shoe for warmth or comfort

insolent adj showing disrespectful rudeness; impudent – **insolence** n, **insolently** adv

insoluble adj 1 having or admitting of no solution or explanation 2 (practically) incapable of being dissolved in liquid – **insoluble** n, **insolubleness** n, **insolubly** adv, **insolubility** n

insolvable adj, chiefly NAm impossible to solve ⟨an apparently ~ problem⟩ – **insolvably** adv

insolvent adj 1 unable to pay debts as they fall due; specif having liabilities in excess of the value of assets held 2 relating to or for the relief of insolvents – **insolvency** n, **insolvent** n

insomnia n prolonged (abnormal) inability to obtain adequate sleep – **insomniac** adj or n

insouciance n lighthearted unconcern – **insouciant** adj, **insouciantly** adv

inspect vt 1 to examine closely and critically; scrutinize 2 to view or examine officially – **inspection** n, **inspective** adj

inspector n a police officer ranking immediately above a sergeant – **inspectorate** n, **inspectorship** n

inspiration n 1a a divine influence or action on a person which qualifies him/her to receive and communicate sacred revelation b the action or power of stimulating the intellect or emotions 2 the drawing of air into the lungs 3a being inspired b an inspired idea ⟨I've had an ~, let's go to the seaside⟩ 4 an inspiring agent or influence – **inspirational** adj, **inspirationally** adv, **inspiratory** adj

inspire vt 1 to inhale 2a to influence or guide by divine inspiration b to exert an animating or exalting influence on ⟨was particularly ~d by the Impressionists⟩ ⟨inspiring music⟩ c to act as a stimulus for ⟨threats don't necessarily ~ people to work harder⟩ ⟨music ~d by a trip to Venice⟩ d to affect – usu + with ⟨seeing the old room again ~d him with nostalgia⟩ 3 to communicate to an agent supernaturally ⟨writings ~d by God⟩ ~ vi to breathe in – **inspirer** n

inspired adj outstanding or brilliant in a way that suggests divine inspiration ⟨gave an ~ rendering of the piano sonata⟩

instability n lack of (emotional or mental) stability

install vt 1 to induct into an office, rank, or order, esp with ceremonies or formalities ⟨~ed the new department chairman⟩ 2 to establish in a specified place, condition, or status 3 to place in usu permanent position for use or service ⟨had a shower ~ed in the bathroom⟩ – **installer** n

installation n 1 a device, apparatus, or piece of machinery fixed or fitted in place to perform some specified function ⟨a new gas central-heating ~⟩ 2 a military base or establishment ⟨US ~s in Europe⟩

instalment, NAm chiefly installment n 1 any of the parts into which a debt is divided when payment is made at intervals 2a any of several parts (e g of a publication) presented at intervals b a single part of a serial story

¹instance n 1 an example cited as an illustration or proof 2 the institution of a legal action ⟨a court of first ~⟩ 3 a situation viewed as 1 stage in a process or series of events ⟨prefers, in this ~, to remain anonymous – TLS⟩ 4 a solicitation, request – fml ⟨am writing to you at the ~ of my client⟩ – **for instance** as an example

²instance vt 1 to exemplify by an instance 2 to put forward as a case or example; cite

¹instant n 1 an infinitesimal space of time; esp a point in time separating 2 states ⟨at the ~ of death⟩ 2 the present or current month

²instant adj 1a present, current ⟨previous felonies not related to the ~ crime⟩ b of or occurring in the present month – used in commercial communications 2 immediate ⟨the play was an ~ success⟩ 3a(1) premixed or precooked for easy final preparation ⟨~ mashed potatoes⟩ (2) appearing (as if) in ready-to-use form ⟨updating your image with ~ beards, moustaches, and sideburns – Playboy⟩ b immediately soluble in water ⟨~ coffee⟩ 4 demanding, urgent – fml

instantaneous adj 1 done, occurring, or acting in an instant or instantly; IMMEDIATE 3 ⟨death was ~⟩ 2 occurring or present at a particular instant ⟨~ velocity⟩ – **instantaneously** adv, **instantaneousness, instantaneity** n

instantly adv immediately; AT ONCE

instead adv as a substitute or alternative ⟨was going to write but called ~⟩ ⟨sent his son ~⟩

instead of prep as a substitute for or alternative to

instep n 1 (the upper surface of) the arched middle portion of the human foot 2 the part of a shoe or stocking over the instep

instigate vt 1 to goad or urge forwards; provoke, incite 2 to initiate (a course of action or procedure, e g a legal investigation) – **instigator** n, **instigation** n

instil, NAm chiefly instill vt -ll- 1 to cause to enter drop by drop ⟨~ medication into the infected eye⟩ 2 to impart gradually ⟨~ling in children a love of learning⟩ – + in or into – **instillment, instillation** n

¹instinct n 1 a natural or inherent aptitude, impulse, or capacity ⟨had an ~ for the right word⟩ 2 (a largely inheritable tendency of an organism to make a complex and specific) response to environmental stimuli without involving reason – **instinctive** adj, **instinctively** adv, **instinctual** adj

²instinct adj imbued, infused – fml ⟨~ with patriotism⟩

¹institute vt 1 to instate 2 to originate and establish; inaugurate ⟨~d many social reforms⟩

²institute n sthg instituted: e g a(1) an elementary principle recognized as authoritative (2) pl a (legal) compendium b (the premises used by) an organization for the promotion of a cause ⟨an ~ for the blind⟩ c an educational institution

institution n 1 an established practice in a culture ⟨the ~ of marriage⟩; also a familiar object 2 an established organization or (public) body (e g a university or hospital) – **institutional** adj

instruct vt 1 to teach 2a to direct authoritatively b COMMAND 1 3 to engage (a lawyer, specif a barrister) for a case

instruction *n* **1a** ORDER 7b, COMMAND 1 – often pl with sing. meaning ⟨*had* ~s *not to admit strangers*⟩ **b** *pl* an outline or manual of technical procedure **c** a code that tells a computer to perform a particular operation **2** teaching – **instructional** *adj*

instructive *adj* carrying a lesson; enlightening – **instructively** *adv*, **instructiveness** *n*

instructor, *fem* **instructress** *n* a teacher: e g **a** a teacher of a technical or practical subject ⟨*a swimming* ~⟩ **b** NAm a college teacher below professorial rank – **instructorship** *n*

¹**instrument** *n* **1a** a means whereby sthg is achieved, performed, or furthered **b** a dupe; TOOL 3 **2** an implement, tool, or device designed esp for delicate work or measurement ⟨*scientific* ~s⟩ **3** a device used to produce music **4** a formal legal document **5** an electrical or mechanical device used in navigating an aircraft

²**instrument** *vt* to orchestrate

¹**instrumental** *adj* **1a** serving as an instrument, means, agent, or tool ⟨*was* ~ *in organizing the strike*⟩ **b** of or done with an instrument or tool **2** relating to, composed for, or performed on a musical instrument **3** of or being a grammatical case or form expressing means or agency – **instrumentally** *adv*

²**instrumental** *n* a musical composition or passage for instruments but not voice

instrumentalist *n* a player on a musical instrument

instrumentality *n* a means, agency

instrumentation *n* the arrangement or composition of music for instruments

insubordinate *adj* unwilling to submit to authority – **insubordinately** *adv*, **insubordination** *n*

insubstantial *adj* **1** lacking substance or material nature; unreal **2** lacking firmness or solidity; flimsy – **insubstantiality** *n*

insufferable *adj* intolerable ⟨*an* ~ *bore*⟩ – **insufferably** *adv*

insufficiency *n* being insufficient; *specif* inability of an organ or body part (e g the heart or kidneys) to function normally

insufficient *adj* deficient in power, capacity, or competence – **insufficiently** *adv*

insular *adj* **1** of or being an island **2a** of island people **b** that results (as if) from lack of contact with other peoples or cultures; narrow-minded **3** of an island of cells or tissue – **insularism** *n*, **insularly** *adv*, **insularity** *n*

insulate *vt* to place in a detached situation; *esp* to separate from conducting bodies by means of nonconductors so as to prevent transfer of electricity, heat, or sound

insulation *n* **1** insulating or being insulated **2** material used in insulating

insulator *n* (a device made from) a material that is a poor conductor of electricity and is used for separating or supporting conductors and to prevent undesired flow of electricity

insulin *n* a protein pancreatic hormone secreted by the islets of Langerhans that is essential esp for the metabolism of carbohydrates and is used in the treatment of diabetes mellitus

¹**insult** *vt* to treat with insolence, indignity, or contempt; *also* to cause offence or damage to ⟨*arguments that* ~ *the reader's intelligence*⟩ – **insultingly** *adv*

²**insult** *n* **1** an act of insulting; sthg that insults **2** (sthg that causes) injury to the body or 1 of its parts ⟨*pollution and other environmental* ~s⟩

insuperable *adj* incapable of being surmounted, overcome, or passed over ⟨~ *difficulties*⟩ – **insuperably** *adv*

insupportable *adj* **1** unendurable ⟨~ *pain*⟩ **2** incapable of being sustained ⟨~ *charges*⟩ – **insupportably** *adv*

insurance *n* **1** insuring or being insured **2a** the business of insuring people or property **b** (the protection offered by) a contract whereby one party undertakes to indemnify or guarantee another against loss by a particular contingency or risk **c**(1) the premium demanded under such a contract (2) the sum for which sthg is insured

insure *vt* **1** to give, take, or procure insurance on or for **2** *chiefly NAm* to ensure ~ *vi* to contract to give or take insurance; *specif* to underwrite – **insurable** *adj*, **insurer** *n*

insured *n*, *pl* **insured** sby whose life or property is insured

insurgent *n* a rebel – **insurgence**, **insurgency** *n*, **insurgent** *adj*

insurmountable *adj* insuperable ⟨~ *problems*⟩ – **insurmountably** *adv*

insurrection *n* (a) revolt against civil authority or established government – **insurrectional** *adj*, **insurrectionary** *adj or n*, **insurrectionist** *n*

intact *adj* **1** untouched, esp by anything that harms or diminishes; whole, uninjured **2a** being a virgin **b** not castrated

intaglio *n*, *pl* **intaglios 1a** (the act or process of producing) an incised or engraved design made in hard material, esp stone, and sunk below the surface of the material **b** printing done from a plate engraved in intaglio **2** sthg (e g a gem) carved in intaglio

intake *n* **1** an opening through which liquid or gas enters an enclosure or system **2a** a taking in **b**(1) *sing or pl in constr* an amount or number taken in (2) sthg taken in

intangible *n or adj* (sthg) not tangible – **intangibly** *adv*, **intangibility** *n*

integer *n* the number 1 or any number (e g 6, 0, -23) obtainable by once or repeatedly adding 1 to or subtracting 1 from the number 1

¹**integral** *adj* **1a** essential to completeness; constituent – chiefly in *integral part* **b** of a mathematical integer, integral, or integration **c** formed as a unit with another part **2** composed of integral parts **3** lacking nothing essential; whole – **integrally** *adv*, **integrality** *n*

²**integral** *n* **1** a mathematical expression denoting a definite integral or an indefinite integral **2** a solution of a differential equation

integral calculus *n* a branch of mathematics dealing with methods of finding indefinite integrals and with their applications (e g to the determination of lengths, areas, and volumes and to the solution of differential equations)

integrate *vt* **1** to form or blend into a whole **2a** to combine together or with sthg else **b** to incorporate into a larger unit – usu + *into* **3** to find the integral of (e g a function or differential equation) **4** to end the segregation of or in ~ *vi* **1** to become integrated **2** to calculate an integral – **integrative** *adj*, **integration** *n*

integrity *n* **1** an unimpaired condition **2** uncompromising adherence to a code of esp moral or artistic values **3** the quality or state of being complete or undivided ⟨*the* ~ *of the Empire was threatened*⟩

integument *n* a skin, membrane, husk, or other covering or enclosure, esp of (part of) a living organism – **integumental** *adj*, **integumentary** *adj*

intellect *n* the capacity for intelligent thought, esp when highly developed

¹**intellectual** *adj* **1a** of the intellect **b** developed or chiefly guided by the intellect rather than by emotion or experience ⟨*a coldly* ~ *artist*⟩ **2** given to or requiring the use

of the intellect – **intellectualize** *vb*, **intellectually** *adv*, **intellectuality** *n*

²**intellectual** *n* an intellectual person

intelligence *n* **1** the ability to learn, apply knowledge, or think abstractly, esp in allowing one to deal with new or trying situations; *also* the skilled use of intelligence or reason **2** the act of understanding **3a** news; INFORMATION 2a, c **b** (a group of people who gather) information concerning an enemy

intelligence quotient *n* a number expressing the ratio of sby's intelligence as determined by a test to the average for his/her age

intelligent *adj* having or indicating esp high intelligence – **intelligently** *adv*

intelligentsia *n sing or pl in constr* the intellectuals who form an artistic, social, or political vanguard

intelligible *adj* **1** capable of being understood **2** able to be apprehended by the intellect only – **intel igibly** *adv*, **intelligibility** *n*

intemperate *adj* not temperate; *esp* going beyond the bounds of reasonable behaviour – **intemperately** *adv*, **intemperateness** *n*

intend *vt* **1** to mean, signify **2a** to have in mind as a purpose or goal **b** to design for a specified use or future ⟨*poems* ~ ed *for reading aloud*⟩

intended *n* one's future spouse ⟨*she was his* ~⟩ – infml

intense *adj* **1a** existing or occurring in an extreme degree **b** having or showing a usual characteristic in extreme degree **2** INTENSIVE a **3a** feeling emotion deeply, esp by nature or temperament **b** deeply felt – **intensely** *adv*, **intenseness** *n*

intensifier *n* a linguistic element (e g *very*) that gives force or emphasis

intensify *vb* to make or become (more) intense – **intensification** *n*

intensity *n* **1** extreme degree of strength, force, or energy **2** the magnitude of force or energy per unit (e g of surface, charge, or mass) **3** SATURATION 1

¹**intensive** *adj* of or marked by intensity or intensification: e g **a** highly concentrated **b** constituting or relating to a method designed to increase productivity by the expenditure of more capital and labour rather than by increase in the land or raw materials used ⟨~ *farming*⟩ – **intensively** *adv*

²**intensive** *n* an intensifier

¹**intent** *n* **1a** the act or fact of intending **b** the state of mind with which an act is done **2** criminal intention ⟨*loitering with* ~⟩ **3** meaning, significance – **to all intents and purposes** in every practical or important respect; virtually

²**intent** *adj* **1** directed with strained or eager attention; concentrated **2** having the mind, attention, or will concentrated *on* sthg or some end or purpose ⟨~ *on his work*⟩ – **intently** *adv*, **intentness** *n*

intention *n* **1** a determination to act in a certain way; a resolve **2** *pl* purpose with respect to proposal of marriage **3a** what one intends to do or bring about; an aim **b** the object for which religious devotion is offered **4** a concept

intentional *adj* done by intention or design – **intentionally** *adv*

¹**inter** *vt* **-rr-** to deposit (a dead body) in the earth or a tomb

²**inter** *n* any of various intermediate examinations – infml

inter- *prefix* **1** between; among; in the midst ⟨*intercity*⟩ ⟨*interpenetrate*⟩ ⟨*interstellar*⟩ **2a** reciprocal ⟨*interrelation*⟩ **b** reciprocally ⟨*intermarry*⟩ **3** located

between ⟨*interface*⟩ **4** carried on between ⟨*international*⟩ **5** occurring between ⟨*interglacial*⟩ ⟨*interlunar*⟩

interact *vi* to act upon each other – **interactant** *n*, **interaction** *n*

inter alia *adv* among other things

interbreed *vb* **interbred** *vi* **1** to crossbreed **2** to breed within a closed population ~ *vt* to cause to interbreed

intercalary *adj* **1a** inserted in a calendar to resynchronize it with some objective time-measure (e g the solar year) **b** *of a year* containing an intercalary period **2** inserted between other elements or layers; interpolated

intercalate *vt* to insert between or among existing items, elements, or layers – **intercalation** *n*

intercede *vi* to beg or plead on behalf of another with a view to reconciling differences

¹**intercept** *vt* **1** to stop, seize, or interrupt in progress, course, or movement, esp from one place to another **2** to intersect – **interception** *n*

²**intercept** *n* **1** the distance from the origin to a point where a graph crosses a coordinate axis **2** an interception

interceptor, intercepter *n* a high-speed fast-climbing fighter plane or missile designed for defence against raiding bombers or missiles

intercession *n* the act of interceding, esp by prayer, petition, or entreaty – **intercessional** *adj*, **intercessor** *n*, **intercessory** *adj*

¹**interchange** *vt* **1** to put each of (2 things) in the place of the other **2** EXCHANGE 1 ~ *vi* to change places reciprocally – **interchangeable** *adj*, **interchangeably** *adv*, **interchangeability** *n*

²**interchange** *n* **1** (an) interchanging **2** a junction of 2 or more roads having a system of separate levels that permit traffic to pass from one to another without the crossing of traffic streams

intercollegiate *adj* between colleges ⟨~ *athletics*⟩

intercom *n* a local communication system (e g in a ship or building) with a microphone and loudspeaker at each station

intercontinental *adj* extending among continents; *also* carried on or (capable of) travelling between continents ⟨~ *ballistic missile*⟩

intercourse *n* **1** connection or dealings between people or groups **2** exchange, esp of thoughts or feelings **3** physical sexual contact between individuals that involves the genitals of at least 1 person ⟨*oral* ~⟩; *esp* SEXUAL INTERCOURSE a

interdepend *vi* to depend on each other – **interdependence, interdependency** *n*, **interdependent** *adj*

¹**interdict** *n* **1** a Roman Catholic disciplinary measure withdrawing most sacraments and Christian burial from a person or district **2** a prohibition

²**interdict** *vt* to forbid in a usu formal or authoritative manner – **interdiction** *n*, **interdictory** *adj*

¹**interest** *n* **1a**(1) right, title, or legal share in sthg **(2)** participation in advantage and responsibility **b** a business in which one has an interest **2** benefit; ADVANTAGE 2; *specif* self-interest ⟨*it is to your* ~ *to speak first*⟩ **3a** a charge for borrowed money, generally a percentage of the amount borrowed **b** sthg added above what is due **4** a financially interested group **5a** readiness to be concerned with, moved by, or have one's attention attracted by sthg; curiosity **b** (the quality in) a thing that arouses interest ⟨*sport doesn't hold much* ~ *for me*⟩ ⟨*has many* ~s⟩

²**interest** *vt* **1** to induce or persuade to participate or engage, esp in an enterprise **2** to concern or engage (sby, esp oneself) *in* an activity or cause **3** to engage the attention or arouse the interest of

interested *adj* **1** having the interest aroused or attention engaged **2** affected or involved; not impartial – **interestedly** adv

interesting adj holding the attention – **interestingly** adv

¹**interface** n **1** a surface forming a common boundary of 2 bodies, regions, or phases ⟨an oil-water ~⟩ **2** the place at which (diverse) independent systems meet and act on or communicate with each other ⟨the man-machine ~⟩ – **interfacial** adj

²**interface** vt **1** to connect by means of an interface ⟨~ a machine with a computer⟩ **2** to serve as an interface for ~ vi **1** to become interfaced **2** to serve as an interface

interfere vi **1** to get in the way of, hinder, or impede another – + with ⟨noise ~s with my work⟩ **2** to enter into or take a part in matters that do not concern one **3** of sound, light, etc waves to act so as to augment, diminish, or otherwise affect one another **4** to claim priority for an invention **5** to hinder illegally an attempt of a player to catch or hit a ball or puck – usu + with

interference n **1** the phenomenon resulting from the meeting of 2 wave trains (e g of light or sound) with an increase in intensity at some points and a decrease at others **2** the illegal hindering of an opponent in hockey, ice hockey, etc **3** (sthg that produces) the confusion of received radio signals by unwanted signals or noise – **interferential** adj

¹**interim** n an intervening time ⟨in the ~⟩

²**interim** adj temporary, provisional

¹**interior** adj **1** lying, occurring, or functioning within the limits or interior **2** away from the border or shore **3** of the mind or soul – **interiorize** vt, **interiorly** adv, **interiority** n

²**interior** n **1** the internal or inner part of a thing; also the inland **2** internal affairs ⟨the minister of the ~⟩ **3** a representation of the interior of a building or room

interject vt to throw in (e g a remark) abruptly among or between other things – **interjector** n, **interjectory** adj

interjection n an ejaculatory word (e g Wonderful) or utterance (e g ah or good heavens) usu expressing emotion – **interjectional** adj, **interjectionally** adv

interlace vt **1** to unite (as if) by lacing together **2** to mingle, blend, or intersperse ⟨narrative ~d with anecdotes⟩ ~ vi to cross one another intricately – **interlacement** n

interlard vt to intersperse, esp with sthg foreign or irrelevant

interleave vt to provide with interleaves

interline vt to provide (a garment) with an interlining

interlinear adj inserted between lines already written or printed

interlock vi to become engaged, interrelated, or interlocked ~ vt **1** to lock together **2** to connect so that motion of any part is constrained by another – **interlock** n or adj

interlocutor, fem **interlocutress** n one who takes part in dialogue or conversation – **interlocution** n

interloper n sby who interferes or encroaches; an intruder – **interlope** vi

interlude n **1** an intervening or interruptive period, space, or event, esp of a contrasting character; an interval **2** a musical composition inserted between the parts of a longer composition, a drama, or a religious service

intermarriage n **1** marriage between members of different families, tribes, etc **2** endogamy

intermarry vi **1** to marry each other or sby from the the same group **2** to become connected by marriage with another group or with each other ⟨the different races ~ freely⟩

intermediary n or adj (sby or sthg) acting as a mediator or go-between

¹**intermediate** adj being or occurring at or near the middle place, stage, or degree or between 2 others or extremes – **intermediately** adv, **intermediacy** n

²**intermediate** n a chemical compound formed as an intermediate step in a reaction

interment n burial

intermezzo n, pl **intermezzi**, **intermezzos 1** a movement coming between the major sections of an extended musical work (e g an opera) **2** a short independent instrumental composition

interminable adj having or seeming to have no end; esp wearisomely long – **interminableness** n, **interminably** adv, **interminability** n

intermingle vb to mix or mingle together or with sthg else

intermission n **1** intermitting or being intermitted **2** an intervening period of time (e g between acts of a performance or attacks of a disease)

intermittent adj coming and going at intervals; not continuous ⟨~ rain⟩ – **intermittence** n, **intermittently** adv

¹**intern** vt to confine, esp during a war ⟨~ enemy aliens⟩ – **internee** n, **internment** n

²**intern, interne** n, NAm an advanced student or graduate in medicine, teaching, etc gaining supervised practical experience (e g in a hospital or classroom) – **intern** vi, **internship** n

internal adj **1** existing or situated within the limits or surface of sthg **2** applied through the stomach by swallowing ⟨an ~ medicine⟩ **3** of or existing within the mind **4** depending only on the properties of the thing under consideration without reference to things outside it ⟨~ evidence of forgery in a document⟩ **5** (present or arising) within (a part of) the body or an organism ⟨an ~ organ⟩ ⟨an ~ stimulus⟩ **6** within a state ⟨~ strife⟩ ⟨~ affairs⟩ – **internally** adv, **internality** n

internal-combustion engine n a heat engine in which the combustion that generates the heat energy takes place inside the engine (e g in a cylinder)

internalize, -ise vt to make internal; specif to incorporate (e g learnt values) within the self as guiding principles – **internalization** n

¹**international** adj **1** affecting or involving 2 or more nations ⟨~ trade⟩ ⟨an ~ movement⟩ **2** known, recognized, or renowned in more than 1 country ⟨an ~ celebrity⟩ – **internationally** adv, **internationality** n

²**international** n **1** (sby who plays or has played in) a sports, games, etc match between 2 national teams **2** also **internationale** often cap any of several socialist or communist organizations of international scope

international date line n, often cap I, D, & L an arbitrary line approximately along the 180th meridian, east and west of which the date differs by 1 calendar day

internationalism n **1** international character, interests, or outlook **2** (an attitude favouring) cooperation among nations – **internationalist** n or adj

internationalize, -ise vb to make or become international; esp to place under international control – **internationalization** n

internecine adj **1** mutually destructive **2** of or involving conflict within a group

interpellate vt to question (e g a minister) formally concerning an action or policy – **interpellator** n, **interpellation** n

interpenetrate vt to penetrate thoroughly ~ vi to penetrate mutually – **interpenetration** n

interplanetary *adj* existing, carried on, or operating between planets

interplay *n* interaction – **interplay** *vi*

Interpol *n* an international police organization for liaison between national police forces

interpolate *vt* **1** to alter or corrupt (e g a text) by inserting new or foreign matter **2** to insert between other things or parts; *esp* to insert (words) into a text or conversation **3** to estimate values of (a function) between 2 known values – **interpolative** *adj*, **interpolator** *n*, **interpolation** *n*

interpose *vt* **1** to place between 2 things or in an intervening position **2** to put forth by way of interference or intervention ⟨*prevented a decision by* interposing *a veto*⟩ **3** to interrupt with (words) during a conversation or argument ~ *vi* **1** to be or come in an intervening position **2** INTERVENE 3 **3** to interrupt – **interposer** *n*, **interposition** *n*

interpret *vt* **1** to expound the meaning of ⟨~ *a dream*⟩ **2** to conceive of in the light of one's beliefs, judgments, or circumstances; construe **3** to represent by means of art; bring to realization by performance ⟨~s *a role*⟩ ~ *vi* to act as an interpreter – **interpretable** *adj*, **interpretive**, **interpretative** *adj*, **interpretatively** *adv*

interpretation *n* an instance of artistic interpreting in performance or adaptation – **interpretational** *adj*

interpreter *n* **1** one who translates orally for people speaking in different languages **2** a computer program that translates an instruction into machine language for immediate execution

interregnum *n*, *pl* **interregnums**, **interregna 1** the time during which **a** a throne is vacant between reigns **b** the normal functions of government are suspended **2** a lapse or pause in a continuous series

interrelate *vb* to bring into or be in a relationship where each one depends upon or is acting upon the other – **interrelation**, **interrelationship** *n*

interrogate *vt* **1** to question formally **2** to give or send out a signal to (e g a computer) to trigger a response – **interrogator** *n*, **interrogation** *n*

¹interrogative, **interrogatory** *adj* **1a** of or being the grammatical mood that expresses a question **b** used in a question **2** questioning – **interrogatively** *adv*

²interrogative *n* **1** an interrogative utterance **2** a word, esp a pronoun, used in asking questions **3** the interrogative mood of a language

interrogatory *n* a formal question; *esp* a written question to be answered under direction of a court

¹interrupt *vt* **1** to break the flow or action of (a speaker or speech) **2** to break the uniformity or continuity of (sthg) ~ *vi* to interrupt an action; *esp* to interrupt another's utterance with one's own – **interrupter** *n*, **interruptible** *adj*, **interruption** *n*, **interruptive** *adj*

²interrupt *n* (a circuit that conveys) a signal to a computer that halts a program while a higher-priority program is carried out

intersect *vt* to pierce or divide (e g a line or area) by passing through or across to meet and cross at a point

intersection *n* **1** a place where 2 or more things (e g streets) intersect **2** the set of elements common to 2 sets; *esp* the set of points common to 2 geometric configurations

intersperse *vt* **1** to insert at intervals among other things ⟨interspersing *drawings throughout the text*⟩ **2** to diversify or vary with scattered things ⟨interspersing *the text with drawings*⟩ – **interspersion** *n*

¹interstate *adj* between 2 or more states, esp of the USA or of Australia ⟨*an ~ highway*⟩

²interstate *adv*, *Austr* to or in another state ⟨*went ~ to live*⟩

interstellar *adj* located or taking place among the stars

interstice *n* a small space between adjacent things – fml

intertwine *vt* to twine together to twine about one another – **intertwinement** *n*

interval *n* **1** an intervening space: e g **a** a time between events or states; a pause **b** a distance or gap between objects, units, or states ⟨*lamp posts placed at regular ~s*⟩ **c** the difference in pitch between 2 notes **2** a set of real numbers between 2 numbers; *also* the set of real numbers greater or less than some number **3** *Br* a break in the presentation of an entertainment (e g a play)

intervene *vi* **1** to enter or appear as sthg irrelevant or extraneous **2** to occur or come between 2 things, esp points of time or events **3** to come in or between so as to hinder or modify **4a** to enter a lawsuit as a third party **b** to interfere in another nation's internal affairs – **intervenor** *n*, **intervention** *n*

intervention *adj*, *of a commodity* purchased from the producer by the European economic community when the market price falls to a specified level ⟨*~ butter*⟩

interview *n* **1** a formal consultation usu to evaluate qualifications (e g of a prospective student or employee) **2** (a report of) a meeting at which information is obtained (e g by a journalist) from sby – **interview** *vt*, **interviewer** *n*, **interviewee** *n*

interweave *vb* **interwove** *also* **interweaved**; **interwoven** *also* **interweaved 1** to weave together **2** to intermingle, blend – **interwoven** *adj*, **interweave** *n*

¹intestate *adj* having made no valid will ⟨*he died ~*⟩ – **intestacy** *n*

²intestate *n* sby who dies intestate

intestinal *adj* of, being, affecting, or occurring in the intestine – **intestinally** *adv*

¹intestine *adj* of the internal affairs of a state or country

²intestine *n* the tubular part of the alimentary canal that extends from the stomach to the anus

intimacy *n* **1** familiarity **2** SEXUAL INTERCOURSE – euph

¹intimate *vt* to make known: e g **a** to announce **b** to hint; IMPLY 2 – **intimation** *n*

²intimate *adj* **1a** intrinsic, essential **b** belonging to or characterizing one's deepest nature **2** marked by very close association, contact, or familiarity **3a** marked by a warm friendship developing through long association **b** suggesting informal warmth or privacy **4** of a very personal or private nature **5** involved in a sexual relationship; *specif* engaging in an act of sexual intercourse ⟨*in six months they were ~ six times in the car and twice on a mountainside – News of the World*⟩ – euph – **intimately** *adv*

³intimate *n* a close friend or confidant

intimidate *vt* to frighten; *esp* to compel or deter (as if) by threats – **intimidator** *n*, **intimidatory** *adj*, **intimidation** *n*

into *prep* **1a** so as to be inside ⟨*come ~ the house*⟩ **b** so as to be ⟨*grow ~ a woman*⟩ ⟨*divide it ~ sections*⟩ ⟨*roll it ~ a ball*⟩ **c** so as to be in (a state) ⟨*get ~ trouble*⟩ ⟨*shocked ~ silence*⟩ **d** so as to be expressed in ⟨*translate it ~ French*⟩, dressed in ⟨*changed ~ his uniform*⟩, engaged in ⟨*go ~ farming*⟩, or a member of ⟨*enter ~ an alliance*⟩ **e** – used in division as the inverse of *by* or *divided by* ⟨*divide 35 ~ 70*⟩ **2** – used to indicate a partly elapsed period of time or a partly traversed extent of space ⟨*far ~ the night*⟩ ⟨*deep ~ the jungle*⟩ **3** in the direction of; *esp* towards the centre of ⟨*look ~ the sun*⟩ ⟨*inquire ~ the matter*⟩ **4** to a position of contact with; against ⟨*ran ~ a wall*⟩ **5** involved with ⟨*they were ~ hard drugs*⟩; *esp* keen on ⟨*are you ~ meditation?*⟩ – infml

intolerable *adj* unbearable – **intolerableness** *n*, **intolerably** *adv*

intolerant *adj* **1** unable or unwilling to endure ⟨*a plant ~ of direct sunlight*⟩ **2** unwilling to grant or share social, professional, political, or religious rights; bigoted – **intolerance** *n*, **intolerantly** *adv*

intonation *n* **1** sthg that is intoned; *specif* the opening notes of a Gregorian chant **2** performance of music with respect to correctness of pitch and harmony **3** the rise and fall in pitch of the voice in speech

intone *vb* to utter (sthg) in musical or prolonged tones; recite in singing tones or in a monotone – **intoner** *n*

in toto *adv* totally, entirely

intoxicate *vt* **1** POISON 1a **2a** to excite or stupefy by alcohol or a drug, esp to the point where physical and mental control is markedly diminished **b** to cause to lose self-control through excitement or elation – **intoxicant** *n or adj*, **intoxicatedly** *adv*, **intoxication** *n*

intra- *prefix* **1** within; inside ⟨intra*uterine*⟩ **2** intro- ⟨*an* intra*muscular injection*⟩

intractable *adj* **1** not easily managed or directed; OBSTINATE 1 **2** not easily manipulated, wrought, or solved **3** not easily relieved or cured ⟨*~ pain*⟩ – **intractableness** *n*, **intractably** *adv*, **intractability** *n*

intramural *adj* within the limits of a community or institution (e g a university) – **intramurally** *adv*

intransigent *adj* refusing to compromise or to abandon an extreme position or attitude, esp in politics; uncompromising – **intransigence** *n*, **intransigent** *n*, **intransigently** *adv*

intransitive *adj* characterized by not having a direct object ⟨*an ~ verb*⟩ – **intransitive** *n*, **intransitively** *adv*

intrauterine device, intrauterine contraceptive device *n* a device inserted and left in the uterus to prevent conception

intravenous *adj* situated or occurring in, or entering by way of a vein; *also* used in intravenous procedures – **intravenously** *adv*

intrench *vb* to entrench

intrepid *adj* fearless, bold, and resolute – **intrepidly** *adv*, **intrepidity** *n*

intricate *adj* **1** having many complexly interrelating parts or elements **2** difficult to resolve or analyse – **intricacy** *n*, **intricately** *adv*

¹intrigue *vt* **1** to arouse the interest or curiosity of **2** to captivate; FASCINATE 1 ⟨*her beauty ~s me*⟩ to carry on an intrigue; *esp* to plot, scheme – **intriguer** *n*

²intrigue *n* **1a** a secret scheme or plot **b** the practice of engaging in or using scheming or underhand plots **2** a clandestine love affair

intrinsic *adj* **1** belonging to the essential nature or constitution of sthg ⟨*an ornament of no ~ worth but of great sentimental value*⟩ **2** originating or situated within the body – **intrinsically** *adv*

intro *n, pl* **intros** INTRODUCTION 1 – infml

intro- *prefix* **1** in; into ⟨intro*jection*⟩ **2** inwards; within ⟨intro*vert*⟩

introduce *vt* **1** to lead or bring in, esp for the first time ⟨*~ a rare plant species into the country*⟩ **2a** to bring into play ⟨*~ a new line of approach into the argument*⟩ **b** to bring into practice or use; institute **3** to lead to or make known by a formal act, announcement, or recommendation: e g **a** to cause to be acquainted; make (oneself or sby) known to another **b** to present formally (e g at court or

into society) **c** to announce formally or by an official reading **d** to make preliminary explanatory or laudatory remarks about (e g a speaker) **4** PLACE 2a, INSERT 2 ⟨*the risk of* introducing *harmful substances into the body*⟩ **5** to bring to a knowledge or discovery of sthg ⟨*~ her to the works of Byron*⟩

introduction *n* **1a** a preliminary treatise or course of study **b** a short introductory musical passage **2** sthg introduced; *specif* a plant or animal new to an area

introductory *adj* of or being a first step that sets sthg going or in proper perspective; preliminary – **introductorily** *adv*

introit *n* a piece of music sung or played at the beginning of a church service; *specif, often cap* the antiphon or psalm sung as the priest approaches the altar to celebrate the Eucharist

introspect *vi* to examine one's own mind or its contents reflectively – **introspection** *n*, **introspective** *adj*

¹introvert *vt* to turn inwards or in on itself or oneself: e g **a** to draw in (a tubular part) usu by invagination **b** to concentrate or direct (the mind, thoughts, or emotions) on oneself – **introversion** *n*

²introvert *n* **1** sthg (e g the eyestalk of a snail) that is or can be drawn in **2** one whose attention and interests are directed towards his/her own mental life

intrude *vi* **1** to thrust oneself in without invitation, permission, or welcome **2** to enter as a geological intrusion ~*vt* **1** to thrust or force in or on, esp without permission, welcome, or suitable reason **2** to cause (e g rock) to intrude – **intruder** *n*

intrusion *n* **1** intruding or being intruded; *specif* wrongfully entering upon the property of another **2** (the forcible entry of) rock or magma forced while molten into or between other rock formations

intrusive *adj* **1** characterized by (a tendency to) intrusion **2** *of a rock* being an intrusion – **intrusively** *adv*

intrust *vt* to entrust

intuit *vt* to apprehend by intuition – **intuitable** *adj*

intuition *n* **1a** (knowledge gained by) immediate apprehension or cognition **b** the power of attaining direct knowledge without evident rational thought and the drawing of conclusions from evidence available **2** quick and ready insight – **intuitional** *adj*, **intuitive** *adj*, **intuitively** *adv*

intumesce *vi* ENLARGE 1, SWELL 1b – **intumescence** *n*, **intumescent** *adj*

inundate *vt* to cover or overwhelm (as if) with a flood – **inundation** *n*

inure *vt* to accustom *to* sthg undesirable – **inurement** *n*

invade *vt* **1** to enter (e g a country) for hostile purposes **2** to encroach on ⟨*a noise ~d his privacy*⟩ **3a** to spread over or into as if invading **b** to affect injuriously and progressively ⟨*gangrene ~s healthy tissue*⟩ – **invader** *n*

¹invalid *adj* **1** without legal force **2** logically inconsistent – **invalidly** *adv*, **invalidity** *n*

²invalid *adj* **1** suffering from disease or disability **2** of or suited to an invalid

³invalid *n* one who is sickly or disabled

⁴invalid *vt* to remove from active duty by reason of sickness or disability ⟨*he was ~ed out of the army*⟩

invalidate *vt* to make invalid; *esp* to weaken or destroy the convincingness of (e g an argument or claim) – **invalidation** *n*

invaluable *adj* valuable beyond estimation; priceless – **invaluably** *adv*

invariable *adj* not (capable of) changing; constant – **invariable** *n*, **invariableness** *n*, **invariably** *adv*, **invariability** *n*

invasion n 1 an invading, esp by an army 2 the incoming or spread of sthg usu harmful – **invasive** adj

invective n abusive or insulting (use of) language; denunciation – **invective** adj, **invectively** adv

inveigh vi to speak or protest bitterly or vehemently against

inveigle vt to win (sby or sthg) over by ingenuity or flattery – **inveiglement** n

invent vt 1 to think up ⟨~ an excuse⟩ 2 to produce (e g sthg useful) for the first time – **inventor** n, **inventress** n

invention n 1 productive imagination; inventiveness 2a sthg invented: e g (1) a (misleading) product of the imagination (2) a contrivance or process devised after study and experiment b a short keyboard composition, usu in double counterpoint

inventive adj 1 creative 2 characterized by invention – **inventively** adv, **inventiveness** n

¹**inventory** n 1a an itemized list (e g of the property of an individual or estate) b a list of traits, preferences, attitudes, etc used to evaluate personal characteristics or skills 2a the items listed in an inventory b NAm the quantity of goods, components, or raw materials on hand; STOCK 5b 3 the taking of an inventory

²**inventory** vt to make an inventory of; catalogue

¹**inverse** adj 1 opposite in order, direction, nature, or effect 2 of a mathematical function expressing the same relationship as another function but from the opposite viewpoint 3 being or relating to an inverse function ⟨~ sine⟩ – **inversely** adv

²**inverse** n 1 a direct opposite 2 an inverse function or operation in mathematics ⟨addition is the ~ of subtraction⟩

inversion n 1 the act or process of inverting 2 a reversal of position, order, form, or relationship: e g a(1) a change in normal word order; esp the placement of a verb before its subject (2) the process or result of changing, converting, or reversing the relative positions of the elements of a musical interval, chord, or phrase b being turned inwards or inside out 3 the operation of forming the inverse of a magnitude, operation, or element 4 homosexuality 5 a conversion of a substance showing dextrorotation into one showing laevorotation or vice versa ⟨~ of sucrose⟩ 6 a conversion of direct current into alternating current 7 a reversal of the normal atmospheric temperature gradient – **inversive** adj

¹**invert** vt 1a to turn inside out or upside down b to turn (e g a foot) inwards 2a to reverse in position, order, or relationship b to subject to musical inversion c to subject to chemical inversion d to express the mathematical inverse, esp the reciprocal, of – **invertible** adj

²**invert** n sby or sthg characterized by inversion; esp a homosexual

invertebrate adj 1 (of animals) lacking a spinal column or notochord 2 lacking in strength or vitality of character – **invertebrate** n

inverted comma n 1 a comma in type printed upside down at the top of the line 2 chiefly Br QUOTATION MARK

¹**invest** vt 1 to confer (the symbols of) authority, office, or rank on 2 to clothe, endow, or cover (as if) with sthg ⟨~ed with an air of mystery⟩ 3 to surround with troops or ships so as to prevent escape or entry

²**invest** vt 1 to commit (money) to a particular use (e g buying shares or new capital outlay) in order to earn a financial return 2 to devote (e g time or effort) to sthg for future advantages ~ vi to make an investment ⟨~ in a new car⟩ – **investable** adj, **investor** n

investigate vb 1 to make a systematic examination or study (of) 2 to conduct an official inquiry (into) – **investigational** adj, **investigative** adj, **investigator** n, **investigatory** adj, **investigation** n

investiture n a formal ceremony conferring an office or honour on sby

¹**investment** n a siege or blockade

²**investment** n (a sum of) money invested for income or profit; also the asset (e g property) purchased

inveterate adj 1 firmly, obstinately, and persistently established 2 habitual ⟨an ~ liar⟩ – **inveteracy** n, **inveterately** adv

invidious adj 1 tending to cause discontent, ill will, or envy 2 of an unpleasant or objectionable nature; of a kind causing or likely to cause harm or resentment – **invidiously** adv, **invidiousness** n

invigilate vb to keep watch (over); specif, Br to supervise (candidates) at (an examination) – **invigilator** n, **invigilation** n

invigorate vt to give fresh life and energy to – **invigoratingly** adv, **invigorator** n, **invigoration** n

invincible adj incapable of being conquered or subdued – **invincibleness** n, **invincibly** adv, **invincibility** n

inviolable adj (to be kept) secure from violation, profanation, or assault – **inviolably** adv, **inviolability** n

inviolate adj not violated or profaned – **inviolacy** n, **inviolately** adv, **inviolateness** n

invisible adj 1 incapable (by nature or circumstances) of being seen 2a not appearing in published financial statements ⟨~ assets⟩ b not reflected in statistics ⟨~ earnings⟩ c of or being trade in services (e g insurance or tourism) rather than goods 3 too small or unobtrusive to be seen or noticed; inconspicuous – **invisible** n, **invisibleness** n, **invisibly** adv, **invisibility** n

invitation n 1 an often formal request to be present or participate 2 an incentive, inducement – **invitational** adj

¹**invite** vt 1a to offer an incentive or inducement to b to (unintentionally) increase the likelihood of ⟨his actions ~ trouble⟩ 2 to request (the presence of) formally or politely – **invitatory** adj, **inviter** n, **invitee** n

²**invite** n an invitation – infml

inviting adj attractive, tempting – **invitingly** adv

invocation n 1 the act or process of petitioning for help or support; specif, often cap an invocatory prayer, esp at the beginning of a church service 2 the performing of magical rites in order to summon spirits – **invocational** adj, **invocatory** adj

¹**invoice** n 1 ⁴BILL 3a; specif an itemized list of goods shipped, usu specifying the price and the terms of sale 2 a consignment of merchandise

²**invoice** vt to submit an invoice for or to

invoke vt 1a to petition (e g a deity) for help or support b to appeal to or cite as an authority 2 to call forth (e g a spirit) by uttering a spell or magical formula 3 to make an earnest request for; SOLICIT 3 4 to put into effect ⟨~ economic sanctions⟩ – **invoker** n

involuntary adj 1 done contrary to or without choice 2 not subject to conscious control; reflex ⟨~ muscle⟩ – **involuntarily** adv, **involuntariness** n

involve vt 1a to cause to be associated or take part b to occupy (oneself) absorbingly; esp to commit (oneself) emotionally 2 to envelop 3 to relate closely 4a to have within or as part of itself b to require as a necessary accompaniment – **involvement** n, **involver** n

involved adj 1 (needlessly or excessively) complex 2 taking part in ⟨workers ~ in building a dam⟩ – **involvedly** adv

invulnerable adj 1 incapable of being injured or harmed

2 immune to or proof against attack – **invulnerableness** *n*, **invulnerably** *adv*, **invulnerability** *n*

inward *adj* **1** situated within or directed towards the inside **2** of or relating to the mind or spirit ⟨*struggled to achieve ~ peace*⟩ – **inwardness** *n*

inwards, *NAm chiefly* **inward** *adv* **1** towards the inside, centre, or interior **2** towards the inner being

in-wrought *adj* **1** *of a fabric* decorated with a pattern woven or worked in **2** *of a pattern* woven or worked in (e g to a fabric)

iodine *n* a (solid blackish grey) halogen element – **iodinate** *vt*, **iodination** *n*

iodize, **-ise** *vt* to treat with iodine or an iodide ⟨*~d salt*⟩

ion *n* **1** an atom or group of atoms that carries a positive or negative electric charge as a result of having lost or gained 1 or more electrons **2** a free electron or other charged subatomic particle

-ion *suffix* (*vb → n*) **1a** act or process of ⟨*validation*⟩ **b** result of (a specified act or process) ⟨*regulation*⟩ **2** quality or condition of ⟨*hydration*⟩ ⟨*ambition*⟩

ionic *adj* **1** of, existing as, or characterized by ions ⟨*~ gases*⟩ **2** functioning by means of ions ⟨*~ conduction*⟩ – **ionicity** *n*

¹**Ionic** *adj* **1** (characteristic) of Ionia **2** of that 1 of the 3 Greek orders of architecture that is characterized esp by the scroll-shaped ornament of its capital

²**Ionic** *n* a dialect of ancient Greek used in Ionia

ionize, **-ise** *vb* to convert or become converted wholly or partly into ions – **ionizable** *adj*, **ionizer** *n*, **ionization** *n*

ionosphere *n* the part of the earth's atmosphere that extends from an altitude above that of the stratosphere out to at least 480km (about 300mi) and consists of several distinct regions containing free ions; *also* a comparable region surrounding another planet – **ionospheric** *adj*, **ionospherically** *adv*

iota *n* **1** the 9th letter of the Greek alphabet **2** an infinitesimal amount

IOU *n* (a written acknowledgment of) a debt

ipso facto *adv* by the very nature of the case

IQ *n* INTELLIGENCE QUOTIENT

ir- – see IN-

Iranian *n* **1** a native or inhabitant of Iran **2** a branch of the Indo-European family of languages that includes Persian – **Iranian** *adj*

irascible *adj* having an easily provoked temper – **irascibleness** *n*, **irascibly** *adv*, **irascibility** *n*

irate *adj* roused to or arising from anger – **irately** *adv*, **irateness** *n*

ire *n* intense and usu openly displayed anger – **ireful** *adj*

iridescence *n* (a display or effect suggestive of) a play of changing colours in a soap bubble, bird's plumage, etc – **iridescent** *adj*, **iridescently** *adv*

iridium *n* a silver-white hard brittle very heavy (tetravalent) metallic element of the platinum group – **iridic** *adj*

iris *n*, *pl* (*1*) **irises, irides**, (*2*) **irises, irides**, *esp collectively* **iris 1a** the opaque contractile diaphragm perforated by the pupil that forms the coloured portion of the eye **b iris, iris diaphragm** an adjustable diaphragm of thin opaque plates that can be moved to control the size of an aperture **2** any of a large genus of plants with long straight leaves and large showy flowers

¹**Irish** *adj* **1** of Ireland or the Irish (language) **2** amusingly illogical – **Irishman** *n*

²**Irish** *n* **1** *pl in constr* the people of Ireland **2 Irish, Irish Gaelic** the Celtic language of Ireland, esp as used since the end of the medieval period

Irish setter *n* (any of) a breed of chestnut-brown or mahogany-red gundogs

irk *vt* to make weary, irritated, or bored

irksome *adj* troublesome, annoying – **irksomely** *adv*, **irksomeness** *n*

¹**iron** *n* **1** a heavy malleable ductile magnetic silver-white metallic element that readily rusts in moist air, occurs in most igneous rocks, and is vital to biological processes **2** sthg (orig) made of iron: e g **a** sthg used to bind or restrain – usu pl **b** a heated metal implement used for branding or cauterizing **c** a metal implement with a smooth flat typically triangular base that is heated (e g by electricity) and used to smooth or press clothing **d** a stirrup **e** any of a numbered series of usu 9 golf clubs with metal heads of varying angles for hitting the ball to various heights and lengths **3** great strength or hardness – **iron in the fire** a prospective course of action; a plan not yet realized ⟨*got several irons in the fire and I'm hoping to land something before very long* – W S Maugham⟩

²**iron** *adj* **1** (made) of iron **2** resembling iron (e g in appearance, strength, solidity, or durability) – **ironness** *n*

³**iron** *vt* **1** to smooth (as if) with a heated iron ⟨*~ed his shirt*⟩ **2** to remove (e g wrinkles) by ironing – often + *out* ~ *vi* to be capable of being ironed ⟨*this skirt ~s well*⟩

Iron Age *n* the period of human culture characterized by the widespread use of iron for making tools and weapons and dating from before 1000 BC

¹**ironclad** *adj* sheathed in iron or steel armour

²**ironclad** *n* an ironclad naval vessel, esp in the 19th c

iron curtain *n*, *often cap I&C* an esp political and ideological barrier between the Communist countries of E Europe and the non-Communist countries of (and those friendly to) W Europe

iron grey *adj or n* dark greenish grey

ironic, ironical *adj* **1** of, containing, or constituting irony **2** given to irony – **ironically** *adv*, **ironicalness** *n*

ironing *n* clothes and cloth articles (e g towels and tablecloths) that are (to be) ironed

ironing board *n* a narrow flat board, on which clothes are ironed, mounted on collapsible and adjustable legs

iron lung *n* a device for artificial respiration that fits over the patient's chest and forces air into and out of the lungs

ironmonger *n*, *Br* a dealer in esp household hardware – **ironmongery** *n*

iron out *vt* to put right or correct (e g a problem or defect); resolve (e g difficulties)

iron pyrites *n* iron disulphide occurring as a lustrous pale brass-yellow mineral

ironstone *n* a hard sedimentary iron ore, esp a siderite

ironware *n* articles, esp vessels and implements for domestic use, made of iron

ironworks *n*, *pl* **ironworks** a mill or building where iron or steel is smelted or heavy iron or steel products are made – often pl with sing. meaning

irony *n* **1a** the use of words to express a meaning other than and esp the opposite of the literal meaning **b** an expression or utterance using irony **2a** (an event or situation showing) incongruity between actual circumstances and the normal, appropriate, or expected result **b** DRAMATIC IRONY **3** an attitude of detached awareness of incongruity ⟨*viewed with ~ the craze for individuality*⟩

irradiate *vt* **1a** to cast rays (of light) upon **b** to give intellectual or spiritual insight to **c** to affect or treat by (exposure to) radiant energy (e g heat) **2** to emit like rays (of light); RADIATE 2 – **irradiance** *n*, **irradiative** *adj*, **irradiator** *n*

¹irrational *adj* not rational: e g **a** not governed by or according to reason **b** being or having a value that is an irrational number ⟨*an ~ root of an equation*⟩ – **irrationalism** *n*, **irrationalist** *n*, **irrationally** *adv*, **irrationality** *n*

²irrational, irrational number *n* a number (e g π) that cannot be expressed as the result of dividing 1 integer by another

¹irreconcilable *adj* impossible to reconcile: e g **a** resolutely opposed **b** INCOMPATIBLE 1 – **irreconcilableness** *n*, **irreconcilably** *adv*, **irreconcilability** *n*

²irreconcilable *n* an opponent of compromise or collaboration

irrecoverable *adj* not capable of being recovered or retrieved – **irrecoverably** *adv*

irredeemable *adj* not redeemable; *esp* beyond remedy; hopeless – **irredeemably** *adv*

irreducible *adj* impossible to bring into a desired, normal, or simpler state ⟨*an ~ matrix*⟩ – **irreducibly** *adv*, **irreducibility** *n*

irrefutable *adj* incontrovertible – **irrefutably** *adv*, **irrefutability** *n*

¹irregular *adj* **1a** contrary to rule, custom, or moral principles **b** not inflected in the normal manner; *specif* STRONG 14 **c** inadequate because of failure to conform **d** *of troops* not belonging to the regular army organization **2** lacking symmetry or evenness **3** lacking continuity or regularity, esp of occurrence or activity – **irregularly** *adv*

²irregular *n* an irregular soldier

irregularity *n* sthg irregular (e g contrary to accepted professional or ethical standards)

irrelevant *adj* not relevant; inapplicable – **irrelevance** *n*, **irrelevancy** *n*, **irrelevantly** *adv*

irreligion *n* hostility to or disregard of religion – **irreligionist** *n*, **irreligious** *adj*, **irreligiously** *adv*

irremediable *adj* not remediable; *specif* incurable – **irremediableness** *n*, **irremediably** *adv*

irreparable *adj* not able to be restored to a previous condition – **irreparableness** *n*, **irreparably** *adv*

irreplaceable *adj* having no adequate substitute – **irreplaceably** *adv*

irrepressible *adj* impossible to restrain or control – **irrepressibly** *adv*, **irrepressibility** *n*

irreproachable *adj* offering no foundation for blame or criticism – **irreproachably** *adv*, **irreproachability** *n*

irresistible *adj* impossible to resist successfully; highly attractive or enticing – **irresistibleness** *n*, **irresistibly** *adv*, **irresistibility** *n*

irresolute *adj* lacking decision or a firm aim and purpose – **irresolutely** *adv*, **irresoluteness** *n*, **irresolution** *n*

irrespective of *prep* without regard or reference to; IN SPITE OF

irresponsible 1 showing no regard for the consequences of one's actions **2** unable to bear responsibility – **irresponsibly** *adv*, **irresponsibility** *n*

irreverence *n* (an act or utterance showing) lack of reverence – **irreverent** *adj*, **irreverently** *adv*

irreversible *adj* unable to be changed back into a previous state or condition – **irreversibly** *adv*, **irreversibility** *n*

irrevocable *adj* incapable of being revoked or altered – **irrevocably** *adv*, **irrevocability** *n*

¹irrigate *vt* to wet, moisten: e g **a** to supply (e g land) with water by artificial means **b** to flush (e g an eye or wound) with a stream of liquid ~*vi* to practise irrigation – **irrigator** *n*, **irrigation** *n*

irritable *adj* capable of being irritated: e g **a** easily exasperated or excited **b** (excessively) responsive to stimuli – **irritableness** *n*, **irritably** *adv*, **irritability** *n*

irritant *n* sthg that irritates or excites – **irritant** *adj*

irritate *vt* **1** to excite impatience, anger, or displeasure in **2** to induce a response to a stimulus in or of ~*vi* to cause or induce displeasure or anger – **irritatingly** *adv*, **irritative** *adj*, **irritation** *n*

irrupt *vi* to rush in forcibly or violently – **irruption** *n*, **irruptive** *adj*, **irruptively** *adv*

is *pres 3 sing of* BE, *dial pres 1&2 sing of* BE, *substandard pres pl of* BE

is-, iso- *comb form* **1** equal; homogeneous; uniform ⟨*isacoustic*⟩ **2** isomeric with (a specified compound or radical) ⟨*isopropyl*⟩

ischaemia *n* local deficiency of blood due to decreased arterial flow

-ise – see -IZE

-ish *suffix* **1** (*n → adj*) of or belonging to (a specified country or ethnic group) ⟨*Finnish*⟩ **2a(1)** (*adj, n → adj*) having a trace of ⟨*summerish*⟩; slightly ⟨*purplish*⟩⟨*biggish*⟩ **(2)** (*n → adj*) having the approximate age of ⟨*fortyish*⟩ **(3)** (*n → adj*) being or occurring at the approximate time of ⟨*eightish*⟩ **b** (*n → adj*) having the characteristics of ⟨*boyish*⟩⟨*mulish*⟩ – often derog ⟨*childish*⟩⟨*bookish*⟩

isinglass *n* a very pure gelatin prepared from the air bladders of sturgeons and other fishes and used esp in jellies and glue

Islam *n* **1** the religious faith of Muslims including belief in Allah as the sole deity and in Muhammad as his prophet **2a** the civilization or culture accompanying Islamic faith **b** the group of modern nations in which Islam is the dominant religion – **Islamic** *n or adj*, **Islamize** *vt*, **Islamization** *n*

island *n* **1** an area of land surrounded by water and smaller than a continent **2** sthg like an island (e g in being isolated or surrounded) **3** TRAFFIC ISLAND **4** an isolated superstructure on the deck of a ship, esp an aircraft carrier – **islander** *n*

isle *n* a (small) island – used in some names

islet *n* **1** a little island **2** a small isolated mass of 1 type of tissue

ism *n* a distinctive doctrine, cause, theory, or practice – often derog

-ism *suffix* (*n, adj → n*) **1a** act, practice, or process of ⟨*plagiarism*⟩ **b** mode of behaviour characteristic of (sby or sthg specified) ⟨*cannibalism*⟩ **2a** state, condition, or property of ⟨*magnetism*⟩ **b** pathological state or condition resulting from excessive use of (a specified drug) ⟨*alcoholism*⟩ or marked by resemblance to (a specified person or thing) ⟨*gigantism*⟩ **3a** doctrine, theory, or cult of ⟨*Buddhism*⟩ **b** adherence to (a specified doctrine or system) ⟨*stoicism*⟩ **c** prejudice on grounds of ⟨*sexism*⟩ **4** characteristic or peculiar feature of (a specified language or variety of language) ⟨*colloquialism*⟩ ⟨*Anglicism*⟩

isn't is not

isobar *n* **1** a line on a chart connecting places where the atmospheric pressure is the same **2** any of 2 or more atoms or elements having the same atomic weights or mass numbers but different atomic numbers – **isobaric** *adj*

isolate *vt* **1** to set apart from others; *also* to quarantine **2** to separate from another substance so as to obtain in a pure form **3** to insulate – **isolatable** *adj*, **isolator** *n*, **isolable** *adj*, **isolation** *n*

isolationism *n* a policy of national isolation by refraining from engaging in international relations – **isolationist** *n or adj*

isosceles *adj, of a triangle* having 2 equal sides

isotherm *n* **1** a line on a chart connecting points having the same temperature at a given time or the same mean temperature for a given period **2** a line on a chart representing changes of volume or pressure under conditions of constant temperature – **isothermal** *adj*

isotope *n* any of 2 or more species of atoms of a chemical element that have the same atomic number and nearly identical chemical behaviour but differ in atomic mass or mass number and physical properties – **isotopic** *adj*, **isotopically** *adv*, **isotopy** *n*

Israeli *adj* (characteristic) of modern Israel – **Israeli** *n*

Israelite *n* any of the descendants of the Hebrew patriarch Jacob; *specif* a member of any of the 10 Hebrew tribes occupying northern Palestine in biblical times – **Israelite** *adj*

¹**issue** *n* **1** the action of going, coming, or flowing out **2** a means or place of going out **3** offspring ⟨*died without* ~⟩ **4** an outcome that usu resolves or decides a problem **5** a matter that is in dispute between 2 or more parties; a controversial topic **6** sthg coming out from a usu specified source **7a** the act of publishing, giving out, or making available ⟨*the next* ~ *of commemorative stamps*⟩ **b** the thing or the whole quantity of things given out, published, or distributed at 1 time ⟨*read the latest* ~⟩ – **issueless** *adj* – **at issue** under discussion or consideration; in dispute – **join/take issue** to take an opposing or conflicting stand; disagree or engage in argument on a point of dispute

²**issue** *vi* **1a** to go, come, or flow out **b** to emerge **2** to descend from a specified parent or ancestor **3** to be a consequence – + *in* **4** to appear or become available through being given out, published, or distributed ~ *vt* **1** to cause to come out **2a** to give out, distribute, or provide officially **b** to send out for sale or circulation – **issuer** *n*

¹**-ist** *suffix* (→ *n*) **1a** one who performs (a specified action) ⟨*cyclist*⟩ **b** one who makes or produces (a specified thing) ⟨*novelist*⟩ **c** one who plays (a specified musical instrument) ⟨*harpist*⟩ **d** one who operates (a specified mechanical instrument or device) ⟨*motorist*⟩ **2** one who specializes in or practises (a specified art, science, skill, or profession) ⟨*geologist*⟩ ⟨*ventriloquist*⟩ **3** one who adheres to or advocates (a specified doctrine, system, or code of behaviour) ⟨*socialist*⟩ ⟨*royalist*⟩ ⟨*hedonist*⟩ ⟨*Calvinist*⟩ **4** one who is prejudiced on grounds of ⟨*sexist*⟩

²**-ist** *suffix* (→ *adj*) **1** relating to, or characteristic of ⟨*dilettantist*⟩ ⟨*obscurantist*⟩ **2** showing prejudice on grounds of ⟨*racist*⟩

isthmus *n* **1** a narrow strip of land connecting 2 larger land areas **2** a narrow anatomical part connecting 2 larger parts

¹**it** *pron* **1a** that thing, creature, or group – used as subject or object ⟨*saw the house and noticed that* ~ *was very old*⟩ ⟨*had a baby but lost* ~⟩; compare HE, ITS, THEY, THERE **2 b** the person in question ⟨*who is* ~? *It's me*⟩ **2** – used as subject of an impersonal verb ⟨~ *'s raining*⟩ ⟨~ *'s not far to London*⟩ **3a** – used as anticipatory subject or object of a verb ⟨~ *'s no fun being a secretary*⟩ ⟨*I take* ~ *that you refuse*⟩ **b** – used to highlight part of a sentence ⟨~ *was the President who arrived yesterday*⟩ ⟨~ *was yesterday that he arrived*⟩ **c** – used with many verbs and prepositions as a meaningless object ⟨*run for* ~⟩ ⟨*footed* ~ *back to camp*⟩ **4a** this, that – used to refer to previous or following information ⟨*She failed. It's a shame*⟩ **b** – used to refer to an explicit or implicit state of affairs ⟨*how's* ~ *going?*⟩ **5** that which is available ⟨*one boiled egg and that's* ~⟩, important ⟨*yes, that's just* ~⟩, or appropriate ⟨*a bit tighter; that's* ~⟩

²**it** *n* **1** the player in a usu children's game who performs a unique role (e g trying to catch others in a game of tag) **2** SEX APPEAL; *also* SEXUAL INTERCOURSE – infml

Italian *n* **1** a native or inhabitant of Italy **2** the Romance language of the Italians – **Italian** *adj*, **Italianate** *adj*

¹**italic** *adj* **1** *cap* (characteristic) of ancient Italy or of Italic **2** of a type style with characters that slant upwards to the right (e g in '*these words are italic*')

²**italic** *n* **1** (a character in) an italic type style **2** *cap* the Italic branch of the Indo-European language family that includes Latin, ancient Italian languages, and the Romance languages descended from Latin

italicize, -ise *vt* to print in italics – **italicization** *n*

Italo- *comb form* Italian; Italian and ⟨*Italo-Austrian*⟩

¹**itch** *vi* **1** to have or produce an itch **2** to have a restless desire ⟨*were* ~ing *to go outside*⟩ ~ – infml ~ *vt* to cause to itch

²**itch** *n* **1a** an irritating sensation in the upper surface of the skin that makes one want to scratch **b** a skin disorder characterized by such a sensation **2** a restless desire – infml – **itchiness** *n*, **itchy** *adj*

it'd it had; it would

¹**-ite** *suffix* (→ *n*) **1a** one who belongs to (a specified place, group, etc) ⟨*Israelite*⟩ ⟨*socialite*⟩ ⟨*Hittite*⟩ **b** adherent or follower of (a specified doctrine or movement) ⟨*Pre-Raphaelite*⟩ ⟨*Thatcherite*⟩ **2a**(1) product of ⟨*metabolite*⟩ ⟨*catabolite*⟩ (2) commercially manufactured product ⟨*ebonite*⟩ -itol ⟨*inosite*⟩ **3** fossil ⟨*ammonite*⟩ **4** mineral ⟨*bauxite*⟩ ⟨*bentonite*⟩ **5** segment or constituent part of (a specified body or organ) ⟨*somite*⟩ ⟨*dendrite*⟩

²**-ite** *suffix* (→ *n*) salt or ester of (a specified acid with a name ending in -ous) ⟨*sulphite*⟩

¹**item** *adv* and in addition – used to introduce each article in a list or enumeration

²**item** *n* **1** a separate unit in an account or series **2** a separate piece of news or information

itemize, -ise *vt* to list ⟨~d *all expenses*⟩ – **itemization** *n*

iterate *vt* to say or do again or repetitively – **iteration** *n*

itinerant *adj* travelling from place to place; *esp* covering a circuit ⟨~ *preacher*⟩ – **itinerant** *n*

itinerary *n* **1** the (proposed) route of a journey **2** a travel diary **3** a traveller's guidebook

-itis *suffix* (→ *n*), *pl* **-itises** *also* **-itides 1** disease or inflammation of ⟨*bronchitis*⟩ **2a** suffering caused by a surfeit or excess of ⟨*electionitis*⟩ **b** infatuation or obsession with ⟨*jazzitis*⟩ *USE* (2) humor

it'll it will; it shall

its *adj* relating to it or itself, esp as possessor ⟨~ *climate*⟩ ⟨*going to* ~ *kennel*⟩, agent ⟨*a child proud of* ~ *first drawings*⟩, or object of an action ⟨~ *final enactment into law*⟩

it's it is; it has

itself *pron* **1** that identical thing, creature, or group emphasis ⟨*the letter* ~ *was missing*⟩; compare ONESELF **2** its normal self – **in itself** intrinsically considered ⟨*not dangerous in itself*⟩

itsy-bitsy *adj* tiny – infml

-ity *suffix* (→ *n*) **1** quality or state of ⟨*authority*⟩ ⟨*theatricality*⟩; *also* instance of (a specified quality or state) ⟨*an obscenity*⟩ **2** amount or degree of ⟨*humidity*⟩ ⟨*salinity*⟩

IUD *n* INTRAUTERINE DEVICE

¹**-ive** *suffix* (→ *adj*) **1** tending to; disposed to ⟨*corrective*⟩ ⟨*sportive*⟩ **2** performing (a specified function) ⟨*descriptive*⟩ ⟨*generative*⟩

²**-ive** *suffix* (→ *n*) **1** sby or sthg that performs or serves to accomplish (a specified action) ⟨*sedative*⟩ ⟨*detective*⟩ **2** sby who is in or affected by (a specified state or condition) ⟨*captive*⟩ ⟨*consumptive*⟩

I've I have

ivied *adj* overgrown with ivy ⟨~ *walls*⟩

ivory *n* **1** the hard creamy-white form of dentine of which the tusks of elephants and other tusked mammals are made **2** a creamy slightly yellowish white colour **3** *pl* things (e g dice or piano keys) made of (sthg resembling) ivory – infml – **ivory** *adj*

ivory tower *n* aloofness from practical concerns; *also* a place encouraging such an attitude

ivy *n* a very common and widely cultivated Eurasian woody climbing plant with evergreen leaves, small yellowish flowers, and black berries

-ize, -ise *suffix* (→ *vb*) **1a(1)** cause to be, conform to, or resemble ⟨*liquidize*⟩ ⟨*popularize*⟩ **(2)** subject to (a specified action) ⟨*plagiarize*⟩ ⟨*criticize*⟩ **(3)** impregnate, treat, or combine with ⟨*albuminize*⟩ ⟨*oxidize*⟩ **b** treat like; make into ⟨*lionize*⟩ ⟨*proselytize*⟩ **c** treat according to the method of ⟨*bowdlerize*⟩ **2a** become; become like ⟨*crystallize*⟩ **b** engage in (a specified activity) ⟨*philosophize*⟩

J

j *n, pl* **j's, js** *often cap* (a graphic representation of or device for reproducing) the 10th letter of the English alphabet

¹jab *vb* **-bb-** *vt* **1a** to pierce (as if) with a sharp object **b** to poke quickly or abruptly **2** to strike with a short straight blow ~ *vi* **1** to make quick or abrupt thrusts (as if) with a sharp or pointed object **2** to strike sby with a short straight blow

²jab *n* **1** a short straight punch in boxing delivered with the leading hand **2** a hypodermic injection – infml

jabber *vi or n* (to engage in) rapid or unintelligible talk or chatter – **jabberer** *n*

¹jack *n* **1a** MAN 1a(1), e, 3 – usu as an intensive in such phrases as *every man jack* **b** a labourer, lumberjack, or steeplejack **2** any of various portable mechanisms for exerting pressure or lifting a heavy object a short distance **3** a male donkey **4a** a small white target ball in lawn bowling **b(1)** *pl but sing in constr* a game in which players toss and pick up small bone or metal objects in a variety of shapes in between throws of a ball **(2)** a small 6-pointed metal object used in the game of jacks **5** a playing card carrying the figure of a soldier or servant and ranking usu below the queen **6a** JACK PLUG **b** JACK SOCKET

²jack *vt* **1** to move or lift (as if) by a jack **2** to raise the level or quality of **3** GIVE UP – usu + *in*; infml ⟨*I was fed up with my job so I ~ed it in*⟩ USE (1&2) usu + *up*

jackal *n* **1** any of several Old World wild dogs smaller than the related wolves **2** sby who collaborates with another in committing immoral acts

jackanapes *n* **1** a monkey, ape **2a** an impudent or conceited person **b** a mischievous child

jackaroo, jackeroo *n, Austr* a young inexperienced worker on a cattle or sheep station

jackass *n* **1** a male ass **2** a stupid person; a fool

jackboot *n* **1** a heavy military leather boot extending above the knee and worn esp during the 17th and 18th c **2a** a laceless military boot reaching to the calf **b** political repression effected by military or paramilitary force – + *the* – **jackbooted** *adj*

jackdaw *n* a common black and grey Eurasian bird that is related to but smaller than the common crow

¹jacket *n* **1** an outer garment for the upper body opening down the full length of the centre front **2a** the natural coat of an animal **b** the skin of a (baked) potato **3a** a thermally insulating cover (e g for a hot water tank) **b(1)** DUST JACKET **(2)** the cover of a paperback book

²jacket *vt* to put a jacket on; enclose in or with a jacket

Jack Frost *n* frost or frosty weather personified

jack-in-the-box *n, pl* **jack-in-the-boxes, jacks-in-the-box** a toy consisting of a small box out of which a figure springs when the lid is raised

¹jackknife *n* **1** a large clasp knife for the pocket **2** a dive in which the diver bends from the waist, touches the ankles with straight knees, and straightens out before hitting the water

²jackknife *vt* to cause to double up like a jackknife ~ *vi* **1** to double up like a jackknife **2** *esp of an articulated lorry* to turn or rise and form an angle of 90 degrees or less

jack-of-all-trades *n, pl* **jacks-of-all-trades** a handy versatile person – sometimes derog

jack-o'-lantern *n* **1** a will-o'-the-wisp **2** a lantern made from a hollowed-out pumpkin cut to look like a human face

jack plug *n* a single-pronged electrical plug for insertion into a jack socket

jackpot *n* **1** (a combination that wins) a top prize on a fruit machine **2** a large prize (e g in a lottery), often made up of several accumulated prizes that have not been previously won

jack socket *n* an electrical socket that is designed to receive a jack plug

jack tar *n* a sailor – infml

jack up *vt, NZ* to settle, fix

Jacobean *adj* of (the age of) James I

Jacobite *n* a supporter of James II or of the Stuarts after 1688 – **Jacobitism** *n*

¹jade *n* **1** a vicious or worn-out old horse **2** *archaic* a flirtatious or disreputable woman

²jade *n* either of 2 typically green hard gemstones

jaded *adj* fatigued (as if) by overwork or dissipation

jaffa *n, often cap* a large type of orange grown esp in Israel

¹jag *vt* **-gg-** **1** to cut or tear unevenly or raggedly **2** to cut indentations into

²jag *n* a sharp projecting part – **jaggy** *adj*

³jag *n* a period of indulgence ⟨*a crying ~*⟩; *esp* a drinking bout – slang

jagged *adj* having a sharply uneven edge or surface – **jaggedly** *adv*, **jaggedness** *n*

jaguar *n* a big cat of tropical America that is typically brownish yellow or buff with black spots

jai alai *n* a court game for 2 or 4 players who use a long curved wicker basket strapped to the wrist to catch and hurl a ball against a wall

¹jail, *Br also* gaol *n* a prison

²jail, *Br also* gaol *vt* to confine (as if) in a jail

jailbird *n* a person who has been (habitually) confined in jail

jailbreak *n* an escape from jail

jailer, jailor *n* **1** a keeper of a jail **2** sby or sthg that restricts another's liberty (as if) by imprisonment

jalopy *n* a dilapidated old vehicle or aircraft – infml

¹jam *vb* **-mm-** *vt* **1a** to press, squeeze, or crush into a close or tight position **b** to cause to become wedged so as to be unworkable ⟨*~ the typewriter keys*⟩ **c** to block passage of or along ⟨*crowds ~ming the streets*⟩ **d** to fill (to excess) ⟨*a book ~med with facts*⟩ **2** CRUSH 1; *also* to bruise by crushing **3** to send out interfering signals or cause reflections so as to make **a** (a radio signal) unintelligible **b** (a radio device) ineffective ~ *vi* **1a** to become blocked or wedged **b** to become unworkable through the jamming of a movable part **2** to crowd or squash tightly together ⟨*they all* ~ med *into the room*⟩ **3** to take part in a jam session – slang

²jam *n* **1** a crowded mass that impedes or blocks ⟨*traffic* ~⟩ **2** the pressure or congestion of a crowd **3** a difficult state of affairs – infml

³jam *n* a preserve made by boiling fruit and sugar to a thick consistency

jamb *n* a straight vertical member or surface forming the side of an opening for a door, window, etc

jamboree *n* **1** a large festive gathering **2** a large gathering of scouts or guides in a camp

jammy *adj, Br* **1** lucky **2** easy *USE* infml

jam on *vt* to apply (brakes) suddenly and forcibly

jam-packed *adj* full to overflowing

jam session *n* an impromptu jazz performance that features group improvisation

jangle *vi* **1** *of the nerves* to be in a state of tense irritation **2** to make a harsh or discordant often ringing noise ~ *vt* **1** to utter or cause to sound in a jangling way **2** to excite (e g nerves) to tense irritation – **jangle** *n*, **jangly** *adj*

janissary *n* **1** *often cap* a soldier of an élite corps of Turkish troops organized in the 14th c and abolished in 1826 **2** a loyal or subservient official or supporter

janitor, *fem* **janitress** *n* **1** a doorkeeper; ¹PORTER **2** *NAm* a caretaker – **janitorial** *adj*

January *n* the 1st month of the Gregorian calendar

¹japan *n* **1** a varnish giving a hard brilliant finish **2** work (e g lacquer ware) finished and decorated in the Japanese manner

²japan *vt* **-nn-** **1** to cover with a coat of japan **2** to give a high gloss to

Japanese *n, pl* **Japanese 1** a native or inhabitant of Japan **2** the language of the Japanese – **Japanese** *adj*

jape *vi or n* (to) jest, joke

japonica *n* a hardy ornamental shrub of the rose family with clusters of scarlet, white, or pink flowers

¹jar *vb* **-rr-** *vi* **1a** to make a harsh or discordant noise **b** to be out of harmony *with* **c** to have a harshly disagreeable effect – + *on* or *upon* **2** to vibrate ~ *vt* to cause to jar, esp by shaking or causing a shock to – **jarringly** *adv*

²jar *n* **1** a jarring noise **2a** a sudden or unexpected shake **b** an unsettling shock (e g to nerves or feelings)

³jar *n* **1a** a usu cylindrical short-necked and wide-mouthed container, made esp of glass **b** the contents of or quantity contained in a jar **2** a glass of an alcoholic drink, esp beer – infml – **jarful** *n*

jargon *n* **1a** confused unintelligible language **b** outlandish or barbarous language **2** the terminology or idiom of a particular activity or group ⟨*scientific* ~⟩ **3** obscure and often pretentious language – **jargonize** *vb*, **jargonistic** *adj*

jasmine *n* **1** any of numerous often climbing shrubs that usu have extremely fragrant flowers; *esp* a high-climbing half-evergreen Asian shrub with fragrant white flowers **2** a light yellow

jasper *n* an opaque quartz which is usu red brown, yellow, or dark green – **jaspery** *adj*

jaundice *n* **1** an abnormal condition marked by yellowish pigmentation of the skin, tissues, and body fluids caused by the deposition of bile pigments **2** a state of prejudice inspired by bitterness, envy, or disillusionment

jaundiced *adj* **1** affected with jaundice **2** mistrustful or prejudiced, esp because of bitterness, envy, or disillusionment

jaunt *vi or n* (to make) a short journey for pleasure

jaunting car *n* a light open 2-wheeled horse-drawn vehicle used formerly in Ireland

jaunty *adj* having or showing airy self-confidence; sprightly – **jauntily** *adv*, **jauntiness** *n*

javelin *n* a light spear thrown as a weapon or in an athletic field event; *also* the sport of throwing the javelin

¹jaw *n* **1a** either of 2 cartilaginous or bony structures that in most vertebrates form a framework above and below the mouth in which the teeth are set **b** any of various organs of invertebrates that perform the function of the vertebrate jaws **2** *pl* **a** the entrance of a narrow pass or channel **b** the 2 parts of a machine, tool, etc between which sthg may be clamped or crushed ⟨*the* ~ s *of a vice*⟩ **c** a position or situation of imminent danger ⟨*stared into the* ~ s *of death*⟩ **3a** continual and esp impudent or offensive talk – infml **b** a friendly chat – infml

²jaw *vi* to talk or gossip for a long time or long-windedly – infml

jawbone *n* the bone of an esp lower jaw

jawbreaker *n* a word which is difficult to pronounce – infml

jay *n* an Old World bird of the crow family with a dull pink body, black, white, and blue wings, and a black-and-white crest

jaywalk *vi* to cross a street carelessly so as to be endangered by traffic – **jaywalker** *n*

jazz *n* **1** music developed esp from ragtime and blues and characterized by syncopated rhythms and individual or group improvisation around a basic theme or melody **2** empty pretentious talk ⟨*spouted a lot of scientific* ~⟩ – infml **3** similar but unspecified things ⟨*planting, weeding, cropping, and all that* ~ – *Evening Argus* (Brighton)⟩ – infml

jazz up *vt* **1** to play (e g a piece of music) in the style of jazz **2** to enliven **3** to make bright, esp in a vivid or garish way *USE* infml

jazzy *adj* **1** having the characteristics of jazz **2** garish, gaudy – infml – **jazzily** *adv*, **jazziness** *n*

jealous *adj* **1a** intolerant of rivalry or unfaithfulness ⟨*the Lord your God is a* ~ *God* – Ex 20:5(AV)⟩ **b** apprehensive of and hostile towards a (supposed) rival **2** resentful, envious *of* **3** vigilant in guarding a possession, right, etc ⟨~ *of his honour*⟩ **4** distrustfully watchful ⟨*kept a* ~ *eye on her husband*⟩ – **jealously** *adv*, **jealousness** *n*, **jealousy** *n*

jeans *n pl in constr, pl* **jeans** casual usu close-fitting trousers, made esp of blue denim

jeep *n* a small rugged general-purpose motor vehicle with 4-wheel drive, used esp by the armed forces

¹jeer *vb* to laugh mockingly or scoff (at) – **jeerer** *n*, **jeeringly** *adv*

²jeer *n* a jeering remark; a taunt

Jehovah *n* GOD **1** ⟨*in the Lord* ~ *is everlasting strength* – Isaiah 26:4 (AV)⟩

Jehovah's Witness *n* a member of a fundamentalist sect practising personal evangelism, rejecting the authority of the secular state, and preaching that the end of the present world is imminent

jejune *adj* **1** lacking nutritive value or substance; *also* barren **2** lacking interest or significance **3** lacking maturity; puerile – **jejunely** *adv*, **jejuneness** *n*

jejunum *n* the section of the small intestine between the duodenum and the ileum – **jejunal** *adj*

jell *vb, chiefly NAm* to gel

¹jelly *n* **1a** a soft fruit-flavoured transparent dessert set with gelatin **b** a savoury food product of similar consistency, made esp from meat stock and gelatin **2** a clear fruit preserve made by boiling sugar and the juice of fruit **3** a substance resembling jelly in consistency

²jelly *vi* to jell ~ *vt* **1** to bring to the consistency of jelly; cause to set **2** to set in a jelly ⟨*jellied beef*⟩

jellyfish *n* **1** a free-swimming marine coelenterate that has a nearly transparent saucer-shaped body and extendable tentacles covered with stinging cells **2** a person lacking firmness of character

jemmy *vt or n, Br* (to force open with) a steel crowbar, used esp by burglars

je ne sais quoi *n* a quality that cannot be adequately described or expressed

jenny *n* **1** a female donkey **2** SPINNING JENNY

jeopardize, -ise *vt* to put in jeopardy

jeopardy *n* **1** exposure to or risk of death, loss, injury, etc; danger **2** liability to conviction faced by a defendant in a criminal trial

jerboa *n* any of several nocturnal Old World desert rodents with long legs adapted for jumping

jeremiad *n* a prolonged lamentation or complaint

¹jerk *vt* **1** to give a quick suddenly arrested push, pull, twist, or jolt to **2** to propel with short abrupt motions **3** to utter in an abrupt or snappy manner ~ *vi* **1** to make a sudden spasmodic motion **2** to move in short abrupt motions – **jerker** *n*

²jerk *n* **1** a single quick motion (e g a pull, twist, or jolt) **2a** an involuntary spasmodic muscular movement due to reflex action **b** *pl* spasmodic movements due to nervous excitement **3** *chiefly NAm* a stupid, foolish, or naive person – *infml*

³jerk *vt* to preserve (e g beef or venison) by cutting into long slices or strips and drying in the sun

jerkin *n* **1** a close-fitting hip-length sleeveless jacket, made esp of leather and worn by men in the 16th and 17th c **2** a man's or woman's sleeveless jacket

jerk off *vb, chiefly NAm* to masturbate – vulg

jerky *adj* **1** marked by irregular or spasmodic movements **2** marked by abrupt or awkward changes – **jerkily** *adv*, **jerkiness** *n*

jeroboam *n* a wine bottle holding 4 to 6 times the usual amount

Jerry *n, chiefly Br* **1** a German; *esp* a German soldier in WW II **2** *sing or pl in constr* the German armed forces in WW II

jerry-build *vt* jerry-built to build (e g houses) cheaply and flimsily – **jerry-builder** *n*, **jerry-built** *adj*

jersey *n* **1** a plain weft-knitted fabric made of wool, nylon, etc and used esp for clothing **2** ²JUMPER 1 **3** *often cap* any of a breed of small short-horned cattle noted for their rich milk

Jerusalem artichoke *n* (an edible sweet-tasting tuber of) a perennial N American sunflower

¹jest *n* **1** an amusing or mocking act or utterance; a joke **2** a frivolous mood or manner ⟨*was just said in* ~⟩

²jest *vi* **1** to speak or act without seriousness **2** to make a witty remark

jester *n* a retainer formerly kept in great households to provide casual amusement and commonly dressed in a brightly coloured costume

Jesuit *n* **1** a member of the Society of Jesus, a Roman Catholic order founded by St Ignatius Loyola in 1534 which is devoted to missionary and educational work **2** one given to intrigue or equivocation – **jesuitism, jesuitry** *n, often cap*, **jesuitize** *vb, often cap*, **jesuitic, jesuitical** *adj, often cap*, **jesuitically** *adv, often cap*

¹jet *n* **1** a hard velvet-black form of coal that is often polished and used for jewellery **2** an intense black

²jet *vb* **-tt-** *vi* to spout forth in a jet or jets ~ *vt* **1** to emit in a jet or jets **2** to direct a jet of liquid or gas at

³jet *n* **1a** a forceful stream of fluid discharged from a narrow opening or a nozzle **b** a nozzle or other narrow opening for emitting a jet of fluid **2** (an aircraft powered by) a jet engine

⁴jet *vi* **-tt-** to travel by jet aircraft

jet-black *adj* of a very dark black

jet engine *n* an engine that produces motion in one direction as a result of the discharge of a jet of fluid in the opposite direction; *specif* an aircraft engine that discharges the hot air and gases produced by the combustion of a fuel to produce propulsion or lift

jet-propelled *adj* moving (as if) by jet propulsion

jet propulsion *n* propulsion of a body produced by the forwardly directed forces resulting from the backward discharge of a jet of fluid; *specif* propulsion of an aeroplane by jet engines

jetsam *n* **1** goods thrown overboard to lighten a ship in distress; *esp* such goods when washed ashore **2** FLOTSAM AND JETSAM

jet set *n sing or pl in constr* an international wealthy elite who frequent fashionable resorts – **jet-set** *adj*, **jetsetter** *n*

¹jettison *n* **1** the act of jettisoning cargo **2** abandonment

²jettison *vt* **1** to throw (e g goods or cargo) overboard to lighten the load of a ship in distress **2** to cast off as superfluous or encumbering; abandon **3** to drop (e g unwanted material) from an aircraft or spacecraft in flight – **jettisonable** *adj*

jetty *n* **1** a structure (e g a pier or breakwater) extending into a sea, lake, or river to influence the current or tide or to protect a harbour **2** a small landing pier

jew *vt* to get the better of financially, esp by hard bargaining – often + *out of*; derog

Jew, fem Jewess *n* **1** a member of a Semitic people existing as a nation in Palestine from the 6th c BC to the 1st c AD, some of whom now live in Israel and others in various countries throughout the world **2** a person whose religion is Judaism **3** sby given to hard financial bargaining – derog – **Jewish** *adj*

jewel *n* **1** an ornament of precious metal often set with stones and worn as an accessory **2** sby or sthg highly esteemed **3** a precious stone **4** a bearing for a pivot (e g in a watch or compass) made of crystal, precious stone, or glass – **jewelled** *adj*

jeweller, NAm chiefly jeweler *n* sby who deals in, makes, or repairs jewellery and often watches, silverware, etc

jewellery, NAm chiefly jewelry *n* jewels, esp as worn for personal adornment

Jew's harp, Jews' harp *n* a small lyre-shaped instrument that is placed between the teeth and sounded by striking a metal tongue with the finger

Jezebel *n, often not cap* a shameless or immoral woman

¹jib *n* a triangular sail set on a stay extending from the top of the foremast to the bow or the bowsprit

²jib *vb* **-bb-** *chiefly NAm* to gybe

³jib *n* the projecting arm of a crane

⁴jib *vi* **-bb-** *esp of a horse* to refuse to proceed further – **jibber** *n* – **jib at** to recoil or baulk at

¹jibe *vb* to gibe

²jibe *vb, chiefly NAm* to gybe

jiffy *n* a moment, instant ⟨*ready in a* ~⟩ – infml

¹jig *n* **1** (a piece of music for) any of several lively springy dances in triple time **2a** any of several fishing lures that jerk up and down in the water **b** a device used to hold a piece of work in position (e g during machining or assembly) and to guide the tools working on it **c** a device in which crushed ore or coal is separated from waste by agitating in water

²jig *vb* **-gg-** *vt* **1** to dance in the rapid lively manner of a jig **2a** to cause to make a rapid jerky movement **b** to separate (a mineral from waste) with a jig **3** to catch (a fish) with a jig **4** to machine by using a jig ~ *vi* **1a** to dance a jig **b** to move with rapid jerky motions **2** to fish with a jig **3** to work with or operate a jig

jigger *n* **1** (a glass container holding) a variable measure of spirits used esp in mixing drinks **2** *chiefly NAm* sthg, esp a gadget or small piece of apparatus, which one is (temporarily) unable to designate accurately – *infml*

jiggered *adj* **1** blowed, damned ⟨*well I'll be* ~⟩ – *infml* **2** *N Eng* tired out; exhausted

jiggery-pokery *n*, *Br* dishonest underhand dealings or scheming – *infml*

jiggle *vb* jiggling to (cause to) move with quick short jerks – *infml* – **jiggle** *n*

jigsaw *n* **1** a power-driven fretsaw **2 jigsaw, jigsaw puzzle** a puzzle consisting of small irregularly cut pieces, esp of wood or card, that are fitted together to form a picture for amusement; *broadly* sthg composed of many disparate parts or elements

jihad *n* **1** a holy war waged on behalf of Islam as a religious duty **2** a crusade for a principle or belief

jilt *vt* to cast off (e g one's lover) capriciously or unfeelingly

jim crow *n*, *often cap J&C, NAm* **1** racial discrimination, esp against black Americans ⟨~ *laws*⟩ **2** a Negro – *derog* ⟨~ *schools*⟩

jimjams *n pl* **1** DELIRIUM TREMENS **2** JITTERS 1 *USE* infml; + *the*

¹**jingle** *vb* jingling to (cause to) make a light clinking or tinkling sound

²**jingle** *n* **1** a light, esp metallic clinking or tinkling sound **2** a short catchy song or rhyme characterized by repetition of phrases and used esp in advertising – **jingly** *adj*

jingo *interj* – used as a mild oath in *by jingo*

jingoism *n* belligerent patriotism; chauvinism – **jingoist** *n*, **jingoistic** *adj*, **jingoistically** *adv*

jink *n* **1** a quick evasive turn **2** *pl* pranks, frolics – esp in *high jinks*

jinn, djinn *n*, *pl* **jinns, jinn 1** any of a class of spirits that according to Muslim demonology inhabit the earth, assume various forms, and exercise supernatural power **2** a spirit, often in human form, which serves whoever summons it

jinx *n* sby or sthg (e g a force or curse) which brings bad luck – *infml* – **jinx** *vt*

jitney *n*, *NAm* NICKEL 2 – *slang*

jitter *vi* **1** to be nervous or act in a nervous way **2** to make continuous fast repetitive movements

jitterbug *n* (one who dances) a jazz variation of the two-step in which couples swing, balance, and twirl

jiu-jitsu *n* ju-jitsu

¹**jive** *n* **1** (dancing or *the* energetic dance performed to) swing music **2** *NAm* **a** glib or deceptive talk **b** a type of jargon used esp by jazz musicians

²**jive** *vi* **1** to dance to or play jive **2** *NAm* to kid ~ *vt,NAm* to cajole; TEASE 2b

¹**job** *n* **1a** a piece of work; *esp* a small piece of work undertaken at a stated rate **b** sthg produced by work **2a**(1) a task (2) sthg requiring unusual exertion ⟨*it was a real* ~ *to talk over that noise*⟩ **b** a specific duty, role, or function **c** a regular paid position or occupation **d** *chiefly Br* a state of affairs – + *bad* or *good* ⟨*make the best of a bad* ~⟩ **3** an object of a usu specified type ⟨*bought myself a brand-new V-8 sports* ~⟩ **4a** a plan or scheme designed or carried out for private advantage ⟨*suspected the whole incident was a put-up* ~⟩ **b** a crime; *specif* a robbery *USE* (*3&4*) *infml* – **jobless** *adj* – **on the job 1** engaged in one's occupation; AT WORK 1 ⟨*this burglar is known to wear black woollen gloves when he is* on the job⟩ **2** in the act of copulation – *vulg*

²**job** *vb* -**bb**- *vi* **1** to do odd or occasional pieces of work,

usu at a stated rate ⟨*a* ~ bing *gardener*⟩ **2** to carry on public business for private gain **3a** to carry on the business of a middleman or wholesaler **b** to work as a stockjobber ~ *vt* **1** to buy and sell (e g shares) for profit **2** to hire or let for a definite job or period of service **3** to get, deal with, or effect by jobbery **4** to subcontract – usu + *out*

Job *n* (a narrative and poetic book of the Old Testament which tells of) a Jewish patriarch who endured afflictions with fortitude and faith – usu in *the patience of Job*

jobber *n* a stockjobber

jobbery *n* corruption in public office

job lot *n* a miscellaneous collection of goods sold as a lot; *broadly* any miscellaneous collection of articles

Job's comforter *n* sby whose attempts to encourage or comfort have the opposite effect

¹**jockey** *n* **1** sby who rides a horse, esp as a professional in races **2** *NAm* sby who operates a specified vehicle, device, or object ⟨*a truck* ~⟩

²**jockey** *vt* **1** to ride (a horse) as a jockey **2** to manoeuvre or manipulate by adroit or devious means ⟨~ ed *me into handing over the money*⟩ **3** *chiefly NAm* to drive or operate; *also* to manoeuvre ~ *vi* **1** to act as a jockey **2** to manoeuvre for advantage ⟨~ ed *for position*⟩

jockstrap *n* a support for the genitals worn by men taking part in strenuous esp sporting activities

jocose *adj* **1** given to joking **2** jocular *USE* fml or poetic – **jocosely** *adv*, **jocoseness** *n*, **jocosity** *n*

jocular *adj* **1** habitually jolly **2** characterized by joking – **jocularly** *adv*, **jocularity** *n*

jocund *adj* marked by or suggestive of high spirits; merry – fml or poetic – **jocundly** *adv*, **jocundity** *n*

jodhpurs *n pl in constr, pl* **jodhpurs** riding trousers cut full at the hips and close-fitting from knee to ankle

¹**jog** *vb* -**gg**- *vt* **1** to give a slight shake or push to; nudge **2** to rouse (the memory) ~ *vi* **1** to move up and down or about with a short heavy motion **2a** to run or ride at a slow trot **b** to go at a slow or monotonous pace

²**jog** *n* **1** a slight shake **2a** a jogging movement or pace **b** a slow trot

joggle *vb* to (cause to) move or shake slightly – *infml* – **joggle** *n*

jog trot *n* **1** a slow regular trot (e g of a horse) **2** a routine or monotonous progression

john *n* **1** *NAm* TOILET **2** – *infml* **2** *chiefly NAm* a prostitute's client – *slang*

John *n* **1** the 4th Gospel in the New Testament **2** any of 3 short didactic letters addressed to early Christians and included in the New Testament

John Barleycorn *n* alcoholic liquor personified

John Bull *n* **1** the English nation personified **2a** a typical Englishman, esp regarded as truculently insular – **John Bullish** *adj*, **John Bullishness** *n*, **John Bullism** *n*

johnny *n*, *often cap* a fellow, guy – *infml*

joie de vivre *n* keen enjoyment of life

¹**join** *vt* **1a** to put or bring together so as to form a unit **b** to connect (e g points) by a line **c** to adjoin; MEET 1c ⟨*where the river* ~ s *the sea*⟩ **2** to put or bring into close association or relationship ⟨~ ed *in marriage*⟩ **3a** to come into the company of ⟨~ ed *us for lunch*⟩ **b** to become a member of ⟨~ ed *the sports club*⟩ ~ *vi* **1** to come together so as to be connected **2** to come into close association: e g **a** to form an alliance **b** to become a member of a group **c** to take part in a collective activity – usu + *in* – **joinable** *adj* – **join battle** to engage in battle or conflict

²**join** *n* JOINT 2a

joiner *n* **1** one who constructs or repairs wooden articles, esp furniture or fittings **2** a gregarious person who joins many organizations – *infml*

joinery n **1** the craft or trade of a joiner **2** woodwork done or made by a joiner

¹**joint** n **1a**(1) a point of contact between 2 or more bones of an animal skeleton together with the parts that surround and support it (2) NODE 3a **b** a part or space included between 2 articulations, knots, or nodes **c** a large piece of meat (for roasting) cut from a carcass **2a** a place where 2 things or parts are joined **b** an area at which 2 ends, surfaces, or edges are attached **c** a crack in rock not accompanied by dislocation **d** the hinge of the binding of a book along the back edge of each cover **3** a shabby or disreputable place of entertainment – infml **4** a marijuana cigarette – slang – **jointed** adj, **jointedly** adv, **jointedness** n – **out of joint 1** of a bone dislocated **2** disordered, disorganized

²**joint** adj **1** united, combined ⟨a ~ effort⟩ **2** common to 2 or more: e g **a** involving the united activity of 2 or more **b** held by, shared by, or affecting 2 or more **3** sharing with another ⟨~ heirs⟩ **4** being a function of or involving 2 or more random variables ⟨a ~ probability density function⟩

³**joint** vt **1** to fit together **2** to provide with a joint **3** to prepare (e g a board) for joining by planing the edge **4** to separate the joints of (e g meat)

jointly adv together

joint-stock company n a company consisting of individuals who own shares representing a joint stock of capital

join up vi to enlist in an armed service

joist n any of the parallel small timbers or metal beams that support a floor or ceiling

¹**joke** n **1a** sthg said or done to provoke laughter; esp a brief oral narrative with a humorous twist **b** the humorous or ridiculous element in sthg **c** an instance of joking or making fun ⟨can't take a ~⟩ **d** a laughingstock **2** sthg of little difficulty or seriousness; a trifling matter ⟨that exam was a ~⟩ – often in neg constructions ⟨no ~ to be lost in the desert⟩ – **jokey, joky** adj

²**joke** vi to make jokes – **jokingly** adv

joker n **1** sby given to joking **2** a playing card added to a pack usu as a wild card **3a** sthg (e g an expedient or stratagem) held in reserve to gain an end or escape from a predicament **b** chiefly NAm an unsuspected or misunderstood clause in a document that greatly alters it **c** chiefly NAm a not readily apparent factor or condition that nullifies a seeming advantage **4** a fellow; esp an insignificant, obnoxious, or incompetent person – infml

jollification n (an instance of) merrymaking

¹**jolly** adj **1a** full of high spirits **b** given to conviviality **c** expressing, suggesting, or inspiring gaiety **2** extremely pleasant or agreeable – infml **3** Br slightly drunk – euph – **jolliness** n, **jollity** n

²**jolly** adv very – infml ⟨~ cold for the time of year⟩

³**jolly** vt **1** to (try to) put in good humour, esp to gain an end – usu + along **2** to make cheerful or bright – + up; infml

jolly boat n a ship's boat of medium size used for general work

Jolly Roger n a pirate's black flag with a white skull and crossbones

¹**jolt** vt **1** to cause to move with a sudden jerky motion **2** to give a (sudden) knock or blow to **3** to abruptly disturb the composure of ⟨crudely ~ed out of that mood – Virginia Woolf⟩ ~ vi to move with a jerky motion

²**jolt** n an unsettling blow, movement, or shock – **jolty** adj

Jonah n (a narrative book of the Old Testament telling of) an Israelite prophet who resisted a divine call to preach repentance to the people of Nineveh, was swallowed and vomited by a great fish, and eventually carried out his mission

jonquil n a Mediterranean plant of the daffodil family that is widely cultivated for its yellow or white fragrant flowers

joss stick n a slender stick of incense (e g for burning in front of a joss)

jostle vb **jostling 1a** to come in contact or into collision (with) **b** to make (one's) way) by pushing **2** to vie (with) in gaining an objective – **jostle** n

¹**jot** n the least bit ⟨not a ~ of evidence⟩

²**jot** vt **-tt-** to write briefly or hurriedly – **jotting** n

jotter n a small book or pad for notes or memoranda

joule n the SI unit of work or energy equal to the work done when a force of 1N moves its point of application through a distance of 1m

journal n **1** a record of current transactions: e g **a** an account of day-to-day events **b** a private record of experiences, ideas, or reflections kept regularly **c** a record of the transactions of a public body, learned society, etc **d** LOG 3, 4 **2a** a daily newspaper **b** a periodical dealing esp with matters of current interest or specialist subjects **3** the part of a rotating shaft, axle, roll, or spindle that turns in a bearing

journalese n a style of writing supposed to be characteristic of newspapers; specif loose or cliché-ridden writing

journalism n **1** (the profession of) the collecting and editing of material of current interest for presentation through news media **2a** writing designed for publication in a newspaper or popular magazine **b** writing characterized by a direct presentation of facts or description of events without an attempt at interpretation

journalist n a person engaged in journalism, esp one working for a news medium – **journalistic** adj

journey n **1** travel from one place to another, esp by land and over a considerable distance **2** the distance involved in a journey, or the time taken to cover it – **journey** vi, **journeyer** n

journeyman n **1** a worker who has learned a trade and is employed by another person, usu by the day **2** an experienced reliable worker or performer, as distinguished from one who is outstanding

¹**joust** vi to fight in a joust or tournament – **jouster** n

²**joust** n a combat on horseback between 2 knights or men-at-arms with lances

Jove n Jupiter, the chief Roman god – often used interjectionally to express surprise or agreement ⟨by ~!⟩

jovial adj markedly good-humoured – **jovially** adv, **joviality** n

¹**jowl** n **1** the jaw; esp a mandible **2** CHEEK 1

²**jowl** n usu slack flesh associated with the lower jaw or throat – often pl with sing. meaning

joy n **1** (the expression of) an emotion or state of great happiness, pleasure, or delight **2** a source or cause of delight **3** Br success, satisfaction ⟨had no ~ at the first shop he went into⟩ – infml – **joyless** adj, **joylessly** adv, **joylessness** n

joyful adj filled with, causing, or expressing joy – **joyfully** adv, **joyfulness** n

joyous adj joyful – **joyously** adv, **joyousness** n

joyride n **1** a ride in a motor car taken for pleasure and often without the owner's consent **2** a short pleasure flight in an aircraft – **joyrider** n, **joyriding** n

joystick n **1** a hand-operated lever that controls an aeroplane's elevators and ailerons **2** a control for any of various devices that resembles an aeroplane's joystick, esp in being capable of motion in 2 or more directions

jubilant adj filled with or expressing great joy – **jubilance** n, **jubilantly** adv

jubilation *n* being jubilant; rejoicing

jubilee *n* 1 *often cap* a year of emancipation and restoration provided by ancient Hebrew law to be kept every 50 years 2 (a celebration of) a special anniversary (e g of a sovereign's accession) ⟨*remembered Queen Victoria's diamond ~*⟩ 3 a period of time, proclaimed by the Pope ordinarily every 25 years, during which a special plenary indulgence is granted to Catholics who perform certain works of repentance and piety 4 a season or occasion of celebration

Judaism *n* 1 a religion developed among the ancient Hebrews and characterized by belief in 1 transcendent God and by a religious life in accordance with Scriptures and rabbinic traditions 2 (conformity with) the cultural, social, and religious beliefs and practices of the Jews – **Judaize** *vt*, **Judaizer** *n*, **Judaic** *adj*

Judas *n* 1 one who betrays, esp under the guise of friendship 2 **judas, judas hole** a peephole in a door

judder *vi, chiefly Br* to vibrate jerkily – **judder** *n*

¹**judge** *vt* 1 to form an opinion about through careful weighing of evidence 2 to sit in judgment on 3 to determine or pronounce after deliberation 4 to decide the result of (a competition or contest) 5 to form an estimate or evaluation of 6 to hold as an opinion ~ *vi* 1 to form a judgment or opinion 2 to act as a judge ⟨*to ~ between us*⟩

²**judge** *n* sby who judges: e g **a** a public official authorized to decide questions brought before a court **b** *often cap* a Hebrew tribal leader in the period after the death of Joshua **c** sby appointed to decide in a competition or (sporting) contest (e g diving) **d** sby who gives an (authoritative) opinion ⟨*a good ~ of character*⟩ ⟨*a good ~ of modern art*⟩ – **judgeship** *n*

judgment, judgement *n* 1 (a formal utterance of) an authoritative opinion 2a a formal decision by a court **b** an obligation (e g a debt) created by a court decision 3a **Judgment, Last Judgment** *the* final judging of mankind by God **b** a calamity held to be sent by God as a punishment 4 (the process of forming) an opinion or evaluation based on discerning and comparing 5 the capacity for judging – **judgmental** *adj*

Judgment Day *n* the day of God's judgment of mankind at the end of the world, according to various theologies

judicature *n* 1 the administration of justice 2 a court of justice 3 JUDICIARY 1 4 (the duration of) a judge's office

judicial *adj* 1 of a judgment, judging, justice, or the judiciary 2 ordered by a court ⟨*~ separation*⟩ 3 of, characterized by, or expressing judgment; CRITICAL 1c – **judicially** *adv*

judiciary *n* 1a a system of courts of law **b** the judges of these courts 2 a judicial branch of the US government – **judiciary** *adj*

judicious *adj* having, exercising, or characterized by sound judgment – **judiciously** *adv*, **judiciousness** *n*

judo *n* a martial art developed from ju-jitsu and emphasizing the use of quick movement and leverage to throw an opponent – **judoist** *n*

¹**jug** *n* 1a(1) *chiefly Br* a vessel for holding and pouring liquids that typically has a handle and a lip or spout (2) *chiefly NAm* a large deep earthenware or glass vessel for liquids that usu has a handle and a narrow mouth often fitted with a cork; FLAGON 1b **b** the contents of or quantity contained in a jug; a jugful 2 prison – infml – **jugful** *n*

²**jug** *vt* **-gg-** 1 to stew (e g a hare) in an earthenware vessel 2 to imprison – infml

juggernaut *n* 1 an inexorable force or object that crushes anything in its path 2 *chiefly Br* a very large, usu

articulated, lorry; *esp* one considered too large for safety

¹**juggle** *vb* **juggling** *vi* 1 to perform the tricks of a juggler 2 to engage in manipulation, esp in order to achieve a desired end ~ *vt* 1 to manipulate, esp in order to achieve a desired end ⟨*~ an account to hide a loss*⟩ 2 to hold or balance precariously 3 to toss in the manner of a juggler

²**juggle** *n* an act or instance of juggling

juggler *n* one skilled in keeping several objects in motion in the air at the same time by alternately tossing and catching them – **jugglery** *n*

jugular vein, jugular *n* any of several veins of each side of the neck that return blood from the head

juice *n* 1 the extractable fluid contents of cells or tissues 2a *pl* the natural fluids of an animal body **b** the liquid or moisture contained in sthg 3 the inherent quality of sthg; *esp* the basic force or strength of sthg 4 a medium (e g electricity or petrol) that supplies power – infml – **juiceless** *adj*

juicy *adj* 1 succulent 2 financially rewarding or profitable – infml 3 rich in interest ⟨*a ~ problem*⟩; *esp* interesting because of titillating content ⟨*~ scandal*⟩ – infml – **juicily** *adv*, **juiciness** *n*

ju-jitsu, jiu-jitsu *n* a martial art employing holds, throws, and paralysing blows to subdue or disable an opponent

juju *n* (a magic attributed to) a fetish or charm of W African peoples

jujube *n* 1 (the edible fruit of) any of several trees of the buckthorn family 2 a fruit-flavoured gum or lozenge

jukebox *n* a coin-operated record player that automatically plays records chosen from a restricted list

julep *n, chiefly NAm* a drink consisting of a spirit and sugar poured over crushed ice and garnished with mint

Julian calendar *n* a calendar introduced in Rome in 46 BC establishing the 12-month year of 365 days with an extra day every fourth year

July *n* the 7th month of the Gregorian calendar

¹**jumble** *vt* **jumbling** to mix *up* in a confused or disordered mass

²**jumble** *n* 1 a mass of things mingled together without order or plan 2 *Br* articles for a jumble sale

jumble sale *n, Br* a sale of donated secondhand articles, usu conducted to raise money for some charitable purpose

jumbo *n, pl* **jumbos** a very large specimen of its kind – **jumbo** *adj*

¹**jump** *vi* 1a to spring into the air, esp using the muscular power of feet and legs **b** to move suddenly or involuntarily from shock, surprise, etc **c** to move quickly or energetically (as if) with a jump; *also* to act with alacrity 2 to pass rapidly, suddenly, or abruptly (as if) over some intervening thing: e g **a** to skip ⟨*~ed to the end of the book*⟩ **b** to rise suddenly in rank or status ⟨*~ed from captain to colonel*⟩ **c** to make a mental leap **d** to come to or arrive at a position or judgment without due deliberation ⟨*~ to conclusions*⟩ **e** to undergo a sudden sharp increase ⟨*prices ~ed sky-high*⟩ 3 to move haphazardly or aimlessly 4 to make a sudden verbal or physical attack – usu + *on* or *upon* 5 *NAm* to bustle with activity ⟨*by midnight the place was really ~ing*⟩ ~ *vt* 1a to (cause to) leap over ⟨*~ a hurdle*⟩ ⟨*~ed his horse over the fence*⟩ **b** to pass over, esp to a point beyond; skip, bypass **c** to act, move, or begin before (e g a signal) 2a to escape or run away from **b** to leave hastily or in violation of an undertaking ⟨*~ed bail*⟩ **c** to depart from (a normal course) ⟨*the train ~ed the rails*⟩ 3a to make a sudden or surprise attack on **b** to occupy without proper legal rights ⟨*~ a mining claim*⟩ 4 *chiefly NAm* to leap aboard, esp so as to travel illegally

– **jump at** to accept eagerly ⟨jump at *the chance*⟩ – **jump the gun 1** to start in a race before the starting signal **2** to act, move, or begin sthg before the proper time – **jump the queue 1** to move in front of others in a queue **2** to obtain an unfair advantage over others who have been waiting longer – **jump to it 1** to make an enthusiastic start **2** to hurry

²**jump** *n* **1a**(1) an act of jumping; a leap (2) a sports contest (e g the long jump) including a jump (3) a space, height, or distance cleared by a jump (4) an obstacle to be jumped over (e g in a horse race) **b** a sudden involuntary movement; a start **2a** a sharp sudden increase (e g in amount, price, or value) **b** a sudden change or transition; *esp* one that leaves a break in continuity **c** any of a series of moves from one place or position to another; a move **3** *pl the* fidgets – infml

jumped-up *adj* recently risen in wealth, rank, or status – derog

¹**jumper** *n* **1** a short wire used to close a break in or cut out part of a circuit **2** a jumping animal; *esp* a horse trained to jump obstacles

²**jumper** *n* **1** *Br* a knitted or crocheted garment worn on the upper body **2** *NAm* PINAFORE 2

jumpy *adj* **1** having jumps or sudden variations **2** nervous, jittery – **jumpiness** *n*

junction *n* **1** joining or being joined **2a** a place of meeting **b** an intersection of roads, esp where 1 terminates **c** a point of contact or interface between dissimilar metals or semiconductor regions (e g in a transistor) **3** sthg that joins – **junctional** *adj*

juncture *n* **1** an instance or place of joining; a connection or joining part **2** a point of time (made critical by a concurrence of circumstances)

June *n* the 6th month of the Gregorian calendar

jungle *n* **1** an area overgrown with thickets or masses of (tropical) trees and other vegetation **2a** a confused, disordered, or complex mass ⟨*the ~ of tax laws*⟩ **b** a place of ruthless struggle for survival ⟨*the blackboard ~*⟩ – **jungly** *adj*

¹**junior** *n* **1** a person who is younger than another ⟨*she is my ~*⟩ **2a** a person holding a lower or subordinate position in a hierarchy of ranks **b** a member of a younger form in a school **3** *NAm* a student in the next-to-the-last year before graduating **4** *NAm* a male child; a son – infml

²**junior** *adj* **1** younger – used, esp in the USA, to distinguish a son with the same name as his father **2** lower in standing or rank **3** for children aged from 7 to 11 ⟨*a ~ school*⟩

juniper *n* any of several evergreen shrubs or trees of the cypress family

¹**junk** *n* **1** pieces of old cable or rope used for mats, swabs, or oakum **2a** secondhand or discarded articles or material; *broadly* RUBBISH 1 **b** sthg of little value or inferior quality **3** narcotics; *esp* heroin – slang – **junky** *adj*

²**junk** *vt* to get rid of as worthless – infml

³**junk** *n* a sailing ship used in the Far East with a high poop and overhanging stem, little or no keel, and lugsails often stiffened with horizontal battens

¹**junket** *n* **1** a dessert of sweetened flavoured milk curdled with rennet **2** a festive social affair (at public or a firm's expense) – chiefly infml

²**junket** *vi* to feast, banquet – infml – **junketer** *n*, **junketeer** *n*

junkie, junky *n* a drug peddler or addict – infml

Junoesque *adj, of a woman* having stately beauty

junta *n sing or pl in constr* **1** a political council or

committee; *esp* a group controlling a government after a revolution **2** a junto

Jupiter *n* the largest of the planets and 5th in order from the sun

juridical *also* **juridic** *adj* **1** JUDICIAL 1 **2** of or being jurisprudence; legal ⟨*~ terms*⟩ – **juridically** *adv*

jurisdiction *n* **1** the power, right, or authority to apply the law **2** the authority of a sovereign power **3** the limits within which authority may be exercised – **jurisdictional** *adj*, **jurisdictionally** *adv*

jurisprudence *n* (the science or philosophy of) a body or branch of law ⟨*criminal ~*⟩ – **jurisprudential** *adj*

jurist *n* **1** sby with a thorough knowledge of law **2** *NAm* a lawyer; *specif* a judge

juror *n* **1** a member of a jury **2** one who takes an oath

¹**jury** *n* **1** a body of usu 12 people who hear evidence in court and are sworn to give an honest verdict, esp of guilty or not guilty, based on this evidence **2** a committee for judging a contest or exhibition

²**jury** *adj* improvised for temporary use (in an emergency) ⟨*a ~ rig for a sailing boat*⟩

juryman, *fem* **jurywoman** *n* JUROR 1

¹**just** *adj* conforming (rigidly) to fact or reason ⟨*a ~ but not a generous decision*⟩ **b** conforming to a standard of correctness; proper **2a**(1) acting or being in conformity with what is morally upright or equitable (2) being what is merited; deserved **b** legally correct – **justly** *adv*, **justness** *n*

²**just** *adv* **1a** exactly, precisely – not following *not* ⟨*~ right*⟩ ⟨*~ the thing for your cold*⟩ **b** at this moment and not sooner ⟨*he's only ~ arrived*⟩ – sometimes used with the past tense ⟨*the bell ~ rang*⟩ **c** only at this moment and not later ⟨*I'm ~ coming*⟩ **2a** by a very small margin; immediately, barely ⟨*~ too late*⟩ ⟨*only ~ possible*⟩ **b** only, simply ⟨*~ a short note*⟩ **3** quite ⟨*not ~ yet*⟩ ⟨*~ as well I asked*⟩ **4** perhaps, possibly **5** very, completely ⟨*~ wonderful*⟩ **6** indeed – sometimes expressing irony ⟨*didn't he ~!*⟩ *USE* (5, 6) infml – **just about 1** almost **2** not more than ⟨*just about room to cook*⟩ – **just in case** as a precaution – **just now 1** at this moment **2** a moment ago – **just on** almost exactly – used with reference to numbers and quantities – **just so 1** tidily arranged **2** – used to express agreement – **just the same** nevertheless; EVEN SO

justice *n* **1a** the maintenance or administration of what is just **b** the administration of law ⟨*court of ~*⟩ **c** JUSTICE OF THE PEACE **2a** the quality of being just, impartial, or fair **b** (conformity to) the principle or ideal of just dealing or right action **3** conformity to truth, fact, or reason **4** *Br* – used as a title for a judge ⟨*Mr Justice Smith*⟩

justice of the peace *n* a lay magistrate empowered chiefly to administer summary justice in minor cases and to commit for trial

justify *vt* **1** to prove or show to be just, right, or reasonable **2** to extend freedom from the consequences of sin to, by Christ's righteousness or by grace **3** to space out (e g a line of printed text) so as to be flush with a margin – **justifier** *n*, **justifiable** *adj*, **justifiably** *adv*, **justificatory** *adj*, **justification** *n*

jut *vi* **-tt-** to extend out, up, or forwards; project, protrude – often + *out*

jute *n* the glossy fibre of either of 2 E Indian plants of the linden family used chiefly for sacking, burlap, and twine

Jute *n* a member of a Germanic people that invaded England and esp Kent along with the Angles and Saxons in the 5th c AD – **Jutish** *adj*

¹**juvenile** *adj* **1** physiologically immature or undeveloped

2 (characteristic) of or suitable for children or young people – **juvenilely** *adv*, **juvenility** *n*

²**juvenile** *n* **1a** a young person **b** a book for young people **2** a young individual resembling an adult of its kind except in size and reproductive activity **3** an actor who plays youthful parts

juxtapose *vt* to place side by side – **juxtaposition** *n*, **juxtapositional** *adj*

K

---

k *n*, *pl* **k's**, **ks**, *often cap* **1** (a graphic representation of or device for reproducing) the 11th letter of the English alphabet **2** a unit of computer storage capacity equal to 1024 bytes ⟨*a memory of 64K*⟩

Kaffir, Kafir *n* **1** a member of a group of southern African Bantu-speaking peoples **2** *often not cap, chiefly SAfr* a S African Black – *derog*

kaftan *n* a caftan

kaiser *n* an emperor of Germany during the period 1871 to 1918 – **kaiserdom** *n*

kale, kail *n* **1** a hardy cabbage with curled often finely cut leaves that do not form a dense head **2** *Scot* a broth of cabbage, esp kale

kaleidoscope *n* **1** a tubular instrument containing loose chips of coloured glass between mirrors so placed that an endless variety of symmetrical patterns is produced as the instrument is rotated and the chips of glass change position **2** sthg that is continually changing; *esp* a variegated changing pattern, scene, or succession of events – **kaleidoscopic, kaleidoscopical** *adj*, **kaleidoscopically** *adv*

kalends *n pl but sing or pl in constr* calends

kampong, campong *n* a hamlet or village in a Malay-speaking country

kangaroo *n*, *pl* **kangaroos** any of various plant-eating marsupial mammals of Australia, New Guinea, and adjacent islands that hop on their long powerful hind legs

kangaroo court *n* an unauthorized or irresponsible court in which justice is perverted

kaolin *n* a fine usu white clay formed from decomposed feldspar and used esp in ceramics

kapok *n* a mass of silky fibres that surround the seeds of a tropical tree and are used esp as a soft (insulating) filling for mattresses, cushions, sleeping bags, etc

kappa *n* the 10th letter of the Greek alphabet

kaput *adj* no longer able to function; broken, exhausted – *infml*

karakul, caracul *n* **1** *often cap* any of a breed of hardy fat-tailed sheep from Bukhara **2** the tightly curled glossy black coat of karakul lambs valued as fur

karat *n*, *NAm* CARAT 2

karate *n* a martial art in which opponents use their hands and feet to deliver crippling blows

karma *n*, *often cap* the force generated by a person's actions, held in Hinduism and Buddhism to determine his/her destiny in his/her next existence – **karmic** *adj*, *often cap*

katydid *n* any of several large green N American long-horned grasshoppers

kayak *n* an Eskimo canoe made of a frame covered with skins; *also* a similar canvas-covered or fibreglass canoe

kazoo *n*, *pl* **kazoos** a musical instrument consisting of a tube into which one sings or hums to vibrate a membrane covering a side hole

kebab *n* cubes of (marinated) meat cooked with onions, mushrooms, etc, usu on a skewer

kedgeree *n* a dish containing rice, flaked fish, and chopped hard-boiled eggs

¹**keel** *n* a flat-bottomed ship; *esp* a barge used on the river Tyne to carry coal

²**keel** *n* **1a** a timber or plate which extends along the centre of the bottom of a vessel and usu projects somewhat from the bottom **b** the main load-bearing member (e g in an airship) **2** a projection (e g the breastbone of a bird) suggesting a keel **3** a ship – *poetic* – **keeled** *adj*, **keelless** *adj*

³**keel** *vt* to cause to turn over ~ *vi* **1** to turn over **2** to fall over (as if) in a faint

keelhaul *vt* **1** to drag (a person) under the keel of a ship as punishment **2** to rebuke severely

¹**keen** *adj* **1a** having or being a fine edge or point; sharp **b** affecting one as if by cutting or piercing ⟨*a ~ wind*⟩ **2a** enthusiastic, eager ⟨*a ~ swimmer*⟩ **b** of emotion or feeling intense ⟨*took a ~ interest*⟩ **3a** intellectually alert; *also* shrewdly astute ⟨*a ~ awareness of the problem*⟩ **b** sharply contested; competitive; *specif, Br,* of prices low in order to be competitive **c** extremely sensitive in perception ⟨*~ eyesight*⟩ **4** *NAm* wonderful, excellent – **keenly** *adv*, **keenness** *n* – **keen on** interested in; attracted to

²**keen** *vi or n* (to utter) a loud wailing lamentation for the dead, typically at Irish funerals – **keener** *n*

¹**keep** *vb* **kept** *vt* **1a** to take notice of by appropriate conduct; fulfil (the obligations of) ⟨*~ a promise*⟩ ⟨*~ the law*⟩ **b** to act fittingly in relation to (a feast or ceremony) ⟨*~ the Sabbath*⟩ **c** to conform to in habits or conduct ⟨*~ late hours*⟩ **d** to stay in accord with (a beat) ⟨*~ time*⟩ ⟨*~ step*⟩ **2a** to watch over and defend; guard ⟨*~ us from harm*⟩ ⟨*~s goal for the local team*⟩ **b(1)** to take care of, esp as an owner; tend ⟨*~s a dog*⟩ **(2)** to support ⟨*earns enough to ~ himself*⟩ **(3)** to maintain in a specified condition – often in combination ⟨*a well-kept garden*⟩ **c** to continue to maintain ⟨*~ order*⟩ ⟨*~ a lookout*⟩ **d(1)** to cause to remain in a specified place, situation, or condition ⟨*~ him waiting*⟩ ⟨*kept him up all night*⟩ ⟨*a net to ~ the birds out*⟩ **(2)** to store habitually for use ⟨*where do you ~ the butter?*⟩ **(3)** to preserve (food) in an unspoilt condition ⟨*how long can you ~ fish in a freezer?*⟩ **e** to have or maintain in one's service, employment, or possession or at one's disposal ⟨*~ a car*⟩ ⟨*~ a mistress*⟩ – often + on ⟨*~ the cook on for another month*⟩ ⟨*~ the flat on over the summer*⟩ **f** to record by entries in a book ⟨*~ accounts*⟩ ⟨*~ a diary*⟩ **g** to have customarily in stock for sale **3a** to delay, detain ⟨*what kept you?*⟩ ⟨*~ children in after school*⟩ **b** to hold back; restrain ⟨*~ him from going*⟩ ⟨*kept him back with difficulty*⟩ **c** to save, reserve ⟨*~ some for later*⟩ **d** to refrain from revealing or releasing ⟨*~ a secret*⟩ ⟨*kept the news back*⟩ **4** to retain possession or control of ⟨*kept the money he found*⟩ ⟨*~ a copy of the letter*⟩ ⟨*~ your temper*⟩ **5a** to continue to follow ⟨*~ the path*⟩ **b** to stay or remain on or in, often against opposition ⟨*kept his ground*⟩ ⟨*~ your seat*⟩ **6** to manage, run ⟨*~s a shop*⟩ ~ *vi* **1a** to maintain a course ⟨*~ right*⟩ **b** to continue, usu without interruption ⟨*~ talking*⟩ ⟨*~ on smiling*⟩ **c** to persist in a practice ⟨*kept bothering them*⟩ ⟨*kept on smoking in spite of warnings*⟩ **2a** to stay or remain in a specified desired place, situation, or condition ⟨*~ warm*⟩ ⟨*~ out of the way*⟩ ⟨*~ off the grass*⟩ **b** to remain in good condition ⟨*meat will ~ in the freezer*⟩ **c** to be or remain with regard to health ⟨*how are you ~ing?*⟩ ⟨*she ~s well*⟩ **d** to call for no immediate action ⟨*the matter will ~ till morning*⟩ **3** to act as wicketkeeper or goalkeeper – *infml* – **keep an/one's eye on** to watch over – **keep at** to persist in doing or concern-

ing oneself with – **keep cave** *Br* to act as a lookout at school – **keep company** to provide with companionship ⟨*won't anyone stay and keep me* company?⟩ – **keep from** to refrain from; help ⟨*can't keep from laughing*⟩ – **keep one's eye in** *chiefly Br* to keep in practice; *specif* to retain ability to judge the speed and direction of a moving ball – **keep one's eyes open/peeled,** *Br* **keep one's eyes skinned** to be on the alert; be watchful – **keep one's feet** to avoid overbalancing – **keep one's fingers crossed** to hope for the best – **keep one's hand in** to remain in practice – **keep one's head above water** to remain solvent; *broadly* to stay out of difficulty – **keep one's nose clean** to keep one's record untarnished by playing safe – **keep one's shirt on,** *Br* **keep one's hair on** to remain calm; keep one's temper – *infml* – **keep the ball rolling** to play one's part (e g in conversation) – **keep to 1** to stay in or on ⟨keep to *the path*⟩ **2** not to deviate from; ABIDE BY ⟨keep to *the rules*⟩ – **keep to oneself 1** to keep secret ⟨kept *the facts* to himself⟩ **2** *also* **keep oneself to oneself** to remain solitary or apart from other people – **keep warm** to occupy (a position) temporarily for another

²keep *n* **1** a castle, fortress, or fortified tower **2** the means (e g food) by which one is kept ⟨*earned his* ~⟩ – **for keeps 1** with the provision that one keeps as one's own what one wins or receives ⟨*he gave it to me* for keeps⟩ – *infml* **2** FOR GOOD ⟨*came home* for keeps⟩ – *infml*

keeper *n* **1a** a protector, guardian **b** a gamekeeper **c** a custodian **d** a curator **2** any of various devices (e g a latch or guard ring) for keeping sthg in position **3a** a goalkeeper **b** a wicketkeeper *USE* (3) chiefly *infml*

keeping *n* custody, care – **out of/in keeping** not/conforming or agreeing with sthg implied or specified – usu + **with**

keep on *vi* to talk continuously; *esp* to nag ⟨kept on *at him to buy her a fur coat*⟩

keepsake *n* sthg (given, to be) kept as a memento, esp of the giver

keep up *vt* **1** to persist or persevere in; continue ⟨keep up *the good work*⟩ **2** to preserve from decline ⟨keep up *appearances*⟩ ~ *vi* **1** to maintain an equal pace or level of activity, progress, or knowledge (e g with another) **2** to continue without interruption ⟨*rain kept up all night*⟩

keg *n, Br* **1** a small barrel having a capacity of (less than) 10gal (about 45.5l); *specif* a metal beer barrel from which beer is pumped by pressurized gas **2** beer from a keg

kelp *n* **1** any of various large brown seaweeds **2** the ashes of seaweed used esp as a source of iodine

kelvin *n* the SI unit of temperature defined by the Kelvin scale

Kelvin *adj* of, conforming to, or being a scale of temperature on which absolute zero is at 0 and water freezes at 273.16K under standard conditions

¹ken *vb* **-nn-** *chiefly Scot* to have knowledge (of); know

²ken *n* the range of perception, understanding, or knowledge – usu + *beyond, outside*

¹kennel *n* **1a** a shelter for a dog **b** an establishment for the breeding or boarding of dogs – often pl with sing. meaning but sing. or pl in constr ⟨*runs a* ~s *in the country*⟩ **2** a pack of dogs

²kennel *vt* **-ll-** (*NAm* **-l-, -ll-**), to put or keep (as if) in a kennel

kepi *n* a round French military cap with a flat top and a horizontal peak

kept *past of* KEEP

keratin *n* any of various fibrous proteins that form the chemical basis of nails, claws, and other horny tissue and hair – **keratinous** *adj*, **keratinize** *vb*

kerb *n, Br* **1** the edging, esp of stone, to a pavement, path,

etc **2** a market for trading in securities not listed on a stock exchange

kerchief *n, pl* **kerchiefs** *also* **kerchieves 1** a square or triangle of cloth used as a head covering or worn as a scarf around the neck **2** a handkerchief

kerfuffle *n, chiefly Br* a fuss, commotion – *infml*

kernel *n* **1** the inner softer often edible part of a seed, fruit stone, or nut **2** a whole seed of a cereal **3** a central or essential part; CORE 2

kerosine, kerosene *n, chiefly NAm* PARAFFIN 3

kersey *n* a heavy compact ribbed or twilled woollen cloth with a short nap

kestrel *n* a small common Eurasian and N African falcon that is noted for its habit of hovering in the air against a wind

ketch *n* a fore-and-aft rigged ship with the mizzenmast stepped forward of the rudder

ketchup, *NAm chiefly* **catchup** *n* any of several sauces made with vinegar and seasonings and used as a relish; *esp* a sauce made from seasoned tomato puree

kettle *n* **1** a metal vessel used esp for boiling liquids; *esp* one with a lid, handle, and spout that is placed on top of a stove or cooker or contains an electric heating-element and is used to boil water **2** a steep-sided hollow in a deposit of glacial drift, caused by the melting of a mass of underlying ice

kettledrum *n* a percussion instrument that consists of a hollow brass or copper hemisphere with a parchment head whose tension can be changed to vary the pitch

¹key *n* **1a** a usu metal instrument by which the bolt of a lock is turned **b** sthg having the form or function of such a key ⟨*a* ~ *for a clock*⟩ **2a** a means of gaining or preventing entrance, possession, or control **b** an instrumental or deciding factor **3a** sthg that gives an explanation or identification or provides a solution **b** a list of words or phrases explaining symbols or abbreviations **c** an arrangement of the important characteristics of a group of plants or animals used for identification **4** a small piece of wood or metal used as a wedge or for preventing motion between parts **5a** any of the levers of a keyboard musical instrument that is pressed by a finger or foot to actuate the mechanism and produce the notes **b** a lever that controls a vent in the side of a woodwind instrument or a valve in a brass instrument **c** a small button or knob on a keyboard (e g of a typewriter) designed to be pushed down by the fingers **6** a (particular) system of 7 notes based on their relationship to a tonic **7** characteristic style or tone **8** a small switch for opening or closing an electric circuit **9** a dry usu single-seeded fruit (e g of an ash or elm tree) **10** the indentation, roughness, or roughening of a surface to improve adhesion of plaster, paint, etc – **keyed** *adj*, **keyless** *adj*

²key *vt* **1** to secure or fasten by a key **2** to roughen (a surface) to provide a key for plaster, paint, etc **3** to bring into harmony or conformity; make appropriate **4** to make nervous, tense, or excited – usu + *up* ⟨*was* ~ *ed up over her impending operation*⟩ **5** to keyboard

³key *adj* of basic importance; fundamental

⁴key *n* a low island or reef, esp in the Caribbean area

¹keyboard *n* **1a** a bank of keys on a musical instrument (e g a piano) typically having 7 usu white and 5 raised usu black keys to the octave **b** any instrument having such a keyboard, esp when forming part of a pop or jazz ensemble **2** a set of systematically arranged keys by which a machine is operated

²keyboard *vi* to operate a machine (e g for typesetting) by means of a keyboard ~ *vt* to capture or set (e g data or text) by means of a keyboard – **keyboarder** *n*

keyhole *n* a hole in a lock into which the key is put

key money *n* a payment made by a tenant to secure occupancy of a rented property

¹keynote *n* 1 the first and harmonically fundamental note of a scale 2 the fundamental or central fact, principle, idea, or mood ·

²keynote *adj* being or delivered by a speaker who presents the issues of primary interest to an assembly ⟨a ~ speech⟩

keypunch *n* a machine with a keyboard used to cut holes or notches in punched cards – **keypunch** *vt*, **keypuncher** *n*

key signature *n* the sharps or flats placed on the musical staff to indicate the key

keystone *n* 1 the wedge-shaped piece at the apex of an arch that locks the other pieces in place 2 sthg on which associated things depend for support

khaki *n* 1 a dull yellowish brown 2 a khaki-coloured cloth made usu of cotton or wool and used esp for military uniforms – **khaki** *adj*

khan *n* a medieval supreme ruler over the Turkish, Tartar, and Mongol tribes – **khanate** *n*

kibbutz *n*, *pl* **kibbutzim** a collective farm or settlement in Israel

kibosh *n* sthg that serves as a check or stop ⟨put the ~ on that⟩ – infml – **kibosh** *vt*

¹kick *vi* 1a to strike out with the foot or feet b to make a kick in football 2 to show opposition; rebel 3 *of a firearm* to recoil when fired ~ *vt* 1 to strike suddenly and forcefully (as if) with the foot 2 to score by kicking a ball 3 to free oneself of (a drug or drug habit) – infml – **kick oneself** to reprove oneself for some stupidity or omission – **kick one's heels** 1 to be kept waiting 2 to be idle – **kick over the traces** to cast off restraint, authority, or control – **kick the bucket** DIE 1 – infml, humor – **kick upstairs** to promote to a higher but less desirable position

²kick *n* 1a a blow or sudden forceful thrust with the foot; *specif* one causing the propulsion of an object b the power to kick c a repeated motion of the legs used in swimming d a sudden burst of speed, esp in a footrace 2 the recoil of a gun 3 power or strength to resist; *broadly* resilience ⟨still has some ~ in him⟩ 4a a stimulating effect or quality ⟨this drink has quite a ~⟩ b a stimulating or pleasurable experience or feeling – often pl ⟨he did it for ~s⟩ c an absorbing or obsessive new interest ⟨on a health food ~ at present⟩

³kick *n* an indentation in the base of a glass vessel, esp a bottle

kick about *vb* KICK AROUND

kick around *vt* 1 to treat inconsiderately or high-handedly 2 to consider (a problem) from various angles, esp in an unsystematic or experimental way ~ *vi* 1 to wander aimlessly or idly 2 to lie unused or unwanted ⟨there's a spare blanket kicking around in one of these rooms⟩ USE (vt & vi) infml

kickback *n* 1 a sharp violent reaction 2 a money return received usu because of help or favours given or sometimes because of confidential agreement or coercion

kicker *n* a horse with a habit of kicking

kickoff *n* 1 a kick that puts the ball into play in soccer, rugby, etc 2 an act or instance of starting or beginning

kick off *vi* 1 to start or resume play with a kickoff 2 to start or begin proceedings – infml

kick out *vt* to dismiss or eject forcefully or summarily – infml

kick-starter *n* a foot-operated starter (eg for a motorcycle) – **kick-start** *vt*

kick up *vt* 1 to cause to rise upwards; raise ⟨clouds of dust kicked up by passing cars⟩ 2 to stir up (a row, a fuss, trouble, etc) – infml

¹kid *n* 1 the young of a goat or related animal 2 the flesh, fur, or skin of a kid 3 a child; *also* a young person (e g a teenager) – infml – **kiddish** *adj* – **with kid gloves** with special consideration

²kid *vi* -dd- *of a goat or antelope* to bring forth young

³kid *vb* -dd- *vt* 1a to mislead as a joke ⟨it's the truth; I wouldn't ~ you⟩ b to convince (oneself) of sthg untrue or improbable 2 to make fun of ~ *vi* to engage in good-humoured fooling USE (vt & vi) infml – **kidder** *n*, **kiddingly** *adv*

kiddie, kiddy *n* a small child – infml

kidnap *vt* -pp-, -p- to seize and detain (a person) by force and often for ransom – **kidnapper, kidnaper** *n*

kidney *n* 1a either of a pair of organs situated in the body cavity near the spinal column that excrete waste products of metabolism in the form of urine b an excretory organ of an invertebrate 2 the kidney of an animal eaten as food 3 sort, kind, or type, esp with regard to temperament

kidney bean *n* (any of the kidney-shaped seeds of) the French bean

kike *n*, *chiefly NAm* a Jew – derog

¹kill *vt* 1 to deprive of life 2a to put an end to b to defeat, veto 3a to destroy the vital, active, or essential quality of ⟨~ed the pain with drugs⟩ b to spoil, subdue, or neutralize the effect of ⟨that colour ~s the room⟩ c(1) to turn off (studio or stage lighting) (2) to remove (a shadow) by adjusting lighting or moving a camera 4 to cause (time) to pass (e g while waiting) 5 to hit (a shot) so hard in a racket game that a return is impossible 6 to cause (e g an engine) to stop 7 to cause extreme pain to ⟨my feet are ~ing me⟩ 8 to overwhelm with admiration or amusement 9 to discard or abandon further investigation of (a story) – journ ~ *vi* to destroy life USE (6, 7, 8) infml – **killer** *n* – **to kill** TO THE NINES ⟨dressed to kill⟩

²kill *n* 1 a killing or being killed ⟨moved in for the ~⟩ 2 sthg killed: e g a animals killed in a shoot, hunt, season, or particular period of time b an enemy aircraft, submarine, etc destroyed by military action

killer whale *n* a flesh-eating gregarious black-and-white toothed whale found in most seas of the world

¹killing *n* a sudden notable gain or profit – infml

²killing *adj* 1 extremely exhausting or difficult to endure 2 highly amusing USE infml – **killingly** *adv*

killjoy *n* one who spoils the pleasure of others

kill off *vt* to destroy totally or in large numbers

kiln *n* an oven, furnace, or heated enclosure used for processing a substance by burning, firing, or drying – **kiln** *vt*

kilo *n*, *pl* **kilos** 1 a kilogram . 2 a kilometre

Kilo – a communications code word for the letter *k*

kilo- *comb form* thousand ⟨kiloton⟩

kilocalorie *n* the quantity of heat required to raise the temperature of 1 kg of water 1°C under standard conditions

kilogram *n* 1 the SI unit of mass and weight equal to the mass of a platinum-iridium cylinder kept near Paris, and approximately equal to the weight of a litre of water (2.205lb) 2 a unit of force equal to the weight of a kilogram mass under the earth's gravitational attraction

kilohertz *n* a unit of frequency equal to 1000 hertz

kilometre *n* 1000 metres

kilowatt *n* 1000 watts

kilt *n* a skirt traditionally worn by Scotsmen that is formed usu from a length of tartan, is pleated at the back and sides, and is wrapped round the body and fastened at the front

kimono *n*, *pl* **kimonos** a loose robe with wide sleeves and a broad sash traditionally worn by the Japanese

¹**kin** *n* **1** a group of people of common ancestry **2** *sing or pl in constr* one's relatives **3** *archaic* kinship

²**kin** *adj* kindred, related

-kin *also* **-kins** *suffix* (→ *n*) small kind of ⟨cat*kin*⟩ ⟨mann*i*kin⟩

¹**kind** *n* **1** fundamental nature or quality **2a** a group united by common traits or interests **b** a specific or recognized variety – often in combination ⟨*how delinquents differ from the rest of juvenile-kind – TLS*⟩ **c** a doubtful or barely admissible member of a category ⟨*a ~ of grey*⟩ – **in kind 1** in goods, commodities, or natural produce as distinguished from money **2** in a similar way or with the equivalent of what has been offered or received ⟨*repaid his generosity in kind*⟩

²**kind** *adj* **1** disposed to be helpful and benevolent **2** forbearing, considerate, or compassionate **3** showing sympathy, benevolence, or forbearance **4** cordial, friendly **5** not harmful; mild, gentle – **kindness** *n*

kindergarten *n* a school or class for small children

kindhearted *adj* marked by a sympathetic nature – **kindheartedly** *adv*, **kindheartedness** *n*

kindle *vb* **kindling** *vt* **1** to set (a fire, wood, etc) burning **2** to stir up (e g emotion) ~ *vi* **1** to catch fire **2** to become animated or aroused

kindling *n* material (e g dry wood and leaves) for starting a fire

¹**kindly** *adj* **1** agreeable, beneficial **2** sympathetic, generous – **kindliness** *n*

²**kindly** *adv* **1** in an appreciative or sincere manner ⟨*I'd take it ~ if you'd put in a good word for the boy*⟩ **2** – used (1) to add politeness or emphasis to a request ⟨*~ fill in the attached questionnaire*⟩ (2) to convey irritation or anger in a command ⟨*will you ~ shut that door*⟩

kind of *adv* **1** to a moderate degree; somewhat ⟨*it's ~ late to begin*⟩ **2** in a manner of speaking ⟨*all you can do is ~ nurse it – SEU S*⟩ **3** roughly, approximately *USE* infml

¹**kindred** *n* **1** *sing or pl in constr* (one's) relatives **2** family relationship

²**kindred** *adj* similar in nature or character

kine *archaic pl of* COW

kinetic *adj* of motion

kinetic art *n* art (e g sculpture) depending for its effect on the movement of surfaces or volumes – **kinetic artist** *n*

kinetic energy *n* energy that a body or system has by virtue of its motion

kinetics *n pl but sing or pl in constr* **1** science that deals with the effects of forces on the motions of material bodies or with changes in a physical or chemical system **2** the mechanism by which a physical or chemical change is effected

king *n* **1** a male monarch of a major territorial unit; *esp* one who inherits his position and rules for life **2** the holder of a preeminent position **3** the principal piece of each colour in a set of chessmen that has the power to move 1 square in any direction and must be protected against check **4** a playing card marked with a stylized figure of a king and ranking usu below the ace **5** a draughtsman that has reached the opposite side of the board and is empowered to move both forwards and backwards – **kingship** *n*

kingbolt *n* a large or major bolt

king cobra *n* a large venomous cobra of southeastern Asia and the Philippines

kingcup *n* MARSH MARIGOLD

kingdom *n* **1** a territorial unit with a monarchical form of government **2** *often cap* the eternal kingship of God **3** an area or sphere in which sby or sthg holds a preeminent

position **4** any of the 3 primary divisions into which natural objects are commonly classified

kingfisher *n* any of numerous small brightly-coloured fish-eating birds with a short tail and a long stout sharp bill

King James Version *n* AUTHORIZED VERSION

kingmaker *n* sby having influence over the choice of candidates for office

kingpin *n* **1** the key person or thing in a group or undertaking **2** a kingbolt

Kings *n pl but sing in constr* any of 2 or, in the Roman Catholic canon, 4 narrative and historical books of the Old Testament

King's Bench *n* QUEEN'S BENCH – used when the British monarch is a man

King's Counsel *n* QUEEN'S COUNSEL – used when the British monarch is a man

King's English *n* standard or correct S British English speech or usage – used when the monarch is a man

king's evil *n*, *often cap K&E* scrofula

kingship *n* the position, office, or dignity of a king

kink *n* **1** a short tight twist or curl caused by sthg doubling or winding on itself **2** an eccentricity or mental peculiarity; *esp* such eccentricity in sexual behaviour or preferences – **kink** *vb*

kinky *adj* **1** closely twisted or curled **2a** offbeat **b** titillatingly unusual or bizarre; *esp* sexually perverted *USE* (2) infml – **kinkiness** *n*

kinsfolk *n pl* relatives

kinship *n* **1** blood relationship **2** similarity

kinsman, *fem* **kinswoman** *n* a (male) relative

kiosk *n* **1** an open summerhouse or pavilion common in Turkey or Iran **2** a small stall or stand used esp for the sale of newspapers, cigarettes, and sweets **3** *Br* a public telephone box

¹**kip** *n*, *pl* **kip, kips** the standard unit of money in Laos

²**kip** *n*, *chiefly Br* **1** a place to sleep **2** a period of sleep *USE* infml

³**kip** *vi* **-pp-** *chiefly Br* **1** to sleep **2** to lie down to sleep – often + *down USE* infml

¹**kipper** *n* a kippered fish, esp a herring

²**kipper** *vt* to cure (split dressed fish) by salting and drying, usu by smoking

kirk *n* **1** *cap the* national Church of Scotland as distinguished from the Church of England or the Episcopal Church in Scotland **2** *chiefly Scot* a church

kirsch *n* a dry colourless spirit distilled from the fermented juice of the black morello cherry

kirtle *n* a man's tunic or coat or a woman's dress worn esp in the Middle Ages

kismet *n*; *often cap* FATE 1, 2a

¹**kiss** *vt* **1a** to touch with the lips, esp as a mark of affection or greeting **b** to express or effect by kissing ⟨*~ed her good night*⟩ **2** to touch gently or lightly ⟨*wind gently ~ing the trees*⟩ ~ *vi* **1** to touch one another with the lips, esp as a mark of love or sexual desire **2** to come into gentle contact – **kissable** *adj*

²**kiss** *n* an act or instance of kissing

kisser *n* the mouth or face – slang

¹**kit** *n* **1** a set of tools or implements **2** a set of parts ready to be assembled ⟨*a model aeroplane ~*⟩ **3** a set of clothes and equipment for use in a specified situation; *esp* the equipment carried by a member of the armed forces

²**kit** *vt* **-tt-** *chiefly Br* to equip, outfit; *esp* to clothe – usu + *out* or *up* ⟨*all ~ted out for camping*⟩

³**kit** *n* a kitten

kitbag *n* a large cylindrical bag carried over the shoulder and used for holding the kit, esp of a member of the armed forces

kitchen *n* a place (e g a room in a house or hotel) where food is prepared

kitchenette *n* a small kitchen or alcove containing cooking facilities

kitchen garden *n* a garden in which vegetables are grown

kite *n* 1 any of various hawks with long narrow wings, a deeply forked tail, and feet adapted for taking insects and small reptiles as prey 2 a light frame covered with thin material (e g paper or cloth), designed to be flown in the air at the end of a long string

kith *n* friends or neighbours ⟨~ *and kin*⟩

kitsch *n* artistic or literary material that is pretentious or inferior and is usu designed to appeal to popular or sentimental taste – **kitschy** *adj*

¹**kitten** *n* the young of a cat or other small mammal

²**kitten** *vi* to give birth to kittens

kittenish *adj* coyly playful or flirtatious

kittiwake *n* any of various gulls that have a short or rudimentary hind toe

¹**kitty** *n* CAT 1a; *esp* a kitten – used chiefly as a pet name or calling name

²**kitty** *n* a jointly held fund of money (e g for household expenses)

kiwi *n* 1 a flightless New Zealand bird with hairlike plumage 2 *cap* a New Zealander

Klaxon *trademark* – used for a powerful electrically operated horn or warning signal

Kleenex *trademark* – used for a paper handkerchief

kleptomania *n* an irresistible desire to steal, esp when not accompanied by economic motives or desire for financial gain – **kleptomaniac** *n*

knack *n* a special ability, capacity, or skill that enables sthg, esp of a difficult or unusual nature, to be done with ease ⟨*skating is easy once you've got the* ~⟩; *broadly* APTITUDE 1 ⟨*has a* ~ *for saying the wrong thing*⟩

¹**knacker** *n*, *Br* 1 sby who buys and slaughters worn-out horses for use esp as animal food or fertilizer ⟨*a* ~ *'s yard*⟩ 2 a buyer of old ships, houses, or other structures for their constituent materials – **knackery** *n*

²**knacker** *vt*, *chiefly Br* to exhaust – *infml* ⟨*after working all night I felt* ~*ed*⟩

knapsack *n* a (soldier's) bag (e g of canvas or leather) strapped on the back and used for carrying supplies or personal belongings

knave *n* 1 an unprincipled deceitful fellow 2 JACK 5 3 *archaic* a male servant – **knavery** *n*, **knavish** *adj*, **knavishly** *adv*

knead *vt* 1 to work and press into a mass (as if) with the hands ⟨~*ing dough*⟩ 2 to manipulate (as if) by kneading ⟨~ *the idea into shape*⟩ – **kneadable** *adj*, **kneader** *n*

¹**knee** *n* 1a (the part of the leg that includes) a joint in the middle part of the human leg that is the articulation between the femur, tibia, and kneecap b a corresponding joint in an animal, bird, or insect 2 sthg (e g a piece of wood or iron) shaped like the human knee – **kneed** *adj*

²**knee** *vt* to strike with the knee

¹**kneecap** *n* a thick flat triangular movable bone that forms the front point of the knee and protects the front of the joint

²**kneecap** *vt* to smash the kneecap of, as a punishment or torture

knee-deep *adj* 1 knee-high 2 immersed *in* (as if) up to the knees ⟨~ *in work*⟩

knee-high *adj* high or deep enough to reach up to the knees

kneel *vi* **knelt, kneeled** to fall or rest on the knee or knees – **kneeler** *n*

¹**knell** *vi* 1 *of a bell* to ring, esp for a death, funeral, etc 2

to sound ominously ~ *vt* to summon, announce, or proclaim (as if) by a knell

²**knell** *n* 1 (the sound of) a bell rung slowly (e g for a funeral or disaster) 2 an indication of the end or failure of sthg

knew *past of* KNOW

knickerbockers *n pl* short baggy trousers gathered on a band at the knee

knickers *n pl* 1 *Br* women's pants 2 *NAm* knickerbockers

knick-knack *n* a small trivial ornament or trinket – *infml*

¹**knife** *n*, *pl* **knives** 1a a cutting implement consisting of a more or less sharp blade fastened to a handle b such an instrument used as a weapon 2 a sharp cutting blade or tool in a machine – **knifelike** *adj* – **at knifepoint** under a threat of death by being knifed

²**knife** *vt* 1 to cut, slash, or wound with a knife 2 to cut, mark, or spread with a knife 3 *chiefly NAm* to try to defeat by underhand means – *infml*

knife-edge *n* 1 a sharp wedge of hard material (e g steel) used as a fulcrum or pivot in a pair of scales, a pendulum, etc 2 sthg sharp and narrow (e g a ridge of rock) resembling the edge of a knife 3 an uncertain or precarious position or condition

¹**knight** *n* 1a(1) a mounted man-at-arms serving a feudal superior; *esp* a man ceremonially inducted into special rank after service as page and squire (2) a man honoured by a sovereign for merit, ranking below a baronet (3) sby equivalent to a knight in rank b a man devoted to the service of a lady (e g as her champion) 2 either of 2 pieces of each colour in a set of chessmen that move from 1 corner to the diagonally opposite corner of a rectangle of 3 by 2 squares over squares that may be occupied – **knightly** *adj or adv*, **knighthood** *n*

²**knight** *vt* to make a knight of

knight-errant *n*, *pl* **knights-errant** 1 a knight travelling in search of chivalrous adventures 2 a quixotic or chivalrous person

¹**knit** *vb* **knit, knitted; -tt-** *vt* 1a to link firmly or closely b to unite intimately 2a to cause to grow together ⟨*time and rest will* ~ *a fractured bone*⟩ b to contract into wrinkles ⟨~*ted her brow in thought*⟩ 3a to form (e g a fabric, garment, or design) by working 1 or more yarns into a series of interlocking loops using 2 or more needles or a knitting machine b to work (e g a specified number of rows) using a knitting stitch, specif knit stitch ⟨~ *1, purl 1*⟩ ~ *vi* 1a to make knitted fabrics or articles b to work yarn or thread in a knitting stitch, specif knit stitch 2a to become compact b to grow together c to become joined or drawn together – **knitter** *n*

²**knit, knit stitch** *n* a basic knitting stitch that produces a raised pattern on the front of the work

knitting *n* work that has been or is being knitted

knob *n* 1a a rounded protuberance b a small rounded ornament, handle, or control (for pushing, pulling, or turning) 2 a small piece or lump (e g of coal or butter) – **knobbed** *adj*, **knobby** *adj* – **with knobs on** to an even greater degree – *infml*

knobble *n* a small rounded irregularity – **knobbly** *adj*

knobkerrie *n* a short wooden club with a knobbed head used esp by S African tribesmen

¹**knock** *vi* 1 to strike sthg with a sharp (audible) blow; *esp* to strike a door seeking admittance 2 to collide with sthg 3 to be in a place, often without any clearly defined aim or purpose – usu + *about* or *around* 4a to make a sharp pounding noise b *of an internal-combustion engine* to make a metallic rapping noise because of a mechanical defect; *also* ²PINK 3 5 to find fault ~ *vt* 1a(1) to strike

sharply (2) to drive, force, make, or take (as if) by so striking ⟨~ed *a hole in the wall*⟩ ⟨*her earnings would be* ~ed *off her mother's benefit – The Times*⟩ **b** to set forcibly in motion with a blow **2** to cause to collide (with each other) ⟨~ed *their heads together*⟩ **3** to find fault with ⟨*always* ~ing *those in authority*⟩ *USE* (vi 5; vt 3) infml – **knock together** to make or assemble, esp hurriedly or shoddily

²**knock** *n* **1a** (the sound of) a knocking or a sharp blow or rap ⟨*the engine has a* ~⟩ **b** a piece of bad luck or misfortune **2** a harsh and often petty criticism **3** INNINGS 1b – infml

knockabout *adj* **1** suitable for rough use ⟨~ *clothes*⟩ **2** (characterized by antics that are) boisterous ⟨*a* ~ *comedy*⟩

knock about *vt* to treat roughly or with physical violence

knock back *vt, chiefly Br* **1** to drink (an alcoholic beverage) rapidly **2** to cost; SET BACK 2 **3** to surprise, disconcert *USE* infml

¹**knockdown** *n* sthg (e g a piece of furniture) that can be easily assembled or dismantled

²**knockdown** *adj* **1** having such force as to strike down or overwhelm **2** easily assembled or dismantled ⟨*a* ~ *table*⟩ **3** *of a price* very low or substantially reduced; *esp* being the lowest acceptable to the seller

knock down *vt* **1** to strike to the ground (as if) with a sharp blow **2** to dispose of (an item for sale at an auction) *to* a bidder **3** to take apart; disassemble **4** to make a reduction in ⟨knock *the price* down *to £4*⟩

knocker *n* a metal ring, bar, or hammer hinged to a door for use in knocking

knockers *n pl* a woman's breasts – vulg

knock-knee *n* a condition in which the legs curve inwards at the knees – often pl with sing. meaning but sing. or pl in constr – **knock-kneed** *adj*

knock off *vi* to stop doing sthg, esp one's work ~ *vt* **1** to do hurriedly or routinely ⟨knocked off *one painting after another*⟩ **2** to discontinue, stop ⟨knocked off *work at 5*⟩ **3** to deduct ⟨knocked off *a pound to make the price more attractive*⟩ **4** to kill; *esp* to murder **5** to steal **6** *Br* to have sexual intercourse with *USE* (4&5) infml, (6) slang

knock-on *n* (an instance of) the knocking of the ball forwards on the ground with the hand or arm in rugby in violation of the rules – **knock on** *vt*

knockout, knock-out *n* **1a** knocking out or being knocked out **b** a blow that knocks out an opponent (or knocks him down for longer than a particular time, usu 10s, and results in the termination of a boxing match) **c** TECHNICAL KNOCKOUT **2** a competition or tournament with successive rounds in which losing competitors are eliminated until a winner emerges in the final **3** sby or sthg that is sensationally striking or attractive – infml – **knockout** *adj*

knock out *vt* **1** to empty (a tobacco pipe) by striking on or with sthg **2** KNOCK UP 1 **3a** to defeat (a boxing opponent) by a knockout **b** to make unconscious **4** to tire out; exhaust **5** to eliminate (an opponent) from a knockout competition **6** to overwhelm with amazement or pleasure – infml

knock up *vt* **1** to make, prepare, or arrange hastily **2** KNOCK OUT 4 **3** to achieve a total of ⟨knocked up *300mi in the first day of travelling*⟩ **4** *Br* to rouse, awaken **5** *chiefly NAm* to make pregnant – infml ~ *vi* to practise informally before a tennis, squash, etc match

knoll *n* a small round hill; a mound

¹**knot** *n* **1a** an interlacing of (parts of) 1 or more strings, threads, etc that forms a lump or knob **b** a piece of ribbon, braid etc tied as an ornament **c** a (sense of) tight constric-

tion ⟨*his stomach was all in* ~s⟩ **2** sthg hard to solve **3** a bond of union; *esp* the marriage bond **4a** a protuberant lump or swelling in tissue **b** (a rounded cross-section in timber of) the base of a woody branch enclosed in the stem from which it arises **5** a cluster of people or things **6a** a speed of 1 nautical mile per hour **b** 1 nautical mile – not used technically

²**knot** *vb* -tt- *vt* **1** to tie in or with a knot **2** to unite closely or intricately ~ *vi* to form a knot or knots – **knotter** *n*

³**knot** *n, pl* **knots,** *esp collectively* **knot** (a bird of) a species of migratory sandpiper

knothole *n* a hole in a board or tree trunk where a knot or branch has come out

knotty *adj* complicated or difficult (to solve) ⟨*a* ~ *problem*⟩ – **knottiness** *n*

knout *n* a whip formerly used in Russia for flogging criminals – **knout** *vt*

¹**know** *vb* **knew; known** *vt* **1a**(1) to perceive directly; have direct cognition of (2) to have understanding of (3) to recognize or identify ⟨*would* ~ *him again*⟩ **b**(1) to be acquainted or familiar with (2) to have experience of **2a** to be aware of the truth or factual nature of; be convinced or certain of **b** to have a practical understanding of ⟨~s *how to write*⟩ **3** *archaic* to have sexual intercourse with ~ *vi* to (come to) have knowledge (of sthg) – **knowable** *adj,* **knower** *n* – **be to know** be expected to discern; have any knowledge of ⟨*how was I to know it wouldn't bite?*⟩ – **not know someone from Adam** have no idea who sby is – **you know** – used for adding emphasis to a statement ⟨*you'll have to try harder,* you know, *if you want to succeed*⟩

²**know** *n* – **in the know** in possession of confidential or otherwise exclusive knowledge or information

know-all *n* one who behaves as if he knows everything

know-how *n* (practical) expertise

knowing *adj* **1** having or reflecting knowledge, information, or intelligence **2** shrewd or astute; *esp* implying (that one has) knowledge of a secret **3** deliberate, conscious – **knowingly** *adv*

knowledge *n* **1a** the fact or condition of knowing sthg or sby through experience or association **b** acquaintance with, or understanding or awareness of, sthg ⟨*some* ~ *of Newtonian physics*⟩ **2a** the range of a person's information, perception, or understanding ⟨*is it true? Not to my* ~⟩ **b** the fact or condition of having information or of being learned ⟨*a man of little* ~⟩ **3** the sum of what is known; the body of truth, information, and principles acquired by mankind (on some subject)

knowledgeable *adj* having or exhibiting knowledge or intelligence; well-informed – **knowledgeably** *adv*

known *adj* generally recognized ⟨*a* ~ *authority on this topic*⟩

¹**knuckle** *n* **1** the rounded prominence formed by the ends of the 2 bones at a joint; *specif* any of the joints between the hand and the fingers or the finger joints closest to these **2** a cut of meat consisting of the lowest leg joint of a pig, sheep, etc with the adjoining flesh – **near the knuckle** almost improper or indecent

²**knuckle** *vi* **knuckling** to place the knuckles on the ground in shooting a marble

knuckle down *vi* to apply oneself earnestly

knuckle-duster *n* a metal device worn over the front of the doubled fist for protection and use as a weapon

knuckle under *vi* to give in, submit ⟨*refused to* knuckle under *to any dictatorship*⟩

¹**KO** *n, pl* **KOs** KNOCKOUT 1 – infml

²**KO** *vt* **KO's; KO'ing; KO'd** to knock out – infml

koala, koala bear *n* an Australian tree-dwelling marsupial mammal that has large hairy ears, grey fur, and sharp claws and feeds on eucalyptus leaves

kohl *n* (a cosmetic preparation made with) a black powder used, orig chiefly by Asian women, to darken the eyelids

kohlrabi *n, pl* **kohlrabies** a cabbage with a greatly enlarged fleshy turnip-shaped edible stem

kookaburra *n* a large Australian kingfisher that has a call resembling loud laughter

kopeck, copeck *also* **kopek** *n* a coin in the USSR, worth 1/100 of a rouble

kopje, koppie *n* a small hill on the S African veld; *broadly, SAfr* a small hill

Koran, Qur'an *n* the book composed of writings accepted by Muslims as revelations made to Muhammad by Allah through the angel Gabriel – **Koranic** *adj*

koruna *n, pl* **koruny, korunas** the standard unit of money in Czechoslovakia

¹kosher *adj* **1a** *of food* prepared according to Jewish law **b** selling kosher food ⟨a ∼ *butcher*⟩ **2** proper, legitimate – *infml* – **kosher** *n*

²kosher *vt* to make (food) kosher

¹kowtow *n* a (Chinese) gesture of deep respect in which one kneels and touches the ground with one's forehead

²kowtow *vi* **1** to make a kowtow **2** to show obsequious deference

¹kraal *n* **1** a village of S African tribesmen **2** an enclosure for domestic animals in S Africa

²kraal *vt* to pen in a kraal

kremlin *n* **1** a citadel within a Russian town or city **2** *cap the* government of the USSR

kris *n* a Malay or Indonesian dagger with a wavy blade

krona *n, pl* **kronor** the standard unit of money in Sweden

króna *n, pl* **kronur** the standard unit of money in Iceland

krone *n, pl* **kroner** the standard unit of money in Denmark and Norway

kudos *n* fame and renown, esp resulting from an act or achievement

Ku Klux Klan *n* **1** a secret society opposing the right of blacks to vote after the US Civil War **2** a secret political organization in the USA that confines its membership to American-born Protestant whites and is hostile to blacks

kukri *n* a short curved knife used esp by Gurkhas

kümmel *n* a colourless aromatic liqueur flavoured with caraway seeds

kumquat, cumquat *n* (any of several trees that bear) any of several small citrus fruits that are used chiefly for preserves

kung fu *n* a Chinese martial art resembling karate

kvass *n* a slightly alcoholic beverage made in E Europe usu by fermenting mixed cereals and adding flavouring

kwashiorkor *n* severe malnutrition in infants and children that is caused by a diet high in carbohydrate and low in protein

kyrie, kyrie eleison *n, often cap* a short liturgical prayer, often set to music, that begins with or consists of the words "Lord, have mercy"

L

l *n, pl* **l's, ls** *often cap* **1a** (a graphic representation of or device for reproducing) the 12th letter of the English alphabet **b** sthg shaped like the letter L **2** fifty **3** *NAm* an elevated railway; an el

l- *prefix* **1** laevorotatory ⟨l-*tartaric acid*⟩ **2** having a similar configuration at an optically active carbon atom to the configuration of laevorotatory glyceraldehyde – usu printed as a small capital ⟨L-*fructose*⟩

la *n* the 6th note of the diatonic scale in solmization

laager *n* a camp; *esp* an encampment protected by a circle of wagons or armoured vehicles – **laager** *vi*

lab *n* a laboratory

¹label *n* **1** a slip (e g of paper or cloth), inscribed and fastened to sthg to give information (e g identification or directions) **2** a descriptive or identifying word or phrase: e g **a** an epithet **b** a word or phrase used with a dictionary definition to provide additional information (e g level of usage) **3** an adhesive stamp **4** TRADE NAME 1b, 2; *specif* a name used by a company producing commercial recordings ⟨*several new record* ∼s⟩

²label *vt* **-ll-** (*NAm* **-l-, -ll-**), **1a** to fasten a label to **b** to describe or categorize (as if) with a label **2** to make (e g an element) traceable, by substitution of a radioactive or other special isotope – **labellable** *adj*, **labeller** *n*

¹labial *adj* **1** of the lips or labia **2** articulated using 1 or both lips – **labially** *adv*, **labialize** *vt*, **labialization** *n*

²labial *n* a labial consonant (e g /f/ and /p/)

laboratory *n* a place equipped for scientific experiment, testing, or analysis; *broadly* a place providing opportunity for research in a field of study

laborious *adj* involving or characterized by effort – **laboriously** *adv*, **laboriousness** *n*

¹labour, NAm chiefly labor *n* **1a** expenditure of effort, esp when difficult or compulsory; toil **b** human activity that provides the goods or services in an economy **c** (the period of) the physical activities involved in the birth of young **2** an act or process requiring labour; a task **3a** *sing or pl in constr* an economic group comprising those who do manual work or work for wages **b** workers ⟨*local* ∼ *isn't suitable*⟩ **4** *sing or pl in constr, cap* the Labour party

²labour, NAm chiefly labor *vi* **1** to exert one's powers of body or mind, esp with great effort; work, strive **2** to move with great effort ⟨*a fat man* ∼*ing up the stairs*⟩ **3** to be in labour when giving birth **4** to suffer from some disadvantage or distress ⟨∼ *under a delusion*⟩ **5** *of a ship* to pitch or roll heavily ∼ *vt* **1** to treat in laborious detail ⟨∼ *the obvious*⟩ **2** *archaic* to spend labour on or produce by labour

Labour *adj* of or being a political party, specif one in the UK, advocating a planned socialist economy and associated with working-class interests

Labour Day *n* a day set aside for special recognition of working people: e g **a** the first Monday in September observed in the USA and Canada as a public holiday **b** MAY DAY

labourer *n* one who does unskilled manual work, esp outdoors

labour exchange *n, often cap L&E* a government office that seeks to match unemployed people and vacant jobs and that is responsible for paying out unemployment benefit

labourite *n, often cap* a member or supporter of the Labour party

labour of love *n* a task performed for the pleasure it yields rather than for personal gain

labrador *n, often cap* LABRADOR RETRIEVER

Labrador retriever *n* a retriever characterized by a dense black or golden coat

laburnum *n* any of a small genus of Eurasian leguminous shrubs and trees with bright yellow flowers and poisonous seeds

labyrinth *n* **1** a place that is a network of intricate passageways, tunnels, blind alleys, etc **2** sthg perplexingly complex or tortuous in structure, arrangement, or character **3** (the tortuous anatomical structure in) the ear or its bony or membranous part – **labyrinthine** *adj*

¹lace *n* **1** a cord or string used for drawing together 2 edges (e g of a garment or shoe) **2** an ornamental braid for trimming coats or uniforms **3** an openwork usu figured fabric made of thread, yarn, etc, used for trimmings, household furnishings, garments, etc

²lace *vt* **1** to draw together the edges of (as if) by means of a lace passed through eyelets **2** to draw or pass (e g a lace) through sthg **3** to confine or compress by tightening laces, esp of a corset **4** to adorn (as if) with lace **5** to beat, lash **6a** to add a dash of an alcoholic drink to **b** to give savour or variety to ⟨a mundane story line ~d with witty repartee⟩ ~ *vi* to be fastened or tied *up* with a lace

lacerate *vt* **1** to tear or rend roughly **2** to cause sharp mental or emotional pain to

laceration *n* a torn and ragged wound

lachrymal, lacrimal *adj* **1** of or constituting the glands that produce tears **2** of or marked by tears

lachrymose *adj* **1** given to weeping **2** tending to cause tears – **lachrymosely** *adv*

¹lack *vi* **1** to be deficient or missing **2** to be short or have need of sthg – usu + *for* ⟨she will not ~ *for* advisers⟩ ~ *vt* to stand in need of; suffer from the absence or deficiency of

²lack *n* **1** the fact or state of being wanting or deficient **2** sthg lacking

lackadaisical *adj* lacking life or zest; *also* (reprehensibly) casual or negligent – **lackadaisically** *adv*

lackey *n* **1** a usu liveried retainer **2** a servile follower

lacklustre *adj* lacking in sheen, radiance, or vitality; dull

laconic *adj* using, or involving the use of, a minimum of words; terse – **laconically** *adv*, **laconicism** *n*

¹lacquer *n* **1** a clear or coloured varnish obtained by dissolving a substance (e g shellac) in a solvent (e g alcohol) **2** a durable natural varnish; *esp* one obtained from an Asian shrub of the sumach family

²lacquer *vt* to coat with lacquer – **lacquerer** *n*

lacrosse *n* a game played on grass by 2 teams of 10 players, whose object is to throw a ball into the opponents' goal, using a long-handled stick that has a triangular head with a loose mesh pouch for catching and carrying the ball

lactation *n* (the period of time given to) the secretion of milk by a mammal – **lactational** *adj*, **lactationally** *adv*

lactic *adj* of milk

lactic acid *n* an organic acid, normally present in living tissue, and used esp in food and medicine and in industry

lactose *n* a sugar that is present in milk

lacuna *n, pl* **lacunae, lacunas** **1** a blank space or a missing part **2** a small cavity in an anatomical structure – **lacunal** *adj*, **lacunar** *adj*, **lacunary** *adj*, **lacunate** *adj*

lacy *adj* resembling or consisting of lace

lad *n* **1** a male person between early boyhood and maturity **2** a fellow, chap **3** *Br* STABLE LAD

¹ladder *n* **1** a structure for climbing up or down that has 2 long sidepieces of metal, wood, rope, etc joined at intervals by crosspieces on which one may step **2a** sthg

that resembles or suggests a ladder in form or use **b** *chiefly Br* a vertical line in hosiery or knitting caused by stitches becoming unravelled **3** a series of ascending steps or stages **4** a means of rising or climbing (e g to a higher status or social position)

²ladder *vb, chiefly Br* to develop a ladder (in) ⟨she ~ed *her* tights⟩ ⟨her tights have ~ed⟩

laddie *n* a (young) lad

lade *vt* **laded, laden** **1** to put a load or burden on or in (e g a ship); load **2** to put or place as a load, esp for shipment **3** to weigh down with sthg

la-di-da, lah-di-dah *adj* affectedly refined, esp in voice and pronunciation – *infml*

ladies *n pl but sing in constr, often cap, chiefly Br* a public lavatory for women – *infml*

ladies' man, lady's man *n* a man who likes to please or to be with women

lading *n* cargo, freight

¹ladle *n* **1** a deep-bowled long-handled spoon used esp for taking up and conveying liquids or semiliquid foods (e g soup) **2** a vessel for carrying molten metal

²ladle *vt* **ladling** to take up and convey (as if) in a ladle

lady *n* **1a** a woman with authority, esp as a feudal superior **b** a woman receiving the homage or devotion of a knight or lover **2a** a woman of refinement or superior social position **b** a woman – often in courteous reference ⟨show the ~ *to a seat*⟩ or usu pl in address ⟨ladies *and* gentlemen⟩ **3** a wife ⟨the captain and his ~⟩ **4a** *cap* any of various titled women in Britain – used as a title **b** *cap a* female member of an order of knighthood

ladybird *n* any of numerous small beetles of temperate and tropical regions; *esp* any of several ladybirds that have red wing cases with black spots

lady-in-waiting *n, pl* **ladies-in-waiting** a lady of a queen's or princess's household appointed to wait on her

lady-killer *n* a man who captivates women

ladylike *adj* **1** resembling a lady, esp in manners; well-bred **2** becoming or suitable to a lady

ladyship *n* – used as a title for a woman having the rank of lady

¹lag *vi* **-gg-** **1a** to stay or fall behind; fail to keep pace – often + *behind* **b** to become retarded in attaining maximum value **2** to slacken or weaken gradually

²lag *n* **1** the act or an instance of lagging **2** comparative slowness or retardation **3** an interval between related events; *specif* TIME LAG

³lag *vt* **-gg-** **1** to send to prison **2** to arrest *USE* slang

⁴lag *n* **1** a convict **2** an ex-convict

⁵lag *n* lagging

⁶lag *vt* **-gg-** to cover or provide with lagging – **lagger** *n*

lager *n* a light beer brewed by slow fermentation

laggard *n* sby who or sthg that lags or lingers – **laggardly** *adv or adj*

lagging *n* material for thermal insulation (e g wrapped round a boiler or laid in a roof)

lagoon *n* a shallow channel or pool usu separated from a larger body of water by a sand bank, reef, etc

lah-di-dah *adj* la-di-da

¹laid *past of* LAY

²laid *n* paper watermarked with fine lines running across the grain

lain *past part of* LIE

¹lair *n* **1** the resting or living place of a wild animal **2** a refuge or place for hiding

²lair *n, Austr* a showily dressed young man – chiefly derog – **lairy** *adj*

laird *n, Scot* a member of the landed gentry

laissez-faire, *Br also* **laisser-faire** *n* a doctrine opposing government interference in economic affairs – **laissez-faire** *adj*

laity *n sing or pl in constr* **1** the people of a religion other than its clergy **2** the mass of the people as distinguished from those of a particular profession

¹**lake** *n* a large inland body of water; *also* a pool of oil, pitch, or other liquid

²**lake** *n* **1a** a deep purplish red pigment orig prepared from lac or cochineal **b** any of numerous usu bright pigments composed essentially of a soluble dye absorbed in or combined with an inorganic carrier **2** CARMINE 2

lam *vt* **-mm-** to beat soundly – *infml*

lama *n* a Lamaist monk

Lamaism *n* the Buddhism of Tibet, marked by a dominant monastic hierarchy headed by the Dalai Lama – **Lamaist** *n or adj*, **Lamaistic** *adj*

lamasery *n* a monastery of lamas

¹**lamb** *n* **1a** a young sheep, esp one that is less than a year old or without permanent teeth **b** the young of various animals (e g the smaller antelopes) other than sheep **2a** a gentle, meek, or innocent person **b** a dear, pet **3** the flesh of a lamb used as food

²**lamb** *vi* to give birth to a lamb ~*vt* to tend (ewes) at lambing time – **lamber** *n*

lambaste, lambast *vt* **1** to beat, thrash **2** to attack verbally; censure

lambent *adj* **1** playing lightly on or over a surface; flickering ⟨~ *flames*⟩ **2** softly bright or radiant ⟨*eyes* ~ *with love*⟩ **3** marked by lightness or brilliance, esp of expression ⟨*a* ~ *wit*⟩ USE *fml* – **lambently** *adv*, **lambency** *n*

lambskin *n* **1** (leather made from) the skin of a lamb or small sheep **2** the skin of a lamb dressed with the wool on

¹**lame** *adj* **1** having a body part, esp a leg, so disabled as to impair freedom of movement; *esp* having a limp caused by a disabled leg **2** weak, unconvincing ⟨*a* ~ *excuse*⟩ – **lamely** *adv*, **lameness** *n*

²**lame** *vt* **1** to make lame **2** to make weak or ineffective

lamé *n* a brocaded clothing fabric made from any of various fibres combined with tinsel weft threads often of gold or silver

lame duck *n* sby or sthg (e g a person or business) that is weak or incapable

¹**lament** *vi* to feel or express grief or deep regret; mourn aloud – often + *for* or *over* ~*vt* to lament or mourn (demonstratively) for – **lamentation** *n*

²**lament** *n* **1** an expression of grief **2** a dirge, elegy

lamentable *adj* that is to be regretted; deplorable – **lamentableness** *n*, **lamentably** *adv*

lamina *n, pl* **laminae, laminas** a thin plate, scale, layer, or flake

¹**laminate** *vt* **1** to roll or compress (e g metal) into a thin plate or plates **2** to separate into laminae **3** to make by uniting superimposed layers of 1 or more materials **4** to overlay with a thin sheet or sheets of material (e g metal or plastic) ~*vi* to separate into laminae

²**laminate** *adj* covered with or consisting of laminae

³**laminate** *n* a product made by laminating

lamp *n* **1** any of various devices for producing visible light: e g **a** a vessel containing an inflammable substance (e g oil or gas) that is burnt to give out artificial light **b** a usu portable electric device containing a light bulb **2** any of various light-emitting devices (e g a sunlamp) which produce electromagnetic radiation (e g heat radiation) **3** a source of intellectual or spiritual illumination

lampblack *n* a pigment made from finely powdered black soot

lampoon *vt or n* (to make the subject of) a harsh vitriolic satire – **lampooner, lampoonist** *n*, **lampoonery** *n*

lamp post *n* a post, usu of metal or concrete, that supports a light which illuminates a street or other public area (e g a park)

lamprey *n* any of several eel-like aquatic vertebrates that have a large sucking mouth with no jaws

lampshade *n* a decorative translucent cover placed round an electric light bulb to reduce glare

¹**lance** *n* **1** a weapon having a long shaft with a sharp steel head carried by horsemen for use when charging **2a** LANCET 1 **b** a spear or harpoon for killing whales **3** LANCER 1

²**lance** *vt* **1** to pierce (as if) with a lance **2** to open (as if) with a lancet ⟨~ *a boil*⟩

lance corporal *n* a noncommissioned officer of the lowest rank in the British army or US marines

lancer *n* **1** a member of a light-cavalry unit (formerly) armed with lances **2** *pl but sing in constr* (the music for) a set of 5 quadrilles each in a different metre

lancet *n* **1** a sharp-pointed and usu 2-edged surgical instrument used to make small incisions **2a** *also* **lancet window** a high narrow window with an acutely pointed head **b** *also* **lancet arch** an acutely pointed arch

¹**land** *n* **1a** the solid part of the surface of a celestial body, esp the earth **b** ground or soil of a specified situation, nature, or quality ⟨*wet* ~⟩ **2** (*the* way of life in) *the* rural and esp agricultural regions of a country ⟨*going back to the* ~⟩ **3** (the people of) a country, region, etc **4** a realm, domain ⟨*in the* ~ *of dreams*⟩ **5** ground owned as property – often *pl* with *sing.* meaning – **landless** *adj*

²**land** *vt* **1** to set or put on shore from a ship **2a** to set down (e g passengers or goods) after conveying **b** to bring to or cause to reach a specified place, position, or condition ⟨*his carelessness* ~*ed him in trouble*⟩ **c** to bring (e g an aeroplane) to a surface from the air **3a** to catch and bring in (e g a fish) **b** to gain, secure ⟨~ *a job*⟩ – *infml* **4** to strike, hit ⟨~ *ed him one on the nose*⟩ – *infml* **5** to present or burden *with* sthg unwanted – *infml* ~*vi* **1a** to go ashore from a ship; disembark **b** *of a boat, ship, etc* to come to shore; *also* to arrive on shore in a boat, ship, etc **2a** to end up – usu + *up* ⟨*took the wrong bus and* ~*ed up on the other side of town*⟩ **b** to strike or come to rest on a surface (e g after a fall) ⟨~*ed on his head*⟩ **c** *of an aircraft, spacecraft, etc* to alight on a surface; *also* to arrive in an aircraft, spacecraft, etc which has alighted on a surface

land agent *n* ESTATE AGENT

landau *n* a 4-wheeled carriage with a folding top divided into 2 sections

land breeze *n* a breeze blowing seawards from the land, generally at night

land crab *n* any of various crabs that live mostly on land and breed in the sea

landed *adj* **1** owning land ⟨~ *proprietors*⟩ **2** consisting of land ⟨~ *property*⟩

landfall *n* an act or instance of sighting or reaching land after a voyage or flight

landing *n* **1** the act of going or bringing to a surface from the air or to shore from the water **2** a place for discharging and taking on passengers and cargo **3** a level space at the end of a flight of stairs or between 2 flights of stairs

landing craft *n* any of numerous naval craft designed for putting troops and equipment ashore

landing stage *n* a sometimes floating platform for landing passengers or cargo

landing strip *n* a runway without normal airfield or airport facilities

landlady n 1 a female landlord 2 the female proprietor of a guesthouse or lodging house

landlocked adj (nearly) enclosed by land

landlord n 1 sby who owns land, buildings, or accommodation for lease or rent 2 sby who owns or keeps an inn; an innkeeper

landlubber n a person unacquainted with the sea or seamanship – **landlubberly** adj

landmark n 1a an object (e g a stone) that marks a boundary b a conspicuous object that can be used to identify a locality 2 an event that marks a turning point or new development ⟨a ~ in the history of aviation⟩

¹landscape n 1 natural, esp inland scenery 2a a picture, drawing, etc of landscape b the art of depicting landscape

²landscape vt to improve or modify the natural beauties of ~ vi to engage in the occupation of landscape gardening – **landscaper** n

landscape gardener n one who designs and arranges the layout of gardens and grounds – **landscape gardening** n

landslide n 1 a usu rapid movement of rock, earth, etc down a slope; also the moving mass 2 an overwhelming victory, esp in an election

landslip n a small landslide

¹lane n 1 a narrow passageway, road, or street 2a a fixed ocean route used by ships b a strip of road for a single line of vehicles c AIR LANE d any of several marked parallel courses to which a competitor must keep during a race (e g in running or swimming) e a narrow hardwood surface down which the ball is sent towards the pins in tenpin bowling

²lane adj, Scot lone

language n 1a those words, their pronunciation, and the methods of combining them used by a particular people, nation, etc ⟨the English ~⟩ b(1) (the faculty of making and using) audible articulate meaningful sound (2) a systematic means of communicating using conventionalized signs, sounds, gestures, or marks (3) the suggestion by objects, actions, or conditions of associated ideas or feelings ⟨body ~⟩ (4) a formal system of signs and symbols (e g a logical calculus or one for use with a computer) together with rules for the formation and transformation of admissible expressions 2a a particular style or manner of verbal expression b the specialized vocabulary and phraseology belonging to a particular group or profession ⟨legal ~⟩

language laboratory n a room, usu divided into booths each equipped with a tape recorder, where foreign languages are learnt by listening and speaking

languid adj 1 drooping or flagging (as if) from exhaustion; weak 2a spiritless or apathetic in character b esp of literary style lacking colour; uninteresting 3 lacking force or quickness, esp of movement; sluggish – **languidly** adv, **languidness** n

languish vi 1 to be or become feeble or enervated 2a to become dispirited or depressed; pine – often + for b to lose intensity or urgency ⟨his interest ~ed⟩ c to suffer hardship or neglect ⟨~ed in prison for 2 years⟩ 3 to assume an expression of emotion appealing for sympathy – **languishingly** adv, **languishment** n

languor n 1 weakness or weariness of body or mind 2 a feeling or mood of wistfulness or dreaminess 3 heavy or soporific stillness – **languorous** adj, **languorously** adv

lank adj 1 lean, gaunt 2 straight, limp, and usu greasy ⟨~ hair⟩ – **lankly** adv, **lankness** n

lanky adj ungracefully tall and thin – **lankily** adv, **lankiness** n

lanolin, lanoline n wool grease, esp when refined for use in ointments and cosmetics

lantern n 1 a portable protective case with transparent windows that houses a light (e g a candle) 2a the chamber in a lighthouse containing the light b a structure above an opening in a roof which has glazed or open sides for light or ventilation 3 MAGIC LANTERN

lanyard n 1 a piece of rope or line for fastening sthg on board ship 2 a cord worn round the neck as a decoration or to hold sthg (e g a knife) 3 a cord used in firing certain types of cannon

¹lap n (the clothing covering) the front part of the lower trunk and thighs of a seated person – **lapful** n – **drop/land (sthg) in someone's lap** to (cause to) become sby's responsibility – **in the lap of luxury** in an environment of great ease, comfort, and wealth – **in the lap of the gods** beyond human influence or control

²lap vb -pp- vt 1a to fold or wrap over or round b to envelop entirely; swathe 2 to surround or hold protectively (as if) in the lap 3a to place or lie so as to (partly) cover (one another) ⟨~ tiles on a roof⟩ b to unite (e g beams or timbers) so as to preserve the same breadth and depth throughout 4a to dress, smooth, or polish (e g a metal surface) to a high degree of refinement or accuracy b to work (2 surfaces) together with or without abrasives until a very close fit is produced 5a to overtake and thereby lead or increase the lead over (another contestant) by a full circuit of a racetrack b to complete a circuit of (a racetrack) ~ vi 1 to overlap 2 to traverse or complete a circuit of a course

³lap n 1a the amount by which one object overlaps another b the part of an object that overlaps another 2 a smoothing and polishing tool (e g for metal or precious stones), usu consisting of a rotating disc covered with abrasive 3 a layer of a flexible substance (e g fibres or paper) wound round sthg, esp a roller 4a (the distance covered during) the act or an instance of moving once round a closed course or track b one stage or segment of a larger unit (e g a journey) c one complete turn (e g of a rope round a drum)

⁴lap vb -pp- vi 1 to take in liquid with the tongue 2 to move in little waves, usu making a gentle splashing sound ⟨the sea ~ped gently against the edge of the quay⟩ ~ vt 1a to take in (liquid) with the tongue b to take in eagerly or quickly – usu + up ⟨the crowd ~ped up every word he said⟩ 2 to flow or splash against in little waves

⁵lap n 1 an act or instance of lapping 2 a thin or weak beverage or food 3 a gentle splashing sound

lapdog n a small dog that may be held in the lap

lapel n a fold of the top front edge of a coat or jacket that is continuous with the collar

¹lapidary n sby who cuts, polishes, or engraves precious stones

²lapidary adj 1a sculptured in or engraved on stone b of or relating to (the cutting of) gems 2 of literary style having the elegance and dignity associated with monumental inscriptions

lapis lazuli n (the colour of) a rich blue semiprecious stone

¹lapse n 1 a slight error (e g of memory or in manners) 2a a drop; specif a drop in temperature, humidity, or pressure with increasing height b an esp moral fall or decline ⟨a ~ from grace⟩ 3a(1) the legal termination of a right or privilege through failure to exercise it (2) the termination of insurance coverage for nonpayment of premiums b a decline into disuse 4 an abandonment of religious faith 5 a continuous passage or elapsed period ⟨returned after a ~ of several years⟩

²lapse vi 1a to fall or depart from an attained or accepted standard or level (e g of morals) – usu + *from* **b** to sink or slip gradually ⟨the guests ~d into silence when the speech began⟩ **2** to go out of existence or use **3** to pass to another proprietor by omission or negligence **4** *of time* to run its course; pass

lapse rate *n* the rate of change of temperature, humidity, or pressure with changing height

lapwing *n* a crested Old World plover noted for its shrill wailing cry

larboard *n, archaic* ⁴PORT – **larboard** *adj*

larceny *n* theft

larch *n* (the wood of) any of a genus of trees of the pine family with short deciduous leaves

¹**lard** *vt* **1a** to dress (e g meat) for cooking by inserting or covering with fat, bacon, etc **b** to cover with grease **2** to intersperse or embellish (e g speech or writing) *with* sthg

²**lard** *n* a soft white solid fat obtained by rendering the esp abdominal fat of a pig – **lardy** *adj*

larder *n* a place where food is stored; a pantry

¹**large** *adj* **1** having more than usual power, capacity, or scope **2** exceeding most other things of like kind (in quantity or size) **3** dealing in great numbers or quantities; operating on an extensive scale ⟨a ~ and highly profitable business⟩ – **largeness** *n*, **largish** *adj*

²**large** *n* – **at large 1** without restraint or confinement; AT LIBERTY ⟨the escaped prisoner is still at large⟩ **2** AS A WHOLE ⟨society at large⟩

large intestine *n* the rear division of the vertebrate intestine that is divided into caecum, colon, and rectum, and concerned esp with the resorption of water and formation of faeces

largely *adv* to a large extent

largess, largesse *n* **1** liberal giving, esp to an inferior **2** sthg (e g money) given generously as a gift

largo *n, adv, or adj, pl* **largos** (a movement to be) played in a very slow and broad manner – used in music

lariat *n, chiefly NAm* a lasso

¹**lark** *n* any of numerous brown singing birds mostly of Europe, Asia, and northern Africa; *esp* a skylark

²**lark** *vi* to have fun – usu + *about* or *around*

³**lark** *n* **1** a lighthearted adventure; *also* a prank **2** *Br* a type of activity; *esp* a business, job ⟨it's a good ~: 80 quid a week, own car, and no questions asked⟩ *USE* infml

larkspur *n* a delphinium; *esp* a cultivated annual delphinium grown for its bright irregular flowers

larrup *vt, Br dial* to beat soundly – infml

larva *n, pl* **larvae 1** the immature, wingless, and often wormlike feeding form that hatches from the egg of many insects and is transformed into a pupa or chrysalis from which the adult emerges **2** the early form (e g a tadpole) of an animal (e g a frog) that undergoes metamorphosis before becoming an adult – **larval** *adj*

laryngeal *n* a nerve, artery, etc that supplies or is associated with the larynx

laryngitis *n* inflammation of the larynx – **laryngitic** *adj*

larynx *n, pl* **larynges, larynxes** the modified upper part of the trachea of air-breathing vertebrates that contains the vocal cords in human beings, most other mammals, and a few lower forms – **laryngeal**

lasagne *n* (a baked dish of minced meat, sauce, and) pasta in the form of broad flat sheets

lascivious *adj* inclined or inciting to lechery or lewdness – **lasciviously** *adv*, **lasciviousness** *n*

laser *n* a device that generates an intense beam of coherent light or other electromagnetic radiation of a single wavelength by using the natural oscillations of atoms or molecules

¹**lash** *vi* **1** to move violently or suddenly **2** to beat, pour ⟨rain ~ed down⟩ **3** to attack physically or verbally, (as if) with a whip – often + *at, against, out* ~ *vt* **1** to strike quickly and forcibly (as if) with a lash **2a** to drive (as if) with a whip; rouse ⟨~ed the crowd into a frenzy⟩ **b** to cause to lash

²**lash** *n* **1a**(1) a stroke (as if) with a whip (2) (the flexible part of) a whip **b** a sudden swinging movement or blow **2** violent beating ⟨the ~ of a north wind⟩ **3** an eyelash **4** *Austr & NZ* an attempt, go – infml

³**lash** *vt* to bind or fasten with a cord, rope, etc – **lasher** *n*

¹**lashing** *n* a physical or verbal beating

²**lashing** *n* sthg used for binding, wrapping, or fastening

lashings *n pl* an abundance – usu + *of* ⟨~ of hot water⟩; infml

lash out *vi* **1** to make a sudden violent physical or verbal attack – usu + *at* or *against* **2** *Br* to spend unrestrainedly – often + *on*; infml

lass, lassie *n* a young woman; a girl

¹**lasso** *n, pl* **lassos, lassoes** a rope or long thong of leather with a running noose that is used esp for catching horses and cattle

²**lasso** *vt* **lassos, lassoes; lassoed; lassoing** to catch (as if) with a lasso – **lassoer** *n*

¹**last** *vi* **1** to continue in time **2a** to remain in good or adequate condition, use, or effectiveness **b** to manage to continue (e g in a course of action) **c** to continue to live ⟨he won't ~ much longer⟩ ~ *vt* **1** to continue in existence or action as long as or longer than – often + *out* ⟨couldn't ~ out the training⟩ **2** to be enough for the needs of ⟨the supplies will ~ them a week⟩ – **laster** *n*

²**last** *adj* **1** following all the rest: e g **a** final, latest **b** being the only remaining ⟨his ~ pound⟩ **2** of the final stage of life ⟨~ rites⟩ **3** next before the present; most recent ⟨~ week⟩ ⟨this is better than his ~ book⟩ **4a** lowest in rank or standing; *also* worst **b** least suitable or likely ⟨he'd be the ~ person to fall for flattery⟩ **5a** conclusive, definitive ⟨the ~ word on the subject⟩ **b** single – used as an intensive ⟨ate every ~ scrap⟩ – **lastly** *adv* – **last but one 1** second most recent **2** penultimate

³**last** *adv* **1** after all others; at the end ⟨came ~ and left first⟩ **2** on the most recent occasion ⟨when we ~ met⟩ **3** in conclusion; lastly ⟨and ~, the economic aspect⟩

⁴**last** *n* sby or sthg last – **at last/at long last** after everything; finally; *esp* after much delay – **to the last** till the end

⁵**last** *n* a form (e g of metal) shaped like the human foot, over which a shoe is shaped or repaired

last-ditch *adj* made as a final effort, esp to avert disaster ⟨a ~ attempt⟩

lasting *adj* existing or continuing for a long while – **lastingly** *adv*, **lastingness** *n*

last straw *n* the last of a series (e g of events or indignities) stretching one's patience beyond its limit

last word *n* **1** the final remark in a verbal exchange **2** the power of final decision **3** the most up-to-date or fashionable example of its kind ⟨the ~ in sports cars⟩

¹**latch** *vi* **1** to attach oneself ⟨~ed onto a rich widow⟩ **2** to gain understanding or comprehension *USE* + *on* or *onto*

²**latch** *n* **1** a fastener (e g for a door) with a pivoted bar that falls into a notch on the door post **2** a fastener (e g for a door) in which a spring slides a bolt into a hole when the door is shut – **latch** *vt*

latchkey *n* a key to an outside (front) door

latchkey child *n, chiefly Br* a child whose mother is regularly out on his/her return from school; *specif* one given a key to let him-/herself in

¹**late** adj **1a** occurring or arriving after the expected time ⟨a ~ spring⟩ **b** of the end of a specified time span ⟨the ~ Middle Ages⟩ **2a** (recently) deceased – used with reference to names, positions or specified relationships ⟨the ~ James Scott⟩ ⟨his ~ wife⟩ ⟨the ~ chairman⟩ **b** just prior to the present, esp as the most recent of a succession ⟨the ~ government⟩ ⟨some ~ news has just arrived⟩ **3** far on in the day or night ⟨it's too ~ to go now⟩ – **lateness** n

²**late** adv **1a** after the usual or proper time ⟨stayed up ~⟩ **b** at or near the end of a period of time or of a process – often + on ⟨~ on in the experiment⟩ **2** until lately ⟨Dr Evans, ~ of Birmingham, now lectures at Durham⟩ – **of late** in the period shortly or immediately before; recently ⟨have not seen him of late⟩

lateen adj of or being a rig characterized by a triangular sail hung from a long spar set obliquely on a low mast

lately adv recently; OF LATE ⟨has been friendlier ~⟩

latent adj present but not manifest ⟨a ~ infection⟩ ⟨his desire for success remained ~⟩ – **latency** n, **latently** adj

latent heat n heat given off or absorbed in a change of phase without a change in temperature

¹**lateral** adj **1** of the side; situated on, directed towards, or coming from the side **2** made by allowing air to escape on either or both sides of the tongue ⟨l is a ~ consonant⟩ – **laterally** adv

²**lateral** n a lateral consonant

latest n **1** the most recent or currently fashionable style or development ⟨the ~ in diving techniques⟩ **2** the latest acceptable time ⟨be home by one at the ~⟩

latex n, pl **latices**, **latexes 1** a milky usu white fluid that is produced by various flowering plants (e g of the spurge and poppy families) and is the source of rubber, gutta-percha, chicle, and balata **2** a water emulsion of a synthetic rubber or plastic – **laticiferous** adj

¹**lath** n, pl **laths**, **lath** a thin narrow strip of wood, esp for nailing to woodwork (e g rafters or studding) as a support (e g for tiles or plaster)

²**lath** vt to cover or line with laths – **lathing** n

¹**lathe** n a former administrative district of Kent

²**lathe** n a machine in which work is rotated about a horizontal axis and shaped by a fixed tool

¹**lather** n **1a** a foam or froth formed when a detergent (e g soap) is agitated in water **b** foam or froth from profuse sweating (e g on a horse) **2** an agitated or overwrought state – **lathery** adj

²**lather** vt **1** to spread lather over **2** to beat severely – infml ~vi to form a (froth like) lather – **latherer** n

¹**Latin** adj **1** of Latium or the Latins **2a** of or composed in Latin **b** Romance **3** of the part of the Christian church using a Latin liturgy; broadly ROMAN CATHOLIC **4** of the peoples or countries using Romance languages **5** chiefly NAm of the peoples or countries of Latin America – **Latinize** vb

²**Latin** n **1** the Italic language of ancient Latium and of Rome **2** a member of the people of ancient Latium **3** a member of any of the Latin peoples **4** chiefly NAm a native or inhabitant of Latin America

latinize, -ise vt **1** to give a Latin form or character to **2** ROMANIZE **2** – **latinization** n

latitude n **1a** the angular distance of a point on the surface of a celestial body, esp the earth, measured N or S from the equator **b** the angular distance of a celestial body from the ecliptic **2** a region as marked by its latitude – often pl with sing. meaning **3** (permitted) freedom of action or choice – **latitudinal** adj, **latitudinally** adv

latitudinarian n or adj (a person) liberal in standards of religious belief and conduct; specif a member of the Church of England favouring freedom of doctrine and practice within it – **latitudinarianism** n

latrine n a small pit used as a toilet, esp in a military camp, barracks, etc; broadly a toilet

-latry comb form (→ n) worship ⟨heliolatry⟩ ⟨idolatry⟩ – **-later** comb form (→ n)

¹**latter** adj **1** of the end; later, final ⟨the ~ stages of a process⟩ **2** recent, present ⟨in ~ years⟩ **3** second of 2 things, or last of several things mentioned or understood ⟨of ham and beef the ~ meat is cheaper today⟩

²**latter** n, pl **latter** the second or last mentioned

latter-day adj of present or recent times

latterly adv **1** towards the end or latter part of a period **2** lately

lattice n **1** (a window, door, etc having) a framework or structure of crossed wooden or metal strips with open spaces between **2** a network or design like a lattice **3a** a regular geometrical arrangement of points or objects over an area or in space **b** the geometrical arrangement of the atoms or ions in a crystal – **lattice** vt, **latticed** adj

¹**laud** n **1** pl but sing or pl in constr, often cap an office usu immediately following matins and forming with it the first of the canonical hours **2** praise – used esp in hymns

²**laud** vt to praise, esp with hymns

laudable adj worthy of praise; commendable – **laudableness** n, **laudably** adv, **laudability** n

laudanum n **1** any of various preparations of opium formerly used in medicine **2** a tincture of opium

laudatory, laudative adj of or expressing praise

¹**laugh** vi **1a** to make the explosive vocal sounds characteristically expressing amusement, mirth, joy, or derision **b** to experience amusement, mirth, joy, or derision ⟨~ed inwardly though her face remained grave⟩ **2** to produce a sound of or like laughter – chiefly poetic ⟨a ~ing brook⟩ ~ vt **1** to influence or bring to a specified state by laughter ⟨~ed him out of his fears⟩ **2** to utter (as if) with a laugh ⟨~ed her consent⟩ **3** to dismiss as trivial – + off or away ⟨you can't ~ off a royal commission – Alan Villiers⟩ – **laugher** n, **laughingly** adv – **laugh up one's sleeve** to be secretly amused

²**laugh** n **1** the act or sound of laughing **2** an expression of mirth or scorn **3** a means of entertainment; a diversion – often pl with sing. meaning **4** a cause for derision or merriment; a joke – infml ⟨swim in that current? That's a ~⟩

laughable adj of a kind to provoke laughter or derision; ridiculous – **laughableness** n, **laughably** adv

laughing gas n NITROUS OXIDE

laughing jackass n the kookaburra

laughingstock n an object of ridicule

laughter n **1** a sound (as if) of laughing **2** the action of laughing

¹**launch** vt **1a** to throw forward; hurl **b** to release or send off (e g a self-propelled object) ⟨~ a rocket⟩ **2a** to set (an esp newly built boat or ship) afloat **b** to start or set in motion (e g on a course or career) **c** to introduce (a new product) onto the market ⟨a party to ~ a new book⟩ ~ vi **1** to throw oneself energetically – + into or out into ⟨~ed into a brilliant harangue⟩ **2** to make a start – usu + out or forth ⟨~ed forth on a long-winded explanation⟩

²**launch** n an act or instance of launching

³**launch** n **1** the largest boat carried by a warship **2** a large open or half-decked motorboat

launching pad n a noninflammable platform from which a rocket can be launched

launder vt **1** to wash (e g clothes) in water **2** to make ready for use by washing, sometimes starching, and ironing **3** to give (sthg, esp money, obtained illegally) the appearance of being respectable or legal ~ vi to become clean by washing, ironing, etc ⟨clothes that ~ well⟩ – **launderer** n, **laundress** n

launderette n a self-service laundry

laundry n **1** clothes or cloth articles that have been or are to be laundered, esp by being sent to a laundry **2** a place where laundering is done; esp a commercial laundering establishment

laureate n a person specially honoured for achievement in an art or science – **laureate** adj, **laureateship** n

laurel n **1** any of a genus of trees or shrubs that have alternate entire leaves, small flowers, and fruits that are ovoid berries **2** a tree or shrub that resembles the true laurel **3** a crown of laurel awarded as a token of victory or preeminence; distinction, honour – usu pl with sing. meaning

lava n (solidified) molten rock that issues from a volcano – **lavalike** adj

lavatory n **1** a toilet **2** NAm a room with facilities for washing and usu with 1 or more toilets – **lavatory** adj

lave vt to wash; BATHE **1** – poetic

lavender n **1** a Mediterranean plant of the mint family widely cultivated for its narrow aromatic leaves and spikes of lilac-purple flowers which are dried and used in perfume sachets **2** pale purple

¹**lavish** adj **1** expending or bestowing profusely **2** expended, bestowed, or produced in abundance – **lavishly** adj, **lavishness** n

²**lavish** vt to expend or bestow with profusion

law n **1a(1)** a rule of conduct formally recognized as binding or enforced by authority **(2)** the whole body of such rules ⟨the ~ of the land⟩ **(3)** COMMON LAW **b** the control brought about by such law – esp in law and order **c** litigation ⟨ready to go to ~⟩ **2a** a rule one should observe **b** control, authority **3a** often cap the revelation of the will of God set out in the Old Testament **b** cap the first part of the Jewish scriptures; the Pentateuch **4** a rule of action, construction, or procedure ⟨the ~s of poetry⟩ **5** the law relating to one subject ⟨company ~⟩ **6** often cap the legal profession **7** jurisprudence **8a** a statement of an order or relation of natural phenomena ⟨the first ~ of thermodynamics⟩ ⟨Boyle's ~⟩ **b** a necessary relation between mathematical or logical expressions **9** sing or pl in constr, often cap the police – infml – **in/at law** according to the law – **law unto him-/her-/itself** sby or sthg that does not follow accepted conventions

law-abiding adj abiding by or obedient to the law

lawbreaker n one who violates the law – **lawbreaking** adj or n

lawful adj **1** allowed by law **2** rightful ⟨your ~ Queen⟩ – **lawfully** adv, **lawfulness** n

lawless adj **1** not regulated by or based on law **2** not restrained or controlled by law – **lawlessly** adv, **lawlessness** n

¹**lawn** n a fine sheer linen or cotton fabric of plain weave that is thinner than cambric – **lawny** adj

²**lawn** n an area of ground (e g around a house or in a garden or park) that is covered with grass and is kept mowed

lawn tennis n tennis played on a grass court

lawsuit n a noncriminal case in a court of law

lawyer n sby whose profession is to conduct lawsuits or to advise on legal matters

lax adj **1** of the bowels loose, open **2** not strict or stringent; negligent ⟨~ morals⟩ ⟨~ in his duties⟩; also deficient in firmness or precision ⟨his ideas are a bit ~⟩ **3a** not tense, firm, or rigid; slack ⟨a ~ rope⟩ **b** not compact or exhibiting close cohesion; loose ⟨a ~ flower cluster⟩ **4** of a speech sound articulated with the muscles in a relatively

relaxed state (e g the vowel /i/ in contrast with the vowel /ee/) – **laxity**, **laxness** n, **laxly** adv, **laxation** n

laxative n or adj (a usu mild purgative) having a tendency to loosen or relax the bowels (to relieve constipation) – **laxativeness** n

¹**lay** vb **laid** vt **1** to beat or strike down with force ⟨a blow that laid him to the ground⟩ ⟨wheat laid flat by the wind and rain⟩ **2a** to put or set down **b** to place for rest or sleep; esp to bury **3** of a bird to produce (an egg) **4** to calm, allay ⟨~ the dust⟩ ⟨~ a ghost⟩ **5** to bet, wager ⟨~ odds on the favourite⟩ ⟨~ my life on it⟩ **6** to press down giving a smooth and even surface ⟨laid tarmac on the road⟩ **7a** to dispose or spread over or on a surface ⟨~ a cloth on the table⟩ **b** to set in order or position ⟨~ a table for dinner⟩ ⟨~ bricks⟩ **c** to put (strands) in place and twist to form a rope, hawser, or cable **8a** to put or impose as a duty, burden, or punishment – esp + on or upon **b** to put as a burden of reproach ⟨laid the blame on him⟩ **c** to advance as an accusation; impute ⟨the disaster was laid to faulty inspection⟩ ⟨laid a charge of manslaughter⟩ **9** to place (sthg immaterial) on sthg ⟨~ stress on grammar⟩ **10** to prepare, contrive ⟨a well-laid plan⟩ **11a** to bring into position or against or into contact with sthg ⟨laid the watch to his ear⟩ ⟨the horse laid his ears back⟩ **b** to prepare or position for action or operation ⟨~ a fire in the fireplace⟩ **c** to adjust (a gun) to the proper direction and elevation **12** to bring to a specified condition ⟨~ waste the land⟩ **13a** to assert, allege ⟨~ claim to an estate⟩ **b** to submit for examination and judgment ⟨laid his case before the tribunal⟩ **14** to place fictitiously; locate ⟨the scene is laid in wartime London⟩ **15** to put aside for future use; store, reserve – + aside, by, in, or up **16** to put out of use or consideration – + aside or by **17** to copulate with – slang ~ vi **1** esp of a hen to produce eggs **2** to wager, bet **3** to apply oneself vigorously ⟨laid to his oars⟩ **4** ¹LIE – nonstandard – **lay about one** to deal blows indiscriminately; lash out on all sides – **lay hands on 1** to seize forcibly **2** to find – **lay into** to attack with words or blows – **lay it on 1** to exaggerate, esp in order to flatter or impress ⟨that was really laying it on a bit thick⟩ **2** to charge an exorbitant price – **lay on the table** to make public; disclose – **lay low 1** to knock or bring down, esp; destroy **2** to cause to be ill or physically weakened – **lay open** to expose: e g **a** to cut ⟨a blow that laid his head open⟩ **b** to explain or make known; UNCOVER 1 ⟨the facts of the case were laid wide open⟩ – **lay siege to 1** to besiege militarily **2** to attempt to conquer or persuade diligently or persistently

²**lay** n **1** (a partner in) sexual intercourse – slang **2** chiefly NAm the position or situation in which sthg lies, esp relative to sthg else ⟨the ~ of the land⟩ – **in lay** esp of a hen in condition to lay eggs

³**lay** past of LIE

⁴**lay** n a simple narrative poem intended to be sung; a ballad

⁵**lay** adj **1** of or performed by the laity **2** of domestic or manual workers in a religious community ⟨a ~ brother⟩ **3** not belonging to a particular profession

layabout n, chiefly Br a lazy shiftless person

lay-by n, pl **lay-bys** Br a branch from or widening of a road to permit vehicles to stop without obstructing traffic

lay down vt **1** to surrender; GIVE UP ⟨laid down her life for the cause⟩ **2a** to begin to construct (e g a ship or railway) **b** to establish, prescribe; esp to dictate ⟨~ the law⟩ **3** to store; specif to store (wine) in a cellar

¹**layer** n **1a** a single thickness of some substance spread or lying over or under another (as part of a series) **b** any of a series of gradations or depths ⟨~s of meaning⟩ **2a** a branch or shoot of a plant treated to induce rooting while

still attached to the parent plant **b** a plant developed by layering

²layer *vt* **1** to propagate (a plant) by means of layers **2** to cut (hair) in layers **3** to arrange or form (as if) in layers ⟨*potato slices* ~ed *with cheese*⟩ **4** to form out of or with layers ~ *vi, of a plant* to form roots where a stem comes in contact with the ground

layette *n* a complete outfit of clothing and equipment for a newborn infant

lay figure *n* **1** a jointed model of the human body used by artists, esp to show the arrangement of drapery **2** a person likened to a dummy or puppet

layman, *fem* **laywoman** *n* **1** a person not of the clergy **2** a person without special (e g professional) knowledge of some field

layoff *n* **1** the laying off of an employee or work force **2** a period of unemployment, inactivity, or idleness

lay off *vt* **1** to cease to employ (a worker), usu temporarily **2a** to let alone **b** to avoid ⟨*lay off pastry and pud – The Times*⟩ ~ *vi* to stop or desist, specif from an activity causing annoyance *USE* (*vt 2; vi*) *infml*

lay on *vt, chiefly Br* **1** to supply (e g water or gas) to a building **2** to supply; organize ⟨*cars were* laid on⟩ ⟨*they* laid on *a good meal*⟩

layout *n* **1** arranging or laying out **2** the plan, design, or arrangement of sthg (e g rooms in a building or matter to be printed) laid out **3** sthg laid out ⟨*a model train* ~⟩

lay out *vt* **1** to prepare (a corpse) for a funeral **2** to arrange according to a plan ⟨*flower beds and lawns were* laid out *in a formal pattern*⟩ **3** to knock flat or unconscious **4** to spend **5** to exert (oneself) for a purpose *USE* (*except 1 & 2*) *infml*

lay reader *n* a lay person authorized to conduct parts of church services

lay up *vt* **1** to store up; have or keep for future use **2** to disable or confine with illness or injury **3** to take out of active service

laze *vi* to act or rest lazily ~ *vt* to pass (time) *away* in idleness or relaxation – **laze** *n*

lazy *adj* **1a** disinclined or averse to activity; indolent; *also* not energetic or vigorous ⟨*a* ~ *manner*⟩ **b** encouraging inactivity or indolence ⟨*a* ~ *afternoon*⟩ **2** moving slowly ⟨*a* ~ *river*⟩ – **lazily** *adv,* **laziness** *n*

L-dopa *n* the laevorotatory form of dopa used in the treatment of Parkinson's disease

lea *n* (an area of) grassland, pasture – chiefly poetic

leach *vt* to separate the soluble components from (a mixture) or remove (sthg soluble) by the action of a percolating liquid ~ *vi* to pass out or through (as if) by percolation – **leach** *n,* **leacher** *n*

¹lead *vb* **led** *vt* **1a(1)** to guide on a way, esp by going in advance (**2**) to cause to go with one (under duress) ⟨led *the condemned man to the scaffold*⟩ **b** to direct or guide on a course or to a state or condition; influence ⟨*reflection* led *him to a better understanding of the problem*⟩ **c** to serve as a channel or route for ⟨*a pipe* ~s *water to the house*⟩ ⟨*the road* led *her to a small village*⟩ **2** to go through; live ⟨~ *a quiet life*⟩ **3a(1)** to direct the operations, activity, or performance of; have charge of ⟨led *a safari into little known territory*⟩ (**2**) to act as or be a leader in or of ⟨~ *fashion*⟩ ⟨~ *an orchestra*⟩ **b** to go or be at the head or ahead of **4** to begin play, esp at a card game, with ~ *vi* **1a(1)** to guide sby or sthg along a way (**2**) to act as or be a leader **b(1)** to lie or run in a specified place or direction ⟨*the path* ~s *uphill*⟩ (**2**) to serve as an entrance or passage ⟨*this door* ~s *to the garden*⟩ **2a** to be first or ahead **b(1)** to begin, open – usu + *off* ⟨led *off with a speech by the chairman*⟩ (**2**) to play the first card of a trick, round, or game **3** to tend or be directed towards

a specified result ⟨*study* ~ing *to a degree*⟩ **4** to direct the first of a series of blows at an opponent in boxing (*with the right or left hand*) – **lead up to** to prepare the way for, esp by using a gradual or indirect approach – **lead someone a dance** to cause sby a lot of trouble

²lead *n* **1a(1)** position at the front or ahead (**2**) the act or privilege of leading in cards; *also* the card or suit led **b** guidance, direction; (an) example **c** a margin or position of advantage or superiority **2a** a channel of water (**1**) leading to a mill (**2**) through an ice field **b** an indication, clue **c** (one who plays) a principal role in a dramatic production **d** a line or strap for leading or restraining an animal (e g a dog) **e** a news story of chief importance **3** an insulated electrical conductor **4** ⁴PITCH 2b(2)

³lead *n* **1** a heavy soft malleable bluish-white metallic element used esp in pipes, cable sheaths, batteries, solder, type metal, and shields against radioactivity **2a** the (lead) weight on a sounding line **b** *pl* lead framing for panes in windows **c** a thin strip of metal used to separate lines of type in printing **3a** a thin stick of graphite or crayon in or for a pencil **b** WHITE LEAD **4** bullets, projectiles ⟨*the* ~ *was flying*⟩ **5** *pl, Br* (a usu flat roof covered with) thin lead sheets – **leadless** *adj*

⁴lead *vt* **1** to fix (window glass) in position with leads **2** to separate lines of (type) with leads **3** to treat or mix with (a compound of) lead ⟨~ed *petrol*⟩

leaden *adj* **1a** made of lead **b** dull grey **2a** oppressively heavy ⟨~ *limbs*⟩ ⟨*a* ~ *silence*⟩ **b** lacking spirit or animation; sluggish ⟨~ *prose*⟩ – **leadenly** *adv,* **leadenness** *n*

leader *n* **1a** a main or end shoot of a plant **b** *pl* dots or hyphens used to lead the eye horizontally **c** a blank section at the beginning or end of a reel of film or recorded tape **2a** sby or sthg that ranks first, precedes others, or holds a principal position **b** sby who has commanding authority or influence **c(1)** the principal officer of a political party ⟨~ *of the opposition*⟩ (**2**) either of 2 government ministers in charge of government business in Parliament ⟨*the* Leader *of the Commons*⟩ (**3**) the principal member of the ruling party in a totalitarian system **3** a horse placed in advance of the other horse or horses of a pair or team **4** *chiefly Br* a newspaper editorial **5a** *Br* the principal first violinist and usu assistant conductor of an orchestra **b** NAm CONDUCTOR 2 – **leaderless** *adj,* **leadership** *n*

lead-in *n* **1** introductory matter **2** the part of the groove on a record before the recording

¹leading *adj* coming or ranking first; foremost, principal ⟨*the* ~ *role*⟩

²leading *n* ¹LEAD 2c; *also* a space between printed lines made (as if) with a lead

leading article *n, chiefly Br* LEADER 4

leading light *n* a prominent and influential person in a particular sphere

leading question *n* a question so phrased as to suggest the expected answer

leading reins *n pl* straps by which children are supported when beginning to walk

leading strings *n pl* **1** LEADING REINS **2** a state of unnecessary or prolonged dependence – chiefly in *in leading strings*

lead-off *n* a beginning or leading action; a start

lead on *vt* **1** to entice or induce to proceed in a (mistaken or unwise) course **2** to cause to believe sthg that is untrue

¹leaf *n, pl* **leaves** **1a(1)** any of the usu green flat and typically broad-bladed outgrowths from the stem of a plant that function primarily in food manufacture by photosynthesis (**2**) a modified leaf (e g a petal or sepal) **b(1)** (the state of having) foliage ⟨*in* ~⟩ (**2**) the leaves of a plant (e g tobacco) as an article of commerce **2a** a part of a book or folded sheet of paper containing a page on each side **b(1)** a part (e g of a window shutter, folding door, or table) that slides or is hinged **(2)** a section that can be inserted into a tabletop to extend it **c(1)** a thin sheet of metal, marble, etc **(2)** metal (e g gold or silver) in sheets, usu thinner than foil – **leafless** *adj*, **leaflike** *adj*

²leaf *vi* to shoot out or produce leaves – **leaf through** to turn over the pages of (e g a book) quickly while only glancing at the contents

leafage *n* FOLIAGE 1

-leafed *comb form* (*adj* → *adj*) -leaved

leaflet *n* **1a** any of the divisions of a compound leaf **b** a small or young foliage leaf **2** a single sheet of paper or small loose-leaf pamphlet containing printed matter (e g advertising)

leaf mould *n* a compost or soil layer composed chiefly of decayed vegetable matter

leafy *adj* **1** having or thick with leaves ⟨~ *woodlands*⟩ **2** consisting chiefly of leaves ⟨*green* ~ *vegetables*⟩ – **leafiness** *n*

¹league *n* any of various units of distance of about 3mi (5km)

²league *n* **1a** an association of nations, groups, or people for a common purpose or to promote a common interest **b** (a competition for an overall title, in which each person or team plays all the others at least once, held by) an association of people or sports clubs **2** a class, category ⟨*the top* ~⟩ – **leaguer** *n* – **in league** in alliance

³league *vb* to form into a league

¹leak *vi* **1** to (let a substance) enter or escape through a crack or hole **2** to become known despite efforts at concealment – often + *out* ~ *vt* **1** to permit to enter or escape (as if) through a leak **2** to give out (information) surreptitiously ⟨~ed *the story to the press*⟩ – **leakage** *n*

²leak *n* **1a** a crack or hole through which sthg (e g a fluid) is admitted or escapes, usu by mistake **b** a means by which sthg (e g secret information) is admitted or escapes, usu with prejudicial effect **c** a loss of electricity due to faulty insulation **2** a leaking or that which is leaked; *esp* a disclosure **3** an act of urinating – slang

leaky *adj* permitting fluid, information, etc to leak in or out; *broadly* not watertight ⟨*a* ~ *argument*⟩ – **leakiness** *n*

¹lean *vb* **leant, leaned** *vi* **1a** to incline or bend from a vertical position ⟨~t *forward to look*⟩ **b** to rest supported *on/against* sthg **2** to rely on for support or inspiration – + *on* or *upon* **3** to incline in opinion, taste, etc **4** to exert pressure; use coercion – + *on*; *infml* ~ *vt* to place *on/against* for support – **lean** *n*

²lean *adj* **1a** lacking or deficient in flesh or bulk **b** *of meat* containing little or no fat **2** lacking richness, sufficiency, or value **3a** deficient in an essential or important quality or ingredient **b** *esp of a fuel mixture* low in the combustible component – **leanly** *adv*, **leanness** *n*

³lean *n* the part of meat that consists principally of fat-free muscular tissue

leaning *n* a definite but weak attraction, tendency, or partiality

lean-to *n*, *pl* **lean-tos** a small building having a roof that rests on the side of a larger building or wall

¹leap *vb* **leapt, leaped** *vi* **1** to jump in or through the air **2a** to pass abruptly from one state or topic to another; *esp* to rise quickly ⟨*the idea* ~t *into his mind*⟩ **b** to seize eagerly *at* an opportunity, offer, etc ~ *vt* to pass over by leaping – **leaper** *n*

²leap *n* **1a** (the distance covered by) a jump **b** a place leapt

over or from **2** a sudden transition, esp a rise or increase

¹leapfrog *n* a game in which one player bends down and another leaps over him/her

²leapfrog *vb* **-gg-** **1** to leap (over) (as if) in leapfrog **2** to go ahead of (each other) in turn

leap year *n* a year with an extra day added to make it coincide with the solar year; *esp* a year in the Gregorian calendar with February 29 as the 366th day

learn *vb* **learnt, learned** *vt* **1a(1)** to gain knowledge of or skill in ⟨~ *a trade*⟩ **(2)** to memorize ⟨~ *the lines of a play*⟩ **b** to come to be able – + infinitive ⟨~ *to dance*⟩ **c** to come to realize or know ⟨*we* ~ed *that he was ill*⟩ **2** to teach – substandard to acquire knowledge or skill – **learnable** *adj*, **learner** *n*

learned *adj* **1** characterized by or associated with learning; erudite **2** acquired by learning ⟨~ *versus innate behaviour patterns*⟩ – **learnedly** *adv*, **learnedness** *n*

learning *n* **1** acquired knowledge or skill **2** modification of a behavioural tendency by experience (e g exposure to conditioning)

¹lease *n* **1** a contract putting the land or property of one party at the disposal of another, usu for a stated period and rent **2** a (prospect of) continuance – chiefly in *lease of life*

²lease *vt* to grant by or hold under lease

leasehold *n* tenure by or property held by lease – **leaseholder** *n*

leash *n* **1a** ²LEAD 2d **b** a restraint, check **2** a set of 3 animals (e g greyhounds, foxes, or hares) – **leash** *vt*

¹least *adj* **1** lowest in rank, degree, or importance **2a** smallest in quantity or extent **b** being (of) a kind distinguished by small size ⟨~ *bittern*⟩ **c** smallest possible; slightest ⟨*haven't the* ~ *idea*⟩ – **at least 1** as a minimum; if not more ⟨*costs at least £5*⟩ **2** if nothing else; IN ANY CASE ⟨*at least it is legal*⟩

²least *n* the smallest quantity, number, or amount ⟨*it's the* ~ *I can do*⟩ ⟨*to say the* ~⟩ – **least of all** especially not ⟨*no one*, least of all *the children paid attention*⟩

³least *adv* to the smallest degree or extent ⟨*least-known*⟩ ⟨*when we* ~ *expected it*⟩

leastways, leastwise *adv*, *chiefly dial* AT LEAST 2

¹leather *n* **1** animal skin dressed for use **2** sthg wholly or partly made of leather; *esp* a piece of chamois, used esp for polishing metal or glass

²leather *vt* to beat with a strap; thrash

Leatherette *trademark* – used for an imitation leather

leathery *adj* resembling leather in appearance or consistency; *esp* tough

¹leave *vb* **left** *vt* **1a(1)** to bequeath **(2)** to have (esp members of one's family) remaining after one's death **b** to cause to remain as an aftereffect **2a** to cause or allow to be or remain in a specified or unaltered condition ⟨*his manner left me cold*⟩ ⟨~ *the washing-up for tomorrow*⟩ **b** to fail to include, use, or take along ⟨*left his notes at home*⟩ – sometimes + *off* or *out* ⟨*left his name off the list*⟩ **c** to have remaining or as a remainder ⟨*10 from 12* ~*s 2*⟩ **d** to permit to be or remain subject to the action or control of a specified person or thing ⟨*just* ~ *everything to me*⟩ ⟨*nothing left to chance*⟩ **e** to allow to do or continue sthg without interference ⟨~ *you to take care of things*⟩ **3a** to go away from ⟨*told him to* ~ *the room*⟩ **b** to desert, abandon ⟨*left his wife*⟩ **c** to withdraw from ⟨*left school at 15*⟩ **4** to put, station, deposit, or deliver, esp before departing ⟨*the postman left a package for you*⟩ ⟨~ *your name with the receptionist*⟩ ~ *vi* to depart; SET OUT – **leaver** *n* – **leave alone/be** LET ALONE/BE – **leave go** LET GO – **leave well alone** to avoid meddling

²leave n 1 permission to do sthg 2 authorized (extended) absence (e g from employment)

-leaved comb form (adj → adj) having (such or so many) leaves ⟨palmate-leaved⟩ ⟨4-leaved clover⟩

¹leaven n 1 a substance (e g yeast) used to produce fermentation or a gas in dough, batter, etc to lighten it; esp a mass of fermenting dough reserved for this purpose 2 sthg that modifies or lightens

²leaven vt to raise or make lighter (as if) with a leaven

leave off vb to stop, cease

leaves pl of leaf

leave-taking n a departure, farewell

leavings n pl remains, residue

lecher n a man who engages in lechery

lechery n inordinate indulgence in sexual activity; debauchery, lasciviousness – **lecherous** adj, **lecherously** adv

lecithin n any of several waxy compounds that are widely distributed in animals and plants and have emulsifying, wetting, and antioxidant properties

lectern n a reading desk; esp one from which the Bible is read in church

¹lecture n 1 a discourse given to an audience, esp for instruction 2 a reproof delivered at length; a reprimand

²lecture vi to deliver a lecture or series of lectures ~ vt 1 to deliver a lecture to 2 to reprove at length or severely – **lecturer** n

lectureship n the office of an academic lecturer

led past of LEAD

LED n a diode that emits light when an electric current is passed through it and that is used esp to display numbers, symbols, etc on a screen (e g in a pocket calculator)

ledge n 1 a (narrow) horizontal surface that projects from a vertical or steep surface (e g a wall or rock face) 2 an underwater ridge or reef 3 a mineral-bearing lode or vein – **ledgy** adj

¹ledger n 1 a book containing (the complete record of all) accounts 2 a horizontal piece of timber secured to the uprights of scaffolding

²ledger vi to fish with ledger tackle

lee n 1 protecting shelter 2 lee, lee side the side (e g of a ship) sheltered from the wind

¹leech n 1 any of numerous flesh-eating or bloodsucking usu freshwater worms 2 one who gains or seeks to gain profit or advantage from another, esp by clinging persistently 3 archaic a physician, surgeon

²leech vt to bleed by the use of leeches

³leech n 1 either vertical edge of a square sail 2 the rear edge of a fore-and-aft sail

leek n a biennial plant of the lily family grown for its mildly pungent leaves and esp for its thick edible stalk

leer vi or n (to give) a lascivious, knowing, or sly look

lees n pl the sediment of a liquor (e g wine) during fermentation and aging

lee shore n a shore lying off a ship's lee side

¹leeward adj or adv in or facing the direction towards which the wind is blowing

²leeward n LEE 2

leeway n 1 off-course sideways movement of a ship in the direction of the wind 2a an allowable margin of freedom or variation; tolerance b a margin of shortcoming in performance ⟨she has a lot of ~ to make up after her absence⟩

¹left adj 1a of, situated on, or being the side of the body in which most of the heart is located b(1) located nearer to the left hand than to the right; esp located on the left hand when facing in the same direction as an observer ⟨the ~ wing of an army⟩ (2) located on the left when

facing downstream ⟨the ~ bank of a river⟩ 2 often cap of the Left in politics – **left** adv

²left n 1a (a blow struck with) the left hand b the location or direction of the left side c the part on the left side 2 sing or pl in constr, often cap the members of a European legislative body occupying the left of a legislative chamber as a result of holding more radical political views than other members 3 sing or pl in constr a cap those professing socialist or radical political views b often cap LEFT WING 1

³left past of LEAVE

left-hand adj 1 situated on the left 2 left-handed

left-handed adj 1 using the left hand habitually or more easily than the right; also swinging from left to right ⟨a ~ batsman⟩ 2 of, designed for, or done with the left hand 3 morganatic 4 clumsy, awkward 5 ambiguous, double-edged ⟨a ~ compliment⟩ 6 anticlockwise – used of a twist, rotary motion, or spiral curve as viewed from a given direction with respect to the axis of rotation – **left-handed, left-handedly** adv, **left-handedness** n

left-hander n 1 a left-handed person 2 a blow struck with the left hand

leftism n, often cap (advocacy of) the principles and policy of the Left – **leftist** n or adj

left-luggage adj, Br of or for the storing of luggage for safekeeping

leftover n an unused or unconsumed residue; esp leftover food – often pl – **leftover** adj

leftward adj towards or on the left

leftwards, chiefly NAm **leftward** adv towards the left

left wing n sing or pl in constr 1 often cap L&W the more socialist division of a group or party 2 cap L&W LEFT 3a – **left-wing** adj, **left-winger** n

¹leg n 1 a limb of an animal used esp for supporting the body and for walking: e g a (an artificial replacement for) either of the lower limbs of a human b a (hind) leg of a meat animal, esp above the hock c any of the appendages on each segment of an arthropod (e g an insect or spider) used in walking and crawling 2a a pole or bar serving as a support or prop ⟨the ~s of a tripod⟩ ⟨a table ~⟩ b a branch of a forked or jointed object ⟨the ~s of a compass⟩ 3 the part of a garment that covers (part of) the leg 4. either side of a triangle as distinguished from the base or hypotenuse 5a LEG SIDE b a fielding position in cricket on the leg side of the pitch – usu in combination ⟨fine ~⟩ ⟨short ~⟩ 6a the course and distance sailed on a single tack b a portion of a trip; a stage c the part of a relay race run by 1 competitor d any of a set of events or games that must all be won to decide a competition – a **leg to stand on** the least support or basis for one's position, esp in a controversy – **on one's last legs** at or near the end of one's resources; on the verge of failure, exhaustion, or ruin

²leg vi -gg- – **leg it** to walk or run fast; esp to hurry

³leg adj 1 esp of a ball bowled in cricket moving or tending to move in the direction of the off side ⟨a ~ break⟩ 2 in, on, through, or towards the leg side of a cricket field ⟨the ~ stump⟩

legacy n 1 a gift by will; a bequest 2 sthg passed on or remaining from an ancestor or predecessor or from the past ⟨the bitter ~ of 2 world wars⟩

legal adj 1 of law 2a deriving authority from law b established by or having a formal status derived from law 3 permitted by law 4 recognized in common law as distinguished from equity – **legalize** vt, **legally** adv, **legalization** n

legal aid n payments from public funds to those who cannot afford legal advice or representation

legal fiction *n* an assertion recognized by the law as fictitious but accepted for convenience as true

legality *n* **1** lawfulness **2** *pl* the requirements and procedures of the law

legal tender *n* currency which a creditor is bound by law to accept as payment of a money debt

legate *n* an official delegate or representative – **legateship** *n*, **legatine** *adj*

legatee *n* one to whom a legacy is bequeathed

legation *n* (the official residence of) a diplomatic mission in a foreign country headed by a minister

legato *n, adv, or adj, pl* **legatos** (a manner of performing or passage of music performed) in a smooth and connected manner

leg bye *n* a run scored in cricket after the ball has touched a part of the batsman's body but not his bat or hands

legend *n* **1a(1)** a story coming down from the past; *esp* one popularly regarded as historical **(2)** a body of such stories ⟨*a character in Celtic* ∼⟩ **b** a person, act, or thing that inspires legends ⟨*a* ∼ *in her own lifetime*⟩ **2a** an inscription or title on an object (e g a coin) **b** CAPTION 2 **c** the key to a map, chart, etc – **legendry** *n*

legendary *adj* (characteristic) of (a) legend; *esp* told of in legend

legerdemain *n* **1** SLEIGHT OF HAND **2** a display of artful skill, trickery, or adroitness ⟨*political* ∼⟩

-legged *comb form* (adj → adj) having (such or so many) legs ⟨*a 4-legged animal*⟩

legging *n* a closely fitting covering (e g of leather) that reaches from the ankle to the knee or thigh

leggy *adj* **1** having disproportionately long legs ⟨*a* ∼ *colt*⟩ **2** *esp of a woman* having attractively long legs **3** *of a plant* spindly

legible *adj* capable of being read or deciphered ⟨∼ *handwriting*⟩ – **legibly** *adv*, **legibility** *n*

¹legion *n sing or pl in constr* **1** the principal unit of the ancient Roman army comprising 3000 to 6000 foot soldiers with cavalry **2** a very large number; a multitude **3** a national association of ex-servicemen ⟨*the Royal British Legion*⟩

²legion *adj* many, numerous ⟨*the problems are* ∼⟩

¹legionary *adj* of or being a legion

²legionary *n* a legionnaire

legislate *vi* to make or enact laws

legislation *n* **1** (the making of) laws **2** a prospective law – **legislative** *adj*, **legislatively** *adv*

legislator *n* a maker of laws – **legislatress, legislatrix** *n*, **legislatorial** *adj*

legislature *n* a body of people having the power to legislate

legit *adj* LEGITIMATE 2, 3a, 4, 5 – infml

¹legitimate *adj* **1** lawfully begotten; *specif* born in wedlock **2** neither spurious nor false; genuine ⟨∼ *grievance*⟩ **3a** in accordance with law ⟨*a* ∼ *government*⟩ **b** ruling by or based on the strict principle of hereditary right ⟨*a* ∼ *king*⟩ **4** conforming to recognized principles or accepted rules and standards **5** relating to plays acted by professional actors but not including revues, music hall, or some forms of musical comedy **6** in accord with reason or logic; following logically ⟨*a* ∼ *deduction*⟩ – **legitimately** *adv*, **legitimacy** *n*

²legitimate, legitimatize, -ise legitimize, -ise *vt* **1a** to give legal status to **b** JUSTIFY 1 **2** to give (an illegitimate child) the legal status of one legitimately born – **legitimation, legitimatization , legitimization** *n*

leg-pull *n* a playful trick or hoax intended to deceive sby

legroom *n* space in which to extend the legs while seated

leg side, leg *n* the part of a cricket field on the side of a line joining the middle stumps in which the batsman stands when playing a ball

legume *n* **1** the (edible) pod or seed of a leguminous plant **2** any of a large family of plants, shrubs, and trees having pods containing 1 or many seeds and including important food and forage plants (e g peas, beans, or clovers) – **leguminous** *adj*

lei *n* a wreath or necklace usu of flowers or leaves that is a symbol of affection in Polynesia

leisure *n* **1** freedom provided by the cessation of activities; *esp* time free from work or duties **2** unhurried ease – **leisureless** *adj* – **at leisure, at one's leisure 1** at an unhurried pace **2** at one's convenience

leisured *adj* **1** having plenty of free time, esp because of not needing to work **2** leisurely

¹leisurely *adv* without haste; deliberately

²leisurely *adj* characterized by leisure; unhurried – **leisureliness** *n*

leitmotiv, leitmotif *n* **1** a musical phrase that accompanies the reappearance of an idea, person, or situation **2** a (dominant) recurring theme, esp in a literary work

lemming *n* any of several small short-tailed furry-footed northern voles; *esp* one of northern mountains that undergoes recurrent mass migrations

lemon *n* **1** (a stout thorny tree that bears) an oval yellow acid citrus fruit **2** a pale yellow colour **3** one who or that which is unsatisfactory or worthless; a dud – infml – **lemony** *adj*

lemonade *n* a (carbonated) soft drink made or flavoured with lemon

lemon sole *n* a flatfish that is found in N Atlantic and European waters and is highly valued for food

lemur *n* any of numerous tree-dwelling chiefly nocturnal mammals, esp of Madagascar, typically having a muzzle like a fox, large eyes, very soft woolly fur, and a long furry tail

lend *vb* **lent** *vt* **1a** to give for temporary use on condition that the same or its equivalent be returned **b** to let out (money) for temporary use on condition of repayment with interest **2a** to give the assistance or support of; afford, contribute ⟨*a dispassionate and scholarly manner which* ∼*s great force to his criticisms* – *TLS*⟩ **b** to adapt or apply (oneself); accommodate ⟨*a topic that* ∼*s itself admirably to class discussion*⟩ ∼*vi* to make a loan – **lender** *n*

length *n* **1a(1)** the longer or longest dimension of an object **(2)** the extent from end to end ⟨*walked the* ∼ *of the street*⟩ **b** a measured distance or dimension ⟨*a 2m* ∼ *of tube*⟩ **c** the quality or state of being long **2a** duration or extent in or with regard to time ⟨*the* ∼ *of a broadcast*⟩ **b** relative duration or stress of a sound **3a** distance or extent in space ⟨*an arm's* ∼ *apart*⟩ **b** the length of sthg taken as a unit of measure ⟨*his horse led by a* ∼⟩ **4** the degree to which sthg (e g a course of action or a line of thought) is carried; a limit, extreme – often pl with long meaning ⟨*went to great* ∼*s to learn the truth*⟩ **5a** a long expanse or stretch ⟨∼*s of hair*⟩ **b** a piece, esp of a certain length (being or usable as part of a whole or of a connected series) ⟨*a* ∼ *of pipe*⟩ **6** the (ideal) distance down a cricket pitch which the bowled ball travels before pitching **7** the vertical extent of sthg (e g an article of clothing), esp with reference to the position it reaches on the body – usu in combination ⟨*shoulder-length hair*⟩ – **at length 1** fully, comprehensively **2** for a long time **3** finally; AT LAST

lengthen *vb* to make or become longer

lengthways, lengthwise *adv or adj* in the direction of the length ⟨*bricks are generally laid* ∼⟩

lengthy *adj* of great or unusual length; long; *also* excessively or tediously protracted – **lengthily** *adv*, **lengthiness** *n*

lenient *adj* **1** of a mild or merciful nature; not severe ⟨~ *laws*⟩ **2** *archaic* exerting a soothing or easing influence – **lenience, leniency** *n*, **leniently** *adv*

lenity *n* gentleness, mercy – *fml*

lens *n* **1a** a piece of glass or other transparent material with 2 opposite regular surfaces, at least 1 of which is curved, that is used either singly or combined in an optical instrument to form an image by focussing rays of light **b** a combination of 2 or more simple lenses **2** a device for directing or focussing radiation other than light (e g sound waves or electrons) **3** sthg shaped like an optical lens with both sides convex **4** a transparent lens-shaped or nearly spherical body in the eye that focuses light rays (e g on the retina) – **lensed** *adj*, **lensless** *adj*

Lent *n* the 40 weekdays from Ash Wednesday to Easter observed by Christians as a period of penitence and fasting – **Lenten** *adj*

lentil *n* (the small round edible seed of) a widely cultivated Eurasian leguminous plant

lento *adv or adj* in a slow manner – used in music

Leo *n* (sby born under) the 5th sign of the zodiac in astrology, pictured as a lion

leonine *adj* resembling a lion; having the characteristics (e g courage) popularly ascribed to a lion

leopard, *fem* **leopardess** *n* **1** a big cat of southern Asia and Africa that is usu tawny or buff with black spots arranged in broken rings or rosettes **2** a heraldic charge that is a lion with the farther forepaw raised and its head turned towards the observer

leotard *n* a close-fitting one-piece garment worn by dancers or others performing physical exercises

leper *n* **1** sby suffering from leprosy **2** a person shunned for moral or social reasons; an outcast

leprechaun *n* a mischievous elf of Irish folklore

leprosy *n* a long-lasting bacterial disease characterized by loss of sensation with eventual paralysis, wasting of muscle, and production of deformities and mutilations – **leprotic** *adj*

lesbian *n, often cap* a female homosexual – **lesbian** *adj*, **lesbianism** *n*

lese majesty, lèse majesté *n* **1a** a crime (e g treason) committed against a sovereign power **b** an offence violating the dignity of a ruler **2** an affront to dignity or importance

lesion *n* **1** injury, harm **2** abnormal change in the structure of an organ or part due to injury or disease

¹less *adj* **1** fewer ⟨~ *than 3*⟩ ⟨*a call for* ~ *government controls*⟩ – disapproved of by some speakers **2** lower in rank, degree, or importance ⟨*James the Less*⟩ ⟨*no* ~ *a person than the president himself*⟩ **3** smaller in quantity or extent ⟨*of* ~ *importance*⟩ ⟨*in* ~ *time*⟩ ⟨*weighs 3 pounds* ~⟩

²less *adv* to a lesser degree or extent ⟨*sleeps* ~ *in summer*⟩ ⟨*much* ~ *angrily*⟩ – **less and less** to a progressively smaller size or extent – **less than** by no means; not at all ⟨*was being* less than *honest in her replies*⟩

³less *prep* diminished by; minus ⟨*£100* ~ *tax*⟩

⁴less *n, pl* **less** a smaller portion or quantity – **less of 1** not so truly ⟨*he's* less of *a fool than I thought*⟩ **2** enough of ⟨less of *your cheek!*⟩ – *infml*

-less *suffix* (→ *adj*) **1a** destitute of; not having ⟨*brainless*⟩ ⟨*childless*⟩ ⟨*hopeless*⟩ **b** free from ⟨*painless*⟩ ⟨*careless*⟩ **2** unable to (so act or be acted on) ⟨*tireless*⟩ ⟨*stainless*⟩

lessee *n* sby who holds property under a lease

lessen *vb* to reduce in size, extent, etc; diminish, decrease

lesser *adj or adv* less in size, quality, or significance ⟨*lesser-known*⟩ ⟨*the* ~ *of 2 evils*⟩ – not used in comparatives

lesson *n* **1** a passage from sacred writings read in a service of worship **2a** a reading or exercise to be studied **b** a period of instruction **3a** sthg, esp a piece of wisdom, learned by study or experience ⟨*her years of travel had taught her valuable* ~s⟩ **b** an instructive or warning example ⟨*the* ~s *history holds for us*⟩

lessor *n* sby who conveys property by lease

lest *conj* **1** so that not; IN CASE ⟨*obeyed her* ~ *she should be angry*⟩ **2** that – used after an expression of fear ⟨*afraid* ~ *she be angry*⟩

¹let *n* **1** a serve or rally in tennis, squash, etc that does not count and must be replayed **2** sthg that impedes; an obstruction – *fml* ⟨*without* ~ *or hindrance*⟩

²let *vt* **let; -tt- 1** to cause to; make ⟨~ *it be known*⟩ **2a** to offer or grant for rent or lease ⟨~ *rooms*⟩ **b** to assign, esp after bids ⟨~ *a contract*⟩ **3a** to give opportunity to, whether by positive action or by failure to prevent; allow to ⟨*he* ~ *his beard grow*⟩ ⟨*please* ~ *me know*⟩ ⟨~ *the prisoner go*⟩ **b** to allow to escape, enter, or pass ⟨~ *the dogs loose*⟩ ⟨~ *them through*⟩ ⟨*she* ~ *out a scream*⟩ **4** – used in the imperative to introduce a request or proposal ⟨~ *us pray*⟩ ⟨~ *me see*⟩, a challenge ⟨*just* ~ *him try*⟩, a command ⟨~ *it be known*⟩, or sthg to be supposed for the sake of argument ⟨~ *AB be equal to BC* – **let alone/be** to stop or refrain from molesting, disturbing, or interrupting ⟨*please* let *the cat* alone⟩ – **let fall/drop** to mention casually as if by accident – **let fly** to aim a blow – **let go** to stop holding ⟨let go *of the handle*⟩ – **let in for** to involve (sby, esp oneself) in sthg undesirable ⟨let *myself* in for *a lot of work*⟩ – **let into** to insert into (a surface) ⟨*a tablet* let into *the wall*⟩ – **let loose on** to give freedom of access to or of action with respect to ⟨*can't* let *him* loose on *the files just yet*⟩ – **let oneself go 1** to behave with relaxed ease or abandonment **2** to allow one's appearance to deteriorate – **let rip** to proceed with abandon ⟨*lost his temper and really* let *rip*⟩ – *infml* – **let slip 1** LET FALL **2** to fail to take ⟨let slip *a chance*⟩ – **let up on** to become less severe towards

³let *n, Br* **1** an act or period of letting premises (e g a flat or bed-sitter) **2** premises rented or for rent

-let *suffix* (→ *n*) **1** -ETTE **1** ⟨*booklet*⟩ ⟨*starlet*⟩ **2** article worn on (a specified part of the body) ⟨*anklet*⟩

letdown *n* a disappointment, disillusionment – *infml*

let down *vt* **1** to make (a garment) longer **2** to fail in loyalty or support; disappoint ⟨let *her friend* down *badly*⟩

lethal *adj* relating to or (capable of) causing death – **lethally** *adv*, **lethality** *n*

lethargic *adj* **1** sluggish **2** indifferent, apathetic – **lethargically** *adv*

lethargy *n* **1** abnormal drowsiness **2** lack of energy or interest

let off *vt* **1** to cause to explode ⟨let *the fireworks* off⟩ **2** to excuse from punishment **3** *chiefly Br* to offer (part of a building) for rent

let on *vi* **1** to reveal or admit sthg; *esp* to divulge secret information ⟨*nobody* let on *about the surprise party*⟩ **2** to pretend ⟨*she* let on *that she was a stranger*⟩ – *infml*

let-out *n* sthg (e g an exclusion clause in a contract) that provides an opportunity to escape or be released from an obligation – *infml*

let out *vt* **1** to make (a garment) wider (e g by inserting an inset) **2** to excuse from an obligation or responsibility **3** *chiefly Br* to express publicly; *esp* to blab **4** *chiefly Br* to rent out (e g property)

¹letter *n* **1** a symbol, usu written or printed, representing a speech sound and constituting a unit of an alphabet **2a** a written or printed message addressed to a person or organization and usu sent through the post **b** a formal written communication containing a grant or authorization – usu pl with sing. meaning **3** *pl but sing or pl in constr* **a** literature; BELLES LETTRES **b** learning; *esp* scholarly knowledge of or achievement in literature ⟨*a man of* ~s⟩ **4** the precise wording; the strict or literal meaning ⟨*obeyed the instructions to the* ~⟩ **5a** a single piece of type **b** a style of type

²**letter** *vt* to set down in or mark with letters

letter box *n, Br* a hole or box (e g in a door) to receive material delivered by post

lettered *adj* learned, educated

letterhead *n* stationery printed with a heading; *also* the heading itself

lettering *n* the letters used in an inscription, esp as regards their style or quality

letterpress *n* **1** (work produced by) printing from an inked raised surface **2** *chiefly Br* text (e g of a book) as distinct from pictorial illustrations

letters patent *n pl* a formal document (e g from a sovereign) conferring on sby the sole right to exploit his/her invention

letting *n, chiefly Br* ³LET

lettuce *n* a common garden vegetable whose succulent edible leaves are used esp in salads

letup *n* a cessation or lessening of effort, activity, or intensity

let up *vi* **1a** to diminish, slow down, or cease **b** to relax or cease one's efforts or activities **2** to become less severe – usu + *on*; *infml*

leucocyte *n* WHITE BLOOD CELL

leucotomy *n* a lobotomy

leukaemia *n* any of several usu fatal types of cancer that are characterized by an abnormal increase in the number of white blood cells in the body tissue, esp the blood, and occur in acute or chronic form

¹**levee** *n* **1** a reception of visitors formerly held by a person of rank on rising from bed **2** a reception, usu in honour of a particular person

²**levee** *n, NAm* **1** an embankment for preventing or confining flooding **2** a river landing place

¹**level** *n* **1** a device (e g a spirit level) for establishing a horizontal line or plane **2a** a horizontal state or condition **b** the equilibrium of a fluid marked by a horizontal surface of even altitude ⟨*water seeks its own* ~⟩ **c** an (approximately) horizontal line, plane, or surface **3a** a position of height in relation to the ground; height ⟨*eye* ~⟩ **b** a practically horizontal or flat area, or surface **4** a position or place in a scale or rank (e g of value or importance) ⟨*a high* ~ *of academic excellence*⟩ **5** (a passage in) an interconnecting series of regularly worked horizontal mine passages **6** the (often measurable) size or amount of sthg specified ⟨*noise* ~⟩ – **on the level** honest; BONA FIDE

²**level** *vb* -**ll**- (*NAm* -**l**-, -**ll**-), *vt* **1a** to make (a line or surface) horizontal; make level, even, or uniform **b** to raise or lower to the same height – often + *up* ⟨~ *up the picture with the one next to it*⟩ **2a** to bring to a horizontal aiming position **b** to aim, direct – + *at* or *against* ⟨~ *led a charge of fraud at her*⟩ **3** to bring to a common level, plane, or standard; equalize ⟨*love* ~*s all ranks* – W S Gilbert⟩ **4** to lay level with the ground; raze **5** to find the heights of different points in (a land area) ~ *vi* **1** to attain or come to a level – usu + *out* or *off* ⟨*the plane* ~ *led off at 10,000ft*⟩ **2** to aim a gun or other weapon horizontally **3** to deal frankly and openly – *infml*

³**level** *adj* **1a** having no part higher than another **b** parallel

with the plane of the horizon; conforming to the curvature of the liquid parts of the earth's surface **2a** even, unvarying ⟨*a* ~ *temperature*⟩ **b** equal in advantage, progression, or standing ⟨*drew* ~ *with the leaders*⟩ **c** steady, unwavering ⟨*spoke in* ~ *tones*⟩ **3** distributed evenly; uniform ⟨~ *stress*⟩ – **levelly** *adv*, **levelness** *n* – **level best** very best ⟨*she did her level best*⟩

level crossing *n, Br* the crossing of railway and road or 2 railways on the same level

leveller, *NAm chiefly* **leveler** *n* **1** *cap* a member of a radical group during the English Civil War who advocated legal equality and religious tolerance **2** an advocate of equality **3** sthg that tends to reduce human differences

¹**lever** *n* **1a** a bar used for prizing up or dislodging sthg **b** an inducing or compelling force; a tool ⟨*attempts to use food as a political* ~ – *Time*⟩ **2a** a rigid bar used to exert a pressure or sustain a weight at one end by applying force at the other and turning it on a fulcrum **b** a projecting part by which a mechanism is operated or adjusted

²**lever** *vt* to prize, raise, or move (as if) with a lever

leverage *n* **1** the action of a lever or the mechanical advantage gained by it **2** power, influence

leveret *n* a hare in its first year

leviathan *n* **1** *often cap* a biblical sea monster **2** sthg large or formidable – **leviathan** *adj*

levitate *vb* to (cause to) rise or float in the air, esp in apparent defiance of gravity – **levitation** *n*, **levitational** *adj*

levity *n* lack of seriousness; *esp* excessive or unseemly frivolity

¹**levy** *n* **1a** the imposing or collection of a tax, fine, etc **b** an amount levied **2a** the enlistment or conscription of men for military service **b** *sing or pl in constr* troops raised by levy

²**levy** *vt* **1** to impose, collect, or demand by legal authority ⟨~ *a tax*⟩ **2** to enlist or conscript for military service **3** to prepare for and make (war) – usu + *on* or *upon* – **leviable** *adj*

lewd *adj* **1** sexually coarse or suggestive **2** obscene, salacious ⟨~ *songs*⟩ – **lewdly** *adv*, **lewdness** *n*

lexical *adj* **1** of words or the vocabulary of a language as distinguished from its grammar and construction **2** of a lexicon – **lexically** *adv*, **lexicality** *n*

lexicography *n* (the principles of) the editing or making of a dictionary – **lexicographer** *n*, **lexicographic, lexicographical** *adj*

lexicon *n, pl* **lexica, lexicons 1** a dictionary, esp of Greek, Latin, or Hebrew **2** the vocabulary of a language, individual, or subject

lexis *n, pl* **lexes** LEXICON 2

liability *n* **1** being liable **2** sthg for which one is liable; *esp, pl* debts **3** a hindrance, drawback – *infml*

liable *adj* **1** legally responsible **2** exposed or subject *to* ⟨~ *to a fine*⟩ ⟨~ *to hurt yourself*⟩ **3** habitually likely *to* ⟨*she's* ~ *to get annoyed*⟩

liaise *vi* **1** to establish a connection and cooperate or act as a liaison officer

liaison *n* **1** a substance or mixture used in cooking to thicken or bind liquids **2a** a close bond or connection **b** an illicit sexual relationship; AFFAIR **3a** the pronunciation (e g in the French *est-il*) of an otherwise silent consonant before a word beginning with a vowel sound **4** communication, esp between parts of an armed force

liana *n* a climbing plant, esp of tropical rain forests, that roots in the ground – **lianoid** *adj*

liar *n* one who (habitually) tells lies

lib *n, often cap* LIBERATION 2 – *infml* ⟨*women's* ~⟩ – **libber** *n*

libation *n* **1** (an act of pouring) a liquid used in a sacrifice to a god **2a** an act or instance of drinking **b** a beverage, esp alcoholic *USE* (2) *fml* or *humor*

¹libel *n* **1** (a) defamation of sby by published writing or pictorial representation as distinguished from spoken words or gestures **2** a false insulting statement – **libellous** *adj*

²libel *vb* **-ll-** (*NAm* -l-, -ll-), to make or publish a libel (against) – **libeller** *n*, **libellist** *n*

¹liberal *adj* **1** of or in liberal studies ⟨~ *education*⟩ **2a** generous, openhanded ⟨*a* ~ *giver*⟩ **b** abundant, ample ⟨*a* ~ *helping*⟩ **3** broad-minded, tolerant; *esp* not bound by authoritarianism, orthodoxy, or tradition **4** *cap* based on or advocating (political) liberalism; *specif* of a political party in the UK advocating economic freedom and moderate reform – **liberally** *adv*, **liberalness**, **liberality** *n*

²liberal *n* **1** one who is not strict in the observance of orthodox ways (e g in politics or religion) **2** *cap* a supporter of a Liberal party **3** a champion of individual rights

liberalism *n* **1** breadth of mind; tolerance, understanding **2a** a political philosophy based on belief in progress and the protection of political and civil liberties **b** *cap* Liberal principles and policies – **liberalist** *n or adj*, **liberalistic** *adj*

liberalize, -ise *vb* to make or become (more) liberal – **liberalization** *n*

liberate *vt* **1** to set free; *specif* to free (e g a country) from foreign domination **2** to free (a molecule, ion, etc) from combination **3** to steal – euph or humor – **liberator** *n*

liberation *n* **1** liberating or being liberated **2** the seeking of equal rights and status ⟨*gay* ~⟩ – **liberationist** *n*

libertarian *n* **1** a believer in free will **2** an advocate of liberty – **libertarian** *adj*, **libertarianism** *n*

libertine *n* a person who is unrestrained by convention or morality; *specif* one leading a dissolute life – **libertinage**, **libertinism** *n*

liberty *n* **1a** the power to do as one pleases **b** freedom from physical restraint or dictatorial control **c** the enjoyment of various rights and privileges ⟨*civil* ~⟩ **d** the power of choice **2** a right or immunity awarded or granted; a privilege **3a** a breach of etiquette or propriety **b** a risk, chance ⟨*took foolish liberties with her health*⟩ – **at liberty 1** free **2** at leisure; unoccupied

libidinous *adj* having or marked by strong sexual desire; lascivious – **libidinously** *adv*, **libidinousness** *n*

libido *n, pl* **libidos** **1** emotional or mental energy derived in psychoanalytic theory from primitive biological urges **2** sexual drive – **libidinal** *adj*

Libra *n* (sby born under) the 7th sign of the zodiac in astrology, pictured as a pair of scales – **Libran** *n or adj*

librarian *n* sby who manages or assists in a library – **librarianship** *n*

library *n* **1a** a place in which books, recordings, films, etc are kept for reference or for borrowing by the public **b** a collection of such books, recordings, etc **2** a series of related books issued by a publisher

libretto *n, pl* **librettos**, **libretti** (the book containing) the text of a work (e g an opera) that is both theatrical and musical – **librettist** *n*

lice *pl of* LOUSE

licence, NAm *chiefly* **license** *n* **1a** permission to act **b** freedom of action **2** (a certificate giving evidence of) permission granted by authority to engage in an otherwise unlawful activity, esp the sale of alcoholic drink **3a** freedom that allows or is used with irresponsibility **b** disregard for rules of propriety or personal conduct **4** freedom claimed by an artist or writer to alter facts or deviate from the rules of an art, esp for the sake of the effect gained ⟨*poetic* ~⟩

license, licence *vt* to give official permission to or for (esp the sale of alcoholic drink)

licensed victualler *n, Br* a publican holding a licence to sell food and alcoholic drink on the premises

licensee *n* the holder of a licence; *esp, Br* a publican

license plate *n, NAm* a renewable number plate showing that the vehicle to which it is attached is licensed

licentiate *n* **1** one licensed to practise a profession **2** an academic degree awarded by some European universities

licentious *adj* behaving in a sexually uncontrolled manner – **licentiously** *adv*, **licentiousness** *n*

lichen *n* **1** any of numerous complex plants made up of an alga and a fungus growing in symbiotic association on a solid surface (e g a rock or tree trunk) **2** any of several skin diseases characterized by raised spots – **lichenous** *adj*, **lichenoid** *adj*

licit *adj* not forbidden (by law); permissible – **licitly** *adv*

¹lick *vt* **1a**(1) to draw the tongue over, esp in order to taste, moisten, or clean ⟨~ *a stamp*⟩ (2) to flicker or play over like a tongue **b** to take into the mouth with the tongue; lap – *usu* + *up* **2a** to strike repeatedly; thrash **b** to get the better of; overcome ⟨*has* ~ed *every problem*⟩ – *vi* to lap (as if) with the tongue; *also* to dart like a tongue ⟨*flames* ~ing *at the windows*⟩ *USE* (*vt 2*) *infml* – **lick into shape** to put into proper form or condition

²lick *n* **1a** an act or instance of licking **b** a small amount; a touch ⟨*a* ~ *of paint*⟩ **2** ³BLOW 1 **3** a place to which animals regularly go to lick a salt deposit **4** speed, pace ⟨*the car was travelling at a good* ~⟩ – *infml* – **a lick and a promise** sthg hastily and not thoroughly done; *esp* a quick wash

licking *n* **1** a sound thrashing; a beating **2** a severe setback; a defeat *USE* infml

licorice *n* liquorice

lid *n* **1** a hinged or detachable cover (for a receptacle) **2** the operculum in mosses – **lidded** *adj*

lido *n, pl* **lidos** **1** a fashionable beach resort **2** a public open-air swimming pool

¹lie *vi* **lying**; **lay**; **lain** **1a** to be or to stay at rest in a horizontal position; rest, recline ⟨~ *motionless*⟩ ⟨~ *asleep*⟩ **b** to assume a horizontal position – *often* + *down* **c** to be or remain in a specified state or condition ⟨~ *in wait*⟩ ⟨*machinery* lying *idle*⟩ **2a** of sthg inanimate to be or remain in a flat or horizontal position on a surface ⟨*books* lying *on the table*⟩ **b** of snow to remain on the ground without melting **3** to have as a direction; ¹LEAD 1b(1) ⟨*the route* lay *to the west*⟩ **4a** to occupy a specified place or position ⟨*hills* ~ *behind us*⟩ ⟨*the responsibility* ~s *with us*⟩ **b** to have an adverse or disheartening effect; weigh ⟨*remorse* lay *heavily on her*⟩ **c** *of an action, claim, etc in a court of law* to be sustainable or admissible **5** to remain at anchor or becalmed – **lie low 1** to stay in hiding; strive to avoid notice **2** to bide one's time

²lie *n* **1** the way, position, or situation in which sthg lies ⟨*the* ~ *of the land*⟩ **2** a haunt of an animal or fish

³lie *vi* **lying 1** to make an untrue statement with intent to deceive; speak falsely **2** to create a false or misleading impression ⟨*the camera never* ~s⟩

⁴lie *n* **1** an untrue or false statement, esp when made with intent to deceive **2** sthg that misleads or deceives

lied *n, pl* **lieder** a German song; *esp* a 19th-c setting of a lyrical poem

lie detector *n* an instrument for detecting physical evidence of the mental tension that accompanies telling lies

lie-down *n, chiefly Br* a brief rest, esp on a bed – infml

lie down *vi* to submit meekly or abjectly to defeat, disappointment, or insult ⟨*won't take that criticism* lying down⟩

lief *adv, archaic* soon, gladly ⟨*I'd as ~ go as not*⟩

¹liege *adj* **1a** entitled to feudal allegiance **b** owing feudal allegiance **2** faithful, loyal

²liege *n* **1a** a feudal vassal **b** a loyal subject **2** a feudal superior

lie in *vi* **1** to be confined to give birth to a child **2** *chiefly Br* to stay in bed until later than usual in the morning – **lie-in** *n*

lien *n* the legal right to hold another's property until a claim is met

lie off *vi, of a ship* to keep a little distance away from the shore or another ship

lie over *vi* to await attention at a later time ⟨*several jobs* lying over *from last week*⟩

lie to *vi, of a ship* to stay stationary with head to wind-ward

lieu *n* – **in lieu** in substitution; instead ⟨*I'm sending this message* in lieu *of a letter*⟩

lie up *vi* **1** to stay in bed, esp for a long period **2** *of a ship* to remain in dock or out of commission **3** to remain inactive or at rest

lieutenant *n* **1** an official empowered to act for a higher official; a deputy or representative **2** an officer of low rank in the navy, army, or US airforce **3** an officer with the rank next below the one named ⟨lieutenant *colonel*⟩

¹life *n, pl* **lives** **1a** the quality that distinguishes a vital and functional being from a dead body **b** a principle or force considered to underlie the distinctive quality of animate beings **c** a state of matter (e g a cell or an organism) characterized by capacity for metabolism, growth, reaction to stimuli, and reproduction **2a** the sequence of physical and mental experiences that make up the existence of an individual **b** an aspect of the process of living ⟨*the sex ~ of the frog*⟩ **3** BIOGRAPHY 1 **4** a state or condition of existence ⟨*~ after death*⟩ **5a** the period from birth to death or to the present time ⟨*I have lived here all my ~*⟩ **b** a specific phase of earthly existence ⟨*adult ~*⟩ **c** the period from an event or the present time until death ⟨*a member for ~*⟩ **d** a sentence of imprisonment for life ⟨*got ~ for the murder*⟩ **6** a way or manner of living ⟨*a holy ~*⟩⟨*a full ~*⟩ **7** a person ⟨*many* lives *were lost in the disaster*⟩ **8** the source of pleasure, interest, or enjoyment in living; the reason for living ⟨*his work was his whole ~*⟩ **9** the living form considered as a model ⟨*painted from ~*⟩ **10** the period of usefulness, effectiveness, or functioning of sthg inanimate ⟨*the expected ~ of torch batteries*⟩ **11** a period of existence (e g of a subatomic particle) **12** living beings (e g of a specified kind or environment) ⟨*forest ~*⟩ **13a** the active part of human existence, esp in a wide range of circumstances or experiences ⟨*left home to see ~*⟩ **b** activity from living things; movement ⟨*stirrings of ~*⟩ **c** the activities of a specified sphere, area, or time ⟨*the political ~ of the country*⟩ **14** (one who provides) interest, animation, or vigour ⟨*the ~ and soul of the party*⟩ **15** any of several chances to participate given to a contestant in some games, 1 of which is forfeited each time he/she loses; *also* a failed chance to get a batsman out ⟨*dropped a catch and gave the batsman a ~*⟩

²life *adj* **1** using a living model ⟨*a ~ class*⟩ **2** of, being, or provided by life insurance ⟨*a ~ policy*⟩

life belt *n* a buoyant belt for keeping a person afloat

lifeblood *n* **1** the blood necessary to life **2** a vital or life-giving force

lifeboat *n* a robust buoyant boat for use in saving lives at sea

life buoy *n* a buoyant often ring-shaped float to which a person may cling in the water

life cycle *n* the series of stages in form and functional activity through which an organism, group, culture, etc passes during its lifetime

lifeguard *n* a usu expert swimmer employed to safeguard other swimmers – **lifeguard** *vi*

life history *n* the changes through which an organism passes in its development from the primary stage to its natural death

life jacket *n* a buoyant device that is designed to keep a person afloat and can be worn continuously as a precaution against drowning

lifeless *adj* **1a** dead **b** inanimate **2** having no living beings ⟨*a ~ planet*⟩ **3** lacking qualities expressive of life and vigour; dull ⟨*a ~ voice*⟩ – **lifelessly** *adv*, **lifelessness** *n*

lifelike *adj* accurately representing or imitating (the appearance of objects in) real life

lifeline *n* **1a** a rope for saving or safeguarding life: e g **(1)** one stretched along the deck of a ship in rough weather **(2)** one fired to a ship in distress by means of a rocket **b** the line by which a diver is lowered and raised **2** sthg, esp the sole means of communication, regarded as indispensable for the maintenance or protection of life

lifelong *adj* lasting or continuing throughout life

life peer, *fem* **life peeress** *n* a British peer whose title is not hereditary – **life peerage** *n*

life preserver *n* **1** *chiefly Br* a small weighted club **2** *chiefly NAm* a life jacket, life buoy, etc

lifer *n* one sentenced to life imprisonment – infml

life-size, **life-sized** *adj* of natural size; of the size of the original ⟨*a ~ statue*⟩

life table *n* a table of life based on the mortality statistics for several years

lifetime *n* the length of time for which a person, living thing, subatomic particle, etc exists

lifework *n* the entire or principal work (filling the whole) of one's lifetime

¹lift *vt* **1a** to raise from a lower to a higher position; elevate **b** to raise in rank or condition **2** to put an end to (a blockade or siege) by withdrawing the surrounding forces **3** to revoke, rescind ⟨*~ an embargo*⟩ **4a** to plagiarize **b** to take out of normal setting ⟨*~ a word out of context*⟩ **5** to take up (e g a root crop) from the ground **6** to hit (e g a cricket ball) or to hit the bowling of (a bowler) into the air **7** to steal ⟨*had her purse ~ed*⟩ – infml ~ *vi* **1** to ascend, rise **2a** to disperse upwards ⟨*until the fog ~s*⟩ **b** *of bad weather* to cease temporarily ⟨*the rain finally ~ed*⟩ **3** *of a bowled ball in cricket* to rise at a sharper angle than expected after pitching – **liftable** *adj*, **lifter** *n*

²lift *n* **1a** (a device for) lifting or (the amount) being lifted **b** the lifting up of a dancer or skater usu by her partner **2** a usu free ride as a passenger in a motor vehicle **3** a slight rise or elevation of ground **4** the distance or extent to which sthg (e g water in a canal lock) rises **5** a usu temporary feeling of cheerfulness, pleasure, or encouragement ⟨*her new haircut gave her a real ~*⟩ **6** the upward part of the aerodynamic force acting on an aircraft or aerofoil that opposes the pull of gravity **7** an organized transport of men, equipment, or supplies; *esp* an airlift **8** any of the ropes by which the yard is suspended from the mast on a square-rigged ship **9** *chiefly Br* a device for conveying people or objects from one level to another, esp in a building

lift-off *n* a vertical takeoff by an aircraft, rocket vehicle, or missile – **lift off** *vi*

ligament *n* a tough band of connective tissue forming the capsule round a joint or supporting an organ (e g the womb) – **ligamentary, ligamentous** *adj*

ligature *n* **1a** sthg that is used to bind; *specif* a thread used in surgery **b** sthg that unites or connects **2** the action of binding or tying **3** [2]SLUR 1 **4** a character consisting of 2 or more letters or characters joined together; *esp* one (e g fr) other than a diphthong

[1]**light** *n* **1a** (the sensation aroused by) sthg that makes vision possible by stimulating the sense of sight **b** an electromagnetic radiation in the wavelength range including infrared, visible, ultraviolet, and X rays; *specif* the part of this range that is visible to the human eye **2** daylight **3** a source of light: e g **a** a celestial body **b** a burning candle **c** an electric light **4a** spiritual illumination **b** INNER LIGHT **c** understanding, knowledge **d** *the* truth ⟨*see the* ~⟩ **5a** public knowledge ⟨*facts brought to* ~⟩ **b** a particular aspect or appearance in which sthg is viewed ⟨*now saw the matter in a different* ~⟩ **6** a particular illumination in a place ⟨*studio with a north* ~⟩ **7** (enlightening) information or explanation ⟨*he shed some* ~ *on the problem*⟩ **8** a medium (e g a window) through which light is admitted **9** *pl* a set of principles, standards, or opinions ⟨*true by your* ~s⟩ **10** LEADING LIGHT **11** a specified expression, perceived as being in sby's eyes ⟨*the* ~ *of love in his eyes*⟩ **12a** a lighthouse **b** TRAFFIC LIGHT **13** the representation in art of the effect of light on objects or scenes **14** a flame or spark for lighting sthg (e g a cigarette) **15** *Br* the answer to 1 of the clues of a crossword – **lightless** *adj*, **lightproof** *adj* – **in the light of** with the insight provided by

[2]**light** *adj* **1** having plenty of light; bright ⟨*a* ~ *airy room*⟩ **2a** pale in colour or colouring **b** *of colours* medium in saturation and high in lightness

[3]**light** *vb* **lit, lighted** *vi* **1** LIGHT UP 1 **2** to catch fire ~ *vt* **1** to set fire to **2a** to conduct (sby) with a light; guide **b** to illuminate ⟨*a room lit by a bay window*⟩

[4]**light** *adj* **1a** having little weight; not heavy **b** designed to carry a comparatively small load ⟨*a* ~ *van*⟩ **c** of the smaller variety ⟨*a* ~ *gun*⟩ **d** (made of materials) having relatively little weight in proportion to bulk ⟨*aluminium is a* ~ *metal*⟩ **e** containing less than the legal, standard, or usual weight ⟨*a* ~ *coin*⟩ **2a** of little importance; trivial **b** not abundant ⟨~ *rain*⟩ ⟨*a* ~ *crop of wheat*⟩ **3a** *of sleep or a sleeper* easily disturbed **b** exerting a minimum of force or pressure; gentle, soft ⟨*a* ~ *touch*⟩ ⟨*a* ~ *breeze*⟩ ⟨*a* ~ *voice*⟩ **c** faint ⟨~ *print*⟩ **4a** easily endurable ⟨~ *taxation*⟩ **b** requiring little effort ⟨~ *work*⟩ **5** nimble ⟨~ *on his feet*⟩ **6** lacking seriousness; frivolous **7** free from care; cheerful ⟨*a* ~ *heart*⟩ **8** intending or intended chiefly to entertain ⟨~ *reading*⟩ **9** *of a drink* having a comparatively low alcoholic content or a mild flavour ⟨*a* ~ *white wine*⟩ **10a** easily digested ⟨*a* ~ *dessert*⟩ **b** well leavened ⟨*a* ~ *cake*⟩ **11** lightly armoured, armed, or equipped ⟨~ *cavalry*⟩ **12** easily pulverized; crumbly ⟨~ *soil*⟩ **13** dizzy, giddy ⟨*felt* ~ *in the head*⟩ **14a** carrying little or no cargo ⟨*the ship returned* ~⟩ **b** producing light usu small goods often for direct consumption ⟨~ *industry*⟩ – **lightish** *adj*, **lightly** *adv*, **lightness** *n*

[5]**light** *adv* **1** lightly **2** with the minimum of luggage ⟨*travel* ~⟩

[6]**light** *vi* **lighted, lit 1** to settle, alight ⟨*a bird lit on the lawn*⟩ **2** to arrive by chance; happen ⟨*lit upon a solution*⟩

light bulb *n* INCANDESCENT LAMP

[1]**lighten** *vt* **1** to make (more) light or clear; illuminate **2** to make (e g a colour) lighter ~ *vi* **1** to grow lighter; brighten **2** to discharge flashes of lightning – **lightener** *n*

[2]**lighten** *vt* **1** to reduce the weight of ⟨~ *the lorry*⟩ ⟨~ *her duties*⟩ **2** to relieve (partly) of a burden ⟨*the news* ~ed *his mind*⟩ **3** to make less wearisome; alleviate ⟨~ed *his gloom*⟩; *broadly* to cheer, gladden ~ *vi* **1** to become lighter or less burdensome **2** to become more cheerful ⟨*his mood* ~ed⟩ – **lightener** *n*

[1]**lighter** *vt or n* (to convey by) a large usu flat-bottomed barge used esp in unloading or loading ships

[2]**lighter** *n* a device for lighting (a cigar, cigarette, etc)

lighterage *n* (the charge for) the loading, unloading, or transport of goods by means of a lighter

light-fingered *adj* **1** adroit in stealing, esp picking pockets **2** having a light and dexterous touch; nimble – **light-fingeredness** *n*

light-headed *adj* **1** mentally disoriented; dizzy **2** frivolous – **light-headedly** *adv*, **light-headedness** *n*

lighthearted *adj* free from care or worry; cheerful – **lightheartedly** *adv*, **lightheartedness** *n*

lighthouse *n* a tower, mast, etc equipped with a powerful light to warn or guide shipping at sea

lighting *n* (the apparatus providing) an artificial supply of light

lightness *n* the attribute of object colours by which more or less of the incident light is reflected or transmitted

[1]**lightning** *n* (the brilliant light flash resulting from) an electric discharge between 2 clouds or between a cloud and the earth

[2]**lightning** *adj* very quick, short, or sudden

lightning conductor *n* a metal rod fixed to the highest point of a building or mast and connected to the earth or water below as a protection against lightning

light out *vi, NAm* to leave in a hurry – *infml* ⟨*lit out for home as soon as he could*⟩

lights *n pl* the lungs, esp of a slaughtered sheep, pig, etc

lightship *n* a moored vessel equipped with a powerful light to warn or guide shipping at sea

lights-out *n* **1** a command or signal for putting out lights **2** a prescribed bedtime for people living in an institution (e g boarding school)

light up *vb* **1** to illuminate or become illuminated or lit (in a sudden or conspicuous manner) ⟨*fireworks* lit up *the night sky*⟩ ⟨*her face* lit up⟩ **2** to ignite (a cigarette, pipe, etc)

lightweight *n or adj* **1** (a boxer) weighing not more than 9st 9lb (61.2kg) if professional or more than 57kg (about 8st 13lb) but not more than 60kg (about 9st 6lb) if amateur **2** (sby) of little ability or importance

light-year *n* a unit of length in astronomy equal to the distance that light travels in 1 year in a vacuum; 9,460 thousand million km (about 5,878 thousand million mi)

lignite *n* a brownish black coal that is harder than peat but usu retains the texture of the original wood – **lignitic** *adj*

lignum vitae *n, pl* **lignum vitaes** (the very hard heavy dark wood of) any of several tropical American trees

likable *also* **likeable** *adj* pleasant, agreeable – **likableness** *n*, **likability** *n*

[1]**like** *vt* **1a** to find agreeable, acceptable, or pleasant; enjoy ⟨~s *games*⟩ ⟨~s '*playing games*⟩ **b** to feel towards; regard ⟨*how would you* ~ *a change?*⟩ **2** to wish or choose to have, be, or do; want ⟨~s *to help*⟩ ⟨~s *us to come early*⟩ ~ *vi* to feel inclined; choose ⟨*you can leave any time you* ~⟩ – **if you like** SO TO SPEAK

[2]**like** *n* a liking, preference ⟨*one's* ~s *and dislikes*⟩

[3]**like** *adj* **1a** alike in appearance, character, or quantity

⟨*suits of* ~ *design*⟩ **b** bearing a close resemblance; *esp* faithful ⟨*his portrait is very* ~⟩ **2** likely

⁴**like** *prep* **1a** having the characteristics of; similar to ⟨*his house is* ~ *a barn*⟩ **b** typical of ⟨*was* ~ *her to do that*⟩ **2a** in the manner of; similarly to ⟨*act* ~ *a fool*⟩ **b** to the same degree as ⟨*fits* ~ *a glove*⟩ **c** close to ⟨*cost something* ~ *£5*⟩ **3** appearing to be, threaten, or promise ⟨*you seem* ~ *a sensible man*⟩ **4** – used to introduce an example ⟨*a subject* ~ *physics*⟩ – **like that 1** in that way ⟨*don't eat like that*⟩ **2** without demur or hesitation ⟨*can't change jobs just* like *that*⟩ – **like anything/crazy** – used to emphasize a verb; *infml* ⟨*run* like *anything*⟩

⁵**like** *n* one who or that which is like another, esp in high value; a counterpart ⟨*never saw the* ~ *of it*⟩ ⟨*had no use for the* ~ *s of him*⟩ ⟨*her* ~ *will never be seen again*⟩ – **the like** similar things ⟨*football, tennis, and the like*⟩

⁶**like** *adv* **1** likely, probably ⟨*he'll come as* ~ *as not*⟩ **2** SO TO SPEAK ⟨*went up to her casually,* ~⟩ – nonstandard

⁷**like** *conj* **1** in the same way as ⟨*if she can sing* ~ *she can dance*⟩ **2** *chiefly NAm* as if ⟨*acts* ~ *he knows what he's doing*⟩

-like *comb form* (*n* → *adj*) resembling or characteristic of ⟨*bell-like*⟩ ⟨*ladylike*⟩

likelihood *n* probability ⟨*in all* ~ *it will rain*⟩

¹**likely** *adj* **1** having a high probability of being or occurring ⟨~ *to succeed*⟩ ⟨*the* ~ *result*⟩ **2a** reliable, credible ⟨*a* ~ *enough story*⟩ **b** incredible – used ironically ⟨*a* ~ *tale!*⟩ **3** seeming appropriate; suitable ⟨*a* ~ *spot*⟩ **4** promising ⟨~ *lads*⟩

²**likely** *adv* probably – often in *most/very/more/quite likely* ⟨*he most* ~ *will give up*⟩

like-minded *adj* having a similar outlook or disposition – **like-mindedly** *adv*, **like-mindedness** *n*

liken *vt* to find or point out similarities in; compare

likeness *n* **1** resemblance **2** a copy, portrait ⟨*a good* ~ *of her*⟩ **3** *archaic* an appearance, semblance

likewise *adv* **1** in like manner; similarly ⟨*go and do* ~⟩ **2** moreover; IN ADDITION **3** similarly so with me ⟨*answered* '~' *to 'Pleased to meet you'*⟩

liking *n* favourable regard; fondness, taste ⟨*took a* ~ *to the newcomer*⟩ ⟨*things were not to his* ~⟩

lilac *n* **1** a European shrub of the olive family with heart-shaped leaves and large clusters of fragrant white or (pale pinkish) purple flowers **2** pale pinkish purple

lilliputian *n or adj, often cap* (sby or sthg) remarkably tiny or diminutive

Li-Lo *trademark* – used for an airbed

¹**lilt** *vb* to sing or speak rhythmically and with varying pitch – **liltingly** *adv*

²**lilt** *n* **1** (a song or tune with) a rhythmic swing, flow, or rising and falling inflection **2** a light springy motion ⟨*a* ~ *in her step*⟩

lily *n* **1** any of a genus of plants that grow from bulbs and are widely cultivated for their variously coloured showy flowers; *also* any of various other plants of the lily or the related daffodil or iris families **2** WATER LILY **3** a calla **4** FLEUR-DE-LIS **2** one resembling a lily in fairness, purity, or fragility – poetic – **liliaceous** *adj*

lily-livered *adj* lacking courage; cowardly

lily of the valley *n* a low perennial plant of the lily family that has usu 2 large leaves and a stalk of fragrant drooping bell-shaped white flowers

lily-white *adj* **1** pure white **2** irreproachable, pure

lima bean *n* (the flat edible seed of) any of various widely cultivated bushy or tall-growing orig tropical American beans

¹**limb** *n* **1** any of the projecting paired appendages of an animal body used esp for movement and grasping but sometimes modified into sensory or sexual organs; *esp* a

leg or arm of a human being **2** a large primary branch of a tree **3** an active member or agent ⟨~ *s of the law*⟩ **4** an extension, branch; *specif* any of the 4 branches or arms of a cross **5** *archaic* a mischievous child – **limbless** *adj* – **out on a limb** in an exposed and unsupported position

²**limb** *vt* to dismember; *esp* to cut off the limbs of (a felled tree)

³**limb** *n* **1** the graduated edge of a quadrant, levelling staff, etc **2** the outer edge of the apparent disc of a celestial body **3** the broad flat part of a petal or sepal furthest from its base

limbed *adj* having (a specified kind or number of) limbs – usu in combination ⟨*strong-limbed*⟩

¹**limber** *n* a 2-wheeled (ammunition-carrying) vehicle to which a gun may be attached

²**limber** *adj* supple in mind or body; flexible – **limberly** *adv*, **limberness** *n*

limber up *vb* to (cause to) become supple, flexible, or prepared for physical action ⟨*limbered up before the match*⟩

¹**limbo** *n, pl* **limbos 1** *often cap* an abode of souls that are according to Roman Catholic theology barred from heaven because of not having received Christian baptism **2a** a place or state of restraint or confinement, or of neglect or oblivion **b** an intermediate or transitional place or state

²**limbo** *n, pl* **limbos** a W Indian acrobatic dance that involves bending over backwards and passing under a low horizontal pole

¹**lime** *n* **1** birdlime **2a** a caustic solid consisting of calcium (and some magnesium) oxide, obtained by heating calcium carbonate (e g in the form of shells or limestone) to a high temperature, and used in building (e g in plaster) and in agriculture **b** calcium hydroxide (occurring as a dry white powder), made by treating caustic lime with water **c** calcium ⟨*carbonate of* ~⟩ – not now used technically – **limy** *adj*

²**lime** *vt* to treat or cover with lime ⟨~ *the soil in the spring*⟩

³**lime** *n* (the light fine-grained wood of) any of a genus of widely planted (ornamental) trees that usu have heart-shaped leaves

⁴**lime** *n* a (spiny tropical citrus tree cultivated for its) small spherical greenish-yellow fruit

limelight *n* **1** (the white light produced by) a stage lighting instrument producing illumination by means of an intense flame directed on a cylinder of lime **2** the centre of public attention ⟨*she's in the* ~ *again*⟩

limerick *n* a humorous and often epigrammatic or indecent verse form of 5 lines with a rhyme scheme of aabba

limestone *n* a widely-occurring rock consisting mainly of calcium carbonate

limey *n, often cap, NAm* a British person, esp a sailor – slang

¹**limit** *n* **1a** a boundary **b** *pl* the place enclosed within a boundary ⟨*must not go off* ~s⟩ **2a** sthg that bounds, restrains, or confines ⟨*worked within the* ~s *of his knowledge*⟩ ⟨*set a* ~ *on his spending*⟩ **b** a line or point that cannot or should not be passed **3** a prescribed maximum or minimum amount, quantity, or number ⟨*a speed* ~⟩ **4** a number which is approached but not reached by the value of **a** a function when the independent variable is made to approach a prescribed number or to increase or decrease indefinitely **b** the sum of a series as the number of terms is increased indefinitely **5** sby or sthg exasperating or intolerable – + *the*; *infml* – **limitless** *adj*, **limitlessly** *adv*, **limitlessness** *n*

²**limit** *vt* **1** to restrict to specific bounds or limits ⟨*the*

specialist can no longer ~ himself to his speciality⟩ 2 to curtail or reduce in quantity or extent; curb ⟨we must ~ the power of aggressors⟩ – **limitable** adj, **limiter** n, **limitative** adj

limitation n 1 (sthg that is) limiting; esp a limit of capability 2 a period defined by statute after which a claimant is barred from bringing a legal action – **limitational** adj

limited adj 1 confined within limits; restricted ⟨~ success⟩ 2 restricted as to the scope of powers ⟨a ~ monarchy⟩ 3 lacking the ability to grow or do better ⟨a bit ~; a bit thick in the head – Virginia Woolf⟩ 4 Br being a limited company – **limitedly** adv, **limitedness** n

limousine n a luxurious motor car (with a glass partition separating the driver from the passengers)

¹limp vi 1 to walk in a manner that avoids putting the full weight of the body on 1 (injured) leg 2 to proceed slowly or with difficulty ⟨the plane ~ed home⟩ – **limper** n

²limp n a limping movement or gait

³limp adj **1a** lacking firmness and body; drooping or shapeless **b** not stiff or rigid ⟨a ~ cover for a book⟩ 2 lacking energy – **limply** adv, **limpness** n

limpet n 1 a marine gastropod mollusc with a low conical shell broadly open beneath, that clings very tightly to rock when disturbed 2 sby or sthg that clings tenaciously 3 an explosive device designed to cling to the hull of a ship, tank, etc ⟨a ~ mine⟩

limpid adj 1 transparent, pellucid ⟨~ streams⟩ 2 clear and simple in style ⟨~ prose⟩ – **limpidly** adv, **limpidness**, **limpidity** n

linchpin, lynchpin n 1 a locking pin inserted crosswise (e g through the end of an axle or shaft) 2 sby or sthg regarded as a vital or coordinating factor ⟨the ~ of the organization⟩

linctus n any of various syrupy usu medicated liquids used to relieve throat irritation and coughing

linden n ³LIME

¹line vt 1 to cover the inner surface of; provide with a lining ⟨~ a cloak with silk⟩ 2 to fill ⟨lining his pockets with other people's money⟩ 3 to serve as the lining of ⟨tapestries ~d the walls⟩

²line n **1a(1)** a (comparatively strong slender) cord or rope **(2)** a rope used on shipboard **b(1)** a device for catching fish consisting of a usu single-filament cord with hooks, floats, a reel, etc **(2)** scope for activity **c** a length of material (e g cord) used in measuring and levelling ⟨a plumb ~⟩ **d** piping for conveying a fluid (e g steam or compressed air) **e(1)** (a connection for communication by means of) a set of wires connecting one telephone or telegraph (exchange) with another **(2)** the principal circuits of an electric power distribution system **2a** a horizontal row of written or printed characters **b** a single row of words in a poem **c** a short letter; a note **d** a short sequence of words spoken by an actor playing a particular role; also, pl all of the sequences making up a particular role **3a** sthg (e g a ridge, seam, or crease) that is distinct, elongated, and narrow **b** a wrinkle (e g on the face) **c(1)** the course or direction of sthg in motion ⟨the ~ of march⟩ **(2)** the trail of scent left by a hunted animal **d** a real or imaginary straight line ⟨lies on a ~ between London and Glasgow⟩ **e** a boundary or limit (of an area) ⟨the state ~⟩ ⟨there's a very fine ~ between punishment and cruelty⟩ **f** (a single set of rails forming) a railway track **4a** a course of conduct, action, or thought **b** a field of activity or interest ⟨what's your ~?⟩ **c** a specified way or theme of talking or writing **5a(1)** a related series of people or things coming one after the other in time; a family, lineage **(2)** a strain produced and maintained by selective breeding **b** a linked series of trenches and fortifi-

cations, esp facing the enemy – usu pl with sing. meaning **c** a military formation in which men, companies, etc are abreast of each other **d** naval ships arranged in a regular order ⟨the fleet changed from ~ ahead to ~ abreast⟩ **e'** the regular and numbered infantry regiments of the army as opposed to auxiliary forces or household troops **f** a rank of objects of 1 kind; a row **g** (the company owning or operating) a group of vehicles, ships, aeroplanes, etc carrying passengers or goods regularly over a route ⟨a shipping ~⟩ **h** an arrangement of operations in manufacturing allowing ordered occurrence of various stages of production **6** a narrow elongated mark drawn, projected, or imagined (e g on a map): e g **a** a boundary, contour, circle of latitude or longitude, etc **b** the equator **c** any of the horizontal parallel strokes on a music staff on or between which notes are placed **d** a mark (e g in pencil) that forms part of the formal design of a picture; also an artist's use of such lines ⟨purity of ~⟩ **e** (a single passage of the scanning spot tracing) a horizontal line on a television screen **f** a narrow part of a spectrum (e g of light from the sun) distinguished by being noticeably more or less bright than neighbouring areas ⟨the sodium ~s occur in the yellow part of the spectrum⟩ **g** a demarcation of a limit with reference to which the playing of some game or sport is regulated – usu in combination ⟨a touchline⟩ **7** a straight or curved geometric element, generated by a moving point (continually satisfying a particular condition), that has length but no breadth **8a** a defining outline; a contour ⟨the ~ of a building⟩ ⟨the clean ~s of a ship⟩ **b** a general plan; a model – usu pl with sing. meaning ⟨writing sthg on the ~s of a guidebook⟩ **9** merchandise or services of the same general class for sale or regularly available **10** an indication (e g of intention) based on insight or investigation ⟨got a ~ on their plans⟩ **11** pl, Br a row of tents or huts in a military camp **12** chiefly Br a pica **13** pl, Br a (specified) number of lines of writing, esp to be copied as a school punishment – **liny** also **liney** adj – **between the lines 1** by concealed implication **2** by way of inference ⟨if you read between the lines, the meaning is different⟩ – **in line for** due or in a position to receive – **into line** into a state of agreement or obedience – **on the line** at risk ⟨put his job on the line because of his principles⟩

³line vt 1 to mark or cover with a line or lines 2 to place or form a line along ⟨pedestrians ~ the streets⟩ 3 to form into a line or lines; LINE UP

lineage n a (group of organisms belonging to the same) line of descent from a common ancestor or source

lineal adj 1 composed of or arranged in lines 2 consisting of or being in a direct line of ancestry or descent – usu contrasted with collateral 3 of, being, or dealing with a lineage – **lineally** adv, **lineality** n

lineament n a distinctive outline, feature, or contour of a body or figure, esp a face – usu pl – **lineamental** adj

linear adj **1a(1)** of, being, or resembling a line **(2)** involving a single dimension **b** of an equation, function, etc containing any number of variables, all of the first degree, and represented graphically by a straight line **c(1)** characterized by an emphasis on line; esp having clearly defined outlines **(2)** esp of writing composed of simply drawn lines with little attempt at pictorial representation **d** consisting of a straight chain of atoms **2** having or being a response or output that is directly proportional to the input ⟨a good amplifier is ~⟩ – **linearly** adv, **linearity** n

linear motor n an electric motor that produces thrust in a straight line by direct induction (e g between a track and a vehicle running on it)

linear perspective n representation in a drawing or

painting of parallel lines as converging in order to give the illusion of depth and distance

linen *n* **1** cloth or yarn made from flax **2** clothing or household articles (e g sheets and tablecloths) made of a usu washable cloth, esp linen

line of sight *n* a straight line from an observer's eye to a distant point towards which he/she is looking

line-out *n* (a method in Rugby Union of returning the ball to play after it has crossed a touchline which involves throwing it in between) a line of forwards from each team

line printer *n* a high-speed printing device (e g for a computer) that prints each line as a unit rather than character by character – **line printing** *n*

¹liner *n* a passenger ship belonging to a shipping company and usu sailing scheduled routes

²liner *n* a replaceable (metal) lining (for reducing the wear of a mechanism) – **linerless** *adj*

linesman *n* an official who assists the referee or umpire in various games, esp in determining if a ball or player is out of the prescribed playing area

lineup *n* (a list of) the players playing for usu 1 side in a game

line-up *n* **1** a line of people arranged esp for inspection or as a means of identifying a suspect **2** a group of people or items assembled for a particular purpose ⟨the ~ for tonight's show⟩

line up *vi* to assume an orderly arrangement in a line ⟨line up *for inspection*⟩ ~*vt* **1** to put into alignment **2** to assemble or organize

¹ling *n* a large food fish of shallow seas off Greenland and Europe

²ling *n* the commonest British heather

¹-ling *suffix* (*adj or n → n*) **1** one connected with ⟨*hire*ling⟩ ⟨*sib*ling⟩ **2** young, small, or lesser kind of ⟨*duck*ling⟩ ⟨*prince*ling⟩ **3** one having (a specified quality or attribute) ⟨*under*ling⟩ ⟨*dar*ling⟩

²-ling *suffix* (*n or adj → adj or adv*) of or in (such) a state, direction, or manner ⟨*dark*ling⟩

linger *vi* **1a** to delay going, esp because of reluctance to leave; tarry **b** to dwell on a subject – usu + *over, on,* or *upon* **2** to continue unduly or unhappily in a failing or moribund state – often + *on* **3** to be slow to act; procrastinate **4** to be protracted or slow in disappearing – **lingerer** *n*, **lingeringly** *adv*

lingerie *n* women's underwear and nightclothes

lingo *n, pl* **lingoes 1** a foreign language **2** JARGON 2 *USE* infml

lingua franca *n, pl* **lingua francas, linguae francae 1** a language spoken in Mediterranean ports that consists of a mixture of Italian with French, Spanish, Greek, and Arabic **2** a language used as a common or commercial tongue among people not speaking the same native language **3** sthg resembling a common language

lingual *adj* **1a** of or resembling the tongue **b** lying near or next to the tongue **c** articulated with the tongue **2** linguistic – **lingually** *adv*

linguist *n* **1** sby accomplished in languages; *esp* POLYGLOT 1 **2** sby who specializes in linguistics

linguistic *adj* of language or linguistics – **linguistically** *adv*

linguistic form *n* a meaningful unit of speech (e g a morpheme, word, or sentence)

linguistics *n pl but sing in constr* the study of human language with regard to its nature, structure, and modification

liniment *n* a liquid preparation that is applied to the skin, esp to allay pain or irritation

lining *n* **1** (a piece of) material used to line sthg (e g a garment) **2** providing sthg with a lining

¹link *n* **1** a connecting structure: e g **a(1)** a single ring or division of a chain **(2)** a unit of length formerly used in surveying equal to 7.92in (about 20.12cm) **b** the fusible part of an electrical fuse **2** sthg analogous to a link of chain: e g **a** a connecting element ⟨sought a ~ between *smoking and cancer*⟩ **b** a unit in a communications system – **linker** *n*

²link *vt* to join, connect ⟨road that ~s 2 towns⟩ ~*vi* to become connected by a link – often + *up*

linkage *n* **1** the manner or style of being joined; *specif* BOND 3a **2** the relationship between genes on the same chromosome that causes them to be inherited together **3a** a system of links **b** the degree of electromagnetic interaction expressed as the product of the number of turns of a coil and the magnetic flux linked by the coil

linkman *n* a broadcaster whose function is to link and introduce separate items, esp in a news programme

links *n pl* **1** GOLF COURSE – often pl with sing. meaning **2** *Scot* sand hills, esp along the seashore

linkup *n* **1** the establishment of contact; a meeting ⟨the ~ of 2 spacecraft⟩ **2a** sthg that serves as a linking device or factor **b** a functional whole that is the result of a linkup

linnet *n* a common small Old World finch having variable reddish brown plumage

linocut *n* (a print made from) a design cut in relief on a piece of linoleum

linoleum *n* a floor covering with a canvas back and a coloured or patterned surface of hardened linseed oil and a filler (e g cork dust)

Linotype *trademark* – used for a keyboard-operated typesetting machine that produces each line of type in the form of a solid metal slug

linseed *n* the seed of flax used esp as a source of linseed oil

linseed oil *n* a yellowish drying oil obtained from flaxseed and used esp in paint, varnish, printing ink, and linoleum and for conditioning cricket bats

lint *n* **1** a soft absorbent material with a fleecy surface that is made from linen and is used chiefly for surgical dressings **2** *chiefly NAm* FLUFF 1a – **linty** *adj*

lintel *n* a horizontal architectural member spanning and usu carrying the load above an opening

lion, *fem* **lioness** *n, pl* **lions**, (**1a**) **lions**, *esp collectively* **lion 1a** a flesh-eating big cat of open or rocky areas of Africa and formerly southern Asia that has a tawny body with a tufted tail and in the male a shaggy blackish or dark brown mane **b** *cap* Leo **2** a person of interest or importance ⟨*literary* ~s⟩

lionhearted *adj* courageous, brave

lionize, -ise *vt* to treat as an object of great interest or importance – **lionizer** *n*, **lionization** *n*

lip *n* **1** either of the 2 fleshy folds that surround the mouth **2a** a fleshy edge or margin (e g of a wound) **b** a labium **3** the edge of a hollow vessel or cavity; *esp* one shaped to make pouring easy **4** an embouchure **5** impudent or insolent talk, esp in reply – slang – **lipless** *adj*, **liplike** *adj*

lip-, lipo- *comb form* fat; fatty tissue; fatty ⟨*lipoma*⟩ ⟨*lipoprotein*⟩

lipid *n* any of various substances that with proteins and carbohydrates form the principal structural components of living cells and that include fats, waxes, and related and derived compounds – **lipidic** *adj*

lipped *adj* having a lip or lips, esp of a specified kind or number – often in combination ⟨tight-lipped⟩

lip reading *n* the interpreting of a speaker's words (e g by the deaf) by watching the movements of the lips – **lip-read** *vb*, **lip-reader** *n*

lip service *n* support in words but not in deeds ⟨*paid ~ to racial equality but still employed only whites*⟩

lipstick *n* (a cased stick of) a waxy solid cosmetic for colouring the lips

liquefaction *n* **1** the process of making or becoming liquid **2** the state of being liquid

liquefy *also* **liquify** *vt* to reduce to a liquid state *~ vi* to become liquid – **liquefiable** *adj*, **liquefier** *n*, **liquefiability** *n*

liquescent *adj* being or tending to become liquid

liqueur *n* any of several usu sweetened alcoholic drinks variously flavoured (e g with fruit or aromatics)

liquid *adj* **1** flowing freely like water **2** neither solid nor gaseous; characterized by free movement of the constituent molecules among themselves but without the tendency to separate like those of gases ⟨*~ mercury*⟩ **3a** shining and clear ⟨*large ~ eyes*⟩ **b** *of a sound* flowing, pure, and free of harshness **c** smooth and unconstrained in movement **d** *of a consonant* (e g /t/ or /l/) articulated without friction and capable of being prolonged like a vowel **4** consisting of or capable of ready conversion into cash ⟨*~ assets*⟩ – **liquid** *n*, **liquidly** *adv*, **liquidness** *n*, **liquidity** *n*

liquid air *n* air in the liquid state that is intensely cold and used chiefly as a refrigerant

liquidate *vt* **1a** to settle (a debt), esp by payment **b** to settle the accounts of (e g a business) and use the assets towards paying off the debts **2** to get rid of; *specif* to kill **3** to convert (assets) into cash *~ vi* **1** to liquidate debts, damages, or accounts **2** to be or become liquidated – **liquidation** *n*

liquidator *n* a person appointed by law to liquidate a company

liquidize, -ise *vt* to cause to be liquid; *esp* to pulverize (e g fruit or vegetables) into a liquid

liquidizer, -iser *n*, *chiefly Br* a domestic electric appliance for grinding, puréeing, liquidizing, or blending foods

¹**liquor** *n* a liquid substance: e g **a** a solution of a drug in water **b** BATH 2c **c** a liquid, esp water, in which food has been cooked **d** *chiefly NAm* a usu distilled rather than fermented alcoholic drink

²**liquor** *vt* **1** to dress (e g leather) with oil or grease **2** to make drunk with alcoholic drink – usu + *up ~ vi* to drink alcoholic drink, esp to excess – usu + *up*

liquorice *n* **1** a European leguminous plant having spikes of blue flowers and grown for its roots **2** the dried root of liquorice; *also* an extract of this used esp in medicine, brewing, and confectionery

lira *n*, *pl* (1) **lire** *also* **liras**, (2) **liras** *also* **lire 1** the standard unit of money in Italy **2** the standard unit of money in Turkey

lisle *n* a smooth tightly twisted thread usu made of long-staple cotton

¹**lisp** *vi* **1** to pronounce /s/ and /z/ imperfectly, esp by giving them the sounds of /th/ and /dh/ **2** to speak with a lisp – **lisper** *n*

²**lisp** *n* a speech defect or affectation characterized by lisping

lissom, lissome *adj* easily flexed; lithe, nimble

¹**list** *n* **1** a band or strip of material; *esp* a selvage **2** *pl but sing or pl in constr* **a** (the fence surrounding) a tiltyard **b** a scene of competition

²**list** *n* a roll or catalogue of words or numbers (e g representing people or objects belonging to a class), usu arranged in order so as to be easily found ⟨*a guest ~*⟩ ⟨*a shopping ~*⟩

³**list** *vt* **1** to make a list of **2** to include on a list; *specif*, *Br*

to include (a building) in an official list as being of architectural or historical importance and hence protected from demolition

⁴**list** *vb* to (cause to) lean to one side ⟨*the ship was ~ing badly*⟩ – **list** *n*

¹**listen** *vi* **1** to pay attention to sound ⟨*~ to music*⟩ **2** to hear or consider with thoughtful attention; heed ⟨*~ to a plea*⟩ **3** to be alert to catch an expected sound ⟨*~ for his step*⟩ – **listener** *n*

²**listen** *n* an act of listening – infml

listen in *vi* to tune in to or monitor a broadcast – **listener-in** *n*

listless *adj* characterized by indifference, lack of energy, and disinclination for exertion; languid – **listlessly** *adv*, **listlessness** *n*

lit *past of* LIGHT

litany *n* a prayer consisting of a series of petitions by the leader with alternate responses by the congregation

litchi, lichee *n* (a Chinese tree that bears) an oval fruit that has a hard scaly outer covering and a small hard seed surrounded by edible pulp

liter *n*, *NAm* a litre

literacy *n* the quality or state of being literate

¹**literal** *adj* **1a** according with the exact letter of a written text; *specif* according with the letter of the scriptures **b** having the factual or ordinary construction or primary meaning of a term or expression; actual **c** characterized by a lack of imagination; prosaic ⟨*a very ~ approach to the subject*⟩ **2** of or expressed in letters **3** reproduced word for word; exact, verbatim ⟨*a ~ translation*⟩ – **literalness, literality** *n*

²**literal** *n* a misprint involving a single letter

literally *adv* **1** in the literal sense; without metaphor or exaggeration **2** with exact equivalence; verbatim ⟨*follow the instructions ~*⟩ **3** – used to intensify a metaphorical or hyperbolic expression ⟨*she was ~ tearing her hair out*⟩; disapproved of by some speakers

literary *adj* **1a** of, being, or concerning literature ⟨*~ criticism*⟩ **b** characteristic of or being in a formal, rather than colloquial, style **2a** well-read **b** producing, well versed in, or connected with literature – **literarily** *adv*, **literariness** *n*

¹**literate** *adj* **1a** educated, cultured **b** able to read and write **2** versed in literature or creative writing – **literately** *adv*, **literateness** *n*

²**literate** *n* a literate person

literati *n pl* the educated class; the intelligentsia

literature *n* **1a** writings in prose or verse; *esp* writings having artistic value or expression and expressing ideas of permanent or universal interest **b** the body of writings on a particular subject ⟨*scientific ~*⟩ **c** printed matter (e g leaflets or circulars) **2** the body of musical compositions ⟨*the piano ~ of Brahms*⟩

lithe *adj* flexible, supple – **lithely** *adv*, **litheness** *n*

lithium *n* a soft silver-white element of the alkali metal group that is the lightest metal known

lithograph *vt or n* (to produce or copy in the form of) a print made by lithography – **lithographic** *adj*, **lithographically** *adv*

lithography *n* the process of printing from a surface (e g a stone or a metal plate) on which the image to be printed is ink-receptive and the blank area ink-repellent

litigate *vi* to carry on a lawsuit *~ vt* to contest (an issue) at law – **litigable** *adj*, **litigant** *n or adj*, **litigation** *n*

litigious *adj* **1** (excessively) inclined to engage in lawsuits **2** subject to litigation **3** tending to argue; disputatious – fml – **litigiously** *adv*, **litigiousness** *n*

litmus *n* a colouring matter from lichens that turns red in acid solutions and blue in alkaline solutions and is used as an acid-alkali indicator

litmus paper *n* absorbent paper coloured with litmus and used as an indicator

litotes *n, pl* **litotes** understatement in which an affirmative is expressed by the negative of its opposite (e g in 'not a bad singer')

litre, *NAm chiefly* **liter** *n* a metric unit of capacity equal to 1.000 028dm³ (about 0.220gal)

¹litter *n* **1a** a covered and curtained couch carried by people or animals **b** a stretcher or other device for carrying a sick or injured person **2a** material used as bedding for animals **b** the uppermost slightly decayed layer of organic matter on the forest floor **3** a group of offspring of an animal, born at 1 birth **4a** rubbish or waste products, esp in a public place **b** an untidy accumulation of objects (e g papers) – **littery** *adj*

²litter *vt* **1** to provide (e g a horse) with litter as a bed **2** to give birth to (young) **3a** to strew with litter, esp scattered articles ⟨~ *the horse's stall*⟩ ⟨~ *the desk-top with papers*⟩ **b** to scatter about in disorder ~ *vi* **1** to give birth to a litter **2** to strew litter

litterateur *also* **littérateur** *n* a literary man; *esp* a professional writer

litterlout *n* one who carelessly drops rubbish in public places – *infml*

¹little *adj* **littler, less, lesser; littlest, least 1a** amounting to only a small quantity ⟨*had* ~ *or no time*⟩ **b** *of a plant or animal* small in comparison with related forms – used in vernacular names **c** small in condition, distinction, or scope **d** narrow, mean ⟨*the pettiness of* ~ *minds*⟩ **2** not much: e g **a** existing only in a small amount or to a slight degree ⟨*unfortunately he has* ~ *money*⟩ **b** short in duration; brief ⟨*wait a* ~ *while*⟩ **c** existing to an appreciable though not extensive degree or amount – + *a* ⟨*fortunately she had a* ~ *money in the bank*⟩ **3** small in importance or interest; trivial – **littleness** *n*

²little *adv* **less; least 1** to no great degree or extent; not much ⟨little-*known*⟩ **2** not at all ⟨*cared* ~ *for his neighbours*⟩

³little *n* **1a** only a small portion or quantity; not much ⟨*understood* ~ *of his speech*⟩ ⟨*do what* ~ *I can*⟩ **b** at least some, though not much – + *a* ⟨*have a* ~ *of this cake*⟩ **2** a short time or distance ⟨*walk for a* ~⟩ – **a little** somewhat, rather ⟨*a little over 50 years*⟩ ⟨*found the play a little boring*⟩

little finger *n* the fourth and smallest finger of the hand counting the index finger as the first

little people *n pl* imaginary beings (e g fairies, elves, etc) of folklore – + *the*

little toe *n* the outermost and smallest digit of the foot

little woman *n* one's wife – humor; often derog

¹littoral *adj* of or occurring on or near a (sea) shore

²littoral *n* a coastal region; *esp* the intertidal zone

liturgical *adj* **1** (having the characteristics) of liturgy **2** using or favouring the use of liturgy – **liturgically** *adv*

liturgy *n* **1** *often cap* the form of service used in the celebration of Communion, esp in the Orthodox church **2** a prescribed form of public worship

livable *also* **liveable** *adj* **1** suitable for living in or with **2** endurable – **livableness** *n*

¹live *vi* **1** to be alive; have the life of an animal or plant **2** to continue alive ⟨*his illness is so serious, he is lucky to* ~⟩ **3** to maintain oneself; subsist ⟨*she* ~d *by writing*⟩ ⟨*he* ~d *by his wits*⟩ **4** to conduct or pass one's life ⟨~d *only for her work*⟩ **5** to occupy a home; dwell ⟨*they had always* ~d *in the country*⟩ **6** to attain eternal life ⟨*though he were dead, yet shall he* ~ – Jn 11:25 (AV)⟩ **7** to have a life rich in experience ⟨*the right to* ~, not

merely *to exist*⟩ **8** to cohabit – + *together* or *with* **9** *chiefly Br, of a thing* to be found in a specified place, esp normally or usually – *infml* ~ *vt* **1** to pass, spend, or experience **2** to enact, practise ⟨~ *a lie*⟩ ⟨*really* ~s *her faith*⟩ – **live in sin** to cohabit – **live it up** to enjoy an exciting or extravagant social life or social occasion ⟨lived it up *with wine and song* – *Newsweek*⟩ – **live up to** to act or be in accordance with (esp a standard expected by sby)

²live *adj* **1** having life **2** containing living organisms ⟨~ *yoghourt*⟩ **3** exerting force or containing energy: e g **a** glowing ⟨~ *coals*⟩ **b** connected to electric power **c** *of ammunition, bombs, etc* unexploded, unfired **d** driven by or imparting motion or power **e** *of a nuclear reactor or nuclear bomb* charged with material capable of undergoing fission **4** of continuing or current interest ⟨~ *issues*⟩ **5** *esp of a rock* not quarried or cut; native **6** in play in a game ⟨*a* ~ *ball*⟩ **7a** of or involving the presence or participation of real people ⟨*a* ~ *audience*⟩ ⟨~ *music*⟩ **b** broadcast while happening ⟨*a* ~ *television programme*⟩

³live *adv* during, from, or at a live production

live down *vt* to cause (e g a crime or mistake) to be forgotten, esp by future good behaviour ⟨*made a mistake and couldn't* live *it* down⟩

live in *vi* to live in one's place of work ⟨*the housekeeper is required to* live in⟩

livelihood *n* a means of support or sustenance

livelong *adj* whole, entire – chiefly poetic ⟨*the* ~ *day*⟩

lively *adj* **1** briskly alert and energetic; vigorous, animated ⟨*a* ~ *discussion*⟩ ⟨~ *children racing home from school*⟩ **2** brilliant, vivid ⟨*a* ~ *flashing wit*⟩ ⟨*a* ~ *colour*⟩ **3** quick to rebound; resilient **4** responding readily to the helm ⟨*a* ~ *boat*⟩ **5** full of life, movement, or incident ⟨*the crowded streets made a* ~ *scene*⟩ **6** full of possibly disagreeable or dangerous action – humor ⟨*given a* ~ *time by enemy artillery*⟩ – **livelily** *adv*, **liveliness** *n*, **lively** *adv*

liven *vb* to make or become lively – often + *up*

live out *vi* to live outside one's place of work ⟨*owing to the shortage of college rooms, some students must* live out⟩ ~ *vt* to live till the end of ⟨*will the sick man* live out *the month?*⟩

¹liver *n* **1a** a large vascular glandular organ of vertebrates that secretes bile and causes changes in the blood (e g by converting blood sugar into glycogen) **b** any of various large digestive glands of invertebrates **2** the liver of an animal (e g a calf or pig) eaten as food **3** a greyish reddish brown **4** *archaic* the seat of the emotions

²liver *n* one who lives, esp in a specified way ⟨*a clean* ~⟩

liverish *adj* **1** suffering from liver disorder; bilious **2** peevish, irascible; *also* glum – **liverishness** *n*

liver sausage *n* a sausage consisting chiefly of cooked minced liver often with pork trimmings

¹livery *n* **1a** the distinctive clothing worn by a member of a livery company or guild **b** the uniform of servants employed by an individual or a single household **c** distinctive colouring or marking; *also* distinctive dress **d** a distinctive colour scheme (e g on aircraft) distinguishing an organization or group **2** the legal delivering of property **3** *chiefly NAm* LIVERY STABLE – **liveried** *adj*

²livery *adj* liverish

livery company *n* any of various London craft or trade associations that are descended from medieval guilds

liveryman *n* a freeman of the City of London who is a member of a livery company

livery stable *n* an establishment where horses are stabled and fed for their owners

lives *pl of* LIFE

livestock *n* **1** animals kept or raised for use or pleasure; *esp* farm animals kept for use and profit **2** *Br* small verminous creatures (e g lice or fleas) – chiefly humor

live wire *n* an alert, active, or aggressive person

livid *adj* **1** discoloured by bruising **2** ashen, pallid ⟨*this cross, thy ~ face, thy pierced hands and feet* – Walt Whitman⟩ **3** reddish **4** very angry; enraged ⟨*was ~ at his son's disobedience*⟩ – **lividness** *n*, **lividity** *n*

¹**living** *adj* **1a** having life; alive **b** existing in use ⟨*a ~ language*⟩ **2** ²LIVE 3a **3a** true to life; exact – esp in *the living image of* **b** suited for living ⟨*the ~ area*⟩ **4** – used as an intensive ⟨*scared the ~ daylights out of him*⟩ **5** *of feelings, ideas, etc* full of power and force ⟨*in ~ colour*⟩ – **livingness** *n*

²**living** *n* **1** the condition of being alive **2** a manner of life **3a** means of subsistence; a livelihood ⟨*earning a ~*⟩ **b** *Br* a benefice

living death *n* a life so full of misery that death would be preferable

living room *n* a room in a residence used for everyday activities

living space *n* lebensraum

living standard *n* STANDARD OF LIVING

living wage *n* **1** a subsistence wage **2** a wage sufficient to provide an acceptable standard of living

lizard *n* any of a suborder of reptiles distinguished from the snakes by 2 pairs of well differentiated functional limbs (which may be lacking in burrowing forms), external ears, and eyes with movable lids

'll *vb* will, shall ⟨*you'll be late*⟩

llama *n* any of several wild and domesticated S American ruminant mammals related to the camels but smaller and without a hump; *esp* the domesticated guanaco

lo *interj*, *archaic* – used to call attention or to express wonder or surprise

¹**load** *n* **1a** an amount, esp large or heavy, that is (to be) carried, supported, or borne; a burden **b** the quantity that can be carried at 1 time by a specified means – often in combination ⟨*a boatload of tourists*⟩ **2** the forces to which a structure is subjected ⟨*the ~ on the arch*⟩ **3** a burden of responsibility, anxiety, etc ⟨*took a ~ off her mind*⟩ **4** external resistance overcome by a machine or other source of power **5a** power output (e g of a power plant) **b** a device to which power is delivered **6** the amount of work to be performed by a person, machine, etc **7** a large quantity or amount; a lot – usu *pl* with sing. meaning; infml ⟨*there's ~s of room on the back seat*⟩ – **get a load of** to pay attention to (sthg surprising) – slang

²**load** *vt* **1a** to put a load in or on ⟨*~ a van with furniture*⟩ **b** to place in or on a means of conveyance ⟨*~ cargo*⟩ **2** to encumber or oppress with sthg heavy, laborious, or disheartening; burden ⟨*a company ~ed down with debts*⟩ **3a** to weight or shape (dice) to fall unfairly **b** to charge with one-sided or prejudicial influences; bias **c** to charge with emotional associations or hidden implications ⟨*a ~ed statement*⟩ **4a** to put a load or charge in (a device or piece of equipment) ⟨*~ a gun*⟩ **b** to place or insert in a device or piece of equipment ⟨*~ a film in a camera*⟩ **5** to affect, often adversely, (the output of a preceding stage of an electrical circuit) – *vi* **1** to receive a load **2** to put a load on or in a carrier, device, or container; *esp* to insert the charge in a firearm – **loader** *n*

loaded *adj* having a large amount of money – infml

loadstar *n* a lodestar

loadstone *n* (a) lodestone

¹**loaf** *n*, *pl* **loaves 1** a mass of bread often having a regular shape and standard weight **2** a shaped or moulded often

symmetrical mass of food (e g sugar or chopped cooked meat) **3** *Br* head, brains – slang; esp in *use one's loaf*

²**loaf** *vi* to spend time in idleness

loafer *n* **1** one who loafs **2** *chiefly NAm* a low leather shoe similar to a moccasin but with a broad flat heel

loam *n* ³SOIL 2a; *specif* crumbly soil consisting of a mixture of clay, silt, and sand – **loamy** *adj*

¹**loan** *n* **1a** money lent at interest **b** sthg lent, usu for the borrower's temporary use **2** the grant of temporary use

²**loan** *vt* to lend ⟨*~ ed to the gallery by an unnamed owner*⟩ – **loanable** *adj*

lo and behold *interj* – used to express wonder or surprise

loanword *n* a word taken from another language and at least partly naturalized

loath, loth *also* **loathe** *adj* unwilling *to* do sthg disliked; reluctant

loathe *vt* to dislike greatly, often with disgust or intolerance; detest – **loather** *n*

loathing *n* extreme disgust; detestation

loathsome *adj* giving rise to loathing; disgusting – **loathsomely** *adv*, **loathsomeness** *n*

loaves *pl of* LOAF

¹**lob** *vb* **-bb-** *vt* **1** to throw, hit, or propel easily or in a high arc **2** to hit a lob against (an opponent, esp in tennis) to hit a ball easily in a high arc, esp in tennis, squash, etc

²**lob** *n* a ball that is lobbed

lob-, lobo- *comb form* lobe ⟨*lobar*⟩ ⟨*lobotomy*⟩

¹**lobby** *n* **1** a porch or small entrance hall **2** an anteroom of a legislative chamber to which members go to vote during a division **3** *sing or pl in constr* a group of people engaged in lobbying

²**lobby** *vi* to try to influence members of a legislative body towards an action – *vt* **1** to secure the passage of (legislation) by influencing public officials **2** to try to influence (e g a member of a legislative body) towards an action – **lobbyer** *n*, **lobbyist** *n*

lobe *n* a curved or rounded projection or division; *esp* such a projection or division of a bodily organ or part – **lobed** *adj*, **lobar** *adj*, **lobate, lobated** *adj*

lobotomy *n* a brain operation used, esp formerly, in the treatment of some mental disorders (e g violent psychoses) in which nerve fibres in the cerebral cortex are cut in order to change behaviour – **lobotomize** *vt*

lobster *n*, *pl* **lobsters**, *esp collectively* **lobster** any of a family of large edible 10-legged marine crustaceans that have stalked eyes, a pair of large claws, and a long abdomen

lobster pot *n* (a basket used as) a trap for catching lobsters

¹**local** *adj* **1** characterized by or relating to position in space **2** (characteristic) of or belonging to a particular place; not general or widespread ⟨*~ news*⟩ **3a** primarily serving the needs of a particular limited district ⟨*~ government*⟩ **b** *of a public conveyance* making all the stops on a route **4** involving or affecting only a restricted part of a living organism – **locally** *adv*

²**local** *n* a local person or thing ⟨*spoke to the friendly ~s*⟩: e g **a** *Br* the neighbourhood pub **b** *NAm* a local public conveyance (e g a train or bus)

local colour *n* the description in a literary work of the features and peculiarities of a particular locality and its inhabitants

locale *n* a place or locality, esp when viewed in relation to a particular event or characteristic; a scene

localism *n* **1** affection or partiality for a particular place, esp to the exclusion of others **2** a local idiom or custom

locality *n* **1** the fact or condition of having a location in space or time **2** a particular place, situation, or location

localize, -ise *vt* **1** to give local characteristics to **2** to assign to or keep within a definite locality to collect in a specific or limited area – **localization** *n*

locate *vt* **1** to determine or indicate the place, site, or limits of **2** to set or establish in a particular spot – **locatable** *adj*, **locater** *n*

location *n* **1** a particular place or position **2** a place outside a studio where a (part of a) picture is filmed – usu in *on location* – **locational** *adj*, **locationally** *adv*

loch *n* a lake or (nearly landlocked) arm of the sea in Scotland

loci *pl of* LOCUS

¹lock *n* **1** a curl, tuft, etc of hair **2** *pl* the hair of the head

²lock *n* **1a** a fastening that can be opened and often closed only by means of a particular key or combination **b** a gunlock **2a** an enclosed section of waterway (e g a canal) which has gates at each end and in which the water level can be raised or lowered to move boats from one level to another **b** AIR LOCK **3a** a locking or fastening together **b** a hold in wrestling secured on a usu specified body part **4** *chiefly Br* the (maximum) extent to which the front wheels of a vehicle are turned to change the direction of travel ⟨*from ~ to ~ is 3⅝ turns of the steering wheel*⟩

³lock *vt* **1a** to fasten the lock of **b** to make fast (as if) with a lock ⟨*~ up the house*⟩ **2a** to shut in or out or make secure or inaccessible (as if) by means of locks ⟨*~ed himself away from the curious world*⟩ ⟨*~ed her husband out*⟩ **b** to hold fast or inactive; fix in a particular situation or method of operation **3a** to make fast by the interlacing or interlocking of parts **b** to hold in a close embrace **c** to grapple in combat; *also* to bind closely – often pass ⟨*administration and students were ~ed in conflict*⟩ **4** to move or permit (e g a ship) to pass by raising or lowering in a lock *~vi* to become locked – **lockable** *adj*

locker *n* **1** a cupboard or compartment that may be closed with a lock; *esp* one for individual storage use **2** a chest or compartment on board ship

locket *n* a small case usu of precious metal that has space for a memento (e g a small picture) and is usu worn on a chain round the neck

lockjaw *n* an early symptom of tetanus characterized by spasm of the jaw muscles and inability to open the jaws; *also* tetanus

lockkeeper *n* sby who looks after a canal or river lock

locknut *n* **1** a nut screwed hard up against another to prevent either of them from moving **2** a nut so constructed that it locks itself when screwed up tight

lockout *n* a whole or partial closing of a business by an employer in order to gain concessions from or resist demands of employees

lock out *vt* to subject (a body of employees) to a lockout

locksmith *n* sby who makes or mends locks as an occupation

lockstitch *n* a sewing machine stitch formed by the looping together of 2 threads, 1 on each side of the material being sewn – **lockstitch** *vb*

lockup *n* **1** (the time of) locking; the state of being locked **2** a (small local) prison **3** *Br* a lock-up shop or garage

lock-up *adj, Br, of a building* (able to be) locked up and left when not in use

¹loco *n, pl* **locos** a locomotive

²loco *adj, chiefly NAm* out of one's mind – slang

locomotion *n* **1** an act or the power of moving from place to place **2** TRAVEL 1, 2a

¹locomotive *adj* **1** of or functioning in locomotion **2** of travel **3** moving, or able to move, by self-propulsion

²locomotive *n* an engine that moves under its own power; *esp* one that moves railway carriages and wagons

locum *n* sby having an office for a time or temporarily taking the place of another – used esp with reference to a doctor or clergyman

locus *n, pl* **loci** *also* **locuses** **1** a place, locality **2** the set of all points whose location is determined by stated conditions **3** the position on a chromosome of a particular gene or allele

locus classicus *n, pl* **loci classici** the best-known and most authoritative passage or work on a particular subject

locust *n* **1** a migratory grasshopper that often travels in vast swarms stripping the areas passed of all vegetation **2** any of various hard-wooded leguminous trees; *esp* a carob

locution *n* **1** a word or expression characteristic of a region, group, or cultural level **2** phraseology

lode *n* an ore deposit

lodestar, loadstar *n* **1** a star that guides; *esp* POLE STAR **2** sthg that serves as a guiding star

lodestone, loadstone *n* **1** (a piece of) magnetized mineral iron oxide **2** sthg that strongly attracts; a magnet

¹lodge *vt* **1a** to provide temporary, esp rented, accommodation for **b** to establish or settle in a place **2** to serve as a receptacle for; contain, house **3** to beat (e g a crop) flat to the ground **4** to fix in place **5** to deposit for safeguard or preservation ⟨*~ your money in the nearest bank*⟩ **6** to place or vest (e g power), esp in a source, means, or agent **7** to lay (e g a complaint) before authority *~vi* **1a** to occupy a place, esp temporarily **b** to be a lodger **2** to come to rest; settle ⟨*the bullet ~d in his chest*⟩ **3** *esp of hay or grain crops* to fall or lie down

²lodge *n* **1** the meeting place of a branch of an esp fraternal organization **2** a house set apart for residence in a particular season (e g the hunting season) **3a** a house orig for the use of a gamekeeper, caretaker, porter, etc **b** a porter's room (e g at the entrance to a college, block of flats, etc) **c** the house where the head of a university college lives, esp in Cambridge **4** a den or lair of an animal or a group of animals (e g beavers or otters) **5** a wigwam

lodger *n* one who occupies a rented room in another's house

lodging *n* **1** a place to live; a dwelling **2a** a temporary place to stay ⟨*a ~ for the night*⟩ **b** a rented room or rooms for residing in, usu in a private house rather than a hotel – usu pl with sing. meaning

lodging house *n* a house where lodgings are provided and let

loess *n* a usu yellowish brown loamy deposit found in Europe, Asia, and N America and believed to be chiefly deposited by the wind – **loessial**

¹loft *n* **1** an attic **2a** a gallery in a church or hall **b** an upper floor in a barn or warehouse used for storage – sometimes in combination ⟨*a hayloft*⟩ **c** a shed or coop for pigeons **3** the backward slant of the face of a golf-club head **4** *NAm* an upper room or floor

²loft *vt* to propel through the air or into space ⟨*~ed the ball over midwicket*⟩

lofty *adj* **1** having a haughty overbearing manner; supercilious **2a** elevated in character and spirit; noble **b** elevated in position; superior **3** rising to a great height; impressively high ⟨*~ mountains*⟩ – **loftily** *adv*, **loftiness** *n*

¹log *n* **1** a usu bulky piece or length of unshaped timber (ready for sawing or for use as firewood) **2** an apparatus for measuring the rate of a ship's motion through the water **3a** the record of the rate of a ship's speed or of her daily progress; *also* the full nautical record of a ship's voyage **b** the full record of a flight by an aircraft **4** any of various records of performance ⟨*a computer* ~⟩

²**log** *vb* -gg- *vt* **1** to cut (trees) for timber **2** to enter details of or about in a log **3a** to move or attain (e g an indicated distance, speed, or time) as noted in a log **b(1)** to sail a ship or fly an aircraft for (an indicated distance or period of time) **(2)** to have (an indicated record) to one's credit; achieve ⟨~ged *about 30,000 miles a year in his car*⟩ ~ *vi* to cut logs for timber

³**log** *n* a logarithm

log-, logo- *comb form* thought; speech ⟨logogram⟩ ⟨logorrhoea⟩

-log *comb form* (→ *n*), *chiefly NAm* -logue

loganberry *n* (the red sweet edible berry of) an upright-growing raspberry hybrid

logarithm *n* the exponent that indicates the power to which a number is raised to produce a given number ⟨*the* ~ *of 100 to the base 10 is 2*⟩ – **logarithmic** *adj*, **logarithmically** *adv*

logbook *n* **1** LOG 3, 4 **2** *Br* a document held with a motor vehicle that gives the vehicle's registration number, make, engine size, etc and a list of its owners – not now used technically

logger *n*, *NAm* a lumberjack

loggerhead *n* **1** any of various very large marine turtles **2** an iron tool consisting of a long handle ending in a ball or bulb that is heated and used to melt tar or to heat liquids – **at loggerheads** in or into a state of quarrelsome disagreement

loggia *n*, *pl* **loggias** *also* **loggie** a roofed open gallery behind a colonnade or arcade

logic *n* **1a(1)** a science that deals with the formal principles and structure of thought and reasoning **(2)** a specified branch or system of logic **b** a particular mode of reasoning viewed as valid or faulty ⟨*couldn't follow his* ~⟩ **c** the interrelation or sequence of facts or events when seen as inevitable or predictable **d** the fundamental principles and the connection of circuit elements for performing Boolean operations (e g those needed for arithmetical computation) in a computer; *also* the circuits themselves **2** sthg that forces a decision apart from or in opposition to reason ⟨*the* ~ *of war*⟩ – **logician**

logical *adj* **1** of or conforming with logic ⟨*a* ~ *argument*⟩ **2** capable of reasoning or of using reason in an orderly fashion ⟨*a* ~ *thinker*⟩ – **logically** *adv*, **logicalness, logicality** *n*

logical positivism *n* a 20th-c philosophical movement stressing linguistic analysis and rejecting metaphysical theories – **logical positivist** *n*

logistics *n pl but sing or pl in constr* **1** the aspect of military science dealing with the transportation, quartering, and supplying of troops in military operations **2** the handling of the details of an operation – **logistic** *adj*, **logistically** *adv*

logjam *n*, *chiefly NAm* a deadlock, impasse

logrolling *n*, *chiefly NAm* the trading of votes by members of a legislature to secure favourable action on projects of mutual interest

-logue, *NAm chiefly* **-log** *comb form* (→ *n*) **1** conversation; talk ⟨duologue⟩ **2** student; specialist ⟨sinologue⟩

-logy *comb form* (→ *n*) **1** oral or written expression ⟨phraseology⟩; *esp* body of writings of (a specified kind) or on (a specified subject) ⟨trilogy⟩ ⟨hagiology⟩ **2** doctrine; theory; science ⟨ethnology⟩ ⟨semiology⟩

loin *n* **1a** the part of a human being or quadruped on each side of the spinal column between the hipbone and the lower ribs **b** a cut of meat comprising this part of one or

both sides of a carcass with the adjoining half of the vertebrae included **2** *pl* **a** the upper and lower abdominal regions and the region about the hips **b(1)** the pubic region **(2)** the genitals

loincloth *n* a cloth worn about the hips and covering the genitals

loiter *vi* **1** to remain in an area for no obvious reason; HANG ABOUT **2** to make frequent pauses while travelling; dawdle – **loiterer** *n*

loll *vi* **1** to hang down loosely ⟨*his tongue* ~ed *out*⟩ **2** to recline, lean, or move in a lazy or excessively relaxed manner; lounge

lollipop, lollypop *n* a large often round flat sweet of boiled sugar on the end of a stick

lollipop man, *fem* **lollipop lady** *n*, *Br* sby controlling traffic to allow (school) children to cross busy roads

lollop *vi* to move or proceed with an ungainly loping motion

lolly *n* **1** a lollipop or ice lolly **2** *Br* money – *infml*

lone *adj* **1** only, sole **2** situated alone or separately; isolated **3** having no company; solitary – *fml* – **loneness** *n*

lonely *adj* **1** cut off from others; solitary **2** not frequented by people; desolate **3** sad from being alone or without friends – **lonelily** *adv*, **loneliness** *n*

lonely hearts *adj* of or for lonely people seeking companions or spouses ⟨*a* ~ *club*⟩

loner *n* a person or animal that prefers solitude

¹**lonesome** *adj* **1** lonely **2** LONE 2 ⟨*on the trail of the* ~ *pine* – Ballard Macdonald⟩ – **lonesomely** *adv*, **lonesomeness** *n*

²**lonesome** *n* self – *infml* ⟨*sat all on his* ~⟩

lone wolf *n* a person who prefers to work, act, or live alone

¹**long** *adj* **1a** extending for a considerable distance **b** having greater length or height than usual **2a** having a specified length ⟨*6ft* ~⟩ **b** forming the chief linear dimension ⟨*the* ~ *side of the room*⟩ **3** extending over a considerable or specified time ⟨*a* ~ *friendship*⟩ ⟨*2 hours* ~⟩ **4** containing a large or specified number of items or units ⟨*a* ~ *list*⟩ ⟨*300 pages* ~⟩ **5a** of a speech sound or syllable of relatively long duration **b** being one of a pair of similarly spelt vowel sounds that is longer in duration ⟨~ *a in* fate⟩ **c** bearing a stress or accent **6a** having the capacity to reach or extend a considerable distance ⟨*a* ~ *left jab*⟩ **b** hit for a considerable distance ⟨*a* ~ *drive from the tee*⟩ **7** *of betting odds* greatly differing in the amounts wagered on each side **8** subject to great odds ⟨*a* ~ *chance*⟩ **9** owning or accumulating securities or goods, esp in anticipation of an advance in prices ⟨*they are now* ~ *on wheat*⟩ – **longish** *adj*, **longness** *n* – **before long** in a short time; soon – **in the long run** in the course of sufficiently prolonged time, trial, or experience – compare IN THE SHORT RUN – **long in the tooth** past one's best days; old – **not by a long chalk** not at all

²**long** *adv* **1** for or during a long or specified time ⟨*not* ~ *returned*⟩ **2** at a point of time far before or after a specified moment or event ⟨*was excited* ~ *before the big day*⟩ **3** after or beyond a specified time ⟨*said it was no* ~ *er possible*⟩ – **so long** goodbye – *infml*

³**long** *n* a long syllable – **the long and (the) short** the gist; the outline ⟨*the long and the short of it was that we had to walk home*⟩

⁴**long** *vi* to feel a strong desire or craving, esp *for* sthg not likely to be attained

longboat *n* the largest boat carried by a sailing vessel

longbow *n* a long wooden bow for shooting arrows, specif that used in medieval England that was about 6ft (1.8m) long, was made of yew or ash, and was drawn by hand

¹long-distance *adj* **1** covering or effective over a long distance **2** *of telephone communication* between points a long distance apart

²long-distance *adv* by long-distance telephone

long division *n* arithmetical division in which the calculations corresponding to the division of parts of the dividend by the divisor are written out

long-drawn-out *adj* extended to a great length; protracted

longevity *n* (great) length of life ⟨*a study of ~*⟩

longhair *n* a person with, or usu thought of as having, long hair; e g **a** a hippie **b** sby of an artistic, esp avant-garde, temperament **c** an unwordly intellectual – **long-hair, long-haired** *adj*

longhand *n* ordinary writing; handwriting

long haul *n* **1** a lengthy usu difficult period of time ⟨*the ~ back to health*⟩ **2** the transport of goods over long distances – **long-haul** *adj*

longheaded *adj* **1** having unusual foresight or wisdom **2** dolichocephalic

long hop *n* an easily hit short-pitched delivery of a cricket ball

longing *n* a strong desire, esp for sthg difficult to attain – **longingly** *adv*

longitude *n* the (time difference corresponding to) angular distance of a point on the surface of a celestial body, esp the earth, measured E or W from a prime meridian (e g that of Greenwich)

longitudinal *adj* **1** of length or the lengthways dimension **2** placed or running lengthways – **longitudinally** *adv*

long johns *n pl* underpants with legs extending usu down to the ankles – *infml*

long jump *n* (an athletic field event consisting of) a jump for distance from a running start – **long jumper** *n*

long-lived *adj* **1** characterized by long life ⟨*a ~ family*⟩ **2** long-lasting, enduring – **long-livedness** *n*

long-range *adj* **1** involving or taking into account a long period of time ⟨*~ planning*⟩ **2** relating to or fit for long distances ⟨*~ rockets*⟩

long run *n* a relatively long period of time – usu in *in the long run* – **long-run** *adj*

longship *n* a long open ship propelled by oars and a sail and used by the Vikings principally to carry warriors

longshoreman *n, chiefly NAm* a docker

long shot *n* **1** (a bet at long odds on) a competitor given little chance of winning **2** a venture that involves considerable risk and has little chance of success – **by a long shot** by a great deal

longsighted *adj* hypermetropic – **longsightedness** *n*

long-standing *adj* of long duration

long stop *n* a now little-used fielding position in cricket near the boundary and directly behind the wicket-keeper

long-suffering *n or adj* (the quality of) patiently enduring pain, difficulty, or provocation – **long-sufferingly** *adv*

long suit *n* the activity or quality in which a person excels

long-term *adj* occurring over or involving a relatively long period of time

long ton *n* a British unit of weight equal to 2240lb (about 1016.05kg)

longueur *n, pl* **longueurs** a dull and tedious part or period

long vacation *n* the long summer holiday of British law courts and universities

long wave *n* a band of radio waves typically used for sound broadcasting and covering wavelengths of 1000m or more

longways *adv* lengthways

long-winded *adj* tediously long in speaking or writing – **long-windedly** *adv*, **long-windedness** *n*

longwise *adv* lengthways

¹loo *n* (money staked at) an old card game in which the winner of each trick takes a portion of the pool while losing players have to contribute to the next pool

²loo *n, chiefly Br* TOILET 2 – *infml*

loofah *n* a dried seed pod of any of several plants of the cucumber family that is used as a bath sponge

¹look *vt* **1** to find out or learn by the use of one's eyes ⟨*~ what time it starts*⟩ ⟨*~ what you've done!*⟩ **2** to regard intensely; examine ⟨*~ him in the eye*⟩ ⟨*~ a gift horse in the mouth*⟩ **3** to express by the eyes or facial expression ⟨*~ed daggers at him*⟩ **4** to have an appearance that befits or accords with ⟨*really ~ed the part*⟩ *~ vi* **1a** to use the power of sight; *esp* to make a visual search *for* **b** to direct one's attention ⟨*~ into the matter*⟩ **c** to direct the eyes ⟨*~ at him!*⟩ **2** to have the appearance of being; appear, seem ⟨*~s very ill*⟩ ⟨*~ed to be crying* – Colin MacInnes⟩ **3** to have a specified outlook ⟨*the house ~ed east*⟩ – **look after** to take care of – **look sharp** to be quick; hurry

²look *n* **1a** the act of looking **b** ²GLANCE **3** **2a** a facial expression ⟨*she had a funny ~ on her face*⟩ **b** (attractive) physical appearance – usu pl with sing. meaning **3** the state or form in which sthg appears ⟨*a new ~ in knitwear*⟩ ⟨*has the ~ of a loser about him*⟩

look-alike *n* sby or sthg that looks like another; a double

look back *vi* **1** to remember – often + *to, on* **2** to fail to make successful progress – in *never look back* ⟨*after his initial success, he never looked back*⟩

look down *vi* to have an attitude of superiority or contempt – usu + *on* or *upon* ⟨*snobbishly looks down on the poor*⟩

looker *n* **1** one having an appearance of a specified kind – often in combination ⟨*a good-*looker⟩ **2** an attractive person, esp a woman – *infml*

look-in *n* a chance to take part; *also* a chance of success – *infml*

look in *vi, Br* to pay a short visit ⟨*will look in on the party*⟩

looking glass *n* a mirror

look on *vi* to be a spectator

lookout *n* **1** one engaged in keeping watch **2** a place or structure affording a wide view for observation **3** a careful looking or watching **4** a matter of care or concern ⟨*it's your ~ if you do such a silly thing*⟩ **5** *chiefly Br* a future possibility; a prospect

look out *vi* **1** to take care – often imper **2** to keep watching ⟨*look out for your parents*⟩ *~vt, chiefly Br* to choose by inspection; select ⟨*look out a suit for the interview*⟩

look over *vt* to examine (quickly) – **lookover** *n*

look up *vi* to improve in prospects or conditions ⟨*business is looking up*⟩ *~ vt* **1** to search for (as if) in a reference work ⟨*look up a phone number in the directory*⟩ **2** to pay a usu short visit to ⟨*looked up my friend while I was there*⟩ **3** to have an attitude of respect – + *to* ⟨*always looked up to their parents*⟩

¹loom *n* a frame or machine for weaving together yarns or threads into cloth

²loom *vi* **1** to come into sight indistinctly, in enlarged or distorted and menacing form, often as a result of atmospheric conditions **2a** to appear in an impressively great or exaggerated form **b** to take shape as an impending occurrence ⟨*exams ~ed large*⟩

¹loon *n* a mad or silly person

²loon *n* any of several large fish-eating diving birds that have the legs placed far back under the body

loony, looney *adj* crazy, foolish – *infml* – **looniness** *n*, **loony** *n*

loony bin *n* MADHOUSE 1 – *humor*

¹loop *n* **1 a** (partially) closed figure that has a curved outline surrounding a central opening **2a** sthg shaped like a loop **b** a manoeuvre in which an aircraft passes successively through a climb, inverted flight, and a dive, and then returns to normal flight **c** a zigzag-shaped intrauterine contraceptive device **3** a ring or curved piece used to form a fastening or handle **4** a piece of film or magnetic tape whose ends are spliced together so as to reproduce the same material continuously **5** a series of instructions (e g for a computer) that is repeated until a terminating condition is reached

²loop *vi* **1** to make, form, or move in a loop or loops **2** to execute a loop in an aircraft ~ *vt* **1a** to make a loop in, on, or about **b** to fasten with a loop **2** to join (2 courses of loops) in knitting **3** to form a loop with ⟨~ed *the wool round the knitting needle*⟩ – **loop the loop** to perform a loop in an aircraft

¹loophole *n* **1** a small opening through which missiles, firearms, etc may be discharged or light and air admitted **2** a means of escape; *esp* an ambiguity or omission in a text through which its intent may be evaded

²loophole *vt* to make loopholes in

¹loose *adj* **1a** not rigidly fastened or securely attached **b** having worked partly free from attachments ⟨*the masonry is ~ at the base of the wall*⟩ **c** of a cough produced freely and accompanied by rising of mucus **d** not tight-fitting ⟨*a ~ cardigan*⟩ **2a** free from a state of confinement, restraint, or obligation ⟨*a lion ~ in the streets*⟩ **b** not brought together in a bundle, container, or binding ⟨*~ hair*⟩ **3** not dense, close, or compact in structure or arrangement **4a** lacking in (power of) restraint ⟨*a ~ tongue*⟩ ⟨*~ bowels*⟩ **b** dissolute, promiscuous ⟨*~ living*⟩ **5** not tightly drawn or stretched; slack **6a** lacking in precision, exactness, or care ⟨*a ~ translation*⟩ **b** permitting freedom of interpretation ⟨*the wording of the document is very ~*⟩ – **loosely** *adv*, **loosen** *vb*, **looseness** *n*

²loose *vt* **1** to let loose; release **b** to free from restraint **2** to make loose; untie ⟨*~ a knot*⟩ **3** to cast loose; detach **4** to let fly; discharge (e g a bullet)

³loose *adv* in a loose manner; loosely ⟨*the rope hung ~*⟩

loose box *n*, *Br* an individual enclosure within a barn or stable in which an animal may move about freely

loose-leaf *adj* bound so that individual leaves can be detached or inserted ⟨*a ~ photograph album*⟩

¹loot *n* **1** goods, usu of considerable value, taken in war; spoils **2** sthg taken illegally (e g by force or deception) ⟨*the robbers' ~*⟩

²loot *vb* **1** to plunder or sack (a place) in war **2** to seize and carry away (sthg) by force or illegally, esp in war or public disturbance – **looter** *n*

¹lop *n* small branches and twigs cut from a tree

²lop *vt* **-pp- 1a** to cut off branches or twigs from **b** to cut from a person **2** to remove or do away with as unnecessary or undesirable – usu + *off* or *away* ⟨*~ped several thousand off the annual budget*⟩ – **lopper** *n*

¹lope *n* an easy bounding gait capable of being sustained for a long time

²lope *vi* to go, move, or ride at a lope – **loper** *n*

lop-eared *adj* having ears that droop

lopsided *adj* **1** having one side heavier or lower than the other **2** lacking in balance, symmetry, or proportion – **lopsidedly** *adv*, **lopsidedness** *n*

loquacious *adj* talkative – *fml* – **loquaciously** *adv*, **loquaciousness** *n*, **loquacity** *n*

loquat *n* (the yellow edible fruit of) an often cultivated Asiatic evergreen tree of the rose family

¹lord *n* **1** one having power and authority over others: e g **a** a (hereditary) ruler **b** sby from whom a feudal fee or estate is held **c** BARON 3 **2** *cap* **a** GOD 1 **b** Jesus – often + *Our* **3** a man of rank or high position: e g **a** a feudal tenant holding land directly from the king **b** a British nobleman: e g **(1)** BARON 2a **(2)** a marquess, earl, or viscount **(3)** the son of a duke or marquess or the eldest son of an earl **(4)** a bishop of the Church of England **4** *pl, cap* HOUSE OF LORDS – often + *the* **5** – used as the title of a lord or as an official title ⟨Lord *Advocate*⟩

²lord *vi* to act like a lord; *esp* to put on airs – usu + *it* ⟨*~s it over his friends*⟩

Lord *interj* – used to express surprise, amazement, or dismay; esp in *Oh Lord!, Good Lord!*, etc

lord chancellor *n, often cap L&C* an officer of state who presides over the House of Lords, serves as head of the judiciary, and is usu a member of the cabinet

lordly *adj* **1a** (having the characteristics) of a lord; dignified **b** grand, noble **2** disdainful and arrogant – **lordliness** *n*, **lordly** *adv*

lordship *n* **1** – used as a title for a lord **2** the authority of a lord

Lord's Prayer *n* *the* prayer taught by Jesus beginning 'Our Father'

¹lore *n* a specified body of knowledge or tradition ⟨*bird ~*⟩ ⟨*ghost ~*⟩

²lore *n* the space between the eye and bill in a bird or the corresponding region in a reptile or fish – **loreal**

lorgnette *n* a pair of glasses or opera glasses with a handle

lorry *n*, *Br* a large motor vehicle for carrying loads by road

lose *vb* **lost** *vt* **1a** to bring to destruction; perish – usu pass ⟨*the ship was lost on the reef*⟩ **b** to damn ⟨*lost souls*⟩ **2** to miss from one's possession or from a customary or supposed place; *also* to fail to find ⟨*lost her glasses*⟩ **3** to suffer deprivation of; part with, esp in an unforeseen or accidental manner ⟨*lost his leg in an accident*⟩ **4** to suffer loss through the death of or final separation from (sby) ⟨*lost a son in the war*⟩ **5a** to fail to use; let slip by ⟨*he lost his chance of a place in the team*⟩ **b(1)** to be defeated in (a contest for) ⟨*~ a battle*⟩ ⟨*~ a prize*⟩ **(2)** to have less of ⟨*the aircraft began to ~ height*⟩ **c** to fail to catch with the senses or the mind ⟨*lost part of what was said*⟩ **6** to cause the loss of ⟨*one careless statement lost her the election*⟩ **7** to fail to keep or maintain ⟨*lost her balance*⟩ **8a** to cause to miss one's way ⟨*lost themselves in the maze of streets*⟩ **b** to withdraw (oneself) from immediate reality ⟨*lost himself in a book*⟩ **9** to fail to keep in sight or in mind ⟨*I lost track of his reasoning*⟩ **10** to free oneself from; get rid of ⟨*dieting to ~ some weight*⟩ **11** to run slow by the amount of – used with reference to a timepiece ⟨*my watch ~s a minute each day*⟩ ~ *vi* **1** to undergo deprivation of sthg of value **2** to undergo defeat **3** *of a timepiece* to run slow – **lose one's head** to lose self-control (e g in anger or panic)

lose out *vi* **1** to make a loss **2** to be the loser, esp unluckily *USE* often + *on*

loser *n* **1** one who loses, esp consistently **2** one who does poorly; a failure

loss *n* **1a** the act or an instance of losing possession **b** the harm or privation resulting from loss or separation **2** a person, thing, or amount lost ⟨*the woman who retired is a great ~ to her firm*⟩: e g **a** *pl* killed, wounded, or captured soldiers **b** the power diminution of a circuit element corresponding to conversion of electric power into heat **3a** failure to gain, win, obtain, or use sthg **b** an amount by which cost exceeds revenue **4** decrease in amount, size, or degree **5** destruction, ruin ⟨*the ship went down with the ~ of many lives*⟩ – **at a loss** uncertain, puzzled

loss leader *n* an article sold at a loss in order to draw customers

lost *adj* **1a** unable to find the way **b** no longer visible **c** bewildered, helpless **2** ruined or destroyed physically or morally **3a** no longer possessed ⟨*one's ~ youth*⟩ **b** no longer known ⟨*the ~ art of letter-writing*⟩ **4a** taken away or beyond reach or attainment; denied **b** insensible, hardened ⟨*~ to shame*⟩ **5** rapt, absorbed ⟨*~ in reverie*⟩

lost cause *n* a cause that has lost all prospect of success

¹lot *n* **1** an object used as a counter in deciding a question by chance ⟨*they drew ~s for who was to go*⟩ **2** (the use of lots as a means of making) a choice **3a** sthg that falls to sby by lot; a share **b** one's way of life or worldly fate; fortune ⟨*it's my ~ to be misunderstood*⟩ **4a** a portion of land; *esp* one with fixed boundaries designated on a plot or survey **b** a film studio and its adjoining property **5** an article or a number of articles offered as 1 item (e g in an auction sale) ⟨*what am I bid for ~ 16?*⟩ **6a** *sing or pl in constr* a number of associated people; a set ⟨*hello you ~* – Margaret Drabble⟩ **b** a kind, sort – chiefly in a *bad lot* **7** a considerable amount or number ⟨*a ~ of illness*⟩ ⟨*has ~s of friends*⟩ – often pl with sing. meaning **8** *chiefly Br* the whole amount or number ⟨*ate up the whole ~*⟩ *USE* (6a&8) *infml* – **a lot 1** lots ⟨*drove a lot faster*⟩ – chiefly *infml* **2** often, frequently ⟨*goes there a lot*⟩ – chiefly *infml*

²lot *vt* **-tt- 1** to form or divide into lots **2** to allot, apportion

loth *adj* loath

lotion *n* a medicinal or cosmetic liquid for external use

lottery *n* **1** (a way of raising money by the sale or) the distribution of numbered tickets some of which are later randomly selected to entitle the holder to a prize **2** an event or affair whose outcome is (apparently) decided by chance ⟨*buying a secondhand car is a ~*⟩

lotto *n* bingo

lotus *n* **1** a fruit considered in Greek legend to cause indolence and dreamy contentment **2** any of various water lilies including several represented in ancient Egyptian and Hindu art and religious symbolism **3** any of a genus of widely distributed upright herbaceous plants (e g bird's-foot trefoil)

lotus-eater *n* sby who lives in dreamy indolence

loud *adj* **1** marked by or producing a high volume of sound **2** clamorous, noisy **3** obtrusive or offensive in appearance; flashy ⟨*a ~ checked suit*⟩ – **loud** *adv*, **louden** *vb*, **loudly** *adv*, **loudness** *n*

loud-hailer *n, chiefly Br* a megaphone

loudmouth *n* a person given to much loud offensive talk – *infml* – **loudmouthed** *adj*

loudspeaker *n* (a cabinet that contains) an electromechanical device that converts electrical energy into acoustic energy and that is used to reproduce audible sounds in a room, hall, etc

lough *n* a loch in Ireland

¹lounge *vi* to act or move idly or lazily; loll – **lounger** *n*

²lounge *n* **1** a room in a private house for sitting in; SITTING ROOM **2** a room in a public building providing comfortable seating; *also* a waiting room (e g at an airport)

lounge bar *n, Br* SALOON BAR

lounge suit *n* a man's suit for wear during the day and on informal occasions

lour *vi or n, chiefly Br* ¹⋅ ²LOWER – **loury** *adj*, **louring** *adj*

louse *n, pl* lice,; *sense 2* louses **1a** any of various small wingless usu flattened insects parasitic on warm-blooded animals **b** any of several small arthropods that are not parasitic – usu in combination ⟨*book ~*⟩ ⟨*wood ~*⟩ **2** a contemptible person – *infml*

louse up *vt* to make a mess of; spoil – *infml*

lousy *adj* **1** infested with lice **2a** very mean; despicable ⟨*a ~ trick to play*⟩ **b** very bad, unpleasant, useless, etc **c** amply or excessively supplied ⟨*~ with money*⟩ ⟨*the place was ~ with police*⟩ *USE* (2) *infml* – **lousily** *adv*, **lousiness** *n*

lout *n* a rough ill-mannered man or youth – **loutish** *adj*

louvre, louver *n* **1** a roof lantern or turret with slatted apertures for the escape of smoke or admission of light **2** an opening provided with 1 or more slanted fixed or movable strips of metal, wood, glass, etc to allow flow of air or sound (e g in a bell louvre) but to exclude rain or sun or to provide privacy – **louvered, louvred** *adj*

lovable *also* **loveable** *adj* having qualities that deserve love; worthy of love – **lovableness** *n*, **lovably** *adv*

¹love *n* **1a(1)** strong affection for another ⟨*maternal ~ for a child*⟩ **(2)** attraction based on sexual desire; strong affection and tenderness felt by lovers **b** any assurance of love ⟨*give her my ~*⟩ **2** warm interest in, enjoyment of, or attraction to sthg ⟨*~ of music*⟩ **3a** the object of interest and enjoyment ⟨*music was his first ~*⟩ **b** a person who is loved; DEAR 1a; *also* DEAR 1b **4a** unselfish loyal and benevolent concern for the good of another **b(1)** the fatherly concern of God for man **(2)** a person's adoration of God **5** a god or personification of love **6** an amorous episode; LOVE AFFAIR ⟨*My Life and* Loves – Frank Harris⟩ **7** a score of zero in tennis, squash, etc **8** SEXUAL INTERCOURSE – *euph* – **for love or money** in any possible way – usu neg ⟨*couldn't get a ticket for love or money*⟩

²love *vt* **1** to hold dear; cherish **2a** to feel a lover's passion, devotion, or tenderness for **b(1)** to caress **(2)** to have sexual intercourse with **3** to like or desire actively; take pleasure in ⟨*~d to play the violin*⟩ **4** to thrive in ⟨*the rose ~s sunlight*⟩ **~** *vi* to feel love or affection or experience desire

love affair *n* **1** an often temporary romantic attachment between lovers, esp a man and a woman **2** a lively enthusiasm

lovebird *n* any of various small usu grey or green parrots that show great affection for their mates

love child *n* an illegitimate child – *euph*

love feast *n* a meal eaten together by a Christian congregation in token of brotherly love

loveless *adj* **1** without love ⟨*a ~ marriage*⟩ **2** unloving **3** unloved – **lovelessly** *adv*, **lovelessness** *n*

lovelorn *adj* sad because of unrequited love – **lovelornness** *n*

¹lovely *adj* **1** delicately or delightfully beautiful **2** very pleasing; fine ⟨*a ~ view*⟩ – **lovelily** *adv*, **loveliness** *n*, **lovely** *adv*

²lovely *n* a beautiful woman – *infml* ⟨*hello, my ~*⟩

lovemaking *n* **1** courtship **2** sexual activity; *esp* SEXUAL INTERCOURSE

lover *n* **1a** a person in love **b** a man with whom a woman has sexual relations, esp outside marriage **c** *pl* 2 people in love with each other; *esp* 2 people who habitually have sexual relations **2** DEVOTEE ⟨*a ~ of the theatre*⟩

lovesick *adj* languishing with love – **lovesickness** *n*

lovey *n, chiefly Br* LOVE 3b – *infml*

loving *adj* feeling or showing love; affectionate ⟨~ *care*⟩ ⟨*a* ~ *glance*⟩ – **lovingly** *adv*

loving cup *n* a large ornamental drinking vessel with 2 or more handles that is passed among a group of people for all to drink from

¹**low** *vi or n* (to make) the deep sustained throat sound characteristic of esp a cow

²**low** *adj* **1a** not measuring much from the base to the top; not high ⟨*a* ~ *wall*⟩ **b** situated or passing little above a reference line, point, or plane ⟨~ *bridges*⟩ ⟨*his work was* ~ *on his list of priorities*⟩ **c** low-necked **2a** situated or passing below the normal level or below the base of measurement ⟨~ *ground*⟩ **b** marking a nadir or bottom ⟨*the* ~ *point of her career*⟩ **3a** *of sound* not shrill or loud; soft **b** depressed in pitch ⟨*a* ~ *note*⟩ **4** near the horizon ⟨*it was evening, and the sun was* ~⟩ **5** humble in character or status ⟨*people of* ~ *birth*⟩ **6a** lacking strength, health, or vitality; weak ⟨*he's been very* ~ *with pneumonia*⟩ **b** lacking spirit or vivacity; depressed ⟨~ *spirits*⟩ **7** of less than usual degree, size, amount, or value ⟨~ *pressure*⟩ ⟨*prices are* ~ *at the moment*⟩ **8a** lacking dignity or formality ⟨*a* ~ *style of writing*⟩ **b** morally reprehensible ⟨*played a* ~ *trick on her*⟩ **c** coarse, vulgar ⟨~ *language*⟩ **9** unfavourable, disparaging ⟨*had a* ~ *opinion of him*⟩ **10** *of a gear* designed for slow speed **11** *of a vowel* open – **lowness** *n*

³**low** *n* **1** sthg low: e g **a** a depth, nadir ⟨*sales have reached a new* ~⟩ **b** a region of low atmospheric pressure **2** *NAm* BOTTOM 4c

⁴**low** *adv* at or to a low place, altitude, or degree

lowborn *adj* born to parents of low social rank

lowbred *adj* rude, vulgar

lowbrow *adj* dealing with, possessing, or having unsophisticated or unintellectual tastes, esp in the arts – often derog – **lowbrow** *n*

Low Church *adj* tending, esp in the Anglican church, to minimize emphasis on the priesthood, sacraments, and ceremonial and often to emphasize evangelical principles – **Low Churchman** *n*

low comedy *n* comedy bordering on farce and depending on physical action and situation rather than wit and characterization

lowdown *n* inside information – usu + *the*; infml

low-down *adj* contemptible, base – infml

¹**lower,** *Br chiefly* **lour** *vi* **1** to look sullen; frown **2** to become dark, gloomy, and threatening – **lowering** *adj*

²**lower,** *Br chiefly* **lour** *n* **1** a lowering look; a frown **2** a gloomy sky or aspect of weather – **lowery** *adj*

³**lower** *adj* **1** relatively low in position, rank, or order **2** less advanced in the scale of evolutionary development ⟨~ *organisms*⟩ **3** constituting the popular, more representative, and often (e g in Britain) more powerful branch of a legislative body consisting of 2 houses ⟨*the* ~ *chamber*⟩ **4a** beneath the earth's surface **b** *often cap* being an earlier division of the named geological period or series ⟨Lower *Carboniferous*⟩

⁴**lower** *vi* to move down; drop; *also* to diminish ~ *vt* **1a** to cause to descend; let down in height ⟨~ed *the boat over the side of the ship*⟩ ⟨~ *your aim*⟩ **b** to reduce the height of ⟨~ed *the ceiling*⟩ **2a** to reduce in value, amount, degree, strength, or pitch ⟨~ *the price*⟩ ⟨~ *your voice*⟩ **b** to bring down; degrade; *also* to humble ⟨*I wouldn't* ~ *myself to speak to them*⟩ **c** to reduce the objective of ⟨~ed *their sights and accepted less*⟩

lower-case *adj, of a letter* of or conforming to the series (e g a, b, c rather than A, B, C) typically used elsewhere than at the beginning of sentences or proper names

lower case *n* **1** a type case containing lower-case letters and usu spaces and quads **2** lower-case letters

lower deck *n* **1** a deck below the main deck of a ship **2** *sing or pl in constr, chiefly Br* the petty officers and men of a ship or navy as distinguished from the officers

lowermost *adj* lowest

low-key *also* **low-keyed** *adj* of low intensity; restrained

Lowland *adj* of the Lowlands of Scotland – **Lowlander** *n*

¹**lowly** *adv* **1** in a humble or meek manner **2** in a low position, manner, or degree

²**lowly** *adj* **1** humble and modest in manner or spirit **2** low in the scale of biological or cultural evolution **3** ranking low in a social or economic hierarchy – **lowliness** *n*

low-lying *adj* lying below the normal level or surface or below the base of measurement or mean elevation ⟨~ *clouds*⟩

low-necked, low-neck *adj* having a low-cut neckline

low-pitched *adj* **1** *of sound* not shrill; deep **2** *of a roof* sloping gently

low profile *n* an inconspicuous mode of operation or behaviour (intended to attract little attention) ⟨*the Government has been keeping a* ~ *over the disturbances* – The Guardian⟩

low-spirited *adj* dejected, depressed – **low-spiritedly** *adv,* **low-spiritedness** *n*

low tide *n* (the time of) the tide when the water reaches its lowest level

low water *n* LOW TIDE

loyal *adj* **1** unswerving in allegiance (e g to a person, country, or cause); faithful **2** showing such allegiance ⟨*her* ~ *determination to help the party*⟩ – **loyally** *adv,* **loyalty** *n*

loyalist *n* sby loyal to a government or sovereign, esp in time of revolt

lozenge *n* **1** (sthg shaped like) a figure with 4 equal sides and 2 acute and 2 obtuse angles **2** a small often medicated sweet

LP *n* a gramophone record designed to be played at 33⅓ revolutions per minute and typically having a diameter of 12in (30.5cm) and a playing time of 20–25min

LSD *n* a drug taken illegally for its potent action in producing hallucinations and altered perceptions

lubber *n* **1** a big clumsy fellow **2** a clumsy seaman – **lubberliness** *n,* **lubberly** *adj or adv*

lubricant *n* **1** a substance (e g grease or oil) capable of reducing friction, heat, and wear when introduced as a film between solid surfaces **2** sthg that lessens or prevents difficulty – **lubricant** *adj*

lubricate *vt* **1** to make smooth or slippery **2** to apply a lubricant to ~ *vi* to act as a lubricant – **lubricator** *n,* **lubricative** *adj,* **lubrication** *n*

lubricious *adj* **1** lecherous, salacious **2** slippery, smooth USE *fml* – **lubriciously** *adv,* **lubricity** *n*

lucerne *also* **lucern** *n, chiefly Br* a deep-rooted European leguminous plant widely grown for fodder

lucid *adj* **1** having full use of one's faculties; sane **2** clear to the understanding; plain – **lucidly** *adv,* **lucidness,** **lucidity** *n*

luck *n* **1** whatever good or bad events happen to a person by chance **2** the tendency for a person to be consistently fortunate or unfortunate **3** success as a result of good fortune

lucky *adj* having, resulting from, or bringing good luck – **luckily** *adv,* **luckiness** *n*

lucky dip *n, Br* an attraction (e g at a fair) in which articles can be drawn unseen from a receptacle

lucrative *adj* producing wealth; profitable – **lucratively** *adv,* **lucrativeness** *n*

lucre *n* financial gain; profit; *also* money – esp in *filthy lucre*

ludicrous *adj* 1 amusing because of obvious absurdity or incongruity 2 meriting derision – **ludicrously** *adv*, **ludicrousness** *n*

ludo *n* a simple game played on a square board with counters and dice in which the first to reach the home square wins

¹**luff** *n* the forward edge of a fore-and-aft sail

²**luff** *vi* to sail nearer the wind – often + *up*

¹**lug** *vt* **-gg-** to drag, pull, or carry with great effort – *infml*

²**lug** *n* a lugsail

³**lug** *n* 1 sthg (e g a handle) that projects like an ear 2 ¹EAR 1a – chiefly dial. or humor

luggage *n* (cases, bags, etc containing) the belongings that accompany a traveller

lugger *n* a small fishing or coasting boat that carries 1 or more lugsails

lughole *n*, *Br* ¹EAR 1a – chiefly dial or humor

lugsail *n* a 4-sided fore-and-aft sail attached to an obliquely hanging yard

lugubrious *adj* (exaggeratedly or affectedly) mournful – **lugubriously** *adv*, **lugubriousness** *n*

lugworm *n* any of a genus of marine worms that are used for bait

lukewarm *adj* 1 moderately warm; tepid 2 lacking conviction; indifferent – **lukewarmly** *adv*, **lukewarmness** *n*

¹**lull** *vt* 1 to cause to sleep or rest; soothe 2 to cause to relax vigilance, esp by deception

²**lull** *n* a temporary pause or decline in activity

lullaby *n* a song to quieten children or lull them to sleep

lumbago *n* muscular pain of the lumbar region of the back

lumbar *adj* of or constituting the loins or the vertebrae between the thoracic vertebrae and sacrum ⟨*the ~ region*⟩

¹**lumber** *vi* to move heavily or clumsily

²**lumber** *n* 1 surplus or disused articles (e g furniture) that are stored away 2 *NAm* timber or logs, esp when dressed for use – **lumber** *adj*

³**lumber** *vt* 1 to clutter (as if) with lumber; encumber, saddle ⟨*parents, ~ed with the unenviable task of guiding choice – The Economist*⟩ 2 *NAm* to cut down and saw the timber of – **lumberer** *n*

lumberjack *n* a person engaged in logging

luminary *n* a source of light or illumination: e g a a natural body that gives light (e g the sun or moon) b a person brilliantly outstanding in some respect – **luminary** *adj*

luminescence *n* (an emission of) light that occurs at low temperatures and that is produced by physiological processes (e g in the firefly), by chemical action, by friction, or by electrical action – **luminescent** *adj*

luminosity *n* 1a being luminous b sthg luminous 2a the relative quantity of light b relative brightness of sthg

luminous *adj* 1a emitting or full of light; bright b of emitting or full of light; bright of light or luminous flux 2 easily understood; *also* explaining clearly – **luminously** *adv*, **luminousness** *n*

luminous paint *n* paint containing a phosphorescent compound causing it to glow in the dark

lumme *interj*, *Br* – used to express surprise; *infml*

lummox *n* a clumsy person – *infml*

¹**lump** *n* 1 a usu compact piece or mass of indefinite size and shape ⟨*a ~ of coal or sugar*⟩ 2a an abnormal swelling b BRUISE 1 3 a heavy thickset person; *specif* one who is stupid or dull 4 *Br the* whole group of casual nonunion building workers

²**lump** *vt* 1 to group without discrimination 2 to make lumps on, in, or of ~ *vi* to become formed into lumps

³**lump** *adj* not divided into parts; entire ⟨*a ~ sum*⟩

⁴**lump** *vt* to put up with – chiefly in *like it or lump it*; *infml*

lumpish *adj* 1 dull, sluggish 2 heavy, awkward – **lumpishly** *adv*, **lumpishness** *n*

lumpy *adj* 1a filled or covered with lumps b characterized by choppy waves 2 having a thickset clumsy appearance – **lumpily** *adv*, **lumpiness** *n*

lunacy *n* 1a insanity (interrupted by lucid intervals) – not now in technical use b insanity amounting to lack of capability or responsibility in law 2 wild foolishness; extravagant folly 3 a foolish act

lunar *adj* 1a of the moon b designed for use on the moon ⟨*~ vehicles*⟩ 2 lunar, lunate shaped like a crescent 3 measured by the moon's revolution ⟨*~ month*⟩

lunar month *n* the period of time, averaging 29½ days, between 2 successive new moons

lunatic *adj* 1a insane b of or designed for the care of insane people ⟨*a ~ asylum*⟩ 2 wildly foolish – **lunatic** *n*

lunatic fringe *n* the extremist or fanatical members of a political or social movement

¹**lunch** *n* (the food prepared for) a light midday meal; *broadly*, *NAm* a light meal

²**lunch** *vi* to eat lunch

luncheon meat *n* a precooked mixture of meat (e g pork) and cereal shaped in a loaf

lung *n* 1 either of the usu paired compound saclike organs in the chest that constitute the basic respiratory organ of air-breathing vertebrates 2 any of various respiratory organs of invertebrates

¹**lunge** *vb* to make a lunge (with)

²**lunge** *n* 1 a sudden thrust or forceful forward movement 2 the act of plunging forward

³**lunge** *n* a long rein used to hold and guide a horse in breaking and training

⁴**lunge** *vt* to guide (a horse) on a lunge in a circular course round the trainer

lungfish *n* any of various fishes that breathe by a modified air bladder as well as gills

lupin *also* **lupine** *n* 1 any of a genus of leguminous plants some of which are cultivated for fertiliser, fodder, their edible seeds, or their long spikes of variously coloured flowers 2 an edible lupin seed

¹**lurch** *n* – **in the lurch** in a vulnerable and unsupported position; deserted – *infml*

²**lurch** *vi* 1 to roll or tip abruptly; pitch 2 to stagger – **lurch** *n*

¹**lure** *n* 1 a bunch of feathers and often meat attached to a long cord and used by a falconer to recall his/her bird 2a sby or sthg used to entice or decoy b the power to appeal or attract ⟨*the ~ of success*⟩ 3 a decoy for attracting animals to capture

²**lure** *vt* 1 to recall (a hawk) by means of a lure 2 to tempt with a promise of pleasure or gain

lurid *adj* 1 wan and ghastly pale in appearance 2a causing horror or revulsion; gruesome b sensational ⟨*~ newspaper reports of the crime*⟩ c highly coloured; gaudy – **luridly** *adv*, **luridness** *n*

lurk *vi* 1a to lie hidden in wait, esp with evil intent b to move furtively or inconspicuously 2 to lie hidden; *esp* to be a hidden threat – **lurker** *n*

luscious *adj* 1 having a delicious taste or smell 2 having sensual appeal; seductive 3 richly luxurious or appealing to the senses; *also* excessively ornate – **lusciously** *adv*, **lusciousness** *n*

¹**lush** *adj* 1 producing or covered by luxuriant growth ⟨*~*

grass⟩⟨~ pastures⟩ **2** opulent, sumptuous – **lushly** *adv*

²lush *n, chiefly NAm* a heavy drinker; an alcoholic

¹lust *n* **1** strong sexual desire, esp as opposed to love **2** an intense longing; a craving – **lustful** *adj*

²lust *vi* to have an intense (sexual) desire or craving

¹lustre, NAm chiefly luster *n* a lustrum

²lustre, NAm chiefly luster *n* **1** (the quality of) the glow of reflected light from a surface ⟨e g of a mineral⟩ **2a** a glow of light (as if) from within **b** radiant beauty **3** glory, distinction **4** a glass pendant used esp to ornament a chandelier **5** a lustrous fabric with cotton warp and a wool, mohair, or alpaca weft – **lustreless** *adj*

³lustre, NAm chiefly luster *vt* to give lustre or distinction to – **lustring** *n*

lustrous *adj* evenly shining ⟨a ~ satin⟩ ⟨the ~ glow of an opal⟩ – **lustrously** *adv*

lusty *adj* **1** full of vitality; healthy **2** full of strength; vigorous – **lustily** *adv*, **lustiness** *n*

lute *n* a stringed instrument with a large pear-shaped body, a neck with a fretted fingerboard, and pairs of strings tuned in unison

lutenist, lutanist *n* a lute player

luxuriant *adj* **1** characterized by abundant growth **2a** exuberantly rich and varied; prolific **b** richly or excessively ornamented ⟨~ prose⟩ – **luxuriance** *n*, **luxuriantly** *adv*

luxuriate *vi* to enjoy oneself consciously; revel – often + *in*

luxurious *adj* **1** fond of luxury or self-indulgence; *also* voluptuous **2** characterized by opulence and rich abundance – **luxuriously** *adv*, **luxuriousness** *n*

luxury *n* **1** great ease or comfort based on habitual or liberal use of expensive items without regard to cost ⟨lived in ~⟩ **2a** sthg desirable but costly or difficult to obtain **b** sthg relatively expensive adding to pleasure or comfort but not indispensable

¹-ly *suffix* (→ *adj*) **1** like in appearance, manner, or nature; having the characteristics of ⟨queenly⟩ ⟨fatherly⟩ **2** recurring regularly at intervals of; every ⟨hourly⟩ ⟨daily⟩

²-ly *suffix* (→ *adv*) **1** in (such) a manner ⟨slowly⟩; like ⟨kingly⟩ **2** from (such) a point of view ⟨musically speaking⟩ **3** with respect to ⟨partly⟩ **4** as is (specified); it is (specified) that ⟨naturally⟩ ⟨regrettably⟩ **5** speaking (in a specified way) ⟨frankly⟩ ⟨briefly⟩

lycée *n* a French public secondary school

lychee *n* a litchi

lych-gate *n* a roofed gate in a churchyard traditionally used as resting place for a coffin during part of a burial service

lye *n* a strong alkaline liquid rich in potassium carbonate, leached from wood ashes, and used esp in making soap; *broadly* a strong alkaline solution

lying-in *n, pl* **lyings-in, lying-ins** confinement for childbirth

lymph *n* a pale fluid resembling blood plasma that contains white blood cells but normally no red blood cells, that circulates in the lymphatic vessels, and bathes the cells of the body

lymph-, lympho- *comb form* lymph; lymphatic tissue ⟨lymphocyte⟩

¹lymphatic *adj* **1** of, involving, or produced by lymph, lymphoid tissue, or lymphocytes **2** conveying lymph ⟨~ vessels⟩

²lymphatic *n* a vessel that contains or conveys lymph

lymphocyte *n* a white blood cell that is present in large numbers in lymph and blood and defends the body by immunological responses to invading or foreign matter (e g by producing antibodies) – **lymphocytic** *adj*

lynch *vt* to put to death illegally by mob action – **lyncher** *n*

lynch law *n* the punishment of presumed crimes or offences usu by death without due process of law

lynx *n, pl* **lynx, lynxes** any of various wildcats with relatively long legs, a short stubby tail, mottled coat, and often tufted ears

lynx-eyed *adj* having keen eyesight

lyre *n* a stringed instrument of the harp family used by the ancient Greeks esp to accompany song and recitation

lyrebird *n* either of 2 Australian birds the male of which displays tail feathers in the shape of a lyre during courtship

¹lyric *adj* **1** suitable for being set to music and sung **2** expressing direct personal emotion ⟨~ poetry⟩

²lyric *n* **1** a lyric poem **2** *pl* the words of a popular song – **lyricist, lyrist** *n*

lyrical *adj* **1** lyric **2** full of admiration or enthusiasm – esp in *wax lyrical* – **lyrically** *adv*

lyricism *n* **1** a directly personal and intense style or quality in an art **2** great enthusiasm or exuberance

M

m *n, pl* **m's, ms** *often cap* **1** (a graphic representation of or device for reproducing) the 13th letter of the English alphabet **2** one thousand **3** sthg shaped like the letter M **4** an em

'm *vb* am ⟨I'm going⟩

ma *n* MOTHER 1a – chiefly as a term of address; infml

ma'am *n* madam – used widely in the USA and in Britain, esp by servants and when addressing the Queen or a royal princess

mac, mack *n, Br* a raincoat – infml

Mac *n* – used informally to address **a** a Scotsman **b** *NAm* an unknown man

macabre *adj* **1** having death as a subject **2** dwelling on the gruesome **3** tending to produce horror in an onlooker

macadam *n* material used in making a macadamized road

macadamize, -ise *vt* to construct or finish (a road) by compacting into a solid mass successive layers of small broken stones

macaroni *n, pl* (2) **macaronis, macaronies 1** pasta made from durum wheat and shaped in hollow tubes that are wider in diameter than spaghetti **2** an English dandy of the late 18th and early 19th c who affected continental ways

macaroon *n* a small cake or biscuit composed chiefly of egg whites, sugar, and ground almonds or occasionally coconut

macaw *n* any of numerous parrots including some of the largest and showiest

¹mace *n* **1** a medieval heavy spiked staff or club **2** an ornamental staff used as a symbol of authority

²mace *n* an aromatic spice consisting of the dried external fibrous covering of a nutmeg

Mace *trademark* – used for a riot control agent containing tear gas

macerate *vt* **1** to cause to waste away (as if) by excessive fasting **2** to cause to become soft or separated into constituent elements (as if) by steeping in fluid ~*vi* to soften and wear away, esp as a result of being wetted – **macerator** n, **maceration** n

Mach n MACH NUMBER ⟨an aeroplane flying at ~ 2⟩

machete n a large heavy knife used for cutting vegetation and as a weapon

Machiavellian adj cunning and deceitful

machination n a scheming or crafty action or plan intended to accomplish some unusu evil end

¹machine n **1a** a combination of parts that transmit forces, motion, and energy one to another in a predetermined manner ⟨a sewing ~⟩ **b** an instrument (e g a lever or pulley) designed to transmit or modify the application of power, force, or motion **c** a combination of mechanically, electrically, or electronically operated parts for performing a task **d** a coin-operated device **e** machinery – + the or in pl ⟨humanity must not become the servant of the ~⟩ **2a** a person or organization that acts like a machine **b** the (controlling or inner) organization (e g of a group or activity) ⟨the war ~⟩ **c** a highly organized political group

²machine vt **1** to shape, finish, or operate on by a machine **2** to act on, produce, or perform a particular operation or activity on, using a machine; esp to sew using a sewing machine ⟨~ the zip in place⟩ – **machinable** also **machineable** adj

machine gun n an automatic gun for rapid continuous fire – **machine-gun** vb, **machine gunner** n

machinery n **1a** machines in general or as a functioning unit **b** the working parts of a machine **2** the means by which sthg is kept in action or a desired result is obtained **3** the system or organization by which an activity or process is controlled

machine tool n a usu power-driven machine designed for cutting or shaping wood, metal, etc

machinist n **1** a craftsman skilled in the use of machine tools **2** one who operates a machine, esp a sewing machine

Mach number, Mach n a number representing the ratio of the speed of a body to the speed of sound in the surrounding atmosphere ⟨a ~ of 2 indicates a speed that is twice that of sound⟩

mackerel n, pl **mackerels**, esp collectively **mackerel** a fish of the N Atlantic that is green with dark blue bars above and silvery below and is one of the most important food fishes; also any of various usu small or medium-sized related fishes

mackintosh also **macintosh** n, chiefly Br a raincoat

macr-, macro- comb form **1** long ⟨macrodiagonal⟩ ⟨macrobiotic⟩ **2** large ⟨macrospore⟩ **3** including or more comprehensive than ⟨Macro-Ge⟩ – used of a language group

macrame, macramé n (the act of making) a coarse lace or fringe made by knotting threads or cords in a geometrical pattern

macro n, pl **macros** a single computer instruction that stands for a sequence of operations

macrobiotic adj of or being a restricted diet, esp one consisting chiefly of whole grains or whole grains and vegetables, that is usu undertaken with the intention of promoting health and prolonging life

macrocosm n **1** the universe **2** a complex that is a large-scale reproduction of 1 of its constituents – **macrocosmic** adj, **macrocosmically** adv

macrophage n any of various large cells that are distributed throughout the body tissues, ingest foreign matter and debris, and may be attached to the fibres of a tissue or mobile – **macrophagic** adj

mad adj **1** mentally disordered; insane – not now used technically **2** utterly foolish; senseless **3** carried away by intense anger **4** carried away by enthusiasm or desire **5** affected with rabies **6** intensely excited or distraught; frantic **7** marked by intense and often chaotic activity ⟨made a ~ dash for cover⟩ – like **mad** very hard, fast, loud, etc ⟨shouted like mad⟩

madam n, pl **madams**, (1) **mesdames 1** a lady – used without a name as a form of respectful or polite address to a woman **2** a mistress – used as a title formerly with the Christian name but now with the surname or esp with a designation of rank or office ⟨Madam Chairman⟩ ⟨Madam President⟩ **3** a female brothel keeper **4** Br a conceited pert young lady or girl ⟨a little ~⟩

madame n, pl **mesdames**, **madames** – used as a title equivalent to Mrs preceding the name of a married woman not of English-speaking nationality or used without a name as a generalized term of direct address

madcap adj marked by impulsiveness or recklessness – **madcap** n

madden vt **1** to drive mad; craze **2** to exasperate, enrage

madder n **1** a Eurasian plant with whorled leaves and small yellowish flowers **2** (a dye prepared from) the root of the madder

made adj **1** assembled or prepared, esp by putting together various ingredients ⟨~ mustard⟩ **2** assured of success ⟨you've got it ~⟩ – infml

Madeira n any of several fortified wines from Madeira

madeira cake n, often cap, Br a very rich sponge cake

mademoiselle n, pl **mademoiselles**, **mesdemoiselles 1** an unmarried French-speaking girl or woman – used as a title equivalent to Miss for an unmarried woman not of English-speaking nationality **2** a French governess or female language teacher

made-to-measure adj, of a garment made according to an individual's measurements in order to achieve a good fit

madhouse n **1** a lunatic asylum – not used technically **2** a place of uproar or confusion

madly adv to a degree suggestive of madness: e g **a** with great energy; frantically **b** without restraint; passionately

madman, fem **madwoman** n a person who is or acts insane

madness n **1a** insanity **b** extreme folly **2** any of several ailments of animals marked by frenzied behaviour; specif rabies

Madonna n VIRGIN MARY

Madonna lily n a white lily with trumpet-shaped flowers

madras n a fine usu cotton plain-woven shirting and dress fabric, usu in brightly coloured checked or striped designs

madrigal n **1** a short medieval love poem **2** an unaccompanied and often complex secular song for several voices – **madrigalian** adj

maelstrom n **1** a powerful whirlpool **2** sthg resembling a maelstrom in turbulence and violence

maenad n **1** a female participant in ritual orgies in honour of Dionysus **2** a distraught woman – **maenadic** adj

maestro n, pl **maestros**, **maestri** a master in an art; esp an eminent composer, conductor, or teacher of music

Mafia n sing or pl in constr **1** a secret society of Sicilian political terrorists **2** an organized secret body originating in Sicily and prevalent esp in the USA that controls illicit activities (e g vice and narcotics) **3** often not cap an

excessively influential coterie of a usu specified kind ⟨*the literary ~*⟩
mag *n* a magazine – infml
magazine *n* **1** a storeroom for arms, ammunition, or explosives (e g gunpowder) **2a** a usu illustrated periodical, bound in paper covers, containing miscellaneous pieces by different authors **b** a television or radio programme containing a number of usu topical items, often without a common theme **3** a supply chamber: e g **a** a holder from which cartridges can be fed into a gun chamber automatically **b** a lightproof chamber for films or plates in a camera or for film in a film projector
magenta *n* **1** fuchsine **2a** a deep purplish red **b** a pinkish red – used in photography with reference to one of the primary colours
maggot *n* a soft-bodied legless grub that is the larva of a 2-winged fly (e g the housefly) – **maggoty** *adj*
magi *pl of* MAGUS
¹magic *n* **1** (rites, incantations, etc used in) the art of invoking supernatural powers to control natural forces by means of charms, spells, etc **2a** an extraordinary power or influence producing results which defy explanation **b** sthg that seems to cast a spell ⟨*the ~ of the voice*⟩ **3** the art of producing illusions by sleight of hand
²magic *adj* **1** of, being, or used in magic **2** having seemingly supernatural qualities **3** – used as a general term of approval; infml ⟨*this new record is really ~*⟩ – **magical** *adj*, **magically** *adv*
³magic *vt* **-ck-** to affect, influence, or take *away* (as if) by magic
magic eye *n* PHOTOELECTRIC CELL
magician *n* **1** one skilled in magic **2** a conjurer
magic lantern *n* an early device for the projection of still pictures from slides
magisterial *adj* **1a** of, being, or having the characteristics of a master or teacher **b** having masterly skill **2** of a magistrate – **magisterially** *adv*
magistrate *n* a civil legislative or executive official: e g **a** a principal official exercising governmental powers **b** a paid or unpaid local judicial officer who presides in a magistrates' court – **magistracy** *n*, **magistrature** *n*, **magistratical** *adj*
magma *n* **1** a thin pasty suspension (e g of a precipitate in water) **2** molten rock material within the earth from which an igneous rock results by cooling – **magmatic** *adj*
magnanimous *adj* **1** showing or suggesting a lofty and courageous spirit **2** showing or suggesting nobility of feeling and generosity of mind; not subject to petty feelings – **magnanimously** *adv*, **magnanimity** *n*
magnate *n* a person of wealth or influence, often in a specified area of business or industry
magnesia *n* **1** a white oxide of magnesium used esp in making cements, insulation, fertilizers, and rubber, and in medicine as an antacid and mild laxative **2** magnesium – **magnesian** *adj*
magnesium *n* a silver-white bivalent metallic element that burns with an intense white light, is lighter than aluminium, and is used in making light alloys
magnet *n* **1a** LODESTONE 1 **b** a body (of iron, steel, etc) that has an (artificially imparted) magnetic field external to itself and attracts iron **2** sthg that attracts
magnet-, magneto- *comb form* magnetic force; magnetism; magnetic ⟨*magnetoelectric*⟩ ⟨*magneton*⟩
magnetic *adj* **1a** of magnetism or a magnet **b** (capable of being) magnetized **c** working by magnetic attraction **2** possessing an extraordinary power or ability to attract or charm – **magnetically** *adv*
magnetic field *n* a region of space (near a body possessing magnetism or carrying an electric current) in which magnetic forces can be detected
magnetic pole *n* either of 2 small nonstationary regions in the N and S geographical polar areas of the earth or another celestial body towards which a magnetic needle points from any direction
magnetic tape *n* a ribbon of thin paper or plastic with a magnetizable coating for use in recording sound, video, etc signals
magnetism *n* **1** (physics dealing with) a class of physical forces and interactions that includes the attraction for iron shown by a permanent magnet or an electromagnet and is believed to be produced by moving electric charges **2** an ability to attract or charm
magnetize, -ise *vt* **1** to attract like a magnet **2** to cause to be a magnet – **magnetizable** *adj*, **magnetizer** *n*, **magnetization** *n*
magneto *n, pl* **magnetos** an alternator with permanent magnets (formerly) used to generate a high voltage for the ignition in an internal-combustion engine
magneto- – see MAGNET-
Magnificat *n* (a musical setting of) the canticle of the Virgin Mary in Luke 1:46–55
magnification *n* **1** a magnifying or being magnified **2** the apparent enlargement of an object by a microscope, telescope, etc
magnificent *adj* **1** marked by stately grandeur and splendour **2a** sumptuous in structure and adornment **b** strikingly beautiful or impressive **3** sublime ⟨*her ~ prose*⟩ **4** exceptionally fine or excellent ⟨*a ~ day*⟩ – **magnificence** *n*, **magnificently** *adv*
magnify *vt* **1** to (falsely) increase in significance **2** to enlarge in fact or in appearance ⟨*a telescope* magnifies *distant objects*⟩ ~ *vi* to have the power of causing objects to appear larger than they are – **magnifier** *n*
magnifying glass *n* a single optical lens for magnifying
magniloquent *adj* grandiloquent – **magniloquence** *n*, **magniloquently** *adv*
magnitude *n* **1a** (great) size or extent **b** a quantity, number **2** the importance or quality of sthg **3** the apparent brightness of a celestial body, esp a star, measured on a logarithmic scale in which a difference of 5 units corresponds to the multiplication or division of the brightness of light by 100
magnolia *n* any of a genus of shrubs and trees with evergreen or deciduous leaves and usu large white, yellow, rose, or purple flowers
magnum *n* a wine bottle holding twice the usual amount (about 1.5l)
magnum opus *n* the greatest achievement of an artist, writer, etc
magpie *n* **1** any of numerous birds of the crow family with a very long tail and black-and-white plumage **2** one who chatters noisily **3** one who collects objects in a random fashion
magus *n, pl* **magi** **1a** a member of a Zoroastrian hereditary priestly class in ancient Persia **b** *often cap* any of the traditionally 3 wise men from the East who paid homage to the infant Jesus **2** a magician, sorcerer
maharajah, maharaja *n* a Hindu prince ranking above a rajah
maharani, maharanee *n* **1** the wife of a maharaja **2** a Hindu princess ranking above a rani
mahatma *n* a person revered for outstanding moral and spiritual qualities – used as a title of honour, esp by Hindus
mah-jong, mah-jongg *n* a game of Chinese origin usu

played by 4 people with 144 tiles that are drawn and discarded until one player secures a winning hand

mahlstick *n* a maulstick

mahogany *n* **1** (any of various tropical, esp W Indian, trees that yield) a durable usu reddish-brown moderately hard and heavy wood, widely used for fine cabinetwork **2** the reddish-brown colour of mahogany

mahout *n* a keeper and driver of an elephant

maid *n* **1** an unmarried girl or woman; *also* a female virgin **2** a female servant

¹**maiden** *n* **1** an unmarried girl or woman **2** a former Scottish beheading device like a guillotine **3** a horse that has never won a race **4 maiden, maiden over** an over in cricket in which no runs are credited to the batsman – **maidenly** *adj,* **maidenliness** *n,* **maidenhood** *n*

²**maiden** *adj* **1a(1)** not married **(2)** VIRGIN 2, 3 **b** *of a female animal* never having borne young or been mated **c** that has not been altered from its original state **2** being the first or earliest of its kind ⟨*the ship's* ∼ *voyage*⟩

maidenhair *n* any of a genus of ferns with fronds that have delicate spreading branches

maidenhead *n* **1** virginity **2** the hymen

maiden name *n* the surname of a woman prior to marriage

maid of honour *n, pl* **maids of honour 1** a bride's principal unmarried wedding attendant **2** a puff pastry tartlet filled with custard

maidservant *n* a female servant

¹**mail** *n* **1a** a bag of posted items conveyed from one post office to another **b** the postal matter that makes up 1 particular consignment **c** a conveyance that transports mail **2** a postal system

²**mail** *vt* ⁴POST 1 – **mailable** *adj*

³**mail** *n* **1** armour made of interlocking metal rings, chains, or sometimes plates **2** a hard enclosing covering of an animal – **mailed** *adj*

⁴**mail** *vt* to clothe (as if) with mail

mailbag *n* a bag used to carry mail

mailbox *n, NAm* a letter box

mailing list *n* an organization's list of the names and addresses to which it regularly sends information

mail order *n* an order for goods that is received and fulfilled by post – **mail-order** *adj*

maim *vt* to mutilate, disfigure, or wound seriously; cripple – **maimer** *n*

¹**main** *n* **1** physical strength – in *with might and main* **2** the chief or essential part – chiefly in *in the main* **3** the chief pipe, duct, or cable of a public service (e g gas, electricity, or water) – often pl with sing. meaning ⟨*turned the electricity off at the* ∼ *s*⟩ **4a** a mainland **b** the high sea *USE* (4) chiefly poetic or archaic

²**main** *adj* **1** chief, principal **2** fully exerted ⟨*used* ∼ *force*⟩ **3** connected with or located near the mainmast or mainsail **4** *of a clause* able to stand alone (e g *he laughed* in *he laughed when he heard*)

³**main** *n* a number from 4 to 9 inclusive called by a player before throwing the dice in the game of hazard

main chance *n* *the* chance that promises most advantage or profit – esp in *have an eye for the main chance*

main deck *n* **1** the highest deck that extends the full width and length of a naval vessel **2** the upper deck of a merchant vessel between the poop and forecastle

mainland *n* the largest land area of a continent, country, etc, considered in relation to smaller offshore islands – **mainlander** *n*

mainline *vb* to inject (a narcotic or other drug of abuse) into a vein – slang – **mainliner** *n*

main line *n* a principal railway line

mainly *adv* in most cases or for the most part; chiefly

mainmast *n* (the lowest section of) a sailing vessel's principal mast

mains *adj* of or (suitable to be) powered by electricity from the mains ⟨*a* ∼ *razor*⟩

mainsail *n* **1** the lowest square sail on the mainmast of a square-rigged ship **2** the principal fore-and-aft sail on the mainmast of a fore-and-aft rigged ship

mainspring *n* **1** the chief spring, esp of a watch or clock **2** the chief motive, agent, or cause

mainstay *n* **1** a rope that stretches forwards from a sailing ship's maintop, usu to the foot of the foremast, and provides the chief support of the mainmast **2** a chief support

mainstream *n* a prevailing current or direction of activity or influence – **mainstream** *adj*

maintain *vt* **1** to keep in an existing state (e g of operation, repair, efficiency, or validity) **2** to sustain against opposition or danger **3** to continue or persevere in **4** to support, sustain, or provide for ⟨*has a family to* ∼⟩ **5** to affirm (as if) in argument – **maintainable** *adj,* **maintainer** *n*

maintenance *n* **1** maintaining or being maintained **2** (payment for) the upkeep of property or equipment **3** *chiefly Br* payments for the support of one spouse by another, esp of a woman by a man, pending or following legal separation or divorce

maisonette *n* **1** a small house **2** a part of a house, usu on 2 floors, let or sold separately

maize *n* (the ears or edible seeds of) a tall widely cultivated cereal grass bearing seeds on elongated ears

majesty *n* **1** sovereign power **2** – used in addressing or referring to a king or queen ⟨*Your* Majesty⟩ **3a** impressive bearing or aspect **b** greatness or splendour of quality or character – **majestic** *adj,* **majestically** *adv*

majolica *n* a type of early Italian tin-glazed earthenware

¹**major** *adj* **1a** greater in importance, size, rank, or degree ⟨*one of our* ∼ *poets*⟩ **b** of considerable importance ⟨*a* ∼ *improvement*⟩ **2** having attained the age of majority **3** notable or conspicuous in effect or scope **4** involving serious risk to life; serious ⟨*a* ∼ *operation*⟩ **5a** *esp of a scale or mode* having semitones between the third and fourth and the seventh and eighth degrees **b** being or based on a (specified) major scale ⟨*in a* ∼ *key*⟩ ⟨*a piece in D* ∼⟩ **c** being an interval (equivalent to that) between the first and the second, third, sixth, or seventh degree of a major scale **d** *of a chord* having an interval of a major third between the root and the next note above it

²**major** *n* **1** one who has attained the age of majority **2** a major musical interval, scale, key, or mode **3** an officer in the army or US airforce ranking below lieutenant colonel

majordomo *n, pl* **majordomos 1** a man having charge of a large household (e g a palace) **2** a butler or steward

majorette *n* a girl or woman who twirls a baton and accompanies a marching band

major general *n* an officer in the army or US airforce ranking below lieutenant general

majority *n* **1** (the status of one who has attained the) age at which full legal rights and responsibilities are acquired **2a** a number greater than half of a total **b** the amount by which such a greater number exceeds the remaining smaller number **3** the greatest in number of 2 or more groups constituting a whole; *specif* (the excess of votes over its rival obtained by) a group having sufficient votes to obtain control **4** the military office, rank, or commission of a major

major suit *n* either of the suits of hearts or spades that are of superior scoring value in bridge

¹**make** vb **made** vt **1a** to create or produce (for someone) by work or action ⟨~ a dress⟩ ⟨made in Korea⟩ ⟨she made herself a cup of coffee⟩ **b** to cause; BRING ABOUT ⟨~ a disturbance⟩ ⟨~ peace⟩ **2** to formulate in the mind ⟨~ plans⟩ ⟨~ no doubt about it⟩ **3** to put together from ingredients or components ⟨butter is made from milk⟩ – often + up **4** to compute or estimate to be ⟨what time do you ~ it?⟩ **5a** to assemble and set alight the materials for (a fire) **b** to renew or straighten the bedclothes on (a bed) **c** to shuffle (a pack of cards) in preparation for dealing **6a** to cause to be or become ⟨made him bishop⟩ ⟨couldn't ~ himself heard⟩ **b** to cause (sthg) to appear or seem to; represent as ⟨in the film they ~ the battle take place in winter⟩ **c(1)** to change, transform ⟨~ the material into a skirt⟩ **(2)** to produce as an end product ⟨the navy will ~ a man of you⟩ **d** to carry on right through (a period) ⟨take sandwiches and ~ a day of it⟩ **7a** to enact, establish ⟨~ laws⟩ **b** to draft or produce a version of ⟨~ a will⟩ **8** to cause (an electric circuit) to be completed **9a** to perform; CARRY OUT ⟨~ a speech⟩ ⟨~ a discovery⟩ ⟨~ a sweeping gesture⟩ ⟨~ a detour⟩ **b** to eat ⟨~ a good breakfast⟩ **c** to put forward for acceptance ⟨~ an offer⟩ ⟨~ a promise⟩ **10** to cause to act in a specified way; compel ⟨rain ~ s the flowers grow⟩ ⟨she was made to give in⟩ **11a** to amount to; count as ⟨4 and 4 ~ 8⟩ ⟨~ s a great difference⟩ **b** to be integral or essential to the existence or success of ⟨it made my day⟩ **c** to combine to form ⟨hydrogen and oxygen ~ water⟩ **12** to be capable of becoming or of serving as ⟨you'll ~ a lexicographer yet⟩ **13** to reach, attain ⟨never ~ the airfield⟩ ⟨the story made the papers⟩ – often + it ⟨you'll never ~ it that far⟩ **14** to gain (e g money) by working, trading, dealing, etc **15a** to act so as to acquire ⟨~ enemies⟩ **b** to score (points, runs, etc) in a game or sport **16a** to fulfil (a contract) in bridge or another card game **b** to win a trick with (a card) **17** to persuade to consent to sexual intercourse – infml ~ vi **1a** to behave so as to seem ⟨made as though he were angry⟩ **b** to behave as if beginning a specified action ⟨made as if to hand it over⟩ **c** to act so as to be ⟨~ ready to leave⟩ **2** to set out or go (in a specified direction) ⟨made towards the door⟩ ⟨we're making for the coast⟩ **3** to undergo manufacture or processing – usu + up ⟨the silk ~ s up beautifully⟩ – **maker** n – **as near as makes no difference** almost exactly – **make a book** to take bets on – **make a meal of** Br to make more of than is necessary or tactful – **make an exhibition of oneself** to behave foolishly in public – **make away with 1** MAKE OFF WITH ⟨the thief made away with her handbag⟩ **2** to destroy – **make believe** to pretend, feign – **make bold** to venture, dare ⟨made so bold as to ask for more⟩ – **make certain/sure 1** to ascertain by enquiry **2** to take measures to ensure ⟨make certain of a seat⟩ – **make do** to get along or manage with the means at hand – **make ends meet** to live within one's income – **make eyes to** ogle – + at – **make fast** to tie or attach firmly – **make for** to be conducive to ⟨courtesy makes for safer driving⟩ – **make free** with to take excessive or disrespectful liberties with – **make friends 1** to acquire friends **2** to become friendly ⟨make friends with a neighbour⟩ – **make fun of** to make an object of amusement or ridicule – **make good 1** MAKE UP vt **4 2** to be successful in life **3** chiefly Br to repair ⟨make good the brickwork under the window⟩ – **make head or tail of** to understand in the least ⟨I can't make head or tail of it⟩ – **make it 1** to be successful ⟨actors trying to make it in the big time⟩ – infml **2** to achieve sexual intercourse – slang – **make like** to act the part of; imitate – slang – **make love 1** to woo, court; also to pet, neck **2** to engage in sexual intercourse – **make no bones** to have no hesitation or shame ⟨makes no bones about

giving her opinion⟩ – **make of 1** to attribute a specified degree of significance to ⟨tends to make too much of his problems⟩ **2** to understand by; conclude as to the meaning of ⟨could make nothing of the play⟩ – **make oneself scarce** to hide or avoid sby or sthg unobtrusively – **make public** to disclose – **make the grade** MAKE IT 1 – **make tracks** to leave ⟨its getting late; we'll have to make tracks⟩ – infml – **make water** to urinate – euph – **make way** to give room ⟨the crowd made way for the ambulance⟩ – **make with** chiefly NAm to produce, perform – usu + the; slang

²**make** n **1a** the manner or style in which sthg is constructed **b** a place or origin of manufacture; BRAND 3a **2** the physical, mental, or moral constitution of a person **3** the type or process of making or manufacturing – **on the make 1** rising or attempting to rise to a higher social or financial status **2** NAm in search of a sexual partner or sexual adventure

make-believe n or adj (sthg) imaginary or pretended

make off vi to leave in haste – **make off with** to take away; steal

make out vt **1** to draw up in writing **2** to complete (e g a printed form or document) by writing information in appropriate spaces **3** to find or grasp the meaning of ⟨tried to make out what had happened⟩ **4** to claim or pretend to be true ⟨made out that he had never heard of me⟩ **5** to identify (e g by sight or hearing) with difficulty or effort ~ vi **1** to fare, manage ⟨how is he making out in his new job?⟩ **2** chiefly NAm to engage in sexual intercourse – slang

make over vt **1** to transfer the title of (property) ⟨made over the estate to his eldest son⟩ **2** chiefly NAm to remake, remodel ⟨made the whole house over⟩

Maker n GOD 1

makeshift adj or n (being) a crude and temporary expedient

make-up n **1a** the way in which the parts of sthg are put together **b** physical, mental, and moral constitution **2a** cosmetics (e g lipstick and mascara) applied, esp to the face, to give colour or emphasis **b** the effect achieved by the application of make-up **c** materials (e g wigs and cosmetics) used for special costuming (e g for a play)

make up vt **1a** to invent (e g a story), esp in order to deceive **b** to set (an account) in order **2a** to arrange typeset matter into (columns or pages) for printing **b** to produce (e g clothes) by cutting and sewing **3a** PREPARE 3a ⟨make up a prescription⟩ **3** to wrap or fasten up ⟨make the books up into a parcel⟩ **4** to compensate for (a deficiency); esp to make (e g a required amount or number) complete **5** to settle, decide ⟨made up his mind to leave⟩ ⟨made up their differences⟩ **6a** to prepare in physical appearance for a role **b** to apply cosmetics to ~ vi **1** to become reconciled **2** to compensate for ⟨we made up for lost time⟩ **3** to put on costumes or make-up (e g for a play) **4** to assemble a finished article; esp to complete a garment by sewing together

making n **1** a process or means of advancement or success **2a** the essential qualities for becoming – often pl with sing. meaning ⟨had the ~ s of a great artist⟩ **b** pl, chiefly NAm & Austr paper and tobacco used for rolling one's own cigarettes – **in the making** in the process of becoming, forming, or developing

mal- comb form **1a** bad ⟨malpractice⟩; faulty ⟨malfunction⟩ **b** badly ⟨malodorous⟩; deficiently ⟨malnourished⟩ **2a** abnormal ⟨malformation⟩ **b** abnormally ⟨malformed⟩ **3** not ⟨malcontent⟩ ⟨maladroit⟩

malacca cane n an often mottled cane from an Asiatic rattan palm used esp for walking sticks

malachite *n* hydrated copper carbonate occurring as a green mineral and used esp for ornaments

maladjusted *adj* poorly or inadequately adjusted, specif to one's social environment and conditions of life – **maladjustment** *n*

maladministration *n* incompetent or corrupt administration, esp in public office – **maladminister** *vt*

maladroit *adj* clumsy, inept

malady *n* an animal disease or disorder

malaise *n* **1** an indeterminate feeling of debility or lack of health, often accompanying the start of an illness **2** a vague sense of mental or moral unease

malapropism *n* (an instance of) an incongruous misapplication of a word (e g in 'always said 'polobears' and 'neonstockings' ' – *Time*)

malaria *n* a disease caused by protozoan parasites in the red blood cells, transmitted by the bite of mosquitoes, and characterized by periodic attacks of chills and fever – **malarious** *adj*, **malarial** *adj*, **malarian** *adj*

Malay *n* (the language of) a member of a people of the Malay peninsula and adjacent islands – **Malay** *adj*, **Malayan** *n or adj*

¹malcontent *n* a discontented person; *esp* sby violently opposed to a government or regime

²malcontent, malcontented *adj* dissatisfied with the existing state of affairs

¹male *adj* **1a(1)** of or being the sex that produces relatively small sperms, spermatozoids, or spermatozoa by which the eggs of a female are made fertile **(2)** *of a plant or flower* having stamens but no ovaries **b(1)** (characteristic) of the male sex **(2)** made up of male individuals **2** designed for fitting into a corresponding hollow part – **maleness** *n*

²male *n* a male person, animal, or plant

malediction *n* a curse – fml – **maledictory** *adj*

malefactor *n* **1** a criminal; *esp* a felon **2** one who does evil – fml

malefic *adj* **1** having malignant influence **2** harmful, malicious *USE* fml – **maleficence** *n*, **maleficent** *adj*

malevolent *adj* having, showing, or arising from an often intense desire to do harm – **malevolence** *n*, **malevolently** *adv*

malfeasance *n* (official) misconduct

malformation *n* anomalous, abnormal, or faulty formation or structure – **malformed** *adj*

malfunction *vi* to fail to operate in the normal manner – **malfunction** *n*

malice *n* conscious desire to harm; *esp* a premeditated desire to commit a crime – **malicious** *adj*, **maliciously** *adv*, **maliciousness** *n*

¹malign *adj* **1a** harmful in nature, influence, or effect **b** *of a disease* malignant, virulent **2** bearing or showing (vicious) ill will or hostility

²malign *vt* to utter injuriously (false) reports about; speak ill of

malignant *adj* **1a** harmful in nature, influence, or effect **b** passionately and relentlessly malevolent **2** *of a disease* very severe or deadly ⟨~ *malaria*⟩; *specif, of a tumour* tending to infiltrate, spread, and cause death – **malignantly** *adv*, **malignancy** *n*

malinger *vi* to pretend illness or incapacity so as to avoid duty or work – **malingerer** *n*

mall *n* **1** a public promenade, often bordered by trees **2** *NAm* a shopping precinct, usu with associated parking space

mallard *n, pl* **mallards,** *esp collectively* **mallard** a common large wild duck that is the ancestor of the domestic ducks

malleable *adj* **1** *esp of metals* capable of being beaten or rolled into a desired shape **2** easily shaped by outside forces or influences – **malleableness** *n*, **malleability** *n*

mallet *n* **1** a hammer with a usu large head of wood, plastic, etc **2** an implement with a large usu cylindrical wooden head for striking the ball in croquet, polo, etc **3** a light hammer with a small rounded or spherical usu padded head used in playing certain musical instruments (e g a vibraphone)

mallow *n* any of various related plants with usu deeply cut lobed leaves and showy flowers

malmsey *n, often cap* the sweetest variety of Madeira

malnutrition *n* faulty or inadequate nutrition

malodorous *adj* smelling bad – fml

malpractice *n* **1** failure to exercise due professional skill or care **2** an instance of improper conduct; malfeasance – **malpractitioner** *n*

¹malt *n* **1** grain softened in water, allowed to germinate, then roasted and used esp in brewing and distilling **2** unblended malt whisky produced in a particular area ⟨*the finest Highland ~s*⟩ – **malty** *adj*

²malt *vt* **1** to convert into malt **2** to make or treat with malt or malt extract ~ *vi* to become malt

Maltese *n, pl* **Maltese** (the language of) a native or inhabitant of Malta – **Maltese** *adj*

Maltese cross *n* a cross consisting of 4 equal arms that widen out from the centre and have their outer ends indented by a V

Malthusian *adj* of Malthus or his theory that population tends to increase faster than its means of subsistence and that widespread poverty inevitably results unless population growth is checked – **Malthusian** *n*

maltreat *vt* to treat cruelly or roughly – **maltreatment** *n*

¹mama, mamma *n* ¹MOTHER 1a – formerly used in address

²mama, mamma *n* mummy – used informally and by children

mamba *n* any of several (tropical) African venomous snakes related to the cobras but with no hood

mambo *n, pl* **mambos** (the music for) a ballroom dance of Haitian origin that resembles the rumba – **mambo** *vi*

mammal *n* any of a class of higher vertebrates comprising humans and all other animals that have mammary glands and nourish their young with milk – **mammalian** *adj or n*, **mammalology** *n*

mammary *adj* of, lying near, or affecting the mammary glands

Mammon *n* material wealth or possessions, esp considered as an evil

¹mammoth *n* any of numerous large hairy long-tailed extinct Pleistocene elephants

²mammoth *adj* of very great size

mammy *n* **1** mamma, mummy – used esp by children **2** *NAm* a Negro nanny of white children, esp formerly in the southern USA

¹man *n, pl* **men 1a(1)** a human being; *esp* an adult male as distinguished from a woman or child **(2)** a man belonging to a usu specified category – usu in combination ⟨*businessman*⟩⟨*horseman*⟩ **(3)** a husband – esp in *man and wife* **(4)** a male sexual partner **b** the human race **c** a member of a family of biped primate mammals anatomically related to the great apes but distinguished esp by greater brain development and a capacity for articulate speech and abstract reasoning; *broadly* any ancestor of modern man **d** one possessing the qualities associated with manhood (e g courage and strength) **e** a fellow, chap – used interjectionally **2a** a feudal vassal **b** *pl* the members of (the ranks of) a military force **c** *pl* the working force as distinguished from the employer and usu the management **d** *pl* the members of a team **3a** an individual, person ⟨*what can a* ~ *do in this situation?*⟩ **b** the most suitable man ⟨*he's your* ~ *for the job*⟩ **4** any of the pieces moved by each player in chess, draughts, etc **5** *often cap, NAm the* police **6** *often cap, NAm the* white establishment – used by Negroes **7** – used interjectionally to express intensity of feeling ⟨~, *what a party!*⟩ *USE* (5, 6 & 7) slang – **manless** *adj*, **manlike** *adj* – **to a man** without exception

²**man** *vt* **-nn-** **1** to supply with the man or men necessary **2** to take up station by ⟨~ *the pumps*⟩ **3** to serve in the force or complement of

¹**manacle** *n* **1** a shackle or handcuff **2** a restraint *USE* usu *pl*

²**manacle** *vb* **1** to confine (the hands) with manacles **2** to subject to a restraint

manage *vt* **1a** to make and keep submissive **b** to use (e g money) economically **2** to succeed in handling (e g a difficult situation or person) **3** to succeed in accomplishing ⟨*she could only* ~ *a smile*⟩ ⟨*always* ~*s to win*⟩ **4** to conduct the running of (esp a business); *also* to have charge of (e g a sports team or athlete) ~ *vi* to be able to cope with difficulties; *esp* to use one's finances to the best advantage – **manageable** *adj*

management *n* **1** the act or art of managing **2** *sing or pl in constr* the collective body of those who manage or direct an enterprise

manager, *fem* **manageress** *n* **1** one who conducts business or household affairs **2** sby who directs a sports team, player, entertainer, etc – **managership** *n*, **managerial** *adj*

man-at-arms *n, pl* **men-at-arms** a (heavily armed and usu mounted) soldier

manatee *n* any of several (tropical) aquatic plant-eating mammals with broad tails

mandarin *n* **1a** a public official in the Chinese Empire ranked according to any of 9 grades **b** a person of position and influence, esp in literary or bureaucratic circles; *esp* an elder and often reactionary member of such a circle **2** *cap* **a** the primarily northern dialect of Chinese used by the court and officials under the Empire **b** the chief dialect of Chinese that has a standard variety spoken in the Peking area **3** **mandarin, mandarin orange** (a small spiny Chinese orange tree that bears) a yellow to reddish orange fruit

mandarin duck *n* a brightly marked crested Asian duck, often found domesticated

¹**mandate** *n* **1** an authoritative command from a superior **2** an authorization to act on the behalf of another; *specif* the political authority given by electors to parliament ⟨*the* ~ *of the people*⟩ **3a** an order granted by the League of Nations to a member nation for the establishment of a responsible government over a conquered territory **b** a mandated territory

²**mandate** *vt* to administer or assign under a mandate

¹**mandatory** *adj* **1** containing or constituting a command **2** compulsory, obligatory

²**mandatory** *n* a nation or person holding a mandate

mandible *n* **1a** JAW **1a** **b** a lower jaw together with its surrounding soft parts **c** the upper or lower part of a bird's bill **2** any of various mouth parts in insects or other invertebrates for holding or biting food – **mandibular** *adj*, **mandibulate** *adj or n*

mandolin *also* **mandoline** *n* a musical instrument of the lute family with a fretted neck

mandrake *n* (the root of) a Mediterranean plant of the nightshade family with whitish or purple flowers and a large forked supposedly man-shaped root formerly used in medicine

mandrill *n* a large gregarious baboon found in W Africa, the male of which has red and blue striped cheeks

mane *n* **1** long thick hair growing about the neck of a horse, male lion, etc **2** long thick hair on a person's head

man-eater *n* a person or animal that eats human flesh – **man-eating** *adj*

maneuver *vb or n, NAm* (to) manoeuvre

manful *adj* having courage and resolution – **manfully** *adv*

manganese *n* a greyish white hard divalent or hexavalent metallic element – **manganic** *adj*, **manganous** *adj*

mange *n* any of various contagious skin diseases affecting domestic animals or sometimes human beings, marked by inflammation and loss of hair and caused by a minute parasitic mite

mangel-wurzel, mangel *n* a large yellow to orange type of beet grown as food for livestock

manger *n* a trough or open box in a stable for holding feed

¹**mangle** *vt* **1** to hack or crush (as if) by repeated blows **2** to spoil by poor work, errors, etc

²**mangle** *vt or n* (to pass through) a machine with rollers for squeezing water from and pressing laundry

mango *n, pl* **mangoes, mangos** (a tropical evergreen tree that bears) a yellowish red fruit with a firm skin, large stone, and juicy edible slightly acid pulp

mangosteen *n* (an E Indian tree that bears) a dark reddish brown fruit with thick rind and edible flesh

mangrove *n* any of a genus of tropical maritime trees or shrubs with prop roots that form dense masses

mangy *adj* **1** suffering or resulting from mange **2** having many worn or bare spots

manhandle *vt* **1** to move or manage by human force **2** to handle roughly

manhole *n* a covered opening through which a person may go, esp to gain access to an underground or enclosed structure (e g a sewer)

manhood *n* **1** manly qualities **2** the condition of being an adult male as distinguished from a child or female **3** *sing or pl in constr* adult males collectively

man-hour *n* a unit of 1 hour's work by 1 person, used esp as a basis for cost accounting and wage calculation

mania *n* **1** abnormal excitement and euphoria marked by mental and physical hyperactivity and disorganization of behaviour **2** excessive or unreasonable enthusiasm – often in combination ⟨*Beatle*mania⟩

maniac *n* one who is or acts as if (violently) insane; a lunatic – not used technically

maniacal *also* **maniac** *adj* **1** affected with or suggestive of madness **2** characterized by ungovernable frenzy

manic *adj* affected by, relating to, or resembling mania – **manic** *n*, **manically** *adv*

manic-depressive *adj* of or affected by a mental disorder characterized by alternating mania and (extreme) depression – **manic-depressive** *n*

¹**manicure** *n* **1** (a) treatment for the care of the hands and fingernails **2** a manicurist

²**manicure** *vt* **1** to give a manicure to **2** to trim closely and evenly – **manicurist** *n*

¹**manifest** *adj* readily perceived by the senses (e g sight) or mind; obvious – **manifestly** *adv*

²**manifest** *vt* to make evident or certain by showing or displaying ~ *vi of a spirit, ghost, etc* to appear in visible form – **manifester** *n*

³**manifest** *n* a list of passengers or an invoice of cargo, esp for a ship

manifestation *n* a sign (e g materialization) of the presence of a spirit

manifesto n, pl **manifestos, manifestoes** a public declaration of intentions, esp by a political party before an election

¹**manifold** adj many and varied – **manifoldly** adv, **manifoldness** n

²**manifold** n **1** a whole that unites or consists of many diverse elements **2** a hollow fitting (e g connecting the cylinders of an internal combustion engine with the exhaust pipe) with several outlets or inlets for connecting 1 pipe with several other pipes

³**manifold** vt to make (many) copies of

manikin, mannikin n **1** a mannequin **2** a little man

manila also **manilla** adj, often cap made of Manila paper or hemp – **manila** n

manipulate vt **1** to handle or operate, esp skilfully **2a** to manage or use skilfully **b** to control or influence by artful, unfair, or insidious means, esp to one's own advantage **3** to examine and treat (a fracture, sprain, etc) by moving bones into the proper position manually – **manipulatable** adj, **manipulator** n, **manipulative** adj, **manipulatory** adj, **manipulation** n

man jack n individual man ⟨every ~⟩

mankind n sing but sing or pl in constr the human race

manly adj (marked by the good qualities) befitting a man – **manliness** n

man-made adj made or produced by human beings rather than nature; also synthetic

manna n **1** food miraculously supplied to the Israelites in their journey through the wilderness **2** a sudden source of benefit

manned adj **1** equipped with men **2** of a spacecraft carrying a human crew

mannequin n **1** an artist's, tailor's, or dressmaker's model of the human figure; also such a model used esp for displaying clothes **2** a woman who models clothing

manner n **1** a kind, sort; also sorts ⟨all ~ of information⟩ **2a** the mode or method in which sthg is done or happens **b** a method of artistic execution; a style **3** pl **a** (rules of) social conduct **b** social behaviour evaluated as to politeness; esp conduct indicating good background ⟨mind your ~s!⟩ **4** characteristic or distinctive bearing, air, or deportment – **mannerless** adj

mannered adj **1** having manners of a specified kind – usu in combination ⟨well-mannered⟩ **2** having an artificial or stilted character

mannerism n **1a** exaggerated or affected adherence to a particular style in art or literature **b** often cap a style of art in late 16th-c Europe characterized by distortion of the human figure **2** a characteristic (unconscious) gesture or trait; an idiosyncrasy – **mannerist** n, **manneristic** adj

mannerly adj showing or having good manners – **mannerliness** n, **mannerly** adv

mannish adj resembling, befitting, or typical of a man rather than a woman – **mannishly** adv, **mannishness** n

¹**manoeuvre,** NAm chiefly **maneuver** n **1a** a military or naval movement **b** a (large-scale) training exercise for the armed forces **2** an intended and controlled deviation from a straight and level flight path in the operation of an aircraft **3** a skilful or dexterous movement **4** an adroit and clever management of affairs, often using deception

²**manoeuvre,** NAm chiefly **maneuver** vi **1** to perform a military or naval manoeuvre (to secure an advantage) **2** to perform a manoeuvre **3** to use stratagems ~ vt **1** to cause (e g troops) to execute manoeuvres **2** to manipulate with adroitness **3** to bring about or secure as a result of contriving – **manoeuvrable** adj, **manoeuvrer** n, **manoeuvrability** n

man-of-war n, pl **men-of-war** a warship (of the days of sail)

manometer n an instrument for measuring the pressure of gases and vapours – **manometry** n, **manometric, manometrical** adj, **manometrically** adv

manor n **1** a landed estate **2a** a medieval estate under a lord who held a variety of rights over land and tenants, including the right to hold court **b** manor, manor house the house of the lord of a manor **3** a district of police administration – slang – **manorial** adj, **manorialism** n

manpower n the total supply of people available for work or service

manqué adj that could have been but failed to be – used after the noun modified ⟨a poet ~⟩

mansard, mansard roof n a roof with a lower steeper slope and a higher shallower one on all 4 sides

manse n the residence of an esp Presbyterian or Baptist clergyman

manservant n, pl **manservants** a male servant, esp a valet

-manship suffix (→ n) art or skill of one who practises ⟨horsemanship⟩ ⟨gamesmanship⟩

mansion n **1a** the house of the lord of a manor **b** a large imposing residence **2** a separate apartment in a large structure **3** archaic a dwelling

manslaughter n the unlawful killing of sby without malicious intent

mantelpiece, mantel n an ornamental structure round a fireplace; also a mantelshelf

mantelshelf, mantel n a shelf forming part of or above a mantelpiece

mantilla n a light scarf worn over the head and shoulders esp by Spanish and Latin-American women

mantis n, pl **mantises, mantes** any of several insects that feed on other insects; esp PRAYING MANTIS

¹**mantle** n **1a** a loose sleeveless garment worn over other clothes; a cloak **b** a mantle regarded as a symbol of preeminence or authority **2a** sthg that covers, envelops, or conceals **b** a fold of a tunicate's, barnacle's, or mollusc's body wall (lining the shell) **3** the feathers covering the back, shoulders,and wings of a bird **4** a lacelike sheath of some reflecting material that gives light by incandescence when placed over a flame **5** the part of the earth or a similar planet that lies between the crust and central core

²**mantle** vt to cover (as if) with a mantle

man-to-man adj **1** characterized by frankness and honesty **2** of or being a defensive system in soccer, basketball, etc in which each player marks 1 specific opponent

mantrap n a trap for catching people

¹**manual** adj **1** of or involving the hands **2** requiring or using physical skill and energy **3** worked or done by hand and not by machine or automatically – **manually** adv

²**manual** n **1** a book of instructions; a handbook **2** the set movements in the handling of a weapon during a military drill or ceremony **3** a keyboard for the hands; specif any of the several keyboards of an organ that control separate divisions of the instrument

¹**manufacture** n **1** the esp large-scale making of wares by hand or by machinery **2** an industry using mechanical power and machinery **3** the act or process of producing sthg

²**manufacture** vt **1** to make (materials) into a product suitable for use **2** to make (wares) from raw materials by hand or by machinery, esp on a large scale **3** to invent, fabricate **4** to produce as if by manufacturing ⟨writers who ~ stories for television⟩ – **manufacturing** n

manufacturer *n* an employer in a manufacturing industry

manumit *vt* **-tt-** to release from slavery – **manumission** *n*

¹manure *vt* to enrich (land) by the application of manure – **manurer** *n*

²manure *n* material that fertilizes land; *esp* the faeces of domestic animals – **manurial** *adj*

manuscript *n or adj* (a composition or document) written by hand or typed as distinguished from a printed copy

¹Manx *adj* (characteristic) of the Isle of Man

²Manx *n* **1** *pl in constr* the people of the Isle of Man **2** the almost extinct Celtic language of the Manx people

Manx cat *n* (any of) a breed of short-haired domestic cats some of which have no external tail

¹many *adj* **more; most 1** consisting of or amounting to a large but unspecified number ⟨*worked for ~ years*⟩ ⟨*many-sided*⟩ **2** being one of a large number ⟨*~ a man*⟩ ⟨*~ is the time I've wondered*⟩ – **as many** the same in number ⟨*saw 3 plays in* as many *days*⟩

²many *pron pl in constr* a large number of people or things ⟨*~ prefer to stay at home*⟩ ⟨*I haven't got as ~ as you*⟩

³many *n pl in constr* **1** a large but indefinite number ⟨*a good ~ of them have already left*⟩ **2** the great majority

⁴many *adv* to a considerable degree or amount; far – with plurals ⟨*~ more cars than usual*⟩

many-sided *adj* **1** having many sides or aspects **2** having many interests or aptitudes – **many-sidedness** *n*

Maoism *n* Marxism-Leninism as developed in China chiefly by Mao Tse-tung – **Maoist** *n or adj*

Maori *n, pl* **Maoris,** *esp collectively* **Maori 1** a member of the indigenous people of New Zealand **2** the Austronesian language of the Maori

¹map *n* **1** a representation, usu on a flat surface, of (part of) the earth's surface, the celestial sphere, etc **2** sthg that represents with a clarity suggestive of a map

²map *vt* **-pp- 1a** to make a map of **b** to delineate as if on a map **c** to survey in order to make a map **2** to assign to every element of (a mathematical set) an element of the same or another set **3** to plan in detail – often + *out* ⟨*~ out a programme*⟩ – **mappable** *adj*, **mapper** *n*

maple *n* (the hard light-coloured close-grained wood, used esp for furniture, of) any of a genus of widely planted trees or shrubs

maple sugar *n* sugar made by boiling maple syrup

maquis *n, pl* **maquis 1** (an area of) thick scrubby underbrush of Mediterranean shores **2a** *often cap* a member of the French Resistance during WW II **b** *sing or pl in constr* a band of maquis

mar *vt* **-rr-** to detract from the perfection or wholeness of

marabou, marabout *n* a large African stork

maraschino *n, pl* **maraschinos** *often cap* **1** a sweet liqueur distilled from the fermented juice of a bitter wild cherry **2** a usu large cherry preserved in true or imitation maraschino

marathon *n* **1** a long-distance race; *specif* a foot race of 26mi 385yd (about 42.2km) that is contested on an open course in major athletics championships **2a** an endurance contest **b** an event or activity characterized by great length or concentrated effort

maraud *vi* to roam about in search of plunder ~ *vt* to raid, pillage – **marauder** *n*

¹marble *n* **1a** (more or less) crystallized limestone that can be highly polished and is used esp in building and sculpture **b** a sculpture or carving made of marble **2a** a little ball made of a hard substance, esp glass, and used in

children's games **b** *pl but sing in constr* any of several games played with marbles, the object of which is to hit a mark or hole, to hit another player's marble, or to knock as many marbles as possible out of a ring **3** marbling **4** *pl* elements of common sense; *esp* sanity – infml ⟨*he's lost his ~!*⟩

²marble *vb* **marbling** to give a veined or mottled appearance to (e g the edges of a book) – **marbling** *n*

marbled *adj* **1a** made of or veneered with marble **b** marked by an extensive use of marble as an architectural or decorative feature ⟨*ancient ~ cities*⟩ **2** *of meat* marked by a mixture of fat and lean

marc *n* **1** the organic residue remaining after an extraction process (e g the pressing of grapes) **2** brandy made from the residue of grapes after pressing

marcasite *n* (a piece of) crystallized iron pyrites or a similar mineral, used esp for jewellery

¹march *n, often cap* a border region; *esp* a tract of land between 2 countries whose ownership is disputed – usu *pl* ⟨*the Welsh ~es*⟩

²march *vi* to have common borders or frontiers ⟨*a region that ~es with Canada in the north*⟩

³march *vi* **1** to move along steadily, usu in step with others **2a** to move in a direct purposeful manner **b** to make steady progress ⟨*time ~es on*⟩ ~ *vt* **1** to cause to march ⟨*~ed him off to the police station*⟩ **2** to cover by marching ⟨*~ed 30 miles*⟩

⁴march *n* **1a** the action of marching **b** the distance covered within a specified period of time by marching **c** a regular measured stride or rhythmic step used in marching **d** steady forward movement **2** a musical composition, usu in duple or quadruple time, that has a strongly accentuated beat and is designed or suitable to accompany marching – **on the march** moving steadily; advancing

March *n* the 3rd month of the Gregorian calendar

marching orders *n pl* **1** official notice for troops to move **2** notice of dismissal ⟨*the player was given his ~ after the brutal foul*⟩

marchioness *n* **1** the wife or widow of a marquess **2** a woman having in her own right the rank of a marquess

Mardi Gras *n* (a carnival period culminating on) Shrove Tuesday often observed (e g in New Orleans) with parades and festivities

¹mare *n* a female equine animal, esp when fully mature or of breeding age; *esp* a female horse

²mare *n, pl* **maria** any of several large dark areas on the surface of the moon or Mars

mare's nest *n, pl* **mare's nests, mares' nests** a false discovery, illusion, or deliberate hoax

margarine *n* a substitute for butter made usu from vegetable oils churned with ripened skimmed milk to a smooth emulsion

¹margin *n* **1** the part of a page outside the main body of printed or written text **2** the outside limit and adjoining surface of sthg **3a** a spare amount or measure or degree allowed (e g in case of error) **b(1)** a bare minimum below which or an extreme limit beyond which sthg becomes impossible or is no longer desirable **(2)** the limit below which economic activity cannot be continued under normal conditions **4** the difference between net sales and the cost of merchandise sold **5** measure or degree of difference – **margined** *adj*

²margin *vt* to provide with a border

¹marginal *adj* **1** written or printed in the margin **2** of or situated at a margin or border **3** close to the lower limit of qualification, acceptability, or function **4** of or providing a nominal profit margin **5** being a constituency where the Member of Parliament was elected with only a small majority – **marginally** *adv*, **marginality** *n*

²**marginal** n a marginal constituency

marguerite n (a single-flowered chrysanthemum like) an oxeye daisy

marigold n any of a genus of composite plants with showy yellow or red flower heads

marijuana, marihuana n 1 HEMP 1 2 a usu mild form of cannabis

marimba n a percussion instrument resembling a large xylophone

marina n a dock or basin providing secure moorings for motorboats, yachts, etc

marinade vt or n (to soak in) a blend of oil, wine or vinegar, herbs, and spices in which meat, fish, etc is soaked, esp to enrich its flavour

marinate vt to marinade

¹**marine** adj 1 of or (living) in the sea 2 of or used in the navigation or commerce of the sea ⟨a ~ chart⟩⟨~ law⟩

²**marine** n 1 seagoing ships (of a specified nationality or class) ⟨the mercantile ~⟩ 2a any of a class of soldiers serving on shipboard or in close association with a naval force **b** a person holding the lowest rank in the Royal Marines 3 a seascape

mariner n a seaman, sailor

marionette n a small-scale usu wooden figure with jointed limbs that is moved from above by attached strings or wires

marital adj of marriage – **maritally** adv

maritime adj 1 MARINE 2 2 of or bordering on the sea

marjoram n any of various plants of the mint family used as herbs; also oregano

¹**mark** n **1a(1)** a conspicuous object serving as a guide for travellers **(2)** sthg (e g a line, notch, or fixed object) designed to record position **b** any of the points on a sounding line that correspond to a depth in whole fathoms **c** TARGET **2a** the starting line or position in a track event **d** a goal or desired object **e** a goal or desired object **f** the point under discussion ⟨that comment was rather off the ~⟩ **g** an established or accepted standard of performance, quality, or condition ⟨his singing was hardly up to the ~⟩ **2a(1)** a sign or token ⟨a ~ of his esteem⟩ **(2)** an impression on the surface of sthg; esp a scratch, stain, etc that spoils the appearance of a surface **(3)** a distinguishing characteristic ⟨bears the ~ of an educated woman⟩ **b(1)** a symbol used for identification or indication of ownership **(2)** a symbol, esp a cross, made in place of a signature **c** a written or printed symbol ⟨punctuation ~s⟩ **d** cap – used with a numeral to designate a particular model of a weapon or machine ⟨Mark II⟩ **e** a symbol representing a judgment of merit, esp one used by a teacher ⟨a point or level (reached) ⟨passed the halfway ~⟩ **3a** attention, notice ⟨nothing worthy of ~ occurred⟩ **b** importance, distinction ⟨a person of little ~⟩ **c** a lasting or strong impression ⟨years of warfare have left their ~ on the country⟩ **d** an assessment of merits ⟨got high ~s for honesty⟩ **4** an object of attack; specif a victim of a swindle – infml

²**mark** vt **1a(1)** to fix or trace out the limits of **(2)** to plot the course of **b** to set apart (as if) by a line or boundary – usu + off **2a(1)** to designate or identify (as if) by a mark ⟨~ed for greatness⟩ **(2)** to make or leave a mark on **(3)** to label (merchandise) so as to indicate price or quality **(4)** to add appropriate symbols, characters, or other marks to or on ⟨~ the manuscript for the printer⟩ – usu + up **b(1)** to indicate by a mark ⟨X ~s the spot⟩ **(2)** to register, record ⟨~ the date in your diary⟩ **(3)** to evaluate by marks ⟨~ examination papers⟩ **c(1)** to characterize, distinguish ⟨the flamboyance that ~s her stage appearance⟩ **(2)** to be the occasion of (sthg notable); to indicate as a particular time ⟨this year ~s the 50th anniversary of

the organization⟩ **3** to take notice of ⟨~ what I say⟩ **4** Br to stay close to (an opposing player) in hockey, soccer, etc so as to hinder the getting or play of the ball ~ vi **1** to become or make sthg stained, scratched, etc ⟨it won't ~ will it?⟩ **2** to evaluate sthg by marks – **marker** n – **mark time 1** to keep the time of a marching step by moving the feet alternately without advancing **2** to function listlessly or unproductively while waiting to progress or advance

³**mark** n **1** often cap (a note or coin representing) the basic money unit of either East or West Germany **2** a markka

Mark n the 2nd Gospel in the New Testament

markdown n (the amount of) a reduction in price – **mark down** vt

marked adj **1a** having natural marks (of a specified type) ⟨wings ~ with white⟩ **b** made identifiable by marking ⟨a ~ card⟩ **2** having a distinctive or emphasized character ⟨a ~ American accent⟩ **3** being an object of attack, suspicion, or vengeance ⟨a ~ man⟩ **4** distinguished from a basic form (e g the singular) by the presence of a particular linguistic feature (e g s indicating the plural form) – **markedly** adv

¹**market** n **1a** a meeting together of people for the purpose of trade, by private purchase and sale **b** an open space, building, etc where a market (e g for trading in provisions or livestock) is held **2a** (a geographical area or section of the community in which there is) demand for commodities ⟨the foreign ~⟩ **b** commercial activity; extent of trading **c** an opportunity for selling ⟨create new ~s for our product⟩ **d** the area of economic activity in which the forces of supply and demand affect prices ⟨~ value⟩ – **in the market** interested in buying ⟨in the market for a house⟩ – **on the market** available for purchase

²**market** vi to deal in a market ~ vt to sell – **marketable** adj, **marketability** n

market garden n a plot in which vegetables are grown for market – **market gardener** n, **market gardening** n

marketing n the skills and functions, including packaging, promotion, and distribution, involved in selling goods

marketplace n **1** an open place in a town where markets are held **2** MARKET 2c, d

market research n research (e g the collection and analysis of information about consumer preferences) dealing with the patterns or state of demand (for a particular product) in a market

marking n **1** (the giving of) a mark or marks **2** arrangement, pattern, or disposition of marks

marking ink n indelible ink for marking fabric

markka n, pl **markkaa, markkas** the standard unit of money in Finland

marksman, fem **markswoman** n, pl **marksmen,** fem **markswomen** a person skilled in hitting a mark or target – **marksmanship** n

markup n (the amount of) an increase in price – **mark up** vt

marl vt or n (to fertilize with) a crumbly earthy deposit (e g of silt or clay) that contains calcium carbonate and is used esp as a fertilizer for lime-deficient soils – **marly** adj

marlinespike, marlinspike n a pointed steel tool used to separate strands of rope or wire

¹**marmalade** n a clear sweetened preserve made from oranges, lemons, etc and usu containing pieces of fruit peel

²**marmalade** adj, esp of cats brownish orange

marmoreal, also **marmorean** adj of or like marble or a marble statue – chiefly poetic

marmoset *n* any of numerous soft-furred S and Central American monkeys

marmot *n* any of several stout-bodied short-legged small-eared burrowing rodents

¹maroon *vt* 1 to abandon on a desolate island or coast 2 to isolate in a helpless state

²maroon *n* 1 a dark brownish red 2 an explosive rocket used esp as a distress signal

Maroon *n* (a descendant of) a fugitive Negro slave of the W Indies and Guiana in the 17th and 18th c

marquee *n* 1 a large tent (e g for an outdoor party or exhibition) 2 *NAm* a permanent canopy projecting over an entrance (e g of a hotel or theatre)

marquess, marquis *n, pl* **marquesses, marquises, marquis** (a European nobleman equivalent in rank to) a member of the British peerage ranking below a duke and above an earl – **marquessate, marquisate** *n*

marquetry *also* **marqueterie** *n* decorative work of pieces of wood, ivory, etc inlaid in a wood veneer that is then applied to a surface (e g of a piece of furniture)

marram grass *n* any of several strong wiry grasses that grow on sandy shores and prevent erosion

marriage *n* 1a the state of being or mutual relation of husband and wife b the institution whereby a man and a woman are joined in a special kind of social and legal dependence 2 an act or the rite of marrying; *esp* the wedding ceremony 3 an intimate or close union – **marriageable** *adj*

¹married *adj* 1a joined in marriage b of married people 2 united, joined

²married *n* a married person ⟨*young* ~*s*⟩

marrow *n* 1a a soft tissue that fills the cavities and porous part of most bones and contains many blood vessels b the substance of the spinal cord 2 the inmost, best, or essential part; the core 3 *chiefly Br* VEGETABLE MARROW – **marrowless** *adj*, **marrowy** *adj*

marrowbone *n* a bone rich in marrow

marrowfat *n* any of several types of large pea

¹marry *vt* 1a to give in marriage b to take as spouse c to perform the ceremony of marriage for d to obtain by marriage ⟨*she* married *money*⟩ 2 to bring together closely, harmoniously, and usu permanently ~ *vi* 1a to take a spouse b to become husband and wife 2 to join in a close or harmonious relationship – **marry into** to become a member of or obtain by marriage ⟨married into a prominent family⟩

²marry *interj, archaic* – used for emphasis, esp to express amused or surprised agreement

Mars *n* the planet 4th in order from the sun and conspicuous for its red colour

Marsala *n* a (sweet) fortified wine from Sicily

marsh *n* (an area of) soft wet land usu covered with sedges, rushes, etc – **marshy** *adj*, **marshiness** *n*

¹marshal *n* 1a a high official in a medieval royal household b one who arranges and directs a ceremony c one who arranges the procedure at races 2a FIELD MARSHAL b an officer of the highest military rank 3a a chief officer in the USA responsible for court processes in a district b the head of a US police or fire department – **marshalcy, marshalship** *n*

²marshal *vb* -ll- (*NAm* -l-, -ll-), *vt* 1 to place in proper rank or position 2 to bring together and order in an effective way ⟨~ *one's thoughts*⟩ 3 to lead ceremoniously or solicitously; usher ~ *vi* to form or collect together (in a proper order)

marshalling yard *n, chiefly Br* a place where railway vehicles are shunted and assembled into trains

Marshal of the Royal Air Force *n* an officer of the highest rank in the Royal Air Force

marsh gas *n* methane

marshmallow *n* 1 a pink-flowered Eurasian marsh plant of the mallow family 2 a light spongy confection made from the root of the marshmallow or from sugar, albumen, and gelatin – **marshmallowy** *adj*

marsh marigold *n* a European and N American marsh plant of the buttercup family with large bright yellow flowers

¹marsupial *adj* 1 of or being a marsupial 2 of or forming a marsupium or pouch

²marsupial *n* any of an order of lower mammals including the kangaroos, wombats, and opossums that have a pouch on the abdomen of the female for carrying young, and do not develop a placenta

mart *n* a place of trade (e g an auction room or market)

marten *n, pl* **martens,** *esp collectively* **marten** any of several slender-bodied flesh-eating tree-dwelling mammals larger than the related weasels

martial *adj* of or suited to war or a warrior; *also* warlike – **martially** *adv*

martial law *n* the law administered by military forces in occupied territory or in an emergency

Martian *adj* of or coming from the planet Mars – **Martian** *n*

martin *n* any of various birds of the swallow family: e g a a house martin b a sand martin

martinet *n* a strict disciplinarian

martini *n* a cocktail made of gin and dry vermouth

Martinmas *n* November 11 celebrated as the feast of St Martin

¹martyr *n* 1 one who is put to death for adherence to a cause, esp a religion 2 a victim, esp of constant (self-inflicted) suffering – **martyrize** *vt*, **martyrdom** *n*, **martyrization** *n*

²martyr *vt* 1 to put to death as a martyr 2 to inflict agonizing pain on

¹marvel *n* one who or that which is marvellous

²marvel *vi* -ll- (*NAm* -l-, -ll-), to become filled with surprise, wonder, or amazed curiosity

marvellous, *NAm chiefly* **marvelous** *adj* 1 causing wonder 2 of the highest kind or quality – **marvellously** *adv*, **marvellousness** *n*

Marxism *n* the political and economic principles and policies advocated by Karl Marx, that stress the importance of human labour in determining economic value, the struggle between classes as an instrument of social change, and dictatorship of the proletariat – **Marxist** *n or adj*, **Marxian** *adj*

Marxism-Leninism *n* a theory and practice of communism developed by Lenin from the doctrines of Marx – **Marxist-Leninist** *n or adj*

marzipan *n* a paste made from ground almonds, sugar, and egg whites, used for coating cakes or shaped into small sweets

mascara *n* a cosmetic for colouring, esp darkening, the eyelashes

mascot *n* a person, animal, or object adopted as a (good luck) symbol

¹masculine *adj* 1a male b having qualities appropriate to a man ⟨*her deep* ~ *voice*⟩ 2 of, belonging to, or being the gender that normally includes most words or grammatical forms referring to males 3 having or occurring in a stressed final syllable – **masculinely** *adv*, **masculineness** *n*, **masculinize** *vt*, **masculinity** *n*

²masculine *n* (a word or morpheme of) the masculine gender

maser *n* a device that works like a laser for amplifying or generating (microwave) radiation

¹**mash** n 1 crushed malt or grain meal steeped and stirred in hot water to ferment 2 a mixture of bran or similar feeds and usu hot water for livestock 3 a soft pulpy mass 4 Br mashed potatoes – infml

²**mash** vt 1 to crush, pound, etc to a soft pulpy state 2 to heat and stir (e g crushed malt) in water to prepare wort – **masher** n

¹**mask** n 1a a (partial) cover for the face used for disguise or protection b(1) a figure of a head worn on the stage in ancient times to identify the character (2) a grotesque false face worn at carnivals or in rituals c a copy of a face made by sculpting or by means of a mould 2a sthg that disguises or conceals; esp a pretence, facade b a translucent or opaque screen to cover part of the sensitive surface in taking or printing a photograph 3 a device covering the mouth and nose used a to promote breathing (e g by connection to an oxygen supply) b to remove noxious gas from air c to prevent exhalation of infective material (e g during surgery) 4 a face-pack 5 the head or face of a fox, dog, etc

²**mask** vt 1 to provide, cover, or conceal (as if) with a mask: e g a to make indistinct or imperceptible ⟨~s the strong flavour⟩ b to cover up ⟨~ed his real purpose⟩ 2 to cover for protection 3 to modify the shape of (e g a photograph) by means of a mask

masochism n 1 a sexual perversion in which pleasure is experienced from being physically or mentally abused 2 pleasure from sthg tiresome or painful – not used technically – **masochist** n, **masochistic** adj, **masochistically** adv

mason n 1 a skilled worker with stone 2 cap a freemason

Mason-Dixon line n the S boundary line of Pennsylvania; also the boundary line between the free N and slave-owning S states of the USA

Masonic adj (characteristic) of Freemasons or Freemasonry

masonry n 1 work done with or sthg constructed of stone; also a brick construction 2 cap FREEMASONRY 1

masque n 1 MASQUERADE 1 2 a short allegorical dramatic entertainment of the 16th and 17th c performed by masked actors

¹**masquerade** n 1 a social gathering of people wearing masks and often fantastic costumes 2 sthg that is merely show

²**masquerade** vi 1 to disguise oneself; also to wear a disguise 2 to assume the appearance of sthg that one is not – usu + as – **masquerader** n

¹**mass** n 1 cap the liturgy or a celebration of the Eucharist, esp in Roman Catholic and Anglo-Catholic churches 2 a musical setting for the ordinary of the Mass

²**mass** n 1a a quantity of matter or the form of matter that holds together in 1 body b(1) an (unbroken) expanse ⟨a mountain ~⟩ ⟨a ~ of colour⟩ (2) the principal part or main body (3) a total, whole – esp in in the mass c the property of a body that is a measure of its inertia, causes it to have weight in a gravitational field, and is commonly taken as a measure of the amount of material it contains 2 a large quantity, amount, or number – often pl with sing. meaning ⟨there was ~es of food left⟩ 3 pl the body of ordinary people as contrasted with the élite – **massless** adj

³**mass** vb to assemble in or collect into a mass

⁴**mass** adj 1a of, designed for, or consisting of the mass of the people ⟨a ~ market⟩ b participated in by or affecting a large number of individuals ⟨~ murder⟩ c large scale 2 viewed as a whole; total

¹**massacre** vt 1 to kill (as if) in a massacre 2 to defeat severely; also MANGLE 2 – infml – **massacrer** n

²**massacre** n 1 the ruthless and indiscriminate killing of large numbers 2 complete defeat or destruction

massage n (an act of) kneading, rubbing, etc of the body in order to relieve aches, tone muscles, give relaxation, etc – **massage** vt, **massager** n

masseur, fem **masseuse** n one who practises massage and physiotherapy

massif n 1 a principal mountain mass 2 a mountainous block bounded by faults or folds and displaced as a unit

massive adj 1a large, solid, or heavy b impressively large or ponderous c of a mineral not obviously crystalline 2a large or impressive in scope or degree b large in comparison to what is typical ⟨a ~ dose of penicillin⟩ c extensive and severe ⟨~ haemorrhage⟩ – **massively** adv, **massiveness** n

mass media n pl broadcasting, newspapers, and other means of communication designed to reach large numbers of people

mass-produce vt to produce (goods) in large quantities by standardized mechanical processes – **mass production** n

massy adj massive, heavy – fml

¹**mast** n 1 a tall pole or structure rising from the keel or deck of a ship, esp for carrying sails 2 a vertical pole or lattice supporting a radio or television aerial – **before the mast** as an ordinary sailor, not an officer

²**mast** vt to give a mast to

³**mast** n beechnuts, acorns, etc accumulated on the forest floor and often serving as food for animals (e g pigs)

mastectomy n excision or amputation of a breast

¹**master** n 1a(1) a male teacher (2) a person holding an academic degree higher than a bachelor's but lower than a doctor's b often cap a revered religious leader c a workman qualified to teach apprentices ⟨a ~ carpenter⟩ d an artist, performer, player, etc of consummate skill 2a one having control or authority over another b one who or that which conquers or masters; a victor c a person qualified to command a merchant ship d(1) an owner, esp of a slave or animal (2) often cap one who directs a hunt and has overall control of the pack of hounds e an employer f the male head of a household 3 cap a youth or boy too young to be called mister – used as a title 4 a presiding officer in an institution or society (e g a Masonic lodge) or at a function 5a a mechanism or device that controls the operation of another b an original from which copies (e g of film or gramophone records) can be made 6 archaic Mr – **mastership** n

²**master** vt 1 to become master of; overcome 2a to become skilled or proficient in the use of b to gain a thorough understanding of

³**master** adj 1 having chief authority; controlling 2 principal, main ⟨the ~ bedroom⟩

master-at-arms n, pl **masters-at-arms** a petty officer responsible for maintaining discipline aboard ship

masterful adj 1 inclined to take control and dominate 2 having or showing the technical, artistic, or intellectual skill of a master – **masterfully** adv, **masterfulness** n

master key n a key designed to open several different locks

masterly adj showing superior knowledge or skill – **masterliness** n

¹**mastermind** n 1 one who masterminds a project 2 a person of outstanding intellect

²**mastermind** vt to be the intellectual force behind (a project)

master of arts n, often cap M&A the recipient of a master's degree, usu in an arts subject

master of ceremonies, fem **mistress of ceremonies** n 1 one who determines the procedure to be observed on a state or public occasion **2** one who acts as host, esp by introducing speakers, performers, etc, at an event

master of science *n, often cap M&S* the recipient of a master's degree in a scientific subject

masterpiece *n* a work done with extraordinary skill; *esp* the supreme creation of a type, period, or person

masterstroke *n* a masterly performance or move

mastery *n* **1a** the authority of a master **b** the upper hand in a contest or competition **2a** possession or display of great skill or technique **b** skill or knowledge that makes one master of a subject

masthead *n* **1** the top of a mast **2** the name of a newspaper displayed on the top of the first page

mastic *n* **1** an aromatic resin that exudes from mastic trees and is used esp in varnishes **2** a pasty substance used as a protective coating or cement

masticate *vt* **1** to grind or crush (food) before swallowing, (as if) with the teeth; to chew **2** to soften or reduce to pulp (e g by crushing) ~ *vi* to chew – **masticator** *n*, **masticatory** *adj or n*, **mastication** *n*

mastiff *n* any of a breed of very large powerful deep-chested smooth-coated dogs used chiefly as guard dogs

mastitis *n* inflammation of the breast or udder, usu caused by infection – **mastitic** *adj*

mastodon *n* any of numerous extinct mammals similar to the related mammoths and elephants – **mastodont** *adj or n*, **mastodontic** *adj*

mastoid *adj or n* (of, near, or being) a somewhat conical part of the temporal bone lying behind the ear – **mastoiditis** *n*

masturbation *n* stimulation of the genitals commonly resulting in orgasm and accomplished by any means except sexual intercourse – **masturbate** *vb*, **masturbatory** *adj*

¹**mat** *n* **1a** a piece of coarse usu woven, felted, or plaited fabric (e g of rushes or rope) used esp as a floor covering; *also* RUG 1 **b** DOORMAT 1 **c** an often decorative piece of material used to protect a surface from heat, moisture, etc caused by an object placed on it **d** a large thick pad used as a protective surface for wrestling, tumbling, gymnastics, etc **2** sthg made up of many intertwined or tangled strands

²**mat** *vb* **-tt-** *vt* **1** to provide with a mat or matting **2** to form into a tangled or compact mass ~ *vi* to become tangled or intertwined

³**mat** *vt, adj, or n* **-tt-** (to) matt

matador *n* one who has the principal role and who kills the bull in a bullfight

¹**match** *n* **1a** one who or that which is equal to or able to contend with another **b** a person or thing exactly like another **2** two people, animals, or things that go well together **3** a contest between 2 or more teams or individuals **4a** a marriage union **b** a prospective partner in marriage

²**match** *vt* **1a** to be equal to (an opponent) **b** to set in competition, opposition, or comparison **2a** to cause to correspond (~ing *life-style to income*) **b(1)** to be, find, or provide the exact counterpart or equal of or for **(2)** to harmonize with **c** to provide funds complementary to **3** *archaic* to join or give in marriage ~ *vi* **1** to be a counterpart or equal **2** to harmonize – **matcher** *n*

³**match** *n* **1** a chemically prepared wick or cord formerly used in firing firearms or powder **2** a short slender piece of wood, cardboard, etc tipped with a mixture that ignites when subjected to friction

matchless *adj* having no equal – **matchlessly** *adv*

matchlock *n* (a musket with) a gunlock with a match for igniting the charge

matchmaker *n* one who arranges marriages; *also* one who derives vicarious pleasure from contriving to arrange marriages – **matchmaking** *n*

match point *n* a situation in tennis, badminton, etc in which a player will win the match by winning the next point

matchstick *n* ³MATCH 2; *specif* one made of wood

matchwood *n* wood suitable for matches; *also* wood splinters

¹**mate** *vt* CHECKMATE 2

²**mate** *n* CHECKMATE 1

³**mate** *n* **1a** an associate, companion – usu in combination (*flatmate*) (*playmate*) **b** an assistant to a more skilled workman (*plumber's* ~) **c** a friend, chum – often used in familiar address, esp to a man by a man **2a** a deck officer on a merchant ship ranking below the captain **3a** either of a pair: e g **(1)** either member of a breeding pair of animals **(2)** either of 2 matched objects **b** a marriage partner

⁴**mate** *vt* **1** to join or fit together; couple **2a** to join together as mates **b** to provide a mate for ~ *vi* **1** to become mated (*gears that* ~ *well*) **2** to copulate

maté, mate *n* **1** a tealike aromatic beverage used chiefly in S America **2** (the leaves and shoots, used in making maté, of) a S American holly

¹**material** *adj* **1a(1)** of, derived from, or consisting of matter; *esp* physical **(2)** bodily **b** of matter rather than form (~ *cause*) **2** important, significant (*facts* ~ *to the investigation*) **3** of or concerned with physical rather than spiritual things – **materially** *adv*, **materiality** *n*

²**material** *n* **1a(1)** the elements, constituents, or substances of which sthg is composed or can be made **(2)** matter that has usu specified qualities which give it individuality (*sticky* ~) **b(1)** data that may be worked into a more finished form **(2)** a person considered with a view to his/her potential for successful training (*I don't think he's officer* ~) **c** cloth **2** *pl* apparatus necessary for doing or making sthg

materialism *n* **1a** a theory that only physical matter is real and that all processes and phenomena can be explained by reference to matter **b** a doctrine that the highest values lie in material well-being and material progress **2** a preoccupation with or stress on material rather than spiritual things – **materialist** *n or adj*, **materialistic** *adj*

materialize, -ise *vb* **1** to (cause to) have existence or tangibility (~ *an idea in words*) **2** to (cause to) appear in or assume bodily form – **materialization** *n*

maternal *adj* **1** (characteristic) of a mother **2** related through a mother – **maternally** *adv*

¹**maternity** *n* **1a** motherhood **b** motherliness **2** a hospital department for the care of women before and during childbirth

²**maternity** *adj* designed for wear during pregnancy (*a* ~ *dress*)

¹**matey** *n, chiefly Br* ³MATE 1c – chiefly in familiar address

²**matey** *adj, chiefly Br* friendly – *infml* – **mateyness, matiness** *n*

mathematical *also* **mathematic** *adj* **1** of, used in, using, or according with mathematics **2** rigorously exact – **mathematically** *adv*

mathematics *n pl but sing or pl in constr* **1** the science of numbers and their operations, interrelations, and combinations and of space configurations and their structure, measurement, etc **2** the mathematics or mathematical operations involved in a particular problem, field of study, etc – **mathematician** n

matinée, matinee n a musical or dramatic performance during the day, esp the afternoon

matinee jacket n, Br a cardigan worn by babies

matins n pl but sing or pl in constr often cap **1** the (night) office forming with lauds the first of the canonical hours **2** MORNING PRAYER

matr-, matri- also **matro-** comb form mother ⟨matriarch⟩ ⟨matronymic⟩

matriarch n a woman who rules a family, group, or state; specif a mother who is the head of her family – **matriarchal** adj

matriarchy n a (system of) social organization in which the female is the head of the family, and descent and inheritance are traced through the female line

matricide n (the act of) one who kills his/her mother – **matricidal** adj

matriculate vt to enrol as a member of a body, esp a college or university ~ vi to become eligible) to be matriculated – **matriculation** n

matrimony n MARRIAGE 1 – **matrimonial** adj, **matrimonially** adv

matrix n, pl **matrices, matrixes 1** a substance, environment, etc within which sthg else originates or develops **2** a mould in which sthg is cast or from which a surface in relief (e g a piece of type) is made by pouring or pressing **3** the (natural) material in which sthg (e g a fossil, gem, or specimen for study) is embedded **4** the substance between the cells of a tissue that holds them together **5** a rectangular array of mathematical elements treated as a unit and subject to special algebraic laws

matron n **1a** a (dignified mature) married woman **b** a woman in charge of living arrangements in a school, residential home, etc **2** Br a woman in charge of the nursing in a hospital – not now used technically – **matronly** adj

¹**matt, mat, matte** vt to make (e g metal or colour) matt

²**matt, mat, matte** adj lacking lustre or gloss; esp having an even surface free from shine or highlights

³**matt, mat, matte** n **1** a border round a picture between the picture and frame or serving as the frame **2** a dull or roughened finish (e g on gilt or paint)

¹**matter** n **1a** a subject of interest or concern or which merits attention **b** an affair, concern ⟨it's no laughing ~⟩ **c** material (for treatment) in thought, discourse, or writing **d** that part of a legal case which deals with facts rather than law **e** a condition (unfavourably) affecting a person or thing ⟨what's the ~?⟩ **2a** the substance of which a physical object is composed **b** material substance that occupies space and has mass **c** sth of a specified kind or for a specified purpose ⟨mineral ~⟩ ⟨reading ~⟩ **d**(1) material (e g faeces or urine) discharged from the living body (2) material discharged by suppuration; pus **3** the formless substratum of all existing things **4** a more or less definite amount or quantity ⟨a ~ of 10 years⟩ – **as a matter of fact** as it happens; actually – often used in correcting a misapprehension – **for that matter** so far as that is concerned – **no matter** it does not matter; irrespective of ⟨would be calm no matter what the provocation⟩

²**matter** vi **1** to be of importance **2** to form or discharge pus

matter of course n sthg routine or to be expected as a natural consequence

matter-of-fact adj keeping to or concerned with fact; esp not fanciful or imaginative – **matter-of-factly** adv, **matter-of-factness** n

matting n material (e g hemp) for mats

mattock n a digging tool with a head like that of a pick and often a blade like that of an axe or adze

mattress n a fabric casing filled with resilient material (e g foam rubber or an arrangement of coiled springs) used esp on a bed

¹**mature** adj **1** based on careful consideration ⟨a ~ judgment⟩ **2a** having completed natural growth and development; ripe **b** having attained a final or desired state **3a** (characteristic) of or having a condition of full or adult development **b** older or more experienced than others of his/her kind ⟨a ~ student⟩ **4** due for payment ⟨a ~ loan⟩ – **maturely** adv, **matureness, maturity** n

²**mature** vt to bring to full development or completion ~ vi **1** to become mature **2** to become due for payment – **maturation** n, **maturational** adj

maudlin adj **1** weakly and effusively sentimental **2** drunk enough to be emotionally silly

¹**maul** vt **1** esp of an animal to attack and tear the flesh of **2** to handle roughly – **mauler** n

²**maul** n **1** a situation in Rugby Union in which 1 or more players from each team close round the player carrying the ball who tries to get the ball out to his own team **2** a confused and noisy struggle

maulstick, mahlstick n a stick used by painters to support and steady the hand while working

maunder vi **1** to act or wander idly **2** to speak in a rambling or indistinct manner; also, Br to grumble – **maunderer** n

Maundy Thursday n the Thursday before Easter observed in commemoration of the Last Supper

mausoleum n, pl **mausoleums** also **mausolea** a large and elaborate tomb

mauve n or adj bluish purple

maverick n **1** an independent and nonconformist individual **2** NAm an unbranded range animal; esp a motherless calf

maw n **1a** an animal's stomach or crop **b** the throat, gullet, or jaws, esp of a voracious flesh-eating animal **2** sthg resembling a maw, esp in gaping or tending to swallow things up

mawkish adj **1** having an insipid often unpleasant taste **2** sickly or feebly sentimental – **mawkishly** adv, **mawkishness** n

maxi n, pl **maxis** a floor-length woman's coat, skirt, etc

maxi- comb form **1** extra long ⟨maxi-skirt⟩ **2** extra large ⟨maxi-budget⟩

maxim n (a succinct expression of) a general truth, fundamental principle, or rule of conduct

maximal adj **1** greatest; most comprehensive **2** being an upper limit – **maximally** adv

maximize, ise vt to increase to a maximum or to the highest possible degree – **maximization** n

maximum n, pl **maxima, maximums 1** the greatest quantity or value attainable or attained **2** the period of highest or most extreme development – **maximum** adj

may verbal auxiliary, pres sing & pl **may**; past **might** va **1a** have permission to ⟨you ~ go now⟩; have liberty to ⟨what's this, ~ I ask?⟩ **b** be in some degree likely to ⟨you ~ be right⟩ ⟨the road ~ well be closed⟩ **2** – used to express a wish or desire, esp in prayer, curse, or benediction ⟨long ~ he reign⟩ **3** – used to express purpose or expectation ⟨sit here so I ~ see you better⟩, contingency ⟨he'll do his duty come what ~⟩, or concession ⟨he ~ be slow but he is thorough⟩; used in questions to emphasize ironic uncertainty ⟨and who ~ you be?⟩

May n **1** the 5th month of the Gregorian calendar **2** not cap (the blossom of) hawthorn

maybe adv perhaps

Mayday – used for an international radiotelephone signal word used as a distress call

May Day n May 1 celebrated as a springtime festival and in many countries as a public holiday in honour of working people

mayfly n any of an order of insects with an aquatic nymph and a short-lived fragile adult with membranous wings

mayhem n 1 needless or wilful damage 2 a state of great confusion or disorder

mayn't may not

mayonnaise n a thick dressing (e g for salad) made with egg yolks, vegetable oil, and vinegar or lemon juice

mayor n the chief executive or nominal head of a city or borough – **mayoral** adj

mayoralty n the (term of) office of a mayor

mayoress n 1 the wife or hostess of a mayor 2 a female mayor

maypole n a tall ribbon-wreathed pole forming a centre for dances, esp on May Day

mayst mayest

¹**maze** vt, archaic to bewilder, perplex

²**maze** n 1a (a drawn representation of) a network of paths designed to confuse and puzzle those who attempt to walk through it b sthg intricately or confusingly complicated 2 archaic a state of bewilderment – **mazy** adj

mazurka also **mazourka** n (music for, or in the rhythm of) a Polish folk dance in moderate triple time

MC n MASTER OF CEREMONIES

¹**me** pron, objective case of I ⟨looked at ~⟩ ⟨fatter than ~⟩ ⟨it's ~⟩

²**me** n sthg suitable for me ⟨that dress isn't really ~⟩

³**me** n the 3rd note of the diatonic scale in solmization

¹**mead** n a fermented alcoholic drink made of water, honey, malt, and yeast

²**mead** n a meadow – archaic or poetic

meadow n (an area of moist low-lying usu level) grassland

meadowsweet n a tall Eurasian plant of the rose family with creamy-white fragrant flowers

meagre, NAm chiefly **meager** adj 1 having little flesh 2 deficient in quality or quantity – **meagrely** adv, **meagreness** n

¹**meal** n 1 the portion of food taken or provided at 1 time to satisfy appetite 2 (the time of) eating a meal

²**meal** n (a product resembling, esp in texture) the usu coarsely ground seeds of a cereal grass or pulse

mealie n, SAfr (an ear of) maize

mealtime n the usual time for a meal

mealy adj 1 soft, dry, and crumbly 2 containing meal 3a covered with meal or fine granules b esp of a horse flecked with another colour

mealybug n any of numerous scale insects with a white powdery covering that are pests, esp of fruit trees

mealy-mouthed adj unwilling to speak plainly or directly, esp when this may offend

¹**mean** adj 1 lacking distinction or eminence; merely ordinary or inferior ⟨a man of ~ estate⟩ ⟨no ~ feat⟩ 2 of poor shabby inferior quality or status 3 not honourable or worthy; base; esp small-minded 4a not generous b characterized by petty malice; spiteful c chiefly NAm particularly bad-tempered, unpleasant, or disagreeable d excellent, impressive – infml ⟨blows a ~ trumpet – Globe & Mail (Toronto)⟩ – **meanly** adv, **meanness** n

²**mean** vb **meant** vt 1 to have in mind as a purpose; intend ⟨she ~t no offence⟩ ⟨I ~ to leave soon⟩ 2 to serve or intend to convey, produce, or indicate; signify ⟨red ~s danger⟩ ⟨this action will ~ war⟩ 3 to intend for a particular use or purpose ⟨it is ~t to relieve pain⟩ ⟨I ~t it as a warning⟩ 4 to have significance or importance to

the extent or degree of ⟨health ~s everything⟩ ~ vi to have an intended purpose – chiefly in to mean well/ill –

I mean – used to introduce and emphasize a clause or sentence or when hesitating ⟨it wasn't too bad. I mean it didn't even hurt⟩ – **mean business** to be in earnest

³**mean** n 1a a middle point between extremes b a value that lies within a range of values and is computed according to a prescribed law; esp ARITHMETIC MEAN 2 pl but sing or pl in constr that which enables a desired purpose to be achieved; also the method used to attain an end 3 pl resources available for disposal; esp wealth ⟨a man of ~s⟩

⁴**mean** adj 1 occupying a middle position; intermediate in space, order, time, kind, or degree 2 being the mean of a set of values ⟨~ temperature⟩

¹**meander** n a turn or winding of a stream – usu pl

²**meander** vi 1 to follow a winding course 2 to wander aimlessly without urgent destination

¹**meaning** n 1 that which is conveyed or which one intends to convey, esp by language 2 significant quality; value ⟨this has no ~ in law⟩ 3 implication of a hidden or special significance ⟨a glance full of ~⟩ – **meaningful** adj, **meaningfully** adv, **meaningfulness** n, **meaningless** adj, **meaninglessly** adv, **meaninglessness** n

²**meaning** adj significant, expressive – **meaningly** adv

means test n an examination into sby's financial state to determine his/her eligibility for public assistance, for a student grant, etc

meant adj, past of MEAN Br expected, supposed ⟨to get a mature student's place you are ~ to have a minimum of five O-levels – Observer Magazine⟩

¹**meantime** n the intervening time ⟨in the ~⟩

²**meantime** adv meanwhile

mean time n time that is based on the motion of the mean sun and that has the mean solar second as its unit

¹**meanwhile** n the meantime

²**meanwhile** adv 1 during the intervening time 2 during the same period ⟨~, down on the farm⟩

measles n pl but sing or pl in constr 1 (German measles or another disease similar to) an infectious virus disease marked by a rash of distinct red circular spots 2 infestation with larval tapeworms, esp in pigs or pork

measly adj 1 infected with measles 2 containing larval tapeworms ⟨~ pork⟩ 3 contemptibly small; also worthless – infml

¹**measure** n 1a(1) an appropriate or due portion ⟨had their ~ of luck⟩ (2) a (moderate) extent, amount, or degree ⟨a ~ of respectability⟩ (3) a fixed, suitable, or conceivable limit ⟨wisdom beyond ~⟩ b(1) the dimensions, capacity, or amount of sthg ascertained by measuring (2) the character, nature, or capacity of sby or sthg ascertained by assessment – esp in get the measure of (3) the width of a full line of type c a measured quantity ⟨a ~ of whisky⟩ ⟨short ~⟩ 2a an instrument or utensil for measuring b(1) a standard or unit of measurement ⟨the metre is a ~ of length⟩ (2) a system of standard units of measure ⟨metric ~⟩ ⟨liquid ~⟩ 3a a (slow and stately) dance b(1) poetic rhythm measured by quantity or accent; specif ²METRE 1 (2) musical time c(1) the notes and rests that form a bar of music (2) a metrical unit; FOOT 4 4 an exact divisor or factor of a quantity 5 a basis or standard of comparison 6a a step planned or taken to achieve an end ⟨we must take ~s to improve sales⟩ b a proposed legislative act ⟨~s to combat unemployment⟩

²**measure** vt 1 to choose or control with cautious restraint; regulate ⟨~d his words to suit the occasion⟩ 2 to take or allot in measured amounts – usu + out ⟨~ out 60g of flour⟩ 3 to mark off by making measurements – often + off 4 to ascertain the measurements of 5 to estimate

or appraise by a criterion – usu + *against* or *by* **6** to serve as a measure of ⟨*a thermometer* ~s *temperature*⟩ ~ *vi* **1** to take or make a measurement **2** to have a specified measurement ⟨~s *2ft from end to end*⟩ – **measurable** *adj*, **measurably** *adv*

measured *adj* **1** rhythmical; *esp* slow and regular **2** carefully thought out ⟨*a* ~ *remark*⟩ – **measuredly** *adv*

measureless *adj* having no observable limit; immeasurable

measurement *n* **1** measuring **2** a figure, extent, or amount obtained by measuring **3** MEASURE 2b

measure up *vi* to have necessary or fitting qualifications – often + *to*

meat *n* **1a** food; *esp* solid food as distinguished from drink **b** the edible part of sthg as distinguished from a husk, shell, or other covering **2** animal tissue used as food; *esp* FLESH 2 **3** the core or essence of sthg **4** *archaic* a meal; *esp* dinner

meaty *adj* **1** full of meat; fleshy **2** rich in matter for thought **3** of or like meat – **meatiness** *n*

mecca *n*, *often cap* a place regarded as a goal (by a specified group of people)

mechanic *n* a skilled worker who repairs or maintains machinery ⟨*a motor* ~⟩

mechanical *adj* **1a** of or using machinery **b** made, operated by, or being a machine or machinery **2** done as if by machine; lacking in spontaneity **3** of, dealing with, or in accordance with (the principles of) mechanics ⟨~ *energy*⟩ ⟨~ *engineering*⟩ **4** caused by or being a physical as opposed to a chemical process – **mechanically** *adv*

mechanics *n pl but sing or pl in constr* **1** the physics and mathematics of (the effect on moving and stationary bodies of) energy and forces **2** the practical application of mechanics to the design, construction, or operation of machines or tools **3** mechanical or functional details

mechanism *n* **1a** a piece of machinery **b** a process or technique for achieving a result **2** mechanical operation or action **3** a theory that all natural processes are mechanically determined and can be explained by the laws of physics and chemistry **4** the physical or chemical processes involved in a natural phenomenon (e g an action, reaction, or biological evolution) – **mechanist** *n*, **mechanistic** *adj*, **mechanistically** *adv*

mechanize, -ise *vt* **1** to make mechanical or automatic **2a** to equip with machinery, esp in order to replace human or animal labour **b** to equip with (armed and armoured) motor vehicles – **mechanization** *n*

medal *n* a piece of metal with a (stamped) design, emblem, inscription, etc that commemorates a person or event or is awarded for excellence or achievement – **medallic** *adj*

medallion *n* **1** a large medal **2** a decorative tablet, panel, etc, often bearing a figure or portrait in relief

medallist, *NAm chiefly* **medalist 1** a designer, engraver, or maker of medals **2** a recipient of a (specified) medal as an award

meddle *vb* **meddling** to interest oneself in what is not one's concern; interfere unduly – usu + *in* or *with* – **meddler** *n*, **meddlesome** *adj*

¹**media** *n*, *pl* **mediae** the middle muscular part of the wall of a blood or lymph vessel

²**media** *pl of* MEDIUM

mediaeval *adj* medieval

medial *adj* being, occurring in, or extending towards the middle; median – **medially** *adv*

¹**median** *n* **1** a median vein, nerve, etc **2** a value in a series above and below which there are an equal number of values **3** a line from a vertex of a triangle to the midpoint of the opposite side

²**median** *adj* **1** in the middle or in an intermediate position **2** lying in the plane that divides an animal into right and left halves

¹**mediate** *adj* acting through an intervening agent or agency – **mediacy** *n*, **mediately** *adv*

²**mediate** *vi* to intervene between parties in order to reconcile them ~ *vt* **1** to bring about (a settlement) by mediation **2a** to act as intermediary agent in or between **b** to transmit or effect by acting as an intermediate mechanism or agency – **mediator** *n*, **mediatory** *adj*, **mediative** *adj*, **mediation** *n*

¹**medic** *n* a medick

²**medic** *n* a medical doctor or student – *infml*

¹**medical** *adj* **1** of or concerned with physicians or the practice of medicine **2** requiring or devoted to medical treatment – **medically** *adv*

²**medical, medical examination** *n* an examination to determine sby's physical fitness

medicament *n* MEDICINE 1

medicare *n* comprehensive medical insurance, esp for the aged, sponsored by the US and Canadian governments

medicate *vt* **1** to treat medicinally **2** to impregnate with a medicinal substance ⟨~d *soap*⟩ – **medication** *n*

medicinal *n or adj* (a substance) tending or used to cure disease or relieve pain – **medicinally** *adv*

medicine *n* **1** a substance or preparation used (as if) in treating disease **2** the science and art of the maintenance of health and the prevention and treatment of disease (using nonsurgical methods)

medicine ball *n* a heavy ball that is usu thrown between people for exercise

medicine man *n* a healer or sorcerer, esp among the N American Indians

medico *n*, *pl* **medicos** ²MEDIC – *infml*

medico- *comb form* medical ⟨medico*psychology*⟩; medical and ⟨medico*legal*⟩

medieval, mediaeval *adj* of or like the Middle Ages – **medievalism** *n*, **medievalist** *n*, **medievally** *adv*

mediocre *adj* **1** neither good nor bad; indifferent; *esp* conspicuously lacking distinction or imagination **2** not good enough; fairly bad – **mediocrity** *n*

meditate *vt* to focus one's thoughts on; consider or plan in the mind ~ *vi* **1** to engage in deep or serious reflection **2** to empty the mind of thoughts and fix the attention on 1 matter, esp as a religious exercise – **meditator** *n*, **meditative** *adj*, **meditatively** *adv*, **meditation** *n*

Mediterranean *adj* **1** of or characteristic of (the region round) the Mediterranean sea **2** of or resembling a physical type of the Caucasian race characterized by medium or short stature, slender build, and dark complexion

¹**medium** *n*, *pl* **mediums**, **media**, (2b(2)) **media**, (2e) **mediums**, (3b) **media** *also* **mediums 1** (sthg in) a middle position or state **2** a means of effecting or conveying sthg: e g **a**(1) a substance regarded as the means of transmission of a force or effect ⟨*air is the* ~ *that conveys sound*⟩ (2) a surrounding or enveloping substance; *esp* MATRIX 3 **b**(1) a channel of communication (2) *pl but sing or pl in constr* MASS MEDIA **c** a mode of artistic expression or communication ⟨*discovered his true* ~ *as a writer*⟩ **d** an intermediary, go-between **e** one through whom others seek to communicate with the spirits of the dead **f** a material or technical means of artistic expression ⟨*found watercolour a satisfying* ~⟩ **3a** a condition or environment in which sthg may function or flourish **b** a nutrient for the artificial cultivation of bacteria and other (single-celled) organisms **c** a liquid with which dry pigment can be mixed

²**medium** *adj* intermediate in amount, quality, position, or degree

medium wave *n* a band of radio waves, typically used for sound broadcasting, covering wavelengths between about 180m and 600m – sometimes pl with sing. meaning

medlar n (a small Eurasian tree of the rose family that bears) a fruit like a crab apple used in preserves

medley n 1a (confused) mixture 2 a musical composition made up of a series of songs or short musical pieces

meek adj 1 patient and without resentment 2 lacking spirit and courage; timid – **meekly** adv, **meekness** n

meerschaum n 1 hydrated magnesium silicate occurring, chiefly in Asia Minor, as a white clayey mineral and used esp for tobacco pipes 2 a tobacco pipe with a bowl made of meerschaum

¹**meet** vb met vt 1a to come into the presence of by accident or design b to be present to greet the arrival of ⟨met the London train⟩ c to come into contact or conjunction with ⟨where the river ~s the sea⟩ d to appear to the perception of ⟨hazy sunshine ~s the eye⟩ 2 to encounter as antagonist or foe 3 to answer, esp in opposition ⟨his speech was met by loud catcalls⟩ 4 to conform to, esp exactly and precisely; satisfy ⟨this should ~ your requirements⟩ 5 to pay fully ⟨~ the cost⟩ 6 to become acquainted with 7 to experience during the course of sthg ⟨met his death during the war⟩ ~ vi 1 to come together a from different directions b for a common purpose c as contestants, opponents, or enemies 2 to join at a fastening ⟨the waistcoat won't ~⟩ 3 to become acquainted – **meet someone halfway** to make concessions to; compromise with

²**meet** n the assembling of participants for a hunt or for competitive sports

³**meet** adj suitable, proper – fml – **meetly** adv

meeting n 1 a coming together: e g a an assembly of people for a common purpose b a session of horse or greyhound racing 2 a permanent organizational unit of the Quakers 3 an intersection, junction

meetinghouse n a building used for Protestant worship

mega-, meg- comb form 1a great; large ⟨megalith⟩ ⟨megaspore⟩ b having (a specified part) of large size ⟨megacephalic⟩ 2 million (10⁶) ⟨megawatt⟩ ⟨megohm⟩

megadeath n one million deaths – used as a unit esp in reference to atomic warfare

megahertz n a unit of frequency equal to 1,000,000 hertz

megalith n a huge undressed block of stone used in prehistoric monuments – **megalithic** adj

megalomania n 1 a mania for grandiose things 2 feelings of personal omnipotence and grandeur occurring as a delusional mental disorder – **megalomaniac** adj or n, **megalomaniacal** adj

megaphone n a hand-held device used to amplify or direct the voice – **megaphonic** adj

megaton n an explosive force (of an atom or hydrogen bomb) equivalent to that of 1,000,000 tons of TNT

¹**megrim** n 1 migraine 2 vertigo, dizziness – usu pl with sing. meaning

²**megrim** n any of several small flounders or other flatfishes

meiosis n, pl **meioses** 1 understatement 2 a specialized cellular process of division in gamete-producing cells by which 1 of each pair of chromosomes passes to each resulting gametic cell which thus has half the number of chromosomes of the original cell – **meiotic** adj, **meiotically** adv

melancholia n feelings of extreme depression and worthlessness occurring as an abnormal mental condition – **melancholiac** n

¹**melancholy** n 1a (a tendency to) irascibility or depression; melancholia b BLACK BILE 2a depression of mind or spirits b a sad pensive mood – **melancholic** adj or n, **melancholically** adv

²**melancholy** adj 1 depressed in spirits; dejected 2 causing, tending to cause, or expressing sadness or depression

mélange n a mixture (of incongruous elements)

¹**meld** vb to declare (a card or combination of cards) for a score in a card game, esp by placing face up on the table

²**meld** n a card or combination of cards that is or can be melded

mêlée, melee n a confused or riotous struggle; esp a general hand-to-hand fight

meliorate vb to ameliorate – **meliorative** adj, **melioration** n

mellifluous, mellifluent adj smoothly or sweetly flowing ⟨a ~ voice⟩ – **mellifluously, mellifluently** adv, **mellifluousness, mellifluence** n

mellow adj 1a of a fruit tender and sweet because ripe b of a wine well aged and pleasingly mild 2a made gentle by age or experience b rich and full but free from harshness ⟨~ lighting⟩ c pleasantly intoxicated – **mellow** vb, **mellowly** adv, **mellowness** n

melodic adj 1 of or forming melody 2 melodious – **melodically** adv

melodious adj of or producing (a pleasing) melody – **melodiously** adv, **melodiousness** n

melodrama n 1a a work (e g a film or play) characterized by crude emotional appeal and by the predominance of plot and action over characterization b the dramatic genre comprising such works 2 sensational or sensationalized events or behaviour – **melodramatic** adj, **melodramatically** adv, **melodramatist** n, **melodramatize** vt

melody n 1 an agreeable succession or arrangement of sounds 2a a rhythmic succession of single notes organized as an aesthetic whole b the chief part in a harmonic composition

melon n (any of various plants of the cucumber family having) a fruit (e g a watermelon) containing sweet edible flesh and usu eaten raw

¹**melt** vi 1 to become altered from a solid to a liquid state, usu by heating 2a to dissolve, disintegrate ⟨food that ~s in the mouth⟩ b to disappear as if by dissolving ⟨his anger ~ed⟩ 3 to be or become mild, tender, or gentle 4 to lose distinct outline; blend ⟨tried to ~ into the background⟩ ~ vt 1 to reduce from a solid to a liquid state, usu by heating 2 to cause to disappear or disperse 3 to make tender or gentle – **meltable** adj, **meltingly** adv

²**melt** n 1a molten material b the mass melted at a single operation 2 (the period of) melting or being melted ⟨the river overflowed during the Spring ~⟩

³**melt** n the spleen, esp when used as food

melting point n the temperature at which a solid melts

melting pot n a place, a situation, or the result of mixing diverse ideas, peoples, traditions, etc

member n 1 a part or organ of the body: e g a a limb b the penis – euph 2a an individual or unit belonging to or forming part of a group or organization b often cap one who is entitled to sit in a legislative body; esp a member of Parliament 3a a constituent part of a whole b a beam or similar (load-bearing) structure, esp in a building c either of the expressions on either side of a mathematical equation or inequality

membership n sing or pl in constr the body of members ⟨an organization with a large ~⟩

membrane n a thin pliable sheet or layer, esp in an animal or plant – **membranous** adj

memento *n, pl* **mementos, mementoes** sthg (e g a souvenir) that serves as a reminder of past events, people, etc

memo *n, pl* **memos** a memorandum

memoir *n* **1a** a narrative written from personal experience **b** an autobiography – usu pl with sing. meaning **c** a biography **2** a learned essay on a particular topic *USE* (*1a&1c*) often pl with sing. meaning – **memoirist** *n*

memorabilia *n pl* (records of) memorable events

memorable *adj* worth remembering; notable – **memorability** *n,* **memorably** *adv*

memorandum *n, pl* **memorandums, memoranda 1** an often unsigned informal record or communication; *also* a written reminder **2** a document recording the terms of an agreement, the formation of a company, etc **3** a usu brief communication for internal circulation (e g within an office)

¹**memorial** *adj* serving to commemorate a person or event – **memorially** *adv,* **memorialize** *vt*

²**memorial** *n* **1** sthg, esp a monument, that commemorates a person or event **2** a historical record – often pl

memorize, -ise *vt* to commit to memory; learn by heart – **memorizable** *adj,* **memorization** *n*

memory *n* **1** (the power or process of recalling or realizing) the store of things learned and retained from an organism's experience ⟨*good visual* ~⟩ **2** commemorative remembrance ⟨*a statue in* ~ *of the hero*⟩ **3a** (the object of) recall or recollection ⟨*had no* ~ *of the incident*⟩ ⟨*left many happy* memories⟩ **b** (posthumous) image or impression ⟨*his* ~ *will stay with us*⟩ **c** the time within which past events can be or are remembered **4** (the capacity of) a device in which information, esp for a computer, can be inserted and stored, and from which it may be extracted when wanted **5** a capacity of a metal, plastic, etc for retaining effects as the result of past treatment, or for returning to a former condition

memsahib *n* a white foreign woman of high social status living in India; *broadly* any woman of rank in India

men *pl of* MAN

men-, meno- *comb form* menstruation ⟨*menorrhagia*⟩

¹**menace** *n* **1** a show of intention to inflict harm; a threat **2a** a source of danger **b** a person who causes annoyance

²**menace** *vb* to threaten or show intent to harm – **menacingly** *adv*

ménage *n* a household

ménage à trois *n* a relationship in which 3 people, esp a married couple and the lover of 1, live together

menagerie *n* a place where animals are kept and trained, esp for exhibition; *also* a zoo

¹**mend** *vt* **1** to improve or rectify ⟨~ *one's ways*⟩ ⟨*attempt to* ~ *matters*⟩ **2a** to restore to sound condition or working order; repair **b** to restore to health; cure ~ *vi* **1** to undergo improvement **2** to improve in health; *also* to heal – **mendable** *adj,* **mender** *n*

²**mend** *n* a mended place or part – **on the mend** improving, esp in health

mendacity *n* (sthg marked by) untruthfulness – fml – **mendacious** *adj,* **mendaciously** *adv*

Mendelian *adj* of or according with the genetic principle that genes occur in pairs, each gamete receives 1 member of each pair, and that an organism thus has 1 gene of each pair randomly selected from each of its parents – **Mendelian** *n,* **Mendelism** *n*

mendicant *n* **1** BEGGAR **1 2** *often cap* a friar living off alms – **mendicant** *adj,* **mendicancy, mendicity** *n*

menfolk *n pl in constr* **1** men in general **2** the men of a family or community

¹**menial** *adj* **1** of servants; lowly **2a** degrading; *also* servile

b lacking in interest or status ⟨*a boring* ~ *job*⟩ – **menially** *adv*

²**menial** *n* a domestic servant or retainer

meningitis *n* bacterial, fungal, or viral inflammation of the meninges – **meningitic** *adj*

meninx *n, pl* **meninges** any of the 3 membranes (the dura mater, pia mater, and arachnoid) that envelop the brain and spinal cord – usu pl

meniscus *n, pl* **menisci** *also* **meniseuses 1** a crescent-shaped body or figure **2** a lens that is concave on one side and convex on the other **3** the curved concave or convex upper surface of a column of liquid

menopause *n* (the time of) the natural cessation of menstruation occurring usu between the ages of 45 and 50 – **menopausal** *adj*

menses *n pl but sing or pl in constr* the menstrual flow

men's room *n, chiefly NAm* a men's toilet

menstruation *n* the discharging of blood, secretions, and tissue debris from the uterus that recurs in nonpregnant primate females of breeding age at approximately monthly intervals; *also* a single occurrence of this – **menstruous** *adj,* **menstruate** *vi,* **menstrual** *adj*

mensuration *n* **1** measurement **2** geometry applied to the computation of lengths, areas, or volumes – **mensurable** *adj,* **mensural** *adj*

-ment *suffix* (*vb → n*) **1a** concrete result, object, or agent of a (specified) action ⟨*embank*ment⟩ ⟨*entangle*ment⟩ **b** concrete means or instrument of a (specified) action ⟨*entertain*ment⟩ **2a** action; process ⟨*encircle*ment⟩ ⟨*develop*ment⟩ **b** place of a (specified) action ⟨*encamp*ment⟩

mental *adj* **1a** of the mind or its activity ⟨~ *health*⟩ ⟨~ *processes*⟩ **b** of intellectual as contrasted with emotional or physical activity ⟨~ *ability*⟩ ⟨*a* ~ *age of 3*⟩ **c** (performed or experienced) in the mind ⟨~ *arithmetic*⟩ ⟨~ *anguish*⟩ **2** of, being, or (intended for the care of people) suffering from a psychiatric disorder ⟨*a* ~ *patient*⟩ ⟨~ *illness*⟩ **3** crazy; *also* stupid – infml – **mentally** *adv*

mental defective *n* one who is mentally deficient

mentality *n* **1** mental power or capacity; intelligence **2** a mode of thought; mental disposition or outlook

menthol *n* an alcohol that occurs esp in mint oils and has the smell and cooling properties of peppermint – **mentholated** *adj*

¹**mention** *n* **1** a brief reference to sthg; a passing remark **2** a formal citation for outstanding achievement

²**mention** *vt* to make mention of; refer to; *also* to cite for outstanding achievement – **mentionable** *adj*

mentor *n* a wise and trusted adviser

menu *n, pl* **menus** (a list of) the dishes that may be ordered (e g in a restaurant) or that are to be served (e g at a banquet)

meow *vi or n* (to) miaow

Mephistopheles *n* a diabolical or fiendish person – **Mephistophelean, Mephistophelian** *adj*

mercantile *adj* **1** of or concerned with merchants or trading ⟨~ *law*⟩ **2** of mercantilism

mercantilism *n* an economic system first prominent in the 17th c that was intended to increase the power and wealth of a nation by strict governmental regulation of the national economy – **mercantilist** *n or adj*

Mercator's projection *n* a map projection showing the lines of longitude as parallel evenly-spaced straight lines and the lines of latitude as parallel straight lines whose distance from each other increases with their distance from the equator

¹**mercenary** *n* a hired soldier in foreign service

²**mercenary** *adj* **1** serving merely for (financial) reward **2**

hired for service in the army of a foreign country – **mercenariness** n, **mercenarily** adv

mercer n, Br a dealer in (fine quality) textile fabrics – **mercery** n

mercerize, -ise vt to give (e g cotton or fabrics) lustre and strength by chemical treatment – **mercerization** n

¹**merchandise** n **1** the commodities that are bought and sold in commerce **2** wares for sale

²**merchandise** vb to buy and sell in business; trade (in) – **merchandiser** n

¹**merchant** n **1** a wholesaler; also, chiefly NAm a shopkeeper **2** a person who is given to a specified activity – chiefly derog ⟨a speed ~⟩

²**merchant** adj of or used in commerce; esp of a merchant navy

merchantman n, pl **merchantmen** a ship used in commerce

merchant navy n, Br (the personnel of) the privately or publicly owned commercial ships of a nation

¹**mercurial** adj **1** of or born under the planet Mercury **2** having qualities of eloquence, ingenuity, or thievishness attributed to Mercury **3** characterized by rapid and unpredictable changes of mood **4** of, containing, or caused by mercury – **mercurially** adv

²**mercurial** n a drug or chemical containing mercury

mercurous chloride n an insoluble compound formerly used as a purgative

mercury n **1** a heavy silver-white poisonous univalent or bivalent metallic element that is liquid at ordinary temperatures and used in thermometers, barometers, etc **2** cap the planet nearest the sun – **mercuric** adj, **mercurous** adj

mercy n **1** compassion or forbearance shown esp to an offender **2a** an act of divine compassion; a blessing **b** a fortunate circumstance ⟨it was a ~ they found her before she froze⟩ **3** compassionate treatment of those in distress – **merciful** adj, **mercifully** adv, **mercifulness** n, **merciless** adj, **mercilessly** adv, **mercilessness** n – **at the mercy of** wholly in the power of; with no way to protect oneself against

mercy killing n euthanasia

¹**mere** n a (small) lake

²**mere** adj being what is specified and nothing else; nothing more than ⟨a ~ child⟩ – **merely** adv

meretricious adj **1** tawdrily and falsely attractive **2** based on pretence or insincerity; specious – **meretriciously** adv, **meretriciousness** n

merge vb **1** to (cause to) combine or unite **2** to blend or (cause to) come together gradually without abrupt change – **mergence** n

merger n **1** the absorption of an estate, contract, or interest in another – used in law **2** a combining or combination, esp of 2 organizations (e g business concerns)

meridian n **1** a great circle passing through the poles of the celestial sphere and the zenith of a given place **2** a high point, esp of success or greatness **3** (a representation on a map or globe of) a circle on the surface of the earth or other celestial body passing through both poles – **meridian** adj

meridional adj **1** of, characteristic of, or (being people) situated in the south, esp of France **2** of a meridian – **meridional** n, **meridionally** adv

meringue n (a small cake, cream-filled shell, etc made with) a mixture of stiffly beaten egg whites and sugar baked until crisp

merino n, pl **merinos** **1** (any of) a breed of fine-woolled white orig Spanish sheep **2** a soft wool or wool and cotton clothing fabric resembling cashmere **3** a fine wool and cotton yarn used for hosiery and knitwear

¹**merit** n **1a** the quality of deserving well or ill ⟨payment by ~⟩ **b** a praiseworthy quality; virtue **c** worth, excellence **2** spiritual credit held to be earned by performance of righteous acts and to ensure future benefits **3** pl the intrinsic rights and wrongs of a (legal) case

²**merit** vt to be worthy of or entitled to

meritocracy n (a social system based on) leadership by the talented – **meritocratic** adj

meritorious adj deserving of reward or honour – **meritoriously** adv, **meritoriousness** n

mermaid n, masc **merman** n, pl masc **mermen** a mythical sea creature usu represented with a woman's body to the waist and a fish's tail

merriment n lighthearted gaiety or fun

merry adj **1** full of gaiety or high spirits **2** marked by festivity **3** slightly drunk; tipsy – infml – **merrily** adv, **merriness** n

merry-go-round n a fairground machine with seats, often shaped like horses, that revolve about a fixed centre

merrymaking n gay or festive activity – **merrymaker** n

mesa n a usu isolated hill, esp in SW USA, with steeply sloping sides and a level top

mescal n **1a** a small cactus with rounded stems covered with mescaline-containing jointed protuberances used as a hallucinogen, esp among the Mexican Indians **2** (a usu colourless Mexican spirit made esp from) the maguey plant

mescal button n any of the dried disc-shaped tops of the mescal

mesdames pl of MADAM or of MADAME or of MRS

mesdemoiselles pl of MADEMOISELLE

¹**mesh** n **1** an open space in a net, network, etc **2a** the cords, wires, etc that make up a net; NETWORK 1 ⟨wire ~⟩ **b** a woven, knitted, or knotted fabric with evenly spaced small holes **3a** an interlocking or intertwining arrangement or construction **b** a web, snare – usu pl with sing. meaning **4** working contact (e g of the teeth of gears) ⟨in ~⟩

²**mesh** vt **1** to catch or entangle (as if) in the openings of a net **2** to cause to engage ~ vi **1** esp of gears to be in or come into mesh **2** to fit or work together properly or successfully

mesmerism n hypnotism – **mesmerist** n, **mesmeric** adj

mesmerize, -ise vt **1** to hypnotize **2** to fascinate, rivet – **mesmerizer** n

¹**mess** n **1** a prepared dish of soft or liquid food; also a usu unappetizing mixture of ingredients eaten together **2a(1)** sing or pl in constr a group of people (e g servicemen or servicewomen) who regularly take their meals together **(2)** a meal so taken **b** a place where meals are regularly served to a group ⟨the officers' ~⟩ **3a** a confused, dirty, or offensive state or condition **b** a disordered situation resulting from misunderstanding, blundering, or misconduct

²**mess** vi **1** to take meals with a mess **2** to make a mess **3a** to dabble, potter **b** to handle or play with sthg, esp carelessly **c** to interfere, meddle USE (3) often + about or around

mess about vb, chiefly Br vi **1a** to waste time **b** to work according to one's whim or mood ⟨messing about in boats⟩ **2** to conduct an affair with ⟨messing about with someone else's husband⟩ ~ vt to treat roughly or without due consideration ⟨he shouldn't mess the men about too much, they know their job – The Lorry Driver⟩

message n **1** a communication in writing, in speech, or by signals **2** a messenger's errand or function **3** a central theme or idea intended to inspire, urge, warn, enlighten, advise, etc

messenger n one who bears a message or does an errand: e g **a** a dispatch bearer in government or military service **b** an employee who carries messages

messiah n **1** often cap **a** the expected king and deliverer of the Jews **b** Jesus **2** a professed leader of some cause – **messiahship** n

messianic adj **1** of a messiah **2** marked by idealistic enthusiasm for a cherished cause **3** of a time of blessedness and peace associated with the Jewish and Christian concept of the end of the world – **messianism** n

messieurs pl of MONSIEUR

messmate n a member of a (ship's) mess

Messrs pl of MR ⟨~ Jones, Brown, and Robinson⟩

messuage n a dwelling house with its outbuildings and land

mess up vt to make a mess of; spoil – infml

messy adj **1** marked by confusion, disorder, or dirt **2** lacking neatness or precision; slovenly **3** unpleasantly or tryingly difficult to conclude – **messily** adv, **messiness** n

mestiza, masc **mestizo** n, pl **mestizas**, masc **mestizos** a person of mixed European and American Indian ancestry

¹**met** past of MEET

²**met** adj meteorological ⟨the ~ office forecast⟩

meta-, met- prefix **1a** situated behind or beyond ⟨metacarpus⟩ ⟨metagalaxy⟩ **b** later or more highly organized or specialized form of ⟨metaxylem⟩ **2** change; transformation ⟨metamorphosis⟩ ⟨metabolism⟩ **3** more comprehensive; transcending; of a higher or second order ⟨metapsychology⟩ – used with the name of a discipline to designate a new but related discipline designed to deal critically with the original one ⟨metalanguage⟩ **4a** related to ⟨metaldehyde⟩ **b** involving substitution at 2 positions in the benzene ring that are separated by 1 carbon atom

metabolism n all the processes (by which a specified substance is dealt with) in the building up and destruction of living tissue; specif the chemical changes in living cells by which energy is provided and new material is assimilated – **metabolize** vb, **metabolic** adj

metacarpal n a metacarpal bone

metacarpus n the part of the hand or forefoot between the wrist and fingers or the ankle and toes – **metacarpal** adj

metal n **1** any of various opaque, fusible, ductile, and typically lustrous substances (e g iron, copper, or mercury), esp chemical elements, that are good conductors of electricity and heat, form positive ions by loss of electrons, and yield basic oxides and hydroxides **2** glass in its molten state **3** either of the heraldic colours gold or silver **4** chiefly Br ROAD METAL – **metalliferous** adj

metalanguage n a language used to talk about language

metallic adj **1** of, containing, like, or being (a) metal **2** yielding metal **3** having an acrid quality – **metallically** adv

metalloid n an element (e g arsenic) having some properties of typical metals and some properties of typical nonmetals

metallurgy n the science and technology of metals – **metallurgist** n, **metallurgical** adj, **metallurgically** adv

metalwork n the craft or product of shaping things out of metal – **metalworker** n

metamorphic adj **1** of or involving metamorphosis **2** of a rock of or produced by metamorphism – **metamorphically** adv

metamorphism n a change in rock effected esp by heat and pressure and resulting in a more compact and crystalline structure

metamorphose vt **1a** to change into a different physical form **b** to change strikingly the appearance or character of; transform **2** to cause (rock) to undergo metamorphism ~ vi to undergo metamorphosis

metamorphosis n, pl **metamorphoses** **1a** change of form, structure, or substance, esp by supernatural means **b** a striking alteration (e g in appearance or character) **2** a marked (abrupt) change in the form or structure of a butterfly, frog, etc occurring in the course of development

metaphor n (an instance of) a figure of speech in which a word or phrase literally denoting one kind of object or idea is applied to another to suggest a likeness or analogy between them (e g in the ship ploughs the sea) – **metaphoric, metaphorical** adj, **metaphorically** adv

metaphysical adj **1** of metaphysics **2** often cap of or being poetry, esp of the early 17th c, marked by elaborate subtleties of thought and expression – **metaphysically** adv

metaphysics n pl but sing in constr **1** a division of philosophy concerned with ultimate causes and the underlying nature of things; esp ontology **2** pure or speculative philosophy – **metaphysician** n

metatarsal n a metatarsal bone

mete vt to assign by measure; allot – usu + out

metempsychosis n the passing of the soul at death into another body

meteor n a phenomenon in the atmosphere; esp (the streak of light produced by the passage of) any of many small particles of matter in the solar system observable only when heated by friction so that they glow as they fall into the earth's atmosphere

meteoric adj **1** of a meteor **2** resembling a meteor in speed or in sudden and temporary brilliance ⟨~ rise to fame⟩ – **meteorically** adv

meteorite n a meteor that reaches the surface of the earth without being completely vaporized – **meteoritic, meteoritical** adj

meteoroid n a particle in orbit round the sun that becomes a meteor when it meets the earth's atmosphere – **meteoroidal** adj

meteorology n **1** the science of the atmosphere and its phenomena, esp weather and weather forecasting **2** the weather or atmospheric phenomena of a region – **meteorologist** n, **meteorologic, meteorological** adj, **meteorologically** adv

¹**meter** n, NAm a metre

²**meter** n an instrument for measuring (and recording) the amount of sthg (e g gas, electricity, or parking time) used

³**meter** vt **1** to measure by means of a meter **2** to supply in a measured or regulated amount

¹**-meter** comb form (→ n) measure or unit of metrical verse ⟨pentameter⟩

²**-meter** comb form (→ n) instrument or means for measuring ⟨barometer⟩

methane n an inflammable gaseous hydrocarbon of the alkane series used as a fuel and as a raw material in chemical synthesis

methanol n a volatile inflammable poisonous liquid alcohol that is added to ethyl alcohol to make it unfit to drink and is used as a solvent and as a raw material in chemical synthesis

methinks vb impersonal **methought** archaic it seems to me

method n **1a** a systematic procedure for doing sthg **b** a regular way of doing sthg **2a** an orderly arrangement or system **b** the habitual practice of orderliness and regularity **3** *cap* a dramatic technique by which an actor seeks to identify closely with the inner personality of the character being portrayed – usu + *the*

methodical, *NAm also* **methodic** *adj* **1** arranged, characterized by, or performed with method or order **2** habitually proceeding according to method; systematic – **methodically** *adv*, **methodicalness** *n*

Methodism *n* (the doctrines and practice of) the Methodist churches

Methodist *n or adj* (a member) of any of the denominations deriving from the Wesleyan revival in the Church of England

methodology *n* (the analysis of) the body of methods and rules employed by a science or discipline – **methodologist** *n*, **methodological** *adj*

meths *n pl but sing in constr*, *Br* METHYLATED SPIRITS – *infml*

Methuselah *n* a champagne bottle holding 8 times the usual amount

methyl alcohol *n* methanol

methylated spirits *n pl but sing or pl in constr* alcohol mixed with an adulterant, esp methanol, to make it undrinkable and therefore exempt from duty

meticulous *adj* marked by extreme or excessive care over detail – **meticulously** *adv*, **meticulousness** *n*

métier *n* one's trade; *also* sthg (e g an activity) in which one is expert or successful

¹metre, *NAm chiefly* **meter** *n* the SI unit of length equal to a certain number of wavelengths of a specific radiation of the krypton isotope $_{36}Kr^{86}$ (about 1.094yd)

²metre, *NAm chiefly* **meter** *n* **1** systematically arranged and measured rhythm in verse ⟨*iambic* ~⟩ **2** a basic recurrent rhythmical pattern of accents and beats per bar in music – **metrist** *n*

metric *adj* **1** **metric**, **metrical** (using or being units) based on the metre, litre, and kilogram as standard of measurement **2** metrical – **metrically** *adv*

-metric, **-metrical** *comb form* (→ *adj*) **1** of, employing, or obtained by (a specified meter) ⟨*galvano*metric⟩ **2** of or relating to the art, process, or science of measuring (sthg specified) ⟨*chrono*metric⟩ ⟨*gravi*metrical⟩

metrical, **metric** *adj* **1** of or composed in metre **2** of measurement – **metrically** *adv*

metricate *vt* to change into or express in the metric system – ~ *vi* to adopt the metric system – **metrication** *n*

metric ton *n* a tonne

metro *n*, *pl* **metros** an underground railway system in a city ⟨*the Leningrad* ~⟩

Metro *adj*, *Can* of or relating to the inner urban area of a Canadian city, esp of Toronto

metronome *n* an instrument designed to mark exact time by a regularly repeated tick – **metronomic** *adj*

metropolis *n* **1** the chief city of a country, state, or region **2** a centre of a usu specified activity **3** a large or important city

¹metropolitan *n* **1** the primate of an ecclesiastical province **2** one who lives in a metropolis

²metropolitan *adj* **1** of or constituting a metropolitan or his see **2** (characteristic) of a metropolis **3** of or constituting a mother country

mettle *n* **1** strength of spirit or temperament **2** staying quality; stamina – **on one's mettle** aroused to do one's best

mettlesome *adj* spirited

¹mew *vi* to utter a miaow or similar sound ⟨*gulls* ~ed *over the bay*⟩ ~ *vt* to miaow – **mew** *n*

²mew *vt* to shut up; confine – often + *up*

mews *n pl but sing or pl in constr*, *pl* **mews** *chiefly Br* (living accommodation adapted from) stables built round an open courtyard

mezzanine *n* a low-ceilinged storey between 2 main storeys, esp the ground and first floors, of a building

mezzo, **mezzo-soprano** *n*, *pl* **mezzos**, **mezzo-sopranos** (a singer with) a woman's voice with a range between that of the soprano and contralto

mezzotint *n* (a print produced by) a method of engraving on copper or steel by scraping or burnishing a roughened surface to produce light and shade

mi *n* the 3rd note of the diatonic scale in solmization

mi-, **mio-** *comb form* less ⟨*Mio*cene⟩

miaow, **meow** *vi or n* (to make) the characteristic cry of a cat

miasma *n*, *pl* **miasmas** *also* **miasmata** **1** a heavy vapour (e g from a swamp) formerly believed to cause disease; *broadly* any heavy or malodorous vapour **2** a pervasive influence that tends to weaken or corrupt – **miasmal** *adj*, **miasmatic** *adj*, **miasmic** *adj*

mica *n* any of various coloured or transparent silicate materials occurring as crystals that readily separate into very thin flexible leaves – **micaceous** *adj*

mice *pl of* MOUSE

Michaelmas *n* September 29 celebrated as the feast of St Michael the Archangel

Michaelmas daisy *n* any of several (Autumn-blooming) asters widely grown as garden plants

mick *n* an Irishman – chiefly derog

mickey *n* – **take the mickey** to make sby an object of amusement by humorous or playful ridicule – *infml*

Mickey Finn *n* an alcoholic drink doctored usu with a hypnotic drug

micr-, **micro-** *comb form* **1a** small; minute ⟨*micro*cosm⟩ **b** used for or involving minute quantities or variations ⟨*micro*barograph⟩ ⟨*micro*calorimeter⟩ **c** microscopic ⟨*micro*organism⟩ **2** one millionth (10^6) part of (a specified unit) ⟨*micro*second⟩ ⟨*micro*gram⟩ ⟨*micro*hm⟩ **3** enlarging; magnifying; amplifying ⟨*micro*phone⟩ **4a** used in or involving microscopy ⟨*micro*dissection⟩ **b** used in or connected with microphotography ⟨*micro*copy⟩ ⟨*micro*film⟩ **5** of a small or localized area ⟨*micro*climate⟩ ⟨*micro*habitat⟩

micro *adj* very small; *esp* microscopic

microbe *n* a microorganism, germ – **microbial**, **microbic** *adj*

microbiology *n* the biology of bacteria and other microscopic forms of life – **microbiologist** *n*, **microbiological**, **microbiologic** *adj*

microcosm *n* **1** a little world; *esp* an individual human being or human nature seen as an epitome of the world or universe **2** a whole (e g a community) that is an epitome of a larger whole – **microcosmic** *adj*

microelectronics *n pl but sing in constr* a branch of electronics that deals with or produces miniaturized electronic circuits and components – **microelectronic** *adj*

microfiche *n*, *pl* **microfiche**, **microfiches** a sheet of microfilm containing rows of very small images of pages of printed matter

microfilm *n* a film bearing a photographic record on a reduced scale of graphic matter (e g printing) – **microfilm** *vb*, **microfilmable** *adj*

micrometer *n* **1** an instrument for measuring distances between objects seen through a microscope or telescope **2** a gauge for making precise measurements of length by means of a spindle moved by a finely threaded screw

micron *n*, *pl* **microns** *also* **micra** one millionth (10^{-6}) part of a metre – not now recommended for technical use

microorganism *n* an organism of (smaller than) microscopic size

microphone *n* a device that converts sounds into electrical signals, esp for transmission or recording – **microphonic** *adj*

microscope *n* an instrument consisting of (a combination of) lenses for making enlarged images of minute objects using light or other radiations

microscopic *also* **microscopical** *adj* 1 of or conducted with the microscope or microscopy 2 resembling a microscope, esp in perception 3a invisible or indistinguishable without the use of a microscope b very small, fine, or precise – **microscopically** *adv*

microwave *n* a band of very short electromagnetic waves of between 1m and 0.1m in wavelength

¹**mid** *adj* 1 being the part in the middle or midst ⟨*in ~ ocean*⟩ – often in combination ⟨*mid-August*⟩ ⟨*in mid-sentence*⟩ 2 occupying a middle position 3 *of a vowel* articulated with the tongue midway between the upper and lower areas of the mouth – **mid** *adv*

²**mid** *prep* amid – poetic

midair *n* a point or region in the air not immediately near the ground

midday *n* the middle part of the day; noon

midden *n* 1 a dunghill 2 a refuse heap; *esp* a heap or stratum of domestic rubbish found on the site of an ancient settlement

¹**middle** *adj* 1 equally distant from the extremes; central 2 at neither extreme 3 *cap* a constituting a division intermediate between those prior and later or upper and lower ⟨*Middle Palaeozoic*⟩ b belonging to a period of a language intermediate between Old and New or Modern forms ⟨Middle *Dutch*⟩

²**middle** *n* 1 a middle part, point, or position 2 the waist 3 the position of being among or in the midst of sthg 4 sthg intermediate between extremes; a mean

³**middle** *vt* to hit (a shot) correctly with the middle of the bat in cricket

middle age *n* the period of life from about 40 to about 60 – **middle-aged** *adj*

Middle Ages *n pl* the period of European history from about AD 500 to about 1500

middlebrow *adj* dealing with or having conventional and often bourgeois intellectual and cultural activities and activities – often derog – **middlebrow** *n*

middle class *n* a class occupying a position between upper and lower; *esp* a fluid heterogeneous grouping of business and professional people, bureaucrats, and some farmers and skilled workers – often pl with sing. meaning – **middle-class** *adj*

middle-distance *adj* of or being a footrace over a distance between 400m and 1mi

middle distance *n* the part of a picture or view between the foreground and the background

middle ear *n* a cavity through which sound waves are transmitted by a chain of tiny bones from the eardrum to the inner ear

middleman *n* an intermediary between 2 parties; *esp* a dealer intermediate between the producer of goods and the retailer or consumer

middle name *n* 1 a name between one's first name and surname 2 a quality of character for which sby is well known ⟨*generosity is her ~*⟩

middle-of-the-road *adj* conforming to the majority in taste, attitude, or conduct; *also* neither right-wing nor left-wing in political conviction – **middle-of-the-roader** *n*, **middle-of-the-roadism** *n*

middle school *n* (part of) a school for pupils aged 8–12 or 9–13

middleweight *n* a boxer who weighs not more than 11st 6lb (72.6kg) if professional or more than 71kg (about 11st 2lb) but not more than 75kg (about 11st 11lb) if amateur

middling *adj* 1 of middle or moderate size, degree, or quality 2 mediocre, second-rate – **middling** *adv*, **middlingly** *adv*

midge *n* a tiny two-winged fly

midget *n* 1 a very small person; a dwarf 2 sthg (e g an animal) much smaller than usual – **midget** *adj*

midi *n* a woman's garment that extends to the mid-calf

midland *n*, *often cap* the central region of a country – usu pl with sing. meaning – **midland** *adj*, *often cap*

midmost *adj* in or near the middle – **midmost** *adv or n*

midnight *n* the middle of the night; *specif* 12 o'clock at night – **midnight** *adj*, **midnightly** *adv or adj*

midnight sun *n* the sun visible at midnight in the arctic or antarctic summer

mid-off *n* a fielding position in cricket near the bowler on the off side of the pitch

mid-on *n* a fielding position in cricket near the bowler on the leg side of the pitch

midpoint *n* a point midway between the beginning and end of sthg

midriff *n* 1 DIAPHRAGM 1 2 the middle part of the human torso

midshipman *n* (the rank of) a young person training to become a naval officer

midships *adv* amidships

midst *n* 1 the inner or central part or point; the middle 2 a position near to the members of a group ⟨*a traitor in our ~*⟩ 3 the condition of being surrounded or beset (e g by problems) 4 a period of time about the middle of a continuing act or state ⟨*in the ~ of the celebrations*⟩ – **midst** *prep*

midsummer *n* the summer solstice

Midsummer Day *n* June 24 celebrated as the feast of the nativity of John the Baptist

midway *adv* halfway

midweek *n* the middle of the week – **midweek** *adj*, **midweekly** *adj or adv*

mid-wicket *n* a fielding position in cricket on the leg side equidistant from each wicket

midwife *n* 1 a woman who assists other women in childbirth 2 sby or sthg that helps to produce or bring forth sthg

midwifery *n* (the art of) assisting at childbirth; *also* obstetrics

mien *n* air or bearing, esp as expressive of mood or personality – fml

miff *n* 1 a brief outburst of bad temper 2 a trivial quarrel *USE* infml

¹**might** *past of* MAY – used to express permission or liberty in the past ⟨*asked whether he ~ come*⟩ ⟨*the king ~ do nothing without parliament's consent*⟩, a past or present possibility contrary to fact ⟨*I ~ well have been killed*⟩ ⟨*if he were older he ~ understand*⟩, purpose or expectation in the past ⟨*wrote it down so that I ~ not forget it*⟩, less probability or possibility than may ⟨*~ get there before it rains*⟩, a polite request ⟨*you ~ post this letter for me*⟩, or as a polite or ironic alternative to may ⟨*who ~ you be?*⟩ or to ought or should ⟨*you ~ at least apologize*⟩ ⟨*he ~ have offered to help*⟩

²**might** *n* 1 power, authority, or resources wielded individually or collectively 2a physical strength b all the power or effort one is capable of

mightily *adv* very much ⟨*it amused us ~* – Charles Dickens⟩

mightn't might not

¹mighty *adj* **1** powerful **2** accomplished or characterized by might ⟨*a ~ thrust*⟩ **3** imposingly great ⟨*the ~ mountains*⟩ – **mightiness** *n*

²mighty *adv* to a great degree; extremely ⟨*a ~ big man*⟩

mignonette *n* an annual garden plant with fragrant greenish yellow flowers or any of various related plants

migraine *n* recurrent severe headache usu associated with disturbances of vision, sensation, and movement often on only 1 side of the body – **migrainous** *adj*

migrant *n* **1** a person who moves regularly in order to find work, esp in harvesting crops **2** an animal that moves from one habitat to another – **migrant** *adj*

migrate *vi* **1** to move from one country or locality to another **2** *of an animal* to pass usu periodically from one region or climate to another for feeding or breeding – **migration** *n*, **migrational** *adj*, **migrator** *n*

migratory *adj* wandering, roving

mikado *n*, *pl* **mikados** – formerly used as a title for the emperor of Japan

mike *n* a microphone – *infml*

Mike – a communications code word for the letter *m*

milady *n* an Englishwoman of noble or gentle birth – often used as a term of address or reference

milch *adj*, *of a domestic animal* bred or used primarily for milk production

¹mild *adj* **1** gentle in nature or manner **2a** not strong in flavour or effect **b** not being or involving what is extreme **3** not severe; temperate ⟨*a ~ climate*⟩ **4** easily worked; malleable ⟨*~ steel*⟩ – **mildly** *adv*, **mildness** *n*

²mild *n*, *Br* a dark-coloured beer not flavoured with hops

¹mildew *n* (a fungus producing) a usu whitish growth on the surface of organic matter (e g paper or leather) or living plants – **mildewy** *adj*

²mildew *vb* to affect or become affected (as if) with mildew

mile *n* **1** any of various units of distance: e g **a** a unit equal to 1760yd (about 1.61km) **b** NAUTICAL MILE **2** a large distance or amount – often pl with sing. meaning – **miles from nowhere** in an extremely remote place

mileage *n* **1** an allowance for travelling expenses at a certain rate per mile **2** total length or distance in miles: e g **a** the number of miles travelled over a period of time **b** the distance, or distance covered, in miles **c** the average distance in miles a vehicle will travel for an amount of fuel

miler *n* a person or horse that competes in mile races

milestone *n* **1** a stone serving as a milepost **2** a crucial stage in sthg's development

milieu *n*, *pl* **milieus, milieux** an environment, setting ⟨*three studies of women, each from a different ~* – Edmund Wilson⟩

militant *adj* **1** engaged in warfare or combat **2** aggressively active (e g in a cause); combative – **militancy** *n*, **militant** *n*, **militantly** *adv*, **militantness** *n*

militarism *n* **1** exaltation of military virtues and ideals **2** a policy of aggressive military preparedness – **militarist** *n*, **militaristic** *adj*, **militaristically** *adv*

militarize, -ise *vt* **1** to equip with military forces and defences **2** to give a military character to – **militarization** *n*

¹military *adj* **1** (characteristic) of soldiers, arms, or war carried on or supported by armed force ⟨*a ~ dictatorship*⟩ **3** of the army or armed forces – **militarily** *adv*

²military *n* **1** *pl in constr* soldiers **2** *sing or pl in constr* the army (as opposed to civilians or police)

military police *n* a branch of an army that carries out police functions within the army

militate *vi* to have significant weight or effect – often + *against*

militia *n sing or pl in constr* a body of citizens with some military training who are called on to fight only in an emergency – **militiaman** *n*

¹milk *n* **1** a (white or creamy) liquid secreted by the mammary glands of females for the nourishment of their young (and used as a food by humans) **2** a milklike liquid: e g **a** the latex of a plant **b** the juice of a coconut **c** a cosmetic lotion, esp a cleanser – **milky** *adj*, **milkiness** *n*

²milk *vt* **1** to draw milk from the breasts or udder of **2** to draw sthg from as if by milking: e g **a** to induce (a snake) to eject venom **b** to compel or persuade to yield illicit or excessive profit or advantage ⟨*opera stars who ~ their audience for applause*⟩ – **milker** *n*

milk float *n*, *Br* a light usu electrically-propelled vehicle for carrying esp milk for domestic delivery

milkmaid *n* a female who works in a dairy

milkman *n* one who sells or delivers milk

milk of magnesia *n* a white suspension of magnesium hydroxide in water, used as an antacid and mild laxative

milk pudding *n* a pudding consisting of rice, tapioca, sago, etc boiled or baked in (sweetened) milk

milk run *n* a regular journey or course

milk shake *n* a thoroughly shaken or blended beverage made of milk and a flavouring syrup

milksop *n* a weak and unmanly male

milk tooth *n* a tooth of a mammal, esp a child, that is replaced later in life

milkweed *n* any of various plants that secrete milky latex

Milky Way *n* a broad irregular band of faint light that stretches completely round the celestial sphere and is caused by the light of the many stars forming the galaxy of which the sun and the solar system are a part

¹mill *n* **1** a building provided with machinery for grinding grain into flour **2a** a machine or apparatus for grinding grain **b** a machine or hand-operated device for crushing or grinding a solid substance (e g coffee beans or peppercorns) **3** a building or collection of buildings with machinery for manufacturing **4** MILLING MACHINE **5** an experience that has a hardening effect on the character – usu in *through the mill*

²mill *vt* **1** to subject to an operation or process in a mill: e g **a** to grind into flour, meal, or powder **b** to shape or dress by means of a rotary cutter **2** to give a raised rim or a ridged edge to (a coin) **3** to cut grooves in the metal surface of (e g a knob) ~ *vi* **1** to move in a confused swirling mass – usu + *about* or *around* **2** to undergo milling

millboard *n* strong cardboard suitable for book covers and for panelling in furniture

milldam *n* a dam to make a millpond

millenarian *adj* **1** of or relating to 1000 years **2** of or having belief in the millennium – **millenarian** *n*, **millenarianism** *n*

millennium *n*, *pl* **millennia, millenniums 1a** a period of 1000 years **b** (the celebration of) a 1000th anniversary **2a** *the* thousand years mentioned in Revelation 20 during which holiness is to prevail and Christ is to reign on earth **b** a (future) golden age – **millennial** *adj*

millepede *n* a millipede

miller *n* sby who owns or works a mill, esp for corn

millet *n* (the seed of) any of various small-seeded annual cereal and forage grasses cultivated for their grain, used as food

milli- *comb form* one thousandth (10⁻³) part of (a specified unit) ⟨milli*ampere*⟩

millibar *n* a unit of pressure equal to ¹/₁₀₀₀ bar

milligram *n* one thousandth of a gram (about 0.015 grain)

millilitre *n* a thousandth of a litre (.002pt)

millimetre *n* one thousandth of a metre (about 0.039in)

milliner *n* sby who designs, makes, trims, or sells women's hats – **millinery** *n*

milling machine *n* a machine tool for shaping metal against rotating milling cutters

million *n, pl* **millions, million 1** (the number) 1,000,000 **2** an indefinitely large number – *infml*; often *pl* with *sing.* meaning ⟨~s of cars in that traffic jam⟩ **3** ¹MASS **3** ⟨appealing to the ~s⟩ – **million** *adj,* **millionth** *adj or n*

millionaire *n* sby whose wealth is estimated at a million or more money units

millipede, millepede *n* any of numerous myriopods usu with a cylindrical segmented body and 2 pairs of legs on each segment

millpond *n* a pond produced by damming a stream to produce a head of water for operating a mill

millrace *n* (the current in) a channel in which water flows to and from a mill wheel

millstone *n* **1** either of a pair of circular stones that rotate against each other and are used for grinding (grain) **2** a heavy or crushing burden

mill wheel *n* a waterwheel that drives a mill

millwright *n* sby who plans, builds, or maintains mills

milometer *n* an odometer calibrated in miles

milord *n* an Englishman of noble or gentle birth – often used in imitation of foreigners

milt *n* the male reproductive glands of fishes when filled with secretion; *also* the secretion of these glands – **milty** *adj*

¹**mime** *n* **1** an ancient dramatic entertainment representing scenes from life usu in a ridiculous manner **2** the art of portraying a character or telling a story by body movement

²**mime** *vi* to act a part with mimic gesture and action, usu without words ~ *vt* **1** to mimic **2** to act out in the manner of a mime – **mimer** *n*

mimetic *adj* **1** imitative **2** relating to, characterized by, or exhibiting mimicry – **mimetically** *adv*

¹**mimic** *adj* **1a** IMITATIVE **1** **b** imitation, mock ⟨a ~ battle⟩ **2** of mime or mimicry – **mimical** *adj*

²**mimic** *vt* **-ck- 1** to imitate slavishly; ape **2** to ridicule by imitation **3** to simulate **4** to resemble by biological mimicry – **mimic** *n*

mimicry *n* **1** the act or an instance of mimicking **2** resemblance of one organism to another that secures it an advantage (e g protection from predation)

mimosa *n* any of a genus of leguminous trees, shrubs, and herbaceous plants of warm regions with globular heads of small white, pink, or esp yellow flowers

minaret *n* a slender tower attached to a mosque and surrounded by 1 or more projecting balconies from which the summons to prayer is made

minatory *adj* menacing, threatening – *fml*

¹**mince** *vt* **1** to cut or chop into very small pieces **2** to keep (one's words) within the bounds of decorum ⟨doesn't ~ his words⟩ ~ *vi* to walk with short affected steps – **mincer** *n*

²**mince** *n* minced meat

mincemeat *n* a finely chopped mixture of raisins, apples, suet, spices, etc (with brandy) which traditionally used to contain meat

mince pie *n* a sweet usu small and round pie filled with mincemeat

mincing *adj* affectedly dainty or delicate ⟨trying to speak in a small ~ treble – George Eliot⟩ – **mincingly** *adv*

¹**mind** *n* **1** the (capabilities of the) organized conscious and unconscious mental processes of an organism that result in reasoning, thinking, perceiving, etc **2a** recollection, memory ⟨keep that in ~⟩ **b** attention, concentration ⟨can't keep her ~ on her work⟩ **3** the normal condition of the mental faculties ⟨lost his ~⟩ **4a** an intention, desire ⟨he changed his ~⟩⟨doesn't know his own ~⟩⟨I've a good ~ to box his ears⟩⟨had half a ~ to leave early⟩ **b** an opinion, view ⟨unwilling to speak his ~⟩⟨they were of the same ~⟩⟨though she's just a child, she has a ~ of her own⟩⟨in two ~s about the problem⟩ **5** a disposition, mood ⟨her state of ~ was calm⟩⟨always has good peace of ~⟩ **6** the mental attributes of a usu specified group ⟨the scientific ~⟩ **7** a person considered as an intellectual being ⟨one of the finest ~s of the academic world⟩ **8a** the intellect and rational faculties as contrasted with the emotions **b** the human spirit and intellect as opposed to the body and the material world ⟨~ over matter⟩ – **bear/keep in mind** to think of, esp at the appropriate time; not forget – **on one's mind** as a preoccupation; troubling one's thoughts ⟨she can't work with the problem of the mortgage on her mind⟩

²**mind** *vt* **1** to attend to closely ⟨~ how you behave⟩⟨~ your manners⟩⟨~ your own business⟩ **2** to pay attention to or follow (advice, instructions, or orders) **3a** to be concerned about; care ⟨I don't ~ what we do⟩⟨Never ~ the hole in your tights: no one will notice⟩ **b** to object to ⟨do you ~ going?⟩⟨I don't ~ the noise⟩ **4a** to be careful ⟨~ you finish your homework!⟩ **b** to be cautious about ⟨~ the step⟩ **5** to give protective care to; look after ⟨~ed the children while their parents were out⟩ ~ *vi* **1** to be attentive or wary – often + *out* **2** to be or become concerned; care ⟨would you prefer tea of coffee? I don't ~⟩⟨I'm sorry, I've spilt my coffee. Never ~!⟩ – **minder** *n* – **mind you** take this fact into account; notice this ⟨mind you, I don't blame him⟩

mindbending *adj* at the limits of understanding or credibility – *infml* – **mindbendingly** *adv,* **mindbender** *n*

mind-blowing *adj* **1** of or causing a psychic state similar to that produced by a psychedelic drug **2** mentally or emotionally exhilarating *USE infml* – **mindblower** *n*

mind-boggling *adj* causing great surprise or wonder – *infml*

minded *adj* **1** having a (specified kind of) mind – usu in combination ⟨narrow-minded⟩ **2** inclined, disposed ⟨was not ~ to report his losses – Herts & Essex Observer⟩ – **mindedness** *n*

mind-expanding *adj* PSYCHEDELIC **1b** – *infml*

mindful *adj* keeping in mind; aware *of* – **mindfully** *adv,* **mindfulness** *n*

mindless *adj* **1** devoid of thought or intelligence; senseless ⟨~ violence⟩ **2** involving or requiring little thought or concentration ⟨the work is routine and fairly ~⟩ **3** inattentive, heedless – usu + *of* ⟨dashed into the burning house ~ of the danger⟩ – **mindlessly** *adv,* **mindlessness** *n*

mind reader *n* sby who can, or is thought to be able to, perceive another's thought directly – **mind reading** *n*

mind's eye *n* the faculty of visual memory or imagination

¹**mine** *adj, archaic* my – used before a vowel or *h* ⟨~ host⟩ or sometimes to modify a preceding noun ⟨mistress ~⟩

²**mine** *pron, pl* **mine** that which or the one who belongs to me – used without a following noun as a pronoun equivalent in meaning to the adjective *my* ⟨children younger than

~⟩ ⟨*that brother of* ~⟩ ⟨*the house became* ~⟩ – **me and mine** I and my family and possessions

³mine *n* **1a** an excavation from which mineral substances are taken **b** an ore deposit **2** an underground passage beneath an enemy position **3** an encased explosive designed to destroy enemy personnel, vehicles, or ships **4** a rich source of ⟨*a* ~ *of information*⟩

⁴mine *vt* **1a** to dig an underground passage to gain access to or cause the collapse of (an enemy position) **b** UNDER-MINE 2 **2** to obtain from a mine **3** to place military mines in, on, or under ⟨~ *a harbour*⟩ **4** to dig into for ore, coal, etc **5** to seek valuable material in ~ *vi* to dig a mine – **miner** *n*, **mining** *n*

minelayer *n* a vessel or aircraft for laying mines

mineral *n* **1** (a synthetic substance resembling) a solid homogeneous crystalline material that results from the inorganic processes of nature; *broadly* any of various naturally occurring substances (e g stone, coal, and petroleum) obtained by drilling, mining, etc **2** sthg neither animal nor vegetable **3** *Br* MINERAL WATER – usu pl – **mineral** *adj*

mineral kingdom *n* the one of the 3 basic groups of natural objects that includes inorganic objects

mineralogy *n* a science dealing with the structure, properties, and classification of minerals – **mineralogist** *n*, **mineralogical** *adj*

mineral oil *n* an oil of mineral as opposed to vegetable origin

mineral water *n* water naturally or artificially impregnated with mineral salts or gases (e g carbon dioxide); *broadly* any effervescent nonalcoholic beverage

minestrone *n* a rich thick vegetable soup usu containing pasta (e g macaroni)

minesweeper *n* a ship designed for removing or neutralizing mines – **minesweeping** *n*

mingle *vb* **mingling** *vt* to bring or mix together or with sthg else ~ *vi* **1** to become mingled **2** to mix with or go among a group of people ⟨*simply will not* ~ *at parties*⟩ ⟨~d *with the crowd*⟩

mingy *adj* mean, stingy – *infml*

mini *n, pl* **minis** **1** sthg small of its kind (e g a motor car) **2** a woman's skirt or dress with the hemline several inches above the knee – **mini** *adj*

mini- *comb form* miniature; of small dimensions ⟨*minicomputer*⟩; *specif* having a hemline several inches above the knee ⟨*miniskirt*⟩

¹miniature *n* **1a** a copy or representation on a much reduced scale **b** sthg small of its kind **2** a painting in an illuminated manuscript **3** the art of painting miniatures **4** a very small painting (e g a portrait on ivory or metal) – **miniaturist** *n*

²miniature *adj* **1** (represented) on a small or reduced scale **2** of still photography using film 35mm wide or smaller

minibus *n* a small bus for carrying usu between 5 and 10 passengers

minim *n* **1** a musical note with the time value of 2 crotchets or ½ of a semibreve **2** a unit of capacity equal to ¹/₆₀ fluid drachm (about 59.19mm³) – **minim** *adj*

minimal *adj* of or being a minimum; constituting the least possible – **minimalize** *vt*, **minimally** *adv*

minimize, -ise *vt* **1** to reduce to a minimum **2** to represent (sby or sthg) at less than true value; PLAY DOWN – **minimizer** *n*, **minimization** *n*

minimum *n, pl* **minima, minimums** **1** the least quantity or value assignable, admissible, or possible **2** the lowest degree or amount reached or recorded – **minimum** *adj*

minimum wage *n* a wage fixed by legal authority or by contract as the least that may be paid either to employees generally or to a particular category of employees

minion *n* **1** a servile attendant **2** FAVOURITE 1 **3** a minor official – *derog*

¹minister *n* **1** AGENT 1a, 2 **2a** one officiating or assisting the officiant in Christian worship **b** a clergyman, esp of a Protestant or nonconformist church **c** the superior of any of several religious orders **3** a high officer of state managing a division of government **4** a diplomatic representative accredited to a foreign state – **ministerial** *adj*, **ministerially** *adv*

²minister *vi* **1** to perform the functions of a minister of religion **2** to give aid or service ⟨~ *to the sick*⟩ – **ministrant** *n or adj*

ministration *n* the act or process of ministering, esp in religious matters

ministry *n* **1** service, ministration **2** the office, duties, or functions of a minister **3** the body of ministers of religion or government **4** the period of service or office of a minister or ministry **5** a government department presided over by a minister

miniver *n* a white fur used chiefly for robes of state

mink *n, pl* **mink, minks** **1** any of several semiaquatic flesh-eating mammals that resemble weasels and have partially webbed feet and a soft thick coat **2** the soft fur or pelt of the mink

minnow *n, pl* **minnows,** *esp collectively* **minnow** **1** a small dark-coloured freshwater fish or any of various small fishes **2** sthg small or insignificant of its kind

¹minor *adj* **1a** inferior in importance, size, rank, or degree ⟨*a* ~ *poet*⟩ **b** comparatively unimportant ⟨*a* ~ *alteration*⟩ **2** not having attained majority **3a** *esp of a scale or mode* having semitones between the second and third, fifth and sixth, and sometimes seventh and eighth steps **b** being or based on a (specified) minor scale ⟨*in a* ~ *key*⟩ ⟨*a piece in A* ~⟩ **c** being an interval less by a semitone than a corresponding major interval **d** *of a chord* having an interval of a minor third between the root and the next note above it **4** not serious or involving risk to life ⟨*a* ~ *illness*⟩

²minor *n* **1** sby who has not attained majority **2** a minor musical interval, scale, key, or mode

minority *n* **1a** the period before attainment of majority **b** the state of being a legal minor **2** the smaller of 2 groups constituting a whole; *specif* a group with less than the number of votes necessary for control **3** *sing or pl in constr* a group of people who share common characteristics or interests differing from those of the majority of a population

minor planet *n* an asteroid

minor suit *n* either of the suits of clubs or diamonds that in bridge are of inferior scoring value

Minotaur *n* a mythological monster shaped half like a man and half like a bull and confined in the labyrinth at Crete

minster *n* a large or important church often having cathedral status

minstrel *n* **1** a medieval singer, poet, or musical entertainer **2** any of a troupe of performers usu with blackened faces giving a performance of supposedly Negro singing, jokes, dancing, etc

minstrelsy *n* **1** the singing and playing of a minstrel **2** *sing or pl in constr* a body of minstrels **3** songs or poems (composed or performed by minstrels)

¹mint *n* **1** a place where money is made **2** a vast sum or amount – *infml*

²mint *vt* **1** to make (e g coins) by stamping metal **2** to fabricate, invent ⟨~ *a new word*⟩ – **minter** *n*

³mint *adj* unspoilt as if fresh from a mint; pristine ⟨*in* ~ *condition*⟩

⁴mint *n* **1** any of a genus of plants that have whorled leaves and foliage with a characteristic strong taste and smell, used esp as a flavouring **2** a sweet, chocolate, etc flavoured with mint

minuet *n* (music for or in the rhythm of) a slow graceful dance in 3_4 time

¹minus *prep* **1** diminished by ⟨*seven ~ four is three*⟩ **2** without ⟨*~ his hat*⟩

²minus *n* **1** a negative quantity **2** a deficiency, defect

³minus *adj* **1** negative ⟨*a ~ quantity*⟩ ⟨*a temperature of ~ 10°C*⟩ **2** having negative qualities; *esp* involving a disadvantage ⟨*a ~ factor*⟩ **3** falling low in a specified range ⟨*a mark of B ~*⟩

¹minuscule *n* (a lower-case letter in) a style of small flowing handwriting

²minuscule *adj* **1** written in minuscules **2** very small

¹minute *n* **1** the 60th part of an hour of time or of a degree **2** the distance one can cover in a minute ⟨*lived 5 ~ s from the station*⟩ **3** a short space of time; a moment **4a** MEMORANDUM **3** **b** *pl* the official record of the proceedings of a meeting

²minute *vb* to make notes or a brief summary (of)

³minute *adj* **1** extremely small **2** of minor importance; petty **3** marked by painstaking attention to detail – **minutely** *adv*, **minuteness** *n*

minute hand *n* the long hand that marks the minutes on the face of a watch or clock

minuteman *n* a member of a group of armed men pledged to take the field at a minute's notice during and immediately before the American Revolution

minutia *n*, *pl* **minutiae** a minor detail – usu *pl*

minx *n* a flirtatious girl

miracle *n* **1** an extraordinary event manifesting divine intervention in human affairs **2** an astonishing or unusual event, thing, or accomplishment **3** a person or thing that is a remarkable example or instance of sthg ⟨*this watch is a ~ of precision*⟩

miracle play *n* a medieval drama based on episodes from the Bible or the life of a saint; *also* MYSTERY PLAY

miraculous *adj* **1** of the nature of a miracle; supernatural **2** evoking wonder like a miracle; marvellous **3** (capable of) working miracles – **miraculously** *adv*, **miraculousness** *n*

mirage *n* **1** an optical illusion appearing esp as a pool of water or as the reflection of distant objects caused by the reflection of rays of light by a layer of heated air (near the ground) **2** sthg illusory and unattainable

¹mire *n* **1** a tract of soft waterlogged ground; a marsh, bog **2** (deep) mud or slush – **miry** *adj*

²mire *vt* to cause to stick fast (as if) in mire; BOG DOWN

¹mirror *n* **1** a smooth surface (e g of metal or silvered glass) that forms images by reflection **2** sthg that gives a true representation – **mirrorlike** *adj*

²mirror *vt* to reflect (as if) in a mirror

mirror image *n* sthg that has its parts reversely arranged in comparison with another similar thing

mirth *n* happiness or amusement accompanied with laughter – **mirthful** *adj*, **mirthfully** *adv*, **mirthfulness** *n*, **mirthless** *adj*

¹mis- *prefix* **1** badly; wrongly; unfavourably ⟨*misjudge*⟩ ⟨*misbehave*⟩ **2** suspicious; apprehensive ⟨*misgiving*⟩ **3** bad; wrong ⟨*misdeed*⟩ ⟨*misfit*⟩ **4** opposite or lack of ⟨*mistrust*⟩ ⟨*misfortune*⟩ **5** not ⟨*misunderstand*⟩

²mis-, miso- *comb form* hatred ⟨*misogamy*⟩

misadventure *n* a misfortune, mishap

misalliance *n* an improper or unsuitable alliance; *esp* a mésalliance

misanthrope, misanthropist *n* one who hates or distrusts people – **misanthropic** *adj*, **misanthropy** *n*

misapply *vt* to apply wrongly – **misapplication** *n*

misapprehend *vt* to misunderstand – **misapprehension** *n*

misappropriate *vt* to appropriate wrongly (e g by theft or embezzlement) – **misappropriation** *n*

misbegotten *adj* **1** having a disreputable or improper origin **2** wretched, contemptible ⟨*a ~ scoundrel*⟩ **3** *archaic* illegitimate, bastard

misbehave *vi* to behave badly – **misbehaviour** *n*

miscalculate *vb* to calculate wrongly – **miscalculation** *n*

miscarriage *n* **1** a failure in administration ⟨*~ of justice*⟩ **2** the expulsion of a human foetus before it is viable, esp after the 12th week of gestation

miscarry *vi* **1** to suffer miscarriage of a foetus **2** to fail to achieve an intended purpose

miscast *vt* **miscast** to cast in an unsuitable role

miscegenation *n* interbreeding of races, esp between sby white and sby nonwhite – **miscegenational** *adj*

miscellaneous *adj* **1** consisting of diverse items or members **2** having various characteristics or capabilities – **miscellaneously** *adv*, **miscellaneousness** *n*

miscellany *n* **1** a mixture of various things **2** a book containing miscellaneous literary pieces – **miscellanist** *n*

mischance *n* (a piece of) bad luck

mischief *n* **1** a specific injury or damage from a particular agent ⟨*did himself a ~ on the barbed wire*⟩ **2** sthg or esp sby that causes harm or annoyance **3** often playful action that annoys or irritates, usu without causing or intending serious harm **4** the quality or state of being mischievous

mischievous *adj* **1** harmful, malicious **2** able or tending to cause annoyance, unrest, or minor injury **3a** playfully provocative; arch **b** disruptively playful – **mischievously** *adv*, **mischievousness** *n*

misconceive *vt* to interpret wrongly; misunderstand – **misconception** *n*

misconduct *n* **1** mismanagement of responsibilities **2** adultery – **misconduct** *vt*

misconstrue *vt* to construe wrongly; misinterpret – **misconstruction** *n*

miscount *vt* to count wrongly ~*vi* to make a wrong count – **miscount** *n*

miscreant *adj or n* (of) one who behaves criminally or maliciously

miscue *vi or n* (to make) a faulty stroke in billiards or snooker in which the cue slips

misdate *vt* to date (e g a letter) wrongly

misdeal *vb* to deal (cards) incorrectly – **misdeal** *n*

misdeed *n* a wrong deed; an offence

misdemeanour *n* **1** a minor crime formerly technically distinguished from a felony **2** a misdeed

misdirect *vt* **1** to give a wrong direction to **2** to address (mail) wrongly – **misdirection** *n*

mise-en-scène *n*, *pl* **mise-en-scènes** **1** the arrangement of actors, props, and scenery on a stage in a theatrical production **2** the environment or setting in which sthg takes place

miser *n* a mean grasping person; *esp* one who hoards wealth – **miserly** *adj*, **miserliness** *n*

miserable *adj* **1a** wretchedly inadequate or meagre **b** causing extreme discomfort or unhappiness **2** in a pitiable state of distress or unhappiness **3** shameful, contemptible ⟨*a ~ failure*⟩ – **miserableness** *n*, **miserably** *adv*

misery *n* **1** (a cause of) physical or mental suffering or discomfort **2** great unhappiness and distress **3** *chiefly Br* a grumpy or querulous person; *esp* a killjoy – *infml*

misfire *vi* **1** *of a motor vehicle, engine, etc* to have the explosive or propulsive charge fail to ignite at the proper time ⟨*the engine* ~d⟩ **2** *esp of a firearm* to fail to fire **3** to fail to have an intended effect – **misfire** *n*

misfit *n* **1** sthg that fits badly **2** a person poorly adjusted to his/her environment

misfortune *n* **1** bad luck **2** a distressing or unfortunate incident or event; *also* the resultant unhappy situation ⟨*feared that some ~ would befall her*⟩ ⟨*sympathized with her in her ~*⟩

misgiving *n* a feeling of doubt, suspicion, or apprehension, esp concerning a future event

misgovern *vt* to govern badly – **misgovernment** *n*

misguide *vt* to lead astray – **misguidance** *n*

misguided *adj* directed by mistaken ideas, principles, or motives – **misguidedly** *adv*, **misguidedness** *n*

mishandle *vt* **1** to treat roughly; maltreat **2** to mismanage (a situation, crisis, etc)

mishap *n* an unfortunate accident

mishear *vb* **misheard** to hear wrongly

mishit *vt* **mishit; -tt-** to hit (a ball or stroke) faultily – **mishit** *n*

mishmash *n* a hotchpotch, jumble – infml

misinform *vt* to give untrue or misleading information to – **misinformation** *n*

misinterpret *vt* to understand or explain wrongly – **misinterpretation** *n*

misjudge *vt* **1** to estimate wrongly **2** to have an unjust opinion of ~ *vi* to make a mistaken judgment – **misjudgment** *n*

mislay *vt* **mislaid** to leave in an unremembered place

mislead *vt* **misled** to lead in a wrong direction or into a mistaken action or belief – **misleadingly** *adv*

mismanage *vt* to manage wrongly or incompetently – **mismanagement** *n*

mismatch *vt* to match incorrectly or unsuitably, esp in marriage – **mismatch** *n*

misname *vt* to call by the wrong name

misnomer *n* (a use of) a wrong name or designation

misogynist *n* one who hates women – **misogynous** *adj*, **misogyny** *n*, **misogynistic** *adj*

misplace *vt* **1a** to put in the wrong place **b** to mislay **2** to direct towards a wrong object or outcome ⟨~d *affections*⟩ ⟨~d *enthusiasm*⟩ **3** to fail to suit to the occasion ⟨~d *humour*⟩ – **misplacement** *n*

misprint *vt* to print wrongly – **misprint** *n*

mispronounce *vt* to pronounce wrongly

mispronunciation *n* (an instance of) mispronouncing

misquote *vt* to quote incorrectly – **misquotation** *n*

misread *vt* **misread** to read or interpret incorrectly

misreport *vt* to report falsely – **misreport** *n*

misrepresent *vt* to represent falsely; give an untrue or misleading account of – **misrepresentation** *n*

¹**misrule** *vt* to rule incompetently

²**misrule** *n* **1** misruling or being misruled **2** disorder, anarchy

¹**miss** *vt* **1** to fail to hit, reach, contact, or attain ⟨~ed *the train*⟩ ⟨*his arrow* ~ed *the mark*⟩ ⟨~ed *her step and fell heavily*⟩ **2** to discover or feel the absence of, esp with regret ⟨*didn't ~ his cheque book for several days*⟩ ⟨~ed *his wife desperately*⟩ **3** to escape, avoid ⟨*narrowly* ~ed *being run over*⟩ **4** to leave out; omit – often + *out* **5** to fail to understand, sense, or experience ⟨*he* ~ed *the point of the speech*⟩ **6** to fail to perform or attend ⟨~ed *his appointment*⟩ **7** to fail to take advantage of ⟨*never* ~es *an opportunity of playing golf*⟩ ~ *vi* **1** to fail to hit sthg **2** to misfire ⟨*the engine* ~ed⟩ – **miss out on** to lose or not to have had (a good opportunity) ⟨*people who* missed out on *further education*⟩ – **miss the boat** to fail to take advantage of an opportunity

²**miss** *n* **1** a failure to hit **2** a failure to attain a desired result **3** a deliberate avoidance or omission of sthg ⟨*felt so full he gave the dessert a ~*⟩

³**miss** *n* **1a** – used as a title preceding the name of an unmarried woman or girl **b** – used before the name of a place or of a line of activity or before some epithet to form a title for a usu young unmarried female who is representative of the thing indicated ⟨Miss *World*⟩ **2** young lady – used without a name as a conventional term of address to a young woman **3** a young unmarried woman or girl – chiefly infml

missal *n* a book containing the order of service of the mass for the whole year

misshape *vt* to shape badly; deform – **misshapen** *adj*, **misshapenly** *adv*

missile *n* an object thrown or projected, usu so as to strike sthg at a distance; *also* a self-propelled weapon that travels through the air

missing *adj* absent; *also* lost ⟨~ *in action*⟩

missing link *n* **1** an item needed to complete a continuous series **2** a supposed intermediate form between man and his anthropoid ancestors

mission *n* **1a** a ministry commissioned by a religious organization to propagate its faith or carry on humanitarian work, usu abroad **b** assignment to or work in a field of missionary enterprise **c** a mission establishment **d** *pl* organized missionary work **e** a campaign to increase church membership or strengthen Christian faith **2a** a group sent to a foreign country to negotiate, advise, etc **b** a permanent embassy or legation **3** a specific task with which a person or group is charged **4a** a definite military, naval, or aerospace task ⟨*a bombing* ~⟩ ⟨*a space* ~⟩ **b** a flight operation of an aircraft or spacecraft in the performance of a mission ⟨*a ~ to Mars*⟩ **5** a calling, vocation

¹**missionary** *adj* **1** relating to, engaged in, or devoted to missions **2** characteristic of a missionary

²**missionary** *n* a person undertaking a mission; *esp* one in charge of a religious mission in some remote part of the world

missive *n* a written communication; a letter – fml

misspell *vt* **misspelt**, *Nam chiefly* **misspelled** to spell incorrectly

misspend *vt* **misspent** to spend wrongly or foolishly; squander ⟨*regretted his* misspent *youth*⟩

misstate *vt* to state incorrectly; give a false account of – **misstatement** *n*

missus, missis *n* **1** a wife – infml or humor ⟨*have you met the ~?*⟩ **2** *chiefly Br* – used to address a married woman; infml

missy *n* a young girl; miss – infml

¹**mist** *n* **1** water in the form of diffuse particles in the atmosphere, esp near the earth's surface **2** sthg that dims or obscures ⟨*the ~s of time*⟩ **3** a film, or of tears, before the eyes **4a** a cloud of small particles suggestive of a mist **b** a suspension of a finely divided liquid in a gas

²**mist** *vi* to be or become misty ~ *vt* to cover (as if) with mist

¹**mistake** *vt* **mistook; mistaken** **1** to choose wrongly ⟨*mistook her way in the dark*⟩ **2a** to misunderstand the meaning, intention, or significance of **b** to estimate wrongly **3** to identify wrongly; confuse with another ⟨*I* mistook *him for his brother*⟩

²**mistake** *n* **1** a misunderstanding of the meaning or significance of sthg **2** a wrong action or statement arising from faulty judgment, inadequate knowledge, or carelessness

mistaken *adj* **1** *of a person* wrong in opinion ⟨*if you think he's honest, you're ~*⟩ **2** *of an action, idea, etc* based on wrong thinking; incorrect ⟨*trusted him in the ~ belief that he was honest*⟩ – **mistakenly** *adv*

mister *n* **1** – used sometimes in writing instead of the usual *Mr* **2** sir – used without a name as a generalized infml term of direct address of a man who is a stranger **3** a man not entitled to a title of rank or an honorific or professional title

mistime *vt* to time badly

mistle thrush, missel thrush *n* a large Eurasian thrush with larger spots on its underparts than the song thrush

mistletoe *n* a European shrub that grows as a parasite on the branches of trees and has thick leaves and waxy white glutinous berries

mistral *n* a strong cold dry northerly wind of S France

mistress *n* **1a** a woman in a position of power or authority **b** the female head of a household **2** a woman who has achieved mastery of a subject or skill **3** sthg personified as female that rules or directs **4** a woman with whom a man has a continuing sexual relationship outside marriage **5** *chiefly Br* a schoolmistress ⟨*thoroughly disliked the maths ~*⟩ **6** *archaic* a sweetheart **7** – used archaically as a title preceding the name of a woman and now superseded by *Mrs, Miss,* and *Ms*

mistrial *n* a trial declared void because of some error in the proceedings

mistrust *vt* **1** to have little trust in; be suspicious of **2** to doubt the reliability or effectiveness of – **mistrust** *n*, **mistrusted** *adj*, **mistrustful** *adj*, **mistrustfully** *adv*

misty *adj* **1** obscured by mist **2** not clear to the mind or understanding; indistinct – **mistily** *adv*, **mistiness** *n*

misunderstand *vt* **1** to fail to understand **2** to interpret incorrectly

misunderstanding *n* **1** a failure to understand; a misinterpretation **2** a disagreement, dispute

misuse *vt* **1** to put to wrong or improper use **2** to abuse or maltreat – **misuse** *n*

mite *n* **1** any of numerous (extremely) small arachnids that often infest animals, plants, and stored foods **2** a small coin or sum of money ⟨*a widow's ~*⟩ **3** a very small object or creature; *esp* a small child – **a mite** to a small extent – infml

mitigate *vt* **1** to cause to become less harsh or hostile **2a** to make less severe or painful; alleviate **b** to extenuate ⟨*mitigating circumstances*⟩ – **mitigatory** *adj*, **mitigation** *n*

mitochondrion *n, pl* **mitochondria** any of several organelles in a cell that are rich in fats, proteins, and enzymes and produce energy through cellular respiration – **mitochondrial** *adj*, **mitochondrially** *adv*

mitosis *n, pl* **mitoses** the formation of 2 new nuclei from an original nucleus, each having the same number of chromosomes as the original nucleus, during cell division; *also* cell division in which this occurs – **mitotic** *adj*

¹**mitre,** *NAm chiefly* **miter** *n* **1** a tall pointed divided headdress with 2 bands hanging down at the back worn by bishops and abbots on ceremonial occasions **2** MITRE JOINT **3** a seam joining 2 parts of a sail whose fabric runs in different directions

²**mitre,** *NAm chiefly* **miter** *vt* **1** to bevel the ends of to make a mitre joint **2** to match or fit together in a mitre joint

mitre box *n* a device for guiding a handsaw at the proper angle in making a mitre joint in wood

mitre joint *n* a joint made by cutting the ends of 2 pieces of wood at an oblique angle so that they form a right angle when fitted together

mitt *n* **1a** a glove that leaves the (ends of the) fingers uncovered **b** MITTEN 1 **c** a baseball catcher's protective glove made in the style of a mitten **2** a hand or paw; *specif* a person's hand – infml

mitten *n* **1** a glove that is divided into one part covering the fingers and another part covering the thumb **2** MITT 1a

¹**mix** *vt* **1a(1)** to combine or blend into a mass **(2)** to combine with another – often + *in* ⟨*prepare the soup and ~ in the herbs*⟩ **b** to bring into close association ⟨*~ business with pleasure*⟩ **2** to prepare by mixing different components or ingredients ⟨*~ a drink*⟩ **3** to control the balance of (various sounds), esp during the recording of a film, broadcast, record, etc ~ *vi* **1a** to become mixed **b** to be capable of mixing **2** to seek or enjoy the society of others **3** to crossbreed **4** to become actively involved ⟨*decided not to ~ in politics*⟩ – **mix it** to fight, brawl – infml

²**mix** *n* **1** an act or process of mixing **2** a product of mixing; *specif* a commercially prepared mixture of food ingredients **3** a combination ⟨*the right ~ of jobs, people, and amenities – The Times*⟩ **4** a combination in definite proportions of 2 or more recordings (e g of a singer and an accompaniment)

mixed *adj* **1** combining diverse elements **2** made up of or involving people of different races, national origins, religions, classes, or sexes **3** including or accompanied by conflicting or dissimilar elements ⟨*~ feelings*⟩ **4** deriving from 2 or more races or breeds ⟨*a person of ~ blood*⟩

mixed bag *n* a miscellaneous collection; an assortment

mixed farming *n* the growing of food crops and the rearing of livestock on the same farm

mixed grill *n* a dish of several meats and vegetables grilled together

mixed metaphor *n* a combination of incongruous metaphors (e g in *iron out bottlenecks*)

mixed-up *adj* marked by perplexity, uncertainty, or disorder; confused – infml

mixer *n* **1a** a set of adjustable electrical resistances or attenuators used to combine signals, esp sound signals, from a number of sources in variable proportions for recording, broadcasting, etc; *also* one who operates such a device **b** a container, device, or machine for mixing sthg (e g food or concrete) **2a** a person considered with respect to his/her sociability ⟨*was shy and a poor ~*⟩ **b** a nonalcoholic beverage intended to be drunk mixed with spirits

mixture *n* **1a** mixing or being mixed **b** the relative proportions of constituents; *specif* the proportion of fuel to air produced in a carburettor **2a** (a portion of) matter consisting of 2 or more components in varying proportions that retain their own properties **b** a fabric woven of different coloured threads **c** a combination of several different kinds; a blend

mix-up *n* a state or instance of confusion

mix up *vt* **1** to make untidy or disordered **2** to mistake or confuse ⟨*it's easy to* mix *her* up *with her sister*⟩

mizzen, mizen *n* (the principal fore-and-aft sail set on) a mizzenmast

mizzenmast *n* the mast behind the mainmast in a sailing vessel

mizzle *vi* **mizzling** to drizzle – **mizzle** *n*, **mizzly** *adj*

¹**mnemonic** *adj* **1** assisting or intended to assist the memory **2** of memory – **mnemonically** *adv*

²**mnemonic** *n* a mnemonic device or code

mnemonics *n pl but sing in constr* the art of improving the memory

mo, mo' *n, chiefly Br* a very short space of time; a moment – infml; often in *half a mo*

moa *n* a very large extinct flightless bird of New Zealand

¹moan n **1** a complaint ⟨*the unflagging stream of* ~s *and queries* – *Honey Magazine*⟩ **2** a low prolonged sound of pain or grief

²moan vt **1** to lament **2** to utter with moans ~ vi **1** to produce (a sound like) a moan **2** to complain, grumble ⟨*always* ~ing *on about something*⟩ – **moaner** n

¹moat n a deep wide trench round a castle, fortified home, etc that is usu filled with water

²moat vt to surround (as if) with a moat ⟨*a* ~ed *grange*⟩

¹mob n **1** *the* masses, populace **2** a disorderly riotous crowd **3** a criminal gang **4** chiefly Austr a flock, drove, or herd of animals **5** *sing or pl in constr, chiefly Br* a crowd, bunch – infml – **mobbish** adj, **mobocracy** n

²mob vt **-bb-** **1** to attack in a large crowd or group **2** to crowd round, esp out of curiosity or admiration

¹mobile adj **1** capable of moving or being moved **2** changing quickly in expression or mood **3** (capable of) undergoing movement into a different social class **4** marked by movement ⟨~ *warfare*⟩ – **mobility** n

²mobile n a structure (e g of cardboard or metal) with usu suspended parts that are moved in different planes by air currents or machinery

mobilize, -ise vt **1a** to put into movement or circulation **b** to release (sthg stored in the body) for use in an organism **2a** to assemble and make ready (e g troops) for active service **b** to marshal (e g resources) for action ~ vi to undergo mobilization – **mobilization** n

mobster n, chiefly NAm a member of a criminal gang

moccasin n a soft leather heelless shoe with the sole brought up the sides of the foot and joined to the upper by a puckered seam

mocha n **1** a coffee of superior quality, specif grown in Arabia **2** a flavouring obtained from a (mixture of cocoa or chocolate with a) strong coffee infusion

¹mock vt **1** to treat with contempt or ridicule **2** to disappoint the hopes of **3** to mimic in fun or derision ~ vi to jeer, scoff – **mocker** n, **mockingly** adv

²mock n a school examination used as a rehearsal for an official one

³mock adj (having the character) of an imitation or simulation ⟨~ *cream*⟩ ⟨*a* ~ *battle*⟩

⁴mock adv in an insincere or pretended manner – usu in combination ⟨mock-*serious*⟩

mockery n **1** jeering or contemptuous behaviour or words **2** an object of laughter or derision **3** a deceitful or contemptible imitation; a travesty **4** sthg insultingly or ridiculously inappropriate

mockingbird n a common bird of esp the southern USA that imitates the calls of other birds

mock turtle soup n a soup made from a calf's head in imitation of green turtle soup

mock-up n a full-sized structural model built accurately to scale

modal adj **1** of modality in logic **2** of or being (in) a mode (e g in music); *specif* being in one of the church modes rather than a major or minor key **3** of general form or structure as opposed to particular substance or content **4** of or being a form or category indicating grammatical mood – **modally** adv

modal auxiliary n an auxiliary verb (e g *can, must, may*) expressing a distinction of mood

modality n **1** a modal quality or attribute; a form **2** the classification of logical propositions according to the possibility, impossibility, contingency, or necessity of their content **3** a procedure (e g massage) or apparatus used in (physical) therapy **4** MOOD

mod con n, Br a modern convenience; esp a household

fitting or device designed to increase comfort or save time – infml; often in *all mod cons*

¹mode n **1a** an arrangement of the 8 diatonic musical notes of an octave in any of several fixed schemes which use different patterns of whole tones and semitones between successive notes **b** a rhythmical scheme, esp in 13th and 14th-c music **2** ²MOOD **3** MODALITY 2 **4a** a particular form or variety of sthg **b** a form or manner of expression; a style **5** a way of doing or carrying out sthg **6** a particular functional arrangement or condition ⟨*a spacecraft in orbiting* ~⟩ **7** the most frequently occurring value in a set of data **8** any of various stationary vibration patterns of which an elastic body or oscillatory system is capable ⟨*the vibration* ~s *of a propeller blade*⟩

²mode n a prevailing fashion or style (e g of dress or behaviour) – fml

¹model n **1** structural design ⟨*built his home on the* ~ *of an old farmhouse*⟩ **2** a replica of sthg in relief or 3 dimensions; *also* a representation of sthg to be constructed **3** an example worthy of imitation or emulation ⟨*this essay is a* ~ *of clarity*⟩ **4** sby or sthg that serves as a pattern for an artist; *esp* one who poses for an artist **5** one who is employed to wear merchandise, esp clothing, in order to display it ⟨*a fashion* ~⟩ **6** a type or design of an article or product (e g a garment or car) **7a** a (simplified) description or analogy used to help visualize sthg (e g an atom) that cannot be directly observed **8** a system of postulates, data, and inferences presented as a mathematical description of an entity or state of affairs **9** a prostitute – euph

²model vb **-ll-** (NAm **-l-, -ll-**), vt **1** to plan or form after a pattern **2** to shape in a mouldable material; *broadly* to produce a representation or simulation of ⟨*using a computer to* ~ *a problem*⟩ **3** to construct or fashion in imitation of a particular model **4** to display, esp by wearing ⟨~-led *hats for a living*⟩ ~ vi **1** to design or imitate forms **2** to work or act as a fashion model – **modeller** n

³model adj **1** (worthy of) being a pattern for others ⟨*a* ~ *student*⟩ **2** being a miniature representation of sthg ⟨*a* ~ *aeroplane*⟩

¹moderate adj **1a** avoiding extremes of behaviour or expression **b** not violent; temperate **2a** being (somewhat less than) average in quality, amount, or degree **b** (done or kept) within reasonable limits ⟨~ *wage demands*⟩ – **moderately** adv, **moderateness** n

²moderate vt **1** to lessen the intensity or extremeness of **2** to preside over ~ vi **1** to act as a moderator **2** to decrease in violence, severity, intensity, or volume – **moderation** n

³moderate n one who holds moderate views or favours a moderate course

Moderations n pl the first honours examination at Oxford in some subjects

moderato adv or adj in a moderate tempo – used in music

moderator n **1** a mediator **2** the presiding officer of a Presbyterian governing body **3** a substance (e g graphite) used for slowing down neutrons in a nuclear reactor – **moderatorship** n

modern adj **1a** (characteristic) of a period extending from a particular point in the past to the present time **b** (characteristic) of the present or the immediate past; contemporary **2** involving recent techniques, styles, or ideas **3** cap constituting the present or most recent period of a language – **modernness, modernity** n

modernism n **1** a practice, usage, or expression characteristic of modern times **2** often cap a tendency in theology to adapt traditional doctrine to contemporary thought by minimizing the role of the supernatural **3** the theory and practices of modern art; *esp* a search for new forms of expression involving a deliberate break with the past – **modernist** *n or adj*, **modernistic** *adj*

modernize, -ise *vt* to adapt to modern needs, style, or standards ~ *vi* to adopt modern views, habits, or techniques – **modernization** *n*

modern pentathlon *n* a contest in which all contestants compete in a 300-m freestyle swimming race, a 4000-m cross-country run, a 5000-m 30-jump equestrian steeplechase, épée fencing, and target shooting at 25m

modest *adj* **1** having a moderate estimate of one's abilities or worth; not boastful or self-assertive **2** (characteristic) of a modest nature **3** carefully observant of proprieties of dress and behaviour **4** small or limited in size, amount, or aim – **modestly** *adv*, **modesty** *n*

modicum *n* a small or limited amount

modification *n* **1** the limiting of a statement **2** the making of a limited change to sthg

modifier *n* a word or word group that modifies another

modify *vt* **1** to make less extreme **2** to limit in meaning; qualify **3a** to make minor changes in **b** to make basic changes in, often for a specific purpose ~ *vi* to undergo change – **modifiable** *adj*

modish *adj* fashionable, stylish – **modishly** *adv*, **modishness** *n*

Mods *n pl* Moderations – *infml*

modular *adj* of or based on a module or modulus – **modularly** *adv*, **modularity** *n*

modulate *vt* **1** to vary in tone; make tuneful ⟨~ *one's voice*⟩ **2** to adjust to or keep in proper measure or proportion **3** to vary the amplitude, frequency, or phase of (a carrier wave or signal) by combining with a wave of a different frequency, so as to transmit a radio, television, etc signal ~ *vi* to pass by regular chord or melodic progression from one musical key or tonality into another – **modulator** *n*, **modulatory** *adj*, **modulation** *n*

module *n* **1** a standard or unit of measure; *esp* one by which the proportions of an architectural composition are regulated **2** a standardized or independent unit used in construction (e g of buildings, electronic systems, or spacecraft)

modus operandi *n*, *pl* **modi operandi** a method of procedure

modus vivendi *n*, *pl* **modi vivendi 1** a practical compromise, esp between opposed or quarrelling parties **2** a manner of living; a way of life

moggie, moggy *n*, *Br* CAT 1a – *infml*

mogul *n* **1** Mogul, Moghul a member of a Muslim dynasty of Turkish and Mongolian origin ruling India from the 16th to the 18th c **2** a great or prominent (business) person

mohair *n* a fabric or yarn made (partly) from the long silky hair of the Angora goat

Mohammedan *adj* Muhammadan

moiety *n* **1** either of 2 (approximately) equal parts **2** any of the portions into which sthg is divided

moiré, moire *n* an irregular wavy sheen on a fabric or metal – **moiré** *adj*

moist *adj* **1** slightly wet; damp **2** highly humid – **moistly** *adv*, **moistness** *n*, **moisten** *vb*

moisture *n* liquid diffused, condensed, or absorbed in relatively small amounts

moisturize, -ise *vt* to add or restore moisture to (e g the skin) – **moisturizer** *n*

moke *n* **1** *Br* a donkey **2** *Austr* a horse, esp of poor appearance *USE* slang

¹molar *n* a grinding tooth with a rounded or flattened

surface; *specif* one lying behind the incisors and canines of a mammal

²molar *adj* of or located near the molar teeth

³molar *adj* **1** of a mass of matter as distinguished from the properties of individual molecules or atoms **2** of or containing 1 gram molecule (of solute) in 1 litre of solution ⟨*a* ~ *solution*⟩ – **molarity** *n*

molasses *n* the darkest most viscous syrup remaining after all sugar that can be separated by crystallization has been removed during the refining of raw sugar

mold *vt or n*, *NAm* (to) mould

¹mole *n* a pigmented spot, mark, or lump on the human body; *esp* a naevus

²mole *n* **1** any of numerous small burrowing insect-eating mammals with minute eyes, concealed ears, and soft fur **2** one who works subversively within an organization, esp to secretly further the interests of a rival organization or government

³mole *n* (a harbour formed by) a massive work of masonry, large stones, etc laid in the sea as a pier or breakwater

⁴mole *n* an abnormal mass in the womb, esp when containing foetal tissues

⁵mole *also* **mol** *n* the basic SI unit of substance; the amount of substance that contains the same number of atoms, molecules, ions, etc as there are atoms in 0.012kg of carbon-12

molecular *adj* of, produced by, or consisting of molecules ⟨~ *oxygen*⟩ – **molecularly** *adv*, **molecularity** *n*

molecule *n* the smallest particle of a substance that retains its characteristic properties, consisting of 1 or more atoms

molehill *n* a mound of earth thrown up by a burrowing mole

molest *vt* to annoy, disturb, or attack; *specif* to annoy or attack (esp a child or woman) sexually – **molester** *n*, **molestation** *n*

moll *n* **1** a prostitute **2** a gangster's girl friend *USE* infml

mollify *vt* **1** to lessen the anger or hostility of **2** to reduce in intensity – **mollification** *n*

mollusc, *NAm chiefly* **mollusk** *n* any of a large phylum of invertebrate animals with soft bodies not divided into segments and usu enclosed in a shell, including the snails, shellfish, octopuses, and squids – **molluscan** *adj*

mollycoddle *vt* mollycoddling to treat with excessive indulgence and attention

Molotov cocktail *n* a crude hand grenade made from a bottle filled with petrol or other inflammable liquid with usu a saturated rag for a wick

molt *vb or n*, *NAm* (to) moult

molten *adj* melted by heat

molto *adv* much, very – used in music ⟨~ *sostenuto*⟩

molybdenum *n* a metallic element resembling chromium and tungsten and used esp in strengthening and hardening steel

mom *n*, *NAm* ²MUM

moment *n* **1** a very brief interval or point of time **2a** present time ⟨*at the* ~⟩ **b** a time of excellence or prominence ⟨*she has her* ~s⟩ **3** importance in influence or effect **4** a stage in historical or logical development **5** (a measure of) the tendency of a force to produce turning motion **6** the product of a force and the distance from its line of action to a particular axis

momentarily *adv* **1** for a moment **2** *chiefly NAm* instantly

momentary *adj* lasting a very short time – **momentariness** *n*

moment of truth *n* **1** the moment of the final sword

thrust in a bullfight 2 a moment of crisis on whose outcome everything depends

momentous adj of great consequence or significance – **momentousness** n

momentum n, pl **momenta, momentums** the product of the mass of a body and its velocity

momma n, NAm ²MUM

Mon n a member, or the language of, the dominant ethnic group of Burma and Thailand

mon-, mono- comb form 1 one; single; alone ⟨mono*plane*⟩ ⟨mono*drama*⟩ ⟨mono*phobia*⟩ 2a containing 1 (specified) atom, radical, or group ⟨mono*hydrate*⟩ ⟨mono*xide*⟩ b monomolecular ⟨mono*layer*⟩

monarch n 1 sby who reigns over a kingdom or empire 2 sby or sthg occupying a commanding or preeminent position 3 a large American butterfly with orange-brown wings with black veins and borders – **monarchal, monarchial, monarchic, monarchical** adj

monarchism n government by or the principles of monarchy – **monarchist** n or adj, **monarchistic** adj

monarchy n (a government or state with) undivided rule by a monarch

monastery n a residence occupied by a religious community, esp of monks

monastic adj of or being monasteries, monks, or nuns – **monastic** n, **monastically** adv, **monasticism** n

Monday n the day of the week following Sunday – **Mondays** adv

monetary adj of money or its behaviour in an economy – **monetarily** adv

money n, pl **moneys, monies** 1 sthg generally accepted as a means of payment; esp officially printed, coined, or stamped currency 2 (one who has) wealth reckoned in terms of money ⟨she refused to marry ∼⟩ 3 a form or denomination of coin or paper money 4 the first, second, and third places in a race on whose result money is betted – usu in in/out of the money

moneybags n, pl **moneybags** a wealthy person – derog

money box n a container for small personal savings, usu with a slot for the insertion of coins

money changer n one whose occupation is the exchanging of kinds or denominations of currency

moneyed, monied adj 1 having much money 2 consisting of or derived from money

money grubber n a person sordidly bent on accumulating money – infml – **money-grubbing** adj or n

moneylender n one whose business is lending money and charging interest on it

money-maker n a product or enterprise that produces much profit – **moneymaking** adj or n

money-spinner n, chiefly Br a money-maker – infml – **money-spinning** adj or n

monger n 1 a trader or dealer ⟨ale*monger*⟩ 2 one who attempts to stir up or spread sthg petty or discreditable ⟨gossip*monger*⟩ ⟨war*monger*⟩ USE usu in combination

Mongol n 1 a member of any of the chiefly pastoral peoples of Mongolia 2 MONGOLIAN 2 3 a person of Mongoloid racial stock 4 often not cap a sufferer from Down's syndrome – **Mongol** adj

Mongolian n 1a MONGOL 1, 3 b a native or inhabitant of Mongolia or of the Mongolian People's Republic 2 the language of the Mongol people – **Mongolian** adj

mongolism n DOWN'S SYNDROME

mongoose n, pl **mongooses** also **mongeese** an agile ferret-sized esp Indian mammal that feeds on snakes and rodents and is related to the civets

mongrel n a dog or other individual (of unknown ancestry) resulting from the interbreeding of diverse breeds –

mongrel, mongrelly adj, **mongrelize** vt, **mongrelization** n

¹**monitor**, fem **monitress** n 1a a pupil appointed to help a teacher b sby or sthg that monitors or is used in monitoring: e g (1) a receiver used to view the picture being picked up by a television camera (2) a device for observing a biological condition or function ⟨a heart ∼⟩ 2 any of various large tropical Old World lizards closely related to the iguanas 3 a small warship with guns heavy in relation to its size – **monitorship** n, **monitorial** adj

²**monitor** vt 1 to keep (a broadcast) under surveillance by means of a receiver, in order to check the quality or fidelity to a frequency or to investigate the content (e g for political significance) 2 to observe or inspect, esp for a special purpose 3 to regulate or control the operation of (e g a machine or process)

monk n a male member of a religious order, living apart from the world under vows of poverty, chastity, etc – **monkhood** n

¹**monkey** n 1 any (small long-tailed) primate mammal with the exception of the human beings and usu also the lemurs and tarsiers 2 the falling weight of a pile driver 3a a mischievous child; a scamp b a ludicrous figure; a fool ⟨made a ∼ of him⟩ 4 £500 or $500 – slang USE (3) infml

²**monkey** vi 1 to act in an absurd or mischievous manner 2 TAMPER 2 – usu + with USE infml; often + about or around

monkey business n mischievous or underhand activity – infml

monkey nut n PEANUT 1

monkey-puzzle n a commonly planted S American evergreen gymnospermous tree with intertwined branches and stiff sharp leaves

monkey wrench n a large spanner with one fixed and one adjustable jaw

mono adj or n monophonic (sound reproduction)

mono- – see MON-

monochrome adj or n (of, using, or being) reproduction or execution in 1 colour, black and white, or shades of grey – **monochromist** n, **monochromic** adj

monocle n an eyeglass for 1 eye – **monocled** adj

monogamy n the state or custom of being married to 1 person at a time – **monogamist** n, **monogamous** adj, **monogamously** adv, **monogamic** adj

monogram vt or n (to mark with) a character usu formed of the interwoven initials of a name – **monogrammatic** adj

monograph n a treatise on a small area of learning – **monographic** adj

monolith n 1 a single large block of stone, often in the form of an obelisk or column 2 a massive structure 3 an organized whole that acts as a single powerful force

monolithic adj 1 formed from or produced in or on a single crystal ⟨a ∼ silicon chip⟩ 2 constituting a massive uniform whole ⟨the ∼ totalitarian state⟩ – **monolithically** adv

monologue, NAm also **monolog** n 1 a dramatic or literary soliloquy; also a dramatic sketch performed by 1 speaker 2 a long speech monopolizing conversation – **monologuist, monologist** n

monomania n obsessional concentration on a single object or idea – **monomaniac** n or adj

monomolecular adj (of a layer) only 1 molecule thick ⟨a ∼ film⟩ – **monomolecularly** adv

mononucleosis n INFECTIOUS MONONUCLEOSIS

monophonic adj of or being a system for sound reproduction in which the sound signal is not split into 2 or more

different channels between the source and the point of use
– **monophonically** *adv*

monophthong *n* a simple nongliding vowel sound (e g /i/ in *bid*) – **monophthongal** *adj*

monoplane *n* an aeroplane with only 1 main pair of wings

monopolist *n* one who has or favours a monopoly – **monopolistic** *adj*

monopolize, -ise *vt* to get a monopoly of; assume complete possession or control of – **monopolizer** *n*, **monopolization** *n*

monopoly *n* **1** (a person or group having) exclusive ownership or control (through legal privilege, command of the supply of a commodity, concerted action, etc) **2** sthg, esp a commodity, controlled by one party

monorail *n* (a vehicle running on) a single rail serving as a track for a wheeled vehicle

monosyllable *n* a word of 1 syllable; *specif* one used by sby intending to be pointedly brief in answering or commenting – **monosyllabic** *adj*, **monosyllabically** *adv*

monotheism *n* the doctrine or belief that there is only 1 God – **monotheist** *n*, **monotheistic** *adj*

¹**monotone** *n* **1** a succession of speech sounds in 1 unvarying pitch **2** a single unvaried musical note **3** a tedious sameness or repetition

²**monotone** *adj* **1** having a uniform colour **2** MONOTONIC 2

monotonic *adj* **1** uttered in a monotone **2** *of a mathematical function* increasing continuously or decreasing continuously as the independent variable increases – **monotonically** *adv*

monotonous *adj* **1** uttered or sounded in 1 unvarying tone **2** tediously uniform or repetitive – **monotonously** *adv*, **monotonousness, monotony** *n*

monotype *n* an impression on paper taken from a painting on glass or metal

Monotype *trademark* – used for a keyboard-operated typesetting machine that casts and sets metal type in separate characters

monsieur *n*, *pl* **messieurs** – used by or to a French-speaking man as a title equivalent to Mr or without a name as a term of direct address

monsignor *n*, *pl* **monsignors, monsignori** – used as a title for certain Roman Catholic prelates and officers of the papal court – **monsignorial** *adj*

monsoon *n* **1** a seasonal wind of S Asia blowing from the SW in summer and the NE in winter **2** the season of the SW monsoon, marked by very heavy rains – **monsoonal** *adj*

monster *n* **1a** an animal or plant of (grotesquely) abnormal form or structure **b** an (imaginary) animal of incredible shape or form that is usu dangerous or horrifying **2** one exceptionally large for its kind ⟨~ tomatoes⟩ **3** sthg monstrous; *esp* a person of appalling ugliness, wickedness, or cruelty

monstrance *n* a vessel in which the consecrated Host is exposed for veneration, esp in a Catholic church

monstrosity *n* **1** MONSTER 1a **2** (the quality or state of being) sthg monstrous

monstrous *adj* **1** having the qualities or appearance of a monster; extraordinarily large **2a** extraordinarily ugly or vicious **b** outrageously wrong or ridiculous – **monstrously** *adv*, **monstrousness** *n*

mons veneris *n*, *pl* **montes veneris** a rounded raised mass of fatty tissue over the pubic bone and above the vulva of the human female

montage *n* **1a** a picture made by combining or overlapping several separate pictures **b** an artistic composition made from different materials combined or juxtaposed **2**

(a film sequence using) a method of film editing in which the chronological sequence of events is interrupted by juxtaposed or rapidly succeeding shots

month *n* **1a** any of the 12 divisions of the year in the Julian or Gregorian calendars corresponding roughly with the period of the moon's rotation; *also* any similar division of the year in other calendars **b** 28 days or 4 weeks; *also* the interval between the same date in adjacent months **2** *pl* an indefinite usu protracted period of time ⟨*he's been gone for* ~s⟩ **3** a ninth of the typical duration of human pregnancy ⟨*in her 8th* ~⟩ – **monthly** *adv or adj*

monthly *n* **1** a monthly periodical **2** *pl* a menstrual period – *infml*

monument *n* **1** a written record **2a** a lasting evidence or reminder of sby or sthg notable or influential **b** a memorial stone, sculpture, or structure erected to commemorate a person or event **3** a structure or site of historical or archaeological importance

monumental *adj* **1a** of, serving as, or resembling a monument **b** occurring or used on a monument ⟨*a* ~ *inscription*⟩ **2** very great in degree; imposing, outstanding ⟨*their* ~ *arrogance*⟩ ⟨*a* ~ *work*⟩ – **monumentally** *adv*

moo *vi or n* ¹LOW

mooch *vi* **1** to wander aimlessly or disconsolately – usu + *around, about*, or *along* **2** *NAm* to sponge, cadge ~ *vt*, *NAm* **1** to steal; MAKE OFF WITH **2** to cadge, beg *USE* infml – **moocher** *n*

¹**mood** *n* **1a** (the evocation, esp in art or literature, of) a predominant emotion, feeling, or frame of mind **b** the right frame of mind ⟨*you must be in the* ~, *or you'll fall asleep* – *The Listener*⟩ **2** a fit of often silent anger or bad temper **3** a prevailing attitude

²**mood** *n* a distinct form or set of inflectional forms of a verb indicating whether the action or state it denotes is considered a fact, wish, possibility, etc ⟨*the subjunctive* ~⟩

moody *adj* **1** sullen or gloomy **2** temperamental – **moodily** *adv*, **moodiness** *n*

¹**moon** *n* **1a** (the appearance or visibility from the earth of) the earth's natural satellite that shines by reflecting the sun's light ⟨*there is a* ~ *tonight*⟩ **b** a satellite **2** LUNAR MONTH – *poetic* – **moonless** *adj*, **moonlet** *n*, **moonlike** *adj* – **over the moon** absolutely delighted

²**moon** *vi* **1** to move about listlessly **2** to spend time in idle gazing or daydreaming *USE* often + *around* or *about*; infml

moonbeam *n* a ray of light from the moon

mooncalf *n* MONSTER 1a

moonlight *vi* **moonlighted** to hold a second job in addition to a regular one – **moonlighter** *n*

moonlit *adj* lighted (as if) by the moon

moonshine *n* **1** the light of the moon **2** empty talk; nonsense **3** (illegally distilled) spirits, esp whisky – infml

moonstone *n* a transparent or translucent opalescent feldspar used as a gem

moonstruck *adj* affected (as if) by the moon; *specif* mentally unbalanced

moony *adj* inanely dreamy; moonstruck – *infml*

¹**moor** *n*, *chiefly Br* an expanse of open peaty infertile usu heath-covered upland

²**moor** *vt* to make (e g a boat or buoy) fast with cables, lines, or anchors ~ *vi* **1** to secure a vessel by mooring **2** to be made fast

Moor *n* a member of the mixed Arab and Berber people that conquered Spain in the 8th c AD – **Moorish** *adj*

moorhen *n* a common red-billed blackish bird of the rail family that nests near fresh water

mooring *n* **1** a place where or an object to which a ship, boat, etc can be made fast **2** the lines, chains, anchors, etc used to make a ship, boat, etc fast ⟨*she may have dragged her* ~ *s*⟩ *USE* usu pl with sing. meaning

moose *n, pl* **moose 1** a large N American ruminant mammal of the deer family with very large flattened antlers **2** the European elk

¹**moot** *n* **1** an early English assembly to decide points of community and political interest **2** a mock court in which law students argue hypothetical cases

²**moot** *vt* to put forward for discussion ⟨*the idea was first* ~*ed years ago*⟩

³**moot** *adj* open to question; debatable – usu in *moot point*

¹**mop** *n* **1** an implement consisting of a head made of absorbent material fastened to a long handle and used esp for cleaning floors **2** (sthg like) a shock of untidy hair

²**mop** *vt* **-pp- 1** to clean (a floor or other surface) with a mop **2** to wipe (as if) with a mop ⟨~*ped his brow with a handkerchief*⟩ – **mopper** *n*

mope *vi* to give oneself up to brooding; become listless or dejected – **moper** *n*

moped *n* a low-powered motorcycle whose engine can be pedal-assisted (e g for starting)

moppet *n* a young child; *esp* a little girl – chiefly infml; apprec

mop up *vt* **1** to eliminate remaining resistance in (e g a previously occupied area in a war) **2** to absorb, take up, or deal with (esp a remnant or remainder) ~*vi* to complete a project or transaction – **mop-up** *n*

moquette *n* a carpet or upholstery fabric with a velvety pile

moraine *n* an accumulation of earth and stones carried and deposited by a glacier – **morainal, morainic** *adj*

¹**moral** *adj* **1a** of or being principles of right and wrong in conduct; ethical **b** expressing or teaching a conception of right conduct ⟨*a* ~ *poem*⟩ **c** conforming to a standard of right conduct ⟨*a* ~ *person*⟩ **d** sanctioned by, resulting from, or operative on one's conscience or (correct) moral judgment ⟨*a* ~ *obligation*⟩⟨*a* ~ *right*⟩ **e** capable of distinguishing right and wrong ⟨*man is a* ~ *being*⟩ **2** very probable though not proved ⟨*a* ~ *certainty*⟩ **3** of, occurring in, or acting on the mind, emotions, or will ⟨*a* ~ *victory*⟩ ⟨~ *support*⟩ – **morally** *adv*

²**moral** *n* **1** (a concluding passage pointing out) the moral significance or practical lesson **2** *pl* **a** moral practices or teachings; standards of esp sexual conduct ⟨*a man of loose* ~*s*⟩ **b** ethics

morale *n* the mental and emotional condition (e g of enthusiasm or loyalty) of an individual or group with regard to the function or tasks at hand

moralist *n* **1** one concerned with moral principles and problems **2** one concerned with regulating the morals of others – often derog – **moralistic** *adj*, **moralistically** *adv*

morality *n* **1** a system or sphere of moral conduct ⟨*Christian* ~ ⟩ **2** (degree of conformity to standards of) right conduct or moral correctness ⟨*questioned the* ~ *of his act*⟩

morality play *n* a form of allegorical drama popular esp in the 15th and 16th c in which the characters personify moral or abstract qualities (e g pride or youth)

moralize, -ise *vt* **1** to interpret morally; draw a moral from **2** to make moral or morally better ~*vi* to make moral reflections – **moralizer** *n*, **moralization** *n*

morass *n* **1** a marsh, swamp **2** sthg that ensnares, confuses, or impedes – **morassy** *adj*

moratorium *n, pl* **moratoriums, moratoria 1** a legally authorized delay in the performance of an obligation or

the payment of a debt **2** a suspension of (a specified) activity – usu + *on*

morbid *adj* **1** of, affected with, induced by, or characteristic of disease ⟨~ *anatomy*⟩ **2** abnormally susceptible to or characterized by gloomy feelings; *esp* having an unnatural preoccupation with death **3** grisly, gruesome ⟨~ *curiosity*⟩ – **morbidly** *adv*, **morbidness** *n*

morbidity *n* the relative incidence of (a) disease

¹**mordant** *adj* **1** caustic or sharply critical in thought, manner, or style ⟨~ *wit*⟩ **2** acting as a mordant **3** burning, pungent – **mordancy** *n*, **mordantly** *adv*

²**mordant** *n* **1** a chemical that fixes a dye by combining with it to form an insoluble compound **2** a corroding substance used in etching

¹**more** *adj* **1** greater in quantity or number ⟨*something* ~ *than she expected*⟩ ⟨*7 is 2* ~ *than 5*⟩ **2** additional, further ⟨*three* ~ *guests arrived*⟩ ⟨*have some* ~ *tea*⟩ ⟨*what* ~ *do you want?*⟩ – **neither/nothing more or/nor less than** simply, plainly

²**more** *adv* **1a** as an additional amount ⟨*not much* ~ *to do*⟩ **b** moreover, again ⟨*summer is here once* ~ ⟩ **2** to a greater degree or extent ⟨*you should practise* ~⟩⟨~ *sad than angry*⟩ ⟨*costs* ~ *than making your own beer – SEU S*⟩ – often used with an adjective or adverb to form the comparative ⟨*much* ~ *evenly matched*⟩ – **more often than not** at most times; usually

³**more** *n, pl* **more 1** a greater or additional quantity, amount, or part ⟨*hope to see* ~ *of her*⟩ ⟨*tell me* ~⟩ ⟨~ *than meets the eye*⟩ **2** *pl* additional ones ⟨*many* ~ *were found as the search continued*⟩ – **more of** nearer to being (sthg specified) ⟨*it's more of a sofa than a bed*⟩

morello *n, pl* **morellos** a cultivated red-skinned sour cherry used esp in jams

more or less *adv* **1** to some extent or degree; somewhat **2** almost, nearly

moreover *adv* in addition to what has been said – used to introduce new matter

mores *n pl* the (morally binding) customs or conventions of a particular group

moresque *adj, often cap* typical of Moorish art or architecture

morganatic *adj* of or being a marriage between people of different rank in which the rank of the inferior partner remains unchanged and the children do not succeed to the titles or property of the parent of higher rank – **morganatically** *adv*

morgue *n* **1a** a mortuary **b** a gloomy dispiriting place **2** a collection of reference works and files in a newspaper office

moribund *adj* dying – **moribundity** *n*

Mormon *n* a member of the Church of Jesus Christ of Latter-Day Saints, founded in 1830 in the USA by Joseph Smith, and following precepts contained in the Book of Mormon, a sacred text that he discovered – **Mormonism** *n*

morn *n* the morning – chiefly poetic

morning *n* **1a** the dawn **b** the time from midnight or sunrise to noon **2** an early period (e g of time or life); the beginning – **in the morning** tomorrow morning

morning coat *n* a man's tailcoat that is worn on formal occasions during the day

morning dress *n* men's dress for formal occasions (e g a wedding) during the day

morning glory *n* any of various usu twining plants of the bindweed family with showy trumpet-shaped flowers

Morning Prayer *n* a daily morning office of the Anglican church

mornings *adv, chiefly NAm* in the morning; on any morning

morning sickness *n* nausea and vomiting occurring esp in the morning during the earlier months of a woman's pregnancy

morning star *n* a bright planet, specif Venus, seen in the eastern sky before or at sunrise

morocco *n* a fine leather made from goatskin tanned with sumach

moron *n* **1** MENTAL DEFECTIVE **2** a very stupid person – *infml* – **moronism** *n*, **moronic** *adj*

morose *adj* (having a disposition) marked by or expressive of gloom – **morosely** *adv*, **moroseness** *n*

morpheme *n* a meaningful linguistic unit that contains no smaller meaningful parts and can be either a free form (e g *pin*) or a bound form (e g the *-s* of *pins*) – **morphemic** *adj*

morphemics *n pl but sing in constr* the study of morphemes and esp of word structure

morphine *n* the principal alkaloid of opium that is an addictive narcotic drug used esp as a powerful painkiller – **morphinism** *n*, **morphinic** *adj*

morphology *n* **1** (the biology of) the form and structure of animals and plants **2a** a study and description of word formation in a language including inflection, derivation, and compounding **b** the system of word-forming elements and processes in a language **3** (a study of) the structure or form of sthg – **morphologist** *n*, **morphological** *adj*

morris dance *n* any of several traditional English dances that are performed by groups of people wearing costumes to which small bells are attached – **morris dancer** *n*

morrow *n* **1** the next day – *fml* **2** *archaic* the morning

Morse, Morse code *n* a signalling code consisting of dots and dashes used to send messages by light or by sound signals or esp by radio – **morse** *vb*

morsel *n* **1** a small piece of food **2** a small quantity; a scrap

¹mortal *adj* **1** causing or about to cause death; fatal **2a** not living forever; subject to death **b** humanly conceivable ⟨*every* ~ *thing*⟩ **3** marked by relentless hostility ⟨*a* ~ *enemy*⟩ **4** very great, intense, or severe **5** of or connected with death **6** very tedious and prolonged ⟨*waited 3* ~ *hours*⟩ – *infml*

²mortal *n* **1** a human being **2** a person of a specified kind

mortality *n* **1** being mortal **2** the death of large numbers of people, animals, etc **3** the human race ⟨*take these tears,* ~ *'s relief* – Alexander Pope⟩ **4a** the number of deaths in a given time or place **b** the ratio of deaths in a given time to population **c** the number lost, or the rate of loss or failure

mortality table *n* LIFE TABLE

mortally *adv* **1** in a deadly or fatal manner **2** to an extreme degree; intensely

mortal sin *n* a sin (e g murder) of such gravity that it totally debars the soul from divine grace – **mortal sinner** *n*

¹mortar *n* **1** a strong usu bowl-shaped vessel (e g of stone) in which substances are pounded or ground with a pestle **2** a usu muzzle-loading artillery gun having a tube short in relation to its calibre, a low muzzle velocity, and a high trajectory

²mortar *n* a mixture of cement, lime, gypsum plaster, etc with sand and water, that hardens and is used to join bricks, stones, etc or for plastering

³mortar *vt* to plaster or make fast with mortar

mortarboard *n* **1** ¹HAWK **2** an academic cap consisting of a close-fitting crown with a stiff flat square attached on top

¹mortgage *n* **1** a transfer of the ownership of property (e g for security on a loan) on condition that the transfer

becomes void on payment **2** the state of the property whose ownership is transferred by a mortgage

²mortgage *vt* **1** to transfer the ownership of (property) by a mortgage **2** to make subject to a claim or obligation

mortgagee *n* sby to whom property is mortgaged

mortgagor *also* **mortgager** *n* sby who mortgages his/her property

mortician *n*, *chiefly NAm* an undertaker

mortify *vt* **1** to subdue (e g bodily needs and desires), esp by abstinence or self-inflicted suffering **2** to subject to feelings of shame or acute embarrassment ~ *vi* to become necrotic or gangrenous – **mortification** *n*

¹mortise *also* **mortice** *n* a usu rectangular cavity cut into a piece of material (e g wood) to receive a protrusion, esp a tenon, of another piece

²mortise *also* **mortice** *vt* **1** to join or fasten securely, specif by a mortise and tenon joint **2** to cut or make a mortise in

mortise lock *n* a lock that is designed to be fitted into a mortise in the edge of a door

¹mortuary *n* a room or building in which dead bodies are kept before burial or cremation

²mortuary *adj* of death or the burial of the dead

mosaic *n* **1** (a piece of) decorative work made from small pieces of different coloured material (e g glass or stone) inlaid to form pictures or patterns **2** sthg like a mosaic **3a** (a part of) an organism composed of cells with different genetic make-up; CHIMERA 3 **b** a virus disease of plants (e g tobacco) characterized esp by diffuse yellow and green mottling of the foliage – **mosaic** *adj*, **mosaicism** *n*, **mosaicist** *n*

Mosaic *adj* of Moses or the institutions or writings attributed to him

Moselle, Mosel *n* a typically light-bodied white table wine made in the valley of the Moselle

mosey *vi*, *NAm* to saunter – *infml*

Moslem *n or adj* (a) Muslim

mosque *n* a building used for public worship by Muslims

mosquito *n*, *pl* **mosquitoes** *also* **mosquitos** any of numerous 2-winged flies with females that suck the blood of animals and often transmit diseases (e g malaria) to them – **mosquitoey** *adj*

mosquito net *n* a net or screen for keeping out mosquitoes

moss *n* **1** (any of various plants resembling) any of a class of primitive plants with small leafy stems bearing sex organs at the tip; *also* many of these plants growing together and covering a surface **2** *chiefly Scot* a (peat) bog – **mosslike** *adj*, **mossy** *adj*

¹most *adj* **1** the majority of ⟨~ *men*⟩ **2** greatest in quantity or extent ⟨*the* ~ *ability*⟩

²most *adv* **1** to the greatest degree or extent ⟨*what I like* ~ *about him*⟩ – often used with an adjective or adverb to form the superlative ⟨*the* ~ *challenging job he ever had*⟩ **2** very ⟨*shall* ~ *certainly come*⟩ ⟨*her argument was* ~ *persuasive*⟩

³most *n*, *pl* **most** the greatest quantity, number, or amount ⟨*it's the* ~ *I can do*⟩ ⟨*spends* ~ *of her time in bed*⟩ ⟨~ *became discouraged and left*⟩ ⟨*she made the* ~ *of the fine weather*⟩ – **at most, at the most 1** as a maximum limit ⟨*took him an hour* at most *to finish the job*⟩ **2** AT BEST

⁴most *adv*, *archaic, dial, or NAm* almost

-most *suffix* (→ *adj*) **1** most; to the highest possible degree ⟨*innermost*⟩ ⟨*utmost*⟩ **2** most towards ⟨*topmost*⟩ ⟨*hindmost*⟩

mostly *adv* for the greatest part; mainly; *also* in most cases; usually

mot n, pl **mots** a pithy or witty saying

MOT also **MoT** n a compulsory annual roadworthiness test in Britain for motor vehicles older than a certain age

mote n a small particle; esp a particle of dust suspended in the air

motel n an establishment which provides accommodation and parking and in which the rooms are usu accessible from an outdoor parking area

motet n a choral composition on a sacred text

moth n 1 CLOTHES MOTH 2 a usu night-flying insect with feathery antennae and a stouter body and duller colouring than the butterflies

mothball n 1 a naphthalene or (formerly) camphor ball used to keep moths from clothing 2 pl a state of indefinitely long protective storage; also a state of having been rejected as of no further use or interest – **mothball** vt

moth-eaten adj 1 eaten into by moth larvae ⟨~ clothes⟩ 2a very worn-out or shabby in appearance b antiquated, outmoded

¹**mother** n 1a a female parent b an old or elderly woman 2 a source, origin ⟨necessity is the ~ of invention⟩ – **motherhood** n, **motherless** adj

²**mother** adj 1a of or being a mother b bearing the relation of a mother 2 derived (as if) from one's mother 3 acting as or providing a parental stock – used without reference to sex

³**mother** vt 1a to give birth to b to give rise to; initiate, produce 2 to care for or protect like a mother – often derog

⁴**mother, mother of vinegar** n a slimy membrane of yeast and bacterial cells that develops on the surface of alcoholic liquids undergoing vinegar-producing fermentation and is added to wine or cider to produce vinegar

Mother Carey's chicken n STORM PETREL

Mother Goose rhyme n, chiefly NAm NURSERY RHYME

mother-in-law n, pl **mothers-in-law** the mother of one's spouse

motherly adj 1 (characteristic) of a mother 2 like a mother; maternal – **motherliness** n

mother-of-pearl n the hard pearly iridescent substance forming the inner layer of a mollusc shell

mother superior n, often cap M&S the head of a religious community of women

mother tongue n 1 one's native language 2 a language from which another language derives

mothproof vt or adj (to make) resistant to attack by the larvae of (clothes) moths

motif n 1 a recurring element forming a theme in a work of art or literature; esp a dominant idea or central theme 2 a single or repeated design or colour 3 a leitmotiv

¹**motion** n 1a a formal proposal made in a deliberative assembly b an application to a court or judge for an order, ruling, or direction 2a an act, process, or instance of changing position; movement b an active or functioning state or condition 3a an act or instance of moving the body or its parts; a gesture b pl actions, movements; esp merely simulated or mechanical actions – often in go through the motions 4 melodic change of pitch 5a an evacuation of the bowels – usu pl with sing. meaning b the matter evacuated – **motional** adj, **motionless** adj, **motionlessness** n

²**motion** vt to direct by a gesture ⟨~ed me to a seat⟩

motion picture n, chiefly NAm a film, movie

motivate vt to provide with a motive or incentive; impel ⟨~d by fear⟩ – **motivation** n

¹**motive** n 1 a need, desire, etc that causes sby to act 2 a recurrent phrase or figure that is developed through the course of a musical composition – **motiveless** adj

²**motive** adj 1 moving or tending to move to action 2 of (the causing of) motion ⟨~ energy⟩

mot juste n, pl **mots justes** the exactly right word or phrasing

¹**motley** adj 1 multicoloured 2 composed of varied (disreputable or unsightly) elements

²**motley** n 1 a woollen fabric of mixed colours made in England between the 14th and 17th c 2 a haphazard mixture (of incompatible elements)

moto-cross n the sport of racing motorcycles across country on a rugged usu hilly closed course

¹**motor** n 1 sthg or sby that imparts motion 2 any of various power units that develop energy or impart motion: e g **a** a small compact engine **b** INTERNAL-COMBUSTION ENGINE **c** a rotating machine that transforms electrical energy into mechanical energy 3 MOTOR VEHICLE; esp MOTOR CAR – **motorless** adj

²**motor** adj 1a causing or imparting motion **b** of or being a nerve (fibre) that conducts an impulse causing the movement of a muscle **c** of or involving muscular movement 2a equipped with or driven by a motor **b** of or involving motor vehicles ⟨the ~ trade⟩

³**motor** vi to travel by motor car; esp DRIVE 2

motor bike n a motorcycle – infml

motorboat n a usu small boat propelled by a motor

motorcade n a procession of motor vehicles

motor car n a usu 4-wheeled motor vehicle designed for transporting a small number of people and typically propelled by an internal-combustion engine

motorcycle n a 2-wheeled motor vehicle that can carry 1 or sometimes 2 people astride the engine – **motorcycle** vi, **motorcyclist** n

motorist n sby who drives a car

motorize, -ise vt 1 to equip (e g a vehicle) with a motor 2 to provide with motor-driven equipment (e g for transport) – **motorization** n

motorman n a driver of a motor-driven vehicle (e g a bus or underground train)

motor scooter n a usu 2-wheeled motor vehicle having a seat so that the driver sits in front of rather than astride the engine

motor vehicle also **motor** n an automotive vehicle not operated on rails; esp one with rubber tyres for use on roads

motorway n, Br a major road designed for high-speed traffic that has separate carriageways for different directions and certain restrictions on the types of vehicle and driver allowed on it

mottle n 1 a coloured spot or blotch 2 an irregular pattern of spots or blotches on a surface – **mottled** adj

motto n, pl **mottoes** also **mottos** 1 a sentence, phrase, or word inscribed on sthg as appropriate to or indicative of its character or use 2 a short expression of a guiding principle; a maxim 3 (a piece of paper printed with) a usu humorous or sentimental saying

¹**mould, NAm chiefly mold** n crumbling soft (humus-rich) soil suited to plant growth

²**mould, NAm chiefly mold** n 1 distinctive character or type ⟨need to recruit more men of his ~⟩ 2 the frame on or round which an object is constructed 3 a cavity or form in which a substance (e g a jelly or a metal casting) is shaped 4 a moulding 5 a fixed pattern or form

³**mould, NAm chiefly mold** vt 1 to give shape to 2 to form in a mould 3 to exert a steady formative influence on 4 to fit closely to the contours of 5 to ornament with moulding or carving ⟨~ed picture frames⟩

⁴**mould, NAm chiefly mold** n (a fungus producing) an often

woolly growth on the surface of damp or decaying organic matter

moulder, *NAm chiefly* **molder** *vi* to crumble into dust or decayed fragments, esp gradually

moulding *n* **1** an article produced by moulding **2** a decorative recessed or embossed surface **3** a decorative band or strip used for ornamentation or finishing (e g on a cornice)

mouldy *adj* **1** of, resembling, or covered with a mould-producing fungus **2** old and mouldering; fusty, crumbling **3a** miserable, nasty **b** stingy *USE* (*3*) *infml*

¹**moult,** *NAm chiefly* **molt** *vb* to shed or cast off (hair, feathers, shell, horns, or an outer layer) periodically

²**moult,** *NAm chiefly* **molt** *n* moulting; *specif* ecdysis

mound *n* **1a(1)** an artificial bank of earth or stones **(2)** the slightly elevated ground on which a baseball pitcher stands **b** a knoll, hill **2** a heap, pile

¹**mount** *n* a high hill; a mountain – usu before a name ⟨Mount *Everest*⟩

²**mount** *vi* **1** to increase in amount, extent, or degree **2** to rise, ascend **3** to get up on or into sthg above ground level; *esp* to seat oneself (e g on a horse) for riding ~ *vt* **1a** to go up; climb **b(1)** to seat or place oneself on ⟨*the speaker* ~ed *the platform*⟩ **(2)** COVER 6a **2a** to lift up; raise, erect **b** to place (e g artillery) in position **c** to initiate and carry out (e g an assault or strike) **3a** to set (sby) on a means of conveyance ⟨~ed *his little daughter on a donkey*⟩ **b** to provide with animals for riding **4** to station for defence or observation or as an escort ⟨~ *guard over the palace*⟩ **5a** to attach to a support **b** to arrange or assemble for use or display **6a** to prepare (e g a specimen) for examination or display **b** to organize and present for public viewing or performance; stage ⟨~ed *a sumptuous opera*⟩

³**mount** *n* **1** an opportunity to ride a horse, esp in a race **2** sthg on which sby or sthg is mounted: e g **a** the material (e g cardboard) on which a picture is mounted **b** a jewellery setting **c** an attachment for an accessory **d** a hinge, card, etc for mounting a stamp in a stamp collection **3** a horse for riding

mountain *n* **1** a landmass that projects conspicuously above its surroundings and is higher than a hill **2a** a vast amount or quantity – often *pl* with *sing.* meaning **b** a supply, esp of a specified usu agricultural commodity, in excess of demand ⟨*a butter* ~⟩

mountain ash *n* a rowan or related tree of the rose family usu with small red fruits

mountaineering *n* the pastime or technique of climbing mountains and rock faces – **mountaineer** *n*

mountain lion *n* a puma

mountainous *adj* **1** containing many mountains **2** resembling a mountain; huge – **mountainously** *adv*

mountebank *n* **1** sby who sells quack medicines from a platform **2** a charlatan – **mountebankery** *n*

Mountie *n* a member of the Royal Canadian Mounted Police

mourn *vi* to feel or express (e g in a conventional manner) grief or sorrow, esp for a death ~ *vt* to feel or express grief or sorrow for – **mourner** *n*

mournful *adj* expressing, causing, or filled with sorrow – **mournfully** *adv,* **mournfulness** *n*

mourning *n* **1** the act or state of one who mourns **2a** an outward sign (e g black clothes or an armband) of grief for a person's death ⟨*is wearing* ~⟩ **b** a period of time during which signs of grief are shown

¹**mouse** *n, pl* **mice** **1** any of numerous small rodents with a pointed snout, rather small ears, and slender tail **2** a timid person

²**mouse** *vi* to hunt for mice ~ *vt, chiefly NAm* to search for carefully – usu + *out* – **mouser** *n*

mousetrap *n* a trap for mice

moussaka, mousaka *n* a Greek dish consisting of layers of minced meat (e g lamb), aubergine or potato, tomato, and cheese with cheese or savoury custard topping

mousse *n* a light sweet or savoury cold dish usu containing cream, gelatin, and whipped egg whites

moustache, *NAm chiefly* **mustache** *n* **1** the hair growing or allowed to grow on sby's upper lip **2** hair or bristles round the mouth of a mammal

mousy, mousey *adj* **1** of or resembling a mouse: e g **a** quiet, stealthy **b** timid; *also* colourless **2** *of hair* light greyish brown

¹**mouth** *n, pl* **mouths** **1a** the opening through which food passes into an animal's body; *also* the cavity in the head of the typical vertebrate animal bounded externally by the lips that encloses the tongue, gums, and teeth **b** a grimace made with the lips **c** a horse's response to pressure on the bit **d** an individual, esp a child, requiring food ⟨*too many* ~s *to feed*⟩ **2a** utterance ⟨*finally gave* ~ *to his feelings*⟩ **b** MOUTHPIECE 3 **3** sthg like a mouth, esp in affording entrance or exit: e g **a** the place where a river enters a sea, lake, etc **b** the opening of a cave, volcano, etc **c** the opening of a container **4a** a tendency to talk too much **b** impertinent language *USE* (*4*) *infml* – **mouthed** *adj,* **mouthlike** *adj* – **down in the mouth** dejected, sulky

²**mouth** *vt* **1** to utter pompously **2** to repeat without comprehension or sincerity **3** to form (words) soundlessly with the lips ~ *vi* to talk pompously

mouthful *n* **1a** a quantity that fills the mouth **b** the amount (of food) put into the mouth at 1 time **2** a small quantity **3a** a word or phrase that is very long or difficult to pronounce **b** *chiefly NAm* a very apt or significant comment or statement – chiefly in *say a mouthful USE* (*3*) *infml*

mouth organ *n* a harmonica

mouthpiece *n* **1** sthg placed at or forming a mouth **2** a part (e g of a musical instrument or a telephone) that goes in the mouth or is put next to the mouth **3** sby or sthg that expresses or interprets another's views

mouth-watering *adj* stimulating or appealing to the appetite; appetizing – **mouth-wateringly** *adv*

movable, moveable *n or adj* (property) able to be removed – often used to distinguish personal property from buildings, land, etc; usu *pl*

movable feast *n* an annual church festival (e g Easter) not celebrated on the same date each year

¹**move** *vi* **1a(1)** to go or pass with a continuous motion **(2)** to proceed or progress towards a (specified) place or condition ⟨*moving up the executive ladder*⟩ – often + *on* ⟨~ *on to the next item*⟩ **b** to go away ⟨*it's time we were moving*⟩ **c(1)** to transfer a piece in a board game **(2)** in chess) from one position to another ⟨*it's your turn to* ~⟩ **(2)** *of a piece in board games* to travel or be capable of travelling to another position ⟨*the bishop* ~s *diagonally*⟩ **d(1)** to change one's residence **(2)** to change one's (official) location **2** to pass one's life in a specified environment ⟨~s *in fashionable circles*⟩ **3** to change position or posture **4** to take action; act **5** to make a formal request, application, or appeal **6** to change hands by being sold or rented – often + *quickly* or *slowly* **7** *of the bowels* to evacuate **8a** to operate or function, esp mechanically **b** to show marked activity or speed – *infml* ⟨*after a brief lull things really began to* ~⟩ ~ *vt* **1a** to change the place or position of **b** to transfer (e g a piece in chess) from one position to another **2a(1)** to cause to go or pass with a continuous motion **(2)** to take (furniture and possessions) from one residence or location to another **b** to cause to

operate or function ⟨*this button* ~s *the whole machine*⟩ 3 to cause (the body or part of the body) to change position or posture 4 to prompt to action 5 to affect in such a way as to lead to a show of emotion or of a specified emotion 6 to propose formally in a deliberative assembly 7 to cause (the bowels) to evacuate – **mover** n

²**move** n **1a** the act of moving a piece (e g in chess) **b** the turn of a player to move **2a** a step taken so as to gain an objective **b** a movement **c** a change of residence or official location – **on the move 1** in a state of moving about from place to place ⟨*a salesman is constantly* on the move⟩ **2** in a state of moving ahead or making progress ⟨*said that civilization is always* on the move⟩

move in vi **1** to take up occupation of a dwelling or place of work **2** to advance aggressively in order to gain control – often + on ⟨*police* moved in *on the criminals hiding in the house*⟩

movement n **1a** the act or process of moving; esp change of place, position, or posture **b** a particular instance or manner of moving **c** an action, activity – usu pl with sing. meaning ⟨*troop* ~s⟩ **2a** a trend, specif in prices **b** an organized effort to promote an end ⟨*the civil rights* ~⟩ **3** the moving parts of a mechanism that transmit motion **4** a unit or division having its own key, rhythmic structure, and themes and forming a separate part of an extended musical composition **5a** the development of the action in a work of literature **b** the quality of a book, play, etc of having a quickly moving plot **6** MOTION 5

move on vi to change one's residence or location for another ~vt to cause to depart ⟨*the squatters were* moved on *by the police*⟩

move out vi to leave a dwelling or place of work

move over vi to make room

movie n FILM 3a, b

moving adj **1a** marked by or capable of movement **b** of a change of residence **2a** producing or transferring motion or action ⟨*the* ~ *spirit behind the scheme*⟩ **b** evoking a deep emotional response – **movingly** adv

moving picture n, chiefly NAm a film, movie

¹**mow** n **1** a stack of hay, grain, fodder, etc (in a barn) **2** the part of a barn where hay or straw is stored

²**mow** vb mowed; mowed, mown vt **1** to cut down (a crop, esp grass) **2** to cut down the standing herbage, esp grass, of (e g a field) ~vi to cut down standing herbage, esp grass – **mower** n

mow down vt **1** to kill, destroy, or knock down, esp in great numbers or mercilessly **2** to overcome swiftly and decisively; rout

Mr n, pl **Messrs 1** – used as a conventional title of courtesy before a man's surname, except when usage requires the substitution of a title of rank or an honorary or professional title **2** – used in direct address before a man's title of office ⟨*may I ask one more question,* ~ *Chairman?*⟩ **3** – used before the name of a place or of a profession or activity or before some epithet (e g *clever*) to form a title applied to a male viewed or recognized as representative of the thing indicated ⟨~ *Football*⟩

Mrs n, pl **Mesdames 1a** – used as a conventional title of courtesy before a married woman's surname, except when usage requires the substitution of a title of rank or an honorary or professional title ⟨*spoke to* ~ *Smith*⟩ **b** – used before the name of a place (e g a country or city) or of a profession or activity (e g a sport) or before some epithet (e g *clever*) to form a title applied to a married woman viewed or recognized as representative of the thing indicated ⟨~ *Tennis 1982*⟩ **2** a wife ⟨*took the* ~ *along to the pub*⟩ – infml

Ms n – used instead of Mrs or Miss, esp when marital status is unknown or irrelevant

mu n the 12th letter of the Greek alphabet

¹**much** adj more; most **1** great in quantity or extent ⟨*not* ~ *money*⟩ ⟨*nothing* ~ *to do*⟩ ⟨*how* ~ *milk is there?*⟩ **2** excessive, immoderate ⟨*it's a bit* ~ *having to work so late*⟩ – **too much 1** wonderful, exciting **2** terrible, awful

²**much** adv more; most **1a(1)** to a great degree or extent; considerably ⟨~ *happier*⟩ ⟨*don't* ~ *like it*⟩ ⟨~ *to my surprise*⟩ ⟨*how* ~ *did it cost?*⟩ **(2)** very – with verbal adjectives ⟨*was* ~ *amused*⟩ **b** frequently, often ⟨~ *married*⟩ **c** by far ⟨~ *the fatter*⟩ ⟨*I'd* ~ *rather not*⟩ ⟨~ *the brightest student*⟩ **2** nearly, approximately ⟨*looks* ~ *the way his father did*⟩ – **as much 1** the same quantity **2** that, so ⟨*I thought* as much⟩ – **much less** and certainly not ⟨*can't even walk,* much less *run*⟩

³**much** n **1** a great quantity, amount, or part ⟨*gave away* ~⟩ ⟨~ *of the night*⟩ ⟨*got too* ~ *to do*⟩ **2** sthg considerable or impressive ⟨*wasn't* ~ *to look at*⟩ ⟨*the film wasn't up to* ~⟩ ⟨*I don't think* ~ *of that idea*⟩ **3** a relative quantity or part ⟨*I'll say this* ~ *for him*⟩ – **too much for 1** more than a match for **2** beyond the endurance of

muchness n – **much of a muchness** very much the same

mucilage n a gelatinous substance obtained esp from seaweeds and similar to plant gums

mucilaginous adj **1** sticky, viscid **2** of, full of, or secreting mucilage

muck n **1** soft moist farmyard manure **2** slimy dirt or filth **3** mire, mud **4a** a worthless or useless thing; rubbish – infml **b** Br – used in *Lord Muck* and *Lady Muck* to designate an arrogantly patronizing person – **mucky** adj

muck about vb, chiefly Br MESS ABOUT – infml

muck in vi, Br to share or join in esp a task ⟨*all mucked in together*⟩; also to share sleeping accommodation – infml

muck out vi to remove manure or filth, esp from an animal's quarters ~vt to clear (e g a stable) of manure

muckrake vi to search out and publicly expose real or apparent misconduct of prominent individuals – **muckraker** n

muck up vt, chiefly Br **1** to dirty (as if) with muck; soil **2** to bungle, spoil USE infml

mucous adj of, like, secreting, or covered (as if) with mucus

mucous membrane n a membrane rich in mucous glands, specif lining body passages and cavities (e g the mouth) with openings to the exterior

mucus n a thick slippery secretion produced by mucous membranes (e g in the nose) which it moistens and protects

mud n **1** (a sticky mixture of a solid and a liquid resembling) soft wet earth **2** abusive and malicious remarks or charges

¹**muddle** vb muddling vt **1** to stupefy, esp with alcohol **2** to mix confusedly in one's mind – often + up **3** to cause confusion to ~vi to proceed or get along in a confused aimless way – + along or on – **muddler** n

²**muddle** n **1** a state of (mental) confusion **2** a confused mess

muddleheaded adj **1** mentally confused **2** inept, bungling – **muddleheadedness** n

muddle through vi to succeed in spite of incompetence or lack of method and planning

¹**muddy** adj **1** lacking in clarity or brightness **2** obscure in meaning; muddled, confused – **muddily** adv, **muddiness** n

²**muddy** vt to make cloudy, dull, or confused

mudflat *n* a muddy area of ground covered at high tide – often pl with sing. meaning

mudguard *n* a metal or plastic guard over the wheel of a bicycle, motorcycle, etc to deflect or catch mud

mudpack *n* a face-pack containing fuller's earth

muesli *n* a (breakfast) dish of Swiss origin consisting of rolled oats, dried fruit, nuts, grated apple, etc

muezzin *n* a mosque official who calls the faithful to prayer at fixed daily times, usu from a minaret

¹muff *n* a warm cylindrical wrap in which both hands are placed

²muff *n* **1** a failure to hold a ball in attempting a catch **2** a timid awkward person, esp in sports – infml ⟨*a hopeless ~ at tennis*⟩

³muff *vt* **1** to handle awkwardly; bungle **2** to fail to hold (a ball) when attempting a catch

muffin *n* a light round yeast-leavened bun usu served hot

¹muffle *vt* **muffling 1** to wrap up so as to conceal or protect **2a** to wrap or pad with sthg to dull the sound **b** to deaden the sound of **3** to keep down; suppress ⟨*~d laughter*⟩

²muffle *n* a chamber in a furnace or kiln where articles can be heated without direct contact with flames or combustion products

muffler *n* **1** a warm scarf worn round the neck **2** *NAm* a silencer for a motor vehicle

¹mufti *n* a professional Muslim jurist

²mufti *n* civilian or ordinary clothes worn by one who is usually in uniform

¹mug *n* **1** a large usu cylindrical drinking cup **2** the face or mouth of sby **3** *Br* sby easily deceived; a sucker *USE* (2 & 3) infml

²mug *vt* **-gg-** to assault, esp in the street with intent to rob – **mugger** *n*

muggins *n, pl* **mugginses, muggins** a fool, simpleton – slang; often used in address ⟨*~ here lost her passport*⟩

muggy *adj, of weather* warm, damp, and close – **muggily** *adv*, **mugginess** *n*

mug's game *n, chiefly Br* a profitless activity – infml

mug up *vt, Br* to study hard – infml

mugwump *n, chiefly NAm* an independent in politics

Muhammadan *adj* of Muhammad or Islam – **Muhammadan** *n*, **Muhammadanism** *n*

mulatto *n, pl* **mulattoes, mulattos** the first-generation offspring of a Negro and a white person

mulberry *n* (any of a genus of trees of the fig family bearing) an edible usu purple multiple fruit

mulch *n* a protective covering (e g of compost) spread on the ground to control weeds, enrich the soil, etc – **mulch** *vt*

¹mulct *n* a fine, penalty

²mulct *vt* **1** to punish by a fine **2a** to swindle **b** to obtain by swindling

¹mule *n* **1** the offspring of a mating between a (female) horse and an ass **2** a very stubborn person **3** a machine for simultaneously drawing and twisting fibre into yarn or thread and winding it onto spindles

²mule *n* a backless shoe or slipper

muleteer *n* sby who drives mules

mulish *adj* unreasonably and inflexibly obstinate – **mulishly** *adv*, **mulishness** *n*

¹mull *vt* to heat, sweeten, and flavour (e g wine or beer) with spices

²mull *n* crumbly soil humus forming a layer of mixed organic matter and mineral soil and merging into the underlying mineral soil

³mull *n* a headland or peninsula in Scotland

mullah *n* a Muslim of a quasi-clerical class trained in traditional law and doctrine – **mullahism** *n*

mullet *n, pl* **mullet,** *esp for different types* **mullets** any of a family of **a** food fishes with elongated bodies **b** red or golden fishes with 2 barbels on the chin

mulligatawny *n* a rich meat soup of Indian origin seasoned with curry

mullion *n* a slender vertical bar placed esp between panes or panels (e g of windows or doors) – **mullion** *vt*

mull over *vt* to consider at length

multi- *comb form* **1a** many; multiple; much ⟨multi-*storey*⟩ **b** more than 2 ⟨multi*lateral*⟩ ⟨multi*valent*⟩ **c** more than 1 ⟨multi*parous*⟩ **2** many times over ⟨multi*millionaire*⟩

multicoloured *adj* of various colours

multifarious *adj* having or occurring in great variety; diverse – **multifariously** *adv*, **multifariousness** *n*

multiform *adj* having many forms or appearances – **multiformity** *n*

multilateral *adj* **1** having many sides **2** participated in by more than 2 parties **3** *of a school* divided into more than 2 separately organized sides offering different curricula – **multilaterally** *adv*

multilingual *adj* **1** POLYGLOT 2 **2** using or able to use several languages ⟨*a ~ stewardess*⟩ – **multilingualism** *n*, **multilingually** *adv*

multimillionaire *n* sby whose wealth is estimated at many millions of money units

¹multiple *adj* **1** consisting of, including, or involving more than 1 **2** many, manifold ⟨*~ achievements*⟩ **3** shared by many ⟨*~ ownership*⟩ **4** *of a fruit* formed by coalescence of the ripening ovaries of several flowers

²multiple *n* **1** the product of a quantity by an integer ⟨*35 is a ~ of 7*⟩ **2 multiple, multiple store** *chiefly Br* CHAIN STORE

multiple sclerosis *n* progressively developing partial or complete paralysis and jerking muscle tremor resulting from the formation of patches of hardened nerve tissue in nerves of the brain and spinal cord that have lost their myelin

¹multiplex *adj* **1** manifold, multiple **2** being or relating to a system allowing several messages to be transmitted simultaneously by the same circuit or channel

²multiplex *vb* to send (messages or signals) by a multiplex system – **multiplexer, multiplexor** *n*

multiplication *n* **1** multiplying or being multiplied **2** a mathematical operation that at its simplest is an abbreviated process of adding an integer to itself a specified number of times and that is extended to other numbers in accordance with laws that are valid for integers – **multiplicative** *adj*, **multiplicatively** *adv*

multiplicity *n* **1** the quality or state of being multiple or various **2** a great number ⟨*a ~ of errors*⟩

multiply *vt* **1** to increase in number, esp greatly or in multiples; augment **2a** to combine by multiplication ⟨*~ 7 and 8*⟩ **b** to combine with (another number) by multiplication – usu pass ⟨*7 multiplied by 8 is 56*⟩ ~ *vi* **1a** to become greater in number; spread **b** to breed or propagate **2** to perform multiplication – **multipliable** *adj*

multiracial *adj* composed of, involving, or representing various races – **multiracialism** *n*

multi-storey *n or adj* (a building, esp a car park) having several storeys

multitude *n* **1** the state of being many **2** a great number; a host **3** a crowd – chiefly fml **4** *the* populace, masses

multitudinous *adj* **1** comprising a multitude of individuals; populous **2** existing in a great multitude **3** existing in or consisting of innumerable elements or aspects *USE* fml – **multitudinously** *adv*, **multitudinousness** *n*

¹**mum** *adj* silent ⟨*keep* ∼⟩ – infml

²**mum** *n, chiefly Br* MOTHER 1a – infml

mumble *vb* **mumbling** to say (words) in an inarticulate usu subdued voice – **mumble** *n*, **mumbler** *n*

mumbo jumbo *n* 1 elaborate but meaningless ritual 2 involved activity or language that obscures and confuses

mummery *n* 1 a performance of mumming 2 an absurd or pretentious ceremony or performance

mummify *vt* 1 to embalm and dry (the body of an animal or human being) 2 to cause to dry up and shrivel ∼ *vi* to dry up and shrivel like a mummy – **mummification** *n*

mumming *n* 1 the practice of performing in a traditional pantomime 2 the custom of going about merrymaking in disguise during festivals – **mummer** *n*

¹**mummy** *n* 1 a body embalmed for burial in the manner of the ancient Egyptians 2 an unusually well-preserved dead body

²**mummy** *n, chiefly Br* MOTHER 1a – used esp by or to children

mumps *n pl but sing or pl in constr* an infectious virus disease marked by gross swelling of esp the parotid glands

munch *vb* to chew (food) with a crunching sound and visible movement of the jaws – **muncher** *n*

mundane *adj* 1 (characteristic) of this world in contrast to heaven 2 practical and ordinary, esp to the point of dull familiarity – **mundanely** *adv*, **mundaneness** *n*

municipal *adj* 1a of a municipality b having local self-government 2 restricted to 1 locality – **municipally** *adv*

municipality *n* (the governing body of) a primarily urban political unit having corporate status and some self-government

munificent *adj* 1 giving or bestowing with great generosity 2 characterized by great liberality *USE* fml – **munificence** *n*, **munificently** *adv*

muniment *n* a document kept as evidence of title or privilege – usu pl

munition *n* armament, ammunition – usu pl with sing. meaning – **munition** *vt*

¹**mural** *adj* of, resembling, or applied to a wall

²**mural** *n* a mural work of art (e g a painting) – **muralist** *n*

¹**murder** *n* 1 the crime of unlawfully and intentionally killing sby 2 sthg very difficult, dangerous, or disagreeable – infml ⟨*it was* ∼ *trying to park*⟩

²**murder** *vt* 1 to kill (sby) unlawfully and intentionally 2 to slaughter brutally 3a to put an end to b to mutilate, mangle ⟨∼ *a sonata*⟩ ∼ *vi* to commit murder – **murderer**, *fem* **murderess** *n*

murderous *adj* 1a having the purpose or capability of murder b characterized by or causing murder or bloodshed 2 capable of overwhelming ⟨∼ *heat*⟩ – **murderously** *adv*, **murderousness** *n*

murk *n* gloom, darkness; *also* fog

murky *adj* dark and gloomy – **murkily** *adv*, **murkiness** *n*

¹**murmur** *n* 1 a half-suppressed or muttered complaint 2a a low indistinct (continuous) sound b a subdued or gentle utterance 3 an atypical sound of the heart indicating an abnormality

²**murmur** *vi* 1 to make a murmur 2 to complain, grumble ∼ *vt* to say in a murmur ⟨∼ ed *an apology for being late*⟩ – **murmurer** *n*

muscat *n* any of several cultivated grapes used in making wine and raisins

muscatel *n* 1 a sweet dessert wine made from muscat grapes 2 a raisin made from muscat grapes

muscle *n* 1 (an organ that moves a body part, consisting of) a tissue made of modified elongated cells that contract when stimulated to produce motion 2 muscular strength; brawn – **muscled** *adj*

muscle-bound *adj* 1 having enlarged muscles with impaired elasticity, often as a result of excessive exercise 2 lacking flexibility; rigid

muscle in *vi* to interfere forcibly – infml; often + *on*

muscovite *n* 1 *cap* a native or inhabitant of (the ancient principality of) Moscow 2 a colourless to pale brown potassium mica – **Muscovite** *adj*

muscular *adj* 1a of, constituting, or performed by muscle or the muscles b having well-developed musculature 2 having strength of expression or character; vigorous – **muscularly** *adv*, **muscularity** *n*

muscular dystrophy *n* progressive wasting of muscles occurring as a hereditary disease

¹**muse** *vi* to become absorbed in thought; *esp* to engage in daydreaming ∼ *vt* to think or say reflectively – **muser** *n*

²**muse** *n* 1 *cap* any of the 9 sister goddesses in Greek mythology who were the patrons of the arts and sciences 2 a source of inspiration; *esp* a woman who influences a creative artist

museum *n* an institution devoted to the acquiring, care, study, and display of objects of interest or value; *also* a place exhibiting such objects

museum piece *n* 1 an object interesting enough for a museum to display 2 sthg absurdly old-fashioned

mush *n* 1 a soft mass of semiliquid material 2 mawkish sentimentality

¹**mushroom** *n* 1 the enlarged, esp edible, fleshy fruiting body of a class of fungus, consisting typically of a stem bearing a flattened cap 2 a fungus

²**mushroom** *vi* 1 to spring up suddenly or multiply rapidly 2 to flatten at the end on impact 3 to pick wild mushrooms ⟨*go* ∼ing⟩

mushy *adj* 1 having the consistency of mush 2 mawkishly sentimental – **mushily** *adv*, **mushiness** *n*

music *n* 1a the science or art of ordering tones or sounds in succession and combination to produce a composition having unity and continuity b vocal, instrumental, or mechanical sounds having rhythm, melody, or harmony 2 an agreeable sound 3 the score of a musical composition set down on paper

¹**musical** *adj* 1 having the pleasing harmonious qualities of music 2 having an interest in or talent for music 3 set to or accompanied by music 4 of music, musicians, or music lovers – **musically** *adv*, **musicality** *n*

²**musical** *n* a film or theatrical production that consists of songs, dances, and dialogue based on a unifying plot

musical box, *chiefly NAm* **music box** *n* a container enclosing an apparatus that reproduces music mechanically when activated

musical chairs *n pl but sing in constr* a game in which players march to music round a row of chairs numbering 1 less than the players and scramble for seats when the music stops

music hall *n* (a theatre formerly presenting) entertainments consisting of a variety of unrelated acts (e g acrobats, comedians, or singers)

musician *n* a composer, conductor, or performer of music; *esp* an instrumentalist – **musicianship** *n*

musk *n* 1a (a synthetic substitute for) a substance with a penetrating persistent smell that is obtained from a gland of the male musk deer and used as a perfume fixative; *also* a similar substance from another animal b the odour of musk 2 any of various plants with musky smells – **musky** *adj*

musk deer n a small heavy-limbed hornless deer of central Asia, the male of which produces musk

musket n a heavy large-calibre shoulder firearm with a smooth bore

musketeer n a soldier armed with a musket

musketry n **1** (troops armed with) muskets **2** musket fire

muskmelon n (an Asiatic plant that bears) a usu sweet musky-smelling edible melon

muskrat n, pl **muskrats**, esp collectively **muskrat** an aquatic rodent of N America with a long scaly tail and webbed hind feet

musk rose n a rose of the Mediterranean region with musky flowers

Muslim n an adherent of Islam – **Muslim** adj

muslin n a plain-woven sheer to coarse cotton fabric

musquash n (the dark glossy brown fur or pelt of) the muskrat

¹muss n, NAm a state of disorder; mess – infml – **mussy** adj

²muss vt, NAm to make untidy; disarrange, dishevel – infml

mussel n **1** a marine bivalve mollusc with a dark elongated shell **2** a freshwater bivalve mollusc whose shell has a lustrous mother-of-pearl lining

¹must verbal auxiliary, pres & past all persons **must 1a** be commanded or requested to ⟨you ~ stop⟩ **b** certainly should; ought by all means to ⟨I ~ read that book⟩ ⟨we mustn't despair⟩ **2** be compelled by physical, social, or legal necessity to ⟨man ~ eat to live⟩ ⟨I ~ say you're looking much better⟩; be required by need or purpose to ⟨we ~ hurry if we want to catch the bus⟩ – past often replaced by had to except in reported speech; used in the negative to express the idea of prohibition ⟨we ~ not park here⟩ **3** ¹WILL **6** ⟨if you ~ go at least wait till morning⟩; esp be unreasonably or perversely compelled to ⟨why ~ you be so stubborn?⟩ ⟨in spite of my advice, she ~ go and do the opposite⟩ **4** be logically inferred or supposed to ⟨it ~ be time⟩ ⟨they mustn't have arrived⟩ **5** was presumably certain to; was or were bound to ⟨if he really was there I ~ have seen him⟩

²must n an essential or prerequisite

³must n grape juice before and during fermentation

mustache n, chiefly NAm a moustache

mustachio n, pl **mustachios** a (large) moustache – **mustachioed** adj

mustang n the small hardy naturalized horse of the western plains of the USA

mustard n (a pungent yellow powder used as a condiment or in medicine, esp as an emetic or counterirritant, and ground from the seeds of) any of several related plants with lobed leaves, yellow flowers, and straight seed pods – **mustardy** adj

mustard gas n an irritant and blister-inducing oily liquid used as a poison gas

¹muster vt **1a** to assemble, convene **b** to call the roll of **2** to summon in response to a need ⟨all the courage he could ~ ⟩ ~ vi to come together; congregate

²muster n **1a** assembling (for military inspection) **b** an assembled group; a collection **2** a critical examination ⟨slipshod work that would never pass ~ ⟩

mustn't must not

musty adj **1** affected by mould, damp, or mildew **2** tasting or smelling of damp and decay – **mustily** adv, **mustiness** n

mutable adj **1** capable of or liable to change or alteration **2** capable of or subject to mutation – **mutableness** n, **mutably** adv, **mutability** n

mutation n **1** (a) significant and fundamental alteration **2** sandhi; specif umlaut **3** (an individual or strain differing from others of its type and resulting from) a relatively permanent change in an organism's hereditary material – **mutational** adj, **mutationally** adv, **mutant** n, **mutate** vb

mutatis mutandis adv with the necessary changes having been made or respective differences considered

¹mute adj **1** unable to speak; dumb **2a** felt but not expressed ⟨~ sympathy⟩ **b** refusing to plead ⟨the prisoner stands ~⟩ **3** of letters (e g the b in plumb) not pronounced – **mutely** adv, **muteness** n

²mute n **1** one who cannot or does not speak **2** STOP 7 **3** a device attached to a musical instrument to reduce, soften, or muffle its tone

³mute vt **1** to muffle or reduce the sound of **2** to tone down (a colour)

⁴mute vi, of a bird to pass waste matter from the body

muted adj **1** silent, subdued **2** provided with or produced or modified by the use of a mute – **mutedly** adv

mutilate vt **1** to cut off or permanently destroy or damage a limb or essential part of **2** to damage or deface ⟨the censors had ~d the script⟩ – **mutilator** n, **mutilation** n

mutineer n sby who mutinies

mutinous adj **1** tending to mutiny; rebellious **2** of or constituting mutiny – **mutinously** adv, **mutinousness** n

mutiny n open resistance to lawful authority; esp concerted revolt (e g of a naval crew) against discipline or a superior officer – **mutiny** vi

mutt n **1** a dull or stupid person **2** a (mongrel) dog

mutter vi **1** to utter sounds or words in a low or indistinct voice **2** to utter muffled threats or complaints ~ vt to utter, esp in a low or indistinct voice **mutter** n, **mutterer** n

mutton n the flesh of a mature sheep used as food – **muttony** adj

muttonchops n pl side-whiskers that are narrow at the temple and broad by the lower jaws

mutual adj **1a** directed by each towards the other ⟨~ affection⟩ **b** having the same specified feeling for each other ⟨they had long been ~ enemies⟩ **2** shared by 2 or more in common – **mutualize** vb, **mutually** adv, **mutuality** n

Muzak trademark – used for recorded background music played in public places

¹muzzle n **1a** the projecting jaws and nose of a dog or other animal **b** a covering for the mouth of an animal used to prevent biting, barking, etc **2** the discharging end of a pistol, rifle, etc

²muzzle vt **muzzling 1** to fit with a muzzle **2** to restrain from free expression; gag – **muzzler** n

muzzle-loader n a firearm that is loaded through the muzzle

muzzy adj mentally confused; befuddled – **muzzily** adv, **muzziness** n

my adj **1** of me or myself, esp as possessor ⟨~ car⟩, agent ⟨~ promise⟩, or object of an action ⟨~ injuries⟩ – sometimes used with vocatives ⟨~ child⟩ ⟨~ lord⟩ and in the opening of a letter ⟨My dear Mrs Jones⟩ **2** – used interjectionally to express surprise and sometimes reduplicated ⟨~ oh ~!⟩, in certain fixed exclamations ⟨~ God!⟩, and with names of certain parts of the body to express doubt or disapproval ⟨~ foot!⟩

my-, myo- comb form muscul- ⟨myograph⟩ ⟨myoneural⟩

mycelium n, pl **mycelia** the mass of interwoven filamentous hyphae that forms the body of a fungus and is usu submerged in another body (e g of soil or the tissues of a host) – **mycelial** adj

mycology n (the biology of) fungal life or fungi – **mycol-**

ogist *n*, **mycological** *also* **mycologic** *adj*, **mycologically** *adv*

myelin *n* a soft white fatty material that forms a thick sheath about the cytoplasmic core of nerve cells adapted for fast conduction of nervous impulses – **myelinic** *adj*

myelitis *n* inflammation of the bone marrow

myna, mynah *also* **mina** *n* any of various Asian starlings; *esp* a largely black one easily taught to pronounce words

myopia *n* defective vision of distant objects resulting from the focussing of the visual images in front of the retina; shortsightedness – **myopic** *adj*, **myopically** *adv*

¹**myriad** *n* **1** ten thousand **2** an indefinitely large number – often pl with sing. meaning

²**myriad** *adj* innumerable, countless

myrrh *n* (a mixture of labdanum with) brown bitter aromatic gum resin obtained from any of several African and Asian trees

myrtle *n* **1** an evergreen S European bushy shrub with shiny leaves, fragrant white or rosy flowers, and black berries, or a related tropical shrub or tree **2** *NAm* ¹PERIWINKLE

myself *pron* **1** that identical one that is I – used reflexively ⟨*I got ~ a new suit*⟩, for emphasis ⟨*I ~ will go*⟩, or in absolute constructions ⟨*~ a tourist, I nevertheless avoided other tourists*⟩ **2** my normal self ⟨*I'm not quite ~ today*⟩

mysterious *adj* **1** difficult to comprehend **2** containing, suggesting, or implying mystery – **mysteriously** *adv*, **mysteriousness** *n*

mystery *n* **1a** a religious truth disclosed by revelation alone **b(1)** any of the 15 events (e g the Nativity, the Crucifixion, or the Assumption) serving as a subject for meditation during the saying of the rosary **(2)** *cap* a Christian sacrament; *specif* the Eucharist **c** a secret religious rite (e g of Eleusinian or Mithraic cults) **2a** sthg not understood or beyond understanding ⟨*his disappearance remains a ~*⟩ ⟨*a ~ illness*⟩ **b** a fictional work dealing usu with the solution of a mysterious crime **3** an enigmatic or secretive quality

mystery play, mystery *n* a medieval religious drama based on episodes from the Scriptures

mystic *n* a person who believes that God or ultimate reality can only be apprehended by direct personal experience (and who orders his/her life towards this goal)

mystical, mystic *adj* **1** having a sacred or spiritual meaning not given by normal modes of thought or feeling **2** of or resulting from a person's direct experience of communion with God or ultimate reality **3** of mysteries or esoteric rites **4** of mysticism or mystics **5a** mysterious, incomprehensible **b** obscure, esoteric **c** arousing awe and wonder – **mystically** *adv*, **mysticism** *n*

mystification *n* mystifying or being mystified

mystify *vt* **1** to perplex, bewilder **2** to cause to appear mysterious or obscure – **mystifier** *n*, **mystifyingly** *adv*

mystique *n* **1** a mystical reverential atmosphere or quality associated with a person or thing **2** an esoteric skill peculiar to an occupation or activity

myth *n* **1** a traditional story that embodies popular beliefs or explains a practice, belief, or natural phenomenon **2** a parable, allegory **3a** a person or thing having a fictitious existence **b** a belief subscribed to uncritically by an (interested) group

mythical *also* **mythic** *adj* **1** based on or described in a myth **2** invented or imagined – **mythically** *adv*

mythological *adj* **1** of or dealt with in mythology or myths **2** lacking factual or historical basis – **mythologically** *adv*

mythology *n* **1** a body of myths, esp those dealing with the gods and heroes of a particular people **2** a branch of knowledge that deals with myth **3** a body of beliefs, usu with little factual foundation, lending glamour or mystique to sby or sthg – **mythologist** *n*

myxoma *n*, *pl* **myxomas, myxomata** a soft tumour made up of gelatinous connective tissue – **myxomatous** *adj*

myxomatosis *n* a severe flea-transmitted virus disease of rabbits that is characterized by the formation of myxomas in the body, and that has been used in their biological control

N

n *n*, *pl* **n's, ns** *often cap* **1** (a graphic representation of or device for reproducing) the 14th letter of the English alphabet **2** an indefinite number **3** the haploid or gametic number of chromosomes **4** an en

-n – see ¹-EN

'n' *also* **'n** *conj* and ⟨*fish ~ chips*⟩

Naafi *n* the organization which runs shops and canteens in British military establishments; *also* any of these shops or canteens

nab *vt* **-bb-** **1** to arrest; apprehend **2** to catch hold of; grab *USE* infml

nabob *n* **1** a provincial governor of the Mogul empire in India **2** a man of great wealth – used orig of an Englishman grown rich in India – **nabobess** *n*

nacelle *n* a housing for an aircraft engine

nacre *n* mother-of-pearl – **nacred** *adj*, **nacreous** *adj*

nadir *n* **1** the point of the celestial sphere that is directly opposite the zenith and vertically downwards from the observer **2** the lowest point

naevus *n* a congenital pigmented area on the skin; a birthmark

¹**nag** *n* a horse; *esp* one that is old or in poor condition

²**nag** *vb* **-gg-** *vi* **1** to find fault incessantly **2** to be a persistent source of annoyance or discomfort ~ *vt* to subject to constant scolding or urging – **nagger** *n*, **nagging** *adj*, **naggingly** *adv*

³**nag** *n* a person, esp a woman, who nags habitually

naiad *n*, *pl* **naiads, naiades** **1** *often cap* a nymph in classical mythology living in lakes, rivers, etc **2** the aquatic larva of a mayfly, dragonfly, damselfly, etc

¹**nail** *n* **1** (a claw or other structure corresponding to) a horny sheath protecting the upper end of each finger and toe of human beings and other primates **2** a slender usu pointed and headed spike designed to be driven in, esp with a hammer, to join materials, act as a support, etc

²**nail** *vt* **1** to fasten (as if) with a nail **2** to fix steadily **3** to catch, trap **4** to detect and expose (e g a lie or scandal) so as to discredit **5** *chiefly NAm* to hit, strike *USE* (*except 1*) infml – **nailer** *n*

nail down *vt* **1** to define or establish clearly **2** to secure a definite promise or decision from

naive, naïve *adj* **1** ingenuous, unsophisticated **2** lacking in worldly wisdom or informed judgment; *esp* credulous **3** PRIMITIVE 3d – **naively** *adv*, **naiveness** *n*

naivety *also* **naïvety** *n* **1** being naive **2** a naive remark or action

naked *adj* **1** having no clothes on **2a** *of a knife or sword* not enclosed in a sheath or scabbard **b** exposed to the air or to full view ⟨*a ~ light*⟩ **c** *of (part of) a plant or animal* lacking hairs or other covering or enveloping parts (e g a shell or feathers) **d** lacking foliage or vegetation **3** without furnishings or ornamentation ⟨*a ~ room*⟩ **4** unarmed, defenceless **5** lacking factual confirmation or support ⟨~ *faith*⟩ **6** not concealed or disguised ⟨*the ~ truth*⟩ **7** unaided by any optical device ⟨*visible to the ~ eye*⟩ – **nakedly** *adv*, **nakedness** *n*

¹**name** *n* **1** a word or phrase designating an individual person or thing **2** a descriptive usu disparaging epithet ⟨*called him ~s*⟩ **3a** reputation ⟨*gave the town a bad ~*⟩ **b** a famous or notorious person or thing **4** family, kindred ⟨*was a disgrace to his ~*⟩ **5** semblance as opposed to reality ⟨*a friend in ~ only*⟩ – **one's name is mud** one is in disgrace

²**name** *vt* **1** to give a name to; call **2** to identify by name **3** to nominate, appoint **4** to decide on; choose ⟨*~ the day for the wedding*⟩ **5** to mention explicitly; specify – **nameable** *adj*, **namer** *n*

name day *n* the feast day of the saint whose name one has taken at baptism

name-dropping *n* seeking to impress others by the apparently casual mention of prominent people as friends – **name-dropper** *n*

nameless *adj* **1** obscure, undistinguished **2** not known by name; anonymous **3** having no legal right to a name; illegitimate **4a** having no name ⟨*a ~ species of moth*⟩ **b** left purposely unnamed ⟨*a certain person who shall remain ~*⟩ **5** not marked with a name ⟨*a ~ grave*⟩ **6a** not capable of being described; indefinable ⟨*~ fears*⟩ **b** too terrible or distressing to describe ⟨*a ~ horror*⟩ – **namelessly** *adv*, **namelessness** *n*

namely *adv* that is to say

nameplate *n* a plate or plaque bearing a name

namesake *n* sby or sthg that has the same name as another

nanny *also* **nannie** *n*, *chiefly Br* a child's nurse; a nurse-maid

nanny goat *n* a female domestic goat – *infml*

¹**nap** *vi* **-pp-** **1** to take a short sleep, esp during the day **2** to be off one's guard ⟨*caught his opponent* ~ping⟩

²**nap** *n* a short sleep, esp during the day

³**nap** *n* a hairy or downy surface (e g on a woven fabric); a pile – **napless** *adj*, **napped** *adj*

⁴**nap** *vt* **-pp-** to raise a nap on (fabric or leather)

⁵**nap** *n* NAPOLEON 2

⁶**nap** *vt* **-pp-** to recommend (a horse) as a possible winner – **nap** *n*

¹**napalm** *n* **1** a thickener consisting of a mixture of aluminium soaps **2** petrol jellied with napalm and used esp in incendiary bombs and flamethrowers

²**napalm** *vt* to attack with napalm

nape *n* the back of the neck

naphtha *n* **1** petroleum **2** any of various liquid hydrocarbon mixtures used chiefly as solvents

naphthalene *n* a hydrocarbon usu obtained by distillation of coal tar and used esp in the synthesis of organic chemicals – **naphthalenic** *adj*

napkin *n* **1** a usu square piece of material (e g linen or paper) used at table to wipe the lips or fingers and protect the clothes **2** *chiefly Br* a nappy – *fml*

napoleon *n* **1** a French 20-franc gold coin **2** (a bid to win all 5 tricks at) a card game played with hands of 5 cards in which players bid to name the numbers of tricks they will take

nappy *n*, *chiefly Br* a square piece of cloth or paper worn by babies to absorb and retain excreta and usu drawn up between the legs and fastened at the waist

narcissism *n* love of or sexual desire for one's own body – **narcissist** *n* or *adj*, **narcissistic** *adj*

narcissus *n* a daffodil; *esp* one whose flowers are borne separately and have a short corona

¹**narcotic** *n* a usu addictive drug, esp (a derivative of) morphine, that dulls the senses, induces prolonged sleep, and relieves pain – **narcotize** *vb*

²**narcotic** *adj* **1a** like, being, or yielding a narcotic **b** inducing mental lethargy; soporific **2** of (addiction to) narcotics – **narcotically** *adv*

¹**nark** *n* **1** *Br* a police informer **2** *chiefly Austr* an annoying person or thing *USE* slang

²**nark** *vb*, *Br vi* to act as an informer – slang; often + *on* ~ *vt* to offend, affront – *infml*

narrate *vt* to recite the details of (a story) – **narrator** *n*

narration *n* **1** (a) narrating **2** a story, narrative – **narrational** *adj*

narrative *n* **1** sthg (e g a story) that is narrated **2** the art or practice of narration – **narrative** *adj*, **narratively** *adv*

¹**narrow** *adj* **1** of little width, esp in comparison with height or length **2** limited in size or scope; restricted **3** inflexible, hidebound **4** only just sufficient or successful ⟨*a ~ escape*⟩ **5** TENSE 3 – **narrowly** *adv*, **narrowness** *n*

²**narrow** *n* a narrow part or (water) passage; *specif* STRAIT 1 – usu pl with sing. meaning

³**narrow** *vt* **1** to make narrow or narrower **2** to restrict the scope or sphere of ~ *vi* to become narrow or narrower

narrow boat *n* a canal barge with a beam of 21m (7ft) or less

narrow gauge *n* a railway gauge narrower than standard gauge

narrow-minded *adj* lacking tolerance or breadth of vision; bigoted – **narrow-mindedly** *adv*, **narrow-mindedness** *n*

narwhal *also* **narwal** *n* a small arctic whale, the male of which has a long twisted ivory tusk

¹**nasal** *n* a nasal speech sound

²**nasal** *adj* **1** of the nose **2a** uttered through the nose with the mouth passage closed (as in English /m, n, ng/) **b** uttered with both the mouth and nose passage open (as in French *en*) **c** characterized by resonance produced through the nose – **nasally** *adv*, **nasality** *n*

nasalize, -ise *vb* to speak or say in a nasal manner – **nasalization** *n*

nascent *adj* in the process of being born; just beginning to develop – *fml* – **nascence** *n*, **nascency** *n*

nasturtium *n* (any of a genus of plants related to) a widely cultivated plant with showy spurred flowers and pungent seeds

nasty *adj* **1a** disgustingly filthy **b** repugnant, esp to smell or taste **2** obscene, indecent **3** mean, tawdry ⟨*cheap and ~ furniture*⟩ **4a** harmful, dangerous ⟨*a ~ accident*⟩ **b** disagreeable, dirty ⟨*~ weather*⟩ **5** giving cause for concern or anxiety ⟨*a ~ suspicion*⟩ **6** spiteful, vicious ⟨*trespassers who turn ~ when challenged*⟩ – **nastily** *adv*, **nastiness** *n*

natal *adj* of, present at, or associated with (one's) birth ⟨*a ~ star*⟩

nation *n* **1** *sing or pl in constr* **a** a people with a common origin, tradition, and language (capable of) constituting a nation-state **b** a community of people possessing a more or less defined territory and government **2** a tribe or federation of tribes (e g of American Indians) – **nationhood** *n*

¹**national** *adj* **1** of a nation **2** belonging to or maintained by the central government **3** of or being a coalition government – **nationally** *adv*

²**national** *n* **1** a citizen of a specified nation **2** a competition that is national in scope – usu pl

national assistance *n*, *Br, often cap N&A* SUPPLEMENTARY BENEFIT – not now used technically

national debt n the amount of money owed by the government of a country

National Guard n a militia force recruited by each state of the USA and equipped by the federal government that can be called up by either

National Health Service, National Health n the British system of medical care, started in 1948, by which every person receives free medical treatment paid for by taxation

national insurance n, often cap N&I a compulsory social-security scheme in Britain funded by contributions from employers, employees, and the government which insures the individual against sickness, retirement, and unemployment

nationalism n loyalty and devotion to a nation; esp the exalting of one nation above all others

nationalist n 1 an advocate of nationalism 2 cap a member of a political group advocating national independence or strong national government – **nationalist, nationalistic** adj, **nationalistically** adv

nationality n 1 national character 2 national status 3 citizenship of a particular nation 4 existence as a separate nation 5a NATION 1a b an ethnic group within a larger unit USE 0

nationalize, -ise vt 1 to make national 2 to invest control or ownership of in the national government – **nationalizer** n, **nationalization** n

national park n an area of special scenic, historical, or scientific importance preserved and maintained by the government

national service n conscripted service in the British armed forces – **national serviceman** n

national socialism n Nazism – **national socialist** adj

nation-state n a sovereign state inhabited by a relatively homogeneous people as opposed to several nationalities

¹**native** adj 1 inborn, innate ⟨~ talents⟩ 2 belonging to a particular place by birth ⟨~ to Yorkshire⟩ 3a belonging to or being the place of one's birth ⟨my ~ language⟩ b of or being one's first language or sby using his/her first language ⟨a ~ speaker⟩ ⟨~ fluency⟩ 4 living (naturally), grown, or produced in a particular place; indigenous 5 found in nature, esp in a pure form ⟨mining ~ silver⟩ 6 chiefly Austr (superficially) resembling a specified British plant or animal – **natively** adv, **nativeness** n

²**native** n 1 one born or reared in a particular place ⟨a ~ of London⟩ 2a an original or indigenous (non-European) inhabitant b a plant, animal, etc indigenous to a particular locality 3 a local resident

nativity n 1 birth; specif, cap the birth of Jesus 2 a horoscope

natter vi or n, chiefly Br (to) chatter, gossip – infml

natty adj neat and trim; spruce – **nattily** adv, **nattiness** n

¹**natural** adj 1 based on an inherent moral sense ⟨~ justice⟩ ⟨~ law⟩ 2 in accordance with or determined by nature 3 related by blood rather than by adoption ⟨his ~ parents⟩ 4 innate, inherent ⟨a ~ talent for art⟩ 5 of nature as an object of study 6 having a specified character or attribute by nature ⟨a ~ athlete⟩ 7 happening in accordance with the ordinary course of nature ⟨death from ~ causes⟩ 8 normal or expected ⟨events followed their ~ course⟩ 9 existing in or produced by nature without human intervention ⟨~ scenery⟩ 10 (as if) in a state unenlightened by culture or morality ⟨~ man⟩ 11a having a physical or real existence b of the physical as opposed to the spiritual world 12a true to nature; lifelike b free from affectation or constraint c not disguised or altered in appearance or form 13a (containing only notes

that are) neither sharp nor flat b having the pitch modified by the natural sign – **naturalness** n

²**natural** n 1 one born mentally defective 2 (a note affected by) a sign placed on the musical staff to nullify the effect of a preceding sharp or flat 3 one having natural skills or talents ⟨as an actor, he was a ~⟩ 4 one who is likely to be particularly suitable or successful USE (3 & 4) infml

natural gas n gas from the earth's crust; specif a combustible mixture of methane and other hydrocarbons used chiefly as a fuel and as raw material in industry

natural history n 1 a treatise on some aspect of nature 2 the natural development of an organism, disease, etc over a period of time 3 the usu amateur study, esp in the field, of natural objects (e g plants and animals), often in a particular area

naturalism n 1 action or thought based on natural desires and instincts 2 a theory discounting supernatural explanations of the origin and meaning of the universe 3 realism in art or literature, esp when emphasizing scientific observation of life without idealization of the ugly – **naturalist** adj, **naturalistic** adj, **naturalistically** adv

naturalist n 1 a follower or advocate of naturalism 2 a student of natural history

naturalize, -ise vt 1a to introduce into common use or into the vernacular b to cause (e g a plant) to become established as if native 2 to make natural 3 to admit to citizenship ~vi to become naturalized – **naturalization** n

naturally adv 1 by nature ⟨~ timid⟩ 2 as might be expected ⟨~, we shall be there⟩ 3 in a natural manner

natural number n the number 1 or any number (e g 3, 12, 432) obtained by repeatedly adding 1 to the number 1

natural resources n pl industrial materials and capacities (e g mineral deposits and waterpower) supplied by nature

natural science n any of the sciences (e g physics or biology) that deal with objectively measurable phenomena – **natural scientist** n

natural selection n a natural process that tends to result in the survival of organisms best adapted to their environment and the elimination of (mutant) organisms carrying undesirable traits

nature n 1a the inherent character or constitution of a person or thing b disposition, temperament 2a a creative and controlling force in the universe b the inner forces in an individual 3 a kind, class ⟨documents of a confidential ~⟩ 4 the physical constitution of an organism 5 the external world in its entirety 6 (a way of life resembling) mankind's original or natural condition 7 natural scenery

naturism n nudism – **naturist** adj or n

naturopathy n treatment of disease emphasizing stimulation of the natural healing processes, including the use of herbal medicines – **naturopathic** adj

naught n 1 nothing 2 NOUGHT 2

naughty adj 1 badly behaved; wicked ⟨you ~ boy!⟩ 2 slightly improper – euph or humor – **naughtily** adv, **naughtiness** n

nausea n 1 a feeling of discomfort in the stomach accompanied by a distaste for food and an urge to vomit 2 extreme disgust – **nauseant** n or adj

nauseate vb to (cause to) become affected with nausea or disgust – **nauseatingly** adv

nauseous adj causing or affected with nausea or disgust – **nauseously** adv, **nauseousness** n

nautch n an entertainment in India performed by professional dancing girls

nautical *adj* of or associated with seamen, navigation, or ships – **nautically** *adv*

nautical mile *n* any of various units of distance used for sea and air navigation based on the length of a minute of arc of a great circle of the earth: e g ,**a** a British unit equal to 6080ft (about 1853.18m) **b** an international unit equal to 1852m (about 6076.17ft)

nautilus *n, pl* **nautiluses, nautili** 1 any of a genus of molluscs related to the octopuses and squids that live in the Pacific and Indian oceans and have a spiral shell 2 PAPER NAUTILUS

naval *adj* 1 of a navy 2 consisting of or involving warships

¹**nave** *n* the hub of a wheel

²**nave** *n* the main body of a church lying to the west of the chancel; *esp* the long central space flanked by aisles

navel *n* 1 a depression in the middle of the abdomen marking the point of former attachment of the umbilical cord 2 the central point

navel orange *n* a seedless orange with a pit at the top enclosing a small secondary fruit

navigable *adj* 1 suitable for ships to pass through or along 2 capable of being steered – **navigableness** *n*, **navigably** *adv*, **navigability** *n*

navigate *vi* 1 to travel by water 2 to steer a course through a medium 3 to perform the activities (e g taking sightings and making calculations) involved in navigation ~ *vt* 1a to sail over, on, or through b to make one's way over or through 2a to steer or manage (a boat) in sailing b to operate or direct the course of (e g an aircraft) – **navigator** *n*

navigation *n* 1 navigating 2 the science of determining position, course, and distance travelled during a journey and hence advising on the best course to be steered or taken 3 ship traffic or commerce – **navigational** *adj*, **navigationally** *adv*

navvy *n, Br* an unskilled labourer

navy *n* 1 a nation's ships of war and support vessels together with the organization needed for maintenance 2 *sing or pl in constr* the personnel manning a navy 3 NAVY BLUE

navy blue *adj or n* deep dark blue

¹**nay** *adv* 1 not merely this but also ⟨*she was happy,* ~, *ecstatic*⟩ 2 *N Eng or archaic* no

²**nay** *n* 1 denial, refusal 2 a vote or voter against

nazi *n, often cap* a member of the German fascist party controlling Germany from 1933 to 1945 – **nazi** *adj*, **nazify** *vt*, **nazification** *n*

Nazism, Naziism *n* the totalitarian and racialist doctrines of the fascist National Socialist German Workers' party in the 3rd German Reich

NCO *n* NONCOMMISSIONED OFFICER

-nd *suffix* (→ *adj*), *chiefly Br* – used after the figure 2 to indicate the ordinal number *second* ⟨2nd⟩ ⟨72nd⟩

ne-, neo- *comb form* 1a new; recent ⟨Neo*cene*⟩ b new, subsequent, or revived period or form of ⟨Neo*platonism*⟩ ⟨neo-*Classicism*⟩ c in a new, subsequent, or revived form or manner ⟨Neo*lithic*⟩ ⟨neo-*Georgian*⟩ 2 New World ⟨Neo*tropical*⟩

Neanderthal *adj* being, relating to, or like Neanderthal man – **Neanderthal** *n*

Neanderthal man *n* a Middle Palaeolithic man known from skeletal remains in Europe, N Africa, and W Asia – **Neanderthaloid** *adj or n*

Neapolitan *n or adj* (a native or inhabitant) of Naples

neap tide *n* a tide of minimum height occurring at the 1st and the 3rd quarters of the moon

¹**near** *adv* 1 in or into a near position or manner ⟨*came* ~ *to tears*⟩ 2 closely approximating; nearly ⟨*a near-perfect*

performance⟩ ⟨*isn't anywhere* ~ *clever enough*⟩ – **near on** CLOSE ON

²**near** *prep* near to ⟨*went too* ~ *the edge*⟩ ⟨*call me* ~ *er the time*⟩

³**near** *adj* 1 intimately connected or associated ⟨*he and I are* ~ *relations*⟩ 2a not far distant in time, space, or degree ⟨*in the* ~ *future*⟩ b close, narrow ⟨*a* ~ *miss*⟩ ⟨*a* ~ *resemblance*⟩ 3a being the closer of 2 ⟨*the* ~ *side*⟩ b being the left-hand one of a pair ⟨*the* ~ *wheel of a cart*⟩ – **nearness** *n*

⁴**near** *vb* to approach

nearby *adv or adj* close at hand ⟨*live* ~⟩ ⟨*a* ~ *café*⟩

nearly *adv* 1 in a close manner or relationship ⟨~ *related*⟩ 2 almost but not quite ⟨*very* ~ *identical*⟩ ⟨~ *a year later*⟩

nearside *n, Br* the left-hand side (e g of a vehicle or road) ⟨*hit a car parked on his* ~⟩ – **nearside** *adj*

nearsighted *adj* able to see near things more clearly than distant ones; myopic – **nearsightedly** *adv*, **nearsightedness** *n*

¹**neat** *n, pl* **neat, neats** *archaic* the common domestic ox or cow

²**neat** *adj* 1a without addition or dilution ⟨~ *gin*⟩ b free from irregularity; smooth 2 elegantly simple 3a precise, well-defined ⟨*a* ~ *solution to the problem*⟩ b skilful, adroit 4 (habitually) tidy and orderly ⟨*a* ~ *room*⟩ ⟨*a* ~ *little man*⟩ 5 *chiefly NAm* fine, excellent – *infml* – **neatly** *adv*, **neatness** *n*

³**neat** *adv* without addition or dilution; straight ⟨*drinks his whisky* ~⟩

neath *prep* beneath – poetic

nebula *n, pl* **nebulas, nebulae** 1 a cloudy patch on the cornea 2a any of many immense bodies of highly rarefied gas or dust in interstellar space b a galaxy – **nebular** *adj*

nebulous *adj* 1 indistinct, vague 2 of or resembling a nebula; nebular – **nebulously** *adv*, **nebulousness** *n*

necessarily *adv* as a necessary consequence; inevitably

¹**necessary** *n* an indispensable item; an essential

²**necessary** *adj* 1a inevitable, inescapable b(1) logically unavoidable ⟨*a* ~ *conclusion*⟩ (2) that cannot be denied without contradiction of some other statement c determined by a previous state of affairs d acting under compulsion; not free ⟨*a* ~ *agent*⟩ 2 essential, indispensable

necessitate *vt* to make necessary or unavoidable – **necessitation** *n*

necessitous *adj* needy, impoverished – *fml* – **necessitously** *adv*, **necessitousness** *n*

necessity *n* 1 the quality of being necessary, indispensable, or unavoidable 2 impossibility of a contrary order or condition ⟨*physical* ~⟩ 3 poverty, want 4a sthg necessary or indispensable ⟨*the bare necessities of life*⟩ b a pressing need or desire – **of necessity** necessarily

¹**neck** *n* 1a the part of an animal that connects the head with the body; *also* a cut of beef, mutton, etc taken from this part b the part of a garment that covers the neck; *also* the neckline 2a a narrow part, esp shaped like a neck ⟨~ *of a bottle*⟩ b the part of a stringed musical instrument extending from the body and supporting the fingerboard and strings c a narrow stretch of land d STRAIT 1 e a column of solidified magma of a volcanic pipe or laccolith 3 a narrow margin ⟨*won by a* ~⟩ – **neck of the woods** area or district in which one lives; locality

²**neck** *vt* to reduce the diameter of ~ *vi* 1 to become constricted 2 to kiss and caress in sexual play – *infml*

neck and neck *adv* evenly matched; running level

necked *adj* having a (specified kind of) neck – often in combination ⟨*long- necked*⟩

neckerchief *n, pl* **neckerchiefs** *also* **neckerchieves** a square of fabric folded and worn round the neck

necklace *n* a string of jewels, beads, etc worn round the neck as an ornament

neckline *n* the upper edge of a garment that forms the opening for the neck and head

necktie *n, chiefly NAm* TIE 5

necromancy *n* 1 the conjuring up of the spirits of the dead in order to predict or influence the future 2 magic, sorcery – **necromancer** *n*, **necromantic** *adj*, **necromantically** *adv*

necrophilia *n* obsession with and usu erotic interest in corpses – **necrophile** *n*, **necrophiliac** *adj or n*, **necrophilic** *adj*, **necrophilism** *n*

necropolis *n, pl* **necropolises, necropoles, necropoleis, necropoli** a cemetery; *esp* a large elaborate cemetery of an ancient city

nectar *n* 1 the drink of the gods in classical mythology; *broadly* a delicious drink 2 a sweet liquid secreted by the flowers of many plants that is the chief raw material of honey – **nectarous** *adj*

nectarine *n* (a tree that bears) a smooth-skinned peach

née, nee *adj* – used to identify a woman by her maiden name ⟨*Mrs Thomson, ~ Wilkinson*⟩

¹**need** *n* **1a** a necessary duty; an obligation **b** reason or grounds for an action or condition **2a** a lack of sthg necessary, desirable, or useful ⟨*socks in ~ of mending*⟩ **b** a physiological or psychological requirement for the well-being of an organism **3** a condition requiring supply or relief ⟨*help in time of ~*⟩ **4** poverty, want – **needful** *adj*, **needfulness** *n*

²**need** *vt* 1 to be in need of; require ⟨*the soup ~s salt*⟩ ⟨*my socks ~ mending*⟩ 2 to be constrained ⟨*I'll ~ to work hard*⟩ *~vi* be under necessity or obligation to ⟨*~ I go?*⟩ ⟨*he ~ not answer*⟩

needful *adj* necessary, requisite ⟨*do whatever is ~*⟩

¹**needle** *n* **1a** a small slender usu steel instrument with an eye for thread at one end and a sharp point at the other, used for sewing **b** any of various similar larger instruments without an eye, used for carrying thread and making stitches (e g in crocheting or knitting) **c** the slender hollow pointed end of a hypodermic syringe for injecting or removing material **2** a slender, usu sharp-pointed, indicator on a dial; *esp* a magnetic needle **3a** a slender pointed object resembling a needle: e g (1) a pointed crystal (2) a sharp pinnacle of rock (3) an obelisk **b** a needle-shaped leaf, esp of a conifer **c** STYLUS **b** **d** a slender pointed rod controlling a fine inlet or outlet (e g in a valve) **4** a beam used to take the load of a wall while supported at each end by shores **5** *Br* a feeling of enmity or ill will – *infml* ⟨*a ~ match*⟩ – **needlelike** *adj*

²**needle** *vt* 1 to sew or pierce (as if) with a needle 2 to provoke by persistent teasing or gibes – **needler** *n*, **needling** *n*

needlepoint *n* 1 lace worked over a paper or parchment pattern 2 embroidery worked on canvas usu in a simple even stitch (e g cross- or tent stitch) – **needlepoint** *adj*

needless *adj* not needed; unnecessary ⟨*~ to say*⟩ – **needlessly** *adv*, **needlessness** *n*

needlewoman *n* a woman who does needlework

needlework *n* sewing; *esp* fancy work (e g embroidery)

needn't need not – **needn't have** was under no necessity to but did ⟨*I needn't have worn this sweater*⟩

needs *adv* necessarily ⟨*must ~ be recognized*⟩

needy *adj* in want, impoverished – **neediness** *n*

ne'er *adv* never – poetic

ne'er-do-well *n* an idle worthless person – **ne'er-do-well** *adj*

nefarious *adj* iniquitous, evil – **nefariously** *adv*, **nefariousness** *n*

negate *vt* 1 to deny the existence or truth of 2 to make ineffective or invalid – **negate** *n*, **negator, negater** *n*

negation *n* **1a** a denial or refusal **b** a negative statement; *esp* an assertion of the falsity of a given proposition **2a** sthg that is merely the absence of sthg actual or positive ⟨*anarchy is the ~ of government*⟩ **b** sthg opposite to sthg regarded as positive – **negational** *adj*

¹**negative** *adj* **1a** marked by denial, prohibition, or refusal **b** expressing negation **2** lacking positive or agreeable features ⟨*a ~ outlook on life*⟩ **3a** less than zero and opposite in sign to a positive number that when added to the given number yields zero ⟨*-2 is a ~ number*⟩ **b** in a direction opposite to an arbitrarily chosen regular direction ⟨*~ angle*⟩ **4a** being, relating to, or charged with electricity as a result of an excess of electrons **b** having lower electric potential and constituting the part towards which the current flows from the external circuit **5a** not showing the presence or existence of the organism, condition, etc in question **b** directed or moving away from a source of stimulation ⟨*~ tropism*⟩ **6** having the light and dark parts in approximately inverse order to those of the original photographic subject – **negatively** *adv*, **negativeness** *n*, **negativity** *n*

²**negative** *n* 1 a proposition by which sthg is denied or contradicted **b** a negative reply 2 sthg that is the negation or opposite of sthg else 3 an expression (e g the word *no*) of negation or denial 4 the side that upholds the contradictory proposition in a debate 5 the plate of a voltaic or electrolytic cell that is at the lower potential 6 a negative photographic image on transparent material used for printing positive pictures

³**negative** *vt* **1a** to refuse to accept or approve **b** to reject, veto 2 to demonstrate the falsity of; disprove

¹**neglect** *vt* 1 to pay insufficient attention to; disregard 2 to leave undone or unattended to – **neglecter** *n*

²**neglect** *n* neglecting or being neglected

neglectful *adj* careless, forgetful – **neglectfully** *adv*, **neglectfulness** *n*

negligee, negligé *n* a woman's light decorative housecoat, often designed to be worn with a matching nightdress

negligence *n* 1 forgetfulness; carelessness 2 failure to exercise the proper care expected of a prudent person

negligent *adj* 1 (habitually or culpably) neglectful 2 pleasantly casual in manner – **negligently** *adv*

negligible *adj* trifling, insignificant – **negligibly** *adv*, **negligibility** *n*

negotiable *adj* 1 transferable to another ⟨*~ securities*⟩ 2 capable of being passed along or through ⟨*a difficult but ~ road*⟩ 3 capable of being dealt with or settled through discussion – **negotiability** *n*

negotiate *vi* to confer with another in order to reach an agreement or settlement *~ vt* 1 to arrange or bring about through discussion **2a** to transfer (e g a bill of exchange) to another by endorsement or delivery **b** to convert into cash or the equivalent value ⟨*~ a cheque*⟩ **3a** to travel successfully along or over **b** to complete or deal with successfully – **negotiant** *n*, **negotiator** *n*, **negotiatory** *adj*

negotiation *n* negotiating or being negotiated; *esp* discussion of a disputed issue – often pl with sing. meaning

Negress *n* a female Negro – chiefly derog and technical

Negro *n, pl* **Negroes** 1 a member of the esp African branch of the black race of mankind 2 a person of Negro descent – **Negro** *adj, often not cap*, **Negroid** *n or adj, often not cap*

negus *n* a drink of wine, hot water, sugar, lemon juice, and nutmeg

neigh *vi* to make the loud prolonged cry characteristic of a horse – **neigh** *n*

¹**neighbour, NAm chiefly neighbor** *n* **1** one living or situated near another **2** a fellow human being ⟨*love thy ~*⟩

²**neighbour, NAm chiefly neighbor** *vt* to adjoin or lie near to

neighbourhood *n* **1** an adjacent or surrounding region **2** an approximate amount, extent, or degree ⟨*cost in the ~ of £300*⟩ **3a** *sing or pl in constr* the neighbours **b** a district lived in by neighbours **c** (the inhabitants of) a district of a town, city etc, forming a distinct community **4** the set of all points whose distances from a given point are not greater than a given positive number

neighbouring *adj* nearby, adjacent

neighbourly *adj* characteristic of congenial neighbours; *esp* friendly

¹**neither** *pron* not the one or the other ⟨*~ of us*⟩

²**neither** *conj* **1** not either ⟨*~ here nor there*⟩ ⟨*~ ate, drank, nor smoked*⟩ **2** also not; nor ⟨*he didn't go and ~ did I*⟩

³**neither** *adj* not either ⟨*~ hand*⟩

⁴**neither** *adv* **1** similarly not; also not ⟨'*I can't swim.*' '*Neither can I.*'⟩ **2** *chiefly dial* either

nelson *n* FULL NELSON; *also* HALF NELSON

nematode *n* any of a phylum of elongated cylindrical worms parasitic in animals or plants or free-living in soil or water

nemesis *n, pl* **nemeses 1a** (an agent of) retribution or vengeance **b** a formidable enemy or opponent **2** downfall, undoing

neo- – see NE-

neoclassic, neoclassical *adj* of or constituting a revival or adaptation of the classical, esp in literature, music, art, or architecture – **neoclassicism** *n*, **neoclassicist** *n or adj*

neocolonialism *n* the economic and political policies by which a great power indirectly extends its influence over other areas – **neocolonial** *adj*, **neocolonialist** *n or adj*

Neolithic *adj* of the last period of the Stone Age characterized by polished stone implements

neologism *n* (the use of) a new word, usage, or expression – **neology** *n*, **neological** *adj*, **neologistic** *adj*

neon *n* **1** a noble gaseous element used esp in electric lamps **2** a discharge lamp in which the gas contains a large proportion of neon – **neon** *adj*, **neoned** *adj*

neonate *n* a newborn child (less than a month old) – **neonatal** *adj*

neophyte *n* **1** a new convert **2** a beginner

neoplasm *n* an abnormal growth of tissue; a tumour – **neoplastic** *adj*

nephew *n* a son of one's brother or sister or of one's brother-in-law or sister-in-law

nephritis *n, pl* **nephritides** inflammation of the kidneys

ne plus ultra *n* **1** the highest point or stage **2** the greatest degree of a quality or state

nepotism *n* favouritism shown to a relative (e g by appointment to office) – **nepotist** *n*

Neptune *n* **1** the ocean personified **2** the planet 8th in order from the sun – **Neptunian** *adj*

¹**nerve** *n* **1** sinew, tendon ⟨*strain every ~*⟩ **2** any of the filaments of nervous tissue that conduct nervous impulses to and from the nervous system and are made up of axons and dendrites **3a** fortitude, tenacity **b** (disrespectful) assurance or boldness **4a** a sore or sensitive subject – esp in *hit/touch a nerve* **b** *pl* acute nervousness or anxiety **5** VEIN 3 **6** the sensitive pulp of a tooth

²**nerve** *vt* **1** to give strength and courage to **2** to prepare (oneself) psychologically *for* – often + *up* ⟨*~d herself up for the confrontation*⟩

nerve cell *n* a neuron

nerve centre *n* **1** CENTRE 3 **2** a source of leadership, control, or energy

nerveless *adj* **1** lacking strength or vigour **2** not agitated or afraid; cool – **nervelessly** *adv*, **nervelessness** *n*

nerve-racking, nerve-wracking *adj* placing a great strain on the nerves

nervous *adj* **1** of, affected by, or composed of (the) nerves or neurons **2a** easily excited or agitated **b** timid, apprehensive ⟨*~ of strangers*⟩ – **nervously** *adv*, **nervousness** *n*

nervous breakdown *n* (an occurrence of) a disorder in which worrying, depression, severe tiredness, etc prevent one from coping with one's responsibilities

nervous system *n* the brain, spinal cord, or other nerves and nervous tissue together forming a system for interpreting stimuli from the sense organs and transmitting impulses to muscles, glands, etc

nervy *adj* **1** suffering from nervousness or anxiety **2** brash, imprudent – infml – **nerviness** *n*

ness *n* a cape or headland

-ness *suffix* (*adj → n*) **1** state or quality of ⟨*good*ness⟩; *also* instance of (a specified state or quality) ⟨*a kind*ness⟩ **2** degree or amount of ⟨*big*ness⟩

¹**nest** *n* **1a** a bed or receptacle prepared by a bird for its eggs and young **b** a place or structure in which animals live, esp in their immature stages ⟨*an ants' ~*⟩ **2a** a place of rest, retreat, or lodging **b** a den or haunt **3a** a group of similar things **b** a hotbed **4** a series of objects made to fit close together or one inside another

²**nest** *vi* **1** to build or occupy a nest **2** to fit compactly together **~** *vt* to pack or fit compactly together – **nester** *n*

nest egg *n* **1** a real or artificial egg left in a nest to induce a fowl to continue to lay there **2** an amount of money saved up as a reserve

nestle nestling *vi* **1** to settle snugly or comfortably **2** to lie in a sheltered position **~** *vt* **1** to shelter or enclose (as if) in a nest **2** to press closely and affectionately

nestling *n* a young bird that has not abandoned the nest

Nestor *n, often not cap* a patriarch or mentor

¹**net** *n* **1a** an open meshed fabric twisted, knotted, or woven together at regular intervals **b** a device for catching fish, birds, or insects **c** a net barricade which divides a tennis, badminton, etc court in half and over which a ball or shuttlecock must be hit to be in play **d** the fabric that encloses the sides and back of a soccer, hockey, etc goal **e**(1) a practice cricket pitch surrounded by nets – usu pl (2) a period of practice in such a net **2** an entrapping situation **3** a network of lines, fibres, etc **4** a ball hit into the net in a racket game – **netless** *adj*, **netlike** *adj*, **netty** *adj*

²**net** *vt* **-tt- 1** to cover or enclose (as if) with a net **2** to catch (as if) in a net **3a** to hit (a ball) into the net for the loss of a point in a game **b** to hit or kick (a ball or puck) into the goal for a score in hockey, soccer, etc – **netter** *n*

³**net, chiefly Br nett** *adj* **1** remaining after all deductions (e g for taxes, outlay, or loss) ⟨*~ earnings*⟩ **b** excluding all tare ⟨*~ weight*⟩ **2** final, ultimate ⟨*the ~ result*⟩

⁴**net, chiefly Br nett** *vt* **-tt- 1** to make by way of profit **2** to get possession of

⁵**net** *n* a net amount, profit, weight, price, or score

netball *n* a game, usu for women, between 2 sides of 7 players each who score goals by tossing an inflated ball through a high horizontal ring on a post at each end of a hard court

nether adj 1 beneath the earth's surface ⟨the ~ regions⟩ 2 lower, under – fml – **nethermost** adj

netting n NETWORK 1

¹**nettle** n 1 any of a genus of widely distributed green-flowered plants covered with stinging hairs 2 any of various plants like the nettle – used in combination ⟨red dead nettle⟩

²**nettle** vt **nettling** 1 to strike or sting (as if) with nettles 2 to arouse to annoyance or anger

nettle rash n urticaria

¹**network** n 1 a fabric or structure of cords or wires that cross at regular intervals and are knotted or secured at the crossings 2 a system of crisscrossing lines or channels 3 an interconnected chain, group, or system 4a a group of radio or television stations linked together so that they can broadcast the same programmes if desired b a radio or television company that produces programmes for broadcast over such a network

²**network** vt to present on or integrate into a radio or television network ⟨~ed programmes⟩

neur-, neuro- comb form 1 nerve; nervous system ⟨neural⟩ ⟨neurology⟩ ⟨neurosurgeon⟩ 2 neural; neural and ⟨neuromuscular⟩

neural adj 1 of or affecting a nerve or the nervous system 2 dorsal – **neurally** adv

neuralgia n intense paroxysms of pain radiating along the course of a nerve without apparent cause – **neuralgic** adj

neurasthenia n severe fatigue, depression, etc occurring as a mental disorder; NERVOUS BREAKDOWN – not now used technically – **neurasthenic** adj, **neurasthenically** adv

neuritis n inflammation or degeneration of a nerve causing pain, sensory disturbances, etc – **neuritic** adj or n

neurology n the study of (diseases of) the nervous system – **neurologist** n, **neurologic, neurological** adj, **neurologically** adv

neurosis n, pl **neuroses** a nervous disorder, unaccompanied by disease of the nervous system, in which phobias, compulsions, anxiety, and obsessions make normal life difficult

neurotic n one who is emotionally unstable or is affected with a neurosis – **neurotic** adj, **neurotically** adv, **neuroticism** n

neurotransmitter n a substance (e g acetylcholine) that is released at a nerve ending and transmits nerve impulses across the synapse – **neurotransmission** n

¹**neuter** adj 1a of or belonging to the gender that is neither masculine nor feminine b intransitive 2 lacking generative organs or having nonfunctional ones ⟨the worker bee is ~⟩

²**neuter** n 1 (a word or morpheme of) the neuter gender 2a WORKER 2 b a castrated animal

³**neuter** vt CASTRATE 1

¹**neutral** adj 1 (of or being a country, person, etc) not engaged on either side of a war, dispute, etc ⟨~ territory⟩ 2a indifferent, indefinite b without colour c NEUTER 2 d neither acid nor alkaline ⟨a ~ solution⟩ e not electrically charged or positive or negative; not live ⟨the ~ wire in a mains plug is blue⟩ 3a produced (e g like the vowel /ʌ/) with the tongue in the position it has when at rest b produced (e g like the vowel /ah/) with the lips neither spread nor rounded – **neutrally** adv, **neutralism** n, **neutralist** n, **neutralistic** rality n

²**neutral** n 1 a neutral country, person, etc 2 a neutral colour 3 a position (of a gear lever) in which gears are disengaged 4 a neutral electrical conductor

neutralize, -ise vt 1 to make (chemically, politically, electrically, etc) neutral 2 to nullify or counteract (the effect of) with an opposing action, force, etc ~vi to become neutralized – **neutralization** n

neutron n an uncharged elementary particle with a mass about that of the proton, present in the nuclei of all atoms except those of normal hydrogen

never adv 1 not ever; at no time ⟨~ saw him before⟩ ⟨~ forgotten⟩ 2 not in any degree; not under any condition ⟨this will ~ do⟩ ⟨~ mind⟩ 3 surely not ⟨you're ~ 18!⟩ ⟨'I said it to his face.' 'Never!'⟩ – chiefly infml – I **never** 1 – used to express amazement ⟨well I never⟩; chiefly infml 2 I didn't do it – nonstandard ⟨no she never⟩

nevermore adv never again

never-never n, Br HIRE PURCHASE – + the; infml

never-never land n an ideal or imaginary place

nevertheless adv in spite of that; yet ⟨true but ~ unkind⟩

¹**new** adj 1 not old; not used previously; recent ⟨a ~ book⟩ ⟨a ~ science⟩ 2a(1) only recently discovered, recognized, or in use; novel ⟨the ~ morality⟩ (2) fresh, unfamiliar ⟨visit ~ places⟩ b different from or replacing a former one of the same kind ⟨a ~ model⟩ 3 having been in the specified condition or relationship for only a short time; unaccustomed ⟨~ to the job⟩ ⟨a ~ member⟩ 4a beginning as the repetition of a previous act or thing ⟨a ~ day⟩ b refreshed, regenerated ⟨awoke, a ~ man⟩ 5 cap MODERN 3; esp in use after medieval times – **newish** adj, **newness** n – **new lease of life** a renewed period of healthy activity, strength, or usefulness

²**new** adv newly, recently – usu in combination ⟨new-mown grass⟩

newborn n or adj, pl **newborn, newborns** (an individual who is) recently born

newcomer n 1 a recent arrival 2 a beginner, novice

New Deal n the programme of economic and social reform in the USA during the 1930s

newel n 1 an upright post about which the steps of a spiral staircase wind 2 also **newel post** a principal post supporting either end of a staircase handrail

newfangled adj modern and unnecessarily complicated or gimmicky – derog or humor – **newfangledness** n

Newfoundland n (any of) a breed of large intelligent dogs with coarse dense usu black hair

New Left n a radical left-wing movement originating in Britain in the late 1950s

newly adv 1 lately, recently ⟨a ~ married couple⟩ 2 anew

newlywed n or adj (one who is) recently married

new moon n the phase of the moon when its dark side is towards the earth; also the thin crescent moon seen a few days after this

new penny n PENNY 1a(2)

news n pl but sing in constr 1 (a report or series of reports of) recent (notable) events; new information about sthg ⟨have you heard the ~?⟩ ⟨there is no ~ of him⟩ 2a news reported in a newspaper, a periodical, or a broadcast b material that is newsworthy 3 a radio or television broadcast of news – **newsless** adj

newsagent n, chiefly Br a retailer of newspapers and magazines

newsboy, fem newsgirl n a paperboy

newscast n NEWS 3 – **newscaster** n, **newscasting** n

newsletter n a printed pamphlet containing news or information of interest chiefly to a special group

newsmonger n a gossip

newspaper n 1 (an organization that publishes) a paper printed and distributed usu daily or weekly and containing news, articles of opinion, features, and advertising 2 the paper on which a newspaper is printed

newsprint *n* cheap paper made chiefly from wood pulp and used mostly for newspapers

newsreel *n* a short film dealing with current events

newsroom *n* a place (e g an office) where news is prepared for publication or broadcast

newsstand *n* a stall where newspapers and periodicals are sold

newsvendor *n* one who sells newspapers, esp in the street at a regular place

newsworthy *adj* sufficiently interesting to warrant reporting

newsy *adj* full of (inconsequential) news – **newsiness** *n*

newt *n* any of various small semiaquatic salamanders

New Testament *n* the second part of the Christian Bible comprising the canonical Gospels and Epistles, the books of Acts, and the book of Revelation

newton *n* the SI unit of force equal to the force that when acting for 1s on a free mass of 1kg will give it a velocity of 1m/s

Newtonian *adj* of, following, or agreeing with (the discoveries of) Isaac Newton ⟨*~ mechanics*⟩

new town *n* any of several towns in Britain planned and built as a unit since 1946

New World *n* the W hemisphere; *esp* the continental landmass of N and S America

New Year *n* the first day or days of a year; *esp* NEW YEAR'S DAY

New Year's Day *n* January 1 observed as a public holiday in many countries

¹**next** *adj* **1** immediately adjacent or following (e g in place or order) ⟨*the ~ house*⟩ **2** immediately after the present or a specified time ⟨*~ week*⟩ ⟨*he left the very ~ Monday*⟩

²**next** *adv* **1** in the time, place, or order nearest or immediately succeeding ⟨*~ we drove home*⟩ ⟨*the ~ closest school*⟩ **2** on the first occasion to come ⟨*when ~ we meet*⟩

³**next** *prep* nearest or adjacent to ⟨*wear wool ~ the skin*⟩

⁴**next** *n* the next occurrence, item, or issue of a kind ⟨*to be contained in our ~*⟩

next-door *adj* situated or living in the next building, room, etc

next door *adv* in or to the next building, room, etc

next of kin *n, pl* **next of kin** the person most closely related to another person

¹**next to** *prep* immediately following or adjacent to ⟨*sit ~ Mary*⟩ ⟨*~ gin I like sherry best*⟩

²**next to** *adv* very nearly; almost ⟨*it was ~ impossible to see in the fog*⟩ ⟨*the article told me ~ nothing*⟩

nexus *n, pl* **nexuses, nexus 1** a connection or link **2** a connected group or series

niacin *n* NICOTINIC ACID

¹**nib** *n* **1** a bill or beak **2a** the sharpened point of a quill pen **b** (each of the 2 equal divisions of) a small thin (detachable) piece of metal at the end of a pen, that tapers to a split point which is placed in contact with the paper or other surface to be marked **3** a small pointed or projecting part or article ⟨*roasted almond ~s*⟩

²**nib** *vt* **-bb-** to make into a nib or give a nib to

¹**nibble** *vb* **nibbling** *vt* **1a** to bite cautiously, gently, or playfully **b** to eat or chew in small bites **2** to produce by repeated small bites *~ vi* **1** to take gentle, small, or cautious bites **2** to show cautious or qualified interest *USE* (*vi*) usu + *at* – **nibbler** *n*

²**nibble** *n* **1** an act of nibbling **2** a very small amount (e g of food) *USE* infml

nibs *n pl but sing in constr* an important or self-important person – infml; chiefly in *his nibs* or *His Nibs*

nice *adj* **1** showing or requiring fine discrimination or treatment ⟨*a ~ distinction*⟩ **2a** pleasant, agreeable **b** well done; well-executed ⟨*~ shot!*⟩ **3** inappropriate or unpleasant – usu ironic ⟨*he's a ~ one to talk*⟩; compare PRETTY 2 **4a** socially acceptable; well-bred **b** decent, proper – **nicely** *adv*, **niceness** *n* – **nice and** to a satisfactory degree ⟨*it's nice and cool*⟩

nicety *n* **1** an elegant or refined feature **2** a fine point or distinction **3** (the showing or requiring of) delicacy, discernment, or careful attention to details – **to a nicety** to the point at which sthg is at its best ⟨*roasted to a nicety*⟩

¹**niche** *n* **1** a recess in a wall, esp for a statue **2a** a place or activity for which a person is best suited **b** the ecological role of an organism in a community, esp in regard to food consumption

²**niche** *vt* to place (as if) in a niche

¹**nick** *n* **1** a small notch or groove **2** the point at which the back or side wall of a squash court meets the floor **3** EDGE 4 **4** *Br* state of health or repair – infml; esp in *in good/bad nick* ⟨*it's not in very good ~*⟩ **5** *Br* a prison or police station – slang ⟨*he's been in the ~ for the last 3 years*⟩ – **in the nick of time** at the final critical moment; just before it would be too late

²**nick** *vt* **1a** to make a nick in **b** to cut into or wound slightly **2** *Br* **a** STEAL 1a **b** ARREST 2 *~ vi esp of domestic animals* to complement one another genetically and produce superior offspring *USE* (*vt* 2) slang

nickel *n* **1** a hard bivalent metallic transition element with magnetic properties like those of iron **2** (a US coin containing 1 part of nickel to 3 of copper and worth) the sum of 5 cents

¹**nicker** *n, pl* **nicker** *Br* the sum of £1 – slang

²**nicker** *vi* to whinny

nicknack *n* a knick-knack

nickname *n* **1** a name used in place of or in addition to a proper name **2** a familiar form of a proper name, esp of a person – **nickname** *vt*

nicotine *n* an alkaloid that is the chief drug in tobacco and has the actions of the neurotransmitter acetylcholine on some of its receptors, esp those in skeletal muscle – **nicotinic** *adj*

nicotinic acid *n* a vitamin of the vitamin B complex that is found widely in animals and plants and whose lack results in pellagra

niece *n* a daughter of one's brother or sister or of one's brother-in-law or sister-in-law

niff *n, Br* an unpleasant smell – slang – **niffy** *adj*

nifty *adj* very good or effective; *esp* cleverly conceived or executed – infml – **nifty** *adv*

niggard *n* a mean and stingy person – **niggard** *adj*

niggardly *adj* **1** grudgingly mean; miserly **2** provided in meagre amounts ⟨*~ praise*⟩ – **niggardliness** *n*, **niggardly** *adv*

nigger *n* a Negro; *broadly* a member of any dark-skinned race – derog

niggle *vb* **niggling** *vi* **1** to waste time or effort on minor details **2** to find fault constantly in a petty way *~vt* to cause slight irritation to; bother – **niggle** *n*, **niggler** *n*, **niggly** *adj*

niggling *adj* **1** petty **2** persistently annoying ⟨*~ doubts*⟩ – **nigglingly** *adv*

nigh *adv, adj, or prep* near (in place, time, or relation) ⟨*~ on 50 years*⟩

night *n* **1** the period of darkness from dusk to dawn caused by the earth's daily rotation **2** an evening characterized by a specified event or activity ⟨*Thursday is bingo ~*⟩ ⟨*opening ~*⟩ **3a** darkness **b** a state of affliction, ignorance, or obscurity

night blindness *n* reduced vision in faint light (e g at night) – **night-blind** *adj*

nightcap *n* **1** a cloth cap worn in bed **2** a drink taken at bedtime

nightclub *n* a place of entertainment open at night that has a floor show, provides music and space for dancing, and usu serves drinks and food

nightdress *n* a woman's or girl's nightgown

nightfall *n* dusk

nighthawk *n* a nightjar, owl, or similar bird that flies at night

nightingale *n* any of several Old World thrushes noted for the sweet usu nocturnal song of the male

nightjar *n* a Eurasian insect-eating bird that is active at night and has a characteristic churring call

nightlife *n* late evening entertainment or social life

night-light *n* a dim light kept burning all night long, esp in sby's bedroom

nightly *adj or adv* (of, occurring, taken, or done) at or by night or every night

nightmare *n* **1** an evil spirit that causes frightening dreams **2** a frightening dream accompanied by a sense of oppression or suffocation that usu awakens the sleeper **3** an experience, situation, or object that causes acute anxiety or terror – **nightmare, nightmarish** *adj*, **nightmarishly** *adv*

nights *adv* in the night repeatedly; on any night

night school *n* classes, often in subjects leading to a qualification, held in the evening

nightshade *n* any of various related usu poisonous plants: e g **a** bittersweet **b** DEADLY NIGHTSHADE

nightshirt *n* a long loose shirt for sleeping in

night soil *n* human excrement collected for fertilizing the soil

nightstick *n, NAm* a club carried by a policeman

night watchman *n* **1** sby who keeps watch (e g over a building) by night **2** a relatively inexpert batsman who is sent in to bat towards the end of a day's play so that a more expert batsman need not face the bowling until the following day

nihilism *n* **1** a view that rejects all values and beliefs as meaningless or unfounded **2a** *often cap* the doctrine that social conditions are so bad as to make destruction desirable for its own sake, adhered to specif by a 19th-c Russian terrorist revolutionary party **b** terrorism – **nihilist** *n or adj*, **nihilistic** *adj*

-nik *suffix* (*n or adj → n*) one connected with or characterized by being ⟨*beat*nik⟩ ⟨*computer*nik⟩

nil *n* nothing, zero ⟨*a score of 2 points to* ~⟩ – **nil** *adj*

Nilotic *adj* of (the inhabitants or languages of) the Nile or Nile region

nimble *adj* **1** quick, light, and easy in movement **2** quick and clever in thought and understanding – **nimbleness** *n*, **nimbly** *adv*

nimbus *n, pl* **nimbi, nimbuses 1** a luminous vapour, cloud, or atmosphere surrounding a god or goddess **2** a luminous circle about the head of a representation of a god, saint, or sovereign **3** a cloud from which rain is falling

nincompoop *n* a silly or foolish person

nine *n* **1** (the number) 9 **2** the ninth in a set or series **3** sthg having 9 parts or members or a denomination of 9 **4** the first or last 9 holes of an 18-hole golf course **5** *pl in constr, cap the* Common Market countries between 1973 and 1981 – **nine** *adj or pron*, **ninefold** *adj or adv* – **to the nines** elaborately in special, formal, or party clothes ⟨*dressed up* to the nines⟩

nine days' wonder *n* sthg that creates a short-lived sensation

nineteen *n* (the number) 19 – **nineteen** *adj or pron*, **nineteenth** *adj or n* – **nineteen to the dozen** very fast and volubly ⟨*talking* nineteen to the dozen⟩

ninety *n* **1** (the number) 90 **2** *pl* (a range of temperatures, ages, or dates within a century characterized by) the numbers 90 to 99 – **ninety** *adj or pron*, **ninetyfold** *adj or adv*, **ninetieth** *adj or n*

ninny *n* a silly or foolish person – humor; infml

ninth *n* **1** number nine in a countable series **2a** (a chord containing) a musical interval of an octave and a second **b** the note separated by this interval from a lower note – **ninth** *adj or adv*

¹nip *vb* **-pp-** *vt* **1** to catch hold of and squeeze sharply; pinch **2a** to sever (as if) by pinching sharply – often + *off* **b** to prevent the growth or development of ⟨*her plans were* ~*ped in the bud*⟩ **3** to injure or make numb with cold ~ *vi chiefly Br* to go quickly or briefly; hurry – infml ⟨*I'll just* ~ *out to the shops*⟩

²nip *n* **1** a sharp stinging cold ⟨*a* ~ *in the air*⟩ **2** (an instance of) nipping; a pinch **3** *chiefly NAm* a pungent flavour; a tang

³nip *n* a small measure or drink of spirits

⁴nip *vb* **-pp-** to take nips of (a drink)

Nip *n* a Japanese – derog

nip and tuck *adj or adv, chiefly NAm* NECK AND NECK

nipper *n* **1** any of various devices (e g pincers) for gripping or cutting – usu pl with sing. meaning **2** *chiefly Br* a child; *esp* a small boy – infml

nipple *n* **1** the small protuberance of a mammary gland (e g a breast) from which milk is drawn in the female **2a** an artificial teat through which a bottle-fed infant feeds **b** a device with a hole through which the discharge of a liquid can be regulated **3** a small projection through which oil or grease is injected into machinery

nippy *adj* **1** nimble and lively; snappy **2** CHILLY 1 – **nippily** *adv*, **nippiness** *n*

nirvana *n, often cap* **1** a Hindu and Buddhist state of final bliss and freedom from the cycle of rebirth, attainable through the extinction of desire and individual consciousness **2** a place or state of relief from pain or anxiety

nisi *adj* taking effect at a specified time unless previously modified or avoided ⟨*a decree* ~⟩

Nissen hut *n* a prefabricated shelter with a semicircular arching roof of corrugated iron and a concrete floor

¹nit *n* (the egg of) a parasitic insect (e g a louse)

²nit *n, chiefly Br* a nitwit – infml

nit-picking *n* petty and usu unjustified criticism – **nit-pick** *vi*

¹nitrate *n* **1** a salt or ester of nitric acid **2** sodium or potassium nitrate used as a fertilizer

²nitrate *vt* to treat or combine with nitric acid or a nitrate – **nitrator** *n*, **nitration** *n*

nitre, *NAm chiefly* **niter** *n* POTASSIUM NITRATE – not now used technically

nitric *adj* of or containing nitrogen (with a relatively high valency) ⟨~ *oxide*⟩

nitric acid *n* a corrosive inorganic liquid acid used esp as an oxidizing agent and in making fertilizers, dyes, etc

nitrogen *n* a trivalent gaseous chemical element that constitutes about 78 per cent by volume of the atmosphere and is found in combined form as a constituent of all living things – **nitrogenous** *adj*

nitroglycerine *n* an oily explosive liquid used chiefly in making dynamite and, as a weak solution in water, in medicine to dilate the blood vessels

nitrous *adj* of or containing **a** potassium nitrate **b** nitrogen (with a relatively low valency)

nitrous oxide *n* a gas used as a general anaesthetic, esp in obstetrics and dentistry

nitty-gritty *n the* important basic realities – infml – **nitty-gritty** *adj*

nitwit *n* a scatterbrained or stupid person – infml – **nit-witted** *adj*

¹**nix**, *fem* **nixie** *n* a water sprite of Germanic folklore

²**nix** *n* nothing – slang

³**nix** *adv, NAm* no – slang

⁴**nix** *vt, NAm* to veto, forbid – slang

¹**no** *adv* 1 – used to negate an alternative choice ⟨*whether you like it or* ~⟩ 2 in no respect or degree – in comparisons ⟨~ *better than before*⟩ 3 – used in answers expressing negation, dissent, denial, or refusal; contrasted with *yes* ⟨~, *I'm not going*⟩ 4 – used like a question demanding assent to the preceding statement ⟨*she's pretty,* ~?⟩ 5 nay ⟨*happy,* ~, *ecstatic*⟩ 6 – used as an interjection to express incredulity ⟨'*She's 17.*' 'No!'⟩ 7 chiefly *Scot* not ⟨*it's* ~ *canny*⟩

²**no** *adj* 1a not any ⟨~ *money*⟩ ⟨*there's* ~ *denying*⟩ ⟨~ *parking*⟩ b hardly any; very little ⟨*I'll be finished in* ~ *time*⟩ 2a not a; quite other than a ⟨*he's* ~ *expert*⟩ b – used before a noun phrase to give force to an opposite meaning ⟨*in* ~ *uncertain terms*⟩; compare NOT 3

³**no** *n, pl* **noes, nos** a negative reply or vote

No, Noh *n, pl* **No, Noh** a classic Japanese (form of) dance-drama

¹**nob** *n* 1 a jack of the same suit as the card turned by the dealer in cribbage, that scores 1 point for the holder – chiefly in *his nob/nobs* ⟨*one for his* ~⟩ 2 a person's head – infml

²**nob** *n, chiefly Br* a wealthy or influential person – infml

¹**no-ball** *interj or n* – (used as a call by an umpire to indicate) an illegal delivery of the ball in cricket which cannot take a wicket and counts 1 run to the batsman's side if the batsman does not score a run off it

²**no-ball** *vt*, *of an umpire in cricket* to declare (a bowler) to have delivered or (a delivery) to be a no-ball ~ *vi* to bowl a no-ball

nobble *vt* **nobbling** *Br* 1 to incapacitate (esp a racehorse), esp by drugging 2a to win over to one's side, esp by dishonest means b to get hold of, esp dishonestly c to swindle, cheat USE (*1*) infml; (*2*) slang – **nobbler** *n*

Nobel prize *n* any of various annual prizes established by the will of Alfred Nobel for the encouragement of people who work for the interests of humanity (e g in the fields of peace, literature, medicine, and physics)

nobility *n* 1 being noble 2 *sing or pl in constr* the people making up a noble class

¹**noble** *adj* 1a gracious and dignified in character or bearing b famous, notable ⟨*a* ~ *victory*⟩ 2 of or being high birth or exalted rank 3 of fine quality; excellent ⟨*a* ~ *vintage*⟩ 4 imposing, stately 5 having or showing a magnanimous character or high ideals ⟨*a* ~ *deed*⟩ – **nobleness** *n*, **nobly** *adv*

²**noble** *n* 1 a person of noble rank or birth 2 a former English gold coin worth £⅓

nobleman, *fem* **noblewoman** *n* a man of noble rank

noblesse oblige *n* the obligation of honourable and responsible behaviour associated with high rank

¹**nobody** *pron* not anybody ⟨~ *likes me*⟩

²**nobody** *n* a person of no influence or consequence

nocturnal *adj* 1 of or occurring in the night 2 active at night ⟨*a* ~ *predator*⟩ – **nocturnally** *adv*

nocturne *n* a work of art dealing with evening or night; *esp* a dreamy pensive composition for the piano

¹**nod** *vb* **-dd-** *vi* 1 to make a short downward movement of the head (e g in assent or greeting) 2 to bend or sway

gently downwards or forwards 3a to become drowsy or sleepy ⟨~ *in front of the fire*⟩ b to make a slip or error in a moment of inattention ⟨*even Homer sometimes* ~s⟩ ~ *vt* 1 to incline (e g the head) in a quick downward movement 2 to express by a nod ⟨~*ded their approval*⟩ – **nodder** *n*

²**nod** *n* 1 (an instance of) nodding 2 an unconsidered indication of agreement, approval, etc – infml ⟨*the motion went through on the* ~⟩

nodding *adj* 1 pendulous or drooping ⟨*a plant with* ~ *flowers*⟩ 2 casual, superficial ⟨*a* ~ *acquaintance with French*⟩

noddle *n* a person's head – infml

node *n* 1 a thickening or swelling (e g of a rheumatic joint) 2 either of the 2 points where the orbit of a a planet or comet intersects the ecliptic b an earth satellite crosses the plane of the equator 3a a point on a stem at which 1 or more leaves are attached b a point at which a curve intersects itself 4 a point, line, etc of a vibrating body at which vibration is at a minimum – **nodal** *adj*, **nodally** *adv*

nodule *n* a small rounded mass: e g a a small rounded lump of a mineral or mineral aggregate b a swelling on the root of a leguminous plant (e g clover) containing symbiotic bacteria that convert atmospheric nitrogen into a form in which it can be used by the plant – **nodular** *adj*, **nodulated** *adj*, **nodulation** *n*

Noel, Noël *n* the Christmas season

noes *pl of* NO

nog *n* (an) eggnog

noggin *n* 1 a small mug or cup 2 a small measure of spirits, usu 0.142 litres (¼ pt) 3 a person's head – infml

no-go *adj* having prohibited or restricted access ⟨*a* ~ *military zone*⟩

nohow *adv* in no way; not at all – chiefly dial or humor

¹**noise** *n* 1 loud confused shouting or outcry 2a a (harsh or unwanted) sound b unwanted signals or fluctuations in an electrical circuit c irrelevant or meaningless information occurring with desired information in the output of a computer 3 a usu trite remark of a specified type – usu pl ⟨*made sympathetic* ~s⟩ – **noiseless** *adj*, **noiselessly** *adv*

²**noise** *vt* to spread by gossip or hearsay – usu + *about* or *abroad*

noisome *adj* repellent, offensive – fml – **noisomely** *adv*, **noisomeness** *n*

noisy *adj* 1 making noise 2 full of or characterized by noise – **noisily** *adv*, **noisiness** *n*

nomad *n* 1 a member of a people that wanders from place to place, usu seasonally and within a well-defined territory 2 one who wanders aimlessly from place to place – **nomad** *adj*, **nomadism** *n*, **nomadic** *adj*

no-man's-land *n* 1a an area of waste or unclaimed land b an unoccupied area between opposing armies 2 an area of anomalous, ambiguous, or indefinite character

nom de plume *n, pl* **noms de plume** a pseudonym under which an author writes

nomenclature *n* 1 a name, designation 2 (an instance of) naming, esp within a particular system 3 a system of terms used in a particular science, discipline, or art – **nomenclatural** *adj*

¹**nominal** *adj* 1 of or being a nominal 2 of or constituting a name 3a being sthg in name only b assigned as a convenient approximation (e g to an actual weight or size) c negligible, insignificant ⟨*a* ~ *rent*⟩ – **nominally** *adv*

²**nominal** *n* a word (group) functioning as a noun

nominate *vt* 1 to designate, specify 2a to appoint or

recommend for appointment **b** to propose for an honour, award, or candidature – **nominator** *n*, **nominee** *n*, **nomination** *n*

nominative *adj* **1** of or being the grammatical case expressing the subject of a verb **2** nominated – **nominative** *n*

non- *prefix* **1** not; reverse of; absence of ⟨non*conformity*⟩ ⟨non*payment*⟩ ⟨non*existence*⟩ ⟨non*alcoholic*⟩ **2** failure to be; refraining from ⟨non*smoker*⟩ ⟨non*violent*⟩ ⟨non*appearance*⟩ **3** lacking the usual characteristics of the thing specified ⟨non*event*⟩ ⟨non*appearance*⟩ **4** proof against; designed to avoid ⟨non*stick*⟩ ⟨non-*iron*⟩ ⟨non*flammable*⟩

nonage *n* a period or state of youth or immaturity

nonagenarian *n* a person between 90 and 99 years old – **nonagenarian** *adj*

nonaligned *adj* not allied with other nations, esp any of the great powers – **nonalignment** *n*

nonce *n* the present occasion, time, or purpose ⟨*for the* ~⟩ ⟨*a* ~ *word*⟩

nonchalant *adj* giving an impression of easy unconcern or indifference – **nonchalance** *n*, **nonchalantly** *adv*

noncombatant *n* a civilian, army chaplain, etc who does not engage in combat – **noncombatant** *adj*

noncommissioned officer *n* a subordinate officer (e g a sergeant) in the armed forces appointed from among the personnel who do not hold a commission

noncommittal *adj* giving no clear indication of attitude or feeling – **noncommittally** *adv*

non compos mentis *adj* not of sound mind

nonconductor *n* a substance that conducts heat, electricity, etc only very slightly under normal conditions

nonconformist *n* **1** *often cap* a person who does not conform to an established church; *specif* a member of a Protestant body separated from the Church of England **2** one who does not conform to a generally accepted pattern of thought or behaviour – **nonconformism** *n*, *often cap*, **nonconformist** *adj*, *often cap*

nonconformity *n* **1** refusal to conform to an established creed, rule, or practice **2** absence of correspondence or agreement

nondescript *adj* **1** (apparently) belonging to no particular class or kind **2** lacking distinctive or interesting qualities; dull – **nondescript** *n*

¹none *pron, pl* **none 1** not any; no part or thing ⟨~ *of the money is missing*⟩ ⟨~ *of the telephones are working*⟩ **2** not one person; nobody ⟨*it's* ~ *other than Tom*⟩ ⟨~ *but a fool*⟩ **3** not any such thing or person ⟨*a bad film is better than* ~ *at all*⟩

²none *adv* **1** by no means; not at all ⟨~ *too soon to begin*⟩ **2** in no way; to no extent ⟨ ~ *the worse for wear*⟩

³none *n*, *often cap* the fifth of the canonical hours that was orig fixed for 3 pm

nonentity *n* **1** sthg that does not exist or exists only in the imagination **2** nonexistence **3** sby or sthg of little importance or interest

nonesuch *also* **nonsuch** *n* a person or thing without an equal; a paragon – **nonesuch** *adj*

nonetheless *adv* nevertheless

nonevent *n* an event that is (unexpectedly) dull or inconsequential

nonflammable *adj* difficult or impossible to set alight – **nonflammability** *n*

nonintervention *n* the state or policy of not intervening – **noninterventionist** *n or adj*

nonpareil *n or adj* (sby or sthg) having no equal

nonplus *vt* **-ss-** (*NAm* **-s-**, **-ss-**) to perplex or disconcert

nonproliferation *adj or n* (providing for) the stoppage of proliferation (e g of nuclear weapons)

nonresident *adj* not residing in a particular place (e g a hotel) – **nonresident** *n*, **nonresidence**, **nonresidency** *n*

nonsense *n* **1a** meaningless words or language **b** (an instance of) foolish or absurd language, conduct, or thought **2** frivolous or insolent behaviour **3** – used interjectionally to express forceful disagreement – **nonsensical** *adj*, **nonsensically** *adv*, **nonsensicalness** *n*

non sequitur *n* **1** a conclusion that does not follow from the premises **2** a statement that does not follow logically from anything previously said

nonskid *adj*, *of a tyre or road* designed or equipped to prevent skidding

nonstandard *adj* not conforming in pronunciation, grammatical construction, idiom, or word choice to accepted usage

nonstarter *n* sby or sthg that is sure to fail or prove impracticable

nonstick *adj* having or being a surface that prevents adherence of food during cooking

nonstop *adj* done or made without a stop – **nonstop** *adv*

non-U *adj* not characteristic of the upper classes

nonunion *adj* not belonging to or connected with a trade union ⟨~ *plumbers*⟩ ⟨*a* ~ *job*⟩

nonviolence *n* **1** refraining from violence on moral grounds **2** passive resistance or peaceful demonstration for political ends – **nonviolent** *adj*, **nonviolently** *adv*

nonwhite *n or adj* (one who is) not Caucasian

¹noodle *n* a silly or foolish person – humor

²noodle *n* a narrow flat ribbon of pasta made with egg

nook *n* a small secluded or sheltered place or part

noon *n* **1** noon, noonday the middle of the day; midday **2** the highest or culminating point

no one *pron* nobody

¹noose *n* a loop with a running knot that tightens as the rope is pulled

²noose *vt* **1** to secure by a noose **2** to make a noose in or of

nope *adv*, *chiefly NAm* no – *infml*

nor *conj* **1** – used to join 2 sentence elements of the same class or function ⟨*neither here* ~ *there*⟩ ⟨*not done by you* ~ *me* ~ *anyone*⟩ **2** also not; neither ⟨*it didn't seem hard,* ~ *was it*⟩

nor' *n* north – often in combination ⟨~-*easter*⟩

¹Nordic *adj* **1** of a tall, fair, longheaded, blue-eyed physical type characteristic of the Germanic peoples of N Europe, esp Scandinavia **2** of competitive ski events consisting of ski jumping and cross-country racing

²Nordic *n* a person of Nordic physical type or of a supposed Nordic division of the Caucasian race; *esp* one from N Europe

Norfolk jacket *n* a man's semifitted belted single-breasted jacket with box pleats

norm *n* **1** an authoritative standard; a model **2** a principle of correctness that is binding upon the members of a group, and serves to regulate action and judgment **3** the average: e g **a** a set standard of development or achievement, usu derived from the average achievement of a large group **b** a pattern typical of a social group

¹normal *adj* **1** PERPENDICULAR 1 **2** conforming to or constituting a norm, rule, or principle **3** occurring naturally ⟨~ *immunity*⟩ **4a** having average intelligence or development **b** free from mental disorder **5** *of a solution* having a concentration of 1 gram equivalent weight of a solute in 1l **6** of, involving, or being a normal curve or normal distribution – **normally** *adv*, **normalcy**, **normality** *n*

²normal *n* **1** a line that is normal **2** sby or sthg that is normal

normalize, -ise *vt* to make normal – **normalizable** *adj*, **normalization** *n*

Norman *n* **1** a native or inhabitant of Normandy: e g **a** any of the Scandinavian conquerors of Normandy in the 10th c **b** any of the Norman-French conquerors of England in 1066 **2** **Norman, Norman-French** the French language of the medieval Normans **3** a style of architecture characterized, esp in its English form, by semicircular arches and heavy pillars – **Norman** *adj*

normative *adj* serving as or prescribing a norm – **normatively** *adv*, **normativeness** *n*

¹Norse *n* **1** *pl in constr* Scandinavians; *specif* Norwegians **2a** the (older forms of the) language of Norway **b** NORTH GERMANIC

²Norse *adj* Scandinavian; *esp* of ancient Scandinavia or Norway

¹north *adj or adv* towards, at, belonging to, or coming from the north

²north *n* **1** (the compass point corresponding to) the direction of the north terrestrial pole **2** *often cap* regions or countries lying to the north of a specified or implied point of orientation – **northward** *adv, adj, or n*, **northwards** *adv*

¹northeast *adj or adv* towards, at, belonging to, or coming from the northeast

²northeast *n* **1** (the general direction corresponding to) the compass point midway between north and east **2** *often cap* regions or countries lying to the northeast of a specified or implied point of orientation – **northeastward** *adv, adj, or n*, **northeastwards** *adv*

¹northeasterly *adj or adv* northeast

²northeasterly, northeaster *n* a wind from the northeast

northeastern *adj* **1** *often cap* (characteristic) of a region conventionally designated Northeast **2** northeast – **northeasternmost** *adj*

¹northerly *adj or adv* north

²northerly *n* a wind from the north

northern *adj* **1** *often cap* (characteristic) of a region conventionally designated North **2** north – **northernmost** *adj*

Northerner *n* a native or inhabitant of the North

northern lights *n pl* AURORA BOREALIS

North Germanic *n* a group of Germanic languages comprising the Scandinavian languages including Icelandic and Faroese

north pole *n* **1a** *often cap N&P* the northernmost point of the rotational axis of the earth or another celestial body **b** the northernmost point on the celestial sphere, about which the stars seem to revolve **2** the northward-pointing pole of a magnet

¹northwest *adj or adv* towards, at, belonging to, or coming from the northwest

²northwest *n* **1** (the general direction corresponding to) the compass point midway between north and west **2** *often cap* regions or countries lying to the northwest of a specified or implied point of orientation – **northwestward** *adv, adj, or n*, **northwestwards** *adv*

¹northwesterly *adj or adv* northwest

²northwesterly, northwester *n* a wind from the northwest

northwestern *adj* **1** *often cap* (characteristic) of a region conventionally designated Northwest **2** northwest

nos-, noso- *comb form* disease ⟨*nosology*⟩

¹nose *n* **1a** the part of the face that bears the nostrils and covers the front part of the nasal cavity (together with the nasal cavity itself) **b** the front part of the head above or

projecting beyond the mouth; a snout, muzzle **2a** the sense or (vertebrate) organ of smell **b** aroma, bouquet **3** the projecting part or front end of sthg **4a** the nose as a symbol of undue curiosity or interference **b** a knack for detecting what is latent or concealed – **through the nose** at an exorbitant rate ⟨*had to pay* through the nose⟩

²nose *vt* **1** to detect (as if) by smell; scent **2** to push (as if) with the nose **3** to touch or rub with the nose; nuzzle ~ *vi* **1** to use the nose in examining, smelling, etc; to sniff or nuzzle **2a** to pry – often + *into* **b** to search or look inquisitively – usu + *about* or *around* **3** to move ahead slowly or cautiously

nose bag *n* a bag for feeding a horse or other animal, that covers the muzzle and is fastened on top of the head

nosebleed *n* an attack of bleeding from the nose

nosed *adj* having a (specified kind of) nose – usu in combination ⟨*snub*-nosed⟩

nose dive *n* **1** a downward nose-first plunge of an aircraft or other flying object **2** a sudden dramatic drop – **nose-dive** *vb*

nosegay *n* a small bunch of flowers; a posy

¹nosh *vt* to chew, munch ~ *vi* to eat – *infml* – **nosher** *n*

²nosh *n* food (in sufficient quantities for a meal); a meal – *infml*

nosh-up *n*, *Br* a large meal – *infml*

nostalgia *n* **1** homesickness **2** a wistful or excessively sentimental yearning for sthg past or irrecoverable – **nostalgic** *adj or n*, **nostalgically** *adv*

nostril *n* the opening of the nose to the outside (together with the adjoining nasal passage)

nostrum *n* **1** a medicine of secret composition recommended by its preparer usu without proof of its effectiveness **2** a facile or questionable remedy

nosy, nosey *adj* inquisitive, prying – *infml* – **nosily** *adv*, **nosiness** *n*

nosy parker *n*, *Br* a busybody – *infml*

not *adv* **1** – used to negate a word or word group ⟨~ thirsty⟩ ⟨~ *to complain*⟩; often *n't* after auxiliary verbs ⟨*can't go*⟩ **2** – used to negate a preceding word or word group ⟨*will it rain? I hope* ~⟩ ⟨*are you ready? If* ~, *hurry up*⟩ **3** – used to give force to an opposite meaning ⟨~ *without reason*⟩ ⟨~ *a few of us*⟩ – compare ²NO **2b** – **not a** not even one – **not at all** – used in answer to thanks or to an apology ⟨*'Sorry to trouble you.' 'Not at all!'*⟩ – **not half 1** *chiefly Br* not nearly ⟨not half *long enough*⟩ **2** very much; totally ⟨*didn't half scold us*⟩ ⟨*'Are you busy?' 'Not half!'*⟩ – *slang*

not-, noto- *comb form* back (part) ⟨*notochord*⟩

notability *n* **1** a notable **2** being notable

¹notable *adj* **1** worthy of note; remarkable **2** distinguished, prominent – **notableness** *n*, **notably** *adv*

²notable *n* **1** a prominent person **2** *pl*, *often cap* a group of people summoned, esp in France when it was a monarchy, to act as a deliberative body

notarize, -ise *vt*, *chiefly NAm* to validate as a notary public

notary, notary public *n*, *pl* **notaries, notaries public, notary publics** a public officer appointed to administer oaths and draw up and authenticate documents

notation *n* **1** (a representation of sthg by) a system or set of marks, signs, symbols, figures, characters, or abbreviated expressions (e g to express technical facts or quantities) **2** *chiefly NAm* an annotation, note – **notational** *adj*

¹notch *n* **1a** a V-shaped indentation **b** a slit or cut used as a record **2** a degree, step **3** *NAm* a deep narrow pass; a gap – **notched** *adj*

²notch *vt* **1** to make a notch in **2a** to mark or record (as if) by a notch – often + *up* **b** to score or achieve – usu + *up*

¹**note** *vt* **1a** to take due or special notice of **b** to notice, observe **c** to record in writing **2** to make special mention of; remark – **noter** *n*

²**note** *n* **1a(1)** a sound having a definite pitch (2) a call, esp of a bird **b** a written symbol used to indicate duration and pitch of a tone by its shape and position on the staff **2a** a characteristic feature of smell, flavour, etc **b** a mood or quality **3a** a memorandum **b(1)** a brief comment or explanation (2) a printed comment or reference set apart from the text **c** a piece of paper money **d(1)** a short informal letter (2) a formal diplomatic communication **e** a short essay **4a** distinction, reputation **b** observation, notice

notebook *n* a book for notes or memoranda

noted *adj* well-known, famous – **notedly** *adv*, **notedness** *n*

noteworthy *adj* worthy of or attracting attention; notable – **noteworthily** *adv*, **noteworthiness** *n*

¹**nothing** *pron* **1** not any thing; no thing ⟨~ *greasy*⟩ ⟨~ *much to eat*⟩ ⟨*eats next to* ~⟩ **2** sthg of no consequence ⟨*it means* ~ *to me*⟩ ⟨*thinks* ~ *of walking 20 miles*⟩ ⟨*would be* ~ *without his title*⟩ **3** no truth or value ⟨*there's* ~ *in this rumour*⟩ – **like nothing on earth 1** severely indisposed or embarrassed **2** grotesque, outlandish

²**nothing** *adv* not at all; in no degree ⟨~ *like as cold*⟩

³**nothing** *n* **1a** sthg that does not exist **b** NOTHINGNESS 2b **2** sby or sthg of no or slight value or size ⟨*whisper sweet* ~s⟩

⁴**nothing** *adj* of no account; worthless

nothingness *n* **1a** nonexistence **b** utter insignificance **2a** a void, emptiness **b** a metaphysical entity opposed to and devoid of being

¹**notice** *n* **1a** warning of a future occurrence **b** notification of intention of terminating an agreement at a particular time **2** attention, heed **3** a written or printed announcement **4** a review (e g of a play)

²**notice** *vt* **1** to comment upon; refer to **2** to take notice of; mark **3** *chiefly NAm* to give a formal notice to

noticeable *adj* **1** worthy of notice **2** capable of being noticed; perceptible – **noticeably** *adv*

notice-board *n*, *chiefly Br* a board on which notices may be (temporarily) displayed

notifiable *adj*, *of a disease* required by law to be reported to official health authorities

notification *n* **1** (an instance of) notifying **2** sthg written that gives notice

notify *vt* **1** to give (official) notice to **2** to make known – **notifier** *n*

notion *n* **1a(1)** a broad general concept (2) a conception, impression ⟨*had no* ~ *of the poem's meaning*⟩ **b** a whim or fancy **2** *pl*, *chiefly NAm* small articles of merchandise (e g haberdashery)

notional *adj* **1** theoretical, speculative **2** existing only in the mind; imaginary – **notionally** *adv*, **notionality** *n*

notochord *n* a longitudinal rod that forms the supporting axis of the body in the lancelet, lamprey, etc and in the embryos of higher vertebrates – **notochordal** *adj*

notoriety *n* the quality or state of being notorious

notorious *adj* well-known, esp for a specified (unfavourable) quality or trait – **notoriously** *adv*, **notoriousness** *n*

¹**notwithstanding** *prep* in spite of

²**notwithstanding** *adv* nevertheless

³**notwithstanding** *conj* although

nougat *n* a sweetmeat of nuts or fruit pieces in a semisolid sugar paste

nought *n* **1** NAUGHT 1 **2** the arithmetical symbol 0; zero

noughts and crosses *n pl but sing in constr* a game in which 2 players alternately put noughts and crosses in usu 9 square spaces arranged in a square in an attempt to get a row of 3 noughts or 3 crosses

noun *n* a word that is the name of a person, place, thing, substance, or state and that belongs to 1 of the major form classes in grammar

nourish *vt* **1** to nurture, rear **2** to encourage the growth of; foster **3a** to provide or sustain with nutriment; feed **b** to cherish, entertain – **nourisher** *n*, **nourishing** *adj*

nourishment *n* **1** food, nutriment **2** nourishing or being nourished

nous *n* **1** mind, reason **2** *chiefly Br* gumption, common sense

nouveau riche *n*, *pl* **nouveaux riches** sby who has recently become rich (and shows it)

nova *n*, *pl* **novas**, **novae** a previously faint star that becomes suddenly very bright and then fades away to its former obscurity over months or years – **novalike** *adj*

¹**novel** *adj* **1** new and unlike anything previously known **2** original and striking, esp in conception or style

²**novel** *n* an invented prose narrative that is usu long and complex and deals esp with human experience and social behaviour – **novelist** *n*, **novelistic** *adj*

novelette *n* a short novel or long short story, often of a sentimental nature – **noveletteish** *adj*

novella *n*, *pl* **novellas** *also* **novelle** a short novel, usu more complex than a short story

novelty *n* **1** sthg new and unusual **2** the quality or state of being novel **3** a small manufactured often cheap article for personal or household adornment

November *n* the 11th month of the Gregorian calendar

novice *n* **1** a person admitted to probationary membership of a religious community **2** a beginner

novitiate *n* **1** (the duration of) the state of being a novice **2** a house where novices are trained

¹**now** *adv* **1a** at the present time **b** in the immediate past **c** in the time immediately to follow; forthwith ⟨*come in* ~⟩ ⟨~ *for tea*⟩ **2** – used with the sense of present time weakened or lost **a** to introduce an important point or indicate a transition ⟨~ *if we turn to the next aspect of the problem*⟩ **b** to express command, request, or warning ⟨*oh, come* ~⟩ ⟨~, ~, *don't squabble*⟩ ⟨~ *then, what's the matter?*⟩ **3** sometimes – linking 2 or more coordinate words or phrases ⟨~ *one and* ~ *another*⟩ **4** under the changed or unchanged circumstances ⟨*he'll never believe me* ~, *after what happened*⟩ **5** at the time referred to ⟨~ *the trouble began*⟩ **6** up to the present or to the time referred to ⟨*haven't been for years* ~⟩

²**now** *conj* in view of the fact that; since ⟨~ *that we are here*⟩

³**now** *n* **1** the present time ⟨*been ill up to* ~⟩ ⟨*goodbye for* ~⟩ **2** the time referred to ⟨*by* ~ *the hints and rumours were fairly thick – The Economist*⟩

nowadays *adv* in these modern times; today

now and again *adv* at occasional intervals; from time to time

noway, **noways** *adv* in no way whatever; not at all – *fml*

no way *interj*, *chiefly NAm* – used to express forceful refusal; *infml*

¹**nowhere** *adv* **1** not anywhere **2** to no purpose or result ⟨*this will get us* ~⟩

²**nowhere** *n* a nonexistent place

nowise *adv* noway

noxious *adj* **1** harmful to living things ⟨~ *industrial* _wastes_〉 **2** having a harmful moral influence; unwholesome – **noxiously** adv, **noxiousness** n

nozzle n a projecting part with an opening that usu serves as an outlet; _esp_ a short tube with a taper or constriction used on a hose, pipe, etc to speed up or direct a flow of fluid

-n't comb form not 〈_isn't_〉

nth adj **1** of or having an unspecified or indefinitely large number **2** extreme, utmost 〈_to the ~ degree_〉

nuance n a subtle distinction or gradation; a shade – **nuanced** adj

nub n **1** a knob, lump 〈_a ~ of coal_〉 **2** the gist or crux

nubile adj, _of a girl_ of marriageable age; _esp_ young and sexually attractive – often humor – **nubility** n

nuclear adj **1** of or constituting a nucleus **2** of, using, or being the atomic nucleus, atomic energy, the atom bomb, or atomic power

nuclear disarmament n the reduction or giving up of a country's nuclear weapons

nucleic acid n RNA, DNA, or another acid composed of a chain of nucleotide molecules linked to each other

nucleotide n any of several compounds that form the structural units of RNA and DNA and consist of a nucleoside combined with a phosphate group

nucleus n, _pl_ **nuclei** _also_ **nucleuses 1** a small bright and dense part of a galaxy or head of a comet **2** a central point, mass, etc about which gathering, concentration, etc takes place: e g **a** a usu round membrane-surrounded cellular organelle containing the chromosomes **b** a (discrete) mass of nerve cells in the brain or spinal cord **c** the positively charged central part of an atom that accounts for nearly all of the atomic mass and consists of protons and usu neutrons

¹nude adj **1** lacking sthg essential to legal validity 〈_a ~ contract_〉 **2a** without clothing; naked **b** without natural covering or adornment; bare – **nudely** adv, **nudeness**, **nudity** n

²nude n **1a** a representation of a nude human figure **b** a nude person **2** the state of being nude 〈_in the ~_〉

nudge vt **1** to touch or push gently; _esp_ to catch the attention of by a push of the elbow **2** to move (as if) by pushing gently or slowly – **nudge** n

nudism n the cult or practice of going nude as much as possible – **nudist** adj or n

nugatory adj **1** trifling, inconsequential **2** inoperative _USE_ fml

nugget n a solid lump, esp of a precious metal in its natural state

nuisance n **1** (legally actionable) harm or injury **2** an annoying or troublesome person or thing

¹null adj **1** having no force in law – esp in _null and void_ **2** amounting to nothing; nil **3** without character or distinction **4** _of an instrument_ indicating (e g by a zero reading on a scale) when current or voltage is zero **5** of or being a method of measurement that uses a null instrument

²null n **1** ZERO 3 **2** a minimum or zero value of an electric current or of a radio signal

nullah n, _Ind_ a gully, ravine

null and void adj completely invalid

nullify vt **1** to make (legally) null **2** to make worthless, unimportant, or ineffective

nullity n **1** (an act or document characterized by) legal invalidity **2** sthg null

numb adj **1** devoid of sensation, esp as a result of cold or anaesthesia **2** devoid of emotion – **numb** vt, **numbingly** adv, **numbly** adv, **numbness** n

¹number n **1a(1)** a total **(2)** _sing or pl in constr_ an indefinite, usu large, total 〈_a ~ of members were absent_〉 **(3)** _pl_ a numerous group; many; _also_ an instance of numerical superiority 〈_there is safety in ~_s〉 **b(1)** any of an ordered set of standard names or symbols (e g 2, 5, 27th) used in counting or in assigning a position in an order; _esp_ NATURAL NUMBER **(2)** an element (e g 6, -3, ⅝, √7) belonging to an arithmetical system based on or analogous to the numbers used in counting and subject to specific rules of addition, subtraction, and multiplication **c** _pl_ arithmetic 〈_teach children their ~_s〉 **2** a distinction of word form denoting reference to singular or plural _also_ a set of forms so distinguished **3a** a word, symbol, letter, or combination of symbols representing a number **b** one or more numerals or digits used to identify or designate 〈_a car ~_〉〈_a telephone ~_〉 **4a** a member of a sequence or collection designated by esp consecutive numbers; _also_ an individual or item (e g a single act in a variety show or an issue of a periodical) singled out from a group **b** a position in a numbered sequence **5** a group of individuals 〈_he is not of our ~_〉 **6** _pl but sing or pl in constr_ a form of US lottery in which bets are made on the appearance of a certain combination of 3 digits in sets of numbers regularly published in newspapers (e g the stock-market receipts) **7a** sthg viewed in terms of the advantage or enjoyment obtained from it 〈_her job is a really cushy ~_〉〈_drives round in a fast little ~_〉 **b** an article of esp women's clothing 〈_wearing a chic little black ~_〉 **c** a person or individual, esp an attractive girl 〈_who's the blonde ~ over there?_〉 **8** insight into a person's motives or character 〈_soon had his ~_〉 _USE_ (7&8) infml – **without number** innumerable

²number vt **1** to count **2** to include as part of a whole or total 〈_proud to ~ her among my friends_〉 **3** to restrict to a definite number; limit – usu pass 〈_knew his days were ~ed_〉 **4** to assign a number to 〈_~ed the team members 1 to 10_〉〈_a ~ed road_〉 **5** to comprise in number; total 〈_the inhabitants ~ed 150,000_〉 ~ vi **1** to be part of a total number 〈_~s among my closest friends_〉 **2** to call off numbers in sequence – **numberable** adj

Number 10 n the British government – infml

numberless adj innumerable, countless

number one n **1** sthg that is first in rank, order, or importance 〈_~ in her list of priorities_〉 **2** one's own interests or welfare – infml 〈_always thinking of ~_〉 **3** an act of urinating – euph; used by or to children

numberplate n, _chiefly Br_ a rectangular identifying plate fastened to a vehicle and bearing the vehicle's registration number

Numbers n _pl but sing in constr_ the mainly narrative 4th book of the Old Testament

numeracy n, _Br_ the quality or state of being numerate

¹numeral adj of or expressing numbers – **numerally** adv

²numeral n a conventional symbol that represents a natural number or zero

numerate adj understanding basic mathematics; able to use numbers in calculation

numeration n **1a** counting **b** designating by a number **2** expressing in words numbers written as numerals **3** a system of numbering or counting – **numerate** vt

numerator n the part of a fraction that is above the line and signifies the number of parts of the denominator that is shown by the fraction

numerical, numeric adj of, expressed in, or involving numbers or a number system 〈_the ~ superiority of the enemy_〉〈_~ standing in a class_〉〈_a ~ code_〉 – **numerically** adv

numerology n the study of the occult significance of numbers – **numerologist** n, **numerological** adj

numerous *adj* consisting of many units or individuals – **numerously** *adv*, **numerousness** *n*

numinous *adj* 1 awe-inspiring, mysterious 2 filled with a sense of the presence of divinity

numismatics *n pl but sing in constr* the study or collection of coinage, coins, paper money, medals, tokens, etc – **numismatic** *adj*, **numismatically** *adv*, **numismatist** *n*

numskull, numbskull *n* a dull or stupid person

nun *n* a female member of a religious order living in a convent under vows of chastity, poverty, etc and often engaged in educational or nursing work

nuncio *n, pl* **nuncios** a papal ambassador to a civil government

nunnery *n* a convent of nuns

¹nuptial *adj* 1 of marriage 2 characteristic of or occurring in the breeding season ⟨*a ~ flight*⟩

²nuptial *n* a wedding – usu pl

¹nurse *n* 1a WET NURSE b a woman employed to take care of a young child 2 sby skilled or trained in caring for the sick or infirm, esp under the supervision of a physician ⟨*she and her brother are both ~*s⟩ 3 a member of the worker caste in an ant, bee, etc society, that cares for the young

²nurse *vt* 1 to suckle 2a to rear, nurture b to encourage the development of; foster ⟨*carefully ~*d *his tomatoes*⟩ 3a to attempt to cure (e g an illness or injury) by appropriate treatment b to care for and wait on (e g a sick person) 4 to hold in one's mind; harbour ⟨*~ a grievance*⟩ 5 to handle carefully in order to conserve or prolong 6 to hold (e g a baby) lovingly or caressingly ~ *vi* 1a to suckle an offspring b to suck at the breast 2 to act or serve as a nurse

nursemaid *n* a girl or woman employed to look after children

nursery *n* 1 a child's bedroom or playroom 2a a place where small children are looked after in their parents' absence b NURSERY SCHOOL 3 a place where young animals (e g fish) grow or are cared for 4 an area where plants, trees, etc are grown for propagation, sale, or transplanting

nurseryman *n* one whose occupation is the cultivation of plants, usu for sale

nursery rhyme *n* a short traditional story in rhyme for children

nursery school *n* a school for children aged usu from 2 to 5

nursing home *n* a usu private hospital or home (where care is provided for the aged, chronically ill, etc)

nursling *n* a child under the care of a nurse, esp in former times

¹nurture *n* 1 training, upbringing 2 food, nourishment 3 all the environmental influences that affect the innate genetic potentialities of an organism

²nurture *vt* 1 to give care and nourishment to 2 to educate or develop

¹nut *n* 1 (the often edible kernel of) a dry fruit or seed with a hard separable rind or shell 2 a difficult person, problem, or undertaking ⟨*a tough ~*⟩ 3 a typically hexagonal usu metal block that has a central hole with an internal screw thread cut on it, and can be screwed onto a piece, esp a bolt, with an external thread to tighten or secure sthg 4 the ridge in a stringed instrument (e g a violin) over which the strings pass on the upper end of the fingerboard 5 a small piece or lump ⟨*a ~ of butter*⟩ 6 pl nonsense – often used interjectionally 7 a person's head 8a an insane or wildly eccentric person b an ardent enthusiast *USE* (6, 7, & 8) infml – **nutlike** *adj*

²nut *vi* -tt- to gather or seek nuts – chiefly in **go nutting**

nut-brown *adj or n* (of) the colour of a ripe hazelnut

nutcase *n* a nut, lunatic – infml

nutcracker *n* an implement for cracking nuts, usu consisting of 2 hinged metal arms between which the nut is held and compressed – often pl with sing. meaning

nuthouse *n* a madhouse – slang; humor

nutmeg *n* (an Indonesian tree that produces) an aromatic seed used as a spice

nutria *n* 1 a coypu 2 the fur of the coypu

nutrient *n or adj* (sthg) that provides nourishment

nutriment *n* sthg that nourishes or promotes growth

nutrition *n* nourishing or being nourished; *specif* all the processes by which an organism takes in and uses food – **nutritional** *adj*, **nutritionally** *adv*, **nutritionist** *n*

nutritious *adj* nourishing – **nutritiously** *adv*, **nutritiousness** *n*

nutritive *adj* 1 of nutrition 2 nourishing – **nutritively** *adv*

nuts *adj* 1 passionately keen or enthusiastic ⟨*he's ~ on ice-hockey*⟩ 2 crazy, mad *USE* infml

nutshell *n* the hard outside covering enclosing the kernel of a nut – **in a nutshell** in a brief accurate account

nutty *adj* 1 having or producing nuts 2 having a flavour like that of nuts 3 eccentric, silly; *also* NUTS 2 – infml – **nuttiness** *n*

nuzzle *vb* **nuzzling** *vi* 1 to push or rub sthg with the nose 2 to lie close or snug; nestle ~ *vt* to root or rub (as if) with the nose

nylon *n* 1 any of numerous strong tough elastic synthetic polyamide materials fashioned into fibres, sheets, etc and used esp in textiles and plastics 2 pl stockings made of nylon

nymph *n* 1 any of the minor female divinities of nature in classical mythology 2 any of various immature insects; *esp* a larva of a dragonfly or other insect with incomplete metamorphosis 3 a girl – poetic – **nymphal** *adj*

nymphet *n* a sexually desirable girl in early adolescence

nymphomania *n* excessive sexual desire in a female – **nymphomaniac** *n or adj*, **nymphomaniacal** *adj*

O

o *n, pl* **o's, os** *often cap* 1 (a graphic representation of or device for reproducing) the 15th letter of the English alphabet 2 sthg shaped like the letter O; *esp* zero

O *interj or n* oh

o-, oo- *comb form* egg ⟨*oology*⟩; *specif* ovum ⟨*oogonium*⟩

-o- – used as a connective vowel to join word elements of Greek and other origin ⟨*milometer*⟩ ⟨*elastomer*⟩

¹-o *suffix* (→ *n or adj*) (sby or sthg) that is, has the qualities of, or is associated with ⟨*cheapo*⟩ ⟨*wino*⟩ ⟨*beano*⟩ – infml

²-o *suffix* (→ *interj*) – in interjections formed from other parts of speech ⟨*cheerio*⟩ ⟨*righto*⟩; infml

o' *also* **o** *prep* 1 of ⟨*one o'clock*⟩ 2 *chiefly dial* on

oaf *n* a clumsy slow-witted person – **oafish** *adj*, **oafishly** *adv*, **oafishness** *n*

oak *n, pl* **oaks, oak** (the tough hard durable wood of) any of various trees or shrubs of the beech family, usu having lobed leaves and producing acorns as fruits – **oaken** *adj*

oak apple *n* a large round gall produced on oak stems or leaves by a gall wasp

oakum *n* hemp or jute fibre impregnated with tar or a tar derivative and used in packing joints and stopping up gaps between the planks of a ship

¹**oar** n **1** a long usu wooden shaft with a broad blade at one end used for propelling or steering a boat **2** an oarsman – **oared** adj

²**oar** vb ¹ROW – poetic

oarlock n, chiefly NAm a rowlock

oarsman n one who rows a boat, esp in a racing crew – **oarsmanship** n

oasis n, pl **oases 1** a fertile or green area in a dry region **2** sthg providing relaxation or relief

Oasis trademark – used for a highly water-absorbent material into which cut flowers and other plants may be stuck for display

oast house n a usu circular building housing a kiln for drying hops or malting barley

oat n **1a** (any of various wild grasses related to) a widely cultivated cereal grass – usu pl **b** pl a crop or plot of oats **2** an oat seed – **oaten** adj

oat cake n a usu crisp unleavened biscuit or bread made of oatmeal

oath n, pl **oaths 1a** a solemn calling upon God or a revered person or thing to witness to the true or binding nature of one's declaration **b** sthg (e g a promise) formally confirmed by an oath ⟨an ~ of allegiance⟩ **c** a form of expression used in taking an oath **2** an irreverent use of a sacred name; broadly a swearword – **on/under oath** bound by a solemn promise to tell the truth

oatmeal n **1** meal made from oats, used esp in porridge **2** a greyish beige colour

¹**obbligato** adj not to be omitted – used in music

²**obbligato** n, pl **obbligatos** also **obbligati** an elaborate, esp melodic, accompaniment, usu played by a single instrument

obdurate adj **1** stubbornly persistent in wrong doing **2** inflexible, unyielding – **obdurately** adv, **obdurateness**, **obduracy** n

obeah n, often cap sorcery and magic ritual as practised among Negroes, esp of the British W Indies

obedient adj submissive to the will or authority of a superior; willing to obey – **obediently** adv, **obedience** n

obeisance n **1** a movement or gesture made as a sign of respect or submission **2** deference, homage – **obeisant** adj, **obeisantly** adv

obelisk n **1** an upright 4-sided usu monolithic pillar that gradually tapers towards the top and terminates in a pyramid **2** DAGGER 2

obese adj excessively fat – **obesity** n

obey vt **1** to submit to the commands or guidance of ⟨~s the teacher⟩ ⟨~ed a whim⟩ **2** to comply with; execute ⟨~ed instructions⟩ ~vi to act obediently

obfuscate vt **1** to make obscure or difficult to understand **2** to confuse, bewilder – **obfuscation** n, **obfuscatory** adj

obiter dictum n, pl **obiter dicta 1** an incidental observation made by a judge which is not material to his judgment and therefore not binding **2** an incidental remark or observation

obituary n a notice of a person's death, usu with a short biography – **obituary** adj

¹**object** n **1** sthg that is (capable of) being sensed physically or examined mentally ⟨an ~ of study⟩ **2a** sthg or sby that arouses an emotion or provokes a reaction or response ⟨an ~ of derision⟩ **b** sby or sthg that is ridiculous, outlandish, or pathetic in appearance ⟨looked a real ~⟩ **3** an end towards which effort, action, etc is directed; a goal ⟨what's the ~ of the exercise?⟩ **4** a noun or noun equivalent appearing in a prepositional phrase or representing the goal or the result of the action of its verb (e g house in we

built a house) **5** sthg of paramount concern ⟨if money's no ~ then buy it⟩ – **objectless** adj

²**object** vi **1** to oppose sthg with words or arguments **2** to feel dislike or disapproval ⟨I ~ to his condescending manner⟩ ~vt to offer in opposition or objection – **objector** n

objection n **1** a reason or argument presented in opposition **2** a feeling or statement of dislike, disapproval, or opposition

objectionable adj unpleasant or offensive – **objectionableness** n, **objectionably** adv

¹**objective** adj **1a** constituting an object: e g **(1)** existing independently of the mind **(2)** belonging to the external world and observable or verifiable **(3)** of a symptom of disease perceptible to other people as well as the affected individual **b** concerned with or expressing the nature of external reality rather than personal feelings or beliefs **c** dealing with facts without distortion by personal feelings or prejudices **2** of or in the case that follows a preposition or a transitive verb – **objectively** adv, **objectiveness**, **objectivity** n

²**objective** n **1** sthg towards which efforts are directed; a goal **2** sthg to be attained or achieved by a military operation **3** (a word in) the objective case **4** a lens or system of lenses that forms an image of an object

object lesson n **1** a lesson that takes a material object as its basis **2** sthg that serves as a concrete illustration of a principle

objet d'art n, pl **objets d'art** a usu small article of some artistic value

oblate adj flattened or depressed at the poles ⟨an ~ spheroid⟩ – **oblateness** n

oblation n **1** cap the act of offering to God the bread and wine used at Communion **2** an offering made for religious purposes

¹**obligate** adj **1** restricted to 1 characteristic mode of life ⟨an ~ parasite⟩ **2** always happening irrespective of environmental conditions ⟨~ parasitism⟩ – **obligately** adv

²**obligate** vt to constrain legally or morally

obligation n **1** sthg (e g a contract or promise) that binds one to a course of action **2** (the amount of) a financial commitment ⟨the company was unable to meet its financial ~s⟩ **3** sthg one is bound to do; a duty **4** (indebtedness for) a service or favour ⟨her kindness has put me under an ~ to her⟩

obligatory adj **1** binding in law or conscience **2** relating to or enforcing an obligation ⟨a writ ~⟩ **3** mandatory, compulsory **4** obligate – **obligatorily** adv

oblige vt **1** to constrain by force or circumstance **2a** to put in one's debt by a favour or service – usu pass ⟨we're much ~d to you for all your help⟩ **b** to do a favour for ⟨~d the assembled company with a song⟩ ~vi to do sthg as a favour; be of service ⟨always ready to ~⟩

obliging adj eager to help; accommodating – **obligingly** adv, **obligingness** n

oblique adj **1a** neither perpendicular nor parallel; inclined **b** having the axis not perpendicular to the base ⟨an ~ cone⟩ **c** having no right angle ⟨an ~ triangle⟩ **d** of an angle greater than but not a multiple of 90° **2** not straightforward or explicit; indirect ⟨~ references to financial difficulties⟩ **3** of a muscle situated obliquely with 1 end not attached to bone – **oblique** n, **obliquely** adv, **obliqueness** n

obliterate vt **1** to make illegible or imperceptible **2** to destroy all trace or indication of **3** to cause (e g a blood vessel or other body part) to collapse or disappear **4** CANCEL **5** – **obliterative** adj, **obliterator** n, **obliteration** n

oblivion n 1 the state of forgetting or being oblivious 2 the state of being forgotten 3 official disregarding of offences

oblivious adj lacking conscious knowledge; completely unaware – usu + of or to – **obliviously** adv, **obliviousness** n

oblong adj deviating from a square by being longer; esp rectangular with adjacent sides unequal – **oblong** n

obloquy n 1 strongly-worded condemnation 2 discredit, disgrace

obnoxious adj highly offensive or repugnant – **obnoxiously** adv, **obnoxiousness** n

oboe n a double-reed woodwind instrument with a conical tube and a usual range from B flat below middle C upwards for about 2½ octaves – **oboist** n

obscene adj 1 offending standards of esp sexual propriety or decency; specif inciting sexual depravity ⟨confiscated various ~ publications⟩ 2 (morally) repugnant – **obscenely** adv

obscenity n 1 the quality or state of being obscene 2 an obscene act or utterance

obscurantism n opposition to the advance of knowledge – **obscurantist** n or adj

¹**obscure** adj 1 hard to understand; abstruse 2 not well-known or widely acclaimed 3 faint, indistinct 4 constituting or representing the unstressed vowel /M/ – **obscurely** adv, **obscureness** n

²**obscure** vt 1 to conceal (as if) by covering 2 to make indistinct or unintelligible – **obscuration** n

obscurity n 1 the quality or state of being obscure 2 an obscure person or thing

obsequious adj showing a servile willingness to oblige – **obsequiously** adv, **obsequiousness** n

obsequy n a funeral ceremony – usu pl with sing. meaning

observable adj capable of being observed; discernible – **observable** n, **observably** adv

observance n 1a a customary practice, rite, or ceremony – often pl b a rule governing members of a religious order 2 an act of complying with a custom, rule, or law

observant adj 1 paying close attention; watchful 2 careful to observe; mindful – + of 3 quick to notice; alert – **observantly** adv

observation n 1 an act or the faculty of observing 2 the gathering of information by noting facts or occurrences ⟨weather ~s⟩ 3 a remark, comment 4 the condition of sby or sth that is observed ⟨under ~ at the hospital⟩ – **observational** adj

observation car n, NAm a railway carriage with large windows and often a partly transparent roof that affords passengers a broad view

observatory n a building or institution for the observation and interpretation of natural phenomena, esp in astronomy

observe vt 1a to act in due conformity with ⟨always ~d the law⟩ ⟨careful to ~ local customs⟩ b to celebrate or perform (e g a ceremony or festival) according to a prescribed or traditional form ⟨~d the fast of Ramadan⟩ 2 to perceive or take note of, esp by concentrated attention 3 to utter as a comment ⟨~d that things weren't what they used to be⟩ 4 to make a scientific observation on or of

observer n 1 sby sent to observe but not participate officially in a gathering 2 sby who accompanies the pilot of an aircraft to make observations

obsess vt to preoccupy intensely or abnormally – **obsessive** adj or n, **obsessively** adv, **obsessiveness** n

obsession n a persistent (disturbing) preoccupation with an often unreasonable idea; also an idea causing such a preoccupation – **obsessional** adj, **obsessionally** adv

obsidian n a usu black volcanic glass which splits to give a convex surface

obsolescent adj going out of use; becoming obsolete – **obsolescence** n

obsolete adj 1 no longer in use 2 outdated, outmoded – **obsoleteness** n

obstacle n sth that hinders or obstructs

obstetrics n pl but sing or pl in constr a branch of medicine dealing with the care and treatment of women before, during, and after childbirth – **obstetrician** n

obstinate adj 1 clinging stubbornly to an opinion or course of action; not yielding to arguments or persuasion 2 not easily subdued, remedied, or removed ⟨an ~ fever⟩ – **obstinately** adv, **obstinacy** n

obstreperous adj 1 aggressively noisy; clamorous 2 vociferously defiant; unruly – **obstreperously** adv, **obstreperousness** n

obstruct vt 1 to block or close up by an obstacle ⟨the road is ~ed by a landslide⟩ ⟨the fence ~s the view⟩ 2 to hinder, impede – **obstructive** adj or n, **obstructiveness** n, **obstructively** adv, **obstructor** n

obstruction n 1 a condition of being clogged or blocked 2 an attempted delay of business in a deliberative body (e g Parliament) 3 sth that obstructs

obstructionism n deliberate interference with (legislative) business – **obstructionist** n, **obstructionistic** adj

obtain vt to acquire or attain ~ vi to be generally accepted or practised – fml – **obtainable** adj, **obtainer** n, **obtainment** n, **obtainability** n

obtrude vt 1 to thrust out 2 to assert without warrant or request ~ vi to thrust oneself forward with unwarranted assertiveness – **obtruder** n, **obtrusion** n

obtrusive adj 1 forward in manner; pushing 2 unduly noticeable – **obtrusively** adv, **obtrusiveness** n

obtuse adj 1 lacking sensitivity or mental alertness 2a being or forming an angle greater than 90° but less than 180° b having an obtuse angle ⟨an ~ triangle⟩ c not pointed or acute 3 of a leaf rounded at the end furthest from the stalk – **obtusely** adv, **obtuseness** n

¹**obverse** adj 1 facing the observer or opponent 2 with the base narrower than the top ⟨an ~ leaf⟩ 3 constituting a counterpart or complement – **obversely** adv

²**obverse** n 1a the side of a coin, medal, or currency note that bears the principal device and lettering; broadly a front or principal surface b the more conspicuous of 2 possible sides or aspects 2 a counterpart to a fact or truth

obviate vt 1 to anticipate and dispose of in advance 2 to make unnecessary – **obviation** n

obvious adj 1 evident to the senses or understanding 2 unsubtle ⟨the symbolism of the novel was rather ~⟩ – **obviously** adv, **obviousness** n

ocarina n a simple wind instrument with an oval body

¹**occasion** n 1 a suitable opportunity or circumstance ⟨this is hardly the ~ for laughter⟩ 2 a state of affairs that provides a reason or grounds ⟨you have no ~ to be annoyed⟩ 3 the immediate or incidental cause 4 a time at which sth occurs ⟨on the ~ of his daughter's marriage⟩ 5 a special event or ceremony ⟨the wedding was a real ~⟩ – **on occasion** from time to time

²**occasion** vt to bring about; cause – fml

occasional adj 1 of a particular occasion 2 composed for a particular occasion ⟨~ verse⟩ 3 occurring at irregular or infrequent intervals 4 acting in a specified capacity from time to time ⟨an ~ golfer⟩ 5 designed for use as the occasion demands ⟨an ~ table⟩ – **occasionally** adv

Occident n WEST 2a

occidental *adj, often cap* of or situated in the Occident; western – **occidentalism** *n, often cap,* **occidentalize** *vt, often cap,* **occidentally** *adv, often cap*

Occidental *n* a member of any of the indigenous peoples of the Occident

¹**occult** *vt* to conceal by occultation

²**occult** *adj* **1** secret; *esp* esoteric **2** not easily understood; abstruse **3** involving (secret knowledge of) supernatural powers **4** not present, manifest, or detectable by the unaided eye ⟨~ *blood loss*⟩ – **occult** *n,* **occultly** *adv*

occultation *n* the eclipsing of one celestial body by another, usu much larger, one

occupancy *n* **1** the act of taking and holding possession of land, a property, etc **2** becoming or being an occupant; *also* being occupied

occupant *n* **1** one who acquires title by occupancy **2** a resident

occupation *n* **1a** an activity in which one engages **b** an activity by which one earns a living **2a** the occupancy of land **b** tenure **3a** the act of taking possession or the holding and control of a place or area, esp by a foreign military force **b** *sing or pl in constr* a military force occupying a country **c** the period of time for which a place or area is occupied

occupational *adj* of or resulting from a particular occupation ⟨~ *hazards*⟩ – **occupationally** *adv*

occupational therapy *n* creative activity used as therapy for promoting recovery or rehabilitation – **occupational therapist** *n*

occupy *vt* **1** to engage the attention or energies of **2** to fill up (a portion of space or time) **3** to take or maintain possession of **4** to reside in or use as an owner or tenant – **occupier** *n*

occur *vi* **-rr-** **1** to be found; exist **2** to become the case; happen **3** to come to mind ⟨*it* ~s *to me that I haven't posted the letter*⟩

occurrence *n* **1** sthg that takes place; an event **2** the action or process of occurring

ocean *n* **1** (any of the large expanses that together constitute) the whole body of salt water that covers nearly ¾ of the surface of the globe **2** *pl* a huge amount – infml ⟨*no need to hurry, we've got* ~s *of time*⟩ – **oceanic** *adj*

oceangoing *adj* of or designed for travel on the ocean

oceanography *n* the science dealing with oceans and their form, biology, and resources – **oceanographer** *n,* **oceanographic** *also* **oceanographical** *adj,* **oceanographically** *adv*

ocelot *n* a medium-sized American wildcat with a yellow or greyish coat dotted and striped with black

ochre, *NAm chiefly* **ocher** *n* **1** the colour of esp yellow ochre **2** an earthy usu red or yellow (impure) iron ore used as a pigment – **ochreous** *adj*

o'clock *adv* **1** according to the clock – used in specifying the exact hour ⟨*the time is 3* ~⟩ **2** – used for indicating position or direction as if on a clock dial that is oriented vertically or horizontally ⟨*an aircraft approaching at 6* ~⟩

octa-, octo- *also* **oct-** *comb form* **1** eight ⟨*octane*⟩ ⟨*octoroon*⟩ **2** containing 8 atoms, groups, or chemical equivalents in the molecular structure

octagon *n* a polygon of 8 angles and 8 sides – **octagonal** *adj,* **octagonally** *adv*

octane *n* a liquid hydrocarbon that occurs esp in petroleum

octave *n* **1** a group of 8 lines of verse, esp the first 8 of a sonnet **2a** (the combination of 2 notes at) a musical interval of 8 diatonic degrees **b** a note separated from a lower note by this interval **c** the whole series of notes or

piano, organ, etc keys within this interval that form the unit of the modern scale **3** a group of 8

octavo *n, pl* **octavos** (a book or page in) the size of a piece of paper cut 8 from a sheet

octet *n* **1** (a musical composition for) 8 instruments, voices, or performers **2** OCTAVE 1

October *n* the 10th month of the Gregorian calendar

octogenarian *n* a person between 80 and 89 years old – **octogenarian** *adj*

octopus *n, pl* **octopuses, octopi** **1** any of a genus of molluscs related to the squids and cuttlefishes with 8 muscular arms equipped with 2 rows of suckers **2** sthg having many radiating branches or far-reaching controlling influence

octosyllable *n* a word or line of 8 syllables – **octosyllabic** *adj*

¹**ocular** *adj* **1** performed or perceived with the eyes **2** of the eye ⟨~ *muscles*⟩

²**ocular** *n* an eyepiece

oculist *n* an ophthalmologist or optician

odalisque *n* a female slave or concubine in a harem

odd *adj* **1a** left over when others are paired or grouped **b** not matching ⟨~ *socks*⟩ **2** not divisible by 2 without leaving a remainder ⟨*1,3,5 are* ~ *numbers*⟩ **3** somewhat more than the specified number – usu in combination ⟨*300-odd pages*⟩ **4** not regular or planned; casual, occasional ⟨~ *jobs*⟩⟨*at* ~ *moments*⟩ **5** different from the usual or conventional; strange – **oddly** *adv,* **oddness** *n*

oddball *n* an eccentric or peculiar person – infml – **oddball** *adj*

oddity *n* **1** an odd person, thing, event, or trait **2** oddness, strangeness

odd man out *n* sby or sthg that differs in some respect from all the others in a set or group

oddment *n* **1** sthg left over; a remnant **2** *pl* ODDS AND ENDS

odds *n pl but sing or pl in constr* **1a** an amount by which one thing exceeds or falls short of another ⟨*won the election against considerable* ~⟩ **b** a difference in terms of advantage or disadvantage ⟨*it makes no* ~⟩⟨*what's the* ~?⟩ **2** the probability (expressed as a ratio) that one thing will happen rather than another ⟨*the* ~ *are that he will be dismissed*⟩⟨*the* ~ *are 50 to 1 against the newcomer*⟩ **3** disagreement, variance ⟨*was at* ~ *with management*⟩ **4** the ratio between the amount to be paid off for a winning bet and the amount of the bet ⟨*gave* ~ *of 3 to 1*⟩

odds and ends *n pl* miscellaneous items or remnants

odds-on *adj* **1** (viewed as) having a better than even chance to win ⟨*the* ~ *favourite*⟩ **2** not involving much risk ⟨*an* ~ *bet*⟩

ode *n* a lyric poem, often addressed to a particular subject, marked by a usu exalted tone and varying meter and length of line

-ode *comb form* (→ *n*) **1** way; path ⟨*electrode*⟩ **2** electrode ⟨*diode*⟩

odious *adj* arousing hatred or revulsion ⟨*an* ~ *crime*⟩ – **odiously** *adv,* **odiousness** *n*

odium *n* general condemnation or disgrace associated with a despicable act – fml

odometer *n* an instrument for measuring the distance travelled (e g by a vehicle)

odoriferous *adj* yielding a scent or odour – **odoriferously** *adv*

odorous *adj* having a scent or odour – **odorously** *adv*

odour, *NAm chiefly* **odor** *n* **1** (the sensation resulting from) a quality of sthg that stimulates the sense of smell **2** repute, favour ⟨*in bad* ~⟩ – fml **3** a characteristic

quality; a savour – chiefly derog ⟨an ~ of sanctity⟩ –
odourless adj
odyssey n a long wandering or quest
oecumenical adj ecumenical
oedema, NAm chiefly **edema** n abnormal accumulation
of liquid derived from serum causing abnormal swelling of
the tissues
Oedipus complex n (an adult personality disorder
resulting from) the sexual attraction developed by a child
towards the parent of the opposite sex with accompanying
jealousy of the parent of the same sex – **Oedipal** adj
o'er adv or prep over – poetic
oesophagus n, pl **oesophagi** the muscular tube leading
from the back of the mouth to the stomach – **oesophageal**
oestrogen n a substance, esp a sex hormone, that stimulates the development of secondary sex characteristics in
female vertebrates and promotes oestrus in lower mammals – **oestrogenic** adj, **oestrogenically** adv
oestrus n a regularly recurrent state of sexual excitability
in the female of most lower mammals when she will
copulate with the male – **oestral, oestrous** adj
oestrus cycle n the series of changes in a female mammal
occurring from one period of oestrus to the next
of prep **1a** – used to indicate origin or derivation ⟨a man
~ noble birth⟩ ⟨they expect it ~ me⟩ **b** – used to indicate
cause, motive, or reason ⟨died ~ pneumonia⟩ ⟨did it ~
her own free will⟩ **c** proceeding from; on the part of ⟨the
approval ~ the minister⟩ ⟨the buzzing ~ the bees⟩ ⟨very
kind ~ him⟩ **d** BY 4a(2) ⟨the plays ~ Shaw⟩ **2a(1)**
composed or made from ⟨a crown ~ gold⟩ ⟨a staff ~
teachers⟩ ⟨a family ~ 5⟩ **(2)** using as a material ⟨what
did he make the crown ~ ?⟩ ⟨made the dress ~ silk rather
than cotton⟩ **b** containing ⟨cup ~ water⟩ **c** – used to
indicate the mass noun or class that includes the part
denoted by the previous word ⟨an inch ~ rain⟩ ⟨a blade
~ grass⟩ **d** from among ⟨most ~ the army⟩ ⟨one ~ his
last poems⟩ ⟨the fattest ~ the girls⟩ ⟨members ~ the
team⟩ ⟨she, ~ all people!⟩ ⟨the elder ~ the two⟩ **3a**
belonging to; related to ⟨the leg ~ the chair⟩ ⟨the colour
~ her dress⟩ ⟨the relatives ~ those who were killed⟩ ⟨the
wife ~ the managing director⟩ ⟨the hat ~ the old gentle-
man⟩ **b** that is or are – used before possessive forms ⟨a
friend ~ John's⟩ ⟨that nose ~ his⟩ **c** characterized by;
with, having ⟨a man ~ courage⟩ ⟨an area ~ hills⟩ ⟨a
woman ~ no importance⟩ ⟨suitcases ~ a suitable size⟩ **d**
connected with ⟨the king ~ England⟩ ⟨a teacher ~
French⟩ ⟨a smell ~ mice⟩ ⟨the time ~ arrival⟩ **e** existing or happening in or on ⟨the battle ~ Blenheim⟩ ⟨my
letter ~ the 19th⟩ **4a** relating to (a topic); concerning
⟨stories ~ his travels⟩ ⟨dreamed ~ home⟩ ⟨what ~ it?⟩
b in respect to ⟨slow ~ speech⟩ ⟨north ~ the lake⟩ ⟨have
hopes ~ him⟩ ⟨fond ~ chocolate⟩ ⟨guilty ~ murder⟩ **c**
directed towards ⟨love ~ nature⟩ ⟨care ~ guinea
pigs⟩ ⟨the shooting ~ seals⟩ ⟨ask a question ~ him⟩ **d**
– used to show separation or removal ⟨eased ~
pain⟩ ⟨cured him ~ mumps⟩ ⟨cheated him ~ his rights⟩
e – used as a function word to indicate a whole or quantity
from which a part is removed or expended ⟨gave ~ his
time⟩ **5** – used to indicate apposition ⟨the city ~
Rome⟩ ⟨the age ~ 8⟩ ⟨the art ~ painting⟩ ⟨a house ~
a specified hour⟩ ⟨a quarter ~ four⟩ **7** in, during ⟨died ~
a Monday⟩ ⟨go there ~ an evening⟩ – infml – **of a** -like
⟨that palace of a house⟩ ⟨that brute of a dog⟩ – used after
expressions of strong feeling

¹**off** adv **1a(1)** from a place or position ⟨march
~⟩ ⟨frighten them ~⟩; specif away from land ⟨ship stood
~ to sea⟩ **(2)** away in space or ahead in time ⟨stood 10
paces ~⟩ ⟨Christmas is a week ~⟩ **b** from a course; aside

⟨turned ~ into a lay-by⟩; specif away from the wind **c**
into sleep or unconsciousness ⟨dozed ~⟩ **2a** so as to be
not supported ⟨rolled to the edge of the table and ~⟩, not
in close contact ⟨took his coat ~⟩, or not attached
⟨handle came ~⟩ **b** so as to be divided ⟨surface marked
~ into squares⟩ ⟨a corner screened ~⟩ **3a** to or in a state
of discontinuance or suspension ⟨shut ~ an
engine⟩ ⟨game was rained ~⟩ ⟨the radio is ~⟩ **b** so as
to be completely finished or no longer existent ⟨finish it
~⟩ ⟨kill them ~⟩ ⟨walk it ~⟩ ⟨sleep it ~⟩ **c** in or into
a state of putrefaction ⟨cream's gone ~⟩ **d** (as if) by heart
⟨know it ~ pat⟩ **4** away from an activity or function ⟨the
night shift went ~⟩ ⟨take time ~ for lunch⟩ **5** offstage
⟨noises ~⟩ **6** to a sexual climax ⟨brought him ~⟩ –
slang

²**off** prep **1a** – used to indicate physical separation or
distance from ⟨take it ~ the table⟩ ⟨jumped ~ his
bicycle⟩ ⟨wear it ~ the shoulder⟩ **b** to seaward of ⟨2
miles ~ shore⟩ **c** lying or turning aside from; adjacent to
⟨a shop just ~ the high street⟩ **d** (slightly) away from –
often in combination ⟨a week ~ work⟩ ⟨completely ~
the point⟩ ⟨off-target⟩ ⟨off-centre⟩ **2** – used to indicate
the source from which sthg derives or is obtained ⟨dined
~ oysters⟩ ⟨bought it ~ a friend⟩ ⟨claim it ~ tax⟩ **3a**
not occupied in ⟨~ duty⟩ **b** tired of; no longer interested
in or using ⟨he's ~ drugs⟩ ⟨I've gone ~ science fiction⟩
c below the usual standard or level of ⟨~ his game⟩

³**off** adj **1a** FAR 3 **b** seaward **c** being the right-hand one of
a pair ⟨the ~ wheel of a cart⟩ **d** situated to one side;
adjoining ⟨bedroom with dressing room ~⟩ **2a** started on
the way ⟨~ on a spree⟩ **b** not taking place or staying in
effect; cancelled ⟨the match is ~⟩ **c** of a dish on a menu
no longer being served **3a** not up to standard; unsatisfactory in terms of achievement ⟨an ~ day⟩ **b** slack ⟨~
season⟩ **4** affected (as if) with putrefaction ⟨this fish is ~⟩
5 provided ⟨well ~⟩ ⟨how are you ~ for socks?⟩ **6a** in,
on, through, or towards the off side of a cricket field **b** esp
of a ball bowled in cricket moving or tending to move in
the direction of the leg side ⟨~ break⟩ **7** of behaviour not
what one has a right to expect; esp rather unkind or
dishonest ⟨it was a bit ~ to leave without a word of
thanks!⟩ – infml

⁴**off** vi to go away; leave

⁵**off** n the start or outset; also a starting signal ⟨ready for
the ~⟩

offal n **1** the by-products of milling used esp for animal
feeds **2** the liver, heart, kidney, etc of a butchered animal
used as food **3** refuse
offbeat adj unusual; esp unconventional – infml
off-colour adj **1** unwell ⟨feeling a bit ~⟩ **2** chiefly NAm
somewhat indecent; risqué
offence, NAm chiefly **offense** n **1** sthg that occasions a
sense of outrage **2** (an) attack, assault **3** displeasure,
resentment **4a** a sin or misdeed **b** an illegal act; a crime
5 chiefly NAm ATTACK **6** – **offenceless** adj
offend vi **1** to break a moral or divine law – often +
against **2** to cause displeasure, difficulty, or discomfort
~ vt **1** to cause pain or displeasure to; hurt ⟨colours that
~ the eye⟩ **2** to cause to feel indignation or disgust –
offender n
¹**offensive** adj **1a** aggressive, attacking **b** of or designed
for attack ⟨~ weapons⟩ **2** arousing physical disgust;
repellent **3** causing indignation or outrage – **offensively**
adv, **offensiveness** n
²**offensive** n **1** the position or attitude of an attacking
party ⟨took the ~⟩ **2** an esp military attack on a large
scale
¹**offer** vt **1** to present (e g a prayer or sacrifice) in an act
of worship or devotion – often + up **2a** to present for

acceptance, rejection, or consideration **b** to present in order to satisfy a requirement ⟨*candidates may* ~ *Welsh as one of their foreign languages*⟩ **3** to declare one's willingness ⟨~ed *to help me*⟩ **4** to put up ⟨~ed *stubborn resistance*⟩ **5a** to make available; afford ⟨*the hotel* ~s *a full range of facilities*⟩ **b** to present (goods) for sale **6** to present in performance or exhibition **7** to tender as payment; bid ~ *vi* **1** to make an offer for consideration, acceptance, etc **2** to present itself; occur

²**offer** *n* **1a** a proposal; *specif* a proposal of marriage **b** an undertaking to do or give sthg on a specific condition **2** a price named by a prospective buyer – **on offer** being offered; *specif* for sale, esp at a reduced price – **under offer** sold subject to the signing of contracts – used in connection with sales of real estate

offering *n* **1** the act of one who offers **2** sthg offered; *esp* a sacrifice ceremonially offered as a part of worship **3** a contribution to the support of a church or other religious organization

offertory *n* **1** *often cap* (a text said or sung during) the offering of the Communion bread and wine to God before consecration **2** (the collection and presentation of) the offerings of the congregation at public worship

offhand *adv or adj* **1** without forethought or preparation **2** without proper attention or respect – **offhanded** *adj*, **offhandedly** *adv*, **offhandedness** *n*

office *n* **1** an esp beneficial service or action carried out for another ⟨*through her good* ~s *I recovered my belongings*⟩ **2a** a position giving authority to exercise a public function ⟨*the* ~ *of Prime Minister*⟩ **b** a position with special duties or responsibilities **3** a prescribed form or service of worship; *esp, cap* DIVINE OFFICE **4a** a place, esp a large building, where the business of a particular organization is carried out **b** (a group of people sharing) a room in which the administrative, clerical, or professional work of an organization is performed **c** a place, esp a small room, where a particular service is provided ⟨*the lost property* ~⟩ **5a** *cap* a major administrative unit in some governments ⟨*the Foreign* Office⟩ **b** a subdivision of some government departments

office boy, *fem* **office girl** *n* a young person employed to run errands in an office

¹**officer** *n* **1** a policeman **2** one who holds a position with special duties or responsibilities (e g in a government or business) **3a** one who holds a position of authority or command in the armed forces; *specif* a commissioned officer **b** a master or any of the mates of a merchant or passenger ship

²**officer** *vt* **1** to supply with officers **2** to command or direct as an officer

¹**official** *n* one who holds an esp public office ⟨*government* ~s⟩ – **officialdom** *n*, **officialese** *n*

²**official** *adj* **1** of an office and its duties **2** holding an office **3a** authoritative, authorized **b** prescribed or recognized as authorized, esp by a pharmacopoeia **4** suitable for or characteristic of a person in office; formal – **officially** *adv*

Official Receiver *n* a public official appointed to administer a bankrupt's property

officiate *vi* **1** to perform an esp religious ceremony, function, or duty ⟨~ *at a wedding*⟩ **2** to act as an official or in an official capacity – **officiant** *n*, **officiation** *n*

officious *adj* **1** given to or marked by overzealousness in exercising authority or carrying out duties **2** *esp of a diplomatic agreement* informal, unofficial – **officiously** *adv*, **officiousness** *n*

offing *n* the part of the deep sea visible from the shore – **in the offing** likely to happen in the near future ⟨*thought more unemployment was* in the offing⟩

offish *adj* inclined to be aloof or distant – infml – **offishly** *adv*, **offishness** *n*

off-licence *n, Br* a shop, part of a public house, etc licensed to sell alcoholic drinks to be consumed off the premises; *also* the licence permitting such sale – **off-licensee** *n*

off-load *vt* UNLOAD 1, 2

off-peak *adj* (used) at a time of less than the maximum demand or activity ⟨~ *electricity*⟩ ⟨~ *travel*⟩

offprint *n* a separately printed excerpt (e g an article from a magazine) – **offprint** *vt*

off-putting *adj, chiefly Br* disagreeable, disconcerting – infml

¹**offset** *n* **1** a short shoot or bulb growing out to the side from the base of a plant **2** an offshoot, esp of a family or race **b** a spur in a range of hills **3** an abrupt bend in an object by which one part is turned aside out of line **4** sthg that serves to compensate for sthg else **5** a printing process in which an inked impression from a plate is first made on a rubber surface and then transferred to paper

²**offset** *vt* **-tt-;** offset **1a** to balance ⟨*credits* ~ *debits*⟩ **b** to compensate or make up for **2** to print (e g a book) by using the offset process

offshoot *n* **1** a branch of a plant's main stem **2a** a lateral branch (e g of a mountain range) **b** a subsidiary branch, descendant, or member

offshore *adj or adv* **1** (coming or moving) away from the shore **2** at a distance from the shore

offside *adv or adj* illegally in advance of the ball or puck in a team game

off side *n* **1** the part of a cricket field on the opposite side of a line joining the middle stumps to that in which the batsman stands when playing a ball **2** *chiefly Br* the right side of a horse, vehicle, etc

offspring *n, pl* offspring the progeny of a person, animal, or plant; young

offstage *adv or adj* **1** on a part of the stage not visible to the audience **2** behind the scenes; away from the public gaze

off-the-record *adj or adv* (given or made) unofficially or in confidence

off-white *n or adj* (a) yellowish or greyish white

oft *adv* often – poetic

often *adv* **1** (at) many times **2** in many cases ⟨*they* ~ *die young*⟩

ogle *vb* ogling to glance or stare with esp sexual interest (at) – **ogle** *n*, **ogler** *n*

ogre, *fem* **ogress** *n* **1** a hideous giant of folklore believed to feed on human beings **2** a dreaded person or thing – **ogreish** *adj*

¹**oh, O** *interj* – used to express surprise, pain, disappointment, etc

²**oh, O** *n* nought

ohm *n* the derived SI unit of electrical resistance equal to the resistance between 2 points of a conductor when a constant potential difference of 1 volt applied to these points produces a current of 1 ampere – **ohmic** *adj*, **ohmically** *adv*

oho *interj* – used to express amused surprise, exultation, etc

¹**-oid** *suffix* (→ *n*) sthg resembling (a specified object) or having (a specified quality) ⟨*globoid*⟩ ⟨*asteroid*⟩

²**-oid** *suffix* (→ *n, adj*) **1** resembling; having the form or appearance of ⟨*petaloid*⟩ ⟨*anthropoid*⟩ **2** bearing an imperfect resemblance to ⟨*humanoid*⟩

¹**oil** *n* **1** any of numerous smooth greasy combustible liquids or low melting-point solids that are insoluble in water but dissolve in organic solvents **2** a substance (e g a cosmetic

preparation) of oily consistency **3a** OIL PAINT ⟨*a portrait done in* ~s⟩ **b** OIL PAINTING **4** petroleum – **oil** *adj*

²**oil** *vt* to treat or lubricate with oil ~ *vi* to change from a solid fat into an oil by melting – **oiler** *n* – **oil the wheels** to help things run smoothly

oil cake *n* the solid residue left after extracting the oil from seeds (e g of cotton)

oilcan *n* a vessel with a nozzle designed to release oil in a controlled flow (e g for lubricating machinery)

oilcloth *n* cloth treated with oil or paint and used for table and shelf coverings

oil colour *n* OIL PAINT

oil field *n* a region rich in petroleum deposits; *esp* one producing petroleum in commercial quantities

oil paint *n* paint consisting of ground pigment mixed with oil

oil painting *n* (a product of) the art of painting with oil paints

oilskin *n* **1** an oiled waterproof cloth used for coverings and garments **2** an oilskin or plastic raincoat **3** *pl* an oilskin or plastic suit of coat and trousers

oil slick *n* a film of oil floating on water

oil well *n* a well drilled in the earth from which petroleum is obtained

oily *adj* **1** of, resembling, containing, or covered with oil **2** unctuous, ingratiating – **oilily** *adv*, **oiliness** *n*

oink *n* the grunt of a pig – *humor* – **oink** *vi*

ointment *n* a soothing or healing salve for application to the skin

¹**OK, okay** *adv, adj, or interj* ALL RIGHT

²**OK, okay** *vt or n* OK's; OK'ing; OK'd (to give) approval or authorization (of); sanction

okapi *n* an African mammal closely related to the giraffe but with a shorter neck and black and cream rings on the upper parts of the legs

okra *n* **1** a tall annual plant of the mallow family cultivated for its mucilaginous green pods used as a vegetable, esp in soups and stews; *also* the pods of this plant **2** GUMBO 1

¹**old** *adj* **1a** dating from the esp remote past ⟨~ *traditions*⟩ **b** persisting from an earlier time ⟨*an* ~ *ailment*⟩ **c** of long standing ⟨*an* ~ *friend*⟩ **2** *cap* constituting an early period in the development of a language ⟨Old *Irish*⟩ **3** having existed for a specified period of time ⟨*3 years* ~⟩ **4** advanced in years or age **5** experienced ⟨*an* ~ *hand*⟩ **6** former **7a** made long ago; *esp* worn with time or use **b** no longer in use; discarded **8a** long familiar ⟨*the same* ~ *story*⟩ **b** – used as an intensive ⟨*a high* ~ *time*⟩ ⟨*any* ~ *time*⟩ – **oldish** *adj*, **oldness** *n*

²**old** *n* **1** old or earlier time ⟨*men of* ~⟩ **2** one of a specified age – usu in combination ⟨*a 3-year-old*⟩

old age *n* the final stage of the normal life span

old age pension *n* a state pension paid to retired people – **old age pensioner** *n*

old boy, *fem* **old girl** *n*, *chiefly Br* **1** a former pupil of a particular, esp public, school **2** a fellow or friend – often used as an informal term of address

old boy network *n*, *chiefly Br* the system of favouritism operating among people of a similar privileged background, esp among former pupils of public schools

old country *n* an immigrant's country of origin

olden *adj* of a bygone era – *poetic*

olde-worlde *adj* (excessively or falsely) old-world

old-fashioned *adj* **1** (characteristic) of a past era; outdated **2** clinging to customs of a past era – **old-fashionedly** *adv*

old guard *n sing or pl in constr, often cap O&G* the (original) conservative members of a group or party

old hand *n* VETERAN 1

old hat *adj* **1** old-fashioned **2** hackneyed, trite

old lady *n* one's wife or mother – *infml*

old maid *n* **1** SPINSTER 2 **2** a simple card game in which each player tries to avoid holding a designated unpaired card at the end **3** a prim fussy person – *infml* – **old-maidish** *adj*

old man *n* **1** one's husband or father **2** one in authority (e g one's employer, manager, or commander) – + *the* USE *infml*

old master *n* (a work by) a distinguished European painter of the 16th to early 18th c

Old Nick *n* – used as an informal or humorous name for the devil

old school *n* adherents of traditional ideas and practices

old school tie *n* **1** a tie displaying the colours of an English public school, worn by former pupils **2** the conservatism and upper-class solidarity traditionally attributed to former members of British public schools

old stager *n* VETERAN 1

oldster *n, chiefly NAm* an old or elderly person – *infml*

Old Testament *n* a collection of writings forming the Jewish canon of Scripture and the first part of the Christian Bible

old-timer *n* **1** VETERAN 1 **2** *chiefly NAm* an old man

old wives' tale *n* a traditional superstitious notion

old woman *n* **1** one's wife or mother **2** a timid, prim, or fussy person, esp a man – *derog* USE *infml*

old-world *adj* **1** of the E hemisphere **2** reminiscent of a past age; *esp* quaintly charming

Old World *n* the E Hemisphere; *specif* Europe, Asia, and Africa

oleaginous *adj* resembling, containing, or producing oil; oily – **oleaginously** *adv*, **oleaginousness** *n*

oleander *n* a poisonous evergreen shrub of the periwinkle family with fragrant white, pink, or red flowers

oleograph *n* a chromolithograph printed on cloth to resemble an oil painting – **oleographic** *adj*, **oleography** *n*

O level *n* ORDINARY LEVEL

olfaction *n* smelling or the sense of smell – **olfactive**, **olfactory** *adj*

oligarch *n* a member of an oligarchy

oligarchy *n* **1** government by a small group **2** a state or organization in which a small group exercises control, esp for its own interests **3** a small group exercising such control – **oligarchic**, **oligarchical** *adj*

¹**olive** *n* **1** (an Old World evergreen tree that grows esp around the Mediterranean and bears) a small stone fruit used as a food and a source of oil **2 olive, olive green** a dull yellowish green colour resembling that of an unripe olive

²**olive, olive green** *adj* of the colour olive

olive branch *n* an offer or gesture of conciliation or goodwill

ology *n* SCIENCE 1a, c – *humor*

olympiad *n, often cap* **1** any of the 4-year intervals between Olympian games by which time was reckoned in ancient Greece **2** OLYMPIC GAMES

¹**Olympian** *adj* of the ancient Greek region of Olympia

²**Olympian** *n, chiefly NAm* a participant in the Olympic Games

³**Olympian** *adj* **1** of Mount Olympus in Thessaly **2** lofty, detached

⁴**Olympian** *n* **1** an inhabitant of the ancient Greek region of Olympia **2** any of the ancient Greek deities dwelling on Olympus **3** a loftily detached or superior person

Olympic *adj* **1** ³OLYMPIAN **2** of or executed in the Olympic Games

Olympic Games *n pl but sing or pl in constr, pl* **Olympic Games** an international sports meeting that is a modified revival of the Olympian games and is held once every 4 years in a different host country

ombre *n* a 3-handed card game popular in Europe in the 17th and 18th c

ombudsman *n* a government official appointed to investigate complaints made by individuals against government or public bodies

omega *n* **1** the 24th and last letter of the Greek alphabet **2** the last one in a series, order, etc

omelette, *NAm chiefly* **omelet** *n* a mixture of beaten eggs cooked until set in a shallow pan and often served folded in half over a filling

omen *n* an event or phenomenon believed to be a sign of some future occurrence

ominous *adj* portentous; *esp* foreboding evil or disaster – **ominously** *adv*, **ominousness** *n*

omission *n* **1** omitting or being omitted ⟨*sins of ~*⟩ **2** sthg neglected or left undone

omit *vt* **-tt- 1** to leave out or unmentioned **2** to fail to do or perform – **omissible** *adj*

omni- *comb form* all; universally ⟨*omnidirectional*⟩

¹omnibus *n* **1** a book containing reprints of a number of works, usu by 1 author ⟨*an ~ edition*⟩ **2** BUS 1 – *fml*

²omnibus *adj* of, containing, or providing for many things at once

omnipotent *adj* having unlimited or very great power or influence; *specif, often cap* ALMIGHTY 1 – **omnipotence** *n*, **omnipotently** *adv*

Omnipotent *n* GOD 1

omnipresent *adj* present in all places at all times – **omnipresence** *n*

omniscient *adj* **1** having infinite awareness or understanding **2** possessed of complete knowledge; all-knowing – **omniscience** *n*, **omnisciently** *adv*

omnivorous *adj* **1** feeding on both animal and vegetable substances **2** avidly taking in, and esp reading, everything – **omnivorously** *adv*, **omnivorousness** *n*, **omnivore** *n*

¹on *prep* **1a(1)** in contact with or supported from below by ⟨*a fly ~ the ceiling*⟩ ⟨*stand ~ 1 foot*⟩ ⟨*a book ~ the table*⟩ **(2)** attached or fastened to ⟨*a dog ~ a lead*⟩ **(3)** carried on the person of ⟨*have you a match ~ you?*⟩ **(4)** very near to, esp along an edge or border ⟨*towns ~ the frontier*⟩ ⟨*Walton-~-Thames*⟩ **(5)** within the limits of a usu specified area ⟨*~ the steppes*⟩ ⟨*~ page 17*⟩ **b** at the usual standard or level of ⟨*~ form*⟩ **c(1)** in the direction of ⟨*~ the right*⟩ ⟨*crept up ~ him*⟩ **(2)** into contact with ⟨*jumped ~ the horse*⟩ **(3)** with regard to; concerning ⟨*keen ~ sports*⟩ ⟨*unfair ~ me*⟩ ⟨*evidence ~ the matter*⟩ **(4)** with a specified person or thing as object ⟨*try it out ~ her*⟩ **(5)** having as a topic; about ⟨*a book ~ India*⟩ **(6)** staked on the success of ⟨*put £5 ~ a horse*⟩ **(7)** doing or carrying out a specified action or activity ⟨*here ~ business*⟩ ⟨*went ~ an errand*⟩ **(8)** working for, supporting, or belonging to ⟨*~ a committee*⟩ ⟨*~ their side*⟩ **(9)** working at; in charge of ⟨*the man ~ the gate*⟩ **2a** having as a basis or source (e g of knowledge or comparison) ⟨*have it ~ good authority*⟩ ⟨*swear ~ the Bible*⟩ ⟨*prices are down ~ last year*⟩ **b** at the expense of ⟨*got it ~ the National Health*⟩ ⟨*drinks are ~ the house*⟩ **3a** in the state or process of ⟨*~ fire*⟩ ⟨*~ strike*⟩ ⟨*~ holiday*⟩ ⟨*~ offer*⟩ ⟨*~ the increase*⟩ in the specified manner ⟨*~ the cheap*⟩ **c** using as a medium ⟨*played it ~ the clarinet*⟩; *esp* OVER 4b ⟨*talking ~ the telephone*⟩ **d** using by way of transport ⟨*arrived ~ foot*⟩ ⟨*left ~ the early train*⟩ **e** sustained or powered by ⟨*live ~ vegetables*⟩ ⟨*car runs ~*

petrol⟩ ⟨*people ~ low incomes*⟩ ⟨*dined out ~ the story*⟩ **f** regularly taking ⟨*~ Valium*⟩ **4** through contact with ⟨*cut himself ~ a piece of glass*⟩ **5a** at the time of ⟨*came ~ Monday*⟩ ⟨*every hour ~ the hour*⟩ ⟨*cash ~ delivery*⟩ **b** on the occasion of or immediately after and usu in consequence of ⟨*shot ~ sight*⟩ ⟨*fainted ~ hearing the news*⟩ **c** in the course of ⟨*~ a journey*⟩ ⟨*~ tour*⟩ ⟨*~ my way*⟩ **d** AFTER 2b ⟨*blow ~ blow*⟩

²on *adv* **1** so as to be supported from below ⟨*put the top ~*⟩, in close contact ⟨*has new shoes ~*⟩, or attached ⟨*sew the buttons ~*⟩ **2a** ahead or forwards in space or time ⟨*went ~ home*⟩ ⟨*do it later ~*⟩ ⟨*40 years ~*⟩ ⟨*getting ~ for 5*⟩ **b** with the specified part forward ⟨*cars crashed head ~*⟩ **c** without interruption ⟨*chattered ~ and ~*⟩ **d** in continuance or succession ⟨*and so ~*⟩ **3a** in or into (a state permitting) operation ⟨*switch the light ~*⟩ ⟨*get the potatoes ~*⟩ ⟨*put a record ~*⟩ **b** in or into an activity or function ⟨*the night shift came ~*⟩

³on *adj* **1a** LEG 2 ⟨*~ drive*⟩ **b** taking place ⟨*the game is ~*⟩ **c** performing or broadcasting ⟨*we're ~ in 10 minutes*⟩ **d** intended, planned ⟨*has nothing ~ for tonight*⟩ **e** worn as clothing ⟨*went out with just a cardigan ~*⟩ **2a** committed to a bet **b** in favour of a win ⟨*the odds are 2 to 1 ~*⟩ **3** *chiefly Br* possible, practicable – usu neg ⟨*you can't refuse, it's just not ~*⟩ **4a** *chiefly Br* nagging ⟨*she's always ~ at him about his hair*⟩ **b** talking dully, excessively, or incomprehensibly ⟨*what's he ~ about?*⟩ *USE* (3&4) *infml*

¹-on *suffix* (→ *n*) chemical compound ⟨*parathion*⟩ ⟨*interferon*⟩

²-on *suffix* (→ *n*) **1** elementary particle ⟨*electron*⟩ ⟨*baryon*⟩ **2a** unit; quantum ⟨*photon*⟩ ⟨*magneton*⟩ **b** basic operational unit of the genetic material ⟨*cistron*⟩ ⟨*operon*⟩

³-on *suffix* (→ *n*) inert gas ⟨*neon*⟩

¹once *adv* **1** one time and no more ⟨*met only ~*⟩ ⟨*shaves ~ a week*⟩ **2** even 1 time; ever ⟨*if ~ we lose the key*⟩ **3** at some indefinite time in the past; formerly ⟨*there ~ lived a king*⟩ **4** by 1 degree of relationship ⟨*2nd cousin ~ removed*⟩ – **once again/more 1** now again as before ⟨*back home once again*⟩ **2** for 1 more time

²once *n* one single time ⟨*~ is enough*⟩ ⟨*just this ~*⟩ – **all at once 1** all at the same time **2** ALL OF A SUDDEN – **at once 1** at the same time; simultaneously ⟨*both spoke at once*⟩ **2** IMMEDIATELY 2 – **once and for all, once for all** for the final or only time; conclusively

³once *conj* from the moment when; as soon as ⟨*~ he arrives we can start*⟩ ⟨*~ over the wall we're safe*⟩

once-over *n* a swift appraising glance – *infml* ⟨*gave him the ~*⟩

oncoming *adj* coming nearer in time or space; advancing

¹one *adj* **1a** being a single unit or thing ⟨*~ day at a time*⟩ **b** being the first – used after the noun modified ⟨*on page ~*⟩ **2** being a particular but unspecified instance ⟨*saw her early ~ morning*⟩ **3a(1)** the same; identical ⟨*both of ~ mind*⟩ ⟨*it's all ~ to me where we go*⟩ **(2)** constituting a unified entity ⟨*all shouted with ~ voice*⟩ ⟨*the combined elements form ~ substance*⟩ **b** being in a state of agreement; united ⟨*I am ~ with the rest of you in this matter*⟩ **4** being some unspecified instance – used esp of future time ⟨*will see you ~ day soon*⟩ ⟨*we might try it ~ weekend*⟩ **5a** being a particular object or person ⟨*close first ~ eye then the other*⟩ **b** being the only individual of an indicated or implied kind ⟨*the ~ and only person she wanted to marry*⟩ – **one and the same** the very same

²one *pron, pl* **ones 1** a single member or specimen of a usu specified class or group ⟨*saw ~ of his friends*⟩ **2** an indefinitely indicated person; anybody at all ⟨*~ has a*

duty to ~'s public⟩ ⟨~ never knows⟩ **3** – used to refer to a noun or noun phrase previously mentioned or understood ⟨2 grey shirts and 3 red ~ s⟩ ⟨if you want a book about bees, try this ~⟩ ⟨the question is ~ of great importance⟩ **USE** used as a subject or object; no pl for senses 2 and 3

³one *n* **1** (the number) 1 **2** the number denoting unity **3** the first in a set or series ⟨takes a ~ in shoes⟩ **4a** a single person or thing **b** a unified entity ⟨is secretary and treasurer in ~⟩ ⟨they all rose up as ~ and clamoured for more pay⟩ **c** a particular example or instance ⟨~ of the coldest nights this year⟩ **d** a certain specified person ⟨~ George Hopkins⟩ **5a** a person with a liking or interest for a specified thing; an enthusiast ⟨he's rather a ~ for baroque music⟩ **b** a bold, amusing, or remarkable character ⟨oh! you are a ~⟩ **6a** a blow, stroke ⟨socked him ~ on the jaw⟩ **b** a drink ⟨just time for a quick ~⟩ **c** a remark; esp a joke ⟨have you heard this ~?⟩ **7** sthg having a denomination of 1 ⟨I'll take the money in ~s⟩ **– at one** in harmony; in a state of agreement **– for one** even if alone; not to mention others **– one by one** singly, successively

-one *suffix* (→ *n*) (compound related or analogous to a) ketone ⟨acetone⟩ ⟨oestrone⟩

one another *pron* each other

one-armed bandit *n* FRUIT MACHINE

one-horse *adj* of little importance or interest – infml ⟨a ~ town⟩

one-man *adj* **1** consisting of only 1 person **2** done or produced by only 1 person

one-night stand *n* **1** a performance given only once in any particular locality **2** (a person with whom one has) a sexual relationship lasting only 1 night

one-piece *adj* consisting of or made in a single undivided piece ⟨a ~ swimming costume⟩

onerous *adj* burdensome, troublesome – **onerously** *adv*, **onerousness** *n*

oneself *pron* **1** a person's self; one's own self – used reflexively ⟨one should wash ~⟩ or for emphasis ⟨to do it ~⟩ **2** one's normal self ⟨not feeling quite ~⟩ **– be oneself** to behave in a normal, unconstrained, or unpretentious manner **– by oneself** ON ONE'S OWN **– to oneself** for one's exclusive use or knowledge

one-sided *adj* **1a** having or occurring on 1 side only **b** having 1 side prominent or more developed **2** partial, biased – **one-sidedly** *adv*, **one-sidedness** *n*

onetime *adj* former, sometime

one-track *adj* interested or absorbed in 1 thing only ⟨a ~ mind⟩

one-upmanship *n* the art of gaining a psychological advantage over others by professing social or professional superiority

one-way *adj* **1** that moves in or allows movement in only 1 direction ⟨~ traffic⟩ **2** one-sided, unilateral

ongoing *adj* **1** actually in progress **2** growing, developing

onion *n* (the pungent edible bulb, eaten as a vegetable, of) an Asian plant of the lily family or any of various related plants

onlooker *n* a passive spectator – **onlooking** *adj*

¹only *adj* **1** unquestionably the best ⟨flying is the ~ way to travel⟩ **2** alone in its class or kind; sole ⟨an ~ child⟩ ⟨the ~ detergent that contains fabric softener⟩

²only *adv* **1a** nothing more than; merely ⟨~ a little one⟩ ⟨if it would ~ rain!⟩ **b** solely, exclusively ⟨known ~ to him⟩ **2** nothing other than ⟨it was ~ too true⟩ **3a** in the final outcome ⟨will ~ make you sick⟩ **b** with nevertheless the final result ⟨won the battle, ~ to lose the

war⟩ **4** no earlier than ⟨~ last week⟩ ⟨has ~ just left⟩

³only *conj* **1** but, however ⟨they look very nice, ~ we can't use them⟩ **2** were it not for the fact that ⟨I'd tell you, ~ you'll just spread it around⟩ **USE** infml

onomatopoeia *n* the formation or use of words intended to be a vocal imitation of the sound associated with the thing or action designated (e g in *buzz, cuckoo*) – **onomatopoeic** *adj*, **onomatopoeically** *adv*

onrush *n* a forceful rushing forwards

onset *n* **1** an attack, assault **2** a beginning, commencement

onshore *adj or adv* **1** (moving) towards the shore **2** on or near the shore

onside *adv or adj* not offside

onslaught *n* a fierce attack

onto, on to *prep* **1** to a position on **2** in or into a state of awareness about ⟨put the police ~ him⟩ **3** – used as a function word to indicate a mathematical set, each element of which is the image of at least 1 element of another set ⟨a function mapping the set S ~ the set T⟩ **4** chiefly Br in or into contact with ⟨been ~ him about the drains⟩; esp on at; nagging

ontology *n* a branch of philosophy concerned with the nature of being – **ontologist** *n*

onus *n* **1a** duty, responsibility **b** blame **2** BURDEN OF PROOF

onward *adj* directed or moving onwards; forward

onwards, onward *adv* towards or at a point lying ahead in space or time; forwards ⟨from his childhood ~⟩

onyx *n* **1** a translucent variety of quartz with layers of different colours, typically green and white or black or brown and white **2 onyx, onyx marble** a translucent or semitranslucent calcium carbonate mineral, usu calcite, with marble-like bands of colour

oodles *n pl but sing or pl in constr* a great quantity; a lot – infml

oomph *n* vitality, enthusiasm – humor

oops *interj* – used to express apology or surprise

¹ooze *n* **1** a soft deposit of mud, slime, debris, etc on the bottom of a body of water **2** (the muddy ground of) a marsh or bog – **oozy** *adj*

²ooze *n* **1** an infusion of vegetable material (e g bark) used for tanning leather **2** sthg that oozes – **oozy** *adj*

³ooze *vi* **1a** to pass or flow slowly through small openings **b** to diminish gradually; dwindle *away* **2** to exude moisture ~ *vt* **1** to emit or give out slowly **2** to display in abundance ⟨positively ~ d vitality⟩

op *n* OPERATION 3, 5 – infml

opacity *n* **1** opaqueness **2** obscurity of meaning; unintelligibility **3** an opaque spot on a normally transparent structure (e g the lens of the eye)

opal *n* a transparent to translucent mineral consisting of a hydrated silica and used in its opalescent forms as a gem

opalescent *adj* reflecting a milky iridescent light – **opalescence** *n*

opaque *adj* **1** not transmitting radiant energy, esp light; not transparent **2** hard to understand; unintelligible – **opaquely** *adv*, **opaqueness** *n*

op art *n* OPTICAL ART – **op artist** *n*

¹open *adj* **1** having no enclosing or confining barrier ⟨the ~ hillside⟩ **2** allowing passage; not shut or locked **3a** exposed to general view or knowledge; public ⟨regarded him with ~ hatred⟩ **b** vulnerable to attack or question; liable ⟨~ to doubt⟩ **4a** not covered or protected ⟨an ~ boat⟩ ⟨an ~ wound⟩ **b** not fastened or sealed **5** not restricted to a particular category of participants; specif contested by both amateurs and professionals **6** presenting no obstacle to passage or view **7** having the parts or surfaces spread out or unfolded **8** articulated with the tongue low in the mouth ⟨*an ~ vowel*⟩ **9a** available ⟨*the only course ~ to us*⟩ **b** not taken up with duties or engagements ⟨*keep an hour ~ on Friday*⟩ **c** not finally decided or settled ⟨*an ~ question*⟩ **d** available for a qualified applicant; vacant **e** remaining available for use or filling until cancelled ⟨*an ~ order for more items*⟩ **10a(1)** willing to consider new ideas; unprejudiced ⟨*an ~ mind*⟩ **(2)** willing to receive and consider ⟨*always ~ to suggestions*⟩ **b** candid, frank **11a** containing many small openings or spaces; *specif* porous **b** having relatively wide spacing between words or lines ⟨*~ type*⟩ **c** of a compound word elements separated by a space in writing or printing (e g in *ski lift*) **12a** of a string on a musical instrument not stopped by the finger **b** of a note produced on a musical instrument without fingering the strings, valves, slides, or keys **13** in operation; *esp* ready for business or use ⟨*the shop is ~ from 9 to 5*⟩ ⟨*the new motorway will be ~ next week*⟩ **14** free from checks or restraints ⟨*an ~ economy*⟩ **15** of a mathematical set containing a neighbourhood of every element ⟨*the interior of a sphere is an ~ set*⟩ **16** *Br*, of a cheque payable in cash to the person, organization, etc named on it; not crossed – **open** *adv*, **openness** *n*

²**open** *vt* **1a** to change or move from a closed position **b** to permit entry into or passage through **c** to gain access to the contents of ⟨*~ a parcel*⟩ **2a** to make available for or active in a particular use or function; *specif* to establish ⟨*~ed a new shop*⟩ **b** to declare available for use, esp ceremonially **c** to make the necessary arrangements for (e g a bank account), esp by depositing money **3a** to disclose, reveal – often + *up* **b** to make more responsive or enlightened **4a** to make 1 or more openings in **b** to loosen and make less compact ⟨*~ the soil*⟩ **5** to spread out; unfold **6** to begin, commence ⟨*~ed the meeting*⟩ **7** to begin (e g the bidding, betting, or play) in a card game **8a** to initiate (a side's innings) as one of the 2 first batsmen **b** to initiate (a side's bowling attack) by bowling one of the first 2 overs of an innings ~*vi* **1** to become open **2** to commence, start ⟨*~ed with a prayer*⟩ **3** to give access – usu + *into* or *onto* **4** to extend, unfold – usu + *out* ⟨*the view ~ed out in front of us*⟩ – **openable** *adj*, **openability** *n*

³**open** *n* **1** OUTDOORS 2 **2** often *cap* an open contest, competition, or tournament – **bring into/be in the open** to (cause to) be generally known

open-air *adj* outdoor

open air *n* OUTDOORS 2

open-and-shut *adj* easily settled ⟨*an ~ case*⟩

opencast *adj, of a mine or mining* worked from or carried out on the earth's surface by removing material covering the mineral mined for

open door *n* a policy of equal commercial relations with all nations – **open-door** *adj*

open-ended *adj* without any definite limits or restrictions (e g of time or purpose) set in advance – **open-endedness** *n*

opener *n* **1a** an instrument that opens sthg – usu in combination ⟨*a bottle ~*⟩ **b** one who opens; *specif* an opening batsman **2** *pl* cards of sufficient value for a player to open the betting in a poker game **3** the first item or event in a series

openhanded *adj* generous in giving – **openhandedly** *adv*, **openhandedness** *n*

open-heart *adj* of or performed on a heart surgically opened whilst its function is temporarily taken over by a heart-lung machine ⟨*~ surgery*⟩

openhearted *adj* **1** candidly straightforward **2** kind, generous – **openheartedly** *adv*, **openheartedness** *n*

open-hearth *adj* of, produced by, or used in the open-hearth steelmaking process

opening *n* **1** an act of making or becoming open **2** a breach, aperture **3a** an often standard series of moves made at the beginning of a game of chess or draughts **b** a first performance **4a** a favourable opportunity; a chance **b** an opportunity for employment; a vacancy

opening time the time at which a business, shop, etc opens; *specif* the statutory time at which a public house may open for the sale of alcohol

open letter *n* a letter, esp of protest, appeal, or explanation, usu addressed to an individual but intended for the general public, and published in a newspaper, periodical, etc

openly *adv* in an open and frank manner

open-minded *adj* receptive to new arguments or ideas – **open-mindedly** *adv*, **open-mindedness** *n*

openmouthed *adj* having the mouth open, esp in surprise

open out *vi* to speak more freely and confidently

open sandwich *n* a sandwich without a top slice of bread

open season *n* a period during which it is legal to kill or catch game or fish protected at other times by law

open secret *n* a supposed secret that is in fact widely known

open sesame *n* a means of gaining access to sthg otherwise inaccessible

open shop *n* an establishment in which eligibility for employment is not dependent on membership of a trade union

Open University *n* the nonresidential British university that caters mainly for adults studying part-time, has no formal entrance requirements, and operates mainly through correspondence and broadcasting

open up *vi* **1** to commence firing **2** OPEN OUT **3** to open a door ⟨*open up, it's the police!*⟩ **4** of a game, competition, etc to become more interesting, esp because more closely contested to make available or accessible ⟨*the deal* opened up *important new possibilities for trade*⟩

open verdict *n* a verdict at an inquest that records a death but does not state its cause

openwork *n* work (e g in fabric or metal) that is perforated or pierced – **open-worked** *adj*

¹**opera** *pl of* OPUS

²**opera** *n* **1** (the performance of or score for) a drama set to music and made up of vocal pieces with orchestral accompaniment and usu other orchestral music (e g an overture) **2** the branch of the arts concerned with such works **3** a company performing operas – **operatic** *adj*, **operatically** *adv*

operable *adj* suitable for surgical treatment ⟨*an ~ cancer*⟩ – **operably** *adv*, **operability** *n*

opera glass *n* small binoculars suitable for use at the opera or theatre – often pl with sing. meaning

opera hat *n* a man's collapsible top hat

opera house *n* a theatre designed for the performance of opera

operate *vi* **1** to exert power or influence; act ⟨*factors* operating *against our success*⟩ **2** to produce a desired effect **3a** to work, function **b** to perform surgery – usu + *on* **c** to carry on a military or naval action or mission **4** to be in action; *specif* to carry out trade or business ~*vt* **1** to effect; BRING ABOUT **2a** to cause to function; work **b** to put or keep in operation; manage

operating theatre *n, Br* a room, usu in a hospital, where surgical operations are carried out

operation *n* **1a** the act, method, or process of operating **b** sthg (to be) done; an activity **2** the state of being functional or operative ⟨*the plant is now in* ~⟩ **3** a procedure carried out on a living body with special instruments, usu for the repair of damage or the restoration of health **4** any of various mathematical or logical processes (e g addition) carried out to derive one expression from others according to a rule **5** a usu military action, mission, or manoeuvre and its planning **6** a business or financial transaction **7** a single step performed by a computer in the execution of a program

operational *adj* **1** of or based on operations **2a** of, involved in, or used for the execution of commercial, military, or naval operations **b** (capable of) functioning – **operationally** *adv*

operational research *n, chiefly Br* the application of scientific, esp mathematical, methods to the study and analysis of problems involving complex systems (e g business management, economic planning, and the waging of war)

¹operative *adj* **1a** producing an appropriate effect; efficacious **b** significant, relevant ⟨*I might come, but might is the* ~ *word*⟩ **2** in force or operation **3** based on, consisting of, or using an esp surgical operation – **operatively** *adv*, **operativeness** *n*

²operative *n* an operator: e g **a** a workman **b** *NAm* PRIVATE DETECTIVE

operator *n* **1a** one who operates a machine or device **b** one who owns or runs a business, organization, etc ⟨*a tour* ~⟩ **c** one who is in charge of a telephone switchboard **2** a mathematical or logical symbol denoting an operation to be performed **3** a shrewd and skilful manipulator – infml

operetta *n* a usu romantic comic opera that includes dancing – **operettist** *n*

ophthalmia *n* inflammation of the conjunctiva or the eyeball

ophthalmic *adj* of or situated near the eye

ophthalmology *n* the branch of medical science dealing with the structure, functions, and diseases of the eye – **ophthalmological** *also* **ophthalmologic** *adj*, **ophthalmologically** *adv*

ophthalmoscope *n* an instrument used to view the retina and other structures inside the eye – **ophthalmoscopic** *adj*, **ophthalmoscopy** *n*

¹opiate *adj* **1** containing or mixed with opium **2** inducing sleep; narcotic

²opiate *n* **1** a preparation or derivative of opium; *broadly* a narcotic **2** sthg that induces inaction or calm

opine *vt* to state as an opinion – fml

opinion *n* **1a** a view or judgment formed about a particular matter **b** an esp favourable estimation ⟨*I have no great* ~ *of his work*⟩ **2a** a belief unsupported by positive knowledge **b** a generally held view **3a** a formal expression by an expert of his/her professional judgment or advice; *esp* a barrister's written advice to a client **b** *chiefly NAm* a formal expression of the principles on which a legal decision is based

opinionated *adj* stubbornly sticking to one's own opinions – **opinionatedly** *adv*, **opinionatedness** *n*

opium *n* the dried juice of the unripe seed capsules of the opium poppy, containing morphine and other addictive narcotic alkaloids

opossum *n, pl* **opossums** *also esp collectively* **opossum** any of various American (tree-dwelling) marsupial mammals; *also* any of several Australian phalangers resembling this

¹opponent *n* one who takes the opposite side in a contest, conflict, etc

²opponent *adj* OPPOSITE 2

opportune *adj* **1** suitable or convenient for a particular occurrence ⟨*an* ~ *moment*⟩ **2** occurring at an appropriate time – **opportunely** *adv*, **opportuneness** *n*

opportunism *n* the taking advantage of opportunities or circumstances, esp with little regard for principles or consequences – **opportunist** *n or adj*, **opportunistic** *adj*

opportunity *n* **1** a favourable set of circumstances **2** a chance for advancement or progress

oppose *vt* **1** to place opposite or against sthg so as to provide counterbalance, contrast, etc **2** to offer resistance to – **opposer** *n*

¹opposite *n* **1** sthg or sby opposed or contrary **2** an antonym

²opposite *adj* **1a** set over against sthg that is at the other end or side of an intervening line or space ⟨~ *ends of a diameter*⟩ **b** of *plant parts* situated in pairs at the same level on opposite sides of an axis ⟨~ *leaves*⟩ **2a** occupying an opposing position ⟨~ *sides of the question*⟩ **b** diametrically different; contrary **3** being the other of a matching or contrasting pair ⟨*the* ~ *sex*⟩ – **oppositely** *adv*, **oppositeness** *n*

³opposite *adv* on or to an opposite side

⁴opposite *prep* **1** across from and usu facing ⟨*sat* ~ *each other*⟩ **2** in a role complementary to ⟨*played* ~ *the leading lady*⟩

opposite number *n* a counterpart

opposition *n* **1** an opposite position of 2 celestial bodies in which their longitude differs by 180 degrees **2** the relation between 2 propositions having the same subject and predicate but differing in quantity or quality or both **3** placing opposite or being so placed **4** hostile or contrary action **5** *sing or pl in constr* **a** the body of people opposing sthg **b** *often cap* a political party opposing the party in power – **oppositional** *adj*

oppress *vt* **1** to crush by harsh or authoritarian rule **2** to weigh heavily on the mind or spirit of – **oppressor** *n*

oppression *n* **1** unjust or harsh exercise of authority or power **2** a sense of being weighed down in body or mind

oppressive *adj* **1** unreasonably harsh or severe **2** tyrannical **3** physically or mentally depressing or overpowering – **oppressively** *adv*, **oppressiveness** *n*

opprobrious *adj* scurrilous and abusive ⟨~ *language*⟩ – fml – **opprobriously** *adv*

opprobrium *n* (a cause of) public infamy or disgrace – fml

opt *vi* to decide in favour of sthg *USE* – usu + *for*

optative *adj* of or belonging to a grammatical mood (e g in Greek) expressing wish or desire – **optative** *n*

¹optic *adj* of vision or the eye

²optic *n* **1** the eye **2** any of the lenses, prisms, or mirrors of an optical instrument

optical *adj* **1** of optics **2a** visual ⟨*an* ~ *illusion*⟩ **b** visible ⟨*an* ~ *galaxy*⟩ **c** designed to aid vision ⟨*an* ~ *instrument*⟩ **3** of or using light ⟨~ *microscopy*⟩ – **optically** *adv*

optical art *n* abstract art that uses linear or geometric patterns to create an optical illusion

optical illusion *n* ILLUSION 2a(1)

optician *n* one who prescribes correctional lenses for eye defects or supplies (lenses for) spectacles on prescription

optics *n pl but sing or pl in constr* **1** the science of the nature, properties, and uses of (radiation or particles that behave like) light **2** optical properties or components

optimism *n* **1** the doctrine that this world is the best possible world **2** a tendency to emphasize favourable aspects of situations or events or to expect the best possible outcome – **optimist** *n*, **optimistic** *adj*, **optimistically** *adv*

optimum *n, pl* **optima** *also* **optimums** (the amount or degree of) sthg that is most favourable to a particular end – **optimum** *adj*, **optimize** *vt*

¹**option** *n* **1** an act of choosing **2a** the power or right to choose **b** (a contract conveying) a right to buy or sell designated securities or commodities at a specified price during a stipulated period **3a** an alternative course of action **b** an item offered in addition to or in place of standard equipment

²**option** *vt* to grant or take an option on

optional *adj* not compulsory; available as a choice – **optionally** *adv*

opt out *vi* to choose not to participate in sthg – often + *of*

opulent *adj* **1** wealthy, rich **2** abundant, profuse – **opulence** *n*, **opulently** *adv*

opus *n, pl* **opera** *also* **opuses** WORK 7; *specif* a musical composition or set of compositions, usu numbered in the order of issue

¹**or** *conj* **1a** – used to join 2 sentence elements of the same class or function and often introduced by *either* to indicate that what immediately follows is another or a final alternative ⟨*either sink ~ swim*⟩ ⟨*red, blue, ~ green*⟩ ⟨*coffee ~ tea ~ whisky*⟩ ⟨*whether you like it ~ not*⟩ **b** – used before the second and later of several suggestions to indicate approximation or uncertainty ⟨*five ~ six days*⟩ ⟨*a place such as Venice ~ Florence ~ somewhere like that – SEU S*⟩ **2** and not – used after a neg ⟨*never drinks ~ smokes*⟩ **3** that is – used to indicate equivalence or elucidate meaning ⟨*lessen ~ abate*⟩ ⟨*a heifer ~ young cow*⟩ **4** – used to indicate the result of rejecting a preceding choice ⟨*hurry ~ you'll be late*⟩ **5** – used to introduce an afterthought ⟨*e=mc²– ~ am I boring you?*⟩ – **or so** – used to indicate an approximation or conjecture ⟨*I've known him 20 years or so*⟩

²**or** *n* a gold colour; *also* yellow – used in heraldry

¹**-or** *suffix* (→ *n*) one that performs (a specified action) ⟨*vendor*⟩

²**-or** *suffix* (→ *n*) quality, condition, or state of ⟨*horror*⟩ ⟨*tremor*⟩; *also* instance of (a specified quality or state) ⟨*an error*⟩

oracle *n* **1a** an often cryptic answer to some question, usu regarding the future, purporting to come from a deity **b** (a shrine housing) a priest or priestess who delivers oracles **2** (a statement by) a person giving wise or authoritative decisions

Oracle *trademark* – used for a service provided by ITV which transmits information (e g the weather or sports results) on usu special channels

oracular *adj* **1** of or being an oracle **2** resembling an oracle (e g in solemnity or obscurity of expression) – **oracularly** *adv*

¹**oral** *adj* **1a** uttered in words; spoken **b** using speech **2a** of, given through, or affecting the mouth ⟨*~ contraceptive*⟩ **b** of or characterized by (passive dependency, aggressiveness, or other personality traits typical of) the first stage of sexual development in which gratification is derived from eating, sucking, and later by biting – **orally** *adv*, **orality** *n*

²**oral** *n* an oral examination

¹**orange** *n* **1a** (a small evergreen tree of the rue family with hard yellow wood and fragrant white flowers that bears) a spherical fruit with a reddish yellow leathery aromatic rind and sweet juicy edible pulp **2** any of several trees or fruits resembling the orange **3** a colour whose hue resembles that of the orange and lies between red and yellow in the spectrum

²**orange** *adj* of the colour orange

Orange *adj* of Orangemen ⟨*an ~ lodge*⟩ – **Orangeism** *n*

Orangeman *n, pl* **Orangemen** **1** a member of a Protestant loyalist society in the north of Ireland **2** a Protestant Irishman, esp of Ulster

orangutan, orangoutan *n* a largely plant-eating tree-dwelling anthropoid ape of Borneo and Sumatra with brown skin and hair and very long arms

oration *n* a speech delivered in a formal and dignified manner

orator *n* **1** one who delivers an oration **2** a skilled public speaker

oratorio *n, pl* **oratorios** a choral work based usu on a religious subject and composed chiefly of recitatives, arias, and choruses without action or scenery

¹**oratory** *n* **1a** a place of prayer; *esp* a private or institutional chapel **2** *cap* an Oratorian congregation, house, or church

²**oratory** *n* **1** the art of public speaking **2** public speaking characterized by (excessive) eloquence

orb *n* **1** a spherical body; *esp* a celestial sphere **2** a sphere surmounted by a cross symbolizing royal power and justice

¹**orbit** *n* **1** the bony socket of the eye **2** (1 complete passage of) a path described by one body in its revolution round another (e g that of the earth round the sun) **3** a sphere of influence **4** the eye – poetic – **orbital** *adj*

²**orbit** *vt* **1** to revolve in an orbit round **2** to send up and make revolve in an orbit to travel in circles

orchard *n* a usu enclosed area in which fruit trees are planted

orchestra *n* **1** the circular space used by the chorus in front of the stage in an ancient Greek theatre **2** the space in front of the stage in a modern theatre that is used by an orchestra **3** a group of musicians including esp string players organized to perform ensemble music

orchestral *adj* of or composed for an orchestra – **orchestrally** *adv*

orchestrate *vt* **1** to compose or arrange (music) for an orchestra **2** to provide with orchestration ⟨*~ a ballet*⟩ – **orchestrator** *n*

orchid *n* a plant or flower of a large family of plants related to the grasses and lilies and usu having striking 3-petalled flowers with an enlarged liplike middle petal

ordain *vt* **1** to invest officially with priestly authority (e g by the laying on of hands) **2a** to order by appointment, decree, or law; enact **b** to destine, foreordain – **ordainment** *n*

ordeal *n* **1** a method formerly used to determine guilt or innocence by submitting the accused to dangerous or painful tests whose outcome was believed to depend on divine or supernatural intervention ⟨*~ by fire*⟩ **2** a severe or testing experience

¹**order** *n* **1a** a religious body or community living under a specific rule and often required to take vows of renunciation of earthly things **2a** any of the several grades of the Christian ministry **b** *pl* the office of a person in the Christian ministry **3a** a rank or group in a community **b** a category in the classification of living things ranking above the family and below the class **4a(1)** a rank or level **(2)** a category or kind **b** arrangement of objects or events according to sequence in space, time, value, importance, etc **c** DEGREE 7a **d** the number of times mathematical differentiation is applied successively ⟨*derivatives of higher ~*⟩ **e** the number of columns or rows in a square matrix **f** the number of elements in a finite mathematical group **5a** (a sphere of) a sociopolitical system ⟨*the present economic ~*⟩ **b** regular or harmoni-

ous arrangement **6a** customary procedure, esp in debate ⟨*point of* ~⟩ **b** a prescribed form of a religious service **7a** the rule of law or proper authority ⟨*law and* ~⟩ **b** a specific rule, regulation, or authoritative direction **8a** a style of building; *esp* any of the classical styles of building ⟨*the Doric* ~⟩ **b** a column and entablature proportioned and decorated according to one of the classical styles **9** a proper, orderly, or functioning condition ⟨*telephone is out of* ~⟩ **10a** a written direction to pay money to sby **b** a direction to purchase, sell, or supply goods or to carry out work **c** goods bought or sold **d** an assigned undertaking – chiefly in *a tall order* **11** the style of dress and equipment for a specified purpose ⟨*troops in full marching* ~⟩ – **in order that** THAT 2a(1) – **in order to** for the purpose of – **in the order of** about as much or as many as; approximately – **on order** having been ordered – **to order** according to the specifications of an order ⟨*furniture made* to order⟩

²**order** *vt* **1** to put in order; arrange **2a** to give an order to; command **b** to command to go or come to a specified place **c** to place an order for ⟨~ *a meal*⟩ ~ *vi* to give or place an order

ordered *adj* **1** well regulated or ordered **2a** having elements succeeding or arranged according to rule **b** having a specified first element ⟨*a set of* ~ *pairs*⟩

¹**orderly** *adj* **1a** arranged in order; neat, tidy **b** liking or exhibiting order; methodical **2** well behaved; peaceful – **orderliness** *n*

²**orderly** *n* **1** a soldier assigned to carry messages, relay orders, etc for a superior officer **2** a hospital attendant who does routine or heavy work (e g carrying supplies or moving patients)

order of the day *n* **1** an agenda **2** the characteristic or dominant feature or activity

order paper *n* a programme of the day's business in a legislative assembly

¹**ordinal** *n* **1a** *cap* (a book containing) the forms of service for ordination **b** a book containing the Roman Catholic services proper to every day of the year **2** ORDINAL NUMBER

²**ordinal** *adj* of a specified order or rank in a series

ordinal number *n* a number designating the place (e g first, second, or third) occupied by an item in an ordered set

ordinance *n* **1** an authoritative decree; *esp* a municipal regulation **2** a prescribed usage, practice, or ceremony

ordinand *n* a candidate for ordination

¹**ordinary** *n* **1** *often cap* the invariable parts of the Mass **2** the regular or customary state of affairs – chiefly in *out of the ordinary* **3** any of the simplest heraldic charges bounded by straight lines (e g a chevron)

²**ordinary** *adj* **1** routine, usual **2** not exceptional; commonplace – **ordinarily** *adv*, **ordinariness** *n*

Ordinary level *n, often cap L* an examination that is the lowest of the 3 levels of the British General Certificate of Education

ordinary seaman *n* a person holding the lowest rank in the British navy

ordinate *n* the coordinate of a point in a plane Cartesian coordinate system obtained by measuring parallel to the y-axis

ordination *n* (an) ordaining; being ordained

ordnance *n* **1** (a branch of government service dealing with) military supplies **2** cannon, artillery

Ordnance Survey *n* (a British or Irish government organization that produces) a survey of Great Britain or Ireland published as a series of detailed maps

ordure *n* excrement

ore *n* a mineral containing a metal or other valuable constituent for which it is mined

oregano *n* a bushy plant of the mint family whose leaves are used as a herb in cooking

organ *n* **1a** a wind instrument consisting of sets of pipes made to sound by compressed air and controlled by keyboards; *also* an electronic keyboard instrument producing a sound approximating to that of an organ **b** REED ORGAN **c** any of various similar cruder instruments **2** a differentiated structure (e g the heart or a leaf) consisting of cells and tissues and performing some specific function in an organism **3** a subordinate organization that performs specialized functions ⟨*the various* ~s *of government*⟩ **4** a periodical – **organist** *n*

organ-, organo- *comb form* **1** organ; organs ⟨*organogenesis*⟩ **2** organic ⟨*organomercurial*⟩

organdie, organdy *n* a very fine transparent muslin with a stiff finish

organelle *n* a part of a cell (e g a mitochondrion) that has a specialized structure and usu a specific function

organ-grinder *n* an itinerant street musician who operates a barrel organ

organic *adj* **1a** of or arising in a bodily organ **b** affecting the structure of the organism ⟨*an* ~ *disease*⟩ **2a** of or derived from living organisms **b** of or being food produced using fertilizer solely of plant or animal origin without the aid of chemical fertilizers, pesticides, etc ⟨~ *farming*⟩ **3a** forming an integral element of a whole **b** having systematic coordination of parts **c** containing carbon compounds, esp those occurring in living organisms; *also* of or being the branch of chemistry dealing with these **d** resembling or developing in the manner of an organism **4** of or constituting the law by which a government exists – **organically** *adv*

organism *n* **1** a complex structure of interdependent and subordinate elements **2** a living being – **organismic** *adj*, **organismal** *adj*

organization, -isation *n* **1a** organizing or being organized **b** the condition or manner of being organized **2a** an association, society **b** an administrative and functional body – **organizational** *adj*

organize, -ise *vt* **1** to cause to develop an organic structure **2** to arrange or form into a complete or functioning whole **3a** to set up an administrative structure for **b** to persuade to associate in an organization; *esp* to unionize ⟨~d *labour*⟩ **4** to arrange by systematic planning and effort ~ *vi* **1** to arrange elements into a whole **2** to form an organization, esp a trade union – **organizer** *n*

orgasm *n* intense or paroxysmal emotional excitement; *esp* (an instance of) the climax of sexual excitement, occurring typically as the culmination of sexual intercourse – **orgasmic** *adj*, **orgastic** *adj*

orgy *n* **1** the secret rites of an ancient Greek or Roman deity, often accompanied by ecstatic singing and dancing **2a** drunken revelry **b** a wild party characterized by sexual promiscuity **3** an excessive or frantic indulgence in a specified activity ⟨*an* ~ *of destruction*⟩ – **orgiastic** *adj*

oriel window *n* a bay window projecting from an upper storey and supported by a corbel or bracket

¹**orient** *n* **1** *cap* EAST **2** a pearl of great lustre

²**orient** *adj* **1** lustrous, sparkling ⟨~ *gems*⟩ **2** *archaic* ORIENTAL 1

³**orient** *vt* **1a** to cause to face or point towards the east; *specif* to build (a church or temple) with the longitudinal axis pointing eastwards **b** to set in a definite position, esp in relation to the points of the compass **c** to ascertain the bearings of **2a** to adjust to an environment or a situation **b** to acquaint (oneself) with the existing situation or environment

oriental adj 1 often cap relating to or characteristic of the Orient 2a of a pearl or other precious stone of superior grade, lustre, or value b being corundum but simulating another specified gem in colour ⟨~ amethyst⟩ 3 often cap relating to or having the characteristics of Orientals 4 cap of or being the biogeographic region that includes Asia S and SE of the Himalayas and part of the Malay archipelago

Oriental n a member of any of the indigenous peoples of the Orient

orientalist n, often cap a specialist in oriental subjects

orientate vt , chiefly Br to orient ~ vi to face east

orientation n 1a orienting or being oriented b an arrangement or alignment 2 a lasting tendency of thought, inclination, or interest 3 change of position by (a part of) an organism in response to an external stimulus – orientational adj

orifice n an opening (e g a vent or mouth) through which sthg may pass – orificial adj

origin n 1 ancestry, parentage 2 a source or starting-point 3 the more fixed, central, or large attachment or part of a muscle 4 the intersection of coordinate axes

¹**original** n 1 that from which a copy, reproduction, or translation is made 2 an eccentric person

²**original** adj 1 initial, earliest 2a not secondary, derivative, or imitative b being the first instance or source of a copy, reproduction, or translation 3 inventive, creative – originally adv

originality n 1 freshness, novelty 2 the power of imaginative and independent thought or creation

original sin n (the doctrine of) man's innate sinfulness resulting from Adam's fall

originate vb to (cause to) begin or come into existence – originator n, origination n

oriole n any of a family of birds with black and either orange or yellow plumage

orison n, archaic a prayer

Orlon trademark – used for an acrylic fibre

ormolu n gilded brass or bronze used to decorate furniture, ornaments, etc

¹**ornament** n 1 sthg that lends grace or beauty; (a) decoration or embellishment 2 a person who adds honour or importance to sthg 3 an embellishing note not belonging to the essential harmony or melody

²**ornament** vt to add ornament to; embellish

ornamental adj or n (of or being) a decorative object, esp a plant cultivated for its beauty – ornamentally adv

ornamentation n 1 ornamenting or being ornamented 2 sthg that ornaments; an embellishment

ornate adj 1 rhetorical or florid in style 2 elaborately or excessively decorated – ornately adv, ornateness n

ornery adj, NAm cantankerous – infml – orneriness n

ornithology n a branch of zoology dealing with birds – ornithologist n, ornithological adj

orotund adj 1 marked by fullness of sound; sonorous 2 pompous, bombastic – orotundity n

¹**orphan** n 1 a child 1 or both of whose parents are dead 2 a young animal that has lost its mother – orphanhood n

²**orphan** vt to cause to be an orphan

orphanage n an institution for the care of orphans

orrery n a clockwork apparatus showing the relative positions and motions of bodies in the solar system

orrisroot n the fragrant rootstock of orris or another iris

orth-, ortho- comb form 1 straight; upright; vertical ⟨orthorhombic⟩ 2 correct; corrective ⟨orthodontics⟩ 3 containing the highest possible number of hydroxyl groups or molecules of water ⟨orthophosphate⟩ 4 ortho-

also orth- involving substitution at 2 neighbouring positions in the benzene ring ⟨ortho-xylene⟩

orthodontics n pl but sing in constr dentistry dealing with (the correction of) irregularities of the teeth – orthodontic adj, orthodontist n

orthodox adj 1a conforming to established, dominant, or official doctrine (e g in religion) b conventional 2a cap (consisting) of the Eastern churches headed by the patriarch of Constantinople which separated from the Western church in the 9th c and have characteristic and separate doctrines, liturgy, and forms of organization b cap relating to Judaism that keeps to strict and conservative interpretation of the Torah and rabbinic tradition – orthodoxly adv

orthodoxy n 1 being orthodox 2 an orthodox belief or practice

orthography n 1 correct spelling 2 the manner of spelling – orthographic adj, orthographically adv

orthopaedics, NAm chiefly orthopedics n pl but sing or pl in constr the correction or prevention of skeletal and muscular deformities, esp by surgery – orthopaedic adj, orthopaedist n

ortolan n a brown and greyish-green European bunting

¹**-ory** suffix (→ n) 1 place of or for ⟨observatory⟩ ⟨refectory⟩ 2 sthg that serves for ⟨directory⟩

²**-ory** suffix (→ adj) 1 of or involving ⟨gustatory⟩ ⟨compulsory⟩ 2 serving for or producing ⟨justificatory⟩

oryx n, pl oryxes, esp collectively oryx any of a genus of large straight-horned African antelopes

¹**Oscar** n a statuette awarded annually by a US professional organization for outstanding achievement in the cinema

²**Oscar** – a communications code word for the letter o

oscillate vi 1a to swing backwards and forwards like a pendulum b to move or travel back and forth between 2 points 2 to vary between opposing beliefs, feelings, or courses of action – oscillatory adj

oscillation n 1 oscillating 2 a variation, fluctuation 3 a flow of electricity periodically changing direction 4 a single swing (e g of sthg oscillating) from one extreme limit to the other

oscillator n 1 sby or sthg that oscillates 2 a device for producing alternating current; esp a radio-frequency or audio-frequency signal generator

oscillograph n an instrument for recording (electrical) oscillations – oscillographic adj, oscillography n

oscilloscope n an instrument in which electrical oscillations register as a temporary visible wave form on the fluorescent screen of a cathode-ray tube – oscilloscopic adj

osculate vt to kiss – humor or fml – osculation n

osier n 1 any of various willows whose pliable twigs are used for furniture and basketry 2 a willow rod used in basketry

-osis suffix, pl -oses, -osises (→ n) 1a action, process, or condition of ⟨hypnosis⟩ ⟨metamorphosis⟩ b abnormal or pathological condition of ⟨thrombosis⟩ 2 increase or formation of ⟨leucocytosis⟩ – -otic adj, -otically adv

osmosis n 1 movement of a solvent through a semipermeable membrane (e g of a living cell) into a solution of higher concentration that tends to equalize the concentrations on the 2 sides of the membrane 2 a process of absorption or diffusion suggestive of osmosis – osmotic adj

osprey n 1 a large fish-eating hawk with dark brown and white plumage 2 a feather trimming used for millinery

osseous adj BONY 1

ossify vi 1 to become bone 2 to become unfeeling,

unimaginative, or rigid ~ *vt* to change (e g cartilage) into bone – **ossification** *n*

oste-, osteo- *comb form* bone ⟨oste*al*⟩ ⟨osteo*myelitis*⟩

ostensible *adj* being such in appearance rather than reality; professed, declared – **ostensibly** *adv*

ostentation *n* unnecessary display of wealth, knowledge, etc designed to impress or attract attention – **ostentatious** *adj*, **ostentatiously** *adv*, **ostentatiousness** *n*

osteoarthritis *n* degenerative arthritis – **osteoarthritic** *adj*

osteopathy *n* a system of treatment of diseases based on the theory that they can be cured by manipulation of bones – **osteopath** *n*, **osteopathic** *adj*

ostler, *chiefly NAm* **hostler** *n* a groom or stableman at an inn

ostracism *n* **1** temporary banishment by popular vote as practised in ancient Greece **2** exclusion by general consent from common privileges or social acceptance

ostracize, -ise *vt* to exile or exclude by ostracism

ostrich *n* **1** a swift-footed 2-toed flightless bird that has valuable wing and tail plumes and is the largest of existing birds **2** one who refuses to face up to unpleasant realities

¹**other** *adj* **1a** being the 1 left of 2 or more ⟨*held on with 1 hand and waved with the ~ one*⟩ **b** being the ones distinct from that or those first mentioned ⟨*taller than the ~ boys*⟩ **c** SECOND 2 ⟨*every ~ day*⟩ **2a** not the same; different ⟨*schools ~ than her own*⟩ **b** far, opposite ⟨*lives the ~ side of town*⟩ **3** additional, further ⟨*John and 2 ~ boys*⟩ **4** recently past ⟨*the ~ evening*⟩

²**other** *pron, pl* **others** *also* **other** **1** the remaining or opposite one ⟨*went from one side to the ~*⟩ ⟨*the ~s came later*⟩ **2** a different or additional one ⟨*some film or ~*⟩ ⟨*some left, but many ~s stayed*⟩

³**other** *adv* otherwise – + *than* ⟨*can't get there ~ than by swimming*⟩

¹**otherwise** *adv* **1** in a different way **2** in different circumstances ⟨*might ~ have left*⟩ **3** in other respects ⟨*an ~ excellent dinner*⟩ **4** if not; or else ⟨*do what I say, ~ you'll be sorry*⟩ **5** not – used to express the opposite ⟨*mothers, whether married or ~*⟩ ⟨*guilty unless proved ~*⟩ **6** alias ⟨*Chee Soo, ~ Cliff Gibbs – Sportsworld*⟩

²**otherwise** *adj* of a different kind ⟨*how can I be ~ than grateful*⟩

otherworldly *adj* concerned with spiritual or intellectual matters rather than the material world – **otherworldliness** *n*

otic *adj* of or located in the region of the ear

-otic *comb form* (→ *adj*) having (a specified relationship to) the ear ⟨*periotic*⟩

otiose *adj* **1** at leisure; idle **2** futile, pointless *USE* fml – **otiosely** *adv*, **otioseness** *n*

otter *n, pl* **otters**, *esp collectively* **otter** **1** (the dark brown fur or pelt of) any of several aquatic fish-eating mammals with webbed and clawed feet, related to the weasels **2a** an otterboard **b** a paravane

ottoman *n* **1** *cap* a Turk **2a** a usu heavily upholstered box or seat without a back or arms **b** a cushioned stool for the feet

Ottoman *adj* TURKISH 1

oubliette *n* a dungeon with an opening only at the top

¹**ouch** *n, archaic* a setting for a precious stone

²**ouch** *interj* – used esp to express sudden sharp pain

¹**ought** *verbal auxiliary* – used to express moral obligation ⟨*~ to pay our debts*⟩, advisability ⟨*~ to be boiled for 10 minutes*⟩, enthusiastic recommendation ⟨*you ~ to hear her sing*⟩, natural expectation ⟨*~ to have arrived by now*⟩, or logical consequence ⟨*the result ~ to be infinity*⟩; used in the negative to express moral condemnation of an action ⟨*you ~ not to treat him like that*⟩; often used with the perfect infinitive to express unfulfilled obligation ⟨*~ never to have been allowed*⟩

²**ought** *n or adj* (a) zero

Ouija *trademark* – used for a board with the alphabet and other signs on it that is used to produce automatic writing in spiritualistic seances

¹**ounce** *n* **1a** a unit of weight equal to 16 drams (28.35g) **b** a small amount ⟨*an ~ of common sense*⟩ **2** FLUID OUNCE

²**ounce** *n* SNOW LEOPARD

our *adj* of us, ourself, or ourselves, esp as possessors or possessor ⟨*~ throne*⟩, agents or agent ⟨*~ discovery*⟩, or objects or object of an action ⟨*~ being chosen*⟩; of everybody ⟨*~ Saviour*⟩

Our Father *n* LORD'S PRAYER

Our Lady *n* VIRGIN MARY

ours *pron, pl* **ours** that which or the one who belongs to us – used without a following noun as a pronoun equivalent in meaning to the adjective *our*; compare phrases at MINE

ourselves *pron, pl in constr* **1** those identical people that are we – used reflexively ⟨*we're doing it solely for ~*⟩ or for emphasis ⟨*we ~ will never go*⟩; compare ONESELF **2** our normal selves ⟨*not feeling quite ~*⟩

-ous *suffix* (→ *adj*) **1** full of; characterized by; possessing the quality of ⟨*clamorous*⟩ ⟨*envious*⟩ **2** having a valency relatively lower than in (specified compounds or ions named with an adjective ending in *-ic*) ⟨*ferrous*⟩ ⟨*mercurous*⟩ – **-ously** *suffix* (→ *adv*)

ousel *n* an ouzel

oust *vt* **1** to remove from or dispossess of property or position **2** to take the place of; supplant

¹**out** *adv* **1a** away from the inside or centre ⟨*went ~ into the garden*⟩ **b** from among other things ⟨*separate ~ the bad apples*⟩ **c** away from the shore, the city, or one's homeland ⟨*~ at sea*⟩ ⟨*go ~ to Africa*⟩ ⟨*live ~ in the country*⟩ **d** away from a particular place, esp of one's home or business ⟨*~ for lunch*⟩ ⟨*~ on strike*⟩ ⟨*move ~ into lodgings*⟩ **e**(1) clearly in or into view ⟨*when the sun's ~*⟩ (2) of a flower in or into full bloom **2a**(1) out of the proper place ⟨*left a word ~*⟩ ⟨*put his shoulder ~*⟩ (2) amiss in reckoning ⟨*more than 4 lb ~ – Punch*⟩ **b** in all directions from a central point of control ⟨*lent ~ money*⟩ **c** from political power ⟨*voted them ~*⟩ **d** into shares or portions ⟨*parcelled ~ the farm*⟩ **e** out of vogue or fashion **3a** to or in a state of extinction or exhaustion ⟨*burn ~*⟩ ⟨*before the year is ~*⟩ **b** to the fullest extent or degree; completely ⟨*all decked ~*⟩ ⟨*hear me ~*⟩ ⟨*clean ~ the attic*⟩ **c** in or into a state of determined effort ⟨*~ to fight pollution*⟩ **4a** aloud ⟨*cried ~*⟩ ⟨*~ with it!*⟩ **b** in existence; ever – with a superlative; infml ⟨*the funniest thing ~*⟩ **5** so as to be put out of a game ⟨*bowled ~*⟩ **6** – used on a 2-way radio circuit to indicate that a message is complete and no reply is expected

²**out** *vi* to become publicly known

³**out** *adj* **1** located outside; external **2** located at a distance; outlying ⟨*the ~ islands*⟩ **3** not being in operation or power ⟨*the fire's ~*⟩ **4** directed or serving to direct outwards ⟨*the ~ tray*⟩ **5** not allowed to continue batting **6** out of the question ⟨*your suggestion's definitely ~*⟩

⁴**out** *prep* OUT OF 1a(1)

⁵**out** *n* a way of escaping from an embarrassing or difficult situation

out- *prefix* **1** forth ⟨*outcry*⟩ ⟨*outburst*⟩ ⟨*outrush*⟩ **2** result; product ⟨*output*⟩ ⟨*outcome*⟩ **3** in a manner that goes beyond, surpasses, or excels ⟨*outmanoeuvre*⟩ ⟨*outstrip*⟩

outback *n* isolated rural (Australian) country

outbalance *vt* to outweigh in value or importance

outbid *vt* **outbid; -dd-** to make a higher bid than

¹**outboard** *adj* **1** situated outboard **2** having, using, or limited to the use of an outboard motor

²**outboard** *adv* **1** in a lateral direction from the hull of a ship or the fuselage of an aircraft **2** in a position closer or closest to either of the wing tips of an aeroplane or of the sides of a motor vehicle

³**outboard** *n* **1** outboard, outboard motor a motor, propeller, and rudder attached as a unit to the stern of a small boat **2** a boat with an outboard

outbreak *n* **1a** a sudden or violent breaking out ⟨*the* ~ *of war*⟩ **b** a sudden increase in numbers of a harmful organism or in sufferers from a disease within a particular area ⟨*an* ~ *of locusts*⟩ ⟨*an* ~ *of measles*⟩ **2** an insurrection, revolt

outbuilding *n* a smaller building (e g a stable or a woodshed) separate from but belonging to a main building

outburst *n* **1** a violent expression of feeling **2** a surge of activity or growth

outcast *n* one who is cast out by society – **outcast** *adj*

outcaste *n* **1** a Hindu who has been ejected from his/her caste **2** one who has no caste

outclass *vt* to excel, surpass

outcome *n* a result, consequence

¹**outcrop** *n* **1** (the emergence of) the part of a rock formation that appears at the surface of the ground **2** an outbreak

²**outcrop** *vi* **-pp-** to project as an outcrop

outcry *n* **1** a loud cry; a clamour **2** a public expression of anger or disapproval

outdated *adj* outmoded

outdistance *vt* to go far ahead of (e g in a race)

outdo *vt* **outdoes; outdid; outdone** to surpass in action or performance

outdoor *also* **outdoors** *adj* **1** of or performed outdoors **2** not enclosed; without a roof ⟨*an* ~ *restaurant*⟩

¹**outdoors** *adv* outside a building; in or into the open air

²**outdoors** *n pl but sing in constr* **1** the open air **2** the world remote from human habitation ⟨*the great* ~ ⟩

outer *adj* **1** existing independently of the mind; objective **2a** situated farther out ⟨*the* ~ *limits*⟩ **b** away from a centre ⟨*the* ~ *planets*⟩ **c** situated or belonging on the outside ⟨*the* ~ *covering*⟩ – **outermost** *adj*

outer space *n* space outside the earth's atmosphere

outface *vt* **1** to cause to waver or submit (as if) by staring **2** to confront unflinchingly; defy

outfall *n* the outlet for a river, lake, drain, sewer, etc

outfield *n* the part of a cricket field beyond the prepared section on which wickets are laid out or of a baseball field furthest from the bases – **outfielder** *n*

¹**outfit** *n* **1a** a complete set of equipment needed for a particular purpose **b** a set of garments worn together, often for a specified occasion or activity **2** *sing or pl in constr* a group that works as a team – *infml*

²**outfit** *vt* **-tt-** to equip with an outfit

outflank *vt* **1** to go round or extend beyond the flank of (an opposing force) **2** to gain an advantage over by doing sthg unexpected

outflow *n* **1** a flowing out **2** sthg that flows out – **outflow** *vi*

outgeneral *vt* **-ll-** (*NAm* **-l-**) to surpass in generalship

outgoing *adj* **1a** going away; departing **b** retiring or withdrawing from a position ⟨*the* ~ *president*⟩ **2** friendly, sociable – **outgoingness** *n*

outgoings *n pl* expenditures; *esp* overheads

outgrow *vt* **outgrew; outgrown 1** to grow or increase faster than **2** to grow too large or too old for

outgrowth *n* **1** a process or product of growing out ⟨*an* ~ *of hair*⟩ **2** a consequence, by-product

out-Herod *vt* to outdo in violence, extravagance, etc – chiefly in *out-Herod Herod*

outhouse *n* an outbuilding; *esp, chiefly NAm* PRIVY 1

outing *n* a short pleasure trip

outlandish *adj* strikingly unusual; bizarre – **outlandishly** *adv*

outlast *vt* to last longer than

¹**outlaw** *n* **1** sby excluded from the protection of the law **2** a fugitive from the law – **outlaw** *adj*

²**outlaw** *vt* **1** to deprive of the protection of law **2** to make illegal – **outlawry** *n*

outlay *n* expenditure, payment

outlet *n* **1a** an exit or vent **b** a means of release or satisfaction for an emotion or drive **2** an agency (e g a shop or dealer) through which a product is marketed **3** *chiefly NAm* POWER POINT

¹**outline** *n* **1a** a line bounding the outer limits of sthg **b** SHAPE 1, 2 **2** (a) drawing with no shading **3a** a condensed treatment of a subject **b** a summary of a written work **4** a preliminary account of a project

²**outline** *vt* **1** to draw the outline of **2** to indicate the principal features of

outlive *vt* **1** to live longer than **2** to survive the effects of

outlook *n* **1** a view from a particular place ⟨*house with a pleasant* ~ ⟩ **2** an attitude; POINT OF VIEW **3** a prospect for the future

outlying *adj* remote from a centre or main point

outmanoeuvre, *NAm* **outmaneuver** *vt* to defeat by more skilful manoeuvring

outmatch *vt* to surpass, outdo

outmoded *adj* **1** no longer in fashion **2** no longer acceptable or usable; obsolete

outnumber *vt* to exceed in number

out of *prep* **1a(1)** from within to the outside of ⟨*walked* ~ *the room*⟩ **(2)** – used to indicate a change in quality, state, or form ⟨*woke up* ~ *a deep sleep*⟩ **b(1)** beyond the range or limits of ⟨ ~ *sight*⟩ ⟨*lived a mile* ~ *the town*⟩ **(2)** – used to indicate a position or state away from a qualification or circumstance ⟨ ~ *practice*⟩ ⟨ ~ *perspective*⟩ **2a** – used to indicate origin or cause ⟨*came* ~ *fear*⟩ ⟨*did well* ~ *the war*⟩ ⟨*what do I get* ~ *it?*⟩ **b** using as a material ⟨*built* ~ *old timber*⟩ **c** having as a mother – used esp of horses ⟨*a colt* ~ *an ordinary mare*⟩; compare BY 4b(1) **3** – used to indicate exclusion from or deprivation of ⟨ ~ *breath*⟩ ⟨*we're right* ~ *soap*⟩ ⟨*cheated him* ~ *his savings*⟩ **4** from among; *also* IN 5 ⟨*one* ~ *4 survived*⟩ – **out of it 1** not part of a group, activity, or fashion **2** hence, away ⟨*get off* out of it⟩

out-of-date *adj* outmoded, obsolete

out-of-pocket *adj* **1** requiring an outlay of cash ⟨ ~ *expenses*⟩ **2** having spent or lost more money than one can afford ⟨*that shopping spree has left me* ~ ⟩

out-of-the-way *adj* **1** off the beaten track; remote **2** unusual

outpatient *n* a patient who is not an inmate of a hospital but visits it for diagnosis or treatment

outplay *vt* to defeat or play better than in a game ⟨ ~ *ed his rival*⟩

outpoint *vt* to score more points than (and so defeat)

outpost *n* **1** a post or detachment established at a distance from a main body of troops, esp to protect it from surprise attack **2a** an outlying or frontier settlement **b** an outlying branch of a main organization or body

outpouring *n* an effusive expression (e g of emotion) – usu pl with sing. meaning

¹**output** *n* **1** mineral, agricultural, or industrial production

⟨*steel* ~⟩ **2** mental or artistic production **3** the amount produced by sby in a given time **4a** sthg (e g energy, material, or data) produced by a machine or system **b** the terminal for the output on an electrical device

²**output** *vt* **-tt-**; **output** to produce as output

¹**outrage** *n* **1** an act of violence or brutality **2** an act that violates accepted standards of behaviour or taste

²**outrage** *vt* **1** to violate the standards or principles of **2** to rape – *euph*

outrageous *adj* **1** not conventional or moderate; extravagant **2** going beyond all standards of propriety, decency, or taste; shocking, offensive – **outrageously** *adv*, **outrageousness** *n*

outrank *vt* to rank higher than

outré *adj* violating convention or propriety; bizarre

outride *vt* **outrode; outridden** to ride out (a storm)

outrider *n* a mounted attendant or motorcyclist who rides ahead of or beside a carriage or car as an escort

outrigger *n* **1** a spar, beam, or framework run out or projecting from a ship's side (e g to help secure a mast or support a float or rowlock) **2** a member projecting from a main structure to provide additional stability or support sthg

¹**outright** *adv* **1** completely **2** instantaneously; ON THE SPOT **2**

²**outright** *adj* being completely or exactly what is stated ⟨*an* ~ *lie*⟩

outrun *vt* **outran; outrun; -nn- 1** to run faster than **2** to exceed, surpass

outsell *vt* **outsold** to surpass in selling, salesmanship, or numbers sold

outset *n* *the* beginning, start

outshine *vb* **outshone, outshined** *vt* **1** to shine brighter than **2** to outdo or excel (in splendour)

¹**outside** *n* **1a** an external part; the region beyond a boundary **b** the area farthest from a point of reference: e g **(1)** the section of a playing area towards the sidelines; *also* a corner **(2)** the side of a pavement nearer the traffic **2** an outer side or surface **3** an outer manifestation; an appearance **4** the extreme limit of an estimation or guess; a maximum ⟨*the crowd numbered 10,000 at the* ~⟩

²**outside** *adj* **1a** of or being on, near, or towards the outside ⟨*an* ~ *lavatory*⟩ ⟨*an* ~ *telephone line*⟩ **b** of or being the outer side of a curve or near the middle of the road ⟨*driving on the* ~ *lane*⟩ **2** maximum **3a** originating elsewhere ⟨*an* ~ *broadcast*⟩ ⟨~ *agitators*⟩ **b** not belonging to one's regular occupation or duties ⟨~ *interests*⟩ **4** barely possible; remote ⟨*an* ~ *chance*⟩

³**outside** *adv* **1** on or to the outside ⟨*wait* ~ *in the passage*⟩ **2** outdoors **3** *chiefly Br* not in prison – *slang*

⁴**outside** *prep* **1** on or to the outside of ⟨*live a mile* ~ *Cambridge*⟩ **2** beyond the limits of ⟨~ *my experience*⟩ **3** except, besides ⟨*few interests* ~ *her children*⟩

outside of *prep, chiefly NAm* outside

outsider *n* **1** sby who does not belong to a particular group **2** a competitor who has only an outside chance of winning

outsize *adj or n* (of) an unusual or above standard size

outskirt *n* an outer area, esp of a town or city – usu pl with sing. meaning

outsmart *vt* to get the better of; outwit

outspoken *adj* direct and open in speech or expression; frank – **outspokenly** *adv*, **outspokenness** *n*

outstanding *adj* **1a** unpaid ⟨*left several bills* ~⟩ **b** continuing, unresolved **2a** standing out from a group; conspicuous **b** marked by eminence and distinction – **outstandingly** *adv*

outstay *vt* **1** to overstay ⟨~ *ed his welcome*⟩ **2** to surpass in staying power

outstretch *vt* to stretch out; extend

outstrip *vt* **-pp- 1** to go faster or farther than **2** to get ahead of; leave behind

outvote *vt* to defeat by a majority of votes

¹**outward** *adj* **1a** situated at or directed towards the outside **b** being or going away from home ⟨*the* ~ *voyage*⟩ **2** of the body or external appearances ⟨~ *calm*⟩

²**outward** *n* external form, appearance, or reality

outwardly *adv* in outward appearance; superficially

outwards *adv* towards the outside

outwear *vt* **outwore; outworn** to last longer than

outweigh *vt* to exceed in weight, value, or importance

outwit *vt* **-tt-** to get the better of by superior cleverness

outwork *n* **1** a minor defensive position constructed outside a fortified area **2** work done for a business or organization off its premises usu by employees based at home – **outworker** *n*

outworn *adj* no longer useful or acceptable; outmoded

ouzel, ousel *n* **1** RING OUZEL **2** a dipper

ouzo *n* an unsweetened Greek spirit flavoured with aniseed that is usu drunk with water

ova *pl of* OVUM

¹**oval** *adj* having the shape of an egg; *also* exactly or approximately elliptical – **ovally** *adv*, **ovalness** *n*

²**oval** *n* an oval figure or object

ovary *n* **1** the typically paired female reproductive organ that produces eggs and female sex hormones **2** the enlarged rounded usu basal female part of a flowering plant that bears the ovules and consists of 1 or more carpels – **ovarian** *adj*, **ovaritis** *n*

ovation *n* an expression of popular acclaim

oven *n* a chamber used for baking, heating, or drying

ovenware *n* heat-resistant dishes (e g casseroles) in which food can be cooked in an oven

¹**over** *adv* **1a** across a barrier ⟨*climb* ~⟩ **b** across an intervening space ⟨*went* ~ *to the States*⟩; *also* ROUND **5** ⟨*ask them* ~ *for drinks*⟩ **c** downwards from an upright position ⟨*fell* ~⟩ ⟨*knocked him* ~⟩ **d** across the brim or brink ⟨*soup boiled* ~⟩ **e** so as to bring the underside up ⟨*turned his cards* ~⟩ ⟨*rolled* ~ *and* ~⟩ **f** so as to be reversed or folded ⟨*change the 2 pictures* ~⟩ ⟨*bend it* ~⟩ **g** from one person or side to another ⟨*hand it* ~⟩ ⟨*won them* ~⟩ ⟨*went* ~ *to the enemy*⟩ **h** ACROSS **3** ⟨*got his point* ~⟩ **2a(1)** beyond some quantity or limit ⟨*£10 or* ~⟩ ⟨*show ran a minute* ~⟩ **(2)** excessively, inordinately – often in combination ⟨over-*optimistic*⟩ ⟨over*value*⟩ **(3)** in excess; remaining ⟨*there wasn't much* ~⟩ ⟨*3 into 7 goes twice and 1* ~⟩ **b** till a later time ⟨*stay* ~ *till Monday*⟩ **3** so as to cover the whole surface ⟨*windows boarded* ~⟩ **4a** at an end ⟨*the day is* ~⟩ **b** – used on a two-way radio circuit to indicate that a message is complete and a reply is expected **5a** – used to show repetition ⟨*10 times* ~⟩ ⟨*told you* ~ *and* ~ *again*⟩ **b** *chiefly NAm* once more ⟨*do one's sums* ~⟩

²**over** *prep* **1a** higher than; above ⟨*towered* ~ *his mother*⟩ **b** vertically above but not touching ⟨*lamp hung* ~ *the table*⟩ **c** – used to indicate movement down upon ⟨*hit him* ~ *the head*⟩ or down across the edge of ⟨*fell* ~ *the cliff*⟩ **d** ACROSS **1** ⟨*climbed* ~ *the gate*⟩ ⟨*flew* ~ *the lake*⟩ **e** so as to cover ⟨*laid a blanket* ~ *the child*⟩ ⟨*curtains drawn* ~ *the windows*⟩ **f** divided by ⟨*6* ~ *2 is 3*⟩ **2a** with authority, power, or jurisdiction in relation to ⟨*respected those* ~ *him*⟩ **b** – used to indicate superiority, advantage, or preference ⟨*a big lead* ~ *the others*⟩ **3** more than ⟨*cost* ~ *£5*⟩ **4a** all through or throughout ⟨*showed me all* ~ *the house*⟩ ⟨*went* ~ *his notes*⟩ **b** by means of (a medium or channel of communication) ⟨~ *the radio*⟩ ⟨~ *the phone*⟩ **5a** in the course of; during ⟨~ *the past 25 years*⟩ ⟨*wrote it* ~ *the weekend*⟩ **b** until the end of ⟨*stay*

~ *Sunday*⟩ **c** past, beyond ⟨*we're* ~ *the worst*⟩ **6a** – used to indicate an object of solicitude or reference ⟨*the Lord watches* ~ *them*⟩ ⟨*laughed* ~ *the incident*⟩ **b** – used to indicate an object of occupation or activity ⟨*sitting* ~ *their wine*⟩ ⟨*spent an hour* ~ *cards*⟩

³over *adj* **1** upper, higher ⟨over*lord*⟩ **2** outer, covering ⟨over*coat*⟩ **3** excessive ⟨over - *imagination*⟩ ⟨over*confidence*⟩ *USE* often in combination

⁴over *n* any of the divisions of an innings in cricket during which 1 bowler bowls 6 or 8 balls from the same end of the pitch

overact *vb* to perform (a part) with undue exaggeration

¹overall *adv* **1** as a whole; IN TOTO **2** from end to end, esp of a ship

²overall *n* **1** *pl* a protective garment resembling a boiler suit or dungarees **2** *chiefly Br* a usu loose-fitting protective coat worn over other clothing

³overall *adj* including everything

overarm *adj or adv* overhand

overawe *vt* to fill with respect or fear

overbalance *vt* to cause to lose balance ~ *vi chiefly Br* to lose one's balance

overbear *vt* overbore; overborne *also* overborn **1** to bring down by superior weight or force **2a** to domineer over **b** to surpass in importance or cogency; outweigh

overbearing *adj* harshly masterful or domineering – **overbearingly** *adv*

overbid *vb* overbid; -dd- *vi* **1** to bid in excess of value **2** to bid more than the scoring capacity of a hand at cards ~ *vt* to bid in excess of; *esp* to bid more than the value of (one's hand at cards) – **overbid** *n*

¹overblown *adj* inflated, pretentious

²overblown *adj* past the prime of bloom ⟨~ *roses*⟩

overboard *adv* **1** over the side of a ship or boat into the water **2** to extremes of enthusiasm ⟨*went* ~ *for the plan*⟩ **3** aside ⟨*threw the plan* ~⟩

¹overburden *vt* to place an excessive burden on

²overburden *n* soil, rock, etc overlying a useful deposit (e g of coal)

overcall *vb* to make a higher bid than (the previous bid or player) in a card game – **overcall** *n*

overcapitalize, -ise *vt* to put a nominal value on the capital of (a company) higher than actual cost or fair market value – **overcapitalization** *n*

overcast *adj* being, having, or characterized by a cloudy sky

overcharge *vt* **1** to charge too much or too fully **2** to fill too full **3** to exaggerate ~ *vi* to make an excessive charge – **overcharge** *n*

overcloud *vt* to cover with clouds

overcoat *n* **1** a warm usu thick coat for wearing outdoors over other clothing **2** a protective coat (e g of paint)

overcome *vb* overcame; overcome *vt* **1** to get the better of; surmount ⟨~ *difficulties*⟩ **2** to overpower, overwhelm ~ *vi* to gain superiority; win

overcompensation *n* excessive reaction to feelings of inferiority, guilt, inadequacy, etc

overcrowd *vb* to (cause to) be too crowded

overdo *vt* overdoes; overdid; overdone **1a** to do or use in excess **b** to exaggerate **2** to cook too much

overdose *vb or n* (to give or take) too great a dose of drugs, medicine, etc

overdraft *n* an act of overdrawing at a bank; the state of being overdrawn; *also* the sum overdrawn

overdraw *vb* overdrew; overdrawn *vt* **1** to draw cheques on (a bank account) for more than the balance ⟨*his account was overdrawn*⟩ **2** to exaggerate, overstate ~ *vi* to make an overdraft

overdrawn *adj* having an overdrawn account

¹overdress *vb* to dress (oneself) too elaborately or formally

²overdress *n* a dress worn over another, or over a jumper, blouse, etc

overdrive *n* a transmission gear in a motor vehicle that provides a ratio higher than the normal top gear and that drives the propeller shaft at a speed greater than the engine speed

overdue *adj* **1a** unpaid when due **b** delayed beyond an appointed time **2** more than ready or ripe

overestimate *vt* **1** to estimate as being more than the actual amount or size **2** to place too high a value on; overrate – **overestimate** *n*, **overestimation** *n*

¹overflow *vt* **1** to cover (as if) with water; inundate **2** to flow over the brim, edge, or limit of ~ *vi* to flow over or beyond a brim, edge, or limit

²overflow *n* **1** a flowing over; an inundation **2** sthg that flows over; *also, sing or pl in constr* the excess members of a group **3** an outlet or receptacle for surplus liquid

overfly *vt* overflew; overflown to fly over, esp in an aircraft

overgrow *vb* overgrew; overgrown *vt* **1** to grow over so as to cover with vegetation **2** to grow beyond; to outgrow ~ *vi* **1** to grow excessively **2** to become overgrown – **overgrowth** *n*

overgrown *adj* **1** grown over or choked with vegetation **2** grown too large

overhand *adj or adv* with the hand brought forwards and down from above shoulder level

¹overhang *vb* overhung *vt* **1** to project over **2** to threaten ~ *vi* to project so as to be over sthg

²overhang *n* **1** sthg that overhangs; *also* the extent by which sthg overhangs **2** a projection of the roof or upper storey of a building beyond the wall of the lower part

overhaul *vt* **1** to examine thoroughly and carry out necessary repairs **2** to overtake – **overhaul** *n*

¹overhead *adv* above one's head

²overhead *adj* **1** operating, lying, or coming from above **2** of overhead expenses

³overhead *n* **1** a business expense (e g rent, insurance, or heating) not chargeable to a particular part of the work or product – often *pl with sing. meaning* **2** a stroke in squash, tennis, etc made above head height; a smash

overhear *vb* overheard to hear (sby or sthg) without the speaker's knowledge or intention

overjoyed *adj* extremely pleased; elated

¹overkill *vt* to obliterate (a target) with more nuclear force than required

²overkill *n* **1** the capability of destroying an enemy or target with a force, esp nuclear, larger than is required **2** an excess of sthg beyond what is required or suitable for a particular purpose

¹overland *adv or adj* by, upon, or across land rather than sea or air

²overland *vb, Austr* to drive (stock) overland for long distances – **overlander** *n*

overlap *vb* -pp- *vt* to extend over and cover a part of ~ *vi* to coincide partly; have sthg in common – **overlap** *n*

¹overlay *vt* overlaid to lay or spread over or across

²overlay *n* sthg (designed to be) laid over sthg else; *esp* a transparent sheet containing graphic matter to be superimposed on another sheet

overleaf *adv* on the other side of the page ⟨*continued* ~⟩

overload *vt* overloaded, overladen to load to excess – **overload** *n*

overlong *adj or adv* too long

overlook *vt* 1 to have or provide a view of from above 2a to fail to notice; miss b to ignore c to excuse

overlord *n* 1 a lord who is superior to other lords 2 an absolute or supreme ruler – **overlordship** *n*

overly *adv, chiefly NAm & Scot* to an excessive degree

overman *vt* **-nn-** to have or provide too many workers for ⟨~ *a ship*⟩

overmaster *vt* to overpower, subdue

overmuch *adj or adv* too much

overnight *adv* 1 during or throughout the evening or night 2 suddenly – **overnight** *adj*

overpass *n* a flyover; *also* the crossing of 2 roads, paths, railways, or combinations of these

overpay *vt* to give excessively high payment to or for

overplay *vt* 1 to exaggerate (e g a dramatic role) 2 to give too much emphasis to – **overplay one's hand** to overestimate one's capacities

overpopulation *n* the condition of having too dense a population, so that the quality of life is impaired – **overpopulated** *adj*

overpower *vt* 1 to overcome by superior force 2 to overwhelm – **overpoweringly** *adv*

overprint *n* a printed marking added to a postage stamp to alter the original or to commemorate a special event – **overprint** *vt*

overrate *vt* to rate too highly

overreach *vt* to defeat (oneself) by trying to do or gain too much ~ *vi, of a horse* to strike the hind foot against the forefoot

¹**override** *vt* **overrode**; **overridden** 1a to prevail over; dominate ⟨*an overriding* consideration⟩ b to set aside or annul; *esp* to neutralize the action of (e g an automatic control) 2 to overlap

²**override** *n* a device or system used to override a control

overrule *vt* to rule against or set aside, esp by virtue of superior authority

overrun *vt* **overran**; **-nn-** 1a to defeat decisively and occupy the positions of b to swarm over; infest 2a to run or go beyond or past b to readjust (set type) by shifting letters or words from one line into another 3 to flow over – **overrun** *n*

¹**overseas, oversea** *adv* beyond or across the seas ⟨*travelled* ~⟩

²**overseas, oversea** *adj* 1 of transport across the seas 2 of, from, or in (foreign) places across the seas ⟨~ *markets*⟩ ⟨~ *students here in London*⟩

oversee *vt* **oversaw**; **overseen** to supervise

overseer *n* a supervisor

oversell *vt* **oversold** 1 to sell too much of 2 to make excessive claims for – **oversell** *n*

oversexed *adj* with an abnormally strong sexual drive

overshadow *vt* 1 to cast a shadow over 2 to exceed in importance; outweigh

overshoe *n* a usu rubber shoe worn over another as protection (e g from rain or snow)

overshoot *vt* **overshot** to shoot or pass over or beyond, esp so as to miss – **overshoot** *n*

oversight *n* 1 supervision 2 an inadvertent omission or error

oversimplify *vb* to simplify (sthg) to such an extent as to cause distortion or error – **oversimplification** *n*

oversleep *vi* **overslept** to sleep beyond the intended time

overspill *n, chiefly Br* people who have moved away from crowded urban areas ⟨~ *towns*⟩; *also* the movement of such people

overstate *vt* to state in too strong terms; exaggerate – **overstatement** *n*

overstay *vt* to stay beyond the time or the limits of

oversteer *n* the tendency of a motor vehicle to steer into a sharper turn than the driver intends – **oversteer** *vb*

overstep *vt* **-pp-** to exceed, transgress – esp in **overstep the mark**

overstrung *adj* too highly strung; too sensitive

overstuff *vt* to cover (e g a chair) thickly with upholstery

oversubscribe *vt* to subscribe for more of than is offered for sale – **oversubscription** *n*

overt *adj* public, manifest – **overtly** *adv*

overtake *vb* **overtook**; **overtaken** *vt* 1a to catch up with b to catch up with and pass beyond 2 to come upon suddenly ~ *vi, chiefly Br* to catch up with and pass by another vehicle going in the same direction

overtax *vt* 1 to tax too heavily 2 to put too great a burden or strain on

¹**overthrow** *vt* **overthrew**; **overthrown** 1 to overturn, upset 2 to cause the downfall of; defeat

overtime *n* 1 time in excess of a set limit; *esp* working time in excess of a standard working day or week 2 the wage paid for overtime – **overtime** *adv*

overtone *n* 1a any of the higher harmonics produced simultaneously with the fundamental in a complex musical note b HARMONIC 2 2 a secondary effect, quality, or meaning; a suggestion – often pl with sing. meaning

overtop *vt* **-pp-** 1 to rise above the top of 2 to surpass

overtrump *vb* to trump with a higher trump card than the highest previously played on the same trick

overture *n* 1a an initiative towards agreement or action – often pl with sing. meaning b sthg introductory; a prelude 2a the orchestral introduction to a musical dramatic work b an orchestral concert piece written esp as a single movement

overturn *vt* 1 to cause to turn over; upset 2 to overthrow; BRING DOWN 1 ~ *vi* TURN OVER 1 – **overturn** *n*

overweening *adj* 1 arrogant, presumptuous 2 immoderate, exaggerated

¹**overweight** *n* weight above what is normal, average, or required

²**overweight** *vt* 1 to give too much weight or consideration to 2 to weight excessively 3 to exceed in weight

³**overweight** *adj* exceeding the expected, normal, or proper (bodily) weight

overwhelm *vt* 1 to cover over completely; submerge 2 to overcome by superior force or numbers 3 to overpower with emotion – **overwhelmingly** *adv*

overwork *vt* 1 to cause to work too hard or too long 2 to make excessive use of ~ *vi* to work too much or too long – **overwork** *n*

overwrought *adj* extremely excited; agitated

oviduct *n* the tube that serves for the passage of eggs from an ovary, esp before laying – **oviductal** *adj*

oviparous *adj* involving or producing eggs that develop and hatch outside the mother's body – **oviparously** *adv*, **oviparousness** *n*, **oviparity** *n*

ovoid, ovoidal *adj* shaped like an egg – **ovoid** *n*

ovulate *vi* to produce eggs or discharge them from an ovary – **ovulation** *n*, **ovulatory** *adj*

ovule *n* 1 an outgrowth of the ovary of a seed plant that develops into a seed after fertilization of the egg cell it contains 2 a small egg, esp one in an early stage of growth – **ovular** *adj*

ovum *n, pl* **ova** an animal's female gamete that when fertilized can develop into a new individual

ow *interj* – used esp to express sudden mild pain

owe *vt* 1a to be under obligation to pay or render b to be indebted to **2** to have or enjoy as a result of the action or existence of sthg or sby else ⟨~s *his fame to luck*⟩ ~ *vi* to be in debt

owing to *prep* BECAUSE OF 1 ⟨*delayed* ~ *a crash*⟩

owl *n* any of an order of chiefly nocturnal birds of prey with large head and eyes and a short hooked bill

owlet *n* a small or young owl

owlish *adj* having a round face or a wide-eyed stare – **owlishly** *adv*

¹own *adj* belonging to, for, or relating to oneself or itself – usu after a possessive pronoun ⟨*cooked his* ~ *dinner*⟩

²own *vt* **1** to have or hold as property; possess **2** to acknowledge, admit ~ *vi* to acknowledge sthg to be true or valid – + *to* – **owner** *n*, **ownership** *n*

³own *pron, pl* **own** one belonging to oneself or itself – usu after a possessive pronoun ⟨*a country with oil of its* ~⟩ – **on one's own 1** in solitude; alone ⟨*live on one's own*⟩ **2** without assistance or control

owner-occupier *n* sby who owns the house he/she lives in

own up *vi* to confess a fault frankly

ox *n, pl* **oxen** *also* **ox 1** a (domestic species of) bovine mammal **2** an adult castrated male domestic ox

ox-, oxo- *comb form* containing a carbonyl group in the molecular structure; ketone ⟨oxo*acetic acid*⟩

Oxbridge *adj or n* (of) the universities of Oxford and Cambridge

oxeye *n* any of several composite plants whose heads have both disc and ray flowers; *esp* OXEYE DAISY

oxeye daisy *n* a leafy-stemmed European composite plant with long white ray florets

Oxford movement *n* a Victorian High Church movement within the Church of England

oxide *n* a compound of oxygen with an element or radical – **oxidic** *adj*

oxidize, -ise *vt* **1** to combine with oxygen **2** to remove hydrogen or 1 or more electrons from (e g an atom, ion, or molecule) ~ *vi* to become oxidized – **oxidizable** *adj*, **oxidizer** *n*, **oxidation** *n*, **oxidative** *adj*

Oxonian *n* a student or graduate of Oxford University – **Oxonian** *adj*

oxtail *n* the tail of cattle (skinned and used for food, esp in soup)

oxyacetylene *adj* of or using a mixture of oxygen and acetylene, esp for producing a hot flame ⟨*an* ~ *torch*⟩

oxygen *n* a bivalent gaseous chemical element that forms about 21 per cent by volume of the atmosphere, is found combined in water, most minerals, and many organic compounds, is required for most burning processes, and is essential for the life of all plants and animals – **oxygenic** *adj*

oxygenate *vt* to impregnate, combine, or supply (e g blood) with oxygen – **oxygenator** *n*, **oxygenation** *n*

oxygen mask *n* a device worn over the nose and mouth through which oxygen is supplied from a storage tank

oxygen tent *n* a canopy placed over sby in bed to maintain a flow of oxygen-enriched air

oyez *vb imper* – uttered by a court official or public crier to gain attention

oyster *n* **1** any of various (edible) marine bivalve molluscs with a rough irregular·shell **2** a small mass of muscle on each side of the back of a fowl

oyster bed *n* a place where oysters grow or are cultivated

oystercatcher *n* any of a genus of usu black-and-white stout-legged wading birds

ozone *n* **1** a form of oxygen with 3 atoms in each molecule that is a bluish irritating gas with a pungent smell and occurs naturally in the upper atmosphere where it is formed by the action of ultraviolet solar radiation on normal oxygen **2** pure and refreshing air – **ozonous** *adj*, **ozonize** *vt*, **ozonic** *adj*, **ozoniferous** *adj*

p *n, pl* **p's, ps** *often cap* **1** (a graphic representation of or device for reproducing) the 16th letter of the English alphabet **2** a grade rating a student's work as passing

pa *n* father – *infml*

pabulum *n* **1** food **2** intellectual sustenance

¹pace *n* **1a** rate of movement **b** parallel rate of growth or development ⟨*wages do not keep* ~ *with inflation*⟩ **c** rate or manner of doing sthg **2** a manner of walking **3a** STEP 2a(1) **b** the distance covered by a single step in walking, usu taken to be about 0.75m (about 30in) **4a** GAIT 2; *esp* a fast 2-beat gait of a horse in which the legs move in lateral pairs **b** *pl* an exhibition of skills or abilities ⟨*put him through his* ~s⟩

²pace *vi* **1** to walk with a slow or measured tread **2** *esp of a horse* to go at a pace ~ *vt* **1a** to measure by pacing – often + *out* or *off* **b** to traverse at a walk **2** *of a horse* to cover (a course) by pacing **3** to set or regulate the pace of; *specif* to go ahead of (e g a runner) as a pacemaker – **pacer** *n*

³pace *prep* with due respect to

pace bowler *n* sby who bowls the ball fast and without spin in cricket

pacemaker *n* **1** sby or sthg that sets the pace for another (e g in a race) **2** (a device for applying regular electric shocks to the heart that reproduces the function of) a part of the heart that maintains rhythmic (coordinated) contractions – **pacemaking** *n*

pacesetter *n* PACEMAKER 1

pachyderm *n* an elephant, rhinoceros, pig, or other usu thick-skinned (hoofed) nonruminant mammal – **pachydermal** *adj*, **pachydermatous** *adj*

pacific *adj* **1** tending to bring about peace; conciliatory **2** having a mild peaceable nature **3** *cap* (of the region round) the Pacific ocean – **pacifically** *adv*

pacifism *n* opposition to war as a means of settling disputes; *specif* refusal to bear arms on moral or religious grounds – **pacifist** *n*

pacify *vt* **1** to allay the anger or agitation of **2a** to restore to a peaceful state; subdue **b** to reduce to submission – **pacifiable** *adj*, **pacifier** *n*, **pacification** *n*

¹pack *n* **1** a bundle or bag of things carried on the shoulders or back; *specif* a knapsack **2a** a large amount or number ⟨*a* ~ *of lies*⟩ **b** a full set of playing cards **3** a method of packing ⟨*vacuum* ~⟩ **4** *sing or pl in constr* **a** a group of people with a common characteristic ⟨*a* ~ *of thieves*⟩ **b** an organized troop (e g of cub scouts) **5** *sing or pl in constr* the forwards in a rugby team, esp when acting together **6** *sing or pl in constr* **a** a group of domesticated animals trained to hunt or run together ⟨*a* ~ *of hounds*⟩ **b** a group of (predatory) animals of the same kind ⟨*a wolf* ~⟩ **7** a concentrated mass; *specif* PACK ICE **8** wet absorbent material for application to the body as treatment (e g for a bruise) **9** *chiefly NAm* a packet

²pack *vt* **1a** to stow (as if) in a container, esp for transport or storage **b** to cover, fill, or surround with protective material **2a** to crowd together so as to fill; cram **b** to force into a smaller volume; compress **3** to bring to an end; finish – + *up* or *in* ⟨*he's* ~*ing up his job next year*⟩ **4** to gather into a pack **5** to cover or surround with a pack **6**

to cause or be capable of making (an impact) ⟨*a book that ~s quite a punch*⟩ ~ *vi* **1** to stow goods or equipment for transporting – often + *up* **2** to crowd together **3** to become compacted in a layer or mass – **packable** *adj*, **packer** *n*, **packability** *n* – **pack it in** to stop doing it; give it up – *infml*

³pack *vt* to influence the composition of (e g a jury) so as to bring about a desired result

¹package *n* **1a** a small or medium-sized pack; a parcel **b** sthg wrapped or sealed **2** a wrapper or container in which sthg is packed **3** PACKAGE DEAL

²package *vt* to make into or enclose in a package – **packager** *n*

package deal *n* an offer or agreement involving a number of related items and making acceptance of one item dependent on the acceptance of all; *also* the items so offered

packed *adj* **1a** that is crowded or stuffed – often in combination ⟨*an action*-packed *story*⟩ **b** compressed ⟨*hard*-packed *snow*⟩ **2** filled to capacity ⟨*played to a ~ house*⟩

packet *n* **1** a small pack or parcel ⟨*a ~ of biscuits*⟩ **2** a passenger boat carrying mail and cargo on a regular schedule **3** *Br* a large sum of money ⟨*cost a ~*⟩ – *infml*

pack ice *n* sea ice crushed together into a large floating mass

packing *n* **1** the action, process, or method of packing sthg **2** material used to pack

packing case *n* a usu wooden crate in which goods are packed for storage or transport

pack off *vt* to send away, esp abruptly or unceremoniously – *infml* ⟨pack *the kids* off *to school*⟩

packsaddle *n* a saddle designed to support a pack on an animal's back

pack up *vi* **1** to finish work **2** to cease to function ⟨*the engine* packed up⟩ *USE infml*

pact *n* an agreement, treaty

¹pad *n* **1** a thin flat mat or cushion: e g **a** a padding used to shape an article of clothing **b** a padded guard worn to shield body parts, esp the legs of a batsman, against impact **c** a piece of absorbent material used as a surgical dressing or protective covering **2a** the foot of an animal **b** the cushioned thickening of the underside of the toes of cats, dogs, etc **3** a large floating leaf of a water plant **4** a number of sheets of paper (e g for writing or drawing on) fastened together at 1 edge **5a** a flat surface for a vertical takeoff or landing **b** LAUNCHING PAD **6** living quarters – *infml*

²pad *vt* **-dd-** **1** to provide with a pad or padding **2** to expand or fill out (speech or writing) with superfluous matter – often + *out*

³pad *vb* **-dd-** *vt* to go along on foot ~ *vi* to walk with a muffled step

padding *n* material used to pad

¹paddle *n* **1a** a usu wooden implement similar to but smaller than an oar, used to propel and steer a small craft (e g a canoe) **b** an implement with a short handle and broad flat blade used for stirring, mixing, hitting, etc **2** any of the broad boards at the circumference of a paddle wheel or waterwheel

²paddle *vb* **paddling** *vi* to go on or through water (as if) by means of paddling a craft ~ *vt* to propel (as if) by a paddle – **paddler** *n*

³paddle *vi* to walk, play, or wade in shallow water – **paddle** *n*, **paddler** *n*

paddle steamer *n* a vessel propelled by a pair of paddle wheels mounted amidships or by a single paddle wheel at the stern

paddle wheel *n* a power-driven wheel with paddles, floats, or boards round its circumference used to propel a boat

paddock *n* **1** a small usu enclosed field, esp for pasturing or exercising animals; *esp* one where racehorses are saddled and paraded before a race **2** an area at a motor-racing track where cars, motorcycles, etc are parked and worked on before a race

paddy *n* **1** (threshed unmilled) rice **2** a paddyfield

Paddy *n* an Irishman – chiefly derog

padlock *n* a portable lock with a shackle that can be passed through a staple or link and then secured – **padlock** *vt*

padre *n* **1** a Christian priest **2** a military chaplain

paean *n* a joyously exultant song or hymn of praise, tribute, thanksgiving, or triumph

paediatrics *n pl but sing or pl in constr* medicine dealing with the development, care, and diseases of children – **paediatric** *adj*, **paediatrician** *n*

paella *n* a saffron-flavoured Spanish dish containing rice, meat, seafood, and vegetables

paeony *n* a peony

pagan *n* **1** a follower of a polytheistic religion **2** an irreligious person – **pagan** *adj*, **paganish** *adj*, **paganism** *n*, **paganize** *vt*

¹page *n* **1a(1)** a youth being trained for the medieval rank of knight and in the personal service of a knight **(2)** a youth attending on a person of rank **b** a boy serving as an honorary attendant at a formal function (e g a wedding) **2** sby employed to deliver messages or run errands

²page *vt* **1** to summon by repeatedly calling out the name of (e g over a public-address system) **2** to summon by a coded signal emitted esp by a short-range radio transmitter

³page *n* **1** (a single side of) a leaf of a book, magazine, etc **2** sthg worth being recorded in writing ⟨*the brightest ~ of her career*⟩ **3** a sizable subdivision of computer memory used chiefly for convenience of reference in programming

⁴page *vt* to paginate

pageant *n* **1** an ostentatious display **2** a show, exhibition; *esp* a colourful spectacle with a series of tableaux, dramatic presentations, or a procession, expressing a common theme **3** PAGEANTRY 1

pageantry *n* **1** pageants and the presentation of pageants **2** colourful or splendid display; spectacle

paginate *vt* to number the sides of the leaves of (e g a book) in a sequence – **pagination** *n*

pagoda *n* a many-storied usu polygonal tower with upturned projecting roofs at the division of each storey and erected esp as a temple or memorial in the Far East

paid *past of* PAY

paid-up *adj* having paid the necessary fees to be a full member of a group or organization; *broadly* showing the characteristic attitudes and behaviour of a specified group to a marked degree ⟨*a ~ member of the awkward squad*⟩

pail *n* (the contents of or quantity contained in) an esp wooden or metal bucket – **pailful** *n*

paillasse *n* a palliasse

¹pain *n* **1a** a basic bodily sensation induced by a noxious stimulus or physical disorder and characterized by physical discomfort (e g pricking, throbbing, or aching) **b** acute mental or emotional distress **2** *pl* the throes of childbirth **3** *pl* trouble or care taken **4** sby or sthg that annoys or is a nuisance – *infml* ⟨*she's a real ~*⟩ – **painless** *adj*, **painlessly** *adv*, **painlessness** *n* – **on/under pain of** subject to penalty or punishment of ⟨*ordered to leave the country* on pain of *death* – **pain in the neck** a source of annoyance; a nuisance – infml

²**pain** vt to make suffer or cause distress to; hurt ~ vi to give or have a sensation of pain

painful adj -ll- **1a** feeling or giving pain **b** irksome, annoying **2** requiring effort or exertion ⟨a long ~ trip⟩ – **painfully** adv, **painfulness** n

painkiller n sthg, esp a drug (e g morphine or aspirin), that relieves pain – **painkilling** adj

painstaking adj showing diligent care and effort – **painstakingly** adv

¹**paint** vt **1a** to apply colour, pigment, paint, or cosmetics to **b** to apply with a movement resembling that used in painting **2a** to represent in colours on a surface by applying pigments **b** to decorate by painting **c** to produce or evoke as if by painting ⟨her novel ~ s glowing pictures of rural life⟩ **3** to depict as having specified or implied characteristics ⟨not as black as he's ~ ed⟩ ~ vi to practise the art of painting

²**paint** n **1a(1)** a mixture of a pigment and a suitable liquid which forms a closely adherent coating when spread on a surface **(2)** pigment, esp in compressed form **b** an applied coat of paint ⟨wet ~⟩ **2** (coloured) make-up – infml – **painty** adj

paintbrush n a brush for applying paint

¹**painter** n **1** an artist who paints **2** sby who applies paint (e g to a building), esp as an occupation

²**painter** n a line used for securing or towing a boat

painting n **1** a product of painting; esp a painted work of art **2** the art or occupation of painting

paintwork n paint that has been applied to a surface; also a painted surface ⟨damaged the ~ of the car⟩

¹**pair** n sing or pl in constr, pl pairs also pair **1a(1)** two corresponding things usu used together ⟨a ~ of shoes⟩ **(2)** two corresponding bodily parts ⟨a beautiful ~ of legs⟩ **b** a single thing made up of 2 connected corresponding pieces ⟨a ~ of trousers⟩ **2a** two similar or associated things: e g **(1)** a couple in love, engaged, or married ⟨were a devoted ~⟩ **(2)** two playing cards of the same value in a hand **(3)** two horses harnessed side by side **(4)** two mated animals **b** a partnership between 2 people, esp in a contest against another partnership **c** two members from opposite sides of a deliberative body who agree not to vote on a specific issue during a time agreed on **d** a failure to score runs in either innings of a match by a batsman in cricket

²**pair** vt **1** to arrange a voting pair between **2** to arrange in pairs ⟨she succeeded in ~ing the socks⟩

pair off vb to (cause to) form pairs, esp male and female ⟨the anxious mothers are trying to pair off their children⟩ ⟨they paired off for the next dance⟩

paisley adj, often cap of a fabric or garment made usu of soft wool and woven or printed with colourful abstract teardrop-shaped figures – **paisley** n

pajamas n pl in constr, pl pajamas chiefly NAm pyjamas – **pajama** adj

Pakistani n **1** a native or inhabitant of Pakistan **2** a descendant of Pakistanis – **Pakistani** adj

pal n **1** a close friend **2** – used as a familiar form of address, esp to a stranger USE infml

¹**palace** n **1** the official residence of a ruler (e g a sovereign or bishop) **2a** a large stately house **b** a large public building **c** a large and often ornate place of entertainment ⟨a picture ~⟩

²**palace** adj **1** of a palace **2** of or involving the intimates of a chief executive ⟨a ~ revolution⟩ ⟨~ politics⟩

paladin n a champion of a medieval prince

palae-, palaeo-, chiefly Nam pale-, paleo- comb form **1** involving or dealing with ancient (e g fossil) forms or conditions ⟨palaeobotany⟩ **2** early; primitive; archaic ⟨Palaeolithic⟩

palaeography n the study of ancient writings and inscriptions – **palaeographer** n

Palaeolithic adj or n (of or being) the 2nd era of the Stone Age characterized by rough or chipped stone implements

palaeontology n a science dealing with the life of past geological periods as inferred from fossil remains – **palaeontologist** n, **palaeontological** adj

Palaeozoic adj or n (of or being) an era of geological history that extends from the beginning of the Cambrian to the close of the Permian

palais, palais de dance n a public dance hall – chiefly infml

palanquin n a litter formerly used in eastern Asia, esp for 1 person, and usu hung from poles borne on the bearers' shoulders

palatable adj **1** pleasant to the taste **2** acceptable to the mind – **palatableness** n, **palatably** adv, **palatability** n

palatal adj **1** of the palate **2** of a speech sound (e g /y/) formed with the front of the tongue near or touching the hard palate – **palatal** n, **palatalize** vt, **palatally** adv, **palatalization** n

palate n **1** the roof of the mouth, separating it from the nasal cavity **2a** the sense of taste **b** a usu intellectual taste or liking

palatial adj **1** of or being a palace **2** suitable to a palace; magnificent – **palatially** adv, **palatialness** n

palatinate n the territory of a palatine

palaver n **1** a long parley or discussion **2** idle talk – **palaver** vi

¹**pale** adj **1** deficient in (intensity of) colour **2** not bright or brilliant; dim ⟨a ~ sun shining through the fog⟩ **3** feeble, faint ⟨a ~ imitation⟩ **4** of a colour not intense ⟨a ~ pink⟩ – **pale** vb, **palish** adj, **palely** adv, **paleness** n

²**pale** n **1** PICKET 1 **2** a territory under a particular jurisdiction – **beyond the pale** in violation of good manners, social convention etc

pale-, paleo- comb form, chiefly NAm palae-, palaeo-

paleface n a white person, esp as distinguished from an American Indian

palette n **1** a thin board held in the hand on which an artist mixes pigments **2** a particular range, quality, or use of colour; esp that of an individual artist

palette knife n a knife with a flexible steel blade and no cutting edge, used esp in cooking or by artists for mixing and applying paints

palfrey n, archaic a saddle horse other than a war-horse, esp for a woman

palimpsest n writing material (e g a parchment or tablet) reused after earlier writing has been erased

palindrome n a word, sentence, etc that reads the same backwards or forwards – **palindromic** adj

paling n (a fence of) stakes or pickets

¹**palisade** n **1** a fence of stakes, esp for defence **2** a long strong stake pointed at the top and set close with others as a defence

²**palisade** vt to surround or fortify with palisades

¹**pall** n **1** PALLIUM 1b **2a** a square of linen used to cover the chalice containing the wine used at Communion **b** a heavy cloth draped over a coffin or tomb **3** sthg heavy or dark that covers or conceals ⟨a ~ of thick black smoke⟩

²**pall** vi to cease to be interesting or attractive

Palladian adj of a neoclassic style of architecture based on the works of Andrea Palladio – **Palladianism** n

pallbearer n a person who helps to carry the coffin at a funeral or is part of its immediate escort

¹pallet n 1 a straw-filled mattress 2 a small hard often makeshift bed

²pallet n 1 a flat-bladed wooden tool used esp by potters for shaping clay 2 a lever or surface in a timepiece that receives an impulse from the escapement wheel and imparts motion to a balance or pendulum 3 a portable platform intended for handling, storing, or moving materials and packages

palliasse, paillasse n a thin straw mattress

palliate vt 1 to lessen the unpleasantness of (e g a disease) without removing the cause 2 to disguise the gravity of (a fault or offence) by excuses or apologies; extenuate 3 to moderate the intensity of ⟨trying to ~ the boredom⟩ – **palliator** n, **palliative** n or adj, **palliation** n

pallid adj 1 lacking colour; wan 2 lacking sparkle or liveliness; dull – **pallidly** adv, **pallidness** n

pallium n, pl **pallia, palliums** 1a a draped rectangular cloth worn as a cloak, esp by men of ancient Rome b a white woollen band in the shape of 2 Y's that meet on the shoulders, worn esp by a pope or archbishop 2 the mantle of a mollusc, bird etc – **pallial** adj

pallor n deficiency of (facial) colour; paleness

pally adj friendly ⟨he was very ~ with the local vicar⟩ – infml

¹palm n 1 any of a family of tropical or subtropical trees, shrubs, or climbing plants related to the lilies, grasses, and orchids and usu having a simple stem and a crown of large leaves 2 a leaf of the palm as a symbol of victory, distinction, or rejoicing; also a branch (e g of laurel) similarly used 3 a symbol of triumph or distinction; also a victory, triumph – **palmlike** adj, **palmaceous** adj

²palm n 1 the concave part of the human hand between the bases of the fingers and the wrist 2 a unit of measurement based on the length (e g about 200mm or 8in) or breadth (e g about 100mm or 4in) of the human hand

³palm vt 1a to conceal in or with the hand b to pick up stealthily 2 to impose by fraud

palmer n a pilgrim wearing 2 crossed palm leaves as a sign of a visit to the Holy Land

palmetto n, pl **palmettos, palmettoes** any of several usu low-growing fan-leaved palms

palmistry n reading a person's character or future from the markings on his/her palms – **palmist** n

palm off vt to get rid of (sthg unwanted or inferior) by deceiving sby into taking it – often + on

palm oil n an edible fat obtained from the fruit of several palms and used esp in soap and candles

Palm Sunday n the Sunday before Easter celebrated in commemoration of Christ's triumphal entry into Jerusalem

palmy adj marked by prosperity; flourishing ⟨~ days⟩

palomino n, pl **palominos** a light tan or cream usu slender-legged horse

palpable adj 1 capable of being touched or felt; tangible 2 easily perceptible by the mind; manifest ⟨a ~ falsehood⟩ – **palpably** adv, **palpability** n

palpate vt to examine, esp medically, by touch – **palpation** n

palpitate vi to beat rapidly and strongly; throb ⟨a palpitating heart⟩ – **palpitation** n

¹palsy n paralysis or uncontrollable tremor of (a part of) the body

²palsy vt to affect (as if) with palsy

palter vi 1 to act insincerely or deceitfully; equivocate 2 to haggle – + with – **palterer** n

paltry adj 1 mean, despicable ⟨a ~ trick⟩ 2 trivial ⟨a ~ sum⟩ – **paltriness** n

pampa n an extensive (grass-covered) plain of temperate S America east of the Andes – usu pl with sing. meaning but sing. or pl in constr

pampas grass n a tall S American grass with large silky flower heads frequently cultivated as an ornamental plant

pamper vt to treat with extreme or excessive care and attention ⟨~ed their guests⟩

pamphlet n a usu small unbound printed publication with a paper cover, often dealing with topical matters ⟨a ~ on nuclear disarmament⟩

pamphleteer n a writer of (political) pamphlets attacking sthg or urging a cause

¹pan n 1a any of various usu broad shallow open receptacles: e g (1) WARMING PAN (2) a dustpan (3) a bedpan (4) a metal or plastic dish in a pair of scales (5) a round metal container or vessel usu with a long handle, used to heat or cook food b any of various similar usu metal receptacles: e g (1) the hollow part of the gunlock in old guns or pistols for receiving the priming (2) a vessel in which gold or a similar metal is separated from waste by washing 2 a hollow or depression in land ⟨a salt ~⟩ 3 hardpan 4a chiefly Br the bowl of a toilet b chiefly NAm TIN 2b

²pan vb -nn- vi 1 to wash earth, gravel, etc in a pan in search of metal (e g gold) 2 to yield precious metal in panning – vt 1a to wash (earth, gravel, etc) in a pan b to separate (e g gold) by panning 2 to criticize severely – infml

³pan n (a substance for chewing consisting of betel nut and various spices etc wrapped in) a betel leaf

⁴pan vb -nn- vi 1 to rotate a film or television camera horizontally so as to keep a moving object in view or obtain a panoramic effect ⟨a camera⟩ to undergo panning – vt to cause (a camera) to pan

⁵pan n the act or process of panning a camera; the movement of the camera in a panning shot

pan- comb form 1 all; completely ⟨panchromatic⟩ 2a of all of (a specified group) ⟨Pan-American⟩ b advocating or involving the union of (a specified group) ⟨Pan-Asian⟩ 3 whole; general ⟨pandemic⟩

panacea n a remedy for all ills or difficulties – **panacean** adj

panache n 1 an ornamental tuft (e g of feathers), esp on a helmet 2 dash or flamboyance in style and action; verve

panama n, often cap a lightweight hat of plaited straw

panatela, panatella n a long slender straight-sided cigar rounded off at the sealed mouth end

pancake n 1 a flat cake made from thin batter and cooked on both sides usu in a frying pan 2 make-up compressed into a flat cake or stick form

Pancake Day n Shrove Tuesday as marked by the eating of pancakes

pancake landing n a landing in which an aircraft descends in an approximately horizontal position with little forward motion

panchromatic adj sensitive to light of all colours in the visible spectrum ⟨~ film⟩

pancreas n a large compound gland in vertebrates that secretes digestive enzymes into the intestines and the hormones insulin and glucagon into the blood – **pancreatic** adj

panda n 1 a long-tailed Himalayan flesh-eating mammal resembling the American raccoon and having long chestnut fur spotted with black 2 a large black-and-white plant-eating mammal of western China resembling a bear but related to the raccoons

panda car n, Br a small car used by police patrols, esp in urban areas

pandemic *n or adj* (a disease) occurring over a wide area and affecting an exceptionally high proportion of the population

pandemonium *n* a wild uproar; a tumult

¹pander *n* **1** a pimp **2** sby who encourages or exploits the weaknesses or vices of others

²pander *vi* to act as a pander; *esp* to provide gratification for others' desires – usu + *to*

pandit *n* a wise or learned man in India – often used as an honorary title

pane *n* **1** a piece, section, or side of sthg; *esp* a framed sheet of glass in a window or door **2** any of the sections into which a sheet of postage stamps is cut for distribution

panegyric *n* a eulogistic oration or piece of writing; *also* formal or elaborate praise – **panegyrical** *adj*, **panegyrically** *adv*, **panegyrist** *n*

¹panel *n* **1a**(1) a list of people summoned for jury service (2) the jury so summoned **b**(1) a group of people selected to perform some service (e g investigation or arbitration) ⟨*a* ~ *of experts*⟩ (2) a group of people who discuss before an audience topics of usu political or social interest (3) a group of entertainers who appear as contestants in a quiz or guessing game on radio or television **2** a separate or distinct part of a surface: e g **a**(1) a thin usu rectangular board set in a frame (e g in a door) (2) a usu sunken or raised section of a surface set off by a margin **b** a vertical section of fabric ⟨*skirt made with 8* ~ s⟩ **3** a thin flat piece of wood on which a picture is painted **4a** a flat often insulated support (e g for parts of an electrical device) usu with controls on 1 face **b** a usu vertical mount for controls or dials (e g in a car or aircraft) *USE* (1a(2) & 1b) sing. or pl in constr

²panel *vt* **-ll-** (*NAm* **-l-, -ll-**), to furnish or decorate with panels ⟨~ led *the living room*⟩

panellist *n* a member of a discussion or advisory panel or of a radio or television panel

pang *n* **1** a brief piercing spasm of pain **2** a sharp attack of mental anguish ⟨~ s *of remorse*⟩

panhandle *vb, NAm* to beg (from) in the street *USE* – *infml* – **panhandler** *n*

¹panic *n* **1** a sudden overpowering fright; *esp* a sudden unreasoning terror that spreads rapidly through a group **2** a sudden widespread fright concerning financial affairs and resulting in a depression in values – **panic** *adj*, **panicky** *adj*

²panic *vb* **-ck-** to (cause to) be affected with panic

panic-stricken *adj* overcome with panic

Panjabi *n or adj* (a) Punjabi

panjandrum *n, pl* **panjandrums** *also* **panjandra** a powerful personage or self-important official – *humor*

pannier, panier *n* **1** a large basket; *esp* either of a pair carried on the back of an animal **2** a hoop petticoat or overskirt that gives extra width to the sides of a skirt at hip level **3** *chiefly Br* either of a pair of bags or boxes fixed on either side of the rear wheel of a bicycle or motorcycle

panoply *n* **1a** a full suit of armour **b** ceremonial dress **2** a magnificent or impressive array ⟨*the full* ~ *of a military funeral*⟩ – **panoplied** *adj*

panorama *n* **1a** a large pictorial representation encircling the spectator **b** a picture exhibited by being unrolled before the spectator **2a** an unobstructed or complete view of a landscape or area **b** a comprehensive presentation or survey of a series of events – **panoramic** *adj*, **panoramically** *adv*

pan out *vi* to turn out as specified; *esp* to succeed

panpipe *n* a primitive wind instrument consisting of a graduated series of short vertical pipes bound together with the mouthpieces in an even row – often pl with sing. meaning

pansy *n* **1** (a flower of) a garden plant derived from wild violets **2** an effeminate male or male homosexual – *derog*

¹pant *vi* **1a** to breathe quickly, spasmodically, or in a laboured manner **b** to run panting ⟨~ ing *along beside the bicycle*⟩ **c** to make a puffing sound **2** to long eagerly; yearn **3** to throb, pulsate ~ *vt* to utter with panting; gasp ⟨~ ed *his apologies for arriving so late*⟩

²pant *n* **1** a panting breath **2** a puffing sound

pant-, panto- *comb form* all ⟨*pantisocracy*⟩

pantaloon *n* **1** a stock character in the commedia dell'arte who is usu a skinny old dotard wearing pantaloons **2** *pl* any of several kinds of men's breeches or trousers; *esp* close-fitting trousers fastened under the calf or instep and worn in the 18th and 19th c

pantechnicon *n, Br* a large van, esp for transporting household possessions, furniture, etc

pantheism *n* **1** a doctrine that equates God with the forces and laws of nature **2** the indiscriminate worship of all the gods of different religions and cults; *also* toleration of such worship (e g at certain periods of the Roman empire) – **pantheist** *n*, **pantheistic, pantheistical** *adj*, **pantheistically** *adv*

pantheon *n* **1** a building serving as the burial place of or containing memorials to famous dead **2** the gods of a people; *esp* the officially recognized gods

panther *n, pl* **panthers** *also esp collectively* **panther 1** a leopard, esp of the black colour phase **2** *NAm* a puma

panties *n pl* pants for women or children; *also* knickers

pantile *n* a roofing tile whose transverse section is a flattened S-shape – **pantiled** *adj*

panto *n, Br* PANTOMIME 1b – *infml*

pantograph *n* **1** an instrument for copying sthg (e g a map) on a predetermined scale consisting of 4 light rigid bars jointed in parallelogram form; *also* any of various extensible devices of similar construction **2** a collapsible and adjustable framework mounted on an electric vehicle (e g a railway locomotive) for collecting current from an overhead wire – **pantographic** *adj*

pantomime *n* **1a** any of various dramatic or dancing performances in which a story is told by bodily or facial movements **b** a British theatrical and musical entertainment of the Christmas season based on a nursery tale with stock roles and topical jokes **2** conveyance of a story by bodily or facial movements, esp in drama or dance – **pantomimic** *adj*

pantry *n* **1** a room or cupboard used for storing provisions or tableware **2** a room (e g in a hotel or hospital) for preparation of cold foods to order

pants *n pl* **1** *chiefly Br* an undergarment that covers the crotch and hips and that may extend to the waist and partly down each leg **2** *chiefly NAm* trousers

panty hose *n pl, chiefly NAm* tights

¹panzer *adj* of, carried out by, or being a (WW II German) armoured unit

²panzer *n* TANK 2; *esp* a German tank of WW II

¹pap *n, chiefly dial* a nipple, teat

²pap *n* **1** a soft food for infants or invalids **2** sthg lacking solid value or substance

¹papa *n, chiefly Br* father – formerly used formally, esp in address

²papa *n* daddy – used informally and by children

papacy *n* **1** the (term of) office of pope **2** *cap* the system of government of the Roman Catholic church of which the pope is the supreme head

papal *adj* of a pope or the Roman Catholic church –
papally *adv*
papaw *n* 1 papaya 2 (a N American tree that bears
purple flowers and) a yellow edible fruit
papaya *n* (a tropical American tree that bears) a large
oblong yellow edible fruit
¹**paper** *n* 1a a sheet of closely compacted vegetable fibres
(e g of wood or cloth) b a piece of paper 2a a piece of
paper containing a written or printed statement; a document ⟨*naturalization* ~s⟩; *specif* a document carried as
proof of identity or status – often pl b a piece of paper
containing writing or print c a formal written composition d the question set or answers written in an examination in 1 subject 3 a paper container or wrapper ⟨*a sweet*
~⟩ 4 a newspaper 5 the negotiable notes or instruments
of commerce 6 wallpaper – **on paper** in theory; hypothetically
²**paper** *vt* 1 to cover or line with paper; *esp* to apply
wallpaper to 2 to give out free tickets for ⟨~ *the theatre
for the opening night*⟩ ~ *vi* to hang wallpaper –
paperer *n*
³**paper** *adj* 1a made of paper, thin cardboard, or
papier-mâché b papery 2 of clerical work or written
communication 3 existing only in theory; nominal 4
issued as paper money 5 finished with a crisp smooth
surface like that of paper ⟨~ *taffeta*⟩
paperback *n* a book with a flexible paper binding –
paperback *adj*
paperboy, *fem* **papergirl** *n* a boy who delivers or sells
newspapers
paper chase *n* a game in which some of the players
scatter bits of paper as a trail which others follow to find
and catch them
paper clip *n* a small clip made from 2 loops of wire, used
for holding sheets of paper together
paperhanger *n* sby who applies wallpaper to walls
paper knife *n* a knife for slitting envelopes or uncut
pages
paper money *n* bank notes
paper nautilus *n* a mollusc related to the octopuses and
squids, the female of which has a delicate papery shell
paper over *vt* 1 to gloss over, explain away, or patch up
(e g major differences), esp in order to maintain a semblance of unity 2 to hide, conceal
paperweight *n* a usu small heavy object used to hold
down loose papers (e g on a desk)
paperwork *n* routine clerical or record-keeping work,
often incidental to a more important task
papery *adj* resembling paper in thinness or consistency
⟨~ *leaves*⟩⟨~ *silk*⟩ – **paperiness** *n*
papier-mâché *n* a light strong moulding material made
of paper pulped with glue that is used for making boxes,
trays, etc – **papier-mâché** *adj*
papist *n, often cap* a Roman Catholic – chiefly derog –
papist *adj*, **papistry** *n*
papoose *n* a young N American Indian child
paprika *n* (a mild to hot red condiment consisting of the
finely ground dried pods of) any of various cultivated
sweet peppers
papyrus *n, pl* **papyruses, papyri** 1 a tall sedge of the Nile
valley 2 the pith of the papyrus plant, esp when made into
a material for writing on 3 a usu ancient manuscript
written on papyrus
par *n* 1a the established value of the monetary unit of one
country expressed in terms of the monetary unit of
another country b the money value assigned to each share
of stock in the charter of a company 2 a common level;
equality – esp in **on a par with** 3a an amount taken as an
average or norm b an accepted standard; *specif* a usual

standard of physical condition or health 4 the standard
score (of a good player) for each hole of a golf course –
par *adj*
para *n, pl* **paras** a paratrooper
¹**para-, par-** *prefix* 1a beside; alongside
⟨para*thyroid*⟩ ⟨par*allel*⟩ b beyond ⟨para-
normal⟩ ⟨para*dox*⟩ 2 involving substitution at 2
opposite positions in the benzene ring that are separated
by 2 carbon atoms ⟨para*dichlorobenzene*⟩ 3a faulty;
abnormal ⟨para*esthesia*⟩ ⟨para*noia*⟩ b associated in a
subsidiary or auxiliary capacity ⟨para*medical*⟩ c closely
resembling or related to ⟨para*typhoid*⟩
²**para-** *comb form* parachute ⟨para*trooper*⟩
-para *comb form* (→ *n*), *pl* **-paras, -parae** woman delivered
of (so many) children ⟨*tripara*⟩
parable *n* a usu short allegorical story illustrating a moral
or religious principle
parabola *n* a plane curve generated by a point moving so
that its distance from a fixed point is equal to its distance
from a fixed line; the intersection of a right circular cone
with a plane parallel to a straight line in the surface of the
cone
¹**parachute** *n* a folding device of light fabric used esp for
ensuring a safe descent of a person or object from a great
height (e g from a aeroplane) – **parachutist** *n*
²**parachute** *vi* to descend by means of a parachute
Paraclete *n* HOLY SPIRIT
¹**parade** *n* 1 an ostentatious show; an exhibition ⟨*made a
~ of his superior knowledge*⟩ 2 the (ceremonial) ordered
assembly of a body of troops before a superior officer 3
a public procession 4 *chiefly Br* a row of shops, esp with
a service road
²**parade** *vt* 1 to cause to manoeuvre or march 2 to exhibit
ostentatiously ~ *vi* 1 to march in a procession 2 to
promenade 3a SHOW OFF b to masquerade ⟨*myths which
~ as modern science* – M R Cohen⟩ – **parader** *n*
paradigm *n* 1 an example or pattern 2 an example of a
conjugation or declension showing a word in all its inflectional forms – **paradigmatic** *adj*
paradise *n* 1 *often cap* a the garden of Eden b Heaven
2 a place of bliss, felicity, or delight – **paradisiacal** *adj*
paradox *n* 1 a tenet contrary to received opinion 2a a
statement that is apparently contradictory or absurd and
yet might be true b a self-contradictory statement that at
first seems true 3 sthg (e g a person, condition, or act)
with seemingly contradictory qualities or phases
paraffin *n* 1 a usu waxy inflammable mixture of hydrocarbons obtained from distillates of wood, coal,
petroleum, etc and used chiefly in candles, chemical
synthesis, and cosmetics 2 an alkane 3 an inflammable
liquid hydrocarbon obtained by distillation of petroleum
and used esp as a fuel – **paraffinic** *adj*
paragon *n* a model of excellence or perfection
paragraph *n* 1a a usu indented division of a written
composition that develops a single point or idea b a
composition or news item that is complete in 1 paragraph
2 a sign (e g ¶) used as a reference mark or to indicate
the beginning of a paragraph – **paragraph** *vt*, **paragraphic**
adj
parakeet, *NAm also* **parrakeet** *n* any of numerous usu
small slender long-tailed parrots
¹**parallel** *adj* 1a extending in the same direction, everywhere equidistant, and not meeting ⟨~ *rows of trees*⟩ b
everywhere equally distant ⟨*concentric spheres are* ~⟩ 2
being or relating to an electrical circuit having a number
of conductors in parallel 3 analogous, comparable
²**parallel** *n* 1a a parallel line, curve, or surface b a circle
or line of latitude on (a globe or map of) the earth c a sign
used as a reference mark – often pl with sing. meaning

2 sby or sthg equal or similar in all essential particulars; a counterpart, analogue 3 a comparison to show resemblance ⟨drew a ~ between the 2 states⟩ 4a the state of being physically parallel b the arrangement of 2-terminal electrical devices in which one terminal of each device is joined to one conductor and the others are joined to another conductor

³**parallel** vt 1 to compare 2a to equal, match ⟨no one has ~ed my success in business⟩ b to correspond to

⁴**parallel** adv in a parallel manner

parallel bars n pl but sing or pl in constr (a men's gymnastic event using) a pair of bars supported horizontally 1.7m (5ft 7in) above the floor usu by a common base

parallelism n 1 the quality or state of being parallel 2 a resemblance, correspondence

parallelogram n a quadrilateral with opposite sides parallel and equal

paralysis n, pl **paralyses** 1 (partial) loss of function, esp when involving motion or sensation in a part of the body 2 loss of the ability to move 3 a state of powerlessness or incapacity to act – **paralyse**, NAm **paralyze** vt, **paralysation** n

¹**paralytic** adj 1 of, resembling, or affected with paralysis 2 chiefly Br very drunk – infml

²**paralytic** n one suffering from paralysis

parameter n 1 an arbitrary constant whose value characterizes a member of a system (e g a family of curves) 2 a characteristic, factor ⟨political dissent as a ~ of modern life⟩ – **parametric** also **parametrical** adj, **parametrically** adv

paramilitary adj formed on a military pattern (as a potential auxiliary military force) ⟨a ~ border patrol⟩

paramount adj superior to all others; supreme

paramour n an illicit lover; esp a mistress

paranoia n 1 a mental disorder characterized by delusions of persecution or grandeur 2 a tendency towards excessive or irrational suspiciousness and distrustfulness of others – **paranoiac** adj or n, **paranoid** adj or n

parapet n 1 a wall, rampart, or elevation of earth or stone to protect soldiers 2 a low wall or balustrade to protect the edge of a platform, roof, or bridge – **parapeted** adj

paraphernalia n pl but sing or pl in constr 1 personal belongings 2a articles of equipment b accessory items

¹**paraphrase** n a restatement of a text, passage, or work giving the meaning in another form

²**paraphrase** vb to make a paraphrase (of) – **paraphrasable** adj, **paraphraser** n

paraplegia n paralysis of the lower half of the body including the legs – **paraplegic** adj or n

paraquat n a very poisonous herbicide used esp as a weedkiller

parasite n 1 an organism living in or on another organism in parasitism 2 sthg resembling a biological parasite in dependence on sthg else for existence or support without making a useful or adequate return – **parasitic** also **parasitical** adj, **parasitically** adv, **parasitology** n, **parasitologist** n

parasitism n an intimate association between organisms of 2 or more kinds in which a parasite benefits at the expense of a host – **parasitize** vt

parasol n a lightweight umbrella used, esp by women, as a protection from the sun

parathyroid, **parathyroid gland** n any of 4 small endocrine glands near the thyroid gland that produce a hormone – **parathyroid** adj

paratroops n pl troops trained and equipped to parachute from an aeroplane – **paratrooper** n

paratyphoid n a disease caused by salmonella that resembles typhoid fever and is commonly contracted by eating contaminated food – **paratyphoid** adj

parboil vt to boil briefly as a preliminary or incomplete cooking procedure

¹**parcel** n 1 a plot of land 2 ¹PACK 2a 3 a wrapped bundle; a package

²**parcel** vt -ll- (NAm -l-, -ll-), 1 to divide into parts; distribute – often + out 2 to make up into a parcel; wrap – often + up 3 to cover (e g a rope) with strips of canvas

parch vt 1 to roast (e g peas) slightly in a dry heat 2 to make dry or scorched ~vi to become dry or scorched

parchment n 1 the skin of an animal, esp of a sheep or goat, prepared for writing on 2 strong paper made to resemble parchment 3 a parchment manuscript

pard n, archaic a leopard

¹**pardon** n 1 INDULGENCE 1 2 a release from legal penalties 3 excuse or forgiveness for a fault, offence, or discourtesy

²**pardon** vt 1 to absolve from the consequences of a fault or crime 2 to allow (an offence) to pass without punishment – **pardonable** adj, **pardonably** adv

pardoner n a medieval preacher delegated to raise money by granting indulgences

pare vt 1 to cut or shave off a (an outer surface) ⟨~ the skin from an apple⟩ b the outer surface of ⟨~ an apple⟩ 2 to diminish gradually (as if) by paring ⟨~ expenses⟩ – **parer** n

¹**parent** n 1 sby who begets or brings forth offspring; a father or mother 2a an animal or plant regarded in relation to its offspring b the material or source from which sthg is derived – **parent** adj, **parenthood** n, **parental** adj, **parentally** adv

²**parent** vt to be or act as the parent of; originate, produce

parentage n descent from parents or ancestors; lineage ⟨a woman of noble ~⟩

parenthesis n, pl **parentheses** 1a an amplifying or explanatory word or phrase inserted in a passage from which, in writing, it is usu set off by punctuation b either or both of the curved marks (or) used in writing and printing to enclose a parenthesis or to group a symbolic unit in a logical or mathematical expression 2 an interlude, interval – **parenthetic**, **parenthetical** adj, **parenthetically** adv

parent-teacher association n sing or pl in constr an organization of teachers at a school and the parents of their pupils, that works for the improvement of the school

par excellence adj being the best example of a kind; without equal – used postpositively ⟨the dictionary ~⟩

parhelion n, pl **parhelia** any one of several bright spots that often appear on the parhelic circle – **parhelic** adj

pariah n 1 a member of a low caste of S India and Burma 2 an outcast

pari-mutuel n 1 a betting pool in which those who bet on the winners of the first 3 places share the total amount bet, minus a percentage for the management 2 NAm a totalizator

paring n 1 the act of cutting away an edge or surface 2 sthg pared off ⟨apple ~s⟩

parish n 1 the subdivision of a diocese served by a single church or clergyman 2 a unit of local government in rural England, often coinciding with an original ecclesiastical parish

parishioner n a member or inhabitant of a parish

¹**parity** n 1 the quality or state of being equal or equivalent 2 equivalence of a commodity price expressed in one currency to its price expressed in another 3a the property

of an integer with respect to being odd or even ⟨*3 and 7 have the same ~*⟩ **b** the state of being odd or even that is the basis of a method of detecting errors in binary-coded data **4** the property whereby a quantity (e g the charge of an elementary particle) changes from positive to negative or vice versa or remains unaltered during a particular interaction or reaction

²**parity** *n* the state or fact of having borne offspring; *also* the number of children previously borne

¹**park** *n* **1** an enclosed area of lawns, woodland, pasture, etc attached to a country house and used as a game reserve or for recreation **2a** an area of land for recreation in or near a city or town **b** an area maintained in its natural state as a public property **3** an assigned space for military animals, vehicles, or materials **4a** *Br* a pitch where professional soccer is played **b** *NAm* an arena or stadium used for ball games

²**park** *vt* **1a** to leave or place (a vehicle) for a time, esp at the roadside or in a car park or garage **b** to land or leave (e g an aeroplane) **c** to establish (e g a satellite) in orbit **2** to assemble (e g equipment or stores) in a military dump or park **3** to set and leave temporarily – *infml* ⟨*~ed her boyfriend at the bar*⟩ to park a vehicle – **parker** *n*

parka *n* **1** a hooded fur garment for wearing in the arctic **2** an anorak

parkin *n* a thick heavy ginger cake made with oatmeal and treacle

parking lot *n, NAm* an outdoor car park

parking meter *n* a coin-operated device which registers the payment and displays the time allowed for parking a motor vehicle

Parkinson's disease *n* tremor, weakness of resting muscles, and a peculiar gait occurring in later life as a progressive nervous disease – **parkinsonian** *adj*

Parkinson's Law *n* an observation in office organization: work expands so as to fill the time available for its completion

parkland *n* land with clumps of trees and shrubs in cultivated condition suitable for use as a park

parky *adj, Br* CHILLY **1** – *infml*

parlance *n* manner of speech and esp choice of words ⟨*in legal ~*⟩

¹**parley** *vi* to speak with another; confer; *specif* to discuss terms with an enemy

²**parley** *n* a conference for discussion of points in dispute; *specif* a conference under truce to discuss terms with an enemy

parliament *n* **1** a formal conference for the discussion of public affairs **2** *often cap* the supreme legislative body of the UK that consists of the House of Commons and the House of Lords and is called together and dissolved by the sovereign; *also* a similar body in another nation or state

parliamentarian *n* **1** *often cap* an adherent of the parliament during the Civil War **2** an expert in parliamentary rules and practice **3** *Br* a Member of Parliament

parliamentary *adj* **1** of, appropriate to, or enacted by a parliament **2** of or supporting the parliament during the Civil War

¹**parlour**, *NAm* **parlor** *n* **1a** a room in a private house for the entertainment of guests **b** a room in an inn, hotel, or club for conversation or semiprivate uses **2** any of various business places ⟨*a funeral ~*⟩ ⟨*a beauty ~*⟩ **3** a place for milking cows

²**parlour** *adj* fostered or advocated in comfortable seclusion without consequent action or application to affairs

parlour game *n* an indoor word game, board game, etc

parlous *adj* full of uncertainty and danger – *fml* or *humor*

Parmesan *n* a very hard dry strongly flavoured cheese that is often used grated

parochial *adj* **1** of a (church) parish **2** limited in range or scope (e g to a narrow area or region); provincial, narrow – **parochially** *adv*

¹**parody** *n* **1** a literary or musical work in which the style of an author is imitated for comic or satirical effect **2** a feeble or ridiculous imitation – **parodic** *adj*, **parodist** *n*

²**parody** *vt* to compose a parody on ⟨*~ a poem*⟩

¹**parole** *n* **1** a pledge of one's honour; *esp* the promise of a prisoner of war to fulfil stated conditions in consideration of release or the granting of privileges **2** a password given only to officers of the guard and of the day **3** a conditional release of a prisoner **4** linguistic behaviour

²**parole** *vt* to put on parole – **parolee** *n*

paroxysm *n* **1** a fit, attack, or sudden increase or recurrence of (disease) symptoms; a convulsion ⟨*a ~ of coughing*⟩ **2** a sudden violent emotion or action ⟨*a ~ of rage*⟩ – **paroxysmal** *adj*

¹**parquet** *vt* **parqueted; parqueting** to furnish with a floor of parquetry

²**parquet** *n* parquetry

parquetry *n* work in the form of usu geometrically patterned wood laid or inlaid esp for floors

parr *n, pl* **parr** *also* **parrs** a young salmon actively feeding in fresh water

parricide *n* (the act of) sby who murders his/her father, mother, or a close relative – **parricidal** *adj*

¹**parrot** *n* **1** any of numerous chiefly tropical birds that have a distinctive stout hooked bill, are often crested and brightly variegated, and are excellent mimics **2** a person who parrots another's words

²**parrot** *vt* to repeat or imitate (e g another's words) without understanding or thought

parry *vi* to ward off a weapon or blow ~ *vt* **1** to ward off (e g a blow) **2** to evade, esp by an adroit answer ⟨*~ an embarrassing question*⟩ – **parry** *n*

parse *vt* **1** to resolve (e g a sentence) into component parts of speech and describe them grammatically **2** to describe grammatically by stating the part of speech and the inflectional and syntactic relationships

Parsi, Parsee *n* a Zoroastrian descended from Persian refugees settled principally in Bombay

parsimonious *adj* frugal to the point of stinginess; niggardly – **parsimoniously** *adv*

parsimony *n* **1** the quality of being careful with money or resources; thrift **2** the quality or state of being niggardly; stinginess

parsley *n* an orig S European plant of the carrot family widely cultivated for its leaves used as a herb or garnish in cooking

parsnip *n* (the long edible tapering root of) a European plant of the carrot family with large leaves and yellow flowers

parson *n* **1** the incumbent of a parish **2** a clergyman

parsonage *n* the house provided by a church for its parson

parson's nose *n* the fatty extension of the rump of a cooked fowl

¹**part** *n* **1a(1)** any of the often indefinite or unequal subdivisions into which sthg is (regarded as) divided and which together constitute the whole **(2)** an essential portion or integral element **b** an amount equal to another amount ⟨*mix 1 ~ of the powder with 3 ~s of water*⟩ **c(1)** an organ, member, or other constituent element of a plant or animal body **(2)** *pl* PRIVATE PARTS **d** a division of a literary work **e(1)** a vocal or instrumental line or melody in

concerted music or in harmony (2) (the score for) a particular voice or instrument in concerted music **f** a constituent member of an apparatus (e g a machine); *also* SPARE PART **2** sthg falling to one in a division or apportionment; a share **3** any of the opposing sides in a conflict or dispute ⟨*took his son's ∼ in the argument*⟩ **4** a portion of an unspecified territorial area ⟨*took off for unknown ∼s*⟩ **5** a function or course of action performed ⟨*the government's ∼ in the strike*⟩⟨*did you take ∼ in the fighting?*⟩ **6a** an actor's lines in a play **b** ROLE 1b **7** a constituent of character or capacity; a talent ⟨*a man of many ∼s*⟩ **8** NAm ¹PARTING 2 **– for the most part** in most cases or respects; mainly **– in part** in some degree; partly **– on the part of** with regard to the one specified

²**part** *vi* **1a** to separate from or take leave of sby **b** to take leave of one another **2** to become separated into parts ⟨*the clouds ∼ed and the sun appeared*⟩ **3** to become separated, detached, or broken ⟨*the strands of the rope ∼ed*⟩ **4** to relinquish possession or control, esp reluctantly ⟨*hated to ∼ with her money*⟩ ∼ *vt* **1a** to divide into parts **b** to separate (the hair) by combing on each side of a line **2a** to remove from contact or association; separate ⟨*till death do us ∼*⟩ **b** to hold (e g combatants) apart

³**part** *adv* partly ⟨*a centaur is ∼ man ∼ horse*⟩

⁴**part** *adj* PARTIAL 3

partake *vi* partook; partaken to take a part or share; participate – usu + *in* or *of*; fml **– partaker** *n*

parterre *n* an ornamental garden with paths between the beds

parthenogenesis *n* reproduction by development of an unfertilized gamete that occurs esp among lower plants and invertebrate animals **– parthenogenetic** *adj*

¹**partial** *adj* **1** inclined to favour one party more than the other; biased **2** markedly fond of sby or sthg – + *to* ⟨*∼ to beans*⟩ **3** of a part rather than the whole; not general or total ⟨*a ∼ solution*⟩ **– partially** *adv*

²**partial** *n* OVERTONE 1a

partiality *n* **1** the quality or state of being partial; a bias **2** a special taste or liking

participate *vi* **1** TAKE PART **2** to have a part or share in sthg **– participator** *n*, **participant** *n*, **participation** *n*, **participatory** *adj*

participle *n* a verbal form (e g *singing* or *sung*) that has the function of an adjective and at the same time can be used in compound verb forms **– participial** *adj*

particle *n* **1** a minute subdivision of matter (e g an electron, atom or molecule) **2** a minute quantity or fragment **3a** a minor unit of speech including all uninflected words or all words except nouns and verbs; *esp* FUNCTION WORD **b** AFFIX 1

parti-coloured *adj* showing different colours or tints ⟨*∼ threads*⟩

¹**particular** *adj* **1** of or being a single person or thing; specific ⟨*the ∼ person I had in mind*⟩ **2** detailed, exact **3** worthy of notice; special, unusual ⟨*there was nothing in the letter of ∼ importance*⟩ **4** *of a proposition in logic* predicating a term of some but not all members of a specified class **5a** concerned over or attentive to details; meticulous **b** hard to please; exacting **– particularity** *n*

²**particular** *n* an individual fact, point, circumstance, or detail ⟨*complete in every ∼*⟩ **– in particular** particularly, especially

particularize, -ise *vt* to state in detail; specify ∼ *vi* to go into details **– particularization** *n*

particularly *adv* **1** in a particular manner; IN DETAIL **2** to an unusual degree

¹**parting** *n* **1** a place or point where a division or separation occurs **2 parting**, *NAm* **part** the line where the hair is parted

²**parting** *adj* given, taken, or performed at parting ⟨*a ∼ kiss*⟩

¹**partisan, partizan** *n* **1** a firm adherent to a party, faction, cause, or person; *esp* one exhibiting blind, prejudiced, and unreasoning allegiance **2** a guerrilla **– partisan** *adj*, **partisanship** *n*

²**partisan, partizan** *n* a weapon of the 16th and 17th c consisting of a broad blade mounted on a long shaft

partita *n* a musical suite

¹**partition** *n* **1a** division into parts **b** separation of a class or whole into constituent elements **2** sthg that divides; *esp* a light interior dividing wall **3** a part or section of a whole **– partitionist** *n*

²**partition** *vt* **1** to divide into parts or shares **2** to divide or separate *off* by a partition ⟨*can we ∼ off part of the room to use as an office?*⟩

partitive *adj* of or denoting a part of a whole **– partitively** *adv*

partly *adv* in some measure or degree; partially

¹**partner** *n* **1a** either of a couple who dance together **b** sby who plays with 1 or more others in a game against an opposing side **c** a person with whom one is having a sexual relationship; a spouse, lover, etc **2** a member of a partnership

²**partner** *vt* **1** to act as a partner to **2** to provide with a partner

partnership *n* **1** the state of being a partner; association **2** (a legal relation between) 2 or more joint principals in a business **3** an association involving close cooperation

part of speech *n* a class of words distinguished according to the kind of idea denoted and the function performed in a sentence

partridge *n*, *pl* **partridges**, *esp collectively* **partridge** any of various typically medium-sized stout-bodied Old World game birds with variegated plumage

part-song *n* a usu unaccompanied song consisting of 2 or more voice parts with 1 part carrying the melody

part-time *adj* involving or working less than customary or standard hours ⟨*a ∼ job*⟩ ⟨*∼ students*⟩ **– part-time** *adv*, **part-timer** *n*

parturition *n* the action or process of giving birth to offspring

party *n* **1a** a person or group taking 1 side of a question, dispute, or contest **b** *sing or pl in constr* a group of people organized to carry out an activity or fulfil a function together ⟨*sent out a search ∼*⟩ **2** *sing or pl in constr* a group organized for political involvement **3** one who is involved; a participant – usu + *to* ⟨*a ∼ to the transaction*⟩ **4** a (festive) social gathering **5** sby who is concerned in an action or activity – chiefly fml ⟨*a third ∼ was involved*⟩ ⟨*is this the guilty ∼?*⟩ **6** a particular individual – infml ⟨*a shameless old ∼*⟩

party line *n* **1** a single telephone line connecting 2 or more subscribers with an exchange **2** the official principles of a political party

party wall *n* a wall which divides 2 adjoining properties and in which each owner has a joint interest

parvenu *n* a person of low social position who has recently or suddenly acquired wealth or power; an upstart **– parvenu, parvenue** *adj*

paschal *adj* **1** of the Passover **2** of or appropriate to Easter

pasha *n* a man of high rank or office (e g in Turkey or N Africa) ⟨*Glubb Pasha*⟩

¹**pass** *vi* **1** to move, proceed **2a** to go away ⟨*the panic ∼ed very quickly*⟩ – often + *off* ⟨*his headache had ∼ed off by lunchtime*⟩ **b** to die – often + *on* or *away*; euph **3a** to go by; move past ⟨*waved from the car window as she ∼ed*⟩ **b** *of time* to elapse ⟨*4 years ∼ed before we met again*⟩ **c**

to overtake another vehicle ⟨*we can ~ once we're round this bend*⟩ **4a** to go across, over, or through ⟨*allow no one to ~*⟩ **b** to go uncensured or unchallenged ⟨*let her remark ~*⟩ **5** to go from one quality, state, or form to another ⟨*~es from a liquid to a gaseous state*⟩ **6a** to pronounce a judgment **b** to be legally pronounced **7** to go from the control or possession of one person or group to that of another ⟨*the throne ~ed to the king's daughter*⟩ **8** to take place as a mutual exchange or transaction ⟨*angry words ~ed between them*⟩ **9a** to become approved by a body (e g a legislature) ⟨*the proposal ~ed*⟩ **b** to undergo an inspection, test, or examination successfully **10a** to be accepted or regarded as adequate or fitting ⟨*it's only a quick repair but it will ~*⟩ **b** to resemble or act the part of so well as to be accepted – usu + *for* **11** to kick, throw, or hit a ball or puck to a teammate **12** to decline to bid, bet, or play in a card game ~ *vt* **1** to go beyond: e g **a** to surpass, exceed ⟨*~es all expectations*⟩ **b** to advance or develop beyond ⟨*societies that have ~ed the feudal stage*⟩ **c** to go by; move past **2a** to go across, over, or through ⟨*~ a barrier*⟩ **b** to spend (time) ⟨*~ed the holidays at her sister's home*⟩ **3a** to secure the approval of (e g a legislative body) **b** to succeed in satisfying the requirements of (a test, inspection, or examination) **4a** to cause or permit to win approval or sanction ⟨*~ a law*⟩ **b** to accept (sby or sthg) after examination ⟨*I can't ~ this bad piece of work!*⟩ **5a** to put in circulation ⟨*~ bad cheques*⟩ **b** to transfer from one person to another ⟨*please ~ the salt*⟩ **c** to move or place, esp in or for a short time ⟨*~ed his hand across his brow*⟩ ⟨*~ a rope round a tree*⟩ **d** to throw, hit, or kick (a ball or puck), esp to a teammate **6a** to pronounce judicially ⟨*~ sentence*⟩ **b** to utter – esp in *pass a comment, pass a remark* **7a** to cause or permit to go past or through a barrier **b** to cause to march or go by in order ⟨*~ the troops in review*⟩ **8** to emit or discharge from a bodily part, esp the bowels or bladder **9** to hit a ball past (an opponent), esp in tennis – **in passing** as a relevant digression; parenthetically – **pass muster** to be found adequate, esp in passing an inspection or examination – **pass the buck** to shift a responsibility to sby else – **past the time of day** to give or exchange friendly greetings – **pass water** to urinate – euph

²pass *n* a narrow passage over low ground in a mountain range

³pass *n* **1** a usu distressing or bad state of affairs – often in *come to a pretty pass* **2a** a written permission to move about freely in a place or to leave or enter it **b** a written leave of absence from a military post or station for a brief period **c** a permit or ticket allowing free transport or free admission **3** a movement of the hands over or along sthg **4** the passing of an examination ⟨*2 A-level ~es*⟩ **5** a single complete mechanical operation (e g in manufacturing or data processing) **6a** an act of passing in cards, soccer, rugby, etc; *also* a ball or puck passed **b** a ball hit to the side and out of reach of an opponent, esp in tennis **7** a single passage or movement of a man-made object (e g an aircraft) over a place or towards a target **8** a sexually inviting gesture or approach – usu in *make a pass at*

passable *adj* **1** capable of being passed, crossed, or travelled on ⟨*~ roads*⟩ **2** barely good enough; tolerable – **passably** *adv*

passage *n* **1** the action or process of passing from one place or condition to another **2a** a way of exit or entrance; a road, path, channel, or course by which sthg passes **b** a corridor or lobby giving access to the different rooms or parts of a building or apartment **3a(1)** a specified act of travelling or passing, esp by sea or air ⟨*a rough ~*⟩ **(2)** a right to be conveyed as a passenger ⟨*secured a ~ to France*⟩ **b** the passing of a legislative measure **4** a right,

liberty, or permission to pass **5a** a brief noteworthy portion of a written work or speech **b** a phrase or short section of a musical composition **6** passing sthg or undergoing a passing **7** incubation of a pathogen (e g a virus) in culture, a living organism, or a developing egg

passageway *n* a corridor

pass away *vi* **1** to go out of existence **2** to die – euph

passbook *n* **1** a (building society) account-holder's book in which deposits and withdrawals are recorded **2** *SAfr* a dompass

passé *adj* **1** outmoded **2** behind the times

passenger *n* **1** sby who travels in, but does not operate, a public or private conveyance **2** *chiefly Br* a member of a group who contributes little or nothing to the functioning or productivity of the group

passe-partout *n* **1** MASTER KEY **2** a strong paper gummed on 1 side and used esp for mounting pictures

passerby *n, pl* **passersby** a person who happens by chance to pass by a particular place

passim *adv* HERE AND THERE 1

passing *adj* **1** going by or past ⟨*a ~ pedestrian*⟩ **2** having a brief duration ⟨*a ~ whim*⟩ **3** superficial **4** of or used in or for passing ⟨*a ~ place in a road*⟩

passion *n* **1** *often cap* **a** the sufferings of Christ between the night of the Last Supper and his death **b** a musical setting of a gospel account of the Passion story **2a** intense, driving, or uncontrollable feeling **b** an outbreak of anger **3a** ardent affection; love **b** (the object of) a strong liking, devotion, or interest **c** strong sexual desire – **passional** *adj*

passionate *adj* **1** easily aroused to anger **2a** capable of, affected by, or expressing intense feeling, esp love, hatred, or anger **b** extremely enthusiastic; keen ⟨*a ~ interest in sport*⟩ – **passionately** *adv*, **passionateness** *n*

passionflower *n* any of a genus of chiefly tropical plants with usu showy flowers and pulpy often edible berries

passion play *n, often cap 1st P* a dramatic representation of the passion and crucifixion of Christ

Passion Sunday *n* the fifth Sunday in Lent

Passion Week *n* the second week before Easter

¹passive *adj* **1a** acted on, receptive to, or influenced by external forces or impressions **b** *of a verb form or voice* expressing an action that is done to the grammatical subject of a sentence (e g *was hit* in 'the ball was hit') **c** *esp of an animal* placid **d** *of a person* lacking in energy, will, or initiative; meekly accepting **2a** not active or operative; inert **b** of or characterized by chemical inactivity; *esp* resistant to corrosion **c** not involving expenditure of chemical energy ⟨*~ transport across a cell membrane*⟩ **d** relating to or being an electronic component (e g a capacitor or resistor) or network of components whose characteristics cannot be controlled electronically and which show no gain **e** operating solely by means of the power of an input signal ⟨*a ~ communication satellite that reflects radio waves*⟩ **f** operating by intercepting signals emitted from a target ⟨*a ~ homing missile*⟩ **3** offering no resistance; submissive ⟨*~ surrender to fate*⟩ – **passively** *adv*, **passiveness** *n*, **passivity** *n*

²passive *n* the passive voice of a verb

passive resistance *n* resistance characterized by nonviolent noncooperation

passkey *n* MASTER KEY

pass off *vt* **1** to present with intent to deceive **2** to give a false identity or character to ⟨*passed herself off as a millionairess*⟩ ~ *vi* to take place and be completed ⟨*his stay in France passed off smoothly – TLS*⟩

pass out *vi* **1** to lose consciousness **2** *chiefly Br* to finish a period of (military) training

Passover *n* the Jewish celebration of the liberation of the Hebrews from slavery in Egypt

pass over *vt* 1 to ignore in passing ⟨*I will pass over this aspect of the book in silence*⟩ 2 to pay no attention to the claims of; disregard ⟨*was passed over for the chairmanship*⟩

passport *n* 1 an official document issued by a government **a** as proof of identity and nationality to one of its citizens for use when leaving or reentering the country and affording some protection when abroad **b** as a safe-conduct to a foreign citizen passing through its territory 2a a permission or authorization to go somewhere **b** sthg that secures admission or acceptance ⟨*education as a ~ to success*⟩

pass up *vt* to decline, reject

password *n* 1 a word or phrase that must be spoken by a person before being allowed to pass a guard 2 WATCH-WORD 1

¹**past** *adj* 1a just gone or elapsed ⟨*for the ~ few months*⟩ **b** having gone by; earlier ⟨*~ generations*⟩ ⟨*in years ~*⟩ 2 finished, ended ⟨*winter is ~*⟩ 3 of or constituting the past tense expressing elapsed time 4 preceding, former ⟨*~ president*⟩

²**past** *prep* 1a beyond the age of or for ⟨*he's ~ 80*⟩ ⟨*~ playing with dolls*⟩ **b** subsequent to in time ⟨*half ~ 2*⟩ 2a at the farther side of; beyond **b** up to and then beyond ⟨*drove ~ the house*⟩ 3 beyond the capacity, range, or sphere of ⟨*~ belief*⟩ ⟨*wouldn't put it ~ her to cheat*⟩ – **past it** no longer effective or in one's prime – *infml*

³**past** *n* 1a time gone by **b** sthg that happened or was done in the past ⟨*regret the ~*⟩ 2 the past tense of a language 3 a past life, history, or course of action; *esp* one that is kept secret ⟨*she has a ~, you know*⟩

⁴**past** *adv* so as to pass by the speaker ⟨*children ran ~*⟩ ⟨*days crawled ~*⟩

pasta *n* any of several (egg or oil enriched) flour and water doughs that are usu shaped and used fresh or dried (e g as spaghetti)

¹**paste** *n* 1a a fat-enriched dough used esp for pastry **b** a usu sweet doughy confection ⟨*almond ~*⟩ **c** a smooth preparation of meat, fish, etc used as a spread 2 a soft plastic mixture or composition: e g **a** a preparation of flour or starch and water used as an adhesive **b** clay or a clay mixture used in making pottery or porcelain 3 a brilliant glass used in making imitation gems

²**paste** *vt* 1 to stick with paste 2 to cover with sthg pasted on

¹**pasteboard** *n* board made by pasting together sheets of paper

²**pasteboard** *adj* 1 made of pasteboard 2 sham, insubstantial

¹**pastel** *n* 1 (a crayon made of) a paste of powdered pigment mixed with gum 2 a drawing in pastel 3 any of various pale or light colours – **pastellist** *n*

²**pastel** *adj* pale and light in colour

pastern *n* (a part of an animal's leg corresponding to) a part of a horse's foot extending from the fetlock to the hoof

paste-up *n* 1 a piece of copy for photographic reproduction consisting of text and artwork in the proper positions 2 DUMMY 4

pasteurization, -isation *n* partial sterilization of a substance, esp a liquid (e g milk), by heating for a short period – **pasteurize** *vt*

pastiche *n* 1 a literary, artistic, or musical work that imitates the style of a previous work 2 a musical, literary, or artistic composition made up of elements borrowed from various sources

pastille *also* **pastil** *n* 1 a small cone of aromatic paste,

burned to fumigate or scent a room 2 an aromatic or medicated lozenge

pastime *n* sthg (e g a hobby, game, etc) that amuses and serves to make time pass agreeably

pasting *n* a beating, trouncing – *infml*

past master *n* one who is expert or experienced (in a particular activity)

pastor *n* one having responsibility for the spiritual welfare of a group (e g a congregation) – **pastorate** *n*, **pastorship** *n*

¹**pastoral** *adj* 1a(1) (composed) of shepherds or herdsmen (2) used for or based on livestock rearing **b** of the countryside; not urban **c** portraying rural life, esp in an idealized and conventionalized manner ⟨*~ poetry*⟩ **d** pleasingly peaceful and innocent; idyllic 2a of or providing spiritual care or guidance, esp of a church congregation **b** of the pastor of a church – **pastoralism** *n*, **pastorally** *adv*

²**pastoral** *n* 1 **pastoral, pastoral letter** a letter addressed by a bishop to his diocese 2a a pastoral literary work **b** an (idealized) depiction of country life **c** a pastorale

pastorale *n* an instrumental composition or opera with a pastoral theme

past participle *n* a participle with past, perfect, or passive meaning

past perfect *adj* of or constituting a verb tense (e g *had finished*) that expresses completion of an action at or before a past time – **past perfect** *n*

pastrami *n* a highly seasoned smoked beef

pastry *n* 1 PASTE 1a; *esp* paste when baked (e g for piecrust) 2 (an article of) usu sweet food made with pastry

pasturage *n* pasture

¹**pasture** *n* 1 plants (e g grass) grown for feeding (grazing) animals 2 (a plot of) land used for grazing 3 the feeding of livestock; grazing

²**pasture** *vi* to graze on pasture ~ *vt* to feed (e g cattle) on pasture

¹**pasty** *n* a small filled usu savoury pie or pastry case baked without a container

²**pasty** *adj* resembling paste; *esp* pallid and unhealthy in appearance – **pastiness** *n*

¹**pat** *n* 1 a light tap, esp with the hand or a flat instrument 2 a light tapping sound 3 a small mass of sthg (e g butter) shaped (as if) by patting

²**pat** *vt* **-tt-** 1 to strike lightly with the open hand or some other flat surface 2 to flatten, smooth, or put into place or shape with light blows ⟨*he ~ted his hair into place*⟩ 3 to tap or stroke gently with the hand to soothe, caress, or show approval

³**pat** *adv* in a pat manner; aptly, promptly

⁴**pat** *adj* 1 prompt, immediate 2 suspiciously appropriate; contrived ⟨*a ~ answer*⟩ 3 learned, mastered, or memorized exactly

pat-ball *n* slow or feeble play (e g in cricket or tennis)

¹**patch** *n* 1 a piece of material used to mend or cover a hole or reinforce a weak spot 2 a tiny piece of black silk worn on the face, esp by women in the 17th and 18th c, to set off the complexion 3a a cover (e g a piece of adhesive plaster) applied to a wound **b** a shield worn over the socket of an injured or missing eye 4a a small piece; a scrap **b** a small area distinct from its surroundings ⟨*damp ~es on the wall*⟩ **c** a small piece of land usu used for growing vegetables ⟨*a cabbage ~*⟩ 5 a piece of cloth sewn on a garment as an ornament or insignia 6 a temporary connection in a communications system 7 a temporary correction in a faulty computer program 8 *chiefly Br* a usu specified period ⟨*poetry is going through a bad ~ – Cyril Connolly*⟩ 9 *chiefly Br* an area for which a particu-

lar individual or unit (e g of police) has responsibility – **not a patch on** not nearly as good as

²patch vt **1** to mend or cover (a hole) with a patch **2** to provide with a patch ⟨a ~ed pair of trousers⟩ **3a** to make from patchwork **b** to mend or put together, esp in a hasty or shabby fashion – usu + **up c** to make a patch in (a computer program); also to make a change in (data stored on a computer) without following the standard routine for this procedure **4** to connect (e g circuits) by a patch cord

patchouli, patchouly n **1** an E Indian shrubby plant of the mint family that yields a fragrant essential oil **2** a heavy perfume made from patchouli

patch pocket n a flat pocket attached to the outside of a garment

patch up vt to bring (a quarrel, dispute, etc) to an end

patchwork n **1** sthg composed of miscellaneous or incongruous parts **2** work consisting of pieces of cloth of various colours and shapes sewn together

patchy adj **1** uneven in quality; incomplete ⟨my knowledge of French is ~⟩ **2** of certain types of weather appearing in patches ⟨~ fog⟩ – **patchily** adv, **patchiness** n

pate n (the crown of) the head – **pated** adj

pâté n a rich savoury paste of seasoned and spiced meat, fish, etc

patella n, pl **patellae, patellas** the kneecap – **patellar** adj

¹patent adj **1a** secured by or made under a patent ⟨~ locks⟩ **b** proprietary ⟨~ drugs⟩ **2a** of patents ⟨a ~ lawyer⟩ **b** made of patent leather ⟨~ shoes⟩ **3** original and ingenious as if protected by patent ⟨a ~ way of pickling onions⟩ **4** affording free passage; unobstructed ⟨a ~ opening⟩ **5** readily visible or intelligible; not hidden or obscure – **patency** n, **patently** adv

²patent n **1** LETTERS PATENT 2a (a formal document securing to an inventor) the exclusive right to make or sell an invention **b** a patented invention **3** a privilege, licence

³patent vt to obtain a patent for (an invention) – **patentable** adj

patentee n sby to whom a grant is made or a privilege secured by patent

patent leather n a leather with a hard smooth glossy surface

patent medicine n a medicine that is made and marketed under a patent, trademark, etc

pater n, chiefly Br a father – now usu humor

paterfamilias n, pl **patresfamilias** the male head of a household

paternal adj **1** fatherly ⟨~ benevolence⟩ **2** received or inherited from one's male parent **3** related through one's father ⟨~ grandfather⟩ – **paternally** adv

paternalism n a system under which a government or organization deals with its subjects or employees in an authoritarian but benevolent way, esp by supplying all their needs and regulating their conduct – **paternalist** n or adj, **paternalistic** adj

paternity n **1** being a father **2** origin or descent from a father

paternoster n, often cap LORD'S PRAYER

path n, pl **paths 1** a track formed by the frequent passage of people or animals **2** a track specially constructed for a particular use ⟨garden ~s⟩ **3a** a course, route ⟨the ~ of a planet⟩ **b** a way of life, conduct, or thought ⟨his ~ through life was difficult⟩ **4** the continuous series of positions or configurations that can be assumed in any motion or process of change by a moving or varying system

path-, patho- comb form pathological state; disease ⟨pathogen⟩

-path comb form (→ n) **1** practitioner of (a specified system of medicine) ⟨naturopath⟩ **2** sufferer from disorder of (such a part or system) ⟨psychopath⟩

Pathan n a member of the principal ethnic group of Afghanistan

pathetic adj **1a** PITIFUL 1 ⟨a ~ lost child⟩ **b** PITIFUL 2 ⟨a ~ performance⟩ ⟨~ attempts to learn German⟩ **2** marked by sorrow or melancholy; sad – **pathetically** adv

pathetic fallacy n the attribution of human characteristics or feelings to inanimate nature (e g in cruel sea)

pathfinder n **1** sby or sthg that explores unexplored regions to mark out a new route **2** sby who discovers new ways of doing things – **pathfinding** n or adj

pathogen n a bacterium, virus, or other disease-causing agent – **pathogenic** adj, **pathogenically** adv, **pathogenicity** n

pathologist n one who studies pathology; specif one who conducts postmortems to determine the cause of death

pathology n **1** the study of (the structure and functional changes produced by) diseases **2** sthg abnormal: **a** the anatomical and physiological abnormalities that constitute or characterize (a particular) disease **b** deviation from an assumed normal state of mentality or morality – **pathological, pathologic** adj, **pathologically** adv

pathos n **1** a quality in experience or in artistic representation evoking pity or compassion **2** an emotion of sympathetic pity

pathway n **1** a path, course **2** the sequence of enzyme-catalysed reactions by which a substance is synthesized or an energy-yielding substance is used by living tissue ⟨metabolic ~s⟩

patience n **1** the capacity, habit, or fact of being patient **2** chiefly Br any of various card games that can be played by 1 person and usu involve the arranging of cards into a prescribed pattern

¹patient adj **1** bearing pains or trials calmly or without complaint **2** manifesting forbearance under provocation or strain **3** not hasty or impetuous **4** steadfast despite opposition, difficulty, or adversity – **patiently** adv

²patient n an individual awaiting or under medical care

patina n, pl **patinas, patinae 1** a (decorative) usu green film formed on copper and bronze by (simulated) weathering and valued as aesthetically pleasing **2** a surface appearance of sthg (e g polished wood) that has grown more beautiful esp with age or use

patio n, pl **patios** a usu paved area adjoining a dwelling

patisserie n **1** PASTRY 2 **2** an establishment where patisserie is made and sold

patois n, pl **patois 1** a provincial dialect other than the standard or literary dialect **2** JARGON 2

patr-, patri-, patro- comb form father ⟨patronymic⟩

patrial n sby who has a legal right to reside in the UK because one of his/her parents or grandparents was born there – **patrial** adj, **patriality** n

patriarch n **1a** any of the biblical fathers of the human race or of the Hebrew people **b** a man who is father or founder (e g of a race, science, religion, or class of people) **c**(1) the oldest member or representative of a group (2) a venerable old man **d** a man who is head of a patriarchy **2a** any of the bishops of the ancient or Orthodox sees of Constantinople, Alexandria, Antioch, and Jerusalem **b** the head of any of various Eastern churches – **patriarchal** adj

patriarchate n the (duration of) office or jurisdiction of a patriarch

patriarchy n a system or an instance of social organization marked by the supremacy of the father in the clan or family, the legal dependence of wives and children, and the reckoning of descent and inheritance in the male line

patrician *n* 1 a member of any of the original citizen families of ancient Rome 2a sby of high birth; an aristocrat **b** sby of breeding and cultivation – **patrician** *adj*

patricide *n* (the act of) sby who kills his/her father – **patricidal** *adj*

patrimony *n* 1a property inherited from one's father or ancestor **b** sthg derived from one's father or ancestors; a heritage 2 an estate or endowment belonging to a church – **patrimonial** *adj*

patriot *n* one who loves and zealously supports his/her country – **patriotism** *n*, **patriotic** *adj*, **patriotically** *adv*

¹**patrol** *n* 1a traversing a district or beat or going the rounds of a garrison or camp for observation or the maintenance of security **b** *sing or pl in constr* a detachment of men employed for reconnaissance, security, or combat 2 *sing or pl in constr* a subdivision of a scout troop or guide company that has 6 to 8 members

²**patrol** *vb* -ll- to carry out a patrol (of) – **patroller** *n*

patrol car *n* a usu high-performance car used by police to patrol esp motorways

patrolman *n, NAm* a policeman assigned to a beat

patrol wagon *n, NAm* an enclosed van used by police to carry prisoners

patron, fem patroness *n* 1a sby chosen, named, or honoured as a special guardian, protector, or supporter **b** a wealthy or influential supporter of an artist or writer 2 sby who uses his/her wealth or influence to help an individual, institution, or cause 3 CUSTOMER 1 4 the holder of the right of presentation to an English ecclesiastical benefice 5 a master in ancient times who freed his slave but retained some rights over him/her 6 the proprietor of an establishment (e g an inn), esp in France

patronage *n* 1 advowson 2 the support or influence of a patron 3 the granting of favours in a condescending way 4 business or activity provided by patrons 5 the power to appoint to government jobs

patronize, -ise *vt* 1 to act as patron of 2 to adopt an air of condescension towards 3 to be a patron of – **patronizingly** *adv*

patron saint *n* a saint regarded as having a particular person, group, church, etc under his/her special care and protection

patronymic *n* a name derived from that of the father or a paternal ancestor, usu by the addition of an affix – **patronymic** *adj*

patten *n* a sandal or overshoe set on a wooden sole or metal device to elevate the foot

¹**patter** *vb* to say or talk glibly and volubly – **patterer** *n*

²**patter** *n* 1 cant 2 the sales talk of a street hawker 3 empty chattering talk 4a the rapid-fire talk of a comedian **b** the talk with which an entertainer accompanies his/her routine

³**patter** *vi* 1 to strike or tap rapidly and repeatedly ⟨*rain* ~ed *against the window pane*⟩ 2 to run with quick light-sounding steps ~ *vt* to cause to patter – **patter** *n*

¹**pattern** *n* 1 a form or model proposed for imitation; an example 2 a design, model, or set of instructions for making things ⟨*a dress* ~⟩ 3 a model for making a mould into which molten metal is poured to form a casting 4 a specimen, sample 5 a usu repeated decorative design (e g on fabric) 6 a natural or chance configuration ⟨*a frost* ~⟩ ⟨*the* ~ *of events*⟩ 7 the grouping on a target by bullets, bombs, etc 8 the flight path prescribed for an aircraft coming in for a landing

²**pattern** *vt* 1 to make or model according to a pattern 2 to decorate with a design

patty *n* 1 a little pie or pasty 2 *NAm* a small flat cake of chopped food ⟨*a hamburger* ~⟩

paucity *n* 1 smallness of number 2 smallness of quantity; scarcity *USE fml*

paunch *n* 1a the belly **b** a potbelly 2 the rumen

paunchy *adj* having a potbelly

pauper *n* a very poor person; *specif* sby supported by charity or from public funds – **pauperism** *n*

pauperize, -ise *vt* to reduce to poverty or destitution

¹**pause** *n* 1 a temporary stop 2 a caesura 3 temporary inaction, esp as caused by uncertainty; hesitation 4 the sign denoting a fermata

²**pause** *vi* 1 to stop temporarily 2 to linger for a time

pavane *also* **pavan** *n* (music for or having the slow duple rhythm of) a stately court dance by couples

pave *vt* 1 to lay or cover with material (e g stone or concrete) to form a firm level surface for walking or travelling on 2 to serve as a covering or pavement of ⟨*palaces* ~d *with marble*⟩ – **paver** *n* – **pave the way** to prepare a smooth easy way; facilitate development

pavé *n or adj* (a setting in which jewels are) set closely together to conceal a metal base

paved *adj* covered with a pavement

pavement *n* a paved surface: e g **a** *chiefly Br* a surfaced walk for pedestrians at the side of a road **b** *NAm* the artificially covered surface of a road

pavement artist *n* sby who draws coloured pictures on the pavement in the hope that passersby will give him/her money

¹**pavilion** *n* 1 a large often sumptuous tent 2 a part of a building projecting from the rest 3a a light sometimes ornamental structure in a garden, park, etc **b** a temporary structure erected at an exhibition by an individual exhibitor 4 the lower faceted part of a cut gem below the girdle 5 *chiefly Br* a permanent building on a sports ground, specif a cricket ground, containing changing rooms and often also seats for spectators

²**pavilion** *vt* to provide with or put in a pavilion

paving stone *n* a thin rectangular stone or concrete block used for paving

¹**paw** *n* 1 the (clawed) foot of a lion, dog, or other (quadruped) animal 2 a human hand – infml; chiefly humor

²**paw** *vt* 1 to feel or touch clumsily, rudely, or indecently 2 to touch or strike at with a paw 3 to scrape or strike (as if) with a hoof ~ *vi* 1 to beat or scrape sthg (as if) with a hoof 2 to touch or strike with a paw

pawky *adj, chiefly Br* artfully shrewd, esp in a humorous way; canny

pawl *n* a pivoted tongue or sliding bolt on one part of a machine that is adapted to fall into notches on another part (e g a ratchet wheel) so as to permit motion in only 1 direction

¹**pawn** *n* 1 sthg delivered to or deposited with another as a pledge or security (e g for a loan) 2 the state of being pledged – usu + *in*

²**pawn** *vt* to deposit in pledge or as security

³**pawn** *n* 1 any of the 8 chessmen of each colour of least value that have the power to move only forwards usu 1 square at a time and to capture only diagonally forwards, and that may be promoted to any piece except a king upon reaching the opposite side of the board 2 sby or sthg that can be used to further the purposes of another

pawnbroker *n* one who lends money on the security of personal property pledged in his/her keeping – **pawnbroking** *n*

pawnshop *n* a pawnbroker's shop

pawpaw *n* PAPAW 2

¹**pay** *vb* **paid**, (7) **paid** *also* **payed** *vt* **1a** to make due return to for services done or property received **b** to engage for money; hire ⟨*you couldn't ~ me to do that*⟩ **2a** to give in return for goods or service ⟨*~ wages*⟩ **b** to discharge indebtedness for; settle ⟨*~ a bill*⟩ **c** to make a disposal or transfer of (money) ⟨*~ money into the bank*⟩ **3** to give or forfeit in reparation or retribution ⟨*~ the penalty*⟩ **4a** to make compensation for **b** to requite according to what is deserved ⟨*~ him back*⟩⟨*~ her out*⟩ **5** to give, offer, or make willingly or as fitting ⟨*~ attention*⟩⟨*~ heed*⟩ **6a** to be profitable to; be worth the expense or effort to ⟨*it ~s shopkeepers to stay open late*⟩ **b** to bring in as a return ⟨*an investment ~ing 5 per cent*⟩ **7** to slacken (e g a rope) and allow to run out – usu + *out* ~ *vi* **1** to discharge a debt or obligation **2** to be worth the expense or effort ⟨*it ~s to advertise*⟩ – **payer** *n*, **payee** *n*

²**pay** *n* **1** the status of being paid by an employer; employ ⟨*was in the ~ of the enemy*⟩ **2** sthg paid as a salary or wage

³**pay** *adj* **1** containing or leading to sthg valuable **2** equipped with a coin slot for receiving a fee for use ⟨*a ~ phone*⟩ **3** requiring payment

⁴**pay** *vt* **payed** *also* **paid** to coat with a waterproof composition

payable *adj* that may, can, or must be paid

payday *n* a regular day on which wages are paid

payload *n* **1** the revenue-producing load that a vehicle of transport can carry **2** the explosive charge carried in the warhead of a missile **3** the load (e g instruments) carried in a spacecraft relating directly to the purpose of the flight as opposed to the load (e g fuel) necessary for operation

paymaster *n* an officer or agent whose duty it is to pay salaries or wages

paymaster general *n, often cap P&G* a British government minister who is often made a member of the cabinet and entrusted with special functions

payment *n* **1** the act of paying **2** sthg that is paid **3** a recompense (e g a reward or punishment)

payoff *n* **1** a profit or reward, esp received by a player in a game **2** a decisive fact or factor resolving a situation or bringing about a definitive conclusion **3** the climax of an incident or chain of events; *specif, chiefly NAm* the denouement of a narrative – *infml*

pay off *vt* **1** to give all due wages to; *esp* to pay in full and discharge (an employee) **2** to pay (a debt or a creditor) in full ~ *vi* to yield returns ⟨*it was a risk but it paid off*⟩

payola *n* an undercover or indirect payment for unofficial promotion of a commercial product

pay-out *n* (the act of making) a usu large payment of money – *infml*

pay-packet *n, Br* (an envelope containing) sby's wages

payroll *n* **1** a list of those entitled to be paid and of the amounts due to each **2** the sum necessary to pay those on a payroll **3** *sing or pl in constr* the people on a payroll

pay up *vb* to pay in full

pea *n, pl* **peas** *also* **pease 1a** (a leguminous climbing plant that bears) an edible rounded protein-rich green seed **b** *pl* the immature pods of the pea with their seeds **2** any of various leguminous plants related to or resembling the pea – usu with a qualifying term ⟨*chick-pea*⟩⟨*sweet ~*⟩

peace *n* **1** a state of tranquillity or quiet: e g **a** freedom from civil disturbance **b** public order and security maintained by law or custom ⟨*a breach of the ~*⟩ **2** freedom from disquieting or oppressive thoughts or emotions ⟨*~ of mind*⟩ **3** harmony in personal relations **4a** mutual concord between countries **b** an agreement to end hostilities **5** – used interjectionally as a command or request for silence or calm or as a greeting or farewell – **at peace** in a state of concord or tranquillity

peaceable *adj* **1a** disposed to peace; not inclined to dispute or quarrel **b** quietly behaved **2** free from strife or disorder – **peaceableness** *n*, **peaceably** *adv*

peace corps *n* a body of trained volunteer personnel sent by the US government to assist developing nations

peaceful *adj* **1** PEACEABLE 1 **2** untroubled by conflict, agitation, or commotion; quiet, tranquil **3** of a state or time of peace – **peacefully** *adv*, **peacefulness** *n*

peace offering *n* sthg given or done to produce peace or reconciliation

peace pipe *n* a calumet

peacetime *n* a time when a nation is not at war

¹**peach** *n* **1** (a low spreading tree of the rose family that grows in temperate areas, has stalkless usu pink spring flowers, and bears) an edible fruit with a large stone, thin downy skin, and sweet white or yellow flesh **2** light yellowish pink **3** a particularly excellent person or thing; *specif* an unusually attractive girl or young woman – *infml*

²**peach** *vi* to turn informer ⟨*~ed on his accomplices*⟩

peacock *n* a male peafowl with very large tail feathers that are usu tipped with eyelike spots and can be erected and spread in a fan shimmering with iridescent colour; *broadly* a peafowl

peacock blue *n* lustrous greenish blue

peafowl *n* a very large ornamental ground-living pheasant of SE Asia and the E Indies

pea green *n* light yellowish green

peahen *n* a female peafowl

¹**peak** *vi* to grow thin or sickly

²**peak** *n* **1** a projecting part on the front of a cap or hood **2** a sharp or pointed end **3a** (the top of) a hill or mountain ending in a point **b** sthg resembling a mountain peak **4a** the upper aftermost corner of a 4-cornered fore-and-aft sail **b** the narrow part of a ship's bow or stern **5a** the highest level or greatest degree **b** a high point in a course of development, esp as represented on a graph

³**peak** *vi* to reach a maximum

⁴**peak** *adj* at or reaching the maximum of capacity, value, or activity ⟨*the factory reached ~ productivity*⟩⟨*~ traffic hours*⟩

¹**peaked** *adj* having a peak; pointed – **peakedness** *n*

²**peaked** *adj* peaky

peaky *adj* looking pale and wan; sickly

¹**peal** *n* **1a** a complete set of changes on a given number of bells **b** a set of bells tuned to the notes of the major scale for change ringing **2** a loud prolonged sound ⟨*~s of laughter*⟩

²**peal** *vi* to give out peals ~ *vt* to utter or give forth loudly

peanut *n* **1** (the pod or oily edible seed of) a low-branching widely cultivated leguminous plant with showy yellow flowers and pods containing 1 to 3 seeds that ripen in the earth **2** *pl* a trifling amount – *infml*

pear *n* (a tree of the rose family that bears) a large fleshy edible fruit wider at the end furthest from the stalk

¹**pearl** *n* **1a** a dense usu milky white lustrous mass of mother-of-pearl layers, formed as an abnormal growth in the shell of some molluscs, esp oysters, and used as a gem **b** mother-of-pearl **2** sby or sthg very rare or precious

²**pearl** *vt* **1** to set or adorn (as if) with pearls **2** to form into small round grains ~ *vi* **1** to form drops or beads like pearls **2** to fish or search for pearls – **pearler** *n*

³**pearl** *adj* **1a** of or resembling pearl **b** made of or adorned with pearls **2** having medium-sized grains ⟨*~ barley*⟩

⁴**pearl** *vt or n, Br* (to) picot

¹**pearly** *adj* resembling, containing, or decorated with pearls or mother-of-pearl

²**pearly** *n, Br* **1** a button made of mother-of-pearl **2** a member of certain cockney families who are traditionally costermongers and entitled to wear a special costume covered with pearlies

pearmain *n* any of various eating apples

peasant *n* **1** a small landowner or farm labourer **2** a usu uneducated person of low social status – **peasantry** *n sing or pl in constr*

pease *n, chiefly Br* PEA 1a – archaic except in attributive use ⟨~ *pudding*⟩

peashooter *n* a toy blowpipe for shooting peas

pea-souper *also* **pea soup** *n* a heavy fog

peat *n* (a piece of) partially carbonized vegetable tissue formed by partial decomposition in water of various plants (e g mosses), found in large bogs, and used esp as a fuel for domestic heating and as a fertilizer – **peaty** *adj*

¹**pebble** *n* **1** a small usu rounded stone, often worn smooth by the action of water **2** rock crystal – **pebbly** *adj*

²**pebble** *vt* to pave or cover with (sthg resembling) pebbles

pebbledash *n* a finish for exterior walls consisting of small pebbles embedded in a stucco base

pecan *n* (the smooth oblong thin-shelled edible nut of) a large hickory tree with roughish bark and hard but brittle wood

peccadillo *n, pl* **peccadilloes, peccadillos** a slight or trifling offence

peccary *n* either of 2 largely nocturnal social American mammals resembling the related pigs

¹**peck** *n* a unit of volume or capacity equal to 2gall (about 9.1l)

²**peck** *vt* **1a** to strike or pierce (repeatedly) with the beak or a pointed tool **b** to make by pecking ⟨~ *a hole*⟩ **c** to kiss perfunctorily **2** to pick up with the beak ~ *vi* **1** to strike, pierce, or pick up sthg (as if) with the beak **2** to eat reluctantly and in small bites ⟨~ *at food*⟩

³**peck** *n* **1** an impression or hole made by pecking **2** a quick sharp stroke **3** a quick perfunctory kiss

⁴**peck** *vi, of a horse* to stumble on landing from a jump

pecker *n* **1** *chiefly Br* courage – in *keep one's pecker up*; *infml* **2** *NAm* a penis – *vulg*

pecking order, peck order *n* **1** the natural hierarchy within a flock of birds, esp poultry, in which each bird pecks another lower in the scale without fear of retaliation **2** a social hierarchy

peckish *adj, chiefly Br* agreeably hungry – *infml*

pectin *n* any of various water-soluble substances that bind adjacent cell walls in plant tissues and yield a gel which acts as a setting agent in jams and fruit jellies – **pectic** *adj*

pectoral *adj* of, situated in or on, or worn on the chest

pectoral cross *n* a cross worn on the chest, esp by a prelate

peculate *vt* to embezzle – **peculator** *n*, **peculation** *n*

¹**peculiar** *adj* **1** belonging exclusively to 1 person or group **2** distinctive **3** different from the usual or normal; strange, curious – **peculiarly** *adv*

²**peculiar** *n* sthg exempt from ordinary jurisdiction; *esp* a church or parish independent of the diocese in which it is situated

peculiarity *n* a distinguishing characteristic

pecuniary *adj* of or measured in money – *fml* – **pecuniarily** *adv*

pedagogue *n* a teacher, schoolmaster – now chiefly derog

pedagogy *n* the science of teaching

¹**pedal** *n* **1** a lever pressed by the foot in playing a musical instrument **2** a foot lever or treadle by which a part is activated in a mechanism

²**pedal** *adj* of the foot

³**pedal** *vb* **-ll-** *(NAm -l- also -ll-)*, *vi* **1** to use or work a pedal or pedals **2** to ride a bicycle ~ *vt* to work the pedals of

pedant *n* one who is unimaginative or unnecessarily concerned with detail, esp in academic matters – **pedantic** *adj*, **pedantry** *n*

peddle *vb* **peddling** *vi* to sell goods as a pedlar ~ *vt* **1** to sell as a pedlar **2** to deal out or seek to disseminate (e g ideas or opinions)

peddler *n* **1** one who peddles dangerous or illicit drugs; a pusher **2** *NAm* a pedlar

pederast, paederast *n* one who practises anal intercourse, esp with a boy – **pederasty** *n*, **pederastic** *adj*

pedestal *n* **1a** a base supporting a late classic or neo-classic column **b** the base of an upright structure (e g a statue) **2** a base, foundation **3** a position of esteem or idealized respect

¹**pedestrian** *adj* **1** commonplace, unimaginative **2a** going or performed on foot **b** of or designed for walking ⟨*a ~ precinct*⟩ – **pedestrianism** *n*

²**pedestrian** *n* sby going on foot; a walker

pedestrian crossing *n* a usu marked stretch of road on which pedestrians crossing the road have priority over the traffic in certain circumstances

pedicel *n* **1** a plant stalk that supports a fruiting or spore-bearing organ **2** a narrow basal attachment of an animal organ or part – **pedicellate** *adj*

pedicure *n* **1** one who practises chiropody **2** (a) treatment for the care of the feet and toenails

¹**pedigree** *n* **1** a register recording a line of ancestors **2a** an esp distinguished ancestral line; a lineage **b** the origin and history of sthg **3** the recorded purity of breed of an individual or strain – **pedigreed** *adj*

²**pedigree** *adj* of, being, or producing pedigree animals

pediment *n* the triangular gable of a 2-pitched roof in classic architecture – **pedimental** *adj*

pedlar, NAm chiefly peddler *n* **1** one who travels about offering small wares for sale **2** one who deals in or promotes sthg intangible – **pedlary** *n*

pedometer *n* an instrument that records the distance a walker covers by responding to body motion at each step

¹**pee** *vi* to urinate – *euph*

²**pee** *n* **1** an act of urinating **2** urine *USE euph*

³**pee** *n, pl* **pee** *Br* PENNY 1a(2) – *infml*

peek *vi* **1** to look furtively – often + *in* or *out* **2** to take a brief look; glance – **peek** *n*

¹**peekaboo** *n* a game for amusing a baby in which one repeatedly hides and comes back into view, typically exclaiming 'Peekaboo!'

²**peekaboo** *adj* trimmed with eyelet embroidery ⟨*a ~ blouse*⟩

¹**peel** *vt* **1** to strip off an outer layer of ⟨~ *an orange*⟩ **2** to remove by stripping ⟨~ *the label off the can*⟩ ~ *vi* **1a** to come off in sheets or scales **b** to lose an outer layer (e g of skin) ⟨*his face is* ~*ing*⟩ **2** to take off one's clothes – usu + *off*; *infml* ⟨*they* ~*ed off and dived into the water*⟩ – **peeler** *n*

²**peel** *n* the skin or rind of a fruit

³**peel** *also* **pele** *n* a small fortified tower built in the 16th c along the Scottish-English border

⁴**peel** *n* a usu long-handled (baker's) shovel for getting bread, pies, etc into or out of an oven

peeler *n, archaic Br* a policeman

peeling *n* a strip of skin, rind, etc that has been stripped off

peel off *vi* **1** to veer away from an aircraft formation, esp when diving or landing **2** to break away from a group or formation (e g of marchers or ships in a convoy)

¹peep *vi* **1** to utter a feeble shrill sound characteristic of a newly hatched bird; cheep **2** to utter a slight sound

²peep *n* **1** a cheep **2** a slight sound, esp spoken – infml ⟨*don't let me hear another ~ out of you*⟩

³peep *vi* **1** to look cautiously or slyly, esp through an aperture; peek **2** to begin to emerge (as if) from concealment; show slightly

⁴peep *n* **1** the first faint appearance ⟨*at the ~ of dawn*⟩ **2** a brief or furtive look; a glance

peeper *n* **1** a voyeur **2** an eye – infml

peephole *n* a hole or crevice to peep through

Peeping Tom *n, often not cap P* a voyeur

peep show *n* an entertainment (e g a film) or object (e g a small painting) viewed through a small opening or a magnifying glass

¹peer *n* **1** sby who is of equal standing with another **2** a duke, marquess, earl, viscount, or baron of the British peerage

²peer *adj* belonging to the same age, grade, or status group ⟨*a ~ group of adolescents*⟩

³peer *vi* to look narrowly or curiously; *esp* to look searchingly at sthg difficult to discern

peerage *n* **1** *sing or pl in constr* the body of peers **2** the rank or dignity of a peer

peeress *n* **1** the wife or widow of a peer **2** a woman having in her own right the rank of a peer

peerless *adj* matchless, incomparable – **peerlessly** *adv*, **peerlessness** *n*

peeve *vt* to make peevish or resentful; annoy – infml

peevish *adj* querulous in temperament or mood; fretful – **peevishly** *adv*, **peevishness** *n*

peewit, pewit *n* a lapwing

¹peg *n* **1** a small usu cylindrical pointed or tapered piece of wood, metal, or plastic used to pin down or fasten things or to fit into or close holes; a pin ⟨*they secured the guy ropes with tent ~s*⟩ **2a** a projecting piece used to hold or support ⟨*he hung his hat on the ~ in the hall*⟩ **b** sthg (e g a fact or opinion) used as a support, pretext, or reason ⟨*the strike was simply a ~ for their prejudices*⟩ **3a** any of the wooden pins set in the head of a stringed instrument and turned to regulate the pitch of the strings **b** a step or degree, esp in estimation – esp in take sby down a peg (or two) **4** *Br* a clothes peg **5** *Br* a drink, esp of spirits ⟨*poured himself out a stiff ~* – Dorothy Sayers⟩ – **off the peg** mass-produced; READY-MADE ⟨*men over 7 feet have difficulty in finding clothes* off the peg *to fit*⟩

²peg *vt* **-gg-** **1** to put a peg into **2** to pin down; restrict **3** to fix or hold (e g prices) at a predetermined level **4** *Br* to fasten (e g washing) to a clothesline with a clothes peg – often + out

peg away *vi, chiefly Br* to work hard and steadily – often + at

peg leg *n* (one who wears) an artificial leg

peg out *vi* **1** to finish a game in croquet by hitting the peg with the ball **2** *chiefly Br* DIE 1 – infml ~*vt* to mark by pegs ⟨*peg out the boundaries of an estate*⟩

pejorative *adj* depreciatory, disparaging – **pejorative** *n*, **pejoratively** *adv*

Pekingese, Pekinese *n, pl* Pekingese, Pekinese **1a** a native or inhabitant of Peking **b** Mandarin **2** (any of) a Chinese breed of small short-legged dogs with a broad flat face and a long thick soft coat

pekoe *n* a black tea of superior quality

pelagic *adj* of, occurring, or living (at or above moderate depths) in the open sea

pelf *n* money, riches

pelican *n* any of a genus of large web-footed birds with a very large bill containing a pouch in which fish are kept

pellagra *n* dermatitis and nervous symptoms associated with a deficiency of nicotinic acid and protein in the diet – **pellagrous** *adj*

pellet *n* **1** a usu small rounded or spherical body (e g of food or medicine) **2** a piece of small shot – **pelletal** *adj*, **pelletize** *vt*

pell-mell *adv* **1** in confusion or disorder **2** in confused haste – **pell-mell** *adj or n*

pellucid *adj* **1** transparent **2** easy to understand *USE* fml or poetic – **pellucidly** *adv*, **pellucidity** *n*

pelmet *n, chiefly Br* a length of board or fabric placed above a window to conceal curtain fixtures

pelota *n* any of various Spanish or Latin-American court games; *specif* JAI ALAI

¹pelt *n* **1** a usu undressed skin with its hair, wool, or fur **2** a skin stripped of hair or wool before tanning

²pelt *vt* **1** to strike with a succession of blows or missiles ⟨*~ed him with stones*⟩ **2** to hurl, throw **3** to beat or dash repeatedly against ⟨*rain ~ing the windows*⟩ ~*vi* **1** of rain to fall heavily and continuously **2** to move rapidly and vigorously; hurry ⟨*the children ~ed down the road*⟩

³pelt *n* – **at full pelt** as fast as possible

pelvis *n, pl* **pelvises, pelves** **1** (the cavity of) a basin-shaped structure in the skeleton of many vertebrates that is formed by the pelvic girdle and adjoining bones of the spine **2** the funnel-shaped cavity of the kidney into which urine is discharged – **pelvic** *adj*

pemmican *also* **pemican** *n* a concentrated food of lean dried pounded meat mixed with melted fat traditionally made by N American Indians; *also* a similar preparation usu of beef and dried fruits used for emergency rations

¹pen *n* **1** a small enclosure for animals **2** a small place of confinement or storage **3** a (heavily fortified) dock or slip for a submarine

²pen *vt* **-nn-** to shut in a pen

³pen *n* **1** an implement for writing or drawing with fluid (e g ink): e g **a** a quill **b** a penholder fitted with a nib **c** FOUNTAIN PEN **d** a ballpoint **2a** a writing instrument as a means of expression ⟨*the ~ is mightier than the sword*⟩ **b** a writer – fml

⁴pen *vt* **-nn-** to write – fml ⟨*~ a letter*⟩

⁵pen *n* a female swan

penal *adj* **1** of punishment **2** liable to punishment ⟨*a ~ offence*⟩ **3** used as a place of punishment ⟨*a ~ colony*⟩ – **penally** *adv*

penalize, -ise *vt* **1** to inflict a penalty on **2** to put at a serious disadvantage – **penalization** *n*

penalty *n* **1** a punishment legally imposed or incurred **2** a forfeiture to which a person agrees to be subject if conditions are not fulfilled **3a** disadvantage, loss, or suffering due to some action ⟨*paid the ~ for his heavy drinking*⟩ **b** a disadvantage imposed for violation of the rules of a sport **4** PENALTY KICK

penalty area *n* a rectangular area 44yd (about 40m) wide and 18yd (about 16m) deep in front of each goal on a soccer pitch

penalty box *n* **1** PENALTY AREA **2** an area alongside an ice hockey rink to which penalized players are confined

penalty kick *n* **1** a free kick in rugby **2** a free kick at the goal in soccer awarded for a serious offence committed in the penalty area and taken from a point 12yd (about 11m) in front of the goal with only the goalkeeper to defend it

penance *n* an act of self-abasement or devotion performed to show repentance for sin; *also* a sacramental rite of the Roman, Orthodox, and some Anglican churches involving confession and a penance directed by the confessor

pence pl of PENNY

penchant n a strong leaning; a liking

¹**pencil** n **1a** an implement for writing, drawing, or marking consisting of or containing a slender cylinder or strip of a solid marking substance (e g graphite) **b** a small medicated or cosmetic roll or stick for local applications **2** a set of light rays, esp when diverging from or converging to a point **3** sthg long and thin like a pencil

²**pencil** vt -ll- (NAm -l-, -ll-), to draw, write, or mark with a pencil – **penciller** n

pendant also **pendent** n **1** sthg suspended (e g an ornament allowed to hang free) **2** a companion piece or supplement **3** chiefly Br a pennant

pendent, pendant adj **1** suspended **2** jutting or leaning over; overhanging ⟨a ~ cliff⟩ **3** remaining undetermined; pending

¹**pending** prep until – fml

²**pending** adj **1** not yet decided or dealt with **2** imminent, impending – **pendency** n

pendulous adj suspended, inclined, or hanging downwards ⟨~ jowls⟩ – **pendulously** adv

pendulum n a body suspended from a fixed point so as to swing freely periodically under the action of gravity and commonly used to regulate movements (e g of clockwork)

penetrate vt **1a** to pass into or through **b** to enter, esp by overcoming resistance; pierce **2** to see into or through; discern **3** to diffuse through or into ~ vi to be absorbed by the mind; be understood ⟨I heard what he said, but it didn't ~⟩ – **penetrable** adj, **penetrability** n, **penetrative** adj

penetrating adj **1** having the power of entering, piercing, or pervading ⟨a ~ shriek⟩⟨the cold is ~⟩ **2** acute, discerning ⟨~ insights into life⟩ – **penetratingly** adv

penetration n **1a** the entering of a country so that influence is established **b** the process of successfully introducing or increasing sales of a product in an existing market **2a** the depth to which sthg penetrates **b** the ability to discern deeply and acutely ⟨a critic gifted with great powers of ~⟩

pen-friend n a person, esp one in another country, with whom a friendship is made through correspondence

penguin n any of various erect short-legged flightless aquatic birds of the southern hemisphere

penicillin n (a salt, ester, or mixture of salts and esters of) any of several antibiotics or antibacterial drugs orig obtained from moulds, that act by interfering with the synthesis of bacterial cell walls and are active against a wide range of bacteria

peninsula n a piece of land jutting out into or almost surrounded by water; esp one connected to the mainland by an isthmus

penis n, pl **penes, penises** the male organ of copulation by which semen is introduced into the female during coitus

¹**penitent** adj feeling or expressing sorrow for sins or offences – **penitence** n, **penitently** adv

²**penitent** n **1** sby who repents of sin **2** sby under church censure but admitted to penance, esp under the direction of a confessor

penitential adj of penitence or penance – **penitentially** adv

¹**penitentiary** n a prison in the USA

²**penitentiary** adj, NAm of or incurring confinement in a penitentiary

penknife n a small pocketknife

penmanship n **1** the art or practice of writing with the pen **2** quality or style of handwriting

pen name n an author's pseudonym

pennant n **1** any of various nautical flags used for identification or signalling **2** a flag that tapers to a point or has a swallowtail

penniless adj lacking money; poor

pennon n a long usu triangular or swallow-tailed streamer typically attached to the head of a lance as a knight's personal flag

penny n, pl **pennies, pence, (3) pennies 1a** (a usu bronze coin representing) (1) a former British money unit worth £½₄₀ (2) a British money unit in use since 1971 that is worth £¹/₁₀₀ **b** (a coin representing) 1/100 of various other units (e g the Irish punt) **2** a denarius **3** NAm a cent – **the penny drops** the true meaning finally dawns

-**penny** comb form (→ adj) costing (so many) pence ⟨ninepenny⟩

penny-farthing n, Br an early type of bicycle having 1 small and 1 large wheel

penny-pinching adj mean, niggardly, stingy – **penny pincher** n, **penny- pinching** n

pennyweight n a unit of troy weight equal to 24grains (about 1.56g)

pennywort n any of various round-leaved plants

penology n criminology dealing with prison management and the treatment of offenders – **penologist** n, **penological** adj

pen pal n a pen-friend – infml

pen pusher n one whose work involves usu boring or repetitive writing at a desk; specif CLERK 2a

¹**pension** n **1** a fixed sum paid regularly to a person (e g following retirement or as compensation for a wage-earner's death) ⟨a widow's ~⟩ **2** (bed and board provided by) a hotel or boardinghouse, esp in continental Europe – **pensionless** adj

²**pension** vt to grant or pay a pension to

pensionable adj (that makes sby) entitled to receive a pension ⟨~ employment⟩⟨a ~ employee⟩

pensioner n one who receives or lives on an esp old-age pension

pension off vt **1** to dismiss or retire from service with a pension ⟨pensioned off his faithful old servant⟩ **2** to set aside or dispense with after long use – infml ⟨pensioned off his old trousers⟩

pensive adj sadly or dreamily thoughtful – **pensively** adv, **pensiveness** n

penta-, pent- comb form **1** five ⟨pentahedron⟩⟨pentavalent⟩⟨pentode⟩ **2** containing 5 atoms, groups, or chemical equivalents in the molecular structure ⟨pentahydrate⟩

pentagon n a polygon of 5 angles and 5 sides – **pentagonal** adj, **pentagonally** adv

Pentagon n sing or pl in constr the US military establishment

pentagram n a 5-pointed star used as a magical symbol

pentameter n a line of verse consisting of 5 metrical feet

Pentateuch n the first 5 books of the Old Testament – **pentateuchal** adj

pentathlon n **1** a (women's) athletic contest in which all contestants compete in the 100m hurdles, shot put, high jump, long jump, and 200m sprint **2** MODERN PENTATHLON

Pentecost n (a Christian festival on the 7th Sunday after Easter commemorating the descent of the Holy Spirit on the apostles at) the Jewish festival of Shabuoth

penthouse n **1** a structure (e g a shed or roof) attached to and sloping from a wall or building **2** a structure or dwelling built on the roof of a (tall) building ⟨*a ~ flat*⟩

pent-up *adj* confined, held in check ⟨*~ emotions*⟩

¹**penultimate** *adj* next to the last ⟨*the ~ chapter of a book*⟩ – **penultimately** *adv*

²**penultimate** *n* a penult

penumbra *n, pl* **penumbrae, penumbras 1** a region of partial darkness (e g in an eclipse) in a shadow surrounding the umbra **2** a less dark region surrounding the dark centre of a sunspot – **penumbral** *adj*

penurious *adj* marked by or suffering from penury – *fml* – **penuriously** *adv*, **penuriousness** *n*

penury *n* a cramping and oppressive lack of resources, esp money; *esp* severe poverty – *fml*

peon *n, pl* **peons, peones, (3) peons 1** an Indian or Sri Lankan infantryman, orderly, or other worker **2** an agricultural labourer in Spanish America **3** a drudge, menial

peony, paeony *n* any of a genus of plants with very large usu double showy red, pink, or white flowers

¹**people** *n pl in constr,* (5) *sing or pl in constr* **1** human beings in general **2** a group of persons considered collectively ⟨*poor ~*⟩ **3** the members of a family or kinship ⟨*his ~ have been farmers for generations*⟩ **4** the mass of a community ⟨*disputes between the ~ and the nobles*⟩ **5** a body of persons that are united by a common culture and that often constitute a politically organized group ⟨*the Jewish ~*⟩ **6** the citizens of a state who are qualified to vote – **of all people** – used to show surprise ⟨*the Archbishop of all people said that?*⟩

²**people** *vt* **1** to supply or fill with people **2** to dwell in; inhabit

pep *vt or n* **-pp-** (to liven up or instil with) brisk energy or initiative and high spirits – **peppy** *adj*, **peppiness** *n*

¹**pepper** *n* **1a(1)** BLACK PEPPER (2) WHITE PEPPER **b** any of a genus of tropical mostly climbing shrubs with aromatic leaves; *esp* one with red berries from which black pepper and white pepper are prepared **2** any of various products similar to pepper; *esp* a pungent condiment obtained from capsicums – used with a qualifying term ⟨*cayenne ~*⟩ **3** (the usu red or green fruit of) a capsicum whose fruits are hot peppers or sweet peppers – **pepper** *adj*

²**pepper** *vt* **1a** to sprinkle, season, or cover (as if) with pepper **b** to shower with shot or other missiles **2** to sprinkle ⟨*~ed his report with statistics*⟩

pepper-and-salt *adj, of a fabric or garment* having black and white or dark and light colour intermingled in small flecks

peppercorn *n* a dried berry of the pepper plant

peppermint *n* **1** (an aromatic essential oil obtained from) a mint with dark green tapering leaves and whorls of small pink flowers **2** a sweet flavoured with peppermint oil – **pepperminty** *adj*

pepper pot *n, Br* a small usu cylindrical container with a perforated top used for sprinkling ground pepper on food

peppery *adj* **1** hot, pungent **2** hot-tempered, touchy ⟨*a ~ old man*⟩ **3** fiery, stinging ⟨*a ~ speech*⟩

pep pill *n* a tablet of a stimulant drug

pepsin *n* an enzyme of the stomach that breaks down most proteins in an acid environment

pep talk *n* a usu brief, high-pressure, and emotional talk designed esp to encourage an audience (e g a sports team)

peptic *adj* **1** of or promoting digestion **2** connected with or resulting from the action of digestive juices ⟨*a ~ ulcer*⟩

peptide *n* a short chain of 2 or more amino acids joined by peptide bonds – **peptidic** *adj*

peptide bond *n* the chemical bond between the carbon of one amino acid and the nitrogen of another that links amino acids in peptides and proteins

per *prep* **1** by the means or agency of; through ⟨*send it ~ rail*⟩ **2** with respect to every; for each ⟨*£30 ~ head a week*⟩ **3** ACCORDING TO 1 ⟨*~ list price*⟩

per- *prefix* **1a** through; throughout ⟨*perambulate*⟩ ⟨*pervade*⟩ **b** thoroughly; very ⟨*perfervid*⟩ ⟨*perfect*⟩ **2** to the bad; to destruction ⟨*perjure*⟩ ⟨*perdition*⟩ **3** containing an atom in a high oxidation state in its molecular structure ⟨*perchloric acid*⟩ ⟨*perchlorate*⟩

peradventure *adv, archaic* perhaps, possibly

perambulate *vt* to travel over or through on foot; traverse ~ *vi* to stroll USE *fml* – **perambulation** *n*, **perambulatory** *adj*

perambulator *n, chiefly Br* a pram

per annum *adv* in or for each year

per capita *adv or adj* per unit of population; by or for each person ⟨*the highest income ~ of any European country*⟩

perceive *vt* **1** to understand, realize **2** to become aware of through the senses; *esp* to see, observe – **perceivable** *adj*, **perceivably** *adv*, **perceiver** *n*

¹**per cent** *adv* in or for each 100 ⟨*50 ~ of our workers are married*⟩

²**per cent** *n, pl* **per cent 1** one part in a 100 ⟨*gave half a ~ of her income to charity*⟩ **2** a percentage ⟨*a large ~ of the total*⟩

³**per cent** *adj* **1** reckoned on the basis of a whole divided into 100 parts ⟨*a 10 ~ increase*⟩ **2** *of bonds, securities, etc* paying interest at a specified per cent

percentage *n* **1** a proportion (expressed as per cent of a whole) ⟨*what ~ of the population own their own houses?*⟩ ⟨*the ~ of car owners has increased to 50*⟩ **2** a share of winnings or profits ⟨*they did him out of his ~*⟩ **3** an advantage, profit – *infml*

percentile *n* a statistical measure (e g used in educational and psychological testing) that expresses a value as a percentage of all the values that are lower than or equal to it

perceptible *adj* capable of being perceived, esp by the senses ⟨*a ~ change in her tone*⟩ ⟨*the light became increasingly ~*⟩ – **perceptibly** *adv*, **perceptibility** *n*

perception *n* **1a** a result of perceiving; an observation **b** a mental image; a concept **2** the mental interpretation of physical sensations produced by stimuli from the external world **3** intuitive discernment; insight, understanding ⟨*has little ~ of what is required*⟩ – **perceptional** *adj*, **perceptual** *adj*

perceptive *adj* **1** capable of or exhibiting (keen) perception; observant, discerning ⟨*a ~ scholar*⟩ **2** characterized by sympathetic understanding or insight – **perceptively** *adv*, **perceptiveness** *n*, **perceptivity** *n*

¹**perch** *n* **1a** a roost for a bird **2** *chiefly Br* ROD 2 **3a** a resting place or vantage point; a seat **b** a prominent position ⟨*his new ~ as president*⟩ USE (3) *infml*

²**perch** *vt* to place on a perch, height, or precarious spot ~ *vi* to alight, settle, or rest, esp briefly or precariously

³**perch** *n, pl* **perches,** *esp collectively* **perch** a small European freshwater spiny-finned fish

perchance *adv* perhaps, possibly – usu poetic or humor

percipient *adj* perceptive, discerning – *fml* – **percipience** *n*

percolate *vt* **1a** to cause (esp a liquid) to pass through a permeable substance, esp for extracting a soluble constituent **b** to prepare (coffee) in a percolator **2** to be diffused through; permeate ~*vi* **1** to ooze or filter through a permeable substance; seep **2** to become percolated **3** to become diffused ⟨*sunlight* ~d *into the room*⟩ – **percolation** *n*

percolator *n* a coffee pot in which boiling water rising through a tube is repeatedly deflected downwards through a perforated basket containing ground coffee beans

percussion *n* **1a** the beating or striking of a musical instrument **b** the tapping of the surface of a body part (e g the chest) to learn the condition of the parts beneath (e g the lungs) by the resultant sound **2** the striking of sound on the ear **3** *sing or pl in constr* percussion instruments that form a section of a band or orchestra – **percussion** *adj*, **percussive** *adj*

percussion cap *n* CAP 6

percussionist *n* one who plays percussion instruments

¹**per diem** *adj or adv* (paid) by the day or for each day

²**per diem** *n, pl* **per diems** a daily allowance or fee

perdition *n* eternal damnation; Hell

peregrination *n* a long and wandering journey, esp in a foreign country – *humor* – **peregrinate** *vb*

peregrine, peregrine falcon *n* a smallish swift widely occurring falcon formerly much used in falconry

peremptory *adj* **1** admitting no contradiction or refusal ⟨*a* ~ *conclusion*⟩⟨*a* ~ *command*⟩ **2** expressive of urgency or command ⟨*a* ~ *call*⟩ **3** (having an attitude or nature) characterized by imperious or arrogant self-assurance ⟨*a* ~ *disregard for safety measures*⟩⟨*a* ~ *tone*⟩ – **peremptorily** *adv*, **peremptoriness** *n*

perennial *adj* **1** present at all seasons of the year **2** *of a plant* living for several years, usu with new herbaceous growth each year **3** lasting for a long time or forever; constant ⟨*politics provide a* ~ *topic of argument*⟩ – **perennial** *n*, **perennially** *adv*

¹**perfect** *adj* **1** expert, proficient ⟨*practice makes* ~⟩ **2a** entirely without fault or defect; flawless ⟨*a* ~ *gemstone*⟩ **b** satisfactory in every respect ⟨*the holiday was* ~⟩ **c** corresponding to an ideal standard or abstract concept ⟨*a* ~ *gentleman*⟩ **3a** accurate, exact ⟨~ *pitch*⟩ ⟨*a* ~ *circle*⟩ **b** lacking in no essential detail; complete **c** absolute, utter ⟨*I felt a* ~ *fool*⟩ **4** of or constituting a verb tense or form that expresses an action or state completed at the time of speaking or at a time spoken of **5a** *of the musical intervals fourth, fifth, and octave* having a character that is retained when inverted; not augmented or diminished **b** *of a cadence* passing from a dominant or subdominant to a tonic chord **6** having the stamens and carpels in the same flower – **perfectness** *n*

²**perfect** *vt* **1** to make perfect; improve, refine **2** to bring to final form – **perfecter** *n*, **perfectible** *adj*, **perfectibility** *n*

perfection *n* **1a** making or being perfect **b** freedom from (moral) fault or defect **c** full development; maturity ⟨*Greek civilization slowly flowered to* ~⟩ **2** (an example of) unsurpassable accuracy or excellence ⟨*the cake was* ~⟩

perfectionism *n* **1** the theological doctrine that a state of freedom from sin is attainable on earth **2** a disposition to regard anything short of perfection, esp in one's own work, as unacceptable – **perfectionist** *adj or n*

perfectly *adv* to an adequate extent; quite ⟨*your dress will be* ~ *suitable for the party*⟩

perfect participle *n* PAST PARTICIPLE

perfidy *n* being faithless or disloyal; treachery – **perfidious** *adj*, **perfidiously** *adv*, **perfidiousness** *n*

perforate *vt* **1** to make a hole through; *specif* to make a line of holes in or between (e g rows of postage stamps in a sheet) to make separation easier **2** to pass through or

into (as if) by making a hole ~*vi* to penetrate or make a hole in a surface – **perforator** *n*, **perforate** *adj*, **perforation** *n*

perforce *adv* by force of circumstances – *fml*

perform *vt* **1** to do; CARRY OUT ⟨~ed *a small service*⟩ **2a** to do in a formal manner or according to prescribed ritual ⟨~ *a marriage ceremony*⟩ **b** to give a rendering of; present ⟨*they* ~ed *a new play*⟩ ~*vi* **1** to carry out an action or pattern of behaviour; act, function **2** to give a performance – **performable** *adj*, **performer** *n*

performance *n* **1a** the execution of an action **b** sthg accomplished; a deed, feat **2** the fulfilment of a claim, promise, etc **3** a presentation to an audience of a (character in a) play, a piece of music, etc ⟨*3* ~s *a night*⟩ ⟨*gave a brilliant* ~ *in the title rôle*⟩ **4** the ability to perform or work (efficiently or well) ⟨*good engine* ~ *requires good tuning*⟩ **5** manner of reacting to stimuli; behaviour ⟨*the* ~ *of the stock market*⟩ **6** language as manifested in actual speech and writing **7a** a lengthy or troublesome process or activity ⟨*going through the customs was such a* ~!⟩ **b** a display of bad behaviour *#USE* (7) *infml*

¹**perfume** *n* **1** a sweet or pleasant smell; a fragrance **2** a pleasant-smelling (liquid) preparation (e g of floral essences)

²**perfume** *vt* to fill or imbue with a sweet smell

perfumery *n* **1** (the manufacture of) perfumes **2** a place where perfumes are made or sold – **perfumer** *n*

perfunctory *adj* characterized by routine or superficiality; mechanical, cursory ⟨*a* ~ *smile*⟩ – **perfunctorily** *adv*, **perfunctoriness** *n*

pergola *n* (an arbour made by training plants over) a support for climbing plants

perhaps *adv* possibly but not certainly; maybe ⟨~ *I'm mistaken*⟩ ⟨~ *you would open it?*⟩

perigee *n* the point in an orbit round the earth that is nearest the centre of the earth – **perigean** *adj*

perihelion *n, pl* **perihelia** the point in the path of a planet, comet, etc that is nearest to the sun – **perihelic** *adj*

peril *n* **1** exposure to the risk of being injured, destroyed, or lost; danger ⟨*fire put the city in* ~⟩ **2** sthg that imperils; a risk – **perilous** *adj*, **perilously** *adv*, **perilousness** *n*

perimeter *n* **1** (the length of) the boundary of a closed plane figure **2a** a line, strip, fence, etc bounding or protecting an area ⟨*a* ~ *fence*⟩ **3** the outer edge or limits of sthg

¹**period** *n* **1** a well-proportioned sentence of several clauses **2a** the full pause at the end of a sentence; *also, chiefly NAm* FULL STOP **b** a stop, end **3a** a portion of time **b** the (interval of) time that elapses before a cyclic motion or phenomenon begins to repeat itself; the reciprocal of the frequency **c** (a single cyclic occurrence of) menstruation **4a** a chronological division; a stage (of history) **b** a division of geological time longer than an epoch and included in an era **5** any of the divisions of **a** a school day **b** the playing time of a game

²**period** *adj* of, representing, or typical of a particular historical period ⟨~ *furniture*⟩

periodic *adj* **1** recurring at regular intervals **2** consisting of or containing a series of repeated stages ⟨~ *decimals*⟩ ⟨*a* ~ *vibration*⟩ – **periodicity** *n*

¹**periodical** *adj* **1** PERIODIC 1 **2** *of a magazine or journal* published at fixed intervals (e g weekly or quarterly) – **periodically** *adv*

²**periodical** *n* a periodical publication

periodic table *n* an arrangement of chemical elements in the order of their atomic numbers, that shows a periodic variation in their properties

period piece *n* a piece (e g of fiction, art, furniture, or music) whose special value lies in its evocation of a historical period

¹peripatetic *n* sby, esp a teacher unattached to a particular school, or sthg that travels about from place to place (on business)

²peripatetic *adj* itinerant – **peripatetically** *adv*

¹peripheral *adj* **1** of, involving, or forming a periphery ⟨~ *nerves*⟩; *also* of minor significance **2** located away from a centre or central portion; external **3** of, using, or being the outer part of the field of vision ⟨*good* ~ *vision*⟩ **4** auxiliary or supplementary ⟨~ *equipment*⟩ – **peripherally** *adv*

²peripheral *n* a device (e g a VDU) connected to a computer to provide communication (e g input and output) or auxiliary functions (e g additional storage)

periphery *n* **1** the perimeter of a closed curve (e g a circle or polygon) **2** the external boundary or surface of a (person's) body, esp as distinguished from its internal regions or centre

periphrasis *n*, *pl* **periphrases** (a) circumlocution

periphrastic *adj* **1** of or characterized by periphrasis **2** formed by the use of function words or auxiliaries instead of by inflection (e g *more fair* as contrasted with *fairer*) – **periphrastically** *adv*

periscope *n* a tubular optical instrument containing lenses, mirrors, or prisms for seeing objects not in the direct line of sight

perish *vi* **1a** to be destroyed or ruined ⟨~ *the thought!*⟩ **b** to die, esp in a terrible or sudden way – poetic or journ **2** chiefly *Br* to deteriorate, spoil ⟨*the rubber had begun to* ~⟩ ~ *vt, of cold or exposure* to weaken, numb ⟨*we were* ~ed *with cold*⟩

perishable *n or adj* (sthg, esp food) liable to spoil or decay ⟨*such* ~ *products as fruit, fish, butter, and eggs*⟩ – **perishability** *n*

perisher *n, Br* an annoying or troublesome person or thing; *esp* a mischievous child – infml

perishing *adj* **1** freezingly cold **2** damnable, confounded – **perishingly** *adv*

peristyle *n* a colonnade surrounding a building or court

peritonitis *n* inflammation of the peritoneum

periwig *n* a peruke – **periwigged** *adj*

¹periwinkle *n* any of several trailing evergreen plants with blue or white flowers

²periwinkle *n* any of various (related) edible marine snails

perjure *vt* to make (oneself) guilty of perjury – **perjurer** *n*

perjury *n* the voluntary violation of an oath, esp by a witness

¹perk *n, chiefly Br* a privilege, gain, or profit incidental to regular salary or wages

²perk *vi, of coffee* to percolate

perk up *vb* to (cause to) recover one's vigour or cheerfulness, esp after a period of weakness or depression ⟨*she perked up when the letter arrived*⟩ ⟨*a drink will perk him up*⟩

perky *adj* **1** briskly self-assured; cocky ⟨*a* ~ *salesman*⟩ **2** jaunty – **perkily** *adv*, **perkiness** *n*

¹perm *n* a long-lasting wave set in the hair by chemicals

²perm *vt, Br* to give a perm to

³perm *vt, Br* to permute; *specif* to pick out and combine (a specified number of teams in a football pool) in all the possible permutations ⟨~ *any 8 from 11*⟩ – **perm** *n*

permafrost *n* a layer of permanently frozen ground in frigid regions

¹permanent *adj* **1** continuing or enduring without fundamental or marked change; lasting, stable **2** not subject to

replacement according to political circumstances ⟨~ *undersecretary at the Home Office*⟩ – **permanence, permanency** *n*, **permanently** *adv*

²permanent *n, NAm* ¹PERM

permanent way *n, Br* the rails, sleepers, and ballast that make up the track of a railway system

permanganate *n* a usu dark purple salt containing manganese

permeable *adj* capable of being permeated; *esp* having pores or openings that permit liquids or gases to pass through ⟨*a* ~ *membrane*⟩ – **permeableness** *n*, **permeably** *adv*

permeate *vi* to diffuse through or penetrate sthg ~ *vt* **1** to spread or diffuse through ⟨*a room* ~d *with tobacco smoke*⟩ **2** to pass through the pores, gaps, cracks, etc of – **permeance** *n*, **permeant** *adj or n*, **permeation** *n*

permissible *adj* allowable – **permissibly** *adv*, **permissibility** *n*

permission *n* formal consent; authorization

permissive *adj* **1** tolerant; *esp* accepting a relaxed social or sexual morality ⟨*the* ~ *age*⟩ **2** allowing (but not enforcing) ⟨~ *legislation*⟩ – **permissively** *adv*, **permissiveness** *n*

¹permit *vb* **-tt-** *vt* **1** to consent to, usu expressly or formally ⟨~ *access to records*⟩ **2** to give leave; authorize **3** to make possible ~ *vi* to give an opportunity; allow ⟨*if time* ~s⟩ ⟨*weather* ~ting⟩ – **permitter** *n*

²permit *n* a written warrant allowing the holder to do or keep sthg ⟨*a gun* ~⟩

permutation *n* **1** a variation or change (e g in character or condition) brought about by rearrangement of existing elements **2** (the changing from one to another of) any of the various possible ordered arrangements of a set of objects, numbers, letters, etc – **permutational** *adj*

permute *vt* to change the order or arrangement of; *esp* to arrange successively in all possible ways

pernicious *adj* highly injurious or destructive; deadly – **perniciously** *adv*, **perniciousness** *n*

pernicious anaemia *n* anaemia marked by a decrease in the number of red blood cells which is caused by a reduced ability to absorb vitamin B_{12}

pernickety *adj* **1** fussy about small details; fastidious ⟨*a* ~ *teacher*⟩ **2** requiring precision and care ⟨*a* ~ *job*⟩

peroration *n* **1** the concluding part of a discourse, in which the main points are summed up **2** a highly rhetorical speech – **perorational** *adj*, **perorate** *vi*

¹peroxide *n* **1** an oxide containing a high proportion of oxygen; *esp* a compound containing the peroxy radical **2** HYDROGEN PEROXIDE – **peroxidic** *adj*

²peroxide *vt* to bleach (hair) with hydrogen peroxide – **peroxidation** *n*

¹perpendicular *adj* **1** being or standing at right angles to the plane of the horizon or a given line or plane **2** extremely steep; precipitous **3** *cap* of, being, or built in a late Gothic style of architecture prevalent in England from the 15th to the 16th c characterized by large windows, fan vaults, and an emphasis on vertical lines – **perpendicularly** *adv*, **perpendicularity** *n*

²perpendicular *n* a line, plane, or surface at right angles to the plane of the horizon or to another line or surface

perpetrate *vt* to be guilty of performing or doing; commit ⟨~ *a fraud*⟩ ⟨~ *a blunder*⟩ – **perpetrator** *n*, **perpetration** *n*

perpetual *adj* **1a** continuing or valid forever; everlasting **b** holding sthg (e g an office) for life or for an unlimited time **2** occurring continually; constant ⟨*a* ~ *complaint*⟩ **3** *of a plant* blooming continuously throughout the season – **perpetually** *adv*

perpetuate vt to make perpetual; cause to last indefinitely ⟨~ *the species*⟩ – **perpetuator** n, **perpetuation** n

perpetuity n (the quality or state of) sthg that is perpetual; eternity ⟨*bequeathed to them in* ~⟩

perplex vt 1 to puzzle, confuse ⟨*her attitude* ~es *me*⟩ ⟨~ing *problem*⟩ 2 to complicate – **perplexedly** adv, **perplexingly** adv

perplexity n (sthg that causes) the state of being perplexed or bewildered

perquisite n 1 sthg held or claimed as an exclusive right or possession 2 a perk – fml

perry n an alcoholic drink made from fermented pear juice

perse adj or n dark greyish blue

per se adv by, of, or in itself; intrinsically

persecute vt 1 to harass in a manner designed to injure or afflict; *specif* to cause to suffer because of race, religion, political beliefs, etc 2 to annoy with persistent or urgent approaches, attacks, pleas, etc; pester – **persecutor** n, **persecution** n, **persecutory** adj

perseverance n 1 persevering, steadfastness 2 continuance in a state of grace

persevere vi to persist in a state, enterprise, or undertaking in spite of adverse influences, opposition, or discouragement

Persian n or adj (a native, inhabitant, or language) of ancient Persia or modern Iran

persiflage n frivolous bantering talk

persimmon n (the orange several-seeded globular fruit of) any of a genus of American and Asian trees of the ebony family with hard fine wood

persist vi 1 to go on resolutely or stubbornly in spite of opposition or warning 2 to be insistent in the repetition or pressing of an utterance (e g a question or opinion) 3 to continue to exist, esp past a usual, expected, or normal time – **persister** n

persistent adj 1 continuing to exist in spite of interference or treatment ⟨*a* ~ *cough*⟩ 2a remaining (1) beyond the usual period ⟨*a* ~ *leaf*⟩ (2) without change in function or structure ⟨~ *gills*⟩ b of a chemical substance broken down only slowly in the environment ⟨~ *pesticides*⟩ – **persistence**, **persistency** n, **persistently** adv

persnickety adj, NAm 1 pernickety 2 snobbish

person n 1 a human being (considered as having a character of his/her own, or as being different from all others) ⟨*you're just the* ~ *I wanted to see*⟩ 2 any of the 3 modes of being in the Trinity as understood by Christians 3 a living human body or its outward appearance ⟨*she was small and neat of* ~⟩ ⟨*insured against damage to* ~ *and property*⟩ 4 an individual, corporation, etc with recognized legal rights and duties 5 any of 3 forms of verb or pronoun that indicate reference to the speaker, to one spoken to, or to sby or sthg spoken of – **in person** in one's own bodily presence ⟨*he appeared* in person *last time*⟩

persona n, pl (1) personae, (2) personas 1 pl the characters in a fictional work 2 an individual's social facade that, esp in Jungian psychology, reflects the role that the individual is playing in life

personable adj pleasing in person; attractive – **personableness** n

personage n 1 a person of rank, note, or distinction; *esp* one distinguished in presence and personal power 2 a dramatic, fictional, or historical character 3 a human individual; a person – fml

personal adj 1 of or affecting a person; private ⟨*done purely for* ~ *financial gain*⟩ 2a done in person without the intervention of another; *also* proceeding from a single person b carried on between individuals directly ⟨*a* ~ *interview*⟩ 3 of the person or body 4 of or referring to (the

character, conduct, motives, or private affairs of) an individual, often in an offensive manner ⟨*don't make* ~ *remarks*⟩ 5 of personal property ⟨*a* ~ *estate*⟩ 6 denoting grammatical person

personality n 1 pl reference, esp critical, to a particular person ⟨*let's keep* personalities *out of this debate*⟩ 2 the totality of an individual's behavioural and emotional tendencies; *broadly* a distinguishing complex of individual or group characteristics 3a (sby having) distinction or excellence of personal and social traits b a person of importance, prominence, renown, or notoriety ⟨*a well-known stage* ~⟩

personality cult n the officially encouraged slavish admiration of a leader

personalize, -ise vt 1 PERSONIFY 1 2 to make personal or individual; *specif* to mark as the property of a particular person ⟨~d *stationery*⟩ – **personalization** n

personally adv 1 IN PERSON ⟨*attend to the matter* ~⟩ 2 as a person; in personality ⟨~ *attractive but not very trustworthy*⟩ 3 for oneself; as far as oneself is concerned ⟨~, *I don't think much of it*⟩ 4 as directed against oneself in a personal way ⟨*don't take my remarks about your plan* ~⟩

personal pronoun n a pronoun (e g *I, you,* or *they*) that expresses a distinction of person

personal property n all property other than freehold estates and interests in land

persona non grata adj personally unacceptable or unwelcome

personification n 1 the personifying of an abstract quality or thing 2 an embodiment, incarnation

personify vt 1 to conceive of or represent as having human qualities or form 2 to be the embodiment of in human form; incarnate ⟨*he was kindness* personified⟩ – **personifier** n

personnel n 1 sing or pl in constr a body of people employed (e g in a factory, office, or organization) or engaged on a project 2 a division of an organization concerned with the employees and their welfare at work

¹**perspective** adj of, using, or seen in perspective ⟨*a* ~ *drawing*⟩ – **perspectively** adv

²**perspective** n 1a (the technique of accurately representing on a flat or curved surface) the visual appearance of solid objects with respect to their relative distance and position b LINEAR PERSPECTIVE 2a the aspect of an object of thought from a particular standpoint ⟨*try to get a different* ~ *on your problem*⟩ b (the capacity to discern) the true relationship or relative importance of things ⟨*get things in* ~⟩ 3 a picture or view giving a distinctive impression of distance; a vista

Perspex trademark – used for a transparent acrylic plastic

perspicacious adj of acute mental vision or discernment; KEEN 3a – fml – **perspicaciously** adv, **perspicaciousness** n, **perspicacity** n

perspiration n 1 sweating 2 ²SWEAT 1 – **perspiratory** adj

perspire vi ¹SWEAT 1

persuade vt 1 to move by argument, reasoning, or entreaty to a belief, position, or course of action 2 to cause to feel certain; convince ⟨*the icy roads* ~d *him of the need to drive carefully*⟩ 3 to get (sthg) with difficulty out of or from ⟨*finally* ~d *an answer out of her*⟩ – **persuadable** adj, **persuader** n

persuasion n 1a persuading or being persuaded b persuasiveness ⟨*she has great powers of* ~⟩ 2a an opinion held with complete assurance b (a group adhering to) a particular system of religious beliefs **3** a kind, sort 〈*people of the same* ~〉

persuasive *adj* tending or able to persuade – **persuasively** *adv*, **persuasiveness** *n*

pert *adj* **1** impudent and forward; saucy **2** trim and chic; jaunty 〈*a* ~ *little hat*〉 – **pertly** *adv*, **pertness** *n*

pertain *vi* **1a** to belong *to* as a part, attribute, feature, function, or right 〈*the destruction and havoc* ~ing *to war*〉 **b** to be appropriate to sthg 〈*the criteria that* ~ *elsewhere do not apply here*〉 **2** to have reference *to* 〈*books* ~ing *to birds*〉

pertinacious *adj* clinging resolutely to an opinion, purpose, or design, often to the point of stubbornness – *fml* – **pertinaciously** *adv*, **pertinaciousness** *n*, **pertinacity** *n*

pertinent *adj* clearly relevant (to the matter in hand) 〈~ *details*〉 – **pertinence**, **pertinency** *n*, **pertinently** *adv*

perturb *vt* **1** to disturb greatly in mind; disquiet **2** to throw into confusion; disorder **3** to cause (a moving object, celestial body, etc) to deviate from a theoretically regular (orbital) motion – **perturbable** *adj*, **perturbation** *n*, **perturbational** *adj*

peruke *n* a long curly wig worn by men in the 17th and 18th c

peruse *vt* **1** to examine or consider with attention and in detail; study – *fml* **2** to look over the contents of (e g a book) – often *humor* – **perusal** *n*, **peruser** *n*

pervade *vt* to become diffused throughout every part of – **pervasion** *n*, **pervasive** *adj*, **pervasively** *adv*, **pervasiveness** *n*

perverse *adj* **1a** obstinate in opposing what is right, reasonable, or accepted; wrongheaded **b** arising from or indicative of stubbornness or obstinacy **2** unreasonably opposed to the wishes of others; uncooperative, contrary – **perversely** *adv*, **perversity**, **perverseness** *n*

perversion *n* **1** perverting or being perverted **2** sthg perverted; *esp* abnormal sexual behaviour – **perversive** *adj*

¹**pervert** *vt* **1** to cause to turn aside or away from what is good, true, or morally right; corrupt **2a** to divert to a wrong end or purpose; misuse **b** to twist the meaning or sense of; misinterpret – **perverter** *n*

²**pervert** *n* a perverted person; *specif* one given to some form of sexual perversion

peseta *n* the standard unit of money in Spain

pesky *adj*, *NAm* troublesome, vexatious – *infml*

peso *n*, *pl* **pesos** **1** a former silver coin of Spain and Spanish America worth 8 reals **2** (a note or coin representing) the basic money unit of certain Spanish-speaking South and Latin American countries (e g Argentina, Chile, Mexico, Uruguay) and the Philippines

pessary *n* **1** a vaginal suppository **2** a device worn in the vagina to support the uterus or prevent conception

pessimism *n* **1** a tendency to stress the adverse aspects of a situation or event or to expect the worst possible outcome **2** the doctrine that this is the worst of all possible worlds – **pessimist** *n*, **pessimistic** *adj*, **pessimistically** *adv*

pest *n* **1** a pestilence **2** a plant or animal capable of causing damage or carrying disease **3** sby or sthg that pesters or annoys; a nuisance

pester *vt* to harass with petty irritations; annoy

pesticide *n* a chemical used to destroy insects and other pests of crops, domestic animals, etc

pestiferous *adj* **1** dangerous to society; pernicious **2** carrying or propagating infection – **pestiferously** *adv*

pestilence *n* a virulent and devastating epidemic disease; *specif* BUBONIC PLAGUE

pestilent *adj* **1** destructive of life; deadly **2** morally harmful; pernicious **3** causing displeasure or annoyance; irritating – **pestilently** *adv*

¹**pestle** *n* **1** a usu club-shaped implement for pounding substances in a mortar **2** any of various devices for pounding, stamping, or pressing

²**pestle** *vb* to pound or pulverize (as if) with a pestle

¹**pet** *n* **1** a domesticated animal kept for companionship rather than work or food **2** sby who is treated with unusual kindness or consideration; a favourite **3** *chiefly Br* DARLING **1** – used chiefly by women as an affectionate form of address

²**pet** *adj* **1a** kept or treated as a pet **b** for pet animals 〈*a* ~ *shop*〉 **2** expressing fondness or endearment 〈*a* ~ *name*〉 **3** favourite 〈*his* ~ *project*〉

³**pet** *vb* **-tt-** *vt* **1** to stroke in a gentle or loving manner **2** to treat with unusual kindness and consideration; pamper ~ *vi* to engage in amorous embracing, caressing, etc – **petter** *n*

⁴**pet** *n* a fit of peevishness, sulkiness, or anger

petal *n* any of the modified often brightly coloured leaves of the corolla of a flower – **petaled**, **petalled** *adj*, **petallike** *adj*, **petaloid** *adj*

petard *n* **1** a case containing an explosive for military demolitions **2** a firework that explodes with a loud report

peter *vi* to diminish gradually and come to an end; give out – usu + *out*

Peter *n* (either of 2 New Testament epistles attributed to) a fisherman of Galilee and one of the 12 apostles

petiole *n* the usu slender stalk by which a leaf is attached to a stem – **petiolated** *adj*, **petioled**, **petiolate** *adj*, **petiolar** *adj*

petit bourgeois *n*, *pl* **petits bourgeois** a member of the petite bourgeoisie – **petit bourgeois** *adj*

petite *adj*, *esp of a woman* having a small trim figure

petit four *n*, *pl* **petits fours**, **petit fours** a small fancy cake or biscuit

¹**petition** *n* **1** an earnest request; an entreaty **2** (a document embodying) a formal written request to a superior **3** sthg asked or requested – **petitionary** *adj*

²**petition** *vb* to make an esp formal written request (to or for) – **petitioner** *n*

petit mal *n* (an attack of) mild epilepsy

petrel *n* any of numerous seabirds; *esp* any of the smaller long-winged birds (e g a storm petrel) that fly far from land

petrifaction *n* **1** the process of petrifying; being petrified **2** sthg petrified

petrify *vt* **1** to convert (as if) into stone or a stony substance **2a** to make lifeless or inactive; deaden **b** to confound with fear, amazement, or awe; paralyse 〈*is petrified of talking in public* – Alan Frank〉 ~ *vi* to become stone or of stony hardness or rigidity

petrochemical *n* a chemical obtained from petroleum or natural gas – **petrochemical** *adj*, **petrochemistry** *n*

petrol *n*, *chiefly Br* a volatile inflammable liquid hydrocarbon mixture refined from petroleum and used as a fuel for internal-combustion engines

petroleum *n* an oily inflammable usu dark liquid composed of a mixture of hydrocarbons, widely occurring in the upper strata of the earth, and refined for use as petrol, naphtha, etc

petroleum jelly *n* a semisolid mixture of hydrocarbons obtained from petroleum and used esp as the basis of ointments

petrology *n* a science that deals with the origin, structure, composition, etc of rocks – **petrologist** *n*, **petrologic**, **petrological** *adj*, **petrologically** *adv*

petrol station *n*, *Br* FILLING STATION

¹**petticoat** n 1 an outer skirt formerly worn by women and small children 2 a skirt designed to be worn as an undergarment – **petticoated** adj

²**petticoat** adj of or exercised by women; female ⟨~ government⟩ – chiefly humor or derog

pettifog vi -gg- 1 to engage in legal chicanery 2 to quibble over insignificant details **pettifogger** n, **pettifoggery** n

petty adj 1 having secondary rank or importance; also trivial 2 small-minded – **pettiness** n, **pettily** adv

petty bourgeois n PETIT BOURGEOIS

petty cash n cash kept on hand for payment of minor items

petty larceny n, NAm larceny involving property below a value specified by law – no longer used technically in the UK

petty officer n a noncommissioned officer in the navy

petulant adj characterized by temporary or capricious ill humour; peevish – **petulance** n, **petulantly** adv

petunia n any of a genus of plants of the nightshade family with large brightly coloured funnel-shaped flowers

pew n 1 a bench fixed in a row for the use of the congregation in a church; also a high compartment with such benches for the accommodation of a group (e g a family) 2 Br a seat ⟨take a ~⟩ – infml

pewit n a peewit

pewter n (utensils, vessels, etc made of) any of various tin-containing alloys; esp one of tin and lead – **pewter** adj

peyote n 1 any of several American cacti; esp MESCAL 1 2 MESCAL BUTTON; also mescaline

pfennig n, pl **pfennigs**, **pfennige** often cap a German coin worth 1/100 of a mark

pH n the negative logarithm of the hydrogen-ion concentration in moles per litre, used to express the acidity or alkalinity of a solution on a scale of 0 to 14 with 7 representing neutrality

phaeton n a light open 4-wheeled carriage

phagocyte n a macrophage, white blood cell, etc that characteristically engulfs foreign material (e g bacteria) and consumes debris (e g from tissue injury) – **phagocyte** adj, **phagocytic** adj, **phagocytically** adv

phalanx n, pl **phalanges**, **phalanxes** 1 sing or pl in constr a body of troops, esp those of ancient Greece, in close array 2 any of the digital bones of the hand or foot of a vertebrate 3 sing or pl in constr a massed arrangement of people, animals, or things; esp a body of people organized for a common purpose

phalarope n, pl **phalaropes**, esp collectively **phalarope** any of various small wading birds that have lobed toes and are good swimmers

phallic adj of or resembling a phallus – **phallically** adv

phallus n, pl **phalli**, **phalluses** (a symbol or representation of) the penis

phantasm n 1 an illusion 2a a ghost, spectre b a figment of the imagination; a fantasy – **phantasmal** adj, **phantasmic** adj

phantasmagoria n 1 an optical effect by which figures on a screen appear to dwindle into the distance or to rush towards the observer with enormous increase of size 2 a constantly shifting, confused succession of things seen or imagined (e g in a dreaming or feverish state) – **phantasmagoric** adj

phantasy vb or n (to) fantasy

¹**phantom** n 1a sthg (e g a ghost) apparent to the senses but with no substantial existence b sthg elusive or unreal; a will-o'-the-wisp c sthg existing only in the imagination ⟨his dreams troubled by ~s of the past⟩ 2 sthg existing in appearance only; a form without substance – **phantom-like** adv or adj

²**phantom** adj 1 of the nature of, suggesting, or being a phantom 2 fictitious, dummy ⟨~ voters⟩

pharaoh n, often cap a ruler of ancient Egypt – **pharaonic** adj, often cap

pharisaic, pharisaical adj 1 cap of the Pharisees 2 marked by hypocritical self-righteousness – **pharisaism** n

pharisee n 1 cap a member of a Jewish party noted for strict adherence to (their own oral traditions interpreting) the Torah 2 a pharisaic person

¹**pharmaceutical** also **pharmaceutic** adj of or engaged in pharmacy or in the manufacture of medicinal substances – **pharmaceutically** adv

²**pharmaceutical** n a medicinal drug

pharmacology n 1 the science of drugs and their effect on living things 2 the properties and effects of a usu specified drug ⟨the ~ of morphine⟩ – **pharmacologist** n, **pharmacologic, pharmacological** adj, **pharmacologically** adv

pharmacopoeia n 1 an (official) book describing drugs, chemicals, and medicinal preparations 2 a stock of drugs – **pharmacopoeial** adj

pharmacy n 1 the preparation, compounding, and dispensing of drugs 2a a place where medicines are compounded or dispensed b CHEMIST 2 – **pharmacist** n

pharynx n, pl **pharynges** also **pharynxes** the part of the vertebrate alimentary canal between the mouth cavity and the oesophagus – **pharyngeal** adj, **pharyngitis** n

¹**phase** n 1 a particular appearance or state in a regularly recurring cycle of changes ⟨~s of the moon⟩ 2a a discernable part or stage in a course, development, or cycle ⟨the early ~s of his career⟩ b an aspect or part (e g of a problem) under consideration 3 a stage of progress in a regularly recurring motion or cyclic process (e g an alternating electric current) with respect to a starting point or standard position 4 a homogeneous and mechanically separable portion of matter present in a complex mixture – **phasic** adj

²**phase** vt 1 to conduct or carry out by planned phases 2 to schedule (e g operations) or contract for (e g goods or services) to be performed or supplied as required ⟨~ a development programme⟩

phase in vt to introduce the practice, production, or use of in gradual stages ⟨phase in a new model⟩

phase out vt to discontinue the practice, production, or use of in gradual stages ⟨phase out the old machinery⟩ – **phaseout** n

pheasant n, pl **pheasants**, esp collectively **pheasant** any of numerous large often long-tailed and brightly coloured Old World (game) birds

phenobarbitone NAm chiefly **phenobarbital** n, chiefly Br a barbiturate used esp as a sedative and anticonvulsant in the treatment of epilepsy

phenol n (any of various derivatives of benzene containing a hydroxyl group and analogous to) a caustic poisonous hydroxy benzene used in dilute solution as a disinfectant – **phenolic** adj

phenomenal adj relating to or being a phenomenon: e g a known through the senses rather than through thought or intuition b concerned with phenomena rather than with hypotheses c extraordinary, remarkable ⟨a ~ success⟩ – **phenomenally** adv

phenomenon n, pl **phenomena** also **phenomenons** 1 an observable fact or event 2a an object of sense perception rather than of thought or intuition b a fact or event that can be scientifically described and explained 3a a rare or significant fact or event ⟨vandalism is a social ~⟩ b an exceptional, unusual, or abnormal person, thing, or event; a prodigy

phew *interj* – used to express shock, relief, or exhaustion

phi *n* the 21st letter of the Greek alphabet

phial *n* a small closed or closable vessel, esp for holding liquid medicine

philander *vi* 1 *of a man* to flirt 2 to have many casual love affairs – **philanderer** *n*

philanthropic *also* **philanthropical** *adj* 1 of or characterized by philanthropy; humanitarian 2 dispensing or receiving aid from funds set aside for humanitarian purposes ⟨a ~ institution⟩ – **philanthropically** *adv*

philanthropy *n* 1 goodwill to one's fellow men; *esp* active effort to promote the welfare of others 2 a philanthropic act or gift – **philanthropist** *n*

philately *n* the study and collection of (postage) stamps – **philatelist** *n*, **philatelic** *adj*, **philatelically** *adv*

-phile, -phil *comb form* (→n) one having a fondness or liking for ⟨Francophile⟩; *also* one having a chemical affinity for ⟨neutrophil⟩ – **-phile** *comb form* (→adj)

Philharmonic *n* SYMPHONY ORCHESTRA

-philia *comb form* (→ n) abnormal appetite or liking for ⟨necrophilia⟩ – **-philiac** *comb form* (→adj)

philippic *n* a speech or declamation full of bitter invective

philistine *n* 1 *cap* a native or inhabitant of ancient Philistia 2 *often cap* a person who professes indifference or opposition to intellectual or aesthetic values – **philistine** *adj*, **philistinism** *n*

philology *n* (historical and comparative) linguistics – **philologist** *n*, **philological** *adj*, **philologically** *adv*

philosopher *n* 1a a scholar, thinker b a specialist in philosophy 2 a person whose philosophical viewpoint enables him/her to meet trouble with equanimity

philosophers' stone *n* a substance believed by alchemists to have the power of transmuting base metals into gold

philosophical *adj* 1 of philosophers or philosophy 2 calm in the face of trouble

philosophize, -ise *vi* 1 to engage in philosophical reasoning 2 to expand a trite or superficial philosophy

philosophy *n* 1a the pursuit of wisdom b the study of the nature of knowledge and existence and the principles of moral and aesthetic value 2 the philosophical principles or teachings of a specified individual, group, or period ⟨Kantian ~⟩ 3a the sum of beliefs and attitudes of a specified individual, group, or period ⟨the vegetarian ~⟩ b equanimity in the face of trouble or stress

philtre, *NAm chiefly* **philter** *n* a potion or drug reputed to have the power to arouse sexual passion

phizog *n* FACE 1 –*infml or humor*

phlebitis *n* inflammation of a vein

phlebotomy *n* the letting or taking of blood in the treatment or diagnosis of disease – **phlebotomize** *vb*, **phlebotomist** *n*

phlegm *n* 1 that one of the 4 humours in medieval physiology that was considered to be cold and moist and to cause sluggishness 2 thick mucus secreted in abnormal quantities in the respiratory passages 3a dull or apathetic coldness or indifference b intrepid coolness; composure – **phlegmy** *adj*

phlegmatic *adj* 1 resembling, consisting of, or producing phlegm 2 having or showing a slow and stolid temperament – **phlegmatically** *adv*

phloem *n* a complex vascular tissue of higher plants that functions chiefly in the conduction of soluble food substances (e g sugars)

phlox *n*, *pl* **phlox**, *esp for different types* **phloxes** any of a

genus of American plants with red, purple, white, or variegated flowers

-phobe *comb form* (→ n) one afraid of or averse to ⟨Francophobe⟩ – **-phobe** *comb form* (→adj)

phobia *n* an exaggerated and illogical fear of sthg

-phobia *comb form* (→ n) abnormal fear or dislike of ⟨claustrophobia⟩

phobic *adj* 1 of or being a phobia 2 motivated by or based on withdrawal from an unpleasant stimulus ⟨a ~ response to light⟩

-phobic, -phobous *comb form* (→ adj) lacking (chemical) affinity for ⟨hydrophobic⟩; having an aversion for ⟨Anglophobic⟩

Phoenician *n* (the language of) a native or inhabitant of ancient Phoenicia – **Phoenician** *adj*

phoenix *n* a mythical bird believed to live for 500 years, burn itself on a pyre, and rise alive from the ashes to live another cycle – **phoenixlike** *adj*

phon *n* the unit of loudness relative to a 1kHz tone measured on a scale corresponding to the decibel scale of sound intensity

phon-, phono- *comb form* sound; voice; speech ⟨phonate⟩ ⟨phonograph⟩

¹phone *n* 1 an earphone 2 a telephone

²phone *vb* to telephone – often + *up*

³phone *n* a simple speech sound

-phone *comb form* (→ n) 1 sound ⟨homophone⟩ – often in names of musical instruments and sound-transmitting devices ⟨radiophone⟩ ⟨xylophone⟩ 2 speaker of (a specified language) ⟨Anglophone⟩

phone-in *n* a broadcast programme in which viewers or listeners can participate by telephone

phoneme *n* the smallest unit of speech that can be used to differentiate the meanings of words

phonemic *adj* 1 of phonemes 2 linguistically distinctive – **phonemically** *adv*

phonemics *n pl but sing in constr* 1 the study of phonemes 2 the phonemic system of a language

phonetic, phonetical *adj* 1a of spoken language or speech sounds b of the study of phonetics 2 representing speech sounds by symbols that each have 1 value only – **phonetically** *adv*

phonetics *n pl* 1 *sing in constr* the study and classification of speech sounds 2 *sing or pl in constr* the system of speech sounds of a language – **phonetician** *n*

phoney, *NAm chiefly* **phony** *adj* not genuine or real: e g a intended to deceive, mislead, or defraud; counterfeit b false, sham ⟨a ~ name⟩ ⟨~ pearls⟩ c *of a person* pretentious – **phoney** *n*

phonic *adj* 1 of or producing sound; acoustic 2a of speech sounds b of phonics – **phonically** *adv*

phonics *n pl but sing in constr* a method of teaching reading and pronunciation through the phonetic value of letters, syllables, etc

phonograph *n* 1 an early device for recording or reproducing sound in which a stylus cuts or follows a groove on a cylinder 2 a gramophone – now chiefly NAm or humor

phonology *n* 1 the science of speech sounds 2 the phonetics and phonemics of a language at a particular time – **phonologist** *n*, **phonological** *also* **phonologic** *adj*

phooey *interj* – used to express scorn or incredulity; *infml*

phosphate *n* 1 a salt or ester of a phosphoric acid 2 any of several phosphates used as fertilizers – **phosphatic** *adj*

phosphorescence *n* 1 light emission that is caused by the absorption of radiations and continues for a noticeable time after these radiations have stopped 2 lasting emission of light without noticeable heat – **phosphorescent** *adj*, **phosphoresce** *vi*

phosphoric *adj* of or containing (high valency) phosphorus

phosphorus *n* **1** a nonmetallic trivalent or pentavalent element of the nitrogen family that occurs widely, esp as phosphates, 1 form of which ignites readily in warm moist air **2** a phosphorescent substance or body; *esp* one that shines or glows in the dark

phot-, photo- *comb form* **1** light; radiant energy ⟨*photography*⟩ ⟨*photophilic*⟩ ⟨*phototaxis*⟩ **2** photograph; photographic ⟨*photoengraving*⟩ **3** photoelectric ⟨*photocell*⟩

¹**photo** *vb or n* **photos; photoing; photoed;** *pl* **photos** (to) photograph

²**photo** *adj* PHOTOGRAPHIC 1

¹**photocopy** *n* a photographic reproduction of graphic matter

²**photocopy** *vb* to make a photocopy (of) – **photocopier** *n*

photoelectric *adj* involving, relating to, or using any of various electrical effects due to the interaction of radiation (e g light) with matter – **photoelectrically** *adv*

photoelectric cell *n* a cell whose electrical properties are modified by the action of light

photo finish *n* **1** a race finish so close that the winner is only revealed (as if) by a photograph of the contestants as they cross the finishing line **2** a close contest

photogenic *adj* **1** producing or generating light; luminescent ⟨*~ bacteria*⟩ **2** suitable for being photographed – **photogenically** *adv*

¹**photograph** *n* a picture or likeness obtained by photography

²**photograph** *vt* to take a photograph of *~ vi* **1** to take a photograph **2** to undergo being photographed – **photographer** *n*

photographic *adj* **1** relating to, obtained by, or used in photography **2** capable of retaining vivid impressions; *esp* eidetic ⟨*~ memory*⟩ – **photographically** *adv*

photography *n* the art or process of producing images on a sensitized surface (e g a film) by the action of radiant energy, esp light

photon *n* a quantum of electromagnetic radiation – **photonic** *adj*

photosensitive *adj* sensitive or sensitized to radiant energy, esp light – **photosensitivity** *n*

photosensitize, -ise *vt* to make (abnormally) sensitive to the influence of radiant energy, esp light – **photosensitive** *adj*, **photosensitization** *n*

photostat *vt* to copy on a Photostat device; *broadly* to photocopy – **photostat** *n*, **photostatic** *adj*

Photostat *trademark* – used for a device for making a photographic copy of graphic matter

photosynthesis *n* the synthesis of organic chemical compounds from carbon dioxide using radiant energy, esp light; *esp* the formation of carbohydrates in the chlorophyll-containing tissues of plants exposed to light – **photosynthesize** *vi*, **photosynthetic** *adj*, **photosynthetically** *adv*

phrasal *adj* (consisting) of a phrase – **phrasally** *adv*

¹**phrase** *n* **1** a mode or form of speech; diction **2** a brief usu idiomatic or pithy expression; *esp* a catchphrase ⟨*good at turning a ~* ⟩ **3** a group of musical notes forming a natural unit of melody that is usu 3 or 4 bars in length **4** a group of 2 or more grammatically related words that do not form a clause; *esp* a preposition with the words it governs

²**phrase** *vt* **1** to express in words or in appropriate or

telling terms ⟨*a politely ~d rejection*⟩ **2** to divide into melodic phrases

phrase book *n* a book containing words and idiomatic expressions of a foreign language and their translation

phraseology *n* **1** a mode of organization of words and phrases into longer elements; a style **2** choice of words – **phraseological** *adj*, **phraseologically** *adv*

phrenetic *adj* frenetic

phrenology *n* the study of the conformation of the skull as a supposed indicator of mental faculties and character – **phrenologist** *n*, **phrenological** *adj*, **phrenologically** *adv*

phthisis *n*, *pl* **phthises** a progressive wasting condition; *esp* lung tuberculosis

¹**phut** *n* a dull sound as of sthg bursting

²**phut** *adv*, *chiefly Br* WRONG 4 – chiefly in **go phut**; *infml* ⟨*steam iron went ~* ⟩

phylloxera *n* any of various plant lice that are destructive to many plants (e g grapevines) – **phylloxeran** *adj or n*

phylum *n*, *pl* **phyla** a major group of related species in the classification of plants and animals

physi-, physio- *comb form* **1** nature ⟨*physiography*⟩ **2** physical ⟨*physiotherapy*⟩

¹**physic** *n* a medicinal preparation (e g a drug); *esp* a purgative

²**physic** *vt* **-ck-** *archaic* to administer medicine to; *esp* to purge

physical *adj* **1a** having material existence; perceptible, esp through the senses, and subject to the laws of nature **b** of material things **2a** of natural science **b** of or involving physics ⟨*~ chemistry*⟩ **3a** of the body ⟨*~ education*⟩ **b** concerned or preoccupied with the body and its needs, as opposed to spiritual matters – **physically** *adv*

physical geography *n* geography that deals with the exterior physical features and changes of the earth

physical jerks *n* bodily exercises – *infml*

physician *n* a person skilled in the art of healing; *specif* a doctor of medicine

physics *n pl but sing or pl in constr* **1** a science that deals with (the properties and interactions of) matter and energy in such fields as mechanics, heat, electricity, magnetism, atomic structure, etc **2** the physical properties and phenomena of a particular system – **physicist** *n*

physiognomy *n* **1** the art of judging character from outward appearance **2** the facial features, esp when revealing qualities of mind or character **3** an external aspect; *also* inner character or quality revealed outwardly ⟨*the ~ of a political party*⟩ – **physiognomic, physiognomical** *adj*, **physiognomically** *adv*

physiological, physiologic *adj* **1** of physiology **2** characteristic of or appropriate to an organism's healthy or normal functioning ⟨*the ~ level of a substance in the blood*⟩ – **physiologically** *adv*

physiology *n* **1** biology that deals with the functions and activities of life or of living matter (e g organs, tissues, or cells) and the physical and chemical phenomena involved **2** the physiological activities of (part of) an organism or a particular bodily function ⟨*the ~ of sex*⟩ – **physiologist** *n*

physiotherapy *n* the treatment of disease by physical and mechanical means (e g massage and regulated exercise) – **physiotherapist** *n*

physique *n* the form or structure of a person's body

¹**pi** *n*, *pl* **pis 1** the 16th letter of the Greek alphabet **2** (the symbol π denoting) the ratio of the circumference of a circle to its diameter with a value, to 8 decimal places, of 3.14159265

²**pi** *vt* **pies; piing; pieing; pied** *chiefly NAm* ³PIE

³**pi** *adj*, *Br* pious – *derog*

pianissimo *adv or adj* very soft – used in music

pianist *n* a skilled or professional performer on the piano

¹piano *adv or adj* in a soft or quiet manner – used in music

²piano *n, pl* **pianos** a stringed instrument having steel wire strings that sound when struck by felt-covered hammers operated from a keyboard

Pianola *trademark* – used for a mechanical piano operated by the pressure of air through perforations in a paper roll

piastre, *NAm* **piaster** *n* (a note or coin representing) a unit worth $^1/_{100}$ of the basic money unit of certain Middle Eastern countries (e g Egypt, Syria)

piazza *n, pl* **piazzas, piazze** 1 an open square, esp in an Italian town 2 *NAm* a veranda

pibroch *n* a set of martial or mournful variations for the Scottish Highland bagpipe

¹pica *n* 1 a unit of 4.23 mm (about 1/6 in) used in measuring typographical material 2 a typewriter type providing 10 characters to the linear inch

²pica *n* the pathological craving for and eating of inappropriate substances (e g chalk or ashes)

picador *n, pl* **picadors, picadores** a horseman who in a bullfight prods the bull with a lance to weaken its neck and shoulder muscles

picaresque *adj* of or being fiction narrating in loosely linked episodes the adventures of a rogue

piccalilli *n* a hot relish of chopped vegetables, mustard, and spices

piccaninny, *chiefly NAm* **picaninny, pickaninny** *n* a small Negro child – chiefly derog

piccolo *n, pl* **piccolos** a small shrill flute whose range is an octave higher than that of an ordinary flute – **piccoloist** *n*

¹pick *vt* 1 to pierce, penetrate, or break up with a pointed instrument ⟨~ed *the hard clay*⟩ 2a to remove bit by bit ⟨~ *meat from bones*⟩ b to remove covering or clinging matter from ⟨~ed *the bones clean*⟩ 3a to gather by plucking ⟨~ed *flowers*⟩ b to choose, select ⟨*tried to* ~ *the shortest route*⟩⟨*she* ~ed *out the most expensive dress*⟩ 4 to pilfer from; rob ⟨~ *pockets*⟩ 5 to provoke ⟨~ *a quarrel*⟩ 6a to dig into, esp in order to remove unwanted matter; probe ⟨~ *his teeth*⟩⟨~ *his nose*⟩ b to pluck with a plectrum or with the fingers ⟨~ *a guitar*⟩ c to loosen or pull apart with a sharp point ⟨~ *wool*⟩ 7 to unlock with a device (e g a wire) other than the key ⟨~ *a lock*⟩ 8 to make (one's way) carefully on foot ~ *vi* to gather or harvest sthg by plucking – **pick and choose** to select with care and deliberation – **pick at** 1 to find fault with, esp in a petty way 2 to eat sparingly and with little interest; toy with – **pick on** 1 to single out for unpleasant treatment or an unpleasant task 2 to single out for a particular purpose or for special attention – **pick someone's brains** to obtain ideas or information from sby – **pick someone/something to pieces** to subject to systematic adverse criticism

²pick *n* 1 the act or privilege of choosing or selecting; a choice ⟨*take your* ~⟩ 2 *sing or pl in constr* the best or choicest ⟨*the* ~ *of the herd*⟩ 3 the portion of a crop gathered at 1 time ⟨*the first* ~ *of grapes*⟩

³pick *vt* to throw (a shuttle) across the loom

⁴pick *n* 1 a throw of the shuttle across a loom 2 one weft thread taken as a unit of fineness of fabric

⁵pick *n* 1 a heavy wooden-handled iron or steel tool with a head that is pointed at one or both ends 2 a toothpick 3 a plectrum

pickaback *n, adv, or adj* (a) piggyback

pickaxe *n* ⁵PICK 1

picked *adj* choice, prime

picker *n* 1 a person or machine that picks sthg, esp crops 2 a person or the part of the loom that threads the shuttle

pickerel *n, pl* **pickerels,** *esp collectively* **pickerel** *dial chiefly Br* a young or small pike

¹picket *n* 1 a pointed or sharpened stake, post, or pale 2 *sing or pl in constr* a a small body of troops detached to guard an army from surprise attack b a detachment kept ready in camp for such duty 3 a person posted by a trade union at a place of work affected by a strike; *also* a person posted for a demonstration or protest

²picket *vt* 1 to enclose, fence, or fortify with pickets 2 to tether 3 to guard with or post as a picket 4a to post pickets at b to walk or stand in front of as a picket ~ *vi* to serve as a picket – **picketer** *n*

picket line *n* a line of people picketing a business, organization, etc

pickings *n pl* sthg picked (up): e g a gleanable or eatable fragments; scraps b yield or return for effort expended; *esp* rewards obtained by dishonest or dubious means

¹pickle *n* 1 a solution or bath for preserving or cleaning: e g a a brine or vinegar solution in which meat, fish, vegetables, etc are preserved b an acidic solution for cleaning metal 2 (an article of) food preserved in a pickle; *also* chutney – often *pl* 3 a difficult situation – *infml* ⟨*I could see no way out of the* ~ *I was in* – R L Stevenson⟩ 4 *Br* a mischievous or troublesome child – *infml*

²pickle *vt* **pickling** to treat, preserve, or clean in or with a pickle

³pickle *n, Scot* a small quantity

pickled *adj* DRUNK 1 – *infml*

pick-me-up *n* sthg that stimulates or restores; a tonic

pick off *vt* to shoot or bring down one by one ⟨*the sniper* picked off *the enemy troops*⟩

pick out *vt* 1 to make clearly visible, esp as distinguished from a background ⟨*the fences were* picked out *in red*⟩ 2 to play the notes of by ear or one by one ⟨*learned to* pick out *tunes on the piano*⟩

pick over *vt* to examine in order to select the best or discard the unwanted ⟨picked over *the berries*⟩

pickpocket *n* one who steals from pockets or bags

pickup *n* 1 the act or process of picking up 2 sby or sthg picked up: e g a a hitchhiker who is given a lift b a temporary casual acquaintance; *esp* one made with the intention of having sex 3 a device (e g on a record player) that converts mechanical movements into electrical signals 4 a device (e g a microphone or a television camera) for converting sound or an image into electrical signals 5 interference (e g to reception) from an adjacent electrical circuit or system 6 a light motor truck having an open body with low sides and tailboard

pick up *vt* 1a to take hold of and lift up ⟨picked up *the pencil*⟩ b to gather together; collect ⟨picked up *all the pieces*⟩ 2 to take (passengers or freight) into a vehicle 3a to acquire casually or by chance ⟨picked up *a valuable antique at a jumble sale*⟩⟨picked up *some money doing odd jobs*⟩ b to acquire by study or experience; learn ⟨picking up *a great deal of information in the process*⟩ c to collect ⟨picked up *his clothes at the cleaners*⟩ d to accept for the purpose of paying ⟨*the government should* pick up *the bill for the damaged ship*⟩ 4 to enter informally into conversation or companionship with (a previously unknown person), usu with the intention of having sex 5a to take into custody b to discover and follow ⟨picked up *the outlaw's trail*⟩ c to bring within range of sight, hearing, or a sensor ⟨picked up *the planes on the radar*⟩ 6 to revive 7 to resume after a break; continue 8 *chiefly NAm* to clean up; tidy ~ *vi*

picky *adj, chiefly NAm* fussy, choosy ⟨*a* ~ *eater*⟩

¹**picnic** n **1** (the food eaten at) an outing that includes an informal meal, usu lunch, eaten in the open **2** a pleasant or amusingly carefree experience ⟨*don't expect marriage to be a ~*⟩; *also* an easily accomplished task or feat – infml – **picnicky** adj

²**picnic** vi **-ck-** to go on a picnic – **picnicker** n

picric acid n an explosive yellow strong acid used esp in powerful explosives and as an antiseptic

pictorial adj **1** of (a) painting or drawing ⟨*~ perspective*⟩ **2** consisting of or illustrated by pictures ⟨*~ records*⟩ **3** suggesting or conveying visual images – **pictorially** adv, **pictorialness** n

¹**picture** n **1** a design or representation made by painting, drawing, etc **2a** a description so vivid or graphic as to suggest a mental image or give an accurate idea of sthg ⟨*painted a vivid ~ of life in Victorian England*⟩ **b** a presentation of the relevant or characteristic facts concerning a problem or situation ⟨*drew an alarming ~ of the economic future*⟩ **3a** an image, copy ⟨*he was the ~ of his father*⟩ **b** the perfect example ⟨*he looked the ~ of health*⟩ **c** a striking or picturesque sight ⟨*his face was a ~ when he heard the news*⟩ **4a** a transitory visible image or reproduction ⟨*adjusted the television for a brighter ~*⟩ **b** FILM 3a, b **c** pl, chiefly Br CINEMA 1b, 2 – infml ⟨*what's on at the ~s?*⟩ **5** a situation ⟨*a look at the overall political ~*⟩ – **in the picture** fully informed and up to date

²**picture** vt **1** to paint or draw a representation, image, or visual conception of; depict **2** to describe graphically in words **3** to form a mental image of; imagine

picture-postcard adj picturesque ⟨*~ villages*⟩

picturesque adj **1** quaint, charming **2** evoking striking mental images; vivid ⟨*~ language*⟩ – **picturesquely** adv, **picturesqueness** n

¹**piddle** vi **piddling 1** to act or work in an idle or trifling manner **2** to urinate USE infml

²**piddle** n **1** urine **2** an act of urinating USE infml

piddling adj trivial, paltry – infml

pidgin n a language based on 2 or more languages and used esp for trade between people with different native languages – **pidginize** vt

¹**pie** n **1** MAGPIE 1 **2** a variegated animal

²**pie** n a dish consisting of a sweet or savoury filling covered or encased by pastry and baked in a container

³**pie**, chiefly NAm **pi** vt to spill or throw (type or typeset matter) into disorder – **pie** n

¹**piebald** adj **1** esp of a horse of different colours; specif spotted or blotched with different colours, esp black and white **2** composed of incongruous parts; heterogeneous

²**piebald** n a piebald horse or other animal

¹**piece** n **1a** a part of a whole; esp a part detached, cut, or broken from a whole ⟨*~ of string*⟩ **b** a portion marked off ⟨*bought a ~ of land*⟩ **2** an object or individual regarded as a unit of a kind or class; an example ⟨*fine teak tables copied from antique ~s*⟩ **3** a standard quantity (e g of length, weight, or size) in which sthg is made or sold **4a** a literary, artistic, dramatic, or musical work **b** a passage to be recited **5** a coin, esp of a specified value ⟨*a 5-pence ~*⟩ **6** a man used in playing a board game; esp a chessman of rank superior to a pawn **7** a gun used for a specified purpose ⟨*an artillery ~*⟩ **8** a person; esp a woman – slang – **piece of one's mind** a severe scolding – **of a piece** alike, consistent – **to pieces 1** into fragments **2** out of control ⟨*went to pieces from shock*⟩

²**piece** vt **1** to repair, renew, or complete by adding pieces; patch – often + up **2** to join into a whole – often + together ⟨*he ~d the story together from the accounts of witnesses*⟩ – **piecer** n

pièce de résistance n, pl **pièces de résistance 1** the

chief dish of a meal **2** an outstanding item; a showpiece

¹**piecemeal** adv **1** one piece at a time; gradually **2** in pieces or fragments; apart

²**piecemeal** adj done, made, or accomplished piece by piece or in a fragmentary way

piece of eight n a peso

piecework n work that is paid for at a set rate per unit – **pieceworker** n

piecrust n the baked pastry covering of a pie

pied adj having patches of 2 or more colours

pied-à-terre n, pl **pieds-à-terre** a temporary or second lodging (e g a flat in a city kept by sby who lives in the country)

pie-eyed adj DRUNK 1 – infml

pier n **1** an intermediate support for the adjacent ends of 2 bridge spans **2** a structure extending into navigable water for use as a landing place, promenade, etc **3** a vertical structural support (e g for a wall)

pierce vt **1** to enter or thrust into sharply or painfully; stab ⟨*the thorn ~d his finger*⟩ **2** to make a hole in or through; perforate **3** to force or make a way into or through ⟨*a light ~d the darkness*⟩ **4** to penetrate with the eye or mind; discern **5** to move or affect the emotions of, esp sharply or painfully ⟨*grief ~d his heart when he heard of his son's death*⟩ **6** to sound sharply through ⟨*a shriek ~d the stillness of the evening*⟩ **7** of cold to penetrate ⟨*the cold ~d them to the bone*⟩ ~ vi to force a way into or through sthg

piercing adj penetrating: e g a loud, shrill ⟨*~ cries*⟩ **b** perceptive ⟨*~ eyes*⟩ **c** penetratingly cold; biting ⟨*a winter wind*⟩ **d** cutting, incisive ⟨*~ sarcasm*⟩ – **piercingly** adv

Pierrot n a stock comic character of old French pantomime usu having a whitened face

pietà n, often cap a representation of the Virgin Mary mourning over the dead body of Christ

piety n **1** the quality or state of being pious; devoutness **2** dutifulness, esp to parents ⟨*inspired by filial ~*⟩ **3** an act inspired by piety

piezoelectricity n electricity or electric polarity due to pressure, esp in a crystalline substance (e g quartz) – **piezoelectric** adj

piffle n trivial nonsense – infml

piffling adj trivial, derisory – infml

¹**pig** n **1a** chiefly Br any of various (domesticated) stout-bodied short-legged omnivorous mammals with a thick bristly skin and a long mobile snout **b** NAm a young pig **2** pork **3** sby like or suggestive of a pig in habits or behaviour (e g in dirtiness, greed, or selfishness) ⟨*a male chauvinist ~*⟩ ⟨*made a ~ of himself by eating all the cake*⟩ **4** an animal related to or resembling the pig – usu in combination ⟨*guinea ~*⟩ **5** a shaped mass of cast crude metal, esp iron **6** a policeman – slang; derog – **piglet** n

²**pig** vb **-gg-** vi **1** to farrow **2** to live like a pig – + it ~ vt **1** to farrow (piglets) **2a** to eat (food) greedily ⟨*~ged all the cream cakes*⟩ **b** to overindulge (oneself) ⟨*~ged himself on cream cakes*⟩ USE (vt 2) infml

pigeon n **1** any of a family of birds with a stout body and smooth and compact plumage, many of which are domesticated or live in urban areas **2** a matter of special concern; business – infml ⟨*that's not my ~; someone else can deal with it*⟩

¹**pigeonhole** n **1** a small open compartment (e g in a desk or cabinet) for letters or documents **2** a neat category which usu fails to reflect actual complexities ⟨*a psychological ~ for every misfit*⟩

²**pigeonhole** vt **1a** to place (as if) in the pigeonhole of a

desk **b** to lay aside; shelve **2** to assign to a category; classify

pigeon-toed *adj* having the toes turned in

piggery *n* **1** a place where pigs are kept **2** dirty or nasty behaviour ⟨*male chauvinist ~*⟩

piggish, piggy *adj* of or resembling a pig, esp in being dirty, greedy, or ill mannered ⟨*embarrassed by his ~ eating habits*⟩ – **piggishly** *adv*, **piggishness** *n*

piggy *n* a pig; *esp* a little pig – used esp by or to children

¹piggyback *adv* up on the back and shoulders ⟨*carried the child ~ up the stairs*⟩

²piggyback *n* a ride on the back and shoulders of another ⟨*gave his injured friend a ~*⟩

³piggyback *adj* **1** being up on the shoulders and back ⟨*children love ~ rides*⟩ **2** being or relating to sthg carried as an extra load on the back of a vehicle (e g an aircraft)

piggy bank *n* a coin bank often in the shape of a pig

pigheaded *adj* obstinate, stubborn – **pigheadedness** *n*

pig iron *n* crude iron from the blast furnace before refining

¹pigment *n* **1** a substance that colours other materials; *esp* a powdered substance that is mixed with a liquid in which it is relatively insoluble and is used to colour paints, inks, plastics, etc **2** (a colourless substance related to) any of various colouring matters in animals and plants – **pigmentary** *adj*

²pigment *vt* to colour (as if) with pigment

pigmentation *n* (excessive) coloration with, or deposition of, (bodily) pigment

pigmy *n* a pygmy

pignut *n* a common plant of the carrot family

pigskin *n* (leather made from) the skin of a pig

pigsticking *n* the hunting of wild boar on horseback with a spear

pigsty *n* **1** an enclosure with a covered shed for pigs **2** a dirty, untidy, or neglected place

pigtail *n* **1** a tight plait of hair, esp when worn singly at the back of the head **2** either of 2 bunches of hair worn loose or plaited at either side of the head by young girls – **pigtailed** *adj*

¹pike *n*, *Br* a mountain or hill, esp in the Lake District, with a peaked summit

²pike *n*, *pl* **pike**, *esp for different types* **pikes** (any of various fishes related to or resembling) a large long-snouted fish-eating bony fish widely distributed in cooler parts of the N hemisphere

³pike *n* a weapon consisting of a long wooden shaft with a pointed steel head that was used by foot soldiers until superseded by the bayonet – **pike** *vt*

⁴pike *n* a body position (e g in diving) in which the hands touch the toes or clasp the legs at the knees, the hips are bent forwards, and the knees are straight

pikestaff *n* **1** a spiked staff for use on slippery ground **2** the staff of a foot soldier's pike

pilaster *n* an upright rectangular column that is usu embedded in a wall

pilau *n* (a) pilaf

pilchard *n* (any of several sardines related to) a fish of the herring family that occurs in great schools along the coasts of Europe

¹pile *n* a beam of timber, steel, reinforced concrete, etc driven into the ground to carry a vertical load

²pile *vt* to drive piles into

³pile *n* **1a** a quantity of things heaped together **b** a heap of wood for burning a corpse or a sacrifice **c** a large quantity, number, or amount ⟨*a ~ of stuff still to be read*⟩ ⟨*~s of friends*⟩ **2** a large building or group of

buildings **3** a great amount of money; a fortune ⟨*now that he has made his ~, he can live in luxury*⟩ **4** a vertical series of alternate discs of 2 dissimilar metals (e g copper and zinc) separated by discs of cloth or paper moistened with an electrolyte for producing an electric current **5** REACTOR 2

⁴pile *vt* **1** to lay or place in a pile; stack – often + up **2** to heap in abundance; load ⟨*~d potatoes on his plate*⟩ ~ *vi* to move or press forwards (as if) in a mass; crowd ⟨*~d into the car*⟩ – **pile it on** to exaggerate

⁵pile *n* **1** soft hair, down, fur, or wool **2** a soft raised surface on a fabric or carpet consisting of cut threads or loops – **piled** *adj*

⁶pile *n* a haemorrhoid – usu pl

pile driver *n* a machine for driving piles into the ground

pileup *n* a collision involving usu several motor vehicles and causing damage or injury

pile up *vi* **1** to accumulate ⟨*his work* piled up *over the holidays*⟩ **2** to become involved in a pileup of vehicles

pileus *n*, *pl* **pilei** the (umbrella-shaped) fruiting body of many fungi (e g mushrooms) – **pileate** *adj*

pilfer *vb* to steal stealthily in small amounts or to small value – **pilferage** *n*, **pilferer** *n*

pilgrim *n* a person making a pilgrimage

pilgrimage *n* **1** a journey to a shrine or sacred place as an act of devotion, in order to acquire spiritual merit, or as a penance **2** the course of life on earth

Pilgrim Fathers *n pl* the English colonists who settled at Plymouth, Massachusetts, in 1620

pill *n* **1a** a small rounded solid mass of medicine to be swallowed whole **b** an oral contraceptive in the form of an (oestrogen- and progestogen-containing) pill taken daily by a woman over a monthly cycle – + the **2** sthg repugnant or unpleasant that must be accepted or endured ⟨*the loss of salary was a bitter ~ to swallow*⟩ **3** sthg resembling a pill in size or shape **4** a disagreeable or tiresome person – *infml*

¹pillage *n* **1** the act of looting or plundering, esp in war **2** sthg taken as booty

²pillage *vb* to plunder ruthlessly; loot – **pillager** *n*

¹pillar *n* **1a** a firm upright support for a superstructure **b** a usu ornamental column or shaft **2** a chief supporter; a prop ⟨*a ~ of the Establishment*⟩ **3** a solid mass of coal, ore, etc left standing to support a mine roof – **from pillar to post** from one place or one situation to another

²pillar *vt* to support or decorate (as if) with pillars

pillar box *n* a red pillar-shaped public letter box

pillbox *n* **1** a box for pills; *esp* a shallow round box made of pasteboard **2** a small low concrete weapon emplacement **3** a small round brimless hat with a flat crown and straight sides, worn esp by women

¹pillion *n* a saddle or seat for a passenger on a motorcycle or motor scooter ⟨*a ~ passenger*⟩

²pillion *adv* (as if) on a pillion ⟨*ride ~*⟩

¹pillory *n* **1** a device for publicly punishing offenders consisting of a wooden frame with holes for the head and hands **2** a means for exposing one to public scorn or ridicule

²pillory *vt* **1** to put in a pillory **2** to expose to public contempt, ridicule, or scorn

¹pillow *n* **1** a usu rectangular cloth bag (e g of cotton) filled with soft material (e g down) and used to support the head of a reclining person **2** sthg resembling a pillow, esp in form

²pillow *vt* **1** to rest or lay (as if) on a pillow **2** to serve as a pillow for

pillowcase *n* a removable washable cover, esp of cotton or nylon, for a pillow

pillow lace *n* lace worked with bobbins over a padded support

¹pilot *n* **1** sby qualified and usu licensed to conduct a ship into and out of a port or in specified waters **2** a guide, leader **3** sby who handles or is qualified to handle the controls of an aircraft or spacecraft **4** a piece that guides a tool or machine part – **pilotage** *n*, **pilotless** *adj*

²pilot *vt* **1** to act as a guide to; lead or conduct over a usu difficult course **2a** to direct the course of ⟨~ *a ship*⟩ **b** to act as pilot of ⟨~ *a plane*⟩

³pilot *adj* serving as a guide, activator, or trial ⟨~ *holes*⟩ ⟨~ *lamps*⟩ ⟨*a* ~ *scheme*⟩

pilot fish *n* an oceanic fish that often swims in company with a shark

pilot light *n* **1** an indicator light showing whether power is on or where a switch or circuit breaker is located **2** a small permanent flame used to ignite gas at a burner

pilot officer *n* an officer of the lowest rank in the Royal Air Force

pimento *n, pl* **pimentos, pimento** **1** a pimiento **2** allspice

pimp *n* a man who solicits clients for a prostitute or brothel – **pimp** *vi*

pimpernel *n* any of several plants of the primrose family: e g **a** SCARLET PIMPERNEL **b** YELLOW PIMPERNEL

pimple *n* (a swelling or protuberance like) a small solid inflamed (pus-containing) elevation of the skin – **pimpled** *adj*, **pimply** *adj*

¹pin *n* **1a** a piece of solid material (e g wood or metal) used esp for fastening separate articles together or as a support **b** sthg resembling a pin, esp in slender elongated form **2a** a small thin pointed piece of metal with a head used esp for fastening cloth, paper, etc **b** sthg of small value; a trifle ⟨*doesn't care a* ~ *for anyone*⟩ **c** an ornament or badge fastened to clothing with a pin **d** SAFETY PIN **3a** any of the wooden pieces constituting the target in various games (e g skittles and tenpin bowling) **b** the peg at which a quoit is pitched **c** the staff of the flag marking a hole on a golf course **4** a projecting metal bar on a plug which is inserted into a socket **5** PEG 3a **6** a leg – infml; usu pl ⟨*wobbly on his* ~ *s*⟩ – **pinned** *adj*

²pin *vt* **-nn-** **1a** to fasten, join, or secure with a pin **b** to hold fast or immobile ⟨~ ned *him against the wall*⟩ **2a** to attach, hang ⟨~ ned *his hopes on a miracle*⟩ **b** to assign the blame or responsibility for ⟨~ *the robbery on a night watchman*⟩ **3** to make (a chess opponent's piece) unable to move without exposing the king to check or a valuable piece to capture

pinafore *n* **1** an apron, usu with a bib **2** *also* **pinafore dress** a sleeveless usu low-necked dress designed to be worn over another garment (e g a blouse)

pinball machine *n* an amusement device for playing pinball and automatically recording the score

pince-nez *n, pl* **pince-nez** glasses clipped to the nose by a spring

pincer *n* **1a** *pl* an instrument having 2 short handles and 2 grasping jaws working on a pivot and used for gripping things **b** a claw (e g of a lobster) resembling a pair of pincers **2** either part of a double military envelopment of an enemy position – **pincerlike** *adj*

¹pinch *vt* **1a** to squeeze or compress painfully (e g between the finger and thumb or between the jaws of an instrument) **b** to prune the tip of (a plant or shoot), usu to induce branching – + *out* or *back* **c** to cause to appear thin or shrunken ⟨*faces* ~ ed *with hunger and fatigue*⟩ **2** to subject to strict economy or want; straiten **3** to sail (a ship) too close to the wind **4a** STEAL 1 – slang **b** ARREST 2 – slang ~ *vi* **1** to compress, squeeze **2** to press painfully

⟨*my new shoes* ~⟩ **3** *of a ship* to sail too close to the wind – **pincher** *n*

²pinch *n* **1a** a critical juncture; an emergency ⟨*when it comes to the* ~ , *he'll let you down*⟩ **b(1)** pressure, stress ⟨*when the* ~ *of foreign competition came at last* – G M Trevelyan⟩ **(2)** hardship, privation ⟨*after a year of sanctions, they began to feel the* ~⟩ **2a** an act of pinching; a squeeze **b** as much as may be taken between the finger and thumb ⟨*a* ~ *of snuff*⟩ – **at a pinch** in an emergency – **with a pinch of salt** with reservations as to the validity of sthg

pinchbeck *n* an alloy of copper and zinc used esp to imitate gold in jewellery – **pinchbeck** *adj*

pincushion *n* a small cushion in which pins are stuck ready for use, esp in sewing

pin down *vt* **1** to force (sby) to state his/her position or make a decision **2** to define precisely ⟨*a vague feeling of unease that she couldn't quite* pin down⟩ **3** to fasten down; prevent from moving

¹pine *vi* **1** to lose vigour or health (e g through grief); languish – often + *away* **2** to yearn intensely and persistently, esp for sthg unattainable; long ⟨*pining for her lost youth*⟩

²pine *n* **1** (any of various trees related to) any of a genus of coniferous evergreen trees which have slender elongated needles **2** the straight-grained white or yellow usu durable and resinous wood of a pine – **piny, piney** *adj*

pineal gland *n* a small appendage of the brain of most vertebrates that has the structure of an eye in a few reptiles, and that secretes melatonin and other hormones – **pineal** *adj*

pineapple *n* **1** (the large oval edible succulent yellow-fleshed fruit of) a tropical plant related to the grasses, lilies, and orchids, with rigid spiny leaves and a dense head of small flowers **2** a hand grenade – slang

pinecone *n* a cone of a pine tree

pine marten *n* a slender Eurasian marten with a yellow patch on the chest and throat

ping *vi* or *n* (to make) a sharp ringing sound

Ping-Pong *trademark* – used for table tennis

pinhead *n* **1** sthg very small or insignificant **2** a very dull or stupid person; a fool – infml

¹pinion *n* **1** (the end section of) a bird's wing **2** a bird's feather; a quill – **pinioned** *adj*

²pinion *vt* **1** to restrain (a bird) from flight, esp by cutting off the pinion of a wing **2a** to disable or restrain by binding the arms **b** to bind fast; shackle

³pinion *n* a gear with a small number of teeth designed to mesh with a larger gear wheel or rack

¹pink *vt* **1** to pierce slightly; stab **2a** to perforate in an ornamental pattern **b** to cut a zigzag or saw-toothed edge on

²pink *n* a sailing vessel with a narrow overhanging stern

³pink *n* any of a genus of plants related to the carnation and widely grown for their white, pink, red, or variegated flowers – **in the pink** in the best of health – infml

⁴pink *adj* **1** of the colour pink **2** holding moderately radical political views – **pinkish** *adj*, **pinkness** *n*

⁵pink *n* **1** any of various shades of pale red **2** (the scarlet colour of) a fox hunter's coat

⁶pink *adv* to a high degree; enormously – in **tickled pink**; infml

⁷pink *vi, Br, of an internal-combustion engine* to make a series of sharp popping noises because of faulty combustion of the fuel-air mixture

pink elephants *n pl* any of various hallucinations arising esp from heavy drinking or use of drugs – infml

pinkeye *n* a highly contagious conjunctivitis of human beings and various domestic animals

pink gin *n* a drink consisting of gin flavoured with angostura bitters

pinkie, pinky *n, NAm & dial Br* LITTLE FINGER

pinking shears *n pl* shears with a saw-toothed inner edge on the blades, used in sewing for making a zigzag cut in cloth to prevent fraying

pinko *n, pl* **pinkos, pinkoes** sby who holds moderately radical political views – chiefly derog

pin money *n* **1a** extra money earned by sby, esp a married woman (e g in a part-time job) **b** money set aside for the purchase of incidentals **2** a trivial amount of money

pinna *n, pl* **pinnae, pinnas 1** a leaflet or primary division of a pinnate leaf or frond **2** a largely cartilaginous projecting portion of the outer ear – **pinnal** *adj*

pinnace *n* any of various ship's boats

¹**pinnacle** *n* **1** an architectural ornament resembling a small spire and used esp to crown a buttress **2** a structure or formation suggesting a pinnacle; *specif* a lofty mountain **3** the highest point of development or achievement

²**pinnacle** *vt* to raise (as if) on a pinnacle

pinnate *adj* resembling a feather, esp in having similar parts arranged on opposite sides of an axis like the barbs on the shaft of a feather ⟨*a ~ leaf*⟩ – **pinnately** *adv*, **pinnation** *n*

pinny *n* PINAFORE 1 – infml

piñon *n* (the edible nut-like seed of) any of various low-growing pines

¹**pinpoint** *vt* **1** to fix, determine, or identify with precision **2** to cause to stand out conspicuously; highlight

²**pinpoint** *adj* **1** extremely small, fine, or precise ⟨*a ~ target*⟩ **2** located, fixed, or directed with extreme precision

³**pinpoint** *n* a very small point or area ⟨*saw a ~ of light at the end of the tube*⟩

pinprick *n* **1** a small puncture made (as if) by a pin **2** a petty irritation or annoyance

pins and needles *n pl* a pricking tingling sensation in a limb recovering from numbness

pinstripe *n* **1** a very thin stripe, esp on a fabric **2** a suit or trousers with pinstripes – often pl with sing. meaning – **pin-striped** *adj*

pint *n* **1** either of 2 units of liquid capacity equal to ⅛gal: **a** a British unit of about 0.568l **b** a US unit of about 0.473l **2** a pint of liquid, esp milk or beer

pintable *n* PINBALL MACHINE

pint-size, pint-sized *adj* small – chiefly derog

pinup *n* (a person whose glamorous qualities make him/her a suitable subject of) a photograph pinned up on an admirer's wall – **pinup** *adj*

pinwheel *n* **1** CATHERINE WHEEL **2** *NAm* WINDMILL 2

¹**pioneer** *n* **1** a member of a military unit (e g engineers) engaging in light construction and defensive works **2a** a person or group that originates or helps open up a new line of thought or activity or a new method or technical development **b** any of the first people to settle in a territory

²**pioneer** *adj* **1** original, earliest **2** (characteristic) of early settlers or their time

³**pioneer** *vi* to act as a pioneer ~ *vt* **1** to open or prepare for others to follow; *esp* to settle **2** to originate or take part in the development of

pious *adj* **1** devout **2** sacred or devotional as distinct from the profane or secular **3** dutiful **4** marked by sham or hypocritical virtue; sanctimonious – **piously** *adv*, **piousness** *n*

¹**pip** *n* **1** (a disorder marked by formation of) a scale or crust on a bird's tongue **2** a fit of irritation, low spirits, or disgust – chiefly infml; esp in *to give one the pip*

²**pip** *n* **1a** any of the dots on dice and dominoes that indicate numerical value **b** SPOT 2c **2** a star worn, esp on the shoulder, to indicate an army officer's rank

³**pip** *vt* **-pp-** to beat by a narrow margin – infml – **pip at the post** to beat at the very last minute (e g in a race or competition)

⁴**pip** *n* a small fruit seed of an apple, orange, etc

⁵**pip** *vt* **-pp-** to remove the pips from (a fruit)

⁶**pip** *n* a short high-pitched tone, esp broadcast in a series as a time signal

pipal *n* a large long-lived Indian fig tree

¹**pipe** *n* **1a** a tubular wind instrument; *specif* a small fipple flute held in and played with one hand, esp while a tabor is played with the other **b**(1) FLUE PIPE (2) REED PIPE **c** a bagpipe – usu pl with sing. meaning **2** a long tube or hollow body for conducting a liquid, gas, etc **3a** a tubular or cylindrical object, part, or passage **b** a roughly cylindrical body of ore **4** a large cask used esp for wine (e g port) and oil **5** (tobacco or other plant material held by the bowl of) a wood, clay, etc tube with a mouthpiece at one end, and at the other a small bowl in which plant material, esp tobacco, is burned for smoking ⟨*he lit his ~*⟩

²**pipe** *vi* **1a** to play on a pipe **b** to convey orders or direct by signals on a boatswain's pipe **2a** to speak in a high or shrill voice **b** to make a shrill sound ~ *vt* **1a** to play (a tune) on a pipe **b** to utter in the shrill tone of a pipe **2** to lead, accompany, or announce ceremonially **3a** to trim with piping **b** to force (e g cream or icing) through a piping tube or nozzle in order to achieve a decorative effect **4** to supply or equip with pipes **5** to convey (as if) by pipes; *specif* to transmit by wire or coaxial cable

pipe-clay *vt* to whiten or clean with pipe clay

pipe clay *n* a fine white clay used esp for making tobacco pipes and for whitening leather

pipe cleaner *n* a piece of flexible wire covered with tufted fabric which is used to clean the stem of a tobacco pipe

piped music *n* recorded background music in public places

pipe down *vi* to stop talking or making noise – infml

pipe dream *n* an illusory or fantastic plan, hope, or story

pipeline *n* **1** a line of pipe with pumps, valves, and control devices for conveying liquids, gases, etc **2a** the processes through which supplies pass from source to user **b** sthg considered as a continuous set of processes which the individual must go through or be subjected to ⟨*children in the educational ~*⟩ ⟨*the housing ~*⟩ **3** *NAm* a direct channel for information

pipe of peace *n* a calumet

piper *n* **1** one who or that which plays on a pipe **2** a maker, layer, or repairer of pipes

pipette, *NAm* **pipet** *n* a narrow tube into which fluid is drawn (e g for dispensing or measuring) by suction and retained by closing the upper end

pipe up *vi* to begin to play or to sing or speak, esp unexpectedly

piping *n* **1a** the music of a pipe **b** a sound, note, or call like that of a pipe **2** a quantity or system of pipes **3a** a narrow trimming consisting of a folded strip of cloth often enclosing a cord, used to decorate upholstery, garments, etc **b** a thin cordlike line of icing piped onto a cake

pipit *n* any of various small birds resembling larks

pippin *n* any of numerous apples with usu yellow skins strongly flushed with red

pip-squeak *n* a small or insignificant person – infml

piquant *adj* **1** agreeably stimulating to the palate; savoury **2** pleasantly stimulating to the mind – **piquancy** *n*, **piquantly** *adv*, **piquantness** *n*

¹**pique** *n* (a fit of) resentment resulting from wounded vanity

²**pique** *vt* **1** to arouse anger or resentment in; *specif* to offend by slighting **2a** to excite or arouse by a provocation, challenge, or rebuff **b** to pride or congratulate (oneself), esp in respect of a particular accomplishment ⟨*he* ~ s *himself on his skill as a cook*⟩

piqué, pique *n* a durable ribbed fabric of cotton, rayon, or silk

piquet *n* **1** a 2-handed card game played with a 32-card pack with no cards below the 7 **2** PICKET 2

piracy *n* **1** robbery or illegal violence on the high seas; *also* a similar act (e g hijacking) against an aircraft in flight **2** the infringement of a copyright, patent, etc **3** an act (as if) of piracy

piranha *n* a small S American fish capable of attacking and (fatally) wounding human beings and large animals

¹**pirate** *n* **1** (a ship used by) sby who commits piracy **2** an unauthorized radio station; *esp* one located on a ship in international waters ⟨*a* ~ *radio station*⟩ – **piratical** *adj*, **piratically** *adv*

²**pirate** *vt* **1** to commit piracy on **2** to take or appropriate by piracy **3** to reproduce without authorization ~ *vi* to commit or practise piracy

pirouette *n* a rapid whirling about of the body; *specif* a full turn on the toe or ball of one foot in ballet – **pirouette** *vi*

piscatory, piscatorial *adj* of or dependent on fishermen or fishing

Pisces *n pl but sing in constr* (sby born under) the 12th sign of the zodiac in astrology, which is pictured as 2 fishes – **Piscean** *adj or n*

pish *interj* – used to express disdain or contempt

¹**piss** *vi* **1** to urinate **2** to rain heavily – often with *down* ~ *vt* **1** to urinate in or on ⟨~ *the bed*⟩ **2** to discharge (as if) as urine ⟨*to* ~ *blood*⟩ *USE* vulg

²**piss** *n* **1** urine **2** an act of urinating *USE* vulg

pissed *adj*, *Br* drunk – slang

piss off *vb*, *Br vi* to go away ~ *vt* to cause to be annoyed or fed up *USE* vulg

pistachio *n*, *pl* **pistachios 1** (the green edible nut of) a small tree of the sumach family **2** the vivid green colour of the pistachio nut

pistil *n* a carpel

pistol *n* a short firearm intended to be aimed and fired with 1 hand

piston *n* **1** a sliding disc or short cylinder fitting within a cylindrical vessel along which it moves back and forth by or against fluid pressure **2a** a sliding valve in a cylinder in a brass instrument that is used to lower its pitch **b** a button on an organ console for bringing in a preselected registration

piston ring *n* a springy split metal ring for sealing the gap between a piston and a cylinder wall

¹**pit** *n* **1a**(1) a hole, shaft, or cavity in the ground (2) a mine **b**(1) an area often sunken or depressed below the adjacent floor area (2) ORCHESTRA 2 **2** Hell – + *the* **3** a hollow or indentation, esp in the surface of a living plant or animal: e g **a** a natural hollow in the surface of the body **b** any of the indented scars left in the skin by a pustular disease (e g smallpox) **4** any of the areas alongside a motor-racing track used for refuelling and repairing the vehicles during a race – usu pl with sing. meaning; + *the* **5** *chiefly Br* the floor of a theatre auditorium; *esp* the area between the stalls and the stage

²**pit** *vb* **-tt-** *vt* **1** to make pits in; *esp* to scar or mark with pits **2a** to set (e g fighting cocks) to fight (as if) in a cockpit – often + *against* **b** to set into opposition or rivalry;

oppose ~ *vi* to become marked with pits; *esp* to preserve for a time an indentation made by pressure

³**pit** *n*, *NAm* STONE 2

⁴**pit** *vt* **-tt-** *chiefly NAm* to remove the pit from (a fruit)

pit-a-pat *n* pitter-patter – **pit-a-pat** *adv or adj*

¹**pitch** *n* **1** (any of various bituminous substances similar to) a black or dark viscous substance obtained as a residue in the distillation of organic materials, esp tars **2** resin obtained from various conifers

²**pitch** *vt* to cover, smear, or treat (as if) with pitch

³**pitch** *vt* **1** to erect and fix firmly in place ⟨~ *a tent*⟩ **2** to throw, fling ⟨~ *hay onto a wagon*⟩ ⟨~ed *a couple of drunks out of the party*⟩: e g **a** to throw (a baseball) to a batter **b** to toss (e g coins) so as to fall at or near a mark **3a**(1) to cause to be at a particular level or of a particular quality (2) to set in a particular musical pitch or key **b** to cause to be set at a particular angle; slope ⟨*a* ~ed *roof*⟩ **4** to hit (a golf ball) in a high arc with backspin **5** to bowl (a ball) in cricket to a specified place or in a specified manner ~ *vi* **1a** to fall precipitately or headlong **b**(1) *of a ship* to move so that the bow is alternately rising and falling (2) *of an aircraft* to turn about a lateral axis so that the nose rises or falls in relation to the tail **c** BUCK 1 **2** to encamp **3** to incline downwards; slope **4** to pitch a baseball or golf ball **5** *of a ball, esp a bowled cricket ball* to bounce

⁴**pitch** *n* **1** pitching; *esp* an up-and-down movement **2a** a slope; *also* the degree of slope **b**(1) distance between one point on a gear tooth and the corresponding point on the next tooth (2) distance from any point on the thread of a screw to the corresponding point on an adjacent thread measured parallel to the axis **c** the distance advanced by a propeller in 1 revolution **d** the number of teeth on a gear or of threads on a screw per unit distance **e** the degree to which a blade of a propeller is slanted in relation to the axis of rotation **3a** the relative level, intensity, or extent of some quality or state ⟨*were at a high* ~ *of excitement*⟩ **b**(1) the property of a sound, esp a musical note, that is determined by the frequency of the waves producing it; highness or lowness of sound (2) a standard frequency for tuning instruments **4** an often high-pressure sales talk or advertisement **5** WICKET 4b **6** *chiefly Br* **a** a usu specially marked area used for playing soccer, rugby, hockey, etc **b** an area or place, esp in a street, to which a person lays unofficial claim for carrying out business or activities – **pitched** *adj*

pitch-black *adj* intensely dark or black

pitchblende *n* a radium-containing uranium oxide occurring as a brown to black lustrous mineral

pitched battle *n* an intense battle; *specif* one fought on previously chosen ground

¹**pitcher** *n* **1** a large deep usu earthenware vessel with a wide lip and a handle or 2 ear-shaped handles, for holding and pouring liquids; *broadly* a large jug **2** a modified leaf of a pitcher plant in which the hollowed stalk and base of the blade form an elongated receptacle

²**pitcher** *n* the player who pitches in a baseball game

¹**pitchfork** *n* a long-handled fork with 2 or 3 long curved prongs used esp for pitching hay

²**pitchfork** *vt* **1** to lift and toss (as if) with a pitchfork ⟨~ed *the hay into the wagon*⟩ **2** to thrust (sby) into a position, office, etc suddenly or without preparation

pitch in *vi* **1** to begin to work **2** to contribute to a common endeavour

piteous *adj* causing or deserving pity or compassion – **piteously** *adv*, **piteousness** *n*

pitfall *n* **1** a trap or snare; *specif* a camouflaged pit used to capture animals **2** a hidden or not easily recognized danger or difficulty

¹pith n **1a** a (continuous) central area of spongy tissue in the stems of most vascular plants **b** the white tissue surrounding the flesh and directly below the skin of a citrus fruit **2a** the essential part; the core ⟨*individuality, which was the very ~ of liberty* – H J Laski⟩ **b** substantial quality (e g of meaning) ⟨*made a speech that lacked ~*⟩

²pith vt **1** to destroy the spinal cord or central nervous system of (e g cattle or a frog) **2** to remove the pith from (a plant part)

pithead n (the ground and buildings adjacent to) the top of a mining pit

pithy adj **1** consisting of or having much pith **2** tersely cogent – **pithily** adv, **pithiness** n

pitiable adj deserving or exciting pity or contempt, esp because of inadequacy ⟨*a ~ excuse*⟩ – **pitiableness** n, **pitiably** adv

pitiful adj **1** deserving or arousing pity or commiseration **2** exciting pitying contempt (e g by meanness or inadequacy) – **pitifully** adv, **pitifulness** n

pitiless adj devoid of pity; merciless – **pitilessly** adv, **pitilessness** n

pitman n, pl (1) **pitmen**, (2) **pitmans 1** a male mine worker **2** NAm CONNECTING ROD

piton n a spike or peg that is driven into a rock or ice surface as a support, esp for a rope, in mountaineering

Pitot tube n a tube with a short right-angled bend that is used with a manometer to measure the velocity of fluid flow

pittance n a small amount or allowance; specif a meagre wage or remuneration

pitter-patter n a rapid succession of light sounds – **pitter-patter** adv or adj, **pitter-patter** vi

pituitary adj or n (of) the pituitary gland

pit viper n any of various mostly New World venomous snakes with a sensory pit on each side of the head and hollow perforated fangs

¹pity n **1a** (the capacity to feel) sympathetic sorrow for one suffering, distressed, or unhappy **b** a contemptuous feeling of regret aroused by the inferiority or inadequacy of another **2** sthg to be regretted ⟨*it's a ~ you can't go*⟩

²pity vb to feel pity (for) – **pitier** n, **pityingly** adv

¹pivot n **1** a shaft or pin on which sthg turns **2a** a person, thing, or factor having a major or central role, function, or effect ⟨*as if the ~ and pole of his life was his Mother* – D H Lawrence⟩ **b** a key player or position; specif ⁶POST 2b

²pivot vi to turn (as if) on a pivot ~ vt **1** to provide with, mount on, or attach by a pivot **2** to cause to pivot – **pivotable** adj

³pivot adj **1** turning (as if) on a pivot **2** pivotal

pivotal adj **1** of or constituting a pivot **2** vitally important; crucial – **pivotally** adv

pixie, pixy n a (mischievous) fairy – **pixieish** adj

pixilated adj, chiefly NAm **1** somewhat unbalanced mentally; also bemused **2** drunk – **pixilation** n

pizza n a round thin cake of baked bread dough spread with a mixture of tomatoes, cheese, herbs, etc

pizzicato n, adv, or adj, pl **pizzicati** (a note or passage played) by means of plucking instead of bowing – used in music

¹placard n a notice for display or advertising purposes, usu printed on or fixed to a stiff backing material

²placard vt **1** to cover (as if) with placards **2** to give public notice of by means of placards

placate vt to soothe or mollify, esp by concessions; appease – **placation** n, **placative** adj, **placatory** adj

¹place n **1a** physical environment; a space **b** physical surroundings; atmosphere **2a** an indefinite region or expanse; an area **b** a building or locality used for a usu specified purpose ⟨*a ~ of amusement*⟩ ⟨*a ~ of worship*⟩ **3a** a particular region or centre of population **b** a house, dwelling ⟨*invited them to his ~ for the evening*⟩ **4** a particular part of a surface or body; a spot **5** relative position in a scale or series: e g **a** a particular part in a piece of writing; esp the point at which a reader has temporarily stopped **b** an important or valued position ⟨*there was never much of a ~ in his life for women*⟩ **c** degree of prestige ⟨*put her in her ~*⟩ **d** a (numbered) point in an argument, explanation, etc ⟨*in the first ~, you're wrong*⟩ **6** a leading place, esp second or third, in a competition **7a** a proper or designated niche ⟨*thought that a woman's ~ was in the home*⟩ ⟨*put it back in its ~*⟩ **b** an appropriate moment or point ⟨*this is not the ~ to discuss legal liability*⟩ **8a** an available seat or accommodation **b** PLACE SETTING ⟨*lay another ~ for our guest*⟩ **9** the position of a figure in relation to others of a row or series; esp the position of a digit within a numeral ⟨*in 316 the figure 1 is in the tens ~*⟩ **10a** remunerative employment; a job; esp public office **b** prestige accorded to one of high rank; status ⟨*an endless quest for preferment and ~* – Time⟩ **c** a duty accompanying a position of responsibility ⟨*it was not his ~ to sack the employee*⟩ **11** a public square **12** chiefly Br an available vacancy ⟨*got a university ~*⟩ – **in place of** so as to replace

²place vt **1** to distribute in an orderly manner; arrange ⟨*~ these documents in their correct order*⟩ **2a** to put into, direct to, or assign to a particular place ⟨*~d her on the right of the host*⟩ ⟨*could always ~ the dart exactly where he wanted to*⟩ **b** to put in a particular state ⟨*~ a performer under contract*⟩ **3** to appoint to a position ⟨*~d him in charge of the class*⟩ **4** to find employment or a home for **5a** to assign to a position in a series or category **b** to estimate ⟨*~d the value of the estate too high*⟩ **c** to identify by connecting with an associated context ⟨*couldn't quite ~ her face*⟩ **d** to put, lay ⟨*the teacher ~s a great deal of stress on correct spelling*⟩ **6a** to give (an order) to a supplier **b** to give an order for ⟨*~ a bet*⟩ – **placeable** adj, **placement** n

placebo n, pl **placebos 1** the Roman Catholic vespers for the dead **2a**(1) a medication that has no physiological effect and is prescribed more for the mental relief of the patient (2) an inert substance against which an active substance (e g a drug) is tested in a controlled trial **b** sthg tending to soothe or gratify

place card n a card indicating the place a guest is to occupy at table during a formal dinner

placed adj, chiefly Br in a leading place, esp second or third, at the end of a competition, horse race, etc

placekick vt or n (to kick or score by means of) a kick at a ball (e g in rugby) placed or held in a stationary position on the ground – **placekicker** n

placenta n, pl **placentas, placentae 1** the organ in all higher mammals that unites the foetus to the maternal uterus and provides for the nourishment of the foetus and the elimination of waste **2** the part of a flowering plant to which the ovules are attached – **placental** adj or n

place setting n a table service for 1 person

placid adj serenely free of interruption or disturbance ⟨*~ summer skies*⟩ ⟨*a ~ disposition*⟩ – **placidly** adv, **placidness, placidity** n

placket n a slit in a garment, esp a skirt, for a fastening or pocket

plagiarism n **1** plagiarizing **2** sthg plagiarized – **plagiarist** n, **plagiaristic** adj

plagiarize, -ise vt to appropriate and pass off (the ideas or words of another) as one's own ~ vi to present as new and original an idea or product derived from an existing source – **plagiarizer** n

¹plague n **1a** a disastrous evil or affliction; a calamity **b** a large destructive influx ⟨a ~ of locusts⟩ **2** any of several epidemic virulent diseases that cause many deaths; esp a fever caused by a bacterium that occurs in several forms **3a** a cause of irritation; a nuisance **b** a sudden unwelcome outbreak ⟨a ~ of burglaries⟩

²plague vt **1** to infest or afflict (as if) with disease, calamity, etc **2a** to cause worry or distress to **b** to disturb or annoy persistently – **plaguer** n

plaguey, plaguy adj causing irritation or annoyance; troublesome – infml

plaice n, pl **plaice** any of various flatfishes; esp a large European flounder

plaid n **1** a rectangular length of tartan worn over the left shoulder as part of Highland dress **2** a usu twilled woollen fabric with a tartan pattern **3** a tartan – **plaid** adj, **plaided** adj

¹plain n **1a** an extensive area of level or rolling treeless country **b** a broad unbroken expanse **2** ²KNIT

²plain adj **1** lacking ornament; undecorated **2** free of added substances; pure **3** free of impediments to view; unobstructed **4a** evident to the mind or senses; obvious ⟨it's perfectly ~ that they will resist⟩ **b** clear ⟨made his intentions ~⟩ **5** free from deceitfulness or subtlety; candid **6** lacking special distinction or affectation; ordinary **7a** characterized by simplicity; not complicated ⟨~ home cooking⟩ **b** not rich or elaborately prepared or decorated **8** unremarkable either for physical beauty or for ugliness **9** of flour not containing a raising agent – **plainly** adv, **plainness** n

³plain adv in a plain manner; clearly, simply; also totally, utterly ⟨it's just ~ daft⟩

plain clothes n ordinary civilian dress as opposed to (police) uniform – often attrib in plain-clothes man

plain dealing n straightforward honesty ⟨a businessman noted for his ~⟩

plain sailing n easy progress along an unobstructed course (e g of action)

plainsong n **1** the nonmetrical monophonic music of the medieval church; esp GREGORIAN CHANT **2** a liturgical chant of any of various Christian rites

plainspoken adj candid, frank – **plainspokenness** n

plaint n a protest

plaintiff n sby who commences a civil legal action

plaintive adj expressive of suffering or woe; melancholy, mournful – **plaintively** adv, **plaintiveness** n

¹plait also **plat** n **1** a pleat **2** a length of plaited material, esp hair

²plait, also plat vt **1** to pleat **2a** to interweave the strands of **b** to make by plaiting – **plaiter** n

¹plan n **1a** a drawing or diagram drawn on a plane: e g **a** a top or horizontal view of an object **b** a large-scale map of a small area **2a** a method for achieving an end **b** an often customary method of doing sthg; a procedure ⟨the usual ~ is to both arrive and leave early⟩ **c** a detailed formulation of a programme of action **d** a goal, aim ⟨his ~ was to get a degree in engineering⟩ – **planless** adj, **planlessly** adv

²plan vb **-nn-** vt **1** to design **2** to arrange in advance **3** to have in mind; intend ~ vi to make plans – **planner** n

plan-, plano- comb form **1** flat ⟨plano*sol*⟩; flat and ⟨plano-*concave*⟩ **2** flatly ⟨plano*spiral*⟩

¹plane vt **1** to make flat or even with a plane ⟨~d the sides of the door⟩ **2** to remove by planing – often + away or down – **planer** n

²plane, plane tree n any of a genus of trees with large deeply cut lobed leaves and flowers in spherical heads

³plane n a tool with a sharp blade protruding from the base of a flat metal or wooden stock for smoothing or shaping a wood surface

⁴plane n **1a** a surface such that any 2 included points can be joined by a straight line lying wholly within the surface **b** a flat or level physical surface **2** a level of existence, consciousness, or development ⟨on the intellectual ~⟩ **3a** any of the main supporting surfaces of an aeroplane **b** an aeroplane

⁵plane adj **1** having no elevations or depressions; flat **2a** of or dealing with geometric planes **b** lying in a plane ⟨a ~ curve⟩

⁶plane vi **1** to fly keeping the wings motionless **2** to skim across the surface of the water

planet n **1** any of the bodies, except a comet, meteor, or satellite, that revolve round a star, esp the sun in our solar system; specif Mercury, Venus, Earth, Mars, Jupiter, Saturn, Uranus, Neptune, or Pluto **2** STAR 2a(1)

planetarium n, pl **planetariums, planetaria 1** a model of the solar system **2** (a building or room housing) an optical projector for projecting images of celestial bodies and effects as seen in the night sky

planetary adj **1a** of or being a planet **b** having a motion like that of a planet ⟨~ electrons⟩ **2** of or belonging to the earth; terrestrial **3** erratic, wandering – poetic

plangent adj **1** loudly reverberating **2** having an expressive, esp plaintive, quality – **plangency** n, **plangently** adv

¹plank n **1a** a long thick piece of wood; specif one 2 to 4in (about 50 to 100mm) thick and at least 8in (about 200mm) wide **2a** an article in a political platform **b** a (principal) item of a policy or programme

²plank vt to cover or floor with planks

plankton n the floating or weakly swimming minute animal and plant organisms of a body of water – **planktonic** adj

planning n the establishment of goals, policies, and procedures for a social or economic unit ⟨town ~⟩

¹plant vt **1a** to put in the ground, soil, etc for growth ⟨~ seeds⟩ **b** to set or sow (land) with seeds or plants **c** to implant **2a** to establish, institute **b** to place (animals) in a new locality **c** to stock with animals **3** to place firmly or forcibly ⟨~ed a hard blow on his chin⟩ **4** to position secretly; specif to conceal in order to observe or deceive ⟨the spy ~ed a microphone in the hotel room⟩ ~ vi to plant sthg – **plantable** adj

²plant n **1a** a tree, vine, etc that is or can be planted; esp a small herbaceous plant **b** any of a kingdom of living things (e g a green alga, moss, fern, conifer, or flowering plant) typically lacking locomotive movement or obvious nervous or sensory organs **2a** the buildings, machinery, etc employed in carrying on a trade or an industrial business **b** a factory or workshop for the manufacture of a particular product **3** an act of planting **4** sthg or sby planted ⟨left muddy footprints as a ~ to confuse the police⟩ – **plantlike** adj

¹plantain n any of a genus of short-stemmed plants bearing dense spikes of minute greenish or brownish flowers

²plantain n (the angular greenish starchy fruit of) a type of banana plant

plantation n **1** (a place with) a usu large group of plants, esp trees, under cultivation **2** a settlement in a new country or region; a colony **3** an agricultural estate, usu worked by resident labour

planter n **1** one who owns or operates a plantation ⟨a tea ~⟩ **2** one who settles or founds a new colony **3** a container in which ornamental plants are grown **4** a planting machine

plant out *vb* to transplant (e g seedlings or a house plant) from a pot, seed tray, etc to open ground

plaque *n* **1a** an ornamental brooch; *esp* the badge of an honorary order **b** a commemorative or decorative inscribed tablet of ceramic, wood, metal, etc **2a** a localized abnormal patch on a body part or surface **b** a film of mucus on a tooth that harbours bacteria

¹plash *n* a shallow or muddy pool

²plash *vt* to interweave (branches and twigs) to form a hedge; *also* to form (a hedge) thus

³plash *vt* to break the surface of (water); splash ~ *vi* to cause a splashing or spattering effect – **plash** *n*

plasma *n* **1** the fluid part of blood, lymph, or milk as distinguished from suspended material **2** protoplasm **3** a highly ionized gas (e g in the atmospheres of stars) containing approximately equal numbers of positive ions and electrons – **plasmatic** *adj*

¹plaster *n* **1** a medicated or protective dressing consisting of a film of cloth, plastic, etc often spread with a medicated substance; STICKING PLASTER **2** a pastelike mixture (e g of lime, water, and sand) that hardens on drying and is used esp for coating walls, ceilings, and partitions **3** **plaster, plaster cast** a rigid dressing of gauze impregnated with plaster of paris for immobilizing a diseased or broken body part – **plastery** *adj*

²plaster *vt* **1** to overlay or cover with plaster **2** to apply a plaster to **3a** to cover over or conceal as if with a coat of plaster **b** to smear (sthg) thickly (on); coat ⟨he ~ ed *butter on his bread*⟩ ⟨she ~ ed *her face with make-up*⟩ **c** to cause to lie flat or stick to another surface ⟨~ ed *his hair down*⟩ ⟨*the rain* ~ ed *his shirt to his body*⟩ **4** to fasten (sthg) (to) or place (sthg) (on), esp conspicuously or in quantity ⟨*walls* ~ ed *with posters*⟩ ⟨~ ed *posters all over the walls*⟩ **5** to inflict heavy damage, injury, or casualties on, esp by a concentrated or unremitting attack – infml ~ *vi* to apply plaster – **plasterer** *n*

plasterboard *n* a board with a plaster core used esp as a substitute for plaster on walls

plastered *adj* drunk – infml

plastering *n* **1** a coating (as if) of plaster **2** a decisive defeat – infml

plaster of paris *n, often cap 2nd P* a white powdery plaster made from gypsum that when mixed with water forms a quicksetting paste used chiefly for casts and moulds

¹plastic *adj* **1** formative, creative ⟨~ *forces in nature*⟩ **2a** capable of being moulded or modelled ⟨~ *clay*⟩ **b** supple, pliant **3** sculptural **4** made or consisting of a plastic **5** capable of being bent or stretched continuously and permanently in any direction without breaking **6** of, involving, or being plastic surgery **7** formed by or adapted to an artificial or conventional standard; synthetic – chiefly derog ⟨*takes a positive effort of will   to avoid ~ food, ~ living, and ~ entertainment* – L E Sissman⟩ – **plastically** *adv*, **plasticize** *vt*, **plasticization** *n*

²plastic *n* any of numerous (synthetic) organic polymers that can be moulded, cast, extruded, etc into objects, films, or filaments

-plastic *comb form* (→ *adj*) of sthg designated by a term ending in *-plasm, -plast, -plasty,* or *-plasy* ⟨*homoplastic*⟩ ⟨*neoplastic*⟩

Plasticine *trademark* – used for a modelling substance that remains plastic for a long period

plasticity *n* **1** being plastic; *esp* capacity for being moulded or altered **2** the ability to retain a shape produced by pressure deformation

plastic surgery *n* surgery concerned with the repair, restoration, or cosmetic improvement of parts of the body chiefly by the grafting of tissue – **plastic surgeon** *n*

plastron *n* **1a** a metal breastplate **b** a quilted pad worn in fencing to protect the chest, waist, and sides **2** the lower part of the shell of a tortoise or turtle – **plastral** *adj*

plat du jour *n, pl* **plats du jour** a dish featured by a restaurant on a particular day

¹plate *n* **1a** a smooth flat thin usu rigid piece of material **b** a very thin layer of metal deposited on a surface of a base metal by plating **c** (armour of) broad metal plates **d** an (external) scale or rigid layer of bone, horn, etc forming part of an animal body **e** any of the huge movable segments into which the earth's crust is divided **2a** domestic utensils and tableware made of or plated with gold, silver, or base metals **b** a shallow usu circular vessel, made esp of china, from which food is eaten or served **c** a plateful **3a** a prepared surface from which printing is done **b** a sheet of material (e g glass) coated with a light-sensitive photographic emulsion **c** an electrode in an accumulator **4** a flat piece or surface bearing letters or a design **5** a horizontal structural member (e g a timber) that provides bearing and anchorage, esp for rafters or joists **6** the part of a denture that fits to the mouth; *broadly* a denture **7** a full-page book illustration, often on different paper from the text pages **8** *NAm* **a** a complete main course served on a plate **b** food and service supplied to 1 person ⟨*a dinner at £5 a ~*⟩ **9** *NAm* the anode of an electron tube – **platelike** *adj* – **on a plate** so as not to require effort – infml

²plate *vt* **1** to cover or equip with plate: e g **a** to arm with armour plate **b** to cover permanently with an adherent layer, esp of metal; *also* to deposit (e g a layer) on a surface **2** to fix or secure with a plate – **plater** *n*

plateau *n, pl* **plateaus, plateaux 1** a usu extensive relatively flat land area raised sharply above adjacent land on at least 1 side **2** a relatively stable level, period, or condition ⟨*a price ~ interrupting an inflationary spiral*⟩

plate glass *n* rolled, ground, and polished sheet glass

platelayer *n, Br* a person who lays and maintains railway track

platform *n* **1** a declaration of (political) principles and policies **2a** a horizontal flat surface, usu higher than the adjoining area; *esp, Br* a raised surface at a railway station to facilitate access to trains **b** a raised flooring (e g for speakers) **c** a raised metal structure secured to the sea bed by posts and serving as a base for the extraction of oil **3** a place or opportunity for public discussion **4** (a shoe with) a thick sole **5** *chiefly Br* the area next to the entrance or exit of a bus

plating *n* **1** a coating of metal plates **2** a thin coating of metal

platinum *n* a heavy precious greyish white noncorroding metallic element used esp as a catalyst and for jewellery

platinum blonde *n* (sby having hair of) a pale silvery blond colour usu produced in human hair by bleach and bluish rinse

platitude *n* a banal, trite, or stale remark, esp when presented as if it were original and significant

platonic *adj* **1** *cap* (characteristic) of Plato or Platonism **2a** of or being a close relationship between 2 people in which sexual desire is absent or has been repressed or sublimated **b** nominal, theoretical – **platonically** *adv*

platoon *n sing or pl in constr* **1** a subdivision of a military company normally consisting of 2 or more sections or squads **2** a group of people sharing a common characteristic or activity ⟨*a ~ of waiters*⟩

platter *n* **1** a large often oval plate used esp for serving meat **2** *NAm* a gramophone record – **platterful** *n*

platypus *n, pl* **platypuses** *also* **platypi** a small aquatic

Australian and Tasmanian primitive mammal that lays eggs and has a fleshy bill resembling that of a duck, webbed feet, and a broad flattened tail

plaudit *n* enthusiastic approval – usu pl with sing. meaning ⟨*received the ~s of the critics*⟩

plausible *adj* **1** apparently fair, reasonable, or valid but often specious ⟨*a ~ pretext*⟩ **2** *of a person* persuasive but deceptive – **plausibleness** *n*, **plausibly** *adv*, **plausibility** *n*

¹play *n* **1** the conduct, course, or (a particular) action in or of a game **2a** (children's) spontaneous) recreational activity **b** the absence of serious or harmful intent; jest ⟨*said it in ~*⟩ **c** a playing on words or speech sounds **d** gaming, gambling **3a** operation, activity ⟨*bringing other forces into ~*⟩ **b** light, quick, transitory, or fitful movement ⟨*the ~ of sunlight and shadows through the trees*⟩ **c** free or unimpeded motion (e g of a part of a machine) **d** scope or opportunity for action **4a** the dramatized representation of an action or story on stage **b** a dramatic composition (for presentation in a theatre) **5** *chiefly NAm* **a** an act or manoeuvre, esp in a game **b** a move or series of moves calculated to arouse friendly feelings – usu + *make* ⟨*made a big ~ for the blonde*⟩ – **in/into play 1** in/into condition or position to be legitimately played **2** in/into operation or consideration – **out of play** not in play

²play *vi* **1a** to engage in sport or recreation **b(1)** to behave aimlessly; toy, trifle ⟨*don't ~ with your food*⟩ **(2)** to deal or behave frivolously, mockingly, or playfully – often + *around* or *about* **(3)** to deal in a light speculative manner ⟨*liked to ~ with ideas*⟩ **(4)** to make use of double meaning or of the similarity of sound of 2 words for stylistic or humorous effect – usu in *play on words* **2a** to take advantage ⟨*~ing on fears*⟩ **b** to move or operate in a lively, irregular, or intermittent manner ⟨*watch the light ~ing on the water*⟩ ⟨*a faint smile ~s on her lips*⟩ **c** to move or function freely within prescribed limits ⟨*a piston rod ~s within cylinders*⟩ **d** to discharge repeatedly or in a stream ⟨*hoses ~ing on a fire*⟩ **3a(1)** to perform music **(2)** to sound in performance ⟨*the organ is ~ing*⟩ **(3)** to reproduce or emit sounds ⟨*his radio is ~ing*⟩ **b(1)** to act in a dramatic production **(2)** to be presented at a place of entertainment (e g a theatre) **c** to act with special consideration so as to gain favour, approval, or sympathy – usu + *up to* **4a** to engage, take part, or make a move in a game **b** to perform (e g in a sport) in a specified position or manner ⟨*the fullbacks are ~ing deep*⟩ **c** to gamble **d(1)** to behave (or conduct oneself) in a specified way ⟨*~ safe*⟩ ⟨*the pitch will ~ well*⟩ **(2)** to feign a specified state or quality ⟨*~ dead*⟩ **(3)** to take part in or assent to some activity; cooperate ⟨*~ along with his scheme*⟩ **5** to have (promiscuous or illicit) sexual relations – euph; usu in *play around* – *vt* **1a(1)** to engage in or occupy oneself with ⟨*~ football*⟩ **(2)** to deal with, handle, or manage ⟨*decided to ~ the dispute another way*⟩ – often + *it* ⟨*trying to ~ it cool*⟩ **(3)** to exploit, manipulate ⟨*~ the stock market*⟩ **b** to pretend to engage in ⟨*children ~ing cops and robbers*⟩ **c(1)** to perform or execute for amusement or to deceive or mock ⟨*~ a trick*⟩ **(2)** to wreak ⟨*~ havoc*⟩ **2a(1)** to put on a performance of (a play) **(2)** to act in the character or part of **(3)** to act or perform in ⟨*~ed leading theatres*⟩ **b** to perform or act the part of ⟨*~ the fool*⟩ **3a(1)** to contend against in a game **(2)** to use as a contestant in a game ⟨*the selectors did not ~ him*⟩ **(3)** to perform the duties associated with (a certain position) ⟨*~ed fullback*⟩ **b(1)** to make bets on ⟨*~ the horses*⟩ **(2)** to operate on the basis of ⟨*~ a hunch*⟩ **c** to put into action in a game ⟨*~ the ace*⟩ ⟨*~ the knight*⟩ **d** to direct the course of (e g a ball); hit **4a** to perform (music) on an instrument ⟨*~ a*

waltz⟩ **b** to perform music on ⟨*~ the violin*⟩ **c** to perform music of (a specified composer) **d** to reproduce sounds, esp music, on (an apparatus) ⟨*~s her radio all day long*⟩ ⟨*~ us your favourite record*⟩ **5a** to aim and fire or set off with continuous effect ⟨*~ed the hose on the burning building*⟩ **b** to cause to move or operate lightly and irregularly or intermittently ⟨*~ed his torch along the fence*⟩ **c** to allow (a hooked fish) to become exhausted by pulling against a line – **playable** *adj*, **player** *n*, **playability** *n* – **play ball** to cooperate – **play by ear** to deal with from moment to moment rather than making plans in advance – **play fast and loose** to act in a reckless, irresponsible, or craftily deceitful way – **play into the hands of** to act so as to prove advantageous to (an opponent) – **play second fiddle** to take a subordinate position – **play the field** to have a number of boyfriends or girl friends rather than committing oneself exclusively to one person – **play the game** to act according to a code or set of standards – **play with oneself** to masturbate – **to play with** at one's disposal ⟨*a lot of funds to play with*⟩

playact *vi* **1** to make believe **2** to behave in a misleading or insincere manner – *vt* ACT OUT 1a

playback *n* (a device that provides for) the reproduction of recorded sound or pictures

play back *vt* to listen to or look at material on (a usu recently recorded disc or tape)

playboy *n* a man who lives a life devoted chiefly to the pursuit of pleasure

play down *n* to cause to seem less important; minimize

played out *adj* worn or tired out

player piano *n* a piano containing a mechanical device that operates the keys automatically

playful *adj* **1** full of fun; frolicsome ⟨*a ~ kitten*⟩ **2** humorous, lighthearted ⟨*the ~ tone of her voice*⟩ – **playfully** *adv*, **playfulness** *n*

playground *n* **1** a piece of land for children to play on **2** an area favoured for recreation or amusement ⟨*that town was a gambler's ~*⟩

playgroup *n, chiefly Br* a supervised group of children below school age who play together regularly

playhouse *n* **1** a theatre **2** *chiefly NAm* WENDY HOUSE

playing card *n* any of a set of usu 52 thin rectangular pieces, usu of cardboard, marked on one side to show one of 13 ranks in one of 4 suits and used in playing any of numerous games

playing field *n* a field used for playing organized games and often divided into several separate pitches – often pl with sing. meaning

playmate *n* a companion in play

play-off *n* a final contest to determine a winner

play off *vt* **1** to decide the winner of (a competition) or break (a tie) by a play-off **2** to set in opposition for one's own gain ⟨*survived by playing his enemies off against each other*⟩

play on words *n* a pun

play out *vt* **1** to finish; USE UP **2** to unreel, unfold

playpen *n* a portable usu collapsible enclosure in which a baby or young child may play

playsuit *n* a garment, esp dungarees, for children to play in

plaything *n* a toy

play up *vt* **1** to give special emphasis or prominence to ⟨*the press played up the divorce story*⟩ **2** *Br* to cause pain or distress to ⟨*my corns have been playing me up again*⟩ – *~vi* to behave in a disobedient or annoying manner; ACT UP

playwright *n* one who writes plays

plaza *n* a public square in a city or town

plea *n* **1** an allegation made by a party in support of his/her case **2** an accused person's answer to an indictment ⟨*a ~ of guilty*⟩ **3** sthg offered by way of excuse or justification **4** an earnest entreaty; an appeal

pleach *vt* to interlace, plash

plead *vb* **pleaded, pled** *vi* **1** to argue a case as an advocate in a court **2** to make or answer an allegation in a legal proceeding **3** to make a specified plea ⟨*~ not guilty*⟩ **4a** to urge reasons for or against sthg **b** to entreat or appeal earnestly; implore *~ vt* **1** to maintain (e g a case) in a court **2** to offer as a (legal) plea ⟨*to ~ ignorance*⟩ – **pleadable** *adj*, **pleader** *n*, **pleadingly** *adv*

pleading *n* **1** advocacy of a case in a court **2** any of the formal usu written allegations made alternately by the parties in a legal action

pleasant *adj* **1** having qualities that tend to give pleasure; agreeable ⟨*a ~ day*⟩ **2** of a person likable, friendly – **pleasantly** *adv*, **pleasantness** *n*

pleasantry *n* **1** an agreeable remark (made in order to be polite) **2** a humorous act or remark; a joke

please *vi* **1** to afford or give pleasure or satisfaction **2** to like, wish ⟨*do as you ~*⟩ **3** to be willing – usu used in the imperative (1) to express a polite request ⟨*coffee, ~*⟩ ⟨*~ come in*⟩ (2) to make polite request for attention ⟨*~, Sir, I don't understand*⟩ (3) to express polite acceptance ⟨*Coffee? Please!*⟩ (4) to turn an apparent question into a request ⟨*can you shut it, ~?*⟩ *~ vt* **1** to give pleasure to; gratify **2** to be the will or pleasure of ⟨*may it ~ your Majesty*⟩ – fml – **pleasing** *adj*, **pleasingly** *adv*

pleasurable *adj* pleasant, enjoyable – **pleasurableness** *n*, **pleasurably** *adv*, **pleasurability** *n*

¹**pleasure** *n* **1** a state of gratification **2a** sensual gratification ⟨*he abandoned the monastery for a life of ~*⟩ **b** enjoyment, recreation ⟨*are you here on business or for ~?*⟩ **3** a source of delight or joy ⟨*it's always a ~ to talk to her*⟩ **4** a wish, desire – fml

²**pleasure** *vt, archaic* to give (sexual) pleasure to

¹**pleat** *vt* to fold; *esp* to arrange in pleats ⟨*~ a skirt*⟩ – **pleater** *n*

²**pleat** *n* a fold in cloth made by doubling material over on itself; *also* sthg resembling such a fold – **pleated** *adj*, **pleatless** *adj*

pleb *n* a plebeian – chiefly derog

¹**plebeian** *n* a member of the (Roman) common people – **plebeianism** *n*

²**plebeian** *adj* **1** of plebeians **2** crude or coarse in manner or style; common – **plebeianly** *adv*

plebiscite *n* a vote by the people of an entire country or district for or against a proposal, esp on a choice of government or ruler – **plebiscitary** *adj*

plectrum *n, pl* **plectra, plectrums** a small thin piece of plastic, metal, etc used to pluck the strings of a stringed instrument

pled *past of* PLEAD

¹**pledge** *n* **1** a chattel delivered as security for an obligation (e g a debt) or for the performance of an act **2** the state of being held as a security ⟨*his watch is in ~*⟩ **3** a token, sign, or earnest of sthg else **4** TOAST 3 **5** a binding promise to do or forbear

²**pledge** *vt* **1** to make a pledge of; *specif* to deposit as security for fulfilment of a contract or obligation **2** to drink the health of **3** to bind by a pledge **4** to give a promise of ⟨*~ allegiance to the flag*⟩ – **pledger, pledgor** *n*

Pleistocene *adj or n* (of or being) the earlier epoch of the Quaternary

plenary *adj* **1** absolute, unqualified ⟨*~ power*⟩ **2** attended by all entitled to be present ⟨*a ~ session*⟩

plenipotentiary *n or adj* (sby, esp a diplomatic agent) invested with full power to transact business

plenitude *n* **1** fullness, completeness **2** abundance *USE* fml

plenteous *adj* plentiful – fml or poetic – **plenteously** *adv*, **plenteousness** *n*

plentiful *adj* **1** containing or yielding plenty ⟨*a ~ land*⟩ **2** characterized by, constituting, or existing in plenty – **plentifully** *adv*, **plentifulness** *n*

¹**plenty** *n* **1a** *sing or pl in constr* a full or more than adequate amount or supply ⟨*had ~ of time to finish the job*⟩ ⟨*there's ~ more*⟩ **b** a large number or amount ⟨*he's in ~ of trouble*⟩ **2** copiousness, plentifulness ⟨*years of ~*⟩

²**plenty** *adj, chiefly NAm* ample ⟨*~ work to be done – Time*⟩

³**plenty** *adv* **1** quite, abundantly ⟨*~ warm enough*⟩ **2** *chiefly NAm* to a considerable or extreme degree; very ⟨*~ hungry*⟩ *USE* infml

pleonasm *n* the use of more words than are necessary to convey the intended sense – **pleonastic** *adj*, **pleonastically** *adv*

plethora *n* **1** an abnormal excess of blood in the body – not now used technically **2** a superfluity, excess ⟨*a ~ of regulations*⟩ – **plethoric** *adj*

pleurisy *n* inflammation of the pleura, usu with fever, painful breathing, and oozing of liquid into the pleural cavity – **pleuritic** *adj*

plexus *n* **1** a network of interlacing blood vessels or nerves **2** a network of parts or elements in a structure or system – **plexiform** *adj*

pliable *adj* **1** easily bent without breaking; flexible **2** yielding readily to others; compliant – **pliableness** *n*, **pliably** *adv*, **pliability** *n*

pliant *adj* PLIABLE 1 – **pliantly** *adv*, **pliantness, pliancy** *n*

pliers *n pl, pl* **pliers** a pair of pincers with long jaws for holding small objects or for bending and cutting wire

¹**plight** *vt* to put or give in pledge; engage ⟨*~ one's troth*⟩

²**plight** *n* an (unpleasant or difficult) state; a predicament

plimsoll *n, Br* a shoe with a rubber sole and canvas top worn esp for sports

Plimsoll line *n* a set of markings indicating the draught levels to which a vessel may legally be loaded in various seasons and waters

plinth *n* **1** a usu square block serving as a base (e g of a pedestal) **2** a part of a structure forming a continuous foundation or base

Pliocene *adj or n* (of or being) the latest epoch of the Tertiary

plod *vb* **-dd-** *vi* **1a** to walk heavily or slowly; trudge **b** to proceed slowly or tediously ⟨*the film just ~s along*⟩ **2** to work laboriously and monotonously ⟨*~ding through stacks of unanswered letters*⟩ *~ vt* to tread slowly or heavily along or over ⟨*~ded the streets all day, looking for work*⟩ – **plod** *n*, **plodder** *n*, **ploddingly** *adv*

¹**plonk** *vt* PLUNK 2

²**plonk** *n, chiefly Br* cheap or inferior wine – infml

plop *vb* **-pp-** *vi* **1** to drop or move suddenly with a sound suggestive of sthg dropping into water **2** to allow the body to drop heavily ⟨*~ped into a chair*⟩ *~ vt* to set, drop, or throw heavily – **plop** *n*

plosion *n* the release of obstructed breath that occurs in the articulation of stop consonants – **plosive** *adj or n*

¹**plot** *n* **1** a small piece of land, esp one used or designated for a specific purpose ⟨*a vegetable ~*⟩ **2** the plan or main story of a literary work **3** a secret plan for accomplishing

a usu evil or unlawful end; an intrigue **4** a chart or other graphic representation **5** *NAm* GROUND PLAN – **plotless** *adj*, **plotlessness** *n*

²**plot** *vb* -tt- *vt* **1a** to make a plot, map, or plan of **b** to mark or note (as if) on a map or chart **2** to lay out in plots **3a** to assign a position to (a point) by means of coordinates **b** to draw (a curve) by means of plotted points **c** to represent (an equation) by means of a curve so constructed **4** to plan or contrive, esp secretly ⟨~ted *his revenge*⟩ **5** to invent or devise the plot of (a literary work) ~ *vi* to form a plot; scheme – **plotter** *n*

¹**plough,** *NAm* **plow** *n* **1** (any of various devices operating like) an implement used to cut, lift, and turn over soil, esp in preparing ground for sowing **2** ploughed land **3** *cap* URSA MAJOR – + *the*

²**plough,** *NAm* **plow** *vi* **1a** to use a plough **b** to bear or undergo ploughing **2** to force a way, esp violently ⟨*the car* ~ed *into a group of spectators*⟩ **3** to proceed steadily and laboriously; plod ⟨*had to* ~ *through a summer reading list*⟩ ~ *vt* **1a** to turn, break up, or work (as if) with a plough **b** to make (e g a furrow) with a plough **2** to cut into, open, or make furrows or ridges in (as if) with a plough – often + *up* – **ploughable** *adj*, **plougher** *n*

plough back *vt* to reinvest (profits) in an industry

ploughman *n* one who guides a plough; *broadly* a farm labourer

ploughman's lunch *n* a cold lunch of bread, cheese, and usu pickled onions often served in a public house

ploughshare *n* the part of a mouldboard plough that cuts the furrow

plover *n, pl* **plovers,** *esp collectively* **plover** any of numerous wading birds with a short beak and usu a stout compact build

ploy *n* sthg devised or contrived, esp to embarrass or frustrate an opponent

¹**pluck** *vt* **1** to pull or pick off or out ⟨*she* ~ed *out a grey hair*⟩ **2** to remove sthg from (as if) by plucking; esp to remove the feathers from (e g a chicken) **3** to pick, pull, or grasp at; *also* to play (an instrument) in this manner ~ *vi* to tug *at* ⟨~ed *at the folds of her skirt*⟩ – **plucker** *n*

²**pluck** *n* **1** an act or instance of plucking or pulling **2** the heart, liver, and lungs of a slaughtered animal, esp as food **3** courage and determination

plucky *adj* marked by courage; spirited – **pluckily** *adv*, **pluckiness** *n*

¹**plug** *n* **1a** a piece used to fill a hole; a stopper **b** an obtruding or obstructing mass of material resembling a stopper ⟨*a volcanic* ~⟩ **2** a flat compressed cake of (chewing) tobacco; *also* a piece cut from this for chewing **3** a small core or segment removed from a larger object **4** a fire hydrant **5a** any of various devices resembling or functioning like an electrical plug **b** a device having usu 3 pins projecting from an insulated case for making electrical connection with a suitable socket; *also* the electrical socket **6** a piece of favourable publicity (e g for a commercial product) usu incorporated in general matter – infml

²**plug** *vb* -gg- *vt* **1** to block, close, or secure (as if) by inserting a plug **2** to hit with a bullet; SHOOT 2a **3** to advertise or publicize insistently ~ *vi* to work doggedly and persistently ⟨~ged *away at his homework*⟩ – **plugger** *n*

plug in *vi* to establish an electric circuit by inserting a plug ~ *vt* to attach to a power point

plum *n* **1** (any of numerous trees and shrubs of the rose family, that bear) an edible globular to oval smooth-skinned fruit with an oblong seed **2** a raisin when used in a pudding, cake, etc ⟨~ *cake*⟩ **3** sthg excellent or

superior; *esp* an opportunity or position offering exceptional advantages ⟨*a* ~ *job*⟩ **4** a dark reddish purple – **plum** *adj*, **plumlike** *adj*

plumage *n* the entire covering of feathers of a bird – **plumaged** *adj*

¹**plumb** *n* **1** a lead weight attached to a cord and used to indicate a vertical line **2** any of various weights (e g a sinker for a fishing line or a lead for sounding)

²**plumb** *adv* **1** straight down or up; vertically **2** exactly, precisely ⟨*his house is* ~ *in the middle of the island*⟩ **3** *chiefly dial NAm* completely, absolutely USE (2&3) chiefly infml

³**plumb** *vt* **1** to measure the depth of with a plumb **2** to examine minutely and critically, esp so as to achieve complete understanding ⟨~ing *the book's complexities*⟩ **3** to adjust or test by a plumb line **4** to supply with or install as plumbing – often + *in*

⁴**plumb** *adj* **1** exactly vertical or true **2** *of a cricket wicket* flat and allowing little or no horizontal or vertical deviation of the bowled ball **3** downright, complete – infml

plumb-, plumbo- *comb form* lead ⟨plumb*ism*⟩

plumbago *n, pl* **plumbagos 1** graphite **2** any of a genus of plants of the thrift family with spikes of showy flowers

plumber *n* **1** sby who installs, repairs, and maintains water piping and fittings **2** *obs* a dealer or worker in lead

plumbing *n* **1** a plumber's occupation or trade **2** the apparatus (e g pipes and fixtures) concerned in the distribution and use of water in a building

¹**plume** *n* **1a** a (large showy) bird's feather **b** a cluster of distinctive feathers **2** a usu large feather or cluster of feathers worn esp as an ornament **3** sthg resembling a feather (e g in shape, appearance, or lightness): e g **a** a feathery or feather-like animal or plant part; *esp* a full bushy tail **b** a trail of smoke, blowing snow, etc – **plumed** *adj*

²**plume** *vt* **1** to provide or deck with plumes **2** to pride or congratulate (oneself) *on* or *upon* **3a** *of a bird* to preen and arrange the feathers of (itself) **b** to preen and arrange (feathers)

¹**plummet** *n* a plumb (line)

²**plummet** *vi* to fall sharply and abruptly ⟨*prices* ~ed⟩

plummy *adj* **1** *of the voice* rich and mellow, often to the point of affectation **2** choice, desirable ⟨*got a* ~ *role in the film*⟩ – infml

¹**plump** *vi* to drop or sink suddenly or heavily ⟨~ed *down in the chair*⟩ ~ *vt* to drop, cast, or place suddenly or heavily – **plump for** to decide on out of several choices or courses of action ⟨plumped *for beer rather than wine*⟩

²**plump** *adv* **1** with a sudden or heavy drop **2** without qualification; directly

³**plump** *n* (the sound of) a sudden plunge, fall, or blow

⁴**plump** *adj* having a full rounded form; slightly fat – **plumpish** *adj*, **plumply** *adv*, **plumpness** *n*

⁵**plump** *vb* to make or become plump – often + *up* or *out*

plum pudding *n* a rich boiled or steamed pudding containing dried fruits (e g raisins) and spices

plump up *vt* to cause to fill or swell out ⟨plumped up *the pillows when she made the bed*⟩

¹**plunder** *vt* **1** to pillage, sack **2** to take, esp by force (e g in war); steal ~ *vi* to commit robbery or looting – **plunderer** *n*

²**plunder** *n* **1** an act of plundering; pillaging **2** sthg taken by force, theft, or fraud; loot

¹**plunge** *vt* **1a** to cause to penetrate quickly and forcibly **b** to sink (a potted plant) in the ground **2** to cause to enter a thing, state, or course of action, usu suddenly, unex-

pectedly, or violently ~ *vi* **1** to thrust or cast oneself (as if) into water **2a** to be thrown headlong or violently forwards and downwards ⟨*the car stopped abruptly and he* ~d *through the windscreen*⟩; *also* to move oneself in such a manner **b** to act with reckless haste; enter suddenly or unexpectedly ⟨*the firm* ~d *into debt*⟩ **3** to descend or dip suddenly **4** to bet or gamble heavily and recklessly – *infml*

²**plunge** *n* a dive; *also* a swim

plunger *n* **1a** a device (e g a piston in a pump) that acts with a plunging or thrusting motion **b** a rubber suction cup on a handle used to free plumbing from blockages **2** a reckless gambler or speculator – *chiefly infml*

plunk *vt* **1** to pluck so as to produce a hollow, metallic, or harsh sound **2** to set down suddenly; plump – *chiefly infml* – **plunk** *n*, **plunker** *n*

plunk down *vi* to drop abruptly; settle into position ~ *vt* **1** to put down usu firmly or abruptly ⟨plunked *his money* down *on the counter*⟩ **2** to settle (oneself) into position ⟨plunked *himself* down *on the bench*⟩ *USE* chiefly *infml*

pluperfect *adj* PAST PERFECT – **pluperfect** *n*

plural *adj* **1** of or being a word form (e g *we, houses, cattle*) denoting more than 1, or in some languages more than 2 or 3, persons, things, or instances **2** consisting of or containing more than 1 (kind or class) ⟨*a* ~ *society*⟩ – **plural** *n*, **plurally** *adv*, **pluralize** *vt*

pluralism *n* **1** the holding of 2 or more offices or positions (e g benefices) at the same time **2** a state of society in which members of diverse social groups develop their traditional cultures or special interests within a common civilization – **pluralist** *adj or n*, **pluralistic** *adj*, **pluralistically** *adv*

plurality *n* **1a** the state of being plural or numerous **b** a large number or quantity **2** (a benefice held by) pluralism

¹**plus** *prep* **1** increased by; with the addition of ⟨*4* ~ *5*⟩⟨*the debt* ~ *interest*⟩ **2** and also ⟨*the job needs experience* ~ *patience*⟩

²**plus** *n, pl* **-s-** *also* **-ss-** **1** an added quantity **2** a positive factor, quantity, or quality **3** a surplus

³**plus** *adj* **1** algebraically or electrically positive **2** additional and welcome ⟨*a* ~ *factor is its nearness to the shops*⟩ **3** greater than that specified ⟨*had a B* ~ *for his essay*⟩

⁴**plus** *conj* and moreover ⟨~ *he has to watch what he says* – *Punch*⟩

plus fours *n pl* loose wide trousers gathered on a band and finishing just below the knee

¹**plush** *n* a fabric with an even pile longer and less dense than that of velvet

²**plush** *adj* **1** (made) of or resembling plush **2** PLUSHY 2 – **plushly** *adv*, **plushness** *n*

plushy *adj* **1** having the texture of or covered with plush **2** luxurious, showy – **plushiness** *n*

Pluto *n* the planet furthest from the sun

plutocracy *n* (government by) a controlling class of wealthy people – **plutocrat** *n*, **plutocratic** *adj*, **plutocratically** *adv*

plutonium *n* a radioactive metallic element similar to uranium that is formed in atomic reactors and is used in weapons and as a fuel for atomic reactors

¹**ply** *vt* to twist together ⟨~ *2 single yarns*⟩

²**ply** *n* **1a** a strand in a yarn, wool, etc **b** any of several layers (e g of cloth) usu sewn or laminated together **2a** (any of the veneer sheets forming) plywood **b** a layer of paper or paperboard

³**ply** *vt* **1a** to use or wield diligently ⟨busily ~ing *his axe*⟩ **b** to practise or perform diligently ⟨~ing *his trade*⟩ **2** to

keep furnishing or supplying sthg to ⟨plied *them with drinks*⟩ **3** to go or travel over or on regularly ~ *vi* **1** to apply oneself steadily **2** *of a boatman, taxi driver, etc* to wait regularly in a particular place for custom – esp in *ply for hire* **3** to go or travel regularly ⟨*a steamer* ~ing *between opposite shores of the lake*⟩

plywood *n* a light structural material of thin sheets of wood glued or cemented together with the grains of adjacent layers arranged crosswise usu at right angles

pneumatic *adj* of or using gas (e g air or wind): **a** moved or worked by air pressure **b** adapted for holding or inflated with compressed air **c** having air-filled cavities – **pneumatically** *adv*

pneumoconiosis *n, pl* **pneumoconioses** a crippling disease of the lungs, esp of miners, caused by the habitual inhalation of irritant mineral or metallic particles

pneumonia *n* localized or widespread inflammation of the lungs with change from an air-filled to a solid consistency, caused by infection or irritants

po *n, pl* **pos** *Br* CHAMBER POT – *infml*

¹**poach** *vt* to cook (e g fish or an egg) in simmering liquid

²**poach** *vt* **1** to trample or cut up (e g turf) (as if) with hoofs **2a** to trespass on ⟨*a field* ~ed *too frequently by the amateur* – *TLS*⟩ **b** to take (game or fish) illegally **c** to take or acquire by unfair or underhand means ~ *vi* **1** *of land* to become soft or muddy when trampled on **2a** to (trespass while attempting to) take game or fish illegally **b** to trespass on or upon ⟨*what happens to a poet when he* ~es *upon a novelist's preserves* – Virginia Woolf⟩ – **poacher** *n*

pock *n* (a spot resembling) a pustule in an eruptive disease (e g smallpox) – **pock** *vt*, **pocky** *adj*

¹**pocket** *n* **1** a small bag that is sewn or inserted in a garment so that it is open at the top or side **2** a supply of money; means ⟨*has houses to suit all* ~s⟩ **3a** a receptacle, container **b** any of several openings at the corners or sides of a billiard table into which balls are propelled **4a** a small isolated area or group ⟨~s *of unemployment*⟩ **b** a cavity (e g in the earth) containing a deposit (e g of gold or water) **c** AIR POCKET **5** *chiefly SAfr* (the amount contained in) a bag – **pocketful** *n* – **in pocket** in the position of having made a profit – **out of pocket** having suffered a financial loss

²**pocket** *vt* **1a** to put or enclose (as if) in one's pocket ⟨~ed *his change*⟩ **b** to appropriate to one's own use; steal ⟨~ed *the money she had collected for charity*⟩ **2** to accept; PUT UP WITH ⟨~ *an insult*⟩ **3** to set aside, suppress ⟨~ed *his pride*⟩ **4** to drive (a ball) into a pocket of a billiard table

³**pocket** *adj* **1** small enough to be carried in the pocket ⟨*a* ~ *camera*⟩ **2** small, miniature ⟨*a* ~ *submarine*⟩

pocketbook *n* **1** a pocket-size container for (paper) money and personal papers **2** *NAm* **a** a small, esp paperback, book that can be carried in the pocket **b** a purse **c** a strapless handbag

pocket-handkerchief *n* a handkerchief

pocketknife *n* a knife that has 1 or more blades that fold into the handle so that it can be carried in the pocket

pocket money *n* money for small personal expenses, esp as given to a child

pockmark *n* a mark or pit (like that) caused by smallpox – **pockmarked** *adj*

¹**pod** *n* **1** a long seed vessel or fruit, esp of the pea, bean, or other leguminous plant **2** an egg case of a locust or similar insect **3** a streamlined compartment under the wings or fuselage of an aircraft used as a container (e g for fuel) **4** a detachable compartment on a spacecraft or aircraft

²**pod** *vb* **-dd-** *vi* to produce pods ~ *vt* to remove (e g peas) from the pod

³**pod** *n* a small group of animals (e g seals) close together

-pod *comb form* (→ *n*) foot; part resembling a foot ⟨pleopod⟩

podgy *adj* short and plump; chubby

podiatry *n*, *NAm* chiropody – **podiatrist** *n*, **podiatric** *adj*

podium *n*, *pl* **podiums, podia 1** a low wall serving as a foundation or terrace wall: e g **a** one round the arena of an ancient amphitheatre **b** the stone base supporting the columns of a classical structure **2** a small raised platform (for an orchestral conductor)

-podium *comb form* (→ *n*), *pl* **-podia** **-pod** ⟨pseudopodium⟩

poem *n* **1** an individual work of poetry **2** a creation, experience, or object suggesting a poem ⟨*the interior was a ~ of chinoiserie*⟩

poesy *n* **1** a poem or body of poems **2** the art or composition of poetry

poet, *fem* **poetess** *n* **1** one who writes poetry **2** a creative artist with special sensitivity to his/her medium ⟨*a ~ of the piano*⟩

poetaster *n* an inferior poet

poetic, poetical *adj* **1a** (characteristic) of poets or poetry **b** having the qualities associated with poetry **2** written in verse – **poetically** *adv*, **poeticism** *n*

poetic justice *n* an outcome in which vice is punished and virtue rewarded in an (ironically) appropriate manner

poet laureate *n*, *pl* **poets laureate, poet laureates 1** a distinguished poet honoured for achievement in his/her art **2** a poet appointed for life by the sovereign as a member of the British royal household and expected to compose poems for state occasions

poetry *n* **1** metrical writing; verse **b** a poet's compositions; poems **2** writing that is arranged to formulate a concentrated imaginative awareness of experience through meaning, sound, and rhythm **3** a quality of beauty, grace, and great feeling ⟨*~ in motion*⟩

po-faced *adj*, *Br* having a foolishly solemn or humourless expression – chiefly *infml*

pogo stick *n* a pole with a spring at the bottom and 2 footrests on which sby stands and can move along with a series of jumps

pogrom *n* an organized massacre, esp of Jews

poignant *adj* **1a** painfully affecting the feelings; distressing **b** deeply affecting; touching **2** designed to make an impression; cutting ⟨*~ satire*⟩ – **poignancy** *n*, **poignantly** *adv*

poinsettia *n* any of various spurges bearing flower clusters opposite brightly coloured bracts

¹**point** *n* **1a(1)** an individual detail; an item **(2)** a distinguishing detail ⟨*tact is one of her strong ~s*⟩ **b** the most important essential in a discussion or matter ⟨*missed the whole ~ of the joke*⟩ **2** an end or object to be achieved; a purpose ⟨*did not see what ~ there was in continuing the discussion*⟩ **3a(1)** a geometric element that has a position but no extent or magnitude **(2)** a geometric element determined by an ordered set of coordinates **b** (a narrowly localized place having) a precisely indicated position ⟨*walked to a ~ 50 yards north of the building*⟩ **c(1)** an exact moment ⟨*at this ~ he was interrupted*⟩ **(2)** a time interval immediately before sthg happened; the verge ⟨*at the ~ of death*⟩ **d(1)** a particular step, stage, or degree in development ⟨*had reached the ~ where nothing seemed to matter anymore*⟩ **(2)** a definite position in a scale ⟨*boiling ~*⟩ **4a** the sharp or narrowly rounded end of

sthg; a tip **b** the tip of the toes – used in ballet; usu *pl* **c** *pl* a contact breaker **5a** a projecting usu tapering piece of land **b(1)** the tip of a projecting body part **(2)** TINE **2 (3)** *pl* (the markings of) the extremities of an animal, esp when of a different colour from the rest of the body **6a** a very small mark **b(1)** PUNCTUATION MARK; *esp* FULL STOP **(2)** DECIMAL POINT **7** any of the 32 evenly spaced compass directions; *also* the 11° 15′ interval between 2 successive points **8a** lace worked with a needle; NEEDLEPOINT **1 b** lace imitating needlepoint worked with bobbins; PILLOW LACE **9a** a unit of counting in the scoring of a game or contest **b** a unit used in evaluating the strength of a bridge hand **c** a unit used in quoting prices (e g of shares, bonds, and commodities) **d** a unit of 0.351mm (about ¹/₇₂in) used to measure the body size of printing type **10a** the action of pointing **b** the rigidly intent attitude of a gundog when marking game for a hunter **11** (the position of) a defensive player in lacrosse **12** a fielding position in cricket near to the batsman and on a direct line with the popping crease on the off side **13** *pl*, *Br* a device made of usu 2 movable rails and necessary connections and designed to turn a locomotive or train from one track to another – **beside the point** irrelevant – **to the point** relevant, pertinent ⟨*a suggestion that was to the point*⟩

²**point** *vt* **1a** to provide with a point; sharpen ⟨*~ing a pencil with a knife*⟩ **b** to give added force, emphasis, or piquancy to ⟨*~ up a remark*⟩ **2** to scratch out the old mortar from the joints of (e g a brick wall) and fill in with new material **3a** to punctuate **b** to mark signs or points in (e g psalms or Hebrew words) **4** *of a gundog* to indicate the presence and place of (game) for a hunter by a point **5** to cause to be turned in a particular direction ⟨*~ a gun*⟩ ⟨*~ed the boat upstream*⟩ ~ *vi* **1a** to indicate the fact or probability of sthg specified ⟨*everything ~s to a bright future*⟩ **b** to indicate the position or direction of sthg, esp by extending a finger ⟨*~ at the map*⟩ **c** to point game ⟨*a dog that ~s well*⟩ **2** to lie extended, aimed, or turned in a particular direction ⟨*the signpost ~ed north*⟩

point-blank *adj* **1** so close to a target that a missile fired will travel in a straight line to the mark **2** direct, blunt ⟨*a ~ refusal*⟩ – **point-blank** *adv*

point-duty *n* traffic regulation carried out usu by a policeman stationed at a particular point

pointed *adj* **1** having a point **2a** pertinent; TO THE POINT **b** aimed at a particular person or group **3** conspicuous, marked ⟨*~ indifference*⟩ – **pointedly** *adv*, **pointedness** *n*

pointer *n* **1** a rod used to direct attention **2** a large strong slender smooth-haired gundog that hunts by scent and indicates the presence of game by pointing **3** a useful suggestion or hint; a tip

pointillism *n* the technique in art of applying small strokes or dots of pure colour to a surface so that from a distance they blend together – **pointillist** *also* **pointilliste** *n or adj*

pointless *adj* devoid of meaning, relevance, or purpose; senseless ⟨*a ~ remark*⟩ – **pointlessly** *adv*, **pointlessness** *n*

point of no return *n* **1** the point in a long-distance journey after which return to the starting point is impossible **2** a critical point (e g in a course of action) at which turning back or reversal is not possible

point of order *n* a question relating to procedure in an official meeting

point of view *n* a position from which sthg is considered or evaluated

point out *vt* to direct sby's attention to ⟨point out a mistake⟩

pointsman n **1** a policeman on point-duty **2** Br a person in charge of railway points

point-to-point n a usu cross-country steeplechase for amateur riders – **point-to-pointer** n

¹**poise** vt **1a** to balance; esp to hold or carry in equilibrium ⟨walked along gracefully with a water jar ~d on her head⟩ **b** to hold supported or suspended without motion in a steady position **2** to hold or carry in a particular way **3** to put into readiness; brace ~ vi to hang (as if) suspended; hover

²**poise** n **1** a stably balanced state ⟨a ~ between widely divergent impulses – F R Leavis⟩ **2a** easy self-possessed assurance of manner **b** a particular way of carrying oneself

³**poise** n a cgs unit of dynamic viscosity

poised adj **1** marked by balance or equilibrium or by easy composure of manner **2** in readiness ⟨~ for flight⟩⟨~ for action⟩

¹**poison** n **1a** a substance that through its chemical action kills, injures, or impairs an organism **b** sthg destructive or harmful **2** a substance that inhibits the activity of another substance or the course of a reaction or process ⟨a catalyst ~⟩ – **poison** adj

²**poison** vt **1a** to injure or kill with poison **b** to treat, taint, or impregnate with poison **2** to exert a harmful influence on; corrupt ⟨~ed their minds⟩ **3** to inhibit the activity, course, or occurrence of – **poisoner** n

poison gas n a poisonous gas or a liquid or solid giving off poisonous vapours designed to kill, injure, or disable by inhalation or contact

poison ivy n (any of several plants related to) a N American climbing plant of the sumach family that has greenish flowers and white berries and produces an oil that causes an intensely itching skin rash

poisonous adj having the properties or effects of poison – **poisonously** adv

poison-pen adj written with malice and spite and usu anonymously ⟨~ letter⟩

¹**poke** n, chiefly dial NAm a bag, sack

²**poke** vt **1a**(1) to prod, jab ⟨~d him in the ribs and grinned broadly⟩ (2) to stir the coals or logs of (a fire) so as to promote burning **b** to produce by piercing, stabbing, or jabbing ⟨~ a hole⟩ **2** to cause to project ⟨~d her head out of the window⟩ **3** to hit, punch ⟨~d him in the nose⟩ – infml **4** of a man to have sexual intercourse with –vulg ~ vi **1** to make a prodding, jabbing, or thrusting movement, esp repeatedly **2a** to look about or through sthg without system; rummage ⟨found it while poking around in the attic⟩ **b** to meddle **3** to move or act slowly or aimlessly; potter ⟨just ~d about at home and didn't accomplish much⟩ **4** to become stuck out or forwards; protrude **5** of a man to have sexual intercourse – vulg – **poke fun at** to mock – **poke one's nose into** to meddle in or interfere with (esp sthg that does not concern one)

³**poke** n **1** a quick thrust; a jab **2** a punch – infml **3** an act of sexual intercourse – vulg

¹**poker** n a metal rod for poking a fire

²**poker** n any of several card games in which a player bets that the value of his/her hand is greater than that of the hands held by others and in which each subsequent player must either equal or raise the last bet or drop out

poker face n an inscrutable face that reveals no hint of a person's thoughts or feelings – **poker-faced** adj

pokerwork n (the art of doing) decorative work burnt into a material by a heated instrument

poky also **pokey** adj small and cramped – infml – **pokily** adv, **pokiness** n

Polack n, archaic or NAm a Pole – now derog

polar adj **1a** of, coming from, or characteristic of (the region round) a geographical pole **b** esp of an orbit passing over a planet's N and S poles **2** of 1 or more poles (e g of a magnet) **3** diametrically opposite **4** exhibiting polarity; esp having (molecules with) groups with opposing properties at opposite ends ⟨a ~ molecule⟩⟨a ~ solvent⟩ **5** resembling a pole or axis round which all else revolves; pivotal **6** of or expressed in polar coordinates ⟨~ equations⟩; also of a polar coordinate system

polar bear n a large creamy-white bear that inhabits arctic regions

polarity n **1** the quality or condition of a body that has opposite or contrasted properties or powers in opposite directions **2** attraction towards a particular object or in a specific direction **3** the particular electrical state of being either positive or negative **4** (an instance of) diametric opposition

polarize, -ise vt **1a** to affect (radiation, esp light) so that the vibrations of the wave assume a definite form (e g restriction to vibration in 1 plane) **b** to give electrical or magnetic polarity to **2** to divide into opposing factions or groupings ~ vi to become polarized – **polarizable** adj, **polarizability** n, **polarization** n

Polaroid trademark – used esp for a light-polarizing material used esp in glasses to prevent glare and in various optical devices

polder n an area of low land reclaimed from a body of water, esp in the Netherlands

¹**pole** n **1a** a long slender usu cylindrical object (e g a length of wood) **b** a shaft which extends from the front axle of a wagon between the draught animals **2** ROD 2 **3** the most favourable front-row position on the starting line of a (motor) race

²**pole** vb to push or propel (oneself or sthg) with poles

³**pole** n **1** either extremity of an axis of (a body, esp the earth, resembling) a sphere **2a** either of 2 related opposites **b** a point of guidance or attraction **3a** either of the 2 terminals of an electric cell, battery, or dynamo **b** any of 2 or more regions in a magnetized body at which the magnetic flux density is concentrated **4** either of the anatomically or physiologically differentiated areas at opposite ends of an axis in an organism or cell

Pole n a native or inhabitant of Poland

¹**poleaxe** n **1** a battle-axe with a short handle and often a hook or spike opposite the blade **2** an axe used, esp formerly, in slaughtering cattle

²**poleaxe** vt to attack, strike, or fell (as if) with a poleaxe

polecat n, pl **polecats**, esp collectively **polecat 1** a European flesh-eating mammal of which the ferret is considered a domesticated variety **2** NAm SKUNK 1

polemic n **1** an aggressive attack on or refutation of the opinions or principles of another **2** the art or practice of disputation or controversy – usu pl with sing. meaning but sing. or pl in constr – **polemic, polemical** adj, **polemicist** n

polestar n **1** a directing principle; a guide **2** a centre of attraction

Pole Star n the star in the constellation Ursa Minor that lies very close to the N celestial pole

pole vault n (an athletic field event consisting of) a jump for height over a crossbar with the aid of a pole – **pole-vault** vi, **pole-vaulter** n

¹**police** n **1** the department of government concerned with maintenance of public order and enforcement of laws **2a** sing or pl in constr POLICE FORCE **b** pl in constr policemen **3** sing or pl in constr an organized body having similar functions to a police force within a more restricted sphere ⟨railway ~⟩

²**police** *vt* 1 to control by use of police 2 to put in order 3 to supervise the operation of

police force *n sing or pl in constr* a body of trained people entrusted by a government with maintenance of public order and enforcement of laws

policeman, *fem* **policewoman** *n* a member of a police force

police state *n* a political unit characterized by repressive governmental control of political, economic, and social life, usu enforced by (secret) police

police station *n* the headquarters of a local police force

¹**policy** *n* 1 procedure based primarily on material interest; wisdom ⟨*it's bad ~ to smoke*⟩ 2a a definite course of action selected from among alternatives to guide and determine present and future decisions b an overall plan embracing general goals and procedures, esp of a governmental body

²**policy** *n* (a document embodying) a contract of insurance

polio *n* poliomyelitis

poliomyelitis *n* an infectious virus disease, esp of children, characterized by inflammation of the nerve cells of the spinal cord, paralysis of the motor nerves, and atrophy of skeletal muscles often with permanent disability and deformity – **poliomyelitic** *adj*

¹**polish** *vt* 1 to make smooth and glossy, usu by friction 2 to refine in manners or condition 3 to bring to a highly developed, finished, or refined state; perfect – often + *up* ~ *vi* to become smooth or glossy (as if) by friction – **polisher** *n*

²**polish** *n* 1a a smooth glossy surface b freedom from rudeness or coarseness 2 the action or process of polishing ⟨*give the table a ~*⟩ 3 a preparation used to produce a gloss and often a colour for the protection and decoration of a surface ⟨*furniture ~*⟩ ⟨*nail ~*⟩

¹**Polish** *adj* (characteristic) of Poland

²**Polish** *n* the language of the Poles

polish off *vt* to dispose of rapidly or completely

politburo *n* the principal committee of a Communist party

polite *adj* 1 showing or characterized by correct social usage; refined 2 marked by an appearance of consideration and deference; courteous – **politely** *adv*, **politeness** *n*

politic *adj* 1 *of a person* shrewd and sagacious in managing, contriving, or dealing 2 *of a policy* expedient

political *adj* 1 of government 2a of (party) politics b sensitive to politics ⟨*highly ~ students*⟩ 3 involving or charged with acts against a government ⟨*~ criminals*⟩ – **politically** *adv*

political economy *n* a social science dealing with the interrelationship of political and economic processes – **political economist** *n*

political science *n* a social science concerned chiefly with political institutions and processes – **political scientist** *n*

politician *n* a person experienced or engaged in politics

politicize, -ise *vi* to discuss politics ~ *vt* to give a political tone to – **politicization** *n*

politico *n, pl* **politicos** *also* **politicoes** a politician – infml

politico- *comb form* political and ⟨*politico-diplomatic*⟩

politics *n pl but sing or pl in constr* 1a the art or science of government b POLITICAL SCIENCE 2a political affairs; *specif* competition between interest groups in a government b political life as a profession 3 sby's political sympathies 4 the total complex of relations between human beings in society

polity *n* (the form of) a politically organized unit

polka *n* (music for or in the rhythm of) a vivacious dance of Bohemian origin in duple time – **polka** *vi*

polka dot *n* any of many regularly distributed dots in a textile design – **polka-dot, polka-dotted** *adj*

¹**poll** *n* 1 (the hairy top or back of) the head 2 the broad or flat end of the head of a striking tool (e g a hammer) 3a the casting of votes b the place where votes are cast – usu pl with sing. meaning ⟨*at the ~s*⟩ c the number of votes recorded ⟨*a heavy ~*⟩ 4 a survey conducted by the questioning of people selected at random or by quota

²**poll** *vt* 1 to cut off or cut short a the hair or wool of b the horns of (a cow) c (e g wool) 2 to remove the top of (e g a tree); *specif* to pollard 3 to receive and record the votes of 4 to receive (votes) 5 to question in a poll ~ *vi* to cast one's vote – **pollee** *n*, **poller** *n*

³**poll** *n* a polled animal

¹**pollard** *n* 1 a hornless animal of a usu horned kind 2 a tree cut back to the main stem to promote the growth of a dense head of foliage

²**pollard** *vt* to make a pollard of (a tree)

pollen *n* (a fine dust of) the minute granular spores discharged from the anther of the flower of a flowering plant that serve to fertilize the ovules – **pollinic** *adj*

pollen count *n* a figure representing the amount of pollen in the air, available as a warning to people allergic to pollen

pollinate *vt* to place pollen on the stigma of and so fertilize – **pollinator** *n*, **pollination** *n*

pollster *n* one who conducts a poll or compiles data obtained by a poll

poll tax *n* a tax of a fixed amount per person levied on adults

pollute *vt* 1 to make morally impure; defile 2 to make physically impure or unclean; *esp* to contaminate (an environment), esp with man-made waste – **pollutant** *n*, **polluter** *n*, **pollutive** *adj*

pollution *n* 1 polluting or being polluted 2 material that pollutes

Pollyanna *n* an irrepressible optimist – **Pollyannaish, Pollyannish** *adj*

polo *n* a game of oriental origin played by teams of usu 4 players on ponies or canoes, bicycles, etc using mallets with long flexible handles to drive a wooden ball into the opponent's goal

polonaise *n* 1 a short-sleeved elaborate dress with a fitted waist and panniers at the sides and back drawn up on cords 2 (music in moderate ¾ time for) a stately Polish processional dance

polo neck *n, chiefly Br* (a jumper with) a very high closely fitting collar worn folded over

polony *n* a dry sausage of partly cooked meat, esp pork; *also* a cooked sausage made from soya and meat and eaten cold

poltergeist *n* a noisy mischievous ghost believed to be responsible for unexplained noises and physical damage

poltroon *n* a spiritless coward

poly *n, pl* **polys** *Br* a polytechnic – infml

poly- *comb form* 1a many; several; much; multi- ⟨*polyphonic*⟩ ⟨*polygyny*⟩ b excessive; abnormally great; hyper- ⟨*polyphagia*⟩ 2a containing 2 or more (specified ions or radicals) in the molecular structure ⟨*polysulphide*⟩ b polymeric; polymer of (a specified monomer) ⟨*polyethylene*⟩ ⟨*polynucleotide*⟩

polyandrous *adj* 1 having many usu free stamens 2 of or practising polyandry

polyandry *n* 1 having more than 1 husband at a time 2 the state of being polyandrous

polyanthus *n, pl* **polyanthuses, polyanthi** any of various cultivated hybrid primroses

polyester *n* a polymer containing ester groups used esp in making fibres, resins, or plastics – **polyesterification** *n*

polyethylene *n* polythene

polygamous, polygamic *adj* **1a** of or practising polygamy **b** having more than 1 mate at a time ⟨*baboons are* ~⟩ **2** bearing both hermaphrodite and unisexual flowers on the same plant – **polygamously** *adv*

polygamy *n* **1** being married to more than 1 person at a time; *esp* marriage to more than 1 wife **2** the state of being polygamous – **polygamist** *n*, **polygamize** *vi*

¹**polyglot** *n* **1** one who is polyglot **2** *cap* a book, esp a bible, containing versions of the same text in several languages **3** a mixture or confusion of languages – **polyglottal** *adj*

²**polyglot** *adj* **1** MULTILINGUAL **2 2** containing matter in several languages ⟨*a* ~ *sign*⟩

polygon *n* a closed plane figure bounded by straight lines – **polygonal** *adj*, **polygonally** *adv*

polyhedron *n, pl* **polyhedrons, polyhedra** a solid formed by plane faces – **polyhedral** *adj*

polymath *n* one who has a wide range of learning or accomplishments – **polymath** *adj*, **polymathic** *adj*, **polymathy** *n*

polymer *n* a chemical compound or mixture of compounds containing repeating structural units and formed by chemical combination of many small molecules – **polymerize** *vb*, **polymerization** *n*, **polymeric** *adj*, **polymerically** *adv*

polymorphic, polymorphous *adj* having, assuming, or occurring in various forms, characters, or styles – **polymorphically, polymorphously** *adv*, **polymorphism** *n*

polyp *n* **1** a coelenterate with a hollow cylindrical body attached at one end and having a central mouth surrounded by tentacles at the other **2** a projecting mass of tissue (e g a tumour) – **polypoid** *adj*, **polypous** *adj*

polyphony *n* a style of musical composition in which 2 or more independent but organically related voice parts sound against one another

polystyrene *n* a rigid transparent polymer of styrene used esp in moulded products, foams, and sheet materials

polysyllabic, polysyllabical *adj* **1** having more than 3 syllables **2** characterized by polysyllables – **polysyllabically** *adv*

polysyllable *n* a polysyllabic word

¹**polytechnic** *adj* relating to or devoted to instruction in many technical arts or applied sciences

²**polytechnic** *n* a polytechnic school; *specif* any of a number of British institutions offering full-time, sandwich, and part-time courses in various subjects but with a bias towards the vocational

polytheism *n* belief in or worship of 2 or more gods – **polytheist** *adj or n*, **polytheistic** *adj*

polythene *n* any of various lightweight ethylene polymers used esp for packaging and bowls, buckets, etc

polyurethane *n* any of various polymers used esp in foams and paints

polyvalent *adj* **1** having a valency greater usu than 2 **2** having more than 1 valency – **polyvalence** *n*

polyvinyl chloride *n* a plastic used esp as a rubber substitute (e g for raincoats and insulation for wires)

pomade *n* a perfumed ointment for the hair or scalp – **pomade** *vt*

pomander *n* a mixture of aromatic substances enclosed in a perforated bag or box and used to scent clothes or linen or formerly carried as a guard against infection

pomegranate *n* (an Old World tree that bears) a

thick-skinned reddish fruit about the size of an orange that contains many seeds each surrounded by a tart edible crimson pulp

Pomeranian *n* (any of) a breed of very small compact long-haired dogs

¹**pommel** *n* **1** the knob on the hilt of a sword **2** the protuberance at the front and top of a saddle **3** either of the pair of removable handles on the top of a pommel horse

²**pommel** *vt* **-ll-** (*NAm* **-l-, -ll-**), to pummel

pommel horse *n* (a men's gymnastic event using) a leather-covered horizontal rectangular or cylindrical form with 2 handles on the top that is supported above the ground and is used for swinging and balancing feats

Pommy, Pommie *n, often not cap, Austr & NZ* a British person; *esp* a British immigrant – **Pommy, Pommie** *adj*

pomp *n* **1** a show of magnificence; splendour **2** ostentatious or specious display

¹**pom-pom** *n* an automatic gun mounted on ships in pairs, fours, or eights

²**pom-pom** *n* an ornamental ball or tuft used esp on clothing, hats, etc

pomposity *n* **1** pompous demeanour, speech, or behaviour **2** a pompous gesture, habit, or act

pompous *adj* **1** self-important, pretentious ⟨*a* ~ *politician*⟩ **2** excessively elevated or ornate ⟨~ *rhetoric*⟩ – **pompously** *adv*, **pompousness** *n*

¹**ponce** *n, Br* **1** a pimp **2** a man who behaves in an effeminate manner – *infml*

²**ponce** *vi, Br* **1** to pimp **2** to act in a frivolous, showy, or effeminate manner – *usu* + *around* or *about*; *infml*

poncho *n, pl* **ponchos** a cloak resembling a blanket with a slit in the middle for the head

poncy, poncey *adj, Br* (characteristic) of a ponce – *infml*

pond *n* a body of (fresh) water usu smaller than a lake

ponder *vt* **1** to weigh in the mind; assess **2** to review mentally; think over ⟨~ *ed the events of the day*⟩ ~ *vi* to think or consider, esp quietly, soberly, and deeply – **ponderer** *n*

ponderous *adj* **1** unwieldy or clumsy because of weight and size **2** oppressively or unpleasantly dull; pedestrian ⟨~ *prose*⟩ – **ponderously** *adv*, **ponderousness** *n*

pong *vi or n, Br* (to emit) an unpleasant smell; stink – *infml*

poniard *n* a small dagger

pontiff *n* a bishop; *specif* the pope

¹**pontifical** *adj* **1** of a pontiff or pontifex **2** pretentiously dogmatic – **pontifically** *adv*

²**pontifical** *n* **1** episcopal dress; *specif* the full vestments of bishophood worn by a prelate when celebrating a pontifical mass – *usu pl with sing. meaning* **2** a book containing the forms for sacraments and rites performed by a bishop

¹**pontificate** *n* the state, office, or term of office of the pope

²**pontificate** *vi* **1** to officiate as a pontiff **2** to deliver oracular utterances or dogmatic opinions – **pontificator** *n*, **pontification** *n*

¹**pontoon** *n* a flat-bottomed boat or portable float (used in building a floating temporary bridge)

²**pontoon** *n* a gambling card game in which the object is to be dealt cards scoring more than those of the dealer up to but not exceeding 21

pony *n* **1** a small horse; *esp* a member of any of several breeds of very small stocky horses under 142 hands in height **2** a racehorse – *usu pl; slang* **3** *Br* the sum of £25 – *slang*

ponytail *n* a hairstyle in which the hair is drawn back tightly and tied high at the back of the head

pony trekking *n* the pastime of riding ponies long distances across country in a group

pooch *n* DOG 1a – slang

poodle *n* (any of) a breed of active intelligent dogs with a thick curly coat which is of 1 colour only

poof, pouf *n*, *Br* an effeminate man or male homosexual – chiefly derog

pooh *interj* – used to express contempt, disapproval, or distaste at an unpleasant smell

pooh-pooh *vb* to express contempt (for)

¹pool *n* **1a** a small and relatively deep body of usu fresh water (e g a still place in a stream or river) **b** sthg resembling a pool (e g in depth or shape) ⟨~s *of light*⟩ **2** a small body of standing liquid; a puddle ⟨*lay in a ~ of blood*⟩ **3** SWIMMING POOL

²pool *n* **1** an aggregate stake to which each player of a game has contributed **2** any of various games played on a billiard table with 6 pockets and often 15 numbered balls **3** a combination of the interests or property of different parties that subjects each party to the same controls and a common liability **4** a readily available supply; *esp* the whole quantity of a particular material present in the body and available for metabolism **5** a facility, service, or group of people providing a service for a number of people (e g the members of a business organization) ⟨*a typing ~*⟩ **6** *pl* FOOTBALL POOLS

³pool *vt* to contribute to a common stock (e g of resources or effort)

¹poop *n* an enclosed superstructure at the stern of a ship above the main deck

²poop *vt* **1** to break over the stern of **2** to receive (a sea or wave) over the stern

³poop *vb*, *chiefly NAm* vt to put out of breath; *also* to tire out ~ *vi* to become exhausted *USE* (*vt & vi*) usu + *out*; infml

poor *adj* **1a** lacking material possessions **b** of or characterized by poverty **2** less than adequate; meagre ⟨*a ~ harvest*⟩ **3** exciting pity ⟨*~ old soul!*⟩ **4** inferior in quality, value, or workmanship ⟨*in ~ health*⟩⟨*a ~ essay*⟩ **5** humble, unpretentious ⟨*in my ~ opinion*⟩ **6** *of land* barren, unproductive – **poorish** *adj*, **poorly** *adv*, **poorness** *n*

poor box *n* a box (e g in a church) into which money for the poor can be put

poorhouse *n* WORKHOUSE 1

poor law *n* a law that in former times provided for the relief of the poor

poorly *adj* somewhat ill

poor-spirited *adj* lacking zest, confidence, or courage – **poor-spiritedly** *adv*, **poor-spiritedness** *n*

poor white *n* a member of an inferior or underprivileged white social group – chiefly derog

poove *n*, *Br* a poof – chiefly derog

¹pop *vb* **-pp-** vt **1** to strike or knock sharply; hit ⟨~ped *him one on the jaw*⟩ **2** to push, put, or thrust suddenly ⟨~ped *a sweet into his mouth*⟩ **3** to cause to explode or burst open **4** to shoot at **5** to take (drugs) orally or by injection ⟨*he ~ped pills*⟩ **6** *Br* to pawn ~ *vi* **1a** to go, come, or enter suddenly or quickly ⟨*just ~ped out to do some shopping*⟩ **b** to escape or break away from sthg (e g a point of attachment) usu suddenly or unexpectedly **2** to make or burst with a sharp explosive sound **3** to protrude from the sockets ⟨*eyes ~ping in amazement*⟩ *USE* (*vt & vi*) infml – **pop the question** to propose marriage – infml

²pop *n* **1** a popping sound **2** a flavoured carbonated beverage **3** *Br* PAWN 2 *USE* (*1 & 3*) infml

³pop *adv* like or with a pop; suddenly – infml

⁴pop *n*, *chiefly NAm* a father – infml

⁵pop *adj* popular: e g **a** of pop music ⟨*~ singer*⟩ **b** of or constituting a mass culture widely disseminated through the mass media ⟨*~ society*⟩

⁶pop *n* POP MUSIC

pop art *n*, *often cap P&A* art that incorporates everyday objects from popular culture and the mass media (e g comic strips) – **pop artist** *n*

popcorn *n* (the popped kernels of) a maize whose kernels burst open when heated to form a white starchy mass

pope *n* **1** *often cap* the prelate who as bishop of Rome is the head of the Roman Catholic church **2** a priest of an Eastern church **3** ¹RUFF

popery *n* ROMAN CATHOLICISM – chiefly derog

pop-eyed *adj* having staring or bulging eyes (e g as a result of surprise or excitement)

popgun *n* a toy gun that shoots a cork or pellet and produces a popping sound; *also* an inadequate or inefficient firearm

popinjay *n* a strutting supercilious person

popish *adj* of popery – chiefly derog – **popishly** *adv*

poplar *n* **1** (the wood of) any of a genus of slender quick-growing trees (e g an aspen) of the willow family **2** TULIP TREE

poplin *n* a strong usu cotton fabric in plain weave with crosswise ribs

pop music *n* modern commercially promoted popular music that is usu short and simple and has a strong beat

pop off *vi* **1** to leave suddenly **2** to die unexpectedly *USE* infml

poppa *n*, *NAm* a father – infml

poppadom *n* a crisp wafer-thin pancake of deep-fried dough eaten with Indian food

popper *n*, *chiefly Br* PRESS-STUD

poppet *n* **1** a valve that rises up and down from its seat **2** *chiefly Br* a lovable or enchanting person or animal – infml

popping crease *n* either of the lines drawn perpendicularly across a cricket pitch 4ft (about 1.22m) in front of each wicket and behind which the batsman must have a foot or his/her bat on the ground to avoid being run out or stumped

poppy *n* any of several genera of plants with showy flowers and capsular fruits including the opium poppy and several other plants cultivated for their ornamental value

poppycock *n* empty talk; nonsense – infml

popsy *n*, *Br* GIRLFRIEND – infml; often derog

populace *n sing or pl in constr* the (cômmon) people; the masses

popular *adj* **1** of the general public **2** suited to the needs, means, tastes, or understanding of the general public ⟨*a ~ history of the war*⟩ **3** having general currency **4** commonly liked or approved ⟨*a very ~ girl*⟩ – **popularly** *adv*, **popularity** *n*

popularize, -ise *vt* **1** to cause to be liked or esteemed **2** to present in a generally understandable or interesting form – **popularizer** *n*, **popularization** *n*

populate *vt* **1** to have a place in; occupy, inhabit **2** to supply or provide with inhabitants; people

population *n* **1** *sing or pl in constr* the whole number of people or inhabitants in a country or region **2** *sing or pl in constr* a body of people or individuals having a quality or characteristic in common ⟨*a floating ~ of drifters*⟩ **3** all the particles in a particular energy level – used esp with reference to atoms in a laser **4** the group of organisms inhabiting a particular area **5** a set (e g of individual people or items) from which samples are taken for statistical measurement

populist *n* **1** a member of a political party claiming to represent the common people **2** a believer in the rights, wisdom, or virtues of the common people – **populism** *n*, **populist** *also* **populistic** *adj*

populous *adj* densely populated – **populously** *adv*, **populousness** *n*

pop-up *adj* of or having a device that causes its contents to spring up or stand out in relief ⟨a ~ toaster⟩ ⟨a ~ book⟩

pop up *vi* to arise suddenly or unexpectedly; CROP UP – *infml*

porcelain *n* **1a** a type of hard nonporous translucent white ceramic ware made from a mixture of kaolin, quartz, and feldspar fired at a high temperature **b** a type of translucent ceramic ware made from a mixture of refined clay and ground glass fired at a low temperature **2** porcelain ware – **porcelaneous, porcellaneous** *adj*

porch *n* **1** a covered usu projecting entrance to a building **2** *NAm* a veranda

porcine *adj* of or like pigs; *esp* obese

porcupine *n* any of various ground-living or tree-dwelling relatively large rodents with stiff sharp erectile bristles mingled with the hair

¹pore *vi* **1** to study closely or attentively **2** to reflect or meditate steadily *USE* usu + *on, over,* or *upon*

²pore *n* a minute opening; *esp* one (e g in a membrane, esp the skin, or between soil particles) through which fluids pass or are absorbed – **pored** *adj*

pork *n* the flesh of a pig used as food

porker *n* PIG 1a; *esp* a young pig fattened for food

porkpie hat a man's hat with a low crown, flat top, and usu a turned-up brim

porky *adj* fat, fleshy ⟨a ~ young man⟩ – *infml*

porn *n* pornography – *infml*

pornography *n* (books, photographs, films, etc containing) the depiction of erotic behaviour intended to cause sexual excitement – **pornographic** *adj*, **pornographically** *adv*

porous *adj* **1** having or full of pores or spaces **2** permeable to liquids – **porously** *adv*, **porousness** *n*, **porosity** *n*

porphyry *n* an igneous rock consisting of crystals (e g of feldspar) embedded in a compact mass of surrounding rock – **porphyritic** *adj*

porpoise *n* (any of several small gregarious toothed whales related to) a blunt-snouted usu largely black whale about 2m (6ft) long

porridge *n* **1** (sthg with the consistency of) a soft food made by boiling a cereal product, esp oatmeal, in milk or water until thick **2** *Br* time spent in prison – *slang*

porringer *n* a small bowl from which esp soft or liquid foods (e g porridge) are eaten

¹port *n* **1** a town or city with a harbour where ships, hovercraft, etc may take on or discharge cargo or passengers **2** a place where goods and people may be permitted to pass into or out of a country

²port *n* **1** an opening (e g in machinery) for intake or exhaust of a fluid **2** an opening in a ship's side to admit light or air or to load cargo **3** a hole in an armoured vehicle or fortification through which guns may be fired

³port *n* the position in which a military weapon is carried at the command *port arms*

⁴port *adj or n* (of or at) the left side of a ship or aircraft looking forwards

⁵port *vt* to turn or put (a helm) to the left – used chiefly as a command

⁶port *n* a fortified sweet wine of rich taste and aroma made in Portugal

portable *n or adj* (sthg) capable of being carried or moved about ⟨a ~ typewriter⟩ ⟨a ~ sawmill⟩ – **portably** *adv*, **portability** *n*

¹portage *n* **1** the carrying of boats or goods overland from one body of water to another **2** the route followed in portage; *also* a place where such a transfer is necessary

²portage *vt* to carry over a portage ~ *vi* to move gear over a portage

¹portal *n* **1a** (a grand or imposing) door or entrance **2** the point at which sthg (e g a disease-causing agent) enters the body

²portal *adj* **1** of the transverse fissure on the underside of the liver where most of the vessels enter **2** of or being a portal vein

portcullis *n* a usu iron or wood grating that can prevent entry through the gateway of a fortified place by sliding down between grooves

portend *vt* **1** to give an omen or anticipatory sign of; bode **2** to indicate, signify

portent *n* **1** sthg foreshadowing a coming event; an omen **2** prophetic indication or significance

portentous *adj* **1** eliciting amazement or wonder; prodigious **2** self-consciously weighty; pompous – **portentously** *adv*, **portentousness** *n*

¹porter, *fem* **portress** *n*, *chiefly Br* a gatekeeper or doorkeeper, esp of a large building, who usu regulates entry and answers enquiries

²porter *n* **1** sby who carries burdens; *specif* sby employed to carry luggage (e g in a hotel or railway station) **2** a heavy dark brown beer **3** *NAm* a sleeping car attendant

porterage *n* (the charge made for) the work performed by a porter

porterhouse *n* a large steak cut from the back end of the sirloin above the ribs and containing part of the fillet

portfolio *n, pl* **portfolios** **1** a hinged cover or flexible case for carrying loose papers, pictures, etc **2** the office of a government minister or member of a cabinet ⟨the defence ~⟩ **3** the securities held by an investor

porthole *n* **1** a usu glazed opening, esp in the side of a ship or aircraft **2** ²PORT 2

portico *n, pl* **porticoes, porticos** a colonnade or covered veranda, usu at the entrance of a building and characteristic of classical architecture

¹portion *n* **1** a part or share of sthg: e g **a** a helping of food **b** *archaic* a dowry **2** an individual's lot or fate

²portion *vt* to divide into portions; distribute – often + *out*

portland cement *n* a hydraulic cement made from lime and clay

portland stone *n* a limestone much used in building

portly *adj* rotund, stout – **portliness** *n*

¹portmanteau *n, pl* **portmanteaus, portmanteaux** a trunk for a traveller's belongings that opens into 2 equal parts

²portmanteau *adj* combining more than 1 use or quality

portmanteau word *n* BLEND 2

port of call *n* **1** a port where ships customarily stop during a voyage **2** a stop included in an itinerary

portrait *n* **1** a pictorial likeness of a person **2** a verbal portrayal or representation – **portraitist** *n*

portraiture *n* the art of making portraits

portray *vt* **1** to make a picture of; depict **2a** to describe in words **b** to play the role of – **portrayer** *n*

portrayal *n* **1** the act or process of portraying; representation **2** a portrait

Portuguese *n*, *pl* **Portuguese 1** a native or inhabitant of Portugal **2** the language of esp Portugal and Brazil – **Portuguese** *adj*

Portuguese man-of-war *n* any of several large floating jellyfishes with very long stinging tentacles

¹**pose** *vt* **1** to place (e g a model) in a studied attitude **2** to put or set forth; offer ⟨*this attitude* ~s *a threat to our hopes for peace*⟩ **3** to present for attention or consideration ⟨*let me* ~ *a question*⟩ ~ *vi* **1** to assume a posture or attitude, usu for artistic purposes **2** to affect an attitude or character; posture ⟨~d *as an honest man*⟩

²**pose** *n* **1** a sustained posture; *esp* one assumed for artistic purposes **2** an assumed attitude of mind or mode of behaviour

¹**poser** *n* a puzzling or baffling question

²**poser** *n* a poseur

poseur *n* an affected or insincere person

¹**posh** *adj* **1** very fine; splendid ⟨*a* ~ *new car*⟩ **2** socially exclusive or fashionable; *broadly* upper-class ⟨*a* ~ *Knightsbridge address*⟩ – often derog *USE* infml

²**posh** *adv* in a posh accent – infml ⟨*talk* ~⟩

posit *vt* to assume or affirm the existence of; postulate

¹**position** *n* **1** the statement of a proposition or thesis **2** an opinion; POINT OF VIEW ⟨*made her* ~ *on the issue clear*⟩ **3** a market commitment in securities or commodities; *also* the inventory of a market trader **4a** the place occupied by sby or sthg ⟨*house in an attractive* ~ *overlooking the sea*⟩; *also* the proper place ⟨*the cars are now in the starting* ~⟩ **b** a disposition or attitude of (a part of) the body ⟨*rose to a standing* ~⟩ **5a** a condition, situation ⟨*is now in a* ~ *to make important decisions on his own*⟩ **b** social or official rank or status **c** a situation that confers advantage or preference ⟨*jockeying for* ~⟩ **6** the disposition of the notes of a chord **7** a post, job – fml

²**position** *vt* to put in a proper or specified position

positional *adj* of or fixed by position ⟨~ *astronomy*⟩

¹**positive** *adj* **1a** expressed clearly or peremptorily ⟨*her answer was a* ~ *no*⟩ **b** fully assured; confident ⟨~ *that he is right*⟩ **2** of or constituting the simple form of an adjective or adverb that expresses no degree of comparison **3** incontestable ⟨~ *proof*⟩ **4** utter ⟨*a* ~ *disgrace*⟩ **5** real, active ⟨*a* ~ *influence for good in the community*⟩ **6a** capable of being constructively applied; helpful ⟨~ *advice*⟩ **b** concentrating on what is good or beneficial; optimistic ⟨*has a* ~ *attitude towards his illness*⟩ **7a** having or expressing actual existence or quality as distinguished from deficiency **b** not speculative; empirical **8** having the light and dark parts similar in tone to those of the original photographic subject **9a** in a direction arbitrarily or customarily taken as that of increase or progression ⟨~ *angles*⟩ **b** directed or moving towards a source of stimulation ⟨*a* ~ *response to light*⟩ **10** numerically greater than zero ⟨+2 *is a* ~ *integer*⟩ **11a** of being, or charged with electricity as a result of a deficiency of electrons **b** having higher electric potential and constituting the part from which the current flows to the external circuit **12a** marked by or indicating acceptance, approval, or affirmation **b** showing the presence of sthg sought or suspected to be present ⟨*a* ~ *test for blood*⟩ **13** of a lens converging light rays and forming a real inverted image – **positively** *adv*, **positiveness** *n*

²**positive** *n* sthg positive: e g **a** the positive degree or form of an adjective or adverb **b** sthg about which an affirmation can be made; reality **c** a positive photograph or a print from a negative

positivism *n* **1** a theory rejecting theology and metaphysics in favour of knowledge based on the scientific observation of natural phenomena **2** LOGICAL POSITIVISM – **positivist** *adj or n*, **positivistic** *adj*

positron *n* a positively charged elementary particle that has the same mass and magnitude of charge as the electron and is the antiparticle of the electron

posse *n sing or pl in constr* **1** a body of people summoned by a sheriff, esp in N America, to assist in preserving the public peace, usu in an emergency **2** a large group, often with a common interest

possess *vt* **1a** to make the owner or holder – + *of* or *with* **b** to have possession of **2a** to have and hold as property; own **b** to have as an attribute, knowledge, or skill **3a** to take into one's possession **b** to influence so strongly as to direct the actions ⟨*whatever* ~ed *her to act like that?*⟩; *also, of a demon, evil spirit, etc* to enter into and control – **possessor** *n*

possessed *adj* **1** influenced or controlled by sthg (e g an evil spirit or a passion) **2** mad, crazed – **possessedly** *adv*, **possessedness** *n*

possession *n* **1a** the act of having or taking into control **b** ownership; *also* control or occupancy (e g of property) without regard to ownership **2a** sthg owned, occupied, or controlled **b** *pl* wealth, property **3** domination by sthg (e g an evil spirit or passion) – **possessional** *adj*

¹**possessive** *adj* **1** manifesting possession or the desire to own or dominate ⟨*a* ~ *mother*⟩ **2** of or being the grammatical possessive – **possessively** *adv*, **possessiveness** *n*

²**possessive** *n* (a form in) a grammatical case expressing ownership or a similar relation

posset *n* a comforting hot beverage of sweetened and spiced milk curdled with ale or wine; *also* a dessert made with cream, eggs, sugar and usu lemon

possibility *n* **1** the condition or fact of being possible **2** sthg possible **3** potential or prospective value – usu pl with sing. meaning ⟨*the house had great* possibilities⟩

¹**possible** *adj* **1** within the limits of ability, capacity, or realization **2** capable of being done or occurring according to nature, custom, or manners **3** that may or may not occur ⟨*it is* ~ *but not probable that he will win*⟩ **4** having a specified potential use, quality, etc ⟨*a* ~ *housing site*⟩

²**possible** *n* **1** sthg possible ⟨*politics is the art of the* ~⟩ **2** sby or sthg that may be selected for a specified role, task, etc ⟨*a* ~ *for the post of Chancellor*⟩

possibly *adv* **1** it is possible that; maybe ⟨~ *there is life on Mars*⟩ ⟨*he may* ~ *have caught a later train*⟩ **2** – used as an intensifier with *can* or *could* ⟨*you can't* ~ *eat all that cake*⟩ ⟨*I'll do all I* ~ *can to have it ready on time*⟩

possum *n* an opossum – not used technically

¹**post** *n* **1** a piece of timber, metal, etc fixed firmly in an upright position, esp as a stay or support **2** a pole marking the starting or finishing point of a horse race **3** a goal-post

²**post** *vt* **1** to fasten to a wall, board, etc in order to make public – often + *up* **2** to publish, announce, or advertise (as if) by use of a placard

³**post** *n* **1** (a single despatch or delivery of) the mail handled by a postal system **2** *chiefly Br* a postal system or means of posting **3** *archaic* (the distance between) any of a series of stations for keeping horses for relays

⁴**post** *vt* **1** to send by post ⟨~ *a letter*⟩ **2a** to transfer or carry from a book of original entry to a ledger **b** to make transfer entries in **3** to provide with the latest news; inform ⟨*kept her* ~ed *on the latest gossip*⟩

⁵**post** *adv* with post-horses; express

⁶**post** *n* **1a** the place at which a soldier is stationed **b** a station or task to which one is assigned **c** the place at which a body of troops is stationed **2a** an office or position to which a person is appointed **b** (the position of) a player

in basketball who provides the focal point of the attack **3** a trading post, settlement **4** *Br* either of 2 bugle calls giving notice of the hour for retiring at night

⁷**post** *vt* **1** to station ⟨*guards were* ~*ed at the doors*⟩ **2** *chiefly Br* to assign to a unit or location

post- *prefix* **1a** after; subsequent; later ⟨post*date*⟩ **b** posterior; following after ⟨post*script*⟩ ⟨post*consonantal*⟩ **2a** subsequent to; later than ⟨post*operative*⟩ ⟨post-*Pleistocene*⟩ **b** situated behind ⟨post*orbital*⟩

postage *n* (markings or stamps representing) the fee for a postal service

postage stamp *n* an adhesive or imprinted stamp used as evidence of prepayment of postage

postal *adj* **1** of or being a system for the conveyance of written material, parcels, etc between a large number of users **2** conducted by post ⟨~ *chess*⟩ – **postally** *adv*

postal order *n, Br* an order issued by a post office for payment of a specified sum of money usu at another post office

postbag *n, Br* **1** a mailbag **2** a single batch of mail usu delivered to 1 address

postbox *n* a secure receptacle for the posting of outgoing mail

postcard *n* a card that can be posted without an enclosing envelope

post chaise *n* a usu closed 4-wheeled carriage seating 2 to 4 people

postcode *n* a combination of letters and numbers that is used in the postal address of a place in the UK to assist sorting

postdate *vt* **1a** to date with a date later than that of execution ⟨~ *a cheque*⟩ **b** to assign (an event) to a date subsequent to that of actual occurrence **2** to follow in time

poster *n* a (decorative) bill or placard for display often in a public place

poste restante *n, chiefly Br* mail that is intended for collection from a post office – **poste restante** *adv*

¹**posterior** *adj* **1** later in time; subsequent **2** situated behind or towards the back: e g **a** *of an animal part* near the tail; caudal **b** *of the human body or its parts* dorsal **3** *of a plant part* (on the side) facing towards the stem or axis; *also* SUPERIOR

²**posterior** *n* the buttocks

posterity *n* **1** *sing or pl in constr* all the descendants of 1 ancestor **2** all future generations

postern *n* a back door or gate – **postern** *adj*

poster paint *n* an opaque watercolour paint containing gum

post-free *adv, chiefly Br* postpaid

postgraduate *n* a student continuing higher education after completing a first degree – **postgraduate** *adj*

posthaste *adv* with all possible speed

post horn *n* a simple wind instrument with cupped mouthpiece used esp by postilions in the 18th and 19th c

posthumous *adj* **1** born after the death of the father **2** published after the death of the author or composer **3** following or occurring after death ⟨~ *fame*⟩ – **posthumously** *adv*, **posthumousness** *n*

postilion, postillion *n* sby who rides as a guide on the near horse of one of the pairs attached to a coach or post chaise, esp without a coachman

¹**posting** *n* the act of transferring an entry to the proper account in a ledger; *also* the resultant entry

²**posting** *n* an appointment to a post or a command

postman *fem* **postwoman** *n* sby who delivers the post

postman's knock *n* a children's game in which a kiss is the reward for the pretended delivery of a letter

postmark *vt or n* (to mark with) a cancellation mark showing the post office and date of posting of a piece of mail

postmaster *fem* **postmistress** *n* sby who has charge of a post office – **postmastership** *n*

postmaster general *n, pl* **postmasters general** an official in charge of a national post office

post meridiem *adj* being after noon – *abbr* **pm**

¹**postmortem** *adj* **1** occurring after death **2** following the event ⟨*a* ~ *appraisal of the game*⟩

²**postmortem** *n* **1** *also* **postmortem examination** an examination of a body after death for determining the cause of death or the character and extent of changes produced by disease **2** an examination of a plan or event that failed, in order to discover the cause of failure

post office *n* **1** a national usu governmental organization that runs a postal system; *specif, cap P&O* the corporation that fulfils this function in the UK **2** a local branch of a national post office **3** *NAm* POSTMAN'S KNOCK

postpaid *adv* with the postage paid by the sender and not chargeable to the receiver

postpone *vt* to hold back to a later time; defer – **postponable** *adj*, **postponement** *n*, **postponer** *n*

postprandial *adj* following a meal – *fml or humor*

postscript *n* **1** a note or series of notes appended to a completed article, a book, or esp a letter **2** a subordinate or supplementary part

postulant *n* a person seeking admission to a religious order – **postulancy** *n*

¹**postulate** *vt* **1** to assume or claim as true **2** to assume as a postulate or axiom – **postulation** *n*, **postulational** *adj*

²**postulate** *n* **1** a hypothesis advanced as a premise in a train of reasoning **2** AXIOM **2a**

¹**posture** *n* **1** the position or bearing of (relative parts of) the body **2** a state or condition, esp in relation to other people or things ⟨*put the country in a* ~ *of defence*⟩ **3** a frame of mind; an attitude ⟨*his* ~ *of moral superiority*⟩ – **postural** *adj*

²**posture** *vi* **1** to assume a posture; *esp* to strike a pose for effect **2** to assume an artificial or insincere attitude; attitudinize – **posturer** *n*

postwar *adj* of or being the period after a war, esp WW I or II

posy *n* a small bouquet of flowers; a nosegay

¹**pot** *n* **1a** any of various usu rounded vessels (e g of metal or earthenware) used for holding liquids or solids, esp in cooking **b** a potful ⟨*a* ~ *of coffee*⟩ **2** an enclosed framework for catching fish or lobsters **3** a drinking vessel (e g of pewter) used esp for beer **4** the total of the bets at stake at 1 time **5** *Br* a shot in billiards or snooker in which an object ball is pocketed **6** *NAm* the common fund of a group **7** a large amount (of money) – usu *pl* with sing. meaning; *infml* **8** a potbelly – *infml* **9** cannabis; *specif* marijuana – *slang*

²**pot** *vb* **-tt-** *vt* **1a** to place in a pot **b** to preserve in a sealed pot, jar, or can ⟨~ *ted chicken*⟩ **2** to shoot (e g an animal) for food **3** to make or shape (earthenware) as a potter **4** to embed (e g electronic components) in a container with an insulating or protective material (e g plastic) **5** to sit (a young child) on a potty ~ *vi* to take a potshot

potable *adj* suitable for drinking – **potableness** *n*, **potability** *n*

potash *n* **1a** potassium carbonate, esp from wood ashes **b** potassium hydroxide **2** potassium or a potassium compound, esp as used in agriculture or industry

potassium *n* a soft light univalent metallic element of the alkali metal group that occurs abundantly in nature, esp combined in minerals – **potassic** *adj*

potassium nitrate *n* a salt that occurs as a product of nitrification in arable soils, is a strong oxidizer, and is used esp in making gunpowder and in preserving meat

potation *n* an act or instance of drinking; *also* a usu alcoholic drink – *fml or humor*

potato *n, pl* **potatoes** 1 SWEET POTATO 2 a plant of the nightshade family widely cultivated in temperate regions for its edible starchy tubers; *also* a potato tuber eaten as a vegetable

potato chip *n* 1 *chiefly Br* CHIP 6a 2 *NAm* a crisp

potbelly *n* an enlarged, swollen, or protruding abdomen – **potbellied** *adj*

potboiler *n* a usu inferior work (e g of art or literature) produced chiefly to make money

pot-bound *adj, of a potted plant* having roots so densely matted as to allow little or no space for further growth

poteen, potheen *n* Irish whiskey illicitly distilled; *broadly* any distilled alcoholic drink made at home

potent *adj* 1 having or wielding force, authority, or influence; powerful ⟨~ *arguments*⟩ 2 achieving or bringing about a particular result; effective 3 chemically or medicinally effective ⟨a ~ *vaccine*⟩ 4 producing an esp unexpectedly powerful reaction; strong ⟨*this whisky is* ~ *stuff*⟩ 5 *esp of a male* able to have sexual intercourse – **potently** *adv*, **potence** *n*, **potency** *n*

potentate *n* one who wields controlling power

¹**potential** *adj* 1 existing in possibility; capable of being made real ⟨~ *benefits*⟩ 2 of or constituting a verb phrase expressing possibility – **potentially** *adv*

²**potential** *n* 1 sthg that can develop or become actual; possible capacity or value ⟨a ~ *for violence*⟩ 2 **potential, potential difference** the difference between the voltages at 2 points (e g in an electrical circuit or in an electrical field)

potentiality *n* POTENTIAL 1

¹**pother** *n* 1 a noisy disturbance; a commotion 2 needless agitation over a trivial matter; fuss

²**pother** *vb* to put into or be in a pother

potherb *n* a herb whose leaves or stems are cooked for use as greens; *also* one (e g parsley) used to season food

¹**pothole** *n* 1 a circular hole worn in the rocky bed of a river by stones or gravel whirled round by the water 2 a natural vertically descending hole in the ground or in the floor of a cave; *also* a system of these usu linked by caves 3 an unwanted hole in a road surface – **potholed** *adj*

²**pothole** *vi* to explore pothole systems – **potholer** *n*

pothunter *n* sby who shoots animals indiscriminately rather than as a sport – **pothunting** *n*

potion *n* a mixed drink, esp of medicine, often intended to produce a specified effect ⟨a love ~⟩

potluck *n* 1 food that is available without special preparations being made 2 whatever luck or chance brings – esp in *take potluck*

potpourri *n* 1 a mixture of dried flowers, herbs, and spices, usu kept in a jar for its fragrance 2 a miscellaneous collection; a medley

pot roast *n* a joint of meat cooked by braising, usu on the top of a cooker – **pot-roast** *vt*

potsherd *n* a pottery fragment

potshot *n* 1 a shot taken in a casual manner or at an easy target 2 a critical remark made in a careless manner

pottage *n* a thick soup of vegetables (and meat)

potted *adj* 1 planted or grown in a pot 2 *chiefly Br* abridged or summarized, usu in a simplified or popular form ⟨~ *biographies*⟩

¹**potter** *n* one who makes pottery

²**potter** *vi* 1 to spend time in aimless or unproductive

activity – often + *around* or *about* ⟨loves to ~ *around at home*⟩ 2 to move or travel in a leisurely or random fashion ⟨avoided the motorways and ~ed *along country lanes*⟩

potter's wheel *n* a horizontal disc revolving on a vertical spindle, on which clay is shaped by a potter

pottery *n* 1 a place where ceramic ware is made and fired 2a the art or craft of the potter **b** the manufacture of pottery 3 articles of fired clay; *esp* coarse or hand-made ceramic ware

¹**potty** *adj, chiefly Br* 1 slightly crazy ⟨that noise is driving me ~⟩ 2 foolish, silly ⟨a ~ *idea*⟩ 3 having a great interest or liking ⟨~ *about her new boyfriend*⟩ USE *infml* – **pottiness** *n*

²**potty** *n* a chamber pot, esp for a small child

¹**pouch** *n* 1 a small drawstring bag carried on the person 2 a bag of small or moderate size for storing or transporting goods; *specif* a lockable bag for mail or diplomatic dispatches 3 an anatomical structure resembling a pouch: e g **a** a pocket of skin in the abdomen of marsupials for carrying their young **b** a pocket of skin in the cheeks of some rodents used for storing food **c** a loose fold of skin under the eyes 4 an arrangement of cloth (e g a pocket) resembling a pouch – **pouched** *adj*

²**pouch** *vt* 1 to put (as if) into a pouch 2 to form (as if) into a pouch ⟨his face was ~ed *and lined from fatigue*⟩ ~ *vi* to form a pouch

pouf *n* a poof

poulterer *n* one who deals in poultry, poultry products, or game

¹**poultice** *n* a soft usu heated and sometimes medicated mass spread on cloth and applied to inflamed or injured parts (e g sores)

²**poultice** *vt* to apply a poultice to

poultry *n* domesticated birds (e g chickens) kept for eggs or meat

¹**pounce** *vi* 1 to swoop on and seize sthg (as if) with talons 2 to make a sudden assault or approach

²**pounce** *n* the act of pouncing

³**pounce** *n* 1 a fine powder formerly used to prevent ink from blotting 2 a fine powder for making stencilled patterns

¹**pound** *n, pl* **pounds** *also* **pound** 1 a unit of mass and weight equal to 16oz avoirdupois (about 0.453kg) 2 the basic money unit of the UK and many other countries

²**pound** *vt* 1 to reduce to powder or pulp by beating or crushing ⟨~ *the meat to a paste*⟩ 2 to strike heavily or repeatedly ⟨~ed *the door with his fists*⟩ 3 to move or run along with heavy steps ⟨the policeman ~s *his beat*⟩ ~ *vi* 1 to strike heavy repeated blows ⟨~ing *angrily on the table*⟩ 2 to move with or make a dull repetitive sound ⟨his heart was ~ing *with fear*⟩

³**pound** *n* an act or sound of pounding

⁴**pound** *n* 1 an enclosure for animals; *esp* a public enclosure for stray or unlicensed animals 2 a place for holding personal property until redeemed by the owner ⟨a car ~⟩

¹**poundage** *n* 1 a charge per pound of weight 2 weight in pounds

²**poundage** *n* impounding or being impounded

pounder *n* 1 one having a usu specified weight or value in pounds – usu in combination ⟨caught a 9-pounder *with his new fly rod*⟩ 2 a gun firing a projectile of a specified weight – in combination ⟨the artillery were using 25-pounders⟩

pound out *vt* to produce (as if) by striking repeated heavy blows ⟨pounded out *a story on the typewriter*⟩

¹**pour** *vt* 1 to cause to flow in a stream ⟨~ *the dirty water down the sink*⟩ 2 to dispense (a drink) into a container

⟨~ *me a whisky*⟩ **3** to supply or produce freely or copiously ⟨*she* ~ed *money into the firm*⟩ ~ *vi* **1** to move or issue with a continuous flow and in large quantities; stream ⟨*people* ~ed *out of the offices at the end of the day*⟩ **2** to rain hard – often + *down* – **pourable** *adj*, **pourer** *n*, **pouringly** *adv* – **pour cold water on** to be critical or unenthusiastic about ⟨*he* poured cold water on *all their proposals*⟩ – **pour oil on troubled waters** to calm or defuse a heated situation

²pour *n* sthg that is poured ⟨*a* ~ *of concrete*⟩

pour out *vt* to speak or express volubly or at length ⟨poured out *his woes*⟩

¹pout *n, pl* **pout,** *esp for different types* **pouts** any of several large-headed fishes (e g a bullhead or eelpout)

²pout *vi* **1a** to show displeasure by thrusting out the lips or wearing a sullen expression **b** to sulk **2** *of lips* to protrude ~ *vt* to cause to protrude, usu in displeasure ⟨~ed *her lips*⟩

³pout *n* **1** an act of pouting **2** *pl* a fit of pique – usu + *the*

poverty *n* **1a** the lack of sufficient money or material possessions **b** the renunciation of individual property by a person entering a religious order **2a** a scarcity, dearth ⟨*a* ~ *of ideas and images*⟩ **b** the condition of lacking desirable elements; deficiency ⟨*the* ~ *of our critical vocabulary*⟩ *USE* (2) *fml*

poverty-stricken *adj* very poor; destitute

¹powder *n* **1** matter reduced to a state of dry loose particles (e g by crushing or grinding) **2a** a preparation in the form of fine particles, esp for medicinal or cosmetic use **b** fine dry light snow **3** any of various solid explosives used chiefly in gunnery and blasting – **powdery** *adj*

²powder *vt* **1** to sprinkle or cover (as if) with powder **2** to reduce or convert to powder ~ *vi* to become powder – **powderer** *n*

powder horn *n* a flask (made from horn) for carrying gunpowder

powder keg *n* an explosive place or situation ⟨*the problem of race is a potential* ~⟩

powder puff *n* a small (fluffy) pad for applying powder to the skin

powder room *n* a public toilet for women in a hotel, department store, etc

¹power *n* **1a** possession of control, authority, or influence over others **b** a sovereign state **c** a controlling group – often in *the powers that be* **2a** ability to act or produce or undergo an effect **b** legal or official authority or capacity ⟨*the police had no* ~ *to intervene*⟩ **3a** physical might **b** mental or moral efficacy; vigour ⟨*the* ~ *and insight of his analysis*⟩ **c** political control or influence ⟨*the balance of* ~⟩ **4a** the number of times, as indicated by an exponent, that a number has to be multiplied by itself ⟨*2 to the* ~ *3 is* $2^3 = 2x2x2$⟩ **b** EXPONENT 1 **5a** a source or means of supplying energy; *specif* electricity **b** the rate at which work is done or energy emitted or transferred **6** MAGNIFICATION 2 **7** a large amount *of* – *infml* ⟨*the walk did him a* ~ *of good*⟩

²power *vt* **1** to supply with esp motive power **2** to make (one's way) in a powerful and vigorous manner ⟨~ed *her way to the top*⟩ ~ *vi* to move in a powerful and rigorous manner ⟨~ing *down the back straight*⟩

³power *adj* driven by a motor ⟨*a* ~ *saw*⟩ ⟨*a* ~ *mower*⟩

power dive *n* a dive of an aircraft accelerated by the power of the engine – **power-dive** *vi*

powerful *adj* having great power, prestige, or influence – **powerfully** *adv*

powerhouse *n* **1** POWER STATION **2** a dynamic individual of great physical or mental force

powerless *adj* **1** devoid of strength or resources; helpless

2 lacking the authority or capacity to act ⟨*the police were* ~ *to intervene*⟩ – **powerlessly** *adv*, **powerlessness** *n*

power of attorney *n* a legal document authorizing one to act as the agent of the grantor

power plant *n* **1** POWER STATION **2** an engine and related parts supplying the motive power of a self-propelled object

power point *n, Br* a set of terminals that are connected to the electric mains and to which an electrical device may be connected

power politics *n pl but sing or pl in constr* international politics characterized by attempts to advance national interests by force

power station *n* an electricity generating station

¹powwow *n* **1** a N American Indian medicine man **2** a N American Indian ceremony **3** a meeting for discussion – *infml*

²powwow *vi* to hold a powwow

pox *n, pl* **pox, poxes 1** a virus disease (e g chicken pox) characterized by eruptive spots **2** syphilis – *infml* **3** *archaic* smallpox **4** *archaic* a disastrous evil; a plague ⟨*a* ~ *on him*⟩

practicable *adj* **1** capable of being carried out; feasible **2** usable ⟨*the road was* ~ *despite the weather conditions*⟩ – **practicableness** *n*, **practicably** *adv*, **practicability** *n*

¹practical *adj* **1a** of or manifested in practice or action ⟨*for all* ~ *purposes*⟩ **b** being such in practice or effect; virtual ⟨*a* ~ *failure*⟩ **2** capable of being put to use or account; useful ⟨*he had a* ~ *knowledge of French*⟩ **3** suitable for use ⟨*a table of* ~ *design*⟩ **4a** disposed to or capable of positive action as opposed to speculation; *also* prosaic **b** qualified by practice or practical training ⟨*a good* ~ *mechanic*⟩ – **practicalness** *n*, **practicality** *n*

²practical *n* a practical examination or lesson

practical joke *n* a trick or prank played on sby to derive amusement from his/her discomfiture – **practical joker** *n*

practically *adv* almost, nearly ⟨~ *everyone went to the party*⟩

practice, NAm also practise *n* **1a** actual performance or application ⟨*ready to carry out in* ~ *what she advocated in principle*⟩ **b** a repeated or customary action; a habit ⟨*he made a* ~ *of going to bed early*⟩ **c** the usual way of doing sthg ⟨*it's wise to conform to local* ~s⟩ **d** the established method of conducting legal proceedings **e** dealings, conduct – esp in *sharp practice* **2** (an instance of) regular or repeated exercise in order to acquire proficiency; *also* proficiency or experience gained in this way ⟨*must get back into* ~⟩ **3a** the continuous exercise of a profession, esp law or medicine **b** a professional business

practise, NAm chiefly practice *vt* **1** to perform or work at repeatedly so as to become proficient ⟨~d *the drums every day*⟩ **2a** to apply; CARRY OUT 1 ⟨~ *what he preaches*⟩ **b** to make a habit or practice of **c** to be professionally engaged in ⟨~ *medicine*⟩ ~ *vi* **1** to exercise repeatedly so as to achieve proficiency **2** to pursue a profession actively ⟨~s *as a lawyer*⟩ – **practiser** *n*

practised, NAm chiefly practiced *adj* **1** experienced, skilled **2** learned by practice – often derog ⟨*a* ~ *smile*⟩

practitioner *n* **1** one who practises a profession, esp law or medicine ⟨*a legal* ~⟩ **2** one who practises a skill or art – sometimes derog ⟨*a* ~ *of fiction*⟩

praesidium *n* a presidium

praetor, chiefly NAm pretor *n* an ancient Roman magistrate ranking below a consul – **praetorship** *n*, **praetorial** *adj*

praetorian *adj, often cap* of the Roman imperial bodyguard – **praetorian** *n, often cap*

pragmatic *adj* concerned with practicalities or expediency rather than theory or dogma; realistic – **pragmatically** *adv*

pragmatism *n* 1 a practical approach to problems and affairs ⟨*tried to strike a balance between principles and* ~⟩ 2 an American philosophical movement asserting that the meaning or truth of a concept depends on its practical consequences – **pragmatist** *adj or n*, **pragmatistic** *adj*

prairie *n* an extensive area of level or rolling (practically) treeless grassland, esp in N America

¹**praise** *vt* 1 to express a favourable judgment of; commend 2 to glorify or extol (e g God or a god) – **praiser** *n*

²**praise** *n* 1 expression of approval; commendation ⟨*won high – for her efforts*⟩ 2 worship

praiseworthy *adj* laudable, commendable – **praiseworthily** *adv*, **praiseworthiness** *n*

praline *n* (sthg, esp a powder or paste, made from) a confection of nuts, esp almonds, caramelized in boiling sugar

¹**pram** *n* a small lightweight nearly flat-bottomed boat with a broad transom and usu squared-off bow

²**pram** *n*, *chiefly Br* a usu 4-wheeled carriage for 1 or 2 babies that is pushed by a person on foot

¹**prance** *vi* 1 *esp of a horse* to spring from the hind legs or move by so doing 2 to walk or move in a gay, lively, or haughty manner – **prancer** *n*, **prancingly** *adv*

²**prance** *n* a prancing movement

prank *n* a mildly mischievous act; a trick

prankster *n* one who plays pranks

prat *n*, *Br* a foolish or contemptible person – slang

prate *vi* to talk foolishly and excessively *about*; chatter ⟨*he* ~*d on about his new car*⟩ – **prater** *n*, **pratingly** *adv*

¹**prattle** *vi* prattling to chatter in an artless or childish manner – **prattler** *n*, **prattlingly** *adv*

²**prattle** *n* idle or childish talk

prawn *n* any of numerous widely distributed edible 10-legged crustaceans that resemble large shrimps

praxis *n*, *pl* **praxes** 1 exercise or practice of an art, science, or skill, as opposed to theory 2 customary practice or conduct – fml

pray *vt* to entreat, implore – often used to introduce a question, request, or plea; fml ⟨~ *tell me*⟩ ~ *vi* 1 to request earnestly or humbly 2 to address prayers to God or a god – **prayer** *n*

prayer *n* 1a(1) an address to God or a god in word or thought, with a petition, confession, thanksgiving, etc (2) a set order of words used in praying **b** an earnest request 2 the act or practice of praying 3 a religious service consisting chiefly of prayers – often pl with sing. meaning 4 sthg prayed for 5 a slight chance ⟨*tried hard but didn't have a* ~⟩ – infml – **prayerful** *adj*

prayer book *n* a book containing directions for worship; *specif, often cap P&B* the official service book of the Anglican church

prayer wheel *n* a revolving cylinder to which written prayers may be attached, used by Tibetan Buddhists

praying mantis *n* a (large green) mantis

pre- *prefix* 1a(1) earlier than; prior to ⟨Precambrian⟩ ⟨prehistoric⟩; *specif* immediately preceding ⟨preadolescence⟩ (2) preparatory or prerequisite to ⟨premedical⟩ **b** in advance; beforehand ⟨precancel⟩ ⟨prefabricate⟩ 2 situated in front of; anterior to ⟨preaxial⟩ ⟨premolar⟩

preach *vi* 1 to deliver a sermon 2 to urge acceptance or abandonment of an idea or course of action, esp in an officious manner ~ *vt* 1 to set forth in a sermon 2 to advocate earnestly ⟨~*ed revolution*⟩ 3 to deliver (e g a sermon) publicly – **preacher** *n*, **preachingly** *adv*

preamble *n* 1 an introductory statement; *specif* that of a constitution or statute 2 an introductory or preliminary fact or circumstance

prearrange *vt* to arrange beforehand ⟨*at a* ~*d signal*⟩ – **prearrangement** *n*

prebend *n* (a clergyman receiving) a stipend furnished by a cathedral or collegiate church to a member of its chapter – **prebendal** *adj*

prebendary *n* a canon in a cathedral chapter, often in receipt of a prebend

precarious *adj* 1 dependent on chance or uncertain circumstances; doubtful 2 characterized by a lack of security or stability; dangerous – **precariously** *adv*, **precariousness** *n*

precast *adj* being concrete that is cast in the form of a panel, beam, etc before being placed in final position

precaution *n* 1 care taken in advance; foresight ⟨*warned of the need for* ~⟩ 2 a measure taken beforehand to avoid possible harmful or undesirable consequences; a safeguard – **precautionary** *adj*

precede *vt* 1 to surpass in rank, dignity, or importance 2 to be, go, or come ahead or in front of 3 to be earlier than 4 to cause to be preceded; preface ⟨*he* ~*d his address with a welcome to the visitors*⟩ ~ *vi* to go or come before – **preceding** *adj*

precedence *also* **precedency** *n* 1 the fact of preceding in time 2 the right to superior honour on a ceremonial or formal occasion 3 priority of importance; preference

¹**precedent** *adj* prior in time, order, arrangement, or significance

²**precedent** *n* 1 an earlier occurrence of sthg similar 2 sthg done or said that may serve as an example or rule to justify a similar subsequent act or statement; *specif* a judicial decision that serves as a rule for subsequent similar cases

precentor *n* 1 a leader of the singing of a choir or congregation 2 the officer of a church, esp a cathedral, who directs choral services – **precentorship** *n*, **precentorial** *adj*

precept *n* a command or principle intended as a general rule of conduct – **preceptive** *adj*

preceptor, *fem* **preceptress** *n* a teacher, tutor – **preceptorial** *adj*

precession *n* a slow movement of the axis of rotation of a spinning body about another line intersecting it caused by the application of a turning force tending to change the direction of the axis of rotation – **precessional** *adj*

precinct *n* 1a an enclosure bounded by the walls of a building – often pl with sing. meaning **b** *pl* the region immediately surrounding a place; environs **c** the boundary – often pl with sing. meaning ⟨*a ruined tower within the* ~*s of the squire's grounds* – T L Peacock⟩ 2 an area of a town or city containing a shopping centre and not allowing access to traffic ⟨*a shopping* ~⟩ 3 *NAm* an administrative district for election purposes or police control

preciosity *n* (an instance of) fastidious or excessive refinement (e g in language)

¹**precious** *adj* 1 of great value or high price ⟨~ *stone*⟩ 2 highly esteemed or cherished; dear ⟨*his friendship was* ~ *to her*⟩ 3 excessively refined; affected 4 highly valued but worthless – used as an intensive ⟨*you can keep your* ~ *Costa Brava: I prefer Blackpool!*⟩ – **preciously** *adv*, **preciousness** *n*

²**precious** *adv* very, extremely ⟨*has* ~ *little to say*⟩

³**precious** *n* a dear one; darling ⟨*my* ~⟩

precipice *n* 1a a very steep, perpendicular, or overhanging surface (e g of a rock or mountain) 2 the brink of disaster

¹**precipitate** *vt* 1 to throw violently; hurl 2 to bring about suddenly, unexpectedly, or too soon ⟨*the failure of government policy* ~d *a general election*⟩ 3a to cause to separate from solution or suspension b to cause (vapour) to condense and fall as rain, snow, etc ~ *vi* 1 to separate from solution or suspension 2 to fall as rain, snow, etc – **precipitable** *adj*, **precipitator** *n*, **precipitative** *adj*

²**precipitate** *n* a substance separated from a solution or suspension by chemical or physical change, usu as an insoluble amorphous or crystalline solid

³**precipitate** *adj* 1 exhibiting violent or undue haste ⟨*a* ~ *departure*⟩ 2 lacking due care or consideration; rash – **precipitately** *adv*, **precipitateness** *n*

precipitation *n* 1 a precipitating or the forming of a precipitate 2 (the amount of) a deposit of rain, snow, hail, etc on the earth 3 a precipitate

precipitous *adj* 1 PRECIPITATE 1 2 resembling a precipice, esp in being dangerously steep or perpendicular – **precipitously** *adv*, **precipitousness** *n*

¹**précis** *n, pl* **précis** a concise summary of essential points, facts, etc

²**précis** *vt* **précising; précised** to make a précis of; summarize

precise *adj* 1 exactly or sharply defined or stated ⟨~ *images*⟩ 2 highly exact ⟨~ *timing*⟩ 3 strictly conforming to a rule, convention, etc; punctilious 4 distinguished from every other; very ⟨*at that* ~ *moment*⟩ – **precisely** *adv*, **preciseness** *n*

¹**precision** *n* 1 being precise; exactness 2 the degree of refinement with which an operation is performed or a measurement stated – **precisionist** *n*

²**precision** *adj* 1 adapted for extremely accurate measurement or operation ⟨~ *instruments*⟩ 2 marked by precision of execution ⟨~ *bombing*⟩

preclude *vt* 1 to make ineffectual or impracticable; exclude 2 to make impossible; prevent – **preclusion** *n*, **preclusive** *adj*, **preclusively** *adv*

precocious *adj* 1 exceptionally early in development or occurrence 2 exhibiting mature qualities at an unusually early age – **precociously** *adv*, **precociousness** *n*, **precocity** *n*

precognition *n* clairvoyance relating to a future event – **precognitive** *adj*

preconceive *vt* to form (e g an opinion) prior to actual knowledge or experience

preconception *n* 1 a preconceived idea 2 a prejudice

precondition *n* a prerequisite

precursor *n* 1a sby or sthg that precedes and signals the approach of sby or sthg else; a forerunner b a predecessor 2 a substance from which another substance is formed

predacious, predaceous *adj* living by preying on other animals; predatory

predation *n* 1 the act of preying or plundering; depredation 2 a mode of life of certain animals in which food is primarily obtained by the killing and consuming of other animals – **predator** *n*

predatory *adj* 1a of or carrying out plunder or robbery b showing a disposition to injure or exploit others for one's own gain 2 living by predation; predacious; *also* adapted to predation – **predatorily** *adv*

predecease *vt* to die before (another person) – **predecease** *n*

predecessor *n* 1 the previous occupant of a position or office to which another has succeeded 2 an ancestor

¹**predestinate** *adj* destined or determined beforehand

²**predestinate** *vt* to predestine – **predestinator** *n*

predestination *n* the doctrine of God's foreknowledge of all events; *esp* the doctrine that salvation or damnation is foreordained

predestine *vt* to destine or determine (e g damnation or salvation) beforehand

predetermine *vt* 1 to determine or arrange beforehand ⟨*at a* ~d *signal*⟩ 2 to impose a direction or tendency on beforehand – **predetermination** *n*

predeterminer *n* a limiting noun modifier (e g *both* or *twice*) occurring before the determiner in a noun phrase

predicament *n* a (difficult, perplexing, or trying) situation

¹**predicate** *n* 1 sthg that is stated or denied of the subject in a logical proposition 2 the part of a sentence or clause that expresses what is said of the subject

²**predicate** *vt* 1 to affirm, declare 2 to assert to be a quality or property ⟨~s *intelligence of man*⟩ 3 to imply 4 chiefly NAm BASE 2 – usu + on or upon ⟨*his theory is* ~d *on recent findings*⟩ USE chiefly fml

predicative *adj* 1 of a predicate 2 joined to a modified noun by a copula (e g *red* in *the dress is red*) – **predicatively** *adv*

predict *vt* to declare in advance; *esp* to foretell (sthg) on the basis of observation, experience, or scientific reason – **predictable** *adj*, **predictably** *adv*, **predictor** *n*, **predictability** *n*

prediction *n* sthg that is predicted; a forecast – **predictive** *adj*, **predictively** *adv*

predigest *vt* to prepare (e g food or a book) in an easier form (for consumption) – **predigestion** *n*

predilection *n* a liking, preference ⟨*has a* ~ *for classical music*⟩

predispose *vt* 1 to incline, esp in advance ⟨*a good teacher* ~s *children to learn*⟩ 2 to make susceptible *to* – **predisposition** *n*

predominant *adj* having superior strength, influence, or authority; prevailing – **predominance** *n*, **predominantly** *adv*

predominate *vi* 1 to exert controlling power or influence; prevail 2 to hold advantage in numbers or quantity – **predomination** *n*

preeminent *adj* excelling all others; paramount – **preeminence** *n*, **preeminently** *adj*

preempt *vt* 1 to acquire by preemption 2 to seize on to the exclusion of others; appropriate ⟨*the movement was then* ~ed *by a lunatic fringe*⟩ 3 to take the place of; replace 4 to invalidate or render useless by taking action or appearing in advance ⟨*the government decision to build an airport* ~ed *the council's plans*⟩ ~ *vi* to make a preemptive bid in bridge – **preemptor** *n*

preemption *n* 1a the right of purchasing before others b a purchase under this right 2 a prior seizure or appropriation

preemptive *adj* 1 (capable) of preemption 2 of or being a bid in bridge high enough to shut out bids by the opponents 3 carried out in order to forestall intended action by others ⟨*a* ~ *attack that disabled the enemy*⟩ – **preemptively** *adv*

preen *vt* 1 to trim or dress (as if) with a beak 2 to dress or smarten (oneself) up 3 to pride or congratulate (oneself) *on* ~ *vi* 1 to smarten oneself, esp in a vain way ⟨~ing *in front of the mirror*⟩ 2 to appear to be congratulating oneself; gloat ⟨*couldn't help* ~ing *after his campaign victory*⟩ 3 *of a bird* to trim and arrange the feathers – **preener** *n*

preexistence *n* existence in a former state or previous to sthg else; *esp* existence of the soul before incarnation – **preexist** *vi*, **preexistent** *adj*

prefab *n* a prefabricated structure or building – **prefab** *adj*

prefabricate *vt* 1 to fabricate the parts of (e g a building) at a factory ready for assembly elsewhere **2** to produce artificially – **prefabricator** *n*, **prefabrication** *n*

¹preface *n* **1** an introduction to a book, speech, etc **2** sthg that precedes or heralds; a preliminary

²preface *vt* **1** to introduce *by* or provide *with* a preface **2** to be a preliminary or preface to – **prefacer** *n*

prefatory *adj* of or constituting a preface; introductory – **prefatorily** *adv*

prefect *n* **1** any of various high officials or magistrates in ancient Rome **2** a chief officer or chief magistrate (e g in France or Italy) **3** a monitor in a secondary school, usu with some authority over other pupils

prefecture *n* the office or official residence of a prefect – **prefectural** *adj*

prefer *vt* **-rr- 1** to choose or esteem above another; like better ⟨~s *sports to reading*⟩ **2** to give (a creditor) priority **3** to bring against sby ⟨*won't* ~ *charges*⟩ **4** to bring forward or submit for consideration – **preferrer** *n*, **preferable** *adj*, **preferably** *adv*

preference *n* **1** the power or opportunity of choosing ⟨*gave him first* ~⟩ **2** sby or sthg preferred; a choice ⟨*which is your* ~?⟩ **3** special favour or consideration ⟨*give* ~ *to those with qualifications*⟩ **4** priority in the settlement of an obligation – **preferential** *adj*, **preferentially** *adv* – **for preference** as being the more desirable; preferably ⟨*use red wine* for preference⟩

preference share *n* a share guaranteed priority over ordinary shares in the payment of dividends and usu in the distribution of assets

preferment *n* (an esp ecclesiastical appointment affording) advancement or promotion in rank, station, etc

prefigure *vt* **1** to represent or suggest in advance; foreshadow **2** to picture or imagine beforehand; foresee – **prefigurement** *n*, **prefigurative** *adj*, **prefiguration** *n*

¹prefix *vt* **1** to attach as a prefix **2** to add to the beginning ⟨~ed *a brief introduction to the article*⟩

²prefix *n* **1** an affix (e g *un* in *unhappy*) placed at the beginning of a word or before a root **2** a title used before a person's name – **prefixal** *adj*, **prefixally** *adv*

pregnancy *n* **1** the condition or quality of being pregnant **2** fertility of mind; inventiveness

pregnant *adj* **1** full of ideas or resourcefulness; inventive **2** rich in significance or implication; meaningful ⟨*a* ~ *pause*⟩ **3** containing unborn young within the body **4** showing signs of the future; portentous ⟨*the* ~ *years of the prewar era*⟩ **5** full, teeming – usu + *with* ⟨*nature* ~ *with life*⟩ – **pregnantly** *adv*

prehensile *adj* adapted for seizing or grasping, esp by wrapping round ⟨*a* ~ *tail*⟩ – **prehensility** *n*

prehistoric, prehistorical *adj* of or existing in times antedating written history – **prehistorically** *adv*

prehistory *n* (the study of) the prehistoric period of human beings' evolution – **prehistorian** *n*

prejudge *vt* to pass judgment on prematurely or before a full and proper examination – **prejudger** *n*, **prejudgment** *n*

¹prejudice *n* **1** disadvantage resulting from disregard of one's (legal) rights **2a** (an instance of) a preconceived judgment or opinion; *esp* a biased and unfavourable one formed without sufficient reason or knowledge **b** an irrational attitude of hostility directed against an individual, group, or race

²prejudice *vt* **1** to injure by some judgment or action **2** to cause (sby) to have an unreasonable bias

prejudiced *adj* having a prejudice or bias in favour of or esp against

prejudicial, prejudicious *adj* **1** detrimental **2** leading to prejudiced judgments – **prejudicially** *adv*, **prejudicialness** *n*, **prejudiciously** *adv*

prelacy *n* **1** the office of a prelate **2** episcopal church government

prelate *n* an ecclesiastic (e g a bishop or abbot) of high rank

prelim *n* a preliminary

¹preliminary *n* sthg that precedes or is introductory or preparatory: e g **a** a preliminary scholastic examination **b** *pl, Br* matter (e g a list of contents) preceding the main text of a book

²preliminary *adj* preceding and preparing for what is to follow; introductory – **preliminarily** *adv*

preliterate *adj* not yet employing writing – **preliterate** *n*

¹prelude *n* **1** an introductory or preliminary performance, action, or event; an introduction **2a** a musical section or movement introducing the theme or chief subject or serving as an introduction (e g to an opera) **b** a short separate concert piece, usu for piano or orchestra – **preludial** *adj*

²prelude *vt* to serve as prelude to; foreshadow – **preluder** *n*

premature *adj* happening, arriving, existing, or performed before the proper or usual time; *esp, of a human* born after a gestation period of less than 37 weeks – **prematureness** *n*, **prematurely** *adv*, **prematurity** *n*

premeditate *vt* to think over and plan beforehand ⟨~d *murder*⟩ – **premeditator** *n*, **premeditative** *adj*, **premeditation** *n*

¹premier *adj* **1** first in position, rank, or importance; principal **2** first in time; earliest

²premier *n* PRIME MINISTER – **premiership** *n*

premiere *n* a first public performance or showing ⟨*the* ~ *of a play*⟩ – **premiere** *vt*

¹premise *n* **1** *Br also* **premiss** a proposition taken as a basis of argument or inference; *specif* either of the first 2 propositions of a syllogism **2** *pl, Br also* **premiss** matters previously stated; *specif* the preliminary and explanatory part of a deed **3** *pl* **a** a piece of land with the buildings on it **b** (part of) a building

²premise *vt* **1** to state as a premise or introduction **2** to presuppose, postulate

¹premium *n* **1a** a reward or recompense for a particular act **b** a sum above a fixed price or remuneration, paid chiefly as an incentive; a bonus ⟨*willing to pay a* ~ *for immediate delivery*⟩ **c** a sum in advance of or in addition to the nominal value of sthg **2** the sum paid for a contract of insurance **3** a high value or a value in excess of that normally expected ⟨*put a* ~ *on accuracy*⟩ – **at a premium** valuable because rare or difficult to obtain ⟨*flats in London are* at a premium⟩

²premium *adj, chiefly NAm* of exceptional quality or amount ⟨*wine made from* ~ *grapes*⟩

premium bond *n* a government bond that is issued in units of £1 and which instead of earning interest is entered into a monthly draw for money prizes

premonition *n* **1** a previous notice or warning; a forewarning ⟨*a* ~ *of the troubles that lay in store*⟩ **2** an anticipation of an event without conscious reason; a presentiment ⟨*felt a* ~ *of danger*⟩ – **premonitory** *adj*

prenatal *adj* occurring or being in a stage before birth – **prenatally** *adv*

preoccupation *n* (sthg that causes) complete mental absorption

preoccupied *adj* lost in thought; engrossed

preoccupy *vt* **1** to engage or engross the attention of to the exclusion of other things **2** to take possession of or occupy in advance or before another

preordain *vt* to decree or determine in advance – **preordainment** *n*, **preordination** *n*

prep *n, Br* homework done at or away from school

preparation *n* **1** preparing **2** a state of being prepared; readiness **3** a preparatory act or measure – usu pl ⟨*made his ~s for the journey*⟩ **4** sthg prepared; *esp* a medicine ⟨*a ~ for colds*⟩

¹**preparatory, preparative** *adj* preparing or serving to prepare for sthg; introductory – **preparatorily** *adv*

²**preparatory** *adv* by way of preparation; in a preparatory manner – usu + *to* ⟨*took a deep breath ~ to drinking*⟩

preparatory school *n* a private school preparing pupils **a** *Br* for public schools **b** *NAm* for college

prepare *vt* **1a** to make ready beforehand for some purpose, use, or activity ⟨*~ food for dinner*⟩ **b** to put into a suitable frame of mind for sthg ⟨*~d her gradually for the shocking news*⟩ **2** to work out the details of; plan in advance ⟨*preparing his strategy for the coming campaign*⟩ **3a** to put together ⟨*~ a prescription*⟩ **b** to draw up in written form ⟨*~ a report*⟩ *~vi* to get ready; make preparations ⟨*preparing for a career in teaching*⟩ – **preparer** *n*

prepared *adj* subjected to a special process or treatment

preparedness *n* adequate preparation (in case of war)

prepay *vt* **prepaid** to pay or pay the charge on in advance ⟨*carriage* prepaid⟩ – **prepayment** *n*

preponderant *also* **preponderate** *adj* **1** having superior weight, force, or influence; predominant **2** occurring in greater number or quantity – **preponderance** *n*, **preponderantly** *adv*

preponderate *vt* **1** to predominate in influence, power, or importance **2** to predominate in number or frequency – **preponderation** *n*

preposition *n* a linguistic form (e g *by*, *of*, *for*) that combines with a noun, pronoun, or noun equivalent to form a phrase with a relation to some other word – **prepositional** *adj*, **prepositionally** *adv*

prepossess *vt* to prejudice, esp in favour of sby or sthg

prepossessing *adj* tending to create a favourable impression; attractive – **prepossessingly** *adv*, **prepossessingness** *n*

prepossession *n* **1** an opinion or impression formed beforehand; a prejudice **2** an exclusive concern with 1 idea or object; a preoccupation

preposterous *adj* contrary to nature or reason; absurd; *also* ridiculous ⟨*look at that ~ outfit*⟩ – **preposterously** *adv*, **preposterousness** *n*

prep school *n* PREPARATORY SCHOOL

prepuce *n* the foreskin; *also* a similar fold surrounding the clitoris – **preputial** *adj*

Pre-Raphaelite *adj or n* (of or relating to) a member of the Pre-Raphaelite Brotherhood – **Pre-Raphaelitism** *n*

prerecord *vt* to record (e g a radio or television programme) in advance of presentation or use

prerequisite *n* a requirement that must be satisfied in advance – **prerequisite** *adj*

prerogative *n* **1** an exclusive or special right or privilege belonging esp to a person or group of people by virtue of rank or status **2** the discretionary power inhering in the Crown – **prerogatived** *adj*

¹**presage** *n* **1** sthg that foreshadows or portends a future event; an omen **2** an intuition of what is going to happen in the future; a presentiment – **presageful** *adj*

²**presage** *vt* **1** to give an omen or warning of; portend **2** to forecast, predict **3** to have a presentiment of *~vi* to make or utter a prediction

presbyter *n* **1** a member of the governing body of an early Christian church **2** ³ELDER **3** – **presbyterate** *n*

¹**Presbyterian** *adj* of or constituting a Christian church governed by elected representative bodies and traditionally Calvinistic in doctrine – **Presbyterianism** *n*

²**Presbyterian** *n* a member of a Presbyterian church

presbytery *n* **1** the part of a church (e g the E end of the chancel) reserved for the officiating clergy **2** a local ruling body in Presbyterian churches **3** the house of a Roman Catholic parish priest

preschool *adj* of the period from infancy to first attendance at primary school

prescience *n* foreknowledge of events; *also* foresight – **prescient** *adj*, **presciently** *adv*

prescribe *vi* **1** to claim a title to sthg by right of prescription **2** to lay down a rule; dictate **3** to write or give medical prescriptions *~vt* **1a** to ordain; LAY DOWN **2b b** to specify with authority **2** to designate or order the use of as a remedy – **prescriber** *n*

prescript *n or adj* (sthg) prescribed as a rule

prescription *n* **1** the establishment of a claim to sthg by use and enjoyment of it over a long period **2** the action of laying down authoritative rules or directions **3** a written direction or order for the preparation and use of a medicine; *also* the medicine prescribed **4** (a claim founded on) ancient or long-standing custom

prescriptive *adj* **1** serving to prescribe **2** established by, founded on, or arising from prescription or long-standing custom **3** authoritarian as regards language use – **prescriptively** *adv*

presence *n* **1** the fact or condition of being present ⟨*requested his ~ at the meeting*⟩ **2a** the immediate vicinity of a specified person ⟨*never looked at ease in my ~*⟩ **b** the vicinity of one of superior, esp royal, rank ⟨*bowed before withdrawing from the ~*⟩ **3a** sby or sthg present; *also* a spirit felt to be present **b** a body of people from a specified place (e g a country), present and playing an influential role in another organization or nation ⟨*the withdrawal of the American ~ in Vietnam*⟩ **4a** a personal magnetism that attracts and holds the attention of others **b** a usu dignified or stately bearing or appearance **5** a quality of poise or distinction that enables a person, esp a performer, to impress, or have a strong effect on, others ⟨*she had great stage ~*⟩

presence of mind *n* the ability to retain one's self-possession and act calmly in emergencies or difficult situations

¹**present** *n* sthg presented; a gift

²**present** *vt* **1a** to introduce (sby) esp to another of higher rank **b** to bring (e g a play) before the public **2** to make a gift to **3** to give or bestow formally **4** to lay (e g a charge) before a court **5** to nominate (a clergyman) to a benefice **6a** to offer for show; exhibit ⟨*~ a bedraggled appearance*⟩ **b** to offer for approval or consideration ⟨*~ this report again next week in greater detail*⟩ **7** to act as a presenter of (e g a television or radio programme) **8** to act the part of **9** to level or aim (e g a weapon) *~vi* to come to notice or into view ⟨*the patient ~ed with abdominal pain*⟩

³**present** *n* PRESENT ARMS ⟨*his gun held at the ~*⟩

⁴**present** *adj* **1** now existing or in progress ⟨*under the ~ system of government*⟩ **2a** in or at a usu specified place ⟨*he wasn't ~ at the meeting*⟩ **b** existing in sthg mentioned or understood ⟨*methane and air had to be ~ in the right quantities for combustion to take place*⟩ **c** vividly felt, remembered, or imagined – usu + *to* or *in* ⟨*the events of a decade ago are still ~ to our minds*⟩ **3** being discussed, dealt with, or considered ⟨*as far as the ~ writer is concerned*⟩ **4** of or being a verb tense that expresses present time or the time of speaking – **presentness** *n*

⁵**present** *n* **1** (a verb form in) the present tense of a

language **2** the present time **3** *pl* the present words or statements – fml

presentable *adj* **1** fit to be seen or inspected **2** fit (e g in dress or manners) to appear in company ⟨*must make myself ~ for dinner*⟩ – **presentableness** *n*, **presentably** *adv*, **presentability** *n*

present arms *n* a saluting position in which the firearm is held vertically in front of the body

presentation *n* **1a** sthg offered or given; a gift **b** sthg put forward for consideration or notice **c** a descriptive or persuasive account (e g by a salesman of a product) **2a** the manner in which sthg is set forth, laid out, or presented ⟨*his ~ of the argument was masterly*⟩ ⟨*the ~ of the final dish is important in cookery*⟩ **b** the position in which the foetus lies in the uterus in labour with respect to the mouth of the uterus **3** an immediate object of perception, cognition, or memory – **presentational** *adj*

present-day *adj* now existing or occurring

presenter *n* one who presents; *specif* a broadcaster who introduces and provides comments on broadcast material during a programme

presentiment *n* a feeling that sthg will or is about to happen; a premonition – **presentimental** *adj*

presently *adv* **1** before long; soon **2** *chiefly NAm & Scot* at the present time; now

present participle *n* a participle (e g *dancing, being*) with present or active meaning

present perfect *adj or n* (of or being) a verb tense (e g *have finished*) that expresses completion of an action at or before the time of speaking

preservative *n or adj* (sthg) that preserves or has the power to preserve; *specif* (sthg) used to protect against decay, discoloration, or spoilage

¹preserve *vt* **1** to keep safe from harm or destruction; protect **2a** to keep alive, intact, or free from decay **b** to maintain ⟨*~s her habitual calm at all times*⟩ **3a** to keep or save from decomposition **b** to can, pickle, or similarly prepare (a perishable food) for future use **c** to make a preserve of (fruit) **4** to keep and protect (e g land or game) for private, esp sporting, use *~ vi* **1** to make preserves **2** to withstand preserving (e g by canning) ⟨*some fruits do not ~ well*⟩ – **preservable** *adj*, **preserver** *n*, **preservation** *n*

²preserve *n* **1** a preparation (e g a jam or jelly) consisting of fruit preserved by cooking whole or in pieces with sugar **2** an area restricted for the preservation of natural resources (e g animals or trees); *esp* one used for regulated hunting or fishing **3** sthg (e g a sphere of activity) reserved for certain people

preset *vt* **-tt-; preset** to set beforehand – **preset** *adj*, **presettable** *adj*

preshrunk *adj* of or being material subjected to a process during manufacture designed to reduce later shrinking

preside *vi* **1** to occupy the place of authority **2** to exercise guidance, authority, or control *over* **3** to perform as featured or chief instrumentalist – usu + *at* ⟨*~d at the organ*⟩ **4** to be prominent ⟨*the presiding genius of the company*⟩ – **presider** *n*

presidency *n* **1** the office of president **2** the term during which a president holds office **3** the action or function of one who presides; superintendence

president *n* **1** an official chosen to preside over a meeting or assembly **2** an elected head of state in a republic **3** *chiefly NAm* the chief officer of an organization (e g a business corporation or university) – **presidential** *adj*, **presidentially** *adv*

presidium *n, pl* **presidia, presidiums** a permanent executive committee in a Communist country

¹press *n* **1** a crowd of people; a throng; *also* crowding **2** an apparatus or machine by which pressure is applied (e g for shaping material, extracting liquid, or compressing sthg) **3** a cupboard; *esp* one for books or clothes **4** an action of pressing or pushing; pressure **5a** PRINTING PRESS **b** the act or process of printing **c** (a building containing) a publishing house or printing firm **6a** *sing or pl in constr, often cap* (**1**) *the* newspapers and magazines collectively (**2**) *the* journalists collectively **b** comment or notice in newspapers and magazines

²press *vt* **1** to push firmly and steadily against **2** to assail, harass – esp in *hard-pressed* **3a** to squeeze out the juice or contents of (e g citrus fruits) **b** to squeeze with apparatus or instruments to a desired density, smoothness, or shape ⟨*~ed flowers*⟩ **c** IRON **1** ⟨*~ed his trousers*⟩ **4a** to exert influence on; constrain **b** to try hard to persuade; entreat **5** to move by means of pressure ⟨*~ this button*⟩ **6** to lay emphasis or insist on ⟨*continued to ~ his point*⟩ **7** to follow through (a course of action) ⟨*~ed his claim*⟩ **8** to clasp in affection or courtesy ⟨*~ed his hand*⟩ **9** to make (a gramophone record) from a matrix *~ vi* **1** to crowd closely; mass **2** to force or push one's way ⟨*~ing through the crowd*⟩ **3** to seek urgently; contend ⟨*~ing for salary increases*⟩ **4** to require haste or speed in action ⟨*time is ~ing*⟩ **5** to exert pressure **6** to come to a desired condition, esp of smoothness, by being pressed – **presser** *n*

³press *vt* **1** to force into military service, esp in an army or navy **2a** to take by authority, esp for public use; commandeer **b** to take and force into any, usu temporary, service

⁴press *n* impressment into service, esp in a navy

press agent *n* an agent employed to establish and maintain good public relations through publicity

press conference *n* an interview given by a public figure to journalists by appointment

press cutting *n, Br* a paragraph or article cut from a newspaper or magazine

press-gang *n sing or pl in constr* a detachment empowered to press men into military or naval service

press gang *vt* to force into service (as if) by a press-gang ⟨*was press ganged into playing cricket in a charity match*⟩

¹pressing *adj* **1** very important; critical **2** earnest, insistent ⟨*a ~ invitation*⟩ – **pressingly** *adv*

²pressing *n* one or more gramophone records produced from a single matrix

pressman, *fem* **presswoman** *n* **1** the operator of a printing press **2** *Br* a newspaper reporter

pressmark *n, chiefly Br* a combination of characters assigned to a book to indicate its place in a library

press on *vi* **1** to continue on one's way ⟨*press on along the Blackpool road*⟩ **2** to proceed in an urgent or resolute manner ⟨*the firm is pressing on with its plans for expansion*⟩

press-stud *n, Br* a metal fastener consisting of 2 parts joined by pressing

press-up *n* an exercise performed in a prone position by raising and lowering the body with the arms while supporting it only on the hands and toes

¹pressure *n* **1a** the burden of physical or mental distress ⟨*the ~ of family anxieties*⟩ **b** trouble or difficulty resulting from social or economic constraints ⟨*under severe financial ~*⟩ **2** the application of force to sthg by sthg else in direct contact with it; compression **3a** the action of a force against an opposing force **b** the force or thrust exerted over a surface divided by its area **4** the stress of urgent matters ⟨*people who work well under ~*⟩ **5a** influence or compulsion directed towards achieving a particular end ⟨*the unions put ~ on the government to* *increase wages*⟩ **b** repeated persistent attack; harassment ⟨*the English batsmen were under ~ from the Australian bowlers*⟩ **6** the atmospheric pressure

²**pressure** *vt* **1** to apply pressure to **2** *chiefly NAm* to pressurize

pressure cooker *n* a metal vessel with an airtight lid in which superheated steam under pressure produces a very high temperature, used for cooking food quickly – **pressure-cook** *vb*

pressure gauge *n* a gauge for indicating the pressure of a fluid

pressure group *n* an interest group organized to influence public, esp governmental, policy

pressurize, -ise *vt* **1** to maintain near-normal atmospheric pressure in (e g an aircraft cabin) **2** to apply pressure to ⟨*the team* ~d *the opponents' goal and eventually scored*⟩; *specif* to coerce ⟨*the prisoner's hunger strike* ~d *the authorities into action*⟩ **3** to design to withstand pressure – **pressurizer** *n*, **pressurization** *n*

prestidigitation *n* conjuring; SLEIGHT OF HAND – **prestidigitator** *n*

prestige *n* **1** high standing or esteem in the eyes of others **2** superiority or desirability in the eyes of society resulting from associations of social rank or material success ⟨*a ~ executive suite*⟩

prestigious *adj* having or conferring prestige – **prestigiously** *adv*, **prestigiousness** *n*

¹**presto** *n, adv, or adj, pl* **prestos** (a musical passage or movement played) at a rapid tempo – used in music

²**presto** *interj* HEY PRESTO

prestress *vt* to introduce internal stresses into (e g a structural beam) to counteract stresses that will result from an applied load – **prestress** *n*

presume *vt* **1** to undertake without leave or justification; dare ⟨*I wouldn't ~ to tell you how to do your job*⟩ **2** to suppose or assume, esp with some degree of certainty **3** to take for granted; imply ~ *vi* **1** to act or proceed on a presumption; take sthg for granted **2** to take liberties **3** to take advantage, esp in an unscrupulous manner – usu + *on* or *upon* ⟨*don't ~ on his kindness*⟩ – **presumable** *adj*, **presumably** *adv*, **presumer** *n*

presumption *n* **1** presumptuous attitude or conduct; effrontery **2a** an attitude or belief based on reasonable evidence or grounds; an assumption **b** a ground or reason for presuming sthg **3** a legal inference as to the existence or truth of a fact

presumptive *adj* **1** giving grounds for reasonable opinion or belief ⟨*~ evidence*⟩ **2** based on probability or presumption ⟨*heir ~*⟩ – **presumptively** *adv*

presumptuous *adj* overstepping due bounds; forward – **presumptuously** *adv*, **presumptuousness** *n*

presuppose *vt* **1** to suppose beforehand **2** to require as an antecedent in logic or fact – **presupposition** *n*

pretence, *NAm chiefly* **pretense** *n* **1** a claim made or implied; *esp* one not supported by fact ⟨*made no ~ to learning*⟩ **2a** mere ostentation; pretentiousness ⟨*a man entirely free of pomp and ~*⟩ **b** a false or feigning act or assertion **3** an outward and often insincere or inadequate show; a semblance ⟨*struggling to maintain some ~ of order in the meeting*⟩ **4** a professed rather than a real intention or purpose; a pretext – esp in **false pretences**

¹**pretend** *vt* **1** to give a false appearance of; feign ⟨*he ~ed deafness*⟩ **2** to claim or assert falsely; profess ⟨*~ing an emotion he could not really feel*⟩ ⟨*~ed affection*⟩ ~ *vi* **1** to feign an action, part, or role (as if) in play **2** to lay claim ⟨*did not ~ to high office*⟩ – **pretended** *adj*, **pretendedly** *adv*

²**pretend** *adj* make-believe – used esp by children

pretender *n* **1** sby who lays claim to sthg; *specif* a (false)

claimant to a throne **2** sby who makes a false or hypocritical show ⟨*a ~ to spirituality*⟩

pretension *n* **1** (an effort to establish) an esp unjustified claim ⟨*have no ~ to be a great writer*⟩ **2** vanity, pretentiousness – **pretensionless** *adj*

pretentious *adj* making usu unjustified or excessive claims (e g of value or standing) – **pretentiously** *adv*, **pretentiousness** *n*

preterite, *chiefly NAm* **preterit** *adj* of or constituting a verb tense that expresses action in the past without reference to duration, continuance, or repetition – **preterite** *n*

preternatural *adj* **1** exceeding what is natural or regular; extraordinary **2** lying beyond or outside normal experience *USE* fml – **preternaturally** *adv*, **preternaturalness** *n*

pretext *n* a false reason given to disguise the real one; an excuse

pretor *n, chiefly NAm* a praetor – **pretorian** *adj*

prettify *vt* to make pretty or depict prettily, esp in an inappropriate way; *also* to palliate ⟨*attempts to ~ criminal violence*⟩ – **prettification** *n*

¹**pretty** *adj* **1a** attractive or aesthetically pleasing, esp because of delicacy or grace, but less than beautiful ⟨*a ~ girl*⟩ **b** outwardly pleasant but lacking strength, purpose, or intensity ⟨*~ words that make no sense* – Elizabeth Barrett Browning⟩ **2** miserable, terrible ⟨*a ~ mess you've got us into*⟩ **3** moderately large; considerable ⟨*a very ~ profit*⟩ **4** *of a man* having delicate features; *specif* effeminate – derog – **prettily** *adv*, **prettiness** *n*, **prettyish** *adj*

²**pretty** *adv* **1a** in some degree; moderately ⟨*~ comfortable*⟩; *esp* somewhat excessively ⟨*felt ~ sick*⟩ **b** very – used to emphasize *much* or *nearly* ⟨*~ nearly ready*⟩ **2** in a pretty manner; prettily – infml

³**pretty** *n, archaic* a dear or pretty child or young woman – in **my pretty**

pretty-pretty *adj* excessively pretty, esp in an insipid or inappropriate way

pretzel *n* a brittle glazed and salted biscuit typically having the form of a loose knot

prevail *vi* **1** to gain ascendancy through strength or superiority; triumph – often + *against* or *over* **2** to persuade successfully – + *on, upon*, or *with* ⟨*~ed on him to sing*⟩ **3** to be frequent; predominate ⟨*the west winds that ~ in the mountains*⟩ **4** to be or continue in use or fashion; persist ⟨*a custom that still ~s*⟩ – **prevailing** *adj*, **prevailingly** *adj*

prevalent *adj* generally or widely occurring or existing; widespread – **prevalently** *adv*, **prevalence** *n*

prevaricate *vi* to speak or act evasively so as to hide the truth; equivocate – **prevaricator** *n*, **prevarication** *n*

prevent *vt* **1** to keep from happening or existing ⟨*steps to ~ war*⟩ **2** to hold or keep back; stop – often + *from* – **preventable** *also* **preventible** *adj*, **preventer** *n*, **prevention** *n*, **preventability** *n*

¹**preventive, preventative** *n* sthg that prevents (disease)

²**preventive, preventative** *adj* **1** intended or serving to prevent; precautionary **2** undertaken to forestall anticipated hostile action ⟨*~ war*⟩ – **preventively** *adv*, **preventiveness** *n*

preventive detention *n, Br* a term of imprisonment for habitual criminals over 30

¹**preview** *vt* to see beforehand; *specif* to view or show in advance of public presentation

²**preview** *n* **1** an advance showing or performance (e g of a film or play) **2** a brief view or foretaste of sthg that is to come **3** *also* **prevue** *chiefly NAm* a film or television trailer

previous *adj* **1** going before in time or order **2** acting too

soon; premature ⟨*she was a bit* ~ *when she said she'd got the job*⟩ – infml – **previously** *adv*, **previousness** *n*
previous to *prep* before; PRIOR TO
prevision *n* **1** foreknowledge, prescience **2** a forecast, prognostication – **previsional** *adj*, **previsionary** *adj*
prewar *adj* of or being the period preceding a war, esp WW I or II
¹**prey** *n* **1a** an animal taken by a predator as food **b** sby or sthg helpless or unable to resist attack; a victim **2** the act or habit of preying
²**prey** *vi* **1** to make raids for booty ⟨*pirates* ~ed *on the coast*⟩ **2a** to seize and devour prey – often – + *on* or *upon* ⟨*kestrels* ~ *upon mice*⟩ **b** to live by extortion, deceit, or exerting undue influence ⟨*confidence tricksters* ~ing *on elderly women*⟩ **3** to have continuously oppressive or distressing effect ⟨*problems that* ~ *on one's mind*⟩ – **preyer** *n*
¹**price** *n* **1** the money, or amount of goods or services, that is exchanged or demanded in barter or sale **2** the terms for the sake of which sthg is done or undertaken: e g **a** an amount sufficient to bribe sby ⟨*believed every man had his* ~⟩ **b** a reward for the catching or killing of sby ⟨*a man with a* ~ *on his head*⟩ **3** the cost at which sthg is done or obtained ⟨*the* ~ *of his carelessness was a broken window*⟩ **4** *archaic* value, worth ⟨*her* ~ *is far above rubies* – Prov 31:10(AV)⟩
²**price** *vt* **1** to set a price on **2** to find out the price of – **pricer** *n*
priceless *adj* **1** having a worth beyond any price; invaluable **2** particularly amusing or absurd ⟨*told me this* ~ *story*⟩ – infml
price tag *n* **1** a label on merchandise showing the price at which it is offered for sale **2** price, cost ⟨*the council was asked to put a* ~ *on the new nursery school*⟩
pricey *also* **pricy** *adj*, *chiefly Br* expensive – infml
¹**prick** *n* **1** a mark or shallow hole made by a pointed instrument **2** a pointed instrument, weapon, etc **3** an instance of pricking or the sensation of being pricked: e g **a** a nagging or sharp feeling of sorrow or remorse **b** a sharp localized pain ⟨*the* ~ *of a needle*⟩ **4** the penis – vulg **5** a disagreeable person – chiefly vulg
²**prick** *vt* **1** to pierce slightly with a sharp point **2** to affect with sorrow or remorse ⟨*his conscience began to* ~ *him*⟩ **3** to mark, distinguish, or note by means of a small mark **4** to trace or outline with punctures **5** to cause to be or stand erect ⟨*a dog* ~ing *his ears*⟩ – often + *up* – *vi* **1** to prick sthg or cause a pricking sensation **2** to feel discomfort as if from being pricked – **pricker** *n* – **prick up one's ears** to start to listen intently
¹**prickle** *n* **1** a sharp pointed spike arising from the skin or bark of a plant **2** a prickling sensation
²**prickle** *vb* **prickling** *vt* to prick slightly ~ *vi* to cause or feel a prickling or stinging sensation; tingle
prickly *adj* **1** full of or covered with prickles **2** marked by prickling; stinging ⟨*a* ~ *sensation*⟩ **3a** troublesome, vexatious ⟨~ *issues*⟩ **b** easily irritated ⟨*had a* ~ *disposition*⟩ – **prickliness** *n*
prickly heat *n* a skin eruption of red spots with intense itching and tingling caused by inflammation round the sweat ducts
prickly pear *n* (the pulpy pearshaped edible fruit of) any of a genus of cacti having yellow flowers and bearing spines or prickly hairs
prick out *vt* to transplant (seedlings) from the place of germination to a more permanent position (e g in a flower bed)
¹**pride** *n* **1a** inordinate self-esteem; conceit **b** a reasonable or justifiable self-respect **c** delight or satisfaction arising from some act, possession, or relationship ⟨*parental* ~⟩

2 a source of pride; *esp*, *sing or pl in constr* the best in a group or class ⟨*this pup is the* ~ *of the litter*⟩ **3** *sing or pl in constr* a group of lions
²**pride** *vt* to be proud of (oneself) – + *on* or *upon* ⟨*he* ~d *himself on his generosity*⟩
prie-dieu *n*, *pl* **prie-dieux** **1** a kneeling bench with a raised shelf, designed for use by a person at prayer **2** a low armless upholstered chair with a high straight back
priest *n* a person authorized to perform the sacred rites of a religion; *specif* a clergyman ranking below a bishop and above a deacon (e g in the Anglican and Roman Catholic churches) – **priestly** *adj*, **priestliness** *n*, **priesthood** *n*
prig *n* one who is excessively self-righteous or affectedly precise about the observance of proprieties (e g of speech or manners) – **priggish** *adj*, **priggishly** *adv*, **priggishness** *n*, **priggery** *n*
prim *adj* **-mm-** **1** stiffly formal and proper; decorous **2** prudish – **primly** *adv*, **primness** *n*
prima ballerina *n* the principal female dancer in a ballet company
primacy *n* **1** the office or rank of an ecclesiastical primate **2** the state of being first (e g in importance, order, or rank); preeminence – fml
prima donna *n*, *pl* **prima donnas** **1** a principal female singer (e g in an opera company) **2** an extremely sensitive or temperamental person
primaeval *adj*, *chiefly Br* primeval
¹**prima facie** *adv* at first view; on the first appearance ⟨*his arguments appear* ~ *true*⟩
²**prima facie** *adj* true, valid, or sufficient at first impression; apparent ⟨*the theory offers a* ~ *solution*⟩
primal *adj* **1** original, primitive ⟨*village life continues in its* ~ *innocence* – Van Wyck Brookes⟩ **2** first in importance; fundamental ⟨*our* ~ *concern*⟩ – **primality** *n*
primarily *adv* **1** for the most part, chiefly **2** in the first place; originally
¹**primary** *adj* **1a** first in order of time or development; primitive **b** of or being formations of the Palaeozoic and earlier periods **2a** of first rank, importance, or value; principal **b** basic, fundamental **c** of *Latin*, *Greek*, or *Sanskrit tense* expressing present or future time **d** of or constituting the strongest degree of stress in speech **3a** direct, firsthand ⟨~ *sources of information*⟩ **b** not derivable from other colours, odours, or tastes **c** preparatory to sthg else in a continuing process; elementary ⟨~ *instruction*⟩ **d** of or at a primary school ⟨~ *education*⟩ **e** belonging to the first group or order in successive divisions, combinations, or ramifications ⟨~ *nerves*⟩ **f** of or being the inducing current or its circuit in an induction coil or transformer **g** of or being the amino acid sequence in proteins ⟨~ *protein structure*⟩ **4** of, involving, or derived directly from plant-forming tissue, *specif* meristem, at a growing point ⟨~ *tissue*⟩ ⟨~ *growth*⟩ **5** of or being an industry that produces raw materials ⟨*mining is a* ~ *industry*⟩
²**primary** *n* **1** sthg that stands first in rank, importance, or value; a fundamental – usu pl **2** any of the usu 9 or 10 strong feathers on the joint of a bird's wing furthest from the body **3** PRIMARY COLOUR **4** a caucus **5** PRIMARY SCHOOL
primary colour *n* **1** any of the 3 spectral bands red, green, and bluish violet from which all other colours can be obtained by suitable combinations **2** any of the 3 coloured pigments red, yellow, and blue that cannot be matched by mixing other pigments
primary school *n* a school usu for pupils from 5 to 11, but sometimes also including nursery school
primate *n* **1** *often cap* a bishop having precedence (e g in a nation) **2** any of an order of mammals including human

beings, the apes, monkeys, and related forms (e g lemurs and tarsiers) – **primateship** n, **primatial** adj, **primatology** n, **primatologist** n, **primatological** adj

¹prime n 1 often cap the second of the canonical hours, orig fixed for 6 am 2 the most active, thriving, or successful stage or period ⟨in the ~ of his life⟩ 3 the chief or best individual or part; the pick ⟨~ of the flock, and choicest of the stall – Alexander Pope⟩ 4 **prime, prime number** a positive integer that has no factor except itself and 1 5 the symbol ′ used in mathematics as a distinguishing mark (e g in denoting derivatives of a function)

²prime adj 1 first in time; original 2 having no factor except itself and 1 ⟨3 is a ~ number⟩ 3a first in rank, authority, or significance; principal b of meat, esp beef of the highest grade or best quality regularly marketed 4 not deriving from sthg else; primary – **primely** adv, **primeness** n

³prime vt 1 to fill, load; esp to fill or ply (a person) with liquor 2 to prepare (a firearm or charge) for firing by supplying with priming or a primer 3 to apply a first coat (e g of paint or oil) to (a surface), esp in preparation for painting 4 to put into working order by filling or charging with sthg, esp a liquid ⟨~ a pump with water⟩ 5 to instruct beforehand; prepare ⟨~d the witness⟩

prime meridian n the meridian (at Greenwich) of 0° longitude from which other longitudes E and W are reckoned

prime minister n 1 the chief minister of a ruler or state 2 the chief executive of a parliamentary government – **prime ministership** n, **prime ministry** n

prime mover n 1 God as the creator of (motion in) the physical universe 2a an initial source of motive power (e g a windmill, water wheel, turbine, or internal-combustion engine) b a powerful tractor or lorry 3 the original or most influential force in a development or undertaking ⟨he was a ~ of the constitutional reform⟩

¹primer n a small book for teaching children to read

²primer n 1 a device (e g a percussion cap) used for igniting a charge 2 material used in priming a surface

primeval, Br also primaeval adj 1 of the earliest age or ages 2 existing in or persisting from the beginning (e g of a universe) – **primevally** adv

priming n the explosive used for igniting a charge

¹primitive adj 1 original, primary 2a of the earliest age or period; primeval b belonging to or characteristic of an early stage of development or evolution ⟨~ technology⟩ 3a elemental, natural b of or produced by a relatively simple people or culture ⟨~ art⟩ c lacking in sophistication or subtlety; crude; also uncivilized d(1) self-taught, untutored (2) produced by a self-taught artist – **primitively** adv, **primitiveness** n, **primitivism** n, **primitivist** n, **primitivistic** adj, **primitivity** n

²primitive n 1a a primitive concept, term, or proposition b a root word 2a(1) an artist of an early, esp pre-Renaissance, period (2) a later imitator of such an artist b an artist, esp self-taught, whose work is marked by directness and naiveté c a primitive work of art 3a a member of a primitive people b an unsophisticated person

primogeniture n 1 the state or fact of being the firstborn of the children of the same parents 2 the principle by which right of inheritance belongs to the eldest son

primordial adj 1a existing from or at the beginning; primeval b earliest formed in the development of an individual or structure 2 fundamental, primary – **primordially** adv

primp vt to dress, adorn, or arrange in a careful or fastidious manner ~vi to dress or groom oneself carefully

primrose n 1 any of a genus of perennial plants with showy, esp yellow, flowers 2 pale yellow

primula n PRIMROSE 1

Primus trademark – used for a portable oil-burning stove used chiefly for cooking (e g when camping)

primus inter pares n first among equals

prince n 1 a sovereign ruler, esp of a principality 2 a foreign nobleman of varying rank and status 3 a person of high rank or standing in his class or profession ⟨a ~ among poets⟩ – **princedom** n, **princeship** n

prince charming n an ideal suitor

prince consort n, pl **princes consort** the husband of a reigning female sovereign – used only after the title has been specif conferred by the sovereign

princely adj 1 of a prince 2 befitting a prince; noble ⟨~ manners⟩ 3 magnificent, lavish ⟨a ~ sum⟩ – **princely** adv, **princeliness** n

¹princess n 1 a female member of a royal family; esp a daughter of a sovereign 2 the wife or widow of a prince 3 a woman having in her own right the rank of a prince 4 a woman, or sthg personified as female, that is outstanding in a specified respect

²princess, princesse adj closely fitting at the top, flared from the hips to the hemline, and having gores or panels ⟨dress with ~ line⟩

¹principal adj most important, consequential, or influential; chief – **principally** adv

²principal n 1 a person who has controlling authority or is in a leading position: e g a the head of an educational institution b one who employs another to act for him/her c the chief or an actual participant in a crime – no longer used technically d the person ultimately liable on a legal obligation e a leading performer 2 a matter or thing of primary importance: e g a a capital sum placed at interest, due as a debt, or used as a fund b a main rafter of a roof – **principalship** n

principal boy n the role of the hero in British pantomime traditionally played by a girl

principality n the office or territory of a prince

principal parts n pl that series of verb forms from which all the other forms of a verb can be derived

principle n 1a a universal and fundamental law, doctrine, or assumption b(1) a rule or code of conduct (2) habitual devotion to right principles ⟨a man of ~⟩ (3) a fundamental implication ⟨he objects to the ~ of the thing, not the method⟩ c the laws or facts of nature underlying the working of an artificial device 2 a primary source; a fundamental element ⟨the ancients emphasized the opposing ~s of heat and cold⟩ 3 an underlying faculty or endowment ⟨such ~s of human nature as greed and curiosity⟩ 4 an ingredient (e g a chemical) that exhibits or imparts a characteristic quality – **in principle** with respect to fundamentals ⟨prepared to accept the proposition in principle⟩

principled adj exhibiting, based on, or characterized by principle – often used in combination ⟨high-principled⟩

prink vb to primp – **prinker** n

¹print n 1a a mark made by pressure; an impression b sthg impressed with a print or formed in a mould 2 printed state or form 3 printed matter or letters 4a(1) a copy made by printing (e g from a photographic negative) (2) a reproduction of an original work of art (e g a painting) (3) an original work of art (e g a woodcut or lithograph) intended for graphic reproduction b (an article made from) cloth with a pattern applied by printing c a photographic copy, esp from a negative – **in print** obtainable from the publisher – **out of print** not obtainable from the publisher

²print vt 1 to stamp (e g a mark or design) in or on sthg

2a to make a copy of by impressing paper against an inked printing surface **b** to impress with a design or pattern **c** to publish in print **3** to write each letter of separately, not joined together **4** to make (a positive picture) on sensitized photographic surface from a negative or a positive ~ *vi* **1** to form a printed image **2a** to work as a printer **b** to produce printed matter **3** to produce sthg by printing **4** to use unjoined letters like those of roman type

printable *adj* **1** capable of being printed or of being printed from or on **2** considered fit to publish – **printability** *n*

printed circuit *n* a circuit for electronic apparatus consisting of conductive material in thin continuous paths from terminal to terminal on an insulating surface

printer *n* **1** a person engaged in printing **2** a machine for printing from photographic negatives **3** a device (e g a line printer) that produces printout

printing *n* **1** reproduction in printed form **2** the art, practice, or business of a printer **3** IMPRESSION 4c

printing press *n* a machine that produces printed copies

printout *n* a printed record produced automatically (e g by a computer) – **print out** *vt*

¹prior *n* **1** the deputy head of a monastery ranking next below the abbot **2** the head (of a house) of any of various religious communities – **priorate** *n*, **priorship** *n*

²prior *adj* **1** earlier in time or order **2** taking precedence (e g in importance) – **priorly** *adv*

priority *n* **1a** being prior **b(1)** superiority in rank **(2)** legal precedence in exercise of rights **2** sthg meriting prior attention

prior to *prep* before in time; in advance of – *fml*

priory *n* (the church of) a religious house under a prior or prioress

prise *vt, chiefly Br* ⁵PRIZE

prism *n* **1** a polyhedron whose ends are similar, equal, and parallel polygons and whose faces are parallelograms **2** a transparent body that is bounded in part by 2 nonparallel plane faces and is used to deviate or disperse a beam of light

prismatic *adj* **1** of, like, or being a prism **2** formed, dispersed, or refracted (as if) by a prism ⟨~ *effects*⟩ ⟨~ *colours*⟩ – **prismatically** *adv*

prison *n* **1** a state of confinement or captivity **2** a place of enforced confinement; *specif* a building in which people are confined for safe custody while on trial or for punishment after conviction – **prison** *vt*

prisoner *n* sby kept under involuntary confinement; *esp* sby on trial or in prison

prisoner of war *n* a person captured in war

prissy *adj* prim and over-precise; finicky – **prissily** *adv*, **prissiness** *n*

pristine *adj* **1** belonging to the earliest period or state **2** free from impurity or decay; fresh and clean as if new – **pristinely** *adv*

prithee *interj, archaic* – used to express a wish or request

privacy *n* **1** being apart from the company or observation of others; seclusion **2** freedom from undesirable intrusions and esp publicity

¹private *adj* **1a** intended for or restricted to the use of a particular person, group, etc ⟨a ~ *park*⟩ **b** belonging to or concerning an individual person, company, or interest ⟨a ~ *house*⟩ **c(1)** restricted to the individual or arising independently of others ⟨*my ~ opinion is that the whole scheme's ridiculous*⟩ **(2)** independent of the usual institutions ⟨~ *study*⟩ **d** not general in effect ⟨a ~ *statute*⟩ **e** of or receiving medical treatment in Britain for which fees are charged and in which the patient has more privileges

than a patient being treated under the National Health Service **f** of or administered by a private individual or organization as opposed to a governmental institution or agency ⟨a ~ *pension scheme*⟩ **2a(1)** not holding public office or employment ⟨a ~ *citizen*⟩ **(2)** not related to one's official position; personal ⟨~ *correspondence*⟩ **b** having the rank of a private ⟨a ~ *soldier*⟩ **3a(1)** withdrawn from company or observation; sequestered **(2)** not seeking or having the companionship of others ⟨*she was a very ~ person*⟩ **b** not (intended to be) known publicly; secret – **privately** *adv*, **privateness** *n*

²private *n* a soldier of the lowest rank – **in private** not openly or in public

private detective *n* a person concerned with the maintenance of legal conduct or the investigation of crime either as a regular employee of a private interest (e g a hotel) or as a contractor for fees

private enterprise *n* FREE ENTERPRISE

privateer *n* **1** an armed private ship commissioned to cruise against the commerce or warships of an enemy **2** the commander or any of the crew of a privateer – **privateer** *vi*

private eye *n* PRIVATE DETECTIVE

private parts *n pl* the external genital and excretory organs

private school *n* an independent school that is not a British public school

privation *n* **1** an act or instance of depriving; deprivation **2** being deprived; *esp* lack of the usual necessities of life

privet *n* an ornamental shrub with half-evergreen leaves widely planted for hedges

¹privilege *n* a right, immunity, or advantage granted exclusively to a particular person, class, or group; a prerogative; *esp* such an advantage attached to a position or office

²privilege *vt* to grant a privilege to

privileged *adj* **1** having or enjoying 1 or more privileges ⟨~ *classes*⟩ **2** not subject to disclosure in court ⟨a ~ *communication*⟩

¹privy *adj* **1** sharing in a secret – + *to* ⟨~ *to the conspiracy*⟩ **2** *archaic* secret, private – **privily** *adv*

²privy *n* **1** a small building containing a bench with a hole in it used as a toilet **2** *NAm* TOILET 2b

Privy Council *n* an advisory council nominally chosen by the British monarch and usu functioning through its committees – **Privy Councillor** *n*

privy purse *n, often cap both Ps* an allowance for the monarch's private expenses

¹prize *n* **1** sthg offered or striven for in competition or in a contest of chance **2** sthg exceptionally desirable or precious

²prize *adj* **1a** awarded or worthy of a prize ⟨a ~ *pupil*⟩ **b** awarded as a prize ⟨a ~ *medal*⟩ **2** outstanding of a kind ⟨a ~ *idiot*⟩

³prize *vt* **1** to estimate the value of; rate **2** to value highly; esteem

⁴prize *n* property or shipping lawfully captured at sea in time of war

⁵prize, *Br also* **prise** *vt* **1** to press, force, or move with a lever **2** to open, obtain, or remove with difficulty ⟨*tried to ~ information out of him*⟩

¹pro *n, pl* **pros 1** an argument or piece of evidence in favour of a particular proposition or view ⟨*an appraisal of the ~s and cons*⟩ **2** one who favours or supports a particular proposition or view

²pro *adv* in favour or affirmation ⟨*much has been written ~ and con*⟩

³pro *prep* for; IN FAVOUR OF 1

⁴pro *n or adj, pl* **pros** (a) professional – *infml*

⁵pro *n, pl* **pros** a prostitute – *slang*

¹pro- *prefix* **1a** earlier than; prior to; before ⟨pro*logue*⟩ **b** rudimentary; prot- ⟨pro*nucleus*⟩ **2** projecting ⟨progna*thous*⟩

²pro- *prefix* **1** taking the place of; substituting for ⟨pro*cathedral*⟩⟨pro*proctor*⟩ **2** favouring; supporting; championing ⟨pro-*American*⟩ **3** onwards; forwards ⟨pro*gress*⟩⟨pro*pel*⟩

pro-am *n* an esp golf competition in which amateurs play professionals

probability *n* **1** being probable **2** sthg (e g an occurrence or circumstance) probable **3** a measure of the likelihood that a given event will occur, usu expressed as the ratio of the number of times it occurs in a test series to the total number of trials in the series

¹probable *adj* **1** supported by evidence strong enough to establish likelihood but not proof **2** likely to be or become true or real ⟨~ *events*⟩ – **probably** *adv*

²probable *n* sby or sthg probable; *esp* sby who will probably be selected ⟨*she's a ~ for the new post*⟩

¹probate *n* the judicial determination of the validity of a will; *also* an official copy of a will certified as valid

²probate *vt, NAm* to establish (a will) by probate

probation *n* **1a** subjection of an individual to a period of testing to ascertain fitness **b** a method of dealing with (young) offenders by which sentence is suspended subject to regular supervision by a probation officer **2** the state or a period of being subject to probation – **probational** *adj*, **probationally** *adv*, **probationary** *adj*

probationer *n* **1** one (e g a newly admitted student nurse) whose fitness for a post is being tested during a trial period **2** an offender on probation

probation officer *n* an officer appointed to supervise the conduct of offenders on probation

¹probe *n* **1** a slender surgical instrument for examining a cavity **2a** a slender pointed metal conductor (e g of electricity or sound) that is temporarily connected to or inserted in the monitored device or quantity **b** a device used to investigate or send back information, esp from interplanetary space **3a** the action of probing **b** a tentative exploratory survey **c** a penetrating or critical investigation; an inquiry – *journ*

²probe *vt* **1** to examine (as if) with a probe **2** to investigate thoroughly – *journ* ~ *vi* to make an exploratory investigation – **prober** *n*

probity *n* adherence to the highest principles and ideals; uprightness – *fml*

¹problem *n* **1a** a question raised for inquiry, consideration, or solution **b** a proposition in mathematics or physics stating sthg to be done **2a** a situation or question that is difficult to understand or resolve **b** sby who is difficult to deal with or understand

²problem *adj* **1** dealing with a social or human problem ⟨*a ~ play*⟩ **2** difficult to deal with; presenting a problem ⟨*a ~ child*⟩

problematic, problematical *adj* **1** difficult to solve or decide; puzzling **2** open to question or debate; questionable **3** *of a proposition in logic* asserted as possible – **problematically** *adv*

proboscis *n, pl* **proboscises** *also* **proboscides** **1** a long flexible snout (e g the trunk of an elephant) **2** any of various elongated or extendable tubular parts (e g the sucking organ of a mosquito) of an invertebrate **3** the human nose – *infml; humor*

procedural *adj* of procedure – **procedurally** *adv*

procedure *n* **1** a particular way of acting or accomplishing sthg **2** a series of ordered steps ⟨*legal ~*⟩ **3** an established method of doing things ⟨*a stickler for ~*⟩

proceed *vi* **1** to arise from a source; originate ⟨*this trouble ~ed from a misunderstanding*⟩ **2** to continue after a pause or interruption **3** to begin and carry on an action, process, or movement **4** to move along a course; advance

proceeding *n* **1** a procedure **2** *pl* events, goings-on **3** *pl* legal action ⟨*divorce ~s*⟩ **4** *pl* an official record of things said or done **5** (an) affair, transaction – *fml* in sing.; usu pl with sing. meaning

proceeds *n pl* **1** the total amount brought in ⟨*the ~ of a sale*⟩ **2** the net amount received

¹process *n* **1a** a moving forwards, esp as part of a progression or development ⟨*the historical ~*⟩ **b** sthg going on; a proceeding **2a** a natural phenomenon marked by gradual changes that lead towards a particular result ⟨*the ~ of growth*⟩ **b** a series of actions or operations designed to achieve an end; *esp* a continuous operation or treatment (e g in manufacture) **3a** a whole course of legal proceedings **b** a summons, writ **4** a prominent or projecting part of a living organism or an anatomical structure ⟨*a bone ~*⟩

²process *vt* **1** to subject to a special process or treatment (e g in the course of manufacture) **2** to take appropriate action on ⟨*~ an insurance claim*⟩ – **processible, processable** *adj*

³process *vi, chiefly Br* to move in a procession

procession *n* **1** a group of individuals moving along in an orderly way, esp as part of a ceremony or demonstration **2** a succession, sequence

¹processional *n* a musical composition (e g a hymn) designed for a procession

²processional *adj* of or moving in a procession – **processionally** *adv*

proclaim *vt* **1** to declare publicly and usu officially; announce **2** to give outward indication of; show – **proclaimer** *n*

proclamation *n* **1** proclaiming or being proclaimed **2** an official public announcement

proclivity *n* an inclination or predisposition towards sthg, esp sthg reprehensible – often pl with sing. meaning

proconsul *n* **1** a governor or military commander of an ancient Roman province **2** an administrator in a modern dependency or occupied area – **proconsulship** *n*, **proconsular** *adj*, **proconsulate** *n*

procrastinate *vi* to delay intentionally and reprehensibly in doing sthg necessary – *fml* – **procrastinator** *n*, **procrastination** *n*

procreate *vb* to beget or bring forth (young) – **procreative** *adj*, **procreator** *n*, **procreation** *n*

proctor *n* a supervisor, monitor; *specif* one appointed to maintain student discipline at Oxford or Cambridge – **proctorship** *n*, **proctorial** *adj*

procurator-fiscal *n, often cap P&F* a local public prosecutor in Scotland

procure *vt* **1** to get and provide (esp women) to act as prostitutes **2** to obtain, esp by particular care and effort **3** to achieve; BRING ABOUT ~ *vi* to procure women USE (*vt 2&3*) *fml* – **procurable** *adj*, **procurance** *n*, **procurement** *n*

procurer, fem procuress *n* sby who procures women for prostitution

¹prod *vb* **-dd-** *vt* **1** to poke or jab (as if) with a pointed instrument **2** to incite to action; stir ~ *vi* to make a prodding or jabbing movement, esp repeatedly – **prodder** *n*

²prod *n* **1** a pointed instrument **2** a prodding action; a jab **3** an incitement to act

¹prodigal *adj* **1** recklessly extravagant or wasteful **2** yielding abundantly; lavish ⟨*~ of new ideas*⟩ – fml – **prodigally** *adv*, **prodigality** *n*

²**prodigal** *n* **1** a repentant sinner or reformed wastrel **2** one who spends or gives lavishly and foolishly

prodigious *adj* **1** exciting amazement or wonder **2** extraordinary in bulk, quantity, or degree; enormous – **prodigiously** *adv*, **prodigiousness** *n*

prodigy *n* **1a** sthg extraordinary, inexplicable, or marvellous **b** an exceptional and wonderful example ⟨*a ~ of patience*⟩ **2** a person, esp a child, with extraordinary talents

¹**produce** *vt* **1** to offer to view or notice; exhibit **2** to give birth or rise to **3** to extend in length, area, or volume ⟨*~ a side of a triangle*⟩ **4** to act as a producer of **5** to give being, form, or shape to; make; *esp* to manufacture **6** to (cause to) accumulate *~ vi* to bear, make, or yield sthg – **producible** *adj*

²**produce** *n* agricultural products; *esp* fresh fruits and vegetables as distinguished from grain and other staple crops

producer *n* **1** an individual or entity that grows agricultural products or manufactures articles **2a** sby who has responsibility for the administrative aspects of the production of a film (e g casting, schedules, and esp finance) **b** *Br* DIRECTOR 3 **3** an organism, usu a photosynthetic green plant, that can synthesize organic matter from inorganic materials and that often serves as food for other organisms – compare CONSUMER

product *n* **1** the result of the multiplying together of 2 or more numbers or expressions **2** sthg produced by a natural or artificial process; *specif* a result of a combination of incidental causes or conditions ⟨*a typical ~ of an arts education*⟩ **3** a salable or marketable commodity ⟨*tourism should be regarded as a ~*⟩

production *n* **1a** sthg produced; a product **b(1)** a literary or artistic work **(2)** a work presented on the stage or screen or over the air **2a** the act or process of producing **b** the creation of utility; *esp* the making of goods available for human wants **3** total output, esp of a commodity or an industry – **productional** *adj*

production line LINE 5h

productive *adj* **1** having the quality or power of producing, esp in abundance ⟨*~ fishing waters*⟩ **2** effective in bringing about; being the cause of **3a** yielding or furnishing results or benefits ⟨*a ~ programme of education*⟩ **b** yielding or devoted to the satisfaction of wants or the creation of utilities – **productively** *adv*, **productiveness** *n*, **productivity** *n*

proem *n* **1** a preface or introduction, esp to a book or speech **2** a prelude – **proemial** *adj*

prof *n* a professor – slang

profanation *n* (a) profaning

¹**profane** *vt* **1** to treat (sthg sacred) with abuse, irreverence, or contempt; desecrate **2** to debase by an unworthy or improper use – **profaner** *n*

²**profane** *adj* **1** not concerned with religion or religious purposes **2** debasing or defiling what is holy; irreverent **3a** not among the initiated **b** not possessing esoteric or expert knowledge – **profanely** *adv*, **profaneness** *n*

profanity *n* **1a** being profane **b** (the use of) profane language **2** a profane utterance

profess *vt* **1** to receive formally into a religious community **2a** to declare or admit openly or freely; affirm **b** to declare falsely; pretend **3** to confess one's faith in or allegiance to **4** to be a professor of (an academic discipline) *~ vi* to make a profession or avowal

professed *adj* **1** openly and freely admitted or declared ⟨*a ~ atheist*⟩ **2** professing to be qualified ⟨*a ~ solicitor*⟩ **3** pretended, feigned ⟨*~ misery*⟩ – **professedly** *adv*

profession *n* **1** the act of taking the vows of a religious community **2** an act of openly declaring or claiming a faith, opinion, etc; a protestation **3** an avowed religious faith **4a** a calling requiring specialized knowledge and often long and intensive academic preparation **b** a principal calling, vocation, or employment **c** *sing or pl in constr* the whole body of people engaged in a particular calling

¹**professional** *adj* **1a** (characteristic) of a profession **b** engaged in 1 of the learned professions **c(1)** characterized by or conforming to the technical or ethical standards of a profession ⟨*~ conduct*⟩ **(2)** characterized by conscientious workmanship ⟨*a sound ~ novel*⟩ ⟨*did a really ~ job on the garden*⟩ **2a** engaging for gain or livelihood in an activity or field of endeavour often engaged in by amateurs **b** engaged in by professionals ⟨*~ football*⟩ **3** following a line of conduct as though it were a profession ⟨*a ~ agitator*⟩ – derog **4** *of a breaking of rules, esp in sport* intentional – euph – **professionalize** *vt*, **professionally** *adv*

²**professional** *n* **1** one who engages in a pursuit or activity professionally **2** one with sufficient experience or skill in an occupation or activity to resemble a professional ⟨*a real ~ when it comes to mending cars*⟩ – infml

professionalism *n* **1** the esp high and consistent conduct, aims, or qualities that characterize a profession or a professional person **2** the following for gain or livelihood of an activity often engaged in by amateurs

professor *n* **1** sby who professes or declares sthg (e g a faith or opinion) **2a** a staff member of the highest academic rank at a university; *esp* the head of a university department **b** sby who teaches or professes special knowledge of an art, sport, or occupation requiring skill **c** *NAm* a teacher at a university, college, or sometimes secondary school – **professorship** *n*, **professorate** *n*, **professorial** *adj*

proffer *vt* to present for acceptance; tender

proficient *adj* well advanced or expert in an art, skill, branch of knowledge, etc – **proficiency** *n*, **proficient** *n*, **proficiently** *adv*

¹**profile** *n* **1** a side view, esp of the human face **2** an outline seen or represented in sharp relief; a contour **3** a side or sectional elevation: e g **a** a drawing showing a vertical section of the ground **b** a vertical section of a soil from the ground surface to the underlying material **4** a concise written or spoken biographical sketch

²**profile** *vt* **1** to represent in profile or by a profile; produce a profile of (e g by drawing or writing) **2** to shape the outline of by passing a cutter round – **profiler** *n*

¹**profit** *n* **1** a valuable return; a gain **2** the excess of returns over expenditure **3** compensation for the assumption of risk in business enterprise, as distinguished from wages or rent – **profitless** *adj*

²**profit** *vi* to derive benefit; gain – usu + *from* or *by* ⟨*~ ed greatly from these lessons*⟩ *~ vt* to be of service to; benefit ⟨*it will not ~ you to start an argument*⟩

profitable *adj* affording financial or other gains or profits – **profitableness** *n*, **profitably** *adv*, **profitability** *n*

profiteer *n* one who makes an unreasonable profit, esp on the sale of scarce and essential goods – **profiteer** *vi*

profit sharing *n* a system or process under which employees receive a part of the profits of an industrial or commercial enterprise

¹**profligate** *adj* **1** utterly dissolute; immoral **2** wildly extravagant; prodigal – **profligacy** *n*, **profligately** *adv*

²**profligate** *n* a person given to wildly extravagant and usu grossly self-indulgent expenditure

profound *adj* **1a** having intellectual depth and insight **b** difficult to fathom or understand **2a** extending far below the surface **b** coming from, reaching to, or situated at a depth; deep-seated ⟨*a ~ sigh*⟩ **3a** characterized by intensity of feeling or quality **b** all encompassing; complete ⟨*~ sleep*⟩ – **profoundly** *adv*, **profoundness** *n*

profundity *n* **1a** intellectual depth **b** sthg profound or abstruse **2** being profound or deep

profuse *adj* **1** liberal, extravagant ⟨*~ in their thanks*⟩ **2** greatly abundant; bountiful ⟨*a ~ harvest*⟩ – **profusely** *adv*, **profuseness** *n*

profusion *n* **1** being profuse **2** a large or lavish amount

progenitor *n* **1a** a direct ancestor; a forefather **b** a biologically ancestral form **2** a precursor, originator

progeny *n* **1** *sing or pl in constr* **a** descendants, children **b** offspring of animals or plants **2** an outcome, product – *fml*

progesterone *n* a steroid progestational hormone

prognathous *adj* having the jaws projecting beyond the upper part of the face

prognosis *n, pl* **prognoses 1** the prospect of recovery as anticipated from the usual course of disease or peculiarities of a particular case **2** a forecast, prognostication – *fml*

prognostic *n* **1** sthg that foretells; a portent **2** prognostication, prophecy *USE* fml – **prognostic** *adj*

prognosticate *vt* **1** to foretell from signs or symptoms; predict **2** to indicate in advance; presage *USE* fml – **prognosticator** *n*, **prognosticative** *adj*, **prognostication** *n*

¹**program** *n* **1a** a plan for the programming of a mechanism (e g a computer) **b** a sequence of coded instructions that can be inserted into a mechanism (e g a computer) or that is part of an organism **2** *chiefly NAm* a programme

²**program** *vt* **-mm-** (*NAm* **-mm-, -m-**) **1** to work out a sequence of operations to be performed by (a computer or similar mechanism); provide with a program **2** *chiefly NAm* to programme – **programmable** *adj*, **programmability** *n*

¹**programme**, *NAm chiefly* **program** *n* **1a** a brief usu printed (pamphlet containing a) list of the features to be presented, the people participating, etc (e g in a public performance or entertainment) **b** the performance of a programme **c** a radio or television broadcast characterized by some feature (e g a presenter, a purpose, or a theme) giving it coherence and continuity **2** a systematic plan of action ⟨*a rehousing ~*⟩ **3** a curriculum **4** a prospectus, syllabus **5** matter for programmed instruction

²**programme**, *NAm chiefly* **program** *vt* **1a** to arrange or provide a programme of or for **b** to enter in a programme **2** to cause to conform to a pattern (e g of thought or behaviour); condition ⟨*our visions of marriage have been ~d by Hollywood*⟩ – **programmable** *adj*, **programming** *n*, **programmability** *n*

programme music *n* music intended to suggest a sequence of images or incidents

programmer, *NAm also* **programer** *n* **1** a person or device that prepares and tests programs for mechanisms **2** a person or device that programs a mechanism (e g a computer) **3** one who prepares educational programmes

¹**progress** *n* **1a** a ceremonial journey; *esp* a monarch's tour of his/her dominions **b** an expedition, journey, or march **2** a forward or onward movement (e g to an objective or goal); an advance **3** gradual improvement; *esp* the progressive development of mankind – **in progress** occurring; going on

²**progress** *vi* **1** to move forwards; proceed **2** to develop to a higher, better, or more advanced stage ~ *vt* **1** to oversee

and ensure the satisfactory progress or running of (e g a project) ⟨*the editor must ~ articles from conception to publication*⟩ **2** to ascertain and attempt to bring forward the delivery or completion date of ⟨*~ these orders*⟩

progression *n* **1** a sequence of numbers in which each term is related to its predecessor by a uniform law **2a** progressing, advance **b** a continuous and connected series; a sequence **3** succession of musical notes or chords – **progressional** *adj*

¹**progressive** *adj* **1a** of or characterized by progress or progression **b** making use of or interested in new ideas, findings, or opportunities **c** of or being an educational theory marked by emphasis on the individual, informality, and self-expression **2** moving forwards continuously or in stages; advancing **3** increasing in extent or severity ⟨*a ~ disease*⟩ **4** of or constituting a verb form (e g *am working*) that expresses action in progress **5** increasing in rate as the base increases ⟨*a ~ tax*⟩ – **progressively** *adv*, **progressiveness** *n*, **progressivism** *n*, **progressivist** *n or adj*, **progressivistic** *adj*

²**progressive** *n* **1** sby or sthg progressive **2** sby believing in moderate political change, esp social improvement; *esp, cap* a member of a political party that advocates these beliefs

prohibit *vt* **1** to forbid by authority **2a** to prevent from doing sthg **b** to preclude

prohibition *n* **1** the act of prohibiting by authority **2** an order to restrain or stop **3** *often cap* the forbidding by law of the manufacture and sale of alcohol **4** a judicial writ prohibiting a lower court from proceeding in a case beyond its jurisdiction – **prohibitionist** *n*

prohibitive, **prohibitory** *adj* **1** tending to prohibit or restrain **2** tending to preclude the use or acquisition of sthg ⟨*the running expenses seemed ~*⟩ – **prohibitively** *adv*, **prohibitiveness** *n*

¹**project** *n* **1** a specific plan or design; a scheme **2** a planned undertaking: e g **a** a definitely formulated piece of research **b** a large undertaking, esp a public works scheme **c** a task or problem engaged in usu by a group of pupils, esp to supplement and apply classroom studies

²**project** *vt* **1a** to devise in the mind; design **b** to plan, figure, or estimate for the future **2** to throw forwards or upwards, esp by mechanical means **3** to present or transport in imagination ⟨*a book that tries to ~ how the world will look in 2100*⟩ **4** to cause to protrude **5** to cause (light or an image) to fall into space or on a surface **6** to reproduce (e g a point, line, or area) on a surface by motion in a prescribed direction **7a** to cause (one's voice) to be heard at a distance **b** to communicate vividly, esp to an audience **c** to present or express (oneself) in a manner that wins approval ⟨*must learn to ~ yourself better if you want the job*⟩ **8** to attribute (sthg in one's own mind) to a person, group, or object ⟨*a nation is an entity on which one can ~ many of the worst of one's instincts* – *TLS*⟩ ~ *vi* **1** to jut out; protrude **2** to attribute sthg in one's own mind to a person, group, or object – **projectable** *adj*

¹**projectile** *n* **1** a body projected by external force and continuing in motion by its own inertia; *esp* a missile (e g a bullet, shell, or grenade) fired from a weapon **2** a self-propelling weapon (e g a rocket)

²**projectile** *adj* **1** projecting or impelling **2** capable of being thrust forwards

projection *n* **1a** a systematic representation on a flat surface of latitude and longitude from the curved surface of the earth, celestial sphere, etc **b** (a graphic reproduction formed by) the process of reproducing a spatial object on a surface by projecting its points **2** the act of throwing or shooting forward; ejection **3a** a jutting out **b** a part that juts out **4** the act of perceiving a subjective mental image as objective **5** the attribution of one's own ideas, feelings, or attitudes to other people or to objects, esp as a defence against feelings of guilt or inadequacy **6** the display of films or slides by projecting an image from them onto a screen **7** an estimate of future possibilities based on a current trend – **projectional** *adj*

projectionist *n* the operator of a film projector or television equipment

projector *n* an apparatus for projecting films or pictures onto a surface

prolapse *n* the falling down or slipping of a body part (e g the uterus) from its usual position or relations – **prolapse** *vi*

prole *n or adj* (a) proletarian – derog

prolegomenon *n, pl* **prolegomena** an introductory section, esp to a learned work – **prolegomenous** *adj*

proletarian *n or adj* (a member) of the proletariat – **proletarianize** *vt*, **proletarianization** *n*

proletariat *n sing or pl in constr* **1** the lowest class of a community **2** WORKING CLASS; *esp* those workers who lack their own means of production and hence sell their labour to live

¹**proliferate** *vi* to grow or increase (as if) by rapid production of new parts, cells, buds, etc – **proliferative** *adj*, **proliferatively** *adv*, **proliferation** *n*

²**proliferate** *adj* increased in number or quantity

prolific *adj* **1** producing young or fruit (freely) **2** marked by abundant inventiveness or productivity ⟨*a ~ writer*⟩ – **prolificacy** *n*, **prolifically** *adv*, **prolificness** *n*, **prolificity** *n*

prolix *adj* **1** unduly prolonged or repetitious ⟨*a ~ speech*⟩ **2** given to verbosity in speaking or writing; long-winded – **prolixity** *n*, **prolixly** *adv*

prologue, NAm also **prolog** *n* **1** the preface or introduction to a literary work **2** (the actor delivering) a speech, often in verse, addressed to the audience at the beginning of a play **3** an introductory or preceding event or development

prolong *vt* **1** to lengthen in time; continue **2** to lengthen in space ⟨*to ~ a line*⟩ – **prolonger** *n*, **prolongation** *n*

prom *n* **1** PROMENADE CONCERT **2** *Br* PROMENADE 2

¹**promenade** *n* **1** a leisurely stroll or ride taken for pleasure, usu in a public place and often as a social custom **2** a place for strolling; *esp, Br* a paved walk along the seafront at a resort

²**promenade** *vi* to take or go on a promenade ~*vt* **1** to walk about in or on **2** to display (as if) by promenading around ⟨*~d his new bicycle in front of his friends*⟩

promenade concert *n* a concert at which some of the audience stand or can walk about

promenade deck *n* an upper deck or an area on a deck of a passenger ship where passengers may stroll

promenader *n* sby attending a promenade concert

prominence *n* **1** being prominent or conspicuous **2** sthg prominent; a projection ⟨*a rocky ~*⟩ **3** a large mass of gas arising from the lower solar atmosphere

prominent *adj* **1** projecting beyond a surface or line; protuberant **2a** readily noticeable; conspicuous **b** widely and popularly known; leading – **prominently** *adv*

promiscuity *n* **1** a miscellaneous mixture or mingling of people or things **2** promiscuous sexual behaviour

promiscuous *adj* **1** composed of a mixture of people or things **2** not restricted to 1 class or person; indiscriminate; *esp* not restricted to 1 sexual partner **3** casual, irregular ⟨*~ eating habits*⟩ – **promiscuously** *adv*,· **promiscuousness** *n*

¹**promise** *n* **1a** a declaration that one will or refrain from doing sthg specified **b** a legally binding declaration

2 grounds for expectation usu of success, improvement, or excellence ⟨*show ~*⟩ **3** sthg promised

²**promise** *vt* **1** to pledge oneself to do, bring about, or provide (sthg for) ⟨*~ aid*⟩ ⟨*but you ~d me*⟩ **2** to assure ⟨*it can be done, I ~ you*⟩ **3** to betroth **4** to suggest beforehand; indicate ⟨*dark clouds ~ rain*⟩ ~*vi* **1** to make a promise **2** to give grounds for expectation, esp of sthg good

promised land *n* a place or condition believed to promise final satisfaction or realization of hopes

promising *adj* full of promise; likely to succeed or to yield good results – **promisingly** *adv*

promissory note *n* a written promise to pay, either on demand or at a fixed or determinable future time, a sum of money to a specified individual or to the bearer

promontory *n* **1** HEADLAND 2 **2** a bodily prominence

promote *vt* **1a** to advance in station, rank, or honour; raise **b** to change (a pawn) into a more valuable piece in chess by moving to the 8th rank **c** to assign to a higher division of a sporting competition (e g a football league) **2a** to contribute to the growth or prosperity of; further ⟨*~ international understanding*⟩ **b** to help bring (e g an enterprise) into being; launch **c** to present (e g merchandise) for public acceptance through advertising and publicity – **promoter** *n*, **promotive** *adj*

promotion *n* **1** the act or fact of being raised in position or rank; preferment **2a** the act of furthering the growth or development of sthg, esp sales or public awareness **b** sthg (e g a price reduction or free sample) intended to promote esp sales of merchandise – **promotional** *adj*

¹**prompt** *vt* **1** to move to action; incite ⟨*curiosity ~ed him to ask the question*⟩ **2** to assist (sby acting or reciting) by saying the next words of sthg forgotten or imperfectly learnt **3** to serve as the inciting cause of; urge ⟨*~s serious anxiety about unemployment*⟩ – **prompter** *n*

²**prompt** *adj* of or for prompting actors

³**prompt** *adj* **1a** ready and quick to act as occasion demands **b** PUNCTUAL 2 **2** performed readily or immediately ⟨*~ assistance*⟩ – **promptly** *adv*, **promptness** *n*

⁴**prompt** *n* **1** the act or an instance of prompting; a reminder **2** (the contract fixing) a limit of time given for payment of an account for goods purchased

promulgate *vt* to make known by open declaration; proclaim – fml – **promulgator** *n*, **promulgation** *n*

prone *adj* **1** having a tendency or inclination; disposed *to* **2** having the front or ventral surface downwards; prostrate – **prone** *adv*, **pronely** *adv*, **proneness** *n*

¹**prong** *n* **1** any of the slender sharp-pointed parts of a fork **2** a subdivision of an argument, attacking force, etc

²**prong** *vt* to stab, pierce, or break up (as if) with a prong

pronged *adj* having or divided into prongs; esp having more than 1 attacking force, each coming from a different direction – usu in combination ⟨*a 3-pronged attack*⟩

pronominal *adj* of, resembling, or constituting a pronoun – **pronominally** *adv*

pronoun *n* a word used as a substitute for a noun or noun equivalent and referring to a previously named or understood person or thing

pronounce *vt* **1** to declare officially or ceremoniously ⟨*the priest ~d them man and wife*⟩ **2** to declare authoritatively or as an opinion ⟨*doctors ~d him fit to resume duties*⟩ **3** to utter the sounds of; esp to say correctly ~*vi* **1** to pass judgment; declare one's opinion definitely or authoritatively – often + *on* or *upon* **2** to produce speech sounds ⟨*she ~s abominably*⟩ – **pronounceable** *adj*, **pronouncer** *n*

pronounced *adj* strongly marked; decided – **pronouncedly** *adv*

pronouncement *n* **1** a usu formal declaration of opinion **2** an authoritative announcement

pronto *adv* without delay; quickly – *infml*

pronunciamento *n, pl* **pronunciamentos, pronunciamentoes** a declaration; *esp* one made by the leaders of a revolt announcing a change of government

pronunciation *n* the act or manner of pronouncing sthg – **pronunciational** *adj*

¹**proof** *n* **1** the cogency of evidence that compels acceptance of a truth or a fact **2** an act, effort, or operation designed to establish or discover a fact or the truth; a test **3** legal evidence **4a** an impression (e g from type) taken for examination or correction **b** a proof impression of an engraving, lithograph, etc **c** a test photographic print **5** a test of the quality of an article or substance **6** the alcoholic content of a beverage compared with the standard for proof spirit

²**proof** *adj* **1** designed for or successful in resisting or repelling; impervious – often in combination ⟨*waterproof*⟩ ⟨*sound*proof⟩ **2** used in proving or testing or as a standard of comparison **3** of standard strength or quality or alcoholic content

³**proof** *vt* **1** to make or take a proof of **2** to give a resistant quality to; make (sthg) proof *against* – **proofer** *n*

proofread *vt* to read and mark corrections on (a proof) – **proofreader** *n*

proof spirit *n* a mixture of alcohol and water containing a standard amount of alcohol, in Britain 57.1% by volume

¹**prop** *n* **1** a rigid usu auxiliary vertical support (e g a pole) ⟨*pit* ~⟩ **2** a source of strength or support ⟨*his son was his chief* ~ *in his old age*⟩ **3** PROP FORWARD

²**prop** *vt* -**pp**- **1** to support by placing sthg under or against **2** to support by placing against sthg *USE* often + *up*; compare PROP UP

³**prop** *n* any article or object used in a play or film other than painted scenery or costumes

⁴**prop** *n* a propeller

propaganda *n* **1** *cap* a division of the Roman curia having jurisdiction over missionary territories and related institutions **2** (the usu organized spreading of) ideas, information, or rumour designed to promote or damage an institution, movement, person, etc

propagandize, -ise *vb* to subject to or carry on propaganda – **propagandism** *n*, **propagandist** *n or adj*, **propagandistic** *adj*, **propagandistically** *adv*

propagate *vt* **1** to reproduce or increase by sexual or asexual reproduction **2** to pass down (e g a characteristic) to offspring **3a** to cause to spread out and affect a greater number or area; disseminate **b** to publicize ⟨~ *the Gospel*⟩ **c** to transmit ~ *vi* **1** to multiply sexually or asexually **2** to increase, extend – **propagator** *n*, **propagable** *adj*, **propagative** *adj*

propagation *n* **1** an increase (e g of a type of organism) in numbers **2** the spreading of sthg (e g a belief) abroad or into new regions **3** an enlargement or extension (e g of a crack) in a solid body – **propagational** *adj*

propane *n* a hydrocarbon of the alkane series used as a fuel

propel *vt* -**ll**- **1** to drive forwards by means of a force that imparts motion **2** to urge on; motivate

propellant *also* **propellent** *n* sthg that propels: e g **a** a fuel for propelling projectiles **b** fuel plus oxidizer used by a rocket engine **c** a gas in a pressurized container for expelling the contents when the pressure is released

propeller *also* **propellor** *n* SCREW PROPELLER

propelling pencil *n, Br* a usu metal or plastic pencil whose lead can be extended by a screw device

propensity *n* a natural inclination or tendency – *fml*

¹**proper** *adj* **1** suitable, appropriate **2** appointed for the liturgy of a particular day **3** belonging to one; own **4** represented heraldically in natural colour **5** belonging characteristically *to* a species or individual; peculiar **6** being strictly so-called ⟨*the borough is not part of the city* ~⟩ **7a** strictly accurate; correct **b** strictly decorous; genteel ⟨*a very prim and* ~ *gentleman*⟩ **8** *chiefly Br* thorough, complete ⟨*I felt a* ~ *Charlie!*⟩ – **properness** *n*

²**proper** *n* the parts of the mass that vary according to the liturgical calendar

³**proper** *adv, chiefly dial* in a thorough manner; completely

proper fraction *n* a fraction in which the numerator is less or of lower degree than the denominator

properly *adv* **1** in a fit manner; suitably **2** strictly in accordance with fact; correctly ⟨~ *speaking*⟩ **3** *chiefly Br* to the full extent; completely

proper noun *n* a noun that designates a particular being or thing and is usu capitalized (e g *Janet, London*)

propertied *adj* possessing property, esp land

property *n* **1a** a quality, attribute, or power inherent in sthg **b** an attribute common to all members of a class **2a** sthg owned or possessed; *specif* a piece of real estate **b** ownership **c** sthg to which a person has a legal title **3** ³PROP – **propertyless** *adj*

prop forward *n* (the position of) either of the 2 players in rugby on either side of the hooker in the front row of the scrum

prophecy *n* **1** the function or vocation of a prophet; (the capacity to utter) an inspired declaration of divine will and purpose **2** a prediction of an event

prophesy *vt* **1** to utter (as if) by divine inspiration **2** to predict with assurance or on the basis of mystic knowledge ~ *vi* **1** to speak as if divinely inspired **2** to make a prediction – **prophesier** *n*

prophet, *fem* **prophetess** *n* **1** a person who utters divinely inspired revelations; *specif, often cap* the writer of any of the prophetic books of the Old Testament **2** one gifted with more than ordinary spiritual and moral insight **3** one who foretells future events; a predictor **4** a spokesman for a doctrine, movement, etc ⟨*a* ~ *of socialism*⟩

prophetic, prophetical *adj* **1** (characteristic) of a prophet or prophecy **2** foretelling events; predictive – **prophetically** *adv*

Prophets *n pl* the second part of the Jewish scriptures

prophylactic *adj* **1** guarding or protecting from or preventing disease **2** tending to prevent or ward off; preventive – *fml* – **prophylactic** *n*, **prophylactically** *adv*

prophylaxis *n, pl* **prophylaxes** measures designed to preserve health and prevent the spread of disease

propinquity *n* **1** nearness of blood; kinship **2** nearness in place or time; proximity *USE* fml

propitiate *vt* to gain or regain the favour or goodwill of; appease – **propitiator** *n*, **propitiable** *adj*, **propitiatory** *adj*, **propitiation** *n*

propitious *adj* **1** favourably disposed; benevolent **2** boding well; auspicious **3** tending to favour; opportune ⟨*a* ~ *moment for the revolt to break out*⟩ – **propitiously** *adv*, **propitiousness** *n*

propjet *n* a turboprop

proponent *n* one who argues in favour of sthg; an advocate

¹**proportion** *n* **1** the relation of one part to another or to the whole with respect to magnitude, quantity, or degree **2** harmonious relation of parts to each other or to the whole; balance **3** a statement of equality of 2 ratios (e g in 4/2 = 10/5) **4a** proper or equal share ⟨*each did his* ~

of the work⟩ **b** a quota, percentage **5** *pl* size, dimension

²**proportion** *vt* **1** to adjust (a part or thing) in proportion to other parts or things **2** to make the parts of harmonious or symmetrical

¹**proportional** *adj* **1a** proportionate – usu + *to* ⟨*a is ~ to* b⟩ **b** having the same or a constant ratio **2** regulated or determined in proportionate amount or degree *USE* (*1*) – **proportionally** *adv*, **proportionality** *n*

²**proportional** *n* a number or quantity in a proportion

proportional representation *n* an electoral system designed to represent in a legislative body each political group in proportion to its voting strength in the electorate

¹**proportionate** *adj* being in due proportion – **proportionately** *adv*

²**proportionate** *vt* to make proportionate; proportion

proposal *n* **1** an act of putting forward or stating sthg for consideration **2a** a proposed idea or plan of action; a suggestion **b** an offer of marriage **3** an application for insurance

propose *vi* **1** to form or put forward a plan or intention ⟨*man ~s, but God disposes*⟩ **2** to make an offer of marriage *~vt* **1a** to present for consideration or adoption ⟨*~d terms for peace*⟩ **b** to establish as an aim; intend ⟨*~d to spend the summer in study*⟩ **2a** to recommend to fill a place or vacancy; nominate **b** to nominate (oneself) for an insurance policy **c** to offer as a toast ⟨*~ the health of the bridesmaids*⟩ – **proposer** *n*

¹**proposition** *n* **1a** sthg offered for consideration or acceptance; *specif* a proposal of sexual intercourse **b** a formal mathematical statement to be proved **2** an expression, in language or signs, of sthg that can be either true or false **3** a project, situation, or individual requiring to be dealt with ⟨*the firm is not a paying ~*⟩ – **propositional** *adj*

²**proposition** *vt* to make a proposal to; *specif* to propose sexual intercourse to

propound *vt* to offer for discussion or consideration – fml – **propounder** *n*

¹**proprietary** *n* a body of proprietors

²**proprietary** *adj* **1** (characteristic) of a proprietor ⟨*~ rights*⟩ **2** made and marketed under a patent, trademark, etc ⟨*a ~ process*⟩ **3** privately owned and managed ⟨*a ~ clinic*⟩

proprietor, *fem* **proprietress** *n* **1** an owner **2** sby having an interest less than absolute right – **proprietorship** *n*, **proprietorial** *adj*

propriety *n* **1** the quality or state of being proper; fitness **2** the standard of what is socially or morally acceptable in conduct or speech, esp between the sexes; decorum **3** *pl* the conventions and manners of polite society *USE* fml

propulsion *n* **1** the action or process of propelling **2** sthg that propels

propulsive *adj* having power to or tending to propel

prop up *vt* to give nonmaterial (e g moral or financial) support to ⟨*government* propping up *ailing industries*⟩

propylene *n* a hydrocarbon of the alkene series used chiefly in organic synthesis

pro rata *adv* proportionately according to an exactly calculable factor – **pro rata** *adj*

prorogue *vt* to terminate a session of (e g a parliament) by royal prerogative *~vi* to suspend a legislative session – **prorogation** *n*

prosaic *adj* **1a** characteristic of prose as distinguished from poetry **1b** dull, unimaginative **2** belonging to the everyday world; commonplace – **prosaically** *adv*

proscenium *n* the stage of an ancient Greek or Roman theatre

proscribe *vt* **1a** to put outside the protection of the law **b** to outlaw, exile; *specif, in ancient Rome* to outlaw by publishing the name of (a person) **2** to condemn or forbid as harmful; prohibit – **proscriber** *n*

proscription *n* **1** proscribing or being proscribed **2** an imposed restraint or restriction; a prohibition – **proscriptive** *adj*, **proscriptively** *adv*

prose *n* **1a** ordinary nonmetrical language **b** a literary medium distinguished from poetry esp by its closer correspondence to the patterns of everyday speech **2** a commonplace quality or character; ordinariness – **prose** *adj*

prosecute *vt* **1a** to institute and pursue criminal proceedings against **b** to institute legal proceedings with reference to ⟨*~ a claim*⟩ **2** to follow through, pursue ⟨*determined to ~ the investigation*⟩ **3** CARRY OUT 1 *~vi* to institute and carry on a prosecution *USE* (*2&3*) fml

prosecution *n* **1** prosecuting; *specif* the formal institution of a criminal charge **2** *sing or pl in constr* the party by whom criminal proceedings are instituted or conducted

prosecutor *n* sby who institutes or conducts an official prosecution

¹**proselyte** *n* a new convert, esp to Judaism

²**proselyte** *vb, chiefly NAm* to proselytize

proselytize, -ise *vt* to convert (sby), esp to a new religion *~vi* to (try to) make converts, esp to a new religion – **proselytizer** *n*, **proselytization** *n*

prose poem *n* a work in prose that has some of the qualities of a poem – **prose poet** *n*

prosody *n* the study of versification and esp of metrical structure – **prosodist** *n*, **prosodic** *adj*

¹**prospect** *n* **1** an extensive view; a scene **2a** a mental picture of sthg to come ⟨*doesn't like the ~ of more examinations*⟩ **b** expectation, possibility ⟨*has a fine career in ~*⟩ **c** *pl* (1) financial and social expectations (2) chances, esp of success **3a** a place showing signs of containing a mineral deposit **b** a partly developed mine **c** the mineral yield of a tested sample of ore or gravel **4** a potential client, candidate, etc

²**prospect** *vb* to explore (an area), esp for mineral deposits – **prospector** *n*

prospective *adj* **1** likely to come about; expected **2** likely to be or become ⟨*a ~ mother*⟩ – **prospectively** *adv*

prospectus *n* a printed statement, brochure, etc describing an organization or enterprise and distributed to prospective buyers, investors, or participants

prosper *vi* to succeed, thrive; *specif* to achieve economic success *~vt* to cause to succeed or thrive ⟨*may the gods ~ our city*⟩

prosperity *n* the condition of being successful or thriving; esp economic well-being

prosperous *adj* marked by esp financial success – **prosperously** *adv*

¹**prostate, prostate gland** *n* a partly muscular, partly glandular body situated around the base of the male mammalian urethra that secretes a major constituent of the ejaculatory fluid

²**prostate** *also* **prostatic** *adj* of or being the prostate gland

prosthesis *n, pl* **prostheses** **1** an artificial device to replace a missing part of the body **2** prothesis

¹**prostitute** *vt* **1** to make a prostitute of **2** to devote to corrupt or unworthy purposes; debase ⟨*~ one's talents*⟩ – **prostitution** *n*

²**prostitute** *n* a person, esp a woman, who engages in sexual practices for money

¹**prostrate** *adj* **1** lying full-length face downwards, esp in

adoration or submission **2a** physically and emotionally weak; overcome ⟨~ *with grief*⟩ **b** physically exhausted **3** *of a plant* trailing on the ground

²**prostrate** *vt* **1** to throw or put into a prostrate position **2** to put (oneself) in a humble and submissive posture or state **3** to reduce to submission, helplessness, or exhaustion; overcome – **prostration** *n*

prosy *adj* dull, commonplace; *esp* tedious in speech or manner – **prosily** *adv*

prot-, proto- *comb form* **1** first in time; earliest; original ⟨proto*lithic*⟩ ⟨proto*type*⟩ **2** first-formed; primary ⟨proto*xylem*⟩ **3** *cap* of or constituting the recorded or assumed language that is ancestral to (a specified language or group of related languages or dialects) ⟨*Proto-Indo-European*⟩

protagonist *n* **1** one who takes the leading part in a drama, novel, or story **2** a leader or notable supporter of a cause

protean *adj* **1** readily assuming different shapes or roles **2** displaying great diversity or variety

protect *vt* **1** to cover or shield *from* injury or destruction; guard *against* **2** to shield or foster (a home industry) by a protective tariff – **protectant** *n*, **protective** *adj*, **protectively** *adv*, **protectiveness** *n*

protection *n* **1** protecting or being protected **2** sthg that protects **3** the shielding of the producers of a country from foreign competition by import tariffs **4a** immunity from threatened violence, often purchased under duress **b** money extorted by racketeers posing as a protective association **5** COVERAGE 3a

protectionist *n* an advocate of government economic protection – **protectionism** *n*, **protectionist** *adj*

protective custody *n* detention of sby (allegedly) for his/her own safety

protector, *fem* **protectress** *n* **1a** a guardian **b** a device used to prevent injury; a guard **2** *often cap* the executive head of the Commonwealth from 1653 to 1659 – **protectorship** *n*

protectorate *n* **1a** government by a protector **b** *often cap* the government of the Commonwealth from 1653 to 1659 **c** the rank or (period of) rule of a protector **2a** the relationship of one state over another dependent state which it partly controls but has not annexed **b** the dependent political unit in such a relationship

protégé, *fem* **protégée** *n* a person under the protection, guidance, or patronage of sby influential

protein *n* any of numerous genetically specified naturally occurring extremely complex combinations of amino acids linked by peptide bonds that are essential constituents of all living cells and are an essential part of the diet of animals and humans – **proteinaceous** *adj*

pro tem *adv* for the time being

¹**protest** *n* **1a** a sworn declaration that a note or bill has been duly presented and that payment has been refused **b** a formal declaration of dissent from an act of esp a legislature **c** a formal declaration of disapproval ⟨*reprieved in response to international* ~s⟩ **2** protesting; *esp* an organized public demonstration of disapproval **3** an objection or display of unwillingness ⟨*went to the dentist under* ~⟩

²**protest** *vt* **1** to make formal or solemn declaration or affirmation of **2** to execute or have executed a formal protest against (e g a bill or note) **3** *NAm* to make a formal protest against **4** *NAm* to remonstrate against ⟨*unwilling to* ~ *the cost of her ticket*⟩ ~ *vi* **1** to make a protestation **2** to enter a protest – **protester, protestor** *n*

protestant *n* **1** *cap* **a** any of a group who protested against an edict of the Diet of Spires in 1529 intended to suppress the Lutheran movement **b** a Christian who denies the universal authority of the pope and affirms the principles of the Reformation **2** one who makes or enters a protest – **Protestantism** *n*

Protestant *adj*, of Protestants, their churches, or their religion

protestation *n* **1** an act of protesting **2** a solemn declaration or avowal

proto- – see PROT-

protocol *n* **1** an original draft or record of a document or transaction **2** a preliminary memorandum often formulated and signed by diplomatic negotiators as a basis for a final treaty **3** a code of correct etiquette and precedence **4** *NAm* the plan of a scientific experiment or treatment

proton *n* an elementary particle that is identical with the nucleus of the hydrogen atom, that along with neutrons is a constituent of all other atomic nuclei, that carries a positive charge numerically equal to the charge of an electron, that has a mass of 1.672×10^{-27} kg, and that is classified as a baryon – **protonic** *adj*

protoplasm *n* **1** the organized complex of organic and inorganic substances (e g proteins and salts in solution) that constitutes the living nucleus, cytoplasm, plastids, and mitochondria of the cell **2** cytoplasm – **protoplasmic** *adj*

prototype *n* **1** an original model on which sthg is based; an archetype **2** sby or sthg that has the essential features of a later type ⟨*the battle chariot is the* ~ *of the modern tank*⟩ **3** sby or sthg that exemplifies the essential or typical features of a type ⟨*mathematics is the* ~ *of logical thinking*⟩ **4** a first full-scale and usu operational form of a new type or design of a construction (e g an aeroplane) – **prototypal** *adj*

protozoan *n* any of a phylum or subkingdom of minute single-celled animals which have varied structure and physiology and often complex life cycles – **protozoal** *adj*, **protozoan** *adj*, **protozoic** *adj*

protozoon *n, pl* **protozoa** a protozoan

protract *vt* **1** to prolong in time or space **2** to lay down the lines and angles of with scale and protractor **3** to extend forwards or outwards – **protraction** *n*, **protractive** *adj*

protractor *n* **1** a muscle that extends a body part **2** an instrument that is used for marking out or measuring angles in drawing

protrude *vb* to (cause to) jut out from the surrounding surface or place – **protrusion** *n*, **protrusive** *adj*

protuberant *adj* thrusting or projecting out from a surrounding or adjacent surface – **protuberance** *n*

proud *adj* **1a** having or displaying excessive self-esteem **b** much pleased; exultant **c** having proper self-respect **2a** stately, magnificent **b** giving reason for pride; glorious ⟨*the* ~est *moment of her life*⟩ **3** projecting slightly from a surrounding surface – **proudly** *adv*

prove *vb* **proved, proven** *vt* **1a** to test the quality of; try out ⟨*the exception* ~s *the rule*⟩ **b** to subject to a testing process **2a** to establish the truth or validity of by evidence or demonstration **b** to check the correctness of (e g an arithmetical operation) **3a** to verify the genuineness of; *specif* to obtain probate of **b** PROOF 1 **4** to allow (bread dough) to rise and become light before baking ~ *vi* **1** to turn out, esp after trial ⟨*the new drug* ~d *to be effective*⟩ **2** of bread dough to rise and become aerated through the action of yeast

provenance *n* an origin, source – used esp with reference to works of art or literature

Provençal *n* **1** a native or inhabitant of Provence **2** a Romance language of SE France – **Provençal** *adj*

provender n **1** dry food for domestic animals **2** food, provisions – humor

proverb n a brief popular epigram or maxim; an adage

proverbial adj **1** of or like a proverb **2** that has become a proverb or byword; commonly spoken of – **proverbially** adv

Proverbs n pl but sing in constr a collection of moral sayings forming a book of the Old Testament

provide vi **1** to take precautionary measures ⟨~d against future loss⟩ **2** to make a proviso or stipulation ⟨the regulations ~ for 2 directors⟩ **3** to supply what is needed for sustenance or support ⟨~s for a large family⟩ ~vt **1a** to furnish, equip with ⟨~ the children with new shoes⟩ **b** to supply, afford ⟨curtains ~ privacy⟩ **2** to stipulate

provided conj providing

providence n **1** cap God conceived as the power sustaining and guiding human destiny **2** being provident

provident adj making provision for the future, esp by saving – **providently** adv

providential adj of or determined (as if) by Providence; lucky – **providentially** adv

provider n one who provides for his/her family

providing conj on condition; if and only if ⟨may come ~ that you pay for yourself⟩

province n **1a** an administrative district of a country **b** pl all of a country except the metropolis – usu + the **2** a territorial unit of religious administration **3a** proper or appropriate function or scope; sphere **b** a field of knowledge or activity

¹provincial n **1** the head of a province of a Roman Catholic religious order **2** one living in or coming from a province **3a** a person with a narrow outlook **b** a person lacking polish or refinement

²provincial adj **1** of or coming from a province **2a** limited in outlook; narrow **b** lacking polish; unsophisticated – **provincialism** n, **provincialize** vt

proving ground n **1** a place designed for or used in scientific experimentation or testing; esp a place for testing vehicles **2** a place where sthg new is tried out

¹provision n **1a** providing **b** a measure taken beforehand; a preparation ⟨no ~ made for replacements⟩ **2** pl a stock of food or other necessary goods **3** a proviso, stipulation

²provision vt to supply with provisions

provisional adj serving for the time being; temporary; specif requiring later confirmation ⟨gave her ~ consent⟩ – **provisionally** adv

Provisional adj of or being the secret terrorist wing of the IRA – **Provisional** n

proviso n, pl provisos, provisoes **1** a clause that introduces a condition **2** a conditional stipulation

provocation n **1** an act of provoking; incitement **2** sthg that provokes or arouses

provocative adj serving or tending to provoke or arouse to indignation, sexual desire, etc – **provocatively** adv, **provocativeness** n

provoke vt **1** to incite to anger; incense **2a** to call forth; evoke **b** to stir up on purpose; induce ⟨always trying to ~ an argument⟩

provoking adj causing mild anger; annoying – **provokingly** adv

provost n **1** the head of a collegiate or cathedral chapter; specif one who is also the incumbent of a parish of which the cathedral is the church **2** the chief magistrate of a Scottish burgh **3** the head of certain colleges at Oxford, Cambridge, etc

provost marshal n an officer who supervises the military police of a command

prow n **1** the bow of a ship **2** a pointed projecting front part

prowess n **1** outstanding (military) valour and skill **2** outstanding ability

¹prowl vb to move about (in) or roam (over) in a stealthy or predatory manner – **prowler** n

²prowl n an act or instance of prowling

proximal adj, esp of an anatomical part next to or nearest the point of attachment or origin – **proximally** adv

proximate adj **1a** very near; close **b** forthcoming; imminent **2** next preceding or following; specif next in a chain of cause and effect USE fml – **proximately** adv, **proximateness** n

proximity n being close in space, time, or association; esp nearness – fml

proximo adj of or occurring in the next month after the present

proxy n **1** (the agency, function, or office of) a deputy authorized to act as a substitute for another ⟨marriage by ~⟩ **2** (a document giving) authority to act or vote for another – **proxy** adj

prude n one who shows or affects extreme modesty or propriety, esp in sexual matters

prudence n **1** discretion or shrewdness in the management of affairs **2** skill and good judgment in the use of resources; frugality **3** caution or circumspection with regard to danger or risk ⟨conservative from ~ – T S Eliot⟩

prudent adj characterized by, arising from, or showing prudence – **prudently** adv

prudential adj **1** of or proceeding from prudence **2** exercising prudence, esp in business matters – **prudentially** adv

prudery n **1** the quality of being a prude **2** a prudish act or remark

prudish adj marked by prudery; priggish – **prudishly** adv, **prudishness** n

¹prune n a plum dried or capable of drying without fermentation

²prune vt **1** to cut off the dead or unwanted parts of (a usu woody plant or shrub) **2a** to reduce by eliminating superfluous matter ⟨~d the text⟩ **b** to remove as superfluous ⟨~ away all ornamentation⟩ ~vi to cut away what is unwanted

prurient adj inclined to, having, or arousing an excessive or unhealthy interest in sexual matters – **prurience** n

pruritus n ITCH 1

Prussian blue n **1** any of numerous blue iron pigments **2** a dark blue hydrated salt of iron and cyanide used as a test for ferric iron **3** a strong greenish blue colour

prussic acid n HYDROCYANIC ACID

¹pry vi **1** to inquire in an overinquisitive or impertinent manner into **2** to look closely or inquisitively at sby's possessions, actions, etc ⟨~ing neighbours⟩

²pry vt, chiefly NAm ⁵PRIZE

psalm n, often cap any of the sacred songs attributed to King David and collected in the Book of Psalms

psalmody n **1** (the practice or art of) singing psalms in worship **2** a collection of psalms

Psalms n pl but sing in constr a collection of 150 sacred poems forming a book of the Old Testament

Psalter n a book containing a collection of Psalms for liturgical or devotional use

psaltery also **psaltry** n an ancient stringed musical instrument similar to the dulcimer but plucked

psephology n the scientific study of elections – **psephologist** n, **psephological** adj

pseud n, chiefly Br an intellectually or socially pretentious person – infml – **pseud** adj, **pseudy** adj

pseudo adj apparent rather than actual; spurious ⟨distinction between true and ~ freedom⟩

pseudo-, pseud- comb form false; sham; spurious ⟨pseudoscience⟩ ⟨pseudaxis⟩ ⟨pseudo-intellectual⟩

pseudonym n a fictitious name; esp one used by an author

pseudonymous adj bearing, using, or being a pseudonym – **pseudonymously** adv

pseudopodium n, pl **pseudopodia** a temporary protrusion of a cell (e g an amoeba) that serves to take in food, move the cell, etc

pshaw interj – used to express irritation, disapproval, or disbelief

psittacosis n a severe infectious disease of birds caused by a rickettsia that causes a serious pneumonia when transmitted to human beings – **psittacotic** adj

psoriasis n a chronic skin condition characterized by distinct red patches covered by white scales – **psoriatic** adj or n

psych, psyche vt 1 NAm to psychoanalyse 2 chiefly NAm a to anticipate correctly the intentions or actions of; outguess b to analyse or work out (e g a problem or course of action) ⟨I ~ ed it all out by myself⟩ 3 chiefly NAm a to make psychologically uneasy; intimidate – often + out b to make (oneself) psychologically ready for some action, test, etc – usu + up ⟨~ ed herself up for the race⟩ USE infml

psych-, psycho- comb form 1 psyche ⟨psychognosis⟩ 2a mind; mental processes ⟨psychoactive⟩ ⟨psychology⟩ b using psychoanalytical methods ⟨psychotherapy⟩ c brain ⟨psychosurgery⟩ d mental and ⟨psychosomatic⟩

psyche n 1 the soul, self 2 the mind

psychedelic adj 1a of drugs capable of producing altered states of consciousness that involve changed mental and sensory awareness, hallucinations, etc b produced by or associated with the use of psychedelic drugs 2a imitating or reproducing effects (e g distorted or bizarre images or sounds) resembling those produced by psychedelic drugs ⟨a ~ light show⟩ b of colours fluorescent

psychiatry n a branch of medicine that deals with mental, emotional, or behavioural disorders – **psychiatrist** n, **psychiatric** adj, **psychiatrically** adv

¹**psychic** also **psychical** adj 1 of or originating in the psyche 2 lying outside the sphere of physical science or knowledge 3 of a person sensitive to nonphysical or supernatural forces and influences – **psychically** adv

²**psychic** n 1 a psychic person 2 MEDIUM 2e

psycho n, pl **psychos** a psychopath, psychotic – infml – **psycho** adj

psychoanalyse vt to treat by means of psychoanalysis

psychoanalysis n a method of analysing unconscious mental processes and treating mental disorders, esp by allowing the patient to talk freely about early childhood experiences, dreams, etc – **psychoanalyst** n, **psychoanalytic, psychoanalytical** adj

psychokinesis n apparent movement in physical objects produced by the power of the mind without physical contact – **psychokinetic** adj

psychological adj 1a of psychology b mental 2 directed towards or intended to affect the will or mind ⟨~ warfare⟩ – **psychologically** adv

psychology n 1 the science or study of mind and behaviour 2 the mental or behavioural characteristics of an individual or group – **psychologist** n

psychopath n a person suffering from a severe emotional and behavioural disorder characterized by antisocial tendencies and usu the pursuit of immediate gratification through often violent acts; broadly a dangerously violent mentally ill person – **psychopathic** adj, **psychopathy** n

psychosis n, pl **psychoses** severe mental derangement (e g schizophrenia) that results in the impairment or loss of contact with reality – **psychotic** adj or n, **psychotically** adv

psychosomatic adj of or resulting from the interaction of psychological and somatic factors, esp the production of physical symptoms by mental processes ⟨~ medicine⟩

psychotherapy n treatment by psychological methods for mental, emotional, or psychosomatic disorders – **psychotherapist** n

ptarmigan n, pl **ptarmigans**, esp collectively **ptarmigan** any of various grouse of northern regions whose plumage turns white in winter

pterodactyl n any of an order of extinct flying reptiles without feathers

Ptolemaic system n the system of planetary motions according to which the sun, moon, and planets revolve round a stationary earth – **Ptolemaist** n

ptomaine n any of various often very poisonous organic compounds formed by the action of putrefactive bacteria on nitrogen-containing matter

pub n an establishment where alcoholic beverages are sold and consumed; esp, chiefly Br PUBLIC HOUSE

pub crawl n, chiefly Br a visit to a series of pubs, usu involving at least 1 drink at each – infml

puberty n 1 the condition of being or the period of becoming capable of reproducing sexually 2 the age at which puberty occurs – **pubertal** adj

pubic adj of or situated in or near the region of the pubis or the pubic hair

¹**public** adj 1a of or affecting all the people or the whole area of a nation or state ⟨~ law⟩ b of or being in the service of the community ⟨~ affairs⟩ 2 general, popular ⟨increasing ~ awareness⟩ 3 of national or community concerns as opposed to private affairs; social 4a accessible to or shared by all members of the community ⟨a ~ park⟩ b capitalized in shares that can be freely traded on the open market ⟨the company has gone ~⟩ 5a exposed to general view; open ⟨a ~ quarrel⟩ b well-known, prominent ⟨~ figures⟩

²**public** n 1 the people as a whole; the populace 2 a group or section of people having common interests or characteristics ⟨the motoring ~⟩ – **in public** in the presence, sight, or hearing of strangers

public-address system n an apparatus including a microphone and loudspeakers used to address a large audience

publican n 1 a Jewish tax collector for the ancient Romans 2 chiefly Br the licensee of a public house

publication n 1 the act or process of publishing 2 a published work

public bar n, Br a plainly furnished and often relatively cheap bar in a public house

public company n a company whose shares are offered to the general public

public convenience n, Br public toilet facilities provided by local government

public corporation n a corporation responsible for running a nationalized service or industry

public house n, chiefly Br an establishment where alcoholic beverages are sold to be drunk on the premises

publicist n an expert or commentator on public affairs

publicity n 1a information with news value issued as a means of gaining public attention or support b paid advertising c the dissemination of information or promotional material 2 public attention or acclaim 3 being public ⟨the ~ of an open court⟩ – fml

publicize, -ise *vt* to give publicity to

publicly *adv* **1** in a manner observable by or in a place accessible to the public; openly **2a** by the people generally; communally **b** by a government ⟨~ *provided medical care*⟩

public prosecutor *n* an official who conducts criminal prosecutions on behalf of the state

public relations *n pl but usu sing in constr* the business of inducing the public to have understanding for and goodwill towards a person, organization, or institution; *also* the degree of understanding and goodwill achieved

public school *n* **1** an endowed independent usu single-sex school in Britain, typically a large boarding school preparing pupils for higher education **2** *NAm & Scot* STATE SCHOOL

public servant *n* a government employee

public-spirited *adj* motivated by concern for the general welfare

public works *n pl* schools, roads, etc constructed for public use, esp by the government

publish *vt* **1a** to make generally known **b** to announce publicly **2a** to produce or release for publication; *specif* to print **b** to issue the work of (an author) ~ *vi* to put out an edition (e g of a newspaper) – **publishing** *n*

publisher *n* a person or company whose business is publishing

puce *adj or n* brownish purple

¹**puck** *n* a mischievous sprite

²**puck** *n* a vulcanized rubber disc used in ice hockey

¹**pucker** *vb* to (cause to) become wrinkled or irregularly creased

²**pucker** *n* a crease or wrinkle in a normally even surface

puckish *adj* impish, whimsical

pud *n, Br* a pudding – *infml*

pudding *n* **1** BLACK PUDDING **2** WHITE PUDDING **3a** any of various sweet or savoury dishes of a soft to spongy or fairly firm consistency that are made from rice, tapioca, flour, etc and are cooked by boiling, steaming, or baking ⟨*sponge* ~⟩ ⟨*steak and kidney* ~⟩ **b** dessert **4** a small podgy person – *infml*

pudding stone *n* (a) conglomerate rock

¹**puddle** *n* **1** a small pool of liquid; *esp* one of usu muddy rainwater **2** a mixture (e g of clay, sand, and gravel) used as a waterproof covering

²**puddle** *vt* **puddling 1** to work (a wet mixture of earth or concrete) into a dense impervious mass **2** to subject (iron) to puddling – **puddler** *n*

pudendum *n, pl* **pudenda** the external genital organs of a (female) human being – usu pl with sing. meaning – **pudendal** *adj*

pudgy *adj* podgy – **pudginess** *n*

pueblo *n, pl* **pueblos** the communal dwelling of an American Indian village of Arizona or New Mexico, consisting of adjoining flat-roofed stone or adobe houses

puerile *adj* **1** juvenile **2** not befitting an adult; childish ⟨~ *remarks*⟩ – **puerilism** *n*, **puerility** *n*

puerperal *adj* of or occurring during (the period immediately following) childbirth

¹**puff** *vi* **1a**(1) to blow in short gusts (2) to exhale or blow forcibly ⟨~ed *into a blowpipe to shape the molten glass*⟩ **b** to breathe hard and quickly; pant **c** to emit small whiffs or clouds (e g of smoke or steam) **2** to become distended; swell – usu + *up* ~ *vt* **1a** to emit, propel, or blow (as if) by puffs; waft **b** to draw on (a pipe, cigarette, etc) with intermittent exhalations of smoke **2a** to distend (as if) with air or gas; inflate **b** to make proud or conceited ⟨*extravagant praise* ~ed *up his ego*⟩ **c** to praise extravagantly and usu exaggeratedly; *also* to advertise by this means **3** to make (one's way) emitting puffs of breath or smoke ⟨~ed *her way up the hill*⟩ USE (2a&b) usu + *up*

²**puff** *n* **1a** an act or instance of puffing **b** a slight explosive sound accompanying a puff **c** a small cloud (e g of smoke) emitted in a puff **d** DRAW 1a **2** a light round hollow pastry made of puff paste **3** a highly favourable notice or review, esp one that publicizes sthg or sby **4** *chiefly Br* BREATH 2a ⟨*sat down until she got her* ~ *back*⟩ – *infml* **5** *NAm* a quilted bed cover; an eiderdown **6** a poof – *slang* – **puffy** *adj*, **puffiness** *n*

puff adder *n* a large venomous African viper that inflates its body and hisses loudly when disturbed

puffball *n* any of various spherical and often edible fungi

puffed *adj, chiefly Br* out of breath – *infml*

puffer *n* a globefish

puffin *n* any of several seabirds that have a short neck and a deep grooved multicoloured bill

puff out *vt* **1** to extinguish by blowing **2** to cause to enlarge, esp by filling or inflating with air ~ *vi* to be enlarged with air

puff pastry *n* a light flaky pastry made with a rich dough containing a large quantity of butter

¹**pug** *n* a small sturdy compact dog with a tightly curled tail and broad wrinkled face

²**pug** *vt* **-gg-** to work and mix (e g clay) when wet

³**pug** *n* a footprint, esp of a wild mammal

pugilism *n* boxing – *fml* – **pugilist** *n*, **pugilistic** *adj*

pugnacious *adj* inclined to fight or quarrel; belligerent – **pugnaciousness** *n*, **pugnacity** *n*

pug nose *n* a nose having a slightly concave bridge and flattened nostrils – **pug-nosed** *adj*

puissance *n* **1** a showjumping competition which tests the horse's power to jump high obstacles **2** strength, power – *fml or poetic* – **puissant** *adj*

puke *vb* to vomit – *slang* – **puke** *n*

pukka *adj* **1** genuine, authentic; *also* first-class **2** *chiefly Br* stiffly formal or proper

pulchritude *n* physical beauty – *fml* – **pulchritudinous** *adj*

pule *vi* to whine, whimper

¹**pull** *vt* **1a** to draw out from the skin ⟨~ *feathers from a cock's tail*⟩ **b** to pick from a plant or pluck by the roots ⟨~ *flowers*⟩ ⟨~ *turnips*⟩ **c** to extract ⟨~ *a tooth*⟩ **2a** to exert force upon so as to (tend to) cause motion towards the force; tug at **b** STRAIN 2b ⟨~ *a tendon*⟩ **c** to hold back (a horse) from winning a race **d** to work (an oar) **3** to hit (e g a ball in cricket or golf) towards the left from a right-handed swing or towards the right from a left-handed swing **4** to draw apart; tear **5** to print (e g a proof) by impression **6** to bring out (a weapon) ready for use ⟨~ed *a knife on him*⟩ **7** to draw from the barrel, esp by pulling a pump handle ⟨~ *a pint*⟩ **8a** to carry out, esp with daring and imagination ⟨~ *a robbery*⟩ ⟨~ed *another financial coup*⟩ **b** to do, perform, or say with a deceptive intent ⟨*been* ~ing *these tricks for years*⟩ **9** to (attempt to) seduce or attract ⟨*spends his weekends* ~ing *the birds*⟩ ⟨~ *votes*⟩ ~ *vi* **1a** to use force in drawing, dragging, or tugging **b** to move, esp through the exercise of mechanical energy ⟨*the car* ~ed *out of the driveway*⟩ **c** to draw or inhale hard in smoking **d** *of a horse* to strain against the bit **2** to be capable of being pulled USE (*vt* 8a, 8b, & 9) *infml* – **pull a fast one** to perpetrate a trick or fraud – *infml* – **pull oneself together** to regain one's self-possession or self-control – **pull one's punches** to refrain from using all the force at one's disposal – **pull one's weight** to do one's full share of the work – **pull out all the stops** to do everything possible to achieve an effect

or action – **pull rank on somebody** to assert one's authority in order to get sthg pleasant – **pull someone's leg** to deceive sby playfully; hoax – **pull strings** to exert (secret) personal influence – **pull the wool over someone's eyes** to blind sby to the true situation; hoodwink sby – **pull together** to work in harmony towards a common goal; cooperate

²**pull** *n* **1a** the act or an instance of pulling **b(1)** a draught of liquid **(2)** an inhalation of smoke (e g from a cigarette) **c** the effort expended in moving ⟨*a long ~ uphill*⟩ **d** an attacking stroke in cricket made by hitting the ball to the leg side with a horizontal bat **e** force required to overcome resistance to pulling **2** (special influence exerted to obtain) an advantage **3** PROOF **4a 4** a force that attracts, compels, or influences

pull away *vi* **1** to draw oneself back or away; withdraw **2** to move off or ahead ⟨pulled away *from the leaders on the last lap*⟩

pull down *vt* to demolish, destroy

pullet *n* a young female domestic fowl less than a year old

pulley *n* **1** a wheel with a grooved rim that is used with a rope or chain to change the direction and point of application of a pulling force; *also* such a wheel together with a block in which it runs **2** a wheel used to transmit power or motion by means of a belt, rope, or chain passing over its rim

pull-in *n, chiefly Br* a place where vehicles may pull in and stop; *also* a roadside café

pull in *vt* **1** to arrest **2** to acquire as payment or profit ⟨pulls in £10,000 *a year*⟩ – infml ~ *vi* **1** *esp of a train or road vehicle* to arrive at a destination or stopping place **2** *of a vehicle or driver* to move to the side of or off the road in order to stop

Pullman *n* a railway passenger carriage with extra-comfortable furnishings, esp for night travel

pull off *vt* to carry out or accomplish despite difficulties

pull-on *n* a garment (e g a hat) that has no fastenings and is pulled onto the head or body – **pull-on** *adj*

pullout *n* **1** a larger leaf in a book or magazine that when folded is the same size as the ordinary pages **2** a removable section of a magazine, newspaper, or book ⟨*see this week's handy TV guide* ~⟩

pull out *vi* **1** *esp of a train or road vehicle* to leave, depart **2a** to withdraw from a military position **b** to withdraw from a joint enterprise or agreement **3** *of an aircraft* to resume horizontal flight after a dive ⟨pulled out *at 400 feet*⟩ **4** *of a motor vehicle* **a** to move into a stream of traffic **b** to move out from behind a vehicle (e g when preparing to overtake)

pullover *n* a garment for the upper body, esp a jumper, put on by being pulled over the head

pull over *vi, of a driver or vehicle* to move towards the side of the road, esp in order to stop

pullthrough *n* a weighted cord with a piece of cloth attached that is passed through a tube (e g the barrel of a rifle or a woodwind instrument) to clean it

pull through *vb* to (cause to) survive a dangerous or difficult situation (e g illness)

pullulate *vi* **1a** to germinate, sprout **b** to breed or produce rapidly and abundantly **2** to swarm, teem – fml – **pullulation** *n*

pull-up *n* **1** an exercise performed by drawing oneself up while hanging by the hands until the chin is level with the support **2** *chiefly Br* a pull-in

pull up *vt* **1** to bring to a stop; halt **2** to reprimand, rebuke ⟨*her manager* pulled *her* up *for her carelessness*⟩ – infml ~ *vi* **1** to come to a halt; stop **2** to draw even with or gain

on others (e g in a race) – **pull one's socks up** *or* **pull up one's socks** to make an effort to show greater application or improve one's performance

pulmonary, pulmonic *adj* of, associated with, or carried on by the lungs

¹**pulp** *n* **1a** the soft juicy or fleshy part of a fruit or vegetable **b** a soft mass of vegetable matter from which most of the water has been pressed **c** the soft sensitive tissue that fills the central cavity of a tooth **d** a material prepared by chemical or mechanical means from rags, wood, etc that is used in making paper **2** pulverized ore mixed with water **3a** a soft shapeless mass, esp produced by crushing or beating ⟨smashed his face to a ~⟩ **4** a magazine or book cheaply produced on rough paper and containing sensational material – **pulpiness** *n*, **pulpy** *adj*

²**pulp** *vt* **1** to reduce to pulp **2** to remove the pulp from **3** to produce or reproduce (written matter) in pulp form ~ *vi* to become pulp or pulpy

pulpit *n* **1** a raised platform or high reading desk in church from which a sermon is preached **2** *the* clergy as a profession

pulsar *n* a celestial source, prob a rotating neutron star, of uniformly pulsating radio waves

pulsate *vi* **1** to beat with a pulse **2** to throb or move rhythmically; vibrate – **pulsatory** *adj*

pulsation *n* rhythmic throbbing or vibrating (e g of an artery); *also* a single beat or throb – **pulsatile** *adj*

¹**pulse** *n* the edible seeds of any of various leguminous crops (e g peas, beans, or lentils); *also* the plant yielding these

²**pulse** *n* **1a** a regular throbbing caused in the arteries by the contractions of the heart; *also* a single movement of such throbbing **b** the number of beats of a pulse in a specific period of time **2a** (an indication of) underlying sentiment or opinion ⟨felt the political ~ *of the nation at Westminster*⟩ **b** a feeling of liveliness; vitality **3a** rhythmical vibrating or sounding **b** a single beat or throb **4a** a short-lived variation of electrical current, voltage, etc whose value is normally constant **b** an electromagnetic wave or sound wave of brief duration

³**pulse** *vi* to pulsate, throb ~ *vt* **1** to drive (as if) by a pulsation **2** to cause to pulsate **3** to produce or modulate (e g electromagnetic waves) in the form of pulses ⟨~d *waves*⟩ – **pulser** *n*

pulverize, -ise *vt* **1** to reduce (e g by crushing or grinding) to very small particles **2** to annihilate, demolish ~ *vi* to become pulverized – **pulverizable** *adj*, **pulverizer** *n*, **pulverization** *n*

puma *n, pl* **pumas**, *esp collectively* **puma** a powerful tawny big cat formerly widespread in the Americas but now extinct in many areas

¹**pumice** *n* a light porous volcanic rock used esp as an abrasive and for polishing – **pumiceous** *adj*

²**pumice** *vt* to dress or polish with pumice

pummel *vb* **-ll-** (*NAm* **-l-, -ll-**), to pound or strike repeatedly, esp with the fists

¹**pump** *n* **1a** a device that raises, transfers, or compresses fluids or that reduces the density of gases, esp by suction or pressure or both **b** a mechanism (e g the sodium pump) for pumping atoms, ions, or molecules **2** the heart **3** an act or the process of pumping

²**pump** *vt* **1a** to raise (e g water) with a pump **b** to draw fluid from with a pump – often + *out* **2** to pour out or inject (as if) with a pump ⟨~ed *money into the economy*⟩ **3** to question persistently ⟨~ed *her for information*⟩ **4** to move (sthg) rapidly up and down as if working a pump handle ⟨~ed *her hand warmly*⟩ **5a** to inflate by means of a pump or bellows – usu + *up* **b** to supply with air by means of a pump or bellows ⟨~ *an organ*⟩ ~ *vi* **1** to work a pump; raise or move a fluid with a pump **2** to move in

a manner resembling the action of a pump handle **3** to spurt out intermittently

³**pump** n **1** a low shoe without fastenings that grips the foot chiefly at the toe and heel **2** Br a plimsoll

pumpernickel n a dark coarse slightly sour-tasting bread made from wholemeal rye

pumpkin n (a usu hairy prickly plant that bears) a very large usu round fruit with a deep yellow to orange rind and edible flesh

pump room n a room at a spa in which the water is distributed and drunk

¹**pun** to consolidate (e g earth, concrete, or hardcore) by repeated ramming or pounding

²**pun** n a humorous use of a word with more than 1 meaning or of words with (nearly) the same sound but different meanings

³**pun** vi **-nn-** to make puns

¹**punch** vt **1** to strike, esp with a hard and quick thrust of the fist **2** to drive or push forcibly (as if) by a punch **3** to hit (a ball) with less than a full swing of a bat, racket, etc **4** to emboss, cut, or make (as if) with a punch ~ vi to punch sthg – **puncher** n

²**punch** n **1** a blow (as if) with the fist **2** effective energy or forcefulness ⟨an opening paragraph that packs a lot of ~⟩

³**punch** n **1** a tool, usu in the form of a short steel rod, used esp for perforating, embossing, cutting, or driving the heads of nails below a surface **2** a device for cutting holes or notches in paper or cardboard

⁴**punch** n a hot or cold drink usu made from wine or spirits mixed with fruit, spices, water, and occas tea

punch ball n, Br a punch-bag

punch bowl n a large bowl in which a beverage, esp punch, is mixed and served

punch-drunk adj **1** suffering brain damage as a result of repeated punches or blows to the head **2** behaving as if punch-drunk; dazed

punched card, punch card n a card used in data processing in which a pattern of holes or notches has been cut to represent information or instructions

punch line n a sentence or phrase, esp a joke, that forms the climax to a speech or dialogue

punch-up n, chiefly Br a usu spontaneous fight, esp with the bare fists – infml

punchy adj having punch; forceful

punctilio n, pl **punctilios 1** a minute detail of ceremony or observance **2** careful observance of forms (e g in social conduct)

punctilious adj strict or precise in observing codes of conduct or conventions – **punctiliously** adv, **punctiliousness** n

punctual adj **1** relating to or having the nature of a point **2** (habitually) arriving, happening, performing, etc at the exact or agreed time – **punctually** adv, **punctuality** n

punctuate vt **1** to mark or divide with punctuation marks **2** to break into or interrupt at intervals ~ vi to use punctuation marks – **punctuator** n

punctuation n the dividing of writing with marks to clarify meaning; also a system of punctuation

punctuation mark n a standardized mark or sign used in punctuation

¹**puncture** n a perforation (e g a hole or narrow wound) made by puncturing; esp a small hole made accidentally in a pneumatic tyre

²**puncture** vt **1** to pierce with a pointed instrument or object **2** to cause a puncture in **3** to make useless or deflate as if by a puncture ⟨failures ~d her confidence⟩ ~ vi to become punctured

pundit n **1** a learned man or teacher; specif a pandit **2** one

who gives opinions in an authoritative manner; an authority – **punditry** n

pungent adj **1** having a stiff and sharp point ⟨~ leaves⟩ **2a** marked by a sharp incisive quality; caustic **b** to the point; highly expressive ⟨~ prose⟩ **3** having a strong sharp smell or taste; esp acrid – **pungency** n

Punic n or adj (the dialect) of Carthage or the Carthaginians

punish vt **1** to impose a penalty on (an offender) or for (an offence) **2** to treat roughly or damagingly ⟨~ an engine⟩ – infml ~ vi to inflict punishment – **punishable** adj, **punisher** n

punishment n **1a** punishing or being punished **b** a judicial penalty **2** rough or damaging treatment – infml ⟨the contender took plenty of ~ in the last round⟩

punitive adj inflicting or intended to inflict punishment ⟨a ~ blow⟩ ⟨a ~ schedule⟩

Punjabi n (the language spoken by) a native or inhabitant of the Punjab of NW India and Pakistan – **Punjabi** adj

¹**punk** n **1** sby following punk styles in music, dress, etc **2** chiefly NAm sby considered worthless or inferior; esp a petty criminal

²**punk** adj **1** of or being a movement among young people of the 1970s and 1980s in Britain characterized by a violent rejection of established society and expressed through punk rock and the wearing of aggressively outlandish clothes and hairstyles **2** chiefly NAm of very poor quality; inferior – slang

³**punk** n a dry spongy substance prepared from fungi and used to ignite fuses

punkah n a fan used esp formerly in India consisting of a cloth-covered frame suspended from the ceiling and swung to and fro by means of a cord

punnet n, chiefly Br a small basket of wood, plastic, etc, esp for soft fruit or vegetables

punster n one who is given to punning

¹**punt** n a long narrow flat-bottomed boat with square ends, usu propelled with a pole

²**punt** vt to propel (e g a punt) with a pole; also to transport by punt ~ vi to propel a punt; go punting

³**punt** vi **1** to play against the banker at a gambling game **2** Br to gamble

⁴**punt** vb to kick (a football) by means of a punt

⁵**punt** n the act of kicking a football with the top or tip of the foot after it is dropped from the hands and before it hits the ground

⁶**punt** n the standard unit of money in the Irish Republic

puny adj slight or inferior in power, size, or importance; weak – **puniness** n

¹**pup** n a young dog; also a young seal, rat, etc

²**pup** vi **-pp-** to give birth to pups

pupa n, pl **pupae, pupas** the intermediate usu inactive form of an insect that undergoes metamorphism (e g a bee, moth, or beetle) that occurs between the larva and the imago stages – **pupal** adj

pupate vi to become a pupa – **pupation** n

¹**pupil** n **1** a child or young person at school or receiving tuition **2** one who has been taught or influenced by a distinguished person

²**pupil** n the contractile usu round dark opening in the iris of the eye – **pupilar** adj, **pupillary** adj

puppet n **1a** a small-scale toy figure (e g of a person or animal) usu with a cloth body and hollow head that fits over and is moved by the hand **b** a marionette **2** one whose acts are controlled by an outside force or influence ⟨a ~ government⟩ – **puppetry** n, **puppeteer** n

puppy n **1** a young dog (less than a year old) **2** a conceited or ill-mannered young man

puppy fat *n* temporary plumpness in children and adolescents

puppy love *n* short-lived romantic affection felt by an adolescent for sby of the opposite sex

purblind *adj* **1** partly blind **2** lacking in vision or insight; obtuse – *fml* – **purblindness** *n*

¹**purchase** *vt* **1a** to acquire (real estate) by means other than inheritance **b** to obtain by paying money or its equivalent; buy **c** to obtain by labour, danger, or sacrifice ⟨~d *life at the expense of honour*⟩ **2** to move or raise by a device (e g a lever or pulley) **3** to constitute the means for buying ⟨*a pound seems to* ~ *less each year*⟩ – **purchasable** *adj*, **purchaser** *n*

²**purchase** *n* **1** sthg obtained by payment of money or its equivalent **2a** a mechanical hold or advantage (e g that applied through a pulley or lever); *broadly* an advantage used in applying power or influence **b** a means, esp a mechanical device, by which one gains such an advantage

purchase tax *n* a tax levied on the sale of goods and services that is usu calculated as a percentage of the purchase price

purdah *n* the seclusion of women from public view among Muslims and some Hindus, esp in India; *also* a screen used for this purpose

pure *adj* **1a**(1) unmixed with any other matter ⟨~ *gold*⟩ (2) free from contamination ⟨~ *food*⟩ (3) spotless; *specif* free from moral fault **b** *of a musical sound* being in tune and free from harshness **c** *of a vowel* monophthongal **2a** sheer, unmitigated ⟨~ *folly*⟩ **b** abstract, theoretical ⟨~ *science*⟩ **3a** free from anything that vitiates or weakens ⟨*the* ~ *religion of our fathers*⟩ **b** containing nothing that does not properly belong ⟨*the* ~ *text*⟩ **c** of unmixed ancestry **4a** chaste **b** ritually clean – **pureness** *n*

pureblood, pure-blooded *adj* PURE 3c – **pureblood** *n*

purebred *adj* bred over many generations from members of a recognized breed, strain, or kind without mixture of other blood – **purebred** *n*

¹**puree, purée** *n* a thick pulp (e g of fruit or vegetable) usu produced by rubbing cooked food through a sieve or blending in a liquidizer; *also* a thick soup made from pureed vegetables

²**puree, purée** *vt* to reduce to a puree

purely *adv* **1** without addition, esp of anything harmful **2** simply, merely ⟨*read* ~ *for relaxation*⟩ **3** in a chaste or innocent manner **4** wholly, completely ⟨*a selection based* ~ *on merit*⟩

purgation *n* the act or result of purging

purgative *n or adj* (a medicine) causing evacuation of the bowels

purgatory *n* **1** a place or state of punishment in which, according to Roman Catholic doctrine, the souls of those who die in God's grace may make amends for past sins and so become fit for heaven **2** a place or state of temporary suffering or misery – *infml* ⟨*the return trip was absolute* ~⟩ – **purgatorial** *adj*

¹**purge** *vt* **1a** to clear of guilt **b** to free from moral or physical impurity **2a** to cause evacuation from (e g the bowels) **b**(1) to rid (e g a nation or party) of unwanted or undesirable members, often summarily or by force (2) to get rid of (e g undesirable people) by means of a purge

²**purge** *n* **1** an (esp political) act of purging **2** a purgative

purify *vt* **1** to free of physical or moral impurity or imperfection **2** to free from undesirable elements ~*vi* to grow or become pure or clean – **purifier** *n*, **purificator** *n*, **purification** *n*

purist *n* one who keeps strictly and often excessively to

established or traditional usage, esp in language – **purism** *n*

puritan *n* **1** *cap* a member of a 16th- and 17th-c mainly calvinist Protestant group in England and New England which wished to purify the Church of England of all very ceremonial worship **2** one who practises or preaches a rigorous or severe moral code – **puritan** *adj*, *often cap*

puritanical *adj* **1** puritan **2** of or characterized by a rigid morality; strict

purity *n* **1** pureness **2** SATURATION 1

¹**purl** *n* **1** a thread of twisted gold or silver wire used for embroidering or edging **2** purl, purl stitch a basic knitting stitch made by inserting the needle into the back of a stitch that produces a raised pattern on the back of the work **3** *Br* an ornamental edging of small loops or picots on lace, ribbon, or braid

²**purl** *vt* **1a** to decorate, edge, or border with gold or silver thread **b** to edge with loops; picot **2** to knit in purl stitch ~*vi* to do knitting in purl stitch

³**purl** *n* a gentle murmur or movement (e g of water)

⁴**purl** *vi, of a stream, brook, etc* to flow in eddies with a soft murmuring sound

purler *n, chiefly Br* a heavy headlong fall – *infml*

purlieus *n pl* **1** environs, neighbourhood **2** confines, bounds – *fml*

purloin *vt* to take dishonestly; steal – *fml*

¹**purple** *adj* **1** of the colour purple **2** highly rhetorical; ornate ⟨~ *prose*⟩

²**purple** *n* **1a** a colour falling about midway between red and blue in hue **b** cloth dyed purple; *also* a purple robe worn as an emblem of rank or authority **c**(1) a mollusc yielding a purple dye, esp the Tyrian purple of ancient times (2) a pigment or dye that colours purple **2** imperial, regal, or very high rank ⟨*born to the* ~⟩

³**purple** *vb* to make or become purple

purple heart *n* a light blue tablet containing the drug phenobarbitone and formerly prescribed as a hypnotic or sedative

purple passage *n* a piece of obtrusively ornate writing

purplish *adj* rather purple

¹**purport** *n* professed or implied meaning; import; *also* substance – *fml*

²**purport** *vt* to (be intended to) seem; profess ⟨*a book that* ~s *to be an objective analysis*⟩

¹**purpose** *n* **1** the object for which sthg exists or is done; the intention **2** resolution, determination – **purposeless** *adj* – **on purpose** with intent; intentionally

²**purpose** *vt* to have as one's intention – *fml*

purpose-built *n, chiefly Br* designed to meet a specific need ⟨*a* ~ *conference centre*⟩

purposeful *adj* **1** full of determination **2** having a purpose or aim ⟨~ *activities*⟩ – **purposefully** *adv*, **purposefulness** *n*

purposely *adv* with a deliberate or express purpose

purposive *adj* **1** serving or effecting a useful function though not necessarily as a result of deliberate intention **2** having or tending to fulfil a conscious purpose; purposeful *USE fml* – **purposively** *adv*, **purposiveness** *n*

purr *vi* **1** to make the low vibratory murmur of a contented cat **2** to make a sound resembling a purr – **purr** *n*

¹**purse** *n* **1** a small flattish bag for money; *esp* a wallet with a compartment for holding change **2a** resources, funds **b** a sum of money offered as a prize or present; *also* the total amount of money offered in prizes for a given event **3** *NAm* a handbag

²**purse** *vt* to pucker, knit

purser *n* an officer on a ship responsible for documents and accounts and on a passenger ship also for the comfort and welfare of passengers

purse strings n pl control over expenditure ⟨she holds the ~⟩

pursuance n a carrying out or into effect (e g of a plan or order); prosecution ⟨in ~ of her duties⟩ – fml

pursue vt 1 to follow in order to overtake, capture, kill, or defeat 2 to find or employ measures to obtain or accomplish ⟨~ a goal⟩ 3 to proceed along ⟨~s a northern course⟩ 4a to engage in ⟨~ a hobby⟩ b to follow up ⟨~ an argument⟩ 5 to continue to afflict; haunt ⟨was ~d by horrible memories⟩ ~ vi to go in pursuit

pursuer n, Scot 1 a plaintiff 2 a prosecutor

pursuit n 1 an act of pursuing 2 an activity that one regularly engages in (e g as a pastime or profession)

purulent adj 1 containing, consisting of, or being pus ⟨a ~ discharge⟩ 2 accompanied by suppuration – **purulence** n

purvey vt to supply (e g provisions), esp in the course of business – **purveyance** n

purveyor n a victualler or caterer

purview n 1 the body or enacting part of a statute 2 the range or limit of authority, responsibility, or concern 3 the range of vision or understanding USE (2&3) fml

pus n thick opaque usu yellowish white fluid matter formed by suppuration (e g in an abscess)

¹**push** vt 1a to apply a force to (sthg) in order to cause movement away from the person or thing applying the force b to move (sthg) away or forwards by applying such a force ⟨to ~ a car uphill⟩ 2 to cause (sthg) to change in quantity or extent as if under pressure ⟨scarcity of labour ~ed up wages⟩ 3a to develop (e g an idea or argument), esp to an extreme degree b to urge or press the advancement, adoption, or practice of; specif to make aggressive efforts to sell ⟨a drive to ~ tinned foods⟩ c to press or urge (sby) to sthg; pressurize ⟨keeps ~ing me to give her a rise⟩ 4 to force towards or beyond the limits of capacity or endurance ⟨poverty ~ed them to breaking point⟩ 5 to hit (a ball) towards the right from a right-handed swing or towards the left from a left-handed swing 6 to approach in age or number ⟨the old man was ~ing 75⟩ – infml 7 to engage in the illicit sale of (drugs) – slang ~ vi 1 to press against sthg with steady force (as if) in order to move it away 2 to press forwards energetically against obstacles or opposition ⟨explorers ~ed out into the Antarctic⟩ 3 to exert oneself continuously or vigorously to achieve an end ⟨unions ~ing for higher wages⟩ – **push one's luck** to take an increasing risk

²**push** n 1a a vigorous effort to attain an end; a drive b a military assault or offensive c an advance that overcomes obstacles 2a an act or action of pushing b a nonphysical pressure; an urge ⟨the ~ and pull of conflicting emotions⟩ c vigorous enterprise or energy ⟨she'll need a lot of ~ to get to the top⟩ 3a an exertion of influence to promote another's interests ⟨his father's ~ took him to the top⟩ b stimulation to activity; an impetus 4 a time for action; an emergency ⟨when it came to the ~ I forgot my lines⟩ 5 Br dismissal – esp in get/give the push ⟨he'll get the ~ if he's late again⟩ USE (4&5) infml – **at a push** chiefly Br if really necessary; if forced by special conditions

push around vt to order about; bully

push-bike n, Br a pedal bicycle

push-button adj 1 operated by means of a push button 2 characterized by the use of long-range weapons rather than physical combat ⟨~ warfare⟩

push button n a small button or knob that when pushed operates or triggers sthg, esp by closing an electric circuit

pushchair n, Br a light folding chair on wheels in which young children may be pushed

pushed adj having difficulty in finding enough time, money, etc ⟨you'll be ~ to finish that by tonight⟩ – infml

pusher n 1 a utensil used by a child for pushing food onto a spoon or fork 2 one who sells drugs illegally – slang

push in vi to join a queue at a point in front of others already waiting, esp by pushing or jostling

push off vi to go away, esp hastily or abruptly – infml

push on vi to continue on one's way, esp despite obstacles or difficulties

pushover n 1 an opponent who is easy to defeat or a victim who is incapable of effective resistance 2 sby unable to resist a usu specified attraction; a sucker ⟨he's a ~ for blondes⟩ 3 sthg accomplished without difficulty; a cinch USE infml

pushy adj self-assertive often to an objectionable degree; forward – infml – **pushily** adv, **pushiness** n

pusillanimous adj lacking courage and resolution; contemptibly timid – fml – **pusillanimity** n

puss n 1a a cat – used chiefly as a pet name or calling name 2 a girl ⟨a saucy little ~⟩ USE infml

¹**pussy** n 1 a catkin of the pussy willow 2 a cat – infml; used chiefly as a pet name

²**pussy** n the vulva – vulg

pussycat n a cat – used chiefly by or to children

pussyfoot vi 1 to tread or move warily or stealthily 2 to avoid committing oneself (e g to a course of action)

pussy willow n any of various willows having grey silky catkins

pustule n 1 a small raised spot on the skin having an inflamed base and containing pus 2 a small raised area like a blister or pimple – **pustular** adj

¹**put** vb put; -tt- vt 1a to place in or move into a specified position or relationship ⟨~ the book on the table⟩ ⟨~ a child to bed⟩ b to thrust (e g a weapon) into or through sthg c to throw (a shot, weight, etc) with a put, esp in the shot put d to bring into a specified condition ⟨~ a rule into effect⟩ ⟨~ the matter right⟩ 2a to cause to endure or undergo; subject ⟨~ me to a lot of expense⟩ b to impose, establish ⟨~ a tax on luxuries⟩ 3a to formulate for judgment or decision ⟨~ the question⟩ ⟨~ the motion⟩ b to express, state ⟨~ting it mildly⟩ 4a to turn into language or literary form ⟨~ her feelings into words⟩ b to adapt, set ⟨lyrics ~ to music⟩ 5a to devote, apply ⟨~ his mind to the problem⟩ b to cause to perform an action; urge ⟨~ the horse at the fence⟩ c to impel, incite ⟨~ them into a frenzy⟩ 6a to repose, rest ⟨~s his faith in reason⟩ b to invest ⟨~ his money into steel⟩ 7 to give as an estimate ⟨~ her age at about 40⟩; also to imagine as being ⟨~ yourself in my place⟩ 8 to write, inscribe ⟨~ their names to what they wrote – Virginia Woolf⟩ 9 to bet, wager ⟨~ £5 on the favourite⟩ ~ vi, of a ship to take a specified course ⟨~ back to port⟩ – **put a foot wrong** to make the slightest mistake – **put a good/bold face on** to represent (a matter) or confront (an ordeal) as if all were well – **put a sock in it** Br to stop talking; SHUT UP – slang – **put a spoke in someone's wheel** to thwart sby's plans – **put forth** 1a to assert, propose b to make public; issue 2 to bring into action; exert 3 to produce or send out by growth ⟨put forth leaves⟩ – **put in mind** to remind – often + of – **put it across someone** Br to deceive sby into believing or doing sthg – compare PUT ACROSS – **put it past someone** to think sby at all incapable or unlikely ⟨wouldn't put it past him to cheat⟩ – **put it there** – used as an invitation to shake hands – **put one's best foot forward** to make every effort – **put one's finger on** to identify ⟨put his finger on the cause of the trouble⟩ – **put**

one's foot down to take a firm stand – **put one's foot in it** to make an embarrassing blunder – **put one's shirt on** to risk all one's money on – **put one's shoulder to the wheel** to make an effort, esp a cooperative effort – **put on the map** to cause to be considered important – **put paid to** Br to ruin; FINISH 1a ⟨St George putting paid to the dragon – Scottish Field⟩ – **put someone's nose out of joint** to supplant sby distressingly – **put the lid on** chiefly Br to be the culminating misfortune of (a series) – **put the wind up** Br to scare, frighten – infml – **put to bed** to make the final preparations for printing (e g a newspaper) – **put together** to create as a united whole; construct – **put to it** to give difficulty to; press hard ⟨had been put to it to keep up⟩ – **put to shame** to disgrace by comparison ⟨their garden puts ours to shame⟩ – **put two and two together** to draw the proper conclusion from given premises – **put wise** to inform, enlighten – infml

²**put** n a throw made with an overhand pushing motion; specif the act or an instance of putting the shot

³**put** adj in the same position, condition, or situation – in stay put

put about vi, of a ship to change direction ∼ vt to cause (a ship) to put about

put across vt to convey (the meaning or significance of sthg) effectively

putative adj 1 commonly accepted or supposed 2 assumed to exist or to have existed USE fml – **putatively** adv

put away vt 1 to discard, renounce 2a to place for storage when not in use ⟨put the knives away in the drawer⟩ b to save (money) for future use 3a to confine, esp in an asylum b to kill; esp PUT DOWN 2 4 to eat or drink up; consume ⟨used to put away a bottle without blinking⟩ – infml

put by vt PUT AWAY 2

put-down n a humiliating remark; a snub – infml

put down vt 1 to bring to an end; suppress ⟨put down a riot⟩ 2 to kill (e g a sick or injured animal) painlessly 3a to put in writing ⟨put it down on paper⟩ b to enter in a list (e g of subscribers) ⟨put me down for £5⟩ 4 to pay as a deposit 5a to place in a category ⟨I put him down as an eccentric⟩ b to attribute ⟨put it down to inexperience⟩ 6 to store or set aside (e g bottles of wine) for future use 7a to disparage, belittle b to humiliate, snub ∼ vi, of an aircraft or pilot to land USE (7) infml

put forward vt 1 to propose (e g a theory) 2 to bring into prominence ⟨have no wish to put myself forward⟩

put in vt 1 to make a formal offer or declaration of ⟨put in a plea of guilty⟩ 2 to come in with; interpose ⟨put in a word for her brother⟩ 3 to spend (time) at an occupation or job ⟨put in 6 hours at the office⟩ ∼ vi 1 to call at or enter a place, harbour, etc 2 to make an application, request, or offer for ⟨decided to put in for a pension⟩

put off vt 1 to disconcert, distract 2a to postpone ⟨decided to put off their departure⟩ b to get rid of or persuade to wait, esp by means of excuses or evasions ⟨put his creditors off for another few days⟩ 3a to repel, discourage b to dissuade ⟨so keen it was impossible to put her off⟩ 4 to take off; rid oneself of

¹**put-on** adj pretended, assumed

²**put-on** n an instance of deliberately misleading sby; also, chiefly NAm a parody, spoof

put on vt 1a to dress oneself in; don b to make part of one's appearance or behaviour c to feign, assume ⟨put on a saintly manner⟩ 2 to cause to act or operate; apply ⟨put on more speed⟩ 3 to come to have an increased amount of ⟨put on weight⟩ 4 to stage, produce (e g a play) 5 to bet (a sum of money) 6 to bring to or cause to speak on

the telephone ⟨is your father there? Put him on, then⟩ 7 to mislead deliberately, esp for amusement – infml

put out vt 1 to extinguish ⟨put the fire out⟩ 2 to publish, issue 3 to produce for sale 4a to disconcert, confuse b to annoy, irritate c to inconvenience ⟨don't put yourself out for us⟩ 5 to cause to be out (in baseball, cricket, etc) 6 to give or offer (a job of work) to be done by another outside the premises ∼ vi 1 to set out from shore 2 to make an effort

put over vt PUT ACROSS

putrefaction n 1 the decomposition of organic matter; esp the breakdown of proteins by bacteria and fungi, typically in the absence of oxygen, with the formation of foul-smelling incompletely oxidized products 2 being putrefied; corruption – **putrefactive** adj

putrefy vb to make or become putrid

putrescent adj of or undergoing putrefaction – **putrescence** n

putrid adj 1a in a state of putrefaction b (characteristic) of putrefaction; esp foul-smelling 2 very unpleasant – slang – **putridness** n, **putridity** n

putsch n a secretly plotted and suddenly executed attempt to overthrow a government

putt n a gentle golf stroke made to roll the ball towards or into the hole on a putting green – **putt** vb

puttee n 1 a long cloth strip wrapped spirally round the leg from ankle to knee, esp as part of an army uniform 2 NAm a usu leather legging secured by a strap or catch or by laces

¹**putter** n a golf club used for putting

²**putter** vi, NAm to potter

put through vt 1 to carry into effect or to a successful conclusion 2a to make a telephone connection for b to obtain a connection for (a telephone call)

putting green n a smooth grassy area at the end of a golf fairway containing the hole into which the ball must be played

putto n, pl **putti** a figure of a Cupid-like boy, esp in Renaissance painting

¹**putty** n 1 a pasty substance consisting of hydrated lime and water 2 a dough-like cement, usu made of whiting and boiled linseed oil, used esp in fixing glass in sashes and stopping crevices in woodwork

²**putty** vt to use putty on or apply putty to

put-up adj contrived secretly beforehand ⟨the vote was obviously a ∼ job⟩ – infml

put up vt 1 to sheathe (a sword) 2 to flush (game) from cover 3 to nominate for election 4 to offer up (e g a prayer) 5 to offer for public sale ⟨put her possessions up for auction⟩ 6 to give food and shelter to; accommodate 7 to build, erect 8a to make a display of; show ⟨desperate as she was, she put up a brave front⟩ b CARRY ON 2 ⟨put up a struggle against considerable odds⟩ 9a to contribute, pay b to offer as a prize or stake 10 to increase the amount of; raise ∼ vi 1 to shelter, lodge ⟨we'll put up here for the night⟩ 2 to present oneself as a candidate in an election – usu + for – **put someone's back up** to annoy or irritate sby – **put up to** to urge on, instigate ⟨they put him up to playing the prank⟩ – **put up with** to endure or tolerate without complaint or protest

put-upon adj imposed upon; taken advantage of

¹**puzzle puzzling** vt to offer or represent a problem difficult to solve or a situation difficult to resolve; perplex; also to exert (e g oneself) over such a problem or situation ⟨they ∼ d their brains to find a solution⟩ ∼ vi to be uncertain as to action, choice, or meaning – usu + over or about – **puzzlement** n, **puzzler** n

²**puzzle** n 1 being puzzled; perplexity 2a sthg that puzzles

b a problem, contrivance, etc designed for testing one's ingenuity

puzzle out *vt* to find (a solution or meaning) by means of mental effort

PVC *n* POLYVINYL CHLORIDE

pygmy *n* **1** *cap* a member of a people of equatorial Africa under 1.5m (about 5ft) in height **2** a very short person; a dwarf **3** one who is insignificant or inferior in a specified sphere or manner ⟨*a political* ∼⟩ – **pygmoid** *adj*

pyjamas, *NAm chiefly* **pajamas** *n pl, chiefly Br* **1** loose lightweight trousers traditionally worn in the East **2** a suit of loose lightweight jacket and trousers for sleeping in – **pyjama** *adj*

pylon *n* **1** either of 2 towers with sloping sides flanking the entrance to an ancient Egyptian temple **2** a tower for supporting either end of a wire, esp electricity power cables, over a long span **3** a rigid structure on the outside of an aircraft for supporting sthg

pyorrhoea *n* an inflammation of the sockets of the teeth leading usu to loosening of the teeth

pyramid *n* **1a** an ancient massive structure having typically a square ground plan and tapering smooth or stepped walls that meet at the top **b** a structure or object of similar form **2** a polyhedron having for its base a polygon and for faces triangles with a common vertex **3** a nonphysical structure or system (e g a social or organizational hierarchy) having a broad supporting base and narrowing gradually to an apex – **pyramidal** *adj*

pyramid selling *n* a fraudulent financial system whereby agents for the sale of a product are induced to recruit further agents on ever-dwindling commissions

pyre *n* a heap of combustible material for burning a dead body as part of a funeral rite; *broadly* a pile of material to be burned

Pyrex *trademark* – used for glass and glassware that is resistant to heat, chemicals, and electricity

pyrexia *n* abnormal elevation of body temperature – **pyrexial** *adj,* **pyrexic** *adj*

pyrites *n, pl* **pyrites** any of various metallic-looking sulphide minerals; *esp* IRON PYRITES – **pyritic** *adj*

pyromania *n* a compulsive urge to start fires – **pyromaniac** *n,* **pyromaniacal** *adj*

pyrotechnic *n* **1** a firework **2** *pl* a brilliant or spectacular display (e g of oratory or extreme virtuosity) ⟨*his verbal* ∼*s are entertaining – TLS*⟩ – **pyrotechnic** *adj,* **pyrotechnist** *n*

Pyrrhic victory *n* a victory won at excessive cost

python *n* a large boa or other constrictor; *esp* any of a genus that includes the largest living snakes – **pythonine** *adj*

pyx *n* **1** a container in which the bread used at Communion is kept; *esp* one used for carrying the Eucharist to the sick **2** a box in a mint for deposit of sample coins reserved for testing

---

Q

q *n, pl* **q's, qs** *often cap* (a graphic representation of or device for reproducing) the 17th letter of the English alphabet

Q *n* a source posited by biblical critics for the material common to the gospels of Matthew and Luke that is not derived from that of Mark

qua *prep* in the capacity or character of; as

¹quack *vi or n* (to make) the characteristic cry of a duck

²quack *n* **1** one who has or pretends to have medical skill **2** CHARLATAN 2 *USE* infml – **quackery** *n,* **quackish** *adj*

³quack *adj* (characteristic) of a quack ⟨∼ *medicines*⟩

¹quad *n* a quadrangle

²quad *n* a type-metal space that is 1 or more ems in width

³quad *n* a quadruplet

⁴quad *adj* quadraphonic

Quadragesima *n* the first Sunday in Lent

quadrangle *n* **1** a quadrilateral **2** a 4-sided enclosure surrounded by buildings – **quadrangular** *adj*

quadrant *n* **1a** an instrument for measuring angles, consisting commonly of a graduated arc of 90° **b** a device or mechanical part shaped like or suggestive of the quadrant of a circle **2** (the area of 1 quarter of a circle that is bounded by) an arc of a circle containing an angle of 90° **3** any of the 4 quarters into which sthg is divided by 2 real or imaginary lines that intersect each other at right angles – **quadrantal** *adj*

quadraphonic *adj* of or being an audio system that uses 4 signal channels by which the signal is conveyed from its source to its final point of use – **quadraphonics** *n,* **quadraphony** *n*

quadratic *n or adj* (an equation or expression) of or involving (terms of) the second power or order – **quadratically** *adv*

quadri-, quadr-, quadru- *comb form* **1** four ⟨quadri*lateral*⟩ ⟨quadri*valent*⟩ **2** square ⟨quadr*ic*⟩ **3** fourth ⟨quadri*centennial*⟩ ⟨quadr*oon*⟩

quadrilateral *n or adj* (a polygon) having 4 sides

quadrille *n* **1** a 4-handed variant of ombre played with a pack of 40 cards and popular esp in the 18th c **2** (the music for) a square dance for 4 couples made up of 5 or 6 figures

quadrillion *n* **1** *Br* a million million million millions (10^{24}) **2** *chiefly NAm* a thousand million millions (10^{15}) – **quadrillion** *adj,* **quadrillionth** *adj or n*

quadroon *n* sby of one-quarter Negro ancestry

quadruped *n* an animal having 4 feet – **quadruped, quadrupedal** *adj*

¹quadruple *vb* to make or become 4 times as great or as many

²quadruple *n* a sum 4 times as great as another

³quadruple *adj* **1** having 4 units or member **2** being 4 times as great or as many **3** marked by 4 beats per bar ⟨∼ *time*⟩ – **quadruply** *adv*

quadruplet *n* **1** any of 4 offspring born at 1 birth **2** a combination of 4 of a kind **3** a group of 4 musical notes performed in the time of 3 notes of the same value

¹quadruplicate *adj* **1** consisting of or existing in 4 corresponding or identical parts or examples ⟨∼ *invoices*⟩ **2** being the fourth of 4 things exactly alike

²quadruplicate *vt* **1** to make quadruple or fourfold **2** to prepare in quadruplicate – **quadruplication** *n*

³quadruplicate *n* **1** any of 4 identical copies **2** 4 copies all alike – + *in* ⟨*typed in* ∼⟩

quaff *vb* to drink (a beverage) deeply in long draughts ⟨∼ed *his ale*⟩ – **quaffer** *n*

quagga *n* a recently extinct wild zebra of southern Africa

quagmire *n* **1** soft miry land that shakes or yields under the foot **2** a predicament from which it is difficult to extricate oneself

¹quail *n, pl* **quails,** *esp collectively* **quail 1** a migratory Old World game bird **2** any of various small American game birds

²**quail** *vi* to shrink back in fear; cower ⟨*the strongest ~ before financial ruin* – Samuel Butler †1902⟩

quaint *adj* **1** unusual or different in character or appearance; odd **2** pleasingly or strikingly old-fashioned or unfamiliar – **quaintly** *adv*, **quaintness** *n*

¹**quake** *vi* **1** to shake or vibrate, usu from shock or instability **2** to tremble or shudder, esp inwardly from fear

²**quake** *n* **1** a quaking **2** an earthquake – infml

Quaker *n* a member of a pacifist Christian sect that stresses Inner Light and rejects sacraments and an ordained ministry – **Quakerish** *adj*, **Quakerism** *n*, **Quakerly** *adj*

qualification *n* **1** a restriction in meaning or application; a limiting modification **2a** a quality or skill that fits a person (e g for a particular task or appointment) ⟨*the applicant with the best ~s*⟩ **b** a condition that must be complied with (e g for the attainment of a privilege) ⟨*a ~ for membership*⟩

qualified *adj* **1a** fitted (e g by training or experience) for a usu specified purpose; competent **b** complying with the specific requirements or conditions (e g for appointment to an office); eligible **2** limited or modified in some way ⟨*~ approval*⟩

qualifier *n* one who or that which qualifies: e g **a** sby or sthg that satisfies requirements or meets a specified standard **b** a grammatical modifier **c** a preliminary heat or contest

qualify *vt* **1a** to reduce from a general to a particular or restricted form; modify **b** to make less harsh or strict; moderate **c** MODIFY **2 2** to characterize or describe *as* ⟨*cannot ~ it as either glad or sad*⟩ **3a** to fit by training, skill, or ability for a special purpose **b** to render legally capable or entitled ⟨*~ vi* **1** to be fit (e g for an office) ⟨*qualifies for the job by virtue of his greater experience*⟩ **2** to reach an accredited level of competence ⟨*has just qualified as a lawyer*⟩ **3** to exhibit a required degree of ability or achievement in a preliminary contest

qualitative *adj* of or involving quality or kind – **qualitatively** *adv*

¹**quality** *n* **1a** peculiar and essential character; nature **b** an inherent feature; a property **2a** degree of excellence; grade ⟨*a decline in the ~ of applicants*⟩ **b** superiority in kind ⟨*proclaimed the ~ of his wife* – Compton Mackenzie⟩ **3** high social position ⟨*a man of ~*⟩ **4** a distinguishing attribute; a characteristic ⟨*listed all her good* qualities⟩ **5** the identifying character of a vowel sound **6** *archaic* a capacity, role ⟨*in the ~ of reader and companion* – Joseph Conrad⟩

²**quality** *adj* **1** concerned with or displaying excellence ⟨*~ control*⟩ ⟨*~ goods*⟩ **2** *of a newspaper* aiming to appeal to an educated readership ⟨*the ~ Sundays*⟩

qualm *n* **1** a sudden and brief attack of illness, faintness, or nausea **2** a sudden feeling of anxiety or apprehension **3** a scruple or feeling of uneasiness, esp about a point of conscience or honour – **qualmish** *adj*

quandary *n* a state of perplexity or doubt

quantify *vt* **1** to specify the logical quantity of **2** to determine, express, or measure the quantity of – **quantifier** *n*, **quantifiable** *adj*, **quantification** *n*

quantitative *adj* **1** (expressible in terms) of quantity **2** of or involving the measurement of quantity or amount **3** *of classical verse* based on the relative duration of sequences of sounds – **quantitatively** *adv*, **quantitativeness** *n*

quantity *n* **1a** an indefinite amount or number **b** a known, measured or estimated amount ⟨*precise* quantities *of 4 ingredients*⟩ **c** the total amount or number **d** a considerable amount or number – often pl with sing.

meaning ⟨*wept like anything to see such* quantities *of sand* – Lewis Carroll⟩ **2a** the aspect in which a thing is measurable in terms of degree of magnitude **b** the number, value, etc subjected to a mathematical operation **c** sby or sthg to take into account or be reckoned with ⟨*an unknown ~ as military leader*⟩ **3** the relative duration of a speech sound or sound sequence, specif a prosodic syllable **4** the character of a logical proposition as universal, particular, or singular

quantity surveyor *n* sby who estimates or measures quantities (e g for builders) – **quantity surveying** *n*

quantum *n*, *pl* **quanta 1a** a quantity, amount **b** a portion, part **2** any of the very small parcels or parts into which many forms of energy are subdivided and which cannot be further subdivided *USE* (*1*) fml

quantum theory *n* a theory in physics based on the acceptance of the idea that all energy can be divided into quanta

¹**quarantine** *n* **1** (the period of) a restraint on the activities or communication of people or the transport of goods or animals, designed to prevent the spread of disease or pests **2** a place in which people, animals, vehicles, etc under quarantine are kept **3** a state of enforced isolation

²**quarantine** *vt* **1** to detain in or exclude by quarantine **2** to isolate from normal relations or communication

quark *n* a hypothetical particle that carries a fractional electric charge and is held to be a constituent of known elementary particles

¹**quarrel** *n* a short heavy square-headed arrow or bolt, esp for a crossbow

²**quarrel** *n* **1** a reason for dispute or complaint ⟨*have no ~ with his reasoning*⟩ **2** a usu verbal conflict between antagonists; a dispute

³**quarrel** *vi* **-ll-** (*NAm* **-l-, -ll-**) **1** to find fault *with* ⟨*the teacher invariably found something to ~ with in her essays*⟩ **2** to contend or dispute actively; argue – **quarreller** *n*

quarrelsome *adj* inclined or quick to quarrel, esp in a petty manner – **quarrelsomely** *adv*, **quarrelsomeness** *n*

¹**quarry** *n* the prey or game of a predator, esp a hawk, or of a hunter

²**quarry** *n* **1** an open excavation from which building materials (e g stone, slate, and sand) are obtained **2** a source from which useful material, esp information, may be extracted

³**quarry** *vt* **1** to obtain (as if) from a quarry **2** to make a quarry in *~ vi* to dig (as if) in a quarry – **quarrier** *n*

quart *n* either of 2 units of liquid capacity equal to 2pt: **a** a British unit equal to about 1.136l **b** a US unit equal to about 0.946l

¹**quarter** *n* **1** any of 4 equal parts into which sthg is divisible **2** any of various units equal to or derived from a fourth of some larger unit; specif a quarter of either an American or British hundredweight **3** a fourth of a measure of time: e g **a** any of 4 3-month divisions of a year **b** a quarter of an hour – used in designation of time ⟨*~ past four*⟩ **4** (a coin worth) a quarter of a (US) dollar **5** a limb of a 4-limbed animal or carcass together with the adjacent parts; *esp* a hindquarter **6a** (the direction of or region round) a (cardinal) compass point **b** a person, group, direction, or place not specifically identified ⟨*had financial help from many ~s*⟩ ⟨*did little trade in that ~*⟩ **7** a division or district of a town or city ⟨*the Chinese ~*⟩ **8a** an assigned station or post – usu pl ⟨*battle ~s*⟩ **b** *pl* living accommodation; lodgings; *esp* accommodation for military personnel or their families **9** merciful consideration of an opponent; *specif* the clemency of not killing a defeated enemy ⟨*gave him no ~*⟩ **10** a fourth part of the moon's periodic cycle **11** any of the 4 or more parts of a

heraldic shield that are marked off by horizontal and vertical lines **12** the part of a ship's side towards the stern; *also* any direction to the rear of abeam and from a specified side ⟨*light on the port* ~⟩ **13** any of the 4 equal periods into which the playing time of some games is divided

²quarter *vt* **1** to divide into 4 (almost) equal parts; *broadly* to divide into parts **2** to provide with lodgings or shelter; *esp* to assign (a member of the armed forces) to accommodation ⟨~ed *his men on the villagers*⟩ **3** *esp of a gun dog* to crisscross (an area) in many directions in search of game, or in order to pick up an animal's scent **4a** to arrange or bear (e g different coats of arms) in heraldic quarters on 1 shield **b** to add (a coat of arms) to others on 1 heraldic shield **c** to divide (a heraldic shield) into 4 or more sections **5** *archaic* to divide (esp a traitor's body) into 4 parts, usu after hanging ~ *vi* **1** to lodge, dwell **2** to strike on a ship's quarter ⟨*the wind was* ~ing⟩
³quarter *adj* consisting of or equal to a quarter

quarter day *n* a day which begins a quarter of the year and on which a quarterly payment often falls due

quarterdeck *n* **1** the stern area of a ship's upper deck **2** *sing or pl in constr, chiefly Br* the officers of a ship or navy

quarterfinal *n* a match whose winner goes through to the semifinals of a knockout tournament; *also, pl* a round made up of such matches – **quarterfinal** *adj*, **quarterfinalist** *n*

quartering *n* the division of a heraldic shield into 4 or more heraldic quarters; *also* any of the heraldic quarters so formed or the coat of arms it bears

¹quarterly *n* a periodical published at 3-monthly intervals

²quarterly *adj* **1** computed for or payable at 3-monthly intervals ⟨*a* ~ *premium*⟩ **2** recurring, issued, or spaced at 3-monthly intervals – **quarterly** *adv*

quartermaster *n* **1** a petty officer or seaman who attends to a ship's compass, tiller or wheel, and signals **2** an army officer who provides clothing, subsistence, and quarters for a body of troops

quarter note *n, NAm* a crotchet

quarter sessions *n pl, often cap Q&S* a former English local court with limited criminal and civil jurisdiction, held quarterly

quarterstaff *n, pl* **quarterstaves** a long stout staff formerly used as a weapon

quartet *also* **quartette** *n* **1** (a musical composition for) a group of 4 instruments, voices, or performers **2** *sing or pl in constr* a group or set of 4

quarto *n, pl* **quartos 1** (a book or page of) the size of a piece of paper cut 4 from a sheet **2** *Br* a size of paper usu 10 × 8in (about 25 × 20cm) – not used technically

¹quartz *n* a mineral consisting of a silicon dioxide occurring in colourless and transparent or coloured hexagonal crystals or in crystalline masses – **quartzose** *adj*

²quartz *adj* controlled by the oscillations of a quartz crystal ⟨*a* ~ *watch*⟩

quasar *n* any of various unusually bright very distant star-like celestial objects that have spectra with large red shifts

quash *vt* **1a** to nullify (by judicial action) **b** to reject (a legal document) as invalid **2** to suppress or extinguish summarily and completely; subdue

quasi *adj* having some resemblance to ⟨*a* ~ *corporation*⟩

quasi- *comb form* to some degree; partly; seemingly ⟨quasi-*officially*⟩ ⟨quasi-*stellar object*⟩

quatercentenary *n* (the celebration of) a 400th anniversary

quatrain *n* a stanza of 4 lines

¹quaver *vi* **1** *esp of the voice* to tremble, shake **2** to speak or sing in a trembling voice ~ *vt* to utter in a quavering voice – **quaveringly** *adv*, **quavery** *adj*

²quaver *n* **1** a musical note with the time value of ½ that of a crotchet **2** a tremulous sound

quay *n* an artificial landing place beside navigable water for loading and unloading ships – **quayage** *n*

quean *n, chiefly Scot* a woman; *esp* one who is young or unmarried

queasy *also* **queazy** *adj* **1** causing or suffering from nausea **2** causing or feeling anxiety or uneasiness – **queasily** *adv*, **queasiness** *n*

¹queen *n* **1** the wife or widow of a king **2** a female monarch **3** (sthg personified as) a woman who is preeminent in a specified respect ⟨*a beauty* ~⟩ ⟨*Paris*, ~ *of cities*⟩ **4** the most powerful piece of each colour in a set of chessmen, which has the power to move any number of squares in any direction **5** a playing card marked with a stylized figure of a queen and ranking usu below the king **6** the fertile fully developed female in a colony of bees, ants, or termites **7** a mature female cat **8** an aging male homosexual – used esp by male homosexuals

²queen *vi*, *of a pawn* to become a queen in chess ~ *vt* to promote (a pawn) to a queen in chess – **queen it** to put on airs

queen consort *n, pl* **queens consort** the wife of a reigning king

queen mother *n* a woman who is the widow of a king and the mother of the reigning sovereign

Queen's Bench, Queen's Bench Division *n* a division of the High Court hearing both civil and criminal cases – used when the British monarch is a queen

Queen's Counsel *n* a barrister who has been appointed by the Crown to a senior rank with special privileges – used when the British monarch is a queen

¹queer *adj* **1a** eccentric, unconventional **b** mildly insane **2** questionable, suspicious ⟨~ *goings-on*⟩ **3** not quite well; queasy – *infml* **4** homosexual – derog – **queerish** *adj*, **queerly** *adv*, **queerness** *n*

²queer *vt* to spoil the effect or success of ⟨~ *one's plans*⟩ – **queer someone's pitch** to prejudice or ruin sby's chances in advance

³queer *n* a usu male homosexual – derog

quell *vt* **1** to overwhelm thoroughly and reduce to submission or passivity **2** to quiet, pacify ⟨~ *fears*⟩ – **queller** *n*

quench *vt* **1a** to put out (the light or fire of) ⟨~ed *the fire by throwing on sand*⟩ ⟨~ed *the glowing coals*⟩ **b** to cool (e g hot metal) suddenly by immersion in oil, water, etc; *broadly* to cause to lose heat or warmth **2a** to bring (sthg immaterial) to an end, esp by satisfying, damping, or decreasing ⟨*the praise that* ~es *all desire to read the book* – T S Eliot⟩ **b** to terminate (as if) by destroying; eliminate ⟨~ *a rebellion*⟩ **c** to relieve or satisfy with liquid ⟨~ed *his thirst at a wayside spring*⟩ – **quenchable** *adj*, **quencher** *n*, **quenchless** *adj*

querulous *adj* habitually complaining; fretful, peevish – **querulously** *adv*, **querulousness** *n*

¹query 1 a question, esp expressing doubt or uncertainty **2** QUESTION MARK; *esp* one used to question the accuracy of a text

²query *vt* **1** to put as a question ⟨'*what's wrong?*' *she queried*⟩ **2** to question the accuracy of (e g a statement) **3** to mark with a query **4** *chiefly NAm* to ask questions of – **querier** *n*

¹quest *n* **1** (the object of) a pursuit or search ⟨*went in* ~ *of gold*⟩ **2** an adventurous journey undertaken by a knight in medieval romance

²quest vi **1** *of a dog* to search for a trail or game **2** to go on a quest ⟨~ing *after gold*⟩ ~ vt to search for – chiefly poetic

¹question n **1a** a command or an interrogative expression used to elicit information or test knowledge ⟨*unable to answer the exam* ~⟩ **b** an interrogative sentence or clause **2** an act or instance of asking; an inquiry **3a** a subject or concern that is uncertain or in dispute; an issue ⟨*the abortion* ~⟩; *broadly* a problem, matter ⟨*it's only a* ~ *of time*⟩ **b** a subject or point of debate or a proposition to be voted on in a meeting ⟨*the* ~ *before the House*⟩ **c** the specific point at issue **4a** (room for) doubt or objection ⟨*her integrity is beyond* ~⟩ ⟨*called into* ~ *the veracity of his statement*⟩ **b** chance, possibility ⟨*no* ~ *of escape*⟩ – **in question** under discussion – **out of the question** preposterous, impossible

²question vt **1a** to ask a question of **b** to interrogate ⟨~ed her as to her whereabouts⟩ **2** to doubt, dispute ⟨~ed the wisdom of his decision⟩ **3** to subject (facts or phenomena) to analysis; examine to ask questions; inquire – **questioner** n

questionable adj **1** open to doubt or challenge; not certain or exact **2** of doubtful morality or propriety; shady – **questionableness** n, **questionably** adv

question mark n a punctuation mark ? used in writing and printing at the end of a sentence to indicate a direct question

question-master n one who puts questions during a quiz

questionnaire n (a form having) a set of questions to be asked of a number of people to obtain statistically useful information

question time n a period during which members of a parliamentary body may put questions to a minister

quetzal n, pl **quetzals, quetzales 1** a Central American bird that has brilliant plumage and the male of which has very long upper tail feathers **2** the standard unit of money in Guatemala

¹queue n **1** a pigtail **2a** a waiting line, esp of people or vehicles **b** WAITING LIST ⟨*a housing* ~⟩

²queue vi **queuing, queueing** to line up or wait in a queue – **queuer** n

¹quibble n a minor objection or criticism, esp used as an equivocation

²quibble vi **quibbling 1** to equivocate **2** to bicker – **quibbler** n

¹quick adj **1a** fast in understanding, thinking, or learning; mentally agile ⟨*a* ~ *mind*⟩ ⟨~ *thinking*⟩ **b** reacting with speed and keen sensitivity **2a** fast in development or occurrence ⟨*a* ~ *succession of events*⟩ **b** done or taking place with rapidity ⟨*gave them a* ~ *look*⟩ **c** marked by speed, readiness, or promptness of physical movement ⟨*walked with* ~ *steps*⟩ **d** inclined to hastiness (e g in action or response) ⟨~ *to find fault*⟩ **e** capable of being easily and speedily prepared ⟨*a* ~ *and tasty dinner*⟩ **3** archaic alive – **quickly** adv, **quickness** n

²quick adv in a quick manner

³quick n **1** painfully sensitive flesh, esp under a fingernail, toenail, etc **2** the inmost sensibilities ⟨*cut to the* ~ *by the remark*⟩

quicken vt **1** to enliven, stimulate **2** to make more rapid; accelerate ⟨~ed *her steps*⟩ ~ vi **1** to come to life **2** to reach the stage of gestation at which foetal motion is felt **3** to become more rapid ⟨*her pulse* ~ed *at the sight*⟩ – **quickener** n

quick-freeze vt **quick-froze; quick-frozen** to freeze (food) for preservation so rapidly that the natural juices and flavour are preserved intact

quickie n sthg done or made in a hurry – infml

quicklime n LIME 2a

quicksand n (a deep mass of) loose sand, esp mixed with water, into which heavy objects readily sink

quickset n, *chiefly Br* plant cuttings, esp hawthorn, set in the ground to grow into a hedgerow; *also* a hedge formed in this way

quicksilver n MERCURY 1 – **quicksilver** adj

quickstep n (a piece of music composed for) a fast fox-trot characterized by a combination of short rapid steps

quick time n a rate of marching of about 120 steps in a minute

quick-witted adj quick in understanding; mentally alert – **quick-wittedly** adv, **quick-wittedness** n

¹quid n, pl **quid** also **quids** Br the sum of £1 – infml – **quids in** in the state of having made a usu large profit – infml ⟨*if we sell them at £5 each, we'll be* quids in⟩

²quid n a wad of sthg, esp tobacco, for chewing

quid pro quo n sthg given or received in exchange for sthg else

quiescent adj **1** causing no trouble **2** at rest; inactive – fml – **quiescence** n, **quiescently** adv

¹quiet n being quiet; tranquillity – **on the quiet** without telling anyone; discreetly, secretly

²quiet adj **1a** marked by little or no motion or activity; calm ⟨*a* ~ *day at the office*⟩ ⟨*business had been very* ~ *recently*⟩ **b** free from noise or uproar; still ⟨*a* ~ *little village in the Cotswolds*⟩ **c** secluded ⟨*a* ~ *nook*⟩ **d** enjoyed in peace and relaxation; undisturbed ⟨*a* ~ *cup of tea*⟩ **e** informal and usu involving small numbers of people ⟨*a* ~ *wedding*⟩ **2a** gentle, reserved ⟨*a* ~ *temperament*⟩ **b** unobtrusive, conservative ⟨~ *clothes*⟩ **3** private, discreet ⟨*can I have a* ~ *word with you?*⟩ – **quietly** adv, **quietness** n

³quiet adv in a quiet manner

⁴quiet vt to calm, soothe ⟨*did nothing to* ~ *her fears*⟩, *chiefly NAm* to become quiet – usu + **down** – **quieter** n

quieten vb, *chiefly Br* to make or become quiet – often + **down**

quietism n (a system of religious mysticism teaching) a passive withdrawn attitude or policy towards the world or worldly affairs – **quietist** adj or n

quietude n being quiet; repose – fml

quietus n removal from activity; esp death

quiff n, Br a lock of hair brushed so as to stand up over the forehead

¹quill n **1a** a bobbin, spool, or spindle on which yarn is wound **b** a hollow shaft often surrounding another shaft and used in various mechanical devices **c** a roll of dried bark ⟨*cinnamon* ~s⟩ **2a** the hollow horny barrel of a feather **b** any of the large stiff feathers of a bird's wing or tail **c** any of the hollow sharp spines of a porcupine, hedgehog, etc **3** sthg made from or resembling the quill of a feather; esp a pen for writing **4** a float for a fishing line

²quill vt to wind (thread or yarn) on a quill

¹quilt n **1** a thick warm top cover for a bed consisting of padding held in place between 2 layers of cloth by lines of stitching **2** a usu thinnish cover for a bed; a bedspread

²quilt vt **1a** to fill, pad, or line like a quilt ⟨*a* ~ed *jacket*⟩ **b** to fasten between 2 pieces of material **2** to stitch or sew together in layers with padding in between to make quilts or quilted work – **quilter** n, **quilting** n

quin n, Br a quintuplet

quince n (a central Asian tree of the rose family that bears) a fruit resembling a hard-fleshed yellow apple, used for marmalade, jelly, and preserves

quinine n an alkaloid with a bitter taste that is obtained from cinchona bark, is used as a tonic, and was formerly the major drug in the treatment of malaria

Quinquagesima n the Sunday before Lent

quinsy n a severe inflammation of the throat or adjacent parts with swelling and fever

quintal n 1 a hundredweight 2 a metric unit of weight equal to 100kg (about 220.5lb)

quintessence n 1 the pure and concentrated essence of sthg; the most significant or typical element in a whole 2 the most typical example or representative (e g of a quality or class) ⟨the ~ of pride⟩ – **quintessential** adj, **quintessentially** adv

quintet also **quintette** n 1 (a musical composition for) a group of 5 instruments, voices, or performers 2 sing or pl in constr a group or set of 5

quintuplet n 1 a combination of 5 of a kind 2 any of 5 offspring born at 1 birth 3 a group of 5 equal musical notes performed in the time given to 3, 4, etc of the same value

quip vi or n (to make) a clever, witty, or sarcastic observation or response – **quipster** n

¹**quire** n 1 twenty-four sheets of paper of the same size and quality 2 a set of folded sheets (e g of a book) fitting one within another

²**quire** n, archaic a choir

quirk 1 an odd or peculiar trait; an idiosyncrasy 2 an accident, vagary ⟨by some ~ of fate⟩ 3 a groove separating a bead or other moulding from adjoining members – **quirky** adj

quisling n a traitor who collaborates with invaders

¹**quit** adj released from obligation, charge, or penalty – + of

²**quit** vb -tt-; **quitted** (NAm chiefly **quit**) vt 1 to leave, depart from (a person or place) ⟨~ted her without a backward glance⟩ ⟨ready to ~ the building at a moment's notice⟩ 2 to relinquish (e g a way of thinking or acting); stop ⟨~ moaning!⟩ 3 to give up (e g an activity or employment) ⟨he ~ his job⟩ 4 archaic to conduct (oneself) in a usu specified way ⟨~ themselves with great courage⟩ ~ vi 1 to cease doing sthg; specif to give up one's job 2 of a tenant to vacate occupied premises ⟨the landlord gave them notice to ~⟩ 3 to admit defeat; GIVE UP – infml

quite adv or adj 1a wholly, completely ⟨not ~ all⟩ ⟨~ sure⟩ b positively, certainly ⟨~ the best I've seen⟩ 2 more than usually; rather ⟨took ~ a while⟩ ⟨that was ~ some party!⟩ 3 chiefly Br to only a moderate degree ⟨~ good but not perfect⟩ – **quite so** JUST SO 2

quits adj on even terms as a result of repaying a debt or retaliating for an injury

quittance n (a document giving proof of) discharge from a debt

quitter n one who gives up too easily; a defeatist

¹**quiver** n a case for carrying or holding arrows

²**quiver** vi to shake or move with a slight trembling motion – **quiver** n

qui vive n the alert, lookout – in on the qui vive

quixotic, quixotical adj idealistic or chivalrous in a rash or impractical way – **quixotically** adv

¹**quiz** n -zz- 1 a public test of (general) knowledge, esp as a television or radio entertainment ⟨a ~ programme⟩ 2 NAm an informal test given by a teacher to a student or class

²**quiz** vt -zz- 1 to question closely – journ 2 NAm to test (a student or class) informally – **quizzer** n

quizzical adj 1 gently mocking; teasing 2 indicating a state of puzzlement; questioning ⟨a ~ glance⟩ – **quizzically** adv, **quizzicality** n

quoit n 1 a ring (e g of rubber or iron) used in a throwing game 2 pl but sing in constr a game in which quoits are thrown at an upright pin in an attempt to ring the pin or come as near to it as possible

quondam adj former, sometime ⟨a ~ friend⟩ – fml

Quonset trademark, NAm – used for a prefabricated shelter similar to a Nissen hut

quorum n the number of members of a body that when duly assembled is constitutionally competent to transact business

quota n 1 a proportional part or share; esp the share or proportion to be either contributed or received by an individual or body ⟨most factories fulfilled their production ~⟩ 2 the number or amount constituting a proportional share 3 a numerical limit set on some class of people or things ⟨an immigration ~⟩

quotable adj 1 fit for or worth quoting 2 made with permission for publication (e g in a newspaper) ⟨were the Minister's remarks ~ or off the record?⟩

quotation n 1 sthg quoted; esp a passage or phrase quoted from printed literature 2 quoting 3a (the naming or publishing of) current bids and offers for or prices of shares, securities, commodities, etc b ESTIMATE 4

quotation mark n either of a pair of punctuation marks ' ' or " " used to indicate the beginning and end of a direct quotation

¹**quote** vt 1a to repeat (a passage or phrase previously said or written, esp by another) in writing or speech, usu with an acknowledgment b to repeat a passage or phrase from, esp in substantiation or illustration ⟨to ~ the Scriptures⟩ 2 to cite in illustration ⟨~ cases⟩ 3a to name (the current or recent buying or selling price) of a commodity, stock, share, etc b to make an estimate of or give exact information on (e g the price of a commodity or service) 4 to set off by quotation marks ~ vi 1 to repeat sthg previously said or written ⟨the Prime Minister said, and I ~, 'We have beaten inflation'⟩ 2 to name one's price

²**quote** n 1 a quotation 2 QUOTATION MARK – often used orally to indicate the beginning of a direct quotation

quoth vb past, archaic said – chiefly in the 1st and 3rd persons with a subject following ⟨~ he⟩

quotidian adj 1 occurring or recurring every day ⟨~ fever⟩ 2 commonplace, ordinary – fml

quotient n 1 the result of the division of one number or expression by another 2 the ratio, usu multiplied by 100, between a test score and a measurement on which that score might be expected largely to depend 3 a quota, share – nonstandard

R

r n, pl **r's, rs** often cap (a graphic representation of or device for reproducing) the 18th letter of the English alphabet

¹**-r** suffix – used to form the comparative degree of adjectives and adverbs of 1 syllable, and of some adjectives and adverbs of 2 or more syllables, that end in e ⟨truer⟩ ⟨freer⟩; compare ¹-ER

²**-r** suffix ²-ER – used with nouns that end in e ⟨old-timer⟩ ⟨teenager⟩ ⟨diner⟩

rabbi n 1 a Jew qualified to expound and apply Jewish law 2 a Jew trained and ordained for professional religious leadership; specif the official leader of a Jewish congregation

rabbinic, rabbinical adj 1 of rabbis or their writings 2 of or preparing for the rabbinate – **rabbinically** adv

¹**rabbit** n, pl **rabbits**, (1) esp collectively **rabbit** 1 (the fur

of) a small long-eared mammal that is related to the hares but differs from them in producing naked young and in its burrowing habits **2** *Br* an unskilful player (e g in golf, cricket, or tennis) – **rabbity** *adj*

²**rabbit** *vi* **1** to hunt rabbits **2** *Br* to talk aimlessly or inconsequentially – *infml; often* + *on* – **rabbiter** *n*

rabbit punch *n* a short chopping blow delivered to the back of the neck

rabble *n* **1** a disorganized or disorderly crowd of people; a mob **2** *the* common people; *the* lowest class of society – *derog*

rabble-rouser *n* one who stirs up the common people (e g to hatred or violence); a demagogue

Rabelaisian *adj* marked by the robust humour, extravagant caricature, or bold naturalism characteristic of Rabelais or his works

rabid *adj* **1** unreasoning or fanatical in an opinion or feeling ⟨a ~ racialist⟩ **2** affected with rabies – **rabidly** *adv*, **rabidness, rabidity** *n*

rabies *n, pl* **rabies** a fatal short-lasting virus disease of the nervous system of warm-blooded animals, transmitted esp through the bite of an affected animal, and characterized by extreme fear of water and convulsions

raccoon, racoon *n, pl* **raccoons,** *esp collectively* **raccoon** (the fur of) a small flesh-eating mammal of N America that has a bushy ringed tail and lives chiefly in trees

¹**race** *n* **1a** a strong or rapid current of water in the sea, a river, etc **b** (the current flowing in) a watercourse used industrially (e g to turn the wheel of a mill) **2a** a contest of speed (e g in running or riding) **b** *pl* a meeting in which several races (e g for horses) are run **c** a contest or rivalry for an ultimate prize or position ⟨*the* ~ *for the league championship*⟩ **3** a track or channel in which sthg rolls or slides; *specif* a groove for the balls in a ball bearing **4** *archaic* the course of life

²**race** *vi* **1** to compete in a race **2** to go or move at top speed or out of control ⟨*his pulse was racing*⟩ **3** *of a motor, engine, etc* to revolve too fast under a diminished load ~ *vt* **1** to have a race with ⟨~d *her brother to the garden gate*⟩ **2a** to enter in a race ⟨*always* ~s *his horses at Chepstow*⟩ **b** to drive at high speed **c** to transport or propel at maximum speed **3** to accelerate (e g an engine) without a working load or with the transmission disengaged – **racer** *n*

³**race** *n* **1** a family, tribe, people, or nation belonging to the same stock **2** an actually or potentially interbreeding group within a species; *also* a category (e g a subspecies) in classification representing such a group **3a** a division of mankind having traits that are transmissible by descent and sufficient to characterize it as a distinct human type **b** human beings collectively ⟨*the human* ~⟩ **4** the division of mankind into races ⟨*the brotherhood of man independent of colour, creed, or* ~⟩

racecourse *n* a place where or the track on which races, esp horse races, are held

raceme *n* a simple stalk of flowers (e g that of the lily of the valley) in which the flowers are borne on short side-stalks of about equal length along an elongated main stem

racial *adj* **1** of or based on a race **2** existing or occurring between (human) races ⟨*strove for* ~ *harmony*⟩; *also* directed towards a particular race ⟨~ *discrimination*⟩ – **racially** *adv*

racialism *n* **1** racial prejudice or discrimination **2** RACISM 1 – **racialist** *n or adj*, **racialistic** *adj*

racism *n* **1** a belief that racial differences produce an inherent superiority of a particular race **2** RACIALISM 1 – **racist** *n or adj*

¹**rack** *n* a wind-driven mass of high often broken clouds

²**rack** *vi, of clouds* to fly or scud in high wind

³**rack** *n* **1** a framework for holding fodder for livestock **2** an instrument of torture on which the victim's body is stretched – usu + *the* **3** a framework, stand, or grating on or in which articles are placed ⟨*a luggage* ~⟩ **4** a bar with teeth on 1 face for meshing with a pinion or worm gear ⟨~ *and pinion*⟩ – **on the rack** under great mental or emotional stress

⁴**rack** *vt* **1** to torture on the rack **2** to cause to suffer torture, pain, or anguish ⟨~ed *by headaches*⟩ **3a** to stretch or strain considerably ⟨~ed *his brains*⟩ **b** to raise (rents) oppressively **4** to place in a rack

⁵**rack** *vt* to draw off (e g wine) from the lees

⁶**rack** *n* the front rib section of lamb used for chops or as a roast

⁷**rack** *n* destruction – chiefly in *rack and ruin*

¹**racket** *also* **racquet** *n* **1** a lightweight implement that consists of a netting stretched in an open frame with a handle attached and that is used for striking the ball or shuttle in any of various games (e g tennis, squash, or badminton) **2** *pl but sing in constr* a game for 2 or 4 players played with a ball and rackets on a 4-walled court

²**racket** *n* **1** a loud and confused noise; a din **2a** a fraudulent enterprise made workable esp by bribery or intimidation **b** an easy and lucrative means of livelihood – *infml* **c** a usu specified occupation or business – *slang* ⟨*he's in the publicity* ~⟩

³**racket** *vi* **1** to engage in an active, esp a dissipated, social life – usu + *about* or *round* **2** to move with or make a racket

racketeer *n* one who extorts money or advantages by threats, blackmail, etc – **racketeer** *vi*

rack railway *n* a railway having between its running rails a rack that meshes with a gear wheel or pinion on a locomotive

rack rent *vt or n* (to subject to) an excessive or unreasonably high rent

raconteur *n* one who excels in telling anecdotes

racoon *n* a raccoon

racy *adj* **1** full of zest or vigour **2** having a strongly marked quality; piquant ⟨*a* ~ *flavour*⟩ **3** risqué, suggestive – **racily** *adv*, **raciness** *n*

radar *n* an electronic device that generates high-frequency radio waves and locates objects in the vicinity by analysis of the radio waves reflected back from them

¹**radial** *adj* **1** (having parts) arranged like rays or radii from a central point or axis **2a** relating to, placed like, or moving along a radius **b** characterized by divergence from a centre **3** of or situated near a radius bone (e g in the human forearm) – **radially** *adv*

²**radial** *n* **1** any line in a system of radial lines **2** a radial body part (e g an artery) **3** radial, **radial tyre** a pneumatic tyre in which the ply cords are laid at a right angle to the centre line of the tread

¹**radiant** *adj* **1a** radiating rays or reflecting beams of light **b** vividly bright and shining; glowing **2** marked by or expressive of love, confidence, or happiness ⟨*a* ~ *smile*⟩ **3a** emitted or transmitted by radiation ⟨~ *energy*⟩ **b** of or emitting radiant heat – **radiance, radiancy** *n*, **radiantly** *adv*

²**radiant** *n* **1** the apparent point of origin of a meteor shower **2** a point or object from which light or heat emanates; *specif* the part of a gas or electric heater that becomes incandescent

¹**radiate** *vi* **1** to send out rays of light, heat, or any other form of radiation **2** to issue in rays **3** to proceed in a direct line from or towards a centre ~ *vt* **1a** to send out in rays

b to show or display clearly ⟨~s *health and vitality*⟩ **2** to disseminate (as if) from a centre

²**radiate** *adj* having rays or radial parts; *specif* having radial symmetry – **radiately** *adv*

radiation *n* **1** the action or process of radiating; *esp* the process of emitting radiant energy in the form of waves or particles **2** energy radiated in the form of waves or particles; *esp* electromagnetic radiation (e g light) or emission from radioactive sources (e g alpha rays) **3** a radial arrangement – **radiational** *adj*

radiation sickness *n* sickness that results from overexposure to ionizing radiation (e g X-rays), commonly marked by fatigue, nausea, vomiting, loss of teeth and hair, and, in more severe cases, leukaemia

radiator *n* **1** a room heater (with a large surface area for radiating heat); *specif* one through which hot water or steam circulates as part of a central-heating system **2** a device with a large surface area used for cooling an internal-combustion engine by means of water circulating through it

¹**radical** *adj* **1a** of or growing from the root or the base of a stem **b** of or constituting a linguistic root **c** of or involving a mathematical root **d** designed to remove the root of a disease or all diseased tissue ⟨~ *surgery*⟩ **2** essential, fundamental **3a** departing from the usual or traditional; extreme **b** affecting or involving the basic composition or nature of sthg; thoroughgoing ⟨~ *changes*⟩ **c** tending or disposed to make extreme changes in existing views, conditions, institutions, etc **d** of or constituting a political group advocating extreme measures ⟨*the* ~ *right*⟩ – **radicalism** *n*, **radicalize** *vt*, **radically** *adv*, **radicalness** *n*, **radicalization** *n*

²**radical** *n* **1** ROOT 6 **2** sby who is a member of a radical party or who holds radical views **3** a group of atoms that is replaceable in a molecule by a single atom and is capable of remaining unchanged during a series of reactions

radicle *n* **1** the lower part of the axis of a plant embryo or seedling, including the embryonic root **2** the rootlike beginning of an anatomical vessel or part **3** a radical – **radicular** *adj*

radii *pl of* RADIUS

¹**radio** *n*, *pl* **radios** **1** (the use of) the system of wireless transmission and reception of signals by means of electromagnetic waves **2** a radio receiver **3a** a radio transmitter (e g in an aircraft) **b** a radio broadcasting organization or station ⟨Radio *London*⟩ **c** the radio broadcasting industry **d** the medium of radio communication

²**radio** *adj* **1** of electric currents or phenomena of frequencies between about 10,000 and 10¹¹Hz **2a** of, used in, or transmitted or received by a radio **b** making or participating in radio broadcasts **c** controlled or directed by or using radio

³**radio** *vb* **radios**; **radioing**; **radioed** *vt* **1** to send or communicate by radio **2** to send a radio message to ~*vi* to send or communicate sthg by radio

radio-, radi- *comb form* **1** radial ⟨radio*symmetrical*⟩ **2a** radiant energy; radiation ⟨radio*dermatitis*⟩ **b** radioactive ⟨radio*element*⟩ ⟨radio*nuclide*⟩ **c** using ionizing radiation ⟨radio*therapy*⟩ **d** radioactive isotopes of (a specified element) ⟨radio*carbon*⟩ **e** radio ⟨radio*telegraphy*⟩

radioactivity *n* the property possessed by some elements (e g uranium) of spontaneously emitting alpha or beta rays and sometimes also gamma rays by the disintegration of the nuclei of atoms – **radioactive** *adj*, **radioactively** *adv*

radio frequency *n* a frequency (e g of electromagnetic waves) intermediate between audio frequencies and infrared frequencies and used esp in radio and television transmission

radiogram *n* **1** a radiograph **2** *Br* a combined radio receiver and record player

radiograph *n* a picture produced on a sensitive surface by a form of radiation other than light; *specif* an X-ray or gamma-ray photograph – **radiograph** *vt*, **radiographic** *adj*, **radiographically** *adv*, **radiographer** *n*

radioisotope *n* a radioactive isotope – **radioisotopic** *adj*, **radioisotopically** *adv*

radiology *n* the study and use of radioactive substances and high-energy radiations; *esp* the use of radiant energy (e g X rays and gamma rays) in the diagnosis and treatment of disease – **radiologist** *n*, **radiological** *adj*

radio telescope *n* a radio receiver connected to a large often dish-shaped aerial for recording and measuring radio waves from celestial bodies

radiotherapy *n* the treatment of disease (e g cancer) by means of X rays or radiation from radioactive substances – **radiotherapist** *n*

radish *n* (a plant of the mustard family with) a pungent fleshy typically dark red root, eaten raw as a salad vegetable

radium *n* an intensely radioactive metallic element that occurs in minute quantities in pitchblende and some other minerals and is used chiefly in luminous materials and in the treatment of cancer

¹**radius** *n*, *pl* **radii** *also* **radiuses** **1** the bone on the thumb side of the human forearm; *also* a corresponding part in forms of vertebrate animals higher than fishes **2** (the length of) a straight line extending from the centre of a circle or sphere to the circumference or surface **3a** the circular area defined by a stated radius **b** a bounded or circumscribed area ⟨*alerted all police cars within a 2 mile* ~⟩ **4** a radial part (e g a spoke of a wheel)

²**radius** *vt* to give a rounded edge to (e g a machine part)

raffia, raphia *n* the fibre of the raffia palm used esp for making baskets, hats, and table mats

raffish *adj* marked by careless unconventionality; rakish – **raffishly** *adv*, **raffishness** *n*

raffle *vt or n* **raffling** (to dispose of by means of) a lottery in which the prizes are usually goods ⟨~ *a turkey*⟩

¹**raft** *n* **1a** a collection of logs or timber fastened together for transport by water **b** a flat usu wooden structure designed to float on water and used as a platform or vessel **2** a foundation slab for a building, usu made of reinforced concrete

²**raft** *vt* **1a** to transport in the form of or by means of a raft **b** to cross (e g a lake or river) by raft **2** to make into a raft ~*vi* to travel by raft

³**raft** *n*, *chiefly NAm* a large collection or quantity ⟨*assembled a* ~ *of facts and figures* – *New Yorker*⟩

¹**rafter** *n* any of the parallel beams that form the framework of a roof

²**rafter** *n* one who manoeuvres logs into position and binds them into rafts

¹**rag** *n* **1a** (a waste piece of) worn cloth **b** *pl* clothes, esp when in poor or ragged condition **2** a scrap or unevenly shaped fragment of sthg ⟨*a* ~ *of cloud*⟩ **3** a usu sensational or poorly written newspaper

²**rag** *n* any of various hard rocks used in building

³**rag** *vb* **-gg-** *vt* to torment, tease ~*vi* to engage in horseplay

⁴**rag** *n*, *chiefly Br* **1** an outburst of boisterous fun; a prank **2** a series of processions and stunts organized by students to raise money for charity ⟨~ *week*⟩

⁵**rag** *n* (a composition or dance in) ragtime

raga *n* (an improvisation based on) any of the ancient traditional melodic patterns or modes in Indian music

ragamuffin *n* a ragged often disreputable person, esp a child

ragbag *n* 1 a dishevelled or slovenly person 2 a miscellaneous collection ⟨a ~ of prejudices⟩ *USE* infml

¹**rage** *n* 1 (a fit or bout of) violent and uncontrolled anger 2 violent action (e g of the wind or sea) 3 an intense feeling; passion 4 (an object of) fashionable and temporary enthusiasm ⟨enormous hats were all the ~⟩ – infml

²**rage** *vi* 1 to be in a rage 2 to be violently stirred up or in tumult ⟨the wind ~d outside⟩ 3 to be unchecked in violence or effect ⟨the controversy still ~s⟩

ragged *adj* 1 having an irregular edge or outline 2 torn or worn to tatters 3 wearing tattered clothes 4a straggly b showing irregularities; uneven – **raggedly** *adv*, **raggedness** *n*

raglan *n* a loose overcoat with raglan sleeves

ragout *n* a well-seasoned stew, esp of meat and vegetables, cooked in a thick sauce

ragtime *n* (music having) rhythm characterized by strong syncopation in the melody with a regularly accented accompaniment

rag trade *n the* clothing trade – infml

¹**raid** *n* 1a a usu hostile incursion made in order to seize sby or sthg ⟨a cattle ~⟩ b a surprise attack by a small force 2 a sudden invasion by the police (e g in search of criminals or stolen goods) 3 an attempt to depress share prices by concerted selling 4 an act of robbery

²**raid** *vt* to make a raid on ~ *vi* to take part in a raid – **raider** *n*

¹**rail** *n* 1a an esp horizontal bar, usu supported by posts, which may serve as a barrier (e g across a balcony) or as a support on or from which sthg (e g a curtain) may be hung b a horizontal structural support (e g in a door) 2a RAILING 1 b either of the fences on each side of a horse-racing track – usu pl with sing. meaning 3a either of a pair of lengths of rolled steel forming a guide and running surface (e g a railway) for wheeled vehicles b the railway ⟨always travels by ~⟩ – **off the rails** 1 away from the proper or normal course; awry 2 mad, crazy

²**rail** *vt* to enclose or separate with a rail or rails – often + off

³**rail** *n, pl* **rails**, *esp collectively* **rail** any of numerous wading birds of small or medium size, usu having very long toes which enable them to run on soft wet ground

⁴**rail** *vi* to utter angry complaints or abuse – often + against or at – **railer** *n*

railcar *n* a self-propelled railway carriage

railhead *n* the farthest point reached by a railway; *also* the point at which goods are transferred to or from road transport

railing *n* 1 a usu vertical rail in a fence or similar barrier 2 (material for making) rails

raillery *n* (a piece of) good-humoured teasing

¹**railroad** *n, NAm* a railway

²**railroad** *vt* 1a to push through hastily or without due consideration b to hustle into taking action or making a decision 2 *NAm* to transport by rail 3 *NAm* to convict with undue haste or by unjust means – **railroader** *n*

railway *n, chiefly Br* 1 a line of track usu having 2 parallel lines or rails fixed to sleepers on which vehicles run to transport goods and passengers; *also* such a track and its assets (e g rolling stock and buildings) constituting a single property 2 an organization which runs a railway network ⟨works as a clerk on the ~⟩

raiment *n* garments, clothing – poetic ⟨the heroine garbed in flowing ~ – New York Times⟩

¹**rain** *n* 1a (a descent of) water falling in drops condensed from vapour in the atmosphere b rainwater 2 *pl* the rainy season 3 rainy weather 4 a dense flow or fall of sthg ⟨a steady ~ of fire from the helicopters⟩ ⟨greeted him with a ~ of abuse⟩

²**rain** *vi* 1 *of rain* to fall in drops from the clouds 2 to fall in profusion ~ *vt* 1 to cause to fall; pour or send down 2 to bestow abundantly – **rain cats and dogs** to rain heavily

rainbow *n* 1 an arch in the sky consisting of a series of concentric arcs of the colours red, orange, yellow, green, blue, indigo, and violet, formed esp opposite the sun by the refraction, reflection, and interference of light rays in raindrops, spray, etc 2 an array of bright colours

rainbow trout *n* a large stout-bodied trout of Europe and western N America

raincoat *n* a coat made from waterproof or water-resistant material

rainfall *n* 1 a fall of rain; a shower 2 the amount of rain that has fallen in a given area during a given time, usu measured by depth

rain forest *n* a dense tropical woodland with an annual rainfall of at least 2500mm (about 100in) and containing lofty broad-leaved evergreen trees forming a continuous canopy

rain gauge *n* an instrument for measuring rainfall

rain off *vt, chiefly Br* to interrupt or prevent (e g a sporting fixture) by rain – usu pass

rainproof *vt or adj* (to make) impervious to rain

rainwater *n* water that has fallen as rain and is therefore usu soft

rainy *adj* 1 having or characterized by heavy rainfall 2 wet with rain ⟨~ streets⟩

¹**raise** *vt* 1 to cause or help to rise to an upright or standing position 2a to awaken, arouse b to stir up; incite c to recall (as if) from death d to establish radio communication with 3a to build, erect b to lift up c to place higher in rank or dignity d to invigorate ⟨~ the spirits⟩ e to end the operation of ⟨~ a siege⟩ 4a to levy, obtain ⟨~ funds⟩ b to assemble, collect ⟨~ an army⟩ 5a to grow, cultivate b to rear (e g a child) 6a to give rise to; provoke ⟨~ a laugh⟩ b to give voice or expression to ⟨~ a cheer⟩ 7 to bring up for consideration or debate ⟨~ an issue⟩ 8a to increase the strength, intensity, degree, or pitch of ⟨~ the temperature⟩ b to cause to rise in level or amount ⟨~ the rent⟩ c(1) to increase the amount of (a poker bet) (2) to bet more than (a previous better) 9 to make light and porous, esp by adding yeast ⟨~ dough⟩ 10 to multiply (a quantity) by the same quantity a number of times so as to produce a specified power ⟨2 ~d to the power 3 equals 8⟩ 11 to bring in sight on the horizon by approaching ⟨~ land⟩ 12a to bring up the nap of (cloth), esp by brushing b to bring (e g a design) into relief c to cause (e g a blister) to form on the skin 13 to pronounce (a vowel sound) with the tongue unusually near the roof of the mouth 14 *chiefly NAm* to increase the nominal value of fraudulently ⟨~ a cheque⟩ – **raiser** *n* – **raise Cain/hell/the roof** to create a usu angry and noisy disturbance; *esp* to complain vehemently – infml – **raise an eyebrow/eyebrows** to cause surprise, doubt, or disapproval ⟨his ideas would raise eyebrows in political circles⟩

²**raise** *n* 1 an act of raising or lifting 2a an increase of a bet or bid b *chiefly NAm* RISE 4b

raisin *n* a dried grape

raison d'être *n* a reason or justification for existence

raj *n* RULE 3; *specif, cap* British rule in India

rajah, raja *n* 1 an Indian or Malay prince or chief 2 a person bearing a Hindu title of nobility

¹**rake** *n* 1 a long-handled implement with a head on which a row of projecting prongs is fixed for gathering hay, grass, etc or for loosening or levelling the surface of the ground;

also any of several implements similar in shape or use (e g a tool used to draw together the money or chips on a gaming table) **2** a mechanical implement, usu with rotating pronged wheels, used for gathering hay

²**rake** *vt* **1** to gather, loosen, or level (as if) with a rake **2** to search through, esp in a haphazard manner – often + *through* or *among* **3** to sweep the length of, esp with gunfire – **raker** *n*

³**rake** *vb* to (cause to) incline from the perpendicular

⁴**rake** *n* **1** inclination from the perpendicular; *esp* the overhang of a ship's bow or stern **2** the angle of inclination or slope, esp of a stage in a theatre

⁵**rake** *n* a dissolute man, esp in fashionable society

rake in *vt* to earn or gain (money) rapidly or in abundance – *infml*

rake-off *n* a share of usu dishonestly gained profits – *infml*

rake up *vt* **1** to uncover, revive ⟨raked up *an old grievance*⟩ **2** to find or collect, esp with difficulty ⟨*managed to* rake up *enough money for the rent*⟩

¹**rakish** *adj* dissolute, licentious

²**rakish** *adj* **1** *of a ship, boat, etc* having a smart stylish appearance suggestive of speed **2** dashing, jaunty ⟨*with her hat at a ~ angle*⟩ – **rakishly** *adv*, **rakishness** *n*

rallentando *n, adj, or adv, pl* **rallentandos, rallentandi** (a passage performed) with a gradual decrease in tempo – used in music

¹**rally** *vt* **1** to bring together for a common cause **2a** to arouse for or recall to order or action ⟨rallied *his wits to face the problem*⟩ **b** to rouse from depression or weakness ⟨rallied *his strength*⟩ ~ *vi* **1** to join in a common cause ⟨*thousands will ~ to the new party*⟩ **2** to come together again to renew an effort ⟨*the troops* rallied *and drove back the enemy*⟩ **3** to recover, revive ⟨*began to ~ after his long illness*⟩

²**rally** *n* **1a** a mustering of scattered forces to renew an effort **b** a recovery of strength or courage after weakness or dejection **c** an increase in price after a decline **2** a mass meeting of people sharing a common interest or supporting a common, usu political, cause **3** a series of strokes interchanged between players (e g in tennis) before a point is won **4** *also* **rallye** a motor race, usu over public roads, designed to test both speed and navigational skills

¹**ram** *n* **1** an uncastrated male sheep **2a** BATTERING RAM **b** a heavy beak on the prow of a warship for piercing enemy vessels; *also* a warship equipped with a ram **3a** the plunger of a hydrostatic press or force pump **b** the weight that strikes the blow in a pile driver

²**ram** *vb* -**mm**- *vi* to strike with violence ⟨*her car ~ med into a tree*⟩ ~ *vt* **1** to force down or in by driving, pressing, or pushing ⟨*~ med his hat down over his ears*⟩ **2** to force passage or acceptance of ⟨*~ home an idea*⟩ **3** to strike against violently and usu head-on – **rammer** *n* – **ram something down someone's throat** to force sby to accept or listen to sthg, esp by constant repetition

Ramadan, Ramadhan *n* the 9th month of the Muslim year, during which fasting is practised daily from dawn to sunset

¹**ramble** *vi* **rambling 1** to walk for pleasure, esp without a planned route **2** to talk or write in a disconnected long-winded fashion **3** to grow or extend irregularly ⟨*a* rambling *old house*⟩ – **ramblingly** *adv*

²**ramble** *n* a leisurely walk taken for pleasure and often without a planned route

rambler *n* any of various climbing roses with small, often double, flowers in large clusters

rambunctious *adj, NAm* rumbustious, unruly – *infml* – **rambunctiously** *adv*, **rambunctiousness** *n*

ramekin, ramequin *n* **1** a preparation of cheese with

breadcrumbs, puff pastry, or eggs baked in an individual mould **2** an individual baking and serving dish

ramification *n* **1a** the act or process of branching out **b** the arrangement of branches (e g on a plant) **2a** a branch, subdivision **b** a branched structure **3** a usu extended or complicated consequence ⟨*the ~s of a problem*⟩

ramify *vb* to (cause to) separate or split up into branches, divisions, or constituent parts

ramjet *n* a jet engine that uses the flow of compressed air produced by the forward movement of the aeroplane, rocket, etc to burn the fuel

ramp *n* **1** a sloping floor, walk, or roadway leading from one level to another **2** a stairway for entering or leaving an aircraft

¹**rampage** *vi* to rush about wildly or violently

²**rampage** *n* – **on the rampage** engaged in violent or uncontrolled behaviour

rampant *adj* **1** *of a heraldic animal* rearing upon the hind legs with forelegs extended – used postpositively **2a** characterized by wildness or absence of restraint (e g of opinion or action) ⟨*a ~ militarist*⟩ **b** spreading or growing unchecked ⟨*a ~ crime wave*⟩ – **rampancy** *n*, **rampantly** *adv*

rampart *n* **1** a broad embankment raised as a fortification (e g around a fort or city) and usu surmounted by a parapet **2** a protective barrier; a bulwark

ramrod *n* **1** a rod for ramming home the charge in a muzzle-loading firearm **2** a rod for cleaning the barrels of rifles and other small arms

ramshackle *adj* badly constructed or needing repair; rickety

ran *past of* RUN

¹**ranch** *n* **1** a large farm for raising livestock esp in N America and Australia **2** *chiefly NAm* a farm or area devoted to raising a particular crop or animal ⟨*a poultry ~*⟩

²**ranch** *vi* to own, work, or live on a ranch – **rancher** *n*

rancid *adj* (smelling or tasting) rank – **rancidness, rancidity** *n*

rancour, *NAm* rancor *n* bitter and deep-seated ill will or hatred – **rancorous** *adj*

rand *n, pl* **rand** the standard unit of money in the Republic of South Africa

¹**random** *n* – **at random** without definite aim, direction, rule, or method

²**random** *adj* **1** lacking a definite plan, purpose, or pattern **2** (of, consisting of, or being events, parts, etc) having or relating to a probability of occurring equal to that of all similar parts, events, etc – **randomly** *adv*, **randomness** *n*

randy *adj* sexually aroused; lustful – *infml*

rang *past of* RING

¹**range** *n* **1a** a series of mountains **b** a number of objects or products forming a distinct class or series **c** a variety, cross-section ⟨*a good ~ of people here*⟩ **2** a usu solid-fuel fired cooking stove with 1 or more ovens, a flat metal top, and 1 or more areas for heating pans **3a** an open region over which livestock may roam and feed, esp in N America **b** the region throughout which a kind of living organism or ecological community naturally lives or occurs **4a(1)** the distance to which a projectile can be propelled **(2)** the distance between a weapon and the target **b** the maximum distance a vehicle can travel without refuelling **c** a place where shooting (e g with guns or missiles) is practised **5a** the space or extent included, covered, or used **b** the extent of pitch within a melody or within the capacity of a voice or instrument **6a** a sequence, series, or scale between limits ⟨*a wide ~ of patterns*⟩ **b** (the difference between) the least and greatest

values of an attribute or series **7** the set of values a function may take; *esp* the values that a dependent variable may have **8** LINE 9

²**range** *vt* **1a** to set in a row or in the proper order ⟨*troops were ~d on either side*⟩ **b** to place among others in a specified position or situation ⟨*~d himself with the radicals in the party*⟩ **2** to roam over or through **3** to determine or give the elevation necessary for (a gun) to propel a projectile to a given distance ~ *vi* **1** to roam at large or freely ⟨*the talk ~d over current topics*⟩ **2** *esp of printing type* to align **3** to extend in a usu specified direction **4** *of a gun or projectile* to have a usu specified range **5** to change or differ within limits ⟨*their ages ~d from 5 to 65*⟩ **6** to live, occur in, or be native to, a specified region

range finder *n* a device for indicating or measuring the distance between a gun and a target or a camera and an object

ranger *n* **1a** the keeper of a British royal park or forest **b** an officer who patrols a N American national park or forest **2a** a member of any of several bodies of armed men in N America who range over a usu specified region, esp to enforce the law **b** a soldier in the US army specially trained in close-range fighting and raiding tactics **3** *often cap* a private in an Irish line regiment **4** *cap* a senior member of the British Guide movement aged from 14 to 19

rani, ranee *n* a Hindu queen or princess; *esp* the wife of a rajah

¹**rank** *adj* **1** (covered with vegetation which is) excessively vigorous and often coarse in growth **2** offensively gross or coarse **3a** shockingly conspicuous; flagrant ⟨*lecture him on his ~ disloyalty*⟩ **b** complete – used as an intensive ⟨*a ~ outsider*⟩ **4** offensive in odour or flavour – **rankly** *adv*, **rankness** *n*

²**rank** *n* **1a** a row, line, or series of people or things **b**(1) *sing or pl in constr* a line of soldiers ranged side by side in close order (2) *pl* RANK AND FILE **c** any of the 8 rows of squares that extend across a chessboard perpendicular to the files **2** an esp military formation – often pl with sing. meaning ⟨*to break ~s*⟩ **3a** a degree or position in a hierarchy or order; *specif* an official position in the armed forces **b** (high) social position ⟨*the privileges of ~*⟩ **4** the number of rows in a mathematical matrix **5** *Br* a place where taxis wait to pick up passengers

³**rank** *vt* **1** to arrange in lines or in a regular formation **2** to determine the relative position of; rate **3** *NAm* to outrank ~ *vi* to take or have a position in relation to others

rank and file *n sing or pl in constr* **1** the body of members of an armed force as distinguished from the officers **2** the individuals constituting the body of an organization, society, or nation as distinguished from the leading or principal members ⟨*~ members of the orchestra*⟩ – **rank and filer** *n*

ranker *n* one who serves or has served in the ranks; *esp* a commissioned officer promoted from the ranks

ranking *adj, chiefly NAm* having a high or the highest position

rankle *vi* **rankling** to cause continuing anger, irritation, or bitterness

ransack *vt* **1** to search in a disordered but thorough manner **2** to rob, plunder – **ransacker** *n*

¹**ransom** *n* **1** a price paid or demanded for the release of a captured or kidnapped person **2** the act of ransoming

²**ransom** *vt* **1** to deliver or redeem, esp from sin or its consequences **2** to free from captivity or punishment by paying a ransom – **ransomer** *n*

¹**rant** *vi* to talk in a noisy, excited, or declamatory manner

~ *vt* to declaim bombastically – **ranter** *n*, **rantingly** *adv*

²**rant** *n* (a) bombastic extravagant speech

¹**rap** *n* **1** (the sound made by) a sharp blow or knock **2** blame, punishment – *infml* ⟨*I ended up taking the ~*⟩

²**rap** *vb* **-pp-** *vt* **1** to strike with a sharp blow **2** to utter (e g a command) abruptly and forcibly – usu + *out* **3** to express or communicate (e g a message) by means of raps – usu + *out* **4** to criticize sharply – journ ⟨*judge ~s police*⟩ ~ *vi* to strike a quick sharp blow – (a) **rap over the knuckles** (to give) a scolding

³**rap** *n* the least bit (e g of care or consideration) – *infml* ⟨*doesn't care a ~*⟩

⁴**rap** *n, chiefly NAm* talk, conversation – slang

⁵**rap** *vi* **-pp-** *chiefly NAm* to talk freely and frankly – slang

rapacious *adj* **1** excessively grasping or covetous **2** *of an animal* living on prey – **rapaciously** *adv*, **rapaciousness, rapacity** *n*

¹**rape** *n* a European plant of the mustard family grown as a forage crop and for its seeds which yield rapeseed oil

²**rape** *vt* **1** to despoil **2** to commit rape on – **rapist** *n*

³**rape** *n* **1** an act or instance of robbing or despoiling ⟨*the ~ of the countryside*⟩ **2** (an instance of) the crime of forcing sby, esp a woman, to have sexual intercourse against his/her will **3** an outrageous violation ⟨*a ~ of Justice*⟩

¹**rapid** *adj* moving, acting, or occurring with speed; swift – **rapidly** *adv*, **rapidness, rapidity** *n*

²**rapid** *n* a part of a river where the water flows swiftly over a steep usu rocky slope in the river bed – usu pl with sing. meaning

rapier *n* a straight 2-edged sword with a narrow pointed blade

rapine *n* pillage, plunder

rapport *n* a sympathetic or harmonious relationship

rapprochement *n* the reestablishment of cordial relations, esp between nations

rapscallion *n* a rascal

rapt *adj* **1** enraptured **2** wholly absorbed – **raptly** *adv*, **raptness** *n*

rapture *n* **1a** a state or experience of being carried away by overwhelming emotion **b** a mystical experience in which the spirit is exalted to a knowledge of divine things **2** an expression or manifestation of ecstasy or extreme delight ⟨*went into ~s over the new car*⟩ – **rapturous** *adj*, **rapturously** *adv*, **rapturousness** *n*

¹**rare** *adj, of meat* cooked so that the inside is still red

²**rare** *adj* **1** lacking in density; thin ⟨*a ~ atmosphere*⟩ **2** marked by unusual quality, merit, or appeal ⟨*to show ~ tact*⟩ **3** seldom occurring or found ⟨*a ~ moth*⟩ **4** superlative or extreme – *infml* ⟨*gave her a ~ fright*⟩ – **rarely** *adv*, **rareness** *n*

rare earth *n* (an oxide of) any of a series of metallic elements that includes the elements with atomic numbers from 58 to 71, usu lanthanum, and sometimes yttrium and scandium – **rare-earth** *adj*

rarefied *also* **rarified** *adj* **1** esoteric, abstruse **2** very high or exalted (e g in rank) ⟨*moved in ~ political circles*⟩

rarefy *also* **rarify** *vt* **1** to make rare, porous, or less dense **2** to make more spiritual, refined, or abstruse ~ *vi* to become less dense

raring *adj* full of enthusiasm or eagerness ⟨*~ to go*⟩

rarity *n* **1** the quality, state, or fact of being rare **2** sby or sthg rare

rascal *n* **1** an unprincipled or dishonest person **2** a mischievous person or animal – usu humor or affectionate – **rascally** *adj or adv*

¹rash *adj* acting with, characterized by, or proceeding from undue haste or impetuosity – **rashly** *adv*, **rashness** *n*

²rash *n* **1** an outbreak of spots on the body **2** a large number of instances of a specified thing during a short period ⟨*a ~ of arrests*⟩

rasher *n* a thin slice of bacon or ham

¹rasp *vt* **1** to rub with sthg rough; *specif* to abrade with a rasp **2** to grate upon; irritate **3** to utter in a grating tone ~ *vi* to produce a grating sound – **rasper** *n*, **raspingly** *adv*

²rasp *n* a coarse file with rows of cutting teeth

raspberry *n* **1** (a widely grown shrub that bears) any of various usu red edible berries **2** a rude sound made by sticking the tongue out and blowing noisily – *slang*

¹rat *n* **1** any of numerous rodents that are considerably larger than the related mice **2a** a contemptible or wretched person; *specif* one who betrays or deserts his party, friends, or associates **b** a blackleg *USE* (2) *infml* – **ratlike** *adj*

²rat *vi* **-tt-** **1** to betray, desert, or inform on one's associates – usu + *on* **2** to catch or hunt rats **3** to work as a blackleg

rat-a-tat, rat-a-tat-tat *n* a sharp repeated knocking or tapping sound

ratchet *n* **1** a mechanism that consists of a bar or wheel having inclined teeth into which a pawl drops so that motion is allowed in 1 direction only **2** *also* **ratchet wheel** a toothed wheel held in position or turned by a pawl

¹rate *vt, archaic* to scold angrily

²rate *n* **1** valuation ⟨*appraised him at a low ~*⟩ **2a** a fixed ratio between 2 things **b** a charge, payment, or price fixed according to a ratio, scale, or standard ⟨*~ of exchange*⟩ ⟨*~ of interest*⟩ **c** *Br* a tax levied by a local authority – usu pl with sing. meaning **3** a quantity, amount, or degree of sthg measured per unit of sthg else – **at any rate** in any case; anyway

³rate *vt* **1** to consider to be; value as ⟨*was ~d an excellent pianist*⟩ **2** to determine or assign the relative rank or class of **3** to assign a rate to **4** to be worthy of; deserve ⟨*now ~s his own show*⟩ **5** to think highly of; consider to be good – *infml* ⟨*doesn't ~ Spurs' chances of avoiding relegation*⟩ ~ *vi* to be estimated at a specified level ⟨*~s as the best show ever staged in London*⟩

-rate *comb form* of the specified level of quality ⟨*fifth-rate*⟩

rateable, ratable *adj* capable of or susceptible to being rated, estimated, or apportioned

ratepayer *n* a taxpayer; *also, Br* a person liable to pay rates

rather *adv or adj* **1** more readily or willingly; sooner ⟨*left ~ than cause trouble*⟩ ⟨*I'd ~ not go*⟩ – often used interjectionally, esp by British speakers, to express enthusiastic affirmation ⟨*'will you come?' 'Rather!'*⟩ **2** more properly, reasonably, or truly ⟨*my father, or ~ my stepfather*⟩ **3** to some degree; somewhat ⟨*it's ~ warm*⟩ ⟨*~ too big*⟩ ⟨*I ~ thought so*⟩; *esp* somewhat excessively ⟨*it's ~ far for me*⟩ **4** on the contrary ⟨*was nothing bettered, but ~ grew worse* – Mk 5:26 (AV)⟩

ratify *vt* to approve or confirm formally – **ratification** *n*

rating *n* **1** a classification according to grade **2** relative estimate or evaluation **3** *pl* any of various indexes which list television programmes, new records, etc in order of popularity – usu + *the* **4** *chiefly Br* ORDINARY SEAMAN

ratio *n, pl* **ratios** **1** the indicated division of one mathematical expression by another **2** the relationship in quantity, number, or degree between 2 things or between one thing and another thing

ratiocinate *vi* to reason logically or formally – *fml* – **ratiocinator** *n*, **ratiocinative** *adj*, **ratiocination** *n*

¹ration *n* a share or amount (e g of food) which one permits oneself or which one is permitted ⟨*the petrol ~*⟩

²ration *vt* **1** to distribute or divide (e g commodities in short supply) in fixed quantities – often + *out* **2a** to limit (a person or commodity) to a fixed ration ⟨*sugar was strictly ~ed*⟩ **b** to use sparingly

¹rational *adj* **1** having, based on, or compatible with reason; reasonable ⟨*~ behaviour*⟩ **2** of, involving, or being (a mathematical expression containing) 1 or more rational numbers – **rationally** *adv*, **rationalness, rationality** *n*

²rational *n* sthg rational; *specif* RATIONAL NUMBER

rationale *n* **1** an explanation of controlling principles of opinion, belief, practice, or phenomena **2** an underlying reason; basis

rationalism *n* **1** reliance on reason for the establishment of religious truth **2** a theory that reason is a source of knowledge superior to and independent of sense perception – **rationalist** *n*, **rationalist, rationalistic** *adj*, **rationalistically** *adv*

rationalize, -ise *vt* **1** to free (a mathematical expression) from irrational parts ⟨*~ a denominator*⟩ **2** to bring into accord with reason or cause to seem reasonable; *specif* to attribute (e g one's actions) to rational and creditable motives without analysis of true, esp unconscious, motives in order to provide plausible but untrue reasons for conduct **3** to increase the efficiency of (e g an industry) by more effective organization ~ *vi* to provide plausible but untrue reasons for one's actions, opinions, etc – **rationalizer** *n*, **rationalization** *n*

rational number *n* a number (e g 2, 5/2, –1/2) that can be expressed as the result of dividing one integer by another

ratline *n* any of the short transverse ropes attached to the shrouds of a ship to form rungs

rat race *n* a fiercely competitive and wearisome activity; *specif* the struggle to maintain one's position in a career or survive the pressures of modern urban life

rattan *n* **1** a climbing palm with very long tough stems **2** a part of the stem of a rattan used esp for walking sticks and wickerwork

¹rattle *vb* **rattling** *vi* **1** to make a rapid succession of short sharp sounds **2** to chatter incessantly and aimlessly – often + *on* **3** to move with a clatter or rattle ~ *vt* **1** to say or perform in a brisk lively fashion – often + *off* ⟨*~d off a long list of examples*⟩ **2** to cause to make a rattling sound **3** to upset to the point of loss of poise and composure ⟨*he looked severely ~d*⟩ – *infml*

²rattle *n* **1** a rattling sound **2a** a child's toy consisting of loose pellets in a hollow container that rattles when shaken **b** a device that consists of a springy tongue in contact with a revolving ratchet wheel which is rotated or shaken to produce a loud noise **3** the sound-producing organ on a rattlesnake's tail **4** a throat noise caused by air passing through mucus and heard esp at the approach of death

rattlesnake *n* any of various American poisonous snakes with horny interlocking joints at the end of the tail that rattle when shaken

¹rattling *adj* lively, brisk ⟨*moved at a ~ pace*⟩ – not now in vogue – **rattlingly** *adv*

²rattling *adv* to an extreme degree; very – *chiefly in* **rattling good**; *infml*

ratty *adj* irritable – *infml*

raucous *adj* disagreeably harsh or strident; noisy – **raucously** *adv*, **raucousness** *n*

raunchy *adj* earthy, gutsy ⟨*a group with a confident ~ sound*⟩ – infml – **raunchily** *adv*, **raunchiness** *n*

¹**ravage** *n* damage resulting from ravaging – usu pl with sing. meaning ⟨*the ~s of time*⟩

²**ravage** *vb* to wreak havoc (on); cause (violent) destruction (to) – **ravagement** *n*, **ravager** *n*

¹**rave** *vi* **1** to talk irrationally (as if) in delirium; *broadly* to rage, storm **2** to talk with extreme or passionate enthusiasm ⟨*~d about her beauty*⟩

²**rave** *n* **1** a raving **2** an extravagantly favourable review ⟨*the play opened to ~ notices*⟩ **3** a wild exciting period, experience, or event – slang ⟨*the party was a real ~*⟩

¹**ravel** *vb* **-ll-** (*NAm* **-l-**, **-ll-**), *vt* **1** to unravel, disentangle – usu + *out* **2** to entangle, confuse ~ *vi* to fray

²**ravel** *n* **1** a tangle or tangled mass **2** a loose thread

¹**raven** *n* a very large glossy black bird of the crow family

²**raven** *adj* glossy black ⟨*~ hair*⟩

³**raven** *vt* **1** to devour greedily **2** to despoil ⟨*men ~ the earth, destroying its resources – New Yorker*⟩ ~ *vi* **1** to (seek after) prey **2** to plunder – **ravener** *n*

ravenous *adj* **1** urgently seeking satisfaction, gratification, etc; grasping, insatiable **2** fiercely eager for food; famished – **ravenously** *adv*, **ravenousness** *n*

raver *n*, *chiefly Br* an energetic and uninhibited person who enjoys a hectic social life; *also* a sexually uninhibited or promiscuous person – slang

rave-up *n*, *chiefly Br* a wild party – slang

ravine *n* a narrow steep-sided valley smaller than a canyon and usu worn by running water

¹**raving** *n* irrational, incoherent, wild, or extravagant utterance or declamation – usu pl with sing. meaning

²**raving** *adj* extreme, marked ⟨*a ~ beauty*⟩ – infml

ravioli *n* little cases of pasta containing meat, cheese, etc

ravish *vt* **1** to overcome with joy, delight, etc ⟨*~ed by the beauty of the scene*⟩ **2** to rape, violate – **ravisher** *n*, **ravishment** *n*

ravishing *adj* unusually attractive or pleasing – **ravishingly** *adv*

¹**raw** *adj* **1** not cooked **2a**(1) not processed or purified; in the natural state ⟨*~ fibres*⟩ ⟨*~ sewage*⟩ (2) not diluted or blended ⟨*~ spirits*⟩ **b** not in a polished, finished, or processed form ⟨*~ data*⟩ ⟨*hem this ~ edge to stop it fraying*⟩ **3** having the surface abraded or chafed ⟨*~ skin*⟩ **4** lacking experience, training, etc; new ⟨*a ~ recruit*⟩ **5** disagreeably damp or cold – **rawly** *adv*, **rawness** *n*

²**raw** *n* a sensitive place or state ⟨*touched her on the ~*⟩ – **in the raw 1** in the natural or crude state ⟨*life in the raw*⟩ **2** naked ⟨*slept in the raw*⟩

rawboned *adj* having a heavy or clumsy frame that seems inadequately covered with flesh

raw deal *n* an instance of unfair treatment

rawhide *n* (a whip of) untanned hide

raw material *n* material that can be converted by manufacture, treatment, etc into a new and useful product

¹**ray** *n* any of numerous fishes having the eyes on the upper surface of a flattened body and a long narrow tail

²**ray** *n* **1a** any of the lines of light that appear to radiate from a bright object **b** a narrow beam of radiant energy (e g light or X rays) **c** a stream of (radioactive) particles travelling in the same line **2a** a thin line suggesting a ray **b** any of a group of lines diverging from a common centre **3a** any of the bony rods that support the fin of a fish **b** any of the radiating parts of the body of a radially symmetrical animal (e g a starfish) **4** RAY FLOWER **5** a slight manifestation or trace (e g of intelligence or hope) – **rayed** *adj*, **rayless** *adj*

³**ray** *vi* **1** to shine (as if) in rays **2** to radiate from a centre ~ *vt* to emit in rays; radiate

ray flower *n* any of the strap-shaped florets forming **a** the outer ring of the head of a composite plant (e g an aster or daisy) having central disc florets **b** the entire flower head of a composite plant (e g a dandelion) lacking disc florets

rayon *n* (a fabric made from) a yarn or fibre produced by forcing and drawing cellulose through minute holes

raze, rase *vt* to destroy or erase completely; *specif* to lay (e g a town or building) level with the ground

razor *n* a sharp-edged cutting implement for shaving or cutting (facial) hair – **razor** *vt*

razor-backed, razorback *adj* having a sharp narrow back ⟨*a ~ whale*⟩

razzle *n*, *chiefly Br* a spree, binge – usu in *on the razzle*; slang

¹**re** *n* the 2nd note of the diatonic scale in solmization

²**re** *prep* WITH REGARD TO; concerning

re- *prefix* **1a** again; anew ⟨*reborn*⟩ ⟨*reprint*⟩ **b**(1) again in a new, altered, or improved way ⟨*rehash*⟩ ⟨*rewrite*⟩ ⟨*rehouse*⟩ (2) repeated, new, or improved version of ⟨*retread*⟩ ⟨*rebroadcast*⟩ ⟨*remake*⟩ **2** back; backwards ⟨*recall*⟩ ⟨*retract*⟩

'**re** *vb* are ⟨*you're right*⟩

¹**reach** *vt* **1** to stretch out ⟨*~ out your hand to her*⟩ **2a** to touch or grasp by extending a part of the body (e g a hand) or an object ⟨*couldn't ~ the apple*⟩ **b** to pick up and draw towards one; pass ⟨*~ me my hat, will you?*⟩ **c**(1) to extend to ⟨*the shadow ~ed the wall*⟩ (2) to get up to or as far as; arrive at ⟨*took 2 days to ~ the mountains*⟩ ⟨*they hoped to ~ an agreement*⟩ **d** to contact or communicate with ⟨*~ed her by phone at the office*⟩ ~ *vi* **1a** to make a stretch (as if) with one's hand ⟨*~ towards the book on the top shelf*⟩ **b** to strain after sthg ⟨*~ing for the unattainable*⟩ **2a** to project, extend ⟨*her land ~es to the river*⟩ **b** to arrive at or come to sthg ⟨*as far as the eye could ~*⟩ **3** to sail on a reach – **reachable** *adj*

²**reach** *n* **1a** the action or an act of reaching **b** the distance or extent of reaching or of ability to reach **c** a range; *specif* comprehension ⟨*an idea well beyond his ~*⟩ **2** a continuous stretch or expanse; *esp* a straight uninterrupted portion of a river or canal **3** the tack sailed by a vessel with the wind blowing more or less from the side **4** *pl* groups or levels in a usu specified activity or occupation; echelons ⟨*the higher ~es of academic life*⟩

reach-me-down *n or adj*, *chiefly Br* (sthg) passed on from another ⟨*~ clothes*⟩ – infml

react *vi* **1** to exert a reciprocal or counteracting force or influence – often + *on* or *upon* **2** to respond to a stimulus **3** to act in opposition to a force or influence – usu + *against* **4** to undergo chemical reaction to cause to react chemically

reaction *n* **1a** a reacting **b** tendency towards a former and usu outmoded (political or social) order or policy **2** bodily response to or activity aroused by a stimulus: e g **a** the response of tissues to a foreign substance (e g an antigen or infective agent) **b** a mental or emotional response to circumstances **3** the force that sthg subjected to the action of a force exerts equally in the opposite direction **4a** a chemical transformation or change; an action between atoms, molecules, etc to form 1 or more new substances **b** a process involving change in atomic nuclei resulting from interaction with a particle or another nucleus

reactionary *also* **reactionist** *n or adj* (a person) opposing radical social change or favouring a return to a former (political) order

reactivate vb to make or become active again – **reactivation** n

reactive adj 1 of or marked by reaction or reactance 2 tending to or liable to react ⟨highly ~ chemicals⟩ – **reactively** adv, **reactiveness, reactivity** n

reactor n 1 a vat for an industrial chemical reaction 2 an apparatus in which a chain reaction of fissile material (e g uranium or plutonium) is started and controlled, esp for the production of nuclear power or elementary particles

¹**read** vb read vt **1a**(1) to look at or otherwise sense (e g letters, symbols, or words) with mental assimilation of the communication represented ⟨can't ~ his handwriting⟩ ⟨to ~ a book⟩ ⟨~ music⟩ ⟨~ braille⟩ (2) to look at, interpret, and understand (signs, communicative movements, etc) ⟨~ lips⟩ ⟨~ semaphore⟩ (3) to utter aloud (interpretatively) the printed or written words of ⟨~ them a story⟩ – often + out **b** to learn or get to know by reading ⟨~ that he had died⟩ **c**(1) to study (a subject), esp for a degree ⟨~ law⟩ (2) to read (the) works of (an author or type of literature) ⟨~s science fiction mainly⟩ **d** to receive and understand (a message) by radio **2a** to understand, comprehend ⟨can ~ you like a book⟩ ⟨~ his thoughts⟩ **b** to interpret the meaning or significance of ⟨~s dreams⟩ ⟨can ~ the situation in 2 ways⟩ **c** to interpret the action of or in so as to anticipate what will happen or what needs doing ⟨in football the sweeper must be able to ~ the game⟩ **d** to attribute (a meaning) to sthg read or considered ⟨~ a nonexistent meaning into her words⟩ **3** to use as a substitute for or in preference to another written or printed word, character, etc ⟨~ hurry for harry⟩ **4** to indicate ⟨the thermometer ~s zero⟩ **5a** to sense the meaning of (information stored or recorded on punched cards, in a computer memory, etc) **b** esp of a computer to take (information) from storage ~ vi **1a** to perform the act of reading; read sthg **b**(1) to learn about sthg by reading – usu + up ⟨~ing up on astronomy⟩ (2) to study a subject in order to qualify for ⟨to ~ for the Bar⟩ **2** to yield a (particular) meaning or impression when read ⟨Hebrew ~s from right to left⟩ ⟨the poem ~s rather badly⟩

²**read** n **1** sthg to read with reference to the interest, enjoyment, etc it provides ⟨the book is a terrific ~⟩ **2** chiefly Br a period of reading ⟨had a ~ and went to bed early⟩

³**read** adj instructed by or informed through reading ⟨well-read⟩ ⟨widely ~ in contemporary literature⟩

readable adj **1** legible **2** pleasurable or interesting to read – **readably** adv, **readability, readableness** n

reader n **1** one appointed to read to others; esp LAY READER **b**(1) one who reads and corrects proofs (2) one who evaluates manuscripts **2** a member of a British university staff between the ranks of lecturer and professor **3** a device that reads or displays coded information on a tape, microfilm, punched cards, etc **4** a usu instructive (introductory) book or anthology

readership n **1** the office, duties, or position of a (university) reader **2** sing or pl in constr a collective body of readers; esp the readers of a particular publication or author

readily adv **1** without hesitating ⟨he ~ accepted advice⟩ **2** without much difficulty ⟨for reasons that anyone could ~ understand⟩

reading n **1a** material read or for reading ⟨his biography makes fine ~⟩ **b** the extent to which a person has read ⟨a man of wide ~⟩ **c** an event at which a play, poetry, etc is read to an audience **d** an act of formally reading a bill that constitutes any of 3 successive stages of approval by a legislature, specif Parliament **2a** a form or version of a particular (passage in a) text ⟨the generally accepted ~⟩

b the value indicated or data produced by an instrument ⟨examined the thermometer ~⟩ **3a** a particular interpretation ⟨what is your ~ of the situation?⟩ **b** a particular performance of sthg (e g a musical work)

reading desk n a desk designed to support a book in a convenient position for a (standing) reader

readout n (a device used for) the removal of information from storage (e g in a computer memory or on magnetic tape) for display in an understandable form (e g as a printout); also the information displayed

¹**ready** adj **1a** prepared mentally or physically for some experience or action **b** prepared or available for immediate use ⟨dinner is ~⟩ ⟨had little ~ cash⟩ **2a**(1) willingly disposed ⟨~ to agree to his proposal⟩ (2) likely or about to do the specified thing ⟨~ to cry with vexation⟩ **b** spontaneously prompt ⟨always has a ~ answer⟩ ⟨a ~ wit⟩ **c** (presumptuously) eager ⟨he is very ~ with his criticism⟩ ⟨~ acceptance⟩ – **readiness** n

²**ready** vt to make ready

³**ready** n (ready) money – sometimes pl with sing. meaning; infml – **at/to the ready 1** of a gun prepared and in the position for immediate aiming and firing **2** ¹READY 1b

⁴**ready** adv in advance ⟨food that is bought ~ cooked⟩

ready-made adj **1** made beforehand, esp for general sale or use rather than to individual specifications ⟨~ suits⟩ **2** lacking originality or individuality ⟨~ opinions⟩ **3** readily available ⟨her illness provided a ~ excuse⟩

ready reckoner n, Br an arithmetical table (e g a list of numbers multiplied by a fixed per cent) or set of tables for aid in calculating

ready-to-wear adj, of a garment off-the-peg

reafforest vt, chiefly Br to renew the forest cover of by seeding or planting – **reafforestation** n

reagent n a substance that takes part in or brings about a particular chemical reaction, used esp to detect sthg

¹**real** adj **1** of or being fixed or immovable property (e g land or buildings) **2a** not artificial, fraudulent, illusory, fictional, etc; also being precisely what the name implies; genuine **b** of practical or everyday concerns or activities ⟨left university to live in the ~ world⟩ **c** belonging to or concerned with the set of real numbers ⟨the ~ roots of an equation⟩ **d** formed by light rays converging at a point ⟨a ~ image⟩ **e** measured by purchasing power rather than the paper value of money ⟨~ income⟩ **f** complete, great – used chiefly for emphasis ⟨a ~ surprise⟩ – **realness** n

²**real** n – **for real** in earnest; seriously ⟨they were fighting for real⟩

³**real** adv, chiefly NAm & Scot very

⁴**real** n, pl **reals, reales** (a coin representing) a former money unit of Spain and Spanish colonies

real estate n property in buildings and land

realign vt to reorganize or make new groupings of – **realignment** n

realism n **1** concern for fact or reality and rejection of the impractical and visionary **2** the belief that objects of sense perception have real existence independent of the mind **3** fidelity in art, literature, etc to nature and to accurate representation without idealization – **realist** adj or n, **realistic** adj, **realistically** adv

reality n **1** being real **2a** a real event, entity, or state of affairs ⟨his dream became a ~⟩ **b** the totality of real things and events ⟨trying to escape from ~⟩ – **in reality** AS A MATTER OF FACT

realize, -ise vt **1a** to convert into actual fact; accomplish ⟨finally ~d his goal⟩ **b** to cause to seem real ⟨a book in which the characters are carefully ~d⟩ **2a** to convert into actual money ⟨~ his assets⟩ **b** to bring or get by sale, investment, or effort ⟨the painting will ~ several thou-

sand pounds⟩ **3** to be fully aware of ⟨*she did not ~ the risk he was taking*⟩ **4** to play or write (music) in full (e g from a figured bass) – **realizable** *adj*, **realization** *n*

really *adv* **1a** in reality, actually ⟨*did he ~ say that?*⟩⟨*not very difficult ~*⟩ **b** without question; thoroughly ⟨*~ cold weather*⟩⟨*~ hates him*⟩ **2** more correctly – used to give force to an injunction ⟨*you should ~ have asked me first*⟩ **3** – expressing surprise or indignation ⟨*'she wants to marry him.' 'Really?'*⟩⟨*~, you're being ridiculous*⟩

realm *n* **1** a kingdom **2** a sphere, domain – often pl with sing. meaning ⟨*within the ~s of possibility*⟩

realpolitik *n* politics based on practical factors rather than on moral objectives

real tennis *n* a game played with a racket and a ball in an irregularly-shaped indoor court divided by a net

real-time *adj* being or involving the almost instantaneous processing, presentation, or use of data by a computer

realtor *n*, *NAm* a real estate agent, esp a member of the National Association of Real Estate Boards

realty *n* REAL ESTATE

¹**ream** *n* **1** a quantity of paper equal to 20 quires or variously 480, 500, or 516 sheets **2** a great amount (e g of sthg written or printed) – usu pl with sing. meaning ⟨*composed ~s of poetry*⟩

²**ream** *vt* **1** to enlarge or widen (a hole) with a reamer **2** *NAm* to press the juice from (a citrus fruit)

reap *vt* **1a** to cut (a crop) with a sickle, scythe, or reaping machine; *also* to harvest thus **b** to clear (e g a field) of a crop by reaping **2** to obtain or win, esp as the reward for effort ⟨*to ~ lasting benefits from study*⟩ to reap sthg – **reaper** *n*

¹**rear** *vt* **1** to build or construct **2** to raise upright **3a** to breed and tend (an animal) or grow (e g a crop) for use or sale **b** BRING UP 1 – *vi* **1** to rise to a height **2** *of a horse* to rise up on the hind legs – **rearer** *n*

²**rear** *n* **1** the back part of sthg: e g **a** the part (e g of an army) away from the enemy **b** the part of sthg located opposite its front ⟨*the ~ of a house*⟩ **c** the buttocks **2** the space or position at the back ⟨*moved to the ~*⟩

³**rear** *adj* at the back ⟨*a ~ window*⟩ – **rearmost** *adj*

rear admiral *n* an officer in the navy ranking below vice admiral

rearguard *adj* of vigorous resistance in the face of defeat ⟨*a ~ action*⟩

rear guard *n* a military detachment for guarding the rear of a main body or force, esp during a retreat

rearm *vt* to arm (e g a nation or military force) again, esp with new or better weapons ~ *vi* to become armed again – **rearmament** *n*

¹**rearward** *n* the rear; *esp* the rear division (e g of an army) ⟨*to ~ of the main column*⟩

²**rearward** *adj* located at or directed towards the rear

rearwards *also* **rearward** *adv* at or towards the rear; backwards

¹**reason** *n* **1a** (a statement offered as) an explanation or justification **b** a rational ground or motive ⟨*a good ~ to act soon*⟩ **c** that which makes some phenomenon intelligible; cause ⟨*wanted to know the ~ for earthquakes*⟩ **2a(1)** the power of comprehending, inferring, or thinking, esp in orderly rational ways; intelligence **(2)** proper exercise of the mind **b** sanity ⟨*lost his ~*⟩ – **within reason** within reasonable limits – **with reason** with good cause

²**reason** *vi* **1** to use the faculty of reason so as to arrive at conclusions **2** to talk or argue *with* another so as to influence his/her actions or opinions ⟨*can't ~ with them*⟩ ~ *vt* **1** to persuade or influence by the use of reason ⟨*~ed myself out of such fears*⟩ **2** to formulate, assume, analyse,

or conclude by the use of reason – often + *out* ⟨*to ~ out a plan*⟩ – **reasoner** *n*

reasonable *adj* **1a** in accord with reason ⟨*a ~ theory*⟩ **b** not extreme or excessive ⟨*~ requests*⟩ **c** moderate, fair ⟨*a ~ boss*⟩⟨*~ weather*⟩ **d** inexpensive **2a** having the faculty of reason; rational **b** sensible – **reasonableness** *n*, **reasonably** *adv*

reasoning *n* the drawing of inferences or conclusions through the use of reason

reassure *vt* **1** to assure anew ⟨*~d him that the work was satisfactory*⟩ **2** to restore confidence to ⟨*I was ~d by his promise*⟩ – **reassurance** *n*, **reassuringly** *adv*

rebarbative *adj* repellent, unattractive – *fml*

¹**rebate** *n* **1** a return of part of a payment ⟨*tax ~*⟩ **2** a deduction from a sum before payment; a discount ⟨*10% ~*⟩

²**rebate** *vt or n* (to) rabbet

¹**rebel** *adj* **1** in rebellion **2** of rebels ⟨*the ~ camp*⟩

²**rebel** *n* one who rebels against a government, authority, convention, etc

³**rebel** *vi* **-ll-** **1a** to oppose or disobey (one in) authority or control **b** to resist by force the authority of one's government **2a** to act in or show opposition ⟨*~led against the conventions of polite society*⟩ **b** to feel or exhibit anger or revulsion ⟨*~led at the injustice of life*⟩

rebellion *n* **1** opposition to (one in) authority or dominance **2** (an instance of) open armed resistance to an established government

rebellious *adj* **1a** in rebellion ⟨*~ troops*⟩ **b** (characteristic) of or inclined towards rebellion ⟨*a ~ speech*⟩ ⟨*a ~ people*⟩ **2** REFRACTORY 1 – **rebelliously** *adv*, **rebelliousness** *n*

rebirth *n* **1a** a new or second birth **b** spiritual regeneration **2** a renaissance, revival ⟨*a ~ of nationalism*⟩

reborn *adj* born again; regenerated; *specif* spiritually renewed

¹**rebound** *vi* **1** to spring back (as if) on collision or impact with another body **2** to return with an adverse effect to a source or starting point ⟨*their hatred ~ed on themselves*⟩

²**rebound** *n* **1a** a rebounding, recoil **b** a recovery ⟨*a sharp ~ in prices*⟩ **2** a shot (e g in basketball or soccer) that rebounds – **on the rebound** (whilst) in an unsettled or emotional state resulting from setback, frustration, or crisis ⟨*on the rebound from an unhappy love affair*⟩

rebuff *vt or n* (to) snub

rebuke *vt or n* (to) reprimand

rebus *n* (a riddle using) a representation of words or syllables by pictures that suggest the same sound

rebut *vt* **-tt-** **1** to drive back; repel **2** to disprove or expose the falsity of; refute – **rebuttable** *adj*, **rebuttal** *n*

recalcitrant *adj* **1** obstinately defiant of authority or restraint **2** difficult to handle or control – **recalcitrance** *n*, **recalcitrant** *n*

¹**recall** *vt* **1a** to call or summon back ⟨*~ed their ambassador*⟩ **b** to bring back to mind ⟨*~s his early years*⟩ **2** to cancel, revoke – **recallable** *adj*

²**recall** *n* **1** a call or summons to return ⟨*a ~ of workers after a layoff*⟩ **2** remembrance of what has been learned or experienced ⟨*had almost perfect visual ~*⟩ **3** the act of revoking or the possibility of being revoked **4** the ability (e g of an information retrieval system) to retrieve stored material

recant *vt* to withdraw or repudiate (a statement or belief) formally and publicly; renounce ~ *vi* to make an open confession of error; *esp* to disavow a religious or political opinion or belief – **recantation** *n*

¹**recap** *vt* **-pp-** *NAm* to partially retread (a worn pneumatic tyre) – **recappable** *adj*

²**recap** *vb* **-pp-** to recapitulate – **recap** *n*

recapitulate *vb* to repeat the principal points or stages of (e g an argument or discourse) in summing up

recapitulation *n* **1** recapping; a concise summary **2** the supposed occurrence in the development of an embryo of successive stages resembling the series of ancestral types from which the organism has evolved **3** a modified repetition of the main themes forming the third section of a musical movement written in sonata form

recapture *vt* **1a** to capture again **b** to experience again ⟨*to ~ the atmosphere of the past*⟩ **2** *NAm* to take (excess earnings or profits) by law – **recapture** *n*

recast *vt* **recast** to cast again ⟨*~ a gun*⟩ ⟨*~ a play*⟩; *also* to remodel, refashion ⟨*~s his political image to fit the times*⟩ – **recast** *n*

¹**recce** *n* a reconnaissance – *infml*

²**recce** *vb* **recceing; recced, recceed** to reconnoitre – *infml*

¹**recede** *vi* **1a** to move back or away; withdraw **b** to slant backwards ⟨*a receding chin*⟩ **2** to grow less, smaller, or more distant; diminish ⟨*fears that demand will ~*⟩ ⟨*hope ~d*⟩

²**recede** *vt* to cede (e g land) back to a former possessor

¹**receipt** *n* **1** the act or process of receiving ⟨*please acknowledge ~ of the goods*⟩ **2** sthg (e g goods or money) received – usu pl with sing. meaning ⟨*took the days's ~s to the bank*⟩ **3** a written acknowledgment of having received goods or money

²**receipt** *vt* to give a receipt for or acknowledge, esp in writing, the receiving of

receive *vt* **1a** to (willingly) come into possession of or be provided with **b** to accept for consideration; give attention to ⟨*had to ~ their unwanted attentions*⟩ ⟨*~ a petition*⟩ **2a** to act as a receptacle or container for; *also* to take (an impression, mark, etc) **b** to assimilate through the mind or senses ⟨*~ new ideas*⟩ **3a** to permit to enter; admit ⟨*~d into the priesthood*⟩ **b** to welcome, greet; *also* to entertain **c** to act in response to ⟨*how did she ~ the offer?*⟩ ⟨*well ~d on his tour*⟩ **4** to accept as authoritative or true ⟨*~d wisdom*⟩ **5a** to take the force or pressure of ⟨*these pillars ~ the weight of the roof*⟩ **b** to suffer the hurt or injury of ⟨*~ a broken nose*⟩ **6** to be the player who returns (the service of his/her opponent) in tennis, squash, etc **7** to convert (an incoming signal, esp radio waves) into a form suitable for human perception ~ *vi* to be a recipient: e g **a** to be at home to visitors **b** to accept stolen goods – **receivable** *adj*

receiver *n* **1** a person appointed to hold in trust and administer property of a bankrupt or insane person or property under litigation **2** one who receives stolen goods **3a** a radio, television, or other part of a communications system that receives the signal **b** the part of a telephone that contains the mouthpiece and earpiece – **receivership** *n*

recent *adj* **1a** of a time not long past ⟨*the ~ election*⟩ **b** having lately come into existence ⟨*the ~ snow*⟩ **2** *cap* of or being the present or post-Pleistocene geological epoch – **recency, recentness** *n*, **recently** *adv*

receptacle *n* **1** an object that receives and contains sthg **2** the end of the flower stalk of a flowering plant upon which the floral organs are borne

reception *n* **1** receiving or being received: e g **a** an admission ⟨*his ~ into the church*⟩ **b** a response, reaction ⟨*the play met with a mixed ~*⟩ **c** the receiving of a radio or television broadcast **2** a formal social gathering during which guests or clients are received **3** *Br* an office or desk where visitors or clients (e g to an office, factory, or hotel) are received on arrival

receptionist *n* one employed to greet and assist callers or clients

reception room *n* **1** a waiting room for dental or medical patients **2** a room used primarily for the reception of guests or visitors

receptive *adj* **1** open and responsive to ideas, impressions, or suggestions **2** able to receive and transmit stimuli; sensory – **receptively** *adv*, **receptiveness** *n*, **receptivity** *n*

receptor *n* **1** a cell or group of cells that receives stimuli; SENSE ORGAN **2** a molecule or group of molecules, esp on the surface of a cell, that have an affinity for a particular chemical (e g a neurotransmitter)

¹**recess** *n* **1** a hidden, secret, or secluded place – usu pl ⟨*illuminating the ~es of American politics – TLS*⟩ **2a** an indentation or cleft (e g in an anatomical or geological structure) **b** an alcove ⟨*a pleasant ~ lined with books*⟩ **3** a suspension of business or activity, usu for a period of rest or relaxation ⟨*Parliament is in ~*⟩; *specif, NAm* a break between school classes

²**recess** *vt* **1** to put in a recess ⟨*~ed lighting*⟩ **2** to make a recess in **3** *chiefly NAm* to interrupt for a recess ~ *vi*, *chiefly NAm* to take a recess

recession *n* **1** a withdrawal **2** the withdrawal of clergy and choir at the end of a church service **3** a period of reduced economic activity – **recessional, recessionary** *adj*

recessional *n* a hymn or musical piece at the conclusion of a church service

recessive *adj* **1** receding or tending to recede **2** being the one of a pair of (genes determining) contrasting inherited characteristics that is suppressed if a dominant gene is present – **recessively** *adv*

recharge *vi* to charge again; *esp* to renew the active materials in (a storage battery) – **recharge** *n*, **rechargeable** *adj*

recherché *adj* **1** exotic, rare ⟨*discusses all manner of words – common, ~, and slang – New Yorker*⟩ **2** precious, affected ⟨*his ~ highbrow talk*⟩

recidivist *n* one who relapses, *specif* into criminal behaviour – **recidivism** *n*, **recidivist, recidivistic** *adj*

recipe *n* **1** PRESCRIPTION 3 **2** a list of ingredients and instructions for making sthg, *specif* a food dish **3** a procedure for doing or attaining sthg ⟨*a ~ for success*⟩

recipient *n* sby who or sthg that receives – **recipient** *adj*

¹**reciprocal** *adj* **1** *esp of mathematical functions* inversely related **2** shared, felt, or shown by both sides ⟨*~ love*⟩ **3** consisting of or functioning as a return in kind ⟨*did not expect ~ benefit*⟩ **4** mutually corresponding; equivalent ⟨*~ trade agreements*⟩ – **reciprocally** *adv*

²**reciprocal** *n* **1** either of a pair of numbers (e g $\frac{2}{3}$, $\frac{3}{2}$) that when multiplied together equal 1 ⟨*the ~ of 2 is 0.5*⟩ **2** the inverse of a number under multiplication

reciprocate *vt* **1** to give and take mutually **2** to return in kind or degree ⟨*~ a compliment gracefully*⟩ ~ *vi* **1** to make a return for sthg ⟨*we hope to ~ for your kindness*⟩ **2** to move forwards and backwards alternately ⟨*a reciprocating valve*⟩ – **reciprocator, reciprocative** *adj*, **reciprocation** *adj*

reciprocating engine *n* an engine in which the to-and-fro motion of a piston is transformed into circular motion of the crankshaft

reciprocity *n* **1** mutual dependence, action, or influence **2** a mutual exchange of privileges, *specif* between countries or institutions

recital *n* **1a** a reciting **b** a detailed account ⟨*a ~ of her troubles*⟩ **c** a discourse, narration **2** a concert or public performance given by a musician, small group of musicians, or dancer – **recitalist** n

recitative n (a passage delivered in) a rhythmically free declamatory style for singing a narrative text – **recitative** adj

recite vt **1** to repeat from memory or read aloud, esp before an audience **2** to relate in detail; enumerate ⟨~d a catalogue of offences⟩ to repeat or read aloud sthg memorized or prepared – **reciter** n, **recitation** n

reck vt **1** to take account of ⟨he little ~ed what the outcome might be⟩ **2** to matter to; concern ⟨what ~s it me that I shall die tomorrow?⟩ USE archaic or poetic

reckless adj marked by lack of proper caution; careless of consequences ⟨~ driving⟩ ⟨~ courage⟩ – **recklessly** adv, **recklessness** n

reckon vt **1a** to count – usu + up **b** to estimate, compute ⟨~ the height of a building⟩ **c** to determine by reference to a fixed basis ⟨the Gregorian calendar is ~ed from the birth of Christ⟩ **2** to consider or think of in a specified way ⟨she is ~ed the leading expert⟩ **3** to suppose, think ⟨I ~ they're not coming⟩ **4** to esteem highly ⟨the boys ~ him because he's one of the lads⟩ – infml ~vi **1** to settle accounts **2** to make a calculation **3** to place reliance ⟨I'm ~ing on your support⟩ – **reckon with** to take into account, esp because formidable – **reckon without** to fail to consider; ignore

reckoning n **1a** a calculation or counting **b** an account, bill **2** a settling of accounts ⟨day of ~⟩ **3** an appraisal

reclaim vt **1** to rescue or convert from an undesirable state; reform **2** to make available for human use by changing natural conditions ⟨~ed marshland⟩ **3** to obtain from a waste product – **reclaimable** adj, **reclamation** n, **reclamator** n

recline vb **1** (to cause or permit) to incline backwards ⟨~d the seat a little⟩ **2** to place or be in a recumbent position; lean, repose ⟨~s her head on the pillow⟩

recluse n or adj (sby) leading a secluded or solitary life – **reclusive** adj, **reclusion** n

recognition n **1** recognizing or being recognized: e g **a** (formal) acknowledgment (e g of a government or claim) **b** perception of sthg as identical with sthg already known in fact or by description ⟨~ of a former friend⟩ ⟨~ of a fine claret⟩ **2** special notice or attention ⟨a writer who has received much ~⟩ **3** the sensing and coding of printed or written data by a machine ⟨optical character ~⟩ ⟨machine ~ of handwritten characters⟩

recognizance n (the sum pledged as a guarantee for) a bond entered into before a court or magistrate that requires a person to do sthg (e g pay a debt or appear in court at a later date)

recognize, -ise vt **1a** to perceive to be sthg or sby previously known or encountered ⟨~d the word⟩ **b** to perceive clearly ⟨~d his own inadequacy⟩ **2a** to show appreciation of (e g by praise or reward) **b** to acknowledge acquaintance with ⟨~ an old crony with a nod⟩ **c** to admit the fact of ⟨~s his obligation⟩ **3a** to admit as being of a particular status or having validity ⟨~d her as legitimate representative⟩ **b** to allow to speak in a meeting – **recognizable** adj, **recognizably** adv, **recognizability** n

¹**recoil** vi **1** to shrink back physically or emotionally (e g in horror, fear, or disgust) **2** to spring back; rebound: e g **a** to fly back into an uncompressed position ⟨the spring ~ed⟩ **b** esp of a firearm to move backwards sharply when fired **3** REBOUND 2

²**recoil** n recoiling; esp the backwards movement of a gun on firing

recollect vt **1** to bring back to the level of conscious awareness; remember, recall **2** to bring (oneself) back to

a state of composure or concentration to call sthg to mind – **recollection** n, **recollective** adj

recommend vt **1a** to declare to be worthy of acceptance or trial ⟨~ed the restaurant⟩ **b** to endorse as fit, worthy, or competent ⟨~s her for the position⟩ **2** to make acceptable ⟨has other points to ~ it⟩ **3** to advise ⟨~ that the matter be dropped⟩ **4** archaic to entrust, commit ⟨~ed his soul to God⟩ – **recommendable** adj, **recommendation** n, **recommendatory** adj

¹**recompense** vt **1** to give sthg to by way of compensation ⟨~d him for his losses⟩ **2** to make or amount to an equivalent or compensation for ⟨a pleasure that ~s our trouble⟩

²**recompense** n an equivalent or a return for sthg done, suffered, or given ⟨offered in ~ for injuries⟩

reconcile vt **1a** to restore to friendship or harmony **b** to settle, resolve ⟨~ differences⟩ **2** to make consistent or congruous ⟨~ an ideal with reality⟩ **3** to cause to submit to or accept ⟨was ~d to hardship⟩ – **reconcilable** adj, **reconciler**, **reconcilement** n, **reconciliation** n, **reconciliatory** adj

recondite adj (of or dealing with sthg) little known, abstruse, or obscure ⟨the ~ literature of the Middle Ages⟩ ⟨a ~ subject⟩ – **reconditely** adv, **reconditeness** n

recondition vt to restore to good (working) condition (e g by replacing parts)

reconnaissance n a preliminary survey to gain information; esp an exploratory military survey of enemy territory or positions

reconnoitre, NAm **reconnoiter** vb to make a reconnaissance (of)

reconsider vb to consider (sthg) again with a view to change, revision, or revocation – **reconsideration** n

reconstitute vt to constitute again or anew; esp to restore to a former condition by adding water ⟨~ powdered milk⟩ – **reconstitution** n

reconstruct vt **1a** to restore to a previous condition **b** RECREATE a ⟨~ing a dinosaur from its bones⟩ **2** to reorganize, reestablish ⟨~ing society during the postwar period⟩ **3** to build up a mental image or physical representation of (e g a crime or a battle) from the available evidence – **reconstructible** adj, **reconstruction** n

¹**record** vt **1a** to commit to writing so as to supply written evidence **b** to state or indicate (as if) for a record ⟨said he wanted to ~ certain reservations⟩ **c(1)** to register permanently by mechanical or other means ⟨earthquake shocks ~ed by a seismograph⟩ **(2)** to indicate, read **2** to give evidence of; show **3** to convert (e g sound) into a permanent form fit for reproduction ~vi to record sthg – **recordable** adj

²**record** n **1** the state or fact of being recorded **2a** sthg recorded or on which information, evidence, etc has been registered **b** sthg that recalls, relates, or commemorates past events or feats **c** an authentic official document **d** the official copy of the papers used in a law case **3a(1)** a body of known or recorded facts regarding sthg or sby **(2)** a list of previous criminal convictions **b** a performance, occurrence, or condition that goes beyond or is extraordinary among others of its kind; specif the best recorded performance in a competitive sport **4** (the sound recorded on) a flat usu plastic disc with a spiral groove whose undulations represent recorded sound for reproduction on a gramophone – **off the record** not for publication ⟨remarks that were off the record⟩ – **on record** in or into the state of being known, published, or documented ⟨he is on record as saying this⟩

record deck n the apparatus including a turntable and stylus on which a gramophone record is played

recorded delivery adv or n (by) a postal service available in the UK in which the delivery of a posted item is recorded

recorder n 1 often cap a magistrate formerly presiding over the court of quarter sessions 2 any of a group of wind instruments consisting of a slightly tapering tube with usu 8 finger holes and a mouthpiece like a whistle

recording n sthg (e g sound or a television programme) that has been recorded electronically

record player n an electronically-operated system for playing records; a gramophone

¹**recount** vt to relate in detail

²**recount** vt to count again

³**recount** n a recounting, esp of votes

recoup vt 1 to rightfully withhold part of (a sum due) 2a to get an equivalent for (e g losses) b to pay (a person, organization, etc) back; compensate 3 to regain ⟨an attempt to ~ his fortune⟩ ~ vi to make up for sthg lost – **recoupable** adj

recourse n 1 (a turning or resorting to) a source of help, strength, or protection ⟨to have ~ to the law⟩ 2 the right to demand payment

recover vt 1 to get back: e g a to regain possession or use of ⟨quickly ~ed his senses⟩ b RECLAIM 2 2 to bring back to a normal position or condition ⟨stumbled, then ~ed himself⟩ 3a to make up for ⟨~ one's costs⟩ b to obtain by legal action ⟨~ damages⟩ 4 to obtain from an ore, waste product, or by-product ~ vi to regain a normal or stable position or condition (e g of health) ⟨~ing from a cold⟩ – **recoverable** adj, **recoverability** n

recovery n a recovering: e g a a return to normal health b a regaining of balance or control (e g after a stumble or mistake) c an economic upturn (e g after a depression)

recreant adj 1 cowardly 2 unfaithful to duty or allegiance USE fml or poetic – **recreant** n

recreate vt to create again: e g a to reproduce so as to resemble exactly ⟨~d an old frontier town for the film⟩ b to visualize or create again in the imagination – **recreatable** adj, **recreation** n

recreation n (a means of) pleasurable activity, diversion, etc ⟨his favourite ~ was spying on his neighbours⟩ – **recreational** adj

recriminate vi to indulge in bitter mutual accusations – **recriminative, recriminatory** adj, **recrimination** n

recrudesce vi, of sthg undesirable, esp a disease to break out or become active again – fml – **recrudescence** n, **recrudescent** adj

¹**recruit** n a newcomer to a field or activity; specif a newly enlisted member of the armed forces

²**recruit** vt 1a(1) to enlist recruits for (e g an army, regiment, or society) (2) to enlist (a person) as a recruit b to secure the services of; hire 2 to replenish, renew ~ vi to enlist new members – **recruiter** n, **recruitment** n

rectal adj of, affecting, or near the rectum – **rectally** adv

rectangle n a parallelogram all of whose angles are right angles; esp one that is not a square

rectangular adj 1 shaped like a rectangle ⟨a ~ area⟩ 2a crossing, lying, or meeting at a right angle ⟨~ axes⟩ b having faces or surfaces shaped like rectangles ⟨volume of a ~ solid⟩ ⟨~ blocks⟩ – **rectangularly** adv, **rectangularity** n

rectifier n a device for converting alternating current into direct current

rectify vt 1 to set right; remedy ⟨to ~ mistakes⟩ 2 to purify (e g alcohol), esp by repeated or fractional distillation 3 to correct by removing errors ⟨~ the calendar⟩ 4 to convert (alternating current) to direct current – **rectifiable** adj, **rectification** n

rectilinear adj 1 (moving) in or forming a straight line ⟨~ motion⟩ 2 characterized by straight lines – **rectilinearly** adv

rectitude n 1 moral integrity 2 correctness in judgment or procedure

recto n, pl **rectos** a right-hand page

rector n 1a a clergyman in charge of a parish; specif one in a Church of England parish where the tithes were formerly paid to the incumbent b a Roman Catholic priest directing a church with no pastor or one whose pastor has other duties 2 the head of a university or college – **rectorship** n, **rectorate, rectorial** adj

rectory n a rector's residence or benefice

rectum n, pl **rectums, recta** the last part of the intestine of a vertebrate, ending at the anus

recumbent adj 1 in an attitude suggestive of repose ⟨comfortably ~ against a tree⟩ 2 lying down – **recumbency** n, **recumbently** adv

recuperate vt to regain ⟨~ financial losses⟩ ~ vi to regain a former (healthy) state or condition – **recuperation** n, **recuperative** adj

recur vi -rr- to occur again, esp repeatedly or after an interval: e g a to come up again for consideration ⟨knew the difficulties would only ~⟩ b to come again to mind ⟨~ring thoughts⟩ – **recurrence** n

recurrent adj 1 esp of nerves and anatomical vessels running or turning back in a direction opposite to a former course 2 returning or happening repeatedly or periodically ⟨~ complaints⟩ – **recurrently** adv

recurved adj curved backwards or inwards

recusancy, recusance n refusal to accept or obey established authority; specif the refusal of Roman Catholics to attend services of the Church of England, a statutory offence from about 15?0 until 1?91 – **recusant** n or adj

recycle vt to pass through a series of changes or treatments so as to return to a previous stage in a cyclic process; specif to process (sewage, waste paper, glass, etc) for conversion back into a useful product ~ vi esp of an electronic device to return to an original condition so that operation can begin again – **recyclable** adj, **recycler** n

¹**red** adj -dd- 1 of the colour red 2a flushed, esp with anger or embarrassment b bloodshot ⟨eyes ~ from crying⟩ c of hair or the coat of an animal in the colour range between a medium orange and russet or bay d tinged with or rather red ⟨a ~ sky⟩ 3 cap of a communist country, esp the Soviet Union 4 failing to show a profit ⟨a ~ financial statement⟩ 5a inciting or endorsing radical social or political change, esp by force b often cap communist USE (5) infml or derog – **reddish** adj, **reddishness** n, **redly** adv, **redness** n

²**red** n 1 a colour whose hue resembles that of blood or of the ruby or is that of the long-wave extreme of the visible spectrum 2 sthg that is of or gives a red or reddish colour 3 the condition of being financially in debt or of showing a loss – usu in in/out of the red; compare BLACK 7 4 a red traffic light meaning 'stop' 5a a revolutionary radical b cap a communist USE (5) chiefly derog

red admiral n a common N American and European butterfly that has broad orange-red bands on the fore wings and feeds on nettles in the larval stage

red blood cell, red cell n any of the haemoglobin-containing cells that carry oxygen to the tissues and are responsible for the red colour of vertebrate blood

red-blooded adj full of vigour; virile

redbreast n a robin

redbrick n or adj (an English university) founded between 1800 and WW II

redcap n 1 Br a military policeman 2 NAm a (railway) porter

red carpet *n* a greeting or reception marked by ceremonial courtesy – usu in *roll out the red carpet* – **red-carpet** *adj*

red cent *n, chiefly NAm* a trivial amount; a whit ⟨*not worth a ~*⟩

redcoat *n* a British soldier, esp formerly when scarlet jackets were worn

redcurrant *n* (the small red edible fruit of) a widely cultivated European currant bush

redden *vt* to make red or reddish *~ vi* to become red; *esp* to blush

redeem *vt* **1a** to repurchase (e g sthg pledged or lodged as security against a sum of money) ⟨*to ~ a pawned ring*⟩ **b** to get or win back ⟨*~ed his losses of the previous night's gambling*⟩ **2** to free from what distresses or harms: e g **a** to free from captivity by payment of ransom **b** to release from blame or debt ⟨*hoped to ~ himself by these heroics*⟩ **c** to free from the consequences of sin **3a** to eliminate another's right to (sthg) by payment of a debt **b(1)** to remove the obligation of (e g a bond) by making a stipulated payment ⟨*the government ~ savings bonds on demand*⟩; *specif* to convert (paper money) into money in coin **(2)** to convert (trading stamps, tokens, etc) into money or goods **c** to make good; fulfil ⟨*~ed his promise*⟩ **4a** to atone for ⟨*to ~ an error*⟩ **b(1)** to offset the bad effect of ⟨*flashes of wit ~ed a dreary speech*⟩ **(2)** to make worthwhile; retrieve ⟨*no efforts of hers could ~ such a hopeless undertaking*⟩ – **redeemable** *adj*

Redeemer *n* Jesus

redemption *n* redeeming or being redeemed; *also* sthg that redeems – **redemptive** *adj*

redeploy *vb* to transfer (e g troops or workers) from one area or activity to another – **redeployment** *n*

red giant *n* a star that has a low surface temperature and a large diameter relative to the sun

red-handed *adv or adj* in the act of committing a crime or misdeed ⟨*caught ~*⟩

redhead *n* a person with red hair – **redheaded** *adj*

red-hot *adj* **1** glowing with heat; extremely hot **2a** ardent, passionate ⟨*~ anger*⟩ **b** sensational; *specif* salacious ⟨*this ~ story of a Regency love affair*⟩ **c** full of energy, vigour, or enterprise ⟨*a ~ band*⟩ **d** arousing enthusiasm; currently extolled ⟨*a ~ favourite for the National*⟩ **3** new, topical ⟨*~ news*⟩

Red Indian *n* a N American Indian

redirect *vt* to change the course or direction of – **redirection** *n*

red lead *n* an orange-red to brick-red lead oxide used in storage battery plates, in glass and ceramics, and as a paint pigment

red-letter *adj* of special (happy) significance

red light *n* **1** a red warning light, esp on a road or railway, commanding traffic to stop **2** a cautionary sign ⟨*saw her warning as a ~ to potential troublemakers*⟩

red-light district *n* a district having many brothels

red meat *n* dark-coloured meat (e g beef or lamb)

redo *vt* **redoes; redoing; redid; redone 1** to do over again **2** to decorate (a room or interior of a building) anew

redolent *adj* **1** full of a specified fragrance ⟨*air ~ of seaweed*⟩ **2** evocative, suggestive ⟨*a city ~ of antiquity*⟩ – **redolence** *n*, **redolently** *adv*

redouble *vb* **redoubling 1** to make or become greater, more numerous, or more intense ⟨*to ~ our efforts*⟩ **2** to double (an opponent's double) in bridge – **redouble** *n*

redoubt *n* **1** a small usu temporary enclosed defensive fortified structure **2** a secure place; a stronghold

redoubtable *adj* **1** formidable ⟨*a ~ adversary*⟩ **2** inspiring or worthy of awe or reverence – **redoubtably** *adv*

redound *vi* **1** to have a direct effect; lead or contribute *to* ⟨*can only ~ to our advantage*⟩ **2** to rebound *on or upon* ⟨*the President's behaviour ~s on his Party*⟩ *USE* fml

red pepper *n* CAYENNE PEPPER

¹redress *vt* **1a** to set right ⟨*to ~ social wrongs*⟩ **b** to make or exact reparation for **2** to adjust evenly; make stable or equal again ⟨*to ~ the balance of power*⟩

²redress *n* **1** compensation for wrong or loss **2** the (means or possibility of) putting right what is wrong

redskin *n* a N American Indian – chiefly derog

red squirrel *n* a reddish brown Eurasian squirrel native to British woodlands that is gradually being replaced by the grey squirrel

red tape *n* excessively complex bureaucratic routine that results in delay

reduce *vt* **1** to diminish in size, amount, extent, or number; make less ⟨*~ taxes*⟩ ⟨*~ the likelihood of war*⟩ **2** to bring or force to a specified state or condition ⟨*was ~d to tears of frustration*⟩ **3** to force to capitulate ⟨*~d Alexandria after a lengthy siege*⟩ **4** to bring to a systematic form or character ⟨*~ natural events to laws*⟩ **5** to correct (e g a fracture) by bringing displaced or broken parts back into normal position **6** to lower in grade, rank, status, or condition ⟨*~d to the ranks*⟩ ⟨*living in ~d circumstances*⟩ **7a** to diminish in strength, density, or value **b** to lower the price of ⟨*shoes ~d in the sale*⟩ **8** to change the denominations or form of without changing the value ⟨*~ fractions to a common denominator*⟩ **9** to break down by crushing, grinding, etc **10a** to convert (e g an ore) to a metal by removing nonmetallic elements **b** to combine with or subject to the action of hydrogen **c** to change (an atom, molecule, ion, etc) from a higher to a lower oxidation state, esp by adding electrons *~ vi* **1** to become diminished or lessened; *esp* to lose weight by dieting **2** to become reduced ⟨*ferric iron ~s to ferrous iron*⟩ – **reducer** *n*, **reducible** *adj*, **reducibility** *n*

reductio ad absurdum *n* proof of the falsity of a proposition by revealing the absurdity of its logical consequences

reduction *n* **1** a reducing or being reduced **2a** sthg made by reducing; *esp* a reproduction (e g of a picture) in a smaller size **b** the amount by which sthg is reduced – **reductive** *adj*

redundancy *n* **1** being redundant **2** the part of a message that can be eliminated without loss of essential information **3** *chiefly Br* dismissal from a job

redundant *adj* **1a** superfluous **b** characterized by or containing an excess; *specif* excessively verbose ⟨*a ~ literary style*⟩ **2** serving as a backup so as to prevent failure of an entire system (e g a spacecraft) in the event of failure of a single component **3** *chiefly Br* unnecessary, unfit, or no longer required for a job – **redundantly** *adv*

reduplication *n* **1** a doubling or reiterating **2** the doubling of (part of) a word with or without partial modification (e g in *hocus pocus* or *dilly-dally*) – **reduplicate** *vt or adj*, **reduplicative** *adj*

redwing *n* a Eurasian thrush with red patches beneath its wings

redwood *n* (the wood of) a commercially important Californian timber tree of the pine family that often reaches a height of 100m (about 300ft)

reecho *vb* **reechoes; reechoing; reechoed** *vi* to repeat or return an echo *~ vt* to echo back; repeat

reed *n* **1a** (the slender, often prominently jointed, stem of) any of various tall grasses that grow esp in wet areas **b** a person or thing too weak to rely on **2** a growth or mass of reeds; *specif* reeds for thatching **3a** a thin elastic tongue or flattened tube (e g of cane or plastic) fastened over an air opening in a musical instrument (e g an organ or clarinet) and set in vibration by an air current **b** a woodwind instrument having a reed ⟨*the ~s of an orchestra*⟩ **4** a device on a loom resembling a comb, used to space warp yarns evenly **5** a semicircular convex moulding that is usu 1 of several set parallel

reed organ *n* a keyboard wind instrument in which the wind acts on a set of reeds

reed pipe *n* an organ pipe producing its tone by vibration of a beating reed in an air current

reeducate *vt* to rehabilitate through education – **reeducative** *adj*, **reeducation** *n*

reedy *adj* **1** full of, covered with, or made of reeds **2** slender, frail **3** having the tonal quality of a reed instrument; *esp* thin and high

¹reef *n* a part of a sail taken in or let out to regulate the area exposed to the wind

²reef *vt* to reduce the area of (a sail) exposed to the wind by rolling up or taking in a portion

³reef *n* **1** a ridge of rocks or sand at or near the surface of water **2** a lode – **reefy** *adj*

¹reefer, reefer jacket *n* a close-fitting usu double-breasted jacket of thick cloth

²reefer *n* JOINT 4

reef knot *n* a symmetrical knot made of 2 half-knots tied in opposite directions and commonly used for joining 2 pieces of material

¹reek *n* **1** a strong or disagreeable smell **2** *chiefly Scot & N Eng* smoke, vapour – **reeky** *adj*

²reek *vi* **1** to emit smoke or vapour **2a** to give off or become permeated with a strong or offensive smell **b** to give a strong impression (of some usu undesirable quality or feature) – + *of* or *with* ⟨*an area that ~s of poverty*⟩ ⟨*man who ~s of charm*⟩

¹reel *n* a revolvable device on which sthg flexible is wound: e g **a** a small wheel at the butt of a fishing rod for winding the line **b** a flanged spool for photographic film, magnetic tape, etc **c** *chiefly Br* a small spool for sewing thread

²reel *vt* **1** to wind (as if) on a reel **2** to draw by reeling a line ⟨*~ a fish in*⟩

³reel *vi* **1** to be giddy; be in a whirl ⟨*his mind was ~ing*⟩ **2** to waver or fall back (e g from a blow) ⟨*~ed back in horror*⟩ **3** to walk or (appear to) move unsteadily (e g from dizziness or intoxication)

⁴reel *n* a reeling motion

⁵reel *n* (the music for) a lively esp Scottish-Highland or Irish dance in which 2 or more couples perform a series of circular figures and winding movements

reel off *vt* **1** to tell or repeat readily and without pause ⟨*reeled off all the facts and figures*⟩ **2** to chalk up, usu as a series ⟨*to reel off 6 wins in succession*⟩

reentry *n* **1** the retaking of possession **2** a second or new entry ⟨*a ~ visa*⟩; *esp* the return to and entry of the earth's atmosphere by a space vehicle – **reenter** *vb*

¹reeve *n* a medieval English manor officer

²reeve *vt* **rove, reeved** **1** to pass (e g a rope) through a hole or opening **2** to fasten by passing through a hole or round sthg **3** to pass a rope through (e g a block)

³reeve *n* the female of the ruff

ref *n* REFEREE 2 – *infml*

refectory *n* a dining hall in an institution (e g a monastery or college)

refer *vb* **-rr-** *vt* **1a** to explain in terms of a general cause ⟨*~s their depression to the weather*⟩ **b** to allot to a specified place, stage, period, or category ⟨*to ~ the fall of Rome to 410* AD⟩ **c** to experience (e g pain) as coming from or located in a different area from its source ⟨*the pain in appendicitis may be ~red to any area of the abdomen*⟩ **2** to send or direct for treatment, aid, information, testimony, or decision ⟨*to ~ a patient to a*

specialist⟩ ⟨*~s students to her other works*⟩ ~ *vi* **1a** to relate *to* sthg **b** to direct attention (by clear and specific mention); allude ⟨*the numbers ~ to footnotes*⟩ ⟨*no one ~red to yesterday's quarrel*⟩ **2** to have recourse; glance briefly for information ⟨*~ frequently to his notes while speaking*⟩ – **referable** *adj*, **referral** *n*

¹referee *n* **1** a person to whom sthg is referred: e g **a** one to whom a legal matter is referred for investigation or settlement **b** one who reviews a (technical) paper before publication **c** REFERENCE 4a **2** an official who supervises the play and enforces the laws in any of several sports (e g football and boxing)

²referee *vb* to act as a referee (in or for)

¹reference *n* **1** referring or consulting ⟨*a manual designed for ready ~*⟩ **2** (a) bearing on or connection with a matter – often in *in/with reference to* **3** sthg that refers: e g **a** an allusion, mention **b** sthg that refers a reader or consulter to another source of information (e g a book or passage) **4** one referred to or consulted: e g **a** a person to whom inquiries as to character or ability can be made **b** a statement of the qualifications of a person seeking employment or appointment given by sby familiar with him/her **c** a source of information (e g a book or passage) to which a reader or inquirer is referred **d** a standard for measuring, evaluating, etc – **referential** *adj*

²reference *vt* to provide (e g a book) with references to authorities and sources of information

reference book *n* a book (e g a dictionary, encyclopedia, or atlas) intended primarily for consultation rather than for consecutive reading

reference mark *n* a conventional sign (e g * or †) to direct the reader's attention, esp to a footnote

referendum *n*, *pl* **referendums** *also* **referenda** the submitting to popular vote of a measure proposed by a legislative body or by popular initiative; *also* a vote on a measure so submitted

referent *n* the thing that a symbol (e g a word or sign) stands for

refill *n* a fresh or replacement supply (for a device) ⟨*a ~ for a ballpoint pen*⟩ – **refill** *vb*, **refillable** *adj*

refine *vt* **1** to free from impurities ⟨*~ sugar*⟩ **2** to improve or perfect by pruning or polishing ⟨*~ a poetic style*⟩ **3** to free from imperfection, esp from what is coarse, vulgar, or uncouth ~ *vi* **1** to become pure or perfected **2** to make improvement by introducing subtleties or distinctions – **refiner** *n*

refined *adj* **1** fastidious, cultivated **2** *esp of food* processed to the extent that desirable ingredients may be lost in addition to impurities or imperfections

refinement *n* **1** refining or being refined **2a** a (highly) refined feature, method, or distinction ⟨*pursued the delicate art of suggestion to its furthest ~s* – Maurice Bowra⟩ **b** a contrivance or device intended to improve or perfect ⟨*a new model of car with many ~s*⟩

refinery *n* a plant where raw materials (e g metals, oil or sugar) are refined or purified

refit *vt* **-tt-** to fit out or supply again; *esp* to renovate and modernize (e g a ship) – **refit** *n*

reflation *n* an expansion in the volume of available money and credit or in the economy, esp as a result of government policy – **reflationary** *adj*, **reflate** *vb*

reflect *vt* **1** to send or throw (light, sound, etc) back or at an angle ⟨*a mirror ~s light*⟩ **2** to show as an image or likeness; mirror ⟨*the clouds were ~ed in the water*⟩ **3** to make manifest or apparent; give an idea of ⟨*the pulse ~s the condition of the heart*⟩ **4** to consider ~ *vi* **1** to throw back light or sound **2** to think quietly and calmly **3a** to tend to bring reproach or discredit – usu + *on* or *upon* ⟨*an investigation that ~s on all the members of the depart-*

ment⟩ **b** to tend to bring about a specified appearance or impression – usu + *on* ⟨*an act which* ~s *favourably on her*⟩

reflecting telescope *n* REFLECTOR 2

reflection, *Br also* **reflexion** *n* **1** a reflecting of light, sound, etc **2** sthg produced by reflecting: e g **a** an image given back (as if) by a reflecting surface **b** an effect produced by or related to a specified influence or cause ⟨*a high crime rate is a* ~ *of an unstable society*⟩ **3** an often obscure or indirect criticism **4** (a thought, opinion, etc formed by) consideration of some subject matter, idea, or purpose ⟨*on* ~ *it didn't seem such a good plan*⟩ **5** a transformation of a figure with respect to a reference line producing a mirror image of the figure – **reflectional** *adj*

reflective *adj* **1** capable of reflecting light, images, or sound waves **2** thoughtful, deliberative **3** of or caused by reflection ⟨*the* ~ *glare of the snow*⟩ – **reflectively** *adv*, **reflectiveness, reflectivity** *n*

reflector *n* **1** a polished surface for reflecting radiation, esp light **2** a telescope in which the principal focussing element is a mirror

¹reflex *n* **1a** reflected heat, light, or colour **b** a mirrored image **c** a reproduction or reflection that corresponds to some usu specified original; *specif* a word (element) in a form determined by development from an earlier stage of the language **2a** an automatic response to a stimulus that does not reach the level of consciousness **b** *pl* the power of acting or responding with adequate speed **c** an (automatic) way of behaving or responding ⟨*lying became a natural* ~ *for him*⟩

²reflex *adj* **1** bent, turned, or directed back ⟨*a stem with* ~ *leaves*⟩ **2** directed back upon the mind or its operations; introspective **3** occurring as an (automatic) response **4** *of an angle* greater than 180° but less than 360° **5** of, being, or produced by a reflex without intervention of consciousness – **reflexly** *adv*

reflex camera *n* a camera in which the image formed by the lens is reflected onto a ground-glass screen or is seen through the viewfinder for focussing and composition

¹reflexive *adj* **1** directed or turned back on itself **2** of, denoting, or being an action (e g in *he perjured himself*) directed back upon the agent or the grammatical subject – **reflexively** *adv*

²reflexive *n* a reflexive verb or pronoun

¹reform *vt* **1** to amend or alter for the better **2** to put an end to (an evil) by enforcing or introducing a better method or course of action **3** to induce or cause to abandon evil ways ⟨~ *a drunkard*⟩ ~*vi* to become changed for the better – **reformable** *adj*, **reformative, reformatory** *adj*

²reform *n* **1** amendment of what is defective or corrupt ⟨*educational* ~⟩ **2** (a measure intended to effect) a removal or correction of an abuse, a wrong, or errors

reformation *n* **1** reforming or being reformed **2** *cap the* 16th-c religious movement marked ultimately by the rejection of papal authority and some Roman Catholic doctrines and practices, and the establishment of the Protestant churches – **reformational** *adj*

reformatory *n, chiefly NAm* a penal institution to which young or first offenders or women are sent for reform – no longer used technically in Br

refract *vt* **1** to deflect (light or another wave motion) from one straight path to another when passing from one medium (e g glass) to another (e g air) in which the velocity is different **2** to determine the refracting power of – **refraction** *n*, **refractive** *adj*, **refractivity** *n*

refracting telescope *n* a refractor

¹refractory *adj* **1** resisting control or authority; stubborn,

unmanageable **2a** resistant to treatment or cure ⟨*a* ~ *cough*⟩ **b** immune ⟨*after recovery they were* ~ *to infection*⟩ **3** difficult to fuse, corrode, or draw out; *esp* capable of enduring high temperatures – **refractorily** *adv*, **refractoriness** *n*

²refractory *n* a heat-resisting ceramic material

¹refrain *vi* to keep oneself from doing, feeling, or indulging in sthg, esp from following a passing impulse – usu + *from*

²refrain *n* (the musical setting of) a regularly recurring phrase or verse, esp at the end of each stanza or division of a poem or song; a chorus

refresh *vt* **1** to restore strength or vigour to; revive (e g by food or rest) **2** to restore or maintain by renewing supply; replenish ⟨*the waiter* ~ed *our glasses*⟩ **3** to arouse, stimulate (e g the memory)

refresher *n* **1** sthg (e g a drink) that refreshes **2 refresher, refresher course** a course of instruction designed to keep one abreast of developments in one's professional field

refreshing *adj* agreeably stimulating because of freshness or newness – **refreshingly** *adv*

refreshment *n* **1** refreshing or being refreshed **2a** sthg (e g food or drink) that refreshes **b** assorted foods, esp for a light meal – usu *pl* with sing. meaning

refrigerate *vb* to make or keep cold or cool; *specif* to freeze or chill (e g food) or remain frozen for preservation – **refrigerant** *n or adj*, **refrigeration** *n*

refrigerator *n* an insulated cabinet or room for keeping food, drink, etc cool

refuel *vb* **-ll-** (*NAm* **-l-, -ll-**) to provide with or take on additional fuel

refuge *n* **1** (a place that provides) shelter or protection from danger or distress ⟨*to seek* ~ *in flight*⟩ ⟨*a mountain* ~⟩ **2** a person, thing, or course of action that offers protection or is resorted to in difficulties ⟨*patriotism is the last* ~ *of a scoundrel* – Samuel Johnson⟩

refugee *n* one who flees for safety, esp to a foreign country to escape danger or avoid political, religious, or racial persecution

refulgence *n* radiance, brilliance – *fml* – **refulgent** *adj*, **refulgently** *adv*

¹refund *vt* **1** to return (money) in restitution, repayment, or balancing of accounts **2** to pay (sby) back – **refundable** *adj*

²refund *n* **1** a refunding **2** a sum refunded

³refund *vt* to fund (a debt) again

refurbish *vt* to renovate – **refurbishment** *n*

refusal *n* **1** a refusing, denying, or being refused **2** the right or option of refusing or accepting sthg before others

¹refuse *vt* **1** to express oneself as unwilling to accept **2a** to show or express unwillingness to do or comply with ⟨*the engine* ~d *to start*⟩ **b** to deny ⟨*they were* ~d *admittance to the game*⟩ **3** to decline to jump over – used esp of a horse ⟨~d *the water jump*⟩ ~*vi* **1** to withhold acceptance, compliance, or permission **2** *of a horse* to decline to jump a fence, wall, etc ⟨~d *at the third fence*⟩ – **refusable** *adj*, **refuser** *n*

²refuse *n* worthless or useless stuff; rubbish, garbage

refute *vt* **1** to prove wrong by argument or evidence **2** to deny the truth or accuracy of – **refutable** *adj*, **refutably** *adv*, **refutation** *n*

regain *vt* to gain or reach again; recover

regal *adj* **1** of or suitable for a king or queen **2** stately, splendid – **regally** *adv*, **regality** *n*

regale *vt* **1** to entertain sumptuously **2** to give pleasure or amusement to ⟨~d *us with stories of her exploits*⟩

regalia *n pl but sing or pl in constr* **1** (the) ceremonial emblems or symbols indicative of royalty **2** special dress; *esp* official finery

¹regard *n* **1** a gaze, look **2a** attention, consideration ⟨*due ~ should be given to all facets of the question*⟩ **b** a protective interest ⟨*ought to have more ~ for his health*⟩ **3a** a feeling of respect and affection ⟨*her hard work won her the ~ of her colleagues*⟩ **b** *pl* friendly greetings ⟨*give him my ~ s*⟩ **4** an aspect to be taken into consideration ⟨*is a small school, and is fortunate in this ~*⟩ – **regardful** *adj* – **in/with regard to** with reference to; on the subject of

²regard *vt* **1** to pay attention to; take into consideration or account **2** to look steadily at **3** to relate to; concern **4** to consider and appraise in a specified way or from a specified point of view ⟨*he is highly ~ ed as a mechanic*⟩ – **as regards** WITH REGARD TO

regarding *prep* WITH REGARD TO

¹regardless *adj* heedless, careless – **regardlessly** *adv*, **regardlessness** *n*

²regardless *adv* despite everything ⟨*went ahead with their plans ~*⟩

regardless of *prep* IN SPITE OF ⟨*regardless of our mistakes*⟩

regatta *n* a series of rowing, speedboat, or sailing races

regency *n* **1** the office, period of rule, or government of a regent or regents **2** *sing or pl in constr* a body of regents

Regency *adj* of or resembling the styles (e g of furniture or dress) prevalent during the time of the Prince Regent

¹regenerate *adj* **1** formed or created again **2** spiritually reborn or converted **3** restored to a better, higher, or more worthy state – **regenerate** *n*, **regeneracy** *n*

²regenerate *vi* **1** to become regenerate or regenerated **2** *of a body or body part* to undergo renewal or regrowth (e g after injury) ~ *vt* **1a** to subject to spiritual or moral renewal or revival **b** to change radically and for the better **2a** to generate or produce anew; *esp* to replace (a body part) by a new growth of tissue **b** to produce from a derivative or modified form, esp by chemical treatment ⟨*~ d cellulose*⟩ **3** to restore to original strength or properties – **regenerator** *n*, **regenerable** *adj*, **regenerative** *adj*, **regeneration** *n*

regent *n* one who governs a kingdom in the minority, absence, or disability of the sovereign – **regent** *adj*

reggae *n* popular music of West Indian origin that is characterized by a strongly accented subsidiary beat

regicide *n* (the act of) one who kills a king – **regicidal** *adj*

regime *also* **régime** *n* **1a** a regimen **b** a regular pattern of occurrence or action (e g of seasonal rainfall) **2a** a form of management or government ⟨*a socialist ~*⟩ **b** a government in power

regimen *n* a systematic plan (e g of diet, exercise, or medical treatment) adopted esp to achieve some end

¹regiment *n sing or pl in constr* **1** a permanent military unit consisting usu of a number of companies, troops, batteries, or sometimes battalions **2** a large number or group – **regimental** *adj*, **regimentally** *adv*

²regiment *vt* **1** to form into a regiment **2** to subject to strict and stultifying organization or control ⟨*~ an entire country*⟩ – **regimentation** *n*

regimentals *n pl* **1** the uniform of a regiment **2** military dress

Regina *n* CROWN 5a – used when a queen is ruling

region *n* **1** an administrative area **2a** an indefinite area of the world or universe **b** a broadly uniform geographical or ecological area ⟨*desert ~ s*⟩ **3** an indefinite area surrounding a specified body part ⟨*the abdominal ~*⟩ **4** a

sphere of activity or interest ⟨*the abstract ~ of higher mathematics*⟩ **5** any of the zones into which the atmosphere is divided according to height or the sea according to depth – **in the region of** approximating to; MORE OR LESS

regional *adj* **1** (characteristic) of a region **2** affecting a particular region; localized – **regionally** *adv*

¹register *n* **1** a written record containing (official) entries of items, names, transactions, etc **2a** a roster of qualified or available individuals ⟨*the electoral ~*⟩ **b** a school attendance record **3a** an organ stop **b** (a part of) the range of a human voice or a musical instrument **4** the language style and vocabulary appropriate to a particular subject matter **5** a device regulating admission of air, esp to solid fuel **6** REGISTRATION 1 **7** an automatic device registering a number or a quantity **8** a condition of correct alignment or proper relative position (e g of the plates used in colour printing) – often in *in/out of register* **9** a device (e g in a computer) for storing and working on small amounts of data

²register *vt* **1a** to make or secure official entry of in a register ⟨*~ ed the birth of their daughter*⟩ **b** to enrol formally **c** to record automatically; indicate ⟨*this dial ~ s speed*⟩ **d** to make a (mental) record of; note **2** to secure special protection for (a piece of mail) by prepayment of a fee **3** to convey an impression of ⟨*~ ed surprise at the telegram*⟩ **4** to achieve, win ⟨*~ ed an impressive victory*⟩ ~ *vi* **1a** to put one's name in a register ⟨*~ ed at the hotel*⟩ **b** to enrol formally (as a student) **2** to make or convey an impression ⟨*the name didn't ~*⟩ – **registrable** *adj*

registered *adj* qualified formally or officially

register office *n* REGISTRY OFFICE

register ton *n* a unit of internal capacity for ships equal to 100ft³ (about 2.83m³)

registrar *n* **1** an official recorder or keeper of records: e g **a** a senior administrative officer of a university **b** a court official who deals with administrative and interlocutory matters and acts as a subordinate judge **2** (the post, senior to that of a senior house officer, of) a British hospital doctor in training

registration *n* **1** registering or being registered **2** an entry in a register

registry *n* **1** REGISTRATION 1 **2** a place of registration; *specif* a registry office

registry office *n*, *Br* a place where births, marriages, and deaths are recorded and civil marriages conducted

regius professor *n* a holder of a professorship founded by royal subsidy at a British university

regnant *adj* reigning ⟨*a queen ~*⟩

¹regress *n* **1** REGRESSION 2a **2** an act of going or coming back – *fml*

²regress *vi* **1** to undergo or exhibit backwards movement, esp to an earlier state **2** to tend to approach or revert to a mean ~ *vt* to induce, esp by hypnosis, a state of psychological regression in

regression *n* **1** the act or an instance of regressing; *esp* (a) retrograde movement **2a** a trend or shift towards a lower, less perfect, or earlier state or condition **b** reversion to an earlier mental or behavioural level **3** the statistical analysis of the association between 2 or more variables, esp so that predictions (e g of sales over a future period of time) can be made – **regressive** *adj*, **regressively** *adv*

¹regret *vt* **-tt-** **1** to mourn the loss or death of **2** to be very sorry about ⟨*~ s his mistakes*⟩ – **regrettable** *adj*

²regret *n* **1** (an expression of) the emotion arising from a wish that some matter or situation could be other than what it is; *esp* grief or sorrow tinged esp with disappointment, longing, or remorse **2** *pl* a conventional expression of disappointment, esp on declining an invitation

⟨*couldn't come to tea, and sent her ~s*⟩ – **regretful** *adj*, **regretfully** *adv*, **regretfulness** *n*

regrettably *adv* **1** in a regrettable manner; to a regrettable extent ⟨*a ~ steep decline in wages*⟩ **2** it is regrettable that ⟨*~, we had failed to consider alternatives*⟩

¹**regular** *adj* **1** belonging to a religious order **2a** formed, built, arranged, or ordered according to some rule, principle, or type ⟨*a ~ curve*⟩ **b(1)** both equilateral and equiangular ⟨*a ~ polygon*⟩ **(2)** having faces that are identical regular polygons with identical angles between them ⟨*a ~ polyhedron*⟩ ⟨*a ~ solid*⟩ **c** perfectly (radially) symmetrical or even **3a** steady or uniform in course, practice, or occurrence; habitual, usual, or constant ⟨*~ habits*⟩ **b** recurring or functioning at fixed or uniform intervals ⟨*a ~ income*⟩ **c** defecating or having menstrual periods at normal intervals **4a** constituted, conducted, or done in conformity with established or prescribed usages, rules, or discipline **b** real, absolute ⟨*the office seemed like a ~ madhouse*⟩ **c** inflecting normally; *specif* WEAK 7 **5** of or being a permanent standing army **6** *chiefly NAm* thinking or behaving in an acceptable manner ⟨*wanted to prove he was a ~ guy*⟩ – *infml* – **regularly** *adv*, **regularize** *vt*, **regularization** *n*, **regularity** *n*

²**regular** *n* **1a** a member of the regular clergy **b** a soldier in a regular army **2** one who is usu present or participating; *esp* one who habitually visits a particular place

regulate *vt* **1** to govern or direct according to rule **2** to bring order, method, or uniformity to ⟨*~ one's habits*⟩ **3** to fix or adjust the time, amount, degree, or rate of ⟨*~ the pressure of a tyre*⟩ – **regulative, regulatory** *adj*, **regulator** *n*

¹**regulation** *n* **1** regulating or being regulated **2a** an authoritative rule dealing with details or procedure ⟨*safety ~s in a factory*⟩ **b** a rule or order having the force of law ⟨*EEC ~s*⟩

²**regulation** *adj* conforming to regulations; official ⟨*~ uniform*⟩

regulo *n, chiefly Br* the temperature in a gas oven expressed as a specified number ⟨*meat cooked on ~ 4*⟩

regurgitate *vb* to vomit or pour back or out (as if) from a cavity – **regurgitation** *n*

rehabilitate *vt* **1** to reestablish the good name of **2a** to restore to a former capacity or state (e g of efficiency, sound condition, or solvency) ⟨*~ slum areas*⟩ **b** to restore to a condition of health or useful and constructive activity (e g after illness or imprisonment) – **rehabilitative** *adj*, **rehabilitation** *n*

¹**rehash** *vt* to present or use again in another form without substantial change or improvement

²**rehash** *n* sthg presented in a new form without change of substance

rehear *vt* **reheard** to hear (a trial or lawsuit) over again – **rehearing** *n*

rehearsal *n* **1** a rehearsing **2** a practice session, esp of a play, concert, etc preparatory to a public appearance

rehearse *vt* **1** to present an account of (again) ⟨*~ a familiar story*⟩ **2** to recount in order ⟨*had ~d their grievances in a letter to the governor*⟩ **3a** to give a rehearsal of; practice **b** to train or make proficient by rehearsal *~vi* to engage in a rehearsal of a play, concert, etc – **rehearser** *n*

rehouse *vt* to establish in new or better-quality housing

reify *vt* to regard (sthg abstract) as a material thing – **reification** *n*

¹**reign** *n* **1a** royal authority; sovereignty **b** the dominion, sway, or influence of one resembling or likened to a monarch ⟨*the ~ of the military dictators*⟩ **2** the time during which sby or sthg reigns

²**reign** *vi* **1a** RULE 1a **b** to hold office as head of state although possessing little governing power ⟨*the queen ~s but does not rule*⟩ **2** to be predominant or prevalent ⟨*chaos ~ed in the classroom*⟩

reign of terror *n* a period of ruthless violence committed by those in power

reimburse *vt* **1** to pay back to sby ⟨*~ travel expenses*⟩ **2** to make restoration or payment to ⟨*~ you*⟩ – **reimbursable** *adj*, **reimbursement** *n*

¹**rein** *n* **1** a long line fastened usu to both sides of a bit, by which a rider or driver controls an animal **2a** a restraining influence **b** controlling or guiding power ⟨*the ~s of government*⟩ **c** opportunity for unhampered activity or use ⟨*gave free ~ to his emotions*⟩ *USE (1 & 2b)* usu pl with sing. meaning

²**rein** *vt* to check or stop (as if) by pulling on reins – often + *in* ⟨*~ed in his horse*⟩ ⟨*couldn't ~ his impatience*⟩

reincarnate *vt* **1** to incarnate again; give a new form or fresh embodiment to **2** to cause (a person or his/her soul) to be reborn in another (human) body after death – usu in pass; compare TRANSMIGRATE – **reincarnate** *adj*, **reincarnation** *n*, **reincarnationist** *n*

reindeer *n* any of several deer that inhabit N Europe, Asia, and America, have antlers in both sexes, and are often domesticated

reinforce *vt* **1** to strengthen by additional assistance, material, or support; make stronger or more pronounced **2** to strengthen or increase (e g an army) by fresh additions **3** to stimulate (an experimental subject) with a reward following a correct or desired performance; *also* to encourage (a response) with a reward – **reinforceable** *adj*, **reinforcement** *n*, **reinforcer** *n*

reinforced concrete *n* concrete in which metal is embedded for strengthening

reinstate *vt* **1** to place again (e g in possession or in a former position) **2** to restore to a previous effective state or condition – **reinstatement** *n*

reinsure *vt* to insure (a risk or person) by reinsurance – **reinsurer** *n*

reissue *vt* to issue again; *esp* to cause to become available again – **reissue** *n*

reiterate *vt* to say or do over again or repeatedly, sometimes with wearying effect – **reiteration** *n*, **reiterative** *adj*, **reiteratively** *adv*

¹**reject** *vt* **1a** to refuse to accept, consider, submit to, or use **b** to refuse to accept or admit ⟨*the underprivileged feel ~ed by society*⟩ **2** to eject; *esp* VOMIT 1 **3** to fail to accept (e g a skin graft or transplanted organ) as part of the organism because of immunological differences – **rejecter, rejector** *n*, **rejection** *n*

²**reject** *n* a rejected person or thing; *esp* a substandard article of merchandise

rejoice *vt* to give joy to; gladden *~vi* to feel or express joy or great delight – **rejoicer** *n*, **rejoicingly** *adv*

rejoin *vt* to say (sharply or critically) in response

rejoinder *n* (an answer to) a reply

rejuvenate *vt* **1** to make young or youthful again **2** to restore to an original or new state ⟨*~ old cars*⟩ *~vi* to cause or undergo rejuvenation – **rejuvenator** *n*, **rejuvenation** *n*

¹**relapse** *n* a relapsing or backsliding; *esp* a recurrence of symptoms of a disease after a period of improvement

²**relapse** *vi* **1** to slip or fall back into a former worse state **2** to sink, subside ⟨*~ into deep thought*⟩

relate *vt* **1** to give an account of; tell **2** to show or establish logical or causal connection between *~vi* **1** to have relationship or connection **2** to respond, esp favourably ⟨*can't ~ to that kind of music*⟩ *USE (vi)* often + *to* – **relatable** *adj*, **relater** *n*

related adj 1 connected by reason of an established or discoverable relation 2 connected by common ancestry or sometimes by marriage – **relatedness** n

relation n 1 the act of telling or recounting 2 an aspect or quality (e g resemblance) that connects 2 or more things as belonging or working together or as being of the same kind 3a RELATIVE 3a b kinship 4 reference, respect, or connection ⟨in ~ to⟩ 5 the interaction between 2 or more people or groups – usu pl with sing. meaning ⟨race ~s⟩ 6 pl a dealings, affairs ⟨foreign ~s⟩ b communication, contact ⟨broke off all ~ with her family⟩ c sexual intercourse – euph – **relational** adj

relationship n 1 the state or character of being related or interrelated ⟨show the ~ between 2 things⟩ 2 (a specific instance or type of) kinship 3 a state of affairs existing between those having relations or dealings ⟨had a good ~ with his family⟩

¹**relative** n 1 a word referring grammatically to an antecedent 2 sthg having or a term expressing a relation to, connection with, or necessary dependence on another thing 3a a person connected with another by blood relationship or marriage b an animal or plant related to another by common descent

²**relative** adj 1 introducing a subordinate clause qualifying an expressed or implied antecedent ⟨a ~ pronoun⟩; also introduced by such a connective ⟨a ~ clause⟩ 2 relevant, pertinent ⟨matters ~ to world peace⟩ 3a not absolute or independent; comparative ⟨the ~ isolation of life in the country⟩ b expressing, having, or existing in connection with or reference to sthg else (e g a standard) ⟨~ density⟩ ⟨supply is ~ to demand⟩ 4 of major and minor keys and scales having the same key signature – **relatively** adv, **relativeness** n

relativism n a theory that knowledge and moral principles are relative and have no objective standard – **relativist** n

relativistic adj 1 of or characterized by relativity or relativism 2 moving at or being a velocity that causes a significant change in properties (e g mass) in accordance with the theory of relativity ⟨a ~ electron⟩ – **relativistically** adv

relativity n 1 being relative 2a also **special theory of relativity** a theory (based on the 2 postulates (1) that the speed of light in a vacuum is constant and independent of the source or observer and (2) that all motion is relative) that leads to the assertion that mass and energy are equivalent and that mass, dimension, and time will change with increased velocity b also **general theory of relativity** an extension of this theory to include gravitation and related acceleration phenomena

relax vt 1 to make less tense or rigid ⟨~ed her muscles⟩ 2 to make less severe or stringent ⟨~ immigration laws⟩ 3 to lessen the force, intensity, or strength of ⟨~ing his concentration⟩ 4 to relieve from nervous tension ~ vi 1 to become lax, weak, or loose 2 to become less intense or severe 3 to cast off inhibition, nervous tension, or anxiety ⟨couldn't ~ in crowds⟩ 4 to seek rest or recreation – **relaxant** adj or n, **relaxer** n

relaxation n 1 relaxing or being relaxed 2 a relaxing or recreational state, activity, or pastime 3 the attainment of an equilibrium state following the abrupt removal of some influence (e g light, high temperature, or stress)

¹**relay** n 1a a fresh supply (e g of horses) arranged beforehand for successive use b a number of people who relieve others in some work ⟨worked in ~s around the clock⟩ 2 a race between teams in which each team member successively covers a specified portion of the course 3 a device set in operation by variation in an electric circuit and operating other devices in turn 4 the act of passing sthg along by stages; also such a stage 5 sthg, esp a message, relayed

²**relay** vt 1 to provide with relays 2 to pass along by relays ⟨news was ~ed to distant points⟩

¹**release** vt 1 to set free from restraint, confinement, or servitude 2 to relieve from sthg that confines, burdens, or oppresses ⟨was ~d from her promise⟩ 3 to relinquish (e g a claim or right) in favour of another 4 to give permission for publication, performance, exhibition, or sale of, on but not before a specified date; also to publish, issue ⟨the commission ~d its findings⟩

²**release** n 1 relief or deliverance from sorrow, suffering, or trouble 2a discharge from obligation or responsibility b (a document effecting) relinquishment or conveyance of a (legal) right or claim 3 freeing or being freed; liberation (e g from jail) 4 a device adapted to release a mechanism as required 5a (the act of permitting) performance or publication b the matter released: e g (1) a statement prepared for the press (2) a (newly issued) gramophone record – **releaser** n

relegate vt 1 to assign to a place of insignificance or oblivion; put out of sight or mind; specif to demote to a lower division of a sporting competition (e g a football league) 2a to assign to an appropriate place or situation on the basis of classification or appraisal b to submit or refer to sby or sthg for appropriate action – **relegation** n

relent vi 1 to become less severe, harsh, or strict, usu from reasons of humanity 2 to slacken; LET UP

relentless adj persistent, unrelenting – **relentlessly** adv, **relentlessness** n

relevant adj 1 having significant and demonstrable bearing on the matter at hand 2 having practical application, esp to the real world – **relevance, relevancy** n, **relevantly** adv

reliable adj suitable or fit to be relied on; dependable – **reliableness** n, **reliably** adv, **reliability** n

reliance n 1 the act of relying; the condition or attitude of one who relies ⟨~ on military power to achieve political ends⟩ 2 sthg or sby relied on – **reliant** adj, **reliantly** adv

relic n 1 a part of the body of or some object associated with a saint or martyr, that is preserved as an object of reverence 2 sthg left behind after decay, disintegration, or disappearance ⟨~s of ancient cities⟩ 3 a trace of sthg past, esp an outmoded custom, belief, or practice 4 pl, archaic remains, corpse

relict n 1 a (type of) plant or animal that is a remnant of an otherwise extinct flora, fauna, or kind of organism 2 a geological or geographical feature (e g a lake or mountain) or a rock remaining after other parts have disappeared or substantially altered 3 archaic a widow

relief n 1a removal or lightening of sthg oppressive, painful, or distressing ⟨sought ~ from asthma by moving to the coast⟩ b aid in the form of money or necessities, esp for the poor ⟨a ~ organization⟩ c military assistance to an endangered or surrounded post or force d a means of breaking or avoiding monotony or boredom ⟨studied medieval theology for light ~⟩ 2 (release from a post or duty by) one who takes over the post or duty of another ⟨a ~ teacher⟩ 3 legal compensation or amends 4 (a method of) sculpture in which the design stands out from the surrounding surface 5 sharpness of outline due to contrast ⟨a roof in bold ~ against the sky⟩ 6 the differences in elevation of a land surface

relief map n a map representing topographical relief a graphically by shading, hachures, etc b by means of a three-dimensional scale model

relieve vt 1a to free from a burden; give aid or help to b to set free from an obligation, condition, or restriction – often + *of* **2** to bring about the removal or alleviation of **3** to release from a post, station, or duty **4** to remove or lessen the monotony of **5** to raise in relief **6** to give relief to (oneself) by urinating or defecating ~ *vi* to bring or give relief – **relievable** *adj*

relieved *adj* experiencing or showing relief, esp from anxiety or pent-up emotions – **relievedly** *adv*

religion *n* **1a(1)** the (organized) service and worship of a god, gods, or the supernatural **(2)** personal commitment or devotion to religious faith or observance **b** the state of a member of a religious order **2** a cause, principle, or system of beliefs held to with ardour and faith; sthg considered to be of supreme importance

¹**religious** *adj* **1** of or manifesting faithful devotion to an acknowledged ultimate reality or deity ⟨*a ~ man*⟩ **2** of, being, or devoted to the beliefs or observances of a religion **3** scrupulously and conscientiously faithful ⟨*~ in his observance of rules of health*⟩ – **religiously** *adv*, **religiousness** *n*

²**religious** *n*, *pl* **religious** a member of a religious order under monastic vows

relinquish *vt* **1** to renounce or abandon; GIVE UP 3b **2a** to stop holding physically ⟨*~ed his grip*⟩ **b** to give over possession or control of ⟨*few leaders willingly ~ power*⟩ – **relinquishment** *n*

reliquary *n* a container or shrine in which sacred relics are kept

¹**relish** *n* **1** characteristic, pleasing, or piquant flavour or quality **2** enjoyment of or delight in sthg (that satisfies one's tastes, inclinations, or desires) ⟨*eat with ~*⟩ ⟨*little ~ for sports*⟩ **3** sthg that adds an appetizing or savoury flavour; *esp* a highly seasoned sauce (e g of pickles or mustard) eaten with plainer food

²**relish** *vt* **1** to add relish to **2** to enjoy; have pleasure from – **relishable** *adj*

relive *vt* to live over again; *esp* to experience again in the imagination

reluctance *n* **1** being reluctant **2** the opposition offered by a magnetic substance to magnetic flux; *specif* the ratio of the magnetic potential difference to the corresponding flux

reluctant *adj* holding back; unwilling ⟨*~ to condemn him*⟩ – **reluctantly** *adv*

rely *vi* **1** to have confidence based on experience ⟨*her husband was a man she could ~ on*⟩ **2** to be dependent ⟨*they ~ on a spring for their water*⟩ USE + *on* or *upon*

remain *vi* **1a** to be sthg or a part not destroyed, taken, or used up ⟨*only a few ruins ~*⟩ **b** to be sthg yet to be shown, done, or treated ⟨*it ~s to be seen*⟩ **2** to stay in the same place or with the same person or group; *specif* to stay behind **3** to continue to be ⟨*~ faithful*⟩

¹**remainder** *n* **1** a future interest in property that is dependent upon the termination of a previous interest created at the same time **2a** a remaining group, part, or trace **b(1)** the number left after a subtraction **(2)** the final undivided part after division, that is less than the divisor **3** a book sold at a reduced price by the publisher after sales have fallen off

²**remainder** *vt* to dispose of (copies of a book) as remainders

remains *n* **1** a remaining part or trace ⟨*threw away the ~ of the meal*⟩ **2** writings left unpublished at a writer's death ⟨*literary ~*⟩ **3** a dead body

¹**remake** *vt* **remade** to make anew or in a different form

²**remake** *n* a new version of a film

remand *vt* **1** to adjourn (a case) for further enquiries **2** to return to custody – **remand** *n*

remand home *n*, *Br* a temporary centre for (juvenile) offenders – not now in technical use

¹**remark** *vt* **1** to express as an observation or comment **2** to take notice of; observe – chiefly *fml* ~ *vi* to notice sthg and make a comment or observation *on* or *upon*

²**remark** *n* **1** mention or notice of that which deserves attention ⟨*would merit ~ in any political history*⟩ **2** a casual expression of an opinion or judgment ⟨*heartily sick of his snide ~s*⟩

remarkable *adj* worthy of being or likely to be noticed, esp as being uncommon or extraordinary – **remarkableness** *n*, **remarkably** *adv*

remedial *adj* **1** intended as a remedy ⟨*~ treatment*⟩ **2** concerned with the correction of faulty study habits ⟨*~ reading courses*⟩ – **remedially** *adv*

¹**remedy** *n* **1** a medicine, application, or treatment that relieves or cures a disease **2** sthg that corrects or counteracts an evil or deficiency ⟨*the firing squad made a simple ~ for discontent*⟩ **3** (legal) compensation or amends

²**remedy** *vt* to provide or serve as a remedy for – **remediable** *adj*

remember *vt* **1** to bring to mind or think of again (for attention or consideration) ⟨*~s the old days*⟩ ⟨*~ me in your prayers*⟩ **2** to give or leave (sby) a present, tip, etc ⟨*was ~ed in the will*⟩ **3** to retain in the memory ⟨*~ the facts until the test is over*⟩ **4** to convey greetings from ⟨*~ me to your mother*⟩ **5** to commemorate ~ *vi* **1** to exercise or have the power of memory **2** to have a recollection or remembrance

remembrance *n* **1** the state of bearing in mind **2** the period over which one's memory extends **3** an act of recalling to mind ⟨*~ of the offence angered him all over again*⟩ **4** a memory of a person, thing, or event ⟨*had only a dim ~ of that night*⟩ **5a** sthg that serves to keep in or bring to mind **b** a commemoration, memorial **c** a greeting or gift recalling or expressing friendship or affection

Remembrance Sunday *n* the Sunday closest to November 11, set aside in commemoration of fallen Allied servicemen and of the end of hostilities in 1918 and 1945

remind *vt* to put in mind of sthg; cause to remember – **reminder** *n*

reminisce *vi* to indulge in reminiscence

reminiscence *n* **1** the process or practice of thinking or telling about past experiences **2a** a remembered experience **b** an account of a memorable experience – often *pl* ⟨*published the ~s of the old settler*⟩ **3** sthg that recalls or is suggestive of sthg else

reminiscent *adj* **1** of (the character of) reminiscence **2** marked by or given to reminiscence **3** tending to remind one (e g of sthg seen or known before) ⟨*a technology ~ of the Stone Age*⟩

remiss *adj* **1** negligent in the performance of work or duty **2** showing neglect or inattention ⟨*service was ~ in most of the hotels*⟩ – **remissly** *adv*, **remissness** *n*

remission *n* **1** the act or process of remitting **2** a state or period during which sthg (e g the symptoms of a disease) is remitted **3** reduction of a prison sentence

¹**remit** *vb* **-tt-** *vt* **1a** to release sby from the guilt or penalty of (sin) **b** to refrain from inflicting or exacting ⟨*~ a tax*⟩ ⟨*~ the penalty of loss of pay*⟩ **c** to give relief from (suffering) **2a** to desist from (an activity) **b** to let (e g attention or diligence) slacken **3** to refer for consideration; *specif* to return (a case) to a lower court. **4** to put back **5** to postpone, defer **6** to send (money) to a person or place ~ *vi* **1a** to moderate **b** *of a disease or abnormality* to become less severe for a period **2** to send money (e g in payment) – **remitment** *n*, **remittable** *adj*, **remitter** *n*

²**remit** n 1 an act of remitting 2 sthg remitted to another person or authority for consideration or judgment

remittance n 1a a sum of money remitted b a document by which money is remitted 2 transmittal of money

remittent adj, of a disease marked by alternating periods of abatement and increase of symptoms – **remittently** adv

remnant n 1a a usu small part or trace remaining b a small surviving group – often pl 2 an unsold or unused end of fabric

remodel vt to reconstruct

remonstrance n an act or instance of remonstrating

remonstrate vt to say or plead in protest, reproof, or opposition ~vi to present and urge reasons in opposition – often + with – **remonstration** n, **remonstrative** adj, **remonstratively** adv, **remonstrator** n

remorse n a deep and bitter distress arising from a sense of guilt for past wrongs – **remorseful** adj, **remorsefully** adv

remote adj 1 far removed in space, time, or relation ⟨the ~ past⟩ ⟨comments ~ from the truth⟩ 2 out-of-the-way, secluded 3 acting on or controlling indirectly or from a distance ⟨~ computer operation⟩ 4 small in degree ⟨a ~ possibility⟩ 5 distant in manner – **remotely** adv, **remoteness** n

remote control n control over an operation (e g of a machine or weapon) exercised from a distance usu by means of an electrical circuit or radio waves

¹**remould** vt to refashion the tread of (a worn tyre)

²**remould** n a remoulded tyre

¹**remount** vt 1 to mount again ⟨~ a picture⟩ 2 to provide (e g a unit of cavalry) with remounts ~vi to mount again

²**remount** n a fresh riding horse; esp one used as a replacement for one which is exhausted

removal n 1 Br the moving of household goods from one residence to another 2 removing or being removed; specif MOVE 2c – fml ⟨our ~ to Hampton Wick⟩

¹**remove** vt 1 to change the location, position, station, or residence of ⟨~ soldiers to the front⟩ 2 to move by lifting, pushing aside, or taking away or off ⟨~s his hat in church⟩ 3 to get rid of ⟨~ a tumour surgically⟩ ~vi to change location, station, or residence – fml ⟨removing from the city to the suburbs⟩ – **remover** n, **removable** adj, **removably** adv

²**remove** n 1a a distance or interval separating one person or thing from another ⟨poems that work best at a slight ~ from the personal⟩ b a degree or stage of separation ⟨a repetition, at many ~s, of the theme of her first book⟩ 2 a form intermediate between 2 others in some British schools

remunerate vt 1 to pay an equivalent for 2 to recompense – **remunerator** n, **remuneration** n, **remunerative** adj

renaissance n 1 cap the (period of the) humanistic revival of classical influence in Europe from the 14th c to the 17th c, expressed in a flowering of the arts and literature and by the beginnings of modern science 2 often cap a movement or period of vigorous artistic and intellectual activity 3 a rebirth, revival

renal adj relating to, involving, or located in the region of the kidneys

renascent adj rising again into being or vigour – fml

rend vb rent vt 1 to wrest, split, or tear apart or in pieces (as if) by violence 2 to tear (the hair or clothing) as a sign of anger, grief, or despair 3a to lacerate mentally or emotionally b to pierce with sound ~vi to become torn or split

render vt 1a to melt down; extract by melting ⟨~ lard⟩ b to treat so as to convert into industrial fats and oils or fertilizer 2a to yield; GIVE UP 1 b to deliver for consideration, approval, or information 3a to give in return or retribution b to restore; give back c to give in acknowledgment of dependence or obligation d to do (a service) for another 4a to cause to be or become ⟨enough rain to ~ irrigation unnecessary⟩ b(1) to reproduce or represent by artistic or verbal means (2) to give a performance of c to translate 5 to direct the execution of; administer ⟨~ justice⟩ 6 to apply a coat of plaster or cement directly to

rendering n a covering material, usu of cement, sand, and a small percentage of lime, applied to exterior walls

rendezvous n, pl **rendezvous** 1 a place (appointed) for assembling or meeting 2 a meeting at an appointed place and time – **rendezvous** vi

rendition n the act or result of rendering: e g a a translation b a performance, interpretation

renegade n 1 a deserter from one faith, cause, or allegiance to another 2 an individual who rejects lawful or conventional behaviour – **renegade** adj

renege vi to go back on a promise or commitment ⟨~d on her contract⟩ – **reneger** n

renew vt 1 to restore to freshness, vigour, or perfection ⟨as we ~ our strength in sleep⟩ 2 to make new spiritually; regenerate 3a to revive b to make changes in; rebuild 4 to make or do again 5 to begin again; resume 6 to replace, replenish ⟨~ water in a tank⟩ 7a to grant or obtain an extension of or on (e g a subscription, lease, or licence) b to grant or obtain a further loan of ⟨~ a library book⟩ ~vi to make a renewal (e g of a lease) – **renewable** adj, **renewably** adv, **renewal** n, **renewer** n, **renewability** n

rennet n 1a the contents of the stomach of an unweaned animal, esp a calf b (a preparation from) the lining membrane of a stomach (e g the fourth of a ruminant) used for curdling milk 2 (a substitute for) rennin

renounce vt 1 to give up, refuse, or resign, usu by formal declaration ⟨~ his errors⟩ 2 to refuse to follow, obey, or recognize any further 3 to fail to follow with a card from (the suit led) in a card game – **renouncement** n, **renouncer** n

renovate vt 1 to restore to life, vigour, or activity 2 to restore to a former or improved state (e g by cleaning, repairing, or rebuilding) – **renovator** n, **renovation** n

renown n a state of being widely acclaimed; fame

renowned adj celebrated, famous

¹**rent** n 1a a usu fixed periodical return made by a tenant or occupant of property or user of goods to the owner for the possession and use thereof b an amount paid or collected as rent 2 the portion of the income of an economy (e g of a nation) attributable to land as a factor of production in addition to capital and labour

²**rent** vt 1 to take and hold under an agreement to pay rent 2 to grant the possession and use of for rent ~vi 1 to obtain the possession and use of a place or article for rent 2 to allow the possession and use of property for rent – **rentable** adj, **rentability** n

³**rent** past of REND

⁴**rent** n 1 an opening or split made (as if) by rending 2 an act or instance of rending

¹**rental** n 1 an amount paid or collected as rent 2 an act of renting 3 NAm sthg (e g a house) that is rented

²**rental** adj of or relating to rent or renting

renter n the lessee or tenant of property

rentier n one who receives a fixed income (e g from land or shares)

rent strike n a refusal by a group of tenants to pay rent

renunciation n the act or practice of renouncing; specif self-denial practised for religious reasons – **renunciative** *adj*, **renunciatory** *adj*

reopen *vt* **1** to open again **2** to resume (discussion or consideration of) ⟨~ *a contract*⟩ **3** to begin again ~ *vi* to open again ⟨*school* ~s *in September*⟩

¹**rep, repp** *n* a plain-weave fabric with raised crosswise ribs

²**rep** *n* a representative; *specif, chiefly Br* SALES REPRESENTA-TIVE – *infml*

³**rep** *n* REPERTORY 2b, c – *infml*

¹**repair** *vi* to betake oneself; go ⟨~ed *to his home*⟩ – *fml*

²**repair** *vt* **1** to restore by replacing a part or putting together what is torn or broken **2** to restore to a sound or healthy state **3** to remedy – **repairer** *n*, **repairable** *adj*, **repairability** *n*

³**repair** *n* **1** an instance or the act or process of repairing **2** relative condition with respect to soundness or need of repairing ⟨*the car is in reasonably good* ~⟩

reparable *adj* capable of being repaired

reparation *n* **1a** the act of making amends, offering expiation, or giving satisfaction for a wrong or injury **b** sthg done or given as amends or satisfaction **2** damages; *specif* compensation payable by a defeated nation for war damages – usu pl with sing. meaning – **reparative** *adj*

repartee *n* **1** a quick and witty reply **2** (skill in) amusing and usu light sparring with words

repast *n* ¹MEAL – *fml*

repatriate *vt* to restore to the country of origin – **repatri-ate** *n*, **repatriation** *n*

repay *vt* **repaid 1a** to pay back ⟨~ *a loan*⟩ **b** to give or inflict in return or requital ⟨~ *evil for evil*⟩ **2** to compensate, requite **3** to recompense ⟨*a company which* ~s *hard work*⟩ – **repayable** *adj*, **repayment** *n*

repeal *vt* to revoke (a law) – **repeal** *n*, **repealable** *adj*

¹**repeat** *vt* **1a** to say or state again **b** to say through from memory **c** to say after another ⟨~ *these words after me*⟩ **2a** to make, do, perform, present, or broadcast again ⟨~ *an experiment*⟩ **b** to experience again **3** to express or present (oneself or itself) again in the same words, terms, or form ~ *vi* **1** to say, do, or accomplish sthg again **2** *of food* to continue to be tasted intermittently after being swallowed – often + *on* – **repeatable** *adj*, **repeatabil-ity** *n*

²**repeat** *n* **1** the act of repeating **2a** sthg repeated; *specif* a television or radio programme that has previously been broadcast at least once **b** (a sign placed before or after) a musical passage to be repeated in performance

repeated *adj* **1** renewed or recurring again and again ⟨~ *changes of plan*⟩ **2** said, done, or presented again

repeatedly *adv* again and again

repeater *n* **1** a watch that strikes the time when a catch is pressed **2** a firearm that fires several times without having to be reloaded

repel *vt* **-ll- 1** to drive back; repulse **2a** to drive away **b** to be incapable of sticking to, mixing with, taking up, or holding ⟨*a fabric that* ~s *moisture*⟩ **c** to (tend to) force away or apart by mutual action at a distance ⟨*2 like electric charges* ~ *one another*⟩ **3** to cause aversion in; disgust

¹**repellent** *also* **repellant** *adj* **1** serving or tending to drive away or ward off **2** repulsive – **repellently** *adv*

²**repellent** *also* **repellant** *n* sthg that repels; *esp* a substance used to prevent insect attacks

¹**repent** *vi* **1** to turn from sin and amend one's life **2** to feel regret or contrition ~ *vt* to feel sorrow, regret, or contri-tion for – **repentance** *n*, **repentant** *adj*, **repenter** *n*

²**repent** *adj*, *of a plant part* creeping, prostrate

repercussion *n* **1** an echo, reverberation **2a** an action or

effect given or exerted in return **b** a widespread, indirect, or unforeseen effect of an act, action, or event – **repercuss-ive** *adj*

repertoire *n* **1a** a list or supply of dramas, operas, pieces, or parts that a company or person is prepared to perform **b** a range of skills, techniques, or expedients **2a** the complete list or range of skills, techniques, or ingredients used in a particular field, occupation, or practice **b** a list or stock of capabilities ⟨*the instruction* ~ *of a com-puter*⟩

repertory *n* **1** a repository **2a** a repertoire **b** (a theatre housing) a company that presents several different plays in the course of a season at one theatre **c** the production and presentation of plays by a repertory company ⟨*acting in* ~⟩

repetition *n* **1** repeating or being repeated **2** a reproduc-tion, copy – **repetitional** *adj*

repetitious *adj* characterized or marked by repetition; *esp* tediously repeating – **repetitiously** *adv*, **repetitious-ness** *n*

repetitive *adj* repetitious – **repetitively** *adv*, **repetitive-ness** *n*

repine *vi* to feel or express dejection or discontent –*fml* – **repiner** *n*

replace *vt* **1** to restore to a former place or position ⟨~ *cards in a file*⟩ **2** to take the place of, esp as a substitute or successor **3** to put sthg new in the place of ⟨~ *a worn carpet*⟩ – **replaceable** *adj*, **replacer** *n*

replacement *n* **1** replacing or being replaced **2** sthg or sby that replaces another

¹**replay** *vt* to play again

²**replay** *n* **1a** an act or instance of replaying **b** the playing of a tape (e g a videotape) **2** a repetition, reenactment ⟨*don't want a* ~ *of our old mistakes*⟩ **3** a match played to resolve a tie in an earlier match

replenish *vt* to stock or fill up again ⟨~ed *his glass*⟩ – **replenishment** *n*

replete *adj* **1** fully or abundantly provided or filled **2** abundantly fed; sated – **repleteness** *n*, **repletion** *n*

replica *n* **1** a close reproduction or facsimile, esp by the maker of the original **2** a copy, duplicate

replicate *vt* **1** to duplicate, repeat ⟨~ *a statistical experi-ment*⟩ **2** to fold or bend back ~ *vi* to produce a replica of itself ⟨*replicating virus particles*⟩ – **replicable** *adj*, **repli-cative** *adj*, **replicability** *n*

¹**reply** *vi* **1a** to respond in words or writing **b** to make a legal replication **2** to do sthg in response ~ *vt* to give as an answer

²**reply** *n* sthg said, written, or done in answer or response

¹**report** *n* **1a** (an account spread by) common talk **b** character or reputation ⟨*a man of good* ~⟩ **2a** a usu detailed account or statement ⟨*a news* ~⟩ **b** an account of a judicial opinion or decision **c** a usu formal record of the proceedings of a meeting or inquiry **d** a statement of a pupil's performance at school usu issued every term to the pupil's parents or guardian **3** a loud explosive noise

²**report** *vt* **1** to give information about; relate **2a** to convey news of **b** to relate the words or sense of (sthg said) **c** to make a written record or summary of **d** to present the newsworthy aspects or developments of in writing or for broadcasting **3a** to announce or relate (as the result of examination or investigation) ⟨~ed *no sign of disease*⟩ **b** to make known to the relevant authorities ⟨~ *a fire*⟩ **c** to make a charge of misconduct against ~ *vi* **1a** to give an account **b** to present oneself ⟨~ *at the main entrance*⟩ **c** to account for oneself as specified ⟨~ed *sick on Friday*⟩

2 to make, issue, or submit a report 3 to act in the capacity of a news reporter – **reportable** *adj*

reportage *n* 1 the act or process of reporting news 2 writing intended to give a usu factual account of events

reportedly *adv* reputedly

reported speech *n* the report of one utterance grammatically adapted for inclusion in another

reporter *n* sby who or sthg that reports: e g **a** one who makes a shorthand record of a proceeding **b** a journalist who writes news stories **c** one who gathers and broadcasts news

¹**repose** *vt* to lay at rest ⟨~ *her head on the cushion*⟩ ~ *vi* **1a** to lie resting **b** to lie dead ⟨reposing *in state*⟩ 2 to take rest 3 to rest for support – chiefly fml ⟨*a bowl* reposing *on the table*⟩

²**repose** *n* 1 a place or state of rest or resting; *esp* rest in sleep **2a** calm, tranquillity **b** a restful effect (e g of a painting or colour scheme) 3 cessation or absence of activity, movement, or animation ⟨*the appearance of his face in* ~⟩ 4 composure of manner – **reposeful** *adj*

repository *n* 1 a place, room, or container where sthg is deposited or stored 2 sby who or sthg that holds or stores sthg nonmaterial (e g knowledge) 3 sby to whom sthg is confided or entrusted

repossess *vt* 1 to regain possession of 2 to resume possession of in default of the payment of instalments due – **repossession** *n*

reprehend *vt* to voice disapproval of; censure

reprehensible *adj* deserving censure; culpable – **reprehensibleness** *n*, **reprehensibly** *adv*, **reprehensibility** *n*

represent *vt* 1 to convey a mental impression of ⟨*a book which* ~s *the character of Tudor England*⟩ 2 to serve as a sign or symbol of ⟨*the snake* ~s *Satan*⟩ 3 to portray or exhibit in art; depict **4a(1)** to take the place of in some respect; stand in for **(2)** to act in the place of **b** to serve, esp in a legislative body, by delegated authority 5 to attribute a specified character or identity to ⟨~s *himself as a friend of the workingman*⟩ 6 to serve as a specimen, exemplar, or instance of 7 to form a mental impression of – **representable** *adj*, **representer** *n*

representation *n* 1 sby who or sthg that represents: e g **a** an artistic likeness or image **b** a statement made to influence opinion – usu pl with sing. meaning **c** a usu formal protest ⟨*a* ~ *in parliament*⟩ 2 representing or being represented: e g **a** the action or fact of one person standing in place of another so as to have the rights and obligations of the person represented **b** representing or being represented on or in some formal, esp legislative, body 3 the people representing a constituency – **representational** *adj*

representational *adj* 1 of representation 2 of realistic depiction of esp physical objects or appearances in the graphic or plastic arts

¹**representative** *adj* 1 serving to represent ⟨*a painting* ~ *of strife*⟩ **2a** standing or acting for another, esp through delegated authority **b** of or based on representation of the people in government by election 3 serving as a typical or characteristic example ⟨*a* ~ *area*⟩ 4 of representation – **representatively** *adv*, **representativeness** *n*

²**representative** *n* 1 a typical example of a group, class, or quality 2 one who represents another or others: e g **a(1)** one who represents a constituency **(2)** a member of a House of Representatives or of a US state legislature **b** a deputy, delegate **c** one who represents a business organization; *esp* SALES REPRESENTATIVE **d** one who represents another as successor or heir

repress *vt* **1a** to curb ⟨*injustice was* ~ed⟩ **b** to put down by force ⟨~ *an insurrection*⟩ **2a** to hold in or prevent the expression of, by self-control ⟨~ed *a laugh*⟩ **b** to exclude

(e g a feeling) from consciousness by psychological repression – **repressible** *adj*, **repressive** *adj*, **repressor** *n*

repression *n* **1a** repressing or being repressed ⟨~ *of unpopular opinions*⟩ **b** an instance of repressing ⟨*racial* ~s⟩ 2 a psychological process by which unacceptable desires or impulses are excluded from conscious awareness

¹**reprieve** *vt* 1 to delay or remit the punishment of (e g a condemned prisoner) 2 to give temporary relief or rest to

²**reprieve** *n* **1a** reprieving or being reprieved **b** (a warrant for) a suspension or remission of a (death) sentence 2 a temporary remission (e g from pain or trouble)

¹**reprimand** *n* a severe (and formal) reproof

²**reprimand** *vt* to criticize sharply or formally censure, usu from a position of authority

reprint *n* 1 a subsequent impression of a book previously published in the same form 2 matter (e g an article) that has appeared in print before – **reprint** *vt*

reprisal *n* 1 (a) retaliation by force short of war 2 the usu forcible retaking of sthg (e g territory) 3 a retaliatory act

reprise *n* 1 a deduction or charge made yearly out of a manor or estate – usu pl 2 a repetition of a musical passage, theme, or performance

¹**reproach** *n* 1 (a cause or occasion of) discredit or disgrace ⟨*the poverty of millions is a constant* ~⟩ 2 the act or action of reproaching or disapproving ⟨*was beyond* ~⟩ 3 an expression of rebuke or disapproval – **reproachful** *adj*, **reproachfully** *adv*, **reproachfulness** *n*

²**reproach** *vt* to express disappointment and displeasure with (a person) for conduct that is blameworthy or in need of amendment – **reproachable** *adj*, **reproacher** *n*, **reproachingly** *adv*

¹**reprobate** *vt* 1 to condemn strongly as unworthy, unacceptable, or evil 2 to predestine to damnation – **reprobation** *n*, **reprobative** *adj*, **reprobatory** *adj*

²**reprobate** *adj* 1 predestined to damnation 2 morally dissolute; unprincipled – **reprobate** *n*

reproduce *vt* 1 to produce (new living things of the same kind) by a sexual or asexual process 2 to cause to exist again or anew 3 to imitate closely ⟨*sound-effects that* ~ *the sound of thunder*⟩ 4 to make an image or copy of 5 to translate (a recording) into sound or an image ~ *vi* 1 to undergo reproduction in a usu specified manner ⟨*the picture* ~s *well*⟩ 2 to produce offspring – **reproducer** *n*, **reproducible** *adj*, **reproducibility** *n*

reproduction *n* 1 the act or process of reproducing; *specif* the sexual or asexual process by which plants and animals give rise to offspring 2 sthg (e g a painting) that is reproduced – **reproductive** *adj*

reproof *n* criticism for a fault

reprove *vt* 1 to call attention to the remissness of ⟨~ *a child's bad manners*⟩ 2 to express disapproval of; censure ⟨~ *a child for her bad manners*⟩ – **reprover** *n*, **reprovingly** *adv*

reptile *n* 1 any of a class of air-breathing vertebrates that include the alligators and crocodiles, lizards, snakes, turtles, and extinct related forms (e g the dinosaurs) and have a bony skeleton and a body usu covered with scales or bony plates 2 a grovelling or despicable person

¹**reptilian** *adj* 1 resembling or having the characteristics of a reptile 2 of the reptiles

²**reptilian** *n* REPTILE 1

republic *n* **1a** a state whose head is not a monarch **b** a state in which supreme power resides in the people and is exercised by their elected representatives governing according to law **c** a (specified) republican government ⟨*the French Fourth* Republic⟩ 2 a body of people freely and equally engaged in a common activity ⟨*the ~ of letters*⟩ **3** a constituent political and territorial unit of the USSR or Yugoslavia

¹**republican** *adj* **1a** of or like a republic **b** advocating a republic **2** *cap* of or constituting a political party of the USA that is usu primarily associated with business, financial, and some agricultural interests and is held to favour a restricted governmental role in social and economic life – **republicanism** *n*

²**republican** *n* **1** one who favours republican government **2** *cap* a member of the US Republican party

repudiate *vt* **1** to refuse to have anything to do with; disown **2a** to refuse to accept; *esp* to reject as unauthorized or as having no binding force **b** to reject as untrue or unjust ⟨*~ a charge*⟩ **3** to refuse to acknowledge or pay ⟨*~ a debt*⟩ – **repudiation** *n*

repugnance *n* **1** the quality or fact or an instance of being contradictory or incompatible **2** strong dislike, aversion, or antipathy

repugnant *adj* **1** incompatible, inconsistent **2** arousing strong dislike or aversion – **repugnantly** *adv*

¹**repulse** *vt* **1** to drive or beat back ⟨*~ the invading army*⟩ **2** to repel by discourtesy, coldness, or denial **3** to cause repulsion in

²**repulse** *n* **1** a rebuff, rejection **2** repelling an assailant or being repelled

repulsion *n* **1** repulsing or being repulsed **2** a force (e g between like electric charges or like magnetic poles) tending to produce separation **3** a feeling of strong aversion

repulsive *adj* **1** tending to repel or reject; forbidding **2** serving or able to repulse **3** arousing strong aversion or disgust – **repulsively** *adv*, **repulsiveness** *n*

reputable *adj* held in good repute; well regarded – **reputably** *adv*, **reputability** *n*

reputation *n* **1a** overall quality or character as seen or judged by others **b** recognition by other people of some characteristic or ability ⟨*has the ~ of being clever*⟩ **2** a place in public esteem or regard; good name

¹**repute** *vt* to believe, consider ⟨*~d to be the oldest specimen*⟩ ⟨*~d honest*⟩

²**repute** *n* **1** the character, quality, or status commonly ascribed **2** the state of being favourably known or spoken of

reputed *adj* being such according to general or popular belief ⟨*the ~ father of the child*⟩ – **reputedly** *adv*

¹**request** *n* **1** the act or an instance of asking for sthg **2** sthg asked for **3** the condition or fact of being requested ⟨*available on ~*⟩ **4** the state of being sought after ⟨*a book in great ~*⟩

²**request** *vt* **1** to make a request to or of ⟨*~ed her to write a paper*⟩ **2** to ask as a favour or privilege ⟨*he ~s to be excused*⟩ **3** to ask for ⟨*~ed a brief delay*⟩

requiem *n* **1** a mass for the dead **2** sthg that resembles a solemn funeral chant in tone or function ⟨'Requiem for a Nun' – William Faulkner⟩ **3** *often cap* **a** a musical setting of the mass for the dead **b** a musical composition in honour of the dead

require *vt* **1** to claim or demand by right and authority **2a** to call for as suitable or appropriate ⟨*the occasion ~s formal dress*⟩ **b** to call for as necessary or essential; have a compelling need for ⟨*all living beings ~ food*⟩ **3** to impose an obligation or command on; compel – **requirement** *n*

requisite *adj* necessary, required ⟨*make the ~ payment*⟩ – **requisite** *n*, **requisiteness** *n*

requisition *n* **1** the act of formally requesting sby to perform an action **2a** the act of requiring sthg to be supplied **b** a formal and authoritative (written) demand or application ⟨*~ for army supplies*⟩ – **requisition** *vt*

requite *vt* **1** to make retaliation for **2a** to make suitable return to (for a benefit or service) **b** to compensate sufficiently for (an injury) – **requital** *n*

reredos *n* a usu ornamental wood or stone screen or partition wall behind an altar

rerun *n* a presentation of a film or television programme after its first run – **rerun** *vt*

rescind *vt* **1** to annul; TAKE BACK ⟨*refused to ~ her harsh order*⟩ **2** to repeal, revoke (e g a law, custom, etc) – **rescinder** *n*, **rescindment** *n*, **rescission** *n*

rescript *n* **1** a written answer (e g of a pope) to a legal inquiry or petition **2** an act or instance of rewriting

rescue *vt* to free from confinement, danger, or evil – **rescue** *n*, **rescuer** *n*

¹**research** *n* **1** careful or diligent search **2** scientific or scholarly inquiry; *esp* study or experiment aimed at the discovery, interpretation, reinterpretation, or application of (new) facts, theories, or laws

²**research** *vt* **1** to search or investigate thoroughly ⟨*~ a problem*⟩ **2** to engage in research on or for ⟨*~ a book*⟩ ⟨*~ the life of Chaucer*⟩ ~*vi* to perform research – **researchable** *adj*, **researcher** *n*

resemble *vt* **resembling** to be like or similar to – **resemblance** *n*

resent *vt* to harbour or express ill will or bitterness at – **resentful** *adj*, **resentfully** *adv*, **resentfulness** *n*, **resentment** *n*

reservation *n* **1** an act of reserving sthg; *esp* (a promise, guarantee, or record of) an arrangement to have sthg (e g a hotel room) held for one's use **2** a tract of land set aside; *specif* one designated for the use of American Indians by treaty **3a** (the specifying of) a limiting condition ⟨*agreed, but with ~s*⟩ **b** a specific doubt or objection ⟨*had ~s about the results*⟩ **4** a strip of land separating carriageways **5** *chiefly NAm* an area in which hunting is not permitted; *esp* one set aside as a secure breeding place

¹**reserve** *vt* **1** to hold in reserve; keep back ⟨*~ grain for seed*⟩ **2** to set aside (part of the consecrated elements) at the Eucharist for future use **3** to defer ⟨*~ one's judgment on a plan*⟩

²**reserve** *n* **1** sthg retained for future use or need **2** sthg reserved or set aside for a particular use or reason: e g **a(1)** a military force withheld from action for later use – usu pl with sing. meaning **(2)** the military forces of a country not part of the regular services; *also* a reservist **b** *chiefly Br* a tract (e g of public land) set apart for the conservation of natural resources or (rare) flora and fauna ⟨*a nature ~*⟩; *also* one used for regulated hunting or fishing ⟨*a game ~*⟩ **3** an act of reserving ⟨*accepted without ~*⟩ **4** restraint, closeness, or caution in one's words and actions **5** money, gold, foreign exchange, etc kept in hand or set apart usu to meet liabilities – often pl with sing. meaning **6** a player or participant who has been selected to substitute for another if the need should arise – **in reserve** held back ready for use if needed

reserved *adj* **1** restrained in speech and behaviour **2** kept or set apart or aside for future or special use – **reservedly** *adv*, **reservedness** *n*

reservist *n* a member of a military reserve

reservoir *n* **1** a place where sthg is kept in store: e g **a** an artificial lake where water is collected and kept in quantity for use **b** a part of an apparatus in which a liquid is held **2** an available but unused extra source or supply ⟨*an untapped ~ of ideas*⟩

reset *vt* **-tt-**; **reset 1** to set again or anew ⟨*~ type*⟩ **2** to change the reading of ⟨*~ a meter*⟩ – **resettable** *adj*

reshuffle *vt* to reorganize by the redistribution of (existing) elements ⟨*the cabinet was* ~d *by the Prime Minister*⟩ – **reshuffle** *n*

reside *vi* **1a** to dwell permanently or continuously; occupy a place as one's legal domicile **b** to make one's home for a time ⟨*the King* ~d *at Lincoln*⟩ **2a** to be present as an element or quality **b** to be vested as a right

residence *n* **1a** the act or fact of dwelling in a place **b** the act or fact of living in or regularly attending some place for the discharge of a duty or the enjoyment of a benefit **2 a** (large or impressive) dwelling **3a** the period of abode in a place ⟨*after a* ~ *of 30 years*⟩ **b** a period of study, teaching, etc at a college or university **4** *chiefly NAm* housing or a unit of housing provided for students – **residency** *n* – **in residence 1** serving in a regular capacity **2** actually living in a usu specified place ⟨*the Queen is* in residence *at Windsor*⟩

¹**resident** *adj* **1a** living in a place, esp for some length of time **b** serving in a regular or full-time capacity ⟨*the* ~ *engineer for a highway department*⟩; *also* being in residence **2** present, inherent **3** *of an animal* not migratory

²**resident** *n* one who resides in a place

residential *adj* **1a** used as a residence or by residents ⟨~ *accommodation*⟩ **b** entailing residence ⟨*a* ~ *course*⟩ **2** given over to private housing as distinct from industry or commerce ⟨*a* ~ *neighbourhood*⟩ **3** of residence or residences – **residentially** *adv*

¹**residual** *adj* of or constituting a residue – **residually** *adv*

²**residual** *n* sthg left over; a remainder, residue: e g **a** the difference between **(1)** results obtained by observation and by computation from a formula **(2)** the mean of several observations and any one of them **b** a residual product or substance

residuary legatee *n* sby who inherits a residue

residue *n* sthg that remains after a part is taken, separated, or designated; a remnant, remainder: e g **a** that part of a testator's estate remaining after the satisfaction of all debts and the payment of all bequests **b** a constituent structural unit of a usu complex molecule (e g a protein or nucleic acid)

resign *vt* **1** to renounce voluntarily; *esp* to relinquish (e g a right or position) by a formal act **2** to reconcile, consign; *esp* to give (oneself) over without resistance ⟨~ed *herself to her fate*⟩ ~ *vi* to give up one's office or position – **resigner** *n*

resignation *n* **1a** an act or instance of resigning sthg **b** a formal notification of resigning ⟨*handed in her* ~⟩ **2** the quality or state of being resigned

resigned *adj* marked by or expressing submission to sthg regarded as inevitable ⟨*a* ~ *look on his face*⟩ – **resignedly** *adv*, **resignedness** *n*

resilience, resiliency *n* **1** the ability of a body to recover its original form after deformation (e g due to stretching or applying pressure) **2** an ability to recover quickly from or adjust easily to misfortune, change, or disturbance

resilient *adj* characterized by or marked by resilience; *esp* capable of withstanding shock without permanent deformation or rupture – **resiliently** *adv*

¹**resin** *n* (a synthetic polymer or plastic with some of the characteristics of) any of various solid or semisolid yellowish to brown inflammable natural plant secretions (e g amber) that are insoluble in water and are used esp in varnishes, sizes, inks, and plastics – **resinoid** *adj or n*, **resinous** *adj*

²**resin** *vt* to treat with resin

¹**resist** *vt* **1** to withstand the force or effect of **2** to strive against ⟨~ed *the enemy valiantly*⟩ **3** to refrain from

⟨*could never* ~ *a joke*⟩ ~ *vi* to exert force in opposition – **resistible** *adj*, **resistibility** *n*

²**resist** *n* sthg (e g a protective coating) applied to a surface to cause it to resist or prevent the action of a particular agent (e g an acid or dye)

resistance *n* **1** an act or instance of resisting **2** the ability to resist **3** an opposing or retarding force **4a** the opposition offered to the passage of a steady electric current through a substance, usu measured in ohms **b** a resistor **5** *often cap* an underground organization of a conquered country engaging in sabotage

resistant *adj* capable of or offering resistance – often in combination ⟨*heat*-resistant *paint*⟩

resistor *n* a component included in an electrical circuit to provide resistance

resolute *adj* **1** firmly resolved; determined **2** bold, unwavering – **resolutely** *adv*, **resoluteness** *n*

resolution *n* **1** the act or process of reducing to simpler form: e g **a** the act of making a firm decision **b** the act of finding out sthg (e g the answer to a problem); solving **c** the passing of a voice part from a dissonant to a consonant note or the progression of a chord from dissonance to consonance **d** the separating of a chemical compound or mixture into its constituents **e** the analysis of a vector into 2 or more vectors of which it is the sum **f** the process or capability (e g of a microscope) of making individual parts or closely adjacent images distinguishable **2** the subsidence of inflammation, esp in a lung **3a** sthg that is resolved **b** firmness of resolve **4** a formal expression of opinion, will, or intent voted by a body or group

¹**resolve** *vt* **1a** to break up or separate into constituent parts **b** to reduce by analysis ⟨~ *the problem into simple elements*⟩ **2** to cause or produce the resolution of **3a** to deal with successfully ⟨~ *doubts*⟩ ⟨~ *a dispute*⟩ **b** to find an answer to **c** to find a mathematical solution of **d** to express (e g a vector) as the sum of 2 or more components **4** to reach a firm decision about ⟨~ *disputed points in a text*⟩ **5** to declare or decide by a formal resolution and vote **6** to make (e g voice parts) progress from dissonance to consonance ~ *vi* **1** to become separated into constituent parts; *also* to become reduced by dissolving or analysis **2** to form a resolution; determine ⟨*he* ~d *against overeating at Christmas*⟩ **3** to progress from dissonance to consonance – **resolvable** *adj*, **resolver** *n*

²**resolve** *n* **1** sthg that is resolved **2** fixity of purpose **3** a legal or official decision; *esp* a formal resolution

resonance *n* **1a** the quality or state of being resonant **b** (the state of adjustment that produces) strong vibration in a mechanical or electrical system caused by the stimulus of a relatively small vibration of (nearly) the same frequency as that of the natural vibration of the system **2a** the intensification and enrichment of a musical tone by supplementary vibration **b** a quality imparted to voiced sounds by a buildup esp of vibrations in the vocal tract **3** the possession by a molecule, radical, etc of 2 or more possible structures differing only in the distribution of electrons

resonant *adj* **1** continuing to sound **2a** capable of inducing resonance **b** relating to or exhibiting resonance **3** intensified and enriched by resonance – **resonant** *n*, **resonantly** *adv*

resonate *vi* to produce or exhibit resonance ~ *vt* to make resonant

resonator *n* sthg that resounds or resonates: e g **a** a device that responds to and can be used to detect a particular frequency **b** a device for increasing the resonance or amplifying the sound of a musical instrument

¹**resort** *n* **1a** sby who or sthg that is looked to for help; a refuge ⟨*saw her as a last* ~⟩ **b** recourse ⟨*have* ~ *to force*⟩

2a frequent, habitual, or general visiting ⟨*a place of popular* ~⟩ **b** a frequently visited place (e g a village or town), esp providing accommodation and recreation for holidaymakers

²**resort** *vi* **1** to go, esp frequently or in large numbers **2** to have recourse ⟨~ *to force*⟩

resound *vi* **1** to become filled with sound **2** to produce a sonorous or echoing sound **3** to become renowned ~ *vt* to extol loudly or widely

resounding *adj* **1a** resonating **b** impressively sonorous **2** vigorously emphatic; unequivocal ⟨*a* ~ *success*⟩ – **resoundingly** *adv*

resource *n* **1a** an available means of support or provision **b** a natural source of wealth or revenue **c** computable wealth **d** a source of information or expertise **2** a means of occupying one's spare time **3** the ability to deal with a difficult situation; resourcefulness *USE* (*1a, b, c*) usu pl

resourceful *adj* skilful in handling situations; capable of devising expedients – **resourcefully** *adv*, **resourcefulness** *n*

¹**respect** *n* **1** a relation to or concern with sthg usu specified; reference – in *with/in respect to* ⟨*with* ~ *to your last letter*⟩ **2a** high or special regard; esteem **b** the quality or state of being esteemed ⟨*achieving* ~ *among connoisseurs*⟩ **c** *pl* expressions of respect or deference ⟨*paid his* ~s⟩ **3** an aspect; detail ⟨*a good plan in some* ~s⟩ – **in respect of 1** from the point of view of **2** in payment of

²**respect** *vt* **1a** to consider worthy of high regard **b** to refrain from interfering with ⟨~ *the sovereignty of a state*⟩ **c** to show consideration for ⟨~ *a person's privacy*⟩ **2** to have reference to – **respecter** *n*

respectability *n* the quality or state of being socially respectable

respectable *adj* **1** worthy of respect **2** decent or conventional in character or conduct **3a** acceptable in size or quantity ⟨~ *amount*⟩ **b** fairly good; tolerable **4** presentable ⟨~ *clothes*⟩ – **respectability** *n*, **respectably** *adv*

respectful *adj* marked by or showing respect or deference – **respectfully** *adv*, **respectfulness** *n*

respecting *prep* with regard to; concerning

respective *adj* of or relating to each; particular, separate ⟨*their* ~ *homes*⟩ – **respectiveness** *n*

respectively *adv* **1** in particular; separately **2** in the order given ⟨*Mary and Anne were 12 and 16 years old* ~⟩

respiration *n* **1a** the process by which air or dissolved gases are brought into intimate contact with the circulating medium of a multicellular organism (e g by breathing) **b** (a single complete act of) breathing **2** the processes by which an organism supplies its cells with the oxygen needed for metabolism and removes the carbon dioxide formed in energy-producing reactions **3** any of various energy-yielding reactions involving oxidation that occur in living cells – **respirational** *adj*, **respiratory** *adj*

respirator *n* **1** a device worn over the mouth or nose to prevent the breathing of poisonous gases, harmful dusts, etc **2** a device for maintaining artificial respiration

respire *vi* **1** to breathe **2** *of a cell or tissue* to take up oxygen and produce carbon dioxide during respiration ~ *vt* to breathe

respite *n* **1** a period of temporary delay; *esp* REPRIEVE 1b, **2** an interval of rest or relief

resplendent *adj* characterized by splendour ⟨*the Queen sat* ~ *on her throne*⟩ – **resplendently** *adv*, **resplendence** *n*

¹**respond** *vi* **1** to write or speak in reply; make an answer ⟨~ *to the appeal for aid*⟩ **2a** to react in response ⟨~ *to*

a stimulus⟩ **b** to show favourable reaction ⟨~ *to surgery*⟩ ~ *vt* to reply – **responder** *n*

²**respond** *n* an engaged pillar or pier supporting an arch or terminating a colonnade or arcade

¹**respondent** *n* one who responds: e g **a** a defendant, esp in an appeal or divorce case **b** a person who replies to a poll

²**respondent** *adj* making response

response *n* **1** an act of responding **2** sthg constituting a reply or reaction: e g **a** sthg (e g a verse) sung or said by the people or choir after or in reply to the officiant in a liturgical service **b** a change in the behaviour of an organism resulting from stimulation **c** the output of a transducer or detecting device that results from a given input and is often considered as a function of some variable (e g frequency)

responsibility *n* **1** the quality or state of being responsible: e g **a** moral or legal obligation **b** reliability, trustworthiness **2** sthg or sby that one is responsible for

responsible *adj* **1a** liable to be required to justify **b(1)** liable to be called to account as the agent or primary cause ⟨*the woman* ~ *for the job*⟩ **(2)** being the reason or cause ⟨*mechanical defects were* ~ *for the accident*⟩ **2a** able to answer for one's own conduct **b** able to discriminate between right and wrong **3** marked by or involving responsibility or liability ⟨~ *financial policies*⟩ ⟨*a* ~ *job*⟩ **4** *esp of the British cabinet* required to submit to the electorate if defeated by the legislature – **responsibleness** *n*, **responsibly** *adv*

responsive *adj* **1** giving response; constituting a response ⟨*a* ~ *glance*⟩ ⟨~ *aggression*⟩ **2** quick to respond or react appropriately or sympathetically – **responsively** *adv*, **responsiveness** *n*

¹**rest** *n* **1** repose, sleep **2a** freedom or a break from activity or labour **b** a state of motionlessness or inactivity **c** the repose of death **3** a place for resting, lodging, or taking refreshment ⟨*sailor's* ~⟩ **4** peace of mind or spirit **5a** (a character representing) a silence in music of a specified duration **b** a brief pause in reading **6** sthg (e g an armrest) used for support – **at rest** resting or reposing, esp in sleep or death

²**rest** *vi* **1a** to relax by lying down; *esp* to sleep **b** to lie dead ⟨~ *in peace*⟩ **2** to cease from action or motion; desist from labour or exertion **3** to be free from anxiety or disturbance **4** to be set or fixed or supported ⟨*a column* ~s *on its pedestal*⟩ **5** to be based or founded ⟨*the verdict* ~ed *on several sound precedents*⟩ **6** to depend for action or accomplishment ⟨*the answer* ~s *with him*⟩ **7** *of farmland* to remain idle or uncropped **8** to stop introducing evidence in a law case ~ *vt* **1** to give rest to **2** to set at rest **3** to place on or against a support **4a** to cause to be firmly based or founded ⟨~ed *all hope in his son*⟩ **b** to stop presenting evidence pertinent to (a case at law) – **rester** *n*

³**rest** *n* a collection or quantity that remains over ⟨*ate the* ~ *of the chocolate*⟩

restate *vt* to state again or in a different way (e g more emphatically) – **restatement** *n*

restaurant *n* a place where refreshments, esp meals, are sold usu to be eaten on the premises

restaurant car *n* DINING CAR

restaurateur *n* the manager or proprietor of a restaurant

restful *adj* **1** marked by, affording, or suggesting rest and repose ⟨*a* ~ *colour scheme*⟩ **2** quiet, tranquil – **restfully** *adv*, **restfulness** *n*

restitution *n* **1** restoration: e g **a** the returning of sthg (e g property) to its rightful owner **b** the making good of or giving a compensation for an injury **2** a legal action serving to cause restoration of a previous state

restive adj **1** stubbornly resisting control **2** restless, uneasy – **restively** adv, **restiveness** n

restless adj **1** affording no rest ⟨a ~ night⟩ **2** continuously agitated ⟨the ~ ocean⟩ **3** characterized by or manifesting unrest, esp of mind ⟨~ pacing⟩; also changeful, discontented – **restlessly** adv, **restlessness** n

restoration n **1** restoring or being restored: e g **a** a reinstatement **b** a handing back of sthg **2** a representation or reconstruction of the original form (e g of a fossil or building) **3** cap the reestablishment of the monarchy in England in 1660 under Charles II; also the reign of Charles II ⟨Restoration drama⟩

restorative n or adj (sthg capable of) restoring esp health or vigour – **restoratively** adv

restore vt **1** to give back ⟨~ the book to its owner⟩ **2** to bring back into existence or use **3** to bring back to or put back into a former or original (unimpaired) state ⟨to ~ a painting⟩ **4** to put again in possession of sthg ⟨newly ~d to health⟩ – **restorable** adj, **restorer** n

restrain vt **1a** to prevent from doing sthg ⟨~ed the boy from jumping⟩ **b** to limit, repress, or keep under control ⟨she found it hard to ~ her anger⟩ **2** to deprive of liberty; esp to place under arrest – **restrainable** adj, **restrainer** n

restrained adj characterized by restraint; being without excess or extravagance – **restrainedly** adv

restraint n **1a** restraining or being restrained **b** a means of restraining; a restraining force or influence **2** moderation of one's behaviour; self-restraint

restrict vt **1** to confine within bounds **2** to regulate or limit as to use or distribution

restricted adj **1a** not general; limited **b** available only to particular groups or for a particular purpose **c** subject to control, esp by law **d** not intended for general circulation ⟨a ~ document⟩ **2** narrow, confined – **restrictedly** adv

restriction n **1** a regulation that restricts or restrains ⟨~s for motorists⟩ **2** restricting or being restricted

restrictive adj **1** restricting or tending to restrict ⟨~ regulations⟩ **2** identifying rather than describing a modified word or phrase ⟨a ~ clause⟩ – **restrictively** adv, **restrictiveness** n

rest room n, NAm public toilet facilities in a public building (e g a restaurant)

restructure vt to change the make-up, organization, or pattern of ⟨~ local government⟩

¹result vi **1** to proceed or arise as a consequence, effect, or conclusion, usu from sthg specified ⟨injuries ~ing from skiing⟩ **2** to have a usu specified outcome or end ⟨errors that ~ in tragedy⟩

²result n **1** sthg that results as a (hoped for or required) consequence, outcome, or conclusion **2** sthg obtained by calculation or investigation ⟨showed us the ~ of the calculations⟩ **3a** a win or tie as the conclusion of a cricket match **b** a win (e g in soccer)

¹resultant adj derived or resulting from sthg else, esp as the total effect of many causes – **resultantly** adv

²resultant n the single vector that is the sum of a given set of vectors

resume vt **1** to take or assume again ⟨~d his seat by the fire – Thomas Hardy⟩ **2** to return to or begin again after interruption ~ vi to begin again after an interruption ⟨the meeting will ~ after lunch⟩ – **resumption** n

résumé, resumé also **resume** n a summary: e g **a** a summing up of sthg (e g a speech or narrative) **b** NAm CURRICULUM VITAE

resurgence n a rising again into life, activity, or influence – **resurge** vi, **resurgent** adj

resurrect vt **1** to bring back to life from the dead **2** to bring back into use or view

resurrection n **1a** cap the rising of Christ from the dead **b** often cap the rising again to life of all the human dead before the last judgment **2** a resurgence, revival, or restoration – **resurrectional** adj

resuscitate vt to revive from apparent death or from unconsciousness; also to revitalize ~ vi to revive; COME TO – **resuscitation** n, **resuscitative** adj, **resuscitator** n

¹retail vt **1** to sell (goods) in carrying on a retail business **2** ¹RECOUNT ~ vi to be sold at retail ⟨tomatoes ~ at a higher price⟩ – **retailer** n

²retail adj, adv, or n (of, being, or concerned with) the sale of commodities or goods in small quantities to final consumers who will not resell them

retain vt **1a** to keep in possession or use **b** to engage by paying a retainer ⟨~ a lawyer⟩ **c** to keep in mind or memory **2** to hold secure or intact; contain in place ⟨lead ~s heat⟩ – **retainable** adj

¹retainer n a fee paid to a lawyer or professional adviser for services

²retainer n an old and trusted domestic servant

retaining wall n a wall built to withstand a mass of earth, water, etc

¹retake vt retook; retaken **1** to recapture **2** to photograph again

²retake n a second photographing or photograph

retaliate vi to return like for like; esp to get revenge – **retaliation** n, **retaliative, retaliatory** adj

retard vt to slow down or delay, esp by preventing or hindering advance or accomplishment – **retardant** adj or n, **retardation** n

retarded adj slow in intellectual or emotional development or academic progress

retch vb to (make an effort to) vomit – **retch** n

retention n **1a** retaining or being retained **b** abnormal retaining of a fluid (e g urine) in a body cavity **2** retentiveness

retentive adj able or tending to retain; esp retaining knowledge easily ⟨a ~ mind⟩ – **retentively** adv, **retentiveness** n

rethink vb rethought to think (about) again; esp to reconsider (a plan, attitude, etc) with a view to changing – **rethinker** n, **rethink** n

reticent adj **1** inclined to be silent or reluctant to speak **2** restrained in expression, presentation, or appearance – **reticence** n, **reticently** adv

reticle n a graticule visible in the eyepiece of an optical instrument

reticulate, reticular also **reticulose** adj resembling a net; esp having veins, fibres, or lines crossing – **reticulately** adv

reticule n **1** a reticle **2** a decorative drawstring bag used as a handbag by women in the 18th and 19th c

retina n, pl retinas, retinae the sensory membrane at the back of the eye that receives the image formed by the lens and is connected with the brain by the optic nerve – **retinal** adj

retinue n a group of retainers or attendants accompanying an important personage (e g a head of state)

retire vi **1** to withdraw a from action or danger ⟨~ from the scene of the crime⟩ **b** for rest or seclusion; go to bed **2** to recede; FALL BACK **3** to give up one's position or occupation; conclude one's working or professional career ⟨has ~d from the civil service⟩ ~ vt **1a** to order (a military force) to withdraw **b** to withdraw (e g currency or shares) from circulation **2** to cause to retire from a position or occupation – **retirement** *n*

retired *adj* **1** remote from the world; secluded **2** having concluded one's career **3** received or due in retirement ⟨~ *pay*⟩

retiring *adj* reserved, shy – **retiringly** *adv*

¹**retort** *vt* **1** to fling back or return aggressively **2** to say or exclaim in reply or as a counter argument **3** to answer (e g an argument) by a counter argument ~ *vi* to answer back sharply or tersely; retaliate

²**retort** *n* a terse, witty, or cutting reply; *esp* one that turns the first speaker's words against him/her

³**retort** *vt or n* (to treat by heating in) a vessel in which substances are distilled or decomposed by heat

retouch *vt* **1** TOUCH UP 1 **2** to alter (e g a photographic negative) to produce a more acceptable appearance ~ *vi* to retouch sthg – **retouch** *n*, **retoucher** *n*

retrace *vt* to trace again or back ⟨~d *her footsteps*⟩

retract *vt* **1** to draw back or in ⟨*cats can* ~ *their claws*⟩ **2a** to withdraw; TAKE BACK ⟨~ *a confession*⟩ **b** to refuse to admit or abide by ~ *vi* **1** to draw back **2** to recant or disavow sthg – **retractable** *adj*

retractile *adj* capable of being retracted – **retractility** *n*

retraction *n* an act of recanting; *specif* a statement made by one retracting

¹**retread** *vt* to replace and vulcanize the tread of (a worn tyre)

²**retread** *n* (a tyre with) a new tread

¹**retreat** *n* **1a** an act or process of withdrawing, esp from what is difficult, dangerous, or disagreeable; *specif* (a signal for) the forced withdrawal of troops from an enemy or position **b** the process of receding from a position or state attained ⟨*the* ~ *of a glacier*⟩ **c** a bugle call sounded at about sunset **2** a place of privacy or safety; a refuge **3** a period of usu group withdrawal for prayer, meditation, and study

²**retreat** *vi* **1** to make a retreat; withdraw **2** RECEDE 1b ~ *vt* to draw or lead back; *specif* to move (a piece) back in chess – **retreater** *n*

retrench *vt* **1** to reduce ⟨~ *company expenditure*⟩ **2a** to cut out; excise ⟨~ *offending paragraphs from an article*⟩ **b** *Austr & WI* to make (a worker) redundant ~ *vi* to make reductions, esp in expenses; economize – **retrenchment** *n*

retribution *n* **1** requital for an insult or injury **2** (the dispensing or receiving of reward or) punishment – used esp with reference to divine judgment – **retributively** *adv*, **retributive, retributory** *adj*

retrieval *n* a retrieving

retrieve *vt* **1** to discover and bring in (killed or wounded game) **2** to call to mind again **3a** to get back again; recover (and bring back) ⟨~d *the keys he left on the bus*⟩ **b** to rescue, save ⟨~ *him from moral ruin*⟩ **4** to return (e g a ball that is difficult to reach) successfully **5** to remedy the ill effects of ⟨~ *the situation*⟩ **6** to recover (e g information) from storage, esp in a computer memory ~ *vi, esp of a dog* to retrieve game; *also* to bring back an object thrown by a person – **retrievable** *adj*, **retrievability** *n*, **retrievably** *adv*

retriever *n* a medium-sized dog with water-resistant coat used esp for retrieving game

retro- *prefix* **1a** back towards the past ⟨*retrospect*⟩ ⟨*retrograde*⟩ **b** backwards ⟨*retrocede*⟩ ⟨*retroflex*⟩ **2** situated behind ⟨*retrochoir*⟩ ⟨*retrosternal*⟩

retroactive *adj* extending in scope or effect to a prior time ⟨*a* ~ *tax*⟩ – **retroactively** *adv*, **retroactivity** *n*

retroflex, retroflexed *adj* articulated with the tongue tip

turned up or curled back just under the hard palate ⟨*a* ~ *vowel*⟩ – **retroflexion, retroflection** *n*

¹**retrograde** *adj* **1a** of orbital or rotational movement in a direction contrary to neighbouring celestial bodies **b** moving or directed backwards **c** ordered in a manner that is opposite to normal ⟨*a* ~ *alphabet*⟩ **2** tending towards or resulting in a worse or less advanced or specialized state – **retrogradely** *adv*

²**retrograde** *vi* **1** to move back; recede ⟨*a glacier* ~s⟩ **2** to undergo retrogression – **retrogradation** *n*

retrogress *vi* to revert, regress. or decline from a better to a worse state – **retrogressive** *adj*, **retrogressively** *adv*

retrogression *n* **1** REGRESSION 3 **2** a reversal in development or condition; *esp* a return to a less advanced or specialized state during the development of an organism

retro-rocket *n* a rocket on an aircraft, spacecraft, etc that produces thrust in a direction opposite to or at an angle to its motion for slowing it down or changing its direction

retrospect *n* a survey or consideration of past events **–in retrospect** in considering the past or a past event

retrospection *n* the act or process or an instance of surveying the past

¹**retrospective** *adj* **1a** of, being, or given to retrospection **b** based on memory ⟨*a* ~ *report*⟩ **2** relating to or affecting things past; retroactive – **retrospectively** *adv*

²**retrospective** *n* an exhibition showing the evolution of an artist's work over a period of years

retroussé *adj, esp of a nose* turned up (at the end)

retroversion *n* the act or process of turning back or regressing

retsina *n* a white resin-flavoured Greek wine

¹**return** *vi* **1a** to go back or come back again ⟨~ed *home*⟩ **b** to go back *to* in thought, conversation, or practice ⟨*soon* ~ed *to her old habits*⟩ **2** to pass back to an earlier possessor ⟨*the estate* ~ed *to a distant branch of the family*⟩ **3** to reply, retort – *fml* ~ *vt* **1a** to state officially, esp in answer to a formal demand ⟨~ed *details of her income*⟩ **b** to elect (a candidate) **c** to bring in (a verdict) **2** to restore to a former or proper place, position, or state ⟨~ *the book to the shelf*⟩ **3** to retort ⟨*she* ~ed *a pretty sharp answer*⟩ **4** to bring in (e g a profit) **5a** to repay ⟨*I cannot* ~ *the compliment*⟩ **b** to give or send back, esp to an owner **6** to lead (a card) or a card of (a suit) in response to one's partner's earlier action, esp in bridge **7** to play (a ball or shuttlecock) hit, esp served, by an opponent – **returnable** *adj*, **returner** *n*

²**return** *n* **1** the act or process of coming back to or from a place or condition **2a** a (financial) account or formal report **b** a report or declaration of the results of an election – usu pl with sing. meaning **3a** the continuation, usu at a right angle, of the facade of a building or of a moulding **b** a means for conveying sthg (e g water) back to its starting point **4** the profit from labour, investment, or business – often pl with sing. meaning **5a** the act of returning sthg, esp to a former place, condition, or owner **b** sthg returned; *esp, pl* unsold newspapers, magazines, etc returned to the publisher for a refund **6** the returning of a ball (e g in tennis) or shuttlecock **7** *Br* a ticket bought for a trip to a place and back again – **by return (of post)** by the next returning post **– in return** in compensation or repayment

³**return** *adj* **1** doubled back on itself ⟨*a* ~ *flue*⟩ **2** played, delivered, or given in return; taking place for the second time ⟨*a* ~ *match*⟩ **3** used or followed on returning ⟨*the* ~ *road*⟩ **4** permitting return ⟨*a* ~ *valve*⟩ **5** of or causing a return to a place or condition

returning officer *n, Br* an official who presides over an election count and declares the result

reunion *n* **1** reuniting or being reunited **2** a gathering of people (e g relatives or associates) after a period of separation

reunite *vb* to come or bring together again ⟨*the child was ~d with its parents*⟩

reuse *vt* to use again, esp after reclaiming or reprocessing ⟨*the need to ~ scarce resources*⟩ – **reusable** *adj*, **reuser** *n*

¹**rev** *n* a revolution of a motor

²**rev** *vb* **-vv-** *vt* to increase the number of revolutions per minute of (esp an engine) – often + *up* ~ *vi* to operate at an increased speed of revolution – usu + *up*

revalue *vt* **1** to change, specif to increase, the exchange rate of (a currency) **2** to reappraise

revamp *vt* **1** to renovate, reconstruct **2** to revise without fundamental alteration – **revamp** *n*

¹**reveal** *vt* **1** to make known through divine inspiration **2** to make known (sthg secret or hidden) ⟨*~ a secret*⟩ **3** to open up to view ⟨*the uncurtained window ~ed a gloomy room*⟩ – **revealable** *adj*, **revealer** *n*, **revealment** *n*

²**reveal** *n* the side of an opening (e g for a window) between a frame and the outer surface of a wall; *also* a jamb

revealing *adj* exposing sthg usu intended to be concealed ⟨*a ~ dress*⟩ ⟨*the answer was ~*⟩

reveille *n* a call or signal to get up in the morning; *specif* a military bugle call

¹**revel** *vi* **-ll-** (*NAm* **-l-, -ll-**), **revelling 1** to take part in a revel **2** to take intense satisfaction *in* ⟨*~led in his discomfiture*⟩ – **reveller** *n*

²**revel** *n* a usu riotous party or celebration – often pl with sing. meaning

revelation *n* **1** (the communicating of) a divine truth revealed by God to man **2** *cap* a prophetic book of the New Testament – often pl with sing. meaning but sing. in constr **3** a revealing or sthg revealed; *esp* a sudden and illuminating disclosure

revelatory *adj* serving to reveal sthg

revelry *n* exuberant festivity or merrymaking

¹**revenge** *vt* **1** to inflict injury in return for (an insult, slight, etc) **2** to avenge (e g oneself) usu by retaliating in kind or degree – **revenger** *n*

²**revenge** *n* **1** (a desire for) retaliating in order to get even ⟨*exacted ~ for the insult*⟩ ⟨*saw ~ in her eyes*⟩ **2** an opportunity for getting satisfaction or requital

revenue *n* **1** the total yield of income; *esp* the income of a national treasury **2** a government department concerned with the collection of revenue

reverberate *vi* **1a** to be reflected **b** to continue (as if) in a series of echoes **2** to produce a continuing strong effect ⟨*the scandal ~d round Whitehall*⟩ ~ *vt* to reflect or return (light, heat, sound, etc) – **reverberator** *n*, **reverberant, reverberative, reverberatory** *adj*, **reverberation** *n*

revere *vt* to regard with deep and devoted or esp religious respect

¹**reverence** *n* **1** honour or respect felt or shown; *esp* profound respect accorded to sthg sacred **2** a gesture (e g a bow) denoting respect **3** being revered ⟨*we hold her in ~*⟩ **4** – used as a title for a clergyman – **reverential** *adj*, **reverentially** *adv*

²**reverence** *vt* to regard or treat with reverence – **reverencer** *n*

¹**reverend** *adj* **1** revered **2** *cap* being a member of the clergy – used as a title, usu preceded by *the* ⟨*the Reverend David Brown*⟩ ⟨*the Reverend Mr Brown*⟩

²**reverend** *n* a member of the clergy – *infml*

reverent *adj* expressing or characterized by reverence – **reverently** *adv*

reverie, revery *n* **1** a daydream **2** the condition of being lost in thought or dreamlike fantasy

revers *n, pl* **revers** a wide turned-back or applied facing along each of the front edges of a garment; *specif* a lapel, esp on a woman's garment

reversal *n* **1** reversing **2** a conversion of a photographic positive into a negative or vice versa **3** a change for the worse ⟨*his condition suffered a ~*⟩

¹**reverse** *adj* **1a** (acting, operating, or arranged in a manner) opposite or contrary to a previous, normal, or usual condition ⟨*put them in ~ order*⟩ **b** having the front turned away from an observer or opponent **2** effecting reverse movement ⟨*the ~ gear*⟩ – **reversely** *adv*

²**reverse** *vt* **1a** to turn or change completely about in position or direction ⟨*~ the order of the words*⟩ **b** to turn upside down **2a** to overthrow (a legal decision) **b** to change (e g a policy) to the contrary **3** to cause (e g a motor car) to go backwards or in the opposite direction ~ *vi* **1** to turn or move in the opposite direction **2** to go or drive in reverse – **reverser** *n* – **reverse the charges** *Br* to arrange for the recipient of a telephone call to pay for it

³**reverse** *n* **1** the opposite of sthg **2** reversing or being reversed **3** a misfortune, REVERSAL 3 **4a** the side of a coin, medal, or currency note that does not bear the principal device **b** the back part of sthg; *esp* the back cover of a book **5** a gear that reverses sthg – **in reverse** backwards

reversion *n* **1** (an owner's future interest in) property temporarily granted to another **2** the right of future possession or enjoyment **3a** the process of reverting **b** (an organism showing) a return to an ancestral type or reappearance of an ancestral character – **reversionary** *adj*

revert *vi* **1a** to return, esp to a lower, worse, or more primitive condition or to an ancestral type **b** to go back in thought or conversation ⟨*~ed to the subject of finance*⟩ **2** *esp of property* to return to (the heirs of) the original owner after an interest granted away has expired – **reverter** *n*, **revertible** *adj*

¹**review** *n* **1** REVISION 1 ⟨*prices are subject to ~*⟩ **2** a formal military or naval inspection **3a** a general survey (e g of current affairs) **b** a retrospective view or survey (e g of one's life) **4** an act of inspecting or examining **5** judicial reexamination of a case **6a** a critical evaluation of a book, play, etc **b** (a part of) a magazine or newspaper devoted chiefly to reviews and essays

²**review** *vt* **1** to take a retrospective view of ⟨*~ the past year*⟩ **2a** to go over (again) or examine critically or thoughtfully ⟨*~ed the results of the study*⟩ **b** to give a review of (a book, play, etc) **3** to hold a review of (troops, ships, etc)

reviewer *n* a writer of critical reviews

revile *vt* to subject to harsh verbal abuse – **revilement** *n*, **reviler** *n*

revise *vt* **1** to look over again in order to correct or improve **2** to make an amended, improved, or up-to-date version of ⟨*~ a dictionary*⟩ **3** *Br* to refresh knowledge of (e g a subject), esp before an exam ⟨*busy revising her physics*⟩ ~ *vi*, *Br* to refresh one's knowledge of a subject, esp in preparation for an exam – **revisable** *adj*, **reviser**, **revisor** *n*

Revised Version *n* a British revision of the Authorized Version of the Bible published in 1881 and 1885

revision *n* **1** the action or an act of revising ⟨*~ of a manuscript*⟩ ⟨*~ for an examination*⟩ **2** a revised version – **revisionary** *adj*

revisionism *n* **1** advocacy of revision (e g of a doctrine) **2** a movement in Marxist socialism favouring an evol-

utionary rather than a revolutionary transition to socialism – chiefly derog – **revisionist** adj or n
revitalize, -ise vt to impart new life or vigour to ⟨~ urban
development⟩ – **revitalization** n
revival n reviving or being revived: e g **a** a renewed attention to or interest in sthg **b** a new presentation or
production (e g of a play) **c** a period of renewed religious
fervour **d** an often emotional evangelistic meeting or
series of meetings **e** restoration of an earlier fashion, style,
or practice
revivalism n the spirit or evangelistic methods characteristic of religious revivals – **revivalist** n or adj, **revivalistic**
adj
revive vb to return to consciousness, life, health, (vigorous) activity, or current use, esp from a depressed, inactive, or unused state ⟨she soon ~d in the fresh air⟩ ⟨~d
an old musical⟩ ⟨~d memories of the war⟩ – **revivable**
adj, **reviver** n
revivify vt to revive – **revivification** n
¹revoke vt to annul, rescind, or withdraw ⟨~ a will⟩ ~ vi
to fail to follow suit when able in a card game, in violation
of the rules – **revoker** n, **revocable** also **revokable** adj,
revocation n
²revoke n an act or instance of revoking in a card game
¹revolt vi **1** to renounce allegiance or subjection to a
government, employer, etc; rebel **2** to experience or recoil
from disgust or abhorrence ⟨~ at their behaviour⟩ ~ vt
to cause to recoil with disgust or loathing; nauseate –
revolter n
²revolt n **1** a (determined armed) rebellion **2** a movement
or expression of vigorous opposition
revolting adj extremely offensive; nauseating
revolution n **1a** the action of or time taken by a celestial
body in going round in an orbit **b** (a single recurrence of)
a cyclic process or succession of related events **c** the
motion of a figure or object about a centre or axis;
ROTATION 1a, b ⟨33⅓ ~ s per minute⟩ **2a** a sudden or
far-reaching change **b** a fundamental (political) change;
esp (activity supporting) the overthrow of one government
and the substitution of another by the governed – **of
revolution** of a solid shape formed by the rotation of a
plane figure or curve about an axis ⟨a cone of revol-
ution⟩
¹revolutionary adj **1a** of or being a revolution ⟨~ war⟩
b promoting or engaging in revolution ⟨a ~ speech⟩; also
extremist ⟨a ~ outlook⟩ **2** completely new and different
– **revolutionarily** adv, **revolutionariness** n
²revolutionary n sby who advocates or is engaged in a
revolution
revolutionize, -ise vt to cause a revolution in; change
fundamentally or completely ⟨an idea that has ~d the
steel industry⟩
¹revolve vt **1** to ponder ⟨~d a scheme in his mind⟩ **2** to
cause to turn round (as if) on an axis ~ vi **1** to recur ⟨the
seasons ~d⟩ **2** to be considered in turn ⟨all sorts of ideas
~d in her head⟩ **3** to move in a curved path round (and
round) a centre or axis; turn round (as if) on an axis **4** to
be centred on a specified theme or main point ⟨the dispute
~d around wages⟩ – **revolvable** adj
²revolve n, Br a device used on a stage to allow a piece of
scenery to be rotated
revolver n a handgun with a revolving cylinder of several
chambers each holding 1 cartridge and allowing several
shots to be fired without reloading
revue n a theatrical production consisting typically of
brief loosely connected often satirical sketches, songs, and
dances
revulsion n **1** a sudden or violent reaction or change **2**
a feeling of utter distaste or repugnance – **revulsive** adj

¹reward vt **1** to give a reward to or for **2** to recompense
– **rewardable** adj, **rewarder** n, **rewardless** adj
²reward n sthg that is given in return for good or evil done
or received; esp sthg offered or given for some service,
effort, or achievement
rewarding adj yielding a reward; personally satisfying ⟨a
very ~ experience⟩
rewire vt to provide (e g a house) with new electric
wiring
reword vt to alter the wording of; also to restate in
different words
¹rewrite vb rewrote; rewritten to revise (sthg previously
written) – **rewriter** n
²rewrite n (the result, esp a rewritten news story, of)
rewriting
rhapsodize, -ise vi to speak or write rhapsodically or
emotionally – **rhapsodist** n
rhapsody n **1** a part of an epic poem suitable for recitation **2a** a highly rapturous or emotional utterance or
literary composition **b** rapture, ecstasy **3** a musical composition of irregular form suggesting improvisation –
rhapsodic, rhapsodical adj, **rhapsodically** adv
rhea n any of several large tall flightless S American birds
like but smaller than the ostrich
rheostat n an adjustable resistor for regulating an electric
current – **rheostatic** adj
rhesus factor n any of several antigens in red blood cells
that can induce intense allergic reactions
rhesus monkey n a pale brown E Indian monkey
rhetoric n **1** the art of speaking or writing effectively;
specif (the study of) the principles and rules of composition **2a** skill in the effective use of speech **b** insincere or
exaggerated language (that is calculated to produce an
effect)
rhetorical adj **1** employed (merely) for rhetorical effect
2 given to rhetoric; grandiloquent – **rhetorically** adv
rhetorical question n a question asked merely for effect
with no answer expected
rhetorician n **1** rhetorician, rhetor **a** a master or teacher
of rhetoric **b** an orator **2** an eloquent or grandiloquent
writer or speaker
rheum n a watery discharge from the mucous membranes
of the eyes, nose, etc – **rheumy** adj
¹rheumatic adj of, being, characteristic of, or suffering
from rheumatism – **rheumatically** adv
²rheumatic n sby suffering from rheumatism
rheumatic fever n inflammation and pain in the joints,
pericardium, and heart valves, occurring together with
fever as a short-lasting disease, esp in children
rheumaticky adj rheumatic – not used technically
rheumatics n pl rheumatism – not used technically
rheumatism n **1** any of various conditions characterized
by inflammation and pain in muscles, joints, or fibrous
tissue **2** RHEUMATOID ARTHRITIS
rheumatoid adj characteristic of or affected with rheumatism or rheumatoid arthritis
rheumatoid arthritis n painful inflammation and swelling of joint structures occurring as a progressively worsen-
ing disease of unknown cause
rhinestone n a lustrous imitation gem made of glass,
paste, quartz, etc
rhinoceros n, pl **rhinoceroses**, esp collectively **rhinoceros**
any of various large plant-eating very thick-skinned
hoofed African or Asian mammals with 1 or 2 horns on
the snout
rhizome n an elongated (thickened and horizontal) underground plant stem distinguished from a true root in having
buds and usu scalelike leaves – **rhizomic, rhizomatous**
adj

rhododendron *n* any of a genus of showy-flowered shrubs and trees of the heath family; *esp* one with leathery evergreen leaves

¹**rhomboid** *n* a parallelogram that is neither a rhombus nor a square

²**rhomboid, rhomboidal** *adj* shaped like a rhombus or rhomboid

rhombus *n, pl* **rhombuses, rhombi** a parallelogram with equal sides but unequal angles; a diamond-shaped figure

rhubarb *n* **1** (the thick succulent stems, edible when cooked, of) any of several plants of the dock family **2** *chiefly Br* – used by actors to suggest the sound of (many) people talking in the background **3** *chiefly Br* nonsense, rubbish – slang or humor **4** *chiefly NAm* a heated or noisy dispute – slang

¹**rhyme** *n* **1a** correspondence in the sound of (the last syllable of) words, esp those at the end of lines of verse **b** a word that provides a rhyme for another **2** (a) rhyming verse – **rhymeless** *adj*

²**rhyme** *vi* **1** to make rhymes; *also* to compose rhyming verse **2** *of a word or (line of) verse* to end in syllables that rhyme **b** to constitute a rhyme ⟨*date* ~s *with fate*⟩ ~ *vt* **1** to put into rhyme **2** to cause to rhyme; use as (a) rhyme – **rhymer** *n*

rhymester *n* a poetaster

rhyming slang *n* slang in which the word actually meant is replaced by a rhyming phrase of which only the first element is usu pronounced (e g 'head' becomes 'loaf of bread' and then 'loaf')

rhythm *n* **1a** the pattern of recurrent alternation of strong and weak elements in the flow of sound and silence in speech **b** ²METRE 1 **2a** (the aspect of music concerning) the regular recurrence of a pattern of stress and length of notes **b** a characteristic rhythmic pattern ⟨*music in rumba*⟩; *also* ²METRE 2 **c rhythm, rhythm section** *sing or pl in constr* the group of instruments in a band (e g the drums, piano, and bass) supplying the rhythm **3** movement or fluctuation marked by a regular recurrence of elements (e g pauses or emphases) **4** a regularly recurrent change in a biological process or state (e g with night and day) **5** the effect created by the interaction of the elements in a play, film, or novel that relate to the development of the action **6 rhythm, rhythm method** birth control by abstinence from sexual intercourse during the period when ovulation is most likely to occur

rhythmic, rhythmical *adj* **1** of or involving rhythm **2** moving or progressing with a pronounced or flowing rhythm **3** regularly recurring – **rhythmically** *adv*, **rhythmicity** *n*

¹**rib** *n* **1a** any of the paired curved rods of bone or cartilage that stiffen the body walls of most vertebrates and protect the heart, lungs, etc **b** a cut of meat including a rib **2** sthg resembling a rib in shape or function: e g **a** a transverse member of the frame of a ship that runs from keel to deck **b** any of the stiff strips supporting an umbrella's fabric **c** an arched support or ornamental band in Romanesque and Gothic vaulting **3** an elongated ridge: e g **a** a vein of a leaf or insect's wing **b** any of the ridges in a knitted or woven fabric; *also* ribbing

²**rib** *vt* **-bb-** **1** to provide or enclose with ribs ⟨~bed vaulting⟩ **2** to form a pattern of vertical ridges in by alternating knit stitches and purl stitches

³**rib** *vt* **-bb-** to tease – infml

ribald *adj* **1** crude, offensive ⟨~ *language*⟩ **2** characterized by coarse or indecent humour ⟨a ~ youth⟩ – **ribaldry** *n*

ribbing *n* an arrangement of ribs; *esp* a knitted pattern of ribs

ribbon *n* **1a** a (length of a) narrow band of decorative fabric used for ornamentation (e g of hair), fastening, tying parcels, etc **b** a piece of usu multicoloured ribbon worn as a military decoration or in place of a medal **2** a long narrow ribbonlike strip; *esp* a strip of inked fabric or plastic used in a typewriter **3** *pl* tatters, shreds ⟨*her coat was in* ~s⟩ – **ribbonlike** *adj*

ribbon development *n* haphazard development of buildings and settlements along main roads

rib cage *n* the enclosing wall of the chest consisting chiefly of the ribs and their connections

riboflavin, riboflavine *n* a yellow vitamin of the vitamin B complex occurring esp in milk and liver

rice *n* (the seed, important as a food, of) a cereal grass widely cultivated in warm climates

rice paper *n* a very thin edible paper made from the pith of an oriental tree

rich *adj* **1** having abundant possessions, esp material and financial wealth **2a** having high worth, value, or quality ⟨a ~ *crop*⟩ **b** well supplied or endowed – often + *in* ⟨~ *in natural talent*⟩ **3** sumptuous **4a** vivid and deep in colour ⟨a ~ *red*⟩ **b** full and mellow in tone and quality ⟨a ~ *voice*⟩ **c** pungent ⟨~ *odours*⟩ **5** highly productive or remunerative; giving a high yield ⟨~ *farmland*⟩ **6a** *of soil* having abundant plant nutrients **b** (of food that is) highly seasoned, fatty, oily, or sweet ⟨a ~ *diet*⟩ **c** *esp of mixtures of fuel with air* high in the combustible component; containing more petrol than normal **7a** highly amusing; *also* laughable – infml **b** full of import ⟨~ *allusions*⟩ – **richen** *vt*, **richness** *n*

riches *n pl* (great) wealth

richly *adv* in full measure; amply ⟨*praise* ~ *deserved*⟩

¹**rick** *n* a stack (e g of hay) in the open air

²**rick** *vt* to pile (e g hay) in ricks

³**rick** *vt, chiefly Br* to wrench or sprain (e g one's neck)

rickets *n pl but sing in constr* soft and deformed bones in children caused by failure to assimilate and use calcium and phosphorus, normally due to a lack of sunlight or vitamin D

rickettsia *n, pl* **rickettsias, rickettsiae** any of a family of microorganisms similar to bacteria that are intracellular parasites and cause various diseases (e g typhus) – **rickettsial** *adj*

rickety *adj* **1** suffering from rickets **2a** feeble in the joints ⟨a ~ *old man*⟩ **b** shaky, unsound ⟨~ *stairs*⟩

rickshaw, ricksha *n* a small covered 2-wheeled vehicle pulled by 1 or more people

¹**ricochet** *n* the glancing rebound of a projectile (e g a bullet) off a hard or flat surface

²**ricochet** *vi* **ricocheting, ricocheted; ricochetting , ricochetted** to proceed (as if) with glancing rebounds

rid *vt* **-dd-; rid** *also* **ridded** to relieve, disencumber ⟨~ *himself of his troubles*⟩

riddance *n* deliverance, relief – often in *good riddance*

-ridden *comb form* (→ *adj*) **1** afflicted or excessively concerned with ⟨*conscience*-ridden⟩ **2** excessively full of or supplied with ⟨*slum*-ridden⟩

¹**riddle** *n* **1** a short and esp humorous verbal puzzle **2** a mystifying problem or fact ⟨*the* ~ *of her disappearance*⟩ **3** sthg or sby difficult to understand

²**riddle** *vi* **riddling** to speak in or propound riddles – **riddler** *n*

³**riddle** *n* a coarse sieve (e g for sifting grain or gravel)

⁴**riddle** *vt* **1** to separate (e g grain from chaff) with a riddle; sift **2** to cover with holes ⟨~d *with bullets*⟩ **3** to spread through, esp as an affliction ⟨*the state was* ~d *with poverty* – Thomas Wood⟩

¹**ride** *vb* **rode; ridden** *vi* **1a** to sit and travel mounted on and usu controlling an animal **b** to travel on or in a vehicle **2**

to be sustained ⟨rode *on a wave of popularity*⟩ **3a** to lie moored or anchored **b** to appear to float ⟨*the moon* rode *in the sky*⟩ **4** to become supported on a point or surface **5** to continue without interference ⟨*let it* ~⟩ **6** to be contingent; depend ⟨*everything* ~s *on her initial success*⟩ **7** to work up the body ⟨*shorts that* ~ *up*⟩ **8** to be bet ⟨*his money is* riding *on the favourite*⟩ **9** to move from a correct or usual position ⟨*the screwdriver tends to* ~ *out of the slot*⟩ **10** *of a racetrack* to be in a usu specified condition for horse riding – *vt* **1a** to travel mounted on and in control of ⟨~ *a bike*⟩ **b** to move with or float on ⟨~ *the waves*⟩ **2a** to traverse by car, horse, etc **b** to ride a horse in ⟨~ *a race*⟩ **3** to survive without great damage or loss; last *out* ⟨*rode out the gale*⟩ **4** *esp of a male animal* to mount in copulation **5** to obsess, oppress ⟨*ridden by anxiety*⟩ **6** to give with (a punch) to soften the impact **7** *NAm* to harass persistently – **ride high** to experience success – **ride roughshod over** to disregard in a high-handed or arrogant way

²**ride** *n* **1** a trip on horseback or by vehicle **2** a usu straight road or path in a wood, forest, etc used for riding, access, or as a firebreak **3** any of various mechanical devices (e g at a funfair) for riding on **4** the quality of travel comfort in a vehicle ⟨*gives a rough* ~⟩ **5** *chiefly NAm* a trip on which gangsters take a victim to murder him/her – euph

rider *n* **1** sby who rides; *specif* sby who rides a horse **2** sthg added by way of qualification or amendment **3** sthg used to overlie another or to move along on another piece

ridge *n* **1a** a range of hills or mountains **b** an elongated elevation of land **2** the line along which 2 upward-sloping surfaces meet; *specif* the top of a roof at the intersection of 2 opposite slopes **3** an elongated part that is raised above a surrounding surface (e g the raised part between furrows on ploughed ground) – **ridge** *vt*, **ridged** *adj*, **ridger** *n*

ridgepole *n* the horizontal pole at the top of a tent

¹**ridicule** *n* exposure to laughter

²**ridicule** *vt* to mock; MAKE FUN OF

ridiculous *adj* arousing or deserving ridicule – **ridiculously** *adv*, **ridiculousness** *n*

riding *n* **1** any of the 3 former administrative jurisdictions of Yorkshire **2** an administrative or electoral district of a Commonwealth dominion

Riesling *n* a typically medium-dry white table wine; *also* the grape variety from which this is made

rife *adj* **1** prevalent, esp to a rapidly increasing degree ⟨*fear was* ~ *in the city*⟩ **2** abundant, common **3** abundantly supplied – usu + *with* ⟨~ *with rumours*⟩

riff *n* (a piece based on) a constantly repeated phrase in jazz or rock music, typically played as a background to a solo improvisation – **riff** *vi*

riffle *n* **1** (the sound made while) shuffling sthg (e g cards) **2** *NAm* a shallow stretch of rough water in a stream **3** *NAm* RIPPLE 1

riffraff *n sing or pl in constr* **1** disreputable people **2** rabble

¹**rifle** *vt* **rifling** to search through, esp in order to steal and carry away sthg – **rifler** *n*

²**rifle** *vt* to cut spiral grooves into the bore of (a rifle, cannon, etc)

³**rifle** *n* **1** a shoulder weapon with a rifled bore **2** *pl* a body of soldiers armed with rifles – **rifleman** *n*

⁴**rifle** *vt* to propel (e g a ball) with great force or speed

¹**rift** *n* **1** a fissure or crack, esp in the earth **2** an opening made by tearing or splitting apart **3** an estrangement

²**rift** *vt* to tear apart; split

rift valley *n* a valley formed by the subsidence of the earth's crust between at least 2 faults

¹**rig** *vt* **-gg-** **1** to fit out (e g a ship) with rigging **2** to clothe, dress up – usu + *out* **3** to supply with special gear **4** to put together, usu for temporary use – usu + *up*

²**rig** *n* **1** the distinctive shape, number, and arrangement of sails and masts of a ship **2** an outfit of clothing worn for an often specified occasion or activity ⟨*in ceremonial* ~⟩ **3** tackle, equipment, or machinery fitted for a specified purpose

³**rig** *vt* **-gg-** to manipulate, influence, or control for dishonest purposes ⟨~ *the election*⟩

rigging *n* **1** lines and chains used aboard a ship, esp for controlling sails and supporting masts and spars **2** a network similar to a ship's rigging used (e g in theatrical scenery) for support and manipulation

¹**right** *adj* **1** in accordance with what is morally good, just, or proper **2** conforming to facts or truth **3** suitable, appropriate ⟨*the* ~ *woman for the job*⟩ **4** straight ⟨*a* ~ *line*⟩ **5a** of, situated on, or being the side of the body that is away from the heart **b** located nearer to the right hand than to the left; *esp* located on the right hand when facing in the same direction as an observer ⟨*stage* ~⟩ **c** located on the right when facing downstream ⟨*the* ~ *bank of a river*⟩ **d** being the side of a fabric that should show or be seen when made up **6** having its axis perpendicular to the base ⟨~ *cone*⟩ **7** of or being the principal or more prominent side of an object **8** acting or judging in accordance with truth or fact; not mistaken **9** in a correct, proper, or healthy state ⟨*not in his* ~ *mind*⟩ **10** conforming to or influencing what is socially favoured or acceptable **11** *often cap* of the Right, esp in politics **12** *chiefly Br* real, utter – infml – **rightness** *n*

²**right** *n* **1** qualities (e g adherence to duty) that together constitute the ideal of moral conduct or merit moral approval **2a** a power, privilege, interest, etc to which one has a just claim **b** a property interest in sthg – often pl with sing. meaning ⟨*mineral* ~s⟩ **3** sthg one may legitimately claim as due **4** the cause of truth or justice ⟨*trust that* ~ *may prevail*⟩ **5a** (a blow struck with) the right hand **b** the location or direction of the right side **c** the part on the right side **6** the quality or state of being factually or morally correct **7** *sing or pl in constr, often cap* the members of a European legislative body occupying the right of a legislative chamber as a result of holding more conservative political views than other members **8a** *sing or pl in constr, cap* those professing conservative political views **b** *often cap* a conservative position – **by rights** with reason or justice; properly – **in one's own right** by virtue of one's own qualifications or properties – **to rights** into proper order

³**right** *adv* **1** in a right, proper, or correct manner ⟨*guessed* ~⟩ ⟨*knew he wasn't doing it* ~⟩ **2** in the exact location or position ⟨~ *in the middle of the floor*⟩ **3** in a direct line or course; straight ⟨*go* ~ *home*⟩ **4** all the way; completely ⟨*blew* ~ *out of the window*⟩ **5a** without delay; straight ⟨~ *after lunch*⟩ **b** immediately ⟨~ *now*⟩ **6** to the full ⟨*entertained* ~ *royally*⟩ – often in British titles **7** on or to the right ⟨*looked left and* ~⟩

⁴**right** *vt* **1** to avenge **2a** to adjust or restore to the proper state or condition; correct **b** to bring or restore (e g a boat) to an upright position – **righter** *n*

right angle *n* the angle bounded by 2 lines perpendicular to each other; an angle of 90° – **right-angled, right-angle** *adj*

right away *adv* without delay or hesitation

righteous *adj* **1** acting in accord with divine or moral law; free from guilt or sin **2a** morally right or justified **b**

arising from an outraged sense of justice – **righteously**
adv, **righteousness** *n*

rightful *adj* **1** just, equitable **2a** having a just claim ⟨*the
~ owner*⟩ **b** held by right ⟨*~ authority*⟩ – **rightfully**
adv, **rightfulness** *n*

right-hand *adj* **1** situated on the right **2** right-handed **3**
chiefly or constantly relied on

right hand *n* **1a** the hand on the right-hand side of the
body **b** a reliable or indispensable person **2a** the right side
b a place of honour

right-handed *adj* **1** using the right hand habitually or
more easily than the left; *also* swinging from right to left
⟨*a ~ batsman*⟩ **2** relating to, designed for, or done with
the right hand **3** clockwise – used of a twist, rotary
motion, or spiral curve as viewed from a given direction
with respect to the axis of rotation – **right-handed** *adv*,
right-handedly *adv*, **right-handedness** *n*

right-hander *n* **1** a blow struck with the right hand **2** a
right-handed person

rightism *n, often cap* (advocacy of) the doctrines of the
Right – **rightist** *n or adj, often cap*

rightly *adv* **1** in accordance with right conduct; fairly **2**
in the right manner; properly **3** according to truth or fact
4 with certainty ⟨*I can't ~ say*⟩

right-minded *adj* thinking and acting by just or honest
principles – **right-mindedness** *n*

right off *adv* RIGHT AWAY, AT ONCE – *infml*

right of way *n, pl* **rights of way** **1** a legal right of passage
over another person's property **2a** the course along which
a right of way exists **b** the strip of land over which a public
road is built **c** the land occupied by a railway for its tracks
3 a precedence in passing accorded to one vehicle over
another by custom, decision, or statute

rightward *adj* being towards or on the right

rightwards, *chiefly NAm* **rightward** *adv* towards or on
the right

right wing *n sing or pl in constr, often cap R&W* the
more conservative division of a group or party –
right-wing *adj*, **rightwinger** *n*

rigid *adj* **1a** deficient in or devoid of flexibility **b** fixed in
appearance ⟨*her face ~ with pain*⟩ **2a** inflexibly set in
opinions or habits **b** strictly maintained ⟨*a ~ schedule*⟩
3 firmly inflexible rather than lax or indulgent **4** precise
and accurate in procedure **5a** having the gas containers
enclosed within compartments of a fixed fabric-covered
framework ⟨*a ~ airship*⟩ **b** having the outer shape
maintained by a fixed framework – **rigidly** *adv*, **rigidness**
n, **rigidify** *vb*, **rigidity** *n*

rigmarole *n* **1** confused or nonsensical talk **2** an absurd
and complex procedure

rigor mortis *n* the temporary rigidity of muscles that
occurs after death

rigorous *adj* **1** manifesting, exercising, or favouring rigour; very strict ⟨*~ standards of hygiene*⟩ **2** harsh, severe
3 scrupulously accurate – **rigorously** *adv*

rigour *n* **1a(1)** harsh inflexibility in opinion, temper, or
judgment **(2)** the quality of being unyielding or inflexible
(3) severity of life; austerity **b** an act or instance of
strictness or severity – often *pl* **2** a condition that makes
life difficult, challenging, or painful; *esp* extremity of cold
– often *pl* **3** strict precision ⟨*logical ~*⟩

rigout *n* a complete outfit of clothing – *infml*

rile *vt* **1** to make angry or resentful **2** *NAm* ROIL 1

¹rill *n* a small brook – chiefly poetic

²rill, rille *n* any of several long narrow valleys on the moon's
surface

¹rim *n* **1** an outer usu curved edge or border **2** the outer
ring of a wheel not including the tyre

²rim *vt* **-mm-** to serve as a rim for; border

¹rime *n* **1** FROST 1b **2** an accumulation of granular ice tufts
on the windward sides of exposed objects at low temperatures – **rimy** *adj*

²rime *vt* to cover (as if) with rime

rimmed *adj* having a rim – usu in combination
⟨*dark-rimmed glasses*⟩

¹rind **1** the bark of a tree **2** a usu hard or tough outer layer
of fruit, cheese, bacon, etc

²rind *vt* to remove the rind or bark from

rinderpest *n* an infectious fever, esp of cattle

¹ring *n* **1** a circular band for holding, connecting, hanging,
moving, fastening, etc or for identification **2** a circlet usu
of precious metal, worn on the finger **3a** a circular line,
figure, or object **b** an encircling arrangement **c** a circular
or spiral course **4a** an often circular space, esp for exhibitions or competitions; *esp* such a space at a circus **b** a
square enclosure in which boxers or wrestlers contest **5**
any of the concentric bands that revolve round some
planets (e g Saturn or Uranus) **6** ANNUAL RING **7** *sing or
pl in constr* an exclusive association of people for a selfish
and often corrupt purpose ⟨*a drug ~*⟩ **8** a closed chain
of atoms in a molecule **9** a set of elements closed under
2 binary operations (e g addition and multiplication)
which is a commutative group under the first operation
and in which the second operation is associative and is
distributive relative to the first **10** boxing as a profession
⟨*retired after 9 years in the ~*⟩ **11** an electric element or
gas burner in the shape of a circle, set into the top of a
cooker, stove, etc, which provides a source of heat for
cooking – **ringlike** *adj*

²ring *vt* **ringed** **1** to place or form a ring round; encircle **2**
to attach a ring to ⟨*~ migrating geese*⟩ **3** GIRDLE 3 **4** to
throw a ring over (the peg) in a game (e g quoits)

³ring *vb* **rang; rung** *vi* **1** to sound resonantly ⟨*the doorbell
rang*⟩ ⟨*cheers rang out*⟩ **2a** to be filled with resonant
sound; resound **b** to have the sensation of a continuous
humming sound **3** to sound a bell as a summons **4a** to be
filled with talk or report **b** to sound repeatedly ⟨*praise
rang in her ears*⟩ **5** *chiefly Br* to telephone – often + *up*
~ *vt* **1** to cause to ring, esp by striking **2** to sound (as if)
by ringing a bell **3** to announce (as if) by ringing – often
+ *in* or *out* **4** *chiefly Br* to telephone – usu + *up* – **ring
a bell** to sound familiar – **ring the changes** to run through
the range of possible variations – **ring true** to appear to
be true or authentic

⁴ring *n* **1** a set of bells **2** a clear resonant sound made by
vibrating metal; *also* a similar sound **3** resonant tone **4** a
loud sound continued, repeated, or reverberated **5** a
sound or character suggestive of a particular quality or
feeling **6a** an act or instance of ringing **b** a telephone call
– usu in *give somebody a ring*

ring binder *n* a loose-leaf binder in which split metal rings
attached to a metal back hold perforated sheets of paper
in place

ringer *n* **1** sby who rings bells **2** *NAm* sby or sthg that
strongly resembles another – often + *dead* ⟨*she's a dead
~ for the senator*⟩ **3** a horse entered in a race under false
representations; *broadly* an impostor – *infml*

ring finger *n* the third finger, esp of the left hand,
counting the index finger as the first

ringleader *n* a leader of a group that engages in objectionable activities

ringlet *n* **1** a small ring or circle **2** a long lock of hair
curled in a spiral

ringmaster *n* one in charge of performances in a ring (e g
of a circus)

ring off *vi, chiefly Br* to terminate a telephone conversation

ring ouzel *n* an Old World thrush, the male of which is black with a broad white bar across the breast

ring road *n, Br* a road round a town or town centre designed to relieve traffic congestion

¹**ringside** *n* 1 the area surrounding a ring, esp providing a close view of a contest 2 a place that gives a close view

²**ringside** *adj or adv* at the ringside

ring up *vt* 1 to record by means of a cash register 2 to record, achieve

ringworm *n* any of several contagious fungous diseases of the skin, hair, or nails in which ring-shaped discoloured blister-covered patches form on the skin

rink *n* 1a (a building containing) a surface of ice for ice-skating b an enclosure for roller-skating 2 part of a bowling green being used for a match

¹**rinse** *vt* 1 to cleanse (e g from soap) with liquid (e g clean water) – often + *out* 2 to remove (dirt or impurities) by washing lightly – **rinser** *n*

²**rinse** *n* 1 (a) rinsing 2a liquid used for rinsing b a solution that temporarily tints the hair

riot *n* 1 unrestrained revelry 2 (a) violent public disorder; *specif* a disturbance of the peace by 3 or more people 3 a profuse and random display ⟨*the woods were a ~ of colour*⟩ 4 sby or sthg wildly funny – **riot** *vi*, **rioter** *n*

riotous *adj* 1 participating in a riot 2a wild and disorderly b exciting, exuberant ⟨*the party was a ~ success*⟩ – **riotously** *adv*, **riotousness** *n*

¹**rip** *vb* -pp- *vi* 1 to become ripped; rend 2 to rush along ⟨*~ped past the finishing post*⟩ 3 to start or proceed without restraint ⟨*let it ~*⟩ – *vt* 1a to tear or split apart, esp in a violent manner b to saw or split (wood) along the grain 2 to slit roughly (as if) with a sharp blade 3 to remove by force – + *out* or *off* – **ripper** *n*

²**rip** *n* a rough or violent tear

³**rip** *n* a body of rough water formed a by the meeting of opposing currents, winds, etc b by passing over ridges

⁴**rip** *n* 1 a worn-out worthless horse 2 a mischievous usu young person

riparian *adj* of or occurring on the bank of a body of water, esp a river

rip cord *n* a cord or wire for releasing a parachute from its pack

ripe *adj* 1 fully grown and developed; mature 2 mature in knowledge, understanding, or judgment 3 of advanced years 4a fully arrived; propitious ⟨*the time seemed ~ for the experiment*⟩ b fully prepared; ready *for* 5 brought by aging to full flavour or the best state; mellow ⟨*~ cheese*⟩ 6 ruddy, plump, or full like ripened fruit 7 smutty, indecent – euph – **ripely** *adv*, **ripen** *vb*, **ripener** *n*, **ripeness** *n*

rip-off *n* 1 an act or instance of stealing 2 an instance of financial exploitation; *esp* the charging of an exorbitant price *USE* infml

rip off *vt* 1 to rob; *also* to steal 2 to defraud *USE* infml

riposte *n* 1 a fencer's quick return thrust following a parry 2 a piece of retaliatory banter 3 a usu rapid retaliatory manoeuvre or measure – **riposte** *vi*

¹**ripple** *vb* **rippling** *vi* 1a to become covered with small waves b to flow in small waves or undulations 2 to flow with a light rise and fall of sound or inflection 3 to proceed with an undulating motion (so as to cause ripples) 4 to spread irregularly outwards, esp from a central point ~ *vt* 1 to stir up small waves on 2 to impart a wavy motion or appearance to ⟨*rippling his muscles*⟩ – **rippler** *n*

²**ripple** *n* 1 a small wave or succession of small waves 2a

RIPPLE MARK b a sound like that of rippling water ⟨*a ~ of laughter*⟩ 3 *NAm* RIFFLE 1

ripple mark *n* any of a series of small ridges produced, esp on sand, by wind or water

rip-roaring *adj* noisily excited or exciting; exuberant

ripsaw *n* a coarse-toothed saw having teeth only slightly bent to alternate sides that is designed to cut wood in the direction of the grain

riptide *n* a strong surface current flowing outwards from a shore

¹**rise** *vi* rose; risen 1a to assume an upright position, esp from lying, kneeling, or sitting b to get up from sleep or from one's bed 2 to return from death 3 to take up arms 4a to respond warmly or readily; applaud – usu + *to* b to respond to nasty words or behaviour, esp by annoyance or anger ⟨*despite the innuendos, he didn't ~*⟩ 5 to end a session; adjourn 6 to appear above the horizon 7a to move upwards; ascend b to increase in height or volume 8 to extend above other objects or people 9a to become cheered or encouraged b to increase in fervour or intensity 10a to attain a higher office or rank b to increase in amount or number 11a to occur; TAKE PLACE b to come into being; originate 12 to show oneself equal to a challenge

²**rise** *n* 1 rising or being risen: e g a a movement upwards b emergence (e g of the sun) above the horizon c the upward movement of a fish to seize food or bait 2 origin ⟨*behaviour that gave ~ to much speculation*⟩ 3 the vertical height of sthg; *specif* the vertical height of a step 4a an increase, esp in amount, number, or intensity b an increase in price, value, rate, or sum; *specif, chiefly Br* an increase in pay 5a an upward slope or gradient b a spot higher than surrounding ground 6 a rising-pitch intonation in speech – **get/take a rise out of** to provoke to annoyance by teasing

riser *n* the upright part between 2 consecutive stair treads

risible *adj* 1 inclined or susceptible to laughter 2 arousing or provoking laughter 3 associated with or used in laughter – **risibility** *n*

¹**rising** *n* an insurrection, uprising

²**rising** *adv* approaching a specified age

¹**risk** *n* 1 possibility of loss, injury, or damage 2 a dangerous element or factor; hazard 3a the chance of loss or the dangers to that which is insured in an insurance contract b sby who or sthg that is a specified hazard to an insurer ⟨*a poor ~ for insurance*⟩ c an insurance hazard from a specified cause ⟨*war ~*⟩ – **risky** *adj*, **riskily** *adv*, **riskiness** *n* – **at risk** in danger (e g of infection or of behaving in ways which are considered antisocial) – **on risk** *of an insurer* having assumed and accepting liability for a risk

²**risk** *vt* 1 to expose to hazard or danger 2 to incur the risk or danger of

risotto *n, pl* risottos an Italian dish of rice cooked in meat stock with onion, green pepper, etc

risqué *adj* verging on impropriety or indecency

rissole *n* a small fried cake or ball of cooked minced food, esp meat

rite *n* 1 (a prescribed form of words or actions for) a ceremonial act or action 2 the characteristic liturgy of a church or group of churches

¹**ritual** *adj* 1 of rites or a ritual; ceremonial ⟨*a ~ dance*⟩ 2 according to religious law or social custom – **ritually** *adv*

²**ritual** *n* 1 the form or order of words prescribed for a religious ceremony 2 (a) ritual observance; *broadly* any formal and customary act or series of acts

ritualism *n* (excessive devotion to) the use of ritual – **ritualist** *n*, **ritualistic** *adj*

ritzy *adj* ostentatiously smart – infml – **ritziness** *n*

¹**rival** *n* **1a** any of 2 or more competing for a single goal **b** sby who tries to compete with and be superior to another **2** sby who or sthg that equals another in desirable qualities – **rivalry** *n*

²**rival** *adj* having comparable pretensions or claims

³**rival** *vt* **-ll-** (*NAm* -l, -ll-), **1** to be in competition with; contend with **2** to strive to equal or excel **3** to possess qualities that approach or equal (those of another)

rive *vb* **rived; riven** *also* **rived** *vt* **1a** to wrench open or tear apart or to pieces **b** to split with force or violence; cleave **2** to rend with distress or dispute ~ *vi* to become split

river *n* **1** a natural stream of water of considerable volume **2a** a flow that matches a river in volume ⟨a ~ of lava⟩ **b** *pl* a copious or overwhelming quality

¹**rivet** *n* a headed metal pin used to unite 2 or more pieces by passing the shank through a hole in each piece and then beating or pressing down the plain end so as to make a second head

²**rivet** *vt* **1** to fasten (as if) with rivets **2** to hammer or flatten the end or point of (e g a metal pin, rod, or bolt) so as to form a head **3** to fix firmly **4** to attract and hold (e g the attention) completely – **riveter** *n*

riviera *n*, *often cap* a coastal region, usu with a mild climate, frequented as a resort

rivulet *n* a small stream

RNA *n* any of various nucleic acids similar to DNA that contain ribose and uracil as structural components instead of deoxyribose and thymine, and are associated with the control of cellular chemical activities

¹**roach** *n*, *pl* **roach** *also* **roaches** a silver-white European freshwater fish of the carp family

²**roach** *n* a concave or convex curvature in the edge of a sail

³**roach** *n*, *NAm* **1** a cockroach **2** the butt of a marijuana cigarette – slang

road *n* **1** a relatively sheltered stretch of water near the shore where ships may ride at anchor – often *pl* with sing. meaning **2a** an open way paved for the passage of vehicles, people, and animals **b** the part of a paved surface used by vehicles **3** a route or path – **roadless** *adj* – **off the road** *of a vehicle* not roadworthy – **on the road** travelling or touring on business

roadbed *n* **1** the bed on which the sleepers, rails, and ballast of a railway rest **2a** the earth foundation of a road prepared for surfacing **b** ROAD 2b

roadblock *n* **1** a road barricade set up by an army, the police, etc **2** an obstruction in a road **3** *chiefly NAm* an obstacle to progress or success

road hog *n* a driver of a motor vehicle who obstructs or intimidates others

roadhouse *n* an inn situated usu on a main road in a country area

roadman *n* one who mends or builds roads

road metal *n* broken stone used in making and repairing roads or ballasting railways

roadside *n* the strip of land beside a road; the side of a road

roadster *n* **1** a horse for riding or driving on roads **2a** an open sports car that seats usu 2 people **b** *Br* a sturdy bicycle for ordinary use on common roads

roadway *n* a road

roadwork *n* **1** conditioning for an athletic contest (e g a boxing match) consisting mainly of long runs **2** *pl, Br* (the site of) the repair or construction of roads

roadworthy *adj, of a vehicle* in a fit condition to be used

on the roads; in proper working order – **roadworthiness** *n*

roam *vi* **1** to go aimlessly from place to place; wander **2** to travel unhindered through a wide area ~ *vt* to range or wander over – **roam** *n*, **roamer** *n*

¹**roan** *adj, esp of horses and cattle* having a coat of a usu reddish brown base colour that is muted and lightened by some white hairs

²**roan** *n* (the colour of) an animal (e g a horse) with a roan, specif a bay roan, coat

¹**roar** *vi* **1a** to give a roar **b** to sing or shout with full force **2a** to make or emit loud reverberations **b** to laugh loudly and deeply **3** to be boisterous or disorderly – usu + *about* **4** *of a horse suffering from roaring* to make a loud noise in breathing ~ *vt* to utter with a roar

²**roar** *n* **1** the deep prolonged cry characteristic of a wild animal **2** a loud cry, call, etc (e g of pain, anger, or laughter) **3** a loud continuous confused sound ⟨*the* ~ *of the waves*⟩

¹**roaring** *n* noisy breathing in a horse occurring during exertion and caused by muscular paralysis

²**roaring** *adj* **1** making or characterized by a sound resembling a roar **2** marked by energetic or successful activity ⟨*did a* ~ *trade*⟩

³**roaring** *adv* extremely, thoroughly – infml ⟨*went and got* ~ *drunk*⟩

roaring forties *n pl* either of 2 areas of stormy westerly winds between latitudes 40° and 50° N and S

¹**roast** *vt* **1a** to cook by exposing to dry heat (e g in an oven) or by surrounding with hot embers **b** to dry and brown slightly by exposure to heat ⟨~ *coffee*⟩ ⟨~ *chestnuts*⟩ **2** to heat (ore or other inorganic material) with air to cause the removal of volatile material, oxidation, etc **3** to heat to excess **4** *chiefly NAm* to criticize severely ~ *vi* **1** to cook food by roasting **2** to be subject to roasting

²**roast** *n* **1** a piece of meat roasted or suitable for roasting **2** *NAm* a party at which food is roasted, esp in the open air

³**roast** *adj* roasted ⟨~ *beef*⟩

roaster *n* **1** a device for roasting **2** a pig, fowl, vegetable, etc suitable for roasting

rob *vb* **-bb-** *vt* **1** to steal sthg from (a person or place), esp by violence or threat **2** to deprive of sthg due, expected, or desired ~ *vi* to commit robbery – **robber** *n*

robbery *n* the act of robbing; *specif* theft accompanied by violence or threat

¹**robe** *n* **1** a long flowing outer garment; *esp* one used for ceremonial occasions or as a symbol of office or profession – sometimes *pl* with sing. meaning **2** *NAm* a woman's dressing gown

²**robe** *vt* to clothe or cover (as if) with a robe ~ *vi* to put on a robe; *broadly* DRESS 1a

robin, robin redbreast *n* **1** a small brownish European thrush resembling a warbler and having an orange red throat and breast **2** a large N American thrush with a dull reddish breast and underparts

robot *n* **1a** (a fictional) humanoid machine that walks and talks **b** sby efficient or clever who lacks human warmth or sensitivity **2** an automatic apparatus or device that performs functions ordinarily ascribed to human beings or operates with what appears to be almost human intelligence **3** sthg guided by automatic controls

robust *adj* **1a** having or exhibiting vigorous health or stamina **b** firm in purpose or outlook **c** strongly formed or constructed **2** earthy, rude **3** requiring strenuous exertion **4** full-bodied ⟨*a* ~ *red wine*⟩ – **robustly** *adv*, **robustness** *n*

¹**rock** *vt* **1** to move gently back and forth (as if) in a cradle **2a** to cause to sway back and forth **b(1)** to daze or stun

(2) to disturb, upset ~ *vi* **1** to become moved rapidly or violently backwards and forwards (e g under impact) **2** to move rhythmically back and forth – **rock the boat** to disturb the equilibrium of a situation ⟨*even though you're right you can't afford to rock the boat*⟩

²**rock, rock and roll, rock 'n' roll** *n* popular music, usu played on electronically amplified instruments and characterized by a persistent heavily accented beat, much repetition of simple phrases, and often country, folk, and blues elements

³**rock** *n* **1** a large mass of stone forming a cliff, promontory, or peak **2** a large concreted mass of stony material **3** consolidated or unconsolidated solid mineral matter **4a** sthg like a rock in firmness; a firm or solid foundation or support **b** sthg that threatens or causes disaster – often pl with sing. meaning **5** a coloured and flavoured sweet produced in the form of a usu cylindrical stick **6** ROCK SALMON – used esp by fishmongers **7** *NAm* a small stone **8** a gem; *esp* a diamond – slang – **rock** *adj*, **rocklike** *adj* – **on the rocks 1** in or into a state of destruction or wreckage ⟨*their marriage was* on the rocks⟩ **2** on ice cubes ⟨*Scotch* on the rocks⟩

rock-bottom *adj* being the lowest possible

rock bottom *n* the lowest or most fundamental part or level

rockbound *adj* surrounded or strewn with rocks; rocky

rock crystal *n* transparent colourless quartz

rocker *n* **1a** either of the 2 curved pieces of wood or metal on which an object (e g a cradle) rocks **b** sthg mounted on rockers; *specif* ROCKING CHAIR **c** any object (with parts) resembling a rocker (e g a skate with a curved blade) **2** a device that works with a rocking motion **3** a member of a group of aggressive leather-jacketed young British motorcyclists in the 1960s who waged war on the mods – **off one's rocker** crazy, mad – infml

rockery *n* a bank of rocks and earth where rock plants are grown

¹**rocket** *n* any of numerous plants of the mustard family

²**rocket** *n* **1a** a firework consisting of a long case filled with a combustible material fastened to a guiding stick and projected through the air by the rearward discharge of gases released in combustion **b** such a device used as an incendiary weapon or as a propelling unit (e g for a lifesaving line or whaling harpoon) **2** a jet engine that carries with it everything necessary for its operation and is thus independent of the oxygen in the air **3** a rocket-propelled bomb, missile, or projectile **4** *chiefly Br* a sharp reprimand – infml – **rocketeer** *n*

³**rocket** *vi* **1** to rise or increase rapidly or spectacularly **2** to travel with the speed of a rocket

rocketry *n* the study of, experimentation with, or use of rockets

rocking chair *n* a chair mounted on rockers

rocking horse *n* a toy horse mounted on rockers

rock 'n' roll *n* ²ROCK

rock plant *n* a small esp alpine plant that grows among rocks or in rockeries

rock salmon *n* a dogfish – not now used technically

rock salt *n* common salt occurring as a solid mineral

¹**rocky** *adj* **1** full of or consisting of rocks **2** filled with obstacles; difficult – **rockiness** *n*

²**rocky** *adj* unsteady, tottering – **rockiness** *n*

¹**rococo** *adj* **1a** (typical) of a style of architecture and decoration in 18th-c Europe characterized by elaborate curved forms and shell motifs **b** of an 18th-c musical style marked by light gay ornamentation **2** excessively ornate or florid

²**rococo** *n* rococo work or style

rod *n* **1a(1)** a straight slender stick **(2)** (a stick or bundle

of twigs used for) punishment **(3)** a pole with a line for fishing **b(1)** a slender bar (e g of wood or metal) **(2)** a wand or staff carried as a sign of office, power, or authority **2** a unit of length equal to 5½yd (about 5m) **3** any of the relatively long rod-shaped light receptors in the retina that are sensitive to faint light **4** an angler – **rodless** *adj*, **rodlike** *adj*

rode *past of* RIDE

rodent *n* any of an order of relatively small gnawing mammals including the mice, rats, squirrels, and beavers – **rodent** *adj*, **rodenticide** *n*

rodeo *n, pl* **rodeos 1** a roundup **2** a public performance featuring the riding skills of cowboys

rodomontade *n* **1** a bragging speech **2** vain boasting or bluster; bombast – **rodomontade** *adj*

roe *n* **1** the eggs of a female fish, esp when still enclosed in a membrane, or the corresponding part of a male fish **2** the eggs or ovaries of an invertebrate (e g a lobster)

roebuck *n, pl* **roebuck, roebucks** a (male) roe deer

roe deer *n* a small Eurasian deer with erect cylindrical antlers that is noted for its nimbleness and grace

roentgen *n* a röntgen

Rogation Day *n* any of the days of prayer, esp for the harvest, observed on the 3 days before Ascension Day and by Roman Catholics also on April 25

¹**roger** *vt* to have sexual intercourse with – slang

¹**rogue** *n* **1** a wilfully dishonest or corrupt person **2** a mischievous person; a scamp **3** sby or sthg that displays a chance variation making it inferior to others – **roguish** *adj*, **roguishly** *adv*, **roguishness** *n*

²**rogue** *vb* **roguing, rogueing** to weed out inferior, diseased, etc plants (from)

³**rogue** *adj, of an animal* (roaming alone and) vicious and destructive ⟨*a* ~ *elephant*⟩

roguery *n* an act characteristic of a rogue

roil *vt* **1a** to make muddy or opaque by stirring up the sediment of **b** to stir up **2** to annoy, rile

role, rôle *n* **1a(1)** a character assigned or assumed **(2)** a socially expected behaviour pattern, usu determined by an individual's status in a particular society **b** a part played by an actor or singer **2** a function

¹**roll** *n* **1a** a written document that may be rolled up; *specif* one bearing an official or formal record **b** a list of names or related items; a catalogue **c** an official list of people (e g members of a school or of a legislative body) **2** sthg rolled up to resemble a cylinder or ball; e g **a** a quantity (e g of fabric or paper) rolled up to form a single package **b** any of various food preparations rolled up for cooking or serving; *esp* a small piece of baked yeast dough **3** ROLLER **1a(1) 4** *NAm* paper money folded or rolled into a wad

²**roll** *vt* **1a** to propel forwards by causing to turn over and over on a surface **b** to cause (sthg fixed) to revolve (as if) on an axis **c** to cause to move in a circular manner **d** to form into a mass by revolving and compressing **e** to carry forwards with an easy continuous motion ⟨*the river* ~s *its waters to the sea*⟩ **2a** to put a wrapping round **b** to wrap round on itself; shape into a ball or roll – often + *up* **3a** to press, spread, or level with a roller; make thin, even, or compact **b** to spread out ⟨~ *out the red carpet*⟩ **4** to move as specified on rollers or wheels **5a** to sound with a full reverberating tone **b** to make a continuous beating sound ⟨~ed *their drums*⟩ **c** to utter with a trill **6** *NAm* to rob (sby sleeping or unconscious) – infml ⟨~ *a drunk*⟩ ~ *vi* **1a** to travel along a surface with a rotary motion **b(1)** to turn over and over **(2)** to luxuriate in an abundant supply; wallow **2a** to move onwards in a regular cycle or succession **b** to shift the gaze continually and erratically ⟨*eyes* ~ing *in terror*⟩ **c** to revolve on an axis **3a** to flow with an undulating motion **b** to flow in an

abundant stream; pour **c** to extend in broad undulations ⟨~*ing hills*⟩ **4a** to become carried on a stream **b** to move on wheels **5** to make a deep reverberating sound ⟨*the thunder ~s*⟩ **6a** to rock from side to side **b** to walk with a swinging gait **c** to move so as to reduce the impact of a blow – + *with* ⟨~*ed with the punch*⟩ **7** to take the form of a cylinder or ball – often + *up* **8a** to begin to move or operate ⟨*let the cameras ~*⟩ **b** to move forwards; develop and maintain impetus

³roll *n* **1a** a sound produced by rapid strokes on a drum **b** a rhythmic sonorous flow (of speech) **c** a reverberating sound **2** (an action or process involving) a rolling movement: e g **a** a swaying movement of the body (e g in walking or dancing) **b** a side-to-side movement (e g of a ship) **c** a flight manoeuvre in which a complete revolution about the longitudinal axis of an aircraft is made with the horizontal direction of flight being approximately maintained

roll back *vt* to cause to retreat or withdraw; push back

roll call *n* the calling out of a list of names (e g for checking attendance)

¹roller *n* **1a(1)** a revolving cylinder over or on which sthg is moved or which is used to press, shape, or apply sthg **(2)** a hair curler **b** a cylinder or rod on which sthg (e g a blind) is rolled up **2** a long heavy wave

²roller *n* **1** any of a group of mostly brightly coloured Old World birds noted for performing aerial rolls in their nuptial display **2** a canary that has a song in which the notes are soft and run together

roller coaster *n* an elevated railway (e g in a funfair) constructed with curves and inclines on which the cars roll

roller skate *n* (a shoe fitted with) a metal frame holding usu 4 small wheels that allows the wearer to glide over hard surfaces – **roller-skate** *vi*, **roller-skater** *n*

roller towel *n* a continuous towel hung from a roller

¹rollicking *adj* boisterously carefree

²rollicking *n*, *Br* a severe scolding – *infml*

roll in *vi* to come or arrive in large quantities

rolling mill *n* an establishment or machine in which metal is rolled into plates and bars

rolling pin *n* a long usu wooden cylinder for rolling out dough

rolling stock *n* **1** the vehicles owned and used by a railway **2** *NAm* the road vehicles owned and used by a company

rolling stone *n* one who leads a wandering or unsettled life

roll-on *n* **1** a woman's elasticated girdle without fastenings **2** a liquid preparation (e g deodorant) applied to the skin by means of a rolling ball in the neck of the container

roll on *interj*, *Br* – used to urge on a desired event ⟨~ *summer!*⟩

rollout *n* the public introduction or unveiling of a new aircraft

rolltop desk *n* a writing desk with a sliding cover often of parallel slats fastened to a flexible backing

roll-up *n*, *Br* a hand-rolled cigarette – *infml*

roll up *vi* **1** to arrive in a vehicle **2** to turn up at a destination, esp unhurriedly

¹roly-poly *n* a dish, esp a pudding, consisting of pastry spread with a filling (e g jam), rolled, and baked or steamed

²roly-poly *adj* short and plump – *infml*

Romaic *n* the modern Greek vernacular – **Romaic** *adj*

¹Roman *n* **1** a native or inhabitant of (ancient) Rome **2** ROMAN CATHOLIC **3** *not cap* roman letters or type

²Roman *adj* **1** (characteristic) of Rome or the (ancient) Romans **2** *not cap*, *of numbers and letters* not slanted;

perpendicular **3** of the see of Rome or the Roman Catholic church

¹Roman Catholic *n* a member of the Roman Catholic church

²Roman Catholic *adj* of the body of Christians headed by the pope, with a hierarchy of priests and bishops under the pope, a liturgy centred on the Mass, and a body of dogma formulated by the church as the infallible interpreter of revealed truth; *specif* of the Western rite of this church marked by a formerly Latin liturgy – **Roman Catholicism** *n*

¹romance *n* **1a(1)** a medieval usu verse tale dealing with chivalric love and adventure **(2)** a prose narrative dealing with imaginary characters involved in usu heroic, adventurous, or mysterious events that are remote in time or place **(3)** a love story **b** such literature as a class **2** sthg lacking any basis in fact **3** an emotional aura attaching to an enthralling era, adventure, or pursuit – LOVE AFFAIR

²romance *vi* **1** to exaggerate or invent detail or incident **2** to entertain romantic thoughts or ideas

³romance *n* a short instrumental piece of music in ballad style

Romance *adj* of or constituting the languages developed from Latin

Romanesque *adj* of a style of architecture developed in Italy and western Europe and characterized after 1000 AD by the use of the round arch and vault, decorative arcading, and elaborate mouldings – **Romanesque** *n*

romanize, -ise *vt* **1** *often cap* to make Roman; Latinize **2** to write or print (e g a language) in the roman alphabet – **romanization** *n*, *often cap*

roman law *n*, *often cap R* the legal system of the ancient Romans which forms the basis of many modern legal codes

Roman numeral *n* a numeral in a system of notation based on the ancient Roman system using the symbols i, v, x, l, c, d, m

¹romantic *adj* **1** consisting of or like a romance **2** having no basis in real life **3** impractical or fantastic in conception or plan **4a** marked by the imaginative appeal of the heroic, remote, or mysterious **b** *often cap* (having the characteristics) of romanticism **c** of or being (a composer of) 19th-c music characterized by an emphasis on subjective emotional qualities and freedom of form **5a** having an inclination for romance **b** marked by or constituting strong feeling, esp love – **romantically** *adv*

²romantic *n* **1** a romantic person **2** *cap* a romantic writer, artist, or composer

romanticism *n*, *often cap* (adherence to) a chiefly late 18th- and early 19th-c literary, artistic, and philosophical movement that reacted against neoclassicism by emphasizing individual aspirations, nature, the emotions, and the remote and exotic – **romanticist** *n*, *often cap*

romanticize, -ise *vt* to give a romantic character to ~ *vi* **1** to hold romantic ideas **2** to present incidents or people in a (misleadingly) romantic way – **romanticization** *n*

Romany *n* **1** GIPSY **1** **2** the Indic language of the Gipsies – **Romany** *adj*

Romish *adj* ROMAN CATHOLIC – *chiefly derog*

¹romp *n* **1** boisterous or bawdy entertainment or play **2** an effortless winning pace

²romp *vi* **1** to play in a boisterous manner **2** to win easily

romper, romper suit *n* a 1-piece child's garment combining a top or bib and short trousers – usu pl with sing. meaning

rondeau *n*, *pl* **rondeaux** (a poem in) a form of verse using only 2 rhymes, in which the opening words of the first line are used as a refrain

rondo *n, pl* **rondos** an instrumental composition, esp a movement in a concerto or sonata, typically having a refrain or recurring theme

Roneo *trademark* – used for a duplicating machine that uses stencils

röntgen, roentgen, rontgen *n* a unit of ionizing radiation equal to the amount that produces ions of 1 sign carrying a charge of 2.58×10^{-4} coulomb in 1kg of air

rood *n* 1 a cross, crucifix; *specif* a large crucifix on a beam or screen at the entrance to the chancel of a medieval church 2 a British unit of land area equal to ¼ acre (about $1011m^2$)

¹roof *n, pl* **roofs** *also* **rooves** 1a the upper usu rigid cover of a building b a dwelling, home ⟨*why not share the same* ~ – *Virginia Woolf*⟩ 2a the highest point or level b sthg resembling a roof in form or function 3 the vaulted or covering part of the mouth, skull, etc – **roofed** *adj*, **roofless** *adj*, **rooflike** *adj*, **roofing** *n*

²roof *vt* 1 to cover (as if) with a roof 2 to serve as a roof over

rooftree *n* a ridgepiece

¹rook *n* a common Old World social bird similar to the related carrion crow but having a bare grey face

²rook *vt* to defraud by cheating (e g at cards) – *infml*

³rook *n* either of 2 pieces of each colour in a set of chessmen having the power to move along the ranks or files across any number of consecutive unoccupied squares

rookery *n* 1a (the nests, usu built in the upper branches of trees, of) a colony of rooks b (a breeding ground or haunt of) a colony of penguins, seals, etc 2 a crowded dilapidated tenement or maze of dwellings

rookie *n* a recruit; *also, chiefly NAm* a novice

¹room *n* 1 an extent of space occupied by, or sufficient or available for, sthg 2a a partitioned part of the inside of a building b such a part used as a separate lodging – often *pl* 3 suitable or fit occasion; opportunity + *for* ⟨~ *for improvement*⟩

²room *vt* to accommodate with lodgings ~*vi, NAm* to occupy a room; lodge

roomed *adj* containing rooms – usu in combination ⟨*a 6-roomed house*⟩

roomer *n, NAm* a lodger

roommate *n* any of 2 or more people sharing the same room (e g in a university hall)

room service *n* the facility by which a hotel guest can have food, drinks, etc brought to his/her room

roomy *adj* spacious – **roominess** *n*

¹roost *n* 1 a support or place where birds roost 2 a group of birds roosting together

²roost *vi, esp of a bird* to settle down for rest or sleep; perch

rooster *n, chiefly NAm* COCK 1a

¹root *n* 1a the (underground) part of a flowering plant that usu anchors and supports it and absorbs and stores food b a (fleshy and edible) root, bulb, tuber, or other underground plant part 2a the end of a nerve nearest the brain and spinal cord b the part of a tooth, hair, the tongue, etc by which it is attached to the body 3a sthg that is an underlying cause or basis (e g of a condition or quality) b one or more progenitors of a group of descendants c the essential core, the heart d *pl* a feeling of belonging established through close familiarity or family ties with a particular place ⟨*the need for* ~ s⟩ ⟨~ *s in Scotland*⟩ 4a a number which produces a given number when taken an indicated number of times as a factor ⟨*2 is a fourth* ~ *of 16*⟩ b a number that reduces an equation to an identity when it is substituted for 1 variable 5a the lower part; the base b the part by which an object is attached to or embedded in sthg else 6 the basis from which a word is derived 7 the tone from whose overtones a chord is composed; the lowest note of a chord in normal position – **rooted** *adj*, **rootedness** *n*, **rootless** *adj*, **rootlet** *n*, **rootlike** *adj*, **rooty** *adj*

²root *vt* 1 to give or enable to develop roots 2 to fix or implant (as if) by roots ~*vi* 1 to grow roots or take root 2 to have an origin or base

³root *vi* 1 *esp of a pig* to dig with the snout 2 to poke or dig about *in*; search (unsystematically) for sthg

⁴root *vi, chiefly NAm* to lend vociferous or enthusiastic support to sby or sthg – + *for* – **rooter** *n*

root crop *n* a crop (e g turnips or sugar beet) grown for its enlarged roots

root out *vt* 1 to discover or cause to emerge by rooting 2 to get rid of or destroy completely

¹rope *n* 1a a strong thick cord composed of strands of fibres or wire twisted or braided together b a long slender strip of material (used) like rope c a hangman's noose 2 a row or string consisting of things united (as if) by braiding, twining, or threading 3 *pl* special methods or procedures

²rope *vt* 1a to bind, fasten, or tie with a rope b to enclose, separate, or divide by a rope c to connect (a party of climbers) with a rope 2 to enlist (sby reluctant) *in* a group or activity 3 *NAm* to lasso ~*vi* to put on a rope for climbing; *also* to climb *down* or *up* – **roper** *n*

ropedancer *n* one who dances, walks, or performs acrobatic feats on a rope high in the air – **ropedancing** *n*

rope ladder *n* a ladder having rope sides and rope, wood, or metal rungs

ropewalk *n* a long covered area where ropes are made

ropeway *n* an endless aerial cable moved by a stationary engine and used to transport goods (e g logs and ore)

ropy, ropey *adj* 1a capable of being drawn out into a thread b gelatinous or slimy from bacterial or fungal contamination ⟨~ *milk*⟩ ⟨~ *flour*⟩ 2 like rope in texture or appearance 3 *Br* a of poor quality; shoddy b somewhat unwell USE (3) *infml* – **ropiness** *n*

Roquefort *trademark* – used for a strong-flavoured crumbly French cheese with bluish green veins, made from the curds of ewes' milk

Rorschach test *n* a personality test based on the interpretation of sby's reactions to a set of standard inkblot designs

rosary *n* a string of beads used in counting prayers

¹rose *past of* RISE

²rose *n* 1 (the showy often double flower of) any of a genus of widely cultivated usu prickly shrubs 2a COMPASS CARD b (the form of) a gem, esp a diamond, with a flat base and triangular facets rising to a point c a perforated outlet for water (e g from a shower or watering can) d an electrical fitting that anchors the flex of a suspended light bulb to a ceiling 3 a pale to dark pinkish colour – **roselike** *adj*

³rose *adj* 1a of, containing, or used for roses b flavoured, sweetly scented, or coloured with or like roses 2 of the colour rose

rosé *n* a light pink table wine made from red grapes by removing the skins after fermentation has begun

roseate *adj* 1 resembling a rose, esp in colour 2 marked by unrealistic optimism – **roseately** *adv*

rosebud *n* the bud of a rose

rosemary *n* a fragrant shrubby Eurasian plant used as a cooking herb

rosette *n* 1 an ornament usu made of material gathered so as to resemble a rose and worn as a badge, trophy, or trimming 2 a stylized carved or moulded rose used as a decorative motif in architecture 3 a rosette-shaped structure or marking on an animal **4** a cluster of leaves in crowded circles or spirals (e g in the dandelion)

rose window *n* a circular window filled with tracery radiating from its centre

rosewood *n* (any of various esp leguminous tropical trees yielding) a valuable dark red or purplish wood, streaked and variegated with black

¹**rosin** *n* a translucent resin that is the residue from the distillation of turpentine and is used esp in making varnish and soldering flux and for rubbing on violin bows

²**rosin** *vt* to rub or treat (e g the bow of a violin) with rosin

roster *n* **1** a list or register giving the order in which personnel are to perform a duty, go on leave, etc **2** an itemized list

rostrum *n, pl* **rostrums, rostra 1a** a stage for public speaking **b** a raised platform (on a stage) **2** a body part (e g an insect's snout or beak) shaped like a bird's bill – **rostral** *adj*

rosy *adj* **1a** ROSE **2 b** having a rosy complexion – often in combination ⟨rosy-*cheeked youngsters*⟩ **2** characterized by or encouraging optimism – **rosily** *adv,* **rosiness** *n*

¹**rot** *vb* **-tt-** *vi* **1a** to undergo decomposition, esp from the action of bacteria or fungi – often + *down* **b** to become unsound or weak (e g from chemical or water action) **2a** to go to ruin **b** to become morally corrupt ~ *vt* to cause to decompose or deteriorate

²**rot** *n* **1** (sthg) rotting or being rotten; decay **2** any of several plant or animal diseases, esp of sheep, with breakdown and death of tissues **3** nonsense, rubbish – often used interjectionally

rota *n, chiefly Br* **1** a list specifying a fixed order of rotation (e g of people or duties) **2** an ordered succession

¹**rotary** *adj* **1a** turning on an axis like a wheel **b** proceeding about an axis ⟨~ *motion*⟩ **2** having a principal part that turns on an axis **3** characterized by rotation **4** of or being a printing press using a rotating curved printing surface

²**rotary** *n* **1** a rotary machine **2** *NAm* a roundabout

¹**rotate** *adj, of a flower* with petals or sepals radiating like the spokes of a wheel

²**rotate** *vi* **1** to turn about an axis or a centre; revolve **2a** to take turns at performing an act or operation **b** to perform an ordered series of actions or functions ~ *vt* **1** to cause to turn about an axis or centre **2** to order in a recurring sequence – **rotatable** *adj,* **rotative** *adj,* **rotatory** *adj*

rotation *n* **1a(1)** a rotating or being rotated (as if) on an axis or centre **(2)** the act or an instance of rotating sthg **b** one complete turn; the angular displacement required to return a rotating body or figure to its original orientation **2a** recurrence in a regular series **b** the growing of different crops in succession in 1 field, usu in a regular sequence **3** the turning of a limb about its long axis – **rotational** *adj*

rote *n* the mechanical use of the memory

rotgut *n* spirits of low quality – *infml*

rotisserie *n* **1** a restaurant specializing in roast and barbecued meats **2** an appliance fitted with a spit on which food is cooked

rotor *n* **1** a part that revolves in a machine; *esp* the rotating member of an electrical machine **2** a complete system of more or less horizontal blades that supplies (nearly) all the force supporting an aircraft (e g a helicopter) in flight

rotten *adj* **1** having rotted; putrid **2** morally or politically corrupt **3** extremely unpleasant or inferior **4** marked by

illness, discomfort, or unsoundness *USE* (*3, 4*) *infml* – **rottenly** *adv,* **rottenness** *n*

rotten borough *n* an election district with very few voters – used esp of certain English constituencies before 1832

rotter *n* a thoroughly objectionable person – often humor

rotund *adj* **1** rounded **2** high-flown or sonorous **3** markedly plump – **rotundity** *n,* **rotundly** *adv,* **rotundness** *n*

rotunda *n* a round building; *esp* one covered by a dome

rouble, ruble *n* the standard unit of money in the USSR

roué *n* a debauched man; *esp* one past his prime

¹**rouge** *n* **1** a red cosmetic, esp for the cheeks **2** ferric oxide as a red powder, used as a pigment and in polishing glass, metal, or gems

²**rouge** *vt* to apply rouge to

¹**rough** *adj* **1** having an irregular or uneven surface: e g **a** not smooth **b** covered with or made up of coarse hair **c** covered with boulders, bushes, etc **2a** turbulent, stormy **b(1)** harsh, violent **(2)** requiring strenuous effort ⟨*had a* ~ *day*⟩ **(3)** unfortunate and hard to bear – often + *on* ⟨*it's rather* ~ *on his wife*⟩ **3** coarse or rugged in character or appearance: e g **a** harsh to the ear **b** crude in style or expression **c** ill-mannered, uncouth **4a** crude, unfinished **b** executed hastily or approximately ⟨*a* ~ *draft*⟩ **5** *Br* poorly or exhausted, esp through lack of sleep or heavy drinking – *infml* – **roughish** *adj,* **roughness** *n*

²**rough** *n* **1** uneven ground covered with high grass, brush, and stones; *specif* such ground bordering a golf fairway **2** the rugged or disagreeable side or aspect **3a** sthg, esp written or illustrated, in a crude or preliminary state **b** broad outline **c** a quick preliminary drawing or layout **4** a hooligan, ruffian

³**rough** *adv, chiefly Br* in want of material comforts; without proper lodging – esp in *live/sleep rough*

⁴**rough** *vt* to roughen – **rough it** to live in uncomfortable or primitive conditions

roughage *n* coarse bulky food (e g bran) that is relatively high in fibre and low in digestible nutrients and that by its bulk stimulates intestinal peristalsis

rough-and-tumble *n* disorderly unrestrained fighting or struggling – **rough-and-tumble** *adj*

¹**roughcast** *n* a plaster of lime mixed with shells or pebbles used for covering buildings

²**roughcast** *vt* **roughcast** to plaster with roughcast

rough-dry *vt* to dry (laundry) without ironing or pressing – **rough-dry** *adj*

roughen *vb* to make or become (more) rough

rough-hewn *adj* **1** in a rough or unfinished state **2** lacking refinement

roughhouse *n* an instance of brawling or excessively boisterous play – *infml* – **roughhouse** *vi*

roughly *adv* **1a** with insolence or violence **b** in primitive fashion; crudely **2** without claim to completeness or exactness

roughneck *n* **1** a worker who handles the heavy drilling equipment of an oil rig **2** *NAm* a ruffian, tough

rough out *vt* **1** to shape or plan in a preliminary way **2** to outline

roughshod *adv* forcefully and without justice or consideration

rough stuff *n* violent behaviour; violence – *infml*

rough up *vt* to beat up – *infml*

roulette *n* **1** a gambling game in which players bet on which compartment of a revolving wheel a small ball will come to rest in **2** any of various toothed wheels or discs

(e g for producing rows of dots on engraved plates or for perforating paper)

¹**round** *adj* **1a(1)** having every part of the surface or circumference equidistant from the centre **(2)** cylindrical ⟨a ~ peg⟩ **b** approximately round ⟨a ~ face⟩ **2** well filled out; plump ⟨~ cheeks⟩ **3a** complete, full ⟨a ~ dozen⟩ **b** approximately correct; *esp* exact only to a specific decimal **c** substantial in amount ⟨a good ~ sum⟩ **4** direct in expression ⟨a ~ oath⟩ **5a** moving in or forming a ring or circle **b** following a roughly circular route ⟨a ~ tour of the Cotswolds⟩ **6** presented with lifelike fullness **7a** having full resonance or tone **b** pronounced with rounded lips; labialized **8** *of handwriting* not angular; curved – **roundness** *n*

²**round** *adv* **1a** in a circular or curved path **b** with revolving or rotating motion ⟨wheels go ~⟩ **c** in circumference ⟨a tree 5 feet ~⟩ **d** in, along, or through a circuitous or indirect route ⟨the road goes ~ by the lake⟩ **e** in an encircling position ⟨a field with a fence all ~⟩ **2a** in close from all sides so as to surround ⟨the children crowded ~⟩ **b** near, about **c** here and there in various places **3a** in rotation or recurrence ⟨your birthday will soon be ~ again⟩ **b** from beginning to end; through ⟨all the year ~⟩ **c(1)** in or to the other or a specified direction ⟨turn ~⟩⟨talk her ~⟩ **(2)** TO **4 (3)** in the specified order or relationship ⟨got the story the wrong way ~⟩ **4** about, approximately ⟨~ 1900⟩ **5** to a particular person or place ⟨invite them ~ for drinks⟩ – **round about 1** approximately; MORE OR LESS **2** in a ring round; on all sides of

³**round** *prep* **1a** so as to revolve or progress about (a centre) **b** so as to encircle or enclose ⟨seated ~ the table⟩ **c** so as to avoid or get past; beyond the obstacle of ⟨got ~ his objections⟩ ⟨lives just ~ the corner⟩ **d** near to; about **2a** in all directions outwards from ⟨looked ~ her⟩ **b** here and there in or throughout ⟨travel ~ Europe⟩ **3** so as to have a centre or basis in ⟨a movement organized ~ the idea of service⟩ **4** continuously during; throughout

⁴**round** *n* **1a** sthg round (e g a circle, curve, or ring) **b** a circle of people or things **2** a musical canon sung in unison in which each part is continuously repeated **3** a rung of a ladder or chair **4a** a circling or circuitous path or course **b** motion in a circle or a curving path **5a** a route or assigned territory habitually traversed (e g by a milkman or policeman) **b** a series of visits made by **(1)** a general practitioner to patients in their homes **(2)** a hospital doctor to the patients under his/her care **c** a series of customary social calls ⟨doing the ~s of her friends⟩ **6** a set of usu alcoholic drinks served at 1 time to each person in a group **7** a recurring sequence of actions or events ⟨a ~ of talks⟩ **8** a period of time that recurs in fixed succession ⟨the daily ~⟩ **9** a unit of ammunition consisting of the parts necessary to fire 1 shot **10a** any of a series of units of action in a game or sport (e g covering a prescribed time) **b** a division of a tournament in which each contestant plays 1 other **11** a prolonged burst (e g of applause) **12a** a cut of beef between the rump and the lower leg **b** a single slice of bread or toast; *also* a sandwich made with 2 whole slices of bread **13** a rounded or curved part *USE (5b, c)* usu pl with sing. meaning – **in the round 1** in full sculptured form unattached to a background **2** with a centre stage surrounded by an audience ⟨theatre in the round⟩

⁵**round** *vt* **1** to make round or rounded **b(1)** to make (the lips) round and protruded **(2)** to produce (e g the vowel /ooh/) with rounded lips; labialize **2** to go round (e g a bend, corner) ⟨the ship ~ed the headland⟩ **3** to encircle, encompass **4** to bring to completion or perfection – often + *off* or *out* **5** to express as a round number – often + *off*,

up, or down ⟨11.3572 ~ed off to 3 decimal places becomes 11.357⟩ ~ *vi* **1a** to become round, plump, or smooth in outline **b** to reach fullness or completion – usu + *off* or *out* **2** to follow a winding or circular course ⟨~ing into the home stretch⟩ – **round on** to turn against and attack; *esp* to suddenly scold

¹**roundabout** *n, Br* **1** a merry-go-round; *also* a rotatable platform that is an amusement in a children's playground **2** a road junction formed round a central island about which traffic moves in 1 direction only; *also* a paved or planted circle in the middle of this

²**roundabout** *adj* circuitous, indirect – **roundaboutness** *n*

round bracket *n, chiefly Br* PARENTHESIS 1b

roundel *n* **1** a round figure or object: e g **a** a circular panel, window, etc **b** a circular mark identifying the nationality of an aircraft, esp a warplane **2** (an English modification of) the rondeau

roundelay *n* **1** a simple song with a refrain **2** a poem with a refrain recurring frequently or at fixed intervals

rounder *n* **1** *pl but sing in constr* a game with bat and ball that resembles baseball **2** a boxing or wrestling match lasting a specified number of rounds ⟨a 10-rounder⟩

Roundhead *n* an adherent of Parliament in its contest with Charles I

roundhouse *n* **1** a cabin or apartment on the after part of a quarterdeck **2** *chiefly NAm* a circular building for housing and repairing locomotives

roundly *adv* **1** in a round or circular form or manner **2** in a blunt or severe manner ⟨~ rebuked him⟩

round robin *n* **1** a written petition or protest; *esp* one on which the signatures are arranged in a circle so that no name heads the list **2** a tournament in which each contestant plays every other contestant in turn

round-shouldered *adj* having stooping or rounded shoulders

roundsman *n* sby (e g a milkman) who takes, orders, sells, or delivers goods on an assigned route

round table *n* a meeting or conference of several people on equal terms – **round-table** *adj*

round-the-clock *adj* lasting or continuing 24 hours a day; constant

round trip *n* a trip to a place and back, usu over the same route

roundup *n* **1a** the collecting in of cattle by riding round them and driving them **b** a gathering in of scattered people or things **2** a summary of information (e g from news bulletins)

round up *vt* **1** to collect (cattle) by a roundup **2** to gather in or bring together from various quarters

roup *n* a virus disease of poultry in which soft whitish lesions form on the mouth, throat, and eyes

rouse *vi* **1** to become aroused **2** to become stirred ~ *vt* **1** to stir up; provoke **2** to arouse from sleep or apathy

rousing *adj* giving rise to enthusiasm; stirring

roustabout *n, Br* **1** a deck hand or docker **2** an unskilled or semiskilled labourer, esp in an oil field or refinery

¹**rout** *n* **1** a disorderly crowd of people; a mob **2** *archaic* a fashionable social gathering

²**rout** *vi* ¹ROOT **1** ~ *vt* to gouge out or make a furrow in

³**rout** *n* **1** a state of wild confusion; *specif* a confused retreat; headlong flight **2** a disastrous defeat

⁴**rout** *vt* **1** to disorganize completely; wreak havoc among **2** to put to headlong flight **3** to defeat decisively or disastrously

¹**route** *n* **1a** a regularly travelled way ⟨the trunk ~ north⟩ **b** a means of access **2** a line of travel **3** an itinerary

²**route** *vt* **1** to send by a selected route; direct **2** to divert in a specified direction

route march n a usu long and tiring march, esp as military training

¹**routine** n **1a** a regular course of procedure **b** habitual or mechanical performance of an established procedure **2** a fixed piece of entertainment often repeated ⟨a dance ~⟩ **3** a particular sequence of computer instructions for carrying out a given task

²**routine** adj **1** commonplace or repetitious in character **2** of or in accordance with established procedure – **routinely** adv

rout out vt ROOT OUT

roux n, pl **roux** a cooked mixture of fat and flour used as a thickening agent in a sauce

¹**rove** vb to wander aimlessly or idly (through or over)

²**rove** past of REEVE

³**rove** vt to join (textile fibres) with a slight twist and draw out into roving

⁴**rove** n roving

¹**rover** n a pirate

²**rover** n a wanderer

¹**roving** adj **1** not restricted as to location or area of concern **2** inclined to ramble or stray ⟨a ~ fancy⟩

²**roving** n a slightly twisted roll or strand of textile fibres

roving eye n promiscuous sexual interests

¹**row** vi **1** to propel a boat by means of oars **2** to move (as if) by the propulsion of oars ~ vt **1a** to propel (as if) with oars **b** to compete against in rowing **2** to transport in a boat propelled by oars **3** to occupy a specified position in a rowing crew – **rower** n

²**row** n an act of rowing a boat

³**row** n **1** a number of objects arranged in a (straight) line; also the line along which such objects are arranged **2** a way, street – **in a row** one after another; successively

⁴**row** n **1** a noisy quarrel or stormy dispute **2** excessive or unpleasant noise

⁵**row** vi to engage in quarrelling

rowan n (the red berry of) a small Eurasian tree of the rose family that bears flat clusters of white flowers

rowdy n or adj (sby) coarse or boisterous – **rowdily** adv, **rowdiness** n, **rowdyism** n

rowel n a revolving disc with sharp marginal points at the end of a spur

rowing boat n, Br a small boat designed to be rowed

rowlock n, chiefly Br a device for holding an oar in place and providing a fulcrum for its action

¹**royal** adj **1a** of monarchical ancestry ⟨the ~ family⟩ **b** of the crown ⟨the ~ estates⟩ **c** in the crown's service ⟨Royal Air Force⟩ **2** suitable for royalty; regal, magnificent **3** of superior size, magnitude, or quality **4** of or being a part of the rigging of a sailing ship next above the topgallant – **royally** adv

²**royal** n **1** a stag of 8 years or more having antlers with at least 12 points **2** a royal sail or mast **3** a size of paper usu 25 x 20in (635 × 508mm) **4** sby of royal blood – infml

royal flush n a straight flush having an ace as the highest card

royalist n, often cap a supporter of a king or of monarchical government (e g a Cavalier) – **royalism** n, **royalist** adj

royal jelly n a highly nutritious secretion of the honeybee that is fed to the very young larvae and to all larvae that will develop into queens

royal prerogative n the constitutional rights of the monarch

royalty n **1a** royal sovereignty **b** a monetary benefit received by a sovereign (e g a percentage of minerals) **2** regal character or bearing **3a** people of royal blood **b** a privileged class of a specified type **4** a right of jurisdiction granted by a sovereign **5a** a share of the product or profit reserved by one who grants esp an oil or mining lease **b** a payment made to an author, composer, or inventor for each copy or example of his/her work sold

¹**rub** vb **-bb-** vi to move along a surface with pressure and friction ~ vt **1** to subject to pressure and friction, esp with a back-and-forth motion **2a** to cause (a body) to move with pressure and friction along a surface **b** to treat in any of various ways by rubbing **3** to bring into reciprocal back-and-forth or rotary contact – **rub shoulders** to associate closely; mingle socially – **rub the wrong way** to arouse the antagonism or displeasure of; irritate

²**rub** n **1a** an obstacle, difficulty – usu + the **b** sthg grating to the feelings (e g a gibe or harsh criticism) **2** the application of friction and pressure

rub along vi **1** to continue coping in a trying situation **2** to remain on friendly terms

¹**rubber** n **1a** an instrument or object used in rubbing, polishing, or cleaning **b** Br a small piece of rubber or plastic used for rubbing out esp pencil marks on paper, card, etc **2** (any of various synthetic substances like) an elastic substance obtained by coagulating the milky juice of the rubber tree or other plant that is essentially a polymer of isoprene and is used, esp when toughened by chemical treatment, in car tyres, waterproof materials, etc **3** sthg like or made of rubber: e g **a** NAm a galosh **b** NAm a condom – **rubber** adj, **rubbery** adj

²**rubber** n a contest consisting of an odd number of games won by the side that takes a majority

rubber band n a continuous band of rubber used for holding small objects together

rubberize, -ise vt to coat or impregnate with (a solution of) rubber

¹**rubberneck** also **rubbernecker** n, NAm **1** an overinquisitive person **2** a tourist, sightseer; esp one on a guided tour – USE derog

²**rubberneck** vi, NAm **1** to show exaggerated curiosity – infml **2** to engage in sightseeing – derog

rubber plant n a tall Asian tree of the fig family frequently dwarfed and grown as an ornamental plant

rubber-stamp vt **1** to imprint with a rubber stamp **2** to approve, endorse, or dispose of as a matter of routine or at the dictate of another

rubber stamp n **1** a stamp of rubber for making imprints **2** sby who unthinkingly assents to the actions or policies of others **3** a routine endorsement or approval

rubber tree n a S American tree of the spurge family that is cultivated in plantations and is the chief source of rubber

rubbing n an image of a raised surface obtained by placing paper over it and rubbing the paper with charcoal, chalk, etc ⟨a brass ~⟩

¹**rubbish** n **1** worthless or rejected articles; trash **2** sthg worthless; NONSENSE 1a, b – often used interjectionally – **rubbishy** adj

²**rubbish** vt **1** to condemn as rubbish **2** to litter with rubbish

rubble n **1** broken fragments of building material (e g brick, stone, etc) **2** rough broken stones or bricks used in coarse masonry or in filling courses of walls **3** rough stone from the quarry

rubdown n a brisk rubbing of the body

rubella n GERMAN MEASLES

Rubicon n a bounding or limiting line; esp one that when crossed commits sby irrevocably

rubicund adj ruddy – **rubicundity** n

rub in vt to harp on (e g sthg unpleasant or embarrassing)

ruble *n* a rouble

rub off *vi* **1** to disappear as the result of rubbing **2** to exert an influence through contact or example

rub out *vt* **1** to remove (e g pencil marks) with a rubber; *broadly* to obliterate **2** *chiefly NAm* to kill, murder – slang

rubric *n* **1** a heading (e g in a book or manuscript) written or printed in a distinctive colour (e g red) or style **2a** a heading under which sthg is classed **b** an authoritative rule; *esp* a rule for the conduct of church ceremonial **c** an explanatory or introductory commentary – **rubric, rubrical** *adj*

rub up *vt* to revive or refresh knowledge of; revise

¹**ruby** *n* **1** a red corundum used as a gem **2a** the dark red colour of the ruby **b** sthg like a ruby in colour

²**ruby** *adj* of or marking a 40th anniversary ⟨~ *wedding*⟩

¹**ruck** *n* **1a** an indistinguishable mass **b** *the* usual run of people or things **2** a situation in Rugby Union in which 1 or more players from each team close round the ball when it is on the ground and try to kick the ball out to their own team

²**ruck** *vb* to wrinkle, crease – often + *up*

rucksack *n* a lightweight bag carried on the back and fastened by straps over the shoulders, used esp by walkers and climbers

ruckus *n, chiefly NAm* a row or disturbance – infml

ruction *n* **1** a violent dispute **2** a disturbance, uproar *USE* infml

rudder *n* **1** a flat piece or structure of wood or metal hinged vertically to a ship's stern for changing course with **2** a movable auxiliary aerofoil, usu attached to the fin, that serves to control direction of flight of an aircraft in the horizontal plane – **rudderless** *adj*

ruddy *adj* **1** having a healthy reddish colour **2** red, reddish **3** *Br* BLOODY **4** – euph – **ruddily** *adv*, **ruddiness** *n*

rude *adj* **1a** in a rough or unfinished state **b** primitive, undeveloped **c** simple, elemental **2** lacking refinement or propriety: e g **a** discourteous **b** vulgar, indecent **c** uncivilized **d** ignorant, unlearned **3** showing or suggesting lack of training or skill **4** robust, vigorous – esp in *rude health* **5** sudden and unpleasant; abrupt ⟨*a* ~ *awakening*⟩ – **rudely** *adv*, **rudeness** *n*, **rudery** *n*

rudiment *n* **1** a basic principle or element or a fundamental skill **2a** sthg as yet unformed or undeveloped **b**(1) a deficiently developed body part or organ; VESTIGE 2 (2) a primordium *USE* usu pl with sing. meaning – **rudimental** *adj*

rudimentary *adj* **1** basic, fundamental **2** of a primitive kind; crude **3** very poorly developed or represented only by a vestige ⟨*the* ~ *tail of a hyrax*⟩ – **rudimentarily** *adv*

¹**rue** *vt* to feel penitence or bitter regret for

²**rue** *n* a strong-scented woody plant with bitter leaves formerly used in medicine

rueful *adj* **1** arousing pity or compassion **2** mournful, regretful; *also* feigning sorrow – **ruefully** *adv*, **ruefulness** *n*

¹**ruff, ruffe** *n* a small freshwater European perch

²**ruff** *n* **1** a broad starched collar of fluted linen or muslin worn in the late 16th and early 17th c **2** a fringe or frill of long hairs or feathers growing round the neck **3** *fem* reeve a Eurasian sandpiper the male of which has a large ruff of erectable feathers during the breeding season – **ruffed** *adj*

³**ruff** *vt* TRUMP 1 – **ruff** *n*

ruffian *n* a brutal and lawless person – **ruffianism** *n*, **ruffianly** *adj*

¹**ruffle** *vb* **ruffling** *vt* **1a** to disturb the smoothness of **b** to trouble, vex ⟨~d *his composure*⟩ **2** to erect (e g feathers) (as if) in a ruff **3** to make into a ruffle ~*vi* to become ruffled

²**ruffle** *n* **1** a disturbance of surface evenness (e g a ripple or crumple) **2a** a strip of fabric gathered or pleated on 1 edge **b** ²RUFF 2

rug *n* **1** a heavy mat, usu smaller than a carpet and with a thick pile, which is used as a floor covering **2a** a woollen blanket, often with fringes on 2 opposite edges, used as a wrap esp when travelling **b** a blanket for an animal (e g a horse)

rugby *n, often cap* a football game that is played with an oval football, that features kicking, lateral hand-to-hand passing, and tackling, and in which forward passing is prohibited

rugged *adj* **1** having a rough uneven surface or outline ⟨~ *mountains*⟩ **2** seamed with wrinkles and furrows ⟨*a* ~ *face*⟩ **3** austere, stern; *also* uncompromising ⟨~ *individualism*⟩ **4a** strongly built or constituted; sturdy **b** presenting a severe test of ability or stamina – **ruggedly** *adv*, **ruggedness** *n*

¹**ruin** *n* **1** physical, moral, economic, or social collapse **2a** the state of being wrecked or decayed ⟨*the city lay in* ~s⟩ **b** the remains of sthg destroyed – usu pl with sing. meaning **3** (a cause of) destruction or downfall ⟨*whisky was his* ~⟩ ⟨*the* ~ *of modern drama* – T S Eliot⟩ **4** a ruined person or structure – **ruination** *n*

²**ruin** *vt* **1** to reduce to ruins **2a** to damage irreparably; spoil **b** to reduce to financial ruin – **ruiner** *n*

ruinous *adj* **1** dilapidated, ruined **2** causing (the likelihood of) ruin ⟨~ *sales performance*⟩ – **ruinously** *adv*, **ruinousness** *n*

¹**rule** *n* **1a** a prescriptive specification of conduct or action **b** the laws or regulations prescribed by the founder of a religious order for observance by its members **c** an established procedure, custom, or habit **d** a legal precept or doctrine **2a**(1) a usu valid generalization (2) a generally prevailing quality, state, or form **b** a standard of judgment **c** a regulating principle, esp of a system ⟨*the* ~s *of grammar*⟩ **3** the exercise or a period of dominion **4** a strip or set of jointed strips of material marked off in units and used for measuring or marking off lengths – **as a rule** generally; FOR THE MOST PART

²**rule** *vt* **1a** to exert control, direction, or influence on **b** to exercise control over, esp by restraining ⟨~d *her appetites firmly*⟩ **2a** to exercise power or firm authority over **b** to be preeminent in; dominate ⟨*an actor who* ~s *the stage*⟩ **3** to lay down authoritatively, esp judicially **4a** to mark with lines drawn (as if) along the straight edge of a ruler **b** to mark (a line) on sthg with a ruler ~*vi* **1** to exercise supreme authority **2** to make a judicial decision

rule out *vt* **1a** to exclude, eliminate **b** to deny the possibility of ⟨*rule out further discussion*⟩ **2** to make impossible; prevent

ruler *n* **1** sby, specif a sovereign, who rules **2** a smooth-edged strip of material that is usu marked off in units (e g centimetres) and is used for guiding a pen or pencil in drawing lines, for measuring, or for marking off lengths – **rulership** *n*

¹**ruling** *n* an official or authoritative decision

²**ruling** *adj* **1** exerting power or authority **2** chief, predominant

¹**rum** *adj* **-mm-** *chiefly Br* queer, strange ⟨*she's a* ~ *customer*⟩ – infml

²**rum** *n* a spirit distilled from a fermented cane product (e g molasses)

rumba, rhumba *n* (the music for) a ballroom dance of

Cuban Negro origin marked by steps with a delayed transfer of weight and pronounced hip movements

¹rumble *vb* **rumbling** *vi* **1** to make a low heavy rolling sound **2** *NAm* to engage in a street fight – *infml* ~ *vt* **1** to utter or emit with a low rolling sound **2** to reveal or discover the true character of – *infml* – **rumbler** *n*

²rumble *n* **1a** a rumbling sound **b** low-frequency noise from a record deck caused by the vibrations of the turntable **2** *NAm* a street fight, esp between gangs – *infml*

rumbustious *adj, chiefly Br* irrepressibly or coarsely exuberant – **rumbustiousness** *n*

¹ruminant *n* a ruminant mammal

²ruminant *adj* **1a** that chews the cud **b** of or being (a member of) a group of hoofed mammals including the cattle, sheep, giraffes, and camels that chew the cud and have a complex 3- or 4-chambered stomach **2** meditative

ruminate *vb* **1** to chew again (what has been chewed slightly and swallowed) **2** to engage in contemplation (of) – **ruminator** *n*, **ruminative** *adj*, **ruminatively** *adv*, **rumination** *n*

¹rummage *n* **1** a thorough search, esp among a jumbled assortment of objects **2a** *chiefly NAm* JUMBLE 2 **b** *NAm* a miscellaneous or confused accumulation

²rummage *vt* **1** to make a thorough search of (an untidy or congested place) **2** to uncover by searching – usu + *out* ~ *vi* to engage in a haphazard search – **rummager** *n*

rummage sale *n, chiefly NAm* JUMBLE SALE

rummy *n* any of several card games for 2 or more players in which each player tries to assemble combinations of 3 or more related cards and to be the first to turn all his/her cards into such combinations

¹rumour, *NAm chiefly* **rumor** *n* **1** a statement or report circulated without confirmation of its truth **2** talk or opinion widely disseminated but with no identifiable source

²rumour, *NAm chiefly* **rumor** *vt* to tell or spread by rumour

rump *n* **1** the rear part of a quadruped mammal, bird, etc; the buttocks **2** a cut of beef between the loin and round **3** a small or inferior remnant of a larger group (e g a parliament)

¹rumple *n* a fold, wrinkle

²rumple *vb* **rumpling** *vt* **1** to wrinkle, crumple **2** to make unkempt; tousle ~ *vi* to become rumpled

rumpus *n* a usu noisy commotion

¹run *vb* **-nn-; ran; run** *vi* **1a** to go faster than a walk; *specif* to go steadily by springing steps so that both feet leave the ground for an instant in each step **b** *of a horse* to move at a fast gallop **c** to flee, escape ⟨*dropped his gun and ran*⟩ **2a** to go without restraint ⟨*let his chickens* ~ *loose*⟩ ⟨~ *about barefoot*⟩ **b** to sail before the wind as distinct from reaching or sailing close-hauled **3a** to hasten with a specified often distressing purpose ⟨~ *and fetch the doctor*⟩ **b** to make a quick, easy, or casual trip or visit ⟨~ *up to town for the day*⟩ **4** to contend in a race; *also* to finish a race in the specified place ⟨*ran third*⟩ **5a** to move (as if) on wheels ⟨*a chair that* ~*s on castors*⟩ **b** to pass or slide freely or cursorily ⟨*a thought ran through my mind*⟩ **6** to sing or play quickly ⟨~ *up the scale*⟩ **7a** to go back and forth; ply ⟨*made the trains* ~ *on time*⟩ **b** *of fish* to migrate or move in schools; *esp* to ascend a river to spawn **8** to function, operate ⟨*don't touch the engine while it's* ~*ning*⟩ ⟨*the engine* ~*s on petrol*⟩ ⟨*everything's* ~*ning smoothly at the office*⟩ **9a** to continue in force ⟨*the lease has 2 more years to* ~⟩ **b** to continue to accumulate or become payable ⟨*interest on the loan* ~*s from July 1st*⟩ **10** to pass, esp by negligence or indulgence, into a specified state ⟨~ *to waste*⟩ ⟨*money ran low*⟩ **11a(1)** to flow,

course ⟨~*ning water*⟩ **(2)** to become by flowing ⟨*the water ran cold*⟩ **(3)** to discharge liquid ⟨*made my nose* ~⟩ ⟨*left the tap* ~*ning*⟩ **(4)** to reach a specified state by discharging liquid ⟨*the well ran dry*⟩ **b** MELT 1 ⟨*butter started to* ~⟩ **c** to spread, dissolve ⟨*colours guaranteed not to* ~⟩ **d** to discharge pus or serum ⟨*a* ~*ning sore*⟩ **12a** to develop rapidly in some specific direction; *esp* to throw out an elongated shoot **b** to have a tendency; be prone ⟨*they* ~ *to big noses in that family*⟩ **13a** to lie or extend in a specified position, direction, or relation to sthg ⟨*the road* ~*s through a tunnel*⟩ **b** to extend in a continuous range ⟨*shades* ~ *from white to dark grey*⟩ **c** to be in a certain form or expression ⟨*the letter* ~*s as follows*⟩ **14a** to occur persistently ⟨*a note of despair* ~*s through the narrative*⟩ **b** to continue to be as specified ⟨*profits were* ~*ning high*⟩ **c** to play or be featured continuously (e g in a theatre or newspaper) ⟨*the musical ran for 6 months*⟩ **15** to spread quickly from point to point ⟨*chills ran up his spine*⟩ **16** to ladder **17** *chiefly NAm* STAND 10 ⟨~ *for President*⟩ ~ *vt* **1a** to bring to a specified condition (as if) by running ⟨*ran himself to death*⟩ **b** to go in pursuit of; hunt ⟨*dogs that* ~ *deer*⟩ ⟨*ran the rumour to its source*⟩ **c** to drive, chase ⟨~ *him out of town*⟩ **d** to enter, register, or enrol as a contestant in a race **e** to put forward as a candidate for office **2a** to drive (livestock), esp to a grazing place **b** to provide pasturage for (livestock) **3a** to cover, accomplish, or perform (as if) by running ⟨*ran 10 miles*⟩ ⟨~ *errands for his mother*⟩ ⟨*ran the whole gamut of emotions*⟩ **b** to slip through or past ⟨~ *a blockade*⟩ **4a** to cause or allow to penetrate or enter ⟨*ran a splinter into his toe*⟩ **b** to stitch **c** to cause to lie or extend in a specified position or direction ⟨~ *a wire in from the aerial*⟩ **d** to cause to collide ⟨*ran his head into a post*⟩ **e** to smuggle ⟨~ *guns*⟩ **5** to cause to pass lightly, freely, or cursorily ⟨*ran a comb through her hair*⟩ **6a(1)** to cause or allow (a vehicle or vessel) to go ⟨~ *his car off the road*⟩ ⟨~ *the ship aground*⟩ **(2)** to cause to ply or travel along a regular route ⟨~ *an extra train on Saturdays*⟩ **(3)** to own and drive ⟨*she* ~*s an old banger*⟩ **(4)** to convey in a vehicle ⟨*can I* ~ *you home?*⟩ **b** to operate ⟨~ *a lathe*⟩ ⟨~ *your razor off the mains*⟩ **c** to carry on, manage, or control ⟨~ *a factory*⟩ **7** to be full of; flow with ⟨*streets ran blood*⟩ **8a** to cause to move or flow in a specified way or into a specified position **b(1)** to cause to pour out liquid ⟨~ *the hot tap*⟩ **(2)** to fill from a tap ⟨~ *a hot bath*⟩ **9a** to melt and cast in a mould **b** to subject to a treatment or process ⟨~ *a problem through a computer*⟩ **10** to make oneself liable to ⟨~ *risks*⟩ **11** to permit (e g charges) to accumulate before settling ⟨~ *an account at the grocer's*⟩ **12a** RUN OFF 1b ⟨*a book to be* ~ *on lightweight paper*⟩ **b** to carry in a printed medium; print – **run across** to meet with or discover by chance – **run after** to pursue, chase; *esp* to seek the company of – **run a temperature** to be feverish – **run foul of 1** to collide with ⟨*run foul of a hidden reef*⟩ **2** to come into conflict with ⟨*run foul of the law*⟩ **b** to merge with **b** to mount up to ⟨*income often runs into five figures*⟩ **2a** to collide with **b** to encounter, meet ⟨*ran into an old friend the other day*⟩ – **run into the ground** to tire out or use up with heavy work – **run it fine** to leave only the irreducible margin – **run on** to be concerned with; dwell on ⟨*her mind keeps running on the past*⟩ – **run rings round** to show marked superiority over; defeat decisively – **run riot 1** to act or function wildly or without restraint ⟨*let one's imagination run riot*⟩ **2** to grow or occur in profusion – **run short 1** to become insufficient **2** to come near the end of available supplies ⟨*we ran short of tea*⟩ – **run somebody off his/her feet 1** to tire sby out with running **2** to keep sby very busy – **run through 1** to squander **2a RUN THROUGH** *vt* 2 ⟨ran through *it quickly*⟩ **b** to deal with rapidly and usu perfunctorily – **run to** 1 to extend to ⟨*the book* runs to *500 pages*⟩ **2a** to afford **b** *of money* to be enough for ⟨*his salary won't* run to *a car*⟩ – **run to earth/ground** to find after protracted search

²**run** *n* **1a** an act or the activity of running; continued rapid movement **b** a quickened gallop; *broadly* the gait of a runner **c** (a school of fish) migrating or ascending a river to spawn **d** a running race ⟨*a mile* ∼⟩ **2a** the direction in which sthg (e g a vein of ore or the grain of wood) lies **b** general tendency or direction ⟨*watching the* ∼ *of the stock market*⟩ **3** a continuous series or unbroken course, esp of identical or similar things ⟨*a* ∼ *of bad luck*⟩: e g **a** a rapid passage up or down a musical scale **b** a number of rapid small dance steps executed in even tempo **c** an unbroken course of performances or showings **d** a set of consecutive measurements, readings, or observations **e** a persistent and heavy commercial or financial demand ⟨*a* ∼ *on gilt-edged securities*⟩ **f** three or more playing cards usu of the same suit in consecutive order of rank **4** the quantity of work turned out in a continuous operation **5** the average or prevailing kind or class ⟨*the general* ∼ *of students*⟩ **6a** the distance covered in a period of continuous journeying **b(1)** a regularly travelled course or route ⟨*ships on the Far East* ∼⟩ **(2)** a short excursion in a car ⟨*went for a Sunday* ∼⟩ **c** the distance a golf ball travels after touching the ground **d** freedom of movement in or access to a place ⟨*has the* ∼ *of the house*⟩ **7a** a way, track, etc frequented by animals **b** an enclosure for domestic animals where they may feed or exercise **c** an inclined passageway **8a** an inclined course (e g for skiing) **b** a support or channel (e g a track, pipe, or trough) along which sthg runs **9** a unit of scoring in cricket made typically by each batsman running the full length of the wicket **10 LADDER 2b** – **runless** *adj* – **on the run** 1 in haste; without pausing **2** in hiding or running away, esp from lawful authority – **run for one's money** the profit or enjoyment to which one is legitimately entitled

runabout *n* a light motor car, aeroplane, or motorboat

run along *vi* to go away; depart – often used as an order or request

runaround *n, chiefly NAm* delaying action, esp in response to a request

¹**runaway** *n* **1** a fugitive **2** sthg (e g a horse) that is running out of control

²**runaway** *adj* **1** fugitive **2** accomplished as a result of running away ⟨*a* ∼ *marriage*⟩ **3** won by a long lead; decisive ⟨*a* ∼ *victory*⟩ **4** out of control ⟨∼ *inflation*⟩

run away *vi* **1a** to take to flight **b** to flee from home; *esp* to elope **2** to run out of control; stampede, bolt – **run away with** 1 to take away in haste or secretly; *esp* to steal **2** to believe too easily ⟨*don't* run away with *the idea that you needn't go*⟩ **3** to carry beyond reasonable limits ⟨*his imagination* ran away with *him*⟩

rundown *n* **1** the running down of sthg ⟨*the* ∼ *of the steel industry*⟩ **2** an item-by-item report; a résumé

run-down *adj* **1** in a state of disrepair **2** in poor health **3** *NAm* completely unwound ⟨*a* ∼ *clock*⟩

run down *vt* **1a** to knock down, esp with a motor vehicle **b** to run against and cause to sink **2a** to chase to exhaustion or until captured **b** to find by searching ⟨run down *a book in the library*⟩ **3** to disparage ⟨*don't* run *him* down; *he's an honest fellow*⟩ **4** to allow the gradual decline or closure of ⟨*the lead mines are being gradually* run down⟩ ∼ *vi* **1** to cease to operate because of the exhaustion of motive power ⟨*that battery* ran down *weeks ago*⟩ **2** to decline in physical condition

rune *n* **1** any of the characters of an alphabet prob derived

from Latin and Greek and used in medieval times, esp in carved inscriptions, by the Germanic peoples **2** a magical or cryptic utterance or inscription – **runic** *adj*

¹**rung** *past part of* RING

²**rung** *n* **1a** a rounded part placed as a crosspiece between the legs of a chair **b** any of the crosspieces of a ladder **2** a level or stage in sthg that can be ascended ⟨*the bottom* ∼ *of the social scale*⟩

run-in *n* **1** the final part of a race(track) **2** *NAm* a quarrel

run in *vt* **1** to make (typeset matter) continuous without a paragraph or other break **2** to use (e g a motor car) cautiously for an initial period **3** to arrest, esp for a minor offence – *infml*

runnel *n* a small stream; a brook

runner *n* **1** an entrant for a race who actually competes in it **2a** a bank or stockbroker's messenger **b** sby who smuggles or distributes illicit or contraband goods – usu in combination ⟨*a dope*-runner⟩ **3** a straight piece on which sthg slides: e g **a** a longitudinal piece on which a sledge or ice skate slides **b** a groove or bar along which sthg (e g a drawer or sliding door) slides **4** a stolon **5a** a long narrow carpet (e g for a hall or staircase) **b** a narrow decorative cloth for a table or dresser top **6 RUNNER BEAN** **7** a player who runs in place of an injured batsman in cricket

runner bean *n, chiefly Br* (the long green edible pod of) a widely cultivated orig tropical American high-climbing bean with large usu bright red flowers

runner-up *n, pl* **runners-up** *also* **runner-ups** a competitor other than the outright winner whose attainment still merits a prize

¹**running** *n* **1** the state of competing, esp with a good chance of winning – in *in/out of the running* **2** management, operation ⟨*the* ∼ *of a small business*⟩ ⟨*the* ∼ *of a company car*⟩

²**running** *adj* **1** runny **2a** having stages that follow in rapid succession ⟨*a* ∼ *battle*⟩ **b** made during the course of a process or activity ⟨*a* ∼ *commentary*⟩ ⟨∼ *repairs*⟩ **3** being part of a continuous length ⟨*cost of timber per* ∼ *metre*⟩ **4** cursive, flowing **5** designed or used for races on foot ⟨*a* ∼ *track*⟩

³**running** *adv* in succession ⟨*for 3 days* ∼⟩

running board *n* a footboard, esp at the side of a motor car

running knot *n* a knot that slips along the rope or line round which it is tied

running mate *n* a candidate standing for a subordinate place in a US election

runny *adj* tending to run ⟨*a* ∼ *nose*⟩

runoff *n* a final decisive race, contest, or election

run off *vt* **1a** to compose rapidly or glibly **b** to produce with a printing press or copier ⟨run off *a few copies*⟩ **c** to decide (e g a race) by a runoff **2** to drain off (a liquid) **3** *NAm* to steal (e g cattle) by driving away ∼ *vi* **RUN AWAY** 1 – **run off with** **RUN AWAY WITH** 1

run-of-the-mill *adj* average, commonplace

run-on *n* sthg (e g a dictionary entry) run on

run on *vi* **1** to keep going without interruption ⟨*the opera* ran on *for 4 hours*⟩ **2** to talk or narrate at length ∼ *vt* **1** to continue (written material) without a break or a new paragraph **2** to place or add (e g an entry in a dictionary) at the end of a paragraphed item

run out *vi* **1a** to come to an end ⟨*time* ran out⟩ **b** to become exhausted or used up ⟨*the petrol* ran out⟩ **2** to finish a course or contest in the specified position ⟨ran out *the winner*⟩ **3** *of a horse* to evade a fence by turning aside ∼ *vt* **1** to dismiss (a batsman who is outside his crease and attempting a run) by breaking the wicket with the ball **2**

chiefly NAm to compel to leave ⟨run *him* out *of town*⟩ – **run out of** to use up the available supply of – **run out on** ³DESERT

runover *n* typeset matter that exceeds the allotted space

run over *vi* **1** to overflow **2** to exceed a limit ⟨*meetings that* run over *into the next day*⟩ ~ *vt* **1** to glance over, repeat, or rehearse quickly **2** to injure or kill with a motor vehicle ⟨*ran the dog* over⟩

runt *n* **1** an animal unusually small of its kind; *esp* the smallest of a litter of pigs **2** a puny person – **runty** *adj*

run-through *n* **1** a cursory reading, summary, or rehearsal **2** a sequence of actions performed for practice

run through *vt* **1** to pierce with a weapon (e g a sword) **2** to perform, esp for practice or instruction

run-up *n* **1** (the track or area provided for) an approach run to provide momentum (e g for a jump or throw) **2** *Br* a period that immediately precedes an action or event ⟨*the* ~ *to the last election*⟩

run up *vt* **1** to make (esp a garment) quickly **2a** to erect hastily **b** to hoist (a flag) **3** to accumulate or incur (debts) – **run up against** to encounter (e g a difficulty)

runway *n* **1a** (a beaten) path made by or for animals **2** an artificially surfaced strip of ground on an airfield for the landing and takeoff of aeroplanes

rupee *n* (a note or coin representing) the basic money unit of various countries of the Indian subcontinent and the Indian Ocean (e g India, Pakistan, Seychelles, and Sri Lanka)

¹**rupture** *n* **1** breach of peace or concord; *specif* open hostility between nations **2a** the tearing apart of a tissue, esp muscle **b** a hernia **3a** a breaking apart or bursting **b** the state of being broken apart or burst

²**rupture** *vt* **1a** to part by violence; break, burst **b** to create a breach of **2** to produce a rupture in ~ *vi* to have or undergo a rupture

rural *adj* of the country, country people or life, or agriculture – **rurally** *adv*

rural dean *n* a priest supervising 1 district of a diocese

Ruritanian *adj* (characteristic) of an imaginary Central European country used as a setting for contemporary cloak-and-dagger court intrigues

ruse *n* a wily subterfuge

¹**rush** *n* any of various often tufted marsh plants with cylindrical (hollow) leaves, used for the seats of chairs and for plaiting mats – **rushy** *adj*

²**rush** *vi* to move forwards, progress, or act quickly or eagerly or without preparation ~ *vt* **1** to push or impel forwards with speed or violence **2** to perform or finish in a short time or at high speed ⟨~ed *his breakfast*⟩ **3** to urge to an excessive speed **4** to run against in attack, often with an element of surprise; charge – **rusher** *n*

³**rush** *n* **1a** a rapid and violent forward motion **b** a sudden onset of emotion ⟨*a quick* ~ *of sympathy*⟩ **2a** a surge of activity; *also* busy or hurried activity ⟨*the bank holiday* ~⟩ **b** a burst of productivity or speed **3** a great movement of people, esp in search of wealth **4** the unedited print of a film scene processed directly after shooting – usu pl **5** ²FLASH 9

⁴**rush** *adj* requiring or marked by special speed or urgency

rush hour *n* a period of the day when traffic is at a peak

rushlight *n* a candle that consists of the pith of a rush dipped in grease

rusk *n* (a light dry biscuit similar to) a piece of sliced bread baked again until dry and crisp

russet *n* **1** a reddish to yellowish brown **2** any of various russet-coloured winter eating apples – **russet** *adj*

Russian *n* **1** a native or inhabitant of Russia; *broadly* a native or inhabitant of the USSR **2** a Slavonic language of the Russians – **Russian** *adj*

Russian roulette *n* an act of bravado consisting of spinning the cylinder of a revolver loaded with 1 cartridge, pointing the muzzle at one's own head, and pulling the trigger

Russo- *comb form* **1** Russian nation, people, or culture ⟨*Russophobia*⟩ **2** Russian; Russian and ⟨*Russo-Japanese*⟩

¹**rust** *n* **1a** brittle reddish hydrated ferric oxide that forms as a coating on iron, esp iron chemically attacked by moist air **b** a comparable coating produced on another metal **c** sthg like rust **2** corrosive or injurious influence or effect **3** (a fungus causing) any of numerous destructive diseases of plants in which reddish brown pustular lesions form **4** a reddish brown to orange colour

²**rust** *vi* **1** to form rust; become oxidized ⟨*iron* ~s⟩ **2** to degenerate, esp through lack of use or advancing age **3** to become reddish brown as if with rust **4** to be affected with a rust fungus ~ *vt* to cause (a metal) to form rust

¹**rustic** *adj* **1** of or suitable for the country **2a** made of the rough limbs of trees ⟨~ *furniture*⟩ **b** finished by rusticating ⟨*a* ~ *joint in masonry*⟩ **3** characteristic of country people – **rustically** *adv*, **rusticity** *n*

²**rustic** *n* an unsophisticated rural person

rusticate *vt* **1** to suspend (a student) from college or university **2** to bevel or cut a groove, channel etc in (e g the edges of stone blocks) to make the joints conspicuous ⟨*a* ~d *stone wall*⟩ **3** to impart a rustic character to – **rusticator** *n*, **rustication** *n*

¹**rustle** *vb* **rustling** *vi* **1a** to make or cause a rustle **b** to move with a rustling sound **2** *chiefly NAm* to steal cattle or horses ~ *vt chiefly NAm* to steal (e g cattle) – **rustler** *n*

²**rustle** *n* a quick succession or confusion of faint sounds

rustproof *adj* able to resist rust

rusty *adj* **1** affected (as if) by rust; *esp* stiff (as if) with rust ⟨*the creaking of* ~ *hinges*⟩ **2** inept and slow through lack of practice or advanced age **3a** of the colour rust **b** dulled in colour by age and use; shabby ⟨*a* ~ *old suit of clothes*⟩ – **rustily** *adv*, **rustiness** *n*

¹**rut** *n* **1** an annually recurrent state of readiness to copulate, in the male deer or other mammal; *also* oestrus, heat **2** the period during which rut normally occurs – often + *the*

²**rut** *n* **1** a track worn by habitual passage, esp of wheels on soft or uneven ground **2** an established practice; *esp* a tedious routine ⟨*get into a* ~⟩

³**rut** *vt* **-tt-** to make a rut in

ruthless *adj* showing no pity or compassion – **ruthlessly** *adv*, **ruthlessness** *n*

-ry – see -ERY

rye *n* (the seeds, from which a wholemeal flour is made, of) a hardy grass widely grown for grain

rye whisky *n* a whisky distilled from rye or from rye and malt

S

s *n, pl* **s's, ss** *often cap* (a graphic representation of or device for reproducing) the 19th letter of the English alphabet

¹-s *suffix* (→ *n pl*) **1a** – used to form the plural of most nouns that do not end in *s, z, sh, ch,* or postconsonantal *y* ⟨*cats*⟩ ⟨*heads*⟩ ⟨*books*⟩ ⟨*boys*⟩ ⟨*beliefs*⟩; compare ¹-ES **1 b** – used with or without a preceding apostrophe to form the plural of abbreviations, numbers, letters, and symbols used as nouns ⟨*MCs*⟩ ⟨*4s*⟩ ⟨*the 1940's*⟩ ⟨*£s*⟩ ⟨*B's*⟩; compare ¹-ES **1 2** *chiefly NAm* – used to form adverbs denoting usual or repeated action or state ⟨*always at home Sundays*⟩ ⟨*mornings he stops by the newsstand*⟩

²-s *suffix* (→ *vb*) – used to form the third person singular present of most verbs that do not end in *s, z, sh, ch,* or postconsonantal *y* ⟨*falls*⟩ ⟨*takes*⟩ ⟨*plays*⟩; compare ²-ES

¹'s *vb* **1** is ⟨*she's here*⟩ **2** has ⟨*he's seen them*⟩ **3** does – in questions ⟨*what's he want?*⟩

²'s *pron* us – + *let* ⟨*let's*⟩

-'s *suffix* (→ *n* or *pron*) – used to form the possessive of singular nouns ⟨*boy's*⟩, of plural nouns not ending in *s* ⟨*children's*⟩, of some pronouns ⟨*anyone's*⟩, and of word groups functioning as nouns ⟨*the man in the corner's hat*⟩ or pronouns ⟨*someone else's*⟩

Sabbatarian *n* **1** a person who observes the Sabbath on Saturday in strict conformity with the 4th commandment **2** an adherent of Sabbatarianism – **Sabbatarian** *adj*

sabbath *n* **1** *often cap* the 7th day of the week observed from Friday evening to Saturday evening as a day of rest and worship by Jews **2** *often cap* Sunday observed among Christians as a day of rest and worship **3** a sabbat

¹sabbatical, sabbatic *adj* **1** of the sabbath ⟨~ *laws*⟩ **2** of or being a sabbatical

²sabbatical *n* a leave, often with pay, granted usu every 7th year (e g to a university teacher)

¹sable *n, pl* **sables,** (1) **sables,** *esp collectively* **sable 1** (the valuable dark brown fur of) a N Asian and European flesh-eating mammal related to the martens **2** BLACK 2 – poetic or used technically in heraldry

²sable *adj* of the colour sable

sabot *n* **1** a wooden shoe worn in various European countries **2** a thrust-transmitting carrier that positions a smaller projectile in a larger gun barrel or launching tube and that prevents the escape of gas ahead of the missile so as to increase the muzzle velocity of the projectile

¹sabotage *n* **1** destructive or obstructive action carried on by a civilian or enemy agent, intended to hinder military activity **2** deliberate subversion (e g of a plan or project)

²sabotage *vt* to practise sabotage on

saboteur *n* one who commits sabotage

sabra *n, often cap* a native-born Israeli

¹sabre, NAm chiefly saber *n* **1** a cavalry sword with a curved blade, thick back, and guard **2** a light fencing or duelling sword having an arched guard that covers the back of the hand and a tapering flexible blade with a full cutting edge along one side

²sabre, NAm chiefly saber *vt* to strike or kill with a sabre

sabre rattling *n* blustering display of military power

sabre-toothed tiger *n* an extinct big cat with long curved upper canines

sac *n* a (fluid-filled) pouch within an animal or plant – **saclike** *adj*

saccharin *n* a compound containing no calories that is

several hundred times sweeter than cane sugar and is used as a sugar substitute (e g in low-calorie diets)

saccharine *adj* **1** of, like, or containing sugar ⟨~ *taste*⟩ **2** excessively sweet; mawkish ⟨~ *sentiment*⟩ – **saccharinity** *n*

sacerdotal *adj* of priests or a priesthood – **sacerdotally** *adv*

sacerdotalism *n* religious belief emphasizing the role of priests as essential mediators between God and human beings – **sacerdotalist** *n*

sachet *n* **1** a small usu plastic bag or packet; *esp* one holding just enough of sthg (e g shampoo or sugar) for use at 1 time **2** a small bag containing a perfumed powder used to scent clothes and linens – **sacheted** *adj*

¹sack *n* **1** a usu rectangular large bag (e g of paper or canvas) **2** the amount contained in a sack **3** a garment without shaping: e g **a** a loosely fitting dress **b** a loose coat or jacket; *esp* one worn by men in the 19th c **4** dismissal from employment – usu + *get* or *give* + *the*; infml – **sackful** *n*

²sack *vt* **1** to place in a sack **2** to dismiss from a job – infml – **sacker** *n*

³sack *n* any of various dry white wines formerly imported to England from S Europe

⁴sack *n* the plundering of a place captured in war

⁵sack *vt* **1** to plunder (e g a town) after capture **2** to strip (a place) of valuables – **sacker** *n*

sackbut *n* the renaissance trombone

sackcloth *n* **1** sacking **2** a garment of sackcloth worn as a sign of mourning or penitence

sack race *n* a jumping race in which each contestant has his/her legs enclosed in a sack

¹sacral *adj* of or lying near the sacrum

²sacral *adj* holy, sacred

sacrament *n* **1** a formal religious act (e g baptism) functioning as a sign or symbol of a spiritual reality **2** *cap* the bread and wine used at Communion; *specif* the consecrated Host

sacramental *adj* (having the character) of a sacrament – **sacramentally** *adv*

sacred *adj* **1a** dedicated or set apart for the service or worship of a god or gods **b** dedicated as a memorial ⟨~ *to his memory*⟩ **2a** worthy of religious veneration **b** commanding reverence and respect **3** of religion; not secular or profane – **sacredly** *adv*, **sacredness** *n*

sacred cow *n* sby or sthg granted unreasonable immunity from criticism

¹sacrifice *n* **1** an act of offering to a deity; *esp* the killing of a victim on an altar **2** sthg offered in sacrifice **3a** destruction or surrender of one thing for the sake of another of greater worth or importance **b** sthg given up or lost ⟨*the ~s made by parents*⟩

²sacrifice *vt* **1** to offer as a sacrifice **2** to give up or lose for the sake of an ideal or end ~ *vi* to offer up or perform rites of a sacrifice – **sacrificer** *n*

sacrificial *adj* of or involving sacrifice – **sacrificially** *adv*

sacrilege *n* **1** a technical violation of what is sacred **2** gross irreverence toward sby or sthg sacred – **sacrilegious** *adj*, **sacrilegiously** *adv*, **sacrilegiousness** *n*

sacristan *n* a person in charge of the sacristy and ceremonial equipment; *also* a sexton

sacristy *n* a room in a church where sacred vessels and vestments are kept and where the clergy put on their vestments

sacrosanct *adj* accorded the highest reverence and respect; *also* regarded with unwarranted reverence – **sacrosanctity** *n*

sacrum *n, pl* **sacra** the part of the vertebral column that is directly connected with or forms part of the pelvis and in humans consists of 5 united vertebrae

sad *adj* **-dd-** **1a** affected with or expressing unhappiness **b(1)** causing or associated with unhappiness (2) deplorable, regrettable ⟨*a ~ decline in standards*⟩ **2** of a dull sombre colour **3** *of baked goods* ¹HEAVY 9b – **sadly** *adv*, **sadness** *n*

sadden *vb* to make or become sad

¹**saddle** *n* **1a(1)** a usu padded and leather-covered seat secured to the back of a horse, donkey, etc for the rider to sit on **(2)** a part of a harness for a draught animal (e g a horse pulling a carriage) comparable to a saddle that is used to keep in place the strap that passes under the animal's tail **b** a seat in certain types of vehicles (e g a bicycle or agricultural tractor) **2** sthg like a saddle in shape, position, or function **3** a ridge connecting 2 peaks **4a** a large cut of meat from a sheep, hare, rabbit, deer, etc consisting of both sides of the unsplit back including both loins **b** the rear part of a male fowl's back extending to the tail **5** a saddle-shaped marking on the back of an animal – **saddleless** *adj* – **in the saddle** in control

²**saddle** *vt* **saddling 1** to put a saddle on **2** to encumber ⟨*got ~d with the paperwork*⟩

saddlebag *n* a pouch or bag on the back of a horse behind the saddle, or either of a pair laid across behind the saddle or hanging over the rear wheel of a bicycle or motorcycle

saddler *n* one who makes, repairs, or sells furnishings (e g saddles) for horses

saddlery *n* **1** the trade, articles of trade, or shop of a saddler **2** a set of the equipment used for sitting on and controlling a riding horse

saddle-stitched *adj* fastened by staples through the fold ⟨*a ~ magazine*⟩

sadhu, saddhu *n* an Indian ascetic usu mendicant holy man

sadism *n* **1** a sexual perversion in which pleasure is obtained by inflicting physical or mental pain on others **2** delight in inflicting pain – **sadist** *adj or n*, **sadistic** *adj*, **sadistically** *adv*

sadomasochism *n* sadism and masochism occurring together in the same person – **sadomasochist** *n*, **sadomasochistic** *adj*

sae *n* a stamped addressed envelope

¹**safari** *n* (the caravan and equipment of) a hunting or scientific expedition, esp in E Africa – **safari** *vi*

²**safari** *adj* made of lightweight material, esp cotton, and typically having 2 breast pockets and a belt

safari park *n* a park stocked with usu big game animals (e g lions) so that visitors can observe them in natural-appearing surroundings

¹**safe** *adj* **1** freed from harm or risk **2** secure from threat of danger, harm, or loss **3** affording safety from danger **4a** not threatening or entailing danger ⟨*is your dog ~?*⟩ **b** unlikely to cause controversy ⟨*keeping to ~ subjects*⟩ **5a** not liable to take risks **b** trustworthy, reliable **6** being a constituency where the MP was elected with a large majority – **safe** *adv*, **safely** *adv*, **safeness** *n*

²**safe** *n* **1** a room or receptacle for the safe storage of valuables **2** a receptacle, esp a cupboard, for the temporary storage of fresh and cooked foods that typically has at least 1 side of wire mesh to allow ventilation while preventing flies from entering

safebreaker *n* a safecracker – **safebreaking** *n*

safe-conduct *n* (a document authorizing) protection given to a person passing through a military zone or occupied area

¹**safeguard** *n* **1** a pass, safe-conduct **2** a precautionary measure or stipulation

²**safeguard** *vt* **1** to provide a safeguard for **2** to make safe; protect

safekeeping *n* keeping safe or being kept safe

safety *n* **1** the condition of being safe from causing or suffering hurt, injury, or loss **2** SAFETY CATCH **3** a billiard shot made with no attempt to score or so as to leave the balls in an unfavourable position for the opponent

safety belt *n* a belt fastening a person to an object to prevent falling or injury

safety catch *n* a device (e g on a gun or machine) designed to prevent accidental use

safety curtain *n* a fireproof curtain which can isolate the stage from the auditorium in case of fire

safety glass *n* glass strengthened by tempering so that when broken, it shatters into relatively safe rounded granules

safety lamp *n* a miner's lamp constructed to avoid ignition of inflammable gas, usu by enclosing the flame in wire gauze

safety match *n* a match capable of being ignited only on a specially prepared surface

safety pin *n* a pin in the form of a clasp with a guard covering its point when fastened

safety razor *n* a razor with a guard for the blade

safety valve *n* **1** an automatic escape or relief valve (e g for a steam boiler) **2** an outlet for pent-up energy or emotion ⟨*a ~ for life's frustrations*⟩

saffron *n* **1** (the deep orange aromatic pungent dried stigmas, used to colour and flavour foods, of) a purple-flowered crocus **2** orange-yellow

¹**sag** *vi* **-gg-** **1** to droop, sink, or settle (as if) from weight, pressure, or loss of tautness **2** to lose firmness or vigour ⟨*spirits ~ging from overwork*⟩ **3** to fail to stimulate or retain interest ⟨*~ged a bit in the last act*⟩

²**sag** *n* **1** a sagging part ⟨*the ~ in a rope*⟩ **2** an instance or amount of sagging ⟨*~ is inevitable in a heavy unsupported span*⟩

saga *n* **1** (a modern heroic narrative resembling) a medieval Icelandic narrative dealing with historic or legendary figures and events **2** a long detailed account **3** a roman-fleuve

sagacious *adj* **1** of keen and farsighted judgment ⟨*~ judge of character*⟩ **2** prompted by or indicating acute discernment ⟨*~ purchase of stock*⟩ – **sagaciously** *adv*, **sagaciousness, sagacity** *n*

¹**sage** *adj* **1** wise on account of reflection and experience **2** proceeding from or indicating wisdom and sound judgment ⟨*~ counsel*⟩ – **sagely** *adv*, **sageness** *n*

²**sage** *n* **1** sby (e g a great philosopher) renowned for wise teachings **2** a venerable man of sound judgment

³**sage** *n* **1** a plant of the mint family whose greyish green aromatic leaves are used esp in flavouring meat **2** sage-brush

sagebrush *n* any of several composite undershrubs that cover large areas of plains in the W USA

Sagittarius *n* (sby born under) the 9th sign of the zodiac in astrology, pictured as a centaur shooting an arrow – **Sagittarian** *adj or n*

sago *n*, *pl* **sagos** a dry powdered starch prepared from the pith of a sago palm and used esp as a food (e g in a milk pudding)

sahib *n* sir, master – used, esp among Hindus and Muslims in colonial India, when addressing or speaking of a European of some social or official status

said *adj* aforementioned

¹**sail** *n*, *pl* **sails, (1b)** **sail** *also* **sails 1a** an expanse of fabric which is spread to catch or deflect the wind as a means of propelling a ship, sand yacht, etc **b** (a ship equipped with) sails **2** sthg like a sail in function or form ⟨*the ~s of a*

windmill⟩ **3** a voyage by ship ⟨*a 5-day ~ from the nearest port*⟩ – **sailed** *adj* – **under sail** in motion with sails set

²**sail** *vi* **1a** to travel in a boat or ship **b** to make journeys in or manage a sailing boat for pleasure **2a** to travel on water, esp by the action of wind on sails **b** to move without visible effort or in a stately manner ⟨*~ed gracefully into the room* – L C Douglas⟩ **3** to begin a journey by water ⟨*~ with the tide*⟩ ~ *vt* **1** to travel over (a body of water) in a ship ⟨*~ the 7 seas*⟩ **2** to direct or manage the operation of (a ship or boat) – **sailable** *adj* – **sail into** to · attack vigorously or sharply ⟨sailed into *his dinner*⟩ ⟨sailed into *me for being late*⟩ – **sail close to the wind 1** to sail as nearly as possible against the main force of the wind **2** to be near to dishonesty or improper behaviour

sailcloth *n* a heavy canvas used for sails, tents, or upholstery; *also* a lightweight canvas used for clothing

sailing boat *n* a boat fitted with sails for propulsion

sailor *n* **1a** a seaman, mariner **b** a member of a ship's crew other than an officer **2** a traveller by water; *esp* one considered with reference to any tendency to seasickness ⟨*a bad ~*⟩

sailplane *n* a glider designed to rise in an upward air current – **sailplane** *vi*, **sailplaner** *n*

saint *n* **1** a person officially recognized through canonization as being outstandingly holy and so worthy of veneration **2a** any of the spirits of the departed in heaven **b** ANGEL 1 ⟨Saint *Michael the Archangel*⟩ **3** any (of various Christian groups regarding themselves as) of God's chosen people **4** a person of outstanding piety or virtue – **sainthood** *n*, **saintlike** *adj*, **saintly** *adj*, **saintliness** *n*

saint's day *n* a day in a church calendar on which a saint is commemorated

saith *archaic pres 3 sing of* SAY

¹**sake** *n* – **for the sake of, for someone's/something's sake 1** for the purpose of ⟨for the sake of *argument*⟩ **2** so as to get, keep, or improve ⟨for *conscience* sake⟩ ⟨study Latin for *its own* sake⟩ **3** so as to help, please, or honour ⟨*to go to the sea* for the sake of *the children*⟩ ⟨for *old times'* sake⟩ **–for God's/goodness/Heaven's/pity's sake** – used in protest or supplication

²**sake, saki** *n* a Japanese alcoholic drink of fermented rice

¹**salaam** *n* **1** a ceremonial greeting in E countries **2** an obeisance made by bowing low and placing the right palm on the forehead

²**salaam** *vb* to perform a salaam (to)

salable, saleable *adj* capable of being or fit to be sold – **salability** *n*

salacious *adj* **1** arousing or appealing to sexual desire **2** lecherous, lustful – **salaciously** *adv*, **salaciousness** *n*

salad *n* **1a** (mixed) raw vegetables (e g lettuce, watercress, or tomato) often served with a dressing **b** a dish of raw or (cold) cooked foods often cut into small pieces and combined with a dressing ⟨*fruit ~*⟩ **2** a vegetable or herb eaten raw (in salad); *esp* lettuce

salad days *n pl* time of youthful inexperience or indiscretion ⟨*my ~ when I was green in judgment* – Shak⟩

salad oil *n* an edible vegetable oil (e g olive oil) used in salad dressings

salamander *n* **1** a mythical animal with the power to endure fire without harm **2** any of numerous scaleless amphibians superficially resembling lizards – **salamandrine** *adj*

salami *n, pl* **salamis** a highly seasoned, esp pork, sausage often containing garlic

salary *n* a fixed usu monthly payment for regular services, esp of a nonmanual kind – **salaried** *adj*

sale *n* **1** the act or an instance of selling; *specif* the transfer

of ownership of and title to property or goods from one person to another for a price **2a** opportunity of selling or being sold ⟨*counting on a large ~ for the new product*⟩ **b** quantity sold – often pl with sing. meaning ⟨*total ~*s *rose last year*⟩ **3** an event at which goods are offered for sale ⟨*an antiques ~*⟩ **4** public disposal to the highest bidder **5** a selling of goods at bargain prices **6a** *pl* operations and activities involved in promoting and selling goods or services ⟨*manager in charge of ~*s⟩ **b** gross receipts obtained from selling – **on/for sale** available for purchase

saleable *adj* salable

saleroom *n, chiefly Br* a place where goods are displayed for sale, esp by auction

sales *adj* of, engaged in, or used in selling

salesclerk *n* SHOP ASSISTANT

salesgirl *n* a female shop assistant

saleslady *n* a female shop assistant

salesman, fem **saleswoman** *n, pl* **salesmen, fem** **saleswomen** a salesperson – **salesmanship** *n*

salesperson *n* sby employed to sell goods or a service (e g in a shop or within an assigned territory)

sales representative *n* a person who travels, usu in an assigned territory, to win orders for his/her firm's goods

¹**salient** *adj* **1** pointing upwards or outwards ⟨*a ~ angle*⟩ **2a** projecting beyond a line or level **b** standing out conspicuously ⟨*~ characteristics*⟩ – **saliently** *adv*, **salience, saliency** *n*

²**salient** *n* an outwardly projecting part of a fortification, trench system, or line of defence

¹**saline** *adj* **1** (consisting) of, containing, or resembling salt ⟨*a ~ solution*⟩ **2** esp of a purgative containing salts of potassium, sodium, or magnesium – **salinity** *n*

²**saline** *n* **1** a purgative salt of potassium, sodium, or magnesium **2a** a saline solution (similar in concentration to body fluids)

saliva *n* a slightly alkaline mixture of water, protein, salts, and often enzymes that is secreted into the mouth by glands, and that lubricates ingested food and often begins the breakdown of starches – **salivary** *adj*

salivate *vi* to have an (excessive) flow of saliva – **salivation** *n*

¹**sallow** *n* any of various Old World broad-leaved willows some of which are important sources of charcoal

²**sallow** *adj* of a sickly yellowish colour – **sallowish** *adj*, **sallowness** *n*

¹**sally** *adj, chiefly dial* sallow

²**sally** *n* **1** a rushing forth; *esp* a sortie of troops from a besieged position **2a** a brief outbreak ⟨*a ~ of rage*⟩ **b** a witty or penetrating remark **3** a short excursion; a jaunt

³**sally** *vi* **1** to rush out or issue forth suddenly **2** to set out (e g on a journey) – usu + *forth*

salmon *n, pl* **salmon, esp for different types** **salmons 1** (any of various fishes related to) a large soft-finned game and food fish of the N Atlantic that is highly valued for its pink flesh **2** orangy-pink – **salmonoid** *adj*

salmonella *n, pl* **salmonellae, salmonellas, salmonella** any of a genus of bacteria that cause diseases, esp food poisoning, in warm-blooded animals – **salmonellosis** *n*

salon *n* **1** an elegant reception room or living room **2** a gathering of literary figures, statesmen, etc held at the home of a prominent person and common in the 17th and 18th c **3** *cap* an exhibition, esp in France, of works of art by living artists **4** a stylish business establishment or shop ⟨*a beauty ~*⟩

saloon *n* **1** a public apartment or hall (e g a ballroom, exhibition room, or shipboard social area) **2** a railway carriage with no compartments **3** *Br* an enclosed motor car having no partition between the driver and passengers **4a** *Br* SALOON BAR **b** *NAm* a room or establishment in which alcoholic beverages are sold and consumed

saloon bar *n*, *Br* a comfortable, well-furnished, and often relatively expensive bar in a public house

salsify *n* (the long tapering edible root of) a European composite plant

¹salt *n* **1a** sodium chloride, occurring naturally esp as a mineral deposit and dissolved in sea water, and used esp for seasoning or preserving **b** any of numerous compounds resulting from replacement of (part of) the hydrogen ion of an acid by a (radical acting like a) metal **c** *pl* **(1)** a mixture of the salts of alkali metals or magnesium (e g Epsom salts) used as a purgative **(2)** SMELLING SALTS **2a** an ingredient that imparts savour, piquancy, or zest **b** sharpness of wit **3** an experienced sailor ⟨*a tale worthy of an old ~*⟩ **4** a saltcellar – **saltlike** *adj* – **above/below the salt** placed, esp seated, in a socially advantageous/disadvantageous position – **worth one's salt** worthy of respect; competent, effective

²salt *vt* **1** to treat, provide, season, or preserve with common salt or brine **2** to give flavour or piquancy to (e g a story) **3** to enrich (e g a mine) fraudulently by adding valuable matter, esp mineral ores **4** to sprinkle (as if) with a salt ⟨*~ing clouds with silver iodide*⟩ – **salter** *n*

³salt *adj* **1a** saline, salty **b** being or inducing a taste similar to that of common salt that is one of the 4 basic taste sensations **2** cured or seasoned with salt; salted ⟨*~ pork*⟩ **3** containing, overflowed by, or growing in salt water ⟨*a ~ marsh*⟩ **4** sharp, pungent ⟨*a ~ wit* – John Buchan⟩ – **saltness** *n*

salt away *vt* to put by in reserve; save ⟨*salted his money away*⟩

saltcellar *n* a cruet for salt

saltire *n* a diagonal heraldic cross

salt lick *n* LICK 3

saltpan *n* a depression (e g made in rock) or vessel for evaporating brine

saltpetre, *NAm* **saltpeter** *n* POTASSIUM NITRATE

saltwater *adj* of, living in, or being salt water

salty *adj* **1** of, seasoned with, or containing salt **2** having a taste of (too much) salt **3a** piquant, witty **b** earthy, coarse – **saltily** *adv*, **saltiness** *n*

salubrious *adj* **1** favourable to health or well-being ⟨*a ~ climate*⟩ **2** RESPECTABLE 2 ⟨*not a very ~ district*⟩ – **salubriously** *adv*, **salubriousness**, **salubrity** *n*

salutary *adj* having a beneficial or edifying effect – **salutariness** *n*, **salutarily** *adv*

salutation *n* **1a** an expression of greeting or courtesy by word or gesture **b** *pl* regards **2** the word or phrase of greeting (e g *Dear Sir*) that conventionally comes immediately before the body of a letter or speech – **salutational**, **salutatory** *adj*

¹salute *vt* **1** to address with expressions of greeting, goodwill, or respect **2a** to honour by a conventional military or naval ceremony **b** to show respect and recognition to (a military superior) by assuming a prescribed position **c** to praise ⟨*~d her courage*⟩ **3** *archaic* to become apparent to (one of the senses) ⟨*~ vi* to make a salute – **saluter** *n*

²salute *n* **1** a greeting, salutation **2a** a sign or ceremony expressing goodwill or respect ⟨*the festival was a ~ to the arts*⟩ **b** an act of saluting a military superior; *also* the position (e g of the hand or weapon) or the entire attitude of a person saluting a superior

¹salvage *n* **1a** compensation paid to those who save property from loss or damage; *esp* compensation paid for saving a ship from wreckage or capture **b** the act of saving

or rescuing a ship or its cargo **c** the act of saving or rescuing property in danger (e g from fire) **2a** property saved from a calamity (e g a wreck or fire) **b** sthg of use or value extracted from waste material

²salvage *vt* to rescue or save (e g from wreckage or ruin) – **salvager** *n*, **salvageable** *adj*, **salvageability** *n*

salvation *n* **1** (an agent or means which effects) deliverance from the power and effects of sin **2** deliverance from danger, difficulty, or destruction – **salvational** *adj*

Salvation Army *n* an international Christian group organized on military lines and founded in 1865 by William Booth for evangelizing and performing social work among the poor

Salvationist *n* a member of the Salvation Army – **salvationist** *adj, often cap*

¹salve *n* **1** an ointment for application to wounds or sores **2** a soothing influence or agency ⟨*a ~ to their hurt feelings*⟩

²salve *vt* **1** to remedy (as if) with a salve **2** to ease ⟨*~ a troubled conscience*⟩

salver *n* a tray; *esp* an ornamental tray (e g of silver) on which food or beverages are served or letters and visiting cards are presented

salvia *n* any of a genus of herbs or shrubs of the mint family; *esp* one grown for its scarlet or purple flowers

salvo *n, pl* **salvos**, **salvoes** **1a** a simultaneous discharge of 2 or more guns or missiles in military or naval action or as a salute **b** the release at one moment of several bombs or missiles from an aircraft **2** a sudden or emphatic burst (e g of cheering or approbation)

sal volatile *n* an aromatic solution of ammonium carbonate in alcohol or ammonia water used as smelling salts

Samaritan *n* **1** a native or inhabitant of ancient Samaria **2a** *often not cap* one who selflessly gives aid to those in distress **b** a member of an organization that offers help to those in despair – **samaritan** *adj, often cap*

samba *n* (the music for) a Brazilian dance of African origin characterized by a dip and spring upwards at each beat of the music – **samba** *vi*

¹same *adj* **1** being 1 single thing, person, or group; identical ⟨*wear the ~ shoes for a week*⟩ – often as an intensive ⟨*born in this very ~ house*⟩ **2** being the specified one or ones – + *as* or *that* ⟨*made the ~ mistake as last time*⟩ **3** corresponding so closely as to be indistinguishable ⟨*2 brothers have the ~ nose*⟩ – **at the same time** for all that; nevertheless

²same *pron, pl* **same** **1** *the* same thing, person, or group ⟨*do the ~ for you*⟩ ⟨*happy Christmas! Same to you!*⟩ **2** sthg previously mentioned ⟨*ordered a drink and refused to pay for ~*⟩

³same *adv* in the same manner – + *the* ⟨*2 words spelt the ~*⟩

sameness *n* **1** identity, similarity **2** monotony, uniformity

samovar *n* a metal urn with a tap at its base and an interior heating tube, that is used, esp in Russia, to boil water for tea

sampan *n* a small flat-bottomed boat used in rivers and harbours in the Far East

¹sample *n* **1** an item serving to show the character or quality of a larger whole or group **2** a part of a statistical population whose properties are studied to gain information about the whole

²sample *vt* **sampling** to take a sample of or from; *esp* to test the quality of by a sample ⟨*~d his output for defects*⟩

³sample *adj* intended as an example

¹sampler *n* a decorative piece of needlework typically having letters or verses embroidered on it in various stitches as an example of skill

²**sampler** n 1 sby or sthg that collects, prepares, or examines samples 2 NAm a collection of representative specimens ⟨a ~ of 18 poets⟩

samurai n, pl **samurai** 1 a military retainer of a Japanese feudal baron 2 the warrior aristocracy of Japan

sanatorium n, pl **sanatoriums, sanatoria** an establishment that provides therapy, rest, or recuperation for convalescents, the chronically ill, etc

sanctify vt 1 to set apart for a sacred purpose or for religious use 2 to free from sin 3 to give moral or social sanction to 4 to make productive of holiness or piety ⟨keep the sabbath day to ~ it – Deut 5:12 (AV)⟩ – **sanctification** n

sanctimonious adj self-righteous – **sanctimoniously** adv, **sanctimoniousness** n

¹**sanction** n 1 a formal ecclesiastical decree 2 sthg that makes an oath or moral precept binding 3 a penalty annexed to an offence 4a a consideration that determines moral action or judgment b a mechanism of social control (e g shame) for enforcing a society's standards c official permission or authoritative ratification 5 an economic or military coercive measure adopted to force a nation to conform to international law

²**sanction** vt 1 to make valid; ratify 2 to give authoritative consent to

sanctity n 1 holiness of life and character 2 the quality or state of being holy or sacred

sanctuary n 1 a consecrated place: e g a the ancient temple at Jerusalem or its holy of holies b the most sacred part of a religious building; esp the part of a Christian church in which the altar is placed c a place (e g a church or a temple) for worship 2a(1) a place of refuge and protection (2) a refuge for (endangered) wildlife where predators are controlled and hunting is illegal ⟨a bird ~⟩ b the immunity from law attached to a sanctuary

sanctum n, pl **sanctums** also **sancta** a place of total privacy and security (e g a study)

Sanctus n a hymn of adoration sung or said before the prayer of consecration in the celebration of the Eucharist

¹**sand** n 1 loose granular particles smaller than gravel and coarser than silt that result from the disintegration of (silica-rich) rocks 2 an area of sand; a beach – usu pl with sing. meaning 3 moments of time measured (as if) with an hourglass – usu pl with sing. meaning ⟨the ~s of this government run out very rapidly – H J Laski⟩ 4 yellowish grey

²**sand** vt 1 to sprinkle (as if) with sand 2 to cover or choke with sand – usu + up 3 to smooth or dress by grinding or rubbing with an abrasive (e g sandpaper) – often + down – **sander** n

sandal n a shoe consisting of a sole held on to the foot by straps or thongs

sandalwood n 1 (the compact close-grained fragrant yellowish heartwood, used in ornamental carving and cabinetwork, of) an Indo-Malayan tree 2 (any of various trees yielding) fragrant wood similar to true sandalwood

¹**sandbag** n a bag filled with sand and used in usu temporary fortifications or constructions, as ballast, or as a weapon

²**sandbag** vt -gg- to barricade, stop up, or weight with sandbags

sandbank n a large deposit of sand, esp in a river or coastal waters

sandbar n a sandbank

sandblast vt or n (to treat with) a high-speed jet of sand propelled by air or steam (e g for cutting or cleaning glass or stone) – **sandblaster** n

sandboy n sby who is cheerfully absorbed or engrossed – chiefly in happy as a sandboy

sandcastle n a model of a castle made in damp sand, esp at the seaside

sand fly n any of various small biting two-winged flies

¹**sandpaper** n paper to which a thin layer of sand has been glued for use as an abrasive; broadly any abrasive paper (e g glasspaper) – **sandpapery** adj

²**sandpaper** vt to rub (as if) with sandpaper

sandpiper n any of numerous small wading birds with longer bills than the plovers

sandpit n an enclosure containing sand for children to play in

sandshoe n, chiefly Br a plimsoll

sandstone n a sedimentary rock consisting of cemented (quartz) sand

sandstorm n a storm driving clouds of sand, esp in a desert

¹**sandwich** n 1a two slices of usu buttered bread containing a layer of any of various sweet or savoury foods (e g meat, cheese, or jam); also a bread roll stuffed with a filling b a sponge cake containing a filling 2 sthg like a sandwich in having a layered or banded arrangement

²**sandwich** vt 1 to insert between 2 things of a different quality or character 2 to create room or time for – often + in or between

³**sandwich** adj 1 of or used for sandwiches ⟨~ bread⟩ 2 Br of a sandwich course

sandwich board n either of 2 boards hung at the front of and behind the body by straps from the shoulders and used esp for advertising

sandwich course n a British vocational course consisting of alternate periods of some months' duration in college and in employment

sandy adj 1 consisting of, containing, or sprinkled with sand 2 resembling sand in colour or texture – **sandiness** n

sane adj (produced by a mind that is) mentally sound; able to anticipate and appraise the effect of one's actions – **sanely** adv, **saneness** n

sang past of SING

sangfroid n imperturbability, esp under strain

sangr'a, sangria n a usu cold punch made of red wine, fruit juice, and soda water

sanguinary adj 1 bloodthirsty, murderous 2 accompanied by bloodshed 3 readily punishing with death USE fml – **sanguinarily** adv

sanguine adj 1 (having the bodily conformation and temperament marked by sturdiness, high colour, and cheerfulness held to be characteristic of sby) having blood as the predominating bodily humour – used in medieval physiology 2 confident, optimistic 3a SANGUINARY 1 b ruddy USE (3) fml – **sanguinity** n

sanitary adj 1 of or promoting health ⟨~ measures⟩ 2 free from danger to health

sanitary towel n a disposable absorbent pad worn after childbirth or during menstruation to absorb the flow from the womb

sanitation n (the promotion of hygiene and prevention of disease by) maintenance or improvement of sanitary conditions – **sanitate** vt

sanity n being sane; esp soundness or health of mind

sank past of SINK

sans prep, archaic without ⟨my love to thee is sound, ~ crack or flaw – Shak⟩

Sanskrit n an ancient sacred Indic language of India and of Hinduism – **Sanskrit** adj

sans serif, sanserif n a letter or typeface with no serifs

Santa Claus n FATHER CHRISTMAS

¹sap *n* **1a** a watery solution that circulates through a plant's vascular system **b** (a fluid essential to life or) bodily health and vigour **2** a foolish gullible person – *infml*

²sap *vt* **-pp-** to drain or deprive of sap

³sap *n* the extension of a trench from within the trench itself to a point near an enemy's fortifications

⁴sap *vb* **-pp-** *vi* to proceed by or dig a sap ~ *vt* **1** to destroy (as if) by undermining ⟨ ~ ped *the morale of their troops*⟩ **2** to weaken or exhaust gradually **3** to operate against or pierce by a sap

sapient *adj* possessing or expressing great wisdom or discernment – *fml* – **sapience** *n*, **sapiently** *adv*

sapless *adj* feeble, lacking vigour – **saplessness** *n*

sapling *n* **1** a young tree **2** YOUTH **2a**

sapper *n* a (private) soldier of the Royal Engineers

¹sapphic *adj* **1** (consisting) of a 4-line stanza made up of chiefly trochaic and dactylic feet **2** lesbian

²sapphic *n* a verse in sapphic stanzas

sapphire *n* **1** a semitransparent corundum of a colour other than red, used as a gem; *esp* a transparent rich blue sapphire **2** deep purplish blue – **sapphire** *adj*

sappy *adj* **1** resembling or consisting largely of sapwood **2** *NAm* SOPPY **2** – **sappiness** *n*

sapwood *n* the younger softer usu lighter-coloured living outer part of wood that lies between the bark and the heartwood

saraband, sarabande *n* **1** a stately court dance resembling the minuet **2** a musical composition or movement in slow triple time with the accent on the second beat

sarcasm *n* (the use of) caustic and often ironic language to express contempt or bitterness, esp towards an individual – **sarcastic** *adj*, **sarcastically** *adv*

sarcophagus *n*, *pl* **sarcophagi** *also* **sarcophaguses** a stone coffin

sardine *n*, *pl* **sardines** *also* **sardine** the young of the European pilchard, or another small or immature fish, when of a size suitable for preserving for food

sardonic *adj* disdainfully or cynically humorous; derisively mocking – **sardonically** *adv*

sarge *n* a sergeant – *infml*

sari *also* **saree** *n* a garment worn by Hindu women that consists of a length of lightweight cloth draped so that one end forms a skirt and the other a head or shoulder covering

sarky *adj*, *Br* sarcastic – *infml*

sarong *n* **1** a loose skirt made of a long strip of cloth wrapped round the body and traditionally worn by men and women in Malaysia and the Pacific islands **2** cloth for sarongs

sarsaparilla *n* **1** (the dried roots, used esp as a flavouring, of) any of various tropical American trailing plants of the lily family **2** *chiefly NAm* a sweetened fizzy drink flavoured with birch oil and sassafras

sartorial *adj* with regard to clothing ⟨ ~ *elegance*⟩ – *fml*; humor; used esp with reference to men – **sartorially** *adv*

¹sash *n* a band of cloth worn round the waist or over 1 shoulder as a dress accessory or as the emblem of an honorary or military order – **sashed** *adj*

²sash *n*, *pl* **sash** *also* **sashes** the framework in which panes of glass are set in a window or door; *also* such a framework together with its panes forming a usu sliding part of a window

sashay *vi*, *NAm* **1a** to saunter **b** to strut ostentatiously **2** to proceed in a zigzag manner *USE infml*

sash window *n* a window having 2 sashes that slide vertically in a frame

sassafras *n* (the dried root bark, used esp as a flavouring, of) a tall N American tree of the laurel family with mucilage-containing twigs and leaves

sat *past of* SIT

Satan *n* the adversary of God and lord of evil in Judaism and Christianity

satanic *adj* **1** (characteristic) of Satan or satanism ⟨ ~ *pride*⟩ ⟨ ~ *rites*⟩ **2** extremely cruel or malevolent – **satanically** *adv*

satanism *n*, *often cap* **1** diabolism **2** obsession with or affinity to evil; *specif* the worship of Satan marked by the travesty of Christian rites – **satanist** *n*, *often cap*

satchel *n* a usu stiff bag often with a shoulder strap; *esp* one carried by schoolchildren – **satchelful** *n*

sate *vt* **1** to surfeit with sthg **2** to satisfy (e g a thirst) by indulging to the full

sateen *n* a smooth durable lustrous fabric in which the weft predominates on the face

satellite *n* **1** an obsequious follower **2a** a celestial body orbiting another of larger size **b** a man-made object or vehicle intended to orbit a celestial body **3** sby or sthg attendant or dependent; *esp* a country subject to another more powerful country **4** an urban community that is physically separate from an adjacent city but dependent on it – **satellite** *adj*

satiable *adj* capable of being satisfied – *fml*

satiate *vt* to satisfy (e g a need or desire) to the point of excess – **satiation** *n*

satiety *n* **1** being fed or gratified to or beyond capacity **2** the aversion caused by overindulgence

¹satin *n* a fabric (e g of silk) in satin weave with lustrous face and dull back

²satin *adj* **1** made of satin **2** like satin, esp in lustrous appearance or smoothness – **satiny** *adj*

satinwood *n* (the lustrous yellowish brown wood of) an E Indian tree of the mahogany family or any of various trees with similar wood

satire *n* **1** a literary work holding up human vices and follies to ridicule or scorn; *also* the genre of such literature **2** biting wit, irony, or sarcasm intended to expose foolishness or vice – **satirical** *adj*

satirize, -ise *vi* to utter or write satire ~ *vt* to censure or ridicule by means of satire

satisfaction *n* **1a** the payment through penance of the temporal punishment incurred by a sin **b** reparation for sin and fulfilment of the demands of divine justice, achieved for mankind by the death of Christ **2a** fulfilment of a need or want **b** being satisfied **c** a source of pleasure or fulfilment **3a** compensation for a loss, insult, or injury **b** the discharge of a legal claim **c** vindication of one's honour, esp through a duel **4** full assurance or certainty

satisfactory *adj* satisfying needs or requirements; adequate – **satisfactorily** *adv*, **satisfactoriness** *n*

satisfy *vt* **1a** to discharge; CARRY OUT **b** to meet a financial obligation to **2a** to make content **b** to gratify to the full **c** to meet the requirements of ⟨ ~ *the examiners*⟩ **3a** to convince **b** to put an end to ⟨ ~ *every objection*⟩ **4a** to conform to (e g criteria) **b** to make valid by fulfilling a condition ~ *vi* to be adequate; suffice; *also* to please ⟨*a taste that satisfies*⟩ – **satisfyingly** *adv*, **satisfiable** *adj*

satsuma *n* a sweet seedless type of mandarin orange

saturate *vt* **1** to treat or provide with sthg to the point where no more can be absorbed, dissolved, or retained ⟨*water* ~ d *with salt*⟩ **2a** to fill completely with sthg that permeates or pervades ⟨*moonglow* ~ s *an empty sky* – Henry Miller⟩ **b** to fill to capacity **3** to cause to combine chemically until there is no further tendency to combine – **saturant** *adj or n*, **saturator** *n*

saturation *n* **1** the chromatic purity of a colour; freedom from dilution with white **2** the point at which a market is supplied with all the goods it will absorb **3** an overwhelming concentration of military forces or firepower

Saturday *n* the day of the week following Friday – **Saturdays** *adv*

Saturn *n* the planet 6th in order from the sun and conspicuous for its rings

saturnalia *n, pl* **saturnalias** *also* **saturnalia 1** *pl but sing or pl in constr* the festival of Saturn in ancient Rome beginning on December 17, observed as a time of general and unrestrained merrymaking **2** an unrestrained (licentious) celebration – **saturnalian** *adj*

saturnine *adj* **1** gloomy **2** sullen **3** of or being lead poisoning – **saturninely** *adv*

satyr *n* **1** *often cap* a Greek minor woodland deity having certain characteristics of a horse or goat and associated with Dionysian revelry **2** a lecherous man (having satyriasis) – **satyric** *adj*

¹sauce *n* **1a** a liquid or soft preparation used as a relish, dressing, or accompaniment to food ⟨*tomato* ~⟩ **b** *NAm* stewed or tinned fruit eaten as a dessert **2** sthg adding zest or piquancy **3** CHEEK **3** – *infml*

²sauce *vt* **1** to dress or prepare with a sauce or seasoning **2** to be impudent to – *infml*

saucepan *n* a deep usu cylindrical cooking pan typically having a long handle and a lid

saucer *n* **1** a small usu circular shallow dish with a central depression in which a cup is set **2** sthg like a saucer; *esp* FLYING SAUCER – **saucerlike** *adj*

saucy *adj* **1a** disrespectfully bold and impudent **b** engagingly forward and flippant **2** smart, trim ⟨*a* ~ *ship*⟩ – **saucily** *adv*, **sauciness** *n*

sauerkraut *n* finely cut cabbage fermented in a brine made from its juice

sauna *n* (a room or building for) a Finnish steam bath in which water is thrown on hot stones

saunter *vi* to walk about in a casual manner – **saunter** *n*, **saunterer** *n*

saurian *n* any of a group of reptiles including the lizards and formerly the crocodiles and dinosaurs – **saurian** *adj*

sausage *n* (sthg shaped like) a fresh, precooked, or dried cylindrical mass of seasoned minced pork or other meat often mixed with a filler (e g bread) and enclosed in a casing usu of prepared animal intestine

sausage roll *n* a small pastry-encased roll or oblong of sausage meat

sauté *vt* **sautéing**; **sautéed, sautéd** to fry in a small amount of fat – **sauté** *n or adj*

Sauternes, *NAm* **Sauterne** *n* a usu sweet golden-coloured Bordeaux made in the commune of Sauternes in France

¹savage *adj* **1a** not domesticated or under human control; untamed **b** lacking in social or moral restraints **2** rugged, rough **3** boorish, rude **4** lacking a developed culture – now usu taken to be offensive – **savagely** *adv*, **savageness**, **savagery** *n*

²savage *n* **1** a member of a primitive society **2** a brutal, rude, or unmannerly person

³savage *vt* to attack or treat brutally; *esp* to maul

savanna, savannah *n* a tropical or subtropical grassland with scattered trees

savant *n* one who has exceptional knowledge of a particular field (e g science or literature)

¹save *vt* **1a** to deliver from sin **b** to rescue from danger or harm **c** to preserve from injury, destruction, or loss **2a** to put aside as a store **b** to put aside for a particular use **c** to keep from being spent, wasted, or lost ⟨~d *time by taking a short cut*⟩ **d** to economize in the use of; conserve

3a to make unnecessary ⟨~s *me going into town*⟩ **b** to prevent an opponent from scoring, winning, or scoring with ⟨~d *the goal*⟩ ⟨~d *the shot*⟩ **4** to maintain ⟨~ *appearances*⟩ ~ *vi* **1** to rescue sby (e g from danger) **2a** to put aside money – often + *up* **b** to be economical in use or expenditure **3** to make a save – **savable, saveable** *adj*, **saver** *n*

²save *n* an action (e g by a goalkeeper) that prevents an opponent from scoring

³save *prep* BUT **1a** – chiefly fml

⁴save *conj* were it not; only ⟨*would have protested* ~ *that he was a friend*⟩ – chiefly fml

saveloy *n* a precooked highly seasoned dry sausage

¹saving *n* **1** preservation from danger or destruction **2** sthg saved ⟨*a* ~ *of 40 per cent*⟩ **3a** *pl* money put by over a period of time **b** the excess of income over expenditures – often *pl*

²saving *prep* **1** except, save **2** without disrespect to

saving grace *n* a redeeming quality or feature

saviour, *NAm chiefly* **savior** *n* **1** one who brings salvation; *specif, cap* Jesus **2** one who saves sby or sthg from danger or destruction

savoir faire *n* polished self-assurance in social behaviour

savory *n* any of several aromatic plants of the mint family used as herbs in cooking

¹savour, *NAm chiefly* **savor** *n* **1** the characteristic taste or smell of sthg **2** a particular flavour or smell **3** a (pleasantly stimulating) distinctive quality ⟨*felt that argument added* ~ *to conversation*⟩

²savour, *NAm chiefly* **savor** *vi* to have a specified smell or quality; smack ⟨*arguments that* ~ *of cynicism*⟩ ~ *vt* **1** to taste or smell with pleasure; relish **2a** to have (pleasurable) experience of, esp at length **b** to delight in; enjoy

¹savoury, *NAm chiefly* **savory** *adj* **1** piquantly pleasant to the mind **2** morally wholesome **3a** pleasing to the palate **b** salty, spicy, meaty, etc, rather than sweet

²savoury, *NAm chiefly* **savory** *n* a dish of piquant or stimulating flavour served usu at the end of a main meal but sometimes as an appetizer

savoy, savoy cabbage *n* a hardy cabbage with compact heads of wrinkled and curled leaves

¹savvy *vb* to know, understand – *slang*

²savvy *n* practical know-how; shrewd judgment – *slang* – **savvy** *adj*

¹saw *past of* SEE

²saw *n* a hand or power tool with a toothed part (e g a blade or disc) used to cut wood, metal, bone, etc – **sawlike** *adj*

³saw *vb* **sawed, sawn** *vt* **1** to cut with a saw **2** to shape by cutting with a saw **3** to cut through as though with a saw ~ *vi* **1a** to use a saw **b** to cut (as if) with a saw **2** to make motions as though using a saw – **sawer** *n*

⁴saw *n* a maxim, proverb

sawbones *n* a doctor; *specif* a surgeon – humor

sawdust *n* fine particles of wood produced in sawing

sawhorse *n* a rack on which wood is laid for sawing

sawmill *n* a factory or machine that cuts wood

sawn-off *adj* having the end removed by sawing; *specif, of a shotgun* having the end of the barrel sawn off

saw-pit *n* the pit in which the lower sawyer stands while timber is being cut with a pit saw

sawyer *n* sby employed to saw timber

saxifrage *n* any of a genus of usu showy-flowered plants often with tufted leaves, many of which are grown in rock gardens

Saxon *n* **1a(1)** a member of a Germanic people that invaded England along with the Angles and Jutes in the 5th c AD and merged with them to form the

Anglo-Saxon people **(2)** an Englishman or Lowlander as distinguished from a Welshman, Irishman, or Highlander **b** a native or inhabitant of Saxony **2** the Germanic language or dialect of any of the Saxon peoples – **Saxon** *adj*

saxophone *n* any of a group of single-reed woodwind instruments having a conical metal tube and finger keys and used esp in jazz and popular music – **saxophonist** *n*

¹say *vb* **says; said** *vt* **1a** to state in spoken words **b** to form an opinion as to ⟨*can't ~ when I met him*⟩ **2a** to utter, pronounce ⟨*can't ~ her 'h''s*⟩ **b** to recite, repeat ⟨*said his prayers*⟩ **3a** to indicate, show ⟨*the clock ~*s *12*⟩ **b** to give expression to; communicate ⟨*I said to myself 'That's funny'*⟩ ⟨*it ~s press button A*⟩ **4a** to suppose, assume **b** to allege – usu pass ⟨*the house is said to be 300 years old*⟩ ~ *vi* **1** to speak, declare ⟨*I'd rather not ~*⟩ **2** *NAm* I SAY – used interjectionally – **sayer** *n* – **I say** *chiefly Br* – used as a weak expression of surprise or to attract attention – **not to say** and indeed; or perhaps even ⟨*impolite*, not to say *rude*⟩ – **say boo to a goose** to brave even trivial dangers – usu neg – **say fairer** *Br* to express oneself any more generously ⟨*you can't say fairer than that*⟩ – **say when** to tell sby when to stop, esp when pouring a drink – **that is to say 1** in other words; IN EFFECT **2** or at least ⟨*he's coming*, that is to say he *promised to*⟩ – **to say nothing of** without even considering; not to mention

²say *n* **1** an expression of opinion – esp in **have one's say 2** a right or power to influence action or decisions; *esp* the authority to make final decisions

³say *adv* **1** at a rough estimate ⟨*the picture is worth*, ~, *£200*⟩ **2** FOR EXAMPLE ⟨*we could leave next week*, ~ *on Monday*⟩

saying *n* a maxim, proverb

say-so *n* **1** one's unsupported assertion **2** the right of final decision

¹scab *n* **1** scabies of domestic animals **2** a crust of hardened blood and serum over a wound **3a** a contemptible person **b** BLACKLEG **3 4** any of various plant diseases characterized by crusted spots; *also* any of these spots – **scabby** *adj*

²scab *vi* **-bb- 1** to become covered with a scab **2** to act as a scab

scabbard *n* a sheath for a sword, dagger, or bayonet

scabies *n*, *pl* **scabies** a skin disease, esp contagious itch or mange, caused by a parasitic mite and usu characterized by oozing scabs – **scabietic** *adj*

¹scabious *n* any of a genus of plants with flowers in dense heads at the end of usu long stalks

²scabious *adj* **1** scabby **2** of or resembling scabies

scabrous *adj* **1** rough to the touch with scales, scabs, raised patches, etc **2** dealing with indecent or offensive themes **3** intractable, knotty *USE (2 & 3) fml* – **scabrously** *adv*, **scabrousness** *n*

scaffold *n* **1a** a temporary platform for workmen to stand or sit on when working at a height above the floor or ground **b** a platform on which a criminal is executed **c** a platform above ground or floor level **2** a supporting framework

scaffolding *n* **1** material used in scaffolds **2** SCAFFOLD 1a, 2

¹scalar *adj* **1** having a continuous series of steps ⟨*~ chain of authority*⟩ **2a** capable of being represented by a point on a scale ⟨*a ~ quantity*⟩ **b** of a scalar or scalar product ⟨*~ multiplication*⟩

²scalar *n* **1** a real number rather than a vector **2** a quantity (e g mass or time) that has a magnitude describable by a real number, and no direction

scalawag *n*, *NAm* a scallywag

¹scald *vt* **1** to burn (as if) with hot liquid or steam **2a** to subject to boiling water or steam **b** to heat to just short of boiling ⟨*~ milk*⟩

²scald *n* an injury to the body caused by scalding **scalding** *adj* **1** boiling hot **2** biting, scathing

¹scale *n* **1a** either pan of a balance **b** a beam that is supported freely in the centre and has 2 pans of equal weight suspended from its ends **2** an instrument or machine for weighing *USE (1b, 2) usu pl with sing. meaning*

²scale *vi* to have a specified weight on scales

³scale *n* **1** (a small thin plate resembling) a small flattened rigid plate forming part of the external body covering of a fish, reptile, etc **2** a small thin dry flake shed from the skin **3** a thin coating, layer, or incrustation: **a** a (black scaly) coating of oxide forming on the surface of metals, esp iron when heated **b** a hard incrustation usu of calcium sulphate or carbonate that is deposited on the inside of a kettle, boiler, etc by the evaporation or constant passage of hard water **4** a usu thin, membranous, chaffy, or woody modified leaf **5** infestation with or disease caused by scale insects – **scaled** *adj*, **scaleless** *adj*

⁴scale *vt* **1** to remove scale or scales from (e g by scraping) **2** to remove in thin layers or scales ⟨*~ paint from a wall*⟩ **3** to cover with scale ⟨*hard water ~s a boiler*⟩ ~ *vi* **1** to shed or separate or come off in scales; flake **2** to become encrusted with scale – **scaler** *n*

⁵scale *n* **1** a graduated series of musical notes ascending or descending in order of pitch according to a specified scheme of their intervals **2** sthg graduated, esp when used as a measure or rule: e g **a** a linear region divided by lines into a series of spaces and used to register or record sthg (e g the height of mercury in a barometer) **b** a graduated line on a map or chart indicating the length used to represent a larger unit of measure **c** an instrument having a scale for measuring or marking off distances or dimensions **3** a graduated system ⟨*a ~ of taxation*⟩ **4** a proportion between 2 sets of dimensions (e g between those of a drawing and its original) **5** a graded series of tests – **scale** *adj* – **to scale** according to the proportions of an established scale of measurement ⟨*floor plans drawn to scale*⟩

⁶scale *vt* **1** to climb up or reach (as if) by means of a ladder **2a** to change the scale of **b** to pattern, make, regulate, set, or estimate according to some rate or standard ⟨*a production schedule ~d to actual need*⟩ ⟨*~ down imports*⟩ *USE (2) often + up or down* – **scaler** *n*

scalene *adj*, *of a triangle* having the 3 sides of unequal length

scallion *n* **1** a leek **2** an onion forming a thick basal part without a bulb; *also* SPRING ONION **3** *chiefly NAm* a shallot

¹scallop *n* **1** (a large muscle, used as food, of) any of various marine bivalve molluscs that have a shell consisting of 2 wavy-edged halves each with a fan-shaped pattern of ridges and that swim by opening and closing the halves of the shell **2** a scallop shell or a similarly shaped dish used for baking esp seafood **3** any of a continuous series of circle segments or angular projections forming a border

²scallop *vt* **1** to bake in a scallop shell or shallow baking dish, usu with a sauce covered with breadcrumbs **2a** to shape, cut, or finish (e g an edge or border) in scallops **b** to form scallops in

scallywag, *NAm chiefly* **scalawag** *n* a troublemaking or dishonest person; a rascal

¹scalp *n* **1** (the part of a lower mammal corresponding to) the skin of the human head, usu covered with hair in both sexes **2a** a part of the human scalp with attached hair cut or torn from an enemy as a trophy, esp formerly by N American Indian warriors **b** a trophy of victory **3** chiefly Scot a projecting rocky mound

²scalp vt **1** to remove the scalp of **2** NAm **a** to buy and sell to make small quick profits **b** to obtain speculatively and resell at greatly increased prices ⟨~ theatre tickets⟩ USE (2) infml – **scalper** n

scalpel n a small very sharp straight thin-bladed knife used esp in surgery

scaly adj **1** covered with or composed of scale or scales **2** flaky – **scaliness** n

¹scamp n an impish or playful young person – **scampish** adj

²scamp vt to perform in a hasty, careless, or haphazard manner

¹scamper vi to run about nimbly and playfully

²scamper n a playful scurry

scampi n, pl scampi a (large) prawn (often prepared with a batter coating)

¹scan vb -nn- vt **1** to read or mark (a piece of text) so as to show metrical structure **2a** to subject to critical examination **b** to examine all parts of in a systematic order **c** to check or read hastily or casually ⟨~ned the small ads⟩ **3a** to traverse (a region) with a controlled beam: e g (1) to observe (a region) using a radar scanner (2) to translate (an image) into an electrical signal by moving an electron beam across it according to a predetermined pattern (e g for television transmission); also to reproduce (an image) from such a signal (3) to make a detailed examination of (e g the human body) using any of a variety of sensing devices (e g ones using ultrasonics, thermal radiation, X-rays, or radiation from radioactive materials) **b** to examine (a computer data source; e g a punched card) for the presence of recorded data ~ vi, of verse to conform to a metrical pattern

²scan n **1** a scanning **2** a radar or television trace

scandal n **1** loss of reputation caused by (alleged) breach of moral or social propriety **2** a circumstance or action that causes general offence or indignation or that disgraces those associated with it **3** malicious or defamatory gossip **4** indignation, chagrin, or bewilderment brought about by a flagrant violation of propriety or religious opinion

scandalize, -ise vt to offend the moral sense of – **scandalizer** n, **scandalization** n

scandalmonger n sby who circulates scandal

scandalous adj **1** libellous, defamatory **2** offensive to propriety – **scandalously** adv, **scandalousness** n

Scandinavian n **1** a native or inhabitant of Scandinavia **2** NORTH GERMANIC – **Scandinavian** adj

scanner n **1** a device that automatically monitors a system or process **2** a device for sensing recorded data **3** the rotating aerial of a radar set

scansion n (the analysis of) the way in which a piece of verse scans

¹scant adj **1a** barely sufficient; inadequate **b** lacking in quantity **2** having a small or insufficient supply – **scantly** adv, **scantness** n

²scant vt to restrict or withhold the supply of

scanty adj scant; esp deficient in coverage – **scantily** adv, **scantiness** n

scape n **1** a leafless flower stalk arising directly from the root of a plant (e g in the dandelion) **2** the shaft of an animal part (e g an antenna or feather)

-scape comb form (→ n) view of (a specified type of scene); also pictorial representation of (such a scene) ⟨seascape⟩

scapegoat n **1** a goat on whose head are symbolically placed the sins of the people after which he is sent into the wilderness in the biblical ceremony for Yom Kippur **2** sby

or sthg made to bear the blame for others' faults – **scapegoat** vt

scapegrace n an incorrigible rascal

scapula n, pl scapulae, scapulas a large flat triangular bone at the upper part of each side of the back forming most of each half of the shoulder girdle; SHOULDER BLADE

¹scar n a steep rocky place on a mountainside

²scar n **1** a mark left (e g on the skin) by the healing of injured tissue **2** CICATRIX 2 **3** a mark of damage or wear **4** a lasting moral or emotional injury – **scarless** adj

³scar vb -rr- vt **1** to mark with a scar **2** to do lasting injury to ~ vi **1** to form a scar **2** to become scarred

scarab n **1** a scarabaeus or other scarabaeid beetle **2** a representation of a beetle, usu made of stone or glazed earthenware, used in ancient Egypt esp as a talisman

¹scarce adj **1** not plentiful or abundant **2** few in number; rare – **scarceness** n, **scarcity** n

²scarce adv, archaic scarcely, hardly

scarcely adv **1a** by a narrow margin; only just ⟨had ~ finished eating⟩ **b** almost not ⟨~ ever went to parties⟩ ⟨could ~ have been better qualified⟩ **2** not without unpleasantness or discourtesy ⟨could ~ interfere in a private dispute⟩

¹scare vt **1** to frighten suddenly **2** to drive off by frightening ~ vi to become scared – **scarer** n

²scare n **1** a sudden or unwarranted fright **2** a widespread state of alarm or panic ⟨a bomb ~⟩ – **scare** adj

scarecrow n **1** an object usu suggesting a human figure, set up to frighten birds away from crops **2** a skinny or ragged person – infml

scaremonger n sby who (needlessly) encourages panic – **scaremongering** n

¹scarf n, pl scarves, scarfs a strip or square of cloth worn round the shoulders or neck or over the head for decoration or warmth

²scarf n, pl scarfs **1** either of the chamfered or cut away ends that fit together to form a scarf joint **2** scarf, scarf joint a joint made by chamfering, halving, or notching 2 pieces to correspond and lapping and bolting them

³scarf, scarph vt **1** to unite by a scarf joint **2** to form a scarf on

scarify vt **1** to make scratches or small cuts in (e g the skin) **2** to wound the feelings of (e g by harsh criticism) **3** to break up and loosen the surface of (e g a field or road) – **scarifier** n, **scarification** n

scarlet adj or n (of) a vivid red colour tinged with orange

scarlet fever n an infectious fever caused by a streptococcus in which there is a red rash and inflammation of the nose, throat, and mouth

scarlet pimpernel n a common pimpernel with usu red flowers that close in cloudy weather

scarlet runner n RUNNER BEAN

scarlet woman n a prostitute – euph

¹scarp n **1** the inner side of a ditch below the parapet of a fortification **2** a steep slope, esp a cliff face, produced by faulting or erosion

²scarp vt to cut down to form a vertical or steep slope

scarper vi, Br to run away (e g from creditors) – infml

scary, scarey adj **1** causing fright; alarming **2** easily scared; timid USE infml

¹scat vi -tt- to depart rapidly – infml

²scat n jazz singing with nonsense syllables – **scat** vi

scathing adj bitterly severe ⟨a ~ condemnation⟩ – **scathingly** adv

scatology n **1** the biologically oriented study of excrement (e g for the determination of diet) **2** (literature characterized by) interest in or treatment of obscene matters – **scatological** *adj*

¹scatter *vt* **1** to cause (a group or collection) to separate widely **2a** to distribute at irregular intervals **b** to distribute recklessly and at random **3** to sow (seed) by casting in all directions **4** to reflect or disperse (e g a beam of radiation or particles) irregularly and diffusely ~ *vi* to separate and go in various directions – **scatterer** *n*, **scatteringly** *adv*

²scatter *n* **1** the act of scattering **2** a small supply or number irregularly distributed **3** the state or extent of being scattered

scatterbrain *n* sby incapable of concentration – **scatterbrained** *adj*

scatty *adj*, *Br* scatterbrained – *infml*

scavenge *vt* **1** to salvage from discarded or refuse material; *also* to salvage usable material from **2** to feed on (carrion or refuse) **3a** to remove (burnt gases) from the cylinder of an internal-combustion engine after a working stroke **b** to remove (e g an undesirable constituent) by chemical or physical means **c** to clean and purify (molten metal) by making foreign elements from chemical compounds ~ *vi* **1** to search for reusable material **2** to obtain food by scavenging ⟨dogs scavenging *on kitchen waste*⟩

scavenger *n* **1** a refuse collector **2** a chemical used to remove or make innocuous an undesirable substance **3** an organism that feeds on refuse or carrion

scenario *n*, *pl* **scenarios** **1** an outline or synopsis of a dramatic work **2a** a screenplay **b** a shooting script **3** an account or synopsis of a projected course of action

scend *vi* to rise upwards on a wave

scene *n* **1** any of the smaller subdivisions of a dramatic work: e g **a** a division of an act presenting continuous action in 1 place **b** an episode, sequence, or unit of dialogue in a play, film, or television programme **2** a vista suggesting a stage setting **3** the place of an occurrence or action ⟨~ *of the crime*⟩ **4** an exhibition of unrestrained feeling ⟨make a ~⟩ **5** a sphere of activity or interest – slang ⟨the drug ~⟩ ⟨philosophy is not my ~⟩ – **behind the scenes** out of the public view; IN SECRET

scenery *n* **1** the painted scenes or hangings and accessories used on a theatre stage **2** landscape, esp when considered attractive

sceneshifter *n* a worker who moves the scenery in a theatre

scenic *also* scenical *adj* **1** of the stage, a stage setting, or stage representation **2** of or displaying (fine) natural scenery **3** representing graphically an action or event – **scenically** *adv*

¹scent *vt* **1a** to perceive by the sense of smell **b** to get or have an inkling of **2** to fill with a usu pleasant smell ~ *vi* to use the nose in seeking or tracking prey

²scent *n* **1** odour: e g **a** a smell left by an animal on a surface it passes over ⟨hounds followed the ~ *of the fox*⟩ **b** a characteristic or particular, esp agreeable, smell **c** PERFUME 2 **2a** power of smelling; the sense of smell ⟨a keen ~⟩ **b** power of detection; a nose ⟨a ~ *for heresy*⟩ **3** a course of pursuit or discovery ⟨threw him off the ~⟩ **4** a hint, suggestion ⟨a ~ *of trouble*⟩ – **scentless** *adj*

sceptic *n* a person disposed to scepticism, esp regarding religion or religious principles

sceptical *adj* relating to, characteristic of, or marked by scepticism

scepticism *n* **1** doubt concerning basic religious principles (e g immortality, providence, or revelation) **2** the doctrine that certain knowledge is unattainable either generally or in a particular sphere **3** an attitude of doubt, esp associated with implied criticism

sceptre, *NAm chiefly* scepter *n* **1** a staff borne by a ruler as an emblem of sovereignty **2** royal or imperial authority

¹schedule *n* **1** a statement of supplementary details appended to a document **2** a list, catalogue, or inventory **3** (the times fixed in) a timetable **4** a programme, proposal **5** a body of items to be dealt with

²schedule *vt* **1a** to place on a schedule **b** to make a schedule of **2** to appoint or designate for a fixed time **3** *Br* to place on a list of buildings or historical remains protected by state legislation – **scheduler** *n*

schema *n*, *pl* **schemata** a diagrammatic representation; a plan

schematic *adj* of a scheme or schema; diagrammatic – **schematically** *adv*

schematize, -ise *vt* **1** to form into a systematic arrangement **2** to express or depict schematically – **schematization** *n*

¹scheme *n* **1** a concise statement or table **2** a plan or programme of action; a project ⟨a hydroelectric ~⟩ **3** a crafty or secret strategy **4** a systematic arrangement of parts or elements

²scheme *vt* to form a scheme for ~ *vi* to make plans; *also* to plot, intrigue – **schemer** *n*

scherzo *n*, *pl* **scherzos**, **scherzi** a lively instrumental musical composition or movement in quick usu triple time

schism *n* **1** separation into opposed factions **2a** formal division in or separation from a religious body **b** the offence of promoting schism

¹schismatic *n* a person who creates or takes part in schism

²schismatic *also* schismatical *adj* **1** (having the character) of schism **2** guilty of schism – **schismatically** *adv*

schist *n* a metamorphic crystalline rock composed of thin layers of minerals and splitting along approx parallel planes – **schistose** *adj*

schizoid *adj* characterized by, resulting from, tending towards, or suggestive of schizophrenia – **schizoid** *n*

schizophrenia *n* a mental disorder characterized by loss of contact with reality and disintegration of personality, usu with hallucinations and disorder of feeling, behaviour, etc – **schizophrenic** *adj or n*, **schizophrenically** *adv*

schmaltz, **schmalz** *n* excessive sentimentalism, esp in music or art – **schmaltzy** *adj*

schnapps *n*, *pl* **schnapps** strong gin as orig made in the Netherlands

schnitzel *n* a veal escalope

schnorkel *vi or n* (to) snorkel

scholar *n* **1** one who attends a school or studies under a teacher **2** one who has done advanced study **3** the holder of a scholarship

scholarly *adj* learned, academic

scholarship *n* **1** a grant of money to a student **2** the character, methods, or attainments of a scholar; learning **3** a fund of knowledge and learning

scholastic *adj* **1a** *often cap* of Scholasticism **b** suggestive or characteristic of a scholar or pedant, esp in specious subtlety or dryness **2** of schools or scholars – **scholastically** *adv*

scholasticism *n* **1** *cap* a chiefly late medieval philosophical movement that applied Aristotelian concepts and principles to the interpretation of religious dogma **2** pedantic adherence to the traditional teachings or methods of a school

¹school *n* **1a** an institution for the teaching of children **b(1)** any of the 4 faculties of a medieval university **(2)** a part of a university ⟨the ~ *of engineering*⟩ **c** an establishment offering specialized instruction ⟨driving ~s⟩ **d** *pl*, *cap* the final honours examination for the Oxford BA **e**

NAm a college, university **2a(1)** the process of teaching or learning, esp at a school **(2)** a session of a school **b** a school building **3a** people with a common doctrine or teacher (e g in philosophy or theology) ⟨*the Frankfurt* ∼⟩ **b** a group of artists under a common stylistic influence **4** a body of people with similar opinions ⟨*a* ∼ *of thought*⟩

²**school** *vt* **1** to educate in an institution of learning **2a** to teach or drill in a specific knowledge or skill ⟨∼ *a horse*⟩ **b** to discipline or habituate to sthg

³**school** *n* a large number of fish or aquatic animals of 1 kind swimming together

⁴**school** *vi* to swim or feed in a school

schoolboy, *fem* **schoolgirl** *n* a schoolchild

schoolhouse *n* a building used as a school; *esp* a country primary school

schooling *n* **1a** instruction in school **b** training or guidance from practical experience **2** the cost of instruction and maintenance at school **3** the training of a horse to service; *esp* the teaching and exercising of a horse and rider in the formal techniques of horse riding

schoolmarm, **schoolma'am** *n* **1** a prim censorious woman **2** *chiefly NAm* a female schoolteacher; *esp* a rural or small-town schoolmistress

schoolmaster, *fem* **schoolmistress** *n* a schoolteacher

schoolmate *n* a companion at school

schoolwork *n* lessons

schooner *n* **1** a fore-and-aft rigged sailing vessel having 2 or more masts **2a** *Br* **(1)** a relatively tall narrow glass used esp for a large measure of sherry or port **(2)** the capacity of a schooner used as a measure (e g for sherry) **b** *chiefly NAm & Austr* a large tall drinking glass, esp for beer

schwa *n* (the symbol /M/ used for) an unstressed vowel that is the usual sound of the first and last vowels of *banana*

sciatic *adj* **1** of or situated near the hip **2** of or caused by sciatica ⟨∼ *pains*⟩

sciatica *n* pain in the back of the thigh, buttocks, and lower back caused esp by pressure on the sciatic nerve

science *n* **1a** a department of systematized knowledge ⟨*the* ∼ *of theology*⟩ **b** sthg (e g a skill) that may be learned systematically ⟨*the* ∼ *of boxing*⟩ **c** any of the natural sciences **2a** coordinated knowledge of the operation of general laws, esp as obtained and tested through scientific method **b** such knowledge of the physical world and its phenomena; NATURAL SCIENCE **3** a system or method (purporting to be) based on scientific principles

science fiction *n* fiction of a type orig set in the future and dealing principally with the impact of science on society or individuals, but now including also works of literary fantasy

scientific *adj* of or exhibiting the methods of science – **scientifically** *adv*

scientist *n* an expert in a science, esp natural science; a scientific investigator

scientology *n, often cap* a religious and psycho-therapeutic movement begun in 1952 by L Ron Hubbard

scimitar *n* a chiefly Middle Eastern sword having a curved blade which narrows towards the hilt and is sharpened on the convex side

scintilla *n* an iota, trace

scintillate *vi* **1** to emit sparks **2** to emit flashes as if throwing off sparks; *also* to sparkle, twinkle **3** to be brilliant or animated ⟨*scintillating wit*⟩ – **scintillant** *adj*

scion *n* **1** a detached living part of a plant joined to a stock

in grafting and usu supplying parts above ground of the resulting graft **2** a (male) descendant or offspring

scissor *vt* to cut (out) (as if) with scissors

scissors *n pl* **1** a cutting instrument with 2 blades pivoted so that their cutting edges slide past each other **2** *sing or pl in constr* a gymnastic feat in which the leg movements suggest the opening and closing of scissors – **scissor** *adj*

sclerosis *n* **1** (a disease characterized by) abnormal hardening of tissue, esp from overgrowth of fibrous tissue **2** the natural hardening of plant cell walls usu by the formation of lignin – **sclerose** *vb*

¹**scoff** *n* an expression of scorn, derision, or contempt

²**scoff** *vi* to show contempt by derisive acts or language – often + *at* ⟨∼ *at conventional wisdom*⟩ – **scoffer** *n*

³**scoff** *vt, chiefly Br* to eat, esp greedily, rapidly, or in an ill-mannered way – *infml*

¹**scold** *n* a woman who habitually nags or quarrels

²**scold** *vi* to find fault noisily and at length ∼*vt* to reprove sharply – **scolder** *n*

scollop *n* a scallop

¹**sconce** *n* a bracket candlestick or group of candlesticks; *also* an electric light fixture patterned on a candle sconce

²**sconce** *n* a detached defensive work (e g a fort or mound)

³**sconce** *n, Br* (the mug used for) a forfeit formerly common at Oxford and Cambridge universities that involves drinking or supplying drink (e g beer) – **sconce** *vt*

scone *n* any of several small light cakes made from a dough or batter containing a raising agent and baked in a hot oven or on a griddle

¹**scoop** *n* **1a** a large ladle for taking up or skimming liquids **b** a deep shovel for lifting and moving granular material (e g corn or sand) **c** a handled utensil of shovel shape or with a hemispherical bowl for spooning out soft food (e g ice cream) **d** a small spoon-shaped utensil for cutting or gouging (e g in surgical operations) **2a** an act or the action of scooping **b** the amount held by a scoop ⟨*a* ∼ *of sugar*⟩ **3** a cavity **4** material for publication or broadcast, esp when obtained ahead or to the exclusion of competitors – **scoopful** *n*

²**scoop** *vt* **1** to take out or up (as if) with a scoop **2** to empty by scooping **3** to make hollow; dig out **4** to obtain a news story in advance or to the exclusion of (a competitor) **5** to obtain by swift action or sudden good fortune – chiefly infml ⟨∼ *the lion's share of an aid programme*⟩

scoot *vi* to go suddenly and swiftly – infml – **scoot** *n*

scooter *n* **1** a child's foot-operated vehicle consisting of a narrow board with usu 1 wheel at each end and an upright steering handle **2** MOTOR SCOOTER

¹**scope** *n* **1** space or opportunity for unhampered action, thought, or development **2a** extent of treatment, activity, or influence **b** extent of understanding or perception

²**scope** *n* a periscope, telescope, or other optical instrument – infml

-scope *comb form* (→ *n*) instrument for viewing or observing ⟨*microscope*⟩

scorbutic *adj* of, resembling, or diseased with scurvy – **scorbutically** *adv*

¹**scorch** *vt* **1** to burn so as to produce a change in colour and texture **2a** to parch (as if) with intense heat **b** to criticize or deride bitterly **3** to devastate completely, esp before abandoning – used in *scorched earth*, of property of possible use to an enemy ∼ *vi* **1** to become scorched **2** to travel at (excessive) speed – **scorchingly** *adv*

²**scorch** *n* a mark resulting from scorching

scorcher *n* a very hot day – infml

¹**score** *n, pl* **scores**, *(1a, b)* **scores, score** **1a** twenty **b** a

group of 20 things – used in combination with a cardinal number ⟨*fivescore*⟩ **c** *pl* an indefinite large number **2a** a line (e g a scratch or incision) made (as if) with a sharp instrument **b** a notch used for keeping a tally **3a** an account or reckoning kept by making incisions **b** an account of debts **c** an amount due **4** a grudge ⟨*settle an old* ~⟩ **5a** a reason, ground ⟨*complain on the* ~ *of maltreatment*⟩ **b** a subject, topic ⟨*have no doubts on that* ~⟩ **6a** the copy of a musical composition in written or printed notation **b** the music for a film or theatrical production **c** a complete description of a dance composition in choreographic notation **7a** a number that expresses accomplishment (e g in a game or test) **b** an act (e g a goal, run, or try) in any of various games or contests that increases such a number **8** the inescapable facts of a situation ⟨*knows the* ~⟩

²**score** *vt* **1a** to record (as if) by notches on a tally **b** to enter (a debt) in an account – usu + *to* or *against* **c** to cancel or strike out (e g record of a debt) with a line or notch – often + *out* **2** to mark with grooves, scratches, or notches **3a(1)** to gain (e g points) in a game or contest ⟨~d *8 runs*⟩ **(2)** to have as a value in a game or contest ⟨*a try* ~s *4 points*⟩ **b** to gain, win ⟨~d *a success with his latest novel*⟩ **4a** to write or arrange (music) for specific voice or instrumental parts **b** to orchestrate **c** to compose a score for (e g a film) ~ *vi* **1** to record the scores or make a score in a game or contest **2** to obtain a rating or grade ⟨~ *high in intelligence tests*⟩ **3a** to gain or have an advantage or a success **b** to obtain illicit drugs – slang **c** to achieve a sexual success – slang – **scorer** *n* – **score off someone** *Br* to get the better of sby in debate or argument

scoreboard *n* a usu large board for displaying the state of play (e g the score) in a game or match

¹**scorn** *n* **1** vigorous contempt; disdain **2** an expression of extreme contempt **3** an object of extreme disdain or derision – **scornful** *adj*

²**scorn** *vt* to reject with outspoken contempt – **scorner** *n*

Scorpio *n* (sby born under) the 8th sign of the zodiac in astrology, which is pictured as a scorpion – **Scorpian** *adj or n*

scorpion *n* **1** any of an order of arachnids having an elongated body and a narrow tail bearing a venomous sting at the tip **2** a whip studded with metal spikes

Scot *n* **1** a member of a Gaelic people orig of N Ireland that settled in Scotland about AD 500 **2** a native or inhabitant of Scotland

¹**scotch** *vt* **1a** to stamp out; crush **b** to hinder, thwart ⟨~ *schemes for sponsorship*⟩ **2** to repudiate by exhibiting as false ⟨~ *rumours*⟩

²**scotch** *n* a slight cut

¹**Scotch** *adj* Scottish

²**Scotch** *n* **1** Scots **2** *pl in constr* the Scots **3** *often not cap* SCOTCH WHISKY; *broadly* (a) whisky

Scotch broth *n* soup made from beef or mutton, vegetables, and barley

Scotch egg *n* a hard-boiled egg covered with sausage meat, coated with breadcrumbs, and deep-fried

Scotch tape *trademark* – used for any of numerous adhesive tapes

Scotch whisky *n* whisky distilled in Scotland, esp from malted barley

Scotch woodcock *n* buttered toast spread with anchovy paste and scrambled egg

scot-free *adj* without any penalty, payment, or injury

Scotland Yard *n sing or pl in constr* the criminal investigation department of the London metropolitan police force

¹**Scottish** *adj* (characteristic) of Scotland – **Scottish-ness** *n*

²**Scottish** *n* Scots

Scottish terrier *n* (any of) a Scottish breed of terrier with short legs and a very wiry coat of usu black hair

scoundrel *n* a wicked or dishonest fellow – **scoundrelly** *adj*

¹**scour** *vt* **1** to move through or range over usu swiftly **2** to make a rapid but thorough search of

²**scour** *vt* **1a** to rub vigorously in order to cleanse **b** to remove by rubbing, esp with rough or abrasive material **2** to clean out by purging **3** to free from impurities (as if) by washing **4** to clear, excavate, or remove (as if) by a powerful current of water ~ *vi* **1** to undertake scouring **2** *esp of cattle* to suffer from diarrhoea or dysentery **3** to become clean and bright by being rubbed – **scourer** *n*

³**scour** *n* **1** scouring action (e g of a glacier) **2** diarrhoea or dysentery, esp in cattle – usu pl with sing. meaning but sing. or pl in constr

¹**scourge** *n* **1** a whip used to inflict punishment **2a** a means of vengeance or criticism **b** a cause of affliction

²**scourge** *vt* **1** to flog **2a** to punish severely **b** to subject to affliction; devastate **c** to subject to scathing criticism – **scourger** *n*

¹**scout** *vi* to make an advance survey (e g to obtain military information) ~ *vt* **1** to observe or explore in order to obtain information **2** to find by making a search – often + *out* or *up*

²**scout** *n* **1** the act or an instance of scouting **2a** sby or sthg sent to obtain (military) information **b** TALENT SCOUT **3** an Oxford university college servant **4** *often cap* a member of a worldwide movement of boys and young men that was founded with the aim of developing leadership and comradeship and that lays stress on outdoor activities; *specif* a British boy member aged from 11 to 15

scoutmaster *n* the adult leader of a troop of scouts – no longer used technically

scow *n* a large flat-bottomed usu unpowered boat used chiefly for transporting ore, sand, refuse, etc

¹**scowl** *vi* **1** to frown or wrinkle the brows in expression of displeasure **2** to exhibit a gloomy or threatening aspect – **scowler** *n*

²**scowl** *n* an angry frown

¹**scrabble** *vi* **scrabbling** **1** to scratch or scrape about **2a** to scramble, clamber **b** to struggle frantically ⟨*urchins scrabbling for leftovers*⟩ *USE* infml – **scrabbler** *n*

²**scrabble** *n* **1** a persistent scratching or clawing **2** a scramble *USE* infml

Scrabble *trademark* – used for a board game of word-building from individual letters

¹**scrag** *n* **1** a scraggy person or animal **2** (the bony end nearest the head of) a neck of mutton or veal

²**scrag** *vt* **-gg-** **1** to kill or execute by hanging, garrotting, or wringing the neck of **2** to attack in anger – infml

scraggly *adj*, *NAm* irregular; *also* ragged, unkempt – infml

scraggy *adj* lean and lanky in growth or build

scram *vi* **-mm-** to go away at once – infml

¹**scramble** *vb* **scrambling** *vi* **1a** to move or climb using hands and feet, esp hastily **b** to move with urgency or panic **2** to struggle eagerly or chaotically for possession of sthg **3a** to spread or grow irregularly **b** *of a plant* to climb over a support **4** *esp of an aircraft or its crew* to take off quickly in response to an alert ~ *vt* **1** to collect by scrambling – + *up* or *together* ⟨~d *up a hasty supper*⟩ **2a** to toss or mix together **b** to prepare (eggs) in a pan by stirring during cooking **3** to cause or order (an aircraft) to scramble **4** to encode (the elements of a telecommuni-

cations transmission) in order to make unintelligible on unmodified receivers

²**scramble** n 1 a scrambling movement or struggle 2 a disordered mess; a jumble 3 a rapid emergency takeoff of aircraft 4 a motorcycle race over very rough ground

¹**scrap** n 1 pl fragments of discarded or leftover food 2a a small detached fragment b an excerpt from sthg written or printed c the smallest piece 3 pl the remains of animal fat after rendering; cracklings 4a the residue from a manufacturing process b manufactured articles or parts, esp of metal, rejected or discarded and useful only for reprocessing

²**scrap** vt -pp- 1 to convert into scrap ⟨~ a battleship⟩ 2 to abandon or get rid of, as without further use ⟨~ outworn methods⟩

³**scrap** vi or n -pp- (to engage in) a minor fight or dispute – infml

scrapbook n a blank book in which miscellaneous items (e g newspaper cuttings or postcards) may be pasted

¹**scrape** vt 1a to remove (clinging matter) from a surface by usu repeated strokes of an edged instrument b to make (a surface) smooth or clean with strokes of an edged or rough instrument 2a to grate harshly over or against b to damage or injure by contact with a rough surface c to draw roughly or noisily over a surface 3 to collect or procure (as if) by scraping – often + up or together ⟨~ up the price of a pint⟩ ~ vi 1 to move in sliding contact with a rough or abrasive surface 2 to accumulate money by small but difficult economies ⟨scraping and saving to educate their children⟩ 3 to draw back the foot along the ground in making a bow – chiefly in bow and scrape 4 to get by with difficulty or succeed by a narrow margin – often + in, through, or by ⟨the candidate ~d through with a majority of 6⟩ – **scraper** n

²**scrape** n 1a an act, process, or result of scraping b the sound of scraping 2 a disagreeable predicament, esp as a result of foolish behaviour – infml

scrap heap n 1 a pile of discarded materials, esp metal 2 the place to which useless things are consigned

scrappy adj consisting of scraps ⟨a ~ education⟩

¹**scratch** vt 1 to scrape or dig with the claws or nails 2 to tear, mark, or cut the surface of with sthg sharp or jagged 3 to scrape or rub lightly (e g to relieve itching) 4 to scrape together ⟨~ a precarious living – Punch⟩ 5 to write or draw on a surface ⟨~ed his initials on the desk⟩ 6a to cancel or erase (as if) by drawing a line through b to withdraw (an entry) from competition ~vi 1 to use the claws or nails in digging, tearing, or wounding 2 to scrape or rub oneself (e g to relieve itching) 3 to acquire money by hard work and saving 4 to make a thin grating sound ⟨this pen ~es⟩ – **scratcher** n

²**scratch** n 1 a mark, injury, or slight wound (produced by scratching) 2 the sound of scratching 3 the most rudimentary beginning – in from scratch 4 standard or satisfactory condition or performance ⟨not up to ~⟩

³**scratch** adj 1 made or done by chance and not as intended ⟨a ~ shot⟩ 2 arranged or put together haphazardly or hastily ⟨a ~ team⟩ 3 without handicap or allowance ⟨a ~ golfer⟩

scratchy adj 1 tending to scratch or irritate ⟨~ wool⟩ 2 making a scratching noise ⟨a ~ pen⟩ 3 made (as if) with scratches ⟨~ drawing⟩ 4 uneven in quality 5 irritable, fractious – **scratchiness** n

scrawl vb to write or draw awkwardly, hastily, or carelessly – **scrawl** n, **scrawler** n, **scrawly** adj

scrawny adj exceptionally thin and slight ⟨~ cattle⟩ – **scrawniness** n

¹**scream** vi 1a(1) to voice a sudden piercing cry, esp in alarm or pain (2) to produce harsh high tones b to move

with or make a shrill noise like a scream 2 to speak or write violently or hysterically ⟨a ~ing headline⟩ 3 to produce a vivid or startling effect ⟨a ~ing red⟩ ~ vt 1 to utter (as if) with a scream or screams 2 to bring to a specified state by screaming ⟨~ oneself hoarse⟩ – **screamer** n

²**scream** n 1 a shrill penetrating cry or noise 2 sby or sthg that provokes screams of laughter ⟨he's a ~ after a drink or 2⟩ – infml

screamingly adv extremely ⟨~ funny⟩

scree n (a mountain slope covered with) loose stones or rocky debris

¹**screech** vi 1 to utter a shrill piercing cry; cry out, esp in terror or pain 2 to make a sound like a screech ⟨the car ~ed to a halt⟩ – **screecher** n

²**screech** n a shrill sound or cry

screech owl n a barn owl or other owl with a harsh shrill cry

screed n 1 an overlong usu dull piece of writing 2 a strip (e g of plaster) serving as a guide to the thickness of a subsequent coat 3 a levelling device drawn over freshly poured concrete

¹**screen** n 1a a usu movable piece of furniture that gives protection from heat or draughts or is used as an ornament ⟨fire ~⟩ b an ornamental partition 2a sthg that shelters, protects, or conceals ⟨a ~ of light infantry⟩ b a shield for secret usu illicit practices 3a a sieve or perforated material set in a frame used to separate coarser from finer parts b a device that shields from interference (e g by electrical or magnetic fields) c a frame holding a netting used esp in a window or door to exclude mosquitoes and other pests 4a a surface on which images are projected or reflected b the surface on which the image appears in a television or radar receiver c a ruled glass plate through which an image is photographed in making a halftone 5a the film industry; films ⟨a star of stage and ~⟩ b the medium of television

²**screen** vt 1 to guard from injury, danger, or punishment 2a to separate (as if) with a screen b to provide with a screen to keep out pests (e g insects) 3a to pass (e g coal, gravel, or ashes) through a screen to separate the fine part from the coarse; also to remove (as if) by a screen b(1) to examine systematically so as to separate into different groups ⟨~ visa applications⟩ (2) to test or check by a screening process 4a to show or broadcast (a film or television programme) b to present in a film or on television – **screenable** adj, **screener** n

screening n 1 pl but sing or pl in constr material (e g waste or fine coal) separated out by a screen 2 metal or plastic mesh (e g for window screens) 3 a showing of a film or television programme

screenplay n the script of a film including description of characters, details of scenes and settings, dialogue, and stage directions

¹**screw** n 1 a simple machine of the inclined plane type in which the applied force acts along a spiral path about a cylinder while the resisting force acts along the axis of the cylinder 2a a usu pointed tapering metal rod having a raised thread along all or part of its length and a usu slotted head which may be driven into a body by rotating (e g with a screwdriver) b a screw-bolt that can be turned by a screwdriver 3a sthg like a screw in form or function; a spiral b a turn of a screw; also a twist resembling such a turn 4 SCREW PROPELLER 5 a thumbscrew 6 backspin, esp when given to a cue ball in billiards, snooker, etc 7 chiefly Br a small twisted paper packet (e g of tobacco) 8 sby who drives a hard bargain – slang 9 a prison guard – slang 10 an act of sexual intercourse – vulg – **screwlike** adj

²screw vt **1a(1)** to attach, close, operate, adjust, etc by means of a screw **(2)** to unite or separate by means of a screw or a twisting motion ⟨~ *the 2 pieces together*⟩ **b** to cause to rotate spirally about an axis **2a(1)** to contort (the face) or narrow (the eyes) (e g with effort or an emotion) – often + *up* **(2)** to crush into irregular folds **b** to make a spiral groove or ridge in **3** to increase the intensity, quantity, or effectiveness of ⟨~ *up one's courage*⟩ **4** to give backwards spin to (a ball) **5a** to make oppressive demands on ⟨~ed *him for every penny he'd got*⟩ **b** to extract by pressure or threat – usu + *from* or *out of* **6** to copulate with ~ vi **1a** to rotate like or as a screw b to become secured (as if) by screwing – usu + *on* or *up* ⟨*panels that* ~ *on*⟩ **2** to turn or move with a twisting motion **3** to copulate *USE* (*vt* 2a(2), 3) usu + *up*; (*vt* 5) slang; (*vt* 6; *vi* 3) vulg – **screwer** n

screwball n or adj, chiefly NAm (sby) crazily eccentric or whimsical – infml

screwdriver n a tool for turning screws

screw propeller n a device that consists of a central hub with radiating blades and is used to propel a vehicle (e g a ship or aeroplane)

screw top n (an opening designed to take) a cover secured by twisting

screw up vt **1** to fasten or lock (as if) by a screw **2** to bungle, botch **3** to cause to become anxious or neurotic *USE* (2, 3) slang

screwy adj crazily absurd, eccentric, or unusual; *also* mad – infml – **screwiness** n

scribble vb **scribbling** to write or draw without regard for legibility or coherence – **scribble** n

scribbler n a minor or worthless author

¹scribe n **1** a member of a learned class of lay jurists in ancient Israel up to New Testament times **2** a copier of manuscripts **3** an author; *specif* a journalist – chiefly humor – **scribal** adj

²scribe vt **1** to mark a line on by scoring with a pointed instrument **2** to make (e g a line) by scratching or gouging

scrimmage vi or n (to take part in) **a** a confused fight or minor battle; a mêlée **b** the interplay between 2 American football teams that begins with the passing back of the ball from the ground and continues until the ball is dead

scrimp vi to be frugal or niggardly – esp in *scrimp and save* ~ vt to be niggardly in providing (for) ⟨~ *provisions*⟩ ⟨~s *his family*⟩ – **scrimpy** adj

scrimshank vi, Br to avoid duties or obligations – infml – **scrimshanker** n

scrimshaw n carved or coloured work made esp by sailors from ivory or whalebone – **scrimshaw** vb

scrip n any of various documents used as evidence that the holder or bearer is entitled to receive sthg

¹script n **1a** sthg written; text ⟨*handed him several pages of* ~⟩ **b** an original document **c** the written text of a stage play, film, or broadcast (used in production or performance) **d** an examination candidate's written answers ⟨*a pile of* ~s *to mark*⟩ **2a** (printed lettering resembling) handwriting **b** the characters used in the alphabet of a particular language ⟨*unable to decipher Cyrillic* ~⟩

²script vt to prepare a script for or from

scriptural adj of, contained in, or according to a sacred writing; *esp* biblical – **scripturally** adv

scripture n **1a** *often cap* the sacred writings of a religion; *esp* the Bible – often pl with sing. meaning **b** a passage from the Bible **2** an authoritative body of writings

scriptwriter n one who writes screenplays or radio or television programmes

scrivener n a notary

scrofula n tuberculosis of lymph glands, esp in the neck

scrofulous adj of or affected (as if) with scrofula or a similar disease

scroll n **1** a written document in the form of a roll **2** a stylized ornamental design imitating the spiral curves of a scroll – **scrolled** adj

scrooge n, *often cap* a miserly person – infml

scrotum n, pl **scrota**, **scrotums** the external pouch of most male mammals that contains the testes – **scrotal** adj

¹scrounge vt to beg, wheedle ⟨*can I* ~ *a cigarette off you?*⟩ ~ vi **1** to hunt *around* **2** to wheedle – **scrounger** n

²scrounge n – **on the scrounge** attempting to obtain sthg by wheedling or cajoling

¹scrub n **1** (an area covered with) vegetation consisting chiefly of stunted trees or shrubs ⟨~ *land*⟩ ⟨~ *vegetation*⟩ **2a** a usu inferior type of domestic animal of mixed or unknown parentage; a mongrel **b** a small or insignificant person; a runt **3** NAm a player not in the first team; *also* a team composed of such players

²scrub vb **-bb-** vt **1a** to clean by rubbing, esp with a stiff brush **b** to remove by scrubbing **2** WASH **6b** **3** to abolish; DO AWAY WITH ⟨*let's* ~ *that idea*⟩ – infml ~ vi to use hard rubbing in cleaning

scrubber n **1** an apparatus for removing impurities, esp from gases **2** Br a girl who is readily available for casual sex; *also* a prostitute **3** Br a coarse or unattractive person *USE* (2, 3) slang

scrubbing brush, NAm **scrub brush** n a brush with hard bristles used for heavy cleaning, esp washing floors

scrubby adj **1** inferior in size or quality; stunted ⟨~ *cattle*⟩ **2** covered with or consisting of scrub **3** lacking distinction; trashy – infml

¹scruff n the back of the neck; the nape

²scruff n an untidily dressed or grubby person – infml

scruffy adj **1** seedy, disreputable ⟨*a* ~ *neighbourhood*⟩ **2** slovenly and untidy, esp in appearance – **scruffiness** n

scrum n **1** a set piece in rugby in which the forwards of each side crouch in a tight formation with the 2 front rows of each team meeting shoulder to shoulder so that the ball can be put in play between them **2** a disorderly struggle – chiefly humor ⟨*the morning* ~ *to board the bus*⟩

scrum-half n the player in rugby who puts the ball into the scrum

scrummage vi or n (to take part in) a scrum

scrumptious adj, *esp of food* delicious – infml – **scrumptiously** adv, **scrumptiousness** n

scrumpy n, Br dry rough cider

scrunch vt **1** to crunch, crush **2** to crumple – often + *up* ⟨~ *up a sheet of cardboard*⟩ ~ vi **1** to move making a crunching sound ⟨*her boots* ~ed *in the snow*⟩ **2** NAm to hunch up – **scrunch** n

¹scruple n **1** a unit of weight equal to 1/24oz apothecary (about 1.296g) **2** *archaic* a minute part or quantity

²scruple n a moral consideration that inhibits action

³scruple vi to be reluctant on grounds of conscience

scrupulous adj **1** inclined to have moral scruples **2** painstakingly exact ⟨*working with* ~ *care*⟩ – **scrupulously** adv, **scrupulousness** n, **scrupulosity** n

scrutineer n, Br sby who examines or observes sthg, esp the counting of votes at an election

scrutinize, -ise vt to examine painstakingly – **scrutinizer** n

scrutiny n **1** a searching study, inquiry, or inspection **2** a searching or critical look **3** close watch ⟨*keep prisoners under* ~⟩

scuba n an aqualung ⟨~ *diving*⟩

¹scud *vi* **-dd-** **1** to move or run swiftly, esp as if swept along ⟨*clouds* ~ding *along*⟩ **2** *of a ship* to run before a gale

²scud *n* **1a** a sudden slight shower **b** ocean spray or loose vaporizing clouds driven swiftly by the wind **2** a gust of wind

¹scuff *vi* **1** to slouch along without lifting the feet **2** to become scratched or roughened by wear ⟨*patent leather soon* ~s⟩ ~ *vt* **1** to shuffle (the feet) along while walking or back and forth while standing **2** to scratch, chip, or abrade the surface of

²scuff *n* **1** (a blemish or injury caused by) scuffing **2** *NAm* a noise (as if) of scuffing

¹scuffle *vi* scuffling **1** to struggle confusedly and at close quarters **2** to move (hurriedly) about with a shuffling gait

²scuffle *n* a confused impromptu usu brief fight

¹scull *n* **1** an oar worked to and fro over the stern of a boat as a means of propulsion **2** either of a pair of light oars used by a single rower

²scull *vt* to propel (a boat) by sculls or by a large oar worked to and fro over the stern ~ *vi* to scull a boat – **sculler** *n*

scullery *n* a room for menial kitchen work (e g washing dishes and preparing vegetables)

scullion *n*, *archaic* a kitchen servant

sculptor, *fem* **sculptress** *n* an artist who sculptures

¹sculpture *n* **1a** the art of creating three-dimensional works of art out of mouldable or hard materials by carving, modelling, casting, etc **b** (a piece of) work produced by sculpture **2** (a pattern of) impressed or raised marks, esp on a plant or animal part – **sculptural** *adj*, **sculpturally** *adv*, **sculpturesque** *adj*

²sculpture *vt* **1a** to represent in sculpture **b** to form (e g wood or stone) into a sculpture **2** to shape by erosion or other natural processes **3** to shape (as if) by carving or moulding

¹scum *n* **1** pollutants or impurities risen to or collected on the surface of a liquid **2** *pl in constr* the lowest class; the dregs ⟨*the* ~ *of the earth*⟩ – **scummy** *adj*

²scum *vi* **-mm-** to become covered (as if) with scum

¹scupper *n* an opening in a ship's side for draining water from the deck

²scupper *vt*, *Br* to wreck; PUT PAID TO ⟨~ed *our plans for a reunion*⟩ – *infml*

scurf *n* thin dry scales detached from the skin; *specif* dandruff – **scurfy** *adj*

scurrilous *adj* **1a** using or given to coarse language **b** wicked and unscrupulous in behaviour ⟨~ *impostors who rob poor people*⟩ **2** containing obscenities or coarse abuse – **scurrilously** *adv*, **scurrilousness** *n*, **scurrility** *n*

scurry *vi* to move briskly, esp with short hurried steps, and often in some agitation or confusion; scamper – **scurry** *n*

¹scurvy *adj* disgustingly mean or contemptible ⟨*a* ~ *trick*⟩ – **scurvily** *adv*, **scurviness** *n*

²scurvy *n* a deficiency disease caused by a lack of vitamin C and marked by spongy gums, loosening of the teeth, and bleeding under the skin

scut *n* a short erect tail (e g of a hare)

¹scuttle *n* a vessel that resembles a bucket and is used for storing, carrying, and dispensing coal indoors

²scuttle *n* **1** a small opening or hatchway with a movable lid in the deck of a ship **2** *Br* the top part of a motor-car body forward of the 2 front doors, to which the windscreen and instrument panel are attached

³scuttle *vt* scuttling **1** to sink (a ship) by making holes in the hull or opening the sea-cocks **2** to destroy, wreck ⟨~ *attempts to reach agreement*⟩

⁴scuttle *vi* to scurry, scamper

⁵scuttle *n* **1** a quick shuffling pace **2** a short swift dash; *esp* a swift departure

¹scythe *n* a long curving blade fastened at an angle to a long handle for cutting standing plants, esp grass

²scythe *vt* to cut (as if) with a scythe

sea *n* **1a** OCEAN 1; *broadly* the waters of the earth as distinguished from the land and air – often pl with sing. meaning **b** a large (partially) landlocked or inland body of salt water **c** a freshwater lake ⟨*the* Sea *of Galilee*⟩ **2** (the direction of) surface motion caused by the wind on a large body of water; *also* a heavy swell or wave **3** sthg vast or overwhelming likened to the sea ⟨*a* ~ *of faces*⟩ **4** the seafaring life ⟨*to run away to* ~⟩ **5** ²MARE – **at sea 1** on the sea; *specif* on a sea voyage **2** unable to understand; bewildered ⟨*he was all at sea, having never done such work before*⟩

sea anchor *n* a device, typically of canvas, thrown overboard to slow the drifting of a ship or seaplane and to keep its head to the wind

sea anemone *n* any of numerous usu solitary and brightly coloured polyps with a cluster of tentacles superficially resembling a flower

seabird *n* a bird (e g a gull or albatross) frequenting the open sea

seaboard *n*, *chiefly NAm* (the land near) a seashore – **seaboard** *adj*

seaborne *adj* conveyed on or over the sea ⟨~ *trade*⟩

sea breeze *n* a cool breeze blowing usu during the day inland from the sea

sea captain *n* the master of a (merchant) vessel

sea change *n* a complete transformation

sea cow *n* **1** a dugong **2** a manatee

seadog *n* a fogbow

sea dog *n* a veteran sailor

seafaring *n* travel by sea; *esp* the occupation of a sailor – **seafaring** *adj*

seafood *n* edible marine fish, shellfish, crustaceans, etc

seafront *n* the waterfront of a seaside town

seagirt *adj* surrounded by the sea – poetic ⟨*this* ~ *isle*⟩

seagoing *adj* of or designed for travel on the sea

sea gull *n* ¹GULL

sea horse *n* **1** a mythical creature half horse and half fish **2** any of numerous small fishes whose head and body are shaped like the head and neck of a horse

seakale *n* **1** a fleshy European plant of the mustard family used as a herb in cooking **2** *also* **seakale beet** chard

¹seal *n*, *pl* **seals**, *esp collectively* **seal** **1** any of numerous marine flesh-eating mammals chiefly of cold regions with limbs modified into webbed flippers for swimming **2** sealskin

²seal *vi* to hunt seal

³seal *n* **1a** sthg that confirms, ratifies, or makes secure **b(1)** an emblem or word impressed or stamped on a document as a mark of authenticity **(2)** an article used to impress such a word or emblem (e g on wax); *also* a disc, esp of wax, bearing such an impression **2a** a closure (e g a wax seal on a document or a strip of paper over the cork of a bottle) that must be broken in order to give access, and so guarantees that the item so closed has not been tampered with **b** a tight and effective closure (e g against gas or liquid) – **under seal** with an authenticating seal attached

⁴seal *vt* **1** to confirm or make secure (as if) by a seal ⟨~ed *the agreement with a handshake*⟩ **2a** to attach an authenticating seal to; *also* to authenticate, ratify **b** to mark with a stamp or seal (e g as evidence of size, accuracy, or quality) **3a** to fasten (as if) with a seal, esp to prevent or disclose interference **b** to close or make secure against access, leakage, or passage by a fastening or coating; *esp* to make airtight **c** to fix in position or close breaks in with a filling (e g of plaster) **4** to determine irrevocably ⟨*that answer ~ed our fate*⟩

sea legs *n pl* bodily adjustment to the motion of a ship, indicated esp by ability to walk steadily and by freedom from seasickness

¹**sealer** *n* **1** a coat (e g of size) applied to prevent subsequent coats of paint or varnish from being too readily absorbed **2** *chiefly NAm* an official who certifies conformity to a standard of correctness

²**sealer** *n* a person or ship engaged in hunting seals

sea level *n* the mean level of the surface of the sea midway between high and low tide

sealing wax *n* a resinous composition that becomes soft when heated and is used for sealing letters, parcels, etc

sea lion *n* any of several large Pacific seals

seal off *vt* to close securely, esp in order to prevent passage ⟨*troops sealed off the airport*⟩

sealskin *n* **1** (leather made from) the skin of a seal **2** a garment of sealskin – **sealskin** *adj*

Sealyham terrier *n* (any of) a breed of short-legged wirehaired chiefly white Welsh terriers

¹**seam** *n* **1** a line of stitching joining 2 separate pieces of fabric, esp along their edges **2** the space between adjacent planks or strakes of a ship **3a** a line, groove, or ridge formed at the meeting of 2 edges **b** a layer or stratum of coal, rock, etc **c** a line left by a cut or wound; *also* a wrinkle – **seamless** *adj*

²**seam** *vt* **1** to join (as if) by sewing **2** to mark with a seam, furrow, or scar

seaman *n* **1** a sailor, mariner **2** a trained person holding a rank below that of a noncommissioned officer in the US navy – **seamanlike** *adj*, **seamanly** *adj*, **seamanship** *n*

sea mile *n* NAUTICAL MILE

seamstress *n* a woman whose occupation is sewing

seamy *adj* unpleasant, sordid ⟨*the ~ side of the building trade*⟩ – **seaminess** *n*

séance *n* a meeting at which spiritualists attempt to communicate with the dead

seaplane *n* an aeroplane designed to take off from and land on the water

seaport *n* a port, harbour, or town accessible to seagoing ships

sea power *n* (a nation that commands) naval strength

¹**sear** *adj* sere

²**sear** *vt* **1** to make withered and dried up **2** to burn, scorch, or injure (as if) with a sudden application of intense heat **3** to mark (as if) with a branding iron ⟨*a sight which was ~ed on my memory*⟩ – **searingly** *adv*

³**sear** *n* a mark or scar left by searing

⁴**sear** *n* the catch that holds the hammer of a gunlock at cock or half cock

¹**search** *vt* **1a** to look through or over carefully or thoroughly in order to find or discover sthg ⟨*~ed the horizon*⟩ ⟨*~ed the house for clues*⟩ **b** to examine (a person) for concealed articles (e g weapons or drugs) **c** to scrutinize, esp in order to discover intention or nature ⟨*~ed her heart*⟩ **2** to uncover or ascertain by investigation – usu + *out* ⟨*~ out the relevant facts*⟩ **3** to cover (an area) with gunfire ~ *vi* **1** to look or inquire carefully or thoroughly ⟨*~ed for the papers*⟩ **2** to make painstaking investigation or examination ⟨*~ed into the matter very thoroughly*⟩ – **searchable** *adj*, **searcher** *n* – **search me** – used to express ignorance of an answer

²**search** *n* **1** an act or process of searching; *esp* an organized act of searching ⟨*the ~ for the escaped convicts is still in progress*⟩ ⟨*a ~ party*⟩ **2** an exercise of the right of search

searching *adj* piercing, penetrating ⟨*a ~ gaze*⟩ – **searchingly** *adv*

searchlight *n* (an apparatus for projecting) a movable beam of light

search warrant *n* a warrant authorizing a search of premises for unlawful possessions

seascape *n* (a picture representing) a view of the sea

seashell *n* the shell of a sea animal, esp a mollusc

seashore *n* land (between high and low water marks) next to the sea

seasick *adj* suffering from the motion sickness associated with travelling by boat or hovercraft – **seasickness** *n*

seaside *n* (a holiday resort or beach on) land bordering the sea

¹**season** *n* **1a** any of the 4 quarters into which the year is commonly divided **b** a period characterized by a particular kind of weather ⟨*the dry ~*⟩ **c** a period of the year characterized by or associated with a particular activity or phenomenon ⟨*the holiday ~*⟩ ⟨*the hunting ~*⟩ ⟨*an animal's mating ~*⟩ **d** the time of year when a place is most frequented ⟨*difficult to find accommodation there at the height of the ~*⟩ **e** the time of a major holiday; *specif* the Christmas season ⟨*send the ~'s greetings*⟩ **2** *archaic* an indefinite length of time – **in season 1** *of food* readily available and in the best condition for eating **2** *of game* legally available to be hunted or caught **3** *of an animal* on heat ⟨*the bitch is in season*⟩ **4** *esp of advice* given when most needed or most welcome ⟨*a word in season*⟩ – **out of season** not in season

²**season** *vt* **1a** to give (food) more flavour by adding seasoning or savoury ingredients **b** to make less harsh or unpleasant; relieve **c** to enliven ⟨*conversation ~ed with wit*⟩ **2a** to treat or expose (e g timber) over a period so as to prepare for use **b** to make fit or expert by experience ⟨*a ~ed veteran*⟩ – **seasoner** *n*

seasonable *adj* **1** occurring in good or proper time; opportune **2** suitable to the season or circumstances – **seasonableness** *n*, **seasonably** *adv*

seasonal *adj* **1** of, occurring, or produced at a particular season ⟨*~ rainfall*⟩ **2** determined by seasonal need or availability ⟨*~ employment*⟩ ⟨*~ industries*⟩ – **seasonally** *adv*

seasoning *n* a condiment, spice, herb, etc added to food primarily for the savour that it imparts

season ticket *n*, *Br* a ticket sold, usu at a reduced price, for an unlimited number of trips over the same route during a limited period

¹**seat** *n* **1a** a piece of furniture (e g a chair, stool, or bench) for sitting in or on **b** the part of sthg on which one rests when sitting ⟨*the ~ of a chair*⟩ ⟨*trouser ~*⟩; *also* the buttocks **c** a place for sitting ⟨*took his ~ next to her*⟩ **d** a unit of seating accommodation ⟨*a ~ for the game*⟩ **2a** a special chair (e g a throne) of sby in authority; *also* the status symbolized by it **b** a right of sitting ⟨*lost her ~ in the Commons*⟩ **c** a large country mansion **3a** a place where sthg is established or practised ⟨*an ancient ~ of learning*⟩ **b** a place from which authority is exercised ⟨*the ~ of government*⟩ **4** a bodily part in which a particular function, disease, etc is centred **5** posture in or a way of sitting on horseback **6a** a part at or forming the base of sthg **b** a part or surface on or in which another part or surface rests ⟨*a valve ~*⟩

²**seat** *vt* **1a** to cause to sit or assist in finding a seat ⟨*~ed her next to the door*⟩ **b** to provide seats for ⟨*a theatre ~ing 1000 people*⟩ **c** to put (e g oneself) in a sitting position **2** to fit correctly on a seat **3** to fit to or with a seat ⟨*~ a valve*⟩ ~ *vi*, *of a garment* to become baggy in

the area covering the buttocks ⟨*your woollen dress has ~ed badly*⟩ – **seater** *n*

seat belt *n* an arrangement of straps designed to secure a person in a seat in an aeroplane, vehicle, etc

seating *n* **1a** the act of providing with seats **b** the arrangement of seats (e g in a theatre) **2a** material for upholstering seats **b** a base on or in which sthg rests ⟨*a valve ~*⟩

sea urchin *n* any of a class of echinoderms usu with a thin shell covered with movable spines

seawall *n* a wall or embankment to protect the shore from erosion or to act as a breakwater

seaway *n* **1** a ship's headway **2** the sea as a route for travel **3** a deep inland waterway that admits ocean shipping

seaweed *n* (an abundant growth of) a plant, specif an alga, growing in the sea, typically having thick slimy fronds

seaworthy *adj* fit or safe for a sea voyage ⟨*a ~ ship*⟩ – **seaworthiness** *n*

sebaceous *adj* of, secreting, or being sebum or other fatty material

sebum *n* fatty lubricant matter secreted by sebaceous glands of the skin

¹sec *n, Br* a second, moment – *infml* ⟨*hang on a ~!*⟩

²sec *adj, of wine* not sweet; dry

secateur *n, chiefly Br* a pair of pruning shears –usu pl with sing. meaning

secede *vi* to withdraw from an organization (e g a church or federation) – **seceder** *n*

secession *n* an act of seceding – **secessionism** *n*, **secessionist** *n*

seclude *vt* to remove or separate from contact with others

secluded *adj* **1** screened or hidden from view **2** living in seclusion – **secludedly** *adv*, **secludedness** *n*

seclusion *n* **1** secluding or being secluded **2** a secluded or isolated place – **seclusive** *adj*, **seclusively** *adv*, **seclusiveness** *n*

¹second *adj* **1a** next to the first in place or time ⟨*was ~ in line*⟩ **b(1)** next to the first in value, quality, or degree **(2)** inferior, subordinate ⟨*was ~ to none*⟩ **c** standing next below the top in authority or importance ⟨*~ mate*⟩ **2** alternate, other ⟨*elects a mayor every ~ year*⟩ **3** resembling or suggesting a prototype ⟨*a ~ Napoleon*⟩ **4** being the forward gear or speed 1 higher than first in a motor vehicle **5** relating to or having a part typically subordinate to or lower in pitch than the first part in concerted or ensemble music – **second, secondly** *adv* – **at second hand** from or through an intermediary ⟨*heard the news* at second hand⟩

²second *n* **1a** number two in a countable series **b** sthg that is next after the first in rank, position, authority, or precedence ⟨*the ~ in line*⟩ **2** sby who aids, supports, or stands in for another; *esp* the assistant of a duellist or boxer **3a** (the combination of 2 notes at) a musical interval of 2 diatonic degrees **b** the supertonic **4** a slightly flawed or inferior article (e g of merchandise) **5a** a place next below the first in a contest **b** *also* **second class** *often cap* the second level of British honours degree **6** the second forward gear or speed of a motor vehicle **7** pl a second helping of food – *infml*

³second *n* **1a** a 60th part of a minute of time or of a minute of angular measure **b** the SI unit of time equal to the duration of a certain number of periods of vibration of a specific radiation of a particular caesium isotope **2** a moment ⟨*wait a ~ will you*⟩

⁴second *vt* **1** to give support or encouragement to **2** to endorse (a motion or nomination) – **seconder** *n*

⁵second *vt, chiefly Br* to release (e g a teacher, businessman, or military officer) from a regularly assigned position for temporary duty with another organization – **secondment** *n*

¹secondary *adj* **1a** of second rank or importance ⟨*~ streams*⟩ **b** of or constituting the second strongest degree of stress in speech **2a** immediately derived from sthg primary or basic; derivative ⟨*~ sources*⟩ **b** of or being the induced current or its circuit in an induction coil or transformer ⟨*a ~ coil*⟩ ⟨*~ voltage*⟩ **3a** not first in order of occurrence or development **b** of the second order or stage in a series or sequence **c** produced away from a growing point by the activity of plant formative tissue, esp cambium ⟨*~ growth*⟩ ⟨*~ phloem*⟩ ⟨*~ thickening*⟩ **d** of or being the (feathers growing on the) second segment of the wing of a bird **e** of a secondary school **4** of or being a manufacturing industry – **secondarily** *adv*, **secondariness** *n*

²secondary *n* **1** a secondary electrical circuit or coil **2** a secondary feather **3** SECONDARY SCHOOL

secondary modern, secondary modern school *n* a secondary school formerly providing a practical rather than academic type of education

secondary school *n* a school intermediate between primary school and higher education

second-best *adj* next after the best

second best *n* sby or sthg that comes after the best in quality or worth

second childhood *n* dotage

¹second-class *adj* **1** of a second class ⟨*a ~ honours degree*⟩ **2** inferior, mediocre; *also* socially, politically, or economically deprived ⟨*~ citizens*⟩

²second-class *adv* **1** in accommodation next below the best ⟨*travel ~*⟩ **2** by second-class mail ⟨*send the letters ~*⟩

second class *n* the second and usu next to highest group in a classification

Second Coming *n* the return of Christ to judge the world on the last day

¹secondhand *adj* **1a** received from or through an intermediary ⟨*~ information*⟩ **b** not original; derivative **2a** acquired after being owned by another ⟨*a ~ car*⟩ **b** dealing in secondhand goods ⟨*a ~ bookshop*⟩

²secondhand *adv* indirectly; AT SECOND HAND

second-in-command *n* one who is immediately subordinate to a commander; a deputy commander

second lieutenant *n* an officer of the lowest rank in the army or US airforce

second nature *n* an action or ability that practice has made instinctive

second person *n* (any of) a set of linguistic forms referring to the person or thing addressed (e g 'you')

second-rate *adj* of inferior quality or value – **secondrateness** *n*, **second-rater** *n*

second sight *n* clairvoyance, precognition

second-string *adj, chiefly NAm* being a substitute as distinguished from a regular player (e g in a football team); *broadly* substitute

secrecy *n* **1** the habit or practice of keeping secrets or maintaining privacy or concealment **2** the condition of being hidden or concealed ⟨*complete ~ surrounded the conference*⟩

¹secret *adj* **1a** kept or hidden from knowledge or view ⟨*determined to keep his mission ~*⟩ **b** marked by the practice of discretion; secretive **c** conducted in secret ⟨*~ negotiations*⟩ **2** retired, secluded **3** revealed only to the initiated; esoteric ⟨*~ rites*⟩ **4** containing information whose unauthorized disclosure could endanger national security – **secretly** *adv*

²**secret** *n* **1a** sthg kept hidden or unexplained **b** a fact concealed from others or shared confidentially with a few ⟨a trade ∼⟩ **2** sthg taken to be the means of attaining a desired end ⟨the ∼ of longevity⟩ – **in secret** in a private place or manner; in secrecy

secret agent *n* a spy

secretariat *n* **1** the office of secretary **2** the clerical staff of an organization **3** a government administrative department

secretary *n* **1** sby employed to handle correspondence and manage routine work for a superior **2a** COMPANY SECRETARY **b** an officer of an organization or society responsible for its records and correspondence **3** an officer of state who superintends a government administrative department – **secretaryship** *n*, **secretarial** *adj*

secretary-general *n, pl* **secretaries-general** a principal administrative officer (e g of the United Nations)

¹**secrete** *vt* to form and give off (a secretion) – **secretory** *adj*

²**secrete** *vt* to deposit in a hidden place ⟨∼ opium about his person⟩

secretion *n* **1** (a product formed by) the bodily process of making and releasing some material either functionally specialized (e g a hormone, saliva, latex, or resin) or isolated for excretion (e g urine) **2** the act of hiding sthg – **secretionary** *adj*

secretive *adj* inclined to secrecy; not open or outgoing in speech or behaviour – **secretively** *adv*, **secretiveness** *n*

secret service *n* a (secret) governmental agency concerned with national security; *esp, cap both Ss* a British government intelligence department

sect *n* **1** a (heretical) dissenting or schismatic religious body **2a** a group maintaining strict allegiance to a doctrine or leader **b** a party; *esp* a faction **3** a denomination – chiefly derog

-sect *comb form* (→ *vb*) cut; divide ⟨bisect⟩

¹**sectarian** *n* **1** a (fanatical) adherent of a sect **2** a bigoted person

²**sectarian** *adj* **1** (characteristic) of a sect or sectarian **2** limited in character or scope; parochial – **sectarianism** *n*, **sectarianize** *vb*

¹**section** *n* **1a** the action or an instance of (separating by) cutting; *esp* the action of dividing sthg (e g tissues) surgically ⟨caesarean ∼⟩ **b** a part separated (as if) by cutting **2** a distinct part or portion of sthg written; *esp* a subdivision of a chapter **3** the profile of sthg as it would appear if cut through by an intersecting plane **4** a sign used in printing as a mark for the beginning of a section **5** a distinct part of an area, community, or group **6** a part when considered in isolation ⟨the northern ∼ of the route⟩ **7** *sing or pl in constr* a subdivision of a platoon, troop, or battery that is the smallest tactical military unit **8** a very thin slice (e g of tissue) suitable for microscopic examination **9** any of several component parts that may be separated and reassembled ⟨a bookcase in ∼s⟩ **10** a division of an orchestra composed of 1 class of instruments **11** a printed sheet that is folded to form part (e g 8 leaves) of a book

²**section** *vt* **1** to cut or separate into sections **2** to represent in sections (e g by a drawing)

sectional *adj* **1** restricted to a particular group or locality ⟨∼ interests⟩ **2** composed of or divided into sections ⟨∼ furniture⟩ – **sectionalize** *vt*, **sectionally** *adv*

sectionalism *n* an excessive concern for the interests of a region or group

sector *n* **1** a part of a circle consisting of 2 radii and the portion of the circumference between them **2a** a portion of a military area of operation **b** a part of a field of

activity, esp of business, trade, etc ⟨employment in the public and private ∼s⟩

¹**secular** *adj* **1a** of this world rather than the heavenly or spiritual **b** not overtly or specifically religious **2** not bound by monastic vows or rules; *specif* of or being clergy not belonging to a particular religious order **3a** taking place once in an age or a century **b** surviving or recurring through ages or centuries – **secularly** *adv*, **secularity** *n*

²**secular** *n, pl* **seculars**, **secular** a layman

secularism *n* disregard for or rejection of religious beliefs and practices – **secularist** *n or adj*, **secularistic** *adj*

secularize, -ise *vt* **1** to transfer (e g property) from ecclesiastical to civil use **2** to release from monastic vows **3** to convert to or imbue with secularism – **secularizer** *n*, **secularization** *n*

¹**secure** *adj* **1a** calm in mind **b** confident in opinion or hope **2a** free from danger **b** free from risk of loss ⟨∼ employment⟩ **c** affording safety ⟨a ∼ hideaway⟩ **d** firm, dependable; *esp* firmly fastened ⟨∼ foundation⟩ **3** assured, certain ⟨when the reinforcements arrived, victory was ∼⟩ **4** *archaic* overconfident – **securely** *adv*, **secureness** *n*

²**secure** *vt* **1a** to make safe from risk or danger ⟨∼d the lid with a padlock⟩ **b** to guarantee against loss or denial ⟨a bill to ∼ the rights of strikers⟩ **c** to give pledge of payment to (a creditor) or of (an obligation) ⟨∼ a note by a pledge of collateral⟩ **2** to make fast; shut tightly ⟨∼ a door⟩ **3** to obtain or bring about, esp as the result of effort ⟨∼d a cabin for the voyage home⟩ ⟨spared no effort to ∼ his ends⟩ – **securement** *n*, **securer** *n*

security *n* **1** being secure: e g **a** freedom from danger, fear, or anxiety **b** stability, dependability **2a** sthg pledged to guarantee the fulfilment of an obligation **b** a surety **3** an evidence of debt or of ownership (e g a stock certificate) **4a** protection **b(1)** measures taken to protect against esp espionage or sabotage **(2)** *sing or pl in constr* an organization whose task is to maintain security

Security Council *n* a permanent council of the United Nations responsible for the maintenance of peace and security

sedan *n, NAm & Austr* SALOON 3

sedan chair *n* a portable often enclosed chair, esp of the 17th and 18th c, designed to seat 1 person and be carried on poles by 2 people

¹**sedate** *adj* calm and even in temper or pace – **sedately** *adv*, **sedateness** *n*

²**sedate** *vt* to give a sedative to

sedation *n* (the induction, esp with a sedative, of) a relaxed easy state

sedative *n or adj* (sthg, esp a drug) tending to calm or to tranquillize nervousness or excitement

sedentary *adj* **1** *esp of birds* not migratory **2** doing or involving much sitting ⟨a ∼ occupation⟩ **3** permanently attached ⟨∼ barnacles⟩

sedge *n* any of a family of usu tufted marsh plants differing from the related grasses esp in having solid stems – **sedgy** *adj*

sediment *n* **1** the matter that settles to the bottom of a liquid **2** material deposited by water, wind, or glaciers – **sediment** *vb*

sedimentary *adj* **1** of or containing sediment ⟨∼ deposits⟩ **2** formed by or from deposits of sediment ⟨∼ rock⟩

sedimentation *n* the forming or depositing of sediment

sedition *n* incitement to defy or rise up against lawful authority – **seditionary** *adj*

seditious *adj* **1** tending to arouse or take part in sedition;

guilty of sedition **2** of or constituting sedition – **seditiously** *adv*, **seditiousness** *n*

seduce *vt* **1** to incite to disobedience or disloyalty **2** to lead astray, *esp* by false promises **3** to effect the physical seduction of – **seducer** *n*

seduction *n* **1** the act of seducing to wrong; *specif* enticement to sexual intercourse **2** a thing or quality that attracts by its charm ⟨*the ~ of riches*⟩ ⟨*the ~s of articles in shop windows*⟩

seductive *adj* tending to seduce; alluring ⟨*a ~ woman*⟩ – **seductively** *adv*, **seductiveness** *n*

sedulous *adj* **1** involving or accomplished with steady perseverance ⟨*~ craftsmanship*⟩ **2** diligent in application or pursuit ⟨*a ~ student*⟩ *USE fml* – **sedulously** *adv*, **sedulousness** *n*

¹see *vb* **saw; seen** *vt* **1a** to perceive by the eye ⟨*looked for her but couldn't ~ her in the crowd*⟩ ⟨*saw that she was in difficulties*⟩ **b** ~ to look at; inspect ⟨*can I ~ your ticket please?*⟩ **2a** to have experience of; undergo ⟨*~ army service*⟩ ⟨*shoes that ~ a lot of wear*⟩ ⟨*a coat that has ~n better days*⟩ **b** ~ to (try to) find out or determine ⟨*~ if you can mend it*⟩ **3a** to form a mental picture of; imagine, envisage ⟨*can't ~ him objecting*⟩ **b** to regard ⟨*couldn't ~ him as a crook*⟩ **4** to perceive the meaning or importance of; understand ⟨*I ~ what you mean*⟩ ⟨*failed to ~ that it was important*⟩ ⟨*couldn't ~ the point of it*⟩ **5a** to observe, watch ⟨*want to ~ how he handles the problem*⟩ **b** to be a witness of ⟨*can't ~ her neglected*⟩ **c(1)** to read ⟨*~ page 17*⟩ **(2)** to read of ⟨*saw it in the paper*⟩ **d** to attend as a spectator ⟨*~ a play*⟩ **6** to ensure; MAKE CERTAIN **2** ⟨*~ that order is kept*⟩ **7a** to prefer to have ⟨*I'll ~ him hanged first*⟩ **b** to find acceptable or attractive ⟨*can't understand what he ~s in her*⟩ **8** of a period of time to be marked by ⟨*the 5th century saw the collapse of the Western Roman Empire*⟩ **9a** to call on; visit ⟨*~ the dentist*⟩ **b(1)** to keep company with ⟨*they've been ~ing each other regularly for some time*⟩ **(2)** to meet to a specified extent ⟨*haven't ~n much of her lately*⟩ **c** to grant an interview to ⟨*the president will ~ you*⟩ **d** to accompany, escort ⟨*~ the girls home*⟩ **10** to meet (a bet) in poker or equal the bet of (a player) ~ *vi* **1a** to have the power of sight **b** to apprehend objects by sight ⟨*too dark to ~*⟩ **2a** to give or pay attention ⟨*~ here!*⟩ **b** to look about ⟨*come to the window and ~*⟩ **3** to have knowledge ⟨*~ into the future*⟩ **4** to make investigation or inquiry; consider, deliberate ⟨*let me ~*⟩ – **see about 1** to deal with **2** to consider further ⟨*we'll see about that*⟩ – **see eye to eye** to have a common viewpoint; agree – **see fit** to consider proper or advisable ⟨*saw fit to warn him of his impending dismissal*⟩ – **see one's way to** to feel capable of – **see red** to become suddenly enraged – **see someone right** to protect and reward (a protégé) – **see someone through** to provide for, support, or help sby until the end of (a time of difficulty) ⟨*enough supplies to see us through the winter*⟩ ⟨*saw him through his divorce*⟩ – **see the light 1a** to be born **b** to be published **2** to undergo conversion – **see the wood for the trees** to grasp the total picture without being confused by detail – **see through** to grasp the true nature of; penetrate ⟨*saw through his deceptions*⟩ – **see to** to attend to; care for

²see *n* a bishopric

¹seed *n, pl* **seeds**, *esp collectively* **seed 1a(1)** the grains or ripened ovules of plants used for sowing **(2)** the fertilized ripened ovule of a (flowering) plant that contains an embryo and is capable of germination to produce a new plant **b** semen or milt **c** SPAT **2 d** the condition or stage of bearing seed ⟨*in ~*⟩ **2** a source of development or growth ⟨*sowed the ~s of discord*⟩ **3** sthg (e g a tiny particle) that resembles a seed in shape or size **4** a

competitor who has been seeded in a tournament **5** *archaic* progeny – **seed** *adj*, **seeded** *adj*, **seedless** *adj*, **seedlike** *adj* – **go/run to seed 1** to develop seed **2** to decay; *also* to become unattractive by being shabby or careless about appearance

²seed *vi* **1** to sow seed **2** *of a plant* to produce or shed seeds ~ *vt* **1a** to plant seeds in; sow **1** ⟨*~ land to grass*⟩ **b** PLANT **1a 2** to treat with solid particles to stimulate crystallization, condensation, etc; *esp* to treat (a cloud) in this way to produce rain, snow, etc **3** to extract the seeds from (e g raisins) **4** to schedule (tournament players or teams) so that superior ones will not meet in early rounds

seedbed *n* a place where sthg specified develops ⟨*the ~ of revolution*⟩

seedcake *n* a sweet cake containing aromatic seeds (e g caraway seeds)

seedling *n* **1** a plant grown from seed rather than from a cutting **2** a young plant; *esp* a nursery plant before permanent transplantation – **seedling** *adj*

seedsman *n* sby who sows or deals in seeds

seedy *adj* **1** containing or full of seeds ⟨*a ~ fruit*⟩ **2a** shabby, grubby ⟨*~ clothes*⟩ **b** somewhat disreputable; run-down ⟨*a ~ district*⟩ **c** slightly unwell – *infml* ⟨*felt ~ and went home early*⟩ – **seedily** *adv*, **seediness** *n*

seeing *conj* in view of the fact that; since – often + *that* or, in nonstandard use, *as how*

seek *vb* **sought** *vt* **1** to resort to; go to ⟨*~ the shade on a hot day*⟩ **2a** to go in search of – often + *out* **b** to try to discover ⟨*~ a solution to the problem*⟩ **3** to ask for ⟨*~s advice*⟩ **4** to try to acquire or gain ⟨*~ fame*⟩ **5** to make an effort; aim – + infinitive ⟨*~ to cater for every taste*⟩ ~ *vi* to make a search or inquiry – **seeker** *n*

seem *vi* **1** to give the impression of being ⟨*he ~s unhappy*⟩ ⟨*she ~s a bore*⟩ **2** to appear to the observation or understanding ⟨*I ~ to have caught a cold*⟩ ⟨*it ~s he lost his passport*⟩ **3** to give evidence of existing ⟨*there ~s no reason*⟩ – **not seem** somehow not ⟨*I don't seem to feel hungry*⟩ ⟨*he can't seem to lift it*⟩ – **would seem** to seem to one ⟨*it would seem to be raining*⟩

seeming *adj* apparent rather than real

seemingly *adv* **1** so far as can be seen or judged **2** to outward appearance only

seemly *adj* in accord with good taste or propriety – **seemliness** *n*

see off *vt* **1** to be present at the departure of ⟨*saw his parents off on holiday*⟩ **2** to avert, repel

see out *vt* **1** to escort to the outside (e g of a room, office, or house) **2** to last until the end of ⟨*enough fuel to see the winter out*⟩

seep *vi* to pass slowly (as if) through fine pores or small openings ⟨*water ~ed in through a crack*⟩ – **seepage** *n*

seer *n* **1a** sby who predicts future events **b** sby credited with exceptional moral and spiritual insight **2** sby who practises divination

seersucker *n* a light slightly puckered fabric of linen, cotton, or rayon

¹seesaw *n* **1** an alternating up-and-down or backwards-and-forwards movement; *also* anything (e g a process or movement) that alternates ⟨*a ~ of shame and defiance*⟩ **2** (a game in which 2 or more children ride on opposite ends of) a plank balanced in the middle so that one end goes up as the other goes down – **seesaw** *adj or adv*

²seesaw *vi* **1a** to move backwards and forwards or up and down **b** to play at seesaw **2a** to alternate **b** to vacillate ~ *vt* to cause to move with a seesaw motion

seethe *vi* **1a** to be in a state of agitated usu confused movement **b** to churn or foam as if boiling **2** to feel or express violent emotion ⟨*he ~d with rage*⟩

see-through *adj* transparent

see through *vt* to undergo or endure to the end ⟨*bravely saw the fight* through⟩

¹segment *n* **1a** a separated piece of sthg ⟨*chop the stalks into short* ∼s⟩ **b** any of the constituent parts into which a body, entity, or quantity is divided or marked off ⟨*all* ∼s *of the population agree*⟩ **2** a portion cut off from a geometrical figure by 1 or more points, lines, or planes: e g **a** a part of a circular area bounded by a chord of that circle and the arc subtended by it **b** a part of a sphere cut off by a plane or included between 2 parallel planes **c** the part of a line between 2 points in the line – **segmentary** *adj*, **segmental** *adj*

²segment *vt* to separate into segments

segmentation *n* the formation of many cells from a single cell (e g in a developing egg)

segregate *vt* **1** to separate or set apart **2** to cause or force separation of (e g criminals from society) or in (e g a community) ∼ *vi* **1** to withdraw **2** to undergo (genetic) segregation – **segregative** *adj*

segregated *adj* **1** set apart from others of the same kind **2** administered separately for different groups or races ⟨∼ *education*⟩

segregation *n* **1a** the separation or isolation of a race, class, or ethnic group **b** the separation for special treatment or observation of individuals or items from a larger group ⟨*the* ∼ *of political prisoners from common criminals*⟩ **2** the separation of pairs of genes controlling the same hereditary characteristic, that occurs during meiotic cell division – **segregationist** *n*

seigneur *n* a feudal lord

seine *vb or n* (to catch with, fish in with, or use) a large net with weights on one edge and floats on the other that hangs vertically in the water and is used to enclose fish when its ends are pulled together or drawn ashore

seismic, seismal *adj* **1** of or caused by an earth vibration, specif an earthquake **2** of a vibration on the moon or other celestial body comparable to a seismic event on earth – **seismicity** *n*

seismograph *n* an apparatus to measure and record earth tremors – **seismographer** *n*, **seismography** *n*, **seismographic** *adj*

seismology *n* a science that deals with earth vibrations, esp earthquakes – **seismologist** *n*, **seismological** *adj*

seize *vt* **1** *also* **seise** /∼/ to put in possession of **2** to confiscate, esp by legal authority **3a** to take possession of by force **b** to take prisoner **4** to take hold of abruptly or eagerly ⟨∼d *his arm and pulled him clear of the fire*⟩ **5a** to attack or afflict physically ⟨∼d *with an attack of arthritis*⟩ **b** to possess (the mind) completely or overwhelmingly **6** to bind or fasten together with a lashing of cord or twine ∼ *vi* **1** to lay hold of sthg suddenly, forcibly, or eagerly – usu + *on* or *upon* ⟨∼d *on her idea for a new TV series*⟩ **2a** of brakes, pistons, *etc* to become jammed through excessive pressure, temperature, or friction – often + *up* **b** *of an engine* to fail to operate owing to the seizing of a part

seizure *n* **1** the taking possession of sby or sthg by legal process **2** a sudden attack (e g of disease)

¹seldom *adv* in few instances; rarely, infrequently

²seldom *adj* rare, infrequent

¹select *adj* **1** picked out in preference to others **2a** of special value or quality **b** exclusively or fastidiously chosen, esp on the basis of social characteristics ⟨*a* ∼ *membership*⟩ **3** judicious in choice ⟨∼ *appreciation*⟩ – **selectness** *n*

²select *vt* to take according to preference from among a number; pick out ∼ *vi* to make a selection or choice

select committee *n* a temporary committee of a legislative body, established to examine 1 particular matter

selection *n* **1** sby or sthg selected; *also* a collection of selected items **2** a range of things from which to choose **3** a natural or artificially imposed process that results in the survival and propagation only of organisms with desired or suitable attributes so that their heritable characteristics only are perpetuated in succeeding generations

selective *adj* of or characterized by selection; selecting or tending to select – **selectively** *adv*, **selectiveness** *n*, **selectivity** *n*

selective service *n*, *NAm* a system under which people are called up for military service

selector *n*, *Br* sby who chooses the members of a sports team

selenium *n* a nonmetallic solid element resembling sulphur and tellurium chemically, 1 form of which varies in electrical conductivity under the influence of light and is used in electronic devices (e g solar cells) – **selenic** *adj*

¹self *pron* myself, himself, herself

²self *adj* identical throughout, esp in colour

³self *n, pl* **selves 1** the entire being of an individual **2** a (part or aspect of a) person's individual character ⟨*his true* ∼ *was revealed*⟩ **3** the body, emotions, thoughts, sensations, etc that constitute the individuality and identity of a person **4** personal interest, advantage, or welfare ⟨*took no thought of* ∼⟩

self- *comb form* **1a** oneself; itself ⟨self-*supporting*⟩ **b** of oneself or itself ⟨self-*abasement*⟩ **c** by oneself or itself ⟨self-*propelled*⟩ ⟨self-*made*⟩ ⟨self-*starting*⟩ **2a** to, with, for, or in oneself or itself ⟨self-*confident*⟩ ⟨self-*addressed*⟩ ⟨self-*love*⟩ **b** of or in oneself or itself inherently ⟨self-*evident*⟩ ⟨self-*explanatory*⟩

self-absorbed *adj* preoccupied with one's own thoughts, activities, or welfare – **self-absorption** *n*

self-abuse *n* masturbation

self-addressed *adj* addressed for return to the sender ⟨*a* ∼ *envelope*⟩

self-assertion *n* the act of asserting oneself or one's own rights, claims, or opinions, esp aggressively or conceitedly – **self-assertive** *adj*

self-assurance *n* self-confidence

self-centred *adj* concerned excessively with one's own desires or needs

self-coloured *adj* of a single colour ⟨*a* ∼ *flower*⟩

self-command *n* self-control

self-confessed *adj* openly acknowledged ⟨*a* ∼ *debauchee*⟩

self-confidence *n* confidence in oneself and one's powers and abilities – **self-confident** *adj*

self-conscious *adj* **1a** conscious of oneself as a possessor of mental states and originator of actions **b** intensely aware of oneself as an object of notice **2** uncomfortably conscious of oneself as an object of notice; ill at ease – **self-consciously** *adv*, **self-consciousness** *n*

self-contained *adj* **1** complete in itself ⟨*a* ∼ *flat*⟩ **2a** showing self-possession **b** formal and reserved in manner – **self-containedly** *adv*

self-contradiction *n* **1** contradiction of oneself **2** a statement that contains 2 contradictory elements or ideas – **self-contradictory** *adj*

self-control *n* restraint of one's own impulses or emotions – **self-controlled** *adj*

self-defeating *adj* having the effect of preventing its own success

self-defence *n* **1** the act of defending or justifying oneself **2** the legal right to defend oneself with reasonable force – **self-defensive** *adj*

self-denial n the restraint or limitation of one's desires or their gratification

self-denying adj showing self-denial

self-determination n 1 free choice of one's own actions or states without outside influence 2 determination by a territorial unit of its own political status – **self-determined** adj, **self-determining** adj

self-discipline n the act of disciplining or power to discipline one's thoughts and actions, usu for the sake of improvement – **self-disciplined** adj

self-drive adj, chiefly Br, of a hired vehicle intended to be driven by the hirer

self-effacement n the act of making oneself inconspicuous, esp because of modesty; humility – **self-effacing** adj, **self-effacingly** adv

self-employed adj earning income directly from one's own business, trade, or profession rather than as salary or wages from an employer – **self-employment** n

self-esteem n 1 confidence and satisfaction in oneself; self-respect 2 vanity

self-evident adj requiring no proof; obvious – **self-evidence** n, **self-evidently** adv

self-examination n the analysis of one's conduct, motives, etc

self-explanatory adj capable of being understood without explanation

self-governing adj having control over oneself; specif having self-government

self-government n control of one's own (political) affairs

self-help n the bettering or helping of oneself without dependence on others

self-importance n 1 an exaggerated sense of one's own importance 2 arrogant or pompous behaviour – **self-important** adj

self-indulgence n excessive or unrestrained gratification of one's own appetites, desires, or whims – **self-indulgent** adj

self-interest n (a concern for) one's own advantage and well-being ⟨acted out of ~ and fear⟩ – **self-interested** adj

selfish adj concerned with or directed towards one's own advantage, pleasure, or well-being without regard for others – **selfishly** adv, **selfishness** n

selfless adj having no concern for self; unselfish – **selflessly** adv, **selflessness** n

self-made adj raised from poverty or obscurity by one's own efforts ⟨a ~ man⟩

self-opinionated adj 1 conceited 2 stubbornly holding to one's own opinion; opinionated

self-pity n a self-indulgent dwelling on one's own sorrows or misfortunes – **self-pitying** adj

self-possessed adj having or showing self-possession; composed in mind or manner; calm – **self-possessedly** adv

self-possession n control of one's emotions or behaviour, esp when under stress; composure

self-preservation n an instinctive tendency to act so as to safeguard one's own existence

self-raising flour n a commercially prepared mixture of flour containing a raising agent

self-reliance n reliance on one's own efforts and abilities; independence – **self-reliant** adj

self-respect n a proper respect for one's human dignity

self-respecting adj having or characterized by self-respect or integrity

self-righteous adj assured of one's own righteousness, esp in contrast with the actions and beliefs of others;

narrow-mindedly moralistic – **self-righteously** adv, **self-righteousness** n

self-sacrifice n sacrifice of oneself or one's well-being for the sake of an ideal or for the benefit of others – **self-sacrificing** adj

selfsame adj precisely the same; identical ⟨he left the ~ day⟩

self-satisfaction n a smug satisfaction with oneself or one's position or achievements

self-satisfied adj feeling or showing self-satisfaction ⟨a ~ smile⟩

self-seeker n sby self-seeking

self-seeking adj seeking only to safeguard or further one's own interests; selfish – **self-seeking** n

self-service n the serving of oneself (e g in a cafeteria or supermarket) with things to be paid for at a cashier's desk, usu upon leaving – **self-service** adj

self-sow vi **self-sown, self-sowed** of a plant to grow from seeds spread naturally (e g by wind or water)

self-starter n an electric motor used to start an internal-combustion engine

self-styled adj called by oneself, esp without justification ⟨~ experts⟩

self-sufficient adj 1 able to maintain oneself or itself without outside aid; capable of providing for one's own needs ⟨a community ~ in dairy products⟩ 2 having unwarranted assurance of one's own ability or worth – **self-sufficiency** n

self-supporting adj 1 meeting one's needs by one's own labour or income 2 supporting itself or its own weight ⟨a ~ wall⟩

self-will n stubborn or wilful adherence to one's own desires or ideas; obstinacy – **self-willed** adj

self-winding adj not needing to be wound by hand ⟨a ~ watch⟩

¹**sell** vb **sold** vt 1 to deliver or give up in violation of duty, trust, or loyalty; betray – often + out **2a**(1) to give up (property) in exchange, esp for money (2) to offer for sale ⟨~s insurance⟩ **b** to give up or dispose of foolishly or dishonourably (in return for sthg else) ⟨juries who sold the verdicts⟩ 3 to cause or promote the sale of ⟨advertising ~s newspapers⟩ 4 to achieve a sale of ⟨a book which sold a million copies⟩ **5a** to make acceptable, believable, or desirable by persuasion ⟨~ an idea⟩ **b** to persuade to accept or enjoy sthg – usu + on; infml ⟨~ children on reading⟩ 6 to deceive, cheat – usu pass; infml ⟨we've been sold!⟩ ~ vi 1 to transfer sthg to another's ownership by sale 2 to achieve a sale; also to achieve satisfactory sales ⟨hoped that the new line would ~⟩ 3 to have a specified price – + at or for – **sellable** adj – **sell down the river** to betray the faith of

²**sell** n 1 the act or an instance of selling 2 a deliberate deception; a hoax – infml

seller n a product offered for sale and selling well, to a specified extent, or in a specified manner ⟨a million-copy ~⟩ ⟨a poor ~⟩

seller's market n a market in which demand exceeds supply

sell off vt to dispose of completely by selling, esp at a reduced price

sellotape vt to fix (as if) with Sellotape

Sellotape trademark – used for a usu transparent adhesive tape

sell-out n 1 a performance, exhibition, or contest for which all tickets or seats are sold 2 a betrayal – infml

sell out vt 1 to dispose of entirely by sale 2 to betray or be unfaithful to (e g one's cause or associates), esp for the sake of money ~ vi 1 SELL UP 2 to betray one's cause or associates – usu + on

sell up *vb, chiefly Br* to sell (e g one's house or business) in a conclusive or forced transaction ⟨sold up *and emigrated to Australia*⟩

selvage, selvedge *n* **1a** the edge on either side of a (woven) fabric, so finished as to prevent unravelling; *specif* a narrow border often of different or heavier threads than the fabric and sometimes in a different weave **b** an edge (e g of wallpaper) meant to be cut off and discarded **2** a border, edge

selves *pl of* SELF

semantic *adj* of meaning in language – **semantically** *adv*

semantics *n pl but sing or pl in constr* **1** the branch of linguistics concerned with meaning **2** a branch of semiotics dealing with the relation between signs and the objects they refer to – **semanticist** *n*

¹**semaphore** *n* **1** an apparatus for conveying information by visual signals (e g by the position of 1 or more pivoted arms) **2** a system of visual signalling by 2 flags held 1 in each hand

²**semaphore** *vt* to convey (information) (as if) by semaphore ∼ *vi* to send signals (as if) by semaphore

semblance *n* outward and often deceptive appearance; a show ⟨wrapped in a ∼ of euphoria⟩

semen *n* a suspension of spermatozoa produced by the male reproductive glands that is conveyed to the female reproductive tract during coitus

semester *n* an academic term lasting half a year, esp in America and Germany

semi *n, Br* a semidetached house – *infml*

semi- *prefix* **1a** precisely half of **b** forming a bisection of ⟨semi*ellipse*⟩ ⟨semi*oval*⟩ **c** occurring halfway through (a specified period of time) ⟨semi*annual*⟩ ⟨semi*centenary*⟩ **2** to some extent; partly; incompletely ⟨semi*civilized*⟩ ⟨semi-*independent*⟩ ⟨semi*dry*⟩ ⟨semi*acid*⟩ **3a** partial; incomplete ⟨semi*consciousness*⟩ ⟨semi*darkness*⟩ **b** having some of the characteristics of ⟨semi*porcelain*⟩ ⟨semi*metal*⟩ **c** quasi ⟨semi*judicial*⟩ ⟨semi*governmental*⟩ ⟨semi*monastic*⟩

semibreve *n* a musical note with the time value of 2 minims or 4 crotchets

semicircle *n* (an object or arrangement in the form of) a half circle – **semicircular** *adj*

semicolon *n* a punctuation mark ; used chiefly to coordinate major sentence elements where there is no conjunction

semiconductor *n* a substance (e g silicon) whose electrical conductivity at room temperature is between that of a conductor and that of an insulator

semidetached *adj* forming 1 of a pair of residences joined into 1 building by a common wall – **semidetached** *n*

¹**semifinal** *adj* **1** next to the last in a knockout competition **2** of or participating in a semifinal

²**semifinal** *n* a semifinal match or round – often pl with sing. meaning – **semifinalist** *n*

seminal *adj* **1** (consisting) of, storing, or conveying seed or semen ⟨∼ duct⟩ ⟨∼ vesicle⟩ **2** containing or contributing the seeds of future development; original and influential ⟨a ∼ book⟩ ⟨one of the most ∼ of the great poets⟩ – **seminally** *adv*

seminar *n* **1** an advanced or graduate class often featuring informality and discussion **2** a meeting for exchanging and discussing information

seminarist *n* a seminarian

seminary *n* **1** an institution of education **2** an institution for the training of candidates for the (Roman Catholic) priesthood

semiology, semeiology *n* the study of signs; *esp* semiotics – **semiological** *adj*

semiotics *n pl but sing or pl in constr* a general philosophical theory of signs and symbols that includes syntactics and semantics – **semiotic** *adj*

semiprecious *adj, of a gemstone* of less commercial value than a precious stone

semiquaver *n* a musical note with time value of 1₂ of a quaver

¹**Semitic** *adj* **1** of or characteristic of the Semites; *specif* Jewish **2** of a branch of the Afro-Asiatic language family that includes Hebrew, Aramaic, Arabic, and Ethiopic

²**Semitic** *n* (any of) the Semitic languages

semitone *n* the musical interval (e g E–F or F–F) equal to the interval between 2 adjacent keys on a keyboard instrument – **semitonic** *adj*

semitropical *adj* subtropical

semivowel *n* (a letter representing) a speech sound (e g /y/ or /w/) intermediate between vowel and consonant

semiweekly *adj or adv* appearing or taking place twice a week ⟨a ∼ news bulletin⟩

semolina *n* the purified hard parts left after milling of (hard) wheat used for pasta and in milk puddings

sempstress *n* a seamstress

senate *n sing or pl in constr* **1a** the supreme council of the ancient Roman republic and empire **b** the 2nd chamber in some legislatures that consist of 2 houses **2** the governing body of some universities

senator *n* a member of a senate – **senatorial** *adj*, **senatorship** *n*

¹**send** *vb* **sent** *vt* **1** to direct or cause to go in a specified direction, esp violently ⟨sent *a blow to his chin*⟩ ⟨the crash sent *them scuttling out of their houses*⟩ **2** of God, fate, etc to cause to be; grant; BRING ABOUT ⟨∼ her victorious⟩ **3** to dispatch by a means of communication ⟨∼ a telegram⟩ **4a** to cause, direct, order, or request to go ⟨sent *her to buy some milk*⟩ **b** to dismiss ⟨was sent home⟩ **5** to cause to assume a specified state ⟨sent him into a rage⟩ **6** to cause to issue: e g **a** to pour out; discharge ⟨clouds ∼ing forth rain⟩ **b** to utter ⟨∼ forth a cry⟩ **c** to emit ⟨sent out waves of perfume⟩ **d** to grow out (parts) in the course of development ⟨a plant ∼ing forth shoots⟩ **7** to consign to a destination (e g death or a place of imprisonment) **8** to delight, thrill – *infml* ⟨that music really ∼s me⟩ ∼ *vi* **1a** to convey a message or do an errand ⟨∼ out for coffee⟩ **b** to dispatch a request or order ⟨have to ∼ to Germany for spares⟩ **2** to scend **3** to transmit – **sender** *n* – **send for** to request by message to come; summon – **send packing** to dismiss roughly or in disgrace

²**send** *n* a scend

send down *vt, Br* **1** to suspend or expel from a university **2** to send to jail – *infml*

send in *vt* **1** to cause to be delivered to an authority, group, or organization ⟨send *in a letter of complaint*⟩ **2** to assign with a view to tackling a crisis or difficulty ⟨send *a receiver* in *to deal with the bankruptcy*⟩

send-off *n* a usu enthusiastic demonstration of goodwill at the beginning of a venture (e g a trip)

send off *vt* **1** to dispatch **2** to attend to the departure of

send on *vt* **1** to dispatch (e g luggage) in advance **2** to forward (readdressed mail)

send out *vt* **1** to issue for circulation ⟨had sent *the invitations* out⟩ **2** to dispatch (e g an order) from a shop or place of storage

send-up *n, Br* a satirical imitation, esp on stage or television; a parody

send up vt 1 chiefly Br to make an object of mockery or laughter; ridicule 2 chiefly NAm SEND DOWN 2

senescence n being or becoming old or withered – senesce vi, senescent adj

seneschal n the agent or bailiff of a feudal lord's estate

senile adj of, exhibiting, or characteristic of (the mental or physical weakness associated with) old age – senility n

¹senior n 1 sby who is older than another ⟨5 years his ~⟩ 2a sby of higher standing or rank b NAm a student in the final year before graduation from school, university, etc

²senior adj 1 elder – used, chiefly in the USA, to distinguish a father with the same name as his son 2 higher in standing or rank ⟨~ officers⟩

senior citizen n sby beyond the usual age of retirement – euph

seniority n a privileged status attained by length of continuous service (e g in a company)

senna n (the dried leaflets or pods, used as a purgative, of) any of a genus of leguminous plants, shrubs, and trees of warm regions

senor, señor n, pl senors, señores a Spanish-speaking man – used as a title equivalent to Mr or as a generalized term of direct address

senora, señora n a married Spanish-speaking woman – used as a title equivalent to Mrs or as a generalized term of direct address

senorita, señorita n an unmarried Spanish-speaking girl or woman – used as a title equivalent to Miss

sensation n 1a a mental process (e g seeing or hearing) resulting from stimulation of a sense organ b a state of awareness of a usu specified type resulting from internal bodily conditions or external factors; a feeling or sense ⟨~s of fatigue⟩ 2a a surge of intense interest or excitement ⟨their elopement caused a ~⟩ b a cause of such excitement; esp sby or sthg in some respect remarkable or outstanding

sensational adj 1 arousing an immediate, intense, and usu superficial interest or emotional reaction 2 exceptionally or unexpectedly excellent or impressive – infml – sensationalize vt, sensationally adv

sensationalism n the use of sensational subject matter or style – sensationalist n

¹sense n 1 a meaning conveyed or intended; esp any of a range of meanings a word or phrase may bear, esp as isolated in a dictionary entry 2 (the faculty of perceiving the external world or internal bodily conditions by means of) any of the senses of feeling, hearing, sight, smell, taste, etc 3 soundness of mind or judgment – usu pl with sing. meaning ⟨when he came to his ~s he was shocked to hear what he had done⟩ 4a an ability to use the senses for a specified purpose ⟨a good ~ of balance⟩ b a definite but often vague awareness or impression ⟨felt a ~ of insecurity⟩ c an awareness that motivates action or judgment ⟨done out of a ~ of justice⟩ d a capacity for discernment and appreciation ⟨her ~ of humour⟩ ⟨a highly-developed critical ~⟩ 5 the prevailing view; a consensus ⟨the ~ of the meeting⟩ 6 an ability to put the mind to effective use; practical intelligence 7 either of 2 opposite directions (of motion)

²sense vt 1a to perceive by the senses b to be or become conscious of ⟨~ danger⟩ 2 to grasp, comprehend ⟨~ the import of a remark⟩ 3 to detect (e g a symbol or radiation) automatically

senseless adj deprived of, deficient in, or contrary to sense: e g a unconscious ⟨knocked ~⟩ b foolish, stupid ⟨it was some ~ practical joke – A Conan Doyle⟩ c

meaningless, purposeless ⟨a ~ murder⟩ – senselessly adv, senselessness n

sense organ n a bodily structure that responds to a stimulus (e g heat or sound waves) by initiating impulses in nerves that convey them to the central nervous system where they are interpreted as sensations

sensibility n 1 ability to have sensations ⟨tactile ~⟩ 2 heightened susceptibility to feelings of pleasure or pain (e g in response to praise or blame) – often pl with sing. meaning ⟨a man of strong sensibilities⟩ 3 the ability to discern and respond freely to sthg (e g emotion in another) 4 (exaggerated) sensitiveness in feelings and tastes

sensible adj 1 capable of sensing ⟨~ to pain⟩ 2 having, containing, or indicative of good sense or sound reason ⟨~ men⟩ ⟨made a ~ answer⟩ 3a perceptible to the senses or to understanding ⟨his distress was ~ from his manner⟩ b large enough to be observed or noticed; considerable ⟨a ~ decrease⟩ 4 aware, conscious of USE (3 & 4) fml – sensibleness n, sensibly adv

sensitive adj 1 capable of being stimulated or excited by external agents (e g light, gravity, or contact) ⟨a photographic emulsion ~ to red light⟩ 2 highly responsive or susceptible: e g a(1) easily provoked or hurt emotionally (2) finely aware of the attitudes and feelings of others or of the subtleties of a work of art b hypersensitive ⟨~ to egg protein⟩ c capable of registering minute differences; delicate ⟨~ scales⟩ d readily affected or changed by external agents (e g light or chemical stimulation) e of a radio receiving set highly responsive to incoming waves 3 concerned with highly classified information ⟨a ~ document⟩ – sensitively adv, sensitiveness n, sensitivity n

sensitize, -ise vb to make or become sensitive or hypersensitive – sensitizer n, sensitization n

sensor n a device that responds to heat, light, sound, pressure, magnetism, etc and transmits a resulting impulse (e g for measurement or operating a control)

sensory adj of sensation or the senses

sensual adj 1 sensory 2 relating to or consisting in the gratification of the senses or the indulgence of appetites 3a devoted to or preoccupied with the senses or appetites, rather than the intellect or spirit b voluptuous – sensualism n, sensualist n, sensualize vt, sensually adv, sensuality n

sensuous adj 1a of (objects perceived by) the senses b providing or characterized by gratification of the senses; appealing strongly to the senses ⟨~ pleasure⟩ 2 suggesting or producing rich imagery or sense impressions ⟨~ verse⟩ 3 readily influenced by sense perception – sensuously adv, sensuousness n, sensuosity n

sent past of SEND

¹sentence n 1a a judgment formally pronounced by a court and specifying a punishment b the punishment so imposed ⟨serve a ~⟩ 2 a grammatically self-contained speech unit that expresses an assertion, a question, a command, a wish, or an exclamation and is usu shown in writing with a capital letter at the beginning and with appropriate punctuation at the end – sentential adj

²sentence vt 1 to impose a judicial sentence on 2 to consign to a usu unpleasant fate ⟨development that ~s rural industries to extinction⟩

sententious adj 1 terse, pithy 2 given to or full of a terse or pithy sayings b pompous moralizing – sententiously adv, sententiousness n

sentient adj 1 capable of perceiving through the senses; conscious 2 keenly sensitive in perception or feeling USE chiefly fml – sentiently adv

sentiment n 1a (an attitude, thought, or judgment prompted or coloured by) feeling or emotion b a specific view or attitude; an opinion – usu pl with sing. meaning

⟨*held similar* ~s *on the matter*⟩ **2a** sensitive feeling; refined sensibility, esp as expressed in a work of art **b** indulgently romantic or nostalgic feeling **3** the emotional significance of a communication as distinguished from its overt meaning ⟨*the* ~ *is admirable, though it is clumsily expressed*⟩

sentimental *adj* **1** resulting from feeling rather than reason ⟨*kept the gift for its* ~ *value*⟩ **2** having an excess of superficial sentiment – **sentimentalism** *n*, **sentimentalist** *n*, **sentimentalize** *vb*, **sentimentally** *adv*, **sentimentality** *n*

¹**sentinel** *n* sby who or sthg that keeps guard

²**sentinel** *vt* **-ll-** (*NAm* **-l-, -ll-**) **1** to watch over as a sentinel **2** to post as a sentinel

sentry *n* a guard, watch; *esp* a soldier standing guard at a gate, door, etc

sentry box *n* a shelter for a standing sentry

sepal *n* any of the modified leaves comprising the calyx of a flower – **sepaloid** *adj*

separable *adj* capable of being separated or dissociated – **separableness** *n*, **separably** *adv*, **separability** *n*

¹**separate** *vt* **1a** to set or keep apart; detach, divide **b** to make a distinction between; distinguish ⟨~ *religion from magic*⟩ **c** to disperse in space or time; scatter ⟨*widely* ~d *hamlets*⟩ **2** to part (a married couple) by separation **3** to isolate, segregate **4a** to isolate from a mixture or compound ⟨~ *cream from milk*⟩ **b** to divide into constituent parts or types **5** *NAm* to discharge ⟨*was* ~d *from the army*⟩ ~ *vi* **1** to become divided or detached; draw or come apart **2a** to sever an association; withdraw ⟨~ *from a federation*⟩ **b** to cease to live together as man and wife, esp by formal arrangement **3** to go in different directions **4** to become isolated from a mixture *USE* (*vt* 4; *vi* 4) often + **out** – **separative** *adj*

²**separate** *adj* **1** set or kept apart; detached, separated **2** not shared with another; individual ⟨~ *rooms*⟩ **3a** existing independently; autonomous **b** different in kind; distinct ⟨*6* ~ *ways of cooking an egg*⟩ – **separately** *adv*, **separateness** *n*

separation *n* **1a** a point, line, or means of division **b** an intervening space; a gap, break **2** cessation of cohabitation between husband and wife by mutual agreement or judicial decree

separatism *n* a belief or movement advocating separation (e g schism, secession, or segregation)

separator *n* a device for separating liquids of different specific gravities (e g cream from milk) or liquids from solids

¹**sepia** *n* **1** (a brown melanin-containing pigment from) the inky secretion of cuttlefishes **2** rich dark brown

²**sepia** *adj* **1** of the colour sepia **2** made of or done in sepia ⟨*a* ~ *print*⟩

sepoy *n* an Indian soldier employed by a European power, esp Britain

sepsis *n*, *pl* **sepses** the spread of bacteria from a focus of infection; *esp* septicaemia

September *n* the 9th month of the Gregorian calendar

septet *n* **1** a musical composition for 7 instruments, voices, or performers **2** *sing or pl in constr* a group or set of 7; *esp* the performers of a septet

septic *adj* **1** putrefactive **2** relating to, involving, or characteristic of sepsis

septicaemia *n* invasion of the bloodstream by microorganisms from a focus of infection with chills, fever, etc

septic tank *n* a tank in which the solid matter of continuously flowing sewage is disintegrated by bacteria

septuagenarian *n* sby between 70 and 79 years old – **septuagenarian** *adj*

Septuagesima *n* the third Sunday before Lent

Septuagint *n* a pre-Christian Greek version of the Jewish Scriptures arranged and edited by Jewish scholars about 300 BC

sepulchral *adj* **1** of the burial of the dead **2** suited to or suggestive of a tomb; funereal ⟨*a* ~ *whisper*⟩ – **sepulchrally** *adv*

sepulchre, *NAm chiefly* **sepulcher** *n* **1** a place of burial; a tomb **2** a receptacle (in an altar) for religious relics

sequel *n* **1** a consequence, result **2a** subsequent development or course of events **b** a play, film, or literary work continuing the course of a narrative begun in a preceding one

¹**sequence** *n* **1** a continuous or connected series: e g **a** an extended series of poems united by theme ⟨*a sonnet* ~⟩ **b** RUN 3f **c** a succession of repetitions of a melodic phrase or harmonic pattern each in a new position **d** a set of elements following the same order as the natural numbers **e** an episode, esp in a film **2a** order of succession **b** the order of amino acids in a protein, nucleotide bases in DNA or RNA, etc **3** a subsequent but not resultant occurrence or course **4** a continuous progression

²**sequence** *vt* **1** to place in ordered sequence **2** to determine the amino acid sequence of (a protein), nucleotide sequence of (a nucleic acid), etc – **sequencer** *n*

sequent *adj* **1** consecutive, succeeding **2** consequent, resultant *USE* fml

sequential *adj* **1** of or arranged in a sequence; serial ⟨~ *file systems*⟩ **2** following in sequence – **sequentially** *adv*

sequester *vt* **1a** to set apart; segregate **b** to seclude, withdraw ⟨~ *oneself from urban life*⟩ ⟨*a quiet* ~ed *spot*⟩ **2** to seize (e g a debtor's property) judicially **3** to chelate

sequestrate *vt* SEQUESTER 2 – **sequestration** *n*

sequin *n* **1** a former gold coin of Italy and Turkey **2** a very small disc of shining metal or plastic used for ornamentation, esp on clothing

sequoia *n* either of 2 huge coniferous Californian trees: **a** BIG TREE **b** a redwood

seraglio *n*, *pl* **seraglios** HAREM 1a

seraph *n*, *pl* **seraphim, seraphs** any of the 6-winged angels standing in the presence of God – **seraphic** *adj*

¹**sere, sear** *adj* shrivelled, withered – chiefly poetic

²**sere** *n* a series of successive ecological communities established in 1 area – **seral** *adj*

¹**serenade** *n* **1** a complimentary vocal or instrumental performance (given outdoors at night for a woman) **2** an instrumental composition in several movements written for a small ensemble

²**serenade** *vb* to perform a serenade (in honour of) – **serenader** *n*

serendipity *n* the faculty of discovering pleasing or valuable things by chance – **serendipitous** *adj*

serene *adj* **1** free of storms or adverse changes; clear, fine ⟨~ *skies*⟩ ⟨~ *weather*⟩ **2** having or showing tranquillity and peace of mind ⟨*a* ~ *smile*⟩ – **serenely** *adv*, **sereneness** *n*, **serenity** *n*

serf *n* a member of a class of agricultural labourers in a feudal society, bound in service to a lord, and esp transferred with the land they worked if its ownership changed hands – **serfage** *n*, **serfdom** *n*

serge *n* a durable twilled fabric having a smooth clear face and a pronounced diagonal rib on the front and the back

sergeant *n* **1** a police officer ranking in Britain between constable and inspector **2** a high-ranking noncommissioned officer in the army, airforce, or marines

sergeant-at-arms *n*, *pl* **sergeants-at-arms** *often cap* S&A

an officer attending the British Speaker or Lord Chancellor; *also* a similar officer in other legislatures

sergeant major *n, pl* **sergeant majors, sergeants major** **1** a noncommissioned officer of the highest rank in the US army or marine corps **2** a warrant officer in the British army or Royal Marines

¹serial *adj* **1** of or constituting a series, rank, or row ⟨~ *order*⟩ **2** appearing in successive instalments ⟨*a* ~ *story*⟩ **3** of or being music based on a series of notes in an arbitrary but fixed order without regard for traditional tonality ⟨~ *technique*⟩ – **serially** *adv*

²serial *n* **1** a work appearing (e g in a magazine or on television) in parts at usu regular intervals **2** a publication issued as 1 of a consecutively numbered continuing series – **serialist** *n*

serialize, -ise *vt* to arrange or publish in serial form – **serialization** *n*

serial number *n* a number used as a means of identification that indicates position in a series

seriatim *adv or adj* in regular order

sericulture *n* the production of raw silk by breeding silkworms – **sericultural** *adj*, **sericulturist** *n*

series *n, pl* **series** **1** a number of things or events of the same kind following one another in spatial or temporal succession ⟨*a concert* ~⟩ ⟨*the hall opened into a* ~ *of small rooms*⟩; *broadly* any group of systematically related items **2** a usu infinite mathematical sequence whose terms are to be added together **3** the coins or currency of a particular country and period **4** a succession of issues of volumes published with continuous numbering or usu related subjects or authors and format **5** a division of rock formations that is smaller than a system and comprises rocks deposited during an epoch **6** a group of chemical compounds or elements related in structure and properties **7** an arrangement of devices in an electrical circuit in which the whole current passes through each device **8** a number of games (e g of cricket) played between 2 teams ⟨*a 5-match* ~ *between England and Australia*⟩

serif *n* a short line stemming from the stroke of a letter – **seriffed** *adj*

seriocomic *adj* having a mixture of the serious and the comic – **seriocomically** *adv*

serious *adj* **1** grave or thoughtful in appearance or manner; sober **2a** requiring careful attention and concentration ⟨~ *study*⟩ **b** of or relating to a weighty or important matter ⟨*a* ~ *play*⟩ **3a** not jesting or deceiving; in earnest **b** deeply interested or committed ⟨~ *fishermen*⟩ **4** having important or dangerous consequences; critical ⟨*a* ~ *injury*⟩ – **seriousness** *n*

seriously *adv* **1a** in a sincere manner; earnestly **b** to speak in a serious way ⟨~, *you should be more careful*⟩ **2** to a serious extent; severely ⟨~ *injured*⟩

sermon *n* **1** a religious discourse delivered in public, usu by a clergyman as a part of a religious service **2** a speech on conduct or duty; *esp* one that is unduly long or tedious

sermonize, -ise *vi* to give moral advice in an officious or dogmatic manner – **sermonizer** *n*

serpent *n* **1** a (large) snake **2** *the* Devil **3** a wily treacherous person **4** an old-fashioned bass woodwind instrument of serpentine form

¹serpentine *adj* **1** of or like a serpent (e g in form or movement) **2** subtly tempting; wily, artful **3** winding or turning one way and another

²serpentine *n* sthg wavy or winding; *specif* a serpentine movement in dressage

³serpentine *n* a usu dull green mottled mineral consisting mainly of hydrated magnesium silicate

¹serrate *vt* to mark or provide with serrations

²serrate *adj* notched or having (forwards-pointing) teeth on the edge ⟨*a* ~ *leaf*⟩

serration *n* **1** a formation resembling the teeth of a saw **2** any of the teeth of a serrated edge

serried *adj* crowded or pressed together; compact ⟨*the crowd collected in a* ~ *mass* – W S Maugham⟩

serum *n, pl* **serums, sera** the watery part of an animal liquid (remaining after coagulation): **a** blood serum, esp when containing specific antibodies **b** whey – **serous** *adj*

serum hepatitis *n* an often fatal inflammation of the liver caused by a virus that is contracted esp by contact with an infected person's blood

serval *n* a long-legged long-eared African wildcat with a tawny black-spotted coat

servant *n* sby who or sthg that serves others; *specif* sby employed to perform personal or domestic duties for another

¹serve *vi* **1a** to act as a servant **b** to do military or naval service **2** to act as server at Mass **3a** to be of use; fulfil a specified purpose – often + *as* **b** to be favourable, opportune, or convenient ⟨*told the story whenever occasion* ~ *d*⟩ **c** to prove reliable or trustworthy ⟨*it was last year, if memory* ~*s*⟩ **d** to hold a post or office; discharge a duty ⟨~ *on a jury*⟩ **4** to prove adequate or satisfactory; suffice ⟨*dress that* ~*s for all occasions*⟩ **5** to distribute drinks or helpings of food **6** to attend to customers in a shop **7** to put the ball or shuttle in play in any of various games (e g tennis or volleyball) ~ *vt* **1a** to act as a servant to **b** to give military or naval service to ⟨~*d France in the last war*⟩ **c** to perform the duties of ⟨~*d his presidency*⟩ **2** to act as server at (Mass) **3a** to work through or perform (a term of service) ⟨~ *d his time as a mate*⟩ **b** to undergo (a term of imprisonment) **4** to supply (food or drink) to (guests or diners) **5a(1)** to provide with sthg needed or desired ⟨*3 schools* ~ *the area*⟩ **(2)** to attend to (a customer) in a shop **b** to supply (sthg needed or desired) ⟨*garages refused to* ~ *petrol*⟩ **6** to prove adequate for; suffice ⟨*a smile would* ~ *him for encouragement*⟩ ⟨*this sharp stone will* ~ *my purposes*⟩ **7** to treat or act towards in a specified way ⟨*he* ~*d me ill*⟩ **8** to make legal service of (e g a writ or summons) or upon (a person there named) **9** *of a male animal* to copulate with **10** to wind yarn or wire tightly round (a rope or stay) for protection **11** to act so as to help or benefit ⟨*the citizen's duty to* ~ *society*⟩ **12** to put (the ball or shuttle) in play – **serve someone right** to be a deserved punishment for sby

²serve *n* the act of putting the ball or shuttle in play in any of various games (e g volleyball, badminton, or tennis); *also* a turn to serve

server *n* **1** sby who serves food or drink **2** the player who serves (e g in tennis) **3** sthg (e g tongs) used in serving food or drink **4** an assistant to the celebrant of a low mass

servery *n* a room, counter, or hatch (e g in a public house) from which food is served

¹service *n* **1a** work or duty performed for sby ⟨*on active* ~⟩ **b** employment as a servant ⟨*entered* ~ *when she was 14*⟩ **2a** the function performed by sby who or sthg that serves ⟨*these shoes have given me good* ~⟩ **b** help, use, benefit ⟨*be of* ~ *to them*⟩ **c** disposal for use or assistance ⟨*I'm always at your* ~⟩ **3a** a form followed in a religious ceremony **b** a meeting for worship **4** the act of serving: e g **a** a helpful act; a favour ⟨*did him a* ~⟩ **b** a piece of useful work that does not produce a tangible commodity – usu pl with sing. meaning ⟨*charge for professional* ~*s*⟩ **c** a serve **5** a set of articles for a particular use; *specif* a set of matching tableware ⟨*a 24-piece dinner* ~⟩ **6a** a administrative division ⟨*the consular* ~⟩ **b** any of a nation's military forces (e g the army or navy) **7a(1)** a facility supplying some public demand ⟨*telephone* ~⟩⟨*bus* ~⟩ **(2)** *pl* utilities (e g gas, water sewage, or electricity) available or connected to a building **b(1)** a facility providing maintenance and repair ⟨*television* ~⟩ **(2)** the usu routine repair and maintenance of a machine or motor vehicle ⟨*the car is due for its 6000 mile* ~⟩ **c** a facility providing broadcast programmes ⟨*East European* Service⟩ **8** the bringing of a legal writ, process, or summons to notice as prescribed **9** the act of copulating with a female animal

²**service** *adj* **1** of the armed services **2** used in serving or delivering ⟨*tradesmen use the* ~ *entrance*⟩ **3** providing services ⟨*the* ~ *industries*⟩

³**service** *vt* to perform services for: e g **a** to repair or provide maintenance for **b** to meet interest and sinking fund payments on (e g government debt) **c** to perform any of the business functions auxiliary to production or distribution of **d** *of a male animal* SERVE 9 – **servicer** *n*

⁴**service, service tree** *n* an Old World tree of the rose family resembling the related mountain ashes but with larger flowers and larger edible fruits

serviceable *adj* **1** fit to use; suited for a purpose **2** wearing well in use; durable – **serviceableness** *n*, **serviceably** *adv*, **serviceability** *n*

service charge *n* a proportion of a bill added onto the total bill to pay for service, usu instead of tips

service flat *n*, *Br* a flat of which the rent includes a charge for certain services (e g cleaning)

serviceman, *fem* **servicewoman** *n* **1** a member of the armed forces **2** *chiefly NAm* sby employed to repair or maintain equipment

service road *n* a road that provides access for local traffic only

service station *n* a retail station for servicing motor vehicles, esp with oil and petrol

serviette *n*, *chiefly Br* a table napkin

servile *adj* **1** of or befitting a slave or a menial position ⟨*a* ~ *task*⟩ **2** slavishly or unctuously submissive; abject, obsequious – **servilely** *adv*, **servility** *n*

serving *n* a single portion of food or drink; a helping

servitude *n* **1** lack of liberty; bondage ⟨*penal* ~⟩ **2** a right by which sthg owned by one person is subject to a specified use or enjoyment by another

servomechanism *n* an automatic device for controlling large amounts of power by means of very small amounts of power and automatically correcting performance of a mechanism

servomotor *n* a power-driven mechanism that supplements a primary control operated by a comparatively feeble force (e g in a servomechanism)

sesame *n* (an E Indian plant with) small flattish seeds used as a source of oil and as a flavouring agent

sesqui- *comb form* **1** one and a half times ⟨sesquicenten-nial⟩ **2** containing 3 atoms or equivalents of a specified element or radical, esp combined with 2 of another ⟨sesquioxide⟩

session *n* **1** a meeting or series of meetings of a body (e g a court or council) for the transaction of business; a sitting **2** the period between the meeting of a legislative or judicial body and the final adjournment of that meeting **3** the period in which a school conducts classes **4** a period devoted to a particular activity, esp by a group of people ⟨*a recording* ~⟩ – **sessional** *adj*

¹**set** *vb* **-tt-;** set, (*vt 10*) setted *vt* **1** to cause to sit; place in or on a seat **2a** to place with care or deliberate purpose and with relative stability ⟨~ *a ladder against the wall*⟩ **b** TRANSPLANT 1 ⟨~ *seedlings*⟩ **c** to make (e g a trap) ready

to catch prey **3** to cause to assume a specified condition ⟨~ *the room to rights*⟩⟨*she* ~ *my mind at rest*⟩ **4a** to appoint or assign to an office or duty ⟨~ *him over them as foreman*⟩ **b** to post, station ⟨~ *sentries*⟩ **5a** to place in a specified relation or position ⟨*a dish to* ~ *before a king*⟩ **b** to place in a specified setting ⟨*the story is* ~ *in 17th-c Spain*⟩ **6a** to fasten **b** to apply ⟨~ *pen to paper*⟩⟨~ *a match to the fire*⟩ **7** to fix or decide on as a time, limit, or regulation; prescribe ⟨~ *a wedding day*⟩ **8a** to establish as the most extreme, esp the highest, level ⟨~ *a new record*⟩ **b** to provide as a pattern or model ⟨~ *an example*⟩⟨~ *a fashion*⟩ **c** to allot as or compose for a task ⟨~ *the children some homework*⟩ **9a** to adjust (a device, esp a measuring device) to a desired position ⟨~ *the alarm for 7:00*⟩ **b** to restore to normal position or connection after dislocation or fracturing ⟨~ *a broken bone*⟩; *also* REDUCE 5 ⟨~ *a fracture*⟩ **c** to spread to the wind ⟨~ *the sails*⟩ **10a** to divide (an age-group of pupils) into sets **b** to teach (a school subject) by dividing the pupils into sets ⟨*maths and science are* ~ted⟩ **11a** to make ready for use ⟨~ *the stage*⟩⟨~ *another place for dinner*⟩ **b** to provide music or instrumentation for (a text) **c(1)** to arrange (type) for printing **(2)** to put into type or its equivalent (e g on film) **12a** to put a fine edge on by grinding or honing ⟨~ *a razor*⟩ **b** to bend slightly the alternate teeth of (a saw) in opposite directions **c** to sink (the head of a nail) below the surface **13** to fix in a desired position **14** to fix (the hair) in a desired style by waving, curling, or arranging, usu while wet **15a** to adorn or surround with sthg attached or embedded; stud, dot ⟨*river all* ~ *about with fever trees* – Rudyard Kipling⟩ **b** to fix (e g a gem) in a metal setting **16a** to fix at a specified amount ⟨~ *bail at £500*⟩ **b** to value, rate ⟨*his promises were* ~ *at naught*⟩ **c** to place as an estimate of worth ⟨~ *a high value on life*⟩ **17** to place in relation for comparison ⟨~ *her beside Michelangelo*⟩; *also* to offset ⟨~ *our gains against our losses*⟩ **18a** to direct to action ⟨~ *her to write a report*⟩ **b** to put into activity or motion ⟨~ *the clock going*⟩⟨*it* ~ *me wondering*⟩ **c** to incite to attack or antagonism ⟨*war* ~s *brother against brother*⟩ **19** *of a gundog* to point out the position of (game) by holding a fixed attitude **20** to defeat (an opponent or his/her contract) in bridge **21** to fix firmly; give rigid form to ⟨~ *his jaw in determination*⟩ **22** to cause to become firm or solid ⟨~ *jelly by adding gelatin*⟩ **23** to cause (e g fruit) to develop ~*vi* **1** – used as an interjection to command runners to put themselves into the starting position before a race **2** *of a plant part* to undergo development, usu as a result of pollination **3** to pass below the horizon; go down ⟨*the sun* ~s⟩ **4** to make an attack – + *on* or *upon* **5** to have a specified direction in motion; flow, tend ⟨*the wind was* ~ting *south*⟩ **6** to apply oneself to some activity ⟨~ *to work*⟩ **7** *of a gundog* to indicate the position of game by crouching or pointing **8** to dance face to face with another in a square dance ⟨~ *to your partner*⟩ **9a** to become solid or thickened by chemical or physical attention ⟨*the cement* ~s *rapidly*⟩ **b** *of a broken bone* to become whole by knitting together **c** *of metal* to acquire a permanent twist or bend from strain **10** *chiefly dial* to sit – **set about 1** to begin to do ⟨*how to* set about *losing weight*⟩ **2** to attack ⟨set about *the intruder with a rolling pin*⟩ – **set foot** to pass over the threshold; enter – + *in, on,* or *inside* – **set in motion** to get (sthg) started; initiate ⟨set *an inquiry* in motion⟩ – **set on** to cause to attack or pursue ⟨set *the dog* on *the trespassers*⟩ – **set one's face against** to oppose staunchly – **set one's hand to** to become engaged in – **set one's heart** to resolve; *also* to want (sthg) very much – + *on* or *upon* ⟨*she* set *her heart* on *succeeding*⟩ – **set one's house in order** to introduce necessary reforms – **set one's sights** to focus one's concentration or intentions; aim – **set one's teeth on edge** to give one an unpleasant sensation (e g that caused by an acid flavour or squeaky noise) – **set sail** to begin a voyage ⟨set sail *for America*⟩ – **set store by** to consider valuable, trustworthy, or worthwhile, esp to the specified degree ⟨*don't* set *much* store by *his advice*⟩ – **set the scene** to provide necessary background information – **set to work** to apply oneself; begin ⟨*he* set to work *to undermine their confidence*⟩

²**set** *adj* **1** intent, determined ⟨~ *on going*⟩ **2** fixed by authority or binding decision; prescribed, specified ⟨*there are 3* ~ *books for the examination*⟩ **3** *of a meal* consisting of a specified combination of dishes available at a fixed price **4** reluctant to change; fixed by habit ⟨~ *in his ways*⟩ **5** immovable, rigid ⟨*a* ~ *frown*⟩ **6** ready, prepared ⟨*all* ~ *for an early morning start*⟩ **7** conventional, stereotyped ⟨*her speech was full of* ~ *phrases*⟩

³**set** *n* **1** setting or being set **2a** a mental inclination, tendency, or habit **b** predisposition to act in a certain way in response to an anticipated stimulus or situation **3** a number of things, usu of the same kind, that belong or are used together or that form a unit ⟨*a chess* ~⟩ ⟨*a* ~ *of Dickens*⟩ ⟨*a good* ~ *of teeth*⟩ **4** direction of flow ⟨*the* ~ *of the wind*⟩ **5** the form or carriage of the body or of its parts ⟨*the graceful* ~ *of his head*⟩ **6** tlie amount of deviation from a straight line; *specif* the degree to which the teeth of a saw have been set **7** permanent change of form due to repeated or excessive stress **8** the arrangement of the hair by curling or waving **9a** a young plant or rooted cutting ready for transplanting **b** a small bulb, corm, or (piece of) tuber used for propagation ⟨*onion* ~s⟩ **10** an artificial setting for a scene of a theatrical or film production **11** a division of a tennis match won by the side that wins at least 6 games beating the opponent by 2 games or that wins a tie breaker **12** the basic formation in a country dance or square dance **13** (the music played at) a session of music (e g jazz or rock music), usu followed by an intermission **14** *sing or pl in constr* a group of people associated by common interests ⟨*the smart* ~⟩ **15** a collection of mathematical elements (e g numbers or points) **16** an apparatus of electronic components assembled so as to function as a unit ⟨*a radio* ~⟩ **17** *sing or pl in constr* a group of pupils of roughly equal ability in a particular subject who are taught together **18** a sett

seta *n, pl* **setae** a slender bristle or similar part of an animal or plant – **setaceous** *adj*, **setaceously** *adv*, **setal** *adj*

set aside *vt* **1** to put to one side; discard **2** to reserve for a particular purpose; save **3** to reject from consideration **4** to annul or overrule (a sentence, verdict, etc)

setback *n* **1** an arresting of or hindrance in progress **2** a defeat, reverse

set back *vt* **1** to prevent or hinder the progress of; impede, delay **2** to cost ⟨*a new suit set him back a full week's wages*⟩ – infml

set down *vt* **1** to place at rest on a surface or on the ground; deposit **2** to cause or allow (a passenger) to alight from a vehicle **3** to land (an aircraft) on the ground or water **4** to put in writing **5a** to regard, consider ⟨set him down *as a liar*⟩ **b** to attribute, ascribe ⟨set her success down *to sheer perseverance*⟩

set-in *adj* cut separately and stitched in ⟨~ *sleeves*⟩

set in *vt* to insert; *esp* to stitch (a small part) into a larger article ⟨set in *a sleeve of a dress*⟩ ~ *vi* **1** to become established ⟨*the rot has* set in⟩ **2** to blow or flow towards the shore ⟨*the wind was beginning to* set in⟩

set-off *n* **1** sthg set off against another thing: **a** a decoration, adornment **b** a counterbalance, compensation **2** the discharge of a debt by setting against it a sum owed by the creditor to the debtor

set off *vt* **1a** to put in relief; show up by contrast **b** to adorn, embellish **c** to make distinct or outstanding; enhance **2** to treat as a compensating item ⟨set off *the 3 totals against one another*⟩ **3a** to set in motion; cause to begin **b** to cause to explode; detonate **4** *chiefly NAm* to compensate for; offset ~ *vi* to start out on a course or journey ⟨set off *for home*⟩

set out *vt* **1** to state or describe at length; expound ⟨*a pamphlet* setting out *his ideas in full*⟩ **2a** to arrange and present graphically or systematically **b** to mark out (e g a design) **c** to create or construct according to a plan or design ⟨set *gardens* out *on waste ground*⟩ **3** to begin with a definite purpose or goal; intend, undertake ⟨*you* set out *deliberately to annoy me*⟩ ~ *vi* to start out on a course, journey, or career

set piece *n* **1** (a part of) a work of art, literature, etc with a formal pattern or style **2** an arrangement of fireworks that forms a pattern while burning **3** any of various moves in soccer or rugby (e g a corner kick or free kick) by which the ball is put back into play after a stoppage

setscrew *n* **1** a screw that is tightened to prevent relative movement between parts (e g of a machine) and keep them in a set position **2** a screw that serves to adjust a machine

set square *n, chiefly Br* a flat triangular instrument with 1 right angle and 2 other precisely known angles, used to mark out or test angles

sett, set *n* **1** the burrow of a badger **2** a usu rectangular block of stone or wood formerly used for paving streets

settee *n* a long often upholstered seat with a back and usu arms for seating more than 1 person; *broadly* a sofa

setter *n* a large gundog trained to point on finding game; *specif* IRISH SETTER

set theory *n* a branch of mathematics or of symbolic logic that deals with the nature and relations of sets

setting *n* **1** the manner, position, or direction in which sthg (e g a dial) is set **2** the (style of) frame in which a gem is mounted **3a** the background, surroundings **b** the time and place of the action of a literary, dramatic, or cinematic work **c** the scenery used in a theatrical or film production **4** the music composed for a text (e g a poem) **5** PLACE SETTING

¹**settle** *n* a wooden bench with arms, a high solid back, and an enclosed base which can be used as a chest

²**settle** *vb* **settling** *vt* **1** to place firmly or comfortably ⟨~ *d herself in an armchair*⟩ **2a** to establish in residence ⟨~ *refugees on farmland*⟩ **b** to supply with inhabitants; colonize **3a** to cause to sink and become compacted ⟨*rain* ~ *d the dust*⟩ **b** to clarify by causing the sediment to sink ⟨*put eggshells in the coffee to* ~ *it*⟩ **4a** to free from pain, discomfort, disorder, or disturbance ⟨*took a drink to* ~ *his nerves*⟩ **b** to make subdued or well-behaved ⟨*one word from the referee* ~ *d him*⟩ **5** to fix or resolve conclusively ⟨~ *the question*⟩ **6a** to bestow legally for life – usu + *on* ⟨~ *d her estate on her son*⟩ **b** to arrange for or make a final disposition of ⟨~ *d her affairs*⟩ **7** to pay (a bill or money claimed) ~ *vi* **1** to come to rest ⟨*a sparrow* ~ *d on the windowsill*⟩ **2a** to sink gradually to the bottom; subside ⟨*let the dust* ~ *before applying paint*⟩ **b** to become clearer by the deposit of sediment or scum **c** *of a building, the ground, etc* to sink slowly to a lower level; subside **3a** to become fixed or permanent ⟨*his mood* ~ *into apathy*⟩ **b** to establish a residence or colony ⟨~ *d in Canada for a few years*⟩ **4a** to become calm or orderly – often + *down* **b** to adopt an ordered or stable life-style – usu + *down* ⟨*marry and* ~ *down*⟩ **5a** to adjust differences

or accounts – often + *with* or *up* **b** to end a legal dispute by the agreement of both parties, without court action ⟨*~d out of court*⟩ – **settle for** to be content with; accept

settle in *vi* to become comfortably established ⟨*children quickly* settle in *at a new school*⟩ ~ *vt* to assist in becoming comfortably established

settlement *n* **1** settling **2a** an act of bestowing possession under legal sanction **b** an estate, income, etc legally bestowed on sby **3a** a newly settled place or region **b** a small, esp isolated, village **4** an organization providing various community services in an underprivileged area **5** an agreement resolving differences ⟨*reached a ~ on the strike*⟩

settler *n* one who settles sthg (e g a new region)

set-to *n, pl* **set-tos** a usu brief and vigorous conflict – chiefly infml

set to *vi* **1** to make an eager or determined start on a job or activity **2** to begin fighting

set-up *n* **1** an arrangement; *also* an organization **2** *chiefly NAm* carriage of the body; bearing **3** *chiefly NAm* a task or contest with a prearranged or artificially easy course – chiefly infml

set up *vt* **1a** to raise into position; erect ⟨set up a *statue*⟩ ⟨set up *road blocks*⟩ **b** to put forward (e g a theory) for acceptance; propound **2a** to assemble and prepare for use or operation ⟨set up *a printing press*⟩ **b** to put (a machine) in readiness or adjustment for operation **3a** to give voice to, esp loudly; raise ⟨set up *a din*⟩ **b** to create; BRING ABOUT ⟨*issues that* set up *personal tensions*⟩ **4** to place in a high office or powerful position ⟨set up *the general as dictator*⟩ **5** to claim (oneself) to be a specified thing ⟨sets *herself* up *as an authority*⟩ **6a** to found, institute ⟨set up *a fund for orphans*⟩ **b** to install oneself in ⟨set up *house together*⟩ **7a** to provide with an independent livelihood ⟨set *her* up *in business*⟩ **b** to provide with what is necessary or useful – usu + *with* or *for* ⟨*we're well* set up *with logs for the winter*⟩ **8** to bring or restore to health or success ⟨*a drink* will set *you* up⟩ **9** to prepare detailed plans for ⟨set up *a bank robbery*⟩ ~ *vi* to start business ⟨set up *as a house agent*⟩ – **set up shop** to establish one's business

seven *n* **1** (the number) 7 **2** the seventh in a set or series ⟨*the ~ of diamonds*⟩ **3** sthg having 7 parts or members or a denomination of 7 **4** *pl but sing or pl in constr* a rugby game played with teams of 7 players each – **seven** *adj or pron*, **sevenfold** *adj or adv*

seventeen *n* (the number) 17 – **seventeen** *adj or pron*, **seventeenth** *adj or n*

seventh *adj or n* (of or being) number seven in a countable series

seventh heaven *n* a state of supreme rapture or bliss ⟨*she was in the ~ with her new train set*⟩

seventy *n* **1** (the number) 70 **2** *pl* the numbers 70 to 79; *specif* a range of temperatures, ages, or dates within a century characterized by those numbers – **seventieth** *adj or n*, **seventy** *adj or pron*

seventy-eight *n* 12 a gramophone record that plays at 78 revolutions per minute – usu written 78 – **seventy-eight** *adj or pron*

seven-year itch *n* marital discontent allegedly leading to infidelity after about 7 years of marriage

sever *vt* **1** to put or keep apart; separate; *esp* to remove (a major part or portion) (as if) by cutting **2** to break off; terminate ⟨*~ economic links*⟩ ~ *vi* to become separated – **severable** *adj*, **severance** *n*

¹several *adj* **1** more than 2 but fewer than many ⟨*~ hundred times*⟩ **2** separate or distinct from one another; respective ⟨*specialists in their ~ fields*⟩ – chiefly fml

²several *pron, pl in constr* an indefinite number more than 2 and fewer than many ⟨*~ of the guests*⟩ – **severalfold** *adj or adv*

severally *adv* each by itself or him-/herself; separately – chiefly fml

severance pay *n* an amount payable to an employee on termination of employment

severe *adj* **1** having a stern expression or character; austere **2** rigorous in judgment, requirements, or punishment; stringent ⟨*~ penalties*⟩ ⟨*~ legislation*⟩ **3** strongly critical or condemnatory; censorious ⟨*a ~ critic*⟩ **4** sober or restrained in decoration or manner; plain **5** marked by harsh or extreme conditions ⟨*~ winters*⟩ **6** requiring much effort; arduous ⟨*a ~ test*⟩ **7** serious, grave ⟨*~ depression*⟩ ⟨*a ~ illness*⟩ – **severely** *adv*, **severity** *n*

sew *vb* **sewed; sewn, sewed** *vt* **1** to unite, fasten, or attach by stitches made with a needle and thread **2** to close or enclose by sewing ⟨*~ the money in a bag*⟩ **3** to make or mend by sewing ~ *vi* to practise or engage in sewing – **sewer** *n*

sewage *n* waste matter carried off by sewers

sewer *n* an artificial usu underground conduit used to carry off waste matter, esp excrement, from houses, schools, towns, etc and surface water from roads and paved areas

sewerage *n* **1** sewage **2** the removal and disposal of surface water by sewers **3** a system of sewers

sewing *n* **1** the act, action, or work of one who sews **2** work that has been or is to be sewn

sew up *vt* **1** to mend, close (e g a hole), or enclose by sewing **2** to bring to a successful or satisfactory conclusion ⟨sew up *pay negotiations*⟩ – chiefly infml

¹sex *n* **1** either of 2 divisions of organisms distinguished as male or female **2** the structural, functional, and behavioural characteristics that are involved in reproduction and that distinguish males and females **3** SEXUAL INTERCOURSE

²sex *vt* to identify the sex of ⟨*~ chicks*⟩

sex-, sexi- *comb form* six ⟨sexivalent⟩ ⟨sexpartite⟩

sexagenarian *n* a person between 60 and 69 years old – **sexagenarian** *adj*

Sexagesima *n* the second Sunday before Lent

sex appeal *n* physical attractiveness for members of the opposite sex

sexed *adj* having sex, sex appeal, or sexual instincts, esp to a specified degree ⟨highly ~⟩ ⟨under ~⟩

sexism *n* **1** a belief that sex determines intrinsic capacities and role in society and that sexual differences produce an inherent superiority of one sex, usu the male **2** discrimination on the basis of sex; *esp* prejudice against women on the part of men – **sexist** *adj or n*

sexless *adj* **1** lacking sexuality or sexual intercourse ⟨*~ marriage*⟩ **2** lacking sex appeal

sextant *n* an instrument for measuring angles that is used, esp in navigation, to observe the altitudes of celestial bodies and so determine the observer's position on the earth's surface

sextet *n* **1** (a musical composition for) a group of 6 instruments, voices, or performers **2** *sing or pl in constr* a group or set of 6

sexton *n* a church officer who takes care of the church property and is often also the gravedigger

sextuplet *n* **1** a combination of 6 of a kind **2** any of 6 offspring born at 1 birth **3** a group of 6 equal musical notes performed in the time ordinarily given to 4 of the same value

sexual *adj* **1** of or associated with sex or the sexes ⟨*~ conflict*⟩ **2** having or involving sex ⟨*~ reproduction*⟩ – **sexually** *adv*, **sexuality** *n*

sexual intercourse *n* intercourse with genital contact **a** involving penetration of the vagina by the penis; coitus **b** other than penetration of the vagina by the penis

sexy *adj* sexually suggestive or stimulating; erotic – **sexily** *adv*, **sexiness** *n*

sforzando *n, adj, or adv, pl* **sforzandos, sforzandi** (a note or chord played) with prominent stress or accent – used in music

sh *interj* – used often in prolonged or reduplicated form to urge or command silence

shabby *adj* **1a** threadbare or faded from wear ⟨*a ~ sofa*⟩ **b** dilapidated, run-down ⟨*a ~ district*⟩ **2** dressed in worn or grubby clothes; seedy ⟨*a ~ tramp*⟩ **3** shameful, despicable ⟨*what a ~ trick, driving off and leaving me to walk home!*⟩ – **shabbily** *adv*, **shabbiness** *n*

shack *n* a small crudely built dwelling or shelter

¹shackle *n* **1** (a metal ring like) a manacle or handcuff **2** sthg that restricts or prevents free action or expression – usu pl with sing. meaning **3** a U-shaped piece of metal with a pin or bolt to close the opening

²shackle *vt* **1a** to bind with shackles; fetter **b** to make fast with shackles **2** to deprive of freedom of thought or action by means of restrictions or handicaps; impede

shack up *vi* to live with and have a sexual relationship with sby; *also* to spend the night as a partner in sexual intercourse – usu + *together* or *with*; infml

shad *n, pl* **shad** any of several fishes of the herring family that have a relatively deep body and are important food fishes of Europe and N America

¹shade *n* **1a** partial darkness caused by the interception of rays of light **b** relative obscurity or insignificance **2** a place sheltered (e g by foliage) from the direct heat and glare of the sun **3** a transitory or illusory appearance **4** *pl* the shadows that gather as night falls **5** GHOST 2 **6** sthg that intercepts or diffuses light or heat: e g **a** a lampshade **b** *chiefly NAm* (1) *pl* sunglasses – infml (2) a window blind **7** the reproduction of shade in a picture **8a** a colour produced by a pigment mixed with some black **b** a particular level of depth or brightness of a colour ⟨*a ~ of pink*⟩ **9** a minute difference or amount ⟨*the ~s of meaning in a poem*⟩ – **a shade** a tiny bit; somewhat ⟨*a shade too much salt*⟩ – **shades of** – used interjectionally to indicate that one is reminded of or struck by a resemblance to a specified person or thing

²shade *vt* **1a** to shelter or screen by intercepting radiated light or heat **b** to cover with a shade **2** to darken or obscure (as if) with a shadow **3a** to represent the effect of shade on **b** to mark with shading or gradations of colour **4** to change by gradual transition ~*vi* to pass by slight changes or imperceptible degrees – usu + *into* or *off into*

shade tree *n* a tree grown primarily to produce shade

shading *n* an area of filled-in outlines to suggest three-dimensionality, shadow, or degrees of light and dark in a picture

¹shadow *n* **1a** partial darkness caused by an opaque body interposed so as to cut off rays from a light source ⟨*the thieves lurked in the ~ of the house*⟩ **b** a dark area resembling shadow ⟨*~s under his eyes from fatigue*⟩ **2a** a faint representation or suggestion ⟨*~s of future difficulties*⟩ **b** a mere semblance or imitation of sthg ⟨*she wore herself to a ~ by studying too hard*⟩ **3** a dark figure cast on a surface by a body intercepting light rays ⟨*the trees cast their ~s on the wall*⟩ **4** a phantom **5** *pl* darkness **6** a shaded or darker portion of a picture **7** an attenuated form; a vestige ⟨*after his illness he was only a ~ of his former self*⟩ **8a** an inseparable companion or follower **b** one (e g a spy or detective) who shadows **9** a small degree or portion; a trace ⟨*without a ~ of doubt*⟩ **10** a source

of gloom or disquiet ⟨*her death cast a ~ on the festivities*⟩ **11** a pervasive and often disabling influence ⟨*governed under the ~ of his predecessor*⟩

²shadow *vt* **1** to cast a shadow over **2** to follow (a person) secretly; keep under surveillance **3** to shade

³shadow *adj* **1** identical with another in form but without the other's power or status ⟨*a ~ government in exile*⟩; *specif* of or constituting the probable cabinet when the opposition party is returned to power ⟨*the ~ spokesman on employment*⟩ **2a** having an indistinct pattern ⟨*~ plaid*⟩ **b** having darker sections of design ⟨*~ lace*⟩ **3** shown by throwing the shadows of performers or puppets on a screen ⟨*a ~ dance*⟩

shadow-box *vi* to box with an imaginary opponent, esp as a form of training – **shadow-boxing** *n*

shadowy *adj* **1a** of the nature of or resembling a shadow; insubstantial **b** scarcely perceptible; indistinct **2** lying in or obscured by shadow ⟨*deep ~ interiors*⟩ – **shadowiness** *n*

shady *adj* **1** producing or affording shade ⟨*a ~ tree*⟩ **2** sheltered from the direct heat or light of the sun ⟨*a ~ spot*⟩ **3a** of questionable merit; uncertain, unreliable ⟨*a ~ deal*⟩ **b** of doubtful integrity; disreputable ⟨*she's a ~ character*⟩ – chiefly infml – **shadily** *adv*, **shadiness** *n*

¹shaft *n* **1a** (the long handle of) a spear, lance, or similar weapon **b** a pole; *specif* either of 2 poles between which a horse is hitched to a vehicle **c** an arrow, esp for a longbow **2** a sharply delineated beam of light shining from an opening **3** sthg resembling the shaft of a spear, lance, etc, esp in having a long slender cylindrical form: e g **a** the trunk of a tree **b** the cylindrical pillar between the capital and the base of a column **c** the handle of a tool or implement (e g a hammer or golf club) **d** a usu cylindrical bar used to support rotating pieces or to transmit power or motion by rotation **e** a man-made vertical or inclined opening leading underground to a mine, well, etc **f** a vertical opening or passage through the floors of a building ⟨*a lift ~*⟩ **g** the central stem of a feather **4** a scornful, satirical, or pithily critical remark; a barb

²shaft *vt, NAm* to treat unfairly or harshly – slang

¹shag *n* **1a** an unkempt or uneven tangled mass or covering (e g of hair) **b** long coarse or matted fibre or nap **2** a strong coarse tobacco cut into fine shreds **3** a European bird smaller than the closely related cormorant – **shaggy** *adj*, **shaggily** *adv*

²shag *vt* -gg- **1** to fuck, screw – vulg **2** *Br* to make utterly exhausted – usu + *out*; slang

³shag *n* an act of sexual intercourse – vulg

shaggy-dog story *n* a protracted and inconsequential funny story whose humour lies in the pointlessness or irrelevance of the conclusion

shagreen *n* **1** an untanned leather covered with small round granulations and usu dyed green **2** the rough skin of various sharks and rays – **shagreen** *adj*

shah *n, often cap* a sovereign of Iran – **shahdom** *n*

¹shake *vb* **shook; shaken** *vi* **1** to move to and fro with rapid usu irregular motion **2** to vibrate, esp from the impact of a blow or shock **3** to tremble as a result of physical or emotional disturbance **4** to shake hands ⟨*if you've agreed then ~ on it*⟩ ~*vt* **1** to brandish, wave, or flourish, esp in a threatening manner **2** to cause to move with a rapidly alternating motion **3** to cause to quake, quiver, or tremble **4** to cause to waver; weaken ⟨*~ one's faith*⟩ **5** to put in a specified state by repeated quick jerky movements ⟨*shook himself free from the woman's grasp*⟩ **6** to dislodge or eject by quick jerky movements of the support or container ⟨*shook the dust from the cloth*⟩ **7** to clasp (hands) in greeting or farewell or to convey goodwill or agreement **8** to agitate the feelings of; upset ⟨*the news* shook *him*⟩ – **shakable, shakeable** *adj* – **shake a leg** to hurry up; hasten – *infml* – **shake one's head** to move one's head from side to side to indicate disagreement, denial, disapproval, etc

²**shake** *n* 1 an act of shaking ⟨*indicated her disapproval with a ~ of the head*⟩ 2 *pl* a condition of trembling (e g from chill or fever); *specif* DELIRIUM TREMENS 3 a wavering, vibrating, or alternating motion caused by a blow or shock 4 TRILL 1 5 *chiefly NAm* MILK SHAKE 6 *chiefly NAm* an earthquake 7 a moment ⟨*I'll be round in 2 ~s*⟩ *USE* (6&7) *infml*

¹**shakedown** *n* 1 a makeshift bed (e g one made up on the floor) 2 *NAm* an act or instance of shaking sby down; *esp* extortion 3 *NAm* a thorough search *USE* (2&3) *infml*

²**shakedown** *adj* designed to test a new ship, aircraft, etc and allow the crew to become familiar with it ⟨*a ~ cruise*⟩

shake down *vi* 1 to stay the night or sleep, esp in a makeshift bed 2 to become comfortably established, esp in a new place or occupation ~ *vt* 1 to settle (as if) by shaking 2 to give a shakedown test to 3 *NAm* to obtain money from in a dishonest or illegal manner 4 *NAm* to make a thorough search of (a person); frisk *USE* (3&4) *infml*

shake off *vt* to free oneself from ⟨shook off *a heavy cold*⟩

shaker *n* 1 a container or utensil used to sprinkle or mix a substance by shaking ⟨*a flour ~*⟩ ⟨*a cocktail ~*⟩ 2 *cap* a member of an American sect practising celibacy and a self-denying communal life, and looking forward to the millennium – **Shaker** *adj*, **Shakerism** *n*

shake-up *n* an act or instance of shaking up; *specif* an extensive and often drastic reorganization (e g of a company) – *infml*

shake up *vt* 1 to jar (as if) by a physical shock ⟨*the collision* shook up *both drivers*⟩ 2 to reorganize by extensive and often drastic measures – *infml*

shako *n, pl* **shakos, shakoes** a stiff military hat with a high crown and plume

shaky *adj* 1a lacking in stability; precarious ⟨*a ~ coalition*⟩ b lacking in firmness (e g of beliefs or principles) 2a unsound in health; poorly b characterized by or affected with shaking 3 likely to give way or break down; rickety ⟨*a ~ chair*⟩ – **shakily** *adv*, **shakiness** *n*

shale *n* a finely stratified or laminated rock formed by the consolidation of clay, mud, or silt

shale oil *n* a crude dark oil obtained from oil shale by heating

shall *verbal auxiliary, pres sing & pl* **shall;** *past* **should** 1 – used to urge or command ⟨*you ~ go*⟩ or denote what is legally mandatory ⟨*it ~ be unlawful to carry firearms*⟩ 2a – used to express what is inevitable or seems likely to happen in the future ⟨*we ~ have to be ready*⟩ ⟨*we ~ see*⟩ b – used in the question form to express simple futurity ⟨*when ~ we expect you?*⟩ or with the force of an offer or suggestion ⟨*~ I open the window?*⟩ 3 – used to express determination ⟨*they ~ not pass*⟩

shallot *n* (any of the small clusters of bulbs, used esp for pickling and in seasoning, produced by) a perennial plant that resembles the related onion

¹**shallow** *adj* 1 having little depth ⟨*~ water*⟩ 2 superficial in knowledge, thought, or feeling 3 not marked or accentuated ⟨*the plane went into a ~ dive*⟩ ⟨*a ~ curve*⟩ – **shallowly** *adv*, **shallowness** *n*

²**shallow** *vi* to become shallow

³**shallow** *n* a shallow place in a body of water – usu *pl* with sing. meaning but sing. or *pl* in constr

shalom *interj* – used as a Jewish greeting and farewell

shalt *archaic pres 2 sing of* SHALL

¹**sham** *n* 1 cheap falseness; hypocrisy ⟨*the ~ of the empty pageant* – Oscar Wilde⟩ 2 an imitation or counterfeit purporting to be genuine 3 a person who shams – **sham** *adj*

²**sham** *vb* -**mm**- *vt* to act so as to counterfeit ⟨*I ~med a headache to get away*⟩ ~ *vi* to create a deliberately false impression

shaman *n* a priest believed to exercise magic power (e g for healing and divination), esp through ecstatic trances – **shamanism** *n*, **shamanist** *n*

¹**shamble** *vi* **shambling** to walk awkwardly with dragging feet; shuffle

²**shamble** *n* a shambling gait

shambles *n, pl* **shambles** 1 a slaughterhouse 2a a place of carnage b a scene or a state of great destruction, chaos, or confusion; a mess ⟨*the place was left a ~ by hooligans*⟩

¹**shame** *n* 1a a painful emotion caused by consciousness of guilt, shortcomings, impropriety, or disgrace b susceptibility to such emotion ⟨*was not upset because she had no ~*⟩ 2 humiliating disgrace or disrepute; ignominy 3 sthg bringing regret or disgrace ⟨*it's a ~ you weren't there*⟩

²**shame** *vt* 1 to bring shame to; disgrace 2 to put to shame by outdoing 3 to fill with a sense of shame 4 to compel by causing to feel guilty ⟨*~d into confessing*⟩

shamefaced *adj* 1 showing modesty; bashful 2 showing shame; ashamed – **shamefacedly** *adv*, **shamefacedness** *n*

shameful *adj* 1 bringing disrepute or ignominy; disgraceful 2 arousing the feeling of shame – **shamefully** *adv*, **shamefulness** *n*

shameless *adj* 1 insensible to disgrace 2 showing lack of shame; disgraceful – **shamelessly** *adv*

shammy *n* CHAMOIS 2

¹**shampoo** *vt* **shampoos; shampooing; shampooed** 1 to clean (esp the hair or a carpet) with shampoo 2 to wash the hair of – **shampooist** *n*

²**shampoo** *n, pl* **shampoos** 1 a washing of the hair esp by a hairdresser 2 a soap, detergent, etc used for shampooing

shamrock *n* any of several plants (e g a wood sorrel or some clovers) whose leaves have 3 leaflets and are used as a floral emblem by the Irish

shandy *n* a drink consisting of beer mixed with lemonade or ginger beer

shanghai *vt* **shanghais; shanghaiing; shanghaied** 1 to compel to join a ship's crew, esp by the help of drink or drugs 2 to put into an awkward or unpleasant position by trickery

Shangri-la *n* a remote imaginary place where life approaches perfection

shank *n* 1a a leg; *specif* the part of the leg between the knee and the ankle in human beings or the corresponding part in various other vertebrates b a cut of beef, veal, mutton, or lamb from the upper or the lower part of the leg 2 a straight narrow usu vital part of an object: e g a the straight part of a nail or pin b the stem or stalk of a plant c the part of an anchor between the ring and the crown d the part of a fishhook between the eye and the bend e the part of a key between the handle and the bit f the narrow part of the sole of a shoe beneath the instep 3 a part of an object by which it can be attached to sthg else: e g a(1) a projection on the back of a solid button (2) a short stem of thread that holds a sewn button away from the cloth b the end (e g of a drill bit) that is gripped in a chuck

shanks's pony *n* one's own feet or legs considered as a means of transport ⟨*went home by ~*⟩ – *humor*

shan't shall not

shantung *n* a silk fabric in plain weave with a slightly irregular surface

¹shanty *n* a small crudely built or dilapidated dwelling or shelter; a shack

²shanty *n* a song sung by sailors in rhythm with their work

shantytown *n* (part of) a town consisting mainly of shanties

¹shape *vt* 1 to form, create; *esp* to give a particular form or shape to ⟨~d *the clay into a cube*⟩ 2 to adapt in shape so as to fit neatly and closely ⟨*a dress* ~d *to fit*⟩ 3 to guide or mould into a particular state or condition ⟨shaping *her plans for the future*⟩ 4a to determine or direct the course of (e g a person's life) b to cause to take a particular form or course ⟨~ *the course of history*⟩ – **shapable, shapeable** *adj*, **shaper** *n*

²shape *n* 1a the visible or tactile form of a particular (kind of) item b(1) spatial form ⟨*all solids have* ~⟩ (2) a circle, square, or other standard geometrical form 2 the contour of the body, esp of the trunk; the figure 3a a phantom, apparition b an assumed appearance; a guise ⟨*the devil in the* ~ *of a serpent*⟩ 4 definite form (e g in thought or words) ⟨*the plan slowly took* ~⟩ 5 a general structure or plan ⟨*the final* ~ *of society*⟩ 6 sthg made in a particular form ⟨*a* ~ *for moulding jellies*⟩ 7a the condition of a person or thing, esp at a particular time ⟨*in excellent* ~ *for his age*⟩ b a fit or ordered condition ⟨*got the car into* ~⟩ – **shaped** *adj*

shapely *adj* having a pleasing shape; well-proportioned – **shapeliness** *n*

shape up *vi* to (begin to) behave or perform satisfactorily

shard *n* 1 a piece or fragment of sthg brittle (e g earthenware) 2 SHERD 2

¹share *n* 1a a portion belonging to, due to, or contributed by an individual b a full or fair portion ⟨*she's had her* ~ *of fun*⟩ 2a the part allotted or belonging to any of a number owning property or interest together b any of the equal portions into which property or invested capital is divided c *pl, chiefly Br* the proprietorship element in a company, usu represented by transferable certificates

²share *vt* 1 to divide and distribute in shares; apportion – usu + *out* 2 to partake of, use, experience, or enjoy with others ~ *vi* to have a share or part – often + *in* – **shareable, sharable** *adj*, **sharer** *n*

³share *n* a ploughshare

sharecropper *n, NAm* a tenant farmer, esp in the southern USA, who lives on credit provided by the landlord and receives an agreed share of the value of the crop – **sharecrop** *vb*

shareholder *n* the holder or owner of a share in property

¹shark *n* any of numerous mostly large typically grey marine fishes that are mostly active, voracious, and predators and have gill slits at the sides and a mouth on the under part of the body

²shark *n* 1 a greedy unscrupulous person who exploits others by usury, extortion, or trickery 2 *NAm* one who excels greatly, esp in a specified field – infml

sharkskin *n* 1 (leather from) the hide of a shark 2 a smooth stiff durable fabric in twill or basket weave with small woven designs

¹sharp *adj* 1 (adapted to) cutting or piercing: e g a having a thin keen edge or fine point b bitingly cold; icy ⟨*a* ~ *wind*⟩ 2a keen in intellect, perception, attention, etc ⟨~ *sight*⟩ ⟨*keep a* ~ *lookout*⟩ b paying shrewd usu selfish attention to personal gain ⟨*a* ~ *trader*⟩ 3a brisk, vigorous ⟨*a* ~ *trot*⟩ b capable of acting or reacting strongly; esp

caustic ⟨*a* ~ *soap*⟩ 4 severe, harsh: e g a marked by irritability or anger; fiery ⟨*a* ~ *temper*⟩ b causing intense usu sudden anguish ⟨*a* ~ *pain*⟩ c cutting in language or implication ⟨*a* ~ *rebuke*⟩ 5 affecting the senses or sense organs intensely: e g a(1) pungent, tart, or acid, esp in flavour (2) acrid b shrill, piercing c issuing in a brilliant burst of light ⟨*a* ~ *flash*⟩ 6a characterized by hard lines and angles ⟨~ *features*⟩ b involving an abrupt change in direction ⟨*a* ~ *turn*⟩ c clear in outline or detail; distinct ⟨*a* ~ *image*⟩ d conspicuously clear ⟨~ *contrast*⟩ 7 *of a musical note* raised a semitone in pitch 8 stylish, dressy – infml – **sharply** *adv*, **sharpness** *n*

²sharp *adv* 1 in an abrupt manner ⟨*the car pulled up* ~⟩ ⟨*turn* ~ *right*⟩ 2 exactly, precisely ⟨*4 o'clock* ~⟩ 3 above the proper musical pitch ⟨*they're playing* ~⟩

³sharp *n* 1a a musical note 1 semitone higher than another indicated or previously specified note b a character on the musical staff indicating a raising in pitch of a semitone 2 a relatively long needle with a sharp point and a small rounded eye for use in general sewing 3 *chiefly NAm* a swindler, sharper

sharpen *vb* to make or become sharp or sharper – **sharpener** *n*

sharper *n* a cheat, swindler; esp a gambler who habitually cheats

sharpshooter *n* a good marksman – **sharpshooting** *n*

shatter *vt* 1a to break into pieces (e g by a sudden blow) b to cause to break down; impair, disable ⟨*his nerves were* ~ed⟩ 2 to have a forceful or violent effect on the feelings of ⟨*she was absolutely* ~ed *by the news*⟩ 3 to cause to be utterly exhausted ⟨*felt* ~ed *by the long train journey*⟩ ~ *vi* to break suddenly apart; disintegrate *USE* (*vt 2&3*) infml – **shatteringly** *adv*

¹shave *vb* **shaved, shaven** *vt* 1a to remove in thin layers or shreds – often + *off* ⟨~ *off a thin slice of cheese*⟩ b to cut off thin layers or slices from c to cut or trim closely ⟨*a closely* ~d *lawn*⟩ 2a to remove the hair from by cutting close to the roots b to cut off (hair or beard) close to the skin 3 to come very close to or brush against in passing ~ *vi* to cut off hair or beard close to the skin

²shave *n* 1 a tool or machine for shaving 2 an act or process of shaving

shaver *n* 1 an electric-powered razor 2 a boy, youngster – infml

shaving *n* sthg shaved off – usu pl ⟨*wood* ~s⟩

shawl *n* a usu decorative square, oblong, or triangular piece of fabric that is worn to cover the head or shoulders

¹she *pron* 1 that female person or creature who is neither speaker nor hearer ⟨~ *is my mother*⟩ 2 – used to refer to sthg regarded as feminine (e g by personification) ⟨~ *was a fine ship*⟩

²she *n* a female person or creature ⟨*is the baby a he or a* ~⟩ – often in combination ⟨*she-cat*⟩

sheaf *n, pl* **sheaves** 1 a quantity of plant material, esp the stalks and ears of a cereal grass, bound together 2 a collection of items laid or tied together ⟨*a* ~ *of papers*⟩

¹shear *vb* **sheared, shorn** *vt* 1a to cut off the hair from ⟨*with shorn scalp*⟩ b to cut or clip (hair, wool, a fleece, etc) from sby or sthg; also to cut sthg from ⟨~ *a lawn*⟩ c to cut (as if) with shears ⟨~ *a metal sheet in 2*⟩ 2 to cut with sthg sharp 3 to deprive of sthg as if by cutting off – usu passive + of ⟨*has been shorn of her authority*⟩ 4 to subject to a shear force ~ *vi* 1 to become divided or separated under the action of a shear force ⟨*the bolt may* ~ *off*⟩ 2 *chiefly Scot* to reap crops with a sickle – **shearer** *n*, **shearing** *n*

²shear *n* 1a a cutting implement similar to a pair of

scissors but typically larger **b** any of various cutting tools or machines operating by the action of opposed cutting edges of metal **c** *also* **sheer** a sheerlegs – usu pl with sing. meaning but sing. or pl in constr **2** an action or force that causes or tends to cause 2 parts of a body to slide on each other in a direction parallel to their plane of contact *USE* (*1a, b*) usu pl with sing. meaning

sheath *n, pl* **sheaths 1** a case or cover for a blade (e g of a knife or sword) **2** a cover or case of a (part of a) plant or animal body ⟨*the leaves of grasses form a ~ round the main stalk*⟩ **3** a cover or support (applied) like the sheath of a blade **4** a condom

sheathe *vt* **1** to put into or provide with a sheath ⟨*~d her dagger*⟩ **2** to withdraw (a claw) into a sheath **3** to encase or cover with sthg protective (e g thin boards or sheets of metal)

sheath knife *n* a knife that has a fixed blade and is carried in a sheath

shebang *n, chiefly NAm* an affair, business ⟨*she's head of the whole ~*⟩ – infml

shebeen *n, chiefly Irish* an unlicensed or illegally operated drinking establishment

¹shed *vb* **-dd-; shed** *vt* **1** to be incapable of holding or absorbing; repel ⟨*a duck's plumage ~s water*⟩ **2a** to cause (blood) to flow by wounding or killing **b** to pour forth; let flow ⟨*~ tears*⟩ **c** to give off or out; cast ⟨*the book ~s some light on this subject*⟩ **3** to cast off or let fall (a natural covering) ~ *vi* to cast off hairs, threads etc; moult ⟨*the dog is ~ding*⟩

²shed *n* WATERSHED 1

³shed *n* a usu single-storied building for shelter, storage, etc, esp with 1 or more sides open

she'd she had; she would

sheen *n* **1** a bright or shining quality or condition; brightness, lustre **2** a subdued shininess or glitter of a surface **3** a lustrous surface imparted to textiles through finishing processes or use of shiny yarns – **sheeny** *adj*

sheep *n, pl* **sheep 1** any of numerous ruminant mammals related to the goats but stockier and lacking a beard in the male; *specif* one domesticated, esp for its flesh and wool **2** an inane or docile person; *esp* one easily influenced or led

sheep-dip *n* a liquid preparation into which sheep are plunged, esp to destroy parasites

sheepdog *n* a dog used to tend, drive, or guard sheep; *esp* BORDER COLLIE

sheepfold *n* a pen or shelter for sheep

sheepish *adj* embarrassed by consciousness of a fault ⟨*a ~ look*⟩ – **sheepishly** *adv*, **sheepishness** *n*

sheepskin *n* **1** (leather from) the skin of a sheep **2** the skin of a sheep dressed with the wool on ⟨*a ~ coat*⟩

¹sheer *adj* **1** transparently fine; diaphanous ⟨*~ tights*⟩ **2a** unqualified, utter ⟨*~ ignorance*⟩ **b** not mixed or mingled with anything else; pure, unadulterated **3** marked by great and unbroken steepness; precipitous ⟨*a ~ cliff*⟩

²sheer *adv* **1** altogether, completely ⟨*his name went ~ out of my head*⟩ **2** straight up or down without a break ⟨*rugged cliffs rose ~ out of the sea*⟩

³sheer *vb* to (cause to) deviate from a course

⁴sheer *n* a turn, deviation, or change in a course (e g of a ship)

⁵sheer *n* the curvature from front to rear of a ship's deck as observed when looking from the side

⁶sheer *n* SHEAR 1c – usu pl with sing. meaning but sing. or pl in constr

¹sheet *n* **1** a broad piece of cloth; *specif* a rectangle of cloth (e g of linen or cotton) used as an article of bed linen **2a** a usu rectangular piece of paper **b** a printed section for a book, esp before it has been folded, cut, or bound – usu

pl **c** the unseparated postage stamps printed by 1 impression of a plate on a single piece of paper **3** a broad usu flat expanse ⟨*a ~ of ice*⟩ **4** a suspended or moving expanse ⟨*a ~ of flame*⟩ ⟨*~s of rain*⟩ **5a** a piece of sthg that is thin in comparison to its length and breadth **b** a flat metal baking utensil

²sheet *vt* to form into, provide with, or cover with a sheet or sheets ~ *vi* to come down in sheets ⟨*the rain ~ed against the windows*⟩

³sheet *adj* rolled into or spread out in a sheet ⟨*~ steel*⟩

⁴sheet *n* **1** a rope that regulates the angle at which a sail is set in relation to the wind **2** *pl* the spaces at either end of an open boat

sheet anchor *n* **1** an emergency anchor formerly carried in the broadest part of a ship **2** a principal support or dependence, esp in danger; a mainstay

sheeting *n* (material suitable for making into) sheets

sheet lightning *n* lightning in diffused or sheet form due to reflection and diffusion by clouds

sheet music *n* music printed on large unbound sheets of paper

sheikh, sheik *n* **1** an Arab chief **2** sheik, sheikh a romantically attractive or dashing man – **sheikhdom** *n*

sheila, sheilah *n, Austr, NZ, & SAfr* a young woman; a girl – infml

shekel *n* **1** an ancient Hebrew gold or silver coin **2** the standard unit of money in Israel **3** *pl* money – infml

shelduck *n* any of various Old World ducks; *esp* a common mostly black and white duck slightly larger than the mallard

shelf *n, pl* **shelves 1** a thin flat usu long and narrow piece of material (e g wood) fastened horizontally (e g on a wall or in a cupboard, bookcase, etc) at a distance from the floor to hold objects **2** sthg resembling a shelf in form or position: e g **a** a (partially submerged) sandbank or ledge of rocks **b** a flat projecting layer of rock **c** CONTINENTAL SHELF **– off the shelf 1** available from stock **2** OFF THE PEG **– on the shelf 1** in a state of inactivity or uselessness **2** *of a single woman* considered as unlikely to marry, esp because too old

¹shell *n* **1a** a hard rigid often largely calcium-containing covering of an animal (e g a turtle, oyster, or beetle) **b** a seashell **c** the hard or tough outer covering of an egg; *esp* a bird's egg **2** the covering or outside part of a fruit or seed, esp when hard or fibrous **3** shell material or shells ⟨*an ornament made of ~*⟩ **4** sthg like a shell: e g **a** a framework or exterior structure; *esp* the outer frame of a building that is unfinished or has been destroyed (e g by fire) **b** a hollow form devoid of substance ⟨*mere effigies and ~s of men* – Thomas Carlyle⟩ **c** an edible case for holding a filling ⟨*a pastry ~*⟩ **5** a cold and reserved attitude that conceals the presence or absence of feeling ⟨*wish she'd come out of her ~*⟩ **6** a narrow light racing rowing boat propelled by 1 or more rowers **7** any of various spherical regions surrounding the nucleus of an atom at various distances from it and each occupied by a group of electrons of approximately equal energy **8a** a projectile for a cannon containing an explosive bursting charge **b** a metal or paper case which holds the charge in cartridges, fireworks, etc – **shelly** *adj*

²shell *vt* **1** to take out of a natural enclosing cover (e g a shell, husk, pod, or capsule) ⟨*~ peanuts*⟩ **2** to fire shells at, on, or into ~ *vi* **1** to fall or scale off in thin pieces **2** to fall out of the pod or husk ⟨*nuts which ~ on falling from the tree*⟩

she'll she will; she shall

¹shellac *n* the purified form of a resin produced by various insects, usu obtained as yellow or orange flakes; *also* a solution of this in alcohol used esp in making varnish

²**shellac** vt **-ck-** to treat, esp by coating, with shellac

shellfish n an aquatic invertebrate animal with a shell; esp an edible mollusc or crustacean

shell out vb to pay (money) – infml

shell shock n a mental disorder characterized by neurotic and often hysterical symptoms that occurs under conditions (e g wartime combat) that cause intense stress – **shell-shock** vt

¹**shelter** n **1** sthg, esp a structure, affording cover or protection 〈an air-raid ~〉 **2** the state of being covered and protected; refuge 〈took ~〉

²**shelter** vt **1** to serve as a shelter for; protect 〈a thick hedge ~ed the orchard〉 **2** to keep concealed or protected 〈~ed her family in a mountain cave〉 ~vi to take shelter

shelve vt **1** to provide with shelves **2** to place on a shelf **3a** to remove from active service; dismiss **b** to put off or aside 〈~ a project〉 ~vi to slope gently

shelving n (material for constructing) shelves

shenanigan n **1** deliberate deception; trickery **2** boisterous mischief; high jinks – usu pl with sing. meaning USE infml

¹**shepherd** n **1** fem **shepherdess** /-des/ one who tends sheep **2** a pastor

²**shepherd** vt **1** to tend as a shepherd **2** to guide, marshal, or conduct (people) like sheep 〈~ed the children onto the train〉

shepherd's pie n a hot dish of minced meat, esp lamb, with a mashed potato topping

Sheraton adj of or being a style of furniture that originated in England around 1800 and is characterized by straight lines and graceful proportions

sherbet n **1** (a drink made with) a sweet powder that effervesces in liquid and is eaten dry or used to make fizzy drinks **2** a water ice with egg white, gelatin, or sometimes milk added

sherd n **1** SHARD 1 **2** fragments of pottery vessels

sheriff n **1** the honorary chief executive officer of the Crown in each English county who has mainly judicial and ceremonial duties **2** the chief judge of a Scottish county or district **3** a county law enforcement officer in the USA – **sheriffdom** n

Sherpa n a member of a Tibetan people living on the high southern slopes of the Himalayas

sherry n a blended fortified wine from S Spain that varies in colour from very light to dark brown

she's she is; she has

Shetland pony n (any of) a breed of small stocky shaggy hardy ponies that originated in the Shetland islands

Shetland wool n (yarn spun from) fine wool from sheep raised in the Shetland islands

shew vb, archaic Br to show

shibboleth n **1a** a catchword, slogan **b** a use of language that distinguishes a group of people **c** a commonplace belief or saying 〈the ~ that crime does not pay〉 **2** a custom that characterizes members of a particular group

¹**shield** n **1** a piece of armour (e g of wood, metal, or leather) carried on the arm or in the hand and used esp for warding off blows **2** sby or sthg that protects or defends; a defence **3** a piece of material or a pad attached inside a garment (e g a dress) at the armpit to protect the garment from perspiration **4** sthg designed to protect people from injury from moving parts of machinery, live electrical conductors, etc **5** a defined area, the surface of which constitutes a heraldic field, on which heraldic arms are displayed; esp one that is wide at the top and rounds to a point at the bottom **6** an armoured screen protecting an otherwise exposed gun **7** a protective structure (e g a

carapace, scale, or plate) of some animals **8** the Precambrian central rock mass of a continent **9** sthg resembling a shield: e g **a** a trophy awarded in recognition of achievement (e g in a sporting event) **b** a decorative or identifying emblem

²**shield** vt **1** to protect (as if) with a shield; provide with a protective cover or shelter **2** to cut off from observation; hide 〈accomplices who ~ a thief〉

¹**shift** vt **1** to exchange for or replace by another; change 〈the traitor ~ed his allegiance〉 **2** to change the place, position, or direction of; move 〈I can't ~ the grand piano〉 **3** to get rid of; dispose of – infml ~vi **1** to change place, position, or direction 〈~ing uneasily in his chair〉 〈the wind ~ed〉 **2a** to assume responsibility 〈had to ~ for herself〉 **b** to resort to expedients; GET BY **3** NAm to change gear in a motor vehicle

²**shift** n **1a** a deceitful or underhand scheme or method; a subterfuge, dodge **b** an expedient tried in difficult circumstances – usu pl **2** a loose unfitted slip or dress **3a** a change in direction 〈a ~ in the wind〉 **b** a change in emphasis, judgment, or attitude **4a** sing or pl in constr a group who work (e g in a factory) in alternation with other groups **b** a scheduled period of work or duty 〈on the night ~〉 **5** a change in place or position: e g **a** the relative displacement of rock masses on opposite sides of a fault **b** a change in position of a line or band in a spectrum **6** systematic sound change as a language evolves **7** NAm the gear change in a motor vehicle

shift key n a key on a keyboard (e g of a typewriter) that when held down permits a different set of characters, esp the capitals, to be printed

shiftless adj **1** lacking resourcefulness; inefficient **2** lacking ambition or motivation; lazy – **shiftlessly** adv, **shiftlessness** n

shifty adj **1** given to deception, evasion, or fraud; slippery **2** indicative of a fickle or devious nature 〈~ eyes〉 – **shiftily** adv, **shiftiness** n

shilling n **1a** (a coin representing) a former money unit of the UK worth 12 old pence or £¹⁄₂₀ **b** a money unit equal to £¹⁄₂₀ of any of various other countries (formerly) in the Commonwealth **2** (a coin or note representing) the basic money unit of certain E African countries

shilly-shally vi to show hesitation or lack of decisiveness – **shilly-shally** n

¹**shimmer** vi **1** to shine with a softly tremulous or wavering light; glimmer **2** to (cause sthg to) appear in a fluctuating wavy form 〈the ~ing heat from the pavement〉

²**shimmer** n **1** a shimmering light **2** a wavering and distortion of the visual image of a far object usu resulting from heat-induced changes in atmospheric refraction – **shimmery** adj

¹**shin** n the front part of the leg of a vertebrate animal below the knee; also a cut of meat from this part, esp from the front leg of a quadruped 〈a ~ of beef〉

²**shin** vb **-nn-** vi to climb by gripping with the hands or arms and the legs and hauling oneself up or lowering oneself down 〈~ned up the tree〉 ~vt **1** to kick on the shins **2** to climb by shinning

shinbone n TIBIA 1

shindig n a usu boisterous social gathering – infml

shindy n, pl **shindys**, **shindies** a quarrel, brawl – infml

¹**shine** vb **shone**, (vt 2) **shined** vi **1** to emit light **2** to be bright with reflected light **3** to be outstanding or distinguished 〈she always ~s in mathematics〉 **4** to have a radiant or lively appearance 〈his face shone with enthusiasm〉 ~vt **1a** to cause to emit light **b** to direct the light of 〈shone her torch into the corner〉 **2** to make bright by polishing 〈~d his shoes〉

²**shine** n **1** brightness caused by the emission or reflection of light **2** brilliance, splendour ⟨*pageantry that has kept its* ~ *over the centuries*⟩ **3** fine weather; sunshine ⟨*come rain, come* ~⟩ **4** an act of polishing shoes **5** *chiefly NAm* a fancy, crush – esp in *take a shine to*; infml

shiner n BLACK EYE – slang

¹**shingle** n **1** a small thin piece of building material for laying in overlapping rows as a covering for the roof or sides of a building **2** a woman's short haircut in which the hair is shaped into the nape of the neck

²**shingle** vt **1** to cover (as if) with shingles **2** to cut (hair) in a shingle

³**shingle** n (a place, esp a seashore, strewn with) small rounded pebbles – **shingly** adj

shingles n pl but sing in constr severe short-lasting inflammation of certain ganglia of the nerves that leave the brain and spinal cord, caused by a virus and associated with a rash of blisters and often intense neuralgic pain

shining adj **1** emitting or reflecting light; bright **2** possessing a distinguished quality; outstanding ⟨*a* ~ *example of bravery*⟩

Shinto n the indigenous animistic religion of Japan, including the veneration of the Emperor as a descendant of the sun-goddess – **Shinto** adj, **Shintoism** n, **Shintoist** n or adj, **Shintoistic** adj

shiny adj **1** bright or glossy in appearance; lustrous, polished ⟨~ *new shoes*⟩ **2** of material, clothes, etc rubbed or worn to a smooth surface that reflects light – **shininess** n

¹**ship** n **1a** a large seagoing vessel **b** a square-rigged sailing vessel having a bowsprit and usu 3 masts **2** a boat (propelled by power or sail) **3** sing or pl in constr a ship's crew **4** an airship, aircraft, or spacecraft – **when one's ship comes in** when one becomes rich

²**ship** vb **-pp-** vt **1** to place or receive on board a ship for transportation **2** to put in place for use ⟨~ *the tiller*⟩ **3** to take into a ship or boat ⟨~ *the gangplank*⟩ **4** to engage for service on a ship **5** to cause to be transported or sent away ⟨~ *ped him off to boarding school*⟩ – infml ~ vi **1** to embark on a ship **2** to go or travel by ship **3** to engage to serve on shipboard – **shippable** adj

-ship suffix (n → n) **1** state, condition, or quality of ⟨*friend*ship⟩ **2a** office, status, or profession of ⟨*professor*-ship⟩ **b** period during which (a specified office or position) is held ⟨*during his dictator*ship⟩ **3** art or skill of ⟨*horseman*ship⟩ ⟨*scholar*ship⟩ **4** sing or pl in constr whole group or body sharing (a specified clan or state) ⟨*reader*ship⟩ ⟨*member*ship⟩ **5** one entitled to (a specified rank, title, or appellation) ⟨*his Lord*ship⟩

¹**shipboard** n – **on shipboard** on board ship

²**shipboard** adj existing or taking place on board a ship

shipbuilder n a person or company that designs or constructs ships – **shipbuilding** n

ship canal n a canal large enough to allow the passage of sea-going vessels

shipmate n a fellow sailor

shipment n **1** the act or process of shipping **2** the quantity of goods shipped ⟨*a* ~ *of oranges*⟩

shipper n a person or company that ships goods

shipping n **1** ships (in 1 place or belonging to 1 port or country) **2** the act or business of a shipper

ship's biscuit n, chiefly Br a type of hard biscuit orig for eating on board ship

shipshape adj trim, tidy

¹**shipwreck** n **1** a wrecked ship or its remains **2** the destruction or loss of a ship **3** an irrevocable collapse or destruction ⟨*suffered the* ~ *of his fortune*⟩

²**shipwreck** vt **1** to cause to undergo shipwreck **2** to ruin

shipwright n a carpenter skilled in ship construction and repair

shire n **1a** an administrative subdivision; specif an English county, esp one with a name ending in -shire **b** pl the English fox-hunting district consisting chiefly of Leicestershire and Northamptonshire **2** any of a British breed of large heavy draught horses

shirk vt to evade or dodge (a duty, responsibility, etc) – **shirker** n

shirring n a decorative gathering, esp in cloth, made by drawing up the material along 2 or more parallel lines of stitching or by stitching in rows of elastic thread or an elastic webbing

shirt n an (esp man's) garment for the upper body; esp one that opens the full length of the centre front and has sleeves and a collar

shirting n fabric suitable for shirts

shirt-sleeve also **shirt-sleeves, shirt-sleeved** adj **1** (having members) without a jacket ⟨*a* ~ *audience*⟩ **2** marked by informality and directness ⟨~ *diplomacy*⟩

shirtwaister n, chiefly Br a fitted dress that fastens down the centre front to just below the waist or to the hem

shirty adj bad-tempered, fractious – infml

shish kebab n kebab cooked on skewers

¹**shit** vb **-tt-; shitted, shit, shat** vb to defecate (in) – vulg

²**shit** n **1** faeces **2** an act of defecation **3a** nonsense, foolishness **b** a despicable person USE vulg

shitty adj nasty, unpleasant – vulg

¹**shiver** n any of the small pieces that result from the shattering of sthg brittle

²**shiver** vb to break into many small fragments; shatter

³**shiver** vi to tremble, esp with cold or fever

⁴**shiver** n an instance of shivering; a tremor – **shivery** adj

¹**shoal** n **1** a shallow **2** an underwater sandbank; esp one exposed at low tide

²**shoal** vi to become shallow or less deep ~ vt to come to a shallow or less deep part of

³**shoal** n a large group (e g of fish)

¹**shock** n a pile of sheaves of grain or stalks of maize set upright in a field – **shock** vt

²**shock** n **1** a violent shaking or jarring ⟨*an earthquake* ~⟩ **2a(1)** a disturbance in the equilibrium or permanence of sthg (e g a system) **(2)** a sudden or violent disturbance of thoughts or emotions **b** sthg causing such disturbance ⟨*the news came as a terrible* ~⟩ **3** a state of serious depression of most bodily functions associated with reduced blood volume and pressure and caused usu by severe injuries, bleeding, or burns **4** sudden stimulation of the nerves and convulsive contraction of the muscles caused by the passage of electricity through the body

³**shock** vt **1a** to cause to feel sudden surprise, terror, horror, or offence **b** to cause to undergo a physical or nervous shock **2** to cause (e g an animal) to experience an electric shock **3** to impel (as if) by a shock ⟨~ *ed her into realizing her selfishness*⟩

⁴**shock** n a thick bushy mass, usu of hair

shock absorber n any of various devices for absorbing the energy of sudden impulses or shocks in machinery, vehicles, etc

shocker n **1** sthg horrifying or offensive (e g a sensational work of fiction or drama) **2** an incorrigible or naughty person (e g a child) – infml

shock-headed adj having a thick bushy mass of hair

shocking adj **1** giving cause for indignation or offence **2** very bad ⟨*had a* ~ *cold*⟩ – infml – **shockingly** adv

shockproof adj resistant to shock; constructed so as to absorb shock without damage ⟨*a* ~ *watch*⟩

shock troops *n pl* troops trained and selected for assault

shod *adj* **1a** wearing shoes, boots, etc **b** equipped with (a specified type of) tyres **2** furnished or equipped with a shoe – often in combination

¹**shoddy** *n* **1** a wool of better quality and longer fibre length than mungo, reclaimed from materials that are not felted **2** a fabric often of inferior quality manufactured wholly or partly from reclaimed wool

²**shoddy** *adj* **1** made wholly or partly of shoddy **2a** cheaply imitative; vulgarly pretentious **b** hastily or poorly done; inferior **c** shabby – **shoddily** *adv*, **shoddiness** *n*

¹**shoe** *n* **1a** an outer covering for the human foot that does not extend above the ankle and has a thick or stiff sole and often an attached heel **b** a metal plate or rim for the hoof of an animal **2** sthg resembling a shoe in shape or function **3** *pl* a situation, position; *also* a predicament ⟨*I wouldn't be in the president's ~s for anything*⟩ **4** the part of a vehicle braking system that presses on the brake drum

²**shoe** *vt* **shoeing; shod** *also* **shoed** **1** to fit (e g a horse) with a shoe **2** to protect or reinforce with a usu metal shoe

shoehorn *n* a curved piece of metal, plastic, etc used to ease the heel into the back of a shoe

shoe-horn *vt* to force into a limited space ⟨*soon be ~ing passengers into the trains – The Guardian*⟩

shoelace *n* a lace or string for fastening a shoe

shoemaker *n* sby whose occupation is making or repairing footwear

¹**shoestring** *n* **1** a shoelace **2** an amount of money inadequate or barely adequate to meet one's needs ⟨*run a business on a ~*⟩

²**shoestring** *adj* operating on, accomplished with, or consisting of a small amount of money ⟨*a ~ budget*⟩

shone *past of* SHINE

¹**shoo** *interj* – used in frightening away an (esp domestic) animal

²**shoo** *vt* to drive away (as if) by crying 'Shoo!'

¹**shook** *past & chiefly dial past part of* SHAKE

²**shook** *n* **1** ¹SHOCK **2** *NAm* a set of wooden staves and end pieces for making a hogshead, cask, or barrel

¹**shoot** *vb* **shot** *vt* **1a** to eject or impel or cause to be ejected or impelled by a sudden release of tension (e g of a bowstring or by a flick of a finger) ⟨*~ an arrow*⟩ ⟨*~ a marble*⟩ **b** to drive forth or cause to be driven forth **(1)** by an explosion (e g of a powder charge in a firearm or of ignited fuel in a rocket) **(2)** by a sudden release of gas or air ⟨*~ darts from a blowpipe*⟩ **c** to drive (e g a ball) forth or away by striking or pushing with the arm, hand, or foot or with an implement **d(1)** to utter (e g words or sounds) rapidly, suddenly, or violently ⟨*~ out a stream of invective*⟩ **(2)** to emit (e g light or flame) suddenly and rapidly **(3)** to send forth with suddenness or intensity ⟨*shot a look of anger at her*⟩ **e** to discharge or empty (e g rubbish) from a container **2a** to strike and esp wound or kill with a bullet, arrow, shell, etc shot from a gun, bow, etc **b** to remove or destroy by use of firearms; *also* to wreck, explode **3a** to push or slide (a bolt) in order to fasten or unfasten a door **b** to pass (a shuttle) through the warp threads in weaving **c** to push or thrust forwards; stick out – usu + *out* ⟨*toads ~ing out their tongues*⟩ **d** to put forth in growing – usu + *out* **4a** to engage in (a sport, game, or part of a game that involves shooting); play ⟨*~ pool*⟩ **b** to score by shooting ⟨*~ a basket*⟩ **5** to hunt over with a firearm or bow ⟨*~ a tract of woodland*⟩ **6a** to cause to move suddenly or swiftly forwards ⟨*shot the car onto the highway*⟩ **b** to send or carry quickly; dispatch **7** to pass swiftly by, over, or along ⟨*~ing rapids*⟩ **8** to plane (e g the edge of a board) straight or true **9** to take a picture or series of pictures or television images of; film; *also* to

make (a film, videotape, etc) **10** to pass through (a road junction or traffic lights) without slowing down or stopping – infml **11** to take (a drug) by hypodermic needle – slang ~ *vi* **1a** to go or pass rapidly or violently ⟨*sparks ~ing up*⟩ **b** to move ahead by superior speed, force, momentum, etc **c** to stream out suddenly; spurt ⟨*blood shot from the wound*⟩ **d** to dart (as if) in rays from a source of light **e** to dart with a piercing sensation ⟨*pain shot up his arm*⟩ **2a** to cause a weapon or other device to discharge a missile **b** to use a firearm or bow, esp for sport **3** to propel a missile ⟨*guns that ~ many miles*⟩ **4** to protrude, project – often + *out* ⟨*a mountain-range ~ing out into the sea*⟩ **5** to grow or sprout (as if) by putting forth shoots **6a** to propel an object (e g a ball) in a particular way **b** to drive the ball or puck in football, hockey, etc towards a goal **7** to slide into or out of a fastening ⟨*a bolt that ~s in either direction*⟩ **8a** to record a series of visual images (e g on cinefilm or videotape); make a film or videotape **b** to operate a camera or set cameras in operation – **shoot a line** to invent romantic or boastful detail – infml – **shoot one's bolt** to exhaust one's capabilities and resources – **shoot one's mouth off** to talk foolishly or indiscreetly

²**shoot** *n* **1a** a stem or branch with its leaves, buds, etc, esp when not yet mature **b** an offshoot **2a** a shooting trip or party **b** (land over which is held) the right to shoot game **c** a shooting match **3** a sudden or rapid advance **4** (a rush of water down) a descent in a stream **5** *chiefly NAm* a momentary darting sensation; a twinge

shoot down *vt* to assert or show the invalidity of; *also* to veto – infml

shooter *n* a repeating pistol – usu in combination ⟨*six-shooter*⟩

shooting brake *n, Br* ESTATE CAR

shooting gallery *n* a usu covered range equipped with targets for practice in shooting with firearms

shooting match *n* an affair, matter – chiefly in *the whole shooting match*; infml

shooting star *n* a meteor appearing as a temporary streak of light in the night sky

shooting stick *n* a spiked stick with a handle that opens out into a seat

shoot-out *n* a usu decisive battle fought with handguns or rifles

shoot up *vi* **1** to grow or increase rapidly ⟨*house prices have shot up in recent months*⟩ **2** to inject a narcotic drug into a vein – slang

¹**shop** *n* **1** a building or room for the retail sale of merchandise or for the sale of services **2** a place or part of a factory where a particular manufacturing or repair process takes place **3** the jargon or subject matter peculiar to an occupation or sphere of interest – chiefly in *talk shop*

²**shop** *vb* **-pp-** *vi* **1** to visit a shop with intent to purchase goods **2** to make a search; hunt ⟨*~ for winning designs*⟩ ~ *vt* to inform on; betray ⟨*the robber who changed sides and ~ped his mates – Daily Mirror*⟩ – slang – **shopper** *n*

shop around *vi* to investigate a market or situation in search of the best buy or alternative

shop assistant *n, Br* one employed to sell goods in a retail shop

shopfloor *n* the area in which machinery or workbenches are located in a factory or mill, esp considered as a place of work; *also, sing or pl in constr* the workers in an establishment as distinct from the management

shopkeeper *n* one who runs a retail shop

shoplift *vb* to steal from a shop – **shoplifter** *n*, **shoplifting** *n*

shopping centre *n* a group of retail shops and service

establishments of different types, often designed to serve a community or neighbourhood

shopsoiled *adj, chiefly Br* **1** deteriorated (e g soiled or faded) through excessive handling or display in a shop **2** no longer fresh or effective; clichéd ⟨*the* ~ *slogans of fascism*⟩

shop steward *n* a union member elected to represent usu manual workers

shopworn *adj, chiefly NAm* shopsoiled

¹**shore** *n* **1** the land bordering the sea or another (large) body of water **2** land as distinguished from the sea

²**shore** *vt* **1** to support with shores; prop **2** to give support to; brace, sustain – usu + *up* ⟨~ *up farm prices*⟩

³**shore** *n* a prop for preventing sinking or sagging

shore leave *n* time granted to members of a ship's crew to go ashore

shorn *past part of* SHEAR

¹**short** *adj* **1** having little or insufficient length or height **2a** not extended in time; brief ⟨*a* ~ *vacation*⟩ **b** *of the memory* not retentive **c** quick, expeditious ⟨*made* ~ *work of the problem*⟩ **d** seeming to pass quickly ⟨*made great progress in just a few* ~ *years*⟩ **3a** *of a speech sound* having a relatively short duration **b** *of a syllable in prosody* (1) of relatively brief duration (2) unstressed **4** limited in distance ⟨*a* ~ *walk*⟩ **5a** not coming up to a measure or requirement ⟨*in* ~ *supply*⟩ ⟨*the throw was* ~ *by 5 metres*⟩ **b** insufficiently supplied ⟨~ *of cash*⟩ **6a** abrupt, curt **b** quickly provoked ⟨*a* ~ *temper*⟩ **7** SHORT-TERM **2 8a** *of pastry, biscuits, etc* crisp and easily broken owing to the presence of fat **b** *of metal* brittle **9** made briefer; abbreviated ⟨*Sue is* ~ *for Susan*⟩ **10** being or relating to a sale of securities or commodities that the seller does not possess at the time of the sale ⟨~ *sale*⟩ **11a** of or occupying a fielding position in cricket near the batsman **b** *of a bowled ball* bouncing relatively far from the batsman – **shortness** *n* – **by the short hairs, by the short and curlies** totally at one's mercy ⟨*if he signs, we've got him* by the short hairs⟩ – **in the short run** for the immediate future

²**short** *adv* **1** curtly ⟨*tends to talk* ~ *with people when he's busy*⟩ **2** for or during a brief time ⟨*short-lasting*⟩ **3** in an abrupt manner; suddenly ⟨*the car stopped* ~⟩ **4** at a point or degree before a specified or intended goal or limit ⟨*the shells fell* ~⟩ ⟨*stopped* ~ *of murder*⟩ – **be taken/caught short** *Br* to feel a sudden embarrassing need to defecate or urinate

³**short** *n* **1** a short sound or signal **2** *pl* a by-product of wheat milling that includes the germ, bran, and some flour **3** *pl* knee-length or less than knee-length trousers **4** *pl* short-term bonds **5** SHORT CIRCUIT **6** a brief often documentary or educational film **7** *Br* a drink of spirits – **for short** as an abbreviation – **in short** by way of summary; briefly

⁴**short** *vt* to short-circuit

shortage *n* a lack, deficit

shortbread *n* a thick biscuit made from flour, sugar, and fat

shortcake *n* **1** shortbread **2** a thick short cake resembling biscuit that is usu sandwiched with a layer of fruit and cream and eaten as a dessert

shortchange *vt* **1** to give less than the correct amount of change to **2** to cheat – *infml*

short-circuit *vt* **1** to apply a short circuit to or cause a short circuit in (so as to render inoperative) **2** to bypass, circumvent

short circuit *n* the accidental or deliberate joining by a conductor of 2 parts of an electric circuit

shortcoming *n* a deficiency, defect ⟨*felt his* ~s *made him unsuited to management*⟩

shortcut *n* a route or procedure quicker and more direct than one customarily followed

shorten *vt* **1** to make short or shorter **2** to add fat to (e g pastry dough) **3** to reduce the area or amount of (sail that is set)

shortening *n* an edible fat (e g butter or lard) used to shorten pastry, biscuits, etc

shortfall *n* (the degree or amount of) a deficit

shorthand *n* **1** a method of rapid writing that substitutes symbols and abbreviations for letters, words, or phrases **2** a system or instance of rapid or abbreviated communication ⟨*verbal* ~⟩ – **shorthand** *adj*

shorthanded *adj* short of the usual or requisite number of staff; undermanned

shorthand typist *n* sby who takes shorthand notes, esp from dictation, then transcribes them using a typewriter

shorthorn *n, often cap* any of a breed of beef cattle originating in the N of England and including good milk-producing strains

shortie *n or adj* (a) shorty – *infml*

short-list *vt, Br* to place on a short list

short list *n, Br* a list of selected candidates (e g for a job) from whom a final choice must be made

short-lived *adj* not living or lasting long

shortly *adv* **1a** in a few words; briefly **b** in an abrupt manner **2a** in a short time ⟨*we will be there* ~⟩ **b** at a short interval ⟨~ *after sunset*⟩

short order *n, NAm* an order for food that can be quickly cooked – **in short order** quickly

short-range *adj* **1** SHORT-TERM **1 2** relating to, suitable for, or capable of travelling (only) short distances ⟨*a* ~ *missile*⟩

short shrift *n* **1** a brief respite for confession before execution **2** summary or inconsiderate treatment

shortsighted *adj* **1** able to see near objects more clearly than distant objects; myopic **2** lacking foresight – **shortsightedly** *adv*, **shortsightedness** *n*

short story *n* a piece of prose fiction usu dealing with a few characters and often concentrating on mood rather than plot

short-term *adj* **1** involving a relatively short period of time ⟨~ *plans*⟩ **2** of or constituting a financial operation or obligation based on a brief term, esp one of less than a year

short time *n* reduced working hours because of a lack of work

short ton *n* a US unit of weight that is equal to 2000lb (about 746.48kg)

shortwave *n* a band of radio waves having wavelengths between about 120m and 20m and typically used for amateur transmissions or long-range broadcasting – often pl with sing. meaning

short-winded *adj* **1** affected with or characterized by shortness of breath **2** brief or concise in speaking or writing

shorty, shortie *n or adj* (sby or sthg) short – *infml*

¹**shot** *n* **1a** an action of shooting **b** a directed propelling of a missile; *specif* a directed discharge of a firearm **c** a stroke or throw in a game (e g tennis, cricket, or basketball); *also* an attempt to kick the ball into the goal in soccer **d** a hypodermic injection **2a**(1) small lead or steel pellets (for a shotgun) (2) a single (nonexplosive) projectile for a gun or cannon **b**(1) a metal sphere that is thrown for distance as an athletic field event (2) this event **3** the distance that a missile is or can be projected **4** one who shoots; *esp* a marksman **5a** an attempt, try ⟨*had a* ~ *at mending the puncture*⟩ **b** a guess, conjecture **6a** a single photographic exposure **b** an image or series of images in

a film or a television programme shot by 1 camera from 1 angle without interruption **7** a charge of explosives **8** a small amount applied at one time; a dose ⟨*a dramatist could inject a ~ of colloquialism into a tragic aria* – Kenneth Tynan⟩ – *infml* – **like a shot** very rapidly – **shot in the arm** a stimulus, boost – **shot in the dark** a wild guess

²**shot** *adj* **1a** *of a fabric* having contrasting and changeable colour effects; iridescent ⟨*~ silk*⟩ **b** suffused or streaked with (a different) colour ⟨*hair ~ with grey*⟩ **c** infused or permeated *with* a quality or element ⟨*~ through with wit*⟩ **2** utterly exhausted or ruined ⟨*her nerves are ~*⟩ – *infml* – **be/get shot of** *chiefly Br* GET RID OF – *infml*

¹**shotgun** *n* an often double-barrelled smoothbore shoulder weapon for firing quantities of metal shot at short ranges

²**shotgun** *adj* enforced ⟨*a ~ merger*⟩ ⟨*a ~ wedding*⟩

shot put *n* SHOT 2b – **shot-putter** *n*, **shot-putting** *n*

should *past of* SHALL **1** – used (e g in the main clause of a conditional sentence) to introduce a contingent fact, possibility, or presumption ⟨*I ~ be surprised if he wrote*⟩ ⟨*it's odd that you ~ mention that*⟩ **2** ought to ⟨*you ~ brush your teeth after every meal*⟩ **3** – used in reported speech to represent shall or will ⟨*she banged on the door and said we ~ be late* – Punch⟩ **4** will probably ⟨*with an early start, they ~ be here by noon*⟩ **5** – used to soften direct statement ⟨*I ~ have thought it was colder than that*⟩ ⟨*who ~ open the door but Fred*⟩

¹**shoulder** *n* **1a** the part of the human body formed of bones, joints, and muscles that connects the arm to the trunk **b** a corresponding part of a lower vertebrate **2** *pl* **a** the 2 shoulders and the upper part of the back ⟨*shrugged his ~s*⟩ **b** capacity for bearing a burden (e g of blame or responsibility) ⟨*placed the guilt squarely on his ~s*⟩ **3** a cut of meat including the upper joint of the foreleg and adjacent parts **4** an area adjacent to a higher, more prominent, or more important part: e g **a(1)** the slope of a mountain near the top **(2)** a lateral protrusion of a mountain **b** that part of a road to the side of the surface on which vehicles travel **5** a rounded or sloping part (e g of a stringed instrument or a bottle) where the neck joins the body – **shouldered** *adj*

²**shoulder** *vt* **1** to push or thrust (as if) with the shoulder ⟨*~ed his way through the crowd*⟩ **2a** to place or carry on the shoulder ⟨*~ed his rucksack*⟩ **b** to assume the burden or responsibility of ⟨*~ the costs*⟩ ~ *vi* to push aggressively with the shoulders; jostle

shoulder blade *n* the scapula

shoulder strap *n* a strap that passes across the shoulder and holds up a garment

shouldest, shouldst *archaic past 2 sing of* SHALL

shouldn't should not

¹**shout** *vi* **1** to utter a sudden loud cry **2** *Austr & NZ* to buy a round of drinks ~ *vt* **1** to utter in a loud voice **2** *Austr & NZ* **a** to buy sthg, esp a drink, for (another person) **b** to buy (sthg, esp a drink) for sby ⟨*dropped in to see if you'd ~ an old friend a drink* – The Sun (Melbourne)⟩ USE (*vi* 2, *vt* 2) *infml* – **shouter** *n*

²**shout** *n* **1** a loud cry or call **2** ʳROUND 6 – *infml*

shout down *vt* to drown the words of (a speaker) by shouting

shove *vt* **1** to push along with steady force **2** to push in a rough, careless, or hasty manner; thrust ⟨*~d the book into his coat pocket*⟩ ~ *vi* **1** to force a way forwards ⟨*bargain hunters shoving up to the counter*⟩ **2** to move sthg by pushing ⟨*you pull and I'll ~*⟩ – **shove** *n*, **shover** *n*

shove-halfpenny *n* a game played on a special flat board on which players shove discs (e g coins) into marked scoring areas

¹**shovel** *n* **1a(1)** an implement consisting of a broad scoop or a dished blade with a handle, used to lift and throw loose material **(2)** (a similar part on) a digging or earth-moving machine **b** sthg like a shovel **2** a shovelful

²**shovel** *vb* **-ll-** (NAm **-l-**, **-ll-**), *vt* **1** to dig, clear, or shift with a shovel **2** to convey clumsily or in a mass as if with a shovel ⟨*~led his food into his mouth*⟩ ~ *vi* to use a shovel

shove off *vi* to go away; leave – *infml*

¹**show** *vb* **shown, showed** *vt* **1** to cause or permit to be seen; exhibit **2** to present as a public spectacle **3** to reveal by one's condition, nature, or behaviour ⟨*was reluctant to ~ his feelings*⟩ **4** to demonstrate by one's achievements ⟨*~ed herself to be a fine pianist*⟩ **5a** to point out to sby ⟨*~ed him where she lived*⟩ **b** to conduct, usher ⟨*~ed me to an aisle seat*⟩ **6** to accord, grant ⟨*~ respect to one's elders*⟩ **7a** to make evident; indicate ⟨*a letter that ~ed his true feelings*⟩ **b** to have as an attribute; manifest ⟨*trade figures ~ed a large deficit*⟩ ⟨*the patient is ~ing some improvement*⟩ **8a** to establish or make clear by argument or reasoning ⟨*~ a plan to be faulty*⟩ **b** to inform, instruct ⟨*~ed me how to solve the problem*⟩ **9** to present (an animal) for judging in a show ~ *vi* **1** to be or come in view; be noticeable ⟨*he has a tear in his coat but it doesn't ~*⟩ **2** to appear in a specified way ⟨*~ to good advantage*⟩ **3** to be staged or presented **4** *chiefly NAm* SHOW UP 2 ⟨*failed to ~ for the award*⟩ – **shower** *n* – **show one's hand** to declare one's intentions or reveal one's resources – **show one's true colours** to show one's real nature or opinions – **show over** *chiefly Br* to take on a tour or inspection of ⟨*prospective buyers were shown over the new house*⟩ – **show someone the door** to tell sby to get out

²**show** *n* **1** a display ⟨*a ~ of hands*⟩ – often + *on* ⟨*all antiques on ~ are genuine*⟩ **2a** a false semblance; a pretence ⟨*he made a ~ of friendship*⟩ **b** a more or less true appearance of sthg; a sign ⟨*a ~ of reason*⟩ **c** an impressive display ⟨*a ~ of strength*⟩ **d** ostentation **3** sthg exhibited, esp for wonder or ridicule; a spectacle **4a** a large display or exhibition arranged to arouse interest or stimulate sales **b** a competitive exhibition of animals, plants, etc to demonstrate quality in breeding, growing, etc **5** a public presentation: e g **a** a theatrical presentation **b** a radio or television programme **6** an enterprise, affair ⟨*he ran the whole ~*⟩ **7** *chiefly NAm* a chance – esp in **give someone a show** USE (6&7) *infml*

show business *n* the arts, occupations, and businesses (e g theatre, films, and television) that comprise the entertainment industry

showcase *n* **1** a case, box, or cabinet with a transparent usu glass front or top used for displaying and protecting articles in a shop or museum **2** a setting or surround for exhibiting sthg to best advantage

showdown *n* the final settlement of a contested issue or the confrontation by which it is settled

¹**shower** *n* **1** a fall of rain, snow, etc of short duration **2** sthg like a rain shower ⟨*a ~ of tears*⟩ ⟨*~s of sparks from a bonfire*⟩ **3** an apparatus that provides a stream of water for spraying on the body; *also* an act of washing oneself using such an apparatus **4** *sing or pl in constr, Br* a motley or inferior collection of people – *infml* – **showery** *adj*

²**shower** *vi* **1** to descend (as if) in a shower ⟨*letters ~ed on him in praise and protest*⟩ **2** to take a shower ~ *vt* **1a** to wet copiously (e g with water) in a spray, fine stream, or drops **b** to cause to fall in a shower ⟨*factory chimneys ~ed soot on the neighbourhood*⟩; *also* to cover (as if) with

a shower **2** to bestow or present in abundance ⟨~ed *him with honours*⟩

showgirl *n* a young woman who dances or sings in the chorus of a theatrical production; *broadly* a female stage performer whose presence is purely decorative

showing *n* **1** an act of putting sthg on view; a display, exhibition **2** performance in competition ⟨*made a good ~ in the finals*⟩ **3** a statement or presentation of a case; evidence

showjumping *n* the competitive riding of horses 1 at a time over a set course of obstacles in which the winner is judged according to ability and speed – **showjumper** *n*

showman *n* **1** one who presents a theatrical show; *also* the manager of a circus or fairground **2** a person with a flair for dramatically effective presentation – **showmanship** *n*

show-off *n* one who shows off; an exhibitionist

show off *vt* to exhibit proudly ⟨*wanted to* show *his new car* off⟩ ~ *vi* to seek attention or admiration by conspicuous behaviour ⟨*boys* showing off *on their bicycles*⟩

showpiece *n* a prime or outstanding example used for exhibition

showplace *n* a place (e g an estate or building) regarded as an example of beauty or excellence

showroom *n* a room where (samples of) goods for sale are displayed

show up *vt* **1** to expose (e g a defect, deception, or impostor) **2** to embarrass ~ *vi* **1a** to be plainly evident; STAND OUT **b** to appear in a specified light or manner ⟨*showed* up *badly in the semifinals*⟩ **2** to arrive ⟨*showed* up *late for his own wedding*⟩ USE (*vt 2; vi 2*) *infml*

showy *adj* **1** making an attractive show; striking ⟨*~ blossoms*⟩ **2** given to or marked by pretentious display; gaudy – **showily** *adv*, **showiness** *n*

shrank *past of* SHRINK

shrapnel *n*, *pl* **shrapnel 1** a hollow projectile that contains bullets or pieces of metal and that is exploded by a bursting charge to produce a shower of fragments **2** bomb, mine, or shell fragments thrown out during explosion

¹**shred** *n* a narrow strip cut or torn off; *also* a fragment, scrap

²**shred** *vb* **-dd-** *vt* to cut or tear into shreds ~ *vi* to come apart in or be reduced to shreds – **shredder** *n*

shrew *n* **1** any of numerous small chiefly nocturnal mammals having a long pointed snout, very small eyes, and velvety fur **2** an ill-tempered nagging woman; a scold

shrewd *adj* **1** marked by keen discernment and hardheaded practicality ⟨*~ common sense*⟩ **2** wily, artful ⟨*a ~ operator*⟩ – **shrewdly** *adv*, **shrewdness** *n*

shrewish *adj* ill-tempered, intractable – **shrewishly** *adv*, **shrewishness** *n*

¹**shriek** *vi* to utter or make a shrill piercing cry; screech ⟨*~ with laughter*⟩ ~ *vt* to utter with a shriek or sharply and shrilly – often + *out*

²**shriek** *n* (a sound similar to) a shrill usu wild cry

shrike *n* any of numerous usu largely grey or brownish birds that often impale their (insect) prey on thorns

¹**shrill** *vi* to utter or emit a high-pitched piercing sound ⟨*alarm bells ~*ed *as the robbers raced away*⟩ ~ *vt* to scream

²**shrill** *adj* having, making, or being a sharp high-pitched sound – **shrillness** *n*, **shrilly** *adv*

¹**shrimp** *n*, *pl* **shrimps**, (*1*) **shrimps**, *esp collectively* **shrimp 1** any of numerous mostly small marine 10-legged crustacean animals with a long slender body, compressed abdomen, and long legs **2** a very small or puny person – infml; humor – **shrimpy** *adj*

²**shrimp** *vi* to fish for or catch shrimps – usu in *go shrimping*

shrine *n* **1a** a receptacle for sacred relics **b** a place in which devotion is paid to a saint or deity **2** a receptacle (e g a tomb) for the dead, **3** a place or object hallowed by its history or associations ⟨*Oxford is a ~ of learning*⟩ – **shrine** *vt*

¹**shrink** *vb* **shrank** *also* **shrunk; shrunk, shrunken** *vi* **1** to draw back or cower away (e g from sthg painful or horrible) **2** to contract to a smaller volume or extent (e g as a result of heat or moisture) **3** to show reluctance (e g before a difficult or unpleasant duty); recoil ~ *vt* to cause to contract; *specif* to compact (cloth) by a treatment (e g with water or steam) that results in contraction – **shrinkable** *adj*, **shrinkage** *n*, **shrinker** *n*

²**shrink** *n* **1** shrinkage **2** a psychoanalyst or psychiatrist – humor

shrive *vt* **shrived, shrove; shriven, shrived** *archaic* to hear the confession of and absolve

shrivel *vb* **-ll-** (*NAm* **-l-, -ll-**), to (cause to) contract into wrinkles, esp through loss of moisture

¹**shroud** *n* **1** a burial garment (e g a winding-sheet) **2** sthg that covers, conceals, or guards **3** any of the ropes or wires giving support, usu in pairs, to a ship's mast

²**shroud** *vt* **1a** to envelop and conceal ⟨*trees ~*ed *by a thick mist*⟩ **b** to obscure, disguise **2** to dress for burial

Shrove Tuesday *n* the Tuesday before Ash Wednesday; PANCAKE DAY

shrub *n* a low-growing usu several-stemmed woody plant – **shrubby** *adj*

shrubbery *n* a planting or growth of shrubs

shrug *vb* **-gg-** to lift and contract (the shoulders), esp to express aloofness, aversion, or doubt – **shrug** *n*

shrug off *vt* to brush aside; disregard, belittle ⟨shrugs *the problem* off⟩

¹**shuck** *n* **1** a pod, husk **2** *NAm* sthg of no value – usu pl with sing. meaning ⟨*not worth ~*s⟩ **3** *pl* – used interjectionally to express mild annoyance or disappointment; infml

²**shuck** *vt*, *NAm* **1** to strip of shucks **2** to remove or dispose of like a shuck – often + *off* ⟨*~* off *clothing*⟩ ⟨*~* off *bad habits*⟩ – **shucker** *n*

shudder *vi* **1** to tremble with a sudden brief convulsive movement **2** to quiver, vibrate – **shudder** *n*

¹**shuffle** *vb* **shuffling** *vt* **1** to mix together in a confused mass; jumble **2** to rearrange (e g playing cards or dominoes) to produce a random order **3** to move (the feet) by sliding clumsily along or back and forth without lifting ~ *vi* **1** to act or speak in a shifty or evasive manner **2a** to move or walk by sliding or dragging the feet **b** to dance in a lazy nonchalant manner with scraping and tapping motions of the feet **3** to mix playing cards by shuffling – **shuffler** *n*

²**shuffle** *n* **1a** shuffling (e g of cards) **b** a right or turn to shuffle ⟨*it's your ~*⟩ **2** (a dance characterized by) a dragging sliding movement

shuffleboard *n* a game in which players use long-handled cues to shove wooden discs into scoring areas of a diagram marked on a smooth surface

shufti *n*, *Br* a look, glance ⟨*have a ~ at the radar screen*⟩ – infml

shun *vt* **-nn-** to avoid deliberately, esp habitually ⟨*actors who ~ publicity*⟩ – **shunner** *n*

¹**shunt** *vt* **1a** to move (e g a train) from one track to another **b** *Br* to move (railway vehicles) to different positions on the same track within terminal areas **2** to provide with or divert by means of an electrical shunt **3** to divert (blood) by means of a surgical shunt ~ *vi* **1** to

move into a side track **2** to travel back and forth ⟨~ed *between the 2 towns*⟩ – **shunter** *n*

²**shunt** *n* **1** a means or mechanism for turning or thrusting aside: e g **a** a conductor joining 2 points in an electrical circuit so as to form a parallel path through which a portion of the current may pass **b** a surgical passage created between 2 blood vessels to divert blood from one part to another **c** *chiefly Br* a siding **2** a usu minor collision of motor vehicles – *infml*

¹**shush** *n* **1** – used interjectionally to demand silence **2** peace and quiet; silence – *infml* ⟨*quiet, please, children! Let's have a bit of ~!*⟩

²**shush** *vt* to tell to be quiet, esp by saying 'Shush!' – *infml*

shut *vb* **-tt-; shut** *vt* **1** to place in position to close an opening ⟨~ *the lid*⟩ ⟨~ *the door*⟩ **2** to confine (as if) by enclosure ⟨~ *him in the cupboard*⟩ **3** to fasten with a lock or bolt **4** to close by bringing enclosing or covering parts together ⟨~ *the eyes*⟩ **5** to cause to cease or suspend operation ⟨~ *up shop*⟩ ~*vi* **1** to become closed ⟨*flowers that ~ at night*⟩ **2** to cease or suspend operation *USE* (*vt* 5; *vi* 2) often + *up* or *down*

shut away *vt* to remove or isolate from others ⟨*governments that shut dissidents away*⟩

shutdown *n* the cessation or suspension of an activity (e g work in a mine or factory)

shut-eye *n* sleep – *infml*

shutoff *n, chiefly NAm* a stoppage, interruption

shut off *vt* **1a** to cut off, stop ⟨shut *the water* off⟩ **b** to stop the operation of (e g a machine) ⟨shut *the motor* off⟩ **2** to isolate, separate – usu + *from* ⟨*a village* shut off *from the rest of the world*⟩ ~*vi* to cease operating; stop ⟨*the heater* shuts off *automatically*⟩

¹**shutter** *n* **1a** a usu hinged outside cover for a window, often fitted as one of a pair **b** a usu movable cover or screen (e g over a door or as part of stage scenery) **2** a device that opens and closes the lens aperture of a camera **3** the movable slots in the box enclosing the swell organ part of a pipe organ, which are opened to increase the volume of the sound – **shutterless** *adj*

²**shutter** *vt* to provide or close with shutters

¹**shuttle** *n* **1a** a usu spindle-shaped device that holds a bobbin and is used in weaving for passing the thread of the weft between the threads of the warp **b** a spindle-shaped device holding the thread in tatting, knotting, or netting **c** a sliding thread holder that carries the lower thread in a sewing machine through a loop of the upper thread to make a stitch **2** a lightweight conical object with a rounded nose that is hit as the object of play in badminton and consists of (a moulded plastic imitation of) a cork with feathers stuck in it **3a** (a route or vehicle for) a regular going back and forth over a usu short route **b** a reusable space vehicle for use esp between earth and outer space

²**shuttle** *vb* **shuttling 1** to (cause to) move to and fro rapidly **2** to transport or be transported (as if) in or by a shuttle – **shuttler** *n*

shuttlecock *n* SHUTTLE 2

shut up *vt* to cause (sby) to be silent; *esp* to force (a speaker) to stop talking ~*vi* to become silent; *esp* to stop talking *USE* *infml*

¹**shy** *adj* **shier, shyer; shiest, shyest 1** easily alarmed; timid, distrustful – often in combination ⟨camera-shy⟩ **2** wary of ⟨~ *of disclosing his age*⟩ **3** sensitively reserved or retiring; *also* expressive of such a state or nature ⟨*spoke in a ~ voice*⟩ **4** *chiefly NAm* lacking, short ⟨*we're 3 points ~ of what we need to win*⟩ – *infml* – **shyly** *adv*, **shyness** *n*

²**shy** *vi* **1** to start suddenly aside in fright or alarm; recoil **2** to move or dodge to evade a person or thing – usu +

away or from ⟨*they shied away from buying the flat when they learnt the full price*⟩ – **shy** *n*

³**shy** *vt* to throw (e g a stone) with a jerking movement; fling ~*vi* to make a sudden throw *USE* *infml*

⁴**shy** *n* **1** a toss, throw **2** a verbal sally ⟨*took a few shies at the integrity of his opponent*⟩ **3** a stall (e g at a fairground) in which people throw balls at targets (e g coconuts) in order to knock them down **4** an attempt *USE* (*1, 2, & 4*) *infml*

shyster *n, chiefly NAm* sby (esp a lawyer) who is professionally unscrupulous

si *n* ti

SI *n* a system of units whose basic units are the metre, kilogram, second, ampere, kelvin, candela, and mole and which uses prefixes (e g micro-, kilo-, and mega-) to indicate multiples or fractions of 10

¹**Siamese** *adj* Thai

²**Siamese** *n, pl* **Siamese 1** Thai **2** *also* **Siamese cat** any of a breed of slender blue-eyed short-haired domestic cats of oriental origin with pale fawn or grey body and darker ears, paws, tail, and face

Siamese twin *n* either of a pair of congenitally joined twins

sib *adj* related by blood

¹**sibilant** *adj* having, containing, or producing a hissing sound (e g /sh, zh, s, z/) – **sibilance, sibilancy** *n*, **sibilantly** *adv*

²**sibilant** *n* a sibilant speech sound

sibling *n* SIB 2; *also* any of 2 or more individuals having 1 parent in common

sibyl *n, often cap* any of several female prophets credited to widely separate parts of the ancient world; *broadly* any female prophet – **sibylline, sibylic, sibyllic** *adj*

sic *adv* intentionally so written – used after a printed word or passage to indicate that it is intended exactly as printed or that it exactly reproduces an original ⟨*said he seed* [~] *it all*⟩

¹**sick** *adj* **1a**(1) ill, ailing ⟨*a ~ child*⟩ (2) of or intended for use in illness ⟨~ *pay*⟩ ⟨*a ~ ward*⟩ **b** queasy, nauseated; likely to vomit ⟨*felt ~ in the car*⟩ – often in combination ⟨carsick⟩ ⟨airsick⟩ **2a** sickened by intense emotion (e g shame or fear) ⟨~ *with fear*⟩ ⟨*worried ~*⟩ **b** disgusted or weary, esp because of surfeit ⟨*gossip that makes one ~*⟩ ⟨~ *of flattery*⟩ **c** distressed and longing for sthg that one has lost or been parted from **3a** mentally or emotionally disturbed; morbid **b** macabre, sadistic ⟨~ *jokes*⟩ **4a** lacking vigour; sickly **b** badly outclassed ⟨*looked ~ in the contest*⟩ – *infml* – **sickish** *adj*, **sickly** *adv* – **be sick** *chiefly Br* to vomit ⟨*was sick on the rug*⟩

²**sick** *n, Br* vomit

sick bay *n* a compartment or room (e g in a ship) used as a dispensary and hospital

sickbed *n* the bed on which one lies sick

sick call *n* a usu daily (army) parade at which individuals report as sick to the medical officer

sicken *vt* **1** to cause to feel ill or nauseous **2** to drive to the point of despair or loathing ~*vi* to become ill; show signs of illness ⟨*looked as if she was ~ing for a cold*⟩

sickening *adj* **1** causing sickness ⟨*a ~ smell*⟩ **2** very horrible or repugnant ⟨*fell to the floor with a ~ thud*⟩ – **sickeningly** *adv*

sick headache *n, chiefly NAm* migraine

¹**sickle** *n* **1** an agricultural implement for cutting plants or hedges, consisting of a curved metal blade with a short handle **2** a cutting mechanism (e g of a combine harvester) consisting of a bar with a series of cutting parts

²**sickle** *adj* having a curve resembling that of a sickle blade ⟨*the ~ moon*⟩

³**sickle** *vt* **1** to mow, reap, or cut with a sickle **2** to form

(a red blood cell) into a crescent shape ~ *vi* to become crescent-shaped ⟨*the ability of red blood cells to* ~⟩

sick leave *n* absence from work because of illness

sickle-cell anaemia *n* a hereditary anaemia occurring primarily in Negroes, in which the sickling of most of the red blood cells causes recurrent short periods of fever and pain

sickly *adj* 1 somewhat unwell; *also* habitually ailing 2 associated with sickness ⟨*a* ~ *complexion*⟩ 3 producing or tending to produce disease ⟨*a* ~ *climate*⟩ 4 suggesting sickness: a strained, uneasy ⟨*a* ~ *smile*⟩ b feeble, weak ⟨*a* ~ *plant*⟩ 5a tending to produce nausea ⟨*a* ~ *taste*⟩ b mawkish, saccharine ⟨~ *sentiment*⟩ – **sickliness** *n*

sickness *n* 1 ill health 2 a specific disease 3 nausea, queasiness

sick pay *n* salary or wages paid to an employee while on sick leave

sickroom *n* a room set aside for or occupied by sick people

sick up *vt, Br* to vomit – infml

¹**side** *n* 1a the right or left part of the wall or trunk of the body ⟨*a pain in the* ~⟩ b the right or left half of the animal body or of a meat carcass 2 a location, region, or direction considered in relation to a centre or line of division ⟨*the south* ~ *of the city*⟩ ⟨*surrounded on all* ~ s⟩ 3 a surface forming a border or face of an object 4 a slope of a hill, ridge, etc 5a a bounding line of a geometrical figure ⟨*each* ~ *of a square*⟩ b FACE 5a(5) c either surface of a thin object ⟨*one* ~ *of a record*⟩ ⟨*the right* ~ *of the cloth*⟩ 6 company ⟨*he never left her* ~⟩ 7a *sing or pl in constr* a person or group in competition or dispute with another b the attitude or activity of such a person or group; a part ⟨*took my* ~ *of the argument*⟩ 8 a line of descent traced through a parent ⟨*the grandfather on his mother's* ~⟩ 9 an aspect or part of sthg viewed in contrast with some other aspect or part ⟨*the better* ~ *of his nature*⟩ 10 a position viewed as opposite to or contrasted with another ⟨2 ~ s *to every question*⟩ 11 the direction of a specified tendency – + *on* ⟨*she was somewhat on the short* ~⟩ 12 *Br* a television channel 13 *Br* sideways spin imparted to a billiard ball – **on the side** 1 in addition to a principal occupation; *specif* as a dishonest or illegal secondary activity 2 *NAm* in addition to the main portion

²**side** *adj* 1 at, from, towards, etc the side 2a incidental, subordinate ⟨*a* ~ *issue*⟩ b made on the side, esp in secret ⟨*a* ~ *payment*⟩ c additional to the main part or portion ⟨*a* ~ *order for more rolls*⟩

³**side** *vi* to take sides; join or form sides ⟨~ d *with the rebels*⟩

side arm *n* a weapon (e g a sword, revolver, or bayonet) worn at the side or in the belt

sideboard *n* 1 a usu flat-topped piece of dining-room furniture having compartments and shelves for holding articles of table service 2 *pl, Br* whiskers on the side of the face that extend from the hairline to below the ears

sidecar *n* a car attached to the side of a motorcycle or motor scooter for 1 or more passengers

sided *adj* having sides, usu of a specified number or kind ⟨*one*-sided⟩ ⟨*glass*-sided⟩ – **sidedness** *n*

side effect *n* a secondary and usu adverse effect (e g of a drug) ⟨*forced to stop taking the drug by the* ~s⟩

sidekick *n, chiefly NAm* sby closely associated with another, esp as a subordinate – infml

sidelight *n* 1 incidental or additional information 2a the red port light or the green starboard light carried by ships travelling at night b a light at the side of a (motor) vehicle

sideline *n* 1 a line at right angles to a goal line or end line

and marking a side of a court or field of play 2a a line of goods manufactured or esp sold in addition to one's principal line b a business or activity pursued in addition to a full-time occupation 3 *pl* the standpoint of people not immediately participating – chiefly in *on the sidelines*

¹**sidelong** *adv* towards the side; obliquely

²**sidelong** *adj* 1 inclining or directed to one side ⟨~ *glances*⟩ 2 indirect rather than straightforward

sidereal *adj* of or expressed in relation to stars or constellations

sidesaddle *n* a saddle for women in which the rider sits with both legs on the same side of the horse – **sidesaddle** *adv*

sideshow *n* 1a a minor show offered in addition to a main exhibition (e g of a circus) b a fairground booth or counter offering a game of luck or skill 2 an incidental diversion

sideslip *vi* -pp- to move sideways through the air in a downward direction – **sideslip** *n*

sidesman *n* any of a group of people in an Anglican church who assist the churchwardens, esp in taking the collection in services

sidesplitting *adj* causing raucous laughter

sidestep *vb* -pp- *vi* 1 to step sideways or to one side 2 to evade an issue or decision ~ *vt* 1 to move quickly out of the way of ⟨~ *a blow*⟩ 2 to bypass, evade ⟨*adept at* ~ *ping awkward questions*⟩

side step *n* 1 a step aside (e g in boxing to avoid a punch) 2 a step taken sideways (e g when climbing on skis)

side street *n* a minor street branching off a main thoroughfare

sidestroke *n* a swimming stroke executed while lying on one's side

sideswipe *n* an incidental deprecatory remark, allusion, or reference – infml

¹**sidetrack** *n* 1 an unimportant line of thinking that is followed instead of a more important one 2 *NAm* a siding

²**sidetrack** *vt* to divert from a course or purpose; distract

sidewalk *n, NAm* a pavement

sidewards, NAm chiefly sideward *adv* towards one side

sideways, NAm also sideway *adv or adj* 1 to or from the side ⟨*a* ~ *movement*⟩; *also* askance 2 with 1 side forward ⟨*turn it* ~⟩ 3 to a position of equivalent rank ⟨*he was promoted* ~⟩

siding *n* a short railway track connected with the main track

sidle *vi* **sidling** 1 to move obliquely 2 to walk timidly or hesitantly; edge along – usu + *up* – **sidle** *n*

siege *n* a military blockade of a city or fortified place to compel it to surrender; *also* the duration of or operations carried out in a siege – **lay siege to** 1 to besiege militarily ⟨*laid siege to the town*⟩ 2 to pursue diligently or persistently

sienna *n* an earthy substance containing oxides of iron and usu of manganese that is brownish yellow when raw and orange red or reddish brown when burnt and is used as a pigment

sierra *n* a range of mountains, esp with a serrated or irregular outline

Sierra – a communication code word for the letter *s*

siesta *n* an afternoon nap or rest

sieva bean *n* any of several small-seeded beans closely related to and sometimes classed as lima beans; *also* the seed of a lima bean

¹**sieve** *n* a device with a meshed or perforated bottom that

will allow the passage of liquids or fine solids while retaining coarser material or solids

²sieve vt to sift

sift vt **1a** to put through a sieve ⟨~ flour⟩ **b** to separate (out) (as if) by passing through a sieve **2** to scatter (as if) with a sieve ⟨~ sugar on a cake⟩ – **sift through** to make a close examination of (things in a mass or group)

sifter n ²CASTOR 2

¹sigh vi **1** to take a long deep audible breath (e g in weariness or grief) **2** esp of the wind to make a sound like sighing **3** to grieve, yearn – usu + for ⟨~ing for the days of his youth⟩ ~vt to express by or with sighs – **sigher** n

²sigh n **1** an act of sighing, esp when expressing an emotion or feeling (e g weariness or relief) **2** a sound of or resembling sighing ⟨~s of the summer breeze⟩

¹sight n **1** sthg seen; esp a spectacle ⟨the familiar ~ of the postman coming along the street⟩ **2a** a thing (e g an impressive or historic building) regarded as worth seeing – often pl ⟨see the ~s of Paris⟩ **b** sthg ridiculous or displeasing in appearance ⟨you must get some sleep, you look a ~⟩ **3a** the process, power, or function of seeing; specif the one of the 5 basic physical senses by which light received by the eye is interpreted by the brain as a representation of the forms, brightness, and colour of the objects of the real world **b** a manner of regarding; an opinion **4a** the act of looking at or beholding sthg ⟨fainted at the ~ of blood⟩ **b** a view, glimpse ⟨got a ~ of the Queen⟩ **c** an observation (e g by a navigator) to determine direction or position **5a** a perception of an object by the eye **b** the range of vision **6a** a device for guiding the eye (e g in aiming a firearm or bomb) **b** a device with a small aperture through which objects are to be seen and by which their direction is ascertained **7** a great deal; a lot ⟨earned a ~ more as a freelance⟩ – infml – **sightless** adj, **sightlessness** n – **at first sight** when viewed without proper investigation ⟨at first sight the place seems very dull⟩ – **at/on sight** as soon as presented to view – **out of sight 1** beyond all expectation or reason ⟨wages have risen out of sight during the past year⟩ **2** chiefly NAm marvellous, wonderful – infml; no longer in vogue – **sight for sore eyes** sby or sthg whose appearance or arrival is an occasion for joy or relief

²sight vt **1** to get or catch sight of ⟨several whales were ~ed⟩ **2** to aim (e g a weapon) by means of sights **3a** to equip (e g a gun) with sights **b** to adjust the sights of ~ vi to take aim (e g in shooting) – **sighting** n

sighted adj having sight, esp of a specified kind – often in combination ⟨clear-sighted⟩

sightly adj **1** pleasing to the eye; attractive **2** chiefly NAm affording a fine view ⟨homes in a ~ location⟩ – **sightliness** n

sight-read vb **sight-read** vt to read (e g a foreign language) or perform (music) without previous preparation or study ~ vi to read at sight; esp to perform music at sight – **sight reader** n

sight screen n a screen placed on the boundary of a cricket field behind the bowler to improve the batsman's view of the ball

sightseeing n the act or pastime of touring interesting or attractive sights – often in go sightseeing ⟨went on holiday ~ in Scotland⟩ ⟨a ~ trip⟩ – **sightseer** n

¹sign n **1a** a motion or gesture by which a thought, command, or wish is made known **b** SIGNAL 1 **2** a mark with a conventional meaning, used to replace or supplement words **3** any of the 12 divisions of the zodiac **4a**(1) a character (e g a flat or sharp) used in musical notation (2) a segno **b** a character (e g ÷) indicating a mathematical operation; also either of 2 characters + and

– that form part of the symbol of a number and characterize it as positive or negative **5** a board or notice bearing information or advertising matter or giving warning, command, or identification **6a** sthg material or external that stands for or signifies sthg spiritual **b** sthg serving to indicate the presence or existence of sby or sthg ⟨saw no ~ of him anywhere⟩ **c** a presage, portent ⟨~s of an early spring⟩ **d** objective evidence of plant or animal disease **7** a remarkable event indicating the will of a deity

²sign vt **1a** to place a sign on **b** to indicate, represent, or express by a sign **2a** to put a signature to **b** to assign formally ⟨~ed over his property⟩ **c**(1) to write down (one's name) (2) to write as the name of (oneself) ⟨~ed herself 'R E Swan'⟩ **3** to warn, order, or request by a sign ⟨~ed him to enter⟩ **4** to engage by securing the signature of on a contract of employment ⟨~ed a new striker from Arsenal⟩ – often + on or up ~vi **1** to write one's signature, esp in token of assent, responsibility, or obligation **2** to make a sign or signal – **signer** n

¹signal n **1** an act, event, or watchword agreed on as the occasion of concerted action ⟨waited for the ~ to begin the attack⟩ **2** sthg that occasions action ⟨his scolding was a ~ for the little girl to start crying⟩ **3** a conventional sign (e g a siren or flashing light) made to give warning or command ⟨a ~ that warns of an air raid⟩ **4a** an object used to transmit or convey information beyond the range of human voice **b** the sound or image conveyed in telegraphy, telephony, radio, radar, or television **c** the variations of a physical quantity (e g pressure or voltage) by which information may be transmitted: e g (1) the wave that is used to modulate a carrier ⟨the video ~⟩ (2) the wave produced by the modulation of a carrier by a signal ⟨a radio ~⟩

²signal vb **-ll-** (NAm **-l-, -ll-**) vt **1** to warn, order, or request by a signal ⟨~led the fleet to turn back⟩ **2** to communicate by signals ⟨~led their refusal⟩ **3** to be a sign of; mark ⟨his resignation ~led the end of a long career⟩ ~ vi to make or send a signal – **signaller**, NAm chiefly **signaler** n

³signal adj **1** used in signalling ⟨a ~ beacon⟩ **2** distinguished from the ordinary; conspicuous ⟨a ~ achievement⟩ – chiefly fml

signalbox n, Br a raised building above a railway line from which signals and points are worked

signalize, -ise vt **1** chiefly NAm to point out carefully or distinctly; draw attention to **2** to make noteworthy; distinguish ⟨a performance ~d by consummate artistry⟩ – fml – **signalization** n

signally adv in a signal manner; remarkably ⟨a ~ tactless decision⟩ – chiefly fml

signalman n, pl **signalmen** sby employed to operate signals (e g for a railway)

signatory n a signer with another or others; esp a government bound with others by a signed convention – **signatory** adj

signature n **1a** the name of a person written with his/her own hand **b** the act of signing one's name **2** a letter or figure placed usu at the bottom of the first page on each sheet of printed pages (e g of a book) as a direction to the binder in gathering the sheets; also the sheet itself

signature tune n a melody, passage, or song used to identify a programme, entertainer, etc

signet n **1** a personal seal used officially in lieu of signature **2** the impression made (as if) by a signet **3** a small intaglio seal (e g in a finger ring)

significance n **1a** sthg conveyed as a meaning, often latently or indirectly **b** the quality of conveying or implying **2a** the quality of being important; consequence **b** the quality of being statistically significant

significant adj 1 having meaning; esp expressive ⟨the painter's task to pick out the ~ details – Herbert Read⟩ 2 suggesting or containing a veiled or special meaning ⟨perhaps her glance was ~⟩ 3a having or likely to have influence or effect; important ⟨the budget brought no ~ changes⟩ b probably caused by sth other than chance ⟨statistically ~ correlation between vitamin deficiency and disease⟩ c being any of the figures that comes before or after the decimal point of a number and is not zero or is the first figure after the decimal point that is an exact zero – **significantly** adv

signification n 1 signifying by symbolic means (e g signs) 2 the meaning that a term, symbol, or character normally conveys or is intended to convey

signify vt 1 to mean, denote 2 to show, esp by a conventional token (e g a word, signal, or gesture) ~ vi to have significance; matter – **signifiable** adj, **signifier** n

sign in vi to record one's arrival by signing a register or punching a card ~ vt to record the arrival of (a person) or receipt of (an article) by signing ⟨all deliveries must be signed in at the main gate⟩

sign language n 1 a system of hand gestures used for communication (e g by the deaf) 2 unsystematic communication chiefly by gesture between people speaking different languages

sign off vi 1 to announce the end of a message, programme, or broadcast and finish broadcasting 2 to end a letter (e g with a signature) – **sign-off** n

sign on vi 1 to commit oneself to a job by signature or agreement ⟨sign on as a member of the crew⟩ 2 Br to register as unemployed, esp at an employment exchange

signor n, pl **signors, signori** an Italian man – used as a title equivalent to Mr

signora n, pl **signoras, signore** an Italian married woman – used as a title equivalent to Mrs or as a generalized term of direct address

signorina n, pl **signorinas, signorine** an unmarried Italian girl or woman – used as a title equivalent to Miss

sign out vi to indicate one's departure by signing in a register ⟨signed out of the hospital⟩ ~ vt to record or approve the release or withdrawal of ⟨sign books out of a library⟩

¹signpost n a post (e g at a road junction) with signs on it to direct travellers

²signpost vt 1 to provide with signposts or guides 2 to indicate, mark

sign up vi to join an organization or accept an obligation by signing a contract; esp to enlist in the armed services ~ vt to cause to sign a contract

Sikh n or adj (an adherent) of a monotheistic religion of India marked by rejection of idolatry and caste – **Sikhism** n

silage n fodder converted, esp in a silo, into succulent feed for livestock

¹silence n 1 forbearance from speech or noise; muteness – often interjectional 2 absence of sound or noise; stillness 3 failure to mention a particular thing ⟨can't understand the government's ~ on such an important topic⟩ 4a oblivion, obscurity ⟨promising writers who vanish into ~⟩ b secrecy

²silence vt 1 to put or reduce to silence; still 2 to restrain from expression; suppress 3 to cause (a gun, mortar, etc) to cease firing by return fire, bombing, etc

silencer n 1 a silencing device for a small firearm 2 chiefly Br a device for deadening the noise of the exhaust gas release of an internal-combustion engine

silent adj 1a making no utterance; mute, speechless b disinclined to speak; not talkative 2 free from sound or noise; still 3a endured without utterance ⟨~ grief⟩ b conveyed by refraining from reaction or comment; tacit ⟨~ assent⟩ 4 making no mention; uninformative ⟨history is ~ about this man⟩ 5 MUTE 3 ⟨~ b in doubt⟩ 6 lacking spoken dialogue ⟨a ~ film⟩ – **silently** adv, **silentness** n

silent partner n, chiefly NAm SLEEPING PARTNER

¹silhouette n 1 a portrait in profile cut from dark material and mounted on a light background 2 the shape of a body as it appears against a lighter background

²silhouette vt to represent by a silhouette; also to project on a background like a silhouette

silica n silicon dioxide occurring in many rocks and minerals (e g quartz, opal, and sand)

silicate n any of numerous insoluble often complex compounds that contain silicon and oxygen, constitute the largest class of minerals, and are used in building materials (e g cement, bricks, and glass)

silicon n a tetravalent nonmetallic element that occurs, in combination with other elements, as the most abundant element next to oxygen in the earth's crust and is used esp in alloys

silicone n any of various polymeric organic silicon compounds obtained as oils, greases, or plastics and used esp for water-resistant and heat-resistant lubricants, varnishes, and electrical insulators

silicosis n a disease of the lungs marked by hardening of the tissue and shortness of breath and caused by prolonged inhalation of silica dusts – **silicotic** adj or n

silk n 1 a fine continuous protein fibre produced by various insect larvae, usu for cocoons; esp a lustrous tough elastic fibre produced by silkworms and used for textiles 2 thread, yarn, or fabric made from silk filaments 3 a King's or Queen's Counsel 4 pl the cap and shirt of a jockey made in the registered racing colour of his/her stable 5 a silky material or filament (e g that produced by a spider)

silken adj 1 made of silk 2 resembling silk, esp in softness or lustre

silk screen, silk-screen printing n a stencil process in which paint or ink is forced onto the material to be printed, through the meshes of a prepared silk or organdie screen – **silk-screen** vt

silkworm n a moth whose larva spins a large amount of strong silk in constructing its cocoon

silky adj 1 silken 2 having or covered with fine soft hairs, plumes, or scales – **silkily** adv, **silkiness** n

sill n 1 a horizontal piece (e g a timber) that forms the lowest member or one of the lowest members of a framework or supporting structure (e g a window frame or door frame) 2 a horizontal sheet of intrusive igneous rock running between strata of other rocks

sillabub n (a) syllabub

silly adj 1a showing a lack of common sense or sound judgment ⟨a very ~ mistake⟩ b trifling, frivolous ⟨a ~ remark⟩ ⟨he's just being ~⟩ 2 stunned, dazed ⟨scared ~⟩ ⟨knocked me ~⟩ 3 of or occupying a fielding position in cricket in front of and dangerously near the batsman ⟨~ mid-off⟩ – **sillily** adv, **silliness** n, **silly** n or adv

silo n, pl **silos** 1 a trench, pit, or esp a tall cylinder (e g of wood or concrete) usu sealed to exclude air and used for making and storing silage 2 an underground structure for housing a guided missile

¹silt n a deposit of sediment (e g at the bottom of a river) – **silty** adj

²silt vb to make or become choked or obstructed with silt – often + up – **siltation** n

silvan adj sylvan

¹silver n 1 a white ductile and malleable metallic element that takes a very high degree of polish, is chiefly univalent in compounds, and has the highest thermal and electrical conductivity of any substance 2 silver as a commodity 3 coins made of silver or cupro-nickel 4 articles, esp tableware, made of or plated with silver; *also* cutlery made of other metals 5 a whitish grey colour 6 SILVER MEDAL

²silver adj 1 made of silver 2a resembling silver, esp in having a white lustrous sheen b giving a soft, clear, ringing sound c eloquently persuasive ⟨a ~ tongue⟩ 3 consisting of or yielding silver ⟨~ ore⟩ 4 relating to or characteristic of silver 5 of or marking a 25th anniversary ⟨~ wedding⟩

³silver vt 1 to cover with (a substance resembling) silver 2 to impart a silvery lustre or whiteness to – **silverer** n

silver birch n a common Eurasian birch with a silvery-white trunk

silverfish n 1 any of various silvery fishes 2 any of various small wingless insects; *esp* one found in houses and sometimes injurious to sized paper (e g wallpaper) or starched fabrics

silver medal n a medal of silver awarded to one who comes second in a competition – **silver medallist** n

silver paper n paper with a coating or lamination resembling silver

silver plate n 1 a plating of silver 2 tableware and cutlery of silver or a silver-plated metal

silverside n, Br a cut of beef from the outer part of the top of the leg below the aitchbone, that is boned and often salted

silversmith n sby who works in silver

silverware n SILVER PLATE 2

silvery adj 1 having a soft clear musical tone 2 having the lustre or whiteness of silver 3 containing or consisting of silver – **silveriness** n

simian adj or n (of or resembling) a monkey or ape

similar adj 1 marked by correspondence or resemblance, esp of a general kind ⟨~ but not identical⟩ 2 alike in 1 or more essential aspects ⟨no 2 signatures are exactly ~⟩ 3 differing in size but not in shape ⟨~ triangles⟩ – **similarly** adv, **similarity** n

simile n a figure of speech explicitly comparing 2 unlike things (e g in *cheeks like roses*)

similitude n (an instance of) correspondence in kind, quality, or appearance – fml

simmer vi 1a of a liquid to bubble gently below or just at the boiling point b of food to cook in a simmering liquid 2a to develop, ferment ⟨ideas ~ing in the back of his mind⟩ b to be agitated by suppressed emotion ⟨~ with anger⟩ ~vt to cook (food) in a simmering liquid

simmer down vi to become calm or less excited

simony n the buying or selling of a church office or ecclesiastical promotion – **simoniac** adj or n, **simoniacal** adj

¹simper vi to smile in a foolish self-conscious manner ~vt to say with a simper ⟨~ed her apologies⟩ – **simperer** n

²simper n a foolish self-conscious smile

¹simple adj 1a free from guile or vanity; unassuming b free from elaboration or showiness; unpretentious ⟨wrote in a ~ style⟩ 2 of humble birth or lowly position ⟨a ~ farmer⟩ 3a lacking intelligence; esp mentally retarded b lacking sophistication; naive 4a sheer, unqualified ⟨the ~ truth of the matter⟩ b free of secondary complications ⟨a ~ fracture⟩ c of a sentence consisting of only 1 main clause and no subordinate clauses b composed essentially of 1 substance e not made up of many like units ⟨a ~ eye⟩ 5a not subdivided into branches or leaflets b consisting of a single carpel c of a fruit developing from a single ovary

6 not limited; unconditional ⟨a ~ obligation⟩ 7 readily understood or performed; straightforward ⟨a ~ task⟩ ⟨the adjustment was ~ to make⟩ – **simpleness** n

²simple n, archaic a medicinal plant

simple-hearted adj having a sincere and unassuming nature; artless

simple interest n interest paid or calculated on only the original capital sum of a loan

simple machine n any of various elementary mechanisms formerly considered as the elements of which all machines are composed and including the lever, the wheel and axle, the pulley, the inclined plane, the wedge, and the screw

simpleminded adj devoid of subtlety; unsophisticated; *also* mentally retarded – **simplemindedly** adv, **simplemindedness** n

simpleton n sby lacking common sense or intelligence

simplicity n 1 the state or quality of being simple 2 lack of subtlety or penetration; naivety 3 freedom from affectation or guile; sincerity, straightforwardness 4a directness of expression; clarity b restraint in ornamentation; austerity, plainness

simplify vt to make simple or simpler: e g a to reduce to basic essentials b to diminish in scope or complexity; streamline ⟨~ a manufacturing process⟩ c to make more intelligible; clarify ~vi to become simple or simpler – **simplifier** n, **simplification** n

simply adv 1a without ambiguity; clearly ⟨a ~ worded reply⟩ b without ornamentation or show ⟨~ furnished⟩ c without affectation or subterfuge; candidly 2a solely, merely ⟨eats ~ to keep alive⟩ b without any question ⟨the concert was ~ marvellous⟩

simulacrum n, pl **simulacra** also **simulacrums** an often superficial or misleading likeness of sthg; a semblance – fml

simulate vt 1 to assume the outward qualities or appearance of, usu with the intent to deceive 2 to make a functioning model of (a system, device, or process) (e g by using a computer) – **simulator** n, **simulation** n

simultaneous adj 1 existing, occurring, or functioning at the same time 2 satisfied by the same values of the variables ⟨~ equations⟩ – **simultaneously** adv, **simultaneousness**, **simultaneity** n

¹sin n 1a an offence against moral or religious law or divine commandments b an action considered highly reprehensible ⟨it's a ~ to waste food⟩ 2 a state of estrangement from God – **sinless** adj, **sinlessly** adv, **sinlessness** n

²sin vi -nn- 1 to commit a sin 2 to commit an offence – often + against ⟨writers who ~ against good taste⟩ – **sinner** n

¹since adv 1 continuously from then until now ⟨has stayed there ever ~⟩ 2 before now; ago ⟨should have done it long ~⟩ 3 between then and now; subsequently ⟨has ~ become rich⟩ USE + tenses formed with *to have*

²since prep in the period between (a specified past time) and now ⟨haven't met ~ 1973⟩; from (a specified past time) until now ⟨it's a long time ~ breakfast⟩ – + present tenses and tenses formed with *to have*

³since conj 1 between now and the past time when ⟨has held 2 jobs ~ he left school⟩; continuously from the past time when ⟨ever ~ he was a child⟩ 2 in view of the fact that; because ⟨more interesting, ~ rarer⟩

sincere adj free from deceit or hypocrisy; honest, genuine ⟨~ interest⟩ – **sincerely** adv, **sincereness**, **sincerity** n

sine n the trigonometric function that for an acute angle in a right-angled triangle is the ratio between the side opposite the angle and the hypotenuse

sinecure n an office or position that provides an income while requiring little or no work

sine die *adv* without any future date being designated (e g for resumption) ⟨*the meeting adjourned ~*⟩

sine qua non *n* an absolutely indispensable or essential thing

sinew *n* **1** a tendon; *also* one prepared for use as a cord or thread **2a** solid resilient strength; vigour ⟨*intellectual and moral ~* – G K Chalmers⟩ **b** the chief means of support; mainstay – usu pl ⟨*the ~s of political stability*⟩ – **sinewy** *adj*

sinful *adj* tainted with, marked by, or full of sin; wicked – **sinfully** *adv*, **sinfulness** *n*

sing *vb* **sang; sung; sung** *vi* **1a** to produce musical sounds by means of the voice **b** to utter words in musical notes and with musical inflections and modulations (as a trained or professional singer) **2** to make a shrill whining or whistling sound **3** to produce musical or melodious sounds **4** to buzz, ring ⟨*a punch that made his ears ~*⟩ **5** to make a loud clear utterance **b** to give information or evidence – *slang ~ vt* **1** to utter with musical inflections; *esp* to interpret in musical notes produced by the voice **2a** to relate or celebrate in verse **b** to express vividly or enthusiastically ⟨*~ his praises*⟩ **3** to chant, intone ⟨*~ a requiem mass*⟩ **4** to bring to a specified state by singing ⟨*~s the child to sleep*⟩ – **singable** *adj*, **singer** *n*

singe *vt* **singeing; singed** to burn superficially or slightly; scorch; *esp* to remove the hair, down, or nap from, usu by brief exposure to a flame – **singe** *n*

Singhalese *n or adj, pl* **Singhalese** (a) Sinhalese

¹**single** *adj* **1a** not married **b** of the unmarried state **2** not accompanied by others; sole ⟨*the ~ survivor of the disaster*⟩ **3a** consisting of or having only 1 part or feature ⟨*use double, not ~ thread*⟩ **b** of a plant or flower having the normal number of petals or ray flowers **4** consisting of a separate unique whole; individual ⟨*food is our most important ~ need*⟩ **5** *of combat* involving only 2 people **6** of, suitable for, or involving only 1 person ⟨*a ~ portion of food*⟩ – **singleness** *n*, **singly** *adv*

²**single** *n* **1a** a single thing or amount; *esp* a single measure of spirits **b** a (young) unmarried adult ⟨*a ~s club*⟩ **2** a flower having the number of petals or ray flowers typical of the species **3** a single run scored in cricket **4** a gramophone record, esp of popular music, with a single short track on each side **5** *Br* a ticket bought for a trip to a place but not back again

³**single** *vt* to select or distinguish from a number or group – usu + *out*

single-breasted *adj* having a centre fastening with 1 row of buttons ⟨*a ~ coat*⟩

single file *n* a line (e g of people) moving one behind the other

single-handed *adj* **1** performed or achieved by 1 person or with 1 on a side **2** working or managing alone or unassisted by others – **single-handed, single-handedly** *adv*, **single-handedness** *n*

single-minded *adj* having a single overriding purpose – **single-mindedly** *adv*, **single-mindedness** *n*

singles *n, pl* **singles** a game (e g of tennis) with 1 player on each side

singlestick *n* one-handed fighting or fencing with a wooden stick; *also* the stick used

singlet *n, chiefly Br* VEST 1; *also* a similar garment worn by athletes

singleton *n* **1** a card that is the only one of its suit in a dealt hand **2** an individual as opposed to a pair or group; *specif* an offspring born singly

singsong *n* **1** a voice delivery characterized by a monotonous cadence or rhythm or rising and falling inflection **2** *Br* a session of group singing

¹**singular** *adj* **1a** of a separate person or thing; individual

b of or being a word form denoting 1 person, thing, or instance **2** distinguished by superiority; exceptional ⟨*a man of ~ attainments*⟩ **3** not general ⟨*a ~ proposition in logic*⟩ **4** very unusual or strange; peculiar ⟨*the ~ events leading up to the murder*⟩ **5** of a mathematical matrix having a determinant equal to zero – **singularize** *vt*, **singularly** *adv*

²**singular** *n* the singular number, the inflectional form denoting it, or a word in that form

Sinhalese *n, pl* **Sinhalese** **1** a member of the predominant people that inhabit Sri Lanka **2** the Indic language of the Sinhalese – **Sinhalese** *adj*

sinister *adj* **1** (darkly or insidiously) evil or productive of vice **2** threatening evil or ill fortune; ominous **3** of or situated on the left hand or to the left of sthg, esp in heraldry – **sinisterly** *adv*, **sinisterness** *n*

¹**sink** *vb* **sank, sunk; sunk** *vi* **1a** to go down below a surface (e g of water or a soft substance) **2a** to fall or drop to a lower place or level ⟨*sank to his knees*⟩ **b** to disappear from view ⟨*a red sun ~ing slowly in the west*⟩ **c** to take on a hollow appearance ⟨*my cakes always ~ in the middle*⟩ **3** to become deeply absorbed ⟨*sank into a reverie*⟩ **4** to go downwards in quality, state, condition, amount, or worth ⟨*sank into apathy*⟩ ⟨*~ing spirits*⟩ **5** to deteriorate physically ⟨*the patient was ~ing fast and hadn't long to live*⟩ – *~ vt* **1a** to cause to sink ⟨*~ a battleship*⟩ **b** to force down, esp into the ground **c** to cause (sthg) to penetrate ⟨*sank the dagger into his chest*⟩ **2** to engage (oneself) completely in ⟨*sank himself in his work*⟩ **3** to dig or bore (a well or shaft) in the earth **4** to overwhelm, defeat ⟨*if we don't reach the frontier by midnight we're sunk*⟩ **5** to pay no heed to; ignore, suppress ⟨*sank their differences*⟩ **6** to invest **7** *Br* to drink down ⟨*sank a couple of pints*⟩ – *infml* – **sinkable** *adj*

²**sink** *n* **1a** a cesspool **b** a sewer **c** a basin, esp in a kitchen, connected to a drain and usu a water supply for washing up **2** a place of vice or corruption **3a** a depression in which water (e g from a river) collects and becomes absorbed or evaporated **b** SINKHOLE 2 **4** a body or process that stores or dissipates sthg (e g energy); *specif* HEAT SINK

sinker *n* a weight for sinking a fishing line, seine, or sounding line

sink hole *n* **1** SINK 3a **2** a hollow, esp in a limestone region, that communicates with an underground cavern or passage

sink in *vi* **1** to enter a solid through the surface ⟨*don't leave the ink to sink in*⟩ **2** to become understood

sinking fund *n* a fund set up and added to for paying off the original capital sum of a debt when it falls due

Sino- *comb form* **1** Chinese nation, people, or culture ⟨*Sinophile*⟩ **2** Chinese and ⟨*Sino-Tibetan*⟩

sinology *n* the study of the Chinese and esp of their language, literature, history, and culture – **sinologist** *n*, **sinological** *adj*

sinuous *adj* **1a** of or having a serpentine or wavy form; winding **b** lithe, supple ⟨*dancers with a ~ grace*⟩ **2** intricate, tortuous ⟨*~ argumentation*⟩ – **sinuously** *adv*, **sinuousness, sinuosity** *n*

sinus *n* a cavity, hollow: e g **a** a narrow passage by which pus is discharged from a deep abscess or boil **b(1)** any of several cavities in the skull that usu communicate with the nostrils and contain air **(2)** a channel for blood from the veins **(3)** a wider part in a body duct or tube (e g a blood vessel) **c** a cleft or indentation between adjoining lobes (e g of a leaf)

¹**sip** *vb* **-pp-** to drink (sthg) delicately or a little at a time – **sipper** *n*

²**sip** *n* (a small quantity imbibed by) sipping

¹siphon, syphon *n* **1a** a tube by which a liquid can be transferred up over the wall of a container to a lower level by using atmospheric pressure **b** a bottle for holding carbonated water that is driven out through a tube by the pressure of the carbon dioxide in the bottle, when a valve in the tube is opened **2** any of various tubular organs in animals, esp molluscs or arthropods

²siphon, syphon *vt* to convey, draw off, or empty (as if) by a siphon ~ *vi* to pass or become conveyed (as if) by a siphon

sir *n* **1a** a man of rank or position **b** a man entitled to be addressed as *sir* – used as a title before the Christian name of a knight or baronet **2a** – used as a usu respectful form of address to a male **b** *cap* – used as a conventional form of address at the beginning of a letter

¹sire *n* **1** the male parent of a (domestic) animal **2** *archaic* **a** a father **b** a male ancestor **3** a man of rank or authority; *esp* a lord – used formerly as a title and form of address

²sire *vt* **1** to beget – esp with reference to a male domestic animal **2** to bring into being; originate

siren *n* **1** *often cap* any of a group of mythological partly human female creatures that lured mariners to destruction by their singing **2** a dangerously alluring or seductive woman; a temptress **3a** an apparatus producing musical tones by the rapid interruption of a current of air, steam, etc by a perforated rotating disc **b** a usu electrically operated device for producing a penetrating warning sound ⟨an ambulance ~⟩ ⟨air-raid ~s⟩

sirloin *n* a cut of beef from the upper part of the hind loin just in front of the rump

sirocco *n*, *pl* **siroccos 1** a hot dust-laden wind from the Libyan deserts that blows onto the N Mediterranean coast **2** a warm moist oppressive southeasterly wind in the same regions

sirrah *also* **sirra** *n*, *obs* – used as a form of address implying inferiority in the person addressed

sis *n*, *chiefly NAm* SISTER 1, 5 – infml; used esp in direct address

-sis *suffix* (→ *n*), *pl* **-ses** process or action of ⟨peristal*sis*⟩ ⟨analy*sis*⟩

sisal *n* (a widely cultivated W Indian agave plant whose leaves yield) a strong white fibre used esp for ropes and twine

sissy *n or adj* (a) cissy – **sissy** *adj*

¹sister *n* **1a** a female having the same parents as another person ⟨Mary and I are ~s⟩ **b** HALF SISTER **2** *often cap* **a** a member of a women's religious order; *specif* (the title given to) a Roman Catholic nun **b** a female fellow member of a Christian church **3** a woman related to another person by a common tie or interest (e g adherence to feminist principles) **4** *chiefly Br* a female nurse; *esp* one who is next in rank below a nursing officer and is in charge of a ward or a small department **5** a girl, woman – used esp in direct address; infml – **sisterly** *adj*

²sister *adj* related (as if) by sisterhood; essentially similar ⟨~ ships⟩

sisterhood *n* **1** the relationship between sisters **2** a society of women bound by religious vows

sister-in-law *n*, *pl* **sisters-in-law 1** the sister of one's spouse **2** the wife of one's brother

¹sit *vb* **-tt-; sat** *vi* **1a** to rest on the buttocks or haunches ⟨~ in a chair⟩ **b** to perch, roost **2** to occupy a place as a member of an official body ⟨~ on the parish council⟩ **3** to be in session for official business ⟨visited London when Parliament was ~ting⟩ **4** to cover eggs for hatching **5a** to take up a position for being photographed or painted **b** to act as a model **6** to lie or hang relative to a wearer ⟨the collar ~s awkwardly⟩ **7** to lie, rest ⟨a kettle ~ting

on the stove⟩ **8** to be situated ⟨the house ~s well back from the road⟩ **9** to remain inactive or unused ⟨the car just ~s in the garage all day⟩ **10** to take an examination **11** to baby-sit ~ *vt* **1** to cause to be seated; place on or in a seat **2** to sit on (eggs) **3** to keep one's seat on ⟨~ a horse⟩ **4** *Br* to take part in (an examination) as a candidate – **sit on 1** to repress, squash **2** to delay action or decision concerning – **sit on one's hands** to fail to take action – **sit on the fence** to adopt a position of neutrality or indecision

²sit *n* an act or period of sitting ⟨had a long ~ at the station between trains⟩

sitar *n* an Indian lute with a long neck and a varying number of strings – **sitarist** *n*

sit back *vi* to relinquish one's efforts or responsibility ⟨magistrates who sit back and accept police objections – Yorkshire Post⟩

¹site *n* **1a** an area of ground that was, is, or will be occupied by a structure or set of structures (e g a building, town, or monument) ⟨an archaeological ~⟩ **b** an area of ground or scene of some specified activity ⟨caravan ~⟩ ⟨battle ~⟩ ⟨building ~⟩ **2** the place, scene, or point of sthg ⟨the ~ of the wound⟩

²site *vt* to place on a site or in position; locate

sit-in *n* a continuous occupation of a building by a body of people as a protest and means towards forcing compliance with demands

sit in *vi* **1** to participate as a visitor or observer – usu + on ⟨sit in on a group discussion⟩ **2** to stage a sit-in

sit out *vt* **1** to remain until the end of or the departure of ⟨sit the film out⟩ **2** to refrain from participating in

sitter *n* **1** sby who sits (e g as an artist's model) **2** a baby-sitter

¹sitting *n* **1** a single occasion of continuous sitting (e g for a portrait or meal) **2** a batch of eggs for incubation **3** a session

²sitting *adj* **1** that is sitting ⟨a ~ hen⟩ **2** in office or actual possession ⟨the ~ member for Leeds East⟩ – **sitting pretty** in a highly favourable or satisfying position

sitting duck *n* an easy or defenceless target for attack, criticism, or exploitation

sitting room *n* a room, esp in a private house, used for recreation and relaxation

situated *adj* **1** located **2** supplied to the specified extent with money or possessions ⟨comfortably ~⟩ **3** being in the specified situation ⟨rather awkwardly ~⟩

situation *n* **1a** the way in which sthg is placed in relation to its surroundings **b** a locality ⟨a house in a windswept ~⟩ **2** position with respect to conditions and circumstances ⟨the military ~ remains obscure⟩ **3a** the circumstances at a particular moment; *esp* a critical or problematic state of affairs ⟨the ~ called for swift action⟩ **b** a particular (complicated) state of affairs at a stage in the action of a narrative or drama **4** a position of employment; a post – chiefly fml ⟨found a ~ as a gardener⟩ – **situational** *adj*

situation comedy *n* a radio or television comedy series that involves the same basic cast of characters in a succession of connected or unconnected episodes

sit up *vi* **1a** to rise from a reclining to a sitting position **b** to sit with the back straight **2** to show interest, alertness, or surprise ⟨news that made him sit up⟩ **3** to stay up after the usual time for going to bed ⟨sat up to watch the late film⟩

six *n* **1** (the number) 6 **2** the sixth in a set or series ⟨the ~ of spades⟩ **3** sthg having 6 parts or members or a denomination of 6: e g **a** a shot in cricket that crosses the boundary before it bounces and so scores 6 runs **b** the smallest unit in a cub-scout or brownie- guide pack **c** *pl*

in constr, cap the Common Market countries before 1973
– **six** *adj or pron,* **sixfold** *adj or adv* – **at sixes and sevens**
in disorder, confused, or in a muddle – **for six** so as to be
totally wrecked or defeated ⟨*trade balance went* for six –
The Economist⟩

six-pack *n* (a container for) 6 bottles or cans bought
together

six-shooter *n* a six-gun

sixteen *n* **1** (the number) 16 **2** *pl but sing in constr* a book
format in which a folded sheet forms 16 leaves – **sixteen**
adj or pron, **sixteenth** *adj or n*

sixteenth note *n, NAm* a semiquaver

sixth *adj or n* (of or being) number six in a countable
series

sixth form *n* the highest section of a British secondary
school – **sixth-former** *n*

sixth sense *n* a keen intuitive power viewed as analogous
to the 5 physical senses

sixty *n* **1** (the number) 60 **2** *pl* the numbers 60-69; *specif*
a range of temperatures, ages, or dates in a century
characterized by those numbers – **sixtieth** *adj or n,* **sixty**
adj or pron, **sixtyfold** *adj or adv*

sizable, sizeable *adj* fairly large; considerable – **sizable-
ness** *n,* **sizably** *adv*

¹**size** *n* **1a** physical magnitude, extent, or bulk; relative or
proportionate dimensions **b** relative amount or number **c**
bigness ⟨*you should have seen the ~ of him*⟩ **2** any of a
series of graduated measures, esp of manufactured articles
(e g of clothing), conventionally identified by numbers or
letters ⟨*a ~ 7 hat*⟩ **3** the actual state of affairs – *infml*
⟨*that's about the ~ of it*⟩

²**size** *vt* **1** to make in a particular size ⟨*systems ~d to fit
anyone's living room*⟩ **2** to arrange or grade according to
size or bulk

³**size** *n* any of various thick and sticky materials (e g
preparations of glue, flour, varnish, or resins) used for
filling the pores in surfaces (e g of paper, textiles, leather,
or plaster) or for applying colour or metal leaf (e g to book
edges or covers)

⁴**size** *vt* to cover, stiffen, or glaze (as if) with size

⁵**size** *adj* SIZED **1** – usu in combination ⟨*a bite-size biscuit*⟩

sized *adj* **1** having a specified size or bulk – usu in
combination ⟨*a small-sized house*⟩ **2** arranged or graded
according to size

size up *vt* to form a judgment of

sizzle *vi* sizzling to make a hissing sound (as if) in frying
– **sizzle** *n,* **sizzler** *n*

¹**skate** *n, pl* skate, *esp for different types* skates any of
numerous rays that have greatly developed pectoral fins
and many of which are important food fishes

²**skate** *n* **1a** ROLLER SKATE **b** ICE SKATE **2** a period of
skating

³**skate** *vi* **1** to glide along on skates propelled by the
alternate action of the legs **2** to glide or slide as if on skates
3 to proceed in a superficial manner ~ *vt* to go along or
through (a place) or perform (an action) by skating –
skater *n*

skateboard *n* a narrow board about 60cm (2ft) long
mounted on roller-skate wheels – **skateboarder** *n,* **skate-
boarding** *n*

skedaddle *vi* skedaddling to run away; *specif* to disperse
rapidly – often *imper; infml*

skeet *n* trapshooting in which clay targets are hurled
across the shooting range from traps on either side

skein *n* **1** a loosely coiled length of yarn or thread; HANK
1 **2** sthg suggesting the twists or coils of a skein; a tangle
⟨*unravel the ~ of evidence*⟩ **3** a flock of wildfowl (e g
geese) in flight

skeleton *n* **1** a supportive or protective usu rigid structure or framework of an organism; *esp* the bony or more
or less cartilaginous framework supporting the soft tissues
and protecting the internal organs of a vertebrate (e g a
fish or mammal) **2** sthg reduced to its bare essentials **3**
an emaciated person or animal **4** a basic structural framework **5** a secret cause of shame, esp in a family – often in
skeleton in the cupboard – **skeleton** *adj,* **skeletonize** *vt,*
skeletonic *adj,* **skeletal** *adj*

skeleton key *n* a key, esp one with most or all of the
serrations absent, that is able to open many simple
locks

skep *n* **1** a farm basket used esp in mucking out stables
2 a beehive (of twisted straw)

skeptic *n, chiefly NAm* a sceptic – **skeptical** *adj,* **skepti-
cally** *adv,* **skepticism** *n*

¹**sketch** *n* **1** a preliminary study or draft; *esp* a rough often
preliminary drawing representing the chief features of an
object or scene **2** a brief description or outline ⟨*gave a ~
of his personality*⟩ **3a** a short discursive literary composition **b** a short musical composition, usu for piano **c** a
short theatrical piece having a single scene; *esp* a comic
variety act

²**sketch** *vt* to make a sketch, rough draft, or outline of ~ *vi*
to draw or paint a sketch – **sketcher** *n*

sketchy *adj* lacking completeness, clarity, or substance;
superficial, scanty – **sketchily** *adv,* **sketchiness** *n*

¹**skew** *vi* to take an oblique course; twist ~ *vt* **1** to cause
to skew **2** to distort from a true value or symmetrical
curve ⟨*~ed statistical data*⟩

²**skew** *adj* **1** set, placed, or running obliquely **2** more
developed on one side or in one direction than another; not
symmetrical – **skewness** *n*

³**skew** *n* a deviation from a straight line or symmetrical
curve

skewbald *n or adj* (an animal) marked with spots and
patches of white and another colour, esp not black

¹**skewer** *n* **1** a long pin of wood or metal used chiefly to
fasten a piece of meat together while roasting or to hold
small pieces of food for grilling (e g for a kebab) **2** sthg
like a meat skewer in form or function

²**skewer** *vt* to fasten or pierce (as if) with a skewer

skew-whiff *adj, Br* askew – *infml*

¹**ski** *n, pl* skis **1a** a long narrow strip usu of wood, metal,
or plastic that curves upwards in front and is typically one
of a pair used esp for gliding over snow **b** WATER SKI **2** a
runner on a vehicle

²**ski** *vb* skiing; skied to glide (over) on skis as a way of
travelling or as a recreation or sport – **skiable** *adj,*
skier *n*

skibob *n* a bicycle-like vehicle with short skis in place of
wheels that is used for gliding downhill over snow by a
rider wearing miniature skis for balance – **skibobber** *n,*
skibobbing *n*

¹**skid** *n* **1** a plank or log used to support or elevate a
structure or object **2** a ship's fender **3** a device placed
under a wheel to prevent its turning or used as a drag **4**
the act of skidding; a slide **5** a runner used as part of the
undercarriage of an aircraft **6** *pl* a road to defeat or
downfall – in *hit the skids, on the skids; infml* – **skiddy**
adj

²**skid** *vb* -dd- *vt* **1** to apply a brake or skid to **2** to haul
along, slide, hoist, or store on skids ~ *vi of a vehicle,
wheel, driver, etc* to slip or slide, esp out of control –
skidder *n*

skid-lid *n, Br* a motorcyclist's crash helmet – *infml*

skidpan *n, chiefly Br* a slippery surface on which vehicle
drivers may practise the control of skids

skid row *n, chiefly NAm* a district frequented by down-and-outs and alcoholics

skiff *n* a light rowing or sailing boat

skiffle *n* jazz or folk music played by a group and using nonstandard instruments or noisemakers (e g washboards or Jew's harps)

skilful, *NAm chiefly* **skillful** *adj* possessing or displaying skill; expert – **skilfully** *adv*

ski lift *n* a power-driven conveyer consisting usu of a series of bars or seats suspended from an endless overhead moving cable and used for transporting skiers or sightseers up and down a long slope or mountainside

skill *n* **1** the ability to utilize one's knowledge effectively and readily **2** a developed aptitude or ability in a particular field ⟨*knitted with remarkable* ~⟩ – **skill-less** *adj*

skilled *adj* **1** having mastery of or proficiency in sthg (e g a technique or trade) **2** of, being, or requiring workers with skill and training in a particular occupation or craft

skillet *n* **1** *chiefly Br* a small saucepan usu having 3 or 4 legs and used for cooking on the hearth **2** *chiefly NAm* FRYING PAN

¹**skim** *vb* **-mm-** *vt* **1a** to clear (a liquid) of floating matter ⟨~ *boiling syrup*⟩ **b** to remove (e g film or scum) from the surface of a liquid **c** to remove cream from by skimming **d**(1) to remove the best or most accessible contents from (2) to remove (the choicest part or members) from sthg; cream **2** to read, study, or examine cursorily and rapidly; *specif* to glance through (e g a book) for the chief ideas or the plot **3** to throw so as to ricochet along the surface of water **4** to pass swiftly or lightly over ~ *vi* **1** to glide lightly or smoothly along or just above a surface **2** to give a cursory glance or consideration *USE* (*vt* 1b & 1d(2)) often + *off*

²**skim** *n* **1** a thin layer, coating, or film **2** the act of skimming

³**skim** *adj* having the cream removed by skimming ⟨~ *milk*⟩

skimmer *n* **1** a flat perforated scoop or spoon used for skimming **2** any of several long-winged sea birds that feed by flying with the elongated lower part of the beak immersed in the sea

skimp *vt* to give insufficient or barely sufficient attention or effort to or money for ~ *vi* to save (as if) by skimping sthg

skimpy *adj* inadequate in quality, size, etc; scanty ⟨*a* ~ *meal*⟩ – **skimpily** *adv*, **skimpiness** *n*

¹**skin** *n* **1a** the external covering of an animal (e g a fur-bearing mammal or a bird) separated from the body, usu with its hair or feathers; pelt **b**(1) the pelt of an animal prepared for use as a trimming or in a garment ⟨*it took 40* ~ *s to make the coat*⟩ (2) a container (e g for wine or water) made of animal skin **2a** the external limiting layer of an animal body, esp when forming a tough but flexible cover **b** any of various outer or surface layers (e g a rind, husk, or film) ⟨*a sausage* ~⟩ **3** the life or welfare of a person – esp in *save one's skin* **4** a sheathing or casing forming the outside surface of a ship, aircraft, etc – **skinless** *adj* – **by the skin of one's teeth** by a very narrow margin – **under the skin** beneath apparent or surface differences; fundamentally

²**skin** *vb* **-nn-** *vt* **1a** to cover (as if) with skin **b** to heal over with skin **2a** to strip, scrape, or rub away an outer covering (e g the skin or rind) of **b** to strip or peel off like skin ⟨~ *the insulation from the wire*⟩ **c** to cut, graze, or damage the surface of ⟨*fell and* ~*ned his knee*⟩ **3** to strip of money or property; fleece – *infml* ~ *vi* to become covered (as if) with skin – usu + *over* ⟨*the wound had* ~*ned over within a*

skin-deep *adj* **1** as deep as the skin **2** superficial ⟨*beauty is only* ~⟩

skin flick *n* a film characterized by nudity and explicit sexual situations – *infml*

skinflint *n* a miser, niggard

skinful *n* an ample or satisfying quantity, esp of alcoholic drink – *infml*

skin game *n, NAm* a swindling game or trick

skin graft *n* a piece of skin that is taken from one area to replace skin in a defective or damaged area – **skin grafting** *n*

skinhead *n* **1** a person whose hair is cut very short **2** any of a group of young British people with very short hair and a distinctive way of dressing

skinned *adj* having skin, esp of a specified kind – usu in combination ⟨*dark*-skinned⟩

skinny *adj* very thin; lean, emaciated – *infml* – **skinniness** *n*

skint *adj, Br* penniless – *infml*

skintight *adj* extremely closely fitted to the body ⟨~ *jeans*⟩

¹**skip** *vb* **-pp-** *vi* **1a**(1) to move or proceed with light leaps and bounds; gambol (2) to swing a rope round the body from head to toe, making a small jump each time it passes beneath the feet **b** to rebound from one point or thing after another; ricochet **2** to leave hurriedly or secretly; abscond ⟨~*ped out without paying his bill*⟩ **3** to pass over or omit an interval, section, or step ⟨*the story* ~*s to the present day*⟩ ~ *vt* **1** to leave out (a step in a progression or series); omit **2** to cause to ricochet across a surface; skim ⟨~ *a stone over a pond*⟩ **3** to fail to attend ⟨*decided to* ~ *church that Sunday*⟩ **4** *chiefly NAm* to depart from quickly and secretly ⟨~*ped town*⟩ – *infml*

²**skip** *n* **1** a light bounding step or gait **2** an act of omission (e g in reading)

³**skip** *n* the captain of a side in some games (e g curling or bowls)

⁴**skip** *n* **1** SKEP 1 **2** a bucket or cage for carrying men and materials (e g in mining or quarrying) **3** a large open container for waste or rubble

¹**skipper** *n* any of numerous small butterflies that differ from the typical butterflies in the arrangement of the veins in the wings and the form of the antennae

²**skipper** *n* **1** the master of a fishing, small trading, or pleasure boat **2** the captain or first pilot of an aircraft **3** *Br* the captain of a sports team *USE* (2&3) *infml*

³**skipper** *vt* to act as skipper of (e g a boat)

skirl *vi or n* (to emit) the high shrill sound of a bagpipe

¹**skirmish** *n* **1** a minor or irregular fight in war, usu between small outlying detachments **2** a brief preliminary conflict; *broadly* any minor or petty dispute

²**skirmish** *vi* to engage in a skirmish – **skirmisher** *n*

¹**skirt** *n* **1a**(1) a free-hanging part of a garment (e g a coat) extending from the waist down (2) a garment or undergarment worn by women and girls that hangs from and fits closely round the waist **b** either of 2 usu leather flaps on a saddle covering the bars on which the stirrups are hung **c** a flexible wall containing the air cushion of a hovercraft **2** the borders or outer edge of an area or group – often pl with sing. meaning **3** a part or attachment serving as a rim, border, or edging **4** *Br* any of various usu membranous and gristly cuts of beef from the flank **5** a girl, woman – slang – **skirted** *adj*

²**skirt** *vt* **1** to extend along or form the border or edge of; border **2** to provide a skirt for **3** to go or pass round; *specif* to avoid through fear of difficulty, danger, or dispute ⟨~*ed the minefield*⟩ ⟨~*ed the crucial issues*⟩

~ *vi* to be, lie, or move along an edge, border, or margin ⟨*~ round the coast*⟩ – **skirter** *n*

skirting board *n, Br* a board, esp with decorative moulding, that is fixed to the base of a wall and that covers the joint of the wall and floor

skit *n* a satirical or humorous story or sketch ⟨*did a ~ on Queen Victoria*⟩

skitter *vi* **1a** to glide or skip lightly or swiftly **b** to skim along a surface **2** to twitch a fishing lure or baited hook through or along the surface of water **~** *vt* to cause to skitter – **skitter** *n*

skittish *adj* **1a** lively or frisky in behaviour; capricious **b** variable, fickle **2** easily frightened; restive ⟨*a ~ horse*⟩ – **skittishly** *adv*, **skittishness** *n*

skittle *n* **1** *pl but sing in constr* any of various bowling games played with 9 pins and wooden balls or discs **2** a pin used in skittles

skittle out *vt* to dismiss (a batting side in cricket) for a low score

skive *vt* to cut off (e g leather or rubber) in thin layers or pieces; pare **~** *vi, Br* to evade one's work or duty, esp out of laziness; shirk – often + *off*; *infml*

¹skivvy *n, Br* a female domestic servant

²skivvy *vi, Br* to perform menial domestic tasks; act as a skivvy

skua *n* any of several large dark-coloured seabirds of northern and southern seas that tend to harass weaker birds until they drop or disgorge the fish they have caught

skulduggery, skullduggery *n* devious trickery; *esp* underhand or unscrupulous behaviour

skulk *vi* **1** to move in a stealthy or furtive manner; slink **2** to hide or conceal oneself, esp out of cowardice or fear or for a sinister purpose; lurk – **skulker** *n*

skull *n* **1** the skeleton of the head of a vertebrate animal forming a bony or cartilaginous case that encloses and protects the brain and chief sense organs and supports the jaws **2** the seat of understanding or intelligence; the brain – usu derog ⟨*get that fact into your thick ~!*⟩ – **skulled** *adj*

skull and crossbones *n, pl* **skulls and crossbones** a representation of a human skull over crossbones, usu used as a warning of danger to life

skullcap *n* **1** a closely fitting cap; *esp* a light brimless cap for indoor wear **2** any of various plants having a helmet-shaped calyx

skunk *n, pl* **skunks**, *esp collectively* **skunk** **1a** any of various common black-and-white New World mammals that have a pair of anal glands from which a foul-smelling secretion is ejected **b** the fur of a skunk **2** a thoroughly obnoxious person – *infml*

¹sky *n* **1** the upper atmosphere when seen as an apparent great vault over the earth; the firmament, heavens **2** HEAVEN **2** **3a** weather as manifested by the condition of the sky ⟨*a clear ~*⟩ **b** climate

²sky *vt* **skied, skyed** *chiefly Br* to throw, toss, or hit (e g a ball) high in the air

sky blue *adj or n* (of) the light blue colour of the sky on a clear day

skydiving *n* jumping from an aeroplane and executing body manoeuvres while in free-fall before pulling the rip cord of a parachute – **sky diver** *n*

sky-high *adv or adj* **1a** very high **b** to a high level or degree ⟨*prices rose ~*⟩ **2** to bits; apart – in **blow sthg sky-high**

skyjack *vt* to hijack (an aircraft) – **skyjacker** *n*

¹skylark *n* a common largely brown Old World lark noted for its song, esp as uttered in vertical flight or while hovering

²skylark *vi* to act in a high-spirited or mischievous manner; frolic – **skylarker** *n*

skylight *n* **1** the diffused and reflected light of the sky **2** a window or group of windows in a roof or ceiling

skyline *n* **1** the apparent juncture of earth and sky; the horizon **2** an outline (e g of buildings or a mountain range) against the background of the sky

¹skyrocket *n* **²**ROCKET **1a**

²skyrocket *vi* to shoot up abruptly ⟨*shares in copper are ~ing*⟩

skyscraper *n* a many-storeyed building; *esp* one containing offices

skywriting *n* (the formation of) writing in the sky by means of a visible substance (e g smoke) emitted from an aircraft

slab *n* a thick flat usu large plate or slice (e g of stone, wood, or bread)

¹slack *adj* **1** insufficiently prompt, diligent, or careful; negligent **2a** characterized by slowness, indolence, or languor ⟨*a ~ pace*⟩ **b** *of tide* flowing slowly; sluggish **3a** not taut; relaxed ⟨*a ~ rope*⟩ **b** lacking in usual or normal firmness and steadiness; lax ⟨*~ muscles*⟩ ⟨*~ supervision*⟩ **4** wanting in activity ⟨*a ~ market*⟩ – **slackly** *adv*, **slackness** *n*

²slack *vt* **1a** to be sluggish or negligent in performing or doing **b** to lessen, moderate ⟨*~ ed his pace as the sun grew hot*⟩ **2** to release tension in; loosen **3a** to cause to abate or moderate **b** SLAKE **2** **~** *vi* **1** to be or become slack ⟨*our enthusiasm ~ ed off*⟩ **2** to shirk or evade work or duty – **slacker** *n*

³slack *n* **1** cessation in movement or flow; *specif* SLACK WATER **2** a part of sthg (e g a sail or a rope) that hangs loose without strain **3** *pl* trousers, esp for casual wear **4** a lull or decrease in activity; a dull season or period

⁴slack *n* the finest particles of coal produced at a mine

slacken *vb* **1** to make or become less active, rapid, or intense – often + *off* **2** to make or become slack

slack water *n* the period at the turn of the tide when there is no apparent tidal motion

slag *n* **1** waste matter from the smelting of metal ores; dross **2** the rough cindery lava from a volcano **3** *Br* a dirty slovenly (immoral) woman – slang

slain *past part of* SLAY

slake *vt* **1** to satisfy, quench ⟨*~ your thirst*⟩ **2** to cause (e g lime) to heat and crumble by treatment with water

slalom *n* a skiing or canoeing race against time on a zigzag or wavy course between obstacles

¹slam *n* GRAND SLAM

²slam *n* a banging noise; *esp* one made by a door

³slam *vb* **-mm-** *vt* **1** to strike or beat vigorously; knock ⟨*~ med him about the head with a book*⟩ **2** to shut forcibly and noisily; bang **3a** to put or throw down noisily and violently ⟨*~ med his books on the table and stomped out*⟩ **b** to force into sudden and violent action ⟨*~ on the brakes*⟩ **4** to criticize harshly – *infml* **~** *vi* **1** to make a banging noise ⟨*the door ~ med to behind him*⟩ **2** to move violently or angrily ⟨*he ~ med out of his office*⟩ – *infml*

¹slander *n* **1** the utterance of false charges which do damage to another's reputation **2** a false defamatory oral statement – **slanderous** *adj*, **slanderously** *adv*, **slanderousness** *n*

²slander *vt* to utter slander against – **slanderer** *n*

¹slang *n* **1** language peculiar to a particular group: e g **a** argot **b** JARGON **2** **2** informal usu spoken vocabulary that is composed typically of coinages, novel senses of words, and picturesque figures of speech – **slang** *adj*, **slangy** *adj*

²slang *vt* to abuse with harsh or coarse language ⟨*the two*

drivers are ~ing each other – Punch⟩ ~ vi to use harsh or vulgar abuse

¹slant vi 1 to turn or incline from a horizontal or vertical line or a level 2 to take a diagonal course, direction, or path ~ vt 1 to give an oblique or sloping direction to 2 to interpret or present in accord with a particular interest; bias ⟨stories ~ed towards youth⟩ – **slantingly** adv

²slant n 1 a slanting direction, line, or plane; a slope ⟨placed the mirror at a ~⟩ 2 SOLIDUS 2 3a a particular or personal point of view, attitude, or opinion b an unfair bias or distortion (e g in a piece of writing) – **slant** adj, **slantways** adv, **slantwise** adv or adj

¹slap n a quick sharp blow, esp with the open hand – **slap in the face** a rebuff, insult

²slap vt -pp- 1 to strike sharply (as if) with the open hand 2 to put, place, or throw with careless haste or force ⟨~ paint on a wall⟩

³slap adv directly, smack ⟨landed ~ on top of a holly bush⟩

slap and tickle n playful lovemaking – infml; humor

slap-bang adv 1 in a highly abrupt or forceful manner 2 precisely ⟨~ in the middle⟩ USE infml

slapdash adj haphazard, slipshod

slap down vt to restrain or quash the initiative of rudely or forcefully

slaphappy adj 1 punch-drunk 2 irresponsibly casual ⟨the ~ state of our democracies – Alistair Cooke⟩ 3 buoyantly carefree; happy-go-lucky

slapstick n 1 a wooden device that makes a loud noise when used by an actor to strike sby 2 comedy stressing farce and horseplay; knockabout comedy – **slapstick** adj

slap-up adj, chiefly Br marked by lavish consumption or luxury – infml ⟨a ~ Christmas nosh – Sunday Mirror⟩

¹slash vt 1a to cut with violent usu random sweeping strokes b to make (one's way) (as if) by cutting down obstacles 2 LASH 1 ⟨~ him with bridle reins – Sir Walter Scott⟩ 3 to cut slits in (e g a garment) so as to reveal an underlying fabric or colour 4 to criticize cuttingly 5 to reduce drastically; cut ~ vi 1 to cut or hit recklessly or savagely 2 esp of rain to fall hard and slantingly – **slasher** n

²slash n 1 the act of slashing; also a long cut or stroke made (as if) by slashing 2 an ornamental slit in a garment 3 chiefly Br an act of urinating – vulg

¹slat n 1 a thin narrow flat strip, esp of wood or metal (e g a lath, louvre, or stave) 2 ¹SLOT 1a – **slat** adj

²slat vt -tt- to make or equip with slats

¹slate n 1 a piece of slate rock used as roofing material 2 a fine-grained metamorphic rock consisting of compressed clay, shale, etc and easily split into (thin) layers 3 a tablet of material, esp slate, used for writing on 4 dark bluish or greenish grey 5 NAm a list of candidates for nomination or election – **slate** adj, **slatelike** adj, **slaty** adj

²slate vt 1 to cover with slate ⟨~ a roof⟩ 2 NAm to designate for action or appointment

³slate vt, chiefly Br to criticize or censure severely – infml

slattern n an untidy slovenly woman; a slut

¹slaughter n 1 the act of killing; specif the butchering of livestock for market 2 killing of many people (e g in battle); carnage

²slaughter vt 1 to kill (animals) for food 2 to kill violently or in large numbers – **slaughterer** n

slaughterhouse n an establishment where animals are killed for food

¹slave n 1 sby held in servitude as the property of another 2 sby who is dominated by a specified thing or person ⟨a ~ to drink⟩ 3 a device whose actions are controlled by

and often mimic those of another 4 a drudge ⟨women who are merely kitchen ~s⟩ – **slave** adj

²slave vi 1 to work like a slave; toil 2 to traffic in slaves

slave driver n 1 an overseer of slaves 2 a harsh taskmaster

¹slaver vi to drool, slobber

²slaver n 1 sby engaged in the slave trade 2 a ship used in the slave trade

slavery n 1 drudgery, toil 2a the state of being a slave b the practice of owning slaves

slave trade n traffic in slaves; esp the transportation of Negroes to America for profit

Slavic adj or n Slavonic – **Slavicist** n, **Slavist** n

slavish adj 1 (characteristic) of a slave; esp abjectly servile 2 obsequiously imitative; devoid of originality 3 archaic despicable, base – **slavishly** adv, **slavishness** n

slay vt slew; slain 1 to kill violently or with great bloodshed; slaughter 2 to affect overpoweringly (e g with awe or delight); overwhelm – infml – **slayer** n

sleazy adj squalid and disreputable – **sleaziness** n

¹sled n, chiefly NAm ²SLEDGE

²sled vb -dd- chiefly NAm to sledge – **sledder** n

¹sledge n a sledgehammer

²sledge n 1 a vehicle with runners that is pulled by reindeer, horses, dogs, etc and is used esp over snow or ice 2 Br a toboggan

³sledge vb, chiefly Br vi to ride or be conveyed in a sledge ~ vt to transport on a sledge

sledgehammer n a large heavy hammer that is wielded with both hands

sledge-hammer adj clumsy, heavy-handed ⟨a ~ package of spending cuts⟩

¹sleek vt to slick

²sleek adj 1a smooth and glossy as if polished ⟨~ dark hair⟩ b having a smooth well-groomed look ⟨a ~ cat⟩ c having a well fed or flourishing appearance 2 excessively or artfully suave; ingratiating 3 elegant, stylish – **sleeken** vt, **sleekly** adv, **sleekness** n

¹sleep n 1 the natural periodic suspension of consciousness that is essential for the physical and mental well-being of higher animals 2 a sleeplike state: e g a torpor b a state marked by a diminution of feeling followed by tingling ⟨his foot went to ~⟩ c the state of an animal during hibernation d death – euph ⟨put a cat to ~⟩ 3 a period spent sleeping ⟨need a good long ~⟩ – **sleeplike** adj

²sleep vb slept vi 1 to rest in a state of sleep 2 to be in a state (e g of quiescence or death) resembling sleep 3 to have sexual relations – + with or together; infml ~ vt 1 to get rid of or spend in sleep ⟨~ away the hours⟩ ⟨~ off a headache⟩ 2 to provide sleeping accommodation for ⟨the boat ~s 6⟩ 3 to be slumbering in ⟨slept the sleep of the dead⟩ – poetic – **sleep on** to consider (sth) fully before discussing again the next day – **sleep rough** SLEEP OUT 1

sleep around vi to be sexually promiscuous – infml

sleeper n 1 a timber, concrete, or steel transverse support to which railway rails are fixed 2 SLEEPING CAR 3 a ring or stud worn in a pierced ear to keep the hole open 4 chiefly NAm sby or sth unpromising or unnoticed that suddenly attains prominence or value – infml

sleep in vi 1 LIVE IN 2 to sleep late, either intentionally or accidentally

sleeping bag n a large thick envelope or bag of warm material for sleeping in esp when camping

sleeping car n a railway carriage divided into compartments having berths for sleeping

sleeping partner n a partner who takes no active part or an unknown part in the running of a firm's business

sleeping pill *n* a drug in the form of a tablet or capsule that is taken to induce sleep

sleeping sickness *n* a serious disease that is prevalent in much of tropical Africa, is marked by fever and protracted lethargy, and is caused by either of 2 trypanosomes and transmitted by tsetse flies

sleepless *adj* 1 not able to sleep 2 unceasingly active – **sleeplessly** *adv*, **sleeplessness** *n*

sleep out *vi* 1 to sleep out of doors 2 LIVE OUT

sleepwalker *n* a somnambulist – **sleepwalk** *vi*

sleepy *adj* 1a ready to fall asleep b (characteristic) of sleep 2 lacking alertness; sluggish, lethargic 3 sleep-inducing – **sleepily** *adv*, **sleepiness** *n*

sleepyhead *n* a sleepy person – humor

¹**sleet** *n* precipitation in the form of partly frozen rain, or snow and rain falling together – **sleety** *adj*

²**sleet** *vi* to send down sleet

sleeve *n* 1 a part of a garment covering the arm 2 a tubular machine part designed to fit over another part 3 a paper or often highly distinctive cardboard covering that protects a gramophone record when not in use – **sleeved** *adj*, **sleeveless** *adj* – **up one's sleeve** held secretly in reserve

¹**sleigh** *n* ²SLEDGE 1

²**sleigh** *vi* to drive or travel in a sleigh

sleight of hand *n* 1 manual skill and dexterity in conjuring or juggling 2 adroitness in deception

slender *adj* 1a gracefully slim b small or narrow in circumference or width in proportion to length or height 2a flimsy, tenuous ⟨a ~ hope⟩ b limited or inadequate in amount; meagre ⟨a man of ~ means⟩ – **slenderly** *adv*, **slenderness** *n*

sleuth *vi or n* (to act as) a detective – infml

¹**slew** *past of* SLAY

²**slew** *vt* to turn or twist (sthg) about a fixed point that is usu the axis ~ *vi* 1 to turn, twist, or swing about 2 to skid – **slew** *n*

³**slew** *n, NAm* a large number or quantity – infml

¹**slice** *n* 1a a thin broad flat piece cut from a usu larger whole ⟨a ~ of ham⟩ b a wedge-shaped piece (e g of pie or cake) 2 an implement with a broad blade used for lifting, turning, or serving food ⟨a fish ~⟩ 3 (a flight of) a ball that deviates from a straight course in the direction of the dominant hand of the player propelling it 4a a portion, share ⟨a ~ of the profits⟩ b a part or section detached from a larger whole ⟨a sizable ~ of the public – Punch⟩

²**slice** *vt* 1 to cut through (as if) with a knife ⟨~ a melon in 2⟩ 2 to cut into slices ⟨~d bread⟩ 3 to hit (a ball) so that a slice results ~ *vi* to slice sthg – **sliceable** *adj*, **slicer** *n*

¹**slick** *vt* to make sleek or smooth

²**slick** *adj* 1 superficially plausible; glib 2a characterized by suave or wily cleverness b deft, skilful ⟨~ goal-keeping⟩ 3 of a tyre having no tread 4 chiefly NAm smooth, slippery – **slickly** *adv*, **slickness** *n*

³**slick** *n* (a patch of water covered with) a smooth film of crude oil

slicker *n, NAm* an artful crook; a swindler – infml

¹**slide** *vb* slid *vi* 1a to move in continuous contact with a smooth surface b to glide over snow or ice (e g on a toboggan) 2 to slip or fall by loss of grip or footing 3 to pass quietly and unobtrusively; steal 4 to take an undirected course; drift ⟨let his affairs ~⟩ 5 to pass by smooth or imperceptible gradations ⟨the economy slid from recession to depression⟩ ~ *vt* 1 to cause to glide or slip 2 to place or introduce unobtrusively or stealthily ⟨slid the bill into his hand⟩ – **slider** *n*

²**slide** *n* 1a an act or instance of sliding b a portamento 2

a sliding part or mechanism: e g a a U-shaped section of tube in the trombone that is pushed out and in to produce notes of different pitch b a moving piece of a mechanism that is guided by a part along which it slides 3 a landslide, avalanche 4a(1) a track or slope suitable for sliding or tobogganing (2) a chute with a slippery surface down which children slide in play b a channel or track down or along which sthg is slid 5a a flat piece of glass on which an object is mounted for examination using a light microscope b a photographic transparency on a small plate or film suitably mounted for projection 6 Br a hair-slide

slide rule *n* an instrument consisting in its simple form of a ruler with a central slide both of which are graduated in such a way that the addition of lengths corresponds to the multiplication of numbers

sliding scale *n* a flexible scale (e g of fees or subsidies) adjusted to the needs or income of individuals

¹**slight** *adj* 1a having a slim or frail build b lacking strength or bulk; flimsy c trivial d not serious or involving risk; minor ⟨caught a ~ chill⟩ 2 small of its kind or in amount; scanty, meagre – **slightly** *adv*, **slightness** *n*

²**slight** *vt* 1 to treat as slight or unimportant ⟨~ed my efforts at reform⟩ 2 to treat with disdain or pointed indifference; snub 3 NAm to perform or attend to carelessly or inadequately

³**slight** *n* 1 an act of slighting 2 a humiliating affront

¹**slim** *adj* -mm- 1 of small or narrow circumference or width, esp in proportion to length or height 2 slender in build 3 scanty, slight ⟨a ~ chance of success⟩ – **slimly** *adv*, **slimness** *n*

²**slim** *vb* -mm- *vt* to cause to be or appear slender ⟨a style that ~s the waist⟩ ~ *vi* to become thinner (e g by dieting)

¹**slime** *n* 1 soft moist soil or clay; esp viscous mud 2 a viscous or glutinous substance; esp mucus or a mucus-like substance secreted by slugs, catfish, etc

²**slime** *vt* to smear or cover with slime

slimy *adj* 1 of or resembling slime; viscous; also covered with or yielding slime 2 characterized by obsequious flattery; offensively ingratiating 3 chiefly NAm vile, offensive USE (2&3) infml – **slimily** *adv*, **sliminess** *n*

¹**sling** *vt* slung 1 to cast with a careless and usu sweeping or swirling motion; fling ⟨slung the coat over her shoulder⟩ 2 to throw (e g a stone) with a sling 3 Br to cast forcibly and usu abruptly ⟨was slung out of the team for misconduct⟩ – infml – **slinger** *n*

²**sling** *n* an act of slinging or hurling a stone or other missile

³**sling** *n* 1 a device that gives extra force to a stone or other missile thrown by hand and usu consists of a short strap that is looped round the missile, whirled round, and then released at 1 end 2a a usu looped line used to hoist, lower, or carry sthg (e g a rifle); esp a bandage suspended from the neck to support an arm or hand b a rope attached to a mast which supports a yard c a device (e g a rope net) for enclosing material to be hoisted by a tackle or crane

⁴**sling** *vt* slung to place in a sling for hoisting or lowering

⁵**sling** *n* a drink of whisky, brandy, or esp gin with water and sugar

slingshot *n, NAm* a catapult

¹**slink** *vb* slunk also slinked *vi* 1 to go or move stealthily or furtively (e g in fear or shame); steal 2 to move in a graceful provocative manner ~ *vt* to give premature birth to – used with reference to an animal

²**slink** *n* (the flesh or skin of) the prematurely born young (e g a calf) of an animal

¹**slip** *vb* -pp- *vi* 1a to move with a smooth sliding motion

b to move quietly and cautiously; steal **2** *of time* to elapse, pass **3a** to slide out of place or away from a support or one's grasp ⟨*I didn't break the vase, it just* ~*ped!*⟩ **b** to slide on or down a slippery surface ⟨~ *on the stairs*⟩ **4** to get speedily *into* or *out of* clothing ⟨~ *into his coat*⟩ **5** to fall off from a standard or accustomed level by degrees; decline ~ *vt* **1** to cause to move easily and smoothly; slide **2a** to free oneself from ⟨*the dog* ~*ped his collar*⟩ **b** to escape from (one's memory or notice) **3** to put (a garment) on hurriedly **4a** to let loose from a restraining leash or grasp **b** to cause to slip open; release, undo ⟨~ *a knot*⟩ **c** to let go of **d** to detach (an anchor) instead of bringing it on board **5a** to insert, place, or pass quietly or secretly **b** to give or pay on the sly ⟨~*ped him a fiver*⟩ **6** to give birth to prematurely; abort – used with reference to an animal **7** to dislocate ⟨~*ped his shoulder*⟩ **8** to transfer (a stitch) from one needle to another in knitting without working a stitch **9** to keep in partial engagement by resting a foot continuously on the pedal ⟨~ *the clutch*⟩ – **slippage** *n*

²**slip** *n* **1** a sloping ramp extending out into the water to serve as a place for landing, repairing, or building ships **2** *the* act or an instance of eluding or evading ⟨*gave his pursuer the* ~⟩ **3a** a mistake in judgment, policy, or procedure; a blunder **b** an inadvertent and trivial fault or error ⟨*a* ~ *of the tongue*⟩ **4** a leash so made that it can be quickly unfastened **5a** the act or an instance of slipping ⟨*a* ~ *on the ice*⟩ **b** (a movement producing) a small geological fault **c** a fall from some level or standard **6a** a women's sleeveless undergarment with shoulder straps that resembles a light dress **b** a case into which sthg is slipped; *specif* a pillowcase **7** a disposition or tendency to slip easily **8** any of several fielding positions in cricket that are close to the batsman and just to the (off) side of the wicketkeeper

³**slip** *n* **1** a small shoot or twig cut for planting or grafting; a scion **2a** a long narrow strip of material (e g paper or wood) **b** a small piece of paper; *specif* a printed form **3** a young and slim person ⟨*a mere* ~ *of a girl*⟩

⁴**slip** *vt* **-pp-** to take cuttings from (a plant); divide into slips

⁵**slip** *n* a semifluid mixture of clay and water used by potters (e g for coating or decorating ware)

slipknot *n* **1** RUNNING KNOT **2** a knot that can be untied by pulling

¹**slip-on** *n* a slip-on shoe

²**slip-on** *adj, esp of a garment* easily slipped on or off

slipped disc *n* a protrusion of 1 of the cartilage discs that normally separate the spinal vertebrae, producing pressure on spinal nerves and usu resulting in intense pain, esp in the region of the lower back

slipper *n* a light shoe that is easily slipped on the foot; *esp* a flat-heeled shoe that is worn while resting at home

slippery *adj* **1a** causing or tending to cause sthg to slide or fall ⟨~ *roads*⟩ **b** tending to slip from the grasp **2** not to be trusted; shifty – **slipperiness** *n*

slippy *adj* slippery – **be/look slippy** *chiefly Br* to be quick; hurry up – infml

slipshod *adj* careless, slovenly ⟨~ *reasoning*⟩

¹**slipstream** *n* **1** a stream of fluid (e g air or water) driven backwards by a propeller **2** an area of reduced air pressure and forward suction immediately behind a rapidly moving vehicle **3** sthg that sweeps one along in its course

²**slipstream** *vi* to drive or ride in a slipstream and so gain the advantage of reduced air resistance (e g in a bicycle race)

slip-up *n* a mistake, oversight

slip up *vi* to make a mistake; blunder

slipway *n* a slip (on which ships are built)

¹**slit** *vt* **-tt-**; **slit 1** to make a slit in **2** to cut or tear into long narrow strips – **slitter** *n*

²**slit** *n* a long narrow cut or opening – **slit** *adj*, **slitless** *adj*

slither *vi* **1** to slide unsteadily, esp (as if) on a slippery surface **2** to slip or slide like a snake ~ *vt* to cause to slide – **slithery** *adj*

¹**sliver** *n* a small slender piece cut, torn, or broken; a splinter

²**sliver** *vt* to cut or break into slivers ~ *vi* to become split into slivers; splinter

slivovitz *n* a dry usu colourless plum brandy

slob *n* a slovenly or uncouth person – infml – **slobbish** *adj*

¹**slobber** *vi* **1** to let saliva dribble from the mouth; drool **2** to express emotion effusively and esp oversentimentally – often + *over* ~ *vt* to smear (as if) with food or saliva dribbling from the mouth ⟨*the baby* ~*ed his bib*⟩ – **slobberer** *n*

²**slobber** *n* **1** saliva drooled from the mouth **2** oversentimental language or conduct – **slobbery** *adj*

sloe *n* (the small dark spherical astringent fruit of) the blackthorn

sloe gin *n* a liqueur consisting of gin in which sloes have been steeped

¹**slog** *vb* **-gg-** *vt* **1** to hit (e g a cricket ball or an opponent in boxing) hard and often wildly **2** to plod (one's way) with determination, esp in the face of difficulty ~ *vi* **1** to walk, move, or travel slowly and laboriously ⟨~*ged through the snow*⟩ **2** to work laboriously; toil – **slogger** *n*

²**slog** *n* **1** a hard and often wild blow **2** persistent hard work **3** an arduous march or tramp

slogan *n* **1** a phrase used to express and esp make public a particular view, position, or aim **2** a brief catchy phrase used in advertising or promotion

sloop *n* a fore-and-aft rigged sailing vessel with 1 mast and a single foresail

¹**slop** *n* **1** thin tasteless drink or liquid food **2** liquid spilt or splashed **3a** waste food or a thin gruel fed to animals **b** liquid household refuse (e g dirty water or urine) **4** mawkish sentiment in speech or writing; gush USE (1&3) usu pl with sing. meaning

²**slop** *vb* **-pp-** *vt* **1a** to cause (a liquid) to spill over the side of a container **b** to splash or spill liquid on **2** to serve messily ⟨~ *soup into a bowl*⟩ **3** to feed slops to ⟨~ *the pigs*⟩ ~ *vi* **1** to tramp through mud or slush **2** to become spilled or splashed **3** to show mawkish sentiment; gush **4** to slouch, flop ⟨*spends his whole day* ~*ping around the house*⟩

slop basin *n, Br* a bowl for receiving the dregs left in tea or coffee cups at table

¹**slope** *vi* **1** to take an oblique course **2** to lie at a slant; incline ~ *vt* to cause to incline or slant

²**slope** *n* **1** a piece of inclined ground **2** upward or downward inclination or (degree of) slant **3** GRADIENT 1

slope off *vi* to go away, esp furtively; sneak off – infml

slop out *vi, of a prisoner* to empty slops from a chamber pot

sloppy *adj* **1a** wet so as to splash; slushy ⟨*a* ~ *racetrack*⟩ **b** wet or smeared (as if) with sthg slopped over **2** slovenly, careless ⟨*she's a* ~ *dresser*⟩ **3** disagreeably effusive ⟨~ *sentimentalism*⟩ – **sloppily** *adv*, **sloppiness** *n*

¹**slosh** *n* **1** slush **2** the slap or splash of liquid **3** *chiefly Br* a heavy blow; a bash – infml

²**slosh** *vi* **1** to flounder or splash through water, mud, etc **2** to flow with a splashing motion ⟨*water* ~*ed all round*

him⟩ ~ *vt* **1** to splash (sthg) about in liquid **2** to splash (a liquid) about, on, or into sthg **3** to make wet by splashing **4** *chiefly Br* to hit, beat ⟨~ed *him on the head with a bucket*⟩ – *infml*
sloshed *adj* – infml
¹**slot** *n* **1a** a narrow opening, groove, or passage; a slit **b** a passage through an aerofoil directing air rearwards from the lower to the upper surface so as to increase lift and delay stalling **2** a place or position in an organization or sequence; a niche
²**slot** *vb* **-tt-** *vt* **1** to cut a slot in **2** to place in or assign to a slot – often + *in* or *into* ⟨~ted *some reading in as he waited*⟩ ~ *vi* to be fitted (as if) by means of a slot or slots ⟨*a do-it-yourself bookcase that* ~s *together in seconds*⟩
³**slot** *n, pl* **slot** the track of an animal (e g a deer)
sloth *n* **1** disinclination to action or work; indolence **2** any of several slow-moving tree-dwelling mammals that inhabit tropical forests of S and Central America, hang face upwards from the branches, and feed on leaves, shoots, and fruits – **slothful** *adj*, **slothfully** *adv*, **slothfulness** *n*
slot machine *n* **1** a machine (e g for selling cigarettes, chocolate, etc or for gambling) whose operation is begun by dropping a coin or disc into a slot **2** *chiefly NAm* FRUIT MACHINE
¹**slouch** *n* **1** a lazy, incompetent, or awkward person **2** a gait or posture characterized by stooping or excessive relaxation of body muscles – **slouchy** *adj*
²**slouch** *vi* **1** to sit, stand, or walk with a slouch ⟨~ed *behind the wheel*⟩ **2** to hang down limply; droop ~ *vt* to cause to droop ⟨~ed *his shoulders*⟩; *specif* to turn down one side of (a hat brim) – **sloucher** *n*
slouch hat *n* a soft usu felt hat with a wide flexible brim
¹**slough** *n* **1a** a place of deep mud or mire **b** a swamp **2** a state of dejection ⟨*a* ~ *of self-pity*⟩
²**slough** *also* **sluff** *n* **1** the cast-off skin of a snake **2** a mass of dead tissue separating from an ulcer **3** sthg that may be shed or cast off ⟨*when shall this* ~ *of sense be cast* – A E Housman⟩
³**slough** *also* **sluff** *vi* **1** to become shed or cast off **2** to cast off a skin **3** to separate in the form of dead tissue from living tissue ~ *vt* **1** to cast off (e g a skin or shell) **2a** to get rid of or discard as irksome or objectionable – usu + *off* **b** to dispose of (a losing card in bridge) by discarding
sloven *n* one habitually negligent of neatness or cleanliness, esp in personal appearance
slovenly *adj* **1** untidy, esp in personal appearance or habits **2** lazily slipshod; careless – **slovenliness** *n*
¹**slow** *adj* **1a** lacking in intelligence; dull **b** naturally inert or sluggish ⟨*a* ~ *imagination*⟩ **2a** lacking in readiness, promptness, or willingness ⟨*a shop with* ~ *service*⟩ **b** not quickly aroused or excited ⟨*was* ~ *to anger*⟩ **3a** flowing or proceeding with little or less than usual speed ⟨*traffic was* ~⟩ **b** exhibiting or marked by retarded speed ⟨*he moved with* ~ *deliberation*⟩ **c** low, feeble ⟨~ *fire*⟩ **4** requiring a long time; gradual ⟨*a* ~ *convalescence*⟩ **5a** having qualities that hinder or prevent rapid movement ⟨*a* ~ *putting green*⟩ **b** (designed) for slow movement ⟨*learner drivers should keep to the* ~ *lane*⟩ **6** registering a time earlier than the correct one ⟨*his clock is* ~⟩ **7** lacking in liveliness or variety; boring – **slowish** *adj*, **slowly** *adv*, **slowness** *n*
²**slow** *adv* in a slow manner; slowly
³**slow** *vb* to make or become slow or slower ⟨~ *a car*⟩ ⟨*production of new cars* ~ed⟩ – often + *down* or *up*
slowcoach *n* one who thinks or acts slowly

slow motion *n* a technique in filming which allows an action to be shown as if it is taking place unnaturally slowly, which usu involves increasing the number of frames exposed in a given time and then projecting the film at the standard speed – **slow-motion** *adj*
slowworm *n* a legless European lizard popularly believed to be blind
sludge *n* **1** (a deposit of) mud or ooze **2** a slimy or slushy mass, deposit, or sediment: e g **a** precipitated solid matter produced by water and sewage treatment processes **b** muddy sediment in a steam boiler **c** a precipitate from a mineral oil (e g in an internal combustion engine) – **sludgy** *adj*
¹**slue** *vb, chiefly NAm* ²SLEW
²**slue** *n, chiefly NAm* a slew
¹**slug** *n* any of numerous slimy elongated chiefly ground-living gastropod molluscs that are found in most damp parts of the world and have no shell or only a rudimentary one
²**slug** *n* **1** a lump, disc, or cylinder of material (e g plastic or metal): e g **a** a bullet – slang **b** *NAm* a disc for insertion in a slot machine; *esp* one used illegally instead of a coin **2a** a strip of metal thicker than a printer's lead **b** a line of type cast as 1 piece **3** a unit of mass being equal to 32.174lb (about 14.59kg) **4** *chiefly NAm* a quantity of spirits that can be swallowed at a single gulp – slang
³**slug** *n* a heavy blow, esp with the fist – infml
⁴**slug** *vt* **-gg-** to hit hard (as if) with the fist or a bat – infml – **slugger** *n*
sluggard *n* a lazy person or animal – **sluggard** *adj*, **sluggardly** *adj*
sluggish *adj* **1** averse to activity or exertion; indolent; *also* torpid **2** slow to respond (e g to stimulation or treatment) ⟨*a* ~ *engine*⟩ **3** markedly slow in movement, flow, or growth – **sluggishly** *adv*, **sluggishness** *n*
¹**sluice** *n* **1a** an artificial passage for water (e g in a millstream) fitted with a valve or gate for stopping or regulating flow **b** a body of water pent up behind a floodgate **2** a dock gate **3** a stream flowing through a floodgate **4** a long inclined trough (e g for washing ores or gold-bearing earth)
²**sluice** *vt* **1** to draw off by or through a sluice **2a** to wash with or in water running through or from a sluice **b** to drench with a sudden vigorous flow; flush ~ *vi* to pour (as if) from a sluice
sluiceway *n* an artificial channel into which water is let by a sluice
¹**slum** *n* **1** a poor overcrowded run-down area, esp in a city – often pl with sing. meaning **2** a squalid disagreeable place to live – **slummy** *adj*
²**slum** *vi* **-mm-** **1** to live in squalor or on very slender means – often + *it* **2** to amuse oneself by visiting a place on a much lower social level; *also* to affect the characteristics of a lower social class – **slummer** *n*
¹**slumber** *vi* **1** to sleep **2** to lie dormant or latent ⟨*a* ~ing *volcano*⟩ – **slumberer** *n*
²**slumber** *n* sleep – often pl with sing. meaning
slumbrous, slumberous *adj* **1** heavy with sleep; sleepy ⟨~ *eyelids*⟩ **2** inducing sleep; soporific **3** marked by or suggestive of a state of sleep or lethargy; drowsy
¹**slump** *vi* **1a** to fall or sink abruptly ⟨*morale* ~ed *with news of the defeat*⟩ **b** to drop down suddenly and heavily; collapse ⟨~ed *to the floor*⟩ **2** to assume a drooping posture or carriage; slouch **3** to go into a slump ⟨*sales* ~ed⟩
²**slump** *n* a marked or sustained decline, esp in economic activity or prices
slung *past of* SLING
slunk *past of* SLINK

¹slur *vb* **-rr-** *vi* to pass *over* without due mention, consideration, or emphasis ⟨~red *over certain facts*⟩ ~ *vt* **1** to perform (successive notes of different pitch) in a smooth or connected manner **2** to run together, omit, or pronounce unclearly (words, sounds, etc)

²slur *n* **1** (a curved line connecting) notes to be sung to the same syllable or performed without a break **2** a slurring manner of speech

³slur *vb* **-rr-** *vt* **1** to cast aspersions on; disparage **2** to make indistinct; obscure ~ *vi of a sheet being printed* to slip so as to cause a slur

⁴slur *n* **1a** an insulting or disparaging remark; a slight **b** a shaming or degrading effect; a stigma **2** a blurred spot in printed matter

slurp *vb* to eat or drink noisily or with a sucking sound – **slurp** *n*

slurry *n* a watery mixture of insoluble matter (e g mud, manure, or lime)

slush *n* **1** partly melted or watery snow **2** liquid mud; mire **3** worthless and usu oversentimental material (e g literature) – **slushy** *adj*

slush fund *n, chiefly NAm* a fund for bribing (public) officials or carrying on corrupting propaganda

slut *n* **1** a dirty slovenly woman **2** an immoral woman; *esp* a prostitute – **sluttish** *adj*, **sluttishly** *adv*, **sluttishness** *n*

sly *adj* **slier** *also* **slyer**; **sliest** *also* **slyest** **1a** clever in concealing one's ends or intentions; furtive **b** lacking in integrity and candour; crafty **2** humorously mischievous; roguish ⟨*gave me a ~ glance*⟩ – **slyly** *adv*, **slyness** *n* –**on the sly** in a manner intended to avoid notice; secretly

¹smack *n* (a slight hint of) a characteristic taste, flavour, or aura

²smack *vi* – **smack of** to have a trace or suggestion of ⟨*a proposal that smacks of treason*⟩

³smack *vt* **1** to slap smartly, esp in punishment **2** to strike or put down with the sound of a smack **3** to open (the lips) with a sudden sharp sound, esp in anticipation of food or drink ~ *vi* to make or give a smack

⁴smack *n* **1** a sharp blow, esp from sthg flat; a slap **2** a noisy parting of the lips **3** a loud kiss **4** *chiefly NAm* heroin – slang

⁵smack *adv* squarely and with force; directly – infml ⟨*drove ~ into the car parked opposite*⟩

⁶smack *n* a small inshore fishing vessel

smacker *n, Br* **1** ¹POUND **2** ⁴SMACK **3** *USE* infml

¹small *adj* **1a** having relatively little size or dimensions **b** immature, young ⟨*~ children*⟩ **2a** little in quantity, value, amount, etc **b** made up of few individuals or units ⟨*a ~ audience*⟩ **3a** lower-case **b** implying a general application rather than a specific reference, esp to a political party ⟨*my philosophy is a liberal one, with a ~ 'l'* – Reg Prentice⟩ **4** lacking in strength ⟨*a ~ voice*⟩ **5a** operating on a limited scale ⟨*a ~ farmer*⟩ **b** minor in power, influence, etc ⟨*only has a ~ say in the matter*⟩ **c** limited in degree ⟨*paid ~ heed to his warning*⟩ **d** humble, modest ⟨*a ~ beginning*⟩ **6** of little consequence; trivial ⟨*a ~ matter*⟩ **7a** mean, petty **b** reduced to a humiliating position – **smallish** *adj*, **smallness** *n*

²small *adv* **1** in or into small pieces **2** in a small manner or size ⟨*write ~*⟩

³small *n* **1** a part smaller and esp narrower than the remainder; *specif* the narrowest part of the back **2** *pl, Br* small articles of underwear – infml; used with reference to laundry

small ad *n, Br* a classified advertisement

small arm *n* a firearm fired while held in the hands – usu pl

small change *n* coins of low denomination

small fry *n pl in constr* young or insignificant people or things; *specif* children – **small-fry** *adj*

smallholding *n, chiefly Br* a small agricultural farm – **smallholder** *n*

small hours *n pl* the hours immediately following midnight

small intestine *n* the part of the intestine that lies between the stomach and colon, consists of duodenum, jejunum, and ileum, secretes digestive enzymes, and is the chief site of the absorption of digested nutrients

small-minded *adj* **1** having narrow interests or outlook; narrow-minded ⟨*a ~ man*⟩ **2** characterized by petty meanness – **small-mindedly** *adv*, **small-mindedness** *n*

smallpox *n* an acute infectious feverish virus disease characterized by skin eruption with pustules, sloughing, and scar formation

small talk *n* light or casual conversation; chitchat

small-time *adj* insignificant in operation and status; petty ⟨*~ hoodlums*⟩ – **small-timer** *n*

smarmy *adj* marked by flattery or smugness; unctuous – infml

¹smart *vi* **1** to be (the cause or seat of) a sharp pain; *also* to feel or have such a pain **2** to feel or endure mental distress ⟨*~ing from a rebuke*⟩ **3** to pay a heavy penalty ⟨*would have to ~ for this foolishness*⟩

²smart *adj* **1** making one smart; causing a sharp stinging ⟨*gave him a ~ blow with the ruler*⟩ **2** forceful, vigorous **3** brisk, spirited ⟨*walking at a ~ pace*⟩ **4a** mentally alert; bright **b** clever, shrewd ⟨*a ~ investment*⟩ **5** witty, persuasive ⟨*a ~ talker*⟩ **6a** neat or stylish in dress or appearance ⟨*a ~ new coat of paint*⟩ **b** characteristic of or frequented by fashionable society ⟨*a ~ restaurant*⟩ – **smartly** *adv*, **smartness** *n*

³smart *adv* in a smart manner; smartly

⁴smart *n* **1** a smarting pain; *esp* a stinging local pain **2** poignant grief or remorse ⟨*was not the sort to get over ~s* – Sir Winston Churchill⟩

smart alec, smart aleck *n* an arrogant person with pretensions to knowledge or cleverness – derog – **smart-alecky, smart-alec** *adj*

smarten *vt* to make smart or smarter; *esp* to spruce ~ *vi* to smarten oneself *USE* usu + *up*

¹smash *vt* **1** to break in pieces by violence; shatter **2a** to drive, throw, or hit violently, esp causing breaking or shattering; crash **b** to hit (e g a ball) with a forceful stroke, specif a smash **3** to destroy utterly; wreck – often + *up* ~ *vi* **1** to crash *into*; collide ⟨*~ed into a tree*⟩ **2** to become wrecked **3** to go to pieces suddenly under collision or pressure **4** to execute a smash (e g in tennis)

²smash *n* **1a**(1) a smashing blow, attack, or collision ⟨*a 5-car ~*⟩ (2) the result of smashing; *esp* a wreck due to collision **b** a forceful overhand stroke (e g in tennis or badminton) **2** the condition of being smashed or shattered **3a** the action or sound of smashing **b** utter collapse; ruin; *esp* bankruptcy **4** SMASH HIT – infml

³smash *adv* with a resounding crash

smash-and-grab *n or adj, chiefly Br* (a robbery) committed by smashing a shop window and snatching the goods on display

smashed *adj* extremely drunk – infml

smasher *n, chiefly Br* sby or sthg very fine or attractive – infml

smash hit *n* an outstanding success ⟨*his latest play is a ~*⟩

smashing *adj* extremely good; excellent ⟨*a ~ film*⟩ – infml – **smashingly** *adv*

smash-up *n* a serious accident; a crash ⟨*a 10-car ~ on the M1*⟩

smattering *n* a piecemeal or superficial knowledge of

¹**smear** n **1** a mark or blemish made (as if) by smearing a substance **2** material smeared on a surface; *also* material taken or prepared for microscopic examination by smearing on a slide ⟨*a vaginal ~*⟩ **3** a usu unsubstantiated accusation ⟨*took the article as a personal ~*⟩

²**smear** vt **1a** to spread with sthg sticky, greasy, or viscous; daub **b** to spread esp thickly over a surface **2a** to stain or dirty (as if) by smearing **b** to sully, besmirch; *specif* to blacken the reputation of **3** to obscure or blur (as if) by smearing ~ vi to become smeared ⟨*don't touch the paint or it will ~*⟩ – **smearer** n, **smeary** adj

¹**smell** vb **smelled, smelt** vt **1** to perceive the odour of (as if) by use of the sense of smell **2** to detect or become aware of by instinct ⟨*I could ~ trouble*⟩ ~ vi **1** to exercise the sense of smell **2a(1)** to have a usu specified smell ⟨*these clothes ~ damp*⟩ **(2)** to have a characteristic aura; be suggestive of ⟨*reports of survivors seemed to ~ of truth*⟩ **b** to have an offensive smell; stink – **smeller** n – **smell a rat** to have a suspicion of sthg wrong

²**smell** n **1a** the process, function, or power of smelling **b** the one of the 5 basic physical senses by which the qualities of gaseous or volatile substances in contact with certain sensitive areas in the nose are interpreted by the brain as characteristic odours **2** an odour **3** a pervading quality; an aura **4** an act or instance of smelling

smelling salts n pl but sing or pl in constr a usu scented preparation of ammonium carbonate and ammonia water sniffed as a stimulant to relieve faintness

smell out vt **1** to detect or discover (as if) by smelling ⟨*the dog* smelt out *the criminal*⟩ **2** to fill with an esp offensive smell ⟨*the cigarettes* smelt out *the room*⟩

smelly adj having an esp unpleasant smell

¹**smelt** n, pl **smelts,** esp collectively **smelt** any of various small fishes that closely resemble the trouts in general structure and have delicate oily flesh with a distinctive smell and taste

²**smelt** vt **1** to melt (ore) to separate the metal **2** to separate (metal) by smelting – **smelter** n, **smeltery** n

¹**smile** vi **1** to have or assume a smile **2a** to look with amusement or scorn ⟨*~d at his own weakness*⟩ **b** to bestow approval ⟨*Heaven seemed to ~ on her labours*⟩ **c** to appear pleasant or agreeable ⟨*a green and smiling landscape*⟩ ~ vt **1** to affect with or change by smiling ⟨*~d away his embarrassment*⟩ **2** to utter or express with a smile ⟨*~d her thanks*⟩ – **smiler** n, **smilingly** adv

²**smile** n **1** a change of facial expression in which the corners of the mouth curve slightly upwards and which expresses esp amusement, pleasure, approval, or sometimes scorn **2** a pleasant or encouraging appearance – **smiley** adj

smirch vt **1** to make dirty or stained, esp by smearing **2** to bring discredit or disgrace on ⟨*~ed his reputation*⟩ – **smirch** n

smirk vi to smile in a fatuous or scornful manner – **smirk** n, **smirkingly** adv

smite vb **smote; smitten, smote** vt **1** to strike sharply or heavily, esp with (an implement held in) the hand **2** to kill, injure, or damage by smiting **3a** to attack or afflict suddenly and injuriously ⟨smitten *by disease*⟩ **b** to have a sudden powerful effect on; afflict ⟨smitten *with grief*⟩; *specif* to attract strongly ⟨smitten *by her beauty*⟩ **4** to cause to strike ⟨smote *his hand against his side*⟩ ~ vi to beat down or come forcibly *on* or *upon* – **smiter** n

smith n **1** a worker in metals; *specif* a blacksmith **2** a maker – often in combination ⟨gun**smith**⟩ ⟨song**smith**⟩

smithereens n pl fragments, bits ⟨*the house was blown to ~ by the explosion*⟩

smithy n the workshop of a smith

¹**smock** n a light loose garment resembling a smock frock, esp in being gathered into a yoke; *also* SMOCK FROCK

²**smock** vt to ornament (e g a garment) with smocking

smock frock n an outer garment worn chiefly by farm labourers, esp in the 18th and 19th c, and resembling a long loose shirt gathered into a yoke

smocking n a decorative embroidery or shirring made by gathering cloth in regularly spaced round or diamond-shaped tucks held in place with ornamental stitching

smog n a fog made heavier and darker by smoke and chemical fumes – **smoggy** adj, **smogless** adj

¹**smoke** n **1a** the gaseous products of burning carbon-containing materials made visible by the presence of small particles of carbon **b** a suspension of particles in a gas **2** fumes or vapour resembling smoke **3** sthg of little substance, permanence, or value **4** sthg that obscures **5a** sthg (e g a cigarette) that is smoked **b** an act or spell of smoking esp tobacco – **smokelike** adj

²**smoke** vi **1** to emit smoke **2** to (habitually) inhale and exhale the fumes of burning plant material, esp tobacco ~ vt **1a** to fumigate **b** to drive out or away by smoke ⟨*~ a fox from its den*⟩ **2** to colour or darken (as if) with smoke ⟨*~d glasses*⟩ **3** to cure (e g meat or fish) by exposure to smoke, traditionally from green wood or peat **4** to inhale and exhale the smoke of (e g cigarettes)

smoke out vt **1** SMOKE 1b **2** to bring to public view or knowledge

smoker n **1** sby who regularly or habitually smokes tobacco **2** a carriage or compartment in which smoking is allowed

smoke screen n **1** a screen of smoke to hinder observation **2** sthg designed to conceal, confuse, or deceive

smokestack n a chimney or funnel through which smoke and gases are discharged, esp from a locomotive or steamship

smoking jacket n a loosely fitting jacket formerly worn by men while smoking

smoky also **smokey** adj **1** emitting smoke, esp in large quantities ⟨*a ~ fire*⟩ **2a** having the characteristics or appearance of smoke **b** suggestive of smoke, esp in flavour, smell, or colour **3a** filled with smoke **b** made black or grimy by smoke – **smokily** adv, **smokiness** n

smolder vi, NAm to smoulder

smooch vi to kiss, caress ⟨*~ing on the dimly lit dance floor*⟩ – infml – **smoocher** n, **smoochy** adj

¹**smooth** adj **1a** having a continuous even surface **b** free from hair or hairlike projections **c** of liquid of an even consistency; free from lumps **d** giving no resistance to sliding; frictionless **2** free from difficulties or obstructions **3** even and uninterrupted in movement or flow **4a** equable, composed ⟨*a ~ disposition*⟩ **b** urbane, courteous **c** excessively and often artfully suave; ingratiating ⟨*a ~ salesman*⟩ **5** not sharp or acid ⟨*a ~ sherry*⟩ – **smooth** adv, **smoothly** adv, **smoothness** n

²**smooth** vt **1** to make smooth **2** to free from what is harsh or disagreeable **3** to dispel or alleviate (e g enmity or perplexity) – often + *away* or *over* **4** to free from obstruction or difficulty **5** to press flat – often + *out* **6** to cause to lie evenly and in order – often + *down* ⟨*~ed down his hair*⟩ **7** to free (e g a graph or data) from irregularities by ignoring random variations ~ vi to become smooth – **smoother** n

³**smooth** n a smooth or agreeable side or aspect ⟨*take the rough with the ~*⟩

smoothie, smoothy n a person, esp a man, who behaves with suave and often excessive self-assurance – infml

smorgasbord n a luncheon or supper buffet offering a variety of foods and dishes (e g hors d'oeuvres, hot and cold meats, smoked and pickled fish, cheeses, salads, and relishes)

smote *past of* SMITE

¹smother *n* **1** a dense cloud of gas, smoke, dust, etc **2** a confused mass of things; a welter – **smothery** *adj*

²smother *vt* **1** to overcome or kill with smoke or fumes **2a** to kill by depriving of air **b** to overcome or discomfort (as if) through lack of air **c** to suppress (a fire) by excluding oxygen **3a** to suppress expression or knowledge of; conceal ⟨~ *a yawn*⟩ **b** to prevent the growth or development of; suppress **4a** to cover thickly; blanket ⟨*snow ~ed the trees and hedgerows*⟩ **b** to overwhelm ⟨*aunts who always ~ed him with kisses*⟩ – *vi* to become smothered

¹smoulder, *NAm chiefly* **smolder** *n* a smouldering fire

²smoulder, *NAm chiefly* **smolder** *vi* **1** to burn feebly with little flame and often much smoke **2** to exist in a state of suppressed ferment ⟨*resentment ~ed in her*⟩ **3** to show suppressed anger, hate, jealousy, etc ⟨*eyes ~ing with hate*⟩

¹smudge *vt* **1** to soil (as if) with a smudge **2a** to smear, daub **b** to make indistinct; blur ⟨*couldn't read the ~d address*⟩ **3** *NAm* to disinfect or protect by means of smoke – *vi* **1** to make a smudge **2** to become smudged

²smudge *n* **1** a blurry spot or streak **2** an indistinct mass; a blur – **smudgily** *adv*, **smudginess** *n*, **smudgy** *adj*

smug *adj* **-gg-** highly self-satisfied and complacent ⟨~ *self-righteous moralists*⟩ – **smugly** *adv*, **smugness** *n*

smuggle *vb* **smuggling** *vt* **1** to import or export secretly contrary to the law, esp without paying duties **2** to convey or introduce surreptitiously ⟨~*d his notes into the examination*⟩ – *vi* to import or export sthg in violation of customs laws – **smuggler** *n*

¹smut *vb* **-tt-** *vt* **1** to stain or taint with smut **2** to affect (a crop or plant) with smut – *vi* to become affected by smut

²smut *n* **1** matter, esp a particle of soot, that soils or blackens; *also* a mark made by this **2** any of various destructive fungous diseases, esp of cereal grasses, marked by transformation of plant organs into dark masses of spores **3** obscene language or matter – **smuttily** *adv*, **smuttiness** *n*, **smutty** *adj*

¹snack *vi, chiefly NAm* to eat a snack

²snack *n* a light meal; food eaten between regular meals – **snack** *adj*

¹snaffle *n* a simple usu jointed bit for a bridle

²snaffle *vt* **snaffling** to appropriate, esp by devious means; pinch – *infml*

¹snag *n* **1a** a stub or stump remaining after a branch has been lopped **b** a tree or branch embedded in a lake or stream bed and constituting a hazard to navigation **2a** a sharp or jagged projecting part **b** any of the secondary branches of an antler **3** a concealed or unexpected difficulty or obstacle ⟨*the ~ is, there's no train on Sundays*⟩ **4** an irregular tear or flaw made (as if) by catching on a snag ⟨*a ~ in her stocking*⟩ – **snaggy** *adj*

²snag *vb* **-gg-** *vt* **1** to catch (as if) on a snag **2** to clear (e g a river) of snags **3** *chiefly NAm* to halt or impede as if by catching on a snag **4** *chiefly NAm* to catch or obtain by quick action ⟨~*ged a taxi*⟩ – *vi* to become snagged

snail *n* **1** a gastropod mollusc; *esp* one that has an external enclosing spiral shell **2** a slow-moving or sluggish person or thing – **snaillike** *adj*

¹snake *n* **1** any of numerous limbless scaly reptiles with a long tapering body and with salivary glands often modified to produce venom which is injected through grooved or tubular fangs **2** a sly treacherous person **3** sthg long, slender, and flexible; *specif* a flexible rod for freeing clogged pipes **4** *often cap* a system in which the values of

the currencies of countries in the European Economic Community are allowed to vary against each other within narrow limits – **snakelike** *adj*

²snake *vt* to wind (e g one's way) in the manner of a snake – *vi* to crawl, move, or extend silently, secretly, or windingly

snake charmer *n* an entertainer who exhibits the power to control venomous snakes supposedly by magic

snaky *adj* **1** (formed) of or entwined with snakes **2** serpentine, snakelike ⟨*the ~ arms of an octopus*⟩ **3** slyly venomous or treacherous **4** full of snakes – **snakily** *adv*

¹snap *vb* **-pp-** *vi* **1a** to make a sudden closing of the jaws; seize sthg sharply with the mouth ⟨*fish ~ping at the bait*⟩ **b** to grasp or snatch at sthg eagerly ⟨~ *at any chance*⟩ **2** to utter sharp biting words; give an irritable retort ⟨~*ped at his pupil when she apologized for being late*⟩ **3a** to make a sharp or cracking sound **b** to break suddenly, esp with a sharp cracking sound ⟨*the twig ~ped*⟩ **c** to close or fit in place with an abrupt movement or sharp sound ⟨*the catch ~ped shut*⟩ – *vt* **1** to seize (as if) with a snap of the jaws ⟨~*ped the food right out of his hand*⟩ **2** to take possession or advantage of suddenly or eagerly – usu + *up* ⟨*shoppers ~ping up bargains*⟩ **3** to utter curtly or abruptly ⟨~*ped out an answer*⟩ **4a** to cause to make a snapping sound ⟨~*ped her fingers*⟩ **b** to cause to break suddenly, esp with a sharp cracking sound ⟨~*ped the end off the twig*⟩ **c** to put into or remove from a particular position with a sudden movement or sharp sound ⟨~ *the lid shut*⟩ **5a** to take photographically ⟨~ *a picture*⟩ **b** to photograph –**snap out of** it to free oneself from sthg (e g a mood) by an effort of will – *infml*

²snap *n* **1** an abrupt closing (e g of the mouth in biting or of scissors in cutting) **2** an act or instance of seizing abruptly; a sudden snatch or bite **3** a brief usu curt retort **4a** a sound made by snapping **b** a sudden sharp breaking of sthg thin or brittle **5** a sudden spell of harsh weather ⟨*a cold ~*⟩ **6** a thin brittle biscuit ⟨*ginger ~*⟩ **7** a snapshot **8** vigour, energy **9** a card game in which each player tries to be the first to shout 'snap' when 2 cards of identical value are laid successively **10** *dial NEng* **a** a small meal or snack; *esp* elevenses **b** food; *esp* the food taken by a workman to eat at work **11** *NAm* sthg that is easy and presents no problems; a cinch – *infml*

³snap *interj, Br* – used to draw attention to an identity or similarity ⟨~! *You're reading the same book as me*⟩

⁴snap *adv* with (the sound of) a snap

⁵snap *adj* **1** performed suddenly, unexpectedly, or without deliberation ⟨*a ~ judgment*⟩ **2** *NAm* very easy or simple ⟨*a ~ course*⟩

snapdragon *n* any of several garden plants of the figwort family having showy white, red, or yellow 2-lipped flowers

snappish *adj* **1a** given to curt irritable speech **b** bad-tempered, testy ⟨*a ~ reply*⟩ **2** inclined to snap or bite ⟨*a ~ dog*⟩ – **snappishly** *adv*, **snappishness** *n*

snappy *adj* **1** SNAPPISH 1 **2a** brisk, quick ⟨*make it ~*⟩ **b** lively, animated ⟨*~ repartee*⟩ **c** stylish, smart ⟨*a ~ dresser*⟩ – **snappily** *adv*, **snappiness** *n*

snapshot *n* a casual photograph made typically by an amateur with a small hand-held camera and without regard to technique

¹snare *n* **1a** a trap often consisting of a noose for catching animals **b** sthg by which one is trapped or deceived **2** any of the catgut strings or metal spirals of a snare drum which produce a rattling sound **3** a surgical instrument consisting usu of a wire loop used for removing tissue masses (e g tonsils)

²snare *vt* **1a** to capture (as if) by use of a snare **b** to procure by artful or skilful actions ⟨~ *a top job*⟩ **2** to entangle or hold as if in a snare – **snarer** *n*

snare drum *n* a small double-headed drum with 1 or more snares stretched across its lower head

¹**snarl** *n* **1** a tangle, esp of hair or thread; a knot **2** a confused or complicated situation; *also, chiefly NAm* a snarl-up – **snarly** *adj*

²**snarl** *vt* **1** to cause to become knotted and intertwined; tangle **2** to make excessively confused or complicated ~ *vi* to become snarled *USE* (*vt2*; *vi*) often + *up* – **snarler** *n*

³**snarl** *vi* **1** to growl with bared teeth **2** to speak in a vicious or bad-tempered manner ~ *vt* to utter or express viciously or in a snarling manner – **snarl** *n*, **snarler** *n*

snarl-up *n* an instance of confusion, disorder, or obstruction; *specif* a traffic jam

¹**snatch** *vi* to attempt to seize sthg suddenly – often + *at* ⟨~ *at a rope*⟩ ~ *vt* **1** to take or grasp abruptly or hastily ⟨~ *a quick glance*⟩ **2** to seize or grab suddenly and usu forcibly, wrongfully, or with difficulty – **snatcher** *n*

²**snatch** *n* **1** a snatching at or of sthg **2a** a brief period of time or activity ⟨*sleep came in* ~ es⟩ **b** sthg fragmentary or hurried ⟨*caught a brief* ~ *of their conversation*⟩ **3** a robbery – *infml*

snazzy *adj* stylishly or flashily attractive – *infml*

¹**sneak** *vb* **sneaked**, *NAm also* **snuck** *vi* **1** to go or leave stealthily or furtively; slink ⟨*boys* ~ ing *over the orchard wall*⟩ **2** to behave in a furtive or servile manner **3** *Br* to tell tales ⟨*pupils never* ~ *on their classmates*⟩ – *infml* ~ *vt* to put, bring, or take in a furtive or artful manner ⟨~ ed *a glance at the report*⟩ – **sneak up on** to approach or act on stealthily

²**sneak** *n* **1** a person who acts in a stealthy or furtive manner **2** the act or an instance of sneaking **3** *Br* a person, esp a schoolchild, who tells tales against others – *infml* – **sneaky** *adj*

sneaker *n, chiefly NAm* a plimsoll – usu pl

sneaking *adj* **1** furtive, underhand **2** mean, contemptible **3a** not openly expressed; secret ⟨*a* ~ *desire for publicity*⟩ **b** instinctively felt but unverified ⟨*a* ~ *suspicion*⟩ – **sneakingly** *adv*

sneak thief *n* a thief who steals without using violence or breaking into buildings

¹**sneer** *vi* **1** to smile or laugh with a curl of the lips to express scorn or contempt **2** to speak or write in a scornfully jeering manner ~ *vt* to utter with a sneer – **sneerer** *n*

²**sneer** *n* a sneering expression or remark

sneeze *vi or n* (to make) a sudden violent involuntary audible expiration of breath – **sneezer** *n*, **sneezy** *adj* – **sneeze at** to make light of

¹**snick** *vt* **1** to cut slightly; nick **2** EDGE 4

²**snick** *n* EDGE 4

snicker *vi or n* (to) snigger – **snickerer** *n*, **snickery** *adj*

snide *adj* **1** slyly disparaging; insinuating ⟨~ *remarks*⟩ **2** *chiefly NAm* mean, low ⟨*a* ~ *trick*⟩ – **snidely** *adv*, **snideness** *n*

¹**sniff** *vi* **1** to draw air audibly up the nose, esp for smelling ⟨~ ed *at the flowers*⟩ **2** to show or express disdain or scorn *at* ⟨*not to be* ~ ed *at*⟩ ~ *vt* **1** to smell or take by inhalation through the nose **2** to utter in a haughty manner **3** to detect or become aware of (as if) by smelling

²**sniff** *n* **1** an act or sound of sniffing **2** a quantity that is sniffed ⟨*a good* ~ *of sea air*⟩

¹**sniffle** *vi* **sniffling** to sniff repeatedly – **sniffler** *n*

²**sniffle** *n* **1** an act or sound of sniffling **2** *often pl* a head cold marked by nasal discharge ⟨*he's got the* ~ s⟩

sniffy *adj* having or expressing a haughty attitude; supercilious – *infml* – **sniffily** *adv*, **sniffiness** *n*

snifter *n* a small drink of spirits – *infml*

snigger *vi* to laugh in a partly suppressed often derisive manner – **snigger** *n*, **sniggerer** *n*

¹**snip** *n* **1a** a small piece snipped off; *also* a fragment, bit **b** a cut or notch made by snipping **c** an act or sound of snipping **2** *pl but sing or pl in constr* shears used esp for cutting sheet metal by hand **3** *Br* a bargain **4** *Br* CINCH 2a – *infml*

²**snip** *vb* -**pp**- *vt* to cut (as if) with shears or scissors, esp with short rapid strokes ~ *vi* to make a short rapid cut (as if) with shears or scissors – **snipper** *n*

¹**snipe** *n, pl* **snipes**, *esp collectively* **snipe** any of various birds that usu have long slender straight bills; *esp* any of several game birds that occur esp in marshy areas and resemble the related woodcocks

²**snipe** *vi* **1** to shoot *at* exposed individuals usu from in hiding at long range **2** to aim a snide or obliquely critical attack *at* – **sniper** *n*

snippet *n* a small part, piece, or item; *esp* a fragment of writing or conversation – **snippety** *adj*

¹**snitch** *vi* to turn informer; squeal on sby – *infml* ~ *vt* to pilfer, pinch – *infml* – **snitcher** *n*

²**snitch** *n* an esp petty theft – *infml*

snivel *vi* -**ll**- (*NAm* -**l**-, -**ll**-), **1** to run at the nose **2** to sniff mucus up the nose audibly **3** to whine, snuffle **4** to speak or act in a whining, tearful, cringing, or weakly emotional manner – **snivel** *n*, **sniveller** *n*

snob *n* **1** one who blatantly attempts to cultivate or imitate those he/she admires as social superiors **2a** one who tends to patronize or avoid those he/she regards as inferior **b** one who has an air of smug superiority in matters of knowledge or taste ⟨*a cultural* ~⟩ – **snobbish**, **snobby** *adj*, **snobbishly** *adv*, **snobbishness** *n*, **snobbism** *n* **snobbery** *n* (an instance of) snobbishness

snog *vi* -**gg**- *Br* to kiss and cuddle – *slang* – **snog** *n*

snood *n* **1** a net or fabric bag, formerly worn at the back of the head by women, to hold the hair **2** *Scot* a ribbon or band for a woman's hair – **snood** *vt*

snook *n* a gesture of derision made by putting the thumb to the nose and spreading the fingers out

¹**snooker** *n* **1** a variation of pool played with 15 red balls and 6 variously coloured balls **2** a position of the balls in snooker in which a direct shot would lose points

²**snooker** *vt* **1** to prevent (an opponent) from making a direct shot in snooker by playing the cue ball so that another ball rests between it and the object ball **2** to present an obstacle to; thwart – *infml* – **snookered** *adj*

snoop *vi* to look or pry in a sneaking or interfering manner – **snoop** *n*, **snooper** *n*

snooty *adj* **1** haughty, disdainful **2** characterized by snobbish attitudes ⟨*a* ~ *neighbourhood*⟩ *USE infml* – **snootily** *adv*, **snootiness** *n*

snooze *vi or n* (to take) a nap – *infml* – **snoozer** *n*

snore *vi or n* (to breathe with) a rough hoarse noise due to vibration of the soft palate during sleep – **snorer** *n*

¹**snorkel** *n* **1** a tube housing an air intake and exhaust pipes that can be extended above the surface of the water from a submerged submarine **2** a J-shaped tube allowing a skin diver to breathe while face down in the water

²**snorkel** *vi* **snorkeled**; **snorkeling** to operate or swim submerged using a snorkel – **snorkeler** *n*

¹**snort** *vi* **1** to force air violently through the nose with a rough harsh sound **2** to express scorn, anger, or surprise by a snort ~ *vt* **1** to utter with or express by a snort ⟨~ ed *his contempt*⟩ **2** to take in (a drug) by inhalation ⟨~ *coke*⟩ – *infml*

²**snort** n 1 an act or sound of snorting 2 a snifter – infml

snorter n sthg extremely powerful, difficult, or impressive – infml

snot n 1 nasal mucus 2 a snotty person – slang

snotty adj 1 soiled with nasal mucus – infml 2 arrogantly or snobbishly unpleasant 3 contemptible, despicable USE (2&3) slang

snout n 1a(1) a long projecting nose (e g of a pig) (2) a forward prolongation of the head of various animals **b** the human nose, esp when large or grotesque 2 tobacco – slang – **snouted** adj, **snoutish** adj, **snouty** adj

¹**snow** n 1a (a descent of) water falling in the form of white flakes consisting of small ice crystals formed directly from vapour in the atmosphere **b** fallen snow 2a any of various congealed or crystallized substances resembling snow in appearance **b** cocaine – slang – **snowless** adj

²**snow** vi to fall in or as snow ~vt 1 to cause to fall like or as snow 2 to cover, shut in, or block (as if) with snow – usu + in or up ⟨found themselves ~ed in after the blizzard⟩ 3 chiefly NAm to deceive, persuade, or charm glibly

¹**snowball** n a round mass of snow pressed or rolled together for throwing

²**snowball** vt to throw snowballs at ~vi 1 to throw snowballs 2 to increase or expand at a rapidly accelerating rate

snowberry n any of several white-berried (garden) shrubs

snow blindness n inflammation and painful sensitiveness to light caused by exposure of the eyes to ultraviolet rays reflected from snow or ice – **snow-blind**, **snow-blinded** adj

snowbound adj confined or surrounded by snow

snowcap n a covering cap of snow (e g on a mountain top) – **snowcapped** adj

snowdrift n a bank of drifted snow

snowdrop n a bulbous European plant of the daffodil family bearing nodding white flowers in spring

snowfall n the amount of snow falling at one time or in a given period

snowflake n a flake or crystal of snow

snow leopard n a big cat of upland central Asia with long heavy fur that is irregularly blotched with brownish black in summer and almost pure white in winter

snow line n the lower margin of a permanent expanse of snow

snowman n a pile of snow shaped to resemble a human figure

¹**snowplough** n 1 any of various vehicles or devices used for clearing snow 2 a turn in skiing with the skis in the snowploughing position

²**snowplough** vi to force the heels of one's ski's outwards, keeping the tips together, in order to descend slowly or to stop

snowshoe n a light oval wooden frame that is strung with thongs and attached to the foot to enable a person to walk on soft snow without sinking

snowstorm n a storm of or with snow

snow under vt 1 to overwhelm, esp in excess of capacity to handle or absorb sthg ⟨snowed under with applications for the job⟩ 2 NAm to defeat by a large margin

snow-white adj spotlessly white

snowy adj 1a composed of (melted) snow **b** characterized by or covered with snow 2a whitened (as if) by snow ⟨ground ~ with fallen blossom⟩ **b** snow-white – **snowily** adv, **snowiness** n

¹**snub** vt -bb- 1 to check or interrupt with a cutting retort; rebuke 2 to restrain (e g a rope) suddenly while running out, esp by wrapping round a fixed object; also to halt the motion of by snubbing a line 3 to treat with contempt, esp by deliberately ignoring

²**snub** n an act or an instance of snubbing; esp a slight

³**snub** adj short and stubby ⟨a ~ nose⟩ – **snubness** n

snub-nosed adj 1 having a short and slightly turned-up nose 2 having a very short barrel ⟨a ~ revolver⟩

¹**snuff** n the charred part of a candle wick

²**snuff** vt 1 to trim the snuff of (a candle) by pinching or by the use of snuffers 2a to extinguish (a flame) by the use of snuffers **b** to make extinct; put an end to – usu + out ⟨an accident that ~ed out a life⟩ – **snuff it** to die – infml

³**snuff** vb or n (to) sniff

⁴**snuff** n a preparation of pulverized often scented tobacco inhaled usu through the nostrils

snuffer n 1 an instrument resembling a pair of scissors for trimming the wick of a candle – usu pl but sing. or pl in constr 2 an instrument consisting of a small hollow cone attached to a handle, used to extinguish candles

snuffle vb **snuffling** vi 1a to sniff, usu audibly and repeatedly **b** to draw air through an obstructed nose with a sniffing sound 2 to speak (as if) through the nose ~vt to utter with much snuffling – **snuffle** n, **snuffler** n

¹**snug** adj -gg- 1 fitting closely and comfortably ⟨a ~ coat⟩ 2a enjoying or affording warm secure comfortable shelter **b** marked by relaxation and cordiality ⟨a ~ evening among friends⟩ 3 affording a degree of comfort and ease ⟨a ~ income⟩ – **snug** adv, **snugly** adv, **snugness** n

²**snug** vi -gg- to snuggle

³**snug** n, Br a small private room or compartment in a pub; also a snuggery

snuggle vb **snuggling** vi to curl up comfortably or cosily; nestle – infml ~vt to draw close, esp for comfort or in affection ⟨the dog ~d his muzzle under his master's arm⟩ – infml

¹**so** adv 1a(1) in this way; thus ⟨since he was ~ high⟩ – often used as a substitute for a preceding word or word group ⟨do you really think ~?⟩ ⟨are you ready? if ~, let's go⟩ (2) most certainly; indeed ⟨I hope to win and ~ I shall⟩ **b**(1) in the same way; also ⟨worked hard and ~ did she⟩ – used after as to introduce a parallel ⟨as the French drink wine, ~ the British like their beer⟩ (2) as an accompaniment – after as ⟨as the wind increased, ~ the sea grew rougher⟩ **c** in such a way – used esp before as or that, to introduce a result ⟨the book is ~ written that a child could understand it⟩ or to introduce the idea of purpose ⟨hid ~ as not to get caught⟩ 2a to such an extreme degree ⟨had never been ~ happy⟩ – used before as to introduce a comparison, esp in the negative ⟨not ~ fast as mine⟩, or, esp before as or that, to introduce a result ⟨was ~ tired I went to bed⟩ **b** very ⟨I'm ~ glad you could come⟩ **c** to a definite but unspecified extent or degree ⟨can only do ~ much in a day⟩ 3 therefore, consequently ⟨the witness is biased and ~ unreliable⟩ 4 then, subsequently ⟨and ~ home and to bed⟩ 5 chiefly dial & NAm – used, esp by children, to counter a negative charge ⟨you did ~!⟩

²**so** conj 1 with the result that ⟨her diction is good, ~ every word is clear⟩ 2 in order that; THAT 2(1) ⟨be quiet ~ he can sleep⟩ 3a for that reason; therefore ⟨don't want to go, ~ I won't⟩ **b**(1) – used as an introductory particle ⟨~ here we are⟩ often to belittle a point under discussion ⟨~ what?⟩ (2) – used interjectionally to indicate awareness of a discovery ⟨~, that's who did it⟩ or surprised dissent

³**so** adj 1 conforming with actual facts; true ⟨said things that were not ~⟩ 2 disposed in a definite order ⟨his books are always exactly ~⟩

⁴**so** pron such as has been specified or suggested; the same

⟨*became chairman and remained* ~⟩ – **or so** – used to indicate an approximation or conjecture ⟨*I've known him 20 years or so*⟩

⁶**so, soh** *n* ¹SOL

¹**soak** *vi* **1** to lie immersed in liquid (e g water), esp so as to become saturated or softened ⟨*put the clothes to* ~⟩ **2a** to enter or pass through sthg (as if) by pores or small openings; permeate **b** to become fully felt or appreciated – usu + *in* or *into* ~ *vt* **1** to permeate so as to wet, soften, or fill thoroughly **2** to place in a surrounding element, esp liquid, to wet or permeate thoroughly **3** to extract (as if) by steeping ⟨~ *the dirt out*⟩ **4a** to draw in (as if) by absorption ⟨~ed *up the sunshine*⟩ **b** to intoxicate (oneself) with alcohol – *infml* **5** to charge an excessive amount of money – *infml* ⟨~ed *the taxpayers*⟩ – **soakage** *n*, **soaker** *n*

²**soak** *n* **1a** soaking or being soaked **b** that (e g liquid) in which sthg is soaked **2** a drunkard – *infml*

so-and-so *n, pl* **so-and-sos, so-and-so's 1** an unnamed or unspecified person or thing ⟨*Miss So-and-so*⟩ **2** a disliked or unpleasant person – *euph* ⟨*the cheeky* ~*!*⟩

¹**soap** *n* **1** a cleansing and emulsifying agent that lathers when rubbed in water and consists essentially of sodium or potassium salts of fatty acids **2** a salt of a fatty acid

²**soap** *vt* **1** to rub soap over or into **2** to flatter – often + *up*; *infml*

soapbox *n* an improvised platform used by an informal orator – **soapbox** *adj*

soap opera *n* a radio or television drama characterized by stock domestic situations and melodramatic or sentimental treatment

soapstone *n* a soft greyish green or brown stone having a soapy feel and composed mainly of magnesium silicate

soapy *adj* **1** containing or combined with soap or saponin **2a** smooth and slippery **b** suave, ingratiating – **soapily** *adv*, **soapiness** *n*

¹**soar** *vi* **1a** to fly high in the air **b**(1) to sail or hover in the air, often at a great height (2) *of a glider* to fly without engine power and without loss of altitude **2** to rise rapidly or to a very high level ⟨*temperatures* ~ed *into the upper 30s*⟩ **3** to rise upwards in position or status ⟨*a* ~ing *reputation*⟩ **4** to be of imposing height or stature; tower ⟨*mountains* ~ed *above us*⟩ – **soarer** *n*

²**soar** *n* (the range, distance, or height attained in) soaring

¹**sob** *vb* **-bb-** *vi* **1** to weep with convulsive catching of the breath **2** to make a sound like that of a sob or sobbing ~ *vt* **1** to bring (e g oneself) to a specified state by sobbing ⟨~bed *himself to sleep*⟩ **2** to express or utter with sobs ⟨~bed *out her grief*⟩

²**sob** *n* an act or sound of sobbing; *also* a similar sound

¹**sober** *adj* **1** not drunk or addicted to drink **2** gravely or earnestly thoughtful **3** calmly self-controlled; sedate **4a** well balanced; realistic ⟨*a* ~ *estimate*⟩ **b** sane, rational **5** subdued in tone or colour – **soberly** *adv*, **soberness** *n*

²**sober** *vb* to make or become sober – usu + *up*

sobriety *n* being sober – *fml*

sobriquet *n* a nickname

sob story *n* a sentimental story or account intended chiefly to elicit sympathy – *infml*

so-called *adj* **1** commonly named; popularly so termed ⟨*involved in* ~ *campus politics*⟩ **2** falsely or improperly so named ⟨*deceived by his* ~ *friend*⟩

soccer *n* a football game that is played with a round ball between teams of 11 players each, that features the kicking and heading of the ball, and in which use of the hands and arms is prohibited except to the goalkeepers

sociable *adj* **1** inclined to seek or enjoy companionship;

companionable 2 conducive to friendliness or cordial social relations ⟨*spent a* ~ *evening at the club*⟩ – **sociableness** *n*, **sociably** *adv*, **sociability** *n*

¹**social** *adj* **1** involving allies or confederates ⟨*the Social War between the Athenians and their allies*⟩ **2a** sociable **b** of or promoting companionship or friendly relations ⟨*a* ~ *club*⟩ **3a** tending to form cooperative relationships; gregarious ⟨*man is a* ~ *being*⟩ **b** living and breeding in more or less organized communities ⟨~ *insects*⟩ **c** *of a plant* tending to grow in patches or clumps so as to form a pure stand **4** of human society ⟨~ *institutions*⟩ **5a** of or based on status in a particular society ⟨*his* ~ *set*⟩ **b** (characteristic) of the upper classes ⟨*writes a column of* ~ *gossip*⟩ – **socially** *adv*

²**social** *n* a social gathering, usu connected with a church or club

social climber *n* one who strives to gain a higher social position or acceptance in fashionable society – *derog* – **social climbing** *n*

social democracy *n* a political movement advocating a gradual and democratic transition to socialism – **social democrat** *n*, **social democratic** *adj*

socialism *n* **1** an economic and political theory advocating, or a system based on, collective or state ownership and administration of the means of production and distribution of goods **2** a transitional stage of society in Marxist theory distinguished by unequal distribution of goods according to work done

¹**socialist** *n* **1** one who advocates or practises socialism **2** *cap* a member of a socialist party or group

²**socialist** *adj* **1** of socialism **2** *cap* of or constituting a party advocating socialism

socialite *n* a socially active or prominent person

socialize, -ise *vt* **1** to make social; *esp* to fit or train for life in society **2** to adapt to social needs or uses ⟨~ *science*⟩ **3** to constitute on a socialist basis ⟨~ *industry*⟩ ~ *vi* to act in a sociable manner ⟨*likes to* ~ *with his students*⟩ – **socializer** *n*, **socialization** *n*

socialized medicine *n, NAm* medical services administered by an organized group (e g a state agency) and paid for by assessments, philanthropy, or taxation

social science *n* **1** the scientific study of human society and the relationships between its members **2** a science (e g economics or politics) dealing with a particular aspect of human society – **social scientist** *n*

social security *n* **1** provision by the state through pensions, unemployment benefit, sickness benefit, etc for its citizens' economic security and social welfare **2** SUPPLEMENTARY BENEFIT

social service *n* activity designed to promote social welfare; *esp* an organized service (e g education or housing) provided by the state

social work *n* any of various professional activities concerned with the aid of the economically underprivileged and socially maladjusted – **social worker** *n*

¹**society** *n* **1** companionship or association with others; company **2** *often cap* **a** the human race considered in terms of its structure of social institutions ⟨~ *cannot tolerate lawlessness*⟩ **b**(1) a community having common traditions, institutions, and collective interests ⟨*the Society of Friends*⟩ (2) an organized group working together or periodically meeting because of common interests, beliefs, or profession ⟨*the Royal Society*⟩ **3a** a clearly identifiable social circle ⟨*literary* ~⟩ **b** a fashionable leisure class ⟨*not seen in the best* ~⟩ **4** a natural group of plants, usu of a single species or habit

²**society** *adj* (characteristic) of fashionable society ⟨*a* ~ *wedding*⟩

socio- *comb form* 1 society ⟨*sociography*⟩ 2 social (and) ⟨*sociopolitical*⟩

sociology *n* the science of social institutions and relationships; *specif* the study of the behaviour of organized human groups – **sociologist** *n*, **sociological** *adj*

¹**sock** *n*, *pl* **socks**, *NAm also* **sox** a knitted or woven covering for the foot usu extending above the ankle and sometimes to the knee

²**sock** *vt* to hit or apply forcefully – *infml* – **sock it to** to subject to vigorous or powerful attack – *infml*

³**sock** *n* a vigorous or forceful blow; a punch ⟨*gave him a ~ on the chin*⟩ – *infml*

¹**socket** *n* an opening or hollow that forms a holder for sthg ⟨*the eye ~*⟩ ⟨*put the plug in the ~*⟩; *also* an electrical plug

²**socket** *vt* to provide with or place in a socket

Socratic irony *n* a pretence of ignorance in order to elicit the false conceptions of another through adroit questioning

¹**sod** *n* 1 TURF 1; *also* the grass-covered surface of the ground 2 one's native land – *infml*

²**sod** *n*, *Br* 1 an objectionable person, esp male 2 a fellow ⟨*he's not a bad little ~* – Noel Coward⟩ *USE* slang

³**sod** *vt* **-dd-** *Br* to damn – usu used as an oath ⟨*~ you!*⟩ or in the present participle as a meaningless intensive; slang

soda *n* (2b) *pl* **sodas** 1a SODIUM CARBONATE **b** SODIUM BICARBONATE **c** SODIUM HYDROXIDE 2a SODA WATER **b** *chiefly NAm* a sweet drink consisting of soda water, flavouring, and often ice cream

soda fountain *n* 1 *chiefly NAm* an apparatus with a delivery tube and taps for drawing soda water 2 *NAm* a counter where sodas, sundaes, and ice cream are prepared and served

soda water *n* a beverage consisting of water highly charged with carbonic acid gas

sodden *adj* 1 full of moisture or water; saturated ⟨*the ~ ground*⟩ 2 heavy, damp, or doughy because of imperfect cooking ⟨*~ bread*⟩ 3 dull or expressionless, esp from habitual drunkenness ⟨*his ~ features*⟩ – **soddenly** *adv*, **soddenness** *n*

sodium *n* a silver white soft ductile element of the alkali metal group that occurs abundantly in nature in combined form and is very active chemically

sodium bicarbonate *n* a white weakly alkaline salt used esp in baking powders, fire extinguishers, and medicine as an antacid

sodium carbonate *n* a sodium salt of carbonic acid used esp in making soaps and chemicals, in water softening, in cleaning and bleaching, and in photography; *also* WASHING SODA

sodium chloride *n* SALT 1a

sodium hydroxide *n* a white brittle solid that is a strong caustic alkali used esp in making soap, rayon, and paper

sod off *vi*, *Br* to go away – slang

sodomite *n* one who practises sodomy

sodomy *n* a sexual act, resembling copulation, other than normal coitus: e g **a** the penetration of the penis into the mouth or esp the anus of another, esp another male **b** sexual relations between a human being and an animal

soever *adv* to any possible or known extent – used after an adjective preceded by *how* ⟨*how fair ~ she may be*⟩; poetic

sofa *n* a long upholstered seat with a back and 2 arms or raised ends that typically seats 2 to 4 people

¹**soft** *adj* 1a yielding to physical pressure ⟨*a ~ mattress*⟩ ⟨*~ ground*⟩ **b** of a consistency that may be shaped, moulded, spread, or easily cut ⟨*~ dough*⟩ ⟨*~ cheese*⟩ **c** relatively lacking in hardness ⟨*~ wood*⟩ **d** easily magnetized and demagnetized **e** deficient in or free from salts (e g of calcium or magnesium) that prevent lathering of soap ⟨*~ water*⟩ **f** having relatively low energy ⟨*~ X rays*⟩ **g** intended to avoid or prevent damage on impact ⟨*~ landing of a spacecraft on the moon*⟩ 2a pleasing or agreeable to the senses; bringing ease or quiet **b** having a bland or mellow taste **c** not bright or glaring; subdued ⟨*a ~ glow*⟩ **d**(1) quiet in pitch or volume; not harsh (2) of *c* and *g* pronounced /s/ and /j/ respectively (e g in *acid* and *age*) – not used technically (3) *of a consonant sound* articulated with or followed by /y/ (e g in Russian) **e**(1) *of the eyes* having a liquid or gentle appearance (2) having a gently curved outline ⟨*~ hills against the horizon*⟩ **f** smooth or delicate in texture ⟨*~ cashmere*⟩ **g**(1) balmy or mild in weather or temperature (2) falling or blowing with slight force or impact ⟨*~ breezes*⟩ 3 marked by a kindness, lenience, or moderation: e g **a**(1) not being or involving harsh or onerous terms ⟨*~ option*⟩ (2) demanding little effort; easy ⟨*a ~ job*⟩ (3) based on negotiation and conciliation rather than on a show of power or on threats ⟨*took a ~ line towards the enemy*⟩ **b**(1) mild, low-key; *specif* not of the most extreme or harmful kind ⟨*~ porn*⟩ (2) *of a drug* considered less detrimental than a hard drug; not (strongly) addictive 4a lacking resilience or strength, esp as a result of having led a life of ease **b** not protected against enemy attack; vulnerable ⟨*a ~ aboveground landing site*⟩ **c** mentally deficient; feebleminded ⟨*~ in the head*⟩ 5a impressionable **b** readily influenced or imposed upon; compliant **c**(1) lacking firmness or strength of character; feeble (2) marked by a gradually declining trend; not firm ⟨*wool prices are increasingly ~*⟩ **d** amorously attracted, esp covertly – *on* ⟨*has been ~ on her for years*⟩ 6 dealing with ideas, opinions, etc, rather than facts and figures ⟨*the ~ sciences*⟩ – **softish** *adj*, **softly** *adv*, **softness** *n*

²**soft** *n* a soft object, material, or part ⟨*the ~ of the thumb*⟩

³**soft** *adv* in a soft or gentle manner; softly

softball *n* a game similar to baseball played on a smaller field with a ball larger than a baseball

soft-boil *vt* to boil (an egg in its shell) to the point at which the white solidifies but the yolk remains unset

soft coal *n* bituminous coal

soften *vt* 1 to make soft or softer 2a to weaken the military resistance or the morale of **b** to impair the strength or resistance of ⟨*~ him up with compliments*⟩ ~ *vi* to become soft or softer *USE* (2) often + *up* – **softener** *n*

soft furnishing *n*, *chiefly Br* (the practice of furnishing with) a cloth article (e g a curtain or chair cover) that increases the comfort, utility, or decorativeness of a room or piece of furniture – usu pl

softhearted *adj* kind, compassionate – **softheartedly** *adv*, **softheartedness** *n*

softie *n* a softy

soft-land *vb* to (cause to) make a soft landing on a celestial body (e g the moon) – **soft-lander** *n*

soft palate *n* the fold at the back of the hard palate that partially separates the mouth and pharynx

soft-pedal *vb* **-ll-** (*NAm* **-l-**, **-ll-**) to attempt to minimize the importance of (sthg), esp by talking cleverly or evasively ⟨*~ the issue of arms sales*⟩

soft pedal *n* a foot pedal on a piano that reduces the volume of sound

soft sell *n* the use of suggestion or gentle persuasion in selling rather than aggressive pressure

soft-soap *vt* to persuade or mollify with flattery or smooth talk – *infml* – **soft-soaper** *n*

soft soap *n* **1** a semifluid soap **2** flattery – infml

soft-spoken *adj* having a mild or gentle voice; *also* suave

soft spot *n* a sentimental weakness ⟨*has a ~ for him*⟩

software *n* **1** the entire set of programs, procedures, and related documentation associated with a system, esp a computer system; *specif* computer programs **2** sthg contrasted with hardware; *esp* materials for use with audiovisual equipment

softwood *n* the wood of a coniferous tree – **softwood** *adj*

softy, softie *n* **1** an excessively sentimental or susceptible person **2** a feeble, effeminate, or foolish person *USE* infml

soggy *adj* **1a** waterlogged, soaked ⟨*a ~ lawn*⟩ **b** SODDEN **2 2** heavily dull ⟨*~ prose*⟩ – **soggily** *adv*, **sogginess** *n*

soigné, *fem* **soignée** *adj* well-groomed; *also* elegant

¹soil *vt* **1** to stain or make unclean, esp superficially; dirty **2** to defile morally; corrupt **3** to blacken or tarnish (e g a person's reputation) ~ *vi* to become soiled or dirty

²soil *n* **1** stain, defilement **2** sthg (e g refuse or sewage) that spoils or pollutes

³soil *n* **1** firm land; earth **2a** the upper layer of earth that may be dug or ploughed and in which plants grow **b** the superficial unconsolidated and usu weathered part of the mantle of a planet, esp the earth **3** country, land ⟨*his native ~*⟩ **4** a medium in which sthg takes hold and develops – **soily** *adj*

soiree, soirée *n* a party or reception held in the evening

sojourn *vi or n* (to make) a temporary stay – fml – **sojourner** *n*

¹sol *n* the 5th note of the diatonic scale in solmization

²sol *n*, *pl* **soles** the standard unit of money in Peru

³sol *n* a fluid colloidal system; *esp* one in which the continuous phase is a liquid

¹solace *n* (a source of) consolation or comfort in grief or anxiety

²solace *vt* **1** to give solace to; console **2** to alleviate, relieve ⟨*~ grief*⟩ – **solacement** *n*, **solacer** *n*

¹solar *adj* **1** of or derived from the sun, esp as affecting the earth **2** (of or reckoned by time) measured by the earth's course in relation to the sun **3** produced or operated by the action of the sun's light or heat; *also* using the sun's rays

²solar *n* an upper room in a medieval house

solar cell *n* a photovoltaic cell or thermopile that is able to convert the energy of sunlight into electrical energy and is used as a power source

solarium *n*, *pl* **solaria** *also* **solariums** a room exposed to the sun (e g for relaxation or treatment of illness)

solar plexus *n* **1** an interlacing network of nerves in the abdomen behind the stomach **2** the pit of the stomach

solar system *n* the sun together with the group of celestial bodies that are held by its attraction and revolve round it

sold *past of* SELL

¹solder *n* an alloy, esp of tin and lead, used when melted to join metallic surfaces

²solder *vt* **1** to unite or make whole (as if) by solder **2** to hold or join together; unite ⟨*a friendship ~ed by common interests*⟩ ~ *vi* to become united or repaired (as if) by solder – **solderer** *n*, **solderability** *n*

soldering iron *n* a usu electrically heated device that is used for melting and applying solder

¹soldier *n* **1a** sby engaged in military service, esp in the army **b** an enlisted man or woman **c** a person of usu specified military skill ⟨*a good ~*⟩ **2** any of a caste of ants or wingless termites having a large head and jaws – **soldierly** *adj or adv*, **soldiership** *n*

²soldier *vi* **1** to serve as a soldier **2** to press doggedly forward – usu + *on* ⟨*~ed on without a windscreen*⟩

soldier of fortune *n* sby who seeks an adventurous, esp military, life wherever chance allows

soldiery *n sing or pl in constr* **1** a body of soldiers **2** a set of soldiers of a specified sort ⟨*a drunken ~*⟩

¹sole *n* **1a** the undersurface of a foot **b** the part of a garment or article of footwear on which the sole rests **2** the usu flat bottom or lower part of sthg or the base on which sthg rests – **soled** *adj*

²sole *vt* to provide with a sole ⟨*~ a shoe*⟩

³sole *n* any of several flatfish including some valued as superior food fishes

⁴sole *adj* **1** being the only one; only ⟨*she was her mother's ~ confidante*⟩ **2** belonging or relating exclusively to 1 individual or group ⟨*~ rights of publication*⟩ **3** *esp of a woman* not married – used in law – **soleness** *n*

solecism *n* **1** a minor blunder in speech or writing **2** a deviation from what is proper or normal; *esp* a breach of etiquette or decorum – **solecistic** *adj*

solely *adv* **1** without another; singly ⟨*was ~ responsible*⟩ **2** to the exclusion of all else ⟨*done ~ for money*⟩

solemn *adj* **1** performed so as to be legally binding ⟨*a ~ oath*⟩ **2** marked by the observance of established form or ceremony; *specif* celebrated with full liturgical ceremony **3a** conveying a deep sense of reverence or exaltation; sublime ⟨*was stirred by the ~ music*⟩ **b** marked by seriousness and sobriety **c** sombre, gloomy – **solemnly** *adv*, **solemnness** *n*, **solemnify** *vt*

solemnity *n* **1** formal or ceremonious observance of an occasion or event **2** a solemn event or occasion **3** solemn character or state ⟨*the ~ of his words*⟩

solemnize, -ise *vt* **1** to observe or honour with solemnity **2** to perform with pomp or ceremony; *esp* to celebrate (a marriage) with religious rites **3** to make solemn or serious; dignify – **solemnization** *n*

sol-fa *n* **1** *also* **sol-fa syllables** the syllables *do, re, mi,* etc used in singing the notes of the scale **2** solmization **3** TONIC SOL-FA

solicit *vt* **1** to make a formal or earnest appeal or request to; entreat **2a** to attempt to lure or entice, esp into evil **b** *of a prostitute* to proposition publicly **3** to try to obtain by usu urgent requests or pleas ⟨*~ military aid*⟩ **4** to require; CALL FOR ⟨*the situation ~s the closest attention*⟩ – fml ~ *vi* **1** to ask earnestly for; importune **2** *of a prostitute* to proposition sby publicly – **solicitant** *n*, **solicitation** *n*

solicitor *n* **1** a qualified lawyer who advises clients, represents them in the lower courts, and prepares cases for barristers to try in higher courts **2** the chief law officer of a US municipality, county, etc – **solicitorship** *n*

solicitor general *n*, *pl* **solicitors general 1** *often cap S&G* a Crown law officer ranking after the attorney general in England **2** a federally appointed assistant to the US attorney general

solicitous *adj* **1** showing consideration or anxiety; concerned ⟨*~ about the future*⟩ **2** desirous of; eager to – fml – **solicitously** *adv*, **solicitousness** *n*

solicitude *n* **1** being solicitous; concern; *also* excessive care or attention **2** a cause of care or concern – usu pl with sing. meaning

¹solid *adj* **1a** without an internal cavity ⟨*a ~ ball of rubber*⟩ **b** having no opening or division ⟨*a ~ wall*⟩ **c**(1) set in type or printed with minimum spacing (e g without leads) between lines **(2)** joined without a hyphen ⟨*a ~ compound*⟩ **2** of uniformly close and coherent texture; compact **3** of good substantial quality or kind ⟨*~ com-*

fort): e g **a** well constructed from durable materials ⟨~ furniture⟩ **b** sound, cogent ⟨~ reasons⟩ **4a** having, involving, or dealing with 3 dimensions or with solids **b** neither gaseous nor liquid **5a** without interruption; full ⟨waited 3 ~ hours⟩ **b** unanimous ⟨had the ~ support of his party⟩ **6** of a single substance or character ⟨~ rock⟩: e g **a** (almost) entirely of 1 metal ⟨~ gold⟩ **b** of uniform colour or tone **7a** reliable, reputable, or acceptable ⟨are his opinions ~?⟩ **b** serious in character or intent ⟨sent the President a ~ memorandum – The Economist⟩ **8** chiefly NAm in staunch or intimate association ⟨~ with his boss⟩ – infml – **solidly** adv, **solidness** n, **solidify** vb, **solidifier** n, **solidity** n, **solidification** n

²**solid** adv in a solid manner ⟨the grease had set ~⟩; also unanimously

³**solid** n **1** a substance that does not flow perceptibly under moderate stress **2** the part of a solution or suspension that when freed from solvent or suspending medium has the qualities of a solid – usu pl with sing. meaning ⟨milk ~s⟩ **3** a geometrical figure (e g a cube or sphere) having 3 dimensions **4** sthg solid; esp a solid colour

solidarity n unity based on shared interests and standards

solid-state adj **1** relating to the properties, structure, or reactivity of solid material; esp relating to the arrangement or behaviour of ions, molecules, nucleons, electrons, and holes in the crystals of a substance (e g a semiconductor) or to the effect of crystal imperfections on the properties of a solid substance ⟨~ physics⟩ **2** using the electric, magnetic, or photic properties of solid materials; not using thermionic valves ⟨a ~ stereo system⟩

solidus n, pl **solidi** **1** an ancient Roman gold coin introduced by Constantine and used until the fall of the Byzantine Empire **2** a punctuation mark / used esp to denote 'per' (e g in feet/second), 'or' (e g in straggler/deserter), or 'cum' (e g in restaurant/bar) or to separate shillings and pence (e g in 2/6 and 7/-), the terms of a fraction, or esp numbers in a list **3** a curve, usu on a temperature and composition graph for a mixture, below which only the solid phase can exist

soliloquy n **1** the act of talking to oneself **2** a dramatic monologue that gives the illusion of being a series of unspoken reflections – **soliloquist** n, **soliloquize** vi

solipsism n a theory holding that only the self exists and that the external world is merely an idea generated by the self – **solipsist** n, **solipsistic** adj

solitaire n **1** a gem, esp a diamond, set by itself **2** a game played by 1 person in which a number of pieces are removed from a cross-shaped pattern according to certain rules **3** chiefly NAm PATIENCE 2

¹**solitary** adj **1a** (fond of) being or living alone or without companions ⟨a ~ disposition⟩ **b** dispirited by isolation; lonely ⟨left ~ by his wife's death⟩ **2** taken, spent, or performed without companions ⟨a ~ weekend⟩ **3** growing or living alone; not gregarious, colonial, social, or compound **4** being the only one; sole ⟨the ~ example⟩ **5** unfrequented, remote ⟨lived in a ~ place⟩ – **solitariness** n, **solitarily** adv

²**solitary** n one who habitually seeks solitude

solitude n **1** being alone or remote from society; seclusion **2** a lonely place; a fastness

solmization n the act, practice, or system of using syllables to denote musical notes or the degrees of a musical scale

¹**solo** n, pl **solos** **1a** (musical composition for) performance by a single voice or instrument with or without accompaniment **2** a flight by 1 person alone in an aircraft; esp a person's first solo flight – **solo** adj, **soloist** n

²**solo** adv without a companion; alone ⟨fly ~⟩

so long as conj **1** during and up to the end of the time that; while **2** provided that

solstice n (the time when the sun passes) either of the 2 points on the ecliptic at which the distance from the celestial equator is greatest and which is reached by the sun each year about June 22nd and December 22nd

soluble adj **1a** capable of being dissolved (as if) in a liquid **b** capable of being emulsified **2** capable of being solved or explained ⟨~ questions⟩ – **solubilize** vt, **solubleness** n, **solubly** adv, **solubility** n

solution n **1a** an act or the process by which a solid, liquid, or gaseous substance is uniformly mixed with a liquid or sometimes a gas or solid **b** a typically liquid uniform mixture formed by this process **c** a liquid containing a dissolved substance **d** the condition of being dissolved **2a** an action or process of solving a problem **b** an answer to a problem

solve vt to find a solution for ⟨~ a problem⟩ ~ vi to solve sthg ⟨substitute the known values of the constants and ~ for x⟩ – **solver** n

¹**solvent** adj **1** able to pay all legal debts; also in credit **2** that dissolves or can dissolve ⟨~ fluids⟩ ⟨~ action of water⟩ – **solvency** n, **solvently** adv

²**solvent** n a usu liquid substance capable of dissolving or dispersing 1 or more other substances

sombre, NAm chiefly somber adj **1** dark, gloomy **2** of a dull, dark, or heavy shade or colour **3a** serious, grave **b** depressing, melancholy ⟨~ thoughts⟩ – **sombrely** adv

sombrero n, pl **sombreros** a high-crowned hat of felt or straw with a very wide brim, worn esp in Mexico

¹**some** adj **1a** being an unknown, undetermined, or unspecified unit or thing ⟨~ film or other⟩ **b** being an unspecified member of a group or part of a class ⟨~ gems are hard⟩ **c** being an appreciable number, part, or amount of ⟨have ~ consideration for others⟩ **d** being of an unspecified amount or number ⟨give me ~ water⟩ – used as an indefinite pl of A ⟨have ~ apples⟩ **2a** important, striking, or excellent ⟨that was ~ party⟩ – chiefly infml **b** no kind of ⟨~ friend you are!⟩ – chiefly infml

²**some** pron **1** sing or pl in constr some part, quantity, or number but not all ⟨~ of my friends⟩ **2** chiefly NAm an indefinite additional amount ⟨ran a mile and then ~⟩

³**some** adv **1** ABOUT 3 ⟨~ 80 houses⟩ **2** somewhat – used in Br English in some more and more widely in NAm – **some little** a fair amount of – **some few** quite a number of

¹**-some** suffix (→ adj) characterized by a (specified) thing, quality, state, or action ⟨awesome⟩ ⟨burdensome⟩ ⟨cuddlesome⟩

²**-some** suffix (→ n) group of (so many) members, esp people ⟨foursome⟩

³**-some** comb form (→ n) **1** intracellular particle ⟨lysosome⟩ **2** chromosome ⟨monosome⟩

¹**somebody** pron some indefinite or unspecified person

²**somebody** n a person of position or importance

somehow adv **1a** by some means not known or designated **b** no matter how ⟨got to get across ~⟩ **2** for some mysterious reason

someone pron somebody

somersault n a leaping or rolling movement in which a person turns forwards or backwards in a complete revolution bringing the feet over the head and finally landing on the feet – **somersault** vi

¹**something** pron **1a** some indeterminate or unspecified thing ⟨look for ~ cheaper⟩ – used to replace forgotten matter or to express vagueness ⟨he's ~ or other in the Foreign Office⟩ **b** some part; a certain amount ⟨seen ~ of her work⟩ **2a** a person or thing of consequence ⟨make ~ of one's life⟩ ⟨their daughter is quite ~⟩ **b** some truth

or value ⟨*there's* ~ *in what you say*⟩ – **something of a** a fairly notable ⟨*is something of a* ra̐conteur⟩

²**something** adv 1 in some degree; somewhat ⟨~ *over £5*⟩ ⟨*shaped* ~ *like a funnel*⟩ – also used to suggest approximation ⟨*there were* ~ *like 1,000 people there*⟩ 2 to an extreme degree ⟨*swears* ~ *awful*⟩ – infml

¹**sometime** adv 1 at some unspecified future time ⟨*I'll do it* ~⟩ 2 at some point of time in a specified period ⟨~ *last night*⟩ ⟨~ *next week*⟩

²**sometime** adj having been formerly; LATE 2b ⟨*the* ~ *chairman*⟩

¹**sometimes** adv at intervals; occasionally; NOW AND AGAIN

²**sometimes** adj, archaic sometime, former

somewhat adv to some degree; slightly

¹**somewhere** adv 1 in, at, or to some unknown or unspecified place 2 to a place or state symbolizing positive accomplishment or progress ⟨*at last we're getting* ~⟩ 3 in the vicinity of; approximately ⟨~ *about 9 o'clock*⟩

²**somewhere** n an undetermined or unnamed place

somnambulist n sby who walks in his/her sleep – **somnambulant** adj, **somnambulism** n, **somnambulate** vi, **somnambulistic** adj, **somnambulistically** adv

somnolent adj 1 inclined to or heavy with sleep 2 tending to induce sleep ⟨*a* ~ *sermon*⟩ – **somnolence** n, **somnolently** adv

son n 1a a male offspring, esp of human beings b a male adopted child c a male descendant – often pl 2 cap the second person of the Trinity; Christ 3 a person closely associated with or deriving from a specified background, place, etc ⟨*a* ~ *of the welfare state*⟩ – **sonless** adj, **sonship** n

sonar n an apparatus that detects the presence and location of a submerged object (by reflected sound waves)

sonata n an instrumental musical composition typically for 1 or 2 players and of 3 or 4 movements in contrasting forms and keys

son et lumière n an entertainment held at night at a historical site (e g a cathedral or stately home) that uses lighting and recorded sound to present the place's history

song n 1 the act, art, or product of singing 2 poetry ⟨*famous in* ~ *and story*⟩ 3 (the melody of) a short musical composition usu with words 4 a very small sum ⟨*sold for a* ~⟩

songbird n 1 a bird that utters a succession of musical tones 2 a passerine bird

songster, fem **songstress** n a skilled singer

song thrush n a common Old World thrush that is largely brown above and white below

sonic adj 1 of waves and vibrations having a frequency within the audibility range of the human ear 2 using, produced by, or relating to sound waves ⟨~ *altimeter*⟩ 3 of or being the speed of sound in air at sea level (about 340 m/s or 741 mph) – **sonically** adv

sonic boom n a sound resembling an explosion produced when a shock wave formed at the nose of an aircraft travelling at supersonic speed reaches the ground

son-in-law n, pl **sons-in-law** the husband of one's daughter

sonnet n (a poem in) a fixed verse form with any of various rhyming schemes, consisting typically of 14 lines of 10 syllables each

sonny n a young boy – usu used in address; infml

son of a bitch n, pl **sons of bitches** BASTARD 3 – slang

sonorous adj 1 giving out sound (e g when struck) 2 pleasantly loud 3 impressive in effect or style ⟨*made a* ~ *speech to the assembly*⟩ – **sonorously** adv, **sonorousness** n, **sonority** n

sonsy, sonsie adj, chiefly Scot buxom, comely

¹**soon** adv 1 before long; without undue time lapse ⟨~ *after sunrise*⟩ 2 in a prompt manner; speedily ⟨*as* ~ *as possible*⟩ ⟨*the* ~*er the better*⟩ 3 in agreement with one's preference; willingly – in comparisons ⟨*I'd* ~*er walk than drive*⟩ ⟨*I'd just as* ~ *not*⟩ – **no sooner** B **than** at the very moment that ⟨*no sooner built than knocked down again*⟩

²**soon** adj advanced in time; early ⟨*the* ~*est date that can be arranged* – The Times⟩

¹**soot** n a fine black powder that consists chiefly of carbon and is formed by combustion, or separated from fuel during combustion

²**soot** vt to coat or cover with soot

soothe vt 1 to calm (as if) by showing attention or concern; placate 2 to relieve, alleviate 3 to bring comfort or reassurance to ~ vi to bring peace or ease – **soother** n, **soothingly** adv

soothsay vi to predict the future; prophesy – **soothsayer** n

¹**sop** n 1 a piece of food, esp bread, dipped, steeped, or for dipping in a liquid (e g soup) 2 sthg offered as a concession, appeasement, or bribe

²**sop** vt -pp- to soak or dip (as if) in liquid ⟨~ *bread in gravy*⟩

sophism n 1 an argument apparently correct but actually fallacious; esp such an argument used to deceive 2 use of sophisms; sophistry – **sophistic, sophistical** adj, **sophistically** adv

sophisticate n a sophisticated person

sophisticated adj 1a highly complicated or developed; complex ⟨~ *electronic devices*⟩ b worldly-wise, knowing ⟨*a* ~ *adolescent*⟩ 2 intellectually subtle or refined ⟨*a* ~ *novel*⟩ 3 not in a natural, pure, or original state; adulterated ⟨*a* ~ *oil*⟩ – **sophisticatedly** adv, **sophistication** n

sophistry n speciously subtle reasoning or argument

sophomore n, NAm a student in his/her second year at college or secondary school – **sophomoric** adj

¹**soporific** adj 1 causing or tending to cause sleep 2 of or marked by sleepiness or lethargy

²**soporific** n a soporific agent; specif HYPNOTIC 1

¹**sopping** adj wet through; soaking

²**sopping** adv to an extreme degree of wetness ⟨~ *wet*⟩

soppy adj 1 weakly sentimental; mawkish ⟨*you get so* ~ *about couples* – Iris Murdoch⟩ 2 chiefly Br silly, inane USE infml – **soppily** adv, **soppiness** n

soprano n, pl **sopranos** 1 the highest part in 4-part harmony 2 (a person with) the highest singing voice of women, boys, or castrati 3 a member of a family of instruments having the highest range – **soprano** adj

sop up vt to mop up (e g water) so as to leave a dry surface

sorbet n WATER ICE; also SHERBET 2

sorcerer, fem **sorceress** n a person who uses magical power, esp with the aid of evil spirits; a wizard

sorcery n the arts and practices of a sorcerer

sordid adj 1a dirty, filthy b wretched, squalid 2 base, vile ⟨~ *motives*⟩ 3 meanly avaricious; niggardly 4 of a dull or muddy colour – **sordidly** adv, **sordidness** n

¹**sore** adj 1a causing pain or distress b painfully sensitive ⟨~ *muscles*⟩ c hurt or inflamed so as to be or seem painful ⟨~ *runny eyes*⟩ 2a causing irritation or offence ⟨*overtime is a* ~ *point with him*⟩ b causing great difficulty or anxiety; desperate ⟨*in* ~ *straits*⟩ 3 chiefly NAm angry, vexed – **soreness** n

²**sore** n 1 a localized sore spot on the body; esp one (e g an ulcer) with the tissues ruptured or abraded and usu infected 2 a source of pain or vexation; an affliction

³**sore** adv, archaic sorely

sorehead n, NAm a person easily angered or disgruntled – infml – **sorehead, soreheaded** adj

sorely adv 1 painfully, grievously 2 much, extremely ⟨~ needed changes⟩

sorghum n any of an economically important genus of Old World tropical grasses similar to maize in habit but with the spikelets in pairs on a hairy stalk

sorority n a club of women students usu living in the same house in some American universities

¹sorrel n 1 brownish orange to light brown 2 a sorrel-coloured animal; esp a sorrel-coloured horse

²sorrel n 1 ¹DOCK 2 WOOD SORREL

¹sorrow n 1 deep distress and regret (e g over the loss of sthg precious) 2 a cause or display of grief or sadness

²sorrow vi to feel or express sorrow – **sorrower** n

sorry adj 1 feeling regret, penitence, or pity ⟨felt ~ for the poor wretch⟩ 2 inspiring sorrow, pity, or scorn ⟨looked a ~ sight in his torn clothes⟩ – **sorriness** n

¹sort n 1a a group constituted on the basis of any common characteristic; a class, kind b an instance of a kind ⟨a ~ of herbal medicine⟩ 2 nature, disposition ⟨people of an evil ~⟩ 3 a letter or piece of type in a fount 4 a person, individual – infml ⟨he's not a bad ~⟩ – **of sorts/of a sort** of an inconsequential or mediocre quality – **out of sorts** 1 somewhat ill 2 grouchy, irritable

²sort vt 1 to put in a rank or particular place according to kind, class, or quality ⟨~ the good apples from the bad⟩ – often + through 2 chiefly Scot to put in working order; mend ⟨~ a vacuum cleaner⟩ – **sortable** adj, **sorter** n – **sort with** to correspond to; agree with – fml

sortie n 1 a sudden issuing of troops from a defensive position 2 a single mission or attack by 1 aircraft 3 a brief trip to a hostile or unfamiliar place – **sortie** vi

sort of adv 1 to a moderate degree; rather 2 KIND OF ⟨~ 7 to half past – SEU S⟩ USE infml

sort-out n, chiefly Br an act of putting things in order ⟨my study needs a good ~⟩

sort out vt 1 to clarify or resolve, esp by thoughtful consideration ⟨sorting out his problems⟩ 2a to separate from a mass or group ⟨sort out the important papers and throw the rest away⟩ b to clear up; tidy ⟨will take ages to sort out this mess⟩ 3 to make (e g a person) less confused or unsettled ⟨hoped the doctor would sort him out⟩ 4 chiefly Br to punish, esp by violent means – infml

SOS n 1 an internationally recognized signal of distress which is rendered in Morse code as – – – 2 a call or request for help or rescue

¹so-so adv moderately well; tolerably

²so-so adj neither very good nor very bad; middling

sot n a habitual drunkard – **sottish** adj

sotto voce adv or adj 1 under the breath; in an undertone; also in a private manner 2 at a very low volume – used in music

sou n, pl **sous** 1 any of various former French coins of low value 2 the smallest amount of money ⟨hadn't a ~ to his name⟩

soubrette n (an actress who plays) a coquettish maid or frivolous young woman in comedies

soubriquet n a sobriquet

¹soufflé n a light fluffy baked or chilled dish made with a thick sauce into which egg yolks, stiffly beaten egg whites, and sometimes gelatin are incorporated

²soufflé, souffléed adj puffed or made light by or in cooking

sough vi to make a sound like that of wind in the trees – **sough** n

sought past of SEEK

sought-after adj greatly desired or courted ⟨the world's most ~ concert entertainers – Saturday Review⟩

¹soul n 1 the immaterial essence or animating principle of an individual life 2 the spiritual principle embodied in human beings, all rational and spiritual beings, or the universe 3 all that constitutes a person's self 4a an active or essential part ⟨minorities are the very ~ of democracy⟩ b a moving spirit; a leader ⟨the ~ of the rebellion⟩ 5 spiritual vitality; fervour 6 a person ⟨she's a kind old ~⟩ 7 exemplification, personification ⟨he's the ~ of integrity⟩ 8a a strong positive feeling esp of intense sensitivity and emotional fervour conveyed esp by American Negro performers b negritude c music that originated in American Negro gospel singing, is closely related to rhythm and blues, and is characterized by intensity of feeling and earthiness – **souled** adj

²soul adj (characteristic) of American Negroes or their culture

soul brother n a male Negro – used esp by other Negroes

soul-destroying adj giving no chance for the mind to work; very uninteresting

soulful adj full of or expressing esp intense or excessive feeling ⟨a ~ song⟩ – **soulfully** adv, **soulfulness** n

soulless adj 1 having no soul or no warmth of feeling 2 bleak, uninviting ⟨a ~ room⟩ – **soullessly** adv, **soullessness** n

soul-searching n scrutiny of one's mind and conscience, esp with regard to aims and motives

¹sound adj 1a healthy b free from defect or decay ⟨~ timber⟩ 2 solid, firm; also stable 3a free from error, fallacy, or misapprehension ⟨~ reasoning⟩ b exhibiting or grounded in thorough knowledge and experience ⟨~ scholarship⟩ c conforming to accepted views; orthodox 4a deep and undisturbed ⟨a ~ sleep⟩ b thorough, severe ⟨a ~ whipping⟩ 5 showing integrity and good judgment – **soundly** adv, **soundness** n

²sound adv fully, thoroughly ⟨~ asleep⟩

³sound n 1a the sensation perceived by the sense of hearing b a particular auditory impression or quality ⟨the ~ of children playing⟩ c mechanical radiant energy that is transmitted by longitudinal pressure waves in a material medium (e g air) and is the objective cause of hearing 2 a speech sound ⟨-cher of 'teacher' and -ture of 'creature' have the same ~⟩ 3 the impression conveyed by sthg ⟨he's having a rough time by the ~ of it⟩ 4 hearing distance; earshot 5 a characteristic musical style ⟨the Liverpool ~ of the 1960s⟩ 6 radio broadcasting as opposed to television – **soundless** adj, **soundlessly** adv

⁴sound vi 1a to make a sound b to resound c to give a summons by sound ⟨the bugle ~s to battle⟩ 2 to have a specified import when heard; seem ⟨his story ~s incredible⟩ ~ vt 1a to cause to emit sound ⟨~ a trumpet⟩ b to give out (a sound) ⟨~ an A⟩ 2 to put into words; voice 3a to make known; proclaim ⟨~ his praises far and wide⟩ b to order, signal, or indicate by a sound ⟨~ the alarm⟩ 4 to examine by causing to emit sounds – **soundable** adj

⁵sound n 1a a long broad sea inlet b a long passage of water connecting 2 larger bodies or separating a mainland and an island 2 the air bladder of a fish

⁶sound vt 1 to measure the depth of ⟨~ a well⟩ 2 to explore or examine (a body cavity) with sound ~ vi 1 to determine the depth of water, esp with a sounding line 2 of a fish or whale to dive down suddenly

⁷sound n a probe for exploring or sounding body cavities

sound barrier n a sudden large increase in aerodynamic drag that occurs as an aircraft nears the speed of sound

soundboard *n* **1** a thin resonant board so placed in a musical instrument as to reinforce its sound by sympathetic vibration **2** SOUNDING BOARD 1a(1)

¹sounding *n* **1a** measurement by sounding **b** the depth so determined **2** the measurement of atmospheric conditions **3** a probe, test, or sampling of opinion or intention – often pl

²sounding *adj* **1** sonorous, resounding **2** making a usu specified sound or impression – usu in combination ⟨*odd* ~⟩ – **soundingly** *adv*

sounding board *n* **1a**(1) a structure behind or over a pulpit, rostrum, or platform to direct sound forwards (2) SOUNDBOARD 1 **b** a device or agency that helps disseminate opinions or ideas **2** sby or sthg used to test reaction to new ideas, plans, etc

sound off *vi* **1** to voice opinions freely and vigorously **2** *chiefly NAm* to speak loudly *USE* infml

sound out *vt* to attempt to find out the views or intentions of ⟨*sound him* out *about the new proposals*⟩

¹soundproof *adj* impervious to sound ⟨~ *glass*⟩

²soundproof *vt* to insulate so as to obstruct the passage of sound

sound track *n* the area on a film that carries the sound recording; *also* the recorded music accompanying a film

soup *n* **1** a liquid food typically having a meat, fish, or vegetable stock as a base and often thickened and containing pieces of solid food **2** an awkward or embarrassing predicament – infml ⟨*he's really in the* ~ *over that business last night*⟩ **3** nitroglycerine – slang – **soupy** *adj*

soupçon *n* a little bit; a dash

soup kitchen *n* an establishment dispensing minimum food (e g soup and bread) to the needy

soup up *vt* **1** to increase the power of (an engine or car) **2** to make more attractive, interesting, etc *USE* infml

¹sour *adj* **1** being or inducing the one of the 4 basic taste sensations that is produced chiefly by acids ⟨~ *pickles*⟩ **2a**(1) having the acid taste or smell (as if) of fermentation ⟨~ *cream*⟩ (2) of or relating to fermentation **b** smelling or tasting of decay; rotten ⟨~ *breath*⟩ **c** wrong, awry ⟨*a project gone* ~⟩ **3a** unpleasant, distasteful **b** morose, bitter **4** *esp of soil* acid in reaction **5** *esp of petroleum products* containing foul-smelling sulphur compounds – **sourish** *adj*, **sourly** *adv*, **sourness** *n*

²sour *n* **1** the primary taste sensation produced by sthg sour **2** *chiefly NAm* a cocktail made with a usu specified spirit, lemon or lime juice, sugar, and sometimes soda water ⟨*a whisky* ~⟩

³sour *vb* to make or become sour

source *n* **1** the point of origin of a stream of water **2a**(1) a generative force; a cause (2) a means of supply ⟨*a secret* ~ *of wealth*⟩ **b**(1) a place of origin; a beginning (2) sby or sthg that initiates (3) a person, publication, etc that supplies information, esp at firsthand **3** *archaic* a spring, fountain – **sourceless** *adj*

sourdough *n, NAm* an old-timer, esp a prospector, of Alaska or NW Canada

sourpuss *n* a habitually gloomy or bitter person – infml

sousaphone *n* a large tuba that has a flared adjustable bell and is designed to encircle the player and rest on the left shoulder

¹souse *vt* **1** to pickle ⟨~d *herring*⟩ **2a** to plunge in liquid; immerse **b** to drench, saturate **3** to make drunk; inebriate – infml ~*vi* to become immersed or drenched

²souse *n* **1** an act of sousing; a wetting **2** *chiefly NAm* sthg pickled; *esp* seasoned and chopped pork trimmings, fish, or shellfish

¹south *adj or adv* towards, at, belonging to, or coming from the south

²south *n* **1** (the compass point corresponding to) the direction of the south terrestrial pole **2** *often cap* regions or countries lying to the south of a specified or implied point of orientation – **southward** *adv, adj, or n*, **southwards** *adv*

¹southeast *adj or adv* towards, at, belonging to, or coming from the southeast

²southeast *n* **1** (the general direction corresponding to) the compass point midway between south and east **2** *often cap* regions or countries lying to the southeast of a specified or implied point of orientation – **southeastward** *adv, adj, or n*, **southeastwards** *adv*

¹southeasterly *adj or adv* southeast

²southeasterly, southeaster *n* a wind from the SE

southeastern *adj* **1** *often cap* (characteristic) of a region conventionally designated Southeast **2** southeast – **southeasternmost** *adj*

¹southerly *adj or adv* south

²southerly *n* a wind from the S

southern *adj* **1** *often cap* (characteristic) of a region conventionally designated South **2** south – **southernmost** *adj*

Southerner *n* a native or inhabitant of the South

southern lights *n pl* AURORA AUSTRALIS

southpaw *n* a left-hander; *specif* a boxer who leads with the right hand and guards with the left – **southpaw** *adj*

south pole *n* **1a** *often cap S&P* the southernmost point of the rotational axis of the earth or another celestial body **b** the southernmost point on the celestial sphere, about which the stars seem to revolve **2** the southward-pointing pole of a magnet

¹southwest *adj or adv* towards, at, belonging to, or coming from the southwest

²southwest *n* **1** (the general direction corresponding to) the compass point midway between south and west **2** *often cap* regions or countries lying to the southwest of a specified or implied point of orientation – **southwestward** *adv, adj, or n*, **southwestwards** *adv*

southwester *n* a southwesterly

¹southwesterly *adj or adv* southwest

²southwesterly, southwester *n* a wind from the SW

southwestern *adj* **1** *often cap* (characteristic) of a region conventionally designated Southwest **2** southwest – **southwesternmost** *adj*

¹souvenir *n* sthg that serves as a reminder (e g of a place or past event); a memento – **souvenir** *adj*

²souvenir *vt, Austr* to steal, pilfer – infml

sou'wester *n* **1** a southwesterly **2a** a long usu oilskin waterproof coat worn esp at sea during stormy weather **b** a waterproof hat with a wide slanting brim longer at the back than in front

¹sovereign *n* **1a** one possessing sovereignty **b** an acknowledged leader ⟨*the rose,* ~ *among flowers*⟩ **2** a former British gold coin worth 1 pound

²sovereign *adj* **1a** possessing supreme (political) power ⟨~ *ruler*⟩ **b** unlimited in extent; absolute ⟨~ *power*⟩ **c** enjoying political autonomy ⟨*a* ~ *state*⟩ **2a** of outstanding excellence or importance ⟨*their* ~ *sense of humour* – Sir Winston Churchill⟩ **b** of an unqualified nature; utmost ⟨~ *contempt*⟩ **3** (characteristic) of or befitting a sovereign – **sovereignly** *adv*, **sovereignty** *n*

soviet *n* **1** an elected council in a Communist country **2** *pl, cap* the people, esp the leaders, of the USSR – **soviet** *adj, often cap*, **sovietism** *n, often cap*

¹sow *n* **1** an adult female pig; *also* the adult female of various other animals (e g the grizzly bear) **2** (a mass of metal solidified in) a channel that conducts molten metal, esp iron, to moulds

²**sow** *vb* **sowed; sown, sowed** *vi* to plant seed for growth, esp by scattering ~ *vt* **1a** to scatter (e g seed) on the earth for growth; *broadly* PLANT 1a **b** to strew (as if) with seed **c** to introduce into a selected environment **2** to implant, initiate ⟨~ *suspicion*⟩ **3** to disperse, disseminate – **sower** *n* – **sow one's wild oats** to indulge in youthful wildness and dissipation, usu before settling down to a steady way of life

soy *n* **1** an oriental brown liquid sauce made by subjecting soya beans to long fermentation and to digestion in brine **2** SOYA BEAN

soya bean *n* (the edible oil-rich and protein-rich seeds of) an annual Asiatic leguminous plant widely grown for its seed and soil improvement

soybean *n* SOYA BEAN

sozzled *adj*, *chiefly Br* drunk – slang; often humor

spa *n* **1** a usu fashionable resort with mineral springs **2** a spring of mineral water

¹**space** *n* **1** (the duration of) a period of time **2a** a limited extent in 1, 2, or 3 dimensions; distance, area, or volume **b** an amount of room set apart or available ⟨*parking* ~⟩ **3** any of the degrees between or above or below the lines of a musical staff **4a** a boundless 3-dimensional extent in which objects and events occur and have relative position and direction **b** physical space independent of what occupies it **5** the region beyond the earth's atmosphere **6** (a piece of type giving) a blank area separating words or lines (e g on a page) **7** a set of mathematical points, each defined by a set of coordinates **8** a brief interval during which a telegraph key is not causing electrical contact to be made – **spaceless** *adj*

²**space** *vt* to place at intervals or arrange with space between – **spacer** *n*

spacecraft *n* a device designed to travel beyond the earth's atmosphere

spaced-out *adj* dazed or stupefied (as if) by a narcotic substance – slang

space heating *n* the heating of spaces (e g by electricity, solar radiation, or fossil fuels), esp for human comfort, with the heater either within the space or external to it – **space heater** *n*

spaceship *n* a manned spacecraft

space suit *n* a suit equipped with life-supporting provisions to make life in space possible for its wearer

space walk *n* a trip outside a spacecraft made by an astronaut in space – **space walk** *vi*, **spacewalker** *n*, **spacewalking** *n*

spacing *n* **1a** the act of providing with spaces or placing at intervals **b** an arrangement in space ⟨*alter the* ~ *of the chairs*⟩ **2** the distance between any 2 objects in a usu regularly arranged series

spacious *adj* **1** containing ample space; roomy **2a** broad or vast in area ⟨*a country of* ~ *plains*⟩ **b** large in scale or space; expansive – **spaciously** *adv*, **spaciousness** *n*

¹**spade** *n* a digging implement that can be pushed into the ground with the foot – **spadeful** *n*

²**spade** *vt* to dig up, shape, or work (as if) with a spade

³**spade** *n* **1a** a playing card marked with 1 or more black figures shaped like a spearhead **b** *pl but sing or pl in constr* the suit comprising cards identified by these figures **2** a Negro – derog – **in spades** in the extreme

spadework *n* the routine preparatory work for an undertaking

spaghetti *n* pasta in the form of thin often solid strings of varying widths smaller in diameter than macaroni

spake *archaic past of* SPEAK

Spam *trademark* – used for a tinned pork luncheon meat

¹**span** *archaic past of* SPIN

²**span** *n* **1** the distance from the end of the thumb to the end of the little finger of a spread hand; *also* a former English unit of length equal to. 9in (about 0.23m) **2** an extent, distance, or spread between 2 limits: e g **a** a limited stretch (e g of time); *esp* an individual's lifetime **b** the full reach or extent ⟨*the remarkable* ~ *of his memory*⟩ **c** the distance or extent between abutments or supports (e g of a bridge); *also* a part of a bridge between supports **d** a wingspan

³**span** *vt* -**nn**- **1** to measure (as if) by the hand with fingers and thumb extended **2a** to extend across ⟨*his career* ~ned *4 decades*⟩ **b** to form an arch over ⟨*a small bridge* ~ned *the pond*⟩ **c** to place or construct a span over

¹**spangle** *n* **1** a sequin **2** a small glittering object or particle ⟨*gold* ~s *of dew* – Edith Sitwell⟩

²**spangle** *vb* **spangling** *vt* to set or sprinkle (as if) with spangles ~ *vi* to glitter as if covered with spangles; sparkle

spaniel *n* **1** any of several breeds of small or medium-sized mostly short-legged dogs usu having long wavy hair, feathered legs and tail, and large drooping ears **2** a fawning servile person

Spanish *n* **1** the official Romance language of Spain and of the countries colonized by Spaniards **2** *pl in constr* the people of Spain – **Spanish** *adj*

Spanish chestnut *n* a large widely cultivated edible chestnut

¹**spank** *vt* to strike, esp on the buttocks, (as if) with the open hand – **spank** *n*

²**spank** *vi* to move quickly or spiritedly ⟨~ing *along in his new car*⟩

¹**spanking** *adj* **1** remarkable of its kind; striking **2** vigorous, brisk ⟨*rode off at a* ~ *pace*⟩ – **spankingly** *adv*

²**spanking** *adv* completely and impressively ⟨*a* ~ *new car*⟩

spanner *n*, *chiefly Br* a tool with 1 or 2 ends shaped for holding or turning nuts or bolts with nut-shaped heads – **(put) a spanner in the works** (to cause) obstruction or hindrance (e g to a plan or operation) – infml

¹**spar** *n* **1** a stout pole **2a** a mast, boom, gaff, yard, etc used to support or control a sail **b** any of the main longitudinal members of the wing or fuselage of an aircraft

²**spar** *vi* -**rr**- **1a** ³BOX; *esp* to gesture without landing a blow to draw one's opponent or create an opening **b** to engage in a practice bout of boxing **2** to skirmish, wrangle **3** FENCE 1b(2)

³**spar** *n* any of various nonmetallic minerals which usu split easily

¹**spare** *vt* **1** to refrain from destroying, punishing, or harming **2** to refrain from using ⟨~ *the rod, and spoil the child*⟩ **3** to relieve of the necessity of doing, undergoing, or learning sthg ⟨~ *yourself the trouble*⟩ **4** to refrain from; avoid ⟨~d *no expense*⟩ **5** to use or dispense frugally – *chiefly neg* ⟨*don't* ~ *the butter*⟩ **6a** to give up as surplus to requirements ⟨*do you have any cash to* ~?⟩ **b** to have left over, unused, or unoccupied ⟨*time to* ~⟩ ~ *vi* to be frugal ⟨*some will spend and some will* ~ – Robert Burns⟩ – **spareable** *adj*

²**spare** *adj* **1** not in use; *esp* reserved for use in emergency ⟨*a* ~ *tyre*⟩ **2a** in excess of what is required; surplus **b** not taken up with work or duties; free ⟨~ *time*⟩ **3** sparing, concise ⟨*a* ~ *prose style*⟩ **4** healthily lean; wiry **5** not abundant; meagre – infml **6** *Br* extremely angry or distraught – infml ⟨*nearly went* ~ *with worry*⟩ – **sparely** *adv*, **spareness** *n*

³**spare** *n* **1** a spare or duplicate item or part; *specif* a spare

part for a motor vehicle **2** the knocking down of all 10 pins with the first 2 balls in a frame in tenpin bowling

spare part *n* a replacement for a component that may cease or has ceased to function ⟨*went to the garage for spare parts*⟩ ⟨*spare-part surgery*⟩

sparerib *n* a pork rib with most of the surrounding meat removed for use as bacon

spare tyre *n* a roll of fat at the waist – infml

sparing *adj* **1** not wasteful; frugal ⟨*we must be ~ with the butter*⟩ **2** meagre, scant – **sparingly** *adv*

¹spark *n* **1a** a small particle of a burning substance thrown out by a body in combustion or remaining when combustion is nearly completed **b** a hot glowing particle struck from a larger mass ⟨*~s flying from under a hammer*⟩ **2** a luminous disruptive electrical discharge of very short duration between 2 conductors of opposite high potential separated by a gas ⟨*e g air*⟩ **3** a sparkle, flash **4** sthg that sets off or stimulates an event, development, etc **5** a trace, esp one which may develop; a germ ⟨*still retains a ~ of decency*⟩ **6** *pl but sing in constr* a radio operator on a ship – infml

²spark *vi* to produce or give off sparks ~ *vt* **1** to cause to be suddenly active; precipitate – usu + *off* ⟨*the question ~ed off a lively discussion*⟩ **2** to stir to activity; incite ⟨*a player can ~ his team to victory*⟩ – **sparker** *n*

³spark *n* a lively and usu witty person – esp in *bright spark* – **sparkish** *adj*

⁴spark *vb, chiefly NAm* to woo, court – **sparker** *n*

sparking plug *n, chiefly Br* a part that fits into the cylinder head of an internal-combustion engine and produces the spark which ignites the explosive mixture

¹sparkle *vb* **sparkling** *vi* **1a** to give off sparks **b** to give off or reflect glittering points of light; scintillate **2** to effervesce ⟨*wine that ~s*⟩ **3** to show brilliance or animation ⟨*the dialogue ~s with wit*⟩ ~ *vt* to cause to glitter or shine

²sparkle *n* **1** a little spark; a scintillation **2** sparkling **3a** vivacity, gaiety **b** effervescence ⟨*a wine full of ~*⟩

sparkler *n* **1** a firework that throws off brilliant sparks on burning **2** a (cut and polished) diamond – infml

sparrow *n* any of several small dull-coloured songbirds related to the finches; *esp* HOUSE SPARROW

sparse *adj* of few and scattered elements; *esp* not thickly grown or settled – **sparsely** *adv*, **sparseness** *n*, **sparsity** *n*

¹Spartan *n* **1** a native or inhabitant of ancient Sparta **2** a person of great courage and endurance – **Spartanism** *n*

²Spartan *adj* **1** of Sparta in ancient Greece **2a** rigorously strict; austere **b** having or showing courage and endurance

spasm *n* **1** an involuntary and abnormal muscular contraction **2** a sudden violent and brief effort or emotion ⟨*~s of helpless mirth – Punch*⟩

spasmodic *adj* **1a** relating to, being, or affected or characterized by spasm **b** resembling a spasm, esp in sudden violence ⟨*a ~ jerk*⟩ **2** acting or proceeding fitfully; intermittent ⟨*~ attempts at studying*⟩ – **spasmodical** *adj*, **spasmodically** *adv*

¹spastic *adj* **1** of or characterized by spasm ⟨*a ~ colon*⟩ **2** suffering from spastic paralysis ⟨*a ~ child*⟩ – **spastically** *adv*, **spasticity** *n*

²spastic *n* **1** one who is suffering from spastic paralysis **2** an ineffectual person – used esp by children

¹spat *past of* SPIT

²spat *n, pl* **spats**, *esp collectively* **spat** a young oyster or other bivalve mollusc

³spat *n* a cloth or leather gaiter covering the instep and ankle

⁴spat *n* **1** *NAm* a light splash ⟨*a ~ of rain*⟩ **2** a petty argument – infml

spatchcock *vt* **1** to cook (a fowl or small game bird) by splitting along the backbone and frying or grilling **2** to insert or put together in a forced or incongruous way

spate *n* **1** flood ⟨*a river in full ~*⟩ **2a** a large number or amount, esp occurring in a short space of time ⟨*the recent ~ of fire bombs – The Guardian*⟩ **b** a sudden or strong outburst; a rush ⟨*a ~ of anger*⟩

spatial *adj* relating to, occupying, or occurring in space – **spatially** *adv*, **spatiality** *n*

¹spatter *vt* **1** to splash or sprinkle (as if) with drops of liquid; *also* to soil in this way ⟨*his coat was ~ed with mud*⟩ **2** to scatter (as if) by splashing or sprinkling ⟨*~ water*⟩ ~ *vi* to spurt out in scattered drops ⟨*blood ~ing everywhere*⟩

²spatter *n* **1** (the sound of) spattering **2** a drop spattered on sthg or a stain due to spattering

spatula *n* a flat thin usu metal implement used esp for spreading, mixing, etc soft substances or powders

spavin *n* a bony enlargement or soft swelling of the hock of a horse associated with strain – **spavined** *adj*

¹spawn *vt* **1** *of an aquatic animal* to produce or deposit (eggs) **2** to bring forth, esp abundantly ~ *vi* **1** to deposit spawn **2** to produce young, esp in large numbers – **spawner** *n*

²spawn *n* **1** the large number of eggs of frogs, oysters, fish, etc **2** *sing or pl in constr* (numerous) offspring **3** mycelium, esp for propagating mushrooms

spay *vt* to remove the ovaries of

speak *vb* **spoke**; **spoken** *vi* **1a** to utter words or articulate sounds with the ordinary voice; talk **b(1)** to give voice to thoughts or feelings ⟨*why don't you ~ for yourself? – H W Longfellow*⟩ **(2)** to be on speaking terms ⟨*still were not ~ing after the dispute*⟩ **c** to address a group ⟨*the professor spoke on his latest discoveries*⟩ **2a** to express thoughts or feelings in writing ⟨*diaries that ~ of his ambition*⟩ **b** to act as spokesman for **3** to communicate by other than verbal means ⟨*actions ~ louder than words*⟩ **4** to make a claim for; reserve ⟨*5 of the 10 new houses are already spoken for*⟩ **5** to make a characteristic or natural sound ⟨*the thunder spoke*⟩ **6** to be indicative or suggestive ⟨*his battered shoes spoke of a long journey*⟩ ~ *vt* **1a** to utter with the speaking voice; pronounce **b** to express orally; declare ⟨*free to ~ their minds*⟩ **2** to make known in writing **3** to (be able to) use in oral communication ⟨*~s Spanish*⟩ – **speakable** *adj* – **so to speak** – used as an apologetic qualification for an imprecise, unusual, ambiguous, or unclear phrase ⟨*this bus service has gone downhill, so to speak*⟩ – **to speak of** worth mentioning – usu neg

speakeasy *n* a place where alcoholic drinks were illegally sold during Prohibition in the USA in the 1920's and 30's

speaker *n* **1a** one who speaks, esp at public functions **b** one who speaks a specified language ⟨*an Italian-speaker*⟩ **2** the presiding officer of a deliberative or legislative assembly **3** a loudspeaker – **speakership** *n*

speaking tube *n* a pipe through which conversation may be conducted (e g between different parts of a building)

speak out *vi* **1** to speak loudly enough to be heard **2** to speak boldly; express an opinion frankly ⟨*spoke out on the issues*⟩

speak up *vi* **1** to speak more loudly – often imper **2** to express an opinion boldly ⟨*speak up for justice*⟩

¹spear *n* **1a** a thrusting or throwing weapon with long shaft and sharp head or blade used esp by hunters or foot soldiers **2** a sharp-pointed instrument with barbs used in spearing fish **3** a spearman

²**spear** *vt* to pierce, strike, or take hold of (as if) with a spear ⟨~ed *a sausage from the dish*⟩

³**spear** *n* a usu young blade, shoot, or sprout (e g of asparagus or grass)

¹**spearhead** *n* **1** the sharp-pointed head of a spear **2** a leading element or force in a development, course of action, etc

²**spearhead** *vt* to serve as leader or leading force of

spearmint *n* a common mint grown esp for its aromatic oil

spec *n* a speculation – *infml* ⟨*one company worth trying as a ~ – The Economist*⟩ – **on spec** *Br* as a risk or speculation ⟨*houses built* on spec⟩; *also* as a risk in the hope of finding or obtaining sthg desired ⟨*the play may be sold out, but it would be worth going to the theatre* on spec⟩ – *infml*

¹**special** *adj* **1** distinguished from others of the same category, esp because in some way superior **2** held in particular esteem ⟨*a ~ friend*⟩ **3** SPECIFIC 4 **4** other than or in addition to the usual ⟨*a ~ day of thanksgiving*⟩ **5** designed, undertaken, or used for a particular purpose or need ⟨*devised a ~ method of restoring paintings*⟩ **6** established or designed for the use or education of the handicapped ⟨*a ~ school*⟩ – **specially** *adv*, **specialness** *n*

²**special** *n* **1** sthg that is not part of a series **2** sby or sthg reserved or produced for a particular use or occasion ⟨*caught the commuter ~ to work*⟩

specialist *n* **1a** one who devotes him-/herself to a special occupation or branch of knowledge **b** a medical practitioner limiting his/her practice to a specific group of complaints ⟨*a child ~*⟩⟨*an ear, nose, and throat ~*⟩ **2** a rank in the US Army enabling an enlisted man/woman to draw extra pay because of technical qualifications – **specialist, specialistic** *adj*

speciality *n* **1** (the state of having) a distinctive mark or quality **2** a product or object of particular quality ⟨*bread pudding was mother's ~*⟩ **3a** a special aptitude or skill **b** a particular occupation or branch of knowledge

specialize, -ise *vt* to apply or direct to a specific end or use – *vi* **1** to concentrate one's efforts in a special or limited activity or field **2** to undergo structural adaptation of a body part to a particular function or of an organism for life in a particular environment – **specialization** *n*

special licence *n* a British form of marriage license permitting marriage without the publication of banns or at a time and place other than those prescribed by law

special pleading *n* **1** the allegation of special or new matter in a legal action, as distinguished from a direct denial of the matter pleaded by the opposite side **2** an argument that ignores the damaging or unfavourable aspects of a case

specie *n* money in coin – **in specie** in the same or similar form or kind ⟨*ready to return insult* in specie⟩

species *n, pl* **species 1a** a class of individuals having common attributes and designated by a common name **b(1)** a category in the biological classification of living things that ranks immediately below a genus, comprises related organisms or populations potentially capable of interbreeding, and is designated by a name (e g *Homo sapiens*) that consists of the name of a genus followed by a Latin or latinized uncapitalized noun or adjective **(2)** an individual or kind belonging to a biological species **c** a particular kind of atomic nucleus, atom, molecule, or ion **2** the consecrated bread and wine of the Roman Catholic or Eastern Orthodox eucharist **3** a kind, sort – *chiefly derog* ⟨*a dangerous ~ of criminal*⟩

¹**specific** *adj* **1a** constituting or falling into a specifiable category **b** being or relating to those properties of sthg that allow it to be assigned to a particular category ⟨*the ~ qualities of a drug*⟩ **2a** confined to a particular individual, group, or circumstance ⟨*a disease ~ to horses*⟩ **b** having a specific rather than a general influence (e g on a body part or a disease) ⟨*antibodies ~ for the smallpox virus*⟩ **3** free from ambiguity; explicit ⟨*~ instructions*⟩ **4** of or constituting a (biological) species **5a** being any of various arbitrary physical constants, esp one relating a quantitative attribute to unit mass, volume, or area **b** imposed at a fixed rate per unit (e g of weight or amount) ⟨*~ import duties*⟩ – **specifically** *adv*, **specificity** *n*

²**specific** *n* **1** a drug or remedy having a specific effect on a disease **2a** a characteristic quality or trait **b** *pl, chiefly NAm* particulars ⟨*haggling over the legal and financial ~s – Time*⟩

specification *n* **1** specifying **2a** a detailed description of sthg (e g a building or car), esp in the form of a plan – usu pl with sing. meaning **b** a written description of an invention for which a patent is sought

specific gravity *n* the ratio of the density of a substance to the density of a substance (e g pure water or hydrogen) taken as a standard when both densities are obtained by weighing in air

specify *vt* **1** to name or state explicitly or in detail **2** to include as an item in a specification ⟨*~ oak flooring*⟩ – **specifiable** *adj*, **specifier** *n*

specimen *n* **1** an item, part, or individual typical of a group or category; an example **2** a person, individual – *chiefly derog*

specious *adj* **1** having deceptive attraction or fascination **2** superficially sound or genuine but fallacious ⟨*~ reasoning*⟩ – **speciously** *adv*, **speciousness** *n*

¹**speck** *n* **1** a small spot or blemish, esp from stain or decay **2** a small particle ⟨*a ~ of sawdust*⟩

²**speck** *vt* to mark with specks

¹**speckle** *n* a little speck (e g of colour)

²**speckle** *vt* **speckling** to mark (as if) with speckles ⟨*the ~d eggs of a thrush*⟩

spectacle *n* **1a** sthg exhibited as unusual, noteworthy, or entertaining; *esp* a striking or dramatic public display or show **b** an object of scorn or ridicule, esp due to odd appearance or behaviour ⟨*made a ~ of himself*⟩ **2** *pl* GLASSES 2b(2)

spectacled *adj* having (markings suggesting) a pair of spectacles ⟨*the ~ salamander*⟩

¹**spectacular** *adj* of or being a spectacle; sensational ⟨*a ~ display of fireworks*⟩ – **spectacularly** *adv*

²**spectacular** *n* sthg (e g a stage show) that is spectacular

spectator *n* **1** one who attends an event or activity in order to watch **2** one who looks on without participating; an onlooker ⟨*rescuers were hampered by ~s*⟩ – **spectator** *adj*

spectral *adj* **1** of or suggesting a spectre **2** of or made by a spectrum – **spectrally** *adv*, **spectralness** *n*, **spectrality** *n*

spectre, NAm chiefly specter *n* **1** a visible ghost **2** sthg that haunts or perturbs the mind; a phantasm ⟨*the ~ of hunger*⟩

spectroscope *n* an instrument for forming and examining optical spectra – **spectroscopic, spectroscopical** *adj*, **spectroscopically** *adv*, **spectroscopist** *n*, **spectroscopy** *n*

spectrum *n, pl* **spectra, spectrums 1** an array of the components of an emission or wave separated and arranged in the order of some varying characteristic (e g wavelength, mass, or energy): e g **a** a series of images formed when a beam of radiant energy is subjected to dispersion and brought to focus so that the component waves are arranged in the order of their wavelengths (e g when a beam of sunlight that is refracted and dispersed by a prism forms a display of colours) **b** ELECTROMAGNETIC SPECTRUM **c** the range of frequencies of sound waves **2** a sequence, range ⟨a wide ~ of interests⟩

speculate vi **1** to meditate on or ponder about sthg; reflect **2** to assume a business risk in the hope of gain; esp to buy or sell in expectation of profiting from market fluctuations – **speculator** n, **speculation** n

speculative adj **1** involving, based on, or constituting speculation; also theoretical rather than demonstrable **2** questioning, inquiring ⟨a ~ glance⟩ – **speculatively** adv

speech n **1a** the communication or expression of thoughts in spoken words **b** conversation **2** a public discourse; an address **3a** a language, dialect **b** an individual manner of speaking **4** the power of expressing or communicating thoughts by speaking

speechify vi to speak or make a speech in a pompous manner

speechless adj **1a** unable to speak; dumb **b** deprived of speech (e g through horror or rage) **2** refraining from speech; silent **3** incapable of being expressed in words ⟨a shape of ~ beauty – P B Shelley⟩ – **speechlessly** adv, **speechlessness** n

¹**speed** n **1a** moving swiftly; swiftness **b** rate of motion; specif the magnitude of a velocity irrespective of direction **2** rate of performance or execution ⟨tried to increase his reading ~⟩ **3a** the sensitivity of a photographic film, plate, or paper expressed numerically **b** the light-gathering power of a lens or optical system **c** the duration of a photographic exposure **4** chiefly NAm a transmission gear in motor vehicles **5** (a drug related to) methamphetamine – slang – **at speed** at a fast speed; while travelling rapidly

²**speed** vb **sped, speeded** vi **1** to move or go quickly ⟨sped to her bedside⟩ **2** to travel at excessive or illegal speed ⟨drivers who are fined for ~ing⟩ ~vt **1** to promote the success or development of **2** to cause to move quickly; hasten – **speeder** n, **speedster** n

speed limit n the maximum speed permitted by law in a given area or under specified circumstances

speedometer n **1** an instrument for indicating speed; a tachometer **2** an instrument for indicating distance travelled as well as speed; also an odometer

speed trap n a stretch of road along which police officers, radar devices, etc are stationed so as to catch vehicles exceeding the speed limit

speed-up n an acceleration

speed up vb to (cause to) move, work, or take place faster; accelerate

speedway n **1** a usu oval racecourse for motorcycles **2** the sport of racing motorcycles usu belonging to professional teams on closed cinder or dirt tracks

speedwell n any of a genus of plants of the figwort family that mostly have slender stems and small blue or whitish flowers

speedy adj swift, quick – **speedily** adv, **speediness** n

speleology n the scientific study of caves – **speleologist** n, **speleological** adj

¹**spell** n **1a** a spoken word or form of words held to have magic power **b** a state of enchantment **2** a compelling influence or attraction

²**spell** vb **spelt, NAm chiefly spelled** vt **1** to name or write the letters of (e g a word) in order; also, of letters to form (e g a word) ⟨c-a-t ~s cat⟩ **2** to amount to; mean ⟨crop failure would ~ famine for the whole region⟩ – chiefly journ ~vi to form words using the correct combination of letters ⟨graduates who still can't ~⟩

³**spell** vb **spelled** vt **1** to give a brief rest to **2** chiefly NAm

to relieve for a time; stand in for ⟨the 2 guards ~ed each other⟩ ~vi, chiefly Austr to rest from work or activity for a time

⁴**spell** n **1** a period spent in a job or occupation ⟨did a ~ in catering⟩ **2** a short or indefinite period or phase ⟨there will be cold ~s throughout April⟩ **3** ²FIT **3a** chiefly Austr a period of rest from work, activity, or use

spellbinder n sby or sthg that holds one spellbound; esp a speaker of compelling eloquence – **spellbinding** adj

spelling n **1** the forming of or ability to form words from letters **2** the sequence of letters that make up a particular word

spell out vt **1** to read slowly and haltingly **2** to come to understand; discern ⟨tried in vain to spell out his meaning⟩ **3** to explain clearly and in detail

spend vb **spent** vt **1** to use up or pay out; expend ⟨spent £90 on a new suit⟩ **2** to wear out, exhaust ⟨the storm gradually spent itself⟩ **3** to cause or permit to elapse; pass ⟨spent the summer at the beach⟩ ~vi to pay out resources, esp money – **spendable** adj, **spender** n – **spend a penny** Br to urinate – euph

spending money n POCKET MONEY

spendthrift n one who spends carelessly or wastefully – **spendthrift** adj

spent adj **1a** used up; consumed **b** exhausted of useful components or qualities ⟨~ grain⟩ ⟨~ matches⟩ **2** drained of energy; exhausted ⟨~ after his nightlong vigil⟩ **3** exhausted of spawn or sperm ⟨a ~ salmon⟩

sperm n, pl **sperms**, esp collectively **sperm 1a** the male fertilizing fluid; semen **b** a male gamete **2** spermaceti, oil, etc from the sperm whale

sperm-, spermo-, sperma-, spermi- comb form seed; germ; sperm ⟨spermatheca⟩ ⟨spermicidal⟩

spermaceti n a waxy solid obtained from the oil of whales, esp sperm whales, and used in ointments, cosmetics, and candles

spermatozoon n, pl **spermatozoa 1** a motile male gamete of an animal, usu with rounded or elongated head and a long tail-like flagellum **2** a spermatozoid – **spermatozoal** adj

sperm whale n a large toothed whale that has a vast blunt head in the front part of which is a cavity containing a fluid mixture of spermaceti and oil

¹**spew** vi **1** to vomit **2** to come forth in a flood or gush ~vt to propel or eject with violence or in great quantity ⟨a volcano ~ing ash and lava⟩ – **spewer** n

²**spew** n **1** vomit **2** material that gushes or is ejected from a source

sphagnum n any of a large genus of atypical mosses that grow only in wet acid areas (e g bogs) where their remains become compacted with other plant debris to form peat

¹**sphere** n **1a** (a globe depicting) the apparent surface of the heavens of which half forms the dome of the visible sky **b** any of the revolving spherical transparent shells in which, according to ancient astronomy, the celestial bodies are set **2a** a globular body; a ball **b** a planet, star **c** (a space or solid enclosed by) a surface, all points of which are equidistant from the centre **3** natural or proper place; esp social position or class **4** a field of action, existence, or influence – **spheral** adj, **spheric** adj, **sphericity** n

²**sphere** vt **1** to place or enclose in a sphere **2** to form into a sphere

spherical adj **1** having the form of (a segment of) a sphere **2** relating to or dealing with (the properties of) a sphere – **spherically** adv

spheroid n a figure resembling a sphere – **spheroidal** adj, **spheroidally** adv

sphincter *n* a muscular ring, surrounding and able to contract or close a bodily opening – **sphincteral** *adj*

sphinx *n, pl* **sphinxes, sphinges 1a** *cap* a female monster in Greek mythology, with a lion's body and a human head, that killed those who failed to answer a riddle she asked **b** an enigmatic or mysterious person **2** an ancient Egyptian image in the form of a recumbent lion, usu with a human head **3** a hawkmoth

¹**spice** *n* **1a** any of various aromatic vegetable products (e g pepper, ginger, or nutmeg) used to season or flavour foods **b** such products collectively **2** sthg that adds zest or relish ⟨*variety's the very ~ of life* – William Cowper⟩ **3** a pungent or aromatic smell

²**spice** *vt* **1** to season with spice **2** to add zest or relish to ⟨*cynicism ~d with wit*⟩

spick-and-span, spic-and-span *adj* spotlessly clean and tidy; spruce

spicy *adj* **1** lively, spirited ⟨*a ~ temper*⟩ **2** piquant, zestful **3** somewhat scandalous; risqué ⟨*~ gossip*⟩ – **spicily** *adv*, **spiciness** *n*

spider *n* any of an order of arachnids having a body with 2 main divisions, 4 pairs of walking legs, and 2 or more pairs of abdominal spinnerets for spinning threads of silk used for cocoons, nests, or webs

spider's web *n* the (geometrically patterned) silken web spun by most spiders and used as a resting place and a trap for small prey

spidery *adj* **1a** resembling a spider in form or manner; *specif* long, thin, and sharply angular like the legs of a spider **b** resembling a spider's web; *esp* composed of fine threads or lines in a weblike arrangement ⟨*~ handwriting*⟩ **2** infested with spiders

¹**spiel** *vb, chiefly NAm vi* to talk volubly or extravagantly *~vt* to utter or express volubly or extravagantly – usu + *off USE* infml – **spieler** *n*

²**spiel** *n, chiefly NAm* a voluble talk designed to influence or persuade; patter – infml

spigot *n* **1** a small plug used to stop up the vent of a cask **2** the part of a tap, esp on a barrel, which controls the flow **3** a plain end of a piece of piping or guttering that fits into an adjoining piece

¹**spike** *n* **1** a very large nail **2a** any of a row of pointed iron pieces (e g on the top of a wall or fence) **b(1)** any of several metal projections set in the sole and heel of a shoe to improve traction **(2)** *pl* a pair of (athletics) shoes having spikes attached **3** the act or an instance of spiking in volleyball **4a** a pointed element in a graph or tracing **b** an unusually high and sharply defined maximum (e g of amplitude in a wave train)

²**spike** *vt* **1** to fasten or provide with spikes ⟨*~ the soles of climbing boots*⟩ **2** to disable (a muzzle-loading cannon) by driving a spike into the vent **3** to pierce with or impale on a spike; *specif* to reject (newspaper copy), orig by impaling on a spike **4** to add spirits to (a nonalcoholic drink) **5** to drive (a volleyball) sharply downwards into an opponent's court **6** *chiefly NAm* to suppress or thwart completely ⟨*~d the rumour*⟩ – **spiker** *n* – **spike someone's guns** to frustrate sby's opposition; foil an opponent

³**spike** *n* **1** an ear of grain **2** an elongated plant inflorescence with the flowers stalkless on a single main axis

spikenard *n* (an E Indian aromatic plant of the valerian family believed to have given rise to) a fragrant ointment of the ancients

spiky *adj* **1** having a sharp projecting point or points **2** caustic, aggressive ⟨*a ~ retort*⟩

¹**spill** *vb* **spilt,** *NAm chiefly* **spilled** *vt* **1** to cause (blood) to be shed **2a** to cause or allow to fall or flow out so as to be lost or wasted, esp accidentally **b** to empty, discharge ⟨*train* spilt *its occupants onto the platform*⟩ **3** to empty (a sail) of wind **4** to throw off or out ⟨*his horse* spilt *him*⟩ **5** to let out; divulge ⟨*~ a secret*⟩ – infml *~vi* **1a** to fall or flow out or over and become wasted, scattered, or lost **b** to cause or allow sthg to spill **2** to spread profusely or beyond limits ⟨*crowds* spilt *into the streets*⟩ – **spillable** *adj*, **spiller** *n* – **spill the beans** to divulge information indiscreetly – infml

²**spill** *n* **1** a fall from a horse or vehicle **2** a quantity spilt

³**spill** *n* a thin twist of paper or sliver of wood used esp for lighting a fire

spillway *n* a passage for surplus water from a dam

¹**spin** *vb* **-nn-; spun** *vi* **1** to draw out and twist fibre into yarn or thread **2** *esp of a spider or insect* to form a thread by forcing out a sticky rapidly hardening fluid **3a** to revolve rapidly; whirl **b** to have the sensation of spinning; reel ⟨*my head is* ~ning⟩ **4** to move swiftly, esp on wheels or in a vehicle **5** to fish with a spinning lure **6** *of an aircraft* to fall in a spin *~vt* **1a** to draw out and twist into yarns or threads **b** to produce (yarn or thread) by drawing out and twisting a fibrous material **2** to form (e g a web or cocoon) by spinning **3** to compose and tell (a usu involved or fictitious story) ⟨*is always* ~ning *yarns*⟩ **4** to cause to revolve rapidly ⟨*~ a top*⟩; *also* to cause (a cricket ball) to revolve in the manner characteristic of spin bowling **5** to shape into threadlike form in manufacture; *also* to manufacture by a whirling process

²**spin** *n* **1a** the act or an instance of spinning sthg **b** the whirling motion imparted (e g to a cricket ball) by spinning **c** a short excursion, esp in or on a motor vehicle **2** an aerial manoeuvre or flight condition consisting of a combination of roll and yaw with the longitudinal axis of the aircraft inclined steeply downwards and its wings in a state of (partial) stall **3** the property of an elementary particle that corresponds to intrinsic angular momentum, that can be thought of as rotation of the particle about its axis, and that is mainly responsible for magnetic properties **4** a state of mental confusion; a panic ⟨*in a ~*⟩ – infml – **spinless** *adj*

spina bifida *n* a congenital condition in which there is a defect in the formation of the spine allowing the meninges to protrude and usu associated with disorder of the nerves supplying the lower part of the body

spinach *n* (the leaves, eaten as food, of) a plant of the goosefoot family cultivated for its edible leaves

spinal *adj* **1** of or situated near the backbone **2** of or affecting the spinal cord ⟨*~ reflexes*⟩ **3** of or resembling a spine – **spinally** *adv*

spinal column *n* the skeleton running the length of the trunk and tail of a vertebrate that consists of a jointed series of vertebrae and protects the spinal cord

spinal cord *n* the cord of nervous tissue that extends from the brain lengthways along the back in the spinal canal, carries impulses to and from the brain, and serves as a centre for initiating and coordinating many reflex actions

¹**spindle** *n* **1a** a round stick with tapered ends used to form and twist the yarn in hand spinning **b** the long slender pin by which the thread is twisted in a spinning wheel **c** any of various rods or pins holding a bobbin in a textile machine **d** the pin in a loom shuttle **e** the bar or shaft, usu of square section, that carries the knobs and actuates the latch or bolt of a lock **2** a spindle-shaped figure seen in microscopic sections of dividing cells along which the chromosomes are distributed **3a** a turned often decorative piece (e g in a baluster) **b** a newel **c** a pin or axis about which sthg turns

²**spindle** *vi* **spindling** to grow into or have a long slender stalk – **spindler** *n*

spindle tree *n* any of a genus of often evergreen shrubs, small trees, or climbing plants typically having red fruits and a hard wood formerly used for spindle making

spindly *adj* having an unnaturally tall or slender appearance, esp suggestive of physical weakness ⟨~ *legs*⟩

spin-dry *vt* to remove water from (wet laundry) by placing in a rapidly rotating drum – **spin-drier** *n*

spine *n* **1a** SPINAL COLUMN **b** sthg like a spinal column or constituting a central axis or chief support **c** the back of a book, usu lettered with the title and author's name **2** a stiff pointed plant part; *esp* one that is a modified leaf or leaf part **3** a sharp rigid part of an animal or fish; *also* a pointed prominence on a bone – **spined** *adj*

spineless *adj* **1** free from spines, thorns, or prickles **2a** having no spinal column; *invertebrate* **b** lacking strength of character – **spinelessly** *adv*, **spinelessness** *n*

spinet *n* a small harpsichord having the strings at an angle to the keyboard

spinnaker *n* a large triangular sail set forward of a yacht's mast on a long light pole and used when running before the wind

spinner *n* **1** a fisherman's lure consisting of a spoon, blade, or set of wings that revolves when drawn through the water **2** a conical fairing attached to an aircraft propeller hub and revolving with it **3** (a delivery bowled by) a bowler of spin bowling

spinney *n*, *Br* a small wood with undergrowth

spinning jenny *n* an early multiple-spindle machine for spinning wool or cotton

spinning wheel *n* a small domestic machine for spinning yarn or thread by means of a spindle driven by a hand- or foot-operated wheel

spin-off *n* a by-product ⟨*household products that are* ~s *of space research*⟩; *also* sthg which is a further development of some idea or product ⟨*a* ~ *from a successful TV series*⟩

spin out *vt* **1** to cause to last longer, esp by thrift ⟨*spinning out their meagre rations*⟩ **2** to extend, prolong ⟨*spin out a repair job*⟩ **3** to dismiss (a batsman in cricket) by spin bowling

spinster *n* **1** an unmarried woman **2** a woman who is past the usual age for marrying or who seems unlikely to marry – **spinsterhood** *n*, **spinsterish** *adj*

spiny *adj* **1** covered or armed with spines; *broadly* bearing spines, prickles, or thorns **2** full of difficulties or annoyances; thorny ⟨~ *problems*⟩ **3** slender and pointed like a spine – **spininess** *n*

spiny lobster *n* any of several edible crustaceans distinguished from the true lobster by the simple unenlarged first pair of legs and the spiny carapace

¹**spiral** *adj* **1a** winding round a centre or pole and gradually approaching or receding from it ⟨*the* ~ *curve of a watch spring*⟩ **b** helical **2** of the advancement to higher levels through a series of cyclical movements ⟨*a* ~ *theory of social development*⟩ – **spirally** *adv*

²**spiral** *n* **1a** the path of a point in a plane moving round a central point while continuously receding from or approaching it **b** a 3-dimensional curve (e g a helix) with 1 or more turns about an axis **2** a single turn or coil in a spiral object **3a** sthg with a spiral form **b** a spiral flight **4** a continuously expanding and accelerating increase or decrease ⟨*wage* ~s⟩

³**spiral** *vb* -**ll**- (*NAm* -**l**-, -**ll**-) *vi* to go, esp to rise, in a spiral course ⟨*prices* ~led⟩ ~*vt* to cause to take a spiral form or course

¹**spire** *n* **1** a slender tapering blade or stalk (e g of grass) **2** the upper tapering part of sthg (e g a tree or antler) **3**

a tall tapering roof or other construction on top of a tower – **spired** *adj*, **spiry** *adj*

²**spire** *vi* to taper up to a point like a spire

³**spire** *n* **1** a spiral, coil **2** the inner or upper part of a spiral gastropod shell – **spired** *adj*

⁴**spire** *vi* to spiral

¹**spirit** *n* **1** an animating or vital principle of living organisms **2** a supernatural being or essence: e g **a** *cap* HOLY SPIRIT **b** SOUL 2 **c** a being that has no body but can become visible; *specif* GHOST 2 **d** a malevolent being that enters and possesses a human being **3** temper or state of mind – often pl with sing. meaning ⟨*in high* ~s⟩ **4** the immaterial intelligent or conscious part of a person **5** the attitude or intention characterizing or influencing sthg ⟨*undertaken in a* ~ *of fun*⟩ **6** liveliness, energy; *also* courage **7** devotion, loyalty ⟨*team* ~⟩ **8** a person of a specified kind or character ⟨*she's such a kind* ~⟩ **9a** distilled liquor of high alcoholic content – usu pl with sing. meaning ⟨*a glass of* ~s⟩ **b** any of various volatile liquids obtained by distillation or cracking (e g of petroleum, shale, or wood) – often pl with sing. meaning **c** ALCOHOL 1 **10a** prevailing characteristic ⟨~ *of the age*⟩ **b** the true meaning of sthg (e g a rule or instruction) in contrast to its verbal expression **11** an alcoholic solution of a volatile substance ⟨~ *of camphor*⟩ – **spiritless** *adj* – **in spirits** in a cheerful or lively frame of mind – **out of spirits** in a gloomy or depressed frame of mind

²**spirit** *vt* to carry off, esp secretly or mysteriously – usu + *away* or *off* ⟨*was* ~ed *away to a mountain hideout*⟩

spirited *adj* **1** full of energy, animation, or courage ⟨*a* ~ *discussion*⟩ **2** having a specified frame of mind – often in combination ⟨*low*-spirited⟩ – **spiritedly** *adv*, **spiritedness** *n*

spirit level *n* a level that uses the position of a bubble in a curved transparent tube of liquid to indicate whether a surface is level

¹**spiritual** *adj* **1** (consisting) of spirit; incorporeal ⟨*man's* ~ *needs*⟩ **2a** of sacred matters **b** ecclesiastical rather than lay or temporal **3** concerned with religious values **4** based on or related through sympathy of thought or feeling **5** of supernatural beings or phenomena – **spiritualize** *vt*, **spiritually** *adv*, **spiritualness** *n*

²**spiritual** *n* a usu emotional religious song of a kind developed esp among Negroes in the southern USA

spiritualism *n* **1** the doctrine that spirit is the ultimate reality **2** a belief that spirits of the dead communicate with the living, esp through a medium or at a séance – **spiritualist** *n*, *often cap*, **spiritualistic** *adj*

spirituality *n* **1** sensitivity or attachment to religious values **2** a practice of personal devotion and prayer

spirituous *adj* containing or impregnated with alcohol obtained by distillation ⟨~ *liquors*⟩

spirochaete, *NAm chiefly* **spirochete** *n* any of an order of slender spirally undulating bacteria including those causing syphilis and relapsing fever – **spirochaetal** *adj*

spirt *vb or n* ² ⁾ ³SPURT

¹**spit** *n* **1** a slender pointed rod for holding meat over a source of heat (e g an open fire) **2** a small point of land, esp of sand or gravel, running into a river mouth, bay, etc

²**spit** *vt* -**tt**- to fix (as if) on a spit; impale

³**spit** *vb* -**tt**-; **spat**, **spit** *vt* **1** to eject (e g saliva) from the mouth **2a** to express (hostile or malicious feelings) (as if) by spitting ⟨*spat his contempt*⟩ **b** to utter vehemently or with a spitting sound ⟨*spat out his words*⟩ **3** to emit as if by spitting ⟨*the guns spat fire*⟩ ~*vi* **1a** to eject saliva from the mouth (as an expression of aversion or contempt) **b** to exhibit contempt **2** to rain or snow slightly or in

flurries **3** to sputter – **spit it out** to utter promptly what is in the mind

⁴**spit** n **1a**(1) spittle, saliva (2) the act or an instance of spitting **b** a frothy secretion exuded by some insects **2** perfect likeness – often in *spit and image* ⟨*he's the very ~ and image of his father*⟩

spit and polish n extreme attention to cleanliness, orderliness, and ceremonial

¹**spite** n petty ill will or malice – **spiteful** adj, **spitefully** adv – **in spite of** in defiance or contempt of ⟨*sorry in spite of himself*⟩

²**spite** vt to treat vindictively or annoy out of spite

spitfire n a quick-tempered or volatile person

spitting image n ⁴SPIT 2

spittle n **1** saliva (ejected from the mouth) **2** ⁴SPIT 1b

spittoon n a receptacle for spit

spiv n, Br a slick individual who lives by sharp practice or petty fraud; *specif* a black marketeer operating esp after WW II – **spivvery** n

¹**splash** vi **1a** to strike and move about a liquid ⟨*~ed about in the bath*⟩ **b** to move through or into a liquid and cause it to spatter ⟨*~ through a puddle*⟩ **2a**(1) to become spattered about (2) to spread or scatter in the manner of splashed liquid ⟨*sunlight ~ed over the lawn*⟩ **b** to flow, fall, or strike with a splashing sound ⟨*a brook ~ing over rocks*⟩ **3** *chiefly Br* to spend money liberally; splurge – usu + *out* ⟨*~ed out on a bottle of champagne*⟩ ~ vt **1a** to dash a liquid or semiliquid substance on or against **b** to soil or stain with splashed liquid; spatter **c** to display very conspicuously ⟨*the affair was ~ed all over the local papers* – Woman's Journal⟩ **2a** to cause (a liquid or semiliquid substance) to spatter about, esp with force **b** to spread or scatter in the manner of a splashed liquid ⟨*sunset ~ed its colours across the sky*⟩ – **splasher** n

²**splash** n **1a** a spot or daub (as if) from splashed liquid ⟨*a mud ~ on the wing*⟩ **b** a usu vivid patch of colour or of sthg coloured ⟨*~es of yellow tulips*⟩ **2a** (the sound of) splashing **b** a short plunge **3** (a vivid impression created esp by) an ostentatious display **4** a small amount, esp of a mixer added to an alcoholic drink; a dash – **splashy** n

splashdown n the landing of a spacecraft in the ocean – **splash down** vi

splat n a single flat often ornamental piece of wood forming the centre of a chair back

splatter vt to spatter – vi to scatter or fall (as if) in heavy drops ⟨*rain ~ed against the windscreen*⟩ – **splatter** n

¹**splay** vt **1** to spread out **2** to make (e g the edges of an opening) slanting ~ vi **1** to become splayed **2** to slope, slant

²**splay** adj turned outwards ⟨*~ knees*⟩

splayfoot n a foot abnormally flattened and spread out – **splayfoot, splayfooted** adj

spleen n **1** a highly vascular ductless organ near the stomach or intestine of most vertebrates that is concerned with final destruction of blood cells, storage of blood, and production of lymphocytes **2** bad temper; spite **3** *archaic* melancholy – **spleeny** adj, **spleenful** adj

splendid adj **1a** shining, brilliant **b** magnificent, sumptuous **2** illustrious, distinguished **3** of the best or most enjoyable kind; excellent ⟨*a ~ picnic*⟩ – **splendidly** adv, **splendidness** n

splendiferous adj splendid – infml ⟨*his ~ eruption of eloquence* – TLS⟩ – **splendiferously** adv, **splendiferousness** n

splendour, NAm chiefly **splendor** n **1a** great brightness or lustre; brilliance **b** grandeur, pomp **2** sthg splendid – **splendorous, splendrous** adj

splenetic adj **1** bad tempered, spiteful **2** *archaic* given to melancholy – **splenetic** n, **splenetically** adv

¹**splice** vt **1a** to join (e g ropes) by interweaving the strands **b** to unite (e g film, magnetic tape, or timber) by overlapping the ends or binding with adhesive tape **2** Br to unite in marriage; marry – infml – **splicer** n

²**splice** n a joining or joint made by splicing

¹**splint** n **1** a thin strip of wood suitable for interweaving (e g into baskets) **2** material or a device used to protect and immobilize a body part (e g a broken arm) **3** a bony enlargement on the upper part of the cannon bone of a horse, usu on the inside of the leg

²**splint** vt to support and immobilize (as if) with a splint

¹**splinter** n **1** a sharp thin piece, esp of wood or glass, split or broken off lengthways **2** a small group or faction broken away from a parent body – **splinter** adj, **splintery** adj

²**splinter** vt **1** to split or rend into long thin pieces; shatter **2** to split into fragments, parts, or factions ~ vi to become splintered

¹**split** vb **-tt-**; **split** vt **1** to divide, esp lengthways **2a**(1) to tear or rend apart; burst (2) to subject (an atom or atomic nucleus) to artificial disintegration, esp by fission **b** to affect as if by shattering or tearing apart ⟨*a roar that ~ the air*⟩ **3** to divide into parts or portions: e g **a** to divide between people; share ⟨*~ a bottle of wine at dinner*⟩ **b** to divide into opposing factions, parties, etc ⟨*the bill ~ the opposition*⟩ **c** to break down (a chemical compound) into constituents ⟨*~ a fat into glycerol and fatty acids*⟩; *also* to remove by such separation **d** NAm to mark (a ballot) or cast (a vote) so as to vote for opposing candidates **4** to separate (constituent parts) by interposing sthg ⟨*~ an infinitive*⟩ ~ vi **1a** to become split lengthways or into layers **b** to break apart; burst **2a** to become divided up or separated off ⟨*~ into factions*⟩ **b** to sever relations or connections – often + *up* ⟨*~ up after 6 months' marriage*⟩ **3** to share sthg (e g loot or profits) with others – often + *with*; infml **4** to let out a secret; act as an informer – often + *on*; slang ⟨*on the point of ~ting on the gang* – Dorothy Sayers⟩ **5** to leave, esp hurriedly; depart – slang – **splitter** n – **split hairs** to make oversubtle or trivial distinctions – **split one's sides** to laugh heartily – **split the difference** to compromise by taking the average of 2 amounts

²**split** n **1** a narrow break made (as if) by splitting **2** a piece broken off by splitting **3** a division into divergent groups or elements; a breach ⟨*a ~ in party ranks*⟩ **4a** splitting **b** *pl but sing in constr* the act of lowering oneself to the floor or leaping into the air with legs extended at right angles to the trunk **5** a wine bottle holding a quarter of the usual amount; *also* a small bottle of mineral water, tonic water, etc **6** a sweet dish composed of sliced fruit, esp a banana, ice cream, syrup, and often nuts and whipped cream

³**split** adj **1** divided, fractured **2** prepared for use by splitting ⟨*~ bamboo*⟩ ⟨*~ hides*⟩

split-level adj divided so that the floor level in one part is less than a full storey higher than an adjoining part ⟨*a ~ house*⟩ – **split-level** n

split pea n a dried pea in which the cotyledons are usu split apart

split personality n a personality composed of 2 or more internally consistent groups of behaviour tendencies and attitudes each acting more or less independently of the other

split ring n a metal ring of 2 flat turns on which keys may be kept

split second n a fractional part of a second; a flash – **split-second** adj

splitting adj causing a piercing sensation ⟨a ~ head-ache⟩

¹**splotch** n a large irregular spot or smear; a blotch – **splotchy** adj

²**splotch** vt to mark with a splotch or splotches

¹**splurge** n 1 an ostentatious display or enterprise 2 an extravagant spending spree *USE* infml

²**splurge** vi 1 to make a splurge 2 to spend money extravagantly – often + on ⟨~ on a slap-up meal⟩ to to spend extravagantly or ostentatiously *USE* infml

splutter vi 1 to make a noise as if spitting 2 SPUTTER 2 ~ vt to utter hastily and confusedly – **splutter** n, **splutterer** n, **spluttery** adj

¹**spoil** n 1a plunder taken from an enemy in war or a victim in robbery; loot – often pl with sing. meaning b sthg gained by special effort or skill – usu pl with sing. meaning 2 earth and rock excavated or dredged

²**spoil** vb **spoilt**, **spoiled** vt 1a to damage seriously; ruin ⟨heavy rain ~t the crops⟩ b to impair the enjoyment of; mar ⟨a quarrel ~t the celebration⟩ 2a to impair the character of by overindulgence or excessive praise ⟨~ an only child⟩ b to treat indulgently; pamper c to cause to be unsatisfied with sthg inferior – usu + for ⟨the good meals at this hotel will ~ us for canteen food⟩ ~ vi 1 to lose good or useful qualities, usu as a result of decay ⟨fruit soon ~s in warm weather⟩ 2 to have an eager desire for – esp in **spoiling for a fight** – **spoilable** adj

spoilage n 1 sthg spoiled or wasted 2 loss by being spoiled

spoilsport n one who spoils the fun of others – infml

¹**spoke** past & archaic past part of SPEAK

²**spoke** n 1 any of the small radiating bars inserted in the hub of a wheel to support the rim 2 a rung of a ladder

³**spoke** vt to provide (as if) with spokes

spoken adj 1a delivered by word of mouth; oral ⟨a ~ request⟩ b used in speaking or conversation; uttered ⟨the ~ word⟩ 2 characterized by speaking in a specified manner – in combination ⟨soft-spoken⟩ ⟨plainspoken⟩

spokeshave n a plane having a blade set between 2 handles and used for shaping curved surfaces

spokesman, fem **spokeswoman** n one who speaks on behalf of another or others

spoliation n 1a the act of plundering b the state of being plundered, esp in war 2 the act of damaging or injuring, esp irreparably – **spoliator** n

spondee n a metrical foot consisting of 2 long or stressed syllables – **spondaic** adj or n

¹**sponge** n 1a(1) an elastic porous mass of interlacing horny fibres that forms the internal skeleton of various marine animals and is able when wetted to absorb water (2) a piece of sponge (e g for cleaning) (3) a porous rubber or cellulose product used similarly to a sponge b any of a phylum of aquatic lower invertebrate animals that are essentially double-walled cell colonies and permanently attached as adults 2 a sponger 3a raised dough (e g for yeast bread) b a sponge cake or sweet steamed pudding made from a sponge-cake mixture c a metal (e g platinum) in the form of a porous solid composed of fine particles

²**sponge** vt 1 to cleanse, wipe, or moisten (as if) with a sponge 2 to remove or erase by rubbing (as if) with a sponge 3 to obtain by sponging on another ⟨~ the price of a pint⟩ 4 to soak up (as if) with or in the manner of a sponge ~ vi to obtain esp financial assistance by exploiting natural generosity or organized welfare facilities – usu + on

sponge bag n, Br a small waterproof usu plastic bag for holding toilet articles

sponge cake n a light sweet cake made with (approxi-

mately) equal quantities of sugar, flour, and eggs but no shortening

spongy adj 1 resembling a sponge, esp in being soft, porous, absorbent, or moist 2 of a metal in the form of a sponge – **sponginess** n

¹**sponsor** n 1 sby who presents a candidate for baptism or confirmation and undertakes responsibility for his/her religious education or spiritual welfare 2 sby who assumes responsibility for some other person or thing 3 sby who or sthg that pays for a project or activity – **sponsorship** n, **sponsorial** adj

²**sponsor** vt to be or stand as sponsor for

spontaneous adj 1 proceeding from natural feeling or innate tendency without external constraint ⟨a ~ expression of gratitude⟩ 2 springing from a sudden impulse ⟨a ~ offer of help⟩ 3 controlled and directed internally 4 developing without apparent external influence, force, cause, or treatment ⟨~ recovery from a severe illness⟩ 5 not contrived or manipulated; natural – **spontaneously** adv, **spontaneousness** n, **spontaneity** n

¹**spoof** vt 1 to deceive, hoax 2 to make good-natured fun of; lampoon *USE* infml

²**spoof** n 1 a hoax, deception 2 a light, humorous, but usu telling parody *USE* infml – **spoof** adj

¹**spook** n a ghost, spectre – chiefly infml – **spookish** adj

²**spook** vb, chiefly NAm vt to make frightened or frantic; esp to startle into violent activity (e g stampeding) ⟨~ed the herd of horses⟩ ~ vi to become frightened

spooky adj causing irrational fear, esp because suggestive of supernatural presences; eerie – chiefly infml

¹**spool** n 1 a cylindrical device on which wire, yarn, film, etc is wound 2 (the amount of) material wound on a spool 3 chiefly NAm ¹REEL c

²**spool** vt to wind on a spool

¹**spoon** n 1a an eating, cooking, or serving implement consisting of a small shallow round or oval bowl with a handle b a spoonful 2 sthg curved like the bowl of a spoon (e g a usu metal or shell fishing lure)

²**spoon** vt 1 to take up and usu transfer (as if) in a spoon ⟨~ed soup into his mouth⟩ 2 to propel (a ball) weakly upwards ~ vi to indulge in caressing and amorous talk – not now in vogue

spoonerism n a transposition of usu initial sounds of 2 or more words (e g in tons of soil for sons of toil)

spoon-feed vt 1 to feed by means of a spoon 2a to present (e g information or entertainment) in an easily assimilable form that precludes independent thought or critical judgment ⟨~ political theory to students⟩ b to present information to in this manner

spoonful n, pl **spoonfuls** also **spoonsful** as much as a spoon will hold

¹**spoor** n a track, a trail, or droppings, esp of a wild animal

²**spoor** vb to track (sthg) by a spoor

sporadic adj occurring occasionally or in scattered instances – **sporadically** adv

spore n a primitive usu single-celled hardy reproductive body produced by plants, protozoans, bacteria, etc and capable of development into a new individual either on its own or after fusion with another spore – **spored** adj, **sporiferous** adj

sporran n a pouch of animal skin with the hair or fur on that is worn in front of the kilt with traditional Highland dress

¹**sport** vt 1 to exhibit for all to see; show off ⟨~ a new hat⟩ 2 to put forth as a sport or bud variation ~ vi 1 to play about happily; frolic ⟨lambs ~ing in the meadow⟩ 2 to speak or act in jest; trifle 3 to deviate or vary abruptly from type

²**sport** *n* **1a** a source of diversion or recreation; a pastime **b(1)** physical activity engaged in for recreation **(2)** a particular activity (e g hunting or athletics) so engaged in **2a** pleasantry, jest ⟨*only made the remark in* ~⟩ **b** mockery, derision **3** sby or sthg manipulated by outside forces ⟨*was made the* ~ *of fate*⟩ **4** sby who is fair, generous, and esp a good loser **5** an individual exhibiting a sudden deviation from type beyond the normal limits of individual variation **6** *chiefly NAm* a playboy **7** *Austr* – used in informal address, chiefly to men

sporting *adj* **1a** concerned with, used for, or suitable for sport **b** marked by or calling for sportsmanship **c** involving such risk as a sports competitor might take or encounter ⟨*a* ~ *chance*⟩ **d** fond of or taking part in sports ⟨~ *nations*⟩ **2** *chiefly NAm* of or for sports that involve betting or gambling – **sportingly** *adv*

sportive *adj* frolicsome, playful – **sportively** *adv*, **sportiveness** *n*

sports, *NAm chiefly* **sport** *adj* of or suitable for sports ⟨~ *equipment*⟩; *esp* styled in a manner suitable for casual or informal wear ⟨~ *coats*⟩

sports car *n* a low fast usu 2-passenger motor car

sportsman, *fem* **sportswoman** *n* **1** sby who engages in sports, esp blood sports **2** sby who is fair, a good loser, and a gracious winner – **sportsmanlike** *adj*

sportsmanship *n* conduct becoming to a sportsman

sporty *adj* **1** fond of sport **2a** notably loose or dissipated; fast ⟨*ran around with a very* ~ *crowd*⟩ **b** flashy, showy ⟨~ *clothes*⟩ **3** suggestive of or capable of giving good sport ⟨*the car had a very* ~ *feel*⟩ *USE* infml – **sportily** *adv*, **sportiness** *n*

¹**spot** *n* **1** a blemish on character or reputation; a stain **2a** a small usu round area different (e g in colour or texture) from the surrounding surface **b(1)** an area marred or marked (e g by dirt) **(2)** a small surface patch of diseased or decayed tissue ⟨*the* ~s *that appear in measles*⟩ ⟨*rust* ~s *on a leaf*⟩; *also* a pimple **c** a conventionalized design used on playing cards to distinguish suits and indicate values **3** a small amount; a bit ⟨*had a* ~ *of bother with the car*⟩ **4** a particular place or area ⟨*a nice* ~ *for a picnic*⟩ **5a** a particular position (e g in an organization or hierarchy) ⟨*a good* ~ *as the director's secretary*⟩ **b** a place on an entertainment programme **6** SPOTLIGHT 1a **7** a usu difficult or embarrassing position; FIX 1 **8** *chiefly NAm* an object having a specified number of spots or a specified numeral on its surface – **on the spot 1** in one place; without travelling away ⟨*running on the spot*⟩ **2** at the place of action; available at the appropriate place and time **3** in an awkward or embarrassing position ⟨*his subordinate's mistake put him on the spot*⟩

²**spot** *vb* **-tt-** *vt* **1** to sully the character or reputation of; disgrace **2** to mark or mar (as if) with spots **3a** to single out; identify **b** to detect, notice ⟨~ *a mistake*⟩ **c** to watch for and record the sighting of ⟨~ *a rare species of duck*⟩ **4** to locate accurately ⟨~ *an enemy position*⟩ **5a** to lie at intervals in or on **b** to fix in or as if in the beam of a spotlight ~ *vi* **1** to become stained or discoloured in spots **2** to cause a spot; leave a stain **3** to act as a spotter; *esp* to locate targets **4** *chiefly Br* to fall lightly in scattered drops ⟨*it's* ~ting *with rain again*⟩ – **spottable** *adj*

³**spot** *adj* **1a** being, originating, or done on the spot or in or for a particular spot **b** available for immediate delivery after sale ⟨~ *commodities*⟩ **c(1)** paid out immediately ⟨~ *cash*⟩ **(2)** involving immediate cash payment ⟨*a* ~ *sale*⟩ **d** broadcast between scheduled programmes ⟨~ *announcements*⟩ **2** given on the spot or restricted to a few random places or instances ⟨*a* ~ *check*⟩ ⟨~ *prizes*⟩; *also* selected at random or as a sample

spot-check *vb* to make a quick or random sampling or investigation (of)

spotless *adj* **1** free from dirt or stains; immaculate ⟨~ *kitchens*⟩ **2** pure, unblemished ⟨~ *reputation*⟩ – **spotlessly** *adv*, **spotlessness** *n*

¹**spotlight** *n* **1a** a projected spot of light used for brilliant illumination of a person or object on a stage **b** full public attention ⟨*held the political* ~⟩ **2a** a light designed to direct a narrow intense beam on a small area **b** sthg that illuminates brightly or elucidates

²**spotlight** *vt* to illuminate (as if) with a spotlight

spot-on *adj, Br* **1** absolutely correct or accurate **2** exactly right ⟨*a shirt that looks* ~ *with jeans*⟩ *USE* infml – **spot-on** *adv*

spotted *adj* **1** marked with spots **2** sullied, tarnished ⟨*inherited a* ~ *name*⟩

spotted dick *n, Br* a steamed or boiled sweet suet pudding containing currants

spotter *n* **1** sby or sthg that makes or applies a spot (e g for identification) **2** sby or sthg that keeps watch or observes; *esp* a person who watches for and notes down vehicles (e g aircraft or trains)

spotty *adj* **1a** marked with spots **b** having spots, esp on the face ⟨*a* ~ *youth*⟩ **2** lacking evenness or regularity, esp in quality ⟨~ *attendance*⟩ – **spottily** *adv*, **spottiness** *n*

spouse *n* a married person; a husband or wife

¹**spout** *vt* **1** to eject (e g liquid) in a copious stream ⟨*wells* ~ing *oil*⟩ **2** to speak or utter in a strident, pompous, or hackneyed manner; declaim ⟨~ *party slogans*⟩ – infml ~ *vi* **1** to issue with force or in a jet; spurt **2** to eject material, esp liquid, in a jet **3** to declaim – infml – **spouter** *n*

²**spout** *n* **1** a projecting tube or lip through which liquid issues from a teapot, roof, kettle, etc **2** a discharge or jet of liquid (as if) from a pipe – **spouted** *adj* – **up the spout 1** beyond hope of improvement; ruined – infml **2** pregnant – slang

¹**sprain** *n* **1** a sudden or violent twist or wrench of a joint with stretching or tearing of ligaments **2** a sprained condition

²**sprain** *vt* to subject to sprain

sprang *past of* SPRING

sprat *n* a small or young herring; *also* the young of a similar fish

¹**sprawl** *vi* **1** to lie or sit with arms and legs spread out carelessly or awkwardly **2** to spread or develop irregularly ⟨*a town that* ~s *across the countryside*⟩ ~ *vt* to cause (e g one's limbs) to spread out

²**sprawl** *n* **1** a sprawling position **2** an irregular spreading mass or group ⟨*a* ~ *of buildings*⟩

¹**spray** *n* **1** a usu flowering branch or shoot **2** a decorative arrangement of flowers and foliage (e g on a dress) **3** sthg (e g a jewelled pin) resembling a spray

²**spray** *n* **1** fine droplets of water blown or falling through the air ⟨*the* ~ *from the waterfall*⟩ **2a** a jet of vapour or finely divided liquid **b** a device (e g an atomizer or sprayer) by which a spray is dispersed or applied **c(1)** an application of a spray ⟨*give the roses a* ~⟩ **(2)** a substance (e g paint or insecticide) so applied **3** sthg (e g a number of small flying objects) resembling a spray

³**spray** *vt* **1** to discharge, disperse, or apply as a spray **2** to direct a spray on – **sprayer** *n*

spray gun *n* an apparatus resembling a gun for applying a substance (e g paint or insecticide) in the form of a spray

¹**spread** *vb* **spread** *vt* **1a** to open or extend over a larger area – often + *out* ⟨~ *out the map*⟩ **b** to stretch out; extend ⟨~ *its wings for flight*⟩ **c** to form (the lips) into a long narrow slit (e g when pronouncing the vowel /ee/)

2a to distribute over an area ⟨~ *manure*⟩ **b** to distribute over a period or among a group ⟨~ *the work over a few weeks*⟩ **c(1)** to apply as a layer or covering **(2)** to cover or overlay with sthg ⟨~ *bread with butter*⟩ **d** to prepare for dining; set ⟨~ *the table*⟩ **3a** to make widely known ⟨~ *the news*⟩ **b** to extend the range or incidence of ⟨~ *a disease*⟩ **c** to diffuse, emit ⟨*flowers* ~ing *their fragrance*⟩ **4** to force apart ~ *vi* **1a** to become dispersed, distributed, or scattered ⟨*a race that* ~ *across the globe*⟩ **b** to become known or disseminated ⟨*panic* ~ *rapidly*⟩ **2** to cover a greater area; expand **3** to be forced apart (e g from pressure or weight) – **spreadable** *adj*, **spreader** *n*, **spreadability** *n*

²**spread** *n* **1** (extent of) spreading **2** sthg spread out: e g **a** a surface area; an expanse **b(1)** a prominent display in a newspaper or periodical **(2)** (the matter occupying) 2 facing pages, usu with printed matter running across the fold **c** a wide obstacle for a horse to jump **3** sthg spread on or over a surface: e g **a** a food product suitable for spreading **b** a sumptuous meal; a feast **c** a cloth cover; *esp* a bedspread

spread-eagle *vb* to (cause to) stand or lie with arms and legs stretched out wide; (cause to) sprawl ⟨*lay* ~ d *on the lawn*⟩

spree *n* a bout of unrestrained indulgence in an activity ⟨*went on a shopping* ~⟩; *esp* a binge

¹**sprig** *n* **1** a small shoot or twig **2** an ornament in the form of a sprig **3** a small headless nail **4** a young offspring; *specif* a youth – chiefly derog; infml

²**sprig** *vt* **-gg-** to decorate with a representation of plant sprigs

sprightly *adj* marked by vitality and liveliness; spirited – **sprightliness** *n*, **sprightly** *adv*

¹**spring** *vb* **sprang, sprung; sprung** *vi* **1a(1)** to dart, shoot **(2)** to be resilient or elastic; *also* to move by elastic force ⟨*the lid* sprang *shut*⟩ **b** to become warped **2** to issue suddenly and copiously; pour out ⟨*the tears* sprang *from her eyes*⟩ **3a** to grow as a plant **b** to issue by birth or descent **c** to come into being; arise ⟨*the project* ~ s *from earlier research*⟩ **4a** to make a leap or leaps ⟨sprang *towards the door*⟩ **b** to rise or jump up suddenly ⟨sprang *to his feet when the bell rang*⟩ **5** to extend in height; rise ⟨*the tower* ~ s *to 90 metres*⟩ ~ *vt* **1** to cause to spring **2** to split, crack ⟨*wind* sprang *the mast*⟩ **3a** to cause to operate suddenly ⟨~ *a trap*⟩ **b** to bring into a specified state by pressing or bending ⟨~ *a bar into place*⟩ **4** to leap over **5** to produce or disclose suddenly or unexpectedly ⟨~ *a surprise on them*⟩ ⟨sprang *a leak*⟩ **6** to release from prison – infml

²**spring** *n* **1a** a source of supply; *esp* an issue of water from the ground **b** an ultimate source, esp of thought or action ⟨*the inner* ~ s *of being*⟩ **2** a time or season of growth or development; *specif* the season between winter and summer comprising, in the northern hemisphere, the months of March, April, and May **3** a mechanical part that recovers its original shape when released after deformation **4a** the act or an instance of leaping up or forward; a bound **b(1)** capacity for springing; resilience **(2)** bounce, energy ⟨*a man with* ~ *in his step*⟩

springboard *n* **1** a flexible board secured at one end that a diver or gymnast jumps off to gain extra height **2** sthg that provides an initial stimulus or impetus

springbok *n, pl* **springboks,** (*l*) **springbok,** *esp collectively* **springbok 1** a swift and graceful southern African gazelle noted for its habit of springing lightly and suddenly into the air **2** *often cap* a sportsman or sportswoman representing S Africa in an international match or tour abroad

spring-clean *vt* **1** to give a thorough cleaning to (e g a

house or furnishings) **2** to put into a proper or more satisfactory order ⟨~ *a government department*⟩ ~ *vi* to spring-clean a house – **spring-clean** *n*

springer spaniel *n* a medium-sized sporting dog of either of 2 breeds that is used chiefly for finding and flushing small game

spring onion *n* an onion with a small mild-flavoured thin-skinned bulb and long shoots that is chiefly eaten raw in salads

spring tide *n* a tide of maximum height occurring at new and full moon

springtime *n* SPRING 2; *also* YOUTH 1

springy *adj* having an elastic or bouncy quality; resilient ⟨*walked with a* ~ *step*⟩ – **springily** *adv*, **springiness** *n*

¹**sprinkle** *vb* **sprinkling** *vt* **1** to scatter in fine drops or particles **2a** to distribute (sthg) at intervals (as if) by scattering **b** to occur at (random) intervals on; dot ⟨*meadows* ~ d *with flowers*⟩ **c** to wet lightly ~ *vi* to rain lightly in scattered drops

²**sprinkle** *n* **1** an instance of sprinkling; *specif* a light fall of rain **2** a sprinkling

sprinkler *n* a device for spraying a liquid, esp water: e g **a** a fire extinguishing system that works automatically on detection of smoke or a high temperature **b** an apparatus for watering a lawn – **sprinklered** *adj*

sprinkling *n* a small quantity or number, esp falling in scattered drops or particles or distributed randomly

¹**sprint** *vi* to run or ride a bicycle at top speed, esp for a short distance – **sprinter** *n*

²**sprint** *n* **1** (an instance of) sprinting **2a** a short fast running, swimming, or bicycle race **b** a burst of speed

sprite *n* a (playful graceful) fairy

sprocket *n* **1** a tooth or projection on the rim of a wheel, shaped so as to engage the links of a chain **2** *also* **sprocket wheel** a wheel or cylinder having sprockets (e g to engage a bicycle chain)

¹**sprout** *vi* **1** to grow, spring up, or come forth as (if) a shoot **2** to send out shoots or new growth ~ *vt* to send forth or up; cause to develop or grow

²**sprout** *n* **1** a (young) shoot (e g from a seed or root) **2** BRUSSELS SPROUT

¹**spruce** *n* any of a genus of evergreen coniferous trees with a conical head of dense foliage and soft light wood

²**spruce** *adj* neat or smart in dress or appearance; trim ⟨*his* ~ *black coat and his bowler hat* – W S Maugham⟩ – **sprucely** *adv*, **spruceness** *n*

³**spruce** *vt* to make spruce ~ *vi* to make oneself spruce USE usu – *up*

sprung *adj*, **1** *past of* SPRING **2** equipped with springs ⟨*a* ~ *mattress*⟩

spry *adj* **sprier, spryer; spriest, spryest** vigorously active; nimble – **spryly** *adv*, **spryness** *n*

¹**spud** *n* **1** a small narrow spade **2** a potato – infml

²**spud** *vb* **-dd-** *vt* **1** to dig up or remove with a spud **2** to begin to drill (an oil well) ~ *vi* to begin to drill an oil well

spume *vi or n* (to) froth, foam – **spumous, spumy** *adj*

spun *past of* SPIN

spunk *n* **1** any of various fungi used to make tinder **2** spirit, pluck **3** *Br* semen – vulg – **spunky** *adj*

¹**spur** *n* **1a** a pointed device secured to a rider's heel and used to urge on a horse **b** recognition and reward for achievement ⟨won *his academic* ~s⟩ **2** a goad to action; a stimulus **3** sthg projecting like or suggesting a spur: e g **a(1)** a stiff sharp spine (e g on the wings or legs of a bird or insect); *esp* one on a cock's leg **(2)** a metal spike fitted to a fighting cock's leg **b** a hollow projection from a plant's petals or sepals (e g in larkspur or columbine) **4** a lateral projection (e g a ridge) of a mountain (range) **5** a

short piece of road or railway connecting with a major route (e g a motorway) – **spurred** adj – **on the spur of the moment** on impulse; suddenly

²spur vb **-rr-** vt **1** to urge (a horse) on with spurs **2** to incite to usu faster action or greater effort; stimulate – usu + *on* ~ *vi* to spur a horse on; ride hard

spurge n any of various mostly shrubby plants with a bitter milky juice

spurious adj **1** of illegitimate birth **2** having a superficial usu deceptive resemblance or correspondence; false **3a** of deliberately falsified or mistakenly attributed origin; forged **b** based on mistaken ideas ⟨*it would be ~ to claim special privileges*⟩ – **spuriously** adv, **spuriousness** n

spurn vt to reject with disdain or contempt; scorn – **spurn** n

¹spurt vi or n (to make) a sudden brief burst of increased effort, activity, or speed

²spurt vb to (cause to) gush out in a jet

³spurt n a sudden forceful gush; a jet

¹sputter vt **1** to utter hastily or explosively in confusion, anger, or excitement; splutter **2** to dislodge (atoms) from the surface of a material by collision with high energy particles (e g electrons); *also* to deposit (a metallic film) by such a process ~ *vi* **1** to eject particles of food or saliva noisily from the mouth **2** to speak in an explosive or incoherent manner **3** to make explosive popping sounds – **sputterer** n

²sputter n **1** confused and excited speech **2** (the sound of) sputtering

sputum n, pl **sputa** matter, made up of discharges from the respiratory passages and saliva, that is coughed up

¹spy vt **1** to keep under secret surveillance, usu for hostile purposes ⟨*~ out the land*⟩ **2** to catch sight of; see ⟨*spied him lurking in the bushes*⟩ **3** to search or look for intently ⟨*~ out a means of escape*⟩ ~ *vi* **1** to observe or search for sthg; look **2** to watch secretly; act as a spy – often + *on* USE (vt 1&3) usu + *out*

²spy n **1** one who keeps secret watch on sby or sthg **2** one who attempts to gain information secretly from a country, company, etc and communicate it to another

spyglass n a small telescope

squab n, pl **squabs**, (1) **squabs**, *esp collectively* **squab** **1** a fledgling bird, esp a pigeon **2** a thick cushion for a chair, car seat, etc

squabble vi or n squabbling (to engage in) a noisy or heated quarrel, esp over trifles – **squabbler** n

squad n sing or pl in constr **1** a small group of military personnel assembled for a purpose ⟨*a drill ~*⟩ **2** a small group working as a team ⟨*a special police ~*⟩

squad car n, chiefly NAm a police car having radio communication with headquarters

squadron n sing or pl in constr a unit of military organization: **a** a unit of cavalry or of an armoured regiment, usu consisting of 3 or more troops **b** a variable naval unit consisting of a number of warships on a particular operation **c** a unit of an air force consisting usu of between 10 and 18 aircraft

squadron leader n an officer in the Royal Air Force ranking below wing commander

squalid adj **1** filthy and degraded from neglect or poverty ⟨*~ ramshackle tenements*⟩ **2** SORDID 2 – **squalidly** adv, **squalidness** n

¹squall vb to cry out raucously; scream – **squall** n, **squaller** n

²squall n **1** a sudden violent wind, often with rain or snow **2** a short-lived commotion ⟨*a minor domestic ~*⟩ – **squally** adj

squalor n the quality or state of being squalid

squander vt to spend hastily, foolishly, or waste-

fully; dissipate ⟨*~ed his earnings on drink*⟩ – **squanderer** n

¹square n **1** an instrument (e g a set square or T square) with at least 1 right angle and 2 straight edges, used to draw or test right angles or parallel lines **2** a rectangle with all 4 sides equal **3** sthg shaped like a square: e g **a** a square scarf **b** an area of ground for a particular purpose (e g military drill) **c** an arrangement of letters, numbers, etc in a square **4** any of the rectangular, square, etc spaces marked out on a board used for playing games **5** the product of a number multiplied by itself **6** an open space in a town, city, etc formed at the meeting of 2 or more streets, and often laid out with grass and trees **7** a solid object or piece approximating to a cube or having a square as its principal face **8** one who is excessively conventional or conservative in tastes or outlook – infml; no longer in vogue – **out of square** not at an exact right angle

²square adj **1a** having 4 equal sides and 4 right angles **b** forming a right angle ⟨*a ~ corner*⟩ **2a** approximating to a cube ⟨*a ~ cabinet*⟩ **b** of a shape or build suggesting strength and solidity; broad in relation to length or height ⟨*~ shoulders*⟩ **c** square in cross section ⟨*a ~ tower*⟩ **3a** of a unit of length denoting the area equal to that of a square whose edges are of the specified length ⟨*a ~ yard*⟩ **b** being of a specified length in each of 2 equal dimensions meeting at a right angle ⟨*10 metres ~*⟩ **4a** exactly adjusted, arranged, or aligned; neat and orderly **b** fair, honest, or straightforward ⟨*~ in all his dealings*⟩ **c** leaving no balance; settled ⟨*the accounts are all ~*⟩ **d** even, tied **5** of, occupying, or passing through a fielding position near or on a line perpendicular to the line between the wickets and level with the batsman's wicket ⟨*~ leg*⟩ **6** excessively conservative; dully conventional – infml; no longer in vogue – **squarely** adv, **squareness** n, **squarish** adj

³square vt **1a** to make square or rectangular ⟨*~ a building stone*⟩ **b** to test for deviation from a right angle, straight line, or plane surface **2** to set approximately at right angles or so as to present a rectangular outline ⟨*~d his shoulders*⟩ **3a** to multiply (a number) by the same number; to raise to the second power **b** to find a square equal in area to ⟨*~ the circle*⟩ **4a** to balance, settle ⟨*~ an account*⟩ **b** to even the score of (a contest) **5** to mark off into squares or rectangles **6a** to bring into agreement; reconcile ⟨*~ theory with practice*⟩ **b** to bribe – infml ~ *vi* **1** to match or agree precisely – usu + *with* **2** to settle matters; *esp* to pay the bill – often + *up* – **square up to 1** to prepare oneself to meet (a challenge) ⟨*squared up to the situation*⟩ **2** to take a fighting stance towards (an opponent)

⁴square adv **1** in a straightforward or honest manner ⟨*told him ~*⟩ **2a** so as to face or be face to face ⟨*the house stood ~ to the road*⟩ **b** at right angles **3** DIRECTLY 1 ⟨*hit the nail ~ on the head*⟩

square away vt, NAm to put in order or readiness – infml

square-bashing n, chiefly Br military drill, esp marching, on a barrack square

square bracket n either of 2 written or printed marks [ ] used to enclose a mathematical expression or other written or printed matter

square dance n a dance for 4 couples who form a hollow square – **square dancer** n, **square dancing** n

square rig n a sailing ship rig in which the principal sails are square sails – **square-rigged** adj, **square-rigger** n

square root n a (positive) number whose square is a usu specified number ⟨*the ~ of 9 is ±3*⟩

¹squash vt **1a** to press or beat into a pulp or a flat mass; crush **b** to apply pressure to by pushing or squeezing ⟨*got*

~ed *on the crowded platform*〉 **2** to reduce to silence or inactivity; PUT DOWN 〈~ed *her with a cutting remark*〉〈~ *a revolt*〉 ~ *vi* **1** to flatten out under pressure or impact **2** to squeeze, press 〈*we* ~ed *into the front row of spectators*〉 – **squashy** *adj*, **squashily** *adv*, **squashiness** *n*

²**squash** *n* **1** the act or soft dull sound of squashing **2** a crushed mass; *esp* a mass of people crowded into a restricted space **3** *also* **squash rackets** a game played in a 4-walled court with long-handled rackets and a rubber ball that can be played off any number of walls **4** *Br* a beverage made from sweetened and often concentrated citrus fruit juice, usu drunk diluted

³**squash** *n, pl* **squashes, squash** any of various (plants of the cucumber family bearing) fruits widely cultivated as vegetables and for livestock feed

¹**squat** *vi* **-tt-** **1** to crouch close to the ground as if to escape detection 〈*a* ~ting *hare*〉 **2** to assume or maintain a position in which the body is supported on the feet and the knees are bent, so that the haunches rest on or near the heels **3** to occupy property as a squatter

²**squat** *n* **1a** squatting **b** the posture of sby or sthg that squats **2** an empty building occupied by or available to squatters – *infml*

³**squat** *adj* **-tt-** **1** with the heels drawn up under the haunches **2** disproportionately short or low and broad – **squatly** *adv*, **squatness** *n*

squatter *n* **1** one who occupies usu otherwise empty property without rights of ownership or payment of rent **2** *Austr* one who owns large tracks of grazing land

squaw *n* a N American Indian (married) woman

squawk *vi or n* **1** (to utter) a harsh abrupt scream **2** (to make) a loud or vehement protest – **squawker** *n*

¹**squeak** *vi* **1** to utter or make a squeak **2** SQUEAL 2a – *infml* ~ *vt* to utter in a squeak – **squeaker** *n*

²**squeak** *n* **1** a short shrill cry or noise **2** an escape – usu in *a narrow squeak*; *infml* – **squeaky** *adj*

¹**squeal** *vi* **1** to utter or make a squeal **2a** to turn informer 〈*bribed to* ~ *on his boss*〉 **b** to complain, protest ~ *vt* to utter with a squeal *USE* (*vi* 2) *infml* – **squealer** *n*

²**squeal** *n* a shrill sharp cry or noise

squeamish *adj* **1** easily nauseated **2a** excessively fastidious in manners, scruples, or convictions **b** easily shocked or offended – **squeamishly** *adv*, **squeamishness** *n*

¹**squeegee** *n* a usu rubber bladed tool used for spreading liquid on or removing it from a surface (e g a window); *also* a roller or other device used similarly in lithography or photography

²**squeegee** *vt* to smooth, wipe, or treat with a squeegee

¹**squeeze** *vt* **1a** to apply physical pressure to; compress the (opposite) sides of **b** to extract or discharge under pressure 〈~ *juice from a lemon*〉 **c** to force, thrust, or cram (as if) by compression 〈~ *clothes into a suitcase*〉〈~d *his way across the room*〉 **2a** to obtain by force or extortion 〈*dictators who* ~ *money from the poor*〉 **b** to reduce by extortion, oppressive measures, etc 〈squeezing *the profits*〉 **c** to cause (economic) hardship to **3** to fit into a limited time span or schedule – usu + *in* or *into* **4** to force (another player) to discard a card to his/her disadvantage, esp in bridge ~ *vi* **1** to force one's way 〈~ *through a door*〉 **2** to pass, win, or get by narrowly 〈*managed to* ~ *through the month on sick pay*〉 – **squeezable** *adj*, **squeezer** *n*

²**squeeze** *n* **1a** a squeezing or compressing **b** a handshake; *also* an embrace **2a** a quantity squeezed out from sthg 〈*a* ~ *of lemon*〉 **b** a condition of being crowded together; a crush 〈*it was a tight* ~ *with 6 in the car*〉 **3a** a financial pressure caused by narrowing margins or by shortages **b** pressure brought to bear on sby – chiefly in *put the squeeze on*; *infml*

squelch *vt* **1** to fall or stamp on so as to crush **2** to suppress completely; quell, squash ~ *vi* **1** to emit a sucking sound like that of an object being withdrawn from mud **2** to walk or move, esp through slush, mud, etc, making a squelching noise – **squelch** *n*, **squelchy** *adj*

squib *n* **1** a small firework that burns with a fizz and finishes with a small explosion **2** a short witty or satirical speech or piece of writing

squid *n, pl* **squids**, *esp collectively* **squid** any of numerous 10-armed cephalopod molluscs, related to the octopus and cuttlefish, that have a long tapered body and a tail fin on each side

squidgy *adj, chiefly Br* soft and squashy – *infml*

squiffy *adj* slightly drunk, tipsy – *infml*

squiggle *vi or n* (to draw) a short wavy twist or line, esp in handwriting or drawing – **squiggly** *adj*

¹**squint** *adj* having a squint; squinting

²**squint** *vi* **1** to have or look with a squint **2** to look or peer with eyes partly closed – **squinter** *n*, **squintingly** *adv*

³**squint** *n* **1** (a visual disorder marked by) inability to direct both eyes to the same object because of imbalance of the muscles of the eyeball **2** a hagioscope **3** a glance, look – esp in *have/take a squint at*; *infml* – **squinty** *adj*

¹**squire** *n* **1** a shield-bearer or armour-bearer of a knight **2** an owner of a country estate; *esp* the principal local landowner **3** *Br* PAL 2 – *infml*

²**squire** *vt* to attend on or escort (a woman)

squirearchy, squirarchy *n sing or pl in constr* the gentry or landed-proprietor class – **squirearchical** *adj*

squirm *vi* **1** to twist about like a worm; wriggle **2** to feel or show acute discomfort at sthg embarrassing, shameful, or unpleasant – **squirm** *n*, **squirmer** *n*

squirrel *n* (the usu grey or red fur of) any of various New or Old World small to medium-sized tree-dwelling rodents that have a long bushy tail and strong hind legs

¹**squirt** *vi* to issue in a sudden forceful stream from a narrow opening ~ *vt* **1** to cause to squirt **2** to direct a jet or stream of liquid at 〈~ed *his sister with a water pistol*〉

²**squirt** *n* **1** a small rapid stream of liquid; a jet **2** a small or insignificant (impudent) person – *infml*

SS *n sing or pl in constr* Hitler's bodyguard and special police force

¹**-st** *suffix* (*adj or adv* → *adj or adv*) – used to form the superlative degree of adjectives and adverbs of 1 syllable, and of some adjectives and adverbs of 2 or more syllables, that end in *e* 〈*surest*〉〈*completest*〉; compare ¹-EST

²**-st** – see ²-EST

¹**stab** *n* **1** a wound produced by a pointed weapon **2a** a thrust (as if) with a pointed weapon **b(1)** a sharp spasm of pain **(2)** a pang of intense emotion 〈*felt a* ~ *of remorse*〉 **3** an attempt, try – *infml*

²**stab** *vb* **-bb-** *vt* **1** to pierce or wound (as if) with a pointed weapon **2** to thrust, jab 〈~bed *his finger at the page*〉 ~ *vi* to thrust *at* sby or sthg (as if) with a pointed weapon – **stabber** *n*

stabilizer, -iser *n* **1** a chemical substance added to another substance or to a system to prevent or retard an unwanted alteration of physical state **2** a device to keep ships steady in a rough sea **3** *chiefly NAm* the horizontal tailplane of an aircraft

¹**stable** *n* **1** a building in which domestic animals, esp horses, are sheltered and fed – often pl with sing. meaning **2** *sing or pl in constr* **a** the racehorses or racing cars owned by one person or organization **b** a group of athletes (e g boxers) or performers under one management **c** a group, collection 〈*a tycoon who owns a* ~ *of newspapers*〉

²stable vt to put or keep in a stable ~ vi to dwell (as if) in a stable

³stable adj **1a** securely established; fixed ⟨a ~ community⟩ **b** not subject to change or fluctuation; unvarying ⟨a ~ population⟩ ⟨a ~ currency⟩ **c** permanent, enduring **2** not subject to feelings of mental or emotional insecurity **3a(1)** placed or constructed so as to resist forces tending to cause (change of) motion **(2)** that develops forces that restore the original condition of equilibrium when disturbed **b(1)** able to resist alteration in chemical, physical, or biological properties **(2)** not spontaneously radioactive ⟨a ~ isotope⟩ – **stably** adv, **stabilize** vb, **stableness**, **stabilization** n, **stability** n

stable lad n a groom in a racing stable

stabling n indoor accommodation for animals

staccato n, adv, or adj, pl **staccatos** (a manner of speaking or performing, or a piece of music performed) in a sharp, disconnected, or abrupt way

¹stack n **1** a large usu circular or square pile of hay, straw, etc **2** an (orderly) pile or heap **3a** CHIMNEY STACK **b** a smokestack **4** a pyramid of 3 interlocked rifles **5** a structure of shelves for compact storage of books – usu pl with sing. meaning **6** a stacked group of aircraft **7** a group of loudspeakers for a public address sound system **8** a high pillar of rock rising out of the sea, that was detached from the mainland by the erosive action of waves **9** a large quantity or number – often pl with sing. meaning ⟨~s of money⟩; infml

²stack vt **1** to arrange in a stack; pile **2** to arrange secretly for cheating ⟨the cards were ~ed⟩ **3** to assign (an aircraft) to a particular altitude and position within a group of aircraft circling before landing – **stackable** adj

stadium n, pl **stadiums** also **stadia** **1** any of various ancient Greek units of length, usu of about 185m **2** a sports ground surrounded by a large usu unroofed building with tiers of seats for spectators **3** a stage in a life history; esp one between successive moults in the development of an insect

¹staff n, pl **staffs**, **staves**, (5) **staffs** **1a** a long stick carried in the hand for use in walking or as a weapon **b** a supporting rod; esp a flagstaff **c** sthg which gives strength or sustains ⟨bread is the ~ of life⟩ **2a** a crosier **b** a rod carried as a symbol of office or authority **3** a set of usu 5 parallel horizontal lines on which music is written **4** any of various graduated sticks or rules used for measuring **5** sing or pl in constr **a** the body of people in charge of the internal operations of an institution, business, etc **b** a group of officers appointed to assist a military commander **c** the teachers at a school or university **d** the personnel who assist a superior

²staff vt **1** to supply with a staff or with workers **2** to serve as a staff member of

staff sergeant n **1** a high-ranking noncommissioned officer in the British army **2** a middle-ranking noncommissioned officer in the US army, airforce, or marines

¹stag n, pl **stags**, (1) **stags**, esp collectively **stag** **1** an adult male red deer; broadly the male of any of various deer **2** Br a person who buys newly issued shares in the hope of selling them to make a quick profit

²stag adj of or intended for men only ⟨a ~ night⟩ ⟨a ~ party⟩

¹stage n **1** any of a series of positions or stations one above the other **2a(1)** a raised platform **(2)** the area of a theatre where the acting takes place, including the wings and storage space **(3)** the acting profession; also the theatre as an occupation or activity **b** a centre of attention or scene of action **3a** a scaffold for workmen **b** the small platform of a microscope on which an object is placed for

examination **4a** a place of rest formerly provided for those travelling by stagecoach **b** the distance between 2 stopping places on a road **c** a stagecoach **5a** a period or step in a progress, activity, or development **b** any of the distinguishable periods of growth and development of a plant or animal ⟨the larval ~ of an insect⟩ **c** any of the divisions (e g 1 day's riding or driving between predetermined points) of a race or rally that is spread over several days **6** a connected group of components in an electrical circuit that performs some well-defined function (e g amplification) and that forms part of a larger electrical circuit **7** a propulsion unit of a rocket with its own fuel and container **8** chiefly Br a bus stop from or to which fares are calculated; a fare stage

²stage vt **1** to produce (e g a play) on a stage **2** to produce and organize, esp for public view ⟨~d the event to get maximum publicity⟩

stagecoach n a horse-drawn passenger and mail coach that in former times ran on a regular schedule between established stops

stage direction n a description (e g of a character or setting) or direction (e g to indicate sound effects or the movement or positioning of actors) provided in the text of a play

stage door n the entrance to a theatre that is used by those who work there

stage fright n nervousness felt at appearing before an audience

stage-manage vt to arrange or direct, esp from behind the scenes, so as to achieve a desired result

stage manager n one who is in charge of the stage during a performance and supervises related matters beforehand

stager n an experienced person; a veteran – chiefly in old stager

stagestruck adj fascinated by the stage; esp having an ardent desire to become an actor or actress

stage whisper n **1** a whisper by an actor, audible to the audience, but supposedly inaudible to others on stage **2** a whisper that is deliberately made audible

¹stagger vi to reel from side to side (while moving); totter ~ vt **1** to dumbfound, astonish **2** to arrange in any of various alternating or overlapping positions or times ⟨~ work shifts⟩ – **staggerer** n

²stagger n **1** pl but sing or pl in constr an abnormal condition of domestic mammals and birds associated with damage to the brain and spinal cord and marked by lack of muscle coordination and a reeling unsteady gait **2** a reeling or unsteady walk or stance

staggering adj astonishing, overwhelming – **staggeringly** adv

staging n **1** a scaffolding or other temporary platform **2** the business of running stagecoaches

stagnant adj **1a** not flowing in a current or stream; motionless ⟨~ water⟩ **b** stale ⟨long disuse had made the air – and foul – Bram Stoker⟩ **2** dull, inactive – **stagnancy** n, **stagnantly** adv

stagnate vi to become or remain stagnant – **stagnation** n

stagy, stagey adj marked by showy pretence or artificiality; theatrical – **stagily** adv, **staginess** n

staid adj sedate and often primly self-restrained; sober – **staidly** adv, **staidness** n

¹stain vt **1** to discolour, soil **2** to suffuse with colour **3** to taint with guilt, vice, corruption, etc; bring dishonour to **4** to colour (e g wood or a biological specimen) by using (chemical) processes or dyes affecting the material itself ~ vi **1** to become stained **2** to cause staining – **stainable** adj, **stainer** n

²stain *n* **1** a soiled or discoloured spot **2** a moral taint or blemish **3a** a preparation (e g of dye or pigment) used in staining; *esp* one capable of penetrating the pores of wood **b** a dye or mixture of dyes used in microscopy to make minute and transparent structures visible, to differentiate tissue elements, or to produce specific chemical reactions

stained glass *n* glass coloured or stained for use in windows

stainless *adj* **1** free from stain or stigma **2** (made from materials) resistant to stain, specif rust – **stainlessly** *adv*

stair *n* **1** a series of (flights of) steps for passing from one level to another – usu pl with sing. meaning **2** any step of a stairway

staircase *n* **1** the structure or part of a building containing a stairway **2** a flight of stairs with the supporting framework, casing, and balusters

stairway *n* one or more flights of stairs, usu with intermediate landings

stairwell *n* a vertical shaft in which stairs are located

¹stake *n* **1** a pointed piece of material (e g wood) for driving into the ground as a marker or support **2a** a post to which sby was bound for execution by burning **b** execution by burning at a stake – + *the* **3a** sthg, esp money, staked for gain or loss **b** the prize in a contest, esp a horse race – chiefly pl with sing. meaning **c** an interest or share in an undertaking (e g a commercial venture) **4** *pl but sing or pl in constr, often cap* a horse race in which all the horses are evenly matched (e g in age and amount of weight carried) – chiefly in names of races – **at stake** in jeopardy; AT ISSUE

²stake *vt* **1** to mark the limits of (as if) by stakes – often + *off* or *out* **2** to tether to a stake **3** to bet, hazard **4** to fasten up or support (e g plants) with stakes **5** *chiefly NAm* to back financially – **stake a/one's claim** to state that sthg is one's by right

stake out *vt, NAm* to conduct a surveillance of (a suspected area, person, etc) – **stakeout** *n*

stalactite *n* an icicle-like deposit of calcium carbonate hanging from the roof or sides of a cavern – **stalactitic** *adj*

stalagmite *n* a deposit of calcium carbonate like an inverted stalactite formed on the floor of a cavern – **stalagmitic** *adj*

¹stale *adj* **1a** tasteless or unpalatable from age **b** *of air* musty, foul **2** tedious from familiarity ⟨~ *jokes*⟩ **3** impaired in legal force through lack of timely action ⟨a ~ *debt*⟩ **4** impaired in vigour or effectiveness, esp from overexertion – **stalely** *adv*, **staleness** *n*

²stale *vb* to make or become stale

³stale *vi, esp of horses and cattle* to urinate

stalemate *vt or n* (to bring into) **a** a drawing position in chess in which only the king can move and although not in check can move only into check **b** a deadlock

¹stalk *vi* **1** to pursue or approach quarry or prey stealthily **2** to walk stiffly or haughtily ~ *vt* **1** to pursue by stalking ⟨~ *deer*⟩ **2** to go through (an area) in search of prey or quarry ⟨~ *the woods for deer*⟩ – **stalker** *n*

²stalk *n* **1** the stalking of quarry or prey **2** a stiff or haughty walk

³stalk *n* **1a** the main stem of a herbaceous plant, often with its attached parts **b** STEM 1b **2** a slender upright supporting or connecting (animal) structure – **stalked** *adj*, **stalkless** *adj*, **stalky** *adj*

¹stall *n* **1** any of usu several compartments for domestic animals in a stable or barn **2a** a wholly or partly enclosed seat in the chancel of a church **b** a church pew **3a** a booth, stand, or counter at which articles are displayed or offered for sale **b** SIDESHOW 1b **4** a protective sheath for a finger or toe **5** a small compartment ⟨a *shower* ~⟩ **6** *Br* a seat on the main floor of an auditorium (e g in a theatre)

²stall *vt* **1** to put or keep in a stall **2a** to bring to a standstill; block **b** to cause (e g a car engine) to stop, usu inadvertently **c** to cause (an aircraft or aerofoil) to go into a stall ~ *vi* **1** to come to a standstill; block **b** *of an engine* to stop suddenly from failure **2** to experience a stall in flying

³stall *n* the condition of an aerofoil or aircraft when the airflow is so obstructed (e g from moving forwards too slowly) that lift is lost

⁴stall *vi* to play for time; delay ~ *vt* to divert or delay, esp by evasion or deception – **stall** *n*

stallholder *n* one who runs a (market) stall

stallion *n* an uncastrated male horse; *esp* one kept for breeding

¹stalwart *adj* **1** strong in body, mind, or spirit **2** dependable, staunch – **stalwartly** *adv*, **stalwartness** *n*

²stalwart *n* a stalwart person; *specif* a staunch supporter

stamen *n* the organ of a flower that produces the male gamete in the form of pollen, and consists of an anther and a filament

stamina *n* (capacity for) endurance

stammer *vb* to speak or utter with involuntary stops and repetitions – **stammer** *n*, **stammerer** *n*

¹stamp *vt* **1** to pound or crush (e g ore) with a pestle or heavy instrument **2a** to strike or beat forcibly with the bottom of the foot **b** to bring down (the foot) forcibly **3a** to impress, imprint ⟨~ '*paid*' *on the bill*⟩ ⟨*an image* ~ed *on his memory*⟩ **b**(1) to attach a (postage) stamp to (2) to mark with an (official) impression, device, etc **4** to cut out, bend, or form with a stamp or die **5a** to provide with a distinctive character ⟨~ed *with an air of worldly wisdom*⟩ **b** CHARACTERIZE 2 ~ *vi* **1** POUND 2 **2** to strike or thrust the foot forcibly or noisily downwards – **stamper** *n*

²stamp *n* **1** a device or instrument for stamping **2** the impression or mark made by stamping or imprinting **3a** a distinctive feature, indication, or mark ⟨*the* ~ *of genius*⟩ **b** a lasting imprint ⟨*the* ~ *of time*⟩ **4** the act of stamping **5** a printed or stamped piece of paper that for some restricted purpose is used as a token of credit or occasionally of debit: e g **a** POSTAGE STAMP **b** a stamp used as evidence that tax has been paid **c** TRADING STAMP

¹stampede *n* **1** a wild headlong rush or flight of frightened animals **2** a sudden mass movement of people

²stampede *vb* to (cause to) run away or rush in panic or on impulse

stamping ground *n* a favourite or habitual haunt

stamp out *vt* to eradicate, destroy ⟨*stamp out crime*⟩

stance *n* **1a** a way of standing or being placed **b** intellectual or emotional attitude ⟨*took an anti-union* ~⟩ **2** the position of body or feet from which a sportsman (e g a batsman or golfer) plays

stanch, staunch *vt* to check or stop the flow of ⟨~ed *her tears*⟩; *also* to stop the flow of blood from (a wound)

stanchion *vt or n* (to provide with) an upright bar, post, or support (e g for a roof)

¹stand *vb* **stood** *vi* **1a** to support oneself on the feet in an erect position **b** to be a specified height when fully erect ⟨~s *6ft 2*⟩ **c** to rise to or maintain an erect or upright position ⟨*his hair* stood *on end*⟩ **2a** to take up or maintain a specified position or posture ⟨~ *aside*⟩ **b** to maintain one's position ⟨~ *firm*⟩ **3** to be in a specified state or situation ⟨~s *accused*⟩ **4** to sail in a specified direction ⟨~ing *into harbour*⟩ **5a** to have or maintain a relative position (as if) in a graded scale ⟨~s *first in his class*⟩ **b**

to be in a position to gain or lose because of an action taken or a commitment made ⟨~s *to make quite a profit*⟩ **6** to occupy a place or location ⟨*the house* ~s *on a hill*⟩ **7** to remain stationary or inactive ⟨*the car* stood *in the garage for a week*⟩ **8** to agree, accord – chiefly in *it stands to reason* **9a** to exist in a definite (written or printed) form ⟨*copy a passage exactly as it* ~s⟩ ⟨*that is how the situation* ~s *at present*⟩ **b** to remain valid or effective ⟨*the order given last week still* ~s⟩ **10** *chiefly Br* to be a candidate in an election ~ *vt* **1a** to endure or undergo ⟨~ *trial*⟩ ⟨*this book will* ~ *the test of time*⟩ **b** to tolerate, bear; PUT UP WITH ⟨*can't* ~ *his boss*⟩ **c** to benefit from; do with ⟨*looks as if he could* ~ *a good sleep*⟩ **2** to remain firm in the face of ⟨~ *a siege*⟩ **3** to perform the duty of ⟨~ *guard*⟩ **4** to cause to stand; set upright **5** to pay the cost of; pay for ⟨*I'll* ~ *you a dinner*⟩ – *infml* – **stand a chance** to have a chance – **stand by** to remain loyal or faithful to ⟨stand by *the agreement*⟩ – **stand for 1** to be a symbol for; represent **2** to permit; PUT UP WITH – **stand on** to insist on ⟨*never* stands on *ceremony*⟩ – **stand one in good stead** to be of advantage or service to one – **stand one's ground** to remain firm and unyielding in the face of opposition – **stand on one's own feet** to think or act independently

²**stand** *n* **1** an act, position, or place of standing ⟨took up *a* ~ *near the exit*⟩ **2a** a standstill; *also* a halt for defence or resistance **b** a usu defensive effort of some length or success ⟨*a* united ~ *against the plans for the new motorway*⟩ ⟨*a last-wicket* ~ *of 53 runs*⟩ **c** a stop made by a touring theatrical company, rock group, etc to give a performance **3** a strongly or aggressively held position, esp on a debatable issue **4a** a structure of tiered seats for spectators – often *pl* with sing. meaning **b** a raised platform serving as a point of vantage or display (e g for a speaker or exhibit) **5** a small usu temporary and open-air stall where goods are sold or displayed ⟨*a hot dog* ~⟩ **6** a place where a passenger vehicle awaits hire ⟨*a taxi* ~⟩ **7** a frame on or in which sthg may be placed for support ⟨*an umbrella* ~⟩ **8** a group of plants or trees growing in a continuous area **9** *NAm* the witness-box

¹**standard** *n* **1** a conspicuous flag, object, etc used to mark a rallying point, esp in battle, or to serve as an emblem **2a** a (long narrow tapering) flag **b** the personal flag of a member of a royal family or of the head of a state **3a** sthg established by authority, custom, or general consent as a model or example; a criterion **b** a (prescribed) degree of quality or worth **c** *pl* moral integrity; principles **4** sthg set up and established by authority as a rule for the measure of quantity, weight, value, or quality **5a** the fineness and legally fixed weight of the metal used in coins **b** the basis of value in a money system **6** an upright support **7a** a shrub or herbaceous plant grown with an erect main stem so that it forms or resembles a tree **b** a fruit tree grafted on a stock that does not induce dwarfing **8** sthg standard: e g **a** a model of car supplied without optional extras **b** a musical composition, specif a popular song, that has become a part of the established repertoire

²**standard** *adj* **1a** being or conforming to a standard, esp as established by law or custom ⟨~ *weight*⟩ **b** sound and usable but not of top quality **2a** regularly and widely used, available, or supplied ⟨*a* ~ *socket*⟩ **b** well established and familiar ⟨*the* ~ *weekend television programmes*⟩ **3** having recognized and permanent value ⟨*a* ~ *reference work*⟩ – **standardize** *vt*, **standardization** *n*

standard-bearer *n* **1** one who carries a standard or banner **2** the leader of an organization, movement, or party

standard lamp *n* a lamp with a tall support that stands on the floor

standard of living *n* a level of welfare or subsistence maintained by an individual, group, or community and shown esp by the level of consumption of necessities, comforts, and luxuries

standard time *n* the officially established time, with reference to Greenwich Mean Time, of a region or country

¹**standby** *n, pl* **standbys** one who or that which is held in reserve and can be relied on, made, or used in case of necessity

²**standby** *adj* **1** held near at hand and ready for use ⟨~ *equipment*⟩ **2** relating to the act or condition of standing by ⟨~ *duty*⟩

stand by *vi* **1** to be present but remain aloof or inactive ⟨*calmly* stood by *and watched those trying to help*⟩ **2** to wait in a state of readiness ⟨stand by *for action*⟩

stand down *vi* **1** to leave the witness-box **2** *chiefly Br* to relinquish (candidature for) an office or position **3** *chiefly Br, of a soldier* to go off duty ~ *vt chiefly Br* to send (soldiers) off duty; *broadly* to dismiss (workers); LAY OFF

stand-in *n* **1** one who is employed to occupy an actor's place while lights and camera are made ready **2** a substitute – **stand in** *vi*

¹**standing** *adj* **1** used or designed for standing in ⟨~ *places*⟩ **2** not yet cut or harvested ⟨~ *timber*⟩ ⟨~ *grain*⟩ **3** not flowing; stagnant ⟨~ *water*⟩ **4** continuing in existence or use indefinitely ⟨*a* ~ *offer*⟩ **5** established by law or custom ⟨*a* ~ *joke*⟩ **6** done from a standing position ⟨*a* ~ *jump*⟩ ⟨*a* ~ *ovation*⟩

²**standing** *n* **1a** length of service or experience, esp as determining rank, pay, or privilege **b** position, status, or condition, esp in relation to a group or other individuals in a similar field; *esp* good reputation ⟨*his* ~ *in the Labour party*⟩ **2** maintenance of position or condition; duration ⟨*a custom of long* ~⟩

standing order *n* **1** a rule governing the procedure of an organization, which remains in force until specifically changed **2** an instruction (e g to a banker or newsagent) in force until specifically changed

standing room *n* space for standing; *esp* accommodation available for spectators or passengers after all seats are filled

standoff *n, NAm* a tie, deadlock

stand-off, stand-off half *n* the player in rugby positioned between the scrum-half and the three-quarter backs

stand off *vi, of a horse* to take off early for a jump

standoffish *adj* reserved, aloof – **standoffishly** *adv*

stand out *vi* **1a** to appear (as if) in relief; project **b** to be prominent or conspicuous **2** to be stubborn in resolution or resistance

standpipe *n* a pipe fitted with a tap and used for outdoor water supply

standpoint *n* a position from which objects or principles are viewed and according to which they are compared and judged

standstill *n* a state in which motion or progress is absent; a stop

stand to *vi* to take up a position of readiness (e g for action or inspection) ⟨*ordered the men to* stand to⟩

stand-up *adj* **1** stiffened to stay upright without folding over ⟨*a* ~ *collar*⟩ **2** performed in or requiring a standing position ⟨*a* ~ *meal*⟩ **3** (having an act) consisting of jokes usu performed solo standing before an audience ⟨*a* ~ *comedian*⟩

stand up *vi* **1** to rise to or maintain a standing or upright position **2** to remain sound and intact under stress, attack, or close scrutiny ~ *vt* to fail to keep an appointment with – **stand up for** to defend against attack or criticism – **stand**

up to 1 to withstand efficiently or unimpaired ⟨*a car which can* stand up to *rough handling*⟩ **2** to face boldly

stank *past of* STINK

stanza *n* a division of a poem consisting of a series of lines arranged together in a usu recurring pattern of metre and rhyme – **stanzaic** *adj*

¹**staple** *vt or n* (to provide with or secure by) **a** a U-shaped metal loop both ends of which can be driven into a surface (e g to secure sthg) **b** a small piece of wire with ends bent at right angles which can be driven through thin sheets of material, esp paper, and clinched to secure the items

²**staple** *n* **1** a chief commodity or production of a place **2a** a commodity for which the demand is constant **b** sthg having widespread and constant use or appeal **c** the sustaining or principal element; substance **3** RAW MATERIAL **4a** a textile fibre (e g wool or rayon) of relatively short length that when spun and twisted forms a yarn rather than a filament **b** the length of a piece of such textile fibre as a distinguishing characteristic of the raw material

³**staple** *adj* **1** used, needed, or enjoyed constantly, usu by many individuals **2** produced regularly or in large quantities ⟨*~ crops such as wheat and rice*⟩ **3** principal, chief

stapler *n* a small usu hand-operated device for inserting wire staples

¹**star** *n* **1** any natural luminous body visible in the sky, esp at night; *specif* any of many celestial bodies of great mass that give out light and are fuelled by nuclear fusion reactions **2a(1)** a planet or a configuration of the planets that is held in astrology to influence a person's destiny – often pl **(2)** *pl* an astrological forecast; a horoscope **b** a waxing or waning fortune or fame ⟨*her ~ was rising*⟩ **3a** a figure with 5 or more points that represents a star; *esp* an asterisk **b** an often star-shaped ornament or medal worn as a badge of honour, authority, or rank or as the insignia of an order **c** any of a group of stylized stars used to place sthg in a scale of value or quality – often in combination ⟨*a 4-star hotel*⟩ **4a** a (highly publicized) performer in the cinema or theatre who plays leading roles **b** an outstandingly talented performer ⟨*a ~ of the running track*⟩ – **starless** *adj*, **starlike** *adj*

²**star** *vb* **-rr-** *vt* **1** to sprinkle or adorn (as if) with stars **2** to mark with a star or an asterisk **3** to advertise or display prominently; feature ⟨*the film ~s a famous stage personality*⟩ *~ vi* to play the most prominent or important role ⟨*now ~ ring in a West-End musical*⟩

³**star** *adj* of, being, or appropriate to a star ⟨*received ~ treatment*⟩

¹**starboard** *adj or n* (of or at) the right side of a ship or aircraft looking forwards

²**starboard** *vt* to turn or put (a helm or rudder) to the right

¹**starch** *vt* to stiffen (as if) with starch

²**starch** *n* **1** an odourless tasteless complex carbohydrate that is the chief storage form of carbohydrate in plants, is an important foodstuff, and is used also in adhesives and sizes, in laundering, and in pharmacy and medicine **2** a stiff formal manner; formality

Star Chamber *n* a court in England that was abolished in 1641, had both civil and criminal jurisdiction, and was noted for its arbitrary and oppressive procedures; *broadly, often not cap* any oppressive tribunal

starchy *adj* **1** of or containing (much) starch ⟨*~ foods*⟩ **2** marked by formality or stiffness – **starchily** *adv*, **starchiness** *n*

star-crossed *adj* not favoured by the stars; ill-fated ⟨*a pair of ~ lovers take their life* – Shak⟩

stardom *n* the status or position of a celebrity or star ⟨*the actress quickly reached ~*⟩

stardust *n* a feeling or impression of romance or magic

¹**stare** *vi* **1** to look fixedly, often with wide-open eyes **2** to stand out conspicuously ⟨*the error ~d from the page*⟩ **3** *esp of an animal's coat* to appear rough and lustreless *~ vt* to bring to a specified state by staring ⟨*~d his opponent into submission*⟩

²**stare** *n* a staring look

starfish *n* any of a class of sea animals that are echinoderms, have a body consisting of a central disc surrounded by 5 equally spaced arms, and feed largely on molluscs (e g oysters)

stargaze *vi* **1** to gaze at stars **2** to gaze raptly, contemplatively, or absentmindedly; *esp* to daydream

stargazer *n* **1** an astrologer **2** an astronomer *USE* chiefly humor

¹**stark** *adj* **1** sheer, utter ⟨*~ nonsense*⟩ **2a(1)** barren, desolate **(2)** having few or no ornaments; bare ⟨*a ~ white room*⟩ **b** harsh, blunt ⟨*the ~ reality of death*⟩ **3** sharply delineated ⟨*a ~ outline*⟩ – **starkly** *adv*, **starkness** *n*

²**stark** *adv* to an absolute or complete degree; wholly ⟨*~ raving mad*⟩

starkers *adj, Br* completely naked – used predicatively; slang

starlet *n* a young film actress being coached and publicized for starring roles

starling *n* any of a family of usu dark social birds; *esp* a dark brown (or in summer, glossy greenish black) European bird that lives in large social groups

starry *adj* **1a** adorned or studded with stars **b** shining like stars; sparkling **2** (seemingly) as high as the stars ⟨*~ speculations*⟩

starry-eyed *adj* given to thinking in a dreamy, impractical, or overoptimistic manner

Stars and Stripes *n pl but sing in constr* the flag of the USA, having 13 alternately red and white horizontal stripes and a blue rectangle in the top left-hand corner with white stars representing the states

star-studded *adj* full of or covered with stars ⟨*a ~ cast*⟩ ⟨*a ~ uniform*⟩

¹**start** *vi* **1a** to move suddenly and violently; spring ⟨*~ed angrily to his feet*⟩ **b** to react with a sudden brief involuntary movement ⟨*~ed when a shot rang out*⟩ **2a** to issue with sudden force ⟨*blood ~ing from the wound*⟩ **b** to come into being, activity, or operation ⟨*when does the film ~?*⟩ **3** to (seem to) protrude ⟨*his eyes ~ing from their sockets*⟩ **4a** to begin a course or journey ⟨*~ed out at dawn*⟩ **b** to range from a specified initial point ⟨*holiday prices ~ from around £80*⟩ **5** to begin an activity or undertaking; *esp* to begin work **6** to be a participant at the start of a sporting contest *~ vt* **1** to cause to leave a place of concealment; flush ⟨*~ a rabbit*⟩ **2** to bring into being ⟨*~ a rumour*⟩ **3** to begin the use or employment of ⟨*~ a fresh loaf of bread*⟩ **4a** to cause to move, act, operate, or do sthg specified ⟨*the noise ~ed the baby crying*⟩ ⟨*~ the motor*⟩ **b** to act as starter of (e g a race) **c** to cause to enter or begin a game, contest, or business activity ⟨*only had £500 to ~ him*⟩; *broadly* to put in a starting position **5** to perform or undergo the first stages or actions of; begin ⟨*~ed studying music at the age of 5*⟩ – **start something** to cause trouble – **to start with 1** at the beginning; initially **2** taking the first point to be considered

²**start** *n* **1** a sudden involuntary bodily movement or reaction (e g from surprise or alarm) **2** a beginning of movement, activity, or development **3a** a lead conceded at the start of a race or competition **b** an advantage, lead;

HEAD START ⟨*gained a 3 days' ~ on the police*⟩ ⟨*his background gave him a good ~ in politics*⟩ **4** a place of beginning

starter *n* **1** one who initiates or sets going; *esp* one who gives the signal to start a race **2a** one who is in the starting lineup of a race or competition **b** one who begins to engage in an activity or process **3** sby who or sthg that causes sthg to begin operating: e g **a** a self-starter **b** material containing microorganisms used to induce a desired fermentation **c** a compound used to start a chemical reaction **4a** sthg that is the beginning of a process, activity, or series **b** *chiefly Br* the first course of a meal – often *pl* with *sing*. meaning

startle *vb* **startling** to (cause to) be suddenly frightened or surprised and usu to (cause to) make a sudden brief movement – **startling** *adj*, **startlingly** *adv*

starve *vi* **1a** to die from lack of food **b** to suffer or feel extreme hunger **2** to suffer or perish from deprivation ⟨*~d for affection*⟩ **3** *archaic or dial* to suffer or perish from cold *~vt* to cause to starve – **starvation** *n*

starveling *n* a person or animal that is thin (as if) from lack of food

¹stash *vt* to store in a usu secret place for future use – often + *away*

²stash *n, chiefly NAm* **1** a hiding place; a cache **2** sthg stored or hidden away

¹state *n* **1a** a mode or condition of being (with regard to circumstances, health, temperament, etc) ⟨*a ~ of readiness*⟩ ⟨*a highly nervous ~*⟩ **b** a condition of abnormal tension or excitement ⟨*don't get in a ~ about it*⟩ **2a** a condition or stage in the physical being of sthg ⟨*the gaseous ~ of water*⟩ **b** any of various conditions characterized by definite quantities (e g of energy, angular momentum, or magnetic moment) in which an atomic system may exist **3a** social position; *esp* high rank **b(1)** luxurious style of living **(2)** formal dignity; pomp – usu + *in* **4** ESTATE **1** **5** a politically organized (sovereign) body, usu occupying a definite territory; *also* its political organization **6** the operations of the government ⟨*matters of ~*⟩ **7** often *cap* a constituent unit of a nation having a federal government – **statehood** *n*

²state *vt* **1** to set, esp by regulation or authority; specify **2** to express the particulars of, esp in words; *broadly* to express in words – **statable**, **stateable** *adj*, **stated** *adj*, **statedly** *adv*

statecraft *n* the art of conducting state affairs

State Enrolled Nurse *n* a nurse who has successfully followed a 2-year course in practical nursing in Britain

stateless *adj* having no nationality ⟨*a ~ person*⟩ – **statelessness** *n*

stately *adj* **1** imposing, dignified ⟨*~ language*⟩ **2** impressive in size or proportions – **stateliness** *n*, **stately** *adv*

stately home *n, Br* a large country residence, usu of historical or architectural interest and open to the public

statement *n* **1** stating orally or on paper **2** sthg stated: e g **a** a report of facts or opinions **b** a single declaration or remark; an assertion **3** PROPOSITION **2** **4** the presentation of a theme in a musical composition **5** a summary of a financial account **6** an outward expression of thought, feeling, etc made without words ⟨*painted the room bright blue to make a definite ~*⟩

State Registered Nurse *n* a fully qualified nurse in Britain

stateroom *n* **1** a large room in a palace or similar building for use on ceremonial occasions **2** a (large and comfortable) private cabin in a ship

States *n pl but sing or pl in constr* the USA

state school *n* a British school that is publicly financed and provides compulsory free education

state's evidence *n, often cap S* (one who gives) evidence for the prosecution in US criminal proceedings

stateside *adj or adv* of, in, or to the USA

statesman, *fem* **statesdoman** *n, pl* **statesmen,** *fem* **stateswomen** **1** one versed in or esp engaged in the business of a government **2** one who exercises political leadership wisely and without narrow partisanship – **statesmanlike, statesmanly** *adj*, **statesmanship** *n*

¹static *also* **statical** *adj* **1** exerting force by reason of weight alone without motion ⟨*~ load*⟩ ⟨*~ pressure*⟩ **2** of or concerned with bodies at rest or forces in equilibrium **3** characterized by a lack of movement, animation, progression, or change ⟨*a ~ population*⟩ **4** of, producing, or being stationary charges of electricity **5** of or caused by radio static – **statically** *adv*

²static *n* (the electrical disturbances causing) unwanted signals in a radio or television system; atmospherics

-static *comb form* (→ *adj*) **1** causing slowing of; inhibiting ⟨*bacteriostatic*⟩ **2** regulating; maintaining in a steady state ⟨*thermostatic*⟩ ⟨*homoeostatic*⟩

statics *n pl but sing or pl in constr* a branch of mechanics dealing with the relations of forces that produce equilibrium among solid bodies

¹station *n* **1** the place or position in which sthg or sby stands or is assigned to stand or remain **2** a stopping place; *esp* (the buildings at) a regular or major stopping place for trains, buses, etc **3a** a post or sphere of duty or occupation **b** a post or area to which a military or naval force is assigned; *also, sing or pl in constr* the officers or society at a station **c** a stock farm or ranch in Australia or New Zealand **4** standing, rank ⟨*a woman of high ~*⟩ **5** a place for specialized observation and study of scientific phenomena ⟨*a marine biology ~*⟩ **6** a place established to provide a public service; *esp* POLICE STATION **7a** (the equipment in) an establishment equipped for radio or television transmission or reception **b** CHANNEL 1F(2)

²station *vt* to assign to or set in a station or position; post

stationary *adj* **1a** having a fixed position; immobile **b** geostationary **2** unchanging in condition

stationer *n* one who deals in stationery

stationery *n* materials (e g paper) for writing or typing; *specif* paper and envelopes for letter writing

stationmaster *n* an official in charge of a railway station

stations of the cross *n pl, often cap S&C* (a devotion involving meditation before) a series of images or pictures, esp in a church, that represent the 14 stages of Christ's sufferings and death

station wagon *n, chiefly NAm* ESTATE CAR

statistic *n* a single term or quantity in or computed from a collection of statistics; *specif* (a function used to obtain) a numerical value (e g the standard deviation or mean) used in describing and analysing statistics

statistics *n pl but sing or pl in constr* **1** a branch of mathematics dealing with the collection, analysis, interpretation, and presentation of masses of numerical data **2** a collection of quantitative data – **statistical** *adj*, **statistically** *adv*, **statistician** *n*

¹statuary *n* statues collectively

²statuary *adj* of or suitable for statues ⟨*~ marble*⟩

statue *n* a likeness (e g of a person or animal) sculptured, cast, or modelled in a solid material (e g bronze or stone) – **statuette** *n*

statuesque *adj* resembling a statue, esp in dignity, shapeliness, or formal beauty – **statuesquely** *adv*, **statuesqueness** *n*

stature n **1** natural height (e g of a person) in an upright position **2** quality or status gained by growth, development, or achievement

status n **1** the condition of sby or sthg (in the eyes of the law) **2** (high) position or rank in relation to others or in a hierarchy

status quo n the existing state of affairs ⟨*seeks to preserve the* ~⟩

statute n **1** a law passed by a legislative body and recorded **2** a rule made by a corporation or its founder, intended as permanent

statute book n the whole body of legislation of a given jurisdiction

statute law n enacted written law

statutory, statutable adj established, regulated, or imposed by or in conformity to statute ⟨*a* ~ *age limit*⟩ – **statutorily, statutably** adv

¹**staunch** vt to stanch

²**staunch** adj steadfast in loyalty or principle – **staunchly** adv, **staunchness** n

¹**stave** n **1** STAFF 1a, 2 **2** any of the narrow strips of wood or iron placed edge to edge to form the sides, covering, or lining of a vessel (e g a barrel) or structure **3** a supporting bar; esp RUNG 1b **4** a stanza **5** STAFF 3

²**stave** vt staved, stove **1** to crush or break inwards – usu + in **2** to provide with staves

stave off vt to ward or fend off, esp temporarily

staves pl of STAFF

¹**stay** n a strong rope, now usu of wire, used to support a ship's mast or similar tall structure (e g a flagstaff)

²**stay** vt to support (e g a chimney) (as if) with stays

³**stay** vi **1** to continue in a place or condition; remain ⟨~ *here*⟩ ⟨~ed *awake*⟩ **2** to take up temporary residence; lodge **3a** to keep even in a contest or rivalry ⟨~ *with the leaders*⟩ **b** of a racehorse to run well over long distances **4** archaic to stop going forwards; pause **5** archaic to stop doing sthg; cease ~ vt **1** to last out (e g a race) **2** to stop or delay the proceeding, advance, or course of; halt ⟨~ *an execution*⟩ – **stay put** to be firmly fixed, attached, or established

⁴**stay** n **1a** stopping or being stopped **b** a suspension of judicial procedure ⟨*a* ~ *of execution*⟩ **2** a residence or sojourn in a place

⁵**stay** n **1** sby who or sthg that serves as a prop; a support **2** a corset stiffened with bones – usu pl with sing. meaning

⁶**stay** vt to provide physical or moral support for; sustain

stay-at-home n or adj (one) preferring to remain in his/her own home, locality, or country

stayer n a racehorse that habitually stays the course

staying power n stamina

staysail n a fore-and-aft sail hoisted on a stay

stead n the office, place, or function ordinarily occupied or carried out by sby or sthg else ⟨*acted in his brother's* ~⟩

steadfast adj **1a** firmly fixed in place or position ⟨*a* ~ *gaze*⟩ **b** not subject to change **2** firm in belief, determination, or adherence; loyal – **steadfastly** adv, **steadfastness** n

¹**steady** adj **1a** firm in position; not shaking, rocking, etc **b** direct or sure; unfaltering ⟨*a* ~ *hand*⟩ **2** showing or continuing with little variation or fluctuation; stable, uniform ⟨~ *prices*⟩⟨*a* ~ *pace*⟩ **3a** not easily moved or upset; calm ⟨~ *nerves*⟩ **b** dependable, constant **c** not given to dissipation; sober – **steadily** adv, **steadiness** n

²**steady** vb to make, keep, or become steady – **steadier** n

³**steady** adv **1** in a steady manner; steadily **2** on the course set – used as a direction to the helmsman of a ship

⁴**steady** n a boyfriend or girlfriend with whom one is going steady – infml

steady state theory n a theory in cosmology: the universe has always existed and has always been expanding with matter being created continuously

steak n **1a** a slice of meat cut from a fleshy part (e g the rump) of a (beef) carcass and suitable for grilling or frying **b** a poorer-quality less tender beef cut, usu from the neck and shoulder, suitable for braising or stewing **2** a cross-sectional slice from between the centre and tail of a large fish

steal vb stole; stolen vi **1** to take the property of another **2** to come or go secretly or unobtrusively ~ vt **1a** to take without leave, esp secretly or by force and with intent to keep **b** to appropriate entirely to oneself or beyond one's proper share ⟨~ *the show*⟩ **2** to accomplish, obtain, or convey in a secretive, unobserved, or furtive manner ⟨~ *a visit*⟩ ⟨stole *a glance at him*⟩ **3** to seize or gain by trickery or skill ⟨*a footballer adept at* ~ing *the ball*⟩ – **stealer** n – **steal a march** to gain an advantage unobserved – usu + on – **steal someone's thunder** to appropriate or adapt sthg devised by another in order to take the credit due to him/her

stealth n **1** the act or action of proceeding furtively or unobtrusively **2** the state of being furtive or unobtrusive

stealthy adj **1** slow, deliberate, and secret in action or character **2** intended to escape observation; furtive – **stealthily** adv, **stealthiness** n

¹**steam** n **1** a vapour given off by a heated substance **2a** the vapour into which water is converted when heated to its boiling point **b** the mist formed by the condensation of water vapour when cooled **3a** energy or power generated (as if) by steam under pressure **b** driving force; power ⟨*got there under his own* ~⟩ – infml – **let/blow off steam** to release pent-up emotions

²**steam** vi **1** to rise or pass off as vapour **2** to give off steam or vapour **3a** to move or travel (as if) by steam power (e g in a steamship) **b** to proceed quickly **4** to become cooked by steam **5** to be angry; boil ⟨~ing *over the insult he had received*⟩ **6** to become covered up or over with steam or condensation ⟨*his glasses* ~ed *up*⟩ ~ vt **1** to give out as fumes; exhale **2** to apply steam to; esp to expose to the action of steam (e g for softening or cooking)

steamboat n a boat propelled by steam power

steamer n **1** a device in which articles are steamed; esp a vessel in which food is cooked by steam **2a** a ship propelled by steam **b** an engine, machine, or vehicle operated or propelled by steam

steam iron n an electric iron with a compartment holding water that is converted to steam by the iron's heat and emitted through the soleplate onto the fabric being pressed

¹**steamroller** n **1** a machine equipped with wide heavy rollers for compacting the surfaces of roads, pavements, etc **2** a crushing force, esp when ruthlessly applied to overcome opposition

²**steamroller** also **steamroll** vt **1** to crush (as if) with a steamroller ⟨~ *the opposition*⟩ **2** to force to a specified state or condition by the use of overwhelming pressure ⟨~ed *the bill through Parliament*⟩ ~ vi to move or proceed with irresistible force

steamship n STEAMER 2a

steam up vt to make angry or excited; arouse

steed n a horse; esp a spirited horse for state or war – chiefly poetic

¹**steel** n **1** commercial iron distinguished from cast iron by

its malleability and lower carbon content **2** an instrument or implement (characteristically) of steel: e g **a** a fluted round steel rod with a handle for sharpening knives **b** a piece of steel for striking sparks from flint **c** a strip of steel used for stiffening **3** a quality (e g of mind or spirit) that suggests steel, esp in strength or hardness ⟨*nerves of ~*⟩

²**steel** *vt* **1** to make unfeeling; harden **2** to fill with resolution or determination

steel band *n* a band that plays tuned percussion instruments cut out of oil drums, developed orig in Trinidad – **steelbandsman** *n*

steel wool *n* long fine loosely compacted steel fibres used esp for scouring and burnishing

steelworks *n, pl* **steelworks** an establishment where steel is made – often pl with sing. meaning – **steelworker** *n*

steely *adj* of or like (the hardness, strength, or colour of) steel – **steeliness** *n*

steelyard *n* a balance in which an object to be weighed is suspended from the shorter arm of a lever and the weight determined by moving a counterbalance along a graduated scale on the longer arm until equilibrium is attained

steenbok, steinbok *n* any of a genus of small antelopes of the plains of S and E Africa

¹**steep** *adj* **1** making a large angle with the plane of the horizon; almost vertical **2** being or characterized by a rapid and severe decline or increase **3** difficult to accept, comply with, or carry out; excessive – *infml* – **steepen** *vb*, **steepish** *adj*, **steeply** *adv*, **steepness** *n*

²**steep** *vt* **1** to soak in a liquid at a temperature below its boiling point (e g for softening or bleaching) **2** to cover with or plunge into a liquid (e g in bathing, rinsing, or soaking) **3** to imbue with or subject thoroughly to – usu + *in* ⟨*~ed in history*⟩ *~vi* to undergo soaking in a liquid

³**steep** *n* **1** being steeped **2** a liquid in which sthg is steeped

steeple *n* (a tower with) a tall spire on a church

steeplechase *n* **1a** a horse race across country **b** a horse race over jumps; *specif* one over a course longer than 2mi (about 3.2km) containing fences higher than 4ft 6in (about 1.4m) **2** a middle-distance running race over obstacles; *specif* one of 3000m over 28 hurdles and 7 water jumps – **steeplechaser** *n*, **steeplechasing** *n*

steeplejack *n* one who climbs chimneys, towers, etc to paint, repair, or demolish them

¹**steer** *n* a male bovine animal castrated before sexual maturity

²**steer** *vt* **1** to direct the course of; *esp* to guide (e g a ship) by mechanical means (e g a rudder) **2** to set and hold to (a course) *~vi* **1** to direct the course (e g of a ship or motor vehicle) **2** to pursue a course of action **3** to be subject to guidance or direction ⟨*a car that ~s well*⟩ – **steerable** *adj*, **steerer** *n* – **steer clear** to keep entirely away – often + *of*

steerage *n* **1** the act or practice of steering; *broadly* direction **2** a large section in a passenger ship for passengers paying the lowest fares

steerage-way *n* a rate of motion sufficient to make a ship or boat respond to movements of the rudder

steering committee *n* a committee that determines the order in which business will be taken up (e g in Parliament)

steering wheel *n* a handwheel by means of which one steers a motor vehicle, ship, etc

steersman *n* a helmsman

stein *n* a usu earthenware beer mug often with a hinged lid

steinbok *n* a steenbok

stele *n* **1** a usu carved or inscribed stone slab or pillar used esp as a gravestone **2** the (cylindrical) central vascular portion of the stem of a vascular plant – **stelar** *adj*

stellar *adj* of or composed of (the) stars

¹**stem** *n* **1a** the main trunk of a plant; *specif* a primary plant axis that develops buds and shoots instead of roots **b** a branch, petiole, or other plant part that supports a leaf, fruit, etc **2** the bow or prow of a vessel; *specif* the principal frame member at the bow to which the sides are fixed **3** a line of ancestry; *esp* a fundamental line from which others have arisen **4** that part of a word which has unchanged spelling when the word is inflected **5** sthg that resembles a plant stem: e g **a** a main (vertical) stroke of a letter or musical note **b** the tubular part of a tobacco pipe from the bowl outwards, through which smoke is drawn **c** the often slender and cylindrical upright support between the base and bowl of a wineglass **d** a shaft of a watch used for winding – **stemless** *adj*, **stemmed** *adj*

²**stem** *vt* **-mm-** **1** to make headway against (e g an adverse tide, current, or wind) **2** to check or go counter to (sthg adverse)

³**stem** *vb* **-mm-** *vi* to originate – usu + *from* *~vt* to remove the stem from

⁴**stem** *vt* **-mm-** to stop or check (as if) by damming ⟨*~ a flow of blood*⟩

Sten, Sten gun *n* a lightweight British submachine gun

stench *n* a stink

¹**stencil** *n* **1** (a printing process using, or a design, pattern, etc produced by means of) an impervious material (e g a sheet of paper or metal) perforated with a design or lettering through which a substance (e g ink or paint) is forced onto the surface below **2** a sheet of strong tissue paper impregnated or coated (e g with paraffin or wax) for use esp in typing a stencil

²**stencil** *vt* **-ll-** (*NAm* **-l-, -ll-**); **stencilling, 1** to produce by means of a stencil **2** to mark or paint with a stencil – **stenciller** *n*

stenography *n* the writing and transcription of shorthand – **stenographer** *n*, **stenographic** *adj*, **stenographically** *adv*

stentorian *adj* extremely loud

¹**step** *n* **1** a rest for the foot in ascending or descending: e g **a** a single tread and riser on a stairway; a stair **b** a ladder rung **2a(1)** (the distance or space passed over in) an advance or movement made by raising the foot and bringing it down at another point **(2)** a combination of foot (and body) movements constituting a unit or a repeated pattern ⟨*a dance ~*⟩ **(3)** manner of walking; stride **b** FOOTPRINT 1 **c** the sound of a footstep ⟨*heard his ~s in the hall*⟩ **3** a short distance ⟨*just a ~ from the beach*⟩ **4** *pl* a course, way ⟨*directed his ~s towards the river*⟩ **5a** a degree, grade, or rank in a scale **b** a stage in a process ⟨*was guided through every ~ of her career*⟩ **6** a block supporting the base of a mast **7** an action, proceeding, or measure often occurring as 1 in a series – often pl with sing. meaning ⟨*is taking ~s to improve the situation*⟩ **8** a steplike offset or part, usu occurring in a series **9** *pl* a stepladder – **steplike** *adj*, **stepped** *adj* – **in step 1** with each foot moving to the same time as the corresponding foot of others or in time to music **2** in harmony or agreement – **out of step** not in step

²**step** *vb* **-pp-** *vi* **1a** to move by raising the foot and bringing it down at another point or by moving each foot in succession **b** to dance **2a** to go on foot; walk **b** to be on one's way; leave – often + *along* **3** to press down on sthg with the foot ⟨*~ on the brake*⟩ *~vt* **1** to take by moving the feet in succession ⟨*~ 3 paces*⟩ **2** to go through the steps of; perform ⟨*~ a minuet*⟩ **3** to make (e g a mast)

erect by fixing the lower end in a step **4** to measure by steps ⟨~ *50 yards*⟩ – usu + *off* or *out* **5** to construct or arrange (as if) in steps ⟨*craggy peaks with terraces* ~ped *up the sides – Time*⟩ – **step into** to attain or adopt (sthg) with ease ⟨stepped into *a fortune*⟩ – **step on it/the gas** to increase one's speed; hurry up – infml

step- *comb form* related by remarriage and not by blood ⟨step*parent*⟩ ⟨step*sister*⟩

stepbrother *n* a son of one's stepparent by a former marriage

stepchild *n, pl* **stepchildren** a child of one's wife or husband by a former marriage

step down *vt* to lower (the voltage at which an alternating current is operating) by means of a transformer ~ *vi* to retire, resign ⟨step down *as chairman*⟩ – **step-down** *adj*

step-in *adj, of clothes* put on by being stepped into

step in *vi* **1** to make a brief informal visit **2** to intervene in an affair or dispute

stepladder *n* a portable set of steps with a hinged frame

step out *vi* **1** to leave or go outside, usu for a short time ⟨stepped out *for a smoke*⟩ **2** to go or march at a vigorous or increased pace

stepparent *n* the husband or wife of one's parent by a subsequent marriage

steppe *n* a vast usu level and treeless plain, esp in SE Europe or Asia

stepping-stone *n* **1** a stone on which to step (e g in crossing a stream) **2** a means of progress or advancement

stepsister *n* a daughter of one's stepparent by a former marriage

step up *vt* **1** to increase (the voltage at which an alternating current is operating) by means of a transformer **2** to increase, augment, or advance by 1 or more steps ⟨step up *production*⟩ ~ *vi* **1** to come forward ⟨step up *to the front*⟩ **2** to undergo an increase – **step-up** *adj*

-ster *comb form* (→ *n*) **1** sby who or sthg that does, handles, or operates ⟨tap*ster*⟩ ⟨team*ster*⟩ **2** sby who or sthg that makes or uses ⟨song*ster*⟩ ⟨pun*ster*⟩ **3** sby who or sthg that is associated with or participates in ⟨game*ster*⟩ ⟨gang*ster*⟩ **4** sby who or sthg that is ⟨young*ster*⟩

¹**stereo** *n, pl* **stereos** **1** a stereoscopic method, system, or effect **2a** stereophonic reproduction **b** a stereophonic sound system

²**stereo** *adj* **1** stereoscopic **2** stereophonic

stereophonic *adj* of or being (a system for) sound reproduction in which the sound is split into and reproduced by 2 different channels to give spatial effect – **stereophonically** *adv*, **stereophony** *n*

stereoscope *n* an optical instrument with 2 eyepieces through which the observer views 2 pictures taken from points of view a little way apart to get the effect of a single three-dimensional picture

stereoscopy *n* the seeing of objects in 3 dimensions – **stereoscopic** *adj*, **stereoscopically** *adv*

¹**stereotype** *n* **1** a plate made by making a cast, usu in type metal, from a mould of a printing surface **2** sby who or sthg that conforms to a fixed or general pattern; *esp* a standardized, usu oversimplified, mental picture or attitude held in common by members of a group – **stereotypical** *also* **stereotypic** *adj*

²**stereotype** *vt* **1** to make a stereotype from **2a** to repeat without variation; make hackneyed **b** to develop a mental stereotype about – **stereotyper** *n*

sterile *adj* **1** failing or not able to produce or bear fruit, crops, or offspring **2a** deficient in ideas or originality **b**

free from living organisms, esp microorganisms **3** bringing no rewards or results; not productive ⟨*the* ~ *search for jobs*⟩ – **sterilely** *adv*, **sterilize** *vt*, **sterilizable** *adj*, **sterilizer** *n*, **sterilant** *n*, **sterilization** *n*, **sterility** *n*

¹**sterling** *n* **1** British money **2** (articles of) sterling silver

²**sterling** *adj* **1** of or calculated in terms of British sterling **2a** *of silver* having a fixed standard of purity; *specif* 92.5 per cent pure **b** made of sterling silver **3** conforming to the highest standard ⟨~ *character*⟩

sterling area *n* a group of countries whose currencies are tied to British sterling

¹**stern** *adj* **1a** hard or severe in nature or manner; austere **b** expressive of severe displeasure; harsh **2** forbidding or gloomy in appearance **3** inexorable, relentless ⟨~ *necessity*⟩ **4** sturdy, firm ⟨*a* ~ *resolve*⟩ – **sternly** *adv*, **sternness** *n*

²**stern** *n* **1** the rear end of a ship or boat **2** a back or rear part; the last or latter part – **sternmost** *adj*, **sternwards** *adv*

sternum *n, pl* **sternums, sterna** a bone or cartilage at the front of the body that connects the ribs, both sides of the shoulder girdle, or both; the breastbone – **sternal** *adj*

steroid *n* any of numerous compounds of similar chemical structure, including the sterols and various hormones (e g testosterone) and glycosides (e g digitalis) – **steroidal** *adj*

sterol *n* any of various solid alcohols (e g cholesterol) widely distributed in animal and plant fats

stertorous *adj* characterized by a harsh snoring or gasping sound – **stertorously** *adv*

stet *vt* **-tt-** to direct retention of (a word or passage previously ordered to be deleted or omitted) by annotating, usu with the word *stet*

stethoscope *n* an instrument used to detect and study sounds produced in the body – **stethoscopic** *adj*, **stethoscopically** *adv*, **stethoscopy** *n*

stetson *n* a broad-brimmed high-crowned felt hat

¹**stevedore** *n* a docker

²**stevedore** *vb* to handle (cargo) as a stevedore; *also* to load or unload the cargo of (a ship) in port

¹**stew** *n* **1a** a savoury dish, usu of meat and vegetables stewed and served in the same liquid **b** a mixture composed of many usu unrelated parts **2** a state of excitement, worry, or confusion – infml

²**stew** *vt* to cook (e g meat or fruit) slowly by boiling gently or simmering in liquid ~ *vi* **1** to become cooked by stewing **2** to swelter, esp from confinement in a hot atmosphere **3** to become agitated or worried; fret *USE* (*vi* 2&3) infml

¹**steward** *n* **1** one employed to look after a large household or estate **2** SHOP STEWARD **3a** one who manages the provisioning of food and attends to the needs of passengers (e g on an airliner, ship, or train) **b** one who supervises the provision and distribution of food and drink in a club, college, etc **4** an official who actively directs affairs (e g at a race meeting) – **stewardship** *n*

²**steward** *vb* to act as a steward (for)

stewardess *n* a woman who performs the duties of a steward; *esp* HOSTESS 2a

stewed *adj* **1** *of tea* bitter-tasting because allowed to infuse for too long **2** DRUNK 1 – infml

¹**stick** *n* **1a** a (dry and dead) cut or broken branch or twig **b** a cut or broken branch or piece of wood gathered esp for fuel or construction material **2a** a long slender piece of wood: e g **(1)** a club or staff used as a weapon **(2)** a walking stick **b** an implement used for striking an object in a game (e g hockey) **c** sthg used to force compliance **d** a baton symbolizing an office or dignity; a rod **3** any of

various implements resembling a stick in shape, origin, or use: e g **a** COMPOSING STICK **b** a joystick **4** sthg prepared (e g by cutting, moulding, or rolling) in a relatively long and slender often cylindrical form ⟨a ~ of toffee⟩ **5** a person of a specified type ⟨a decent old ~ – Robert Graves⟩ **6** a stick-shaped plant stalk (e g of rhubarb or celery) **7** several bombs, parachutists, etc released from an aircraft in quick succession **8** pl the wooded or rural and usu backward districts **9** a piece of furniture **10** Br hostile comment or activity ⟨gave the Local Authority plenty of ~⟩ USE (8, 9, &10) infml

²**stick** vt to provide a stick as a support for (e g a plant)

³**stick** vb stuck vt **1a** to pierce with sthg pointed; stab **b** to kill by piercing ⟨~ a pig⟩ **2a** to push or thrust so as or as if to pierce **b** to fasten in position (as if) by piercing ⟨stuck a pistol in his belt⟩ **3** to push, thrust ⟨stuck his head out of the window⟩ **4** to cover or adorn (as if) by sticking things on ⟨a crown stuck with rubies⟩ **5** to attach (as if) by causing to adhere to a surface **6a** to halt the movement or action of **b** to baffle, stump ⟨got stuck doing his maths homework⟩ **7** to put or set in a specified place or position ⟨~ your coat over there⟩ **8** to refrain from granting, giving, or allowing (sthg indignantly rejected by the speaker); stuff ⟨you can ~ the job for all I care!⟩ **9** to saddle with sthg disadvantageous or disagreeable ⟨why do I always get stuck with the gardening?⟩ **10** chiefly Br to bear, stand ⟨can't ~ his voice⟩ ~ vi **1a** to become fixed in place by means of a pointed end **b** to become fast (as if) by adhesion ⟨stuck in the mud⟩ **2a** to remain in a place, situation, or environment ⟨don't want to ~ in this job for the rest of my life⟩ **b** to hold fast or adhere resolutely; cling ⟨~ to the truth⟩ **c** to remain effective ⟨the charge will not ~⟩ **d** to keep close in a chase or competition ⟨~ing with the leaders⟩ **3** to become blocked, wedged, or jammed **4a** to hesitate, stop ⟨would ~ at nothing to get what they wanted⟩ **b** to be unable to proceed **5** to project, protrude – often + out or up USE (vt 7, 8, 9, &10) infml – **stick by** to continue to support – **stick one's neck out** to take a risk (e g by saying sthg unpopular) and make oneself vulnerable – infml – **stuck on** infatuated with ⟨he's really stuck on her⟩ – infml

⁴**stick** n adhesive quality or substance

stick around vi to stay or wait about; linger – infml

sticker n **1** sby who or sthg that pierces with a point **2a** sby who or sthg that sticks or causes sticking **b** a slip of paper with gummed back that, when moistened, sticks to a surface

sticking plaster n an adhesive plaster, esp for covering superficial wounds

stick-in-the-mud n one who dislikes and avoids change

stickleback n any of numerous small scaleless fishes that have 2 or more spines in front of the dorsal fin

stickler n one who insists on exactness or completeness in the observance of sthg ⟨a ~ for obedience⟩

stick out vi **1** to be prominent or conspicuous – often in stick out a mile, stick out like a sore thumb **2** to be persistent (e g in a demand or an opinion) – usu + for ~ vt to endure to the end – often + it

stick up vt to rob at gunpoint – infml – **stickup** n – **stick up for** to speak or act in defence of; support

sticky adj **1a** adhesive ⟨~ tape⟩ **b(1)** viscous, gluey **(2)** coated with a sticky substance ⟨~ hands⟩ **2** humid, muggy; also clammy **3a** disagreeable, unpleasant ⟨came to a ~ end⟩ **b** awkward, stiff ⟨after a ~ beginning became good friends⟩ **c** difficult, problematic ⟨a rather ~ question⟩ – **stickily** adv, **stickiness** n

sticky wicket n **1** a cricket pitch drying after rain and therefore difficult to bat on **2** a difficult situation – infml; often in on a sticky wicket

¹**stiff** adj **1a** not easily bent; rigid **b** lacking in suppleness and often painful ⟨~ muscles⟩ **c** of a mechanism impeded in movement **d** incapable of normal alert response ⟨scared ~⟩ **2a** firm, unyielding **b(1)** marked by reserve or decorum; formal **(2)** lacking in ease or grace; stilted **3** hard fought ⟨a ~ match⟩ **4a** exerting great force; forceful ⟨a ~ wind⟩ **b** potent ⟨a ~ drink⟩ **5** of a dense or glutinous consistency; thick **6a** harsh, severe ⟨a ~ penalty⟩ **b** arduous ⟨a ~ climb⟩ **7** expensive, steep ⟨paid a ~ price⟩ – **stiffen** vb, **stiffener** n, **stiffening** n, **stiffish** adj, **stiffly** adv, **stiffness** n

²**stiff** adv in a stiff manner; stiffly

³**stiff** n a corpse – slang

stiff-necked adj haughty, stubborn

¹**stifle** n the joint next above the hock in the hind leg of a quadruped (e g a horse) corresponding to the knee in human beings

²**stifle** vb stifling vt **1a** to overcome or kill by depriving of oxygen; suffocate, smother **b** to muffle ⟨~ noises⟩ **2a** to cut off (e g the voice or breath) **b** to prevent the development or expression of; check, suppress ⟨~d his anger⟩ ⟨~ a revolt⟩ ~ vi to become suffocated (as if) by lack of oxygen – **stiflingly** adv

stigma n, pl stigmata, stigmas, **(2)** stigmata **1a** a mark of shame or discredit **b** an identifying mark or characteristic; specif a specific diagnostic sign of a disease **2** pl marks resembling the wounds of the crucified Christ, believed to be impressed on the bodies of holy or saintly people **3a** a small spot, scar, or opening on a plant or animal **b** the portion of the female part of a flower which receives the pollen grains and on which they germinate – **stigmatic** adj, **stigmatically** adv

stigmatize, -ise vt **1** to describe or identify in disparaging terms **2** to mark with the stigmata of Christ – **stigmatization** n

¹**stile** n **1** a step or set of steps for passing over a fence or wall **2** a turnstile

²**stile** n any of the vertical members in a frame or panel into which the secondary members are fitted

stiletto n, pl stilettos, stilettoes **1** a slender rodlike dagger **2** a pointed instrument for piercing holes (e g for eyelets) in leather, cloth, etc **3** Br an extremely narrow tapering high heel on a woman's shoe

¹**still** adj **1a** devoid of or abstaining from motion ⟨~ water⟩ **b** having no effervescence; not carbonated ⟨~ orange⟩ **c** of, being, or designed for taking a static photograph as contrasted with a moving picture **2a** uttering no sound; quiet **b** low in sound; subdued **3a** calm, tranquil **b** free from noise or turbulence – **stillness** n

²**still** vt **1a** to allay, calm **b** to put an end to; settle **2** to arrest the motion or noise of; quiet ⟨~ the wind⟩ ~ vi to become motionless or silent; quiet USE chiefly poetic

³**still** adv **1** as before; even at this or that time ⟨drink it while it's ~ hot⟩ **2** in spite of that; nevertheless ⟨very unpleasant; ~, we can't help it⟩ **3a** EVEN 2b ⟨a ~ more difficult problem⟩ **b** YET 1a

⁴**still** n **1** a still photograph; specif a photograph of actors or of a scene from a film **2** quiet, silence – chiefly poetic

⁵**still** n an apparatus used in distillation, esp of spirits, consisting of either the chamber in which the vaporization is carried out or the entire equipment

stillbirth n the birth of a dead infant

stillborn adj **1** dead at birth **2** failing from the start; abortive – **stillborn** n

still life n, pl still lifes a picture showing an arrangement of inanimate objects (e g fruit or flowers)

¹stilly *adv* in a calm manner

²stilly *adj* still, quiet – poetic

stilt *n pl* stilts, (2) stilts, *esp collectively* stilt **1a** either of 2 poles each with a rest or strap for the foot, that enable the user to walk along above the ground **b** any of a set of piles, posts, etc that support a building above ground or water level **2** any of various notably long-legged 3-toed wading birds related to the avocets

stilted *adj* stiffly formal and often pompous – **stiltedly** *adv*, **stiltedness** *n*

Stilton *n* a cream-enriched white cheese that has a wrinkled rind and is often blue-veined

stimulant *n* **1** sthg (e g a drug) that produces a temporary increase in the functional activity or efficiency of (a part of) an organism **2** STIMULUS 1 – **stimulant** *adj*

stimulate *vt* **1** to excite to (greater) activity **2a** to function as a physiological stimulus to **b** to arouse or affect by the action of a stimulant (e g a drug) ~ *vi* to act as a stimulant or stimulus – **stimulator** *n*, **stimulative** *adj*, **stimulation** *n*

stimulus *n, pl* **stimuli 1** sthg that rouses or incites to activity; an incentive **2** sthg (e g light) that directly influences the activity of living organisms (e g by exciting a sensory organ or evoking muscular contraction or glandular secretion)

¹sting *vb* stung *vt* **1a** to give an irritating or poisonous wound to, esp with a sting ⟨stung *by a bee*⟩ **b** to affect with sharp quick pain ⟨hail stung *their faces*⟩ **2** to cause to suffer acute mental pain ⟨stung *with remorse*⟩; *also* to incite or goad thus ⟨stung *into action*⟩ **3** to overcharge, cheat ⟨stung *by a street trader*⟩ – infml ~ *vi* **1** to use a sting; to have stings ⟨nettles ~⟩ **2** to feel a sharp burning pain – **stingingly** *adv*

²sting *n* **1a** a stinging; *specif* the thrust of a sting into the flesh **b** a wound or pain caused (as if) by stinging **2** *also* **stinger** a sharp organ of a bee, scorpion, stingray, etc that is usu connected with a poison gland or otherwise adapted to wound by piercing and injecting a poisonous secretion **3** a stinging element, force, or quality ⟨a joke with a ~ *in the tail*⟩ – **stingless** *n*

stingo *n, chiefly Br* a strong beer

stingray *n* any of numerous rays with a whiplike tail having 1 or more large sharp spines capable of inflicting severe wounds

stingy *adj* **1** mean or ungenerous in giving or spending **2** meanly scanty or small – **stingily** *adv*, **stinginess** *n*

¹stink *vi* stank, stunk; stunk **1** to emit a strong offensive smell **2** to be offensive; *also* to be in bad repute or of bad quality **3** to possess sthg to an offensive degree – usu + with ⟨he ~ s *with money*⟩ USE (except 1) infml – **stinky** *adj*

²stink *n* **1** a strong offensive smell; a stench **2** a public outcry against sthg offensive – infml

¹stinking *adj* **1** severe and unpleasant ⟨a ~ *cold*⟩ – infml **2** offensively drunk – slang

²stinking *adv* to an extreme degree ⟨got ~ *drunk*⟩ – infml

stink out *vt* **1** to cause to stink or be filled with a stench ⟨the leaking gas stank *the house* out⟩ **2** to drive out (as if) by subjecting to an offensive or suffocating smell

¹stint *vt* to restrict to a small share or allowance; be frugal with ~ *vi* to be sparing or frugal – **stinter** *n*

²stint *n* **1** restraint, limitation **2** a definite quantity or period of work assigned

³stint *n, pl* stints, *esp collectively* stint any of several small sandpipers

stipend *n* a fixed sum of money paid periodically (e g to a clergyman) as a salary or to meet expenses

¹stipendiary *adj* of or receiving a stipend

²stipendiary *n* one who receives a stipend

¹stipple *vt* stippling **1a** to paint, engrave, or draw in stipple **b** to apply (e g paint) in stipple **2** to speckle, fleck – **stippler** *n*

²stipple *n* (the effect produced by) a method of painting using small points, dots, or strokes to represent degrees of light and shade

stipulate *vt* **1** to specify as a condition or requirement of an agreement or offer ⟨~ *quality and quantity*⟩ **2** to give a guarantee of in making an agreement – **stipulator** *n* – **stipulate for** to demand as an express term in an agreement ⟨we stipulated for *marble*⟩

stipulation *n* sthg (e g a condition) stipulated – **stipulatory** *adj*

¹stir *vb* **-rr-** *vt* **1a** to cause a slight movement or change of position of ⟨the breeze ~ red *the leaves*⟩ **b** to disturb the quiet of; agitate **2a** to disturb the relative position of the particles or parts of (a fluid or semifluid), esp by a continued circular movement in order to make the composition homogeneous ⟨~ *one's tea*⟩ **b** to mix (as if) by stirring ⟨~ *pigment into paint*⟩ **3** to bestir, exert ⟨unable to ~ *himself to wash the car*⟩ **4a** to rouse to activity; produce strong feelings in ⟨the news ~ red *him to action*⟩ **b** to provoke – often + up ⟨~ *up trouble*⟩ ~ *vi* **1a** to make a slight movement **b** to begin to move (e g in waking) **2** to (begin to) be active or busy **3** to pass an implement through a substance with a circular movement – **stirrer** *n*

²stir *n* **1a** a state of disturbance, agitation, or brisk activity **b** widespread notice and discussion ⟨caused quite a ~ *in the neighbourhood*⟩ **2** a slight movement **3** a stirring movement

³stir *n* prison – slang

stirring *adj* rousing, inspiring

stirrup *n* **1** STIRRUP IRON **2** the stapes **3** a short rope by which another rope is suspended from the yard of a sailing ship for seamen to walk along

stirrup cup *n* a farewell usu alcoholic drink; *specif* one taken on horseback

stirrup iron *n* either of a pair of D-shaped metal frames that are attached by a strap to a saddle and in which the rider's feet are placed

¹stitch *n* **1** a local sharp and sudden pain, esp in the side **2a** a single in-and-out movement of a threaded needle in sewing, embroidering, or suturing **b** a portion of thread left in the material after 1 stitch **3a** a single loop of thread or yarn round a stitching implement **b** such a loop after being worked to form 1 of a series of links in a fabric **4** a series of stitches that are formed in a particular manner or constitute a complete step or design **5** a method of stitching **6** the least scrap of clothing – usu neg ⟨without a ~ *on*⟩; infml – **in stitches** in a state of uncontrollable laughter

²stitch *vt* **1** to fasten, join, or close (as if) with stitches; sew **2** to work on or decorate (as if) with stitches ~ *vi* to sew – **stitcher** *n*

stoat *n, pl* stoats, *esp collectively* stoat a European weasel with a long black-tipped tail

¹stock *n* **1** a supporting framework or structure: e g **a** *pl* the frame or timbers holding a ship during construction **b** *pl* a wooden frame with holes for the feet (and hands) in which offenders are held for public punishment **c(1)** the part to which the barrel and firing mechanism of a gun are attached **(2)** the butt (e g of a whip or fishing rod) **d** the beam of a plough to which handles, cutting blades, and mouldboard are attached **2a** the main stem of a plant or tree **b(1)** a plant (part) consisting of roots and lower trunk onto which a scion is grafted **(2)** a plant from which cuttings are taken **3** the crosspiece of an anchor **4a** the original (e g a man, race, or language) from which others derive; a source **b(1)** the descendants of an individual; family, lineage **(2)** a compound organism **c** ^{3}RACE 2, 3a **d** a group of closely related languages **5a** *sing or pl in constr* livestock **b** a store or supply accumulated (e g of raw materials or finished goods) **6a** a debt or fund due (e g from a government) for money loaned at interest; *also, Br* capital or a debt or fund which continues to bear interest but is not usually redeemable as far as the original sum is concerned **b** (preference) shares – often *pl* **7** any of a genus of plants of the mustard family with usu sweet-scented flowers **8** a wide band or scarf worn round the neck, esp by some clergymen **9a** the liquid in which meat, fish, or vegetables have been simmered that is used as a basis for soup, gravy, etc **b** raw material from which sthg is made **10a** an estimate or appraisal of sthg ⟨*take ~ of the situation*⟩ **b** the estimation in which sby or sthg is held ⟨*his ~ with the electorate remains high – Newsweek*⟩ **11** a type of brick – **in stock** in the shop and ready for delivery; ON HAND – **out of stock** having no more on hand; sold out

^{2}**stock** *vt* **1** to fit to or with a stock **2** to provide with (a) stock; supply ⟨*~ a stream with trout*⟩ **3** to procure or keep a stock of ⟨*we don't ~ that brand*⟩ *~ vi* to take in a stock – often + *up* ⟨*~ up on tinned food*⟩

^{3}**stock** *adj* **1a** kept in stock regularly ⟨*clearance sale of ~ goods*⟩ **b** regularly and widely available or supplied ⟨*dresses in all the ~ sizes*⟩ **2** used for (breeding and rearing) livestock ⟨*a ~ farm*⟩ **3** commonly used or brought forward; standard – chiefly derog ⟨*the ~ answer*⟩

^{1}**stockade** *n* **1** a line of stout posts set vertically to form a defence **2** an enclosure or pen made with posts and stakes

^{2}**stockade** *vt* to fortify or surround with a stockade

stockbreeder *n* one who breeds livestock – **stockbreeding** *n*

stockbroker *n* a broker who buys and sells securities – **stockbroking, stockbrokerage** *n*

stock car *n* a racing car having the chassis of a commercially produced assembly-line model

stock exchange *n* (a building occupied by) an association of people organized to provide an auction market among themselves for the purchase and sale of securities

stockfish *n* cod, haddock, etc dried in the open air without salt

stockinet, stockinette *n* a soft elastic usu cotton fabric used esp for bandages

stocking *n* **1** a usu knitted close-fitting often nylon covering for the foot and leg **2** an area of distinctive colour on the lower part of the leg of an animal – **stockinged** *adj*

stock-in-trade *n* **1** the equipment necessary to or used in a trade or business **2** sthg like the standard equipment of a tradesman or business ⟨*the tact and charm that are the ~ of a successful society hostess*⟩

stockist *n, Br* one (e g a retailer) who stocks goods, esp of a particular kind or brand

stockjobber *n* a stock-exchange member who deals only with brokers or other jobbers

stockman *n, Austr & NAm* one who owns or takes care of livestock

^{1}**stockpile** *n* an accumulated store; esp a reserve supply of sthg essential accumulated for use during a shortage

^{2}**stockpile** *vt* **1** to place or store in or on a stockpile **2** to accumulate a stockpile of

stockpot *n* a pot in which stock is prepared or kept

stock-still *adj* completely motionless ⟨*stood ~*⟩

stocktaking *n* **1** the checking or taking of an inventory of goods or supplies on hand (e g in a shop) **2** estimating a situation at a given moment (e g by considering past progress and resources)

stocky *adj* short, sturdy, and relatively thick in build – **stockily** *adv*, **stockiness** *n*

stockyard *n* a yard in which cattle, pigs, horses, etc are kept temporarily for slaughter, market, or shipping

stodge *n* **1** filling (starchy) food **2** turgid and unimaginative writing – *infml*

stodgy *adj* **1** of food heavy and filling **2** dull, boring ⟨*a ~ novel*⟩ – *infml* – **stodgily** *adv*, **stodginess** *n*

^{1}**stoic** *n* **1** *cap* a member of an ancient Greek or Roman school of philosophy equating happiness with knowledge and holding that wisdom consists in self-mastery and submission to natural law **2** sby apparently or professedly indifferent to pleasure or pain

^{2}**stoic, stoical** *adj* **1** *cap* (characteristic) of the Stoics or their doctrines **2** not affected by or showing passion or feeling; *esp* firmly restraining response to pain or distress ⟨*a ~ indifference to cold*⟩ – **stoically** *adv*

stoicism *n* **1** *cap* the philosophy of the Stoics **2a** indifference to pleasure or pain **b** repression of emotion

stoke *vt* **1** to poke or stir up (e g a fire); *also* to supply with fuel **2** to feed abundantly *~ vi* to stir up or tend a fire (e g in a furnace); supply a furnace with fuel

stokehold *n* a compartment containing a steamship's boilers and furnaces

stoker *n* one employed to tend a furnace, esp on a ship, and supply it with fuel

^{1}**stole** *past of* STEAL

^{2}**stole** *n* **1** an ecclesiastical vestment consisting of a long usu silk band worn traditionally over both shoulders and hanging down in front by bishops and priests, and over the left shoulder by deacons **2** a long wide strip of material worn by women usu across the shoulders, esp with evening dress

stolen *past part of* STEAL

stolid *adj* difficult to arouse emotionally or mentally; unemotional – **stolidly** *adv*, **stolidity** *n*

^{1}**stomach** *n* **1a** (a cavity in an invertebrate animal analogous to) a saclike organ formed by a widening of the alimentary canal of a vertebrate, that is between the oesophagus at the top and the duodenum at the bottom and in which the first stages of digestion occur **b** the part of the body that contains the stomach; belly, abdomen **2a** desire for food; appetite **b** inclination, desire – usu neg ⟨*had no ~ for an argument*⟩

^{2}**stomach** *vt* **1** to find palatable or digestible ⟨*can't ~ rich food*⟩ **2** to bear without protest or resentment ⟨*couldn't ~ her attitude*⟩ *USE* usu neg

stomach pump *n* a suction pump with a flexible tube for removing liquids from the stomach or injecting liquids into it

^{1}**stomp** *vi* to walk or dance with a heavy step – *infml*

^{2}**stomp** *n* a jazz dance characterized by heavy stamping

^{1}**stone** *n, pl* **stones, (3) stone** *also* **stones** **1** a concretion of earthy or mineral matter: **a(1)** a piece of this, esp one smaller than a boulder **(2)** rock **b** a piece of rock for a specified function: e g **(1)** a building or paving block **(2)** a gem **(3)** a sharpening stone **(4)** a smooth flat surface on which a printing forme is made up **c** CALCULUS 1a **2** the hard central portion of a fruit (e g a peach or date) **3** an imperial unit of weight equal to 14lb (about 6.35kg)

^{2}**stone** *vt* **1** to hurl stones at; *esp* to kill by pelting with stones **2** to face, pave, or fortify with stones **3** to remove the stones or seeds of (a fruit) **4** to rub, scour, or polish with or on a stone

^{3}**stone** *adj* (made) of stone

stone- *comb form* completely ⟨stone-*dead*⟩ ⟨stone-*cold*⟩
Stone Age *n* the first known period of prehistoric human culture characterized by the use of stone tools and weapons
stoned *adj* intoxicated by alcohol or a drug (e g marijuana) – *infml*
stone fruit *n* a fruit with a (large) stone; a drupe
stone's throw *n* a short distance
stonewall *vi, chiefly Br* **1** to bat excessively defensively and cautiously in cricket; *broadly* to behave obstructively **2** to obstruct or delay parliamentary debate – **stone-waller** *n*
stone wall *n* a wall-like resistance or obstruction (e g in politics or public affairs)
stoneware *n* opaque ceramic ware that is fired at a high temperature and is nonporous
stonework *n* masonry – **stoneworker** *n*
stony *also* **stoney** *adj* **1** containing many stones or having the nature of stone **2a** insensitive to pity or human feeling **b** showing no movement or reaction; dumb, expressionless ⟨a ~ *glance*⟩ **3** stony-broke – *infml* – **stonily** *adv*, **stoniness** *n*
stony-broke *adj, Br* completely without funds; broke – *infml*
stood *past of* STAND
¹stooge *n* **1** one who usu speaks the feed lines in a comedy duo **2** one who plays a subordinate or compliant role to another **3** *chiefly NAm* a nark; STOOL PIGEON *USE* (2&3) *infml*
²stooge *vi* **1** to act as a stooge – usu + *for* **2** to move, esp fly, aimlessly to and fro or at leisure – usu + *around* or *about USE infml*
¹stool *n* **1a** a seat usu without back or arms supported by 3 or 4 legs or a central pedestal **b** a low bench or portable support for the feet or for kneeling on **2** a discharge of faecal matter **3** (a shoot or growth from) a tree stump or plant crown from which shoots grow out
²stool *vi* to throw out shoots from a stump or crown
stool pigeon *n, chiefly NAm* sby acting as a decoy; *esp* a police informer
¹stoop *vi* **1a** to bend the body forwards and downwards, sometimes simultaneously bending the knees **b** to stand or walk with a temporary or habitual forward inclination of the head, body, or shoulders **2a** to condescend ⟨the gods ~ *to intervene in the affairs of men*⟩ **b** to lower oneself morally ⟨~ed *to spying*⟩ **3** *of a bird* to fly or dive down swiftly, usu to attack prey ~ *vt* to bend (a part of the body) forwards and downwards
²stoop *n* **1a** an act of bending the body forwards **b** a temporary or habitual forward bend of the back and shoulders **2** the descent of a bird, esp on its prey
³stoop *n, chiefly NAm* a porch, platform, entrance stairway, or small veranda at a house door
¹stop *vb* **-pp-** *vt* **1a** to close by filling or obstructing **b** to hinder or prevent the passage of ⟨~ *the flow of blood*⟩ **2a** to close up or block off (an opening) **b** to make impassable; choke, obstruct **c** to cover over or fill in (a hole or crevice) **3a** to restrain, prevent **b** to withhold; CUT OFF ⟨~ped *his wages*⟩ **4a** to cause to cease; check, suppress **b** to discontinue ⟨~ *running*⟩ **5a** to deduct or withhold (a sum due) **b** to instruct one's bank not to honour or pay ⟨~ *a cheque*⟩ **6a** to arrest the progress or motion of; cause to halt ⟨~ped *the car*⟩ **b** to beat in a boxing match by a knockout **7** to change the pitch of **a** (e g a violin string) by pressing with the finger **b** (a woodwind instrument) by closing 1 or more finger holes **c** (a French horn) by putting the hand into the bell **d** (e g a trumpet) by putting a mute into the bell **8** to get in the way of, esp so as to be wounded or killed ⟨~ped *a bullet*⟩ – *infml* ~ *vi*

1a to cease activity or operation **b** to come to an end, esp suddenly; close, finish **2a** to cease to move on; halt **b** to pause, hesitate **3a** to break one's journey – often + *off* ⟨~ped *off at Lisbon*⟩ **b** *chiefly Br* to remain ⟨~ *at home*⟩ **c** *chiefly NAm* to make a brief call; DROP IN – usu + *by* – **stoppable** *adj*
²stop *n* **1** a cessation, end ⟨soon put a ~ *to that*⟩ **2a** (a switch or handle operating) a graduated set of organ pipes of similar design and tone quality **b** a corresponding set of vibrators or reeds of a reed organ **3a** sthg that impedes, obstructs, or brings to a halt; an impediment, obstacle **b** (any of a series of markings, esp f-numbers, for setting the size of) the circular opening of an optical system (e g a camera lens) **c** sthg for arresting or limiting motion **5** stopping or being stopped **6a** a halt in a journey ⟨made a brief ~ *to refuel*⟩ **b** a stopping place ⟨a bus ~⟩ **7** a consonant in the articulation of which there is a stage (e g in the /p/ of *apt* or the /g/ of *tiger*) when the breath passage is completely closed **8** – used in telegrams and cables to indicate a full stop **9** *chiefly Br* any of several punctuation marks; *specif* FULL STOP
³stop *adj* serving or designed to stop ⟨~ *line*⟩ ⟨~ *signal*⟩
stopcock *n* a cock for stopping or regulating flow (e g of fluid through a pipe)
stopgap *n* sthg that serves as a temporary expedient; a makeshift
stop-go *adj* alternately active and inactive
stop-off *n* a stopover
stopover *n* a stop at an intermediate point in a journey
stoppage *n* **1** a deduction from pay **2** a concerted cessation of work by a group of employees that is usu more spontaneous and less serious than a strike
¹stopper *n* **1** sby or sthg that brings to a halt or causes to stop operating or functioning; a check **2** sby or sthg that closes, shuts, or fills up; *specif* sthg (e g a bung or cork) used to plug an opening
²stopper *vt* to close or secure (as if) with a stopper
stopping *adj, of a train* that stops at most intermediate stations
stop press *n* (space reserved for) late news added to a newspaper after printing has begun
stopwatch *n* a watch that can be started and stopped at will for exact timing
storage *n* **1a** (a) space for storing **b** MEMORY 4 **2a** storing or being stored (e g in a warehouse) **b** the price charged for keeping goods in storage
storage cell *n* one or a connected set of secondary cells; an accumulator
¹store *vt* **1** to supply; *esp* to provide with a store for the future ⟨~ *a ship with provisions*⟩ **2** to collect as a reserve supply ⟨~ *vegetables for winter use*⟩ – often + *up* or *away* **3** to place or leave in a location (e g a warehouse, library, or computer memory) for preservation or later use or disposal **4** to provide storage room for; hold ⟨boxes for storing *the surplus*⟩ – **storable** *adj*
²store *n* **1a** sthg stored or kept for future use **b** *pl* articles accumulated for some specific object and drawn on as needed ⟨military ~s⟩ **c** sthg accumulated **d** a source from which things may be drawn as needed; a reserve fund **2** storage – usu + *in* ⟨furniture kept in ~⟩ **3** a large quantity, supply, or number **4** a warehouse **5a** DEPARTMENT STORE **b** *chiefly NAm* SHOP 1 **6** *chiefly Br* MEMORY 4 – **in store** about to happen; imminent ⟨there's a nasty surprise in store for *you*⟩
³store *adj* of, kept in, or used for a store
storehouse *n* **1** a warehouse **2** an abundant supply or source

storekeeper *n* **1** sby who keeps and records stock (e g in a warehouse) **2** *NAm* a shopkeeper

storeroom *n* a place for the storing of goods or supplies

storey, *NAm chiefly* **story** *n* (a set of rooms occupying) a horizontal division of a building

storeyed, *NAm chiefly* **storied** *adj* having a specified number of storeys ⟨a 2-storeyed *house*⟩

storied *adj* celebrated in story or history

stork *n* any of various large mostly Old World wading birds that have long stout bills and are related to the ibises and herons

¹**storm** *n* **1a** a violent disturbance of the weather marked by high winds, thunder and lightning, rain or snow, etc **b**(1) wind having a speed of 113 to 117km/h (64 to 72mph) (2) WHOLE GALE **2** a disturbed or agitated state; a sudden or violent commotion **3** a violent shower of objects (e g missiles) **4** a tumultuous outburst ⟨a ~ of *abuse*⟩ **5** a violent assault on a defended position – **by storm** (as if) by using a bold frontal movement to capture quickly

²**storm** *vi* **1a** *of wind* to blow with violence **b** to rain, hail, snow, or sleet ⟨it was ~ing *in the mountains*⟩ **2** to move in a sudden assault or attack ⟨~ed *ashore at zero hour*⟩ **3** to be in or to exhibit a violent passion; rage ⟨~ing *at the unusual delay*⟩ **4** to rush about or move impetuously, violently, or angrily ⟨the mob ~ed *through the streets*⟩ ~ *vt* to attack or take (e g a fortified place) by storm

stormbound *adj* confined or delayed by a storm or its effects

storm lantern *n, chiefly Br* HURRICANE LAMP

storm petrel *n* a small sooty black and white petrel frequenting the N Atlantic and Mediterranean

storm trooper *n* **1** a member of a Nazi party militia **2** a member of a force of shock troops

stormy *adj* marked by turmoil or fury ⟨a ~ *life*⟩ ⟨a ~ *conference*⟩ – **stormily** *adv*, **storminess** *n*

stormy petrel *n* **1** STORM PETREL **2** sby fond of strife

¹**story** *n* **1a** an account of incidents or events **b** a statement of the facts of a situation in question ⟨according to their ~⟩ **c** an anecdote; *esp* an amusing one **2a** a short fictional narrative **b** the plot of a literary work **3** a widely circulated rumour **4** a lie **5** a legend, romance **6** a news article or broadcast

²**story** *n, chiefly NAm* a storey

storybook *adj* fairy-tale

storyteller *n* **1** a relator of tales or anecdotes **2** a liar

stoup *n* **1** a large drinking mug or glass **2** a basin for holy water at the entrance of a church

¹**stout** *adj* **1** firm, resolute ⟨~ *resistance*⟩ **2** physically or materially strong: **a** sturdy, vigorous **b** staunch, enduring **c** solid, substantial **3** forceful ⟨a ~ *attack*⟩; *also* violent ⟨a ~ *wind*⟩ **4** corpulent, fat – *chiefly euph* – **stoutish** *adj*, **stoutly** *adv*, **stoutness** *n*

²**stout** *n* a dark sweet heavy-bodied beer

stouthearted *adj* courageous – **stoutheartedly** *adv*

¹**stove** *n* **1a** an enclosed appliance that burns fuel or uses electricity to provide heat chiefly for domestic purposes **b** a cooker **2** *chiefly Br* a hothouse

²**stove** *past of* STAVE

stovepipe *n* (metal) piping used as a stove chimney or to connect a stove with a flue

stow *vt* **1** to put away; store **2a** to pack away in an orderly fashion in an enclosed space **b** to fill (e g a ship's hold) with cargo **3** to cram in (e g food) – usu + *away* ⟨~ed *away a huge dinner*⟩; *infml* **4** to stop, desist – *slang*; *esp* in *stow it*

stowage *n* **1** goods in storage or to be stowed **2a** storage

capacity **b** a place for storage **3** the state of being stored

¹**stowaway** *n* sby who stows away

²**stowaway** *adj* designed to be dismantled or folded for storage ⟨~ *tables and chairs*⟩

stow away *vi* to hide oneself aboard a vehicle, esp a ship, as a means of travelling without payment or escaping from a place undetected

straddle *vb* **straddling** *vi* to stand or esp sit with the legs wide apart – *vt* **1** to stand, sit, or be astride ⟨~ *a horse*⟩ **2** to bracket (a target) with missiles (e g shells or bombs) **3** to be on land on either side of ⟨the village ~s the frontier⟩ – **straddle** *n*, **straddler** *n*

strafe *vt* to rake (e g ground troops) with fire at close range, esp with machine-gun fire from low-flying aircraft – **strafe** *n*, **strafer** *n*

straggle *vi* **straggling 1** to lag behind or stray away from the main body of sthg, esp from a line of march **2** to move or spread untidily away from the main body of sthg ⟨straggling *branches*⟩ – **straggle** *n*, **straggler** *n*

straggly *adj* loosely spread out or scattered irregularly ⟨a ~ *beard*⟩

¹**straight** *adj* **1a** free from curves, bends, angles, or irregularities ⟨~ *hair*⟩ ⟨~ *timber*⟩ ⟨a ~ *stream*⟩ **b** generated by a point moving continuously in the same direction ⟨a ~ *line*⟩ **c** of, occupying, or passing through a fielding position in front of the batsman and near the line between the wickets or its extension behind the bowler ⟨a ~ *drive*⟩ **2** direct, uninterrupted: e g **a** holding to a direct or proper course or method ⟨a ~ *thinker*⟩ **b** candid, frank ⟨gave me a ~ *answer*⟩ ⟨~ *talking*⟩ **c** coming directly from a trustworthy source ⟨a ~ *tip on the horses*⟩ **d** consecutive ⟨6 ~ *wins*⟩ **e** having the cylinders arranged in a single straight line ⟨a ~ *8-cylinder engine*⟩ **f** upright, vertical ⟨the picture isn't quite ~⟩ **3a** honest, fair ⟨~ *dealing*⟩ **b** properly ordered or arranged (e g with regard to finance) ⟨be ~ *after the end of the month*⟩ ⟨set us ~ *on that issue*⟩ **c** correct ⟨get the facts ~⟩ **4** unmixed ⟨~ *gin*⟩ **5a** not deviating from the general norm or prescribed pattern ⟨preferred acting in ~ *dramas to musicals or comedies*⟩ **b** accepted as usual, normal, or proper **6** *chiefly NAm* marked by no exceptions or deviations in support of a principle or party ⟨a ~ *ballot*⟩ **7a** conventional in opinions, habits, appearance etc **b** heterosexual *USE* (7) *infml* – **straightish** *adj*, **straightness** *n*

²**straight** *adv* **1** in a straight manner **2** without delay or hesitation; immediately ⟨~ *after breakfast*⟩

³**straight** *n* **1** sthg straight: e g **a** a straight line or arrangement **b** a straight part of sthg; *esp* HOME STRAIGHT **2** a poker hand containing 5 cards in sequence but not of the same suit **3a** a conventional person **b** a heterosexual *USE* (3) *infml*

straight and narrow *n the* way of life that is morally and legally irreproachable

straightaway *adv* without hesitation or delay; immediately

straightedge *n* a piece of wood, metal, etc with an accurate straight edge for testing surfaces and (drawing) straight lines

straighten *vb* to make or become straight – usu + *up* or *out* – **straightener** *n*

straight fight *n* a contest, esp an election contest, between 2 candidates only

straightforward *adj* **1** free from evasiveness or ambiguity; direct, candid ⟨a ~ *account*⟩ **2** presenting no hidden difficulties ⟨a perfectly ~ *problem*⟩ **3** clear-cut, precise – **straightforwardly** *adv*, **straightforwardness** *n*

straight-out *adj, NAm* **1** forthright, blunt ⟨gave him a

~ *answer*⟩ **2** outright, thoroughgoing ⟨*a* ~ *Democrat*⟩

straight up *adv, Br* truly, honestly – *infml*; used esp in asking or replying to a question ⟨*'This car's worth a good £1500.' 'Straight up?' 'Straight up.'*⟩

straightway *adv, archaic* immediately, forthwith ⟨~ *the clouds began to part*⟩

¹**strain** *n* **1a** a lineage, ancestry **b** a group of plants, animals, microorganisms, etc at a level lower than a species ⟨*a high-yielding* ~ *of winter wheat*⟩ **c** a kind, sort ⟨*discussions of a lofty* ~⟩ **2** a trace, streak ⟨*a* ~ *of fanaticism*⟩ **3** a passage of verbal or musical expression – usu pl with sing. meaning **4** the tone or manner of an utterance or of a course of action or conduct ⟨*he continued in the same* ~⟩

²**strain** *vt* **1a** to draw tight ⟨~ *the bandage over the wound*⟩ **b** to stretch to maximum extension and tautness ⟨~ *a canvas over a frame*⟩ **2a** to exert (e g oneself) to the utmost **b** to injure by overuse, misuse, or excessive pressure ⟨~ed *a muscle*⟩ **c** to cause a change of form or size in (a body) by application of external force **3** to squeeze or clasp tightly: e g **a** to hug **b** to compress painfully; constrict **4a** to cause to pass through a strainer; filter **b** to remove by straining ⟨~ *lumps out of the gravy*⟩ **5** to stretch beyond a proper limit ⟨*that story* ~s *my credulity*⟩ ~ *vi* **1a** to make (violent) efforts ⟨*has to* ~ *to reach the high notes*⟩ **b** to sustain a strain, wrench, or distortion **c** to contract the muscles forcefully in physical exertion **2** to show great resistance; resist strongly **3** to show signs of strain; continue with considerable difficulty or effort ⟨~ing *under the pressure of work*⟩

³**strain** *n* straining or being strained: e g **a** (a force, influence, or factor causing) physical or mental tension **b** excessive or difficult exertion or labour **c** a wrench, twist, or similar bodily injury resulting esp from excessive stretching of muscles or ligaments **d** the deformation of a body subjected to stress

strained *adj* **1** done or produced with excessive effort **2** subjected to considerable tension ⟨~ *relations*⟩

strainer *n* **1** a device (e g a sieve) to retain solid pieces while a liquid passes through ⟨*tea* ~⟩ **2** any of various devices for stretching or tightening sthg

¹**strait** *adj, archaic* narrow – **straitly** *adv*, **straitness** *n*

²**strait** *n* **1** a narrow passageway connecting 2 large bodies of water – often pl with sing. meaning but sing. or pl in constr **2** a situation of perplexity or distress – usu pl with sing. meaning ⟨*in dire* ~s⟩

straiten *vt* **1** to subject to severely restricting difficulties, esp of a financial kind – often in **straitened circumstances 2** *archaic* to restrict in range or scope

straitjacket, straightjacket *n* **1** a cover or outer garment of strong material used to bind the body and esp the arms closely, in restraining a violent prisoner or patient **2** sthg that restricts or confines like a straitjacket – **straitjacket** *vt*

straitlaced, *NAm also* **straightlaced** *adj* excessively strict in manners or morals

¹**strand** *n* a shore, beach

²**strand** *vt* **1** to run, drive, or cause to drift onto a shore; run aground **2** to leave in a strange or unfavourable place, esp without funds or means to depart

³**strand** *n* **1a** any of the threads, strings, or wires twisted or laid parallel to make a cord, rope, or cable **b** sthg (e g a molecular chain) resembling a strand **2** an elongated or twisted and plaited body resembling a rope ⟨*a* ~ *of pearls*⟩ **3** any of the elements interwoven in a complex whole ⟨*follow the* ~s *of the story*⟩ – **stranded** *adj*

⁴**strand** *vt* to break a strand of (a rope) accidentally

strange *adj* **1** not native to or naturally belonging in a place; of external origin, kind, or character **2a** not known, heard, or seen before **b** exciting wonder or surprise **3** lacking experience or acquaintance; unaccustomed *to* – **strangely** *adv*

stranger *n* **1a** a foreigner, alien **b** sby who is unknown or with whom one is unacquainted **2** one ignorant of or unacquainted with sby or sthg ⟨*a* ~ *to books*⟩

strangle *vb* **strangling** *vt* **1** to choke (to death) by compressing the throat; throttle **2** to suppress or hinder the rise, expression, or growth of ~ *vi* to die (as if) from being strangled – **strangler** *n*

stranglehold *n* a force or influence that prevents free movement or expression

strangulate *vt* **1** to strangle **2** to constrict or compress (a blood vessel, loop of intestine, etc) in a way that interrupts the ability to act as a passage ⟨*a* ~d *hernia*⟩ ~ *vi* to become strangulated – **strangulation** *n*

¹**strap** *n* **1** a strip of metal or a flexible material, esp leather, for holding objects together or in position **2** (the use of, or punishment with) a strip of leather for flogging ⟨*gave him the* ~⟩ – **strapping** *n*

²**strap** *vt* **-pp- 1a** to secure with or attach by means of a strap **b** to support (e g a sprained joint) with adhesive plaster **2** to beat with a strap

straphanger *n* a passenger in a train, bus, etc who has to hold a strap or handle for support while standing – **straphanging** *n*

strapping *adj* big, strong, and sturdy in build

strata *pl of* STRATUM

stratagem *n* **1** an artifice or trick for deceiving and outwitting the enemy **2** a cleverly contrived trick or scheme

strategic, strategical *adj* **1** of, marked by, or important in strategy ⟨*a* ~ *retreat*⟩ **2a** required for the conduct of war ⟨~ *materials*⟩ **b** of great importance within an integrated whole or to a planned effect **3** designed or trained to strike an enemy at the sources of its power ⟨*a* ~ *bomber*⟩ – **strategically** *adv*

strategist *n* one skilled in strategy

strategy *n* **1a**(1) the science and art of employing all the resources of a (group of) nation(s) to carry out agreed policies in peace or war **(2)** the science and art of military command exercised to meet the enemy in combat under advantageous conditions **b** a variety of or instance of the use of strategy **2a** a clever plan or method **b** the art of employing plans towards achieving a goal

stratify *vt* to form, deposit, or arrange in strata to become arranged in strata – **stratification** *n*

stratosphere *n* the upper part of the atmosphere above about 11km (7mi) in which the temperature changes little and clouds are rare – **stratospheric** *adj*

stratum *n, pl* **strata 1** a horizontal layer or series of layers of any homogeneous material: e g **a** a sheetlike mass of rock or earth deposited between beds of other rock **b** a layer of the sea or atmosphere **c** a layer of tissue **d** a layer in which archaeological remains are found on excavation **2** a socioeconomic level of society – often pl with sing. meaning ⟨*this strata of society*⟩

¹**straw** *n* **1** (a single stem of) dry stalky plant residue, specif stalks of grain after threshing, used for bedding, thatching, fodder, making hats, etc **2** a dry coarse stem, esp of a cereal grass **3a** sthg of small value or importance ⟨*she doesn't care a* ~⟩ **b** sthg too insubstantial to provide support or help ⟨*clutching at* ~s⟩ **4** a tube of paper, plastic, etc for sucking up a drink **5** pale yellow – **strawy** *adj* – **straw in the wind** a hint or apparently insignificant fact that is an indication of a coming event

²**straw** *adj* of or resembling (the colour of) straw

³**straw** *vt* to cover (as if) with straw

strawberry *n* (the juicy edible usu red fruit of) any of several white-flowered creeping plants of the rose family

strawberry mark *n* a usu red and elevated birthmark composed of small blood vessels

strawboard *n* coarse cardboard made of straw pulp and used usu for boxes and book covers

straw poll *n* an assessment made by an unofficial vote

¹stray *vi* **1** to wander from a proper place, course, or line of conduct or argument **2** to roam about without fixed direction or purpose

²stray *n* **1** a domestic animal wandering at large or lost **2** a person or animal that strays

³stray *adj* **1** having strayed; wandering, lost **2** occurring at random or sporadically ⟨*a few* ~ *hairs*⟩ **3** not serving any useful purpose; unwanted ⟨~ *light*⟩

¹streak *n* **1** a line or band of a different colour from the background **2** a sample containing microorganisms (e g bacteria) implanted in a line on a solid culture medium (e g agar jelly) for growth **3a** an inherent quality; *esp* one which is only occasionally manifested ⟨*had a mean* ~ *in him*⟩ **b** a consecutive series ⟨*on a winning* ~⟩

²streak *vt* to make streaks on or in ~ *vi* **1** to move swiftly ⟨*a jet* ~*ing across the sky*⟩ **2** to run through a public place while naked – *infml* – **streaker** *n*

streaky *adj* **1** marked with streaks **2** *of meat, esp bacon* having lines of fat and lean **3** *of a shot in cricket* hit off the edge of the bat – **streakily** *adv*, **streakiness** *n*

¹stream *n* **1a** a body of running water, esp one smaller than a river, flowing in a channel on the earth **b** a body of flowing liquid or gas **2a** a steady succession of words, events, etc **b** a continuous moving procession **3** an unbroken flow (e g of gas or particles of matter) **4** a prevailing attitude or direction of opinion – esp in *go against/with the stream* **5** *Br* a group of pupils of the same general academic ability ⟨*the A* ~⟩

²stream *vi* **1** to flow (as if) in a stream **2** to run with a fluid ⟨*her eyes* ~*ing with the cold*⟩ ⟨*walls* ~*ing with condensation*⟩ **3** to trail out at full length ⟨*hair* ~*ing in the wind*⟩ **4** to pour in large numbers in the same direction **5** *Br* to practise the division of pupils into streams ~ *vt* **1** to emit freely or in a stream **2** *Br* to divide (a school or an age-group of pupils) into streams

streamer *n* **1a** a pennant **b** a strip of coloured paper used as a party decoration **c** BANNER **2** **2** a long extension of the sun's corona visible only during a total eclipse

¹streamline *n* **1** the path of a fluid (e g air or water) relative to a solid body past which the fluid is moving smoothly without turbulence **2** a contour given to a car, aeroplane, etc so as to minimize resistance to motion through a fluid (e g air)

²streamline *vt* **1** to design or construct with a streamline **2** to make simpler, more efficient, or better integrated

streamlined *adj* **1a** having a streamline contour **b** effectively integrated; organized **2** having flowing lines

stream of consciousness *n* (a literary technique used to express) individual conscious experience considered as a continuous flow of reactions and experiences

street *n* **1** a thoroughfare, esp in a town or village, with buildings on either side ⟨*lives in a fashionable* ~⟩ **2** the part of a street reserved for vehicles – **on the street** idle, homeless, or out of a job – **on the streets** earning a living as a prostitute – **up/down one's street** suited to one's abilities or tastes

streetcar *n, NAm* a tram

streetwalker *n* a prostitute who solicits in the streets – **streetwalking** *n*

strength *n* **1** the quality of being strong; capacity for exertion or endurance **2** solidity, toughness **3a** legal, logical, or moral force **b** a strong quality or inherent asset ⟨*his* ~*s and weaknesses*⟩ **4a** degree of potency of effect or of concentration **b** intensity of light, colour, sound, or smell **5** force as measured in members ⟨*an army at full* ~⟩ **6** firmness of, or a rising tendency in, prices ⟨*stock markets were displaying remarkable drive and* ~ – *Financial Times*⟩ **7** a basis – chiefly in *on the strength of* – **strengthless** *adj* – **from strength to strength** with continuing success and progress

strengthen *vb* to make or become stronger – **strengthener** *n*

strenuous *adj* **1** vigorously active **2** requiring effort or stamina – **strenuously** *adv*, **strenuousness**, **strenuosity** *n*

streptococcus *n, pl* **streptococci** any of a genus of chiefly parasitic bacteria that occur in pairs or chains and include some that cause diseases in human beings and domestic animals – **streptococcal, streptococcic** *adj*

streptomycin *n* an antibiotic obtained from a soil bacterium and used esp in the treatment of tuberculosis

¹stress *n* **1a** the force per unit area producing or tending to produce deformation of a body; *also* the state of a body under such stress **b** (a physical or emotional factor that causes) bodily or mental tension **c** strain, pressure **2** emphasis, weight **3a** intensity of utterance given to a speech sound, syllable, or word so as to produce relative loudness **b** relative force or prominence given to a syllable in verse **c** ACCENT **2b** – **stressful** *adj*, **stressfully** *adv*, **stressless** *adj*

²stress *vt* **1** to subject to phonetic stress; accent **2** to subject to physical or mental stress **3** to lay stress on; emphasize – **stressor** *n*

¹stretch *vt* **1** to extend in a reclining position – often + *out* ⟨~*ed himself out on the carpet*⟩ **2** to extend to full length **3** to extend (oneself or one's limbs), esp so as to relieve muscular stiffness **4** to pull taut ⟨*canvas was* ~*ed on a frame*⟩ **5a** to enlarge or distend, esp by force **b** to strain ⟨~*ed his already thin patience*⟩ **6** to cause to reach (e g from one point to another or across a space) **7** to enlarge or extend beyond natural or proper limits ⟨~ *the rules*⟩ **8** to fell (as if) with a blow – often + *out*; *infml* – *vi* **1a** to extend in space; reach ⟨*broad plains* ~*ing to the sea*⟩ **b** to extend over a period of time **2** to become extended without breaking **3a** to extend one's body or limbs **b** to lie down at full length – **stretchable** *adj*, **stretchy** *adj* – **stretch a point** to go beyond what is strictly warranted in making a claim or concession – **stretch one's legs** to take a walk in order to relieve stiffness caused by prolonged sitting

²stretch *n* **1** an exercise of the understanding, imagination, etc beyond ordinary or normal limits **2** the extent to which sthg may be stretched ⟨*at full* ~⟩ **3** stretching or being stretched **4** a continuous expanse of time or space **5** the capacity for being stretched; elasticity **6** a term of imprisonment – *infml*

stretcher *n* **1** a mechanism for stretching or expanding sthg **2a** a brick or stone laid with its length parallel to the face of the wall **b** a timber or rod used, esp when horizontal, as a tie (e g a tie-beam) in a load-bearing frame (e g for a building) **3** a device, consisting of a sheet of canvas or other material stretched between 2 poles, for carrying a sick, injured, or dead person **4** a rod or bar extending between 2 legs of a chair or table

strew *vt* **strewed, strewn** **1** to spread by scattering **2** to cover (as if) with sthg scattered **3** to become dispersed over

strewth *interj* struth

stria *n, pl* **striae** **1** a minute groove on the surface of a rock, crystal, etc **2** a narrow groove, ridge, line of colours, etc, esp when one of a parallel series – **striate** *vt*, **striate**, **striated** *adj*

striation *n* **1a** being striated **b** an arrangement of striae **2** a stria

stricken *adj* afflicted or overwhelmed (as if) by disease, misfortune, or sorrow

strickle *n* **1** an instrument for levelling off measures of grain **2** a tool for sharpening scythes

strict *adj* **1a** stringent in requirement or control ⟨*under* ~ *orders*⟩ **b** severe in discipline ⟨*a* ~ *teacher*⟩ **2a** inflexibly maintained or kept to; complete ⟨~ *secrecy*⟩ **b** rigorously conforming to rules or standards **3** exact, precise ⟨*in the* ~ *sense of the word*⟩ – **strictly** *adv*, **strictness** *n*

stricture *n* **1** an abnormal narrowing of a bodily passage **2** sthg that closely restrains or limits; a restriction **3** an unfavourable criticism; a censure *USE (2&3)* usu pl with sing. meaning

¹**stride** *vb* **strode; stridden** *vi* to walk (as if) with long steps to move over or along (as if) with long steps – **strider** *n*

²**stride** *n* **1** a long step **2** an advance – often pl with sing. meaning ⟨*technology has made great* ~s⟩ **3a** (the distance covered in) an act of movement completed when the feet regain the initial relative positions **b** a state of maximum competence or capability ⟨*get into one's* ~⟩ **4** a striding gait ⟨*her loose-limbed* ~⟩ – **in one's stride** without becoming upset ⟨*took the dangers in her stride*⟩

strident *adj* characterized by harsh and discordant sound; *also* loud and obtrusive ⟨~ *slogans*⟩ – **stridence, stridency** *n*, **stridently** *adv*

stridulate *vi*, esp of crickets, grasshoppers, etc to make a shrill creaking noise by rubbing together special bodily structures – **stridulatory** *adj*, **stridulation** *n*

strife *n* bitter conflict or dissension – **strifeless** *adj*

¹**strike** *vb* **struck; struck** *also* **stricken** *vt* **1a** to strike at; hit **b** to make an attack on **c** to inflict ⟨~ *a blow*⟩ **2a** to haul down ⟨~ *a flag*⟩ **b** to dismantle (e g a stage set) **c** to take down the tents of (a camp) **3** to afflict suddenly ⟨stricken *by a heart attack*⟩ **4** to delete, cancel ⟨~ *a name from a list*⟩ **5a** to send down or out ⟨trees struck *roots deep into the soil*⟩ **b** to penetrate painfully ⟨*the news* struck *him to the heart*⟩ **6** to indicate by sounding ⟨*the clock* struck *7*⟩ **7a** *of light* to fall on **b** *of a sound* to become audible to **8** to cause suddenly to become ⟨struck *him dead*⟩ **9** to produce by stamping ⟨~ *a medal*⟩ **10a** to produce (fire) by striking **b** to cause (a match) to ignite **11a** to make a mental impact on ⟨*they were* struck *by its speed*⟩ ⟨*how does that* ~ *you?*⟩ **b** to occur suddenly to **12** to make and ratify (a bargain) **13** to produce (as if) by playing an instrument ⟨~ *a chord*⟩ ⟨~ *a gloomy note*⟩ **14a** to hook (a fish) by a sharp pull on the line **b** *of a fish* to snatch at (bait) **15** to arrive at (a balance) by computation **16** COME ACROSS ⟨~ *gold*⟩ **17** to assume (a pose) **18a** to place (a plant cutting) in a medium for growth and rooting **b** to propagate (a plant) in this manner **19** to cause (an arc) to form (e g between electrodes of an arc lamp) **20** to play or produce on keys or strings **21** *NAm* to engage in a strike against (an employer) *~vi* **1** to take a course ⟨struck *off across the field*⟩ **2a** to aim a blow to make an attack **3** to collide forcefully **4a** *of the time* to become indicated by a clock, bell, or chime ⟨*the hour had just* struck⟩ **b** to make known the time by sounding ⟨*the clock* struck⟩ **5** *of a fish* to seize bait or a lure **6** *of a plant cutting* to take root **7** to engage in a strike – **strike oil** to achieve financial success

²**strike** *n* **1** STRICKLE 1 **2** an act of striking **3** a work stoppage by a body of workers, made as a protest or to

force an employer to comply with demands **4** the direction of a horizontal line formed at the angle of intersection of an upward-sloping stratum and a horizontal plane **5** a pull on a line by a fish in striking **6** a success in finding or hitting sthg; *esp* a discovery of a valuable mineral deposit ⟨*a lucky oil* ~⟩ **7** a pitched ball in baseball that is either missed by the batter or hit outside the foul lines and that counts against him **8** the knocking down of all 10 pins with the first bowl in a frame in tenpin bowling **9** the opportunity to receive the bowling by virtue of being the batsman at the wicket towards which the bowling is being directed **10** an (air) attack on a target

strikebound *adj* subjected to a strike

strikebreaker *n* one hired to replace a striking worker

strikebreaking *n* action designed to break up a strike

strike off *vt* **1** to sever with a stroke **2** to forbid (sby) to continue in professional practice usu because of misconduct or incompetence ⟨struck *the doctor* off *for malpractice*⟩

strike out *vt* to delete *~vi* to set out vigorously ⟨struck out *towards the coast*⟩

strike pay *n* an allowance paid by a trade union to its members on strike

striker *n* **1** a games player who strikes; *esp* a soccer player whose main duty is to score goals **2** a worker on strike

strike up *vi* to begin to sing or play *~vt* **1** to cause to begin singing or playing **2** to cause to begin ⟨strike up *a conversation*⟩

striking *adj* attracting attention, esp because of unusual or impressive qualities – **strikingly** *adv*

¹**string** *n* **1** a narrow cord used to bind, fasten, or tie **2** a plant fibre (e g a leaf vein) **3a** the gut or wire cord of a musical instrument **b** a stringed instrument of an orchestra – usu pl **4a** a group of objects threaded on a string ⟨*a* ~ *of beads*⟩ **b** a set of things arranged (as if) in a sequence **c** a group of usu scattered business concerns ⟨*a* ~ *of shops*⟩ **d** the animals, persons, belonging to or used by sby **5** one who is selected (e g for a sports team) for the specified rank; *also, sing or pl in constr* a group of players so selected ⟨*usually plays for the first* ~⟩ ⟨*a second-string player*⟩ **6** a succession, sequence **7a** either of the inclined sides of a stair supporting the treads and risers **b** STRING COURSE **8** *pl* conditions or obligations attached to sthg – **stringed** *adj*, **stringless** *adj*

²**string** *vt* **strung** **1** to equip with strings **2a** to thread (as if) on a string **b** to tie, hang, or fasten with string **3** to remove the strings of ⟨~ *beans*⟩ **4** to extend or stretch like a string

³**string** *adj* made with wide meshes and usu of string ⟨~ *vest*⟩ ⟨~ *bag*⟩

string along *vi* **1** to accompany sby, esp reluctantly ⟨string along *with the crowd*⟩ **2** to agree; GO ALONG – usu + *with* *~vt* to deceive, fool ⟨string *him* along *with false promises*⟩ *USE* infml

string bean *n* a French bean or runner bean with stringy fibres on the lines of separation of the pods

string course *n* a horizontal ornamental band (e g of bricks) in a building

stringent *adj* **1** rigorous or strict, esp with regard to rules or standards **2** marked by money scarcity and credit strictness – **stringency** *n*, **stringently** *adv*

string up *vt* to hang; *specif* to kill by hanging ⟨*they* strung *him* up *from the nearest tree*⟩

stringy *adj* **1a** containing or resembling fibrous matter or string ⟨~ *hair*⟩ **b** sinewy, wiry **2** capable of being drawn out to form a string – **stringiness** *n*

¹**strip** *vb* **-pp-** *vt* **1a** to remove clothing, covering, or surface or extraneous matter from **b** to deprive of possessions, privileges, or rank **2** to remove furniture, equipment, or

accessories from **3** to press the last available milk from the teats of (esp a cow) **4a** to remove cured leaves from the stalks of (tobacco) **b** to remove the midrib from (tobacco leaves) **5** to damage the thread or teeth of (a screw, cog, etc) ~ *vi* **1** to undress **2** to perform a striptease

²**strip** *n* **1a** a long narrow piece of material **b** a long narrow area of land or water **2** LANDING STRIP **3** *Br* clothes worn by a rugby or soccer team

strip cartoon *n* a series of drawings (e g in a magazine) in narrative sequence

stripe *n* **1** a line or narrow band differing in colour or texture from the adjoining parts **2** a bar, chevron, etc of braid or embroidery worn usu on the sleeve of a uniform to indicate rank or length of service **3** *chiefly NAm* a distinct variety or sort; a type ⟨*men of the same political* ~⟩ – **striped** *adj*, **stripeless** *adj*

strip lighting *n* lighting provided by 1 or more strip lights

stripling *n* an adolescent boy

stripper *n* **1** sby who performs a striptease **2** a tool or solvent for removing sthg, esp paint

striptease *n* an act or entertainment in which a performer, esp a woman, undresses gradually in view of the audience – **stripteaser** *n*

stripy *adj* striped

strive *vi* strove *also* strived; striven, strived **1** to struggle in opposition; contend **2** to endeavour; try hard – **striver** *n*

stroboscope *n* an instrument for measuring or observing motion, esp rotation or vibration, by allowing successive views of very short duration so that the motion appears slowed or stopped: e g **a** a lamp that flashes intermittently at varying frequencies **b** a disc with marks to be viewed under intermittent light, used to set up the speed of a record player turntable – **stroboscopic** *adj*, **stroboscopically** *adv*

strode *past of* STRIDE

¹**stroke** *vt* to pass the hand over gently in 1 direction – **stroker** *n*

²**stroke** *n* **1** the act of striking; *esp* a blow with a weapon or implement **2** a single unbroken movement; *esp* one that is repeated **3** a striking of the ball in a game (e g cricket or tennis); *specif* an (attempted) striking of the ball that constitutes the scoring unit in golf **4a** an action by which sthg is done, produced, or achieved ⟨*a* ~ *of genius*⟩ **b** an unexpected occurrence ⟨*a* ~ *of luck*⟩ **5** (an attack of) sudden usu complete loss of consciousness, sensation, and voluntary motion caused by rupture, thrombosis, etc of a brain artery **6a** (the technique or mode used for) a propelling beat or movement against a resisting medium ⟨*what* — *does she swim?*⟩ ⟨*rowed a fast* ~⟩ **b** an oarsman who sits at the stern of a racing rowing boat and sets the pace for the rest of the crew **7** a vigorous or energetic effort ⟨*never does a* ~⟩ **8** (the distance of) the movement in either direction of a reciprocating mechanical part (e g a piston rod) **9** the sound of a striking clock ⟨*at the* ~ *of 12*⟩ **10** an act of stroking or caressing **11a** a mark or dash made by a single movement of an implement **b** *Br* a solidus – **at a stroke** by a single action – **off one's stroke** in a situation where one performs below a usual standard ⟨*it put him off his stroke*⟩

³**stroke** *vt* **1** to set the stroke for (a rowing crew) or for the crew of (a rowing boat) **2** to hit (a ball) with a controlled swinging blow ~ *vi* to row at a specified number of strokes a minute

stroll *vi* to walk in a leisurely or idle manner – **stroll** *n*

stroller *n*, *NAm* a pushchair

strolling *adj* going from place to place, esp in search of work ⟨~ *players*⟩

strong *adj* **1** having or marked by great physical power **2** having moral or intellectual power **3** having great resources of wealth, talent, etc ⟨*a film with a* ~ *cast*⟩ **4** of a specified number ⟨*an army ten thousand* ~⟩ **5a** striking or superior of its kind ⟨*a* ~ *resemblance*⟩ **b** effective or efficient, esp in a specified area ⟨~ *on logic*⟩ **6** forceful, cogent ⟨~ *evidence*⟩ **7a** rich in some active agent (e g a flavour or extract) ⟨~ *tea*⟩ **b** *of a colour* intense **c** *of an acid or base* ionizing to a great extent in solution **d** magnifying by refracting greatly ⟨*a* ~ *lens*⟩ **8** moving with vigour or force ⟨*a* ~ *wind*⟩ **9** ardent, zealous ⟨*a* ~ *supporter*⟩ **10** well established; firm ⟨~ *beliefs*⟩ **11** not easily upset or nauseated ⟨*a* ~ *stomach*⟩ **12** having a pungent or offensive smell or flavour **13** tending to steady or higher prices ⟨*a* ~ *market*⟩ **14** of or being a verb that forms inflections by internal vowel change (e g *drink, drank, drunk*) – **strongish** *adj*, **strongly** *adv*

strongarm *adj* using or involving undue force ⟨~ *tactics*⟩

strongbox *n* a strongly made chest for money or valuables

stronghold *n* **1** a fortified place **2a** a place of refuge or safety **b** a place dominated by a specified group ⟨*a Tory* ~⟩

strong language *n* offensive language; esp swearing

strong-minded *adj* marked by firmness and independence of judgment – **strong-mindedly** *adv*, **strong-mindedness** *n*

strongpoint *n* a small fortified defensive position

strong point *n* sthg in which one excels

strong room *n* a (fireproof and burglarproof) room for money and valuables

strontium *n* a soft bivalent metallic element of the alkaline-earth group chemically similar to calcium

strontium 90 *n* a radioactive isotope of strontium present in the fallout from nuclear explosions and hazardous because it can replace calcium in bone

¹**strop** *n* sthg, esp a leather band, for sharpening a razor

²**strop** *vt* **-pp-** to sharpen on a strop

strophe *n* **1** (the part of a chorale ode sung to accompany) a turning movement made by the classical Greek chorus **2** a rhythmic system composed of 2 or more lines repeated as a unit

stroppy *adj*, *Br* quarrelsome, obstreperous – *infml*

strove *past of* STRIVE

structural *adj* **1a** of or affecting structure **b** used in or suitable for building structures ⟨~ *steel*⟩ **c** involved in or caused by structure, esp of the economy ⟨~ *unemployment*⟩ **2** of the physical make-up of a plant or animal body – **structurally** *adv*

¹**structure** *n* **1a** sthg (e g a building) that is constructed **b** sthg organized in a definite pattern **2** manner of construction **3a** the arrangement of particles or parts in a substance or body ⟨*soil* ~⟩ ⟨*molecular* ~⟩ **b** arrangement or interrelation of elements ⟨*economic* ~⟩ – **structureless** *adj*

²**structure** *vt* to form into a structure

strudel *n* a pastry made from a thin sheet of dough rolled up with filling and baked ⟨*apple* ~⟩

¹**struggle** *vi* **struggling** **1** to make violent or strenuous efforts against opposition **2** to proceed with difficulty or great effort – **struggler** *n*

²**struggle** *n* **1** a violent effort; a determined attempt in adverse circumstances **2** a hard-fought contest

strum *vb* **-mm-** *vt* **1** to brush the fingers lightly over the strings of (a musical instrument) in playing ⟨~ *a guitar*⟩; *also* to thrum **2** to play (music) on a guitar ⟨~ *a tune*⟩ ~ *vi* to strum a stringed instrument – **strummer** *n*

strumpet *n* a prostitute

strung *past of* STRING

¹strut *vi* **-tt-** **1** to walk with a proud or erect gait **2** to walk with a pompous air; swagger – **strutter** *n*

²strut *n* **1** a structural piece designed to resist pressure in the direction of its length **2** a pompous step or walk

³strut *vt* **-tt-** to provide or stiffen with a strut

strychnine *n* a poisonous alkaloid obtained from nux vomica and related plants and used as a poison (e g for rodents) and medicinally as a stimulant to the central nervous system

¹stub *n* **1** ¹STUMP **2** **2** a short blunt part of a pencil, cigarette, etc left after a larger part has been broken off or used up **3a** a small part of a leaf or page (e g of a chequebook) left on the spine as a record of the contents of the part torn away **b** the part of a ticket returned to the user after inspection

²stub *vt* **-bb-** **1a** to grub up by the roots **b** to clear (land) by uprooting stumps **2** to extinguish (e g a cigarette) by crushing – usu + *out* **3** to strike (one's foot or toe) against an object

stubble *n* **1** the stalky remnants of plants, esp cereal grasses, which remain rooted in the soil after harvest **2** a rough growth (e g of beard) resembling stubble – **stubbly** *adj*

stubborn *adj* **1** (unreasonably) unyielding or determined **2** refractory, intractable ⟨*a ~ cold*⟩ – **stubbornly** *adv*, **stubbornness** *n*

stubby *adj* short and thick like a stub

¹stucco *n, pl* **stuccos, stuccoes** a cement or fine plaster used in the covering and decoration of walls

²stucco *vt* **stuccoes, stuccos; stuccoing; stuccoed** to coat or decorate with stucco

stuck *past of* STICK

stuck-up *adj* superciliously self-important or conceited – *infml*

¹stud *n* **1** *sing or pl in constr* a group of animals, esp horses, kept primarily for breeding **2a** a male animal, esp a stallion, kept for breeding **b** a sexually active man – *vulg* – **at stud** for breeding as a stud ⟨*retired racehorses standing* at stud⟩

²stud *n* **1** any of the smaller upright posts in the walls of a building to which panelling or laths are fastened **2a** a rivet or nail with a large head used for ornament or protection **b** a solid button with a shank or eye on the back inserted through an eyelet in a garment as a fastener or ornament **3a** a piece (e g a rod or pin) projecting from a machine and serving chiefly as a support or axis **b** a metal cleat inserted in a horseshoe or snow tyre to increase grip **4** *NAm* the height from floor to ceiling

³stud *vt* **-dd-** **1** to provide (e g a building or wall) with studs **2** to decorate, cover, or protect with studs **3** to set thickly with a number of prominent objects ⟨*sky ~ded with stars*⟩

studbook *n* an official record of the pedigree of purebred horses, dogs, etc

student *n* **1** a scholar, learner; *esp* one who attends a college or university **2** an attentive and systematic observer ⟨*a ~ of human nature*⟩

studied *adj* **1** carefully considered or prepared **2** deliberate, premeditated ⟨*~ indifference*⟩ – **studiedly** *adv*

studio *n, pl* **studios** **1a** the workroom of a painter, sculptor, or photographer **b** a place for the study of an art (e g dancing, singing, or acting) **2** a place where films are made; *also, sing or pl in constr* a film production company including its premises and employees **3** a room equipped for the production of radio or television programmes

studio couch *n* an upholstered usu backless couch that can be converted into a double bed by sliding from underneath it the frame of a single bed

studious *adj* **1** of, concerned with, or given to study **2a** marked by or suggesting serious thoughtfulness or diligence; earnest ⟨*a ~ expression on his face*⟩ **b** STUDIED **2** – **studiously** *adv*, **studiousness** *n*

¹study *n* **1** a state of deep thought or contemplation – esp in *a brown study* **2a** the application of the mind to acquiring (specific) knowledge ⟨*the ~ of Latin*⟩ **b** a careful examination or analysis of a subject **3** a room devoted to study **4** a branch of learning **5** a literary or artistic work intended as a preliminary or experimental interpretation **6** an étude

²study *vi* to engage in study ~*vt* **1** to engage in the study of ⟨*~ medicine*⟩ **2** to consider attentively or in detail

¹stuff *n* **1a** materials, supplies, or equipment used in various activities ⟨*the plumber brought his ~*⟩ **b** personal property; possessions **2** a finished textile suitable for clothing; *esp* wool or worsted material **3a** an unspecified material substance ⟨*sold tons of the ~*⟩ **b** a group of miscellaneous objects ⟨*pick that ~ up off the floor*⟩ **4** the essence of a usu abstract thing ⟨*the ~ of greatness*⟩ **5a** subject matter ⟨*a teacher who knows his ~*⟩ **b** a task involving special knowledge or skill ⟨*the firemen were called on to do their ~*⟩ **6** worthless ideas, opinion, or writing; rubbish *USE* (5&6) *infml*

²stuff *vt* **1a** to fill (as if) by packing things in; cram **b** to gorge (oneself) with food **c** to fill (e g meat or vegetables) with a stuffing **d** to fill with stuffing or padding **e** to fill out the skin of (an animal) for mounting **f** to stop up (a hole); plug **2** to choke or block *up* (the nasal passages) **3** to force into a limited space; thrust **4** *Br, of a male* to have sexual intercourse with – *vulg* – **stuffer** *n*

stuffed shirt *n* a smug, pompous, and usu reactionary person

stuffing *n* material used to stuff sthg; *esp* a seasoned mixture used to stuff meat, eggs, etc

stuffy *adj* **1a** badly ventilated; close **b** stuffed up ⟨*a ~ nose*⟩ **2** stodgy, dull **3** prim, straitlaced – **stuffily** *adv*, **stuffiness** *n*

stultify *vt* to make futile or absurd – **stultification** *n*

¹stumble *vi* **stumbling** **1** to trip in walking or running **2a** to walk unsteadily or clumsily **b** to speak or act in a hesitant or faltering manner **3** to come unexpectedly or by chance – + *upon, on,* or *across* – **stumbler** *n*, **stumblingly** *adv*

²stumble *n* an act of stumbling

stumbling block *n* an obstacle to progress or understanding

¹stump *n* **1a** the part of an arm, leg, etc remaining attached to the trunk after the rest is removed **b** a rudimentary or vestigial bodily part **2** the part of a plant, esp a tree, remaining in the ground attached to the root after the stem is cut **3** a remaining part; a stub **4** any of the 3 upright wooden rods that together with the bails form the wicket in cricket

²stump *vt* **1** *of a wicketkeeper* to dismiss (a batsman who is outside his popping crease but not attempting to run) by breaking the wicket with the ball before it has touched another fieldsman **2** *NAm* to travel over (a region) making political speeches or supporting a cause **3** to baffle, bewilder – *infml* ⟨*was ~ ed by her question*⟩ ~*vi* **1** to walk heavily or noisily **2** *chiefly NAm* to travel about making political speeches

³stump *vt or n* (to treat with) a short thick roll of leather, paper, etc usu pointed at both ends and used to soften lines in a drawing

stumper *n* **1** a wicketkeeper **2** a puzzling question; a teaser

stump up *vb, chiefly Br* to pay (what is due), esp unwillingly – *infml*

stumpy adj short and thick; stubby

stun vt -nn- 1 to make dazed or dizzy (as if) by a blow 2 to overcome, esp with astonishment or disbelief

stung past of STING

stunk past of STINK

stunner n an unusually beautiful or attractive person or thing – infml

stunning adj strikingly beautiful or attractive – infml – **stunningly** adv

¹**stunt** vt to hinder or arrest the growth or development of – **stuntedness** n

²**stunt** n an unusual or difficult feat performed to gain publicity

stunt man, fem **stunt woman** n sby employed, esp as a substitute for an actor, to perform dangerous feats

stupefy vt 1 to make groggy or insensible 2 to astonish – **stupefaction** n

stupendous adj of astonishing size or greatness; amazing, astounding – **stupendously** adv, **stupendousness** n

stupid adj 1 slow-witted, obtuse 2 dulled in feeling or perception; torpid 3 annoying, exasperating – infml ⟨this ~ torch won't work⟩ – **stupidly** adv, **stupidness, stupidity** n

stupor n a state of extreme apathy, torpor, or reduced sense or feeling (e g resulting from shock or intoxication) – **stuporous** adj

sturdy adj 1 strongly built or constituted; stout, hardy 2a having physical strength or vigour; robust b firm, resolute – **sturdily** adv, **sturdiness** n

sturgeon n any of various usu large edible fishes whose roe is made into caviar

¹**stutter** vi to speak with involuntary disruption or blocking of speech (e g by spasmodic repetition or prolongation of vocal sounds) ~ vt to say, speak, or sound (as if) with a stutter – **stutterer** n

²**stutter** n (a speech disorder involving) stuttering

¹**sty** n, pl sties also styes a pigsty

²**sty, stye, stye** n, pl sties, styes an inflamed swelling of a sebaceous gland at the margin of an eyelid

stygian adj, often cap extremely dark or gloomy – fml

¹**style** n 1a a stylus b a prolongation of a plant ovary bearing a stigma at the top c a slender elongated part (e g a bristle) on an animal 2a a manner of expressing thought in language, esp where characteristic of an individual, period, etc b the custom or plan followed in spelling, capitalization, punctuation, and typographic arrangement and display 3 mode of address; a title 4a a distinctive or characteristic manner of doing sthg b a fashionable or elegant life-style ⟨lived in ~⟩ c excellence or distinction in social behaviour, manners, or appearance – **stylar** adj, **styleless** adj

²**style** vt 1 to designate by an identifying term; name 2 to fashion according to a particular mode – **styler** n

³**style** n a stile

¹**-style** comb form (→ adj) resembling ⟨leather-style briefcase⟩

²**-style** comb form (→ adv) in the style or manner of ⟨seated on the floor Indian-style⟩

stylish adj fashionably elegant – **stylishly** adv, **stylishness** n

stylist n 1 a writer who cultivates a fine literary style 2 one who develops, designs, or advises on styles

stylistic adj of esp literary or artistic style – **stylistically** adv

stylistics n pl but sing or pl in constr the study of style, esp in literature

stylize, -ise vt to make (e g a work of art) conform to a conventional style rather than to nature – **stylization** n

stylus n, pl styli, styluses an instrument for writing, marking, incising, or following a groove: e g a an instrument used by the ancients for writing on clay or waxed tablets b a tiny piece of material (e g diamond) with a rounded tip used in a gramophone to follow the groove on a record

¹**stymie** n a condition on a golf green where a ball nearer the hole lies in the line of play of another ball

²**stymie** vt to present an obstacle to; thwart

styptic adj tending to contract, bind, or check bleeding; astringent – **styptic** n

styrene n a liquid unsaturated hydrocarbon used chiefly in making rubber, plastics, etc

suave adj smoothly though often superficially affable and polite – **suavely** adv, **suavity** n

¹**sub** n a substitute – infml

²**sub** vb -bb- vi to act as a substitute ~ vt 1 to subedit 2 to subcontract USE infml

³**sub** n a submarine – infml

⁴**sub** n, Br 1 a small loan or advance 2 SUBSCRIPTION 2b USE infml

⁵**sub** n a subeditor – infml

sub- prefix 1 under; beneath; below ⟨subsoil⟩ ⟨submarine⟩ ⟨subabdominal⟩ 2a subordinate; secondary; next in rank below ⟨subeditor⟩ b subordinate portion of; subdivision of ⟨subcommittee⟩ ⟨subfamily⟩ ⟨subgenus⟩ ⟨subphylum⟩ ⟨suborder⟩ ⟨subkingdom⟩ c repeated or further instance of (a specified action or process) ⟨subcontract⟩ ⟨sublet⟩ 3 bearing an incomplete, partial, or inferior resemblance to; approximately ⟨subdominant⟩ ⟨sub-Victorian⟩ ⟨subliterature⟩ 4a almost; nearly ⟨suberect⟩ b adjacent to; bordering on ⟨subarctic⟩

¹**subaltern** adj low in rank or status; subordinate

²**subaltern** n sby holding a subordinate position; specif, Br a commissioned Army officer ranking below captain

subatomic adj of the inside of an atom or of particles smaller than atoms

subcommittee n a subdivision of a committee usu organized for a specific purpose

¹**subconscious** adj 1 existing in the mind but not immediately available to consciousness ⟨his ~ motive⟩ 2 imperfectly or incompletely conscious ⟨a ~ state⟩ – **subconsciously** adv, **subconsciousness** n

²**subconscious** n the mental activities below the threshold of consciousness

subcontinent n 1 a landmass (e g Greenland) of great size but smaller than any of the generally recognized continents 2 a vast subdivision of a continent; specif, often cap the Indian subcontinent – **subcontinental** adj

¹**subcontract** vt 1 to engage a third party to perform under a subcontract all or part of (work included in an original contract) 2 to undertake (work) under a subcontract ~ vi to let out or undertake work under a subcontract – **subcontractor** n

²**subcontract** n a contract between a party to an original contract and a third party; esp one to provide all or a specified part of the work or materials required in the original contract

subcutaneous adj being, living, used, or made under the skin ⟨~ fat⟩ – **subcutaneously** adv

subdivide vt to divide the parts of into more parts ~ vi to separate or become separated into subdivisions – **subdivision** n

subdue vt 1 to conquer and bring into subjection 2 to bring under control; curb ⟨~d her fears⟩ 3 to bring under cultivation 4 to reduce the intensity or degree of (e g colour) – **subduer** n

subdued adj 1 brought under control (as if) by military

conquest **2** reduced or lacking in force, intensity, or strength – **subduedly** *adv*

subeditor *n* **1** an assistant editor **2** *chiefly Br* one who edits sthg (e g newspaper copy) in preparation for printing – **subedit** *vt*, **subeditorial** *adj*

subhead, subheading *n* a subordinate caption, title, heading, or headline

subhuman *adj* less than human: e g **a** below the level expected of or suited to normal human beings **b** of animals lower than humans; *esp* anthropoid

¹**subject** *n* **1a** a vassal **b(1)** sby subject to a ruler and governed by his/her law **(2)** sby who enjoys the protection of and owes allegiance to a sovereign power or state **2a** that of which a quality, attribute, or relation may be stated **b** the entity (e g the mind or ego) that sustains or assumes the form of thought or consciousness **3a** a department of knowledge or learning **b(1)** an individual whose reactions are studied **(2)** a dead body for anatomical study and dissection **c(1)** sthg concerning which sthg is said or done ⟨*a ~ of dispute*⟩ **(2)** sby or sthg represented in a work of art **d(1)** the term of a logical proposition denoting that of which sthg is stated, denied, or predicated **(2)** the word or phrase in a sentence or clause denoting that of which sthg is predicated or asserted **e** the principal melodic phrase on which a musical composition or movement is based – **subjectless** *adj*

²**subject** *adj* **1** owing obedience or allegiance to another ⟨*~ nations*⟩ ⟨*~ to higher authority*⟩ **2a** liable or exposed to **b** having a tendency or inclination; prone to ⟨*~ to colds*⟩ **3** dependent or conditional on sthg ⟨*the plan is ~ to approval*⟩ *USE* usu + *to*

³**subject** *vt* **1** to bring under control or rule **2** to make liable; expose **3** to cause to undergo sthg *USE* usu + *to* – **subjection** *n*

subjective *adj* **1** of or being a grammatical subject **2a** relating to, determined by, or arising from the mind or self ⟨*~ reality*⟩ **b** characteristic of or belonging to reality as perceived rather than as independent of mind; phenomenal **3a** peculiar to a particular individual; personal **b** arising from conditions within the brain or sense organs and not directly caused by external stimuli ⟨*~ sensations*⟩ **c** lacking in reality or substance; illusory – **subjectively** *adv*, **subjectivize** *vt*, **subjectivity** *n*

subject matter *n* matter presented for consideration in speech, writing, or artistic form

subject to *prep* depending on; conditionally upon ⟨*~ your approval, I will go*⟩

subjoin *vt* to annex, append – *fml*

sub judice *adv* before a court; not yet judicially decided

subjugate *vt* to conquer and hold in subjection – **subjugator** *n*, **subjugation** *n*

¹**subjunctive** *adj* of or being a grammatical mood that represents the denoted act or state not as fact but as contingent or possible or viewed emotionally (e g with doubt or desire)

²**subjunctive** *n* (a verb form expressing) the subjunctive mood

¹**sublease** *n* a lease to a subtenant

²**sublease** *vt* to make or obtain a sublease of

¹**sublet** *vb* **-tt-**; **sublet** to lease or rent (all or part of a property) to a subtenant

²**sublet** *n* property for subletting

sublieutenant *n* an officer in the British navy ranking below lieutenant

sublimate *vt* **1** SUBLIME 1 **2** to divert the expression of (an instinctual desire or impulse) from a primitive form to a socially or culturally acceptable one – **sublimation** *n*

¹**sublime** *vt* **1** to cause to pass from the solid to the vapour state (and recondense to the solid form) **2** to make finer or of higher worth **~** *vi* to pass directly from the solid to the vapour state

²**sublime** *adj* **1** lofty, noble, or exalted in thought, expression, or manner **2** tending to inspire awe, usu because of elevated quality **3** outstanding as such ⟨*~ indifference*⟩ – **sublimely** *adv*, **sublimity** *n*

subliminal *adj* **1** *of a stimulus* inadequate to produce a sensation or perception **2** existing, functioning, or having effects below the level of conscious awareness ⟨*the ~ mind*⟩ ⟨*~ advertising*⟩ – **subliminally** *adv*

submachine gun *n* an automatic or semiautomatic portable rapid-firing firearm of limited range using pistol-type ammunition

¹**submarine** *adj* being, acting, or growing under water, esp in the sea ⟨*~ plants*⟩

²**submarine** *n* a vessel designed for undersea operations; *esp* a submarine warship that is typically armed with torpedoes or missiles and uses electric, diesel, or nuclear propulsion

submariner *n* a crewman of a submarine

submerge *vt* **1** to put under water **2** to cover (as if) with water; inundate **~** *vi* to go under water – **submergence** *n*

¹**submersible** *adj* capable of going under water

²**submersible** *n* sthg submersible; *esp* a vessel used for undersea exploration and construction work that is either navigable or attached to a surface ship by cable

submission *n* **1** an act of submitting sthg for consideration, inspection, etc **2** the state of being submissive, humble, or compliant **3** an act of submitting to the authority or control of another

submissive *adj* willing to submit to others – **submissively** *adv*, **submissiveness** *n*

submit *vb* **-tt-** *vt* **1a** to yield to the authority or will of another **b** to subject to a process or practice **2a** to send or commit to another for consideration, inspection, etc **b** to put forward as an opinion; suggest ⟨*we ~ that the charge is not proved*⟩ **~** *vi* **1** to yield oneself to the authority or will of another **2** to allow oneself to be subjected to sthg

subnormal *adj* **1** lower or smaller than normal **2** having less of sthg, esp intelligence, than is normal – **subnormally** *adj*, **subnormality** *n*

suborbital *adj* **1** situated beneath the orbit of the eye **2** being or involving less than 1 complete orbit ⟨*a spacecraft's ~ flight*⟩; *also* intended for suborbital flight ⟨*a ~ rocket*⟩

¹**subordinate** *adj* **1** occupying a lower class or rank; inferior **2** subject to or controlled by authority **3** *of a clause* functioning as a noun, adjective, or adverb in a complex sentence (e g the clause 'when he heard' in 'he laughed when he heard') – **subordinate** *n*, **subordinately** *adv*

²**subordinate** *vt* **1** to place in a lower order or class **2** to make subject or subservient; subdue – **subordinative** *adj*, **subordination** *n*

suborn *vt* to induce to commit perjury or another illegal act – **suborner** *n*

subplot *n* a subordinate plot in fiction or drama

¹**subpoena** *n* a writ commanding sby to appear in court

²**subpoena** *vt* **subpoenaing; subpoenaed** to serve with a subpoena

sub rosa *adv* in strict confidence; secretly

subscribe *vt* **1** to write (one's name) underneath **2a** to sign with one's own hand **b** to give a written pledge to contribute **~** *vi* **1a** to give consent or approval to sthg written by signing **b** to give money (e g to charity) **c** to pay regularly in order to receive a periodical or service **2**

to agree to purchase and pay for securities, esp of a new issue ⟨~d *for 1000 shares*⟩ **3** to feel favourably disposed *to USE* (*vi 1*) usu + *to*

subscriber *n* sby who subscribes; *specif* the owner of a telephone who pays rental and call charges

subscription *n* **1** a sum subscribed **2a** a purchase by prepayment for a certain number of issues (e g of a periodical) **b** *Br* membership fees paid regularly **3** a signature – fml

subsequent *adj* following in time or order; succeeding – **subsequently** *adv*

subservience *n* obsequious servility

subservient *adj* **1** useful in an inferior capacity; subordinate **2** obsequiously submissive – **subserviently** *adv*

subside *vi* **1** to sink or fall to the bottom; settle **2a** to descend; *esp* to sink so as to form a depression **b** *of ground* to cave in; collapse **3** to sink down; settle ⟨~d *into a chair*⟩ **4** to become quiet; abate – **subsidence** *n*

¹**subsidiary** *adj* **1** serving to assist or supplement; auxiliary **2** of secondary importance

²**subsidiary** *n* sby or sthg subsidiary; *esp* a company wholly controlled by another

subsidize, -ise *vt* to provide with a subsidy: e g **a** to purchase the assistance of by payment of a subsidy **b** to aid or promote (e g a private enterprise) with public money – **subsidizer** *n*, **subsidization** *n*

subsidy *n* a grant or gift of money (e g by a government to a person or organization, to assist an enterprise deemed advantageous to the public)

subsist *vi* **1** to have or continue in existence **2** to have the bare necessities of life; be kept alive

subsistence *n* **1** the state of subsisting **2** the minimum (e g of food and shelter) necessary to support life – **subsistent** *adj*

subsoil *n* the layer of weathered material that underlies the surface soil

subsonic *adj* **1** of, being, moving at, or using air currents moving at, a speed less than that of sound in air **2** infrasonic – **subsonically** *adv*

substance *n* **1a** a fundamental or essential part or import ⟨*the* ~ *of his argument*⟩ **b** correspondence with reality ⟨*the allegations were without* ~⟩ **2** ultimate underlying reality **3a** (a) physical material from which sthg is made ⟨*an oily* ~⟩ **b** matter of particular or definite chemical constitution **4** material possessions; property ⟨*a man of* ~⟩ – **in substance** in respect to essentials

substandard *adj* deviating from or falling short of a standard or norm: e g **a** of a quality lower than that prescribed **b** in widespread use but not accepted as linguistically correct by some

substantial *adj* **1a** having material existence; real **b** important, essential **2** ample to satisfy and nourish ⟨*a* ~ *meal*⟩ **3a** well-to-do, prosperous **b** considerable in quantity; significantly large **4** firmly constructed; solid **5** being largely but not wholly the specified thing ⟨*a* ~ *lie*⟩ – **substantial** *n*, **substantially** *adv*, **substantialize** *vb*, **substantiality** *n*

substantiate *vt* to establish (e g a statement or claim) by proof or evidence; verify – **substantiative** *adj*, **substantiation** *n*

¹**substantive** *n* a noun; *broadly* a word or phrase functioning syntactically as a noun – **substantivize** *vt*, **substantival** *adj*

²**substantive** *adj* **1** being a totally independent entity; not inferred or derived **2a** indicating or expressing existence ⟨*the* ~ *verb* to be⟩ **b** not requiring or involving a mordant ⟨*a* ~ *dyeing process*⟩ **3** relating to or functioning as a noun **4** defining rights and duties ⟨~ *law*⟩ **5** permanent

and definite rather than temporary or acting ⟨~ *rank of colonel*⟩ – **substantively** *adv*

substation *n* a subsidiary station in which (the voltage of an) electric current is transformed for use

substituent *n* an atom or group that replaces another atom or group in a molecule – **substituent** *adj*

¹**substitute** *n* sby or sthg that takes the place of another – **substitute** *adj*, **substitutive** *adj*

²**substitute** *vt* **1a** to exchange for another **b** to introduce (an atom or group) as a substituent; *also* to alter (e g a compound) by introduction of a substituent ⟨*a* ~d *benzene ring*⟩ **2** to take the place of; *also* to introduce a substitute for ⟨~d *their centre forward in the second half*⟩ ~ *vi* to serve as a substitute – **substitutable** *adj*, **substitution** *n*, **substitutional**, **substitutionary** *adj*

substratum *n*, *pl* **substrata** an underlying support; a foundation: e g **a** a matter considered as the enduring basis for all the qualities that can be perceived by the senses (e g colour) **b** a foundation, basis ⟨*his argument has a* ~ *of truth*⟩ **c** the subsoil

substructure *n* the foundation or groundwork – **substructural** *adj*

subsume *vt* to include as a member of a group or type – **subsumption** *n*

subtenant *n* sby who rents from a tenant

subtend *vt* **1a** to define in a given context by extending from one side to the other of ⟨*a hypotenuse* ~s *a right angle*⟩ ⟨*an arc* ~ed *by a chord*⟩ **b** to fix the angular extent of with respect to a fixed point ⟨*the angle* ~ed *at the eye by an object*⟩ **2** to be lower than, esp so as to embrace or enclose ⟨*a bract that* ~s *a flower*⟩

subterfuge *n* **1** deception or trickery used as a means of concealment or evasion **2** a trick or ruse

subterranean, subterraneous *adj* **1** being or operating under the surface of the earth **2** hidden or out of sight – **subterraneanly** *adv*

subtitle *n* **1** a secondary or explanatory title **2** a printed explanation (e g a fragment of dialogue or a translation) that appears on the screen during a film – **subtitle** *vt*

subtle *adj* **1a** delicate, elusive ⟨*a* ~ *fragrance*⟩ **b** difficult to understand or distinguish **2** showing keen insight and perception **3** cleverly contrived; ingenious **4** artful, cunning – **subtleness** *n*, **subtly** *adv*

subtlety *n* **1** the quality of being subtle **2** sthg subtle; *esp* a fine distinction

subtract *vt* to take away by subtraction ⟨~ *5 from 9*⟩ ~ *vi* to perform a subtraction – **subtracter** *n*

subtraction *n* the operation of finding for 2 given numbers a third number which when added to the first yields the second

subtropical *also* **subtropic** *adj* of or being the regions bordering on the tropical zone – **subtropics** *n pl*

suburb *n* **1** an outlying part of a city or large town **2** *pl* the residential area on the outskirts of a city or large town – **suburban** *adj or n*, **suburbanize** *vt*, **suburbanization** *n*

suburbanite *n* a person who lives in the suburbs

suburbia *n* (the inhabitants of) the suburbs of a city

subvention *n* the provision of assistance or financial support: e g **a** an endowment **b** a subsidy – **subventionary** *adj*

subversion *n* a systematic attempt to overthrow or undermine a government by people working secretly within the country – **subversionary** *adj*, **subversive** *adj or n*, **subversively** *adv*, **subversiveness** *n*

subvert *vt* to overthrow or undermine the power of – **subverter** *n*

subway *n* an underground way: e g **a** a passage under a street (e g for pedestrians, power cables, or water or gas mains) **b** *chiefly NAm* the underground

succeed vi **1a** to inherit sthg, esp sovereignty, rank, or title **b** to follow after another in order **2a** to have a favourable result; turn out well **b** to achieve a desired object or end – ~ vt **1** to follow (immediately) in sequence **2** to come after as heir or successor – **succeeder** n

success n **1** a favourable outcome to an undertaking **2** the attainment of wealth or fame **3** sby or sthg that succeeds ⟨he was an overnight ~⟩

successful adj **1** resulting in success ⟨a ~ experiment⟩ **2** having gained success ⟨a ~ banker⟩ – **successfully** adv, **successfulness** n

succession n **1a** the order or right of succeeding to a property, title, or throne **b** the line having such a right **2a** the act of following in order; a sequence **b** the act or process of becoming entitled to a deceased person's property or title **c** the change in the composition of an ecological system as the competing organisms respond to and modify the environment **3** sing or pl in constr a number of people or things that follow each other in sequence – **successional** adj, **successionally** adv

successive adj following one after the other in succession – **successively** adv, **successiveness** n

successor n sby or sthg that follows another; esp a person who succeeds to throne, title, or office

succinct adj clearly expressed in few words; concise – **succinctly** adv, **succinctness** n

¹succour, NAm chiefly succor n relief; also aid, help

²succour, NAm chiefly succor vt to go to the aid of (sby in need or distress)

succubus n, pl **succubi** a female demon believed to have sexual intercourse with men in their sleep

¹succulent adj **1** full of juice; juicy **2** of a plant having juicy fleshy tissues – **succulence** n, **succulently** adv

²succulent n a succulent plant (e g a cactus)

succumb vi **1** to yield or give in to **2** to die

¹such adj or adv **1a** of the kind, quality, or extent ⟨his habits are ~ that we rarely meet⟩ – used before as to introduce an example or comparison ⟨~ trees as oak or pine⟩ **b** of the same sort ⟨there's no ~ place⟩ **2** of so extreme a degree or extraordinary a nature ⟨ever ~ a lot of people⟩ ⟨in ~ a hurry⟩ – used before as to suggest that a name is unmerited ⟨we forced down the soup, ~ as it was⟩

²such pron, pl **such 1** pl such people; those ⟨~ as wish to leave may do so⟩ **2** that thing, fact, or action ⟨~ was the result⟩ **3** pl similar people or things ⟨tin and glass and ~⟩ – **as such** intrinsically considered; in him-/herself, itself, or themselves ⟨as such the gift was worth little⟩

such and such adj not named or specified – infml

¹suchlike adj of like kind; similar

²suchlike pron, pl **suchlike** a similar person or thing

¹suck vt **1a** to draw (e g liquid) into the mouth by the suction of the contracted lips and tongue **b** to eat by means of sucking movements of the lips and tongue **c** to take into the mouth as if sucking out a liquid ⟨~ed his finger⟩ **2** to draw in or up (as if) by suction ⟨plants ~ing moisture from the soil⟩ – ~ vi **1** to draw sthg in (as if) by suction; esp to draw milk from a breast or udder with the mouth **2** to make a sound associated with suction ⟨~ed at his pipe⟩ **3** to act in an obsequious manner – infml ⟨~ing up to his boss⟩

²suck n **1** the act of sucking **2** a sucking movement

¹sucker n **1a** a human infant or young animal that sucks, esp at a breast or udder; a suckling **b** a device for creating or regulating suction (e g a piston or valve in a pump) **c** a pipe or tube through which sthg is drawn by suction **d** a mouth (e g of a leech) or other animal organ adapted for sucking or sticking **e** a device, esp of rubber, that can cling to a surface by suction **2** a shoot from the roots or lower part of the stem of a plant **3** any of numerous freshwater fishes closely related to the carps and usu having thick soft lips **4a** a gullible person – infml **b** a person irresistibly attracted by sthg specified ⟨a ~ for chocolate⟩ – infml

²sucker vt to remove suckers from ⟨~ tobacco⟩ ~ vi to send out suckers

sucking adj not yet weaned; broadly very young

suckle vt **suckling 1** to give milk to from the breast or udder ⟨a mother suckling her child⟩ **2** to draw milk from the breast or udder of ⟨lambs suckling the ewes⟩

suckling n a young unweaned animal

sucrose n the disaccharide sugar obtained from sugarcane and sugar beet and occurring in most plants

suction n **1** the act of sucking **2** the action of exerting a force on a solid, liquid, or gaseous body by means of reduced air pressure over part of its surface – **suctional** adj

suction pump n a pump in which liquid is raised by suction under a retreating piston

¹sudden adj **1a** happening or coming unexpectedly ⟨a ~ shower⟩ **b** abrupt, steep **2** marked by or showing haste – **suddenly** adv, **suddenness** n

²sudden n – **all of a sudden** sooner than was expected; suddenly

suds n pl but sing or pl in constr (the lather on) soapy water – **sudsless** adj

sue vt to bring a legal action against ~ vi **1** to make a request or application – usu + for or to **2** to take legal proceedings in court – **suer** n

suede, suède n leather with a napped surface

suet n the hard fat round the kidneys and loins in beef and mutton, that yields tallow and is used in cooking

suffer vt **1** to submit to or be forced to endure **2** to undergo, experience **3** to allow, permit ⟨~ the little children to come unto me⟩ ~ vi **1** to endure pain, distress, or death **2** to sustain loss or damage **3** to be handicapped or at a disadvantage – **sufferable** adj, **sufferably** adv, **sufferer** n

sufferance n tacit permission; tolerance implied by a lack of interference or objection ⟨he was only there on ~⟩

suffering n the state of one who suffers

suffice vi to meet a need; be enough ⟨a brief note will ~⟩ ⟨~ it to say he has resigned⟩ ~ vt to be enough for

sufficiency n **1** sufficient means to meet one's needs **2** the quality of being sufficient; adequacy

sufficient adj enough to meet the needs of a situation – **sufficiently** adv

¹suffix n an affix (e g -ness in happiness) appearing at the end of a word or phrase or following a root – **suffixal** adj

²suffix vt to attach as a suffix – **suffixation** n

suffocate vt **1** to stop the breathing of (e g by asphyxiation) **2** to deprive of oxygen **3** to make uncomfortable by want of cool fresh air ~ vi **1** to become suffocated: **a** to die from being unable to breathe **b** to be uncomfortable through lack of air – **suffocatingly** adv, **suffocative** adj, **suffocation** n

suffragan adj or n (of or being) **1** a diocesan bishop subordinate to a metropolitan **2** an Anglican bishop assisting a diocesan bishop and having no right of succession

suffrage n **1** a vote given in favour of a question or in the choice of sby for an office **2** the right of voting

suffragette n a woman who advocates suffrage for her sex

suffuse vt to spread over or through, esp with a liquid or colour; permeate – **suffusion** n, **suffusive** adj

¹sugar n **1a** a sweet crystallizable material that consists (essentially) of sucrose, is colourless or white when pure tending to brown when less refined, is obtained commercially esp from sugarcane or sugar beet, and is important as a source of dietary carbohydrate and as a sweetener and preservative of other foods **b** any of a class of water-soluble carbohydrate compounds containing many hydroxyl groups that are of varying sweetness and include glucose, ribose, and sucrose 2 DEAR 1b

²sugar vt **1** to make palatable or attractive **2** to sprinkle or mix with sugar

sugar beet n a white-rooted beet grown for the sugar in its root

sugarcane n a stout tall grass widely grown in warm regions as a source of sugar

sugar-coated adj **1** covered with a hard coat of sugar **2** having its unpleasantness concealed

sugar daddy n a usu elderly man who lavishes gifts and money on a young woman in return for sex or companionship – infml

sugary adj **1** containing, resembling, or tasting of sugar **2** exaggeratedly or cloyingly sweet

suggest vt **1** to put forward as a possibility or for consideration **2a** to call to mind by thought or association; evoke **b** to indicate the presence of ⟨her look ∼ed irritation⟩ – **suggester** n

suggestible adj easily influenced by suggestion – **suggestibility** n

suggestion n **1a** the act of suggesting **b** sth suggested; a proposal **2a** indirect means (e g the natural association of ideas) to evoke ideas or feeling **b** the impressing of an idea, attitude, desired action, etc on the mind of another **3** a slight indication; a trace

suggestive adj **1a** conveying a suggestion; indicative **b** conjuring up mental associations; evocative **2** suggesting sth improper or indecent; risqué – **suggestively** adv, **suggestiveness** n

suicidal adj **1** relating to or of the nature of suicide **2** marked by an impulse to commit suicide **3a** dangerous, esp to life **b** harmful to one's own interests – **suicidally** adv

suicide n **1a** (an) act of taking one's own life intentionally **b** ruin of one's own interests ⟨political ∼⟩ **2** one who commits or attempts suicide

¹suit n **1** a legal action **2** a petition or appeal; specif courtship **3** a group of things forming a unit or constituting a collection – used chiefly with reference to armour, sails, and counters in games **4a** an outer costume of 2 or more matching pieces that are designed to be worn together **b** a costume to be worn for a specified purpose or under particular conditions **5a** all the playing cards in a pack bearing the same symbol (i e hearts, clubs, diamonds, or spades) **b** all the cards in a particular suit held by 1 player ⟨a 5-card ∼⟩ **c** the suit led ⟨follow ∼⟩

²suit vi **1** to be appropriate or satisfactory ⟨these prices don't ∼⟩ **2** to put on specially required clothing (e g a uniform or protective garb) – usu + up ∼ vt **1** to accommodate, adapt **2a** to be good for the health or well-being of **b** to be becoming to; look right with **3** to satisfy, please ⟨∼s me fine⟩ – **suit someone down to the ground** to suit sby extremely well

suitable adj appropriate, fitting – **suitableness** n, **suitably** adv, **suitability** n

suitcase n a rectangular usu rigid case with a hinged lid and a handle, used for carrying articles (e g clothes)

suite n **1** sing or pl in constr a retinue; esp the personal staff accompanying an official or dignitary on business **2a** a group of rooms occupied as a unit **b**(1) a 17th- and 18th-c instrumental musical form consisting of a series of dances (2) a modern instrumental composition in several

movements of different character **(3)** an orchestral concert arrangement in suite form of material drawn from a longer work (e g a ballet) **c** a set of matching furniture (e g a settee and 2 armchairs) for a room ⟨a 3-piece ∼⟩

suiting n fabric suitable for suits

suitor n one who courts a woman with a view to marriage

¹sulk vi to be moodily silent

²sulk n a fit of sulking – usu pl with sing. meaning

¹sulky adj sulking or given to fits of sulking – **sulkily** adv, **sulkiness** n

²sulky n a light 2-wheeled 1-horse vehicle for 1 person used esp in trotting races

sullen adj **1** silently gloomy or resentful; ill-humoured and unsociable **2** dismal, gloomy – **sullenly** adv, **sullenness** n

sully vt to mar the purity of; tarnish

sulpha drug n any of various synthetic drugs chemically related to sulphanilamide that are used to kill or inhibit the growth of bacteria

sulphate n **1** a salt or ester of sulphuric acid **2** the bivalent group or ion $SO_4{}^{2+}$ characteristic of sulphuric acid and sulphates

sulphide n a binary compound of sulphur, usu with a more electropositive element

¹sulphur n **1** a nonmetallic element chemically resembling oxygen that occurs esp as yellow crystals and is used esp in rubber vulcanization and in medicine for treating skin diseases **2** pale greenish yellow

²sulphur vt to treat with (a compound of) sulphur

sulphuret vt -tt- (NAm -t-, -tt-) to combine or impregnate with sulphur

sulphuric acid n a corrosive oily strong acid that is a vigorous oxidizing and dehydrating agent

sulphurous adj **1** of or containing (low valency) sulphur **2** resembling or coming from (burning) sulphur

sultan n a sovereign of a Muslim state – **sultanate** n

sultana n **1** a female member of a sultan's family; esp a sultan's wife **2** (the raisin of) a pale yellow seedless grape

sultry adj **1** oppressively hot and humid **2** (capable of) exciting strong sexual desire; sensual – **sultrily** adv, **sultriness** n

¹sum n **1** a (specified) amount of money **2** the whole amount; the total **3** the gist – esp in the sum and substance **4a**(1) the result of adding numbers ⟨∼ of 5 and 7 is 12⟩ (2) the limit of the sum of the first n terms of an infinite series as n increases indefinitely **b** numbers to be added; broadly a problem in arithmetic **c** UNION **3** – **in sum** briefly

²sum vt -mm- to calculate the sum of

sumach, sumac n (the dried powdered leaves and flowers, used in tanning and dyeing, of) any of a genus of trees, shrubs, and climbing plants (e g poison ivy) with feathery leaves turning to brilliant colours in the autumn and red or whitish berries

summarize, -ise vt to express as or reduce to a summary – **summarizer** n, **summarization** n

¹summary adj **1** concise but comprehensive **2a** done quickly without delay or formality **b** of or using a summary proceeding; specif tried or triable in a magistrates' court ⟨a ∼ offence⟩ – **summarily** adv

²summary n a brief account covering the main points of sth

summat pron, dial N Eng something

summation n **1** the act or process of forming a sum **2** a total **3** cumulative action or effect **4** (a) summing up of an argument – **summational** adj

¹summer n **1** the season between spring and autumn

comprising in the northern hemisphere the months of June, July, and August 2 a period of maturity 3 a year ⟨*a girl of 17* ~s⟩ – chiefly poetic

²**summer** *adj* sown in the spring and harvested in the same year as sown ⟨~ *wheat*⟩

³**summer** *vi* to pass the summer ~ *vt* to provide (e g cattle or sheep) with pasture during the summer

⁴**summer** *n* a large horizontal beam or stone used esp in building

summerhouse *n* a small building in a garden designed to provide a shady place in summer

summer school *n* a course of teaching held during the summer vacation, esp on university premises

summertime *n* the summer season

summery *adj* of, suggesting, or suitable for summer

summing-up *n* 1 a concluding summary 2 a survey of evidence given by a judge to the jury before it considers its verdict

summit *n* 1 a top; *esp* the highest point or peak 2 the topmost level attainable; the pinnacle 3 a conference of highest-level officials

summon *vt* 1 to convene, convoke 2 to command by a summons to appear in court 3 to call upon to come; SEND FOR ⟨~ *a doctor*⟩ 4 to call up or muster ⟨~ed *up his courage*⟩ – **summoner** *n*

¹**summons** *n, pl* **summonses** 1 a call or order by authority to appear at a particular place or to attend to sthg 2 a written notification warning sby to appear in court

²**summons** *vt* SUMMON 2

sump *n* 1 a pit or reservoir serving as a drain or receptacle for esp waste liquids: e g **a** a cesspool **b** *chiefly Br* the lower section of the crankcase used as a lubricating-oil reservoir in an internal-combustion engine 2 the lowest part of a mine shaft, into which water drains

sumptuary *adj* designed to regulate personal expenditures and habits ⟨~ *laws*⟩

sumptuous *adj* lavishly rich, costly, or luxurious – **sumptuously** *adv*, **sumptuousness** *n*

sum up *vt* 1 to summarize 2 to form or express a rapid appraisal of ~ *vi* to present a summary

¹**sun** *n* 1a the star nearest to the earth, round which the earth and other planets revolve **b** a star or other celestial body that emits its own light 2 the heat or light radiated from the sun – **sunless** *adj* – **under the sun** in the world; ON EARTH ⟨*he was the last person* under the sun *I expected to see*⟩

²**sun** *vb* **-nn-** to expose (e g oneself) to the rays of the sun

sunbaked *adj* baked hard by exposure to sunshine

sunbathe *vi* to expose the body to the rays of the sun or a sunlamp – **sunbathe** *n*

sunbeam *n* a ray of light from the sun

sunblind *n, chiefly Br* an awning or a shade on a window (e g a venetian blind) that gives protection from the sun's rays

sunbonnet *n* a bonnet with a wide brim framing the face and usu having a ruffle at the back to protect the neck from the sun

¹**sunburn** *vb* **sunburnt, sunburned** to burn or tan by exposure to sunlight

²**sunburn** *n* inflammation of the skin caused by overexposure to sunlight

sundae *n* an ice cream served with a topping of fruit, nuts, syrup, etc

¹**Sunday** *n* 1 the day of the week falling between Saturday and Monday, observed by Christians as a day of worship 2 a newspaper published on Sundays ⟨*further scandal in the* ~s⟩ – **Sundays** *adv*

²**Sunday** *adj* 1 of or associated with Sunday 2 amateur ⟨~ *painters*⟩ – derog

Sunday best *n sing or pl in constr* one's best clothes – infml

Sunday school *n* a class usu of religious instruction held, esp for children, on Sundays

sunder *vt* to break apart or in two; sever

sundew *n* any of a genus of bog plants with long glistening hairs on the leaves that attract and trap insects

sundial *n* an instrument to show the time of day by the shadow of a pointer on a graduated plate or cylindrical surface

sun dog *n* 1 a parhelion 2 a small nearly round halo on the parhelic circle

sundown *n* sunset

sundrenched *adj* exposed to much hot sunshine

¹**sundry** *adj* miscellaneous, various ⟨~ *articles*⟩

²**sundry** *pron pl in constr* an indeterminate number – chiefly in *all and sundry*

³**sundry** *n* 1 *pl* miscellaneous small articles or items 2 *Austr* EXTRA c

sunfish *n* a large marine bony fish with a nearly oval body, a length of up to 3m (about 10ft), and a weight of 2 tonnes (about 2 tons)

sunflower *n* any of a genus of composite plants with large yellow-rayed flower heads bearing edible seeds that are often used as animal feed and yield an edible oil

sung *past of* SING

sunglasses *n pl* glasses to protect the eyes from the sun

sunk *past of* SINK

sunken *adj* 1 submerged; *esp* lying at the bottom of a body of water 2a hollow, recessed **b** lying or constructed below the surrounding or normal level ⟨*a* ~ *bath*⟩

sunlamp *n* an electric lamp that emits esp ultraviolet light and is used esp for tanning the skin

sunlight *n* sunshine

sunlit *adj* lit (as if) by the sun

sunlounge *n, Br* a room having a large glazed area placed to admit much sunlight

sunny *adj* 1 bright with sunshine 2 cheerful, optimistic ⟨*a* ~ *disposition*⟩ 3 exposed to or warmed by the sun – **sunnily** *adv*, **sunniness** *n*

sunrise *n* (the time of) the rising of the topmost part of the sun above the horizon as a result of the rotation of the earth

sunroof *n* a motor-car roof having an opening or removable panel

sunset *n* (the time of) the descent of the topmost part of the sun below the horizon as a result of the rotation of the earth

sunshade *n* sthg used as a protection from the sun's rays: e g **a** a parasol **b** an awning

sunshine *n* 1 the sun's light or direct rays 2 a place or surface receiving the warmth and light of the sun ⟨*sat in the* ~⟩ – **sunshiny** *adj*

sunspot *n* a transient dark marking on the visible surface of the sun caused by a relatively cooler area

sunstroke *n* heatstroke caused by direct exposure to the sun

suntan *n* a browning of the skin from exposure to the sun

suntrap *n* a sheltered place that receives a large amount of sunshine

¹**sup** *vb* **-pp-** *chiefly dial* to drink (liquid) in small mouthfuls

²**sup** *n, chiefly dial* a mouthful, esp of liquid; a sip

³**sup** *vi* **-pp-** 1 to eat the evening meal 2 to make one's supper – + *on* or *off*

'super *n* **1** a superfine grade or extra large size **2** a police or other superintendent – *infml*

²super *adj* – used as a general term of approval; *infml* ⟨*a ~ time*⟩ ⟨*it was just ~*⟩

super- *prefix* **1a(1)** higher in quantity, quality, or degree than; more than ⟨super*human*⟩ **(2)** in addition; extra ⟨super*tax*⟩ **b(1)** exceeding or so as to exceed a norm ⟨super*heat*⟩ ⟨super*saturate*⟩ **(2)** to an excessive degree ⟨super*subtle*⟩ ⟨super*sensitive*⟩ **c** surpassing all or most others of its kind (e g in size or power) ⟨super*tanker*⟩ **2** situated or placed above, on, or at the top of ⟨super*lunary*⟩ ⟨super*script*⟩ **3** having (the specified atom or radical) present in an unusually large proportion ⟨super*phosphate*⟩ **4** constituting a more inclusive category of ⟨super*family*⟩ **5** superior in status, title, or position ⟨super*power*⟩

superabundant *adj* more than ample; excessive – **superabundance** *n*, **superabundantly** *adv*

superannuate *vt* **1** to make or declare obsolete or out-of-date **2** to retire on a pension, esp because of age or infirmity – **superannuation** *n*

superannuated *adj* incapacitated or disqualified for work, use, or continuance by advanced age: e g **a** obsolete **b** retired on a pension

superb *adj* **1** marked by grandeur or magnificence **2** of excellent quality ⟨*the meal was ~*⟩ – **superbly** *adv*, **superbness** *n*

supercharge *vt* **1** to charge greatly or excessively (e g with energy or tension) ⟨*~d rhetoric*⟩ **2** to supply a charge to (e g an engine) at a pressure higher than that of the surrounding atmosphere – **supercharge** *n*

supercharger *n* a device supplying fuel or air to an internal-combustion engine at a pressure higher than normal for greater efficiency

supercilious *adj* coolly disdainful – **superciliously** *adv*, **superciliousness** *n*

superconductivity *n* a complete disappearance of electrical resistance in various metals and alloys at temperatures near absolute zero – **superconducting** *adj*, **superconductive** *adj*, **superconductor** *n*

superego *n* the one of the 3 divisions of the mind in psychoanalytic theory that is only partly conscious, reflects social rules, and functions as a conscience to reward and punish

superficial *adj* **1a** of a surface **b** not penetrating below the surface ⟨*~ wounds*⟩ **2a** not thorough or profound; shallow **b** apparent rather than real ⟨*~ differences*⟩ – **superficially** *adv*, **superficialness** *n*, **superficiality** *n*

superficies *n*, *pl* **superficies 1** a surface **2** the external aspect or appearance of a thing *USE* fml

superfine *adj* **1** of extremely fine size or texture ⟨*~ toothbrush bristles*⟩ **2** esp of merchandise of high quality or grade

superfluity *n* **1** an excess; a supply exceeding what is required **2** sthg unnecessary or superfluous

superfluous *adj* exceeding what is sufficient or necessary

superhuman *adj* **1** being above the human; divine ⟨*~ beings*⟩ **2** exceeding normal human power, size, or capability ⟨*a ~ effort*⟩ – **superhumanly** *adv*, **superhumanness**, **superhumanity** *n*

superimpose *vt* to place or lay over or above sthg – **superimposable** *adj*, **superimposition** *n*

superintend *vt* to be in charge of; direct

superintendent *n* **1** one who supervises or manages sthg **2** a British police officer ranking next above a chief inspector – **superintendent** *adj*

'superior *adj* **1** situated higher up; upper **2** of higher rank or status **3** indifferent or unyielding to pain, temptation,

etc **4a** greater in quality, amount, or worth **b** excellent of its kind **5a** *of an animal or plant part* situated above or at the top of another (corresponding) part **b(1)** *of a calyx* attached to and apparently arising from the ovary **(2)** *of an ovary* free from and above a floral envelope (e g the calyx) **6** *of a planet* further from the sun than the earth is **7** thinking oneself better than others; supercilious – **superiority** *n*

²superior *n* **1** a person who is above another in rank or office; *esp* the head of a religious house or order **2** sby or sthg that surpasses another in quality or merit

'superlative *adj* **1** of or constituting the degree of grammatical comparison expressing an extreme or unsurpassed level or extent **2** surpassing all others; of the highest degree ⟨*he spoke with ~ ease*⟩ – **superlatively** *adv*, **superlativeness** *n*

²superlative *n* **1** the superlative degree or form in a language **2** an exaggerated expression, esp of praise ⟨*talked in ~s*⟩

superman *n* a person of extraordinary power or achievements – *infml*

supermarket *n* a usu large self-service retail shop selling foods and household merchandise

supernatural *adj* **1** of an order of existence or an agency (e g a god or spirit) not bound by normal laws of cause and effect **2a** departing from what is usual or normal, esp in nature **b** attributed to an invisible agent (e g a ghost or spirit) – **supernatural** *n*, **supernaturalism** *n*, **supernaturally** *adv*, **supernaturalness** *n*

supernova *n* any of the rarely observed nova outbursts in which the luminosity reaches 100 million times that of the sun

'supernumerary *adj* exceeding the usual or stated number ⟨*a ~ tooth*⟩

²supernumerary *n* **1** a person employed as an extra assistant or substitute **2** an actor employed to play a walk-on

superscription *n* words written on the surface of, outside, or above sthg else; an inscription

supersede *vt* **1** to take the place of (esp sthg inferior or outmoded) ⟨*buses ~d trams*⟩ **2** to displace in favour of another; supplant – **superseder** *n*, **supersedure** *n*, **supersession** *n*

supersonic *adj* **1** (using, produced by, or relating to waves or vibrations) having a frequency above the upper threshold of human hearing of about 20,000Hz **2** of, being, or using speeds from 1 to 5 times the speed of sound in air **3** of supersonic aircraft or missiles ⟨*the ~ age*⟩ – **supersonically** *adv*

superstition *n* **1** a belief or practice resulting from ignorance, fear of the unknown, trust in magic or chance, or a false conception of causation **2** an irrational abject attitude of mind towards the supernatural, nature, or God resulting from superstition – **superstitious** *adj*, **superstitiously** *adv*

superstructure *n* **1a** the part of a building above the ground **b** the structural part of a ship above the main deck **2** an entity or complex based on a more fundamental one – **superstructural** *adj*

supertax *n* a tax paid in addition to normal tax by people with high incomes

supervene *vi* to happen in a way that interrupts some plan or process – fml – **supervenience** *n*, **supervenient** *adj*, **supervention** *n*

supervise *vt* to superintend, oversee – **supervisor** *n*, **supervisory** *adj*, **supervision** *n*

'supine *adj* **1a** lying on the back or with the face upwards **b** marked by supination **2** mentally or morally lazy; lethargic – **supinely** *adv*, **supineness** *n*

²**supine** n a Latin verbal noun formed from the stem of the past participle

supper n **1** (the food for) a usu light evening meal or snack **2** a (fund-raising) social affair featuring a supper

supplant vt to take the place of (another), esp by force or treachery – **supplanter** n, **supplantation** n

¹**supple** adj **1** compliant, often to the point of obsequiousness **2a** capable of easily being bent or folded; pliant **b** able to perform bending or twisting movements with ease and grace; lithe – **suppleness** n, **supplely**, **supply** adv

²**supple** vb to make or become flexible or pliant

¹**supplement** n **1** sthg that completes, adds, or makes good a deficiency, or makes an addition ⟨dietary ~s⟩ **2** a part issued to update or extend a book or periodical **3** an angle or arc that when added to a given angle or arc equals 180°

²**supplement** vt to add a supplement to – **supplementer** n, **supplementation** n

supplementary adj **1** additional **2** being or relating to a supplement or an angle that is a supplement

supplementary benefit n British social-security benefit paid to those who do not qualify for unemployment benefit

suppliant adj humbly imploring or entreating – **suppliant** n, **suppliantly** adv

supplicant n or adj (a) suppliant – **supplicantly** adv

supplicate vi to beg humbly; esp to pray to God ~ vt to ask humbly and earnestly of or for – **supplicatory** adj, **supplication** n

¹**supply** vt **1** to provide for; satisfy ⟨supplies a long-felt need⟩ **2** to provide, furnish – **supplier** n

²**supply** n **1a** the quantity or amount needed or available ⟨in short ~⟩ **b** provisions, stores – usu pl with sing. meaning **2** the act of filling a want or need ⟨~ and demand⟩ **3** the quantities of goods and services offered for sale at a particular time or at one price **4** **supply, supply teacher** Br a teacher who fills a temporary vacancy

³**supply** adj of or for the raising of government revenue ⟨a ~ bill⟩

¹**support** vt **1** to bear, tolerate ⟨could not ~ such behaviour⟩ **2a**(1) to promote the interests of; encourage (2) to defend as valid or right (3) to argue or vote for ⟨~s the Labour Party⟩ **b**(1) to assist, help (2) to act with (a principal actor or actress) **c** to substantiate, corroborate **3a** to pay the costs of **b** to provide livelihood or subsistence for **4a** to hold up or serve as a foundation or prop for ⟨steel girders ~ the building⟩ **b** to maintain (a price) at a desired level by purchases or loans; also to maintain the price of by purchases or loans – **supportable** adj, **supportably** adv

²**support** n **1** supporting or being supported **2** maintenance, sustenance ⟨without visible means of ~⟩ **3** a device that supports sthg **4** sing or pl in constr a body of supporters

supporter n **1** an adherent or advocate ⟨a Chelsea ~⟩ **2** either of 2 figures (e g of men or animals) placed one on each side of a heraldic shield as if holding or guarding it

supporting adj **1** that supports ⟨a ~ wall⟩ **2** of or being a film other than the main feature on a cinema programme

supportive adj providing support; esp sustaining morale

suppose vt **1a** to lay down tentatively as a hypothesis, assumption, or proposal ⟨~ a fire broke out⟩ ⟨~ we wait a bit⟩ **b**(1) to hold as an opinion; believe (2) to think probable or in keeping with the facts (3) to conjecture, think ⟨when do you ~ he'll arrive?⟩ **2** to devise for a purpose; intend ⟨it's ~d to cure acne⟩ **3** to presuppose

4 to allow, permit – used negatively ⟨you're not ~d to go in there⟩ **5** to expect because of moral, legal, or other obligations ⟨drivers are ~d to wear seat belts⟩ **USE** (2, 4, & 5) chiefly in be supposed to – **supposable** adj

supposed adj believed or imagined to be such ⟨her ~ wealth⟩ – **supposedly** adv

supposing conj by way of hypothesis

supposition n a hypothesis – **suppositional** adj, **suppositionaly** adv, **suppositive** adj, **suppositively** adv

suppository n a readily meltable cone or cylinder of medicated material for insertion into a bodily passage or cavity (e g the rectum)

suppress vt **1** to put down by authority or force **2** to stop the publication or revelation of **3a** (deliberately) exclude a thought, feeling, etc from consciousness **b** to hold back, check ⟨~ed his impulse to laugh⟩ **4** to inhibit the growth or development of – **suppressible** adj, **suppression** n, **suppressive** adj, **suppressively** adv, **suppressibility** n

suppressor n an electrical component (e g a capacitor) added to a circuit to suppress oscillations that would otherwise cause radio interference

suppurate vi to form or discharge pus – **suppurative** adj, **suppuration** n

supranational adj transcending national boundaries or interests – **supranationalism** n, **supranationalist** n

supremacy n the state of being supreme; supreme authority, power, or position

supreme adj **1** highest in rank or authority ⟨the ~ commander⟩ **2** highest in degree or quality – **supremely** adv

Supreme Court n the highest judicial tribunal in a nation or state

sur- prefix above; over; beyond ⟨surtax⟩ ⟨surreal⟩ ⟨surface⟩

¹**surcharge** vt **1** to subject to an additional or excessive charge **2** to overprint or mark with a new denomination or surcharge

²**surcharge** n **1a** an additional tax or cost **b** an extra fare **2** surcharging or being surcharged **3** an overprint; esp one on a stamp that alters the denomination

surcoat n an outer coat or cloak; specif a loose tunic worn over armour

¹**surd** adj, of a speech sound voiceless

²**surd** n **1** an irrational root (e g √2); also an algebraic expression containing irrational roots ⟨√2 + 5i is a ~⟩ **2** a surd speech sound

¹**sure** adj **1** firm, secure **2** reliable, trustworthy **3** assured, confident ⟨felt ~ it was right⟩ **4** bound, certain ⟨it's ~ to rain⟩ – **sureness** n – **for sure** as a certainty – **to be sure** it must be acknowledged; admittedly

²**sure** adv, chiefly NAm surely, certainly – infml ⟨I ~ am tired⟩

surefire adj certain to succeed – infml

surefooted adj not liable to stumble or fall – **surefootedly** adv, **surefootedness** n

surely adv **1a** without danger; safely ⟨slowly but ~⟩ **b** without doubt; certainly **2** it is to be believed, hoped, or expected that ⟨~ you like beer⟩

surety n **1** a guarantee **2** sby who assumes legal liability for the debt, default, or failure in duty (e g appearance in court) of another – **suretyship** n

surf n the foam and swell of waves breaking on the shore

¹**surface** n **1** the external or upper boundary or layer of an object or body **2** (a portion of) the boundary of a three-dimensional object ⟨~ of a sphere⟩ **3** the external or superficial aspect of sthg – **on the surface** to all outward appearances; superficially

²**surface** *vt* to apply the surface layer to ⟨~ *a road*⟩ ~ *vi* 1 to come to the surface; emerge 2 to wake up; *also* GET UP 1a – infml ⟨*he never* ~s *before 10*⟩ – **surfacer** *n*

³**surface** *adj* 1 situated or employed on the surface, esp of the earth or sea 2 lacking depth; superficial

surfboard *n* a usu long narrow buoyant board used in surfing – **surfboard** *vi*, **surfboarder** *n*

surfboat *n* a boat for use in heavy surf

¹**surfeit** *n* 1 an excessive amount 2 excessive indulgence in food, drink, etc

²**surfeit** *vt* to fill to excess; satiate – **surfeiter** *n*

surfing *n* the activity or sport of planing on the front part of a wave, esp while standing or lying on a surfboard – **surfer** *n*

¹**surge** *vi* 1 to rise and move (as if) in waves or billows ⟨*the crowd* ~d *past her*⟩ ⟨*felt the blood* surging *to her cheeks*⟩ 2 *esp of current or voltage* to rise suddenly to an excessive or abnormal value

²**surge** *n* 1 the motion of swelling, rolling, or sweeping forwards like a wave 2 a large rolling wave or succession of waves 3 a short-lived sudden rise of current or voltage in an electrical circuit

surgeon *n* a medical specialist who practises surgery

surgery *n* 1 medicine that deals with diseases and conditions requiring or amenable to operative or manual procedures 2a the work done by a surgeon b OPERATION 3 3 *Br* (the hours of opening of) a doctor's, dentist's, etc room where patients are advised or treated 4 *Br* a session at which a member of a profession (e g a lawyer) or esp an elected representative (e g an MP) is available for usu informal consultation

surgical *adj* 1a of surgeons or surgery b used in (connection with) surgery ⟨*a* ~ *stocking*⟩ 2 following or resulting from surgery – **surgically** *adv*

surgical spirit *n*, *Br* a mixture consisting mainly of methylated spirits and used esp as a skin disinfectant

surly *adj* irritably sullen and churlish – **surlily** *adv*, **surliness** *n*

¹**surmise** *vt* to infer on scanty evidence; guess – **surmiser** *n*

²**surmise** *n* a conjecture or guess – fml

surmount *vt* 1 to overcome, conquer ⟨~ *an obstacle*⟩ 2 to get over or above 3 to stand or lie on the top of – **surmountable** *adj*

surname *n* the name shared in common by members of a family – **surname** *vt*

surpass *vt* 1 to go beyond in quality, degree, or performance; exceed 2 to transcend the reach, capacity, or powers of ⟨*her beauty* ~es *description*⟩ – **surpassable** *adj*

surpassing *adj* greatly exceeding others – **surpassingly** *adv*

surplice *n* a loose white outer ecclesiastical vestment usu of knee length with large open sleeves

surplus *n* 1a the amount in excess of what is used or needed b an excess of receipts over disbursements 2 the excess of a company's net worth over the par or stated value of its capital stock – **surplus** *adj*

¹**surprise** *n* 1 an act of taking unawares 2 sthg unexpected or surprising 3 the feeling caused by an unexpected event; astonishment

²**surprise** *vt* 1 to attack unexpectedly; *also* to capture by such action 2 to take unawares ⟨*to* ~ *someone in the act*⟩ 3 to fill with wonder or amazement – **surpriser** *n*

surprising *adj* causing surprise; unexpected – **surprisingly** *adv*

surreal *adj* 1 having a dreamlike irrational quality 2 SURREALISTIC 1

surrealism *n*, *often cap* a 20th-c movement in art and literature seeking to use the incongruous images formed

by the unconscious to transcend reality as perceived by the conscious mind; *also* surrealistic practices or atmosphere – **surrealist** *n or adj*

surrealistic *adj* 1 of surrealism 2 SURREAL 1 – **surrealistically** *adv*

¹**surrender** *vt* 1a to hand over to the power, control, or possession of another, esp under compulsion b to relinquish; GIVE UP 2 to abandon (oneself) to sthg unrestrainedly ~ *vi* to give oneself up into the power of another; yield

²**surrender** *n* 1 the act or an instance of surrendering oneself or sthg 2 the voluntary cancellation of an insurance policy by the party insured in return for a payment

surreptitious *adj* done, made, or acquired by stealth; clandestine – **surreptitiously** *adv*, **surreptitiousness** *n*

surrey *n*, *NAm* a 4-wheeled 2-seat horse-drawn carriage

surrogate *n* 1a a deputy b a local judicial officer in the USA who has jurisdiction over probate and the appointment of guardians 2 sthg that serves as a substitute

¹**surround** *vt* 1a to enclose on all sides b to be part of the environment of; be present round ⟨~ed *by luxury*⟩ c to form a ring round; encircle 2 to cause to be encircled or enclosed by sthg

²**surround** *n* a border or edging

surroundings *n pl* the circumstances, conditions, or objects by which one is surrounded

surtax *n* a graduated income tax formerly imposed in the UK in addition to the normal income tax if one's net income exceeded a specified sum

surveillance *n* close watch kept over sby or sthg – **surveillant** *n*

¹**survey** *vt* 1a to look over and examine closely b to examine the condition of and often give a value for (a building) 2 to determine and portray the form, extent, and position of (e g a tract of land) 3 to view as a whole or from a height ⟨~ed *the panorama below him*⟩

²**survey** *n* a surveying or being surveyed; *also* sthg surveyed

surveyor *n* sby whose occupation is surveying land

survival *n* 1a the condition of living or continuing ⟨*the* ~ *of the soul after death*⟩ b the continuation of life or existence ⟨*problems of* ~ *in arctic conditions*⟩ 2 sby or sthg that survives, esp after others of its kind have disappeared

survival of the fittest *n* NATURAL SELECTION

survive *vi* to remain alive or in existence; live on ⟨*managed to* ~ *on bread and water*⟩ ~ *vt* 1 to remain alive or in being after the death of ⟨*his son* ~d *him*⟩ 2 to continue to exist or live after ⟨~d *the earthquake*⟩ – **survivable** *adj*, **survivor** *n*, **survivability** *n*

susceptibility *n* 1 being susceptible 2 *pl* feelings, sensibilities 3 the ratio of the magnetization in a substance to the corresponding magnetizing force

susceptible *adj* 1 capable of submitting to an action, process, or operation 2 open, subject, or unresistant to some stimulus, influence, or agency 3 easily moved or emotionally affected; impressionable – **susceptibleness** *n*, **susceptibly** *adv*

¹**suspect** *adj* (deserving to be) regarded with suspicion

²**suspect** *n* sby who is suspected

³**suspect** *vt* 1 to be suspicious of; distrust 2 to believe to be guilty without conclusive proof 3 to imagine to be true, likely, or probable

suspend *vt* 1 to debar temporarily from a privilege, office, membership, or employment 2 to make temporarily inoperative ⟨~ *the rules*⟩ 3 to defer till later on certain conditions ⟨*a* ~ed *sentence*⟩ 4 to withhold ⟨~

judgment⟩ **5a** to hang, esp so as to be free on all sides **b** to hold immobile in a liquid or air ⟨*dust* ~ed *in the air*⟩

suspender *n* **1** an elasticated band with a fastening device for holding up a sock **2** *Br* any of the fastening devices on a suspender belt **3** *NAm* BRACE 4c – usu pl with sing. meaning

suspender belt *n*, *Br* a garment consisting of 2 pairs of short straps hanging from a belt or girdle to which are attached fastening devices for holding up a woman's stockings

suspense *n* a state of uncertain expectation as to a decision or outcome – **suspenseful** *adj*

suspension *n* **a** temporary removal from office or privileges **b** temporary withholding or postponement **c** temporary abolishing of a law or rule **d** (the sustaining of) 1 or more notes of a chord held over into the following chord producing a momentary discord **2a** hanging or being hung **b** (the state of or a system consisting of) a solid that is dispersed, but not dissolved, in a solid, liquid, or gas, usu in particles of larger than colloidal size **3** the system of devices supporting the upper part of a vehicle on the axles

suspension bridge *n* a type of bridge that has its roadway suspended from 2 or more cables

suspicion *n* **1a** suspecting or being suspected ⟨*arrested on* ~ *of spying*⟩ **b** a feeling of doubt or mistrust **2** a slight touch or trace ⟨*just a* ~ *of garlic*⟩

suspicious *adj* **1** tending to arouse suspicion; dubious **2** inclined to suspect; distrustful ⟨~ *of strangers*⟩ **3** expressing or indicating suspicion – **suspiciously** *adv*, **suspiciousness** *n*

sustain *vt* **1** to give support or relief to **2** to provide with sustenance **3** to cause to continue; prolong **4** to support the weight of **5** to buoy up the spirits of **6a** to bear up under; endure **b** to suffer, undergo **7** to allow as valid ⟨*the court* ~ed *the motion*⟩ – **sustainable** *adj*, **sustainer** *n*

sustenance *n* **1a** means of support, maintenance, or subsistence **b** food, provisions; *also* nourishment **2** sustaining

suttee *n* the custom of a Hindu widow willingly being cremated on the funeral pile of her husband; *also* such a widow

¹suture *n* **1a** (a strand or fibre used in) the sewing together of parts of the living body **b** a stitch made with a suture **2a** the solid join between 2 bones (e g of the skull) **b** a furrow at the junction of animal or plant parts – **sutural** *adj*, **suturally** *adv*

²suture *vt* to unite, close, or secure with sutures ⟨~ *a wound*⟩

suzerain *n* **1** a feudal overlord **2** a dominant state controlling the foreign relations of an internally autonomous vassal state – **suzerainty** *n*

svelte *adj* slender, lithe – **svelteness** *n*

¹swab *n* **1** a wad of absorbent material used for applying medication, cleaning wounds, taking bacterial specimens, etc **2** a specimen taken with a swab

²swab *vt* **-bb-** **1** to clean (a wound) with a swab **2** to clean (a surface, esp a deck) by washing (e g with a mop) – often + *down* – **swabber** *n*

swaddle *vt* **swaddling** **1** to wrap (an infant) in swaddling clothes **2** to swathe, envelop

swaddling clothes *n pl* narrow strips of cloth wrapped round an infant to restrict movement

¹swag *vt* **-gg-** to hang (e g tapestries or curtains) in heavy folds

²swag *n* **1a** sthg (e g a moulded decoration) hanging in a curve between 2 points **b** a suspended cluster (e g of flowers) **c** an arrangement of fabric hanging in a heavy

curve or fold **2** *chiefly Austr* a pack or roll of personal belongings **3** goods acquired, esp by unlawful means; loot – *infml*

¹swagger *vi* to behave in an arrogant or pompous manner; *esp* to walk with an air of overbearing self-confidence or self-satisfaction – **swaggerer** *n*, **swaggeringly** *adv*

²swagger *n* **1** an act or instance of swaggering **2** arrogant or conceitedly self-assured behaviour

swain *n* **1** a male admirer or suitor **2** a peasant; *specif* a shepherd – chiefly poetic

¹swallow *n* any of numerous small long-winged migratory birds noted for their graceful flight, that have a short bill, a forked tail, and feed on insects caught while flying

²swallow *vt* **1** to take through the mouth and oesophagus into the stomach **2** to envelop, engulf ⟨~ed *up by the shadows*⟩ **3** to accept without question or protest; *also* believe naively **4** to refrain from expressing or showing **5** to utter indistinctly ~ *vi* **1** to receive sthg into the body through the mouth and oesophagus **2** to perform the action of swallowing sthg, esp under emotional stress – **swallowable** *adj*, **swallower** *n*

³swallow *n* **1** an act of swallowing **2** an amount that can be swallowed at one time

swallow dive *n*, *Br* a forward dive executed with the back arched and arms spread sideways

swallowtail *n* **1** a deeply forked and tapering tail (e g of a swallow) **2** a tailcoat **3** any of various large butterflies with the hind wing lengthened to resemble a tail – **swallow-tailed** *adj*

swam *past of* SWIM

swami *n* a Hindu ascetic or religious teacher – used as a title

¹swamp *n* (an area of) wet spongy land sometimes covered with water – **swamp** *adj*, **swampy** *adj*, **swampiness** *n*

²swamp *vt* **1** to inundate, submerge **2** to overwhelm by an excess of work, difficulties, etc

¹swan *n* any of various heavy-bodied long-necked mostly pure white aquatic birds that are larger than geese and are graceful swimmers

²swan *vi* **-nn-** to wander or travel aimlessly – *infml*

swan dive *n*, *NAm* SWALLOW DIVE

¹swank *vi* to swagger, SHOW OFF – *infml*

²swank *n* (one given to) pretentiousness or swagger – *infml*

swanky *adj* **1** showy, ostentatious **2** fashionably elegant; smart *USE infml*

swansdown *n* **1** the soft downy feathers of the swan used esp as trimming on articles of dress **2** a heavy cotton flannel that has a thick nap on one face

swan song *n* **1** a song said to be sung by a dying swan **2** a farewell appearance or final work or pronouncement

¹swap *vb* **-pp-** *vt* to give in exchange; barter ~ *vi* to make an exchange ⟨~ *over to a metric system*⟩ – **swapper** *n*

²swap *n* **1** the act of exchanging one thing for another **2** sthg exchanged for another

sward *n* (a piece of ground covered with) a surface of short grass – **swarded** *adj*

swarf *n* material (e g metallic particles and abrasive fragments) removed by a cutting or grinding tool

¹swarm *n* **1a** a colony of honeybees, esp when emigrating from a hive with a queen bee to start a new colony elsewhere **b** a cluster of free-floating or free-swimming zoospores or other single-celled organisms **2** *sing or pl in constr* a group of animate or inanimate things, esp when massing together ⟨~s *of sightseers*⟩

²swarm *vi* **1** to collect together and depart from a hive **2** to move or assemble in a crowd **3** to contain a swarm; teem ⟨*streets* ~ing *with cars*⟩ – **swarmer** *n*

¹swarm *vi* to climb, esp with the hands and feet – usu + up ⟨*~ up a tree*⟩

swarthy *adj* of a dark colour, complexion, or cast – **swarthiness** *n*

swashbuckler *n* a swaggering adventurer or daredevil

swashbuckling *adj* characteristic of or behaving like a swashbuckler

swastika *n* an ancient symbol in the shape of a cross with the ends of the arms extended at right angles in a clockwise or anticlockwise direction

¹swat *vt* **-tt-** to hit with a sharp slapping blow; *esp* to kill (an insect) with such a blow

²swat *n* **1** a quick crushing blow **2** a swatter

swatch *n* a sample piece (e g of fabric)

swath *n* **1a** a row of cut grain or grass left by a scythe or mowing machine **b** the path cut in 1 passage (e g of a mower) **2** a long broad strip **3** a space cleared as if by a scythe

¹swathe *vt* **1** to bind or wrap (as if) with a bandage **2** to envelop – **swather** *n*

²swathe *n* a swath

swatter *n* a flyswatter

¹sway *vi* **1a(1)** to swing slowly and rhythmically back and forth (2) to walk in a swaying manner **b** to move gently from an upright to a leaning position **2** to fluctuate or alternate between one attitude or position and another *~ vt* **1** to cause to swing, rock, or oscillate **2a** to exert a controlling influence on **b** to change the opinions of, esp by eloquence or argument **3** to hoist in place ⟨*~ up a mast*⟩ – **swayer** *n*

²sway *n* **1** swaying or being swayed **2a** controlling influence or power ⟨*the Church held ~*⟩ **b** rule, dominion

swayback *n* (the abnormal condition, esp in horses, of having) a sagging back – **swaybacked** *adj*

swear *vb* **swore; sworn** *vt* **1** to utter or take (an oath) solemnly **2a** to assert as true or promise under oath ⟨*a sworn affidavit*⟩ **b** to promise emphatically or earnestly ⟨*she swore not to be late*⟩ **3a** to administer an oath to **b** to bind by an oath ⟨swore *him to secrecy*⟩ *~ vi* **1** to take an oath **2** to use profane or obscene language – **swearer** *n* – **swear by** to place great confidence in – **swear to** to have any positive conviction of ⟨*couldn't* swear to *his being the same man*⟩

swear in *vt* to induct into office by administration of an oath

¹sweat *vb* **sweated,** *NAm chiefly* **sweat** *vi* **1** to excrete sweat in visible quantities **2a** to emit or exude moisture ⟨*cheese ~*s *in ripening*⟩ **b** to gather surface moisture as a result of condensation **c** *esp of tobacco* FERMENT 1 **3** to undergo anxiety or tension *~ vt* **1** to (seem to) emit from pores; exude **2** to get rid of (as if) by sweating ⟨*~ out a fever*⟩ **3a** to cause (a patient) to sweat **b** to exact work from under sweatshop conditions **4** to cause to exude or lose moisture: e g **a** to subject (esp tobacco) to fermentation **b** to cook (e g vegetables) gently in melted fat until the juices run out **5** to heat (e g solder) so as to melt and cause to run, esp between surfaces to unite them; *also* to unite by such means ⟨*~ a pipe joint*⟩ – **sweat blood** to work or worry intensely

²sweat *n* **1** the fluid excreted from the sweat glands of the skin; perspiration **2** moisture gathering in drops on a surface **3a** the state of one sweating ⟨*in a cold ~*⟩ **b** a spell of sweating **4** hard work; drudgery **5** a state of anxiety or impatience *USE* (4&5) *infml* – **no sweat** not a problem or difficulty – *infml* ⟨*I can do that all right,* no sweat⟩

sweatband *n* a band of material worn round the head or wrist or inserted in a hat or cap to absorb sweat

sweated *adj* of or produced under a sweatshop system ⟨*~ labour*⟩ ⟨*~ goods*⟩

sweater *n* ²JUMPER 1

sweat gland *n* a tubular gland in the skin that secretes sweat through a minute pore on the surface of the skin

sweat out *vt* to endure or wait through the course of

sweat shirt *n* a loose collarless pullover of heavy cotton jersey

sweatshop *n* a place of work in which workers are employed for long hours at low wages and under unhealthy conditions

sweaty *adj* **1** covered with or smelling of sweat **2** causing sweat – **sweatily** *adv*, **sweatiness** *n*

swede *n* **1** *cap* a native or inhabitant of Sweden **2** a large type of turnip with edible yellow flesh

¹sweep *vb* **swept** *vt* **1a** to remove or clean (as if) by brushing **b** to destroy completely; WIPE OUT – usu + *away* **c** to remove or take with a single forceful action ⟨swept *the books off the desk*⟩ **d** to drive or carry along with irresistible force **2** to move through or along with overwhelming speed or violence ⟨*a new craze ~*ing *the country*⟩ **3** to move lightly over with a rapid continuous movement **4** to cover the entire range of ⟨*his eyes swept the horizon*⟩ **5** to play a sweep in cricket at *~ vi* **1a** to clean a surface (as if) by brushing **b** to move swiftly, forcefully, or devastatingly **2** to go with stately or sweeping movements ⟨*she swept out of the room*⟩ **3** to move or extend in a wide curve ⟨*the hills ~ down to the sea*⟩ **4** to play a sweep in cricket – **sweep someone off his/her feet** to gain immediate and unquestioning support, approval, or acceptance by sby; *esp* to cause sby to fall in love with one – **sweep the board** to win convincingly; win everything (e g in a contest)

²sweep *n* **1a** a long oar **b** a windmill sail **2** a clearing out or away (as if) with a broom **3** a military reconnaissance or attack ranging over a particular area **4a** a curving course or line **b** the compass of a sweeping movement **c** a broad extent ⟨*unbroken ~ of woodland*⟩ **5** a sweepstake **6** obliquity with respect to a reference line **7** an attacking stroke in cricket played on one knee with a horizontal bat and designed to send the ball behind the batsman on the leg side

sweeper *n* a defensive player in soccer who plays behind the backs as a last line of defence before the goalkeeper

sweeping *adj* **1** extending in a wide curve or over a wide area **2** extensive, wide-ranging ⟨*~ reforms*⟩ **b** marked by wholesale and indiscriminate inclusion – **sweepingly** *adv*, **sweepingness** *n*

sweepings *n pl* refuse, rubbish, etc collected by sweeping

sweepstake *n* **1** a race or contest in which the entire prize is awarded to the winner **2** a lottery *USE* often pl with sing. meaning but sing. or pl in constr

¹sweet *adj* **1a** being or inducing the one of the 4 basic taste sensations that is typically induced by sucrose **b** *of a beverage* containing a sweetening ingredient; not dry **2a** delightful, charming **b** marked by gentle good humour or kindliness **c** fragrant **d** pleasing to the ear or eye **3** much loved **4a** not sour, rancid, decaying, or stale **b** not salt or salted; fresh ⟨*~ butter*⟩ ⟨*~ water*⟩ **c** free from noxious gases and smells **d** free from excess of acid, sulphur, or corrosive salts ⟨*~ petroleum*⟩ – **sweetish** *adj*, **sweetly** *adv*, **sweetness** *n*

²sweet *n* **1** a darling or sweetheart **2** *Br* **a** dessert **b** a toffee, truffle, or other small piece of confectionery prepared with (flavoured or filled) chocolate or sugar; *esp* one made chiefly of (boiled and crystallized) sugar

sweet-and-sour *adj* seasoned with a sauce containing sugar and vinegar or lemon juice ⟨*~ pork*⟩

sweetbread *n* the pancreas or thymus of a young animal (e g a calf) used for food

sweetbrier *n* an Old World rose with stout prickles and white to deep rosy pink flowers

sweet corn *n* (the young kernels of) a maize with kernels that contain a high percentage of sugar and are eaten as a vegetable when young and milky

sweeten *vt* **1** to make (more) sweet **2** to soften the mood or attitude of **3** to make less painful or trying **4** to free from sthg undesirable; *esp* to remove sulphur compounds from ⟨∼ *natural gas*⟩ ∼ *vi* to become sweet – **sweetener** *n*

sweetheart *n* a darling, lover

sweetie *n* **1** SWEETIE **2** *Br* SWEET 2b *USE* infml

sweetmeat *n* a crystallized fruit, sugar-coated nut, or other sweet or delicacy rich in sugar

sweet pea *n* a leguminous garden plant with slender climbing stems and large fragrant flowers

sweet pepper *n* (a pepper plant bearing) a large mild thick-walled capsicum fruit

sweet potato *n* (the large sweet edible tuberous root of) a tropical climbing plant of the bindweed family with purplish flowers

sweet tooth *n* a craving or fondness for sweet food

sweet william *n*, *often cap W* a widely cultivated Eurasian pink with small (mottled or striped) white to deep red or purple flowers

¹**swell** *vb* **swollen, swelled** *vi* **1a** to expand gradually beyond a normal or original limit **b** to be distended or puffed up ⟨*her ankle is badly* swollen⟩ **c** to curve outwards or upwards; bulge **2** to become charged with emotion ∼ *vt* **1** to affect with a powerful emotion **2** to increase the size, number, or intensity of

²**swell** *n* **1** a rounded protuberance or bulge **2a** (massive) surge of water, often continuing beyond or after its cause (e g a gale) **3a** swelling **b**(1) a gradual increase and decrease of the loudness of a musical sound (2) a device used in an organ for governing loudness (3) *also* **swell organ** a division of an organ in which the pipes are enclosed in a box with shutters that open or shut to regulate the volume of sound **4** a person of fashion or high social position – infml

³**swell** *adj, chiefly NAm* excellent

swelling *n* **1** sthg swollen; *specif* an abnormal bodily protuberance or enlargement **2** being swollen

¹**swelter** *vi* to suffer, sweat, or be faint from heat

²**swelter** *n* a state of oppressive heat

sweltering *adj* oppressively hot – **swelteringly** *adv*

swept-back *adj* possessing sweepback

swerve *vb* to (cause to) turn aside abruptly from a straight line or course – **swerve** *n*

¹**swift** *adj* **1** (capable of) moving at great speed **2** occurring suddenly or within a very short time **3** quick to respond; ready – **swift** *adv*, **swiftly** *adv*, **swiftness** *n*

²**swift** *n* **1** any of several lizards that run swiftly **2** any of numerous dark-coloured birds noted for their fast darting flight in pursuit of insects, that superficially resemble swallows but are related to the hummingbirds and night-jars

¹**swig** *n* a quantity drunk in 1 draught – infml

²**swig** *vb* **-gg-** to drink (sthg) in long draughts – infml – **swigger** *n*

¹**swill** *vt* **1** to wash, esp by flushing with water **2** to drink greedily ∼ *vi* to drink or eat freely or greedily – **swiller** *n*

²**swill** *n* **1** a semiliquid food for animals (e g pigs) composed of edible refuse mixed with water or skimmed or sour milk **2** RUBBISH 1

¹**swim** *vb* **-mm-; swam; swum** *vi* **1** to propel oneself in water

by bodily movements (e g of the limbs, fins, or tail) **2** to surmount difficulties; not go under ⟨*sink or* ∼⟩ **3** to become immersed (as if) in a liquid ⟨*liver* ∼ *ming in gravy*⟩ **4** to have a floating or dizzy effect or sensation ∼ *vt* **1a** to cross by swimming **b** to use (a stroke) in swimming **2** to cause to swim or float – **swimmer** *n* – **swim against the tide** to move counter to the prevailing or popular trend

²**swim** *n* **1** an act or period of swimming **2a** an area frequented by fish **b** the main current of events ⟨*be in the* ∼⟩

swimming *adj* capable of, adapted to, or used in or for swimming

swimming bath *n, Br* a usu indoor swimming pool – often pl with sing. meaning but sing. or pl in constr

swimming costume *n, chiefly Br* a close-fitting usu woman's garment for swimming

swimmingly *adv* very well; splendidly – infml ⟨*everything went* ∼⟩

swimming pool *n* an artificial pool made for people to swim in

¹**swindle** *vb* **swindling** to obtain property or take property from by fraud – **swindler** *n*

²**swindle** *n* a fraud, deceit

swine *n, pl* **swine 1** PIG 1a – used esp technically or in literature **2** a contemptible person **3** sthg unpleasant ⟨*a* ∼ *of a job*⟩ *USE* (2 & 3) infml – **swinish** *adj*

swineherd *n* sby who tends pigs

¹**swing** *vb* **swung** *vt* **1a** to cause to move vigorously through a wide arc or circle **b**(1) to cause to pivot or rotate (2) to cause to face or move in another direction ⟨∼ *the car into a side road*⟩ **c** to make (a delivery of a cricket ball) swing **2** to suspend so as to allow to sway ⟨*to* ∼ *a hammock*⟩ **3** to play or sing (e g a melody) in the style of swing music **4a** to influence decisively ⟨∼ *a lot of votes*⟩ **b** to manage; BRING ABOUT ⟨*wasn't able to* ∼ *that trip to Vienna*⟩ ∼ *vi* **1a** to move freely to and fro, esp when hanging from an overhead support **b** *of a bowled ball* to deviate from a straight path while travelling through the air before reaching the batsman **2** to die by hanging **3a** to turn (as if) on a hinge or pivot ⟨*she swung on her heel*⟩ **b** to convey oneself by grasping a fixed support **4** to play or sing with a lively compelling rhythm; *specif* to play swing music **5** to shift or fluctuate between 2 moods, opinions, etc **6a** to move along rhythmically ⟨∼ *ing down the street*⟩ **b** to start up in a smooth rapid manner ⟨*ready to* ∼ *into action*⟩ **7** to engage freely in sex, specif wife-swapping – slang *USE* (*vt* 4; *vi* 2) infml – **swingable** *adj*, **swinger** *n*

²**swing** *n* **1a**(1) a stroke or blow delivered with a sweeping arm movement (2) a sweeping or rhythmic movement of the body or a bodily part **b** the regular movement of a freely suspended object to and fro along an arc **c** a steady vigorous rhythm or action ⟨*soon got into the* ∼ *of it*⟩ **d**(1) a trend towards a high or low point in a fluctuating cycle (e g of business activity) (2) a shift from one condition, form, position, or object of attention or favour to another **2** the progression of an activity; course ⟨*the work is in full* ∼⟩ **3** the arc or range through which sthg swings ⟨*a* ∼ *of 10% to Labour*⟩ **4** a suspended seat on which one may swing to and fro **5** jazz played usu by a large dance band and characterized by a steady lively rhythm, simple harmony, and a basic melody often submerged in improvisation – **swing** *adj*

swingeing, swinging *adj, chiefly Br* severe, drastic ⟨∼ *cuts in public expenditure*⟩

swinging *adj* lively and up-to-date – infml

swing-wing *adj* of or being an aircraft having movable

wings giving the best angles of sweepback for both low and high speeds

¹swipe *n* a strong sweeping blow – infml

²swipe *vi* to strike or hit out with a sweeping motion ~ *vt* 1 to strike or wipe with a sweeping motion 2 to steal, pilfer *USE* infml

¹swirl *n* 1 a whirling mass or motion 2 a twisting shape, mark, or pattern – **swirly** *adj*

²swirl *vi* to move in eddies or whirls – **swirlingly** *adv*

¹swish *vb* to move with (the sound of) a swish ⟨*windscreen wipers* ~ ing⟩ ⟨*a cow* ~ ing *its tail*⟩ – **swisher** *n*, **swishingly** *adv*

²swish *n* 1a a sound as of a whip cutting the air b a light sweeping or brushing sound 2 a swishing movement – **swishy** *adj*

³swish *adj* smart, fashionable – infml

¹Swiss *n*, *pl* **Swiss** a native or inhabitant of Switzerland

²Swiss *adj* (characteristic) of Switzerland

Swiss chard *n* chard

Swiss roll *n* a thin sheet of sponge cake spread with jam and rolled up

¹switch *n* 1 a slender flexible twig or rod 2 a shift or change from one to another 3 a tuft of long hairs at the end of the tail of an animal (e g a cow) 4 a device for making, breaking, or changing the connections in an electrical circuit 5 a tress of hair attached to augment a hairstyle 6 *NAm* railway points

²switch *vt* 1 to strike or beat (as if) with a switch 2 to whisk, lash 3 to shift, change 4a to shift to another electrical circuit by means of a switch b to operate an electrical switch so as to turn *off* or *on* 5 *chiefly NAm* to turn from one railway track to another ~ *vi* 1 to lash from side to side 2 to change, shift – **switchable** *adj*, **switcher** *n*

switchback *n* 1 a zigzag road or railway in a mountainous region 2 *chiefly Br* any of various amusement rides; *esp* ROLLER COASTER

switchblade *n*, *NAm* a flick-knife

switchboard *n* an apparatus consisting of a panel or frame on which switching devices are mounted; *specif* an arrangement for the manual switching of telephone calls

switched-on *adj* alive to experience; *also* swinging – infml

switchgear *n* equipment used for the switching of esp large electrical currents

switchman *n* sby who works a switch (e g on a railway)

switchover *n* a conversion to a different system or method

¹swivel *n* a device joining 2 parts so that the moving part can pivot freely

²swivel *vb* -ll- (*NAm* -l-, -ll-), to turn (as if) on a swivel

swiz *n*, *pl* -zz- *Br* sthg that does not live up to one's hopes or expectations – infml

swizzle stick *n* a thin rod used to stir mixed drinks

swollen *past part of* SWELL

¹swoon *vi* to faint – **swooningly** *adv*

²swoon *n* a partial or total loss of consciousness

¹swoop *vi* to make a sudden attack or downward sweep ~ *vt* to carry off abruptly; snatch

²swoop *n* an act of swooping ⟨*arrested in a drug-squad* ~⟩

swop *vb or n* -pp- (to) swap

sword *n* 1 a cutting or thrusting weapon having a long usu sharp-pointed and sharp-edged blade 2 the use of force ⟨*the pen is mightier than the* ~ – E G Bulwer-Lytton⟩ 3 death caused (as if) by a sword – usu

+ *the* 4 sthg (e g the beak of a swordfish) that resembles a sword – **swordlike** *adj*

sword dance *n* a dance performed over, round, or brandishing swords; *esp* a Scottish-Highland solo dance usu performed in the angles formed by 2 swords crossed on the ground – **sword dancer** *n*

swordfish *n* a very large oceanic food fish that has a long swordlike beak formed by the bones of the upper jaw

sword of Damocles *n*, *often cap S* an impending disaster

swordplay *n* the art, skill, or practice of wielding a sword – **swordplayer** *n*

swordsman *n* one skilled in swordplay

swordsmanship *n* swordplay

swordstick *n* a walking stick in which a sword blade is concealed

swore *past of* SWEAR

sworn *past part of* SWEAR

¹swot *n*, *Br* one who studies hard or excessively – infml

²swot *vb* -tt- *Br* *vi* to study hard ~ *vt* to study (a subject) intensively – usu + *up* *USE* infml

swum *past part of* SWIM

swung *past of* SWING

sybarite *n*, *often cap* a voluptuary, sensualist – **sybaritism** *n*, **sybaritic** *adj*

sycamore *n* 1 a tree of Egypt and Asia Minor that is the sycamore of Scripture and has a sweet edible fruit 2 a Eurasian maple widely planted as a shade tree 3 *NAm* ²PLANE

sycophant *n* a self-seeking flatterer; a toady – **sycophancy** *n*, **sycophant** *adj*, **sycophantic** *adj*

¹syllabic *adj* 1 constituting (the nucleus of) a syllable 2 enunciated with separation of syllables 3 of or constituting a type of verse (e g some French poetry) in which the metre is based on a count of syllables – **syllabically** *adv*

²syllabic *n* a syllabic character or sound

syllabify *vt* to form or divide into syllables – **syllabification** *n*

syllable *n* (a letter or symbol representing) an uninterruptible unit of spoken language that usu consists of 1 vowel sound either alone or with a consonant sound preceding or following – **syllabled** *adj*

syllabub, sillabub *n* a cold dessert usu made by curdling sweetened cream or milk with wine, cider, or other acidic liquid

syllabus *n*, *pl* **syllabi, syllabuses** a summary of a course of study or of examination requirements

syllogism *n* a pattern of deductive reasoning consisting of 2 premises and a conclusion (e g 'all men are mortal; Socrates is a man; therefore Socrates is mortal') – **syllogistic** *adj*

sylph *n* a slender graceful woman or girl – **sylphlike** *adj*

sylvan, silvan *adj* 1 of, located in, or characteristic of the woods or forest 2 full of woods or trees

sym- – see SYN-

symbiosis *n*, *pl* **symbioses** the living together of 2 dissimilar organisms in intimate association (to their mutual benefit) – **symbiotic** *adj*

symbol *n* 1 sthg that stands for or suggests sthg else by reason of association, convention, etc 2 a sign used in writing or printing to represent operations, quantities, elements, relations, or qualities in a particular field (e g chemistry or music) – **symbology** *n*

symbolic, symbolical *adj* of, using, constituting, or exhibiting a symbol or symbols – **symbolically** *adv*

symbolism *n* 1 the literary and artistic mode of

expression of the symbolists **2** a system of symbols – **symbolistic** *adj*

symbolist *n* **1** one who employs symbols or symbolism **2** any of a group of esp 19th-c French writers and artists who used symbols to convey a subjective view of reality and esp immaterial or intangible states or truths (e g by exploiting the nonliteral figurative resources of language) – **symbolist** *adj*

symbolize, -ise *vt* **1** to serve as a symbol of **2** to represent, express, or identify by a symbol – **symbolization** *n*

symmetrical, symmetric *adj* **1a** having the same proportions, design, shape, etc on both sides; *specif* capable of division by a longitudinal plane into similar halves **b** *of a flower* having the same number of members in each whorl of floral leaves **2** *of a chemical compound* having symmetry in the molecular structure – **symmetrically** *adv*

symmetry *n* **1** (beauty of form arising from) balanced proportions **2** the property of being symmetrical; *esp* correspondence in size, shape, and relative position of parts on opposite sides of a dividing line or median plane or about a centre or axis SYMMETRY – **symmetrize** *vt*

sympathetic *adj* **1** existing or operating through an affinity, interdependence, or mutual association **2** appropriate to one's mood or temperament; congenial **3** given to or arising from compassion and sensitivity to others' feelings ⟨a ~ *gesture*⟩ **4** favourably inclined ⟨*not* ~ *to the idea*⟩ **5** of, being, mediated by, or acting on (the nerves of) the sympathetic nervous system **6** relating to musical sounds produced, or strings sounded, by sympathetic vibration – **sympathetically** *adv*

sympathize, -ise *vi* **1** to react or respond in sympathy **2** to share in distress or suffering; commiserate – **sympathizer** *n*

sympathy *n* **1a** relationship between people or things in which each is simultaneously affected in a similar way **b** unity or harmony in action or effect **2a** inclination to think or feel alike **b** tendency to favour or support – often pl with sing. meaning ⟨*Tory* sympathies⟩ **3** (the expression of) pity or compassion

symphonic *adj* relating to or having the form or character of a symphony ⟨~ *music*⟩ – **symphonically** *adv*

symphonic poem *n* an extended orchestral composition, based on a legend, tale, etc and usu freer in form than a symphony

symphony *n* **1a** a usu long and complex sonata for symphony orchestra **b** a composition of similar proportions **2** sthg of great harmonious complexity or variety ⟨*the room was a* ~ *in blue*⟩ **3** *chiefly NAm* SYMPHONY ORCHESTRA

symphony orchestra *n* a large orchestra of wind instruments, strings, and percussion that plays symphonic works

symposium *n, pl* **symposia symposiums** **1** a party (e g after a banquet in ancient Greece) with music and conversation **2a** a formal meeting at which several specialists deliver short addresses on a topic **b** a published collection of opinions on a subject

symptom *n* **1** sthg giving (subjective) evidence or indication of disease or physical disturbance **2** sthg that indicates the existence of sthg else – **symptomless** *adj*, **symptomatology** *n*

symptomatic *adj* **1** being a symptom of a disease **2** concerned with, affecting, or acting on symptoms ⟨~ *treatment for influenza*⟩ **3** characteristic, indicative – **symptomatically** *adv*

syn-, sym- *prefix* **1** with; along with; together

⟨sym*pathy*⟩ ⟨syn*thesis*⟩ **2** at the same time ⟨syn*aesthesia*⟩

synagogue *n* (the house of worship and communal centre of) a Jewish congregation – **synagogal** *adj*

synapse *n* the point (between 2 nerves) across which a nervous impulse is transmitted – **synaptic** *adj*

¹sync *also* **synch** *n* synchronization, synchronism ⟨*out of* ~⟩ – infml

²sync *also* **synch** *vt* to match film and magnetic track so that they run exactly in synchronization ⟨*are these rushes for* ~*ing?*⟩ – often + *up*; infml

synchromesh *adj* designed for effecting synchronized gear changing – **synchromesh** *n*

synchronize, -ise *vi* to happen at the same time ~*vt* **1** to arrange so as to indicate coincidence or coexistence **2** to make synchronous in operation ⟨~ *watches*⟩ **3** to make (sound) exactly simultaneous with the action in a film or a television programme – **synchronizer** *n*, **synchronization** *n*

synchrotron *n* an apparatus that imparts very high speeds to charged particles by combining a high-frequency electric field and a low-frequency magnetic field

syncopate *vt* to modify or affect (musical rhythm) by syncopation – **syncopator** *n*

syncopation *n* (a rhythm or passage characterized by) a temporary displacement of the regular metrical accent in music caused typically by stressing the weak beat – **syncopative** *adj*

syncope *n* **1** temporary loss of consciousness; fainting **2** the dropping of 1 or more sounds or letters in a word (e g in *fo'c'sle* for *forecastle*) – **syncopal** *adj*

syndic *n* an agent who transacts business for a university or corporation

syndicalism *n* **1** a revolutionary doctrine according to which workers should seize control of the economy and the government by direct means (e g a general strike) **2** a system of economic organization in which industries are owned and managed by the workers – **syndical** *adj*, **syndicalist** *adj or n*

¹syndicate *n* **1a** the office of a syndic **b** *sing or pl in constr* a council or body of syndics **2** *sing or pl in constr* a group of people or concerns who combine to carry out a particular transaction (e g buying or renting property) or to promote some common interest **3** a business concern that supplies material for simultaneous publication in many newspapers or periodicals

²syndicate *vt* **1** to form into or manage as a syndicate **2** to sell (e g a cartoon) to a syndicate for simultaneous publication in many newspapers or periodicals – **syndicator** *n*, **syndication** *n*

syndrome *n* **1** a group of signs and symptoms that occur together and characterize a particular (medical) abnormality **2** a set of concurrent emotions, actions, etc that usu form an identifiable pattern

synod *n* **1** a formal meeting to decide ecclesiastical matters **2** a church governing or advisory council **3** the ecclesiastical district governed by a synod – **synodal** *adj*

synonym *n* any of 2 or more words or expressions in a language that are used with (nearly) the same meaning – **synonymic, synonymical** *adj*, **synonymity** *n*

synonymous *adj* alike in meaning – **synonymously** *adv*

synopsis *n, pl* **synopses** a condensed statement or outline (e g of a narrative)

synoptic *also* **synoptical** *adj* **1** affording a comprehensive view of a whole **2** *often cap* of or being the first 3 Gospels of the New Testament **3** relating to or displaying meteorological conditions existing simultaneously over a broad area – **synoptically** *adv*

syntactic, syntactical *adj* of or conforming to the rules of syntax or syntactics – **syntactically** *adv*

syntax *n* (the part of grammar dealing with) the way in which words are put together to form phrases, clauses, or sentences

synthesis *n, pl* **syntheses 1a** the composition or combination of separate or diverse elements into a coherent whole **b** the artificial production of a substance by chemical reaction **2** the third and final stage of a reasoned argument, based on the thesis and antithesis – **synthesist** *n*, **synthesize** *vt*

synthesizer, -iser *n* an extremely versatile electronic musical instrument that produces a sound that can be altered in many ways (e g to mimic other instruments) and is usu played by means of a keyboard

¹**synthetic** *also* **synthetical** *adj* **1** asserting of a subject a predicate that is not part of the meaning of that subject **2** characterized by inflection rather than analysis ⟨~ *languages*⟩ **3** produced artificially; man-made ⟨~ *dyes*⟩ ⟨~ *drugs*⟩ ⟨~ *silk*⟩ – **synthetically** *adv*

²**synthetic** *n* a product of (chemical) synthesis

syphilis *n* a contagious usu venereal and often congenital disease caused by a spirochaetal bacterium – **syphilitic** *adj or n*

syphon *vb or n* to siphon

¹**syringe** *n* a device used to inject fluids into or withdraw them from sthg (e g the body or its cavities); *esp* one that consists of a hollow barrel fitted with a plunger and a hollow needle

²**syringe** *vt* to irrigate or spray (as if) with a syringe

syrup *n* **1a** a thick sticky solution of (flavoured, medicated, etc) sugar and water **b** the concentrated juice of a fruit or plant (e g the sugar maple); *esp* the raw sugar juice obtained from crushed sugarcane after evaporation and before crystallization in sugar manufacture **2** cloying sweetness or sentimentality – **syrupy** *adj*

system *n* **1a** a group of body organs that together perform 1 or more usu specified functions ⟨*the digestive* ~⟩ **b** the body considered as a functional unit **c** a group of interrelated and interdependent objects or units **d** a group of devices or an organization that serves a common purpose ⟨*a telephone* ~⟩ ⟨*a heating* ~⟩ ⟨*a highway* ~⟩ ⟨*a data processing* ~⟩ **e** a major division of rocks including those formed during a period or era **f** a form of social, economic, or political organization ⟨*the capitalist* ~⟩ **2** an organized set of doctrines or principles usu intended to explain the arrangement or working of a systematic whole ⟨*the Newtonian* ~ *of mechanics*⟩ **3a** an organized or established procedure ⟨*the touch* ~ *of typing*⟩ **b** a manner of classifying, symbolizing, or formalizing ⟨*a taxonomic* ~⟩ ⟨*the decimal* ~⟩ **4** orderly methods **5** ESTABLISHMENT 2 – + *the* – **systemless** *adj*

systematic *also* **systematical** *adj* **1** relating to, consisting of, or presented as a system **2** methodical in procedure or plan; thorough ⟨~ *investigation*⟩ **3** of or concerned with classification; *specif* taxonomic – **systematically** *adv*

systematize, -ise *vt* to arrange according to a set method; order systematically – **systematizer** *n*, **systematization** *n*

systemic *adj* **1** affecting the body generally **2** *of an insecticide, pesticide, etc* making the organism, esp a plant, toxic to a pest by entering the tissues – **systemically** *adv*

T

t *n, pl* **t's, ts** *often cap* (a graphic representation of or device for reproducing) the 20th letter of the English alphabet

t' *definite article, NEng dial* the

't *pron* it

ta *n, Br* thanks – *infml*

¹**tab** *n* **1a** a flap, loop, etc fixed to or projecting from sthg and used for gripping or suspending or to aid identification **b** a small auxiliary aerofoil hinged to a control surface (e g an aileron) **2** close surveillance; watch – usu pl with sing. meaning ⟨*the police are keeping* ~s *on him*⟩ **3** a tabulator **4** *Br* ¹TAG 2 **5** *chiefly NAm* a statement of money owed; a bill – *infml* ⟨*the company will pick up the* ~⟩

²**tab** *vt* **-bb-** to provide or decorate with tabs

tabard *n* a short loosely fitting sleeveless or short-sleeved coat or cape: e g **a** an emblazoned tunic worn by a knight over his armour **b** a herald's official cape or coat emblazoned with his lord's arms **c** a straight-hanging sleeveless outer garment; *esp* one with slits at the sides for part or all of its length, worn by women

Tabasco *trademark* – used for a pungent condiment sauce made from hot peppers

tabby, tabby cat *n* **1** a domestic cat with a usu buff and black striped and mottled coat **2** a female domestic cat

tabernacle *n* **1** *often cap* a tent sanctuary used by the Israelites during the Exodus **2** a receptacle for the consecrated bread and wine used at Communion, often forming part of an altar **3** a support in which a mast is stepped and pivoted so that it can be lowered (e g to negotiate a bridge) – **tabernacular** *adj*

¹**table** *n* **1a** a piece of furniture consisting of a smooth flat slab (e g of wood) fixed on legs **b** the food served at a meal; fare ⟨*keeps a good* ~⟩ **2** either of the 2 leaves of a backgammon board or either half of a leaf **3** a systematic arrangement of data usu in rows and columns **4** the upper flat surface of a gem **5** sthg having a flat level surface – **on the table** *chiefly Br* under or put forward for discussion ⟨*so far the management have put nothing* on the table⟩ – **under the table 1** into a stupor ⟨*can drink you* under the table⟩ **2** not aboveboard

tableau *n, pl* **tableaux** *also* **tableaus 1** a graphic representation of a group or scene **2** a depiction of a scene usu presented on a stage by silent and motionless costumed participants

tablecloth *n* an often decorative cloth spread over a dining table before the places are set

table d'hôte *n* a meal often of several prearranged courses served to all guests at a stated hour and fixed price

tableland *n* a broad level area elevated on all sides

table linen *n* linen (e g tablecloths and napkins) for the table

tablemat *n* a small often decorative mat placed under a hot dish to protect the surface of a table from heat

tablespoon *n* **1** a large spoon used for serving **2** a tablespoonful

tablespoonful *n, pl* **tablespoonfuls** *also* **tablespoonsful** as much as a tablespoon can hold

tablet *n* **1** a flat slab or plaque suitable for or bearing an inscription **2a** a compressed block of a solid material ⟨*a* ~ *of soap*⟩ **b** a small solid shaped mass or capsule of medicinal material

table tennis *n* a game resembling lawn tennis that is played on a tabletop with bats and a small hollow plastic ball

tableware *n* utensils (e g glasses, dishes, plates, and cutlery) for table use

tabloid *n* a newspaper of which 2 pages make up 1 printing plate and which contains much photographic matter

¹**taboo** *also* **tabu** *adj* **1a** too sacred or evil to be touched, named, or used **b** set apart as unclean or accursed **2** forbidden, esp on grounds of morality, tradition, or social usage

²**taboo** *also* **tabu** *n*, *pl* **taboos** *also* **tabus** **1** a prohibition against touching, saying, or doing sthg for fear of harm from a supernatural force **2** a prohibition imposed by social custom

³**taboo** *also* **tabu** *vt* **1** to set apart as taboo **2** to avoid or ban as taboo

tabor *also* **tabour** *n* a small drum with 1 head of soft calfskin used to accompany a pipe or fife played by the same person

tabular *adj* **1a** having a broad flat surface **b** laminar **c** *of a crystal* having 2 parallel flat faces **2a** of or arranged in a table **b** computed by means of a table – **tabularly** *adv*

tabulate *vt* to arrange in tabular form – **tabulation** *n*

tabulator *n* **1** a business machine that sorts and selects information from marked or perforated cards **2** an attachment to a typewriter that is used for arranging data in columns

tacit *adj* implied or understood but not actually expressed – **tacitly** *adv*

taciturn *adj* not communicative or talkative – **taciturnity** *n*

¹**tack** *n* **1** a small short sharp-pointed nail, usu with a broad flat head **2** the lower forward corner of a fore-and-aft sail **3a** the direction of a sailing vessel with respect to the direction of the wind ⟨*starboard* ~, *with the wind to starboard*⟩ **b** the run of a sailing vessel on 1 tack **c** a change of course from one tack to another **d** a course of action ⟨*off on a new* ~⟩ **4** a long loose straight stitch usu used to hold 2 or more layers of fabric together temporarily **5** a sticky or adhesive quality **6** SADDLERY 2

²**tack** *vt* **1a** to fasten or attach with tacks **b** to sew with long loose stitches in order to join or hold in place temporarily before fine or machine sewing **2** to add as a supplement ⟨~ *a postscript on a letter*⟩ **3** to change the course of (a close-hauled sailing vessel) from one tack to the other by turning the bow to windward ~*vi* **1a** to tack a sailing vessel **b** *of a sailing vessel* to undergo being tacked **2a** to follow a zigzag course **b** to change one's policy or attitude abruptly – **tacker** *n*

¹**tackle** *n* **1** a set of equipment used in a particular activity ⟨*fishing* ~⟩ **2a** a ship's rigging **b** an assembly of ropes and pulleys arranged to gain mechanical advantage for hoisting and pulling **3** an act of tackling

²**tackle** *vb* **tackling** *vt* **1** to attach or secure with or as if with tackle – often + *up* **2a** to take hold of or grapple with, esp in an attempt to stop or restrain **b(1)** to (attempt to) take the ball from (an opposing player) in hockey or soccer **(2)** to seize and pull down or stop (an opposing player with the ball) in rugby or American football **3** to set about dealing with ⟨~ *the problem*⟩ ~*vi* to tackle an opposing player – **tackler** *n*

¹**tacky** *adj* slightly sticky to the touch ⟨~ *varnish*⟩ – **tackiness** *n*

²**tacky** *adj*, *NAm* shabby, shoddy – slang – **tackily** *adv*, **tackiness** *n*

tact *n* a keen sense of how to handle people or affairs so as to avoid friction or giving offence – **tactful** *adj*, **tact-**fully *adv*, **tactfulness** *n*, **tactless** *adj*, **tactlessly** *adv*, **tactlessness** *n*

tactic *n* **1** a method of employing forces in combat **2** a device for achieving an end

tactical *adj* **1a** involving operations of local importance or brief duration **b** of or designed for air attack in close support of friendly ground forces **2a** of small-scale actions serving a wider aim **b** characterized by adroit planning or manoeuvring to accomplish an end – **tactically** *adv*

tactician *n* sby skilled in tactics

tactics *n pl but sing or pl in constr* **1a** the science and art of disposing and manoeuvring forces in combat **b** the art or skill of employing available means to accomplish an end **2** a system or mode of procedure

tactile *adj* of or perceptible by (the sense of) touch – **tactilely** *adv*, **tactility** *n*

tactual *adj* tactile – **tactually** *adv*

tadpole *n* the larva of an amphibian; *specif* a frog or toad larva with a rounded body, a long tail, and external gills

taffeta *n* a crisp plain-woven lustrous fabric of various fibres used esp for women's clothing

taffrail *n* a rail round the stern of a ship

taffy *n*, *NAm* a porous and light-coloured toffee

Taffy *n*, *Br* a Welshman – chiefly derog

¹**tag** *n* **1** a loose hanging piece of torn cloth **2** a rigid binding on an end of a shoelace **3** a piece of hanging or attached material; *specif* a flap on a garment that carries information (e g washing instructions) **4a** a trite quotation used for rhetorical effect **b** a recurrent or characteristic verbal expression **c** a final speech or line (e g in a play) usu serving to clarify a point or create a dramatic effect **5** a marker of plastic, metal, etc used for identification or classification

²**tag** *vb* -**gg**- *vt* **1a** to provide with an identifying marker **b** to label, brand ⟨*had him* ~*ged as a chauvinist from the start*⟩ **2** to attach, append **3** LABEL 2 ~*vi* to follow closely ⟨~ *ging along behind*⟩

³**tag** *n* a game in which one player chases others and tries to make one of them it by touching him/her

⁴**tag** *vt* -**gg**- to touch (as if) in a game of tag

¹**tail** *n* **1** (an extension or prolongation of) the rear end of the body of an animal **2** sthg resembling an animal's tail in shape or position ⟨*the* ~ *of a comet*⟩ **3** *pl* a tailcoat; *broadly* formal evening dress for men including a tailcoat and a white bow tie **4** the last, rear, or lower part of sthg **5** the reverse of a coin – usu pl with sing. meaning ⟨~*s, you lose*⟩; compare HEAD 3 **6** *sing or pl in constr* the group of relatively inexpert batsmen who bat towards the end of a side's innings **7** the stabilizing assembly (e g fin, rudder, and tailplane) at the rear of an aircraft **8** sby who follows or keeps watch on sby – infml **9** the trail of a fugitive ⟨*had the police on her* ~⟩ – infml **10a** women as sexual objects – vulg **b** *NAm* the buttocks – slang – **tailed** *adj*, **tailless** *adj*, **taillike** *adj*

²**tail** *vt* **1** to connect at an end or end to end **2a** to remove the tail of (an animal) **b** to remove the stalk of (e g a gooseberry) **3** to fasten an end of (a tile, brick, or timber) into a wall or other support **4** to follow for purposes of surveillance – infml ~*vi* **1** to diminish gradually in strength, volume, quantity, etc – usu + *off* or *away* **2** to follow closely

³**tail** *adj* entailed

⁴**tail** *n* ENTAIL 1 – often in *in tail*

tailback *n* a long queue of motor vehicles, esp when caused by an obstruction that blocks the road

tailboard *n* a hinged or removable board or gate at the rear of a vehicle

tailcoat *n* a coat with tails; *esp* a man's formal evening coat with 2 long tapering skirts at the back – **tailcoated** *adj*

tail end *n* **1** the back or rear end **2** the concluding period

¹**tailor**, *fem* **tailoress** *n* sby whose occupation is making or altering esp men's garments

²**tailor** *vi* to do the work of a tailor ~ *vt* **1a** to make or fashion as the work of a tailor; *specif* to cut and stitch (a garment) so that it will hang and fit well **b** to make or adapt to suit a special need or purpose **2** to style with trim straight lines and finished handwork

tailor-made *adj* made or fitted for a particular use or purpose

tailpiece *n* **1** a piece added at the end; an appendage **2** a triangular piece from which the strings of a stringed instrument are stretched to the pegs **3** an ornament placed below the text on a page (e g at the end of a chapter)

tailspin *n* SPIN 2

tail wind *n* a wind having the same general direction as the course of an aircraft or ship

¹**taint** *vt* **1** to touch or affect slightly with sthg bad ⟨*people* ~ *ed with prejudice*⟩ **2** to affect with putrefaction; spoil **3** to contaminate morally; corrupt ~ *vi* to become affected with putrefaction; spoil

²**taint** *n* a contaminating mark or influence – **taintless** *adj*

¹**take** *vb* **took**; **taken** *vt* **1a** to seize or capture physically ⟨*took 1500 prisoners*⟩ **b** to get possession of (e g fish or game) by killing or trapping **c(1)** to capture and remove from play ⟨*took my pawn*⟩ **(2)** to win in a card game ⟨*able to* ~ *12 tricks with that hand*⟩ **2** to grasp, grip ⟨*took his arm and led him across the road*⟩ **3a** to catch or attack through a sudden effect ⟨~ *n ill*⟩ **b** to surprise; come upon suddenly ⟨*her death took us by surprise*⟩ **c** to attract, delight ⟨*was quite* ~ *n with him*⟩ **4a** to receive into one's body, esp through the mouth ⟨~ *medicine*⟩ **b** to eat or drink habitually ⟨*I don't* ~ *milk in my tea*⟩ **5a** to bring or receive into a relationship or connection ⟨*Mr Burton took us for French*⟩ ⟨*took her as his wife*⟩ **b** to copulate with (a passive partner) **6a** to acquire, borrow, or use without authority or right ⟨*took someone's hat by mistake*⟩ **b(1)** to pay to have (e g by contract or subscription) ⟨~ *a cottage for the summer*⟩ **(2)** to buy ⟨*the salesman persuaded him to* ~ *the estate car*⟩ **7a** to assume ⟨~ *shape*⟩ ⟨*took the name of Phillips*⟩ **b** to perform or conduct (e g a lesson) as a duty, task, or job ⟨*Miss Jones* ~ *s Physics*⟩ **c** to commit oneself to ⟨~ *a vow*⟩ ⟨~ *a decision*⟩ **d** to involve oneself in ⟨~ *the trouble to learn Chinese*⟩ **e** to consider or adopt as a point of view ⟨~ *a more lenient view*⟩ ⟨~ *Shakespeare, now*⟩ **f** to claim as rightfully one's own ⟨~ *the credit*⟩ ⟨~ *the liberty of refusing*⟩ **8** to obtain by competition ⟨*took third place*⟩ **9** to pick out; choose ⟨~ *any card*⟩ **10** to adopt or avail oneself of for use ⟨~ *an opportunity*⟩: e g **a** to have recourse to as an instrument for doing sthg ⟨~ *a scythe to the weeds*⟩ **b** to use as a means of transport or progression ⟨~ *a plane to Paris*⟩ ⟨~ *the third turning on the right*⟩ **c(1)** to turn to for safety or refuge ⟨~ *cover*⟩ **(2)** to proceed to occupy or hold ⟨~ *a seat*⟩ ⟨~ *office*⟩ **d(1)** to need, require ⟨~ *s a long time to dry*⟩ ⟨*that* ~ *s some believing*⟩ **(2)** to govern ⟨*transitive verbs* ~ *an object*⟩ **11a** to derive, draw ⟨~ *s its title from the name of the hero*⟩ **b(1)** to obtain or ascertain by testing, measuring, etc ⟨~ *his temperature*⟩ **(2)** to record in writing; WRITE DOWN 1 ⟨~ *notes*⟩ **(3)** to get or record by photography ⟨~ *some slides*⟩ ⟨~ *the children in their party clothes*⟩ **(4)** to get by transference from one surface to another ⟨~ *fingerprints*⟩ **12** to receive or accept either willingly or reluctantly ⟨~ *a bribe*⟩ ⟨~ *a risk*⟩: e g **a** to

receive when bestowed or tendered ⟨~ *a degree*⟩ **b(1)** to endure, undergo ⟨*took a terrible beating*⟩ ⟨*can't* ~ *it any longer*⟩ **(2)** to support, withstand ⟨*won't* ~ *my weight*⟩ ⟨*I can* ~ *a lot of Mozart*⟩ **c(1)** to accept as true; believe ⟨*took her word for it*⟩ ⟨~ *it from me*⟩ **(2)** to follow ⟨~ *my advice*⟩ **(3)** to respond to in a specified way ⟨~ *things as they come*⟩ ⟨~ *the news calmly*⟩ **d** to indulge in and enjoy ⟨~ *one's ease*⟩ ⟨~ *a holiday*⟩ **e** to accept in payment, compensation, or recompense ⟨*they won't* ~ *dollars*⟩ **13a** to accommodate ⟨*the suitcase wouldn't* ~ *another thing*⟩ **b** to be affected injuriously by (e g a disease) ⟨~ *cold*⟩ **14a** to apprehend, understand ⟨*slow to* ~ *his meaning*⟩ **b** to look upon; consider ⟨~ *it as settled*⟩ **c** to feel, experience ⟨~ *pleasure*⟩ **15a** to lead, carry, or remove with one to another place ⟨~ *her a cup of tea*⟩ **b** to require or cause to go ⟨*her ability will* ~ *her to the top*⟩ **16a** to obtain by removing ⟨~ *eggs from a nest*⟩ **b** to subtract ⟨~ *2 from 4*⟩ **17** to undertake and make, do, or perform ⟨~ *a walk*⟩ ⟨~ *legal action*⟩ ⟨~ *one's revenge*⟩ **18a** to deal with ⟨~ *the comments one at a time*⟩ **b** to consider or view in a specified relation ⟨~ *n together, the details were significant*⟩ **c** to apply oneself to the study of or undergo examination in ⟨~ *music lessons*⟩ ⟨~ *6 subjects at O Level*⟩ **d** to succeed in passing or surmounting ⟨*the horse took the fence easily*⟩ **19** to cheat, swindle ⟨*was* ~ *n for £5000 by a con man*⟩ **20** to remove by death – euph ⟨*was* ~ *n in his prime*⟩ ~ *vi* **1a** to receive property in law ⟨*b of a fish* to receive a lure or bait **2a** to have the natural or intended effect or reaction ⟨*did your vaccination* ~ *?*⟩ ⟨*glue that* ~ *s well on cloth*⟩ **b** to begin to grow; strike root ⟨*have the seeds* ~ *n yet?*⟩ **3a** to be adversely affected as specified ⟨*took ill*⟩ **b** to be capable of being moved in a specified way ⟨*the table* ~ *s apart for packing*⟩ **c** to admit of being photographed **4** *chiefly dial* – used as an intensifier or redundantly with a following verb ⟨*took and ducked her in the pond*⟩ – **taker** *n* – **take account of** TAKE INTO ACCOUNT – **take action 1** to begin to act **2** to begin legal proceedings – **take advantage of 1** to use to advantage; profit by **2** to impose upon; exploit – **take after** to resemble (an older relative) in appearance, character, or aptitudes – **take against** *chiefly Br* to take sides against; come to dislike – **take apart 1** to disassemble, dismantle **2** to analyse, dissect **3** to treat roughly or harshly – *infml* – **take as read** to accept as axiomatic – **take a toss** to fall off a horse – **take care** to be careful; exercise caution or prudence; be watchful – **take care of** to attend to or provide for the needs, operation, or treatment of – **take charge** to assume care, custody, command, or control – **take effect 1** to become operative **2** to produce a result – **take exception** to object, demur ⟨*took exception to his critic's remarks*⟩ – **take five** to take a brief intermission – *infml* – **take for** to suppose, esp mistakenly, to be – **take for a ride** to deceive wilfully; hoodwink – *infml* – **take for granted 1** to assume as true, real, or certain to occur **2** to value too lightly – **take from** to detract from ⟨*irritations that took from their general satisfaction*⟩ – **take heart** to gain courage or confidence – **take hold 1** to grasp, grip, seize **2** to become attached or established; TAKE EFFECT – **take in good part** to accept without offence – **take in hand** to embark on the control or reform of – **take into account** to make allowances for ⟨*took the boy's age into account*⟩ – **take into consideration** TAKE INTO ACCOUNT; *specif* to take account of (additional offences admitted by a defendant) so that the sentence to be imposed will preclude any chance of subsequent prosecution ⟨*Smith asked for 21 other offences to be* taken into consideration⟩ – **take into one's head** to conceive as a sudden notion or resolve – **take in vain** to use (a name) profanely or without proper respect – **take it upon oneself** to venture, presume – **take offence** to be offended – **take on board** *Br* to apprehend fully; grasp – *infml* – **take one all one's time** *Br* to be the utmost one can manage ⟨*it takes me all my time to afford shoes for them all*⟩ – **take one's leave** to bid farewell – often + *of* – **take one's time** to be leisurely about doing sthg – **take part** to join, participate, share – **take place** to happen; COME ABOUT – **take root** 1 to become rooted 2 to become fixed or established – **take silk** to become a Queen's or King's Counsel – **take someone at his/her word** to believe sby literally – **take someone out of him-/herself** to provide sby with needful diversion – **take someone to task** to rebuke or scold sby – **take stock** 1 to make an inventory 2 to make an assessment – **take the biscuit** *Br* to be the most astonishing or preposterous thing heard of or seen, esp concerning a particular issue – *infml* – **take the field** 1 to go onto the playing field 2 to enter on a military campaign – **take the floor** 1 to rise (e g in a meeting) to make a formal address 2 to begin dancing – **take the gilt off the gingerbread** to take away the part that makes the whole attractive – **take the law into one's own hands** to seek redress by force – **take the mickey** to behave disrespectfully; mock – *infml* – **take the wind out of someone's sails** to frustrate sby by anticipating or forestalling him/her – **take the words out of someone's mouth** to utter the exact words about to be used by sby – **take to** 1 to betake oneself to, esp for refuge ⟨take to *the woods*⟩ 2 to apply or devote oneself to (e g a practice, habit or occupation) ⟨take to *begging*⟩ 3 to adapt oneself to; respond ⟨takes to *water like a duck*⟩ 4 to conceive a liking or affectionate concern for – **take to heart** to be deeply affected by – **take to one's heels** to run away; flee – **take to task** to call to account for a shortcoming – **take to the cleaners** *Br* 1 to rob, defraud – *infml* 2 to criticize harshly – *infml* – **take turns, take it in turns** to act by turns – **what it takes** the qualities or resources needed for success or for attainment of a goal

²**take** *n* **1a** the action of killing or catching sthg (e g game or fish) **b** the uninterrupted recording, filming, or televising of sthg (e g a gramophone record or film sequence); *also* the recording or scene produced **2a** proceeds, takings **b** a share, cut ⟨*wanted a bigger* ~⟩ **c** the number or quantity (e g of animals or fish) taken at 1 time

takeaway *n, Br* **1** a cooked meal that is eaten away from the premises from which it was bought ⟨*a Chinese* ~ *for supper*⟩ **2** a shop or restaurant that sells takeaways

take back *vt* to retract, withdraw

take down *vt* **1** to pull to pieces **2** WRITE DOWN **3** to lower without removing ⟨took down *his trousers*⟩

take-home pay *n* the part of gross salary or wages remaining after deductions (e g for income tax)

take in *vt* **1a** to furl **b** to make (a garment) smaller (e g by altering the positions of the seams or making tucks) **2** to offer accommodation or shelter to **3** to receive (paid work) into one's house ⟨take in *washing*⟩ **4** to include ⟨*the holiday* took in *Venice*⟩ **5** to perceive, understand **6** to deceive, trick – *infml*

takeoff *n* **1** an imitation; esp a caricature **2** an act of leaving or a rise from a surface (e g in making a jump, dive, or flight or in the launching of a rocket) **3** a starting point; a point at which one takes off

take off *vt* **1** to remove ⟨take *your shoes* off⟩ **2a** to release ⟨take *the brake* off⟩ **b** to discontinue, withdraw ⟨took off *the morning train*⟩ **c** to deduct ⟨took *10 per cent* off⟩ **3** to take or spend (a period of time) as a holiday, rest, etc **4** to mimic ⟨*mannerisms that her critics delighted in* taking off⟩ ~ *vi* **1** to start off or away; SET OUT ⟨took off *without delay*⟩ **2** to begin a leap or spring **3** to leave the surface; begin flight

take on *vt* **1a** to agree to undertake ⟨took on *new responsibilities*⟩ **b** to contend with as an opponent ⟨took on *the neighbourhood bully*⟩ **2** to engage, hire **3** to assume or acquire (e g an appearance or quality) ⟨*the city* takes on *a carnival air*⟩ ~ *vi* to become emotional or distraught – *infml*

take out *vt* **1a** to extract ⟨took *the appendix* out⟩ **b** to give vent to – usu + *on* ⟨take out *their frustrations on one another*⟩ **2** to escort or accompany in public **3a** to obtain officially or formally ⟨take out *a warrant*⟩ **b** to acquire (insurance) by making the necessary payment **4** to overcall (a bridge partner) in a different suit – **take it out on** to vent anger, vexation, or frustration on – **take it out of** **1** TAKE IT OUT ON **2** to fatigue, exhaust

takeover *n* the action or an act of taking over; esp an act of gaining control of a business company by buying a majority of the shares – **take-over** *adj*

take over *vb* to assume control or possession (of) or responsibility (for) ⟨*military leaders* took over *the government*⟩

take up *vt* **1** to remove by lifting or pulling up ⟨*the council's* taking *the old tramlines* up⟩ **2** to receive internally or on the surface and hold ⟨*plants* take up *nutrients*⟩ **3a** to begin to engage in or study ⟨took up *Greek*⟩ ⟨*when did he* take up *sailing?*⟩ **b** to raise (a matter) for consideration ⟨took *her case* up *with a lawyer*⟩ **4** to occupy (e g space or time) entirely or exclusively ⟨*outside activities* took up *too much of his time*⟩ **5** to shorten (e g a garment) ⟨*will have to* take *that dress* up⟩ **6** to respond favourably to a bet, challenge, or proposal made by ⟨*I'll take you* up *on that*⟩ **7** to begin again or take over from another ⟨*she* took up *the story where she left off*⟩ ~ *vi* to begin again; resume – **take up the cudgels** to engage vigorously in a defence – **take up with** to begin to associate with; consort with

taking *adj* attractive, captivating

takings *n pl* receipts, esp of money

talc *n* **1** a soft usu greenish or greyish mineral consisting of a magnesium silicate **2** TALCUM POWDER – **talcose** *adj*

talcum powder *n* a powder for toilet use consisting of perfumed talc

tale *n* **1** a series of events or facts told or presented; an account **2a** a usu fictitious narrative; a story **b** a lie, a falsehood **c** a malicious report or piece of gossip

talebearer *n* a telltale, gossip – **talebearing** *adj or n*

talent *n* **1a** any of several ancient units of weight **b** a unit of money equal to the value of a talent of gold or silver **2a** a special often creative or artistic aptitude **b** general ability or intelligence **3** a person or people of talent in a field or activity **4** *sing or pl in constr* sexually attractive members of the opposite sex ⟨*sat eyeing up the local* ~⟩ – *slang* – **talented** *adj*, **talentless** *adj*

talent scout *n* a person engaged in discovering and recruiting people with talent in a specialized field of activity

taler *n* any of numerous silver coins issued by various German states from the 15th to the 19th c

talisman *n, pl* **talismans** **1** an engraved object believed to act as a charm **2** sthg believed to produce magical or miraculous effects – **talismanic** *adj* **talismanically** *adv*

¹**talk** *vt* **1** to express in speech; utter ⟨~ *nonsense*⟩ **2** to make the subject of conversation; discuss ⟨~ *business*⟩ **3** to bring to a specified state by talking; esp to persuade by talking ⟨~ed *them into agreeing*⟩ **4** to use (a language) for conversing or communicating ⟨~ *French*⟩ ~ *vi* **1** to express or exchange ideas verbally or by other means ⟨~ed *till daybreak*⟩ ⟨*they* ~ed *by using sign language*⟩ **2** to use speech; speak **3** to imitate human speech ⟨*her*

budgie can ~⟩ **4a** to gossip ⟨*you know how people* ~⟩ **b** to reveal secret or confidential information ⟨*we have ways of making you* ~⟩ **5** to give a talk or lecture – **talker** *n* – **talk shop** to talk about one's job, esp outside working hours – **talk through one's hat** to voice irrational, or erroneous ideas, esp in attempting to appear knowledgeable – **talk turkey** *chiefly NAm* to speak frankly or bluntly

²**talk** *n* **1** a verbal exchange of thoughts or opinions; a conversation **2** meaningless speech; verbiage ⟨*it's all* ~⟩ **3** a formal discussion or exchange of views – often pl with sing. meaning **4** (the topic of) interested comment or gossip ⟨*the* ~ *of the town*⟩ **5** an often informal address or lecture **6** communicative sounds or signs functioning as talk ⟨*baby* ~⟩

talkative *adj* given to talking – **talkatively** *adv*, **talkativeness** *n*

talk down *vt* **1** to defeat or silence by argument or by loud talking **2** to radio instructions to (a pilot) to enable him/her to land when conditions are difficult ~ *vi* to speak in a condescending or oversimplified fashion *to*

talkie *n* a film with a synchronized sound track

talking point *n* a subject of conversation or argument

talking-to *n* a reprimand, scolding

talk out *vt* to clarify or settle by discussion ⟨*tried to talk out their differences*⟩

talk over *vt* to review or consider in conversation

tall *adj* **1a** of above average height ⟨*a* ~ *woman*⟩ ⟨~ *trees*⟩ **b** of a specified height ⟨*5 feet* ~⟩ **2** of a plant of a higher growing variety or species **3** unreasonably difficult to perform ⟨*a* ~ *order*⟩ **4** highly exaggerated; incredible ⟨*a* ~ *story*⟩ – **tall** *adv*, **tallish** *adj*, **tallness** *n*

tallboy *n* **1** a tall chest of drawers supported on a low legged base **2** a double chest of drawers usu with the upper section slightly smaller than the lower

tallow *n* the solid white rendered fat of cattle and sheep used chiefly in soap, candles, and lubricants – **tallowy** *adj*

¹**tally** *n* **1** a device for visibly recording or accounting esp business transactions; *specif* a wooden rod notched with marks representing numbers and split lengthways through the notches so that each of 2 parties may have a record of a transaction **2a** a record or account (e g of items or charges) ⟨*keep a daily* ~ *of accidents*⟩ **b** a record of the score (e g in a game) **3** a part or person that corresponds to an opposite or companion object or member; a counterpart

²**tally** *vt* **1a** to mark (as if) on a tally; tabulate **b** to list or check off (e g a cargo) by items **2** to make a count of ~ *vi* **1a** to make a tally (as if) by tabulating **b** to register a point in a contest **2** to correspond, match ⟨*their stories* ~⟩

tally-ho *n* a call of a huntsman at the sight of a fox

tallyman *n* **1** one who checks or keeps an account or record (e g of receipt of goods) **2** *Br* one who sells goods on credit; *also* one who calls to collect hire purchase payments

Talmud *n* the authoritative body of Jewish tradition comprising the Mishnah and Gemara – **talmudic** *also* **talmudical** *adj*, *often cap*, **talmudism** *n*, *often cap*

talon *n* a claw of an animal, esp a bird of prey – **taloned** *adj*

tamarind *n* (a tropical leguminous tree with) a fruit with an acid pulp used for preserves or in a cooling laxative drink

tamarisk *n* any of a genus of chiefly tropical or Mediterranean shrubs and trees having tiny narrow leaves and masses of minute flowers

¹**tambour** *n* **1** ¹**DRUM 1 2** (embroidery made on) a frame consisting of a set of 2 interlocking hoops between which

cloth is stretched before stitching **3** a rolling top or front (e g of a rolltop desk) consisting of narrow strips of wood glued on canvas

²**tambour** *vt* to embroider (e g cloth) using a tambour – **tambourer** *n*

tambourine *n* a shallow one-headed drum with loose metallic discs at the sides that is held in the hand and played by shaking, striking with the hand, or rubbing with the thumb

¹**tame** *adj* **1** changed from a state of native wildness, esp so as to be trainable and useful to human beings **2** made docile and submissive **3** lacking spirit, zest, or interest – **tamely** *adv*, **tameness** *n*

²**tame** *vt* **1a** to make tame; domesticate **b** to subject to cultivation **2** to deprive of spirit; subdue – **tamable**, **tameable** *adj*, **tamer** *n*

Tammany *adj*, *chiefly NAm* of or constituting a group exercising municipal political power by corruption and autocratic control – **Tammanyism** *n*

tam-o'-shanter *n* a round flat woollen or cloth cap of Scottish origin, with a tight headband, a full crown, and usu a pom-pom on top

tamp *vt* **1** to fill up (a drill hole above a blasting charge) with material (e g clay) to confine the force of the explosion **2** to drive in or down by a succession of light or medium blows – often + *down* – **tamper** *n*

tamper *vi* **1** to carry on underhand or improper negotiations (e g by bribery) **2** to interfere or meddle without permission ⟨*the car lock had been* ~*ed with*⟩ *USE* usu + *with* – **tamperer** *n*, **tamperproof** *adj*

tampon *vt or n* (to plug with) an absorbent plug put into a cavity (e g the vagina) to absorb secretions, arrest bleeding, etc

¹**tan** *vb* -nn- *vt* **1** to convert (hide) into leather, esp by treatment with an infusion of tannin-rich bark **2** to make (skin) tan-coloured, esp by exposure to the sun **3** to thrash, beat – infml ~ *vi* to get or become tanned – **tan someone's hide** *or* **tan the hide off someone** to beat sby severely; THRASH 2a –infml

²**tan** *n* **1** a brown colour given to the skin by exposure to sun or wind **2** (a) light yellowish brown – **tannish** *adj*

³**tan** *adj* of the colour tan

¹**tandem** *n* **1** (a 2-seat carriage drawn by) horses harnessed one before the other **2** a bicycle or tricycle having 2 or more seats one behind the other – **in tandem 1** in a tandem arrangement **2** in partnership or conjunction

²**tandem** *adv* one behind the other ⟨*ride* ~⟩

¹**tang** *n* **1** a projecting shank or tongue (e g on a knife, file, or sword) that connects with and is enclosed by a handle **2a** a sharp distinctive flavour **b** a pungent or distinctive smell **3** a faint suggestion; a trace – **tanged** *adj*, **tangy** *adj*

²**tang** *n* any of various large coarse seaweeds

Tang *n* a Chinese dynasty (AD 618 to 907) under which printing developed and poetry and art flourished

¹**tangent** *adj* **1** touching a curve or surface at only 1 point ⟨*straight line* ~ *to a curve*⟩ **2** having a common tangent at a point ⟨~ *curves*⟩

²**tangent** *n* **1** the trigonometric function that for an acute angle in a right-angled triangle is the ratio between the shorter sides opposite and adjacent to the angle **2** a straight line tangent to a curve **3** an upright flat-ended metal pin at the inner end of a clavichord key that strikes the string to produce the note – **fly/go off at/on a tangent** to change suddenly from one subject, course of action, etc, to another

tangential *adj* **1** of (the nature of) a tangent **2** acting along or lying in a tangent ⟨~ *forces*⟩ **3a** divergent, digressive **b** incidental, peripheral – **tangentially** *adv*

tangerine *n* **1** (a tree that produces) any of various mandarin oranges with deep orange skin and pulp; *broadly* MANDARIN 3 **2** (a) bright reddish orange

tangible *adj* **1a** capable of being perceived, esp by the sense of touch **b** substantially real; material **2** capable of being appraised at an actual or approximate value ⟨~ *assets*⟩ – **tangibleness** *n*, **tangibly** *adv*, **tangibility** *n*

¹**tangle** *vb* **tangling** *vt* **1** to involve so as to be trapped or hampered **2** to bring together or intertwine in disordered confusion ~ *vi* **1** to become tangled **2** to engage in conflict or argument – usu + *with*; *infml*

²**tangle** *n* **1** a confused twisted mass **2** a complicated or confused state

tango *n*, *pl* **tangos** (the music for) a ballroom dance of Latin-American origin in **4**₄ time, characterized by long pauses and stylized body positions – **tango** *vi*

Tango – a communications code word for the letter *t*

¹**tank** *n* **1** a large receptacle for holding, transporting, or storing liquids or gas **2** an enclosed heavily armed and armoured combat vehicle that moves on caterpillar tracks – **tankful** *n*

²**tank** *vt* to place, store, or treat in a tank

tankard *n* a tall one-handled drinking vessel; *esp* a silver or pewter mug with a lid

tanked-up *adj* DRUNK 1 – *infml*

tanker *n* a ship, aircraft, or road or rail vehicle designed to carry fluid, esp liquid, in bulk (e g an aircraft used for transporting fuel and usu capable of refuelling other aircraft in flight)

tanner *n*, *Br* a coin worth 6 old pence – *infml*

tannery *n* a place where tanning is carried out

tannin *n* any of various soluble astringent complex phenolic substances of plant origin used esp in tanning, dyeing, and making ink

tanning *n* a beating, thrashing – *infml*

Tannoy *trademark* – used for a loudspeaker apparatus that broadcasts to the public, esp throughout a large building

tansy *n* an aromatic composite plant with finely divided leaves that is a common weed

tantalize, -ise *vt* to tease or frustrate by presenting sthg desirable that is just out of reach – **tantalizer** *n*, **tantalizing** *adj*

tantamount *adj* equivalent in value, significance, or effect *to*

tantrum *n* a fit of childish bad temper

Taoism *n* a Chinese philosophy traditionally founded by Lao-tzu in the 6th c BC that teaches action in conformity with nature rather than striving against it; *also* a religion developed from this philosophy together with folk and Buddhist religion and concerned with obtaining long life and good fortune often by magical means – **Taoist** *adj or n*, **Taoistic** *adj*

¹**tap** *n* **1a** a plug designed to fit an opening, esp in a barrel **b** a device consisting of a spout and valve attached to a pipe, bowl, etc to control the flow of a fluid **2** a removal of fluid from a body cavity **3** a tool for forming an internal screw thread **4** the act or an instance of tapping a telephone, telegraph, etc; *also* an electronic listening device used to do this **5** a small piece of metal attached to the sole or heel of tap-dancing shoes – **on tap 1** *of beer* on draught **2** readily available

²**tap** *vt* **-pp-** **1** to let out or cause to flow by piercing or by drawing a plug from the containing vessel **2a** to pierce so as to let out or draw off a fluid (e g from a body cavity) **b** to draw from or upon ⟨~ *new sources of revenue*⟩ **c** to connect an electronic listening device to (e g a telegraph or telephone wire), esp in order to acquire secret information **3** to form an internal screw thread in (e g a nut) by

means of a special tool **4** to get money from as a loan or gift – *infml* – **tapper** *n*

³**tap** *vb* **-pp-** *vt* **1a** to strike lightly, esp with a slight sound **b** to produce by striking in this manner – often + *out* ⟨~ *ped out a tune*⟩ **2** to give a light blow with ⟨~ *a pencil on the table*⟩ ~ *vi* to strike a light audible blow; rap – **tapper** *n*

⁴**tap** *n* **1** (the sound of) a light blow **2** any of several usu rapid drumbeats on a snare drum

tap dance *n* a step dance tapped out audibly by means of shoes with hard soles or soles and heels to which taps have been added – **tap-dance** *vi*, **tap dancer** *n*, **tap dancing** *n*

¹**tape** *n* **1** a narrow band of woven fabric **2** the string stretched above the finishing line of a race **3** a narrow flexible strip or band; *esp* MAGNETIC TAPE **4** a tape recording

²**tape** *vt* **1** to fasten, tie, or bind with tape **2** to record on tape, esp magnetic tape ⟨~ *an interview*⟩ ~ *vi* to record sthg on esp magnetic tape – **have someone/something taped** to have fully understood or learnt how to deal with sby or sthg – *infml*

tape deck *n* a mechanism or self-contained unit that causes magnetic tape to move past the heads of a magnetic recording device in order to generate electrical signals or to make a recording

tape measure *n* a narrow strip (e g of a limp cloth or steel tape) marked off in units (e g inches or centimetres) for measuring

¹**taper** *n* **1a** a slender candle **b** a long waxed wick used esp for lighting candles, fires, etc **2** gradual diminution of thickness, diameter, or width

²**taper** *vi* **1** to decrease gradually in thickness, diameter, or width towards one end **2** to diminish gradually ⟨*his voice* ~ *ed off*⟩ ~ *vt* to cause to taper

tape recorder *n* a device for recording signals, esp sounds, on magnetic tape and for subsequently reproducing them

tapestry *n* **1** a heavy handwoven textile used for hangings, curtains, and upholstery, characterized by complicated pictorial designs **2** a machine-made imitation of tapestry used chiefly for upholstery – **tapestried** *adj*

tapeworm *n* any of numerous cestode worms, which when adult are parasitic in the intestine of human beings or other vertebrates

tapioca *n* (a milk pudding made with) a usu granular preparation of cassava starch used esp in puddings and as a thickening in liquid food

tapir *n*, *pl* **tapirs**, *esp collectively* **tapir** any of several large chiefly nocturnal hoofed mammals with long snouts found in tropical America and Asia that are related to the horses and rhinoceroses

tappet *n* a lever or projection moved by or moving some other piece (e g a cam)

taproom *n* a barroom

taproot *n* a main root of a plant that grows vertically downwards and gives off small side roots

taps *n pl but sing or pl in constr*, *chiefly NAm* the last bugle call at night, blown as a signal that lights are to be put out; *also* a similar call blown at military funerals and memorial services

¹**tar** *n* **1a** a dark bituminous usu strong-smelling viscous liquid obtained by heating and distilling wood, coal, peat, etc **b** a residue present in smoke from burning tobacco that contains resins, acids, phenols, etc **2** a sailor – *infml*

²**tar** *vt* **-rr-** to smear with tar – **tar and feather** to smear (a person) with tar and cover with feathers as a punishment or humiliation – **tarred with the same brush** having the same faults

tarantella *n* (music suitable for) a vivacious folk dance of southern Italy in ¾ time

tarantula *n*, *pl* **tarantulas** *also* **tarantulae** **1** a European wolf spider formerly held to be the cause of tarantism **2** any of various large hairy spiders that can bite sharply but are not significantly poisonous to human beings

tarboosh *also* **tarbush** *n* a usu red hat similar to the fez worn esp by Muslim men

tardy *adj* **1** moving or progressing slowly; sluggish **2** delayed beyond the expected time; late – **tardily** *adv*, **tardiness** *n*

¹tare *n* **1** any of several vetches **2** *pl* a weed found in cornfields which is usu held to be darnel – used in the Bible

²tare *n* **1a** the weight of the wrapping material or container in which goods are packed **b** a deduction from the gross weight of a substance and its container made in allowance for the weight of the container **2** the weight of an unloaded goods vehicle **3** a container used as a counterweight in calculating the net weight of goods

³tare *vt* to weigh in order to determine the tare

target *n* **1** a small round shield **2a** an object to fire at in practice or competition; *esp* one consisting of a series of concentric circles with a bull's-eye at the centre **b** sthg (e g an aircraft or installation) fired at or attacked **3a** an object of ridicule, criticism, etc **b** a goal, objective **4** a body, surface, or material bombarded with nuclear particles or electrons, esp to produce X rays

¹tariff *n* **1** a duty or schedule of duties imposed by a government on imported or in some countries exported goods **2** a schedule of rates or prices

²tariff *vt* to subject to a tariff

¹tarmac *n* **1** tarmacadam **2** a runway, apron, or road made of tarmac

²tarmac *vt* to apply tarmac to

tarn *n* a small mountain lake

¹tarnish *vt* **1** to dull the lustre of (as if) by dirt, air, etc **2a** to mar, spoil **b** to bring discredit on ~ *vi* to become tarnished – **tarnishable** *adj*

²tarnish *n* a film of chemically altered material on the surface of a metal (e g silver)

taro *n*, *pl* **taros** (the edible starchy tuberous rootstock of) a tropical plant of the arum family

tarot *n* any of a set of 78 pictorial playing cards, including 22 trumps, used esp for fortune-telling

tarpaulin *n* (a piece of) heavy waterproof usu tarred canvas material used for protecting objects or ground exposed to the elements

tarragon *n* (a small European wormwood with) pungent aromatic leaves used as a flavouring (e g in chicken dishes and vinegar)

tarry *vi* **1** to delay or be slow in acting or doing **2** to stay in or at a place

tarsus *n*, *pl* **tarsi** **1** (the small bones that support) the back part of the foot of a vertebrate that includes the ankle and heel **2** the part of the limb of an arthropod furthest from the body **3** the plate of dense connective tissue that stiffens the eyelid – **tarsal** *adj or n*

¹tart *adj* **1** agreeably sharp or acid to the taste **2** caustic, cutting ⟨a ~ *rejoinder*⟩ – **tartish** *adj*, **tartishly** *adv*, **tartly** *adv*, **tartness** *n*

²tart *n* **1** a pastry shell or shallow pie containing a usu sweet filling (e g jam or fruit) **2** a prostitute; *broadly* a sexually promiscuous girl or woman – *infml* – **tarty** *adj*, **tartiness** *n*, **tartlet** *n*

tartan *n* (a usu twilled woollen fabric with) a plaid textile design of Scottish origin consisting of checks of varying width and colour usu patterned to designate a distinctive clan

¹tartar *n* **1** a substance consisting essentially of cream of tartar that is derived from the juice of grapes and deposited in wine casks as a reddish crust or sediment **2** an incrustation on the teeth consisting esp of calcium salts

²tartar *n* **1** *cap*, *NAm chiefly* **Tatar** a member of a group of people found mainly in the Tartar Republic of the USSR, the north Caucasus, Crimea, and parts of Siberia **2** *cap*, *NAm chiefly* **Tatar** the language of the Tartars **3** an irritable, formidable, or exacting person – **Tartar** *adj*, **Tartarian** *adj*

tartaric acid *n* a strong carboxylic acid from plants that is usu obtained from tartar, and is used esp in food and medicines

tartar sauce, tartare sauce *n* mayonnaise with chopped pickles, olives, capers, and parsley

tart up *vt*, *chiefly Br* to dress up, esp cheaply or gaudily – *infml*

task *n* **1** an assigned piece of work; a duty **2** sthg hard or unpleasant that has to be done; a chore

task force *n* a temporary grouping under 1 leader for the purpose of accomplishing a definite objective

taskmaster *n* one who assigns tasks ⟨a hard ~⟩

¹tassel *n* **1** a dangling ornament (e g for a curtain or bedspread) consisting of a bunch of cords or threads usu of even length fastened at 1 end **2** the tassel-like flower clusters of some plants, esp maize

²tassel *vb* **-ll-** (*NAm* **-l-**, **-ll-**), **tasselling** *vt* to decorate with tassels ~ *vi* to form tassel flower clusters

¹taste *vt* **1** to experience, undergo ⟨has ~d *defeat*⟩ **2** to test the flavour of by taking a little into the mouth **3** to eat or drink, esp in small quantities ⟨*the first food she has* ~d *in 2 days*⟩ **4** to perceive or recognize (as if) by the sense of taste ⟨*could* ~ *the salt on his lips*⟩ ~ *vi* **1** to test the flavour of sthg by taking a little into the mouth **2** to have perception, experience, or enjoyment – usu + *of* **3** to have a specified flavour – often + *of* ⟨*the milk* ~s *sour*⟩ ⟨*this drink* ~s *of aniseed*⟩

²taste *n* **1a** the act of tasting **b** a small amount tasted **c** a first acquaintance or experience of sthg ⟨*her first* ~ *of success*⟩ **2** (the quality of a dissolved substance as perceived by) the 1 of the 5 basic physical senses by which the qualities of dissolved substances in contact with taste buds on the tongue are interpreted by the brain as 1 or a combination of the 4 basic taste sensations sweet, bitter, sour, or salt **3** individual preference; inclination **4** (a manner or quality indicative of) critical judgment or discernment esp in aesthetic or social matters ⟨*a remark in bad* ~⟩ ⟨*his choice in furnishing showed* ~⟩

taste bud *n* any of the small organs, esp on the surface of the tongue, that receive and transmit the sensation of taste

tasteful *adj* showing or conforming to good taste – **tastefully** *adv*, **tastefulness** *n*

tasteless *adj* **1** having no taste; insipid **2** showing poor taste – disapproved of by some speakers – **tastelessly** *adv*, **tastelessness** *n*

taster *n* sby who tests food or drink by tasting, esp in order to assess quality

tasty *adj* **1** having an appetizing flavour **2** arousing interest ⟨a ~ *bit of gossip*⟩ – *infml* – **tastily** *adv*, **tastiness** *n*

¹tat *vb* **-tt-** *vi* to work at tatting ~ *vt* to make by tatting

²tat *n*, *Br* low quality material or goods – *infml*

ta-ta *interj*, *chiefly Br* goodbye – *infml*

tatter *n* **1** an irregular torn shred, esp of material **2** *pl* tattered clothing; rags – **in tatters 1** torn in pieces; ragged **2** in disarray; useless

tattered *adj* (dressed in clothes which are) old and torn

tatting *n* (the act or art of making) a delicate handmade lace formed usu by making loops and knots using a single cotton thread and a small shuttle

¹tattle *vb* **tattling** *vi* to chatter, gossip ~ *vt* to disclose (e g secrets) by gossiping – **tattler** *n*

²tattle *n* chatter, gossip

¹tattoo *n, pl* **tattoos 1a** an evening drum or bugle call sounded as notice to soldiers to return to quarters **b** an outdoor military display given by troops as a usu evening entertainment **2** a rapid rhythmic beating or rapping

²tattoo *n, pl* **tattoos** (an indelible mark made by) tattooing

³tattoo *vt* **1** to mark (the body) by inserting pigments under the skin **2** to mark (a design) on the body by tattooing – **tattooer** *n,* **tattooist** *n*

tatty *adj* shabby, dilapidated – *infml*

taught *past & past part of* TEACH

¹taunt *vt* to provoke in a mocking way; jeer at – **taunter** *n,* **tauntingly** *adv*

²taunt *n* a sarcastic provocation or insult

Taurus *n* (sby born under) the 2nd sign of the zodiac in astrology which is pictured as a bull – **Taurean** *adj or n*

taut *adj* **1a** tightly drawn; tensely stretched **b** showing anxiety; tense **2** kept in good order ⟨*a ~ ship*⟩ – **tautly** *adv,* **tautness** *n*

taut-, tauto- *comb form* same ⟨*tautomerism*⟩ ⟨*tautonym*⟩

tautology *n* **1** (an instance of) needless repetition of an idea, statement, or word **2** a statement that is true by virtue of its logical form; an analytic proposition – **tautological, tautologous** *adj,* **tautologically, tautologously** *adv*

tavern *n* INN 1a, b

tawdry *adj* cheap and tastelessly showy in appearance – **tawdrily** *adv,* **tawdriness** *n*

tawny *adj* of a warm sandy or brownish orange colour like that of well-tanned skin – **tawniness** *n*

tawse *n, chiefly Scot* a leather strap slit into strips at the end, used for beating children

¹tax *vt* **1** to assess (legal costs) **2** to levy a tax on **3** to charge, accuse *with* **4** to make strenuous demands on – **taxable** *adj,* **taxingly** *adv,* **taxer** *n*

²tax *n* **1** a charge, usu of money, imposed by a government on individuals, organizations, or property, esp to raise revenue **2** a heavy demand or strain – **after tax** net – **before tax** gross

tax-, taxo- *also* **taxi-** *comb form* arrangement ⟨*taxeme*⟩ ⟨*taxidermy*⟩

taxation *n* **1** the action of taxing; *esp* the imposition of taxes **2** revenue obtained from taxes **3** the amount assessed as a tax

tax-free *adj* exempted from tax

tax haven *n* a country with a relatively low level of taxation, esp on incomes

¹taxi *n, pl* **taxis** *also* **taxies** a taxicab

²taxi *vb* **taxis, taxies; taxiing, taxying; taxied** *vi* **1** to ride in a taxi **2** *of an aircraft* to go at low speed along the surface of the ground or water ~ *vt* **1** to transport by taxi **2** to cause (an aircraft) to taxi

taxidermy *n* the art of preparing, stuffing, and mounting the skins of animals – **taxidermist** *n,* **taxidermic** *adj*

taximeter *n* a meter fitted in a taxi to calculate the charge for each journey, usu determined by the distance travelled

taxonomy *n* (the study of the principles of) classification, specif of plants and animals according to their presumed natural relationships – **taxonomist** *n,* **taxonomic** *adj,* **taxonomically** *adv*

TB *n* tuberculosis

T-bone, T-bone steak *n* a thick steak from the thin end of a beef sirloin containing a T-shaped bone

tea *n* **1a** a shrub cultivated esp in China, Japan, and the E Indies **b** the leaves of the tea plant prepared for the market, classed according to method of manufacture (e g green tea or oolong), and graded according to leaf size (e g pekoe) **2** an aromatic beverage prepared from tea leaves by infusion with boiling water **3** any of various plants somewhat resembling tea in appearance or properties; *also* an infusion of their leaves used medicinally or as a beverage ⟨*chamomile ~*⟩ **4a** refreshments including tea with sandwiches, cakes, etc served in the late afternoon **b** a late-afternoon or early-evening meal that is usu less substantial than the midday meal

tea bag *n* a cloth or filter paper bag holding enough tea for an individual serving when infused

tea cake *n* a round yeast-leavened (sweet) bread bun that often contains currants and is usu eaten toasted with butter

teach *vb* **taught** *vt* **1** to cause to know (how), esp by showing or instructing ⟨*is ~ing me to drive*⟩ **2** to guide the studies of **3** to impart the knowledge of ⟨*~ algebra*⟩ **4** to instruct by precept, example, or experience **5** to cause to suffer the usu disagreeable consequences of sthg – *infml* ⟨*I'll ~ you to come home late*⟩ ~ *vi* to provide instruction

teacher *n* sby whose occupation is teaching

tea chest *n* a large square box used for exporting tea ⟨*stored her books in a ~*⟩

teach-in *n* **1** an informally structured conference on a usu topical issue **2** an extended meeting for lectures, demonstrations, and discussions on a topic

teaching *n* **1** the profession of a teacher **2** sthg taught; *esp* a doctrine ⟨*the ~s of Confucius*⟩

teaching hospital *n* a hospital that is affiliated to a medical school and provides medical students with the opportunity of gaining practical experience under supervision

teaching machine *n* any of various mechanical devices for presenting instructional material

tea cloth *n* **1** a small cloth for a table or trolley on which tea is to be served **2** TEA TOWEL

teahouse *n* a restaurant, esp in China or Japan, where tea and light refreshments are served

teak *n* (a tall E Indian tree of the vervain family with) hard yellowish brown wood used for furniture and shipbuilding

teal *n, pl* **teals,** *esp collectively* **teal** (any of several ducks related to) a small Old World dabbling duck the male of which has a distinctive green and chestnut head

¹team *n* **1a** two or more draught animals harnessed together **b** one or more draught animals together with harness and vehicle **2** *sing or pl in constr* a group formed for work or activity: e g **a** a group on 1 side (e g in a sporting contest or debate) **b** a crew, gang

²team *vt* **1** to yoke or join in a team **2** to combine so as to form a harmonizing arrangement ⟨*~ the shoes with the dress*⟩ ~ *vi* **1** to come together (as if) in a team – often + *up* ⟨*let's ~ up with them for a night out*⟩ **2** to form a harmonizing combination

team spirit *n* willingness to subordinate personal aims to group objectives

teamster *n* **1** sby who drives a team of horses **2** *NAm* a lorry driver

teamwork *n* mutual cooperation in a group enterprise

teapot *n* a usu round pot with a lid, spout, and handle in which tea is brewed and from which it is served

¹tear *n* **1** a drop of clear salty fluid secreted by the lachrymal gland that lubricates the eye and eyelids and is often shed as a result of grief or other emotion **2** a transparent drop of (hardened) fluid (e g resin) – **tearless** *adj* – **in tears** crying, weeping

²tear *vb* **tore; torn** *vt* **1a** to pull apart by force **b** to wound by tearing; lacerate **2** to cause division or distress to ⟨*a mind torn with doubts*⟩ **3** to remove by force ⟨tore *the child from him*⟩ **4** to make or effect (as if) by tearing ⟨~ *a hole in the paper*⟩ ~ *vi* **1** to separate on being pulled ⟨*this cloth* ~s *easily*⟩ **2** to move or act with violence, haste, or force ⟨*went* ~*ing down the street*⟩ – **tearer** *n* – **tear a strip off** to rebuke angrily – *infml* – **tear at** to cause distress or pain to ⟨tore at *my heartstrings to see her go*⟩ – **tear into** to attack physically or verbally without restraint or caution – **tear one's hair** to experience or express grief, rage, desperation, or anxiety

³tear *n* **1** damage from being torn – chiefly in *wear and tear* **2** a hole or flaw made by tearing

tearaway *n, Br* an unruly and reckless young person – *infml*

tear away *vt* to remove (oneself or another) reluctantly ⟨*she could hardly tear herself away from the book*⟩

tear down *vt* to pull down, esp violently; demolish

teardrop *n* ¹TEAR 1

tearful *adj* **1** flowing with or accompanied by tears ⟨~ *entreaties*⟩ **2** causing tears **3** inclined or about to cry ⟨*was feeling a bit* ~⟩ – **tearfully** *adv*, **tearfulness** *n*

tear gas *n* a solid, liquid, or gaseous substance that on dispersion in the atmosphere blinds the eyes with tears and is used chiefly in dispelling crowds

tearjerker *n* an excessively sentimental play, film, etc designed to provoke tears – *infml* – **tear-jerking** *adj*

tearoom *n* a restaurant where light refreshments are served

tear up *vt* **1** to tear into pieces **2** to cancel or annul, usu unilaterally ⟨tore up *the treaty*⟩

¹tease *vt* **1** to disentangle and straighten by combing or carding ⟨~ *wool*⟩ **2a** to (attempt to) disturb or annoy by persistently irritating or provoking **b** to persuade to acquiesce, esp by persistent small efforts; coax; *also* to obtain by repeated coaxing ⟨~d *the money out of her father*⟩ ~ *vi* to tease sby or sthg – **teasingly** *adv*

²tease *n* sby or sthg that teases

¹teasel, teazel, teazle *n* **1** (a flower head of) a tall Old World plant of the scabious family with flower heads that are covered with stiff hooked bracts and were formerly used, when dried to raise a nap on woollen cloth **2** a wire substitute for the teasel

²teasel *vt* **-ll-** (*NAm*, **-l-**, **-ll-**), to nap (cloth) with teasels

teaser *n* **1** a frustratingly difficult problem **2** sby who derives malicious pleasure from teasing

teaspoon *n* **1** a small spoon used esp for eating soft foods and stirring beverages **2** a teaspoonful

teaspoonful *n, pl* **teaspoonfuls** *also* **teaspoonsful** as much as a teaspoon will hold

teat *n* **1** NIPPLE 1 **2** a small projection or a nib (e g on a mechanical part); *specif* a rubber mouthpiece with usu 2 or more holes in it, attached to the top of a baby's feeding bottle – **teated** *adj*

teatime *n* the customary time for tea; late afternoon or early evening

tea towel *n* a cloth for drying the dishes

tea tray *n* a tray on which a tea service is carried

tea trolley *n, chiefly Br* a small trolley used in serving tea or light refreshments

tech *n, Br* a technical school or college – *infml*

technical *adj* **1a** having special and usu practical knowledge, esp of a mechanical or scientific subject **b** marked by or characteristic of specialization **2** of a particular subject; *esp* of a practical subject organized on scientific principles **3** in the strict legal interpretation **4** of technique **5** of or produced by ordinary commercial processes without being subjected to special purification – **technically** *adv*, **technicalness** *n*

technicality *n* sthg technical; *esp* a detail meaningful only to a specialist ⟨*a legal* ~⟩

technical knockout *n* the termination of a boxing match when a boxer is declared by the referee to be unable (e g because of injuries) to continue the fight

technician *n* **1** a specialist in the technical details of a subject or occupation ⟨*a medical* ~⟩ **2** sby who has acquired the technique of an area of specialization (e g in art) ⟨*a superb* ~ *and an artist of ingenuity*⟩

technique *n* **1** the manner in which an artist, performer, or athlete displays or manages the formal aspect of his/her skill **2a** a body of technical methods (e g in a craft or in scientific research) **b** a method of accomplishing a desired aim

techno- *comb form* technical; technological ⟨*technocracy*⟩

technocracy *n* (management of society by) a body of technical experts; *also* a society so managed – chiefly derog – **technocrat** *n*, **technocratic** *adj*

technology *n* **1** (the theory and practice of) applied science **2** the totality of the means and knowledge used to provide objects necessary for human sustenance and comfort – **technologist** *n*, **technological** *adj*, **technologically** *adv*

techy *adj* tetchy

teddy bear *n* a stuffed toy bear

teddy boy *n* any of a cult of (British) youths, esp in the 1950s, adopting the dress of the early 20th c and often having a reputation for unruly behaviour

Te Deum *n, pl* **Te Deums** a liturgical Christian hymn of praise to God

tedious *adj* tiresome because of length or dullness – **tediously** *adv*, **tediousness** *n*

tedium *n* tediousness; *also* boredom

¹tee *n* **1** sthg shaped like a capital T **2** a mark aimed at in various games (e g curling)

²tee *n* **1** a peg or a small mound used to raise a golf ball into position for striking at the beginning of play on a hole **2** the area from which a golf ball is struck at the beginning of play on a hole

³tee *vt* to place (a ball) on a tee – often + *up*

¹teem *vi* **1** to abound ⟨*lakes that* ~ *with fish*⟩ **2** to be present in large quantities

²teem *vi, Br* to rain hard

teenage, teenaged *adj* of or being people in their teens – **teenager** *n*

teens *n pl* the numbers 13 to 19 inclusive; *specif* the years 13 to 19 in a lifetime

teeny, teeny-weeny *adj* tiny – *infml*

teenybopper *n* a young teenage girl who zealously follows the latest trends in clothes, pop music, etc

tee off *vi* to drive a golf ball from a tee

tee shirt *n* a T-shirt

teeter *vi* to move unsteadily; wobble, waver

teeth *pl of* TOOTH

teethe *vi* to cut one's teeth; grow teeth – **teething** *n*

teething troubles *n pl* temporary problems occurring with new machinery or during the initial stages of an activity

teetotal *adj* practising complete abstinence from alcoholic drinks – **teetotalism** *n*

teetotaller, NAm chiefly teetotaler *n* sby teetotal

Teflon *trademark* – used for polytetrafluoroethylene

tegument *n* an integument – **tegumental** *adj*, **tegumentary** *adj*

tele-, tel- *comb form* **1** distant; at a distance; over a distance ⟨*telegram*⟩⟨*telepathy*⟩ **2a** telegraph ⟨*teleprinter*⟩ **b** television ⟨*telecast*⟩ ⟨*telecamera*⟩

telecast *vb* to televise – **telecast** *n*, **telecaster** *n*

telecommunication *n* **1** communication at a distance (e g by telegraph) **2** a science that deals with telecommunication – usu pl with sing. meaning

telegram *n* a message sent by telegraph and delivered as a written or typed note

¹telegraph *n* an apparatus or system for communicating at a distance, esp by making and breaking an electric circuit

²telegraph *vt* **1** to send or communicate (as if) by telegraph **2** to make known by signs, esp unknowingly and in advance ⟨*~ a punch*⟩ – **telegrapher** *n*, **telegraphist** *n*

telegraphese *n* the terse and abbreviated language characteristic of telegrams

telegraphic *adj* **1** of the telegraph **2** concise, terse – **telegraphically** *adv*

telegraphy *n* the use or operation of a telegraphic apparatus or system

telemeter *n* an electrical apparatus for measuring a quantity (e g pressure or temperature) and transmitting the result to a distant point – **telemeter** *n*, **telemetric** *adj*, **telemetry** *n*

teleology *n* **1** a doctrine explaining phenomena by reference to goals or purposes **2** the character attributed to nature or natural processes of being directed towards an end or designed according to a purpose – **teleologist** *n*, **teleological** *adj*

telepathy *n* communication directly from one mind to another without use of the known senses – **telepathist** *n*, **telepathic** *adj*

¹telephone *n* **1** a device for reproducing sounds at a distance; *specif* one for converting sounds into electrical impulses for transmission, usu by wire, to a particular receiver **2** the system of communications that uses telephones ⟨*get in touch by ~*⟩ – **telephonic** *adj*, **telephony** *n*

telephone *vi* to make a telephone call ~ *vt* **1** to send by telephone ⟨*~ a message*⟩ **2** (to attempt to) speak to by telephone – **telephoner** *n*

telephone directory *n* a book giving the telephone numbers of subscribers

telephonist *n*, *Br* a telephone switchboard operator

telephoto *adj* **1** of telephotography **2** being a camera lens system designed to give a large image of a distant object

telephotography *n* the photography of distant objects (e g by a camera provided with a telephoto lens) – **telephotographic** *adj*

teleprinter *n* a typewriter keyboard that transmits telegraphic signals, a typewriting device activated by telegraphic signals, or a machine that combines both these functions

TelePrompTer *trademark* – used for a device for unrolling a magnified script in front of a speaker on television

¹telescope *n* **1** a usu tubular optical instrument for viewing distant objects by means of the refraction of light rays through a lens or the reflection of light rays by a concave mirror **2** RADIO TELESCOPE

²telescope *vi* **1** to slide one part within another like the cylindrical sections of a hand telescope **2** to become compressed under impact **3** to become condensed or

shortened ~ *vt* **1** to cause to telescope **2** to condense, shorten

telescopic *adj* **1a** of or performed with a telescope **b** suitable for seeing or magnifying distant objects **2** able to discern objects at a distance **3** having parts that telescope – **telescopically** *adv*

televise *vt* to broadcast (an event or film) by television

television *n* **1** an electronic system of transmitting changing images together with sound along a wire or through space by converting the images and sounds into electrical signals **2** a television receiving set **3a**(1) the television broadcasting industry (2) a television broadcasting organization or station ⟨*Tyne-Tees* Television⟩ **b** the medium of television communication

televisual *adj*, *chiefly Br* of or suitable for broadcast by television

telex *n* a communications service involving teleprinters connected by wire through automatic exchanges; *also* a message by telex – **telex** *vb*

tell *vb* **told** *vt* **1** to count, enumerate ⟨*all* told *there were 27 present*⟩ **2a** to relate in detail; narrate ⟨*~ me a story*⟩ **b** to give utterance to; express in words **3** to make known; divulge **4a** to report to; inform **b** to assure emphatically ⟨*he did not do it, I ~ you*⟩ **5** to order ⟨*told her to wait*⟩ **6a** to ascertain by observing ⟨*can never ~ whether he's lying or not*⟩ **b** to distinguish, discriminate ⟨*can't ~ Bach from the Beatles*⟩ ~ *vi* **1** to give an account **2** to make a positive assertion; decide definitely ⟨*you can never ~ for certain*⟩ **3** to act as an informer – often + *on* **4** to take effect ⟨*the worry began to ~ on her nerves*⟩ **5** to serve as evidence or indication ⟨*will ~ against you in court*⟩

teller *n* **1** sby who relates or communicates ⟨*a ~ of stories*⟩ **2** sby who counts: e g **a** sby appointed to count votes **b** a member of a bank's staff concerned with the direct handling of money received or paid out

telling *adj* carrying great weight and producing a marked effect ⟨*the most ~ evidence against him*⟩ – **tellingly** *adv*

tell off *vt* **1** to number and set apart; *esp* to assign to a special duty ⟨*told off a detail and put them to digging a trench*⟩ **2** to give a telling-off to

telltale *n* **1** sby who spreads gossip or rumours; *esp* an informer **2** a device for indicating or recording sthg (e g the position of a vessel's rudder) – **telltale** *adj*

telly *n*, *chiefly Br* (a) television – *infml*

temerity *n* unreasonable disregard for danger or opposition; *broadly* cheek, nerve

¹temp *n* sby (e g a typist or secretary) employed temporarily – *infml*

²temp *vi* to work as a temp – *infml*

¹temper *vt* **1** to moderate (sthg harsh) *with* the addition of sthg less severe ⟨*~ justice with mercy*⟩ **2** to bring to a suitable state, esp by mixing in or adding a liquid ingredient; *esp* to mix (clay) with water or a modifier and knead to a uniform texture **3** to bring (esp steel) to the right degree of hardness by reheating (and quenching) after cooling **4** to strengthen the character of through hardship ⟨*troops ~ed in battle*⟩ **5** to adjust the pitch of (a note, chord, or instrument) to a temperament – **temperable** *adj*, **temperer** *n*

²temper *n* **1** characteristic tone ⟨*the ~ of the times*⟩ **2** the state of a substance with respect to certain desired qualities (e g the degree of hardness or resilience given to steel by tempering) **3a** a characteristic cast of mind or state of feeling **b** composure, equanimity **c** (proneness to displays of) an uncontrolled and often disproportionate rage ⟨*he has/is in a terrible ~*⟩

tempera *n* (a work produced by) a method of painting

using pigment ground and mixed with an emulsion (e g of egg yolk and water)

temperament n **1a** a person's peculiar or distinguishing mental or physical character (which according to medieval physiology was determined by the relative proportions of the humours) **b** excessive sensitiveness or irritability **2** the modification of the musical intervals of the pure scale to produce a set of 12 fixed notes to the octave which enables a keyboard instrument to play in more than 1 key

temperamental adj **1** of or arising from individual character or constitution 〈~ peculiarities〉 **2a** easily upset or irritated; liable to sudden changes of mood **b** unpredictable in behaviour or performance – **temperamentally** adv

temperance n **1** moderation, self-restraint **2** habitual moderation in the indulgence of the appetites; specif moderation in or abstinence from the use of alcoholic drink

temperate adj **1** moderate: e g **a** not extreme or excessive 〈a ~ climate〉 〈a ~ speech〉 **b** moderate in indulgence of appetite or desire; esp abstemious in the consumption of alcohol **2a** having a moderate climate **b** found in or associated with a temperate climate – **temperately** adv, **temperateness** n

temperature n **1a** degree of hotness or coldness as measured on an arbitrary scale (e g in degrees Celsius) **b** the degree of heat natural to the body of a living being **2** an abnormally high body heat

tempered adj **1a** having the elements mixed in satisfying proportions **b** qualified or diluted by the mixture or influence of an additional ingredient **2** having a specified temper – in combination 〈short-tempered〉

tempest n **1** a violent storm **2** a tumult, uproar

tempestuous adj turbulent, stormy 〈~ weather〉 〈a ~ debate〉 – **tempestuously** adv, **tempestuousness** n

template, templet n **1** a short piece or block placed horizontally in a wall under a beam to distribute its weight or pressure (e g over a door) **2a** a gauge, pattern, or mould used as a guide to the form of a piece being made **b** a molecule (e g of RNA) in a biological system that carries the genetic code for protein or other macromolecules **c** an overlay

¹temple n **1a** a building dedicated to worship among any of various ancient civilizations (e g the Egyptians, the Greeks, and the Romans) and present-day non-Christian religions (e g Hinduism and Buddhism) **b** often cap any of 3 successive national sanctuaries in ancient Jerusalem **2** a place devoted or dedicated to a specified purpose **3** chiefly NAm a Reform or Conservative synagogue

²temple n the flattened space on either side of the forehead of some mammals (e g human beings)

³temple n a device in a loom for keeping the cloth stretched

tempo n, pl **tempi, tempos 1** the speed of a musical piece or passage indicated by any of a series of directions and often by an exact metronome marking **2** rate of motion or activity

temporal adj **1a** of time as opposed to eternity or space; esp transitory **b** of earthly life **c** of lay or secular concerns **2** of grammatical tense or a distinction of time 〈when is a ~ conjunction〉 – **temporally** adv

¹temporary adj lasting for a limited time – **temporarily** adv, **temporariness** n

²temporary n a temp

temporize, -ise vi **1** to comply temporarily with the demands of the time or occasion **2** to draw out negotiations so as to gain time – **temporizer** n, **temporization** n

tempt vt **1** to entice, esp to evil, by promise of pleasure or gain **2** to risk provoking the disfavour of 〈shouldn't ~ fate〉 **3a** to induce to do sthg **b** to cause to be strongly inclined 〈he was ~ed to call it quits〉 **c** to appeal to; entice 〈the idea ~s me〉 – **temptable** adj, **tempter, temptress** n

temptation n **1** tempting or being tempted, esp to evil **2** sthg tempting

ten n **1** (the number) 10 **2** the tenth in a set or series 〈the ~ of diamonds〉 **3** sthg having 10 parts or members or a denomination of 10 **4** the number occupying the position 2 to the left of the decimal point in the Arabic notation; also, pl this position – **ten** adj or pron, **tenfold** adj or adv, **tenth** adj or n

tenable adj capable of being held, maintained, or defended – **tenableness** n, **tenably** adv, **tenability** n

tenacious adj **1** tending to stick or cling, esp to another substance **2a** persistent in maintaining or keeping to sthg valued as habitual **b** retentive 〈a ~ memory〉 – **tenaciously** adv, **tenaciousness** n, **tenacity** n

¹tenant n **1a** a holder of real estate by any kind of right **b** an occupant of lands or property of another; specif sby who rents or leases a house or flat from a landlord **2** an occupant, dweller – **tenantless** adj, **tenancy** n

²tenant vt to hold or inhabit as a tenant – **tenantable** adj

tenant farmer n a farmer who works land owned by another and pays rent

tenantry n sing or pl in constr tenants collectively

tench n, pl **tench, tenches** a Eurasian freshwater fish related to the dace and noted for its ability to survive outside water

Ten Commandments n pl the commandments given by God to Moses on Mt Sinai, recorded in Ex 20:1–17

¹tend vt to have charge of; take care of

²tend vi **1** to move, direct, or develop one's course in a specified direction **2** to show an inclination or tendency – + to, towards, or to and an infinitive

tendency n **1a** a general trend or movement 〈the growing ~ for prices to rise faster than wages〉 **b** an inclination or predisposition to some particular end, or towards a particular kind of thought or action 〈his books show a ~ to drop into sentimentality〉 **2** the purposeful trend of sthg written or said

tendentious also **tendencious** adj marked by a tendency in favour of a particular point of view – chiefly derog – **tendentiously** adv, **tendentiousness** n

¹tender adj **1a** having a soft or yielding texture; easily broken, cut, or damaged **b** easily chewed **2a** physically weak **b** immature, young 〈children of ~ years〉 **3** fond, loving 〈a ~ lover〉 **4a** showing care 〈~ regard〉 **b** highly susceptible to impressions or emotions 〈a ~ conscience〉 **5a** gentle, mild 〈~ breeding〉 〈~ irony〉 **b** delicate or soft in quality or tone 〈~ skin〉 **6a** sensitive to touch **b** sensitive to injury or insult 〈~ pride〉 **c** demanding careful and sensitive handling 〈a ~ situation〉 – **tenderly** adv, **tenderness** n

²tender n **1a** a ship employed to attend other ships (e g to supply provisions) **b** a boat or small steamer for communication between shore and a larger ship **2** a vehicle attached to a locomotive for carrying a supply of fuel and water

³tender vt **1** to make a tender of **2** to present for acceptance 〈~ed his resignation〉 ~vi to make a bid 〈the company ~s for and builds dams〉 – **tenderer** n

⁴tender n **1** an unconditional offer in satisfaction of a debt or obligation, made to avoid a penalty for nonpayment or nonperformance **2** an offer, proposal: e g **a** a formal esp written offer or bid for a contract **b** a public expression of willingness to buy not less than a specified number of shares at a fixed price from shareholders **3** sthg that may be offered in payment; *specif* money

tenderfoot *n, pl* **tenderfeet** *also* **tenderfoots** an inexperienced beginner

tenderhearted *adj* easily moved to love, pity, or sorrow – **tenderheartedly** *adv*

tenderize, -ise *vt* to make (meat or meat products) tender by beating or adding an enzyme that breaks down fibrous tissue – **tenderizer** *n*, **tenderization** *n*

tenderloin *n* a pork or beef fillet

tendon *n* a tough cord or band of dense white fibrous connective tissue that connects a muscle with a bone or other part and transmits the force exerted by the muscle – **tendinous** *adj*

tendril *n* a slender spirally coiling sensitive organ that attaches a plant to its support – **tendriled, tendrilled** *adj*

tenement *n* **1** land or other property held by one person from another **2** (a flat in) a large building; *esp* one meeting minimum standards and typically found in the poorer parts of a large city

tenet *n* a principle, belief, or doctrine; *esp* one held in common by members of an organization or group

tenner *n, Br* a £10 note; *also* the sum of £10 – *infml*

tennis *n* **1** REAL TENNIS **2** a singles or doubles game that is played with rackets and a light elastic ball on a flat court divided by a low net

tennis elbow *n* inflammation and pain of the elbow, usu resulting from excessive twisting movements of the hand

¹**tenon** *n* a projecting part of a piece of material (e g wood) for insertion into a mortise

²**tenon** *vt* **1** to unite by a tenon **2** to cut or fit for insertion in a mortise

tenor *n* **1** the course of thought of sthg spoken or written **2a** the next to the lowest part in 4-part harmony **b** (sby with) the highest natural adult male singing voice **c** a member of a family of instruments having a range next lower than that of the alto **3** a continuance in a course or activity – **tenor** *adj*

tenpin *n* a bottle-shaped pin used in tenpin bowling

tenpin bowling *n* an indoor bowling game using 10 pins and a large ball in which each player is allowed to bowl 2 balls in each of 10 frames

¹**tense** *n* (a member of) a set of inflectional forms of a verb that express distinctions of time

²**tense** *adj* **1** stretched tight; made taut **2a** feeling or showing nervous tension **b** marked by strain or suspense **3** articulated with relatively tense muscles – used e g of the vowel /ee/ in contrast with the vowel /i/ – **tensely** *adv*, **tenseness** *n*

³**tense** *vb* to make or become tense – often + *up*

tensile *adj* **1** ductile **2** of or involving tension – **tensility** *n*

¹**tension** *n* **1a** stretching or being stretched to stiffness **b** STRESS 1a **2a** either of 2 balancing forces causing or tending to cause extension **b** the stress resulting from the elongation of an elastic body **c** gas pressure **3a** inner striving, unrest, or imbalance, often with physiological indication of emotion **b** latent hostility **c** a balance maintained in an artistic work between opposing forces or elements **4** electrical potential ⟨*high* ~⟩ – **tensional** *adj*, **tensionless** *adj*

²**tension** *vt* to tighten to a desired or appropriate degree – **tensioner** *n*

¹**tent** *n* **1** a collapsible shelter (e g of canvas) stretched and supported by poles **2** a canopy or enclosure placed over

the head and shoulders to retain vapours or oxygen during medical treatment – **tented** *adj*, **tentless** *adj*

²**tent** *vi* to live in a tent ~ *vt* to cover (as if) with a tent

tentacle *n* **1** any of various elongated flexible animal parts, chiefly on the head or about the mouth, used for feeling, grasping, etc **2a** sthg like a tentacle (e g in grasping or feeling out) **b** a sensitive hair on a plant (e g the sundew) – **tentacled** *adj*, **tentacular** *adj*

tentative *adj* **1** not fully worked out or developed **2** hesitant, uncertain ⟨*a* ~ *smile*⟩ – **tentative** *n*, **tentatively** *adv*

tenter *n* an apparatus used for drying and stretching cloth

tenterhook *n* a sharp hooked nail used esp for fastening cloth on a tenter – **on tenterhooks** in a state of uneasiness, strain, or suspense

tenth *adj or n* (of or being) number ten in a countable series

tenuous *adj* **1** not dense in consistency ⟨*a* ~ *fluid*⟩ **2** not thick ⟨*a* ~ *rope*⟩ **3** having little substance or strength ⟨*a* ~ *hold on reality*⟩ – **tenuously** *adv*, **tenuousness** *n*, **tenuity** *n*

tenure *n* **1a** the holding of property, an office, etc **b** *chiefly NAm* freedom from summary dismissal, esp from a teaching post **2** grasp, hold – *fml* – **tenured** *adj*, **tenurial** *adj*

tepee *n* a N American Indian conical tent, usu made of skins

tepid *adj* **1** moderately warm ⟨*a* ~ *bath*⟩ **2** not enthusiastic ⟨*a* ~ *interest*⟩ – **tepidly** *adv*, **tepidness** *n*, **tepidity** *n*

tequila *n* **1** a Mexican agave plant cultivated as a source of mescal **2** a Mexican spirit made by redistilling mescal

tercentenary *n* a 300th anniversary or its celebration – **tercentenary** *adj*

tercentennial *n* a tercentenary – **tercentennial** *adj*

¹**term** *n* **1a** an end, termination; *also* a time assigned for sthg (e g payment) **b** the time at which a pregnancy of normal length ends ⟨*had her baby at full* ~⟩ **2a** a limited or definite extent of time; *esp* the time for which sthg lasts ⟨*medium*-term *credit*⟩ **b** an estate or interest held for a term **c** any one of the periods of the year during which the courts are in session **3** any of the usu 3 periods of instruction into which an academic year is divided **4a** a mathematical expression connected to another by a plus or minus sign **b** an expression that forms part of a fraction or proportion or of a series or sequence **5** a concept, word, or phrase appearing as subject or predicate in a logical proposition **6a** a word or expression with a precise meaning; *esp* one peculiar to a restricted field ⟨*legal* ~s⟩ **b** *pl* diction of a specified kind ⟨*spoke in flattering* ~s⟩ **7** *pl* provisions relating to an agreement ⟨~s *of sale*⟩; *also* agreement on such provisions **8** *pl* mutual relationship ⟨*on good* ~s *with him*⟩ – **in terms** expressly, explicitly – **in terms of** in relation to; concerning

²**term** *vt* to apply a term to; call ⟨*wouldn't* ~ *it difficult*⟩

termagant *n* **1** *cap* a violent character in English miracle plays representing an Islamic deity **2** an overbearing or nagging woman

terminable *adj* capable of being terminated – **terminableness** *n*

¹**terminal** *adj* **1a** of or being an end, extremity, boundary, or terminus **b** growing at the end of a branch or stem ⟨*a* ~ *bud*⟩ **2a** of or occurring in a term or each term **b** occurring at or causing the end of life ⟨~ *cancer*⟩ **3** occurring at or being the end of a period or series – **terminally** *adv*

²**terminal** *n* **1** a device attached to the end of a wire or cable or to an electrical apparatus for convenience in making connections **2** the end of a carrier line (e g shipping line or airline) with its associated buildings and facilities ⟨*the West London air* ~⟩ **3** a device (e g a teleprinter) through which a user can communicate with a computer

terminate *vt* **1a** to bring to an end **b** to form the conclusion of **2** to serve as an ending, limit, or boundary of ~ *vi* **1** to extend only to a limit (e g a point or line); *esp* to reach a terminus ⟨*this train* ~s *at Glasgow*⟩ **2** to come to an end in time – often + *in* or *with* ⟨*the coalition* ~d *with the election*⟩ **3** to form an ending or outcome – often + *in* or *with* ⟨*the match* ~d *with the champion winning*⟩ – **termination** *n*

terminology *n* the technical terms used in a particular subject – **terminological** *adj*, **terminologically** *adv*

terminus *n*, *pl* **termini, terminuses 1** a finishing point; an end **2** a post or stone marking a boundary **3** (the station, town, or city at) the end of a transport line or travel route **4** an extreme point or element

termite *n* any of numerous often destructive pale-coloured soft-bodied insects that live in colonies and feed on wood

terms of reference *n pl* the precise delineation of competence (e g of a committee)

tern *n* any of numerous water birds that are smaller than the related gulls and have a black cap, a white body, and often forked tails

terpsichorean *adj* of dancing

¹**terrace** *n* **1** a relatively level paved or planted area adjoining a building **2** a raised embankment with a level top **3** a level usu narrow and steep-fronted area bordering a river, sea, etc **4a** a row of houses or flats on raised ground or a sloping site **b** a row of similar houses joined into 1 building by common walls **c** a street

²**terrace** *vt* to make into a terrace

terracotta *n* **1** an unglazed brownish red fired clay used esp for statuettes and vases and as a building material **2** brownish orange

terra firma *n* dry land; solid ground

terrain *n* **1** (the physical features of) an area of land **2** an environment, milieu

terrapin *n* any of several small edible freshwater reptiles of the same order as, and similar to, tortoises but adapted for swimming

terrestrial *adj* **1a** of the earth or its inhabitants **b** mundane, prosaic **2a** of land as distinct from air or water **b** *of organisms* living on or in land or soil **3** *of a planet* like the earth in density, composition, etc – **terrestrial** *n*, **terrestrially** *adv*

terrible *adj* **1a** exciting intense fear; terrifying **b** formidable in nature ⟨*a* ~ *responsibility*⟩ **c** requiring great fortitude ⟨*a* ~ *order*⟩; *also* severe ⟨*a* ~ *winter*⟩ **2** extreme, great ⟨*a* ~ *amount of trouble arranging all this*⟩ **3** of very poor quality; awful ⟨*a* ~ *performance*⟩; *also* highly unpleasant *USE* (2&3) infml – **terribleness** *n*

terribly *adv* very ⟨~ *lucky*⟩ – infml

terrier *n* **1** (a member of) any of various breeds of usu small dogs, orig used by hunters to drive out small furred game from underground **2** *usu cap, Br* a territorial

terrific *adj* **1** exciting fear or awe **2** extraordinarily great or intense **3** unusually fine *USE* (2&3) infml – **terrifically** *adv*

terrify *vt* **1** to fill with terror or apprehension **2** to drive or impel by menacing; scare, deter – **terrifyingly** *adv*

¹**territorial** *adj* **1a** of territory or land **b** of private property ⟨~ *magnates*⟩ **2a** of or restricted to a particular area or district **b** exhibiting territoriality ⟨~ *birds*⟩ – **territorially** *adv*

²**territorial** *n* a member of a territorial army, esp the Territorial Army and Volunteer Reserve

territorial army *n* a voluntary force organized by a locality to provide a trained army reserve that can be mobilized in an emergency

territorial waters *n pl* the waters under the sovereign jurisdiction of a nation

territory *n* **1a** a geographical area under the jurisdiction of a government **b** an administrative subdivision of a country **c** a part of the USA not included within any state but with a separate legislature **2a** an indeterminate geographical area **b** a field of knowledge or interest **c** a geographical area having a specified characteristic ⟨*in Rolls Royce* ~ – *Annabel*⟩ **3a** an assigned area; *esp* one in which an agent or distributor operates **b** an area, often including a nesting site or den, occupied and defended by an animal or group of animals

terror *n* **1** a state of intense fear **2** sby or sthg that inspires fear **3** REIGN OF TERROR **4** revolutionary violence (e g the planting of bombs) **5** an appalling person or thing; *esp* a brat – infml

terrorism *n* the systematic use of terror, esp as a means of coercion – **terrorist** *adj or n*, **terroristic** *adj*

terrorize, -ise *vt* **1** to fill with terror or anxiety **2** to coerce by threat or violence – **terrorization** *n*

terror-stricken *adj* overcome with an uncontrollable terror

terry *n* an absorbent fabric with uncut loops on both faces – **terry** *adj*

terse *adj* concise; *also* brusque, curt – **tersely** *adv*, **terseness** *n*

tertian *adj, of malarial symptoms* recurring at approximately 48-hour intervals

¹**tertiary** *n* **1** sby belonging to a monastic third order **2** *cap* the Tertiary period or system of rocks

²**tertiary** *adj* **1a** of third rank, importance, or value **b** of higher education **c** of or being a service industry **2** *cap* of or being the first period of the Cainozoic era or the corresponding system of rocks **3** occurring in or being a third stage

Terylene *trademark* – used for a synthetic polyester textile fibre

tessellated *adj* chequered

¹**test** *n* **1a** a critical examination, observation, or evaluation **b** a basis for evaluation **2** a means or instance of testing: e g **a** a procedure used to identify a substance ⟨*iodine* ~ *for the presence of starch*⟩ **b** a series of questions or exercises for measuring the knowledge, intelligence, etc of an individual or group **c** TEST MATCH **3** *chiefly Br* a cupel

²**test** *vt* to put to the test; try ⟨~s *my patience*⟩ ⟨*wet roads that* ~ *a car's tyres*⟩ ~ *vi* to apply a test as a means of analysis or diagnosis – often + *for* – **testable** *adj*, **tester** *n*

³**test** *n* an external hard or firm covering (e g a shell) of an invertebrate (e g a mollusc)

testament *n* **1** *cap* either of the 2 main divisions of the Bible **2** a tangible proof or tribute **3** a will **4** *archaic* a covenant between God and man – **testamentary** *adj*

testate *adj* having made a valid will

testator, *fem* **testatrix** *n* sby who leaves a will

test ban *n* a self-imposed ban on the atmospheric testing of nuclear weapons

test case *n* a representative case whose outcome is likely to serve as a precedent

tester *n* the canopy over a bed, pulpit, or altar

testicle *n* a testis, esp of a mammal and usu with its enclosing structures (e g the scrotum) – **testicular** *adj*

testify *vi* **1a** to make a statement based on personal knowledge or belief **b** to serve as evidence or proof **2** to make a solemn declaration under oath ~ *vt* **1a** to bear witness to **b** to serve as evidence of **2** to make known (a personal conviction) **3** to declare under oath – **testifier** *n*

¹testimonial *adj* **1** of or constituting testimony **2** expressive of appreciation, gratitude, or esteem ⟨a ~ *dinner*⟩

²testimonial *n* **1** a letter of recommendation **2** an expression of appreciation or esteem (e g in the form of a gift)

testimony *n* **1a** firsthand authentication of a fact **b** an outward sign; evidence ⟨*is* ~ *of his abilities*⟩ **c** a sworn statement by a witness **2** a public declaration of religious experience

testis *n, pl* **testes** a male reproductive gland

test match *n* any of a series of international matches, esp cricket matches

test pilot *n* a pilot who specializes in putting new or experimental aircraft through manoeuvres designed to test them by producing strains in excess of normal

test-tube *adj, of a baby* conceived by artificial insemination, esp outside the mother's body

test tube *n* a thin glass tube closed at 1 end and used in chemistry, biology, etc

testy *adj* impatient, ill-humoured – **testily** *adv*, **testiness** *n*

tetanus *n* **1** (the bacterium, usu introduced through a wound, that causes) an infectious disease characterized by spasm of voluntary muscles, esp of the jaw **2** prolonged contraction of a muscle resulting from rapidly repeated motor impulses – **tetanize** *vt*

tetchy *adj* irritably or peevishly sensitive – **tetchily** *adv*, **tetchiness** *n*

¹tête-à-tête *adv or adj* (in) private

²tête-à-tête *n* **1** a private conversation between 2 people **2** a seat (e g a sofa) designed for 2 people to sit facing each other

¹tether *n* **1** a rope, chain, etc by which an animal is fastened so that it can move only within a set radius **2** the limit of one's strength or resources – chiefly in *the end of one's tether*

²tether *vt* to fasten or restrain (as if) by a tether

tetravalent *adj* having a valency of 4

Teutonic *n* Germanic

text *n* **1** (a work containing) the original written or printed words and form of a literary composition **2** the main body of printed or written matter, esp on a page or in a book **3a** a passage of Scripture chosen esp for the subject of a sermon or in authoritative support of a doctrine **b** a passage from an authoritative source providing a theme (e g for a speech) **4** a textbook **5** a theme, topic

¹textbook *n* a book used in the study of a subject; *specif* one containing a presentation of the principles of a subject and used by students

²textbook *adj* conforming to the principles or descriptions in textbooks: e g **a** ideal ⟨*tried hard to be a* ~ *Mum*⟩ **b** typical

textile *n* **1** CLOTH 1; *esp* a woven or knitted cloth **2** a fibre, filament, or yarn used in making cloth

textual *adj* of or based on a text – **textually** *adv*

¹texture *n* **1** the structure formed by the threads of a fabric **2** identifying quality; character ⟨*the* ~ *of American culture*⟩ **3a** the size or organization of the constituent particles of a body or substance ⟨*a soil that is coarse in* ~⟩ **b** the visual or tactile surface characteristics of sthg, esp

fabric ⟨*the* ~ *of an oil painting*⟩ ⟨*the roughish* ~ *of tweed*⟩ **4a** the distinctive or identifying part or quality ⟨*the rich* ~ *of his prose*⟩ **b** a pattern of musical sound created by notes or lines played or sung together – **textural** *adj*, **textured** *adj*

²texture *vt* to give a particular texture to

¹-th, -eth *suffix* (→ *adj*) – used in forming ordinal numbers ⟨*hundredth*⟩ ⟨*fortieth*⟩

²-th, -eth *suffix* (→ *n*) – used in forming fractions ⟨*a fortieth*⟩ ⟨*two hundred*ths *of an inch*⟩

³-th *suffix* (→ *n*) **1** act or process of ⟨*growth*⟩ ⟨*birth*⟩ **2** state or condition of ⟨*dearth*⟩ ⟨*filth*⟩

thalidomide *adj or n* (of or affected by) a sedative and hypnotic drug found to cause malformation of infants born to mothers using it during pregnancy

¹than *conj* **1a** – used with comparatives to indicate the second member or the member taken as the point of departure in a comparison ⟨*older* ~ *I am*⟩ ⟨*easier said* ~ *done*⟩ **b** – used to indicate difference of kind, manner, or degree ⟨*would starve rather* ~ *beg*⟩ **2** rather than – usu only after *prefer, preferable* **3** other than; but ⟨*no alternative* ~ *to sack him*⟩ **4** chiefly NAm from – usu only after *different, differently*

²than *prep* in comparison with ⟨*older* ~ *me*⟩ ⟨*less* ~ *£1000*⟩

thane *also* **thegn** *n* **1** a free retainer of an Anglo-Saxon lord; *esp* one holding lands in exchange for military service **2** a Scottish feudal lord – **thaneship** *n*

thank *vt* **1** to express gratitude to – used in *thank you*, usu without a subject, to express gratitude politely ⟨~ *you for the loan*⟩; used in such phrases as *thank God, thank heaven*, usu without a subject, to express the speaker's or writer's pleasure or satisfaction in sthg **2** to hold responsible ⟨*had only himself to* ~ *for his loss*⟩ – **thanker** *n*

thankful *adj* **1** conscious of benefit received; grateful **2** feeling or expressing thanks **3** well pleased; glad ⟨*he was* ~ *that the room was dark*⟩ – **thankfulness** *n*

thankless *adj* **1** not expressing or feeling gratitude **2** not likely to obtain thanks; unappreciated; *also* unprofitable, futile ⟨*it's a* ~ *job trying to grow tomatoes in England out of doors*⟩ – **thanklessly** *adv*, **thanklessness** *n*

thanks *n pl* **1** kindly or grateful thoughts; gratitude **2** an expression of gratitude ⟨*received with* ~ *the sum of £50*⟩ – often in an utterance containing no verb and serving as a courteous and somewhat informal expression of gratitude ⟨*many* ~⟩ – **no thanks to** not as a result of any benefit conferred by ⟨*he feels better now*, no thanks to *you*⟩ – **thanks to 1** with the help of ⟨thanks to *modern medicine, man's life span is growing longer*⟩ **2** owing to ⟨*our arrival was delayed*, thanks to *the fog*⟩

thanksgiving *n* **1** an expression of gratefulness, esp to God **2** a prayer of gratitude

thank-you *n* a polite expression of one's gratitude

¹that *pron, pl* **those 1a** the thing or idea just mentioned ⟨*after* ~ *he went to bed*⟩ **b** a relatively distant person or thing introduced for observation or discussion ⟨*who is* ~ *?*⟩ ⟨*those are chestnuts and these are elms*⟩ **c** the thing or state of affairs there ⟨*look at* ~ *?*⟩ – sometimes used disparagingly of a person **d** the kind or thing specified as follows ⟨*the purest water is* ~ *produced by distillation*⟩ **e** what is understood from the context ⟨*take* ~ *!*⟩ ⟨*how's* ~ *?*⟩ **2** one of such a group; such ⟨~ *'s life*⟩ **3** – used to indicate emphatic repetition of an idea previously presented ⟨*is he capable? He is* ~⟩ **4** *pl* the people; such ⟨*those who think the time has come*⟩ THAT IS TO SAY – **that's a** THERE'S A – **that's that** that concludes the matter

²that *adj, pl* **those 1** being the person, thing, or idea specified, mentioned, or understood ⟨~ *cake we bought*⟩

2 the farther away or less immediately under observation ⟨*this chair or ~ one*⟩

³that *conj* **1a** – used to introduce a noun clause (1) as subject, object, or complement of a verb ⟨*said ~ he was afraid*⟩, (2) anticipated by *it* ⟨*it is unlikely ~ he'll be in*⟩, or (3) as complement to a noun or adjective ⟨*the fact ~ you're here*⟩ **b** – used to introduce a clause modifying an adverb or adverbial expression ⟨*will go anywhere ~ he's invited*⟩ **c** – used to introduce an emotional exclamation ⟨*~ it should come to this!*⟩ or express a wish ⟨*oh, ~ he would come!*⟩ **2** – used to introduce a subordinate clause expressing (1) purpose ⟨*worked harder ~ he might win esteem*⟩, (2) reason ⟨*glad ~ you are free of it*⟩, or (3) result ⟨*walked so fast ~ we couldn't keep up*⟩

⁴that *pron* **1** – used to introduce a usu restrictive relative clause in reference to a person, thing, or group as subject ⟨*it was George ~ told me*⟩ or as object of a verb or of a following preposition ⟨*the house ~ Jack built*⟩ **2a** at, in, on, by, with, for, or to which ⟨*the reason ~ he came*⟩ ⟨*the way ~ he spoke*⟩ **b** according to what; to the extent of what – used after a negative ⟨*has never been here ~ I know of*⟩

⁵that *adv* **1** to the extent indicated or understood ⟨*a nail about ~ long*⟩ **2** very, extremely – usu with the negative ⟨*not really ~ expensive*⟩ **3** *dial Br* to such an extreme degree ⟨*I'm ~ hungry I could eat a horse*⟩

¹thatch *vt* to cover (as if) with thatch – **thatcher** *n*

²thatch *n* **1** plant material (e g straw) used as a roof covering **2** the hair of one's head – often humor; *broadly* anything resembling the thatch of a house

¹thaw *vt* to cause to thaw – often + *out* ~ *vi* **1a** to go from a frozen to a liquid state **b** to become free of the effect (e g stiffness, numbness, or hardness) of cold as a result of exposure to warmth – often + *out* **2** to be warm enough to melt ice and snow – + *it*; used in reference to the weather **3** to become less hostile ⟨*relations with E Germany have ~ed*⟩ **4** to become less aloof, cold, or reserved

²thaw *n* **1** the action, fact, or process of thawing ⟨*the ~ in relations with Western Europe*⟩ **2** a period of weather warm enough to thaw ice

¹the *definite article* **1a** – used before nouns when the referent has been previously specified by context or circumstance ⟨*put ~ cat out*⟩ ⟨*ordered bread and cheese, but didn't eat ~ cheese*⟩ **b** – indicating that a following noun is unique or universally recognized ⟨*~ Pope*⟩ ⟨*~ south*⟩ ⟨*~ future*⟩ **c** – used before a noun denoting time to indicate the present or the period under consideration ⟨*book of ~ month*⟩ **d** – used before certain proper names ⟨*~ Mayflower*⟩ ⟨*~ Rhine*⟩ ⟨*~ Alhambra*⟩ ⟨*~ Alps*⟩ **e** – used before the name of a familiar accessory of daily life to indicate a service at hand ⟨*talked on ~ telephone*⟩ ⟨*turned off ~ gas*⟩ **f** – used before the names of certain diseases or conditions ⟨*~ jitters*⟩ ⟨*~ mumps*⟩ **g** – used before the names of parts of the body or of the clothing instead of a possessive adjective ⟨*inflammation of ~ bladder*⟩ ⟨*took him by ~ sleeve*⟩ **h** – used before the name of a branch of human endeavour or proficiency ⟨*play ~ piano*⟩ ⟨*study ~ arts*⟩ **i** – indicating an occupation or pursuit symbolically associated with a following noun ⟨*~ pulpit*⟩ ⟨*~ bottle*⟩ **J** – designating 1 of a class as the best or most worth singling out ⟨*this is ~ life*⟩ ⟨*you can't be ~ Elvis Presley!*⟩ **k** – used before the name of a Scottish clan to denote its chief ⟨*~ McTavish*⟩ **l** – used in prepositional phrases to indicate that the following noun serves as a basis for computation ⟨*sold by ~ dozen*⟩ **m** – used before the pl form of a number that is a multiple of 10 to denote a particular decade of a century or of a person's life ⟨*life in ~ twenties*⟩ **2a** which or who is –

limiting the application of a modified noun to what is specified ⟨*~ right answer*⟩ ⟨*Peter ~ Great*⟩ **b** – used before a noun to limit its application to that specified by what follows ⟨*~ University of London*⟩ ⟨*~ man on my right*⟩ ⟨*didn't have ~ time to write*⟩ **3** – used before a singular noun to indicate generic use ⟨*~ dog is a mammal*⟩ ⟨*a history of ~ novel*⟩ **4a** that which is ⟨*nothing but ~ best*⟩ **b** those who are ⟨*~ elite*⟩ ⟨*~ British*⟩ **c** he or she who is ⟨*~ accused stands before you*⟩ **5** – used after *how*, *what*, *where*, *who*, and *why* to introduce various expletives ⟨*who ~ devil are you?*⟩

²the *adv* **1** than before; than otherwise – with comparatives ⟨*none ~ wiser for attending*⟩ ⟨*so much ~ worse*⟩ **2a** to what extent ⟨*~ sooner the better*⟩ **b** to that extent ⟨*the sooner ~ better*⟩ **3** beyond all others – with superlatives ⟨*likes this ~ best*⟩ ⟨*with ~ greatest difficulty*⟩

³the *prep* PER 2

the-, theo- *comb form* god; God ⟨*theism*⟩ ⟨*theocentric*⟩

theatre, *NAm chiefly* **theater** *n* **1a** an outdoor structure for dramatic performances or spectacles in ancient Greece and Rome **b** a building for dramatic performances; *also* a cinema **2** a room with rising tiers of seats (e g for lectures) **3** a place of enactment of significant events or action ⟨*the ~ of public life*⟩ ⟨*the ~ of war*⟩ **4a** dramatic literature or performance **b** dramatic effectiveness ⟨*the effect is pure ~*⟩ **5** *the* theatrical world **6** *Br* OPERATING THEATRE

theatrical *adj* **1** of the theatre or the presentation of plays ⟨*a ~ costume*⟩ **2** marked by artificiality (e g of emotion) **3** marked by exhibitionism; histrionic ⟨*a ~ gesture*⟩ – **theatrically** *adv*, **theatricalism** *n*, **theatricality** *n*

theatricals *n pl* the performance of plays ⟨*amateur ~*⟩

thee *pron, archaic or dial* **1a** *objective case of* THOU **b** thou – used by Quakers, esp among themselves, in contexts where the subjective form would be expected ⟨*is ~ ready?*⟩ **2** thyself

theft *n* the act of stealing; *specif* dishonest appropriation of property with the intention of keeping it

thegn *n* THANE 1

their *adj* **1** of them or themselves, esp as possessors ⟨*~ furniture*⟩, agents ⟨*~ verses*⟩, or objects of an action ⟨*~ being seen*⟩ **2** his or her; his, her, its ⟨*anyone in ~ senses – W H Auden*⟩ *USE* used attributively

theirs *pron, pl* **theirs 1** that which or the one who belongs to them – used without a following noun as a pronoun equivalent in meaning to the adjective *their* **2** his or hers; his, hers ⟨*I will do my part if everybody else will do ~*⟩

theism *n* belief in the existence of a creator god immanent in the universe but transcending it – **theist** *n or adj*, **theistic, theistical** *adj*

-theism *comb form* (→ *n*) belief in (such) a god or (such or so many) gods ⟨*pantheism*⟩ ⟨*monotheism*⟩ – **-theist** *comb form* (→ *n*)

¹them *pron, objective case of* THEY

²them *adj* those ⟨*~ blokes*⟩ – nonstandard

theme *n* **1** a subject of artistic representation or a topic of discourse **2** STEM 4 **3** a melodic subject of a musical composition or movement **4** *NAm* a written exercise; a composition

theme song *n* **1** a recurring melody in a musical play or in a film that characterizes the production or one of its characters **2** a signature tune

themselves *pron pl in constr* **1a** those identical people, creatures, or things that are they – used reflexively ⟨*nations that govern ~*⟩ or for emphasis ⟨*the team ~ were delighted*⟩ **b** himself or herself; himself, herself

⟨*hoped nobody would hurt* ~⟩ **2** their normal selves ⟨*soon be* ~ *again*⟩

¹then *adv* **1** at that time **2a** soon after that; next in order (of time) ⟨*walked to the door,* ~ *turned*⟩ **b** besides; IN ADDITION ⟨~ *there is the interest to be paid*⟩ **3a** in that case ⟨*take it,* ~, *if you want it so much*⟩ **b** as may be inferred ⟨*your mind is made up,* ~?⟩ **c** accordingly, so – indicating casual connection in speech or writing ⟨*our hero,* ~, *was greatly relieved*⟩ **d** as a necessary consequence ⟨*if the angles are equal,* ~ *the complements are equal*⟩ **e** – used after *but* to offset a preceding statement ⟨*he lost the race, but* ~ *he never expected to win*⟩

²then *n* that time ⟨*since* ~, *he's been more cautious*⟩

³then *adj* existing or acting at that time ⟨*the* ~ *secretary of state*⟩

thence *adv* **1** from there ⟨*fly to London and* ~ *to Paris*⟩ **2** from that preceding fact or premise ⟨*it* ~ *transpired*⟩ – chiefly *fml*

thenceforth *adv* from that time or point on – chiefly *fml*

theo- –see THE-

theocracy *n* (a state having) government by immediate divine guidance or by officials regarded as divinely guided – **theocrat** *n*, **theocratic** *also* **theocratical** *adj*

theodolite *n* a surveyor's instrument for measuring horizontal and usu also vertical angles – **theodolitic** *adj*

theologian *n* a specialist in theology

theology *n* **1** the study of God, esp by analysis of the origins and teachings of an organized religion **2** a theological theory, system, or body of opinion ⟨*Catholic* ~⟩ – **theological** *adj*

theorem *n* **1** a proposition in mathematics or logic deducible from other more basic propositions **2** an idea proposed as a demonstrable truth, often as a part of a general theory; a proposition – **theorematic** *adj*

theoretical *also* **theoretic** *adj* **1a** relating to or having the character of theory; abstract **b** confined to theory or speculation; speculative ⟨~ *mechanics*⟩ **2** existing only in theory; hypothetical – **theoretically** *adv*

theorist *n* a theoretician

theorize, **-ise** *vi* to form a theory; speculate – **theorizer** *n*

theory *n* **1a** a belief, policy, or procedure forming the basis for action ⟨*her method is based on the* ~ *that children want to learn*⟩ **b** an ideal or supposed set of facts, principles, or circumstances – often in *in theory* ⟨*in* ~, *we have always advocated freedom for all, but in practice* ...⟩ **2** the general or abstract principles of a subject ⟨*music* ~⟩ **3** a scientifically acceptable body of principles offered to explain a phenomenon ⟨*wave* ~ *of light*⟩ **4a** a hypothesis assumed for the sake of argument or investigation **b** an unproved assumption; a conjecture **c** a body of theorems presenting a concise systematic view of a subject ⟨~ *of equations*⟩

theosophy *n* **1** teaching about God and the world stressing the validity of mystical insight **2** *often cap* the teachings of a modern movement originating in the USA in 1875 and following chiefly Buddhist and Brahmanic theories, esp of pantheistic evolution and reincarnation – **theosophist** *n*, **theosophical** *adj*

therapeutic *adj* of the treatment of disease or disorders by remedial agents or methods – **therapeutically** *adv*

therapeutics *n pl but sing or pl in constr* medicine dealing with the application of remedies to diseases

therapist *n* sby trained in methods of treatment and rehabilitation other than the use of drugs or surgery ⟨*a speech* ~⟩

therapy *n* therapeutic treatment of bodily, mental, or social disorders

¹there *adv* **1** in or at that place ⟨*stand over* ~⟩ – often used to draw attention or to replace a name ⟨~ *goes John*⟩ ⟨*hello* ~!⟩ **2** thither ⟨*went* ~ *after church*⟩ **3a** now ⟨~ *goes the hooter*⟩ **b** at or in that point or particular ⟨~ *is where I disagree with you*⟩ **4** – used interjectionally to express satisfaction, approval, encouragement, or defiance ⟨~, *it's finished*⟩ ⟨~ *won't go, so* ~⟩ ⟨~, ~, *don't cry*⟩ – **there and back** for a round trip – **there it is** such is the unfortunate fact – **there's a** – used when urging a course of action ⟨*don't sulk, there's a dear!*⟩ – **there you are 1** HERE YOU ARE 1 **2** I told you so

²there *pron* – used to introduce a sentence or clause expressing the idea of existence ⟨*what is* ~ *to eat?*⟩ ⟨~ *shall come a time*⟩

³there *n* that place or point

⁴there *adj* **1** – used for emphasis, esp after a demonstrative ⟨*those men* ~ *can tell you*⟩ **2** – used for emphasis between a demonstrative and the following noun ⟨*that* ~ *cow*⟩; substandard

thereabouts, *NAm also* **thereabout** *adv* **1** in that vicinity **2** near that time, number, degree, or quantity ⟨*a boy of 18 or* ~⟩

thereafter *adv* after that

thereby *adv* **1** by that means; resulting from which **2** in which connection ⟨~ *hangs a tale* – Shak⟩

therefore *adv* **1** for that reason; to that end ⟨*We must go. I will* ~ *call a taxi*⟩ **2** by virtue of that; consequently ⟨*was tired and* ~ *irritable*⟩ **3** as this proves ⟨*I think,* ~ *I exist*⟩

therein *adv* in that; esp in that respect ⟨~ *lies the problem*⟩ – *fml*

thereof *adv* **1** of that or it **2** from that or it USE *fml*

thereon *adv* on or onto that or it ⟨*a text with a commentary* ~⟩ – *fml*

thereto *adv* to that matter or document ⟨*conditions attaching* ~⟩ – *fml*

thereunder *adv* under that or it ⟨*the heading and the items listed* ~⟩ – *fml*

thereupon *adv* **1** on that matter ⟨*if all are agreed* ~⟩ **2** immediately after that USE *fml*

therm *n* a quantity of heat equal to 100,000Btu (about 105,506MJ)

therm-, **thermo-** *comb form* heat ⟨*thermion*⟩ ⟨*thermo*stat⟩

-therm *comb form* (→ *n*) animal having (such) a body temperature ⟨*ectotherm*⟩

¹thermal, *adj* **1** thermal, thermic /1thuhmik/ of or caused by heat ⟨~ *stress*⟩ ⟨~ *insulation*⟩ **2** designed (e g with insulating air spaces) to prevent the dissipation of body heat ⟨~ *underwear*⟩ – **thermally** *adv*

²thermal *n* a rising body of warm air

thermion *n* an electrically charged particle, specif an electron, emitted by an incandescent substance

thermionic *adj* of or being (a device, esp a valve using) thermions

thermodynamics *n pl but sing or pl in constr* (physics that deals with) the mechanical action of, or relations between, heat and other forms of energy – **thermodynamic** *adj*, **thermodynamically** *adv*, **thermodynamicist** *n*

thermometer *n* an instrument for determining temperature; esp a glass bulb attached to a fine graduated tube of glass and containing a liquid (e g mercury) that rises and falls with changes of temperature – **thermometry** *n*, **thermometric** *adj*

thermonuclear *adj* of, using, or being (weapons using) transformations occurring in the nucleus of low atomic weight atoms (e g hydrogen) at very high temperatures ⟨*a* ~ *reaction*⟩ ⟨~ *bombs*⟩

thermoplastic *adj* capable of softening or melting when heated and of hardening again when cooled ⟨~ *synthetic resins*⟩ – **thermoplastic** *n*

thermos *n* THERMOS FLASK

Thermos *trademark* – used for a Thermos flask

thermosetting *adj* capable of becoming permanently rigid when heated ⟨*a* ~ *plastic*⟩

Thermos flask *n, often not cap T* a cylindrical container with a vacuum between an inner and an outer wall used to keep material, esp liquids, either hot or cold for considerable periods

thermostat *n* an automatic device for regulating temperature – **thermostatic** *adj*

thesaurus *n, pl* **thesauri, thesauruses** a book of words or of information about a particular field or set of concepts; *esp* a book of words and their synonyms

these *pl of* THIS

thesis *n, pl* **theses 1a** a proposition that a person offers to maintain by argument **b** a proposition to be proved or one advanced without proof; a hypothesis **2** the first stage of a reasoned argument presenting the case **3** a dissertation embodying the results of original research; *specif* one submitted for a doctorate in Britain **4** the unstressed part of a metrical foot

¹**thespian** *adj, often cap* relating to the drama

²**thespian** *n* an actor – chiefly *fml or humor*

thew *n* **1** muscle, sinew – usu *pl* **2a** muscular power or development **b** strength, vitality ⟨*the naked* ~ *and sinew of the English language* – G M Hopkins⟩

they *pron pl in constr* **1a** those people, creatures, or things ⟨~ *taste better with sugar*⟩; *also, chiefly Br* that group ⟨*ask the committee whether* ~ *approve*⟩ **b** HE 2 ⟨*if anyone knows,* ~ *will tell you*⟩ **2a** PEOPLE 1 ⟨~ *say we'll have a hard winter*⟩ **b** the authorities ⟨~ *took my licence away*⟩

they'd they had; they would

they'll they will; they shall

they're they are

they've they have

¹**thick** *adj* **1a** having or being of relatively great depth or extent between opposite surfaces ⟨*a* ~ *plank*⟩ **b** of comparatively large diameter in relation to length ⟨*a* ~ *rod*⟩ **2a** closely-packed; dense ⟨*the air was* ~ *with snow*⟩ ⟨*a* ~ *forest*⟩ **b** great in number **c** viscous in consistency ⟨~ *syrup*⟩ **d** foggy or misty ⟨~ *weather*⟩ **e** impenetrable to the eye ⟨~ *darkness*⟩ **3** measuring in thickness ⟨*12 centimetres* ~⟩ **4a** imperfectly articulated ⟨~ *speech*⟩ **b** plainly apparent; marked ⟨*a* ~ *French accent*⟩ **5a** sluggish, dull ⟨*my head feels* ~ *after too little sleep*⟩ **b** obtuse, stupid **6** on close terms; intimate ⟨*was quite* ~ *with his boss*⟩ **7** unreasonable, unfair ⟨*called it a bit* ~ *to be fired without warning*⟩ USE (5b, 6, & 7) *infml* – **thick** *adv,* **thicken** *vb,* **thickener** *n,* **thickish** *adj,* **thickly** *adv*

²**thick** *n* **1** the most crowded or active part ⟨*in the* ~ *of the battle*⟩ **2** the part of greatest thickness ⟨*the* ~ *of the thumb*⟩

thicket *n* **1** a dense growth of shrubbery or small trees **2** sthg like a thicket in density or impenetrability

thickhead *n* a stupid person – *infml* – **thick-headed** *adj*

thickness *n* **1** the smallest of the 3 dimensions of a solid object **2** the thick part of sthg **3** a layer, ply ⟨*a single* ~ *of canvas*⟩

thickset *adj* **1** closely placed; *also* growing thickly **2** heavily built; burly

thick-skinned *adj* callous, insensitive

thief *n, pl* **thieves** sby who steals, esp secretly and without violence – **thievery** *n,* **thievish** *adj,* **thievishness** *n*

thieve *vb* to steal, rob

thigh *n* the segment of the vertebrate hind limb nearest the body that extends from the hip to the knee and is supported by a single large bone – **thighed** *adj*

thimble *n* **1** a pitted metal or plastic cap or cover worn to protect the finger and to push the needle in sewing **2a** a thin metal grooved ring used to fit in a spliced loop in a rope as protection from chafing **b** a movable ring, tube, or lining in a hole

thimbleful *n* as much as a thimble will hold; *broadly* a very small quantity

¹**thin** *adj* **-nn- 1a** having little depth between opposite surfaces ⟨*a* ~ *book*⟩ **b** measuring little in cross section ⟨~ *rope*⟩ **2** not dense or closely-packed ⟨~ *hair*⟩ **3** without much flesh; lean **4a** more rarefied than normal ⟨~ *air*⟩ **b** few in number **c** with few bids or offerings ⟨*a* ~ *market*⟩ **5** lacking substance or strength ⟨~ *broth*⟩ ⟨*a* ~ *plot*⟩ **6** flimsy, unconvincing ⟨*a* ~ *disguise*⟩ **7** somewhat feeble and lacking in resonance ⟨*a* ~ *voice*⟩ **8** lacking in intensity or brilliance ⟨~ *colour*⟩ **9** lacking sufficient photographic contrast **10** disappointingly poor or hard – *infml* ⟨*had a* ~ *time of it*⟩ – **thin** *adv,* **thinly** *adv,* **thinness** *n,* **thinnish** *adj* – **thin end of the wedge** sthg apparently insignificant that is the forerunner of a more important development

²**thin** *vb* **-nn- vt 1** to reduce in thickness or depth; attenuate **2** to reduce in strength or density **3** to reduce in number or bulk ~ *vi* **1** to become thin or thinner **2** to diminish in strength, density, or number

¹**thine** *adj, archaic* thy – used esp before a vowel or *h*

²**thine** *pron, pl* **thine** *archaic or dial* that which belongs to thee – used without a following noun as a pronoun equivalent in meaning to the adjective *thy;* capitalized when addressing God; still surviving in the speech of Quakers, esp among themselves

thing *n* **1a** a matter, affair, concern ⟨~s *are not improving*⟩ **b** an event, circumstance ⟨*that shooting was a terrible* ~⟩ **2a**(1) a deed, act, achievement ⟨*do great* ~s⟩ **(2)** an activity, action ⟨*abusive moralizing ... is about the least productive* ~ *to do* – Nation Review (Melbourne)⟩ **b** a product of work or activity ⟨*likes to make* ~s⟩ **c** the aim of effort or activity ⟨*the* ~ *is to get well*⟩ **d** sthg necessary or desirable ⟨*I've got just the* ~ *for you*⟩ **3a** a separate and distinct object of thought (e g a quality, fact, idea, etc) **b** the concrete entity as distinguished from its appearances **c** an inanimate object as distinguished from a living being **d** *pl* imaginary objects or entities ⟨*see* ~s⟩ ⟨*hear* ~s⟩ **4a** *pl* possessions, effects ⟨*pack your* ~s⟩ **b** an item of property – used in law **c** an article of clothing ⟨*not a* ~ *to wear*⟩ **d** *pl* equipment or utensils, esp for a particular purpose ⟨*bring the tea* ~s⟩ **5** an object or entity not (capable of being) precisely designated ⟨*what's that* ~ *you're holding?*⟩ **6a** a detail, point ⟨*checks every little* ~⟩ **b** a material or substance of a specified kind ⟨*avoid starchy* ~s⟩ **7a** a spoken or written observation or point ⟨*there are some good* ~s *in his essay*⟩ **b** an idea, motion ⟨*says the first* ~ *he thinks of*⟩ ⟨*for one* ~⟩ **c** a piece of news or information ⟨*couldn't get a* ~ *out of him*⟩ **8** an individual, creature ⟨*poor* ~*!*⟩ **9** the proper or fashionable way of behaving, talking, or dressing ⟨*it's the latest* ~⟩ **10a** a preoccupation (e g a mild obsession or phobia) of a specified type ⟨*has a* ~ *about driving*⟩ **b** an intimate relationship; *esp* LOVE AFFAIR 1 ⟨*had a* ~ *going with her boss*⟩ **c** sthg (e g an activity) that offers special interest and satisfaction to the individual – *infml* ⟨*letting students do their own* ~ – Newsweek⟩ USE (10a, 10b, & 10c) *infml* – **of all things** – used to show surprise ⟨*wants a xylophone of all things*⟩

Thing *n* a legislative or deliberative assembly in a Scandinavian country

thingamajig, thingumajig n sthg or sby that is hard to classify or whose name is unknown or forgotten – infml

¹**think** vb **thought** vt **1** to form or have in the mind **2** to have as an opinion; consider **3a** to reflect on – often + over ⟨~ the matter over⟩ **b** to determine by reflecting – often + out ⟨~ it out for yourself⟩ **4** to call to mind; remember ⟨I didn't ~ to ask his name⟩ **5** to devise by thinking – usu + up ⟨thought up a plan to escape⟩ **6** to have as an expectation ⟨we didn't ~ we'd have any trouble⟩ **7** to have one's mind full of ⟨talks and ~s business⟩ **8** to subject to the processes of logical thought – usu + out or through ⟨~ things out⟩ ~ vi **1a** to exercise the powers of judgment, conception, or inference **b** to have in mind or call to mind a thought or idea – usu + of **2** to have the mind engaged in reflection – usu + of or about **3** to hold a view or opinion – usu + of ⟨~s of himself as a poet⟩ **4** to have consideration – usu + of ⟨a man must ~ first of his family⟩ **5** to expect, suspect ⟨better than he ~s possible⟩ – **thinkable** adj, **thinker** n – **think better of** to decide on reflection to abandon (a plan) – **think much of** to have at all a high opinion of ⟨didn't think much of the new car⟩

²**think** n an act of thinking ⟨if he thinks he can fool me, he's got another ~ coming⟩ – infml

¹**thinking** n **1** the action of using one's mind to produce thoughts **2** opinion that is characteristic (e g of a period, group, or individual) ⟨the current ~ on immigration⟩ – **put/have on one's thinking cap** to ponder or reflect on sthg

²**thinking** adj marked by use of the intellect

think over vt to ponder the advantages or disadvantages of; consider ⟨think it over⟩

think tank n sing or pl in constr a group of people formed as a consultative body to evolve new ideas and offer expert advice

thinner n liquid (e g turpentine) used esp to thin paint

thin-skinned adj unduly susceptible to criticism or insult

¹**third** adj **1a** next after the second in place or time ⟨the ~ man in line⟩ **b** ranking next to second in authority or precedence ⟨~ mate⟩ **c** being the forward gear or speed 1 higher than second in a motor vehicle **2a** being any of 3 equal parts into which sthg is divisible **b** being the last in each group of 3 in a series ⟨take out every ~ card⟩ – **third, thirdly** adv

²**third** n **1a** number three in a countable series **b** sthg or sby that is next after second in rank, position, authority, or precedence ⟨the ~ in line⟩ **c** third, **third class** often cap the third and usu lowest level of British honours degree **2** any of 3 equal parts of sthg **3a** (the combination of 2 notes at) a musical interval of 3 diatonic degrees **b** a mediant **4** the third forward gear or speed of a motor vehicle

third degree n the subjection of a prisoner to torture to obtain information

third-degree burn n a burn characterized by destruction of the skin and possibly the underlying tissues, loss of fluid, and sometimes shock

third-party adj of a third party; specif of insurance covering loss or damage sustained by sby other than the insured

third party n **1** sby other than the principals ⟨a ~ to a divorce proceeding⟩ **2a** a major political party in addition to 2 others in a state normally characterized by a 2-party system **b** a political party whose electoral strength is so small that it can rarely gain control of a government

third person n a set of linguistic forms (e g verb forms or pronouns) referring neither to the speaker or writer of the

utterance in which they occur nor to the one to whom that utterance is addressed

third rail n CONDUCTOR RAIL

third-rate adj third in quality or value; broadly of extremely poor quality – **third-rater** n

third world n, often cap T&W, sing or pl in constr **1** a group of nations, esp in Africa and Asia, that are not aligned with either the communist or the capitalist blocs **2** the underdeveloped nations of the world

¹**thirst** n **1** (the sensation of dryness in the mouth and throat associated with) a desire or need to drink **2** an ardent desire; a craving

²**thirst** vi **1** to feel thirsty **2** to crave eagerly

thirsty adj **1a** feeling thirst **b** deficient in moisture; parched ⟨~ land⟩ **2** having a strong desire; avid – **thirstily** adv, **thirstiness** n

thirteen n (the number) 13 – **thirteen** adj or pron, **thirteenth** adj or n

thirty n **1** (the number) 30 **2** pl the numbers 30 to 39; specif a range of temperatures, ages, or dates in a century characterized by these numbers – **thirtieth** adj or n, **thirty** adj or pron, **thirtyfold** adj or adv

¹**this** pron, pl **these 1a** the thing or idea that has just been mentioned ⟨who told you ~?⟩ **b** what is to be shown or stated ⟨do it like ~⟩ **c** this time or place ⟨expected to return before ~⟩ **2a** a nearby person or thing introduced for observation or discussion ⟨~ is iron and that is tin⟩ ⟨hello! ~ is Anne Fry speaking⟩ **b** the thing or state of affairs here ⟨please carry ~⟩ ⟨what's all ~?⟩

²**this** adj, pl **these 1a** being the person, thing, or idea that is present or near in time or thought ⟨early ~ morning⟩ ⟨who's ~ Mrs Fogg anyway?⟩ **b** the nearer at hand or more immediately under observation ⟨~ country⟩ ⟨~ chair or that one⟩ **c** constituting the immediate past or future period ⟨have lived here these 10 years⟩ **d** constituting what is to be shown or stated ⟨have you heard ~ one?⟩ **2** a certain ⟨there was ~ Irishman ... ⟩

³**this** adv **1** to this extent ⟨known her since she was ~ high⟩ **2** to this extreme degree – usu + the negative ⟨didn't expect to wait ~ long⟩

thistle n any of various prickly composite plants with (showy) heads of mostly tubular flowers – **thistly** adj

thistledown n the fluffy hairs from the ripe flower head of a thistle

thither adv to or towards that place – chiefly fml

thole, tholepin n a peg, pin; esp either of a pair of wooden pegs serving as rowlocks on a boat

thong n a narrow strip, esp of leather – **thonged** adj

thorax n, pl **thoraxes, thoraces** (a division of the body of an insect, spider, etc corresponding to) the part of the mammalian body between the neck and the abdomen; also its cavity in which the heart and lungs lie – **thoracic** adj

thorn n **1** a woody plant (of the rose family) bearing sharp prickles of thorns **2** a short hard sharp-pointed plant part, specif a leafless branch **3** sby or sthg that causes irritation ⟨he's been a ~ in my flesh for years⟩ **4** an orig runic letter þ used in Old and Middle English for either of the sounds /th/ or /dh/ – **thorned** adj, **thornless** adj

thorny adj **1** full of or covered in thorns **2** full of difficulties or controversial points ⟨a ~ problem⟩ – **thorniness** n

¹**thorough** prep or adv, archaic through

²**thorough** adj **1** carried through to completion ⟨a ~ search⟩ **2a** marked by full detail ⟨a ~ description⟩ **b** painstaking ⟨a ~ scholar⟩ **c** complete in all respects ⟨~ pleasure⟩ **d** being fully and without qualification as specified ⟨a ~ rogue⟩ – **thoroughly** adv, **thoroughness** n

¹**thoroughbred** adj **1** bred from the best blood through a

long line; purebred **2a** *cap* of or being a Thoroughbred **b** having the characteristics associated with good breeding or pedigree

²**thoroughbred** *n* **1** *cap* any of an English breed of horses kept chiefly for racing that originated from crosses between English mares of uncertain ancestry and Arabian stallions **2** a purebred or pedigree animal **3** *sby* or *sthg* with the characteristics associated with good breeding

thoroughfare *n* **1** a public way (e g a road, street, or path); *esp* a main road **2** passage, transit ⟨*no* ∼⟩

thoroughgoing *adj* **1** extremely thorough or zealous **2** absolute, utter ⟨*a* ∼ *villain*⟩

those *pl of* ¹, ²THAT

¹**thou** *pron, archaic or dial* the one being addressed; you – capitalized when addressing God; sometimes used by Quakers as the universal form of address to 1 person

²**thou** *n, pl* **thou, thous** **1** a thousand (of sthg, esp money) **2** a unit of length equal to ¹/₁₀₀₀in (about 25.4mm)

¹**though** *also* **tho** *adv* however, nevertheless ⟨*it's hard work. I enjoy it* ∼⟩

²**though** *also* **tho** *conj* **1** in spite of the fact that; while ⟨∼ *it's hard work, I enjoy it*⟩ **2** in spite of the possibility that; even if **3** and yet; but ⟨*it works,* ∼ *not as well as we hoped*⟩

¹**thought** *past of* THINK

²**thought** *n* **1a** thinking ⟨*lost in* ∼⟩ **b** serious consideration ⟨*gave no* ∼ *to the danger*⟩ **2** reasoning or conceptual power **3a** an idea, opinion, concept, or intention **b** the intellectual product or the organized views of a period, place, group, or individual **c** hope, expectation ⟨*gave up all* ∼ *of winning*⟩ **4** a slight amount – in the adverbial phrase *a thought* ⟨*there's a* ∼ *too much seasoning in the stew*⟩

thoughtful *adj* **1a** having thoughts; absorbed in thought **b** showing careful reasoned thinking ⟨*a* ∼ *analysis of the problem*⟩ **2** showing concern for others – **thoughtfully** *adv*, **thoughtfulness** *n*

thoughtless *adj* **1** lacking forethought; rash **2** lacking concern for others – **thoughtlessly** *adv*, **thoughtlessness** *n*

thousand *n, pl* **thousands, thousand** **1** (the number) 1000 **2** the number occupying the position 4 to the left of the decimal point in the Arabic notation; *also, pl* this position **3** an indefinitely large number ⟨∼s *of ants*⟩ – often pl with sing. meaning – **thousand** *adj*, **thousandth** *adj or n*

thrall *n* **1a** a bondman **b** (sby in) a state of (moral) servitude **2** a state of complete absorption or enslavement ⟨*her beauty held him in* ∼⟩ – **thrall** *adj*, **thraldom,** *NAm chiefly* **thralldom** *n*

¹**thrash** *vt* **1** THRESH 1 **2a** to beat soundly (as if) with a stick or whip **b** to defeat heavily or decisively **3** to swing, beat, or strike wildly or violently ⟨∼*ing his arms*⟩ ∼ *vi* **1** THRESH 1 **2** to deal repeated blows (as if) with a flail or whip **3** to move or stir about violently; toss about – usu + *around* or *about* ⟨∼ *around in bed with a fever*⟩ – **thrasher** *n*, **thrashing** *n*

²**thrash** *n* **1** an act of thrashing, esp in swimming **2** a wild party – *infml*

thrash out *vt* to discuss (e g a problem) exhaustively with a view to finding a solution; *also* to arrive at (e g a decision) in this way

¹**thread** *n* **1** a filament, group of filaments twisted together, or continuous strand formed by spinning and twisting together short textile fibres **2a** any of various natural filaments ⟨*the* ∼s *of a spider's web*⟩ **b** sthg (e g a thin stream of liquid) like a thread in length and narrowness **c** a projecting spiral ridge (e g on a bolt or pipe) by which parts can be screwed together **3** sthg continuous or drawn out: e g **a** a train of thought ⟨*I've*

lost the ∼ *of this argument*⟩ **b** a pervasive recurring element ⟨*a* ∼ *of melancholy marked all his writing*⟩ **4** a precarious or weak support ⟨*to hang by a* ∼⟩ – **threadless** *adj*, **threadlike** *adj*, **thready** *adj*

²**thread** *vt* **1a** to pass a thread through the eye of (a needle) **b** to arrange a thread, yarn, or lead-in piece in working position for use in (a machine) **2a(1)** to pass sthg through the entire length of ⟨∼ *a pipe with wire*⟩ **(2)** to pass (e g a tape or film) into or through sthg ⟨∼ed *elastic into the waistband*⟩ **b** to make one's way cautiously through or between ⟨∼ing *narrow alleys*⟩ **3** to string together (as if) on a thread ⟨∼ *beads*⟩ **4** to intermingle (as if) with threads ⟨*dark hair* ∼ed *with silver*⟩ **5** to form a screw thread on or in ∼ *vi* **1** to make one's way *through* **2** to form a thread when poured from a spoon – **threader** *n*

threadbare *adj* **1** having the nap worn off so that the threads show; worn, shabby **2** hackneyed ⟨∼ *phrases*⟩ – **threadbareness** *n*

threat *n* **1** an indication of sthg, usu unpleasant, to come **2** an expression of intention to inflict punishment, injury, or damage **3** sthg that is a source of imminent danger or harm; MENACE 2a

threaten *vt* **1** to utter threats against ⟨*he* ∼ed *his employees with the sack*⟩ **2a** to give ominous signs of ⟨*the clouds* ∼ *rain*⟩ **b** to be a source of harm or danger to **3** to announce as intended or possible ⟨*the workers* ∼ed *a strike*⟩ ∼ *vi* **1** to utter threats **2** to appear menacing ⟨*the sky* ∼ed⟩ – **threatener** *n*, **threateningly** *adv*

three *n* **1** (the number) 3 **2** the third in a set or series ⟨*the* ∼ *of hearts*⟩ **3** sthg having 3 parts or members or a denomination of 3 – **three** *adj or pron*, **threefold** *adj or adv*

three-D, 3-D *n* three-dimensional form

three-decker *n* sthg with 3 tiers, layers, etc; *esp* a sandwich with 3 slices of bread and 2 fillings

three-dimensional *adj* **1** having 3 dimensions **2** giving the illusion of depth – used of an image or pictorial representation, esp when this illusion is enhanced by stereoscopic means **3** describing or being described in great depth; *esp* lifelike ⟨*a story with* ∼ *characters*⟩ – **three-dimensionality** *n*

three-legged race *n* a race between pairs in which each contestant has 1 leg tied to 1 of his/her partner's legs

three-line whip *n* an instruction from a party to its Members of Parliament that they must attend a debate and vote in the specified way

three-quarter *adj* **1** consisting of 3 fourths of the whole **2** *esp of a view of a rectangular object* including 1 side and 1 end ⟨*a* ∼ *view of a vehicle*⟩

three R's *n pl the* fundamentals taught in primary school; *esp* reading, writing, and arithmetic

threnody *n* a song of lamentation, esp for the dead

thresh *vt* **1** to separate the seeds from (a harvested plant) by (mechanical) beating **2** to strike repeatedly ∼ *vi* **1** to thresh grain **2** THRASH 2, 3

thresher *n* a large shark reputed to thresh the water to round up fish on which it feeds using the greatly elongated curved upper lobe of its tail

threshold *n* **1** the plank, stone, etc that lies under a door **2a** the doorway or entrance to a building **b** the point of entering or beginning ⟨*on the* ∼ *of a new career*⟩ **3** the point at which a physiological or psychological effect begins to be produced by a stimulus of increasing strength **4** a level, point, or value above which sthg is true or will take place

threw *past of* THROW

thrice *adv* **1** three times **2a** in a threefold manner or degree **b** to a high degree – usu in combination ⟨*thrice-blessed*⟩

thrift *n* **1** careful management, esp of money; frugality **2** any of a genus of tufted herbaceous plants; *esp* a sea-pink – **thriftless** *adj*, **thrifty** *adj*, **thriftily** *adv*, **thriftiness** *n*

thrill *vt* **1a** to cause to experience a sudden feeling of excitement **b** to cause to have a shivering or tingling sensation **2** to cause to vibrate or tremble perceptibly ~ *vi* **1** to experience a sudden tremor of excitement or emotion **2** to tingle, throb – **thrill** *n*, **thrillingly** *adv*

thriller *n* a work of fiction or drama characterized by a high degree of intrigue or suspense

thrive *vi* **throve, thrived; thriven** *also* **thrived 1** to grow vigorously **2** to gain in wealth or possessions – **thriver** *n*

throat *n* **1a** the part of the neck in front of the spinal column **b** the passage through the neck to the stomach and lungs **2a** sthg throatlike, esp in being a constricted passageway **b** the opening of a tubular (plant) organ **3** the upper forward corner of a fore-and-aft 4-cornered sail – **throated** *adj*

throaty *adj* uttered or produced low in the throat; hoarse, guttural – **throatily** *adv*, **throatiness** *n*

¹throb *vi* **-bb- 1** to pulsate with unusual force or rapidity **2** to (come in waves that seem to) beat or vibrate rhythmically ⟨*a* ~*bing pain*⟩ – **throbber** *n*

²throb *n* a beat, pulse

throe *n* **1** a pang or spasm – usu pl ⟨*death* ~s⟩ ⟨~s *of childbirth*⟩ **2** *pl* a hard or painful struggle ⟨*in the* ~s *of revolutionary change*⟩

thrombosis *n*, *pl* **thromboses** the formation or presence of a blood clot within a blood vessel during life – **thrombotic** *adj*

throne *n* **1** the chair of state of a sovereign or bishop **2** sovereignty

¹throng *n* *sing or pl in constr* **1** a multitude of assembled people, esp when crowded together **2** a large number

²throng *vt* **1** to crowd upon (esp a person) **2** to crowd into ⟨*shoppers* ~ing *the streets*⟩ ~ *vi* to crowd together in great numbers

throstle *n* SONG THRUSH

¹throttle *vt* **throttling 1a(1)** to compress the throat of; choke **(2)** to kill by such action **b** to prevent or check expression or activity of; suppress **2a** to control the flow of (e g steam or fuel to an engine) by means of a valve **b** to regulate, esp reduce the speed of (e g an engine), by such means – usu + *back* or *down* – **throttler** *n*

²throttle *n* **1a** THROAT 1a **b** TRACHEA 1 **2** (the lever or pedal controlling) a valve for regulating the supply of a fluid (e g fuel) to an engine

¹through *also* **thro**, *NAm also* **thru** *prep* **1a(1)** into at one side or point and out at the other ⟨*drove a nail* ~ *the board*⟩ ⟨*a path* ~ *the woods*⟩ **(2)** past ⟨*saw* ~ *the deception*⟩ **b** – used to indicate passage into and out of a treatment, handling, or process ⟨*flashed* ~ *my mind*⟩ ⟨*the matter has already passed* ~ *his hands*⟩ **2** – used to indicate means, agency, or intermediacy: e g **a** by means of; by the agency of **b** because of ⟨*failed* ~ *ignorance*⟩ **c** by common descent from or relationship with ⟨*related* ~ *their grandfather*⟩ **3a** over the whole surface or extent of ⟨*homes scattered* ~ *the valley*⟩ **b** – used to indicate movement within a large expanse ⟨*flew* ~ *the air*⟩ **c** among or between the parts or single members of ⟨*search* ~ *my papers*⟩ **d** – used to indicate exposure to a set of conditions ⟨*put her* ~ *hell*⟩ **4a** during the entire period of ⟨*all* ~ *her life*⟩ **b** against and in spite of (a noise) ⟨*heard his voice* ~ *the howling of the storm*⟩ **5a** – used to indicate completion, exhaustion, or accomplishment ⟨*got* ~ *the book*⟩ ⟨*went* ~ *a fortune in a year*⟩ **b** – used to indicate acceptance or approval, esp by an official body ⟨*got the bill* ~ *Parliament*⟩ **6** chiefly NAm up till and including ⟨*Monday* ~ *Friday*⟩

²through, *NAm also* **thru** *adv* **1** from one end or side to the other ⟨*squeezed* ~⟩ **2a** all the way from beginning to end ⟨*read the letter* ~⟩ ⟨*train goes right* ~ *to London*⟩ **b** to a favourable or successful conclusion ⟨*see it* ~⟩ ⟨*I failed the exam, but he got* ~⟩ **3** to the core; completely ⟨*wet* ~⟩ **4** into the open; out ⟨*break* ~⟩ **5** *chiefly Br* in or into connection by telephone ⟨*put me* ~ *to him*⟩

³through, *NAm also* **thru** *adj* **1a** extending from one surface to the other ⟨*a* ~ *beam*⟩ **b** direct ⟨*a* ~ *road*⟩ **2a** allowing a continuous journey from point of origin to destination without change or further payment ⟨*a* ~ *train*⟩ ⟨*a* ~ *ticket*⟩ **b** starting at and destined for points outside a local zone ⟨~ *traffic*⟩ **3** arrived at completion, cessation, or dismissal; finished ⟨*you're* ~: *that was your last chance*⟩ ⟨*I'm* ~ *with women*⟩

¹throughout *adv* **1** in or to every part; everywhere ⟨*of 1 colour* ~⟩ **2** during the whole time or action; from beginning to end ⟨*remained loyal* ~⟩

²throughout *prep* **1** in or to every part of; THROUGH 3a ⟨*cities* ~ *Europe*⟩ **2** during the entire period of; THROUGH 4a ⟨*troubled him* ~ *his life*⟩

throughput *n* the amount of material put through a process ⟨*the* ~ *of a computer*⟩

¹throw *vb* **threw; thrown** *vt* **1** to propel through the air in some manner, esp by a forward motion of the hand and arm **2a** to cause to fall ⟨*threw his opponent*⟩ **b** UNSEAT 1 **3a** to fling (oneself) abruptly **b** to hurl violently ⟨*the ship was* ~n *against the rocks*⟩ **4a(1)** to put in a specified position or condition, esp suddenly ⟨*the news threw him into confusion*⟩ **(2)** to put on or off hastily or carelessly **b** to exert; BRING TO BEAR ⟨*threw all his weight behind the proposal*⟩ **c** to build, construct ⟨*threw a pontoon bridge over the river*⟩ **5** to shape by hand on a potter's wheel **6** to deliver (a punch) **7** to twist 2 or more filaments of (e g silk) into a thread or yarn **8** to make a cast of (dice or a specified number on dice) **9** to send forth; cast, direct ⟨*the setting sun threw long shadows*⟩ ⟨*he threw me a glance*⟩ **10** to commit (oneself) for help, support, or protection ⟨*threw himself on the mercy of the court*⟩ **11** to bring forth; produce ⟨*threw large litters*⟩ **12** to move (a lever or switch) so as to connect or disconnect parts of a mechanism **13** to project (the voice) **14** to give by way of entertainment ⟨~ *a party*⟩ **15** to disconcert; *also* THROW OFF 4 – *infml* ⟨*the problem didn't* ~ *her*⟩ **16** *chiefly NAm* to lose intentionally – *infml* ⟨~ *a game*⟩ ~ *vi* to cast, hurl – **thrower** *n* – **throw one's weight about/around** to exercise influence or authority, esp to an excessive degree or in an objectionable manner – *infml* – **throw together 1** KNOCK TOGETHER ⟨*threw together a delicious curry in no time*⟩ **2** to bring into casual association

²throw *n* **1a** an act of throwing **b** a method or instance of throwing an opponent in wrestling or judo **2** the distance sthg may be thrown ⟨*lived within a stone's* ~ *from school*⟩ **3** the amount of vertical displacement produced by a geological fault **4** (the distance of) the extent of movement of a cam, crank, or other pivoted or reciprocating piece

¹throwaway *n* a line of dialogue (e g in a play) made to sound incidental by casual delivery

²throwaway *adj* **1** designed to be discarded after use; disposable ⟨~ *containers*⟩ **2** written or spoken (e g in a play) with deliberate casualness ⟨*a* ~ *remark*⟩

throw away *vt* **1** to get rid of as worthless or unnecessary **2a** to use in a foolish or wasteful manner **b** to fail to take advantage of **3** to make (e g a line in a play) unemphatic by casual delivery

throwback *n* (an individual exhibiting) reversion to an earlier genetic type or phase

throw back *vt* 1 to delay the progress or advance of 2 to cause to rely; make dependent – + *on* or *upon*; usu pass ⟨thrown back *on his own resources*⟩ ~ *vi* to revert to an earlier genetic type or phase

throw-in *n* a throw made from the touchline in soccer to put the ball back in play after it has gone over the touchline

throw in *vt* 1 to add as a gratuity or supplement 2 to introduce or interject in the course of sthg ⟨threw in *a casual remark*⟩ 3 to cause (e g gears) to mesh ~ *vi* to enter into association or partnership *with* ⟨agrees *to* throw in *with a crooked ex-cop* – *Newsweek*⟩ – **throw in the sponge/towel** to abandon a struggle or contest; acknowledge defeat

throw off *vt* 1a to cast off, often in an abrupt or vigorous manner ⟨throw off *the oppressors*⟩ ⟨throw *a cold* off⟩ b to divert, distract ⟨dogs thrown off *by a false scent*⟩ 2 to emit; GIVE OFF ⟨stacks throwing off *plumes of smoke*⟩ 3 to produce or execute in an offhand manner ⟨a review thrown off *in an odd half hour*⟩ 4 to cause to deviate or err ~ *vi* to begin hunting with a pack of hounds

throw out *vt* 1a to remove from a place or from employment, usu in a sudden or unexpected manner b THROW AWAY 1 2 to give expression to ⟨threw out *a remark that utterly foxed them*⟩ 3 to refuse to accept or consider ⟨the assembly threw out *the proposed legislation*⟩ 4 to give forth from within ⟨in spring new shoots will be thrown out *from the main stem*⟩ 5 to cause to extend from a main body ⟨throw out *a screen of cavalry*⟩ ⟨rebuilt the house, throwing out *a new wing to the west*⟩ 6 to confuse, disconcert ⟨the question quite threw *him* out⟩

throw over *vt* to forsake or abandon (esp a lover)

throw up *vt* 1 to raise quickly ⟨threw up *his hands in horror*⟩ 2 GIVE UP 3b ⟨the urge to throw up *all intellectual work* – Norman Mailer⟩ 3 to build hurriedly 4 to bring forth ⟨science *will continue to* throw up *discoveries which threaten* society – *TLS*⟩ 5 to mention repeatedly by way of reproach 6 to vomit – infml ~ *vi* to vomit – infml – **throw up the sponge** THROW IN THE SPONGE/TOWEL

thru *prep, adv, or adj, NAm* through

thrum *vb* -mm- *vi* 1 to play or pluck a stringed instrument idly 2 to drum or tap idly 3 to sound with a monotonous hum ~ *vt* to play (e g a stringed instrument) in an idle or relaxed manner

¹**thrush** *n* any of numerous small or medium-sized mostly drab-coloured birds many of which are excellent singers: e g a SONG THRUSH b MISTLE THRUSH

²**thrush** *n* 1 a whitish intensely irritating fungal growth occurring on mucous membranes, esp in the mouth or vagina 2 a suppurative disorder of the feet in various animals, esp horses

¹**thrust** *vb* **thrust** *vt* 1 to push or drive with force 2 to push forth ⟨~ *out roots*⟩ 3 to stab, pierce 4 to put (an unwilling person) into a course of action or position ⟨was ~ *into power*⟩ 5 to press, force, or impose the acceptance of *on* or *upon* sby ~ *vi* 1 to force an entrance or passage – often + *into* or *through* 2 to make a thrust, stab, or lunge (as if) with a pointed weapon – **thruster, thrustor** *n*

²**thrust** *n* 1a a push or lunge with a pointed weapon b(1) a verbal attack (2) a concerted military attack 2a a strong continued pressure b the sideways force of one part of a structure against another c the force exerted by a propeller, jet engine, etc to give forward motion 3a a forward or upward push b a movement (e g by a group of people) in a specified direction

¹**thud** *vi* -dd- to move or strike with a thud

²**thud** *n* 1 ³BLOW 1 2 a dull thump

thug *n* 1 *often cap* a member of a former religious sect in India given to robbery and murder 2 a violent criminal – **thuggish** *adj*, **thuggery** *n*

¹**thumb** *n* 1 the short thick digit of the human hand that is next to the forefinger and is opposable to the other fingers; *also* the corresponding digit in lower animals 2 the part of a glove or mitten that covers the thumb – **all thumbs** extremely awkward or clumsy ⟨dropped everything he picked up and was all thumbs⟩ – **under someone's thumb** under sby's control; in a state of subservience to sby ⟨her father had her completely under his thumb⟩

²**thumb** *vt* 1a to leaf through (pages) with the thumb b to soil or wear (as if) by repeated thumbing 2 to request or obtain (a lift) in a passing vehicle ~ *vi* 1 to turn over pages 2 to travel by thumbing lifts; hitchhike

thumbnail *adj* brief, concise ⟨a ~ *sketch*⟩

thumbscrew *n* an instrument of torture for squeezing the thumb

thumbtack *n, NAm* DRAWING PIN

¹**thump** *vt* 1 to strike or knock with a thump 2 to thrash; BEAT 1a 3 to produce (music) mechanically or in a mechanical manner ⟨~ed *out a tune on the piano*⟩ ~ *vi* 1 to inflict a thump 2 to produce a thumping sound ⟨his heart ~ed⟩ – **thumper** *n*

²**thump** *n* (a sound of) a blow or knock (as if) with sthg blunt or heavy

³**thump** *adv* with a thump

thumping *adv, Br* VERY 1 – chiefly in *thumping great* and *thumping good*; infml

¹**thunder** *n* 1 the low loud sound that follows a flash of lightning and is caused by sudden expansion of the air in the path of the electrical discharge 2 a loud reverberating noise ⟨the ~ *of big guns*⟩ – **thunderous** *adj*, **thunderously** *adv*

²**thunder** *vi* 1a to give forth thunder – usu impersonally ⟨it ~ed⟩ b to make a sound like thunder ⟨horses ~ed *down the road*⟩ 2 to roar, shout ~ *vt* to utter in a loud threatening tone – **thunderer** *n*

thunderbolt *n* 1a a single discharge of lightning with the accompanying thunder b an imaginary bolt or missile cast to earth in a flash of lightning 2a sthg like lightning in suddenness, effectiveness, or destructive power b a vehement threat or censure

thunderclap *n* (sthg loud or sudden like) a clap of thunder

thundercloud *n* a cloud charged with electricity and producing lightning and thunder

thundering *adv, Br* very, thumping ⟨a ~ *great bore*⟩ – infml – **thunderingly** *adv*

thunderstorm *n* a storm accompanied by lightning and thunder

thunderstruck *adj* dumbfounded, astonished

thundery *adj* producing or presaging thunder ⟨a ~ *sky*⟩

thurible *n* a censer

Thursday *n* the day of the week following Wednesday – **Thursdays** *adv*

thus *adv* 1 in the manner indicated; in this way 2 to this degree or extent; so ⟨~ *far*⟩ 3 because of this preceding fact or premise; consequently 4 as an example

thwack *vb* or *n* (to) whack

¹**thwart** *vt* to defeat the hopes or aspirations of – **thwarter** *n*

²**thwart** *n* a seat extending across a boat

thy *adj, archaic or dial* of thee or thyself – capitalized when addressing God; sometimes used by Quakers, esp among themselves; used attributively

thyme *n* any of a genus of plants of the mint family with small pungent aromatic leaves; *esp* a garden plant used in cooking as a seasoning and formerly in medicine

¹thyroid *also* **thyroidal** *adj* of or being (an artery, nerve, etc associated with) **a** the thyroid gland **b** the chief cartilage of the larynx

²thyroid *n* **1 thyroid, thyroid gland** a large endocrine gland that lies at the base of the neck and produces hormones (e g thyroxine) that increase the metabolic rate and influence growth and development **2** a preparation of mammalian thyroid gland containing thyroid hormones used in treating conditions in which the thyroid gland produces insufficient quantities of hormones – **thyroidectomy** *n*

thyself *pron, archaic or dial* that identical person that is thou; yourself – sometimes used by Quakers, esp among themselves

ti *n* the 7th note of the diatonic scale in tonic sol-fa

tiara *n* **1** the 3-tiered crown worn by the pope **2** a decorative usu jewelled band worn on the head by women' on formal occasions

tibia *n, pl* **tibiae** *also* **tibias 1** the inner and usu larger of the 2 bones of the vertebrate hind limb between the knee and ankle; the shinbone **2** the 4th joint of the leg of an insect between the femur and tarsus – **tibial** *adj*

tic *n* **1** (a) local and habitual spasmodic motion of particular muscles, esp of the face; twitching **2** a persistent trait of character or behaviour ⟨*'you know' is a verbal ~ of many inexperienced speakers*⟩

¹tick *n* **1** any of numerous related bloodsucking arachnids that feed on warm-blooded animals and often transmit infectious diseases **2** any of various usu wingless parasitic insects (e g the sheep ked)

²tick *n* **1** a light rhythmic audible tap or beat; *also* a series of such sounds **2** a small spot or mark, typically √; *esp* one used to mark sthg as correct, to draw attention to sthg, to check an item on a list, or to represent a point on a scale **3** *Br* a moment, second – infml

³tick *vi* **1** to make the sound of a tick **2** to function or behave characteristically ⟨*I'd like to know what makes him ~*⟩ ~ *vt* **1** to mark with a written tick **2** to mark or count (as if) by ticks ⟨*a meter ~ing off the cab fare*⟩

⁴tick *n* **1** a strong coarse fabric case of a mattress, pillow, or bolster **2** ticking

⁵tick *n* credit, trust ⟨*bought it on ~*⟩ – infml

ticker *n* sthg that produces a ticking sound: e g **a** a watch **b** HEART 1a – infml

ticker tape *n* a paper tape on which a certain type of telegraphic receiving instrument prints out its information

ticket *n* **1a** a document that serves as a certificate, licence, or permit; *esp* a mariner's or pilot's certificate **b** a tag, label **2** an official notification issued to sby who has violated a traffic regulation **3** a usu printed card or piece of paper entitling its holder to the use of certain services (e g a library), showing that a fare or admission has been paid, etc **4** *Br* a certificate of discharge from the armed forces **5** *chiefly NAm* a list of candidates for nomination or election; *also* PLATFORM 1 **6** the correct, proper, or desirable thing – infml ⟨*hot sweet tea is just the ~* – Len Deighton⟩

ticking *n* a strong linen or cotton fabric used esp for a case for a mattress or pillow

¹tickle *vb* **tickling** *vi* to have or cause a tingling or prickling sensation ~ *vt* **1a** to excite or stir up agreeably **b** to provoke to laughter **2** to touch (e g a body part) lightly and repeatedly so as to excite the surface nerves and cause uneasiness, laughter, or spasmodic movements

²tickle *n* **1** a tickling sensation **2** the act of tickling

ticklish *adj* **1** sensitive to tickling **2** easily upset **3** requiring delicate handling – **ticklishly** *adv*, **ticklishness** *n*

tick off *vt* to scold, rebuke ⟨*his father ticked him off for his impudence*⟩

tick over *vi* to operate at a normal or reduced rate of activity

ticktacktoe *also* **tic-tac-toe** *n, NAm* NOUGHTS AND CROSSES

tidal *adj* of, caused by, or having tides – **tidally** *adv*

tidal wave *n* **1** an unusually high sea wave that sometimes follows an earthquake **2** an unexpected, intense, and often widespread reaction (e g a sweeping majority vote or an overwhelming impulse)

tidbit *n, chiefly NAm* a titbit

tiddler *n, Br* sby or sthg small in comparison to others of the same kind; *esp* a minnow, stickleback, or other small fish

tiddly *adj, Br* **1** very small ⟨*a ~ bit of food*⟩ **2** slightly drunk *USE* infml

tiddlywinks *n* a game whose object is to flick small discs from a flat surface into a small container

¹tide *n* **1a(1)** (a current of water resulting from) the periodic rise and fall of the surface of a body of water, specif the sea, that occurs twice a day and is caused by the gravitational attraction of the sun and moon **(2)** a periodic movement of water in the earth's crust caused by the same forces that produce ocean tides **(3)** a tidal distortion on one celestial body caused by the gravitational attraction of another **b** the level or position of water on a shore with respect to the tide; *also* the water at its highest level **2** sthg that fluctuates like the tides ⟨*the ~ of public opinion*⟩ **3** a flowing stream; a current – **tideless** *adj*

²tide *vi* to drift with the tide, esp in navigating a ship into or out of an anchorage, harbour, or river

tidemark *n* **1** a mark left by or indicating the (highest) position of the tide **2** a mark left on a bath that shows the level reached by the water; *also* a mark left on the body showing the limit of washing – chiefly infml

tide over *vt* to enable to surmount or withstand a difficulty

tidewater *n* **1a** water overflowing land at flood tide **b** water affected by the ebb and flow of the tide **2** low-lying coastal land

tideway *n* (a current in) a channel in which the tide runs

tiding *n* a piece of news – usu pl with sing. meaning

¹tidy *adj* **1a** neat and orderly in appearance or habits; well ordered and cared for **b** methodical, precise ⟨*a ~ mind*⟩ **2** large, substantial – infml ⟨*a ~ profit*⟩ – **tidily** *adv*, **tidiness** *n*

²tidy *vb* to put (things) in order; make (things) neat or tidy – **tidier** *n*

³tidy *n* **1** a receptacle for odds and ends (e g sewing materials) **2** *chiefly NAm* a usu decorative cover used to protect the back, arms, or headrest of a chair or sofa from wear or dirt

¹tie *n* **1a** a line, ribbon, or cord used for fastening or drawing sthg together **b** a structural element (e g a rod or angle iron) holding 2 pieces together **2** sthg that serves as a connecting link: e g **a** a moral or legal obligation to sby or sthg that restricts freedom of action **b** a bond of kinship or affection **3** a curved line that joins 2 musical notes of the same pitch to denote a single sustained note with the time value of the 2 **4a** a match or game between 2 teams, players, etc ⟨*a cup ~*⟩ **b** (a contest that ends in) a draw or dead heat **5** a narrow length of material designed to be worn round the neck and tied in a knot in the front **6** *NAm* a railway sleeper – **tieless** *adj*

²**tie** *vb* **tying, tieing** *vt* **1a** to fasten, attach, or close by knotting **b** to form a knot or bow in **c** to make by tying constituent elements ⟨~d *a wreath*⟩ ⟨~ *a fishing fly*⟩ **d** to make a bond or connection **2a** to unite in marriage **b** to unite (musical notes) by a tie **3** to restrain from independence or from freedom of action or choice; constrain (as if) by authority or obligation – often + *down* ⟨~d *down by his responsibilities*⟩ **4a** to even (the score) in a game or contest **b** to even the score of (a game) ~ *vi* to make a tie; *esp* to make an equal score ⟨*they* ~d *for first place*⟩

tie break, tie breaker *n* a contest or game used to select a winner from among contestants with tied scores at the end of a previous (phase of a) contest

tied cottage *n, Br* a house owned by an employer (e g a farmer) and reserved for occupancy by an employee

tied house *n* a public house in Britain that is bound to sell only the products of the brewery that owns or rents it out

tie-dye *n* tie-dyeing

tie-in *n* **1** sthg that ties in, relates, or connects **2** a book published to coincide with a film or television production to which it is related in some way; *also* the act of publishing such a book

tie in *vt* to bring into connection with sthg relevant; *esp* to coordinate so as to produce balance and unity ⟨*the illustrations were cleverly* tied in *with the text*⟩ ~ *vi* to be closely connected; *esp* to correspond ⟨*that ties in with what I know already*⟩

tiepin *n* a decorative pin used to hold a tie in place

¹**tier** *n* any of a series of levels (e g in an administration) ⟨*the top* ~ *of local government*⟩

²**tier** *vb* to place, arrange, or rise in tiers

tie-up *n* a connection, association ⟨*a political* ~ *with gangsters*⟩

tie up *vt* **1** to attach, fasten, or bind securely; *also* to wrap up and fasten **2** to connect closely; link **3** to place or invest in such a manner as to make unavailable for other purposes ⟨*his money was* tied up *in stocks*⟩ **4** to keep busy ⟨*was* tied up *in conference all day*⟩ **5** *NAm* to restrain from operation or progress ⟨*traffic was* tied up *for miles*⟩ ~ *vi* **1** to dock **2** to assume a definite relationship ⟨*this* ties up *with what you were told before*⟩

tiff *vi or n* (to have) a petty quarrel

tiffin *n* a meal or snack taken at midday or in the middle of the morning, esp by the British in India

tiger, *fem* **tigress** *n, pl* **tigers,** *(1)* **tigers,** *esp collectively* **tiger 1** a very large Asiatic cat having a tawny coat transversely striped with black **2** a fierce and often bloodthirsty person – **tigerish** *adj*, **tigerishly** *adv*, **tigerishness** *n*, **tigerlike** *adj*

tiger lily *n* an Asiatic lily commonly grown for its drooping orange-coloured lily densely spotted with black

¹**tight** *adj* **1** so close or solid in structure as to prevent passage (e g of a liquid or gas) ⟨*a* ~ *roof*⟩ – often in combination ⟨*an airtight compartment*⟩ **2a** fixed very firmly in place **b** firmly stretched, drawn, or set **c** fitting (too) closely **3** set close together ⟨*a* ~ *defensive formation in soccer*⟩ **4** difficult to get through or out of ⟨*in a* ~ *situation*⟩ ⟨*a* ~ *spot*⟩ **5** firm in control; close ⟨*a* ~ *ship*⟩ **6** evenly contested ⟨*a* ~ *match*⟩ **7** packed, compressed or condensed to (near) the limit ⟨*a* ~ *bale*⟩⟨*a* ~ *literary style*⟩; ⟨~ *schedule*⟩ **8** scarce in proportion to demand ⟨~ *money*⟩; *also* characterized by such a scarcity ⟨*a* ~ *labour market*⟩ **9** playing in unison ⟨*his three week old band was surprisingly* ~ – *The Age (Melbourne)*⟩ **10** stingy, miserly **11**

intoxicated, drunk *USE* (*10&11*) *infml* – **tightly** *adv*, **tightness** *n*

²**tight** *adv* **1** fast, tightly ⟨*the door was shut* ~⟩ **2** in a sound manner ⟨*sleep* ~⟩

tighten *vb* to make or become tight or tighter or more firm or severe – often + *up* – **tightener** *n*

tighten up *vi* to enforce regulations more stringently – usu + *on* ⟨*the government is* tightening up *on tax-dodgers*⟩

tightfisted *adj* reluctant to part with money

tight-lipped *adj* **1** having the lips compressed (e g in determination) **2** reluctant to speak; taciturn

tightrope *n* **1** a rope or wire stretched taut for acrobats to perform on **2** a dangerously precarious situation

tights *n pl* a skintight garment covering each leg (and foot) and reaching to the waist – **tight** *adj*

tigress *n* a female tiger; *also* a tigerish woman

tike *n* a tyke

tilde *n* **1** a mark ˜ placed esp over the letter *n* (e g in Spanish *señor*) to denote the sound /ny/ or over vowels (e g in Portuguese *irmã*) to indicate nasality **2** a swung dash, esp as used in mathematics to indicate similarity or equivalence

¹**tile** *n* **1** a thin slab of fired clay, stone, or concrete shaped according to use: e g **a** a flat or curved slab for use on roofs **b** a flat and often ornamented slab for floors, walls, or surrounds **c** a tube-shaped or semicircular and open slab for constructing drains **2** a thin piece of resilient material (e g cork or linoleum) used esp for covering floors or walls **–on the tiles** enjoying oneself socially, esp in an intemperate or wild manner ⟨*looks terrible this morning after a night out* on the tiles⟩

²**tile** *vt* to cover with tiles – **tiler** *n*, **tiling** *n*

¹**till** *prep* **1** until **2** *chiefly Scot* to

²**till** *conj* until

³**till** *vt* to work (e g land) by ploughing, sowing, and raising crops – **tillable** *adj*, **tillage** *n*, **tiller** *n*

⁴**till** *n* **1a** a receptacle (e g a drawer or tray) in which money is kept in a shop or bank **b** CASH REGISTER **2** the money contained in a till

⁵**till** *n* glacial drift consisting of clay, sand, gravel, and boulders not deposited in distinct layers

¹**tiller** *n* a lever used to turn the rudder of a boat from side to side

²**tiller** *n* a sprout or stalk (from the base of a plant)

³**tiller** *vi, of a plant* to put forth tillers

¹**tilt** *vt* **1** to cause to slope ⟨*don't* ~ *the boat*⟩ **2** to point or thrust (as if) in a joust ⟨~ *a lance*⟩ ~ *vi* **1** to shift so as to lean or incline **2a** to engage in combat with lances **b** to make an impetuous attack ⟨~ *at wrongs*⟩ – **tiltable** *adj*, **tilter** *n*

²**tilt** *n* **1** a military exercise in which a mounted person charges at an opponent or mark **2** speed – in *at full tilt* **3** a written or verbal attack – + *at* **4a** tilting or being tilted **b** a sloping surface

³**tilt** *n* a canopy for a wagon, boat, lorry, or stall

¹**timber** *n* **1a** growing trees or their wood **b** – used interjectionally to warn of a falling tree **2** wood suitable for carpentry or woodwork **3** material, stuff; *esp* personal character or quality **4** *Br* wood or logs, esp when dressed for use – **timber** *adj*, **timberman** *n*

²**timber** *vt* to frame, cover, or support with timbers

timbered *adj* having walls framed by exposed timbers

timbre *also* **timber** *n* the quality given to a sound by its overtones: e g **a** the resonance by which the ear recognizes a voiced speech sound **b** the quality of tone distinctive of a particular singing voice or musical instrument

timbrel *n* a small hand drum or tambourine

¹**time** *n* **1a** the measurable period during which an action,

process, or condition exists or continues **b** a continuum in which events succeed one another ⟨*stand the test of* ~⟩ **c** leisure ⟨~ *for reading*⟩ **2a** the point or period when sthg occurs ⟨*at the* ~ *of writing*⟩ **b** the period required for an action ⟨*the winner's* ~ *was under 4 minutes*⟩ **3a** a period set aside or suitable for an activity or event ⟨*now is the* ~⟩⟨*a* ~ *for celebration*⟩ **b** an appointed, fixed, or customary moment for sthg to happen, begin, or end; *esp, Br* closing time in a public house as fixed by law ⟨*hurry up please, it's* ~ – T S Eliot⟩ **4a** a historical period – often pl with sing. meaning ⟨*modern* ~s⟩ **b** conditions or circumstances prevalent during a period – usu pl with sing. meaning ⟨~s *are hard*⟩ **c** *the* present time ⟨*issues of the* ~⟩ **d** the expected moment of giving birth or dying ⟨*her* ~ *is near*⟩ **e** the end or course of a future period ⟨*only* ~ *will tell*⟩⟨*will happen in* ~⟩ **5a** a period of apprenticeship **b** a term of imprisonment – *infml* **6** a season ⟨*very hot for this* ~ *of year*⟩ **7a** a tempo **b** the grouping of the beats of music; a rhythm, metre **8a** a moment, hour, day, or year as measured or indicated by a clock or calendar **b** any of various systems (e g sidereal or solar) of reckoning time **9a** any of a series of recurring instances or repeated actions ⟨*you've been told many* ~s⟩ **b** *pl* (1) multiplied instances ⟨*5* ~s *greater*⟩ (2) equal fractional parts of which a specified number equal a comparatively greater quantity ⟨*7* ~s *smaller*⟩ **10** a person's usu specified experience, esp on a particular occasion ⟨*a good* ~⟩ **11a** the hours or days occupied by one's work ⟨*make up* ~⟩ **b** an hourly rate of pay ⟨*on double* ~⟩ **12** the end of the playing time of a (section of a) game – often used as an interjection – **at times** at intervals; occasionally – **behind the times** old-fashioned – **for the time being** for the present – **from time to time** at irregular intervals – **in time 1** sufficiently early **2** eventually **3** in correct tempo ⟨*learn to play* in time⟩ – **on time** at the appointed time – **time and (time) again** frequently, repeatedly

²**time** *vt* **1** to arrange or set the time of **2** to regulate the moment, speed, or duration of, esp to achieve the desired effect ⟨*an ill-*timed *remark*⟩ **3** to cause to keep time with sthg **4** to determine or record the time, duration, or speed of ⟨~ *a journey*⟩ ~ *vi* to keep or beat time – **timer** *n*

³**time** *adj* **1** of or recording time **2** (able to be) set to function at a specific moment ⟨*a* ~ *bomb*⟩⟨*a* ~ *switch*⟩

time exposure *n* (a photograph taken by) exposure of a photographic film for a relatively long time, usu more than 0.5s

time-honoured *adj* sanctioned by custom or tradition

time immemorial *n* time beyond living memory or historical record

timekeeper *n* sby who records the time worked by employees, elapsed in a race, etc – **timekeeping** *n*

time lag *n* an interval of time between 2 related phenomena

timeless *adj* **1a** unending, eternal **b** not restricted to a particular time or date **2** not affected by time; ageless – **timelessly** *adv*, **timelessness** *n*

timely *adv or adj* at an appropriate time – **timeliness** *n*

timepiece *n* a clock, watch, etc that measures or shows progress of time; *esp* one that does not chime

times *prep* multiplied by ⟨*2* – *2 is 4*⟩

timeserver *n* sby who fits behaviour and ideas to prevailing opinions or to his/her superiors' views

time-sharing *n* **1** simultaneous access to a computer by many users **2** a method of sharing holiday accommodation whereby each of a number of people buys a share of

a lease on a property, entitling him/her to spend a proportionate amount of time there each year

time signature *n* a sign placed on a musical staff being usu a fraction whose denominator indicates the kind of note taken as the time unit for the beat (e g 4 for a crotchet or 8 for a quaver) and whose numerator indicates the number of beats per bar

¹**timetable** *n* **1** a table of departure and arrival times of public transport **2** a schedule showing a planned order or sequence of events, esp of classes (e g in a school)

²**timetable** *vt* to arrange or provide for in a timetable

timeworn *adj* **1** worn or impaired by time **2** ancient, age-old

time zone *n* a geographical region within which the same standard time is used

timid *adj* lacking in courage, boldness, or self-confidence – **timidly** *adv*, **timidness**, **timidity** *n*

timing *n* selection for maximum effect of the precise moment for doing sthg

timorous *adj* timid – **timorously** *adv*, **timorousness** *n*

timothy *n* a European grass widely grown for hay

Timothy *n* (either of 2 New Testament Pastoral Epistles addressed to) a disciple of the apostle Paul

timpani *n pl but sing or pl in constr* a set of 2 or 3 kettledrums played by 1 performer (e g in an orchestra) – **timpanist** *n*

¹**tin** *n* **1** a soft lustrous metallic element that is malleable and ductile at ordinary temperatures and is used as a protective coating, in tinfoil, and in soft solders and alloys **2** a box, can, pan, vessel, or sheet made of tinplate: e g **a** a hermetically sealed tinplate container for preserving foods **b** any of various usu tinplate or aluminium containers of different shapes and sizes in which food is cooked, esp in an oven ⟨*roasting* ~⟩⟨*loaf* ~⟩ **3** a strip of resonant material below the board on the front wall of a squash court – **tinful** *n*

²**tin** *vt* **-nn-** **1** to cover or plate with tin or a tin alloy **2** *chiefly Br* ³CAN 1a

¹**tincture** *n* **1a** a substance that colours or stains **b** a colour, hue **2a** a slight addition; a trace **3** a heraldic metal, colour, or fur **4** a solution of a substance in alcohol for medicinal use ⟨~ *of iodine*⟩

²**tincture** *vt* to tint or stain with a colour

tinder *n* any combustible substance suitable for use as kindling – **tindery** *adj*

tinderbox *n* **1a** a metal box for holding tinder and usu a flint and steel for striking a spark **b** a highly inflammable object or place **2** a potentially unstable place, situation, or person

tine *n* **1** a prong (e g of a fork) **2** a pointed branch of an antler – **tined** *adj*

tinfoil *n* a thin metal sheeting of tin, aluminium, or a tin alloy

¹**tinge** *vt* **tingeing, tinging** **1** to colour with a slight shade **2** to impart a slight smell, taste, or other quality to

²**tinge** *n* **1** a slight staining or suffusing colour **2** a slight modifying quality; a trace

tingle *vi or n* **tingling** (to feel or cause) a stinging, prickling, or thrilling sensation – **tinglingly** *adv*, **tingly** *adj*

tin god *n* **1** a pompous and self-important person **2** sby unjustifiably esteemed or venerated *USE infml*

tin hat *n* a present-day military metal helmet – *infml*

¹**tinker** *n* **1a** a usu itinerant mender of household utensils **2** *chiefly Scot & Irish* a gipsy

²**tinker** *vi* to repair, adjust, or work with sthg in an unskilled or experimental manner – usu + *at* or *with* – **tinkerer** *n*

¹**tinkle** *vb* **tinkling** *vi* to make (a sound suggestive of) a

tinkle ~ *vt* **1** to sound or make known (the time) by a tinkle **2** to cause to (make a) tinkle – **tinkly** *adj*

²tinkle *n* **1** a series of short light ringing or clinking sounds **2** a jingling effect in verse or prose **3** *Br* a telephone call – *infml* **4** *Br* an act of urinating – *euph*

tinny *adj* **1** of, containing, or yielding tin **2a** having the taste, smell, or appearance of tin **b** not solid or durable; shoddy ⟨*a* ~ *car*⟩ **3** having a thin metallic sound – **tinnily** *adv*, **tinniness** *n*

Tin Pan Alley *n* a district that is a centre for composers and publishers of popular music; *also, sing or pl in constr* the body of such composers and publishers

tinplate *n* thin sheet iron or steel coated with tin – **tin-plate** *vt*

¹tinsel *n* **1** a thread, strip, or sheet of metal, plastic, or paper used to produce a glittering and sparkling effect (e g in fabrics or decorations) **2** sthg superficial, showy, or glamorous ⟨*the* ~ *of stardom*⟩ – **tinselled**, *NAm* **tinseled, tinselled** *adj*

²tinsel *adj* cheaply gaudy; tawdry

¹tint *n* **1a** a usu slight or pale coloration; a hue **b** any of various lighter or darker shades of a colour; *esp* one produced by adding white **2** a shaded effect in engraving produced by fine parallel lines close together **3** a panel of light colour serving as background for printing on

²tint *vt* to apply a tint to; colour – **tinter** *n*

tintinnabulation *n* **1** the ringing of bells **2** a sound as if of bells *USE* fml

tiny *adj* very small or diminutive – **tinily** *adv*, **tininess** *n*

¹tip *n* **1** the usu pointed end of sthg **2** a small piece or part serving as an end, cap, or point ⟨*a filter-tip cigarette*⟩ – **tipped** *adj* – **on the tip of one's tongue** about to be uttered ⟨*it was* on the tip of my tongue *to tell him exactly what I thought*⟩

²tip *vt* **-pp-** **1a** to supply with a tip **b** to cover or adorn the tip of **2** to attach (an insert) in a book – usu + *in*

³tip *vb* **-pp-** *vt* **1** to overturn, upset – usu + *over* **2** to cant, tilt **3** *Br* to deposit or transfer by tilting ~ *vi* **1** to topple **2** to lean, slant – **tip the scales 1** to register weight ⟨tips the scales *at 8 stone 4 ounces*⟩ **2** to shift the balance of power or influence ⟨*his greater experience* tipped the scales *in his favour*⟩

⁴tip *n* a place for tipping sthg (e g rubbish or coal); a dump

⁵tip *vt* **-pp-** to strike lightly

⁶tip *vb or n* **-pp-** (to give or present with) a sum of money in appreciation of a service performed

⁷tip *n* **1** a piece of useful or expert information **2** a piece of inside information which, acted upon, may bring financial gain (e g by betting or investment)

⁸tip *vt* **-pp-** to mention as a prospective winner, success, or profitable investment

tip-off *n* a tip given usu as a warning

tip off *vt* to give a tip-off to ⟨*the police were* tipped off *about the raid*⟩

tippet *n* **1** a shoulder cape of fur or cloth often with hanging ends **2** a long black scarf worn over the surplice by Anglican clergymen during morning and evening prayer

¹tipple *vb* **tippling** *vt* to drink (esp spirits), esp continuously in small amounts ~ *vi* DRINK **2** *USE* infml – **tippler** *n*

²tipple *n* DRINK 1b – *infml*

tipstaff *n, pl* **tipstaves** an officer in certain lawcourts

tipster *n* one who gives or sells tips, esp for gambling or speculation

tipsy *adj* **1** unsteady, staggering, or foolish from the effects of alcoholic drink **2** askew ⟨*a* ~ *angle*⟩ – **tipsily** *adv*, **tipsiness** *n*

¹tiptoe *n* the tip of a toe; *also* the ends of the toes ⟨*walk on* ~⟩

²tiptoe *adv* (as if) on tiptoe

³tiptoe *adj* **1** standing or walking (as if) on tiptoe **2** cautious, stealthy

⁴tiptoe *vi* **tiptoeing 1** to stand, walk, or raise oneself on tiptoe **2** to walk silently or stealthily as if on tiptoe

tip-top *adj* excellent, first-rate ⟨*in* ~ *condition*⟩ – *infml* – **tip-top** *adv*

tirade *n* a long vehement speech or denunciation

¹tire *vi* to become tired ~ *vt* **1** to fatigue **2** to wear out the patience of

²tire *n* a woman's headband or hair ornament

³tire *vt* to adorn (the hair) with an ornament

⁴tire *n, chiefly NAm* a tyre

tired *adj* **1** weary, fatigued **2** exasperated; FED UP ⟨~ *of listening to your complaints*⟩ **3a** trite, hackneyed ⟨*the same old* ~ *themes*⟩ **b** lacking freshness ⟨*a* ~ *skin*⟩ ⟨~, overcooked asparagus⟩ – **tiredly** *adv*, **tiredness** *n*

tireless *adj* indefatigable, untiring – **tirelessly** *adv*, **tirelessness** *n*

tiresome *adj* wearisome, tedious – **tiresomely** *adv*, **tiresomeness** *n*

tiro *n* a tyro

tissue *n* **1a** a fine gauzy often sheer fabric **b** a mesh, web ⟨*a* ~ *of lies*⟩ **2** a paper handkerchief **3** a cluster of cells, usu of a particular kind, together with their intercellular substance that form any of the structural materials of a plant or animal – **tissuey** *adj*

¹tit *n* **1** a teat or nipple **2** a woman's breast – *infml*

²tit *n* any of various small tree-dwelling insect-eating birds (e g a blue tit); *broadly* any of various small plump often long-tailed birds

titan, *fem* **titaness** *n* sby or sthg very large or strong; *also* sby notable for outstanding achievement

titan-, titano- *comb form* titanium ⟨titan*ate*⟩

¹titanic *adj* colossal, gigantic – **titanically** *adv*

²titanic *adj* of or containing titanium, esp when tetravalent

titanium *n* a light strong metallic element used esp in alloys and combined in refractory materials and in coatings

titbit, *chiefly NAm* **tidbit** *n* a choice or pleasing piece (e g of food or news)

titfer *n, Br* a hat – *infml*

tit for tat *n* an equivalent given in retaliation (e g for an injury)

¹tithe *vi* to pay a tithe or tithes ~ *vt* to levy a tithe on – **tithable** *adj*, **tither** *n*

²tithe *n* a tax or contribution of a 10th part of sthg (e g income) for the support of a religious establishment; *esp* such a tax formerly due in an English parish to support its church

titillate *vt* to excite pleasurably; arouse by stimulation – **titillating** *adj*, **titillatingly** *adv*, **titillation** *n*, **titillative** *adj*

titivate, tittivate *vb* to smarten up (oneself or another) – **titivation** *n*

¹title *n* **1** (a document giving proof of) legal ownership **2a** sthg that justifies or substantiates a claim **b** an alleged or recognized right **3a** a descriptive or general heading (e g of a chapter in a book) **b** the heading of a legal document or statute **c** a title page and the printed matter on it **d** written material introduced into a film or television programme to represent credits, dialogue, or fragments of narrative – usu pl with sing. meaning **4** the distinguishing name of a work of art (e g a book, picture or musical composition) **5** a descriptive name **6** a division of a legal document; *esp* one larger than a section or article **7** a literary work as distinguished from a particular copy ⟨*published 25* ~s *last year*⟩ **8** designation as champion ⟨*the world heavyweight* ~⟩ **9** a hereditary or acquired appellation given to a person or family as a mark of rank, office, or attainment

²title *vt* **1** to provide a title for **2** to designate or call by a title

titled *adj* having a title, esp of nobility

title deed *n* the deed constituting evidence of ownership

title page *n* a page of a book giving the title, author, publisher, and publication details

title role *n* the role in a production (e g a play) that has the same name as the title of the production

titmouse *n*, *pl* **titmice** ²TIT

titter *vi* to giggle, snigger – **titter** *n*

tittle *n* **1** a point or small sign used as a diacritical mark in writing or printing **2** a very small part

tittle-tattle *vi or n* (to) gossip, prattle

titty *n* ¹TIT – *infml*

titular *adj* **1** in title only; nominal ⟨*the* ~ *head of a political party*⟩ **2** of or constituting a title ⟨*the* ~ *hero of the play*⟩ – **titularly** *adv*

tizzy *n* a highly excited and confused state of mind – *infml*

TNT *n* trinitrotoluene

¹to *prep* **1** – used to indicate a terminal point or destination: e g **a** a place where a physical movement or an action or condition suggestive of movement ends ⟨*drive* ~ *the city*⟩ ⟨*invited them* ~ *lunch*⟩ **b** a direction ⟨*the road* ~ *London*⟩ ⟨*turned his back* ~ *the door*⟩ **c** a terminal point in measuring or reckoning or in a statement of extent or limits ⟨*10 miles* ~ *the nearest town*⟩ ⟨*cost from £5* ~ *£10*⟩ ⟨*wet* ~ *the skin*⟩ ⟨*not* ~ *my knowledge*⟩ ⟨*add salt* ~ *taste*⟩ **d** a point in time before which a period is reckoned ⟨*5 minutes* ~ *5*⟩ ⟨*how long* ~ *dinner?*⟩ **e** a point of contact or proximity ⟨*pinned it* ~ *my coat*⟩ ⟨*applied polish* ~ *the table*⟩ **f** a purpose, intention, tendency, result, or end ⟨*a temple* ~ *Mars*⟩ ⟨*broken* ~ *pieces*⟩ ⟨*held them* ~ *ransom*⟩ ⟨*much* ~ *my surprise*⟩ **g** the one to or for which sthg exists or is done or directed ⟨*kind* ~ *animals*⟩ ⟨*my letter* ~ *John*⟩ **2** – used **a** to indicate addition, attachment, connection, belonging, or possession ⟨*add 17* ~ *20*⟩ ⟨*the key* ~ *the door*⟩ **b** to indicate accompaniment or response ⟨*danced* ~ *live music*⟩ ⟨*rose* ~ *the occasion*⟩ **3** – used to indicate relationship or conformity: e g **a** relative position ⟨*next door* ~ *me*⟩ **b** proportion or composition ⟨*400* ~ *the box*⟩ ⟨*won by 17 points* ~ *11*⟩ **c** correspondence to a standard ⟨*second* ~ *none*⟩ ⟨*compared him* ~ *a god*⟩ ⟨*true* ~ *type*⟩ **4a** – used to indicate that the following verb is an infinitive ⟨*wants* ~ *go*⟩ ⟨*got work* ~ *do*⟩; now often used with an intervening adverb ⟨~ *really understand*⟩ in spite of the disapproval of many; often used by itself at the end of a clause in place of an infinitive suggested by the preceding context ⟨*knows more than he seems* ~⟩ **b** for the purpose of ⟨*did it* ~ *annoy them*⟩

²to *adv* **1a** – used to indicate direction towards; chiefly in **to and fro** **b** close to the wind ⟨*the ship hove* ~⟩ **2** of a door or window into contact, esp with the frame ⟨*the door slammed* ~⟩ **3** – used to indicate application or attention; compare FALL TO, TURN TO **4** back into consciousness or awareness ⟨*brings her* ~ *with smelling salts*⟩ **5** AT HAND ⟨*saw her close* ~⟩

toad *n* **1** any of numerous tailless leaping amphibians that differ from the related frogs by living more on land and in having a shorter squatter body with a rough, dry, and warty skin **2** a loathsome and contemptible person or thing

toad-in-the-hole *n* a dish of sausages baked in a thick Yorkshire-pudding batter

toadstool *n* a (poisonous or inedible) umbrella-shaped fungus

toady *vi or n* (to behave as) a sycophant – **toadyism** *n*

to-and-fro *n or adj* (activity involving alternating movement) forwards and backwards

to and fro *adv* from one place to another; BACK AND FORTH

¹toast *vt* **1** to make (e g bread) crisp, hot, and brown by heat **2** to warm thoroughly (e g at a fire) ~ *vi* to become toasted; *esp* to become thoroughly warm

²toast *n* **1** sliced bread browned on both sides by heat **2a** sthg in honour of which people drink **b** a highly popular or admired person ⟨*she's the* ~ *of London*⟩ **3** an act of drinking in honour of sby or sthg

³toast *vt* to drink to as a toast

toaster *n* an electrical appliance for toasting esp bread

toasting fork *n* a long-handled fork on which bread is held for toasting in front of or over a fire

toastmaster, *fem* **toastmistress** *n* sby who presides at a banquet, proposes toasts, and introduces after-dinner speakers

tobacco *n*, *pl* **tobaccos** **1** any of a genus of chiefly American plants of the nightshade family; *esp* a tall erect annual S American herb cultivated for its leaves **2** the leaves of cultivated tobacco prepared for use in smoking or chewing or as snuff; *also* cigars, cigarettes, or other manufactured products of tobacco

tobacconist *n* a seller of tobacco, esp in a shop

toboggan *vi or n* (to ride on) a long light sledge, usu curved up at the front and used esp for gliding downhill over snow or ice – **tobogganist** *n*

toby, toby jug *n* a small jug or mug generally used for beer and shaped somewhat like a stout man with a cocked hat for the brim

toccata *n* a musical composition in a free style and characterized by rapid runs, usu for organ or harpsichord

tocsin *n* an alarm bell rung as a warning

¹tod *n*, chiefly Scot & NEng a fox

²tod *n*, *Br* – **on one's tod** alone – *slang*

today *adv or n* **1** (on) this day **2** (at) the present time or age

toddle *vi* **toddling** **1** to walk haltingly in the manner of a young child **2a** to take a stroll; saunter **b** *Br* to depart ⟨*I'll just* ~ *off home*⟩ USE (2) *infml* – **toddle** *n*

toddler *n* a young child

toddy *n* a usu hot drink consisting of spirits mixed with water, sugar, and spices

to-do *n*, *pl* **to-dos** bustle, fuss – *infml*

¹toe *n* **1a(1)** any of the digits at the end of a vertebrate's foot **(2)** the fore end of a foot or hoof **b** the front of sthg worn on the foot **2a** a part like a toe in position or form ⟨*the* ~ *of Italy*⟩ **b** the lowest part (e g of an embankment, dam, or cliff)

²toe *vt* **toeing** **1** to provide with a toe; *esp* to renew the toe of ⟨~ *a shoe*⟩ **2** to touch, reach, or drive with the toe – **toe the line** to conform rigorously to a rule or standard

toe cap *n* a piece of material (e g steel or leather) attached to the toe of a shoe or boot to reinforce or decorate it

toehold *n* **1a** a hold or place of support for the toes (e g in climbing) **b** a slight footing ⟨*the firm had a* ~ *in the export market*⟩ **2** a wrestling hold in which the aggressor bends or twists his opponent's foot

toff *n*, chiefly *Br* an upper-class usu well-dressed person – *infml*

toffee, toffy *n* a sweet with a texture ranging from chewy to brittle, made by boiling sugar, water, and often butter

toffee-apple n a toffee-covered apple held on a stick

toffee-nosed adj, Br stuck-up – infml

tog vt -gg- to dress, esp in fine clothing – usu + up or out; infml

toga n a loose outer garment worn in public by citizens of ancient Rome – **togaed** adj

together adv **1a** in or into 1 place, mass, collection, or group ⟨the men get ~ every Thursday for poker⟩ **b** in joint agreement or cooperation; as a group ⟨students and staff ~ presented the petition⟩ **2a** in or into contact (e g connection, collision, or union) ⟨mix these ingredients ~⟩⟨tie the ends ~⟩ **b** in or into association, relationship, or harmony ⟨colours that go well ~⟩ **3a** at one time; simultaneously ⟨everything happened ~⟩ **b** in succession; without intermission ⟨was depressed for days ~⟩ **4** of a single unit in or into an integrated whole ⟨pull yourself ~⟩ **5a** to or with each other ⟨eyes too close ~⟩ – used as an intensive after certain verbs ⟨add ~⟩⟨confer ~⟩ **b** considered as a unit; collectively ⟨these arguments taken ~ make a convincing case⟩ – **together with** with the addition of

togetherness n the feeling of belonging together

¹**toggle** n **1** a piece or device for holding or securing; esp a crosspiece attached to the end of or to a loop in a chain, rope, line, etc, usu to prevent slipping, to serve as a fastening, or as a grip for tightening **2** (a device having) a toggle joint

²**toggle** vt **toggling** to provide or fasten (as if) with a toggle

togs n pl clothes – infml

¹**toil** n long strenuous fatiguing labour – **toilful** adj, **toilsome** adj

²**toil** vi **1** to work hard and long **2** to proceed with laborious effort ⟨~ing wearily up the hill⟩ – **toiler** n

³**toil** n sthg by or with which one is held fast or inextricably involved – usu pl with sing. meaning ⟨caught in the ~s of the law⟩

toilet n **1** the act or process of dressing and grooming oneself **2a** a fixture or arrangement for receiving and disposing of faeces and urine **b** a room or compartment containing a toilet and sometimes a washbasin **3** cleansing in preparation for or in association with a medical or surgical procedure **4** formal or fashionable (style of) dress – fml

toilet paper n a thin usu absorbent paper for sanitary use after defecation or urination

toiletry n an article or preparation (e g cologne) used in washing, grooming, etc – usu pl

toilet water n (a) liquid containing a high percentage of alcohol used esp as a light perfume

to-ing and fro-ing n, pl **to-ings and fro-ings** bustling unproductive activity

Tokay n a usu sweet dark gold wine made near Tokaj in Hungary

¹**token** n **1** an outward sign or expression (e g of an emotion) **2a** a characteristic mark or feature ⟨a white flag is a ~ of surrender⟩ **b** an instance of a linguistic expression **3a** a souvenir, keepsake **b** sthg given or shown as a guarantee (e g of authority, right, or identity) **4** a coinlike piece issued **a** as money by anyone other than a government **b** for use in place of money (e g for a bus fare) **5** a certified statement redeemable for a usu specified form of merchandise to the amount stated thereon ⟨a book ~⟩ – **by the same token** furthermore and for the same reason

²**token** adj **1** done or given as a token, esp in partial

fulfilment of an obligation or engagement ⟨a ~ payment⟩ **2** done or given merely for show ⟨~ resistance⟩

token money n **1** money of regular government issue having a greater face value than intrinsic value **2** a medium of exchange consisting of privately issued tokens

told past of TELL

tolerable adj **1** capable of being borne or endured ⟨~ pain⟩ **2** moderately good or agreeable ⟨a ~ singing voice⟩ – **tolerably** adv, **tolerability** n

tolerance n **1** the ability to endure or adapt physiologically to the effects of a drug, virus, radiation, etc **2a** indulgence for beliefs or practices differing from one's own **b** the act of allowing sthg; toleration **3** an allowable variation from a standard dimension

tolerant adj inclined to tolerate; esp marked by forbearance or endurance – **tolerantly** adv

tolerate vt **1** to endure or resist the action of (e g a drug) without grave or lasting injury **2** to allow to be (done) without prohibition, hindrance, or contradiction – **tolerator** n, **tolerative** adj

toleration n a government policy of permitting forms of religious belief and worship not officially established

¹**toll** n **1** a fee paid for some right or privilege (e g of passing over a highway or bridge) or for services rendered **2** a grievous or ruinous price; esp cost in life or health

²**toll** vt **1** to sound (a bell) by pulling the rope **2** to signal, announce, or summon (as if) by means of a tolled bell ~ vi to sound with slow measured strokes

³**toll** n the sound of a tolling bell

tollgate n a barrier across a road to prevent passage until a toll is paid

tollhouse n a house or booth where tolls are paid

toluene n a toxic inflammable hydrocarbon that is used esp as a solvent and in organic synthesis

tomahawk n a light axe used by N American Indians as a throwing or hand weapon

tomato n, pl **tomatoes 1** any of a genus of S American plants of the nightshade family; esp one widely cultivated for its edible fruits **2** the usu large and rounded red, yellow, or green pulpy fruit of a tomato

tomb n **1a** an excavation in which a corpse is buried **b** a chamber or vault for the dead, built either above or below ground and usu serving as a memorial **2** a tomblike structure; esp a large gloomy building – **tombless** adj

tombola n a lottery in which people buy tickets which may entitle them to a prize

tomboy n a girl who behaves in a manner conventionally thought of as typical of a boy – **tomboyish** adj, **tomboyishly** adv, **tomboyishness** n

tombstone n a gravestone

tomcat n a male cat

tome n a (large scholarly) book

-tome comb form (→ n) cutting instrument ⟨microtome⟩

tomfoolery n foolish trifling; nonsense

tommyrot n utter foolishness or nonsense – infml

tomorrow adv or n **1** (on) the day after today **2** (in) the future ⟨the world of ~⟩

tomtit n any of various small active birds; esp a blue tit

tom-tom n a usu long and narrow small-headed drum commonly beaten with the hands

¹**ton** n, pl **tons** also **ton 1a** LONG TON **b** SHORT TON **c** a tonne **2** REGISTER TON **b** a unit approximately equal to the volume of 1 long ton of seawater, used in reckoning the displacement of ships, and equal to 0.991m³ (35ft³) **3a** a great quantity – often pl with sing. meaning ⟨~s of room on the back seat⟩ **b** a great weight ⟨this bag weighs

a ~〉 **4** a group, score, or speed of 100 *USE (3&4)* infml

²ton *n* **1** the prevailing fashion **2** the quality or state of being fashionable

tonal *adj* **1** of tone, tonality, or tonicity **2** having tonality – **tonally** *adv*

tonality *n* **1** tonal quality **2a** KEY 7 **b** the organization of all the notes and chords of a piece of music in relation to a tonic

¹tone *n* **1** a vocal or musical sound; *esp* one of a specified quality 〈*spoke in low* ~s〉 **2a** a sound of a definite frequency with relatively weak overtones **b** WHOLE TONE **3** an accent or inflection of the voice expressive of a mood or emotion **4** (a change in) the pitch of a word often used to express differences of meaning **5** style or manner of verbal expression 〈*seemed wise to adopt a conciliatory* ~〉 **6a** colour quality or value **b** the colour that appreciably modifies a hue or white or black **7** the general effect of light, shade, and colour in a picture **8a** the state of (an organ or part of) a living body in which the functions are healthy and performed with due vigour **b** normal tension or responsiveness to stimuli **9a** prevailing character, quality, or trend (e g of morals) 〈*lowered the* ~ *of the discussion*〉 **b** distinction, style; ²TON **c** FRAME OF MIND **10** *chiefly NAm* NOTE 1a(1)

²tone *vt* **1** to impart tone to 〈*medicine to* ~ *up the system*〉 **2** to soften in colour, appearance, or sound ~ *vi* **1** to assume a pleasing colour quality or tint **2** to blend or harmonize in colour – **toner** *n*

toned *adj* **1** having a (specified) tone; characterized or distinguished by a tone – often in combination 〈*shrill*-toned〉 **2** *of paper* having a slight tint

tone-deaf *adj* relatively insensitive to differences in musical pitch – **tone deafness** *n*

tone down *vt* to reduce in intensity, violence, or force 〈*he was told to* tone down *his views*〉

tone language *n* a language (e g Chinese) in which variations in tone distinguish words of different meaning

toneless *adj* lacking in expression – **tonelessly** *adv*, **tonelessness** *n*

tone poem *n* SYMPHONIC POEM – **tone poet** *n*

tong *n* a Chinese secret society or fraternal organization formerly notorious for gang warfare

tongs *n pl* any of various grasping devices consisting commonly of 2 pieces joined at 1 end by a pivot or hinged like scissors

¹tongue *n* **1a** a fleshy muscular movable organ of the floor of the mouth in most vertebrates that bears sensory end organs and small glands and functions esp in tasting and swallowing food and in human beings as a speech organ **b** a part of various invertebrate animals that is analogous to the tongue of vertebrates **2** the tongue of an ox, sheep, etc used as food **3** the power of communication through speech **4a** a (spoken) language **b** manner or quality of utterance 〈*a sharp* ~〉 **c** ecstatic usu unintelligible utterance, esp in Christian worship – usu pl with sing. meaning 〈*the gift of* ~s〉 **d** the cry (as if) of a hound pursuing or in sight of game – esp in *give tongue* **5** a long narrow strip of land projecting into a body of water **6** sthg like an animal's tongue (e g elongated and fastened at 1 end only):e g **a** a movable pin in a buckle **b** a piece of metal suspended inside a bell so as to strike against the sides as the bell is swung **c** the pole of a (horse-drawn) vehicle **d** the flap under the lacing or buckles on the front of a shoe or boot **7** the rib on one edge of a board that fits into a corresponding groove in an edge of another board to make a flush joint **8** a tapering cone – in *tongue of flame/fire* – **tonguelike** *adj*

²tongue *vt* **1** to touch or lick (as if) with the tongue **2** to articulate (notes) by tonguing ~ *vi* to articulate notes on a wind instrument by successively interrupting the stream of wind with the action of the tongue

tongued *adj* having a tongue of a specified kind – often in combination 〈*sharp*-tongued〉

tongue-tied *adj* **1** affected with tongue-tie **2** unable to speak freely (e g because of shyness)

tongue twister *n* a word or phrase difficult to articulate because of several similar consonantal sounds (e g 'she sells seashells on the seashore')

¹tonic *adj* **1** marked by prolonged muscular contraction 〈~ *convulsions*〉 **2** increasing or restoring physical or mental tone **3** of or based on the first note of a scale **4** *of a syllable* bearing a principal stress or accent – **tonically** *adv*

²tonic *n* **1a** sthg (e g a drug) that increases body tone **b** sthg that invigorates, refreshes, or stimulates 〈*a day in the country was a* ~ *for him*〉 〈*a skin* ~〉 **c** tonic, tonic water a carbonated drink flavoured with a small amount of quinine, lemon, and lime **2** the first note of a diatonic scale **3** an instance of tonic accent

tonic sol-fa *n* a system of solmization that replaces the normal notation with sol-fa syllables

tonight *adv or n* (on) this night or the night following today

tonnage *n* **1** a duty formerly levied on every cask of wine imported into England **2a** a duty or tax on vessels based on cargo capacity **b** a duty on goods per ton transported **3** ships considered in terms of the total number of tons registered or carried or of their carrying capacity **4** the carrying capacity of a merchant ship in units of 100ft³ (about 2.83m³) **5** total weight in tons shipped, carried, or produced

tonne *n* a metric unit of weight equal to 1000kg

tonsil *n* **1** either of a pair of prominent oval masses of spongy lymphoid tissue that lie 1 on each side of the throat at the back of the mouth **2** any of various masses of lymphoid tissue that are similar to tonsils – **tonsillar** *adj*

tonsillitis *n* inflammation of the tonsils

tonsorial *adj* of a barber or his work – usu humor

¹tonsure *n* **1** the Roman Catholic or Eastern rite of admission to the clerical state by the shaving of a portion of the head **2** the shaved patch on a monk's or other cleric's head

²tonsure *vt* to shave the head of; *esp* to confer the tonsure on

tontine *n* a financial arrangement whereby a group of participants share various advantages on such terms that on the death or default of any member his/her advantages are distributed among the remaining members until 1 member remains or an agreed period has elapsed; *also* the share or right of each individual

ton-up *adj, Br* of or being sby who has achieved a score, speed, etc of 100 〈*the local motorcycle* ~ *boys*〉 〈*darts* ~ *boys are in record-breaking mood – The Sun*〉 – infml

too *adv* **1** also; IN ADDITION 〈*sell the house and furniture* ~〉 **2a** to a regrettable degree; excessively 〈~ *large a house for us*〉 **b** to a higher degree than meets a standard 〈~ *pretty for words*〉 **3** indeed, so – used to counter a negative charge 〈'*I didn't do it.*' '*You did* ~.'〉

took *past of* TAKE

¹tool *n* **1a** an implement that is used, esp by hand, to carry out work of a mechanical nature (e g cutting, levering, or digging) – not usu used with reference to kitchen utensils or cutlery **b** (the cutting or shaping part in) a machine tool **2** sthg (e g an instrument or apparatus) used in performing an operation, or necessary for the practice of a vocation or profession ⟨*books are the* ~s *of a scholar's trade*⟩ **3** sby who is used or manipulated by another **4 a** penis – *vulg*

²**tool** *vt* **1** to work, shape, or finish with a tool; *esp* to letter or ornament (e g leather) by means of hand tools **2** to equip (e g a plant or industry) with tools, machines, and instruments for production – often + *up* ~ *vi* **1** to get tooled up for production – usu + *up* **2** to drive, ride ⟨~ed *round the neighbourhood in a small car*⟩ – *infml*

toot *vi* **1** to produce a short blast or similar sound ⟨*the horn* ~ed⟩ **2** to cause an instrument to toot ~ *vt* to cause to produce a short blast ⟨~ *a whistle*⟩ – **toot** *n*, **tooter** *n*

¹**tooth** *n, pl* **teeth 1a** any of the hard bony structures that are borne *esp* on the jaws of vertebrates and serve *esp* for the seizing and chewing of food and as weapons **b** any of various usu hard and sharp projecting parts about the mouth of an invertebrate **2** a taste, liking ⟨*a sweet* ~⟩ **3a** a projection like the tooth of an animal (e g in shape, arrangement, or action) ⟨*a saw* ~⟩ **b** any of the regular projections on the rim of a cogwheel **4** *pl* effective means of enforcement – **toothlike** *adj*, **toothless** *adj* – **in the teeth of** in direct opposition to ⟨*rule had been imposed by conquest* in the teeth of *obstinate resistance* – A J Toynbee⟩

²**tooth** *vt* to provide with teeth, esp by cutting notches ⟨~ *a saw*⟩ ~ *vi*, *esp of cogwheels* to interlock

toothache *n* pain in or about a tooth

toothbrush *n* a brush for cleaning the teeth

toothcomb *n, Br* a comb with fine teeth

toothed *adj* having teeth, esp of a specified kind or number – often in combination ⟨*sharp*-toothed⟩

toothpaste *n* a paste for cleaning the teeth

toothpick *n* a pointed instrument for removing food particles lodged between the teeth

tooth powder *n* a powder for cleaning the teeth

toothsome *adj* **1** delicious ⟨*crisp* ~ *fried chicken*⟩ **2** (sexually) attractive – **toothsomely** *adv*, **toothsomeness** *n*

toothy *adj* having or showing prominent teeth ⟨*a* ~ *grin*⟩ – **toothily** *adv*

tootle *vi* **tootling 1** to toot gently or continuously **2** to drive or move along in a leisurely manner – *infml* – **tootle** *n*, **tootler** *n*

tootsy *also* **tootsie** *n* FOOT 1 – used chiefly to children

¹**top** *n* **1a(1)** the highest point, level, or part of sthg **(2)** the (top of the) head – esp in *top to toe* **(3)** the head of a plant, esp one with edible roots ⟨*beet* ~s⟩ **(4)** a garment worn on the upper body **b(1)** the highest or uppermost region or part **(2)** the upper end, edge, or surface **2** a fitted or attached part serving as an upper piece, lid, or covering **3** a platform surrounding the head of a lower mast serving to spread the topmast rigging, or to mount guns **4** the highest degree or pitch conceivable or attained **5** the part nearest in space or time to the source or beginning **6** (sby or sthg in) the highest position (e g in rank or achievement) ⟨~ *of the class*⟩ **7** *Br* the transmission gear of a motor vehicle giving the highest ratio of propeller-shaft to engine-shaft speed and hence the highest speed of travel – **topped** *adj* – **off the top of one's head** in an impromptu manner ⟨*can't give the figures* off the top of my head⟩ – **on top of 1a** in control of ⟨*keep on top of my job*⟩ **b** informed about **2** in sudden and unexpected proximity to **3** in addition to ⟨*a bad idea to get chilled* on top of *getting wet* – Sylvia Townsend Warner⟩ – **on top of the world** in high spirits; in a state of exhilaration and well-being

²**top** *vt* **-pp- 1a** to cut the top off **b** to shorten or remove the top of (a plant); *also* to remove the calyx of (e g a strawberry) **2a** to cover with a top or on the top; provide,

form, or serve as a top for **b** to supply with a decorative or protective finish or final touch **c** to complete the basic structure of (e g a high-rise building) by putting on a cap or uppermost section – usu + *out* or *off* **3a** to be or become higher than; overtop ⟨~s *the previous record*⟩ **b** to be superior to ⟨~s *everything of its kind in print*⟩ **c** to gain ascendancy over **4a** to rise to, reach, or be at the top of **b** to go over the top of; clear, surmount **5** to strike (a ball) above the centre, thereby imparting top spin

³**top** *adj* **1** of or at the top **2** foremost, leading ⟨*one of the world's* ~ *journalists*⟩ **3** of the highest quality, amount, or degree ⟨~ *form*⟩

⁴**top** *n* a child's toy that has a tapering point on which it is made to spin

top-, **topo-** *comb form* place; locality ⟨*topology*⟩ ⟨*toponymy*⟩

topaz *n* **1** a mineral that is predominantly a silicate of aluminium, usu occurs in variously coloured translucent or transparent crystals, and is used as a gem **2a** a yellow sapphire **b** a yellow quartz (e g cairngorm or citrine)

top boot *n* a high boot often with light-coloured leather bands round the upper part

top brass *n sing or pl in constr* BRASS HATS

topcoat *n* **1** a (lightweight) overcoat **2** a final coat of paint

top dog *n* a person in a position of authority, esp through victory in a hard-fought competition – *infml*

top drawer *n* the highest level, esp of society – esp in *out of the top drawer* – **top-drawer** *adj*

top-dress *vt* to scatter fertilizer over (land) without working it in – **topdressing** *n*

¹**tope** *vi* to drink alcoholic drink to excess – **toper** *n*

²**tope** *n* a small shark with a liver very rich in vitamin A

topee, topi *n* a lightweight helmet-shaped sunhat made of pith or cork

top-flight *adj* of the highest grade or quality; best

¹**topgallant** *adj* of or being a part next above the topmast ⟨~ *sails*⟩ ⟨*the* ~ *mast*⟩

²**topgallant** *n* a topgallant mast or sail

top hat *n* a man's tall-crowned hat usu of beaver or silk

top-heavy *adj* **1** having the top part too heavy for or disproportionate to the lower part **2** capitalized beyond what is prudent

topiary *adj or n* (of or being) the practice or art of training, cutting, and trimming trees or shrubs into odd or ornamental shapes; *also* (characterized by) such work

topic *n* **1a** a heading in an outlined argument or exposition **b** the subject of a (section of a) discourse **2** a subject for discussion or consideration

topical *adj* **1a** of a place **b** designed for local application ⟨*a* ~ *remedy*⟩ **2a** of or arranged by topics ⟨*set down in* ~ *form*⟩ **b** referring to the topics of the day; of current interest – **topically** *adv*, **topicality** *n*

topknot *n* **1** an ornament (e g of ribbons) worn as a headdress or as part of a hairstyle **2** an arrangement or growth of hair or feathers on top of the head

topless *adj* **1** nude above the waist; *esp* having the breasts exposed **2** featuring topless waitresses or entertainers

topmast *n* a mast that is next above the lowest mast

topmost *adj* highest of all

top-notch *adj* of the highest quality – *infml* – **top-notcher** *n*

topographical, topographic *adj* **1** of or concerned with topography **2** of or concerned with the artistic representation of a particular locality ⟨*a* ~ *poem*⟩ ⟨~ *painting*⟩ – **topographically** *adv*

topography *n* **1** (the mapping or charting of) the configuration of a land surface, including its relief and the position of its natural and man-made features **2** the physical or natural features of an object or entity and their structural relationships – **topographer** *n*

topper *n* **1** TOP HAT **2** sthg (e g a joke) that caps everything preceding – *infml*

¹topping *n* sthg that forms a top; *esp* a garnish or edible decoration on top of a food

²topping *adj, chiefly Br* excellent – not now in vogue

topple *vb* **toppling** *vi* **1** to fall (as if) from being top-heavy **2** to be or seem unsteady ~ *vt* **1** to cause to topple **2** to overthrow

topsail *also* **tops'l** *n* **1** the sail next above the lowest sail on a mast in a square-rigged ship **2** the sail set above and sometimes on the gaff in a fore-and-aft rigged ship

top secret *adj* **1** demanding the greatest secrecy **2** containing information whose unauthorized disclosure could result in exceptionally grave danger to the nation

¹topside *n* **1** *pl* the sides of a ship above the waterline **2** a lean boneless cut of beef from the inner part of a round

²topside *adv or adj* on deck

topsoil *n* surface soil, usu including the organic layer in which plants form roots and which is turned over in ploughing

top spin *n* a rotary motion imparted to a ball that causes it to rotate forwards in the direction of its travel

topsy-turvy *adj or adv* **1** UPSIDE DOWN **2** in utter confusion or disorder – **topsy-turvily** *adv,* **topsy-turvydom** *n*

top up *vt* **1** to make up to the full quantity, capacity, or amount **2** to increase (a money sum set aside for a specific purpose)

toque *n* a woman's small soft brimless hat

tor *n* a high rock or rocky mound

Torah *n* **1** *the* Pentateuch; *broadly* Jewish Scripture and other sacred Jewish literature and oral tradition **2** a leather or parchment scroll of the Pentateuch used in a synagogue

torch *n* **1** a burning stick of resinous wood or twist of tow used to give light **2** sthg (e g wisdom or knowledge) that gives enlightenment or guidance **3** *Br* a small portable electric lamp powered by batteries

tore *past of* TEAR

toreador *n* a torero

¹torment *n* **1** extreme pain or anguish of body or mind **2** a source of vexation or pain

²torment *vt* to cause severe usu persistent distress of body or mind to – **tormentor** *also* **tormenter** *n*

torn *past part of* TEAR

tornado *n, pl* **tornadoes, tornados** a violent or destructive whirlwind, usu progressing in a narrow path over the land and accompanied by a funnel-shaped cloud – **tornadic** *adj*

¹torpedo *n, pl* **torpedoes** **1** ELECTRIC RAY **2** a self-propelling cigar-shaped submarine explosive projectile used for attacking ships **3** *NAm* a charge of explosive in a container or case

²torpedo *vt* **torpedoing; torpedoed** **1** to hit or destroy by torpedo **2** to destroy or nullify (e g a plan) – *infml*

torpedo boat *n* a small fast warship armed primarily with torpedoes

torpid *adj* **1a** having temporarily lost the power of movement or feeling (e g in hibernation) **b** sluggish in functioning or acting **2** lacking in energy or vigour – **torpidly** *adv,* **torpidity** *n*

torpor *n* **1a** a state of mental and motor inactivity with partial or total insensibility **b** extreme sluggishness of action or function **2** apathy

¹torque *n* a twisted metal collar or neck chain worn by the ancient Gauls, Germans, and Britons

²torque *n* **1** (a measure of the effectiveness of) a force that produces or tends to produce rotation or torsion ⟨*a car engine delivers* ~ *to the drive shaft*⟩ **2** a turning or twisting force

torrent *n* **1** a violent stream of water, lava, etc **2** a raging tumultuous flow

torrential *adj* **1** resulting from the action of rapid streams **2** of, caused by, or resembling a torrent – **torrentially** *adv*

torrid *adj* **1a** parched with heat, esp of the sun **b** giving off intense heat **2** ardent, passionate ⟨~ *love letters*⟩ – **torridly** *adv,* **torridness** *n,* **torridity** *n*

torsion *n* **1** the act or process of twisting or turning sthg, esp by forces exerted on one end while the other is fixed or twisted in the opposite direction **2** the state of being twisted **3** the twisting of a bodily organ on its own axis – **torsional** *adj*

torso *n, pl* **torsos, torsi** **1** (a sculptured representation of) the human trunk **2** sthg (e g a piece of writing) that is mutilated or left unfinished

tort *n* a wrongful act, other than breach of contract, for which a civil action for damages may be brought

tortilla *n* a round thin cake of unleavened maize bread, usu eaten hot with a topping or filling of minced meat or cheese

tortoise *n* **1** any of an order of land and freshwater (and marine) reptiles with a toothless horny beak and a bony shell which encloses the trunk and into which the head, limbs, and tail may be withdrawn; *esp* a land tortoise commonly kept as a pet **2** sby or sthg slow or laggard

¹tortoiseshell *n* **1** the mottled horny substance of the shell of some marine turtles used in inlaying and in making various ornamental articles **2** any of several butterflies with striking orange, yellow, brown, and black coloration

²tortoiseshell *adj* mottled black, brown, and yellow ⟨~ *cat*⟩

tortuous *adj* **1** marked by repeated twists, bends, or turns **2a** marked by devious or indirect tactics **b** circuitous, involved – **tortuously** *adv,* **tortuousness** *n,* **tortuosity** *n*

¹torture *n* **1** the infliction of intense physical or mental suffering as a means of punishment, coercion, or sadistic gratification **2** (sthg causing) anguish of body or mind

²torture *vt* **1** to subject to torture **2** to cause intense suffering to **3** to twist or wrench out of shape; *also* to pervert (e g the meaning of a word) – **torturer** *n*

Tory *n* **1a** a member of a major British political group of the 18th and early 19th c favouring at first the Stuarts and later royal authority and the established church and seeking to preserve the traditional political structure and defeat parliamentary reform **b** CONSERVATIVE 1 **2** an American upholding the cause of the crown during the American Revolution – **Tory** *adj,* **Toryism** *n*

¹toss *vt* **1a** to fling or heave repeatedly about ⟨*a ship* ~*ed by waves*⟩ **b** BANDY 1 **2a** to throw with a quick, light, or careless motion ⟨~ *a ball around*⟩ **b** to throw up in the air ⟨~*ed by a bull*⟩ **c** to flip (a coin) to decide an issue **3** to lift with a sudden jerking motion ⟨~*es her head angrily*⟩ ~ *vi* **1** to move restlessly or turbulently; *esp* to twist and turn repeatedly ⟨~*ed sleeplessly all night*⟩ **2** to decide an issue by flipping a coin – often + *up* – **tosser** *n*

²toss *n* **1a** being tossed **b** a fall, esp from a horse – chiefly in *take a toss* **2** an act or instance of tossing: e g **a** an abrupt tilting or upward fling **b** an act or instance of deciding by chance, esp by tossing a coin **c** a throw **3** *Br* DAMN 2 – chiefly in *not give a toss*

toss off *vt* **1** to perform or write quickly and easily **2** to consume quickly; *esp* to drink in a single draught ~ *vi*, *Br* to masturbate – *infml*

toss-up *n* **1** TOSS 2b **2** an even chance or choice – *infml*

tot *n* **1** a small child; a toddler **2** a small amount or allowance of alcoholic drink ⟨a ~ *of rum*⟩

¹**total** *adj* **1** comprising or constituting a whole; entire **2** complete ⟨a ~ *success*⟩ **3** concentrating all available personnel and resources on a single objective ⟨~ *war*⟩ – **totally** *adv*

²**total** *n* **1** a product of addition **2** an entire quantity

³**total** *vt* **-ll-** (*NAm* **-l-**, **-ll-**), **1** to add up **2** to amount to

totalitarian *adj* **1** authoritarian, dictatorial **2** of or constituting a political regime based on subordination of the individual to the state and strict control over all aspects of the life and productive capacity of the nation – **totalitarianism** *n*

totality *n* **1** an entire amount; a whole **2a** wholeness **b** a period during which one body is completely obscured by another during an eclipse

totalizator, -isator *n* a machine for registering bets and calculating winnings in pari-mutuel betting

¹**tote** *vt* **1** to carry by hand or on the person **2** to transport, convey *USE* infml

²**tote** *n* a totalizator

totem *n* **1** a natural object serving as the emblem of a family or clan; *also* a carved or painted representation of this **2** sthg that serves as an emblem or revered symbol – **totemic** *adj*

totem pole *n* **1** a pole carved and painted with a series of totemic symbols erected before the houses of some N American Indian tribes **2** an order of rank; a hierarchy

¹**totter** *vi* **1a** to tremble or rock as if about to fall **b** to become unstable; threaten to collapse **2** to move unsteadily; stagger

²**totter** *n* an unsteady gait – **tottery** *adj*

tot up *vt* to add together ⟨tot up *the score*⟩ ~ *vi* to increase by additions ⟨*the money soon* tots up⟩

toucan *n* any of a family of fruit-eating birds of tropical America with brilliant colouring and a very large but light beak

¹**touch** *vt* **1** to bring a bodily part into contact with, esp so as to perceive through the sense of feeling; feel **2** to strike or push lightly, esp with the hand or foot or an implement **3** to lay hands on (sby afflicted with scrofula) with intent to heal **4a** to take into the hands or mouth ⟨*never* ~es *alcohol*⟩ **b** to put hands on in any way or degree ⟨*don't* ~ *anything before the police come*⟩; *esp* to commit violence against ⟨*swears he never* ~ed *the child*⟩ **5** to concern oneself with **6** to cause to be briefly in contact with sthg ⟨~ *a match to the wick*⟩ **7a**(**1**) to meet without overlapping or penetrating (**2**) to get to; reach ⟨*the speedometer needle* ~ed *80*⟩ **b** to be tangent to **8** to affect the interest of; concern **9a** to leave a mark or impression on ⟨*few reagents will* ~ *gold*⟩ **b** to harm slightly (as if) by contact; blemish ⟨*fruit* ~ed *by frost*⟩ **c** to give a delicate tint, line, or expression to ⟨a *smile* ~ed *her lips*⟩ **10** to draw or delineate with light strokes **11** to move to esp sympathetic feeling ⟨~ed *by the loyalty of her friends*⟩ **12** to speak or tell of, esp in passing **13** RIVAL **3 14** to induce to give or lend ⟨~ ed *him for 10 quid*⟩ ~ *vi* **1a** to feel sthg with a body part (e g the hand or foot) **b** to lay hands on sby to cure disease (e g scrofula) **2** to be in contact **3** to come close ⟨*his actions* ~ *on treason*⟩ **4** to have a bearing – + *on* or *upon* **5a** to make a brief or incidental stop on shore during a trip by water ⟨~ed *at several ports*⟩ **b** to treat a topic in a brief or casual manner

– + *on* or *upon* *USE* (*vt* 12) fml; (*vt* 13&14) infml – **touchable** *adj*, **toucher** *n* – **touch wood 1** with a certain feeling of luck ⟨*everything will be all right now*, touch wood⟩ **2** *Br* to touch a wooden surface as a gesture to bring luck

²**touch** *n* **1** a light stroke, tap, or push **2** the act or fact of touching **3** the sense of feeling, esp as exercised deliberately with the hands, feet, or lips **4** mental or moral sensitivity, responsiveness, or tact ⟨*has a wonderful* ~ *with children*⟩ **5** a specified sensation conveyed through the sense of touch ⟨*the velvety* ~ *of a fabric*⟩ **6** the testing of gold or silver on a touchstone **7** sthg slight of its kind: e g **a** a light attack ⟨a ~ *of fever*⟩ **b** a small amount; a trace ⟨a ~ *of spring in the air*⟩ **c** a bit, little – in the adverbial phrase *a touch* ⟨*aimed a* ~ *too low and missed*⟩ **8a** a manner or method of touching or striking esp the keys of a keyboard instrument **b** the relative resistance to pressure of the keys of a keyboard (e g of a piano or typewriter) **9** an effective and appropriate detail; *esp* one used in an artistic composition **10** a distinctive or characteristic manner, trait, or quality ⟨a *woman's* ~⟩ **11** the state or fact of being in contact or communication ⟨*out of* ~ *with modern times*⟩ **12** the area outside the touchlines in soccer or outside and including the touchlines in rugby **13a** an act of soliciting or receiving a gift or loan of money **b** sby who can be easily induced to part with money – chiefly in *a soft/easy touch USE* (13) slang

touch and go *n* a highly uncertain or precarious situation

touchdown *n* **1** the act of touching down a football **2** (the moment of) touching down (e g of an aeroplane or spacecraft)

touch down *vt* to place (the ball in rugby) by hand on the ground either positioned on or over an opponent's goal line in scoring a try, or behind one's own goal line as a defensive measure ~ *vi* to reach the ground

touché *interj* – used to acknowledge a hit in fencing or the success of an argument, accusation, or witty point

touched *adj* **1** emotionally moved (e g with gratitude) **2** slightly unbalanced mentally – *infml*

¹**touching** *prep* in reference to; concerning – *fml*

²**touching** *adj* capable of arousing tenderness or compassion – **touchingly** *adv*

touchline *n* either of the lines that bound the sides of the field of play in rugby and soccer

touch off *vt* **1** to cause to explode (as if) by touching with a naked flame **2** to release with sudden intensity

touchstone *n* **1** a black flintlike siliceous stone that when rubbed by gold or silver showed a streak of colour and was formerly used to test the purity of these metals **2** a test or criterion for determining the genuineness of sthg

touch-type *vi* to type without looking at the keyboard, using a system that assigns a particular finger to each key

touch up *vt* **1** to improve or perfect by small alterations; make good the minor defects of **2** to stimulate (as if) by a flick of a whip **3** to make often unwelcome physical advances to; touch with a view to arousing sexually – slang

touchy *adj* **1** ready to take offence on slight provocation **2** calling for tact, care, or caution ⟨*sexism was a* ~ *subject with his wife*⟩ – **touchily** *adv*, **touchiness** *n*

¹**tough** *adj* **1a** strong and flexible; not brittle or liable to cut, break, or tear **b** not easily chewed **2** severe or uncompromisingly determined ⟨a ~ *and inflexible foreign policy* – *New Statesman*⟩ **3** capable of enduring great hardship or exertion **4** very hard to influence **5** extremely difficult or testing ⟨a ~ *question to answer*⟩ **6** aggressive or threatening in behaviour **7** without softness

or sentimentality **8** unfortunate, unpleasant – infml ⟨~ *luck*⟩ – **toughly** *adv*, **toughness** *n*

²**tough** *n* a tough person; *esp* sby aggressively violent

³**tough** *adv* in a tough manner ⟨*talk* ~⟩

toughen *vb* to make or become tough

toupee *n* a wig or hairpiece worn to cover a bald spot

¹**tour** *n* **1** a period during which an individual or unit is engaged on a specific duty, esp in 1 place ⟨*his regiment did a* ~ *in N Ireland*⟩ **2a** a journey (e g for business or pleasure) in which one returns to the starting point **b** a visit (e g to a historic site or factory) for pleasure or instruction ⟨*a guided* ~ *of the castle*⟩ **c** a series of professional engagements involving travel ⟨*a theatrical company on* ~⟩

²**tour** *vi* to make a tour ~ *vt* **1** to make a tour of **2** to present (e g a theatrical production or concert) on a tour

tour de force *n*, *pl* **tours de force** a feat of strength, skill, or ingenuity

tourism *n* **1** the practice of travelling for recreation **2** the organizing of tours for commercial purposes **3a** the promotion or encouragement of touring, esp at governmental level **b** the provision of services (e g accommodation) for tourists

tourist *n* **1** sby who makes a tour for recreation or culture **2** a member of a sports team that is visiting another country to play usu international matches – **tourist** *adj*

tourist class *n* the lowest class of accommodation (e g on a ship)

tournament *n* **1** a contest between 2 parties of mounted knights armed with usu blunted lances or swords **2** a series of games or contests for a championship

¹**tourney** *vi* to take part in a tournament, esp in the Middle Ages

²**tourney** *n* a tournament, esp in the Middle Ages

tourniquet *n* a bandage or other device for applying pressure to check bleeding or blood flow

tousle *vt* to dishevel, rumple

¹**tout** *vi* to solicit for customers ~ *vt* **1a** to solicit or peddle importunately **b** *Br* to sell (tickets in great demand) at exploitative prices **2a** *Br* to spy out information about (e g a racing stable or horse) **b** *NAm* to give a tip or solicit bets on (a racehorse)

²**tout** *n* sby who touts: e g **a** sby who solicits custom, usu importunately **b** *Br* sby who offers tickets for a sold-out entertainment (e g a concert or football match) at vastly inflated prices

³**tout** *vt* to praise or publicize loudly or extravagantly ⟨~ *ed as the most elaborate suburban shopping development – Wall Street Journal*⟩

¹**tow** *vt* to draw or pull along behind, esp by a rope or chain

²**tow** *n* **1** a rope or chain for towing **2** towing or being towed **3** sthg towed (e g a boat or car) – **in tow 1** being towed ⟨*a breakdown lorry with a car in tow*⟩ **2a** under guidance or protection ⟨*taken in tow by a friendly neighbour*⟩ **b** in the position of a dependent or devoted follower or admirer ⟨*a young man passed with a good-looking girl in tow*⟩

³**tow** *n* short or broken fibre (e g of flax or hemp) prepared for spinning

towards *prep* **1** moving or situated in the direction of ⟨*driving* ~ *town*⟩ **2a** along a course leading to ⟨*a long stride* ~ *disarmament*⟩ **b** in relation to ⟨*an attitude* ~ *life*⟩ **3** turned in the direction of ⟨*his back was* ~ *me*⟩ **4** not long before ⟨~ *the end of the afternoon*⟩ **5** for the partial financing of ⟨*will put it* ~ *a record*⟩

¹**towel** *n* **1** an absorbent cloth or paper for wiping or drying sthg (e g crockery or the body) after washing **2** SANITARY TOWEL

²**towel** *vt* **-ll-** (*NAm* **-l-**, **-ll-**) to rub or dry (e g the body) with a towel

towelling, *NAm chiefly* **toweling** *n* a cotton or linen fabric often used for making towels

¹**tower** *n* **1** a building or structure typically higher than its diameter and high relative to its surroundings that may stand apart or be attached to a larger structure and that may be fully walled in or of skeleton framework **2** a citadel, fortress **3 tower block, tower** a tall multi-storey building, often containing offices – **towered** *adj*, **towerlike** *adj*

²**tower** *vi* to reach or rise to a great height

towering *adj* **1** impressively high or great ⟨~ *pines*⟩ **2** reaching a high point of intensity ⟨*a* ~ *rage*⟩ **3** going beyond proper bounds ⟨~ *ambitions*⟩ – **toweringly** *adv*

towline *n* a towrope

town *n* **1a** a compactly settled area as distinguished from surrounding rural territory; *esp* one larger than a village but smaller than a city **b** a city **2** a neighbouring city, capital city, or metropolis ⟨*travels into* ~ *daily*⟩ **3** the city or urban life as contrasted with the country or rural life – **town** *adj* – **on the town** in usu carefree pursuit of entertainment or amusement (e g city nightlife)

town clerk *n* the chief official of a British town who until 1974 was appointed to administer municipal affairs and to act as secretary to the town council

town crier *n* a town officer who makes public proclamations

town hall *n* the chief administrative building of a town

town house *n* **1** the city residence of sby having a country seat **2** a terrace house typically of 3 storeys

townscape *n* the overall visual aspect of a town

township *n* **1** an ancient unit of administration in England identical in area with or being a division of a parish **2** an urban area inhabited by nonwhite citizens in S Africa

townsman, *fem* **townswoman** *n* **1** a native or resident of a town or city **2** a fellow citizen of a town

townspeople *n pl* the inhabitants of a town or city

toxaemia *n* **1** an abnormal condition associated with the presence of toxic substances in the blood **2** pre-eclampsia

toxic *adj* **1** of or caused by a poison or toxin **2** poisonous – **toxicity** *n*

toxic-, toxico- *comb form* tox- ⟨*toxicology*⟩ ⟨*toxicosis*⟩

toxicology *n* a branch of biology that deals with poisons and their effects and with medical, industrial, legal, or other problems arising from them – **toxicologist** *n*

toxin *n* an often extremely poisonous protein produced by a living organism (e g a bacterium), esp in the body of a host

¹**toy** *n* **1** a trinket, bauble **2a** sthg for a child to play with **b** sthg designed for amusement or diversion rather than practical use ⟨*an executive* ~⟩ **3** sthg tiny; *esp* an animal of a breed or variety of exceptionally small size – **toylike** *adj*

²**toy** *vi* **1** to act or deal *with* sthg without purpose or conviction **2** to amuse oneself as if with a toy – **toyer** *n*

³**toy** *adj* **1** designed or made for use as a toy ⟨*a* ~ *stove*⟩ **2** toylike, esp in being small

¹**trace** *n* **1** a mark or line left by sthg that has passed; *also* a footprint **2** a vestige of some past thing; *specif* an engram **3** sthg traced or drawn (e g the graphic record made by a seismograph) **4** (the path taken by) the spot

that moves across the screen of a cathode-ray tube **5** a minute and often barely detectable amount or indication, esp of a chemical ⟨*a ~ of a smile*⟩

²**trace** *vt* **1a** to delineate, sketch **b** to write (e g letters or figures) painstakingly **c** to copy (e g a drawing) by following the lines or letters as seen through a semitransparent superimposed sheet **2a** to follow the trail of **b** to follow back or study in detail or step by step ⟨*~ the history of the labour movement*⟩ **c** to discover signs, evidence, or remains of *~ vi* to be traceable historically – **traceable** *adj*

³**trace** *n* either of 2 straps, chains, or lines of a harness for attaching a vehicle to a horse

trace element *n* a chemical element present in minute quantities; *esp* one essential to a living organism for proper growth and development

tracer *n* **1** ammunition containing a chemical composition to mark the flight of projectiles by a trail of smoke or fire **2** a substance, esp a labelled element or atom, used to trace the course of a chemical or biological process

tracery *n* ornamental stone openwork in architecture, esp in the head of a Gothic window – **traceried** *adj*

trachea *n, pl* **tracheae** *also* **tracheas 1** the main trunk of the system of tubes by which air passes to and from the lungs in vertebrates; the windpipe **2** VESSEL **3b 3** any of the small tubes carrying air in most insects and many other arthropods – **tracheal** *adj*, **tracheate** *adj*

trachoma *n* a chronic contagious eye disease that is caused by a rickettsia and commonly causes blindness if left untreated – **trachomatous** *adj*

tracing *n* sthg traced: e g **a** a copy (e g of a design or map) made on a superimposed semitransparent sheet **b** (a map of) the ground plan of a military installation

tracing paper *n* a semitransparent paper for tracing drawings

¹**track** *n* **1a** detectable evidence (e g a line of footprints or a wheel rut) that sthg has passed **b** a path beaten (as if) by feet **c** a specially laid-out course, esp for racing **d(1)** the parallel rails of a railway **(2)** a rail or length of railing along which sthg, esp a curtain, moves or is pulled **e(1)** any of a series of parallel elongated regions on a magnetic tape on which a recording is made **(2)** a more or less independent sequence of recording (e g a single song) visible as a distinct band on a gramophone record **2** a recent or fossil footprint ⟨*the huge ~ of a dinosaur*⟩ **3a** the course along which sthg moves **b** the projection on the earth's surface of the path along which sthg (e g a missile) has flown **4** the condition of being aware of a fact or development ⟨*keep ~ of the costs*⟩ **5a** the width of a wheeled vehicle from wheel to wheel, usu from the outside of the rims **b** either of 2 endless usu metal belts on which a tracklaying vehicle travels – **trackless** *adj* – **in one's tracks** where one stands or is at the moment ⟨*was stopped in his tracks*⟩

²**track** *vt* **1** to follow the tracks or traces of **2** to observe or plot the course of (e g a spacecraft) instrumentally **3a** to make tracks on **b** *NAm* to carry on the feet and deposit ⟨*~ mud into the house*⟩ *~ vi* **1a** of a gramophone needle to follow the groove of a record **b** *of a rear wheel of a vehicle* to follow accurately the corresponding fore wheel on a straight track **2** to move a film or television camera towards, beside, or away from a subject while shooting a scene **3** *NAm* to leave tracks (e g on a floor) – **tracker** *n*

track down *vt* to search for until found ⟨*track a criminal down*⟩ ⟨*track down their new telephone number*⟩

track suit *n* a warm loose-fitting suit worn by athletes when training

¹**tract** *n* a short practical treatise; *esp* a pamphlet of religious propaganda

²**tract** *n* **1** a region or area of land of indefinite extent **2** a system of body parts or organs that collectively serve some often specified purpose ⟨*the digestive ~*⟩

tractable *adj* **1** easily taught or controlled ⟨*a ~ horse*⟩ **2** easily handled or wrought – **tractableness** *n*, **tractably** *adv*, **tractability** *n*

traction *n* **1** pulling or being pulled; *also* the force exerted in pulling **2** the drawing of a vehicle by motive power; *also* the motive power employed **3a** the adhesive friction of a body on a surface on which it moves ⟨*the ~ of a wheel on a rail*⟩ **b** a pulling force exerted on a skeletal structure (e g in treating a fracture) by means of a special device – **tractional** *adj*, **tractive** *adj*

traction engine *n* a large steam- or diesel-powered vehicle used to draw other vehicles or equipment over roads or fields and sometimes to provide power (e g for sawing or ploughing)

¹**tractor** *n* **1** TRACTION ENGINE **2a** a 4-wheeled or tracklaying vehicle used esp for pulling or using farm machinery **b** a truck with a short chassis and no body except a driver's cab, used to haul a large trailer or trailers

²**tractor** *adj* pulling or pulled through the air with force exerted from the front ⟨*a ~ monoplane is pulled by its propeller*⟩

¹**trad** *adj, chiefly Br* traditional – *infml*

²**trad** *n* traditional jazz

¹**trade** *n* **1a** the business or work in which one engages regularly **b** an occupation requiring manual or mechanical skill; a craft **c** the people engaged in an occupation, business, or industry **d** (the social group deriving its income from) commerce as opposed to the professions or landed property **2a** the business of buying and selling or bartering commodities **b** business, market ⟨*when ~ was brisk*⟩ ⟨*novelties for the tourist ~*⟩ **3** *sing or pl in constr* the people or group of firms engaged in a particular business or industry **4** TRADE WIND – usu pl **5** *chiefly NAm* a transaction; *also* an exchange of property usu without use of money

²**trade** *vt* to give in exchange for another commodity; *also* to make an exchange of ⟨*~d secrets*⟩ *~ vi* **1** to engage in the exchange, purchase, or sale of goods **2** to give one thing in exchange for another – **tradable** *also* **tradeable** *adj* – **trade on** to take often unscrupulous advantage of ⟨*they traded on her good nature*⟩

³**trade** *adj* **1** of or used in trade ⟨*a ~ agreement*⟩ **2** intended for or limited to people in a business or industry ⟨*a ~ publication*⟩ ⟨*~ discount*⟩

trade gap *n* the value by which a country's imports exceed its exports

trade-in *n* an item of merchandise (e g a car or refrigerator) that is traded in

trade in *vt* to give as payment or part payment for a purchase or bill

trademark *n* **1** a name or distinctive symbol or device attached to goods produced by a particular firm or individual and legally reserved to the exclusive use of the owner of the mark as maker or seller **2** a distinguishing feature firmly associated with sby or sthg

trade name *n* **1a** the name used for an article by the trade **b** a name given by a manufacturer or seller to an article or service to distinguish it as his/hers **2** the name under which a concern does business

trader *n* **1** a retail or wholesale dealer **2** a ship engaged in trade

tradesman *n* **1a** a shopkeeper **b** one who delivers goods to private houses **2** a workman in a skilled trade

trade union *also* **trades union** *n* an organization of workers formed for the purpose of advancing its members' interests – **trade unionism** n, **trade unionist** n

trade wind, trade n a wind blowing almost continually towards the equator from the NE in the belt between the N horse latitudes and the doldrums and from the SE in the belt between the S horse latitudes and the doldrums

trading estate n INDUSTRIAL ESTATE

trading stamp n a printed stamp of a certain value given by a retailer to a customer, to be accumulated and redeemed in merchandise or cash

tradition n 1 the handing down of information, beliefs, and customs by word of mouth or by example from one generation to another 2a an inherited practice or opinion b conventions associated with a group or period ⟨*the title poem represents a complete break with 19th-c ~* – F R Leavis⟩ 3 cultural continuity in attitudes and institutions – **traditionless** adj

traditional adj 1 of or handed down by tradition 2 of or being a style of jazz orig played in New Orleans in the early 1900s – **traditionally** adv

traditionalism n respect for tradition as opposed to modernism or liberalism – **traditionalist** n or adj, **traditionalistic** adj

traduce vt to (attempt to) damage the reputation or standing of, esp by misrepresentation – fml – **traducement** n, **traducer** n

¹**traffic** n 1a import and export trade b the business of bartering or buying and selling c illegal or disreputable trade ⟨*drug ~*⟩ 2 exchange ⟨*a lively ~ in ideas* – F L Allen⟩ 3a the movement (e g of vehicles or pedestrians) through an area or along a route b the vehicles, pedestrians, ships, or aircraft moving along a route c the information or signals transmitted over a communications system 4a the passengers or cargo carried by a transport system b the business of transporting passengers or freight 5 dealings between individuals or groups – fml

²**traffic** vb **-ck-** vi to carry on traffic ~ vt to trade, barter – **trafficker** n

trafficator n, Br INDICATOR 1c; esp a hinged retractable illuminated arm on the side of an old motor car

traffic circle n, NAm a roundabout

traffic island n a paved or planted island in a road designed to guide the flow of traffic and provide refuge for pedestrians

traffic light n an automatically operated signal of coloured lights for controlling traffic – usu pl

tragedian n 1 a writer of tragedies 2 fem **tragedienne** an actor who plays tragic roles

tragedy n 1 (a) serious drama in which destructive circumstances result in adversity for and usu the deaths of the main characters 2 a disastrous event; a calamity 3 tragic quality or element

tragic also **tragical** adj 1 (expressive) of tragedy ⟨*the ~ significance of the atomic bomb* – H S Truman⟩ 2 of, appropriate to, dealing with, or treated in tragedy 3a deplorable, lamentable ⟨*the ~ disparity between the actual and the ideal*⟩ b marked by a sense of tragedy – **tragically** adv

tragicomedy n a literary work in which tragic and comic elements are mixed in a usu ironic way; also a situation or event of such a character – **tragicomic** also **tragicomical** adj

¹**trail** vi 1a to hang down so as to sweep the ground b of a plant, branch, etc to grow to such length as to droop over towards the ground 2a to walk or proceed draggingly or wearily – usu + along b to lag behind; do poorly in relation to others 3 to move or extend slowly in thin streams ⟨*smoke ~ing from chimneys*⟩ 4a to extend in an erratic course or line b to dwindle ⟨*voice ~ing off*⟩ 5 to

follow a trail; track game ~ vt 1a to drag loosely along a surface; allow to sweep the ground b to haul, tow 2a to drag (e g a limb or the body) heavily or wearily b to carry or bring along as an addition c to draw along in one's wake ⟨*~ing clouds of glory do we come* – William Wordsworth⟩ 3a TRACK 1a b to follow behind, esp in the footsteps of c to lag behind (e g a competitor)

²**trail** n 1 the part of a gun carriage that rests on the ground when the piece is unlimbered 2a sthg that follows as if being drawn behind b the streak of light produced by a meteor 3a a trace or mark left by sby or sthg that has passed or is being followed ⟨*a ~ of blood*⟩ b(1) a track made by passage, esp through a wilderness (2) a marked path through a forest or mountainous region – **trailless** adj

trailer n 1 a trailing plant 2 a wheeled vehicle designed to be towed (e g by a lorry or car); specif, NAm CARAVAN 2 3 a set of short excerpts from a film shown in advance for publicity purposes

¹**train** n 1 a part of a gown that trails behind the wearer 2a a retinue, suite b a moving file of people, vehicles, or animals 3 the vehicles, men, and sometimes animals that accompany an army with baggage, supplies, ammunition, or siege artillery 4 a connected series of ideas, actions, or events 5 a line of gunpowder laid to lead fire to a charge 6 a series of connected moving mechanical parts (e g gears) 7 a connected line of railway carriages or wagons with or without a locomotive – **trainful** n

²**train** vt 1 to direct the growth of (a plant), usu by bending, pruning, etc 2a to form by instruction, discipline, or drill b to teach so as to make fit or proficient 3 to prepare (e g by exercise) for a test of skill 4 to aim at an object or objective ⟨*~ed his rifle on the target*⟩ ~ vi 1 to undergo training 2 to go by train – **trainable** adj

trainbearer n an attendant who holds the train of a robe or gown (e g on a ceremonial occasion)

trainee n one who is being trained for a job

training n 1 the bringing of a person or animal to a desired degree of proficiency in some activity or skill 2 the condition of being trained, esp for a contest ⟨*an athlete out of ~*⟩

training college n, Br a school offering specialized instruction ⟨*a ~ for traffic wardens*⟩

traipse vi to walk or trudge about, often to little purpose – **traipse** n

trait n a distinguishing (personal) quality or characteristic

traitor, fem **traitress** n 1 sby who betrays another's trust 2 sby who commits treason – **traitorous** adj, **traitorously** adv

trajectory n 1 the curve that a planet, projectile, etc follows 2 a path, progression, or line of development like a physical trajectory

tram n any of various vehicles: e g a a boxlike wagon running on rails (e g in a mine) b chiefly Br a passenger vehicle running on rails and typically operating on urban streets

tramline n, Br 1 a track on which trams run 2 pl (the area between) either of the 2 pairs of sidelines on a tennis court that mark off the area used in doubles play

¹**trammel** n 1 a net for catching birds or fish; esp one having 3 layers with the middle one finer-meshed and slack so that fish passing through carry some of the centre net through the coarser opposite net and are trapped 2 sthg that impedes freedom of action – usu pl with sing. meaning ⟨*the ~s of convention*⟩ 3a an instrument for drawing ellipses b a compass for drawing large circles that consists of a beam with 2 sliding parts – usu pl with sing. meaning

²trammel *vt* **-ll-** (*NAm* **-l-**, **-ll-**), **1** to enmesh **2** to impede the free play of

¹tramp *vi* **1** to walk or tread, esp heavily **2a** to travel about on foot **b** to journey as a tramp ~ *vt* **1** to trample **2** to travel or wander through on foot – **tramper** *n*

²tramp *n* **1** a wandering vagrant who survives by taking the occasional job or by begging or stealing money and food **2** a usu long and tiring walk **3** the heavy rhythmic tread of feet **4** an iron plate to protect the sole of a shoe **5** a merchant vessel that does not work a regular route but carries general cargo to any port as required **6** *chiefly NAm* a promiscuous woman

trample *vb* **trampling** *vi* **1** to tread heavily so as to bruise, crush, or injure **2** to treat destructively with ruthlessness or contempt – usu + *on, over,* or *upon* ⟨trampling *on the rights of others*⟩ ~ *vt* to press down, crush, or injure (as if) by treading – **trample** *n*, **trampler** *n*

trampoline *n* a resilient sheet or web supported by springs in a frame and used as a springboard in tumbling – **trampoliner** *n*, **trampolining** *n*

trance *n* **1** a state of semiconsciousness or unconsciousness with reduced or absent sensitivity to external stimulation **2** a usu self-induced state of altered consciousness or ecstasy in which religious or mystical visions may be experienced **3** a state of profound abstraction or absorption – **trancelike** *adj*

tranny *n*, *chiefly Br* TRANSISTOR RADIO – infml

tranquil *adj* free from mental agitation or from disturbance or commotion – **tranquilly** *adv*, **tranquillity** *n*

tranquillize, -ise, *NAm chiefly* **tranquilize** *vt* to make tranquil or calm; *esp* to relieve of mental tension and anxiety by drugs ~ *vi* to become tranquil

tranquilizer, -iser, *NAm chiefly* **tranquilizer** *n* a drug (e g diazepam) used to tranquilize

trans *adj* characterized by having identical atoms or groups on opposite sides of the molecule – usu ital; often in combination ⟨trans-*dichloroethylene*⟩

trans- *prefix* **1** on or to the other side of; across; beyond ⟨trans*atlantic*⟩ ⟨trans*continental*⟩ **2** beyond (a specified chemical element) in the periodic table ⟨trans*uranic*⟩ **3** through ⟨trans*cutaneous*⟩ ⟨trans-*sonic*⟩ **4** so or such as to change or transfer ⟨trans*literate*⟩ ⟨trans*location*⟩ ⟨trans*ship*⟩

transact *vt* to perform; CARRY OUT 1; *esp* to conduct ⟨*business to be* ~ed *by experts*⟩ – **transactor** *n*

transaction *n* **1** transacting **2a** sthg transacted; *esp* a business deal **b** *pl* the (published) record of the meeting of a society or association – **transactional** *adj*

transalpine *adj* north of the Alps

transatlantic *adj* **1** crossing or extending across the Atlantic ocean ⟨*a* ~ *cable*⟩ **2** situated beyond the Atlantic ocean **3** (characteristic) of people or places situated beyond the Atlantic ocean; *specif, chiefly Br* American ⟨*a* ~ *accent*⟩

transcend *vt* **1a** to go beyond the limits of **b** to be or extend beyond and above (the universe or material existence) **2** to surpass, excel ~ *vi* to rise above or extend notably beyond ordinary limits

transcendent *adj* **1a** exceeding usual limits; surpassing **b** beyond the limits of ordinary experience **c** beyond the limits of possible experience and knowledge – used in Kantianism **2** transcending the universe or material existence – **transcendence, transcendency** *n*, **transcendently** *adv*

transcendental *adj* **1** of or employing the basic categories (e g space and time) presupposed by knowledge and experience ⟨*a* ~ *proof*⟩ **2** TRANSCENDENT 1a **3a** of or being a transcendental number **b** being, involving, or representing a function (e g sin x, log x, e Cx) that

cannot be expressed by a finite number of algebraic operations ⟨~ *curves*⟩ **4a** TRANSCENDENT 1b **b** supernatural **c** abstruse, abstract **d** of transcendentalism – **transcendentally** *adv*

transcendentalism *n* **1** a philosophy that emphasizes the basic categories of knowledge and experience, or asserts fundamental reality to be transcendent **2** a philosophy that asserts the primacy of the spiritual over the material – **transcendentalist** *adj or n*

transcendental number *n* a number (e g e or π) that cannot be the root of an algebraic equation with rational coefficients

transcontinental *adj* crossing or extending across a continent

transcribe *vt* **1a** to make a written copy or version of (e g sthg written or printed) **b** to write in a different medium; transliterate ⟨~ *a word in phonetics*⟩ ⟨~ *shorthand*⟩ **c** to write down, record **2** to transfer (data) from one recording form to another **3** to make a musical transcription of – **transcriber** *n*

transcript *n* **1** a written, printed, or typed copy, esp of dictated or recorded material **2** an official written copy ⟨*a court reporter's* ~⟩

transcription *n* **1** transcribing **2** a copy, transcript: e g **a** an often free arrangement of a musical composition for some instrument or voice other than the original **b** a sound recording suitable for broadcasting and thus usu of high quality **3** the naturally occurring process of constructing a molecule of nucleic acid (e g messenger RNA) using a DNA molecule as a template, with resulting transfer of genetic information to the newly formed molecule – **transcriptional** *adj*

transept *n* (either of the projecting arms of) the part of a cross-shaped church that crosses the E end of the nave at right angles – **transeptal** *adj*

¹transfer *vb* **-rr-** *vt* **1a** to convey or cause to pass from one person, place, or situation to another **b** to move or send to another location ⟨~red *her business to the capital*⟩; *specif* to move (a professional soccer player) to another football club **2** to make over the possession or control of **3** to copy (e g a design) from one surface to another by contact ~ *vi* **1** to move to a different place, region, or situation **2** to change from one vehicle or transport system to another – **transferable, transferrable** *adj*, **transferral** *n*, **transferor, transferrer** *n*, **transferee** *n*

²transfer *n* **1** conveyance of right, title, or interest in property **2a** transferring **b** transference **3** sthg or sby that transfers or is transferred; *esp* a design or picture transferred by contact from one surface (e g specially prepared paper) to another **4** *NAm* a ticket entitling a passenger on a public conveyance to continue a journey on another route

transference *n* the redirection of feelings and desires, esp those unconsciously retained from childhood, towards a new object (e g towards a psychoanalyst conducting therapy) – **transferential** *adj*

transfiguration *n* **1a** a change in form or appearance; a metamorphosis **b** an exalting, glorifying, or spiritual change **2** *cap* August 6 observed as a Christian festival in commemoration of the transfiguration of Christ as described in Mt 17:2 and Mk 9:2–3

transfigure *vt* to give a new appearance to; transform outwardly and usu for the better

transfix *vt* **1** to pierce through (as if) with a pointed weapon **2** to hold motionless (as if) by piercing ⟨~ed *by horror*⟩ – **transfixion** *n*

¹transform *vt* **1** to change radically (e g in structure, appearance, or character) **2** to subject to mathematical transformation **3** to change (a current) in potential (e g

from high voltage to low) or in type (e g from alternating to direct) **4** to cause (a cell) to undergo transformation ~ *vi* to become transformed – **transformable** *adj*, **transformative** *adj*
²transform *n* a mathematical element or linguistic structure producible by (a) transformation
transformation *n* **1** the operation of changing one configuration or expression into another in accordance with a mathematical rule **2** any of a set of rules for transforming the supposed underlying structures of (a) language into actual sentences **3** modification of plant or animal cell culture (e g by a cancer-producing virus) resulting in unlimited cell growth and division – **transformational** *adj*
transformer *n* an electrical device making use of the principle of mutual induction to convert variations of current in a primary circuit into variations of voltage and current in a secondary circuit
transfuse *vt* **1** to diffuse into or through; *broadly* to spread across **2** to transfer (e g blood) into a vein – **transfusible, transfusable** *adj*, **transfusion** *n*
transgress *vt* **1** to go beyond limits set or prescribed by ⟨~ *the divine law*⟩ **2** to pass beyond or go over (a boundary) ~ *vi* to violate a command or law – **transgressive** *adj*, **transgressor** *n*
tranship *vb* to transship
¹transient *adj* **1** passing quickly away; transitory **2** making only a brief stay ⟨*a* ~ *summer migrant*⟩ – **transience, transiency** *n*, **transiently** *adv*
²transient *n* **1** a transient guest or worker **2a** a temporary oscillation that occurs in a circuit because of a sudden change of voltage or load **b** a transient current or voltage
transistor *n* **1** any of several semiconductor devices that have usu 3 electrodes and make use of a small current to control a larger one **2** TRANSISTOR RADIO
transistorize, -ise *vt* to construct (a device) using transistors – **transistorization** *n*
transistor radio *n* a radio using transistorized circuitry
¹transit *n* **1a** passing or conveying through or over **b** a change, transition **2** passage of a smaller celestial body across the disc of a larger one **b** over a meridian or through the field of a telescope **3** *NAm* conveyance of people or things from one place to another – **in transit** in passage ⟨*goods lost in transit*⟩
²transit *vi* to make a transit ~ *vt* to traverse
transition *n* **1a** passage from one state or stage to another **b** a movement, development, or evolution from one form, stage, or style to another ⟨*a* ~ *from the inorganic to the organic* – W R Inge⟩ **2a** a musical modulation **b** a musical passage leading from one section of a piece to another **3** an abrupt change in energy state or level (e g of an atomic nucleus or a molecule), usu accompanied by loss or gain of a single quantum of energy – **transitional** *adj*, **transitionally** *adv*
transitive *adj* **1** having or containing a direct object ⟨*a* ~ *verb*⟩⟨*a* ~ *construction*⟩ **2** of or being a relation such that if the relation holds between a first element and a second and between the second element and a third, it holds between the first and third elements **3** of or characterized by transition – **transitive** *n*, **transitively** *adv*, **transitiveness, transitivity** *n*
transitory *adj* **1** tending to pass away **2** of brief duration – **transitorily** *adv*, **transitoriness** *n*
translate *vt* **1a** to bear, remove, or change from one place, state, form, or appearance to another ⟨*a country boy* ~ *d to the city*⟩⟨~ *ideas into action*⟩ **b** to convey to heaven or to a nontemporal condition without death **c** to

transfer (a bishop) from one see to another **2a** to turn into another language **b** to turn from one set of symbols into another **c** to express in different or more comprehensible terms **3** to subject (genetic information, esp messenger RNA) to translation ~ *vi* **1** to practise or make (a) translation **2** to undergo (a) translation – **translatable** *adj*, **translator** *n*
translation *n* **1a** (a version produced by) a rendering from one language into another **b** a change to a different substance or form **c** uniform motion of a body in a straight line **2** the process of forming a protein synthesis from information contained usu in messenger RNA – **translational** *adj*
transliterate *vt* to represent or spell in the characters of another alphabet – **transliteration** *n*
translucent *adj* permitting the passage of light: e g **a** transparent **b** transmitting and diffusing light so that objects beyond cannot be seen clearly ⟨*a* ~ *window of frosted glass*⟩⟨~ *porcelain*⟩ – **translucence, translucency** *n*, **translucently** *adv*
transmigrate *vi* of a soul to pass at death from one body or being to another **2** to migrate – **transmigrator** *n*, **transmigration** *n*, **transmigratory** *adj*
transmission *n* **1** transmitting ⟨~ *of a nerve impulse across a synapse*⟩; *esp* transmitting by radio waves or over a wire **2** the assembly by which the power is transmitted from a motor vehicle engine to the axle **3** sthg transmitted – **transmissive** *adj*
transmit *vb* -tt- *vt* **1a** to send or transfer from one person or place to another **b(1)** to convey (as if) by inheritance or heredity **(2)** to convey (infection) abroad or to another **2a(1)** to cause (e g light or force) to pass or be conveyed through a medium **(2)** to allow the passage of ⟨*glass* ~ *s light*⟩ **b** to send out (a signal) either by radio waves or over a wire ~ *vi* to send out a signal by radio waves or over a wire – **transmissible** *adj*, **transmittable** *adj*, **transmittal** *n*
transmitter *n* **1** the portion of a telegraphic or telephonic instrument that sends the signals **2** a radio or television transmitting station or set **3** a neurotransmitter
transmogrify *vt* to transform, often with grotesque or humorous effect – **transmogrification** *n*
transmutation *n* **1** the conversion of base metals into gold or silver **2** the natural or artificial conversion of one element or nuclide into another – **transmutative** *adj*
transmute *vt* **1** to change in form, substance, or characteristics **2** to subject (e g an element) to transmutation to undergo transmutation – **transmutable** *adj*
transom *n* a transverse piece in a structure: e g **a** a lintel **b** a horizontal crossbar in a window, over a door, or between a door and a window or fanlight above it **c** any of several transverse timbers or beams secured to the sternpost of a boat
transparency *n* **1** being transparent **2a** a picture or design on glass, film, etc viewed by a light shining through it from behind; *esp* SLIDE 5b **b** a framework covered with thin cloth or paper bearing a device for public display (e g for advertisement) and lit from within
transparent *adj* **1a(1)** transmitting light without appreciable scattering so that bodies lying beyond are entirely visible **(2)** penetrable by a specified form of radiation (e g X rays or ultraviolet) **b** fine or sheer enough to be seen through **2a** free from pretence or deceit ⟨~ *sincerity*⟩ **b** easily detected or seen through ⟨*a* ~ *lie*⟩ **c** readily understood ⟨*the meaning of this word is* ~⟩ – **transparence** *n*, **transparently** *adv*, **transparentness** *n*
transpire *vt* to pass off or give passage to (a gas or liquid) through pores or interstices; *esp* to excrete (e g water vapour) through a skin or other living membrane ~ *vi* **1**

to give off a vapour; *specif* to give off or exude water vapour, esp from the surfaces of leaves **2** to pass in the form of a vapour, esp from a living body **3** to become known; come to light **4** to occur; TAKE PLACE – disapproved of by some speakers

¹transplant *vt* **1** to lift and reset (a plant) in another soil or place **2** to remove from one place and settle or introduce elsewhere **3** to transfer (an organ or tissue) from one part or individual to another – **transplantable** *adj*, **transplanter** *n*, **transplantation** *n*

²transplant *n* **1** transplanting **2** sthg transplanted

¹transport *vt* **1** to transfer or convey from one place to another ⟨*mechanisms of* ~*ing ions across a living membrane*⟩ **2** to carry away with strong and often pleasurable emotion **3** to send to a penal colony overseas – **transportable** *adj*

²transport *n* **1** the conveying of goods or people from one place to another **2** strong and often pleasurable emotion – often pl with sing. meaning ⟨~*s of joy*⟩ **3a** a ship or aircraft for carrying soldiers or military equipment **b** a lorry, aeroplane, etc used to transport people or goods **4** a mechanism for moving a tape, esp a magnetic tape, or disk past a sensing or recording head

transportation *n* **1** the act of transporting **2** banishment to a penal colony **3** *NAm* means of conveyance or travel from one place to another

transport café *n, Br* an inexpensive roadside cafeteria catering mainly for long-distance lorry drivers

transporter *n* a vehicle for transporting large or heavy loads ⟨*a tank* ~⟩⟨*a car* ~⟩

¹transpose *vt* **1** to transfer from one place or period to another **2** to change the relative position of; alter the sequence of ⟨~ *letters to change the spelling*⟩ **3** to write or perform (music) in a different key **4** to bring (a term) from one side of an algebraic equation to the other with change of sign ~*vi* to transpose music – **transposable** *adj*

²transpose *n* a matrix formed by interchanging the rows of a given matrix with its corresponding columns

transship, tranship *vb* to transfer from one ship or conveyance to another for further transportation – **transshipment** *n*

transubstantiation *n* the miraculous change by which, according to Roman Catholic and Eastern Orthodox dogma, bread and wine used at communion become the body and blood of Christ when they are consecrated, although their appearance remains unchanged

transverse *adj* lying or being across; set or made crosswise – **transversely** *adv*

transvestism *n* the adoption of the dress and often the behaviour of the opposite sex – **transvestite** *adj or n*

¹trap *n* **1** a device for taking animals; *esp* one that holds by springing shut suddenly **2a** sthg designed to catch sby unawares; *also* PITFALL 1 **b** a situation from which it is impossible to escape ⟨*caught in a poverty* ~⟩; *also* a plan to trick a person into such a situation ⟨*police laid a* ~ *for the criminal*⟩ **3a** a trapdoor **b** a device from which a greyhound is released at the start of a race **4a** a device for hurling clay pigeons into the air **b** BUNKER 2b **5** a light usu 1-horse carriage with springs **6** any of various devices for preventing passage of sthg often while allowing other matter to proceed; *esp* a device for drains or sewers consisting of a bend or partitioned chamber in which the liquid forms a seal to prevent the passage of sewer gas **7** *pl* a group of percussion instruments used esp in a dance or jazz band **8** the mouth – *slang*

²trap *vb* **-pp-** *vt* **1** to catch or take (as if) in a trap **2** to provide or set (a place) with traps **3** to stop, retain ⟨*these mountains* ~ *the rain*⟩ **4** to stop and control (the ball)

with the foot in soccer ~*vi* to engage in trapping animals – **trapper** *n*

³trap, traprock *n* any of various dark-coloured fine-grained igneous rocks (e g basalt) used esp in road making

trapdoor *n* a lifting or sliding door covering an opening in a floor, ceiling, etc

trapeze *n* a gymnastic or acrobatic apparatus consisting of a short horizontal bar suspended by 2 parallel ropes

trapezium *n, pl* **trapeziums, trapezia** *Br* a quadrilateral having only 2 sides parallel

trapezoid *n, chiefly NAm* a trapezium – **trapezoidal** *adj*

trappings *n pl* outward decoration or dress; *also* outward signs and accessories ⟨*all the* ~ *of power with none of the substance*⟩

Trappist *n* a member of a reformed branch of the Roman Catholic Cistercian Order established in 1664 at the monastery of La Trappe in Normandy and noted for its vow of silence – **Trappist** *adj*

trapshooting *n* shooting at clay pigeons sprung into the air from a trap so as to simulate the angles of flight of birds – **trapshooter** *n*

trash *n* **1** sthg of little or no value: e g **a** junk, rubbish **b(1)** empty talk **(2)** inferior literary or artistic work **2** sthg in a crumbled or broken condition or mass **3** a worthless person; *also, sing or pl in constr* such people as a group – *infml*

trash can *n, NAm* a dustbin

trashy *adj* of inferior quality or worth ⟨*a* ~ *novel*⟩ – **trashiness** *n*

trauma *n, pl* **traumata, traumas 1a** an injury (e g a wound) to living tissue caused by an outside agent **b** a disordered mental or behavioural state resulting from mental or emotional stress or shock **2** an agent, force, or mechanism that causes trauma – **traumatic** *adj*

¹travail *n* **1** physical or mental exertion, esp of a painful or laborious nature **2** *archaic* labour pains

²travail *vi* **1** to labour hard – *fml* **2** *archaic* to suffer labour pains

¹travel *vb* **-ll-** (*NAm* **-l-, -ll-**) *vi* **1a** to go (as if) on a tour **b** to go as if by travelling ⟨*my mind* ~*led back to our last meeting*⟩ **c** to go from place to place as a sales representative ⟨~*s in cosmetics*⟩ **2a** to move or be transmitted from one place to another ⟨*wine* ~*s badly*⟩ **b** *esp of machinery* to move along a specified direction or path ⟨*the stylus* ~*s in a groove*⟩ **c** to move at high speed – *infml* ⟨*a car that can really* ~⟩ ~*vt* **1a** to journey through or over ⟨~ *the world*⟩ **b** to follow (a course or path) as if by travelling **2** to traverse (a specified distance) **3** to cover (a place or region) as a sales representative – **travel light** to travel with a minimum of equipment or baggage

²travel *n* **1** a journey, esp to a distant or unfamiliar place – often pl ⟨*set off on her* ~*s*⟩ **2a** movement, progression ⟨*the* ~ *of satellites round the earth*⟩ **b** the motion of a piece of machinery

travel agent *n* sby engaged in selling and arranging personal transport, tours, or trips for travellers – **travel agency** *n*

travelled, NAm chiefly traveled *adj* **1** experienced in travel ⟨*a widely* ~ *journalist*⟩ **2** used by travellers ⟨*a well*-travelled *route*⟩

traveller, NAm chiefly traveler *n* **1** SALES REPRESENTATIVE **2** any of various devices for handling sthg that is being moved laterally **3** *dial Br* a gipsy

traveller's cheque, NAm traveler's check *n* a cheque that is purchased from a bank or express company and that may be exchanged abroad for foreign currency

travelling fellowship *n* a fellowship enabling the holder to travel for study or research

travelogue, *NAm also* **travelog** *n* **1** a film or illustrated talk or lecture on some usu exotic or remote place **2** a narrated documentary film about travel

¹**traverse** *n* **1** sthg that crosses or lies across **2** a transverse gallery in a large building (e g a church) **3** a route or way across or over: e g **a** a curving or zigzag way up a steep slope **b** the course followed in traversing **4** (a) traversing **5a** a lateral movement (e g of the saddle of a lathe carriage) **b** the lateral movement of a gun to change direction of fire **6** a survey consisting of a series of measured lines whose bearings are known

²**traverse** *vt* **1** to pass or travel across, over, or through ⟨~ *a terrain*⟩ ⟨*light rays* traversing *a crystal*⟩ **2** to lie or extend across ⟨*the bridge* ~s *a brook*⟩ **3a** to move to and fro over or along **b** to ascend, descend, or cross (a slope or gap) at an angle **c** to move (a gun) to right or left ~ *vi* **1** to move back and forth or from side to side **2** to climb or ski across rather than straight up or down a hill – **traversable** *adj*, **traversal** *n*, **traverser** *n*

³**traverse** *adj* lying across

¹**travesty** *n* **1** a crude or grotesque literary or artistic parody **2** a debased, distorted, or grossly inferior imitation\⟨*a* ~ *of justice*⟩

²**travesty** *vt* to make a travesty of

¹**trawl** *vb* to fish (for or in) with a trawl

²**trawl** *n* **1** a large conical net dragged along the sea bottom to catch fish **2** *NAm* a setline

trawler *n* a boat used in trawling

tray *n* an open receptacle with a flat bottom and a low rim for holding, carrying, or exhibiting articles – **trayful** *n*

treacherous *adj* **1** characterized by treachery; perfidious **2a** of uncertain reliability **b** providing insecure footing or support ⟨*a* ~ *surface of black ice*⟩ **c** marked by hidden dangers or hazards ⟨*the* ~ *waters round the coast*⟩ – **treacherously** *adv*, **treacherousness** *n*

treachery *n* (an act of) violation of allegiance; (a) betrayal of trust

treacle *n*, *chiefly Br* **1** any of the edible grades of molasses that are obtained in the early stages of sugar refining **2** GOLDEN SYRUP

¹**tread** *vb* **trod** *also* **treaded**; **trodden, trod** *vt* **1a** to step or walk on or over **b** to walk along **2a** to beat or press with the feet **b** to subdue or repress as if by trampling **3** *of a male bird* to copulate with **4a** to form by treading ⟨~ *a path*⟩ **b** to execute by stepping or dancing ⟨~ *a measure*⟩ ~ *vi* **1** to move on foot **2a** to set foot **b** to put one's foot ⟨trod *on a stone*⟩ – **treader** *n* – **tread on someone's toes/corns** to give offence or hurt sby's feelings, esp by encroaching on his/her rights – **tread water** to keep the body nearly upright in the water and the head above water by a treading motion of the feet, usu aided by the hands

²**tread** *n* **1** an imprint made (as if) by treading **2a** the action or an act of treading **b** the sound or manner of treading ⟨*the heavy* ~ *of feet*⟩ **3a** the part of a wheel or tyre that makes contact with a road or rail **b** the pattern of ridges or grooves made or cut in the face of a tyre **4** (the width of) the upper horizontal part of a step – **treadless** *adj*

¹**treadle** *n* a lever pressed by the foot to drive a machine (e g a sewing machine)

²**treadle** *vi* to operate a treadle

treadmill *n* **1a** a mill used formerly in prison punishment that was worked by people treading on steps inside a wide wheel with a horizontal axis **b** a mill worked by an animal treading an endless belt **2** a wearisome or monotonous routine

treason *n* **1** the betrayal of a trust **2** the offence of violating the duty of allegiance owed to one's crown or government – **treasonous** *adj*

treasonable *adj* of or being treason – **treasonably** *adv*

¹**treasure** *n* **1** wealth, esp in a form which can be accumulated or hoarded ⟨*buried* ~⟩ **2** sthg of great worth or value; *also* sby highly valued or prized

²**treasure** *vt* to hold or preserve as precious ⟨~d *those memories*⟩

treasurer *n* the financial officer of an organization (e g a society) – **treasurership** *n*

treasure trove *n* treasure that anyone finds; *specif* gold or silver money, plate, or bullion which is found hidden and whose ownership is not known

treasury *n* **1** a place in which stores of wealth are kept **b** the place where esp public funds that have been collected are deposited and disbursed **2** *often cap* (the building which houses) a government department in charge of finances, esp the collection, management, and expenditure of public revenues **3** a source or collection of treasures ⟨*a* ~ *of poems*⟩

treasury bill *n* a bill issued by the treasury in return for money lent to the government

¹**treat** *vi* **1** to discuss terms of accommodation or settlement **2** to deal with a matter, esp in writing – usu + *of*; *fml* ⟨*a book* ~ing *of conservation*⟩ ~ *vt* **1** to deal with ⟨*food is plentiful and* ~ed *with imagination* – Cecil Beaton⟩ **2a** to behave oneself towards ⟨~ *a horse cruelly*⟩ **b** to regard and deal with in a specified manner – usu + *as* ⟨~ed *it as a serious matter*⟩ **3a** to provide with free food, drink, or entertainment – usu + *to* **b** to provide with enjoyment – usu + *to* **4** to care for or deal with medically or surgically ⟨~ *a disease*⟩ **5** to act on with some agent, esp so as to improve or alter **6** to deal with in speech or writing – *fml* – **treatable** *adj*, **treater** *n*

²**treat** *n* **1** an entertainment given free of charge to those invited **2** a source of pleasure or amusement; *esp* an unexpected one ⟨*the cold beer on a hot day was a* ~⟩ – **a treat** very well or successfully ⟨*the speech went down a treat*⟩ – *infml*

treatise *n* a formal written exposition on a subject ⟨*a* ~ *on higher education*⟩

treatment *n* **1a** treating sby or sthg **b** the actions customarily applied in a particular situation ⟨*the author got the standard* ~ *of cocktail parties and interviews*⟩ **2** a substance or technique used in treating

treaty *n* **1** the action of treating, esp of negotiating – chiefly in *in treaty* **2** (a document setting down) an agreement or contract made by negotiation (e g between states)

treaty port *n* any of numerous ports and inland cities in China, Japan, and Korea formerly open by treaty to foreign commerce

¹**treble** *n* **1a** the highest voice part in harmonic music; *also* sby, esp a boy, who performs this part **b** a member of a family of instruments having the highest range **c** a high-pitched voice or sound **d** the upper half of the whole vocal or instrumental tonal range **e** the higher part of the audio frequency range considered esp in relation to its electronic reproduction **2** sthg treble in construction, uses, amount, number, or value: e g **a** a type of bet in which the winnings and stake from a previous race are bet on the next of 3 races **b** (a throw landing on) the middle narrow ring on a dart board counting treble the stated score

²**treble** *adj* **1a** having 3 parts or uses **b** TRIPLE 2 **2a** relating to or having the range or part of a treble **b** high-pitched, shrill – **trebly** *adv*

³**treble** *vb* to increase to 3 times the size, amount, or number

treble chance n a method of competing in football pools in which the chances of winning are based on the numbers of home wins, away wins, and draws

treble clef n a clef that places the note G above middle C on the second line of the staff

¹tree n **1a** a tall woody perennial plant having a single usu long and erect main stem, generally with few or no branches on its lower part **b** a shrub or herbaceous plant having the form of a tree ⟨rose ~s⟩ ⟨a banana ~⟩ **2** a device for inserting in a boot or shoe to preserve its shape when not being worn **3a** a diagram or graph that branches, usu from a single stem ⟨genealogical ~⟩ **b** a much-branched system of channels, esp in an animal or plant body ⟨the vascular ~⟩ **4** archaic **a** the cross on which Jesus was crucified **b** the gallows – **treeless** adj, **treelike** adj

²tree vt to drive to or up a tree ⟨~d by a bull⟩

tree fern n a treelike fern with a woody stem

trefoil n **1a** (a) clover; broadly any of several leguminous plants having leaves of 3 leaflets **b** a leaf consisting of 3 leaflets **2** a stylized figure or ornament in the form of a 3-lobed leaf or flower

trek vi or n **-kk-** (to make) **1** a journey; esp an arduous one **2** chiefly SAfr a journey by ox wagon

¹trellis n a frame of latticework used as a screen or as a support for climbing plants – **trellised** adj

²trellis vt to provide with a trellis; esp to train (e g a vine) on a trellis

¹tremble vi **trembling 1** to shake involuntarily (e g with fear or cold) **2** to be affected (as if) by a quivering motion ⟨the building ~d from the blast⟩ ⟨his voice ~d with emotion⟩ **3** to be affected with fear or apprehension – **trembler** n

²tremble n **1a** a fit or spell of involuntary shaking or quivering **b** a tremor or series of tremors **2** pl but sing in constr a severe disorder of livestock, esp cattle, characterized by muscular tremors, weakness, and constipation – **trembly** adj

tremendous adj **1** such as to arouse awe or fear **2** of extraordinary size, degree, or excellence – **tremendously** adv, **tremendousness** n

tremolo n, pl **tremolos 1a** the rapid reiteration of a musical note or of alternating notes to produce a tremulous effect **b** a perceptible rapid variation of pitch in the (singing) voice; vibrato **2** a mechanical device in an organ for causing a tremulous effect

tremor n **1** a trembling or shaking, usu from physical weakness, emotional stress, or disease **2** a (slight) quivering or vibratory motion, esp of the earth **3** a thrill, quiver ⟨experienced a sudden ~ of fear⟩

tremulous adj **1** characterized by or affected with trembling or tremors **2** uncertain, wavering – **tremulously** adv, **tremulousness** n

¹trench n **1** a deep narrow excavation (e g for the laying of underground pipes); esp one used for military defence **2** a long narrow usu steep-sided depression in the ocean floor

²trench vb to dig a trench (in) – **trencher** n

trenchant adj **1** keen, sharp **2** vigorously effective and articulate **3a** incisive, penetrating **b** clear-cut, distinct – **trenchancy** n, **trenchantly** adv

trench coat n **1** a waterproof overcoat with a removable lining, designed for wear in trenches **2** a double-breasted raincoat with deep pockets, a belt, and epaulettes

trencher n a wooden platter for serving food

trencherman n a hearty eater

¹trend vi **1** to show a general tendency to move or extend in a specified direction **2** to deviate, shift ⟨opinions ~ing towards conservatism⟩

²trend n **1** a line of general direction **2a** a prevailing tendency or inclination **b** a general movement, esp in taste or fashion

trendsetter n sby who starts new trends, esp in fashion – **trendsetting** n or adj

¹trendy adj, chiefly Br very fashionable; also characterized by uncritical adherence to the latest fashions or progressive ideas ⟨his concern for good composition prevents the up-to-date from dwindling into the merely ~ – The Listener⟩ – infml

²trendy n, chiefly Br sby trendy – chiefly derog ⟨educational trendies⟩

¹trepan n **1** a primitive trephine **2** a heavy tool used in boring mine shafts

²trepan vt **-nn-** to use a trephine on (the skull)

trephine vt or n (to operate on with, or extract by means of) a surgical instrument for cutting out circular sections, esp of bone or the cornea of the eye

trepidation n nervous agitation or apprehension

¹trespass n **1a** a violation of moral or social ethics; esp a sin **b** an unwarranted infringement **2** any unlawful act that causes harm to the person, property, or rights of another; esp wrongful entry on another's land

²trespass vi **1a** to err, sin **b** to make an unwarranted or uninvited intrusion on **2** to commit a trespass; esp to enter sby's property unlawfully – **trespasser** n

tress n **1** a plait of hair **2** a long lock of hair – usu pl

trestle n **1** a (braced) frame serving as a support (e g for a table top) **2** a braced framework of timbers, piles, or girders for carrying a road or railway over a depression

trestle table n a table consisting of a board or boards supported on trestles

trews n pl in constr, pl **trews** trousers; specif tartan trousers

tri- comb form **1** three ⟨tripartite⟩; having 3 elements or parts ⟨trigraph⟩ **2** into 3 ⟨trisect⟩ **3a** thrice ⟨triweekly⟩ **b** every third ⟨trimonthly⟩

triad n **1** a union or group of 3 (closely) related or associated persons, beings, or things **2** a chord of 3 notes consisting of a root with its third and fifth and constituting the harmonic basis of tonal music **3** often cap any of various Chinese secret societies, esp engaging in drug trafficking – **triadic** adj

¹trial n **1a** trying or testing **b** a preliminary contest or match (e g to evaluate players' skills) **2** the formal examination and determination by a competent tribunal of the matter at issue in a civil or criminal cause **3** a test of faith, patience, or stamina by suffering or temptation; broadly a source of vexation or annoyance **4** an experiment to test quality, value, or usefulness **5** an attempt, effort **6a** a competition of vehicle-handling skills, usu over rough ground **b** a competition in which a working animal's skills are tested ⟨a sheepdog ~⟩

²trial adj **1** of a trial **2** made or done as, or used or tried out in, a test or experiment

trial run n an exercise to test the performance of sthg (e g a vehicle or vessel); also EXPERIMENT 1

triangle n **1** a polygon of 3 sides and 3 angles **2** a percussion instrument consisting of a steel rod bent into the form of a triangle open at 1 angle and sounded by striking with a small metal rod **3** TRIAD 1 **4** NAm SET SQUARE

triangular adj **1a** (having the form) of a triangle ⟨a ~ plot of land⟩ **b** having a triangular base or principal surface ⟨a ~ table⟩ ⟨a ~ pyramid⟩ **2** between or involving 3 elements, things, or people ⟨a ~ love affair⟩ – **triangularly** adv, **triangularity** n

tribal adj (characteristic) of a tribe – **tribally** adv

tribalism *n* **1** tribal consciousness and loyalty **2** strong loyalty or attachment to a group

tribe *n sing or pl in constr* **1a** a social group comprising numerous families, clans, or generations living together with slaves, dependants, or adopted strangers **b** any of orig 3 political divisions of the ancient Roman people **2** a group of people having a common character or interest **3** a category in the classification of living things ranking above a genus and below a family; *also* a natural group irrespective of taxonomic rank ⟨*the cat* ~⟩

tribesman, *fem* **tribeswoman** *n* a member of a tribe

tribulation *n* distress or suffering resulting from oppression

tribunal *n* **1** a court of justice; *specif* a board appointed to decide disputes of a specified kind ⟨*rent* ~⟩ **2** sthg that arbitrates or determines ⟨*the* ~ *of public opinion*⟩

tribune *n* **1** an official of ancient Rome with the function of protecting the plebeian citizens from arbitrary action by the patrician magistrates **2** an unofficial defender of the rights of the individual – **tribuneship** *n*, **tribunate** *n*

¹tributary *adj* **1** paying tribute to another; subject **2** paid or owed as tribute **3** providing with material or supplies

²tributary *n* **1** a tributary ruler or state **2** a stream feeding a larger stream or a lake

tribute *n* **1** a payment by one ruler or nation to another in acknowledgment of submission or as the price of protection **2a** sthg (e g a gift or formal declaration) given or spoken as a testimonial of respect, gratitude, or affection **b** evidence of the worth or effectiveness of sthg specified – chiefly in *a tribute to* ⟨*the vote was a* ~ *to their good sense*⟩

¹trice *vt* to haul up or in and lash or secure – usu + *up*

²trice *n* a brief space of time – chiefly in *in a trice*

triceps *n, pl* **tricepses** *also* **triceps** a muscle with 3 points of attachment; *specif* the large muscle along the back of the upper arm that acts to straighten the arm at the elbow

trichina *n, pl* **trichinae** *also* **trichinas** a small slender nematode worm that in the larval state is parasitic in the muscles of flesh-eating mammals (e g human beings and pigs) – **trichinal** *adj*

trichinosis *n* infestation with or disease caused by trichinae and marked esp by muscular pain, fever, and oedema

¹trick *n* **1a** a crafty practice or stratagem meant to deceive or defraud **b** a mischievous act ⟨*played a harmless* ~ *on me*⟩ **c** a deceptive, dexterous, or ingenious feat designed to puzzle or amuse ⟨*a conjurer's* ~ *s*⟩ **2a** a habitual peculiarity of behaviour or manner ⟨*had a* ~ *of stammering slightly*⟩ **b** a deceptive appearance, esp when caused by art or sleight of hand ⟨*a mere* ~ *of the light*⟩ **3a** a quick or effective way of getting a result **b** a technical device or contrivance (e g of an art or craft) ⟨~ *s of the trade*⟩ **4** the cards played in 1 round of a card game, often used as a scoring unit **5** a turn of duty at the helm

²trick *adj* **1** of or involving tricks or trickery ⟨*a* ~ *question*⟩ **2** skilled in or used for tricks ⟨*a* ~ *horse*⟩

³trick *vt* **1** to deceive by cunning or artifice – often + *into, out of* **2** to dress or embellish showily – usu + *out* or *up* ⟨~ *ed out in a gaudy uniform*⟩

trickery *n* the use of crafty underhand ingenuity to deceive

¹trickle *vi* **trickling** **1** to flow in drops or a thin slow stream **2a** to move or go gradually or one by one ⟨*the audience* ~ *d out of the hall*⟩ **b** to dissipate slowly ⟨*time* ~ *s away*⟩

²trickle *n* a thin slow stream or movement

trickster *n* one who tricks: e g **a** a person who defrauds

others by trickery **b** a person (e g a stage magician) skilled in the performance of tricks

tricky *adj* **1** inclined to or marked by trickery **2** containing concealed difficulties or hazards ⟨*a* ~ *path through the swamp*⟩ **3** requiring skill, adroitness, or caution (e g in doing or handling) ⟨~ *gadgets*⟩ – **trickily** *adv*, **trickiness** *n*

¹tricolour, NAm tricolor *n* a flag of 3 colours

²tricolour, tricoloured, NAm tricolor, tricolored *adj* having or using 3 colours

tricycle *vi or n* (to ride or drive) a 3-wheeled pedal-driven vehicle – **tricyclist** *n*

¹trident *n* a 3-pronged (fish) spear **a** serving as the attribute of a sea god **b** used by ancient Roman gladiators

²trident *adj* having 3 prongs or points

tried *adj* **1** found to be good or trustworthy through experience or testing ⟨*a* ~ *recipe*⟩ **2** subjected to trials or severe provocation – often in combination ⟨*a sorely*-tried *father*⟩

triennial *adj* **1** consisting of or lasting for 3 years **2** occurring every 3 years – **triennial** *n*, **triennially** *adv*

trier *n* **1** sby who makes an effort or perseveres **2** an implement (e g a tapered hollow tube) used in obtaining samples of bulk material, esp foodstuffs, for examination and testing

¹trifle *n* **1** sthg of little value or importance; *esp* an insignificant amount (e g of money) **2** *chiefly Br* a dessert typically consisting of sponge cake soaked in wine (e g sherry), spread with jam or jelly, and topped with custard and whipped cream – **a trifle** to some small degree ⟨*a trifle annoyed at the delay*⟩

²trifle *vb* **trifling** *vi* **1** to act heedlessly or frivolously – often + *with* ⟨*not a woman to be* ~ *d with*⟩ **2** to handle sthg idly – ~ *vt* to spend or waste in trifling or on trifles ⟨*trifling his time away*⟩ – **trifler** *n*

trifling *adj* lacking in significance or solid worth: e g **a** frivolous **b** trivial, insignificant

¹trigger *n* **1** a device (e g a lever) connected with a catch as a means of release; *esp* the tongue of metal in a firearm which when pressed allows the gun to fire **2** a stimulus that initiates a reaction or signal in an electronic apparatus – **trigger** *adj*, **triggered** *adj*

²trigger *vt* **1a** to release, activate, or fire by means of a trigger **b** to cause the explosion of ⟨~ *a missile with a proximity fuse*⟩ **2** to initiate or set off as if by pulling a trigger ⟨*an indiscreet remark that* ~ *ed a fight*⟩ – often + *off* ~ *vi* to release a mechanical trigger

trigger-happy *adj* **1** irresponsible in the use of firearms **2a** aggressively belligerent **b** too prompt in one's response

trigonometric function *n* **1** a function (specif the sine, cosine, tangent, cotangent, secant, or cosecant) of an arc or angle most simply expressed in terms of the ratios of pairs of sides of a right-angled triangle **2** the inverse (e g the arc sine) of a trigonometric function

trigonometry *n* the study of the properties of triangles and trigonometric functions and of their applications – **trigonometric** *also* **trigonometrical** *adj*

trilateral *adj* having 3 sides ⟨*a triangle is* ~⟩ – **trilaterally** *adv*

trilby *n, chiefly Br* a soft felt hat with an indented crown

trilingual *adj* **1** of, containing, or expressed in 3 languages **2** using or able to use 3 languages, esp with the fluency of a native – **trilingually** *adv*

¹trill *n* **1** the alternation of 2 musical notes **2** semitones apart **2** a sound resembling a musical trill **3** (a speech sound made by) the rapid vibration of the tip of the tongue against the ridge of flesh behind the front teeth, or of the uvula against the back of the tongue

²**trill** *vt* to utter as or with a trill ⟨~ *the* r⟩ ~ *vi* to play or sing with a trill – **triller** *n*

trillion *n* **1a** *Br* a million million millions (10¹⁸) **b** *chiefly NAm* a million millions (10¹²) **2** an indefinitely large number; a zillion – often pl with sing. meaning – **trillion** *adj*, **trillionth** *adj or n*

trilobite *n* any of numerous extinct Palaeozoic marine arthropods that had a 3-lobed body

trilogy *n* a group of 3 closely related works (e g novels)

¹**trim** *vb* **-mm-** *vt* **1** to decorate (e g clothes) with ribbons, lace, or ornaments; adorn **2** to make trim and neat, esp by cutting or clipping **3** to remove (as if) by cutting ⟨~*med* thousands *from the running costs of the department*⟩ **4a** to cause (e g a ship, aircraft, or submarine) to assume a desired position by arrangement of ballast, cargo, passengers, etc **b** to adjust (e g a sail) to a desired position ~ *vi* to maintain a neutral attitude towards opposing parties or favour each equally

²**trim** *adj* **-mm-** appearing neat or in good order; compact or clean-cut in outline or structure ⟨~ *houses*⟩ ⟨*a* ~ *figure*⟩ – **trimly** *adv*, **trimness** *n*

³**trim** *n* **1** the readiness or fitness of a person or thing for action or use; *esp* physical fitness **2a** one's clothing or appearance **b** material used for decoration or trimming **c** the decorative accessories of a motor vehicle **3a** the position of a ship or boat, esp with reference to the horizontal **b** the inclination of an aircraft or spacecraft in flight with reference to a fixed point (e g the horizon), esp with the controls in some neutral position **4** (sthg removed by) trimming

trimaran *n* a sailing vessel used for cruising or racing that has 3 hulls side by side

trimester *n* a period of (approximately) 3 months – **trimestral** *also* **trimestrial** *adj*

trimmer *n* **1** a short beam or rafter fitted at 1 side of an opening to support the free ends of floor joists, studs, or rafters **2** a person who modifies his/her policy, position, or opinions out of expediency

trimming *n* **1** *pl* pieces cut off in trimming sthg; scraps **2a** a decorative accessory or additional item (e g on the border of a garment) that serves to finish or complete **b** an additional garnish or accompaniment to a main item ⟨*turkey and all the* ~s⟩ – usu pl

trinitrotoluene *n* an inflammable derivative of toluene used as a high explosive and in chemical synthesis

Trinity *n* **1** the unity of Father, Son, and Holy Spirit as 3 persons in 1 Godhead according to Christian theology **2** *not cap* TRIAD 1 **3** the Sunday after Whitsunday observed as a festival in honour of the Trinity

trinket *n* a small (trifling) article; *esp* an ornament or piece of (cheap) jewellery – **trinketry** *n*

trio *n, pl* **trios 1a** (a musical composition for) 3 instruments, voices, or performers **b** the secondary or episodic division of a minuet, scherzo, etc **2** *sing or pl in constr* a group or set of 3

¹**trip** *vb* **-pp-** *vi* **1a** to dance, skip, or walk with light quick steps **b** to proceed smoothly, lightly, and easily; flow ⟨*words that* ~ *off the tongue*⟩ **2** to catch the foot against sthg so as to stumble **3** to make a mistake or false step (e g in morality or accuracy) **4** to stumble in articulation when speaking **5** to make a journey **6** to become operative or activated ⟨*the circuit breaker* ~s *when the voltage gets too high*⟩ **7** to get high on a psychedelic drug (e g LSD); TURN ON 2a – *slang* ~ *vt* **1a** to cause to stumble **b** to cause to fail **2** to detect in a fault or blunder; CATCH OUT – usu + *up* **3** to raise (an anchor) from the bottom so as to hang free **4** to release or operate (a device or mechanism), esp

by releasing a catch or producing an electrical signal **5** to perform (e g a dance) lightly or nimbly – archaic except in *trip the light fantastic USE* (vi 2, 3, & 4; vt 1) often + *up*

²**trip** *n* **1a** a voyage, journey, or excursion **b** a single round or tour (e g on a business errand) **2** an error, mistake **3** a quick light step **4** a faltering step caused by stumbling **5** a device (e g a catch) for tripping a mechanism **6a** an intense, often visionary experience undergone by sby who has taken a psychedelic drug (e g LSD) **b** a highly charged emotional experience ⟨*his divorce was a really bad* ~⟩ **7** a self-indulgent or absorbing course of action, way of behaving, or frame of mind ⟨*on a nostalgia* ~⟩ ⟨*gave up the whole super-star* ~⟩ *USE* (6&7) *infml*

tripartite *adj* **1** divided into or composed of 3 (corresponding) parts **2** made between or involving 3 parties ⟨*a* ~ *treaty*⟩ – **tripartitely** *adv*, **tripartition** *n*

tripe *n* **1** the stomach tissue of an ox, cow, etc for use as food **2** sthg inferior, worthless, or offensive – *infml*

¹**triple** *vb* **tripling** to make or become 3 times as great or as many

²**triple** *n* **1** a triple sum, quantity, or number **2** a combination, group, or series of 3

³**triple** *adj* **1** having 3 units or members **2** being 3 times as great or as many **3** marked by 3 beats per bar of music ⟨~ *metre*⟩ **4** having units of 3 components – **triply** *adv*

triple jump *n* an athletic field event consisting of a jump for distance combining a hop, a step, and a jump in succession

triplet *n* **1** a unit of 3 lines of verse **2** a combination, set, or group of 3 **3** any of 3 children or animals born at 1 birth **4** a group of 3 musical notes performed in the time of 2 of the same value

triplex *adj* threefold, triple

¹**triplicate** *adj* **1** consisting of or existing in 3 corresponding or identical parts or examples ⟨~ *invoices*⟩ **2** being the third of 3 things exactly alike ⟨*file the* ~ *copy*⟩

²**triplicate** *vt* **1** to make triple **2** to prepare in triplicate – **triplication** *n*

³**triplicate** *n* **1** any of 3 things exactly alike; *specif* any of 3 identical copies **2** three copies all alike – + *in* ⟨*typed in* ~⟩

tripod *n* **1** a stool, table, or vessel (e g a cauldron) with 3 legs **2** a 3-legged stand (e g for a camera) – **tripodal** *adj*

tripos *n* either part of the honours examination for the Cambridge BA degree

tripper *n, chiefly Br* one who goes on an outing or pleasure trip, esp one lasting only 1 day – often used disparagingly ⟨*in the summer the village pub is usually full of* ~s, *so we stay at home*⟩

trippingly *adv* nimbly; *also* fluently

triptych *n* a picture or carving on 3 panels side by side; *esp* an altarpiece consisting of a central panel hinged to 2 flanking panels that fold over it

trip wire *n* a concealed wire placed near the ground that is used to trip up an intruder or to actuate an explosive or warning device when pulled

trireme *n* a galley with 3 banks of oars

trisect *vt* to divide into 3 (equal) parts – **trisection** *n*, **trisector** *n*

trite *adj* hackneyed from much use – **tritely** *adv*, **triteness** *n*

¹**triumph** *n* **1** a ceremony attending the entering of ancient Rome by a general who had won a decisive victory over a foreign enemy **2** the joy or exultation of victory or success **3** (a) notable success, victory, or achievement – **triumphal** *adj*

²triumph *vi* **1** to celebrate victory or success boastfully or exultantly **2** to obtain victory – often + *over*

triumphant *adj* **1** victorious, conquering **2** rejoicing in or celebrating victory – **triumphantly** *adv*

triumvir *n, pl* **triumvirs** *also* **triumviri** a member of a commission or ruling body of 3 – **triumviral** *adj*

triumvirate *n* **1** the office of triumvirs **2** *sing or pl in constr* **a** a body of triumvirs **b** a group of 3

trivalent *adj* having a valency of 3

trivet *n* **1** a three-legged (iron) stand for holding cooking vessels over or by a fire; *also* a bracket that hooks onto a grate for this purpose **2** a (metal) stand with 3 feet for holding a hot dish at table

trivia *n pl but sing or pl in constr* unimportant matters or details

trivial *adj* **1** commonplace, ordinary **2a** of little worth or importance; insignificant **b** of or being the mathematically simplest case ⟨*a ~ solution to an equation*⟩ – **trivialness** *n*, **trivially** *adv*, **trivialize** *vt*, **trivialization** *n*, **triviality** *n*

trochee *n* a metrical foot consisting of 1 long or stressed syllable followed by 1 short or unstressed syllable (e g in *apple*) – **trochaic** *adj or n*

trod *past of* TREAD

trodden *past part of* TREAD

troglodyte *n* **1** CAVE DWELLER **2** a person resembling a troglodyte, esp in being solitary or unsocial or in having primitive or outmoded ideas **3** APE 1 – **troglodytic** *adj*

troika *n* **1** (a Russian vehicle drawn by) a team of 3 horses abreast **2** TRIAD 1; *esp* an administrative or ruling body of 3 people

Trojan *n* **1** a native of Troy **2** one who shows qualities (e g pluck or endurance) attributed to the defenders of ancient Troy – chiefly in *work like a Trojan* – **Trojan** *adj*

¹troll *vt* **1** to sing loudly **2** to fish for or in with a hook and line drawn through the water behind a moving boat ~ *vi* **1** to sing or play an instrument in a jovial manner **2** to fish, esp by drawing a hook through the water **3** to move about; stroll, saunter ⟨*travel writers ~ing around from free hotel to free hotel – The Bookseller*⟩ – **troller** *n*

²troll *n* (a line with) a lure used in trolling

³troll *n* a dwarf or giant of Germanic folklore inhabiting caves or hills

trolley *also* **trolly** *n* **1** a device (e g a grooved wheel or skid) attached to a pole that collects current from an overhead electric wire for powering an electric vehicle **2** *chiefly Br* **a** a shelved stand mounted on castors used for conveying sthg (e g food or books) **b** a basket on wheels that is pushed or pulled by hand and used for carrying goods (e g purchases in a supermarket) **3** *Br* a small 4-wheeled wagon that runs on rails **4** *NAm* TRAM b

trolleybus *n* an electrically propelled bus running on a road and drawing power from 2 overhead wires via a trolley

trollop *n* a slovenly or immoral woman – **trollopy** *adj*

trombone *n* a brass instrument consisting of a long cylindrical metal tube with a movable slide for varying the pitch and a usual range 1 octave lower than that of the trumpet – **trombonist** *n*

troop *n* **1** *sing or pl in constr* **a** a military subunit (e g of cavalry) corresponding to an infantry platoon **b** a collection of people or things **c** a unit of scouts under a leader **2** *pl* the armed forces

troop *vi* to move in a group, esp in a way that suggests regimentation ⟨*everyone ~ed into the meeting*⟩

trooper *n* **1a** a cavalry soldier; *esp* a private soldier in a cavalry or armoured regiment **b** the horse of a cavalry soldier **2** *chiefly NAm & Austr* a mounted policeman

trope *n* a figurative use of a word or expression

trophy *n* **1a** a memorial of an ancient Greek or Roman victory raised on or near the field of battle **b** a representation of such a memorial (e g on a medal); *also* an architectural ornament representing a group of military weapons **2** sthg gained or awarded in victory or conquest, esp when preserved as a memorial

tropic *n* **1** either of the 2 small circles of the celestial sphere on each side of and parallel to the equator at a distance of 23½ degrees, which the sun reaches at its greatest declination N or S **2a(1)** TROPIC OF CANCER **(2)** TROPIC OF CAPRICORN **b** *pl, often cap* the region between the 2 terrestrial tropics

tropical *adj* **1** *also* **tropic** of, occurring in, or characteristic of the tropics **2** *of a sign of the zodiac* beginning at either of the tropics – **tropically** *adv*

tropic of Cancer *n* the parallel of latitude that is 23½ degrees N of the equator

tropic of Capricorn *n* the parallel of latitude that is 23½ degrees S of the equator

¹trot *n* **1** a moderately fast gait of a horse or other quadruped in which the legs move in diagonal pairs **2** an instance or the pace of trotting or proceeding briskly **3** *pl but sing or pl in constr* diarrhoea – usu + *the*; humor – **on the trot** in succession – *infml*

²trot *vb* **-tt-** *vi* **1** to ride, drive, or proceed at a trot **2** to proceed briskly ~ *vt* **1** to cause to go at a trot **2** to traverse at a trot

Trot *n* a Trotskyite; *broadly* any adherent of the extreme left – chiefly derog

troth *n, archaic* one's pledged word; *also* betrothal – chiefly in *plight one's troth*

trot out *vt* **1** to produce or bring forward (as if) for display or scrutiny **2** to produce or utter in a trite or predictable manner ⟨*trotted out all the old clichés*⟩

Trotskyism *n* the political, economic, and social principles advocated by Trotsky; *esp* adherence to the concept of permanent worldwide revolution – **Trotskyist, Trotskyite** *n or adj*

trotter *n* **1** a horse trained for trotting races **2** the foot of an animal, esp a pig, used as food

troubadour *n* any of a class of lyric poets and poet-musicians, chiefly in France in the 11th to 13th c, whose major theme was courtly love

¹trouble *vb* **troubling** *vt* **1a** to agitate mentally or spiritually; worry **b** to produce physical disorder or discomfort in ⟨*~d with deafness*⟩ **c** to put to exertion or inconvenience ⟨*could I ~ you to close the door?*⟩ **2** to make (e g the surface of water) turbulent ~ *vi* **1** to become mentally agitated ⟨*refused to ~ over trifles*⟩ **2** to make an effort; be at pains ⟨*don't ~ to come*⟩

²trouble *n* **1a** being troubled **b** an instance of distress, annoyance, or disturbance **2** a cause of disturbance, annoyance, or distress: e g **a** public unrest or demonstrations of dissatisfaction – often pl with sing. meaning **b** effort made; exertion **c(1)** a disease, ailment, or condition of physical distress ⟨*heart ~*⟩ **(2)** a malfunction ⟨*engine ~*⟩ **d** pregnancy out of wedlock – chiefly in *in/into trouble* **3** a problem, snag ⟨*that's the ~ with these newfangled ideas*⟩ – **troublous** *adj, archaic or poetic*

troublemaker *n* one who causes trouble

troubleshooter *n* **1** a skilled workman employed to locate faults and make repairs in machinery and technical equipment **2** one who specializes or is expert in resolving disputes – **troubleshooting** *n*

troublesome *adj* giving trouble or anxiety; annoying or burdensome ⟨*a ~ cough*⟩ ⟨*a ~ neighbour*⟩ – **troublesomely** *adv*, **troublesomeness** *n*

trough *n* **1a** a long shallow receptacle for the drinking water or feed of farm animals **b** a long narrow container used for domestic or industrial purposes **2a** a conduit, drain, or channel for water **b** a long narrow or shallow trench between waves, ridges, etc **3a** the (region round the) lowest point of a regularly recurring cycle of a varying quantity (e g a sine wave) **b** an elongated area of low atmospheric pressure **c** a low point (in a trade cycle)

trounce vt **1** to thrash or punish severely **2** to defeat decisively

troupe n a company or troop (of theatrical performers)

trouper n **1** a member of a troupe **2** a loyal or dependable person

trousers n pl, pl **trousers** a 2-legged outer garment extending from the waist to the ankle or sometimes only to the knee – **trouser** adj

trousseau n, pl **trousseaux, trousseaus** the personal outfit of a bride including clothes, accessories, etc

trout n, pl **trouts**, (1) **trout**, esp for different types **trouts** **1** any of various food and sport fishes of the salmon family restricted to cool clear fresh waters; esp any of various Old World or New World fishes some of which ascend rivers from the sea to breed **2** an ugly unpleasant old woman – slang

trove n TREASURE TROVE

¹**trowel** n any of various smooth-bladed hand tools used to apply, spread, shape, or smooth loose or soft material; also a scoop-shaped or flat-bladed garden tool for taking up and setting small plants

²**trowel** vt -ll- (NAm -l-, -ll-), to smooth, mix, or apply (as if) with a trowel

troy weight n the series of units of weight based on the pound of 12oz and the ounce of 20 pennyweights or 480 grains

truant n one who shirks duty; esp one who stays away from school without permission – **truant** adj, **truanting** n, **truancy** n

truce n a (temporary) suspension of fighting by agreement of opposing forces

¹**truck** vt to give in exchange; barter ~ vi **1** to trade, barter **2** to negotiate or traffic, esp in an underhand way

²**truck** n **1** (commodities suitable for) barter or small trade **2** close association; dealings – chiefly in **have no truck with** **3** payment of wages in goods instead of cash **4** miscellaneous small articles; also rubbish – infml

³**truck** n **1** a small strong wheel **2** a small wooden cap at the top of a flagstaff or masthead, usu having holes for flag or signal halyards **3a** a usu 4- or 6-wheeled vehicle for moving heavy loads; a lorry **b** a usu 2- or 4-wheeled cart for carrying heavy articles (e g luggage at railway stations) **4** Br an open railway goods wagon

⁴**truck** vt to load or transport on a truck ~ vi, NAm to be employed as a lorry driver – **truckage** n

truckle vi to act in a subservient or obsequious manner – usu + to – **truckler** n

truckle bed n a low bed, usu on castors, that can be slid under a higher bed

truculent adj aggressively self-assertive; belligerent – **truculence, truculency** n, **truculently** adv

¹**trudge** vb to walk steadily and laboriously (along or over) – **trudger** n

²**trudge** n a long tiring walk

¹**true** adj **1** steadfast, loyal ⟨a ~ friend⟩ **2a** in accordance with fact or reality ⟨a ~ story⟩ **b** essential ⟨the ~ nature of socialist economics⟩ **c** being that which is the case rather than what is claimed or assumed ⟨the ~ dimensions of the problem⟩ **d** consistent, conforming ⟨~ to expectations⟩ ⟨~ to type⟩ **3a**(1) properly so called ⟨the ~ faith⟩ (2) genuine, real ⟨~ love⟩ **b**(1) possessing the basic characters of and belonging to the same natural

group as ⟨a whale is a ~ but not a typical mammal⟩ (2) typical ⟨the ~ cats⟩ **4a** accurately fitted, adjusted, balanced, or formed **b** exact, accurate ⟨a ~ voice⟩⟨a ~ copy⟩ **5** determined with reference to the earth's axis rather than the magnetic poles ⟨~ north⟩

²**true** n the state of being accurate (e g in alignment or adjustment) – chiefly in in/out of true

³**true** vt to bring or restore to a desired mechanical accuracy or form – **truer** n

⁴**true** adv **1** TRULY 1 **2a** without deviation; straight **b** without variation from type ⟨breed ~⟩

true-blue adj staunchly loyal; specif, Br being a staunch supporter of the Conservative party – **true-blue** n

truelove n a sweetheart – poetic

truffle n **1** (any of several European fungi with) a usu dark and wrinkled edible fruiting body that grows under the ground and is eaten as a delicacy **2** a rich soft creamy sweet made with chocolate – **truffled** adj

trug n, Br a shallow rectangular wooden basket for carrying garden produce

truism n an undoubted or self-evident truth – **truistic** adj

truly adv **1** in accordance with fact or reality; truthfully **2** accurately, exactly **3a** indeed **b** genuinely, sincerely ⟨he was ~ sorry⟩ **4** properly, duly ⟨well and ~ beaten⟩

¹**trump** n a trumpet (call) – chiefly poetic

²**trump** n **1a** a card of a suit any of whose cards will win over a card that is not of this suit **b** pl the suit whose cards are trumps for a particular hand **2** a worthy and dependable person – infml – **come/turn up trumps** to prove unexpectedly helpful or generous

³**trump** vb to play a trump on (a card or trick) when another suit was led

trump card n **1** ²TRUMP 1a **2** a telling or decisive factor; a clincher – esp in play one's trump card

trumpery adj **1** worthless, useless **2** cheap, tawdry – **trumpery** n

¹**trumpet** n **1** a wind instrument consisting of a usu metal tube, a cup-shaped mouthpiece, and a flared bell; specif a valved brass instrument having a cylindrical tube and a usual range from F sharp below middle C upwards for 2½ octaves **2** sthg that resembles (the flared bell or loud penetrating sound of) a trumpet: e g **a** a megaphone **b** the loud cry of an elephant – **trumpetlike** adj

²**trumpet** vi **1** to blow a trumpet **2** to make a sound as of a trumpet ~ vt to sound or proclaim loudly (as if) on a trumpet

trump up vt to concoct, fabricate ⟨charges trumped up by the police⟩

¹**truncate** vt to shorten (as if) by cutting off a part – **truncation** n

²**truncate** adj having the end square or even ⟨the ~ leaves of the tulip tree⟩

truncheon n **1** a staff of office or authority **2** a short club carried esp by policemen

¹**trundle** n a small wheel or roller

²**trundle** vb **trundling** to move heavily or pull along (as if) on wheels

trundle bed n TRUCKLE BED

trunk n **1a** the main stem of a tree as distinguished from branches and roots **b** the human or animal body apart from the head and limbs **c** the main or central part of sthg (e g an artery, nerve, or column) **2** a large rigid box used usu for transporting clothing and personal articles **3a** a proboscis; esp the long muscular proboscis of the elephant **4** pl men's usu close-fitting shorts worn chiefly for swimming or sports **5** a chute, shaft, or similar (major) supply channel **6** TRUNK LINE **7** NAm ³BOOT 4

trunk call n a telephone call made on a trunk line

trunk line *n* a major route of communication: e g **a** a main line of a railway system **b** a telephone line between towns

trunk road *n* a road of primary importance, esp for long distance travel

¹truss *vt* **1a** to secure tightly; bind – often + *up* **b** to bind the wings or legs of (a fowl) closely in preparation for cooking **2** to support or stiffen (e g a bridge) with a truss

²truss *n* **1a** a corbel; BRACKET 1 **b** a usu triangular assemblage of members (e g beams) forming a rigid framework (e g in a roof or bridge) **2** a device worn to reduce a hernia by pressure **3** a compact flower or fruit cluster (e g of tomatoes) – **trussing** *n*

¹trust *n* **1** confident belief in or reliance on (the ability, character, honesty, etc of) sby or sthg ⟨*take it on* ~⟩ **2** financial credit **3a** a property interest held by one person for the benefit of another **b** a combination of companies formed by a legal agreement **4a** a charge or duty imposed in faith or as a condition of some relationship **b** responsible charge or office ⟨*in a position of* ~⟩ **c** care, custody ⟨*child committed to his* ~⟩ – **trustful** *adj*, **trustfully** *adv* – **in trust** in the care or possession of a trustee

²trust *vi* **1** to place confidence; depend ⟨~ *in God*⟩ **2** to be confident; hope ⟨*we'll see you soon, I* ~⟩ ~ *vt* **1a** to place in sby's care or keeping **b** to permit to do or be without fear or misgiving ⟨*won't* ~ *it out of his sight*⟩ **2a** to place confidence in; rely on – also used ironically ⟨~ *him to arrive late!*⟩ **b** to expect or hope, esp confidently ⟨*I* ~ *you are well?*⟩ **3** to extend credit to – **trustable** *adj*, **trusting** *adj*, **trustingly** *adv*

trustee *n* **1** a country charged with the supervision of a trust territory **2a** a natural or legal person appointed to administer property in trust for a beneficiary **b** any of a body of people administering the affairs of a company or institution and occupying a position of trust – **trusteeship** *n*

trustworthy *adj* dependable, reliable – **trustworthily** *adv*, **trustworthiness** *n*

¹trusty *adj* trustworthy – **trustily** *adv*, **trustiness** *n*

²trusty *n* a trusted person; *specif* a convict considered trustworthy and allowed special privileges

truth *n*, *pl* **truths** **1** sincerity, honesty **2a(1)** the state or quality of being true or factual ⟨*there's* ~ *in what she says*⟩ **(2)** reality, actuality ⟨~ *is stranger than fiction*⟩ **(3)** *often cap* a transcendent (e g spiritual) reality **b** a judgment, proposition, idea, or body of statements that is (accepted as) true ⟨*scientific* ~s⟩ **3** conformity to an original or to a standard – **truthful** *adj*, **truthfully** *adv*, **truthfulness** *n*

¹try *vt* **1a** to investigate judicially **b** to conduct the trial of **2a(1)** to test by experiment or trial – often + *out* **(2)** to investigate the state, capabilities, or potential of, esp for a particular purpose ⟨~ *the shop next door*⟩ **b** to subject to sthg that tests the patience or endurance **3** to melt down and obtain in a pure state – usu + *out* ⟨~ *out whale oil from blubber*⟩ **4** to make an attempt at ~ *vi* to make an attempt – **try for size** to test for appropriateness or fittingness – **try one's hand** to make an attempt for the first time

²try *n* **1** an experimental trial; an attempt **2** a score in rugby that is made by touching down the ball behind the opponent's goal line and that entitles the scoring side to attempt a kick at the goal for additional points

try on *vt* **1** to put on (a garment) in order to examine the fit or appearance **2** *Br* to attempt to impose on sby ⟨*don't go trying anything on with me, mate*⟩ – *infml* – **try-on** *n*

tryout *n* an experimental performance or demonstration;

specif a test of the ability of sby (e g an actor or athlete) or sthg to meet requirements

¹tryst *n* **1** an agreement, esp by lovers, to meet **2** an appointed meeting or meeting place *USE* poetic

²tryst *vi*, *chiefly Scot* to make a tryst – poetic

tsar, czar, tzar *n* **1** a male ruler of Russia before 1917 **2** one having great power or authority – **tsarism** *n*, **tsarist** *n or adj*

tsarina *n* the wife of a tsar

tsetse, tsetse fly *n*, *pl* **tsetse, tsetses** any of several two-winged flies that occur in Africa south of the Sahara desert and transmit diseases, esp sleeping sickness, by bites

T-shirt *n* a collarless upper garment of light stretchy fabric for casual wear

T square *n* a ruler with a crosspiece or head at 1 end used in making parallel lines

¹tub *n* **1a** any of various wide low often round vessels typically made of wood, metal, or plastic, and used industrially or domestically (e g for washing clothes or holding soil for shrubs) **b** a small round (plastic) container in which cream, ice cream, etc may be bought **2** BATH 2b **3** an old or slow boat – *infml* – **tubful** *n*

²tub *vb* **-bb-** to wash or bath in a tub

tuba *n* a large brass instrument having valves, a conical tube, a cup-shaped mouthpiece, and a usual range an octave lower than that of the euphonium

tubby *adj* podgy, fat – **tubbiness** *n*

tube *n* **1a** a hollow elongated cylinder; *esp* one to convey fluids **b** a slender channel within a plant or animal body **2** any of various usu cylindrical structures or devices: e g **a** a small cylindrical container of soft metal or plastic sealed at one end, and fitted with a cap at the other, from which a paste is dispensed by squeezing **b** TEST TUBE **c** the basically cylindrical section between the mouthpiece and bell of a wind instrument **3** ELECTRON TUBE; *specif*, *chiefly NAm* a thermionic valve **4** *Br* (a train running in) an underground railway running through deep bored tunnels **5** *chiefly Austr* a can of beer – *infml* – **tubelike** *adj*

tubeless *adj* being a pneumatic tyre that does not depend on an inner tube to be airtight

tuber *n* (a root resembling) a short fleshy usu underground stem (e g a potato) that is potentially able to produce a new plant – **tuberous** *adj*

tubercle *n* **1** a small knobby prominence, esp on a plant or animal **2** a small abnormal lump in an organ or in the skin; *esp* one characteristic of tuberculosis – **tubercled** *adj*, **tuberculate** *also* **tuberculated** *adj*

tubercular *adj* **1** of, resembling, or being a tubercle **2** tuberculous – **tubercularly** *adv*

tuberculosis *n* a serious infectious disease of human beings and other vertebrates caused by the tubercle bacillus and characterized by fever and the formation of abnormal lumps in the body – **tuberculoid** *adj*

tubing *n* **1** (a length of) material in the form of a tube **2** a series or system of tubes

tub-thumper *n* an impassioned or ranting public speaker – **tub-thumping** *n or adj*

tubular *also* **tubulous** *adj* **1** having the form of or consisting of a tube ⟨*a* ~ *calyx*⟩ **2** made of or fitted with tubes or tube-shaped pieces – **tubularly** *adv*, **tubularity** *n*

¹tuck *vt* **1a** to draw into a fold or folded position **b** to make a tuck or series of tucks in **2** to place in a snug often concealed or isolated spot ⟨*cottage* ~ *ed away in the hills*⟩ **3a** to push in the loose end or ends of so as to make secure or tidy **b** to cover snugly by tucking in bedclothes ⟨~ *ed up in bed*⟩ **4** to eat – usu + *away* ~ *vi* to eat heartily – usu + *in* or *into* *USE* (*vt* 4; *vi*) infml

²tuck *n* **1 a** (narrow) fold stitched into cloth to shorten, decorate, or reduce fullness **2** the part of a vessel where the ends of the lower planks meet under the stern **3** (an act of) tucking **4** a body position (e g in diving) in which the knees are bent, the thighs drawn tightly to the chest, and the hands clasped round the shins **5** *Br* food, esp chocolate, pastries, etc, as eaten by schoolchildren ⟨*a ~ shop*⟩ – infml

¹**tucker** *n, Austr & NZ* food ⟨*a ~ bag*⟩ – infml

²**tucker** *vt, chiefly NAm* to exhaust – often + *out*

tuck-in *n, chiefly Br* a hearty meal – infml

-tude *suffix* (→ *n*) -ness ⟨*pleni*tude⟩ ⟨*alti*tude⟩

Tuesday *n* the day of the week following Monday – **Tuesdays** *adv*

¹**tuft** *n* **1a** a small cluster of long flexible hairs, feathers, grasses, etc attached or close together at the base **b** a bunch of soft fluffy threads cut off short and used for ornament **2** a clump, cluster – **tufted** *adj*, **tufty** *adj*

²**tuft** *vt* **1** to adorn with a tuft or tufts **2** to make (e g a mattress) firm by stitching at intervals and sewing on tufts

¹**tug** *vb* **-gg-** to pull hard (at)

²**tug** *n* **1a** a hard pull or jerk **b** a strong pulling force ⟨*felt the ~ of the past*⟩ **2** a struggle between 2 people or opposite forces **3a** tug, tugboat a strongly built powerful boat used for towing or pushing large ships (e g in and out of dock) **b** an aircraft that tows a glider

tug-of-war *n, pl* **tugs-of-war 1** a struggle for supremacy **2** a contest in which teams pulling at opposite ends of a rope attempt to pull each other across a line marked between them

tuition *n* teaching, instruction – **tuitional** *adj*

tulip *n* (the flower of) any of a genus of Eurasian bulbous plants of the lily family widely grown for their showy flowers

tulip tree *n* a tall N American tree of the magnolia family with large tulip-shaped flowers and soft white wood used esp for cabinetwork and wooden utensils; *broadly* any of various trees with tulip-shaped flowers

tulle *n* a sheer, often silk, net used chiefly for veils and dresses

¹**tumble** *vb* **tumbling** *vi* **1a** to perform gymnastic feats in tumbling **b** to turn end over end in falling or flight **2a** to fall suddenly and helplessly **b** to suffer a sudden overthrow or defeat **c** to decline suddenly and sharply ⟨*the stock market ~d*⟩ **3** to roll over and over, to and fro, or around **4** to move hurriedly and confusedly ⟨*~d into his clothes*⟩ **5** to realize suddenly – often + *to*; infml *~ vt* **1** to cause to tumble (e g by pushing) **2** to rumple, disorder **3** to whirl in a tumbler (e g in drying clothes)

²**tumble** *n* **1** a confused heap **2** an act of tumbling; *specif* a fall ⟨*took a nasty ~*⟩

tumbledown *adj* dilapidated, ramshackle

tumbler *n* **1a** an acrobat **b** any of various domestic pigeons that tumble or somersault backwards in flight or on the ground **2** a relatively large drinking glass without a foot, stem, or handle **3a** a movable obstruction (e g a lever, wheel, or pin) in a lock that must be adjusted to a particular position (e g by a key) before the bolt can be moved **b** a lever that when released by the trigger forces the hammer of a firearm forwards **4a** a tumble-drier **b** a revolving drum; often lined with abrasive material, in which gemstones, castings, etc are polished by friction – **tumblerful** *n*

tumbleweed *n* a plant that breaks away from its roots in the autumn and is blown about by the wind

tumbrel, tumbril *n* **1** a farm cart that can be tipped to empty the contents **2** a vehicle used to carry condemned people to a place of execution during the French Revolution

tumescent *adj* somewhat swollen; *esp, of the penis or clitoris* engorged with blood in response to sexual stimulation – **tumescence** *n*

tumid *adj* **1** *esp of body parts* swollen, protuberant, or distended **2** bombastic, turgid – **tumidly** *adv*, **tumidity** *n*

tummy *n* STOMACH 1b – infml

tumour, NAm chiefly tumor *n* an abnormal mass of tissue that arises without obvious cause from cells of existing tissue and possesses no physiological function – **tumorous** *adj*

tumult *n* **1a** commotion, uproar (e g of a crowd) **b** a turbulent uprising; a riot **2** violent mental or emotional agitation

tumultuous *adj* **1** marked by commotion; riotous **2** marked by violent turbulence or upheaval ⟨*~ passions*⟩ – **tumultuously** *adv*, **tumultuousness** *n*

tumulus *n, pl* **tumuli** an ancient grave; a barrow

tun *n* **1** a large cask, esp for wine **2** any of various units of liquid capacity of about 954l

¹**tuna** *n* (the edible fruit of) any of various prickly pears

²**tuna** *n, pl* **tuna,** *esp for different types* **tunas 1** any of numerous large vigorous food and sport fishes related to the mackerels **2 tuna, tuna fish** the flesh of a tuna, often canned for use as food

tundra *n* a level or undulating treeless plain with a permanently frozen subsoil that is characteristic of arctic and subarctic regions

¹**tune** *n* **1a** a pleasing succession of musical notes; a melody **b** *the* dominant tune in a musical composition **2** correct musical pitch (with another instrument, voice, etc) **3a** accord, harmony ⟨*in ~ with the times*⟩ **b** general attitude; approach ⟨*soon changed his ~*⟩ **4** amount, extent – chiefly in *to the tune of* USE (2&3a) chiefly in *in/out of tune*

²**tune** *vi* **1** to bring a musical instrument or instruments into tune, esp with a standard pitch – usu + *up* **2** to become attuned **3** to adjust a receiver for the reception of a particular broadcast or station – + *in* or *to* ⟨*~ in again next week*⟩ *~ vt* **1** to adjust the musical pitch of; *esp* to cause to be in tune **2a** to bring into harmony; attune **b** to adjust for optimum performance – often + *up* ⟨*~d up the engine*⟩ **3** to adjust (a radio or television receiver) to respond to signals of a particular frequency – often + *in* – **tunable, tuneable** *adj*, **tuner** *n*

tuneful *adj* melodious, musical – **tunefully** *adv*, **tunefulness** *n*

tuneless *adj* without an intended or recognizable melody; not tuneful – **tunelessly** *adv*, **tunelessness** *n*

tungsten *n* a hard polyvalent metallic element with a high melting point that is used esp for electrical purposes and in hard alloys (e g steel)

tunic *n* **1** a simple (hip- or knee-length) slip-on garment usu belted or gathered at the waist **2** an enclosing or covering membrane or tissue ⟨*the ~ of a seed*⟩ **3** a close-fitting jacket with a high collar worn esp as part of a uniform ⟨*a soldier's ~*⟩

tuning fork *n* a 2-pronged metal implement that gives a fixed tone when struck and is useful for tuning musical instruments and setting pitches for singing

¹**tunnel** *n* **1** a hollow conduit or recess (e g for a propeller shaft) **2a** a man-made horizontal passageway through or under an obstruction **b** a subterranean passage (e g in a mine)

²**tunnel** *vb* **-ll-** (*NAm* **-l-, -ll-**), *vt* **1** to make a passage through or under **2** to make (e g one's way) by excavating a tunnel *~ vi* **1** to make or pass through a tunnel **2** to pass through an electric potential barrier ⟨*electrons ~ling through an insulator between semiconductors*⟩

tunny *n, pl* **tunnies**, *esp collectively* **tunny** ²TUNA

¹**tup** *n* **1** the heavy metal head of a steam hammer, pile driver, etc **2** *chiefly Br* RAM 1

²**tup** *vt* -pp- *chiefly Br, of a ram* to copulate with (a ewe)

tuppence *n* (a) twopence – **tuppenny** *adj*

turban *n* (a headdress, esp for a lady, resembling) a headdress worn esp by Muslims and Sikhs and made of a long cloth wound round a cap or directly round the head – **turbaned, turbanned** *adj*

turbid *adj* **1a** opaque (as if) with disturbed sediment; cloudy **b** thick with smoke or mist **2** (mentally or emotionally) confused – **turbidly** *adv*, **turbidness, turbidity** *n*

turbine *n* a rotary engine whose central driving shaft is fitted with vanes whirled round by the pressure of water, steam, exhaust gases, etc

turbojet *n* (an aircraft powered by) a turbojet engine

turboprop *n* (an aircraft powered by) an engine that has a turbine-driven propeller for providing the main thrust

turbot *n, pl* **turbot**, *esp for different types* **turbots** a large European flatfish that is a highly valued food fish

turbulence *n* **1** wild commotion or agitation **2** irregular atmospheric motion, esp when characterized by strong currents of rising and falling air **3** the formation of disturbances that interfere with the smooth flow of a liquid or gas

turbulent *adj* **1** causing unrest, violence, or disturbance ⟨a ~ *crowd*⟩ **2** agitated, stormy, or tempestuous ⟨~ *water*⟩ ⟨a ~ *childhood*⟩ **3** exhibiting physical turbulence – **turbulently** *adv*

turd *n* **1** a piece of excrement **2** a despicable person USE *vulg*

tureen *n* a deep (covered) dish from which a food, esp soup, is served at table

¹**turf** *n, pl* **turfs, turves 1** (a piece of or an artificial substitute for) the upper layer of soil bound by grass and plant roots into a thick mat **2** (a piece of dried) peat **3** *the* sport or business of horse racing or the course on which horse races are run – **turfy** *adj*

²**turf** *vt* to cover with turf

turf accountant *n, Br* a bookmaker

turf out *vt, chiefly Br* to dismiss or throw out forcibly – *infml*

turgid *adj* **1** distended, swollen; *esp* exhibiting excessive turgor **2** in a pompous inflated style; laboured – **turgidly** *adv*, **turgidness** *n*, **turgescence** *n*, **turgescent** *adj*, **turgidity** *n*

turkey *n pl* **turkeys**, *esp collectively* **turkey** (the flesh of) a large orig American bird that is farmed for its meat in most parts of the world

Turkic *adj* **1** of a branch of the Altaic language family including Turkish **2** of the peoples who speak Turkic languages – **Turkic** *n*

¹**Turkish** *adj* **1** (characteristic) of Turkey or the Turks **2** TURKIC 1

²**Turkish** *n* **.1** the Turkic language of the Republic of Turkey **2 Turkish, Turkish tobacco** an aromatic tobacco grown chiefly in Turkey and Greece

Turkish bath *n* a steam bath followed by a rubdown, massage, and cold shower

Turkish delight *n* a jellylike confection, usu cut in cubes and dusted with sugar

turmeric *n* **1** an E Indian plant of the ginger family **2** the cleaned, boiled, dried, and usu powdered underground stem of the turmeric plant used as a colouring agent or condiment

turmoil *n* an extremely confused or agitated state

¹**turn** *vt* **1a** to make rotate or revolve ⟨~ *a wheel*⟩ **b(1)**

to cause to move through an arc of a circle ⟨~ *a key*⟩ **(2)** to alter the functioning of (as if) by turning a knob ⟨~ *the oven to a higher temperature*⟩ **c** to perform by rotating or revolving ⟨~ *cartwheels*⟩ **2a** to reverse the sides or surfaces of so as to expose another side ⟨~ *the page*⟩: e g **(1)** to dig or plough so as to bring the lower soil to the surface **(2)** to renew (e g a garment) by reversing the material and resewing ⟨~ *a collar*⟩ **b** to throw into disorder or confusion ⟨*everything* ~ed *topsy-turvy*⟩ **c** to disturb the mental balance of; unsettle ⟨*a mind* ~ed *by grief*⟩ **d** to cause to change or reverse direction ⟨~ed *his car in the street*⟩ ⟨~ed *his steps towards home*⟩ **3a** to bend or change the course or outcome of ⟨~ *the tide of history*⟩ **b** to go round or about ⟨~ed *the corner at full speed*⟩ **c** to reach or go beyond (e g an age or time) ⟨*he's just* ~ed *21*⟩ **4a** to direct, present, or point (e g the face) in a specified direction **b** to aim, train ⟨*cannon were* ~ed *on the troops*⟩ **c** to direct, induce, or influence in a specified direction, esp towards or away from sby or sthg ⟨~ed *his thoughts inwards*⟩ ⟨~ed *the boy against his parents*⟩ **d** to apply, devote ⟨~ed *his hand to plumbing*⟩ **e(1)** to drive, send ⟨~ed *hunters off his land*⟩ ⟨~ed *them out of their home*⟩ **(2)** to direct into or out of a receptacle (as if) by inverting ⟨~ *the meat into a pot*⟩ ⟨~ed *the contents of her handbag out*⟩ **5a** to make acid or sour **b** to cause to become by change; transform, convert ⟨*illness* ~ed *his hair white*⟩ ⟨~ *pounds into drachmas*⟩ **6a** to give a rounded form to ⟨~ *the heel of a sock*⟩ ⟨~ing *wood on a lathe*⟩ **b** to fashion elegantly or neatly ⟨*well* ~ed *ankles*⟩ ⟨*a knack for* ~ing *a phrase*⟩ **7** to fold, bend ⟨~ *his collar up*⟩ **8** to gain in the course of business – esp in **turn an honest penny** ~ *vi* **1a** (to appear to) move round (as if) on an axis or through an arc of a circle ⟨*I tossed and* ~ed *all night*⟩ **b(1)** to become giddy or dizzy **(2)** *of the stomach* to feel nauseated **c** to centre or hinge on sthg ⟨*the argument* ~s *on this point*⟩ **2a** to direct one's course ⟨*didn't know which way to* ~⟩ **b(1)** to change or reverse direction ⟨*the main road* ~s *sharply to the right*⟩ ⟨*his luck* ~ed⟩ **(2)** to become reversed or inverted **3a** to change position so as to face another way ⟨*they* ~ed *to stare at him*⟩ ⟨*he* ~ed *away and refused to look*⟩ **b** to change one's attitude to one of hostility ⟨*the worm will* ~⟩ ⟨~ed *against his parents*⟩ **c** to make a sudden violent physical or verbal assault – usu + *on* or *upon* ⟨*she* ~ed *on him with ferocity*⟩ **4a** to direct one's attention, efforts, or interests to or away from sby or sthg ⟨~ed *to studying law*⟩ ⟨~ *to chapter 4*⟩ **b** to have recourse; resort ⟨~ed *to a friend for help*⟩ **5a** to become changed, altered, or transformed: e g **(1)** to change colour ⟨*the leaves have* ~ed⟩ **(2)** to become acid or sour ⟨*the milk had* ~ed⟩ **b** to become by change ⟨*water had* ~ed *to ice*⟩ ⟨~ *traitor*⟩ **6** to become folded or bent – **turnable** *adj* – **turn a blind eye** to refuse to see; be oblivious – **turn a deaf ear** to refuse to listen – **turn a hair** to show any reaction (e g of surprise or alarm) ⟨*did not* turn *a hair when told of the savage murder – TLS*⟩ – **turn back the clock** to revert to an earlier or past state or condition – **turn colour** to change colour; *esp* to grow pale or red – **turn in one's grave** to be disturbed at goings-on that would have shocked one when alive – said of a dead person ⟨*Malthus would* turn *in his grave at your opinions*⟩ – **turn King's/Queen's evidence** *Br, of an accomplice* to testify for the prosecution in court – **turn one's back on** to reject, deny ⟨*turned his back on the past*⟩ – **turn one's hand** to apply oneself; SET TO WORK – **turn someone's head** to cause sby to become infatuated or to harbour extravagant notions of conceit ⟨*success had not turned his head*⟩ – **turn someone's stomach 1** to disgust sby completely ⟨*that sort of conduct turns my stomach*⟩ **2** to sicken, nauseate ⟨*the foul smell* turned his stomach⟩ – **turn tail** to run away; flee – **turn the other cheek** to respond to injury or unkindness with patience; forgo retaliation – **turn the scale/scales 1** to register a usu specified weight 2 to prove decisive ⟨*air support might just* turn the scale⟩ – **turn the tables** to bring about a reversal of the relative conditions or fortunes of 2 contending parties – **turn turtle** to capsize, overturn

²**turn** *n* **1a** a turning about a centre or axis; (a) rotation **b** any of various rotating or pivoting movements (in dancing) **2a** a change or reversal of direction, stance, position, or course ⟨*illegal left* ∼s⟩ ⟨*an about* ∼⟩ **b** a deflection, deviation ⟨*the twists and* ∼s *of the story*⟩ **c** the place of a change in direction; a turning **3** a short trip out and back or round about ⟨*took a* ∼ *through the park*⟩ **4** an act or deed of a specified kind ⟨*one good* ∼ *deserves another*⟩ **5a** a place, time, or opportunity granted in succession or rotation ⟨*waiting his* ∼ *in the queue*⟩ **b** a period of duty, action, or activity **c** (the performer who gives) a short act or performance (e g in a variety show) **6** a musical ornament played on the principal note and the notes next above and below **7a** an alteration, change ⟨*an unusual* ∼ *of events*⟩ ⟨*a* ∼ *for the better*⟩ **b** a point of change in time ⟨*the* ∼ *of the century*⟩ **8** a style of expression ⟨*an odd* ∼ *of phrase*⟩ **9a** the state or manner of being coiled or twisted **b** a single coil (e g of rope wound round an object) **10** a bent, inclination ⟨*an optimistic* ∼ *of mind*⟩ **11a** a spell or attack of illness, faintness, etc **b** a nervous start or shock ⟨*gave me quite a* ∼⟩ – **at every turn** on every occasion; constantly, continually – **by turns** one after another in regular succession – **in turn** in due order of succession; alternately – **on the turn** at the point of turning ⟨*tide is* on the turn⟩ ⟨*milk is* on the turn⟩ – **out of turn 1** not in due order of succession ⟨*play* out of turn⟩ **2** at a wrong time or place ⟨*spoke* out of turn⟩ – **to a turn** to perfection ⟨*roasted* to a turn⟩ – **turn and turn about** BY TURNS

turnabout *n* a change or reversal of direction, trend, etc

turn away *vt* to refuse admittance or acceptance to

turncoat *n* one who switches to an opposing side or party; a traitor

turndown *adj* worn turned down ⟨∼ *collar*⟩

turn down *vt* **1** to reduce the intensity, volume, etc of (as if) by turning a control ⟨turn *the radio* down⟩ **2** to decline to accept; reject

turner *n* one who forms articles on a lathe – **turnery** *n*

turn in *vt* **1** to deliver, hand over; *esp* to deliver up to an authority **2** to give, execute ⟨turned in *a good performance*⟩ – ∼ *vi* to go to bed – infml

turning *n* **1** a place of turning, turning off, or turning back, esp on a road ⟨*take the third* ∼ *on the right*⟩ **2a** a forming or being formed by use of a lathe **b** *pl* waste produced in turning sthg on a lathe **3** the width of cloth that is folded under for a seam or hem

turning point *n* a point at which a significant change occurs

turnip *n* (a plant of the mustard family with) a thick white-fleshed root eaten as a vegetable or fed to stock

turnkey *n* a prison warden

turnoff *n* **1** a turning off **2** a place where one turns off; *esp* a motorway junction

turn off *vt* **1** to stop the flow or operation of (as if) by turning a control ⟨turn *the radio* off⟩ **2** to cause to lose (sexual) interest – infml ∼ *vi* to deviate from a straight course or from a main road ⟨turned off *into a side road*⟩

turn on *vt* **1** to cause to flow or operate (as if) by turning a control ⟨turn *the water* on *full*⟩ ⟨turned on *the charm*⟩ **2a** to cause to undergo an intense often visionary experience by taking a drug; *broadly* to cause to get high **b** to excite or interest pleasurably and esp sexually ∼ *vi* to become turned on *USE* (*vt* 2) infml – **turn-on** *n*

turnout *n* **1** a turning out **2** people in attendance (e g at a meeting) ⟨*a good* ∼ *tonight*⟩ **3** manner of dress; getup **4** quantity of produce yielded

turn out *vt* **1** to put (e g a horse) to pasture **2a** to turn inside out **b** to empty the contents of, esp for cleaning **3** to produce often rapidly or regularly (as if) by machine **4** to equip or dress in a specified way ⟨*he was nicely* turned out⟩ **5** to put out (esp a light) by turning a switch **6** to call (e g a guard) out from rest or shelter and into formation ∼ *vi* **1** to leave one's home for a meeting, public event, etc ⟨*voters* turned out *in droves*⟩ **2** to prove to be ultimately ⟨*the play* turned out *to be a flop*⟩ **3** to get out of bed – infml

turnover *n* **1** a small semicircular filled pastry made by folding half of the crust over the other half **2a** the total sales revenue of a business **b** the ratio of sales to average stock for a stated period **3** (the rate of) movement (e g of goods or people) into, through, and out of a place

turn over *vt* **1** to cause (an internal-combustion engine) to revolve and usu to fire **2** to think over; meditate on **3** to deliver, surrender **4a** to receive and dispose of (a stock of merchandise) **b** to do business to the amount of ⟨turning over *£1000 a week*⟩ ∼ *vi* **1** *of an internal combustion engine* to revolve at low speed **2** *of merchandise* to be stocked and disposed of – **turn over a new leaf** to make a change for the better, esp in one's way of living

turnpike *n* **1** *chiefly NAm* a road on which a toll is payable **2** *archaic* a tollgate

turnstile *n* a gate with arms pivoted on the top that turns to admit 1 person at a time

turntable *n* **1** a circular platform for turning wheeled vehicles, esp railway engines **2** the platform on which a gramophone record is rotated while being played

turn to *vi* to apply oneself to work

turn-up *n* **1** *chiefly Br* a turned-up hem, esp on a pair of trousers **2** an unexpected or surprising event – esp in *turn-up for the book*; infml

turn up *vt* **1** to find, discover **2** to increase the intensity, volume, etc of (as if) by turning a control ⟨turn *the sound* up⟩ ∼ *vi* **1** to come to light unexpectedly **2** to appear, arrive **3** to happen or occur unexpectedly **4** *of a sailing vessel* TACK 1b – **turn up one's nose** to show scorn or disdain

¹**turpentine** *n* **1a** a yellow to brown semifluid oleoresin exuded from the terebinth tree **b** an oleoresin obtained from various conifers **2a** an essential oil obtained from turpentines by distillation and used esp as a solvent and paint thinner **b** WHITE SPIRIT

²**turpentine** *vt* to apply turpentine to

turpitude *n* baseness, depravity ⟨*moral* ∼⟩

turquoise *n* **1** a sky blue to greenish mineral consisting of a hydrated copper aluminium phosphate and used as a gem **2** light greenish blue

turret *n* **1** a little tower, often at the corner of a larger building **2** a rotatable holder (e g for a tool or die) in a lathe, milling machine, etc **3** a usu revolving armoured structure on warships, forts, tanks, aircraft, etc in which guns are mounted – **turreted** *adj*

turtle *n* any of several marine reptiles of the same order as and similar to tortoises but adapted for swimming; *broadly, NAm* any of the land, freshwater, and sea reptiles of this order

turtledove *n* any of several small wild pigeons noted for plaintive cooing

turtleneck *n* a high close-fitting neckline, esp of a sweater

tush *interj* – used to express disdain or reproach

tusk *vt or n* (to dig up or gash with) a long greatly enlarged tooth of an elephant, boar, walrus, etc, that projects when the mouth is closed and serves for digging food or as a weapon – **tusked** *adj*, **tusklike** *adj*

tusker *n* an animal with tusks; *esp* a male elephant with 2 large tusks

¹**tussle** *vi* **tussling** to struggle roughly; scuffle

²**tussle** *n* a (physical) contest or struggle

tussock *n* a compact tuft of grass, sedge, etc – **tussocky** *adj*

¹**tut, tut-tut** *interj* – used to express disapproval or impatience

²**tut, tut-tut** *vi* **-tt-** to express disapproval or impatience by uttering 'tut' or 'tut-tut'

tutelage *n* **1** guardianship **2** the state or period of being under a guardian or tutor **3** instruction, esp of an individual

tutelary *also* **tutelar** *adj* **1** having the guardianship of sby or sthg ⟨*a ~ deity*⟩ **2** of a guardian

¹**tutor** *n* **1** a private teacher **2** a British university teacher who **a** gives instruction to students, esp individually **b** is in charge of the social and moral welfare of a group of students **3** *Br* an instruction book – **tutorship** *n*

²**tutor** *vt* to teach or guide usu individually; coach ~ *vi* to do the work of a tutor

¹**tutorial** *adj* of or involving (individual tuition by) a tutor – **tutorially** *adv*

²**tutorial** *n* a class conducted by a tutor for 1 student or a small number of students

tutti-frutti *n* (a confection, esp an ice cream, containing) a mixture of chopped, dried, or candied fruits

tutu *n* a very short projecting stiff skirt worn by a ballerina

tu-whit tu-whoo *n* the cry of a (tawny) owl

tuxedo *n, pl* **tuxedos, tuxedoes** *NAm* DINNER JACKET

TV *n* television

twaddle *vi or n* **twaddling** (to speak or write) rubbish or drivel – **twaddler** *n*

twain *n, adj, or pron, archaic* two

¹**twang** *n* **1** a harsh quick ringing sound like that of a plucked bowstring **2** nasal speech or resonance – **twangy** *adj*

²**twang** *vi* to speak or sound with a twang ~ *vt* **1** to utter or cause to sound with a twang **2** to pluck the string of

twat *n* **1** the female genitals **2** *Br* an unpleasant or despicable person *USE* vulg

tweak *vb* to pinch and pull with a sudden jerk and twist – **tweak** *n*

twee *adj* excessively sentimental, pretty, or coy – **tweeness** *n*

tweed *n* **1** a rough woollen fabric made usu in twill weaves and used esp for suits and coats **2** *pl* tweed clothing; *specif* a tweed suit

tweedy *adj* **1** of or resembling tweed **2a** given to or associated with wearing tweeds **b** suggesting the outdoors in taste or habits; *esp* brisk and healthy in manner – **tweediness** *n*

tween *prep* between – chiefly poetic

tweet *vi or n* (to) chirp

tweeter *n* a small loudspeaker that responds mainly to the higher frequencies

tweezers *n pl, pl* **tweezers** a small metal instrument that is usu held between thumb and forefinger, is used for plucking, holding, or manipulating, and consists of 2 prongs joined at 1 end

twelfth *n* **1** number twelve in a countable series **2** *often cap, Br the* twelfth of August on which the grouse-shooting season begins – **twelfth** *adj or adv*, **twelfthly** *adj*

twelve *n* **1** (the number) 12 **2** the twelfth in a set or series **3** sthg having 12 parts or members or a denomination of 12 – **twelve** *adj or pron*, **twelvefold** *adj or adv*

twelvemonth *n* a year – archaic or poetic

twenty *n* **1** (the number) 20 **2** *pl the* numbers 20 to 29; *specif* a range of temperature, ages, or dates in a century characterized by those numbers **3** sthg (e g a bank note) having a denomination of 20 – **twentieth** *adj or n*, **twenty** *adj or pron*, **twentyfold** *adj or adv*

twenty-one *n* **1** (the number) 21 **2** pontoon – **twenty-one** *adj or pron*

twerp *also* **twirp** *n* a silly, insignificant, or contemptible person – infml

twice *adv* **1** on 2 occasions ⟨*~ a week*⟩ **2** two times;in doubled quantity or degree ⟨*~ 2 is 4*⟩⟨*~ as much*⟩

twice-told *adj* familiar, well-known – chiefly in *a twice-told tale*

¹**twiddle** *vi* to play negligently with sthg ~ *vt* to rotate lightly or idly ⟨*~d the knob on the radio*⟩

²**twiddle** *n* a turn, twist

¹**twig** *n* a small woody shoot or branch, usu without its leaves – **twigged** *adj*, **twiggy** *adj*

²**twig** *vb* **-gg-** to catch on (to); understand – infml

twilight *n* **1a** the light from the sky between full night and sunrise or esp between sunset and full night **b** the period between sunset and full night **2a** a shadowy indeterminate state **b** a period or state of decline ⟨*elderly ladies in their ~ years*⟩

twill *n* (a fabric with) a textile weave in which the weft threads pass over 1 and under 2 or more warp threads to give an appearance of diagonal lines – **twilled** *adj*

¹**twin** *adj* **1** born with one other or as a pair at 1 birth ⟨*~ brother*⟩⟨*~ girls*⟩ **2a** having or made up of 2 similar, related, or identical units or parts **b** being one of a pair, esp of officially associated towns

²**twin** *n* **1** either of 2 offspring produced at 1 birth **2** either of 2 people or things closely related to or resembling each other **3** **twin, twin crystal** a compound crystal composed of 2 or more (parts of) related crystals grown together in an oriented manner – **twinship** *n*

³**twin** *vb* **-nn-** *vt* **1** to bring together in close association **2** to form into a twin crystal ~ *vi* **1** to become paired or closely associated **2** to give birth to twins **3** to grow as a twin crystal

twin bed *n* either of 2 matching single beds

¹**twine** *n* **1** a strong string of 2 or more strands twisted together **2** a coil, twist **3** an act of twining or interlacing

²**twine** *vt* **1a** to twist together **b** to form by twisting; weave **2** to twist or coil round sthg ~ *vi* to coil round a support – **twiner** *n*

twinge *vi or n* **twinging, twingeing** (to feel) **1** a sudden sharp stab of pain **2** an emotional pang ⟨*a ~ of conscience*⟩

¹**twinkle** *vi* **1** to shine with a flickering or sparkling light **2** to appear bright with gaiety or amusement ⟨*his eyes ~d*⟩ ~ *vt* to cause to shine (as if) with a flickering light – **twinkler** *n*

²**twinkle** *n* **1** an instant, twinkling **2** an (intermittent) sparkle or gleam – **twinkly** *adj*

twinkling *n* a very short time; a moment

twin set *n* a jumper and cardigan designed to be worn together, usu by a woman

¹**twirl** *vi* to revolve rapidly ~ *vt* **1** to cause to rotate rapidly; spin **2** TWINE 2

²twirl *n* **1** an act of twirling **2** a coil, whorl – **twirly** *adj*

twirp *n* a twerp

¹twist *vt* **1a** to join together by winding; *also* to mingle by interlacing **b** to make by twisting strands together **2** to wind or coil round sthg **3a** to wring or wrench so as to dislocate or distort ⟨~ed *my ankle*⟩ **b** to distort the meaning of; pervert **c** to contort ⟨~ed *his face into a grin*⟩ **d** to pull off, turn, or break by a turning force **e** to cause to move with a rotating motion **f** to form into a spiral **g** WARP 1b ⟨*a* ~ed *mind*⟩ ~ *vi* **1** to follow a winding course; snake **2a** to turn or change shape by a turning force **b** to take on a spiral shape **c** to dance the twist **3** *of a ball* to rotate while following a curving path **4** TURN 3a ⟨~ed *round to see behind him*⟩ – **twist someone's arm** to bring strong pressure to bear on sby ⟨*he decided to come with us, but we had to* twist *his arm a bit first*⟩

²twist *n* **1** sthg formed by twisting: e g **a** a thread, yarn, or cord formed by twisting 2 or more strands together **b** tobacco twisted into a thick roll **c** a screw of paper used as a container **d** a curled strip of citrus peel used to flavour a drink ⟨ *gin, ice, bitters and a* ~ *of lemon*⟩ **2a** a twisting or being twisted **b** a dance popular esp in the 1960s and performed with gyrations, esp of the hips **c** a spiral turn or curve **3a** torsional strain **b** the angle through or amount by which a thing is twisted **4a** a turning off a straight course; a bend **b** a (personal) eccentricity or idiosyncrasy **c** a distortion of meaning or sense **5** an unexpected turn or development ⟨*a strange* ~ *of fate*⟩ **6** a dive in which the diver twists the body sideways for 1 or more half or full turns before entering the water – **twisty** *adj*

twister *n* **1** *NAm* a tornado, waterspout, etc in which the rotatory ascending movement of a column of air is very apparent **2** a dishonest person; a swindler – *infml*

¹twit *vt* **-tt-** to tease, taunt

²twit *n, Br* an absurd or silly person

¹twitch *vt* to move or pull with a sudden motion ~ *vi* **1** to pull, pluck ⟨~ed *at my sleeve*⟩ **2** to move jerkily or involuntarily – **twitcher** *n*

²twitch *n* **1** a short sudden pull or jerk **2** a physical or mental pang **3** a loop of rope or a strap that is tightened over a horse's upper lip as a restraining device **4** (the recurrence of) a short spasmodic contraction or jerk; a tic – **twitchily** *adv*, **twitchy** *adj*

³twitch *n* COUCH GRASS

¹twitter *vi* **1** to utter twitters **2** to talk in a nervous chattering fashion **3** to tremble with agitation; flutter ~ *vt* to utter (as if) in twitters

²twitter *n* **1** a nervous agitation – esp in *all of a twitter* **2** a small tremulous intermittent sound characteristic of birds – **twittery** *adj*

twixt *prep* between – chiefly poetic

¹two *pron, pl in constr* **1** two unspecified countable individuals ⟨*only* ~ *were found*⟩ **2** a small approximate number of indicated things ⟨*only a shot or* ~ *were fired*⟩

²two *n, pl* **twos** **1** (the number) 2 **2** the second in a set or series ⟨*the* ~ *of spades*⟩ **3** sthg having 2 parts or members or a denomination of 2 – **two** *adj*, **twofold** *adj or adv*

two-bit *adj, NAm* petty, small-time

two-edged *adj* double-edged

two-faced *adj* double-dealing, hypocritical – **two-facedness** *n*

two-handed *adj* **1** used with both hands ⟨*a* ~ *sword*⟩ **2** requiring 2 people ⟨*a* ~ *saw*⟩ **3** ambidextrous

twopence *also* **tuppence** *n* (a coin worth) 2 pence

twopenny *also* **tuppenny** *adj* costing or worth twopence

two-piece *n or adj* (a suit of clothes, swimming costume, etc) consisting of 2 matching pieces

two-ply *adj* consisting of 2 strands, layers, or thicknesses ⟨~ *wool*⟩

twosome *n* **1** a group of 2 people or things **2** a golf single

two-step *n* (a piece of music for) a ballroom dance in either 2_4 or 4_4 time

two-time *vb* to be unfaithful to (a spouse or lover) by having a secret relationship with another – **two-timer** *n*

two-tone *adj* **1** *also* **two-toned** having 2 colours or shades **2** of or being popular music played by groups consisting of black, esp W Indian, and white musicians and including elements of reggae and new wave – **two-tone** *n*

two-way *adj* **1** moving or allowing movement or use in 2 (opposite) directions ⟨*a* ~ *road*⟩⟨~ *traffic*⟩ **2a** *of a radio, telephone, etc* designed for both sending and receiving messages **b** involving mutual responsibility or a reciprocal relationship **3** involving 2 participants **4** usable in either of 2 ways

two-winged fly *n* any of a large order of insects including the housefly, mosquito, and gnat with functional front wings and greatly reduced rear wings used to control balance

tycoon *n* a businessman of exceptional wealth and power – **tycoonery** *n*

tying *pres part of* TIE

tyke, tike *n* **1** a (mongrel) dog **2** *chiefly Br* a boorish churlish person **3** a small child **4** a native of Yorkshire USE (3&4) *infml*

tympanic membrane *n* a thin membrane separating the outer ear from the middle ear that functions in the mechanical reception of sound waves and in their transmission to the site of sensory reception; the eardrum

tympanum *n, pl* **tympana, tympanums 1a(1)** TYMPANIC MEMBRANE **(2)** MIDDLE EAR **b** a thin tense membrane covering the hearing-organ of an insect **2a** the recessed triangular face of a pediment **b** the space within an arch and above a lintel (e g in a medieval doorway) – **tympanic** *adj*

¹type *n* **1a** a person or thing (e g in the Old Testament) regarded as foreshadowing another (e g in the New Testament) **b** a model, exemplar, or characteristic specimen (possessing the distinguishable or essential qualities of a class) **c** a lower taxonomic category selected as reference for a higher category ⟨*a* ~ *genus*⟩ **2a** (any of) a collection of usu rectangular blocks or characters bearing a relief from which an inked print can be made **b** a typeface ⟨*italic* ~⟩ **c** printed letters **3a** a set of qualities common to a number of individuals that distinguish them as an identifiable class (e g the form common to all instances of a linguistic expression **b(1)** a member of a specified class or variety of people ⟨*sporting* ~*s*⟩ **(2)** a person of a specified nature ⟨*he's a peculiar* ~⟩ **c** a particular kind, class, or group with distinct characteristics **d** sthg distinguishable as a variety; a sort – **typal** *adj*

²type *vt* **1** to represent beforehand as a type; prefigure **2** to represent in terms of typical characteristics; typify **3** to write with a typewriter; *also* to keyboard **4a** to identify as belonging to a type **b** to determine the natural type of (e g a blood sample) ~ *vi* to use a typewriter

-type *comb form* (*n* → *adj*) of (such) a type; resembling ⟨*Cheddar-type cheese*⟩

typecast *vt* **typecast** to cast (an actor) repeatedly in the same type of role; *broadly* to stereotype

typeface *n* (the appearance of) a single design of printing type

typescript *n* a typewritten manuscript (e g for use as printer's copy)

typeset *vt* -tt-; **typeset** to set in type; compose – **typesetter** *n*, **typesetting** *n*

typewrite *vb* **typewrote; typewritten** to write with a typewriter

typewriter *n* a machine with a keyboard for writing in characters resembling type

¹typhoid *adj* **1** (suggestive) of typhus **2** of or being typhoid

²typhoid, typhoid fever *n* a serious communicable human disease caused by a bacterium and marked esp by fever, diarrhoea, headache, and intestinal inflammation

typhoon *n* a tropical cyclone occurring in the Philippines or the China sea

typhus *n* a serious human disease marked by high fever, stupor alternating with delirium, intense headache, and a dark red rash, caused by a rickettsia, and transmitted esp by body lice

typical *adj* **1** *also* **typic** being or having the nature of a type; symbolic, representative **2a** having or showing the essential characteristics of a type ⟨~ *suburban houses*⟩ **b** showing or according with the usual or expected (unfavourable) traits ⟨*just* ~ *of him to get so annoyed*⟩ – **typically** *adv*, **typicalness, typicality** *n*

typify *vt* **1a** to represent in symbolic fashion (e g by an image or model) **b** to constitute a typical instance of **2** to embody the essential characteristics of – **typification** *n*

typist *n* one who uses a typewriter, esp as an occupation

typographer *n* **1** a compositor **2** a specialist in the design, choice, and arrangement of typographical matter

typography *n* the style, arrangement, or appearance of typeset matter – **typographic, typographical** *adj*, **typographically** *adv*

tyrannical *also* **tyrannic** *adj* characteristic of a tyrant or tyranny; oppressive, despotic – **tyrannically** *adv*

tyrannize, -ise *vb* to exercise power (over) with unjust and oppressive cruelty

tyrannosaur, tyrannosaurus *n* a very large flesh-eating dinosaur of the Cretaceous period having small forelegs and walking on its hind legs

tyranny *n* **1** a government in which absolute power is vested in a single ruler **2** oppressive power (exerted by a tyrant) **3** sthg severe, oppressive, or inexorable in effect – **tyrannous** *adj*

tyrant *n* **1** a ruler who exercises absolute power, esp oppressively or brutally **2** one who exercises authority harshly or unjustly

tyre, NAm chiefly tire *n* a continuous solid or inflated hollow rubber cushion set round a wheel to absorb shock

tyro, tiro *n, pl* **tyros, tiros** a beginner, novice

tzar *n* a tsar

U

u *n, pl* **u's, us** *often cap* (a graphic representation of or device for reproducing) the 21st letter of the English alphabet

¹U *adj, chiefly Br* upper-class

²U *n or adj* (a film that is) certified in Britain as suitable for all age groups

ubiquitous *adj* existing or being everywhere at the same time; omnipresent – **ubiquitously** *adv*, **ubiquitousness, ubiquity** *n*

U-boat *n* a German submarine

udder *n* a large pendulous organ consisting of 2 or more mammary glands enclosed in a common envelope and each having a single nipple

UFO *n, pl* **UFO's, UFOs** an unidentified flying object; *esp* FLYING SAUCER

ugh *interj* – used to express disgust or horror

ugly *adj* **1** frightful, horrible ⟨*an* ~ *wound*⟩ **2** offensive or displeasing to any of the senses, esp to the sight **3** morally offensive or objectionable **4a** ominous, threatening ⟨*an* ~ *customer*⟩⟨~ *weather*⟩ **b** surly, quarrelsome ⟨*an* ~ *disposition*⟩ – **uglily** *adv*, **ugliness** *n*, **uglify** *vt*

ugly duckling *n* sby who or sthg that appears unpromising but turns out successful

ukulele *n* a small usu 4-stringed guitar of Portuguese origin

-ular *suffix* (→ *adj*) of, relating to, or resembling ⟨*angular*⟩

ulcer *n* **1** a persistent open sore in skin or mucous membrane that often discharges pus **2** sthg that festers and corrupts – **ulcerous** *adj*

ulcerate *vb* to (cause to) become affected (as if) with an ulcer – **ulcerative** *adj*, **ulceration** *n*

ullage *n* the amount by which a container (e g a tank or bottle) is less than full

ulna *n* the bone of the human forearm on the little-finger side; *also* a corresponding part of the forelimb of vertebrates above fishes – **ulnar** *adj*

ulterior *adj* going beyond what is openly said or shown; intentionally concealed ⟨~ *motives*⟩ – **ulteriorly** *adv*

¹ultimate *adj* **1a** last in a progression or series ⟨*their* ~ *destination was Paris*⟩ **b** eventual **2a** fundamental, basic ⟨~ *reality*⟩ **b** incapable of further analysis, division, or separation **3** maximum, greatest ⟨*the* ~ *sacrifice*⟩ – **ultimateness** *n*

²ultimate *n* sthg ultimate; *the* highest point ⟨*the* ~ *in stupidity*⟩

ultimately *adv* finally; AT LAST

ultimatum *n, pl* **ultimatums, ultimata** a final proposition or demand; *esp* one whose rejection will end negotiations and cause a resort to direct action

ultimo *adj* of or occurring in the previous month

ultra *adj* going beyond others or beyond due limit

ultra- *prefix* **1** beyond in space; on the other side of; trans- ⟨*ultramontane*⟩ ⟨*ultraplanetary*⟩ **2** beyond the range or limits of; super- ⟨*ultramicroscopic*⟩ ⟨*ultrasound*⟩ **3** excessively; extremely ⟨*ultramodern*⟩ ⟨*ultraconservative*⟩

ultrahigh frequency *n* a radio frequency in the range between 300 megahertz and 3000 megahertz

¹ultramarine *n* **1** a deep blue pigment **2** vivid deep blue

²ultramarine *adj* situated across the sea

¹ultrasonic *adj* supersonic: **a** of waves and vibrations having a frequency above about 20,000Hz **b** using, produced by, or relating to ultrasonic waves or vibrations ⟨*an* ~ *dog whistle*⟩ – **ultrasonically** *adv*

²ultrasonic *n* an ultrasonic wave or frequency

¹ultraviolet *n* electromagnetic radiation having a wavelength between the violet end of the visible spectrum and X rays

²ultraviolet *adj* relating to, producing, or employing ultraviolet ⟨*an* ~ *lamp*⟩

¹umber *n* **1** a brown earth used as a pigment **2** dark or yellowish brown

²umber *adj* of the colour of umber

³umber *vt* to darken (as if) with umber

umbilical cord *n* **1** a cord arising from the navel that connects the foetus with the placenta **2** a cable conveying power to a rocket or spacecraft before takeoff; *also* a tethering or supply line (e g for an astronaut outside a spacecraft or a diver underwater)

umbrage *n* **1** a feeling of pique or resentment ⟨took ~ at the chairman's comment⟩ **2** *archaic* shady branches; foliage

umbrella *n* **1** a collapsible shade for protection against weather, consisting of fabric stretched over hinged ribs radiating from a central pole **2** the bell-shaped or saucer-shaped largely gelatinous structure that forms the chief part of the body of most jellyfishes **3** sthg which provides protection ⟨the American nuclear ~⟩ **4** sthg that embraces a broad range of elements or factors ⟨the Electricity Council: ~ of the area electricity boards – The Economist⟩

umlaut *n* (a mark¨ placed over a letter in some Germanic languages to indicate) the change of a vowel caused by the influence of a following vowel or semivowel

¹**umpire** *n* **1** one having authority to settle a controversy or question between parties **2** a referee in any of several sports (e g cricket, table tennis, badminton, and hockey)

²**umpire** *vb* to act as or supervise (e g a match) as umpire

umpteen *adj* very many; indefinitely numerous – *infml* – **umpteen** *n*, **umpteenth** *adj*

un *pron, dial* one

¹**un-** *prefix* **1** not; in-, non- ⟨unskilled⟩ ⟨undressed⟩ ⟨unbelief⟩ **2** opposite of; contrary to ⟨ungrateful⟩ ⟨unthinking⟩ ⟨unrest⟩

²**un-** *prefix* **1** do the opposite of; reverse (a specified action); DE- 1a, DIS- 1a ⟨unbend⟩ ⟨undress⟩ ⟨unfold⟩ **2a** deprive of; remove (sthg specified) from; remove ⟨unfrock⟩ ⟨unsex⟩ ⟨unnerve⟩ **b** release from; free from ⟨unhand⟩ ⟨untie⟩ **c(1)** remove from; extract from; take out of ⟨unearth⟩ ⟨unsheathe⟩ **(2)** dislodge from ⟨unhorse⟩ ⟨unseat⟩ **d** cause to cease to be ⟨unman⟩ **3** completely ⟨unloose⟩

unabashed *adj*

unabated *adj*

unable *adj* not able; incapable: **a** unqualified, incompetent **b** impotent, helpless

unabridged *adj*

unaccompanied *adj*

unaccountable *adj* **1** inexplicable, strange **2** not to be called to account; not responsible – **unaccountably** *adv*, **unaccountability** *n*

unaccustomed *adj* **1** not customary; not usual or common **2** not used to – **unaccustomedly** *adv*

unadopted *adj, Br* not looked after by local authority ⟨an ~ road⟩

unadulterated *adj* unmixed, esp with anything inferior; pure – **unadulteratedly** *adv*

unadvised *adj* not prudent; indiscreet, rash ILL-ADVISED – **unadvisedly** *adv*

unaffected *adj* **1** not influenced or changed mentally, physically, or chemically **2** free from affectation; genuine – **unaffectedly** *adv*, **unaffectedness** *n*

un-American *adj* not consistent with US customs, principles, or traditions

unanimous *adj* **1** being of one mind; agreeing **2** characterized by the agreement and consent of all ⟨a ~ decision⟩ – **unanimously** *adv*, **unanimity** *n*

unannounced *adj*

unanswerable *adj* not answerable; *esp* irrefutable – **unanswerably** *adv*, **unanswerabillty** *n*

unapproachable *adj* **1** physically inaccessible **2** reserved, unfriendly – **unapproachably** *adv*, **unapproachability** *n*

unarmed *adj* **1** not armed or armoured **2** having no spines, spurs, claws, etc

unasked *adj* **1** not asked or invited **2** not sought or asked for ⟨~ advice⟩

unassuming *adj* not arrogant or presuming; modest – **unassumingness** *n*

unattached *adj* **1** not assigned or committed; *esp* not married or engaged **2** not joined or united ⟨~ polyps⟩ ⟨~ buildings⟩

unavailing *adj* futile, useless – **unavailingly** *adv*, **unavailingness** *n*

unawares *adv* **1** without noticing or intending **2** suddenly, unexpectedly

unbalance *vt* to put out of balance; *esp* to derange mentally

unbar *vt* **-rr-** to remove a bar from; unlock, open

unbearable *adj* not endurable; intolerable – **unbearably** *adv*

unbeknown *adj* happening without one's knowledge – usu + *to*

unbelief *n* incredulity or scepticism, esp in matters of religious faith

unbelievable *adj* too improbable for belief; incredible – **unbelievably** *adv*

unbeliever *n* one who does not believe, esp in a particular religion

unbelieving *adj* marked by unbelief; sceptical – **unbelievingly** *adv*

unbend *vb* **unbent** *vt* **1** to put into or allow to return to a straight position **2a** to unfasten (e g a sail) from a spar or stay **b** to cast loose or untie (e g a rope) ~*vi* **1** to become more relaxed, informal, or outgoing in manner **2** to become straight

unbending *adj* **1** unyielding, inflexible ⟨an ~ will⟩ **2** aloof or unsociable in manner

unbidden *adj* unasked, uninvited

unbind *vt* **unbound 1** to untie, unfasten **2** to set free; release

unblushing *adj* shameless, unabashed – **unblushingly** *adv*

unborn *adj* **1** not yet born **2** still to appear; future ⟨~ ages⟩

unbosom *vt* to disclose the thoughts or feelings of (oneself)

unbounded *adj* having no limits or constraints – **unboundedness** *n*

unbowed *adj* not bowed down; *esp* not subdued

unbridled *adj* **1** not confined by a bridle **2** unrestrained, ungoverned

unbuckle *vt* to loose the buckle of; unfasten

unburden *vt* to free or relieve from anxiety, cares, etc

uncalled-for *adj* **1** unnecessary **2** offered without provocation or justification; gratuitous ⟨an ~ display of temper⟩

uncanny *adj* **1** eerie, mysterious **2** beyond what is normal or expected ⟨an ~ sense of direction⟩ – **uncannily** *adv*, **uncanniness** *n*

unceremonious *adj* **1** not ceremonious; informal **2** abrupt, rude ⟨an ~ dismissal⟩ – **unceremoniously** *adv*, **unceremoniousness** *n*

uncertain *adj* **1** not reliable or trustworthy **2a** not definitely known; undecided, unpredictable ⟨the outcome is ~⟩ **b** not confident or sure; doubtful ⟨~ of the truth⟩ **3** variable, changeable ⟨~ weather⟩ – **uncertainly** *adv*, **uncertainness** *n*

uncertainty *n* the state of being uncertain; doubt

uncharitable adj severe in judging others; harsh – **uncharitableness** n, **uncharitably** adv

unchecked adj

unchristian adj 1 contrary to the Christian spirit or character 2 barbarous, uncivilized

uncle n 1a the brother of one's father or mother b the husband of one's aunt 2 a man who is a very close friend of a young child or its parents

unclean adj 1 morally or spiritually impure 2a ritually prohibited as food b ceremonially unfit or defiled 3 dirty, filthy – **uncleanness** n

Uncle Sam n the American nation, people, or government

Uncle Tom n a black American eager to win the approval of white people and willing to cooperate with them – chiefly derog

uncomfortable adj 1 causing discomfort 2 feeling discomfort; ill at ease – **uncomfortably** adv

uncommitted adj not pledged to a particular belief, allegiance, or course of action

uncommon adj 1 not normally encountered; unusual 2 remarkable, exceptional – **uncommonly** adv, **uncommonness** n

uncompromising adj not making or accepting a compromise; unyielding – **uncompromisingly** adv

unconcerned adj 1 not involved or interested 2 not anxious or worried – **unconcernedly** adv, **unconcernedness** n

unconditional adj absolute, unqualified – **unconditionally** adv

unconscionable adj 1 unscrupulous, unprincipled 2 excessive, unreasonable – **unconscionably** adv

¹**unconscious** adj 1 not knowing or perceiving 2a not possessing mind or having lost consciousness ⟨~ *matter*⟩ ⟨~ *for 3 days*⟩ b not marked by or resulting from conscious thought, sensation, or feeling ⟨~ *motivation*⟩ 3 not intentional or deliberate ⟨~ *bias*⟩ – **unconsciously** adv, **unconsciousness** n

²**unconscious** n the part of the mind that does not ordinarily enter a person's awareness but nevertheless influences behaviour and may be manifested in dreams or slips of the tongue

unconsidered adj 1 disregarded, unnoticed 2 not carefully thought out ⟨~ *opinions*⟩

uncork vt 1 to draw a cork from 2 to release from a pent-up state; unleash

uncouple vt 1 to release (dogs) from a couple 2 to detach, disconnect – **uncoupler** n

uncouth adj awkward and uncultivated in speech or manner; boorish – **uncouthly** adv, **uncouthness** n

uncover vt 1 to disclose, reveal 2a to remove the cover from b to remove the hat from (one's head)

uncritical adj lacking in discrimination or critical analysis – **uncritically** adv

uncrowned adj 1 not having yet been crowned 2 having a specified status in fact but not in name ⟨the ~ *champion*⟩

unction n the act of anointing as a rite of consecration or healing

unctuous adj 1 fatty, oily, or greasy in texture or appearance 2 marked by ingratiating smoothness and false sincerity – **unctuously** adv, **unctuousness** n

uncut adj 1 not cut down or into 2 not shaped by cutting ⟨an ~ *diamond*⟩ 3 *of a book* not having the folds of the leaves trimmed off 4 not abridged or curtailed

undaunted adj not discouraged by danger or difficulty – **undauntedly** adv

undeceive vt to free from deception, illusion, or error

undecided adj 1 in doubt 2 without a result ⟨the match was left ~⟩ – **undecidedly** adv, **undecidedness** n

undeniable adj 1 plainly true; incontestable ⟨~ *evidence*⟩ 2 unquestionably excellent or genuine – **undeniably** adv

¹**under** adv 1 in or to a position below or beneath sthg 2a in or to a lower rank or number ⟨£10 or ~⟩ b to a subnormal degree; deficiently – often in combination ⟨under-*staffed*⟩ 3 in or into a condition of subjection, subordination, or unconsciousness 4 so as to be covered, buried, or sheltered 5 BELOW 3

²**under** prep 1a below or beneath so as to be overhung, surmounted, covered, protected, or hidden ⟨~ *cover of darkness*⟩ b using as a pseudonym or alias ⟨wrote ~ the name 'George Eliot'⟩ 2a(1) subject to the authority, control, guidance, or instruction of ⟨served ~ the general⟩ (2) during the rule or control of ⟨India ~ the Raj⟩ b receiving or undergoing the action or effect of ⟨~ pressure⟩ ⟨courage ~ fire ⟩⟨~ ether⟩⟨~ discussion⟩ ⟨~ sail⟩ 3 within the group or designation of ⟨~ this heading⟩ 4 less than or inferior to ⟨~ an hour⟩; esp falling short of (a standard or required degree)

³**under** adj 1a lying or placed below, beneath, or on the lower side b facing or pointing downwards 2 lower in rank or authority; subordinate 3 lower than usual, proper, or desired in amount or degree USE often in combination

underact vt 1 to perform (a dramatic part) without adequate force or skill 2 to perform with restraint for greater dramatic impact or personal force ~ vi to perform feebly or with restraint

¹**underarm** adj 1 under or on the underside of the arm ⟨~ seams⟩ 2 made with the hand brought forwards and up from below shoulder level

²**underarm** vt or adv (to throw) with an underarm motion ⟨bowl ~⟩

³**underarm** n the part of a garment that covers the underside of the arm

underbelly n 1 the underside of an animal, object, etc 2 a vulnerable area ⟨the soft ~ of capitalism⟩

underbrush n, NAm undergrowth in a wood or forest

undercarriage n 1 a supporting framework (e g of a motor vehicle) 2 the part of an aircraft's structure that supports its weight, when in contact with the land or water

undercharge vb to charge (e g a person) too little – **undercharge** n

underclothes n pl underwear

undercoat n 1 a growth of short hair or fur partly concealed by a longer growth ⟨a dog's ~⟩ 2 a coat (e g of paint) applied as a base for another coat

undercover adj acting or done in secret; specif engaged in spying

undercurrent n 1 a current below the upper currents or surface 2 a hidden opinion, feeling, or tendency

¹**undercut** vt -tt-; **undercut** 1 to cut away the underpart of ⟨~ a vein of ore⟩ 2 to cut away material from the underside of so as to leave a portion overhanging 3 to offer sthg at lower prices than or work for lower wages than (a competitor)

²**undercut** n 1 the action or result of undercutting 2 Br the underside of sirloin; a beef tenderloin 3 NAm a notch cut in a tree to determine the direction of falling during felling

underdeveloped adj 1 not normally or adequately developed ⟨~ muscles⟩ ⟨an ~ film⟩ 2 failing to realize a potential economic level – **underdevelopment** n

underdog n 1 an (expected) loser in a contest 2 a victim of injustice or persecution

underdone *adj* not thoroughly cooked

underestimate *vt* 1 to estimate as being less than the actual size, quantity, etc 2 to place too low a value on; underrate – **underestimate** *n*, **underestimation** *n*

underfelt *n* a thick felt underlay placed under a carpet

underfoot *adv* 1 under the feet, esp against the ground ⟨*trampled ~*⟩ 2 in the way ⟨*children always getting ~*⟩

undergarment *n* a garment to be worn under another

undergo *vt* **underwent; undergone** to be subjected to; experience

undergraduate *n* a college or university student who has not taken a first degree

¹**underground** *adv* 1 beneath the surface of the earth 2 in or into hiding or secret operation

²**underground** *adj* 1 growing, operating, or situated below the surface of the ground 2a conducted in hiding or in secret **b** existing or operated outside the establishment, esp by the avant-garde

³**underground** *n* 1 *sing or pl in constr* **a** a secret movement or group esp in an occupied country, for concerted resistive action **b** a conspiratorial organization set up for disruption of a civil order **c** a usu avant-garde group or movement that functions outside the establishment 2 *Br* a usu electric underground urban railway; *also* a train running in an underground

undergrowth *n* shrub, bushes, saplings, etc growing under larger trees in a wood or forest

¹**underhand** *adv* 1 in an underhand manner; secretly 2 underarm

²**underhand** *adj* 1 not honest and aboveboard; sly 2 UNDERARM 2

underhung *adj* 1 *of a lower jaw* projecting beyond the upper jaw 2 having an underhung jaw

¹**underlay** *vt* **underlaid** 1 to cover or line the bottom of; give support to on the underside or below 2 to raise by sthg laid under

²**underlay** *n* sthg that is (designed to be) laid under sthg else ⟨*a carpet with foam ~*⟩

underlie *vt* **underlying; underlay; underlain** 1 to lie or be situated under 2 to form the basis or foundation of 3 to be concealed beneath the exterior of ⟨*underlying hostility*⟩

underline *vt* 1 to mark (a word or passage) with a line underneath 2 to emphasize, stress – **underline** *n*

underling *n* a subordinate or inferior

undermanned *adj* inadequately staffed

undermentioned *adj*, *Br* referred to at a later point in a text

undermine *vt* 1 to form a mine under; sap 2 to weaken or destroy gradually or insidiously

¹**underneath** *prep* directly below; close under

²**underneath** *adv* 1 under or below an object or a surface; beneath 2 on the lower side

³**underneath** *n* the bottom part or surface ⟨*the ~ of the bowl*⟩

undernourished *adj* supplied with less than the minimum amount of the foods essential for sound health and growth – **undernourishment** *n*

underpants *n pl* men's pants

underpass *n* a tunnel or passage taking a road and pavement under another road or a railway

underpin *vt* **-nn-** to form part of, strengthen, or replace the foundation of ⟨*~ a sagging building*⟩

underplay *vt* 1 to underact (a role) 2 to play down the importance of

underprivileged *adj* deprived of some of the fundamental social or economic rights of a civilized society ⟨*~ children*⟩

underproof *adj* containing less alcohol than proof spirit

underquote *vt* 1 to quote a lower price than (another person) 2 to quote a price for (e g goods or services) that is lower than another's offer or the market price

underrate *vt* to rate too low; undervalue

underscore *vt* to underline – **underscore** *n*

undersecretary *n* a secretary immediately subordinate to a principal secretary

undersell *vt* **undersold** 1 to be sold cheaper than ⟨*imported cars that ~ domestic ones*⟩ 2 to make little of the merits of ⟨*he undersold himself*⟩; *esp* to promote or publicize in a (deliberately) low-key manner

undersexed *adj* deficient in sexual drive or interest

underside *n* the side or surface lying underneath

undersigned *n*, *pl* **undersigned** the one who signs his/her name at the end of a document

undersized *also* **undersize** *adj* of less than average size

underslung *adj*, *of a vehicle frame* suspended below the axles

understaffed *adj* undermanned

understand *vb* **understood** *vt* 1a to grasp the meaning of; comprehend **b** to have a thorough knowledge of or expertise in ⟨*~ finance*⟩ 2 to assume, suppose ⟨*we ~ that he is abroad*⟩ 3 to interpret in one of a number of possible ways ⟨*as I ~ it*⟩ 4 to supply mentally (sthg implied though not expressed) *~ vi* 1 to have a grasp or understanding of sthg 2 to believe or infer sthg to be the case 3 to show a sympathetic or tolerant attitude ⟨*if he loves her he'll ~*⟩ – **understandable** *adj*, **understandably** *adv*, **understandability** *n*

¹**understanding** *n* 1 a mental grasp; comprehension 2 the power of comprehending; intelligence; *esp* the power to make experience intelligible by applying concepts 3a a friendly or harmonious relationship **b** an informal mutual agreement

²**understanding** *adj* tolerant, sympathetic – **understandingly** *adv*

understate *vt* 1 to state as being less than is the case 2 to present with restraint, esp for greater effect – **understatement** *n*

¹**understudy** *vi* to study another actor's part in order to take it over in an emergency *~ vt* to prepare (e g a part) as understudy; *also* to prepare a part as understudy to

²**understudy** *n* one who is prepared to act another's part or take over another's duties

undertake *vt* **undertook; undertaken** 1 to take upon oneself as a task 2 to put oneself under obligation to do; contract 3 to guarantee, promise

undertaker *n* sby whose business is preparing the dead for burial and arranging and managing funerals

undertaking *n* 1 the business of an undertaker 2 an enterprise 3 a pledge, guarantee

under-the-counter *adj* surreptitious and usu illicit – *infml*

undertone *n* 1 a subdued utterance 2 an underlying quality (e g of emotion) 3 a subdued colour; *specif* one seen through and modifying another colour

undertow *n* 1 an undercurrent that flows in a different direction from the surface current, esp out to sea 2 a hidden tendency often contrary to the one that is publicly apparent

underwater *adj* 1 situated, used, or designed to operate below the surface of the water 2 being below the waterline of a ship – **underwater** *adv*

underwear *n* clothing worn next to the skin and under other clothing

underweight *adj or n* (of a) weight below average or normal

underworld *n* **1** the place of departed souls; Hades **2** the world of organized crime

underwrite *vb* **underwrote; underwritten** *vt* **1** to write under or at the end of sthg else **2** to set one's signature to (an insurance policy) thereby assuming liability in case of specified loss or damage; *also* to assume (a sum or risk) by way of insurance **3** to subscribe to; agree to **4a** to agree to purchase (a security issue) usu on a fixed date at a fixed price with a view to public distribution **b** to guarantee financial support of ~ *vi* to carry on the business of an underwriter

underwriter *n* **1** one who underwrites sthg, esp an insurance policy **2** one who selects risks to be solicited or rates the acceptability of risks solicited

undesirable *n or adj* (sby or sthg) unwanted or objectionable ⟨~ *elements in society*⟩ – **undesirably** *adv*, **undesirability** *n*

undeveloped *adj*

undies *n pl* underwear; *esp* women's underwear – *infml*

undistinguished *adj*

undivided *adj*

undo *vb* **undid; undone** *vt* **1** to open or loosen by releasing a fastening **2** to reverse or cancel out the effects of **3** to destroy the standing, reputation, hopes, etc of ~ *vi* to come open or apart – **undoer** *n*

undoing *n* (a cause of) ruin or downfall

¹**undone** *past part of* UNDO

²**undone** *adj* not performed or finished

undoubted *adj* not disputed; genuine – **undoubtedly** *adv*

undreamed *also* **undreamt** *adj* not conceived of; unimagined – usu + *of*

¹**undress** *vt* to remove the clothes or covering of ~ *vi* to take off one's clothes

²**undress** *n* **1** ordinary dress **2** a state of having little or no clothing on

undressed *adj* **1** partially or completely unclothed **2** not fully processed or finished ⟨~ *hides*⟩ **3** not cared for or tended ⟨*an* ~ *wound*⟩

undue *adj* **1** not yet due **2** excessive, immoderate

¹**undulate, undulated** *adj* having a wavy surface, edge, or markings ⟨*the* ~ *margin of a leaf*⟩

²**undulate** *vi* **1** to rise and fall in waves; fluctuate **2** to have a wavy form or appearance

undulation *n* **1a** a gentle rising and falling (as if) in waves **b** a wavelike motion; *also* a single wave or gentle rise **2** a wavy appearance, outline, or form

unduly *adv* excessively

undying *adj* eternal, perpetual

unearth *vt* **1** to dig up out of the ground **2** to make known or public

unearthly *adj* **1** not terrestrial ⟨~ *radio sources*⟩ **2** exceeding what is normal or natural; supernatural ⟨*an* ~ *light*⟩ **3** weird, eerie **4** unreasonable, preposterous ⟨*getting up at an* ~ *hour*⟩ – **unearthliness** *n*

unease *n* a feeling of disquiet or awkwardness

uneasy *adj* **1** marked by lack of physical or mental ease; uncomfortable, awkward **2** apprehensive, worried **3** precarious, unstable ⟨*an* ~ *truce*⟩ – **uneasily** *adv*, **uneasiness** *n*

uneconomic *also* **uneconomical** *adj* not economically practicable

uneducated *adj*

unemployed *adj* **1** not engaged in a job **2** not invested – **unemployed** *n pl in constr*

unemployment *n* the state of being unemployed; lack of available employment

unenviable *adj*

unequal *adj* **1a** not of the same measurement, quantity, or number as another **b** not like in quality, nature, or status **c** not the same for every member of a group, class, or society ⟨~ *rights*⟩ **2** badly balanced or matched **3** not uniform **4** incapable of meeting the requirements of sthg – + *to* – **unequally** *adv*

unequalled *adj* not equalled; unparalleled

unequivocal *adj* clear, unambiguous – **unequivocally** *adv*

unerring *adj* faultless, unfailing ⟨~ *judgment*⟩ – **unerringly** *adv*

uneven *adj* **1a** not level, smooth, or uniform **b** varying from the straight or parallel **c** irregular, inconsistent **d** varying in quality ⟨*an* ~ *performance*⟩ **2** UNEQUAL 2 ⟨*an* ~ *contest*⟩ – **unevenly** *adv*, **unevenness** *n*

uneventful *adj* without any noteworthy or untoward incidents – **uneventfully** *adv*

unexceptionable *adj* beyond reproach or criticism; unimpeachable – **unexceptionableness** *n*, **unexceptionably** *adv*

unexpected *adj* not expected or foreseen – **unexpectedly** *adv*, **unexpectedness** *n*

unfailing *adj* that can be relied on; constant ⟨*a subject of* ~ *interest*⟩ – **unfailingly** *adv*, **unfailingness** *n*

unfaithful *adj* **1** disloyal, faithless **2** not faithful to a marriage partner, lover, etc, esp in having sexual relations with another person – **unfaithfully** *adv*, **unfaithfulness** *n*

unfaltering *adj* not wavering or hesitating; firm – **unfalteringly** *adv*

unfavourable *adj* **1** expressing disapproval; negative **2** disadvantageous, adverse ⟨*an* ~ *economic climate*⟩ – **unfavourably** *adv*

unfeeling *adj* not kind or sympathetic; hardhearted – **unfeelingly** *adv*, **unfeelingness** *n*

unfetter *vt* **1** to release from fetters ⟨~ *a prisoner*⟩ **2** to free from restraint; liberate

unfit *adj* **1** unsuitable, inappropriate **2** incapable, incompetent ⟨~ *for duty*⟩ **3** physically or mentally unsound – **unfitness** *n*

unflagging *adj* never flagging; tireless – **unflaggingly** *adv*

unflappable *adj* remaining calm and composed; imperturbable – **unflappability** *n*

unflinching *adj* not flinching or shrinking; steadfast – **unflinchingly** *adv*

unfold *vt* **1** to open the folds of; spread or straighten out **2** to disclose gradually ~ *vi* **1** to open from a folded state **2** to open out gradually to the mind or eye

unforeseen *adj*

unforgettable *adj* incapable of being forgotten; memorable – **unforgettably** *adv*

¹**unfortunate** *adj* **1a** unsuccessful, unlucky **b** accompanied by or resulting in misfortune ⟨*an* ~ *decision*⟩ **2** unsuitable, inappropriate ⟨*an* ~ *choice of words*⟩

²**unfortunate** *n* an unfortunate person

unfortunately *adv* **1** in an unfortunate manner **2** as is unfortunate ⟨~ *the matter is not so simple*⟩

unfounded *adj* lacking a sound basis; groundless

unfrequented *adj* not often visited or travelled over

unfrock *vt* to deprive (esp a priest) of the right to exercise the functions of office

unfurl *vb* to (cause to) open out from a furled state; unroll

ungainly *adj* lacking in grace or dexterity; clumsy – **ungainliness** *n*

ungenerous *adj* **1** petty, uncharitable **2** stingy, mean – **ungenerously** *adv*

ungodly *adj* **1a** denying God or disobedient to him;

heathen **b** sinful, wicked **2** indecent, outrageous ⟨*gets up at an ~ hour*⟩ – **ungodliness** *n*

ungovernable *adj* not capable of being controlled or restrained

ungracious *adj* rude, impolite – **ungraciously** *adv*, **ungraciousness** *n*

ungrateful *adj* **1** showing no gratitude **2** disagreeable, unpleasant – **ungratefully** *adv*, **ungratefulness** *n*

ungrudging *adj* generous, wholehearted ⟨*~ praise*⟩ – **ungrudgingly** *adv*

unguarded *adj* **1** vulnerable to attack **2** showing lack of forethought or calculation; imprudent – **unguardedly** *adv*, **unguardedness** *n*

unguent *n* a soothing or healing salve; ointment

unhand *vt* to remove the hands from; let go

unhappily *adv* **1** in an unhappy manner **2** UNFORTUNATELY **2**

unhappy *adj* **1** not fortunate; unlucky **2** sad, miserable **3** unsuitable, inappropriate ⟨*an ~ remark*⟩ – **unhappiness** *n*

unhealthy *adj* **1** not in or conducive to good health **2** unnatural; *esp* morbid ⟨*an ~ interest in death*⟩ – **unhealthily** *adv*, **unhealthiness** *n*

unheard *adj* **1** not perceived by the ear **2** not given a hearing

unheard-of *adj* previously unknown; unprecedented

unhinge *vt* **1** to remove (e g a door) from hinges **2** to make unstable; unsettle ⟨*her mind was ~*d *by grief*⟩

unholy *adj* **1** wicked, reprehensible ⟨*an ~ alliance*⟩ **2** terrible, awful – *infml* ⟨*making an ~ racket*⟩ – **unholiness** *n*

unhook *vt* **1** to remove from a hook **2** to unfasten the hooks of

unhorse *vt* to dislodge (as if) from a horse

uni- *prefix* one; single ⟨*unicellular*⟩

unicorn *n* a mythical animal usu depicted as a white horse with a single horn in the middle of the forehead

unidentified *adj*

¹uniform *adj* **1** not varying in character, appearance, quantity, etc ⟨*a ~ speed*⟩ **2** conforming to a rule, pattern, or practice; consonant – **uniformly** *adv*, **uniformness** *n*, **uniformity** *n*

²uniform *vt* to clothe in a uniform ⟨*a ~*ed *officer*⟩

³uniform *n* dress of a distinctive design or fashion worn by members of a particular group and serving as a means of identification

Uniform – a communications code word for the letter *u*

unify *vt* to make into a unit or a coherent whole; unite – **unifier** *n*, **unifiable** *adj*, **unification** *n*

unilateral *adj* **1a** done or undertaken by 1 person or party ⟨*~ disarmament*⟩ **b** of or affecting 1 side **2** produced or arranged on or directed towards 1 side ⟨*a stem bearing ~ flowers*⟩ **3** having only 1 side – **unilaterally** *adv*

unimpeachable *adj* **1** not to be doubted; beyond question **2** irreproachable, blameless – **unimpeachably** *adv*

uninhibited *adj* acting spontaneously without constraint or regard for what others might think – **uninhibitedly** *adv*, **uninhibitedness** *n*

uninterested *adj*

uninterrupted *adj*

¹union *n* **1a(1)** the formation of a single political unit from 2 or more separate and independent units **(2)** a uniting in marriage; *also* SEXUAL INTERCOURSE **b** combination, junction **2a(1)** an association of independent individuals (e g nations) for some common purpose **(2)** a political unit made up from previously independent units **b** TRADE UNION **3** the set of all elements belonging to 1 or more of

a given collection of 2 or more sets **4** a coupling for pipes (and fittings)

²union *adj* of, dealing with, or constituting a union

unionism *n* **1** adherence to the principles of trade unions **2** *cap* adherence to the policy of union between the states of the USA, esp during the Civil War **3** *cap* the principles and policies of the Unionist party

unionist *n* an advocate or supporter of union or unionism

Unionist *adj* of or constituting a political party of N Ireland that supports the union with Britain and draws support generally from the Protestant community

unionize, -ise *vt* to cause to become a member of or subject to the rules of a trade union; form into a trade union – **unionization**

Union Jack *n* the national flag of the UK combining crosses representing England, Scotland, and N Ireland

unique *adj* **1a** sole, only ⟨*his ~ concern*⟩ **b** producing only 1 result ⟨*the ~ factorization of a number into prime factors*⟩ **2** without a like or equal; unequalled **3** very rare or unusual – disapproved of by some speakers – **uniquely** *adv*, **uniqueness** *n*

unisex *adj* **1** able to be worn by both sexes ⟨*a ~ hair style*⟩ **2** dealing in unisex products or styles ⟨*a ~ barber's*⟩

unison *n* **1a** (the state of) identity in musical pitch; the interval between 2 notes of the same pitch **b** the writing, playing, or singing of parts in a musical passage at the same pitch or in octaves **2** harmonious agreement or union – **unison** *adj*

unit *n* **1a(1)** the first and lowest natural number; one **(2)** a single quantity regarded as a whole in calculation **b** the number occupying the position immediately to the left of the decimal point in the Arabic notation; *also, pl* this position **2** a determinate quantity (e g of length, time, heat, value, or housing) adopted as a standard of measurement **3a** a single thing, person, or group that is a constituent of a whole **b** a part of a military establishment that has a prescribed organization (e g of personnel and supplies) **c** a piece of apparatus serving to perform 1 particular function – **unit** *adj*, **unitive** *adj*, **unitize** *vt*

unitarian *n* **1** *often cap* a person who rejects the doctrine of the Trinity and believes in one god who is a single being **2** *cap* a member of a Christian denomination that stresses individual freedom of belief, the free use of reason in religion, a united world community, and liberal social action – **unitarian** *adj, often cap*, **unitarianism** *n, often cap*

unite *vt* **1** to join together to form a single unit **2** to bind by a legal or moral bond ⟨*~*d *by marriage*⟩ *~vi* **1** to become (as if) 1 unit **2** to act in concert – **uniter** *n*

united *adj* **1** combined, joined **2** relating to or produced by joint action ⟨*a ~ effort*⟩ **3** in agreement; harmonious – **unitedly** *adv*

unit trust *n* an investment company that minimizes the risk to investors by collective purchase of shares in many different enterprises

unity *n* **1a** the state of being 1 or united ⟨*strength lies in ~*⟩ **b(1)** a definite amount taken as 1 or for which 1 is made to stand in calculation ⟨*in a table of natural sines the radius of the circle is regarded as ~*⟩ **(2)** a number by which any element of an arithmetical or mathematical system can be multiplied without change in the resultant value **2a** concord, harmony **b** continuity and agreement in aims and interests ⟨*~ of purpose*⟩ **3** singleness of effect or symmetry in a literary or artistic work **4** a whole made up of related parts

univalent *adj* **1** having a valency of 1 **2** *of a chromosome* not pairing with another chromosome at meiotic cell division

¹universal *adj* **1** including or covering all or a whole without limit or exception **2** present or occurring everywhere or under all conditions **3** including a major part or the greatest portion (e g of mankind) ⟨~ *practices*⟩ **4** affirming or denying sthg of, or denoting, every member of a class ⟨*'no man knows everything' is a* ~ *negative*⟩ – **universalize** *vt,* **universally** *adv,* **universalness** *n,* **universality** *n*

²universal *n* **1** a universal proposition in logic **2** a general concept or term

universal joint *n* a shaft coupling capable of transmitting rotation from one shaft to another at an angle

universe *n* **1a(1)** all things that exist; the cosmos **(2)** a galaxy **b** the whole world; everyone **2** POPULATION 5

university *n* (the premises of) an institution of higher learning that provides facilities for full-time teaching and research, is authorized to grant academic degrees, and in Britain receives a Treasury grant ⟨*she's at* ~⟩

unkempt *adj* **1** not combed; dishevelled ⟨~ *hair*⟩ **2** not neat or tidy

unkind *adj* **1** not pleasing or mild ⟨*an* ~ *climate*⟩ **2** lacking in kindness or sympathy; harsh – **unkindly** *adv,* **unkindness** *n*

unknowing *adj* not knowing – **unknowingly** *adv*

¹unknown *adj* not known; *also* having an unknown value ⟨*an* ~ *quantity*⟩

²unknown *n* **1** a person who is little known (e g to the public) **2** a symbol in a mathematical equation representing an unknown quantity

unlawful *adj* **1** illegal **2** not morally right or conventional – **unlawfully** *adv,* **unlawfulness** *n*

unlearn *vt* to put out of one's knowledge or memory

unleash *vt* to free (as if) from a leash; loose from restraint or control

unleavened *adj*

unless *conj* **1** except on the condition that ⟨*won't work* ~ *you put in some money*⟩ **2** without the necessary accompaniment that; except when ⟨*we swim* ~ *it's very cold*⟩

unlettered *adj* illiterate

¹unlike *prep* **1** different from **2** not characteristic of ⟨~ *him to be late*⟩ **3** in a different manner from

²unlike *adj* **1** marked by dissimilarity; different **2** unequal – **unlikeness** *n*

unlikely *adj* **1** having a low probability of being or occurring ⟨*an* ~ *possibility*⟩ **2** not believable; improbable ⟨*an* ~ *story*⟩ **3** likely to fail; unpromising **4** not foreseen ⟨*the* ~ *result*⟩ – **unlikelihood** *n,* **unlikeliness** *n*

unload *vt* **1a(1)** to take off or out **(2)** to take the cargo from **b** to give vent to; pour forth **2** to relieve of sthg burdensome **3** to draw the charge from **4** DUMP 2 ~ *vi* to perform the act of unloading – **unloader** *n*

unlock *vt* **1** to unfasten the lock of **2** to open, release **3** to provide a key to; disclose ⟨~ *the secrets of nature*⟩ ~ *vi* to become unlocked

unlooked-for *adj* not foreseen or expected

unloose *vt* **1** to relax the strain of ⟨~ *a grip*⟩ **2** to release (as if) from restraints; set free **3** to loosen the ties of

unloosen *vt* to unloose

unmade *adj, of a bed* not put in order ready for sleeping

unmannerly *adj* discourteous, rude – **unmannerliness** *n*

unmarried *adj*

unmask *vt* **1** to remove a mask from **2** to reveal the true nature of; expose

unmentionable *adj* not fit to be mentioned; unspeakable

unmentionables *n pl* underwear – euph or humor

unmindful *adj* not taking into account; forgetful *of*

unmistakable *adj* clear, obvious – **unmistakably** *adv*

unmitigated *adj* **1** not diminished in severity, intensity, etc **2** out-and-out, downright ⟨*the evening was an* ~ *disaster*⟩ ⟨*an* ~ *evil*⟩ – **unmitigatedly** *adv*

unnatural *adj* **1** not in accordance with nature or a normal course of events **2a** not in accordance with normal feelings or behaviour; perverse **b** artificial or contrived in manner – **unnaturally** *adv,* **unnaturalness** *n*

unnecessary *adj* not necessary – **unnecessarily** *adv*

unnerve *vt* to deprive of nerve, courage, or the power to act – **unnervingly** *adv*

unnumbered *adj* **1** innumerable **2** without an identifying number ⟨~ *pages*⟩

unobtrusive *adj* not too easily seen or noticed; inconspicuous – **unobtrusively** *adv,* **unobtrusiveness** *n*

unofficial *adj*

unorthodox *adj* not conventional in behaviour, beliefs, doctrine, etc – **unorthodoxly** *adv,* **unorthodoxy** *n*

unpack *vt* **1** to remove the contents of **2** to remove or undo from packing or a container ~ *vi* to set about unpacking sthg – **unpacker** *n*

unparalleled *adj* having no equal or match; unique

unparliamentary *adj* not in accordance with parliamentary practice

unperson *n, pl* **unpersons** a person who, usu for political or ideological reasons, is officially unrecognized

unpick *vt* to undo (e g sewing) by taking out stitches

unplaced *adj, chiefly Br* having failed to finish in a leading place in a competition, esp a horse race

unplayable *adj*

unpleasant *adj* not pleasant or agreeable; displeasing – **unpleasantly** *adv*

unplumbed *adj* not thoroughly explored

unprecedented *adj* having no precedent; novel – **unprecedentedly** *adv*

unprejudiced *adj* impartial, fair

unpretentious *adj* not seeking to impress others by means of wealth, standing, etc; not affected or ostentatious – **unpretentiously** *adv,* **unpretentiousness** *n*

unprincipled *adj* without moral principles; unscrupulous – **unprincipledness** *n*

unprintable *adj* unfit to be printed

unprovoked *adj*

unqualified *adj* **1** not having the necessary qualifications **2** not modified or restricted by reservations ⟨~ *approval*⟩ – **unqualifiedly** *adv*

unquestionable *adj* not able to be called in question; indisputable ⟨~ *evidence*⟩ – **unquestionably** *adv*

unquestioning *adj* not expressing doubt or hesitation ⟨~ *obedience*⟩ – **unquestioningly** *adv*

unquiet *adj* **1** agitated, turbulent **2** physically or mentally restless; uneasy – **unquietly** *adv,* **unquietness** *n*

unquote *n* – used orally to indicate the end of a direct quotation

unravel *vb* **-ll-** (*NAm* **-l-, -ll-**), *vt* **1** to disentangle **2** to clear up or solve (sthg intricate or obscure) ~ *vi* to become unravelled

unreal *adj*

unreasonable *adj* **1** not governed by or acting according to reason ⟨~ *people*⟩ **2** excessive, immoderate ⟨~ *demands*⟩ – **unreasonableness** *n,* **unreasonably** *adv*

unreasoning *adj* not moderated or controlled by reason ⟨~ *fear*⟩ – **unreasoningly** *adv*

unrelenting *adj* **1** not weakening in determination; stern

2 not letting up in vigour, pace, etc – **unrelentingly** adv

unrelieved adj

unremitting adj constant, incessant – **unremittingly** adv

unrequited adj

unreserved adj 1 entire, unqualified ⟨~ *enthusiasm*⟩ 2 frank and open in manner – **unreservedly** adv, **unreservedness** n

unrest n agitation, turmoil

unrestrained adj not held in check; uncontrolled – **unrestrainedly** adv, **unrestrainedness** n

unrivalled, NAm chiefly **unrivaled** adj unequalled, unparalleled

unroll vt to open out; uncoil ~vi to be unrolled; unwind

unruffled adj 1 poised, serene 2 smooth, calm ⟨~ *water*⟩

unruly adj difficult to discipline or manage – **unruliness** n

unsaddle vt 1 to take the saddle from 2 to throw from the saddle ~vi to remove the saddle from a horse

unsaid adj not said or spoken

unsavoury adj disagreeable, distasteful; esp morally offensive

unscathed adj entirely unharmed or uninjured

unschooled adj untaught, untrained

unscramble vt 1 to separate into original components 2 to restore (scrambled communication) to intelligible form – **unscrambler** n

unscrew vt 1 to remove the screws from 2 to loosen or withdraw by turning ~vi to become unscrewed

unscrupulous adj without moral scruples; unprincipled – **unscrupulously** adv, **unscrupulousness** n

unseat vt 1 to dislodge from one's seat, esp on horseback 2 to remove from a (political) position

unseeing adj

unseemly adj not conforming to established standards of good behaviour or taste

¹**unseen** adj done without previous preparation ⟨an ~ *translation*⟩

²**unseen** n, chiefly Br a passage of unprepared translation ⟨doing Latin ~s⟩

unserviceable adj

unsettle vt 1 to move from a settled state or condition 2 to perturb or agitate ~vi to become unsettled – **unsettlingly** adv

unsettled adj 1a not calm or tranquil; disturbed b variable, changeable ⟨~ *weather*⟩ 2 not resolved or worked out; undecided 3 not inhabited or populated ⟨~ *land*⟩ 4 not paid or discharged ⟨~ *debts*⟩ – **unsettledness** n

unsex vt to deprive of sexual power or the typical qualities of one's sex

unshakable, **unshakeable** adj

unsightly adj not pleasing to the eye; ugly

unskilled adj 1 of, being, or requiring workers who are not skilled in any particular branch of work 2 showing a lack of skill

unsociable adj not liking social activity; reserved, solitary – **unsociableness** n, **unsociably** adv, **unsociability** n

unsocial adj 1 marked by or showing a dislike for social interaction 2 Br worked at a time that falls outside the normal working day and precludes participation in normal social activities ⟨~ *hours*⟩ – **unsocially** adv

unsophisticated adj 1 pure, unadulterated 2 not socially or culturally sophisticated 3 simple, straightforward – **unsophistication** n

unsound adj 1 not healthy or whole 2 mentally abnormal ⟨of ~ *mind*⟩ 3 not firmly made, placed, or fixed 4 not valid or true; specious ⟨an ~ *premise*⟩ – **unsoundly** adv, **unsoundness** n

unsparing adj 1 not merciful; hard, ruthless 2 liberal, generous – **unsparingly** adv

unspeakable adj 1 incapable of being expressed in words 2 too terrible or shocking to be expressed – **unspeakably** adv

unspotted adj morally blameless

unstop vt -pp- 1 to free from an obstruction 2 to remove a stopper from

unstressed adj 1 not bearing a stress or accent ⟨~ *syllables*⟩ 2 not subjected to stress ⟨~ *wires*⟩

unstring vt unstrung 1 to loosen or remove the strings of 2 to make mentally disordered or unstable ⟨was unstrung by the news⟩

unstuck adj – **come unstuck** to go wrong; be unsuccessful

unstudied adj 1 not acquired by study 2 not done or planned for effect

unsung adj not celebrated or praised (e g in song or verse)

unswerving adj not deviating; constant ⟨~ *loyalty*⟩

untangle vt to loose from tangles or entanglement; unravel

untapped adj 1 not yet tapped ⟨an ~ *keg*⟩ 2 not drawn on or exploited ⟨as yet ~ *markets*⟩

untenable adj not able to be defended ⟨an ~ *opinion*⟩ – **untenability** n

unthinkable adj contrary to what is acceptable or probable; out of the question – **unthinkably** adv, **unthinkability** n

unthinking adj not taking thought; heedless, unmindful – **unthinkingly** adv

unthought adj not anticipated; unexpected – often + of or on

untie vt 1 to free from sthg that fastens or restrains 2a to separate out the knotted parts of b to disentangle, resolve ~vi to become untied

¹**until** prep 1 up to as late as ⟨not available ~ *tomorrow*⟩ 2 up to as far as ⟨stay on the train ~ *Birmingham*⟩

²**until** conj up to the time that; until such time as

untimely adj 1 occurring before the natural or proper time; premature ⟨~ *death*⟩ 2 inopportune, unseasonable ⟨an ~ *joke*⟩ ⟨~ *frost*⟩ – **untimeliness** n

unto prep, archaic TO 1, 2, 3

untold adj 1 incalculable, vast 2 not told or related

¹**untouchable** adj 1 that may not be touched 2 lying beyond reach ⟨~ *mineral resources buried deep within the earth*⟩ – **untouchability** n

²**untouchable** n sby or sthg untouchable; specif, often cap a member of a large formerly segregated hereditary group in India who in traditional Hindu belief can defile a member of a higher caste by contact or proximity

untoward adj not favourable; adverse, unfortunate – **untowardly** adv, **untowardness** n

untrue adj 1 not faithful; disloyal 2 not level or exact ⟨~ *doors and windows*⟩ 3 inaccurate, false – **untruly** adv

untruth n 1 lack of truthfulness 2 sthg untrue; a falsehood

untruthful adj not telling the truth; false, lying – **untruthfully** adv, **untruthfulness** n

untutored adj 1 having no formal learning or education 2 not produced by instruction; native ⟨his ~ *shrewdness*⟩

unused adj 1 unaccustomed – usu + to 2a fresh, new b not used up ⟨~ *sick leave*⟩

unusual *adj* **1** uncommon, rare **2** different, unique ⟨*an ~ painting*⟩ – **unusually** *adv*, **unusualness** *n*

unutterable *adj* **1** beyond the powers of description; inexpressible **2** out-and-out, downright ⟨*an ~ fool*⟩ – **unutterably** *adv*

unvarnished *adj* not adorned or glossed; plain ⟨*told the ~ truth*⟩

unveil *vt* **1** to remove a veil or covering from **2** to make public; divulge ~ *vi* to remove a veil or protective cloak

unvoiced *adj* **1** not expressed in words **2** voiceless

unwarranted *adj* not justified; (done) without good reason

unwell *adj* in poor health

unwieldy *adj* difficult to move or handle; cumbersome – **unwieldily** *adv*, **unwieldiness** *n*

unwind *vb* **unwound** *vt* to cause to uncoil; unroll ~ *vi* **1** to become unwound **2** to become less tense; relax

unwitting *adj* **1** not intended; inadvertent ⟨*an ~ mistake*⟩ **2** ignorant, unaware ⟨*an ~ accomplice*⟩ – **unwittingly** *adv*

unwonted *adj* out of the ordinary; unusual – **unwontedly** *adv*, **unwontedness** *n*

unwritten *adj* **1** not (formally) written down **2** containing no writing; blank

unyielding *adj* **1** lacking in softness or flexibility **2** firm, obdurate – **unyieldingly** *adv*

unzip *vb* **-pp-** to open (as if) by means of a zip

¹**up** *adv* **1a** at or towards a relatively high level ⟨*live ~ in the mountains*⟩ **b** from beneath the ground or water to the surface **c** above the horizon **d** upstream **e** in or to a raised or upright position ⟨*hands ~!*⟩; *specif* out of bed ⟨*soon be ~ and about*⟩ **f** off or out of the ground or a surface ⟨*pull ~ a daisy*⟩ **g** UPWARDS 1b **h** to the top; *esp* so as to be full ⟨*top ~ the radiator*⟩ **2a** into a state of, or with, greater intensity or activity ⟨*speak ~*⟩ **b** into a faster pace or higher gear **3a** in or into a relatively high condition or status ⟨*family went ~ in the world*⟩ – sometimes used interjectionally as an expression of approval ⟨*~ BBC 2! – The Listener*⟩ **b** above a normal or former level ⟨*sales are ~*⟩: e g **(1)** UPWARDS 2b **(2)** higher in price **c** ahead of an opponent ⟨*we're 3 points ~*⟩ **4a(1)** in or into existence, evidence, prominence, or prevalence ⟨*new houses haven't been ~ long*⟩ **(2)** in or into operation or full power ⟨*get ~ steam*⟩ **b** under consideration or attention; *esp* before a court ⟨*~ for robbery*⟩ **5** so as to be together ⟨*add ~ the figures*⟩ **6a** entirely, completely ⟨*eat ~ your spinach*⟩ **b** so as to be firmly closed, joined, or fastened **c** so as to be fully inflated **7** in or into storage **8** in a direction conventionally the opposite of down: **a(1)** to windward **(2)** with rudder to leeward – used with reference to a ship's helm **b** in or towards the north **c** so as to arrive or approach ⟨*walked ~ to her*⟩ **d** to or at the rear of a theatrical stage **e** *chiefly Br* to or in the capital of a country or a university city ⟨*~ in London*⟩ **9** in or into parts ⟨*chop ~*⟩ **10** to a stop – usu + *draw, bring, fetch,* or *pull*

²**up** *adj* **1** moving, inclining, bound, or directed upwards or up **2** ready, prepared ⟨*dinner's ~!*⟩ **3** going on, taking place; *esp* being the matter ⟨*what's ~?*⟩ **4** at an end ⟨*time's ~*⟩; *esp* hopeless ⟨*it's all ~ with him now*⟩ **5a** well informed **b** ABREAST 2 ⟨*~ on her homework*⟩ **6** of a road being repaired; having a broken surface **7** ahead of an opponent ⟨*2 strokes ~ after 9 holes*⟩ **8** of a ball in court games having bounced only once on the ground or floor after being hit by one's opponent and therefore playable ⟨*not ~*⟩ **9** *Br*, of a train travelling towards a large town; *specif* travelling towards London – **up against**

faced with; confronting – **up against it** in great difficulties

³**up** *vb* **-pp-** *vi* – used with *and* and another verb to indicate that the action of the following verb is either surprisingly or abruptly initiated ⟨*he ~ped and married*⟩ ~ *vt* **1** to increase ⟨*they ~ped the price of milk*⟩ **2** RAISE 8c

⁴**up** *prep* **1a** up along, round, through, towards, in, into, or on ⟨*walk ~ the hill*⟩ ⟨*water ~ my nose*⟩ **b** at the top of ⟨*the office is ~ those stairs*⟩ **2** *Br* (up) to ⟨*going ~ the West End*⟩ – nonstandard

⁵**up** *n* **1** (sthg in) a high position or an upward incline **2** a period or state of prosperity or success ⟨*has had some ~s and downs*⟩ **3** the part of a ball's trajectory in which it is still rising after having bounced ⟨*hit the ball on the ~*⟩

up-and-coming *adj* likely to advance or succeed

up-and-up *n*, *chiefly Br* a potentially or increasingly successful course – chiefly in *on the up-and-up*

¹**upbeat** *n* an unaccented (e g the last) beat in a musical bar

²**upbeat** *adj*, *chiefly NAm* optimistic, cheerful – *infml*

upbraid *vt* to scold or reproach severely – **upbraider** *n*

upbringing *n* a particular way of bringing up a child ⟨*had a strict Calvinist ~*⟩

upcoming *adj*, *NAm* about to happen; forthcoming

up-country *adj* **1** (characteristic) of an inland, upland, or outlying region **2** not socially or culturally sophisticated – **up-country** *n*, **up-country** *adv*

¹**update** *vt* to bring up to date

²**update** *n* an act of updating ⟨*a computer file ~*⟩

upend *vt* **1** to cause to stand on end **2** to knock down

upgrade *vt* to raise or improve the grade of; *esp* to advance to a job requiring a higher level of skill, esp as part of a training programme

upheaval *n* **1** an upheaving, esp of part of the earth's crust **2** (an instance of) extreme agitation or radical change

¹**uphill** *n* rising ground

²**uphill** *adv* upwards on a hill or incline

³**uphill** *adj* **1** situated on elevated ground **2** going up; ascending **3** difficult, laborious ⟨*an ~ struggle*⟩

uphold *vt* **upheld 1** to give support to; maintain **2** to support against an opponent or challenge ⟨*~ the ruling of the lower court*⟩ – **upholder** *n*

upholster *vt* to provide with upholstery – **upholsterer** *n*

upholstery *n* materials (e g fabric, padding, and springs) used to make a soft covering, esp for a seat

upkeep *n* (the cost of) maintaining or being maintained in good condition

upland *n* (an area of) high (inland) land – often pl with sing. meaning – **upland** *adj*, **uplander** *n*

¹**uplift** *vt* **1** to raise, elevate **2** to improve the spiritual, social, or intellectual condition of – **uplifter** *n*

²**uplift** *n* **1** a moral or social improvement **2** influences intended to uplift

upon *prep* on – *chiefly fml*

¹**upper** *adj* **1a** higher in physical position, rank, or order **b** farther inland ⟨*the ~ Thames*⟩ **2** being the branch of a legislature consisting of 2 houses that is usu more restricted in membership, is in many cases less powerful, and possesses greater traditional prestige than the lower house **3** *cap* being a later division of the specified geological period or series ⟨*Upper Carboniferous*⟩

²**upper** *n* the parts of a shoe or boot above the sole – **on one's uppers** at the end of one's means

³**upper** *n* a stimulant drug; *esp* amphetamine – *infml*

upper-case *adj* CAPITAL 2

upper case *n* **1** a type case containing capitals and usu small capitals, fractions, symbols, and accents **2** capital letters

upper class *n* the class occupying the highest position in a society; *esp* the wealthy or the aristocracy – **upper-class** *adj*

upper crust *n sing or pl in constr* the highest social class – infml

uppercut *n* a swinging blow directed upwards with a bent arm – **uppercut** *vb*

upper hand *n* mastery, advantage – + *the*

uppermost *adv* in or into the highest or most prominent position – **uppermost** *adj*

uppish *adj* **1** hit up and travelling far in the air **2** uppity – infml – **uppishly** *adv*, **uppishness** *n*

uppity *adj* putting on airs of superiority; supercilious – infml – **uppityness** *n*

¹upright *adj* **1a** perpendicular, vertical **b** erect in carriage or posture **c** having the main part perpendicular ⟨an ~ freezer⟩ **2** marked by strong moral rectitude – **uprightly** *adv*, **uprightness** *n*

²upright *adv* in an upright or vertical position

³upright *n* **1** sthg that stands upright **2 upright, upright piano** a piano with vertical frame and strings

uprising *n* a usu localized rebellion

uproar *n* a state of commotion or violent disturbance

uproarious *adj* **1** marked by noise and disorder **2** extremely funny ⟨an ~ comedy⟩ – **uproariously** *adv*, **uproariousness** *n*

uproot *vt* **1** to remove by pulling up by the roots **2** to displace from a country or traditional habitat or environment – **uprooter** *n*

ups and downs *n pl* alternating rises and falls, esp in fortune

¹upset *vb* **-tt-; upset** *vt* **1** to thicken and shorten (e g a heated iron bar) by hammering on the end **2** to overturn, knock over **3a** to trouble mentally or emotionally **b** to throw into disorder **4** to make somewhat ill ~ *vi* to become overturned – **upsetter** *n*

²upset *n* **1** a minor physical disorder ⟨a stomach ~⟩ **2** an emotional disturbance **3** an unexpected defeat (e g in politics)

upshot *n* the final result; the outcome – infml

upside down *adv* **1** with the upper and the lower parts reversed **2** in or into great disorder or confusion – **upside-down** *adj*

¹upstage *adv* at the rear of a theatrical stage; *also* away from the audience or film or television camera

²upstage *adj* **1** of or at the rear of a stage **2** haughty, aloof

³upstage *n* the part of a stage that is farthest from the audience or camera

⁴upstage *vt* **1** to force (an actor) to face away from the audience by holding a dialogue with him/her from an upstage position **2** to steal attention from

¹upstairs *adv* **1** up the stairs; to or on a higher floor **2** to or at a higher position

²upstairs *adj* situated above the stairs, esp on an upper floor

³upstairs *n pl but sing or pl in constr* the part of a building above the ground floor

upstanding *adj* **1** erect, upright **2** marked by integrity; honest – **upstandingness** *n*

upstart *n* one who has risen suddenly (e g from a low position to wealth or power); *esp* one who claims more personal importance than he/she warrants – **upstart** *adj*

upstream *adv or adj* in the direction opposite to the flow of a stream

upsurge *n* a rapid or sudden rise

upswing *n* **1** an upward swing **2** a marked increase or rise

uptake *n* **1** an absorbing and incorporating, esp into a living organism **2** understanding, comprehension ⟨quick on the ~⟩ – infml

uptight *adj* **1** tense, nervous, or uneasy **2** angry, indignant *USE* infml – **uptightness** *n*

up to *prep* **1** – used to indicate an upward limit or boundary ⟨sank ~ his knees in mud⟩ ⟨~ 50,000 copies a month⟩ **2** as far as; until **3a** equal to ⟨didn't feel ~ par⟩ **b** good enough for ⟨my German isn't ~ reading Schiller⟩ **4** engaged in (a suspect activity) ⟨what's he ~?⟩ **5** being the responsibility of ⟨it's ~ me⟩

up-to-date *adj* **1** including the latest information **2** abreast of the times; modern – **up-to-dateness** *n*

up-to-the-minute *adj* **1** including the very latest information **2** completely up-to-date

uptown *adv, adj, or n, chiefly NAm* (to, towards, or in) the upper part or residential district of a town or city

¹upturn *vt* **1** to turn up or over **2** to direct upwards ~ *vi* to turn upwards

²upturn *n* an upward turn, esp towards better conditions or higher prices

upward *adj* moving or extending upwards; ascending ⟨an ~ movement⟩ – **upwardly** *adv*

upwards *adv* **1a** from a lower to a higher place, condition, or level; in the opposite direction from down **b** so as to expose a particular surface ⟨held out his hand, palm ~⟩ **2a** to an indefinitely greater amount, price, figure, age, or rank ⟨from £5 ~⟩ **b** towards a higher number, degree, or rate ⟨attendance figures have risen ~⟩

upwards of *adv* more than; IN EXCESS OF ⟨they cost ~ £25⟩

uranium *n* a heavy radioactive polyvalent metallic element found in pitchblende

Uranus *n* the planet 7th in order from the sun

urban *adj* (characteristic) of or constituting a city or town

urbane *adj* notably polite or smooth in manner; suave – **urbanely** *adv*, **urbanity** *n*

urbanize, -ise *vt* **1** to cause to take on urban characteristics **2** to impart an urban way of life to – **urbanization** *n*

urchin *n* **1** a hedgehog **2** a mischievous and impudent young boy, esp one who is scruffy **3** SEA URCHIN

-ure *suffix* (vb → n) **1** act or process of ⟨exposure⟩ ⟨closure⟩ **2** body performing (a specified function) ⟨legislature⟩

¹urge *vt* **1** to advocate or demand earnestly or pressingly **2** to undertake the accomplishment of with energy or enthusiasm **3a** to try to persuade **b** to serve as a motive or reason for **4** to force or impel in a specified direction or to greater speed ~ *vi* to urge an argument, claim, etc – **urger** *n*

²urge *n* a force or impulse that urges

urgent *adj* **1** calling for immediate attention; pressing ⟨~ appeals⟩ **2** conveying a sense of urgency – **urgency** *n*, **urgently** *adv*

uric *adj* of or found in urine

urinal *n* a fixture used for urinating into, esp by men; *also* a room, building, etc containing a urinal

urinary *adj* **1** relating to (or occurring in or constituting the organs concerned with the formation and discharge of) urine **2** excreted as or in urine

urinate *vi* to discharge urine – **urination** *n*

urine *n* waste material that is secreted by the kidney in vertebrates and forms a clear amber and usu slightly acid fluid in mammals but is semisolid in birds and reptiles – **urinous** *adj*

urn *n* **1** an ornamental vase on a pedestal used esp for preserving the ashes of the dead after cremation **2** a large closed container, usu with a tap at its base, in which large quantities of tea, coffee, etc may be heated or served

Ursa Major *n* the most conspicuous of the N constellations that is situated near the N pole of the heavens and contains 7 stars pictured as a plough, 2 of which are in a line indicating the direction of the Pole Star

Ursa Minor *n* a constellation that includes the N pole of the heavens and 7 stars which resemble Ursa Major with the Pole Star at the tip of the handle

urticaria *n* an allergic disorder marked by raised itching patches of skin and caused by contact with a specific factor (e g a food or drug) – **urticarial** *adj*

us *pron* **1** objective case of WE ⟨*please let ~ go*⟩ **2** chiefly Br me ⟨*give ~ a kiss*⟩ – nonstandard

usage *n* **1a** (an instance of) established and generally accepted practice or procedure **b** (an instance of) the way in which words and phrases are actually used in a language **2** the action, amount, or manner of using

¹use *n* **1a** using or being used ⟨*in daily ~*⟩ ⟨*made good ~ of his time*⟩ **b** a way of using sthg ⟨*a machine with many different ~s*⟩ **2a** habitual or customary usage **b** a liturgical form or observance; *esp* a liturgy having modifications peculiar to a local church or religious order **3a** the right or benefit of using sthg ⟨*gave him the ~ of her car*⟩ **b** the ability or power to use sthg (e g a limb) **c** the legal enjoyment of property **4a** a purpose or end ⟨*put learning to practical ~*⟩ **b** practical worth or application ⟨*saving things that might be of ~*⟩ **5** a favourable attitude; a liking ⟨*had no ~ for modern art*⟩

²use *vb* used *vt* **1** to put into action or service **2** to consume or take (e g drugs) regularly **3** to carry out sthg by means of ⟨*~ tact*⟩ **4** to expend or consume **5** to treat in a specified manner ⟨*~d the prisoners cruelly*⟩ ~ *vi* – used in the past with *to* to indicate a former fact or state ⟨*~d to dislike fish*⟩ ⟨*didn't ~d to be so pernickety*⟩ – **user** *n*, **usable** *adj*, **usably** *adv*

used *adj* **1** employed in accomplishing sthg **2** that has endured use; *specif* secondhand **3** accustomed ⟨*I'm not ~ to drinking – SEU S*⟩

useful *adj* **1** having utility, esp practical worth or applicability; *also* helpful **2** of highly satisfactory quality – **usefully** *adv*, **usefulness** *n*

useless *adj* **1** having or being of no use **2** inept – *infml* – **uselessly** *adv*, **uselessness** *n*

use up *vt* **1** to consume completely **2** to deprive wholly of strength or useful properties; exhaust

¹usher *n* **1** an officer or servant who acts as a doorkeeper (e g in a court of law) **2** an officer who walks before a person of rank **3** *fem* **usherette** /-1ret/ one who shows people to their seats (e g in a theatre)

²usher *vt* **1** to conduct to a place **2** to precede as an usher **3** to inaugurate, introduce ⟨*~ in a new era*⟩

usual *adj* **1** in accordance with usage, custom, or habit; normal **2** commonly or ordinarily used ⟨*followed his ~ route*⟩ – **usually** *adv*, **usualness** *n* – **as usual** in the accustomed or habitual way ⟨*as usual he was late*⟩

usurer *n* one who lends money, esp at an exorbitant rate

usurp *vt* to seize and possess by force or without right ⟨*~ a throne*⟩ ~ *vi* to seize possession wrongfully – **usurper** *n*, **usurpation** *n*

usury *n* **1** the lending of money at (exorbitant) interest **2** an exorbitant or illegal rate or amount of interest – **usurious** *adj*, **usuriously** *adv*

utensil *n* **1** an implement, vessel, or device used in the household, esp the kitchen **2** a useful tool or implement

uterine *adj* **1a** born of the same mother but by a different father **b** matrilineal **2** of or affecting the uterus

uterus *n*, *pl* **uteri** *also* **uteruses** **1** an organ of the female mammal for containing and usu for nourishing the young during development before birth **2** a structure in some lower animals analogous to the uterus in which eggs or young develop

¹utilitarian *n* an advocate of utilitarianism

²utilitarian *adj* **1** marked by utilitarian views or practices **2a** of or aiming at utility **b** made for or aiming at practical use rather than beautiful appearance

utilitarianism *n* **1** a doctrine that the criterion for correct conduct should be the usefulness of its consequences; *specif* a theory that the aim of action should be the greatest happiness of the greatest number **2** utilitarian character, spirit, or quality

¹utility *n* **1** fitness for some purpose; usefulness **2** sthg useful or designed for use **3** a business organization performing a public service

²utility *adj* **1** capable of serving as a substitute in various roles or positions ⟨*a ~ player*⟩ **2** serving primarily for utility rather than beauty; utilitarian ⟨*~ furniture*⟩ **3** designed or adapted for general use

utilize, -ise *vt* to make use of; turn to practical use or account – **utilizable** *adj*, **utilizer** *n*, **utilization** *n*

¹utmost *adj* **1** situated at the farthest or most distant point; extreme **2** of the greatest or highest degree ⟨*a matter of ~ concern*⟩

²utmost *n* **1** the highest point or degree **2** the best of one's abilities, powers, etc ⟨*did his ~ to help*⟩

utopia *n* **1** often cap a place or state of ideal (political and social) perfection **2** an impractical scheme for social or political improvement

¹utopian *adj*, *often cap* **1** impossibly ideal, esp in social and political organization **2** proposing impractically ideal social and political schemes – **utopianism** *n*

²utopian *n* **1** a believer in human perfectibility **2** an advocate of utopian schemes

¹utter *adj* absolute, total ⟨*~ desolation*⟩ – **utterly** *adv*

²utter *vt* **1a** to emit as a sound **b** to give (verbal) expression to **2** to put (e g currency) into circulation; *specif* to circulate (e g a counterfeit note) as if legal or genuine – used technically – **utterer** *n*, **utterable** *adj*

utterance *n* **1** an oral or written statement **2** vocal expression; speech – esp in **give utterance to**

U-turn *n* **1** a turn executed by a motor vehicle without reversing that takes it back along the direction from which it has come **2** a total reversal of policy ⟨*a ~ on wage controls – The Economist*⟩

uvula *n*, *pl* **uvulas, uvulae** the fleshy lobe hanging in the middle of the back of the soft palate

uvular *adj* **1** of the uvula ⟨*~ glands*⟩ **2** produced with the aid of the uvula ⟨*a French ~ /r/*⟩ – **uvularly** *adv*

uxorious *adj* (excessively) fond of or submissive to one's wife – fml – **uxoriously** *adv*, **uxoriousness** *n*

V

v *n*, *pl* **v's** *or* **vs** *often cap* **1** (a graphic representation of or device for reproducing) the 22nd letter of the English alphabet **2** five

V-1 *n* a flying bomb used by the Germans in WW II, esp against targets in England

V-2 *n* a long-range rocket used by the Germans in WW II, esp against targets in England

vac *n, Br* a vacation, esp from college or university – *infml*

vacancy *n* 1 physical or mental inactivity; idleness 2 a vacant office, post, or room 3 an empty space 4 the state of being vacant

vacant *adj* 1 not occupied by an incumbent or officer ⟨*a ~ office*⟩ 2 without an occupant ⟨*a ~ room*⟩ 3 free from activity or work ⟨*~ hours*⟩ 4a stupid, foolish ⟨*a ~ mind*⟩ b expressionless ⟨*a ~ look*⟩ 5 not lived in ⟨*~ houses*⟩ – **vacantly** *adv,* **vacantness** *n*

vacant possession *n* availability (e g of a house) for immediate occupation

vacate *vt* 1 to annul legally 2 to give up the possession or occupancy of 3 to make vacant; leave empty ⟨*with instructions to ~ the cinema*⟩

¹vacation *n* 1 a scheduled period during which activity (e g of a university) is suspended 2 an act of vacating 3 *chiefly NAm* a holiday ⟨*had a restful ~ at the beach*⟩

²vacation *vi, chiefly NAm* to take or spend a holiday – **vacationer** *n*

vaccinate *vt* 1 to inoculate with cowpox virus in order to produce immunity to smallpox 2 to administer a vaccine to, usu by injection ~ *vi* to perform or practise the administration of vaccine – **vaccinator** *n,* **vaccination** *n*

¹vaccine *adj* of cowpox or vaccination ⟨*a ~ pustule*⟩

²vaccine *n* material (e g a preparation of killed or modified virus or bacteria) used in vaccinating – **vaccinal** *adj*

vacillate *vi* 1a to sway through imperfect balance b to fluctuate, oscillate 2 to hesitate or waver in choosing between opinions or courses of action – **vacillatingly** *adv,* **vacillator** *n,* **vacillation** *n*

vacuity *n* 1 an empty space 2 vacuousness, meaninglessness 3 sthg (e g an idea) that is stupid or inane

vacuous *adj* 1 empty 2 stupid, inane ⟨*a ~ expression*⟩ 3 idle, aimless – **vacuously** *adv,* **vacuousness** *n*

¹vacuum *n, pl* **vacuums, vacua** 1a a space absolutely devoid of matter b a space from which as much air or other substance as possible has been removed (e g by an air pump) c an air pressure below atmospheric pressure 2a a vacant space; a void b a state of isolation from outside influences 3 VACUUM CLEANER

²vacuum *adj* of, containing, producing, or using a partial vacuum

³vacuum *vb* to clean using a vacuum cleaner

vacuum cleaner *n* an (electrical) appliance for removing dust and dirt (e g from carpets or upholstery) by suction – **vacuum-clean** *vb*

vacuum flask *n, chiefly Br* a cylindrical container with a vacuum between an inner and an outer wall used to keep material, esp liquids, either hot or cold for considerable periods

vacuum-packed *adj* packed in a wrapping from which most of the air has been removed ⟨*~ bacon*⟩

vacuum pump *n* a pump for producing a vacuum

vade mecum *n, pl* **vade mecums** 1 a book for ready reference 2 sthg regularly carried about by a person

¹vagabond *adj* 1 (characteristic) of a wanderer 2 leading an unsettled, irresponsible, or disreputable life – **vagabondish** *adj*

²vagabond *n* a wanderer; *esp* a tramp – **vagabondage** *n,* **vagabondism** *n*

vagary *n* an erratic, unpredictable, or extravagant notion, action, etc – **vagarious** *adj*

vagina *n, pl* **vaginae, vaginas** 1 a canal in a female mammal that leads from the uterus to the external orifice of the genital canal 2 a sheath; *esp* a leaf base that forms a sheath, usu round the main stem – **vaginal** *adj*

¹vagrant *n* 1 one who has no established residence or lawful means of support 2 a wanderer, vagabond

²vagrant *adj* 1 wandering about from place to place, usu with no means of support 2 having no fixed course; random – **vagrancy** *n,* **vagrantly** *adv*

vague *adj* 1a not clearly defined, expressed, or understood; indistinct ⟨*a ~ idea*⟩ b not clearly felt or sensed ⟨*a ~ longing*⟩ 2 not thinking or expressing one's thoughts clearly ⟨*~ about dates and places*⟩ – **vaguely** *adv,* **vagueness** *n*

vain *adj* 1 idle, worthless 2 unsuccessful, ineffectual 3 having or showing excessive pride in one's appearance, ability, etc; conceited – **vainly** *adv,* **vainness** *n* – **in vain** to no end; without success or result

vainglorious *adj* boastful – **vaingloriously** *adv,* **vaingloriousness** *n*

vainglory *n* 1 excessive or ostentatious pride 2 vanity

valance *n* 1 a piece of drapery hung as a border, esp along the edge of a bed, canopy, or shelf 2 a pelmet

vale *n* VALLEY 1a – poetic or in place-names

valediction *n* 1 an act of bidding farewell 2 an address or statement of farewell or leave-taking *USE* fml

¹valedictory *adj* expressing or containing a farewell – fml

²valedictory *n* VALEDICTION 2 – fml

valency, *NAm chiefly* **valence** *n* 1 the degree of combining power of an element or radical as shown by the number of atomic weights of a univalent element (e g hydrogen) with which the atomic weight of the element will combine or for which it can be substituted or with which it can be compared 2 a unit of valency ⟨*the 4 valencies of carbon*⟩

valentine *n* 1 a sweetheart chosen on St Valentine's Day 2 a gift or greeting card sent or given, esp to a sweetheart, on St Valentine's Day

valerian *n* any of several usu perennial plants, many of which possess medicinal properties

valet *n* a gentleman's male servant who performs personal services (e g taking care of clothing); *also* an employee (e g of a hotel) who performs similar services for patrons

valetudinarian *n* a person of a weak or sickly constitution; *esp* a hypochondriac – fml – **valetudinarian** *adj,* **valetudinarianism** *n*

valiant *adj* characterized by or showing valour; courageous – **valiance** *n,* **valiant** *n,* **valiantly** *adv,* **valiantness** *n*

valid *adj* 1 having legal efficacy; *esp* executed according to the proper formalities ⟨*a ~ contract*⟩ 2a well-grounded or justifiable; relevant and meaningful b logically sound – **validly** *adv,* **validness** *n,* **validity** *n*

validate *vt* 1 to make legally valid 2 to corroborate, authenticate ⟨*experiments to ~ his hypothesis*⟩ – **validation** *n*

valley *n* 1a an elongated depression of the earth's surface, usu between hills or mountains b an area drained by a river and its tributaries 2a a hollow, depression b the internal angle formed at the meeting of 2 roof surfaces

valour, *NAm chiefly* **valor** *n* strength of mind or spirit that enables sby to encounter danger with firmness; personal bravery

valse *n* a (concert) waltz

¹valuable *adj* 1 having (high) money value 2 of great use or worth ⟨*~ advice*⟩ – **valuableness** *n,* **valuably** *adv*

²valuable *n* a usu personal possession of relatively great money value – usu pl

valuation *n* 1 the act of valuing sthg, esp property 2 the estimated or determined value, esp market value, of a thing 3 judgment or appraisal of worth or character – **valuational** *adj,* **valuationally** *adv*

¹value *n* 1 a fair return or equivalent for sthg exchanged 2 the worth in money or commodities of sthg 3 relative worth, utility, or importance 〈*had nothing of* ~ *to say*〉 **4a** a numerical quantity assigned or computed **b** the magnitude of a physical quantity **5** the relative duration of a musical note **6a** relative lightness or darkness of a colour **b** the relation of one part in a picture to another with respect to lightness and darkness **7** sthg (e g a principle or quality) intrinsically valuable or desirable **8** DENOMINATION 3

²value *vt* **1a** to estimate the worth of in terms of money 〈~ *a necklace*〉 **b** to rate in terms of usefulness, importance, etc **2** to consider or rate highly; esteem 〈*a* ~d *helper*〉 – **valuer** *n*

value-added tax *n, often cap V, A, & T* a tax levied at each stage of the production and distribution of a commodity and passed on to the consumer as a form of purchase tax

valve *n* **1** a structure, esp in the heart or a vein, that closes temporarily to obstruct passage of material or permits movement of fluid in 1 direction only **2a** any of numerous mechanical devices by which the flow of liquid, gas, or loose material in bulk may be controlled, usu to allow movement in 1 direction only **b** a device in a brass musical instrument for quickly varying the tube length in order to change the fundamental tone by a definite interval **3** any of the separate joined pieces that make up the shell of an (invertebrate) animal; *specif* either of the 2 halves of the shell of a bivalve mollusc **4** any of the segments or pieces into which a ripe seed capsule or pod separates **5** *chiefly Br* a vacuum- or gas-filled device for the regulation of electric current by the control of free electrons or ions – **valved** *adj*, **valveless** *adj*

valvular *adj* **1** resembling or functioning as a valve; *also* opening by valves **2** of a valve, esp of the heart

vamoose *vi, chiefly NAm* to depart quickly – slang

¹vamp *n* **1** the part of a shoe or boot covering the front of the foot **2** a simple improvised musical accompaniment

²vamp *vt* **1** to provide (a shoe) with a new vamp **2** to patch (sthg old) with a new part 〈~ *up old sermons*〉 ~ *vi* to play a musical vamp – **vamper** *n*

³vamp *n* a woman who uses her charm to seduce and exploit men

vampire *n* **1** a dead person believed to come from the grave at night and suck the blood of sleeping people **2** any of various S American bats that feed on blood and are dangerous to human beings and domestic animals, esp as transmitters of disease (e g rabies); *also* any of several other bats that do not feed on blood but are sometimes reputed to do so

¹van *n, dial Eng* a winnowing device (e g a fan)

²van *n* the vanguard

³van *n* **1** an enclosed motor vehicle used for transport of goods, animals, furniture, etc **2** *chiefly Br* an enclosed railway goods wagon

vanadium *n* a malleable polyvalent metallic element found combined in minerals and used esp to form alloys

vandal *n* **1** *cap* a member of a Germanic people who overran Gaul, Spain, and N Africa in the 4th and 5th c AD and in 455 sacked Rome **2** one who wilfully or ignorantly destroys or defaces (public) property – **vandal** *adj, often cap*, **Vandalic** *adj*

vandalism *n* wilful destruction or defacement of property – **vandalize** *vt*, **vandalistic** *adj*

vane *n* **1** WEATHER VANE **2** a thin flat or curved object that is rotated about an axis by wind or water 〈*the* ~s *of a windmill*〉; *also* a device revolving in a similar manner and moving in water or air 〈*the* ~s *of a propeller*〉 **3** the flat expanded part of a feather **4a** the target of a levelling staff

b any of the sights of a compass or quadrant – **vaned** *adj*

vanguard *n* **1** *sing or pl in constr* the troops moving at the head of an army **2** the forefront of an action or movement

vanilla *n* **1** any of a genus of tropical American climbing orchids whose long capsular fruits yield an important flavouring; *also* VANILLA POD **2** a commercially important extract of the vanilla pod that is used esp as a flavouring

vanish *vi* **1a** to pass quickly from sight; disappear **b** to cease to exist **2** to assume the value zero ~ *vt* to cause to disappear – **vanisher** *n*

vanishing cream *n* a light cosmetic cream used chiefly as a foundation for face powder

vanishing point *n* **1** a point at which receding parallel lines seem to meet when represented in linear perspective **2** a point at which sthg disappears or ceases to exist

vanity *n* **1** sthg vain, empty, or worthless **2** the quality of being vain or futile; worthlessness **3** excessive pride in oneself; conceit

vanity case *n* a small bag used by women for carrying toilet articles and cosmetics

vanquish *vt* **1** to overcome, conquer 〈*the* ~ed *foe*〉 **2** to gain mastery over (an emotion, passion, etc) – **vanquishable** *adj*, **vanquisher** *n*

vantage *n* **1** a position giving a strategic advantage or commanding perspective **2** *Br* ADVANTAGE 3

vapid *adj* lacking liveliness, interest, or force; insipid – **vapidly** *adv*, **vapidness** *n*, **vapidity** *n*

vaporize, -ise *vt* **1** to convert (e g by the application of heat) into vapour **2** to destroy by conversion into vapour ~ *vi* to become vaporized – **vaporizable** *adj*, **vaporizer** *n*, **vaporization** *n*

vaporous *adj* **1** resembling, consisting of, or characteristic of vapour **2** producing vapours; volatile **3** containing or obscured by vapours; misty – **vaporously** *adv*, **vaporousness** *n*

¹vapour, *NAm chiefly* **vapor** *n* **1** smoke, fog, etc suspended floating in the air and impairing its transparency **2** a substance in the gaseous state; *esp* such a substance that is liquid under normal conditions **3** *pl, archaic* a depressed or hysterical condition

²vapour, *NAm chiefly* **vapor** *vi* **1** to rise or pass off in vapour **2** to emit vapour

vapour trail *n* a contrail

¹variable *adj* **1** subject to variation or changes 〈~ *winds*〉 **2** having the characteristics of a variable 〈*a* ~ *number*〉 **3** *of a biological group or character* not true to type; aberrant – **variableness** *n*, **variably** *adv*, **variability** *n*

²variable *n* **1** sthg (e g a variable star) that is variable **2** (a symbol representing) a quantity that may assume any of a set of values

variance *n* **1** a discrepancy **2** dissension, dispute – esp in *at variance* **3** the square of the standard deviation – *at variance* not in harmony or agreement

¹variant *adj* varying (slightly) from the standard form 〈~ *readings*〉

²variant *n* any of 2 or more people or things displaying usu slight differences: e g **a** sthg that shows variation from a type or norm **b** any of 2 or more different spellings, pronunciations, or forms of the same word

variation *n* **1a** varying or being varied **b** an instance of varying **c** the extent to which or the range in which a thing varies **2** DECLINATION 3 **3** a change in the mean motion or orbit of a celestial body **4** the repetition of a musical theme with modifications in rhythm, tune, harmony, or key **5a** divergence in characteristics of an organism or genotype from those typical or usual of its group **b** an individual or group exhibiting variation **6** a solo dance in ballet – **variational** *adj*, **variationally** *adv*

varicoloured *adj* having various colours

varicose *also* **varicosed** *adj* abnormally swollen or dilated ⟨~ *veins*⟩ – **varicosity** *n*

varied *adj* **1** having numerous forms or types; diverse **2** variegated – **variedly** *adv*

variegate *vt* to diversify in appearance, esp with patches of different colours; dapple – **variegator** *n*, **variegation** *n*

variety *n* **1** the state of having different forms or types; diversity **2** an assortment of different things, esp of a particular class **3a** sthg differing from others of the same general kind; a sort **b** any of various groups of plants or animals ranking below a species **4** theatrical entertainment consisting of separate performances (e g of songs, skits, acrobatics, etc)

variety meat *n*, *chiefly NAm* edible offal of a slaughtered animal

variform *adj* varied in form

variorum *n* an edition or text with notes by different people

various *adj* **1a** of differing kinds; diverse ⟨~ *remedies*⟩ **b** dissimilar in nature or form; unlike **2** having a number of different aspects or characteristics ⟨~ *genius*⟩ **3** more than one; several ⟨*stop at ~ towns*⟩ – **variousness** *n*

variously *adv* in various ways; at various times

varlet *n* a base unprincipled person

varmint *n*, *dial or NAm* **1** an animal or bird considered a pest **2** a rascal

¹**varnish** *n* **1** a liquid preparation that forms a hard shiny transparent coating on drying **2** outside show; VENEER **3** – **varnishy** *adj*

²**varnish** *vt* **1** to apply varnish to **2** to cover (sthg unpleasant) with a fair appearance; gloss *over* – **varnisher** *n*

varsity *n*, *Br* university – now chiefly humor

vary *vt* **1** to make a (partial) change in **2** to ensure variety in; diversify ~*vi* **1** to exhibit or undergo change **2** to deviate **3** to take on values ⟨*y varies inversely with x*⟩ **4** to exhibit biological variation – **varyingly** *adv*

vascular *adj* of or being a channel or system of channels conducting blood, sap, etc in a plant or animal; *also* supplied with or made up of such channels, esp blood vessels ⟨*a ~ tumour*⟩ – **vascularity** *n*

vase *n* an ornamental vessel usu of greater depth than width, used esp for holding flowers – **vaselike** *adj*

vasectomy *n* surgical cutting out of a section of the vas deferens, usu to induce permanent sterility – **vasectomize** *vt*

Vaseline *trademark* – used for petroleum jelly

vassal *n* **1** sby under the protection of another who is his/her feudal lord **2** sby in a subservient or subordinate position – **vassal** *adj*

vast *adj* very great in amount, degree, intensity, or esp in extent or range – **vastly** *adv*, **vastness** *n*

¹**vat** *n* **1** a tub, barrel, or other large vessel, esp for holding liquids undergoing chemical change or preparations for dyeing or tanning **2** a liquid containing a dye in a soluble form, that, on textile material being steeped in the liquor and then exposed to the air, is converted to the original insoluble dye by oxidation and is precipitated in the fibre

²**vat** *vt* **-tt-** to put into or treat in a vat

³**vat** *n*, *often cap*, *Br* VALUE-ADDED TAX

Vatican *n* the official residence of the Pope and the administrative centre of Roman Catholicism – **Vatican** *adj*

vaudeville *n* **1** a light often comic theatrical piece fre-

quently combining pantomime, dialogue, dancing, and song **2** *NAm* VARIETY **4**

¹**vault** *n* **1a** an arched structure of masonry, usu forming a ceiling or roof **b** sthg (e g the sky) resembling a vault **2a** an underground passage, room, or storage compartment **b** a room or compartment for the safekeeping of valuables **3a** a burial chamber, esp beneath a church or in a cemetery **b** a prefabricated container, usu of metal or concrete, into which a coffin is placed at burial – **vaulted** *adj*, **vaulty** *adj*

²**vault** *vt* to form or cover (as if) with a vault

³**vault** *vb* to bound vigorously (over); *esp* to execute a leap (over) using the hands or a pole – **vaulter** *n*

⁴**vault** *n* an act of vaulting

¹**vaulting** *n* vaulted construction

²**vaulting** *adj* **1** reaching for the heights ⟨~ *ambition*⟩ **2** designed for use in vaulting

vaulting horse *n* an apparatus like a pommel horse without pommels that is used for vaulting in gymnastics

vaunt *vt* to call attention to, proudly and often boastfully – **vaunter** *n*, **vauntingly** *adv*

VD *n* VENEREAL DISEASE

've *vb* have ⟨*we've been there*⟩

veal *n* the flesh of a young calf used as food – **vealy** *adj*

¹**vector** *n* **1a** a quantity (e g velocity or force) that has magnitude and direction and that is commonly represented by a directed line segment whose length represents the magnitude and whose orientation in space represents the direction **b** a course or compass direction, esp of an aircraft **2** an organism (e g an insect) that transmits a disease-causing agent – **vectorial** *adj*

²**vector** *vt* to change the direction of (the thrust of a jet engine) for steering

¹**veer** *vt* to let or pay out (e g a rope)

²**veer** *vi* **1** to change direction, position, or inclination **2** *of the wind* to shift in a clockwise direction **3** to wear ship ~*vt* to direct to a different course; *specif* WEAR **7** – **veeringly** *adv*

³**veer** *n* a change in direction, position, or inclination

veg *n*, *pl* **veg** *Br* a vegetable ⟨*meat and two ~*⟩ – *infml*

vegan *n* a strict vegetarian who avoids food or other products derived from animals – **vegan** *adj*, **veganism** *n*

¹**vegetable** *adj* **1a** of, constituting, or growing like plants **b** consisting of plants **2** made or obtained from plants or plant products – **vegetably** *adv*

²**vegetable** *n* **1** PLANT **1b 2** a usu herbaceous plant (e g the cabbage, bean, or potato) grown for an edible part which is usu eaten with the principal course of a meal; *also* this part of the plant **3a** a person with a dull undemanding existence **b** a person whose physical and esp mental capacities are severely impaired by illness or injury

vegetable marrow *n* (any of various large smooth-skinned elongated fruits, used as a vegetable, of) a cultivated variety of a climbing plant of the cucumber family

¹**vegetarian** *n* one who practises vegetarianism

²**vegetarian** *adj* **1** of vegetarians or vegetarianism **2** consisting wholly of vegetables ⟨*a ~ diet*⟩

vegetarianism *n* the often ethically based theory or practice of living on a diet that excludes the flesh of animals and often other animal products and that is made up of vegetables, fruits, cereals, and nuts

vegetate *vi* **1a** to grow in the manner of a plant **b** to produce vegetation **2** to lead a passive monotonous existence

vegetation *n* **1** plant life or total plant cover (e g of an area) **2** an abnormal outgrowth on a body part (e g a heart valve) – **vegetational** *adj*, **vegetationally** *adv*

vehement *adj* **1** intensely felt; impassioned **2** forcibly expressed – **vehemently** *adv*, **vehemence** *n*

vehicle *n* **1** any of various usu liquid media acting esp as solvents, carriers, or binders for active ingredients (e g drugs) or pigments **2** a means of transmission; a carrier **3** a medium through which sthg is expressed or communicated **4** MOTOR VEHICLE **5** a work created to display the talents of a particular performer

vehicular *adj* of or designed for vehicles, esp motor vehicles

¹veil *n* **1a** a length of cloth worn by women as a covering for the head and shoulders and often, esp in eastern countries, the face; *specif* the outer covering of a nun's headdress **b** a piece of sheer fabric attached for protection or ornament to a hat or headdress **c** any of various liturgical cloths; *esp* one used to cover the chalice **2** *the* cloistered life of a nun **3** a concealing curtain or cover of cloth **4a** sthg that hides or obscures like a veil **b** a disguise, pretext ⟨*under the* ~ *of national defence preparations for war began*⟩ **5** a velum

²veil *vt* to cover, provide, or conceal (as if) with a veil ~ *vi* to put on or wear a veil

veiled *adj* **1** indistinct, muffled **2** disguised ⟨~ *threats*⟩

¹vein *n* **1** a deposit of ore, coal, etc, esp in a rock fissure **2a** BLOOD VESSEL – not used technically **b** any of the tubular converging vessels that carry blood from the capillaries towards the heart **3a** any of the vascular bundles forming the framework of a leaf **b** any of the thickened cuticular ribs that serve to stiffen the wings of an insect **4** a streak or marking suggesting a vein (e g in marble) **5** a distinctive element or quality; a strain **6** a frame of mind; a mood – **veinal** *adj*, **veinlet** *n*, **veiny** *adj*

²vein *vt* to pattern (as if) with veins

veining *n* a pattern of veins

velar *adj* **1** of or forming a velum, esp the soft palate **2** formed with the back of the tongue touching or near the soft palate ⟨*the* ~ /k/ *of* cool⟩ – **velar** *n*, **velarize** *vt*

veld, veldt *n* a (shrubby or thinly forested) grassland, esp in southern Africa

vellum *n* **1** a fine-grained skin (e g calf) prepared esp for writing on or binding books **2** a strong cream-coloured paper

velocipede *n* **1** an early type of bicycle propelled by the rider's feet in contact with the ground **2** *NAm* a child's tricycle

velocity *n* **1** speed, esp of inanimate things **2** speed in a given direction

velour, velours *n*, *pl* **velours 1** any of various fabrics with a pile or napped surface resembling velvet **2** a fur felt finished with a long velvety nap, used esp for hats

velum *n*, *pl* **vela** a curtainlike membrane or anatomical partition; *esp* SOFT PALATE

velvet *n* **1** a fabric (e g of silk, rayon, or cotton) characterized by a short soft dense pile **2** sthg suggesting velvet in softness, smoothness, etc **3** the soft skin that envelops and nourishes the developing antlers of deer

velveteen *n* a fabric made with a short close weft pile in imitation of velvet

velvety *adj* soft and smooth like velvet

venal *adj* open to corrupt influence, esp bribery – **venally** *adv*, **venality** *n*

vend *vi* to sell ~ *vt* **1** to sell, esp in a small way **2** to sell by means of a vending machine – **vendable** *adj*, **vendee** *n*, **vendible** *adj*

vendetta *n* **1** a blood feud arising from the murder or

injury of a member of one family by a member of another **2** a prolonged bitter feud

vending machine *n* a coin-operated machine for selling merchandise

vendor, vender *n* **1** a seller; *specif, Br* the seller of a house **2** VENDING MACHINE

¹veneer *n* **1** a thin layer of wood of superior appearance or hardness used esp to give a decorative finish (e g to joinery) **2** a protective or ornamental facing (e g of brick or stone) **3** a superficial or deceptively attractive appearance

²veneer *vt* **1** to overlay (e g a common wood) with veneer; *broadly* to face with a material giving a superior surface **2** to conceal under a superficial and deceptive attractiveness – **veneerer** *n*

venerable *adj* **1** – used as a title for an Anglican archdeacon, or for a Roman Catholic who has been accorded the lowest of 3 degrees of recognition for sanctity **2** made sacred, esp by religious or historical association **3a** commanding respect through age, character, and attainments **b** impressive by reason of age ⟨*under* ~ *pines*⟩ – **venerableness** *n*, **venerably** *adv*, **venerability** *n*

venerate *vt* to regard with reverence or admiring deference – **venerator** *n*, **veneration** *n*

venereal *adj* **1** of sexual desire or sexual intercourse **2a** resulting from or contracted during sexual intercourse ⟨~ *infections*⟩ **b** of or affected with venereal disease ⟨*a high* ~ *rate*⟩

venereal disease *n* a contagious disease (e g gonorrhoea or syphilis) that is typically acquired during sexual intercourse

venetian blind *n* a blind (e g for a window) made of horizontal slats that may be adjusted so as to vary the amount of light admitted

vengeance *n* punishment inflicted in retaliation for injury or offence – **with a vengeance 1** with great force or vehemence **2** to an extreme or excessive degree

vengeful *adj* revengeful, vindictive – **vengefully** *adv*, **vengefulness** *n*

venial *adj* forgivable, pardonable – **venially** *adv*, **venialness** *n*

venison *n* the flesh of a deer as food

venom *n* **1** poisonous matter normally secreted by snakes, scorpions, bees, etc and transmitted chiefly by biting or stinging **2** ill will, malevolence

venomous *adj* **1a** poisonous **b** spiteful, malevolent ⟨~ *criticism*⟩ **2** able to inflict a poisoned wound – **venomously** *adv*, **venomousness** *n*

venous *adj* **1** having or consisting of veins ⟨*a* ~ *system*⟩ **2** *of blood* containing carbon dioxide rather than oxygen – **venously** *adv*, **venosity** *n*

¹vent *vt* **1** to provide with a vent **2** to give (vigorous) expression to

²vent *n* **1** a means of escape or release; an outlet – chiefly in *give vent to* **2a** the anus, esp of the cloaca of a bird or reptile **b** an outlet of a volcano; a fumarole **c** a hole at the breech of a gun through which the powder is ignited – **ventless** *adj*

³vent *n* a slit in a garment; *specif* an opening in the lower part of a seam (e g of a jacket or skirt)

ventilate *vt* **1** to examine freely and openly; expose publicly **2** to expose to (a current of fresh) air; oxygenate **3a** *of a current of air* to pass or circulate through so as to freshen **b** to cause fresh air to circulate through – **ventilative** *adj*

ventilation *n* **1** the act or process of ventilating **2** a system or means of providing fresh air

ventilator *n* an apparatus or aperture for introducing fresh air or expelling stagnant air

ventral *adj* **1a** abdominal **b** relating to or situated near or on the front or lower surface of an animal or aircraft opposite the back **2** being or located on the lower or inner surface of a plant structure – **ventrally** *adv*

ventricle *n* a cavity of a bodily part or organ: e g a chamber of the heart which receives blood from a corresponding atrium and from which blood is pumped into the arteries **b** any of the system of communicating cavities in the brain that are continuous with the central canal of the spinal cord – **ventricular** *adj*

ventriloquism *n* the production of the voice in such a manner that the sound appears to come from a source other than the vocal organs of the speaker and esp from a dummy manipulated by the producer of the sound – **ventriloquist** *n*, **ventriloquial** *adj*

¹**venture** *vt* **1** to expose to hazard; risk, gamble **2** to face the risks and dangers of; brave **3** to offer at the risk of opposition or censure ⟨~ *an opinion*⟩ ~*vi* to proceed despite danger; dare to go or do

²**venture** *n* **1** an undertaking involving chance, risk, or danger, esp in business **2** sthg (e g money or property) at risk in a speculative venture

venturesome *adj* **1** ready to take risks; daring **2** involving risk; hazardous – **venturesomely** *adv*, **venturesomeness** *n*

venue *n* **1** the place in which a legal case is to be tried and from which the jury is drawn **2** the place where a gathering takes place

Venus *n* the planet second in order from the sun

veracious *adj* **1** reliable in testimony; truthful **2** true, accurate – **veraciously** *adv*, **veraciousness** *n*, **veracity** *n*

veranda, verandah *n* a usu roofed open gallery or portico attached to the outside of a building

verb *n* any of a class of words that characteristically are the grammatical centre of a predicate and express an act, occurrence, or mode of being

¹**verbal** *adj* **1** of, involving, or expressed in words **2** of or formed from a verb **3** spoken rather than written; oral ⟨a ~ *contract*⟩ **4** verbatim, word-for-word – **verbally** *adv*

²**verbal** *n* **1** a word that combines characteristics of a verb with those of a noun or adjective **2** *Br* a spoken statement; *esp* one made to the police admitting or implying guilt and used in evidence

verbalize, -ise *vi* **1** to speak or write verbosely **2** to express sthg in words ~ *vt* **1** to convert into a verb **2** to name or describe in words – **verbalizer** *n*, **verbalization** *n*

verbal noun *n* a noun derived from, and having some of the constructions of, a verb; *esp* a gerund

verbatim *adv or adj* in the exact words

verbiage *n* wordiness, verbosity

verbose *adj* **1** containing more words than necessary **2** given to wordiness – **verbosely** *adv*, **verboseness** *n*, **verbosity** *n*

verdant *adj* **1a** green in tint or colour ⟨~ *grass*⟩ **b** green with growing plants ⟨~ *fields*⟩ **2** immature, unsophisticated – **verdancy** *n*, **verdantly** *adv*

verdict *n* **1** the decision of a jury on the matter submitted to them **2** an opinion, judgment

verdigris *n* **1a** a green or greenish blue poisonous pigment resulting from the action of acetic acid on copper **b** normal copper acetate **2** a green or bluish deposit formed on copper, brass, or bronze surfaces

verdure *n* **1** (the greenness of) growing vegetation **2** a condition of health, freshness, and vigour – **verdureless** *adj*, **verdurous** *adj*, **verdurousness** *n*

¹**verge** *n* **1** a rod or staff carried as an emblem of authority or symbol of office **2** sthg that borders, limits, or bounds:

e g **a** an outer margin of an object or structural part **b** the edge of a roof projecting over the gable **3** the brink, threshold **4** *Br* a surfaced or planted strip of land at the side of a road

²**verge** *vi* – verge on to be near to; border on

³**verge** *vi* **1** *of the sun* to incline towards the horizon; sink **2** to move or extend *towards* a specified condition

verger *n* **1** a church official who keeps order during services or serves as an usher or sacristan **2** *chiefly Br* an attendant who carries a verge (e g before a bishop or justice)

verify *vt* **1** to substantiate in law, esp formally or on oath **2** to ascertain the truth, accuracy, or reality of **3** to bear out, fulfil ⟨*my fears were* verified⟩ – **verifier** *n*, **verifiable** *adj*, **verification** *n*

verily *adv*, *archaic* **1** indeed, certainly **2** truly, confidently

verisimilitude *n* **1** the quality or state of appearing to be true **2** a statement that has the appearance of truth *USE fml* – **verisimilitudinous** *adj*

veritable *adj* being in fact the thing named and not false or imaginary – often used to stress the aptness of a metaphor ⟨a ~ *mountain of references*⟩ – **veritableness** *n*, **veritably** *adv*

verity *n* **1** the quality or state of being true or real **2** sthg (e g a statement) that is true; *esp* a permanently true value or principle

vermicelli *n* **1** pasta in the form of long thin solid threads smaller in diameter than spaghetti **2** small thin sugar strands that are used as a decoration (e g on iced cakes)

vermiculite *n* any of various minerals of hydrous silicates derived from mica that expand on heating to form a lightweight highly water-absorbent material

vermiform *adj* resembling a worm in shape

vermiform appendix *n* a narrow short blind tube that extends from the caecum in the lower right-hand part of the abdomen

vermilion, vermillion *adj or n* (of the brilliant red colour of) mercuric sulphide used as a pigment

vermin *n, pl* **vermin 1** *pl* **a** lice, rats, or other common harmful or objectionable animals **b** birds and mammals that prey on game **2** an offensive person – **verminous** *adj*, **verminously** *adv*

vermouth *n* a dry or sweet alcoholic drink that has a white wine base and is flavoured with aromatic herbs

¹**vernacular** *adj* **1a** expressed or written in a language or dialect native to a region or country rather than a literary, learned, or foreign language **b** of or being the normal spoken form of a language **2** of or being the common building style of a period or place – **vernacularly** *adv*

²**vernacular** *n* **1** the local vernacular language **2** the mode of expression of a group or class – **vernacularism** *n*

vernal *adj* **1** of or occurring in the spring ⟨~ *equinox*⟩ **2** fresh, youthful – **vernally** *adv*

Veronal *trademark* – used for barbitone

veronica *n* speedwell

verruca *n, pl* **verrucas** also **verruccae 1** a wart or warty skin growth **2** a warty prominence on a plant or animal – **verrucose** *adj*

versatile *adj* **1** embracing a variety of subjects, fields, or skills; *also* turning with ease from one thing to another **2** capable of moving easily forwards or backwards, or esp up and down ⟨~ *antennae*⟩ ⟨~ *anther*⟩ **3** having many uses or applications ⟨~ *building material*⟩ – **versatilely** *adv*, **versatileness** *n*, **versatility** *n*

verse *n* **1** a line of metrical writing **2a** (an example of) metrical language or writing, distinguished from poetry esp by its lower level of intensity **b** POETRY **2 c** a body of metrical writing (e g of a period or country) ⟨*Elizabethan* ~⟩ **3** a stanza **4** any of the short divisions into which a chapter of the Bible is traditionally divided

versed *adj* possessing a thorough knowledge (of) or skill *in* – chiefly in *well versed in*

versify *vi* to compose verses ~ *vt* to turn into verse – **versifier** *n*, **versification** *n*

version *n* **1** a translation from another language; *esp, often cap* a translation of (part of) the Bible **2a** an account or description from a particular point of view, esp as contrasted with another account **b** an adaptation of a work of art into another medium ⟨*the film* ~ *of the novel*⟩ **c** an arrangement of a musical composition **3** a form or variant of a type or original ⟨*an experimental* ~ *of the plane*⟩ **4** manual turning of a foetus in the uterus to aid delivery – **versional** *adj*

verso *n, pl* **versos** a left-hand page – contrasted with *recto*

versus *prep* **1** against **2** in contrast to or as the alternative of ⟨*free trade* ~ *protection*⟩

vertebra *n, pl* **vertebrae**, **vertebras** any of the bony or cartilaginous segments composing the spinal column – **vertebral** *adj*

¹vertebrate *adj* **1** having a spinal column **2** of the vertebrates

²vertebrate *n* any of a large group of animals (e g mammals, birds, reptiles, amphibians, and fishes) with a segmented backbone, together with a few primitive forms in which the backbone is represented by a notochord

vertex *n, pl* **vertices** *also* **vertexes** **1a**(1) the point opposite to and farthest from the base in a figure **(2)** the termination or intersection of lines or curves ⟨*the* ~ *of an angle*⟩ **(3)** a point where an axis of an ellipse, parabola, or hyperbola intersects the curve **b** ZENITH 1 **2** the top of the head **3** the highest point; the summit

vertical *adj* **1** situated at the highest point; directly overhead or in the zenith **2** perpendicular to the plane of the horizon or to a primary axis **3** of, involving, or integrating discrete elements (e g from lowest to highest) ⟨*a* ~ *business organization*⟩ ⟨*the* ~ *arrangement of society*⟩ **4** of or concerning the relationships between people of different rank in a hierarchy – **vertical** *n*, **vertically** *adv*, **verticalness** *n*, **verticality** *n*

vertiginous *adj* **1** characterized by or suffering from vertigo **2** inclined to frequent and often pointless change; inconstant **3** causing or tending to cause dizziness ⟨*the* ~ *heights*⟩ **4** marked by turning; rotary – **vertiginously** *adv*

vertigo *n* a disordered state in which the individual loses balance and the surroundings seem to whirl dizzily

verve *n* **1** the spirit and enthusiasm animating artistic work **2** energy, vitality

¹very *adj* **1** properly so called; actual, genuine ⟨*the* ~ *man you met*⟩ **2** absolute ⟨*the* ~ *thing for the purpose*⟩ ⟨*the veriest fool alive* – John Milton⟩ **3** being no more than; mere ⟨*the* ~ *thought terrified me*⟩ *USE* used attributively

²very *adv* **1** to a high degree; exceedingly **2** – used as an intensive to emphasize *same*, *own*, or the superlative degree ⟨*the* ~ *best shop in town*⟩

very high frequency *n* a radio frequency in the range between 30MHz and 300MHz

Very light *n* a white or coloured ball of fire that is projected from a Very pistol and that is used as a signal flare

vesicle *n* **1a** a membranous usu fluid-filled pouch (e g a cyst, vacuole, or cell) in a plant or animal **b** a blister **c** a pocket of embryonic tissue that is the beginning of an organ **2** a small cavity in a mineral or rock – **vesicular** *adj*, **vesiculate** *adj*, **vesicularity** *n*

¹vesper *n* **1** *cap* EVENING STAR **2** *archaic* evening, eventide

²vesper *adj* of vespers or the evening

vespers *n pl but sing or pl in constr, often cap* **1** the sixth of the canonical hours that is said or sung in the late afternoon **2** a service of evening worship

vessel *n* **1a** a hollow utensil (e g a jug, cup, or bowl) for holding esp liquid **b** sby into whom some quality (e g grace) is infused **2** a large hollow structure designed to float on and move through water carrying a crew, passengers, or cargo **3a** a tube or canal (e g an artery) in which a body fluid is contained and conveyed or circulated **b** a conducting tube in a plant

¹vest *vt* **1a** to give (e g property or power) into the possession or discretion of another **b** to clothe with a particular authority, right, or property **2** to clothe (as if) with a garment; *esp* to robe in ecclesiastical vestments ~ *vi* to become legally vested

²vest *n* **1** *chiefly Br* a usu sleeveless undergarment for the upper body **2** *chiefly NAm* a waistcoat – **vested** *adj*, **vestlike** *adj*

¹vestal *adj* **1** of a vestal virgin **2** chaste; *esp* virgin – **vestally** *adv*

²vestal, vestal virgin *n* a priestess of the Roman goddess Vesta, responsible for tending the sacred fire perpetually kept burning on her altar

vested interest *n* **1a** an interest carrying a legal right **b** an interest (e g in an existing political or social arrangement) in which the holder has a strong personal commitment **2** sby or sthg having a vested interest in sthg; *specif* a group enjoying benefits from an existing privilege

vestibule *n* **1** a lobby or chamber between the outer door and the interior of a building **2** any of various bodily cavities, esp when serving as or resembling an entrance to some other cavity or space: e g **a** the central cavity of the bony labyrinth of the ear **b** the part of the mouth cavity outside the teeth and gums – **vestibuled** *adj*, **vestibular** *adj*

vestige *n* **1a** a trace or visible sign left by sthg vanished or lost **b** a minute remaining amount **2** a small or imperfectly formed body part or organ that remains from one more fully developed in an earlier stage of the individual, in a past generation, or in closely related forms – **vestigial** *adj*, **vestigially** *adv*

vestment *n* **1** an outer garment; *esp* a robe of ceremony or office **2** any of the ceremonial garments and insignia worn by ecclesiastical officiants and assistants as appropriate to their rank and to the rite being celebrated – **vestmental** *adj*

vestry *n* **1a** a sacristy **b** a room used for church meetings and classes **2a** the business meeting of an English parish **b** an elective administrative body in an Episcopal parish in the USA

vesture *n* clothing, apparel – fml

¹vet *n* sby qualified and authorized to treat diseases and injuries of animals

²vet *vt* **-tt-** **1** to subject (a person or animal) to a physical examination or checkup **2** *chiefly Br* to subject to careful and thorough appraisal ⟨~ *your application*⟩

³vet *adj or n, NAm* (a) veteran

vetch *n* any of a genus of climbing or twining leguminous plants including valuable fodder and soil-improving plants

veteran *n* **1** sby who has had long experience of an occupation, skill, or (military) service **2** **veteran, veteran car** *Br* an old motor car; *specif* one built before 1916 **3** *NAm* a former serviceman – **veteran** *adj*

Veterans Day n a day set aside in the USA and Canada in commemoration of the end of hostilities in 1918 and 1945; esp November 11 observed as a public holiday in Canada and some states of the USA

¹**veterinary** adj of or being the medical care of animals, esp domestic animals

²**veterinary**, Br chiefly **veterinary surgeon** n ¹VET

¹**veto** n, pl **vetoes** 1 an authoritative prohibition 2 a right to declare inoperative decisions made by others; esp a power vested in a chief executive to prevent permanently or temporarily the enactment of measures passed by a legislature

²**veto** vt **vetoing; vetoed** to subject to a veto – **vetoer** n

vex vt **vexed** also **vext** 1a to bring distress, discomfort, or agitation to **b** to irritate or annoy by petty provocations; harass 2 to puzzle, baffle

vexation n a cause of trouble; an affliction

vexatious adj 1 causing vexation; distressing 2 intended to harass – **vexatiously** adv, **vexatiousness** n

vexed question n a question that has been discussed at length, usu without a satisfactory solution being reached

via prep 1 passing through or calling at (a place) on the way 2 through the medium of; also by means of

viable adj 1 (born alive and developed enough to be) capable of living 2 capable of growing or developing ⟨~ seeds⟩ ⟨~ eggs⟩ 3 capable of working; practicable ⟨~ alternatives⟩ – **viably** adv, **viability** n

viaduct n a usu long bridge, esp on a series of arches, that carries a road, railway, canal, etc over a deep valley

vial n a phial

viand n 1 a (choice or tasty) item of food 2 pl provisions, food USE fml

vibes n pl 1 sing or pl in constr a vibraphone 2 VIBRATIONS 3 USE infml – **vibist** n

vibrant adj 1a oscillating or pulsating rapidly **b** pulsating with life, vigour, or activity ⟨a ~ personality⟩ 2 sounding as a result of vibration; resonant ⟨a ~ voice⟩ – **vibrantly** adv

vibraphone n a percussion instrument resembling the xylophone but having metal bars and motor-driven resonators for sustaining its sound and producing a vibrato – **vibraphonist** n

vibrate vt 1 to cause to swing or move to and fro; cause to oscillate 2 to emit (e g sound) (as if) with a vibratory motion 3 to mark or measure by oscillation ⟨a pendulum vibrating seconds⟩ 4 to set in vibration ~ vi 1 to move to and fro; oscillate 2 to have an effect as of vibration; throb ⟨music vibrating in the memory⟩ 3 to be in a state of vibration; quiver – **vibrative** adj, **vibratory** adj

vibration n 1a a periodic motion of the particles of an elastic body or medium in alternately opposite directions from a position of equilibrium **b** an oscillation or quivering 2 an instance of vibrating 3a a characteristic aura or spirit felt to emanate from sby or sthg and instinctively sensed or experienced **b** a distinctive usu emotional atmosphere capable of being sensed – usu pl with sing. meaning – **vibrational** adj, **vibrationless** adj

vibrato n, pl **vibratos** a slightly tremulous effect imparted to musical tone to add expressiveness, by slight and rapid variations in pitch

vibrator n a vibrating electrical apparatus used in massage, esp to provide sexual stimulation

vicar n 1 a Church of England incumbent receiving a stipend but formerly not the tithes of a parish 2 a clergyman exercising a broad pastoral responsibility as the representative of a prelate – **vicarship** n

vicarage n the benefice or house of a vicar

vicarious adj 1a serving instead of another **b** delegated ⟨~ authority⟩ 2 performed or suffered by one person as a substitute for, or to the benefit of, another ⟨a ~ sacrifice⟩ 3 experienced through imaginative participation in the experience of another ⟨~ pleasure⟩ – **vicariously** adv, **vicariousness** n

¹**vice** n 1a moral depravity or corruption; wickedness **b** a grave moral fault **c** a habitual and usu minor fault or shortcoming 2 habitual abnormal behaviour in a domestic animal detrimental to its health or usefulness 3 sexual immorality; esp prostitution

²**vice**, NAm chiefly **vise** n any of various tools, usu attached to a workbench, that have 2 jaws that close for holding work by operation of a screw, lever, or cam – **vicelike** adj

³**vice**, NAm chiefly **vise** vt to hold, force, or squeeze (as if) with a vice

⁴**vice** prep in the place of; succeeding

vice- prefix 1 person next in rank below or qualified to act in place of; deputy ⟨vice-president⟩ ⟨viceroy⟩ 2 office next in rank below ⟨vice-admiralty⟩

vice admiral n an officer in the navy ranking below admiral

vice-chancellor n an officer ranking next below a chancellor; esp the administrative head of a British university

viceregal adj of a viceroy – **viceregally** adv

vicereine n 1 the wife of a viceroy 2 a woman viceroy

viceroy n the governor of a country or province who rules as the representative of his sovereign – **viceroyalty** n, **viceroyship** n

vice squad n sing or pl in constr a police department enforcing laws concerning gambling, pornography, and prostitution

vice versa adv with the order changed and relations reversed; conversely ⟨Ann hates Jane and ~⟩

vicinity n 1 a surrounding area or district 2 NEIGHBOURHOOD 3b 3 being near; proximity – fml

vicious adj 1 having the nature or quality of vice; depraved ⟨~ habits⟩ 2 esp of language or reasoning defective, faulty 3a dangerous, refractory ⟨a ~ horse⟩ **b** unpleasantly fierce, malignant, or severe ⟨a ~ form of flu⟩ 4 malicious, spiteful ⟨~ gossip⟩ 5 worsened by internal causes that reciprocally augment each other ⟨a ~ wage-price spiral⟩ – **viciously** adv, **viciousness** n

vicious circle n 1 a chain of events in which the apparent solution of 1 difficulty creates a new problem that makes the original difficulty worse 2 the logical fallacy of using 1 argument or definition to prove or define a second on which the first depends

vicissitude n 1 a change or alteration (e g in nature or human affairs) 2 an accident of fortune – usu pl ⟨the ~ s of daily life⟩ 3 the quality of being changeable; mutability – fml – **vicissitudinous** adj

victim n 1 a living animal offered as a sacrifice in a religious rite 2 sby or sthg that is adversely affected by a force or agent: e g **a** one who or that which is injured, destroyed, or subjected to oppression or mistreatment ⟨a ~ of cancer⟩ ⟨a ~ of the car crash⟩ ⟨a ~ of frequent political attacks⟩ **b** a dupe, prey

victimize, -ise vt 1 to make a victim of 2 to punish selectively (e g by unfair dismissal) – **victimizer** n, **victimization** n

victor n a person, country, etc that defeats an enemy or opponent; a winner – **victor** adj

Victor – a communications code word for the letter v

victoria n 1 a low 4-wheeled carriage for 2 with a folding hood 2 any of a genus of S American water lilies with large spreading leaves and immense bright white flowers **3** a large red sweet type of plum

Victoria Cross *n* a bronze Maltese cross that is the highest British military decoration

¹**Victorian** *adj* **1** (characteristic) of the reign of Queen Victoria or the art, letters, or taste of her time **2** typical of the moral standards or conduct of the age of Queen Victoria, esp in being prudish or hypocritical **3** of a place called Victoria (e g the State in Australia or the capital of British Columbia)

²**Victorian** *n* sby living during Queen Victoria's reign

victorious *adj* **1a** having won a victory **b** (characteristic) of victory **2** successful, triumphant – **victoriously** *adv*, **victoriousness** *n*

victory *n* **1** the overcoming of an enemy or antagonist ⟨~ *was ours*⟩ **2** achievement of mastery or success in a struggle or endeavour

¹**victual** *n* **1** food usable by human beings **2** *pl* supplies of food; provisions

²**victual** *vb* **-ll-** (*NAm* **-l-, -ll-**), *vb* to supply with or lay in food

victualler, *NAm also* **victualer** *n* **1** PUBLICAN 2 **2** sby who or sthg that provisions an army, a navy, or a ship with food **3** a provisioning ship

vicuña, vicuna *n* **1** (the wool from the fine undercoat of) a wild ruminant mammal of the Andes related to the domesticated llama and alpaca **2** a fabric made of vicuña wool; *also* a sheep's wool imitation of this

vide *vb imper* see – used to direct a reader to another item

videlicet *adv* that is to say; namely – used to introduce 1 or more examples

¹**video** *adj* **1** of television; *specif* of reproduction of a television image or used in its transmission or reception ⟨a ~ *signal*⟩ **2** of a form of magnetic recording for reproduction on a television screen

²**video** *n* **1** video, **1**video**re**0**corder, **0**video**cas**1**sette re**0**corder** a machine for videotaping **2** *chiefly NAm* television

videotape *vt* to make a recording of (e g sthg that is televised) on magnetic tape – **videotape** *n*

vie *vi* **vying; vied** to strive for superiority; contend ⟨~d *with each other for the prize*⟩ – **vier** *n*

¹**view** *n* **1** the act of seeing or examining; inspection; *also* a survey ⟨a ~ *of English literature*⟩ **2** a way of regarding sthg; an opinion ⟨*in my ~ the conference has no chance of success*⟩ **3** a scene, prospect ⟨*the lovely ~ from the balcony*⟩; *also* an aspect ⟨*the rear ~ of the house*⟩ **4** extent or range of vision; sight ⟨*tried to keep the ship in* ~⟩ **5** an intention, object ⟨*bought a gun with a ~ to murdering his mother*⟩ **6** the foreseeable future ⟨*no hope in* ~⟩ **7** a pictorial representation – **in view of 1** taking the specified feature into consideration ⟨*in view of his age, the police have decided not to prosecute*⟩ **2** able to be seen by or from ⟨*in full view of interested spectators*⟩ – **on view** open to public inspection

²**view** *vt* **1a** to see, watch **b** to look on in a specified way; regard ⟨*doesn't ~ himself as a rebel*⟩ **2** to look at attentively; inspect ⟨~ ed *the house but decided not to buy it*⟩ **3** to survey or examine mentally; consider ⟨~ *all sides of a question*⟩ **4** to see (a hunted animal) break cover ~ *vi* to watch television – **viewable** *adj*

viewer *n* **1** an optical device used in viewing **2** sby who watches television

viewfinder *n* a device on a camera for showing what will be included in the picture

viewless *adj* **1** affording no view **2** holding no opinions – **viewlessly** *adv*

viewpoint *n* a standpoint; POINT OF VIEW

vigil *n* **1a** a devotional watch formerly kept on the night before a religious festival **b** the day before a religious festival, observed as a day of spiritual preparation **2** the act of keeping awake at times when sleep is customary; *also* a period of wakefulness **3** an act or period of watching or surveillance; a watch

vigilant *adj* alert and watchful, esp to avoid danger – **vigilance** *n*, **vigilantly** *adv*

vigilante *n, NAm* a member of a vigilance committee

vignette *n* **1** a decorative design (e g of vine leaves, tendrils, and grapes) on a title page or at the beginning or end of a chapter **2** a picture (e g an engraving or photograph) that shades off gradually into the surrounding background **3a** a short descriptive literary sketch **b** a brief incident or scene (e g in a play or film) – **vignettist** *n*

vigorous *adj* **1** possessing or showing vigour; full of active strength **2** done with vigour; carried out forcefully and energetically ⟨~ *exercises*⟩ – **vigorously** *adv*, **vigorousness** *n*

vigour, *NAm* **vigor** *n* **1** active physical or mental strength or force **2** active healthy well-balanced growth, esp of plants **3** intensity of action or effect; force

Viking *n* **1a** a Norse trader and warrior of the 8th to 10th c **2** a Scandinavian

vile *adj* **1a** morally despicable or abhorrent **b** physically repulsive; foul **2** tending to degrade ⟨~ *employments*⟩ **3** disgustingly or utterly bad; contemptible ⟨*in a ~ temper*⟩ – **vilely** *adv*, **vileness** *n*

vilify *vt* to utter slanderous and abusive statements against; defame – **vilifier** *n*

villa *n* **1** a country mansion **2** an ancient Roman mansion and the surrounding agricultural estate **3** *Br* a detached or semidetached suburban house, usu having a garden and built before WW I

village *n* **1** a group of dwellings in the country, larger than a hamlet and smaller than a town **2** *sing or pl in constr* the residents of a village **3** sthg (e g a group of burrows or nests) suggesting a village

villager *n* **1** an inhabitant of a village **2** a rustic

villain *n* **1** a scoundrel, rascal; *also* a criminal **2** a character in a story or play whose evil actions affect the plot

villainous *adj* **1** being, befitting, or characteristic of a villain; evil ⟨a ~ *attack*⟩ **2** highly objectionable ⟨~ *weather*⟩ – **villainously** *adv*, **villainousness** *n*

villainy *n* **1** villainous conduct; *also* a villainous act **2** depravity

-ville *suffix* (*adj, n → n*) place or thing of (such) a nature ⟨*dulls*ville⟩ – *infml*

villein *n* **1** a free village peasant **2** an unfree peasant standing as the slave of his feudal lord

villeinage, villenage *n* the tenure or status of a villein

vim *n* robust energy and enthusiasm – *infml*

vinaigrette *n* **1** a small ornamental box or bottle with a perforated top used for holding an aromatic preparation (e g smelling salts) **2** (a dish made with) a sharp sauce of oil and vinegar flavoured with salt, pepper, mustard, herbs, etc and used esp on green salads

vindicate *vt* **1a** to exonerate, absolve **b** to provide justification for; justify **2** to maintain the existence of; uphold ⟨~ *his honour*⟩ – **vindicator** *n*

vindication *n* justification against denial or censure; defence

vindictive *adj* **1a** disposed to seek revenge; vengeful **b** intended as revenge ⟨~ *punishments*⟩ **2** intended to cause anguish; spiteful – **vindictively** *adv*, **vindictiveness** *n*

vine *n* **1** the climbing plant that bears grapes **2** (a plant with) a stem that requires support and that climbs by tendrils or twining – **viny** *adj*

vinegar *n* a sour liquid obtained esp by acetic fermentation of wine, cider, etc and used as a condiment or preservative

vinegary *adj* 1 containing or resembling vinegar; sour 2 bitter or irascible in character or manner

vinery *n* an area or building in which vines are grown

vineyard *n* a plantation of grapevines

vino *n* wine – *infml*

vinous *adj* 1 of or made with wine ⟨~ *medications*⟩ 2 (showing the effects of being) addicted to wine – **vinously** *adv*, **vinosity** *n*

¹vintage *n* 1a(1) a season's yield of grapes or wine from a vineyard (2) wine, specif one of a particular type, region, and year and usu of superior quality that is dated and allowed to mature **b** *sing or pl in constr* a collection of contemporaneous and similar people or things; a crop 2 the act or time of harvesting grapes or making wine 3 a period of origin or manufacture ⟨*a piano of 1845* ~⟩

²vintage *adj* 1 of a vintage; *esp* being a product of 1 particular year rather than a blend of wines from different years 2 of enduring interest or quality; classic 3 of the best and most characteristic – with a proper noun ⟨~ *Shaw: a wise and winning comedy* – *Time*⟩ 4 *Br*, of a motor vehicle built between 1917 and 1930 ⟨*a* ~ *Rolls*⟩

vintner *n* WINE MERCHANT

vinyl *n* (a plastic that is a polymer of a derivative of) a univalent radical $CH_2=CH$ derived from ethylene by removal of 1 hydrogen atom – **vinylic** *adj*

viol *n* any of a family of bowed stringed instruments chiefly of the 16th and 17th c with usu 6 strings and a fretted fingerboard, played resting on or between the player's knees

¹viola *n* a musical instrument of the violin family that is intermediate in size and range between the violin and cello and is tuned a 5th below the violin – **violist** *n*

²viola *n* VIOLET 1; *esp* any of various cultivated violets with (variegated) flowers resembling but smaller than those of pansies

violate *vt* 1 to fail to comply with; infringe ⟨~ *the law*⟩ 2 to do harm to; *specif* to rape 3 to fail to respect; desecrate ⟨~ *a shrine*⟩ 4 to interrupt, disturb ⟨~ *your privacy*⟩ – **violator** *n*, **violable** *adj*, **violative** *adj*, **violation** *n*

violence *n* 1 (an instance of) exertion of physical force so as to injure or abuse 2 unjust or unwarranted distortion; outrage ⟨*did* ~ *to her feelings*⟩ 3a intense or turbulent action or force ⟨*the* ~ *of the storm*⟩ **b** (an instance of) vehement feeling or expression; fervour 4 distortion or misinterpretation of meaning ⟨*editor did* ~ *to the text*⟩

violent *adj* 1 marked by extreme force or sudden intense activity ⟨*a* ~ *attack*⟩ 2a notably furious or vehement ⟨*a* ~ *denunciation*⟩; *also* excited or mentally disordered to the point of loss of self-control ⟨*the patient became* ~ *and had to be restrained*⟩ **b** extreme, intense ⟨~ *pain*⟩ 3 caused by force; not natural ⟨*a* ~ *death*⟩ – **violently** *adv*

violet *n* 1 any of a genus of plants with often sweet-scented flowers, usu of all 1 colour, esp as distinguished from the usu larger-flowered violas and pansies 2 bluish purple

violin *n* a bowed stringed instrument having a fingerboard with no frets, 4 strings, and a usual range from G below middle C upwards for more than 4½ octaves – **violinist** *n*

violoncello *n* a cello – **violoncellist** *n*

VIP *n, pl* **VIPs** a person of great influence or prestige ⟨*a* ~ *lounge*⟩

viper *n* **1a** (any of various Old World snakes related to) the adder **b** PIT VIPER 2 a malignant or treacherous person

virago *n, pl* **viragoes, viragos** 1 a loud overbearing woman; a termagant 2 *archaic* a woman of great stature, strength, and courage – **viraginous** *adj*

¹virgin *n* 1 an unmarried girl or woman 2 *often cap* (a statue or picture of) *the* Virgin Mary 3 a person, esp a girl, who has not had sexual intercourse 4 a female animal that has never copulated – **virginity** *n*

²virgin *adj* 1 free of impurity or stain; unsullied 2 being a virgin 3 characteristic of or befitting a virgin; modest 4 untouched, unexploited; *specif* not altered by human activity ⟨*a* ~ *forest*⟩ 5 *of metal* produced directly from ore; not scrap

¹virginal *adj* 1 (characteristic) of a virgin or virginity; *esp* pure, chaste 2 fresh, untouched, uncorrupted – **virginally** *adv*

²virginal *n* a small rectangular harpsichord popular in the 16th and 17th c – often pl with sing. meaning

virgin birth *n* 1 birth from a virgin 2 *often cap V&B* the doctrine that Jesus was born of a virgin mother

Virginia *n* a usu mild-flavoured flue-cured tobacco grown orig in N America and used esp in cigarettes

Virginia creeper *n* a climbing plant of the grape family with reddish leaves composed of 5 leaflets and bluish black berries

Virgin Mary *n* *the* mother of Jesus

Virgo *n* (sby born under) the 6th sign of the zodiac in astrology, which is pictured as a woman holding an ear of corn – **Virgoan** *adj or n*

virile *adj* 1 having the nature, properties, or qualities (often thought of as typical) of a man; *specif* capable of functioning as a male in copulation 2 vigorous, forceful 3 characteristic of or associated with adult males; masculine

virility *n* 1 power to procreate 2 manly vigour; masculinity

virology *n* a branch of science that deals with viruses – **virologic, virological** *adj*, **virologically** *adv*, **virologist** *n*

virtual *adj* 1 that is such in essence or effect though not formally recognized or admitted ⟨*a* ~ *dictator*⟩ 2 formed by the apparent convergence of light rays ⟨*a* ~ *image*⟩

virtually *adv* almost entirely; for all practical purposes

virtue *n* **1a** conformity to a standard of right; morality **b** a particular moral excellence ⟨*truthfulness is a* ~⟩ 2 a beneficial or commendable quality ⟨*has the* ~ *of being easily assembled*⟩ 3 a capacity to act; potency 4 chastity, esp in a woman – **virtueless** *adj* – **by virtue of** 1 through the force of; having as a right 2 as a result of; because of

virtuosity *n* great technical skill, esp in the practice of a fine art

¹virtuoso *n, pl* **virtuosos, virtuosi** 1 one skilled in or having a taste for the fine arts 2 one who excels in the technique of an art, esp in musical performance – **virtuosic** *adj*

²virtuoso *adj* (characteristic) of a virtuoso; having the manner or style of a virtuoso

virtuous *adj* 1 having or exhibiting virtue; *esp* morally excellent; righteous 2 chaste – **virtuously** *adv*, **virtuousness** *n*

virulence, virulency *n* 1 extreme bitterness or malignity of temper; rancour 2 malignancy, venomousness 3 the relative capacity of a pathogen to overcome body defences

virulent *adj* **1a** *of a disease* severe and developing rapidly

b able to overcome bodily defensive mechanisms ⟨*a ~ strain of bacterium*⟩ **2** extremely poisonous or venomous **3** full of malice; malignant **4** objectionably harsh or strong ⟨*a ~ purple*⟩ – **virulently** *adv*

virus *n* **1a** the causative agent of any infectious disease – not now used technically **b** (a disease caused by) any of a large group of submicroscopic often disease-causing agents that typically consist of a protein coat surrounding an RNA or DNA core and that multiply only in living cells **2** sthg that poisons the mind or soul ⟨*the ~ of racism*⟩ – **viral** *adj*, **viricide** *n*, **viricidal** *adj*, **viricidally** *adv*

¹visa *n* an endorsement made on a passport by the proper authorities (e g of a country at entrance or exit) denoting that the bearer may proceed

²visa *vt* **visaing; visaed** to provide (a passport) with a visa

visage *n* **1** a face, countenance **2** an aspect, appearance ⟨*grimy ~ of a mining town*⟩ *USE* fml or poetic – **visaged** *adj*

vis-à-vis *prep* **1** face to face with; opposite **2** in relation to

viscera *n pl* the internal body organs collectively

visceral *adj* **1** deeply or intensely felt ⟨*~ sensation*⟩ **2** of or located on or among the viscera **3** instinctive, unreasoning ⟨*a ~ conviction*⟩ – fml – **viscerally** *adv*

viscosity *n* **1** being viscous **2** (a measure of the force needed to overcome) the property of a liquid, gas, or semifluid that enables it to offer resistance to flow

viscount *n* a member of the peerage in Britain ranking below an earl and above a baron – **viscountcy** *n*, **viscounty** *n*

viscountess *n* **1** the wife or widow of a viscount **2** a woman having the rank of a viscount

viscous *adj* **1** viscid **2** having or characterized by (high) viscosity ⟨*~ flow*⟩ – **viscously** *adv*, **viscousness** *n*

vise *vt or n, chiefly NAm* (to hold with) a mechanical vice

visibility *n* **1** being visible **2** the clearness of the atmosphere as revealed by the greatest distance at which prominent objects can be identified visually with the naked eye

visible *adj* **1** capable of being seen ⟨*stars ~ to the naked eye*⟩ ⟨*~ light*⟩ **2a** exposed to view ⟨*the ~ horizon*⟩ **b** in the public eye; prominent ⟨*a panel of highly ~ people*⟩ **3** capable of being perceived; noticeable ⟨*her ~ impatience*⟩ **4** tangibly or implicitly present **5** of or being trade in goods rather than services ⟨*~ exports*⟩ – **visibleness** *n*, **visibly** *adv*

vision *n* **1a** sthg (revelatory) seen in a dream, trance, or ecstasy **b** a mental image of sthg immaterial ⟨*had ~s of missing the train*⟩ **2a** the power of imagination; *also* the manner of perceiving mental images ⟨*an artist's ~*⟩ **b** discernment, foresight ⟨*a man of ~*⟩ **c** a supernatural apparition **3a** the act or power of seeing; SIGHT **3a b** the sense by which the qualities of an object (e g colour, luminosity, shape, and size) constituting its appearance are perceived and which acts through the eye **4a** sthg seen **b** a lovely or charming sight – **visional** *adj*, **visionally** *adv*, **visionless** *adj*

¹visionary *adj* **1a** able or likely to see visions **b** disposed to daydreaming or imagining; dreamy **2a** of the nature of a vision; illusory **b** impracticable, utopian ⟨*a ~ scheme*⟩ **3** of or characterized by visions or the power of vision – **visionariness** *n*

²visionary *n* **1** one who sees visions; a seer **2** one whose ideas or projects are impractical; a dreamer

¹visit *vt* **1a** *archaic, of God* to comfort ⟨*~ us with Thy salvation* – Charles Wesley⟩ **b** to afflict ⟨*a city frequently ~ed by the plague*⟩ **c** to inflict punishment for ⟨*~ed the sins of the fathers upon the children*⟩ **2a** to pay a call on for reasons of kindness, friendship, ceremony, or business ⟨*~ing the sick*⟩ **b** to reside with temporarily as a guest **c** to go or come to look at or stay at (e g for business or sightseeing) **d** to go or come officially to inspect or oversee ⟨*a bishop ~ing the parish*⟩ to make a visit or visits – **visitable** *adj*

²visit *n* **1a** an act of visiting; a call **b** a temporary residence as a guest **c** an extended but temporary stay ⟨*his annual ~s abroad*⟩ **2** an official or professional call; a visitation

visitant *n* **1** a (supernatural) visitor **2** VISITOR 2 – **visitant** *adj*

visitation *n* **1** the act or an instance of visiting; *esp* an official visit (e g for inspection) **2a** a special dispensation of divine favour or wrath **b** a severe trial; an affliction **3** *cap* the visit of the Virgin Mary to Elizabeth recounted in Luke 1:39–56 and celebrated on July 2 by a Christian festival – **visitational** *adj*

visiting card *n* a small card of introduction bearing the name and sometimes the address and profession of the owner

visitor *n* **1** sby who or sthg that makes (formal) visits **2** a migratory bird that visits a locality for a short time at regular intervals

visitors' book *n* a book in which visitors (e g to a place of interest or hotel) write their names and addresses and sometimes comments

visor, vizor *n* **1** the (movable) part of a helmet that covers the face **2** a usu movable flat sunshade attached at the top of a vehicle windscreen **3** *chiefly NAm* a peak on a cap – **visored** *adj*, **visorless** *adj*

vista *n* **1** a distant view esp through or along an avenue or opening; a prospect **2** an extensive mental view (e g over a stretch of time or a series of events) – **vistaless** *adj*

visual *adj* **1** of, used in, or produced by vision ⟨*~ organs*⟩ ⟨*~ impressions*⟩ **2** visible ⟨*a ~ equivalent for his feelings*⟩ **3** producing mental images; vivid **4** done or executed by sight only ⟨*~ navigation*⟩ – **visually** *adv*

visual aid *n* an instructional device (e g a chart or film) that appeals chiefly to vision

visualize, -ise *vt* **1** to make visible **2** to see or form a mental image of – **visualization** *n*

vital *adj* **1** concerned with or necessary to the maintenance of life ⟨*~ organs*⟩ **2** full of life and vigour; animated **3** concerned with, affecting, or being a manifestation of life or living beings **4a** tending to renew or refresh the living; invigorating **b** of the utmost importance; essential to continued worth or well-being – **vitally** *adv*

vitality *n* **1a** the quality which distinguishes the living from the dead or inanimate **b** capacity to live and develop; *also* physical or mental liveliness **2** power of enduring ⟨*the ~ of an idiom*⟩

vitalize, -ise *vt* to endow with vitality; animate – **vitalization** *n*

vitals *n pl* **1** the vital organs (e g the heart, liver, or brain) **2** essential parts

vital statistics *n pl* **1** statistics relating to births, deaths, health, etc **2** facts considered to be interesting or important; *specif* a woman's bust, waist, and hip measurements

vitamin *n* any of various organic compounds that are essential in minute quantities to the nutrition of most animals and act esp as (precursors of) coenzymes in the regulation of metabolic processes

vitiate *vt* **1** to make faulty or defective; debase ⟨*a spirit ~d by luxury*⟩ **2** to invalidate – **vitiator** *n*

viticulture *n* (the science of) the cultivation of grapevines – **viticultural** *adj*, **viticulturist** *n*

vitreous *adj* **1a** resembling glass in colour, composition, brittleness, etc ⟨~ *rocks*⟩ **b** characterized by low porosity and usu translucence ⟨~ *china*⟩ **2** of or being the vitreous humour – **vitreously** *adv*, **vitreousness** *n*

vitrify *vb* to convert into or become glass or a glassy substance (by heat and fusion) – **vitrifiable** *adj* **vitrification** *n*

vitriol *n* **1a** a (hydrated) sulphate of iron, copper, zinc, etc **b** concentrated sulphuric acid **2** virulent speech, expression, feeling, etc – **vitriolic** *adj*

vituperate *vt* to subject to severe or abusive censure; berate ~ *vi* to use harsh condemnatory language – **vituperator** *n*, **vituperative** *adj*, **vituperation** *n*

vivacious *adj* lively in temper or conduct; sprightly – **vivaciously** *adv*, **vivaciousness** *n*, **vivacity** *n*

vivarium *n*, *pl* **vivaria, vivariums** an enclosure for keeping and observing plants or esp terrestrial animals indoors

viva voce *n*, *adj*, *or adv* (an examination conducted) by word of mouth

vivid *adj* **1** full of vigorous life or freshness; lively ⟨~ *personality*⟩ **2** of a *colour* very intense **3** producing a strong or clear impression on the senses; *specif* producing distinct mental images ⟨*a ~ description*⟩ – **vividly** *adv*, **vividness** *n*

viviparous *adj* **1** producing living young, instead of eggs, from within the body in the manner of nearly all mammals, many reptiles, and a few fishes **2** germinating while still attached to the parent plant ⟨*the ~ seed of the mangrove*⟩ – **viviparously** *adv*, **viviparousness** *n*, **viviparity** *n*

vivisect *vb* to perform vivisection (on) – **vivisector** *n*

vivisection *n* operation or (distressful) experimentation on a living animal, usu in the course of medical or physiological research – **vivisectional** *adj*, **vivisectionally** *adv*, **vivisectionist** *n*

vixen *n* **1** a female fox **2** a scolding ill-tempered woman – **vixenish** *adj*, **vixenishly** *adv*

vizier *n* a high executive officer of various Muslim countries, esp of the former Ottoman Empire – **vizierate** *n*, **vizierial** *adj*, **viziership** *n*

V neck *n* (a garment with) a V-shaped neck

vocabulary *n* **1** a list of words, and sometimes phrases, usu arranged alphabetically and defined or translated ⟨*a ~ at the back of the book*⟩ **2a** the words employed by a language, group, or individual or in a field of work or knowledge ⟨*her limited ~*⟩ **b** a list or collection of terms or codes available for use (e g in an indexing system) **3** a supply of expressive techniques or devices (e g of an art form)

¹**vocal** *adj* **1** uttered by the voice; oral **2** of, composed or arranged for, or sung by the human voice **3a** having or exercising the power of producing voice, speech, or sound **b** given to strident or insistent expression; outspoken – **vocally** *adv*, **vocality** *n*

²**vocal** *n* **1** a vocal sound **2** a usu accompanied musical composition or passage for the voice

vocal cords *n pl* either of 2 pairs of mucous membrane folds in the cavity of the larynx whose free edges vibrate to produce sound

vocalist *n* a singer

vocalize, -ise *vt* to give voice to; utter; *specif* to sing ~ *vi* **1** to utter vocal sounds **2** to sing (without words) – **vocalizer** *n*, **vocalization** *n*

vocation *n* **1a** a summons or strong inclination to a particular state or course of action; *esp* a divine call to the religious life **b** an entry into the priesthood or a religious order **2** the work in which a person is regularly employed; a career **3** the special function of an individual or group

vocational *adj* of or being training in a skill or trade to be pursued as a career ⟨~ *courses*⟩ – **vocationally** *adv*

vocative *n* (a form in) a grammatical case expressing the one addressed – **vocative** *adj*, **vocatively** *adv*

vociferate *vb* to cry out or utter loudly; clamour, shout – **vociferant** *n*, **vociferator** *n*, **vociferation** *n*

vociferous *adj* marked by or given to vehement insistent outcry – **vociferously** *adv*, **vociferousness** *n*

vodka *n* a colourless and unaged neutral spirit distilled from a mash (e g of rye or wheat)

vogue *n* **1** the prevailing, esp temporary, fashion ⟨*long skirts were in ~*⟩ **2** popular acceptance or favour; popularity ⟨*book enjoyed a great ~ about 1960*⟩ – **vogue** *adj*

¹**voice** *n* **1a** sound produced by humans, birds, etc by forcing air from the lungs through the larynx in mammals or syrinx in birds **b(1)** (the use, esp in singing or acting, of) musical sound produced by the vocal cords and resonated by the cavities of the head, throat, lungs, etc **(2)** the power or ability to sing **(3)** any of the melodic parts in a vocal or instrumental composition **(4)** condition of the vocal organs with respect to singing ⟨*be in good ~*⟩ **c** expiration of air with the vocal cords drawn close so as to vibrate audibly (e g in uttering vowels or consonant sounds such as /v/ or /z/) **d** the faculty of utterance; speech **2** a sound suggesting vocal utterance ⟨*the ~ of a foghorn*⟩ **3** an instrument or medium of expression ⟨*the party became the ~ of the workers*⟩ **4a** the expressed wish or opinion ⟨*claimed to follow the ~ of the people*⟩ **b** right of expression; say ⟨*I have no ~ in this matter*⟩ **c** expression – chiefly in *give voice to* **5** distinction of form or a particular system of inflections of a verb to indicate whether it is the subject of the verb that acts ⟨*the passive ~*⟩

²**voice** *vt* **1** to express (a feeling or opinion) in words; utter **2** to adjust (e g an organ pipe) in manufacture, for producing the proper musical sounds **3** to pronounce with voice

voice box *n* the larynx

voiced *adj* **1** having a usu specified type of voice ⟨*soft-voiced*⟩ **2** uttered with vocal cord vibration (e g in /b/) – **voicedness** *n*

voiceless *adj* not voiced (e g in /p/) – **voicelessly** *adv*, **voicelessness** *n*

voice-over *n* the voice of an unseen narrator in a film or television programme; *also* the voice of a visible character indicating his thoughts

¹**void** *adj* **1** containing nothing; unoccupied **2a** devoid ⟨*a nature ~ of all malice*⟩ **b** having no members or examples; *specif, of a suit* having no cards represented in a particular hand **3** vain, useless **4** of no legal effect **5** having no holder or occupant; vacant ⟨*a ~ bishopric*⟩ – *fml* – **voidness** *n*

²**void** *n* **1a** empty space; vacuum **b** an opening, gap **2** a feeling of lack, want, or emptiness

³**void** *vt* **1** to make empty or vacant; clear **2** to discharge or emit ⟨~ *excrement*⟩ **3** to nullify, annul ⟨~ *a contract*⟩ – **voidable** *adj*, **voider** *n*

voile *n* a fine soft sheer fabric used esp for women's summer clothing or curtains

¹**volatile** *n* a volatile substance

²**volatile** *adj* **1** capable of being readily vaporized at a relatively low temperature ⟨*alcohol is a ~ liquid*⟩ **2a** lighthearted, lively **b** dangerously unstable; explosive ⟨*a ~ social situation*⟩ **3a** frivolously changeable; fickle **b** characterized by rapid change **4** evanescent, transitory – **volatility** *n*

vol-au-vent *n* a round case of puff pastry filled with a mixture of meat, poultry, or fish in a thick sauce

volcanic *adj* **1a** of or produced by a volcano **b** characterized by volcanoes **2** explosively violent; volatile ⟨~ *emotions*⟩ – **volcanically** *adv*

volcano *n, pl* **volcanoes, volcanos 1** (a hill or mountain surrounding) an outlet in a planet's crust from which molten or hot rock and steam issue **2** a dynamic or violently creative person; *also* a situation liable to become violent – **volcanology** *n*, **volcanologist** *n*

vole *n* any of various small plant-eating rodents usu with a stout body, blunt nose, and short ears

volition *n* **1** (an act of making) a free choice or decision **2** the power of choosing or determining; will – **volitional** *adj*

¹volley *n* **1a** a flight of arrows, bullets, or other missiles **b** simultaneous discharge of a number of missile weapons **c**(1) (the course of) the flight of the ball, shuttle, etc before striking the ground; *also* a return or succession of returns made by hitting the ball, shuttle, etc before it touches the ground (2) a kick of the ball in soccer before it touches the ground **2** a burst or emission of many things at once or in rapid succession ⟨a ~ *of oaths*⟩

²volley *vb* **volleying; volleyed** *vt* **1** to discharge (as if) in a volley **2** to propel (an object that has not yet hit the ground), esp with an implement or the hand or foot ~ *vi* **1** to be discharged (as if) in a volley **2** to make a volley – **volleyer** *n*

volleyball *n* a game between 2 teams of usu 6 players who volley a ball over a high net in the centre of a court

volt *n* the derived SI unit of electrical potential difference and electromotive force equal to the difference of potential between 2 points in a conducting wire carrying a constant current of 1 ampere when the power dissipated between these 2 points is equal to 1 watt

voltage *n* an electric potential difference; electromotive force

volte-face *n* a sudden reversal of attitude or policy; an about-face

voluble *adj* characterized by ready or rapid speech; talkative – **volubleness** *n*, **volubly** *adv*, **volubility** *n*

volume *n* **1a** a series of printed sheets bound typically in book form; a book **b** a series of issues of a periodical **2** space occupied as measured in cubic units (e g litres); cubic capacity **3a** an amount; *also* a bulk, mass **b** the amount of a substance occupying a particular volume **c** (the representation of) mass in art or architecture **d** a considerable quantity; a great deal – often *pl* with sing. meaning; esp in *speak volumes for* **4** the degree of loudness or the intensity of a sound – **volumed** *adj*

voluminous *adj* **1** having or containing a large volume; *specif, of a garment* very full **2a** consisting of or (capable of) filling a large volume or several volumes ⟨a ~ *correspondence*⟩ **b** writing much or at great length – **voluminously** *adv*, **voluminousness** *n*, **voluminosity** *n*

¹voluntary *adj* **1** proceeding from free choice or consent **2** acting without compulsion and without payment ⟨~ *workers*⟩ **3** intentional ⟨~ *manslaughter*⟩ **4** of, subject to, or regulated by the will ⟨~ *behaviour*⟩ **5** having power of free choice ⟨*man is a ~ agent*⟩ **6** provided or supported by voluntary action ⟨a ~ *hospital*⟩ – **voluntarily** *adv*, **voluntariness** *n*

²voluntary *n* an organ piece played before or after a religious service

¹volunteer *n* one who undertakes a service of his/her own free will; *esp* sby who enters into military service voluntarily

²volunteer *adj* being, consisting of, or engaged in by volunteers ⟨a ~ *army*⟩

³volunteer *vt* **1** to offer or bestow voluntarily ⟨~ *one's services*⟩ **2** to communicate voluntarily; say ~ *vi* to offer oneself as a volunteer

voluptuary *n* one whose chief interest is luxury and sensual pleasure – **voluptuary** *adj*

voluptuous *adj* **1** causing delight or pleasure to the senses; conducive to, occupied with, or arising from sensual gratification ⟨a ~ *dance*⟩ **2** suggestive of sensual pleasure ⟨a ~ *mouth*⟩; *broadly* sexually attractive, esp owing to shapeliness – **voluptuously** *adv*, **voluptuousness** *n*

volute *n* **1** a form that is shaped like a spiral or curled over on itself like a scroll **2** an ornament characteristic of classical architecture that is shaped like a roll of material or a scroll **3** (the short-spined thick shell of) any of numerous marine gastropod molluscs – **volute, voluted** *adj*

¹vomit *n* **1** a vomiting; *also* the vomited matter **2** an emetic

²vomit *vb* **1** to disgorge (the contents of the stomach) through the mouth **2** to eject (sthg) violently or abundantly; spew – **vomiter** *n*

¹voodoo *n, pl* **voodoos 1** a set of magical beliefs and practices, mainly of W African origin, practised chiefly in Haiti and characterized by communication by trance with deities **2a** one skilled in (voodoo) spells and necromancy **b** a voodoo spell – **voodoo** *adj*, **voodooism** *n*

²voodoo *vt* to bewitch (as if) by means of voodoo

voracious *adj* **1** having a huge appetite; ravenous **2** excessively eager; insatiable ⟨a ~ *reader*⟩ – **voraciously** *adv*, **voraciousness** *n*, **voracity** *n*

vortex *n, pl* **vortices** *also* **vortexes 1a** a mass of whirling water, air, etc that tends to form a cavity or vacuum in the centre of the circle into which material is drawn; *esp* a whirlpool or whirlwind **b** a region within a body of fluid in which the fluid is rotating **2** sthg that resembles a whirlpool in violent activity or in engulfing or overwhelming – **vortical** *adj*, **vorticity** *n*

votary, votarist *n* a staunch admirer, worshipper, or advocate; a devotee

¹vote *n* **1a** a (formal) expression of opinion or will in response to a proposed decision **b** BALLOT 1 **2** the collective verdict of a body of people expressed by voting **3** *the* franchise **4** a definable group of voters ⟨*getting the Labour ~ to the polls*⟩ **5** a sum of money voted for a special use

²vote *vi* **1** to cast one's vote; *esp* to exercise a political franchise **2** to express an opinion ~ *vt* **1** to choose, decide, or authorize by vote **2a** to judge by general agreement; declare ⟨*concert was ~ d a flop*⟩ **b** to offer as a suggestion; propose ⟨*I ~ we all go home*⟩ – *infml* – **voter** *n*

votive *adj* **1** offered or performed in fulfilment of a vow and often in gratitude or devotion **2** consisting of or expressing a religious vow, wish, or desire – **votively** *adv*, **votiveness** *n*

vouch *vi* **1** to give or act as a guarantee *for* **2** to supply supporting evidence or personal assurance *for*

voucher *n* **1a** a documentary record of a business transaction **b** a written certificate or authorization **2** *Br* a ticket that can be exchanged for specific goods or services

vouchsafe *vt* **1** to grant as a special privilege or in a gracious or condescending manner **2** to condescend, deign *to* do sthg – **vouchsafement** *n*

¹vow *n* a solemn and often religiously binding promise or assertion; *specif* one by which a person binds him-/herself to an act, service, or condition

²vow *vt* **1** to promise solemnly; swear **2** to dedicate or consecrate by a vow **3** to resolve to bring about ⟨~ *revenge*⟩ ~ *vi* to make a vow – **vower** *n*

³vow *vt* to avow, declare

vowel *n* (a letter, in English usu *a, e, i, o, u*, and sometimes *y*, representing) any of a class of speech sounds (e g /ee/ or /i/) characterized by lack of closure in the breath channel or lack of audible friction

vox populi *n* the opinion of the general public

¹voyage *n* a considerable course or period of travelling by other than land routes; *broadly* a journey

²voyage *vb* to make a voyage (across) – **voyager** *n*

voyeur *n* **1** one who obtains sexual gratification by visual means, specif by looking at sexual organs and sexual acts **2** a prying observer who is usu seeking the sordid or the scandalous – **voyeurism** *n*, **voyeuristic** *adj*, **voyeuristically** *adv*

V sign *n* a gesture made by raising the index and middle fingers in a V **a** with the palm outwards signifying victory **b** with the palm inwards signifying insult or contempt

vulcanization, -isation *n* the process of chemically treating rubber or similar material to give it elasticity, strength, stability, etc – **vulcanize** *vb*

vulgar *adj* **1** generally used, applied, or accepted **2a** of or being the common people; plebeian **b** generally current; public ⟨~ *opinion*⟩ **3a** lacking in cultivation, breeding, or taste; coarse **b** ostentatious or excessive in expenditure or display; pretentious **4** lewdly or profanely indecent; obscene – **vulgarly** *adv*, **vulgarity** *n*

vulgar fraction *n* a fraction in which both the denominator and numerator are explicitly present and are separated by a horizontal or slanted line

vulgarian *n* a vulgar and esp rich person

vulgarism *n* **1** a word or expression originated or used chiefly by illiterate people **2** vulgarity

vulgarize, -ise *vt* **1** to diffuse generally; popularize **2** to make vulgar; coarsen – **vulgarizer** *n*, **vulgarization** *n*

Vulgar Latin *n* the informal Latin of ancient Rome, established as the chief source of the Romance languages

vulgate *n* **1** *cap the* Latin version of the Bible authorized and used by the Roman Catholic church **2** a commonly accepted text or reading

vulnerable *adj* **1** capable of being physically or mentally wounded **2** open to attack or damage; assailable – **vulnerableness** *n*, **vulnerably** *adv*, **vulnerability** *n*

vulpine *adj* **1** of or resembling a fox **2** foxy, crafty

vulture *n* **1** any of various large usu bald-headed birds of prey that are related to the hawks, eagles, and falcons and feed on carrion **2** a rapacious or predatory person – **vulturous** *adj*, **vulturine** *adj*

vulva *n, pl* **vulvas, vulvae** the (opening between the projecting) external parts of the female genital organs – **vulval, vulvar** *adj*

vying *pres part of* VIE

W

w *n, pl* **w's, ws** *often cap* (a graphic representation of, or device for reproducing,) the 23rd letter of the English alphabet

Wac *n* a member of the Women's Army Corps established in the USA during WW II

wack *n, N Eng* – used as a familiar form of address

wacky *adj, chiefly NAm* absurdly or amusingly eccentric or irrational; crazy – *infml* – **wackily** *adv*, **wackiness** *n*

¹wad *n* **1a** a soft mass, esp of a loose fibrous material, variously used (e g to stop an aperture or pad a garment) **b(1)** a soft plug used to retain a powder charge, esp in a muzzle-loading cannon or gun **(2)** a felt or paper disc that separates the components of a shotgun cartridge **2** a roll of paper money **3** *chiefly NAm* a considerable amount – *infml; often pl with sing. meaning* ⟨*getting* ~s *of publicity*⟩

²wad *vt* **-dd-** **1** to form into a wad or wadding **2a** to insert a wad into ⟨~ *a gun*⟩ **b** to hold in by a wad ⟨~ *a bullet in a gun*⟩ **3** to stuff, pad, or line with some soft substance **4** *chiefly NAm* to roll or crush tightly ⟨~ *his shirt up into a ball*⟩ – **wadder** *n*

wadding *n* stuffing or padding in the form of a soft mass or sheet of short loose fibres

¹waddle *vi* **waddling** **1** to walk with short steps swinging the forepart of the body from side to side **2** to move clumsily in a manner suggesting a waddle ⟨*car* ~d *out of the drift* – Len Deighton⟩ – **waddler** *n*

²waddle *n* an awkward clumsy swaying gait

¹wade *vi* **1** to walk through a medium (e g water) offering more resistance than air **2** to proceed with difficulty or effort ⟨~ *through a dull book*⟩ **3** to attack with determination or vigour – + *in* or *into* ⟨~ *into a task*⟩ ~ *vt* to cross by wading – **wadable** *adj*

²wade *n* an act of wading ⟨*a* ~ *in the brook*⟩

wader *n* **1** *pl* high waterproof boots used for wading **2** any of many long-legged birds (e g sandpipers and snipes) that wade in water in search of food

wadge *n, Br* a thick bundle; a wad – *infml*

wadi *n* the bed of a stream in regions of SW Asia and N Africa that is dry except during the rainy season

wading bird *n* WADER 2

wafer *n* **1a** a thin crisp biscuit; *also* a biscuit consisting of layers of wafer sometimes sandwiched with a filling **b** a round piece of thin unleavened bread used in the celebration of the Eucharist **2** an adhesive disc of dried paste used, esp formerly, as a seal

¹waffle *n* a cake of batter that is baked in a waffle iron and has a crisp dimpled surface

²waffle *vi* **waffling** *chiefly Br* to talk or write foolishly, inconsequentially, and usu at length; blather – *infml* ⟨*can* ~ *tiresomely off the point* – TLS⟩ – **waffler** *n*

³waffle *n, chiefly Br* empty or pretentious words – *infml* – **waffly** *adj*

waffle iron *n* a cooking utensil with 2 hinged metal parts that shut on each other and impress surface projections on the waffle being cooked

¹waft *vb* to convey or be conveyed lightly (as if) by the impulse of wind or waves – **wafter** *n*

²waft *n* **1** sthg (e g a smell) that is wafted; a whiff **2** a slight breeze; a puff

¹wag *vb* **-gg-** *vi* **1** to move to and fro, esp with quick jerky motions **2** to move in chatter or gossip ⟨*tongues* ~ged⟩ ~ *vt* **1** to cause to swing to and fro, esp with quick jerky motions; *esp* to nod (the head) or shake (a finger) in assent or mild reproof – often + *at* **2** to move (e g the tongue) animatedly in conversation – **wagger** *n*

²wag *n* an act of wagging; a shake

³wag *n* a wit, joker

¹wage *vt* to engage in or carry on (a war, conflict, etc)

²wage *n* **1a** a payment for services, esp of a manual kind, usu according to contract and on an hourly, daily, weekly, or piecework basis – usu pl with sing. meaning; *compare* SALARY **b** *pl* the share of the national product attributable to labour as a factor in production **2** a recompense, reward – usu pl with sing. meaning but sing. or pl in constr ⟨*the* ~s *of sin is death* – Rom 6:23 (RSV)⟩ – **wageless** *adj*

¹wager *n* **1** sthg (e g a sum of money) risked on an uncertain event **2** sthg on which bets are laid ⟨*do a stunt as a ~*⟩

²wager *vb* to lay as or make a bet – **wagerer** *n*

wage slave *n* a person dependent on wages or a salary for his/her livelihood

waggery *n* **1** mischievous merriment **2** a jest; *esp* PRACTICAL JOKE

waggish *adj* befitting or characteristic of a wag; humorous ⟨*a ~ disposition*⟩ – **waggishly** *adv*, **waggishness** *n*

waggle *vb* **waggling** to (cause to) sway or move repeatedly from side to side; wag – **waggle** *n*, **waggly** *adj*

wagon, *chiefly Br* **waggon** *n* **1a** a usu 4-wheeled vehicle for transporting bulky or heavy loads, often having a removable canopy, and drawn orig by animals **2** TROLLEY 2a; *esp* one used in a dining room or for serving light refreshments (e g afternoon tea) **3** *Br* a railway goods vehicle – **on/off the wagon** abstaining/no longer abstaining from alcoholic drinks – *infml*

wagonette *n* a light horse-drawn wagon with 2 inward-facing seats along the sides behind a forward-facing front seat

wagon-lit *n*, *pl* **wagons-lits, wagon-lits** a sleeping car on a continental train

wagtail *n* any of numerous chiefly Old World birds with trim slender bodies and very long tails that they habitually jerk up and down

waif *n* **1** a piece of property found but unclaimed **2** a stray helpless person or animal; *esp* a homeless child

¹wail *vi* **1** to express sorrow by uttering mournful cries; lament **2** to make a sound suggestive of a mournful cry **3** to express dissatisfaction plaintively; complain – **wailer** *n*

²wail *n* **1** a usu loud prolonged high-pitched cry expressing grief or pain **2** a sound suggestive of wailing ⟨*the ~ of an air-raid siren*⟩

wain *n* **1** a usu large and heavy wagon for farm use **2** *cap* URSA MAJOR

¹wainscot *n* **1a** a usu panelled wooden lining of an interior wall **b** the lower part of an interior wall when finished differently from the remainder of the wall **2** *Br* a fine grade of oak imported for woodwork

²wainscot *vt* **-t-, -tt-** to line (as if) with boards or panelling

waist *n* **1a** the (narrow) part of the body between the chest and hips **b** the greatly constricted part of the abdomen of a wasp, fly, etc **2** the part of sthg corresponding to or resembling the human waist: e g **a**(1) the part of a ship's deck between the poop and forecastle (2) the middle part of a sailing ship between foremast and mainmast **b** the middle section of the fuselage of an aircraft **3** the part of a garment covering the body at the waist or waistline

waistband *n* a band (e g on trousers or a skirt) fitting round the waist

waistcoat *n*, *chiefly Br* a sleeveless upper garment that fastens down the centre front and usu has a V-neck; *esp* such a garment worn under a jacket as part of a man's suit – **waistcoated** *adj*

waistline *n* **1** an imaginary line encircling the narrowest part of the waist; *also* the part of a garment corresponding to this line or to the place where fashion dictates this should be **2** body circumference at the waist

¹wait *vt* **1a** to stay in place in expectation of; await ⟨*~ your turn*⟩ **b** to delay in hope of a favourable change in ⟨*~ out a storm*⟩ **2** to delay serving (a meal), esp in expectation of further arrivals – *infml* ~ *vi* **1a** to remain stationary in readiness or expectation ⟨*~ for a train*⟩ **b** to pause for another to catch up **2a** to look forward

expectantly ⟨*just ~ing to see his rival lose*⟩ **b** to hold back expectantly ⟨*have to ~ till Thursday*⟩ **3** to serve at meals – usu in *wait at table* or *NAm wait on table* **4** to be ready and available ⟨*slippers ~ing by the bed*⟩ – **wait on/upon 1** to act as an attendant to; serve **2** to await **3** *archaic* to make a formal call on

²wait *n* **1** any of a group who serenade for gratuities, esp at the Christmas season **2** an act or period of waiting ⟨*a long ~ for the bus*⟩

waiter *n* **1** *fem* **waitress** one who waits at table (e g in a restaurant), esp as a regular job **2** a salver, tray

waiting list *n* a list of those waiting (e g for a vacancy or for sthg to become available), arranged usu in order of application

waiting room *n* a room for the use of people who are waiting (e g for a train or to see a doctor)

waive *vt* **1** to refrain from demanding or enforcing; relinquish, forgo **2** to put off from immediate consideration; postpone

waiver *n* (a document giving proof of) the relinquishing of a right

¹wake *vb* **waked, woke; waked, woken, woke** *vi* **1** to be or remain awake ⟨*her waking hours*⟩ **2** to awake – often + *up* ~ *vt* **1** to rouse (as if) from sleep; awake – often + *up* **2** to arouse, evoke ⟨*~ memories*⟩ **3** to arouse conscious interest in; alert – usu + *to* ⟨*~ him to the fact of her existence*⟩ – **waker** *n*

²wake *n* **1a** an annual English parish festival formerly held in commemoration of the church's patron saint **b** VIGIL 1a **2** a watch held over the body of a dead person prior to burial and sometimes accompanied by festivity; *broadly* any festive leavetaking **3** *Br* an annual holiday in northern England – usu pl but sing. or pl in constr ⟨*we all go off to Blackpool during ~s week*⟩

³wake *n* the track left by a moving body (e g a ship) in a fluid (e g water)

wakeful *adj* **1** not sleeping or able to sleep **2** spent without sleep ⟨*a ~ night*⟩ – **wakefully** *adv*, **wakefulness** *n*

waken *vi* to awake – often + *up* ~ *vt* to rouse out of sleep; wake – **wakener** *n*

¹walk *vi* **1** *of a spirit* to move about in visible form; appear **2a** to move along on foot; advance by steps, in such a way that at least 1 foot is always in contact with the ground **b** to go on foot for exercise or pleasure **c** to go at a walk **3** *of an inanimate object* to move in a manner suggestive of walking **4** *archaic* to pursue a course of action or way of life; conduct oneself ⟨*~ in darkness* – Jn 8:12 (AV)⟩ ~ *vt* **1** to pass on foot through, along, over, or on ⟨*~ the streets*⟩ ⟨*~ a tightrope*⟩ **2a** to cause (an animal) to go at a walk ⟨*~ a horse*⟩ **b** to take (an animal) for a walk ⟨*~ing a dog*⟩ **c** to cause (an inanimate object) to move in a manner suggestive of walking **3** to accompany on foot; walk with ⟨*~ed her home*⟩ **4** to bring to a specified condition by walking ⟨*~ed us off our feet*⟩ **5** to follow on foot for the purposes of examining, measuring, etc ⟨*~ed the horse before the jump-off*⟩ – **walk off with 1a** to steal and take away **b** to take away unintentionally **2** to win or gain, esp by outdoing one's competitors without difficulty ⟨*walked off with first prize*⟩ – **walk over** to treat contemptuously – **walk tall** to bear oneself proudly – **walk the plank** to be forced to walk, esp blindfold, along a board laid over the side of a ship until one falls into the sea

²walk *n* **1a** an act or instance of going on foot, esp for exercise or pleasure ⟨*go for a ~*⟩ **b** SPACE WALK **2** a route for walking ⟨*many delightful ~s in the neighbourhood*⟩ **3** a place designed for walking: e g **a** a path specially arranged or surfaced for walking; a footpath **b** a railed or colonnaded platform **c** a promenade **4** a place where animals (e g sheep) are kept with minimal restraint **5** distance to be walked ⟨*a quarter of a mile's ~ from here*⟩ **6a** the gait of a 2-legged animal in which the feet are lifted alternately with 1 foot always (partially) on the ground **b** the slow 4-beat gait of a quadruped, specif a horse, in which there are always at least 2 feet on the ground **c** a low rate of speed ⟨*the shortage of raw materials slowed production to a ~*⟩ **7** a route regularly traversed by a person (e g a postman or policeman) in the performance of a particular activity **8** a manner of walking ⟨*his ~ is just like his father's*⟩ **9** an occupation, calling – chiefly in *walk of life* **10** a journey undertaken on foot along a usu agreed route to earn money promised by sponsors for charity – esp in *sponsored walk, charity walk*

walkabout n **1** a short period of wandering bush life engaged in occasionally by an Australian aborigine for ceremonial reasons **2** an informal walk among the crowds by a public figure ⟨*the Queen on her Jubilee ~*⟩

walker n sthg used in walking; specif a framework designed to support a baby learning to walk or a cripple who cannot walk unaided

walkie-talkie n a compact battery-operated transceiver

walk-in adj large enough for a person to enter and move around in ⟨*a ~ safe*⟩

¹walking n the condition of a surface as it will affect sby going on foot ⟨*the ~ is slippery*⟩

²walking adj **1a** animate; esp human ⟨*a ~ encyclopedia*⟩ **b** able to walk; ambulatory **c** that moves in a manner suggestive of walking ⟨*a ~ toy*⟩ **d** guided or operated by a walker ⟨*a ~ plough*⟩ **2a** used for or in walking ⟨*~ shoes*⟩ **b** characterized by or consisting of walking ⟨*a ~ tour*⟩

walking papers n pl, chiefly NAm MARCHING ORDERS – infml

walk-on n (sby who has) a small usu nonspeaking part in a dramatic production

walkout n **1** STRIKE 3 **2** the action of leaving a meeting or organization as an expression of protest

walk out vi **1** to go on strike **2** to depart suddenly, often as an expression of protest **3** chiefly Br COURT 1 – often + with; no longer in vogue – **walk out on** to leave in the lurch; abandon

walkover n an easily won contest; also an advance from one round of a competition to the next without contest, due to the withdrawal or absence of other entrants

¹wall n **1** a usu upright and solid structure, esp of masonry or concrete, having considerable height and length in relation to width and serving esp to divide, enclose, retain, or support: e g **a** a structure bounding a garden, park, or estate **b** any of the upright enclosing structures of a room or house **c** RETAINING WALL **d** the surface of a wall ⟨*the ~ is painted cream*⟩ **2** a material layer enclosing space ⟨*the ~ of a container*⟩ **3** sthg resembling a wall: e g **a** an almost vertical rock surface **b** sthg that acts as a barrier or defence ⟨*tariff ~*⟩ – **walled** adj, **wall-less** adj, **wall-like** adj – **to the wall** into a hopeless position ⟨*small businesses being driven to the wall by government policy*⟩ – **up the wall** Br into a state of exasperation – infml

²wall vt **1a** to protect or surround (as if) with a wall ⟨*a lake ~ed in by mountains*⟩ **b** to separate or shut out (as if) by a wall ⟨*~ed off half the house*⟩ **2a** to immure **b** to close (an opening) (as if) with a wall USE (2) usu + up – **waller** n, **walling** n

wallaby n, pl **wallabies** also esp collectively **wallaby** any of various small or medium-sized and usu less dull-coloured kangaroos

wallah n a person who does a specified type of work or performs a specified duty – usu in combination; infml ⟨*the book ~ was an itinerant peddler* – George Orwell⟩

wallet n **1** a holder for paper money, usu with compartments for other items (e g credit cards and stamps) **2** a flat case or folder ⟨*a ~ of maps*⟩

walleye n **1** an eye with a whitish iris or opaque white (area in the) cornea **2** (a squint marked by) an eye that turns outwards – **walleyed** adj

wallflower n **1** any of several Old World perennial plants of the mustard family; esp a hardy erect plant with showy fragrant flowers **2** sby who from shyness or unpopularity remains on the sidelines of a social activity; esp a woman who fails to get partners at a dance – infml

¹wallop n **1** a powerful body blow; ²PUNCH 2 – sometimes used interjectionally; infml **2** emotional or psychological force; impact – infml **3** Br beer – slang

²wallop vt **1** to hit with force; thrash **2** to beat by a wide margin; trounce USE infml – **walloper** n, **walloping** n

walloping adj large, whopping – infml

¹wallow vi **1** to roll or lie around lazily or luxuriously ⟨*pigs ~ing in mud*⟩ **2** to indulge oneself immoderately; revel in ⟨*~ing in sentiment*⟩ **3** of a ship to struggle laboriously in or through rough water; broadly to pitch ⟨*ship ~ed down the coast*⟩ – **wallower** n

²wallow n **1** an act or instance of wallowing **2a** a muddy or dusty area used by animals for wallowing **b** a depression formed (as if) by the wallowing of animals

wall painting n (a) representational or decorative painting directly on (some surface in immediate contact with) a wall (e g in encaustic, fresco, or tempera)

¹wallpaper n decorative paper for the walls of a room

²wallpaper vb to apply wallpaper to (the walls of a room)

Wall Street n the influential financial interests of the US economy

wall-to-wall adj, of carpeting covering the whole floor of a room

walnut n (an edible nut or the wood of) any of a genus of trees with richly grained wood used for cabinetmaking and veneers

walrus n, pl **walruses**, esp collectively **walrus** either of 2 large sea mammals of northern seas, related to the seals, and hunted for their tough heavy hide, ivory tusks, and the oil yielded by the blubber

¹waltz n (music for or in the tempo of) a ballroom dance in ¾ time with strong accent on the first beat

²waltz vi **1** to dance a waltz **2** to move along in a lively or confident manner **3** to proceed easily or boldly; breeze ⟨*~ed through his finals*⟩ ~ vt **1** to dance a waltz with ⟨*~ed her round the room*⟩ **2** to grab and lead (e g a person) unceremoniously; march – usu + off USE (vi 2&3; vt 2) infml – **waltzer** n

wampum n beads of polished shells strung together and used by N American Indians as money and ornaments

wan adj **-nn-** **1a** suggestive of poor health; pallid **b** lacking vitality; feeble **2** of light dim, faint – **wanly** adv, **wanness** n

wand n a slender rod **a** carried as a sign of office **b** used by conjurers and magicians

wander vi **1** to go or travel idly or aimlessly ⟨*~ across the room*⟩ **2** to follow or extend along a winding course; meander ⟨*road ~s across the plain*⟩ **3a** to deviate (as if) from a course; stray ⟨*eyes ~ed from the page*⟩ **b** to lose concentration; stray in thought ⟨*as the lecturer droned on, the student's mind began to ~*⟩ **c** to think or speak incoherently or illogically ⟨*as the fever worsened, the patient began to ~*⟩ ~ vt to roam over ⟨*~ed the hillside in search of shelter*⟩ – **wander** n, **wanderer** n

¹wandering n **1** a going about from place to place **2**

movement away from the proper or usual course or place
USE often pl with sing. meaning

²wandering *adj* **1** winding, meandering ⟨*a ~ course*⟩ **2** not keeping a rational or sensible course ⟨*~ thoughts*⟩ **3** nomadic ⟨*~ tribes*⟩

wanderlust *n* eager longing for or impulse towards travelling

¹wane *vi* **1** to decrease in size or extent; dwindle: e g *a of the moon, satellites, etc* to diminish in phase or intensity **b** *of light or colour* to become less brilliant; dim **2** to fall gradually from power, prosperity, or influence; decline

²wane *n* **1a** the act or process of waning **b** a time of waning; *specif* the period from full phase of the moon to the new moon **2** a defect in prepared timber characterized by bark or lack of wood at a corner or edge – **waney, wany** *adj* – **on the wane** in a state of decline; waning

wangle *vt* **wangling 1** to adjust or manipulate for personal or fraudulent ends **2** to bring about or get by devious means ⟨*~ an invitation*⟩ *USE* infml – **wangler** *n*

wank *vi, Br* to masturbate – vulg – **wank** *n*

wanker *n* **1** one who masturbates – vulg **2** a foolish or superficial fellow – slang

¹want *vt* **1** to fail to possess, esp in customary or required amount; lack ⟨*his answer ~s courtesy*⟩ **2a** to have a desire for ⟨*he ~s to go*⟩ **b** to have an inclination to; like ⟨*say what you ~, he is efficient*⟩ **3a** to have need of; require ⟨*the room ~s decorating*⟩ **b** to suffer from the lack of; need ⟨*thousands still ~ food and shelter*⟩ **4** to wish or demand the presence of ⟨*the boss ~s you*⟩ **5** ought – + *to* and infinitive ⟨*you ~ to see a doctor about that cold*⟩ ~ *vi* **1** to be deficient or short by a specified amount ⟨*it ~s 3 minutes to 12*⟩ **2** to be needy or destitute **3** to have need; be lacking in the specified respect ⟨*never ~s for friends*⟩ **4** chiefly NAm to desire to come or go ⟨*~s out of the syndicate*⟩

²want *n* **1a** the quality or state of lacking sthg required or usual ⟨*he suffers from a ~ of good sense*⟩ **b** extreme poverty **2** sthg wanted; a need ⟨*supply your ~s*⟩

wanting *adj* **1** not present or in evidence; absent **2a** not up to the required standard or expectation ⟨*a candidate tested and found ~*⟩ **b** lacking in the specified ability or capacity; deficient ⟨*~ in gratitude*⟩

¹wanton *adj* **1** mischievous **2** sexually unbridled; promiscuous **3** having no just foundation or provocation; malicious ⟨*~ indifference to the needs of others*⟩ **4** uncontrolled, unbridled ⟨*~ inflation*⟩ **5** luxuriant, lavish – now chiefly poetic – **wantonly** *adv*, **wantonness** *n*

²wanton *n* a wanton person; *esp* a lewd or lascivious woman

wapiti *n, pl* **wapitis**, *esp collectively* **wapiti** an American deer similar to the European red deer but larger

¹war *n* **1** a state or period of usu open and declared armed hostile conflict between states or nations **2** a struggle between opposing forces or for a particular end ⟨*a ~ against disease*⟩

²war *vi* **-rr- 1** to engage in warfare **2a** to be in active or vigorous conflict **b** to be opposed or inconsistent ⟨*~ring principles*⟩

¹warble *vb* **warbling** *vi* to sing or sound in a trilling manner or with many turns and variations ~ *vt* to render musically, esp in an ornamented or trilling manner – **warble** *n*

²warble *n* (a swelling under the hide of cattle, horses, etc caused by) the maggot of a warble fly – **warbled** *adj*

warbler *n* any of numerous small Old World birds (e g a whitethroat) which are related to the thrushes and many of which are noted songsters

war bride *n* a woman who marries a (foreign) serviceman met during a time of war

war crime *n* a crime (e g genocide or maltreatment of prisoners) committed during or in connection with war – **war criminal** *n*

war cry *n* **1** a cry used during charging or rallying by a body of fighters in war **2** a slogan used esp to rally people to a cause

ward *n* **1** the inner court of a castle or fortress **2** a division of a prison or hospital **3** a division of a city or town for electoral or administrative purposes **4** a projecting ridge of metal in a lock casing or keyhole allowing only a key with a corresponding notch to operate; *also* a corresponding notch on a key **5** a person under guard, protection, or surveillance; *esp* one under the care or control of a legal guardian ⟨*~ of court*⟩ – **warded** *adj*

¹-ward *also* **-wards** *suffix* (→ *adj*) **1** facing or tending in (such) a direction ⟨*home*ward⟩ ⟨*north*ward⟩ **2** occurring or situated in (such) a direction ⟨*left*ward⟩

²-ward *suffix* (→ *adv*), *chiefly NAm* **-wards**

war dance *n* a dance performed esp by primitive peoples as preparation for battle or in celebration of victory

warden *n* **1** one having care or charge of sthg; a guardian **2** the governor of a town, district, or fortress **3** an official charged with special supervisory duties or with the enforcement of specified laws or regulations ⟨*game ~*⟩ ⟨*air-raid ~*⟩ ⟨*traffic ~*⟩ **4** any of various British college officials **5** NAm a prison governor – **wardenship** *n*

¹warder, fem wardress *n* **1** Br a prison guard **2** archaic a watchman, guard – **wardership** *n*

²warder *n* a staff formerly used by a king or commander in chief to signal orders

ward off *vt* to deflect, avert

wardrobe *n* **1** a room or (movable) cupboard, esp fitted with shelves and a rail or pegs, where clothes are kept **2a** a collection of clothes (e g belonging to 1 person) **b** a collection of stage costumes and accessories **3** the department of a royal or noble household entrusted with the care of clothes, jewels, and personal articles

wardroom *n* the space in a warship allotted to the commissioned officers excepting the captain

-wards *suffix* (→ *adv*) **1** in (such) a spatial or temporal direction ⟨*up*wards⟩ ⟨*after*wards⟩ **2** towards (such) a point, position, or place ⟨*earth*wards⟩

¹ware *vt* to beware of – used chiefly as a command to hunting animals

²ware *n* **1a** manufactured articles or products of art or craft; goods – often in combination ⟨*tin*ware⟩ **b** *pl* goods for sale **2** articles of fired clay; *esp* a specified make of pottery or china ⟨*Parian ~*⟩

warehouse *vt or n* (to deposit, store, or stock in) a structure or room for the storage of merchandise or commodities – **warehouser** *n*

warfare *n* **1** hostilities, war **2** struggle, conflict

warhead *n* the section of a missile containing the explosive, chemical, or incendiary charge

war-horse *n* **1** a powerful horse used in war **2** a veteran soldier or public figure **3** a work of art (e g a musical composition) that has become hackneyed from repetition in the standard repertoire

warlike *adj* **1** fond of war **2** of or useful in war **3** hostile

warlock *n* a man practising black magic; a sorcerer

warlord *n* a supreme military leader

¹warm *adj* **1a** having or giving out heat to a moderate or adequate degree ⟨*a ~ bath*⟩; *also* experiencing heat to this degree ⟨*are you ~ enough?*⟩ **b** serving to maintain or preserve heat, esp to a satisfactory degree ⟨*a ~ sweater*⟩

c feeling or causing sensations of heat brought about by strenuous exertion ⟨a ~ climb⟩ **2a** marked by enthusiasm; cordial ⟨a ~ welcome⟩ **b** marked by excitement, disagreement, or anger ⟨a ~ debate⟩ **3** affectionate and outgoing in temperament ⟨a ~ personality⟩ **4** dangerous, hostile **5** of a trail, scent, etc newly made; fresh **6** of a colour producing an impression of being warm; specif in the range yellow to red **7** near to a goal, object, or solution sought – chiefly in children's games – **warmish** adj, **warmness** n, **warmly** adv

²warm vt **1** to make warm **2** to infuse with a feeling of love, friendship, well-being, or pleasure **3** to reheat (cooked food) for eating – often + up in Br or over in NAm ~ vi **1** to become warm **2** to become filled with interest, enthusiasm, or affection – + to or towards ⟨did not ~ to the newcomer⟩ ⟨~ ing to his theme⟩ – **warm the cockles of one's heart** to make one happy; cheer, encourage

³warm n **1** an act of getting or making warm ⟨come to the fire for a ~⟩ **2** Br a warm place or state ⟨sit here in the ~⟩

warm-blooded adj **1** having a relatively high and constant body temperature more or less independent of the environment **2** fervent or ardent in spirit – **warm-bloodedness** n

warmhearted adj marked by ready affection, cordiality, generosity, or sympathy – **warmheartedly** adv, **warm-heartedness** n

warming pan n a usu long-handled flat covered pan (e g of brass) filled with hot coals, formerly used to warm a bed

warmonger n one who attempts to stir up war – **warmongering** n

warmth n the quality or state of being warm **a** in temperature **b** in feeling ⟨a child needing human ~⟩

warm-up n the act or an instance of warming up; also a procedure (e g a set of exercises) used in warming up

warm up vi **1** to engage in exercise or practice, esp before entering a game or contest; broadly to get ready **2** HOT UP ~ vt HOT UP; esp to put (an audience) into a receptive mood (e g before a show), esp by telling jokes, singing, etc

warn vt **1a** to give notice to beforehand, esp of danger or evil ⟨~ them of the floods⟩ **b** to give admonishing advice to; counsel ⟨~ them not to open the door⟩ **c** to notify, inform ⟨~ them of my intentions⟩ **2** to order to go or stay away – often + off or away ~ vi to give a warning – **warner** n

warning n sthg that warns; also NOTICE 1b – **warning** adj, **warningly** adv

war of nerves n (a conflict characterized by) the use of psychological tactics (e g bluff, threats, or intimidation) designed to destroy the enemy's morale

¹warp n **1a** a series of yarns extended lengthways in a loom and crossed by the weft **b** the cords forming the carcass of a pneumatic tyre **2** a rope for warping a ship or boat **3** sediment deposited by (standing) water **4a** a twist or curve that has developed in sthg formerly flat or straight ⟨a ~ in a door panel⟩ **b** a mental twist or aberration – **warpage** n

²warp vt **1a** to turn or twist (e g planks) out of shape, esp out of a plane **b** to cause to think or act wrongly; pervert **2** to arrange (yarns) so as to form a warp **3** to manoeuvre (e g a ship) by hauling on a line attached to a fixed object ~ vi **1** to become warped **2** to move a ship by warping – **warper** n

war paint n **1** paint put on the body by N American Indians as a sign of going to war **2** ceremonial dress; regalia **3** cosmetics USE (2&3) infml

warpath n the route taken by a war party of N American

Indians – **on the warpath** pursuing an angry or hostile course; taking or starting to take action in a struggle or conflict

¹warrant n **1a** a sanction, authorization; also evidence for or token of authorization **b** a guarantee, security **c** a ground, justification; also proof ⟨his assertion was totally without ~⟩ **2** a commission or document giving authority: e g **a** a document authorizing sby to receive money or other consideration ⟨travel ~⟩ **b** a document authorizing an officer to make an arrest, a search, etc **c** an official certificate of appointment issued to a noncommissioned officer **d(1)** a short-term obligation of a governmental body (e g a municipality) issued in anticipation of revenue **(2)** a document issued by a company giving to the holder the right to purchase the capital stock of the company at a stated price either prior to a stipulated date or at any future time – **warrantless** adj

²warrant vt **1a** to declare or maintain with certainty ⟨I'll ~ he'll be here by noon⟩ **2** to guarantee to be as represented **3** to give sanction to ⟨the law ~s this procedure⟩ **4a** to prove or declare the authenticity or truth of **b** to give assurance of the nature of or for the undertaking of; guarantee **5** to serve as or give adequate ground or reason for ⟨the situation ~s dramatic action⟩ – **warrantable** adj, **warrantor, warranter** n

warrantee n sby to whom a warranty is made

warrant officer n an officer in the army, airforce, marines, or US navy, ranking between noncommissioned officer and commissioned officer

warranty n **1** a collateral undertaking that a fact regarding the subject of a contract is or will be as declared **2** sthg that authorizes, supports, or justifies; a warrant **3** a usu written guarantee of the soundness of a product and of the maker's responsibility for repair or replacement

warren n **1** an area of ground (or a structure) where rabbits breed **2a** a crowded tenement or district **b** a maze of narrow passageways or cubbies; broadly anything intricate or confused

warrior n a man engaged or experienced in warfare

warship n an (armed) ship for use in warfare

wart n **1a** a horny projection on the skin, usu of the hands or feet, caused by a virus; also a protuberance, esp on a plant, resembling this **2** an ugly or objectionable man or boy – chiefly Br schoolboy slang **3** a blemish – often in warts and all – **warty** adj

warthog n any of a genus of African wild pigs with 2 pairs of rough warty lumps on the face and large protruding tusks

wartime n a period during which a war is in progress

wary adj marked by caution and watchful prudence in detecting and escaping danger – **warily** adv, **wariness** n

was past 1 & 3 sing of BE

¹wash vt **1a** to cleanse (as if) by the action of liquid (e g water) **b** to remove (e g dirt) by applying liquid **2** of an animal to cleanse (fur or a furry part) by licking or by rubbing with a paw moistened with saliva **3a** to flush or moisten (a body part or injury) with liquid **b** to suffuse with light **c** to pass water over or through, esp so as to carry off material from the surface or interior **4** to flow along, over, or against ⟨waves ~ ing the shore⟩ **5** to move, carry, or deposit (as if) by the force of water in motion ⟨houses ~ ed away by the flood⟩ **6a** to agitate (e g crushed ore) in water to separate valuable material; also to separate (particles) thus **b** to pass (e g a gas) through or over a liquid to carry off impurities or soluble components **7** to cover or daub lightly with a thin coating (e g of paint or varnish) **8** to cause to swirl ⟨~ ing coffee round in his cup⟩ ~ vi **1a** to wash oneself or a part of one's body **b** to wash articles; do the washing **2** to bear washing without damage ⟨*does this dress* ~?⟩ **3** to drift along on water **4** to pour or flow in a stream or current **5** to gain acceptance; inspire belief ⟨*his story didn't* ~ *with me*⟩ ⟨*an interesting theory, but it just won't* ~⟩ – *infml* – **wash one's hands of** to disclaim interest in, responsibility for, or further connection with

²**wash** *n* **1a** (an instance of) washing or being washed **b** articles for washing **c** an area or structure equipped with facilities for washing a vehicle ⟨*a car* ~⟩ **2** the surging action of waves **3a** a piece of ground washed by the sea or river **b** a shallow body of water **4a** worthless esp liquid waste; *also* swill **b** vapid writing or speech **5a** a thin coat of paint (e g watercolour) **b** a thin liquid used for coating a surface (e g a wall) **6** a lotion **7** loose or eroded surface soil, rock debris, etc transported and deposited by running water **8a** BACKWASH 1 **b** a disturbance in the air produced by the passage of an aircraft

washable *adj* capable of being washed without damage – **washability** *n*

washbasin *n* a basin or sink usu connected to a water supply for washing the hands and face

washboard *n* a corrugated board for scrubbing clothes on when washing

washbowl *n* a washbasin

washcloth *n, NAm* FLANNEL 3

wash down *vt* **1** to send downwards by action of a liquid; *esp* to facilitate the swallowing of (food) by taking gulps of liquid **2** to wash the whole surface of ⟨washed down *and scrubbed the front step*⟩

wash drawing *n* (a) watercolour painting done (mainly) in washes, esp in black, white, and grey tones only

washed-out *adj* **1** faded in colour **2** listless, exhausted – *infml*

washed-up *adj* no longer successful or useful; finished – *infml* ⟨*all* ~ *as a footballer at the age of 28*⟩

washer *n* **1** WASHING MACHINE **2** a thin flat ring (e g of metal or leather) used to ensure tightness or prevent friction in joints and assemblies

washerwoman, *masc* **washerman** *n* a woman who takes in washing

washhouse *n* a building used or equipped for washing clothes

washing *n* articles, esp clothes, that have been or are to be washed

washing machine *n* a machine for washing esp clothes and household linen

washing soda *n* a transparent crystalline hydrated sodium carbonate

washing-up *n, chiefly Br* the act or process of washing dishes and kitchen utensils; *also* the dishes and utensils to be washed

wash-leather *n* a soft leather similar to chamois

washout *n* **1** the washing out or away of a road, railway line, etc by a large amount of water; *also* a place where this has occurred **2** a failure, fiasco

wash out *vt* **1a** to wash free of a usu unwanted substance (e g dirt) ⟨washed *the milk bottles* out *before putting them on the doorstep*⟩ **b** to remove (e g a stain) by washing ⟨washed *the tea stain* out *of the tablecloth*⟩ **2a** to cause to fade by laundering **b** to deplete the strength or vitality of ⟨*feeling very* washed out⟩ ~ *vi* to become depleted of colour or vitality; fade

washroom *n, NAm* TOILET 2b – *euph*

washstand *n* a piece of furniture used, esp formerly, to hold a basin, jug, etc needed for washing one's face and hands

wash up *vi* **1** *Br* to wash used dishes and kitchen utensils, esp after a meal **2** *NAm* to wash one's face and hands ~ *vt* **1** to bring into the shore ⟨*a dead whale was* washed up *on*

the sand⟩ **2** *Br* to wash (the dishes and utensils) after a meal

washwoman *n, NAm* a washerwoman

washy *adj* **1** weak, watery ⟨~ *tea*⟩ **2** deficient in colour; pallid **3** lacking in vigour, individuality, or definite form – **washiness** *n*

wasn't was not

wasp *n* any of numerous largely flesh-eating slender narrow-waisted insects many of which have an extremely painful sting; *esp* a very common social wasp with black and yellow stripes – **wasplike** *adj*

WASP, Wasp *n* an American of N European, esp British, stock and of Protestant background; *esp* one in North America considered to be a member of the dominant and most privileged class – **Waspish** *adj*, **Waspy** *adj*

waspish *adj* resembling a wasp in behaviour; *esp* snappish – **waspishly** *adv*, **waspishness** *n*

wasp waist *n* a very slender waist – **wasp-waisted** *adj*

¹**wassail** *n* **1** a toast to sby's health made in England in former times **2 wassail, wassail bowl, wassail cup** a liquor made of spiced ale or wine and often baked apples, and served in a large bowl, esp formerly, at Christmas and other festive occasions **3** *archaic* revelry, carousing

²**wassail 1** to carouse **2** *dial Eng* to sing carols from house to house at Christmas – **wassailer** *n*

wast *archaic past 2 sing of* BE

wastage *n* **1a** loss, decrease, or destruction of sthg (e g by use, decay, or leakage); *esp* wasteful or avoidable loss of sthg valuable **b** waste, refuse **2** reduction or loss in numbers (e g of employees or students), usu caused by individuals leaving or retiring voluntarily - esp in *natural wastage*

¹**waste** *n* **1a** a sparsely settled, barren, or devastated region; a desert **b** uncultivated land **c** a broad and empty expanse (e g of water) **2** wasting or being wasted **3** gradual loss or decrease by use, wear, or decay **4** damaged, defective, or superfluous material produced by a manufacturing process: e g **a** material rejected during a textile manufacturing process and used usu for wiping away dirt and oil **b** fluid (e g steam) allowed to escape without being used **5** human or animal refuse

²**waste** *vt* **1** to lay waste; devastate **2** to cause to be reduced in physical bulk or strength; enfeeble **3** to wear away gradually; consume **4** to spend or use carelessly or inefficiently; squander ~ *vi* **1** to lose weight, strength, or vitality – often + *away* **2** to become consumed gradually and esp wastefully – **waste one's breath** to accomplish nothing by speaking

³**waste** *adj* **1a** uninhabited, desolate **b** not cultivated or used; not productive ⟨~ *energy*⟩ ⟨~ *land*⟩ **2** ruined, devastated **3** discarded as refuse ⟨~ *material*⟩ **4** serving to conduct or hold refuse material; *specif* carrying off superfluous fluid ⟨~ *pipe*⟩

wasteful *adj* given to or marked by waste; prodigal – **wastefully** *adv*, **wastefulness** *n*

wastepaper *n* paper discarded as used or unwanted

wastepaper basket *n* a receptacle for refuse, esp wastepaper

waste product *n* **1** debris resulting from a process (e g of manufacture) that is of no further use to the system producing it **2** material (e g faeces) discharged from, or stored in an inert form in, a living body as a by-product of metabolic processes

waster *n* **1** one who spends or consumes extravagantly without thought for the future **2** a good-for-nothing, idler

wastrel *n* **1** a vagabond, waif **2** a waster

¹**watch** *vi* **1** to remain awake during the night, esp in order to keep vigil ⟨~ *by his bedside*⟩ **2a** to be attentive or

vigilant; wait *for* ⟨*~ed for a chance to get her revenge*⟩ **b** to keep guard ⟨*~ over their flocks*⟩ **3** to be closely observant of an event or action *~vt* **1** to keep under protective guard **2a** to observe closely, esp in order to check on action or change ⟨*being ~ed by the police*⟩ **b** to look at (an event or moving scene) ⟨*~ television*⟩⟨*~ed the train till it went out of sight*⟩ **3a** to take care of; tend ⟨*~ the baby*⟩ **b** to be careful of ⟨*~es his diet*⟩ **c** to take care that ⟨*~ you don't spill it*⟩ **4** to be on the alert for; bide ⟨*~ed his opportunity*⟩ – **watcher** *n* – **watch** it to be careful; LOOK OUT – **watch one's step** to proceed with extreme care; act or talk warily – **watch over** to have charge of; superintend

²**watch** *n* **1a** the act of keeping awake or alert to guard, protect, or attend ⟨*kept ~ by the patient's bedside*⟩⟨*kept a close ~ on his movements*⟩ **b** a state of alert and continuous attention; lookout **2** a wakeful interval during the night – usu pl ⟨*the silent ~es of the night*⟩ **3** a watchman; *also, sing or pl in constr* a body of watchmen, specif those formerly assigned to patrol the streets of a town at night **4a** a period of keeping guard **b**(1) a period of time during which a part of a ship's company is on duty while another part rests **(2)** *sing or pl in constr* the part of a ship's company on duty during a particular watch **5** a small portable timepiece powered esp by a spring or battery and usu worn on a wrist – **on the watch** on the alert

watchdog *n* **1** a dog kept to guard property **2** a person or group (e g a committee) that guards against inefficiency, undesirable practices, etc

watchful *adj* carefully observant or attentive; ON THE WATCH ⟨*kept a ~ eye on the proceedings*⟩ – **watchfully** *adv*, **watchfulness** *n*

watchmaking *n* the making or repairing of watches or clocks – **watchmaker** *n*

watchman *n, pl* **watchmen** sby who keeps watch; a guard ⟨*a night ~*⟩

watch out *vi* **1** to be on the lookout *for* **2** to be careful; take care – often imper

watchtower *n* a tower from which a lookout can keep watch

watchword *n* **1** a word or phrase used as a sign of recognition among members of the same group **2** a motto that embodies a guiding principle

¹**water** *n* **1a** the colourless odourless liquid that descends from the clouds as rain, forms streams, lakes, and seas, is a major constituent of all living matter, and is an oxide of hydrogen which freezes at 0°C and boils at 100°C **b** a natural mineral water – usu pl with sing. meaning ⟨*went to Bath to take the ~s*⟩ **2a(1)** *pl* the water occupying or flowing in a particular bed ⟨*the ~s of the Nile*⟩ **(2)** *chiefly Br* a body of water (e g a river or lake) ⟨*Derwent ~*⟩ **b**(1) *pl* a stretch of sea surrounding and controlled by a country ⟨*territorial ~s*⟩ **(2)** the sea of a specified part of the earth – often pl with sing. meaning ⟨*in tropical ~s*⟩ **c** a water supply ⟨*threatened to turn off the ~*⟩ **3** travel or transport by water ⟨*we went by ~*⟩ **4a** the level of water at a specified state of the tide **b** the surface of the water ⟨*swam under ~*⟩ **5** liquid containing or resembling water: e g **a** a pharmaceutical or cosmetic preparation (e g a toilet water) made with water **b** a watery solution of a gaseous or readily volatile substance ⟨*ammonia ~*⟩ **c** a watery fluid (e g tears, urine, or sap) formed or circulating in a living body **6** degree of excellence ⟨*a scholar of the first ~*⟩ **7** a wavy lustrous pattern (e g of a textile) – **waterless** *adj* – **water under the bridge** past events which it is futile to attempt to alter

²**water** *vt* **1** to moisten, sprinkle, or soak with water ⟨*~ the garden*⟩ **2a** to supply with water for drink ⟨*~ the*

horses⟩ **b** to supply water to ⟨*~ a ship*⟩ **3** to be a source of water for ⟨*land ~ed by the Thames*⟩ **4** to impart a lustrous appearance and wavy pattern to (cloth) by calendering ⟨*~ed silk*⟩ **5a** to dilute (as if) by the addition of water ⟨*~ the programme to suit the Radicals – The Times*⟩ – often + *down* **b** to add to the total par value of (securities) without a corresponding addition to the assets represented by the securities *~vi* **1** to form or secrete water or watery matter (e g tears or saliva) **2a** to take on a supply of water **b** *of an animal* to drink water – **waterer** *n*

water biscuit *n* an unsweetened biscuit made with flour and water

water blister *n* a blister with a clear watery content that does not contain pus or blood

waterborne *adj* supported or carried by water ⟨*~ commerce*⟩⟨*~ infection*⟩

water buffalo *n* an often domesticated Asiatic buffalo

water cannon *n* a device for shooting out a jet of water with great force (e g to disperse a crowd)

water cart *n* a cart or truck equipped with a tank or barrels for hauling or sprinkling water

water closet *n* (a room or structure containing) a toilet with a bowl that can be flushed with water

watercolour *n* **1** a paint made from pigment mixed with water rather than oil **2** (a work produced by) the art of painting with watercolours

watercourse *n* (a natural or man-made channel for) a stream of water

watercress *n* any of several cresses of wet places widely grown for use in salads

waterfall *n* a vertical or steep descent of the water of a river or stream

waterfowl *n, pl* **waterfowls**, *esp collectively* **waterfowl 1** a bird, esp a duck, that frequents water **2** *pl* swimming game birds (e g duck) as distinguished from upland game birds (e g grouse)

waterfront *n* land or a section of a town fronting or bordering on a body of water

water hen *n* any of various birds (e g a coot or moorhen) related to the rails

water hole *n* a natural hollow in which water collects, used esp by animals as a drinking place

water ice *n* a frozen dessert of water, sugar, and flavouring

watering can *n* a vessel having a handle and a long spout often fitted with a rose, used for watering plants

watering place *n* **1** a place where water may be obtained; *esp* one where animals, esp livestock, come to drink **2** a health or recreational resort featuring mineral springs or bathing; *esp* a spa

water jacket *n* an outer casing which holds water or through which water circulates, esp for cooling

water jump *n* an obstacle (e g in a steeplechase) consisting of a pool or ditch of water

water level *n* **1** the level reached by the surface of a body of water **2** WATER TABLE

water lily *n* any of a family of aquatic plants with floating leaves and usu showy colourful flowers

waterline *n* the level on the hull of a vessel to which the surface of the water comes when it is afloat; *also* any of several lines marked on the hull to correspond with this level

waterlogged *adj* filled or soaked with water ⟨*~ soil*⟩; *specif, of a vessel* so filled with water as to be (almost) unable to float – **waterlog** *vt*

waterloo *n, pl* **waterloos** *often cap* a decisive defeat

water main *n* a major pipe for conveying water

waterman *n* a man who works on or near water or who

engages in water recreations; *esp* a boatman whose boat and services are available for hire

¹**watermark** *n* **1** a mark indicating the height to which water has risen **2** (the design or the metal pattern producing) a marking in paper visible when the paper is held up to the light

²**watermark** *vt* to mark (paper) with a watermark

water meadow *n* a meadow kept fertile by a regular influx of water (e g from the flooding of a bordering river)

watermelon *n* (an African climbing plant of the cucumber family that bears) a large oblong or roundish fruit with a hard green often striped or variegated rind, a sweet watery pink pulp, and many seeds

water mill *n* a mill whose machinery is moved by water

water pipe *n* **1** a pipe for conveying water **2** a large chiefly oriental smoking apparatus consisting of a bowl containing tobacco or other smoking material mounted on a vessel of water through which smoke is drawn and cooled before reaching the mouth

water polo *n* a game played in water by teams of 7 swimmers using a ball that is thrown or dribbled with the object of putting it into a goal

waterpower *n* the power derived from movement of a body of water; *also* a fall of water suitable for such use

¹**waterproof** *adj* impervious to water; *esp* covered or treated with a material to prevent passage of water – **waterproofness** *n*

²**waterproof** *n* (a garment made of) waterproof fabric

³**waterproof** *vt* to make waterproof – **waterproofer** *n*, **waterproofing** *n*

water rate *n* the charge made to a British householder for the use of the public water supply

watershed *n* **1** a dividing ridge between 2 drainage areas **2** a crucial turning point

waterside *n* the margin of a body of water

water ski *n* a board used singly or in pairs for standing on and planing over water while being towed at speed – **water-ski** *vi*, **water-skier** *n*

water-skiing *n* the sport of planing and jumping on water skis

water-softener *n* a substance or device for softening hard water

water spaniel *n* a rather large spaniel with a heavy curly coat, used esp for retrieving waterfowl

waterspout *n* a funnel-shaped column of rotating wind usu extending from the underside of a cumulus or cumulonimbus cloud down to a cloud of spray torn up from the surface of a sea, lake, etc

water supply *n* the source, means, or process of supplying water (e g to a town or house), usu including reservoirs, tunnels, and pipelines

water table *n* the level below which the ground is wholly saturated with water

watertight *adj* **1** of such tight construction or fit as to be impermeable to water **2** *esp of an argument* impossible to disprove; without loopholes **3** isolated from other ideas, influences, etc; discrete ⟨*experiences cannot be divided into ∼ compartments*⟩ – **watertightness** *n*

water tower *n* **1** a tower supporting a raised water tank to provide the necessary steady pressure to distribute water **2** a fire fighting apparatus that can supply water at various heights and at great pressure

water vapour *n* water in a vaporous form, esp when below boiling temperature and diffused (e g in the atmosphere)

water vole *n* a common large vole of W Europe that inhabits river banks and often digs extensive tunnels

waterway *n* **1** a navigable route or body of water **2** a groove at the edge of a ship's deck for draining the deck

waterwheel *n* **1** a wheel made to rotate by direct action of water, and used esp to drive machinery **2** a wheel for raising water

water wings *n pl* a pair of usu air-filled floats worn to give support to the body of sby learning to swim

waterworks *n, pl* **waterworks** **1** the reservoirs, mains, building, and pumping and purifying equipment by which a water supply is obtained and distributed (e g to a city) – often pl with sing. meaning **2** *chiefly Br* the urinary system – euph or humor **3** (the shedding of) tears – infml ⟨*turns on the ∼ whenever she wants her own way*⟩

watery *adj* **1a** consisting of or filled with water **b** containing, sodden with, or yielding water or a thin liquid ⟨*a ∼ solution*⟩ ⟨*∼ vesicles*⟩ **c** containing too much water ⟨*∼ soup*⟩ **d** secreting water, esp tears ⟨*∼ eyes*⟩ **2a** pale, faint ⟨*∼ sun*⟩ ⟨*a ∼ smile*⟩ **b** vapid, wishy-washy ⟨*a ∼ writing style*⟩ – **waterily** *adv*, **wateriness** *n*

watt *n* the SI unit of power equal to the power that in 1s gives rise to an energy of 1J

wattage *n* amount of power expressed in watts

¹**wattle** *n* **1** (material for) a framework of poles interwoven with slender branches or reeds and used, esp formerly, in building **2a** a fleshy protuberance usu near or on the head or neck, esp of a bird **b** ²BARBEL **3** *Austr* ACACIA 1 – **wattled** *adj*

²**wattle** *vt* **wattling** **1** to form or build of or with wattle **2a** to interlace to form wattle **b** to unite or make solid by interweaving light flexible material

wattle and daub *n* a framework of wattle covered and plastered with clay and used in building construction

¹**wave** *vi* **1** to flutter or sway to and fro ⟨*flags waving in the breeze*⟩ ⟨*corn ∼d to and fro in the wind*⟩ **2** to give a signal or salute by moving (sthg held in) the hand ⟨*∼d cheerily to them*⟩ **3** to be flourished to and fro ⟨*his sword ∼d and flashed*⟩ **4** to follow a curving line or form; undulate ∼ *vt* **1** to cause to swing to and fro **2** to direct by waving; signal ⟨*∼ the car to a halt*⟩ **3a** to move (the hand or an object) to and fro in greeting, farewell, or homage **b** to convey by waving ⟨*∼d farewell*⟩ **4** to brandish, flourish ⟨*∼d a pistol menacingly*⟩ **5** to give a curving or undulating shape to ⟨*∼d her hair*⟩ – **waver** *n* – **wave aside** to dismiss or put out of mind; disregard

²**wave** *n* **1a** a moving ridge or swell on the surface of a liquid (e g the sea) **b** open water – usu pl with sing. meaning; chiefly poetic **2a** a shape or outline having successive curves **b** a waviness of the hair **c** an undulating line or streak **3** sthg that swells and dies away: e g **a** a surge of sensation or emotion ⟨*a ∼ of anger swept over her*⟩ **b** a movement involving large numbers of people in a common activity ⟨*∼s of protest*⟩ **c** a sudden increase or wide occurrence of a specified activity ⟨*a ∼ of house-buying*⟩ **4** a sweep of the hand or arm or of some object held in the hand, used as a signal or greeting **5** a rolling or undulatory movement or any of a series of such movements passing along a surface or through the air **6** a movement like that of an ocean wave: e g **a** a surging movement; an influx ⟨*a sudden ∼ of new arrivals*⟩ **b** *sing or pl in constr* a line of attacking or advancing troops, aircraft, etc **7** (a complete cycle of) a periodic variation of pressure, electrical or magnetic intensity, electric potential, etc by which energy is transferred progressively from point to point without a corresponding transfer of a medium ⟨*light ∼*⟩ ⟨*radio ∼*⟩ ⟨*sound ∼*⟩ **8** an undulating or jagged line constituting a graphic representation of an action ⟨*a sine ∼*⟩ **9** a marked change in temperature;

a period of hot or cold weather – **wavelet** *n*, **wavelike** *adj*

wave band *n* a band of radio frequency waves

wavelength *n* the distance in the line of advance of a wave from any 1 point to the next point of corresponding phase (e g from 1 peak to the next) – **be on somebody's/the same wavelength** to have the same outlook, views, etc as sby else

waver *vi* **1** to vacillate between choices; fluctuate **2a** to sway unsteadily to and fro; reel **b** to quiver, flicker ⟨*~ing flames*⟩ **c** to hesitate as if about to give way; falter **3** to make a tremulous sound; quaver – **waverer** *n*, **waveringly** *adv*

wavy *adj* **1** having waves ⟨*~ hair*⟩ **2** having a wavelike form or outline ⟨*~ line*⟩ – **wavily** *adv*, **waviness** *n*

¹**wax** *n* **1** beeswax **2a** any of numerous plant or animal substances that are harder, more brittle, and less greasy than fats **b** a solid substance (e g ozocerite or paraffin wax) of mineral origin consisting usu of higher hydrocarbons **c** a pliable or liquid composition used esp for sealing, taking impressions, or polishing **d** a resinous preparation used by shoemakers for rubbing thread **3** a waxy secretion; *esp* cerumen – **waxlike** *adj*

²**wax** *vt* to treat or rub with wax

³**wax** *vi* **1** to increase in size and strength; *esp, of the moon, satellites, etc* to increase in phase or intensity **2** *archaic* to assume a specified quality or state; become ⟨*~ed lyrical*⟩

⁴**wax** *n* a fit of temper – *infml*

waxed paper, wax paper *n* paper coated or impregnated with wax to make it resistant to water and grease, used esp as a wrapping for food

waxen *adj* **1** made of or covered with wax **2** resembling wax, esp in being pliable, smooth, or pallid

waxwork *n* **1** an effigy in wax, usu of a person **2** *pl but sing or pl in constr* an exhibition of wax effigies

waxy *adj* **1** made of, full of, or covered with wax **2** resembling wax, esp in smooth whiteness or pliability – **waxiness** *n*

¹**way** *n* **1a** a thoroughfare for travel or transport from place to place ⟨*lives across the ~*⟩ ⟨*the Pennine Way*⟩ **b** an opening for passage ⟨*this door is the only ~ out*⟩ **c** space or room, esp for forward movement ⟨*move that chair, please, it's in my ~*⟩ ⟨*get out of the ~!*⟩ **2** the course to be travelled from one place to another;a route ⟨*ask one's ~ to the station*⟩ ⟨*lost her ~*⟩ **3a** a course leading in a direction or towards an objective ⟨*took the easy ~ out*⟩ **b** the course of one's life ⟨*puts opportunities in her ~*⟩ **c** what one desires, or wants to do ⟨*always manages to get her own ~*⟩ **4a** the manner in which sthg is done or happens ⟨*the British ~ of life*⟩ ⟨*don't like the ~ he's breathing*⟩ **b** a method of doing or accomplishing; a means ⟨*the best ~ to make coffee*⟩ **c** a characteristic, regular, or habitual manner or mode of being, behaving, or happening ⟨*knows nothing of the ~s of the world*⟩ ⟨*endearing little ~s*⟩ **d** a feature, respect ⟨*useful in more ~s than one*⟩ **5** a category, kind ⟨*porridge is all right in its ~*⟩ **6** the distance to be travelled in order to reach a place or point ⟨*a long ~ from home*⟩ ⟨*Christmas is still a long ~ off*⟩ **7** an advance accompanied by or achieved through a specific action ⟨*working her ~ through college*⟩ ⟨*hacked his ~ through the jungle*⟩ **8a** a direction – often in combination ⟨*come this ~*⟩ ⟨*split it 4 ~s*⟩ ⟨*a one-way street*⟩ **b** (the direction of) the area in which one lives ⟨*do drop in if you're ever down our ~*⟩ **9** a state of affairs; a condition ⟨*that's the ~ things are*⟩ ⟨*my finances are in a bad ~*⟩ **10** *pl but sometimes sing in constr* an inclined structure on which a ship is built or supported in launching **11** motion or speed of a ship

or boat through the water – **by the way** incidentally – usu used to introduce or to comment on the introduction of a new subject – **by way of 1** to be considered as; as a sort of ⟨*by way of light relief*⟩ **2** by the route through; via **3** in the form of ⟨*money recovered by way of grants*⟩ – **in a way** from one point of view; to some extent – **in the way of** in the form of ⟨*what have we in the way of food?*⟩ – **no way** under no circumstances – *infml* – **on one's way** ON THE WAY **1** – **on the way 1** while moving along a course; in the course of travelling **2** coming, approaching; *specif* conceived but not yet born – **on the way out** about to disappear or die ⟨*many of these old customs are* on the way out⟩ – **out of the way 1** unusual, remarkable ⟨*didn't know he'd said anything* out of the way⟩ ⟨*the house wasn't anything* out of the way⟩ **2** in or to a secluded or remote place **3** done, completed ⟨*got his homework* out of the way⟩ – **under way** in progress; started

²**way** *adv* **1** AWAY **7** ⟨*is ~ ahead of the class*⟩ **2** *chiefly NAm* all the way ⟨*pull the switch ~ back*⟩ – **way back** long ago ⟨*friends from* way back⟩

waybill *n* a document showing the number of passengers or parcels carried and the fares charged

wayfarer *n* a traveller, esp on foot

waylay *vt* **waylaid 1** to attack from ambush **2** to accost ⟨*waylaid me after the lesson and asked where I'd been the week before*⟩

way-out *adj* far-out – *infml*

ways *n pl but sing in constr, NAm* WAY **6** ⟨*a long ~ from home*⟩

-ways *suffix* (→ *adv*) in (such) a way, direction, or manner ⟨*sideways*⟩ ⟨*lengthways*⟩

ways and means *n pl* **1** methods and resources for accomplishing sthg, esp for paying expenses **2** *often cap W&M* methods and resources for raising revenue for the use of government

wayside *n* the side of or land adjacent to a road – **wayside** *adj*

wayward *adj* **1** following one's own capricious or wanton inclinations; ungovernable **2** following no clear principle or law; unpredictable – **waywardly** *adv*, **waywardness** *n*

we *pron pl in constr* **1** I and the rest of a group; you and I; you and I and another or others; I and another or others not including you ⟨*may ~ go, sir?*⟩ **2** I – used, esp formerly, by sovereigns; used by writers to maintain an impersonal character **3** YOU **1** – used esp to children and the sick ⟨*how are ~ feeling today, Mr Jones?*⟩

weak *adj* **1a** deficient in physical vigour; feeble **b** not able to sustain or exert much weight, pressure, or strain **c** not able to resist external force or withstand attack **2a** lacking determination or decisiveness; ineffectual **b** unable to withstand temptation or persuasion **3** not factually grounded or logically presented ⟨*a ~ argument*⟩ **4a** unable to function properly ⟨*~ eyes*⟩ **b** lacking skill or proficiency **c** wanting in vigour or strength **5a** deficient in a specified quality or ingredient ⟨*~ in trumps*⟩ **b** lacking normal intensity or potency ⟨*~ strain of virus*⟩ **c** mentally or intellectually deficient **d** deficient in strength or flavour; dilute ⟨*~ coffee*⟩ **6** not having or exerting authority or political power ⟨*~ government*⟩ **7** of or constituting a verb (conjugation) that in English forms inflections by adding the suffix *-ed* or *-d* or *-t* **8** UNSTRESSED **1 9** characterized by falling prices ⟨*a ~ market*⟩ **10** ionizing only slightly in solution ⟨*~ acids and bases*⟩ – **weaken** *vb*, **weakish** *adj*, **weakly** *adv*

weak-kneed *adj* lacking in resolution; easily intimidated

weakling *n* a person or animal weak in body, character, or mind

weakness *n* **1** a fault, defect **2** (an object of) a special desire or fondness ⟨*have a ~ for ice cream*⟩

weal, wheal *n* WELT 3, ²SCAR 1

Weald *n the* area of open grassland, once wooded, covering parts of Sussex, Kent, and Surrey

wealth *n* **1** the state of being rich **2** abundance of money and valuable material possessions **3** abundant supply; a profusion ⟨*a ~ of detail*⟩ – **wealthy** *adj*, **wealthily** *adv*, **wealthiness** *n*

wean *vt* **1** to accustom (a child or other young mammal) to take food other than mother's milk **2** to cause to abandon a state of usu unwholesome dependence or preoccupation ⟨*to ~ your minds from hankering after false standards* – A T Quiller-Couch⟩ **3** to cause to become acquainted with an idea, writer, etc at an early age; bring up *on*

weapon *n* **1** an instrument of offensive or defensive combat **2** a means used to further one's cause in conflict ⟨*his caustic wit was his best ~*⟩

weaponry *n* (the science of designing and making) weapons

¹**wear** *vb* wore; worn *vt* **1a** to have or carry on the body as clothing or adornment ⟨*wore a coat*⟩ **b** to dress in (a particular manner, colour, or garment), esp habitually ⟨*~ green*⟩ **c** to have (hair) in a specified style **2** to hold the rank, dignity, or position signified by (an ornament) ⟨*~ the royal crown*⟩ **3a** to have or show on the face ⟨*wore a happy smile*⟩ **b** to show or fly (a flag or colours) on a ship **4** to impair, damage, or diminish by use or friction ⟨*letters on the stone worn away by weathering*⟩ **5** to produce gradually by friction or attrition ⟨*~ a hole in the rug*⟩ **6** to exhaust or lessen the strength of; weary **7** to cause (a ship, esp a square-rigged vessel) to go about with the stern presented to the wind **8** *chiefly Br* to find (a claim, proposal etc) acceptable; STAND FOR – *infml* ⟨*just won't ~ that feeble excuse*⟩ *~ vi* **1a** to endure use, esp to a specified degree; last ⟨*this material ~s well*⟩ **b** to retain vitality or young appearance to a specified degree ⟨*you've worn well*⟩ **2a** to diminish or decay through use **b** to go by slowly or tediously ⟨*the day ~s on*⟩ **c** to grow or become by attrition, use, or the passage of time ⟨*hair ~ing thin*⟩ **3** of a ship, esp a square-rigged vessel to change to an opposite tack by turning the stern to the wind – **wearable** *adj*, **wearer** *n* – **wear the trousers** to have the controlling authority in a household – **wear thin 1** to become weak or ready to give way ⟨*his patience was wearing thin*⟩ **2** to become trite, unconvincing, or out-of-date ⟨*that argument's wearing a bit thin*⟩

²**wear** *n* **1** wearing or being worn ⟨*clothes for everyday ~*⟩ **2** clothing, usu of a specified kind ⟨*men's ~*⟩; esp clothing worn for a specified occasion – often in combination ⟨*swimwear*⟩ **3** capacity to withstand use; durability ⟨*plenty of ~ left in it*⟩ **4** minor damage or deterioration through use

wear and tear *n* the normal deterioration or depreciation which sthg suffers in the course of use

wear down *vt* to weary and overcome by persistent resistance or pressure

wearing *adj* causing fatigue; tiring – **wearingly** *adv*

wearisome *adj* causing weariness; tiresome – **wearisomely** *adv*, **wearisomeness** *n*

wear off *vi* to decrease gradually and finally end ⟨*the effect of the drug wore off*⟩

wear out *vt* **1** to make useless by long or excessive wear or use **2** to tire, exhaust *~ vi* to become useless from long or excessive wear or use

¹**weary** *adj* **1** exhausted, tired **2** expressing or characteristic of weariness ⟨*a ~ smile*⟩ **3** having one's patience,

tolerance, or pleasure exhausted – + *of* **4** wearisome – **wearily** *adv*, **weariness** *n*

²**weary** *vb* to make or become weary

weasel *n, pl* **weasels**, *esp collectively* **weasel** any of various small slender flesh-eating mammals with reddish brown fur which, in northern forms, turns white in winter

¹**weather** *n* the prevailing (bad) atmospheric conditions, esp with regard to heat or cold, wetness or dryness, calm or storm, and clearness or cloudiness – **under the weather** mildly ill or depressed; not fully well – *infml*

²**weather** *adj* windward

³**weather** *vt* **1** to expose or subject to atmospheric conditions **2** to sail or pass to the windward of **3** to bear up against and come safely through ⟨*~ a storm*⟩ *~ vi* to undergo or be resistant to change by weathering ⟨*wood ~s better if creosoted*⟩

weather-beaten *adj* **1** worn or damaged by exposure to weather **2** toughened or tanned by the weather

weatherboard *n* **1** a board fixed horizontally and usu overlapping the board below to form a protective outdoor wall covering that will throw off water **2** a sloping board fixed to the bottom of a door for excluding rain, snow, etc

weather-bound *adj* unable to proceed or take place because of bad weather

weathercock *n* WEATHER VANE; *esp* one in the figure of a cockerel

weatherglass *n* a barometer

weatherman *n* sby, esp a meteorologist, who reports and forecasts the weather, usu on the radio or television

weatherproof *adj* able to withstand exposure to weather without damage or loss of function – **weatherproof** *vt*, **weatherproofness** *n*

weather ship *n* a ship that makes observations on weather conditions for use by meteorologists

weather station *n* a station for taking, recording, and reporting meteorological observations

weather vane *n* a movable device attached to an elevated structure (e g a spire) in order to show the direction of the wind

¹**weave** *vb* wove, weaved; woven, weaved *vt* **1a** to form (cloth) by interlacing strands (e g of yarn), esp on a loom **b** to interlace (e g threads) into a fabric, design, etc **c** to make (e g a basket) by intertwining **2** of spiders and insects SPIN **2 3a** to produce by elaborately combining elements into a coherent whole **b** to introduce; work in – usu + *in* or *into* *~ vi* to work at weaving; make cloth

²**weave** *n* a pattern or method for interlacing the threads of woven fabrics

³**weave** *vb* weaved *vt* to direct (e g the body or one's way) in a winding or zigzag course, esp to avoid obstacles *~ vi* to move by weaving

weaver *n* **1** sby who weaves, esp as an occupation **2** **weaver, weaverbird** any of numerous Old World birds that resemble finches and usu construct elaborate nests of interlaced vegetation

¹**web** *n* **1** a woven fabric; *esp* a length of fabric still on the loom **2** SPIDER'S WEB; *also* a similar network spun by various insects **3** a tissue or membrane; *esp* that uniting fingers or toes either at their bases (e g in human beings) or for most of their length (e g in many water birds) **4** a thin metal sheet, plate, or strip (e g joining the upper and lower flanges of a girder or rail) **5** an intricate structure suggestive of sthg woven; a network **6** a continuous sheet of paper for use in a printing press – **webbed** *adj*, **webby** *adj*, **weblike** *adj*

²**web** *vb* **-bb-** *vt* **1** to cover with a web or network **2** to entangle, ensnare *~ vi* to construct or form a web

webbing *n* a strong narrow closely woven tape used esp for straps, upholstery, or harnesses

webfoot *n* a foot with webbed toes – **web-footed** *adj*

web offset *n* offset printing by web press

web press *n* a press that prints a continuous roll of paper

wed *vb* **-dd-**; **wedded** *also* **wed** *vt* **1** to marry **2** to unite as if by marriage ~ *vi* to enter into matrimony

we'd we had; we would; we should

wedded *adj* **1** joined in marriage **2** conjugal, connubial ⟨~ *bliss*⟩ **3** strongly emotionally attached; committed *to*

wedding *n* **1** a marriage ceremony, usu with its accompanying festivities; nuptials **2** a joining in close association **3** a wedding anniversary or its celebration – usu in combination ⟨*golden* ~⟩

wedding breakfast *n* a celebratory meal that follows a marriage ceremony

wedding ring *n* a ring usu of plain metal (e g gold) given by 1 marriage partner to the other during the wedding ceremony and worn thereafter to signify marital status

¹**wedge** *n* **1** a piece of wood, metal, etc tapered to a thin edge and used esp for splitting wood or raising heavy objects **2a** sthg wedge-shaped ⟨*a* ~ *of pie*⟩ **b** (a shoe with) a wedge-shaped sole raised at the heel and tapering towards the toe **c** an iron golf club with a broad face angled for maximum loft **3** sthg causing a breach or separation

²**wedge** *vt* **1** to fasten or tighten by driving in a wedge **2** to force or press into a narrow space; cram – usu + *in* or *into* **3** to split or force apart (as if) with a wedge

wedged *adj* shaped like a wedge

Wedgwood *trademark* – used for a type of fine ceramic ware made orig by Josiah Wedgwood and typically decorated with a classical cameo-like design in white relief

wedlock *n* the state of being married; marriage – **out of wedlock** with the natural parents not legally married to each other ⟨*born* out of wedlock⟩

Wednesday *n* the day of the week following Tuesday – **Wednesdays** *adv*

¹**wee** *adj* very small; diminutive – often used to or by children or to convey an impression of Scottishness

²**wee** *n* (an act of passing) urine – used esp by or to children – **wee** *vi*

¹**weed** *n* **1** an unwanted wild plant which often overgrows or chokes out more desirable plants **2a** an obnoxious growth or thing **b** an animal, esp a horse, unfit to breed from **3** *Br* a weedy person – infml **4a** TOBACCO **2** – chiefly humor; usu + *the* **b** MARIJUANA **2** – slang; usu + *the* – **weedless** *adj*

²**weed** *vi* to remove weeds or sthg harmful ~ *vt* **1** to clear of weeds ⟨~ *a garden*⟩ **2** to remove the undesirable parts of ⟨~ *the files*⟩ – **weeder** *n*

weed out *vt* to get rid of (sby or sthg harmful or unwanted); remove

weeds *n pl* MOURNING 2A

weedy *adj* **1** covered with or consisting of weeds ⟨~ *pastures*⟩ **2** noticeably weak, thin, and ineffectual – infml – **weediness** *n*

week *n* **1a** any of several 7-day cycles used in various calendars **b** a week beginning with a specified day or containing a specified event ⟨*Easter* ~⟩ **2a** a period of 7 consecutive days **b** the working days during each 7-day period ⟨*stays in London during the* ~⟩ **c** a weekly period of work ⟨*works a 40-hour* ~⟩ **3** a time 7 days before or after a specified day ⟨*next Sunday* ~⟩ – **week in, week out** for an indefinite or seemingly endless number of weeks

weekday *n* any day of the week except (Saturday and) Sunday

¹**weekend** *n* the end of the week; *specif* the period from Friday night to Sunday night

²**weekend** *vi* to spend the weekend (e g at a place) – **weekender** *n*

¹**weekly** *adv* every week; once a week; by the week

²**weekly** *adj* **1** occurring, appearing, or done weekly **2** calculated by the week

³**weekly** *n* a weekly newspaper or periodical

weeknight *n* a night of any day of the week except Saturday and Sunday

weeny *also* **weensy** *adj* exceptionally small; tiny – infml

¹**weep** *vb* **wept** *vt* **1** to express deep sorrow for, usu by shedding tears; bewail **2** to pour forth (tears) from the eyes **3** to exude (a fluid) slowly; ooze **4** to bring to a specified condition by shedding tears ⟨*wept herself to sleep*⟩ ~ *vi* **1a** to express passion (e g grief) by shedding tears **b** to mourn *for* sby or sthg **2** to give off or leak fluid slowly; ooze

²**weep** *n* a fit of weeping

weeping *adj, of a tree* (being a variety) having slender drooping branches ⟨~ *willow*⟩

weepy *adj* inclined to weep; tearful

weevil *n* any of numerous usu small beetles with a long snout bearing jaws at the tip, many of which are injurious, esp as larvae, to grain, fruit, etc – **weevily**, **weevilly** *adj*

weft *n* the thread or yarn that interlaces the warp in a fabric; the crosswise yarn in weaving

weigh *vt* **1** to ascertain the weight of (as if) on a scale **2** to consider carefully; evaluate – often + *up* ⟨~ *the pros and cons*⟩ **3** to measure (a definite quantity) (as if) on a scale – often + *out* ~ *vi* **1a** to have weight or a specified weight **b** to register a weight (e g on a scale) – + *in* or *out*; compare WEIGH IN 1, WEIGH OUT **2** to merit consideration as important; count ⟨*evidence will* ~ *heavily against him*⟩ **3** to be a burden or cause of anxiety to – often + *on* or *upon* ⟨*her responsibilities* ~ed *upon her*⟩ – **weighable** *adj*, **weigher** *n* – **weigh anchor** to pull up an anchor preparatory to sailing

weighbridge *n* a large scale used for weighing vehicles which usu consists of a plate level with the surface of a road onto which the vehicles are driven

weigh down *vt* **1** to make heavy; weight **2** to oppress, burden

weigh in *vi* **1** to have oneself or one's possessions (e g luggage) weighed; *esp* to be weighed after a horse race or before a boxing or wrestling match **2** to make a contribution; join in ⟨*a bystander* weighed in *to stop the fight*⟩ – **weigh-in** *n*

weigh out *vi* to be weighed after a boxing or wrestling match

¹**weight** *n* **1a** the amount that a quantity or body weighs, esp as measured on a particular scale **b(1)** any of the classes into which contestants in certain sports (e g boxing and wrestling) are divided according to body weight **(2)** a horse carrying a usu specified weight in a handicap race ⟨*the top* ~ *won the race*⟩ **(3)** poundage required to be carried by a horse in a handicap race **2a** a quantity weighing a certain amount ⟨*equal* ~s *of flour and sugar*⟩ **b** a heavy object thrown or lifted as an athletic exercise or contest **3a** a system of units of weight ⟨*troy* ~⟩ **b** any of the units of weight used in such a system **c** a piece of material (e g metal) of known weight for use in weighing articles **4a** sthg heavy; a load **b** a heavy object to hold or press sthg down or to counterbalance ⟨*the* ~s *of the clock*⟩ **5a** a burden, pressure ⟨*took a* ~ *off my mind*⟩

corpulence **6a** relative heaviness ⟨~ *is a quality of material substances*⟩ **b** the force with which a body is attracted towards a celestial body (e g the earth) by gravitation and which is equal to the product of the mass of the body and the local gravitational acceleration **7a** relative importance, authority, or influence ⟨*his views don't carry much* ~⟩ **b** *the* main force or strength ⟨*the* ~ *of the argument*⟩ **8** a numerical value assigned to an item to express its relative importance in a frequency distribution

²**weight** vt **1** to load or make heavy (as if) with a weight **2** to oppress with a burden ⟨~ed *down with cares*⟩ **3** to assign a statistical weight to **4** to arrange in such a way as to create a bias ⟨*a wage structure* ~ed *heavily in favour of employees with long service*⟩

weighting n, Br an additional sum paid on top of wages; esp one paid to offset the higher cost of living in a particular area ⟨*a London* ~ *of £500*⟩

weightless adj having little weight; lacking apparent gravitational pull – **weightlessly** adv, **weightlessness** n

weight-lifter n one who lifts heavy weights, esp barbells, in competition or as an exercise – **weight-lifting** n

weighty adj **1** of much importance, influence, or consequence; momentous **2** heavy, esp in proportion to bulk ⟨~ *metal*⟩ **3** burdensome, onerous ⟨*the* ~ *cares of state*⟩ – **weightily** adv, **weightiness** n

weir n **1** a fence or enclosure set in a waterway for trapping fish **2** a dam in a stream to raise the water level or control its flow

weird adj **1** of or caused by witchcraft or the supernatural **2** of a strange or extraordinary character; odd – infml – **weirdly** adv, **weirdness** n

weirdie, weirdy n sby who is very strange or eccentric – infml

weirdo n, pl **weirdos** a weirdie – infml

welch vi to welsh – **welcher** n

Welch adj Welsh – now only in names ⟨*the Royal* ~ *Fusiliers*⟩

¹**welcome** interj – used to express a greeting to a guest or newcomer on his/her arrival

²**welcome** vt **1** to greet hospitably and with courtesy **2** to greet or receive in the specified, esp unpleasant, way ⟨*they* ~d *the intruder with a hail of bullets*⟩ **3** to receive or accept with pleasure ⟨~s *danger*⟩ ⟨~d *the appearance of his new book*⟩ – **welcomer** n – **welcome with open arms** to greet or accept with great cordiality or pleasure

³**welcome** adj **1** received gladly into one's presence or companionship ⟨*was always* ~ *in their home*⟩ **2** giving pleasure; received with gladness, esp because fulfilling a need ⟨*a* ~ *relief*⟩ **3** willingly permitted or given the right ⟨*you're* ~ *to read it*⟩ **4** – used in the phrase 'You're welcome' as a reply to an expression of thanks – **welcomely** adv, **welcomeness** n

⁴**welcome** n **1** a greeting or reception on arrival or first appearance **2** the hospitable treatment that a guest may expect ⟨*outstayed their* ~⟩

¹**weld** vi to become or be capable of being welded ~ vt **1a** to fuse (metallic parts) together by heating and allowing the metals to flow together or by hammering or compressing with or without previous heating **b** to unite (plastics) in a similar manner by heating or by using a chemical solvent **c** to repair, produce, or create (as if) by such a process **2** to unite closely or inseparably – **weldable** adj, **welder** n, **weldability** n

²**weld** n a welded joint

welfare n **1** well-being ⟨*concerned for her child's* ~⟩ **2** WELFARE WORK **3** aid in the form of money or necessities for those not well able to provide for themselves (e g through poverty, age, or handicap)

welfare state n (a country operating) a social system based on the assumption by the state of responsibility for the individual and social welfare of its citizens

welfare work n organized efforts to improve the living conditions of the poor, elderly, etc – **welfare worker** n

welkin n **1a** *the* sky, firmament **b** heaven **2** the upper atmosphere USE poetic

¹**well** n **1** (a pool fed by) a spring of water **2** a pit or hole sunk into the earth to reach a supply of water **3** an enclosure round the pumps of a ship **4** a shaft or hole sunk in the earth to reach a natural deposit (e g oil or gas) **5** an open space extending vertically through floors of a structure ⟨*a stair* ~⟩ **6** a vessel, space, or hole having a construction or shape suggesting a well for water **7** a source from which sthg springs; a fountainhead **8** Br the open space in front of the judge in a law court

²**well** vi **1** to rise to the surface and usu flow forth ⟨*tears* ~ed *from her eyes*⟩ **2** to rise to the surface like a flood of liquid ⟨*longing* ~ed *up in his breast*⟩

³**well** adv **better; best 1** in a good or proper manner; rightly **2** in a way appropriate to the circumstances: e g **a** satisfactorily, advantageously **b** with good appearance or effect ⟨*carried himself* ~⟩ **c** with skill or aptitude ⟨~ *caught!*⟩ **d** with prudence; sensibly ⟨*would do* ~ *to ask*⟩ ⟨*we may* ~ *wonder*⟩ **3** in a kind or friendly manner; favourably ⟨*spoke* ~ *of your idea*⟩ **4** in a prosperous manner ⟨*he lives* ~⟩ **5a** to an extent approaching completeness; thoroughly ⟨*after being* ~ *dried with a towel*⟩ **b** on a close personal level; intimately ⟨*knew her* ~⟩ **6a** easily, fully ⟨~ *worth the price*⟩ **b** much, considerably ⟨~ *over a million*⟩ **c** in all likelihood; indeed ⟨*may* ~ *be true*⟩ – **as well 1** also; IN ADDITION ⟨*there were other features as well*⟩ ⟨*she's pretty* as well⟩ **2** to the same extent or degree ⟨*open as well to the poor as to the rich*⟩ **3** with equivalent or preferable effect ⟨*might just as well have stayed at home*⟩ ⟨*you may* as well *tell him*⟩ **4** ³WELL **2, 4** – **as well as** ²BESIDES **2** ⟨*skilful* as well as *strong*⟩ – **well and truly** totally, completely – **well away 1** making good progress **2** (almost) DRUNK **1** – infml – **well out of** lucky to be free from

⁴**well** interj **1** – used to express surprise, indignation, or resignation **2** – used to indicate a pause in talking or to introduce a remark

⁵**well** adj **1** satisfactory, pleasing ⟨*all's* ~ *that ends* ~⟩ **2** advisable, desirable ⟨*it's* ~ *to ask*⟩ **3** prosperous, well-off **4** HEALTHY **1 5** being a cause for thankfulness; fortunate ⟨*it is* ~ *that this has happened*⟩ – **wellness** n

we'll we will; we shall

well-advised adj **1** acting with wisdom; prudent **2** resulting from or showing wisdom ⟨~ *plans*⟩

well-appointed adj having good and complete facilities, furniture, etc ⟨*a* ~ *house*⟩

well-being n the state of being happy, healthy, or prosperous

wellborn adj born of a respected and esp noble family

well-bred adj **1** having or indicating good breeding; refined **2** of good pedigree

well-connected adj having useful social or family contacts

well-disposed adj having a favourable or sympathetic disposition ⟨*was* ~ *towards his workmates*⟩

well-done adj cooked thoroughly

well-favoured adj good-looking; handsome – not now in vogue

well-found adj properly equipped ⟨*a* ~ *ship*⟩

well-founded adj based on good grounds or reasoning ⟨*a* ~ *argument*⟩

well-groomed adj well dressed and scrupulously neat

well-grounded adj 1 having a good basic knowledge ⟨~ in Latin and Greek⟩ 2 well-founded

well-heeled adj having a great deal of money; wealthy – infml

well-hung adj 1 having large breasts 2 having a large penis USE vulg

well-informed adj 1 having a good knowledge of a wide variety of subjects 2 having reliable information on a usu specified topic, event, etc

wellington boot, wellington n, chiefly Br a waterproof rubber boot that usu reaches the knee

well-intentioned adj well-meaning

well-knit adj well constructed; esp having a compact usu muscular physique ⟨a ~ athlete⟩

well-known adj fully or widely known; specif famous

well-lined adj full of money – infml ⟨~ pockets⟩

well-meaning adj having or based on good intentions though often failing ⟨~ but misguided idealists⟩

well-meant adj based on good intentions

well-nigh adv almost, nearly

well-off adj 1 well-to-do, rich 2 in a favourable or fortunate situation ⟨you don't know when you're ~⟩ 3 well provided ⟨not very ~ for sheets⟩

well-oiled adj, chiefly Br DRUNK 1 – infml

well-preserved adj retaining a youthful appearance

well-read adj well-informed through much and varied reading

well-rounded adj 1 having a pleasantly curved or rounded shape ⟨a ~ figure⟩ 2 having or consisting of a background of broad experience or education ⟨a ~ person⟩ 3 agreeably complete and well-constructed

well-spoken adj 1 speaking clearly, courteously, and usu with a refined accent 2 spoken in a pleasing or fitting manner ⟨~ words⟩

wellspring n 1 a source of continual supply 2 FOUNTAIN-HEAD 1

well-thought-of adj of good repute

well-timed adj said or done at an opportune moment; timely

well-to-do adj moderately rich; prosperous

well-tried adj thoroughly tested and found reliable

well-turned adj 1 pleasingly formed; shapely ⟨a ~ ankle⟩ 2 concisely and appropriately expressed ⟨a ~ compliment⟩

well-wisher n one who feels goodwill towards a person, cause, etc – well-wishing adj or n

well-worn adj 1 having been much used or worn ⟨~ shoes⟩ 2 made trite by overuse; hackneyed

welsh vi 1 to evade an obligation, esp payment of a debt 2 to break one's word USE usu + on – welsher n

Welsh n 1 pl in constr the people of Wales 2 the Celtic language of the Welsh – Welsh adj, Welshman n

Welsh rabbit n WELSH RAREBIT

Welsh rarebit n a snack of melted cheese (and ale) on toast

¹welt n 1 a strip, usu of leather, between a shoe sole and upper through which they are fastened together 2 a doubled edge, strip, insert, or seam (e g on a garment) for ornament or reinforcement 3 (a ridge or lump raised on the body usu by) a heavy blow

²welt vt 1 to provide with a welt 2a to raise a welt on the body of b to hit hard

weltanschauung n, pl weltanschauungs, weltanschauungen often cap a particular conception of the nature and purpose of the world; a philosophy of life

¹welter vi 1 to writhe, toss; also to wallow 2 to become soaked, sunk, or involved in sthg

²welter n 1 a state of wild disorder; a turmoil 2 a chaotic mass or jumble ⟨a bewildering ~ of data⟩

welterweight n a boxer who weighs not more than 10st 7lb (66.7kg) if professional or above 63.5kg (about 10st) but not more than 67kg (about 10st 8lb) if amateur

wen n 1 a cyst formed by obstruction of a sebaceous gland and filled with fatty material 2 an abnormally large overcrowded city, esp London

¹wench n 1 a female servant or rustic working girl 2 a young woman; a girl – now chiefly humor or dial

²wench vi, of a man to have sexual relations habitually with women, esp prostitutes – wencher n

wend vt to proceed on (one's way)

Wend n a member of a Slavonic people of eastern Germany – Wendish adj

wendy house n, often cap W, chiefly Br a small toy house for children to play in

Wensleydale n a crumbly mild-flavoured English cheese

went past of GO

were past 2 sing, past pl, substandard past 1 & 3 sing, or past subjunctive of BE

we're we are

werewolf n, pl werewolves a person transformed into a wolf or capable of assuming a wolf's form

wert archaic past 2 sing of BE

Wesleyanism n Methodism – Wesleyan adj or n

¹west adj or adv towards, at, belonging to, or coming from the west

²west n 1 (the compass point corresponding to) the direction 90° to the left of north that is the general direction of sunset 2 often cap regions or countries lying to the west of a specified or implied point of orientation: e g a the part of the USA to the west of the Mississippi b the non-Communist countries of Europe and America 3 European civilization in contrast with that of the Orient – westward adv, adj, or n, westwards adv

West Country n the West of England

West End n the western part of central London where the main shopping centres, theatres, etc are located – West-End adj

¹westerly adj or adv west

²westerly n a wind from the west

¹western adj 1 often cap (characteristic) of a region conventionally designated West: e g a of or stemming from European traditions in contrast with those of the Orient b of the non-Communist countries of Europe and America c of the American West 2 west 3 cap of the Roman Catholic or Protestant segment of Christianity – westernmost adj

²western n, often cap a novel, film, etc dealing with cowboys, frontier life, etc in the W USA, esp during the latter half of the 19th c

Westerner n, chiefly NAm a native or inhabitant of the West, esp the W USA

westernize, -ise vb to imbue or be imbued with qualities associated with the West – westernization n

West Indian n 1 a native or inhabitant of the W Indies 2 a descendant of W Indians – West Indian adj

¹wet adj -tt- 1 consisting of, containing, or covered or soaked with liquid (e g water) 2 rainy 3 still moist enough to smudge or smear ⟨~ paint⟩ 4 involving the use or presence of liquid ⟨~ processes⟩ 5 of an aircraft wing containing fuel tanks 6 chiefly Br feebly ineffectual or dull – infml 7 chiefly NAm permitting the sale or consumption of alcoholic drink ⟨a ~ State⟩ – wetly adv, wetness n, wettish adj – wet behind the ears immature, inexperienced – infml

²wet n 1 moisture, wetness 2 rainy weather; rain 3 chiefly Br a wet person; a drip – infml

³wet vt -tt-; (2) wet 1 to make wet 2 to urinate in or on

– wettable *adj*, **wettability** *n* – **wet one's whistle** to take an esp alcoholic drink – *infml*

wet blanket *n* one who quenches or dampens enthusiasm or pleasure

wet dream *n* an erotic dream culminating in orgasm

wether *n* a male sheep castrated before sexual maturity

wet-nurse *vt* **1** to act as wet nurse to **2** to give constant and often excessive care to

wet nurse *n* a woman who cares for and suckles another's children

wet suit *n* a close-fitting suit made of material, usu rubber, that admits water but retains body heat so as to insulate its wearer (e g a skin diver), esp in cold water

wetting agent *n* a substance that prevents a surface from being repellent to a wetting liquid

we've we have

¹**whack** *vt* **1** to strike with a smart or resounding blow **2** *chiefly Br* to get the better of; defeat *USE* *infml* – **whacker** *n*

²**whack** *n* **1** (the sound of) a smart resounding blow **2** a portion, share **3** an attempt, go 〈*have a ~ at it*〉 *USE infml*

whacked *adj*, *chiefly Br* completely exhausted; DONE IN – *infml*

¹**whacking** *adj* extremely big; whopping – *infml*

²**whacking** *adv* very, extremely – *infml* 〈*a ~ great oil tanker*〉

¹**whale** *n*, *pl* **whales**, *esp collectively* **whale** any of an order of often enormous aquatic mammals that superficially resemble large fish, have tails modified as paddles, and are frequently hunted for oil, flesh, or whalebone – **whale of a time** an exceptionally enjoyable time

²**whale** *vi* to engage in whale fishing and processing

³**whale** *vt*, *NAm* to hit or defeat soundly – *infml*

whalebone *n* a horny substance found in 2 rows of plates up to 4m (about 12ft) long attached along the upper jaw of whalebone whales and used for stiffening things

whaler *n* a person or ship engaged in whaling

whaling *n* the occupation of catching and processing whales for oil, food, etc

¹**wham** *n* (the sound made by) a forceful blow – *infml*

²**wham** *interj* – used to express the noise of a forceful blow or impact; *infml*

³**wham** *vb* **-mm-** *vt* to throw or strike with a loud impact ~ *vi* to crash or explode with a loud impact *USE infml*

wharf *n*, *pl* **wharves** *also* **wharfs** a structure built along or out from the shore of navigable water so that ships may load and unload

¹**what** *pron*, *pl* **what** **1a(1)** – used as an interrogative expressing inquiry about the identity, nature, purpose, or value of sthg or the character, nature, occupation, position, or role of sby 〈*~ is this?*〉 **(2)** – used to ask for repetition of sthg not properly heard or understood 〈*he bought ~?*〉 **b** – used as an exclamation expressing surprise or excitement and frequently introducing a question 〈*~, no breakfast?*〉 **c** – used to direct attention to a statement that the speaker is about to make 〈*guess ~*〉〈*you know ~*〉 **d** *chiefly Br* – used in demanding assent 〈*a clever play, ~?*〉; not now in vogue **2** ¹THAT **1**, WHICH **1**, WHO **2** 〈*gilded rat-holes ~ pass for public hostelries – Punch*〉 – substandard **3** that which; the one that 〈*no income but ~ he gets from his writing*〉 **4a** WHATEVER **1a** 〈*say ~ you will*〉 **b** how much – used in exclamations 〈*~ it must cost!*〉 – **or what** – used at the end of a question to express inquiry about additional possibilities 〈*is it raining, or snowing, or what?*〉 – **what about 1** what news or plans have you concerning **2** *also*

what do you say to, **what's wrong with** let's; HOW ABOUT – **what for 1** for what purpose or reason; why – usu used with the other words of a question between *what* and *for* 〈*what did you do that for?*〉 except when used alone **2** punishment, esp by blows or by a sharp reprimand 〈*gave him what for in violent Spanish – New Yorker*〉 – **what have you** any of various other things that might also be mentioned 〈*paper clips, pins, and* what have you〉 – **what if 1** what will or would be the result if **2** what does it matter if – **what it takes** the qualities or resources needed for success or for attainment of a usu specified goal 〈*she's really got* what it takes *to get to the top*〉 – **what not** WHAT HAVE YOU – **what of 1** what is the situation with respect to **2** what importance can be assigned to – **what of it** what does it matter – **what's what** the true state of things 〈*knows* what's what *when it comes to fashion*〉

²**what** *adv* in what respect?; how much? 〈*~ does he care?*〉

³**what** *adj* **1a** – used with a following noun as an adjective equivalent in meaning to the interrogative pronoun *what* 〈*~ minerals do we export?*〉 **b** WHICH **1** 〈*~ size do you take?*〉 **c** how remarkable or striking – used esp in exclamatory utterances and dependent clauses 〈*~ a suggestion!*〉 **2** the that; as much or as many as 〈*told him ~ little I knew*〉

¹**whatever** *pron* **1a** anything or everything that 〈*take ~ you want*〉 **b** no matter what **2** what in the world? – *infml* 〈*~ do you mean?*〉 – **or whatever** or anything else at all – *infml* 〈*buffalo or rhinoceros* or whatever – *Alan Moorehead*〉

²**whatever** *adj* **1a** any that; all that 〈*buy peace on ~ terms could be obtained – C S Forester*〉 **b** no matter what **2** of any kind at all – used after a noun with *any* or with a negative 〈*of any shape ~*〉〈*no food ~*〉

whatnot *n* **1** a lightweight open set of shelves for bric-a-brac **2** other usu related goods, objects, etc 〈*carrying all his bags and ~*〉 **3** a whatsit *USE* (*2&3*) *infml*

whatsit *n* sby or sthg that is of unspecified, nondescript, or unknown character, or whose name has been forgotten – *infml*

what with *prep* having as a contributory circumstance or circumstances 〈*very busy* what with *all these guests to feed*〉

wheat *n* (any of various grasses cultivated in most temperate areas for) a cereal grain that yields a fine white flour and is used for making bread and pasta, and in animal feeds

wheaten *adj* made of (the grain, meal, or flour of) wheat

wheat germ *n* the embryo of the wheat kernel separated in milling and used esp as a source of vitamins

wheedle *vb* **wheedling** *vt* **1** to influence or entice by soft words or flattery **2** to cause to part with sthg by wheedling – + *out of* 〈*~ her out of her last £5*〉 ~ *vi* to use soft words of flattery

¹**wheel** *n* **1** a circular frame of hard material that may be (partly) solid or spoked and that is capable of turning on an axle **2** a contrivance or apparatus having as its principal part a wheel: e g **a** a chiefly medieval instrument of torture to which the victim was tied while his/her limbs were broken by a metal bar **b** any of various revolving discs or drums that produce an arbitrary value on which to gamble, usu by stopping at a particular number 〈*roulette ~*〉 **3** sthg resembling a wheel in shape or motion; *esp* CATHERINE WHEEL **4a** a curving or circular movement **b** a rotation or turn, usu about an axis or centre; *specif* a turning movement of troops or ships in line in which the units preserve alignment and relative positions **5a** *pl* the workings or controlling forces of sthg 〈*the ~s of govern-*

ment⟩ **b** *chiefly NAm* a person of importance, esp in an organization ⟨*a big* ~⟩ **6** *pl* a motor vehicle, esp a motor car *USE* (5b&6) *infml* – **wheelless** *adj*

²**wheel** *vi* **1** to turn (as if) on an axis; revolve **2** to change direction as if revolving on a pivot ⟨~ed *round and walked away*⟩ **3** to move or extend in a circle or curve ⟨*birds in* ~*ing flight*⟩ **4** to alter or reverse one's opinion – often + *about* or *round* ~ *vt* **1** to cause to turn (as if) on an axis; rotate **2** to convey or move (as if) on wheels; *esp* to push (a wheeled vehicle or its occupant) ⟨~ *the baby into the shade*⟩ **3** to cause to change direction as if revolving on a pivot **4** to make or perform in a circle or curve – **wheel and deal** to pursue one's own usu commercial interests, esp in a shrewd or unscrupulous manner

wheelbarrow *n* a load-carrying device that consists of a shallow box supported at 1 end by usu 1 wheel and at the other by a stand when at rest or by handles when being pushed

wheelbase *n* the distance between the front and rear axles of a vehicle

wheelchair *n* an invalid's chair mounted on wheels

wheeler *n* **1** a maker of wheels **2** a draught animal (e g a horse) pulling in the position nearest the front wheels of a wagon **3** sthg (e g a vehicle or ship) that has wheels – esp in combination ⟨*side*-wheeler⟩

wheelhouse *n* a deckhouse for a vessel's helmsman

wheelwright *n* sby who makes or repairs wheels, esp wooden ones for carts

¹**wheeze** *vi* **1** to breathe with difficulty, usu with a whistling sound **2** to make a sound like that of wheezing ~ *vt* to utter wheezily

²**wheeze** *n* **1** a sound of wheezing **2** a cunning trick or expedient – *infml* – **wheezy** *adj*, **wheezily** *adv*, **wheeziness** *n*

¹**whelk** *n* any of numerous large marine snails; *esp* one much used as food in Europe

²**whelk** *n* a pustule, pimple

¹**whelp** *n* **1** any of the young of various flesh-eating mammals, esp a dog **2** a disagreeable or impudent child or youth

²**whelp** *vt* to give birth to (esp a puppy) ~ *vi, esp of a bitch* to bring forth young

¹**when** *adv* **1** at what time? **2a** at or during which time ⟨*the day* ~ *we met*⟩ **b** and then; WHEREUPON 1

²**when** *conj* **1a** at or during the time that ⟨*went fishing* ~ *he was a boy*⟩ **b** as soon as ⟨*will look nice* ~ *finished*⟩ **c** whenever ⟨~ *he listens to music, he falls asleep*⟩ **2** in the event that; if **3a** considering that ⟨*why smoke* ~ *you know it's bad for you?*⟩ **b** in spite of the fact that; although ⟨*gave up politics* ~ *he might have done well*⟩

³**when** *pron* what or which time ⟨*since* ~ *have you known that?*⟩

⁴**when** *n* a date, time ⟨*worried about the wheres and* ~*s*⟩

whence *adv or conj* **1a** from where?; from which place, source, or cause? **b** from which place, source, or cause **2** to the place from which ⟨*returned* ~ *they came*⟩ *USE* chiefly fml

¹**whenever** *conj* **1** at every or whatever time ⟨*roof leaks* ~ *it rains*⟩ ⟨*can go* ~ *he likes*⟩ **2** in any circumstance ⟨~ *possible, he tries to help*⟩ – **or whenever** or at any similar time – *infml* ⟨*in 1922* or whenever⟩

²**whenever** *adv* when in the world? – *infml* ⟨~ *did you find the time?*⟩

¹**where** *adv* **1a** at, in, or to what place? ⟨~ *is the house?*⟩ **b** at, in, or to what situation, direction, circumstances, or respect? ⟨~ *does this plan lead?*⟩ **2** at, in, or to which (place) ⟨*has reached the size* ~ *traffic is a problem*⟩ ⟨*the town* ~ *she lives*⟩

²**where** *conj* **1a** t, in, or to the place at which ⟨*stay* ~ *you are*⟩ **b** ²WHEREVER ⟨*goes* ~ *he likes*⟩ **c** in a case, situation, or respect in which ⟨*outstanding* ~ *endurance is called for*⟩ **2** whereas, while ⟨*he wants a house,* ~ *I would prefer a flat*⟩ – **where it's at** the real scene of the action – *slang*

³**where** *n* **1** what place or point? ⟨~ *are you from?*⟩ **2** a place, point ⟨*bought from any old* ~⟩ – *infml*

¹**whereabouts** *also* **whereabout** *adv or conj* in what vicinity ⟨*do you know* ~ *he lives?*⟩

²**whereabouts** *n pl but sing or pl in constr* the place or general locality where a person or thing is ⟨*his present* ~ *are a secret*⟩

whereas *conj* **1** in view of the fact that; since – used, esp formally, to introduce a preamble **2** while on the contrary; although

whereat *conj, archaic* **1** at or towards which **2** in consequence of which; whereupon

whereby *conj* **1** in accordance with which ⟨*a law* ~ *children receive cheap milk*⟩ **2** by which means – chiefly fml

¹**wherefore** *adv* **1** for what reason; why **2** for that reason; therefore *USE* chiefly fml

²**wherefore** *n* a reason, cause – chiefly in *the whys and wherefores* ⟨*wants to know all the whys and* ~*s*⟩

¹**wherein** *adv* in what; how ⟨*showed him* ~ *he was wrong*⟩ – chiefly fml

²**wherein** *conj* in which; where ⟨*the city* ~ *he lived*⟩ – chiefly fml

whereof *conj, pron, or adv, archaic* of what, which, or whom

whereon *adv or conj, archaic* on which or what ⟨*the base* ~ *it rests*⟩

whereto *adv or conj* to which or what; whither ⟨~ *tends all this* – Shak⟩ – chiefly fml

whereupon *adv or conj* **1** closely following and in consequence of which ⟨*he saw me coming,* ~ *he offered me his seat*⟩ **2** on which; whereon – chiefly fml

¹**wherever** *adv* where in the world? – chiefly infml ⟨~ *have you been?*⟩ – **or wherever** or anywhere else at all – chiefly infml ⟨*go to China* or *wherever*⟩

²**wherever** *conj* at, in, or to every or whatever place ⟨*he can sleep* ~ *he likes*⟩

wherewithal *n* means, resources; *specif* money ⟨*didn't have the* ~ *for an expensive dinner*⟩

wherry *n* **1** a long light rowing boat used to transport passengers on rivers and about harbours **2** a large light barge, lighter, or fishing boat used in Britain

¹**whet** *vt* -tt- **1** to sharpen by rubbing on or with sthg (e g a stone) **2** to make keen or more acute; stimulate ⟨~ *the appetite*⟩ – **whetter** *n*

²**whet** *n* **1** a goad, incitement **2** an appetizer

whether *conj* – used usu with correlative *or* or with *or whether* to indicate **a** an indirect question involving alternatives ⟨*decide* ~ *he should agree or protest*⟩ or a choice between 2 alternatives ⟨*I wonder* ~ *he heard*⟩ **b** indifference between alternatives ⟨*seated him next to her* ~ *by accident or design*⟩

whetstone *n* **1** a stone for sharpening an edge (e g of a chisel) **2** sthg that stimulates or makes keen

whew *n* a half-formed whistle uttered as an exclamation expressing amazement, discomfort, or relief

whey *n* the watery part of milk separated from the curd, esp in cheese-making, and rich in lactose, minerals, and vitamins – **wheyey** *adj*

¹**which** *adj* **1** being what one or ones out of a known or limited group? ⟨~ *tie should I wear?*⟩ **2** whichever ⟨*it will not fit, turn it* ~ *way you like*⟩ **3** – used to introduce a nonrestrictive relative clause by modifying the noun

which refers either to a preceding word or phrase or to a whole previous clause ⟨*he may come, in* ~ *case I'll ask him*⟩

²which *pron, pl* **which 1** what one out of a known or specified group? ⟨~ *of those houses do you live in?*⟩ **2** whichever ⟨*take* ~ *you like*⟩ **3** – used to introduce a relative or esp a nonrestrictive relative clause; used in any grammatical relation except that of a possessive; used esp in reference to an animal, thing, or idea ⟨*the office in* ~ *I work*⟩ ⟨*a large dog,* ~ *bit me*⟩, or to a human group, esp when a singular verb follows ⟨*this tribe,* ~ *has aroused much interest among anthropologists*⟩; often used in reference to a whole previous clause or even to a preceding sentence ⟨*can sing,* ~ *is an advantage*⟩ ⟨*can be overcome by basing these programs on need not race. Which is fine – Nation Review (Melbourne)*⟩

¹whichever *pron, pl* **whichever 1** whatever one out of a group ⟨*take 2 of the 4 optional papers,* ~ *you prefer*⟩ **2** no matter which **3** which in the world? – chiefly infml ⟨~ *did you choose?*⟩

²whichever *adj* being whatever one or ones out of a group; no matter which ⟨*its soothing   effect will be the same* ~ *way you take it – Punch*⟩

¹whiff *n* **1** a quick puff, slight gust, or inhalation, esp of air, a smell, smoke, or gas **2** a slight trace ⟨*a* ~ *of scandal*⟩

²whiff *vi* **1** to emit whiffs; puff **2** to inhale an odour; sniff **3** to smell unpleasant

Whig *n or adj* **1** (a member) of a major British political group of the 18th and early 19th c seeking to limit royal authority and increase parliamentary power **2** *NAm* (a member) of an American political party formed about 1834 and succeeded about 1854 by the Republican party – **Whiggery, Whiggism** *n*, **Whiggish** *adj*

¹while *n* **1** a period of time, esp when short and marked by the occurrence of an action or condition; a time ⟨*stay here for a* ~⟩ **2** the time and effort used; trouble ⟨*it's worth your* ~⟩

²while *conj* **1a** during the time that **b** providing that; as long as ⟨~ *there's life there's hope*⟩ **2a** when on the other hand; whereas **b** in spite of the fact that; although ⟨~ *respected, he is not liked*⟩

³while *prep, archaic or dial* until

while away *vt* to pass (time) in a leisurely, often pleasant, manner ⟨*while away the afternoon*⟩

whilst *conj, chiefly Br* while

whim *n* **1** a sudden, capricious, or eccentric idea or impulse; a fancy **2** a large capstan formerly used in mines for raising ore or water

whimper *vi or n* **1** (to make) a low plaintive whining sound **2** (to make) a petulant complaint or protest

whimsical *adj* **1** full of whims; capricious **2** resulting from or suggesting whimsy; *esp* quizzical, playful ⟨*a* ~ *smile*⟩ – **whimsically** *adv*, **whimsicalness, whimsical-ity** *n*

whimsy, whimsey *n* **1** a whim, caprice **2** an affected or fanciful device, creation, or style, esp in writing or art

whin *n* furze

¹whine *vi* to utter or make a whine ~ *vt* to utter or express (as if) with a whine – **whiner** *n*, **whiningly** *adv*

²whine *n* **1** (a sound like) a prolonged high-pitched cry, usu expressive of distress or pain **2** a querulous or peevish complaint – **whiny, whiney** *adj*

whinny *vb or n* (to make or utter with or as if with) a low gentle neigh or similar sound

¹whip *vb* **-pp-** *vt* **1** to take, pull, jerk, or move very quickly ⟨~*ped out a gun*⟩ **2a** to strike with a whip or similar slender flexible implement, esp as a punishment; *also* to spank **b** to drive or urge on (as if) by using a whip **c** to

strike as a whip does ⟨*rain* ~*ping the pavement*⟩ **3a** to bind or wrap (e g a rope or rod) with cord for protection and strength **b** to wind or wrap (e g cord) round sthg **4** to oversew (an edge, hem, or seam) using a whipstitch; *also* to hem or join (e g ribbon or lace) by whipping **5** to beat (e g eggs or cream) into a froth with a whisk, fork, etc **6** to overcome decisively; defeat – infml **7** to snatch suddenly; *esp* STEAL 1 – slang ~ *vi* to move, go, or come quickly or violently ⟨~*ped out of the turning at top speed*⟩ – **whipper** *n* – **whip into shape** to bring (sby or sthg) into a desired state, esp by hard work or practice

²whip *n* **1** an instrument consisting usu of a lash attached to a handle, used for driving and controlling animals and for punishment **2** a dessert made by whipping some of the ingredients ⟨*prune* ~⟩ **3** a light hoisting apparatus consisting of a single pulley, a block, and a rope **4** one who handles a whip: e g **a** a driver of horses; a coachman **b** a whipper-in **5a** a member of Parliament or other legislative body appointed by a political party to enforce discipline and to secure the attendance and votes of party members **b** *often cap* an instruction (e g a three-line whip or a two-line whip) to each member of a political party in Parliament to be in attendance for voting **c** (the privileges and duties of) membership of the official parliamentary representation of a political party ⟨*was deprived of the Labour* ~⟩ **6** a whipping or thrashing motion **7** the quality of resembling a whip, esp in being flexible – **whiplike** *adj*

whipcord *n* **1** a thin tough cord made of tightly braided or twisted hemp or catgut **2** a usu cotton or worsted cloth with fine diagonal cords or ribs

whip hand *n* a controlling position; *the* advantage

whip in *vt* to keep (hounds in a pack) from scattering by use of a whip

whiplash *n* **1** the lash of a whip **2 whiplash, whiplash injury** injury to the neck resulting from a sudden sharp whipping movement of the neck and head (e g in a car collision)

whipper-in *n, pl* **whippers-in** a huntsman's assistant who whips in the hounds

whippersnapper *n* an insignificant but impudent person, esp a child

whippet *n* (any of) a breed of small swift slender dogs related to greyhounds

whipping *n* **1** a severe beating or chastisement **2a** stitching with or stitches made using whipstitch **b** material used to whip or bind

whipping boy *n* **1** a boy formerly educated with a prince and punished in his stead **2** a scapegoat

whippoorwill *n* a N American nightjar

whippy *adj* unusually resilient; springy ⟨*a* ~ *fishing rod*⟩

whip-round *n, chiefly Br* a collection of money made usu for a benevolent purpose – infml ⟨*had a* ~ *to buy him a leaving present*⟩

whip up *vt* **1** to stir up; stimulate ⟨*whipped up the emotions of the crowd*⟩ **2** to produce in a hurry ⟨*I'll whip a meal up in no time*⟩

¹whirl *vi* **1** to move along a curving or circling course, esp with force or speed ⟨*planets* ~*ing in their orbits*⟩ **2** to turn abruptly or rapidly round (and round) on an axis; rotate, wheel ⟨*he* ~*ed round to face me*⟩ **3** to pass, move, or go quickly ⟨*she* ~*ed down the hallway*⟩ **4** to become giddy or dizzy; reel ⟨*my head's* ~*ing*⟩ ~ *vt* **1** to convey rapidly; whisk ⟨*the ambulance* ~*ed him away*⟩ **2** to cause to turn usu rapidly round (and round) on an axis; rotate – **whirler** *n*, **whirly** *adj*

²whirl *n* **1** (sthg undergoing or having a form suggestive of) a rapid rotating or circling movement **2a** a confused tumult; a bustle ⟨*the social* ~⟩ **b** a confused or disturbed mental state; a turmoil ⟨*my mind is in a* ~ *all the time* – Arnold Bennett⟩ **3** an experimental or brief attempt; a try – infml ⟨*I'll give it a* ~⟩

whirligig *n* **1** a child's toy (e g a top) that whirls **2a** sthg that continuously whirls, moves, or changes **b** a whirling or circling course (e g of events)

whirlpool *n* **1** (sthg resembling, esp in attracting or engulfing power) a circular eddy of rapidly moving water with a central depression into which floating objects may be drawn **2** WHIRL 2a

whirlwind *n* **1** a small rapidly rotating windstorm of limited extent marked by an inward and upward spiral motion of the lower air round a core of low pressure **2** a confused rush; a whirl

whirlybird *n* a helicopter – infml; not now in vogue

whirr, whir *vi or n* **-rr-** (to make or revolve or move with) a continuous buzzing or vibrating sound made by sthg in rapid motion

¹whisk *n* **1** a quick light brushing or whipping motion **2a** any of various small usu hand-held kitchen utensils used for whisking food **b** a small bunch of flexible strands (e g twigs, feathers, or straw) attached to a handle for use as a brush

²whisk *vi* to move lightly and swiftly ~*vt* **1** to convey briskly ⟨~ed *the children off to bed*⟩ **2** to mix or fluff up (as if) by beating with a whisk **3** to brush or wipe off (e g crumbs) lightly **4** to brandish lightly; flick ⟨~ed *its tail*⟩

whisker *n* **1a** a hair of the beard or sideboards **b** a hairs breadth ⟨*lost the race by a* ~⟩ **2** any of the long projecting hairs or bristles growing near the mouth of an animal (e g a cat) **3** a thin hairlike crystal (e g of sapphire or a metal) of exceptional mechanical strength – **whiskered** *adj,* **whiskery** *adj,* **whiskeriness** *n*

whiskey *n* whisky produced in Ireland or the USA

Whiskey – used as a communications code word for the letter *w*

whisky *n* a spirit distilled from fermented mash of rye, corn, wheat, or esp barley

¹whisper *vi* **1** to speak softly with little or no vibration of the vocal cords **2** to make a hissing or rustling sound like whispered speech ~*vt* **1** to address or order in a whisper **2** to utter in a whisper **3** to report or suggest confidentially ⟨*it is* ~ed *that he will soon resign*⟩ – **whisperer** *n*

²whisper *n* **1a** whispering; *esp* speech without vibration of the vocal cords **b** a hissing or rustling sound like whispered speech **2** sthg communicated (as if) by whispering: e g **a** a rumour ⟨~s *of scandal*⟩ **b** a hint, trace

¹whist *vi, dial Br* to be silent; hush – often used as an interjection to call for silence

²whist *n* (any of various card games similar to) a card game for 4 players in 2 partnerships in which each trick made in excess of 6 tricks scores 1 point

whist drive *n, Br* an evening of whist playing with a periodic change of partners, usu with prizes at the finish

¹whistle *n* **1** a device (e g a small wind instrument) in which the forcible passage of air, steam, the breath, etc through a slit or against a thin edge in a short tube produces a loud sound ⟨*a police* ~⟩⟨*a factory* ~⟩ **2** (a sound like) a shrill clear sound produced by whistling or by a whistle ⟨*the* ~ *of the wind*⟩

²whistle *vb* **whistling** *vi* **1** to utter a (sound like a) whistle (by blowing or drawing air through the puckered lips) **2** to make a whistle by rapid movement; *also* to move rapidly (as if) with such a sound ⟨*the train* ~d *by*⟩ **3** to blow or sound a whistle ~*vt* **1** to send, bring, call, or signal to (as if) by whistling **2** to produce, utter, or express

by whistling ⟨~ *a tune*⟩ – **whistleable** *adj,* **whistler** *n* –

whistle for to demand or request in vain ⟨*did a sloppy job so he can* whistle for *his money*⟩

whistle-stop *n* **1** *NAm* **a** a small station at which trains stop only on signal **b** a small community **2** *chiefly NAm* a brief personal appearance (to give an election speech) by a politician during a tour – **whistle-stop** *adj*

whit *n* the smallest part imaginable; a bit ⟨*not a* ~ *abashed*⟩

Whit *n* Whitsuntide

¹white *adj* **1a** free from colour **b** of the colour white **c** light or pallid in colour ⟨*lips* ~ *with fear*⟩ **d** *of wine* light yellow or amber in colour **e** *Br, of coffee* served with milk or cream **2a** of a group or race characterized by reduced pigmentation **b** of or for white people ⟨~ *schools*⟩ **3** free from spot or blemish: e g **a**(1) free from moral impurity; innocent (2) *of a wedding* in which the woman wears white clothes as a symbol of purity **b** not intended to cause harm ⟨*a* ~ *lie*⟩ **4a** dressed in white **b** accompanied by snow ⟨*a* ~ *Christmas*⟩ **5** notably ardent; passionate ⟨*in a* ~ *rage*⟩ **6** reactionary, counterrevolutionary **7** *of light, sound, electromagnetic radiation, etc* consisting of a wide range of frequencies simultaneously ⟨~ *noise*⟩ – **whitely** *adv,* **whitish** *adj,* **whiteness** *n*

²white *n* **1** the achromatic and lightest colour that belongs to objects that reflect diffusely nearly all incident light **2** a white or light-coloured part of sthg: e g **a** the mass of albumin-containing material surrounding the yolk of an egg **b** the white part of the ball of the eye **c** (the player playing) the light-coloured pieces in a two-handed board game **3** sby or sthg that is or approaches the colour white: e g **a** *pl* white (sports) clothing ⟨*tennis* ~s⟩ **b** a white animal (e g a butterfly or pig) **4** *pl* leucorrhoea **5** sby belonging to a light-skinned race

white ant *n* a termite

whitebait *n* (any of various small food fishes similar to) the young of any of several European herrings (e g the common herring or the sprat) eaten whole

white blood cell, white cell *n* any of the white or colourless blood cells that have nuclei, do not contain haemoglobin, and are primarily concerned with body defence mechanisms and repair

white-collar *adj* of or being the class of nonmanual employees whose duties do not call for the wearing of work clothes or protective clothing

whited sepulchre *n* a hypocrite

white dwarf *n* a small whitish star of high surface temperature, low brightness, and high density

white elephant *n* **1** a property requiring much care and expense and yielding little profit **2** sthg that is no longer of value (to its owner)

white feather *n* a mark or symbol of cowardice

white flag *n* **1** a flag of plain white used as a flag of truce or as a token of surrender **2** a token of weakness or yielding

Whitehall *n* the British government

white heat *n* **1** a temperature higher than red heat, at which a body emits white light **2** a state of intense mental or physical activity or strain

white hope *n* a person expected to bring fame and glory to his/her group, country, etc

white horse *n* **1** a usu prehistoric figure of a horse made by cutting away the turf from a chalk hillside **2** a wave with a crest breaking into white foam – usu pl

White House *n the* executive branch of the US government

white lead *n* any of several white lead-containing pigments; *esp* a heavy poisonous carbonate of lead used formerly in exterior paints

white-livered *adj* lily-livered

white magic *n* magic used for good purposes (e g to cure disease)

white meat *n* light-coloured meat (e g poultry breast or veal)

white metal *n* any of several alloys based on tin or sometimes lead used esp for bearings, type metal, and domestic utensils

whiten *vb* to make or become white or whiter; bleach – **whitener** *n*, **whitening** *n*

white paper *n, often cap W&P* a (British) government report usu less extensive than a blue book

white pepper *n* a condiment prepared from the husked dried berries of an E Indian plant used either whole or ground

white pudding *n* a sausage made from minced pork meat and fat

white sauce *n* a sauce made with milk, cream, or a chicken, veal, or fish stock

white slave *n* a woman or girl held unwillingly, esp abroad, and forced to be a prostitute – **white slavery** *n*

white spirit *n* an inflammable liquid distilled from petroleum and used esp as a solvent and thinner for paints

whitethroat *n* an Old World warbler with a white throat, reddish-brown wings, and buff underparts tinged with pink

white-tie *adj* characterized by or requiring the wearing of formal evening dress by men ⟨a ~ *dinner*⟩

¹**whitewash** *vt* **1** to apply whitewash to **2a** to gloss over or cover up (e g vices or crimes) **b** to exonerate by concealment or through biased presentation of data **3** to defeat overwhelmingly in a contest or game – *infml* – **whitewasher** *n*

²**whitewash** *n* **1** a liquid mixture (e g of lime and water or whiting, size, and water) for whitening outside walls or similar surfaces **2** a whitewashing

whither *adv or conj* **1** to or towards what place? – also used in rhetorical questions without a verb ⟨~ *democracy?*⟩ **2** to the place at, in, or to which ⟨go ~ *you wish*⟩ **3** to which place *USE* chiefly fml

¹**whiting** *n* any of various marine food fishes; *esp* one related to the cod

²**whiting** *n* washed and ground chalk used esp as a pigment and in paper coating

whitlow *n* a deep usu pus-producing inflammation of the finger or toe, esp round the nail

Whitsun *adj or n* (of, being, or observed on or at) Whitsunday or Whitsuntide

Whitsunday *n* a Christian feast on the 7th Sunday after Easter commemorating the descent of the Holy Spirit at Pentecost

Whitsuntide *n* Whitsunday and Whitmonday and/or the days of public holiday celebrated together with or in place of these days

¹**whittle** *n, archaic or dial* a large knife

²**whittle** *vb* **whittling** *vt* **1a** to pare or cut off chips from the surface of (wood) with a knife **b** to shape or form by so paring or cutting **2** to reduce, remove, or destroy gradually as if by cutting off bits with a knife; pare – usu + *down* or *away* ⟨~ *down expenses*⟩ ~ *vi* to cut or shape sthg, esp wood, (as if) by paring it with a knife – **whittler** *n*

¹**whiz, whizz** *vi* **-zz-** **1** to (move with a) buzz, whirr, or hiss like an arrow or ball passing through air **2** to move swiftly – *infml* – **whiz** *n*, **whizzer** *n*

²**whiz** *n* WIZARD 2 – *infml*

whiz kid, whizz kid *n* sby who is unusually intelligent, clever, or successful, esp at an early age

who *pron, pl* **who** **1** what or which person or people? **2** – used to introduce a restrictive or nonrestrictive relative clause in reference to a person or animal ⟨*my father,* ~ *was a lawyer*⟩, or to a human group, esp when a pl verb follows ⟨*an orchestra* ~ *play the wartime hits* – The *Observer*⟩ **3** *archaic* the person or people that; whoever *USE* often used as object of a verb or of a following preposition though still disapproved of by some ⟨*a character* ~ *we are meant to pity* – TLS⟩ – **who is/was who** the identity of or the noteworthy facts about each of a number of people

whoa *interj* – used as a command (e g to a draught animal) to stand still

whodunit *also* **whodunnit** *n* a play, film, or story dealing with the detection of crime or criminals

whoever *pron* **1** whatever person **2** no matter who **3** who in the world? – chiefly *infml* ⟨~ *can it be?*⟩ *USE* (1&2) used in any grammatical relation except that of a possessive

¹**whole** *adj* **1a** free of wound, injury, defect, or impairment; intact, unhurt, or healthy **b** restored **2** having all its proper constituents; unmodified ⟨~ *milk*⟩ **3** each or all of; entire ⟨*made the* ~ *class stay in*⟩ **4a** constituting an undivided unit; unbroken ⟨*the snake swallowed the rabbit* ~⟩ **b** directed to (the accomplishment of) 1 end or aim ⟨*we have concentrated our* ~ *efforts on it*⟩ **5** very great – in *a whole lot* ⟨*feels a* ~ *lot better now*⟩ **6** having the same parents as another ⟨a ~ *brother*⟩ – **wholeness** *n*

²**whole** *n* **1** a complete amount or sum; sthg lacking no part, member, or element ⟨*the* ~ *of society*⟩ **2** sthg constituting a complex unity; a coherent system or organization of parts – **as a whole** considered all together as a body rather than as individuals – **on the whole** **1** in view of all the circumstances **2** in most instances; typically

whole gale *n* wind having a speed of 89 to 102km/h (55 to 63mph)

wholehearted *adj* earnestly committed or devoted; free from all reserve or hesitation – **wholeheartedly** *adv*

wholemeal *adj* made with (flour from) ground entire wheat kernels

whole note *n, NAm* a semibreve

whole number *n* an integer

¹**wholesale** *n* the sale of commodities in large quantities usu for resale (by a retailer)

²**wholesale** *adj or adv* **1** (sold or selling) at wholesale **2** (performed) on a large scale, esp without discrimination ⟨~ *slaughter*⟩

wholesaler *n* one who sells chiefly to retailers, merchants, or industrial, institutional, and commercial users mainly for resale or business use – **wholesale** *vb*

wholesome *adj* **1** promoting health or well-being of mind or spirit ⟨*things that aren't* ~ *for the young*⟩ **2** promoting health of body ⟨a light ~ *diet*⟩; *also* healthy ⟨~*-looking children*⟩ **3** based on well-grounded fear; prudent ⟨a ~ *respect for the law*⟩ – **wholesomely** *adv*, **wholesomeness** *n*

whole tone *n* a musical interval (e g C-D or G-A) comprising 2 semitones

wholly *adv* **1** to the full or entire extent; completely ⟨~ *incompetent*⟩ **2** to the exclusion of other things; solely ⟨a book dealing ~ *with herbs*⟩

whom *pron, objective case of* WHO – used as an interrogative or relative; used as object of a preceding preposition ⟨*to know for* ~ *the bell tolls* – John Donne⟩; or less frequently as object of a verb or of a following preposition ⟨*the man* ~ *you wrote to*⟩ though now often considered stilted, esp as an interrogative and esp in oral use; occas used in the environment of a verb of which it might mistakenly be considered the subject ⟨*taking no* *bets on* ~ *The Sex Symbol   is supposed to be* – *The Sun*⟩

¹**whoop** *vi* to utter or make a whoop ~*vt* **1** to utter or express with a whoop **2** to urge or cheer on with a whoop – **whoop it up** to celebrate riotously; carouse – *infml*

²**whoop** *n* **1** a loud yell expressive of eagerness, exuberance, or jubilation **2** the hoot of an owl, crane, etc **3** the crowing intake of breath following a paroxysm in whooping cough

¹**whoopee** *interj* – used to express exuberance

²**whoopee** *n* boisterous convivial fun – in *make whoopee*; *infml*

whooping cough *n* an infectious bacterial disease, esp of children, marked by a convulsive spasmodic cough sometimes followed by a crowing intake of breath

whoosh *vi or n* (to move quickly with) a swift or explosive rushing sound ⟨*cars* ~*ing along the motorway*⟩

whop *vt* **-pp-** **1** to beat, strike **2** to defeat totally *USE infml*

whopper *n* **1** sthg unusually large or otherwise extreme of its kind **2** an extravagant or monstrous lie *USE infml*

¹**whopping** *adj* extremely big – *infml* ⟨*won by a* ~ *majority*⟩

²**whopping** *adv* very, extremely – *infml* ⟨*a* ~ *great oil tanker*⟩

¹**whore** *n* a prostitute

²**whore** *vi* **1** to have sexual intercourse outside marriage, esp with a prostitute **2** to pursue an unworthy or idolatrous desire ⟨*growth was a false god which had been* ~*d after for too long* – *The Guardian*⟩

whorehouse *n* a brothel

whoremonger *n* a whoremaster

whorl *n* **1** an arrangement of similar anatomical parts (e g leaves) in a circle round a point on an axis (e g a stem) **2** sthg spiral in form or movement; a swirl ⟨~*s of smoke*⟩ **3** a single turn of a spiral (shape) **4** a fingerprint in which the central ridges turn through at least 1 complete circle – **whorled** *adj*

whortleberry *n* a bilberry

¹**whose** *adj* of whom or which, esp as possessor or possessors ⟨~ *hat is this?*⟩, agent or agents ⟨*the courts,* ~ *decisions I uphold*⟩, or object or objects of an action ⟨*the factory in* ~ *construction they were involved*⟩

²**whose** *pron, pl* **whose** that which belongs to whom – used without a following noun as a pronoun equivalent in meaning to the adjective *whose* ⟨*tell me* ~ *it was* – Shak⟩

whosoever *pron, archaic* whoever

¹**why** *adv* for what cause, reason, or purpose? – **why not** – used in making a suggestion ⟨why not *boil them?*⟩

²**why** *conj* **1** the cause, reason, or purpose for which ⟨*that's* ~ *I'm so tired*⟩ **2** on which grounds ⟨*the reason* ~ *I left*⟩

³**why** *n, pl* **whys** a reason, cause – chiefly in *the whys and wherefores* ⟨*wants to know the* ~*s and wherefores*⟩

⁴**why** *interj* – used to express mild surprise, hesitation, approval, disapproval, or impatience ⟨~, *here's what I was looking for*⟩

wick *n* a cord, strip, or cylinder of loosely woven material through which a liquid (e g paraffin, oil, or melted wax) is drawn by capillary action to the top in a candle, lamp, oil stove, etc for burning

wicked *adj* **1** morally bad; evil **2** disposed to mischief; roguish ⟨*a* ~ *grin*⟩ **3** very unpleasant, vicious, or dangerous ⟨*a* ~ *waste*⟩ – *infml* – **wickedly** *adv*, **wickedness** *n*

wicker *adj or n* (made of) interlaced osiers, twigs, canes, or rods ⟨*a* ~ *basket*⟩

wickerwork *n* (work consisting of) wicker

wicket *n* **1** a small gate or door; *esp* one forming part of or placed near a larger one **2** an opening like a window; *esp* a grilled or grated window through which business is transacted (e g at a bank) **3** a small gate for emptying the chamber of a canal lock or regulating the amount of water passing through a channel **4a** either of the 2 sets of stumps set 22yd (20.12m) apart, at which the ball is bowled and which the batsman defends in cricket **b** the area 12ft (3.66m) wide bounded by these wickets **c** a terminated innings of a batsman; *also* a partnership between 2 batsmen who are in at the same time ⟨*the 4th* ~ *put on 57 runs*⟩ **d** an innings of a batsman that is not completed or never begun ⟨*won by 5* ~*s*⟩ **5** situation or set of circumstances – in *on a good/bad wicket, on a sticky wicket*; *infml*

wicketkeeper *n* the fieldsman in cricket who is stationed behind the batsman's wicket and whose object is to catch balls missed or hit with the edge of the bat by the batsman and to stump him if possible – **wicketkeeping** *n*

¹**wide** *adj* **1a** having great horizontal extent; vast ⟨*a* ~ *area*⟩ **b** embracing much; COMPREHENSIVE **1** ⟨*reaches a* ~ *public*⟩ **2a** having a specified width ⟨*3ft* ~⟩ **b** having much extent between the sides; broad ⟨*a* ~ *doorway*⟩ **c** fully opened ⟨*wide-eyed*⟩ **3a** extending or fluctuating over a considerable range ⟨*a* ~ *variation*⟩ **b** distant or deviating from sthg specified ⟨*his remark was* ~ *of the truth*⟩ **4** of, occupying, passing through, or being a fielding position in cricket near a line perpendicular to and equidistant from each wicket ⟨~ *mid-off*⟩ **5** *Br* shrewd, astute – slang ⟨*the* ~ *boys*⟩ – **widely** *adv*, **widen** *vb*, **wideness** *n*, **widish** *adj*

²**wide** *adv* **1** over a great distance or extent; widely ⟨*searched far and* ~⟩ **2a** so as to leave much space or distance between ⟨*legs* ~ *apart*⟩ **b** so as to miss or clear a point by a considerable distance ⟨*the bullet went* ~⟩ **3** to the fullest extent; completely – often as an intensive + *open*

³**wide** *n* a ball bowled in cricket that is out of reach of the batsman in his normal position and counts as 1 run to his side

-wide *comb form* (*n* → *adj*) over (a specified distance, area, or extent); throughout (a specified area or scope) ⟨*a nation*wide *business*⟩ ⟨*expanded the business country*wide⟩

wide-angle *adj* (having or using a camera with a lens) that has an angle of view wider than the ordinary

wide-awake *adj* **1** fully awake **2** alertly watchful, esp for advantages or opportunities

wide-eyed *adj* **1** amazed, astonished **2** marked by uncritical acceptance or admiration; naive ⟨~ *innocence*⟩

widespread *adj* **1** widely extended or spread out **2** widely diffused or prevalent ⟨~ *public interest*⟩

widgeon *also* **wigeon** *n, pl* **widgeons**, *esp collectively* **widgeon** (a duck related to) an Old World freshwater dabbling duck the male of which has a chestnut head

¹**widow** *n* **1a** a woman whose husband has died (and who has not remarried) **b** a woman whose husband spends much time away from her pursuing a specified (sporting) activity ⟨*a golf* ~⟩ **2** an extra (part of a) hand of cards dealt face down and usu placed at the disposal of the highest bidder **3** a single usu short last line (e g of a paragraph) at the top of a printed page or column

²**widow** *vt* **1** to cause to become a widow **2** to deprive of sthg greatly valued or needed

widower *n* a man whose wife has died (and who has not remarried)

widowhood *n* (the period during which a woman remains in) the state of being a widow

width *n* **1** the measurement taken at right angles to the length **2** largeness of extent or scope **3** a measured and cut piece of material ⟨*a ~ of calico*⟩

wield *vt* **1** to handle (e g a tool) effectively ⟨*~ a broom*⟩ **2** to exert, exercise ⟨*~ influence*⟩ – **wielder** *n*

wife *n, pl* **wives** **1** a woman acting in a specified capacity – in combination ⟨*fish*wife⟩ **2** a married woman, esp in relation to her husband ⟨*John's ~*⟩ **3** *dial* a woman – **wifehood** *n*, **wifeless** *adj*

wifely *adj* of or befitting a good wife – **wifeliness** *n*

wig *n* a manufactured covering of natural or synthetic hair for the (bald part of a) head – **wigged** *adj*, **wigless** *adj*

wigging *n* a severe scolding – *infml*

¹**wiggle** *vb* **wiggling** to (cause to) move with quick jerky or turning motions or smoothly from side to side ⟨*his toes ~d*⟩ – **wiggler** *n*

²**wiggle** *n* **1** a wiggling movement **2** a wavy line; a squiggle – **wiggly** *adj*

wigwam *n* a N American Indian hut having a framework of poles covered with bark, rush mats, or hides

wilco *interj* – used esp in radio and signalling to indicate that a message received will be complied with

¹**wild** *adj* **1a** (of organisms) living in a natural state and not (ordinarily) tame, domesticated, or cultivated **b(1)** growing or produced without the aid and care of humans ⟨*~ honey*⟩ **(2)** related to or resembling a corresponding cultivated or domesticated organism ⟨*~ strawberries*⟩ **2** not (amenable to being) inhabited or cultivated **3a(1)** free from restraint or regulation; uncontrolled **(2)** emotionally overcome ⟨*~ with grief*⟩; *also* passionately eager or enthusiastic ⟨*was ~ about jazz*⟩ **(3)** very angry; infuriated ⟨*drove me ~ with his whining*⟩ **b** marked by great agitation ⟨*~ frenzy*⟩; *also* stormy ⟨*a ~ night*⟩ **c** going beyond reasonable or conventional bounds; fantastic ⟨*beyond my ~est dreams*⟩ **d** indicative of strong passion or emotion ⟨*a ~ gleam in his eyes*⟩ **4** uncivilized, barbaric **5a** deviating from the intended or regular course ⟨*the throw was ~*⟩ **b** having no logical basis; random ⟨*a ~ guess*⟩ **6** *of a playing card* able to represent any card designated by the holder – **wildish** *adj*, **wildly** *adv*, **wildness** *n*

²**wild** *n* **1** WILDERNESS 1a **2** a wild, free, or natural state or existence ⟨*living in the ~*⟩

³**wild** *adv* in a wild manner: e g **a** without regulation or control ⟨*rhododendrons growing ~*⟩ **b** off an intended or expected course

wild boar *n* an Old World wild pig from which most domestic pigs have derived

¹**wildcat** *n, pl* **wildcats**, *(1b)* **wildcats**, *esp collectively* **wildcat** **1a** either of 2 cats that resemble but are heavier in build than the domestic cat and are usu held to be among its ancestors **b** any of various small or medium-sized cats (e g the lynx or ocelot) **2** a savage quick-tempered person **3** a wildcat oil or gas well

²**wildcat** *adj* **1** operating, produced, or carried on outside the bounds of standard or legitimate business practices ⟨*a ~ insurance scheme*⟩ **2** of or being an oil or gas well drilled in territory not known to be productive **3** initiated by a group of workers without formal union approval or in violation of a contract ⟨*a ~ strike*⟩

³**wildcat** *vi* **-tt-** to prospect and drill an experimental oil or gas well – **wildcatter** *n*

wildebeest *n, pl* **wildebeests**, *esp collectively* **wildebeest** a gnu

wilderness *n* **1a** a (barren) region or area that is (essentially) uncultivated and uninhabited by human beings **b** an empty or pathless area or region ⟨*the remote ~es of*

space⟩ **c** a part of a garden or nature reserve devoted to wild growth **2** a confusing multitude or mass **3** *the* state of exclusion from office or power

wildfire *n* **1** sthg that spreads very rapidly – usu in *like wildfire* **2** a phosphorescent glow (e g will-o'-the-wisp)

wildfowl *n* a wild duck, goose, or other game bird, esp a waterfowl – **wildfowler** *n*, **wildfowling** *n*

wild-goose chase *n* a hopeless pursuit after sthg unattainable

wildlife *n* wild animals

wild oat *n* **1** a wild grass common as a weed in meadows **2** *pl* offences and indiscretions of youth; *esp* premarital promiscuity – usu in *sow one's wild oats*

¹**wile** *n* a deceitful or beguiling trick or stratagem – usu pl

²**wile** *vt* **1** to lure; entice **2** to while

wilful, *NAm chiefly* **willful** *adj* **1** obstinately and often perversely self-willed **2** done deliberately; intentional – **wilfully** *adv*, **wilfulness** *n*

¹**will** *vb, pres sing & pl* **will**; *pres neg* **won't**; *past* **would** *va* **1** – used to express choice, willingness, or consent or in negative constructions refusal ⟨*can find no one who ~ take the job*⟩ ⟨*if we ~ all do our best*⟩; used in the question form with the force of a request ⟨*~ you please stop talking*⟩ or of an offer or suggestion ⟨*~ you have some tea?*⟩ **2** – used to express custom or inevitable tendency ⟨*accidents ~ happen*⟩; used with emphatic stress to express exasperation ⟨*he ~ call the record player the 'gramophone'* – John Fowles⟩ **3** – used to express futurity ⟨*tomorrow morning I ~ wake up in this first-class hotel suite* – Tennessee Williams⟩ **4** can ⟨*the back seat ~ hold 3 passengers*⟩ **5** – used to express logical probability ⟨*that ~ be the milkman*⟩ **6** – used to express determination to command or urge ⟨*I have made up my mind to go, and go I ~*⟩ ⟨*you ~ do as I say, at once*⟩ ~ *vi* **1** to wish, desire ⟨*whether we ~ or no*⟩ **2** *archaic* to be about to go ⟨*thither ~ I then* – Sir Walter Scott⟩

²**will** *n* **1** a desire, wish: e g **a** a resolute intention ⟨*where there's a ~ there's a way*⟩ **b** an inclination ⟨*I did it against my ~*⟩ **c** a choice, wish ⟨*the ~ of the people*⟩ **2** what is wished or ordained by the specified agent ⟨*God's ~ be done*⟩ **3a** a mental power by which one (apparently) controls one's wishes, intentions, etc ⟨*has a ~ of her own*⟩ **b** an inclination to act according to principles or ends ⟨*the ~ to believe*⟩ **c** a specified attitude towards others ⟨*bear him no ill ~*⟩ **4** willpower, self-control ⟨*a man of iron ~*⟩ **5** a (written) legal declaration of the manner in which sby would have his/her property disposed of after his/her death – **will-less** *adj* – **at will** as one wishes; as or when it pleases or suits oneself

³**will** *vt* **1** to bequeath **2a** to determine deliberately; purpose **b** to decree, ordain ⟨*Providence ~s it*⟩ **c** to (attempt to) cause by exercise of the will ⟨*~ ed her to go away*⟩ ~ *vi* to exercise the will – **willer** *n*

willies *n pl* nervousness, jitters – + *the*; *infml*

¹**willing** *adj* **1** inclined or favourably disposed in mind; ready ⟨*~ to work*⟩ **2** prompt to act or respond ⟨*a ~ horse*⟩ **3** done, borne, or given without reluctance ⟨*~ help*⟩ – **willingly** *adv*, **willingness** *n*

²**willing** *n* cheerful alacrity – in *show willing*

will-o'-the-wisp *n* **1** a phosphorescent light sometimes seen over marshy ground and often caused by the combustion of gas from decomposed organic matter **2** an enticing but elusive goal **3** an unreliable or elusive person

willow *n* **1** any of a genus of trees and shrubs bearing catkins of petal-less flowers **2** an object made of willow wood; *esp* a cricket bat – *infml* – **willowlike** *adj*

willow pattern *n* china tableware decorated with a usu blue-and-white story-telling design of oriental style

willowy adj 1 full of willows 2a supple, pliant b gracefully tall and slender

willpower n self-control, resoluteness

willy-nilly adv or adj 1 by compulsion; without choice 2 (carried out or occurring) in a haphazard or random manner ⟨distributed the gifts ~ among the crowd⟩

¹**wilt** archaic pres 2 sing of ¹WILL

²**wilt** vi 1 of a plant to lose freshness and become flaccid; droop 2 to grow weak or faint; languish ~ vt to cause to wilt

³**wilt** n a disease of plants marked by wilting

wily adj full of wiles; crafty – **wilily** adv, **wiliness** n

wimple vt or n wimpling (to cover with or as if with) a cloth covering worn over the head and round the neck and chin, esp by women in the late medieval period and by some nuns

Wimpy trademark – used for a fried hamburger served in a plain bread bun

¹**win** vb -nn-; won vi 1a to gain the victory in a contest; succeed ⟨always ~s at chess⟩ b to be right in an argument, dispute, etc; also to have one's way ⟨OK, you ~, we'll go to the theatre⟩ 2 to succeed in arriving at a place or a state – esp in to win free ~ vt 1a to get possession of by qualities or fortune ⟨~ their approval⟩ ⟨won £10⟩ b to obtain by effort; earn ⟨striving to ~ a living from the soil⟩ 2a to gain (as if) in battle or contest ⟨~ the victory⟩ b to be the victor in ⟨won the war⟩ 3a to solicit and gain the favour of; also to persuade – usu + over or round b to induce (a woman) to accept oneself in marriage 4 to obtain (e g ore, coal, or clay) by mining 5 to reach by expenditure of effort ⟨~ the summit⟩ – **winnable** adj

²**win** n 1 a victory or success, esp in a game or sporting contest 2 first place at the finish, esp of a horse race

wince vi to shrink back involuntarily (e g from pain); flinch – **wince** n

winceyette n a lightweight usu cotton fabric napped on 1 or both sides

¹**winch** n 1 any of various machines or instruments for hoisting or pulling; a windlass 2 a crank or handle for giving motion to a machine (e g a grindstone)

²**winch** vt to hoist (as if) with a winch – often + up – **wincher** n

¹**wind** n 1 a (natural) movement of air, esp horizontally 2 a force or agency that carries along or influences; a trend ⟨the ~s of change⟩ 3a BREATH 4 ⟨the fall knocked the ~ out of him⟩ b BREATH 2a ⟨soon recovered his ~⟩ c the pit of the stomach 4 gas generated in the stomach or the intestines 5 mere talk; idle words 6 air carrying a scent (e g of a hunter or game) 7a musical wind instruments collectively, esp as distinguished from stringed and percussion instruments b sing or pl in constr the group of players of such instruments 8 (a compass point corresponding to) a direction from which the wind may blow – **windless** adj, **windlessly** adv, **windlessness** n – **before the wind** in the same direction as the main force of the wind – **close to the wind** 1 as nearly as possible against the main force of the wind 2 close to a point of danger; near the permissible limit – **have the wind up** to be scared or frightened – **in the wind** about to happen; astir, afoot – **off the wind** away from the direction from which the wind is blowing – **on the wind** towards the direction from which the wind is blowing – **put the wind up** to scare, frighten – **under the wind** 1 to leeward 2 in a place protected from the wind; under the lee

²**wind** vt 1 to detect or follow by scent 2 to make short of breath 3 to rest (e g a horse) in order to allow the breath to be recovered

³**wind** vt winded, wound to sound (e g a call or note) on a horn

⁴**wind** vb wound also winded vi 1 to bend or warp 2 to have a curving course; extend or proceed in curves ⟨path ~s down the hill⟩ 3 to coil, twine 4 to turn when lying at anchor 5 to undergo winding ⟨car window won't ~⟩ ~ vt 1a to surround or wrap with sthg pliable ⟨~ the baby in a shawl⟩ b to turn completely or repeatedly, esp about an object; coil ⟨~ wool into a ball⟩ c(1) to hoist or haul by means of a rope or chain and a windlass (2) to move (a ship) by hauling on a capstan d(1) to tighten the spring of ⟨~ the clock⟩ (2) to put into the specified state or position by winding ⟨~ the speedometer back⟩ e to raise to a high level (e g of excitement or tension) – usu + up ⟨wound himself up into a frenzy⟩ 2 to make (one's way or course) (as if) by a curving route – **winder** n

⁵**wind** n a coil, turn

windbag n an excessively talkative person – infml

windbreak n sthg (e g a growth of trees or a fence) that breaks the force of the wind

windcheater n, chiefly Br a weatherproof or windproof coat or jacket; an anorak

wind down vi to become gradually more relaxed; unwind ~ vt to bring to an end gradually; cause to cease ⟨are winding down their operations in France⟩

windfall n 1 sthg, esp a fruit, blown down by the wind 2 an unexpected gain or advantage; esp a legacy

winding n 1 material (e g wire) wound or coiled about an object (e g an armature); also a single turn of the wound material 2 the manner of winding sthg 3 a curved course, line, or progress ⟨the ~s of the path⟩ – **windingly** adv

winding-sheet n a sheet in which a corpse is wrapped for burial

wind instrument n a musical instrument (e g a trumpet, clarinet, or organ) sounded by wind; esp a musical instrument sounded by the player's breath

windjammer n 1 a large fast square-rigged sailing vessel 2 Br a windcheater

¹**windlass** n any of various machines for hoisting or hauling: e g a a horizontal drum supported on vertical posts and turned by a crank so that the hoisting rope is wound round the drum b a steam, electric, etc winch with a horizontal or vertical shaft and 2 drums, used to raise a ship's anchor

²**windlass** vt to hoist or haul with a windlass

¹**windmill** n 1 a mill operated by vanes that are turned by the wind 2 a toy consisting of lightweight vanes that revolve at the end of a stick

²**windmill** vb to (cause to) move like a windmill

window n 1 an opening, esp in the wall of a building, for admission of light and air that is usu fitted with a frame containing glass and capable of being opened and shut 2 a pane (e g of glass) in a window 3 sthg (e g a shutter, opening, or valve) suggestive of or functioning like a window 4 a transparent panel in an envelope, through which the address on the enclosure is visible 5 a range of wavelengths in the electromagnetic spectrum that can pass through a planet's atmosphere 6 an interval of time within which a rocket or spacecraft must be launched to accomplish a particular mission 7 an area at the limits of the earth's atmosphere through which a spacecraft must pass for successful reentry – **windowless** adj

window box n a box for growing plants on the (outside) sill of a window

window dressing n 1 the display of merchandise in a shop window 2 the means by which sthg is made superficially more attractive or favourable – **window dresser** n

window-shop vi to look at the displays in shop windows for amusement or to assess goods, prices, etc – **window-shopper** n

windpipe *n* the trachea – not used technically

windscreen *n*, *Br* a transparent screen, esp of glass, at the front of a (motor) vehicle

windshield *n*, *NAm* a windscreen

wind-sock *n* a truncated cloth cone that is open at both ends and mounted on a pole and is used to indicate the direction of the wind, esp at airfields

windswept *adj* **1** swept by wind ⟨*a ~ beach*⟩ **2** dishevelled (as if) from being exposed to the wind ⟨*a ~ appearance*⟩

wind tunnel *n* a tunnel-like apparatus through which air is blown at a known velocity to determine the effects of wind pressure on an object placed in the apparatus

wind up *vt* **1** to bring to a conclusion; *specif* to bring (a business) to an end by liquidation **2** to put in order; settle **3** WIND 1d(1) **4** *Br* to deceive playfully; pull (someone's) leg – slang ~ *vi* **1a** to come to a conclusion **b** to arrive in a place, situation, or condition at the end of or because of a course of action ⟨*wound up a millionaire*⟩ **2** to give a preliminary swing to the arms (e g before bowling)

windward *adj, adv, or n* (in or facing) the direction from which the wind is blowing

windy *adj* **1a** windswept **b** marked by strong or stormy wind **2** FLATULENT 1 **3** verbose, bombastic **4** *chiefly Br* frightened, nervous – infml – **windily** *adv*, **windiness** *n*

¹wine *n* **1** fermented grape juice containing varying percentages of alcohol together with ethers and esters that give it bouquet and flavour **2** the usu fermented juice of a plant or fruit used as a drink ⟨*rice ~*⟩ **3** sthg that invigorates or intoxicates **4** the colour of red wine

²wine *vb* to entertain with or drink wine – usu in *wine and dine*

wineglass *n* any of several variously shaped and sized drinking glasses for wine, that usu have a rounded bowl and are mounted on a stem and foot

wine merchant *n*, *Br* a usu wholesale dealer in alcoholic drinks, esp wine

¹wing *n* **1a** (a part of a nonflying bird or insect corresponding to) any of the movable feathered or membranous paired appendages by means of which a bird, bat, or insect flies **b** any of various body parts (e g of a flying fish or flying lemur) providing means of limited flight **2** an appendage or part resembling a wing in shape, appearance, or position: e g **a** any of various projecting anatomical parts **b** a sidepiece at the top of a high-backed armchair **c** a membranous, leaflike, or woody expansion of a plant, esp along a stem or on a seed pod **d** any of the aerofoils that develop a major part of the lift which supports a heavier-than-air aircraft **e** *Br* a mudguard, esp when forming an integral part of the body of a motor vehicle **3** a means of flight – usu pl with sing. meaning ⟨*fear lent me ~s*⟩ **4** a part of a building projecting from the main or central part **5a** any of the pieces of scenery at the side of a stage **b** *pl* the area at the side of the stage out of sight of the audience **6a** a left or right flank of an army or fleet **b(1)** any of the attacking positions or players on either side of a centre position in certain team sports **(2)** the left or right section of a playing field that is near the sidelines **7** *sing or pl in constr* a group or faction holding distinct opinions or policies within an organized body (e g a political party) **8** *pl* a pilot's badge, esp in the British armed forces **9** an operational and administrative unit of an air force; *specif* a unit of the Royal Air Force higher than a squadron and lower than a group – **wingless** *adj*, **winglike** *adj*, **winglet** *n* – **in the wings** in the background; in readiness to act – **on the wing** in flight; flying – **under one's wing** under one's protection; in one's care

²wing *vt* **1a** to fit with wings **b** to enable to fly or move

swiftly **2a** to wound in the wing **b** to wound (e g with a bullet) without killing ⟨*~ed by a sniper*⟩ **3a** to traverse (as if) with wings **b** to make (one's way) by flying ~ *vi* to go (as if) with wings; fly

wing commander *n* an officer in the Royal Air Force ranking below group captain

winger *n*, *chiefly Br* a player (e g in soccer) in a wing position

wing nut *n* a nut that has projecting wings or flanges so that it may be turned by finger and thumb

wingspan *n* the distance from the tip of one of a pair of wings to that of the other

¹wink *vi* **1** to shut 1 eye briefly as a signal or in teasing; *also, of an eye* to shut briefly **2** to avoid seeing or noting sthg – usu + *at* ⟨*~ at his absence*⟩ **3** to gleam or flash intermittently; twinkle ~ *vt* to cause (one's eye) to wink

²wink *n* **1** a brief period of sleep; a nap ⟨*didn't get a ~ all night*⟩ **2** an act of winking **3** the time of a wink; an instant ⟨*quick as a ~*⟩ **4** a hint or sign given by winking – infml ⟨*the bloke ... tipped him the ~* – Richard Llewellyn⟩

winkle *n* ²PERIWINKLE

winkle out *vt* **winkling** *chiefly Br* to displace or extract from a position; *also* to discover or identify with difficulty ⟨*winkling out the facts about the country's stocks of coal* – The Observer⟩

winner *n* sthg (expected to be) successful ⟨*this new scheme is a real ~*⟩ – infml

¹winning *n* **1a** the act of sby or sthg that wins; victory **b** acquisition, gaining **2** *pl* money won by success in a game or competition

²winning *adj* tending to please or delight ⟨*a ~ smile*⟩ – **winningly** *adv*

winnow *vt* **1a** to get rid of (sthg undesirable or unwanted); remove – often + *out* **b** to separate, sift ⟨*~ a mass of evidence*⟩ **2** to remove waste matter from (e g grain) by exposure to a current of air **3** to blow on; fan ⟨*the wind ~ing his thin white hair* – Time⟩ ~ *vi* **1** to separate chaff from grain by exposure to a current of air **2** to separate desirable and undesirable elements – **winnower** *n*

winsome *adj* pleasing and engaging, often because of a childlike charm and innocence – **winsomely** *adv*, **winsomeness** *n*

¹winter *n* **1** the season between autumn and spring comprising in the N hemisphere the months December, January, and February **2** the colder part of the year **3** a year – usu pl ⟨*happened many ~s ago*⟩ **4** a period of inactivity or decay – **winterless** *adj*, **winterlike** *adj*

²winter *adj* **1** of, during, or suitable for winter ⟨*a ~ holiday*⟩ **2** sown in autumn and harvested the following spring or summer ⟨*~ wheat*⟩

³winter *vi* to pass or survive the winter ~ *vt* to keep or feed (e g livestock) during the winter

winter garden *n* a garden, either outside or in a conservatory, containing plants that flourish in winter

wintergreen *n* **1** any of several perennial evergreen plants related to the heaths **2** (the flavour of) an essential oil from a wintergreen

winter sport *n* a usu open-air sport on snow or ice (e g skiing or tobogganing)

win through *vi* to reach a desired or satisfactory end, esp after overcoming difficulties

wintry, wintery *adj* **1** characteristic of winter; cold, stormy **2a** weathered (as if) by winter; aged, hoary **b** chilling, cheerless ⟨*a bitter ~ smile*⟩ – **wintrily** *adv*, **wintriness** *n*

¹wipe *vt* **1a** to clean or dry by rubbing, esp with or on sthg soft ⟨*~ the dishes*⟩ **b** to draw or pass for rubbing or cleaning ⟨~d *a cloth over the table*⟩ **c** to put into the specified state by rubbing ⟨~ *your hands dry*⟩ **2a** to remove (as if) by rubbing ⟨~ *that smile off your face*⟩ **b** to erase completely; obliterate ⟨~ *the scene from his memory*⟩ **3** to spread (as if) by wiping ⟨~ *grease on my skates*⟩ – **wipe the floor with** to defeat decisively

²**wipe** *n* **1** an act or instance of wiping **2** power or capacity to wipe

wipeout *n* a fall from a surfboard caused usu by loss of control

wipe out *vt* **1** to clean the inside of (sthg hollow) by wiping **2** to destroy completely; annihilate **3** to obliterate, cancel

wiper *n* **1a** sthg (e g a towel or sponge) used for wiping **b** a mechanically operated rubber strip for cleaning windscreens **2** a cam; *also* a tappet

¹**wire** *n* **1** metal in the form of a usu very flexible thread or slender rod **2a** a line of wire for conducting electrical current **b** a telephone or telegraph wire or system **c** a telegram, cablegram **3** a barrier or fence of usu barbed wire **4** *pl, chiefly NAm* strings ⟨*that woman behind the president pulling the ~s*⟩ – **wirelike** *adj*

²**wire** *vt* **1** to provide or connect with wire or wiring **2** to send or send word to by telegraph ~ *vi* to send a telegraphic message – **wirable** *adj*, **wirer** *n*

wirehaired *adj, esp of a dog* having a stiff wiry coat of hair

¹**wireless** *adj, chiefly Br* of radiotelegraphy, radiotelephony, or radio

²**wireless** *n* **1** WIRELESS TELEGRAPHY **2** *chiefly Br* RADIO 1, 2, 3d

³**wireless** *vt, chiefly Br* to radio

wireless telegraphy *n* the wireless transmission and reception of signals, usu voice communications, by means of electromagnetic waves

wire netting *n* a network of coarse woven wire

wiretap *n* an electrical connection for wiretapping

wiretapping *n* the act or an instance of tapping a telephone or telegraph wire

wire wool *n* an abrasive material consisting of fine wire strands woven into a mass and used for scouring esp kitchen utensils (e g pans)

wireworm *n* the slender hard-coated larva of various click beetles, destructive esp to plant roots

wiring *n* a system of wires; *esp* an arrangement of wires that carries electric currents

wiry *adj* **1** resembling wire, esp in form and flexibility **2** lean and vigorous; sinewy – **wirily** *adv*, **wiriness** *n*

wisdom *n* **1a** accumulated learning; knowledge **b** the thoughtful application of learning; insight **c** good sense; judgment ⟨*had the ~ to refuse*⟩ **2** the teachings of the ancient wise men

wisdom tooth *n* any of the 4 molar teeth in humans which are the last to erupt on each side at the back of each jaw

¹**wise** *n* manner, way ⟨*in any ~*⟩

²**wise** *adj* **1a** characterized by or showing wisdom; marked by understanding, discernment, and a capacity for sound judgment **b** judicious, prudent ⟨*not ~ to eat oysters*⟩ **2** well-informed ⟨*I'm none the ~r*⟩ **3** possessing inside knowledge; shrewdly cognizant – often + *to* ⟨*was ~ to what was happening*⟩ **4** *archaic* skilled in magic or divination – **wisely** *adv*, **wiseness** *n*

-**wise** *comb form* (*n → adv*) **1a** in the manner of ⟨*entered the room crabwise*⟩ **b** in the position or direction of ⟨*a clockwise movement*⟩ ⟨*laid it out lengthwise*⟩ **2** with regard to; in respect of ⟨*careerwise it's a good idea*⟩

wisecrack *vi or n* (to make) a sophisticated or knowing witticism – *infml* – **wisecracker** *n*

wise guy *n* a conceited and self-assertive person; *esp* a know-it-all – *infml* ⟨*OK ~, you try and fix it*⟩

wise up *vb* to (cause to) become informed or aware – *infml*

¹**wish** *vt* **1** to express the hope that sby will have or attain (sthg) ⟨*I ~ them success*⟩; *esp* to bid ⟨~ *him good night*⟩ **2a** to give form to (a wish) **b** to feel or express a wish for; want ⟨*I ~ to be alone*⟩ **c** to request in the form of a wish; order ⟨*he ~es us to leave*⟩ ~ *vi* **1** to have a desire – usu + *for* **2** to make a wish ⟨~ *on a star*⟩ – **wisher** *n* – **wish on/upon 1** to hope or will that (sby else) should have to suffer (a difficult person or situation) **2** to confer or foist (sthg unwanted) on (sby)

²**wish** *n* **1a** an act or instance of wishing or desire; a want ⟨*his ~ to become a doctor*⟩ **b** an object of desire; a goal ⟨*you got your ~*⟩ **2a** an expressed will or desire ⟨*obeyed their ~es*⟩ **b** an expressed greeting – usu *pl* ⟨*send my best ~es*⟩ **3** a ritual act of wishing ⟨*made a ~*⟩

wishbone *n* a forked bone in front of the breastbone of a bird consisting chiefly of the 2 clavicles fused at their lower ends

wishful *adj* **1a** expressive of a wish **b** having a wish; desirous **2** according with wishes rather than reality ⟨~ *thinking*⟩ – **wishfully** *adv*, **wishfulness** *n*

wishy-washy *adj* **1** lacking in strength or flavour **2** lacking in character or determination; ineffectual *USE infml*

wisp *n* **1** a small handful; *esp, chiefly Br* a pad of hay or straw for grooming an animal **2a** a thin separate streak or piece ⟨*a ~ of smoke*⟩ **b** sthg frail, slight, or fleeting ⟨*a ~ of a girl*⟩ **3** a flock of birds (e g snipe) – **wispish** *adj*, **wispily** *adv*, **wisplike** *adj*, **wispy** *adj*

wisteria, wistaria *n* any of a genus of chiefly Asiatic climbing plants with showy blue, white, purple, or rose flowers like those of the pea

wistful *adj* full of unfulfilled desire; yearning **2** musingly sad; pensive – **wistfully** *adv*, **wistfulness** *n*

wit *n* **1** reasoning power; intelligence ⟨*past the ~ of man to understand*⟩ ⟨*slow ~s*⟩ **2a** mental soundness; sanity ⟨*frightened her out of her ~s*⟩ **b** mental resourcefulness; ingenuity ⟨*was at my ~s end*⟩ **3a** the ability to relate seemingly disparate things so as to illuminate or amuse **b(1)** a talent for banter or raillery **(2)** repartee, satire **4** a witty individual **5** *archaic* a person of superior intellect; a thinker **6** *archaic* SENSE 2 – usu *pl* ⟨*alone and warming his five ~s, the white owl in the belfry sits* – Alfred Tennyson⟩ *USE (1&2)* often *pl* with sing. meaning

witch *n* **1** one who is credited with supernatural powers; *esp* a woman practising witchcraft **2** an ugly old woman; a hag **3** a charming or alluring woman – no longer in vogue – **witchlike** *adj*, **witchy** *adj*

witchcraft *n* (the use of) sorcery or magic

witch doctor *n* a professional sorcerer, esp in a primitive tribal society

witchery *n* witchcraft

witch hazel *n* (a soothing mildly astringent lotion made from the bark of) any of a genus of shrubs with slender-petalled yellow flowers borne in late autumn or early spring

witch-hunt *n* the searching out and harassment of those with unpopular views – **witch-hunter** *n*, **witch-hunting** *n or adj*

witching *adj* of or suitable for witchcraft ⟨*the very ~ time of night* – Shak⟩

with *prep* **1a** in opposition to; against ⟨*had a fight ~ his brother*⟩ **b** so as to be separated or detached from ⟨*I disagree ~ you*⟩ **2a** in relation to ⟨*the Italian frontier ~ Yugoslavia*⟩ **b** – used to indicate the object of attention, behaviour, or feeling ⟨*in love ~ her*⟩ **c** in respect to; so far as concerns ⟨*the trouble* ~ *this machine*⟩ – sometimes used redundantly ⟨*get it finished* ~⟩ **d** – used to indicate the object of an adverbial expression of imperative force ⟨*off* ~ *his head*⟩ **3a** – used to indicate accompaniment or association ⟨*live* ~ *the gipsies*⟩ **b** – used to indicate one to whom a usu reciprocal communication is made ⟨*talking* ~ *a friend*⟩ **c** – used to express agreement or sympathy ⟨*must conclude,* ~ *him, that the painting is a forgery*⟩ **d** able to follow the reasoning of ⟨*are you* ~ *me?*⟩ **4a** on the side of; for ⟨*vote* ~ *the government*⟩ **b** employed by ⟨*he's a salesman* ~ *ICI*⟩ **5a** – used to indicate the object of a statement of comparison, equality, or harmony ⟨*level* ~ *the street*⟩ ⟨*dress doesn't go* ~ *her shoes*⟩ **b** as well as ⟨*can ride* ~ *the best of them*⟩ **c** in addition to – used to indicate combination ⟨*his money,* ~ *his wife's, comes to a million*⟩ **d** inclusive of ⟨*costs £5* ~ *tax*⟩ **6a** by means of; using **b** through the effect of ⟨*pale* ~ *anger*⟩ **7a** – used to indicate manner of action ⟨*ran* ~ *effort*⟩ **b** – used to indicate an attendant or contributory circumstance ⟨*stood there* ~ *his hat on*⟩ **c** in possession of; having, bearing ⟨*came* ~ *good news*⟩ **d** in the possession or care of ⟨*the decision rests* ~ *you*⟩ **e** so as to have or receive ⟨*got off* ~ *a light sentence*⟩ **8a** – used to indicate a close association in time ⟨~ *the outbreak of war they went home*⟩ **b** in proportion to ⟨*the pressure varies* ~ *the depth*⟩ **9a** notwithstanding; IN SPITE OF ⟨*love her* ~ *all her faults*⟩ **b** EXCEPT FOR 2 ⟨*very similar,* ~ *1 important difference*⟩ **10** in the direction of ⟨~ *the wind*⟩

withal *adv* **1** together with this; besides **2** on the other hand; nevertheless

withdraw *vb* **withdrew; withdrawn** *vt* **1a** to draw back, away, or aside; remove ⟨~ *one's hand*⟩ **b** to remove (money) from a place of deposit or take back; retract ⟨~ *my offer*⟩ ~ *vi* **1a** to go back or away; retire from participation **b** to retreat **2** to become socially or emotionally detached ⟨*had* ~n *into himself*⟩ **3** to retract a statement – **withdrawable** *adj*

withdrawal *n* **1a** the act or an instance of withdrawing **b(1)** social or emotional detachment **(2)** a pathological retreat from objective reality (e g in some schizophrenic states) **2a** removal of money or other assets from a place of deposit or investment **b** the discontinuance of use of a drug, often accompanied by unpleasant side effects

withdrawn *adj* **1** secluded, isolated **2** socially detached and unresponsive; *also* shy – **withdrawnness** *n*

withe *n* a slender flexible branch or twig used esp for binding things together

wither *vi* **1** to become dry and shrivel (as if) from loss of bodily moisture **2** to lose vitality, force, or freshness ~ *vt* **1** to cause to wither **2** to make speechless or incapable of action; stun ⟨~ed *him with a look* – Dorothy Sayers⟩ – **withering** *adj,* **witheringly** *adv*

withers *n pl* the ridge between the shoulder bones of a horse or other quadruped

withhold *vt* **withheld 1** to hold back from action; check **2** to refrain from granting or giving ⟨~ *permission*⟩ – **withholder** *n*

¹within *adv* **1** in or into the interior; inside ⟨*enquire* ~⟩ **2** in one's inner thought, mood, or character

²within *prep* **1** inside – used to indicate enclosure or containment, esp in sthg large ⟨~ *the castle walls*⟩ **2** – used to indicate situation or circumstance in the limits or compass of: e g **a(1)** before the end of ⟨*gone* ~ *a week*⟩ **(2)** since the beginning of ⟨*been there* ~ *the last week*⟩ **b(1)** not beyond the quantity, degree, or limitations of ⟨*lives* ~ *his income*⟩ **(2)** in or into the scope or sphere of ⟨~ *his rights*⟩ **(3)** in or into the range of ⟨~ *reach*⟩ **(4)** – used to indicate a specific difference or margin ⟨~ *a mile of the town*⟩ **3** to the inside of; into

³within *n* an inner place or area ⟨*revolt from* ~⟩

¹without *prep* **1** – used to indicate the absence or lack of or freedom from sthg ⟨*go* ~ *sleep*⟩ ⟨*did it* ~ *difficulty*⟩ **2** outside – now chiefly poetic

²without *adv* **1** with sthg lacking or absent ⟨*has learned to do* ~⟩ **2** on or to the exterior; outside – now chiefly poetic

³without *conj, chiefly dial* unless ⟨~ *you have a stunt, what is there?* – Punch⟩

⁴without *n* an outer place or area ⟨*seen from* ~⟩

withstand *vt* **withstood 1** to resist with determination; esp to stand up against successfully **2** to be proof against ⟨*boots won't* ~ *the wet*⟩

withy *n* **1** OSIER 1 **2** a withe of osier

witless *adj* **1** lacking wit or understanding; foolish **2** CRAZY 1

¹witness *n* **1** testimony **2** sby who gives evidence, specif before a tribunal **3** sby asked to be present at a transaction so as to be able to testify to its having taken place **4** sby who personally sees or hears an event take place **5a** sthg serving as evidence; a sign ⟨*these low marks are* ~ *to their lack of application*⟩ **b** public affirmation by word or example of usu religious faith or conviction **6** *cap* a member of the Jehovah's Witnesses

²witness *vt* **1** to testify to **2** to act as legal witness of (e g by signing one's name) **3** to give proof of; betoken ⟨*his appearance* ~es *what he has suffered*⟩ – often in the subjunctive ⟨*has suffered badly, as* ~ *his appearance*⟩ **4** to observe personally or directly; see for oneself ⟨~ed *the historic event*⟩ **5** to be the scene or time of ⟨*structures which this striking Dorset hilltop once* ~ed – *TLS*⟩ ~ *vi* **1** to bear witness **2** to bear witness to one's religious convictions ⟨*opportunity to* ~ *for Christ* – Billy Graham⟩

witness-box *n, chiefly Br* an enclosure in which a witness testifies in court

-witted *comb form (adj → adj)* having wit or understanding of the specified kind ⟨*dull*-witted⟩

witticism *n* a witty and often ironic remark

witty *adj* **1** amusingly or ingeniously clever in conception or execution ⟨*a* ~ *musical theme*⟩ **2** having or showing wit ⟨*a* ~ *speaker*⟩ **3** quick to see or express illuminating or amusing relationships or insights – **wittily** *adv*, **wittiness** *n*

wives *pl of* WIFE

¹wizard *n* **1** a man skilled in magic **2** one who is very clever or skilful, esp in a specified field ⟨*a* ~ *at maths*⟩ – infml

²wizard *adj, chiefly Br* great, excellent – infml

wizardry *n* the art or practices of a wizard; sorcery

wizen *vb* to (cause to) become dry, shrunken, and wrinkled, often as a result of aging – usu in past part

woad *n* (a European plant of the mustard family formerly grown for) the blue dyestuff yielded by its leaves

¹wobble *vb* **wobbling** *vi* **1a** to proceed with an irregular swerving or staggering motion ⟨~d *down the road on his bicycle*⟩ **b** to rock unsteadily from side to side **c** to tremble, quaver **2** to waver, vacillate ~ *vt* to cause to wobble – **wobbler** *n*, **wobbliness** *n*, **wobbly** *adj*

²wobble *n* **1** an unequal rocking motion **2** an act or instance of vacillating or fluctuating

¹woe *interj* – used to express grief, regret, or distress

²woe *n* **1** great sorrow or suffering caused by misfortune, grief, etc **2** a calamity, affliction – usu pl ⟨*economic* ~⟩

woebegone *adj* expressive of great sorrow or misery ⟨*a* ~ *look*⟩

woeful *also* **woful** *adj* **1** feeling or expressing woe ⟨~ *prophecies*⟩ **2** inspiring woe; grievous ⟨*it was* ~ *to see*

him spoiling it – Henry James⟩ – **woefully** *adv*, **woeful-
ness** *n*

wog *n, chiefly Br* a nonwhite person; *broadly* any
dark-skinned foreigner – derog

woke *past of* WAKE

woken *past part of* WAKE

wold *n* 1 an upland area of open country 2 *pl, cap* a hilly
or rolling region – in names of various English geographical areas ⟨*the Yorkshire* Wolds⟩

¹**wolf** *n, pl* wolves, (*I*) wolves, *esp collectively* wolf 1 (the
fur of) any of various large predatory flesh-eating mammals that resemble the related dogs, prey on livestock, and
usu hunt in packs 2 a fiercely rapacious person 3a
dissonance in some chords produced on instruments with
fixed notes tuned by unequal temperament (e g organs and
pianos) b a harshness due to faulty vibration in various
notes in a bowed instrument 4 a man who pursues women
in an aggressive way – infml – **wolflike** *adj* – **keep the wolf
from the door** to avoid or prevent starvation or want –
wolf in sheep's clothing one who cloaks a hostile intention
with a friendly manner

²**wolf** *vt* to eat greedily; devour – often + *down*

wolfhound *n* any of several large dogs used, esp formerly,
in hunting large animals (e g wolves)

wolfram *n* 1 tungsten 2 wolframite

wolfsbane *n* a (yellow-flowered Eurasian) aconite

wolf whistle *n* a distinctive whistle sounded by a man to
express sexual admiration for a woman –
wolf-whistle *vi*

woman *n, pl* women 1a an adult female human as
distinguished from a man or child b a woman belonging
to a particular category (e g by birth, residence, membership, or occupation) – usu in combination ⟨*council-
woman*⟩ 2 womankind 3 distinctively feminine nature;
womanliness ⟨*there's something of the ~ in him*⟩ 4a a
charwoman ⟨*the daily ~*⟩ b a personal maid, esp in
former times 5a a female sexual partner; *esp* a mistress b
GIRLFRIEND 1 – chiefly derog – **womanless** *adj*

womanhood *n* 1a the condition of being an adult female
as distinguished from a child or male b the distinguishing
character or qualities of a woman or of womankind 2
women, womankind

womanish *adj* unsuitable to a man or to a strong character of either sex; effeminate ⟨*~ fears*⟩ – **womanishly** *adv*,
womanishness *n*

womanize, -ise *vi* to associate with many women habitually, esp for sexual relations – **womanizer** *n*

womankind *n sing or pl in constr* female human beings;
women as a whole, esp as distinguished from men

womanly *adj* having or exhibiting the good qualities
befitting a woman – **womanliness** *n*

womb *n* 1 the uterus 2a a hollow enveloping cavity or
space b a place where sthg is generated – **wombed** *adj*

wombat *n* any of several stocky Australian marsupial
mammals resembling small bears

womenfolk *also* **womenfolks** *n pl* 1 women in general 2
the women of a family or community

¹**won** *past of* WIN

²**won** *n, pl* won the standard unit of money in Korea

¹**wonder** *n* 1a a cause of astonishment or admiration; a
marvel ⟨*it's a ~ he wasn't killed*⟩ b a miracle 2 rapt
attention or astonishment at sthg unexpected, strange,
new to one's experience, etc ⟨*gazed in ~ at the snow*⟩

²**wonder** *adj* noted for outstanding success or achievement
⟨*~ drugs*⟩

³**wonder** *vi* 1a to be in a state of wonder; marvel *at* b to
feel surprise ⟨*I shouldn't ~ if he's late*⟩ 2 to feel curiosity
or doubt; speculate ⟨*~ about his motives*⟩ *~vt* to be

curious or in doubt about – with a clause ⟨*~ who she is*⟩
– **wonderer** *n*

wonderful *adj* 1 exciting wonder; astonishing ⟨*a sight ~
to behold*⟩ 2 unusually good; admirable – **wonderfully**
adv, **wonderfulness** *n*

wonderland *n* 1 a fairylike imaginary place 2 a place
that excites admiration or wonder

wonderment *n* 1 astonishment, marvelling 2 a cause of
or occasion for wonder 3 curiosity

wondrous *adj* wonderful – poetic – **wondrous** *adv,
archaic*, **wondrously** *adv*, **wondrousness** *n*

wonky *adj, Br* awry, crooked; *also* shaky, unsteady ⟨*he's
still a bit ~ after the flu*⟩ – infml

¹**wont** *adj* 1 accustomed, used ⟨*places where people are ~
to meet*⟩ 2 inclined, apt ⟨*her letters are ~ to be tedious*⟩
USE + *to* and infin; fml

²**wont** *n* customary practice – fml ⟨*according to my ~*⟩

won't will not

wonted *adj* customary, habitual – used attributively; fml
⟨*spoke with his ~ slowness*⟩ – **wontedly** *adv*, **wonted-
ness** *n*

woo *vt* 1 to try to win the affection of and a commitment
of marriage from (a woman); court 2 to solicit or entreat,
esp with importunity *~vi* to court a woman –
wooer *n*

¹**wood** *n* 1 a dense growth of trees, usu greater in extent
than a copse and smaller than a forest – often pl with sing.
meaning 2a a hard fibrous plant tissue that is basically
xylem and makes up the greater part of the stems and
branches of trees or shrubs beneath the bark b wood
suitable or prepared for some use (e g burning or building)
3 sthg typically made of wood: e g a a golf club with a
wooden head b a wooden cask ⟨*wine from the ~*⟩ c
²BOWL 1 – **not see the wood for the trees** to be unable to
see broad outlines because of a mass of detail – **out of the
wood** *Br* escaped from peril or difficulty

²**wood** *adj* 1 WOODEN 1 2 suitable for cutting, storing, or
carrying wood ⟨*a ~ saw*⟩

wood alcohol *n* methanol

woodbine *n* 1 honeysuckle 2 VIRGINIA CREEPER

¹**woodblock** *n* a woodcut – **wood-block** *adj*

²**woodblock** *adj, of a floor* made of parquet

woodcock *n, pl* woodcocks, *esp collectively* woodcock an
Old World long-billed wading bird of wooded regions that
is related to the sandpipers and shot as game

woodcraft *n* 1 skill and practice in anything relating to
woods or forests, esp in surviving, travelling, and hunting
2 skill in shaping or making things from wood

woodcut *n* (a print taken from) a relief-printing surface
consisting of a wooden block with a design cut esp in the
direction of the grain

woodcutter *n* one who chops down trees

wooded *adj* covered with growing trees

wooden *adj* 1 made or consisting of or derived from
wood 2 lacking ease or flexibility; awkwardly stiff –
woodenly *adv*, **woodenness** *n*

woodenheaded *adj* dense, stupid

wooden spoon *n* a consolation or booby prize

woodland *n* land covered with trees, scrub, etc – often pl
with sing. meaning – **woodland** *adj*, **woodlander** *n*

woodlouse *n, pl* woodlice a small ground-living crustacean with a flattened elliptical body often capable of
rolling into a ball in defence

woodpecker *n* any of numerous usu multicoloured birds
with very hard bills used to drill holes in the bark or wood
of trees to find insect food or to dig out nesting cavities

woodpile *n* a pile of wood (e g firewood) – **in the**

woodpile doing or responsible for secret mischief ⟨*the No 1 villain* in the woodpile – Howard Whitman⟩
wood pulp *n* pulp from wood used in making cellulose derivatives (e g paper or rayon)
woodshed *n* a shed for storing wood, esp firewood
woodsman *n* one who lives in, frequents, or works in the woods
wood sorrel *n* any of a genus of plants with acid sap; *esp* a stemless plant of shady places with leaves made up of 3 leaflets that is sometimes held to be the original shamrock
woodwind *n* **1** any of a group of wind instruments (e g a clarinet, flute, or saxophone) that is characterized by a cylindrical or conical tube of wood or metal, usu with finger holes or keys, that produces notes by the vibration of a single or double reed or by the passing of air over a mouth hole **2** *sing or pl in constr* the woodwind section of a band or orchestra – often pl with sing. meaning
woodwork *n* **1** work made of wood; *esp* wooden interior fittings (e g mouldings or stairways) **2** the craft of constructing things from wood – **woodworker** *n*, **woodworking** *adj*
woodworm *n* an insect larva, esp that of the furniture beetle, that bores in dead wood; *also* an infestation of woodworm
woody *adj* **1** overgrown with or having many woods **2a** of or containing (much) wood, wood fibres, or xylem ⟨~ *plants*⟩ **b** *of a plant stem* tough and fibrous **3** characteristic of or suggestive of wood ⟨*wine with a* ~ *flavour*⟩ – **woodiness** *n*
¹**woof** *n* **1** the weft **2** a basic or essential element or material
²**woof** *vi or n* (to make) the low gruff sound characteristic of a dog
woofer *n* a loudspeaker that responds mainly to low frequencies
wool *n* **1** the soft wavy coat of various hairy mammals, esp the sheep, that is made up of keratin fibres covered with minute scales **2** sthg, esp a garment or fabric, made of wool ⟨*I always wear* ~ *in the winter*⟩ **3a** a dense felted hairy covering, esp on a plant **b** a wiry or fibrous mass (e g of steel or glass) – usu in combination – **woolled, wooled** *adj*
woolgathering *n* indulging in idle daydreaming – **woolgather** *vi*, **woolgatherer** *n*
¹**woollen,** NAm chiefly **woolen** *adj* **1** made of wool **2** of or for the manufacture or sale of woollen products ⟨~ *mills*⟩ ⟨*the* ~ *industry*⟩
²**woollen,** NAm chiefly **woolen** *n* **1** a fabric made of wool **2** *pl* garments of woollen fabric
¹**woolly,** NAm also **wooly** *adj* **1** (made) of or resembling wool; *also* bearing (sthg like) wool **2a** lacking in clearness or sharpness of outline ⟨*a* ~ *TV picture*⟩ **b** marked by mental vagueness or confusion ⟨~ *thinking*⟩ **3** boisterously rough – chiefly in *wild and woolly* – **woollily** *adv*, **woolliness** *n*
²**woolly, woolie,** NAm also **wooly** *n*, chiefly Br a woollen jumper or cardigan
woolsack *n* the official seat of the Lord Chancellor in the House of Lords
woozy *adj* **1** mentally unclear or hazy **2** dizzy or slightly nauseous USE infml – **woozily** *adv*, **wooziness** *n*
wop *n*, often cap an Italian – chiefly derog
Worcester sauce *n* a pungent sauce containing soy sauce, vinegar, and spices
¹**word** *n* **1a** sthg that is said **b** *pl* **(1)** talk, discourse ⟨*putting one's feelings into* ~ *s*⟩ **(2)** the text of a vocal musical composition **c** a short remark, statement, or conversation ⟨*would like to have a* ~ *with you*⟩ **2a** a

meaningful unit of spoken language that can stand alone as an utterance and is not divisible into similar units; *also* a written or printed representation of a spoken word that is usu set off by spaces on either side ⟨*the number of* ~ s *to a line*⟩ **b** a string of adjacent binary digits that is typically longer than a byte and is processed by a computer as a unit ⟨*a 16-bit* ~⟩ **3** an order, command ⟨*don't move till I give the* ~⟩ **4** often cap **a** the divine wisdom manifest in the creation and redemption of the world, and identified in Christian thought with the second person of the Trinity **b** GOSPEL 1 **c** the expressed or manifested mind and will of God **5a** news, information ⟨*sent* ~ *that he would be late*⟩ **b** rumour ⟨~ *has it that they're leaving*⟩ **6** the act of speaking or of making verbal communication ⟨*in* ~ *and deed*⟩ **7** a promise ⟨*kept her* ~⟩ **8** *pl* a quarrelsome utterance or conversation ⟨*been having* ~ s *with my wife*⟩ **9** a verbal signal; a password **10** *the* most appropriate description ⟨*'hot' wasn't the* ~ *for it*⟩ – **wordless** *adj* – **from the word go** from the beginning – **in a word** IN SHORT – **in so many words** in exactly those terms ⟨*implied that such actions were criminal but did not say so in so many words*⟩ – **my word** – used to express surprise or astonishment – **of one's word** that can be relied on to keep a promise – used only after *man* or *woman* ⟨*a man of his word*⟩
²**word** *vt* to express in words; phrase
word-blindness *n* **1** alexia **2** dyslexia
word-for-word *adj, of a report or translation* in or following the exact words; verbatim – **word for word** *adv*
wording *n* the act or manner of expressing in words ⟨*the exact* ~ *of the will*⟩
word of mouth *n* oral communication
word-perfect *adj* having memorized sthg perfectly
wordplay *n* verbal wit
wordy *adj* using or containing (too) many words – **wordily** *adv*, **wordiness** *n*
wore past of WEAR
¹**work** *n* **1** activity in which one exerts strength or faculties to do or produce sthg: **a** sustained physical or mental effort to achieve a result **b** the activities that afford one's accustomed means of livelihood **c** a specific task, duty, function, or assignment **2a** (the result of) expenditure of energy by natural phenomena **b** the transference of energy that is produced by the motion of the point of application of a force and is measured by the product of the force and the distance moved along the line of action **3a** (the result of) a specified method of working ⟨*the* ~ *of many hands*⟩ – often in combination ⟨*can't do needle*work⟩ ⟨*clever camera* ~⟩ **b** sthg made from a specified material – often in combination ⟨*iron*work⟩ ⟨*porcelain* ~⟩ **4a** a fortified structure (e g a fort, earthen barricade, or trench) **b** *pl* structures in engineering (e g docks, bridges, or embankments) or mining (e g shafts or tunnels) **5** *pl but sing or pl in constr* a place where industrial activity is carried out; a factory – often in combination ⟨*a water*works⟩ ⟨*a tile*works⟩ **6** *pl* the working or moving parts of a mechanism ⟨*the* ~ s *of a clock*⟩ **7** an artistic production or creation **8** *pl* performance of moral or religious acts ⟨*salvation by* ~ s⟩ **9a** effective operation; an effect, result ⟨*wait for time to do its healing* ~⟩ **b** activity, behaviour, or experience of the specified kind ⟨*dancing reels is thirsty* ~⟩ **10** a workpiece **11** *pl* **a** everything possessed, available, or belonging – infml; + *the* **b** subjection to all possible abuse – infml; usu + *get* ⟨*get the* ~ s⟩ *or* give ⟨*gave him the* ~ s⟩ – **workless** *adj* – **at work 1** engaged in working; busy; *esp* engaged in one's regular occupation **2** at one's place of work – **in the works** in process of preparation, development, or completion – **one's work cut out** as much as one

can do – **out of work** without regular employment; unemployed

²work *adj* **1** suitable for wear while working ⟨~ *clothes*⟩ **2** used for work ⟨~ *elephant*⟩

³work *vb* **worked, wrought** *vt* **1** to bring to pass; effect ⟨~ *miracles*⟩ **2a** to fashion or create sthg by expending labour on; forge, shape ⟨~ *flint into tools*⟩ **b** to make or decorate with needlework; embroider ⟨~ *a sampler*⟩ **3** to prepare or form into a desired state for use by kneading, hammering, etc **4** to operate ⟨*a pump* ~ed *by hand*⟩ ⟨*switches are* ~ed *from a central tower*⟩ **5** to solve (a problem) by reasoning or calculation – usu + *out* **6** to cause to labour ⟨~ed *his horses nearly to death*⟩ **7** to carry on an operation in (a place or area) ⟨*the salesman* ~ed *both sides of the street*⟩ **8** to finance by working ⟨~ed *his way through college*⟩ **9a** to manoeuvre (oneself or an object) gradually or with difficulty into or out of a specified condition or position ⟨*the screw* ~ed *itself loose*⟩ **b** to contrive, arrange ⟨*we can* ~ *it so that you can take your holiday early*⟩ **10** to excite, provoke ⟨~ed *himself into a rage*⟩ ~ *vi* **1a** to exert oneself, esp in sustained, purposeful, or necessary effort ⟨~ed *all day over a hot stove*⟩ ⟨~ing *for the cause*⟩ **b** to perform work or fulfil duties regularly for wages or a salary **2** to operate, function ⟨*the lifts don't* ~ *at night*⟩ **3** to exert an influence or have a tendency ⟨*events have* ~ed *in our favour*⟩ **4** to produce a desired effect; succeed ⟨*hope your plan will* ~⟩ **5a** to make one's way slowly and with difficulty; move or progress laboriously ⟨*just* ~ing *through her own teenage rebellion thing* – *Annabel*⟩ **b** to sail to windward **6** to produce artefacts by shaping or fashioning a specified material ⟨*she* ~s *in copper*⟩ **7a** to be in agitation or restless motion ⟨*her mouth* ~ed *nervously*⟩ **b** FERMENT 1 **c** to move slightly in relation to another part **d** to get into a specified condition by slow or imperceptible movements ⟨*the knot* ~ed *loose*⟩ – **work on** to strive to influence or persuade; affect – **work to rule** to obey the rules of one's work precisely and so reduce efficiency, esp as a form of industrial action

workable *adj* **1** capable of being worked ⟨~ *vein of coal*⟩ **2** practicable, feasible – **workableness** *n*, **workability** *n*

workaday *adj* **1** of or suited for working days **2** prosaic, ordinary

workbag *n* a bag for implements or materials for work, esp needlework

workbasket *n* a basket for needlework implements and materials

workbench *n* a bench on which work, esp of mechanics or carpenters, is performed

workbook *n* an exercise book of problems to be solved directly on the pages

worked up *adj* emotionally aroused; excited

worker *n* **1a** one who works, esp at manual or industrial work or with a particular material – often in combination **b** a member of the working class **2** any of the sexually underdeveloped usu sterile members of a colony of ants, bees, etc that perform most of the labour and protective duties of the colony

workforce *n sing or pl in constr* the workers engaged in a specific activity or potentially available ⟨*the factory's* ~⟩

workhouse *n* **1** *Br* an institution formerly maintained at public expense to house paupers **2** *NAm* a house of correction for minor offenders

work-in *n* a continuous occupation of a place of employment by employees continuing to work normally as a protest, usu against the threat of factory closure

work in *vt* **1** to cause to penetrate by persistent effort ⟨*work the ointment thoroughly* in⟩ **2** to insinuate unobtrusively ⟨worked in *a few topical jokes*⟩; *also* to find room for

¹working *adj* **1a** that functions or performs labour ⟨*a* ~ *model*⟩ **b** of a domestic animal trained or bred for useful work ⟨*a* ~ *dog*⟩ **2** adequate to permit effective work to be done ⟨*a* ~ *majority*⟩ **3** serving as a basis for further work ⟨~ *draft*⟩ **4** during which one works ⟨~ *hours*⟩; *also* during which one discusses business or policy ⟨*a* ~ *lunch*⟩

²working *n* **1** (a part of) a mine, quarry, or similar excavation **2** the fact or manner of functioning or operating – usu pl with sing. meaning ⟨*the* ~s *of his mind*⟩

working class *n sing or pl in constr* the class of people who work (manually) for wages – often pl with sing. meaning; compare PROLETARIAT – **working-class** *adj*

working day *n* **1** a day on which work is done as distinguished from Sunday or a holiday **2** the period of time in a day during which work is performed

working party *n, chiefly Br* a committee set up (e g by a government) to investigate and report on a particular problem

workman, fem workwoman *n* an artisan

workmanlike *also* **workmanly** *adj* worthy of a good workman: a skilful **b** efficient in appearance

workmanship *n* the relative art or skill of a workman; craftsmanship; *also* the quality or finish exhibited by a thing ⟨*a vase of exquisite* ~⟩

work off *vt* to dispose of or get rid of by work or activity ⟨work off *a debt*⟩ ⟨work off *one's anger*⟩

workout *n* a practice or exercise to test or improve fitness, ability, or performance, esp for sporting competition

work out *vt* **1a** to find out by calculation ⟨*couldn't* work out *how the prices stayed so low* – *Cosmopolitan*⟩ **b** to devise by resolving difficulties ⟨work out *an agreement*⟩ **c** to elaborate in detail ⟨work out *a scheme*⟩ **2** to discharge (e g a debt) by labour **3** to exhaust (e g a mine) by working ~ *vi* **1a** to prove effective, practicable, or suitable ⟨*their marriage didn't* work out⟩ **b** to amount to a total or calculated figure – often + *at* or *to* ⟨works out *at £17.50*⟩ ⟨*gas heating might* work out *expensive*⟩ **c** of a sum to yield a result **2** to engage in a workout

work over *vt* **1** to subject to thorough examination, study, or treatment **2** to beat up thoroughly; manhandle – *infml*

workpeople *n pl, chiefly Br* workers, employees

workroom *n* a room used for esp manual work

works *adj* of a place of industrial labour ⟨~ *council*⟩ ⟨~ *doctor*⟩

workshop *n* **1** a room or place (e g in a factory) in which manufacture or repair work is carried out **2** a brief intensive educational programme for a relatively small group of people in a given field that emphasizes participation

workshy *adj* disliking work; lazy

worktop *n* a flat surface (e g of Formica) on a piece of esp kitchen furniture (e g a cupboard or dresser) suitable for working on

work-to-rule *n* an instance of industrial action designed to reduce output by deliberately keeping very rigidly to rules and regulations

work up *vt* **1** to stir up; rouse ⟨*can't* work up *much interest*⟩ **2** to produce by mental or physical work ⟨worked up *a comedy act*⟩ ⟨worked up *a sweat in the gymnasium*⟩ **3** to improve, esp by mental work ⟨work up *your French*⟩ ~ *vi* to rise gradually in intensity or emotional tone ⟨work up *to a climax*⟩

¹world *n* **1** the earth with its inhabitants and all things on it ⟨*travel round the* ~⟩ **2** the course of human affairs ⟨*knowledge of the* ~⟩ **3** the human race **4** the concerns of earthly existence or secular affairs as distinguished from heaven and the life to come or religious and ecclesiastical matters **5** the system of created things; the universe **6a** a division, section, or generation of the inhabitants of the earth distinguished by living together at the same place or at the same time ⟨*the medieval ~*⟩ **b** a distinctive class of people or their sphere of interest ⟨*the academic ~*⟩⟨*woman's ~*⟩ **7a** human society as a whole ⟨*all the ~ knows*⟩⟨*withdraw from the ~*⟩; *also* the public ⟨*announced his discovery to the ~*⟩ **b** fashionable or respectable people; public opinion **8** a part or section of the earth that is a separate independent unit ⟨*the third ~*⟩ **9a** one's personal environment in the sphere of one's life or work ⟨*the external ~*⟩⟨*the ~ of Van Gogh*⟩ **b** a particular aspect of one's life ⟨*the ~ of dreams*⟩ **10** an indefinite multitude or a great quantity or amount ⟨*makes a ~ of difference*⟩ **11** KINGDOM 4 ⟨*the animal ~*⟩ **12** a planet; *esp* one that is inhabited *USE* (*except 10 & 12*) + *the* – **best of both worlds** the benefit of the advantages of 2 alternatives, esp without their disadvantages – **for all the world** in every way; exactly ⟨*copies which look for all the world like the original*⟩ **–for the world** in any circumstances; for anything ⟨*wouldn't hurt her feelings for the world*⟩ – **in the world** among innumerable possibilities; ever ⟨*what in the world is it?*⟩ – **out of this world** of extraordinary excellence; superb

²world *adj* **1** of the whole world ⟨*a ~ championship*⟩ **2** extending or found throughout the world; worldwide ⟨*a ~ state*⟩⟨*brought about ~ peace*⟩

world-class *adj* of the highest quality in the world, esp in playing a sport or game ⟨*a ~ polo player*⟩

worldly *adj* of or devoted to this world and its pursuits rather than to religion or spiritual affairs ⟨*my ~ goods*⟩ – **worldliness** *n*

worldly-wise *adj* possessing a practical and often shrewd and materialistic understanding of human affairs; sophisticated

world-shaking *adj* earthshaking

world war *n* a war engaged in by (most of) the principal nations of the world; *esp, cap both Ws* either of 2 such wars of the first half of the 20th c

world-weary *adj* bored with the life of the world and its material pleasures – **world-weariness** *n*

worldwide *adj* extended throughout or involving the entire world – **worldwide** *adv*

¹worm *n* **1a** an annelid worm; *esp* an earthworm **b** any of numerous relatively small elongated soft-bodied invertebrate animals: e g **(1)** a (destructive) caterpillar, maggot, or other insect larva **(2)** a shipworm **(3)** a blindworm **2** a human being who is an object of contempt, loathing, or pity; a wretch **3** infestation with or disease caused by parasitic worms – usu pl with sing. meaning but sing. or pl in constr **4a** the thread of a screw **b** a short revolving screw whose threads engage with a worm wheel or a rack **c** a spiral condensing tube used in distilling – **wormlike** *adj*

²worm *vi* to proceed windingly or insidiously ~ *vt* **1** to free (e g a dog) from worms **2a** to cause to move or proceed (as if) in the manner of a worm **b** to insinuate or introduce (oneself) by devious or subtle means **c** to make (one's way) insidiously or deviously ⟨*tried to ~ her way out of the situation*⟩ **3** to obtain or extract by artful or insidious questioning or by pleading, asking, or persuading – usu + *out of* ⟨*~ed the secret out of her*⟩ – **wormer** *n*

wormcast *n* a small heap of earth excreted by an earthworm on the soil surface

worm-eaten *adj* **1** eaten or burrowed into (as if) by worms ⟨*~ timber*⟩ **2** worn-out, antiquated ⟨*~ regulations*⟩

worm gear *n* **1** WORM WHEEL **2** a gear consisting of a worm and a worm wheel working together

wormhole *n* a hole or passage burrowed by a worm

worm wheel *n* a toothed wheel gearing with the thread of a worm

wormwood *n* **1** a European composite plant yielding a bitter slightly aromatic dark green oil used in absinthe **2** sthg bitter or mortifying; bitterness

wormy *adj* containing, infested with, having, or damaged by (many) worms

worn *past part of* WEAR

worn-out *adj* exhausted or used up (as if) by wear

worrisome *adj* **1** causing distress or worry **2** inclined to worry or fret – **worrisomely** *adv*, **worrisomeness** *n*

¹worry *vt* **1a** to harass by tearing, biting, etc, esp at with the throat ⟨*a dog ~ing sheep*⟩ **b** to shake or pull at with the teeth ⟨*a terrier ~ing a rat*⟩ **c** to touch or disturb repeatedly **2** to subject to persistent or nagging attention or effort **3** to afflict with mental distress or agitation; make anxious ~ *vi* **1** to work at sthg difficult ⟨*he worried away at the problem till he found a solution*⟩ **2** to feel or experience concern or anxiety; fret – **worriedly** *adv*, **worrier** *n* – **not to worry** *Br* do not worry; do not feel anxious, dispirited, or troubled – *infml*

²worry *n* **1** mental distress or agitation resulting from concern, usu for sthg impending or anticipated; anxiety **2** a cause of worry; a trouble, difficulty

¹worse *adj, comparative of* BAD *or* ILL **1** of lower quality **2** in poorer health – **worsen** *vb* – **the worse for** harmed by ⟨*none the worse for his fall*⟩

²worse *n, pl* **worse** sthg worse

³worse *adv, comparative of* BAD, BADLY, *or* ILL in a worse manner; to a worse extent or degree ⟨*raining ~ than ever*⟩

¹worship *n* **1** (an act of) reverence offered to a divine being or supernatural power **2** a form of religious practice with its creed and ritual **3** extravagant admiration for or devotion to an object of esteem ⟨*~ of the dollar*⟩ **4** *chiefly Br* a person of importance – used as a title for various officials (e g magistrates and some mayors)

²worship *vb* **-pp-** (*NAm* **-p-, -pp-**) *vt* **1** to honour or reverence as a divine being or supernatural power **2** to regard with great, even extravagant respect, honour, or devotion ~ *vi* to perform or take part in (an act of) worship – **worshipper** *n*

worshipful *adj* **1** rendering worship or veneration **2** *chiefly Br* – used as a title for various people or groups of rank or distinction – **worshipfully** *adv*, **worshipfulness** *n*

¹worst *adj, superlative of* BAD *or* ILL **1** most productive of evil ⟨*the ~ thing you could have done*⟩ **2** most wanting in quality ⟨*the ~ student*⟩

²worst *n, pl* **worst 1** the worst state or part ⟨*always at my ~ before breakfast*⟩ **2** sby or sthg that is worst **3** the utmost harm of which one is capable ⟨*do your ~*⟩ – **at worst, at the worst** under the worst circumstances; seen in the worst light – **if the worst comes to the worst** if the very worst thing happens

³worst *adv, superlative of* BAD, BADLY, *or* ILL in the worst manner; to the worst extent or degree ⟨*the worst-dressed woman*⟩

⁴worst *vt* to get the better of; defeat

worsted *n* **1** a smooth compact yarn from long wool fibres used esp for firm napless fabrics, carpeting, or knitting **2** a fabric made from worsted yarns – **worsted** *adj*

¹wort *n* a (herbaceous) plant – now used only in combination ⟨*stinkwort*⟩

²**wort** *n* a dilute solution containing sugars obtained typically from malt by infusion and fermented to form beer

¹**worth** *vi, archaic* – **woe worth** cursed be

²**worth** *prep* **1a** equal in value to **b** having property equal to ⟨he's ~ £1,000,000⟩ **2** deserving of ⟨well ~ the effort⟩ – **worth it** worthwhile

³**worth** *n* **1a** (money) value **b** the equivalent of a specified amount or figure ⟨3 quidsworth of petrol⟩ **2** moral or personal merit, esp high merit ⟨proved his ~⟩

worthless *adj* **1a** lacking worth; valueless ⟨~ currency⟩ **b** useless ⟨~ to continue searching⟩ **2** contemptible, despicable – **worthlessly** *adv,* **worthlessness** *n*

worthwhile *adj* worth the time or effort spent

¹**worthy** *adj* **1a** having moral worth or value ⟨a ~ cause⟩ **b** honourable, meritorious ⟨they were all honoured and ~ men⟩ **2** important enough; deserving ⟨a deed ~ to be remembered⟩⟨a ~ opponent⟩ – **worthily** *adv,* **worthiness** *n*

²**worthy** *n* a worthy or prominent person – often humor

-**worthy** *comb form* (*n* → *adj*) **1** fit or safe for ⟨a seaworthy vessel⟩ **2** deserving of ⟨praiseworthy⟩ ⟨noteworthy⟩

wotcher *interj, Br* – used as a greeting; slang

would *past of* WILL **1a** to desire, wish ⟨as ye ~ that men should do to you – Lk 6:31 (AV)⟩ **b** – used in auxiliary function with *rather* or *soon, sooner* to express preference ⟨~ sooner die than face them⟩ **2a** – used in auxiliary function to express wish, desire, or intent ⟨those who ~ forbid gambling⟩ or, in negative constructions, reluctance ⟨~ not hurt a fly⟩; used in the question form with the force of a polite request ⟨~ you please help me?⟩ or of an offer or suggestion ⟨~ you like some tea?⟩ **b** – used in auxiliary function in reported speech or writing to represent *shall* or *will* ⟨said he ~ come⟩ ⟨knew I ~ enjoy the trip⟩ **3a** used to ⟨we ~ meet often for lunch⟩ – used with emphatic stress to express exasperation ⟨she ~ keep complaining⟩ **b** – used in auxiliary function with emphatic stress as a comment on the annoyingly typical ⟨you ~ say that⟩ **4** – used in auxiliary function to introduce a contingent fact, possibility, or presumption (1) in the main clause of a conditional sentence ⟨it ~ break if you dropped it⟩ ⟨he ~ have won if he hadn't tripped⟩ (2) after a verb expressing desire, request, or advice ⟨wish he ~ go⟩ **5** could ⟨door wouldn't open⟩ **6** – used in auxiliary function to soften direct statement ⟨~ be glad to know⟩ ⟨that ~ be the milkman⟩

would-be *adj* desiring or intended to be ⟨a ~ rapist – Daily Mirror⟩

wouldn't would not

wouldst, wouldest *archaic past 2 sing of* WILL

¹**wound** *n* **1** an injury to the body or to a plant (e g from violence or accident) that involves tearing or breaking of a membrane (e g the skin) and usu damage to underlying tissues **2** a mental or emotional hurt or blow

²**wound** *vt* to cause a wound to or in ~ *vi* to inflict a wound

³**wound** *past of* WIND

¹**wove** *past of* WEAVE

²**wove** *n* paper made in such a way that no fine lines run across the grain

woven *past part of* WEAVE

¹**wow** *interj* – used to express strong feeling (e g pleasure or surprise); slang

²**wow** *n* a striking success; a hit – slang

³**wow** *vt* to excite to enthusiastic admiration or approval – slang

⁴**wow** *n* a distortion in reproduced sound that is heard as a slow rise and fall in the pitch of the sound and is caused by variations in the speed of the reproducing system

¹**wrack** *n* **1** destruction ⟨~ and ruin⟩ **2** (a remnant of) sthg destroyed

²**wrack** *n* (dried) marine vegetation; esp kelp

³**wrack** *vt* ¹RACK

⁴**wrack** *vt* ¹RACK

wraith *n, pl* **wraiths** an apparition of a living person in his/her exact likeness seen before or after death

¹**wrangle** *vb* **wrangling** *vi* to dispute angrily or peevishly; bicker ~ *vt, NAm* to herd and care for (livestock, esp horses) on the range

²**wrangle** *n* an angry, noisy, or prolonged dispute or quarrel

wrangler *n* **1** a bickering disputant **2** the holder of a Cambridge first in mathematics – **wranglership** *n*

¹**wrap** *vb* **-pp-** *vt* **1a** to envelop, pack, or enfold in sthg flexible **b** to fold round sthg specified ⟨~ a blanket round her⟩ **2a** to obscure or surround with the specified covering ⟨~ped in mist⟩ ⟨the affair was ~ped in scandal⟩ **b** to involve completely; engross – usu + *up* ⟨~ped up in his daughter⟩ ~ *vi* to curl round sthg; be a wraparound ⟨skirt that ~s over⟩

²**wrap** *n* **1** a wrapping; *specif* a waterproof wrapping placed round food to be frozen, esp in a domestic freezer **2** an article of clothing that may be wrapped round a person; *esp* an outer garment (e g a shawl) – **under wraps** secret

wrapper *n* that in which sthg is wrapped: e g **a** a fine quality tobacco leaf used for the covering of a cigar **b** DUST JACKET

wrapping *n* material used to wrap an object

wrap up *vt* to bring to a usu successful conclusion; end – infml ~ *vi* **1** to protect oneself with outer garments ⟨wrap up warm⟩ **2** *Br* to stop talking; SHUT UP – slang

wrath *n* **1** strong vengeful anger or indignation **2** retributory, esp divine, chastisement – **wrathful** *adj*

wreak *vt* **1** to give free play to (malevolent feeling); inflict ⟨~ed his wrath on her⟩ ⟨~ed her revenge⟩ **2** to cause or create (havoc or destruction)

wreath *n, pl* **wreaths 1** sthg intertwined into a circular shape; *esp* a garland ⟨lay a ~ on the coffin⟩ **2** a representation of a wreath (e g in heraldry) **3** a drifting and coiling whorl ⟨~s of smoke⟩

wreathe *vt* **1** to cause (the face) to take on a happy joyful expression – usu pass ⟨face ~d in smiles⟩ **2a** to shape (e g flowers) into a wreath **b** to coil about sthg **3** to encircle (as if) with a wreath ⟨bust ~d with laurel⟩ to twist or move in coils; writhe ⟨smoke ~d from the chimney⟩

¹**wreck** *n* **1** sthg cast up on the land by the sea, esp after a shipwreck **2a** (a) shipwreck **b** wrecking or being wrecked; destruction ⟨after the ~ of our hopes⟩ **3a** the broken remains of sthg (e g a building or vehicle) wrecked or ruined **b** a person or animal of broken constitution, health, or spirits ⟨a mere ~ of his former self⟩

²**wreck** *vt* **1** to cast ashore **2a** to reduce to a ruinous state by violence ⟨~ a train⟩ **b** to cause (a vessel) to be shipwrecked **c** to involve in disaster or ruin ⟨~ one's marriage⟩ to become wrecked

wreckage *n* **1** wrecking or being wrecked **2** broken and disordered parts or material from a wrecked structure

wrecker *n* **1a** sby who wrecks ships (e g by false lights) for plunder **b** sby whose work is the demolition of buildings **2a** sby who searches for or works on the wrecks of ships (e g for rescue or plunder) **b** *NAm* a breakdown lorry **c** *NAm* a dealer in scrap, esp scrapped motor vehicles

wren *n* a very small European bird that has a short erect tail and is noted for its loud song

Wren *n* a woman serving in the Women's Royal Naval Service

¹**wrench** *vi* to pull or strain at sthg with violent twisting ⟨*he ~ed at the handle*⟩ ~ *vt* **1** to pull or twist violently ⟨*~ the door open*⟩ **2** to injure or disable by a violent twisting or straining **3** to distort, pervert ⟨*~ language*⟩ **4** to snatch forcibly; wrest ⟨*~ the knife from her hand*⟩

²**wrench** *n* **1a** a violent twisting or a sideways pull **b** (a sharp twist or sudden jerk causing) a strain to a muscle, ligament, etc (e g of a joint) **c** (sthg causing) acute emotional distress or violent mental change **2a** a spanner with jaws adjustable for holding nuts of different sizes **b** *NAm* a spanner

wrest *vt* **1** to obtain or take away by violent wringing or twisting **2** to obtain with difficulty by force or determined labour ⟨*~ a living from the stony soil*⟩ **3** WRENCH 3

¹**wrestle** *vb* **wrestling** *vi* **1** to contend with an opponent in wrestling **2** to engage in a violent or determined struggle; grapple ⟨*wrestling with cumbersome luggage*⟩ ⟨*~ with a problem*⟩ ~ *vt* **1** to wrestle with **2** to push, pull, or manhandle by force – **wrestler** *n*

²**wrestle** *n* the action or an instance of wrestling; *esp* a wrestling bout

wretch *n* **1** a profoundly unhappy or unfortunate person **2** a base, despicable, or vile person or animal

wretched *adj* **1** deeply afflicted, dejected, or unfortunate **2** deplorably bad ⟨*was in ~ health*⟩ ⟨*~ workmanship*⟩ **3** (appearing) mean, squalid, or contemptible ⟨*dressed in ~ old clothes*⟩ **4** causing annoyance; damned – used as a general expression of annoyance ⟨*lost my ~ socks*⟩ – **wretchedly** *adv*, **wretchedness** *n*

¹**wriggle** *vb* **wriggling** *vi* **1** to move the body or a bodily part to and fro with short writhing motions; squirm **2** to move or advance by twisting and turning **3** to extricate or insinuate oneself by manoeuvring, equivocation, evasion, or ingratiation ⟨*managed to ~ out of a difficult question*⟩ ~ *vt* **1** to cause to move in short quick contortions ⟨*she ~d her hips*⟩ **2** to manoeuvre into a state or place by wriggling **3** to make (one's way) by wriggling – **wriggler** *n*, **wriggly** *adj*

²**wriggle** *n* a short or quick writhing motion or contortion

wright *n* a craftsman – usu in combination ⟨*ship*wright⟩ ⟨*play*wright⟩

wring *vt* **wrung** **1** to twist or compress, esp so as to extract liquid ⟨*~ the towel dry*⟩ **2a** to expel or obtain (as if) by twisting and compressing ⟨*~ the water from the towel*⟩ **b** to exact or extort by coercion or with difficulty ⟨*~ a confession from the suspect*⟩ **3a** to twist so as to strain, sprain, or break ⟨*~ a chicken's neck*⟩ **b** to twist together (one's clasped hands) as a sign of anguish **4** to distress, torment ⟨*a tragedy that ~s the heart*⟩ **5** to shake (sby's hand) vigorously in greeting – **wring** *n*

wringer *n* a mangle

¹**wrinkle** *n* **1** a small ridge, crease, or furrow formed esp in the skin due to aging or stress or on a previously smooth surface (e g by shrinkage or contraction) **2** a valuable trick or dodge for effecting a result – *infml* – **wrinkly** *adj*

²**wrinkle** *vb* **wrinkling** *vi* to become marked with or contracted into wrinkles to contract into wrinkles

wrist *n* **1** (a part of a lower animal corresponding to) the (region of the) joint between the human hand and the arm **2** the part of a garment or glove covering the wrist

wristband *n* a band (e g on the sleeve of a garment) encircling the wrist

wristwatch *n* a small watch attached to a bracelet or strap and worn round the wrist

wristy *adj* characterized by or tending to use a lot of wrist

movement (e g in hitting a ball with a bat or club) – **wristily** *adv*

writ *n* **1a** an order in writing issued under seal in the name of the sovereign or of a court or judicial officer commanding or forbidding an act specified in it ⟨*~ of habeas corpus*⟩ **b** a written order constituting a symbol of the power and authority of the issuer ⟨*over the border where the king's ~ did not run*⟩ **2** *archaic* sthg written; writing – esp in *holy writ, sacred writ*

write *vb* **wrote; written** *also* **writ** *vt* **1a** to form (legible characters, symbols, or words) on a surface, esp with an instrument ⟨*~ an inscription*⟩ ⟨*~ 'I love you'*⟩ **b** to spell in writing ⟨*words written alike but pronounced differently*⟩ **c** to cover, fill, or fill in by writing ⟨*wrote ten pages*⟩ ⟨*~ a cheque*⟩ **2** to set down in writing: e g **a** to be the author of; compose ⟨*~s poems and essays*⟩ ⟨*~ a string quartet*⟩ **b** to use (a specific script or language) in writing ⟨*~ a clear hand*⟩ ⟨*~ shorthand*⟩ ⟨*~ Braille*⟩ ⟨*~ French*⟩ **3** to express, record, or reveal (as if) in writing ⟨*it is written*⟩ ⟨*written on my heart*⟩ **4** to make (a quality or condition) evident – usu pass ⟨*guilt was written all over his face*⟩ **5** to introduce or remove by writing ⟨*~ a clause into a contract*⟩ ⟨*~ a character out of a serial*⟩ **6** to introduce or transfer (information) into or from a computer memory **7** *chiefly NAm* to communicate with in writing ⟨*wrote them on his arrival*⟩ ~ *vi* **1** to make significant written characters, inscriptions, words, or sentences ⟨*learning to ~*⟩ ⟨*~ in ink*⟩; *also* to be adapted to writing ⟨*pen ~s badly*⟩ **2** to compose, communicate by, or send a letter ⟨*~ back*⟩ ⟨*~ for information*⟩ **3** to produce or compose a written work, esp professionally, for publication or performance ⟨*~ for 'The Times'*⟩ ⟨*~ for woodwind*⟩ ⟨*his wife ~s*⟩ – **writable** *adj*

write-down *n* a deliberate reduction in the book value of an asset (e g to reflect the effect of obsolescence or deflation)

write down *vt* **1** to record in written form **2** to disparage, injure, or minimize by writing to write so as to appeal to a lower level of taste, comprehension, or intelligence – usu + *to*

write-off *n* sthg written off as a total loss ⟨*he survived, but the car was a ~*⟩

write off *vt* **1** to cancel ⟨*write off a bad debt*⟩ **2** to concede to be irreparably lost, useless, or dead ⟨*this two square miles isn't being written off as a ghetto* – Colin MacInnes⟩ **3** to write and send a letter

write out *vt* to put in writing; *esp* to put into a full and complete written form

writer *n* **1** one who writes as an occupation; an author **2** *Scot* WRITER TO THE SIGNET

writer's cramp *n* a painful spasmodic cramp of the hand or finger muscles brought on by excessive writing

Writer to the Signet *n* a Scottish solicitor

write-up *n* a written, esp flattering, account

write up *vt* **1a** to write an account of; describe ⟨*wrote up the fire*⟩ **b** to put into finished written form ⟨*write up my notes*⟩ **2** to bring up to date the writing of (e g a diary) **3** to praise or maximize in writing

writhe *vt* to twist (the body or a bodily part) in pain ~ *vi* **1** to proceed with twists and turns **2** to twist (as if) from pain or struggling **3** to suffer keenly ⟨*~ under an insult*⟩ – **writhe** *n*

writing *n* **1** the act, practice, or occupation of literary composition **2a** written letters or words; *esp* handwriting ⟨*put it in ~*⟩ ⟨*I can't read your ~*⟩ **b** a written composition ⟨*the ~s of Marx*⟩ **c** a written or printed letter, notice, document, or inscription – **writing on the wall** an omen of one's unpleasant fate

writing desk *n* a desk often with a sloping top for writing on

writing paper *n* a sized paper that can be written on with ink; *esp* notepaper

¹**wrong** *n* **1** an injurious, unfair, or unjust act; action or conduct inflicting harm without due provocation or just cause ⟨suffer ~ at their hands⟩ ⟨did him a great ~⟩ **2** what is wrong, immoral, or unethical ⟨the difference between right and ~⟩ ⟨to do no ~⟩ **3a** the state of being mistaken or incorrect ⟨my guess was hopelessly in the ~⟩ **b** the state of being or appearing to be the offender ⟨put me in the ~⟩

²**wrong** *adj* **1** against moral standards; evil ⟨thought that war was ~⟩ **2** not right or proper according to a code, standard, or convention; improper ⟨it was ~ not to thank your host⟩ **3** not according to truth or facts; incorrect ⟨gave a ~ date⟩; *also* in error; mistaken ⟨you're quite ~⟩ **4** not satisfactory (e g in condition, results, health, or temper) ⟨sthg ~ with my toe⟩ **5** not in accordance with one's needs, intent, or expectations ⟨took the ~ bus⟩ **6** of or being the side of sthg not meant to be used or exposed or thought the less desirable ⟨put it on ~ side out⟩ ⟨on the ~ side of 40⟩ – **wrongly** *adv*, **wrongness** *n*

³**wrong** *adv* **1** without accuracy; incorrectly ⟨guessed ~⟩ **2** without regard for what is proper ⟨acted ~⟩ **3** on a mistaken course; astray ⟨steered ~⟩ **4** out of proper working order ⟨washing machine went ~⟩

⁴**wrong** *vt* **1** to do wrong to; injure, harm **2** to mistakenly impute a base motive to; misrepresent – **wronger** *n*

wrongdoer *n* one who transgresses (moral) laws – **wrongdoing** *n*

wrongful *adj* **1** wrong, unjust **2** unlawful – **wrongfully** *adv*, **wrongfulness** *n*

wrongheaded *adj* stubborn in adherence to wrong opinion or principles; perverse – **wrongheadedly** *adv*, **wrongheadedness** *n*

wrote *past of* WRITE

wroth *adj* wrathful – poetic or humor

wrought *adj* **1** worked into shape by artistry or effort ⟨carefully ~ essays⟩ **2** processed for use; manufactured ⟨~ silk⟩ **3** of metals beaten into shape by tools **4** deeply stirred; excited – usu + up ⟨gets easily ~ up over nothing⟩

wrought iron *n* a tough malleable iron containing very little carbon and 1 or 2 per cent slag

wrung *past of* WRING

wry *adj* **1** bent or twisted, esp to one side ⟨a ~ smile⟩ **2** ironically or grimly humorous ⟨~ wit⟩ – **wryly** *adv*, **wryness** *n*

X

x *n, pl* **x's, xs** *often cap* **1** (a graphic representation of or device for reproducing) the 24th letter of the English alphabet **2** ten **3** one designated *x*, esp as the 24th in order or class or the 1st in a series that includes x, y, and sometimes z **4** sby or sthg whose identity is unknown or withheld

X *n or adj*, (a film that is) certified in Britain as suitable only for people over 18

X chromosome *n* a sex chromosome that in humans occurs paired in each female cell and single in each male cell

xenon *n* a heavy noble gaseous element used esp in specialized flashtubes

xenophobe *n* one who hates or fears foreigners – **xenophobia** *n*, **xenophobic** *adj*

xerography *n* a process for copying graphic matter by the action of light on an electrically charged photoconductive surface in which the latent image is developed with a resinous powder – **xerographic** *adj*

xerox *vt, often cap* to copy on a Xerox machine

Xerox *trademark* – used for a xerographic copier

Xmas *n* Christmas

Xray – a communications code word for the letter x

x-ray *vt, often cap* to examine, treat, or photograph with X rays

X ray *n* **1** an electromagnetic radiation of extremely short wavelength that has the properties of ionizing a gas when passing through it and of penetrating various thicknesses of all solids **2** an examination or photograph made by means of X rays

xylem *n* a complex vascular tissue of higher plants that functions chiefly in the conduction of water, gives support, and forms the woody part of many plants

xylophone *n* a percussion instrument that has a series of wooden bars graduated in length and sounded by striking with 2 small wooden hammers – **xylophonist** *n*

Y

y *n, pl* **y's, ys** *often cap* **1** (a graphic representation of or device for reproducing) the 25th letter of the English alphabet **2** one designated *y*, esp as the 2nd in a series that includes x, y, and sometimes z

¹**-y** *also* **-ey** *suffix* (*n, vb* → *adj*) **1a** covered with; full of ⟨blossomy⟩ ⟨dirty⟩ ⟨hairy⟩ **b** having the quality of ⟨waxy⟩ ⟨weary⟩ ⟨merry⟩ **c** addicted to; enthusiastic about ⟨horsy⟩ **d** like; like that of ⟨wintry⟩ – often derog ⟨stagy⟩ **2** tending or inclined to ⟨sleepy⟩ ⟨sticky⟩ ⟨curly⟩ **3** slightly; rather; -ish ⟨chilly⟩

²**-y** *suffix* (→ *n*) **1** state, condition, or quality of ⟨beggary⟩ ⟨courtesy⟩ **2** whole body or group sharing a specified class or state) ⟨soldiery⟩ ⟨company⟩

³**-y** *suffix* (*n* → *n*) instance of (a specified action) ⟨entreaty⟩ ⟨inquiry⟩

⁴**-y** *suffix* (→ *n*) little; dear ⟨doggy⟩ ⟨granny⟩ – used esp in pet names by or to children

¹**yacht** *n* any of various relatively small sailing or powered vessels that characteristically have a sharp prow and graceful lines and are used for pleasure cruising or racing

²**yacht** *vi* to race or cruise in a yacht – **yachting** *n*

yachtsman *n* sby who owns or sails a yacht

yahoo *n, pl* **yahoos** an uncouth, rowdy, or degraded person

¹**yak** *n, pl* **yaks**, *esp collectively* **yak** a large long-haired wild or domesticated ox of Tibet and nearby mountainous regions

²**yak, yack** *n* persistent or voluble talk – slang

³**yak, yack** *vi* -kk- to talk persistently; chatter – slang

yam *n* **1** (any of various related plants with) an edible starchy tuberous root used as a staple food in tropical areas **2** *NAm* a moist-fleshed usu orange sweet potato

yammer *vi* **1** to wail, whimper **2** to complain, grumble ⟨~ing at the umpire⟩ **3** to talk volubly; clamour to say in voluble complaint *USE* infml – **yammer** *n*

yang *n* the masculine active principle in nature that in Chinese thought eternally interacts with its opposite and complementary principle, yin

yank *vb* to pull or extract (sthg) with a quick vigorous movement ⟨~ *a tooth out*⟩ – *infml* – **yank** *n*

¹Yankee *n* a native or inhabitant of **a** *chiefly Br* the USA **b** *chiefly NAm* the N USA **c** *NAm* New England – **Yankee** *adj*

²Yankee *n* – a communications code word for the letter *y*

¹yap *vi* **-pp-** **1** to bark snappishly; yelp **2** to talk in a shrill insistent querulous way; scold – *infml* – **yapper** *n*

²yap *n* **1** a quick sharp bark; a yelp **2** (foolish) chatter – *infml*

¹yard *n* **1a** a unit of length equal to 3ft (about 0.914m) **b** a unit of volume equal to 1yd³ (about 0.765m³) **2** a long spar tapered towards the ends to support and spread a sail

²yard *n* **1a** a small usu walled and often paved area open to the sky and adjacent to a building; a courtyard **b** the grounds of a specified building or group of buildings – in combination ⟨a *farm*yard⟩ ⟨a *church*yard⟩ **2a** an area with its buildings and facilities set aside for a specified business or activity – often in combination ⟨a *brick*yard⟩ **b** a system of tracks for the storage and maintenance of railway carriages and wagons and the making up of trains **3** *cap, Br* SCOTLAND YARD – ➤ the **4** *NAm* a garden of a house

³yard *vt* to drive into or confine in a restricted area; herd, pen

¹yardage *n* (the charge for) the use of a livestock enclosure at a railway station

²yardage *n* the length, extent, or volume of sthg as measured in yards

yardarm *n* either end of the yard of a square-rigged ship

yardstick *n* **1** a graduated measuring stick 1yd long **2** a standard basis of calculation or judgment; a criterion

¹yarn *n* **1a** THREAD 1; *esp* a spun thread (e g of wool, cotton, or hemp) as prepared and used for weaving, knitting, and rope-making **b** a similar strand of metal, glass, asbestos, paper, or plastic **2a** a narrative of adventures; *esp* a tall tale **b** a conversation, chat *USE* (2) *infml*

²yarn *vi* to tell a yarn; *also* to chat garrulously – *infml*

yarrow *n* a strong-scented Eurasian composite plant with dense heads of small usu white flowers

yashmak *also* **yasmak** *n* a veil worn over the face by Muslim women, so that only the eyes remain exposed

¹yaw *n* the action of yawing; *esp* a side-to-side movement

²yaw *vi* **1** to deviate erratically from a course **2** *of an aircraft, spacecraft, or projectile* to deviate from a straight course by esp side-to-side movement

yawl *n* **1** a small boat carried on a ship **2** a fore-and-aft rigged sailing vessel with sails set from a mainmast and a mizzenmast that is situated aft of the rudder

¹yawn *vi* **1** to open wide; gape ⟨a ~*ing chasm*⟩ **2** to open the mouth wide and inhale, usu in reaction to fatigue or boredom to utter with a yawn – **yawner** *n*, **yawningly** *adv*

²yawn *n* **1** a deep usu involuntary intake of breath through the wide open mouth **2** a boring thing or person – *slang* ⟨thought the cathedral a big ~ – Kenneth Tynan⟩

yaws *n pl but sing or pl in constr* an infectious tropical disease caused by a spirochaetal bacterium and marked by ulcerating sores

Y chromosome *n* a sex chromosome that in humans occurs paired with an X chromosome in each male cell and does not occur in female cells

¹ye *pron, archaic or dial* the ones being addressed; you – used orig only as a nominative pl pron

²ye *definite article, archaic* the ⟨Ye Olde Gifte Shoppe⟩

¹yea *adv* **1** more than this; indeed ⟨*boys*, ~ *and girls too*⟩ **2** *archaic* yes

²yea *n* **1** affirmation, assent **2** *chiefly NAm* (a person casting) an affirmative vote

yeah *adv* yes – used in writing to represent a casual pronunciation

year *n* **1a** the period of about 365¼ solar days required for 1 revolution of the earth round the sun **b** the time required for the apparent sun to return to an arbitrary fixed or moving reference point in the sky **2a** a cycle in the Gregorian calendar of 365 or 366 days divided into 12 months beginning with January and ending with December **b** a period of time equal to 1 year of the Gregorian calendar but beginning at a different time **3** a calendar year specified usu by a number **4** *pl* age ⟨a man in ~ s *but a child in understanding*⟩; *also* old age ⟨*beginning to show his* ~s⟩ **5** a period of time (e g that in which a school is in session) other than a calendar year **6** *sing or pl in constr* the body of students who enter a school, university, etc in 1 academic year – **year in, year out** for an indefinite or seemingly endless number of successive years

yearbook *n* a book published yearly as a report or summary of statistics or facts

yearling *n* sby or sthg 1 year old: e g **a** an animal 1 year old or in its second year **b** a racehorse between January 1st of the year following its birth and the next January 1st – **yearling** *adj*

yearly *adj* **1** reckoned by the year **2** done or occurring once every year; annual – **yearly** *adv*

yearn *vi* **1** to long persistently, wistfully, or sadly ⟨~ *for home*⟩ ⟨~ *to travel*⟩ **2** to feel tenderness or compassion ⟨*her heart* ~ed *towards the child*⟩ – **yearner** *n*, **yearningly** *adv*

yeast *n* **1** a (commercial preparation of) yellowish surface froth or sediment that consists largely of fungal cells, occurs esp in sweet liquids in which it promotes alcoholic fermentation, and is used esp in making alcoholic drinks and as a leaven in baking **2** a minute fungus that is present and functionally active in yeast, usu has little or no mycelium, and reproduces by budding

yeasty *adj* **1** of or resembling yeast **2a** churning with growth and change; turbulent **b** trivial, frivolous – **yeastily** *adv*, **yeastiness** *n*

¹yell *vi* to utter a sharp loud cry, scream, or shout ⟨~ *for help*⟩ ⟨~ *with laughter*⟩ to utter or declare (as if) with a scream; shout ⟨~ *curses*⟩ – **yeller** *n*

²yell *n* a scream, shout

¹yellow *adj* **1a** of the colour yellow **b** yellowish through age, disease, or discoloration; sallow **c** having a yellow or light brown complexion or skin **2a** featuring sensational or scandalous items or ordinary news sensationally distorted ⟨~ *journalism*⟩ **b** dishonourable, cowardly – *infml* ⟨*too* ~ *to fight*⟩ – **yellowish** *adj*, **yellowy** *adj*

²yellow *vb* to make or become yellow

³yellow *n* **1** a colour whose hue resembles that of ripe lemons or dandelions and lies between green and orange in the spectrum **2** sthg yellow: e g **a** sby with yellow or light brown skin **b** the yolk of an egg **c** a yellow ball (e g in snooker) **3** *pl but sing in constr* any of several plant diseases caused esp by viruses and marked by yellowing of the foliage and stunting

yellow bile *n* the one of the 4 humours in medieval physiology believed to be secreted by the liver and to cause irascibility

yellow fever *n* an often fatal infectious disease of warm regions caused by a mosquito-transmitted virus and marked by fever, jaundice, and often bleeding

yellow peril *n, often cap Y&P* a danger to Western

civilization held to arise from expansion of the power and influence of Oriental peoples

yellow pimpernel *n* a common European pimpernel with nearly prostrate stems and bright yellow flowers

yelp *vi or n* (to utter) a sharp quick shrill cry ⟨*dogs* ∼⟩ – **yelper** *n*

¹yen *n, pl* **yen** the standard unit of money in Japan

²yen *n* a strong desire or propensity; a longing – *infml*

³yen *vi* -**nn**- to yearn

yeoman *n, pl* **yeomen** **1** a petty officer who **a** carries out visual signalling in the British navy **b** carries out clerical duties in the US navy **2** a small farmer who cultivates his own land

yeoman of the guard *n* a member of a military corps attached to the British Royal Household who serve as ceremonial attendants of the sovereign and as warders of the Tower of London

yeomanry *n sing or pl in constr* **1** the body of small landed proprietors **2** a British volunteer cavalry force created from yeomen in 1761 as a home defence force and reorganized in 1907 as part of the territorial force

¹yes *adv* **1** – used in answers expressing affirmation, agreement, or willingness; contrasted with *no* ⟨*are you ready? Yes, I am*⟩ **2** – used in answers correcting or contradicting a negative assertion or direction ⟨*don't say that! Yes, I will*⟩ **3** YEA 1 **4** – indicating uncertainty or polite interest or attentiveness ⟨*Yes? What do you want?*⟩

²yes *n* an affirmative reply or vote; an aye

yes-man *n* one who endorses or supports everything said to him, esp by a superior; a sycophant – *infml*

¹yesterday *adv* on the day before today ⟨*saw him* ∼⟩

²yesterday *n* **1** the day before today **2** recent time; time not long past

yesteryear *n* **1** last year **2** the recent past *USE* poetic – **yesteryear** *adv*

¹yet *adv* **1a** again; IN ADDITION ⟨*gives* ∼ *another reason*⟩ **b** EVEN **2b** ⟨*a* ∼ *higher speed*⟩ **2a** up to this or that time; so far – not in affirmative statements ⟨*hasn't had breakfast* ∼⟩ **b** STILL 1, 2 ⟨*have* ∼ *to learn the truth*⟩ **c** at some future time and despite present appearances ⟨*we may win* ∼⟩ **3** nevertheless ⟨*strange and* ∼ *true*⟩ – **yet again** still 1 more time

²yet *conj* but nevertheless

yeti *n* ABOMINABLE SNOWMAN

yew *n* (the wood of) any of a genus of evergreen coniferous trees and shrubs with stiff straight leaves and red fruits

yid *n, often cap* a Jew – chiefly derog

Yiddish *n* a High German language containing elements of Hebrew and Slavonic that is usu written in Hebrew characters and is spoken by Jews chiefly in or from E Europe – **Yiddish** *adj*

¹yield *vt* **1** to give or render as fitting, rightfully owed, or required ⟨∼*ed allegiance to his master*⟩ **2** to give up possession of on claim or demand: e g **a** to surrender or submit (oneself) to another **b** to give (oneself) up to an inclination, temptation, or habit **c** to relinquish (e g a position of advantage or point of superiority) ⟨∼ *precedence*⟩ **3a** to bear or bring forth as a natural product ⟨*the tree* ∼s *good fruit*⟩ **b** to give as a return or in result of expended effort ⟨*properly handled this soil should* ∼ *good crops*⟩ **c** to produce as revenue ⟨*the tax is expected to* ∼ *millions*⟩ ⟨*a bond that* ∼s *12 per cent*⟩ ∼ *vi* **1** to be fruitful or productive **2** to give up and cease resistance or contention; submit, succumb **3** to give way to pressure or influence; submit to urging, persuasion, or entreaty **4** to give way under physical force (e g bending, stretching, or breaking) **5** to give place or precedence; acknowledge the superiority of another – **yielder** *n*

²yield *n* **1** (the amount of) sthg yielded or produced ⟨∼ *of wheat per acre*⟩ **2** the capacity of yielding produce ⟨*high* ∼ *strain of wheat*⟩

yielding *adj* lacking rigidity or stiffness; flexible

yin *n* the feminine passive principle in nature that in Chinese thought eternally interacts with its opposite and complementary principle, yang

yippee *interj* – used to express exuberant delight or triumph

yob *n, Br* a loutish youth; *esp* a hooligan – slang

yobbo *n, Br* a yob – slang

¹yodel *vb* -**ll**- (*NAm* -**l**-, -**ll**-), to sing, shout, or call (a tune) by suddenly changing from a natural voice to a falsetto and back – **yodeller** *n*

²yodel *n* a yodelled song, shout, or cry

yoga *n* **1** *cap* a Hindu philosophy teaching the suppression of all activity of body, mind, and will so that the self may attain liberation from them **2** a system of exercises for attaining bodily or mental control and well-being – **yogic** *adj, often cap*

yoghourt, yoghurt, yogurt *n* a slightly acid semisolid food made of milk fermented by bacteria

yogi *n* **1** sby who practises or is a master of yoga **2** *cap* an adherent of Yoga philosophy

¹yoke *n* **1a** a bar or frame by which 2 draught animals (e g oxen) are joined at the heads or necks for working together **b** an arched device formerly laid on the neck of a defeated person **c** a frame fitted to sby's shoulders to carry a load in 2 equal portions **d** a crosspiece on a rudder to which steering lines are attached **2** *sing or pl in constr* **2** animals yoked or worked together **3a** an oppressive agency **b** a tie, link; *esp* marriage **4** a fitted or shaped piece at the top of a garment from which the rest hangs

²yoke *vt* **1** to attach (a draught animal) to (sthg) **2** to join (as if) by a yoke

yokel *n* a naive or gullible rustic; a country bumpkin

yolk *also* **yoke** *n* **1** the usu yellow spheroidal mass of stored food that forms the inner portion of the egg of a bird or reptile and is surrounded by the white **2** a mass of protein, lecithin, cholesterol, etc that is stored in an ovum as food for the developing embryo – **yolked** *adj*, **yolky** *adj*

yonder *adj or adv* over there

yonks *n, Br* a long time; ages – *infml*

yore *n* time (long) past – usu in *of yore*

yorker *n* a ball bowled in cricket that is aimed to bounce on the popping crease and so pass under the bat

Yorkshire pudding *n* a savoury baked pudding made from a batter and usu eaten before or with roast beef

Yorkshire terrier *n* a compact toy terrier with long straight silky hair mostly bluish grey but tan on the head and chest

you *pron, pl* **you** **1** the one being addressed – used as subject or object ⟨*can I pour* ∼ *a cup of tea?*⟩; sometimes used as an exclamation with vocatives ⟨∼ *angel*⟩ ⟨∼ *scoundrels*⟩ **2** a person; one ⟨*funny, when* ∼ *come to think of it*⟩ – **you get** there is or are ⟨*within the Chinese language* you get *quite different sounds – SEU S*⟩

you-all *pron, chiefly S US* you – usu used in addressing 2 or more people or sometimes 1 person as representing also another or others

you'd you had; you would

you'll you will; you shall

¹young *adj* younger; youngest **1a** in the first or an early stage of life, growth, or development **b** JUNIOR 1 **c** of an early or tender age for eating or drinking ⟨*fresh* ∼ *lamb*⟩ **2** recently come into being; new ⟨*a* ∼ *industry*⟩ ⟨*the night is* ∼⟩ **3** of or having the characteristics (e g vigour or gaiety) of young people ⟨*a* ∼ *style of dress*⟩ **4** tending towards the size of ⟨*the chapel was a ~ cathedral*⟩ – **youngish** *adj*, **youngness** *n*

²young *n pl* **1** young people; youth **2** immature offspring, esp of an animal – **with young** *of a female animal* pregnant

younger *adj* inferior in age; junior – used before or after sby's name to distinguish him/her from his/her father or mother ⟨*William Pitt the* Younger⟩

youngster *n* **1** a young person or creature **2** a child, baby

your *adj* **1** of you or yourself or yourselves, esp as possessor or possessors ⟨*~ bodies*⟩, agent or agents ⟨*~ contributions*⟩, or object or objects of an action ⟨*~ injury*⟩ –used with certain titles in the vocative ⟨*~ Eminence*⟩ **2** of one or oneself ⟨*when you face north, east is on ~ right*⟩ **3** – used for indicating sthg well-known and characteristic; infml ⟨*~ typical commuter*⟩ USE used attributively

you're you are

yours *pron, pl* **yours** that which or the one who belongs to you – used without a following noun as a pronoun equivalent in meaning to the adjective *your*; often used in the complimentary close of a letter ⟨*~ truly*⟩ – **yours truly 1** I, me, myself ⟨*I can take care of* yours truly⟩ **2** your letter ⟨yours truly *of the 19th*⟩

yourself *pron, pl* **yourselves 1a** that identical person or creature that is you – used reflexively ⟨*enjoy* yourselves, *everyone*⟩, for emphasis ⟨*carry it ~*⟩, or in absolute constructions **b** your normal self ⟨*soon be ~ again*⟩ **2** oneself

youth *n, pl* **youths 1** the time of life when one is young; esp adolescence ⟨*lived there in his ~*⟩ **2a** a young male adolescent **b** young people – often pl in constr ⟨*modern ~*⟩ **3** the quality of being youthful ⟨*preserved her ~*⟩

youthful *adj* **1** (characteristic) of youth ⟨*~ complexion*⟩⟨*~ optimism*⟩ **2** not yet mature or old; young ⟨*~ dancers*⟩ – **youthfully** *adv*, **youthfulness** *n*

youth hostel *n* a lodging typically providing inexpensive bed and breakfast accommodation for members of the YHA, esp young travellers or hikers – **youth-hosteller** *n*, **youth-hostelling** *n*

you've you have

yowl *vi or n* (to utter) the loud long wail of a cat or dog in pain or distress

yo-yo *n, pl* **yo-yos** a toy that consists of 2 discs separated by a deep groove in which a string is attached and wound and that is made to fall and rise when held by the string

yucca *n* any of a genus of sometimes treelike plants of the lily family with long often rigid leaves and a large cluster of white flowers

yule *n, often cap, archaic* Christmas

Yule log *n* a large log formerly put on the hearth on Christmas Eve as the foundation of the fire

Z

z *n, pl* **z's, zs** *often cap* **1** (a graphic representation of or device for reproducing) the 26th letter of the English alphabet **2** one designated z, esp as the 3rd in a series that includes x, y, and z

¹zany *n* one who acts the buffoon to amuse others

²zany *adj* fantastically or absurdly ludicrous – **zanily** *adv*, **zaniness** *n*

zeal *n* eagerness and ardent interest in pursuit of sthg; keenness

zealot *n* a zealous person; esp a fanatical partisan – **zealot** *adj*, **zealotry** *n*

zealous *adj* filled with or characterized by zeal ⟨*~ missionaries*⟩ – **zealously** *adv*, **zealousness** *n*

zebra *n, pl* **zebras**, esp collectively **zebra** any of several black and white striped fast-running African mammals related to the horse – **zebrine** *adj*, **zebroid** *adj*

zebra crossing *n* a crossing in Britain marked by a series of broad white stripes to indicate that pedestrians have the right of way across a road

zebu *n* an ox of any of several breeds of domesticated Asiatic oxen with a large fleshy hump over the shoulders

zed *n, chiefly Br* the letter z

zeitgeist *n* the general intellectual and moral character or cultural climate of an era

Zen *n* a Japanese sect of Mahayana Buddhism that aims at enlightenment by direct intuition through meditation (e g on paradoxes)

zenana *n* the women's quarters in an eastern, esp Muslim, house

zenith *n* **1** the point of the celestial sphere that is directly opposite the nadir and vertically above the observer **2** the highest point reached in the heavens by a celestial body **3** the culminating point or stage ⟨*at the ~ of his powers* – John Buchan⟩

zephyr *n* **1** a gentle breeze, esp from the west **2** any of various lightweight fabrics or articles of clothing

zeppelin *n, often cap* a large rigid cigar-shaped airship of a type built in Germany in the early 20th c; *broadly* an airship

¹zero *n, pl* **zeros** *also* **zeroes 1** the arithmetical symbol 0 or ø denoting the absence of all magnitude or quantity **2** (the number) 0 **3** the point of departure in reckoning; *specif* the point from which the graduation of a scale begins **4a** nothing ⟨*slow down to ~ in the traffic*⟩ **b** the lowest point ⟨*his spirits fell to ~*⟩

²zero *adj* **1** having zero magnitude or quantity ⟨*~ growth*⟩ **2a** *of a cloud ceiling* limiting vision to 15m (about 50ft) or less **b** *of horizontal visibility* limited to 50m (about 165ft) or less

³zero *vt* to adjust the sights of (e g a rifle) ~*vi* **1** to concentrate firepower on a specified target **2** to move near to or focus attention as if on a target; close ⟨*reporters ~ed in on Miss World*⟩ USE (vi) usu + on or in on

zero hour *n* the time at which an event is scheduled to take place

zest *n* **1** the outer peel of a citrus fruit used as flavouring **2** piquancy, spice ⟨*danger added ~ to the proceedings*⟩ **3** keen enjoyment; gusto ⟨*her ~ for living*⟩ – **zestful** *adj*, **zesty** *adj*

ziggurat *n* a temple tower of ancient Mesopotamia in the form of a stepped pyramid

¹zigzag *n* a line, course, or pattern consisting of a series of sharp alternate turns or angles ⟨*a blue shirt with red ~s*⟩

²zigzag *adj* forming or going in a zigzag; consisting of zigzags ⟨*a ~ path up the hill*⟩ – **zigzag** *adv*

³zigzag *vb* **-gg-** *vt* to form into a zigzag to proceed along or consist of a zigzag course

¹zinc *n* a bluish white bivalent metallic element that occurs abundantly in minerals and is used esp as a protective coating for iron and steel – **zincic** *adj*, **zincous** *adj*

²zinc *vt* **-c-, -ck-** to treat or coat with zinc

zinnia *n* any of a small genus of tropical American composite plants with showy flower heads and long-lasting ray flowers

Zionism *n* a movement for setting up a Jewish homeland in Palestine – **Zionist** *adj or n*

¹**zip** *vb* **-pp-** *vi* **1** to move with speed and vigour ⟨*waitresses* ~*ped by*⟩ **2** to become open, closed, or attached by means of a zip **3** to travel with a sharp hissing or humming sound ~ *vt* **1a** to close or open (as if) with a zip **b** to enclose by means of a zip ⟨~ *him into his wet suit*⟩ **c** to cause (a zip) to open or shut **2** to add zest or life to – often + *up*

²**zip** *n* **1** a light sharp hissing sound **2** energy, liveliness **3** *chiefly Br* a fastener that joins 2 edges of fabric by means of 2 flexible spirals or rows of teeth brought together by a sliding clip – **zippy** *adj*, **zippily** *adv*

³**zip** *adj* zip-up ⟨*a* ~ *jacket*⟩

zip code *n, often cap Z&I&P* a 5-digit number that is used in the postal address of a place in the USA to assist sorting

zipper *n, chiefly NAm* ZIP 3

zip-up *adj* fastened by means of a zip

zither *n* a stringed instrument having usu 30 to 40 strings over a shallow horizontal soundboard and played with plectrum and fingers – **zitherist** *n*

zizz *vi or n, Br* (to) nap, doze – *infml*

zo-, zoo- *comb form* animal; animal kingdom ⟨*zooid*⟩ ⟨*zoology*⟩

zodiac *n* an imaginary belt in the heavens that encompasses the apparent paths of all the principal planets except Pluto, has the ecliptic as its central line, and is divided into 12 constellations or signs each taken for astrological purposes to extend 30 degrees of longitude – **zodiacal** *adj*

zombie, *NAm also* **zombi** *n* **1** a human in the W Indies capable only of automatic movement who is held, esp in Haitian voodooism, to have died and been reanimated **2** a person resembling the walking dead; *esp* a shambling automaton – **zombielike** *adj*

¹**zone** *n* **1a** any of 5 great divisions of the earth's surface with respect to latitude and temperature **b** a portion of the surface of a sphere included between 2 parallel planes **2a** a subdivision of a biogeographic region that supports a similar fauna and flora throughout its extent **b** a distinctive layer of rock or other earth materials **3** an area distinct from adjoining parts ⟨*an erogenous* ~⟩ **4** any of the sections into which an area is divided for a particular purpose ⟨*a smokeless* ~⟩ – **zonal** *adj*, **zonate, zonated** *adj*

²**zone** *vt* **1** to arrange in, mark off, or partition into zones **2** to assign to a zone ⟨*neighbourhood has been* ~d *as residential*⟩ – **zoner** *n*

zonked *adj* **1** highly intoxicated by alcohol, LSD, etc – often + *out* **2** completely exhausted *USE* slang

zoo *n, pl* **zoos** a zoological garden or collection of living animals usu open to the public

zoo- – see ZO-

zoological garden *n* a garden or park where wild animals are kept for exhibition – often pl with sing. meaning

zoology *n* (biology that deals with) animals and animal life, usu excluding human beings – **zoologist** *n*, **zoological** *also* **zoologic** *adj*, **zoologically** *adv*

¹**zoom** *vi* **1** to move with a loud low hum or buzz **2** to rise sharply ⟨*retail sales* ~ed⟩ to operate the zoom lens of (e g a camera)

²**zoom** *n* **1** an act or process of zooming **2** ZOOM LENS

zoom lens *n* a lens (e g in a camera) in which the image size can be varied continuously so that the image remains in focus at all times

zoophyte *n* a coral, sponge, or other (branching or treelike) invertebrate animal resembling a plant – **zoophytic** *adj*

Zouave *n* a member of a French infantry unit, orig composed of Algerians, wearing a brilliant uniform

zucchini *n, pl* **zucchini, zucchinis** *chiefly NAm* a courgette

¹**Zulu** *n* **1** a member of a Bantu-speaking people of Natal **2** a Bantu language of the Zulus – **Zulu** *adj*

²**Zulu** – a communications code word for the letter *z*

zygote *n* (the developing individual produced from) a cell formed by the union of 2 gametes – **zygotic** *adj*

Common Abbreviations

A

a 1 acceleration **2** acre **3** answer **4** are—a metric unit of area **5** area
A 1 ampere **2** Associate
AA 1 Alcoholics Anonymous **2** antiaircraft **3** Automobile Association
AAA 1 Amateur Athletic Association **2** American Automobile Association
A and M ancient and modern—used of hymns
AB 1 able seaman; able-bodied seaman **2** *NAm* bachelor of arts
ABA Amateur Boxing Association
ABC 1 American Broadcasting Company **2** Australian Broadcasting Commission
ABM antiballistic missile
Abp archbishop
AC 1 alternating current **2** appellation contrôlée **3** athletic club
a/c account
ACA Associate of the Institute of Chartered Accountants
ACAS Advisory Conciliation and Arbitration Service
acc 1 according to **2** account **3** accusative
acct account; accountant
ACV air-cushion vehicle
ACW aircraftwoman
AD anno domini
ADAS Agricultural Development and Advisory Service
ADC 1 aide-de-camp **2** amateur dramatic club
ad inf ad infinitum
adj 1 adjective **2** adjustment — used in banking **3** adjutant
Adm admiral
adv 1 adverb; adverbial **2** against
AEA Atomic Energy Authority
AERE Atomic Energy Research Establishment
aet, aetat of the specified age; aged
AEU Amalgamated Engineering Union — now AEUW
AEW airborne early warning
AF 1 Anglo-French **2** audio frequency
AFM Air Force Medal
Afr Africa; African
AG 1 adjutant general **2** attorney general **3** joint-stock company
agcy agency
AGM *chiefly Br* annual general meeting
AGR advanced gas-cooled reactor
AI artificial insemination
AIA Associate of the Institute of Actuaries
AIB Associate of the Institute of Bankers
AID 1 Agency for International Development—a US agency **2** artificial insemination by donor
AIH artificial insemination by husband
AKA also known as
ALA Associate of the Library Association
ald alderman
alt 1 alternate **2** altitude **3** alto
am ante meridiem
AM 1 Albert Medal **2** amplitude modulation **3** associate member **4** *NAm* master of arts
AMDG to the greater glory of God
anon anonymous
A/O account of
aob any other business
AOC Air Officer Commanding

AP Associated Press
APEX Association of Professional, Executive, Clerical, and Computer Staff
app 1 apparent; apparently **2** appendix **3** appointed
appro approval
approx approximate; approximately
Apr April
APT Advanced Passenger Train
ARA Associate of the Royal Academy
ARAM Associate of the Royal Academy of Music
ARC Agricultural Research Council
ARCA Associate of the Royal College of Art
Arch archbishop
ARCM Associate of the Royal College of Music
ARCS Associate of the Royal College of Science
ARIBA Associate of the Royal Institute of British Architects
ARP air-raid precautions
arr 1 arranged by—used in music **2** arrival; arrives
art 1 article **2** artificial **3** artillery
arty artillery
AS 1 airspeed **2** Anglo-Saxon **3** antisubmarine
asap as soon as possible
ASLEF Associated Society of Locomotive Engineers and Firemen
assoc association
ASSR Autonomous Soviet Socialist Republic
asst assistant
ASTMS Association of Scientific, Technical and Managerial Staffs
ATC 1 air traffic control **2** Air Training Corps
attn for the attention of
ATV Associated Television
AUEW Amalgamated Union of Engineering Workers
Aug August
AUT Association of University Teachers
av 1 average **2** avoirdupois
Av avenue
AV 1 audiovisual **2** Authorized Version (of the Bible)
avdp avoirdupois
Ave avenue
AVM Air Vice Marshal

B

b 1 born **2** bowled by—used in cricket **3** breadth **4** bye—used in cricket
B 1 bachelor **2** bishop—used in chess **3** black—used esp on lead pencils
BA 1 Bachelor of Arts **2** British Academy **3** British Airways **4** British Association
b and b, *often cap B & B, Br* bed and breakfast
b and w black and white
BAOR British Army of the Rhine
Bart baronet
BB 1 Boys' Brigade **2** double black—used on lead pencils
BBBC British Boxing Board of Control
BBC British Broadcasting Corporation

BC 1 before Christ **2** British Columbia **3** British Council
BCh Bachelor of Surgery
BCom Bachelor of Commerce
BD 1 Bachelor of Divinity **2** bank draft **3** barrels per day **4** brought down
BDA British Dental Association
BDS Bachelor of Dental Surgery
BEA British European Airways—now BA
BEd Bachelor of Education
Beds Bedfordshire
BEF British Expeditionary Force
BEM British Empire Medal
BEng Bachelor of Engineering
Berks Berkshire
BeV billion electron volts
BFPO British Forces Post Office
bk book
BL 1 Bachelor of Law **2** bill of lading **3** British Legion **4** British Leyland **5** British Library
BLitt Bachelor of Letters
BM 1 Bachelor of Medicine **2** bench mark **3** British Medal **4** British Museum
BMA British Medical Association
BMC British Medical Council
BMJ British Medical Journal
BMus Bachelor of Music
BO body odour—euph
BOAC British Overseas Airways Corporation—now BA
BOC British Oxygen Company
BOSS Bureau of State Security—a SAfr organization
BOT Board of Trade
BOTB British Overseas Trade Board
Bp bishop
BP 1 boiling point **2** British Petroleum **3** British Pharmacopoeia
BPC British Pharmaceutical Codex
BPhil Bachelor of Philosophy
Br 1 British **2** brother
BR British Rail
Brig brigade; brigadier
Brig-Gen brigadier-general
Brit Britain; British
bros, Bros brothers
BRS British Road Services
BS 1 Bachelor of Surgery **2** balance sheet **3** bill of sale **4** British Standard **5** *NAm* Bachelor of Science
BSA Building Societies Association
BSc Bachelor of Science
BSC 1 British Steel Corporation **2** British Sugar Corporation
BSI 1 British Standards Institution **2** Building Societies Institute
BST British Standard Time; British Summer Time
Bt Baronet
BTh Bachelor of Theology
Btu British thermal unit
Bucks Buckinghamshire
BUPA British United Provident Association
BV Blessed Virgin
BVM Blessed Virgin Mary

C

c 1 canine—used in dentistry **2** carat **3** caught by—used in cricket **4** centi- **5** century **6** chapter **7** circa **8** cloudy **9** cold

10 college **11** colt **12** copyright **13** cubic

C 1 calorie **2** castle—used in chess **3** Catholic **4** Celsius **5** centigrade **6** *Br* Conservative **7** corps

ca circa

CA 1 California **2** chartered accountant **3** chief accountant **4** Consumers' Association **5** current account

CAA Civil Aviation Authority

CAB Citizens' Advice Bureau

cal 1 calibre **2** (small) calorie

Cal 1 California **2** (large) calorie

Cambs Cambridgeshire

Can Canada; Canadian

c and b caught and bowled by—used in cricket

C and G City and Guilds

C and W country and western

Cantab of Cambridge—used with academic awards ‹MA~›

Cantuar of Canterbury—used chiefly in the signature of the Archbishop of Canterbury

caps 1 capital letters **2** capsule

Capt captain

Card cardinal

CAT 1 College of Advanced Technology **2** computerized axial tomography

CB 1 Citizens' Band **2** Companion of the (Order of the) Bath

CBC Canadian Broadcasting Corporation

CBE Commander of the (Order of the) British Empire

CBI Confederation of British Industry

CBS Columbia Broadcasting System

cc 1 carbon copy **2** chapters **3** cubic centimetre

CC 1 Chamber of Commerce **2** County Council **3** Cricket Club

CD 1 civil defence **2** diplomatic corps

Cdr Commander

Cdre Commodore

CE 1 Church of England **2** civil engineer **3** Council of Europe

CEGB Central Electricity Generating Board

CENTO Central Treaty Organization

cf compare

CFE College of Further Education

cgs centimetre-gram-second (system)

ch 1 chain—a unit of length **2** central heating **3** chapter **4** check—used in chess **5** child; children **6** church

CH 1 clubhouse **2** Companion of Honour

chap 1 chaplain **2** chapter

ChB Bachelor of Surgery

Ches Cheshire

ChM Master of Surgery

CI Channel Islands

CIA Central Intelligence Agency

cia company

CID Criminal Investigation Department

cie company

C in C Commander in Chief

cl 1 centilitre **2** clerk

Cllr *Br* councillor

Clo close—used in street names

cm centimetre

Cmdr Commander

Cmdre Commodore

CMG Companion of (the Order of) St Michael and St George

CND Campaign for Nuclear Disarmament

CO 1 commanding officer **2** Commonwealth Office **3** conscientious objector

c/o 1 care of **2** carried over

COD 1 cash on delivery **2** Concise Oxford Dictionary

C of E 1 Church of England **2** Council of Europe

C of S Church of Scotland

COHSE Confederation of Health Service Employees

COI Central Office of Information

col 1 colour; coloured **2** column

Col 1 Colonel **2** Colorado

coll 1 college **2** colloquial

Com, Comm 1 Commander **2** Commodore **3** Commonwealth **4** Communist

Comdr Commander

Comdt Commandant

Con, Cons Conservative

cont 1 containing **2** contents **3** continent; continental **4** continued

contd continued

Corp 1 Corporal **2** corporation

coy company—used esp for a military company

cp 1 candlepower **2** compare

CP 1 Communist Party **2** Country Party—an Australian political party

Cpl corporal

CPR Canadian Pacific Railway

CPRE Council for the Preservation of Rural England

cresc, cres 1 crescendo **2** *often cap* crescent—used esp in street names

CRO 1 cathode ray oscilloscope **2** Criminal Records Office

CRT cathode-ray tube

CS 1 chartered surveyor **2** Civil Service **3** Court of Session–the supreme civil court of Scotland

CSE Certificate of Secondary Education

CSM Company Sergeant Major

CSO 1 Central Statistical Office **2** Community Service Order

cu cubic

Cumb Cumbria

CV curriculum vitae

CVO Commander of the (Royal) Victorian Order

Cwlth Commonwealth

CWS Cooperative Wholesale Society

cwt hundredweight

D

d 1 date **2** daughter **3** day **4** deca- **5** deci- **6** delete **7** penny; pence—used before introduction of decimal currency **8** density **9** departs **10** diameter **11** died **12** dose **13** drizzle

DA 1 deposit account **2** *NAm* district attorney

D & C dilatation and curettage

dB decibel

DBE Dame Commander of the (Order of the) British Empire

DC 1 from the beginning **2** Detective Constable **3** direct current **4** District of Columbia **5** District Commissioner

DCB Dame Commander of the (Order of the) Bath

DCh Doctor of Surgery

DCL 1 Distillers Company Limited **2** Doctor of Civil Law

DCM Distinguished Conduct Medal

DCMG Dame Commander of (the Order of) St Michael and St George

DCVO Dame Commander of the (Royal) Victorian Order

DD 1 direct debit **2** Doctor of Divinity

DDS Doctor of Dental Surgery

DE 1 Delaware **2** Department of Employment

dec 1 deceased **2** declared—used esp in cricket **3** declension **4** declination **5** decrease **6** decrescendo

Dec December

dep 1 departs; departure **2** deposed **3** deposit **4** depot **5** deputy

dept department

DES Department of Education and Science

det detached; detachment

Det Detective

DF Defender of the Faith

DFC Distinguished Flying Cross

DFM Distinguished Flying Medal

DG 1 by the grace of God **2** director general

DHSS Department of Health and Social Security

DI Detective Inspector

Dip Diploma

Dip Ed Diploma in Education

Dip HE Diploma in Higher Education

dir director

div 1 divergence **2** divide; divided **3** dividend **4** division **5** divorced

DIY do-it-yourself

DLitt Doctor of Letters

DM Doctor of Medicine

DMus Doctor of Music

do ditto

DOA dead on arrival—used chiefly in hospitals

DOE Department of the Environment

DoT Department of Trade

doz dozen

DP 1 data processing **2** displaced person

dpc damp proof course

DPhil Doctor of Philosophy

DPP Director of Public Prosecutions

dpt department

dr 1 debtor **2** drachm **3** dram **4** drawer

Dr 1 doctor **2** drive—used in street names

DS 1 from the sign **2** Detective Sergeant

DSc doctor of science

DSC Distinguished Service Cross

DSM Distinguished Service Medal

DSO Distinguished Service Order

dsp 1 died without issue **2** dessertspoon; dessertspoonful

DST daylight saving time

DTh, DTheol doctor of theology

DV God willing

DVLC Driver and Vehicle Licensing Centre

dz dozen

E

E 1 Earl **2** earth—used esp on electrical plugs **3** East; Easterly; Eastern **4** energy **5** English

E and OE errors and omissions excepted

EC East Central—a London postal district

ECG electrocardiogram; electrocardiograph

ECT electroconvulsive therapy

ed, edit edited; edition; editor

EDP electronic data processing

EEC European Economic Community

EEG electroencephalogram; electroencephalograph

EFTA European Free Trade Association

EFL English as a foreign language

eg for example

EHF extremely high frequency

EHT extremely high tension

ELF extremely low frequency

ELT English language teaching

EMI Electrical and Musical Industries

Emp Emperor; Empress

ENE east-northeast

ENEA European Nuclear Energy Agency

Eng England; English

ENSA Entertainments National Service Association

ENT ear, nose, and throat

EO Executive Officer

EOC Equal Opportunities Commission
ep en passant
EPNS electroplated nickel silver
eq equal
equiv equivalent
ER 1 Eastern Region **2** King Edward **3** Queen Elizabeth
ESA European Space Agency
ESE east-southeast
ESL English as a second language
ESN educationally subnormal
Esq also **Esqr** esquire
est 1 established **2** estate **3** estimate; estimated
EST 1 Eastern Standard Time **2** electro-shock treatment
ETA estimated time of arrival
ETD estimated time of departure
et seq 1 and the following one **2** and the following ones
ETU Electrical Trades Union
EVA extravehicular activity
ex 1 examined **2** example **3** except **4** exchange

F

f 1 fathom **2** female **3** femto- **4** force **5** forte **6** frequency **7** focal length **8** folio **9** following (eg page) **10** foot
F 1 Fahrenheit **2** false **3** farad **4** Fellow **5** filial generation **6** fine—used esp on lead pencils **7** forward **8** French
FA Football Association
Fahr Fahrenheit
F and F fixtures and fittings
FBI Federal Bureau of Investigation
FBR fast breeder reactor
FC 1 Football Club **2** Forestry Commission
FCA Fellow of the (Institute of) Chartered Accountants
FCII Fellow of the Chartered Insurance Institute
FCIS Fellow of the Chartered Institute of Secretaries
FCO Foreign and Commonwealth Office
FCS Fellow of the Chemical Society
FD Defender of the Faith
Feb February
ff 1 folios **2** following (eg pages) **3** fortissimo
FIFA International Football Federation
fig 1 figurative; figuratively **2** figure
fl 1 floor **2** flourished—used to indicate a period of renown of sby whose dates of birth and death are unknown **3** fluid
FL 1 Florida **2** focal length
fl oz fluid ounce
Flt Lt Flight Lieutenant
Flt Off Flight Officer
Flt Sgt Flight Sergeant
fm fathom
FM Field Marshal
fo, fol folio
FO 1 Field Officer **2** Flying Officer **3** Foreign Office
FOC Father of the Chapel (in a Trade Union)
FOE Friends of the Earth
fpm feet per minute
fps 1 feet per second **2** foot-pound-second
Fr 1 Father **2** French **3** Friar
FRCM Fellow of the Royal College of Music
FRCOG Fellow of the Royal College of Obstetricians and Gynaecologists
FRCP Fellow of the Royal College of Physicians
FRCS Fellow of the Royal College of Surgeons
FRCVS Fellow of the Royal College of Veterinary Surgeons

Fri Friday
FRIBA Fellow of the Royal Institute of British Architects
FRIC Fellow of the Royal Institute of Chemistry
FRICS Fellow of the Royal Institution of Chartered Surveyors
FRS Fellow of the Royal Society
FSA Fellow of the Society of Actuaries
ft 1 feet; foot **2** fort
FT Financial Times
fth, fthm fathom
FWD 1 four-wheel drive **2** front-wheel drive

G

g 1 gauge **2** giga **3** good **4** gram
G acceleration due to gravity
gal, gall gallon
GB Great Britain
GBE Knight/Dame Grand Cross of the (Order of the) British Empire
GBH Br grievous bodily harm
GC George Cross
GCB Knight/Dame Grand Cross of the (Order of the) Bath
GCE General Certificate of Education
GCHQ Government Communications Headquarters
GCMG Knight/Dame Grand Cross of (the Order of) St Michael and St George
GCVO Knight/Dame Grand Cross of the (Royal) Victorian Order
gd good
Gdns Gardens—used esp in street names
GDP gross domestic product
GDR German Democratic Republic
GHQ general headquarters
gi gill
Gib Gibraltar
Glam Glamorgan
GLC Greater London Council
Glos Gloucestershire
gm gram
GM 1 general manager **2** George Medal **3** guided missile
GMC 1 General Medical Council **2** general management committee
GMT Greenwich Mean Time
GMWU General and Municipal Workers Union
GNP gross national product
GOC General Officer Commanding
gov 1 government **2** governor
govt government
GP 1 general practitioner **2** Grand Prix
Gp Capt Group Captain
GPI general paralysis of the insane
GPO general post office
GQ general quarters
gr 1 grade **2** grain **3** gram **4** gravity **5** gross
GR King George
gro gross
Gro Grove—used in street names
gt great
GT grand tourer

H

h 1 hect-; hecto **2** height **3** high **4** hot **5** hour **6** husband
H 1 harbour **2** hard—used esp on lead pencils **3** hardness
ha hectare
h and c hot and cold (water)

Hants Hampshire
HB hard black—used on lead pencils
HBM His/Her Britannic Majesty
HCF highest common factor
HE 1 high explosive **2** His Eminence **3** His/Her Excellency
HEO Higher Executive Officer
Here, Heref Herefordshire
Herts Hertfordshire
HF high frequency
HG 1 His/Her Grace **2** Home Guard
HGV Br heavy goods vehicle
HH 1 double hard—used on lead pencils **2** His/Her Highness **3** His Holiness
HIH His/Her Imperial Highness
HIM His/Her Imperial Majesty
HM 1 headmaster **2** headmistress **3** His/Her Majesty
HMF His/Her Majesty's Forces
HMG His/Her Majesty's Government
HMI His/Her Majesty's Inspector (of Schools)
HMS His/Her Majesty's Ship
HMSO His/Her Majesty's Stationery Office
HMV His Master's Voice
HNC Higher National Certificate
HND Higher National Diploma
HO Home Office
Hon (the) Honourable
Hons Br honours
Hon Sec Br Honorary Secretary
HP 1 high pressure **2** hire purchase **3** horsepower **4** Houses of Parliament
HQ headquarters
hr hour
HRH His/Her Royal Highness
HSO Higher Scientific Officer
HST high speed train
ht height
HT 1 high-tension **2** under this title
HV 1 high velocity **2** high-voltage
HW 1 high water **2** hot water
Hz hertz

I

I 1 inductance **2** island; isle
IAEA International Atomic Energy Agency
IAM Institute of Advanced Motorists
IATA International Air Transport Association
ib ibidem
IBA Independent Broadcasting Authority
ibid ibidem
IBM International Business Machines
i/c in charge
IC integrated circuit
ICA Institute of Contemporary Arts
ICBM intercontinental ballistic missile
ICC International Cricket Conference
ICE 1 Institute of Civil Engineers **2** internal-combustion engine
ICI Imperial Chemical Industries
ICL International Computers Limited
id idem
ID 1 Idaho **2** (proof of) identification **3** inner diameter **4** intelligence department
IDA International Development Association
i e that is
IHS Jesus
ILEA Inner London Education Authority
ill, illus, illust illustrated; illustration
ILO 1 International Labour Organization **2** International Labour Office
ILP Independent Labour Party
IMF International Monetary Fund
imp 1 Emperor; Empress **2** imperative **3** imperfect **4** imperial
in inch
inc 1 increase **2** chiefly NAm incorporated

incl included; including; inclusive

ind 1 independent **2** indicative **3** industrial; industry

INRI Jesus of Nazareth, King of the Jews

insp inspector

inst 1 instant **2** institute; institution

int 1 integral **2** interior **3** intermediate **4** internal **5** international **6** interpreter **7** intransitive

intro introduction

I/O input/output

IOC International Olympic Committee

IOM Isle of Man

IOW Isle of Wight

IPA International Phonetic Alphabet

IPC International Publishing Corporation

IPM 1 inches per minute **2** Institute of Personnel Management

IPS inches per second

IR 1 information retrieval **2** infrared **3** Inland Revenue

IRA Irish Republican Army

IRBM intermediate range ballistic missile

IRO 1 Inland Revenue Office **2** International Refugee Organization

ISBN International Standard Book Number

ISD international subscriber dialling

ISO 1 Imperial Service Order **2** International Standardization Organization

ita initial teaching alphabet

ITA Independent Television Authority—now IBA

ital italic; italicized

ITN Independent Television News

ITT International Telephone and Telegraph (Corporation)

ITU International Telecommunications Union

ITV Independent Television

IU international unit

IUD intrauterine device

IVR International Vehicle Registration

IWW Industrial Workers of the World

J

J 1 joule **2** Judge **3** Justice

JA, J/A joint account

Jan January

JC 1 Jesus Christ **2** Julius Caesar

JCD 1 Doctor of Canon Law **2** Doctor of Civil Law

JCR Junior Common Room

jnr junior

JP Justice of the Peace

Jr junior

jt, jnt joint

Jul July

Jun June

K

k 1 carat **2** kilo- **3** kitchen **4** knot **5** kosher

K 1 kelvin **2** king—used in chess **3** knit

KB 1 King's Bench **2** Knight Bachelor

KBE Knight (Commander of the Order of the) British Empire

KC 1 Kennel Club **2** King's Counsel

KCB Knight Commander of the (Order of the) Bath

KCIE Knight Commander of the (Order of the) Indian Empire

KCMG Knight Commander of (the Order of) St Michael and St George

KCSI Knight Commander of the (Order of the) Star of India

KCVO Knight Commander of the (Royal) Victorian Order

kg 1 keg **2** kilogram

KG Knight of the (Order of the) Garter

KGB (Soviet) State Security Committee

kHz kilohertz

KKK Ku Klux Klan

kl kilolitre

km kilometre

kn knot

kph kilometres per hour

kt karat

KT 1 knight—used in chess **2** Knight Templar **3** Knight of the (Order of the) Thistle

kV kilovolt

kW kilowatt

kWh, kwh kilowatt-hour

L

l 1 Lady **2** lake **3** large **4** left **5** length **6** Liberal **7** pound **8** lightning **9** line **10** litre **11** little **12** long **13** last **14** lower

L 1 Latin **2** live—used esp on electrical plugs **3** *Br* learner (driver)

La 1 lane—used esp in street names **2** Louisiana

LA 1 law agent **2** Library Association **3** *Br* local authority **4** Los Angeles **5** Louisiana

Lab 1 Labour **2** Labrador

Lancs Lancashire

lat latitude

lb 1 pound **2** leg bye

LBC London Broadcasting Company

lbw leg before wicket

lc 1 letter of credit **2** in the place cited **3** lowercase

LCC London County Council

lcd 1 liquid crystal display **2** lowest (*or* least) common denominator

LCM lowest (*or* least) common multiple

LCpl lance corporal

Ld Lord

LDS Licentiate in Dental Surgery

LEA Local Education Authority

led light emitting diode

leg legato

Leics Leicestershire

LEM lunar excursion module

LF low frequency

lh left hand

LHA Local Health Authority

LHD Doctor of Letters; Doctor of Humanities

Lieut Lieutenant

Lincs Lincolnshire

lit 1 litre **2** literature

Litt D doctor of letters; doctor of literature

ll lines

LLB Bachelor of Laws

LLD Doctor of Laws

LLM Master of Laws

LOB Location of Offices Bureau

loc cit in the place cited

long longitude

LPG liquefied petroleum gas

LPO London Philharmonic Orchestra

LRAM Licentiate of the Royal Academy of Music

LSE London School of Economics

LSO London Symphony Orchestra

lt light

Lt 1 lieutenant **2** low-tension

LTA Lawn Tennis Association

Lt Cdr Lieutenant Commander

Lt Col Lieutenant Colonel

Ltd limited

Lt Gen Lieutenant General

LV 1 low velocity **2** low voltage **3** *Br* luncheon voucher

LVT 1 landing vehicle, tracked **2** landing vehicle (tank)

LW 1 long wave **2** low water

LWR light water reactor

LWT London Weekend Television

M

m 1 maiden (over)—used in cricket **2** male **3** married **4** masculine **5** mass **6** metre **7** middle **8** mile **9** thousand **10** milli- **11** million **12** minute—used for the unit of time **13** molar **14** month

M 1 Mach **2** Master **3** mega- **4** Member **5** Monsieur **6** motorway

MA 1 Massachusetts **2** Master of Arts **3** Middle Ages **4** Military Academy

MAFF Ministry of Agriculture, Fisheries, and Food

Maj Major

Maj Gen Major General

M & S Marks and Spencer

Mar March

Marq Marquess; Marquis

MASH *NAm* mobile army surgical hospital

max maximum

MB Bachelor of Medicine

MBE Member of the (Order of the) British Empire

MC 1 Master of Ceremonies **2** Member of Congress **3** Military Cross

MCC Marylebone Cricket Club

mcg microgram

MCh, MChir Master of Surgery

MD 1 Managing Director **2** Doctor of Medicine **3** right hand—used in music

MDS Master of Dental Surgery

MEP Member of the European Parliament

met 1 meteorological; meteorology **2** metropolitan

mf 1 medium frequency **2** mezzo forte

MFH Master of Foxhounds

mg milligram

Mgr 1 Monseigneur **2** Monsignor

MHz megahertz

mi mile; mileage

MI 1 Michigan **2** military intelligence

Middx Middlesex

min 1 minimum **2** minor **3** minute—used for the unit of time

Min Minister; Ministry

misc miscellaneous; miscellany

ml 1 mile **2** millilitre

MLitt Master of Letters

Mlle mademoiselle

MLR minimum lending rate

mm millimetre

MM 1 Maelzel's metronome **2** messieurs **3** Military Medal

Mme madame

Mmes mesdames

MN 1 Merchant Navy **2** Minnesota

MO 1 Medical Officer **2** Missouri **3** modus operandi **4** money order

mod 1 moderate **2** moderato **3** modern **4** modulus

MoD Ministry of Defence

MOH Medical Officer of Health

mol 1 molecular; molecule **2** mole

Mon Monday

MP 1 Member of Parliament **2** Metropolitan Police **3** Military Police; Military Policeman

mpg miles per gallon

mph miles per hour

MPhil Master of Philosophy

Mr *see entry in main text*

MRCP Member of the Royal College of Physicians

MRCS Member of the Royal College of Surgeons

MRCVS Member of the Royal College of Veterinary Surgeons
Mrs *see entry in main text*
Ms *see entry in main text*
MS 1 left hand—used in music 2 manuscript 3 Mississippi 4 multiple sclerosis
MSc Master of Science
Msgr *chiefly NAm* Monseigneur; Monsignor
MSS manuscripts
Mt 1 Matthew 2 Mount
mth month
MW 1 medium wave 2 megawatt
mW milliwatt

N

n 1 name 2 nano- 3 born 4 net 5 new 6 neuter 7 nominative 8 noon 9 noun 10 numerical aperture
N 1 knight—used in chess 2 newton 3 North; Northerly; Northern 4 neutral—used esp on electric plugs
n/a no account—used in banking
NA 1 North America 2 not applicable
NAAFI Navy, Army, and Air Force Institutes
NALGO National and Local Government Officers Association
NAm North America; North American
NASA National Aeronautics and Space Administration—a US government organization
NATO North Atlantic Treaty Organization
NATSOPA National Society of Operative Printers, Graphical and Media Personnel
nb no ball—used in cricket
NB 1 Nebraska 2 New Brunswick 3 note well
NCB National Coal Board
NCC Nature Conservancy Council
NCO non-commissioned officer
NCP National Car Parks
NCR National Cash Register (Company)
nd no date
NE 1 modern English [*New English*] 2 New England 3 Northeast; Northeastern
NEB 1 National Enterprise Board 2 New English Bible
NEC National Executive Committee
NEDC National Economic Development Council
neg negative
NERC Natural Environment Research Council
NF 1 National Front 2 Newfoundland 3 no funds
NFU National Farmers' Union
NFWI National Federation of Women's Institutes
ng no good
NGA National Graphical Association
NHS National Health Service
NI 1 National Insurance 2 Northern Ireland
NLF National Liberation Front
NNE north-northeast
NNW north-northwest
no 1 not out—used in cricket 2 number 3 *NAm* north
Norf Norfolk
Northants Northamptonshire
Northumb Northumberland
nos numbers
Notts Nottinghamshire
Nov November
np new paragraph
nr near
NSB National Savings Bank
NSPCC National Society for the Prevention of Cruelty to Children
NSW New South Wales
NT 1 National Trust 2 New Testament 3 no trumps

NUJ National Union of Journalists
NUM National Union of Mineworkers
NUPE National Union of Public Employees
NUR National Union of Railwaymen
NUS 1 National Union of Seamen 2 National Union of Students
NUT National Union of Teachers
NW Northwest; Northwestern
NY New York
NYC New York City
NZ New Zealand

O

o 1 ohm 2 old
O & M organization and methods
OAP *Br* old-age pensioner
OB 1 outside broadcast 2 *Br* old boy
OBE Officer of the (Order of the) British Empire
OC *Br* Officer Commanding
Oct October
OCTU Officer Cadets Training Unit
OECD Organization for Economic Cooperation and Development
OG *Br* old girl
OHMS On His/Her Majesty's Service
OM Order of Merit
ONC Ordinary National Certificate
OND Ordinary National Diploma
ono or near offer—used with prices of goods for sale
op opus
op cit in the work cited
OPEC Organization of Petroleum Exporting Countries
orig original; originally; originator
OS 1 ordinary seaman 2 Ordnance Survey 3 out of stock 4 outsize
O/S outstanding
OT 1 occupational therapy; Occupational Therapist 2 Old Testament 3 overtime
OTC Officers' Training Corps
OU Open University
OXFAM Oxford Committee for Famine Relief
Oxon 1 Oxfordshire 2 of Oxford—used chiefly with academic awards ‹MA~›
oz ounce; ounces

P

p 1 page 2 participle 3 past 4 pence; penny 5 per 6 piano—used as an instruction in music 7 pico- 8 pint 9 power 10 premolar 11 pressure
pa per annum
Pa 1 Pennsylvania 2 pascal
PA 1 Pennsylvania 2 personal assistant 3 press agent 4 public address (system) 5 purchasing agent
PABX *Br* private automatic branch (telephone) exchange
P & O Peninsular and Oriental (Steamship Company)
p & p *Br* postage and packing
par 1 paragraph 2 parallel 3 parish
PAX *Br* private automatic (telephone) exchange
PAYE pay as you earn
PBX private branch (telephone) exchange
pc 1 per cent 2 postcard
PC 1 police constable 2 Privy Councillor
Pde parade—used in street names
PDSA People's Dispensary for Sick Animals
PE physical education

PEP *Br* Political and Economic Planning
PER Professional Employment Register
per pro by the agency (of)
PGA Professional Golfers' Association
PhB Bachelor of Philosophy
PhD Doctor of Philosophy
pk 1 *often cap* park—used esp in street names 2 peck
pl 1 *often cap* place—used esp in street names 2 platoon 3 plural
plc public limited company
PLO Palestine Liberation Organization
PLP Parliamentary Labour Party
PLR Public Lending Right
pm 1 post meridiem 2 premium
PM 1 postmortem 2 Prime Minister 3 Provost Marshal
PO 1 Petty Officer 2 Pilot Officer 3 postal order 4 Post Office
POB Post Office box
POE 1 port of embarkation 2 port of entry
pop population
POP *Br* Post Office Preferred
POW prisoner of war
pp 1 pages 2 past participle 3 by proxy 4 pianissimo
PPE Philosophy, Politics, and Economics
PPS 1 Parliamentary Private Secretary 2 further postscript
Pr 1 Priest 2 Prince
PR 1 proportional representation 2 public relations 3 Puerto Rico
prec preceding
pref 1 preface 2 preferred 3 prefix
prelim preliminary
prep 1 preparation; preparatory 2 preposition
Pres President
PRO 1 Public Records Office 2 public relations officer
Prof Professor
PROM programmable read-only memory
PS 1 Police Sergeant 2 postscript 3 Private Secretary 4 prompt side—used to designate part of the theatrical stage
pseud pseudonym; pseudonymous
psf pounds per square foot
psi pounds per square inch
PSV *Br* public service vehicle
pt 1 part 2 pint 3 point 4 port
PT 1 Pacific time 2 physical training
PTA Parent-Teacher Association
Pte Private
PTO please turn over
Pty *chiefly Austr, NZ, and SAfr* Proprietary
PVC polyvinyl chloride
Pvt *chiefly NAm* Private
pw per week
PW *Br* policewoman
PX post exchange

Q

q 1 quarto 2 quintal 3 quire
Q queen—used in chess
QB Queen's Bench
QC Queen's Counsel
QED which was to be demonstrated
QM quartermaster
QMG Quartermaster General
QMS Quartermaster Sergeant
QPR Queen's Park Rangers
qq which (*pl*) see
QSO quasi-stellar object
qt quart
qto quarto
qty quantity
qv which see

R

r 1 radius **2** railway **3** recto **4** resistance **5** right **6** runs—used in cricket
R 1 rabbi **2** radical—used in chemistry **3** rain **4** Réaumur **5** rector **6** queen **7** registered (as a trademark) **8** king **9** ring road **10** river **11** röntgen **12** rook—used in chess **13** Royal
RA 1 Rear Admiral **2** Royal Academician; Royal Academy **3** Royal Artillery
RAAF Royal Australian Air Force
RAC 1 Royal Armoured Corps **2** Royal Automobile Club
RADA Royal Academy of Dramatic Art
RAF Royal Air Force
RAM 1 random access memory **2** Royal Academy of Music
RAMC Royal Army Medical Corps
R and A Royal and Ancient—used as the title of St Andrews Golf Club
R & B rhythm and blues
R and D research and development
RAOC Royal Army Ordnance Corps
RC 1 Red Cross **2** reinforced concrete **3** Roman Catholic
RCAF Royal Canadian Air Force
RCM Royal College of Music
RCMP Royal Canadian Mounted Police
RCN 1 Royal Canadian Navy **2** Royal College of Nursing
rd *often cap R* road
RDC Rural District Council
RE 1 religious education **2** Royal Engineers
ref 1 reference **2** referred
reg 1 regiment **2** register; registered **3** registrar; registry **4** regulation **5** regulo
regd registered
regt regiment
rel relating; relation; relative
Rev 1 Revelation—used for the book of the Bible **2** Reverend
Revd Reverend
RF 1 radio frequency **2** Rugby Football
RFC 1 Royal Flying Corps **2** Rugby Football Club
RFU Rugby Football Union
rh 1 relative humidity **2** right hand
RH Royal Highness
RHS 1 Royal Historical Society **2** Royal Horticultural Society **3** Royal Humane Society
RI 1 refractive index **2** religious instruction **3** Rhode Island
RIBA Royal Institute of British Architects
RIC Royal Institute of Chemistry
RICS Royal Institute of Chartered Surveyors
RIP 1 may he rest in peace **2** may they rest in peace
RK religious knowledge
RL Rugby League
RM 1 Royal Mail **2** Royal Marines
RMA Royal Military Academy (Sandhurst)
RN Royal Navy
RNAS Royal Naval Air Service
RNIB Royal National Institute for the Blind
RNLI Royal National Lifeboat Institution
RNR Royal Naval Reserve
RNVR Royal Naval Volunteer Reserve
ROC Royal Observer Corps
RoSPA Royal Society for the Prevention of Accidents
RPI *Br* retail price index
rpm 1 *Br, often cap* retail price maintenance **2** revolutions per minute
rps revolutions per second
rpt 1 repeat **2** report
RS 1 right side **2** Royal Society
RSC Royal Shakespeare Company

RSM 1 Regimental Sergeant Major **2** Royal Society of Medicine
RSPB Royal Society for the Protection of Birds
RSPCA Royal Society for the Prevention of Cruelty to Animals
RSV Revised Standard Version (of the Bible)
RSVP please answer
Rt Hon Right Honourable
Rt Rev, Rt Revd Right Reverend
RU Rugby Union
RUC Royal Ulster Constabulary
RV Revised Version (of the Bible)

S

s 1 school **2** scruple **3** second **4** shilling **5** singular **6** sire **7** small **8** snow **9** son **10** succeeded
S 1 saint **2** sea **3** siemens **4** Signor **5** society **6** South; Southerly; Southern **7** sun
SA 1 Salvation Army **2** sex appeal **3** small arms **4** limited liability company; Ltd **5** Society of Actuaries **6** South Africa **7** South America
sae stamped addressed envelope
SALT Strategic Arms Limitation Talks
SAM surface-to-air missile
SAS Special Air Service
Sat Saturday
SATB soprano, alto, tenor, bass
SAYE save-as-you-earn
SBN Standard Book Number
sc 1 scene **2** scilicet **3** small capitals
s/c self-contained
Sc Scots
ScD Doctor of Science
SCE Scottish Certificate of Education
SCF Save the Children Fund
SCR 1 senior common room **2** script **3** scripture
SDLP Social Democratic and Labour Party
SDP Social Democratic Party
SE southeast; southeastern
SEATO Southeast Asia Treaty Organization
sec 1 second; secondary **2** secretary **3** section **4** according to **5** secant
SEN State Enrolled Nurse
Sep, Sept September
seq the following
seqq the following
Serg, Sergt sergeant
SF science fiction
SG 1 Solicitor General **2** *often not cap* specific gravity
sgd signed
Sgt Sergeant
Sgt Maj Sergeant Major
SHAPE Supreme Headquarters Allied Powers Europe
SI International System of Units
Sig Signor
SIS Secret Intelligence Service
SJ Society of Jesus
SLADE Society of Lithographic Artists, Designers and Etchers
SLP Scottish Labour Party
SM Sergeant Major
SNP Scottish National Party
snr senior
So south
soc society
SOGAT Society of Graphical and Allied Trades
Som Somerset
sop soprano
SP 1 without issue **2** starting price
SPCK Society for Promoting Christian Knowledge

SPQR the Senate and the People of Rome
sq square
Sqn Ldr Squadron Leader
Sr 1 senior **2** Senor **3** Sir **4** Sister
SRC Science Research Council
SRN State Registered Nurse
SS 1 saints **2** steamship **3** Sunday School
SSE south-southeast
SSgt staff sergeant
SSM surface-to-surface missile
SSR Soviet Socialist Republic
SSRC Social Science Research Council
SSW south-southwest
st 1 stanza **2** stitch **3** stone **4** stumped by
St 1 Saint **2** street
Staffs Staffordshire
STD 1 doctor of sacred theology **2** subscriber trunk dialling
sth south
STOL short takeoff and landing
STP standard temperature and pressure
STUC Scottish Trades Union Congress
Sun Sunday
supp, suppl supplement; supplementary
supt superintendent
SW 1 shortwave **2** southwest; southwestern
SWALK sealed with a loving kiss
SWAPO South-West Africa People's Organization
Sx Sussex

T

t 1 time **2** ton; tonne **3** transitive
T temperature
TA Territorial Army
T & AVR Territorial and Army Volunteer Reserve
TASS the official news agency of the Soviet Union
TB tubercle bacillus
tbs, tbsp tablespoon; tablespoonful
TCCB Test and County Cricket Board
Tce *Br* terrace—used esp in street names
tech 1 technical; technically; technician **2** technological; technology
temp 1 temperature **2** temporary **3** in the time of
Ter, Terr 1 terrace—used esp in street names **2** territory
TGWU Transport and General Workers' Union
Th Thursday
Thur, Thurs Thursday
TIR International Road Transport
TM 1 trademark **2** transcendental meditation
TOPS Training Opportunities Scheme
tot total
trans 1 transitive **2** translated; translation translator
transl translated; translation
trs transpose
TSB Trustee Savings Bank
tsp teaspoon; teaspoonful
TT 1 teetotal; teetotaller **2** Tourist Trophy **3** tuberculin tested
Tue, Tues Tuesday
TU trade union
TUC Trades Union Congress
TV television
TVP textured vegetable protein
TWA Trans-World Airlines

U

u 1 unit **2** upper
UAE United Arab Emirates

UAR United Arab Republic
UAU Universities Athletic Union
uc upper case
UCCA Universities Central Council on
  Admissions
UCL University College, London
UDA Ulster Defence Association
UDI unilateral declaration of independence
UDR Ulster Defence Regiment
UEFA Union of European Football
  Associations
UHF ultrahigh frequency
UHT ultrahigh temperature
UK United Kingdom
UKAEA United Kingdom Atomic Energy
  Authority
ult 1 ultimate **2** ultimo
UN United Nations
UNA United Nations Association
UNESCO United Nations Educational,
  Scientific, and Cultural Organization
UNICEF United Nations Children's Fund
  [*United Nations Children's Emergency
  Fund*, its former name]
univ 1 universal **2** university
UNO United Nations Organization
US United States
USA 1 United States Army **2** United
  States of America
USAF United States Air Force
USN United States Navy
USS United States Ship
USSR Union of Soviet Socialist Republics
UU Ulster Unionist
UV ultraviolet
UVF Ulster Volunteer Force

V

v 1 vector **2** verb **3** verse **4** versus **5** very **6**
  verso **7** vice **8** vide **9** von— used in
  German personal names
V 1 velocity **2** volt; voltage **3** volume
V & A Victoria and Albert Museum
var 1 variable **2** variant **3** variation **4**
  variety **5** various
VAT value-added tax
VC 1 Vice Chairman **2** Vice Chancellor **3**
  Vice Consul **4** Victoria Cross
VCR video cassette recorder
VD venereal disease
VDU visual display unit
VE Victory in Europe
Ven Venerable
Vet MB Bachelor of Veterinary Medicine
VG 1 very good **2** Vicar General
VHF very high frequency
vi 1 verb intransitive **2** see below
viz videlicet
VLF very low frequency
vol 1 volume **2** volunteer
VR 1 Queen Victoria **2** Volunteer Reserve
VSO Voluntary Service Overseas
VSOP Very Special Old Pale—a type of
  brandy
vt verb transitive
VTOL vertical takeoff and landing
VTR video tape recorder
vv 1 verses **2** vice versa **3** volumes

W

w 1 week **2** weight **3** white **4** wicket **5** wide
  6 width **7** wife **8** with
W 1 Watt **2** West; Westerly; Western
WAAC 1 Women's Army Auxiliary
  Corps—the women's component of the

British Army from 1914 to 1918 **2**
Women's Army Auxiliary Corps—the
women's component of the US army from
1942 to 1948
WAAF Women's Auxiliary Air Force—the
  women's component of the RAF
WAC Women's Army Corps—the
  women's component of the US army
WAF Women in the Air Force—the
  women's component of the USAF
War, Warw Warwickshire
WBA World Boxing Association
WBC 1 white blood cells; white blood
  count **2** World Boxing Council
WC 1 water closet **2** West Central—a
  London postal district
WCT World Championship Tennis
WEA Workers' Education Association
Wed, Weds Wednesday
wf wrong fount
WHO World Health Organization
WI 1 West Indies **2** Wisconsin **3** Women's
  Institute
Wilts Wiltshire
wk 1 week **2** work
wkly weekly
wkt wicket
Wlk walk—used in street names
Wm William
WNP Welsh National Party
WNW west-northwest
w/o without
WO Warrant Officer
Worcs Worcestershire
WOW War on Want
wpb wastepaper basket
WPC Woman Police Constable
wpm words per minute
WPS Woman Police Sergeant
WR Western Region
WRAC Women's Royal Army Corps
WRAF Women's Royal Air Force
WRNS Women's Royal Naval Service
WRVS Women's Royal Voluntary Service
WSW west-southwest
wt weight
WW World War

X

x 1 ex **2** extra
X Christ
XL extra large
XT Christ

Y

y year
yd yard
YHA Youth Hostels Association
YMCA Young Men's Christian Association
YMHA Young Men's Hebrew Association
Yorks Yorkshire
yr 1 year **2** younger **3** your
YWCA Young Women's Christian
  Association
YWHA Young Women's Hebrew
  Association

Z

ZANU Zimbabwe African National Union
ZAPU Zimbabwe African People's Union